CHILDREN'S CATALOG

EIGHTEENTH EDITION

STANDARD CATALOG SERIES

JULIETTE YAAKOV, GENERAL EDITOR

CHILDREN'S CATALOG
FICTION CATALOG
MIDDLE AND JUNIOR HIGH SCHOOL LIBRARY CATALOG
PUBLIC LIBRARY CATALOG
SENIOR HIGH SCHOOL LIBRARY CATALOG

CHILDREN'S CATALOG

EIGHTEENTH EDITION

EDITED BY

ANNE PRICE

AND

JULIETTE YAAKOV

NEW YORK AND DUBLIN

THE H. W. WILSON COMPANY

2001

Printed in the United States of America

Abridged Dewey Decimal Classification and Relative Index, Edition 13 is © 1997-2001 OCLC Online Computer Library Center, Incorporated. Portions reprinted with Permission. DDC, Dewey, Dewey Decimal Classification and Forest Press are registered trademarks of OCLC.

Library of Congress Cataloging-in-Publication Data

Children's catalog— 18th ed. / edited by Anne Price and Juliette Yaakov.
    p. cm. — (Standard catalog series)
  Includes index.

  ISBN 0-8242-1009-3 (alk. paper)

  1. Children's literature—Bibliography. 2 Children's libraries—United States—Book lists. 3. School libraries—United States—Book lists. I. Price, Anne, 1946- II. Yaakov, Juliette. III. Series

Z1037 .C5443 2001
011.62—dc21   2001046599

CONTENTS

PREFACE

Children's Catalog is a comprehensive list of fiction and nonfiction books, magazines, and Web resources for children from preschool through grade six, along with review sources and other professional aids for children's librarians and school media specialists.

In this Edition. This eighteenth edition of *Children's Catalog* includes 6,738 titles and 6,421 analytical entries. Of special note in this edition are a new abundance of books on minorities, ecology, natural sciences, and natural history. The sections for fairy tales and picture books have also been expanded. A separate section listing recommended Web resources has been added, replacing the list of reference works on CD-ROM in the previous edition. Also new in this edition is the mention of audiobook versions of books included and a list of such audiobooks in the index.

Preparation. In preparing this edition The H.W. Wilson Company has benefited from the work of two groups of experts in library service to children. An advisory committee of distinguished librarians re-evaluated the previous edition of the Catalog and its supplements and proposed many new titles. The list that resulted from the committee's deliberations was then submitted to a group of experienced librarians familiar with the needs of children. This group, representing diverse geographical areas, elected the titles included. In most cases their vote represents the composite judgment of a number of their colleagues.

Scope and Purpose. The Catalog is aimed at the needs of children, teachers, and librarians in the elementary school setting, through sixth grade. Sources for the librarian or school media specialist are included among both the print and the Web resources. They are works on the history and development of children's literature; literary criticism; bibliographies; selection aids; guides to the operation of media centers; and periodicals relating to library science, reviewing, and education.

Four annual supplements, to be published in 2002, 2003, 2004, and 2005, are intended for use with this volume. Libraries and media centers serving large systems or users with special needs will undoubtedly wish to augment this list. To accommodate the precocious child the reader is referred to *Middle and Junior High School Library Catalog*.

Books listed were published in the United States, or published in Canada or the United Kingdom and distributed in the United States. A small number of out-of-print titles that were considered essential to a well-rounded collection have been retained at the suggestion of the advisory committee. They are noted as o.p. All other titles were in print at the time of listing. Original paperback editions are included, and information is provided on paperback reprints of hardcover editions. Those concerned about the durability of paperbound editions may wish to utilize a commercial rebinding service.

The convention of citing the first book in a fiction series in full with brief listings for other works in the series has been retained. In cases where more than one edition of a work illustrated by a notable artist is available, a listing of editions is provided with complete ordering information. Notes specify prizes or medals won, indicate the availability of large print editions or audiobook versions, and identify sequels or companion volumes.

The catalog excludes the following: textbooks; pop-up and similar novelty items; and non-English-language materials, except for dictionaries and bilingual works. A non-English version of an English-language work is cited in the main entry for the work and is also listed in the Index under an appropriate heading such as "Spanish-language editions."

Organization. The Catalog consists of four parts. Part 1, the Classified Catalog, is arranged according to the Dewey Decimal Classification. Fiction (Fic), Story Collections (SC), and Easy Books (E) follow the nonfiction classes. Here the user will find complete bibliographical information, including price, grade level designation, suggested subject headings, a descriptive annotation, and an evaluation.

Part 2, List of Recommended Web Resources, is new to the Catalog, replacing the List of Recommended CD-ROM Reference Works in the previous edition.

Part 3, Author, Title, Subject, and Analytical Index, serves as a comprehensive key to the classified list. Entries under publishers' series are also given in this index, as well as titles of Web resources.

Part 4, Directory of Publishers and Distributors, includes fuller information about the publishers of the books listed.

The section that follows, How to Use Children's Catalog, contains more detailed information about the uses, content, and arrangement of the Catalog.

Acknowledgments

The H. W. Wilson Company is indebted to the publishers who supplied copies of their books and information about editions and prices.

The subscription-based Web resources in Part 2 were compiled by Gerry Solomon, Assistant Section Chief, Instructional Resources Evaluation Services, North Carolina Department of Public Instruction. The free Web resources were compiled by Coleman Ridge, Editor of Vertical File Index, H.W. Wilson Co.

This Catalog could not have been published without the efforts of the advisory committee and the consultants who gave so generously of their time and expertise. Their names appear below.

The advisory committee consisted of:

Joan L. Atkinson, Chair
    Director and Professor
    Library & Information Studies
    University of Alabama
    Tuscaloosa, Ala.

Mary Clark
    Director of Library Media
    Greenwich Country Day School
    Greenwich, Conn.

Josephine Fulcher-Anderson
    Librarian
    South End Branch
    Ferguson Library
    Stamford, Conn.

Suzanne W. Hawley
    Media Specialist
    Laurel Oak Elementary School
    Naples, Fla.

Barbara Howell
Librarian
Increase Miller Elementary School
Goldens Bridge, N.Y.

Amy Kellman
Program Specialist
Children's Services
Carnegie Library of Pittsburgh
Pittsburgh, Pa.

Linda Perkins
Children's Librarian
Berkeley Public Library
Berkeley, Calif.

The following consultants participated in the voting:

Barbara Barstow
Children's Services Manager
Cuyahoga County Public Library
Parma, Ohio

Paula Kiley
Coordinator of Children's Services
Milwaukee Public Library
Milwaukee, Wis.

Elaine Drew
Selection Service Section Manager
Indianapolis Marion County Public Library
Library Service Center
Indianapolis, Ind.

Susan Link
Library Media Specialist
Colony Bend Elementary School
Sugar Land, Tex.

Eileen Dunne
Coordinator of Library Services
Abilene Independent School District
Abilene, Tex.

Linda Perkins
Children's Librarian
Berkeley Public Library
Berkeley, Calif.

Randall Enos
Children's Services Consultant
Ramapo Catskill Library System
Middletown, N.Y.

Jennifer Ralston,
Children's Collection Manager
Harford County Library
Belcamp, Md.

Crystal Faris
Youth Services Manager
Nassau Library System
Uniondale, N.Y.

Connie Rockman,
Children's Literature Consultant
Stratford, Conn.

Susan Faust,
Librarian
Katherine Delmer Burke School
San Francisco, Calif.

Judith Rovenger
Youth Services Consultant
Westchester Library System
Ardsley, N.Y.

Helma Hawkins
Director, Children's Services
Kansas City Public Library
Kansas City, Mo.

Grace Ruth
Children's Materials Selection
Specialist
San Francisco Public Library
San Francisco, Calif.

Linda Ward-Callaghan
Children's Services Coordinator
Oak Park Public Library
Oak Park, Ill.

HOW TO USE CHILDREN'S CATALOG

Children's Catalog is arranged in four parts: Part 1. Classified Catalog; Part 2. List of Recommended Web Resources; Part 3. Author, Title, Subject, and Analytical Index; and Part 4. Directory of Publishers and Distributors.

USES OF THE CATALOG

Children's Catalog is designed to serve these purposes:

As an aid in purchasing. The annotations and grade level designation provided for each work in the Classified Catalog, along with information concerning publisher, ISBN, price, and availability, are intended to assist in the selection and ordering of titles. Arrangement of the Classified Catalog according to the Dewey Decimal Classification expedites the process of identifying elements of the collection that should be strengthened or updated. Evaluation of the suitability of any particular work will always take into account the special character of the children, the school, and the community that the library or media center serves.

As an aid in user service. Every item in this Catalog is a highly recommended work of its kind and can be given with confidence to a user who expresses a need based on topic, genre, etc. Reference work and user service are furthered by information about grade level, sequels, and companion volumes; by the descriptive and critical annotations in the Classified Catalog; and by the series and subject approach in the Index. In addition, the Index includes entries under names of illustrators, form headings such as "Large print books," and headings for Newbery and Caldecott medal winners. Analytical entries augment the local catalog by providing access to parts of composite works.

As an aid in verification of information. Full bibliographical data, recommended subject headings based upon *Sears List of Subject Headings*, a suggested classification derived from the *Abridged Dewey Decimal Classification and Relative Index,* and notes that describe editions available, awards, and publication history are provided for this purpose.

As an aid in curriculum support. The classified approach, subject indexing, annotations, and grade level designations are helpful in identifying materials appropriate for classroom use. In areas where few monographs exist, or where those that do are outdated, inaccurate, or unavailable—as in the history and geography of some countries—the user should consult current reference sources, periodical literature, and the Internet to supply the lack.

As an aid in collection maintenance. Items elected to this edition of the Catalog comprise newly published works along with works listed in the previous edition or its supplements that have retained their usefulness. Information about the range of titles available in a field facilitates decisions to rebind, replace, or discard materials in the library's collection. That a book was in a previous edition of Children's Catalog and is not in this edition should not necessarily be interpreted to mean that the book is no longer useful or that it should be weeded from the collection.

As an aid in professional development. The Catalog is useful in courses that deal with children's literature and book selection, particularly on the preschool and elementary level.

DESCRIPTION OF THE CATALOG

Part 1. Classified Catalog

The Classified Catalog is arranged with the nonfiction books first, classified by the Dewey Decimal Classification in numerical order from 000 to 999. Individual biographies are classed in 92 and follow the 920s (collective biography). Three sections follow the nonfiction: Fiction (Fic), Story Collections (S C); and Easy Books (E), consisting chiefly of picture books of interest to children from preschool to grade three.

An Outline of Classification, which serves as a table of contents to the Classified Catalog, is reproduced on page 2. Many books may properly be classified in more than one discipline. If a particular title is not found where it might be expected, the Index should be consulted to determine if the work is classified elsewhere.

Within classes, works are arranged alphabetically under main entry, usually the author. An exception is made for works of individual biography, classed in 92, which are arranged alphabetically under the name of the person written about.

Following is a sample entry and a description of the components of a typical entry:

> **Silverstein, Alvin**
> Common colds; [by] Alvin Silverstein, Virginia Silverstein and Laura Silverstein Nunn. Watts 1999 48p il (My health) lib bdg $22.50; pa $6.95 (3-5)   **616.2**
> 1. Cold (Disease)
> ISBN 0-531-11579-8 (lib bdg); 0-531-16410-1 (pa)
> LC 98-22025
> Explains how people catch colds, how the body fights the germs, how colds are spread, and what precautions people can take against them
> This is "attractively designed, with plenty of sidebars containing fascinating facts and color photographs." Booklist
> Includes glossary and bibliographical references

The name of the author, which is inverted and printed in bold face type, is given in conformity with *Anglo-American Cataloguing Rules*, 2nd edition, 1998 revision, with 1999 Amendments. It is followed by the title, responsibility statement, and publisher. For further information about the publisher, refer to the Directory of Publishers and Distributors. Next are the date of publication, pagination, illustration note, series note, price, binding and grade level. Prices given were current when the Catalog went to press. As time passes they should be confirmed with the publisher. The availability of a CD-ROM version or an audiobook version of a print equivalent is also indicated in the entry for the print version.

The figure printed in bold face on the last line of type in the body of the entry is the classification number derived from the 13th edition of the *Abridged Dewey Decimal Classification*. A numbered term is a recommended subject heading for this book. In some instances subject headings assigned to the entire book will not show that portions of the book deal with more specific topics. In such cases subject analytic entries are made. All subject headings are based on the 17th edition of *Sears List of Subject Headings.*

The ISBN (International Standard Book Number) or ISSN (International Standard Serial Number) is included to facilitate ordering. The Library of Congress control (card) number is provided when available.

Notes supply additional information about the book. Most entries include both a note describing the book's content and a critical note, which is useful in evaluating books for selection and in determining which of several books on the same subject is best suited for the individual reader. Other notes list special features or describe sequels and companion volumes, editions available, awards, and publication history.

Part 2. List of Recommended Web Resources

This section consists of two kinds of Web resources, commercial subscription-based databases, and free Web sites, all listed in a single alphabet. All of them have been chosen for their excellence of content and appropriate age level. The list includes professional resources.

Bibliographic information about Web resources includes the title, publisher's name and telephone number, an indication of the price range for subscription resources, grade level, and URL. This is followed by a descriptive annotation and in some cases a quotation from a reviewing source.

Part 3. Author, Title, Subject, and Analytical Index

This is an alphabetical index of all the books entered in the Catalog. Each book is entered under author; title, if distinctive; and subject, with added entries for joint author, illustrator, editor, and publisher's series as necessary. Also included are subject, author, and title analytics for parts of composite works. Analytical entries are an important feature of the Catalog. Subject analytics afford access to parts of books not covered by the subject headings for the whole, while author and title analytics provide an approach to anthologies and collections, especially of stories and tales. In a time of restricted funding analytic entries aid in maximizing use of the library's holdings.

The classification number in bold face type is the key to the location of the main entry of the book in the Classified Catalog. Works classed in 92, individual biography, will be found under the name of the person written about.

Entries are also made under headings that indicate form or publication characteristics such as "Large print books," "American Library Association publications," "Caldecott medal titles," and "Spanish language editions." Books that are also published in a CD-ROM version are listed under "CD-ROMs."

"See" references are made from forms of names or subjects not used as headings. "See also" references are made to related or more specific headings. The suggested grade level of a book is repeated in the Index.

Examples of entries for the book cited above:

Author	**Silverstein, Alvin** Common colds (3-5)	**616.2**
Title	**Common** colds. Silverstein, A.	**616.2**
Subject	**Cold (Disease)** Silverstein, A. Common colds (3-5)	**616.2**
Publisher's series	**My health** [series] Silverstein, A. Common colds	**616.2**

Examples of other types of entries:

Joint authors	**Nunn, Laura Silverstein** (jt. auth) Silverstein, A. Common colds	**616.2**
	Silverstein, Virginia B. (jt. auth) Silverstein, A. Common colds	**616.2**
Illustrator	**Dillon, Leo, 1933-** (il) Hamilton, V. The girl who spun gold	**398.2**
Editor	**Hall, Donald, 1928-** (ed) The Oxford book of children's verse in America. *See* The Oxford book of children's verse in America	**811.008**
Author analytic	**Mahy, Margaret** A lion in the meadow *In* The Oxford treasury of children's stories p 4-6	**S C**
Title analytic	A **lion** in the meadow. Mahy, M. *In* The Oxford treasury of children's stories p 4-6	**S C**
Subject analytic	**Elizabeth I, Queen of England, 1533-1603** *See/See also pages in the following book(s):* Meltzer, M. Ten queens p73-83 (5 and up)	**920**

Part 4.   Directory of Publishers and Distributors

This Directory provides the full name, address, telephone number, and other pertinent information about the publisher or distributor of the books listed.

PART 1

CLASSIFIED CATALOG

Outline of Classification

Reproduced below is the Second Summary of the Dewey Decimal Classification.* It will serve as a table of contents for the nonfiction section of the Classified Catalog. (Fiction, Story Collections, and Easy Books follow the nonfiction.) Note that the inclusion of this outline is not to be considered a substitute for consulting the Dewey Decimal Classification itself.

CHILDREN'S CATALOG

EIGHTEENTH EDITION

CLASSIFIED CATALOG

000 GENERALITIES

001.4 Research; statistical methods

Duncan, Donna
 I-Search, you search, we all learn to research; a how-to-do-it manual for teaching elementary school students to solve information problems; [by] Donna Duncan, Laura Lockhart. Neal-Schuman 2000 159p (How-to-do-it manuals for librarians) pa $45 **001.4**
 1. Research 2. Libraries 3. Report writing
 ISBN 1-55570-381-X LC 99-89993
 "This manual introduces teachers and librarians to strategies to get students to move away from traditional research in which they merely restate information to a higher order of thinking. . . . Along the way, they will learn about choosing topics, evaluating sources, note taking, presenting findings, and working with peers to develop better skills." SLJ

Markle, Sandra, 1946-
 Discovering graph secrets; experiments, puzzles, and games exploring graphs. Atheneum Bks. for Young Readers 1997 36p il $18 (3-6) **001.4**
 1. Graphic methods
 ISBN 0-689-31942-0 LC 96-15435
 Contains activities dealing with charts and graphs, showing how to construct them, what can be plotted, and how they illustrate mathematical concepts
 "This slim volume could be a dream come true for students looking for math projects or teachers looking for enrichment activities." Bull Cent Child Books

001.9 Controversial knowledge

Campbell, Peter A.
 Alien encounters; written and illustrated by Peter A. Campbell. Millbrook Press 2000 48p il lib bdg $23.90 (4 and up) **001.9**
 1. Unidentified flying objects
 ISBN 0-7613-1402-4 LC 99-25360
 "Arranged chronologically, these eight simply told stories about contacts with UFOs span a 20-year period from 1953 to 1973. . . . Dramatic paintings and drawings and sketches of crafts and creatures appear on almost every page." SLJ
 Includes bibliographical references

Guiberson, Brenda Z.
 Tales of the haunted deep. Holt & Co. 2000 70p il map $15.95 (4 and up) **001.9**
 1. Curiosities and wonders 2. Sea stories 3. Ghost stories
 ISBN 0-8050-6057-X LC 99-34976
 "Guiberson retells ghost stories of the sea—tales of pirate ghosts, lighthouse ghosts, sea monsters, and ships with a mind of their own. . . . The text is nicely illustrated with Guiberson's own occassional black-and-white pictures as well as prints and photos from various maritime museums." Booklist
 Includes bibliographical references

Herbst, Judith
 The mystery of UFOs; illustrated by Greg Clarke. Atheneum Bks. for Young Readers 1997 unp il $16; pa $6.99 (2-4) **001.9**
 1. Unidentified flying objects
 ISBN 0-689-31652-6; 0-689-83893-X (pa)
 LC 95-45845
 Relates the stories of a number of famous UFO sightings, including the purported crash of an alien spaceship in Roswell, New Mexico, in 1947
 This "is a respectable mix of the factual and the speculative. . . . A thought-provoking and useful introduction to the facts." Publ Wkly

Simon, Seymour, 1931-
 Strange mysteries from around the world. Morrow Junior Bks. 1997 58p il $16; pa $6.95 (4-6) **001.9**
 1. Curiosities and wonders
 ISBN 0-688-14636-8; 0-688-14637-6 (pa)
 LC 96-2693
 A revised edition of the title first published 1980 by Four Winds Press
 Describes ten strange natural phenomena and possible explanations for them, including the day it rained frogs, an atomic explosion that occurred forty years before the atom bomb, and an eerie crystal skull
 "Simon's enticingly simple and clear descriptions make the subjects accessible with no unsubstantiated speculations. Worn-out copies of the 1980 edition can be safely replaced with this updated version." SLJ

Wilson, Colin, 1931-
 Mysteries of the universe. DK Pub. 1997 37p il (Unexplained) $14.95 (4 and up) **001.9**
 1. Curiosities and wonders
 ISBN 0-7894-2165-8 LC 97-15424
 Explores such mysteries as Bigfoot, the Loch Ness Monster, weird weather, and black holes

Wilson, Colin, 1931-—*Continued*
This book "has a few tantalizing words to say about everything from the Turin shroud to showers of fish to life on Mars." Booklist

UFOs and aliens. DK Pub. 1997 37p il (Unexplained) $14.95 (4 and up)   **001.9**
1. Unidentified flying objects 2. Extraterrestrial beings
ISBN 0-7894-2166-6   LC 97-15425
Examines various explanations and evidence related to UFO sightings and alien encounters throughout history
"The photographs, often in color, are a browser's dream come true. . . . [This book] doesn't get into the scientific pros and cons, focusing instead on the occurrences that suggest alien visitations, including stories of abduction and UFO sightings, and a few headline-making hoaxes." Booklist

004 Data processing. Computer science

Spencer, Donald D., 1931-
Illustrated computer dictionary for young people. 2nd ed. Camelot 1999 117p il $16.95   **004**
1. Computers—Dictionaries 2. Data processing—Dictionaries
ISBN 0-89218-323-3   LC 98-47643
First published 1995
This dictionary contains over 700 entries covering various aspects of computer science, including artificial intelligence, computer graphics, networks, and desktop publishing

Webster's New World dictionary of computer terms; compiled by Donald Spencer. Hungry Minds pa $11.65   **004**
1. Computers—Dictionaries 2. Data processing—Dictionaries

First edition compiled by Laura Darcy and Louise Boston published 1983 by Simon & Schuster. (8th edition 1999) Frequently revised
"This dictionary defines more than 5,000 of the most frequently used computer terms." Choice [review of 1992 edition]
"A useful desk reference for all levels of readers." Choice [review of 1992 edition]

004.6 Interfacing and communications. Networks

Benson, Allen C.
Connecting kids and the Internet; a handbook for librarians, teachers, and parents; [by] Allen C. Benson, Linda M. Fodemski. 2nd ed. Neal-Schuman 1999 398p (Neal-Schuman net-guide series) pa $49.95   **004.6**
1. Internet 2. Computer-assisted instruction
ISBN 1-55570-348-8   LC 99-16424
First published 1996

This is a "resource for questions about browsers, search engines, e-mail, news groups, Web pages, virtual field trips, and filters. Fourteen lesson plans suggest practical ideas for teaching students to become skilled, savvy Internet users. Packed with information and ideas, the book is accompanied by a useful CD-ROM. . . . A useful addition to school and public libraries." Booklist
Includes bibliographical references

Berger, Pam
Internet for active learners; curriculum-based strategies for K.12. American Lib. Assn. 1998 189p il pa $30   **004.6**
1. Internet 2. Computer-assisted instruction
ISBN 0-8389-3487-0   LC 98-23102
The author "starts by discussing the different roles school librarians will have to play in the 21st century. She then shows readers how the Internet can help them meet these challenges successfully. . . . A useful chapter covers creating a home page for the library, and the book ends with ideas for teaching the Internet to faculty and parents." SLJ
"If you can afford only one Internet manual for your school library, this one should fill the spot." Book Rep
Includes bibliographical references

Brimner, Larry Dane, 1949-
E-mail. Children's Press 1997 47p il lib bdg $22 (2-4)   **004.6**
1. Electronic mail systems 2. Internet
ISBN 0-516-20332-0   LC 96-29053
"A True book"
A simple explanation of what e-mail is and how to use it to communicate with others through the Internet and the Information Superhighway
"The format is attractive, with many full-color photographs and pictures of screens using Eudora software to locate mailing lists on particular topics. Netiquette is also discussed." SLJ
Includes glossary and bibliographical references

The World Wide Web. Children's Press 1997 47p il lib bdg $22 (2-4)   **004.6**
1. World Wide Web
ISBN 0-516-20345-2   LC 96-29054
"A True book"
The author describes how to use the World Wide Web, with a history of its development, and "explains terms such as Hypertext Transfer Protocol, Internet service providers, hyperlinks, HTML coding, URLs, search engines, bookmarks, and safe surfing. Interesting URLs (or addresses) for Web sites are sprinkled throughout." SLJ
Includes glossary and bibliographical references

Jefferis, David
Cyberspace; virtual reality and the World Wide Web. Crabtree 1999 32p il (Megatech) $15.45; pa $8.06 (4 and up)   **004.6**
1. Computers 2. Computer simulation 3. Virtual reality 4. World Wide Web
ISBN 0-7787-0047-X; 0-7787-0057-7 (pa)
    LC 98-48512

Jefferis, David—*Continued*

Surveys digital technology from the early days of computers to virtual reality and the World Wide Web, describing the uses of computer simulation in flight, battle, hazardous environments, and entertainment

Junion-Metz, Gail, 1947-

Coaching kids for the Internet; a guide for librarians, teachers, and parents. Library Solutions Press 2000 306p il (Internet workshop series) $60

004.6

1. Internet
ISBN 1-88220-829-3

This work presents instructions and excercises to help students access the Internet and work with the World Wide Web. Accompanied by computer disc

Kalbag, Asha

Build your own Web site. EDC 1999 48p (Usborne computer guides series) pa $9.95 (4 and up)

004.6

1. Internet
ISBN 0-7460-3293-5

This book "focuses not only on the hows but also on the whys, whens, and wheres of creating Web pages. It explains how to create a Web site with a text editor, but the aesthetic and content advice hold true no matter what program is being used." SLJ

Kazunas, Charnan

The Internet for kids; [by] Charnan and Tom Kazunas. Children's Press 1997 47p il lib bdg $22 (2-4)

004.6

1. Internet
ISBN 0-516-20334-7   LC 96-49661
"A True book"
New edition in preparation

This explains "how networks operate, what function servers play, URLs (Uniform Resource Locators) and addresses, search and retrieval tools, and the parts of the Internet (e-mail, chat sessions, and news groups). Safety tips and cautions are also presented. The colorful photographs include clearly reproduced screens from Netscape. . . . A good starting place for young surfers who wish to venture into cyberspace." SLJ

Includes glossary and bibliographical references

Miller, Elizabeth B.

The Internet resource directory for K-12 teachers and librarians. Libraries Unlimited pa $27.50

004.6

1. Internet 2. Information systems—Directories

Annual. First published 1994 for 1994-1995

This directory "provides details on accessing more than 400 discussion groups, electronic books and newspapers, lesson plans, and a variety of other teaching resources by E-mail, gopher, telnet, and FTP. . . . The directory proper is arranged under broad curricular areas plus resources for educators, reference, and school library media applications. Each of these is further divided by narrower disciplines. . . . Recommended for all school library media centers." Booklist

Murray, Laura K.

Basic Internet for busy librarians; a quick course for catching up. American Lib. Assn. 1998 137p il pa $26

004.6

1. Internet 2. Library information networks
ISBN 0-8389-0725-3   LC 98-14067

The author "presents step-by-step exercises on accessing the Internet, working with the World Wide Web, creating Web pages, and using such other Internet aspects as electronic lists, e-mail, telnet, and FTP. One chapter is devoted to searching. All exercises are accompanied by screen images." Booklist

"If you are still looking for an on-ramp to the information superhighway, this is the book for you." SLJ

Pedersen, Ted

Internet for kids! a beginner's guide to surfing the Net; written by Ted Pedersen and Francis Moss. new updated ed. Price/Stern/Sloan 1997 219p il pa $8.95 (5 and up)

004.6

1. Internet
ISBN 0-8431-7937-6   LC 96-38116
First published 1995

This work "provides information for readers to connect to and surf the Information Superhighway. . . . Getting Outfitted, which is primarily for parents, lists the major service providers and software programs for extending the capabilities of Web browsers. Another chapter suggests specific sites to visit." Book Rep

Trumbauer, Lisa

Homework help for kids on the Net. Millbrook Press 2000 75p il (Cool sites series) lib bdg $17.90; pa $4.95 (4 and up)

004.6

ISBN 0-7613-1655-8 (lib bdg); 0-7613-1291-9 (pa)
LC 99-55372

A compendium of "curriculum-related Web sites. Divided by subject, it covers sites for general reference, math, language arts, history, geography, and science. For the most part, a single page is devoted to each site, with a brief description, a black-and-white picture of either the home page or a sample screen, and some student reviews." SLJ

006   Special computer methods

Baker, Christopher W., 1956-

Scientific visualization; the new eyes of science. Millbrook Press 2000 48p il lib bdg $22.90 (5 and up)

006

1. Science—Methodology 2. Computer simulation
ISBN 0-7613-1351-6

This work "explores the ways that computers enable scientists to study the universe beyond the range of our eyes. Examples include studying the interaction of molecules or even atoms when an egg is heated in a pan, viewing the human brain through MRI images, and simulating events such as the creation of a black hole or the collision of two galaxies." Booklist

Baker, Christopher W., 1956-—*Continued*

Virtual reality; experiencing illusion. Millbrook Press 2000 48p il (New century technology) lib bdg $24.90 (5 and up)   **006**

1. Virtual reality

ISBN 0-7613-1350-8   LC 99-34200

The author "explains how digital imaging synthesizes human sensory experiences, a process with applications in medicine, military training, and robotics, not to mention the more familiar field of computer gaming." Booklist

Includes bibliographical references

011.6 General bibliographies of works for specific kinds of users

Adventuring with books; a booklist for pre-K—grade 6; Kathryn Mitchell Pierce, editor; with Cathy Beck [et al.] and the Committee to Revise the Elementary School Booklist; with a foreword by Jane Yolen. 12th ed. National Council of Teachers of English 1999 xxv, 605p il (NCTE bibliography series) pa $32.95 **011.6**

1. Children's literature—Bibliography 2. Best books

ISBN 0-8141-0077-5   LC 00-267046

First published 1950. Editors vary

"An annotated bibliography of fiction and nonfiction arranged by subject area and cross-referenced in other applicable subjects. The focus is on books published in 1996, 1997, and 1998 for children from preschool to grade six, though many books are appropriate through grade eight." Booklist

Ammon, Bette D.

Worth a thousand words; an annotated guide to picture books for older readers; [by] Bette D. Ammon and Gale W. Sherman. Libraries Unlimited 1996 210p pa $28   **011.6**

1. Picture books for children—Bibliography 2. Children's literature—Bibliography 3. Books and reading

ISBN 1-56308-390-6   LC 96-31489

This is a bibliography of approximately 640 titles. "Arranged alphabetically by author, each entry briefly describes a book. The description is accompanied by a subject list that includes themes, genres, and topics to enhance the book's potential classroom use, as well as to help match books with readers. Following the annotations are specific suggestions for including each book in the curriculum. Icons representing the curriculum ideas indicate classroom applications and suitable curriculum areas. Author/illustrator, title, and subject indexes help users locate specific works." Publisher's note

Barstow, Barbara

Beyond picture books; a guide to first readers; [by] Barbara Barstow, Judith Riggle. 2nd ed. Bowker 1995 501p $59   **011.6**

1. Children's literature—Bibliography 2. Best books

ISBN 0-8352-3519-X   LC 94-49731

First published 1989

This "annotated bibliography, arranged by author's last name, provides full bibliographic information (except price) as well as series note, subjects, and reading category. If a title is out of print, it is so noted. The annotations are brief, ranging from 20 to 50 words. They give a brief summary of contents, note illustrations, and occasionally have a critical comment." Booklist

Best books for children; preschool through grade 6; John T. Gillespie, editor. 6th ed. Bowker 1998 1537p $65   **011.6**

1. Children's literature—Bibliography 2. Best books

ISBN 0-8352-4099-1   LC 98-35713

First published 1978

This work includes nearly 18,000 titles. Entries are grouped in subject areas with bibliographic information, suggested reading level, and an annotation. Includes Author, Title, Illustrator, and Subject/Grade level indexes

Culturally diverse videos, audios, and CD-ROMS for children and young adults; edited by Irene Wood. Neal-Schuman 1999 276p $35   **011.6**

1. Motion pictures—Catalogs 2. Videotapes—Catalogs 3. CD-ROMs—Catalogs

ISBN 1-55570-377-1   LC 99-48572

"A chapter on multicultural videos is followed by chapters on videos by and/or about African Americans, Asian Americans, Hispanic Americans, and Native Americans. Also included are chapters about audio materials: music, storytelling and folklore, audiobooks, and Spanish-language read-alongs. Another section lists CD-ROMs available in languages other than English and those that address multicultural themes. The book concludes with a comprehensive list of distributors and subject and title indexes." SLJ

Denman-West, Margaret W., 1926-

Children's literature: a guide to information sources. Libraries Unlimited 1998 187p (Reference sources in the humanities series) $38.50   **011.6**

1. Children's literature—Bibliography 2. Teenagers—Books and reading—Bibliography 3. Young adults' libraries—Bibliography

ISBN 1-56308-448-1   LC 98-10177

This "is an annotated bibliography of more than 400 bibliographies and other reference works published from 1985 to 1997. Young-adult-related resources are included despite the book's title. It is arranged in chapters on subjects such as award-winning books, multicultural literature, core periodicals, reference books, nonprint media, special collections, professional associations, and the Internet." Booklist

The **Elementary** school library collection; a guide to books and other media, phases 1-2-3. Brodart $139.95   **011.6**

1. Classified catalogs 2. Children's literature—Bibliography 3. Audiovisual materials—Catalogs 4. School libraries—Catalogs

Also available CD-ROM version

First published 1965. Revised biennially

"This collection recommends items for preschool to grade six . . . it includes media and professional materi-

The Elementary school library collection—*Continued*

als. The annotations are largely descriptive; but items are recommended for purchase in phases from one to three. Entries include bibliographic information, both reading and interest level and purchase phase recommendation." Stafford. Guide to Ref Materials for Sch Libr Media Cent. 5th edition

Fiction, folklore, fantasy & poetry for children, 1876-1985. Bowker 1986 2v o.p. **011.6**
1. Children's literature—Bibliography
LC 84-20474

Contents: v 1 Authors; illustrators; v2 Titles; awards

This "is a comprehensive listing of children's literature published over the last century. The 133,000 entries, taken from the *Publisher's Trade List Annual* and verified in other sources, are listed by author, title, and illustrator. A fourth section lists the year-by-year winners of 20 major children's-book awards. Entries, in a format similar to Bowker's *Books in Print*, give the title, author or editor, illustrator, their birth and death dates, series, pagination, publication date, LC card number, ISBN, publisher, and other information when available." Am Libr

Freeman, Judy
More books kids will sit still for; a read-aloud guide. Bowker 1995 869p il $59 **011.6**
1. Children's literature—Bibliography 2. Best books
ISBN 0-8352-3520-3 LC 95-36760

Beginning with a manual on reading aloud, booktalking, storytelling and other ways to use books with children, this book goes on to list more than 1,400 titles, mostly from 1990-1995

"This annotated compilation is an excellent stand-alone acquisition. . . . What distinguishes this volume and its previous companion work from other similar compilations are the refreshing, enticing annotations." Am Ref Books Annu, 1996

Gillespie, John Thomas, 1928-
Guides to collection development for children and young adults; [by] John T. Gillespie, Ralph J. Folcarelli. Libraries Unlimited 1998 191p pa $37 **011.6**
1. Children's literature—Bibliography 2. Young adult literature—Bibliography
ISBN 1-56308-532-1 LC 98-12944

Based in part upon sections of Guides to library collection development (1994), this "provides in-depth annotations for more than 800 books and periodicals about children's and young adult materials, print and nonprint, including CD-ROMs and online services. From preschool read-alouds to YA genre fiction and self-help, this will help librarians find resources for programming, readers' advisory, and selection." Booklist

Harms, Jeanne McLain
Picture books to enhance the curriculum; [by] Jeanne McLain Harms, Lucille J. Lettow. Wilson, H.W. 1996 521p $45 **011.6**
1. Picture books for children—Indexes 2. Picture books for children—Bibliography
ISBN 0-8242-0867-6 LC 94-42653

This is "a list of approximately 1,500 picture-book titles for use in literature-based programs in elementary schools implementing the whole language concept. The focus rests on language arts, graphic and performing arts, social studies, and science. Chapters cover a key to themes; a themes index listing related titles; a picture book index containing bibliographic information, a brief annotation of contents, and a list of themes; and a title index." Choice

Kaleidoscope; a multicultural booklist for grades K-8; Rosalinda B. Barrera, Verlinda D. Thompson, and Mark Dressman, editors, and the Committee to Revise the Multicultural Booklist of the National Council of Teachers of English. 2nd ed, covering books published 1993-95. National Council of Teachers of English 1998 xxi, 215p il pa $16.95 **011.6**
1. Multiculturalism—Bibliography 2. Children's literature—Bibliography 3. Best books 4. Minorities—Bibliography
ISBN 0-8141-2541-7

First published 1994

"An annotated bibliography of selected books about or related to African Americans, Asian Americans, Latinos or Hispanic Americans, and Native Americans." Introduction

Lima, Carolyn W.
A to Zoo; subject access to children's picture books; [by] Carolyn W. Lima, John A. Lima. 5th ed. Bowker 1998 xxvii, 1398p $76.75 **011.6**
1. Picture books for children—Bibliography
ISBN 0-8352-3916-0 LC 98-11920

First published 1982

This work provides subject accessibility to over 18,000 picture books. Arranged under more than 1000 subject headings, entries list only authors and titles. Complete bibliographic information is given in a separate bibliographic section arranged alphabetically by author, and there are title and illustrator indexes

For a review see: Booklist, Sept. 1, 1998

Magazines for kids and teens; Donald R. Stoll, editor. rev ed. Educational Press Assn. of Am. 1997 118p pa $15.95 **011.6**
1. Periodicals—Bibliography
ISBN 0-87207-243-6 LC 97-139394

First published 1990 with title: Magazines for children

"The almost 300 periodical listings include a great variety of choices—from hair styling to softball to French instruction magazines. Moreover, many cultures are represented with periodicals from groups outside the United States. For each title, the author gives a specific audience level along with address, circulation figures, and subscription costs. An age and a broad-based subject index and a list of periodicals that publish readers' works follow." Recomm Ref Books in Paperback. 3d edition

Middle and junior high school library catalog; edited by Anne Price and Juliette Yaakov; managing editor, Zaida Nidza Padró. 8th ed. Wilson, H.W. 2000 1021p $210 **011.6**
1. Classified catalogs 2. School libraries—Catalogs
ISBN 0-8242-0996-6 LC 00-63316

Middle and junior high school library catalog—
Continued

"Standard catalog series"

First published 1965 with title: Junior high school library catalog

Kept up to date by annual supplements which are included in price of main volume

This collection of recommended materials includes 4,520 titles and 4,492 analytical entries of books for grades five through nine. Entries contain full bibliographic information, Dewey decimal classification number, subject headings, descriptive, and when possible, critical annotations. A special section includes entries for a selection of CD-ROMs devoted to reference and educational materials

Rochman, Hazel

Against borders; promoting books for a multicultural world. American Lib. Assn. 1993 288p il pa $25   **011.6**

1. Young adult literature—Bibliography 2. Books and reading 3. Minorities—Bibliography

ISBN 0-8389-0601-X   LC 93-17840

"Starting with her personal immigrant's journey from South Africa to the U.S., Rochman's essays focus on using books across cultures. The second part of the book is made up of bibliographies—many of them updated and expanded from *Booklist*—on specific ethnic groups and cultural issues." Booklist

"The subject access by ethnic group and nationality will prove useful for doing reader's advisory work as well as developing units on ethnic and cultural identity." SLJ

Safford, Barbara Ripp

Guide to reference materials for school media centers. 5th ed. Libraries Unlimited 1998 353p $47
     011.6

1. Reference books—Bibliography 2. School libraries—Catalogs 3. Instructional materials centers

ISBN 1-56308-545-3   LC 98-29867

First edition by Christine Gehrt Wynar published 1973 with title: Guide to reference books for school media centers

"This guide contains critical annotations with full bibliographical information for 1,672 reference materials that are currently available and appropriate for elementary, middle, and senior high schools. Entries include titles published between 1992 and 1997 and older titles that still contain accurate information. Materials focus on the United States and include print, CD-ROM, and on-line resources. Criteria for inclusion are usefulness for curricular applications, interest for students, readability, clarity, accuracy, and currency of information." Voice Youth Advocates

Schon, Isabel

The best of the Latino heritage; a guide to the best juvenile books about Latino people and cultures. Scarecrow Press 1997 285p $37.50
     011.6

1. Children's literature—Bibliography 2. Latin America—Bibliography 3. Spain—Bibliography

ISBN 0-8108-3221-6   LC 96-24249

"This is a bibliography of the books on the topic [Schon] considers the best from the last forty years or so; they range from picture books to novels to biographies to political analyses. The collection is divided by country and region, and each entry includes necessary bibliographic information and a pithy, well-turned annotation that often includes evaluative comments." Bull Cent Child Books

Recommended books in Spanish for children and young adults, 1996 through 1999. Scarecrow Press 2000 362p $45   **011.6**

1. Latin American literature—Bibliography 2. Spanish literature—Bibliography 3. Children's literature—Bibliography 4. Young adult literature—Bibliography

ISBN 0-8108-3840-0   LC 00-38761

Previous volume covering years 1991-1995 published 1997

An "annotated bibliography of nearly 1000 books in Spanish for young readers of all ages. Sections include reference and series titles as well as nonfiction and fiction (each broken down additionally into more specific subsections); books come from all over the globe, with some translated into Spanish (and not just from English) and some written in the language." Horn Book

015.73   Bibliographies and catalogs of works issued or printed in the United States

Children's books in print. Bowker $179.95
     015.73

1. Children's literature—Bibliography

ISSN 0069-3480

Also available CD-ROM version

Annual. First published 1969

"Gives current publisher's information for juvenile titles listed in their catalogs as 'in print.' Useful, but not complete." N Y Public Libr. Ref Books for Child Collect. 2d edition

Subject guide to Children's books in print. Bowker $179.95   **015.73**

1. Children's literature—Bibliography 2. Subject catalogs

ISSN 0000-0167

Also available CD-ROM version

Annual. First published 1970

This publication provides a subject approach to its companion work: Children's books in print. The headings used are based on the Sears list of subject headings supplemented by headings from LC. Entries include author, title, publisher, year of publication, binding, price, ISBN, and, in some cases, grade level. A directory of publishers and distributors is included

016.2 Bibliographies of religion

Dole, Patricia Pearl, 1927-
Children's books about religion. Libraries
Unlimited 1999 230p $32   **016.2**
1. Religions
ISBN 1-56308-515-1   LC 98-33707
"A compilation of books with overt spiritual themes
for preschoolers through young adults. These titles represent a variety of genres, including retellings of Bible stories, prayer books, creation stories, songbooks, holiday
tales, mysteries, and biographies from both religious and
trade publishers. All have been published since 1990."
SLJ
For a fuller review see: Booklist, July, 1999

016.3 Bibliographies of the social sciences

Notable children's trade books in the field of
social studies. Children's Bk. Council pa $2
016.3
1. Social sciences—Bibliography 2. Best books

An annual annotated list, reprinted from an issue of
the periodical Social Education, of the preceding year's
best trade books in the field of social studies of interest
to children in grades K-8. Prepared by the Book Review
Panel of the National Council for the Social Studies—
Children's Book Council Joint Committee. Titles are selected for emphasis on human relations, originality, readability and, when appropriate, illustrations. General reading levels (primary, intermediate, advanced) are indicated

016.3058 Bibliographies of racial, ethnic, national groups

The **Black** experience in children's books; selected
by the New York Public Library, Black
Experience in Children's Books Committee.
New York Public Lib. pa $8   **016.3058**
1. African Americans—Bibliography 2. Blacks—Bibliography

First published 1946 with title: Books about Negro life
for children. (1999 edition) Periodically revised
An annotated bibliography of approximately 500 titles
portraying African American life in the United States and
the Black experience in Africa and the Caribbean. Includes picture books, fiction, folklore, poetry, history, biography, and other nonfiction books for children from
preschool through junior high school

Rand, Donna
Black Books Galore!—guide to great African
American children's books about boys; [by] Donna
Rand, Toni Trent Parker. Wiley 2001 209p il pa
$15.95   **016.3058**
1. African Americans—Bibliography 2. Children's lit-
erature—Bibliography 3. Boys
ISBN 0-471-37527-6   LC 00-42257

An annotated bibliography of approximately 300
recommended titles, divided by age group, with illustrations of the titles covered. An index of titles by topic is
included

Black Books Galore!—guide to great African
American children's books about girls; by Donna
Rand, Toni Trent Parker. Wiley 2000 211pp il pa
$15.95   **016.3058**
1. African Americans—Bibliography 2. Children's lit-
erature—Bibliography 3. Girls
ISBN 0-471-37526-8   LC 00-42258
An annotated bibliography to books arranged by age
from infants and preschoolers through middle-readers.
Photographs, jacket illustrations, and 'spotlight' quotes
from authors and artists highlight the text

016.5 Bibliographies of science

Appraisal; science books for young people.
Children's Science Bk. Review Com.   **016.5**
1. Science—Bibliography—Periodicals 2. Books—Reviews
First published 1967. Ceased publication as a print
product 2000; subscriptions to electronic version with annual CD-ROM $40 from Northeastern University
This periodical "reviews almost all science and math
books published each year that are written for children
and young adults. . . . Some 70 trade books and series
are reviewed in each quarterly issue; two signed reviews,
100-200 words each, by two reviewers, a librarian and a
subject specialist; complete bibliographic and order information and grade level; five rating codes." Safford.
Guide to Ref Books for Sch Media Cent. 5th edition

Outstanding science trade books for children.
Children's Bk. Council pa $2   **016.5**
1. Science—Bibliography 2. Best books

An annual annotated list, reprinted from an issue of
the periodical Science and Children, of the preceding
year's best trade books in the field of science of interest
to children in grades K-8. Prepared by a Book Review
Committee appointed by the National Science Teachers
Association in cooperation with the Children's Book
Council. Titles are selected for accuracy, readability and
pleasing format. General reading levels (primary, intermediate, advanced) are indicated

Science Books & Films. American Assn. for the
Advancement of Science $40 per year   **016.5**
1. Science—Bibliography—Periodicals 2. Books—Reviews 3. Audiovisual materials—Reviews
ISSN 0098-342X
Bimonthly. First published 1965 with title: Science
Books, a quarterly review
"This magazine is an indispensable tool for librarians
in all types of libraries who wish to make informed collection development decisions in the area of science. . . .
Arranged by Dewey decimal class numbers, the reviews
cover books, audiovisual (AV) materials, and even software." Katz. Mag for Libr. 8th edition

016.8   Bibliographies of literature

Colborn, Candy, 1942-
What do children read next? a reader's guide to
fiction for children. Gale Res. $95   **016.8**
1. Best books 2. Children's literature—Bibliography
ISSN 1525-3740

Biennial. First published 1994
Each volume contains over 1,000 entries arranged alphabetically by author, for fiction for children in grades
one through eight. Each annotation includes basic bibliographic information, suggested age range, subject(s) and
genre, names and descriptions of major characters, time
period, locale(s), plot summary, citations of selected reviews, awards received and additional titles on a similar
theme

From biography to history; best books for
children's entertainment and education; edited
by Catherine Barr; foreword by James Cross
Giblin; contributors, Rebecca L. Thomas,
Deanna McDaniel. Bowker 1998 508p il $71
016.8
1. Biography—Bibliography 2. History—Bibliography
ISBN 0-8352-4012-6   LC 98-23147
"This annotated bibliography recommends biographies
and related books that provide information about nearly
300 people of historical interest and the time periods in
which they lived. The entries are arranged alphabetically;
a brief paragraph about the individual is followed by
suggested titles for 'Older Readers' (grades six to nine)
and 'Younger Readers' (grades three to five). The bibliographic information is complete and most of the titles
have been published in the last 10 years." SLJ

Hall, Susan, 1940-
Using picture storybooks to teach literary
devices; recommended books for children and
young adults. 2nd ed. Oryx Press 1994 239p pa
$38.50   **016.8**
1. Children's literature—Bibliography 2. Picture
books for children—Bibliography 3. Literature—Study
and teaching
ISBN 0-89774-849-2   LC 89-8574
Original volume published 1990 available $38.50
(ISBN 0-89774-582-5)
This edition, designated volume 2, contains 300 titles
which expand the coverage of the original volume. The
author advocates the use of picture books in language
arts programs at all grade levels. Entries are listed alphabetically under the literary device they illustrate
"This is a well conceived and functional bibliography.
. . . It will encourage one to take a longer look at the
picture storybook genre and its application to older
youth. An excellent addition to the reference collection
of any school or public library." Voice Youth Advocates
[review of 1990 edition]

Hit list: frequently challenged books for children;
Donna Reidy Pistolis, editor; for the Office for
Intellectual Freedom of the American Library
Association. American Lib. Assn. 1996 61p pa
$22   **016.8**
1. Censorship 2. Children's literature—Bibliography
ISBN 0-8389-3458-7   LC 96-5759
This volume "focuses on 23 titles, ranging from Mau-
rice Sendak's *In the Night Kitchen* and Shel Silverstein's
A Light in the Attic to Brock Cole's *The Goats* and Lois
Lowery's [sic] *The Giver*, as well as three of Alvin
Schwartz's scary stories collections and Michael
Wilhoite's *Daddy's Roommate*. Each entry contains a
long annotation, examples of recent challenges, and cita-
tions of reviews, articles about the book, awards and
prizes, author references, and sources recommending the
book. . . . [Also included is] an appended note on what
ALA can do to help librarians combat censorship."
Booklist

Lynn, Ruth Nadelman, 1948-
Fantasy literature for children and young adults;
an annotated bibliography. 4th ed. Bowker 1995
lxxix, 1092p $55   **016.8**
1. Fantasy fiction—Bibliography 2. Fairy tales—Bibliography
ISBN 0-8352-3456-8   LC 94-42529
First published 1979 with title: Fantasy for children
This volume is divided into two parts. Part One is an
annotated bibliography of 4,800 fantasy novels and story
collections, published between 1900 and 1994, for children and young adults in grades 3-12. Part Two is a research guide to some 10,500 articles, books and disserta-
tions about the authors who write fantasy literature for
children and young adults

Sands, Karen
Back in the spaceship again; juvenile science
fiction series since 1945; [by] Karen Sands and
Marietta Frank. Greenwood Press 1999 152p
(Contributions to the study of science fiction and
fantasy) $55   **016.8**
1. Science fiction—Bibliography
ISBN 0-313-30192-1   LC 99-17848
"The authors delve into the elements of juvenile and
young adult science-fiction series such as 'Animorphs'
'Tom Swift,' and 'Danny Dunn.' The introduction traces
the history of these books and the impact that World
War II and the development of rocket and atomic science
had on the genre. Chapters deal with the inclusion of robots, androids, and artificial intelligence as stock conventions; animals, strange and familiar; the female presence;
the role of humor; the absence or presence of scientific
theory; utopias and dystopias; aliens; and coming-of-age
stories." SLJ

Volz, Bridget Dealy
Junior genreflecting; a guide to good reads and
series fiction for children; [by] Bridget Dealy
Volz, Lynda Blackburn Welborn, and Cheryl
Perkins Scheer. Libraries Unlimited 2000 187p
(Genreflecting advisory series) $28   **016.8**
1. Children's literature—Bibliography 2. Books and
reading
ISBN 1-56308-556-9   LC 99-38135

Volz, Bridget Dealy—*Continued*
"Chapters include contemporary life, fantasy, animals, historical fiction, and mystery. Within these categories books are arranged under specific topics (e.g., girlfriends and friendship, ethnic groups, problem novels). Focusing on books published after 1990, popular paperback series, and the . . . classics, the authors have selected titles noted for quality. A brief historical background of each genre is given, and useful Web sites on children's fiction are listed." Publisher's note

016.9 Bibliographies of geography and history

Adamson, Lynda G.
Literature connections to world history, K-6; resources to enhance and entice. Libraries Unlimited 1998 326p pa $34   **016.9**
1. History—Bibliography 2. Audiovisual materials—Catalogs 3. CD-ROMs—Reviews
ISBN 1-56308-504-6   LC 97-35952
Companion volume to Literature connections to American history, K-6
This bibliography "identifies novels, biographies, history books, CD-ROMs, and videotapes to supplement history courses." Booklist

016.94053 Bibliographies of World War II, 1939-1945

Sullivan, Edward T.
The Holocaust in literature for youth; a guide and resource book. Scarecrow Press 1999 259p $29.50   **016.94053**
1. Holocaust, 1933-1945—Bibliography
ISBN 0-8108-3607-6   LC 98-48768
A "guide to literature of the Holocaust for youth ages ten to seventeen. . . . Each entry contains a synopsis, evaluation of the work's quality, grade level, and notes on special features such as indexes. . . . Fully one-half of the book is devoted to appendixes that include lists of professional resources for the teaching of the Holocaust (including ERIC citations), electronic resources, Holocaust museums and organizations, and a section of booktalks and classroom activities related to the books." Voice Youth Advocates

016.973 Bibliographies of United States history

Adamson, Lynda G.
Literature connections to American history, K-6; resources to enhance and entice. Libraries Unlimited 1998 542p pa $37   **016.973**
1. United States—History—Bibliography 2. Audiovisual materials—Catalogs 3. CD-ROMS—Reviews
ISBN 1-56308-502-X   LC 97-14283
Companion volume to Literature connections to world history, K-6

This bibliography is divided "into two main parts. The first part lists authors and titles in the categories of historical fiction, biography, collective biography, history trade book, CD-ROM, and videotape within specific time periods according to grade levels. The second part contains annotated bibliographies of titles listed in the first part: books, CD-ROMs, and videotapes." Introduction

021.2 Relationships with the community

Scheps, Susan G.
The librarian's guide to homeschooling resources. American Lib. Assn. 1998 151p $25   **021.2**
1. Libraries 2. Home schooling
ISBN 0-8389-0737-7   LC 98-6218
First published 1993 with title: Homeschoolers and the public library
"Schep's book is divided into two sections. The first, 'Serving Homeschoolers', contains information on potential problems encountered in serving homeschoolers, such as staff bias against homeschoolers. . . . Part two contains a directory of resources that includes a listing of national, state, regional, and provincial homeschooling organizations in the U.S. and Canada." J Youth Serv Libr

021.7 Promotion of libraries, information centers

Flowers, Helen F., 1931-
Public relations for school library media programs; 500 ways to influence people and win friends for your school library media center. Neal-Schuman 1998 158p pa $43   **021.7**
1. Libraries—Public relations 2. School libraries
ISBN 1-55570-320-8   LC 98-11470
The author recommends "techniques for promoting the use of the library media services by students, faculty, building administrators, and school support staff. Readers will also learn how to target administrators, the board of education, parents, community, and legislators to maintain and increase suppport for staff, materials, equipment, and space." Publisher's note
"Writing with a sense both of purpose and of humor, Flowers turns a book of excellent lists into a good, entertaining read." Voice Youth Advocates
Includes bibliographical references

025.04 Automated information storage and retrieval systems

McElmeel, Sharron L.
WWW almanac; making curriculum connections to special days, weeks, months; by Sharon L. McElmeel and Carol Smallwood. Linworth Pub. 1999 227p (Professional growth series) pa $36.95   **025.04**
1. World Wide Web 2. Holidays
ISBN 0-938865-78-1   LC 99-41399

McElmeel, Sharron L.—*Continued*

This work provides "Internet sites to link up with various important days—and some less important—throughout the year. Along with the expected holidays, such as New Year's Day, Martin Luther King Jr.'s birthday, and Halloween, there are observances like School Nurse Day, Stephen Foster Memorial Day, and Universal Letter-Writing Week. The name, address, sponsor, and a summary of each site is provided." Booklist

Includes bibliographical references

Minkel, Walter

Delivering Web reference services to young people; [by] Walter Minkel and Roxanne Hsu Feldman. American Lib. Assn. 1998 121p il $32

                                          025.04

1. Children's libraries 2. World Wide Web 3. Library information networks

ISBN 0-8389-0743-1   LC 98-26112

"Minkel and Feldman have written a book designed to guide both school and public librarians through using, teaching, and developing the Web for youth. . . . Descriptions of search tools are given in a manner that anyone trained in research will be able to understand and use easily." J Youth Serv Libr

Includes bibliographical references

025.1   Library administration

Grantsmanship for small libraries and school library media centers; [by] Sylvia D. Hall-Ellis [et al.]; edited by Frank W. Hoffman. Libraries Unlimited 1999 173p pa $32.50   **025.1**

1. Fund raising 2. Subsidies 3. Library finance

ISBN 1-56308-484-8   LC 98-31247

This "guide outlines each step of the process for obtaining grants, providing examples and definitions along the way. . . . This helpful and easy-to-use handbook should be a part of every professional collection." SLJ

Includes bibliographical references

025.2   Acquisitions and collection development

Building a special collection of children's literature in your library; identifying, maintaining, and sharing rare or collectible items; [edited by] Dolores Blythe Jones. American Lib. Assn. 1998 170p pa $40   **025.2**

1. Libraries—Special collections 2. Children's literature

ISBN 0-8389-0726-1   LC 97-43144

"Ten essays that offer advice on many aspects of collection development, acquisition, preservation, funding, and promotion of special collections of children's books in academic or public libraries. The informative discussions cover topics such as acquiring out-of-print materials, securing a professional appraisal of rare books, the elements of a complete catalog record, archival preparation of original materials, organizing a Friends group, preservation and security, and public relations and programming." SLJ

Includes bibliographical references

Ross, Calvin

The frugal youth cybrarian; bargain computing for kids. American Lib. Assn. 1997 321p il pa $35

                                          025.2

1. School libraries 2. Internet 3. Computer software—Catalogs

ISBN 0-8389-0694-X   LC 96-45724

"Ross focuses on helping youth librarians find freeware and shareware programs on the Internet. Part 1 offers an explanation of the advantages (price) and disadvantages (viruses) of downloaded software as well as suggestions for getting connected and bargain hunting. Part 2 includes listings of recommended software for Macintosh and IBM-PC computers and a directory of educational sites located on the World Wide Web, gopher, and FTP. . . . Dedicated shoppers will appreciate Ross' thorough evaluations and comprehensive downloading directions." Booklist

Van Orden, Phyllis J.

Selecting books for the elementary school library media center; a complete guide. Neal-Schuman 2000 212p il pa $49.95   **025.2**

1. School libraries 2. Instructional materials centers

ISBN 1-55570-368-2   LC 99-56394

"The first four chapters give an overview of the selection process and general guidelines for establishing and applying criteria. The remaining nine chapters present measures for evaluating specific genres, including picture books (with color plates illustrating artistic considerations), fiction (including classics and series), genre fiction, folk literature, poetry, informational literature, reference, and professional books." SLJ

025.3   Bibliographic analysis and control

ALA filing rules; [prepared by the] Filing Committee, Resources and Technical Services Division, American Library Association. American Lib. Assn. 1980 50p pa $15   **025.3**

1. Files and filing 2. Library catalogs

ISBN 0-8389-3255-X   LC 80-22186

Successor to ALA Rules for filing catalog cards, second edition

"The rules set forth in *ALA Filing Rules*, which apply to the arrangement of bibliographic records of library materials in card, book, or online format, are based on the 'file-as-is' principle." Nichols. Guide to Ref Books for Sch Media Cent. 4th edition

According to a 1981 announcement of the American Library Association, this may be considered as an alternative to, rather than a definite replacement for, the 1968 edition of ALA Rules for filing catalog cards. Libraries may choose to continue using the earlier publication

Cataloging correctly for kids; an introduction to the tools; Sharon Zuiderveld, editor. 3rd ed. American Lib. Assn. 1998 116p pa $20   **025.3**

1. Cataloging

ISBN 0-8389-3476-5   LC 97-41145

First published 1989 by the Cataloging of Children's Materials Committee

Cataloging correctly for kids—*Continued*
Among the topics discussed are: cataloging nonbook materials; authority control; cataloging Internet sources; curriculum-enhanced MARC; search and retrieval strategies; vendors of cataloging for children's materials
Includes bibliographical references

Gorman, Michael, 1941-
The concise AACR2, 1998 revision; prepared by Michael Gorman. American Lib. Assn. 1999 168p pa $32   **025.3**
1. Anglo-American cataloguing rules 2. Cataloging
ISBN 0-8389-3494-3   LC 98-55150
First published 1988
This practical guide for beginning catalogers incorporates the 1993-1997 Amendments to the Anglo-American cataloguing rules

025.4 Subject analysis and control

Dewey, Melvil, 1851-1931
Abridged Dewey decimal classification and relative index; devised by Melvil Dewey. ed 13, edited by Joan S. Mitchell, Julianne Beall, Winton E. Matthews, Jr., Gregory R. New. Forest Press (Albany) 1997 1023p $90   **025.4**
1. Dewey Decimal Classification
ISBN 0-910608-59-8   LC 97-10791
First abridged edition published 1894
The 13th Abridged Edition is an abridgment of the four volume 21st Edition. Adapted to the needs of small and growing libraries, the 13th Abridged Edition is designed primarily for school and public libraries with collections of up to 20,000 titles

Sears list of subject headings. 17th ed, edited by Joseph Miller. Wilson, H.W. 2000 xlvi, 770p $65   **025.4**
1. Subject headings
ISBN 0-8242-0989-3
Also available Canadian companion to 17th edition $35 (ISBN 0-8242-0979-6)
First published 1923 with title: List of subject headings for small libraries, by Minnie Earl Sears
"A major feature of this seventeenth edition of the Sears List is the revision of the headings for the native peoples of the Western Hemisphere. . . . Also in this edition many new subdivisions have been added to those provided for in the List. . . . The new terms in the present edition represent developments in many different areas, especially computers, personal relations, politics, and popular culture." Preface

Subject headings for children; a list of subject headings used by the Library of Congress with abridged Dewey numbers added; edited by Lois Winkel; numbers verified by Winton E. Matthews, Jr. 2nd ed. Forest Press (Albany) 1998 2v $111.25   **025.4**
1. Subject headings 2. Dewey Decimal Classification
ISBN 0-910608-58-X   LC 98-37183
First published 1994

Contents: v1 List of headings; v2 Keyword index
"A boon to catalogers and customers alike." SLJ

025.5 Services to users

Eisenberg, Michael
Teaching information & technology skills; the Big6 in elementary schools; by Michael B. Eisenberg and Robert E. Berkowitz; with Barbara A. Jansen and Tami J. Little. Linworth Pub. 1999 Xl, 144p il pa $39.95   **025.5**
1. Computer-assisted instruction 2. Research
ISBN 0-938865-81-1   LC 99-29894
The six steps the authors "prescribe are: 'Task Definition,' 'Information Seeking Strategies,' 'Location & Access,' 'Use of information,' 'Synthesis,' and 'Evaluation.' . . . Sample lessons demonstrate how to integrate the Big6 into the curriculum and to teach students how to select appropriate resources, discriminate between needed and superfluous information, and evaluate their progress and success." SLJ
Includes bibliographical references

Heiligman, Deborah
The New York Public Library kid's guide to research. Scholastic Ref. 1998 134p il $14.95; pa $8.95 (5 and up)   **025.5**
1. Research 2. Libraries
ISBN 0-590-30715-0; 0-590-30716-9 (pa)
                                        LC 97-28939
Provides guidance on how to do research, including how to use libraries and their resources, the Internet, and other sources such as interviews and surveys
"Short and complete, this book contains a wealth of material for young researchers. . . . A book that is appealing and informative, with content appeal across the grades." SLJ

027 General libraries, information centers

Munro, Roxie, 1945-
The inside-outside book of libraries; paintings by Roxie Munro; text by Julie Cummins. Dutton Children's Bks. 1996 unp il $15.99 (2-4)   **027**
1. Libraries
ISBN 0-525-45608-2   LC 96-12111
Illustrations and brief text present various types of libraries, from bookmobiles and home libraries to the New York Public Library and the Library of Congress
"Cummins's text flows smoothly and is easy to comprehend, and the vast array of facilities discussed will add greatly to children's understanding of the concept of library services. Munro's excellent watercolor illustrations are extremely detailed and reveal an incredible sense of each architectural space." SLJ

027.62 Libraries for children and young people

Bauer, Caroline Feller, 1935-
Leading kids to books through crafts. American Lib. Assn. 2000 145p $30   **027.62**
1. Children's libraries 2. Book talks 3. Handicraft 4. Children's literature—Bibliography
ISBN 0-8389-0769-5   LC 99-41387
"Bauer gives basic, practical information on presenting programs that introduce preschool and primary-grade youngsters to stories and poems and demonstrates related crafts that are easy to prepare and execute." SLJ

Leading kids to books through magic; illustrated by Richard Laurent. American Lib. Assn. 1996 128p il (Mighty easy motivators) $29   **027.62**
1. Children's libraries 2. Books and reading 3. Children's literature—Bibliography 4. Magic tricks
ISBN 0-8389-0684-2   LC 95-53049
"Bauer shows how she uses magic tricks to entertain children as she leads them to good books. . . . Each section includes instructions for performing at least one trick as well as a short, annotated list of related books and, occasionally, a story or poem to present as part of the magician's patter." Booklist
The author's "concise yet thorough directions accompanied by Richard Laurent's delightful line drawings make this book a useful tool for teachers and librarians looking for ways to promote children's enthusiasm for reading." J Youth Serv Libr

Leading kids to books through puppets; illustrated by Richard Laurent. American Lib. Assn. 1997 156p il (Mighty easy motivators) pa $22   **027.62**
1. Children's libraries 2. Books and reading 3. Puppets and puppet plays 4. Children's literature—Bibliography
ISBN 0-8389-0706-7   LC 97-1357
This "book suggests ways to promote books and reading to children through simple puppetry. . . . [It offers] a number of theme-based programs complete with stories to act out, poems, and lists of related books." Booklist
"Even the most reluctant performer will be encouraged by this practical, concise, easy-to-use book." SLJ

Read for the fun of it; active programming with books for children; drawings by Lynn Gates Bredeson. Wilson, H.W. 1992 xx, 372p il $55   **027.62**
1. Books and reading 2. Children's literature 3. Children's libraries
ISBN 0-8242-0824-2   LC 91-31450
"Among the topics covered are reading aloud, reaching parents, author visits, storytelling with visual aids, teaching children to present stories and poetry, and using puppetry and magic tricks in storytelling." Booklist
"Diagrams, artwork, and word games are . . . scattered appropriately throughout the book. All are reproducible and available for reader use. . . . *Read for the Fun of It* emphasizes Bauer's obvious passion for reading, making this book a delightful addition to the professional collection." J Youth Serv Libr
Includes bibliographical references

Benne, Mae, 1924-
Principles of children's services in public libraries. American Lib. Assn. 1991 332p $45   **027.62**
1. Children's libraries 2. Public libraries 3. Books and reading
ISBN 0-8389-0555-2   LC 90-47427
The author's discussion of public library services to children "falls into four major areas: organizational patterns, design of services, collection development, and facilities. Appendices include examples of budgeting and program forms, and annotated bibliographies of aids for selection, reference services, and programming services to special audiences." Publisher's note

Briggs, Diane
52 programs for preschoolers; the librarian's year-round planner. American Lib. Assn. 1997 217p il pa $30   **027.62**
1. Storytelling 2. Children's libraries
ISBN 0-8389-0705-9   LC 96-52415
"Briggs has outlined 52 programs in thematic units that include 'Celebrations,' 'Multicultural Programs,' 'Animals,' and 'Hodge Podge.' The program outlines suggest books, finger plays, rhymes, flannel-board patterns, videos, crafts, and songs. Full-text rhymes and musical chords are included. . . . Public and school librarians should add the Briggs book to their collections not only for its program value, but as a reference tool for rhymes and songs and as an aid for generating themes." SLJ
Includes discography and bibliographical references

Cullum, Carolyn N.
The storytime sourcebook; a compendium of ideas and resources for storytellers. 2nd ed. Neal-Schuman 1999 469p pa $45   **027.62**
1. Storytelling 2. Children's libraries
ISBN 0-55570-360-7   LC 99-46420
First published 1990
A guide to 146 topics and 2,200 picture books. Appropriate videos and CDs are discussed. A "Topical Calendar," arranged chronologically, suggests holidays or notable events that can be related to a storyhour theme
Includes bibliographical references

DeSalvo, Nancy
Beginning with books; library programming for infants, toddlers, and preschoolers; [by] Nancy N. DeSalvo; foreword by Faith Hektoen. Library Professional Publs. 1993 186p pa $27.50   **027.62**
1. Children's libraries 2. Books and reading
ISBN 0-208-02318-6   LC 92-14858
This is a "presentation of the professional philosophy and practical logistics of library programming for children from infancy through the age of five. . . . [This is] a solid, eminently practical book filled with programming ideas that can be easily adapted to any library setting or budget. A variety of useful information is appended." Booklist

Fasick, Adele M., 1930-
Managing children's services in the public library. 2nd ed. Libraries Unlimited 1998 218p il pa $37   **027.62**
1. Children's libraries 2. Public libraries 3. Books and reading
ISBN 1-56308-526-7   LC 97-41688
First published 1991
The author offers "advice on the many responsibilities of children's services managers in public libraries. She includes all of the basics of administration—from budgeting and creating goals and objectives to hiring new staff. . . . In addition, she devotes several pages to Web-page design, children's list-servs, and other technological innovations." Booklist
Includes bibliographical references

Feinberg, Sandra, 1946-
Running a parent/child workshop; a how-to-do-it manual for librarians; [by] Sandra Feinberg, Kathleen Deere; with special assistance from the staff of the Middle Country Public Library. Neal-Schuman 1995 166p il (How-to-do-it manuals for librarians) pa $32.50   **027.62**
1. Children's libraries
ISBN 1-55570-189-2   LC 94-46345
"The goals of the workshop, Feinberg says, are to increase parents' awareness of library services and materials, to tell them about child development and community agencies, and to provide a comfortable place for parent-child interaction. The authors provide bibliographies of materials for both children and parents. . . . Also included are sample program forms, publicity ideas, suggestions for workshop content, floor plans for workshop space, a list of references, and an index." SLJ

Fiore, Carole D.
Running summer library reading programs; a how-to-do-it manual. Neal-Schuman 1998 xx, 158p il (How-to-do-it manuals for librarians) pa $55
                                               027.62
1. Children's libraries 2. Books and reading
ISBN 1-55570-312-7   LC 97-49204
"Fiore's text combines theory, step-by-step instructions, and case studies to help librarians implement and improve children's and teens' summer reading programs, including staffing, budgeting, using teen volunteers, incorporating multicultural materials, and working with children with disabilities." Booklist
Includes bibliographical references

Jeffery, Debby Ann
Literate beginnings; programs for babies and toddlers. American Lib. Assn. 1995 162p il pa $30
                                               027.62
1. Children's libraries 2. Books and reading
ISBN 0-8389-0640-0   LC 95-10691
The author "begins with a section devoted to successful baby/toddler programming, including discussions of child development, program planning and presentation, tips for success, and suggestions for content. The main part of the book is made up of 52 program sheets (with

instructions) that cover familiar themes from families to animals to holidays. Anyone designing programs for the youngest library customers will appreciate this book." SLJ
Includes bibliographical references

MacDonald, Margaret Read
Bookplay; 101 creative themes to share with young children; with drawings by Julie Liana MacDonald. Library Professional Publs. 1995 xx, 225p il music $35   **027.62**
1. Children's libraries 2. Books and reading
ISBN 0-208-02280-5   LC 94-25146
The author offers "suggestions for library programs for the younger patrons. She demonstrates an appealing combination of pragmatism and lack of inhibition, offering thematically linked sessions ranging from whales to self-esteem involving finger plays, songs, readalouds, art projects, and various other activities. Musical notation for songs, a bibliography (cross-referenced to program numbers), and an index are included." Bull Cent Child Books

Marino, Jane
Mother Goose time; library programs for babies and their caregivers; by Jane Marino and Dorothy F. Houlihan; music arrangements by Jane Marino; photographs by Susan G. Drinker. Wilson, H.W. 1992 172p il music $40   **027.62**
1. Children's libraries 2. Nursery rhymes
ISBN 0-8242-0850-1   LC 91-46986
"The book was inspired by a program designed by the authors, librarians . . . who conducted 'Mother Goose Time' sessions for more than five years at the White Plains, New York, Public Library. These interactive sessions involved sharing songs and rhymes with babies and adults. . . . There are musical arrangements for the songs; bibliographies of picture books, display books, and resource books; an evaluation of form; and various indexes categorizing the rhymes and songs by title, first line, and developmental level." J Youth Serv Libr

Nespeca, Sue McCleaf
Library programming for families with young children. Neal-Schuman 1994 180p il (How-to-do-it manuals for librarians) $47 **027.62**
1. Children's libraries
ISBN 1-55570-181-7   LC 94-37894
The author "outlines the developmental characteristics of young children, providing book-sharing ideas for different age groups, sample family programs, current bibliographies of suggested titles, and places to write for additional information. Multicultural, intergenerational, institutional, and outreach programs are discussed separately, with suggestions for their implementation." SLJ
Includes bibliographical references

Nichols, Judy
Storytimes for two-year-olds; illustrated by Lori D. Sears. 2nd ed. American Lib. Assn. 1998 248p il pa $28   **027.62**
1. Storytelling 2. Children's libraries
ISBN 0-8389-0719-9   LC 97-44295

Nichols, Judy—*Continued*
First published 1987
The author describes 50 library programs for children aged 18 months to 36 months which center on picture books and include "rhythms, rhymes, and finger plays; crafts; and parents' follow-up suggestions. . . . Storytelling devices, such as the professional bibliography and discography, four indexes, and black-and-white illustrations, increase the value of this accessible professional resource." Booklist
Includes bibliographical references

Sierra, Judy
The flannel board storytelling book. 2nd ed rev & expanded. Wilson, H.W. 1997 241p il music $45   **027.62**
1. Children's libraries 2. Storytelling
ISBN 0-8242-0932-X   LC 97-15107
First published 1987
"Fifty stories, poems, and songs and over three hundred patterns are included for presenting stories to children in a flannel board medium, including classic children's stories, nursery rhymes, folk tales, and songs. . . . Sierra's experience telling stories with children is reflected throughout her book." J Youth Serv Libr

Wadham, Tim
Programming with Latino children's materials; a how-to-do-it manual for librarians. Neal-Schuman 1999 314p (How-to-do-it manuals for librarians) pa $39.95   **027.62**
1. Children's libraries 2. Children's literature—Bibliography 3. Hispanic Americans 4. Latin America—Civilization
ISBN 1-55570-352-6   LC 98-52056
"Wadham first discusses various groups comprising Latinos in the U.S. and such related topics as language variations, national origins, cultural holidays, and bilingualism—always turning back to what it all means to practicing professionals. He then provides a country-by-country summary of Latino children's literature. . . . Following a review of Latino folklore, he offers a treasure trove of programming—bilingual finger plays, puppet shows, performance-tested scripts—and information on various types of Latino literature. . . . [An] invaluable resource that may well become the standard." Booklist
Includes bibliographical references

Walter, Virginia A.
Output measures for public library service to children; a manual of standardized procedures. American Lib. Assn. 1992 129p pa $25   **027.62**
1. Children's libraries 2. Public libraries
ISBN 0-8389-3404-8   LC 91-44354
"This manual has been designed as a tool for quantifying and measuring the results of public library service to children. . . . Among the many topics covered are material use measures, in-library use of children's materials, and children's library visits. Other management techniques, such as focus groups and user surveys, add an extra dimension." Booklist
Includes bibliographical references

027.6205   Libraries for children and young people—Serial publications

Journal of Youth Services in Libraries. American Lib. Assn. $40 per year   **027.6205**
1. Young adults' libraries—Periodicals 2. Children's libraries—Periodicals 3. Books—Reviews
ISSN 0894-2498
Quarterly. Formerly Top of the News
"This publication includes news, columns, bibliographic essays, refereed feature articles, and reviews of professional reading." Katz. Mag for Libr. 10th edition

027.8   School libraries

American Association of School Librarians
Information power; building partnerships for learning; prepared by the American Association of School Librarians [and] Association for Educational Communications and Technology. American Lib. Assn. 1998 205p il pa $35   **027.8**
1. School libraries 2. Instructional materials centers
ISBN 0-8389-3470-6   LC 98-23291
First published 1988
This resource "relates the library-media program to the entire educational infrastructure. The authors explicate their themes in terms of standards, indicators, levels of proficiency, goals, principles, and examples of student activities. The appendixes contain essential information on Library Power, AASL's ICON-nect project, the Library Bill of Rights, confidentiality, censorship, access equity, and ethics." SLJ
Includes bibliographical references

Bradburn, Frances Bryant
Output measures for school library media programs. Neal-Schuman 1999 95p pa $49.95   **027.8**
1. School libraries 2. Instructional materials centers
ISBN 1-55570-326-7   LC 98-45557
"Bradburn's handbook is intended to guide school library specialists in collecting data on budgets, staff, and services and in using the data to evaluate programs and argue for increased funding. Forms and work sheets as well as three case studies are included." Booklist
Includes bibliographical references

Bucher, Katherine Toth, 1947-
Information technology for schools. 2nd ed. Linworth Pub. 1998 400p il (Professional growth series) pa $39.95   **027.8**
1. School libraries 2. Instructional materials centers
ISBN 0-938865-65-X   LC 97-41032
First published 1994 with title: Computers & technology in school library media centers
Among the topics discussed are: instructional technology, library management, telecommunications, television and distance learning, multi-media presentations, CD-Roms, videodiscs, and local area networks. Diagrams, sample record-keeping forms, and instructions for using equipment accompany the text
Includes bibliographical references

Exploring science in the library; resources and activities for young people; edited by Maria Sosa and Tracy Gath. American Lib. Assn. 1999 236p pa $32 **027.8**
1. Elementary school libraries 2. Science—Study and teaching
ISBN 0-8389-0768-7 LC 99-41496
This "resource helps public and school librarians develop science, math, and technology resources for K-12 students, supporting the recent national efforts toward achieving science literacy." SLJ

School Library Journal's best; a reader for children's, young adult & school librarians; edited by Lillian N. Gerhardt; compiled by Marilyn L. Miller & Thomas W. Downen. Neal-Schuman 1997 474p il $49.95 **027.8**
1. School libraries 2. Children's libraries 3. Young adults' libraries
ISBN 1-55570-203-1 LC 96-23856
This is a collection of articles and columns culled from issues of SLJ from 1971 to the present. Contributors include Ursula Nordstrom, Margaret McElderry, Zena Sutherland, and June Jordan
"A useful overview of professional writing of the last quarter-century." Bull Cent Child Books
Includes bibliographical references

Zweizig, Douglas
Lessons from Library Power; enriching teaching and learning: final report of the evaluation of the national library power initiative: an initiative of the DeWitt Wallace-Reader's Digest Fund; [by] Douglas L. Zweizig and Dianne McAfee Hopkins; with Norman Lott Webb and Gary Wehlage. Libraries Unlimited 1999 281p $37.50 **027.8**
1. Library Power (Program) 2. School libraries
ISBN 1-56308-833-9 LC 99-52025
The authors "examine the specific goals and accomplishments of Library Power, the school library funding project initiated in 1988 by the DeWitt Wallace—Reader's Digest Fund. Having analyzed surveys collected from teachers, librarians, and principals, and case studies of media center practices, they conclude that collaborative planning, flexible scheduling, collection development, and professional growth can make a positive difference in libraries and the students that they support." Booklist
Includes bibliographical references

027.805 School libraries—Serial publications

Library Talk; the magazine for elementary school library media and technology specialists. Linworth Pub. $49 per year **027.805**
1. School libraries—Periodicals
Five issues per year. First published 1988
Provides articles, tips and ideas for day-to-day school library management. Each issue highlights a particular concern of the school librarian
"The articles are practical and full of useful ideas that school librarians can try. The book and media reviews are numerous and of good quality." Katz. Mag for Libr. 8th edition

School Library Journal; the magazine of children's, young adult, and school libraries. Bowker $97.50 per year **027.805**
1. School libraries—Periodicals 2. Books—Reviews
ISSN 0362-8930
Monthly. First published 1954 with title: Junior Libraries
In addition to the feature articles this journal includes "a calendar of events, news from the field, notes on people, columns . . . as well as many reviews of professional reading, books for children and young adults, audiovisuals, and computer software. The annual 'Reference Books Roundup' is an indispensable selection tool. This is an essential professional journal for school and public librarians." Katz. Mag for Libr. 10th edition

School Library Media Annual. Libraries Unlimited lib bdg $45 **027.805**
1. School libraries—Periodicals 2. Instructional materials centers—Periodicals
ISSN 0739-7712
Annual. First published 1983
This annual "is designed to keep practitioners abreast of new developments in the school media area. It is an essential source for school media specialists. Part 1 contains articles of current interest. . . . Part 2 has reports from professional organizations and governing bodies; a list of institutions that offer degree programs in library and information science, school library media services, and educational media; and award recipients. The final part lists the best books and software and award-winning books for the previous year." Nichols. Guide to Ref Books for Sch Media Cent. 4th edition

028.1 Reviews of books and other media

AudioFile; the audiobook review. AudioFile Publs. $60 per year **028.1**
1. Audiobooks—Reviews
ISSN 1063-0244
Bimonthly. First published 1992 as monthly
Price of subscription includes *AudioFile* issues, the *Audiobook Reference Guide* and the *Annual Index of Titles* (published in May)
"AudioFile reviews unabridged and abridged audiobooks, original audio programs, commentary and dramatizations in the spoken-word format. Our focus is the audio presentation, not the critique of the written material." Publisher's note

Bauermeister, Erica
Let's hear it for the girls; 375 great books for readers 2-14; [by] Erica Bauermeister and Holly Smith. Penguin Bks. 1997 224p pa $10.95 **028.1**
1. Girls—Books and reading 2. Children's literature—Bibliography
ISBN 0-14-025732-2 LC 96-9791
This bibliography attempts to address "the need to provide children with strong female role models. . . . [This guide] is organized by reading level and includes fiction, nonfiction, biography, poetry, and picture books by both women and men writers from all over the world. Cross-referenced indexes by author, title, date, country, genre, and subject." Publisher's note

Baxter, Kathleen A.

Gotcha! nonfiction booktalks to get kids excited about reading; by Kathleen A. Baxter [and] Marcia Agness Kochel. Libraries Unlimited 1999 183p pa $24.50   **028.1**
1. Books and reading
ISBN 1-56308-683-2   LC 99-34279
This guide to booktalking discusses more than 350 titles for grades one through eight
The books are presented in a "conversational style that is extremely readable and entertaining; useful bibliographies following each section assign appropriate grade levels to the books. The authors also give general tips on organizing booktalks." SLJ

The **Best** in children's books; the University of Chicago guide to children's literature, 1966-1972—1985-1990; written and edited by Zena Sutherland. University of Chicago Press 1973-1991 4v   **028.1**
1. Children's literature—Bibliography 2. Best books 3. Books—Reviews

Successor to Good books for children; a selection of outstanding children's books published 1950-65, compiled by Mary K. Eakin
1985-1990 volume written by Zena Sutherland, Betsy Hearne, and Roger Sutton
Volumes available are: 1966-1972 $39 (ISBN 0-226-78057-0); 1973-1978 $39 (ISBN 0-226-78059-7); 1979-1984 $50 (ISBN 0-226-78060-0); 1985-1990 $50 (ISBN 0-226-78064-3)
These volumes bring together reviews originally published in The Bulletin of the Center for Children's Books. Some 1400 recommended titles from each period are covered in each volume. The listings are arranged alphabetically by author, with title, developmental values, curricular use, reading level, subject, and type of literature indexes

Booklist. American Lib. Assn. $74.50 per year   **028.1**
1. Books—Reviews 2. Best books
ISSN 0006-7385
Semimonthly September through June; monthly July and August. First published 1905 with title: A.L.A. Booklist. Merged with Subscription Books Bulletin in 1956
The Reference Books Bulletin section is also available separately in an annual cumulation for $28.50
"Intended chiefly as a guide for librarians in public and school libraries, each issue covers titles in five major areas: forthcoming titles, adult books, books for youth, audiovisual media, and reference books. . . . Because of its selectivity, its early reviews, and its broad coverage of popular non-print media, *Booklist* is essential reading for public, school, and many academic libraries." Katz. Mag for Libr. 10th edition

Bulletin of the Center for Children's Books. University of Ill. Press $50 per year   **028.1**
1. Books—Reviews 2. Children's literature—Periodicals
ISSN 0008-9036
Monthly except August. First published 1945 for the University of Chicago, Graduate Library School

"This highly regarded reviewing source covers selected titles from the thousands of children's books published each year. In addition to complete bibliographic information, the critical annotations are supplemented by an indication of suitable age and/or grade level 2nd a shorthand code noting a range of quality, from 'books of special distinction' to 'NR' for not recommended. . . . Librarians in schools, public libraries, and academic libraries with children's literature collections will find this an indispensable guide." Katz. Mag for Libr. 10th edition

Cianciolo, Patricia J., 1929-

Informational picture books for children. American Lib. Assn. 2000 205p pa $38   **028.1**
1. Picture books for children—Bibliography
ISBN 0-8389-0774-1   LC 99-39597
"Cianciolo lists the criteria for inclusion and discusses trends in informational picture books. Subsequent chapters provide lengthy critical annotations, including recommended age levels, divided into categories such as 'The Natural World,' 'Numbers and Arithmetic,' 'Peoples and Cultures,' And 'Arts and Crafts.' The approximately 250 titles are up-to-date, and though most of them would be considered nonfiction, a handful of titles are classified as fiction or include fictionalized elements." SLJ
Includes bibliographical references

Horning, Kathleen T.

From cover to cover; evaluating and reviewing children's books. HarperCollins Pubs. 1997 230p $24.95; pa $13.95   **028.1**
1. Books—Reviews 2. Children's literature—History and criticism
ISBN 0-06-024519-0; 0-06-446167-X (pa)
         LC 96-27281
The author "begins with an overview of how children's books are published in the United States, the physical parts of the book, and categories of children's books. The next six chapters are devoted to the definition and scope of those categories." Bull Cent Child Books
"Anyone entering the field of children's book reviewing, or indeed, the wider field of children's literature, will find *From Cover to Cover* an excellent guide to analyzing books and presenting clear, useful reviews." Booklist
Includes bibliographical references

Odean, Kathleen

Great books for boys; more than 600 books for boys 2 to 14. Ballantine Bks. 1998 384p pa $12.95   **028.1**
1. Boys—Books and reading 2. Children's literature—Bibliography 3. Young adult literature—Bibliography
ISBN 0-345-42083-7   LC 97-45926
This annotated bibliography offers recommended titles and strategies for parents, teachers, and librarians to promote reading among boys
"An excellent resource!" SLJ

Great books for girls; over 600 books to inspire today's girls and tomorrow's women. Ballantine Bks. 1997 420p pa $14   **028.1**
1. Girls—Books and reading 2. Children's literature—Bibliography 3. Young adult literature—Bibliography
ISBN 0-345-40484-X   LC 96-44392

Odean, Kathleen—*Continued*
This bibliography "introduces 600 titles, ranging from picture-story books for toddlers to biographies and novels for adolescents that depict girls and women who are self-sufficient, decisive, and assertive. . . . Odean's background as a children's book expert is apparent in her well-crafted, descriptive annotations. . . . The introduction and last chapter provide advice about locating good children's books, reading aloud, etc." Libr J

028.5 Reading and use of other information media by children and young people

Author talk; conversations with Judy Blume [et al.]; compiled and edited by Leonard S. Marcus. Simon & Schuster Bks. for Young Readers 2000 103p il $22 (4 and up) **028.5**
1. Authors
ISBN 0-689-81383-X   LC 99-39777
Presents interviews with fifteen well-known children's writers, including Judy Blume, Karen Cushman, Russell Freedman, James Howe, Lois Lowry, Gary Paulsen, and Laurence Yep
"In addition to the editor's well-crafted introductions to the writers, the volume contains contemporary photos and childhood snapshots, reproductions of edited manuscript pages and a selected bibliography of each author's oeuvre. An excellent choice for aspiring writers and avid readers." Publ Wkly

Bauer, Caroline Feller, 1935-
This way to books; drawings by Lynn Gates. Wilson, H.W. 1983 363p il $55   **028.5**
1. Books and reading 2. Children's literature
ISBN 0-8242-0678-9   LC 82-19985
"Designed to involve children in books, this compendium is chock-full of ideas for programs, booktalks, games, crafts, and exhibits. Bauer's upbeat tone lends enthusiasm, and her numerous suggestions, which include easy-to-implement activities, short poems, directions for crafts, recipes, and unusual but effective bibliographies, will inspire readers with new ideas. . . . Teachers, librarians, and other adults working with children will find the collection worthwhile and helpful as a springboard to their own variations." Booklist

Booktalk! 2-5. Wilson, H.W. 1985-1993 4v ea pa $40   **028.5**
1. Books and reading
ISBN 0-8242-0716-5 (v2); 0-8242-0764-5 (v3); 0-8242-0835-8 (v4); 0-8242-0836-6 (v5)
Original Booktalk! published 1980 o.p.
Edited by Joni Bodart-Talbot
Volume 2 explains what booktalks are and contains 250 examples; volume 3 offers 500 booktalks and has a combined index to booktalks in volumes 2-3; volume 4 is a collection of 350 booktalks and 5 articles which appeared in the Booktalker section of Wilson Library Bulletin between September 1989 and May 1992; volume 5 adds 320 more talks and 4 articles on booktalking

Caldecott Medal books, 1938-1957; with the artist's acceptance papers & related material chiefly from The Horn Book Magazine; edited by Bertha Mahony Miller and Elinor Whitney Field. Horn Bk. 1957 329p il o.p.   **028.5**
1. Children's literature—History and criticism 2. Illustrators

Companion volume to Newbery Medal books, 1922-1955
"Horn Book papers"
"A short study of Randolph Caldecott, for whom the award is named, prefaces the chronological listing of the award books. With this listing are given the acceptance speech of each artist and a biographical sketch of each." Booklist
Followed by Newbery and Caldecott Medal books, 1956-1965 (o.p.)

Cameron, Eleanor, 1912-1996
The seed and the vision; on the writing and appreciation of children's books. Dutton Children's Bks. 1993 xx, 362p o.p.   **028.5**
1. Children's literature—History and criticism
2. Books and reading
LC 92-8220
A series of essays examining the writing, themes, influence, range, and critical appreciation of children's books
"Thoughtful and probing, Cameron's critiques bring a broad range of reading and a rigorous intellect to bear on children's books." Booklist

Children's books and their creators; Anita Silvey, editor. Houghton Mifflin 1995 800p il $40
028.5
1. Children's literature—Bio-bibliography 2. Children's literature—History and criticism
ISBN 0-395-65380-0   LC 95-19049
This volume "compiles, in alphabetical order, 823 articles, most of them essays on contemporary creators of children's books. Writers as early as Aesop and as varied as Anna Sewell and Mark Twain are also included. . . . Each essay focuses on the subject's importance to the field of children's books and notes major contributions. . . . Silvey's editorial judgment is sound, and the entries, although varying in quality and depth, are usually well done." SLJ

Children's books: awards & prizes; includes prizes and awards for young adult books; compiled & edited by the Children's Book Council. Children's Bk. Council $60   **028.5**
1. Literary prizes—Bibliography 2. Children's literature—Bibliography 3. Young adult literature—Bibliography
ISSN 0069-3472

First published 1969. (1996 edition) Periodically revised
This publication lists approximately 200 awards divided as follows: Part I: United States awards selected by adults; Part II: United States awards selected by young readers; Part III: Australian, Canadian, New Zealand, and

Children's books: awards & prizes—*Continued*
United Kingdom (UK) awards; Part IV: Selected international and multinational awards; Part V: Awards classified; Part VI: Publications and lists for selecting U. S. children's and young adult books. A brief history of each award precedes the list of winners

The **Coretta** Scott King Awards book, 1970-1999; edited by Henrietta M. Smith. American Lib. Assn. 1999 135p pa $32   **028.5**
1. Coretta Scott King Award 2. Children's literature—History and criticism 3. American literature—African American authors 4. African Americans in literature
ISBN 0-8389-3496-X   LC 99-25046
First published 1994
This work begins with discussions of the 1994-1999 award winners and honor books and then goes back year by year to 1969
"The text is broken up with quotes from the winning titles, and the book ends with photos and biographies of the authors and artists. An essential resource." Booklist

Dresang, Eliza T.
Radical change; books for youth in a digital age. Wilson, H.W. 1999 xxiv, 344p il $50   **028.5**
1. Children's literature—History and criticism 2. Youth—Books and reading 3. Literature and technology 4. Publishers and publishing
ISBN 0-8242-0953-2   LC 98-34791
The author offers a "look at YA and children's contemporary literature that shows how 'handheld' books are changing in today's digital world. . . . She addresses how today's youth, the Net Generation, thinks and learns; the types of handheld books they are reading; their access to the digital world. . . . Each chapter closes with valuable lists: one of books for youth, the other, professional resources. . . . Professionals who work with youth will come away from this with a new understanding of contemporary youth literature and how to evaluate it." Booklist

Gillespie, John Thomas, 1928-
Juniorplots 4; a book talk guide for use with readers ages 12-16; by John T. Gillespie and Corinne J. Naden. Bowker; distributed by Greenwood Press 1993 450p $42   **028.5**
1. Books—Reviews 2. Stories, plots, etc.—Collections 3. Books and reading
ISBN 0-8352-3167-4   LC 92-35670
Continues Gillespie's Juniorplots (1967), More juniorplots (1977), and Juniorplots 3 (1987)
This volume provides entries for 80 contemporary fiction and nonfiction titles arranged by genre. Cumulative author, title and subject indexes for the earlier Juniorplots volumes are included in this volume

Middleplots 4; a book talk guide for use with readers ages 8-12; by John T. Gillespie and Corinne J. Naden. Bowker 1994 434p $45 **028.5**
1. Books—Reviews 2. Stories, plots, etc.—Collections 3. Books and reading
ISBN 0-8352-3446-0   LC 93-21146
Continues Gillespie's Introducing books (1970), Introducing more books, by D. L. Spirt (1978), and Introducing bookplots 3, by D. L. Spirt (1988)

"The selections are organized thematically in eight interest categories such as 'Adventure and Mystery' and 'Other Lands and Times.' Each selection is organized under six sections: plot summary, thematic material, booktalk suggestions, similar books, review citations, and books and articles about the author. . . . Author, title, and subject indexes for this volume are followed by cumulative author, title, and subject indexes to the series." Booklist
Includes bibliographical references

The Newbery companion; booktalk and related materials for Newbery medal and honor books; [by] John T. Gillespie, Corinne J. Naden. Libraries Unlimited 1996 406p $56   **028.5**
1. Newbery Medal 2. Children's literature—History and criticism 3. Authors
ISBN 1-56308-356-6   LC 96-23699
"For each winning title there is a detailed plot summary, a discussion of themes and subjects, passages for booktalking and reading aloud, related children's books for follow-up reading, biographical references about the author, and sources for the acceptance speech. For each Honor book there is a brief plot summary. An introductory essay covers the history of the award, and there's a final general bibliography. This will be a much used reference by teachers, librarians, and students." Booklist

Hearne, Betsy Gould
Choosing books for children; a commonsense guide; [by] Betsy Hearne with Deborah Stevenson. 3rd ed. University of Ill. Press 1999 229p il $27.95; pa $14.95   **028.5**
1. Books and reading 2. Children's literature—Bibliography
ISBN 0-252-02516-4; 0-252-06928-5 (pa)
                         LC 99-6144
First published 1981 by Delacorte Press
"The focus is on books since 1950; the 14 chapter-opening illustrations mainly represent books of the last decade. Chapters divide books by age and genre; one chapter considers the value of controversial books while another affectionately revisits classics." Publ Wkly

Hey! listen to this; stories to read aloud; edited by Jim Trelease. Viking 1992 414p hardcover o.p. paperback available $13.95   **028.5**
1. Books and reading 2. Literature—Collections 3. Authors
ISBN 0-14-014653-9 (pa)   LC 91-37668
"Divided into categories such as 'Animal Tales,' 'Children of Courage,' or 'Classic Tales,' the forty-eight selections cover a wide spectrum from folktales to fantasy, classics to contemporary stories. More than half are complete stories, while the remainder are one or two chapters from longer books. Trelease skillfully weaves his choices into a cohesive whole. Beyond merely categorizing them, he refers to other authors or stories in the discussions that precede and follow each story." J Youth Serv Libr
Includes bibliographies

Huck, Charlotte S.
Children's literature in the elementary school; [by] Charlotte S. Huck, Susan Hepler, Janet Hickman. Harcourt Brace College Pubs. $81.30
028.5
1. Children's literature—History and criticism

First published 1961. (7th edition 2000) Periodically revised
This resource "provides criteria for evaluation of various kinds of genres and discusses favorite books of children at various developmental levels as well as children's responses to literature. It also suggests ideas on how to plan and extend the literature program in the classroom. Lists Book Awards and Book Selection Aids and includes subject and author/illustrator/title indexes." N Y Public Libr. Ref Books for Child Collect. 2d edition

Jones, Raymond E.
Characters in children's literature. Gale Res. 1997 529p il $86
028.5
1. Children's literature—History and criticism 2. Characters and characteristics in literature
ISBN 0-7876-0400-3
LC 97-4999
This work features essays which describe more than 1,700 characters from 230 works of childrens fiction. Each essay includes a plot summary and an analysis of the character's role in the story
Includes bibliographical references

Knowles, Elizabeth, 1946-
More reading connections; bringing parents, teachers, and librarians together; [by] Elizabeth Knowles and Martha Smith. Libraries Unlimited 1999 148p il pa $26.50
028.5
1. Books and reading
ISBN 1-56308-723-5
Also available Reading connections pa $23 (ISBN 0-56308-436-8)
The authors present "information about starting and participating in elementary and middle school book clubs. The authors introduce 13 topics such as the arts, humor, families in transition, folklore and mythology, sports fiction, the Internet, and banned books. Each chapter contains guided reading questions, a related journal article . . . and an additional annotated list of articles." SLJ

Konigsburg, E. L.
TalkTalk; a children's book author speaks to grown-ups. Atheneum Pubs. 1995 198p il $29.95
028.5
1. Children's literature—History and criticism
ISBN 0-689-31993-2
LC 94-32341
"A Jean Karl book"
"Nine entertaining and provocative speeches, ranging from the author's 1968 Newbery acceptance to a reassuring rationale for the continuing significance of children's books in the multimedia nineties." J Youth Serv Libr

Leonhardt, Mary
Keeping kids reading; how to raise avid readers in the video age. Crown 1996 264p $23; pa $12
028.5
1. Reading 2. Books and reading
ISBN 0-517-70114-6; 0-517-88849-1 (pa)
LC 96-4
The author "offers practical guidance to parents who want to instill in their kids a love of reading and an appreciation of literature. . . . Leonhardt explains not only why it's necessary but also, in very down-to-earth terms, how it can be done—for teens, perhaps the toughest to teach, but especially for young children who are just becoming acqainted with books." Booklist
Includes bibliographical references

Lewis, Valerie V.
Valerie & Walter's best books for children; a lively, opinionated guide; [by] Valerie V. Lewis and Walter M. Mayes. Avon Bks. 1998 708p pa $15.95
028.5
1. Children's literature—Bibliography 2. Books and reading
ISBN 0-380-79438-1
LC 98-7711
"Written by children's bookstore owner and a storyteller, this volume offers readers a pep talk and a guide to sharing literature. . . . More than 2000 entries include paragraph summaries and evaluations of nonfiction and fiction titles for children from birth to adolescence. Arranged by interest and reading levels, the listings are identified by several themes." SLJ
"The writing style is casual and chatty, and the tone is animated and enthusiastic throughout, with both compilers contributing their feelings and impressions of specific titles, authors, illustrators, and issues." Bull Cent Child Books

The **Newbery** & Caldecott medal books, 1986-2000; a comprehensive guide to the winners; [by] the Horn Book, Association for Library Service to Children. American Lib. Assn. 2001 368p il pa $38
028.5
1. Newbery Medal 2. Caldecott Medal 3. Children's literature—History and criticism 4. Authors 5. Illustrators
ISBN 0-8389-3505-2
LC 00-53430
This volume "chronologically presents the Newbery and Caldecott acceptance speeches, biographical essays on the authors and artists, and the original *Horn Book Magazine* and *Booklist* reviews of the award winners." Horn Book
Includes bibliographical references

The **Newbery** and Caldecott awards; a guide to the medal and honor books; [by] Association for Library Service to Children. American Lib. Assn. il pa $18
028.5
1. Newbery Medal 2. Caldecott Medal
ISSN 1070-4493

Annual
"An annotated listing of winning titles since the inception of the awards (1922 and 1938 respectively). . . . Annotations serve as a reliable guide for colllection development, reader's advisory, curriculum development, and a host of other programs." Publisher's note

Newbery and Caldecott Medal books, 1966-1975; with acceptance papers, biographies, and related material chiefly from The Horn Book magazine; edited by Lee Kingman. Horn Bk. 1975 xx, 321p il $22.95   **028.5**
1. Newbery Medal 2. Caldecott Medal 3. Children's literature—History and criticism 4. Authors 5. Illustrators
ISBN 0-87675-003-X
Continues Newbery Medal books, 1922-1955, Caldecott Medal books, 1938-1957, and Newbery and Caldecott Medal books, 1956-1965 (o.p.)
"Gives for each Newbery or Caldecott award winner his acceptance speech, a biographical note, and a book note. An excerpt from each Newbery book gives an example of the writer's style; a sample illustration from each Caldecott book is supplemented by notes on size, medium, printing process, number of illustrations and type used." Choice

Newbery and Caldecott Medal books, 1976-1985; with acceptance papers, biographies, and related material chiefly from The Horn Book magazine; edited by Lee Kingman. Horn Bk. 1986 358p il $24.95   **028.5**
1. Newbery Medal 2. Caldecott Medal 3. Children's literature—History and criticism 4. Authors 5. Illustrators
ISBN 0-87675-004-8   LC 86-15223
This volume "compiles the winning speeches, biographies and book notes for the 1976 through 1985 awards. It includes essays by Barbara Bader, Ethel Heins and Zena Sutherland." Bookbird

Newbery Medal books, 1922-1955; with their authors' acceptance papers & related material chiefly from The Horn Book magazine; edited by Bertha Mahony Miller and Elinor Whitney Field. Horn Bk. 1955 458p il $22.95   **028.5**
1. Newbery Medal 2. Children's literature—History and criticism 3. Authors
ISBN 0-87675-000-5
Companion volume to Caldecott Medal books, 1938-1957
"Largely biographical notes about award recipients and the acceptance papers." Ref Sources for Small & Medium-sized Libr. 5th edition

Only connect: readings on children's literature; edited by Sheila Egoff [et al.] 3rd ed. Oxford Univ. Press 1996 416p il pa $24.95   **028.5**
1. Children's literature—History and criticism
ISBN 0-19-541024-6
First published 1969 and analyzed in Essay and general literature index
This volume "presents a completely new selection of more than 40 essays and brief studies on history and criticism, literary standards, changing tastes, science fiction, young adult literature, fantasy, the problem novel, racism, and sexism. Among the essayists are Joan Aiken, Margaret Mahy, P.L. Travers, Perry Nodelman, Brian Attebery, John Rowe Townsend, Myra Cohn Livingston, Peter Hunt, and Jane Yolen." Publisher's note

Stephens, Claire Gatrell
Coretta Scott King Award books; using great literature with children and young adults. Libraries Unlimited 2000 238p pa $26   **028.5**
1. Coretta Scott King Award 2. Children's literature—History and criticism 3. Young adult literature—History and criticism 4. American literature—African American authors 5. African Americans in literature
ISBN 1-56308-685-9   LC 99-51955
"Both author and illustrator award lists are followed by annotated bibliographies. Twelve of the author entries also feature biographical information. The book is chock-full of curricular units for 15 selected titles. The units include discussion questions, crossword puzzles, vocabulary exercises, performance activities, and integrated curriculum ideas. Additionally, lists of related materials and Internet sites are provided." Book Rep
Includes bibliographical references

Sutherland, Zena, 1915-
Children and books; [by] Zena Sutherland, May Hill Arbuthnot; chapters contributed by Dianne L. Monson. HarperCollins Pubs. il $78   **028.5**
1. Children's literature—History and criticism

First edition by May Hill Arbuthnot published 1947 by Scott, Foresman. (9th edition 1997) Periodically revised
"This children's literature textbook emphasizes the best books and authors. The introductory sections about children and books in general are followed by genre overviews which emphasize the major authors in each category. A third section discusses ways to bring children and books together, while a final section covers issues such as censorship. Lavish color illustrations, viewpoint boxes, extensive bibliographies and useful appendices make this an attractive and stimulating work." Safford. Guide to Ref Materials for Sch Libr Media Cent. 5th edition

Trelease, Jim
The read-aloud handbook. 4th ed. Penguin Bks. 1995 xxvi, 387p pa $13.95   **028.5**
1. Books and reading 2. Children's literature—Bibliography
ISBN 0-14-046971-0   LC 95-2269
First published 1982
"Trelease shares his firm belief in books. A pep talk, with new research on the value of reading aloud and new methods for its encouragement, is followed by the 'Treasury of Read-Alouds,' featuring 300 children's books . . . all nicely annotated and with notes leading to even more titles. An essential library book, of value to parents and professionals." Booklist [review of 1989 edition]
Includes bibliographical references

Yolen, Jane
Touch magic; fantasy, faerie & folklore in the literature of childhood. Expanded ed. August House 2000 128p pa $11.95   **028.5**
1. Children's literature—History and criticism 2. Folklore
ISBN 0-87483-591-7   LC 00-27565

Yolen, Jane—*Continued*

First published 1981 by Philomel Bks.

The author provides perspectives on reading, appreciating, and preserving fantasy and folklore for children. Among topics discussed are the morality of fairy tales, the definition of story, and the theme of time travel

Includes bibliographical references

028.505 Children and young people's reading—Serial publications

Book Links; connecting books, libraries, and classrooms. American Lib. Assn. $29.95

028.505

1. Children's literature—Periodicals 2. Best books
ISSN 1055-4742

Bimonthly. First issued as an insert in Booklist, Nov. 15, 1990

This periodical "offers feature articles on children's books (e.g., best books of the year, a Newbery/Caldecott retrospective) and regular columns that suggest ways to incorporate fine children's literature into the curriculum and day-care and nursery school programming. Background information on special topics . . . is accompanied by an annotated bibliography, complete with appropriate grade level. Columns devoted to specific children's books and interviews with authors and illustrators are a plus for the adult who wants to read to or select books for children." Katz. Mag for Libr. 10th edition

Bookbird; world of children's books. $50 per year

028.505

1. Children's literature—Periodicals 2. Books—Reviews 3. Best books
ISSN 0006-7377

Quarterly. First published 1962

Issued by the International Board on Books for Young People. For subscriptions write to P.O. Box 3156, West Lafayette, IN 47906

Articles, criticism, and occasional brief book reviews survey the best of children's literature from an international perspective

Five Owls; a publication for readers personally and professionally involved in children's literature. 2004 Sheridan Ave. S., Minneapolis, MN 55405 $35 per year **028.505**

1. Children's literature—Periodicals 2. Books—Reviews
ISSN 0892-6735

Bimonthly. First published 1986

"Each issue is approximately 22 pages and contains black-and-white photographs and illustrations. In addition to book reviews, there are articles about books and reading, and interviews with authors and illustrators. The reviews are comprehensive and include age recommendations. This would be useful selection tool for a school or public library." Katz. Mag for Libr. 10th edition

The Horn Book Guide to Children's and Young Adult Books. Horn Bk. $47 per year **028.505**

1. Children's literature—Periodicals 2. Books—Reviews
ISSN 1044-405X

Biannual. First published 1990

"This offshoot of *The Horn Book Magazine* provides critical annotations on all hardcover trade children's and young adult books published in the United States during the previous six months. Fiction is arranged by grade level and genre (e.g., picture books, readers), nonfiction by the ten broad Dewey classes and then narrower topics. . . . Numerous indexes (author, illustrator, title, series, subject, and reissues) help the librarian track down particular titles." Katz. Mag for Libr. 10th edition

The Horn Book Magazine. Horn Bk. $45 per year

028.505

1. Children's literature—Periodicals 2. Best books
3. Books—Reviews
ISSN 0018-5078

Bimonthly. First published 1924 with title: The Horn Book

"One of the first magazines to treat children's literature as serious material for discussion and review. . . . The book reviews, most of which are for recommended titles, are grouped by age level and/or format (picture books, folklore, etc.). Other sections of the magazine include lists of new paperbacks and, reissues, books in Spanish, and audiobooks" Katz. Mag for Libr. 10th edition

031 American encyclopedias

Compton's encyclopedia & fact-index. Success Pub. Group, P.O. Box 1167, Elmhurst, Il 60126 26v il maps set $649 **031**

1. Encyclopedias and dictionaries

First published 1922 with title: Compton's pictured encyclopedia. Frequently revised

Supplemented by: Compton's yearbook

"Recommended for home and school use by young people ages nine through eighteen. The main text, consisting of more than 5,000 articles, is supported by nearly 30,000 brief articles among the 70,000 entries in the 'fact-index.' This volume presents brief dictionary entries, biographical sketches, statistics, and capsule treatments of topics not considered in the main text." Ref Sources for Small & Medium-sized Libr. 6th edition

For a fuller review see: Booklist, Sept. 15, 2000

The New book of knowledge; the children's encyclopedia. Grolier 21v il maps apply to publisher for price **031**

1. Encyclopedias and dictionaries

First published 1966 as successor to The Book of knowledge. Frequently revised

Supplemented by The New book of knowledge annual

"Intended to interest a wide range of readers from those in early childhood to students nearly ready to use an adult encyclopedia; thus, articles are written at various levels of understanding, with the main emphasis being for children in grades three to six. Longer articles are signed by contributors or consultants. Suggested activities or projects are incorporated into some articles to further the educational value." Guide to Ref Books. 11th edition

For a fuller review see: Booklist, Sept. 15, 2000

The **World** Book encyclopedia. World Bk. 22v il maps apply to publisher for price   **031**
1. Encyclopedias and dictionaries

Also available CD-ROM version, The World Book multimedia encyclopedia
First published 1917-1918 by Field Enterprises. Frequently revised
Supplemented by The World Book year book; another available supplement is Science year; 2001 set accompanied by extra volume entitled World Book Election 2000
"A good juvenile encyclopedia, one of the leading American works in the field; approximates the form and treatment of the standard works for adults, so is especially good for the older child nearly ready to use adult material. . . . Children's librarians generally agree that *World book* continues to be the most popular general encyclopedia for readers 10 years of age and older." Guide to Ref Books. 11th edition

031.02   American books of miscellaneous facts

Ash, Russell
Incredible comparisons; written by Russell Ash. DK Pub. 1996 63p il $19.95 (4 and up)   **031.02**
1. Measurement 2. Size 3. Shape
ISBN 0-7894-1009-5   LC 96-13875
Offers a visual guide, with brief explanatory text, to comparative sizes, heights, weights, and numbers in such areas as capacity, population, growth, weather, disasters, speed, and others
"An incredible and fascinating book. . . . Brilliant illustrations, sometimes to scale, and succinct text demonstrate unique characteristics of thousands of facts." Sci Child

Information please almanac, atlas & yearbook. Houghton Mifflin $24.95; pa $10.95   **031.02**
1. Almanacs 2. Statistics 3. United States—Statistics
ISSN 0073-7860

Annual. First published 1947 by Doubleday. Publisher varies
"Statistical and factual material organized by subject area; contains special articles by experts. Illustrated, with a color map section and detailed index." N Y Public Libr. Book of How & Where to Look It Up

Kane, Joseph Nathan, 1899-
Famous first facts; a record of first happenings, discoveries, and inventions in American history; by Joseph Nathan Kane, Steven Anzovin, Janet Podell. Wilson, H.W. $95   **031.02**
1. Encyclopedias and dictionaries 2. United States—History—Dictionaries
LC 97-31252
Also available CD-ROM version and Famous first facts, international edition by Steven Anzovin and Janet Podell (2000) $95 (ISBN 0-8242-0958-3)
First published 1933. (5th edition 1997) Periodically revised

"Aims to establish the earliest date of various occurrences, achievements, inventions, etc. Dictionary arrangement with many cross-references. Gives brief description or explanation together with the date; some references to sources." Guide to Ref Books. 11th edition

Pascoe, Elaine
Scholastic kid's almanac for the 21st century; written by Elaine Pascoe and Deborah Kops; illustrated by Bob Italiano and David C. Bell. Scholastic Ref. 1999 352p $18.95; pa $12.95 (4 and up)   **031.02**
1. Encyclopedias and dictionaries
ISBN 0-590-30723-1; 0-590-30724-X (pa)
LC 98-48739
"A Blackbirch graphics book"
"A compilation of facts and lots of visuals on 38 topics that will appeal to children. Some of the subjects included are aerospace, animals, astronomy, chemistry, computers, energy, geography, health, plants, religion, sports, weather, and the zodiac. . . . Though selective, there is a lot of information here. The book is terrific for browsing and there is great graphic material to support reports." SLJ

The **World** almanac and book of facts. World Almanac il maps $29.95; pa $10.95   **031.02**
1. Almanacs 2. Statistics 3. United States—Statistics
ISSN 0084-1382

Annual. First published 1868. Publisher varies
"This is the most comprehensive and well-known of almanacs. . . . Contains a chronology of the year's events, consumer information, historical anniversaries, annual climatological data, and forecasts. Color section has flags and maps. Includes detailed index." N Y Public Libr. Book of How & Where to Look It Up

The **World** almanac for kids. World Almanac il maps $18.95; pa $10.95   **031.02**
1. Almanacs

Annual. First published 1995 for 1996
This volume contains information on animals, art, religion, sports, books, law, language, science and computers. Includes a section of full-color maps and flags. Illustrated throughout with pictures, diagrams, and charts

032.02   English books of miscellaneous facts

Guinness book of records. Guinness Media Inc.; distributed by Mint Pubs. il $26.95   **032.02**
1. Curiosities and wonders
ISSN 1057-4557

Annual. First published 1955 in the United Kingdom; in the United States 1962. Variant title: Guinness book of world records
Editors vary
"Ready reference for current record holders in all fields, some esoteric. Index provides access to information arranged in broad subject categories. Must be replaced annually." N Y Public Libr. Ref Books for Child Collect

051 American general serial publications and their indexes

Children's Magazine Guide; subject index to children's magazines. Bowker $65 per year

051

1. Periodicals—Indexes
ISSN 0743-9873
Nine issues a year. First published 1949 with title: Subject index to Children's Magazines. Publisher and frequency vary

This publication "indexes 53 magazines for children ages 8 to 12. Entries are arranged under subject headings in alphabetical order by the title of the article. Bibliographic information includes article and journal titles, author's name (when available), issue month and year, and page numbers." Katz. Mag for Libr. 10th edition

Cricket; the magazine for children. Carus $35.97

051

1. Children's literature—Periodicals
ISSN 0090-6034
Monthly. First published 1973 by Open Court Publishing

A general-interest magazine for ages 9 to 14 with "stories and poetry about people and events throughout the world. Activities found in *Cricket* include crossword puzzles and recipes. . . . *Cricket* is also available on audio cassette." Katz. Mag for Libr. 10th edition

Highlights for Children. P.O. Box 182346, Columbus, OH 43272-2167 $26.04 per year

051

1. Children's literature—Periodicals
ISSN 0018-165X
Monthly. First published 1946

This magazine "is intended for children of all ages . . . and carries stories, articles, and regular items appropriate to various reading and interest levels. The diversity of subject matter places this magazine among the few general-interest ones available for children. . . . [Included in each issue are] crafts and projects; puzzles, hidden pictures, and word games; and contributions from children." Richardson. Mag for Child. 2d edition

Ladybug; the magazine for young children. Carus $35.97 **051**
1. Children's literature—Periodicals
ISSN 1051-4961
Monthly. First published 1990

A "beginning literary magazine for young children ages 2-6. The stories, poetry, and illustrations are engaging and new information is presented in stories and articles that are delightful. A parent section offers parent-child art activities. A 'Meet the Author' page and a list of book titles by the featured author are also included." Katz. Mag for Libr. 10th edition

Spider; the magazine for children. Carus $32.97

051

1. Children's literature—Periodicals
ISSN 1070-2911
Monthly. First published 1994

"A general-interest magazine with fiction, fairy and folk tales, poetry, crafts, and puzzles to interest early elementary age boys and girls. The large, lovely illustrations enhance the printed material. Opportunities are available for reader input and participation." Katz. Mag for Libr. 10th edition

069 Museology

Norris, Joann, 1947-
Children's museums; an American guidebook. McFarland & Co. 1998 217p il pa $32.50 **069**
1. Museums
ISBN 0-7864-0443-4 LC 97-42194
"This is a listing of 242 children's museums, large and small, valid as of 1997. . . . The entries consist of a brief description, location, hours, admissions, and other sites of interest nearby, concluding with contact information, including Web sites and e-mail addresses. . . . Norris' volume should prove a useful and informative guide for school and public libraries." Booklist

070.1 News media

Bentley, Nancy
The young journalist's book; how to write and produce your own newspaper; [by] Nancy Bentley and Donna Guthrie; illustrated by Katy Keck Arnsteen. Millbrook Press 1998 64p il lib bdg $24.40; pa $8.95 (3-6) **070.1**
1. Journalism 2. Newspapers
ISBN 0-7613-0360-X (lib bdg); 0-7613-1377-X (pa) LC 97-43692
Describes the various functions and elements of a newspaper, giving practical advice on writing, producing, and distributing

"The full-color cartoons are appealing. Inspirational, practical fare for writers and would-be reporters." SLJ

070.5 Publishing

Brookfield, Karen
Book; written by Karen Brookfield; photographed by Laurence Pordes. Knopf 1993 63p il (Eyewitness books) (4 and up) **070.5**
1. Books LC 93-18833
Available DK Pub. edition $15.95; lib bdg $19.99 (ISBN 0-7894-5892-6; 0-7894-6597-3)
"A Dorling Kindersley book"

Text and photographs trace the evolution of the written word, how the alphabet grew out of pictures, the development of papermaking, bookbinding, children's books, and more

"The text is augmented heavily with numerous high-quality photographs, which are, perhaps, the crowning touch. They make the text come alive." Sci Books Films

071   Journalism and newspapers— North America

Granfield, Linda
Extra! Extra! the who, what, where, when and why of newspapers; written by Linda Granfield; illustrated by Bill Slavin. Orchard Bks. 1994 72p il hardcover o.p. paperback available $7.95 (4-6)
071
1. Newspapers
ISBN 0-531-07049-2 (pa)   LC 93-11807
The author "analyzes the different departments and components of a typical paper. Next, she takes readers behind the scenes to catch cameo glimpses of reporters, editors, designers, fact checkers, press workers, and delivery kids at work. The third section shows readers how to publish their own papers. . . . In the final chapter, she offers a series of crafts and other new uses for old newspapers. . . . Cartoonlike drawings enliven every page. This volume packs a lot of newspaper facts and lore into an appealing, though busy, format." Booklist

100   PHILOSOPHY & PSYCHOLOGY

Weate, Jeremy
A young person's guide to philosophy; "I think, therefore I am". DK Pub. 1998 64p il $16.95 (5 and up)
100
1. Philosophy 2. Philosophers
ISBN 0-7894-3074-6   LC 97-33454
Socrates, Aquinas, Descartes, Nietzsche, Simone de Beauvoir and Herbert Marcuse are among the thinkers discussed. Schools of thought and philosophical concepts are covered
"Teens who have thought about and questioned the hows, whats, and whys of human existence will find this introduction fascinating." Booklist

133.1   Apparitions

Cohen, Daniel, 1936-
Ghost in the house; illustrated by John Paul Caponigro. Cobblehill Bks. 1993 60p il $13.99 (4 and up)
133.1
1. Ghosts
ISBN 0-525-65131-4   LC 92-37858
Also available in paperback from Scholastic
Includes nine stories about some of the best known haunted houses in the world, including the Octagon in Washington, D.C., and the Weir house in Edinburgh, Scotland
"The stories are very simply told in very simple language and will serve to whet the appetite for additional information." Booklist

Great ghosts; illustrated by David Linn. Cobblehill Bks. 1990 48p il $15 (4 and up)
133.1
1. Ghosts
ISBN 0-525-65039-3   LC 90-34333

"Nine retellings of encounters with ghosts—six English, one Dutch, one Greek, and one Middle Eastern. Each succinct, concisely told story is from three to four pages long, and sports an illustration. While most of the tales can be found in other sources, here they are lively and easily read, without clutter." SLJ

133.3   Divinatory arts

Krull, Kathleen, 1952-
They saw the future; oracles, psychics, scientists, great thinkers, and pretty good guessers; illustrated by Kyrsten Brooker. Atheneum Bks. for Young Readers 1999 108p il $19.99 (4 and up)
133.3
1. Prophets 2. Prophecies
ISBN 0-689-81295-7   LC 97-51705
"An Anne Schwartz book"
Discusses the work and predictions of those who have speculated about or claimed to see the future, from the oracles of ancient Greece to such modern figures as Edgar Cayce and Jeane Dixon
"Krull's sweeping chronicle of people reputed to have personal pipelines to the future . . . makes fascinating, illuminating reading." Booklist
Includes bibliographical references

133.4   Demonology and witchcraft

Hill, Douglas, 1935-
Witches & magic-makers; written by Douglas Hill; photographed by Alex Wilson. Knopf 1997 59p il (Eyewitness books) (4 and up)   **133.4**
1. Witchcraft
     LC 96-42958
Available DK Pub. edition $15.95; lib bdg $19.95 (ISBN 0-7894-5878-0; 0-7894-6679-8)
"A Dorling Kindersley book"
This book on "witchcraft, shamanism, and mysticism . . . introduces magical charms, talismans, and amulets from around the world. . . . Sharply reproduced color photographs of people and objects float against white backgrounds. One-or-two sentence captions identify the pictures and form the bulk of the text. . . . This title gives a colorful overview of the topic." SLJ

Jackson, Shirley, 1919-1965
The witchcraft of Salem Village. Random House 1987 c1956 146p hardcover o.p. paperback available $5.95 (4 and up)   **133.4**
1. Witchcraft 2. Salem (Mass.)—History
ISBN 0-394-89176-7 (pa)   LC 87-4543
"Landmark books"
A reissue of the title first published 1956
"A simple, chilling account of the witchcraft trials of 1692 and '93 when, because of testimony given by a group of little girls, twenty persons were executed as witches and others died in jail. There is good introductory background and though the story's subject is by nature horrifying the book does not play on the emotions. . . . It presents a difficult theme lucidly and without condescension." Horn Book

Meltzer, Milton, 1915-
Witches and witch-hunts; a history of persecution. Blue Sky Press (NY) 1999 128p $16.95 (4 and up) **133.4**
1. Witchcraft
ISBN 0-590-48517-2   LC 97-36999
Traces the origins and progression of hysteria, fear, and persecution associated with witches and witchcraft in western societies
The author "crams a lot of ideas and insights into this ambitious, unusually meaty survey." Publ Wkly
Includes bibliographical references

Roach, Marilynne K.
In the days of the Salem witchcraft trials. Houghton Mifflin 1996 92p il maps $15 (4 and up) **133.4**
1. Witchcraft 2. Salem (Mass.)—History
ISBN 0-395-69704-2   LC 94-32383
"After discussing the Salem Witchcraft trials in one short chapter, this attractive volume explores the social history of the times to show the context that made such events possible. Topics include the law and punishment, magic, social status, clothing, food, household goods, occupations, recreation, common activities, government, and the political troubles leading to widespread tension and unrest. Readers will come away with a much fuller picture of who lived in Salem and how they lived. Small ink drawings decorate the pages." Booklist
Includes bibliographical references

152.1   Sensory perception

Cobb, Vicki, 1938-
How to really fool yourself; illusions for all your senses; illustrated by Jessica Wolk-Stanley. Wiley 1999 120p il pa $12.95 (5 and up) **152.1**
1. Senses and sensation 2. Perception 3. Optical illusions
ISBN 0-471-31592-3   LC 98-27723
A newly illustrated edition of the title first published 1981 by Lippincott
"The book begins with an explanation of perception and explores many different sensory aspects of it through experiments, definitions of important terms (italicized), background information and how illusions affect us in everyday life." SLJ

152.14   Visual perception

Dispezio, Michael A.
Optical illusion magic; visual tricks & amusements; [by] Michael DiSpezio. Sterling 1999 80p il $17.95 (4 and up) **152.14**
1. Optical illusions
ISBN 0-8069-6581-9   LC 99-21113
This introduction to optical illusions "explains how the eye is deceived by visual tricks. Many examples are effectively used to illustrate different patterns and types of illusions, including spirals, slants, afterimages, broken lines, and 3-D." SLJ
"This entertaining, enlightening volume will be helpful for projects and fun for browsing." Booklist

Simon, Seymour, 1931-
Now you see it, now you don't; the amazing world of optical illusions; drawings by Constance Ftera. rev ed. Morrow Junior Bks. 1998 64p il $17 (4 and up) **152.14**
1. Optical illusions
ISBN 0-688-16152-9   LC 97-49855
First published 1976 by FourWinds Press with title: The optical illusion book
The author explains optical illusions involving lines and spaces, changeable figures, depth and distance, brightness and contrast, and color
"One of the clearest and most interesting discussions of optical illusions ever written for children." Booklist

Westray, Kathleen
Picture puzzler. Ticknor & Fields Bks. for Young Readers 1994 unp il $16 (2-4) **152.14**
1. Optical illusions
ISBN 0-395-70130-3   LC 94-4066
This "explanation of assorted optical illusions employs . . . gouache sketches in the style of American folk art to demonstrate the visual phenomena—afterimages, blind spots, incomplete pictures, the arrangement of lines and shapes to alter perspective, color deceptions, and reversible drawings." Horn Book
"The layout and ample white space will snare reluctant readers; explanations of the illusions and how they work are adequate, although not detailed. A fresh presentation for young puzzlers." SLJ

Wick, Walter
Walter Wick's Optical tricks. Cartwheel Bks. 1998 43p il $13.95 (4 and up) **152.14**
1. Optical illusions
ISBN 0-590-22227-9   LC 97-35672
Presents a series of optical illusions and explains what is seen
The author "has produced a stunning picture book of optical illusions. With crystal-clear photographs, he creates a series of scenes that fool the eye and the brain." Booklist

152.4   Emotions and feelings

Aliki
Feelings. Greenwillow Bks. 1984 32p il $16; pa $5.95 (k-3) **152.4**
1. Emotions
ISBN 0-688-03831-X; 0-688-06518-X (pa)
          LC 84-4098
"Small pen-and-ink cartoons with vivid coloring depict boys and girls interacting and experiencing the full range of feelings which evolve in everyday settings. This creative, unique book would be ideal for parent/child interaction or use by elementary teachers in language arts classes. Children will enjoy the comic book 'frame' format." Child Book Rev Serv

153.4   Thought, thinking, reasoning

Burns, Marilyn

The book of think; or, How to solve a problem twice your size; written by Marilyn Burns; illustrated by Martha Weston. Little, Brown 1976 125p il hardcover o.p. paperback available $14.20 (4 and up)   **153.4**

1. Thought and thinking 2. Problem solving
ISBN 0-316-11743-9 (pa)   LC 76-17848
"A Brown paper school book"

"A provocative text invites the reader to solve problems by looking for alternatives, sharpening the senses, studying people, and expressing ideas in words. Brainteasers, riddles, and suggested projects are interpolated and represented by black-and-white line drawings." Child Books, 1976

155.9   Environmental psychology

Brown, Laurene Krasny

When dinosaurs die; a guide to understanding death; [by] Laurie Krasny Brown and Marc Brown. Little, Brown 1996 32p il lib bdg $14.95; pa $5.95 (k-3)   **155.9**

1. Death 2. Bereavement
ISBN 0-316-10917-7 (lib bdg); 0-316-11955-5 (pa)
    LC 95-14511

"The text explains the inevitability of death, various reasons for death (including old age, sickness, accident, and suicide), and the difference between death and sleep; it then goes on to examine feelings about death and ways, both individual and cultural, of dealing with the loss of loved ones. . . .The simple watercolor illustrations help to make some scary situations more approachable. Quiet, respectful, and unthreatening, this will probably become a primary-grades standard on the subject." Bull Cent Child Books

Includes glossary

Fry, Virginia Lynn, 1952-

Part of me died, too; stories of creative survival among bereaved children and teenagers; illustrated with the children's own artwork, with a foreword by Katherine Paterson. Dutton Children's Bks. 1995 xx, 218p il $19.99 (5 and up)   **155.9**

1. Death 2. Bereavement
ISBN 0-525-45068-8   LC 94-36536

The author "tells stories of children and teenagers who have lost a loved one and how they coped. The types of death experienced are on all levels from that of a beloved pet to the death of parents, siblings and friends. Suicide, murder and AIDs-related deaths are included. Each story is resolved through therapy involving people close to the youngsters and art activities that help them cope with the pain." Book Rep

"Highly compelling, compassionate and comforting, this powerful book should be part of libraries, counseling centers and anywhere else where adults help those who deal with death." Child Book Rev Serv

Gellman, Marc

Lost & found; a kid's book for living through loss; [by] Marc Gellman and Thomas Hartman; illustrated by Debbie Tilley. Morrow Junior Bks. 1999 176p il $15 (4-6)   **155.9**

1. Loss (Psychology)
ISBN 0-688-15752-1   LC 98-27779

Describes different kinds of losses—losing possessions, competitions, health, trust, and the permanent loss because of death—and discusses how to handle these situations

The authors' "informal text is aimed straight at kids and incorporates lots of examples children can relate to. . . . A practical, heartfelt exploration." Booklist

Includes bibliographical references

Krementz, Jill

How it feels when a parent dies. Knopf 1981 110p il hardcover o.p. paperback available $15 (4 and up)   **155.9**

1. Death 2. Bereavement
ISBN 0-394-75854-4 (pa)   LC 80-8808
Also available in hardcover from P. Smith

This book is "a hopeful tribute to the healing power sustained by young survivors, who are competently interviewed and photographed in their widely varied reactions and situations. The subjects range in age from 7 to 16 and cope with a variety of deaths by suicide, accident, and illness. Adults helping children through a hard time will better understand their charges' problems through the honest opinions expressed here, and young readers might feel less alone." Booklist

158   Applied psychology

Brown, Laurene Krasny

How to be a friend; a guide to making friends and keeping them; [by] Laurie Krasny Brown and Marc Brown. Little, Brown 1998 31p il $14.95 (k-3)   **158**

1. Friendship
ISBN 0-316-10913-4   LC 97-10179

Dinosaur characters illustrate the value of friends, how to make friends, and how to be and not to be a good friend

"Dialogue balloons personalize, enrich, and add humor to the main text. . . . How to Be a Friend will be very useful to parents, teachers, and other caregivers of young children." Horn Book

Rogers, Fred

Making friends; photographs by Jim Judkis. Putnam 1987 unp il hardcover o.p. paperback available $6.95 (k-1)   **158**

1. Friendship
ISBN 0-698-11409-4 (pa)   LC 86-12353

"From its opening lines ('When people like each other and like to do things together, they're friends. Can you think of someone who's your friend?'), Rogers's inimitable voice reaches out to his small readers with understanding and reassurance. He describes the pleasures of friendship as well as potential problem areas. . . . Judkis's large color photos capture the range of emotions Rogers writes about." Publ Wkly

Scott, Elaine, 1940-
Friends! photographs by Margie Miller. Atheneum Bks. for Young Readers 2000 unp il lib bdg $16 (k-3)   **158**
1. Friendship
ISBN 0-689-82105-0   LC 99-10357
This book "explores the joys and dilemmas of friendship and encourages children to think about what they do in similar situations. Economical text sets the scenes and full-color photographs show various groups of racially diverse children interacting socially." SLJ
"Scott outlines the situations in straightforward, lucid text and Miller (*Where Does It Go?*) stages them in clear, colorful photographs. . . . This is a solid choice for a discussion-starter on some of the more challenging aspects of making and keeping friends." Publ Wkly

179   Other ethical norms

Young, Ed
Voices of the heart. Scholastic 1997 unp il $17.95   **179**
1. Ethics 2. Emotions 3. Chinese language
ISBN 0-590-50199-2   LC 96-7595
"Young lists 26 emotions with their modern Chinese characters. He then devotes a page to each emotion, breaking each character into its parts and creating a collage out of the parts and the figure of a heart to express the feeling of the emotion. . . . Emotions include panic, rudeness, mercy and loyalty." Booklist
"This is a powerful combination of words and imagery that lends itself to a number of uses both in the library and the classroom, but it will need the intercession of a knowledgeable adult to make this a part of a language, art, or religion curriculum." Bull Cent Child Books

200   RELIGION

Birdseye, Debbie Holsclaw
What I believe; kids talk about faith; by Debbie Holsclaw Birdseye and Tom Birdseye; photographs by Robert Crum. Holiday House 1996 32p il $15.95 (4 and up)   **200**
1. Religions
ISBN 0-8234-1268-7   LC 96-11240
Six children of different religious backgrounds tell about their faith and what it means to them; includes background information on each religious tradition
"These simple personal portraits show kids who have made a strong place for religion in their everyday world. . . . An affirmation of faith that goes beyond any single faith." Booklist
Includes bibliographical references

Gellman, Marc
How do you spell God? answers to the big questions from around the world; [by] Marc Gellman & Thomas Hartman; illustrated by Jos. A. Smith; with a foreword by his Holiness the Dalai Lama. Morrow Junior Bks. 1995 206p il $16.95 (5 and up)   **200**
1. Religions
ISBN 0-688-13041-0   LC 94-28770

The authors "show how the various religions—Judaism, Christianity, Islam, Buddhism, and Hinduism—deal with the soul-searching questions central to all people. . . . There is also information on each religion's teachers, holy days and places, sanctuaries, and prayers, among other topics." Booklist
This book "is warm, friendly and, most of all, respectful of the importance and variety of belief." Book Rep

220.5   Bible—Modern versions

Bible
The Holy Bible; containing the Old and New Testaments; translated out of the original tongues; and with the former translations diligently compared and revised by King James's special command, 1611. Oxford Univ. Press prices vary   **220.5**

Available in various bindings and editions
The authorized or King James Version originally published 1611

The Holy Bible: new revised standard version; containing the Old and New Testaments with the Apocryphal/Deuterocanonical books. Nelson, T. maps prices vary   **220.5**

Available in various bindings and editions
This version first published 1989
"Intended for public reading, congregational worship, private study, instruction, and meditation, it attempts to be as literal as possible while following standard American English usage, avoids colloquialism, and prefers simple, direct terms and phrases." Sheehy. Guide to Ref Books. 10th edition. suppl

220.8   Nonreligious subjects treated in Bible

Bible. Selections
Animals of the Bible; a picture book by Dorothy P. Lathrop; with text selected by Helen Dean Fish from the King James Bible. Harper & Row 1987 65p il $17.95; lib bdg $16.89 (1-4)   **220.8**
1. Bible—Natural history 2. Animals
ISBN 0-397-31536-8; 0-397-30047-6 (lib bdg)
Awarded the Caldecott Medal, 1938
A reissue of the title first published 1937 by Lippincott
"Dorothy Lathrop's love and understanding of animals, the sensitiveness and joy with which she draws them, make her the ideal artist for such a volume. It is more than a beautiful picture book, for she has studied the fauna and flora of Bible lands until each animal and bird, each flower and tree, is true to natural history." NY Times Book Rev

Paterson, John Barstow, 1932-

Consider the lilies; plants of the Bible; [by] John and Katherine Paterson; paintings by Anne Ophelia Dowden. Crowell 1986 96p il o.p.; Houghton Mifflin paperback available $7.95 (5 and up)   **220.8**

1. Bible—Natural history 2. Plants

ISBN 0-395-88828-X (pa)   LC 85-43603

This book gives information "on forty-five shrubs, crops, trees, weeds, fruits and flowers mentioned in the Old and New Testaments with emphasis on the . . . symbolic values of each. Divided into three groups—plants of Revelation, Necessity, and Celebration—each plant is cited in a Bible story or passage (quoted from the King James, New English, or Revised Standard versions of the Bible or paraphrased)." SLJ

"The quality of the art and intelligent explanations coupled with carefully selected examples from both Old and New Testaments will make the book prime read-aloud material for family sharing, Sunday School classes, and religious reports." Bull Cent Child Books

220.9 Bible—Geography, history, biography, stories

Armstrong, Carole

Women of the Bible; with paintings from the great art museums of the world. Simon & Schuster Bks. for Young Readers 1998 45p il $18 (5 and up)   **220.9**

1. Women in the Bible 2. Bible stories

ISBN 0-689-81728-2   LC 97-17059

Presents several prominent women from the Bible, including Eve, Sarah, Bathsheba, Ruth, Mary, Elizabeth, and Martha

"Gracefully written. . . . Grandly illustrated with large, full-page reproductions of appropriate Renaissance paintings by artists such as Giorgione, Filippo Lippi, Cranach, Poussin, and Caravaggio, as well as one more recent work by Dante Gabriel Rossetti. The final paragraph of each selection tells something about the technique, symbolism, point of view, or history of the artwork itself. . . . Includes Scripture citations and an index of artists and paintings." SLJ

Bible. Selections

Tomie dePaola's book of Bible stories. Putnam 1989 127p il $24.99   **220.9**

1. Bible stories

ISBN 0-399-21690-1   LC 88-26468

"A collection of 17 stories from the Old Testament, 15 from the New Testament, and 4 psalms. The text is from the New International Version. . . . De Paola uses the text as written with some abridgement to make the stories an appropriate length. Done in his typical style, the illustrations feature stylized people and objects. . . . There are several illustrations for each story, many of which are full page, and most make dramatic use of color. The large format enhances the impact of the pictures." SLJ

Words of gold; a treasury of the Bible's poetry and wisdom; selected and introduced by Lois Rock; illustrated by Sarah Young. Eerdmans 1999 48p il $18 (4 and up)   **220.9**

1. Bible stories

ISBN 0-8028-5199-1   LC 99-37903

First published 1997 in the United Kingdom

Presents passages from both the Old and New Testaments as lessons on life for young children

"Well organized and beautifully presented. . . . The quotations are short; printed in a clear, varied, handsome typeface; and attractively arranged among a multitude of charming illustrations, ranging from vignettes to half-page scenes. Done in a delicate folk-art technique, using gold and rich, stained-glass colors." SLJ

221.9 Bible. Old Testament—Geography, history, biography, stories

Bible. O.T.

Stories from the Old Testament; with masterwork paintings inspired by the stories. Simon & Schuster Bks. for Young Readers 1996 45p il lib bdg $18 (5 and up)   **221.9**

1. Bible stories 2. Religious art

ISBN 0-689-80955-7   LC 95-48105

A collection of well-known stories from the Old Testament, including the story of The Creation, Noah's Ark, Joseph and his Brothers, and The Ten Commandments, with illustrations by such artists as Raphael, Bruegel, and Rosselli

"The Bible stories have been carefully excerpted to retain essential dramatic action. . . . Full-color reproductions are of excellent quality. An index of paintings includes a short biographical paragraph about each artist and a small reproduction of the entire painting." Voice Youth Advocates

Kimmel, Eric A.

Be not far from me; the oldest love story: legends from the Bible; retold by Eric A. Kimmel; illustrated by David Diaz. Simon & Schuster Bks. for Young Readers 1998 256p il maps $25 (5 and up)   **221.9**

1. Bible stories

ISBN 0-689-81088-1   LC 97-24543

A collection of stories drawn from the Bible and the Midrash telling of twenty heroes and heroines including Abraham, Moses, Samson, Deborah, Elijah, and six other prophets

"The retellings of the stories . . . are quite wonderful. . . . The collage-style art, featuring cut silhouettes of black and light papers set against softer backgrounds, is dynamic." Booklist

Includes bibliographical references

McCaughrean, Geraldine, 1951-

God's people; stories from the Old Testament; retold by Geraldine McCaughrean; illustrated by Anna C. Leplar. Margaret K. McElderry Bks. 1997 120p il $19.95 (4-6) **221.9**
1. Bible stories
ISBN 0-689-81366-X LC 97-2191
Companion volume to God's kingdom
Retells twenty-two stories from the Old Testament, including "Noah and the Flood," "Jacob's Ladder," "Samson and Delilah," and "Esther Speaks for Her People"
This "book remains true to the King James Version but develops it and fleshes it out, offering explanations and tying together themes. The watercolors depict the people and events with historical accuracy, creativity, and tenderness." Booklist

McKissack, Patricia C., 1944-

Let my people go; Bible stories told by a freeman of color to his daughter, Charlotte, in Charleston, South Carolina, 1806-16; by Patricia and Fredrick McKissack; illustrated by James Ransome. Atheneum Bks. for Young Readers 1998 134p il $20 (4 and up) **221.9**
1. African Americans—Fiction 2. Bible stories
3. Slavery—Fiction
ISBN 0-689-80856-9 LC 97-19983
"An Anne Schwartz book"
Charlotte, the daughter of a free black man who worked as a blacksmith in Charleston, South Carolina, in the early 1800s recalls the stories from the Bible that her father shared with her, relating them to the experiences of African Americans
"The poignant juxtaposition of the Biblical characters and Charlotte's personal narrative is authentic and moving. . . . The occasional illustrations are powerful oil paintings in rich colors, emotional and evocative." SLJ
Includes bibliographical references

Sasso, Sandy Eisenberg, 1947-

But God remembered; stories of women from creation to the promised land; illustrated by Bethanne Andersen. Jewish Lights Pub. 1995 31p il $16.95 (3-5) **221.9**
1. Women in the Bible 2. Bible stories
ISBN 1-879045-43-5 LC 95-3591
The author "weaves together the stories of: Lilith, the first woman in the garden of Eden, . . . Serach the musician, who, with her song, reveals to her grandfather Jacob that his son is still alive, . . . Bityah, who draws the baby Moses from the Nile, . . . and the bold-spirited Daughters of Z, who struggle against discrimination." Publisher's note
"Although part of the pleasure of the book lies in its strong feminist voice, Sasso also tells good stories; and these will have even more value for the discussions they can generate. Andersen's evocative paintings are beautiful additions to this carefully designed book." Booklist

222 Historical books of Old Testament

Bible. O.T. Genesis

Genesis; art by Ed Young; adapted from the King James version. HarperCollins Pubs. 1997 unp il $16.95 **222**
1. Creation 2. Bible stories
ISBN 0-06-025356-8 LC 94-18698
"A Laura Geringer book"
This "adapted version of the first book of Genesis is distinguished . . . by the artistic interpretation of Ed Young. The familiar text is on the left-hand page, cream against glossy black, while the facing page is a pastel illustration on colored paper. The strongly horizontal compositions comprise sophisticated, abstract images. . . . Young's adaptation of the King James text retains the poetic rhythms of the well-known chapter and verses. . . . This is a carefully designed and executed piece of picture-book art." Bull Cent Child Books

The story of the creation; words from Genesis; [pictures by] Jane Ray. Dutton Children's Bks. 1993 c1992 unp il $16 (k-3) **222**
1. Creation 2. Bible stories
ISBN 0-525-44946-9 LC 92-20862
First published 1992 in the United Kingdom
Illustrates the story of creation, from the book of Genesis of the King James version of the Bible
"Folk-art exuberance, sapphire and emerald hues, and decorative detail mark Ray's style and reflect Creation's rich abundance." SLJ

Chaikin, Miriam, 1928-

Exodus; adapted from the Bible by Miriam Chaikin; illustrated by Charles Mikolaycak. Holiday House 1987 unp il $15.95 (2-4) **222**
1. Moses (Biblical figure) 2. Bible stories
ISBN 0-8234-0607-5 LC 85-27361
"Oversize pages, lavishly illustrated, provide a visual interpretation of the Biblical story of the plagues in Egypt that led to a pharaoh's reluctant permission for the departure of the Hebrew slaves and of their journey to the promised land. Chaikin has done a good job of adapting the story so that it is simplified and coherent yet preserves the flow of Biblical language. Mikolaycak's paintings, in his distinctively bold and flowing style, are carefully integrated with textual references; they extend the story and add excitement to its inherent drama." Bull Cent Child Books

De Regniers, Beatrice Schenk

David and Goliath; illustrated by Scott Cameron. Orchard Bks. 1996 unp il $15.95; lib bdg $16.99 **222**
1. David, King of Israel 2. Goliath (Biblical figure)
3. Bible stories
ISBN 0-531-09496-0; 0-531-08796-4 (lib bdg)
LC 95-22025
The biblical tale of the young shepherd who uses a slingshot to do battle with a giant and eventually becomes a king

Fisher, Leonard Everett, 1924-
David and Goliath; adapted from the Bible and
illustrated by Leonard Everett Fisher. Holiday
House 1993 unp il $15.95 (k-3)   **222**
1. David, King of Israel 2. Goliath (Biblical figure)
3. Bible stories
ISBN 0-8234-0997-X   LC 92-24063
Retells the Bible story in which a Hebrew shepherd
boy kills the giant Philistine warrior Goliath with a slingshot
"Fisher has created majestic images that reflect the
grandeur of the story in all its mythic proportions. The
concise telling works in counterpoint to the thickly painted images, which Fisher has chosen carefully." Booklist

Moses; retold from the Bible and illustrated by
Leonard Everett Fisher. Holiday House 1995 unp
il $15.95 (k-3)   **222**
1. Moses (Biblical figure) 2. Bible stories
ISBN 0-8234-1149-4   LC 94-12131
"Fisher's version of the biblical story of Moses and
the Exodus from Egypt suggests a great staged pageant.
. . . Each double-page spread captures a mythic drama,
with the Old Testament figures bold against mountain,
desert, and sky, from the hiding of the baby in the bul-
rushes to the coming of the plagues, the parting of the
waters, the wandering in the desert, and the receiving of
the Ten Commandments." Booklist

Geisert, Arthur
The ark. Houghton Mifflin 1988 48p il lib bdg
$17.95; pa $7.95 (k-3)   **222**
1. Noah's ark 2. Bible stories
ISBN 0-395-43078-X (lib bdg); 0-618-00608-7 (pa)
LC 88-15889
"Beginning with God's decision to destroy his creation—except for Noah and his family—Geisert details
the story on buff-colored pages. The illustrator employs
intricate cross hatching and unusual perspectives to show
Noah building the ark and housing all the creatures of
the earth. . . . As a result of its astonishing illustrations,
as well as its compact text, this book can be used with
a wide range of audiences, all of whom will no doubt
want to look closely at the meticulous detail that abounds
on every spread." Booklist

Gelman, Rita Golden, 1937-
Queen Esther saves her people; retold by Rita
Golden Gelman; illustrated by Frané Lessac.
Scholastic 1998 unp il $15.95 (k-3)   **222**
1. Esther, Queen of Persia 2. Bible stories
ISBN 0-590-47025-6   LC 97-2568
Retells the story of how a beautiful Jewish girl be-
came the Queen of Persia and saved her people from
death at the hands of the evil Hamen
"This energetic retelling of the Purim story is framed
with flat, detailed illustrations that set a 'once upon a
time' mood." Horn Book Guide

Gerstein, Mordicai, 1935-
Queen Esther the morning star; the story of
Purim. Simon & Schuster Bks. for Young Readers
2000 unp il $16 (1-3)   **222**
1. Esther, Queen of Persia 2. Bible stories 3. Purim
ISBN 0-689-81372-4   LC 97-29653

A retelling of the "biblical tale of how Esther, Jewish
Queen of Persia, saved her people from the genocidal
whim of wicked prime minister Haman." Bull Cent Child
Books
Gerstein's "dynamic, evocatively illustrated retelling
mines the tale of Purim for its rich stores of drama and
suspense." Publ Wkly

Goldin, Barbara Diamond
Journeys with Elijah; eight tales of the Prophet;
retold by Barbara Diamond Goldin; paintings by
Jerry Pinkney. Harcourt Brace & Co. 1999 77p il
$20 (4 and up)   **222**
1. Elijah (Biblical figure) 2. Jewish legends 3. Bible
stories
ISBN 0-15-200445-9   LC 96-9278
"Gulliver books"
Presents eight stories about the Old Testament prophet
Elijah, set in a variety of time periods and in places all
over the world where Jews have lived
"Goldin's storytelling is every bit as colorful as
Pinkney's radiant, masterfully composed paintings, and
both text and art testify to careful historical research."
Publ Wkly
Includes bibliographical references

Kassirer, Sue
Joseph and his coat of many colors; retold by
Susan Kassirer; illustrated by Danuta Jarecka.
Simon & Schuster 1997 unp il $15; pa $3.99 (k-2)
222
1. Joseph (Biblical figure) 2. Bible stories
ISBN 0-689-81227-2; 0-689-81226-4 (pa)
LC 96-20807
"Ready-to-read"
After being sold into slavery in Egypt by his jealous
brothers, Joseph becomes an important man and is able
to come to his family's rescue during a famine
"Even with its limited easy-reader vocabulary, this abbreviated version of Joseph's adventures is lively and
reads well aloud or alone. . . . The unusual illustrations,
combining surrealism with folk art, have a textured surface resembling oilcloth and are painted in sweeps of
brilliant, glowing colors." SLJ

Manushkin, Fran
Miriam's cup; a Passover story; illustrated by
Bob Dacey. Scholastic 1998 unp il $15.95 (k-3)
222
1. Miriam (Biblical figure) 2. Passover 3. Bible stories
ISBN 0-590-67720-9   LC 96-2480
A Jewish mother preparing for Passover tells her
young children, the story of Miriam, the Biblical woman
who prophesied the birth of Moses
"The text and the lush double-spread watercolors,
which are painted to reflect a child's perspective, are
framed on a papyrus background. Each illustration bursts
with movement, immersing readers and pre-readers alike
in the sequence and drama of the story." Booklist

Paterson, Katherine
The angel and the donkey; retold by Katherine Paterson; illustrated by Alexander Koshkin. Clarion Bks. 1996 34p il $15.95 (3-5)   **222**
1. Balaam (Biblical figure) 2. Bible stories
ISBN 0-395-68969-4   LC 94-22430
"Paterson retells the story from the Book of Numbers in which the Moab king Balak summons soothsayer Balaam to curse the Israelites, but through the intervention of God, an angel, and a talking donkey, Balaam is inspired to bless this people instead." Bull Cent Child Books
"This faithful, graceful retelling is embellished with many equally graceful watercolor, tempera, and gouache paintings executed in a detailed and realistic manner." SLJ

Segal, Lore Groszmann
The book of Adam to Moses; [by] Lore Segal and Leonard Baskin. Knopf 1987 115p il o.p.; Schocken Bks. paperback available $11.95 (4-6)
          222
1. Bible stories
ISBN 0-8052-0961-1 (pa)   LC 87-2581
A modern English version of the stories of the five books of Moses
"What Segal has done is simplify the language and give cohesion to the narrative without sacrificing sonority, sequence, or flow. The tone is reverent, the language comprehensible. Baskin's black-and-white illustrations are handsome in their dramatic sweep and strength." Bull Cent Child Books

Spier, Peter, 1927-
Noah's ark; illustrated by Peter Spier. Doubleday 1977 unp il hardcover o.p. paperback available $7.99 (k-2)   **222**
1. Noah's ark 2. Bible stories
ISBN 0-440-40693-5 (pa)   LC 76-43630
Awarded the Caldecott Medal, 1978
"A seventeenth-century Dutch poem, 'The Flood' by Jacobus Revius, opens the otherwise almost wordless book. Skillfully translated by the artist and set in a readable, appropriately archaic type, the artlessly reverent verses add an unexpected dimension to the full-color pictures. Peter Spier's characteristic panoramas are marvels of minute detail, activity, vitality, and humor." Horn Book

Wiesel, Elie, 1928-
King Solomon and his magic ring; paintings by Mark Podwal. Greenwillow Bks. 1999 51p il $16 (3-5)   **222**
1. Solomon, King of Israel 2. Bible stories
ISBN 0-688-16959-7   LC 98-45433
Recounts some of the stories of the wisdom and folly in the life of the legendary King Solomon
The stories are told "in an intimate, conversational tone. . . . Mark Podwal's full-page paintings in gouache, acrylics, and colored pencil leave space for the mystery and evoke the playful exaggeration of the brief, legendary stories." Booklist

Wildsmith, Brian, 1930-
Exodus. Eerdmans Bks. for Young Readers 1999 c1998 unp il $20   **222**
1. Moses (Biblical figure) 2. Bible stories
ISBN 0-8028-5175-4   LC 98-18066
First published 1998 in the United Kingdom
Describes how God sent Moses to lead his people out of slavery in Egypt and into the promised land of Canaan
"The storytelling is formal but understandable to a young reader. The illustrations are dramatic, and each page is bordered in gold, with God depicted as a prismatic star." Horn Book Guide

Wolkstein, Diane
Esther's story; illustrated by Juan Wijngaard. Morrow Junior Bks. 1996 unp il hardcover o.p. paperback available $4.95 (3-5)   **222**
1. Esther, Queen of Persia 2. Bible stories
ISBN 0-688-15844-7 (pa)   LC 94-15473
"The story of the Jewish girl chosen by King Ahasuerus to replace his deposed queen Vashti and destined to save her people from massacre is recounted from Esther's own point of view. . . . Although the voice and perspective are clearly fictionalized, Wolkstein clings closely to a Scriptural outline, with the notable exception of Esther's bold flirtation with the king upon their first meeting. Although the opulent, jeweled, and gilded gouache paintings . . . will attract a younger audience, the political machinations and court cabals which give rise to Esther's act of heroism are accessible only to a more attentive readership." Bull Cent Child Books

223   Poetic books of Old Testament

Bible. O.T. Ecclesiastes
To every thing there is a season; verses from Ecclesiastes; illustrations by Leo and Diane Dillon. Blue Sky Press (NY) 1998 unp il $15.95   **223**
ISBN 0-590-47887-7   LC 97-35124
Presents that selection from Ecclesiastes which relates that everything in life has its own time and season
"The Dillons compellingly convey the relevance of the Ecclesiastes verse throughout history, via a stunning array of artwork that embraces motifs from cultures the world over." Publ Wkly

Sing a new song; a book of Psalms; [compiled by] Bijou Le Tord. Eerdmans 1997 unp il $15 (k-3)
          223
1. Bible. O.T. Psalms
ISBN 0-8028-5139-8   LC 96-33231
"Excerpts from several different Psalms are combined harmoniously to form a new, beautiful, simple poem describing the attributes of God, who blesses the Earth; is as free as a flying dove; is like a mountain in his love. All nature and humankind praise Him. Le Tord's watercolors, both childlike and subtle, glow with a warm radiance expressive of her subject matter." SLJ

225.9 Bible. New Testament—Geography, history, biography, stories

McCaughrean, Geraldine, 1951-

God's kingdom; stories from the New Testament; retold by Geraldine McCaughrean; illustrated by Anna C. Leplar. Margaret K. McElderry Bks. 1999 120p il map $20 (4-6)
225.9

1. Jesus Christ 2. Bible stories

ISBN 0-689-82488-2   LC 98-68536

Companion volume to God's people

"The stories include the Annunciation, the Nativity, the Magi, etc.; Simeon and Anna, John the Baptist, Nicodemus, Zacchaeus, Lazarus, and the Samaritan woman; Jesus's temptations in the wilderness . . . parables and miracles. . . . The eye-catching watercolor illustrations, ranging in size from vignettes to quarter, half, and full pages, are done in a folk-art style." SLJ

231 God

Fitch, Florence Mary, 1875-1959

A book about God; illustrated by Henri Sorensen. Lothrop, Lee & Shepard Bks. 1998 24p il $16; lib bdg $15.93 (k-3)   **231**

1. God

ISBN 0-688-16128-6; 0-688-16129-4 (lib bdg)

     LC 97-48682

A newly illustrated edition of the title first published 1953

The "text explains how people can understand God's nature by observing the world he created. Fitch describes the ways that characteristics of the sun, air, trees, mountains, and oceans reflect the character of God. Proponents of many faiths will embrace this book's message." Horn Book Guide

Paterson, John Barstow, 1932-

Images of God; by John and Katherine Paterson; illustrated by Alexander Koshkin. Clarion Bks. 1998 112p il $20 (5 and up)   **231**

1. God 2. Bible stories

ISBN 0-395-70734-X   LC 97-21637

Explores some of the images which biblical writers use to teach about God; images include light, rock, and wind as well as a gardener, father, and architect

"The commentary is both explanation and storytelling. It is simple yet profound. Koshkin's paintings in watercolor, tempera and gouache live up to the writing. They are full of movement, color and realistic detail." Child Book Rev Serv

232.9 Family and life of Jesus

Bible. N.T. Selections

The Christmas story; according to the Gospels of Matthew and Luke from the King James Version; paintings by Gennady Spirin. Holt & Co. 1998 32p il $19.95   **232.9**

1. Jesus Christ—Nativity

ISBN 0-8050-5292-5   LC 97-50417

Presents the story of the birth of Christ, from Mary's meeting with the angel Gabriel to the birth of baby Jesus in a stable and the visit of the shepherds and three Wise Men

"The beautiful illustrations, with angels everywhere and Christian symbols such as lilies, are illuminated by an appropriate golden glow that gives an air of religiosity and holiness to the art." Booklist

The Easter story; according to the Gospels of Matthew, Luke & John; illustrated by Gennady Spirin. Holt & Co. 1999 31p il $19.95; lib bdg $19.95   **232.9**

1. Jesus Christ 2. Bible stories 3. Easter

ISBN 0-8050-5052-3; 0-8050-6333-1 (lib bdg)

     LC 98-7087

By combining verses from the gospels of Matthew, Luke, and John, tells the Easter story from Jesus' triumphant entry into Jerusalem through his passion and resurrection to his appearance to his disciples

"From the elaborate architectural details to the stunning use of color and light, the artist's prodigious command of the page inspires awe." Publ Wkly

The first Christmas; illustrated with paintings from the National Gallery, London. Simon & Schuster Bks. for Young Readers 1992 29p il $17 (4 and up)   **232.9**

1. Jesus Christ—Nativity

ISBN 0-671-79364-0   LC 92-11580

The story of the birth of Jesus is illustrated with paintings from the National Gallery in London

"A showcase of ornately beautiful art from 13th, 14th, and 15th century Italy, France, and the Netherlands. . . . The paintings are an apt match for the classic words of the King James Version of the Bible. This book starts with the Annunciation by the Angel Gabriel and ends with the Holy Family returning home by way of Egypt. This is a handsome book in terms of layout, quality of reproduction, and selection of paintings." SLJ

De Paola, Tomie, 1934-

The miracles of Jesus; retold from the Bible and illustrated by Tomie dePaola. Holiday House 1987 unp il $16.95; pa $8.95 (k-3)   **232.9**

1. Jesus Christ 2. Bible stories

ISBN 0-8234-0635-0; 0-8234-1211-3 (pa)

     LC 86-18297

"Thirteen miracles, with the Biblical texts only slightly shortened and simplified, are retold with the beauty and dignity of the original. The artist's typical stylized, flat, highly decorative illustrations of sturdy, pensive figures, their faces often expressing awe, in soft, warm tones, have a still, timeless quality particularly appropriate to the spirituality and eternity of the subject." SLJ

Mayer, Marianna, 1945-
Young Jesus of Nazareth. Morrow Junior Bks.
1999 32p il $16; lib bdg $15.93 (4 and up)
232.9
1. Jesus Christ
ISBN 0-688-14061-0; 0-688-14062-9 (lib bdg)
LC 98-47474
Presents a picture of the early life of Jesus and the
signs that revealed him as a very extraordinary child
"Beautiful reproductions of some of Europe's finest
sacred art complement Mayer's . . . mellifluous account
of Jesus' childhood. Blending accounts from Matthew
and Luke with stories from the apocrypha and other religious writings, Mayer presents a fully dimensional extended portrait of the Holy Family." Publ Wkly
Includes bibliographical references

Osborne, Mary Pope, 1949-
The life of Jesus in masterpieces of art. Viking
1998 48p il $17.99
232.9
1. Jesus Christ 2. Religious art
ISBN 0-670-87313-6
LC 98-60316
In this "introduction to the life and times of Jesus, Osborne links scenes from Scripture to paintings by artists
ranging from Giotto to Botticelli, and explains their historical religious significance." Publ Wkly
"This simplified, rhythmic text is printed in a large,
elegant typeface and is sumptuously illustrated with an
interesting variety of art reproductions." SLJ

Thompson, Lauren
Love one another; the last days of Jesus; retold
by Lauren Thompson; illustrated by Elizabeth
Uyehara. Scholastic Press 2000 unp il lib bdg
$15.95 (1-3)
232.9
1. Jesus Christ 2. Easter 3. Bible stories
ISBN 0-590-31830-6
LC 99-25157
"Drawing from all four Evangelists, Thompson retells
events from the life of Jesus from his public role as
preacher and teacher through the aftermath of his death
and the continuing mission of his disciples." Bull Cent
Child Books
"The text has a fine read-aloud rhythm. . . . The oil-
on-canvas illustrations, with a sweep and agitation reminiscent of van Gogh, are almost overpowering with their
bold lines, gleaming stained-glass colors, and dramatic
movement." SLJ

Winthrop, Elizabeth
He is risen: the Easter story; adapted from the
New Testament by Elizabeth Winthrop; illustrated
by Charles Mikolaycak. Holiday House 1985 unp
il lib bdg $16.95 (k-3)
232.9
1. Jesus Christ 2. Easter 3. Bible stories
ISBN 0-8234-0547-8
LC 84-15869
"The Easter story, adapted from the King James Version of the Gospels of John and Matthew, has been
slightly altered and some of the obscure passages omitted
for the benefit of young readers." Child Book Rev Serv
"Mikolaycak's potent, yet emotionally controlled compositions are enclosed along with the text in narrow,
rust-colored borders that echo the earthy tones of the pic-

tures themselves. . . . The text is lengthy, and adults
may want to paraphrase the story in parts to hold youngsters' attention, but older listeners will be moved by the
timelessness of the language and the reverent beauty of
Mikolaycak's spellbinding interpretation." Booklist

232.91   Mary, mother of Jesus

De Paola, Tomie, 1934-
Mary, the mother of Jesus. Holiday House 1995
unp il $16.95 (3-5)
232.91
1. Mary, Blessed Virgin, Saint 2. Bible stories
ISBN 0-8234-1018-8
LC 92-54491
"Based on the New English Bible and legends about
the mother of Jesus, this picture book tells the story of
Mary's life in words and full-color artwork." Booklist
"The writing style is restrained, elegant, and expressive. Handsome, framed, full-page paintings; harmoniz-
ing, rectangular spot illustrations on the pages of text;
and a clear, attractive typeface give a balanced, dignified
appearance to the book." SLJ

Mayer, Marianna, 1945-
Young Mary of Nazareth. Morrow Junior Bks.
1998 32p il $16; lib bdg $15.93 (4 and up)
232.91
1. Mary, Blessed Virgin, Saint
ISBN 0-688-14061-0; 0-688-14062-9 (lib bdg)
LC 97-38944
An account of the life of the Virgin Mary, from her
own birth through her early years and education at the
Temple to the birth of Jesus in Bethlehem
"The account of Mary's early life reads fluidly and
evenly, and the artistic reproductions from masters such
as Rosetti, Giotto, Titian and Barocci contribute to a
well-rounded portrayal of this essential personage in
Christianity." Publ Wkly
Includes bibliographical references

242   Devotional literature

All God's children; a book of prayers; selected by
Lee Bennett Hopkins; illustrated by Amanda
Schaffer. Harcourt Brace & Co. 1998 48p il $15
(k-3)
242
1. Prayers 2. Religious poetry
ISBN 0-15-201499-3
LC 96-40944
Presents traditional prayers, such as "Now I Lay Me
Down To Sleep," and "The Lord's Prayer," as well as
prayers from such authors as Lois Duncan, Margaret
Wise Brown, and Carl Sandburg
"People of many faiths will appreciate the familiar and
new passages celebrating God's hand in creation and expressing thankfulness for blessings received. Schaffer's
oil paintings show children of various ethnicities engaged
in everyday activities." Horn Book Guide

Beckett, Wendy
A child's book of prayer in art. Dorling
Kindersley 1995 32p il $14.95 (3-6)
242
1. Prayers 2. Art appreciation
ISBN 1-56458-875-0
LC 94-40362

Beckett, Wendy—*Continued*

"Linking the work of 15 different artists, from Michelangelo to Millet, to a spiritual value such as respect or forgiveness, Sister Wendy Beckett introduces children to art as a means of discovering faith. . . . With appeal to older as well as middle readers, this is a remarkable book, not only for its innate spirituality and wisdom, but also for its harmonious partnership of great art and astute interpretation." Booklist

Field, Rachel, 1894-1942

Prayer for a child; pictures by Elizabeth Orton Jones. Macmillan 1944 unp il $14; pa $5.95 (k-3)
242

1. Prayers
ISBN 0-02-735190-4; 0-02-043070-1 (pa)
Awarded the Caldecott Medal, 1945

One of Rachel Field's "greatest legacies to [children] has been this [brief] prayer. It was written for her own daughter, but now belongs to all boys and girls everywhere. It is a prayer, beautifully written and . . . bespeaking the faith, love, hopes, and the trust of little children." Libr J

"The pictures have a freshness and childlikeness which match the text perfectly." Boston Globe

Goble, Paul

I sing for the animals. Bradbury Press 1991 unp il $9.95
242

1. Creation
ISBN 0-02-737725-3　　　　　　LC 90-19812

Reflects on how we are all connected to everything in nature and how all things in nature relate to their Creator

The author's "hallmark artistic technique, bold outlines and clean colors, are used to good effect, and the random thoughts are expressed in a careful and sensitive way." SLJ

Lindbergh, Reeve

The circle of days; from Canticle of the sun by Saint Francis of Assisi; illustrated by Cathie Felstead. Candlewick Press 1998 unp il $15.99 (k-3)
242

1. Prayers
ISBN 0-7636-0357-0　　　　　　LC 96-49848

Rhyming text gives praise and thanks for all of creation including wind and sun, plants and animals, desert, rocks, and sea

"The poem is accessible . . . and quite lyrical. Felstead uses collage and paint to create a benevolent and varied world to complement the poem." Horn Book Guide

One earth, one spirit; a child's book of prayers from many faiths and cultures; compiled by Tessa Strickland. Sierra Club Bks. for Children 1997 unp il $14.95
242

1. Prayers
ISBN 0-87156-978-7　　　　　　LC 96-40387

Photographs of children from around the world are combined with more than fifteen prayers from different times and places to celebrate the natural world

"Poignant children's images accompany poetic expressions that reflect a reverence for the oneness of all living things. Last-page notes provide insights into each prayer's cultural source." Kobrin Letter

289　Other denominations and sects

Bial, Raymond

Shaker home. Houghton Mifflin 1994 37p il $15.95 (3-5)
289

1. Shakers
ISBN 0-395-64047-4　　　　　　LC 93-17917

Text and photographs depict the way of life of the Shakers

"Bial's color photographs are well composed, and his writing is crisp, yet thoughtful. Readers finish the book with a clear understanding of how the Shakers and their idealistic belief in a utopian society have enriched our lives." Horn Book Guide

Includes bibliographical references

289.7　Mennonite churches

Ammon, Richard

An Amish wedding; illustrated by Pamela Patrick. Atheneum Bks. for Young Readers 1998 unp il $17 (k-3)
289.7

1. Amish 2. Weddings
ISBN 0-689-81677-4　　　　　　LC 97-9740
Also available An Amish Christmas (1996)

"Narrated by the bride's younger sister, this picture-book account of an Amish wedding describes the exciting events that take place before, during, and after the special day. . . . Patrick's realistic illustrations . . . are nicely done, showing authentic Amish dress and capturing the simple grace and peaceful way of life of the people." Booklist

An Amish year; illustrated by Pamela Patrick. Atheneum Bks. for Young Readers 2000 unp il lib bdg $16.95 (k-3)
289.7

1. Amish
ISBN 0-689-82622-2　　　　　　LC 98-52806

"Ammon relates the seasonal rhythms of Amish life through a girl's account of the foods, quiet celebrations, farm chores, and games from Easter and spring cleaning through fall canning, Christmas, and Valentine's Day. . . . Patrick's pastel illustrations feature realistic figures in traditional garb, outlined against impressionistic backgrounds." SLJ

Bial, Raymond

Amish home. Houghton Mifflin 1993 40p il $17; pa $5.95 (3-5)
289.7

1. Amish
ISBN 0-395-59504-5; 0-395-72021-4 (pa)
LC 92-4406

Text and photographs depict the way of life of the Amish

The full-color photos depict "cozy kitchens, lovingly tended gardens, prized horses, and rolling landscapes. As well as being informative, these photographs create a mood through which readers enter another lifestyle." SLJ

Includes bibliographical references

Kenna, Kathleen
A people apart; photographs by Andrew Stawicki. Somerville House Pub.; Houghton Mifflin 1995 64p il $17.95 (4 and up)   **289.7**
1. Mennonites
ISBN 0-395-67344-5   LC 94-18545
"A Nick Harris book"
This photo-essay "shows various aspects of life in Old Order Mennonite communities, including home, work, education, and worship. The well-written text does a good job of explaining the Mennonites' lifestyle and the reasons they choose to live as they do. It also explains how groups splinter off or individuals leave or are expelled because of disagreements about what is acceptable and unacceptable. . . . The full-page black-and-white photographs are marvelous and reflect the same respect for the way of life expressed in the narrative." SLJ
Includes bibliographical references

291   Comparative religion and religious mythology

Maestro, Betsy, 1944-
The story of religion; illustrated by Giulio Maestro. Clarion Bks. 1996 48p il map $14.95 (3-5)   **291**
1. Religions
ISBN 0-395-62364-2   LC 92-38980
Also available in paperback from Mulberry Bks.
"Beginning with early polytheistic beliefs in multiple spirits of gods and goddesses, and their usual strong link to nature, the author moves on to introduce Taoism and teachings of Confucius, Hinduism and Buddhism, Judaism, Christianity and Islam." SLJ
"Each religion is presented in only a couple of illustrated pages of text that manage to emphasize important points. The artwork, executed in colored pencil, ink, and water color, is varied and lively, with the illustrator looking to each religion's artistic traditions for inspiration." Booklist

Osborne, Mary Pope, 1949-
One world, many religions; the ways we worship. Knopf 1996 86p il map $25 (4 and up)   **291**
1. Religions
ISBN 0-679-83930-5   LC 96-836
This is an "overview of major world religions—Judaism, Christianity, Islam, Hinduism, Buddhism, Confucianism, and Taoism. . . . Each of six essay-styled chapters addresses themes of religious tenets, deities, morality, and ritual only as they are pertinent to a particular faith." Bull Cent Child Books
"The presentation is notable for its respect to each group, succinctness, and clarity. . . . The artful, full-page, color and black-and-white photographs tell much of the story." SLJ
Includes glossary and bibliographical references

291.1   Religious mythology

Bulfinch, Thomas, 1796-1867
Bulfinch's mythology (6 and up)   **291.1**
1. Mythology 2. Folklore—Europe 3. Chivalry

Hardcover and paperback editions available from various publishers
First combined edition published 1913 by Crowell. First published in three separate volumes 1855, 1858 and 1862 respectively
Contents: The age of fable; The age of chivalry; Legends of Charlemagne
"The basic work on classical mythology. Includes information on Greek, Roman, Norse, Egyptian, Asian, Germanic myths, as well as the Arthurian cycle and other heroic epics." N Y Public Libr. Ref Books for Child Collect

Ganeri, Anita, 1961-
Out of the ark; stories from the world's religions; illustrated by Jackie Morris. Harcourt Brace & Co. 1996 96p il $18 (4 and up)   **291.1**
1. Religions 2. Mythology
ISBN 0-15-200943-4   LC 95-7269
The author retells "traditional stories from seven major world religions in a straightforward and respectful manner. They are arranged thematically, such as 'Flood Stories' or 'Birth, Courtship, and Marriage,' and each section includes from 5-10 selections. The reteller places each tale in the context of its religious tradition but does not allow doctrine to dominate story. Similarities between certain tales are noted, but usually readers are left to draw their own comparisons. Appendixes offer basic facts about each religion represented and brief identifications of characters." SLJ

Hamilton, Virginia, 1936-
In the beginning; creation stories from around the world; told by Virginia Hamilton; illustrated by Barry Moser. Harcourt Brace Jovanovich 1988 161p il lib bdg $26; pa $14.95 (5 and up) **291.1**
1. Creation 2. Mythology
ISBN 0-15-238740-4 (lib bdg); 0-15-238742-0 (pa)
LC 88-6211
A Newbery Medal honor book, 1989
"Hamilton has gathered 25 creation myths from various cultures and retold them in language true to the original. Images from the tales are captured in Moser's 42 full-page illustrations, tantalizing oil paintings that are rich with somber colors and striking compositions. Included in the collection are the familiar stories (biblical creation stories, Greek and Roman myths), and some that are not so familiar (tales from the Australian aborigines, various African and native American tribes, as well as from countries like Russia, China, and Iceland). At the end of each tale, Hamilton provides a brief commentary on the story's origin and originators." Booklist
Includes bibliographical references

Philip, Neil

The illustrated book of myths; tales & legends of the world; retold by Neil Philip; illustrated by Nilesh Mistry. Dorling Kindersley 1995 192p il $19.95 (5 and up)   **291.1**

1. Mythology

ISBN 0-7894-0202-5   LC 95-2156

"This collection represents a wide variety of world cultures and stories. Selections are grouped by type (creation myths, fertility and cultivation, visions of the end), which helps readers understand the commonality of the tales. The standard Greek and Norse myths are here, but what makes this volume special is its inclusion of less frequently anthologized stories of the Aztecs, Haitians, Africans, and Japanese, to name a few." SLJ

291.4 Religious experience, life, practice

Baylor, Byrd, 1924-

The way to start a day; by Byrd Baylor; illustrated by Peter Parnall. Scribner 1978 unp il lib bdg $17; pa $5.99 (1-4)   **291.4**

1. Worship 2. Sun worship

ISBN 0-684-15651-2 (lib bdg); 0-689-71054-2 (pa)
LC 78-113

A Caldecott Medal honor book, 1979

Text and illustrations describe how people all over the world celebrate the sunrise

"While the format is that of a picture book, the concepts in the poetic text of this handsome volume are more appropriate for independent readers who can grasp the historic and ritual values of Baylor's thoughts." Bull Cent Child Books

In every tiny grain of sand; a child's book of prayers and praise; collected by Reeve Lindbergh; illustrated by Christine Davenier [et al.] Candlewick Press 2000 77p il $21.99 (2-5)
291.4

1. Prayers 2. Worship

ISBN 0-7636-0176-4   LC 99-89379

A "collection of 77 poems and prayers, illustrated by four different artists. There are excerpts from Native American, Hindu, Jewish, Buddhist, Christian, African, and Baha'i prayers and meditations as well as offerings from individual poets." SLJ

"This is a prayerful, powerful collection." Booklist

292 Classical religion and religious mythology

Aliki

The gods and goddesses of Olympus; written and illustrated by Aliki. HarperCollins Pubs. 1994 48p il $16; pa $6.95 (2-5)   **292**

1. Classical mythology

ISBN 0-06-023530-6; 0-06-446189-0 (pa)
LC 93-17834

"After the Uranus-Gaea, Cronus-Rhea background is sketched, the occupants of the 12 golden thrones are each described, along with Hades (underground), Hestia (hearth-bound) and Eros (hovering). The author outlines the deities' characters and attributes, sometimes including a brief incident from their lives." SLJ

"This large-format book provides a quick, brightly illustrated introduction to the ancient Greek gods and goddesses." Booklist

Burleigh, Robert, 1936-

Hercules; illustrated by Raúl Colón. Silver Whistle Bks. 1999 unp il $16 (3-6)   **292**

1. Hercules (Legendary character)

ISBN 0-15-201667-8   LC 98-4989

Retells the story of the final, and most difficult, labor of Hercules, known as Heracles in Greek mythology, in which he must go to Underworld and bring back the three-headed dog, Cerberus

"The narrative is spare, broken into short, poetic lines. . . . The success of this version depends heavily on Colón's watercolor and colored-pencil illustrations. His characteristically golden hues work well for the Mediterranean and mythical setting." SLJ

Colum, Padraic, 1881-1972

The Golden Fleece and the heroes who lived before Achilles; illustrated by Willy Pogany. Macmillan 1962 c1921 316p il $18; pa $9.95 (5 and up)   **292**

1. Argonauts (Greek mythology) 2. Classical mythology

ISBN 0-02-723620-X; 0-02-042260-1 (pa)

A reissue of the title first published 1921

Contents: The voyage to Colchis; The return to Greece; The heroes of the quest

"Mr. Colum preserves the spirit of the Greek tales and weaves them into a magic whole. In this he is aided by the spirited drawings." Booklist

Craft, Marie

Cupid and Psyche; as told by M. Charlotte Craft; illustrated by K. Y. Craft. Morrow Junior Bks. 1996 unp il $16 (4 and up)   **292**

1. Eros (Greek deity) 2. Psyche (Greek deity) 3. Classical mythology

ISBN 0-688-13163-8   LC 95-14895

"In this Greek myth, Cupid falls in love with Psyche and treats her royally but does not reveal himself. When Psyche tries to discover his identity, Cupid leaves her, but she wins him back by accomplishing three difficult tasks. Recalling an earlier artistic era, the occasionally ornate romantic paintings—some of them quite dramatic—feature detailed landscapes and beautiful figures in flowing drapery." Horn Book Guide

Daly, Kathleen N.

Greek and Roman mythology A to Z; a young reader's companion. Facts on File 1992 132p il map lib bdg $19.95 (5 and up)   **292**

1. Classical mythology—Dictionaries

ISBN 0-8160-2151-1   LC 91-43037

Daly, Kathleen N.—*Continued*
Presents the gods, goddesses, heroes, places, and other aspects of Greek and Roman mythology in alphabetically arranged entries

"The format is accessible, making the book useful for school assignments, as well as enjoyable for general reading. . . . The broad coverage, ample cross-references, and extensive index enable readers to recognize the many connections and interrelationships between characters and myths." SLJ

Includes bibliographical references

Fisher, Leonard Everett, 1924-
Cyclops; written and illustrated by Leonard Everett Fisher. Holiday House 1991 unp il map hardcover o.p. paperback available $5.95 (3-5)
292
1. Cyclopes (Greek mythology) 2. Odysseus (Greek mythology) 3. Classical mythology
ISBN 0-8234-1062-5 (pa)   LC 90-29317
Describes the encounter between the Cyclops Polyphemus and Odysseus and his men after the end of the Trojan War

"Fisher's narrative is compressed and direct; the illustrations, in rich, saturated oils complement its simplified and dramatic qualities." SLJ

Includes bibliographical references

Theseus and the Minotaur; written and illustrated by Leonard Everett Fisher. Holiday House 1988 unp il map hardcover o.p. paperback available $5.95 (3-5)   292
1. Theseus (Greek mythology) 2. Minotaur (Greek mythology)
ISBN 0-8234-0954-6 (pa)   LC 88-1970
Retells the Greek myth of the hero Theseus and his battle with the bull-headed monster called the Minotaur

"Fisher's paintings, styled in monumental proportions, somber colors, and simple compositions, are well suited to a Greek tale of heroic deeds and death. . . . Fisher has also done a careful job of selecting and consolidating various versions, for which he cites sources in the beginning. An impressive meeting of myth and picture book." Bull Cent Child Books

Geringer, Laura
The pomegranate seeds; a classic Greek myth; retold by Laura Geringer; illlustrated by Leonid Gore. Houghton Mifflin 1995 48p il $15.95 (3-5)
292
1. Persephone (Greek deity)
ISBN 0-395-68192-8   LC 94-11772
"King Hades is so lonely that he kidnaps his niece, Persephone, and brings her to his kingdom in the underworld. But Persephone's mother, the earth-goddess Demeter, decrees that nothing—not even a blade of grass—will grow on earth until her beloved daughter is returned to her." Publisher's note

"Geringer's smoothly written text constructs a version of the tale that is at once contemporarily relevant and solidly classic. . . . Gore's illustrations are emotional and luminescent, perfect for the alternately bright and brooding qualities of the tale." SLJ

Hamilton, Edith, 1867-1963
Mythology; illustrated by Steele Savage. Little, Brown 1942 497p il $27.95; pa $13 (6 and up)
292
1. Classical mythology 2. Norse mythology
ISBN 0-316-34114-2; 0-316-34151-7 (pa)
Contents: The gods, the creation and the earliest heroes; Stories of love and adventure; Great heroes before the Trojan War; Heroes of the Trojan War; Great families of mythology; Less important myths; Mythology of the Norsemen; Genealogical tables

Hutton, Warwick
Odysseus and the Cyclops; retold and illustrated by Warwick Hutton. Margaret K. McElderry Bks. 1995 unp il $15 (3-5)   292
1. Odysseus (Greek mythology) 2. Cyclopes (Greek mythology) 3. Classical mythology
ISBN 0-689-80036-3   LC 94-31303
A retelling of how Odysseus and his companions outwit the giant one-eyed Cyclops and escape from his cave

"Hutton's spare text and storytelling style suggest preliterary origins, but his illustrations give a sense of times past and the all-pervading influence of sea and sky. . . . Emphasis is more on ingenuity than on gore. . . . An appeal to the mind rather than merely to the emotions." Horn Book

Perseus; retold and illustrated by Warwick Hutton. Margaret K. McElderry Bks. 1993 unp il $14.95 (3-5)   292
1. Perseus (Greek mythology) 2. Medusa (Greek mythology) 3. Classical mythology
ISBN 0-689-50565-5   LC 92-7639
Retells the Greek myth in which the hero Perseus beheads Medusa, the most horrible of the Gorgons

"Children will be caught up in the action-packed adventure. The watercolor art is as typically graceful as that on a Greek vase—blue, green, and gold with touches of russet." SLJ

Theseus and the Minotaur; retold and illustrated by Warwick Hutton. Margaret K. McElderry Bks. 1989 unp il $14.95 (3-5)   292
1. Theseus (Greek mythology) 2. Minotaur (Greek mythology)
ISBN 0-689-50473-X   LC 88-26875
Recounts how Theseus killed the monster, Minotaur, with the help of Ariadne

Hutton "makes specific use of patterns and designs of Minoan artifacts, architecture, and costume. And whether he depicts action viewed from daring perspectives or in broad panoramas or whether he reveals character in close-ups, his narrative paintings carry emotional intensity and are imbued with personal as well as with universal meanings." Horn Book

Low, Alice, 1926-
The Macmillan book of Greek gods and heroes; illustrated by Arvis Stewart. Macmillan 1985 184p il $18 (3-6)   292
1. Classical mythology
ISBN 0-02-761390-9   LC 85-7170

Low, Alice, 1926——*Continued*

Retellings of ancient Greek myths including the legends of Odysseus, Pandora, Pygmalion, Heracles, and Perseus

"The tales are clearly told, without embroidery. A useful index not only refers the reader to a page or pages, but briefly identifies the character or subject as well. Watercolors in glowing earth tones with touches of blue and decorative pen-and-ink drawings enhance the book's appeal." Booklist

Mayer, Marianna, 1945-

Pegasus; as told by Marianna Mayer; illustrated by K.Y. Craft. Morrow Junior Bks. 1998 unp il lib bdg $15.93 (4-6)   **292**

1. Pegasus (Greek mythology) 2. Classical mythology

ISBN 0-688-13383-5   LC 96-32442

Retells how Bellerophon, son of the king of Corinth, secures the help of the winged horse Pegasus in order to fight the monstrous Chimera

"Dark, painterly illustrations set in gold frames heighten the mysticism in this lyrical interpretation of the Greek myth." Horn Book Guide

McCaughrean, Geraldine, 1951-

Greek gods and goddesses; retold by Geraldine McCaughrean; illustrated by Emma Chichester Clark. Margaret K. McElderry Bks. 1998 108p il $20 (4-6)   **292**

1. Classical mythology

ISBN 0-689-82084-4

"McCaughrean uses the literary device of a story within a story to relate tales of Greek gods and goddesses. . . . The lively narrative offers accurate accounts of Artemis, Apollo, Demeter, Hephaestus, Aphrodite, and others. Chichester Clark has incorporated stylistic Greek art into her bright watercolor interpretations of the Olympians as they frolic on nearly every page." SLJ

Greek myths; retold by Geraldine McCaughrean; illustrated by Emma Chichester Clark. Margaret K. McElderry Bks. 1993 c1992 96p il $19.95 (4-6)   **292**

1. Classical mythology

ISBN 0-689-50583-3   LC 92-61748

First published 1992 in the United Kingdom

Retells sixteen tales from Greek mythology, including Pandora's box, King Midas, The twelve labors of Heracles, and Orpheus and Eurydice

"McCaughrean's style is fresh and lively, dynamic and direct. She is faithful in essentials, but not afraid to edit. . . . The text is matched by clear, rainbow-bright illustrations. Clark's watercolors are lighthearted and engaging, and a picture or decoration enlivens every page." SLJ

Osborne, Mary Pope, 1949-

Favorite Greek myths; retold by Mary Pope Osborne; illustrated by Troy Howell. Scholastic 1989 81p il lib bdg $18.95 (3-6)   **292**

1. Classical mythology

ISBN 0-590-41338-4   LC 87-32332

Retells twelve tales from Greek mythology, including the stories of King Midas, Echo and Narcissus, the Golden Apples, and Cupid and Psyche

"Osborne's retellings are both lively and descriptive, while Howell's full-color, often iridescent illustrations set the scene and mood at the start of each tale." Publ Wkly

Includes glossary and bibliographical references

Vinge, Joan D., 1948-

The Random House book of Greek myths; illustrated by Oren Sherman. Random House 1999 152p il $25; lib bdg $26.99 (4 and up)   **292**

1. Classical mythology

ISBN 0-679-82377-8; 0-679-92377-2 (lib bdg)

     LC 99-19080

Retells some of the most famous Greek myths about gods, goddesses, humans, heroes, and monsters, explaining the background of the tales and how they have survived

293   Germanic religion and religious mythology

Climo, Shirley, 1928-

Stolen thunder; a Norse myth; retold by Shirley Climo; illustrated by Alexander Koshkin. Clarion Bks. 1994 32p il lib bdg $15.95 (3-5)   **293**

1. Norse mythology

ISBN 0-395-64368-6   LC 93-24627

"In order to retrieve Thor's powerful hammer, which has been stolen by the giant Thrym, Thor - the thunder god - and the trickster Loki disguise themselves as bride and handmaiden and travel to the land of the blue-skinned frost giants." Horn Book Guide

Climo's "dramatic text, jammed with snappy dialogue and colorful emotions, is framed in gold. The lovely full- and half-page paintings, also neatly framed, heighten both the distinctive characters and the fast-moving plot." Booklist

Osborne, Mary Pope, 1949-

Favorite Norse myths; retold by Mary Pope Osborne; illustrated by Troy Howell. Scholastic 1996 87p il hardcover o.p. paperback available $7.99 (4 and up)   **293**

1. Norse mythology

ISBN 0-590-48047-2 (pa)   LC 94-34222

A collection of rarely retold tales from the "Elder Edda" and the "Younger Edda," two six-hundred-year-old Norse manuscripts

The tales are "retold with clarity and grace. The unusual artwork combines acrylic paintings with line drawings reminiscent of Norse carvings in their simplicity and vigor. . . . The informative appendixes include glossaries of the gods, goddesses, giants, giantesses, dwarves, worlds, events, places, and things as well as discussions of symbols and runes." Booklist

Includes bibliographical references

Philip, Neil
Odin's family; myths of the Vikings; retold by
Neil Philip; illustrated by Maryclare Foa. Orchard
Bks. 1996 124p il $19.95 (4-6)   **293**
1. Norse mythology
ISBN 0-531-09531-2   LC 96-1965
"Philip tells the stories of the origin of the gods and
frost giants, how Odin got his wisdom, the death of
Baldur, the coming of Ragnarok, and eleven other Norse
myths. What distinguishes Philip's anthology is its design: large print, a generous amount of white space, and
full-page color art make this an eminently accessible,
easily promoted collection. Foa's oil paintings (with a
preponderance of red, gold and blue) have a primitive
vigor." Bull Cent Child Books
Includes bibliographical references

294.3   Buddhism

Chödzin, Sherab
The wisdom of the crows and other Buddhist
tales; retold by Sherab Chödzin & Alexandra
Kohn; illustrated by Marie Cameron. Tricycle
Press 1998 c1997 80p il pa $16.95 (4 and up)
                                           294.3
1. Buddhism
ISBN 1-883672-68-6   LC 97-30441
First published 1997 in the United Kingdom with title:
The Barefoot book of Buddhist tales
A collection of thirteen retold Buddhist tales from all
over Asia, illustrating various aspects of Buddhist
thought
"Folktale lovers will find much to like here. Marie
Cameron's clear, fresh watercolors, incorporating Asian
artistic motifs and bordered with waves and origami, are
handsomely rendered." Booklist
Includes bibliographical references

Demi, 1942-
Buddha. Holt & Co. 1996 unp il $18.95 (4-6)
                                           294.3
1. Gautama Buddha
ISBN 0-8050-4203-2   LC 95-16906
The author "tells the story of Siddhartha's birth and
the prophecies surrounding it, touches upon his childhood, and then follows his path to enlightenment." Booklist
Demi "uses clear, uncomplicated storytelling to
present complex philosophical concepts. . . . The gilded
illustrations (based, according to the jacket, on "Indian,
Chinese, Japanese, Burmese, and Indonesian paintings,
sculptures, and sutra illustrations") are delicate, yet the
colors and composition are bold, with central figures and
action cascading beyond the careful borders." Bull Cent
Child Books

Buddha stories. Holt & Co. 1997 unp il $20
(3-6)   **294.3**
1. Jataka stories
ISBN 0-8050-4886-3   LC 96-31253
This "is a picture-book collection of eleven Jataka
tales retold in a formal yet straightforward style. . . . An

author's note gives the source of the tales as well as the
historical basis for the design concept behind the elegantly sophisticated artwork. Both text and illustrations are
done in gold ink on deep indigo paper, resulting in a
striking visual impact." Bull Cent Child Books

Lee, Jeanne M.
I once was a monkey; stories Buddha told.
Farrar, Straus & Giroux 1999 unp il $16 (2-5)
                                           294.3
1. Jataka stories
ISBN 0-374-33548-6   LC 98-17651
A retelling of six Jatakas, or birth stories, which illustrate some of the central tenets of Buddha's teachings,
such as compassion, honesty, and thinking clearly before
acting
"The appealing character of the monkey will pull children into the tales, which convey lessons in a direct yet
gentle way that is never preachy. The accompanying li-
nocut illustrations are lovely." Booklist

296   Judaism

Fisher, Leonard Everett, 1924-
To bigotry, no sanction; the story of the oldest
synagogue in America. Holiday House 1998 64p il
$16.95 (4 and up)   **296**
1. Touro Synagogue (Newport, R.I.) 2. Jews—United
States
ISBN 0-8234-1401-9   LC 98-12834
The author discusses "the history of the Jews in
America in general and the building of the Touro Syna-
gogue, the oldest in the U.S. in particular. Fisher does
his usual excellent job of bringing history to life." Book-
list
Includes bibliographical references

296.1   Judaism—Sources

Chaikin, Miriam, 1928-
Clouds of glory; legends and stories about Bible
times; illustrations by David Frampton. Clarion
Bks. 1997 118p il $19 (4 and up)   **296.1**
1. Jewish legends 2. Bible stories
ISBN 0-395-74654-X   LC 97-5042
"The stories in this book are largely based on Rashi's
commentary on the book of Genesis, and on midrashic
threads found in Louis Ginzberg's Legends of the Bible
and in Raphael Patai's Gates of the Old City." Acknowl-
edgments
Presents twenty-one stories, in a single narrative,
about God's relationship with His creation, from creating
angels on the second day to testing Abraham's love
"The stories are told in an involving narrative style
and the book lends itself to discussions about values and
historical development. The woodcuts are few in number,
but provide authenticity to the stories." Child Book Rev
Serv
Includes bibliographical references

Cooper, Ilene
The Dead Sea scrolls; illustrated by John Thompson. Morrow Junior Bks. 1997 58p il $15 (5 and up)   **296.1**
1. Dead Sea scrolls
ISBN 0-688-14300-8   LC 96-21983
Details the important archaeological discovery of the ancient manuscripts known as the Dead Sea Scrolls and discusses efforts to translate them, the battle over their possession, and the people who have figured in their history
"The text's seven brief chapters are clear and accessible. In covering the events from 1947 to the present, Cooper also manages to get in a good bit of the ancient history relevant to readers' understanding of the whole picture, all the while conveying the intrigue of the many questions that still mystify scholars." Horn Book
Includes glossary and bibliographical references

Jaffe, Nina
While standing on one foot; puzzle stories and wisdom tales from the Jewish tradition; [by] Nina Jaffe and Steve Zeitlin; pictures by John Segal. Holt & Co. 1993 120p il hardcover o.p. paperback available $7.95 (4 and up)   **296.1**
1. Jewish legends
ISBN 0-8050-5073-6 (pa)   LC 93-13750
"Each of seventeen tales is divided into two sections: the first poses a dilemma for the main character; the second describes the clever solution. . . . The entire collection is of general interest because of the solve-it-yourself aspect . . . and the suspense or humor of the difficulties. . . . Wash drawings in black and white are whimsically stylized with figures that have a humorous, paper-doll quality." Bull Cent Child Books
Includes glossary and bibliographical references

Lester, Julius
When the beginning began; stories about God, the creatures, and us; illustrations by Emily Lisker. Silver Whistle Bks. 1999 100p il $17 (4 and up)   **296.1**
1. Creation 2. Bible stories 3. Jewish legends
ISBN 0-15-201238-9   LC 97-37352
A collection of traditional and original Jewish tales interpreting the Biblical story of the creation of the world
"Lester fuses two traditions here—the 'loving irreverence' of African-American storytelling and the imaginative inquiry of midrashim. . . . Lisker's paintings capture the stories' primal essence (and a bit of their playfulness) in bold, archetypal forms. A reverent, wise, witty, and wonderfully entertaining book." Horn Book Guide
Includes bibliographical references

Schwartz, Howard, 1945-
Next year in Jerusalem; 3,000 years of Jewish stories; retold by Howard Schwartz; illustrated by Neil Waldman. Viking 1996 56p il $16.99 (4 and up)   **296.1**
1. Jewish legends 2. Jerusalem
ISBN 0-670-86110-3   LC 95-31213

"A collection of 11 Jewish folktales and legends from around the world, all centering on the city of Jerusalem. Stories are taken from the Talmud and Midrash, from folklore, or from mystical or Hasidic sources." SLJ
"Sidebars set the tales in a factual framework, and all are lovingly illustrated by Waldman in a dreamy style colored with the golds, pinks, and blues that shine from the real city of Jerusalem." Booklist
Includes glossary and bibliographical references

296.4   Judaism—Traditions, rites, public services

Berger, Gilda
Celebrate! stories of the Jewish holidays; paintings by Peter Catalanotto. Scholastic 1998 114p il $17.95 (4 and up)   **296.4**
1. Jewish holidays
ISBN 0-590-93503-8   LC 97-40150
"Berger examines the history of the major holidays of the Jewish faith and the Bible story that lies behind the celebration of each, as well as the customs that make these special days. The lively writing coupled with Catalanotto's dramatic watercolors ensure that this volume will become a treasured family favorite." Publ Wkly

Chaikin, Miriam, 1928-
Menorahs, mezuzas, and other Jewish symbols; illustrated by Erika Weihs. Clarion Bks. 1990 102p il $17 (5 and up)   **296.4**
1. Jewish art and symbolism 2. Judaism—Customs and practices
ISBN 0-89919-856-2   LC 89-77719
Explains the history and significance of many Jewish symbols, such as the Shield of David, the menorah, and the mezuza, and discusses holiday symbols and rituals
"Embellished with bibliographical references as well as Weihs' simple yet elegant and wonderfully dramatic scratchboard illustrations, this smoothly woven patchwork of history and culture is a fine introduction that will attract browsers and be useful for children investigating the subject of symbolism in school." Booklist

Fishman, Cathy, 1951-
On Hanukkah; by Cathy Goldberg Fishman; illustrated by Melanie W. Hall. Atheneum Bks. for Young Readers 1998 unp il $16 (k-3)   **296.4**
1. Hanukkah
ISBN 0-689-80643-4   LC 96-44696
"Fishman and Hall focus on a family's celebration of a Jewish holiday. The writing is simple and direct, yet the coverage is ample. . . . The fanciful, mixed-media paintings feature strong texturing and glowing, gilt-edged colors." Booklist

On Passover; by Cathy Goldberg Fishman; illustrated by Melanie W. Hall. Atheneum Bks. for Young Readers 1997 unp il $16; pa $5.99 (k-3)   **296.4**
1. Passover
ISBN 0-689-80528-4; 0-689-83264-6 (pa)
LC 97-114611

Fishman, Cathy, 1951— *Continued*

"A young girl shares the preparations and the rituals that are part of the traditional Passover seder." SLJ

"This is illustrated in beautiful Chagall-like pictures that are rooted in both the practicalities of Passover preparation and the joyful spirit of this holiday of freedom. . . . The book is a lovely introduction to the holiday." Booklist

On Purim; [by] Cathy Goldberg Fishman; illustrated by Melanie W. Hall. Atheneum Bks. for Young Readers 2000 unp il lib bdg $16 (k-3)
296.4
1. Purim
ISBN 0-689-82392-4   LC 98-36389
Uses the story of a family's preparations for the Jewish holiday of Purim to explain the traditions connected with this celebration
Provides an "inclusive view of the celebration, buttressed by a strong sense of family togetherness. The flowing, vibrantly colored artwork, handsomely rendered, glows with warm purples, pinks, greens, and golds." Booklist

On Rosh Hashanah and Yom Kippur; by Cathy Goldberg Fishman; illustrated by Melanie W. Hall. Atheneum Bks. for Young Readers 1997 unp il $16; pa $5.99 (k-3)   **296.4**
1. Rosh ha-Shanah 2. Yom Kippur
ISBN 0-689-80526-8; 0-689-83892-1 (pa)
LC 96-23258
"Fishman explores and explains the traditions associated with the Jewish High Holidays. She focuses mainly on Rosh Hashanah . . . and in a quiet, almost reverent way uses the voice of a little girl to make readers party to a family's celebrations. . . . Hall's beautiful, rosy, expressionistic pictures are a fine complement to Fishman's text. They capture the warm glow of a family celebrating together." Booklist

Goldin, Barbara Diamond
The Passover journey; a Seder companion; illustrated by Neil Waldman. Viking 1994 56p il $15.99; pa $7.99 (4 and up)   **296.4**
1. Passover
ISBN 0-670-82421-6; 0-14-056131-5 (pa)
LC 93-5133
Retells the story of the Israelites' fight for liberation from slavery in Egypt and explains the traditions of the Passover Seder
"Goldin speaks simply, warmly, and directly throughout the book and lets her own love of the holiday shine through. . . . The many illustrations are an attractive mix of bold graphics and soft colors. The geometric borders and pastels characteristic of Waldman's work are . . . combined with stylized, classic Egyptian hieroglyphic figures and set against softly tinted pages that actually glow." Booklist
Includes glossary and bibliographical references

While the candles burn; eight stories for Hanukkah; illustrated by Elaine Greenstein. Viking 1996 60p il $16.99; pa $6.99 (4 and up)   **296.4**
1. Hanukkah
ISBN 0-670-85875-7; 0-14-037341-1 (pa)
LC 95-50310

"In her introduction Goldin discusses the celebratory customs of Hanukkah, noting similarities and differences around the world and pointing out the themes of her selected eight tales, including faith, religious freedom, charity, and miracles. The tales are folkloric, biblical, and original. . . . Greenstein's cheerful, boldly celebratory scratchboard and watercolor illustrations are generously interspersed throughout. . . . This is a solid addition to collections looking for something a little more unusual than typical holiday fare." Bull Cent Child Books
Includes bibliographical references

A **Hanukkah** treasury; edited by Eric A. Kimmel; illustrated by Emily Lisker. Holt & Co. 1998 99p il $19.95   **296.4**
1. Hanukkah
ISBN 0-8050-5293-3   LC 97-24428
Presents stories, songs, recipes, and activities related to the celebration of Hanukkah
"Emily Lisker's vibrant acrylic paintings accent the text in small and full-page illustrations. Her colors and fluid lines are dramatic and joyful." Booklist

Hildebrandt, Ziporah, 1956-
This is our Seder; illustrated by Robin Roraback. Holiday House 1999 unp il $15.95 (k-3)
296.4
1. Passover
ISBN 0-8234-1436-1   LC 98-4194
A simple description of the food and activities at a Seder, the ritual meal of Passover, including an explanation of their historical and symbolic significance
"The compositions are calm but busy, with plenty of background action. . . . Despite the explanatory note at the end, however, terms like 'afikomen' and rites like opening the door (for Elijah) go undefined, so that this book is best enjoyed by families who already know the special significance of Passover." Publ Wkly

Hoyt-Goldsmith, Diane
Celebrating Hanukkah; photographs by Lawrence Migdale. Holiday House 1996 31p il $16.95; pa $6.95 (3-5)   **296.4**
1. Hanukkah
ISBN 0-8234-1252-0; 0-8234-1411-6 (pa)
LC 96-5110
"Leora, the 11-year-old daughter of a San Francisco rabbi, explains the history of Hanukkah and describes how her family observes it." Publ Wkly
The photographs "are warm and inviting, with Migdale catching celebrations at home, at school, and in the synagogue. . . . The text is equally fine, well organized and rich in detail but also friendly." Booklist
Includes glossary

Celebrating Passover; photographs by Lawrence Migdale. Holiday House 2000 32p il lib bdg $16.95 (3-5)   **296.4**
1. Passover
ISBN 0-8234-1420-5   LC 99-49006
Uses one family's celebration of Passover to describe the religious significance, traditions, customs, and symbols of this Jewish holiday
"An attractive and useful choice for the holiday shelf; recipes, songs, and a glossary are a bonus." Booklist

Jaffe, Nina

The uninvited guest and other Jewish holiday tales; illustrated by Elivia. Scholastic 1993 72p il $16.95 (4-6)   **296.4**

1. Jewish holidays 2. Jewish legends
ISBN 0-590-44653-3   LC 92-36308

Includes background information and retellings of traditional tales from Jewish folklore and legend related to major holidays, such as Yom Kippur, Sukkot, Hanukkah, and Purim

"Elivia's bright, flowing artwork, in a rainbow of colors, reflects both the magic and the joy of the seven splendid Jewish holiday tales simply and beautifully retold here." Booklist

Includes glossary and bibliographical references

Kimmel, Eric A.

Bar mitzvah; a Jewish boy's coming of age; illustrated by Erika Weihs. Viking 1995 143p il $15 (5 and up)   **296.4**

1. Bar mitzvah
ISBN 0-670-85540-5   LC 94-34956

"Kimmel imparts basic information about Judaism, including some comparisons between Judaism and Catholicism and Islam, and discusses ritual objects, important texts, the Shabbat service, and the actual responsibilities of the bar mitzvah child." Booklist

"Children with no previous exposure to Jewish beliefs and rituals will find the explanations here both clear and enticing, respectful of different religious traditions. . . . Kimmel also accommodates Jewish readers from a variety of backgrounds, from Reform to Orthodox." Publ Wkly

Days of Awe; stories for Rosh Hashanah and Yom Kippur; adapted from traditional sources by Eric A. Kimmel; illustrated by Erika Weihs. Viking 1991 47p il $14.50 (3-6)   **296.4**

1. Rosh ha-Shanah 2. Yom Kippur
ISBN 0-670-82772-X   LC 91-50198

"The three themes central to the Jewish High Holidays of Rosh Hashanah and Yom Kippur are charity, prayer, and repentance. Eric Kimmel uses three stories from very old sources and, adding some of his own touches as a storyteller, beautifully illustrates the essence of each of these concepts. . . . Erika Weihs's paintings add warmth and quiet dignity to the moving tales." Horn Book

Musleah, Rahel

Why on this night? a Passover haggadah for family celebration; illustrated by Louise August. Simon & Schuster Bks. for Young Readers 2000 112p $24.95; pa $12.99   **296.4**

1. Passover
ISBN 0-689-81356-2; 0-689-83313-X (pa)
LC 97-2570

Includes the basic elements of a traditional seder as well as many creative facets intended to involve children in this Jewish liturgy through song, dance, drama, explanation, and action

"A useful addition to Jewish holiday collections." SLJ

Podwal, Mark H., 1945-

The menorah story. Greenwillow Bks. 1998 unp il $15; lib bdg $14.89 (k-3)   **296.4**

1. Hanukkah
ISBN 0-688-15758-0; 0-688-15759-9 (lib bdg)
LC 97-36300

Discusses the story of the Hanukkah menorah which commemorates the miraculous victory of the Maccabees over King Antiochus and his army

"In his distinctive paintings, Podwal incorporates traditional symbols within masterfully simplified compositions." Publ Wkly

Includes bibliographical references

Rosen, Michael J., 1954-

Our eight nights of Hanukkah; illustrated by DyAnne DiSalvo-Ryan. Holiday House 2000 unp il lib bdg $16.95 (k-3)   **296.4**

1. Hanukkah
ISBN 0-8234-1476-0   LC 99-11001

A child describes how one family celebrates Hanukkah, including polishing the silver menorah, lighting the candles, having a special family dinner, and sharing gifts

"DiSalvo-Ryan's watercolors match the text in their warmth and wealth of familial detail. It's the inclusive message and the sharing across cultures, however, that may strike the most responsive chord with children." Booklist

Schecter, Ellen

The family Haggadah; illustrated by Neil Waldman. Viking 1999 66p il music pa $13.99
296.4

1. Passover
ISBN 0-670-88341-7   LC 98-28597

"This book interweaves original writing with traditional Haggadah, prayer book, and biblical texts, as well as with midrash (rabbinic stories and commentaries)." Verso of title page

"Although really intended for parents to use with their children at a family Passover seder, this attractive book may also be useful to children wanting to plan their own model celebration." Booklist

Schwartz, Lynne Sharon

The four questions; text by Lynne Sharon Schwartz; paintings by Ori Sherman. Dial Bks. 1989 unp il hardcover o.p. paperback available $5.99 (k-3)   **296.4**

1. Passover
ISBN 0-14-055269-3 (pa)   LC 88-18881

This book explores the meaning of Passover by explicating the symbolism of the seder and the four questions

"Framed by the rituals of a Seder, an excellent text gives brief background on the celebration of Passover. . . . The stunningly stylized illustrations facing each page of text are a sophisticated carnival of animals that reflect a kind of Chagallian surrealism grounded by strongly outlined shapes, deep colors, and dense compositions." Bull Cent Child Books

Simon, Norma, 1927-
The story of Hanukkah; illustrated by Leonid Gore. HarperCollins Pubs. 1997 unp il $15.95; pa $5.95 (2-4) **296.4**
1. Hanukkah
ISBN 0-06-027419-0; 0-06-027420-4 (pa)
LC 96-5141
A newly illustrated edition of Hanukkah, first published 1966 by Crowell
Explains the history and traditions that are a part of the Jewish holiday of Hanukkah
"A straightforward . . . text is followed by instructions for playing dreidel, a recipe for potato pancakes, and a quick overview of the Jewish calendar. . . . [This] edition features textured softly colored illustrations that seem to glow like the candles of the holiday." Horn Book

The story of Passover; illustrated by Erica Weihs. HarperCollins Pubs. 1997 unp $15.95; pa $5.95 (2-4) **296.4**
1. Passover
ISBN 0-06-027062-4; 0-06-027063-2 (pa)
LC 95-41201
A newly illustrated edition of the title first published 1965 by Crowell
Describes the origins and traditions of Passover, in particular the special meal called the Seder
"Biblically accurate and factual, Simon's book brings the Passover celebration to life for both Jewish and Gentile children." SLJ

297.1 Sources of Islam

Oppenheim, Shulamith Levey
Iblis; retold by Shulamith Levey Oppenheim; illustrated by Ed Young. Harcourt Brace Jovanovich 1994 unp il $15.95 (2-4) **297.1**
1. Adam (Biblical figure) 2. Eve (Biblical figure)
ISBN 0-15-238016-7
LC 92-15060
An Islamic version of the story of Adam and Eve and the fall from Paradise
"Young's dramatic pastels and watercolor artwork juxtaposes the dark shadows of evil with neon-bright swaths and splotches of electric color. . . . Based on a 9th century scholarly version, the text is charged with the tension, while Young's rich paintings bridge our temporal and cultural distance from the source to bring its message powerfully home." SLJ

297.3 Islamic worship

Ghazi, Suhaib Hamid
Ramadan; illustrated by Omar Rayyan. Holiday House 1996 unp il $16.95; pa $6.95 (k-3) **297.3**
1. Ramadan 2. Islam
ISBN 0-8234-1254-7; 0-8234-1275-X (pa)
LC 96-5154
"The month of Ramadan, an Islamic time of fasting, feasting, sharing, and prayer, is seen through the eyes of young Hakeem. . . . Ghazi gives just the right amount

of background information, along with interesting details. . . . Rayyan incorporates into his paintings Islamic symbols and architectural motifs, as well as a lively, ethnically diverse group of people." Booklist
Includes glossary

Marchant, Kerena
Id-ul-Fitr. Millbrook Press 1998 32p il (Festivals) lib bdg $21.90 (3-5) **297.3**
1. Islam
ISBN 0-7613-0963-2
LC 97-46035
Looks at some of the ways Muslims around the world celebrate the joyous festival of Id-ul-Fitre
Includes bibliographical references

299 Other religions

Fisher, Leonard Everett, 1924-
The gods and goddesses of ancient Egypt. Holiday House 1997 unp il $16.95; pa $6.95 (3-6) **299**
1. Egyptian mythology
ISBN 0-8234-1286-5; 0-8234-1508-2 (pa)
LC 96-42068
Relates the history of the gods and goddesses worshipped by the ancient Egyptians and describes how they were depicted
"Simple profiles of Ra, Osiris, Isis, Nut, and others are accompanied by vivid paintings with bold outlines that recall hieroglyphic symbols. . . . A family tree and pronunciation guide help budding Egyptologists keep the figures straight." SLJ
Includes bibliographical references

Gods and goddesses of the ancient Maya. Holiday House 1999 unp il $16.95 (3-6) **299**
1. Mayas—Religion 2. Native Americans—Religion
ISBN 0-8234-1427-2
LC 99-19900
Gives the history of the principal gods and goddesses of the ancient Mayans, including Hunab Ku, Itzamna, Ixtab, and Ah Puch
"Facing the pages of text are full-page paintings inspired by Mayan glyphs and stelae depicting profiled figures with sloped foreheads holding or wearing representative objects or clothing. Bold, vibrant tones highlight the features of these heavily outlined figures and form backdrops for the pages. . . . A visual treat from cover to cover." SLJ
Includes bibliographical references

Morley, Jacqueline
Egyptian myths; retold by Jacqueline Morley; illustrated by Giovanni Caselli. Bedrick Bks. 2000 64p il $22.50 (4 and up) **299**
1. Egyptian mythology
ISBN 0-87226-589-7
LC 99-44979
First published 1999 in the United Kingdom
"Stories based on ancient temple inscriptions, hieroglyphic texts, and tomb paintings. . . . The creation tale of Ra, explanations of the moon's phases and of how mummies came to be, and the story of the first pyramid are just some of the stories included. . . . The fresh, accessible storytelling style makes this a fine choice." SLJ

Swamp, Jake, 1941-

Giving thanks; a Native American good morning message; by Chief Jake Swamp; illustrated by Erwin Printup, Jr. Lee & Low Bks. 1995 unp il $15.95; pa $5.95 (k-3)   **299**

1. Mohawk Indians 2. Native Americans
ISBN 1-880000-15-6; 1-880000-54-7 (pa)

LC 94-5955

"Drawing on Six Nation (Iroquois) ceremonial tradition, the text speaks concise thanks to Mother Earth, to water, grass, fruits, animals, to the wind and rain, sun, moon and stars, to the Spirit Protectors of our past and present, 'for showing us ways to live in peace and harmony',and to the Great Spirit, giver of all. . . . The entire text is reproduced in Mohawk on the last page." SLJ

"Its simple, timeless language bears witness to the Native American reverence for the natural world and sense of unity with all living things. . . . The gifts of the earth . . . are richly depicted in paintings of wildlife and bountiful harvests. Horizontal bands of color suggest receding landscapes, pristine skies and oceans." Publ Wkly

300   SOCIAL SCIENCES

302   Social interaction

Erlbach, Arlene

The kids' volunteering book. Lerner Publs. 1998 64p il lib bdg $23.54; pa $9.95 (4-6)   **302**

1. Volunteer work
ISBN 0-8225-2415-5 (lib bdg); 0-8225-9820-5 (pa)

LC 97-23356

Presents some opportunities for young people to perform volunteer service, and briefly profiles some children who are volunteers

"The profiles are interesting and inspiring, and substantial information is provided on the practical details of . . . a volunteer enterprise." Horn Book Guide

Includes glossary and bibliographical references

Hoose, Phillip M., 1947-

It's our world, too! stories of young people who are making a difference; by Phillip Hoose. Little, Brown 1993 166p il hardcover o.p. paperback available $13.95 (5 and up)   **302**

1. Volunteer work 2. Social action 3. Community development
ISBN 0-316-37245-5 (pa)   LC 92-24873

"Joy Street books"

"Hoose tells fourteen stories of children and young adolescents who have stood up to gangs, pitted their wits against corporate interests, performed volunteer service, or organized for ecological causes. This fine, large handbook includes a background chapter on the history of 'young activists who went before you' and a substantial concluding section on techniques of organizing for social activism." Horn Book

302.2   Communication

Aliki

Communication. Greenwillow Bks. 1993 unp il $14; pa $4.95 (k-3)   **302.2**

1. Communication
ISBN 0-688-10529-7; 0-688-17116-8 (pa)

LC 91-48156

"The text considers not only the telling and listening aspects of person-to-person exchange, but also the importance of responding. Aliki relies on various combinations of handwritten and typeset text, large drawings, and cartoon strips to introduce some of the ways communication is accomplished—writing, speaking, braille—and to offer a glimpse of the subtle, emotional aspects of interchange." Booklist

Samoyault, Tiphaine

Give me a sign! what pictograms tell us without words. Viking 1997 unp il $13.99 (4 and up)   **302.2**

1. Signs and symbols 2. Picture writing
ISBN 0-670-87466-3   LC 96-51985

Original French edition, 1995

"A brief overview defines pictograms and the ways they have historically been used in various cultures. This . . . discussion is followed by a look at figurative, schematic, and abstract pictograms and how they are used to convey information and facilitate communication throughout the modern world. . . . Pictograms likely to be seen on the road, on vacation, traveling, and in public places are reviewed, as are those for dangerous or fragile products." SLJ

Includes glossary

305.23   Young people

Colman, Penny

Girls! the history of growing up female in America. Scholastic 2000 192p il $18.95 (5 and up)   **305.23**

1. Girls
ISBN 0-590-37129-0   LC 99-28150

Traces the history of growing up female in America as told by the girls themselves in journals, household manuals, letters, slave narratives, and other primary sources

"The author's thorough research, inclusiveness, and accessible style make this book an essential resource for libraries serving young people." SLJ

Includes bibliographical references

Jukes, Mavis

It's a girl thing; how to stay healthy, safe, and in charge; illustrations by Debbie Tilley. Knopf 1996 135p il $12; lib bdg $16.99; pa $5.99 (5 and up)   **305.23**

1. Adolescence 2. Girls 3. Sex education
ISBN 0-679-87392-9; 0-679-94325-0 (lib bdg); 0-679-88771-7 (pa)   LC 93-40296

Jukes, Mavis—*Continued*

"Jukes discusses a wide variety of subjects from buying a bra to sexual harassment and abuse. In a warm, conversational style, she covers body changes in both boys and girls, menstruation, general health, drinking and drugs, sexual feelings, pregnancy, contraceptives, and sexually transmitted diseases including AIDS. The text is sometimes humorous, but always conveys caring, respect, and concern." SLJ

Includes bibliographical references

Kindersley, Barnabas

Children just like me; by Barnabas & Anabel Kindersley. Dorling Kindersley 1995 79p il maps $19.95 (3-6)   **305.23**

1. Children—Pictorial works
ISBN 0-7894-0201-7   LC 95-10199

At head of title: In association with United Nations Children's Fund

This is a "compilation of facts, photographs, and interviews with thirty-seven children from thirty-two countries, including the U.S. Each child gets a full-page or double spread built around a large color photograph of the child and, often, his or her siblings; smaller photos show other family members, home and school, favorite foods and toys, homework or schoolbooks, and file photos of famous sights." Bull Cent Child Books

"A delightful, attractive look at children from around the world. . . . This book is factual, respectful, and insightful. It provides just the right balance of information and visual interest for the intended audience." SLJ

305.4   Women

Blumberg, Rhoda, 1917-

Bloomers! illustrated by Mary Morgan. Bradbury Press 1993 unp il $14.95; pa $5.99 (k-3)   **305.4**

1. Women's rights 2. Costume
ISBN 0-02-711684-0; 0-689-80455-5 (pa)
                                            LC 92-27154

Explains how the new-fashioned outfit, bloomers, helped Amelia Bloomer, Elizabeth Cady Stanton, and Susan B. Anthony spread the word about women's rights

"Young audiences will get a full sense of what life and attitudes were like in the mid-19th century, as Blumberg makes these historical characters real. Morgan's bright, cheerful, watercolor paintings convey a sense of time and place while they carry the narrative along." SLJ

Heinemann, Sue, 1948-

The New York Public Library amazing women in American history; a book of answers for kids. Wiley 1998 192p (New York Public Library answer books for kids series) pa $12.95 (5 and up)   **305.4**

1. Women—United States—History
ISBN 0-471-19216-3   LC 97-18465

"A Stonesong Press book"

Consists of short answers to questions about the roles and achievements of women in America from prehistory to the end of the twentieth century

"The text is succinct, easy to read, and informative. . . . Pertinent black-and-white photos appear throughout." SLJ

Includes glossary and bibliographical references

305.8   Racial, ethnic, national groups

Ancona, George, 1929-

Barrio; José's neighborhood. Harcourt Brace & Co. 1998 unp il $18; pa $9   **305.8**

1. Mexican Americans 2. San Francisco (Calif.)
ISBN 0-15-201049-1; 0-15-201048-3 (pa)
                                            LC 97-29667

Presents life in a barrio in San Francisco, describing the school, recreation, holidays, and family life of an eight-year-old boy who lives there

"A fond and fascinating photo-essay focusing on the richness of the Latino experience." Booklist

Includes glossary

Ashabranner, Brent K., 1921-

The new African Americans; by Brent Ashabranner; photographs by Jennifer Ashabranner. Linnet Bks. 1999 107p lib bdg $21 (4 and up)   **305.8**

1. Africans—United States 2. United States—Immigration and emigration
ISBN 0-208-02420-4   LC 99-31388

This is a look at "contemporary immigrants from sub-Saharan Africa. . . . Reporting on immigrants from Nigeria, Sierra Leone, Ethiopia, and Liberia (among others). Ashabranner is optimistic about their lives in this country, and insistent upon the positive effect they have had on the economy and American culture." Horn Book

"The writing is strongest when revealing the voices of individual immigrants and their traditional values. . . . Captioned black-and-white photographs are interspersed throughout." Bull Cent Child Books

Includes bibliographical references

Birdseye, Debbie Holsclaw

Under our skin; kids talk about race; by Debbie Holsclaw Birdseye and Tom Birdseye; photographs by Robert Crum. Holiday House 1997 30p il $15.95 (4 and up)   **305.8**

1. United States—Race relations 2. Ethnic relations
ISBN 0-8234-1325-X   LC 97-9395

Six young people discuss their feelings about their own ethnic backgrounds and about their experiences with people of different races

"This book provides an excellent starting point for discussion. It gives readers a chance to see what life is like through someone else's eyes, and in someone else's skin." SLJ

Includes bibliographical references

The **Black** Americans: a history in their own words, 1619-1983; edited by Milton Meltzer. Crowell 1984 306p il o.p.; HarperCollins Pubs. paperback available $10.95 (6 and up)   **305.8**
1. African Americans—History—Sources
ISBN 0-06-446055-X (pa)   LC 83-46160
This is a revised and updated edition of In their own words: a history of the American Negro, edited by Milton Meltzer and published in three volumes, 1964-1967

A history of black people in the United States, as told through letters, speeches, articles, eyewitness accounts, and other documents

Brown, Tricia
Konnichiwa! I am a Japanese-American girl; photographs by Kazuyoshi Arai. Holt & Co. 1995 unp il $15.95 (1-4)   **305.8**
1. Japanese Americans 2. San Francisco (Calif.)—Social life and customs
ISBN 0-8050-2353-4   LC 94-36107
The author provides an "introduction to the Japanese American experience told from the point of view of a child named Lauren Seiko Kamiya. Lauren guides readers through San Francisco's Japantown and shows how her family takes part in the annual Cherry Blossom Festival." Booklist
"While the most obvious audience for this title is children of Japanese extraction or teachers needing multicultural materials, this book has great visual appeal and will be readily picked up by browsers." SLJ
Includes glossary and bibliographical references

Cha, Dia, 1962-
Dia's story cloth; written by Dia Cha; stitched by Chue and Nhia Thao Cha. Lee & Low Bks. 1996 unp il $15.95; pa $6.95 (3-5)   **305.8**
1. Hmong (Asian people)
ISBN 1-880000-34-2; 1-880000-63-6 (pa)
      LC 95-41465
The story cloth made for her by her aunt and uncle chronicles the life of the author and her family in their native Laos and their eventual emigration to the United States
"An interesting and unusual title that resists neat categorization. . . . Part autobiography, part history, part description of a changing culture adapting life and art to new circumstances, the book serves as a brief introduction to the Hmong people." SLJ
Includes bibliographical references

Garza, Carmen Lomas
In my family; pictures and stories by Carmen Lomas Garza; as told to Harriet Rohmer; edited by David Schecter; Spanish translation by Francisco X. Alarcón. Children's Bk. Press 1996 unp il $15.95; pa $7.95 (k-3)   **305.8**
1. Mexican Americans 2. Bilingual books—English-Spanish
ISBN 0-89239-138-3; 0-89239-163-4 (pa)
      LC 96-7471
Companion volume to Family pictures, entered in E section
Text in English and Spanish

"Lomas Garza uses her narrative paintings to relate her memories of growing up in Kingsville, Texas, near the Mexican border, and to reflect her pride in her Mexican American heritage. The artist portrays everyday events as well as special moments of family history in crisply colorful, vibrantly peopled paintings and provides brief, bilingual background stories for each of the 13 paintings." Booklist

Magic windows; cut-paper art and stories by Carmen Lomas Garza; as told to Harriet Rohmer; edited by David Schecter; Spanish translation by Francisco X. Alarcón. Children's Bk. Press 1999 30p il $15.95   **305.8**
1. Mexican Americans—Social life and customs 2. Mexico—Social life and customs 3. Bilingual books—English-Spanish
ISBN 0-89239-157-X   LC 98-38379
"Garza creates paper windows that depict scenes from her family life, the desert, and Mexican culture. She places seventeen papercuttings, mostly made from black paper, against vibrant backgrounds of turquoise, tangerine, lime and other tropical colors. Opposite the *papel picado*, text in English and Spanish explains the artistic process, providing cultural or personal information related to the papercutting." Bull Cent Child Books

Hamanaka, Sheila
The journey; Japanese Americans, racism and renewal; painting and text by Sheila Hamanaka; book design by Steve Frederick. Orchard Bks. 1990 39p il $19.95; lib bdg $20.99; pa $8.95 (5 and up)   **305.8**
1. World War, 1939-1945—United States 2. Japanese Americans—Evacuation and relocation, 1942-1945
ISBN 0-531-05849-2; 0-531-08449-3 (lib bdg); 0-531-07060-3 (pa)   LC 89-22877
"A Richard Jackson book"
"Hamanaka has created a five-panel mural depicting the Japanese-American experience with particular emphasis on the watershed of that experience, the concentration camps. Here the mural is reproduced detail by detail with amplifying text. . . . There are other books on this subject . . . but none with the punch and universality of this one." SLJ

Haskins, James, 1941-
Out of the darkness; the story of Blacks moving North, 1890-1940; by James Haskins and Kathleen Benson. Benchmark Bks. (Tarrytown) 2000 112p (Great journeys) lib bdg $31.36 (5 and up) **305.8**
1. African Americans—History 2. United States—Race relations
ISBN 0-7614-0970-X   LC 99-19882
Uses the experiences of two individuals, Ada "Bricktop" Smith and Joe Jones, to present the story of the Great Migration of Southern Blacks to northern cities from the late 1800s to the years after World War I
This "delivers a compelling account of the 'Great Migration' from the South to the North. . . . Black-and-white photos and quotes greatly enhance the narrative." SLJ
Includes bibliographical references

Hoobler, Dorothy

The African American family album; [by] Dorothy and Thomas Hoobler; introduction by Phylicia Rashad. Oxford Univ. Press 1995 127p il (American family albums) $19.95; lib bdg $25; pa $12.95 (5 and up)   **305.8**

1. African Americans
ISBN 0-19-509460-3; 0-19-508128-5 (lib bdg); 0-19-512419-7 (pa)   LC 94-34697
This work "traces the history of African Americans from their homeland in West Africa at least 2,500 years ago to the achievements of contemporary African Americans such as Nobel Prize-winning novelist Toni Morrison. This book is an 'album' in the sense that the story is told in a unique collection of photographs as well as in first-hand accounts." Voice Youth Advocates
Includes bibliographical references

The Chinese American family album; [by] Dorothy and Thomas Hoobler; introduction by Bette Bao Lord. Oxford Univ. Press 1994 128p il map (American family albums) lib bdg $25; pa $14.95 (5 and up)   **305.8**

1. Chinese Americans
ISBN 0-19-508130-7 (lib bdg); 0-19-512421-9 (pa)   LC 93-11873
"This sourcebook on the Chinese immigrant experience is divided into six topics: the homeland, the voyage to America, arrival in America, first-generation life, the integration of successing generations, and Chinese Americans today. The authors introduce each chapter with a summary essay, then let the immigrants and their descendents speak for themselves in excerpts from oral reminiscences, written histories, and fiction spanning the years from the Gold Rush to the 1980s. Period photographs and drawings, maps, and sidebars enhance the text. The result resembles a well-organized, handsomely designed scrapbook. . . . A valuable resource." SLJ
Includes bibliographical references

The Cuban American family album; [by] Dorothy and Thomas Hoobler; introduction by Oscar Hijuelos. Oxford Univ. Press 1996 127p il (American family albums) $19.95; lib bdg $25; pa $12.95 (5 and up)   **305.8**

1. Cuban Americans
ISBN 0-19-510340-8; 0-19-508132-3 (lib bdg); 0-19-512425-1 (pa)   LC 95-38103
Interviews, excerpts from diaries and letters, newspaper accounts, profiles of famous individuals, and pictures from family albums portray the Cuban American experience
Includes bibliographical references

The German American family album; [by] Dorothy and Thomas Hoobler; introductions by Werner Klemperer. Oxford Univ. Press 1996 127p il (American family albums) $19.95; pa $12.95 (5 and up)   **305.8**

1. German Americans
ISBN 0-19-510341-6; 0-19-512422-7 (pa)   LC 95-14448
Traces the history of German immigrants to the United States through letters, diaries and newspaper accounts
Includes bibliographical references

The Irish American family album; [by] Dorothy and Thomas Hoobler; introduction by Joseph P. Kennedy II. Oxford Univ. Press 1995 128p il (American family albums) $19.95; pa $12.95 (5 and up)   **305.8**

1. Irish Americans
ISBN 0-19-509461-1; 0-19-512418-9 (pa)   LC 94-19569
"Selections from diaries, letters, interviews, newspaper and magazine articles, and books provide an arresting picture of what it has meant to be of Irish heritage in America. . . . Topics such as prejudice, working conditions and labor unions; politics; and the importance of family, friends, and the Catholic Church are touched upon." SLJ
Includes bibliographical references

The Italian American family album; [by] Dorothy and Thomas Hoobler; introduction by Governor Mario M. Cuomo. Oxford Univ. Press 1994 127p il map (American family albums) $19.95; lib bdg $25; pa $12.95 (5 and up) **305.8**

1. Italian Americans
ISBN 0-19-509124-8; 0-19-508126-9 (lib bdg); 0-19-512420-0 (pa)   LC 93-46918
This volume includes selections from "diaries, letters, and oral histories. . . . Each of the six chapters begins with background information and then goes on to discuss life in the old country, coming to America, first impressions, working, forming a new life, and becoming a part of America." SLJ
Includes bibliographical references

The Japanese American family album; [by] Dorothy and Thomas Hoobler. Oxford Univ. Press 1996 127p il map (American family albums) lib bdg $25; pa $12.95 (5 and up)   **305.8**

1. Japanese Americans
ISBN 0-19-508131-5 (lib bdg); 0-19-512423-5 (pa)   LC 94-43466
This book describes "the Japanese-American experience. Each of the six chapters offers a succinct historical presentation followed by first-person accounts. Relying on oral histories and original documents, both pictorial and written, the Hooblers have truly humanized historical events. . . . Like a family album, the pages of the book are filled with fine quality archival black-and white photographs that tell a story." SLJ
Includes bibliographical references

The Jewish American family album; [by] Dorothy and Thomas Hoobler; introduction by Mandy Patinkin. Oxford Univ. Press 1995 127p il (American family albums) $19.95; lib bdg $25; pa $12.95 (5 and up)   **305.8**

1. Jews—United States
ISBN 0-19-509935-4; 0-19-508135-8 (lib bdg); 0-19-512417-0 (pa)   LC 94-43460
This volume "begins with a five-page thumbnail sketch of Jewish history from Abraham to the rise of the State of Israel. Successive chapters detail Jewish life in 'the old country', immigration to America, and the contributions Jews have made to their new homeland." Book Rep

Hoobler, Dorothy—*Continued*

"What makes this title unique is the high quality of the carefully researched and varied historical information and the Hooblers' judicious selection of primary-source excerpts, many of which are by well-known writers, politicians, and celebrities." SLJ

Includes bibliographical references

The Mexican American family album; [by] Dorothy and Thomas Hoobler; introduction by Henry G. Cisneros. Oxford Univ. Press 1994 127p il (American family albums) $19.95; pa $14.95 (5 and up)   **305.8**
1. Mexican Americans
ISBN 0-19-509459-X; 0-19-512426-X (pa)
                                LC 94-7785

"Using almost exclusively first-person accounts, the Hooblers present vignettes of history, culture, and experience from the first Mexican American settlers to the Chicano Movement. . . . Gathered together, these accounts present a powerful portrait of a strong people, rich in history and culture. A must for multicultural studies." Book Rep

Includes bibliographical references

The Scandinavian American family album; [by] Dorothy and Thomas Hoobler; introduction by Hubert H. Humphrey, III. Oxford Univ. Press 1997 127p il (American family albums) $19.95; pa $12.95 (5 and up)   **305.8**
1. Scandinavian Americans
ISBN 0-19-510579-6; 0-19-512424-3 (pa)
                                LC 95-45540

"The Hooblers begin with a chapter on life in Scandinavia and the conditions that caused people to emigrate. Scandinavian-Americans who have played an influential role in our society are featured throughout the book. . . . Photographs and captions add personal narratives that explain what life was like for Scandinavian Americans." Book Rep

Includes bibliographical references

Hoyt-Goldsmith, Diane

Hoang Anh; a Vietnamese-American boy; photographs by Lawrence Migdale. Holiday House 1992 30p il map $16.95 (3-5)   **305.8**
1. Vietnamese Americans
ISBN 0-8234-0948-1   LC 91-28880

A Vietnamese American boy describes the daily activities of his family in San Rafael, California, and the traditional culture and customs that shape their lives

"Color photographs of good quality are carefully placed in relation to a text that is direct, informative, and convincing." Bull Cent Child Books

Includes glossary

The **Jewish** Americans: a history in their own words, 1650-1950; edited by Milton Meltzer. Crowell 1982 174p il o.p. (6 and up)   **305.8**
1. Jews—United States—History—Sources
                                LC 81-43886

"Excerpts from letters, journals, books, documents, and assorted other sources provide a varied, firsthand look at Jewish experience in America from colonial times to 1950 when Holocaust survivors made their way to the U.S. . . . [The author] offers commentary before each [selection] helping to clarify context or define perspective by illuminating the times contemporary to the writing." Booklist

"The book has multiple curriculum uses and will be a welcome addition to any library. Interesting historical photographs and a comprehensive index add to [its] usefulness." SLJ

Includes bibliographical references

Kuklin, Susan

How my family lives in America. Bradbury Press 1992 unp il $16; pa $5.99 (k-3)   **305.8**
1. African Americans 2. Chinese Americans 3. Puerto Ricans—United States
ISBN 0-02-751239-8; 0-689-82221-9 (pa)
                                LC 91-22949

"Sanu's father was born in Senegal, Eric's father came from Puerto Rico, and both of April's parents were born in Taiwan. Each section provides special words, foods, games, clothes, music and other ways in which families transmit their heritages and integrate them with the lifestyles of the United States. The photographs provide insights as to how cultures are cherished and continued." Child Book Rev Serv

"Each child's first-person narration is simple and uncomplicated, with occasional humorous touches. . . . The full-color photographs are well composed and serviceable." SLJ

Myers, Walter Dean, 1937-

Now is your time! the African-American struggle for freedom. HarperCollins Pubs. 1991 292p il hardcover o.p. paperback available $11.95 (6 and up)   **305.8**
1. African Americans—History
ISBN 0-06-446120-3 (pa)   LC 91-314
Coretta Scott King Award for text, 1992

A history of the African-American struggle for freedom and equality, beginning with the capture of Africans in 1619, continuing through the American Revolution, the Civil War, and into contemporary times

"Myers's unique episodic approach makes this history a compelling exploration of the African-American experience. . . . This fascinating book will engender pride in heritage for young African Americans and provide insight into American history for all of us." Horn Book

Includes bibliographical references

Patrick, Diane, 1955-

The New York Public Library amazing African American history. Wiley 1998 170p il (New York Public Library answer books for kids series) pa $12.95 (5 and up)   **305.8**
1. African Americans—History
ISBN 0-471-19217-1   LC 97-16938
"A Stonesong Press book"

Presents questions and answers relating to important periods in African American history including the Revolution, Civil War, Reconstruction, Migration, and the Civil Rights Movement

Patrick, Diane, 1955-—_Continued_
"Enhanced by black-and-white photographs, this useful resource provides information in a formal but readable style. . . . A well-organized, objective, accessible guide for students." SLJ
Includes glossary and bibliographical references

Stanley, Jerry, 1941-
I am an American; a true story of Japanese internment. Crown 1994 102p il $18 (5 and up)
305.8
1. Japanese Americans—Evacuation and relocation, 1942-1945 2. World War, 1939-1945—United States
ISBN 0-517-59786-1   LC 93-41330
The author discusses "the internment of Japanese-Americans during World War II. He has spun a cogent narrative of the shameful events, focusing them through the experiences of Shi Nomura, a high school student sent with his family to Manzanar in 1942. . . . This is a first-rate, readable introduction to this particular part of history, and it's complemented by a spacious page design, numerous black-and-white photos, an exemplary bibliographic note, and an index." Bull Cent Child Books

306 Culture and institutions

Junior Worldmark encyclopedia of world cultures. U.X.L 1999 9v il maps set $250 (5 and up)
306
1. Ethnology—Encyclopedias 2. Human geography—Encyclopedias
ISBN 0-7876-1756-3   LC 98-13810
Timothy L. Gall and Susan Bevans Gall, editors
Arranges countries around the world alphabetically, subdivides these countries into 250 culture groups, and provides information about the ethnology and human geography of each group
"The short and engaging articles are based on entries in the _Worldmark Encyclopedia of Cultures and Daily Life_ and targeted to appeal to a younger audience. . . . This is a valuable and timely resource with considerable assignment value." SLJ

Morris, Ann
Work. Lothrop, Lee & Shepard Bks. 1998 29p il $15; lib bdg $14.93 (k-1)
306
1. Work
ISBN 0-688-14866-2; 0-688-14867-0 (lib bdg)
LC 97-21607
Also available Play $15 (ISBN 0-688-14552-3)
Photographs and brief text show people all over the world at work. A section identifies the country in which each photo was taken and describes the activity portrayed
"The language is clear and straightforward, and, for the most part, the photographs support the [text] well." SLJ

306.05 Culture and institutions— Serial publications

Faces; people, places, and culture. Cobblestone Pub. $29.95 per year
306.05
1. Anthropology—Periodicals
ISSN 0749-1387

Nine issues a year. First published 1984
Published with the cooperation of the American Museum of Natural History
A magazine for young people designed to introduce them "to the fascination of natural history and anthropology. There are some 8 to 10 articles in each well-illustrated number. Some issues concentrate on a particular subject. . . . Numerous projects for children are scattered throughout the magazine." Katz. Mag for Sch Libr

306.8 Marriage and family

Cole, Joanna
The new baby at your house; photographs by Margaret Miller. rev ed. Morrow Junior Bks. 1998 unp il $16; lib bdg $15.93 (k-3)
306.8
1. Infants 2. Siblings
ISBN 0-688-13897-7; 0-688-13898-5 (lib bdg)
LC 97-29267
A revised and newly illustrated edition of the title first published 1985
Describes the activities and changes involved in having a new baby in the house and the feelings experienced by the older brothers and sisters
"Miller captures many intimate and touching moments with her pictures. . . . There is a good balance of families from varied ethnic backgrounds. . . . This book opens with a clear and precise note to parents that gives honest, practical advice." SLJ
Includes bibliographical references

Morris, Ann
Families. HarperCollins Pubs. 2000 29p il $15.95; lib bdg $15.89 (k-1)
306.8
1. Family
ISBN 0-688-17198-2; 0-688-17199-0 (lib bdg)
LC 99-37036
A simple explanation of families, how they function, how they are different, and how they are alike
"Through spare, simple text and appealing color photographs, Morris shows readers that 'all children . . . are part of families' and that they come in all sizes, nationalities, and configurations. . . . The book depicts family interactions in the United Kingdom, the United States, Ethiopia, Canada, Vietnam, South Korea, Brazil, Saudi Arabia, Russia, Japan, and India." SLJ

Rogers, Fred
Stepfamilies; photographs by Jim Judkis. Putnam 1997 unp il (Let's talk about it) $15.95; pa $7.95 (k-2)
306.8
1. Stepfamilies
ISBN 0-399-23144-7; 0-399-23145-5 (pa)
LC 96-34176
Discusses the changes involved in becoming part of a stepfamily and ways to deal with the new situation
"This title, written in simple language and accompanied by full-color photographs, offers a reassuring discussion of stepfamilies." SLJ

Rotner, Shelley

About twins; by Shelley Rotner and Sheila M. Kelly; photographs by Shelley Rotner. DK Ink 1999 unp il $16.95 (k-2)   **306.8**
  1. Twins
  ISBN 0-7894-2556-4   LC 98-3060

Examines the different kinds of twins and discusses the delights, difficulties, and complexities of being a twin

"Packed with full-color photos of smiling siblings . . . this appealing photo-essay is a good discussion starter for families of twins and a fine introduction for children curious about them." SLJ

Scott, Elaine, 1940-

Twins! photographs by Margaret Miller. Atheneum Bks. for Young Readers 1998 unp il $16 (k-2)   **306.8**
  1. Twins
  ISBN 0-689-80347-8   LC 97-5049

"The text introduces subjects such as fraternal and identical twins, dressing alike and differently, siblings of twins, and sharing toys." Booklist

"A handsome design and crisp, over-sized full-color photographs contribute to an appealing package." Horn Book Guide

306.89 Separation and divorce

Brown, Laurene Krasny

Dinosaurs divorce; a guide for changing families; [by] Laurene Krasny Brown and Marc Brown. Atlantic Monthly Press 1986 31p il $15.95; pa $7.95 (k-3)   **306.89**
  1. Divorce
  ISBN 0-316-11248-8; 0-316-10996-7 (pa)
                LC 86-1079

Text and illustrations of dinosaur characters introduce aspects of divorce such as its causes and effects, living with a single parent, spending holidays in two separate households, and adjusting to a stepparent

"The picture-book, almost comic-book, format, the touches of humor, and the distancing effect of the dinosaurs as surrogate humans may make the book accessible to young or extremely anxious children. A thoughtful, useful book." Horn Book

Krementz, Jill

How it feels when parents divorce. Knopf 1984 115p il hardcover o.p. paperback available $15 (4 and up)   **306.89**
  1. Divorce
  ISBN 0-394-75855-2 (pa)   LC 83-48856

In a personal interview format "19 boys and girls, ranging in age from 7 to 16 years, tell of their parents' divorces and of the effects the divorce has had on them and their families." SLJ

"The full-page portraits that precede each piece are exceptionally expressive. While the accounts have many similarities, experiences and personalities are unique; Krementz' ear for language ensures that the children project their own individuality." Horn Book

Rogers, Fred

Divorce; photographs by Jim Judkis. Putnam 1996 unp il (Lets talk about it) $16.99; pa $6.99 (k-2)   **306.89**
  1. Divorce
  ISBN 0-399-22449-1; 0-698-11670-4 (pa)
                LC 94-2312

Rogers "defines a family as anyone who gives a child food, care, love, and a place to feel safe. He explains that these main ingredients should remain constant even in the event of a divorce. Children are advised to ask about changes in living arrangements and other aspects of their lives. . . . The author prescribes activities like talking, drawing, and playing with friends to deal with normal feelings of sadness, anger, and crying. . . . Judkis's sensitive full-color photographs of three families work well with the text." SLJ

323.1 Civil and political rights of nondominant groups

Duncan, Alice Faye

The National Civil Rights Museum celebrates everyday people; photos by J. Gerard Smith. BridgeWater Bks. 1995 63p il hardcover o.p. paperback available $6.95 (3-6)   **323.1**
  1. National Civil Rights Museum (Memphis, Tenn.)
  2. African Americans—Civil rights 3. United States—Race relations
  ISBN 0-8167-3503-4 (pa)   LC 94-15831

"Once the site of Dr. King's assassination, the Lorraine Motel is now the National Civil Rights Museum. This instructive and inspirational book takes readers through an exhibit on the civil rights movement from 1954 to 1968. Photos featuring students visiting the museum are included." Soc Educ

Includes bibliographical references

Haskins, James, 1941-

Freedom Rides; journey for justice. Hyperion Bks. for Children 1995 99p il $14.95; lib bdg $15.89 (5 and up)   **323.1**
  1. African Americans—Civil rights 2. Southern States—Race relations
  ISBN 0-7868-0048-8; 0-7868-2037-3 (lib bdg)
                LC 94-7996

The author discusses the efforts of the people who tested the series of court decisions aimed at desegregating buses and trains in the United States. The story begins in the 1850's with a New York City incident and trial, but the focus is mainly on the events of the 1940's, 1950's and 1960's and the freedom riders of those years

"Good-quality black-and-white photographs are scattered throughout. Haskins has . . . given YAs an important source of information on African American history with this well-researched, well-documented book." SLJ

Includes bibliographical references

King, Casey

Oh, freedom! kids talk about the Civil Rights Movement with the people who made it happen: illustrated with photographs; by Casey King and Linda Barrett Osborne; foreword by Rosa Parks; portraits by Joe Brooks. Knopf 1997 137p il lib bdg $19; pa $10.99 (5 and up) **323.1**

1. African Americans—Civil rights 2. United States—Race relations

ISBN 0-679-85856-3 (lib bdg); 0-679-89005-X (pa)

LC 96-13014

Interviews between young people and people who took part in the civil rights movement accompany essays that describe the history of efforts to make equality a reality for African Americans

"King and Osborne present a carefully unbiased overview of the civil rights movement. . . . But most impressive is the way the authors use interesting interviews by students . . . [that] humanize history and add depth to the bare facts of the historical account." Book Rep

Includes bibliographical references

King, Martin Luther, 1929-1968

I have a dream; foreword by Coretta Scott King; paintings by fifteen Coretta Scott King Award and Honor Book artists, Ashley Bryan [et al.] Scholastic 1997 40p il $16.95 **323.1**

1. African Americans—Civil rights 2. United States—Race relations

ISBN 0-590-20516-1 LC 95-45189

"Martin Luther King, Jr.'s classic speech is creatively illustrated by 15 Coretta Scott King Award-winning artists. Signed statements from the artists explain the emotions they were trying to capture and why and how they used certain colors and tones. . . . From cover to cover this is a beautiful book." SLJ

323.44 Freedom of action (Liberty)

Intellectual freedom manual; compiled by the Office for Intellectual Freedom of the American Library Association. American Lib. Assn. il pa $38 **323.44**

1. Intellectual freedom 2. Libraries—Censorship

First published 1974 (5th edition 1996). Periodically revised

This guide to preserving intellectual freedom includes: ALA interpretations of the Library Bill of Rights; recommendations for special libraries and specific situations; information about legal decisions affecting school and public libraries; a section on the ALA's Intellectual Freedom Action Network

Includes bibliographical references

Symons, Ann K.

Protecting the right to read; a how-to-do-it manual for school and public librarians; [by] Ann K. Symons, Charles Harmon; illustrations by Pat Race. Neal-Schuman 1995 211p il (How-to-do-it manuals for librarians) pa $55 **323.44**

1. Libraries—Censorship 2. Intellectual freedom

ISBN 1-55570-216-3 LC 95-42444

"The authors take readers from discussion of the policies and principles of intellectual freedom to considerations specific to school and public libraries to the protection of freedom on the Internet. . . . Appendixes consist of reprints of documents put out by the ALA and the Minnesota Coalition Against Censorship." Book Rep

"Intellectual freedom issues and guiding principles get a thorough and comprehensive treatment. . . . An essential book." Voice Youth Advocates

Includes bibliographical references

West, Mark I.

Trust your children; voices against censorship in children's literature. 2nd ed. Neal-Schuman 1997 xx, 235p il pa $36.75 **323.44**

1. Books and reading 2. Books—Censorship 3. Intellectual freedom

ISBN 1-55570-251-1 LC 96-2648

First published 1988

This is "a collection of interviews with authors and publishers who have been at the front lines of censorship—they have all had personal experiences with their works being censored. Included are some of the most censored authors of today, such as Judy Blume, Katherine Paterson, and Robert Cormier . . . Phyllis Reynolds Naylor and Gail Haley. . . . Also included are people who are active in the anti-censorship movement such as Judith King of the ALA, Leanne Katz of the National Coalition Against Censorship, and Barbara Parker of People for the American Way. This book is a great asset and a great inspiration." Booklist

Includes bibliographical references

324 The political process

Maestro, Betsy, 1944-

The voice of the people; American democracy in action; [by] Betsy Maestro & Giulio Maestro. Lothrop, Lee & Shepard Bks. 1996 48p il maps lib bdg $15.93 (3-5) **324**

1. Elections 2. United States—Politics and government

ISBN 0-688-10679-X LC 95-12672

"The Maestros first explain how our system of government differs from those of other nations. Next there is a history of the Constitution and the amendments, a description of the three branches of government, and then a detailed section on how a presidential election works." SLJ

"Colorful, amply detailed scenes will lure readers into this fact-filled book. . . . The text, straightforward without being stiff, does a masterful job of distilling a complicated subject." Booklist

325.73　Immigration to the United States

Bierman, Carol
Journey to Ellis Island; how my father came to America; by Carol Bierman with Barbara Hehner; illustrated by Laurie McGaw. Hyperion Bks. for Children; Madison Press Bks. 1998 48p il $17.95 (3-5)　　　　325.73
1. Weinstein, Julius 2. Ellis Island Immigration Station 3. United States—Immigration and emigration 4. Jews—United States
ISBN 0-7868-0377-0　　　　LC 98-10987
An account of the ocean voyage and arrival at Ellis Island of twelve-year-old Julius Weinstein who, along with his mother and younger sister, immigrated from Russia in 1922
Includes glossary

Freedman, Russell
Immigrant kids. Dutton 1980 72p il hardcover o.p. paperback available $7.99 (4 and up) 325.73
1. Children of immigrants 2. United States—Immigration and emigration 3. City and town life
ISBN 0-14-037594-5 (pa)　　　　LC 79-20060
The author has "assembled an interesting collection of old photographs for a book that gives a broad view of the experiences of immigrant children in an urban environment. The text is divided into such areas as the journey to America, schools, play, work (much of it illegal), and home life. Photographs are carefully placed in relation to textual references, and the text itself is enlivened by quotations from the reminiscences of several people about their first days in the United States as child immigrants. Large, clear print and an index add to the book's usefulness." Horn Book

I was dreaming to come to America; memories from the Ellis Island Oral History Project; selected and illustrated by Veronica Lawlor; foreword by Rudolph W. Giuliani. Viking 1995 38p il $15.99; pa $6.99 (4 and up)　　325.73
1. Ellis Island Immigration Station 2. United States—Immigration and emigration
ISBN 0-670-86164-2; 0-14-055622-2 (pa)
　　　　LC 95-1281
In their own words, coupled with hand-painted collage illustrations, immigrants recall their arrival in the United States. Includes brief biographies and facts about the Ellis Island Oral History Project
"There is a flavor of Chagall in the peasant figures dancing above the ship or hopping ashore near the turreted towers of the huge building on Ellis Island. The elegant rendering offers a timeless view of this significant journey that is at once personal and universal." Horn Book

Kroll, Steven
Ellis Island; doorway to freedom; illustrated by Karen Ritz. Holiday House 1995 32p il maps $16.95 (3-5)　　　　325.73
1. Ellis Island Immigration Station 2. United States—Immigration and emigration
ISBN 0-8234-1192-3　　　　LC 95-714

Describes how the immigration station on Ellis Island served as a gateway into the United States for more than sixteen million immigrants between 1892 and 1954
This is an "informative, approachable introduction. . . . Illustrations done in pen and ink and in pencil and watercolor give an authentic, old-fashioned feeling to the artwork." Horn Book Guide
Includes glossary

Levine, Ellen
. . . if your name was changed at Ellis Island; illustrated by Wayne Parmenter. Scholastic 1993 80p hardcover o.p. paperback available $5.99 (3-5)
　　　　325.73
1. Ellis Island Immigration Station 2. United States—Immigration and emigration
ISBN 0-590-43829-8 (pa)　　　　LC 92-27940
Describes, in question and answer format, the great migration of immigrants to New York's Ellis Island, from the 1880s to 1914. Features quotes from children and adults who passed through the station
The author "writes in a clear, direct style that's packed with information and lively case histories. . . . There are many illustrations, sometimes full-page, sometimes small, in acrylic earth colors . . . they are an attractive part of a clear and accessible design." Booklist

Maestro, Betsy, 1944-
Coming to America: the story of immigration; illustrated by Susannah Ryan. Scholastic 1996 unp il $15.95 (k-3)　　　　325.73
1. United States—Immigration and emigration
ISBN 0-590-44151-5　　　　LC 94-31110
"In an introductory look at immigration, all inhabitants of the United States are considered immigrants or descendants of immigrants, whether they crossed the land bridge from Asia, came across the oceans voluntarily, or were brought as slaves. The clear, simple text and bright, animated illustrations convey excitement and adventure as well as hardship and loss." Horn Book Guide

326　Slavery and emancipation

Bial, Raymond
The strength of these arms; life in the slave quarters. Houghton Mifflin 1997 40p il $16 (4 and up)　　　　326
1. Slavery—United States 2. Plantation life 3. African Americans—Social life and customs
ISBN 0-395-77394-6　　　　LC 96-39860
Describes how slaves were able to preserve some elements of their African heritage despite the often brutal treatment they experienced on Southern plantations
"This volume features clear, color photographs of plantation sites and artifacts, as well as a few early photos of people living under slavery. . . . This makes slavery in America more concrete than many other books on the subject." Booklist
Includes bibliographical references

The Underground Railroad. Houghton Mifflin 1995 48p il map $16; pa $5.95 (4 and up)　　326
1. Underground railroad 2. Slavery—United States
ISBN 0-395-69937-1; 0-395-97915-3 (pa)
　　　　LC 94-19614

Bial, Raymond—Continued

Using first-person accounts, historical documents, and his own photographs, the author "focuses on the history of the Underground Railroad, building on the experiences of both riders and conductors as he outlines the political climate and the moral beliefs that allowed slavery to thrive and those that helped bring about its downfall." Publ Wkly

"Although the text covers ground often trodden by other works on this popular subject, Bial's shots of places and things which now appear tidy and innocent conjure spirits of desperate freedom-seekers as handily as do more detailed narratives." Bull Cent Child Books

Includes bibliographical references

Hamilton, Virginia, 1936-

Many thousand gone; African Americans from slavery to freedom; illustrated by Leo and Diane Dillon. Knopf 1993 151p il lib bdg $18.99; pa $12 (5 and up) **326**

1. Underground railroad 2. Slavery—United States

ISBN 0-394-92873-3 (lib bdg); 0-679-87936-6 (pa)

LC 89-19988

In this book the author tells "the story of slavery through a series of dramatic biographical vignettes. . . . Her book includes such famous historical figures as Frederick Douglass, Sojourner Truth and Harriet Tubman. She also presents some more obscure individuals. . . . All of these profiles drive home the sickening realities of slavery in a personal way. . . . These are powerful stories eloquently told." N Y Times Book Rev

Includes bibliographical references

Haskins, James, 1941-

Bound for America; the forced migration of Africans to the New World; [by] James Haskins & Kathleen Benson; illustrated by Floyd Cooper. Lothrop, Lee & Shepard Bks. 1999 48p il $18; lib bdg $17.93 (5 and up) **326**

1. Slave trade 2. Slavery—History

ISBN 0-688-10258-1; 0-688-10259-X (lib bdg)

LC 98-24101

Discusses the European enslavement of Africans, including their capture, branding, conditions on slave ships, shipboard mutinies, and arrival in the Americas

"This combination of clear text and judicious use of primary-source material makes crystalline the inhumanity and commercialism that kept the trade in slaves alive for 350 years." SLJ

Includes bibliographical references

Get on board: the story of the Underground Railroad. Scholastic 1993 152p il map $13.95; pa $4.50 (5 and up) **326**

1. Underground railroad 2. Slavery—United States

ISBN 0-590-45418-8; 0-590-45419-6 (pa)

LC 92-13247

The author "relates the history of the Underground Railroad in the U.S., and introduces those who made it a success." SLJ

"Weaving together poignant personal stories and carefully researched historical data, Haskins has produced a stirring account of the founding and the workings of the Underground Railroad." Publ Wkly

Includes bibliographical references

Jurmain, Suzanne

Freedom's sons; the true story of the Amistad mutiny. Lothrop, Lee & Shepard Bks. 1998 128p il $15.95 (4 and up) **326**

1. Amistad (Schooner) 2. Slavery—United States

ISBN 0-688-11072-X

LC 97-37258

This is an "account of the 1839 *Amistad* mutiny and the trial that followed. . . . [The author] places the event in the historical context of a pre-Civil War United States." SLJ

"With meticulous research and a storyteller's knack for pace and well-placed detail, Jurmain re-creates a fascinating chapter in American history." Booklist

Includes bibliographical references

Lester, Julius

From slave ship to freedom road; paintings by Rod Brown. Dial Bks. 1998 40p il $17.99; pa $6.99 (4 and up) **326**

1. Slavery—United States

ISBN 0-8037-1893-4; 0-14-056669-4 (pa)

LC 96-44422

"Lester uses empathy-provoking exercises, open-ended questions, and the paintings of Rod Brown to help readers understand the experience of African-American slaves." Bull Cent Child Books

"Lester's impassioned questions grow from his visceral response to Brown's narrative paintings. . . . The combination of history, art, and commentary demands interaction." Booklist

To be a slave; paintings by Tom Feelings. 30th anniversary ed. Dial Bks. 1998 160p il $20; pa $5.99 (6 and up) **326**

1. Slavery—United States

ISBN 0-8037-2347-4; 0-14-131001-4 (pa)

LC 98-5213

"Through the words of the slave, interwoven with strongly sympathetic commentary, the reader learns what it is to be another man's property; how the slave feels about himself; and how he feels about others. Every aspect of slavery, regardless of how grim, has been painfully and unrelentingly described." Read Ladders for Hum Relat. 6th edition

Includes bibliographical references

McKissack, Patricia C., 1944-

Rebels against slavery; by Patricia C. McKissack and Fredrick McKissack. Scholastic 1996 181p il $14.95; pa $4.50 (5 and up) **326**

1. Slavery—United States

ISBN 0-590-45735-7; 0-590-45736-5 (pa)

LC 94-41089

A Coretta Scott King honor book for text, 1997

The authors "explore slave revolts and the men and women who led them, weaving a tale of courage and defiance in the face of tremendous odds. Readers learn not only about Nat Turner and Denmark Vesey, but also about Cato, Gabriel Prosser, the maroons, and the relationship between escaped slaves and Seminole Indians. The activities of abolitionists are described as well. The authors' careful research, sensitivity, and evenhanded style reveal a sad, yet inspiring story of the will to be free." SLJ

Myers, Walter Dean, 1937-

Amistad: a long road to freedom. Dutton Children's Bks. 1998 99p il maps $16.99; pa $5.99 (5 and up)   **326**

1. Amistad (Schooner) 2. Slavery—United States

ISBN 0-525-45970-7; 0-14-30004-3 (pa)

This is an "account of the capture in West Africa, the hellish journey aboard the slave ship on the Middle Passage, the sale in Cuba, the mutiny led by Sengbe on the *Amistad* as it sailed from Cuba, the forced landing in Connecticut, the subsequent court trials in the U.S., and the final struggle to return home. The design is clear and readable. . . . Myers includes considerable detail drawn from primary reports. . . . The narrative is exciting, not only the account of the uprising but also the tension of the court arguments." Booklist

Includes bibliographical references

328.73   The legislative process in the United States

Stein, R. Conrad, 1937-

The powers of Congress. Children's Press 1995 30p il (Cornerstones of freedom) lib bdg $12.98 (4-6)   **328.73**

1. United States. Congress 2. Separation of powers—United States

ISBN 0-516-06696-X   LC 94-36913

First published 1985 with title: The story of the powers of Congress

"Stein uses the Marbury decision, the impeachment of Andrew Johnson, the resignation of Richard Nixon, and the struggle between Congress's ability to declare war versus the President's authority as Commander-in-Chief to illustrate the shifting balance among the three branches of government and the roots of the doctrine of separation of powers." SLJ

Includes glossary

330.973   United States—Economic conditions

Collins, Mary, 1961-

The Industrial Revolution. Children's Press 2000 30p il (Cornerstones of freedom) lib bdg $20.50; pa $5.95 (4 and up)   **330.973**

1. Industrial revolution

ISBN 0-516-21596-5 (lib bdg); 0-516-27036-2 (pa)   LC 99-14954

A history of the Industrial Revolution focusing primarily on the United States during the nineteenth century and on the change from an agrarian society to one based on machines and factories

331.3   Workers by age group

Bartoletti, Susan Campbell, 1958-

Growing up in coal country. Houghton Mifflin 1996 127p il $16.95; pa $7.95 (5 and up)   **331.3**

1. Child labor 2. Coal mines and mining

ISBN 0-395-77847-6; 0-395-97914-5 (pa)   LC 96-3142

This is an "account of working and living conditions in Pennsylvania coal towns. The first half of the volume details various duties in the mines, from jobs performed by the youngest boys to the tasks of adult miners, while the second half describes the company village, common customs and recreational activities, and the accidents and diseases that frequently beset the workers." Horn Book

"With compelling black-and-white photographs of children at work in the coal mines of northeastern Pennsylvania about 100 years ago, this handsome, spacious photo-essay will draw browsers as well as students doing research on labor and immigrant history." Booklist

Includes bibliographical references

Freedman, Russell

Kids at work; Lewis Hine and the crusade against child labor; with photographs by Lewis Hine. Clarion Bks. 1994 104p il $20; pa $9.95 (5 and up)   **331.3**

1. Hine, Lewis Wickes, 1874-1940 2. Child labor

ISBN 0-395-58703-4; 0-395-79726-8 (pa)   LC 93-5989

"Using the photographer's work throughout, Freedman provides a documentary account of child labor in America during the early 1900s and the role Lewis Hine played in the crusade against it. He offers a look at the man behind the camera, his involvement with the National Child Labor Committee, and the dangers he faced trying to document unjust labor conditions." SLJ

Freedman "does an outstanding job of integrating historical photographs with meticulously researched and highly readable prose." Publ Wkly

Includes bibliographical references

331.4   Women workers

Colman, Penny

Rosie the riveter; women working on the home front in World War II. Crown 1995 120p il $19; pa $10.99 (5 and up)   **331.4**

1. Women—Employment 2. World War, 1939-1945—United States

ISBN 0-517-59790-X; 0-517-88567-0 (pa)   LC 94-3614

This is an account of women's employment in wartime industry during the Second World War. "Colman looks at the jobs women took, the impact women had on the workplace, and what happened to working women at war's end. . . . [She also discusses] the public relations campaign that not only 'wooed' women into the workplace, but also sought to change firmly entrenched attitudes about women's role in society." Booklist

"A thoughtfully prepared look at women's history and wartime society, this dynamic book is characterized by extensive research." Horn Book

Includes bibliographical references

331.5 Special categories of workers other than by age or sex

Atkin, S. Beth
Voices from the fields; children of migrant farmworkers tell their stories; interviews and photographs by S. Beth Atkin. Little, Brown 1993 96p il $17.95; pa $12.95 (5 and up)   331.5
1. Migrant labor 2. Agricultural laborers 3. Mexican Americans 4. Children's writings
ISBN 0-316-05633-2; 0-316-05620-0 (pa)
                                    LC 92-32248
"Joy Street books"
Photographs, poems in Spanish and English, and interviews with children reveal the hardships and hopes of Mexican American migrant farm workers and their families
"The Spanish is accurate, the English expressive, and the whole is a thoughtful tribute to the migrant experience. The black-and-white photographs are crisp and clear, frequently transcending the representational to achieve art." SLJ
Includes bibliographical references

Hoyt-Goldsmith, Diane
Migrant worker; a boy from the Rio Grande valley; photographs by Lawrence Migdale. Holiday House 1996 32p il $15.95 (3-5)   331.5
1. Mexican Americans 2. Migrant labor 3. Agricultural laborers
ISBN 0-8234-1225-3   LC 95-36779
This is a "photo essay covering an 11-year-old boy's daily life in the fields and at school as well as general information about migrant workers. The text introduces Ricky and his family in both their celebrations and struggles. . . . The full-color photos are crisp, engaging, and attractively positioned to support the text." SLJ
Includes glossary

331.8 Labor unions and labor-management relations

Bartoletti, Susan Campbell, 1958-
Kids on strike! Houghton Mifflin 1999 208p il $20 (5 and up)   331.8
1. Strikes 2. Child labor
ISBN 0-395-88892-1   LC 98-50575
Describes the conditions and treatment that drove workers, including many children, to various strikes, from the mill workers strikes in 1828 and 1836 and the coal strikes at the turn of the century to the work of Mother Jones on behalf of child workers
"This well-researched and well-illustrated account creates a vivid portrait of the working conditions of many American children in the 19th and early 20th centuries." SLJ
Includes bibliographical references

332.024 Personal finance

Godfrey, Neale S.
Neale S. Godfrey's ultimate kids' money book; illustrated by Randy Verougstraete. Simon & Schuster Bks. for Young Readers 1998 122p il $19 (5 and up)   332.024
1. Personal finance 2. Money
ISBN 0-689-81717-7   LC 97-35433
Provides an overview of economics and money, including earning, spending, saving, checks and credit cards, banks, and the history of money
"Facts, fables, advice, strategies, games, history, vocabulary, and more are energetically packaged with cartoon art, photos, and archival documents in this exciting treatment of money and economics for kids. The eye-catching pages playfully combine bold colors and varied sizes of print with lighthearted illustrations and commendably cogent text." Booklist
Includes glossary

Otfinoski, Steven, 1949-
The kid's guide to money; earning it, saving it, spending it, growing it, sharing it. Scholastic 1996 128p il hardcover o.p. paperback available $4.95 (4 and up)   332.024
1. Personal finance
ISBN 0-590-53853-5 (pa)   LC 95-38767
After presenting "moneymaking ideas, Otfinoski covers budgeting and standard consumer advice. Other useful information includes the difference between simple and compound interest; a succinct explanation of stocks, bonds, and mutual funds; and the three golden rules of using a credit card. A chapter on sharing encourages charitable giving of both cash and personal effort." SLJ
"A concise, very useful and accessible guide to handling personal finances that covers a lot of ground." Voice Youth Advocates
Includes glossary and bibliographical references

332.4 Money

Cribb, Joe
Money. Knopf 1990 63p il (Eyewitness books) $19 (4 and up)   332.4
1. Money
ISBN 0-679-80438-2   LC 89-15589
Examines, in text and photographs, the symbolic and material meaning of money, from shekels, shells, and beads to gold, silver, checks, and credit cards. Also discusses how coins and banknotes are made, the value of money during wartime, and how to collect coins

Maestro, Betsy, 1944-
The story of money; illustrated by Giulio Maestro. Clarion Bks. 1993 43p il maps $17 (3-5)   332.4
1. Money
ISBN 0-395-56242-2   LC 91-24997
Also available in paperback from Mulberry Bks.

Maestro, Betsy, 1944-—*Continued*

A history of money, beginning with the barter system in ancient times, to the first use of coins and paper money, to the development of modern monetary systems

"A successful, readable presentation of a complicated subject. . . . Guilio Maestro's meticulously drawn watercolor illustrations brighten each page." SLJ

McMillan, Bruce

Jelly beans for sale; written and photo-illustrated by Bruce McMillan. Scholastic 1996 unp il $15.95 (k-2) **332.4**

1. Money 2. Arithmetic
ISBN 0-590-86584-6   LC 95-25864

The author offers an "introduction to coin values and simple addition. Beginning with the equation '1c = 1 jelly bean,' he shows a parade of children using different coin combinations to purchase the candies from a neighborhood stand. . . . It is the combination of artful design, attention to detail, and gorgeous photography that makes the book stand out. Supplements of interest include information on how jelly beans are made and a toll-free number for teachers who would like to obtain a free classroom kit on the subject." Booklist

333.7   Natural resources and energy

Graham, Ian, 1953-

Nuclear power. Raintree Steck-Vaughn Pubs. 1999 48p il (Energy forever?) lib bdg $27.15 (4-6) **333.7**

1. Nuclear energy
ISBN 0-8172-5363-2   LC 98-38725

Discusses how nuclear power is generated and the history of its use and examines both its potential benefits and possible hazards

Includes glossary and bibliographical references

333.75   Forest lands

Parker, Edward, 1961-

Forests for the future. Raintree Steck-Vaughn Pubs. 1998 48p il (Protecting our planet) $27.12 (4-6) **333.75**

1. Forests and forestry 2. Forest conservation
ISBN 0-8172-4934-6   LC 97-1258

Describes northern, temperate, and tropical forests, the problems of preserving them, and their future prospects

Includes glossary and bibliographical references

333.79   Energy

Parker, Steve

Fuels for the future. Raintree Steck-Vaughn Pubs. 1998 48p il maps (Protecting our planet) $27.12 (4-6) **333.79**

1. Fuel 2. Energy resources
ISBN 0-8172-4937-0   LC 97-17983

First published 1997 in the United Kingdom

Describes the availability and uses of various fuels including petrol, diesel, gas, wood, and coal, and discusses the future prospects of these as power resources

This book "is loaded with a wealth of information, wonderful color photographs, and easy-to-read charts, graphs, and maps. The information is clear and concise." Voice Youth Advocates

Includes glossary and bibliographical references

333.8   Subsurface resources

Graham, Ian, 1953-

Geothermal and bio-energy. Raintree Steck-Vaughn Pubs. 1999 48p il (Energy forever?) lib bdg $27.12 (4 and up) **333.8**

1. Geothermal resources 2. Biomass energy
ISBN 0-8172-5367-X   LC 98-38726

Defines geothermal and bio energies, and explains their advantages and disadvantages

Includes bibliographical references

333.95   Biological resources

Galan, Mark A.

There's still time; the success of the endangered species act; by Mark Galan; with a foreword by Bruce Babbitt. National Geographic Soc. 1997 40p il $15 (3-6) **333.95**

1. Endangered species 2. Wildlife conservation 3. Plant conservation
ISBN 0-7922-7092-4   LC 97-11564

Photoessay showing how environmental action has saved various plants and animals from extinction

Patent, Dorothy Hinshaw

Biodiversity; photographs by William Muñoz. Clarion Bks. 1996 109p il $17.95 (5 and up) **333.95**

1. Biological diversity 2. Nature conservation
ISBN 0-395-68704-7   LC 95-49982

Provides a global perspective on environmental issues while demonstrating the concept which encompasses the many forms of life on earth and their interdependence on one another for survival

"Patent imbues her lucid scientific discussion with many examples of her personal experience both in childhood and as an adult, and she employs a wide array of examples from many parts of the world to demonstrate current problems and scientific and conservation activity. Illustrated with plentiful and helpful photos." Horn Book

Includes glossary

Places of refuge; our national wildlife refuge system; photographs by William Muñoz. Clarion Bks. 1992 80p il map $15.95 (4 and up) **333.95**

1. Wildlife refuges 2. National parks and reserves
ISBN 0-89919-846-5   LC 91-29273

Examines some of the popular wildlife refuges, in such states as Texas, North Dakota, and California, and

Patent, Dorothy Hinshaw—*Continued*
focuses on the different methods used to help maintain a natural balance there

"The tight organization, clear writing, handsome format and handy map, list of addresses for more information, and index add up to a book that will be useful for reports and can serve as background for less generalized coverage." Bull Cent Child Books

Swinburne, Stephen R.
Once a wolf; how wildlife biologists fought to bring back the gray wolf; with photographs by Jim Brandenburg. Houghton Mifflin 1999 48p il $16 (4 and up) **333.95**
1. Wolves 2. Wildlife conservation
ISBN 0-395-89827-7   LC 98-16865
Surveys the history of the troubled relationship between wolves and humans, examines the view that these predators are a valuable part of the ecosystem, and describes the conservation movement to restore them to the wild

The "crisp color photographs showing wolves in their natural environment are exceptional. Swinburne's text adds suspense and excitement to the story. . . . This is an involving study . . . which makes fascinating reading." Bull Cent Child Books
Includes bibliographical references

342 Constitutional and administrative law

Fritz, Jean
Shhh! we're writing the Constitution; illustrated by Tomie dePaola. Putnam 1987 64p il $15.99; pa $5.99 (2-4)   **342**
1. Constitutional history—United States
ISBN 0-399-21403-8; 0-698-11624-0 (pa)
LC 86-22528
"This book discusses how the Constitution came to be written and ratified. It includes the full text of the document produced by the Constitutional Convention of 1787." Bull Cent Child Books

"Jean Fritz gives a vivid, vibrant picture of the 1787 Constitutional Convention. The wonderful, full-color illustrations are a perfect match for the captivating text." Child Book Rev Serv

Krull, Kathleen, 1952-
A kid's guide to America's Bill of Rights; curfews, censorship, and the 100-pound giant; illustrated by Anna DiVito. Avon Bks. 1999 226p il $16 (4 and up)   **342**
1. United States. Constitution. 1st-10th amendments
2. Civil rights
ISBN 0-380-97497-5   LC 99-17324
"After describing how the first 10 amendments came to be added to the Constitution, the book considers each one from a historical point of view, examining Supreme Court cases and famous challenges, and explaining in what ways each amendment applies to children and teenagers. Anna Divito's cartoonlike drawings add a visually appealing touch." Booklist
Includes bibliographical references

Maestro, Betsy, 1944-
A more perfect union; the story of our Constitution; illustrated by Giulio Maestro. Lothrop, Lee & Shepard Bks. 1987 48p il hardcover o.p. paperback available $7.95 (2-4)
342
1. Constitutional history—United States
ISBN 0-688-10192-5 (pa)   LC 87-4083
Also available Spanish language edition
The Maestros "cover the birth of the Constitution from the initial decision to hold the convention, through the summer meetings in Philadelphia, the ratification struggle, the first election, and the adoption of the Bill of Rights." SLJ

"A simple, straightforward account using an oversize format with full-color illustration throughout. There is an excellent, fact-filled addenda that also includes the Preamble, chronologies and summaries of the Articles of the Constitution, the Bill of Rights, the Amendments and the Connecticut Compromise. This fine book places important events in historical context." Publ Wkly

347 Civil procedure and courts

Stein, R. Conrad, 1937-
The powers of the Supreme Court. Children's Press 1995 30p il (Cornerstones of freedom) lib bdg $20.50 (4-6)   **347**
1. United States. Supreme Court
ISBN 0-516-06697-8   LC 94-38266
First published 1989 with title: The story of the powers of the Supreme Court

Stein "cites several landmark cases, such as Marbury v. Madison, Plessy v. Ferguson, Brown v. Board of Education of Topeka, Roe v. Wade, and Miranda v. Arizona, to illustrate the evolution of the Court's powers. He also explains how cases get their names and the impact of some of these decisions." SLJ
Includes glossary

355 Military science

Meltzer, Milton, 1915-
Weapons & warfare; from the stone age to the space age; illustrated by Sergio Martinez. HarperCollins Pubs. 1996 85p il $16.95; lib bdg $16.89 (5 and up)   **355**
1. Weapons 2. Military art and science
ISBN 0-06-024875-0; 0-06-024876-9 (lib bdg)
LC 95-48464
Highlights some weapons of war explaining how and why they were developed, various responses people have had to them, and the impact they have had upon society

"A concise, tautly written, introductory survey of an ever-popular subject. In straightforward, seemingly effortless prose, Meltzer presents readers with essential facts and figures." SLJ
Includes bibliographical references

Robertshaw, Andrew
A soldier's life; a visual history of soldiers through the ages. Lodestar Bks. 1997 48p il $16.99 (4 and up) **355**
1. Soldiers—History
ISBN 0-525-67550-7 LC 96-44309
This "photo history of soldiering features contemporary models posed in the historic garb of those who fought in the Crusades, the Civil War, the two world wars, and several other conflicts. A concise text accompanies the clear color photographs and explains the details of the various uniforms, weapons, and equipment used in each war. A time line and list of battle sites and museums are included." Horn Book Guide
Includes glossary

355.1 Military life and customs

The **Visual** dictionary of military uniforms. Dorling Kindersley 1992 64p il (Eyewitness visual dictionaries) $18.95; lib bdg $15.99 (4 and up) **355.1**
1. Military uniforms
ISBN 1-56458-010-5; 1-56458-011-3 (lib bdg)
LC 91-58206
Labeled illustrations with explanatory text show the parts of various military uniforms that have been used from ancient Roman times to the twentieth century
"The book uses beautiful color photographs of actual or reproduced military uniforms. Each uniform has been taken apart in minute detail, and all relevant parts are labeled clearly and accurately." Sci Books Films

355.7 Military installations

Macdonald, Fiona
A Roman fort; illustrated by Gerald Wood. Bedrick Bks. 1993 48p il maps (Inside story) $18.95 (5 and up) **355.7**
1. Fortification 2. Rome—Antiquities
ISBN 0-87226-370-3 LC 93-16397
Text and illustrations describe the construction of an ancient Roman fort and the lives of the soldiers who manned it in defense of the Empire
"Full-color, detailed drawings and diagrams are an integral part of the presentation. A wealth of information can be obtained from the blocks of text and numerous cutaways showing the inside and outside of buildings." SLJ
Includes glossary

355.8 Military equipment and supplies. Weapons

Byam, Michèle
Arms & armor. Knopf 1988 63p il (Eyewitness books) $16; lib bdg $16.99 (4 and up) **355.8**
1. Armor
ISBN 0-394-89622-X; 0-394-99622-4 (lib bdg)
LC 87-26449
Available DK Pub. edition $15.95; lib bdg $19.99 (ISBN 0-7894-5836-5; 0-7894-6553-1)

A photo essay examining the design, construction, and uses of hand weapons and armor from a Stone Age axe to the revolvers and rifles of the Wild West
"The brilliantly colored photos have a luminous sheen, imparting an almost three-dimensional quality." Booklist

Yue, Charlotte
Armor; [by] Charlotte and David Yue. Houghton Mifflin 1994 92p il $16 (4 and up) **355.8**
1. Armor 2. Knights and knighthood
ISBN 0-395-68101-4 LC 93-50601
The authors "discuss European knighthood, the historical development of armor as new weapons called for new defenses, the armorer's craft, the complicated task of dressing a knight, armor for horses, jousts, and the end of knighthood. . . . The text makes the distinction between what historians know from evidence and what they surmise. Black-and-white drawings illustrate the text." Booklist
Includes bibliographical references

359.1 Naval life and customs

Biesty, Stephen
Stephen Biesty's cross-sections: Man-of-war; illustrated by Stephen Biesty; written by Richard Platt. Dorling Kindersley 1993 27p il $16.95 (4 and up) **359.1**
1. Great Britain. Royal Navy 2. Seafaring life 3. Ships
ISBN 1-56458-321-X LC 92-21227
Text and cutaway illustrations depict life aboard a British warship of the Napoleonic era, covering such topics as work, leisure, discipline, navigating, and fighting
"The intriguing text, presented in brief, anecdotal notes, is accompanied by smaller drawings, making this meticulously presented book a treasure of factual content and visual imagery." Booklist
Includes glossary

361.2 Social action

Lewis, Barbara A., 1943-
The kid's guide to social action; how to solve the social problems you choose—and turn creative thinking into positive action; edited by Pamela Espeland and Caryn Pernu. rev, expanded, updated ed. Free Spirit 1998 211p il pa $18.95 (4 and up) **361.2**
1. Social problems
ISBN 1-57542-038-4 LC 98-11036
"A Do something! book"
First published 1991
Resource guide for children for learning political action skills that can help them make a difference in solving social problems at the community, state, and national levels
"Clearly but informally written, the book is packed with well-organized, practical information and includes

Lewis, Barbara A., 1943-—*Continued*

plenty of inspiring quotes and anecdotes. . . . This is an exemplary reference and curricular resource that works as enlightening browsing material as well." Bull Cent Child Books

Includes bibliographical references

362.1 Physical illness

Peacock, Carol Antoinette

Sugar was my best food; diabetes and me; [by] Carol Antoinette Peacock, Adair Gregory, and Kyle Carney Gregory; illustrated by Mary Jones. Whitman, A. 1998 55p il $13.95; pa $4.95 (3-6)
362.1
1. Diabetes
ISBN 0-8075-7646-8; 0-8075-7648-4 (pa)
LC 97-27869
Adair Gregory, an eleven-year-old boy describes how he learned that he had diabetes, the effect of this disease on his life, and how he learned to cope with the changes in his life

"What is truly exceptional here is the boy's emotional candor. . . . This appealing book is packaged with a colorful cover and has charming black-and-white illustrations. . . . A useful title for children with this disease and those who want to know more about it." SLJ

Rogers, Fred

Going to the hospital; photographs by Jim Judkis. Putnam 1988 unp il hardcover o.p. paperback available $5.99 (k-2)
362.1
1. Hospitals 2. Medical care
ISBN 0-698-11574-0 (pa)
LC 87-19170
Describes what happens during a stay in the hospital, including some of the common forms of medical treatment

"The author's style is just right for this level of information book: reassuring yet candid, matter-of-fact about those aspects of hospitalization that may be frightening or painful, yet not in itself alarming." Bull Cent Child Books

Rosenberg, Maxine B., 1939-

Mommy's in the hospital having a baby; photographs by Robert Maass. Clarion Bks. 1997 28p il $14.95 (k-1)
362.1
1. Childbirth 2. Hospitals 3. Infants
ISBN 0-395-71813-9
LC 96-12442
Describes the care that mothers and babies receive in the hospital and tells children what to expect if they go to visit their new brother or sister

"Full-color photographs of several families and babies appear throughout, and the tone is generally upbeat and positive." SLJ

Westcott, Patsy

Living with leukemia. Raintree Steck-Vaughn Pubs. 2000 32p il lib bdg $25.69 (3-5)
362.1
1. Leukemia
ISBN 0-8172-5743-8
LC 99-27219

Describes the condition of leukemia, how it affects the lives of those who have it, and how to cope with or recover from it

"The author does a commendable job of explaining the nature of the disease and its symptoms in the types affecting the young subjects." Sci Books Films

Includes glossary and bibliographical references

362.29 Substance abuse

Pringle, Laurence P.

Smoking; a risky business. Morrow Junior Bks. 1996 124p il $16 (5 and up)
362.29
1. Tobacco habit 2. Smoking
ISBN 0-688-13039-9
LC 96-5359
The author describes "the harmful effects of smoking and then takes on the advertising strategies used to discredit such claims. Beginning with a history of tobacco, he jumps into a forthright discussion of nicotine and other ingredients of cigarettes, also considering pipes and smokeless tobacco, the effects of second-hand smoke, and smoking during pregnancy. . . . The involvement of the federal government in agricultural subsidies, and interest in tobacco as a growth industry are laid out, as well as FDA regulations, congressional bills, and class-action suits." SLJ

"Condemnatory but still restrained and with an excellent array of illustrations, this well-researched volume will satisfy curiosity and be a good source for reports." Booklist

Includes glossary and bibliographical references

362.292 Alcoholism

Pringle, Laurence P.

Drinking; a risky business; [by] Laurence Pringle. Morrow Junior Bks. 1997 112p il $16 (5 and up)
362.292
1. Alcoholism
ISBN 0-688-15044-6
LC 97-7807
Describes the history of alcohol, its effects on the body and personality, how to deal with peer pressure to drink, and how to get help for alcoholism

"Pringle's chapters on the history of the U.S. temperance movement and the economic side of the alcohol industry set his book apart. . . . Readable and well organized." SLJ

Includes glossary and bibliographical references

362.4 Problems of and services to people with physical disabilities

Alexander, Sally Hobart

Do you remember the color blue? and other questions kids ask about blindness. Viking 2000 78p il $16.99 (4 and up)
362.4
1. Blind
ISBN 0-670-88043-4
LC 99-34130

Alexander, Sally Hobart—*Continued*

Children ask questions of an author who lost her vision at the age of twenty-seven, including "How did you become blind?" "How can you read?" and "Was it hard to be a parent when you couldn't see your kids?"

"The author's clearheaded and pragmatic approach . . . refreshingly resists mythologizing, and her balanced account will give kids a feeling for a life that on the one hand seems very different and on the other could be anybody's." Bull Cent Child Books

Carter, Alden R.

Stretching ourselves; kids with cerebral palsy; photographs by Carol S. Carter. Whitman, A. 2000 unp il lib bdg $14.95 (1-3)   **362.4**
1. Cerebral palsy
ISBN 0-8075-7637-9   LC 99-40085
Describes cerebral palsy and focuses on the daily lives of three children with varying degrees of this condition
"Told with multiple full-color photographs . . . this solid introduction to the disability provides just enough information for younger children." SLJ

Haughton, Emma

Living with deafness. Raintree Steck-Vaughn Pubs. 2000 32p il lib bdg $25.69 (3-5)   **362.4**
1. Deafness 2. Deaf
ISBN 0-8172-5742-X   LC 98-32231
The author offers an "explanation of the anatomy of the ear to help children understand various types of hearing loss and their causes, from infection to fluid in the ear. Hearing aids, cochlear implants, and TTYs are described, as are various methods of communication, such as sign language, finger spelling, and lip reading." SLJ
Includes glossary

Pimm, Paul

Living with cerebral palsy. Raintree Steck-Vaughn Pubs. 2000 32p il lib bdg $25.69 (3-5)   **362.4**
1. Cerebral palsy
ISBN 0-8172-5744-6   LC 99-27202
Describes the varying effects of cerebral palsy, how different people manage to live with this condition, and where to get more information
The "book conveys a strong sense of individuals finding it difficult at first to cope with the limitations of the condition and accept the recommended therapies. . . . Young readers will become aware that those affected by cerebral palsy have many of the same desires to be liked, to learn, and to have fun as they themselves have." Sci Books Films
Includes glossary and bibliographical references

Rogers, Fred

Extraordinary friends; photographs by Jim Judkis. Putnam 2000 unp il (Let's talk about it) lib bdg $16.99 (k-2)   **362.4**
1. Handicapped children
ISBN 0-399-23146-3   LC 99-17615

Focuses on people who are different, who might use equipment such as wheelchairs or special computers, who are more like you than you might think, and suggests ways to interact with them

This volume "will be in high demand from early childhood educators and parents who want to give young children positive attitudes toward people with disabilities. . . . Engaging color photographs show three pairs of friends throughout, including a boy with cerebal palsy, a boy who uses a walker, and a girl with Down syndrome." Horn Book

Westcott, Patsy

Living with blindness. Raintree Steck-Vaughn Pubs. 2000 32p il lib bdg $25.69 (3-5)   **362.4**
1. Blind
ISBN 0-8172-5741-1   LC 98-32230
Explains the condition of blindness, its possible causes, and how it affects the everyday lives of those who are dealing with it
"The explanations are clear and straightforward, without creating anxiety. . . . Future prospects for treating blindness and how those affected learn to cope are treated very sensitively." Sci Books Films
Includes glossary and bibliographical references

362.5   Problems of and services to the poor

Wolf, Bernard, 1930-

Homeless; written and photographed by Bernard Wolf. Orchard Bks. 1995 unp il $16.95; lib bdg $17.99 (2-4)   **362.5**
1. Henry Street Settlement (New York, N.Y.) 2. Homeless persons 3. New York (N.Y.)—Social conditions
ISBN 0-531-06886-2; 0-531-08736-0 (lib bdg)
      LC 94-27293
This photoessay "focuses on a New York City family that faces difficulties in finding affordable housing. The book begins as eight-year-old Mikey and his family . . . receive assistance in the form of a temporary rent-free apartment in the Henry Street Settlement Urban Family Center, one of the United States' first transitional housing projects for the homeless." Horn Book
"Crisp color photos of the threadbare but 'squeaky clean' apartment, long lines for the check-cashing office, and expectant young faces at the charity Christmas party will speak as eloquently as the narration does to an audience of kids more fortunate than Mikey." Bull Cent Child Books

362.7   Problems of and services to young people

Krementz, Jill

How it feels to be adopted. Knopf 1982 107p il hardcover o.p. paperback available $15 (4 and up)
     362.7
1. Adoption
ISBN 0-394-75853-6 (pa)   LC 82-48011

Krementz, Jill—*Continued*

"Nineteen youngsters ranging in age from 8 to 16 voice their feelings about being adopted. . . . Several of the accounts are by youngsters who 'have' found their birth mothers and are in the process of getting to know them. Single-parent adoptees are included, too." Booklist

This "is an important contribution to literature on adoption and the question of searching for biological parents." SLJ

Includes bibliographical references

Warren, Andrea

Orphan train rider; one boy's true story. Houghton Mifflin 1996 80p il $16; pa $7.95 (4 and up)   **362.7**

1. Nailling, Lee, 1917- 2. Orphans 3. Abandoned children

ISBN 0-395-69822-7; 0-395-91362-4 (pa)

LC 94-43688

"From 1854 to 1930, the orphan trains took homeless children from cities in the East to new homes in the West, the Midwest, and the South. In Warren's book, one man's memories of his childhood abandonment and adoption give a personal slant on the subject. Chapters telling the story of Lee Nailing, who took an orphan train west in 1926, alternate with chapters filling in background information about the trains and the experiences of other children who rode them to their destinies." Booklist

"An excellent introduction to researching or discussing children-at-risk in an earlier generation. The book is clearly written and illustrated with numerous black-and-white photographs and reproductions." SLJ

Includes bibliographical references

363.2 Police services

Jackson, Donna, 1958-

The wildlife detectives; how forensic scientists fight crimes against nature; by Donna M. Jackson; photographs by Wendy Shattil and Bob Rozinski. Houghton Mifflin 2000 47p il $16 (4 and up)   **363.2**

1. National Fish and Wildlife Forensics Laboratory 2. Forensic sciences 3. Game protection

ISBN 0-395-86976-5   LC 99-34857

Describes how the wildlife detectives at the National Fish and Wildlife Forensics Laboratory in Ashland, Oregon, analyze clues to catch and convict people responsible for crimes against animals

This book features "a smoothly written text that unfolds almost like a mystery novel. . . . Engaging full-color photographs help clarify the text and will appeal to browsers. A list of follow-up suggestions and a glossary of terms are appended. A book that will be welcomed by mystery fans and anyone who cares about animals." Booklist

363.34 Disasters

Gibbons, Gail

Emergency! Holiday House 1994 unp il $16.95; pa $6.95 (k-3)   **363.34**

1. Vehicles

ISBN 0-8234-1128-1; 0-8234-1201-6 (pa)

LC 94-2109

The author "covers emergency vehicles, from ambulances and fire engines to helicopters, boats and planes, distinguishing . . . between the different types of fire trucks and including utility trucks sent out after storms." Bull Cent Child Books

"Gibbons's stylistic, flat, colorful illustrations accurately depict the events described in the text and add more for observant readers to interpret." SLJ

363.7 Environmental problems

Berger, Melvin, 1927-

Oil spill! illustrated by Paul Mirocha. HarperCollins Pubs. 1994 31p il (Let's-read-and-find-out science) $15; pa $4.95 (k-3)   **363.7**

1. Oil spills

ISBN 0-06-022909-8; 0-06-445121-6 (pa)

LC 92-34779

Explains why oil spills occur and how they are cleaned up and suggests strategies for preventing them in the future

"The text is simple and clear. . . . Subtle in texture and deep in tone, the colorful artwork effectively illustrates marine animals and oil tankers. . . . A good introduction to the subject." Booklist

Brown, Laurene Krasny

Dinosaurs to the rescue! a guide to protecting our planet; [by] Laurie Krasny Brown and Marc Brown. Little, Brown 1992 unp il hardcover o.p. paperback available $7.95 (k-3)   **363.7**

1. Environmental protection

ISBN 0-316-11397-2 (pa)   LC 91-27177

"Joy Street books"

Text and illustrations of dinosaur characters introduce the earth's major environmental problems and suggest ways children can help

"Information is presented in a straightforward way, enlivened by energetic, brightly colored, cartoon-style illustrations. Irreverent and often humorous comments . . . appear in conversational balloons and help to lighten the decidedly earnest tone of the narrative. With plenty of practical suggestions and projects . . . this book is an ideal and upbeat way to introduce the problems in our environment and to inspire children to make a difference in the health of our planet." Horn Book

Gibbons, Gail

Recycle! a handbook for kids. Little, Brown 1992 unp il hardcover o.p. paperback available $6.95 (k-3)   **363.7**

1. Recycling

ISBN 0-316-30943-5 (pa)   LC 91-4317

Gibbons, Gail—*Continued*

Explains the process of recycling from start to finish and discusses what happens to paper, glass, aluminum cans, and plastic when they are recycled into new products

"An eminently readable and well-organized offering that's filled with information. . . . The top two-thirds of each page is devoted to illustrations that perfectly complement the brief text below." SLJ

Glaser, Linda

Compost! growing gardens from your garbage; pictures by Anca Hariton. Millbrook Press 1996 unp il lib bdg $22.90; $8.95 (k-2)   **363.7**
1. Compost
ISBN 1-56294-659-5 (lib bdg); 0-76130-030-9
                  LC 95-10421
"A child tells how her family uses leftovers to create compost, explaining how garbage, added to dirt in a bin, makes rich soil for growing healthy plants. The book begins and ends with a picture of the family garden in full glory. Soft watercolor washes and borders grace the book's pages. 'Questions and Answers about Composting' fact sheet included." Horn Book Guide

Maass, Robert

Garbage. Holt & Co. 2000 unp $16.95 (k-3)
                           363.7
1. Refuse and refuse disposal
ISBN 0-8050-5951-2   LC 99-32144
An introduction to the problems of waste management and the various ways we dispose of garbage. Includes tips on recycling

"The last two pages contain a longer text, which discusses disposal of hazardous waste and creating compost heaps. An attractive book that will be useful for introductory units on garbage and recycling." Booklist

Markle, Sandra, 1946-

After the spill; the Exxon Valdez disaster, then and now. Walker & Co. 1999 30p il $16.95 (4 and up)   **363.7**
1. Exxon Valdez (Ship) 2. Oil spills
ISBN 0-8027-8610-3   LC 98-38550
Examines the impact of the 1989 Exxon Valdez oil spill on the environment and people of Prince William Sound and describes the steps taken to minimize the damage and prevent a recurrence

"The easy-to-read text, child-friendly format, and attractive photos will appeal to students writing reports and to teachers looking for material on environmental issues." SLJ

Includes glossary

Paladino, Catherine

One good apple; growing our food for the sake of the earth. Houghton Mifflin 1999 48p il $15 (4 and up)   **363.7**
1. Pesticides 2. Organic farming
ISBN 0-395-85009-6   LC 97-45866

Discusses the problems created by the use of pesticides to grow food crops and the benefits of organic farming

The author's "information is well organized and her message is straightforward and accessible. . . . This is nonfiction writing at its best." SLJ

Includes bibliographical references

Pringle, Laurence P.

The environmental movement; from its roots to the challenges of a new century; [by] Laurence Pringle. Morrow Junior Bks. 2000 144p il $16.95 (5 and up)   **363.7**
1. Environmental protection
ISBN 0-688-15626-6   LC 99-32110
"Topics covered include the rise of the conservation movement, the roles of legislation, big business, and eco-warriors. There's also a brief look at the struggles ahead. . . . Well-chosen photographs and a comprehensive resource section round out this engaging, useful title." Booklist

Includes bibliographical references

Oil spills; damage, recovery, and prevention; [by] Laurence Pringle. Morrow Junior Bks. 1993 56p il maps lib bdg $14.93 (4 and up)   **363.7**
1. Oil spills 2. Petroleum
ISBN 0-688-09861-4   LC 92-30348
"A Save-the-earth book"

Describes petroleum and its uses, examines the harmful effects of oil spills, and discusses how such environmental disasters can be cleaned up or prevented

"Photographs of the areas and animals affected by spills reinforce the written descriptions. This small book contains a wealth of well-organized and clearly stated information." Booklist

Includes glossary and bibliographical references

Vanishing ozone; protecting earth from ultraviolet radiation; [by] Laurence Pringle. Morrow Junior Bks. 1995 64p il $16; lib bdg $15.93 (4 and up)   **363.7**
1. Ozone layer
ISBN 0-688-04157-4; 0-688-04158-2 (lib bdg)
                  LC 94-25928
"A Save-the-earth book"

This is an "introduction to the science and politics of the ozone layer. A history of the scientific study of ozone includes names of major scientists and the titles of their published articles. The political side of the debate includes reactions of elected officials and members of the chemical industry." Horn Book Guide

"The organization is excellent. . . . Technical terms are well balanced. . . . Crisp black-and-white photographs, diagrams, and maps illustrate the text. Concluding chapters offer suggestions for taking action and include addresses for government agencies and environmental groups." SLJ

Includes glossary and bibliographical references

Showers, Paul, 1910-1999
Where does the garbage go? illustrated by
Randy Chewning. rev ed. HarperCollins Pubs.
1994 32p il (Let's-read-and-find-out science book)
lib bdg $14.89; pa $4.95 (k-3)   **363.7**
1. Refuse and refuse disposal 2. Recycling
ISBN 0-06-021057-5 (lib bdg); 0-06-445114-3 (pa)
LC 91-46115
First published 1974 by Crowell
"A class of grade-school students learns about waste
disposal and recycling in a simple, accessible text. The
clear, color illustrations are particularly effective in
showing the recycling process for paper, aluminum, and
glass." Horn Book Guide

364 Criminology

Lane, Brian
Crime & detection; written by Brian Lane;
photographed by Andy Crawford. Knopf 1998 59p
il (Eyewitness books) (4 and up)   **364**
1. Crime 2. Forensic sciences 3. Criminal investigation
LC 97-32376
Available DK Pub. edition $15.95; lib bdg $19.99
(ISBN 0-7894-5882-9; 0-7894-6622-8)
Explores the many different methods used to solve
crimes, covering such topics as criminal, detectives, and
forensics

364.1 Criminal offenses

St. George, Judith, 1931-
In the line of fire; presidents' lives at stake.
Holiday House 1999 144p il lib bdg $18.95 (4 and
up)   **364.1**
1. Presidents—United States—Assassination
ISBN 0-8234-1428-0   LC 98-39030
"The first of the two main sections concerns the four
slain U.S. presidents as well as their respective assassins,
and also discusses the effects of these fatal events on the
country. Each chapter preface relays the day's events
preceding the murder in a dramatic fashion. The second
half concerns the assassination attempts on six presidents
and their would-be assassins. St. George includes intriguing anecdotes. . . . Nicely placed illustrations and photos
add power to the text." SLJ
Includes bibliographical references

370 Education

Coles, Robert
The story of Ruby Bridges; illustrated by
George Ford. Scholastic 1995 unp il lib bdg
$15.95 (1-3)   **370**
1. Bridges, Ruby 2. School integration 3. New Or-
leans (La.)—Race relations
ISBN 0-590-57281-4   LC 92-33674

"Ruby Bridges was the first African American child to
attend an all-white elementary school in New Orleans in
1960. Coles tells the brief story of her daily walk past
. . . white adults, her time alone with her teacher in an
otherwise empty classroom because white parents kept
their children home, and the . . . moment when she
prays in front of the . . . crowd for God to forgive
them." SLJ
Coles "tells one girl's heroic story, part of the history
of ordinary people who have changed the world. . . .
Ford's moving watercolor paintings mixed with acrylic
ink are predominantly in sepia shades of brown and red.
They capture the physical warmth of Ruby's family and
community, the immense powers against her, and her
shining inner strength." Booklist

O'Neill, Laurie, 1949-
Little Rock; the desegregation of Central High.
Millbrook Press 1994 64p il (Spotlight on
American history) lib bdg $24.90 (5 and up)
370
1. Central High School (Little Rock, Ark.) 2. School
integration 3. African Americans—Civil rights 4. Ar-
kansas—Race relations
ISBN 1-56294-354-5   LC 93-29057
This is an "account of a year in the life of the group
of nine brave African-American teenagers who integrated
Central High School in Little Rock, Arkansas, in 1957.
O'Neill's well-written narrative documents human nature
at its best and worst." SLJ
Includes bibliographical references

370.9 Education—Historical and geographic treatment

Bial, Raymond
One-room school. Houghton Mifflin 1999 48p il
$15 (3-5)   **370.9**
1. Schools—United States—History 2. Education—
United States—History
ISBN 0-395-90514-1   LC 98-43241
Presents a brief history of the one-room schools that
existed in the United States from the 1700s to the 1950s
"Clear, beautifully composed photos on every page
transport readers back to bygone days." Booklist
Includes bibliographical references

Loeper, John J., 1929-
Going to school in 1776. Atheneum Pubs. 1973
79p il $16 (4 and up)   **370.9**
1. Education—United States—History 2. Schools—
United States—History 3. United States—Social life
and customs—1600-1775, Colonial period
ISBN 0-689-30089-1   LC 72-86940
The author tells what it was like to be a child and to
go to school in America in 1776. He describes children's
dress, schools, teachers, school books, lessons, discipline
and after-school recreation
Includes bibliographical references

371.1   Teachers, teaching, and related activities

Fisher, Leonard Everett, 1924-
The schoolmasters; written & illustrated by Leonard Everett Fisher. Benchmark Bks. (Tarrytown) 1997 47p il $21.36 (4 and up) **371.1**
1. Teaching 2. Education—United States—History 3. United States—Social life and customs—1600-1775, Colonial period
ISBN 0-7614-0480-5   LC 96-16609
A reissue of the title first published 1967 by Watts
An account of the historical background of education in the United States, telling what the colonial schoolmasters were like, where they taught, how they taught, and what they taught

371.3025   Audiovisual materials— Directories

AV market place; the complete business directory of: audio, audiovisual, computer systems, film, video, programming, with industry yellow pages. Bowker il pa $206.75   **371.3025**
1. Audiovisual materials—Directories
ISSN 1044-0445

Annual. First published 1969 with title: Audiovisual market place
This volume identifies more than "6,300 companies that create, supply, or distribute an extraordinary range of audiovisual equipment and services. An index of . . . products and services is cross-referenced to companies in the main body. The products, services, and company index identifies all firms geographically. . . . Companies are also indexed by name." Nichols. Guide to Ref Books for Sch Media Cent. 4th edition

371.305   Methods of instruction and study—Serial publications

MultiMedia schools; a practical journey of technology for education, including multimedia, CD-ROM, online, internet, & hardware in k-12. Information Today $39.95 per year   **371.305**
1. Teaching—Aids and devices—Periodicals
ISSN 1075-0479

6 issues per year. First published 1994
"Professional materials reviewed in a column called 'Reference Shelf.' Items may be in any format, but books predominate; there are 8-10 critical annotations per issue. Entries include bibliographic information and features. 'Title Watch' lists new products by curriculum area. 'Product Reviews in Brief' are original reviews of CD-ROMs, videodiscs, magnetic media and Web sites written by practicing educators. Reviews are long and cover the company, price, audience, format, system requirements, a description, comments about installation, contents and features, ease of use, and product support, and a final recommendation." Safford. Guide to Ref Materials for Sch Libr Media Cent. 5th edition

371.9   Special education

Stanley, Jerry, 1941-
Children of the Dust Bowl; the true story of the school at Weedpatch Camp. Crown 1992 85p il maps lib bdg $15.99; pa $8.95 (5 and up) **371.9**
1. Migrant labor 2. Great Depression, 1929-1939 3. Education—Social aspects
ISBN 0-517-58782-3 (lib bdg); 0-517-88094-6 (pa)
     LC 92-393
Describes the plight of the migrant workers who traveled from the Dust Bowl to California during the Depression and were forced to live in a federal labor camp and discusses the school that was built for their children
"Stanley's text is a compelling document. . . . The story is inspiring and disturbing, and Stanley has recorded the details with passion and dignity." Booklist
Includes bibliographical references

372   Elementary education

Cole, Ann
I saw a purple cow, and 100 other recipes for learning; [by] Ann Cole [et al.]; illustrated by True Kelley. Little, Brown 1972 96p il hardcover o.p. paperback available $10.95   **372**
1. Preschool education 2. Amusements
ISBN 0-316-15175-0 (pa)
"Based on research done in Project Headstart, this book serves as a guide to the effective use of throwaway objects found in the house and environs as creative learning devices for young children. It is geared to the important first six years of children's lives and attempts to help the untrained mother during this period." Libr J

372.05   Elementary education— Serial publications

Childhood Education; infancy through early adolescence. Association for Childhood Educ. Int. $65 per year   **372.05**
1. Elementary education—Periodicals
ISSN 0009-4056
Six issues a year. First published 1924
"The articles are well written and would provide valuable information to educators, education students, parents, and childcare workers. The book review section includes a section for children's books, professional reading, and special publications pertaining to this area." Katz. Mag for Libr. 10th edition

Instructor. Scholastic $19.95 per year   **372.05**
1. Elementary education—Periodicals
ISSN 1049-5851
Eight issues a year. First published 1891. Title and publisher vary
Topical articles for the elementary classroom teacher. Contains illustrative material, booklists, activity guides and a section on electronic learning
"This is a basic title for academic libraries serving elementary teacher education programs and should be available to all K-6 teachers." Katz. Mag for Libr. 10th edition

Teaching K-8; the professional magazine for teachers. Early Years, 40 Richards Ave., Norwalk, CT 06854-2309 $23.97 **372.05**
1. Elementary education—Periodicals
ISSN 0891-4508
Eight issues a year. Continues Early Years (ceased publication 1987)
Also known as Teaching Pre-K-8
This magazine "offers a wealth of information and should be a basic title for libraries serving elementary and middle schools and teacher preparation programs." Katz. Mag for Libr. 10th edition

372.2 Specific levels of elementary education

Howe, James, 1946-
When you go to kindergarten; text by James Howe; photographs by Betsy Imershein. rev & updated ed. Morrow Junior Bks. 1994 unp il $15; pa $5.95 (k-1) **372.2**
1. Kindergarten
ISBN 0-688-12912-9; 0-688-14387-3 (pa)
LC 93-48152
First published 1986 by Knopf
"The author tells youngsters what school might look like and how they might get there, and describes some of the possible activities. . . . Multicultural children are welcomed and taught by both male and female teachers. Smiling, busy kids engaged in many activities portray school as an exciting, interesting, and happy place." SLJ

372.4 Reading

Herb, Steven
Using children's books in preschool settings; a how-to-do-it manual; [by] Steven Herb and Sara Willoughby-Herb. Neal-Schuman 1994 181p (How-to-do-it manuals for school and public librarians) pa $45.25 **372.4**
1. Reading 2. Books and reading
ISBN 1-55570-156-6
LC 94-8238
Includes sections on child and language development, literary genres and setting up a storybook corner. Problems posed by restless listeners, disliked books, and language barriers are addressed
"The treatment is a nice mixture of the theoretical and the pragmatic." Bull Cent Child Books
Includes bibliographical references

372.405 Reading—Serial publications

The **Reading** Teacher. International Reading Assn. $45 per year **372.405**
1. Reading—Periodicals
ISSN 0034-0561
Eight issues a year. First published 1947

This journal "explores reading and literacy education in an intelligent and professional way. . . . Elementary teachers' and students' voices are clearly heard in articles, adding a personal and authentic note. This journal is important for reading and literacy teachers." Katz. Mag for Libr. 10th edition

372.6 Language arts (Communication skills)

Bauer, Caroline Feller, 1935-
Caroline Feller Bauer's new handbook for storytellers; with stories, poems, magic, and more; illustrations by Lynn Gates Bredeson. American Lib. Assn. 1993 550p il music hardcover o.p. paperback available $45 **372.6**
1. Storytelling
ISBN 0-8389-0664-8 (pa)
LC 93-14959
First published 1977 with title: Handbook for storytellers
Bauer's introduction "incorporates a broad variety of media and props into the storytelling process. . . . Beginners and veterans alike can benefit from this practical approach to program planning and promotion, story selection and preparation, and activities extending various themes or occasions." Bull Cent Child Books
Includes bibliographical references

The poetry break; an annotated anthology with ideas for introducing children to poetry; illustrations by Edith Bingham. Wilson, H.W. 1995 xxv, 347p il $55 **372.6**
1. Poetry—Study and teaching
ISBN 0-8242-0852-8
LC 93-42069
This book serves as a "do-it-yourself poetry-break packet, including ideas for presentation, settings, and general poetry activities; she includes a good 250 pages of poems, suggesting a poem-specific project or topic-extending book after most of the verses." Bull Cent Child Books
Includes bibliographical references

Bruchac, Joseph, 1942-
Tell me a tale; a book about storytelling. Harcourt Brace & Co. 1997 117p $16 (5 and up) **372.6**
1. Storytelling 2. Folklore
ISBN 0-15-201221-4
LC 96-21697
Storyteller Joseph Bruchac incorporates many of his favorite tales in this discussion of the four basic components of storytelling: listening, observing, remembering, and sharing
"Youngsters will find this to be a clear guide to the age-old art form. A 'Note to Parents' about the power of stories, as well as the book's readable style, make this a useful resource for teachers and librarians as well." SLJ
Includes bibliographical references

Buzzeo, Toni

Terrific connections with authors, illustrators, and storytellers; real space and virtual links; by Toni Buzzeo, Jane Kurtz. Libraries Unlimited 1999 185p pa $26.50   **372.6**

1. Children's literature—Study and teaching 2. Book talks 3. Internet

ISBN 1-563-08744-8   LC 99-28468

This book explains "how to choose the right guest, successfully contact bookpeople to make arrangements for your event, and make the most of the visit with curriculum connections and learning extensions." Publisher's note

Includes bibliographical references

Carlson, Ann D., 1952-

Flannelboard stories for infants and toddlers; [by] Ann Carlson and Mary Carlson, illustrator. American Lib. Assn. 1999 196p il pa $25   **372.6**

1. Storytelling

ISBN 0-8389-0759-8   LC 98-54724

"Designed for use with children from 12 to 30 months old, this large paperback provides words and illustrations for storytellers to place on a flannelboard. . . . The introduction provides details for two methods of transferring the large, simple ink drawings from the page to the flannelboard. Well designed for practical use, this book provides helpful ideas for librarians meeting the challenge of programming for the very young." Booklist

Champlin, Connie

Storytelling with puppets. 2nd ed. American Lib. Assn. 1998 249p il pa $35   **372.6**

1. Storytelling 2. Puppets and puppet plays

ISBN 0-8389-0709-1   LC 97-24810

First published 1985 under the authorship of Connie Champlin and Nancy Renfro

This book covers "such topics as puppet types and styles, developing a puppet collection, participatory storytelling, and presentation formats. . . . A very useful choice for professional shelves in both school and public libraries." Booklist

Includes bibliographical references

Greene, Ellin, 1927-

Storytelling; art and technique; foreword by Augusta Baker. 3rd ed. Bowker 1996 xxi, 333p il $39   **372.6**

1. Storytelling

ISBN 0-8352-3458-4   LC 96-11602

First published 1977 under the authorship of Augusta Baker and Ellin Greene

"The first part of the work gives a history of storytelling in U.S. libraries . . . followed by a chapter on the purpose and values of storytelling. Several chapters are devoted to the practice of storytelling, with attention given to selection of the stories, preparation for story hour and the actual presentation." Am Libr [review of 1987 edition]

Includes bibliographical references

Hopkins, Lee Bennett, 1938-

Pass the poetry, please! 3rd ed. HarperCollins Pubs. 1998 277p $25; pa $13.95   **372.6**

1. Poetry—Study and teaching

ISBN 0-06-027746-7; 0-06-446199-8 (pa)

     LC 98-19617

First published 1972

"Written for teachers and librarians seeking ways of getting poetry into the lives of children. . . . Throughout, many poets are cited, from Langston Hughes to Nikki Giovanni and from Jack Prelutsky to Robert Frost." Booklist

"This a must-purchase." SLJ

Includes bibliographical references

Juba this and Juba that; selected by Virginia Tashjian; illustrated by Nadine Bernard Westcott. 2nd ed. Little, Brown 1995 106p il o.p.; Simon & Schuster paperback available $10   **372.6**

1. Storytelling 2. Literature—Collections

ISBN 0-684-80781-5 (pa)   LC 94-27143

A revised and newly illustrated edition of the title first published 1969

"A useful source of chants, poetry and rhyme, stories, finger plays, riddles, songs, tongue twisters, and jokes. The selections accompanied by lively orange and black illustrations, are all suitably silly. They require and inspire audience participation." SLJ [review of 1969 edition]

Livingston, Myra Cohn

Poem-making; ways to begin writing poetry. HarperCollins Pubs. 1991 162p $16.95 (4 and up)

    372.6

1. Poetry—Study and teaching 2. Creative writing

ISBN 0-06-024019-9   LC 90-5012

"A Charlotte Zolotow book"

Introduces the different kinds of poetry and the mechanics of writing poetry, providing an opportunity for the reader to experience the joy of making a poem

"As a writing guide, this book will be most useful in creative writing groups with a teacher or leader. . . . What Livingston does communicate on every page is the excitement of poetry and its strange power to 'arrest our senses' and help us see the world in a new way." Booklist

Includes bibliographical references

MacDonald, Margaret Read

Celebrate the world; twenty tellable folktales for multicultural festivals; illustrations by Roxane Murphy Smith. Wilson, H.W. 1994 225p il $50

    372.6 ·

1. Storytelling 2. Folklore 3. Festivals

ISBN 0-8242-0862-5   LC 94-6682

In this collection of twenty folktales the author "has interwoven the stories with holidays and festivals from various countries and presented tips on how to present both the story and the holiday in a storytelling program. . . . *Celebrate the World* is a thorough and wide-ranging work that will prove valuable to most collections." J Youth Serv Libr

Includes bibliographical references

MacDonald, Margaret Read—*Continued*

Look back and see; twenty lively tales for gentle tellers; illustrations by Roxane Murphy. Wilson, H.W. 1991 178p il $45   **372.6**
1. Storytelling 2. Folklore
ISBN 0-8242-0810-2   LC 91-2539

The author presents twenty non-violent folktales from around the world, with background notes and suggestions for storytelling uses

"Delightfully varied in mood, the tales range from silly and rowdy to contemplative and touching. . . . MacDonald's useful, informative, and entertaining notes follow each story. . . . The notes alone are worth the price of the book." J Youth Serv Libr

Includes bibliographical references

The storyteller's start-up book; finding, learning, performing, and using folktales including twelve tellable tales. August House 1993 215p $26.95; pa $14.95   **372.6**
1. Storytelling 2. Folklore
ISBN 0-87483-304-3; 0-87483-305-1 (pa)
    LC 93-1580

The author's advice on storytelling "covers the practical ground, from selection, learning (in one hour!), performance, and setting to classroom applications. . . . A dozen texts of proven success follow, with performance tips and source notes. Equally valuable are the selected and annotated bibliographies appended to every chapter." Libr J

Twenty tellable tales; audience participation folktales for the beginning storyteller; drawings by Roxane Murphy. Wilson, H.W. 1986 220p il $45; pa $30   **372.6**
1. Storytelling 2. Folklore 3. Fairy tales
ISBN 0-8242-0719-X; 0-8242-0822-6 (pa)
    LC 85-26565

"Dividing her book into three sections—tales, notes, and sources—MacDonald gives instructions for selecting, shaping, learning, and telling each tale and includes notes on their origin as well as comments on audience participation and performance style in other cultures. All the tales are short and include repetitive verses, making them highly suitable for telling aloud." Booklist

Includes bibliographical references

When the lights go out; twenty scary tales to tell; illustrations by Roxane Murphy. Wilson, H.W. 1988 176p il $45; pa $30   **372.6**
1. Storytelling 2. Horror fiction 3. Folklore
ISBN 0-8242-0770-X; 0-8242-0823-4 (pa)
    LC 88-14197

"Divided into six sections—Not Too Scary, Scary in the Dark, Gross Stuff, Jump Tales, Tales to Act Out, and Tales to Draw or Stir Up—the selections will be especially useful around Halloween, although, as the author points out, the book can be used year round. Following each inclusion are helpful notes on telling the stories and a section that gives sources on origins and variants. Murphy's decorative drawings introduce chapters and are scattered throughout the text. Several concluding chapters list bibliographies and provide other helpful information." Booklist

Pellowski, Anne, 1933-

The storytelling handbook; a young people's collection of unusual tales and helpful hints on how to tell them; illustrated by Martha Stoberock. Simon & Schuster 1995 129p il $16   **372.6**
1. Storytelling
ISBN 0-689-80311-7   LC 95-2991

This work "addresses the young person who wants to tell stories in a public setting. It is similar in format to many adult books on storytelling how-tos, with sections on getting started and selecting and preparing stories, as well as a selection of sample tales. Pellowski's notes are extensive and will be very useful to novices looking for ways to research stories." Booklist

Includes bibliographical references

The world of storytelling. expanded and rev ed. Wilson, H.W. 1990 xxi, 311p il $50   **372.6**
1. Storytelling
ISBN 0-8242-0788-2   LC 90-31151
First published 1977

This guide "reviews the oral traditions from which literature for children grew, addresses the controversy between storytellers and folklorists, and offers a modern-day definition for storytelling. *The world of storytelling* also includes chapters on: types of storytelling—bardic, folk, religious, theatrical, library and institutional, campground and playground, hygienic and therapeutic storytelling; format and style of storytelling—opening and closing of a story session; language, voice, and audience response; musical accompaniment; pictures and objects used; training of storytellers—history and survey of training methods; visuality, orality, and literacy; storytelling festivals." Publisher's note

"This is an important work for collections serving adult students of storytelling and the oral tradition." J Youth Serv Libr

Includes bibliographical references

Sawyer, Ruth, 1880-1970

The way of the storyteller. Viking 1962 360p il hardcover o.p. paperback available $12.95   **372.6**
1. Storytelling 2. Literature—Collections
ISBN 0-14-004436-1 (pa)
First published 1942

"This is not primarily a book on how to tell stories; it is rather the whole philosophy of story telling as a creative art. From her own rich experience the author writes inspiringly of the background, experience, creative imagination, technique and selection essential to this art. A part of the book is devoted to a few well-loved stories with suggestions and comments." Booklist

Includes bibliographical references

Shedlock, Marie L., 1854-1935

The art of the story-teller; foreword by Anne Carroll Moore. 3d ed rev, with a new bibliography by Eulalie Steinmetz. Dover Publs. 1951 xxi, 290p pa $8.95   **372.6**
1. Storytelling 2. Literature—Collections
ISBN 0-486-20635-1
First published 1915

Shedlock, Marie L., 1854-1935—_Continued_

"This has long been considered one of the . . . standard books on storytelling. . . . Suggestions for selecting and for telling stories are included as well as eighteen of Miss Shedlock's own favorites." Horn Book

Includes bibliographical references

372.605   Language arts—Serial publications

Language Arts. National Council of Teachers of English $60 per year   **372.605**
1. English language—Study and teaching—Periodicals
ISSN 0360-9170

Bimonthly. First published 1924 with title: Elementary English Review. Also published previously with title: Elementary English

This journal "explores language issues in a thematically arranged format. Articles tend to be conceptual, are grounded in the literature, and frequently allow the teachers' and students' voices to be heard in their own words. . . . Also included are sections titled 'Focus on Research,' 'Current Issues,' 'Roundtable on Books,' and 'Talking About Books.' _LA_ is an intelligent journal that gives press to thoughtful issues related to the teaching of language arts." Katz. Mag for Libr. 10th edition

379   Public policy issues in education

Haskins, James, 1941-

Separate, but not equal; the dream and the struggle. Scholastic 1998 184p il $15.95 (5 and up)   **379**
1. African Americans—Education 2. School integration 3. Segregation in education
ISBN 0-590-45910-4   LC 96-51507

The author traces "the history of the African American struggle for equal rights to education, from the enforced illiteracy of slavery times to the present debate about affirmative action." Booklist

"With his knack for blending historical facts and thoughtful interpretation, Haskins offers an informative, closeup look at the course of black education in America." SLJ

Includes bibliographical references

381   Internal commerce (Domestic trade)

Fisher, Leonard Everett, 1924-

The peddlers; written & illustrated by Leonard Everett Fisher. Benchmark Bks. (Tarrytown) 1998 47p il (Colonial craftsmen) lib bdg $14.95 (4 and up)   **381**
1. Peddlers and peddling 2. United States—Social life and customs—1600-1775, Colonial period
ISBN 0-7614-0511-9   LC 96-38412

A reissue of the title first published 1968 by Watts

Describes the enterprise and commercial development that peddlers brought to the colonies before the establishment of general stores

Lewin, Ted, 1935-

Market! Lothrop, Lee & Shepard Bks. 1996 unp il $16.95; pab bdg $5.95 (k-3)   **381**
1. Markets
ISBN 0-688-12161-6; 0-688-17520-1 (pa)
    LC 95-7439

"An Irish horse market, New York City's Fulton Fish Market, a countryside market in Uganda, and a city market square in Nepal are among the six venues visited in this thoughtful exploration of long-standing social practices. Lewin's richly detailed watercolors convey the color and bustle of the marketplace as a human arena common worldwide, yet having distinctive characteristics according to country." Horn Book Guide

383   Postal communication

Harness, Cheryl

They're off! the story of the Pony Express. Simon & Schuster Bks. for Young Readers 1996 unp il $17 (3-5)   **383**
1. Pony express
ISBN 0-689-80523-3   LC 95-43534

Relates the history of the Pony Express from when it began to carry messages across the American West in April 1860 until the telegraph replaced it in October 1861

"Harness's text is involving and filled with lively detail. Her busy and elaborate illustrations also create a panorama of the age." SLJ

Includes bibliographical references

Kroll, Steven

Pony Express! illustrated by Dan Andreasen. Scholastic 1996 40p il maps $16.95; pa $5.99 (3-5)   **383**
1. Pony express
ISBN 0-590-20239-1; 0-590-20240-5 (pa)
    LC 95-10853

"Kroll begins with an explanation of the California gold rush and shows how the growth of settlements resulted in a demand for faster mail service between Sacramento and the East; he then explores the history of the Pony Express in this handsome, informative picture book. . . . Dan Andreasen's vivid oil paintings, rendered with near photographic quality, clearly convey the human cost of this effort, while portraying the landscape and equipment in sharp detail." Booklist

Includes bibliographical references

385.09   Railroad transportation— Historical and geographic treatment

Blumberg, Rhoda, 1917-

Full steam ahead; the race to build a transcontinental railroad. National Geographic Soc. 1996 159p il maps $18.95 (5 and up)   **385.09**
1. Union Pacific Railroad Company 2. Central Pacific Railroad 3. Railroads—History 4. Frontier and pioneer life—West (U.S.)
ISBN 0-7922-2715-8   LC 94-34979

Blumberg, Rhoda, 1917-—*Continued*

The author "offers not only an assiduously documented, spikes-and-bolts chronicle of the 'great race' to create the first cross-country railroad by laying track between Sacramento and Omaha, but an absorbing panorama of the project's dramatic effect on the American frontier. Lacing her narrative with often amusing anecdotes and ample quotes, Blumberg spins a tale thick with intrigue and controversy. . . . Attractively designed, the volume contains numerous period illustrations and on-site photos of the mammoth undertaking." Publ Wkly

Includes bibliographical references

386   Inland waterway and ferry transportation

Gibbons, Gail

The great St. Lawrence Seaway. Morrow Junior Bks. 1992 unp il maps $17.95 (k-3) **386**

1. Saint Lawrence Seaway

ISBN 0-688-06984-3 LC 91-9851

Tells the story of this inland waterway from the earliest explorers' dream of an Orient passage to today's vast computer-operated system of canals, locks, and gates, and the ships that traverse them

"Gibbons's crisp, detailed pictures and explicit yet animated text enable readers to absorb her well-researched facts with ease. . . . Concise definitions and clearly labeled maps and illustrations make this journey informative as well as entertaining." Publ Wkly

Harness, Cheryl

The amazing impossible Erie Canal. Macmillan Bks. for Young Readers 1995 unp il maps $17.99; pa $5.99 (3-5) **386**

1. Erie Canal (N.Y.)

ISBN 0-02-742641-6; 0-689-82584-6 (pa)

LC 94-11114

"Focusing on the celebration that marked the completion of the Erie Canal in 1825, Harness uses words, maps, and pictures to explain the history and commerce of the canal. The book discusses the need for the canal, the politics of its planning and building, the workings of the locks and canals, the pleasure and pride people took in the accomplishment of this engineering feat, and the reasons for its demise." Booklist

"Harness has done a wonderful job of making the history and construction of the Erie Canal come alive. . . . The narrative is matched with illustrations that cover each page." SLJ

Includes bibliographical references

387.1   Ports. Lighthouses

Gibbons, Gail

Beacons of light: lighthouses. Morrow Junior Bks. 1990 unp il $16 (k-3) **387.1**

1. Lighthouses

ISBN 0-688-07379-4 LC 89-33884

The author traces the development of lighthouses "from hilltop bonfires to the electronically controlled beacons that flash warnings to today's passing ships. Drawings of specific lighthouses grace every page. . . . Readers are told of lighthouse keepers' duties, the changing technology of lighthouses, and their status today as high-tech markers." Booklist

"The history of lighthouses is told in a picture book format for independent readers. Although the narrative is simple, the vocabulary and some of the concepts are more difficult than is typical in picture books. . . . However, each difficult concept is clarified with supplementary illustrations or text." Bull Cent Child Books

Guiberson, Brenda Z.

Lighthouses; watchers at sea. Holt & Co. 1995 70p il $15.95 (3-5) **387.1**

1. Lighthouses

ISBN 0-8050-3170-7 LC 95-4204

"A Redfeather book"

Recounts the history of lighthouses from the struggle to build invincible towers, through heroic rescues of lost ships, to the haunted tales surrounding these isolated structures

This is a "fascinating and readable narrative. . . . Black-and-white photographs and many detailed sketches help to clarify the information and enhance the book's appeal." SLJ

Includes bibliographical references

387.2   Ships

Barton, Byron

Boats. Crowell 1986 unp il lib bdg $14.89 (k-1) **387.2**

1. Boats and boating 2. Ships

ISBN 0-690-04536-0 LC 85-47900

Depicts a variety of boats and a cruise ship docking and unloading passengers

"Thick black outlines contain vivid colors . . . clean lines, bright hues, and undemanding text." Booklist

Gibbons, Gail

Boat book. Holiday House 1983 unp il lib bdg $16.95; pa $5.95 (k-3) **387.2**

1. Boats and boating 2. Ships

ISBN 0-8234-0478-1 (lib bdg); 0-8234-0709-8 (pa)

LC 82-15851

An introduction to "all sorts of seafaring craft . . . [including] speedboats, sailboats, canoes, cruise ships, police and fire boats, and commercial and military vessels. Various means of propulsion (wind, oars and paddles, engine power) are explained, as are the uses of each type of boat." Publ Wkly

"The text, though stilted, is logically presented in a non-condescending manner. Bright color illustrations throughout show an array of boats moving through the water. . . . Most of the illustrations are full page, and all of them are playfully bordered with a scalloped edge that resembles an ocean wave." SLJ

Kentley, Eric
Boat; written by Eric Kentley. Knopf 1992 63p il (Eyewitness books) (4 and up)   **387.2**
1. Ships 2. Boats and boating
                     LC 91-53136
Available DK Pub. edition $15.95; lib bdg $19.99 (ISBN 0-7894-5758-X; 0-7894-6585-X)
"A Dorling Kindersley book"
A history of the development and uses of boats, ships, and rafts, from birch-bark canoes to luxury liners

Macaulay, David, 1946-
Ship. Houghton Mifflin 1993 96p il $19.95; pa $8.95 (4 and up)   **387.2**
1. Shipwrecks 2. Underwater exploration 3. Caribbean region—Antiquities
ISBN 0-395-52439-3; 0-395-74518-7 (pa)
                     LC 92-1346
This book "opens with an underwater find in the Caribbean and, in story and illustration, follows the work of marine archeologists in studying the wreck. As part of the background research in Spain, one of the team finds a diary recording the building of a caravel in 1504. The rest of the book contains a 'translation' of the diary with accompanying illustrations. Though a fictional account, the narrative gives a good feel for the maritime technology of the early 16th century." Sci Books Films

The **Visual** dictionary of ships and sailing. Dorling Kindersley 1991 64p il (Eyewitness visual dictionaries) $18.95 (4 and up)   **387.2**
1. Boats and boating 2. Ships
ISBN 1-879431-20-3   LC 91-60900
This is a visual guide to nautical terminology with brief text describing ships and boats from ancient times to the present
"*Ships and Sailing* is intriguing. The pages proceed from the ships of Greece, Rome, and the Vikings through wooden and iron ships of all kinds to knots, signals, flags, and gear used and worn by sailors. The detailed cutaways are works of art." Booklist

387.7   Air transportation

Barton, Byron
Airplanes. Crowell 1986 unp il lib bdg $15.89 (k-1)   **387.7**
1. Airplanes
ISBN 0-690-04532-8   LC 85-47899
Brief text and illustrations present a variety of airplanes and what they do, "as well as some of the usual scenes surrounding each (e.g., workers checking a passenger plane). Brightly colored illustrations outlined in heavy black convey a bold and simple first impression, yet they portray a good number of accurate details that preschoolers find so fascinating." SLJ

Airport. Crowell 1982 unp il lib bdg $14.89; pa $5.95 (k-1)   **387.7**
1. Airports 2. Airplanes
ISBN 0-690-04169-1 (lib bdg); 0-06-443145-2 (pa)
                     LC 79-7816
"In a brightly illustrated book, the author/artist captures the hustle and bustle of passenger traffic from arrival at the terminal to take off." Kobrin Letter

388.3   Vehicular transportation

Ammon, Richard
Conestoga wagons; illustrated by Bill Farnsworth. Holiday House 2000 unp il lib bdg $16.95   **388.3**
1. Carriages and carts 2. Transportation
ISBN 0-8234-1475-2   LC 99-19726
Explains how Conestoga wagons were built and driven as well as their historical significance and importance to the early American economy
Includes bibliographical references

391   Costume and personal appearance

Chernoff, Goldie Taub
Easy costumes you don't have to sew; costumes designed and illustrated by Margaret A. Hartelius. Four Winds Press 1975 41p il $15.50 (3-5)   **391**
1. Costume 2. Paper crafts
ISBN 0-02-718230-4
"Garbage bags, cartons, cardboard, paper bags, and old white sheets provide the basis for a variety of easy-to-make costumes. At-hand materials (newspaper, milk cartons, string) and clear directions result in simply constructed snowmen, mice, shaggy dogs, turtles, ladybugs, bats, skeletons, robots, totem poles, and even a group dragon. Each two-page spread is devoted to one costume, with careful diagrams, lists of necessary materials, precise instructions for each part, and guidelines for putting on the costume." Booklist

Finley, Carol
The art of African masks; exploring cultural traditions. Lerner Publs. 1999 64p il map (Art around the world) $23.93 (5 and up)   **391**
1. Masks (Facial) 2. African art
ISBN 0-8225-2078-8   LC 98-10570
Describes how different types of masks are made and used in Africa and how they reflect the culture of their ethnic groups
"Clear, sharp full-color photographs of museum artifacts are well placed on the pages. . . . Pictures of modern members of still-existing cultures add to the attractiveness of this volume." SLJ
Includes bibliographical references

Fisher, Leonard Everett, 1924-
The wigmakers; written & illustrated by Leonard Everett Fisher. Benchmark Bks. (Tarrytown) 2000 c1965 44p il (Colonial craftsmen) $21.36 (4 and up)   **391**
1. Wigs 2. United States—Social life and customs—1600-1775, Colonial period
ISBN 0-7614-0933-5   LC 99-16261
A reissue of the title first published 1965 by Watts
Describes the advent of the wig as a fashion necessity in France and England, illustrates popular styles of eighteenth-century wigs, and explains the colonial wigmaker's technique in construction and care of the wig
Includes bibliographical references

Lawlor, Laurie

Where will this shoe take you? a walk through the history of footwear. Walker & Co. 1996 132p il $17.95 (5 and up)   **391**

1. Shoes

ISBN 0-8027-8434-8   LC 96-3718

The author "traces footwear from the Ice Age to Air Jordans. . . . An initial chapter chronicling the early development of footwear is followed by thematic chapters on topics such as shoes as protection, status symbol, fashion statement, play equipment, and shoes in literature." Horn Book Guide

"Sketches and photos enhance the book throughout. . . . This is a rich, in-depth study of a simple topic." Booklist

Includes bibliographical references

Morris, Ann

Hats, hats, hats; photographs by Ken Heyman. Lothrop, Lee & Shepard Bks. 1989 unp il $16; pa $4.95 (k-1)   **391**

1. Hats

ISBN 0-688-06338-1; 0-688-12274-4 (pa)

LC 88-26676

This book introduces a variety of hats worn around the world

"The vivid color photographs, one or two per page, show people engaged in lively activities while . . . wearing their hats. Each picture offers a strong ethnic identity or a thought-provoking human interaction, with captions of only a few words in large print. An unusual index . . . gives background information about the pictures, citing the countries of origin and a few facts about each . . . kind of hat." SLJ

Shoes, shoes, shoes. Lothrop, Lee & Shepard Bks. 1995 32p il $16; pa $4.95 (k-1)   **391**

1. Shoes

ISBN 0-688-13666-4; 0-688-16166-9 (pa)

LC 94-46649

"Morris gives a world-tour of shoes . . . in [a] picture book illustrated by various photographers. In rhyming text, she talks about shoes for all kinds of activities. . . . [The] book includes a map and a photograph key of the places visited." Bull Cent Child Books

Rowland-Warne, L.

Costume; written by L. Rowland-Warne. Knopf 1992 63p il (Eyewitness books) (4 and up)   **391**

1. Costume 2. Clothing and dress

LC 91-53135

Available DK Pub. edition $15.95 (ISBN 0-7894-5586-2)

"A Dorling Kindersley book"

Photographs and text document the history and meaning of clothing, from loincloths to modern children's clothes

This "fascinating historical overview . . . blends close-up, full-color photographs of period clothing and accessories with brief snippets of text that explain the item's significance and purpose." SLJ

Yue, Charlotte

Shoes; their history in words and pictures; [by] Charlotte and David Yue. Houghton Mifflin 1997 92p il $14.95 (4 and up)   **391**

1. Shoes

ISBN 0-395-72667-0   LC 96-17220

Relates the history and lore of many of the kinds of shoes worn by men, women, and children throughout the world

"Filled with vignettes . . . and interesting, little-known facts. . . . The short chapters are chronologically arranged, providing a good historical overview of classical to modern times with just the right scope for the intended audience. Ample black-and-white drawings illustrate almost every style of footwear mentioned in the text." SLJ

Includes bibliographical references

392   Customs of life cycle and domestic life

King, Elizabeth, 1953-

Quinceañera; celebrating fifteen. Dutton Children's Bks. 1998 40p il $15.99 (5 and up)

392

1. Quinceañera (Social custom) 2. Mexican Americans—Social life and customs

ISBN 0-525-45638-4   LC 97-44539

Also available Spanish language edition

Focuses on describing the celebration of this rite of passage in the life of a specific Mexican American girl, while also presenting historical background for the occasion

"The photographs are so full of spectacle and genuine warmth that we feel as though we have been invited, too." Booklist

Morris, Ann

Weddings. Lothrop, Lee & Shepard Bks. 1995 25p il map $15; lib bdg $14.93 (k-1)   **392**

1. Marriage customs and rites

ISBN 0-688-13272-3; 0-688-13273-1 (lib bdg)

LC 94-48040

This photographic look at weddings includes a Shinto rite in Japan, an Orthodox Jewish service in Russia, a Catholic mass in Slovakia and a ceremony at City Hall in Los Angeles

393   Death customs

Perl, Lila

Mummies, tombs, and treasure; secrets of ancient Egypt; drawings by Erika Weihs. Clarion Bks. 1987 120p il lib bdg $15.95; pa $8.95 (4 and up)   **393**

1. Mummies 2. Funeral rites and ceremonies 3. Egypt—Antiquities

ISBN 0-89919-407-9 (lib bdg); 0-395-54796-2 (pa)

LC 86-17646

Perl, Lila—*Continued*

The author incorporates "information on burial customs, religious beliefs, and historical background along with specifics of the mummification process and the archeological finds that have kept the study of the dead a dynamic one." Bull Cent Child Books

This "book is attractive, readable, plentifully illustrated with drawings and black-and-white photographs. There are sufficient grisly details to keep the pages turning, and readers will come away with a healthy understanding of Egyptian religion, scientific accomplishments, and architectural skills. Phonetic pronunciations throughout make this easily accessible." Appraisal

Includes bibliographical references

Putnam, James

Mummy; written by James Putnam; photographed by Peter Hayman. Knopf 1993 c1992 63p il (Eyewitness books) (4 and up)   **393**

1. Mummies 2. Funeral rites and ceremonies

LC 92-1591

Available DK Pub. edition $15.95; lib bdg $19.99 (ISBN 0-7894-5856-X; 0-7894-6593-0); Spanish language edition also available

"A Dorling Kindersley book"

First published 1992 in the United Kingdom

Documents the history and significance of mummies, both natural and man-made, and describes the principles and ceremonies associated with them

"A great collection of mummy information and specimens. . . . The full-color photographs and illustrations are well lit, and captions add additional information." SLJ

Tanaka, Shelley

Secrets of the mummies; uncovering the bodies of ancient Egyptians; illustrations by Greg Ruhl; historical consultation by Peter Brand. Hyperion Bks. for Children 1999 48p il $16.99; pa $7.99 (4 and up)   **393**

1. Mummies 2. Egypt—Civilization

ISBN 0-7868-0473-4; 0-7868-1539-6 (pa)

LC 99-11012

"An I was there book"

Describes the ancient Egyptian practice of preserving the dead through the process of mummification and explains what scientists have learned from unwrapping and examining mummies

Wilcox, Charlotte

Mummies & their mysteries. Carolrhoda Bks. 1993 64p il lib bdg $23.95; pa $7.95 (4-6)   **393**

1. Mummies 2. Antiquities

ISBN 0-87614-767-8; 0-87614-643-4 (pa)

LC 92-32160

Discusses mummies found around the world, including Peru, Denmark, and the Italian Alps, and explains how studying them provides clues to past ways of life

The author's "tone is respectful, and she addresses the controversial issue of educational display and scientific research on bodies of persons who have been revered in life and death by their own peoples. . . . Captioned, full-color photographs on every page inject rich personality into the discussion, while an open format, arresting cover, and large print will encourage browsers to pick this up for more than reports." Bull Cent Child Books

Includes glossary

394   General customs

Gibbons, Gail

Knights in shining armor. Little, Brown 1995 unp il lib bdg $15.95; pa $4.95 (k-3)   **394**

1. Knights and knighthood 2. Medieval civilization

ISBN 0-316-30948-6; 0-316-30038-1 (pa)

LC 94-35525

The author "covers tournaments, chivalry, and what happened when a bad knight was caught. Legendary knights such as Sir Gawain and the knights of the Round Table are briefly described, as is St. George and the dragon, and Gibbons also discusses present-day knights. The watercolor-and-ink pictures are some of Gibbons' liveliest and most attractive." Booklist

Lewin, Ted, 1935-

Fair! Lothrop, Lee & Shepard Bks. 1997 unp il $16; lib bdg $15.93 (k-3)   **394**

1. Fairs 2. United States—Social life and customs

ISBN 0-688-12850-5; 0-688-12851-3 (lib bdg)

LC 96-51146

Describes the sights, sounds, and smells of a county fair, from the setting up of the Ferris wheel to the animal, craft, and food judging

"This superbly illustrated visit to a county fair resembles a photo-essay in its remarkable realism." SLJ

394.1   Eating, drinking; using drugs

Aliki

A medieval feast; written and illustrated by Aliki. Crowell 1983 unp il lib bdg $15.89; pa $6.95 (2-5)   **394.1**

1. Dining—History 2. Courts and courtiers 3. Medieval civilization 4. Festivals—History

ISBN 0-690-04246-9 (lib bdg); 0-06-446050-9 (pa)

LC 82-45923

"In pictures of minute, charming detail and vibrant, translucent colors, Aliki takes us through the ritual of preparation and the enthusiastic consumption of a medieval feast served to a king and his retinue when they stop for a few days at Camdenton Manor. Not to be outdone by the art, the text has its own various facets. There is the fictional story set in type outside the art and there is within the paintings a collection of delightful historical, gastronomical, agricultural, and zoological facts printed by hand. And throughout the spendid whole are border decorations worthy of the great illuminated manuscripts." Child Book Rev Serv

Lauber, Patricia, 1924-

What you never knew about fingers, forks, & chopsticks; illustrated by John Manders. Simon & Schuster Bks. for Young Readers 1999 unp il (Around-the-house history) $16 (2-4)   **394.1**

1. Tableware 2. Table etiquette 3. Eating customs

ISBN 0-689-80479-2   LC 97-17041

Lauber, Patricia, 1924-—*Continued*

Describes changes in eating customs throughout the centuries and the origins of table manners

"A delicious blend of humor and fascinating facts. . . . The lively, linear drawings incorporate amusing asides in dialogue balloons that will entertain readers as the text enlightens them about the subject." SLJ

Includes bibliographical references

394.2 Customs—Special occasions

Gibbons, Gail

Happy birthday! Holiday House 1986 unp il $16.95 (k-3)   **394.2**

1. Birthdays
ISBN 0-8234-0614-8   LC 86-297

Examines the historical beliefs, traditions, and celebrations associated with birthdays

"Simple text explains that everybody has one and tells why the traditional cake is round, why there's a candle for each year, why the candles are blown out and other historical birthday customs. . . . The story is accompanied by brightly colored artwork, complete with ribbons, confetti, party hats and decorations, making this book as festive and fun as the day it describes." Publ Wkly

394.25 Carnivals

Ancona, George, 1929-

Carnaval. Harcourt Brace & Co. 1999 unp il $18; pa $9 (3-6)   **394.25**

1. Carnival 2. Brazil—Social life and customs
ISBN 0-15-201793-3; 0-15-201792-5 (pa)
                    LC 98-47297

Text and photographs present the traditions and rituals of the annual celebration of Carnaval as experienced in the small Brazilian city of Olinda

"The prose is superb—scenes and traditions are clearly presented in a language rich with description and imagery. Stunning photographs capture the spirit of the festival." SLJ

Hoyt-Goldsmith, Diane

Mardi Gras: a Cajun country celebration; photographs by Lawrence Migdale. Holiday House 1995 32p il music $15.95 (3-5)   **394.25**

1. Cajuns—Social life and customs
ISBN 0-8234-1184-2   LC 94-42707

This is a "photo essay and introduction to a Cajun Mardi Gras celebration in Eunice, Louisiana. The text follows Joel, a young fiddle player, as he prepares for and participates in the festivities. This lively and informative look at an ethnic and regional holiday is presented with clear text and bright, attractive photographs." Horn Book Guide

Includes glossary

394.26 Holidays

The **American** book of days. 4th ed, Compiled and edited by Stephen G. Christianson. Wilson, H.W. 2000 xxvi, 945p $105   **394.26**

1. Holidays 2. Festivals—United States
ISBN 0-8242-0954-0   LC 99-86611

First edition, by George William Douglas, published 1937

"This source complements other calendar sources by giving more in-depth information about fewer events. It gives the names of most legal and public holidays, both federal and state, with extended narratives about major political, religious, scientific and social events as well as birthdays and anniversaries. There are notes about moveable holidays and an extensive topical index which permits tracing developments; e.g., all possible dates of significance for a study of the American Revolution." Safford. Guide to Ref Materials for Sch Libr Media Cent. 5th edition [entry for 3rd edition]

For a review see: Booklist, April 1, 2001

Ancona, George, 1929-

Fiesta fireworks. Lothrop, Lee & Shepard Bks. 1998 unp il lib bdg $15.93 (k-3)   **394.26**

1. Festivals 2. Fireworks 3. Mexico—Social life and customs
ISBN 0-688-14818-2   LC 97-21608

Describes the preparation of fireworks as well as the festival honoring San Juan de Dios, the patron saint of Tultepec, Mexico, which is famous for its master pyrotechnics

"An informative tribute to an enduring Mexican tradition, with exciting visuals." SLJ

Includes glossary

Fiesta U.S.A. Lodestar Bks. 1995 unp il $17.99 (k-3)   **394.26**

1. Hispanic Americans—Social life and customs
2. Festivals—United States
ISBN 0-525-67498-5   LC 94-34828

"An introduction to four Hispanic holidays celebrated in the U.S.—*El Día de los Muertos* (Day of the Dead); the processions of *Las Posadas,* which reenact Mary and Joseph's search for a place to stay in Bethlehem; the New Year's Day dance of *Los Matachines;* and *La Fiesta de los Reyes Magos,* which revolves around the story of the Three Wise Kings. . . . Ancona gives children the opportunity to view the distinctive flavors of different Hispanic communities, from San Francisco to a small town in New Mexico to New York City. The text shares the excitement and meaning of the celebrations, and focuses on how young people participate in them. Colorful, eye-catching photographs capture the mood and reinforce the narrative." SLJ

Includes glossary

Pablo remembers; the fiesta of the Day of the Dead. Lothrop, Lee & Shepard Bks. 1993 42p il $16.95; lib bdg $16.89 (k-3)   **394.26**

1. All Souls' Day 2. Mexico—Social life and customs
ISBN 0-688-11249-8; 0-688-11250-1 (lib bdg)
                    LC 92-22819

During the three-day celebration of the Day of the Dead, a young Mexican boy and his family make elaborate preparations to honor the spirits of the dead

"The photography has the intimacy of high-quality family snapshots, and the tone of the text is clear and natural." Bull Cent Child Books

Includes glossary

Barth, Edna

Hearts, cupids, and red roses; the story of the valentine symbols; illustrated by Ursula Arndt. Clarion Bks. 2001 64p il $16; pa $7.95 (3-6)

394.26

1. Valentine's Day 2. Signs and symbols
ISBN 0-618-06789-2; 0-618-06791-4 (pa)

LC 2001-265787

A reissue of the title first published 1974 by Seabury Press

The history of Valentine's Day and the little-known stories behind its symbols

This offers "interesting and concise text along with lists of stories, poems, and sources." SLJ

Includes bibliographical references

Holly, reindeer, and colored lights; the story of the Christmas symbols; illustrated by Ursula Arndt. Clarion Bks. 2000 96p il $16; pa $7.95 (3-6)

394.26

1. Christmas 2. Signs and symbols
ISBN 0-618-06786-8; 0-618-06788-4 (pa)

LC 00-702874

A reissue of the title first published 1971 by Seabury Press

Examines the origins of Christmas symbols—trees, ornaments, Yule logs, Santa Claus, cards, Christmas colors, and many other holiday observances

"The well-written text is concise and interesting and the two-colored marginal drawings are festive. A selected list of books containing Christmas stories and poems is appended." Booklist

Includes bibliographical references

Lilies, rabbits, and painted eggs; the story of the Easter symbols; illustrated by Ursula Arndt. Clarion Bks. c1998 63p il $16; pa $7.95 (3-6)

394.26

1. Easter 2. Signs and symbols
ISBN 0-618-09646-9; 0-618-09648-5 (pa)

A reissue of the title first published 1970 by Seabury Press

Traces the history of Easter symbols from their Christian and pagan origins to such present-day additions as rabbits and new clothes

"The small pen drawings which illustrate the symbols and the celebrations will please the children, and an index and a bibliography of other Easter books will please the librarian." Horn Book

Shamrocks, harps, and shillelaghs; the story of the St. Patrick's Day symbols; illustrated by Ursula Arndt. Clarion Bks. 2001 95p il $16; pa $7.95 (3-6)

394.26

1. Saint Patrick's Day 2. Signs and symbols
ISBN 0-618-09649-3; 0-618-09651-5 (pa)

A reissue of the title first published 1977 by Seabury Press

"Irish history, lore, and legend are part of a wealth of information provided about Patrick the real missionary, St. Patrick's Day, and its celebration. Includes lists of stories for St. Patrick's Day and sources." LC. Child Books, 1977

Turkeys, Pilgrims, and Indian corn; the story of the Thanksgiving symbols; illustrated by Ursula Arndt. Clarion Bks. 2000 96p il $16; pa $7.95 (3-6)

394.26

1. Thanksgiving Day 2. Pilgrims (New England colonists) 3. Signs and symbols
ISBN 0-618-06783-3; 0-618-06785-X (pa)

LC 00-702873

A reissue of the title first published 1975 by Seabury Press

This book provides "information about the Pilgrims' voyage to and life in America and their dealings with the Indians. (The point is made, but not belabored, that the settled land was taken from the Indians.) Interesting sidelights are included about prominent men and women, myths such as Plymouth Rock, and harvest feasts in cultures around the world." SLJ

Includes bibliographical references

Witches, pumpkins, and grinning ghosts; the story of the Halloween symbols; illustrated by Ursula Arndt. Clarion Bks. 2000 95p il $16; pa $7.95 (3-6)

394.26

1. Halloween 2. Signs and symbols
ISBN 0-618-06780-9; 0-618-06782-5 (pa)

LC 00-712796

A reissue of the title first published 1972 by Seabury Press

Explains the origins of and relates stories associated with familiar Halloween symbols

"A diverting as well as useful account appropriately illustrated with drawings in black and orange." Booklist

Includes bibliographical references

Bernhard, Emery

Happy New Year! illustrated by Durga Bernhard. Lodestar Bks. 1996 unp il $15.99 (3-5)

394.26

1. New Year
ISBN 0-525-67532-9   LC 95-25572

This "describes how people celebrate the new year, not only in the U.S., but also in such varied places as Bali, Ethiopia, India, China, and Japan. Discussion of historical perspective and the significance of the holiday in different religions lends authority to the text. Bright, bold illustrations enhance the multicultural theme." SLJ

Includes glossary

Branch, Muriel Miller

Juneteenth; freedom day; photographs by Willis Branch. Cobblehill Bks. 1998 54p il $15.99 (5 and up)

394.26

1. African Americans—History
ISBN 0-525-65222-1   LC 97-9656

Discusses the origin and present-day celebration of Juneteenth, a holiday marking the day Texan slaves realized they were free

"Branch provides a lengthy bibliography for further research, as well as a wealth of holiday enthusiasm that is hard to ignore." Booklist

Bulla, Clyde Robert, 1914-
The story of Valentine's Day; illustrated by Susan Estelle Kwas. newly il ed. HarperCollins Pubs. 1999 unp il $14.95; lib bdg $14.89; pa $5.95 (k-3)   394.26
1. Valentine's Day
ISBN 0-06-027883-8; 0-06-027884-6 (lib bdg); 0-06-443626-8 (pa)   LC 97-37195
A newly illustrated edition of St. Valentine's Day, published 1965
Relates the history and describes the customs of this holiday from its beginning in Roman times to the present. Includes directions for making a paper valentine and sugar cookies
"Bulla's informative and entertaining guide to the holiday of romance . . . here receives fresh treatment— jazzy color-saturated illustrations with a touch of the abstract and a handsome book design." Horn Book Guide

Chase's calendar of events. Contemporary Bks. $59.95   394.26
1. Calendars 2. Almanacs 3. Holidays
ISSN 0740-5286

Annual. First published 1958 with title: Chase's calendar of annual events, under the editorship of William D. and Helen M. Chase. Variant title: Chase's annual events
"The standard chronological calendar is supplemented with spotlights of major events in history, education, and religion, world wide. Each calendar entry supplies the date and day, where the day is in the yearly cycle, and an alphabetic listing of births, anniversaries, events, special weeks and other notables. A special entry of birthdays today completes the day's listing. There is also an almanac-like section of information that is likely to be useful, and a good alphabetical index. No school library of any size should be without this source." Safford. Guide to Ref Materials for Sch Libr Media Cent. 5th edition

Chocolate, Debbi, 1954-
Kwanzaa; illustrations by Melodye Rosales. Children's Press 1990 31p il lib bdg $18; pa $4.95 (3-5)   394.26
1. Kwanzaa 2. African Americans—Social life and customs
ISBN 0-516-03991-1 (lib bdg); 0-516-43991-X (pa)
                LC 89-25418
Discusses the holiday in which Afro-Americans celebrate their roots and cultural heritage from Africa
"Using clear and direct language, Chocolate provides a wealth of detail as she shares her family's Kwanzaa festival. . . . Rosales's brightly colored paintings in a realistic style draw readers into the warmth and joy of this celebration." SLJ

My first Kwanzaa book; illustrated by Cal Massey. Scholastic 1992 unp il $10.95; pa $5.99 (k-2)   394.26
1. Kwanzaa 2. African Americans—Social life and customs
ISBN 0-590-45762-4; 0-439-12926-5 (pa)
                LC 92-1200
"Cartwheel books"

Introduces Kwanzaa, the holiday in which Afro-Americans celebrate their cultural heritage
"The book effectively conveys the spirit of the holiday through the text and the acrylic paint and colored-pencil illustrations, all outlined in a thin line of earthy brown." SLJ
Includes glossary

Christmas gif'; an anthology of Christmas poems, songs, and stories, written by and about African-Americans; compiled by Charlemae Rollins; illustrated by Ashley Bryan; a new introduction by Augusta Baker. Morrow Junior Bks. 1993 xxii, 106p $14 (3-6)   394.26
1. Christmas 2. American literature—African American authors—Collections 3. African Americans in literature
ISBN 0-688-11667-1   LC 92-18976
A newly illustrated edition of the title first published 1963 by Follett
A collection of Christmas poems, songs, stories and recipes. Langston Hughes, Frederick Douglass, Gwendolyn Brooks and Countee Cullen are among the authors included
"Bryan's black-and-white woodcuts are a fitting complement to this classic anthology." Horn Book

Cooney, Barbara, 1917-2000
The story of Christmas; illustrated by Loretta Krupinski. HarperCollins Pubs. 1995 unp il $14.95; pa $5.95 (2-4)   394.26
1. Christmas
ISBN 0-06-023433-4; 0-06-443512-1 (pa)
                LC 94-18687
A revised and newly illustrated edition of the author's Christmas, published 1967 by Crowell
"Central to this story of winter celebrations is Jesus' birth, but the evolution of other cultural traditions and customs associated with and even predating Christmas also receive attention: the Roman Saturnalia, Twelfth Night, the origin of the Christmas tree, the different incarnations of Santa Claus. Attractive gouache and colored-pencil illustrations capture the festive moods of the season." Horn Book Guide

Demi, 1942-
Happy New Year! Kung-hsi fa-ts'ai! Crown 1997 unp il $16; lib bdg $17.99; pa $6.99 (k-3)
                394.26
1. Chinese New Year 2. China—Social life and customs
ISBN 0-517-70957-0; 0-517-70958-9 (lib bdg); 0-517-88592-0 (pa)   LC 97-11692
Examines the customs, traditions, foods, and lore associated with the celebration of Chinese New Year
"Demi's characteristic tiny, lively figures illustrate each page, with several spreads devoted to small, labeled pictures identifying things associated with the holiday, such as the 14 heavenly beings. Infused with joy and filled with information." Booklist

Encyclopedia of Christmas; edited by Tanya Gulevich. Omnigraphics 1999 729p il $48; pa $24.95   **394.26**
1. Christmas
ISBN 0-7808-0387-6; 0-7808-0455-4 (pa)
LC 99-52285

"Nearly 200 alphabetically arranged entries covering all aspects of Christmas, including folk customs, religious observances, history, legends, symbols, and related days from Europe, America, and around the world." Title page

For a review see: Booklist, June 15, 2000

Fisher, Aileen Lucia, 1906-
The story of Easter; by Aileen Fisher; illustrated by Stefano Vitale. HarperCollins Pubs. 1997 unp il $15.95; pa $5.95 (3-5)   **394.26**
1. Jesus Christ—Resurrection 2. Easter
ISBN 0-06-027296-1; 0-06-443490-7 (pa)
LC 96-17395

A newly illustrated edition of Easter published 1968 by Crowell

"This book begins with the story of Jesus' crucifixion and resurrection, but focuses on the origins of various Easter and vernal equinox traditions, with an emphasis on the history of egg decorating. . . . The folk-art illustrations are defined by strong black outlines, simple shapes, and natural colors." Horn Book Guide

The **Folklore** of world holidays; Robert Griffin and Ann H. Shurgin, editors. 2nd ed. Gale Res. 1998 c1999 841p $151.75   **394.26**
1. Holidays 2. Festivals 3. Folklore
ISBN 0-8103-8901-0   LC 98-37030

First published 1992 under the editorship of Margaret Read MacDonald

This volume "provides descriptive information on nearly 2,000 beliefs, stories, superstitions, proverbs, recipes, games, pageants, fairs, processions and other lore related to more than 350 special dates from 150 countries." Publisher's note

Gibbons, Gail
Easter. Holiday House 1989 unp il lib bdg $16.95; pa $6.95 (k-3)   **394.26**
1. Easter
ISBN 0-8234-0737-3 (lib bdg); 0-8234-0866-3 (pa)
LC 88-23292

Examines the background, significance, symbols, and traditions of Easter

Gibbons "simplifies complex beliefs and traditions in a straightforward way, though transitions are occasionally abrupt. Pleasing watercolors outlined in black ink illustrate the text." Booklist

Halloween. Holiday House 1984 unp il lib bdg $16.95; pa $6.95 (k-3)   **394.26**
1. Halloween
ISBN 0-8234-0524-9 (lib bdg); 0-8234-0577-X (pa)
LC 84-519

The author "describes the origins of Halloween beliefs and observances, and discusses the many ways it is celebrated today: the costumes, parties, carved pumpkins, trick-or-treat visiting, games, visits to 'haunted' houses, and costume contests. The text is terse, the subject one in which most children will be interested. . . . The illustrations are bright and bold, with filled pages but no fussy details." Bull Cent Child Books

St. Patrick's Day. Holiday House 1994 unp il lib bdg $16.95; pa $6.95 (k-3)   **394.26**
1. Saint Patrick's Day
ISBN 0-8234-1119-2 (lib bdg); 0-8234-1173-7 (pa)
LC 93-29570

"A basic introduction to the holiday—how it began, the life and works of St. Patrick, and the various ways in which the day is celebrated. The text is clear and concise, and the pages are full of information. Gibbons's simple, clean, full-page watercolor-and-ink illustrations flow logically from one to the next." SLJ

Thanksgiving Day. Holiday House 1983 unp il lib bdg $16.95; pa $6.95 (k-3)   **394.26**
1. Thanksgiving Day
ISBN 0-8234-0489-7 (lib bdg); 0-8234-0576-1 (pa)
LC 83-175

Also available Audiobook version

This book presents information about the first Thanksgiving and the way that holiday is celebrated today

"Cheery shades of gold and orange and other hues animate the scenes illustrating Gibbon's incisive history of the American holiday." Publ Wkly

Valentine's Day. Holiday House 1986 unp il $16.95; pa $6.95 (k-3)   **394.26**
1. Valentine's Day
ISBN 0-8234-0572-9; 0-8234-0764-0 (pa)
LC 85-916

The author "briefly describes the history, meaning, and customs of Valentine's Day in picture-book format. Simple line drawings are brightened with the bright, crisp colors that are the artist's hallmark. . . . On the last two pages she shows how to make valentines and a valentine box. A useful addition to a holiday collection for young children and a serviceable read-aloud choice for classrooms where Valentine's Day is celebrated." Booklist

Giblin, James, 1933-
Fireworks, picnics, and flags; [by] James Cross Giblin; illustrated by Ursula Arndt. Clarion Bks. 1983 90p il $16; pa $8.95 (3-6)   **394.26**
1. Fourth of July
ISBN 0-89919-146-0; 0-89919-174-6 (pa)
LC 82-9612

Traces the social history behind America's celebration of Independence Day and explains the background of such national symbols as the flag, the bald eagle, the Liberty Bell, and Uncle Sam

"Giblin was the editor of Edna Barth's books on holiday symbols; according to his author's note, he knew that Barth intended to write about the Fourth of July and took on the project himself after her death. The result is consistent in both format and spirit with the well-known Barth series, complete with Arndt's unpretentious two-color drawings." Booklist

Hoyt-Goldsmith, Diane

Celebrating Chinese New Year; photographs by Lawrence Migdale. Holiday House 1998 32p il $16.95; pa $6.95 (3-5)   **394.26**
1. Chinese New Year 2. Chinese Americans—Social life and customs
ISBN 0-8234-1393-4; 0-8234-1520-1 (pa)
                                              LC 98-17028
Depicts a San Francisco boy and his family preparing for and enjoying their celebration of the Chinese New Year, their most important holiday
This book offers "big, bright photographs and a clear, easy-to-follow text. . . . Hoyt-Goldsmith's excellent book makes the Chinese New Year celebration accessible and understandable." SLJ
Includes glossary

Day of the Dead; a Mexican-American celebration; photographs by Lawrence Migdale. Holiday House 1994 30p il $16.95 (3-5)   **394.26**
1. All Souls' Day 2. Mexican Americans—Social life and customs
ISBN 0-8234-1094-3   LC 93-42106
"Ten-year-old twins from Sacramento, California, tell the story of their family's Day of the Dead celebration. . . . Aztec beliefs and their intermingling with Catholic rituals are explained, and descriptions of dancing, art, and prayer repeatedly illustrate the unity of past and present during festival days." Booklist
"The excellent-quality, full-color photographs, drawings, and cut-paper illustrations are well placed and appealing. . . . Hoyt-Goldsmith provides a good deal of background, making *Day of the Dead* a solid report source." SLJ
Includes glossary

Las Posadas; an Hispanic Christmas celebration; photographs by Lawrence Migdale. Holiday House 1999 32p il music $16.95; pa $6.95 (3-5) **394.26**
1. Christmas 2. Hispanic Americans—Social life and customs
ISBN 0-8234-1449-3; 0-8234-1635-6 (pa)
                                              LC 99-17337
Follows a Hispanic American family in a small New Mexican community as they prepare for and celebrate the nine-day religious festival which occurs just before Christmas
"Numerous clear, colorful photos bring the text to life. . . . A recipe for Las Posadas cookies, biscochitos, is provided, along with *The Song of Las Posadas* in both Spanish and English." Booklist
Includes glossary

Jones, Lynda

Kids around the world celebrate! the best feasts and festivals from many lands. Wiley 1999 c2000 124p il pa $12.95 (4-6)   **394.26**
1. Festivals 2. Holidays
ISBN 0-471-34527-X   LC 99-14639
Introduces a variety of festivals celebrated around the world. Includes recipes and hands-on activities to give a taste of what it is like to be part of a feast or ceremony in another country

Kindersley, Anabel

Celebrations; written by Anabel Kindersley; photographed by Barnabas Kindersley. DK Pub. 1997 63p il (Children just like me) $17.95 (3-5)
                                              394.26
1. Festivals 2. Holidays
ISBN 0-7894-2027-9   LC 97-20108
Published in association with UNICEF
"The celebrations are arranged by season and include: Christmas in Germany, Halloween in Canada, Hanukkah in the U.S., Diwali in India, Hina Matsuri in Japan, and Egemenlik Bayrami in Turkey. Each holiday is shown on a two-page spread with a large photograph of a featured child or children and many smaller captioned photographs of the festivities and the culture. . . . A superb addition to country/cultural teaching units." SLJ

Lankford, Mary D., 1932-

Christmas around the world; illustrated by Karen Dugan. Morrow Junior Bks. 1995 47p il map $16; lib bdg $16.89; pa $5.95 (3-5)   **394.26**
1. Christmas
ISBN 0-688-12166-7; 0-688-12167-5 (lib bdg); 0-688-16323-8 (pa)   LC 93-38566
This book "looks at the rich diversity of Christmas traditions found in 12 distinctly different cultures. A small amount of pertinent background information serves as an introduction to each entry, but the majority of the text discusses the special ways each culture celebrates the holiday. The book's attractive layout effectively uses repetition of color and theme, with each double-page spread of text and art surrounded by a decorative border. . . . The book features a small selection of craft activities. . . . A helpful pronunciation guide, and an interesting selection of Christmas superstitions." Booklist
Includes bibliographical references

Lasky, Kathryn

Days of the Dead; photographs by Christopher G. Knight. Hyperion Bks. for Children 1994 48p il lib bdg $16.49; pa $5.95 (4-6)   **394.26**
1. All Souls' Day 2. Mexico—Social life and customs
ISBN 0-7868-2018-7 (lib bdg); 0-7868-1055-6 (pa)
                                              LC 93-47957
The author "details the history and customs associated with this traditional Mexican celebration, briefly tells how it is linked to practices in ancient cultures, and describes a contemporary rural family's preparations and observances. . . . Large, bold, and often dramatic full-color photographs fill the pages, amplifying and extending the text." SLJ

McKissack, Patricia C., 1944-

Christmas in the big house, Christmas in the quarters; by Patricia C. McKissack and Fredrick L. McKissack; illustrated by John Thompson. Scholastic 1994 68p il $17.95 (4-6)   **394.26**
1. Plantation life 2. Christmas 3. Slavery—United States
ISBN 0-590-43027-0   LC 92-33831
Coretta Scott King award for text, 1995

McKissack, Patricia C., 1944——*Continued*

"The authors view the holiday from the perspectives of both slaveholder and his household in the 'Big House' and the slaves in the 'Quarters.' Rich descriptions of preparations fill the text—recipes and menus from both groups are provided—and colorful paintings reflect the antebellum period. Sprinkled throughout the book are lyrics of traditional spirituals, carols, and poetry. . . . Use of authentic language of the time helps the narrative flow, and carefully documented notes illuminate the interesting text." Horn Book

Includes bibliographical references

Moehn, Heather

World holidays; a Watts guide for children. Watts 2000 123p il lib bdg $26.80; pa $19.95 (3-6)   **394.26**

1. Holidays 2. Festivals

ISBN 0-531-11714-6 (lib bdg); 0-531-16490-X (pa)
       LC 99-14673

An illustrated alphabetical guide to celebrations and holidays around the world, including religious, civic, and cultural practices

"This will be just the ticket for short reports—and for young researchers studying connections between human cultures." Booklist

Includes bibliographical references

Perl, Lila

Piñatas and paper flowers; holidays of the Americas in English and Spanish; illustrated by Victoria de Larrea. Clarion Bks. 1983 91p il hardcover o.p. paperback available $7.95 (4 and up)   **394.26**

1. Holidays 2. Folklore—Latin America 3. Bilingual books—English-Spanish

ISBN 0-89919-155-X (pa)   LC 82-1211

Text and title page in English and Spanish; Spanish version by Alma Flor Ada

A brief overview of eight holidays and their customs as celebrated in the Americas. Holidays covered include: The New Year, Three Kings' Day; Carnival and Easter; St. John the Baptist Day; Columbus Day; Halloween; The Festival of the Sun; and Christmas

Pinkney, Andrea Davis

Seven candles for Kwanzaa; pictures by Brian Pinkney. Dial Bks. for Young Readers 1993 unp il $15.99; lib bdg $14.89; pa $5.99 (k-3) **394.26**

1. Kwanzaa 2. African Americans—Social life and customs

ISBN 0-8037-1292-8; 0-8037-1293-6 (lib bdg); 0-14-056428-4 (pa)   LC 92-3698

Describes the origins and practices of Kwanzaa, the seven-day festival during which people of African descent rejoice in their ancestral values

The "joyful text is accompanied by equally joyful scratchboard illustrations, set within colorful textilelike borders, depicting a family preparing for and celebrating the holiday." Booklist

Includes bibliographical references

Trawicky, Bernard

Anniversaries and holidays. 5th ed. American Lib. Assn. 2000 311p $68   **394.26**

1. Holidays 2. Calendars 3. Birthdays

ISBN 0-8389-0695-8   LC 99-56166

First edition by Mary Emogene Hazeltine published 1928

"Covers, in calendar form, the names of important people, holidays, religious festivals and special events for nearly 200 countries. Annotated bibliographies about holidays, etc." N Y Public Libr. Ref Books for Child Collect. 2d edition [entry for 4th edition]

Walter, Mildred Pitts, 1922-

Kwanzaa: a family affair. Lothrop, Lee & Shepard Bks. 1995 95p il $15; pa $3.99 (4 and up)   **394.26**

1. Kwanzaa 2. African Americans—Social life and customs

ISBN 0-688-11553-5; 0-380-72735-8 (pa)

This is a "guide to preparing for and celebrating Kwanzaa that encourages early planning and the sharing of family histories. The principles and symbols are clearly explained, and the directions for making simple gifts are accompanied by adequate line drawings. Walter's enthusiasm for her subject brightens this modest effort." Booklist

Includes glossary and bibliographical references

Waters, Kate

Lion dancer: Ernie Wan's Chinese New Year; by Kate Waters and Madeline Slovenz-Low; photographs by Martha Cooper. Scholastic 1990 unp il hardcover o.p. paperback available $4.99 (k-3)   **394.26**

1. Chinese New Year 2. Chinese Americans—Social life and customs

ISBN 0-590-43047-5 (pa)   LC 89-6423

Describes six-year-old Ernie Wan's preparations, at home and in school, for the Chinese New Year celebrations and his first public performance of the lion dance

"While some of the pictures look posed, the marvelously colorful photographs successfully capture Ernie's pride and anticipation as he is dressed in his gorgeous costume and the excitement and swirling movement of the subsequent parade. Illustrations of a Chinese lunar calendar and a Chinese horoscope are extra dividends in a useful and appealing book." Horn Book

395   Etiquette (Manners)

Aliki

Hello! good-bye! Greenwillow Bks. 1996 unp il $15; lib bdg $14.93 (k-3)   **395**

1. Etiquette 2. Communication

ISBN 0-688-14333-4; 0-688-14334-2 (lib bdg)
       LC 95-25090

Describes some of the many ways, both verbal and nonverbal, that people say hello and good-bye

"Vivid cartoons rendered in watercolors and colored pencils show plenty of action and accurately reflect the

Aliki—*Continued*

concise text. . . . While entertaining readers, the author offers vocabulary by providing synonyms, and then explains that sometimes words are not necessary if gestures are used. Illustrations of people from far-away lands in traditional dress are found throughout." SLJ

Manners. Greenwillow Bks. 1990 unp il $16; lib bdg $15.93; pa $5.95 (k-3)   395
1. Etiquette
ISBN 0-688-09198-9; 0-688-09199-7 (lib bdg); 0-688-04579-0 (pa)   LC 89-34622
The author discusses etiquette and good manners
"Aliki makes manners accessible to children through colorful cartoon-style illustrations. . . . Her lively primer sparkles with examples of the proper and the poor." Booklist

Joslin, Sesyle

What do you do, dear? pictures by Maurice Sendak. Harper & Row 1985 c1961 unp il hardcover o.p. paperback available $6.95 (k-2)   395
1. Etiquette
ISBN 0-06-443113-4 (pa)   LC 84-43139
Also available Audiobook version
First published 1961 by Addison-Wesley
A "handbook of etiquette for young ladies and gentlemen to be used as a guide for everyday social behavior." The Author
"The propriety of what the well-mannered child will do is related to extraordinary situations, as for example: The Sheriff of Nottingham interrupts you while you are reading, to take you to jail; you will, naturally, 'Find a bookmark to save your place.'" Horn Book
A "wonderful spoof on manners in a hilarious picture-book made for laughing aloud." Child Study Assoc of Am

What do you say, dear? pictures by Maurice Sendak. Harper & Row 1986 c1958 unp il lib bdg $15.89; pa $5.95 (k-2)   395
1. Etiquette
ISBN 0-06-023074-6 (lib bdg); 0-06-443112-6 (pa)   LC 84-43140
Also available Audiobook version
A Caldecott Medal honor book, 1959
First published 1958 by Addison-Wesley
A "handbook of etiquette for young ladies and gentlemen to be used as a guide for everyday social behavior." The Author
"A rollicking introduction to manners for the very young. A series of delightfully absurd situations—being introduced to a baby elephant, bumping into a crocodile, being rescued from a dragon—are posed and appropriately answered. The illustrations are among Sendak's best—and funniest." Bull Cent Child Books

398   Folklore

Beeler, Selby B.

Throw your tooth on the roof; tooth traditions from around the world; illustrated by G. Brian Karas. Houghton Mifflin 1998 unp il $16 (k-3)   398
1. Teeth—Folklore
ISBN 0-395-89108-6   LC 97-46042
Consists of brief statements relating what children from around the world do with a tooth that has fallen out. Includes facts about teeth
"This book will be an eye-opener for young Americans who may have assumed that the Tooth Fairy holds a worldwide visa." Publ Wkly

Gibbons, Gail

Behold . . . the dragons! Morrow Junior Bks. 1999 unp il $16; lib bdg $15.89 (k-3)   398
1. Dragons 2. Folklore
ISBN 0-688-15526-X; 0-688-15527-8 (lib bdg)
          LC 98-20205
Explains how myths about dragons developed, different types of dragons, what draconologists do, and how different cultures portray dragons
"Numerous bright illustrations accompany the well-researched text. This is a solid, informative presentation." Horn Book Guide

Hunt, Jonathan

Bestiary; an illuminated alphabet of medieval beasts. Simon & Schuster Bks. for Young Readers 1998 unp il $17 (4 and up)   398
1. Mythical animals 2. Alphabet
ISBN 0-689-81246-9   LC 96-42102
An alphabet bestiary featuring mythical animals such as the amphisbaena, basilisk, and catoblepas
"The author's extensive research into the history of bestiaries (as evidenced by his appended note and the lengthy bibliography) has yielded 26 brightly colored, action-filled illustrations of wondrous, and mostly fearsome, creatures." SLJ

MacDonald, Margaret Read

The storyteller's sourcebook; a subject, title, and motif index to folklore collections for children, 1983-1999; by Margaret Read MacDonald and Brian W. Sturm. Gale Group 2001 712p $125   398
1. Folklore—Indexes
ISBN 0-8103-5485-3   LC 00-48395
Also available original volume covering the years 1961-1982 $125 (ISBN 0-8103-0471-6)
This sourcebook "provides descriptions of folktales and references to more than 700 published sources of folktales. . . . [Includes] indexing by subject, motif, title, ethnic group and country of origin and a comprehensive bibliography." Publisher's note

Mayer, Marianna, 1945-

Women warriors; myths and legends of heroic women; illustrated by Julek Heller. Morrow Junior Bks. 1999 80p il $18 (4 and up)   **398**

1. Heroes and heroines 2. Women—Folklore

ISBN 0-688-15522-7   LC 98-45697

A collection of twelve traditional tales about female military leaders, war goddesses, women warriors, and heroines from around the world, including such countries as Japan, Ireland, and Zimbabwe

These stories "are told in accessible, rhythmic prose. . . . Each three-to six page selection is prefaced by comments on its origin and history and accompanied by a full-page watercolor painting showing the protagonist in action." SLJ

Includes bibliographical references

Opie, Iona Archibald

The lore and language of schoolchildren; by Iona and Peter Opie. Oxford Univ. Press 1960 c1959 417p il maps o.p.; New York Review of Bks. paperback available $14.95   **398**

1. Folklore—Great Britain

ISBN 0-940322-69-2 (pa)

A collection of the "rhymes, riddles, incantations, jeers, torments, parodies, nicknames, holiday customs, and other types of lore that is . . . transmitted orally, some of it over a period of hundreds of years. The basic study was made in Great Britain and detailed analysis of geographic usage is made for Great Britain but some usage in other countries is also noted. Chiefly of interest to folklorists, teachers, librarians, and others who work with children but nostalgic appeal for the general reader." Booklist

Van Laan, Nancy

With a whoop and a holler; a bushel of lore from way down south; illustrated by Scott Cook. Atheneum Bks. for Young Readers 1998 102p il map $19.95 (3-6)   **398**

1. Folklore—Southern States

ISBN 0-689-81061-X   LC 96-24336

"An Anne Schwartz book"

A collection of tales, rhymes, riddles, superstitions, and sayings organized around the three distinct regions of the South: the Bayou, the Deep South, and Appalachia

"Cook's caricature-like illustrations draw out the fun-loving humor with an affectionate wink-and-a-nod style." Horn Book Guide

398.2   Folk literature

Sagas, romances, legends, ballads, and fables in prose form, and fairy tales, folk tales, and tall tales are included here, instead of with the literature of the country of origin, to keep the traditional material together and to make it more readily accessible. Modern fairy tales are classified with Fiction, Story collections (SC), or Easy books (E)

Aardema, Verna

Anansi does the impossible! an Ashanti tale; retold by Verna Aardema; illustrated by Lisa Desimini. Atheneum Bks. for Young Readers 1997 unp il $16; pa $5.99 (k-3)   **398.2**

1. Anansi (Legendary character) 2. Folklore—West Africa

ISBN 0-689-81092-X; 0-689-83933-2 (pa)

LC 96-20033

"An Anne Schwartz book"

"Anansi the Spider is determined to buy back the stories taken from the people and kept by the Sky God. With the assistance of his clever wife, Aso, he takes the Sky God the live python, the real fairy, and the 47 stinging hornets required to regain the stories." SLJ

"Vivid, stylized collage illustrations convey the frightening force and power of the Sky God yet also reveal Anansi's own pluck and boldness. Perfect for reading or telling aloud." Booklist

Includes glossary and bibliographical references

Bimwili & the Zimwi; a tale from Zanzibar; retold by Verna Aardema; pictures by Susan Meddaugh. Dial Bks. for Young Readers 1985 unp il hardcover o.p. paperback available $5.99 (k-3)   **398.2**

1. Folklore—Zanzibar

ISBN 0-14-054608-1 (pa)   LC 85-4449

Text adapted from Little sister and the Zimwi, published 1969 in Tales for the third ear. Another version: The children and the Zimwi, published 1896 in Swahili stories

A Swahili girl is abducted by Zimwi, an ugly ogre, and told to be the voice inside his singing drum

"Making the most of each dramatic situation, the bright watercolor and pencil illustrations are well suited to sharing with a group of children. . . . A tightly written, slightly scary story with a heroine who uses her wits and courage to overcome a powerful enemy, this could become a favorite for reading aloud to children in the primary grades." Booklist

Borreguita and the coyote; a tale from Ayutla, Mexico; retold by Verna Aardema; illustrated by Petra Mathers. Knopf 1991 unp il hardcover o.p. paperback available $6.99 (k-3)   **398.2**

1. Folklore—Mexico 2. Coyote (Legendary character) 3. Sheep—Fiction

ISBN 0-679-88936-1 (pa)   LC 90-33302

A little lamb uses her clever wiles to keep a coyote from eating her up

This folk tale "is energetically told and comfortably packed with many recognizable motifs. Mathers enlarges upon the humorous elements of the story in her boldly colored paintings. . . . Aardema and Mathers are felicitously paired in a tale of trickery rewarded that begs to be read aloud." Horn Book

Includes glossary

Aardema, Verna—_Continued_

Bringing the rain to Kapiti Plain; a Nandi tale; retold by Verna Aardema; pictures by Beatriz Vidal. Dial Bks. for Young Readers 1981 unp il $16.99; pa $5.99 (k-3) **398.2**
1. Folklore—Africa 2. Stories in rhyme 3. Droughts—Fiction
ISBN 0-8037-0809-2; 0-8037-0904-8 (pa)
LC 80-25886
Also available Audiobook version
"Retold from an African folk tale, this is a cumulative rhyming tale with the rhythm and repetition of 'The House that Jack Built.' It tells of how Ki-pat, the herdsman, works out a clever method to save the plain from a long drought." SLJ
"Effective both in the rhythm of its metered storytelling and in the brilliance of its stylized paintings, the panoramic picture book quickly engages both eye and ear." Horn Book

Koi and the kola nuts; a tale from Liberia; illustrated by Joe Cepeda. Atheneum Bks. for Young Readers 1999 unp il $16.95 (k-3) **398.2**
1. Folklore—Liberia
ISBN 0-689-81760-6
LC 97-46713
"An Anne Schwartz book"
Originally published 1960 in Aardema's Tales from the story hat
A Liberian folktale in which the son of the chief must make his way in the world with only a sackful of kola nuts and the help of some creatures that he has treated with kindness
"Aardema's crisp retelling . . . is given additional humor by Cepeda's jauntily irreverent illustrations. Oil paintings with backdrops of lime, apricot, and grape give a feeling of spacious plains and skies." Bull Cent Child Books

The lonely lioness and the ostrich chicks; a Masai tale; retold by Verna Aardema; illustrated by Yumi Heo. Knopf 1996 unp il lib bdg $18.99 (k-3) **398.2**
1. Masai (African people)—Folklore 2. Folklore—Africa
ISBN 0-679-96934-9
LC 94-48449
In this retelling of a Masai tale, a mongoose helps an ostrich get her chicks back from the lonely lioness who has stolen them
"This traditional tale of cleverness winning out over strength is retold in an understated but satisfying manner. Heo's enormously appealing, stylized artwork captures the expansiveness and colors of the sun-drenched veld and offers unusual perspectives of the animal characters, rendered in expressive cartoon style." SLJ
Includes bibliographical references

Misoso; once upon a time tales from Africa; retold by Verna Aardema; illustrated by Reynold Ruffins. Knopf 1994 87p il $18 (3-5) **398.2**
1. Folklore—Africa
ISBN 0-679-83430-3
LC 92-43288
"An Apple Soup book"
A collection of twelve folktales from different parts of Africa

"Aardema's usual attention to detail and the rhythm and structure of the oral folk style make the stories a particular pleasure to read aloud. Vibrant illustrations in pencil and acrylic paints, notes about each story, a map of Africa, and a glossary for each tale complete this exceptional collection." Horn Book Guide
Includes bibliographical references

Oh, Kojo! How could you! an Ashanti tale; retold by Verna Aardema; pictures by Marc Brown. Dial Bks. for Young Readers 1984 unp il hardcover o.p. paperback available $5.99 (k-3)
398.2
1. Ashanti (African people)—Folklore 2. Anansi (Legendary character)
ISBN 0-14-054669-3 (pa)
LC 84-1710
"An adaptation of the author's earlier book, 'The Na of Wa' [1960]." Horn Book
"An Ananse story that explains why cats are favored over dogs in Ashantiland. The text and full-color illustrations combine to make a fun book that is sure to be enjoyed by many." Child Book Rev Serv

Rabbit makes a monkey of lion; a Swahili tale; retold by Verna Aardema; pictures by Jerry Pinkney. Dial Bks. for Young Readers 1989 unp il hardcover o.p. paperback available $5.99 (k-3)
398.2
1. Folklore—Zanzibar 2. Animals—Fiction
ISBN 0-14-054593-X (pa)
LC 86-11523
Text adapted from The hare and the lion, published 1901 in Zanzibar tales
With the help of his friends Bush-rat and Turtle, smart and nimble Rabbit makes a fool of the mighty but slow-witted king of the forest
"Aardema's version of the tale reinforces the amusing trickster qualities of rascally Rabbit, making it a sure-fire choice for sharing with groups of children, who will instantly root for her success. Pinkney's lovely watercolor and pencil paintings in hues of green, brown, and gold fill the pages with lush scenes which evoke the East African setting." Horn Book

This for that; a Tonga tale; retold by Verna Aardema; pictures by Victoria Chess. Dial Bks. for Young Readers 1997 unp il $14.99 (k-3) **398.2**
1. Folklore—Zambia
ISBN 0-8037-1553-6
LC 93-32309
"Rabbit tries to muscle in on the water from a well dug by Lion and Elephant, but she is chased away. She encounters Ostrich and . . . tricks him out of his share of the juicy berries they have found. . . . Rabbit proceeds to take advantage of everyone in sight but ultimately gets her comeuppance." Bull Cent Child Books
"Aardema's storytelling is highly readable, spiced with original sound effects. . . . Chess interprets the tale nicely in her devilishly droll style. The characters' facial expressions are hilarious. . . . Watercolors in the bright earth tones of the African plain are detailed with light, textural hatching." SLJ

Traveling to Tondo; a tale of the Nkundo of Zaire; retold by Verna Aardema; illustrated by Will Hillenbrand. Knopf 1991 unp il hardcover o.p. paperback available $5.99 (k-3) **398.2**
1. Folklore—Africa 2. Animals—Fiction
ISBN 0-679-85309-X (pa)
LC 90-39419

Aardema, Verna—*Continued*

On his way to his wedding, with his friends as attendants, a civet cat meets with extraordinary and unexpected delays

"This satisfying tale owes its success to a clean, straightforward telling and beautiful illustrations in blues, browns, greens, and gold. . . . Told with a steady ryhthm that's perfect for reading aloud, this is a traveling tale for all collections." SLJ

Includes glossary

Who's in Rabbit's house? a Masai tale; retold by Verna Aardema; pictures by Leo and Diane Dillon. Dial Bks. for Young Readers 1977 unp il hardcover o.p. paperback available $6.99 (k-3)
398.2
1. Masai (African people)—Folklore 2. Animals—Fiction 3. Folklore—East Africa
ISBN 0-14-054724-X (pa)   LC 77-71514
This "tale relates the attempts of Rabbit to regain possession of her house after it is taken over by an intruder. Rabbit's friends offer suggestions on how to solve the problem, but the solution comes from 'an unexpected source.' The story, adapted from the Masai tale 'The Long One,' uses repetition of key phrases to produce a rhythmic read-aloud text. The Dillons skillfully present their artistry in a vivid, colorful and impressive manner which contributes to the story and sets the tone." Child Book Rev Serv

Why mosquitoes buzz in people's ears; a West African tale retold; pictures by Leo and Diane Dillon. Dial Bks. for Young Readers 1975 unp il $16.99; pa $6.99 (k-3)
398.2
1. Folklore—West Africa 2. Mosquitoes—Fiction 3. Animals—Fiction
ISBN 0-8037-6089-2; 0-14-054905-6 (pa)
Awarded the Caldecott Medal, 1976
This tale relates "how a mosquito's silly lie to an iguana sets in motion a cumulative series of events that finally causes Mother Owl not to call up the sun. The resulting hardship ends only after King Lion traces the problem back to its source." Booklist
"Stunning full-color illustrations—watercolor sprayed with air gun, overlayed with pastel, cut out and re-pasted—give an eye-catching abstract effect and tell the story with humor and power." SLJ

Ada, Alma Flor, 1938-

The rooster who went to his uncle's wedding; a Latin American folktale; retold by Alma Flor Ada; illustrated by Kathleen Kuchera. Putnam 1993 unp il hardcover o.p. paperback available $5.99 (k-3)
398.2
1. Folklore—Latin America
ISBN 0-698-11682-8 (pa)   LC 92-14087
"A Whitebird book"
In this cumulative folktale from Latin America, the sun sets off a chain of events which results in the cleaning of Rooster's beak in time for his uncle's wedding
"The story . . . will delight young children with the sheer joy of its repetitive rhythms, and it is particularly appropriate to be told aloud. The illustrations, bright with tropical colors, depict a Latin American setting." Booklist

The three golden oranges; written by Alma Flor Ada; illustrated by Reg Cartwright. Atheneum Pubs. 1999 unp il $16 (k-3)   **398.2**
1. Folklore—Spain
ISBN 0-689-80775-9   LC 97-47570
Acting on the advice of the old woman on the cliff by the sea, three brothers who wish to find brides go in search of three golden oranges
"The telling is lively, the message is light, and the stylized oil paintings in bright colors combine magic and personality, rhythm and character, with a strong sense of drama." Booklist

Adler, David A., 1947-

Chanukah in Chelm; [illustrated by] Kevin O'Malley. Lothrop, Lee & Shepard Bks. 1997 unp il lib bdg $15.89 (k-3)   **398.2**
1. Jews—Folklore 2. Hanukkah—Fiction
ISBN 0-688-09953-X   LC 96-53127
When the rabbi tells Mendel to get a table for the Chanukah menorah, Mendel makes the task more difficult than it should be
"Adler's witty text finds able companionship in O'Malley's old-worldly crosshatched pen and watercolor illustrations, which capture the folly of the residents of Chelm with both humor and respectful affection." Horn Book Guide

Afanas´ev, A. N. (Aleksandr Nikolaevich), 1826-1871

Russian fairy tales; translated by Norbert Guterman from the collections of Aleksandr Afanas´ev; illustrated by Alexander Alexeieff; folkloristic commentary by Roman Jakobson. Pantheon Bks. 1975 c1945 661p il hardcover o.p. paperback available $18 (4 and up)   **398.2**
1. Folklore—Russia 2. Fairy tales
ISBN 0-394-73090-9 (pa)
A reprint of the title first published 1945
Afanas´ev's "tales carry the reader to faraway Russian villages, long winter nights, deep snow, thatched huts, forests teeming with wild animals and muzhiks (peasants), who have never progressed beyond the very beginnings of human civilization. . . . [This is a] beautiful book. I recommend it to all readers, young and old who are interested in the folktale and its unique qualities." N Y Times Book Rev
Includes bibliographical references

Alderson, Brian

The Arabian nights; or, Tales told by Sheherezade during a thousand nights and one night; retold by Brian Alderson; illustrated by Michael Foreman. Books of Wonder; Morrow Junior Bks. 1995 c1992 191p il $20 (6 and up)
398.2
1. Fairy tales 2. Arabs—Folklore
ISBN 0-688-14219-2   LC 94-40945
First published 1992 in the United Kingdom
This collection includes the stories of Sindbad, Ali Baba, and Aladdin, as well as shorter, lesser known stories such as The fable of the mongoose and the mouse, and The tale of the ruined man and his dream

Alderson, Brian—*Continued*

The tale of the turnip; illustrated by Fritz Wegner. Candlewick Press 1999 unp il $12.99 (k-3)   398.2
1. Folklore—Great Britain
ISBN 0-7636-0494-1   LC 98-35831
When a poor farmer grows a gigantic turnip and the king pays him handsomely for it, the envious town squire tries to get an even bigger reward for one of his horses
"Not the cumulative Russian story but 'a traditional English tale'. . . . Alderson's telling is spare, witty, and engagingly informal. . . . Wegner's pen-and-watercolor art is charmingly detailed." Horn Book

Andreasen, Dan
Rose Red and the bear prince; adapted and illustrated by Dan Andreasen. HarperCollins Pubs. 2000 unp il $16.95; lib bdg $16.89 (k-3)   398.2
1. Fairy tales 2. Folklore—Germany
ISBN 0-06-027966-4; 0-06-027967-2 (lib bdg)
                                      LC 98-47525
"Adapted from Snow White and Rose Red by the Brothers Grimm." Verso of title page
"Clever Rose Red rescues a trapped and ungrateful dwarf by cutting off his beard, hair, and mustache. Doing so frees her friend the bear prince from the Dwarf's enchantment. The elegant illustrations in warm earth tones are framed with gold and textured with small patterns of squares that create a tapestry-like effect." Horn Book Guide

The **Arabian** nights entertainments; selected and edited by Andrew Lang; with numerous illustrations by H. J. Ford. Dover Publs. 1969 424p il pa $9.95 (5 and up)   398.2
1. Arabs—Folklore 2. Fairy tales
ISBN 0-486-22289-6
First published 1898 in the United Kingdom
"A collection of popular tales assembled over many centuries, and well known in Europe from the 18th cent. It contains the stories of 'Aladdin, Alibaba, and Sindbad the sailor'. . . . The framing story in which the tales are set concerns Scheherazade, who is determined to delay her royal husband's plan of killing her—he has taken to murdering his wives because the first was unfaithful to him—by telling him a story every evening. She leaves each evening's tale incomplete until the next day, so that he has to spare her life in order to hear its conclusion. He is so entertained that he finally abandons his murderous plan." Oxford Companion to Child Lit

Aylesworth, Jim, 1943-
Aunt Pitty Patty's piggy; retold by Jim Aylesworth; illustrated by Barbara McClintock. Scholastic Press 1999 unp il lib bdg $15.95 (k-3)
                                          398.2
1. Folklore
ISBN 0-590-89987-2   LC 98-46263
A cumulative tale in which Aunt Pitty Patty's niece Nellie tries to get piggy to go through the gate
This "folktale is great for reading aloud and joining

in. McClintock's delicately detailed double-page spreads in brown pencil and watercolor set the cozy farce in a Randolph Caldecott-style, bucolic farmyard landscape." Booklist

The Gingerbread man; retold by Jim Aylesworth; illustrated by Barbara McClintock. Scholastic 1998 unp il $15.95 (k-3)   398.2
1. Folklore
ISBN 0-590-97219-7   LC 96-52781
A freshly baked gingerbread man escapes when he is taken out of the oven and eludes a number of pursuers until he meets a clever fox
"This hearty retelling of the well-known tale is distinguished by cheery, lively illustrations. . . . The scenery resembles that of the eighteenth-century English artist Thomas Bewick. With even a recipe included, this is altogether an old-fashioned and enjoyable version of a favorite tale." Horn Book Guide

Babbitt, Natalie
Ouch! a tale from Grimm; retold by Natalie Babbitt; illustrated by Fred Marcellino. HarperCollins Pubs. 1998 unp il $14.95; lib bdg $15.89 (k-3)   398.2
1. Fairy tales 2. Folklore—Germany
ISBN 0-06-205066-4; 0-06-205067-2 (lib bdg)
"Michael di Capua books"
"A fortuneteller predicts that Marco will marry a princess and this comes to pass in short order. . . . The youth still must placate his evil father-in-law, the king, who demands three golden hairs from the head of the Devil." Publ Wkly
"Babbitt's language is perfect: neither too archaic nor too modern. Throughout the story, words and pictures work together to underscore the humor in the tale. . . . With comic perspectives and sly expression Marcellino introduces a farcical cast." SLJ

Balit, Christina
Atlantis; the legend of a lost city; adapted and retold by Christina Balit; with a note by Geoffrey Ashe. Holt & Co. 2000 c1999 unp il $16.95 (2-4)
                                          398.2
1. Atlantis
ISBN 0-8050-6334-X   LC 99-27943
First published 1999 in the United Kingdom
In this retelling of Plato's legend, "the city founded by Poseidon flourishes, then falters and is finally destroyed when its inhabitants start acting more like greedy mortals than like gods. Exquisitely detailed illustrations, rich in geometric patterns, capture the tragic core of the story. A historical note is included." Horn Book Guide

Bang, Molly, 1943-
Wiley and the Hairy Man; adapted from an American folk tale. Macmillan 1976 64p il hardcover o.p. paperback available $3.99 (1-4)
                                          398.2
1. African Americans—Folklore 2. Folklore—Southern States
ISBN 0-689-81142-X (pa)
Also available Audiobook version

Bang, Molly, 1943——*Continued*

"A Ready-to-read book"

In this adaptation of an Alabama folk yarn "the swamp-dwelling Hairy Man must be tricked three times before a person is safe from being caught and carried off by him. Wiley, a Black boy, twice meets the Hairy Man in the swamp, and both times quick thinking and his hound dogs save him. On the critical third time, Wiley's mother traps the conjure man into taking a piglet instead of her son." SLJ

Barton, Byron

The little red hen. HarperCollins Pubs. 1993 unp il $15.95; lib bdg $15.89 (k-2)   **398.2**

1. Folklore 2. Chickens—Fiction

ISBN 0-06-021675-1; 0-06-021676-X (lib bdg)
         LC 91-4051

Also available Board book edition and Big book edition

The little red hen finds none of her lazy friends willing to help her plant, harvest, or grind wheat into flour, but all are eager to eat the bread she makes from it

"Barton here skillfully pares down a well-known tale for the youngest readers and listeners. Vibrant hues abound in his full-page, collage-like illustrations." Publ Wkly

The three bears. HarperCollins Pubs. 1991 unp il $15.95; lib bdg $15.89 (k-1)   **398.2**

1. Folklore 2. Bears—Fiction

ISBN 0-06-020423-0; 0-06-020424-9 (lib bdg)
         LC 90-43151

Also available Board book edition

"Here's the familiar tale of the three bears and their blond gal pal drawn for the very youngest. Byron uses large simple shapes, bright colors, and a spare text to tell his story. . . . The size of the art makes this a good choice for mother-toddler story hours." Booklist

Behan, Brendan, 1923-1964

The King of Ireland's son; illustrated by P.J. Lynch. Orchard Bks. 1997 31p il $16.95 (3-5)
         398.2

1. Fairy tales 2. Folklore—Ireland

ISBN 0-531-09549-5   LC 96-28377

First published 1996 in the United Kingdom

Sent to find the source of the heavenly music heard throughout the kingdom, the youngest son of the King of Ireland finds a beautiful maiden held captive by a fierce giant

"By contrasting light with dark and large with small, Lynch creates dramatic illustrations for this lively, amusing retelling by the well-known Irish playwright." Horn Book Guide

Ben-'Ezer, Ehud, 1936-

Hosni the dreamer; an Arabian tale; pictures by Uri Shulevitz. Farrar, Straus & Giroux 1997 unp il $16 (2-4)   **398.2**

1. Arabs—Folklore 2. Shepherds—Fiction 3. Deserts—Fiction

ISBN 0-374-33340-8   LC 96-18608

"Hosni is regarded as a fool by his fellow shepherds when during his trip to the city he spends all his money on a verse. But his purchase saves his life and secures his happiness and fortune." Horn Book

"Ben-Ezer uses crisp, vivid language throughout; he includes descriptions and phrases that suggest the tale's setting. Shulevitz's illustrations add a light, comic touch." SLJ

Beneduce, Ann

Jack and the beanstalk; retold by Ann Keay Beneduce; illustrated by Gennady Spirin. Philomel Bks. 1999 32p il $16.99 (2-4)   **398.2**

1. Fairy tales 2. Folklore—Great Britain

ISBN 0-399-23118-8   LC 98-5722

A boy climbs to the top of a giant beanstalk, where he uses his quick wits to outsmart an ogre and make his and his mother's fortune

"Beneduce bases her version of Jack and the Beanstalk on a Victorian version, complete with a fairy guardian. . . . Spirin contributes some glorious borders for the text as well as many impressively detailed paintings, notable for their dark muted colors and mysterious, foggy look." Booklist

Bernier-Grand, Carmen T.

Juan Bobo; four folktales from Puerto Rico; retold by Carmen T. Bernier-Grand; pictures by Ernesto Ramos Nieves. HarperCollins Pubs. 1994 58p il hardcover o.p. paperback available $3.95 (k-2)   **398.2**

1. Folklore—Puerto Rico

ISBN 0-06-444185-7 (pa)   LC 93-12936

"An I can read book"

Four folktales from rural Puerto Rico about the comical Juan Bobo's nonsensical shenanigans

The tales "are told with immediacy and spirit. The exuberant folk-style illustrations in bright tropical colors reflect the island setting and the scenes of comic confrontation. . . . A Spanish translation is provided in small print at the back." Booklist

Bierhorst, John

Doctor Coyote; a native American Aesop's fables; retold by John Bierhorst; pictures by Wendy Watson. Macmillan 1987 unp il $15.95; pa $5.99 (1-4)   **398.2**

1. Aztecs—Folklore 2. Coyote (Legendary character) 3. Fables

ISBN 0-02-709780-3; 0-689-80739-2 (pa)
         LC 86-8669

"These stories, printed for the first time in English, are taken from an early copy of Aesop found in Mexico where the fables were translated into Aztec by a 16th century scribe. Coyote, a perpetual trickster who appears in various North American Indian tales, becomes the main character in the fables." Child Book Rev Serv

"Elaborate cartoons . . . take such vast liberties with lore (a modern gas station, a chicken in a sleeping bag, everyone decked out in squash blossom necklaces) that you're back in a secret garden of delight. Don't miss this unique, perfectly turned-out book." Read Teach

Bierhorst, John—*Continued*

The people with five fingers; a native Californian creation tale; retold by John Bierhorst; illustrated by Robert Andrew Parker. Marshall Cavendish 2000 unp il $15.95 (k-3)   **398.2**

1. Native Americans—Folklore

ISBN 0-7614-5058-0   LC 99-28795

A tale shared by the different native peoples of California tells how Coyote and other animals created the world and the people who came to live in it

"The spare watercolor illustrations complement this quietly appealing story." Horn Book Guide

Blia Xiong

Nine-in-one, Grr! Grr! a folktale from the Hmong people of Laos; told by Blia Xiong; adapted by Cathy Spagnoli; illustrated by Nancy Hom. Children's Bk. Press 1989 30p il $14.95; pa $7.95 (k-2)   **398.2**

1. Folklore—Laos 2. Tigers—Fiction

ISBN 0-89239-048-4; 0-89239-110-3 (pa)

LC 89-9891

When the great god Shao promises Tiger nine cubs each year, Bird comes up with a clever trick to prevent the land from being overrun by tigers

"Simply and eloquently told, this *pourquoi* tale from a minority Laotian culture is boldly illustrated in a style adapted from the multi-imaged embroidered story cloths of the Hmong people. Its rhythmic text and appealing, brightly colored pictures make it a good choice for pre-school story hours." Booklist

The **Blue** fairy book; edited by Andrew Lang; with numerous illustrations by H. J. Ford and G. P. Jacob Hood. Dover Publs. 1965 390p il pa $8.95 (4-6)   **398.2**

1. Folklore 2. Fairy tales

ISBN 0-486-21437-0

Also available in hardcover from P. Smith

Companion volume to The Green fairy book, The Red fairy book, and The Yellow fairy book, also available: The Pink fairy book pa $8.95 (ISBN 0-486-21792-2) and in hardcover from P. Smith

A reprint of the title first published 1889 by Longmans

A collection of thirty-seven fairy tales from various countries, consisting largely of old favorites from such sources as Perrault, the Brothers Grimm, Madame D'Aulnoy, Asbjörnsen and Möe, the Arabian Nights and Swift's Gulliver's travels

Bodkin, Odds

The crane wife; retold by Odds Bodkin; illustrated by Gennady Spirin. Gulliver Bks. 1998 unp il $16 (3-5)   **398.2**

1. Folklore—Japan

ISBN 0-15-201407-1   LC 96-35488

A retelling of the traditional Japanese tale about a poor sail maker who gains a beautiful but mysterious wife skilled at weaving magical sails

"Capturing the tale's mystery and tragedy, Spirin's watercolor-and-gouache paintings take their inspiration from Japanese art. Delicate shades of tawny gray and burnished gold predominate in the illustrations." Booklist

Bowden, Joan Chase, 1925-

Why the tides ebb and flow; illustrated by Marc Brown. Houghton Mifflin 1979 unp il $16; pa $7.95 (k-2)   **398.2**

1. Folklore 2. Tides—Fiction

ISBN 0-395-28378-7; 0-395-54952-3 (pa)

LC 79-12359

In this folktale explaining why the sea has tides, an old woman threatens to pull the rock from the hole in the ocean floor if Sky Spirit does not honor his promise to give her shelter

"The lyrical text, perfect for reading aloud, is touched with humor and lightly seasoned with onomatopoeic expressions. The elegant illustrations sweep in broad strokes across buff-colored pages." Horn Book

Brett, Jan, 1949-

Beauty and the beast; retold and illustrated by Jan Brett. Clarion Bks. 1989 unp il lib bdg $16; pa $6.95 (1-3)   **398.2**

1. Folklore—France 2. Fairy tales

ISBN 0-89919-497-4 (lib bdg); 0-395-55702-X (pa)

LC 88-16965

Through her great capacity to love, a kind and beautiful maid releases a handsome prince from the spell which has made him an ugly beast

"A Beauty of distinguished appearance, a delightful set of animal servants, and a suitably hideous Beast are presented in Jan Brett's distinctive, decorative style. Small details, such as tapestries mirroring the action of the tale, add to the effect of the simply written story." Horn Book Guide

Gingerbread baby. Putnam 1999 unp il $16.99 (k-3)   **398.2**

1. Folklore

ISBN 0-399-23444-6   LC 98-52310

A young boy and his mother bake a gingerbread baby that escapes from their oven and leads a crowd on a chase

"Although the story remains true to the original tale, Brett has added her own touches and a surprise ending. . . . The illustrations are pure Brett and feature warm colors against a snow-white landscape." SLJ

The mitten; a Ukrainian folktale; adapted and illustrated by Jan Brett. Putnam 1989 unp il $16.99 (k-2)   **398.2**

1. Folklore—Ukraine 2. Animals—Fiction

ISBN 0-399-21920-X   LC 88-32198

Also available Board book edition

"Grandmother knits snow-white mittens that Nikki takes on an adventure. Readers will enjoy the charm and humor in the portrayal of the animals as they make room for each newcomer in the mitten and sprawl in the snow after the big sneeze." Horn Book Guide

Town mouse, country mouse. Putnam 1994 unp il $16.99 (k-3)   **398.2**

1. Fables 2. Mice—Fiction

ISBN 0-399-22622-2   LC 93-41227

A retelling of the Aesop fable. After trading houses, the country mice and the town mice discover there's no place like home

Brett, Jan, 1949——*Continued*

"In Brett's version, the town mice are as charming and naive as their country cousins. . . . Brett's narrative alternates the parallel mishaps of the two sets of mice with lively, smooth writing and a deft touch of humor. . . . The illustrations are rich with meticulous detail." SLJ

Brown, Marcia, 1918-

Once a mouse; a fable cut in wood. Atheneum Pubs. 1961 unp il $16; pa $5.99 (k-3)   **398.2**

1. Folklore—India 2. Fables
ISBN 0-684-12662-1; 0-689-71343-6 (pa)
Awarded the Caldecott Medal, 1962
At head of title: From ancient India

A "fable from the Indian 'Hitopadesa.' There is lively action in spreads showing how a hermit 'thinking about big and little' suddenly saves a mouse from a crow and then from larger enemies by turning the little creature into the forms of bigger and bigger animals—until as a royal tiger it has to be humbled." Horn Book

"The illustrations are remarkably beautiful. The emotional elements of the story . . . are conveyed with just as much intensity as the purely visual ones." New Yorker

Stone soup; an old tale; told and pictured by Marcia Brown. Scribner 1947 unp il $16 (k-3)
    398.2

1. Folklore—France
ISBN 0-684-92296-7
Also available with cassette in hardcover and paperback editions from Live Oak Media
A Caldecott Medal honor book, 1948

"When the people in a French village heard that three soldiers were coming, they hid all their food for they knew what soldiers are. However, when the soldiers began to make soup with water and stones the pot gradually filled with all the vegetables which had been hidden away. The simple language and quiet humour of this folktale are amplified and enriched by gay and witty drawings of clever light-hearted soldiers, and the gullible 'light-witted' peasants." Ont Libr Rev

Bruchac, Joseph, 1942-

Between earth & sky; legends of Native American sacred places; written by Joseph Bruchac; illustrated by Thomas Locker. Harcourt Brace & Co. 1996 unp il map $16; pa $7 (3-5)
    398.2

1. Native Americans—Folklore
ISBN 0-15-200042-9; 0-15-202062-4 (pa)
    LC 95-10862

"In response to Little Turtle's questions about places sacred to the Delaware Indians, Old Bear explains that all people have sacred places and shares 10 legends from different tribes." Booklist

"Each tale is a model of economy, gracefully distilling its message, while Locker's landscapes capture the mysticism inherent in each setting." Horn Book Guide

The first strawberries; a Cherokee story; retold by Joseph Bruchac; pictures by Anna Vojtech. Dial Bks. for Young Readers 1993 unp il $15.99; pa $6.99 (k-3)   **398.2**

1. Cherokee Indians—Folklore 2. Strawberries—Fiction
ISBN 0-8037-1331-2; 0-14-05409-8 (pa)
    LC 91-31058

A quarrel between the first man and the first woman is reconciled when the Sun causes strawberries to grow out of the earth

"This retelling . . . is simply and clearly written, and as sweet as the berries the woman stops to taste. The attractive watercolors and colored-pencil illustrations show an idealized pastoral world." SLJ

Flying with the eagle, racing the great bear; stories from Native North America; told by Joseph Bruchac. BridgeWater Bks. 1993 128p il $13.95; pa $5.95 (5 and up)   **398.2**

1. Native Americans—Folklore
ISBN 0-8167-3026-1; 0-8167-3027-X (pa)
    LC 93-21966

"This collection of Native American folktales revolves around the central theme of journeying from boyhood to manhood. . . . The stories are excellent and could be used for independent reading or as read-alouds." Book Rep

Includes bibliographical references

The girl who married the Moon; tales from Native North America; told by Joseph Bruchac and Gayle Ross. BridgeWater Bks. 1994 127p il o.p.; Troll Assocs. paperback available $5.95 (5 and up)   **398.2**

1. Native Americans—Folklore
ISBN 0-8167-3481-X (pa)   LC 93-43824

"This anthology focuses on the role of women in traditional Indian cultures. The 16 stories, collected from tribes representing all areas of North America, range from female rites of passage to cautionary and *pourquoi* tales. . . . Striking black-and-white stylized drawings as well as background information about the region and the stories introduce each section. . . . An excellent addition for storytelling collections." Booklist

Includes bibliographical references

Gluskabe and the four wishes; retold by Joseph Bruchac; illustrated by Christine Nyburg Shrader. Cobblehill Bks. 1995 unp il $15.99 (k-3)   **398.2**

1. Abnaki Indians—Folklore
ISBN 0-525-65164-0   LC 93-26924

"Four Abenaki men paddle to the fog-enshrouded island of the reclusive god-hero Gluskabe to make wishes. Impressed by their determination, Gluskabe hands each a bag of his granted wishes inside, but warns them not to open the bags until they reach home." Bull Cent Child Books

"The impeccably sourced, well-told tale . . . is illustrated with dramatic, atmospheric oil paintings that aptly suggest an inchoate new world." Horn Book

Bruchac, Joseph, 1942——*Continued*

The great ball game; a Muskogee story; retold by Joseph Bruchac; illustrated by Susan L. Roth. Dial Bks. for Young Readers 1994 unp il $15 (k-3) **398.2**

1. Creek Indians—Folklore 2. Animals—Fiction

ISBN 0-8037-1539-0 LC 93-6269

Bat, who has both wings and teeth, plays an important part in a game between the Birds and the Animals to decide which group is better

"Roth's dynamic collages combine cut papers of varied textures and hues to create a series of effective illustrations. Short and well told, this appealing *pourquoi* tale lends itself to reading aloud." Booklist

The story of the Milky Way; a Cherokee tale; by Joseph Bruchac and Gayle Ross; paintings by Virginia A. Stroud. Dial Bks. for Young Readers 1995 unp il $15.99 (k-3) **398.2**

1. Cherokee Indians—Folklore 2. Milky Way—Fiction

ISBN 0-8037-1737-7 LC 94-20926

When cornmeal is stolen from an elderly couple, the others in a Cherokee village find a way to drive off the thief, creating the Milky Way in the process

"Stroud illustrates this gracefully told tale with her trademark acrylic paintings full of the rich blues of the night and the vivid greens of the fields. Bruchac, Ross, and Stroud have contributed notes on the story's origin and on the choice of the historical setting." Horn Book Guide

When the Chenoo howls; native American tales of terror; [by] Joseph and James Bruchac; illustrations by William Sauts Netamux̌we Bock. Walker & Co. 1998 136p $16.95; lib bdg $17.85; pa $8.95 (4-6) **398.2**

1. Native Americans—Folklore

ISBN 0-8027-8638-3; 0-8027-8639-1 (lib bdg); 0-8027-7576-4 (pa) LC 97-48715

"Twelve monster tales from a variety of American Indian tribes. . . . These pithily retold tales are short enough for reading aloud and easy enough to learn to tell quickly. Brief notes at the end of each tale give cultural context as well as specific written and oral sources. Full-page black-and-white pen and ink drawings and spot art effectively evoke the spooky but concrete creepiness of the tales. . . . A successful, accessible collection." Bull Cent Child Books

Includes bibliographical references

Brusca, María Cristina

When jaguars ate the moon and other stories about animals and plants of the Americas; retold by María Cristina Brusca and Tona Wilson; illustrated by María Cristina Brusca. Holt & Co. 1995 unp il $16.95 (2-4) **398.2**

1. Native Americans—Folklore 2. Animals—Fiction

ISBN 0-8050-2797-1 LC 93-50197

"This alphabetically arranged anthology features stories based on the folklore of North and South American native cultures. A typical page has a wide, horizontal border with a letter in large type and several small pictures of animals and plants whose names begin with that letter." Booklist

"The watercolor and ink paintings are charming and interesting, and are a perfect match for the tales. The retellings are short, but each makes a complete story, and any of them would be enjoyed by listeners." SLJ

Includes bibliographical references

Bryan, Ashley, 1923-

Ashley Bryan's African tales, uh-huh; retold and illustrated by Ashley Bryan. Atheneum Bks. for Young Readers 1998 198p il $22 (4-6) **398.2**

1. Folklore—Africa

ISBN 0-689-82076-3 LC 97-77743

This volume combines three previously published titles: The ox of the wonderful horns and other African folktales (1971), Beat the story-drum, pum-pum (1980), Lion and the ostrich chicks and other African folktales (1986)

This collection of African folktales is "told with Bryan's distinctive rhythmic word patterns and filled with humor, life lessons, and the antics of trickster Ananse. . . . Quality reproductions of the original woodcuts enrich this handsome volume." Horn Book Guide

The story of Lightning & Thunder. Atheneum Pubs. 1993 unp il $16; pa $5.99 (3-5) **398.2**

1. Folklore—Africa

ISBN 0-689-31836-7; 0-689-82450-5 (pa)

LC 92-40509

"A Jean Karl book"

In this retelling of a West African tale, Ma Sheep Thunder and her impetuous son Ram Lightning are forced to leave their home on Earth because of the trouble Ram causes

"Bryan tells the story . . . with playful, rhythmic prose that rhymes intermittently and begs to be read aloud. . . . Bryan's vibrant watercolors are delightful." SLJ

Byrd, Robert, 1942-

Finn MacCoul and his fearless wife; a giant of a tale from Ireland; retold and illustrated by Robert Byrd. Dutton Children's Bks. 1999 unp il $16.99 (k-3) **398.2**

1. Finn MacCumhaill, 3rd cent.—Fiction 2. Folklore—Ireland 3. Giants—Fiction

ISBN 0-525-45971-5 LC 98-26132

With the help of his brave and clever wife, Finn MacCoul bests the fearsome giant, Cucullin

"Cartoonish figures almost burst out of the illustrations, playing up the humor in this tall tale." Horn Book Guide

Caduto, Michael J.

Keepers of the night; Native American stories and nocturnal activities for children; [by] Michael J. Caduto and Joseph Bruchac; story illustrations by David Kanietakeron Fadden; chapter illustrations by Jo Levasseur and Carol Wood; foreword by Merlin D. Tuttle. Fulcrum 1994 146p il pa $15.95 **398.2**

1. Native Americans—Folklore 2. Nature study 3. Night—Fiction

ISBN 1-55591-177-3 LC 94-2602

Caduto, Michael J.—*Continued*

Also available Keepers of the Earth (1988); Keepers of the animals (1991) and Keepers of life (1994)

"Caduto and Bruchac use stories from various American Indian tribes as the basis for activities and lessons about the nighttime world. Written as a guide for teachers, outdoor education leaders, and other adults working with children in a nature setting, the guide gives detailed instructions for preparing, conducting, and evaluating a variety of activities that focus on the nocturnal habits of animals, on astronomy and nighttime weather, and on campfire activities, such as storytelling, dances, and games." Booklist

"The well-written chapters include discussions with illuminating scientific information." Sci Books Films

Includes glossary and bibliographical references

Carpenter, Frances

Tales of a Chinese grandmother; illustrated by Malthé Hasselriis. Tuttle 1973 261p pa $8.95 (4 and up)   **398.2**

1. Folklore—China 2. Fairy tales
ISBN 0-8048-1042-7

Also available in hardcover from Amereon

"Tut books"

First published 1937 by Doubleday

"Thirty Chinese folk stories and legends from various sources are retold with the full flavor of the Orient. . . . They are told to a boy and girl by their grandmother on occasions in their daily life which suggest a story. Useful for storytelling." Booklist

"Phrased with grace and charm, the stories are revelatory of Chinese beliefs in years past, and of customs and home life. Drawings in color and black and white." N Y Libr

Casanova, Mary

The hunter; a Chinese folktale; retold by Mary Casanova; illustrations by Ed Young. Atheneum Bks. for Young Readers 2000 unp il $16.95 (k-3)   **398.2**

1. Folklore—China
ISBN 0-689-82906-X   LC 99-32166

After learning to understand the language of animals, Hai Li Bu the hunter sacrifices himself to save his village

Casanova "tells the tale in a dignified yet moving way that is complemented by the stark artwork. Arid-looking, dun-colored paper is the background for Young's masterful brush strokes." Booklist

Chang, Margaret Scrogin

The beggar's magic; a Chinese tale; retold by Margaret & Raymond Chang; illustrated by David Johnson. Margaret K. McElderry Bks. 1997 unp il $16 (2-4)   **398.2**

1. Folklore—China
ISBN 0-689-81340-6   LC 96-20865

"Fu Nan and his friends befriend an old man who comes to their village. . . . Soon they notice that he can work miracles. His most wondrous feat is to punish a rich and covetous farmer by planting a fast-growing pear tree whose fruit he shares with all the villagers. . . . The prose is simple and elegant with just the right elaboration and matter-of-fact tone to put the tale across convincingly. Johnson's watercolor-and-ink illustrations, in warm brown and orange pastels, lovingly evoke the dustiness of much of rural Imperial China." SLJ

Da Wei's treasure; a Chinese tale; retold by Margaret and Raymond Chang; illustrated by Lori McElrath-Eslick. Margaret K. McElderry Bks. 1999 unp il $16 (k-3)   **398.2**

1. Folklore—China
ISBN 0-689-81835-1   LC 97-26848

In this retelling of a traditional Chinese tale, a boy finds a treasure in an unexpected place

"The narrative is long and involved but never ceases to be intriguing and it rings emotionally true. . . . The paintings, done with thick brush strokes, carry the mood of the story." SLJ

Christmas fairy tales; selected by Neil Philip; illustrated by Isabelle Brent. Viking 1996 140p il $19.99 (4-6)   **398.2**

1. Fairy tales 2. Christmas—Fiction
ISBN 0-670-86805-1   LC 95-62373

"An Albion book"

"Tales both familiar ('The Nutcracker' by E.T.A. Hoffman, 'Schnitzle, Schnotzle, and Schnootzle' by Ruth Sawyer) and less so ('The Last Dream of the Old Oak Tree' by Hans Christian Andersen) are at home on these elegantly edged pages. . . . Brent's trademark rich, delicate watercolors accented with touches of gold paint . . . exude an old-world feel that is perfectly suited to the classic storytelling tradition upheld by this collection." Publ Wkly

The **Classic** fairy tales; [edited by] Iona and Peter Opie. Oxford Univ. Press 1974 336p il $35; pa $15.95   **398.2**

1. Fairy tales
ISBN 0-19-211559-6; 0-19-520219-8 (pa)

This book "contains the earliest published English texts of the tales selected, together with notes on the history and analogues of the stories." Oxford Companion to Child Lit

"Helpful indexing, bibliography, list of sources of illustrations." Choice

Climo, Shirley, 1928-

The Egyptian Cinderella; illustrated by Ruth Heller. Crowell 1989 unp il $15.95; pa $5.95 (k-3)   **398.2**

1. Folklore—Egypt 2. Fairy tales
ISBN 0-690-04822-X; 0-06-443279-3 (pa)
LC 88-37547

In this version of Cinderella set in Egypt in the sixth century B.C., Rhodopes, a slave girl, eventually comes to be chosen by the Pharaoh to be his queen

"The beauty of the language is set off to perfection by Heller's arresting full-color illustrations." SLJ

The **Korean** Cinderella; illustrated by Ruth Heller. HarperCollins Pubs. 1993 unp il $15.95; pa $6.95 (k-3)   **398.2**

1. Folklore—Korea 2. Fairy tales
ISBN 0-06-020432-X; 0-06-443397-8 (pa)
LC 91-23268

Climo, Shirley, 1928-—*Continued*

In this version of Cinderella set in ancient Korea, Pear Blossom, a stepchild, eventually comes to be chosen by the magistrate to be his wife

"Heller's paintings are exotically lush and colorful as well as engaging. Climo includes an explanatory note about Cinderella variants (the Korean version in particular), and Heller explains the decorations, costumes, and settings she used in the illustrations. An agreeable retelling of the Cinderella story." Booklist

Magic & mischief; tales from Cornwall; retold by Shirley Climo; illustrated by Anthony Bacon Venti. Clarion Bks. 1999 127p il $17 (4 and up)
398.2
1. Folklore—Great Britain
ISBN 0-395-86968-4   LC 97-34091
"Ten tales of Cornwall featuring supernatural beings (giants, piskies, spriggans, knackers, changelings, etc.) are accompanied by explanatory bits of traditional lore (how to please piskies, ways to scare spriggans, etc.) in this handsomely presented volume. . . . Climo's style is polished and literary, and her selection of tales to retell from detailed sources leans toward the humorous happy ending with just the occasional creepy shiver." Bull Cent Child Books

Coburn, Jewell Reinhart

Domitila; a Cinderella tale from the Mexican tradition; adapted by Jewell Reinhart Coburn; illustrated by Connie McLennan. Shen's Bks. 2000 unp il $16.95 (2-4)   **398.2**
1. Folklore—Mexico
ISBN 1-88500-813-9   LC 99-56173
By following her mother's admonition to perform every task with care and love, a poor young Mexican girl wins the devotion of the governor's son

"The full-page oil-on-cavas illustrations are bright, sumptuous, and visually enticing. The text is bordered by proverbs rendered in both Spanish and English. Well-written and strongly illustrated." SLJ

Cohen, Caron Lee

The mud pony; a traditional Skidi Pawnee tale retold by Caron Lee Cohen; illustrated by Shonto Begay. Scholastic 1988 unp il hardcover o.p. paperback available $4.99 (k-3)   **398.2**
1. Pawnee Indians—Folklore 2. Horses—Fiction
ISBN 0-590-41526-3 (pa)   LC 87-23451
A poor boy becomes a powerful leader when Mother Earth turns his mud pony into a real one, but after the pony turns back to mud, he must find his own strength

"The text is powerful because it is spare and unadorned. It is extended well by the softly toned, full-color, impressionistic pictures." Helbig. This land is our land

Cole, Joanna

Bony-Legs; pictures by Dirk Zimmer. Four Winds Press 1983 unp il o.p.; Scholastic paperback available $3.99 (k-3)   **398.2**
1. Folklore—Russia 2. Fairy tales
ISBN 0-590-40516-0 (pa)   LC 82-7424

"Based on the tale 'Baba-Yaga' in Russian fairy tales by Aleksandr Afanas'ev." Verso of title page

When a terrible witch vows to eat her for supper, a little girl escapes with the help of a mirror and comb given to her by the witch's cat and dog

"The rich text leaves out some of the grisly details of the original without castrating the story, and it is matched by clear yet densely lined drawings that borrow some from Ivan Bilibin's earlier illustrations, yet add amusing detail and fine design and layout of their own." SLJ

Cooper, Susan, 1935-

The silver cow: a Welsh tale; retold by Susan Cooper; illustrated by Warwick Hutton. Atheneum Pubs. 1983 unp il hardcover o.p. paperback available $5.99 (1-4)   **398.2**
1. Folklore—Wales 2. Cattle—Fiction
ISBN 0-689-71512-9 (pa)   LC 82-13928
"A Margaret K. McElderry book"
A young Welsh boy is rewarded for his beautiful harp playing with a silver cow, the gift of the magic people living in the lake. The cow makes his family rich but when his father becomes greedy the magic people take their revenge

"A lilting text, complemented by luminous watercolor illustrations, captures the enchantment inherent in a traditional tale explaining the genesis of the water lilies fringing Llyn Barfog, 'the bearded lake,' set high in the Welsh hills." Horn Book

Tam Lin; retold by Susan Cooper; illustrated by Warwick Hutton. Margaret K. McElderry Bks. 1991 unp il $14.95 (1-4)   **398.2**
1. Folklore—Scotland 2. Fairy tales
ISBN 0-689-50505-1   LC 90-5571
A retelling of the old Scottish ballad in which a young girl rescues the human knight Tam Lin from his bondage to the Elfin Queen

"Susan Cooper's prose rendering, based on several versions, is a beautifully paced literary fairy tale, told and pictured with precision and restraint. . . . Warwick Hutton is a masterful watercolorist, and his paintings literally and figuratively illuminate the story of faithfulness, heroism, and love. Close-ups lend immediacy to the dramatic action, and panoramic scenes, often with the use of chiaroscuro, convey emotion and establish atmosphere—idyllic, eerie, fearful, and ultimately triumphant." Horn Book

Courlander, Harold, 1908-1996

Cow-tail switch, and other West African stories; [by] Harold Courlander and George Herzog; drawings by Madye Lee Chastain. Holt & Co. 1947 143p il hardcover o.p. paperback available $9.95 (4-6)   **398.2**
1. Folklore—West Africa 2. Ashanti (African people)—Folklore
ISBN 0-80500298-7 (pa)
A Newbery Medal honor book, 1948
"The seventeen stories mostly gathered in the Ashanti country, are fresh to collections and are told with humor and originality. Their themes, chosen with discrimination, are frequently primitive explanations of the origin of folk sayings and customs, or show examples of animal trickery and ingenuity." Horn Book

Craft, Charlotte

King Midas and the golden touch; as told by Charlotte Craft; illustrated by K.Y. Craft. Morrow 1999 32p il $16   **398.2**

1. Midas (Legendary character)

ISBN 0-688-13165-4   LC 98-24035

A king finds himself bitterly regretting the consequences of his wish that everything he touches would turn to gold

"This sophisticated retelling, set in the Middle Ages, places King Midas in a sumptuous palace. . . . The elaborate oil-over-watercolor illustrations show the wondrous, tragic effects of the golden touch." Horn Book Guide

Creswick, Paul, 1866-1947

Robin Hood; illustrated by N.C. Wyeth. Scribner 1984 362p il $28 (5 and up)   **398.2**

1. Robin Hood (Legendary character)

ISBN 0-684-18162-2   LC 84-10662

A reissue of a title first published 1917 by McKay

Recounts the life and adventures of Robin Hood, who, with his band of followers, lived as an outlaw in Sherwood Forest dedicated to fight against tyranny

Cruz, Alejandro

The woman who outshone the sun; the legend of Lucia Zenteno; from a poem by Alejandro Cruz Martinez; pictures by Fernando Olivera; story by Rosalma Zubizarreta, Harriet Rohmer, David Schecter. Children's Bk. Press 1991 30p $14.95; pa $7.95 (k-3)   **398.2**

1. Zapotec Indians—Folklore 2. Bilingual books—English-Spanish

ISBN 0-89239-101-4; 0-89239-126-X (pa)

LC 91-16646

Title page and text in English and Spanish

Retells the Zapotec legend of Lucia Zenteno, a beautiful woman with magical powers who is exiled from a mountain village and takes its water away in punishment

This "Hispanic folktale is skillfully told, and is solid and colorfully steeped with imagery of the earth and sky. Both the Spanish and English read gracefully, and the poetic use of language suits the story well for telling. The illustrations have a sense of volume that is reminiscent of Orozco." SLJ

Curry, Jane Louise, 1932-

Back in the beforetime; tales of the California Indians; retold by Jane Louise Curry; illustrated by James Watts. Margaret K. McElderry Bks. 1987 134p il $16 (4-6)   **398.2**

1. Native Americans—Folklore 2. Coyote (Legendary character)

ISBN 0-689-50410-1   LC 86-21339

A retelling of twenty-two legends about the creation of the world from a variety of California Indian tribes

"The predominantly humorous tone of the stories is highlighted by the black-and-white illustrations, each with its geometrically patterned border. Curry's rhythmic prose lends itself well to storytelling or reading aloud." SLJ

Turtle Island: tales of the Algonquian nations; illustrated by James Watts. Margaret K. McElderry Bks. 1999 145p il $17 (4-6)   **398.2**

1. Algonquian Indians—Folklore

ISBN 0-689-82233-2   LC 98-20393

A collection of twenty-seven tales from the different tribes that are part of the Algonquian peoples who lived from the Middle Atlantic States up through eastern Canada

"Every story is written in simple, easily flowing language that's perfect for telling." SLJ

Includes bibliographical references

Dabcovich, Lydia, 1935-

The polar bear son; an Inuit tale; retold and illustrated by Lydia Dabcovich. Clarion Bks. 1997 37p il $16; pa $5.95 (k-3)   **398.2**

1. Inuit—Folklore 2. Polar bear—Fiction

ISBN 0-395-72766-9; 0-395-97567-0 (pa)

LC 96-4780

An old woman adopts and raises a polar bear cub which grows up and provides for her even after she has had to send it away to save it from the jealous men of the village

"Illustrated in muted pastel colors, the pictures capture this stark, yet beautiful, winter world." SLJ

Daly, Jude

Fair, Brown & Trembling; an Irish Cinderella story. Farrar, Straus & Giroux 2000 unp il $16 (k-3)   **398.2**

1. Fairy tales 2. Folklore—Ireland

ISBN 0-374-32247-3   LC 99-34315

This version of the Cinderella story, in which a young girl overcomes the wickedness of her older sisters to become the bride of a prince, is based on a Irish folktale

This offers "bright illustrations in folk-art style. . . . The fairy godmother is an old henwife, who provides Trembling with splendid clothes and a milk-white horse to carry her to church—not the palace ball. . . . In a nice variation, there are many princes; they fight over Trembling, and the best one wins." Booklist

Daly, Niki, 1946-

Why the Sun & Moon live in the sky. Lothrop, Lee & Shepard Bks. 1995 unp il $15 (k-3) **398.2**

1. Folklore—Nigeria 2. Sun—Fiction 3. Moon—Fiction

ISBN 0-688-13331-2   LC 93-47304

"Sun, an adventurous roamer, lives on earth with Moon, a domestic homebody. Sun invites Sea and all her children to visit, but Sea floods the house, causing great distress for Moon. The flooding forces Sun and Moon into the sky, where they have been to this day." Booklist

"Daly's witty illustrations immerse this Nigerian tale in offbeat charm. His sophisticated watercolors showcase sketchy images borrowed from Renaissance motifs." Publ Wkly

Dayrell, Elphinstone, 1869-1917

Why the Sun and the Moon live in the sky; an African folktale; illustrated by Blair Lent. Houghton Mifflin 1968 26p il $16; pa $6.95 (k-3)
398.2
1. Folklore—Nigeria 2. Sun—Fiction 3. Moon—Fiction
ISBN 0-395-29609-9; 0-395-53963-3 (pa)
A Caldecott Medal honor book, 1969
First told by the author in his book: Folk stories from Southern Nigeria, West Africa, published 1910 in England
"When the Sun and the Moon extended an invitation to Water and his people to visit their earthly home, they underestimated the number of Water's followers and thus were forced to seek a habitation in the sky." SLJ
"The beautifully detailed and stylized art work is based on African sources; the artist uses cool colors for the water, a pale blue-grey for the moon, and shades of gold and white for the sun." Sutherland. The Best in Child Books

De Paola, Tomie, 1934-

Christopher, the holy giant. Holiday House 1994 unp il $16.95; pa $6.95 (k-3)
398.2
1. Christopher, Saint, 3rd cent.?
ISBN 0-8234-0862-0; 0-8234-1169-9 (pa)
LC 90-49926
As Reprobus carries a child across a river one stormy night, the boy gets heavier and heavier until Reprobus feels he is carrying the world on his shoulders—thus goes the legend of the name Christ-bearer, or Christopher
"DePaola's prose is simple and eloquent, and his expressive folk art style, here rendered in the intense but muted shades of the desert, is perfectly attuned to the legend's reverent tone." Publ Wkly

The clown of God; an old story; told and illustrated by Tomie de Paola. Harcourt Brace Jovanovich 1978 unp il $16; pa $7 (k-3) **398.2**
1. Legends 2. Miracles—Fiction 3. Christmas—Fiction
ISBN 0-15-219175-5; 0-15-618192-4 (pa)
LC 78-3845
"An orphan whose juggling skill led him to a career as a traveling entertainer has grown old and clumsy and returns as a hungry beggar to his birthplace. On Christmas Eve in the monastery church a miracle occurs as he summons his last strength to make his only possible offering
"Mr. de Paola has written the tale with love, tenderness, and joy. He has executed authentic Renaissance illustrations that are magnificent in design and beauty." Child Book Rev Serv

Jamie O'Rourke and the big potato; an Irish folktale; retold and illustrated by Tomie dePaola. Putnam 1992 unp il $16.99; pa $5.99 (k-3) **398.2**
1. Folklore—Ireland
ISBN 0-399-22257-X; 0-698-11603-8 (pa)
LC 91-10626
The laziest man in all of Ireland catches a leprechaun, who offers a potato seed instead of a pot of gold for his freedom

"Illustrated in dePaola's signature style, this has an inviting look. Buoyant watercolors are framed by thin orange borders, but the potato simply can't be contained and bulges beyond the boundaries, graphic proof of its enormous size, an engaging read-aloud choice for Saint Patrick's Day." Booklist

The legend of Old Befana; an Italian Christmas story; retold and illustrated by Tomie de Paola. Harcourt Brace Jovanovich 1980 unp il lib bdg $16; pa $6 (k-3) **398.2**
1. Befana (Legendary character) 2. Folklore—Italy 3. Christmas—Fiction
ISBN 0-15-243816-5 (lib bdg); 0-15-243817-3 (pa)
LC 80-12293
Because Befana's household chores kept her from finding the Baby King, she searches to this day, leaving gifts for children on the Feast of the Three Kings
This version of the Italian legend "is attractively designed with rich colors and decorative detail. The tale is told in simple but effective language." SLJ

The legend of the Indian paintbrush; retold and illustrated by Tomie dePaola. Putnam 1988 unp il lib bdg $16.99; pa $6.99 (k-3) **398.2**
1. Native Americans—Folklore
ISBN 0-399-21534-4 (lib bdg); 0-399-21777-0 (pa)
LC 87-20160
A "folktale of the Plains Indians that reveals how the Indian Paintbrush, the state flower of Wyoming, first bloomed. An Indian boy's dream to recreate the colors of the sunset comes true when he discovers paintbrushes filled with the colors he needs. A voice in the night had promised him this because he had shared his artistic talent with his people." Child Book Rev Serv
"The native American motifs are rendered simply and authentically; the night sky and glorious sunset spreads are truly beautiful with line, color, and form perfectly balanced to capture the text." Horn Book

The legend of the poinsettia; retold and illustrated by Tomie de Paola. Putnam 1994 unp il $16.99 (k-3) **398.2**
1. Folklore—Mexico 2. Flowers—Fiction 3. Christmas—Fiction
ISBN 0-399-21692-8
LC 92-20459
When Lucida is unable to finish her gift for the Baby Jesus in time for the Christmas procession, a miracle enables her to offer the beautiful flower we now call the poinsettia
"dePaola establishes a sense of place in his use of glowing colors and architectural details as he retells another legend of miraculous transcendence." Horn Book

Tony's bread: an Italian folktale. Putnam 1989 unp il hardcover o.p. paperback available $5.99 (k-3) **398.2**
1. Folklore—Italy
ISBN 0-689-11371-3 (pa)
LC 88-7687
"A Whitebird book"
"This tale captures the flavor of an Italian folk tale with both textual and visual humor. The story of Angelo—a rich, young nobleman from Milan who attempts to win the hand of his true love, the beautiful daughter of Tony the baker—explains the origin of *panettone*, the delicious Milanese Christmas bread made with eggs, raisins, and candied fruit. . . . The pictures and story combine to make a delectable Christmas treat." Horn Book

Delacre, Lulu, 1957-

Golden tales; myths, legends, and folktales from Latin America; [retold by] Lulu Delacre. Scholastic 1996 73p $17.95 (4 and up)   **398.2**
1. Folklore—Latin America 2. Native Americans—Folklore
ISBN 0-590-48186-X   LC 94-36724

This includes 12 "stories from four native cultures (Taino, Zapotec, Muisca, and Quechua), including *pourquio* tales, legends of the conquistadores, and folktales from before and after the age of Columbus. . . . [The author's] . . . retellings are done in a clear and confident voice and are accompanied by her robust, colorful oil paintings. . . . This impressively presented and referenced collection will inspire readers and tellers alike." Booklist

Includes bibliographical references

Demi, 1942-

The donkey and the rock. Holt & Co. 1999 unp il $16.95 (k-3)   **398.2**
1. Folklore—Tibet (China)
ISBN 0-8050-5959-8   LC 98-14743

In this version of a tale with many Asian variations, a wise king, who rules a town full of foolish people in the mountains of Tibet, puts a donkey and a rock on trial to settle the dispute between two honest men

"The story is told with Demi's usual deft humor, and the illustrations, reminiscent of Chinese paper cut-outs, are aptly supplemented by Tibetan details." Horn Book Guide

The empty pot. Holt & Co. 1990 unp il $16.95; pa $6.95 (k-3)   **398.2**
1. Folklore—China
ISBN 0-8050-1217-6; 0-8050-4900-2 (pa)
LC 89-39062

"Ping is a Chinese boy with an emerald green thumb; he can make anything grow 'as if by magic.' One day the Emperor announces that he needs a successor. . . . He gives each child one seed, and the one who grows the best flower will take over after him. . . . On the day of the competition, [Ping] is the only child with an empty pot; all the others bring lush plants. But the Emperor has tricked everyone by distributing cooked seeds, unable to grow; and Ping, with his empty pot, is the only honest gardener—and the winner." Publ Wkly

"This simple story with its clear moral is illustrated with beautiful paintings. . . . A beautifully crafted book that will be enjoyed as much for the richness of its illustrations as for the simplicity of its story." SLJ

The greatest treasure. Scholastic 1998 unp il $16.95 (k-3)   **398.2**
1. Folklore—China
ISBN 0-590-31339-8   LC 97-10825

In this traditional Chinese tale, a poor man receives a treasure of gold and discovers the true value of simple pleasures

"Demi's pictures, on marbled paper backgrounds, with the distinct line and color of Chinese artwork, are in perfect harmony with the story, which is at once intricate and simple." Booklist

One grain of rice; a mathematical folktale. Scholastic 1997 unp il $19.95 (2-4)   **398.2**
1. Folklore—India
ISBN 0-590-93998-X   LC 96-7002

"A resourceful village girl outsmarts a greedy raja, turning a reward of one grain of rice into a feast for a hungry nation. Delicate paintings emblazoned with touches of gold give this Indian folktale an exotic air." SLJ

Diane Goode's book of scary stories & songs. Dutton Children's Bks. 1994 64p il music $15.99; pa $6.99 (2-5)   **398.2**
1. Ghost stories 2. Folklore 3. Folk songs
ISBN 0-525-45175-7; 0-14-056432-2 (pa)
LC 93-32610

Selections collected by Lucia Monfried

This "anthology of mildly scary stories, songs, and verse includes folktales from English and American (including Native American and African American) sources. Varied in tone and subject, the selections are consistently entertaining. Appealing, full-color illustrations, from the weird to the wonderful, appear throughout the book, lending more of a sense of humor than a sense of menace." Booklist

Includes bibliographical references

Early, Margaret, 1951-

William Tell; retold and illustrated by Margaret Early. Abrams 1991 unp il $17.95   **398.2**
1. Tell, William 2. Legends—Switzerland
ISBN 0-8109-3854-5

This is a retelling of the legend of the Swiss archer who saved his country from the oppressive Austrian emperor Gessler

"Early's illustrations, lavishly embellished with gold, reflect the medieval period in which the events took place. A unique border decorates each page, framing the elaborate paintings with elegant repetitive designs, lending a fittingly mannered feeling to the art. Even the skies, the water, and the trees are made up of minutely executed patterns. A welcome new retelling that makes this inspiring story of freedom accessible to a new generation of young people." Horn Book

Echewa, T. Obinkaram

The magic tree; a folktale from Nigeria; illustrated by E.B. Lewis. Morrow 1999 unp il $16; lib bdg $15.89 (k-3)   **398.2**
1. Folklore—Nigeria 2. Orphans—Fiction
ISBN 0-688-16231-2; 0-688-16232-0 (lib bdg)
LC 91-19770

Mbi, an orphan boy, is constantly asked to "do this" and "do that" by his many unkind relatives until a special tree grows, just for him

"Echewa's storytelling is direct and lively, and Lewis' beautiful watercolors set the action in a contemporary village." Booklist

Egielski, Richard

The gingerbread boy. HarperCollins Pubs. 1997 unp il $15.95; pa $5.95 (k-3)   **398.2**
1. Folklore 2. New York (N.Y.)—Fiction
ISBN 0-06-026030-0; 0-06-443708-6 (pa)
LC 95-50026

Egielski, Richard—*Continued*

"A Laura Geringer book"

The "Gingerbread Boy pops out of an oven in an apartment somewhere in lower Manhattan. As he runs down the New York City streets, the arrogant little cookie is chased by his family, a rat, construction workers, subway musicians, and a mounted policeman." Horn Book

"Egielski's retelling is straightforward and retains the traditional refrain: 'Run run run as fast as you can'—it sounds just right, making a satisfying modern variation. The illustrations . . . adroitly evoke the city setting while giving a solid three-dimensionality and unique individuality to the Gingerbread Boy and his pursuers." SLJ

Ehlert, Lois, 1934-

Cuckoo. Cucú; a Mexican folktale; translated into Spanish by Gloria de Aragón Andújar. Harcourt Brace & Co. 1997 unp il $16; pa $7 (k-3) **398.2**

1. Mayas—Folklore 2. Folklore—Mexico 3. Bilingual books—English-Spanish

ISBN 0-15-200274-X; 0-15-202428-X (pa)

LC 95-39560

A traditional Mayan tale which reveals how the cuckoo lost her beautiful feathers

"This tale, charmingly told in both English and Spanish, is boldly illustrated with large, brightly colored, cutpaper pictures. Inspired by folk art and crafts, the images evoke the tin work and cutout fiesta banners of Mexico." SLJ

Moon rope. Un lazo a la luna; a Peruvian folktale; translated into Spanish by Amy Prince. Harcourt Brace Jovanovich 1992 unp il $17 (k-3) **398.2**

1. Folklore—Peru 2. Moon—Fiction 3. Bilingual books—English-Spanish

ISBN 0-15-255343-6 LC 91-36438

An adaptation of the Peruvian folktale in which Fox and Mole try to climb to the moon on a rope woven of grass

"Designed as a bilingual book from title page to the concluding double-page spread, this handsome addition to material for multicultural education impels young audiences to try reading the story in both languages. . . . The text moves smoothly, just right for reading aloud; the pictures are dramatic abstractions that glow like jewels against richly toned, calendared pages." Horn Book

Emberley, Rebecca

Three cool kids. Little, Brown 1995 unp il lib bdg $15.95 (k-3) **398.2**

1. Folklore 2. Goats—Fiction

ISBN 0-316-23666-7 LC 93-40113

"In this modernized urban version of the 'Three Billy Goats Gruff,' Big, Little and Middle Kid want to move to 'greener pastures' in a different vacant lot, but must first cross a sewer grating where a ferocious rat lives." Child Book Rev Serv

"Large, crisp collages made from paper, corrugated cardboard, and natural objects bring the goats to vibrant life and create the perfect backdrop for the action. . . . The text is witty, the illustrations whimsical, and the combination utterly charming." SLJ

Ernst, Lisa Campbell, 1957-

Little Red Riding Hood: a newfangled prairie tale. Simon & Schuster Bks. for Young Readers 1995 unp il $16; pa $5.99 (k-3) **398.2**

1. Folklore 2. Wolves—Fiction

ISBN 0-689-80145-9; 0-689-82191-3 (pa)

LC 94-45723

In this "contemporary rendering of the old tale, Little Red Riding Hood wears a hooded sweatshirt and rides her bicycle, while Grandma is a robust farmer who turns the tables on the wolf. Ernst's inventive plot, enjoyable characters, and characteristic cartoon-style drawings demonstrate her mastery of the picture-book form." Horn Book Guide

Esbensen, Barbara Juster

The star maiden: an Ojibway tale; retold by Barbara Juster Esbensen; illustrated by Helen K. Davie. Little, Brown 1988 unp il hardcover o.p. paperback available $5.95 (k-3) **398.2**

1. Ojibwa Indians—Folklore

ISBN 0-316-24955-6 (pa) LC 87-3247

"Based on an Ojibway or Chippewa Native American legend, this tells why there are water lilies. It is a lovely retelling which keeps the dignity and wonder associated with Native American attitudes towards nature. The watercolor illustrations are remarkable for their authentic details and the borders which are based on Ojibway pattern. This is a must for units on American Indians." Child Book Rev Serv

Fang, Linda

The Ch'i-lin purse; a collection of ancient Chinese stories; retold by Linda Fang; pictures by Jeanne M. Lee. Farrar, Straus & Giroux 1994 127p il $16; pa $5.95 (5 and up) **398.2**

1. Folklore—China

ISBN 0-374-31241-9; 0-374-41189-1 (pa)

LC 94-9909

A collection of "Chinese stories derived from the history of the Warring States Period (770-221 B.C.E.) and from operatic versions of popular tales. Retellings are vivid, lively, and read aloud well. Many have a moral, and all are entertaining. . . . The black-and-white illustrations—one per selection—are graceful, depicting widely different epochs with amazing accuracy." SLJ

Includes glossary and bibliographical references

Fischer, Hans, 1909-1958

Puss in boots; a fairy tale by Charles Perrault; retold and supplemented with necessary explanations and illustrations by Hans Fischer; translated by Anthea Bell; afterword by Hans ten Doornkaat. North-South Bks. 1996 unp il lib bdg $15.88 (k-3) **398.2**

1. Fairy tales 2. Folklore—France

ISBN 1-55858-643-1 LC 96-15963

A reissue of the title first published 1959 by Harcourt, Brace & Co.

A clever cat helps his poor master win fame, fortune, and the hand of a beautiful princess

"Fischer's whimsical depiction of the enterprising cat should delight children and cat lovers young and old." Booklist

Fisher, Leonard Everett, 1924-

William Tell. Farrar, Straus & Giroux 1996 unp
il $16 (k-3)   **398.2**
  1. Tell, William 2. Legends—Switzerland
ISBN 0-374-38436-3   LC 95-13861
Recounts how the legendary Swiss folk hero was
forced to shoot an apple from his son's head by the tyrannical Austrian governor Gessler
"Fisher's richly textured paintings bring a distinctive
sense of drama to this traditional tale. He uses light and
varying perspectives to highlight the human dimensions
of the story, while vivid colors underscore the emotional
tensions and move the exciting plot to its swift denouement." SLJ

Forest, Heather

The baker's dozen; a colonial American tale;
retold by Heather Forest; illustrated by Susan
Gaber. Harcourt Brace Jovanovich 1988 unp il
hardcover o.p. paperback available $6 (k-3) **398.2**
  1. Folklore—United States
ISBN 0-15-205687-4 (pa)   LC 87-17103
"Gulliver books"
"A seventeenth-century legend describes the rise and
fall of a prosperous baker whose famous St. Nicholas
cookies bring him a booming business until he begins to
cheat his customers. . . . A mysterious old woman
curses him for his greed, and thereafter everything goes
wrong. Only on her return visit, when he adds an extra
cookie to her dozen, does good fortune return." Bull
Cent Child Books
"Gaber's elegant watercolors are vivid and stylized,
showing a dusted palette of burgundies with charcoal and
burnished oranges. This is a fine explanation of a long-
standing custom, and Forest backs it up with an author's
note on the facts." Publ Wkly

The woman who flummoxed the fairies; an old
tale from Scotland; retold by Heather Forest;
illustrated by Susan Gaber. Harcourt Brace
Jovanovich 1990 unp il hardcover o.p. paperback
available $5 (k-3)   **398.2**
  1. Folklore—Scotland 2. Cake—Fiction
ISBN 0-15-201275-3 (pa)   LC 88-28448
"Gulliver books"
Asked to make a cake for the fairies, a clever
bakerwoman must figure out a way to prevent the fairies
from wanting to keep her with them always to bake her
delicious cakes
"While depicting a strong, resourceful heroine, Forest's graceful retelling perfectly captures the story's
fairy-tale flavor. Using deep tones of violet, blue and
green, Gaber's haunting paintings range from the wonderfully eerie to the comfortably reassuring." Publ Wkly

Fox, Paula

Amzat and his brothers: three Italian tales;
remembered by Floriano Vecchi and retold by
Paula Fox; illustrations by Emily McCully.
Orchard Bks. 1993 67p il $16.95 (3-5)   **398.2**
  1. Folklore—Italy
ISBN 0-531-05462-4   LC 92-19494
Also available in paperback from Dell

"In the first tale, clever Amzat and his wife foil his
greedy brothers' schemes to cheat him out of his property. The second story is a variation of 'The Bremen Town
Musicians.' . . . And in the final story, this one in the
noodlehead tradition, the author introduces Olimpia and
her simpleton son Cucol. . . . Paula Fox has retained the
darker elements that are as much a part of folktales in
their original forms as the humor. . . . Emily McCully's
drawings, with their heavy deep brown lines and animated characters, pick up both aspects of these intriguing
tales." Horn Book

Fritz, Jean

Brendan the Navigator; a history mystery about
the discovery of America; illustrated by Enrico
Arno. Coward, McCann & Geoghegan 1979 31p il
$15.99; pa $5.99 (3-5)   **398.2**
  1. Brendan, Saint, the Voyager, ca. 483-577 2. America—Exploration
ISBN 0-698-20473-5; 0-698-11759-X (pa)
                LC 78-13247
Recounts St. Brendan's life and voyage to North
America long before the Vikings arrived
"Jean Fritz's narrative is beautifully cadenced, lively
and wry. Her historical postscript is all right, too, and the
two-color illustrations are appropriately convoluted and
Celtic." N Y Times Book Rev

Galdone, Joanna

The tailypo; a ghost story; told by Joanna
Galdone; illustrated by Paul Galdone. Clarion Bks.
1984 unp il hardcover o.p. paperback available
$6.95 (k-3)   **398.2**
  1. Folklore—United States
ISBN 0-395-30084-3 (pa)   LC 77-23289
Also available with Audiobook
First published by Seabury Press
"An old man lives in the Tennessee backwoods with
his three hunting dogs, Uno, Ino and Cumptico-Calico.
. . . The old man sees an odd animal squeezing through
a crack in his cabin and grabs it. All he gets is its tail
but he makes a snack of that and gets into bed with a
satisfied appetite. But the dismembered [creature] wants
its tail back. When he haunts the old man with his
keening, 'Tailypo, tailypo, all I want is my tailypo' in
vain, he settles for vengeance instead." Publ Wkly
"The energetic postures of the old man and his dogs
form a strong accompaniment to the clean, vigorous storytelling, and the subtly underplayed color in the paintings not only suggests the ghostliness of the story but is
pleasing in itself." Horn Book

Galdone, Paul, 1914-1986

The elves and the shoemaker; retold and
illustrated by Paul Galdone. Clarion Bks. 1984 unp
il hardcover o.p. paperback available $6.95 (k-2)
               398.2
  1. Folklore—Germany 2. Fairy tales
ISBN 0-89919-422-2 (pa)   LC 83-14979
"Based on Lucy Crane's translation from the German
of the Brothers Grimm." Title page

Galdone, Paul, 1914-1986—*Continued*

A pair of elves help a poor shoemaker become successful, and the shoemaker and his wife reward them with elegant outfits

"The pictures in flashing hues emphasize the secret helpers' impishness; they seem to be performing the service more for a lark than in the name of sweet charity." Publ Wkly

The gingerbread boy. Clarion Bks. 1975 unp il $16; pa $6.95 (k-2)   **398.2**
1. Folklore 2. Fairy tales
ISBN 0-395-28799-5; 0-89919-163-0 (pa)
First published by Seabury Press
"A lively version of the tale of the gingerbread boy who sprang into action as soon as he was baked and gleefully eluded all would-be captors until he was finally outwitted by a fox. The artist's gingerbread boy is a strong-legged, cocky individual, who sets out on a merry race through the countryside. The action of the tale is well-paced; large, humorous illustrations with stone fences, a covered bridge, and hearty rural folk suggest a New England background, while the triumphant fox is the epitome of all slyness." Horn Book

Henny Penny; retold and illustrated by Paul Galdone. Clarion Bks. 1968 unp il $16; pa $6.95 (k-2)   **398.2**
1. Folklore 2. Animals—Fiction
ISBN 0-395-28800-2; 0-89919-225-4 (pa)
First published by Seabury Press
A folktale also popularly known as Chicken Little. "The simple retelling has a different ending which makes the fox seem somewhat less villainous—when Henny Penny and her credulous friends follow Foxy Loxy into the cave they are never seen again and the king is never told that the sky is falling, but Foxy Loxy, his wife, and seven little foxes (appealingly portrayed in a picture as a family group) still remember the fine feast they had that day." Booklist

The little red hen. Clarion Bks. 1973 unp il $15; pa $5.95 (k-2)   **398.2**
1. Folklore 2. Chickens—Fiction
ISBN 0-395-28803-7; 0-89919-349-8 (pa)
Also available with Audiobook
First published by Seabury Press
"In a light-hearted interpretation of the old tale, a domesticated little hen, complete with mobcap and apron, busies herself in a picturesquely shabby cottage while her three house mates—a cat, a dog, and a mouse—doze blissfully. The industry of the little hen produces a cake; and only when 'a delicious smell filled the cozy little house,' do her lazy companions come to life." Horn Book
"The large, clear, colorful pictures perfectly suit the book for pre-school story hours; the simple text, with one or two lines per page, will make it a success with beginning readers." SLJ

The monkey and the crocodile; a Jataka tale from India. Clarion Bks. 1969 unp il hardcover o.p. paperback available $6.95 (k-2)   **398.2**
1. Folklore—India 2. Fables 3. Animals—Fiction 4. Jataka stories
ISBN 0-89919-524-5 (pa)

First published by Seabury Press
Illustrated by Galdone, this is a retelling of one of the Jataka fables about Buddha in his animal incarnations. "The crocodile wants a meal of monkey, but the intended prey is far wilier than his antagonist." SLJ
The story "has the humor, plot, and movement to make it a good book for any young child, even one unused to stories: the brilliant colors, clear pictures, and brief text should make it very successful for sharing with groups of children." Horn Book

Puss in boots. Clarion Bks. 1976 unp il hardcover o.p. paperback available $6.95 (k-2)   **398.2**
1. Folklore—France 2. Fairy tales
ISBN 0-89919-192-4 (pa)
First published by Seabury Press
"Galdone follows Perrault's story line faithfully, as Puss works mischief to obtain a fortune for his master. The writing, fluid and readable, makes even this familiar tale sound fresh—no mean feat. Galdone's large, humorous caricatures—easily seen for story hour—have great gusto, and Puss is the embodiment of cleverness and knavery." SLJ

The teeny-tiny woman; a ghost story. Clarion Bks. 1984 unp il $16; pa $5.95 (k-2)   **398.2**
1. Folklore—Great Britain 2. Ghost stories
ISBN 0-89919-270-X; 0-89919-463-X (pa)
LC 84-4311
Also available with Audiobook
Retold and illustrated by Galdone, this is an English folk tale about a "teeny-tiny woman who lives in a teeny-tiny house in a teeny-tiny village goes for a teeny-tiny walk, etc. Opening the gates to a churchyard, she finds a bone that will add flavor to the soup she plans for supper. Back home, she goes to bed but is alarmed by a voice . . . demanding, 'Give me back my bone!'" Publ Wkly
"Quarter-inch type will attract reticent readers, and the comfortable, cozy country and cottage scenes defuse whatever scariness young readers might conjure up. Fences, trees, balustrades and cupboards in murky, inky tones are designed to suggest watchful faces and add to the atmospheric tension of the narrative." SLJ

The three bears. Clarion Bks. 1972 unp il $15; pa $6.95 (k-2)   **398.2**
1. Folklore 2. Bears—Fiction
ISBN 0-395-28811-8; 0-89919-401-X (pa)
Also available Spanish language edition and Audiobook version
First published by Seabury Press
In Galdone's illustrations for his retelling of the tale of Goldilocks, "his three bears are beautifully groomed, civilized creatures, living a life of rustic contentment in an astonishingly verdant forest, while his Goldilocks is a horrid, be-ringletted, overdressed child who rampages wantonly through the bears' tidy home." Times Lit Suppl

The three Billy Goats Gruff. Clarion Bks. 1973 unp il $16; pa $6.95 (k-2)   **398.2**
1. Folklore—Norway 2. Goats—Fiction
ISBN 0-395-28812-6; 0-89919-035-9 (pa)
Also available with Audiobook
First published by Seabury Press

Galdone, Paul, 1914-1986—*Continued*

In this retelling of the old Norwegian folk tale, "the goats flummox the wicked troll and send him over the rickety bridge to a watery grave." Publ Wkly

"Galdone's illustrations are in his usual bold, clear style. The three Billy Goats Gruff are expressively drawn, and the troll looks appropriately ferocious and ugly. The large, lively, double-page spreads are sure to win a responsive audience at story hour." SLJ

Gershator, Phillis, 1942-

Zzzng! Zzzng! Zzzng! a Yoruba tale; retold by Phillis Gershator; illustrated by Theresa Smith. Orchard Bks. 1998 unp il $15.95 (k-3)   **398.2**
  1. Mosquitoes—Fiction 2. Yoruba (African people)—Folklore 3. Folklore—Africa
  ISBN 0-531-09523-1   LC 95-51565
When Ear, Leg, and Arm refuse to marry Mosquito, she shows them that she is not to be ignored

"Gershator's economical but engaging text has repetitive refrains and opportunities for group participation galore; Smith's pastel and crayon illustrations, with their saturated colors and uncluttered compositions, suit the readaloud, showabout nature of the tale." Bull Cent Child Books

Gerson, Mary-Joan

Why the sky is far away; a Nigerian folktale; retold by Mary-Joan Gerson; pictures by Carla Golembe. Little, Brown 1992 unp il hardcover o.p. paperback available $5.95 (k-3)   **398.2**
  1. Folklore—Nigeria
  ISBN 0-316-30874-9 (pa)   LC 91-24949
"Joy Street books"

A revised and newly illustrated edition of the title first published 1974 by Harcourt

The sky was once so close to the Earth that people cut parts of it to eat, but their waste and greed caused the sky to move far away

"Golembe's simple, theatrical illustrations combine monotype prints and collages in brilliant colors. . . . With its playfulness and drama, this is a fine book for story hour, especially in an ecology program." Booklist

Giblin, James, 1933-

The dwarf, the giant, and the unicorn; a tale of King Arthur; retold by James Cross Giblin; illustrated by Claire Ewart. Clarion Bks. 1996 47p il $15.95 (3-5)   **398.2**
  1. Arthur, King 2. Arthurian romances
  ISBN 0-395-60520-2   LC 92-34031
When his ship runs aground on a strange island during a storm, Arthur sets off on his charger to look for help and meets a dwarf who tells a curious story about his son and the unicorn who has befriended them both

"Ewart's impressionistic watercolor-and-colored-pencil artwork sensitively expresses the characters' emotions and creates richly colored and convincing settings. This good read-aloud is one of the few stories that show King Arthur's realm as a peaceful kingdom." Booklist

Ginsburg, Mirra

The Chinese mirror; adapted from a Korean folktale by Mirra Ginsburg; illustrated by Margot Zemach. Harcourt Brace Jovanovich 1988 unp il hardcover o.p. paperback available $6 (k-3) **398.2**
  1. Folklore—Korea
  ISBN 0-15-21708-3 (pa)   LC 86-22940
"Gulliver books"

"A man brings a mirror—an object unknown to his fellow villagers—home from a trip to China. He secretes it in a chest, but when his curious family each indulge in a peek and see a different image (his or her own face, of course), each has a different reaction." Booklist

"This elegantly simple little story is a seamless blend of folk-tale adaptation with illustrations that were inspired by Korean genre paintings of the eighteenth century." Horn Book

Clay boy; adapted from a Russian folk tale by Mirra Ginsburg; pictures by Jos. A. Smith. Greenwillow Bks. 1997 unp il $16; lib bdg $15.89 (k-3)   **398.2**
  1. Folklore—Russia
  ISBN 0-688-14409-8; 0-688-14410-1 (lib bdg)
                            LC 96-33820
Wanting a son, an old man and woman make a clay boy who comes to life and begins eating everything in sight until he meets a clever goat

"The tale is adapted from a Russian folktale, and the storytelling voice is very simple and immediate. . . . In their play with scale, the illustrations express a wonderful combination of the monstrous and the cozy." Booklist

Goble, Paul

Adopted by the eagles; a Plains Indian story of friendship and treachery; told & illustrated by Paul Goble. Bradbury Press 1994 unp il $15.95; pa $5.99 (2-4)   **398.2**
  1. Dakota Indians—Folklore
  ISBN 0-02-736575-1; 0-689-82086-0 (pa)
                            LC 93-24047
"Two young warriors swear friendship, but when they become rivals for the same maiden, one abandons the other on a rocky ledge. Saved by eagles, the abandoned warrior returns to his village and shames his former friend into leaving, then marries the girl. The illustrations are vintage Goble—stylized figures in historically accurate clothing, outlined in white and set against landscapes of vast sky or dark, slanting rock." Booklist
Includes bibliographical references

Buffalo woman; story and illustrations by Paul Goble. Bradbury Press 1984 unp il $16; pa $5.99 (2-4)   **398.2**
  1. Native Americans—Folklore 2. Bison—Fiction
  ISBN 0-02-737720-2; 0-689-71109-3 (pa)
                            LC 83-15704
A young hunter marries a female buffalo in the form of a beautiful maiden, but when his people reject her he must pass several tests before being allowed to join the buffalo nation

"Each page sparkles with the lupins and yuccas of the Southwest and teems with native birds, butterflies, and small animals, the richness of detail never detracting

Goble, Paul—*Continued*

from the overall design of the handsome illustrations. The author-artist successfully combines a compellng version of an old legend with his own imaginative and striking visual interpretation." Horn Book

Includes bibliography

Crow chief; a Plains Indian story; told and illustrated by Paul Goble. Orchard Bks. 1992 unp il $16.95; pa $5.95 (2-4) **398.2**
    1. Native Americans—Folklore
    ISBN 0-531-05947-2; 0-531-07064-6 (pa)
                        LC 90-28457

"A Richard Jackson book"

Crow Chief always warns the buffalo that hunters are coming, until Falling Star, a savior, comes to camp, tricks Crow Chief, and teaches him that all must share and live like relatives together

"Stylized, stylish, and strongly decorative, Goble's distinctive paintings use symbol, design, and repetition to illustrate a retelling of a Plains Indians myth that is both a pourquoi story and a hero tale. . . . Goble discusses the legend of Falling Star, 'the Savior,' in a prefatory note that should be of special interest to storytellers." Bull Cent Child Books

The gift of the sacred dog; story and illustrations by Paul Goble. Bradbury Press 1980 unp il hardcover o.p. paperback available $5.99 (2-4) **398.2**
    1. Native Americans—Folklore 2. Horses—Fiction
    ISBN 0-02-043280-1 (pa)   LC 80-15843

The author "presents one of the common myths of how the Plains Indians got horses. In this case, a boy from a tribe whose members are starving because they cannot find buffalo goes to a high mountain to talk to the Great Spirit. From heaven the boy gets sacred dogs (horses) for hunting the buffalo." Child Book Rev Serv

"Goble's handsome paintings, vigorous in composition and often delicate in style, often stylized, always reflect his identification with the Native American way of life and his empathy with their respect for natural things. . . . The text, which can be read aloud to younger children, ends with Sioux songs about horses and buffalo." Bull Cent Child Books

The girl who loved wild horses; story and illustrations by Paul Goble. Bradbury Press 1978 unp il $14.95; pa $5.99 (k-3) **398.2**
    1. Native Americans—Folklore 2. Horses—Fiction
    ISBN 0-02-736570-0; 0-689-71696-6 (pa)
                        LC 77-20500

Awarded the Caldecott Medal, 1979

"After becoming lost in a storm, a young Indian girl joins and lives with a herd of wild horses until finally, she becomes one herself." SLJ

"Elaborate double-page spreads burst with life, revealing details of flowers and insects, animals and birds. . . . The story is told in simple language, and the author has included verses of a Navaho and Sioux song about horses. Both storytelling and art express the harmony with and the love of nature which characterize Native American culture." Horn Book

The great race of the birds and animals; story and illustrations by Paul Goble. Bradbury Press 1985 unp il hardcover o.p. paperback available $5.99 (2-4) **398.2**
    1. Native Americans—Folklore
    ISBN 0-689-71452-1 (pa)   LC 85-4202

A retelling of the Cheyenne and Sioux myth about the Great Race, a contest called by the Creator to settle the question whether man or buffalo should have supremacy and thus become the guardians of Creation

"With variety in color, pattern, and page design, the brilliant illustrations strengthen the drama and powerfully depict the animals—their massed effects and their individual characteristics." Horn Book

Her seven brothers; story and illustrations by Paul Goble. Bradbury Press 1988 unp il hardcover o.p. paperback available $5.99 (2-4) **398.2**
    1. Cheyenne Indians—Folklore 2. Stars—Fiction
    ISBN 0-689-71730-X (pa)   LC 86-31776

Retells the Cheyenne legend in which a girl and her seven chosen brothers become the Big Dipper

"The story is lovely: the retelling echoes its delicate and gentle charm. The illustrations . . . emphasize the flora and fauna associated with hope and spring. The pages are filled with detail. . . . The author's note not only gives the sources for his art and for his retelling but also describes the particular techniques employed for the illustrations." Horn Book

Iktomi and the boulder; a Plains Indian story; retold and illustrated by Paul Goble. Orchard Bks. 1988 unp il hardcover o.p. paperback available $6.95 (k-3) **398.2**
    1. Dakota Indians—Folklore
    ISBN 0-531-07023-9 (pa)   LC 87-35789

"A Richard Jackson book"

Iktomi, a Plains Indian trickster, attempts to defeat a boulder with the assistance of some bats, in this story which explains why the Great Plains are covered with small stones

"Goble has adapted his usually formal narrative style to suit this boisterous trickster tale. The type is large, the narrative voice is informal, offering numerous asides from Iktomi and the storyteller. Goble's signature ink and vivid watercolor illustrations contain more movement than usual, and fewer stylized symbols are in evidence. . . . A deft blending of text and illustration which will appeal to a wide audience." SLJ

Other available titles about Iktomi are:
Iktomi and the berries (1989)
Iktomi and the buffalo skull (1991)
Iktomi and the buzzard (1994)
Iktomi and the coyote (1998)
Iktomi loses his eyes (1999)

The legend of the White Buffalo Woman. National Geographic Soc. 1998 unp il $16.95 (3-5) **398.2**

    1. Native Americans—Folklore
    ISBN 0-7922-7074-6   LC 97-24086

A Lakota Indian legend in which the White Buffalo Woman presents her people with the Sacred Calf Pipe which gives them the means to pray to the Great Spirit

"In his fluid retelling of the legend of the first peace

Goble, Paul—*Continued*

pipe, Goble . . . handles sweeping Lakota history succinctly and assuredly, largely due to his compelling artwork." Publ Wkly

Includes bibliographical references

Love flute; story and illustrations by Paul Goble. Bradbury Press 1992 unp il hardcover o.p. paperback available $5.99 (2-4)   **398.2**

1. Native Americans—Folklore

ISBN 0-689-81683-9 (pa)   LC 91-19716

A gift to a shy young man from the birds and animals helps him to express his love to a beautiful girl

"Goble's measured prose brings this Santee Dakota myth to life. The lyricism of the romantic story is highlighted by the restraint and dignity of his writing. His familiar painting style is both rich and formal as befits the telling of a myth. . . . A note on sources and historical information on courtship rituals is a welcome plus." SLJ

Paul Goble gallery; three Native American stories. Simon & Schuster Bks. for Young Readers 1999 unp il $19.95 (2-4)   **398.2**

1. Native Americans—Folklore

ISBN 0-689-82219-7   LC 98-88492

Omnibus edition of three titles entered separately

Contents: Her seven brothers; The gift of the sacred dog; The girl who loved wild horses

Remaking the earth; a creation story from the Great Plains of North America; written and illustrated by Paul Goble. Orchard Bks. 1996 unp il lib bdg $16.99 (2-4)   **398.2**

1. Native Americans—Folklore 2. Creation—Fiction

ISBN 0-531-08874-X   LC 96-4243

In this creation myth, the water birds and animals left behind when the old world was flooded dive for mud so that the Creator can make dry land again

The narrative "is based on elements taken from several Native American tribal groups. Goble has included an extensive reference list and a detailed introductory note, and he supplies additional notes by using asterisks. His double-page spreads are saturated with the richness of nature and the splendor of everyday animals." Booklist

Includes bibliographical references

Star Boy; retold and illustrated by Paul Goble. Bradbury Press 1983 unp il hardcover o.p. paperback available $5.99 (2-4)   **398.2**

1. Siksika Indians—Folklore

ISBN 0-689-71499-8 (pa)   LC 82-20599

Relates the Blackfoot Indian legend in which Star Boy gains the Sun's forgiveness for his mother's disobedience and is allowed to return to the Sky World

"This strong sense of design, the restrained and effective use of color, and the stylized use of Native American motifs in bold composition contribute to the distinctive work that won Goble the Caldecott Medal." Bull Cent Child Books

Goldin, Barbara Diamond

Coyote and the firestick; a Pacific Northwest Indian tale; retold by Barbara Diamond Goldin; illustrated by Will Hillenbrand. Harcourt Brace & Co. 1996 unp il $16 (3-5)   **398.2**

1. Native Americans—Folklore 2. Coyote (Legendary character)

ISBN 0-15-200438-6   LC 94-5747

"Gulliver books"

"In this tale, the People are cold and hungry, so they ask Coyote to steal Fire, burning on a snowy mountaintop guarded by three evil spirits." SLJ

"A well-told story with inventive oil and oil pastel illustrations of the sturdy People, the helpful animals, and the serio-comic evil spirits, green and bulbous. Accenting all are the sharp portraits of the scrawny yet supple trickster hero, prancing with admiration for himself." Horn Book

González, Lucía M., 1957-

Señor Cat's romance and other favorite stories from Latin America; retold by Lucía M. González; illustrated by Lulu Delacre. Scholastic 1997 46p il $17.95 (2-4)   **398.2**

1. Folklore—Latin America

ISBN 0-590-48537-7   LC 95-34144

"González and Delacre introduce six . . . folktales popular throughout Latin America." Booklist

González tells these tales "with style and humor. The retellings are peppered with Spanish words, all of which are easily understood through context. Each story is followed by a short glossary and an author's note with information on the tale's origins and its variants. The vivid, sprightly paintings contain many regional details." Horn Book Guide

Grandfather tales; American-English folk tales; selected and edited by Richard Chase; illustrated by Berkeley Williams, Jr. Houghton Mifflin 1948 239p il $18; pa $7.95 (4 and up)   **398.2**

1. Folklore—Southern States

ISBN 0-395-06692-1; 0-395-56150-7 (pa)

Folklore gathered in Alabama, "North Carolina, Virginia and Kentucky. Written down only after many tellings, these [twenty-four] humorous tales are told in the vernacular of the region with added touches of local color or provided by the storytellers as they meet together to keep Old-Christmas Eve. . . . Of special interest to storytellers." Booklist

Green, Roger Lancelyn, 1918-1987

King Arthur and his Knights of the Round Table; retold out of the old romances; with illustrations by Aubrey Beardsley. Knopf 1993 355p il $14.95 (5 and up)   **398.2**

1. Arthur, King 2. Arthurian romances

ISBN 0-679-42311-7   LC 92-55073

Also available in paperback from Puffin Bks.

"Everyman's library children's classics"

A newly illustrated edition of the title first published 1953 in the United Kingdom

Relates the exploits of King Arthur and his knights from the birth of Arthur to the destruction of Camelot

The **Green** fairy book; edited by Andrew Lang; with numerous illustrations by H. J. Ford. Dover Publs. 1965 366p il pa $8.95 (4-6)   **398.2**
1. Folklore 2. Fairy tales
ISBN 0-486-21439-7
A reprint of the title first published 1892 by Longmans
This collection of forty-two fairy tales from various countries includes many from the Brothers Grimm and several by the Comte de Caylus. Other sources include Madame D'Aulnoy, Paul Sebillot, Charles Deulin, Fénelon, and traditional tales from Spain and China

Greene, Ellin, 1927-
The little golden lamb; retold by Ellin Greene; illustrated by Roseanne Litzinger. Clarion Bks. 2000 32p il $15 (k-3)   **398.2**
1. Folklore
ISBN 0-395-71526-1   LC 99-36025
A retelling of the traditional tale in which a poor, but good-hearted lad finds his fortune with the aid of a little golden lamb to which everyone that touches it sticks
"Greene's storytelling style is at once classic and relaxed, and the illustrations, in a soft, springtime palette, are fittingly buoyant." Horn Book Guide

Gregorowski, Christopher, 1940-
Fly, eagle, fly! an African tale; retold by Christopher Gregorowski; pictures by Niki Daly. Margaret K. McElderry Bks. 2000 unp il $16 (k-3)   **398.2**
1. Folklore—Africa
ISBN 0-689-82398-3   LC 98-45302
Original two-color illustrated edition published 1982 in South Africa
A farmer finds an eagle and raises it to behave like a chicken, until a friend helps the eagle learn to find its rightful place in the sky
This "is a powerful celebration of the human spirit and its need for independence. It is beautifully complemented by watercolors, rich in the vibrant tones of earth and sky." Booklist

Grifalconi, Ann
The village of round and square houses. Little, Brown 1986 unp il lib bdg $16.95 (k-3)   **398.2**
1. Folklore—Africa
ISBN 0-316-32862-6   LC 85-24150
A Caldecott Medal honor book, 1987
A grandmother explains to her listeners why in their village on the side of a volcano the men live in square houses and the women in round ones
The author "illustrates her own tale, told to her by a young girl who grew up in Tos. The resting purple volcano, suddenly erupting into orange; the eerie orange sun; the villagers covered with ash; the fiery colored skies; the dense, lush jungles—all are captured beautifully by Grifalconi's art." Publ Wkly

Grimm, Jacob, 1785-1863
The Bremen town musicians; a tale; by Jacob and Wilhelm Grimm; illustrated by Hans Fischer; translated by Anthea Bell. North-South Bks. 1998 unp il $15.95; lib bdg $15.88 (k-3)   **398.2**
1. Folklore—Germany
ISBN 1-55858-893-0; 1-55858-894-9 (lib bdg)
          LC 97-34512
Original Swiss edition 1944; this is a reissue of the 1955 edition published by Harcourt with title: The traveling musicians
While on their way to Bremen, four aging animals who are no longer of any use to their masters find a new home after outwitting a gang of robbers
This offers "sprightly, imaginative drawings that match the humor of this favorite fairy tale." Booklist

Hansel and Gretel; [by] the Brothers Grimm; pictures by Susan Jeffers. Dial Bks. 1980 unp il hardcover o.p. paperback available $6.99 (k-3)
          398.2
1. Folklore—Germany 2. Fairy tales
ISBN 0-14-054636-7 (pa)   LC 80-15079
"A simple, crisply stated translation tells this timeless story of innocence pitted against evil. . . . Jeffers's stunning full-color illustrations expand both the children's purity and the malevolence of the stepmother/witch in an atmosphere that is flawlessly and beautifully executed." Booklist

Hansel and Gretel; [by] the Brothers Grimm; illustrated by Lisbeth Zwerger; translated by Elizabeth D. Crawford. Picture Bk. Studio 1988 unp il $16 (k-3)   **398.2**
1. Folklore—Germany 2. Fairy tales
ISBN 0-88708-068-5   LC 87-32833
Also available Spanish language edition
"A Michael Neugebauer book"
First published 1979 by Morrow
When they are left in the woods by their parents, two children find their way home despite an encounter with a wicked witch
"Working from a faithful translation of the original text, Zwerger has created rosy-cheeked, appealing children who look as if they have just descended the Alps. The witch, by contrast, is a shapeless, fiery-eyed ghoul with real scare potential." Publ Wkly

Little Red Cap; [by] the Brothers Grimm; illustrated by Lisbeth Zwerger; translated from the German by Elizabeth D. Crawford. North-South Bks. 1995 c1983 unp il $14.95; pa $6.95 (k-3)
          398.2
1. Folklore—Germany 2. Wolves—Fiction
ISBN 1-55858-382-3; 1-55858-430-7 (pa)
          LC 94-32154
"A Michael Neugebauer book"
A reissue of the title first published 1983 by Morrow
In this translation of Little Red Riding Hood "Little Red Cap strays from the path while taking wine and cake to grandmother. The wolf then gobbles up grandmother and Red Cap. Justice ultimately prevails when the hunter cuts open the wolf, frees the child and grandmother and finishes off the wolf." SLJ

Grimm, Jacob, 1785-1863—*Continued*

This translation "gives the text a smooth pace and natural-sounding dialogue. . . . Washes in muted earth tones provide suggestions of backgrounds against which expressively drawn figures play out their familiar roles." Horn Book

Snow White & Rose Red; by Jakob and Wilhelm Grimm; illustrated by Gennady Spirin. Philomel Bks. 1992 31p il hardcover o.p. paperback available $6.95 (1-4)   **398.2**
    1. Folklore—Germany 2. Fairy tales
    ISBN 0-698-11585-6 (pa)   LC 91-29414

A newly illustrated version of the classic tale about two kind sisters' experiences with an enchanted bear and an ungrateful gnome

"Spirin's romantic watercolor-and-pencil illustrations recall books of hours with their medieval setting, their delightful interpretations of flowers, trees, and forest animals, and their arched borders that contain the text and main illustrations on every page. . . . This Russian illustrator's distinctive style lends an other-worldly quality that is well suited to the 'long ago and far away' spirit of fairy tales." Booklist

Haley, Gail E.

A story, a story; an African tale retold and illustrated by Gail E. Haley. Atheneum Pubs. 1970 unp il lib bdg $17; pa $5.99 (k-3)   **398.2**
    1. Folklore—Africa 2. Anansi (Legendary character)
    ISBN 0-689-20511-2 (lib bdg); 0-689-71201-4 (pa)

Awarded the Caldecott Medal, 1971

"The story explains the origin of that favorite African folk material, the spider tale. Here Ananse, the old spider man, wanting to buy the Sky God's stories, completes by his cleverness three seemingly impossible tasks set as the price for the golden box of stories which he takes back to earth." Sutherland. The Best in Child Books

Hamanaka, Sheila

Screen of frogs; an old tale; retold and illustrated by Sheila Hamanaka. Orchard Bks. 1993 unp il $16.95 (k-3)   **398.2**
    1. Folklore—Japan
    ISBN 0-531-05464-0   LC 92-24172
    "A Richard Jackson book"

A giant frog convinces rich lazy Koji not to sell his estate because of the harm it would do to the land and animals

"Hamanaka's fluid retelling guides readers smoothly through the detailed proceedings, providing an air of anticipation and occasional humor. . . . Collage and acrylic illustrations, rendered on handmade paper, are liberally adorned with Asian motifs, while the figures' stark black outlines suggest the strokes of Japanese lettering." Publ Wkly

Hamilton, Virginia, 1936-

The girl who spun gold; illustrated by Leo & Diane Dillon. Blue Sky Press (NY) 2000 unp il $16.95 (k-3)   **398.2**
    1. Fairy tales 2. Folklore—West Indies
    ISBN 0-590-47378-6   LC 99-86365

In this West Indian retelling of "Rumpelstiltskin," Lit'mahn spins thread into gold cloth for the Quashiba, the King's new bride

"The source of this folktale is apparent in the distinctive and lilting West Indian dialect that pervades this humorous and, at times, scary telling. The lavish use of gold within the acrylic illustrations and their frames is sumptuous." SLJ

Her stories; African American folktales, fairy tales, and true tales; told by Virginia Hamilton; illustrated by Leo & Diane Dillon. Blue Sky Press (NY) 1995 112p il $19.95 (4 and up)   **398.2**
    1. African American women—Folklore
    ISBN 0-590-47370-0   LC 94-33055
    Coretta Scott King award for text, 1996

"Nineteen African-American fairy tales, animal stories, supernatural tales, legends and true narratives of a female kind are presented in this single volume." Child Book Rev Serv

"Retold from a variety of sources, the stories flow smoothly in Hamilton's expertly measured prose. The full-color illustrations, one per story, are lush and detailed. . . . These are tales to be read over and over again." Publ Wkly

Includes bibliographical references

The people could fly: American black folktales; told by Virginia Hamilton; illustrated by Leo and Diane Dillon. Knopf 1985 178p il lib bdg $18.99; pa $13 (4 and up)   **398.2**
    1. African Americans—Folklore
    ISBN 0-394-96925-1 (lib bdg); 0-679-84336-1 (pa)
                                LC 84-25020

Also available with Audiobook

Coretta Scott King Award for text, 1986

"Hamilton retells 24 representative black folktales. . . . The stories are organized into four sections: tales of animals; the supernatural; the real, extravagant, and fanciful; and freedom tales." Booklist

The author "has been successful in her efforts to write these tales in the Black English of the slave storytellers. Her scholarship is unobtrusive and intelligible. She has provided a glossary and notes concerning the origins of the tales and the different versions in other cultures. Handsomely illustrated." N Y Times Book Rev

A ring of tricksters; animal tales from America, the West Indies, and Africa; illustrated by Barry Moser. Blue Sky Press (NY) 1997 111p il $19.95   **398.2**
    1. Folklore 2. Animals—Fiction
    ISBN 0-590-47374-3   LC 96-37543

"Divided into sections on American, West Indian, and African tricksters, these eleven tales each feature an animal trickster either getting his comeuppance or giving as good as he gets." Bull Cent Child Books

"Hamilton's prose infuses the dialogue with depth and dimension, while Moser's spectacular, lively watercolors nearly render the impish creatures human." Publ Wkly

Hamilton, Virginia, 1936—— *Continued*

When birds could talk & bats could sing; the adventures of Bruh Sparrow, Sis Wren, and their friends; told by Virginia Hamilton; illustrated by Barry Moser. Blue Sky Press (NY) 1996 63p il $17.95 (3-5) **398.2**

1. African Americans—Folklore 2. Birds—Fiction

ISBN 0-590-47372-7 LC 95-15307

A collection of stories, featuring sparrows, jays, buzzards, and bats, based on those African American tales originally written down by Martha Young on her father's plantation in Alabama after the Civil War

"Moser's finely detailed watercolors have an inherent humor that makes the characters especially vivid, and the jacket illustration is a wonderful, slyly funny collection of bird personalities. The text, the layout, and the illustrations work together seamlessly in this beautifully designed, well-crafted collection." Booklist

Han, Suzanne Crowder, 1953-

The rabbit's escape; illustrated by Yumi Heo. Holt & Co. 1995 unp il $15.95 (k-3) **398.2**

1. Folklore—Korea 2. Bilingual books—English-Korean

ISBN 0-8050-2675-4 LC 94-36516

"This adaptation of a Korean folktale is bilingual, with text appearing in both Korean and English. When the Dragon King of the East Sea falls ill, the court physician declares the only cure to be the liver of a rabbit. . . . The tale is illiustrated with large, whimsical paintings in pencil and oil. Characters are drawn in a two-dimensional, naive style against backgrounds of swirling sea creatures." Booklist

The rabbit's tail; a story from Korea; illustrated by Richard Wehrman. Holt & Co. 1999 unp il $16.95 (k-3) **398.2**

1. Folklore—Korea

ISBN 0-8050-4580-5 LC 98-16627

Tiger is afraid of being eaten by a fearsome dried persimmon, but when Rabbit tries to convince him he is wrong, Rabbit loses his long tail

"The tale is vividly retold. . . . An amusing entertainment about misperceptions." SLJ

Hastings, Selina

Sir Gawain and the loathly lady; retold by Selina Hastings; illustrated by Juan Wijngaard. Lothrop, Lee & Shepard Bks. 1985 unp il hardcover o.p. paperback available $4.95 (3 and up) **398.2**

1. Arthurian romances 2. Gawain (Legendary character)

ISBN 0-688-07046-9 (pa) LC 85-63

After a horrible hag saves King Arthur's life by answering a riddle, Sir Gawain agrees to marry her to save the King's honor and thus releases her from an evil enchantment

"This version of the old romance . . . is charmingly retold and gloriously illustrated. . . . Wijngaard combines the illuminator's precision with a modern miniaturist's detailed perspective; each page of text is framed with manuscript-inspired designs of lacy leaves in scarlet, blue and gold, inset with wonderful, naturalistic paintings. These are full of details for readers to discover." SLJ

Hausman, Gerald

Dogs of myth; tales from around the world; [by] Gerald and Loretta Hausman; illustrated by Barry Moser. Simon & Schuster Bks. for Young Readers 1999 83p il $19.95 (3-6) **398.2**

1. Dogs—Folklore

ISBN 0-689-80696-5 LC 98-15817

A collection of traditional tales about dogs from around the world, arranged in such categories as "The Trickster Dog," "The Enchanted Dog," and "The Super Dog"

"Moser's portraits could serve as nature studies, and . . . his watercolors are rooted in realism and lovingly evoked." Publ Wkly

Hayes, Joe, 1945-

Little Gold Star; a Cinderella cuento/Estrellita de oro; retold in Spanish & English by Joe Hayes; illustrated by Gloria Osuna Perez & Lucia Angela Perez. Cinco Puntos Press 2000 30p il $15.95 (k-3) **398.2**

1. Fairy tales 2. Hispanic Americans—Folklore 3. Bilingual books—English-Spanish

ISBN 0-938317-49-0 LC 99-57104

In this variation of the Cinderella story, coming from the Hispanic tradition in New Mexico, Arciá and her wicked stepsisters have different encounters with a magical hawk and are left physically changed in ways that will affect their meeting with the prince

"The English text, which is made full-bodied by its many details, appears with a Spanish translation. The impressive acrylic illustrations, done in a sturdy folk-art style, are thick with color and bright with humor." Booklist

Heins, Ethel L., 1918-1997

The cat and the cook and other fables of Krylov; retold by Ethel Heins; pictures by Anita Lobel. Greenwillow Bks. 1995 32p il $15; lib bdg $14.93 (1-4) **398.2**

1. Fables

ISBN 0-688-12310-4; 0-688-12311-2 (lib bdg)

LC 94-4116

In this "collection, 12 Russian fables warn against pride, show the importance of cooperation and counsel moderation. Includes notes about the fabulist Krylov (1768-1844) and sources for this volume." Publ Wkly

Lobel "outdoes herself with watercolor-and-gouache paintings that are brilliantly colored and wonderfully composed. . . . Heins' prose retellings . . . are elegant. Based on scholarly sources in translation, these brief morality tales are more subtle and complex than the more familiar ones attributed to Aesop." Booklist

Heo, Yumi

The green frogs; a Korean folktale; retold by Yumi Heo. Houghton Mifflin 1996 unp il $16 (k-3) **398.2**

1. Folklore—Korea 2. Frogs—Fiction

ISBN 0-395-68378-5 LC 95-19129

"Two young frogs delight in being contrary whenever their mother asks them to do something. . . . When she

Heo, Yumi—*Continued*

is dying, she asks to be buried by the creek, thinking they will contrarily bury her on a sunny hill. But the saddened frogs decide to carry out her wish." Child Book Rev Serv

"Using delicate tones, flat perspectives, and somewhat abstract figures set against busy backgrounds, [Heo] creates a quaint, comic effect. . . . This is a quirkier pourquoi tale than most, but it's too mischievous to be morbid." Horn Book

Hickox, Rebecca

The golden sandal; a Middle Eastern Cinderella story; illustrated by Will Hillenbrand. Holiday House 1998 unp il $16.95; pa $6.95 (k-3) **398.2**
1. Fairy tales 2. Folklore—Iraq
ISBN 0-8234-1331-4; 0-8234-1513-9 (pa)
LC 97-5071

An Iraqi version of the Cinderella story in which a kind and beautiful girl who is mistreated by her stepmother and stepsister finds a husband with the help of a magic fish

"The story is charmingly told and illustrated with paintings on vellum, giving the pictures a soft, luxurious quality." N Y Times Book Rev

Hodges, Margaret

The hero of Bremen; retold by Margaret Hodges; with illustrations by Charles Mikolaycak. Holiday House 1993 unp il $16.95; pa $6.95 (3-5)
398.2
1. Folklore—Germany
ISBN 0-8234-0934-1; 0-8234-1236-9 (pa)
LC 91-22357

Retells the German legend in which a shoemaker who cannot walk helps the town of Bremen, aided by the spirit of the great hero Roland

"Mikolaycak's realistic watercolor and colored pencil drawings have powerful lines, sculptural forms, and a strong narrative quality. . . . This eloquent retelling of a gentle, little-known tale honoring the chivalric virtues of service and sacrifice is all the more beautiful for its understated quality; the documentation is detailed and scholarly." Booklist

The kitchen knight; a tale of King Arthur; retold by Margaret Hodges and illustrated by Trina Schart Hyman. Holiday House 1990 unp il $16.95 (3 and up) **398.2**
1. Gareth (Legendary character) 2. Arthurian romances
ISBN 0-8234-0787-X
LC 89-11215

A retelling of the Arthurian legend of how Sir Gareth becomes a knight and rescues the lady imprisoned by the fearsome Red Knight of the Red Plain

"Hyman's richly romantic illustrations are lush watercolors, framed and broken with framed insets for closeups and framed text inside the panoramic picture. The format is horizontal, capturing the sweep of the story. While not a tale of King Arthur, it's a wonderful taste of Arthurian legend, hopefully whetting young appetites for more." SLJ

Saint George and the dragon; a golden legend; adapted by Margaret Hodges from Edmund Spenser's Faerie Queene; illustrated by Trina Schart Hyman. Little, Brown 1984 32p il $16.95; pa $6.95 (2-5) **398.2**
1. George, Saint, d. 303 2. Knights and knighthood—Fiction 3. Dragons—Fiction
ISBN 0-316-36789-3; 0-316-36795-8 (pa)
LC 83-19980

Awarded the Caldecott Medal, 1985

Retells the segment from Spenser's The Faerie Queene, in which George, the Red Cross Knight, slays the dreadful dragon that has been terrorizing the countryside for years and brings peace and joy to the land

"Hyman's illustrations are uniquely suited to this outrageously romantic and appealing legend. . . . The paintings are richly colored, lush, detailed and dramatic. . . . This is a beautifully crafted book, a fine combination of author and illustrator." SLJ

Saint Patrick and the peddler; story by Margaret Hodges; paintings by Paul Brett Johnson. Orchard Bks. 1993 unp il $16.95; pa $6.95 (k-3) **398.2**
1. Patrick, Saint, 373?-463? 2. Folklore—Ireland
ISBN 0-531-05489-6; 0-521-07089-1 (pa)
LC 92-44522

"A Richard Jackson book"

When a poor Irish peddler follows the instructions given to him by Saint Patrick in a dream, his life is greatly changed. Includes background on Saint Patrick and on the origin of the story

"Johnson's lovely acrylic paintings display the Irish countryside and the city of Dublin with a strong sense of place. The muted colors match the overall tone of the story, and the eerie ghost of Saint Patrick adds a dramatic touch." Booklist

Hoffman, Mary, 1945-

Sun, moon, and stars; illustrated by Jane Ray. Dutton Children's Bks. 1998 74p il $22.50 (3-6)
398.2
1. Mythology
ISBN 0-525-46004-7
LC 98-21452

"Following an introduction that explains how the ancients looked at the sky, the book is divided by each element in the title. Stories from various cultures, including the Egyptian, Korean, Chinese, Aztec, and Navajo, are augmented by bits of information and lore that enrich the book. Hoffman's story selection is excellent and carefully sourced. . . . [Ray's pictures] . . . soar. Spreads, sidebars, and full-page pictures are intricately designed and executed, touched as usual with bits of silver and gold." Booklist

Includes bibliographical references

Hogrogian, Nonny

The contest; adapted and illustrated by Nonny Hogrogian. Greenwillow Bks. 1976 unp il lib bdg $15.89 (k-3) **398.2**
1. Folklore—Armenia
ISBN 0-688-84042-6

A Caldecott Medal honor book, 1977

Hogrogian, Nonny—_Continued_

A "gently humorous retelling of an Armenian folk tale about two robbers who not only share the same occupation but are engaged to the same girl." SLJ

"The symmetrical elements of the tale, which create arabesques of humor, are well-served by the full-color, full-page illustrations and by the pencil drawings scattered through the text. Some of the colored illustrations are bordered by oriental rug patterns, and all of the paintings and drawings are strong in their depiction of Armenian physiognomy." Horn Book

One fine day. Macmillan 1971 unp il $16; pa $5.99 (k-3) **398.2**

1. Folklore—Armenia 2. Foxes—Fiction

ISBN 0-02-744000-1; 0-02-043620-3 (pa)

Awarded the Caldecott Medal, 1972

When a fox drinks the milk in an old woman's jug, she chops off his tail and refuses to sew it back on unless he gives her milk back. The author-illustrator's cumulative tale, based on an Armenian folktale, tells of the many transactions the fox must go through before his tail is restored

"A charming picture book that is just right for reading aloud to small children, the scale of the pictures also appropriate for group use." Sutherland. The Best in Child Books

Hong, Lily Toy, 1958-

How the ox star fell from heaven; retold and illustrated by Lilly Toy Hong. Whitman, A. 1991 unp il hardcover o.p. paperback available $6.95 (k-3) **398.2**

1. Folklore—China

ISBN 0-8075-3429-3 (pa) LC 90-38978

A Chinese folk tale which explains why the ox was banished from heaven to become the farmer's beast of burden

"Hong's clear, simple text is strongly illustrated in airbrushed acrylics and gouache. The images are formed by large and small blocks of deep color, joined rather like tiles with thick defining lines of contrasting colors between them. The resulting pictures are intriguingly variegated yet clean and fresh." Booklist

Two of everything; a Chinese folktale; retold and illustrated by Lily Toy Hong. Whitman, A. 1993 unp il $15.95 (k-3) **398.2**

1. Folklore—China

ISBN 0-8075-8157-7 LC 92-29880

A poor old Chinese farmer finds a magic brass pot that doubles or duplicates whatever is placed inside it, but his efforts to make himself wealthy lead to unexpected complications

The author "here paints with muted colors, defining rounded forms with broad outlines. Retold with verve and gentle humor, this Chinese folktale could become a read-aloud favorite." Booklist

Hooks, William H.

Moss gown; illustrations by Donald Carrick. Clarion Bks. 1987 48p il hardcover o.p. paperback available $6.95 (k-3) **398.2**

1. Fairy tales

ISBN 0-395-54793-8 (pa) LC 86-17199

After failing to flatter her father as much as her two evil sisters, Candace is banished from his plantation and only after much time and meeting her Prince Charming, is her father able to appreciate her love

"Many children and most adults will recognize in 'Moss Gown' the Cinderella story, while the most astute may note its resemblance to 'King Lear.' But everyone will enjoy this beautifully told North Carolina tale from the oral tradition. Carrick, a master of the dark and mysterious, has created haunting illustrations that are a wonderful complement to the story." Child Book Rev Serv

The three little pigs and the fox; illustrated by S.D. Schindler. Macmillan 1989 unp il hardcover o.p. paperback available $5.99 (k-3) **398.2**

1. Folklore—United States 2. Pigs—Folklore

ISBN 0-689-80962-X (pa) LC 88-29296

In this Appalachian version of the classic tale, Hamlet, the youngest pig, rescues her two greedy brothers from the clutches of the mean, tricky old drooly-mouth fox

"With an ear for colloquial wit and an eye on the family dynamic that sends these characters on their journey of maturation, Hooks has found a perfect fit in Schindler's watercolor scenes. Drafted with ease of proportion, colored with rural blends, and elegantly underplayed in expression, the animals are fresh and funny without being self-conscious." Bull Cent Child Books

Huck, Charlotte S.

Princess Furball; retold by Charlotte Huck; illustrated by Anita Lobel. Greenwillow Bks. 1989 unp il hardcover o.p. paperback available $6.95 (1-3) **398.2**

1. Fairy tales

ISBN 0-688-13107-7 (pa) LC 88-18780

This book is about a "princess who rebels against her tyrannical father and makes the most of her gifts to survive in another kingdom and win the hand of the king. This narrative focuses on the ingenuity of a girl who plots her own destiny." N Y Times Book Rev

"The paintings glimmer with intense colors—Lobel's flair for both historical and humorous detail has never been more apparent, nor more luxuriously bold." SLJ

Hyman, Trina Schart, 1939-

Little Red Riding Hood; by the Brothers Grimm retold and illustrated by Trina Schart Hyman. Holiday House 1983 unp il lib bdg $16.95; pa $6.95 (k-2) **398.2**

1. Folklore—Germany 2. Wolves—Fiction

ISBN 0-8234-0470-6 (lib bdg); 0-8234-0653-9 (pa)

LC 82-7700

This retelling "basically follows the Grimm story, although the text has been fleshed out with some extraneous details (for instance, the little girl is called Elisabeth). . . . The illustrations seem to be a labor of love; richly colored paintings of the forest teem with exquisitely detailed plant and animal life, and the interior scenes, awash with atmospheric light, are beautifully composed and executed." Horn Book

Index to fairy tales; including folklore, legends, and myths in collections. Scarecrow Press 1985-1994 4v   **398.2**
1. Folklore—Indexes 2. Fairy tales—Indexes 3. Legends—Indexes 4. Mythology—Indexes

Volumes covering 1949-1972 and 1973-1977 first published by Faxon 1973 and 1979 respectively
A continuation of Index to fairy tales, myths and legends and its two supplements, compiled by Mary Huse Eastman, published 1926-1952 by Faxon (o.p.)
Volume covering 1949-1972 compiled by Norma Olin Ireland $65 (ISBN 0-8108-2011-0); volume covering 1973-1977 compiled by Norma Olin Ireland $45 (ISBN 0-8108-1855-8); volume covering 1978-1986 compiled by Norma Olin Ireland and Joseph W. Sprug $70 (ISBN 0-8108-2194-X); volume covering 1987-1992 compiled by Joseph W. Sprug $70 (ISBN 0-8108-2750-6)
"An invaluable reference source for locating specific tales in collections." Peterson. Ref Books for Child. 4th edition

The **Jack** tales; with an appendix compiled by Herbert Halpert; and illustrations by Berkeley Williams, Jr. Houghton Mifflin 1943 201p il $16; pa $5.95 (4-6)   **398.2**
1. Folklore—Southern States
ISBN 0-395-06694-8; 0-395-66951-0 (pa)
"Told by R. M. Ward and his kindred in the Beech Mountain section of Western North Carolina and by other descendants of Council Harmon (1803-1896) elsewhere in the Southern mountains; with three tales from Wise County, Virginia. Set down from these sources and edited by Richard Chase." Title page
"Humor, freshness, colorful American background, and the use of one character as a central figure in the cycle mark these 18 folk tales, told here in the dialect of the mountain country of North Carolina. A scholarly appendix by Herbert Halpert, giving sources and parallels, increases the book's value as a contribution to American folklore. Black-and-white illustrations in the spirit of the text." Booklist

Jacobs, Joseph, 1854-1916
English fairy tales; with illustrations by John Batten. Knopf 1993 428p il $13.95 (4-6)   **398.2**
1. Fairy tales 2. Folklore—Great Britain
ISBN 0-679-42809-7   LC 93-13878
Also available in paperback from Dover Pubs.
"Everyman's library children's classics"
A reissue in one volume of the author's English fairy tales (1891) and More English fairy tales (1894)
A collection of more than eighty traditional stories that recount the adventures of giants, witches, princes, princesses, and animals

Jaffe, Nina
The cow of no color: riddle stories and justice tales from around the world; [by] Nina Jaffe and Steve Zeitlin; pictures by Whitney Sherman. Holt & Co. 1998 159p il $17 (4 and up)   **398.2**
1. Folklore
ISBN 0-8050-3736-5   LC 98-14167

In each of these stories, collected from around the world, a character faces a problem situation which requires that he make a decision about what is fair or just
"Sherman's black-and-white line drawings have a stark gracefulness that complements the tales' form and structure; the tales themselves are simply told with little embellishment." Bull Cent Child Books
Includes bibliographical references

The mysterious visitor; stories of the Prophet Elijah; illustrated by Elivia Savadier. Scholastic 1997 112p il $19.95 (4-6)   **398.2**
1. Elijah (Biblical figure) 2. Jews—Folklore
ISBN 0-590-48422-2   LC 96-7534
"Eight stories from German-Jewish traditions, Yiddish folklore, Morocco, and ancient Palestine have as their central character the Biblical prophet, Elijah. . . . The stories are told in a gentle voice that is well suited to reading aloud. . . . The full-page art is colorful and sets each story's mood with an appealing mix of concrete and abstract imagery. Jaffe provides a thoughtful introduction and notes on the origin of each selection." SLJ
Includes glossary and bibliographical references

The way meat loves salt; a Cinderella tale from the Jewish tradition; illustrated by Louise August. Holt & Co. 1998 unp il music $15.95 (k-3)   **398.2**
1. Jews—Folklore
ISBN 0-8050-4384-5   LC 97-41286
The youngest daughter of a rabbi is sent away from home in disgrace, but thanks to the help of the prophet Elijah, marries the son of a renowned scholar and is reunited with her family. Includes words and music to a traditional Yiddish wedding song
"Vibrant oils of reds, yellows, and blues set off the inky black, which defines the trees and rocks, and the sashes on the women's provincial gowns. Both the writing and the art contribute to the abundant good spirit." Horn Book

Johnston, Tony
The tale of Rabbit and Coyote; illustrated by Tomie de Paola. Putnam 1994 unp il $15.99; pa $5.99 (k-3)   **398.2**
1. Zapotec Indians—Folklore 2. Rabbit (Legendary character) 3. Coyote (Legendary character)
ISBN 0-399-22258-8; 0-698-11630-5 (pa)
                    LC 92-43652
Rabbit outwits Coyote in this Zapotec tale which explains why coyotes howl at the moon
"DePaola's vivid, spicy palette of gold, red, and turquoise tones and his use of folk-art borders evoke the desert setting and complement the broad humor of Johnston's text. A glossary of the Spanish phrases that pepper the illustrations is appended." Booklist

Joseph, Lynn
The mermaid's twin sister: more stories from Trinidad; illustrated by Donna Perrone. Clarion Bks. 1994 63p il $13.95; pa $5.95 (4 and up)   **398.2**
1. Folklore—Trinidad and Tobago
ISBN 0-395-64365-1; 0-395-81311-5 (pa)
                    LC 93-28436

Joseph, Lynn—*Continued*

"Tantie, Amber's great-aunt, passes the traditions and values of their Trinidad culture to the many children in the extended family. She has chosen Amber to be her successor, and it is Amber who faithfully records these stories, giving them the flavor of the Trinidad patois but keeping them completely intelligible to the American reader." Booklist

"Accompanied by striking black-and-white illustrations in chalk pastel. . . . The authentic folklore is told with flair, and a fine afterword sets each story in context." Horn Book Guide

A wave in her pocket; stories from Trinidad; illustrated by Brian Pinkney. Clarion Bks. 1991 51p il $15; pa $5.95 (4 and up)   **398.2**
  1. Folklore—Trinidad and Tobago
  ISBN 0-395-54432-7; 0-395-81309-3 (pa)
                          LC 90-39359
On the island of Trinidad, Tantie tells the children six stories, some originating in the countries of West Africa, some in Trinidad, and some in her own imagination

"Fresh and warm as an island breeze, these six stories combine Trinidad's traditional folklore with a child's view of island life. . . . Pinkney's distinctive drawings in white crosshatch on a black background echo the mysterious side of island life. This wonderful addition to the folklore shelf is spiced with magic and suspense." Booklist

Includes glossary

Kajikawa, Kimiko

Yoshi's feast; illustrated by Yumi Heo. DK Ink 2000 unp il $15.95 (k-3)   **398.2**
  1. Folklore—Japan
  ISBN 0-7894-2607-2   LC 99-14754
"A Melanie Kroupa book"
When Yoshi's neighbor, Sabu, the eel broiler, attempts to charge him for the delicious smelling aromas he has been enjoying, Yoshi hatches a plan to enrich them both

"Heo's dazzling collages of painting, pencil, and handmade papers bring out the outrageous action and humor in Yoshi and Sabu's conflict, extending the lively dialogue and rich text." Booklist

Keats, Ezra Jack, 1916-1983

John Henry; an American legend; story and pictures by Ezra Jack Keats. Pantheon Bks. 1965 unp il hardcover o.p. paperback available $5.99 (k-3)   **398.2**
  1. John Henry (Legendary character) 2. African Americans—Folklore 3. Folklore—United States
  ISBN 0-394-89052-3 (pa)   LC 86-27453
This is a picture book retelling of the legend of the Black American folk hero who drove spikes for the railroads

"The dynamic power with which John Henry wields his hammer is matched by the strong illustrations: brilliant oranges and reds contrast with grays and blacks that are often silhouettes; unusual backgrounds produce startling effects. A good picture-story to show to a group." Horn Book

Kellogg, Steven, 1941-

Chicken Little; retold & illustrated by Steven Kellogg. Morrow 1985 unp il hardcover o.p. paperback available $5.95 (k-3)   **398.2**
  1. Folklore 2. Animals—Fiction
  ISBN 0-688-07045-0 (pa)   LC 84-25519
Also available Spanish language edition
Chicken Little and his feathered friends, alarmed that the sky seems to be falling, are easy prey to hungry Foxy Loxy when he poses as a police officer in hopes of tricking them into his truck

"Kellogg has enlivened the text [by] giving it some modern touches (Turkey Lurkey carries golf clubs, Foxy Loxy is caught when a 'hippoliceman' tumbles out of a patrol helicopter to land him). Children have always enjoyed the repetition and cumulation of the story, as well as the silliness of the fowls who believe the sky is falling; here there's added fun." Bull Cent Child Books

Jack and the beanstalk; retold and illustrated by Steven Kellogg. Morrow Junior Bks. 1991 unp il $16; lib bdg $16.89; pa $6.95 (k-3)   **398.2**
  1. Fairy tales 2. Folklore—Great Britain 3. Giants—Fiction
  ISBN 0-688-10250-6; 0-688-10251-4 (lib bdg); 0-688-15281-3 (pa)   LC 90-45990
A boy climbs to the top of a giant beanstalk, where he uses his quick wits to outsmart a giant and make his and his mother's fortune

"Seldom has the ogre at the top of the beanstalk been depicted with such gusto! The warty, fanged, pug-nosed lout dressed in animal skins and a necklace of teeth is a wonder to behold. Steven Kellogg's humorous detail provides witty embellishment for savoring. His story line is quite faithful to the Joseph Jacobs version of the story, the sturdy text offering a strong framework for the energetic illustrations." Horn Book

Mike Fink; a tall tale; retold and illustrated by Steven Kellogg. Morrow Junior Bks. 1992 unp il $16; pa $6.95 (k-3)   **398.2**
  1. Fink, Mike, 1770-1823?—Fiction 2. Tall tales
  ISBN 0-688-07003-5; 0-688-13577-3 (pa)
                          LC 91-46014
Relates the extraordinary deeds of the frontiersman who became King of the Keelboatmen on the Mississippi River

"Steven Kellogg's ebullient retelling of Mike's tall-tale feats—illustrated with large, glowing scenes suffused with blue and yellow and with smaller vignettes emphasizing comic detail—follows Mike's prodigious childhood exploits, his teenage wrestling practice with Rocky Mountain grizzlies, and his years as King of the Keelboatmen, and closes with a final showdown with enormous steamboats taking over the river trade." Horn Book

Paul Bunyan; a tall tale; retold and illustrated by Steven Kellogg. Morrow 1984 unp il lib bdg $16.89; pa $5.95 (k-3)   **398.2**
  1. Bunyan, Paul (Legendary character) 2. Tall tales
  ISBN 0-688-03850-6 (lib bdg); 0-688-05800-0 (pa)
                          LC 83-26684
"Numerous events from the legendary north woodsman's life have been linked together as Bunyan and Babe, his big blue ox, traverse the U.S." Booklist

Kellogg, Steven, 1941-—*Continued*
"Kellogg uses oversize pages for busy, detail-crowded illustrations that have vitality and humor, echoing the exaggeration and ebullience of the story." Bull Cent Child Books

Pecos Bill; a tall tale; retold and illustrated by Steven Kellogg. Morrow 1986 unp il $17; pa $5.95 (k-3)   **398.2**
1. Pecos Bill (Legendary character) 2. Tall tales
ISBN 0-688-05871-X; 0-688-09924-6 (pa)
LC 86-784
Incidents from the life of Pecos Bill, from his childhood among the coyotes to his unusual wedding day
"Although there's a lot going on in these pictures, they're not cluttered; both the gradations of color and the page design smooth the lines of continuous action and tumult of humorous detail. Kellogg's portrayal of Pecos Bill as a perpetual boy will appeal to children. The retelling is a smooth adaptation for introducing young listeners to longer versions or to accompany storytelling sessions centered around tall-tale heroes." Bull Cent Child Books

Sally Ann Thunder Ann Whirlwind Crockett; a tall tale; retold and illustrated by Steven Kellogg. Morrow Junior Bks. 1995 unp il $17; lib bdg $16.93; pa $5.95 (k-3)   **398.2**
1. Crockett, Sally Ann Thunder Ann Whirlwind—Fiction 2. Tall tales
ISBN 0-688-14042-4; 0-688-14043-2 (lib bdg); 0-688-17113-3 (pa)   LC 94-43782
Sally Ann is "Davy's wife and a match for any bear, alligator, or macho man in the West. As retold (and scrupulously sourced) by Kellogg, Sally Ann's early life outracing and outswimming her nine big brothers and beating all comers at the state fair . . . is but a prelude to her flight to the frontier and subsequent rescue of and marriage to Davy Crockett. . . . Kellogg's characteristically energetic paintings meet their match in this story's kinetic hyperbole; the fact that his Sally Ann and Davy look like rambunctious big kids will only add to their story-hour appeal." Bull Cent Child Books

The three little pigs; retold and illustrated by Steven Kellogg. Morrow Junior Bks. 1997 unp il $16; lib bdg $15.93 (k-3)   **398.2**
1. Folklore 2. Pigs—Fiction
ISBN 0-688-08731-0; 0-688-08732-9 (lib bdg)
LC 96-34434
In this retelling of a well-known tale, Serafina Sow starts her own waffle-selling business in order to enable her three offspring to prepare for the future, which includes an encounter with a surly wolf
"Much of the broad humor is carried in the lively, colorful illustrations, though there's wordplay aplenty in the text and pictures too." Booklist

The three sillies. Candlewick Press 1999 unp il $16.99 (k-3)   **398.2**
1. Folklore—Great Britain
ISBN 0-7636-0811-4   LC 98-30646
A retelling of Joseph Jacobs' folk tale
A young man believes his sweetheart and her family are the three silliest people in the world until he meets three others who are even sillier
"Kellogg's ink-and-watercolor illustrations are wonderfully suited to the goofy goings-on. . . . While the telling itself is simple and straightforward, the dialogue balloons and plentiful asides add greatly to the humor." SLJ

Kherdian, David, 1931-
The golden bracelet; retold by David Kherdian; illustrated by Nonny Hogrogian. Holiday House 1998 unp il $16.95 (2-4)   **398.2**
1. Folklore—Armenia
ISBN 0-8234-1362-4   LC 95-25051
In order to win the hand of his love, indolent Prince Haig learns to weave beautiful golden cloth, a craft that later saves his life
"The illustrations' vibrant colors, flat perspectives, and decorative patterns suit this story's light touch." Horn Book Guide

Kimmel, Eric A.
The adventures of Hershel of Ostropol; retold by Eric A. Kimmel; with drawings by Trina Schart Hyman. Holiday House 1995 64p il $15.95; pa $7.95 (3-5)   **398.2**
1. Ostropoler, Hershele, 18th cent.—Legends 2. Jewish legends
ISBN 0-8234-1210-5; 0-8234-1404-3 (pa)
LC 95-8907
"Kimmel retells ten stories about Hershel of Ostropol, a Jewish folk hero who lived during the first part of the nineteenth century. A man quick with a humorous saying or jest, Hershel lived by his wits, traveling from town to town in Eastern Europe." Horn Book Guide
"Hyman's wild, beautifully detailed drawings . . . capture Hershel's farcical interchange with the village creatures and characters, including the miser, the bandit, and the rabbi. With their wry idiom, these are stories for telling across generations." Booklist

Anansi and the talking melon; retold by Eric A. Kimmel; illustrated by Janet Stevens. Holiday House 1994 unp il $16.95; pa $6.95 (k-3) **398.2**
1. Folklore—Africa 2. Anansi (Legendary character)
ISBN 0-8234-1104-4; 0-8234-1167-2 (pa)
LC 93-4239
Anansi the Spider tricks Elephant and some other animals into thinking the melon in which he is hiding can talk
"The snappy narration is well suited for individual reading or group sharing. The colorful line-and-wash illustrations are filled with movement and playful energy." SLJ

Anansi goes fishing; retold by Eric A. Kimmel; illustrated by Janet Stevens. Holiday House 1992 unp il $16.95; pa $6.95 (k-3)   **398.2**
1. Folklore—Africa 2. Anansi (Legendary character)
ISBN 0-8234-0918-X; 0-8234-1022-6 (pa)
LC 91-17813
Anansi the spider plans to trick Turtle into catching a fish for his dinner, but Turtle proves to be smarter and ends up with a free meal. Explains the origin of spider webs

Kimmel, Eric A.—*Continued*

"Children able to comprehend the wordplay will be delighted when the lazy but lovable trickster figure is outwitted by the clever turtle, and Stevens' colorful, comical illustrations are perfect for this contemporary rendition of the tale." Booklist

Bearhead; a Russian folktale; adapted by Eric A. Kimmel with illustrations by Charles Mikolaycak. Holiday House 1991 unp il $16.95; pa $8.95 (k-3)
398.2
1. Folklore—Russia 2. Fairy tales
ISBN 0-8234-0902-3; 0-8234-1302-0 (pa)
LC 91-55026
Bearhead succeeds in outwitting the witch Madame Hexaba and a frog-headed goblin
"Kimmel's lively text plays up the broad, almost slapstick humor of the story. Mikolaycak's watercolor-and-colored-pencil illustrations are deftly drawn." SLJ

The birds' gift; a Ukrainian Easter story; retold by Eric A. Kimmel; illustrated by Katya Krenina. Holiday House 1999 unp il $16.95 (k-3)   **398.2**
1. Easter—Fiction 2. Folklore—Ukraine
ISBN 0-8234-1384-5   LC 97-50209
Villagers take in a flock of golden birds nearly frozen by an early snow and are rewarded with beautifully decorated eggs the next spring
"Exquisitely detailed illustrations complete this engaging tale: pale yellow backgrounds reflect the birds' golden feathers, borders echo the designs on the eggs, and the Ukrainian costumes are lovingly rendered." Horn Book Guide

Gershon's monster; a story for the Jewish New Year; retold by Eric A. Kimmel; illustrated by Jon J Muth. Scholastic Press 2000 unp il $16.95 (k-3)
398.2
1. Jews—Folklore
ISBN 0-439-10839-X   LC 99-46986
When his sins threaten the lives of his beloved twin children, a Jewish man finally repents of his wicked ways
"This presentation of a Hasidic legend has everything a reader could want: a suspenseful story, an insightful lesson and brilliantly conceived, airy pictures that accelerate the delivery of both." Publ Wkly

The gingerbread man; retold by Eric A. Kimmel; illustrated by Megan Lloyd. Holiday House 1993 unp il $16.95 (k-2)   **398.2**
1. Folklore
ISBN 0-8234-0824-8   LC 90-33202
Also available with Audiobook
A freshly baked gingerbread man escapes when he is taken out of the oven and eludes a number of animals until he meets a clever fox
"This version softens the ending with a final page of fresh, recently baked gingerbread men. This is a story that calls for energetic art, and Lloyd provides just that in warm-toned watercolors that feature the gingerbread man zipping across the pages. A compact text and suitably large pictures make this just right for groups." Booklist

Iron John; adapted from the Brothers Grimm by Eric A. Kimmel; illustrated by Trina Schart Hyman. Holiday House 1994 unp il $16.95; pa $6.95 (2-5)   **398.2**
1. Fairy tales 2. Folklore—Germany
ISBN 0-8234-1073-0; 0-8234-1248-2 (pa)
LC 93-7534
With help of Iron John, the wild man of the forest who is under a curse, a young prince makes his way in the world and finds his true love
"Abridged and, as the afterword explains, somewhat changed from the Grimms' tale, Kimmel's dramatic narrative flows from scene to scene with a clear sense of adventure and romance and an underlying sense of mystery. Hyman's beautifully composed illustrations . . . are notable for their rich colors and subtle interplay of light and darkness." Booklist

The rooster's antlers; a story of the Chinese zodiac; retold by Eric A. Kimmel; illustrated by YongSheng Xuan. Holiday House 1999 unp il $16.95 (k-3)   **398.2**
1. Folklore—China 2. Zodiac
ISBN 0-8234-1385-3   LC 97-46854
Relates how the Jade Emperor chose twelve animals to represent the years in his calendar. Also discusses the Chinese calendar, zodiac, the qualities associated with each animal, and what animal rules the year in which the reader was born
"Xuan's illustrations, with their thick black outlines and bold colors, capture the simplicity and strength of Kimmel's telling." Booklist

Seven at one blow; a tale from the Brothers Grimm; retold by Eric A. Kimmel; illustrated by Megan Lloyd. Holiday House 1998 unp il $16.95 (k-3)   **398.2**
1. Fairy tales 2. Folklore—Germany
ISBN 0-8234-1383-7   LC 97-44200
Relates how a tailor who kills seven flies at one blow manages to become king
"Lloyd's watercolor illustrations are a treat for the eye and perfectly complement the rollicking humor of the tale." SLJ

The spotted pony: a collection of Hanukkah stories; retold by Eric A. Kimmel; illustrated by Leonard Everett Fisher. Holiday House 1992 70p il $15.95 (3-6)   **398.2**
1. Jews—Folklore 2. Hanukkah—Fiction
ISBN 0-8234-0936-8   LC 91-24214
This is a collection of "stories for Hanukkah. There are eight tales, one for each night, and each has a *shammes* or 'servant' story preceding it. All of the selections are rich in plot, character, and tradition. . . . Perfect for any occasion, this collection will truly shine when its selections are told or read aloud." SLJ

Ten suns; a Chinese legend; retold by Eric A. Kimmel; illustrated by YongSheng Xuan. Holiday House 1998 unp il $15.95 (2-4)   **398.2**
1. Folklore—China
ISBN 0-8234-1317-9   LC 96-30044
When the ten sons of Di Jun walk across the sky together causing the earth to burn from the blazing heat,

Kimmel, Eric A.—*Continued*
their father looks for a way to stop the destruction
"The dramatic retelling is enhanced by the vibrant colors and sweeping lines of the illustrations." Horn Book Guide

The three princes; a tale from the Middle East; retold by Eric A. Kimmel; illustrated by Leonard Everett Fisher. Holiday House 1994 unp il $16.95; pa $6.95 (k-3)   **398.2**
  1. Folklore—Middle East
  ISBN 0-8234-1115-X; 0-8234-1553-8 (pa)
                                    LC 93-25862
A princess promises to marry the prince who finds the most precious treasure
"Sly humor and high spirits buoy Kimmel's text. . . . Fisher . . . suggests the exotic Arabian setting with a rich palette of striking tones—pink desert skies, violet vistas—and by incorporating unexpected closeups and unusual angles in his compositions. The play of light and shadow is spectacular." Publ Wkly

Three sacks of truth; a story from France; adapted by Eric A. Kimmel; illustrated by Robert Rayevsky. Holiday House 1993 unp il $15.95 (2-4)   **398.2**
  1. Fairy tales 2. Folklore—France
  ISBN 0-8234-0921-X   LC 91-19265
With the aid of a perfect peach, a silver fife, and his own resources, Petit Jean outwits a dishonest king and wins the hand of a princess
"In this crisp and sprightly interpretation, storyteller Kimmel takes full advantage of the plot's sly humor, which he accentuates through many colorful, deft turns of phrase. . . . Rayevsky adds rich, predominantly earthtoned illustrations that emphasize character and expression with a slight ironic bite." Publ Wkly

The two mountains; an Aztec legend; retold by Eric A. Kimmel; illustrated by Leonard Everett Fisher. Holiday House 2000 unp il $16.95 (3-5)
                                    398.2
  1. Aztecs—Folklore 2. Folklore—Mexico
  ISBN 0-8234-1504-X   LC 99-32881
Two married gods disobey their orders and visit Earth, are turned into mortals as punishment, and eventually become mountains so that they will always stand side by side
"Acrylic paintings of large figures in Aztec clothing posed against wide skies have a spareness that accentuates this tale's stark drama." Horn Book Guide

Knutson, Barbara
  How the guinea fowl got her spots; a Swahili tale of friendship; retold and illustrated by Barbara Knutson. Carolrhoda Bks. 1990 unp il lib bdg $19.95; pa $6.95 (k-3)   **398.2**
  1. Folklore—Africa 2. Guinea fowl—Fiction
  ISBN 0-87614-416-4 (lib bdg); 0-87614-537-3 (pa)
                                    LC 89-25191
"In this traditional Swahili folktale, Guinea Fowl twice saves her friend Cow from Lion. In return, Cow sprinkles milk over the formerly all-black guinea fowl, disguising her from the lion and allowing her to easily

hide in the grasses. . . . Knutson's scratchboard illustrations . . . perfectly match the content and tone of the story. . . . The placement of the drawings and the exquisite design create a harmony that makes this a strikingly handsome addition to folktale collections." SLJ

Krishnaswami, Uma, 1956-
  Shower of gold: girls and women in the stories of India; retold by Uma Krishnaswami; with illustrations by Maniam Selven. Linnet Bks. 1999 125p il $19.95 (5 and up)   **398.2**
  1. Folklore—India
  ISBN 0-208-02484-0   LC 98-43142
A collection of stories featuring strong female figures from Hindu mythology, Buddhist tales, and others from the history and folklore of the Indian subcontinent. Each piece is accompanied by background information
"Retold with immediacy and verve. . . . Krishnaswami's informal introduction is eloquent about themes, ideas, women's roles, and cultural traditions in the stories she has chosen, and also about the way all stories move through time and place." Booklist

Kurtz, Jane
  Fire on the mountain; illustrated by E. B. Lewis. Simon & Schuster Bks. for Young Readers 1994 unp il hardcover o.p. paperback available $5.99 (1-4)   **398.2**
  1. Folklore—Ethiopia
  ISBN 0-689-81896-3 (pa)   LC 93-11477
A clever young shepherd boy uses his wits to gain a fortune for himself and his sister from a haughty rich man
"Lewis uses color to achieve intriguing contrast and articulates characters' faces with expression and power. Kurtz, who heard the story as a child in Ethiopia, retells it in a strong narrative voice: her language is simple and spare yet evocative." Booklist

Lattimore, Deborah Nourse
  Medusa. HarperCollins Pubs. 2000 unp il $15.95; lib bdg $15.89 (3-6)   **398.2**
  1. Medusa (Greek mythology) 2. Classical mythology
  ISBN 0-06-027904-4; 0-06-027905-2 (lib bdg)
                                    LC 99-29244
"Joanna Cotler books"
A retelling of the myth of Medusa, turned by Athena's curse into a gorgon whose gaze turned men to stone, and Perseus' quest to vanquish her in order to save his mother's life
"Large print and simple sentence structures and word choices make the text accessible to young readers. . . . The plot moves quickly. The formal language and the ornate illustrations suit the myth, giving it stateliness. The deep-hued colors and rich textures on the cover will attract readership." SLJ

Lee, Jeanne M.
  The song of Mu Lan. Front St. 1995 unp il $15.95   **398.2**
  1. Chinese poetry 2. Folklore—China 3. Bilingual books—English-Chinese
  ISBN 1-886910-00-6   LC 95-9594

Lee, Jeanne M.—*Continued*

"The bilingual edition of a 1500-year-old ballad celebrates the bravery of a Chinese woman. When the emperor calls her ailing father to battle, Mu Lan, having no elder brother, answers the call herself. . . . The story is told through terse, rhythmic, unrhymed stanzas, combining narration with Mu Lan's own words. Lee's art, influenced by classic Chinese painting, illuminates and amplifies the spare poetic text." SLJ

Toad is the uncle of heaven; a Vietnamese folk tale; retold and illustrated by Jeanne M. Lee. Holt & Co. 1985 unp il hardcover o.p. paperback available $6.95 (k-3)   398.2

1. Folklore—Vietnam 2. Toads—Fiction
ISBN 0-8050-1147-1 (pa)   LC 85-5639

Toad leads a group of animals to ask the King of Heaven to send rain to the parched earth

"The story is simple and reminiscent of motifs common to many cultures. . . . The author's simple prose and beautiful page design, far from being static or stilted, are fluid and convey movement and earthy humor. Her tale of courage born of common sense and perseverance will satisfy a wide audience." Horn Book

Lelooska, 1934-1996

Echoes of the elders; the stories and paintings of Chief Lelooska; edited by Christine Normandin. DK Pub. 1997 38p il $24.95 (4-6)   398.2

1. Native Americans—Folklore
ISBN 0-7894-2455-X   LC 97-34242

This "compendium showcases five traditional legends of the Kwakiutl people, one of the Northwest Coast Peoples." Publ Wkly

"Lelooska's paintings command as much attention as his words. The images, rendered in the flat colors and bold patterns familiar from coastal masks and totem poles, are placed for maximum impact. . . . A CD featuring Lelooska's animated tellings accompanies the book. A celebration of centuries of culture that will delight and give pause for generations to come." SLJ

Spirit of the cedar people; more stories and paintings of Chief Lelooska; edited by Christine Normandin; designed by Jennifer Wagner. DK Ink 1998 38p il $24.95 (4-6)   398.2

1. Native Americans—Folklore
ISBN 0-7894-2571-8   LC 98-3522

This is a "book of five Kwakiutl stories from the American northwest coast." Bull Cent Child Books

"Honed by a master storyteller, the tales are designed for reading aloud or telling. For hesitant performers, a CD of the author himself presenting his work is cleverly packaged into the endpapers. The words are mesmerizing; the artwork is stunning." Horn Book

Lesser, Rika

Hansel and Gretel; illustrated by Paul O. Zelinsky; retold by Rika Lesser. Dutton Children's Bks. 1999 unp il $16.99; pa $6,99 (k-3)   398.2

1. Fairy tales 2. Folklore—Germany
ISBN 0-525-46152-3; 0-698-11407-8 (pa)
                LC 99-10198

A Caldecott Medal honor book, 1985

A reissue of the edition first published 1984 by Dodd, Mead

A retelling of the well-known tale in which two children are left in the woods but find their way home despite an encounter with a wicked witch

"Direct and unembellished, Lesser's retelling resembles that of the earliest German edition of Grimm, published in 1812. . . . A visual feast, the illustrations frequently recall Flemish and French genre painting of the seventeenth century, while the idyllic woodland scenes reflect a later Romantic mood." Horn Book Guide

Lester, Julius

John Henry; pictures by Jerry Pinkney. Dial Bks. for Young Readers 1994 unp il $17.99; pa $6.99 (k-3)   398.2

1. John Henry (Legendary character) 2. African Americans—Folklore 3. Folklore—United States
ISBN 0-8037-1606-0; 0-14-056622-8 (pa)
                LC 93-34583

A Caldecott Medal honor book, 1995

"The original legend of John Henry and how he beat the steam drill with his sledgehammer has been enhanced and enriched, in Lester's retelling, with wonderful contemporary details and poetic similes that add humor, beauty, and strength. Pinkney's evocative illustrations—especially the landscapes, splotchy and impressionistic, yet very solid and vigorous—are little short of magnificent." Horn Book Guide

The knee-high man, and other tales; pictures by Ralph Pinto. Dial Bks. 1972 28p il hardcover o.p. paperback available $5.99 (k-3)   398.2

1. African Americans—Folklore 2. Animals—Fiction
ISBN 0-14-054810-6 (pa)

The author retells six animal stories from African American folklore

"These are excellent for story telling and should be so presented for the greatest impact." N Y Times Book Rev

The last tales of Uncle Remus; as told by Julius Lester; illustrated by Jerry Pinkney. Dial Bks. 1994 156p il $18.99 (4-6)   398.2

1. African Americans—Folklore 2. Animals—Fiction
ISBN 0-8037-1303-7   LC 93-7531

Also available Uncle Remus: the complete tales $30 (ISBN 0-8037-2451-9)

A retelling of thirty-nine African American tales

Other available Uncle Remus tales:
Further tales of Uncle Remus (1989)
More tales of Uncle Remus (1988)
The tales of Uncle Remus (1987)

Levine, Arthur A., 1962-

The boy who drew cats; a Japanese folktale; retold by Arthur A. Levine; pictures by Frédéric Clément. Dial Bks. for Young Readers 1994 unp il $16.99; lib bdg $15.89 (k-3)   398.2

1. Folklore—Japan 2. Cats—Fiction
ISBN 0-8037-1172-7; 0-8037-1173-5 (lib bdg)
                LC 91-46232

An artistic young boy's love for drawing cats gets him into trouble and leads him to a mysterious experience

Levine, Arthur A., 1962-—*Continued*

"The unembellished, smooth narrative nicely complements Clément's elegant acrylics. A source note is included, as well as a chart giving the pronunciation and meanings of the Japanese characters that appear at the top of each page of text." Horn Book Guide

Lewis, J. Patrick

At the wish of the fish; an adaptation of a Russian folktale; illustrated by Katya Krenina. Atheneum Bks. for Young Readers 1999 unp il $16 (k-3)   **398.2**

1. Fairy tales 2. Folklore—Russia

ISBN 0-689-81336-8   LC 97-42238

In this adaptation of a traditional Russian tale, Emelya the simpleton catches an enchanted fish which promises him that every wish he ever makes will come true

"Lewis has a skillful sense of pacing and conversation, and Krénina's gouache-and-watercolor folk-style pictures are bright, humorous, and full of movement." SLJ

Louie, Ai-Ling, 1949-

Yeh-Shen; a Cinderella story from China; retold by Ai-Ling Louie; illustrated by Ed Young. Philomel Bks. 1982 unp il $16.99; pa $6.99 (2-4)   **398.2**

1. Folklore—China 2. Fairy tales

ISBN 0-399-20900-X; 0-698-11388-8 (pa)

     LC 80-11745

This version of the Cinderella story, in which a young girl overcomes the wickedness of her stepsister and stepmother to become the bride of a prince, is based on ancient Chinese manuscripts written 1000 years before the earliest European version

"The reteller has cast the tale in well-cadenced prose, fleshing out the spare account with elegance and grace. In a manner reminiscent of Chinese scrolls and of decorated folding screens, the text is chiefly set within vertical panels, while the luminescent illustrations—less narrative than emotional—often increase their impact by overspreading the narrow framework or appearing on pages of their own." Horn Book

Lowell, Susan, 1950-

The bootmaker and the elves; pictures by Tom Curry. Orchard Bks. 1997 unp il $16.95; lib bdg $17.99; pa $6.95 (k-3)   **398.2**

1. West (U.S.)—Fiction 2. Folklore 3. Fairy tales

ISBN 0-531-30044-7; 0-531-33044-3 (lib bdg); 0-531-07138-3 (pa)   LC 96-53303

A retelling, set in the Old West, of the traditional story about two elves who help a poor shoemaker, or in this case a bootmaker, and his wife

"Curry's acrylic rendering of these western characters is the perfect accompaniment to Lowell's laconically funny text, and it's just bigger than life enough to make this a believable tall-tale fairy tale." Bull Cent Child Books

Lunge-Larsen, Lise

The troll with no heart in his body and other tales of trolls from Norway; retold by Lise Lunge-Larsen; woodcuts by Betsy Bowen. Houghton Mifflin 1999 92p il $18 (3-6)   **398.2**

1. Folklore—Norway

ISBN 0-395-91371-3   LC 98-43244

"Lunge-Larsen presents nine Norwegian tales about the greed and foolishness of trolls in a casual style that makes these stories ripe for reading aloud and storytelling. Her liveliness of language and easy turn of phrase give these retellings a comforting tone despite the sometimes scary events. Bowen's colored-ink woodblock prints, inspired by traditional Norwegian woodcarving and design, suit the monumental nature of the subject." Bull Cent Child Books

Includes bibliographical references

Lurie, Alison

The black geese; a Baba Yaga story from Russia; retold by Alison Lurie; illustrated by Jessica Souhami. DK Pub. 1999 unp il $14.95 (k-3)   **398.2**

1. Fairy tales 2. Folklore—Russia

ISBN 0-7894-2558-0   LC 98-3681

"A DK Ink book"

When her little brother is taken away by the black geese belonging to the terrible witch, Baba Yaga, Elena searches for him in the great dark forest

"Souhami's bright illustrations are as spare and lively as Lurie's beautifully honed narrative." Horn Book Guide

MacDonald, Margaret Read

The girl who wore too much; a folktale from Thailand; retold by Margaret Read MacDonald with Thai text by Supaporn Vathanaprida; illustrated by Yvonne Davis. August House LittleFolk 1998 unp il $15.95 (k-3)   **398.2**

1. Folklore—Thailand 2. Bilingual books—English-Thai

ISBN 0-87483-503-8   LC 97-38807

Spoiled and vain, Aree cannot decide which of her many silken dresses and lavish jewels to wear to the dance, so she wears them all

"The story is told in rhythmic, cadenced sentences, ideal for reading aloud. The illustrations substitute modern rural Thailand for the archaic setting of the original tale and depict the characters as somewhat stylized figures dressed in brightly colored Thai silks." SLJ

Pickin' peas; retold by Margaret Read MacDonald; pictures by Pat Cummings. HarperCollins Pubs. 1998 unp il music $15.95; lib bdg $15.89 (k-3)   **398.2**

1. Rabbits—Fiction 2. Folklore—Southern States

ISBN 0-06-027235-X; 0-06-027970-2 (lib bdg)

     LC 95-26133

Because a pesky rabbit picks peas from her garden, a little girl catches it and puts it in a box, but the rabbit outwits her

"Fans of Brer Rabbit stories will have a very good time with this classic tale. The retelling is fresh and is anchored by the repetition of the bouncy, catchy refrain. The illustrations are bold, bright, and action-packed." Booklist

The **Magic** orange tree, and other Haitian folktales; collected by Diane Wolkstein; drawings by Elsa Henriquez. Knopf 1978 212p il music o.p.; Schocken Bks. paperback available $14 (5 and up)   398.2

1. Folklore—Haiti

ISBN 0-8052-1077-6 (pa)   LC 77-15003

"A rare collection of folktales and songs is presented in this volume. Miss Wolkstein travelled throughout Haiti listening to the many storytellers in all areas. Each of the twenty-eight tales is preceded by an introduction which details the circumstances surrounding the collection of each story. The blend of cultures found in Haiti is well-depicted in her selections. The introduction in itself is as spellbinding as are the stories. . . . An added delight is the inclusion of music and words in both English and Creole." Bibliophile

Mahy, Margaret

The seven Chinese brothers; illustrated by Jean and Mou-Sien Tseng. Scholastic 1990 unp hardcover o.p. paperback available $5.99 (1-3)   398.2

1. Folklore—China 2. Fairy tales

ISBN 0-590-42057-7 (pa)   LC 88-33668

A story about "seven brothers, each of whom was blessed with an extraordinary power. Together, they use their amazing talents to avoid death at the hands of Emperor Ch'in Shih Huang, while trying to help the exhausted conscripted laborers working on the Great Wall." Child Book Rev Serv

"The handsome watercolor illustrations show a sensitivity to landscape and character portrayal . . . a hint of humor, and a flair for the dramatic. Written with Mahy's accustomed storytelling skill, this book will find an eager audience as a read-aloud for elementary school children." Booklist

Manna, Anthony L.

Mr. Semolina-Semolinus; a Greek folktale; retold by Anthony L. Manna and Christodoula Mitakidou; illustrated by Giselle Potter. Atheneum Bks. for Young Readers 1997 unp il $16 (1-3)   398.2

1. Folklore—Greece

ISBN 0-689-81093-8   LC 96-1924

"An Anne Schwartz book"

Areti, a Greek princess, makes a man fit for her to love from almonds, sugar, and semolina, but when he is stolen away by a jealous queen, Areti searches the world for him

"This engaging tale, told in flowing prose with the charming authenticity of oral tradition, is enhanced by Potter's use of colored ink and pencil." Booklist

Mark, Jan

The Midas touch; illustrated by Juan Wijngaard. Candlewick Press 1999 unp il $16.99   398.2

1. Midas (Legendary character)

ISBN 0-7636-0488-7   LC 98-21922

A retelling of the classic story of King Midas, who foolishly wishes that everything he touch be turned to gold, and only then realizes his horrible mistake

"The story and Wijngaard's illustrations are set against intricate double-spread mosaics that change from swirling leaves, grapes, and butterflies to glaring, lifeless gold. Within each mosaic spread, a small framed watercolor painting focuses the narrative on the king, the god, and the stiffening, dying landscape. There's shivery appeal in the combination of classical beauty and horror." Booklist

Marshall, James, 1942-1992

Goldilocks and the three bears; retold and illustrated by James Marshall. Dial Bks. for Young Readers 1988 unp il $15.99; pa $5.99 (k-2)   398.2

1. Folklore 2. Bears—Fiction

ISBN 0-8037-0542-5; 0-14-056366-0 (pa)

LC 87-32983

A Caldecott Medal honor book, 1989

"Marshall's Goldilocks, the naughty little girl who disrupts a placid bear household, is no adorable blond moppet led more by curiosity than by mischievous intent. Instead, she is a sturdy, brazen, mini-hussy who stomps over the doorsill with a determined set to her mouth and a confident bounce in her step. . . . The big cartoonlike pictures depict a cozy modern setting for the respectable, suburban bears with snug rooms cluttered with books, bulbous upholstered furniture and a messy little bear's room. . . . The story contains a genuine enjoyment of Goldilock's adventures as they are reflected in Marshall's usual slapdash and rollicking illustrations." Horn Book

Hansel and Gretel; retold and illustrated by James Marshall. Dial Bks. for Young Readers 1990 unp il hardcover o.p. paperback available $5.99 (k-2)   398.2

1. Folklore—Germany 2. Fairy tales

ISBN 0-14-050836-8 (pa)   LC 89-26011

A poor woodcutter's children, lost in the forest, come upon a house made of cookies, cakes, and candy, occupied by a wicked witch who likes to have children for dinner

"Marshall's trademark wit and slyness mark every page of this effervescent interpretation. Never has there been a more horribly magnificent witch than his—an overstuffed, cackling harridan resplendent in scarlet costume, lipstick and rouge, her hair bedecked with incongruously delicate bows." Publ Wkly

Red Riding Hood; retold and illustrated by James Marshall. Dial Bks. for Young Readers 1987 unp il $15.99; pa $5.99 (k-2)   398.2

1. Folklore—Germany 2. Wolves—Fiction

ISBN 0-8037-0344-9; 0-14-054693-6 (pa)

LC 86-16722

Also available with Audiobook

A "retelling of the familiar tale . . . maintaining the integrity of the Grimm Brothers' version, with both Grandma and Red Riding Hood eaten and later rescued by a hunter." SLJ

This version "will have both children and their parents gripped with the drama and amused by the up-to-date dialogue. . . . The humorous, slightly sinister illustrations display Marshall's wacky style to its best advantage. Funny and wonderful for reading aloud." Horn Book

Marshall, James, 1942-1992—*Continued*

The three little pigs; retold and illustrated by James Marshall. Dial Bks. for Young Readers 1989 unp il $15.99 (k-2)   **398.2**
  1. Folklore—Great Britain   2. Pigs—Fiction
3. Wolves—Fiction
  ISBN 0-8037-0591-3   LC 88-33411

"In his spiffed-up version of the story, the three porkers follow the traditional course of straw, sticks, and bricks with the traditional results, but the players and accoutrements have a bit more zip than those in other versions. . . . The large, exuberant, cartoonlike illustrations provide much additional entertainment, jouncing readers along delightfully from one amusing scene to the next." Horn Book

Martin, Rafe, 1946-

The boy who lived with the seals; illustrated by David Shannon. Putnam 1993 unp il $16.99 (1-4)
                                    398.2
  1. Chinook Indians—Folklore   2. Seals (Animals)—Fiction
  ISBN 0-399-22413-0   LC 91-46023

In this Chinook legend, a lost boy who has grown up in the sea with seals returns to his tribe but is strangely changed

"Shannon's dark, romantic paintings are dramatically stylized. . . . Martin's retelling employs lyrical language while carefully retaining a clarity appropriate for the intended audience." Publ Wkly

The language of birds; illustrations by Susan Gaber. Putnam 2000 unp il $15.99 (2-4)   **398.2**
  1. Fairy tales   2. Folklore—Russia
  ISBN 0-399-22925-6   LC 98-48917

A retelling of the Russian folktale in which Ivan, the younger son of a merchant, marries the czar's daughter and gains wealth by learning to understand the language of birds

"The text maintains a rolling pace and lends itself easily to reading aloud or storytelling. Acrylic paintings echo Russian folk art, with borders of birds, feathers, and bird feet running around the edges of the full-and double-page images. . . . This is an unusually robust, inviting folktale setting." Bull Cent Child Books

Mysterious tales of Japan; illustrated by Tatsuro Kiuchi. Putnam 1996 74p il $19.99 (4 and up)
                                    398.2
  1. Folklore—Japan
  ISBN 0-399-22677-X   LC 94-43464

"Some of these 10 stories, such as 'The Boy Who Drew Cats,' will be familiar to readers; others will not. . . . Most of the tales focus on the spiritual powers within nature. A woman falls in love with a pine tree; a man marries a dangerous snow maiden; a priest is granted a wish to live three days as a carp." Booklist

The author retells these "well-chosen tales in the lively voice of a talented storyteller. . . . Shivery, mysterious, and cool as moonlight, these retellings respect both their sources and their audience, while doing what stories do best—entertain." SLJ

Includes bibliographical references

Mayer, Marianna, 1945-

Baba Yaga and Vasilisa the brave; as told by Marianna Mayer; illustrated by K. Y. Craft. Morrow Junior Bks. 1994 unp il $16.95 (3-5)
                                    398.2
  1. Fairy tales   2. Folklore—Russia
  ISBN 0-688-08500-8   LC 90-38514

A retelling of the old Russian fairy tale in which beautiful Vasilisa uses the help of her doll to escape from the clutches of the witch Baba Yaga, who in turn sets in motion the events which lead to the once ill-treated girl's marrying the tzar

"Mayer's graceful prose conveys both the wonder and power of the tale. Complementing the text are Craft's illustrations done in a mixture of watercolor, gouache, and oils. The palette of red and gold set against a dark background resembles Russian folk-art paintings on black-lacquered wood." SLJ

Beauty and the beast; retold by Marianna Mayer; illustrated by Mercer Mayer. Four Winds Press 1978 unp il $15.95 (1-4)   **398.2**
  1. Folklore—France   2. Fairy tales
  ISBN 0-02-765270-X   LC 78-54679

Through her great capacity to love, a kind and beautiful maid releases a handsome prince from the spell which has made him an ugly beast

"This fresh, new version of the classic French tale is a valid condensation of its lengthier ancestors. Ms. Mayer's clear, crisp style perfectly complements the book's visual qualities. Mercer Mayer's illustrations are, quite simply, superb. They are dramatic and evocative, rich in warm, earth tones and exotic detail." Child Book Rev Serv

Iron John; [as told by] Marianna Mayer; [illustrated by] Winslow Pels. Morrow Junior Bks. 1999 unp il $16; lib bdg $14.93 (3-6)   **398.2**
  1. Fairy tales   2. Folklore—Germany
  ISBN 0-688-11554-3; 0-688-11555-1 (lib bdg)
                                  LC 97-45664

With the help of Iron John, also known as the wild man of the forest, a young prince makes his way in the world and finds his true love

"This is a highly enjoyable tale for modern readers and Mayer's masterful narrative abilities are in full evidence here. Pel's dramatic paintings add to the power of the story and accentuate its lyricism, while providing their own elegant charm." SLJ

Includes bibliographical references

Mayo, Margaret, 1935-

Magical tales from many lands; retold by Margaret Mayo; illustrated by Jane Ray. Dutton Children's Bks. 1993 126p il $22.99 (3-6) **398.2**
  1. Folklore
  ISBN 0-525-45017-3   LC 93-12164

"Mayo presents 14 traditional tales from around the world. . . . As retold by Mayo, the stories read aloud well, and that makes them a pleasure to read silently as well. Ray's striking, full-color artwork appears on every page, illustrating the tales with richly patterned, well-composed illustrations that will draw readers to the book." Booklist

Includes bibliographical references

Mayo, Margaret, 1935——*Continued*

Mythical birds & beasts from many lands; retold by Margaret Mayo; illustrated by Jane Ray. Dutton Children's Bks. 1997 c1996 108p il $19.99 (3-6)

398.2

1. Animals—Fiction 2. Folklore 3. Mythology
ISBN 0-525-45788-7   LC 96-36798
First published 1996 in the United Kingdom with title: The Orchard book of mythical birds & beasts

"Mayo retells ten stories, among them tales of Pegasus and the Chimera, the Thunderbird, Quetzalcoatl, and the Nagini, a Burmese Cobra-Woman." Bull Cent Child Books

The "stories are from a variety of cultures and are narrated in an informal yet smooth storytelling style, often with light, effective touches of humor. . . . Ray's distinctive textured paintings are lush and full paged. . . . The earthy palette adds mystery and magic to the text, and her restrained use of gold highlighting is . . . highly effective." SLJ

Includes bibliographical references

McCaughrean, Geraldine, 1951-

The bronze cauldron: myths and legends of the world; illustrated by Bee Willey. Margaret K. McElderry Bks. 1998 c1997 130p il $19.95 (4-6)

398.2

1. Folklore
ISBN 0-689-81758-4   LC 97-72081
First published 1997 in the United Kingdom

"This collection presents twenty-seven elegantly retold stories, gleaned from sources as diverse as the Mayan *Popul Vuh*, French *Chansons de geste*, Russian *byliny*, as well as Greek, Indian, Chinese, Polynesian, Australian, and Inuit folklore. Willey's playful, brightly colored illustrations are a perfect match for this celebration of story around the world." Horn Book Guide

The crystal pool: myths and legends of the world; illustrated by Bee Willey. Margaret K. McElderry Bks. 1999 c1998 138p il $20 (4-6)

398.2

1. Folklore
ISBN 0-689-82266-9
First published 1998 in the United Kingdom

This is a "collection of twenty-eight legends, myths, and stories from a variety of cultures including Inuit, Maori, Sumerian, Egyptian, Hindu, and Bantu." Bull Cent Child Books

"Bee Willey's stylized paintings seem lit from within, intensifying the sense of mystery that underlies even the jocular tales. Unsurpassed for range, language, and presentation." Booklist

The golden hoard: myths and legends of the world; illustrated by Bee Willey. Margaret K. McElderry Bks. 1996 c1995 130p il $19.95 (4-6)

398.2

1. Folklore
ISBN 0-689-80741-4
First published 1995 in the United Kingdom

This collection of 22 tales includes the story of King Midas, an Anansi story, Polynesian, Mexican, and Native American myths and a Robin Hood story

"This is a resource anthology for reading aloud or storytelling and for readers to dip into for themselves, one story at a time. Mixed media illustrations in brilliantly colored folk-art style extend the action, romance, and magic of the stories." Booklist

Grandma Chickenlegs; illustrated by Moira Kemp. Carolrhoda Bks. 1999 unp il $15.95 (k-3)

398.2

1. Folklore—Russia
ISBN 1-57505-415-9   LC 99-19161
In this variation of the traditional Baba Yaga story, a young girl must rely on the advice of her dead mother and her special doll when her wicked stepmother sends her to get a needle from Grandma Chickenlegs

"McCaughrean's well-paced narrative is rich in imagery and humor. . . . Kemp's colored-pencil illustrations are rendered with accessibly childlike simplicity, but she also uses sophisticated composition and perspectives to enhance the drama." Horn Book

The silver treasure: myths and legends of the world; illustrated by Bee Willey. Margaret K. McElderry Bks. 1997 c1996 130p il $21 (4-6)

398.2

1. Folklore
ISBN 0-689-81322-8   LC 96-76845
Also available Audiobook version
First published 1996 in the United Kingdom

"In this collection of 23 myths and legends, some stories are as familiar as Rip Van Winkle and the Tower of Babel, whereas others may be new to most readers." Booklist

"These tales are truly marvels—in both their meaningful content and in the teller's lyrical mastery of language." SLJ

McClintock, Barbara, 1955-

Animal fables from Aesop; adapted and illustrated by Barbara McClintock. Godine 1991 unp il hardcover o.p. paperback available $10.95 (1-4)

398.2

1. Fables 2. Animals—Fiction
ISBN 1-56792-144-2 (pa)   LC 91-55368
The fables "are framed at the beginning and end by scenes from a stage set, with the actors posing as animals introducing themselves to us on the opening page and bowing at our expected applause on the last. The graceful full-color illustrations are both delicate and theatrical, as the limited cast reappears in various tales . . . dressed as 18th- or 19th-century townspeople, with the dramatic gestures and facial expressions of humans. . . . The whole feel of this book is in the tradition of La Fontaine: gay, witty, full of charm and foible." N Y Times Book Rev

McDermott, Gerald

Anansi the spider; a tale from the Ashanti; adapted and illustrated by Gerald McDermott. Holt & Co. 1972 unp il $16.95; pa $6.95 (k-3) **398.2**

1. Folklore—Ghana 2. Ashanti (African people)—Folklore 3. Anansi (Legendary character)
ISBN 0-8050-0310-X; 0-8050-0311-8 (pa)

McDermott, Gerald—*Continued*

A Caldecott Medal honor book, 1973

The adaptation of this traditional tale of Ghana is based on an animated film by McDermott. It tells of Anansi, a spider, who is saved from terrible fates by his six sons and is unable to decide which of them to reward. The solution to his predicament is also an explanation for how the moon was put into the sky

This offers "brief poetic text, complemented by geometric African folk-style illustrations in pure, bold colors." SLJ

Arrow to the sun; a Pueblo Indian tale; adapted and illustrated by Gerald McDermott. Viking 1974 unp il $16.99; pa $6.99 (k-3)   **398.2**

1. Pueblo Indians—Folklore

ISBN 0-670-13369-8; 0-14-050211-4 (pa)

Also available Spanish language edition and Audiobook version

Awarded the Caldecott Medal, 1975

This myth tells how Boy searches for his immortal father, the Lord of the Sun, in order to substantiate his paternal heritage. Shot as an arrow to the sun, Boy passes through the four chambers of ceremony to prove himself. Accepted by his father, he returns to earth to bring the Lord of the Sun's spirit to the world of men

"The simple, brief text—which suggests similar stories in religion and folklore—is amply illustrated in full-page and doublespread pictures. . . . The strong colors and the bold angular forms powerfully accompany the text." Horn Book

Coyote: a trickster tale from the American Southwest; told and illustrated by Gerald McDermott. Harcourt Brace & Co. 1994 unp il $15; pa $6 (k-3)   **398.2**

1. Native Americans—Folklore 2. Coyote (Legendary character)

ISBN 0-15-220724-4; 0-15-200032-1 (pa)

LC 92-32979

"Coyote persuades the crows to help him fly, but he becomes so obnoxious and boastful that they abandon him in midair, so he falls back to earth. Told with playful illustrations against the glowing orange of a desert sky, the humorous Zuni tale explains how Coyote, who once had blue fur, got his dust-colored coat and black-tippped tail." Horn Book Guide

Musicians of the sun. Simon & Schuster Bks. for Young Readers 1997 unp il $17; pa $6.99 (k-3)   **398.2**

1. Mexico—Folklore

ISBN 0-689-80706-6; 0-689-93907-3 (pa)

LC 96-19891

In this retelling of an Aztec myth, Lord of the Night sends Wind to free the four musicians that the Sun is holding prisoner so they can bring joy to the world

"This work bears the hallmarks of McDermott's style: vivid colors, illustrations informed by cultural iconography and mythology, an engaging story, and complete source notes." Bull Cent Child Books

Raven; a trickster tale from the Pacific Northwest; told and illustrated by Gerald McDermott. Harcourt Brace Jovanovich 1993 unp il $16 (k-3)   **398.2**

1. Native Americans—Folklore

ISBN 0-15-265661-8   LC 91-14563

A Caldecott Medal honor book, 1994

Raven, a Pacific Coast Indian trickster, sets out to find the sun

"Raven, whether he appears as a bird or child, is always marked with a distinctive design of clear-cut red, green, and blue on black, sharply contrasting with the softer hues and forms of the backgrounds and the other characters. In this way, Raven is always recognizable, even when he shifts his shape to human form. . . . Read this picture book aloud for the full effect of its simple, rhythmic text and striking artwork." Booklist

Zomo the Rabbit; a trickster tale from West Africa; told and illustrated by Gerald McDermott. Harcourt Brace Jovanovich 1992 unp il $14.95; pa $6 (k-3)   **398.2**

1. Folklore—Africa 2. Rabbits—Fiction

ISBN 0-15-299967-1; 0-15-201010-6 (pa)

LC 91-14558

"Zomo the Rabbit, an African trickster . . . goes to Sky God and requests wisdom. Sky God informs him that he must earn it and assigns him three impossible tasks." Child Book Rev Serv

"Like the spare text, the shapes here are boldly controlled—ideal for sharing with a group of very young children. Because of their rich patterns and sharp color contrasts, the images in the gouache paintings, although simple, never become simplistic." Bull Cent Child Books

McGovern, Ann

Too much noise; illustrated by Simms Taback. Houghton Mifflin 1967 44p il $16; pa $6.95 (k-3)   **398.2**

1. Folklore

ISBN 0-395-18110-0; 0-395-62985-3 (pa)

"The too crowded house of a familiar old tale becomes a too noisy house in this entertaining picture-book story. Bothered by the noises in his house, an old man follows the advice of the village wise man by first acquiring and then getting rid of a cow, donkey, sheep, hen, dog, and cat. Only then can he appreciate how quiet his house is. The simplicity and straightforwardness of the folktale are evident in both the telling of the cumulative story and in the amusing colored illustrations." Booklist

Mollel, Tololwa M. (Tololwa Marti)

Ananse's feast; an Ashanti tale; retold by Tololwa M. Mollel; illustrated by Andrew Glass. Clarion Bks. 1997 31p il $14.95 (k-3)   **398.2**

1. Anansi (Legendary character) 2. Ashanti (African people)—Folklore 3. Folklore—Ghana

ISBN 0-395-67402-6   LC 95-17358

Unwilling to share his feast, Ananse the spider tricks Akye the turtle so that he can eat all the food himself, but Akye finds a way to get even

"Varied in composition and bright with layers of color, the oil-and-colored-pencil artwork captures the actions, reactions, and emotions of the two main characters with a great sense of playfulness and humor." Booklist

Mollel, Tololwa M. (Tololwa Marti)—*Continued*

The orphan boy; a Maasai story; illustrated by Paul Morin. Clarion Bks. 1990 unp il $16; pa $6.95 (k-3) **398.2**
1. Masai (African people)—Folklore 2. Folklore—Africa
ISBN 0-89919-985-2; 0-395-72079-6 (pa)

LC 90-2358

"A solitary old man on the wide plains welcomes into his compound an orphan boy, Kileken, who helps with the work and the cattle and brings prosperity even in times of drought. But when the old man insists on knowing the boy's secret, Kileken returns to his place in the sky. He is the steadily shining star . . . that is the planet Venus." Booklist

"Infused with an aura of mystery, Mollel's compelling story is told skillfully and dramatically. Morin's richly textured paintings, evoking in bold colors an Africa of both parched desert and lush vegetation, are worthy companions." Publ Wkly

Moroney, Lynn

Baby rattlesnake; told by Te Ata; adapted by Lynn Moroney; illustrated by Veg Reisberg. Children's Bk. Press 1989 30p il $14.95; pa $7.95 (k-2) **398.2**
1. Chickasaw Indians—Folklore 2. Rattlesnakes—Fiction
ISBN 0-89239-049-2; 0-89239-111-1 (pa)

LC 89-9892

Also available Spanish language edition
In this Chickasaw Indian tale, willful Baby Rattlesnake throws tantrums to get his rattle before he's ready, but he misuses it and learns a lesson

"The short sentences, onomatopoeia, and repetition will hold the attention of the youngest listeners as will the boldly colored, stylized gouache and cut-paper illustrations that depict the endearing Rattlesnake family." Booklist

Mosel, Arlene

The funny little woman; retold by Arlene Mosel; pictures by Blair Lent. Dutton 1972 unp il hardcover o.p. paperback available $5.99 (k-2) **398.2**
1. Folklore—Japan
ISBN 0-14-054753-3 (pa)
Awarded the Caldecott Medal, 1973
Based on Lafcadio Hearn's The old woman and her dumpling

While chasing a dumpling, a little lady is captured by wicked creatures from whom she escapes with the means of becoming the richest woman in Japan

"The tale unfolds in a simple tellable style. . . . Using elements of traditional Japanese art, the illustrator has made marvelously imaginative pictures. . . . All the inherent drama and humor of the story are manifest in the illustrations." Horn Book

Tikki Tikki Tembo; retold by Arlene Mosel; illustrated by Blair Lent. Holt & Co. 1968 unp il $16.95; pa $6.95 (k-2) **398.2**
1. Folklore—China 2. Personal names—Fiction
ISBN 0-8050-0662-1; 0-8050-1166-8 (pa)

Also available Big book edition and Spanish language edition

A "Chinese folk tale about a first son with a very long name. When Tikki Tikki Tembo-No Sa Rembo-Chari Bari Ruchi-Pip Peri Pembo fell into the well, it took his little brother so long to say his name and get help that Tikki almost drowned." Hodges. Books for Elem Sch Libr

"In this polished version of a story hour favorite, beautifully stylized wash drawings of serene Oriental landscapes are in comic contrast to amusingly visualized folk and the active disasters accruing to the possessor of a 21-syllable, irresistibly chantable name." Best Books of the Year, 1968

Nolan, Dennis, 1945-

Androcles and the lion; retold and illustrated by Dennis Nolan. Harcourt Brace & Co. 1997 unp il $15 (1-3) **398.2**
1. Fables 2. Lions—Fiction
ISBN 0-15-203355-6

LC 95-47578

"This retelling of Androcles's flight from a cruel master into the Egyptian desert, his ministering to a wounded lion, and their resultant friendship derives its power from its succinct language and compelling illustrations. . . . The cream-colored paper and golden-hued sketches with irregular borders resemble antique parchment." SLJ

Norman, Howard

The girl who dreamed only geese, and other tales of the Far North; told by Howard Norman; illustrated by Leo & Diane Dillon. Harcourt Brace & Co. 1997 147p il $22 (4 and up) **398.2**
1. Inuit—Folklore
ISBN 0-15-230979-9

LC 96-20880

"Gulliver books"
A collection of stories retold from Inuit folklore

"The narratives have a marvelous vitality and excitement. They capture the sound and cadence of the spoken word. . . . The plots reflect the diversity and humor of Inuit culture. . . . Each tale is accompanied by several large, full-color acrylic illustrations in addition to outstanding black-and-white friezes that run across the top of each page." SLJ

Trickster and the fainting birds; told by Howard Norman; illustrated by Tom Pohrt. Harcourt Brace & Co. 1999 82p il $20 (4 and up) **398.2**
1. Algonquian Indians—Folklore
ISBN 0-15-200888-8

LC 97-9457

"Gulliver books"
"Norman has gathered these seven Algonquian tales from Native storytellers in Manitoba, Canada." SLJ

"The stories are funny and related in a lively, understated manner, perfect for storytelling. . . . The pen, ink, and watercolor illustrations accurately capture the northern pine forest setting from which the stories spring, adding significantly to their appeal and providing a sense of their culture of origin." Horn Book

Includes bibliographical references

Olaleye, Isaac

In the Rainfield; who is the greatest? [by] Isaac O. Olaleye; illustrated by Ann Grifalconi. Blue Sky Press (NY) 2000 unp il $16.95 (k-3)   **398.2**
1. Yoruba (African people)—Folklore 2. Folklore—Nigeria
ISBN 0-590-48363-3   LC 97-39861
When Wind, Fire, and Rain meet in the land of the Yoruba to decide which of them is the greatest, Wind and Fire make great shows of strength, but Rain demonstrates the power of gentleness
"The story is simple and direct, told with sound effects integrated into the text. . . . Grifalconi's illustrations—collage with cutout photos and paint—are scary and sophisticated." Booklist

Olson, Arielle North, 1932-

Ask the bones: scary stories from around the world; selected and retold by Arielle North Olson and Howard Schwartz; illustrated by David Linn. Viking 1999 145p il $15.99 (4 and up)   **398.2**
1. Folklore
ISBN 0-670-87581-3   LC 98-19108
A collection of scary folktales from countries around the world including China, Russia, Spain, and the United States
"David Linn's bone-chilling black-and-white illustrations. . . will stay with the reader long after the book is closed. Excellent for reading aloud, this collection will satisfy even jaded genre fans." Booklist
Includes bibliographical references

Oram, Hiawyn

Baba Yaga & the wise doll; a traditional Russian folktale; retold by Hiawyn Oram; illustrated by Ruth Brown. Dutton Children's Bks. 1998 c1997 unp il $15.99 (k-3)   **398.2**
1. Folklore—Russia
ISBN 0-525-45947-2   LC 98-124555
First published 1997 in the United Kingdom
"Too Nice Child is driven out of the house by Horrid and Very Horrid, who order her to bring them one of Baba Yaga's toads with its jeweled jacket. Too Nice is terrified, but with the help of her sensible doll . . . she is able to perform the arduous tasks that the witch demands of her." Booklist
"This snappy retelling features plenty of dialogue. . . . Dramatic illustrations contrast the big-eyed, innocent Too Nice with a tangibly—and glamorously—demonic Baba Yaga." Horn Book Guide

Osborne, Mary Pope, 1949-

American tall tales; wood engravings by Michael McCurdy. Knopf 1991 115p il map $22 (3-6)   **398.2**
1. Tall tales 2. Folklore—United States
ISBN 0-679-90089-1   LC 89-37235
A collection of tall tales about such American folk heroes as Sally Ann Thunder Ann Whirlwind, Pecos Bill, John Henry, and Paul Bunyan
"As tantalizing as Osborne's storytelling are McCurdy's . . . elaborate, full-color wood engravings, which in their robust stylization dramatically render the grandeur of these engrossing yarns." Publ Wkly
Includes bibliographical references

Favorite medieval tales; retold by Mary Pope Osborne; illustrated by Troy Howell. Scholastic 1998 86p il $17.95 (4 and up)   **398.2**
1. Folklore—Europe
ISBN 0-590-60042-7   LC 96-17285
A collection of well-known tales from medieval Europe, including "Beowulf," "The Sword in the Stone," "The Song of Roland," and "Gudren and the Island of the Lost Children"
"Inspired by medieval art and illuminated manuscripts, Howell's paintings complement the well-researched text." Horn Book Guide
Includes bibliographical references

Kate and the beanstalk; written by Mary Pope Osborne; illustrated by Giselle Potter. Atheneum Bks. for Young Readers 2000 unp il $16 (k-3)   **398.2**
1. Fairy tales 2. Folklore—Great Britain 3. Giants—Fiction
ISBN 0-689-82550-1   LC 99-27029
"An Anne Schwartz book"
In this version of the classic tale, a girl climbs to the top of a giant beanstalk, where she uses her quick wits to outsmart a giant and make her and her mother's fortune
"The text is straightforward but punctuated by some delicious dialogue. . . . Using a variety of mediums—pencil, ink, gouache, and watercolor—the illustrations are executed in Potter's signature folk-art style. They are immediate, innovative, and just the right size for story hours." Booklist

Mermaid tales from around the world; retold by Mary Pope Osborne; illustrated by Troy Howell. Scholastic 1993 84p il hardcover o.p. paperback available $7.99 (4-6)   **398.2**
1. Mermaids and mermen 2. Folklore
ISBN 0-439-04781-1 (pa)   LC 92-30527
A collection of twelve mermaid tales from around the world, featuring such sources as France, Greece, and North Africa
"Howell's noteworthy illustrations render each painting in a style reflective of the traditional artwork from the tale's place of origin. . . . Both author and illustrator provide extensive source notes for their work. A great choice for primary read-alouds and a welcome compilation for folk-tale units." Booklist

The **Oxford** companion to fairy tales; edited by Jack Zipes. Oxford Univ. Press 2000 xxxii, 601p $49.95   **398.2**
1. Fairy tales—History and criticism
ISBN 0-19-860115-8   LC 99-14271
This is a "collection of brief essays on classic tales, both modern and ancient. In alphabetical order, the companion profiles noted authors, illustrators, filmmakers, choreographers, and composers; more broadly, it covers film, art, opera, ballet, music, and commercial use. . . . Attractive, well written, and approachable, this solid guide to the fairy-tale world is without equal." Libr J

Paterson, Katherine

Parzival; the quest of the Grail Knight; retold by Katherine Paterson. Lodestar Bks. 1998 127p $15.99; pa $4.99 (5 and up)   **398.2**
   1. Arthurian romances
   ISBN 0-525-67579-5; 0-14-130573-8 (pa)
                                          LC 97-23891
A retelling of the Arthurian legend in which Parzival, unaware of his noble birth, comes of age through his quest for the Holy Grail
"Nearly 800 years old, the story has freshness, humor, grace, and depth. . . . Paterson clarifies much of the Christian doctrine that is the basis of the story, but she is never dull or pedantic." SLJ

The tale of the mandarin ducks; illustrated by Leo & Diane Dillon. Lodestar Bks. 1989 unp il $16.99; pa $6.99 (1-3)   **398.2**
   1. Folklore—Japan 2. Ducks—Fiction
   ISBN 0-525-67283-4; 0-14-055739-3 (pa)
                                          LC 88-30484
"A Japanese fairy tale, in picture-book format, about a Mandarin duck caught and caged at the whim of a wealthy Japanese lord. Separated from his mate, the bird languishes in captivity until a compassionate servant girl sets him free. The lord sentences the girl and her beloved to death, but they in turn are freed and rewarded with happiness." Booklist
"Paterson's story is rich with magic, compassion and love. The Dillons' elegantly detailed watercolor and pastel drawings, in the style of 18th-century Japanese woodcuts, are exquisite." Publ Wkly

Perrault, Charles, 1628-1703

Cinderella; or, The little glass slipper; a free translation from the French of Charles Perrault; with pictures by Marcia Brown. Scribner 1954 unp il $16; pa $5.99 (k-3)   **398.2**
   1. Folklore—France 2. Fairy tales
   ISBN 0-684-12676-1; 0-689-81474-7 (pa)
   Awarded the Caldecott Medal, 1955
This is the classic story of the poor, good-natured girl who works for her selfish step-sisters until a fairy godmother transforms her into a beautiful 'princess' for just one night
"With soft, delicate colors and lines that subtly suggest, Miss Brown creates a thoroughly fairyland atmosphere, at the same time recreating the sophistication of the French Court with its golden coach, canopied bed, dazzling chandeliers, liveried footmen, curled and pompadoured ladies, and peruked (bewigged) courtiers." Libr J

Cinderella, Puss in Boots, and other favorite tales; as told by Charles Perrault; translated from the French by A.E. Johnson. Abrams 2000 163p il $24.95 (k-4)   **398.2**
   1. Folklore—France 2. Fairy tales
   ISBN 0-8109-4014-0   LC 98-53961
"New translations of often-adapted Perrault tales. . . . Johnson provides a fresh look at 'Little Red Riding Hood,' 'The Fairies' (also known as 'Diamonds and Toads'), 'Puss in Boots,' 'Blue Beard,' 'Cinderella,' 'Ricky of the Tuft,' 'The Sleeping Beauty,' and 'Little Tom Thumb.'. . . Perrault's morals in verse also allow readers to rethink the tales. Each story is illustrated by a different French artist on partial spreads and in spot art on every page." SLJ

The complete fairy tales of Charles Perrault; illustrated by Sally Holmes; newly translated by Neil Philip and Nicoletta Simborowski; with an introduction and notes on the stories by Neil Philip. Clarion Bks. 1993 156p il $25 (4-6)   **398.2**
   1. Folklore—France 2. Fairy tales
   ISBN 0-395-57002-6   LC 92-17781
An illustrated collection of eleven tales including such familiar titles as "Cinderella" and "Sleeping Beauty" and less familiar ones such as "Tufty Ricky" and "The Fairies"
"This new edition, with its simple, unembroidered language; attractive illustrations; terse, informative commentary; and extensive bibliography deserves to be among the first books considered for a core collection." SLJ

Puss in boots; illustrated by Fred Marcellino; translated by Malcolm Arthur. Farrar, Straus & Giroux 1990 unp il $16; pa $8.95 (k-3)   **398.2**
   1. Folklore—France 2. Fairy tales
   ISBN 0-374-36160-6; 0-374-46034-5 (pa)
                                          LC 90-82136
A Caldecott Medal honor book, 1991
"Opulently designed and handsomely illustrated, this picture book provides a fitting showcase for Perrault's artful tale of deceit and resourcefulness. Unsullied by type, the striking front of the book features a close-up portrait of the cat's face. Befitting a fairy tale, the artwork inside is suffused with a golden light that proclaims the story to be from a sunnier, more dreamlike world." Booklist

Philip, Neil

The Arabian nights; retold by Neil Philip; illustrated by Sheila Moxley. Orchard Bks. 1994 157p il $19.95 (4 and up)   **398.2**
   1. Arabs—Folklore 2. Fairy tales
   ISBN 0-531-06868-4   LC 94-9137
"Sixteen of the classic stories are retold, each accompanied by one full-page and several smaller illustrations rendered in jewel-toned acrylics. A worthy addition to any collection, the volume includes a helpful explanation of the origins of the tales." Horn Book Guide

Celtic fairy tales; retold with an introduction by Neil Philip; illustrated by Isabelle Brent. Viking 1999 137p il $21.99 (4 and up)   **398.2**
   1. Fairy tales 2. Celts—Folklore 3. Folklore—Great Britain
   ISBN 0-670-88387-5   LC 98-50081
An illustrated collection of twenty stories from many Celtic regions, including "The Battle of the Birds," "Finn MacCool and the Scotch Giant," and "The Ship that Went to America."
"There's a mix of the almost familiar and nicely exotic in this collection, which is lavishly illustrated with a glowing full-page painting for each tale and Celtic motifs on every page." Booklist

Pinkney, Jerry, 1939-

Aesop's fables. SeaStar Bks. 2000 87p il $19.95
398.2

1. Fables

ISBN 1-58717-000-0   LC 00-24194

A collection of nearly sixty fables from Aesop, including such familiar ones as "The Grasshopper and the Ants," "The North Wind and the Sun," "Androcles and the Lion," "The Troublesome Dog," and "The Fox and the Stork"

Pinkney brings "vivid new life to these ancient fables by creating pencil, colored pencil, and watercolor illustrations that are subtle and delicate in color but dynamic and dramatic in composition and in size. . . . Pinkney's text proves equal to his art. His language, though formal, is subtly witty and begs to be read aloud." Booklist

Polacco, Patricia

Luba and the wren. Philomel Bks. 1999 unp il $16.99 (k-3)   **398.2**

1. Fairy tales 2. Folklore—Russia

ISBN 0-399-23168-4   LC 98-16353

In this variation on the story of "The Fisherman and His Wife," a young Ukrainian girl must repeatedly return to the wren she has rescued to relay her parents' increasingly greedy demands

"Polacco's signature illustrations are lush and vibrant. The regal colors of royal blue and crimson play against deep green, dappled brown, and ocher of the natural world." SLJ

Pollock, Penny, 1935-

The Turkey Girl; a Zuni Cinderella story; retold by Penny Pollock; illustrated by Ed Young. Little, Brown 1996 unp il lib bdg $16.95 (3-5)   **398.2**

1. Zuni Indians—Folklore

ISBN 0-316-71314-7   LC 93-28947

In this Indian variant of a familiar story, some turkeys make a gown of feathers for the poor girl who tends them so that she can participate in a sacred dance, but they desert her when she fails to return as promised

"The bleakness of the tale is softened by Young's elegantly evocative pastel and oil crayon illustrations. . . . Pollock's retelling is steady and solid, and her source is clearly indicated in an author's note that gives some background on the tale." Booklist

Poole, Amy Lowry

The ant and the grasshopper; retold and illustrated by Amy Lowry Poole. Holiday House 2000 unp il $16.95 (k-3)   **398.2**

1. Fables

ISBN 0-8234-1477-9   LC 99-18820

Retells the fable about a colony of industrious ants which busily prepares for the approaching winter while a grasshopper makes no plans for the cold weather to come

"This graceful retelling of Aesop's fable . . . is set 'in the old Summer Palace at the edge of the Emperor's courtyard.' . . . The simple, rhythmic text . . . is enriched by the strong figures, muted colors, and subtle details of each double-page spread. Ink and gouache illus-

trations on rice paper both literally and figuratively provide another layer; not only do they depict above-ground action, they also delineate outlines of the animals that live beneath the soil in which the ants toil." Bull Cent Child Books

How the rooster got his crown; retold and illustrated by Amy Lowry Poole. Holiday House 1999 unp il $15.95 (k-3)   **398.2**

1. Folklore—China

ISBN 0-8234-1389-6   LC 98-12311

In the early days of the world, when the sun refuses to come out for fear of a skillful archer's arrows, a small rooster saves the day by coaxing the sun out with his crowing

"The illustrations reflect the traditions of ancient scroll paintings; the pacing of the story is synchronized with the pictures so that the visual and verbal elements form a seamless unit." Horn Book Guide

Poole, Josephine, 1933-

Snow White; retold by Josephine Poole and illustrated by Angela Barrett. Knopf 1992 c1991 unp il $15.95 (3-5)   **398.2**

1. Fairy tales 2. Folklore—Germany

ISBN 0-679-82656-4   LC 91-18411

First published 1991 in the United Kingdom

A princess takes refuge from her wicked stepmother in the cottage of seven dwarfs

This "features Poole's cool, limpid, flowing text and Barrett's elegant, mysterious illustrations—delicate yet strong, in deep, muted colors. A splendid work, with the flavor of eighteenth-century German Romanticism." Horn Book Guide

Prose, Francine, 1947-

The angel's mistake; stories of Chelm; pictures by Mark Podwal. Greenwillow Bks. 1997 unp il lib bdg $14.93 (k-3)   **398.2**

1. Jews—Folklore

ISBN 0-688-14906-5   LC 96-7465

"Two angels, given bags of intelligent and foolish souls to distribute throughout the world, accidentally spill all the foolish souls into the town of Chelm." Horn Book Guide

"Like the storytelling, Podwal's gouache and colored-pencil illustrations are deadpan, wild, solemn, and absurd." Booklist

Includes bibliographical references

You never know; a legend of the Lamed-vavniks; pictures by Mark Podwal. Greenwillow Bks. 1998 unp il $15; lib bdg $14.93 (k-3)   **398.2**

1. Jews—Folklore

ISBN 0-688-15806-4; 0-688-15807-2 (lib bdg)
LC 97-24764

Though mocked by the rest of the villagers of Plotchnik, poor Schmuel the shoemaker turns out to be a very special person

"Podwal's gouache and colored-pencil illustrations bring Plotchnik to vivid life in a clean, unmuddy palette. . . . Prose has the language and rhythms of the oral storyteller down pat, and her text is a readaloud gem." Bull Cent Child Books

Pyle, Howard, 1853-1911

King Stork; illustrated by Trina Schart Hyman. Morrow Junior Bks. 1998 48p il lib bdg $16 (2-4)

398.2

1. Fairy tales

ISBN 0-688-15813-7   LC 97-36307

Text originally published 1888 in the author's collection The wonder clock; this is a reissue of the Little, Brown edition published 1973

Pyle's story of a poor drummer youth who wins a beautiful but wicked princess "with the help of King Stork's magic and 'tames' her . . . is fluidly illustrated with medieval scenes." Booklist

"The illustrations fit the various moods of the story. . . . The princess is scantily-clad yet certainly beautiful. Children will enjoy the detailed illustrations and the simplicity and magical qualities of the story." SLJ

Quayle, Eric

The shining princess, and other Japanese legends; illustrated by Michael Foreman. Arcade Pub. 1989 111p il o.p. (5 and up)   **398.2**

1. Folklore—Japan

LC 89-84076

Available paperback United Kingdom edition published by Andersen Press

A "collection of Japanese legends drawn from the two earliest-known English translations." Publisher's note

This "collection of ten exciting tales is surely destined to become a standard source of Japanese folktales. . . . Each tale is sure to enthrall read-aloud audiences as well as independent readers. Foreman's remarkable watercolors, perfectly suited to each text, complete the package." SLJ

Ransome, Arthur, 1884-1967

The Fool of the World and the flying ship; a Russian tale retold by Arthur Ransome; pictures by Uri Shulevitz. Farrar, Straus & Giroux 1968 unp il $16; pa $6.95 (k-3)   **398.2**

1. Folklore—Russia

ISBN 0-374-32442-5; 0-374-42438-1 (pa)

Awarded the Caldecott Medal, 1969

"An Ariel book"

Text first published 1916 in Ransome's Old Peter's Russian tales

The Fool of the World was the third and youngest son whose parents thought little of him. When the Czar announced that his daughter would marry the hero who could bring him a flying ship, Fool of the World went looking and found one. Aided in surprising ways by eight peasants with magical powers, he then had to outwit the treacherous Czar

This "is a fascinating tale, told with humor and grace and brought vividly to life by Uri Shulevitz's illustrations." N Y Times Book Rev

Raw Head, bloody bones; African-American tales of the supernatural; selected by Mary E. Lyons. Scribner 1991 88p il $15 (4-6)   **398.2**

1. African Americans—Folklore 2. Folklore—United States 3. Folklore—Caribbean region

ISBN 0-684-19333-7   LC 91-10690

Fifteen black and African-American tales of the supernatural from various states and several Caribbean countries. Includes commentary on black folklore in the New World

"In retelling these delightfully eerie and gruesome stories, Lyons has preserved the richness and immediacy of the African and African-American oral traditions. Vigorously told in rhythmic and colorful language, the stories demand to be read aloud." SLJ

Includes bibliographical references

Riordan, James, 1936-

King Arthur; retold by James Riordan; illustrated by Victor G. Ambrus. Oxford Univ. Press 1998 95p il $25; pa $12.95 (5 and up)

398.2

1. Arthur, King 2. Arthurian romances

ISBN 0-19-274176-4; 0-19-274177-2 (pa)

LC 98-192703

This retelling covers "the life of Arthur from his boyhood with Merlin to his death in the final battle with Mordred." Voice Youth Advocates

"Riordan draws from a number of traditional sources to create his own version of Arthurian legend. . . . Victor G. Ambrus' ink drawings with washes appear on every spread. Black-and-white pictures alternate with those brightened by brilliant watercolors, which complement the energy of Ambrus' drawing style." Booklist

Robbins, Ruth

Baboushka and the three kings; illustrated by Nicolas Sidjakov; adapted from a Russian folk tale. Houghton Mifflin 1960 unp il $16; pa $6.95 (1-4)   **398.2**

1. Folklore—Russia 2. Christmas—Fiction

ISBN 0-395-27673-X; 0-395-42647-2 (pa)

Awarded the Caldecott Medal, 1961

First published by Parnassus Press

A retelling of the Christmas legend about the old woman who declined to accompany the three kings on their search for the Christ Child and has ever since then searched for the Child on her own. Each year as she renews her search she leaves gifts at the homes she visits, acting, in this respect, as a Russian equivalent to Santa Claus

"Mystery and dignity are in the retelling. . . . At the end of the book is the story in verse set to original music." Horn Book

Rockwell, Anne F., 1934-

The boy who wouldn't obey: a Mayan legend; story and pictures by Anne Rockwell. Greenwillow Bks. 2000 unp il $15.95 (2-4)   **398.2**

1. Mayas—Folklore 2. Folklore—Mexico

ISBN 0-688-14881-6   LC 99-15201

When Chac, the great lord who makes rain, takes a disobedient boy as his servant, they are both in for trouble

"Inspired by the art on Mayan ceramic vases, the pen and watercolor illustrations rendered in a mellow palette of blues, pinks, and greens, with flat perspectives and decorative borders, are an attractive match for this traditional tale." Horn Book Guide

Rogasky, Barbara

The golem; a version; illustrated by Trina Schart Hyman. Holiday House 1996 96p il $18.95 (4 and up)   **398.2**

1. Jewish legends
ISBN 0-8234-0964-3   LC 94-13040

This is "the legend of the golem—a monster created of clay—who, under the guidance of the chief rabbi of Prague, rescued the Jews from persecution by anti-Semitic Christians in the late 16th century. Rogasky's strong storytelling skills are evident. . . . Hyman's colorful, fairy tale-like illustrations bring the story to life." SLJ

Rapunzel; from the Brothers Grimm; retold by Barbara Rogasky; with illustrations by Trina Schart Hyman. Holiday House 1982 unp il hardcover o.p. paperback available $5.95 (1-3)   **398.2**

1. Folklore—Germany 2. Fairy tales
ISBN 0-8234-0652-0 (pa)   LC 81-6419

A retelling of the folktale "about the beautiful girl whose lover climbs her rope of golden hair and whose cruel treatment by a possessive witch ends when Rapunzel, her prince, and their infant twins are united." Bull Cent Child Books

"Some of Hyman's familiar specialities . . . appear again to advantage. . . . Most engaging of all are the lovely borders and vignettes on every page, filled with fruits, flowers, small landscapes and decorative patterns. The highly organized layout and borders, attractive in themselves, enhance Hyman's art by imposing a kind of discipline on her romantic style." SLJ

The water of life; a tale from the Brothers Grimm; retold by Barbara Rogasky; illustrated by Trina Schart Hyman. Holiday House 1986 unp il $16.95 (1-3)   **398.2**

1. Folklore—Germany 2. Fairy tales
ISBN 0-8234-0552-4   LC 84-19226

A prince searching for the Water of Life to cure his dying father finds an enchanted castle, a lovely princess, and treachery from his older brothers

"This traditional tale with all the trappings of magical elements, romance, and underlying psychological truth, is brought to life by Rogasky's spirited telling and Hyman's lush illustrations." SLJ

Rohmer, Harriet

The invisible hunters; a legend from the Miskito Indians of Nicaragua; [by] Harriet Rohmer, Octavio Chow, Morris Vidaure; illustrations, Joe Sam; version in Spanish Rosalma Zubizarreta & Alma Flor Ada. Children's Bk. Press 1987 32p il (Stories from Central America) $15.95; pa $6.95 (2-4)   **398.2**

1. Mosquito Indians—Folklore 2. Bilingual books—English-Spanish
ISBN 0-89239-031-X; 0-89239-109-X (pa)
      LC 86-32658

Title page and text in English and Spanish

This Miskito Indian legend set in seventeenth-century Nicaragua concerns the impact of the first European traders on traditional life. "Three hunters eat a vine of invisibility, the Dar, which they use initially to bag more wari to feed their tribe but eventually to betray their hungry people and become rich off traders' money. . . . The hunters are punished by wandering forever invisible." Bull Cent Child Books

"The lavish collage-style illustrations evoke a sense of movement and are in perfect step with the rhythm of the text." Horn Book

Uncle Nacho's hat; adapted by Harriet Rohmer; illustrations by Veg Reisberg; Spanish version, Rosalma Zubizarreta. Children's Bk. Press 1989 31p il hardcover o.p. paperback available $7.95 (k-3)   **398.2**

1. Folklore—Nicaragua 2. Bilingual books—English-Spanish
ISBN 0-89239-112-X (pa)   LC 88-37090

Title page and text in English and Spanish

"Adaptation of a Nicaraguan folktale. . . . When his niece, Ambrosia, gives Uncle Nacho a new hat, he tries unsuccessfully several times to get rid of the old, holey one. Seeing him dejected because his hat keeps coming back, Ambrosia suggests he put his mind on the new one instead. Flattened primitive paintings in brilliant, clear tropical colors and motifs enhance the fun of this comedy of errors." Helbig. This land is our land

Ross, Gayle

How Turtle's back was cracked; a traditional Cherokee tale; retold by Gayle Ross; illustrated by Murv Jacob. Dial Bks. for Young Readers 1995 unp il $15.99 (k-3)   **398.2**

1. Cherokee Indians—Folklore
ISBN 0-8037-1728-8   LC 93-40657

"When Turtle's friend Possum kills a greedy wolf, Turtle not only takes all the credit for the deed, but boasts and flaunts his trophies. The wolves take revenge on him, but they are stupid and quarrelsome, and Turtle tricks them into throwing him into the river instead of a fire. Although he escapes death, he hits a rock and his shell is cracked into pieces." SLJ

"Ross, a storyteller of Cherokee descent, retains a sense of the oral tradition through the language and rhythm of the text. . . . Jacob . . . illustrates the tale with warm paintings full of pattern and texture, echoing the patterns on the clothing and jewelry that the animals wear." Horn Book

Roth, Susan L.

The biggest frog in Australia; [by] Susan Roth. Simon & Schuster Bks. for Young Readers 1996 unp il $15; pa $5.99 (k-3)   **398.2**

1. Frogs—Fiction 2. Folklore—Australia
ISBN 0-689-80490-3; 0-689-83314-8 (pa)
      LC 95-9721

When a thirsty frog drinks up all the water in Australia, the other animals must think of a way to make him give it up

This story "contains familiar motifs presented with fresh energy. Appropriately, the crayon-bright red frog overflows the edges of most pages. Brilliantly colored cut-paper collages feature a multitude of textures." SLJ

Rounds, Glen, 1906-

Ol' Paul, the mighty logger. Holiday House 1976 93p il hardcover o.p. paperback available $5.95 (3-6)   **398.2**
  1. Bunyan, Paul (Legendary character)
  ISBN 0-8234-0713-6 (pa)
  First published 1936
  "Being a true account of the seemingly incredible exploits and inventions of the great Paul Bunyan, profusely illustrated by drawings made at the scene by the author, Glen Rounds, and now republished in this special fortieth anniversary edition." Subtitle

Three billy goats Gruff; retold and illustrated by Glen Rounds. Holiday House 1993 unp il $16.95; pa $5.95 (k-3)   **398.2**
  1. Folklore—Norway 2. Goats—Fiction
  ISBN 0-8234-1015-3; 0-8234-1136-2 (pa)
                    LC 92-23951
  Retells the folktale about three billy goats who trick a troll that lives under a bridge
  "Spare and straightforward in text and illustrations, this interpretation of the old tale has an energy lacking in more elaborate versions. . . . Shaded, mottled crayon markings color the scenes here and there with good effect, and the broad white pages make a bright, clean background for the action." Booklist

Sabuda, Robert

Arthur and the sword; retold and illustrated by Robert Sabuda. Atheneum Bks. for Young Readers 1995 unp il $16; pa $5.99 (k-3)   **398.2**
  1. Arthur, King 2. Arthurian romances
  ISBN 0-689-31987-8; 0-689-82031-3 (pa)
                    LC 95-9968
  "Sabuda retells the story of young Arthur, who pulls Excalibur from the anvil and becomes the long-awaited king of England." Booklist
  "Sabuda's stunning illustrations for this best known Arthurian story make it an extraordinary effort. The retelling is solid with language that conveys the voice of the legend while remaining easily readable. . . . The artwork is actually painted on glass, done predominantly in purples, blues, and russets with gold." SLJ

San Souci, Robert, 1946-

Brave Margaret; by Robert D. San Souci; illustrated by Sally Wern Comport. Simon & Schuster Bks. for Young Readers 1999 unp il $17 (k-3)   **398.2**
  1. Fairy tales 2. Folklore—Ireland
  ISBN 0-689-81072-5   LC 98-16794
  In this retelling of an Irish folktale, a brave young woman battles a sea serpent and rescues her true love from a giant
  "San Souci's text is smoothly written, dramatic, and rhythmic enough to please a storyteller. Full of rich colors and textures, the large-scale illustrations, rendered in pastels, almost jump off the pages." Booklist

Cendrillon; a Caribbean Cinderella; [by] Robert D. San Souci; illustrated by Brian Pinkney. Simon & Schuster Bks. for Young Readers 1998 unp il $17 (k-3)   **398.2**
  1. Fairy tales 2. Folklore—Martinique
  ISBN 0-689-80668-X   LC 96-53142

A Creole variant of the familiar Cinderella tale set in Martinique and narrated by the godmother who helps Cendrillon find true love
  "The narrative is full of French Creole words and phrases. . . . A *fruit à pain* (breadfruit) is transformed into the coach; six agoutis (a kind of rodent) become the horses. . . . Pinkney's art perfectly conveys the lush beauty and atmosphere of the island setting." SLJ

Cut from the same cloth; American women of myth, legend, and tall tale; collected and told by Robert D. San Souci; illustrated by Brian Pinkney; introduction by Jane Yolen. Philomel Bks. 1993 140p il $21.99; pa $6.99 (4-6)   **398.2**
  1. Folklore—United States 2. Tall tales 3. Women—Folklore
  ISBN 0-399-21987-0; 0-698-11811-1 (pa)
                    LC 92-5233
  A collection of fifteen stories about legendary American women from Anglo-American, African American, and Native American folklore
  "San Souci's language is vigorous and action verbs abound; Pinkney's black-and-white block prints match the strength of the telling. The inclusion of notes on the sources and a general bibliography make this an academic resource as well as a good collection of rolicking stories." Child Book Rev Serv

Even more short & shivery; thirty spine-tingling stories; retold by Robert D. San Souci; illustrated by Jacqueline Rogers. Delacorte Press 1997 162p il $14.95; pa $10.95 (4 and up)   **398.2**
  1. Ghost stories 2. Folklore
  ISBN 0-385-32252-6; 0-385-32639-4 (pa)
                    LC 96-35365
  A collection of scary traditional tales from all over the world
  "San Souci groups together 30 tales that not only read well but also work as splendid choices for oral telling around a campfire, on a trip, in school, or at a sleepover." Booklist
  Includes bibliographical references

Fa Mulan; the story of a woman warrior; [by] Robert D. San Souci; illustrated by Jean & Mou-sien Tseng. Hyperion Bks. for Children 1998 unp il $15.45; lib bdg $16.49; pa $6.99 (2-4)
                    398.2
  1. Folklore—China
  ISBN 0-7868-0346-0; 0-7868-2287-2 (lib bdg); 0-7868-1421-7 (pa)   LC 97-19291
  A retelling of the original Chinese poem in which a brave young girl masquerades as a boy and fights the Tartars in the Khan's army

The faithful friend; [by] Robert D. San Souci; illustrated by Brian Pinkney. Simon & Schuster Bks. for Young Readers 1995 unp il $16; pa $5.99 (2-4)   **398.2**
  1. Folklore—Martinique
  ISBN 0-02-786131-7; 0-689-82458-0 (pa)
                    LC 93-40672
  A Caldecott Medal honor book, 1996
  "A West Indian folktale from Martinique. . . . When Clement seeks the lovely Pauline as his wife, it is

San Souci, Robert, 1946-—*Continued*

Hippolyte who protects the couple from the zombies and her vengeful uncle." Child Book Rev Serv

"Pinkney's scratchboard and oil artwork switches from bright daytime hues for most of the book to purples and grays for scenes with the zombies and snakes, which are very effective. . . . This excellent title contains all the elements of a well-researched folktale, and convincingly conveys the richness of the West Indian culture." SLJ

Includes bibliographical references

The hired hand; an African-American folktale; retold by Robert D. San Souci; pictures by Jerry Pinkney. Dial Bks. for Young Readers 1997 unp il $15.99 (2-4)   **398.2**
1. African Americans—Folklore 2. Folklore—Southern States
ISBN 0-8037-1296-0   LC 93-36285

"In a tale set 'down Virginia way' a century before the Emancipation Proclamation, a successful, free black sawmill owner, at the instigation of his lazy son, takes on a hired hand, who turns out to have remarkable powers. Executed in pencil and watercolor, the illustrations set the plot in a particular time and place without sacrificing the sense of magic and wonder." Horn Book Guide

The Hobyahs; [by] Robert D. San Souci; illustrated by Alexi Natchev. Doubleday Bks. for Young Readers 1994 unp il hardcover o.p. paperback available $5.99 (k-3)   **398.2**
1. Fairy tales 2. Folklore—Great Britain
ISBN 0-440-41212-9 (pa)   LC 92-28655

A version of the folktale about five faithful dogs who rescue their mistress from the goblinlike Hobyahs

"The addition of rhyming quatrains at key moments in the plot turns the book into a storytelling treat, and Natchev's just-a-little-scary illustrations are great for showing to groups during reading aloud." Booklist

More short & shivery; thirty terrifying tales; retold by Robert D. San Souci; illustrated by Katherine Coville and Jacqueline Rogers. Delacorte Press 1994 163p il hardcover o.p. paperback available $10.95 (4 and up)   **398.2**
1. Folklore 2. Ghost stories
ISBN 0-385-32250-X (pa)   LC 94-479

A collection of scary folktales from the United States, China, England, Italy, Russia, and other countries around the world

Includes bibliographical references

The samurai's daughter; a Japanese legend retold by Robert D. San Souci; pictures by Stephen T. Johnson. Dial Bks. for Young Readers 1992 unp il hardcover o.p. paperback available $6.99 (1-4)   **398.2**
1. Folklore—Japan
ISBN 0-14-056284-2 (pa)   LC 91-15585

A Japanese folk tale about the brave daughter of a samurai warrior and her journey to be reunited with her exiled father

"San Souci's retelling of this Kamakura Period folktale is smooth, lively, and makes a resonant read-aloud. Johnson's pastel and ink illustrations capture authentic small details yet remain dreamily impressionistic." SLJ

The secret of the stones; a folktale; retold by Robert D. San Souci; pictures by James Ransome. Phyllis Fogelman Bks. 2000 unp il $16.99 (k-3)   **398.2**
1. African Americans—Folklore 2. Folklore—United States
ISBN 0-8037-1640-0   LC 93-43952

When they try to find out who is doing their chores while they are working in the field, a childless couple discovers that the two stones they have brought home are actually two bewitched orphans

"Based on a tale found in both the Bantu and African-American cultures . . . the clearly told tale (which includes dialect in the dialogue) is accompanied by expressive, deep-toned illustrations." Horn Book Guide

Short & shivery; thirty chilling tales; retold by Robert D. San Souci; illustrated by Katherine Coville. Doubleday 1987 175p il hardcover o.p. paperback available $9.95 (4 and up)   **398.2**
1. Folklore 2. Ghost stories
ISBN 0-385-26426-7 (pa)   LC 86-29067

"A collection of spooky stories, competently adapted and retold (sometimes quite freely) from world folklore, including Japan, Africa, and Latin America, as well as Europe and the U.S. . . . The stories drawn from collections of regional American folklore are not only the freshest, but often the scariest. Sources are fully documented. . . . There are some delicious shivers here, with plenty of fodder for an active imagination, as well as excitement." SLJ

Six foolish fishermen; [by] Robert D. San Souci; illustrated by Doug Kennedy. Hyperion Bks. for Children 2000 unp il $14.99 (k-3)   **398.2**
ISBN 0-7868-0385-1   LC 98-39040

Six silly friends spend a day trying to figure out how to proceed with their fishing trip when one thing after another goes wrong

"The setting and lavish Cajun dialect give the tale a strong regional flavor, while the cartoonlike illustrations of the fishermen's antics (which are observed by a frog, a turtle, and an alligator) play up the humor in this entertaining, ridiculous tale." Horn Book Guide

Sootface; an Ojibwa Cinderella story; retold by Robert D. San Souci; illustrated by Daniel San Souci. Doubleday Bks. for Young Readers 1994 unp il hardcover o.p. paperback available $6.99 (1-4)   **398.2**
1. Ojibwa Indians—Folklore
ISBN 0-440-41363-X (pa)   LC 93-10553

Although she is mocked and mistreated by her two older sisters, Sootface, an Ojibwa Indian maiden, wins a mighty invisible warrior for her husband with her kind and honest heart

"The San Souci version reads aloud well, and the watercolor artwork illustrates the story with quiet grace." Booklist

Sukey and the mermaid; [by] Robert D. San Souci; illustrated by Brian Pinkney. Four Winds Press 1992 unp il $16; pa $5.95 (1-4)   **398.2**
1. Mermaids and mermen 2. African Americans—Folklore
ISBN 0-02-778141-0; 0-689-80718-X (pa)
LC 90-24559

San Souci, Robert, 1946——*Continued*

Unhappy with her life at home, Sukey receives kindness and wealth from Mama Jo the mermaid

San Souci "outdoes himself here with pungent, lyrical prose that reverberates with the cadences of the South Carolina islands. . . . The supple lines of Pinkney's fluid scratchboard technique capture the grace and spirit of this magical tale and serve as the perfect foil to its darker undertones." Publ Wkly

The talking eggs; a folktale from the American South; retold by Robert D. San Souci; pictures by Jerry Pinkney. Dial Bks. for Young Readers 1989 unp il $16 (k-3)   **398.2**
　　1. Folklore—Southern States
　　ISBN 0-8037-0619-7   LC 88-33469
　　A Caldecott Medal honor book, 1990

A Southern folktale in which kind Blanche, following the instructions of an old witch, gains riches, while her greedy sister makes fun of the old woman and is duly rewarded

"Adapted from a Creole folk tale originally included in a collection of Louisiana stories by folklorist Alcee Fortier, this tale captures the flavor of the nineteenth-century South in its language and story line. . . . Jerry Pinkney's watercolors are chiefly responsible for the excellence of the book; his characters convey their moods with vivid facial expressions." Horn Book

A terrifying taste of short & shivery; thirty creepy tales; retold by Robert D. San Souci; illustrated by Lenny Wooden. Delacorte Press 1998 159p il $14.95; pa $10.95 (4 and up) **398.2**
　　1. Ghost stories 2. Folklore
　　ISBN 0-385-32635-1; 0-385-32255-0 (pa)
　　　　　　　　　　　　　　　　　LC 98-5551

"Drawing on urban legends, myths, folktales, and ghost stories from around the world and across time, the reteller serves up 30 tales of the supernatural that range from eerie to downright scary. . . . Suspenseful, accessible, and energetic, the tales are uniformly brief and gripping." SLJ

Includes bibliographical references

Two bear cubs; a Miwok legend from California's Yosemite Valley; retold by Robert D. San Souci; illustrated by Daniel San Souci. Yosemite Assn. 1997 unp il $14.95 (k-3)   **398.2**
　　1. Miwok Indians—Folklore
　　ISBN 0-939666-87-1   LC 97-17226

Retells the Miwok Indian legend in which a little measuring worm saves two bear cubs stranded at the top of the rock known as El Capitan

"Watercolor illustrations portray gently anthropomorphized animals in spare but traditional garb (the females wear buckskin skirts) and with amusing, humanlike poses and facial expressions. . . . Endnotes concerning Miwok customs add heft to this expertly rendered tale." Publ Wkly

A weave of words; an Armenian tale; retold by Robert D. San Souci; illustrated by Raúl Colón. Orchard Bks. 1998 unp il $16.95; lib bdg $17.99 (3-5)   **398.2**
　　1. Fairy tales 2. Folklore—Armenia
　　ISBN 0-531-30053-6; 0-531-33053-2 (lib bdg)
　　　　　　　　　　　　　　　　　LC 97-5046

A reworking of Armenian folktales in which a lazy prince learns to read, write, and weave to win his love only to have these very talents later save him from a three-headed monster

"Rich with subtle colors and strong composition, Colón's textured paintings create a fantasy world that reflects the tale's subtlety and its dramatic force." Booklist

The white cat; an Old French fairy tale; retold by Robert D. San Souci; illustrated by Gennady Spirin. Orchard Bks. 1989 unp il lib bdg $17.99; pa $6.95 (2-4)   **398.2**
　　1. Folklore—France 2. Fairy tales
　　ISBN 0-531-08409-4 (lib bdg); 0-531-07170-7 (pa)
　　　　　　　　　　　　　　　　　LC 88-19698

"Based on Madame D'Aulnoy's 1698 literary tale, which in turn draws on a folktale in which a king sends his three sons on three tests to decide their inheritance. The youngest son produces, at the end of the first year, the tiniest dog and, at the end of the second year, the finest linen—both with the help of a magical white cat who becomes his human bride when he breaks a spell bewitching her." Bull Cent Child Books

"San Souci's retelling is suitably magical and mysterious, and his words flow like music. Spirin's sumptuous paintings, each abounding with meticulous detail from foreground to furthest distance, glow with light and expression." Publ Wkly

Sanderson, Ruth, 1951-

The crystal mountain; retold and illustrated by Ruth Sanderson. Little, Brown 1999 unp il $15.95 (3-5)   **398.2**
　　1. Fairy tales 2. Folklore
　　ISBN 0-316-77092-2   LC 97-46991

The youngest of three sons outwits the fairy thieves who stole his mother's tapestry and marries one of the fairies he has rescued

"The story combines bits of drama, suspense, romance and magic, with some surprises, too. The oil paintings, set in 15th-century Europe, depict a rugged rolling countryside as well as the ornate tapestries of the era." Publ Wkly

Papa Gatto; an Italian fairy tale; retold and illustrated by Ruth Sanderson. Little, Brown 1995 unp il $15.95; pa $5.95 (3-5)   **398.2**
　　1. Fairy tales 2. Folklore—Italy
　　ISBN 0-316-77073-6; 0-316-77112-0 (pa)
　　　　　　　　　　　　　　　　　LC 94-16725

Seeking someone to care for his motherless kittens, Sir Gatto, advisor to the Prince, hires a beautiful, but lazy girl, and then her plain, but loving stepsister

"A lovely, lucid retelling of an Italian folktale. . . . The oil paintings glow with warm, rich tones. Sanderson pays meticulous attention to detail and captures the mood perfectly." SLJ

Sanfield, Steve

The adventures of High John the Conqueror; illustrated by John Ward. Orchard Bks. 1988 113p il o.p.; August House paperback available $8.95 (4 and up)   **398.2**
　　1. African Americans—Folklore
　　ISBN 0-87483-433-3 (pa)   LC 88-17946

Sanfield, Steve—*Continued*

"A Richard Jackson book"

"A competent retelling of 16 African-American folktales about the black trickster hero who always manages to outwit others, particularly his white master. Simply told in language comprehensible to very young readers, these tales are short, funny, and entertaining. . . . Fourteen full-page black-and-white pencil drawings illustrate some of the more dramatic moments in the stories." SLJ

Includes bibliographical references

Bit by bit; illustrated by Susan Gaber. Philomel Bks. 1995 unp il $16.99; pa $5.99 (k-3)   **398.2**
1. Jews—Folklore
ISBN 0-399-22736-9; 0-698-71775-1 (pa)
              LC 94-8752

"When his old winter coat wears out, Zundel the tailor makes himself a replacement out of a beautiful piece of cloth with red, gold, blue, and green threads. He loves the coat so much that he wears it morning and night until it, too, wears out. The cloth is subsequently made into a jacket, a vest, a cap, a pocket, and a button. Finally, when there seems to be nothing left of Zundel's favorite fabric, it becomes the threads of a story, this story." SLJ

"Based on a Yiddish song that Sanfield's grandmother brought with her from Russia, this is a kind of cumulative story, told with a joyful rhythm and repetition, and illustrated with bright, clear, large figures that make it great for group sharing." Booklist

Schwartz, Alvin, 1927-1992

All of our noses are here, and other noodle tales; retold by Alvin Schwartz; pictures by Karen Ann Weinhaus. Harper & Row 1985 64p il lib bdg $15.89 (k-2)   **398.2**
1. Folklore 2. Wit and humor
ISBN 0-06-025288-X (lib bdg)   LC 84-48330

"An I can read book"

This companion volume to There is a carrot in my ear, and other noodle tales, contains additional stories about members of the Brown family

"The illustrations show them looking very much like mice and always smiling and cheerful. Cousins, no doubt, to the Stupids, the family is bound to be as appealing to young readers. With a list of sources." Horn Book

And the green grass grew all around; folk poetry from everyone; illustrations by Sue Truesdell. HarperCollins Pubs. 1992 195p il music hardcover o.p. paperback available $10   **398.2**
1. Folklore
ISBN 0-06-446214-5 (pa)   LC 89-26722

This collection includes "chants and teases, wishes and warnings, jokes and riddles, skip-rope rhymes and stories, fun and games." Booklist

"Full of vigorous, swinging rhythms and funny, often nasty, sentiments, the pages are filled with well-known rhymes as well as new discoveries. . . . Sue Truesdell's cartoon drawings dance and tumble across the pages as a perfect accompaniment to the rhymes they illustrate. . . . A wonderful collection for reading, singing, and laughing out loud, this book is strongly recommended for sharing in groups." Horn Book

Includes bibliographical references

Ghosts! ghostly tales from folklore; retold by Alvin Schwartz; illustrated by Victoria Chess. HarperCollins Pubs. 1991 63p il lib bdg $15.89; pa $3.95 (k-2)   **398.2**
1. Ghost stories 2. Folklore
ISBN 0-06-021797-9; 0-06-444170-9 (pa)
             LC 90-21746

Also available Audiobook version

"An I can read book"

Presents seven, easy-to-read ghost stories based on traditional folk tales and legends from various countries

"All of the pen-and-watercolor illustrations are tidy and cheery and creepy. . . . Retold in a style that is simple but not choppy . . . and accompanied by a page of brief notes, all the tales will lend themselves to elaboration and innovation." Bull Cent Child Books

I saw you in the bathtub, and other folk rhymes; collected by Alvin Schwartz; pictures by Syd Hoff. Harper & Row 1989 64p il hardcover o.p. paperback available $3.95 (k-2)   **398.2**
1. Folklore
ISBN 0-06-444151-2 (pa)   LC 88-16111

"An I can read book"

Presents an illustrated collection of traditional folk rhymes, some composed by children

"Kids may be surprised to see their recess yells on the printed page but will relish the confirmation of significance. Hoff's full-color cartoons interpret the rhymes literally, an approach that leads to some pretty surreal results." Bull Cent Child Books

In a dark, dark room, and other scary stories; retold by Alvin Schwartz; illustrated by Dirk Zimmer. Harper & Row 1984 63p il $15.95; pa $3.95 (k-2)   **398.2**
1. Folklore 2. Ghost stories 3. Horror fiction
ISBN 0-06-025271-5; 0-06-444090-7 (pa)
             LC 83-47699

"An I can read book"

This is a collection of "seven traditional tales from around the world retold in simple yet effective language. . . . The chill here springs from suspense, an eerie setting or a ghostly surprise, rather than from blood and gore. Though pared down somewhat from longer versions, the stories retain their genuine creepiness. . . . The colorfully dark illustrations are sinister without being gruesome and add a comic touch." SLJ

More scary stories to tell in the dark; collected & retold from folklore by Alvin Schwartz; drawings by Stephen Gammell. Lippincott 1984 100p il $14.95; pa $4.95 (4 and up)   **398.2**
1. Ghost stories 2. Horror fiction 3. Folklore—United States
ISBN 0-397-32081-7; 0-06-440177-4 (pa)
             LC 83-49494

Also available Audiobook version

This volume contains stories of ghosts, murders, graveyards and other horrors

"The stories are all short and lively, very tellable, and greatly enhanced by the gray, ghoulish, horrifying illustrations of dismembered bodies, hideous creatures, and mysterious lights. A fine compendium by a well-known collector, easily accessible to young readers." Horn Book

Includes bibliographical references

Schwartz, Alvin, 1927-1992—*Continued*

Scary stories 3; more tales to chill your bones; collected from folklore and retold by Alvin Schwartz; drawings by Stephen Gammell. HarperCollins Pubs. 1991 115p il music $15.95; lib bdg $15.89; pa $4.95 (4 and up) **398.2**
1. Ghost stories 2. Horror fiction 3. Folklore—United States
ISBN 0-06-021794-4; 0-06-021795-2 (lib bdg); 0-06-440418-8 (pa) LC 90-47474
Traditional and modern-day stories of ghosts, haunts, superstitions, monsters, and horrible scary things
"The book is well paced and continually captivates, surprises, and entices audiences into reading just one more page. Gammell's gauzy, cobwebby, black-and-white pen-and-ink drawings help to sustain the overall creepy mood." SLJ
Includes bibliographical references

Scary stories to tell in the dark; collected from American folklore by Alvin Schwartz; with drawings by Stephen Gammell. Lippincott 1981 111p il $15.95; lib bdg $15.89; pa $4.95 (4 and up) **398.2**
1. Ghost stories 2. Horror fiction 3. Folklore—United States
ISBN 0-397-31926-6; 0-397-31927-4 (lib bdg); 0-06-440170-7 (pa) LC 80-8728
"A collection of scary, semi-scary, and humorous stories about ghosts and witches collected from American folklore. Most of the stories (poems and songs also) are very short and range from the traditional to the modern. The author includes suggestions on how to tell scary stories effectively." Bull Cent Child Books
"The scholarship in the source notes and bibliography will be useful to serious literature students." SLJ

There is a carrot in my ear, and other noodle tales; retold by Alvin Schwartz; pictures by Karen Ann Weinhaus. Harper & Row 1982 64p il lib bdg $15.89; pa $3.95 (k-2) **398.2**
1. Folklore 2. Wit and humor
ISBN 0-06-025234-0 (lib bdg); 0-06-444103-2 (pa) LC 80-8442
"An I can read book"
This "is a collection of six stories from sources . . . as diverse as American 'Little Moron' stories, ancient Greek tales and vaudeville pieces. Explaining in his foreword that a 'noodle is a silly person,' reteller Alvin Schwartz goes on to introduce the noodly Brown family and reveal their various foibles. . . . Most of the stories don't appear in other beginning noodle collections and will provide laughs for readers who catch the puns and absurdities the stories hinge on. The drawings by Karen Ann Weinhaus . . . show funny, pointy-proboscised folk blissfully unaware of their own goofiness." SLJ

Schwartz, Howard, 1945-
A coat for the moon and other Jewish tales; selected and retold by Howard Schwartz and Barbara Rush; illustrated by Michael Iofin. Jewish Publ. Soc. 1999 81p il $14.95 (4 and up) **398.2**
1. Jews—Folklore
ISBN 0-8276-0596-X LC 98-52704

A collection of Jewish folktales from around the world, including "The Lamp on the Mountain," "The Witch Barusha," "The Sabbath Walking Stick," and "The Fisherman and the Silver Fish"
"These tales incorporate everything from the magical to the bizarre, all the while imparting specific Jewish values that have transcended time and cultural dispersion. . . . Each retelling opens with a delightfully detailed pen-and-ink illustration encircled by a key sentence or phrase from the text that gives a hint of what's to come." SLJ

The diamond tree; Jewish tales from around the world; selected and retold by Howard Schwartz and Barbara Rush; illustrated by Uri Shulevitz. HarperCollins Pubs. 1991 120p il hardcover o.p. paperback available $4.95 (3-5) **398.2**
1. Jews—Folklore
ISBN 0-06-440695-4 (pa) LC 90-32420
This collection "comprises fifteen Jewish tales that span many centuries and come for the most part from countries of the Middle East, Africa, and eastern Europe." Horn Book
"Schwartz and Rush weave a rich tapestry that shows the diversity of Jewish culture. . . . The language is simple and vivid, and the narrative moves along at a good pace. . . . Ten tales are accompanied by Shulevitz's bright, dramatic watercolor paintings." SLJ
Includes bibliographical references

A journey to paradise and other Jewish tales; retold by Howard Schwartz; illustrated by Giora Carmi. Pitspopany Press 2000 48p il $16.95; pa $9.95 (3-5) **398.2**
1. Jews—Folklore
ISBN 0-943706-21-1; 0-943706-16-5 (pa)
"This collection of traditional tales from the world's far-flung Jewish community is ably selected by a well-known scholar. . . . The volume is abundantly illustrated with both spot and full-spread drawings in subdued colors." Horn Book Guide
Includes bibliographical references

Sewall, Marcia, 1935-
The Green Mist; adapted and illustrated by Marcia Sewall. Houghton Mifflin 1999 unp il $15 (k-3) **398.2**
1. Folklore—Great Britain
ISBN 0-395-90013-1 LC 97-42615
A retelling of a Lincolnshire, England, tale, probably eighteenth-century, in which a dying child is made well by the spring rituals intended to placate the mischievous beings hiding in the earth
"Sewall's beautifully cadenced telling is accompanied by unassuming illustrations that suggest the harmony between those who till the soil and the rhythm of the seasons." Horn Book Guide

Shannon, George, 1952-
More stories to solve; fifteen folktales from around the world; told by George Shannon; illustrated by Peter Sis. Greenwillow Bks. 1991 64p il hardcover o.p. paperback available $4.95 (3 and up) **398.2**
1. Folklore 2. Riddles
ISBN 0-380-73261-0 (pa)

Shannon, George, 1952-—*Continued*

"Shannon combines the folktale and the riddle in a brief collection that brings together 15 international stories." Booklist

Includes bibliographical references

Still more stories to solve; fourteen folktales from around the world; told by George Shannon; pictures by Peter Sis. Greenwillow Bks. 1994 64p il hardcover o.p. paperback available $4.95 (3 and up)   **398.2**

1. Folklore 2. Riddles

ISBN 0-688-814743-7 (pa)   LC 93-26529

This volume contains folktales in which there is a mystery or problem that the reader is invited to solve before the resolution is presented

Stories to solve; folktales from around the world; told by George Shannon; illustrated by Peter Sis. Greenwillow Bks. 1985 55p il $17; pa $4.95 (3 and up)   **398.2**

1. Folklore 2. Riddles

ISBN 0-688-04303-8; 0-688-10496-7 (pa)

LC 84-18656

"Each of these 14 delightful folktales is a short puzzle to be solved through cleverness, common sense or careful observations of details in the text. . . . Sis' pointillistic pen-and-ink drawings illustrate each puzzle, and sometimes clarify the solutions." SLJ

Includes bibliographical references

Shepard, Aaron

The crystal heart; a Vietnamese legend; retold by Aaron Shepard; illustrated by Joseph Daniel Fiedler. Atheneum Bks. for Young Readers 1998 unp il $16 (2-4)   **398.2**

1. Folklore—Vietnam

ISBN 0-689-81551-4   LC 97-3016

The sheltered and privileged daughter of a mandarin comes to understand the consequences of her naive, yet cruel, words to a fisherman

"Shepard's simple yet elegant prose meshes well with Fiedler's dramatic artwork. Featuring a palette of earth tones accented with red and blue, the paintings have a traditional feel." Booklist

Forty fortunes; a tale of Iran; illustrated by Alisher Dianov. Clarion Bks. 1999 32p il $15 (2-4)   **398.2**

1. Folklore—Iran 2. Fairy tales 3. Arabs—Folklore

ISBN 0-395-81133-3   LC 97-19804

A well-intentioned fortune-telling peasant unwittingly tricks a band of local thieves into returning the king's stolen treasure

"Shepard's version of this story is a well-paced combination of humor and action. Watercolors in bright tones capture the amusing situations and accurately depict the setting." SLJ

The sea king's daughter; a Russian legend; retold by Aaron Shepard; illustrated by Gennady Spirin. Atheneum Bks. for Young Readers 1997 28p il $17 (3-6)   **398.2**

1. Folklore—Russia 2. Musicians—Fiction

ISBN 0-689-80759-7   LC 96-3391

A talented musician from Novgorod plays so well that the Sea King wants him to marry one of his daughters

"The telling is descriptive yet very accessible, with the art, in Spirin's majestic signature style, evoking both the mythical feel of the legend and the folk-music roots from which the story sprang." Booklist

Sherlock, Sir Philip Manderson, 1902-

West Indian folk-tales; retold by Philip Sherlock; illustrated by Joan Kiddell-Monroe. Oxford Univ. Press 1966 151p il (Oxford myths and legends) hardcover o.p. paperback available $12.95 (4-6)   **398.2**

1. Folklore—West Indies

ISBN 0-19-274127-6 (pa)   LC 66-701268

"Twenty-one tales of the ancient peoples, the Caribs and the Arawaks, are intertwined here with the folklore of the African slaves. Simply structured and ably retold, the collection includes the familiar 'pourquoi' (why) stories, several tales of Anansi, the spiderman, and other legends that recount the trials and successes of the West Indian birds and animals." SLJ

Shulevitz, Uri, 1935-

The golden goose; [by] the brothers Grimm; retold and with pictures by Uri Shulevitz. Farrar, Straus & Giroux 1995 unp il $16; pa $5.95 (k-3)   **398.2**

1. Fairy tales 2. Folklore—Germany

ISBN 0-374-32695-9; 0-374-42748-8 (pa)

LC 94-44358

"The youngest of three sons is rewarded for his kindheartedness with a gleaming golden goose to which a chain of unwilling companions becomes attached. He makes a sad princess laugh with his silly procession and, after completing a task set by her disgruntled father, wins her hand." SLJ

"This is a lively rendition of an appealing tale, complemented with illustrations done in an angular, puppetlike style that recalls the story's folk origins. The skillful incorporation of an insistent refrain begs for audience participation." Horn Book Guide

The treasure. Farrar, Straus & Giroux 1978 unp il $16; pa $5.95 (k-3)   **398.2**

1. Folklore

ISBN 0-374-37740-5; 0-374-47955-0 (pa)

A Caldecott Medal honor book, 1980

This is the "tale of a poor man, here named Isaac, who three times dreams of a voice telling him to go to the capital and look for a treasure under the bridge by the palace. When he gets to the capital, the captain of the guard tells him of his dream: a treasure is buried under the stove of a man named Isaac back in Isaac's home city. So Isaac returns home, finds the treasure under his own stove, and lives happily ever after." SLJ

"Although the story is known in many cultures the retelling suggests the Hassidic tradition. . . . The eastern European influence is extended in the illustrations." Horn Book

Sierra, Judy

The beautiful butterfly; a folktale from Spain; retold by Judy Sierra; illustrated by Victoria Chess. Clarion Bks. 2000 32p il $15 (k-3) **398.2**

1. Folklore—Spain

ISBN 0-395-90015-8   LC 99-16616

After choosing a husband for his sweet singing voice, a beautiful butterfly mourns the fact that he is swallowed by a fish, until a king in his underwear reunites the two

"Chess adds a madcap atmosphere with gouache scenes of staring, sunken-eyed, richly dressed figures posing in a grassy, sunlit glade. Sierra. . . . tells the tale in a simple, straightforward way that will make it equally easy to read or learn." Booklist

The dancing pig; illustrated by Jesse Sweetwater. Harcourt Brace & Co. 1999 unp il $16 (k-3) **398.2**

1. Folklore—Indonesia

ISBN 0-15-201594-9   LC 97-27983

"Gulliver books"

After being snatched by a terrible ogress who locks them in a trunk, two sisters are rescued by the animals that they have always treated with great kindness

Sierra "deftly catches the rhythm, humor, and suspense of an oral tale. Her well-paced prose is sprinkled with Balinese words; a pronunciation guide is thoughtfully included. Sweetwater's bright, patterned illustrations . . . lovingly depict the warmth between mother and daughters, as well as the whimsy inherent in a dancing pig and four frog musicians." Booklist

Nursery tales around the world; selected and retold by Judy Sierra; illustrated by Stefano Vitale. Clarion Bks. 1996 114p il $20 **398.2**

1. Folklore

ISBN 0-395-67894-3   LC 93-2068

Presents eighteen simple stories from international folklore, grouped around six themes, such as "Runaway Cookies," "Slowpokes and Speedsters," and "Chain Tales." Includes background information and storytelling hints

"This richly illustrated compendium of folktales does double duty as a nursery story book for lap-sharing and as a sourcebook for parents and professionals. . . . Most entries feature strong rhythms and repetition that invite audience participation and develop memory. . . . Top this engaging text with Vitale's lavish oil-on-wood ethnic borders, motif vignettes, and full-page illustrations, and you have a handsome work to be valued by readers and treasured by listeners." Bull Cent Child Books

Includes bibliographical references

Tasty baby belly buttons; a Japanese folktale; illustrated by Meilo So. Knopf 1998 unp il $17; lib bdg $18.99; pa $6.99 (k-3) **398.2**

1. Folklore—Japan

ISBN 0-679-89369-5; 0-679-99369-X (lib bdg); 0-440-41738-4 (pa)   LC 98-22524

Urikohime, a girl born from a melon, battles the monstrous onis, who steal babies to eat their tasty belly buttons

"Graced with occasional delicate brushwork that seems distinctly Japanese, So's fluid, sweeping watercolors add freshness to a traditional tale of swashbuckling heroics." Booklist

Silverman, Erica

Raisel's riddle; story by Erica Silverman; pictures by Susan Gaber. Farrar, Straus & Giroux 1999 unp il $16 (k-3) **398.2**

1. Fairy tales 2. Jews—Fiction

ISBN 0-374-36168-1   LC 97-29421

A Jewish version of the Cinderella story, in which a poor but educated young woman captivates her "Prince Charming" a rabbi's son, at a Purim ball

"Gaber's softly stippled spreads evoke a quiet seriousness appropriate to this thoughtful retelling." Bull Cent Child Books

Simms, Laura, 1947-

The Bone Man; a Native American Modoc tale; illustrated by Michael McCurdy. Hyperion Bks. for Children 1997 unp il lib bdg $29.75 (2-4) **398.2**

1. Modoc Indians—Folklore

ISBN 0-7868-2074-8   LC 96-7904

This story "focuses on the struggles of Nulwee, a young Modoc Indian, who must both accept and fulfill his grandmother's prediction of his heroic destiny. Nulwee's challenge is to confront the Bone Man, and by defeating the monster, he is able to bring the gift of life-giving rain back to the land." Booklist

This tale "is retold in powerful language and arresting visual images. . . . McCurdy's hand-colored woodcuts are remarkably evocative." Bull Cent Child Books

Singer, Isaac Bashevis, 1904-1991

Mazel and Shlimazel; or, The milk of a lioness; pictures by Margot Zemach; translated from the Yiddish by the author and Elizabeth Shub. Farrar, Straus & Giroux 1967 42p il $17; pa $6.95 (2-5) **398.2**

1. Jews—Folklore

ISBN 0-374-34884-7; 0-374-44786-1 (pa)

"An Ariel book"

The happiness of Tam, a poor peasant lad, and lovely Crown Princess Nesika depends upon the outcome of a battle of wits between Mazel, the spirit of good luck, and Shlimazel, the spirit of bad luck

This story "is based on a Jewish folk tale. . . . The way Shlimazel contrives to win the wager is a witty surprise, and how, moreover, the story-teller arranges to have the story end happily after all is also ingenious and satisfying. The colored illustrations . . . have the flavor of folk art but, like the text, are anything but artless." New Yorker

When Shlemiel went to Warsaw & other stories; pictures by Margot Zemach; translated by the author and Elizabeth Shub. Farrar, Straus & Giroux 1968 115p il $13.95 (4 and up) **398.2**

1. Jews—Folklore

ISBN 0-374-38316-2

A Newbery Award honor book, 1969

"An Ariel book"

"A fine collection of five retold traditional Yiddish folk tales and three original stories. . . . The original stories—'Tsirtsur and Peziza,' 'Rabbi Leib and the Witch Cunegunde,' and 'Menaseh's Dream'—blend well with the reworked tales, and Margot Zemach's delightful black-and-white illustrations fittingly capture moods and protagonists." SLJ

Singer, Isaac Bashevis, 1904-1991—*Continued*

Zlateh the goat, and other stories; pictures by
Maurice Sendak; translated from the Yiddish by
the author and Elizabeth Shub. Harper & Row
1966 90p il $15.95; pa $6.95 (4 and up)   **398.2**
   1. Jews—Folklore
   ISBN 0-06-028477-3; 0-06-440147-2 (pa)
A Newbery Award honor book, 1967
"Seven tales drawn from middle-European Jewish village life, with illustrations which extend the humor and
subtlety of the situations." Hodges. Books for Elem Sch
Libr

Snyder, Dianne
The boy of the three-year nap; illustrated by
Allen Say. Houghton Mifflin 1988 32p il $16.95;
pa $6.95 (1-3)   **398.2**
   1. Folklore—Japan
   ISBN 0-395-44090-4; 0-395-66957-X (pa)
                           LC 87-30674
A Caldecott Medal honor book, 1989
"Japan's contribution to the trickster folktale, in which
a lazy son cons a rich man, only to be outsmarted by his
own, even trickier mother. Lilting prose and shimmering
illustrations combine in perfect harmony." SLJ

Steig, Jeanne
A handful of beans; six fairy tales; retold by
Jeanne Steig; with pictures by William Steig.
HarperCollins Pubs. 1998 142p il $17.95 (k-3)
                                 398.2
   1. Fairy tales 2. Folklore
   ISBN 0-06-205162-8   LC 97-78385
"Michael di Capua books"
"Six familiar fairy tales—'Rumpelstiltskin,' 'Beauty
and the Beast,' 'Hansel and Gretel,' 'Little Red Riding
Hood,' 'The Frog Prince,' and 'Jack and the
Beanstalk'—are retold in a sprightly, energetic style.
Jeanne Steig has a knack for slipping humor into simple
language . . . and providing silly rhymes as welcome re-
frains and pithy conclusions." Bull Cent Child Books

Steptoe, John, 1950-1989
Mufaro's beautiful daughters; an African tale.
Lothrop, Lee & Shepard Bks. 1987 unp il $15.95;
lib bdg $15.89 (k-3)   **398.2**
   1. Folklore—Africa
   ISBN 0-688-04045-4; 0-688-04046-2 (lib bdg)
                            LC 84-7158
Also available Big book edition
A Caldecott Medal honor book, 1988; Coretta Scott
King award for illustration, 1988
Mufaro's two beautiful daughters, one bad-tempered,
one kind and sweet, go before the king, who is choosing
a wife
"The pace of the text matches the rhythm of the illustrations—both move in dramatic unity to the climax. By
changing perspective the artist not only captures the lush,
rich background but also the personalities of the characters with revealing studies of their faces." Horn Book

The story of Jumping Mouse; a native American
legend; retold and illustrated by John Steptoe.
Lothrop, Lee & Shepard Bks. 1984 unp il $15.95;
pa $5.95 (1-3)   **398.2**
   1. Native Americans—Folklore
   ISBN 0-688-01902-1; 0-688-08740-X (pa)
                            LC 82-14848
A Caldecott Medal honor book, 1985
"By keeping hope alive within himself, a mouse is
successful in his quest for the far-off land. Steptoe's retelling of an unattributed tribal legend is exquisite in its
use of language and in its expansive drawings which employ dazzling subtleties of light and shadow." SLJ

Stevens, Janet
Coyote steals the blanket; an Ute tale; retold
and illustrated by Janet Stevens. Holiday House
1993 unp il hardcover o.p. paperback available
$6.95 (k-3)   **398.2**
   1. Ute Indians—Folklore 2. Coyote (Legendary character)
   ISBN 0-8234-1129-X (pa)   LC 92-54415
"When Coyote swipes a blanket, thus angering the
spirit of the desert, he is pursued by a rock on a ram-
page. This traditional trickster tale features a scraggly,
scruffy yet lovable character, a narrative that will roll
right off storytellers' tongues, and hilarious pictures of
boastful animals trying to halt the furious boulder." SLJ

Old bag of bones; a Coyote tale; retold and
illustrated by Janet Stevens. Holiday House 1996
unp il $16.95; pa $6.95 (k-3)   **398.2**
   1. Shoshoni Indians—Folklore 2. Coyote (Legendary
character)
   ISBN 0-8234-1215-6; 0-8234-1337-3 (pa)
                            LC 95-31443
"Now an aging, decidedly mangy creature who yearns
for youth, Coyote begs a stalwart young buffalo for 'a
drop of strength.' Transformed into a strapping 'Buffote,'
Coyote misjudges the extent of his new powers, as well
as the virtues of age, and is stripped of his buffalo
guise." Publ Wkly
"Expressive, darkly hued illustrations complement the
lively retelling, loosely based on a Shoshoni tale, which
blends dialogue and a clipped narration for an animated,
appealing story." Horn Book Guide

Tops and bottoms; adapted and illustrated by
Janet Stevens. Harcourt Brace & Co. 1995 unp il
$16 (k-3)   **398.2**
   1. African Americans—Folklore 2. Rabbits—Fiction
3. Bears—Fiction
   ISBN 0-15-292851-0   LC 93-19154
A Caldecott Medal honor book, 1996
"Bear agrees to enter into a farming partnership with
Hare, but first Hare makes Bear choose which half he
will receive at harvest time: tops or bottoms. Because
Bear picks tops, Hare sows all root vegetables. For the
second crop, Bear chooses bottoms; this time Hare grows
lettuce, broccoli, and celery. Finally, the frustrated Bear
demands tops and bottoms from the final season's crop.
But Hare is still the winner: he grows corn [and] keeps
the ears 'in the middle' for his family. . . . Steven's
bold, well-composed watercolor, pencil, and gesso illus-

Stevens, Janet—*Continued*

trations cover every inch of each vertically oriented double-page spread. . . . The story contains enough sly humor and reassuring predictability to captivate listeners." Horn Book

Stewig, John W.

King Midas; a golden tale; told by John Warren Stewig; pictured through the mind of Omar Rayyan. Holiday House 1999 unp il $15.95

398.2

1. Midas (Legendary character)
ISBN 0-8234-1423-X   LC 98-21222

A king finds himself bitterly regretting the consequences of his wish that everything he touches would turn to gold

"Rayyan's watercolors are a phantasmagoria of irreverent details, from the statue of a fresh minotaur sticking his tongue out to a rubber duck floating in a fountain." Bull Cent Child Books

Stockings of buttermilk: American folktales; edited by Neil Philip; illustrated by Jacqueline Mair. Clarion Bks. 1999 124p il $20 (4 and up)

398.2

1. Folklore—United States
ISBN 0-395-84980-2   LC 98-54366

These "stories and anecdotes, rooted in Europe but harvested in America, and often from African American tellers, are nearly all surprising variants on familiar folktales. . . . Philip generally lays editorial hands on the tales lightly, if at all, learnedly discusses tale types and other matters in appended notes. . . . Jacqueline Mair's small paintings add atmosphere by mimicking folk art patchwork and embroidery patterns." Booklist

Includes bibliographical references

Sturges, Philemon

The Little Red Hen (makes a pizza); retold by Philemon Sturges; illustrated by Amy Walrod. Dutton Children's Bks. 1999 unp il $15.99 (k-3)

398.2

1. Folklore 2. Chickens—Fiction
ISBN 0-525-45953-7   LC 99-20066

In this version of the traditional tale, the duck, the dog, and the cat refuse to help the Little Red Hen make a pizza but do get to participate when the time comes to eat it and then they wash the dishes

"There's a keen sense of the absurd here, and the hilarious cut-paper illustrations are right in tune with the zany plot." SLJ

Sutcliff, Rosemary, 1920-1992

The light beyond the forest; the quest for the Holy Grail; decorations by Shirley Felts. Dutton 1980 143p hardcover o.p. paperback available $4.99 (4 and up)

398.2

1. Arthur, King 2. Grail—Fiction 3. Arthurian romances
ISBN 0-14-037150-8 (pa)   LC 79-23396

First published 1979 in the United Kingdom

This is a retelling of the adventures of King Arthur's knights as they search for the Holy Grail. "After a vision of the Cup from the Last Supper appears, Sir Lancelot, Sir Galahad, Sir Bors, and Sir Percival quit Camelot to look for the Grail, knowing that only the world's most perfect knight will succeed. The individual adventures, which take on a loftier meaning as the journeys also become the knights' personal searches for God, will be most appreciated by special readers interested in King Arthur and his time." Booklist

Followed by The sword and the circle

The road to Camlann; decorations by Shirley Felts. Dutton 1982 142p hardcover o.p. paperback available $4.99 (4 and up)   **398.2**

1. Arthur, King 2. Arthurian romances
ISBN 0-14-037147-8 (pa)   LC 82-9481

First published 1981 in the United Kingdom

"This book completes Rosemary Sutcliff's Arthurian trilogy, begun with 'The Light Beyond the Forest' and 'The Sword and the Circle'. Here Sutcliff describes the events from the coming of Mordred to the death of Lancelot. The title refers to The Last Battle, in which Arthur and his civilization perish. Sutcliff writes with her usual economy and rich prose, with a touch of archaic diction in the speeches. . . . Other than Malory, I can think of no better introduction to the whole sweep of Arthurian stories and values." SLJ

The sword and the circle; King Arthur and the Knights of the Round Table. Dutton 1981 260p hardcover o.p. paperback available $5.99 (4 and up)   **398.2**

1. Arthur, King 2. Arthurian romances
ISBN 0-14-037149-4 (pa)   LC 81-9759

The second volume in the author's Arthurian trilogy, begun with: The light beyond the forest. The events in this volume precede those in the earlier volume

"The author has brought together thirteen stories associated with the Arthurian cycle, beginning with 'The Coming of Arthur' and concluding not with the passing of Arthur but with 'The Coming of Perceval.' Although she has relied on Malory's 'Morte d'Arthur' for most of her material, she has drawn upon other medieval sources for some of her best storytelling: For example 'Sir Gawain and the Green Knight' comes from a Middle English poem, and the twenty-nine-page 'Tristan and Iseult' is indebted to Godfrey of Strasburg's version." Horn Book

Followed by The road to Camlann

Talbott, Hudson

Excalibur; written and illustrated by Hudson Talbott. Books of Wonder; Morrow Junior Bks. 1996 unp il $16 (3-5)   **398.2**

1. Arthur, King 2. Arthurian romances
ISBN 0-688-13380-0   LC 95-35388

The young King Arthur asks for and receives the noble sword Excalibur from the Lady of the Lake and promises to be deserving of it through acts of valor

"The particulars of costumes, weapons, and heraldic emblems captured in the watercolors may intrigue many youngsters; others will relish Talbott's abundant detailing of bloody battles or enjoy the story for its fantasy and drama." Booklist

Talbott, Hudson—*Continued*

King Arthur and the Round Table; written and illustrated by Hudson Talbott. Books of Wonder; Morrow Junior Bks. 1995 unp il $16 (3-5) **398.2**
1. Arthur, King 2. Arthurian romances
ISBN 0-688-11340-0 LC 94-43766

"Talbott recounts the battles immediately following Arthur's accession to the throne, the young king's fateful meeting with beautiful Guinevere, and the acquisition of the Round Table." Horn Book Guide

"The rich watercolor tableaux . . . paint war as bloody and painful, not all glorious. The love scenes glow golden. The Round Table, huge and decorated with the signs of the zodiac, exhibits its power more than the words do. Overall, this is a rousing addition to the current pickings of Arthurian stories." SLJ

Taylor, Harriet Peck

Brother Wolf; a Seneca tale; retold and illustrated by Harriet Peck Taylor. Farrar, Straus & Giroux 1996 unp il $15 (k-3) **398.2**
1. Seneca Indians—Folklore
ISBN 0-374-30997-3 LC 95-30775

"This Seneca tale relates how Wolf and Raccoon are friends, but they enjoy teasing each other. After the teasing has turned to insults, Raccoon comes upon the sleeping Wolf and covers his eyes with tar and clay. The mixture hardens, and Wolf has to beg the birds to peck away the seal so that he can see again. . . . Wolf shows his gratitude to the birds by painting their feathers with bright dyes and offers his forgiveness to Raccoon by painting stripes on his tail. . . . The large-scale batik illustrations, with their distinctive look, will please young children with their clarity and freshness. A satisfying read-aloud." Booklist

Coyote places the stars; retold and illustrated by Harriet Peck Taylor. Bradbury Press 1993 unp il hardcover o.p. paperback available $5.99 (k-3)
398.2
1. Chinook Indians—Folklore 2. Coyote (Legendary character) 3. Stars—Fiction
ISBN 0-689-81535-2 (pa) LC 92-46431

"Based on a Wasco Native American legend, this . . . pourquoi tale explains the designs of the constellations. It is the curious coyote who decides to discover the secrets of the heavens by creating a ladder of arrows he shoots into the sky. Once in the heavens, he moves the stars around forming the shapes of his animal friends." SLJ

"Taylor's batik-and-dye paintings are a good match for the casual, playful rhythm of her retelling." Booklist

When Bear stole the chinook; a Siksika tale; retold and illustrated by Harriet Peck Taylor. Farrar, Straus & Giroux 1997 unp il $16 (k-3)
398.2
1. Siksika Indians—Folklore 2. Bears—Fiction
ISBN 0-374-10947-8 LC 96-33843

Because the long, hard winter caused scarcity of firewood and food, a poor Indian boy and his animal friends journey to the lodge of the Great Bear to release the chinook (warm spring wind)

"Handsome batiks illustrate a simply written Siksikan (Blackfoot) Indian tale. . . . Combining cool winter landscapes and warm characters, Ayliffe's subtly patterned artwork is both eye-catching and soothing." Booklist

Includes bibliographical references

Te Kanawa, Kiri

Land of the long white cloud; Maori myths, tales and legends; illustrated by Michael Foreman. Arcade Pub. 1990 118p il o.p.; Trafalgar Sq. paperback available $17.95 (3-6) **398.2**
1. Maoris—Folklore
ISBN 0-86205-075-9 (pa) LC 89-45534

"Opera singer Dame Kiri Te Kanawa retells the Maori folktales she remembers from her childhood in New Zealand." Booklist

"Lively and full of action, adventure, and magic, the collection is well balanced with myths, hero legends, fairy tales, and *pourquoi* stories. . . . Jewel-toned watercolor illustrations capture the vibrant quality of the stories and convey the changing moods of sea and sky. This book is a rich source of Pacific island material." SLJ

Temple, Frances, 1945-1995

Tiger soup; an Anansi story from Jamaica; retold and illustrated by Frances Temple. Orchard Bks. 1994 unp il lib bdg $16.99; pa $6.95 (k-3)
398.2
1. Folklore—Jamaica 2. Anansi (Legendary character)
ISBN 0-531-08709-3 (lib bdg); 0-531-07097-2 (pa)
LC 93-48834

"A Richard Jackson book"

After tricking Tiger into leaving the soup he has been cooking, Anansi the spider eats the soup himself and manages to put the blame on the monkeys

"Temple's retelling is filled with the easy rhythm of the Jamaican dialect and begs to be read—even partly sung—aloud. The story moves along at a pleasant pace and provides opportunities for participation. . . . The torn-and-painted paper collages convey the warmth and color of the tropical setting and suggests a real sense of movement." SLJ

Terada, Alice M., 1928-

Under the starfruit tree; folktales from Vietnam; told by Alice M. Terada; illustrations by Janet Larsen; introduction and notes by Mary C. Austin. University of Hawaii Press 1989 136p il hardcover o.p. paperback available $12.95 (4-6) **398.2**
1. Folklore—Vietnam
ISBN 0-8248-1553-X (pa) LC 89-5123

"A Kolowalu book"

"Twenty-seven tales culled from North and South Vietnam and translated by native speakers are grouped in four sections: foibles and quirks; tales from the lowlands and the highlands; the spirit world; and food, love and laughter. . . . Each narration is followed by an afterword that . . . reveals customs, beliefs and values." Publ Wkly

"Although the book's format is not particularly attractive, these 27 stories from Vietnam will certainly find a place on library shelves. . . . Occasional black-and-white drawings add some visual interest." Booklist

Includes bibliographical references

Tomie dePaola's Favorite nursery tales. Putnam 1986 127p il $24.99 (k-3) **398.2**
1. Folklore 2. Fables
ISBN 0-399-21319-8　　　　　LC 85-28302

The book begins "with a verse about reading picture books from Stevenson's *Child's Garden of Verses*, followed by Longfellow's 'Children's Hour.' The story selections—'Johnny Cake,' 'The Little Red Hen,' 'Rumpelstiltskin,' 'The Princess and the Pea,' 'The Tortoise and the Hare,' 'The House on the Hill,' and 22 more." Booklist

"DePaola's droll, witty, and very funny illustrations capture the essence of each story from a child's point of view. . . . The beautiful layout of these pages, in which the print and pictures are perfectly at ease with one another, invites confident new readers as well as adults for reading aloud." SLJ

Tresselt, Alvin R., 1916-2000
The mitten; an old Ukrainian folktale; retold by Alvin Tresselt; illustrated by Yaroslava; adapted from the version by E. Rachev. Lothrop, Lee & Shepard Bks. 1964 unp il hardcover o.p. paperback available $5.95 (k-2) **398.2**
1. Folklore—Ukraine 2. Animals—Fiction
ISBN 0-688-09238-1 (pa)

"On the coldest day of the year a little Ukrainian boy loses his fur-lined mitten, which becomes so overcrowded with animals seeking a snug shelter that it finally bursts. Brightly colored pictures show the animals dressed in typical Ukrainian costumes." Hodges. Books for Elem Sch Libr

Tseng, Grace
White tiger, blue serpent; illustrated by Jean and Mou-Sien Tseng. Lothrop, Lee & Shepard Bks. 1999 unp il $16; lib bdg $16.84 (2-4) **398.2**
1. Fairy tales 2. China—Fiction
ISBN 0-688-12515-8; 0-688-12516-6 (lib bdg)
　　　　　LC 94-9757
Based on tale from Drung tribe of Yunnan Province
When his mother's beautiful brocade is snatched away by a greedy goddess, a young Chinese boy faces many perils as he attempts to get it back

"Lush paintings in the manner of fifteenth-century Chinese art animate a full-bodied folktale retelling about the search for beauty." Booklist

Uchida, Yoshiko, 1921-1992
The magic purse; retold by Yoshiko Uchida; illustrated by Keiko Narahashi. Margaret K. McElderry Bks. 1993 unp il $15.95 (k-3) **398.2**
1. Folklore—Japan
ISBN 0-689-50559-0　　　　　LC 92-30132
After facing danger and demons to help a young woman, a poor farmer receives a magic purse that always refills itself with gold

The author's elegant retelling is well paced and dotted with lyrical imagery. . . . Narahashi clearly evokes Japanese scroll paintings through her boldly outlined, seemingly spontaneous watercolors. Her luminous art sets the mood perfectly for Uchida's magical tale." Publ Wkly

Vagin, Vladimir Vasil′evich, 1937-
The enormous carrot; [by] Vladimir Vagin. Scholastic Press 1998 unp il $15.95 (k-2) **398.2**
1. Folklore—Russia
ISBN 0-590-45491-9　　　　　LC 97-14770
A group learns the value of teamwork as one animal after another joins in the effort to pull a giant carrot out of the ground. Based on a Russian folktale

"The artist clothes his menagerie in comfortable, colorful, modern dress and puts it in a sunny, rural landscape lush with flowers. . . . It's a classic tale about the value of cooperation, in a fresh, cheerful garb." Booklist

Van Laan, Nancy
The magic bean tree; a legend from Argentina; retold by Nancy Van Laan; paintings by Beatriz Vidal. Houghton Mifflin 1998 unp il $15 (k-3)
　　　　　398.2
1. Native Americans—Folklore 2. Folklore—Argentina
ISBN 0-395-82746-9　　　　　LC 96-38632
A young Quechuan boy sets out on his own to bring the rains back to his parched homeland and is rewarded by a gift of carob beans that come to be prized across Argentina

"Vidal's shimmering, folk art-style paintings are well matched to the elegant simplicity and drama of Van Laan's retelling." Booklist

Includes glossary and bibliographical references

Shingebiss; an Ojibwe legend; retold by Nancy Van Laan; woodcuts by Betsy Bowen. Houghton Mifflin 1997 unp il $16 (2-4) **398.2**
1. Ojibwa Indians—Folklore 2. Ducks—Fiction
ISBN 0-316-89627-6　　　　　LC 95-40274
Shingebiss the duck bravely challenges the Winter Maker and manages to find enough food to survive a long, harsh winter

Van Laan's "lyric text flows like a soft drum beat and, although lengthy, wastes no words. . . . The artist's rustic, spirited woodcuts appear within circular frames of thick, loose lines that give one the sense of peering through ice holes." Publ Wkly

Includes glossary and bibliographical references

The tiny, tiny boy and the big, big cow; a Scottish folk tale; pictures by Marjorie Priceman. Knopf 1993 unp il hardcover o.p. paperback available $6.99 (k-3) **398.2**
1. Folklore—Scotland 2. Cattle—Fiction
ISBN 0-375-80478-1 (pa)　　　　　LC 91-33738
"An Umbrella book"
A cumulative story in which a tiny, tiny boy tries to milk a big, big cow who will not stand still

"Hilarious full-page pen-and-ink and watercolor illustrations in warm, rosy tones are delightfully detailed and rush the exuberant action forward to its sensible, satisfying conclusion." SLJ

Vuong, Lynette Dyer, 1938-

The brocaded slipper and other Vietnamese tales; illustrations by Vo-Dinh Mai. HarperCollins Pubs. 1982 111p il hardcover o.p. paperback available $4.95 (4-6)   **398.2**

1. Folklore—Vietnam 2. Fairy tales
ISBN 0-06-440440-4 (pa)   LC 81-19139
First published by Addison-Wesley

"The title story is a 'Cinderella' variant. 'Little Finger of the Watermelon Patch' is similar to 'Thumbelina.' 'The Fairy Grotto,' in which a man enters fairyland and then comes back to a world that is 300 years older, has a protagonist not unlike Rip van Winkle. In 'Master Frog' the frog heroine must survive in cruel and humble circumstances before she is reunited with her true love." Booklist

"The stories . . . are often more satisfyingly complex than their Western counterparts. . . . The simple, fluid ink-wash illustrations are captioned in both English and Vietnamese. An excellent and unusual addition to folklore collections." SLJ

Wagué Diakité, Baba

The hatseller and the monkeys; a West African folktale; retold and illustrated by Baba Wagué Diakité. Scholastic Press 1999 unp il $15.95 (k-3)
                                                      398.2

1. Folklore—West Africa
ISBN 0-590-96069-5   LC 98-16250

An African version of the familiar story of a man who sets off to sell his hats, only to have them stolen by a treeful of mischievous monkeys

"Ceramic-tile paintings on each spread depict the action in fluid, bold brushwork. . . . In this retelling, Diakité's use of language is as colorful and unusual as his artwork." Publ Wkly

The hunterman and the crocodile; a West African folktale; retold and illustrated by Baba Wagué Diakité. Scholastic 1997 unp il $15.95 (2-4)   **398.2**

1. Folklore—West Africa
ISBN 0-590-89828-0   LC 95-25975

"After Donso rescues a crocodile family, they turn on him and threaten to eat him. Several creatures . . . refuse his appeals for help, saying that Man has always misused them in the past. Only clever Rabbit is willing to assist him. Bold figures painted on ceramic tiles illustrate this teaching tale about 'living in harmony with nature.'" Horn Book Guide

Includes bibliographical references

Walker, Barbara K.

A treasury of Turkish folktales for children; retold by Barbara K. Walker. Linnet Bks. 1988 155p $25 (4 and up)   **398.2**

1. Folklore—Turkey
ISBN 0-208-02206-6   LC 88-6859

"The 34 stories are organized into sections on animals, fables, Keloglan tales, Nasreddin Hoca tales, witch/giant/jinn/dragon tales, trickster tales, tales of fate, and stories of wish fulfillment. The tonal range offers great variety for storytelling, reading aloud, or just plain entertainment among children fond of folktales, though the format is formidable for young readers." Bull Cent Child Books

Includes glossary

Walker, Paul Robert

Big men, big country; a collection of American tall tales; written by Paul Robert Walker; illustrated by James Bernardin. Harcourt Brace Jovanovich 1993 79p il hardcover o.p. paperback available $10 (4-6)   **398.2**

1. Tall tales 2. Folklore—United States
ISBN 0-15-202625-8 (pa)   LC 91-45126

A collection of American tall tales featuring such legendary characters as Davy Crockett, Paul Bunyan, and Pecos Bill

"Walker's informal style and easygoing humor make a natural fit for these nine stories of larger-than-life heroes, and he's done a thorough job of researching the background for them and telling us about it. . . . Bernardin has captured this cast with strong black-and-white drawings, plus full-color pictures with a kind of muscular Frederic Remington energy." Bull Cent Child Books

Includes bibliographical references

Ward, Helen, 1962-

The hare and the tortoise; a fable from Aesop; retold & illustrated by Helen Ward. Millbrook Press 1999 unp il $16.95; lib bdg $24.90 (k-3)
                                                      398.2

1. Fables 2. Folklore
ISBN 0-761-30988-8; 0-7613-1318-4 (lib bdg)
                                              LC 98-26100

Retells the events of the famous race between the boastful hare and the persevering tortoise. Includes a key to the various animals pictured in the illustrations

"A straightforward, elegant, witty retelling of an old favorite. . . . With black ink outlines meticulously delineating the creatures' fur and markings, Ward's watercolor-and-gouache paintings show each animal as both warmly cuddly and realistic." Booklist

The king of the birds; written and illustrated by Helen Ward. Millbrook Press 1997 unp il $15.95; lib bdg $24.90 (k-3)   **398.2**

1. Folklore 2. Birds—Fiction
ISBN 0-7613-0288-3; 0-7613-0313-8 (lib bdg)
                                              LC 97-2129

When chaos reigns among the birds, the oldest and wisest birds declare a contest to determine who will be their king

"Ward's brief and lyrical retelling works hand in hand with her glowing artwork. . . . The pen-and-ink illustrations colored with watercolors and gouache take full advantage of the spectacle and beauty of the avian world." SLJ

Wardlaw, Lee, 1955-

Punia and the King of Sharks; a Hawaiian folktale; adapted by Lee Wardlaw; pictures by Felipe Davalos. Dial Bks. for Young Readers 1997 unp il $16.99 (k-3)   **398.2**

1. Folklore—Hawaii
ISBN 0-8037-1682-6   LC 93-43955

Wardlaw, Lee, 1955-—*Continued*

Clever Punia, a Hawaiian fisherman's son, finds different ways to trick the King of Sharks and take his tasty lobsters away from him

"The involving story contains comforting folktale elements and an engaging protagonist. The illustrations have an appropriate folk-art flatness as well as vigor and humor." Horn Book Guide

Includes glossary

Watson, Richard Jesse, 1951-

Tom Thumb; retold and illustrated by Richard Jesse Watson. Harcourt Brace Jovanovich 1989 unp il hardcover o.p. paperback available $6 (k-3) **398.2**

1. Folklore 2. Fairy tales

ISBN 0-15-289281-8 (pa)   LC 87-12045

After many adventures, a tiny boy, no bigger than his father's thumb, earns a place as the smallest Knight of the Round Table

"Although it is not stated, this is a loose adaptation of an English variant of the tale. . . . However, Watson's heroic ending, in which Tom Thumb replaces the giant's beloved broken shell, is not mentioned in other variants available. The writing borders on the flowery, but is quite readable. The realistic, microscopically detailed tempera and watercolor illustrations are particularly suitable for this tale." SLJ

Wattenberg, Jane

Henny-Penny; retold and illustrated by Jane Wattenberg. Scholastic Press 2000 unp il lib bdg $15.95 (k-3) **398.2**

1. Folklore

ISBN 0-439-07817-2   LC 99-28806

While on their way to tell the king that the sky is falling, Henny Penny and her friends meet the very hungry Foxy-Loxy

"This is a hip, updated version of the old folktale. The colorful photo-collage art places Henny-Penny in locations around the world from Stonehenge to the Egyptian pyramids to the Taj Mahal." SLJ

Wildsmith, Brian, 1930-

The Bremen Town Band. Oxford Univ. Press c1999 unp il $16.95 (k-2) **398.2**

1. Folklore—Germany 2. Fairy tales

ISBN 0-19-279034-X

Four old mistreated animals set out for Bremen to become musicians and encounter a den of thieves

"With line-and-watercolor paintings both delicate and lush, Wildsmith retells the Grimms' fairy tale in a glowing pastoral setting of butterflies, birds, flowers, and wild foliage." Booklist

The hare and the tortoise; based on the fable by La Fontaine. Oxford Univ. Press 1966 unp il hardcover o.p. paperback available $8.95 (k-2) **398.2**

1. Fables 2. Rabbits—Fiction 3. Turtles—Fiction

ISBN 0-19-272398-7 (pa)

"Wildsmith tells, simply and eloquently, his version of the La Fontaine fable about the slow and steady tortoise who wins the race from the quick and careless hare. The paintings are astonishing creations in all the colors of the spectrum. The vistas of a countryside bursting with blooms, birds soring overhead as interested observers like the animals gathered along the route; every one of the scenes is a wonder." Publ Wkly

The miller, the boy and the donkey. Oxford Univ. Press 1969 unp il hardcover o.p. paperback available $8.95 (k-2) **398.2**

1. Fables

ISBN 0-19-272400-2 (pa)

Adapted and illustrated by Brian Wildsmith

The miller and his son take their donkey to market to sell him. To keep him clean they decide to carry him, but a passing farmer laughs at them and they ride the donkey instead. Thus begins a series of suggestions from other people they meet as to who should ride the donkey. The poor miller is utterly confused trying to please everyone and in the end decides that next time he will only please himself

"A spirited and attractive picture book." Child Books, 1970

Willard, Nancy

Beauty and the beast; wood engravings by Barry Moser. Harcourt Brace Jovanovich 1992 67p il $19.95 (5 and up) **398.2**

1. Folklore—France 2. Fairy tales

ISBN 0-15-206052-9   LC 91-28398

Through her great capacity to love, a kind and beautiful young woman releases a handsome young man from the spell which has made him into an ugly beast

"This elegant, handsomely packaged retelling, set in turn-of-the-century New York, is graced by Moser's quietly dramatic woodcuts and Willard's sure command of language." Publ Wkly

Winthrop, Elizabeth

The little humpbacked horse; a Russian tale; adapted by Elizabeth Winthrop; illustrated by Alexander Koshkin. Clarion Bks. 1997 24p il $14.95 (4-6) **398.2**

1. Fairy tales 2. Folklore—Russia 3. Horses—Fiction

ISBN 0-395-65361-4   LC 95-43994

In this adaptation of a story by P. P. Ershov, a young peasant, with the help of his faithful horse, captures magical beasts, marries the woman he loves, and becomes Tsar of Russia

"Winthrop pairs the conventions and cadences of a traditional tale with passages that are rich with poetic images. . . . Koshkin's paintings in watercolor, tempera, and gouache are a perfect match, providing the ornate patterns and symmetrical compositions of folk art." SLJ

Wisniewski, David

Golem; story and pictures by David Wisniewski. Clarion Bks. 1996 unp il $15.95 (3-5) **398.2**

1. Jewish legends

ISBN 0-395-72618-2   LC 95-21777

Awarded the Caldecott Medal, 1997

Wisniewski, David—*Continued*

This "is the tale of a clay giant formed in the image of man to protect the Jewish people of medieval Prague from destruction by their enemies." SLJ

"The fiery, crisply layered paper illustrations, portraying with equal drama and precision the ornamental architecture of Prague and the unearthly career of the Golem, match the specificity and splendor of the storytelling." Publ Wkly

Wolkstein, Diane

The banza; a Haitian story; pictures by Marc Brown. Dial Bks. for Young Readers 1981 unp il hardcover o.p. paperback available $5.99 (k-3)
                              398.2
   1. Folklore—Haiti
   ISBN 0-14-054605-7 (pa)

"Cabree the goat becomes friends with a young tiger named Teegra. . . . Teegra gives Cabree a 'banza' (an old African instrument something like a banjo), which belonged to his uncle, for protection. When Cabree is surrounded by ten hungry tigers, she plays the banza, mobilizing her own resources to frighten the tigers away." Interracial Books Child Bull

"Told with rich economy, this brief tale is laced with action and humor; . . . Brown's solid, textured drawings in bright Caribbean colors are a fine extension of the text, and their size and clarity make the book excellent for sharing with groups." SLJ

White wave; a Chinese tale; retold by Diane Wolkstein; illustrated by Ed Young. Harcourt Brace & Co. 1996 unp il $16 (k-3)   **398.2**
   1. Folklore—China
   ISBN 0-15-200293-6   LC 95-451
   "Gulliver books"
   First published 1979 by Crowell

Kuo Ming's discovery of a moon goddess inside a snail shell changes his lonely life

"An enchanting story and a great introduction for young children to Chinese folktales. Charcoal shaded drawings complement the tale beautifully." Child Book Rev Serv

Womenfolk and fairy tales; edited by Rosemary Minard; illustrated by Suzanna Klein. Houghton Mifflin 1975 163p il $18 (3-6)   **398.2**
   1. Folklore 2. Fairy tales
   ISBN 0-395-20276-0

This collection features stories by the Brothers Grimm, Lafcadio Hearn, Andrew Lang, Joseph Jacobs, and others

"Although the tales are available in a multitude of collections, this handsomely illustrated volume brings them together in a convenient form for those searching for feminist folklore." Horn Book

Wooldridge, Connie Nordhielm, 1950-

Wicked Jack; adapted by Connie Nordhielm Wooldridge; illustrated by Will Hillenbrand. Holiday House 1995 unp il $16.95; pa $6.95 (k-3)
                              398.2
   1. Folklore—Southern States
   ISBN 0-8234-1101-X; 0-8234-1292-X (pa)
                            LC 93-13248

"The mean blacksmith defeats the devil and his young sons with a chair that won't stop rocking, a sledgehammer that won't stop pounding, and a fire bush that keeps on sticking. In the delectable ending, Jack, now deceased, is turned away from the underworld by terrified demons. . . . Hillenbrand's imaginative mixed-media paintings (with smudges of coal) have thin, robust lines, angular figures, subtle colors, and a distinctive style." Booklist

The **Yellow** fairy book; edited by Andrew Lang; with numerous illustrations by H. J. Ford. Dover Publs. 1966 321p il pa $8.95 (4-6)   **398.2**
   1. Folklore 2. Fairy tales
   ISBN 0-486-21674-8

Also available in hardcover from P. Smith

A reprint of the title first published 1894 by Longmans

A collection of more than 40 tales, including many by Andersen and the Brothers Grimm, and others from the folklore of Hungary, Russia, Poland, Iceland, Germany, France, England, and the American Indians

Yeoman, John

The Seven voyages of Sinbad the Sailor; illustrated by Quentin Blake; retold by John Yeoman. Margaret K. McElderry Bks. 1997 c1996 119p il $19.95 (5 and up)   **398.2**
   1. Fairy tales 2. Arabs—Folklore
   ISBN 0-689-81368-6

First published 1996 in the United Kingdom

"Yeoman's first-person narration . . . leads readers through Sinbad's seven shipwrecks while introducing them to the amazing inhabitants of the islands on which the sailor is inevitably stranded." SLJ

"Blake's ink drawings with watercolors . . . illustrate the story with style and grace. A handsome edition in every way, this book features good storytelling, lively illustrations, and excellent design." Booklist

Yep, Laurence

The Khan's daughter; a Mongolian folktale; illustrated by Jean and Mou-Sien Tseng. Scholastic 1996 unp il $16.95 (3-5)   **398.2**
   1. Folklore—Mongolia
   ISBN 0-590-48389-7   LC 95-25150

A simple shepherd must pass three tests in order to marry the Khan's beautiful daughter

"Yep's strong folkloric narrative is amplified by splendid watercolor illustrations. . . . With engaging human characters, frightful monsters, dramatic tension within a warrior-based society, powerful illustrations, and plenty of action, this is the sort of book that will appeal to diverse ages and sensibilities." Booklist

Yolen, Jane

Not one damsel in distress; world folktales for strong girls; collected and told by Jane Yolen; With illustrations by Susan Guevara. Silver Whistle Bks. 2000 116p il $17 (4 and up) **398.2**
   1. Fairy tales 2. Women—Folklore
   ISBN 0-15-202047-0   LC 99-18509

Yolen, Jane—*Continued*

A collection of thirteen traditional tales from various parts of the world, each of whose main character is a fearless, strong, heroic, and resourceful woman

"This is a spirited collection with a lively pace. . . . The stories sing and soar in Yolen's supple language, and each is contained enough for a read-aloud." Booklist

Includes bibliographical references

Tam Lin; an old ballad; retold by Jane Yolen and illustrated by Charles Mikolaycak. Harcourt Brace Jovanovich 1990 unp hardcover o.p. paperback available $6 (3-6)   398.2

1. Folklore—Scotland 2. Fairy tales
ISBN 0-15-201697-X (pa)   LC 88-2280

In this retelling of an old Scottish ballad, a Scottish lass, on the Halloween after her sixteenth birthday, reclaims her family home which has been held for years by the fairies and at the same time effects the release of Tam Lin, a human held captive by the Queen of the Fey

"Yolen's prose is both vivid and economical—it reads aloud very well, and Mikolaycak's brooding pictures swirl with motion, drama, and a compelling play of pattern and color." Booklist

Young, Ed

Cat and Rat; the legend of the Chinese zodiac. Holt & Co. 1995 unp il $15.95; pa $6.95 (k-3)
398.2

1. Folklore—China 2. Zodiac
ISBN 0-8050-2977-X; 0-8050-6049-9 (pa)
LC 94-49147

"Cat and Rat were best friends, according to this Chinese legend, until the Jade Emperor of Heaven held a race to determine which animals would be included in the zodiac. . . . In the author's note, Young comments on the Chinese New Year, the 12 traditional signs, and the birth years and personality traits for each one." Booklist

"Young tells the story in lively, spare prose. . . . His charcoal and pastel drawings on dark blue and buff rice paper are elegant and full of action." SLJ

Donkey trouble. Atheneum Bks. for Young Readers 1995 unp il hardcover o.p. paperback available $5.99 (k-3)   398.2

1. Fables
ISBN 0-689-82010-0 (pa)   LC 95-2135

In this retelling of the traditional fable, a kind but simple man and his grandson, on their way to market with their donkey, find it impossible to please everyone they meet

"Young has given the story an appealing and unique interpretation, evoking a desert setting in handsome impressionistic studies of landscapes changing to show the passage of time." Horn Book Guide

Lon Po Po; a Red-Riding Hood story from China; translated and illustrated by Ed Young. Philomel Bks. 1989 unp il $16.99; pa $6.99 (1-3)
398.2

1. Folklore—China 2. Wolves—Fiction
ISBN 0-399-21619-7; 0-698-11382-9 (pa)
LC 88-15222

Awarded the Caldecott Medal, 1990

Three sisters staying home alone are endangered by a hungry wolf who is disguised as their grandmother

"The text possesses that matter-of-fact veracity that characterizes the best fairy tales. The watercolor and pastel pictures are remarkable: mystically beautiful in their depiction of the Chinese countryside, menacing in the exchanges with the wolf, and positively chilling in the scenes inside the house." SLJ

Seven blind mice. Philomel Bks. 1992 unp il $17.99 (k-3)   398.2

1. Fables 2. Elephants—Fiction 3. Folklore—India 4. Mice—Fiction
ISBN 0-399-22261-8   LC 90-35396

A Caldecott Medal honor book, 1993

"In Young's version of the familiar Indian folktale of the blind men and the elephant, seven blind *mice* approach an elephant, ask what it is, explore various parts of the beast, and arrive at different conclusions. . . . Many preschool and primary grade teachers will find that the book reinforces their students' learning of colors, days of the week, and ordinal numbers, while heeding the story's admonition not to lose sight of the whole in their enthusiasm for identifying the parts. Graphically, this picture book is stunning, with the cut-paper figures of the eight characters dramatically silhouetted against black backgrounds. . . . At once profound and simple, intelligent and playful." Booklist

Zelinsky, Paul O.

Rapunzel; retold and illustrated by Paul O. Zelinsky. Dutton Children's Bks. 1997 unp il $16.99 (3-5)   398.2

1. Fairy tales 2. Folklore
ISBN 0-525-45607-4   LC 96-50260

Awarded the Caldecott Medal, 1998

A retelling of the folktale in which a beautiful girl with long golden hair is kept imprisoned in a lonely tower by a sorceress

"An elegant and sophisticated retelling that draws on early French and Italian versions of the tale. Masterful oil paintings capture the Renaissance setting and flesh out the tragic figures." SLJ

Rumpelstiltskin; from the German of the Brothers Grimm; retold & illustrated by Paul O. Zelinsky. Dutton 1986 unp il lib bdg $16.99; pa $6.99 (k-4)   398.2

1. Folklore—Germany 2. Fairy tales
ISBN 0-525-44265-0 (lib bdg); 0-14-055864-0 (pa)
LC 86-4482

Also available Spanish language edition

A Caldecott Medal honor book, 1987

"The paintings feature a realistic miller's daughter who gets unexpected help in turning her bunches of hay into shimmering gold thread from a gnomelike little man outfitted in medieval garb. Zelinsky makes thoughtful use of composition and provides strong interplay between light and shadow. . . . Zelinsky's story uses an . . . ending in which the little man runs off rather than tearing himself in half when his name is discovered. . . . A lush and substantial offering." Booklist

Zemach, Margot

The little red hen; an old story. Farrar, Straus & Giroux 1983 unp il $14; pa $4.95 (k-2)   **398.2**
    1. Folklore 2. Chickens—Fiction
ISBN 0-374-34621-6; 0-374-44511-7 (pa)
                    LC 83-14159

A retelling of the traditional tale about the little red hen whose lazy friends are unwilling to help her plant, harvest, or grind the wheat into flour, but all are willing to help her eat the bread that she makes from it

"The pleasingly retold, rhythmical text is appropriately extended by scrappy, cartoonish, softly glowing color illustrations. The animals are anthropomorphized just enough, and their characters perfectly caught." Child Book Rev Serv

The three little pigs; an old story. Farrar, Straus & Giroux 1989 unp il $14; pa $5.95 (k-2)   **398.2**
    1. Folklore—Great Britain   2. Pigs—Fiction
3. Wolves—Fiction
ISBN 0-374-37527-5; 0-374-47717-5 (pa)
                    LC 87-73488

"Michael di Capua books"

Zemach "has brought a familiar, often-told tale to life with marvelous ink-and-watercolor illustrations. Her wolf, wearing a dapper green hat and radiating slyness with every inch of his furry self, cuts a spendidly sinister figure as he attempts to wile his way to three pork chop dinners. With simple, lively sentences Zemach has related the complete story, including the apple-picking and country fair episodes." Horn Book

The three wishes; an old story. Farrar, Straus & Giroux 1986 unp il $16; pa $4.95 (k-2)   **398.2**
    1. Folklore 2. Wishes—Fiction
ISBN 0-374-37529-1; 0-374-47728-0 (pa)
                    LC 86-80956

In this "version of the familiar folk tale, a woodcutter and his wife rescue an imp in the forest. He gives them three wishes, which they foolishly manage to squander on a long chain of sausages." N Y Times Book Rev

This "is a natural for the picture-book format, and Zemach has taken full advantage of the humor with her watercolor illustrations. . . . The characters are homely and affectionate, their dog an amusing echo of their own lively expressions." Bull Cent Child Books

Ziefert, Harriet

Little Red Riding Hood; retold by Harriet Ziefert; illustrated by Emily Bolam. Viking 2000 unp il $13.89; pa $3.99 (k-2)   **398.2**
    1. Fairy tales 2. Folklore—Germany
ISBN 0-670-88389-1; 0-14-056529-9 (pa)
                    LC 99-23210

"Viking easy-to-read"

A little girl meets a hungry wolf in the forest while on her way to visit her grandmother

This adaptation of the Grimm's fairy tale "tells the story in a brisk, straightforward style . . . [with] simple, colorful illustrations. . . . The vocabulary is appropriate for beginning readers. The lively illustrations and familiarity of the story should provide a successful reading experience." SLJ

398.8   Rhymes and rhyming games

Anna Banana: 101 jump-rope rhymes; compiled by Joanna Cole; illustrated by Alan Tiegreen. Morrow Junior Bks. 1989 64p il hardcover o.p. paperback available $7.95   **398.8**
    1. Jump rope rhymes 2. Games
ISBN 0-688-08809-0 (pa)   LC 88-29108

An illustrated collection of jump rope rhymes arranged according to the type of jumping they are meant to accompany

"Heavily inked drawings provide cartoon-style humor; sources for jump-rope rhymes and an index of first lines are appended." Booklist

The **Arnold** Lobel book of Mother Goose. Knopf 1997 176p il $21; lib bdg $22.99 (k-2)   **398.8**
    1. Nursery rhymes
ISBN 0-679-88736-9; 0-679-98736-3 (lib bdg)
                    LC 97-1762

First published 1986 with title: The Random House book of Mother Goose

This nursery rhyme collection is "a true classic, with more than three hundred verses and Lobel's vigorous, lively, narrative-filled illustrations." Horn Book Guide

Aylesworth, Jim, 1943-

The completed hickory dickory dock; illustrated by Eileen Christelow. Atheneum Pubs. 1990 unp il hardcover o.p. paperback available $5.99   **398.8**
    1. Nursery rhymes
ISBN 0-689-71862-4 (pa)   LC 89-38484

"This extended version of the familiar nursery rhyme successfully combines simple counting concepts, the numbers one through 12 and a gentle introduction to telling time. Laced with phonetic harmonies, the additional verses have a nonsensical, bouncing quality that offer a fun-filled challenge for little ones to master. . . . The endearingly chubby mouse and his family are humorously portrayed in Christelow's colorful, frantic cartoons." Publ Wkly

The **Baby's** lap book; [compiled and illustrated by] Kay Chorao. rev ed. Dutton 1990 58p il lib bdg $17.99   **398.8**
    1. Nursery rhymes
ISBN 0-525-44604-4   LC 89-23273

First published 1977

A collection of more than fifty traditional nursery rhymes accompanied by "Chorao's soft, eminently careful pencil drawings of the characters and their situations. Innocence is all pervasive, in the alternating pastel pink and yellow pages that nicely counter the light grays of the framed drawings; in the young faces, both animal and human; and in the fullness of cozy interiors and bucolic outdoor field and forest scenes. The artist's light hand is right for her interpretation, unabashedly, uncloyingly sweet, and admirably suited to its purpose." Booklist [review of 1977 edition]

Baker, Keith, 1953-

Big fat hen; illustrated by Keith Baker. Harcourt Brace & Co. 1994 unp il $15   **398.8**
    1. Nursery rhymes 2. Counting 3. Chickens—Fiction
ISBN 0-15-292869-3   LC 93-19160

Baker, Keith, 1953-—*Continued*

Also available Board book edition

"The text is the old rhyme, 'One, two, buckle my shoe,' and the double-page spreads show the hen and her chicks (first appearing as eggs) enacting the words. . . . Children who want to skip the counting altogether can just enjoy the singsong text and the pictures executed in acrylic paints. The big fat hen is very large and quite beautiful, with iridescent green feathers accented with purple and red; her friends are just as lovely, all colors, some with delicate patterns in their feathers." Booklist

Chorao, Kay, 1936-

Knock at the door and other baby action rhymes. Dutton Children's Bks. 1999 32p il $15.99 **398.8**

1. Nursery rhymes 2. Finger play

ISBN 0-525-45969-3 LC 98-43958

"A collection of 20 fingerplays or action rhymes. . . . Each line or two is accompanied by a simple line-drawing icon to suggest the actions." SLJ

"Some of the most joyous finger and bouncing plays are gathered here. . . . The beautifully detailed and patterned pictures are full of ducks and bunnies, kittens and teddy bears, delectable children, and a profusion of flora and fauna." Booklist

The **Comic** adventures of Old Mother Hubbard and her dog; illustrated by Tomie de Paola. Harcourt Brace Jovanovich 1981 unp il hardcover o.p. paperback available $7 **398.8**

1. Nursery rhymes

ISBN 0-15-219542-4 (pa) LC 80-19270

This "version of the popular, early-nineteenth-century nursery rhyme places two familiar and beloved characters in a theatrical setting lavish with magnificent costumes and props. Spectators in box seats attending to the trials of the solicitous, beribboned dame and her mischievous poodle include Humpty Dumpty, the King and Queen of Hearts, and Little Bo Peep, while the stage curtains are decorated with scenes from the stories of still other well-known Mother Goose characters. The fun and action of the story are captured perfectly in a series of large, framed illustrations." Child Book Rev Serv

Dunn, Opal

Hippety-hop, hippety-hay; growing with rhymes from birth to age three; illustrated by Sally Anne Lambert. Holt & Co. 1999 46p il music $16.95 **398.8**

1. Nursery rhymes

ISBN 0-8050-6081-2 LC 98-8105

A "collection of rhymes and finger plays complete with music, movement suggestions, and information for parents and caregivers on childhood developmental stages. . . . Filled with warm colors and appealing details, Lambert's watercolor illustrations pleasantly support the verses." SLJ

Emberley, Barbara

Drummer Hoff; adapted by Barbara Emberley; illustrated by Ed Emberley. Simon & Schuster 1987 c1967 unp il $16; pa $5.95 **398.8**

1. Nursery rhymes

ISBN 0-671-66248-1; 0-671-66249-X (pa)

LC 87-35755

Also available Board book edition and with Audiobook

Awarded the Caldecott Medal, 1968

First published 1967 by Prentice-Hall

"A cumulative folk rhyme is adapted in spirited style and illustrated with arresting black woodcuts accented with brilliant color. The characters who participate in the building and firing of a cannon—'Sergeant Crowder brought the powder, Corporal Farrell brought the barrel,' etc.—are hilariously rugged characters, while 'Drummer Hoff who fired it off stands by, deadpan, waiting to touch off the marvelously satisfying explosion." Hodges. Books for Elem Sch Libr

Galdone, Paul, 1914-1986

The cat goes fiddle-i-fee; adapted and illustrated by Paul Galdone. Clarion Bks. 1985 unp il hardcover o.p. paperback available $6.95 (k-1) **398.8**

1. Nursery rhymes

ISBN 0-89919-705-1 (pa) LC 85-2686

An old English rhyme names all the animals a farm boy feeds on his daily rounds

"Galdone's line-and-watercolor illustrations have all the verve and accessible good humor associated with his work, and the varied and irresistible rhythm of the verses carries the nonsense along at a good pace, enhancing its appeal to the very young. Whether told or sung, this is a diverting selection for preschool story times." Booklist

Three little kittens. Clarion Bks. 1986 unp il $15 **398.8**

1. Nursery rhymes 2. Cats—Poetry

ISBN 0-89919-426-5 LC 86-2655

Also available in paperback with Audiobook

Three little kittens lose, find, soil, and wash their mittens

"Galdone's characteristically exuberant pen-and-wash drawings fill these pages with feline faces, first rueful then joyful, then repentant, and finally excited about the prospects of catching 'a rat close by.' This is one of those sustained nursery rhymes that initiates youngest listeners into the concentration required for stories, and there's enough dramatic movement and color contrast in the art to hold toddlers' attention." Bull Cent Child Books

The **Glorious** Mother Goose; selected by Cooper Edens; with illustrations by the best artists from the past. Atheneum Bks. for Young Readers 1998 88p il $18 **398.8**

1. Nursery rhymes

ISBN 0-689-82050-X LC 97-38444

A reissue of the title first published 1988

A collection of nursery rhymes, including those about Humpty Dumpty, Jack and Jill, Little Jack Horner, and Little Miss Muffet

The Glorious Mother Goose—*Continued*

"Drawing from a rich store of nineteenth -and early-twentieth-century illustrations, Edens has made a splendid selection that will evoke nostalgia in older readers and provide joyous images for future generations of youngsters." Horn Book Guide

Here comes Mother Goose; edited by Iona Opie; illustrated by Rosemary Wells. Candlewick Press 1999 107p il $21.99   **398.8**
1. Nursery rhymes
ISBN 0-7636-0683-9   LC 99-14256

Presents more than sixty traditional nursery rhymes, including "Old Mother Hubbard," "I'm a Little Teapot," and "One, Two, Buckle My Shoe"

"Wells's watercolor-and-ink pictures of somersaulting guinea pigs, mischievous rabbits, and fluffy ducklings capture the sheer joy and exuberance of the rhymes. . . . Make room on the shelves for this must-have title." SLJ

Hoberman, Mary Ann, 1930-

Miss Mary Mack; a hand-clapping rhyme; adapted by Mary Ann Hoberman; illustrated by Nadine Bernard Westcott. Little, Brown 1998 unp il music $14.95   **398.8**
1. Nursery rhymes
ISBN 0-316-93118-7   LC 96-34829

"In this expanded version of the popular hand-clapping rhyme, the elephant (who's 'jumped so high' . . ./ He reached the sky/ . . . lands in the middle of a picnic where Mary Mack promises him her silver buttons if he doesn't go back to the zoo. Westcott's loose and humorous illustrations add to the necessarily limited text. A melody line and instructions for hand-clapping are included on the front endpapers." Horn Book Guide

I saw Esau; the schoolchild's pocket book; edited by Iona and Peter Opie; illustrated by Maurice Sendak. Candlewick Press 1992 160p il $19.99; pa $9.99   **398.8**
1. Folklore—Great Britain 2. English poetry—Collections
ISBN 1-56402-046-0; 0-7636-1199-9 (pa)
     LC 91-71845

A revised and newly illustrated edition of the title first published 1947 in the United Kingdom

A collection of rhymes and riddles traditionally passed on orally from child to child

"From lamentation, pun, and insult to rebuttal, tongue-twister, and comic complaint, these schoolyard folk rhymes are vulgar, absurd, fierce, and utterly compelling. . . . [The book features] Sendak's wicked, joyful illustrations. Blending the factual and the surreal, the pictures (most in color, some in sepia or in black and white) extend the rhymes with characters and scenarios that are gross and tender. Sendak knows kids' ferocity and their fear." Booklist

James Marshall's Mother Goose. Farrar, Straus & Giroux 1979 unp il hardcover o.p. paperback available $6.95   **398.8**
1. Nursery rhymes
ISBN 0-374-43723-8 (pa)   LC 79-2574

"Clean, translucent pastel colors and jolly cartoon figures give this limited collection [of thirty-five rhymes] a cheerful countenance. . . . Several of the old favorites are here, plus a number of lesser known rhymes such as little Poll Parrot and Little Tommy Tittlemouse. The illustrations depict the action in a literal way, with a breezy, occasionally offbeat humor." Booklist

Mother Goose; nursery rhymes; illustrated by Brian Wildsmith. Oxford Univ. Press 1964 80p il hardcover o.p. paperback available $11.95
     398.8
1. Nursery rhymes
ISBN 0-19-272180-1 (pa)

Has also been published with title: Brian Wildsmith's Mother Goose

These eighty-six verses "are well selected and include many quaint and lesser-known verses." Book Week

"The artist's wholly original, sophisticated yet childlike interpretation of long-familiar material is revealed in his clever composition, unconventional humor, and characteristic watercolor technique with its use of geometric patterns and brilliant chromatic modulations." Horn Book

My very first Mother Goose; edited by Iona Opie; illustrated by Rosemary Wells. Candlewick Press 1996 107p il $21.99   **398.8**
1. Nursery rhymes
ISBN 1-56402-620-5   LC 96-4904

"The 60 plus rhymes in this collection are mostly the old-time favorites, but include some more recent ones such as 'Shoo Fly' and 'Down by the Station.' Wells illustrates the selections with her usual winsome, quirky, anthropomorphic mice, rabbits, cats, pigs, bears, etc., and even includes some people. The lavish ink-and-watercolors are filled with action and delightful details." SLJ

Old Mother Hubbard and her wonderful dog; illustrated by James Marshall. Farrar, Straus & Giroux 1991 unp il hardcover o.p. paperback available $4.95   **398.8**
1. Nursery rhymes
ISBN 0-374-45611-9 (pa)   LC 90-56145

"This adaptation of a favorite nursery rhyme is a romp of rhythm and will bring on the smiles because of the inimitable style of Marshall's cartoons and tongue-in-cheek humor." SLJ

The Orchard book of nursery rhymes; rhymes chosen by Zena Sutherland; pictures by Faith Jaques. Orchard Bks. 1990 88p il $22.95 **398.8**
1. Nursery rhymes
ISBN 0-531-05903-0   LC 89-71002

"A collection of familiar short verses, including Mother Goose rhymes, tongue twisters, and nonsense poems, with illustrations set in 18th-century England and France." SLJ

"Sutherland's collection is a particularly fresh and satisfying entry in a crowded field. The selections are sequenced with care. . . . Sprinkled throughout the verses, Jaques's bustling illustrations brim with pleasingly old-fashioned details." Publ Wkly

Includes bibliographical references

The **Oxford** dictionary of nursery rhymes; edited by Iona and Peter Opie. 2nd ed. Oxford Univ. Press 1997 xxix, 559p il $49.95 **398.8**
1. Nursery rhymes—Dictionaries
ISBN 0-19-860088-7   LC 98-140995
First published 1951
An anthology of "over 500 rhymes, songs, nonsense jingles, and lullabies. . . . Complementing the rhymes are nearly a hundred illustrations, including reproductions of early art found in ballad sheets and music books, which highlight the development of children's illustrations over the last two centuries. . . . [The editors note] the earliest known publications of the rhyme, describing how it originated, illustrating changes in wording over time, and indicating variations and parallels in other languages." Publisher's note
"The novice as well as the professional will find it an enjoyable read, as well as a learning experience." Am Ref Books Annu, 1999

Pat-a-cake and other play rhymes; compiled by Joanna Cole and Stephanie Calmenson; illustrated by Alan Tiegreen. Morrow Junior Bks. 1992 48p il $14; pa $6.95   **398.8**
1. Nursery rhymes 2. Finger play
ISBN 0-688-11038-X; 0-688-11533-0 (pa)
LC 91-32264
A collection of nursery rhymes and action rhymes, in such categories as finger and hand rhymes, tickling rhymes, and knee-and-foot-riding rhymes
"A charming source of bounce-and-tickle rhymes, this book features a good choice of games, an inviting format, and illustrations that make the most of the fun. . . . The simple line drawings, one to four on a page, combine an appealing informality of line with the delicacy of watercolor washes." Booklist
Includes bibliographical references

Patz, Nancy
Moses supposes his toeses are roses and 7 other silly old rhymes; retold and illustrated by Nancy Patz. Harcourt Brace Jovanovich 1983 unp il $13.95; pa $6   **398.8**
1. Nursery rhymes
ISBN 0-15-255690-7; 0-15-255691-5 (pa)
LC 82-3099
"Eight English and American nonsense rhymes have lilt, nonsense, and humor. On each page, the ebullient paintings erupt from their tidy frames with vigorous and at times grotesque people and animals painted in the style of eighteenth and nineteenth century Pennsylvania Dutch pictures." Bull Cent Child Books

Polacco, Patricia
Babushka's Mother Goose. Philomel Bks. 1995 64p il $18.99; pa $6.99   **398.8**
1. Nursery rhymes
ISBN 0-399-22747-4; 0-698-11860-X (pa)
LC 94-32332
"The collection includes original rhymes written by Polacco as well as Ukrainian folktales and retellings from Mother Goose and Aesop that Polacco heard as a child from her own Babushka. The distinctive and humorous folk-art illustrations and delightful verses and stories make this book a joy to share with children." Horn Book Guide

The **Real** Mother Goose; illustrated by Blanche Fisher Wright. Checkerboard Press 1987 c1944 128p il   **398.8**
1. Nursery rhymes
LC 87-13778
Available Scholastic edition $9.95 (ISBN 0-590-22517-0)
First published 1916 by Rand McNally
A comprehensive collection of over three-hundred traditional nursery rhymes

Sylvia Long's Mother Goose. Chronicle Bks. 1999 109p il $22.95   **398.8**
1. Nursery rhymes
ISBN 0-8118-2088-2   LC 98-52311
"Human beings are replaced by animals, reptiles, and insects, all elegantly dressed, in this exuberant nursery-rhyme collection, which includes 82 familiar and less familiar verses." SLJ

Tomie dePaola's Mother Goose. Putnam 1985 127p il $24.99   **398.8**
1. Nursery rhymes
ISBN 0-399-21258-2   LC 84-26314
This "is a large, ample, unfussy edition of every child's first staple of literature. . . . The neat, flat illustrations are darkly outlined and colored generally in the illustrator's favorite palette of clear pinks, blues, and violets and surrounded with a lot of white space. Each verse is pictured in a simple and unmistakable interpretation. . . . A perfectly basic and lovely Mother Goose, lavish yet simple, and a splendid beginning for the youngest listener." Horn Book

Tortillitas para mamá and other nursery rhymes; Spanish and English; selected and translated by Margot C. Griego [et al.]; illustrated by Barbara Cooney. Holt & Co. 1981 unp il hardcover o.p. paperback available $5.95   **398.8**
1. Nursery rhymes 2. Folklore—Latin America 3. Bilingual books—English-Spanish
ISBN 0-8050-0317-7 (pa)   LC 81-4823
A bilingual collection of 13 popular Latin American nursery rhymes
The purpose of this book "is to preserve a unique aspect of Hispanic culture which deserves to be passed down to all children. . . . The illustrations are strikingly beautiful, capturing the rich color and texture of some parts of South America. . . . [But their] homogenized view of Latin Americans can easily lead to the perpetuation of some familiar stereotypes." Interracial Books Child Bull

Wilner, Isabel
The baby's game book; pictures by Sam Williams. Greenwillow Bks. 2000 47p il $15.95   **398.8**
1. Games 2. Finger play 3. Nursery rhymes
ISBN 0-688-15916-8   LC 98-22120
Rhymes, illustrations, and instructions present a variety of simple games to play with babies, including foot tapping, knee rides, finger play, peek-a-boo, and tickle games
"Simple instructions for the movements accompany

Wilner, Isabel—*Continued*
the rhymes; gentle pencil and watercolor illustrations depict adult and child at play as well as more whimsical scenes of animals or countryside." Horn Book

Winter, Jeanette
The house that Jack built. Dial Bks. for Young Readers 2000 unp il $13.99   **398.8**
1. Nursery rhymes
ISBN 0-8037-2524-8   LC 99-36344
Simple rebus illustrations are used to present the familiar cumulative nursery rhyme about the antics that go on in the house built by an unsuspecting Jack
"Readers can predict who will enter the story next by watching for visual clues. The small trim size of the book and the clear, vibrant colors and simple shapes of the artwork are appealing." Horn Book Guide

398.9   Proverbs

The **Night** has ears; African proverbs; selected and illustrated by Ashley Bryan. Atheneum Bks. for Young Readers 1999 unp il $16 (k-3)   **398.9**
1. Proverbs 2. Folklore—Africa
ISBN 0-689-82427-0   LC 98-48772
"A Jean Karl book"
A collection of twenty-six proverbs, some serious and some humorous, from a variety of African tribes
"Illustrated in Bryan's distinctive multishape, multicolor style, the tempera-and-gouache art resembles stained glass. . . . A worthy supplement to cultural studies, this will also inspire students to write and illustrate their own proverbs." Booklist

400   LANGUAGE

413   Dictionaries

Feder, Jane
Table, chair, bear; a book in many languages. Ticknor & Fields Bks. for Young Readers 1995 unp hardcover o.p. paperback available $5.95 (k-2)   **413**
1. Polyglot materials 2. Vocabulary
ISBN 0-395-85075-4 (pa)   LC 92-40529
Presents illustrations of objects found in a child's room, labeled in thirteen different languages, including Spanish, Vietnamese, Japanese, and French
"Adults and children will find many ways to explore this deceptively simple concept book, from trying to pronounce the unfamiliar words to investigating the many lettering styles. Feder's clear acrylic illustrations, done in vivid primary colors, and the book's clean design make this a particularly handsome contribution to picture-book shelves." Horn Book

419   Verbal language not spoken and written

Baker, Pamela J., 1947-
My first book of sign; illustrations by Patricia Bellan Gillen. Gallaudet Univ. Press 1986 76p il $11.96 (k-3)   **419**
1. Sign language
ISBN 0-930323-20-3   LC 86-14937
"A Kendall Green publication"
Pictures of children demonstrate the forming in sign language of 150 basic alphabetically arranged words, accompanied by illustrations of the words themselves. Includes a discussion of fingerspelling and general rules for signing
"Looking like an ABC book, this is both appealing and useful. . . . Illustrations are brightly colored and have an even mixture of boys and girls of various racial backgrounds, some with hearing aids, some without." SLJ

Rankin, Laura
The handmade alphabet. Dial Bks. 1991 unp il $16.99; pa $5.99   **419**
1. Sign language 2. Alphabet
ISBN 0-8037-0974-9; 0-14-055876-4 (pa)
      LC 90-24593
Presents the handshape for each letter of the American manual alphabet accompanied by an object whose name begins with that letter
"This [is] an excellent introduction to American sign, as well as an engaging ABC book. The art work is multiethnic, visually appealing, anatomically correct, and full of life. Clever use of props, light, and reflections add to the enjoyment." SLJ

The handmade counting book. Dial Bks. 1998 unp il $15.99; lib bdg $15.89   **419**
1. Sign language 2. Counting
ISBN 0-8037-2309-1; 0-8037-2311-3 (lib bdg)
      LC 97-38463
Shows how to count from one to twenty and twenty-five, fifty, seventy-five, and one hundred using American Sign Language
"Easily recognizable and child-appealing objects, such as toy boats, dinosaurs, and origami cranes, accumulate on the pages and are identified in the back of the book. . . . This is a valuable and attractive contribution to the available literature that introduces American Sign Language to young people." Horn Book

423   English language—Dictionaries

The **American** Heritage children's dictionary; by the editors of the American Heritage dictionaries. Houghton Mifflin 1998 856p il maps $17   **423**
1. English language—Dictionaries
ISBN 0-395-85739-2   LC 98-21414
First published 1986
Also available CD-ROM version
This illustrated reference includes an A-Z vocabulary listing, a thesaurus, and special sections on synonyms, word histories, vocabulary builders, and phonics

The **American** Heritage picture dictionary; by the editors of the American Heritage dictionaries. Houghton Mifflin $13 (k-1)   **423**
1. English language—Dictionaries 2. Picture dictionaries

First published 1986 (1998 printing)
A dictionary for preschool and early elementary grades, with each of the approximately 900 words defined by a sentence using the word to describe the object or activity portrayed in the accompanying illustration
"The almost 650 illustrations are in bright, clear colors. There are several family groupings of different races whose members and pets appear frequently in the illustrations and example sentences. The illustrations are nonsexist." Booklist

Bollard, John K.
Scholastic children's thesaurus; illustrated by Mike Reed. Scholastic Ref. 1998 256p il $15.95 (4 and up)   **423**
1. English language—Synonyms and antonyms
ISBN 0-590-96785-1   LC 97-25049
This work contains more than 500 headwords and 2,500 synonyms. Each entry includes part of speech, a definition, and sample sentences. Information boxes and full-color illustrations accompany the text

The **Cat** in the Hat beginner book dictionary; by the Cat himself and P. D. Eastman. Beginner Bks. 1964 133p il $14.95 (k-3)   **423**
1. Picture dictionaries 2. English language—Dictionaries
ISBN 0-394-81009-0
Also available Spanish-English edition
"This alphabetically arranged dictionary, illustrated with rollicking funny drawings, explains word meanings with sentences and pictures. It intends to help preschoolers 'recognize, remember, and really enjoy a basic vocabulary of 1,350 words.' Despite its age, this book will still appeal to young children." Peterson. Ref Books for Child. 4th edition

DK illustrated Oxford dictionary. DK Pub. 1998 1008p il maps $34.95   **423**
1. Picture dictionaries 2. English language—Dictionaries
ISBN 0-7894-3557-8   LC 98-3664
Over 4,500 full-cover images accompany the 180,000 definitions and entries covering general English vocabulary from around the world. Grammar, style, and usage notes are provided. New words and phrases as well as specialized, technical, and rare words are covered

DK Merriam Webster children's dictionary. DK Pub. 2000 911p il maps $17.95   **423**
1. English language—Dictionaries 2. Picture dictionaries
ISBN 0-7894-5238-3   LC 99-43274
Presents definitions for over 35,000 entries and includes some 4,000 illustrations interspersed throughout the text
For a review see: Booklist, Oct. 15, 2000

Encarta world English dictionary. St. Martin's Press 1999 xxxii, 2078p il $50   **423**
1. English language—Dictionaries
ISBN 0-312-22222-X   LC 99-15350
This dictionary includes "many words representing *world English*, defined (in its entry in the dictionary) as 'the English language in all its varieties as it is spoken and written all over the world.' . . . Not only does *Encarta* offer clearly articulated usage notes, it also offers cultural notes. These explain a word's significance in popular culture." Booklist

The **Facts** on File student's thesaurus; [edited by] Marc McCutcheon. 2nd ed. Facts on File 2000 504p (Facts on File library of language and literature) $39.95   **423**
1. English language—Synonyms and antonyms
ISBN 0-8160-4058-3   LC 99-30711
First published 1991
Provides synonyms and antonyms and usage examples for more than 7000 words listed in alphabetical order

The **Harcourt** Brace student thesaurus. 2nd ed. Harcourt Brace & Co. 1994 312p il $18 (4 and up)   **423**
1. English language—Synonyms and antonyms
ISBN 0-15-200186-7   LC 94-15603
Replaces The HBJ student thesaurus, published 1991
Editor, Christopher Morris
"The 800 main entries are all given part-of-speech, one-line definitions, and four to six synonyms, each of which is used in a sentence. Full-color illustrations in a variety of cartoon styles appear with about 150 of the entries." SLJ

Macmillan dictionary for children; Judith S. Levey, editor-in-chief. Macmillan il $16.95 (3-6)   **423**
1. English language—Dictionaries

Also available CD-ROM version
First published 1975. (1997 edition) Periodically revised
"A good choice for elementary school libraries. Clear definitions for 35,000 words include frequent color pictures to assist in clarifying meaning. Syllabication, pronunciation, parts of speech, and different word forms are provided. Pronunciation guides are clear and well placed, and highlighted guidewords assist the reader in finding the proper page. There are also a 10-page section on how to use a dictionary and a reference section that consists of U.S. and world history timelines, pictures of the presidents, national flags, world maps, and tables of weights and measures." Nichols. Guide to Ref Books for Sch Media Cent. 4th edition

Macmillan first dictionary; Judith S. Levey, editor in chief. Macmillan 1990 402p il $16 (1-3)   **423**
1. English language—Dictionaries
ISBN 0-02-761731-9   LC 90-6062
Replaces Macmillan very first dictionary, published 1983

Macmillan first dictionary—*Continued*

"This work focuses on the most common words in the English language. An introduction outlines the development of words and explains how to use a dictionary. Simple definitions for each of the 2,200 words are often supported by illustrative sentences. Nearly 550 pictures in color explain concepts and abstract words." Nichols. Guide to Ref Books for Sch Media Cent. 4th edition

Merriam-Webster's elementary dictionary. Merriam-Webster 1994 20a, 587p il $15.95 (4-6)   **423**

1. English language—Dictionaries
ISBN 0-87779-575-4   LC 93-41502

Replaces Webster's elementary dictionary, published 1986

This illustrated dictionary for grades four to six includes some 32,000 entries; a color-keyed guide to using the dictionary; word history and synonym paragraphs; abbreviations; signs and symbols; U.S. presidents and vice-presidents; and geographical names

Merriam-Webster's intermediate dictionary. [rev. ed] Merriam-Webster 1998 14, 941p il $15.95 (6 and up)   **423**

1. English language—Dictionaries
ISBN 0-87779-479-0   LC 98-4995

First published 1994 as a replacement for Webster's intermediate dictionary (1986)

The approximately 65,000 entries provide definitions, pronunciation, etymology and part of speech designation. Reference features include abbreviations as well as geographical, biographical, biblical, and mythological names

For a review see: Booklist, Oct. 15, 2000

Roget's children's thesaurus. rev ed. HarperCollins Pubs. 1994 240p il $15 (3-5)   **423**

1. English language—Synonyms and antonyms
ISBN 0-06-275013-5

Replaces the edition published 1991 under the authorship of Andrew Schiller and William A. Jenkins

Published also under titles: In other words, a beginning thesaurus and Scott Foresman beginning thesaurus

Under alphabetically arranged entries are more than a thousand words with illustrative sentences to help the middle grader in choosing the exact word from several synonyms

Roget's student thesaurus. rev ed. Scott Foresman-Addison Wesley 1994 536p il $16 (5 and up)   **423**

1. English language—Synonyms and antonyms
ISBN 0-673-12437-1

Replaces the edition published 1991 under the authorship of Andrew Schiller and William A. Jenkins

"This book also appears under the titles In Other Words, a Junior thesaurus and Scott Foresman Junior thesaurus." Verso of title page

An illustrated alphabetical list of words, their synonyms, antonyms, and the shades of meaning between them. Entries include such features as idioms, words at play, word stories, and writing tips

Scholastic children's dictionary; by the editors of Scholastic Inc. Scholastic 1996 648p il $16.95 (3-5)   **423**

1. English language—Dictionaries
ISBN 0-590-25271-2   LC 95-26237

This work contains approximately 30,000 entries and 1,000 illustrations. "Definitions include homophones and sample sentences; highlighted boxes provide information about prefixes, suffixes, synonyms, and word histories. . . . The reference section inclues the Braille and American Sign Language alphabets, as well as information about countries and U.S. states and presidents." Booklist

Scholastic first dictionary; Judith S. Levey, editor in chief. Scholastic Ref. 1998 224p il $14.95 (1-3)   **423**

1. English language—Dictionaries
ISBN 0-590-96786-X   LC 97-25050

Entries include pronuciations, simple definitions, sentences, and plurals and other forms of the words

"With a crisp layout, bright colors, and a large typeface, this dictionary is appealing and accessible. The 1500 main entries are well suited to use by young readers and writers. There are at least two full-color photographs on each page." SLJ

Terban, Marvin

Scholastic dictionary of idioms. Scholastic 1996 245p il hardcover o.p. paperback available $8.95 (4 and up)   **423**

1. English language—Idioms
ISBN 0-590-38157-1 (pa)   LC 95-16593

"Terban explains the meanings and origins (if known) of more than 600 idioms and proverbs. . . . Each page includes one lightly comical line drawing of a child expressing feelings such as quizzical, annoyed, amused, or distressed. Not only is this a good resource for teachers who discuss idioms in the classroom but it also has some appeal for browsers." Booklist

Webster's New World children's dictionary; editor in chief, Michael Agnes. 2nd ed. Macmillan 1999 16, 928p il maps $16.95 (3-5)   **423**

1. English language—Dictionaries
ISBN 0-02-862766-0   LC 99-21174

First published 1991

This dictionary contains approximately 33,000 entries and 750 illustrations. "Bright colors highlight boxes providing synonyms, word histories, spelling tips, and similar features. . . . Material at the back of the book includes a thesaurus, a basic atlas, and information about American history, presidents, states, and weights and measures." Booklist

427   English language variations

Terban, Marvin

Mad as a wet hen! and other funny idioms; illustrated by Giulio Maestro. Clarion Bks. 1987 64p il hardcover o.p. paperback available $7.95 (3-5)   **427**

1. English language—Idioms 2. English language—Terms and phrases
ISBN 0-89919-479-6 (pa)   LC 86-17575

Terban, Marvin—*Continued*

Illustrates and explains over 100 common English idioms, in categories including animals, body parts, and colors

"Maestro's two-color cartoonlike illustrations are amusing and informative themselves, providing visual clues that support the textual explanations. . . . Although some of the expressions included are dated, the alphabetical index enables teachers and librarians to pick and choose. This book might be particularly beneficial in schools having a large ESL program, especially for older, more advanced students." SLJ

428 Standard English usage

Cleary, Brian P., 1959-

Hairy, scary, ordinary; what is an adjective? illustrated by Jenya Prosmitsky. Carolrhoda Bks. 2000 32p il $12.95; pa $5.95 (k-3)   **428**
1. English language—Grammar
ISBN 1-57505-401-9; 1-57505-419-1 (pa)

LC 98-32132

"Descriptive words of many kinds are presented in bouncy, rhyming text. . . . The adjectives are colorfully highlighted and readers will see their function demonstrated in a wide variety of contexts. Little round cats and quirky humans, both with fat noses and wide eyes, humorously illustrate the meanings." SLJ

Heller, Ruth

Behind the mask; a book about prepositions; written and illustrated by Ruth Heller. Grosset & Dunlap 1995 unp il $17.99; pa $6.99 (k-2)   **428**
1. English language—Terms and phrases
ISBN 0-448-41123-7; 0-698-11698-4 (pa)

LC 95-9535

Explores through rhyming text the subject of prepositions and how they're used

"Large, colorful drawings illustrate the words imaginatively." Booklist

A cache of jewels and other collective nouns; written and illustrated by Ruth Heller. Grosset & Dunlap 1987 unp il $17.99; pa $6.99 (k-2)   **428**
1. English language—Terms and phrases
ISBN 0-448-19211-X; 0-698-11354-3 (pa)

LC 87-80254

"In light verse and brightly colored pictures, Heller provides an introduction to a specialized part of speech, the collective noun. She lists and depicts more than 25, including such familiar terms as 'batch of bread' and 'bunch of bananas,' as well as more unusual phrases. . . . The concept will stimulate the curiosity and imaginations of children with an ear for language. The illustrations, containing large, bold objects in simple yet striking compositions, ensure a visually inspiring exploration as well." Publ Wkly

Fantastic! wow! and unreal! a book about interjections and conjunctions; written and illustrated by Ruth Heller. Grosset & Dunlap 1998 unp il lib bdg $17.99; pa $6.99 (k-2)   **428**
1. English language—Grammar
ISBN 0-448-41862-2; 0-698-11875-8 (pa)

LC 98-36361

Rhyming text and illustrations introduce and explain various interjections and conjunctions, including "awesome," "alas," and "yet."

Kites sail high: a book about verbs; written and illustrated by Ruth Heller. Grosset & Dunlap 1988 unp il $17.99; pa $6.99 (k-2)   **428**
1. English language—Grammar
ISBN 0-448-10480-6; 0-698-11389-6 (pa)

LC 87-82718

This "book explicates and celebrates verbs of all kinds, in ebullient verses which themselves sail and soar. . . . The verses are accompanied by bold, gaily colored graphics that are especially striking for their skillful use of pattern and design." Publ Wkly

Many luscious lollipops: a book about adjectives; written and illustrated by Ruth Heller. Grosset & Dunlap 1989 unp il lib bdg $17.99; pa $6.99 (k-2)   **428**
1. English language—Grammar
ISBN 0-448-03151-5 (lib bdg); 0-698-11641-0 (pa)

LC 88-83045

"The text begins: 'An adjective's terrific/when you want to be specific/It easily identifies/by number, color or by size/TWELVE LARGE, BLUE, GORGEOUS butterflies.' And there they are, blue and yellow, filling a double-page spread. . . . There is great diversity and technical brilliance in the art work, and the text has rhyme, rhythm, humor, and a very clear presentation of the concepts of different kinds of adjectives and what they do." Bull Cent Child Books

Merry-go-round; a book about nouns; written and illustrated by Ruth Heller. Grosset & Dunlap 1990 unp il $17.99; pa $6.99 (k-2)   **428**
1. English language—Terms and phrases
ISBN 0-448-40085-5; 0-698-11642-9 (pa)

LC 90-80645

Rhyming text and illustrations present explanations of various types of nouns and rules for their usage

"While the text will be helpful to children struggling with noun usage, the large, bountiful illustrations will appeal to everyone." Horn Book Guide

Mine, all mine; a book about pronouns; written and illustrated by Ruth Heller. Grosset & Dunlap 1997 unp il $17.99; pa $6.99 (k-2)   **428**
1. English language—Grammar
ISBN 0-448-41606-9; 0-698-11797-2 (pa)

LC 97-10051

Introduces various types of pronouns, explains how and when to use them, and provides whimsical glimpses of what our language would be without them

"Heller has taken a part of speech and made its function perfectly and entertainingly clear. . . . The stylishly drawn, brilliantly colored, double-paged illustrations grab readers and don't let go. The exceptionally fluent, rhythmic text is printed in an unobtrusive font with pronouns highlighted in bright blue." SLJ

Up, up and away; a book about adverbs; written and illustrated by Ruth Heller. Grosset & Dunlap 1991 unp il $17.99; pa $6.99 (k-2)   **428**
1. English language—Grammar
ISBN 0-448-40249-1; 0-698-11663-1 (pa)

LC 91-70668

Heller, Ruth—*Continued*

"Here the author explains concisely how adverbs answer precisely the questions of How? How often? When? and Where? The adverbs, in capital letters, stand out boldly and cannot be missed. . . . In the large, appealing illustrations, her penguins stand proudly, her pandas eat daintily, and her cat stares piercingly. . . . The cheerful volume . . . offers a clever introduction to kinds of words." Booklist

Terban, Marvin

Punctuation power! Scholastic 2000 96p il (Scholastic guides) $12.95 (4 and up)   **428**

1. Punctuation

ISBN 0-590-38673-5   LC 99-19179

Explains the purpose and importance of punctuation and how it is used, covering apostrophes, colons, commas, exclamation points, hyphens, parentheses, slashes, and more

"Children will find this book helpful as they try to craft writing assignments. The examples and the pictures help keep the tone light." SLJ

Scholastic dictionary of spelling; over 15,000 words. Scholastic Ref. 1998 223p il $15.95; pa $8.95 (4 and up)   **428**

1. Spellers

ISBN 0-590-30697-9; 0-439-14496-5 (pa)

                      LC 97-18020

The words in this speller are "arranged alphabetically (i.e., ladies comes before lady) broken into syllables with the accented syllables in boldface, on attractively laid-out pages, with occasional cartoonish illustrations. Homophones include pronunciation help, and a parenthetical sentence illustrates proper use. The first 26 pages are a treasure trove of helpful hints. . . . The book concludes with the 'Misspeller's Dictionary,' 600 words with tricky beginnngs listed in matched pairs of the common misspelling and the correct one." Book Rep

463   Spanish language—Dictionaries

Elya, Susan Middleton, 1955-

Say hola to Spanish, otra vez; illustrated by Loretta Lopez. Lee & Low Bks. 1997 unp il $15.95 (1-4)   **463**

1. Spanish language

ISBN 1-88000-059-8   LC 97-6851

Also available: Say hola to Spanish $15.95 (ISBN 1-88000-029-6); pa $6.95 (ISBN 1-88000-064-4) and Say hola to Spanish at the circus $15.95 (ISBN 1-88000-092-X)

"A rhyming text and bright cartoon illustrations introduce 72 Spanish words." SLJ

"The playful design scatters the text throughout Lopez's gouache and colored-pencil two-page spreads; the most effective scenes group the words thematically. . . . Lopez provides images bound to aid early elementary students' retention and recall of these Spanish words." Publ Wkly

Includes glossary

493   Non-Semitic Afro-Asiatic languages

Donoughue, Carol

The mystery of the hieroglyphs; the story of the Rosetta stone and the race to decipher Egyptian hieroglyphs. Oxford Univ. Press 1999 48p il $16.95; lib bdg $18.95 (3-6)   **493**

1. Rosetta stone inscription 2. Egyptian language 3. Hieroglyphics

ISBN 0-19-521554-0; 0-19-521553-2 (lib bdg)

This is a history of the discovery and deciphering of the Rosetta stone which led to the understanding of Egyptian hieroglyphics

"What makes this book so involving is that readers must do their own learning, translating, and reading of hieroglyphics. . . . Crisp color photos, reproductions, and sidebars enrich the text. An enticing volume." SLJ

Includes glossary and bibliographical references

Giblin, James, 1933-

The riddle of the Rosetta Stone; key to ancient Egypt; [by] James Cross Giblin. Crowell 1990 85p il hardcover o.p. paperback available $6.95 (5 and up)   **493**

1. Rosetta stone 2. Egyptian language 3. Hieroglyphics

ISBN 0-06-446137-8 (pa)   LC 89-29289

Describes how the discovery and deciphering of the Rosetta Stone unlocked the secret of Egyptian hieroglyphics

"Suspense keeps the reader glued to this fine piece of nonfiction as the mystery of hieroglyphs is slowly unraveled. . . . The author has done a masterful job of distilling information, citing the highlights, and fitting it all together in an interesting and enlightening look at a puzzling subject." Horn Book

Includes bibliography

495.1   Chinese language

Lee, Huy Voun

At the beach; written and illustrated by Huy Voun Lee. Holt & Co. 1994 unp il $16.95; pa $6.95 (k-3)   **495.1**

1. Chinese language

ISBN 0-8050-2768-8; 0-8050-5822-2 (pa)

                      LC 93-25462

A mother amuses her young son at the beach by drawing in the sand Chinese characters, many of which resemble the objects they stand for

"The intricate, visually captivating cut-paper collages have borders with sea motifs. Useful for beginning language study and interesting due to its artistic innovation, the book includes a pronunciation guide." Horn Book Guide

495.6 Japanese language

Wells, Ruth
A to Zen; a book of Japanese culture; illustrated by Yoshi. Picture Bk. Studio 1992 unp il map $17 (3-5) **495.6**
1. Japanese language 2. Alphabet 3. Japan—Social life and customs 4. Bilingual books—English-Japanese
ISBN 0-88708-175-4   LC 91-14183
"The format of the alphabet book is used here to introduce young readers to aspects of Japanese life. Each page contains a Japanese term (printed both in English letters and in Japanese characters), a defining paragraph, and a richly colored painting. . . . Among the topics covered are aikido, the bunraku puppet theater, Japanese writing systems, and the tea ceremony." Booklist
"The selections are meaningfully described in lively prose and will add pleasant detail to a child's knowledge of Japan. Readers studying the language will be pleased at the vocabulary enrichment offered. The illustrations in ink and watercolors are bright, vibrant, and culturally accurate." SLJ

496 African languages

Wilson-Max, Ken, 1965-
Furaha means happy; a book of Swahili words. Jump at the Sun; Hyperion Bks. for Children 2000 26p il $12.99 (k-2) **496**
1. Swahili language 2. Kenya—Social life and customs
ISBN 0-7868-0552-8   LC 99-25776
"Using a family outing as a back-drop, Wilson-Max introduces young readers to a handful of Swahili words. . . . Wilson-Max's choice of rich, full-bodied color and the use of bold black outlines give his spirited illustrations instant appeal." SLJ

Halala means welcome! a book of Zulu words; written and illustrated by Ken Wilson-Max. Hyperion Bks. for Children 1998 unp il $11.95 (k-2) **496**
1. Zulu language 2. South Africa—Social life and customs
ISBN 0-7868-0414-9   LC 98-11003
"A small boy named Chidi welcomes his light-skinned friend, Michael, and they speak Zulu as they play together in Chidi's home. . . . The big, exuberant pictures in bright colors with thick black lines show the kids in jeans and T-shirts playing. . . . After each double-page scenario, the English and Zulu words are printed next to the objects, and there's a pronunciation guide at the back. . . . The book begins with a big, clear map of Africa. . . . Kids in the U.S. will recognize the universal friendship story even as they have fun learning the simple vocabulary." Booklist

500 NATURAL SCIENCES & MATHEMATICS

Barnes-Svarney, Patricia
The New York Public Library science desk reference. Macmillan 1995 668p il maps $39.95 (5 and up) **500**
1. Science 2. Technology
ISBN 0-02-860403-2   LC 94-40445
"A Stonesong Press book"
"Thirteen chapters cover major divisions of science (e.g., astronomy, biology, chemistry, computer and environmental sciences, technology) listing basic facts, formulas, terms, and processes. One additional chapter lists 'useful resources' such as books, organizations, museums, zoos, national parks, and planetariums." Libr J

502.8 Science—Auxiliary techniques and procedures; apparatus, equipment, materials

Cobb, Vicki, 1938-
Dirt & grime, like you've never seen. Scholastic 1998 32p il pa $4.99 (4-6) **502.8**
1. Microscopes 2. Cleaning
ISBN 0-590-92666-7   LC 97-9336
Using scanning electron microscopy, studies household dirt, dust, and germs, and the substances that are used to get rid of them

Levine, Shar
Fun with your microscope; [by] Shar Levine & Leslie Johnstone; illustrations by Jason Coons; photomicrographs by James Humphreys & the authors. Sterling 1998 80p il hardcover o.p. paperback available $14.95 **502.8**
1. Microscopes 2. Science—Experiments
ISBN 0-8069-9946-2 (pa)   LC 97-27609
Presents basic techniques for using a microscope to observe and investigate a variety of materials that might be found around the house. Also includes experiments and ideas for science fair projects
"A very interesting, scientifically accurate, and stimulating book." Appraisal

Simon, Seymour, 1931-
Out of sight; pictures of hidden worlds. SeaStar Bks. 2000 unp il $15.95; lib bdg $15.88 (4 and up) **502.8**
1. Science—Pictorial works 2. Photography—Scientific applications
ISBN 1-58717-011-6; 1-58717-012-4 (lib bdg)
    LC 00-25684
Shows pictures of objects which are too small, too far away, or too fast to see without mechanical assistance such as microscopes, telescopes, X-rays, and other techniques
"The text serves primarily as extended captions to the

Simon, Seymour, 1931-—*Continued*

photos, providing information on the ways the pictures were taken and a basic explanation of what the images represent. The large, bright illustrations are beautifully reproduced and present some fascinating views of the world." SLJ

Tomb, Howard, 1959-

Microaliens; dazzling journeys with an electron microscope; [by] Howard Tomb and Dennis Kunkel; with drawings by Tracy Dockray. Farrar, Straus & Giroux 1993 79p il $16 (5 and up)

502.8

1. Electron microscopes 2. Science—Pictorial works
ISBN 0-374-34960-6   LC 93-1403

Text and photographs taken with an electron microscope examine such items as bird feathers, fleas, skin, mold, and blood

"Tomb's short introduction is a good overview of the history of the electron microscope and how it works. . . . [This is] a fascinating look at a relatively unknown world." Booklist

Includes bibliographical references

503   Science—Encyclopedias and dictionaries

The **DK** science encyclopedia. new rev ed. DK Pub. 1998 448p il maps $39.95; pa $9.99 (5 and up)

503

1. Science—Encyclopedias
ISBN 0-7894-2190-9; 0-7894-2871-7 (pa)

LC 97-20881

First published 1993 with title: The Dorling Kindersley science encyclopedia

"Entries are grouped into 12 topical sections ('Weather,' 'Ecology,' 'Reactions,' etc.). Each one-to-two page article is drizzled with small, clipped color photos and paintings supplemented by boxed capsule biographies, brief side excursions, and see-also references. The book concludes with a relatively dense 'Fact Finder Section' into which are gathered charts, statistics, and specialized terms." SLJ

For a fuller review see: Booklist, Feb. 1, 1998

The **New** book of popular science. Grolier 6v il maps apply to publisher for price   503

1. Science—Dictionaries 2. Technology—Dictionaries 3. Natural history—Dictionaries

First published 1924 with title: The Book of popular science. Changed to present title 1978. Annually revised

The information in this set is classified under such broad categories as astronomy & space science, computers & mathematics, earth sciences, energy, environmental sciences, physical sciences, general biology, plant life, animal life, mammals, human sciences and technology

505   Science—Serial publications

Chickadee. 25 Boxwood Lane, Buffalo, NY 14227-2707 $16.95 per year   505

1. Natural history—Periodicals
ISSN 0707-4611

Monthly except July and August. First published 1979

This "is a nature-oriented magazine for early elementary age children. It is bright, colorful, and filled with interesting content. Each issue follows a single theme through several avenues of interest. . . . The web site has a sampling of word games, activities, games, and some links to other web sites." Katz. Mag for Libr. 10th edition

Contact Kids. Sesame Workshop $21.97 per year

505

1. Science—Periodicals 2. Technology—Periodicals
ISSN 1098-0938

Monthly except February and August. First published 1979 with title: 3-2-1 Contact

This "science magazine for middle-grade children, is a publication of the Children's Television Workshop. The magazine publishes informational articles on many areas of science, including the physical and biological sciences, technology, and astronomy. Colorful photographs and illustrations enhance articles and regular features." Katz. Mag for Libr. 10th edition

Owl; the discovery magazine for children. 25 Boxwood Lane, Buffalo, NY 14227-2707 $22 per year   505

1. Natural history—Periodicals
ISSN 0382-6627

Monthly except July and August. First published 1976 as successor to The Young Naturalist

"*Owl* is a discovery magazine written for children ages 8 and up and is a companion magazine to *Chickadee*. *Owl* contains entertaining and informative articles, projects, and lots of activities to interest readers. Each page is filled with things to make and do. There are pen pal opportunities, photography contests, an opinion page, and usually a centerfold poster." Katz. Mag for Libr. 10th edition

Ranger Rick. National Wildlife Federation $17 per year   505

1. Natural history—Periodicals
ISSN 0738-6656

Monthly. First published 1967 with title: Ranger Rick's Nature Magazine

This magazine about animals and the environment for elementary school children "is filled with short stories and articles that are accompanied by colorful pictures and illustrations, often full-page." Katz. Mag for Libr. 10th edition

Your Big Backyard. National Wildlife Federation $15 per year   505

1. Natural history—Periodicals
ISSN 0886-5299

Monthly. First published 1979

This is a nature magazine "for preschool children. Each 20-page issue is full of color pictures of animals that children should find appealing, along with stories and activities designed to teach word and number recognition. Most of the text is written at a low reading level; one story in each issue is designed to be read to the child. The magazine is wrapped by four pages of information for parents or teachers relating to the issue." Katz. Mag for Libr. 8th edition

507 Science—Education and related topics

Kramer, Stephen
How to think like a scientist; answering questions by the scientific method; [by] Stephen P. Kramer; illustrated by Felicia Bond. Crowell 1987 44p il lib bdg $15.89 (3-5) **507**
1. Science—Methodology
ISBN 0-690-04565-4   LC 85-43604
An "exploration of the ways questions are asked and how scientists try to make sure that the questions are answered correctly. Relying on concrete story examples, Kramer shows how observed information can result in different or incorrect conclusions. Examples are also used to explain the principles of the scientific method." Booklist
"This is a pleasant book with an open format; an amusing halftone cartoon on almost every page illustrates the child oriented experiments and supports the light tone of the book." SLJ

507.05 Science—Education and related topics—Serial publications

Science and Children. National Science Teachers Assn. $62 per year   **507.05**
1. Science—Study and teaching—Periodicals
ISSN 0036-8148
Eight issues a year, September through May. First published 1963 as successor to: Elementary School Science Bulletin
"A magazine for preschool through middle-level science teachers. The emphasis is on practical classroom activities, interdisciplinary learning, and current issues in elementary science education. . . . News excerpts of science discoveries or teaching and book and software reviews are also included." Katz. Mag for Libr. 10th edition

507.8 Science—Use of apparatus and equipment in study and teaching

Ardley, Neil, 1937-
The science book of air. Harcourt Brace Jovanovich 1991 29p il $9.95 (3-5)   **507.8**
1. Air—Experiments 2. Flight—Experiments
ISBN 0-15-200578-1   LC 90-36103
"Gulliver books"
Simple experiments demonstrate basic principles of air and flight
"Although most of these activities have appeared in other publications, it is the visual execution of the information which makes this an outstanding and highly recommended purchase. The directions are easy to follow and children (both black and white) are shown engaged in the experiments giving a message of success." Appraisal

Cobb, Vicki, 1938-
Don't try this at home! science fun for kids on the go; [by] Vicki Cobb and Kathy Darling; illustrated by True Kelley. Morrow Junior Bks. 1998 175p il lib bdg $15; pa $4.50 (4-6)   **507.8**
1. Science—Experiments 2. Scientific recreations
ISBN 0-688-14856-5 (lib); 0-380-72810-9 (pa)
          LC 97-20481
Provides instructions for a variety of science activities outside, arranged by such categories as school, parks, and vehicles
"Good ideas and good presentation combine for an appealing book of hands-on science." Booklist

Science experiments you can eat; illustrated by David Cain. rev & updated. HarperCollins Pubs. 1994 214p il lib bdg $15.89; pa $5.95 (5 and up)   **507.8**
1. Science—Experiments 2. Cooking
ISBN 0-06-023551-9 (lib bdg); 0-06-446002-9 (pa)
          LC 93-13679
First published 1972
Experiments with food demonstrate various scientific principles and produce an eatable result. Includes rock candy, grape jelly, cupcakes, and popcorn
Includes glossary

You gotta try this! absolutely irresistible science; by Vicki Cobb and Kathy Darling; illustrated by True Kelly. Morrow Junior Bks. 1999 144p il $16 (4 and up)   **507.8**
1. Science—Experiments 2. Scientific recreations
ISBN 0-688-15740-8   LC 98-29556
A collection of science experiments and activities, arranged in such categories as "Physical Attractions," "Curious Chemistry," and "Freaky Fluids"
"True Kelley's line-and-gray-wash illustrations clarify the directions and add their own good-natured visual appeal. A fine addition to science collections." Booklist

Diehn, Gwen, 1943-
Science crafts for kids; 50 fantastic things to invent & create; [by] Gwen Diehn & Terry Krautwurst. Sterling 1994 144p il hardcover o.p. paperback available $14.95 (5 and up)   **507.8**
1. Science projects 2. Handicraft
ISBN 0-8069-0284-1 (pa)   LC 93-39112
"A Sterling/Lark book"
This "hands-on guide introduces a number of different branches of science. The projects range from the fairly simple (clay pot wind chimes, pinwheel helicopter) to the complex (model grist mill, powered model boats, xylophone). The detailed instructions include a list of materials needed and explanatory line drawings." SLJ
"The book is laid out quite well, with lots of excellent color photographs and easy-to-read and -follow directions. This book offers an excellent opportunity for youngsters to do independent work and is a resource for teachers, parents, and children." Sci Books Films

Friedhoffer, Robert

Science lab in a supermarket; by Bob Friedhoffer; illustrated by Joe Hosking. Watts 1998 95p il (Physical science labs) $25 (5 and up)

507.8

1. Science—Experiments 2. Supermarkets

ISBN 0-531-11335-3   LC 96-37285

Presents a variety of experiments using items you can buy in the supermarket. Also explains the scientific basis for such things as the flexible plastic strips that cover doorways leading into the meat departments in many large markets

"Explanations are clear and thought provoking, and the writing style is lively and humorous." SLJ

Includes glossary and bibliographical references

Gardner, Robert, 1929-

Science projects about physics in the home. Enslow Pubs. 1999 112p il lib bdg $19.95 (5 and up)

507.8

1. Physics 2. Science—Experiments 3. Science projects

ISBN 0-89490-948-7   LC 98-6822

Presents instructions for physics projects and experiments that can be done at home and exhibited at science fairs

"This volume is well organized with lots of hands-on activities that use relatively simple pieces of equipment. . . . A good starting point in the understanding of the physics of objects and events in our daily life." Sci Books Films

Includes bibliographical references

Hauser, Jill Frankel

Super science concoctions; 50 mysterious mixtures for fabulous fun; illustrations by Michael Kline. Williamson 1997 160p il pa $12.95 (3-5)

507.8

1. Science—Experiments 2. Scientific recreations

ISBN 1-885593-02-3   LC 95-47894

"A Williamson kids can! book"

Over 75 science experiments with mixtures that illustrate changes in form and chemical composition

"The sequential logic of the text make[s] this title valuable for teaching basic chemistry principles. Pen-and-ink cartoon illustrations are well placed, informative, and humorous. Safety precautions are emphasized." SLJ

Markle, Sandra, 1946-

Icky, squishy science; illustrated by Cecile Schoberle. Hyperion Bks. for Children 1996 70p il hardcover o.p. paperback available $3.95 (3-5)

507.8

1. Science—Experiments 2. Scientific recreations

ISBN 0-7868-1087-4 (pa)   LC 95-46173

In another collection of "spooky" experiments and activities "Markle encourages readers to foam at the mouth, blow up marshmallows, and think about cockroaches, worms, and dead fish. The science explanations accompanying the experiments, although primarily macroscopic, are thorough in promoting understanding." Horn Book Guide

Muller, Eric Paul, 1961-

While you're waiting for the food to come; a tabletop science activity book: experiments and tricks that can be done at a restaurant or wherever food is served; by Eric Muller; illustrated by Eldon Doty. Orchard Bks. 1999 84p il $15.95; pa $8.95 (3-6)

507.8

1. Science—Experiments

ISBN 0-531-30199-0; 0-531-07144-8 (pa)

LC 99-17168

A collection of science experiments and activities that can be done where food is served, exploring such topics as the senses, gravity, and water

"A delightful book. . . . An 'Attention-Attraction Factor Key' indicates whether people at other tables will notice what you're up to. The black-and-white cartoons provide information and entertainment. A winner." SLJ

Includes glossary and bibliographical references

Murphy, Pat, 1955-

The science explorer; family experiments from the world's favorite hands-on science museum; [by] Pat Murphy, Ellen Klages, Linda Shore, and the staff of the Exploratorium; illustrated by Jason Gorski. Holt & Co. 1996 127p il (Exploratorium science-at-home book) pa $14 (5 and up) **507.8**

1. Science—Experiments

ISBN 0-8050-4536-8   LC 96-16847

Also available: The science explorer out and about $12.95 (ISBN 0-8050-4537-6)

"An Owl book"

This book "contains over 50 activities, organized into nine sections. The sections deal with topics such as bubbles; light, color, and seeing; paper airplanes; static electricity; sound, music, and hearing; and mixtures. Each activity includes an icon, indicating the time required to perform it; a list of materials needed; and steps to be followed. The steps are well illustrated with clear diagrams. . . . This is an excellent book, and one that should be of interest not only to children and their families, but also to elementary school teachers, scout leaders, and others working with young people." Sci Books Films

Includes bibliographical references

Science experiments on file; experiments, demonstrations, and projects for school and home; edited by Judith A. Bazler. rev ed. Facts on File 2000 2v il loose-leaf set $300 **507.8**

1. Science—Experiments

ISBN 0-8160-3998-4   LC 99-52951

First published 1988

Contents: v1 Earth science; weather; space; biology; v2 Chemistry; physics

This offers 200 science experiments, listing time required, safety precautions, materials, procedure, principles illustrated, data tables, connections, and additional activities, which may be reproduced for classroom use

Science fair project index, 1973-1980/1985-1989. Scarecrow Press 1983-1992 3v   **507.8**

1. Science—Experiments—Indexes   2. Science projects

Science fair project index, 1973-1980/1985-1989—*Continued*

Volume covering 1960-1972, published 1975, o.p.; volume covering 1973-1980 $65 (ISBN 0-8108-1605-9); volume covering 1981-1984 $55 (ISBN 0-8108-1892-2); volume covering 1985-1989 $60 (ISBN 0-8108-2555-4)

Prepared by the Science and Technology staff of the Akron-Summit County Public Library

"An index, based on Library of Congress subject headings, to books and general science periodicals that describe projects, experiments, and display techniques useful for teachers and secondary school students. References are alphabetical by article titles, or by authors when an entire book is cited. A bibliography provides complete citation for monographs." Guide to Ref Books. 11th edition

VanCleave, Janice Pratt

Janice VanCleave's 201 awesome, magical, bizarre & incredible experiments. Wiley 1994 118p il pa $12.95 (4 and up)   **507.8**
1. Science—Experiments
ISBN 0-471-31011-5   LC 93-29807
The experiments in this book "are organized by field: astronomy, biology, chemistry, earth science, and physics; the purpose, materials needed, procedure, results, and an explanation are included for each demonstration. The author writes in a clear, easy-to-understand style. . . . The book will be especially useful to teachers looking for ideas that can be adapted as hands-on activities." SLJ
Includes glossary

Janice VanCleave's 202 oozing, bubbling, dripping & bouncing experiments. Wiley 1996 120p il pa $12.95 (4 and up)   **507.8**
1. Science—Experiments
ISBN 0-471-14025-2   LC 95-46398
Provides instructions for over 200 short experiments in astronomy, biology, chemistry, earth science, and physics
"Some activities consist merely of observation, such as 'To study parts of a feather.' Some are more complex, but all are clearly and concisely explained. Many are repeats from prior VanCleave books, but 40 are supposedly new." SLJ
Includes glossary

Janice VanCleave's 203 icy, freezing, frosty, cool & wild experiments. Wiley 1999 122p il pa $12.95 (4 and up)   **507.8**
1. Science—Experiments
ISBN 0-471-25223-9   LC 98-49721
This includes "experiments in astronomy, biology, chemistry, earth science, and physics. . . . Each activity includes a purpose, a list of materials, a step-by-step procedure, results, and an explanation. Experiments address such topics as the Moon's 'changing' size, how environment affects body temperature, and why ice pops are softer than ice. An excellent resource." SLJ

Janice VanCleave's guide to more of the best science fair projects. Wiley 2000 156p il pa $14.95 (4 and up)   **507.8**
1. Science projects 2. Science—Experiments
ISBN 0-471-32627-5   LC 99-25575

This volume includes "fifty experiments . . . in the areas of astronomy, biology, earth science, engineering, physical science, and mathematics. . . . A valuable addition to science collections." SLJ

Includes bibliographical references

Janice VanCleave's guide to the best science fair projects; [by] Janice VanCleave. Wiley 1997 156p il pa 14.95 (4 and up)   **507.8**
1. Science projects 2. Science—Experiments
ISBN 0-471-14802-4   LC 96-27512
"In the first section, VanCleave discusses scientific methodology: how to organize a project from selecting a topic through the investigatory process, the importance of keeping records, writing a final report, and the value of a nicely crafted presentation. . . . The next section—the largest by far—presents a number of double-page projects in a variety of fields. . . . A clear and informative addition." SLJ

Includes glossary and bibliographical references

508 Natural history

Arnosky, Jim

Crinkleroot's nature almanac. Simon & Schuster Bks. for Young Readers 1999 64p il $16 (k-3)   **508**
1. Seasons 2. Animals 3. Nature study
ISBN 0-689-80534-9   LC 98-27191
Crinkleroot the forest dweller describes the changes that take place in animals and plants throughout the four seasons
"The book combines chatty prose sprinkled with facts and watercolor illustrations—some of which are realistic (like the wildflowers) and others, like Crinkleroot himself, that are more cartoonlike." SLJ

Björk, Christina

Linnea's almanac; text [by] Christina Björk; drawings [by] Lena Anderson. R & S Bks. 1989 61p il $13 (2-5)   **508**
1. Nature study
ISBN 91-29-59176-7   LC 89-83540
Original Swedish edition, 1982
Linnea, featured in Linnea in Monet's garden and Linnea's windowsill garden, "is inspired by the *Old Farmer's Almanac* to track the growing things in her city world. Month by month, the round-faced girl with stick-straight hair never lacks for activities, whether making flower garlands, identifying birds or creating a Christmas-present collage out of beach debris." Publ Wkly
"The book is unusually fresh and charming in its approach; the many facts are presented agreeably and lightened by the child's pleasure in activities which young readers could copy." Grow Point

DK nature encyclopedia. DK Pub. 1998 304p il maps $29.95   **508**
1. Natural history—Encyclopedias
ISBN 0-7894-3411-3   LC 98-16657
"The book is divided into six sections. 'The Natural World' describes the origins and evolution of life on

DK nature encyclopedia—_Continued_

earth. 'How Living Things Work' examines the basic characteristics shared by all living things—respiration, reproduction, life cycles, etc. 'Ecology' surveys the major types of habitats around the world and discusses topics such as food chains and endangered species. A short section explains 'How Living Things Are Classified,' while the final chapters look at specific groups of plants. . . . Well organized, clearly written, and with an amazing scope, this encyclopedia makes a valuable guide to nature." SLJ

Lang, Susan S.

Nature in your backyard; simple activities for children; by Susan Lang with the staff of Cayuga Nature Center; illustrated by Sharon Lane Holm. Millbrook Press 1995 47p il lib bdg $22.90 (2-4)
508

1. Nature study 2. Science projects
ISBN 1-56294-451-7　　　　　LC 94-9278

"This book presents simple science-related projects that children will have fun duplicating. Six sections explore insects, worms, birds, other creatures, seeds, plants, soil, air, and water. Each activity is deftly and attractively designed, including a list of materials needed, procedures, full-color illustrations, results, explanations, and further comments." SLJ

Includes bibliographical references

McMillan, Bruce

Summer ice; life along the Antarctic peninsula; written and photo-illustrated by Bruce McMillan. Houghton Mifflin 1995 48p il maps $16 (3-6)
508

1. Natural history—Antarctica 2. Antarctica
ISBN 0-395-66561-2　　　　　LC 93-38831

"This photo-essay introduces readers to the animals and plants of the Antarctic Peninsula. . . . After showing the landforms and glacial iceforms there, McMillan turns to the unexpected wealth of summer wildlife: algae and moss, plankton and krill, humpback whales and orcas, skuas and shags, seals and (of course) penguins." Booklist

"The full-color photography is brilliant in its beauty and attention to detail. However, the text is lively and knowledgeable, and could stand alone and still catch readers' interest." SLJ

Includes glossary and bibliographical references

Myers, Lynne Born

Galápagos: islands of change; text by Lynne Born Myers and Christopher A. Myers; photographs by Nathan Farb. Hyperion Bks. for Children 1995 48p il maps $16.95; lib bdg $17.49 (4 and up)
508

1. Natural history—Galapagos Islands 2. Galapagos Islands
ISBN 0-7868-0074-7; 0-7868-2061-6 (lib bdg)
　　　　　LC 94-26173

This tells the "story of the Galápagos—the formation of the islands, how they came to be inhabited, and the amazing evolutionary changes taking place there. Diffi-

cult concepts, such as plate tectonics and Darwin's theory of evolution, are explained in simple-to-understand terms and accompanied by appropriate examples. . . . Covering subjects as varied as volcanoes, plant and animal life, evolution, erosion, and human exploitation of the environment, this will be a useful research tool as well as a rich supplement for the science curriculum." Booklist

Includes glossary

Potter, Jean, 1947-

Nature in a nutshell for kids; over 100 activities you can do in ten minutes or less. Wiley 1995 136p il pa $12.95 (2-4)
508

1. Nature study
ISBN 0-471-04444-X　　　　　LC 94-28953

"Each of the 102 experiments is easy, uses safe and mostly readily available household supplies, and is fun at the same time. Divided into seasonal sections, the activities have catchy titles, state hypotheses, list materials, lay out procedures, and finish with clear explanations. Among the noteworthy investigations are: how duck feathers react to water, how mountains are formed, what keeps a seal from freezing in icy weather, whether ants prefer sugar or aspertame, and more." SLJ

Includes glossary and bibliographical references

Wright-Frierson, Virginia, 1949-

An island scrapbook; dawn to dusk on a barrier island; written and illustrated by Virginia Wright-Frierson. Simon & Schuster 1998 unp $16 (3-5)
508

1. Natural history—North Carolina 2. Barrier islands 3. Ecology
ISBN 0-689-81563-8　　　　　LC 97-17998

An artist and her daughter explore a North Carolina barrier island and tell of all they observe during the course of a September day

"The accurately rendered, muted watercolors and pencil drawings on glossy paper present a vivid portrait of island ecology and convey the author's keen sense of observation. . . . A carefully detailed look at a unique ecosystem, sensitively described and beautifully rendered." SLJ

508.2　Seasons

Hirschi, Ron

Fall; photographs by Thomas D. Mangelsen. Cobblehill Bks. 1991 unp il $15.99 (k-2)　**508.2**

1. Autumn
ISBN 0-525-65053-9　　　　　LC 90-19595

Spring; photographs by Thomas D. Mangelsen. Cobblehill Bks. 1990 unp il $15.99; pa $6.99 (k-2)
508.2

1. Spring
ISBN 0-525-65037-7; 0-14-055786-5 (pa)
　　　　　LC 89-49039

Summer; photographs by Thomas D. Mangelsen. Cobblehill Bks. 1991 unp il $15.99 (k-2)　**508.2**

1. Summer
ISBN 0-525-65054-7　　　　　LC 90-19596

Hirschi, Ron—*Continued*

Winter; photographs by Thomas D. Mangelsen. Cobblehill Bks. 1990 unp il hardcover o.p. paperback available $5.99 (k-2)   **508.2**
1. Winter
ISBN 0-14-055785-7 (pa)   LC 89-23935
"A Wildlife seasons book"
Simple text and color photographs introduce each season by focusing on animal behavior and the changing scenery

Maass, Robert
When spring comes. Holt & Co. 1994 unp il hardcover o.p. paperback available $6.95 (k-2)   **508.2**
1. Spring
ISBN 0-8050-4705-0 (pa)   LC 93-29816
Companion volumes: When autumn comes (1990), When summer comes (1993), When winter comes (1993)
Color photographs and brief text introduce activities of the spring season
"The spirit of hope and renewal unfolds in the uncomplicated text, which is accompanied by large and small photographs warmly expressing the feelings of this special time of year." Booklist

Simon, Seymour, 1931-
Autumn across America. Hyperion Bks. for Children 1993 unp il $14.95 (3-5)   **508.2**
1. Autumn 2. Natural history—North America
ISBN 1-56282-467-8   LC 92-55043
Describes the signs of autumn that are seen in different parts of the United States, such as leaves changing color, migration of birds and insects, harvesting of crops, and changes in weather
"Simon's first book in a series about the changing seasons introduces autumn as a 'season of memory and change.'. . . Throughout this tribute, each double-page spread contains at least one, sometimes two, four-color photographs of a typical fall scene opposite two or three paragraphs of Simon's information-packed text, all appearing on a brilliant background color." Booklist

509 Science—Historical and geographic treatment

Beshore, George W.
Science in ancient China; [by] George Beshore. Watts 1998 63p il map (Science of the past) lib bdg $25; pa $8.95 (4 and up)   **509**
1. Science—China—History 2. Science and civilization
ISBN 0-531-11334-5 (lib bdg); 0-531-15914-0 (pa)
LC 97-3519
First published 1988 in the First book series
Surveys the achievements of the ancient Chinese in science, medicine, astronomy, and cosmology, and describes such innovations as rockets, wells, the compass, water wheels, and movable type
Includes glossary and bibliographical references

Science in early Islamic culture; [by] George Beshore. Watts 1998 64p il maps (Science of the past) lib bdg $25; pa $8.95 (4 and up)   **509**
1. Science—History 2. Science and civilization 3. Islamic countries—Civilization
ISBN 0-531-20355-7 (lib bdg); 0-531-15917-5 (pa)
LC 97-5012
First published 1988 in the First book series
Discusses the extraordinary scientific discoveries and advancements in the Islamic world after the birth of Mohammed in 570 and their impact on Western civilization in subsequent centuries and today
"The writing is crisp and lively. . . . Numerous full-color and black-and-white photographs, reproductions, and drawings illuminate the text." SLJ
Includes glossary and bibliographical references

Gay, Kathlyn
Science in ancient Greece. Watts 1998 64p il (Science of the past) lib bdg $25; pa $8.95 (4 and up)   **509**
1. Science—Greece—History 2. Science and civilization
ISBN 0-531-20357-3 (lib bdg); 0-531-15929-9 (pa)
LC 97-24029
First published 1988 in the First book series
Discusses the theories of ancient Greek philosopher-scientists such as Ptolemy, Pythagoras, Hippocrates, and Aristotle, and describes some of the scientific discoveries attributed to the Greeks and their impact on modern science
"Useful for reports, and there's also much to interest science students." SLJ
Includes glossary and bibliographical references

Harris, Jacqueline L., 1929-
Science in ancient Rome. Watts 1998 64p il map (Science of the past) lib bdg $25; pa $8.95 (4 and up)   **509**
1. Science—Rome—History 2. Science and civilization
ISBN 0-531-20354-9 (lib bdg); 0-531-15916-7 (pa)
LC 97-1901
First published 1988 in the First book series
Describes how the Romans put to use and expanded the scientific achievements of earlier civilizations
This "includes clear, easy-to-read text; simple yet effective topic headings; excellent-quality, full-color photographs and reproductions; and Internet sites." SLJ
Includes glossary and bibliographical references

January, Brendan, 1972-
Science in colonial America. Watts 1999 64p il (Science of the past) lib bdg $25; pa $8.95 (4 and up)   **509**
1. Science—United States—History 2. Science and civilization
ISBN 0-531-11525-9 (lib bdg); 0-531-15940-X (pa)
LC 98-10450
Describes the scientific contributions made by people in colonial America, including natural history, medicine, astronomy, and electricity
"Attractive and accessible. . . . Plentiful, accurate material." SLJ
Includes glossary and bibliographical references

January, Brendan, 1972-—*Continued*

Science in the Renaissance. Watts 1999 64p il (Science of the past) lib bdg $25 (4 and up)
509

1. Science—History 2. Science and civilization 3. Renaissance
ISBN 0-531-11526-7　　　　　LC 97-38633

Describes advances in scientific knowledge that occurred during the Renaissance in Europe during the 15th and 16th centuries

"Many colorful photographs as well as reproductions of period art illustrate [this] attractive and interesting [book]." Booklist

Includes glossary and bibliographical references

Moss, Carol (Carol Marie)

Science in ancient Mesopotamia. Watts 1998 63p il (Science of the past) hardcover o.p. paperback available $8.95 (4 and up)　　**509**

1. Science—Iraq—History 2. Science and civilization
ISBN 0-531-15930-2 (pa)　　　　　LC 97-24030

First published 1988 in the First book series

Describes the enormous accomplishments of the Sumerians and Babylonians of ancient Mesopotamia in every scientific area, a heritage which affects our own everyday lives

"Clearly written. . . . Black-and-white and full-color photographs and reproductions . . . are well captioned." SLJ

Includes glossary and bibliographical references

Stewart, Melissa, 1968-

Science in ancient India. Watts 1999 64p il map (Science of the past) lib bdg $25 (4 and up)
509

1. Science—India—History 2. Science and civilization
ISBN 0-531-11626-3　　　　　LC 98-18536

An overview of the scientific contributions of ancient India including Arabic numerals, ayurveda, basic chemistry and physics, and celestial observations

"A useful and unique resource." SLJ

Includes glossary and bibliographical references

Woods, Geraldine, 1948-

Science in ancient Egypt. Watts 1998 64p il (Science of the past) lib bdg $25; pa $8.95 (4 and up)　　**509**

1. Science—Egypt—History 2. Science and civilization
ISBN 0-531-20341-7 (lib bdg); 0-531-15915-9 (pa)
LC 97-649

First published 1988 in the First book series

Discusses the achievements of the ancient Egyptians in science, mathematics, astronomy, medicine, agriculture, and technology

"Well-researched and easy-to-understand. . . . Woods offers a fascinating look at the ancient Egyptians' accomplishments." SLJ

Includes glossary and bibliographical references

Science of the early Americas. Watts 1999 64p il (Science of the past) lib bdg $25; pa $8.95 (4 and up)　　**509**

1. Science—History 2. Science and civilization 3. Native Americans
ISBN 0-531-11524-0 (lib bdg); 0-531-15941-8 (pa)
LC 97-44047

Discusses the scientific accomplishments in such fields as medicine, mathematics, engineering, and astronomy of various groups of American Indians

Includes glossary and bibliographical references

510　Mathematics

Merriam, Eve, 1916-1992

12 ways to get to 11; written by Eve Merriam; illustrated by Bernie Karlin. Simon & Schuster Bks. for Young Readers 1993 unp il hardcover o.p. paperback available $6.99 (k-3)　　**510**

1. Mathematics 2. Counting
ISBN 0-689-80892-5 (pa)　　　　　LC 91-25810

Uses ordinary experiences to present twelve combinations of numbers that add up to eleven. Example: At the circus, six peanut shells and five pieces of popcorn

"Some of the double-page spreads are simpler to solve than others, which allows children to progress as they learn more about counting. The huge, vibrant cut-paper and colored-pencil pictures make the book fun, lively, and painlessly educational." Horn Book Guide

Schwartz, David M., 1951-

G is for googol; a math alphabet book; written by David M. Schwartz; illustrated by Marissa Moss. Tricycle Press 1998 57p il $15.95 (4 and up)　　**510**

1. Mathematics 2. Alphabet
ISBN 1-883672-58-9　　　　　LC 98-15162

Explains the meaning of mathematical terms which begin with the different letters of the alphabet from abacus, binary, and cubit to zillion

"The text is lively and clear and will appeal to even those who think math is as dull as the kitchen floor. . . . The cartoon illustrations are colorful, amusing, and informative." SLJ

Includes glossary

510.7　Mathematics—Education and related topics

Teaching Children Mathematics. National Council of Teachers of Mathematics $65　　**510.7**

1. Arithmetic—Study and teaching—Periodicals
ISSN 1073-5836

Monthly September through May. Supersedes Arithmetic Teacher (ceased publication May 1994)

"This journal for teachers of math in grades K-6 presents articles on curriculum, learning, and instruction, reviews research and suggests practical ways to integrate the findings into the classroom. Regular columns review books for children and teachers, computer software, and other teaching materials." Katz. Mag for Libr. 10th edition

511.3 Mathematical (Symbolic) logic

Murphy, Stuart J., 1942-
Dave's down-to-earth rock shop; illustrated by Cat Bowman Smith. HarperCollins Pubs. 2000 33p il (MathStart) $15.95; lib bdg $15.89; pa $4.95 (k-3)   **511.3**
1. Set theory 2. Rocks—Collectors and collecting
ISBN 0-06-028018-2; 0-06-028019-0 (lib bdg); 0-06-446729-5 (pa)   LC 98-32128
As they consider sorting their rock collection by color, size, type, and hardness, Josh and Amy learn that the same objects can be organized in many different ways
"Murphy's forte is explaining complex topics in a down-to-earth manner, and that's just what he's done here. Along the way, he also includes a good deal of information about rocks, minerals, and the scientific method. Smith's full-color illustrations capture the excitement of rock hunting and include many geological and equipment details." Booklist

512 Algebra, number theory

Anno, Masaichiro
Anno's mysterious multiplying jar; [by] Masaichiro and Mitsumasa Anno; illustrated by Mitsumasa Anno. Philomel Bks. 1983 unp il $19.99; pa $7.99 (2-5)   **512**
1. Factorials 2. Mathematics
ISBN 0-399-20951-4; 0-698-11753-0 (pa)
                                              LC 82-22413
Simple text and pictures introduce the mathematical concept of factorials
This book "begins with a painting of a handsome blue and white lidded jar, moves into fantasy with pictures of the water in the jar becoming a sea on which an old sailing ship is moving, transfers to an island on the sea, and goes on to describe the rooms in the houses in the kingdoms on the mountains in the countries on the island. Each time the number grows: one island, two countries, three mountains, etc. How many jars, then, were in the boxes that were in the cupboards in the rooms? . . . The explanation is in itself clear, and is expanded by other examples of factorials." Bull Cent Child Books

513 Arithmetic

Adler, David A., 1947-
Fraction fun; illustrated by Nancy Tobin. Holiday House 1996 unp il $16.95; pa $6.95 (2-4)
                                              513
1. Fractions
ISBN 0-8234-1259-8; 0-8234-1341-1 (pa)
                                              LC 96-10773
"Adler presents the concept of fractions with the tried-and-true example of dividing a pie (pizza pie, in this case), then directs readers to draw lines across paper plates and color the eight resultant wedges in various color combinations. . . . Adler doesn't shy away from

correct terminology—numerators and denominators—in this primary-grade introduction. Next he launches into some hands-on experimentation. . . . Tobin supplies a jazzy, eye-popping color scheme and diagrams of exceptional clarity to illuminate the straightforward text." Bull Cent Child Books

Roman numerals; illustrated by Byron Barton. Crowell 1977 33p il lib bdg $15.89 (2-4)   **513**
1. Numerals
ISBN 0-690-01302-7   LC 77-2270
"Adler provides exercises on how to write Roman numerals and handle the subscription principle involved in writing the symbols representing four and nine. He also explains the historical origins of the symbols for five and ten plus the uses and development of Roman numerals." SLJ
"A simple demonstration with labeled cards clearly explains how the symbols are ordered; another practice lesson tests readers' comprehension of when to use subtraction symbols. . . . A jaunty cartoon figure acts out textual descriptions against an orange-and-brown backdrop. It's a light, lucid, good-humored lesson." Booklist

Anno, Mitsumasa, 1926-
Anno's magic seeds; written and illustrated by Mitsumasa Anno. Philomel Bks. 1995 unp il $19.99; pa $6.99 (k-3)   **513**
1. Mathematics
ISBN 0-399-22538-2; 0-698-11618-6 (pa)
                                              LC 92-39309
The reader is asked to perform a series of mathematical operations integrated into the story of a lazy man who plants magic seeds and reaps an increasingly abundant harvest
"Anno has succeeded in combining both the moral issue of conservation of resources and arithmetical games in a charming story for young readers. A tour de force from a most original author-illustrator." Horn Book

Anno's math games. Philomel Bks. 1987 104p il hardcover o.p. paperback available $12.95 (k-3)
                                              513
1. Mathematics
ISBN 0-698-11671-2 (pa)   LC 86-30513
"From extremely simple 'what is different?' pictures, Anno quickly builds in complexity to tables, mapping, bar graphs, and visual presentations of proportions." SLJ
Anno leads "the reader into an enchanting world full of interesting observations of things that are different and the same, that combine and come apart, and turn out to be an introduction to mathematics so sophisticated it is absolutely simple and clear. The watercolor illustrations are cheery." N Y Times Book Rev

Anno's math games II. Philomel Bks. 1989 103p il hardcover o.p. paperback available $13 (k-3)   **513**
1. Mathematics
ISBN 0-698-11672-0 (pa)   LC 86-30513
"The book presents mathematics and a great deal more with many pictures and very little to read. There are sections on counting, numeration, and measurement as well as left-right orientation, conservation, block building, comparing and contrasting, and other types of picture

Anno, Mitsumasa, 1926-—*Continued*
puzzles." Sci Child

"In an excellent afterword to parents and teachers, Anno discusses his ideas and approach to each section. Best used one-on-one, the book stimulates children to develop their thinking, creativity, and organizational skills." Booklist

Anno's math games III. Philomel Bks. 1991 103p il hardcover o.p. paperback available $13 (k-3)   **513**
1. Mathematics
ISBN 0-698-11673-9 (pa)   LC 90-35398

Picture puzzles, games, and simple activities introduce the mathematical concepts of abstract thinking, circuitry, geometry, and topology

"The humor, brightness, and simplicity of the illustrations make these math games irresistible." Booklist

Burns, Marilyn

The I hate mathematics! book; illustrated by Martha Hairston. Little, Brown 1975 127p il hardcover o.p. paperback available $13.95 (4 and up)   **513**
1. Mathematics
ISBN 0-316-11741-2 (pa)

"A Brown paper school book"

"This lively collection of puzzles, riddles, magic tricks, and brain teasers provides a painless introduction to mathematical concepts and terms through the process of experimentation and discovery. The cartoon-like illustration and breezy titles . . . should appeal to the not-so-mathematically inclined as well as to puzzle devotees. Required materials are readily available and inexpensive; the techniques described are educationally sound and exciting. An excellent resource for parents, teachers, and children." Horn Book

Geisert, Arthur

Roman numerals I to MM; Numerabilia romana uno ad duo mila: liber de difficillimo computando numerum. Houghton Mifflin 1996 xxxiip $16 (k-3)   **513**
1. Roman numerals 2. Counting
ISBN 0-395-74519-5   LC 95-36247

"Seven Roman numerals are introduced, accompanied by very detailed illustrations of . . . pigs engaged in a variety of activities. What little text there is . . . explains the concept of Roman numerals and how they build on one another." Child Book Rev Serv

"Geisert's detailed etchings reward extended perusal, and children will revel in the sheer abundance of pigs. A great lesson in Roman numerals." Publ Wkly

Leedy, Loreen, 1959-

2 x 2 = boo! a set of spooky multiplication stories; written and illustrated by Loreen Leedy. Holiday House 1995 32p il $15.95 (k-3)   **513**
1. Multiplication
ISBN 0-8234-1190-7   LC 94-46711

This is an "introduction to basic multiplication, with witches, cats, and monsters demonstrating the conse-

quences of multiplying numbers from 0 to 5. The illustrations are done in muted, autumnal tones of black, blue, orange, and mustard, and arranged in a comic-strip format. . . . The concepts are clear and understandable. . . . Leedy's book presents an entertaining alternative to rote memorization." SLJ

Fraction action; written and illustrated by Loreen Leedy. Holiday House 1994 31p il $16.95; pa $6.95 (k-3)   **513**
1. Fractions
ISBN 0-8234-1109-5; 0-8234-1244-X (pa)
     LC 93-22800

Miss Prime and her animal students explore fractions by finding many examples in the world around them

"Thickly pigmented paintings loaded with sporty animal figures add to the humorous presentation, which should make fractions not only more understandable, but also more fun for young children." Bull Cent Child Books

Mission: addition; written and ullustrated by Loreen Leedy. Holiday House 1997 unp il $16.95; pa $6.95 (k-3)   **513**
1. Addition
ISBN 0-8234-1307-1; 0-8234-1412-4 (pa)
     LC 96-37149

Miss Prime and her animal students explore addition by finding many examples in the world around them

"Flat chalk-box colors predominate in the illustrations, which will please kids with their liveliness, their informality, and their cartoonlike speech balloons. . . . An attractive picture book to support the math curriculum." Booklist

Subtraction action. Holiday House 2000 32p il $16.95; pa $6.95 (k-3)   **513**
1. Subtraction
ISBN 0-8234-1454-X; 0-8234-1244-X (pa)
     LC 99-49803

Introduces subtraction through the activities of animal students at a school fair. Includes problems for the reader to solve

This is "an action-packed volume that is perfectly suited to its audience. The softly hued cartoon animals and dialogue balloons are skillfully combined on pages divided into framed sequences." SLJ

McMillan, Bruce

Eating fractions; cooked, written, drafted, and photo-illustrated by Bruce McMillan. Scholastic 1991 unp il $15.95 (k-2)   **513**
1. Fractions 2. Cooking
ISBN 0-590-43770-4   LC 90-9139

Food is cut into halves, quarters, and thirds to illustrate how parts make a whole. Simple recipes included

"A mouth-watering introduction to fractions is served up by McMillan in this concept book. . . . The excellent photographs owe their appeal not only to their bright colors, clear focus, and good framing, but also to their winsome subjects, two infectiously happy children and a strawberry-pie eating shaggy dog." SLJ

Murphy, Stuart J., 1942-
Divide and ride; illustrated by George Ulrich. HarperCollins Pubs. 1997 32p il (MathStart) $14.95; lib bdg $15.89; pa $4.95 (1-3)   513
1. Division
ISBN 0-06-026776-3; 0-06-026777-1 (lib bdg); 0-06-446710-4 (pa)   LC 95-26134
"Eleven friends climb aboard the Dare-Devil roller coaster and three other rides, but before each ride can begin, all of the seats must be filled. Readers follow the children as they solve each problem by dividing and then filling the empty seats with new friends. Watercolor, pen, and ink illustrations and follow-up activities accompany the story." Horn Book Guide

Elevator magic; illustrated by G. Brian Karas. HarperCollins Pubs. 1997 32p il (MathStart) lib bdg $15.89; pa $4.95 (k-2)   513
1. Subtraction
ISBN 0-06-026775-5 (lib bdg); 0-06-446709-0 (pa)
LC 96-5672
"A boy meets his mother on the 10th floor of a high rise. On the way down, Mom needs to do some errands. The first stop, two floors down, is to cash a check at the Farm Bank and Trust, which is (lo and behold!) filled with horses, barns, and hay fields. Farther down is the Hard Rock Candy Store, which is not only full of candy but also the sounds and lights of a heavy metal band. Karas's zany illustrations support the main concept being taught, while picking up on the humor in the word play." SLJ

Henry the fourth; illustrated by Scott Nash. HarperCollins Pubs. 1999 33p il (MathStart) $15.95; lib bdg $15.89; pa $4.95 (k-1)   513
1. Numbers
ISBN 0-06-027610-X; 0-06-027611-8 (lib bdg); 0-06-446719-8 (pa)   LC 98-4960
A simple story about four dogs at a dog show introduces the ordinal numbers: first, second, third, and fourth
"The numerical concepts are sequential and simple enough for young children to follow. The watercolor cartoons fill the pages with action." SLJ

Jump, kangaroo, jump! illustrated by Kevin O'Malley. HarperCollins Pubs. 1999 unp il (MathStart) $15.95; pa $4.95 (1-3)   513
1. Division 2. Fractions
ISBN 0-06-027614-2; 0-06-446721-X (pa)
LC 97-45814
Kangaroo and his Australian animal friends divide themselves up into different groups for the various field day events at camp
"The simple story line presents a real-world application of fractions and division, neatly reinforced by O'Malley's expressive illustrations. Related activities are suggested." Horn Book Guide

Just enough carrots; illustrated by Frank Remkiewicz. HarperCollins Pubs. 1997 31p il (MathStart) $14.95; lib bdg $15.89; pa $4.95 (k-1)   513
1. Counting
ISBN 0-06-026778-X; 0-06-026779-8 (lib bdg); 0-06-446711-2 (pa)   LC 96-19495

While a bunny and his mother shop in a grocery store for lunch guests, the reader may count and compare the amounts of carrots, peanuts, and worms in the grocery carts of other shoppers
"Bright, colorful illustrations, a surprise ending, and two pages of activities for adults and children extend and enhance the book's appeal." SLJ

Packard, Edward, 1931-
Big numbers; and pictures that show just how big they are! illustrated by Salvatore Murdocca. Millbrook Press 2000 unp il $14.95; lib bdg $22.40 (k-3)   513
1. Numbers
ISBN 0-7613-1280-3; 0-7613-1570-5 (lib bdg)
LC 99-32242
Uses illustrations of exponentially increasing peas to present the concept of numbers from one to a million, billion, trillion
"A rollicking, cartoon-style expression of big numbers shown in different ways. . . . Bright and sassy, Murdocca's line-and-wash illustrations create an atmosphere of fun that could break through all but the strongest math anxiety." Booklist

Schmandt-Besserat, Denise
The history of counting; illustrated by Michael Hays. Morrow Junior Bks. 1999 45p il $17; lib bdg $16.93 (4 and up)   513
1. Counting 2. Mathematics
ISBN 0-688-14118-8; 0-688-14119-6 (lib bdg)
LC 96-35316
"Beginning with a look at primitive expressions of numbers, the text goes on to explain abstract counting and the methods used by the Sumerians, the Phoenicians, the Greeks, the Romans, and finally the Arabs, who brought Hindu numerals from India to Europe about 1,000 years ago. . . . Imaginatively conceived and well composed, Hays' acrylic paintings feature warm, harmonious colors and delicate plays of light and shadow against textured-linen backings. Cogently written and beautifully made." Booklist
Includes glossary

Scholastic explains math homework. Scholastic 1998 64p il (Scholastic explains homework series) $14.95; pa $6.95 (1-3)   513
1. Mathematics
ISBN 0-590-39754-0; 0-590-39757-5 (pa)
LC 97-38782
Explains the facts and procedures of basic math concepts likely to be found in homework for second and third grades such as rounding numbers and drawing congruent figures

Schwartz, David M., 1951-
On beyond a million; an amazing math journey; illustrated by Paul Meisel. Doubleday Bks. for Young Readers 1999 unp il $15.95 (2-4)   513
1. Counting
ISBN 0-385-32217-8   LC 98-52990

Schwartz, David M., 1951-—*Continued*
"Schwartz helps youngsters conceptualize enormous numbers by introducing them to counting by powers of ten. Professor X, along with his dog Y, comes to the rescue of some children with an out-of-control popcorn popper as they futilely attempt to count the kernels." SLJ

"The design is busy, with sidebars and balloon comments. Each double-page spread is clearly meant to be talked about, and the discussions aren't overwhelming. . . . Awesome and yet accessible." Booklist

VanCleave, Janice Pratt
Janice VanCleave's play and find out about math; easy activities for young children. Wiley 1998 122p il $29.95; pa $12.95 (k-2)   **513**
1. Mathematics
ISBN 0-471-12937-2; 0-471-12938-0 (pa)
LC 96-53002
"Fifty simple activities that involve basic arithmetic such as using one's fingers to do simple addition and subtraction. . . . Most procedures are between four and eight steps and are clearly written and accompanied by pencil drawings." SLJ

515   Analysis

Murphy, Stuart J., 1942-
Beep beep, vroom vroom! illustrated by Chris Demarest. HarperCollins Pubs. 2000 33p il (MathStart) $15.93; lib bdg $15.89; pa $4.95 (k-1)
515
1. Patterns (Mathematics)
ISBN 0-06-028016-6; 0-06-028017-4 (lib bdg); 0-06-446728-7 (pa)   LC 98-51907
"Molly loves playing with cars, but her brother, Kevin, tells her she's too young. He lines up his 12 cars—four red, four green, four yellow—in special order on the shelf and tells her not to touch them while he's gone. . . . At the back are practical suggestions for adults and kids to find patterns on the pages and make their own patterns with pebbles, buttons, coins, and kitchen utensils. Demarest's clear, simple pastel pictures express the fun of playing with cars as the vrooming action reveals the patterns in everyday things." Booklist
Includes bibliographical references

516   Geometry

Adler, David A., 1947-
Shape up! illustrated by Nancy Tobin. Holiday House 1998 unp il $16.95; pa $6.95 (2-4)   **516**
1. Geometry 2. Shape
ISBN 0-8234-1346-2; 0-8234-1638-0 (pa)
LC 97-22236
Uses cheese slices, pretzel sticks, a slice of bread, graph paper, a pencil, and more to introduce various polygons, flat shapes with varying numbers of straight sides
"Tobin's colorful diagrams and lanky, baseball-capped tour guide make each definition and direction crystal clear, making this a useful and appealing title for extending classroom lessons or encouraging beginners to charge beyond circle-square-triangle." Bull Cent Child Books

VanCleave, Janice Pratt
Janice VanCleave's geometry for every kid; easy activities that make learning geometry fun; [by] Janice VanCleave. Wiley 1994 221p il $29.95; pa $12.95 (4 and up)   **516**
1. Geometry
ISBN 0-471-31142-1; 0-471-31141-3 (pa)
LC 93-43049
This "introductory text covers many topics in geometry, from lines, optical illusions, and art-related activities to applications with protractors and the construction of basic solids. Terms are presented in a simplified fashion and are easily understood. Graphics are clear. The hands-on activities encourage learning, creativity, and excitement." Sci Books Films
Includes glossary

519.5   Statistical mathematics

Murphy, Stuart J., 1942-
Betcha! illustrated by S.D. Schindler. HarperCollins Pubs. 1997 33p il (MathStart) $15.95; lib bdg $15.89; pa $4.95 (1-3)   **519.5**
1. Approximate computation 2. Arithmetic
ISBN 0-06-026768-2; 0-06-026769-0 (lib bdg); 0-06-446707-4 (pa)   LC 96-15486
Two friends "want to guess the number of jelly beans in a jar so that they can win a contest for two free tickets for the All-Star Game. They practice their estimating skills. One boy is good at figuring things out, one counts precisely, as they work out the number of people on the bus, the number of cars stuck on the block, the cost of the cool gear in the store window." Booklist
"This title will be especially useful for classroom use as it provides many possibilities for related activities." SLJ

520   Astronomy and allied sciences

Bond, Peter, 1948-
DK guide to space. DK Pub. 1999 63p il $19.95 (4 and up)   **520**
1. Astronomy
ISBN 0-7894-3946-8   LC 98-42054
Presents discoveries, observations, and theories about the planets and other phenomena in our solar system and as well as in outer space, using text, illustrations, and photographs from NASA
"This book demonstrates both the author's enthusiasm and his knowledge of astronomy. The photographs are beautiful, well chosen, and up to date." Sci Books Films

Campbell, Ann
The New York Public Library amazing space; a book of answers for kids; [by] Ann-Jeanette Campbell; illustrated by Jessica Wolk-Stanley. Wiley 1997 186p il pa $12.95 (5 and up)   **520**
1. Astronomy 2. Outer space
ISBN 0-471-14498-3   LC 96-29785
"A Stonesong Press book"

Campbell, Ann—*Continued*

"Arranged in chapters by major topics, the author states and then addresses questions on general astronomy, celestial objects, our solar system, and space exploration. . . . The material is up to date and presented clearly, with simple illustrations sprinkled in that are sure to catch a child's attention." Sci Books Films

Includes glossary and bibliographical references

Ford, Harry

The young astronomer. DK Pub. 1998 37p il $15.95 (4 and up) **520**

1. Astronomy

ISBN 0-7894-2061-9   LC 97-39623

Introduces the basics of astronomy through a variety of projects, including a model of a lunar eclipse and a chart of a comet's path

"Outstanding charts listing a variety of useful information are included. . . . Both browsers and astronomy buffs will find something of interest." Booklist

Includes glossary

Hirst, Robin

My place in space; by Robin and Sally Hirst; illustrated by Roland Harvey with Joe Levine. Orchard Bks. 1990 unp il hardcover o.p. paperback available $6.95 (2-4) **520**

1. Astronomy

ISBN 0-531-07030-1 (pa)   LC 89-37893

First published 1988 in Australia

"Little drawings of a small Australian town serve as foreground for dramatic paintings of the universe—all illustrating exactly where Henry Wilson and his sister Rosie live. The science is sound, presented in enough detail to be interesting but with enough simplicity to be recalled and repeated aloud." Bull Cent Child Books

Mechler, Gary

National Audubon Society first field guide: night sky; sky maps by Wil Tirion. Scholastic 1999 159p il maps $17.95; pa $8.95 (4 and up) **520**

1. Astronomy

ISBN 0-590-64085-2; 0-590-64086-0 (pa)

LC 98-51876

A field guide to the night sky, explaining through text and maps how to locate and identify stars, planets, meteors, comets, and constellations

Includes bibliographical references

Mitton, Jacqueline

The Scholastic encyclopedia of space; [by] Jacqueline Mitton and Simon Mitton. Scholastic Ref. 1999 80p $14.95 **520**

1. Astronomy 2. Outer space—Exploration

ISBN 0-590-59227-0   LC 98-22852

Discusses the many aspects of space, including the origin and nature of the universe, space travel, the solar system, and methods of observing the night sky

"The straightforward, accessible narrative accurately covers numerous relevant and timely topics." SLJ

Stott, Carole

Night sky; written by Carole Stott. Dorling Kindersley 1993 61p il (Eyewitness explorers) hardcover o.p. paperback available $5.95 (3-5) **520**

1. Astronomy

ISBN 0-7894-2214-X (pa)   LC 93-644

Describes and illustrates the astronomical aspects of the sky, including constellations, planets, moons, and the astronomer's role in observing these

This book "does an excellent job of conveying the fact that there is still so much to be learned about the Universe and encourages the reader to join in the search for knowledge." Appraisal

The **Visual** dictionary of the universe. Dorling Kindersley 1993 64p il (Eyewitness visual dictionaries) $18.95 (4 and up) **520**

1. Astronomy

ISBN 1-56458-336-8   LC 93-22419

"Thousands of astronomy terms are defined with full-color photographs and illustrations in logical groups, easy to understand with related information. A great book for browsing or for reference if the comprehensive index is used." Sci Child

520.3 Astronomy—Encyclopedias and dictionaries

Wilsdon, Christina

The solar system: an A-Z guide. Watts 2000 96p il lib bdg $27; pa $16.95 **520.3**

1. Astronomy—Dictionaries

ISBN 0-531-11710-3 (lib bdg); 0-531-116489-6 (pa)

LC 99-34215

A dictionary of terms, concepts, people, and places related to the solar system, astronomy, and the exploration of space

"With its colorful photos and illustrations and simple descriptions, this visually appealing dictionary should attract armchair astronomers. . . . There are cross-references to related articles and a good list for further reading and Web sites is also included." SLJ

520.5 Astronomy—Serial publications

Odyssey; adventures in science. Cobblestone Pub. $29.95 **520.5**

1. Astronomy—Periodicals

ISSN 0163-0946

Monthly September through May. First published 1979 by AstroMedia Corp.

Sub-title varies

This publication focuses "on science, especially astronomy. It is written for upper elementary and junior high school students. Each issue has a single theme that is explored in some depth. Color pictures and illustrations throughout each issue add interest. There are regular features as well as opportunities for reader input." Katz. Mag for Libr. 10th edition

522 Techniques, equipment, materials of astronomy

Cole, Michael D.
Hubble Space Telescope; exploring the universe. Enslow Pubs. 1999 48p il (Countdown to space) lib bdg $18.95 (4 and up)   **522**
1. Astronomy   2. Hubble   Space   Telescope
3. Astronautics
ISBN 0-7660-1120-8   LC 98-3298
Details the initiation of the Hubble Space Telescope in April 1990 and the repair and servicing missions which followed; explains the telescope's role in answering questions about the universe
"Illustrated with color photographs, the book provides solid basic information." Horn Book
Includes glossary and bibliographical references

Scott, Elaine, 1940-
Adventure in space; the flight to fix the Hubble; [by] Elaine Scott; [photographs by] Margaret Miller. Hyperion Bks. for Children 1995 64p il hardcover o.p. paperback available $7.95 (4 and up)   **522**
1. Hubble Space Telescope 2. Outer space—Exploration
ISBN 0-7868-1039-4 (pa)   LC 94-7756
This "book tells the story of the space shuttle *Endeavor's* 1993 mission to repair the Hubble telescope. After explaining 'Hubble's troubles' and scientists' plans to repair the telescope, the book introduces the astronauts and shows them at home with their families as well as at work, practicing every movement of their tasks and anticipating anything that could go wrong." Booklist
"The astronauts are portrayed as three-dimensional people, which helps readers identify with them. There are many full-color photographs throughout; those taken from the shuttle are breathtaking, showing closeups of the astronauts with the Earth featuring prominently in the background." SLJ

523 Specific celestial bodies and phenomena

Berger, Melvin, 1927-
Do stars have points? questions and answers about stars and planets; [by] Melvin and Gilda Berger; illustrated by Vincent Di Fate. Scholastic Ref. 1998 48p il (Scholastic question and answer series) lib bdg $12.95; pa $5.95 (2-4)   **523**
1. Astronomy 2. Stars 3. Solar system
ISBN 0-590-13080-3 (lib bdg); 0-590-13087-0 (pa)
LC 97-36005
Questions and answers explore various aspects of stars and our solar system, including the sun, planets, moons, comets, and asteroids
This book "organizes the material well, it asks questions that children may actually have posed, and the answers are clear and precise. . . . Often dramatic and beautiful, the paintings illustrate the text quite effectively." Booklist

Cole, Joanna
The magic school bus, lost in the solar system; illustrated by Bruce Degen. Scholastic 1990 unp il hardcover o.p. paperback available $4.99 (2-4)
523
1. Astronomy 2. Outer space—Exploration 3. Planets
ISBN 0-590-41429-1 (pa)   LC 89-10185
Also available Spanish language edition and CD-ROM version
"The planetarium is closed for repairs, so the Magic School Bus blasts off on a real tour of the solar system. After their previous field trips, the children in Ms. Frizzle's class are all blasé about such things; as they land on the Moon, Venus, and Mars, and fly by the other planets and the Sun, they comment on what they see, generate a blizzard of one- or two-sentence reports on special topics and—even while Ms. Frizzle is temporarily left behind in the asteroid belt—crack terrible jokes." SLJ

Simon, Seymour, 1931-
The universe. Morrow Junior Bks. 1998 unp il $16.95; lib bdg $16.89; pa $6.95 (3-6)   **523**
1. Cosmology
ISBN 0-688-15301-1; 0-688-15302-X (lib bdg);
0-06-443752-3 (pa)   LC 97-20489
"Matching full-color, full- and double-page-spread-sized light and radio photographs of nebulas, galaxies, and sundry deep-space phenomena with two or three paragraphs of explanatory text [Simon] covers a wide range of topics, from the Big Bang to quasars, from star formation to extrasolar planets. . . . The choice of detail is guaranteed to whet youngster's appetites for a more thorough, narrowly focused treatment." SLJ

523.1 The universe, galaxies, quasars

Simon, Seymour, 1931-
Galaxies. Morrow Junior Bks. 1988 unp il $18; pa $6.95 (3-6)   **523.1**
1. Galaxies
ISBN 0-688-08002-2; 0-688-10992-6 (pa)
LC 87-23967
"This is a step-by-step introduction to and description of the many galaxies in the universe. . . . He includes discussions of the ways in which astronomers classify galaxies, black holes, smaller satellite galaxies such as the Magellanic Clouds and supernovas. The terms are explained within the text." Publ Wkly
"This fine introduction to an awe-inspiring subject will surely stimulate interest in stargazing, further reading, and investigation." Horn Book

523.2 Solar system

Branley, Franklyn Mansfield, 1915-
The sun and the solar system; [by] Franklyn M. Branley. 21st Cent. Bks. (NY) 1996 64p il (Secrets of space) lib bdg $23.90 (4-6)   **523.2**
1. Planets 2. Solar system 3. Sun
ISBN 0-8050-4475-2   LC 96-2836

Branley, Franklyn Mansfield, 1915-—*Continued*

Discusses the sun and the solar system, comparing how they were perceived in earlier times with what is known about them now

"Many colorful illustrations, photographs as well as diagrams and paintings, complement the succinctly written text." Booklist

Includes bibliographical references

Simon, Seymour, 1931-

Our solar system. Morrow Junior Bks. 1992 64p il $19.95; lib bdg $19.93 (3-6)   **523.2**
1. Solar system
ISBN 0-688-09992-0; 0-688-09993-9 (lib bdg)
                  LC 91-36665

"With a variety of full-color photographs, the solar system and its characteristics are described, including the sun, asteroids, meteoroids, and comets. This book is a wonderful introduction into the mysteries surrounding the solar system." Sci Child

Vogt, Gregory

The solar system; facts and exploration; [by] Gregory L. Vogt. 21st Cent. Bks. (Brookfield) 1995 96p il (Scientific American sourcebooks) lib bdg $26.90 (5 and up)   **523.2**
1. Solar system 2. Outer space—Exploration
ISBN 0-8050-3249-5   LC 95-941

This book serves as a "guide to the planets and moons as well as an introduction to asteroids, comets, and meteoroids. Accounts of discoveries and disappointments in the space program give readers a feel for the ongoing challenge of understanding the solar system. The excellent full-color illustrations include many recent images from the Hubble space telescope." Booklist

Includes bibliographical references

523.3   Moon

Branley, Franklyn Mansfield, 1915-

The moon seems to change; by Franklyn M. Branley; illustrations by Barbara and Ed Emberley. rev ed. Crowell 1987 29p il (Let's-read-and-find-out science book) hardcover o.p. paperback available $4.95 (k-3)   **523.3**
1. Moon
ISBN 0-06-445065-1 (pa)   LC 86-47747

A revised and newly illustrated edition of the title first published 1960

The author "explains the waxing and waning of the moon and compares the length of a day on earth and on the moon. Each page has colorful explanatory illustrations. . . . Branley's brief-easy-to-read text and the Emberleys' diagrams make this book a welcome addition to science collections for young children or the picture book section." SLJ

What the moon is like; by Franklyn M. Branley; illustrated by True Kelley. Newly illustrated ed. HarperCollins Pubs. 2000 30p il (Let's-read-and-find-out science) $15.95; lib bdg $15.89; pa $4.95 (k-3)   **523.3**
1. Moon
ISBN 0-06-027992-3; 0-06-027993-1 (lib bdg); 0-06-445185-2 (pa)   LC 98-54072

A revised and newly illustrated edition of the title first published 1963 by Crowell

This book "invites readers simply to observe the moon from Earth before it delves into facts. . . . The following pages, all illustrated with clear, colorful pictures of astronauts and the lunar landscape, explore the moon's actual surface, climate, and temperature; briefly discuss lunar landings (with a map); and draw comparisons between the moon and Earth." Booklist

Bredeson, Carmen

The moon. Watts 1998 63p il lib bdg $23; pa $6.95 (4 and up)   **523.3**
1. Project Apollo 2. Moon
ISBN 0-531-20308-5 (lib bdg); 0-531-15911-6 (pa)
                 LC 96-40226

"A First book"

Describes what people have believed about the moon and what has been learned over time and presents an overview of the Apollo space program

"Clear, effective illustrations, most in color, appear throughout the book. . . . A good resource for science collections." Booklist

Includes glossary and bibliographical references

Gibbons, Gail

The moon book. Holiday House 1997 unp il $16.95; pa $6.95 (k-3)   **523.3**
1. Moon
ISBN 0-8234-1297-0; 0-8234-1364-0 (pa)
                 LC 96-36826

Identifies the moon as our only natural satellite, describes its movement and phases, and discusses how we have observed and explored it over the years

"Gibbons presents a great deal of information in a deceptively simple format by combining inviting illustrations with clear writing." Horn Book Guide

523.4   Planets

Branley, Franklyn Mansfield, 1915-

The planets in our solar system; by Franklyn M. Branley; illustrated by Kevin O'Malley. HarperCollins Pubs. 1998 31p il (Let's-read-and-find-out science) $15.95; lib bdg $15.89; pa $4.95 (k-3)   **523.4**
1. Planets 2. Solar system
ISBN 0-06-027769-6; 0-06-027770-X (lib bdg); 0-06-445178-X (pa)   LC 97-1174

First published 1981

Describes the nine planets and other bodies of the solar system; includes directions for making models showing the size of the planets and their distance from the sun

"Branley makes his points briefly and precisely." SLJ

Brimner, Larry Dane, 1949-
Jupiter. Children's Press 1999 47p il lib bdg
$22; pa $6.95 (2-4)   **523.4**
1. Jupiter (Planet)
ISBN 0-516-21153-6 (lib bdg); 0-516-26495-8 (pa)
LC 98-2951

Neptune. Children's Press 1999 47p il lib bdg
$22; pa $6.95 (2-4)   **523.4**
1. Neptune (Planet)
ISBN 0-516-21157-9 (lib bdg); 0-516-26496-6 (pa)
LC 98-22039

Pluto. Children's Press 1999 47p il lib bdg $22;
pa $6.95 (2-4)   **523.4**
1. Pluto (Planet)
ISBN 0-516-21155-2 (lib bdg); 0-516-26499-0 (pa)
LC 98-26740

Saturn. Children's Press 1999 47p il lib bdg
$22; pa $6.95 (2-4)   **523.4**
1. Saturn (Planet)
ISBN 0-516-21154-4 (lib bdg); 0-516-26501-6 (pa)
LC 98-14006

Uranus. Children's Press 1999 47p il lib bdg
$22; pa $6.95 (2-4)   **523.4**
1. Uranus (Planet)
ISBN 0-516-21156-0 (lib bdg); 0-516-26508-3 (pa)
LC 98-22451

"A True book"
"These simply written texts provide solid, up-to-date
information about current knowledge of the outer planets,
acquired mostly from space probes. The captioned color
photos are generally well chosen, and the odd nature of
the interiors of the gas giants is well described for the
intended audience. Lists of organizations and online sites
for more information are provided. [Also included are
bibliographies and glossaries]." Horn Book Guide

Fradin, Dennis B.
The planet hunters; the search for other worlds;
[by] Dennis Brindell Fradin. Margaret K.
McElderry Bks. 1997 148p il $19.95 (5 and up)
523.4
1. Astronomers 2. Astronomy 3. Planets
ISBN 0-689-81323-6   LC 96-29721
Provides historical information on astronomy, the discovery of the planets, and the people who have made
such discoveries
This is "a well-researched book. . . . Black-and-white
photographs appear throughout the book, with a section
of color plates inserted in the middle. . . . The immediacy of the writing will carry readers along in the narrative
flow of this often dramatic story." Booklist
Includes bibliographical references

Gibbons, Gail
The planets. Holiday House 1993 unp il $16.95;
pa $6.95 (k-3)   **523.4**
1. Planets
ISBN 0-8234-1040-4; 0-8234-1138-8 (pa)
LC 92-44429

Discusses the movements, location, and characteristics
of the nine known planets of our solar system
"Well designed and laid out, the pages feature appealing full-color illustrations." Booklist

Kraske, Robert
Asteroids; invaders from space. Atheneum Pubs.
1995 90p il maps hardcover o.p. paperback
available $5.99 (5 and up)   **523.4**
1. Asteroids
ISBN 0-689-82456-4 (pa)   LC 94-8072
"Readers will learn about land formations caused by
asteroids, how future collisions might be averted, the solar system, comets, meteors, and more. Featuring highly
readable prose, strong visual aids, and vivid description,
this title makes the mindboggling accessible." Booklist
Includes bibliographical references

Ride, Sally K.
The mystery of Mars; [by] Sally Ride and Tam
O'Shaughnessy. Crown 1999 48p il $17.95; lib
bdg $19.99 (4-6)   **523.4**
1. Mars (Planet)
ISBN 0-517-70971-6; 0-517-70972-4 (lib bdg)
LC 98-52929
"This survey draws illuminating parallels and contrasts
between the history, structure, and current state of both
Earth and Mars. . . . The material includes information
gathered from the 1997 *Pathfinder* mission and a mention of the *Mars Climate Orbiter*. . . . The book is
capped by a time line of Mars missions through 2001
and a . . . list of Web sites." SLJ
"An excellent introduction to the red planet. . . . The
book's visuals are stunning; photographs taken from
space pop off the black pages, and there are charts and
sophisticated artist renderings throughout." Booklist

Simon, Seymour, 1931-
Destination: Jupiter. rev ed. Morrow Junior Bks.
1998 unp il $16; pa $6.95 (3-6)   **523.4**
1. Jupiter (Planet)
ISBN 0-688-15620-7; 0-06-443759-0 (pa)
LC 97-20488
First published 1985 with title: Jupiter
This is a "guide to the planet and its four Galilean
moons, Io, Europa, Ganymede, and Callisto. The com-
plete planetary portrait is achieved by combining classic
Voyager spacecraft images and more recent *Galileo* mis-
sion photographs." Horn Book Guide
"Expertly balancing the verbal and visual presentation,
Simon . . . demonstrates his ability to inform and enter-
tain simultaneously." SLJ

Destination: Mars. HarperCollins Pubs. 2000
unp il $15.95; lib bdg $15.89 (3-6)   **523.4**
1. Mars (Planet)
ISBN 0-688-15770-X; 0-688-15771-8 (lib bdg)
LC 99-15523
First published 1987 by Morrow with title: Mars
"The descriptions and explanations of Mars—its geological and meteorological features, and historical speculation about them—present a coherent picture of what

Simon, Seymour, 1931—*Continued*

scientists know about the planet. Also included within the text are vital statistics, such as Mars's distance from the earth and sun, orbit position, and gravity. . . . [Includes] remarkable new color photographs from the Global Surveyor and Pathfinder missions . . . and from the Hubble telescope. . . . *Destination Mars* presents a comprehensive and informative survey of the planet." Horn Book

523.5 Meteoroids, solar wind, zodiacal light

Aronson, Billy

Meteors; the truth behind shooting stars. Watts 1996 63p il lib bdg $23; pa $6.95 (4 and up)

    523.5

1. Meteors

ISBN 0-531-20242-9 (lib bdg); 0-531-15813-6 (pa)

    LC 95-48846

"A First book"

Explains such things as the difference between a meteor, a meteoroid, and a meteorite and what happens when an asteroid or comet gets too close to the earth

"Offers a clear and concise explanation of a . . . common phenomenon. . . . The well-chosen photographs of assorted meteorites and their effects will appeal to readers." SLJ

Includes glossary and bibliographical references

523.6 Comets

Bonar, Samantha

Comets. Watts 1998 63p il lib bdg $23; pa $6.95 (4 and up)

    523.6

1. Comets

ISBN 0-531-20301-8 (lib bdg); 0-531-15907-8 (pa)

    LC 96-53502

"A First book"

Describes what has been learned about the composition, orbits, and the existence of several well-known comets

"Attractive, colorful illustrations are numerous and complement the text. . . . An excellent reference book for young readers." Sci Books Films

Includes glossary and bibliographical references

Marsh, Carole S., 1946-

Asteroids, comets, and meteors; [by] Carole Marsh. 21st Cent. Bks. (NY) 1996 64p il (Secrets of space) lib bdg $23.90 (4-6)

    523.6

1. Comets 2. Meteors 3. Asteroids

ISBN 0-8050-4473-6

    LC 96-8882

This "discusses the discovery of the nature of comets, asteroids, and meteors, from the observations and beliefs of ancient Greek and Chinese astronomers to the first sighting of comet Hyakutake. . . . Many colorful illustrations, photographs as well as diagrams and paintings, complement the succinctly written [text]." Booklist

Includes glossary and bibliographical references

Simon, Seymour, 1931-

Comets, meteors, and asteroids. Morrow Junior Bks. 1994 unp il hardcover o.p. paperback available $6.95 (3-6)

    523.6

1. Comets 2. Meteors 3. Asteroids

ISBN 0-688-15843-9 (pa)

    LC 93-51251

"Simon presents basic information about comets, meteors, and asteroids in an attractive oversize book. . . . Blocks of text appear in fairly large type, usually facing a full-page illustration. . . . Simon writes in plain language, without talking down to his audience. The intriguing photographs include shots of comets and meteor showers in the sky, a meteorite in Antarctica, and an enormous impact crater in Arizona." Booklist

Vogt, Gregory

Asteroids, comets, and meteors; [by] Gregory L. Vogt. Millbrook Press 1996 31p il (Gateway solar system) lib bdg $20.90 (2-4)

    523.6

1. Comets 2. Asteroids 3. Meteors

ISBN 1-56294-601-3

    LC 95-19735

Presents information on the different types of celestial matter known as asteroids, comets, and meteors and on what scientists learned from the impact of a comet on the surface of Jupiter

This "is a relatively thorough, reliable introduction to its subject. . . . [It features] plenty of clear full-color photos and art from NASA." SLJ

Includes glossary and bibliographical references

523.7 Sun

Gallant, Roy A.

When the sun dies. Marshall Cavendish 1999 128p il $14.95 (6 and up)

    523.7

1. Stars 2. Sun

ISBN 0-7614-5036-X

    LC 98-9430

Discusses what is known about the sun in particular and stars in general and describes some possible effects of the sun's gradual demise on life on earth

"Serious students of astrophysics, stellar evolution, climatology, the search for extra-solar planets, and other related topics will be well served by this title." SLJ

Includes glossary and bibliographical references

Gibbons, Gail

Sun up, sun down; written and illustrated by Gail Gibbons. Harcourt Brace Jovanovich 1983 unp il $16; pa $6 (k-3)

    523.7

1. Sun

ISBN 0-15-282781-1; 0-15-282782-X (pa)

    LC 82-23420

The author explains "the sun and its effect on the earth. Narrated by a little girl who notices the sun shining when she wakes up one morning, this . . . [book covers] what the sun does, what makes shadows, how the sun helps form rain clouds, and how it keeps the planet warm." Booklist

"The illustrations clarify the text with bold, clear drawings in full color." SLJ

523.8 Stars

Apfel, Necia H., 1930-
Orion, the Hunter. Clarion Bks. 1995 48p il
$16.95 (4 and up)   **523.8**
   1. Stars
   ISBN 0-395-68962-7   LC 94-44268
"Color photographs from the Hubble Space Telescope
portray the splendor of the constellation Orion, its nebu-
la, and other nearby constellations. Origins of stars such
as blue-white giants and red supergiants are explained in
easy-to-understand terms." Sci Child
  "Large pages allow the spectacular photographs, which
are supplemented by diagrams, to be fully appreciated."
Booklist

Branley, Franklyn Mansfield, 1915-
The Big Dipper; by Franklyn M. Branley;
illustrated by Molly Coxe. rev ed. HarperCollins
Pubs. 1991 32p il (Let's-read-and-find-out science
book) hardcover o.p. paperback available $4.95
(k-1)   **523.8**
   1. Ursa Major
   ISBN 0-06-445100-3 (pa)   LC 90-31199
A revised and newly illustrated edition of the title first
published 1962
Explains basic facts about the Big Dipper, including
which stars make up the constellation, how its position
changes in the sky, and how it points to the North Star

Couper, Heather
Black holes; [by] Heather Couper and Nigel
Henbest; illustrated by Luciano Corbella. DK Pub.
1996 45p il $16.95 (5 and up)   **523.8**
   1. Black holes (Astronomy)
   ISBN 0-7894-0451-6   LC 95-44391
"The authors cover such topics as the discovery of
black holes, Einstein's theory of relativity, gravitation,
time travel and wormholes." Book Rep
  "Deftly distilled brief blocks of text and captions accompany technically sophisticated photographs and painstakingly detailed, realistic art, while diagrams further
clarify the concepts introduced." Publ Wkly
  Includes glossary

Rey, H. A. (Hans Augusto), 1898-1977
Find the constellations. rev ed. Houghton
Mifflin 1976 72p il $20; pa $9.95   **523.8**
   1. Stars
   ISBN 0-395-24509-5; 0-395-24418-8 (pa)
First published 1954
"Constellation diagrams are presented with and without connecting lines and are drawn for 40° N. Latitude
to cover the continental United States. . . . Scientific accuracy is stressed, stellar magnitudes are indicated on the
diagrams, and the concept of light year is discussed.
Some of the myths surrounding the names of the constellations are given." Sci Books Films
  "This is unquestionably a readable, enjoyable, and informative guide." SLJ

Rockwell, Anne F., 1934-
Our stars; written and illustrated by Anne
Rockwell. Silver Whistle Bks. 1999 unp il $13
(k-2)   **523.8**
   1. Stars 2. Planets 3. Outer space
   ISBN 0-15-201868-9   LC 97-49518
A simple introduction to the stars, planets, and outer
space
  "This book clearly explains many science facts without 'talking down' to youngsters. The storybook-style illustrations, . . . invite children to look at the night sky
and think about the information presented in the text."
Sci Books Films

VanCleave, Janice Pratt
Janice VanCleave's constellations for every kid;
easy activities that make learning science fun.
Wiley 1997 247p il maps $29.95; pa $12.95 (4
and up)   **523.8**
   1. Constellations 2. Astronomy
   ISBN 0-471-15981-6; 0-471-15979-4 (pa)
                    LC 96-35309
Describes twenty of the most prominent constellations,
including the Big Dipper, Orion, and Cancer, explains
how to locate them, and provides instructions for related
activities
  "Much more than a connect-the-dots stargazer guide,
this comprehensive book is packed with information on
locating constellations that goes far beyond what is found
in most books on the subject." Booklist
  Includes glossary

525 Earth (Astronomical geography)

Gallant, Roy A.
Earth's place in space. Benchmark Bks.
(Tarrytown) 1999 80p il (Story of science) lib bdg
$28.50 (5 and up)   **525**
   1. Earth 2. Universe
   ISBN 0-7614-0963-7   LC 98-28043
Relates the history of the struggle to understand
earth's place in the universe, from earliest mythmaking
to today's discoveries via the Hubble telescope
  This book is "highly useful. . . . [It is] richly illustrat-
ed with color photos, drawings, and charts." Booklist
  Includes glossary and bibliographical references

Gibbons, Gail
The reasons for seasons. Holiday House 1995
unp il $16.95; pa $6.95 (k-3)   **525**
   1. Seasons
   ISBN 0-8234-1174-5; 0-8234-1238-5 (pa)
                    LC 94-32904
"Gibbons uses simple words and clear, colorful pictures to explain the seasons, the solstices, and the equi-
noxes. Besides discussing the earth's tilt and orbit, she
also comments on what people and animals do in each
season of the year." Booklist

529 Chronology

Branley, Franklyn Mansfield, 1915-
Keeping time; from the beginning and into the 21st century; [by] Franklyn M. Branley; illustrated by Jill Weber. Houghton Mifflin 1993 105p il $16 (4-6)   **529**
1. Time 2. Clocks and watches 3. Calendars
ISBN 0-395-47777-8   LC 92-6783
"From the history of timekeeping and calendars to the theory of relativity to the reasons we divide time as we do, Branley challenges readers with difficult, abstract concepts and offers simple, concrete projects. . . . Weber's cartoonlike ink drawings appear on nearly every page . . . providing an upbeat counterpoint to the text." Booklist
Includes bibliographical references

Hewitt, Sally
Time. Children's Press 1999 30p il (It's science!) lib bdg $20.50 (k-3)   **529**
1. Time
ISBN 0-516-21655-4   LC 98-47632
Discusses the different aspects of time and how it is measured, including days and nights, years, calendars, and clocks. Provides suggestions for related activities
"The text encourages children to actively investigate the concept of time. Color photographs of different clocks and other familiar objects illustrate the text." Horn Book

Maestro, Betsy, 1944-
The story of clocks and calendars; marking a millennium; illustrated by Giulio Maestro. Lothrop, Lee & Shepard Bks. 1999 48p il $16; lib bdg $15.89 (3-6)   **529**
1. Calendars 2. Clocks and watches 3. Time
ISBN 0-688-14548-5; 0-688-14549-3 (lib bdg)
                                           LC 98-21305
"This overview of timekeeping begins with prehistoric 'calendar sticks' and stone structures, and continues through today's ultra-precise atomic clocks. The text takes a broad multicultural approach, showing how science, history, and societal differences have influenced the calendar; the color illustrations are executed in styles that match the eras and cultures discussed in the volume." Horn Book Guide

Older, Jules
Telling time; how to tell time on digital and analog clocks! written by Jules Older; illustrated by Megan Halsey. Charlesbridge Pub. 2000 unp il $16.95; pa $6.95 (k-3)   **529**
1. Time 2. Clocks and watches
ISBN 0-88106-396-7; 0-88106-397-5 (pa)
                                           LC 99-18764
Humorous text explains the concept of time, from seconds to hours on both analog and digital clocks, from years to millennia on the calendar
"The cartoon illustrations, showing children and many, many types of clocks are colorful, plentiful, and inviting. . . . This jovial look at time and time telling is as handy as they come." SLJ

Skurzynski, Gloria
On time; from seasons to split seconds. National Geographic Soc. 2000 41p il $17.95 (4 and up)
                                                    529
1. Time
ISBN 0-7922-7503-9   LC 99-33927
Examines the ways humans have measured time throughout history and discusses the various units that are used to keep track of it
"This attractive offering is brimming with information. . . . The conversational tone helps readers get through the more difficult concepts. . . . The book is heavily illustrated with full-color drawings, photographs, and diagrams." SLJ

530 Physics

Challoner, Jack
The visual dictionary of physics; written by Jack Challoner. DK Pub. 1995 64p il (Eyewitness visual dictionaries) $18.95 (4 and up)   **530**
1. Physics
ISBN 0-7894-0239-4   LC 95-11937
"This book offers a bit about a wide variety of topics, from Newton's Laws to Feynman diagrams. It is an enticing choice for browsing that may inspire further research, or that might possibly supply just the information needed for an assignment." SLJ
Includes glossary

Friedhoffer, Robert
Physics lab in a hardware store; illustrated by Joe Hosking. Watts 1996 112p il (Physical science labs) lib bdg $25; pa $6.95 (5 and up)   **530**
1. Physics 2. Science—Experiments
ISBN 0-531-11292-6 (lib bdg); 0-531-15824-1 (pa)
                                           LC 96-15828
Examines such topics in physics as mass, weight, gravity, buoyancy, and pressure with experiments using common household tools
"Clearly written and illustrated with line drawings [this makes] scientific principles understandable by providing hands-on experiences related to familiar phenomena." Booklist
Includes glossary and bibliographical references

530.4 States of matter

Hewitt, Sally
Solid, liquid, or gas? Children's Press 1998 30p il (It's science!) lib bdg $20.50; pa $6.95 (k-3)
                                                  530.4
1. Matter
ISBN 0-516-20794-6 (lib bdg); 0-516-26393-5 (pa)
                                           LC 97-5308
Presents information about the properties of solids, liquids, and gases, using observation and activities

Zoehfeld, Kathleen Weidner

What is the world made of? all about solids, liquids, and gases; illustrated by Paul Meisel. HarperCollins Pubs. 1998 32p il (Let's-read-and-find-out science) $15.95; lib bdg $15.89; pa $4.95 (k-3)   **530.4**

1. Matter

ISBN 0-06-027143-4; 0-06-027144-2 (lib bdg); 0-06-445163-1 (pa)   LC 97-30658

In simple text, presents the three states of matter, solid, liquid, and gas, and describes their attributes

"The explanations are clear with a simple, informal text for the new reader, and the lively line-and-watercolor pictures bring in humor and common-sense." Booklist

530.8   Measurement

Adler, David A., 1947-

How tall, how short, how faraway; illustrated by Nancy Tobin. Holiday House 1999 unp il $16.95; pa $6.95 (k-3)   **530.8**

1. Measurement

ISBN 0-8234-1375-6; 0-8234-1632-1 (pa)

LC 98-18802

Introduces several measuring systems such as the Egyptian system, the inch-pound system, and the metric system

"In this wonderful hands-on concept book, easy technological measuring tools are superbly introduced and explained. . . . The informative text and colorful illustrations clearly explain the difference between customary and metric systems." Sci Child

Leedy, Loreen, 1959-

Measuring Penny; written and illustrated by Loreen Leedy. Holt & Co. 1997 unp il $16.95; pa $6.95 (1-3)   **530.8**

1. Measurement

ISBN 0-8050-5360-3; 0-8050-6572-5 (pa)

LC 97-19108

"For a measuring project, Lisa decides to measure her dog, Penny, and a cast of other dogs at the park. Noses, tails, ears, paws—nothing escapes her measuring zeal. Also, time, temperature, cost, and even value are creatively calculated throughout a day spent caring for Penny. Leedy cleverly incorporates Lisa's notebook recordings into the illustrations, which depict a wide range of shapes and sizes for easy visual comparison." Horn Book Guide

Markle, Sandra, 1946-

Measuring up! experiments, puzzles, and games exploring measurement. Atheneum Bks. for Young Readers 1995 44p il $17 (4 and up)   **530.8**

1. Measurement

ISBN 0-689-31904-5   LC 94-19240

This "book presents ideas and methods for measuring all sorts of things, from distances to weights to temperatures, from trees and flagpoles to public opinion and the strength of toilet tissue. The directions are clear and the activities creative. . . . Full-color photographs and diagrams fit the text." SLJ

Murphy, Stuart J., 1942-

Room for Ripley; illustrated by Sylvie Wickstrom. HarperCollins Pubs. 1999 33p il (MathStart) lib bdg $15.89; pa $4.95 (1-3)   **530.8**

1. Measurement 2. Aquariums

ISBN 0-06-027621-5 (lib bdg); 0-06-446724-4 (pa)

LC 98-26109

Uses a story about a young boy who is getting a fish bowl ready for his new pet to introduce various units of liquid measure

"The writing is breezy and reads like a story about a boy who wants a pet, but the text constantly reinforces the mathematical concepts (how many cups in a pint, a quart, etc.). The illustrations are painted in muted primary colors against a lot of white space. . . . A fun, painless math lesson." SLJ

531   Classical mechanics. Solid mechanics

Cobb, Vicki, 1938-

Why doesn't the earth fall up? and other not such dumb questions about motion; illustrated by Ted Enik. Lodestar Bks. 1988 40p il $14.99 (3-5)   **531**

1. Motion

ISBN 0-525-67253-2   LC 88-11108

"Four cartoon kids and an omniscient narrator explore nine questions about motion: motions which children can cause and watch, how they can detect motions that they cannot feel, Newton's laws, center of gravity, orbits, and pendula. Along the way, there are simple experiments and brief mention of Newton, Galileo, and Copernicus. It's all very short and simple, in an open, appealing format, and for the most part the science does not suffer from the simplification." SLJ

534   Sound and related vibrations

Pfeffer, Wendy, 1929-

Sounds all around; illustrated by Holly Keller. HarperCollins Pubs. 1999 32p il (Let's-read-and-find-out science) $15.95; lib bdg $15.89 (k-3)   **534**

1. Sound

ISBN 0-06-027711-4; 0-06-027712-2 (lib bdg)

LC 97-17993

This "surveys the topic of sound by discussing vibration, communication, echolocation, radar, and the measurement of loudness by decibels. . . . The last three pages offer instructions for activities and games related to sound. Like the writing, the attractive line-and-watercolor illustrations are clear and simple." Booklist

535 Light and paraphotic phenomena

Branley, Franklyn Mansfield, 1915-
Day light, night light; where light comes from; by Franklyn M. Branley; illustrated by Stacey Schuett. Newly il ed. HarperCollins Pubs. 1998 32p col il (Let's-read-and-find-out science) $14.95; lib bdg $15.89; pa $4.95 (k-3)   535
1. Light
ISBN 0-06-027294-5; 0-06-027295-3 (lib bdg); 0-06-445171-2 (pa)   LC 96-33316
First published 1975 with title: Light and darkness
Discusses the properties of light, particularly its source in heat
"This is a beautifully illustrated children's book about a basic concept in science. The pictures add to the clearly written text." Sci Books Films

Bulla, Clyde Robert, 1914-
What makes a shadow? illustrated by June Otani. rev ed. HarperCollins Pubs. 1994 32p il (Let's-read-and-find-out science) lib bdg $15.89 (k-1)   535
1. Shades and shadows
ISBN 0-06-022916-0   LC 92-36350
A revised and newly illustrated edition of the title first published 1962 by Crowell
"Using short sentences and developmentally appropriate language, the author explains how shadows are formed, gives numerous examples of shadows, and describes how to make shadow pictures on the wall. Each page is illustrated with bright, colorful drawings, and the gender and cultural representation is excellent." Sci Books Films

Burnie, David
Light. Dorling Kindersley 1992 64p il (Eyewitness science) $15.95; lib bdg $19.99 (4 and up)   535
1. Light
ISBN 0-7894-4885-8; 0-7894-6709-7 (lib bdg)   LC 92-7661
A guide to the origins, principles, and historical study of light
"Each double-page spread is lavishly illustrated with full-color photographs and diagrams, and each contains a wealth of information." Booklist

Cobb, Vicki, 1938-
Light action! amazing experiments with optics; [by] Vicki Cobb and Josh Cobb; illustrated by Theo Cobb. HarperCollins Pubs. 1993 198p il lib bdg $15.89 (5 and up)   535
1. Optics 2. Light
ISBN 0-06-021437-6   LC 92-25528
Explains what light is and explores the basic principles of optics through experiments
"The activities are simple and well designed and will give students basic knowledge. Cheerful line drawings and diagrams illustrate the text." Booklist

Levine, Shar
The optics book; fun experiments with light, vision & color; [by] Shar Levine & Leslie Johnstone; illustrated by Jason Coons. Sterling 1998 80p il lib bdg $21.95; pa $10.95 (4 and up)   535
1. Optics 2. Color 3. Science—Experiments
ISBN 0-8069-9947-0 (lib bdg); 0-8069-9942-X (pa)   LC 98-26732
Explores the properties of light and color by means of experiments and analysis of various optical instruments including periscopes, and telescopes
"Illustrated in full color with cartoon-like drawings and diagrams as well as photographs of equipment and results, the pages have a more inviting look than most books of science projects." Booklist
Includes glossary

537 Electricity and electronics

Berger, Melvin, 1927-
Switch on, switch off; illustrated by Carolyn Croll. Crowell 1989 32p il (Let's-read-and-find-out science book) lib bdg $15.89; pa $4.95 (k-3)   537
1. Electricity
ISBN 0-690-04786-X (lib bdg); 0-06-445097-X (pa)   LC 88-17638
"This book presents rudimentary exploration of electricity and how electrical current flows to the light switch in a child's room. Follow the current from the generator to a power plant to the switch on the wall. Includes instructions for a simple generator. A good, first look at a topic that mystifies young scientists." Sci Child

Dispezio, Michael A.
Awesome experiments in electricity & magnetism; [by] Michael Dispezio; illustrated by Catherine Leary. Sterling 1998 160p il lib bdg $17.95; pa $7.95 (5 and up)   537
1. Electricity 2. Magnetism 3. Science—Experiments
ISBN 0-8069-9819-9 (lib bdg); 0-8069-9820-2 (pa)   LC 98-22439
"DiSpezio presents over 70 experiments that explore electrical charges, static electricity, currents, circuits, switches, and magnetism. . . . Thought-provoking questions for further investigation appear in a 'Check It Out' section. The experiments are informative and, given the readily available parts and simple assembly, occasionally amazing." SLJ

Levine, Shar
Shocking science; fun & fascinating electrical experiments; [by] Shar Levine & Leslie Johnstone; illustrated by Emily S. Edliq. Sterling 1999 80p il $19.95; pa $10.95 (5 and up)   537
1. Electricity 2. Science—Experiments
ISBN 0-8069-3946-X; 0-8069-2271-0 (pa)   LC 99-43501
Suggested experiments studying static electricity and electrical circuits, with easily obtained supplies. Includes

Levine, Shar—*Continued*
historical information and glossary
"The organization and writing as a whole is clear and purposeful. . . . Small color photographs illustrate the text in a useful and attractive manner. . . . A practical and informative book of science experiments." Booklist

Parker, Steve
Electricity; written by Steve Parker. Dorling Kindersley 1992 64p il (Eyewitness science) $15.95; lib bdg $19.99 (4 and up)   **537**
1. Electricity
ISBN 0-7894-5577-3; 0-7894-6711-9 (lib bdg)
               LC 92-6926
Discusses the properties of electricity and describes how it is made and used
"Pictures and text work together to offer a lucid chronicle of pertinent experiments, discoveries and inventions from ancient times to the present." Publ Wkly

VanCleave, Janice Pratt
Janice VanCleave's electricity; mind-boggling experiments you can turn into science fair projects; [by] Janice VanCleave. Wiley 1994 89p il $10.95 (4 and up)   **537**
     1. Electricity—Experiments 2. Science projects
     ISBN 0-471-31010-7   LC 93-40913
     "The experiments move from the simple, which do not require the use of batteries, to those that require small batteries, sizes AA, AAA, C, or D. An appendix shows how to make strips of aluminum foil that can be used to form the electrical circuits that are part of some of the experiments. By encouraging students to move beyond the basic problems (with adult supervision), the author encourages them to be creative in designing science fair projects." Booklist
Includes glossary

538   Magnetism

Branley, Franklyn Mansfield, 1915-
What makes a magnet? by Franklyn M. Branley; illustrated by True Kelley. HarperCollins Pubs. 1996 31p il (Let's-read-and-find-out science) $15.95; pa $4.95 (k-3)   **538**
1. Magnets
ISBN 0-06-026441-1; 0-06-445148-8 (pa)
               LC 95-32181
Describes how magnets work and includes instructions for making a magnet and a compass
"Kelley's happy line drawings incorporate a humorous mouse to add safety warnings and goofy side comments. The clear diagrams and lucid explanations are both informative and engaging." Horn Book

Souza, D. M. (Dorothy M.)
Northern lights. Carolrhoda Bks. 1994 48p il (Nature in action) lib bdg $21.27 (4-6)   **538**
     1. Auroras
     ISBN 0-87614-799-6   LC 93-3027

Discusses the origins, characteristics, and lore of the Northern and Southern Lights known as auroras
This "is written in a clear, concise style and is illustrated with magnificent color photographs and accurate paintings." Sci Books Films
Includes glossary

539.2   Radiation

Skurzynski, Gloria
Waves; the electromagnetic universe. National Geographic Soc. 1996 48p il $16.95 (3-6) **539.2**
1. Electromagnetic waves 2. Radiation
ISBN 0-7922-3520-7   LC 96-11976
Examines different kinds of electromagnetic waves, including radio waves, microwaves, light, x-rays and gamma rays
"This short, colorful book is packed with easy-to-understand scientific principles about wave theory. . . . A great source for beginning research as well as an interesting read for the inquiring young mind." Booklist
Includes glossary

539.7   Atomic and nuclear physics

Gallant, Roy A.
The ever changing atom. Benchmark Bks. (Tarrytown) 1999 80p (Story of science) lib bdg $28.50 (5 and up)   **539.7**
1. Atoms 2. Atomic theory 3. Nuclear physics
ISBN 0-7614-0961-0   LC 98-35420
Introduces atoms, the tiny particles which make up everything in the world, discussing their different parts, how they were discovered, and how they can be used as a source of energy
Includes glossary and bibliographical references

540   Chemistry & allied sciences

Challoner, Jack
The visual dictionary of chemistry; written by Jack Challoner. DK Pub. 1996 64p il (Eyewitness visual dictionaries) $18.95 (4 and up)   **540**
1. Chemistry
ISBN 0-7894-0444-3   LC 95-52796
Text and illustrations present the fundamentals of chemistry, including such topics as atomic bonds, catalysts, chemical reactions, and various elements
"This book succeeds in making the non-visual perceivable and easy to understand. . . . The pages are well organized and illustrated with brightly colored, labeled photographs and diagrams." SLJ
Includes glossary

Newmark, Ann
Chemistry; written by Ann Newmark. Dorling Kindersley 1993 64p il (Eyewitness science) $15.95; lib bdg $19.99 (4 and up)   **540**
1. Chemistry
ISBN 0-7894-4881-5; 0-7894-6713-5 (lib bdg)
               LC 92-54480

Newmark, Ann—*Continued*

Explores the world of chemical reactions and shows the role that chemistry plays in our world

"The book is an inspiration for demonstrations or experiments. The brightly colored illustrations are appealing, and . . . the snippets of information are a useful way to introduce many topics or examples relating to the themes under discussion." Sci Books Films

540.7 Chemistry—Education and related topics

Gardner, Robert, 1929-

Science projects about kitchen chemistry. Enslow Pubs. 1999 128p il lib bdg $20.95 (5 and up)   **540.7**
1. Chemistry 2. Science projects 3. Science—Experiments
ISBN 0-89490-953-3   LC 98-35050
Presents experiments suitable for science fair projects, dealing with the chemistry involved with foods and activities related to the kitchen

"The author has assembled some very engaging and safe experiments for middle-school-aged children." Sci Books Films

Includes bibliographical references

Kramer, Alan

How to make a chemical volcano and other mysterious experiments. Watts 1989 111p il hardcover o.p. paperback available $6.95 (4-6)
                                            540.7
1. Chemistry—Experiments
ISBN 0-531-115610-9 (pa)   LC 89-8994
The author presents various experiments, using household chemicals or materials, in order to demonstrate chemical principles

"The easy-to-follow, clearly illustrated instructions include 'Caution' warnings for steps which suggest adult supervision. . . . Kramer's low-key enthusiasm makes this ideal for the reluctant scientist." Bull Cent Child Books

Includes bibliographical references

546 Inorganic chemistry

Elements. Grolier Educ. 1996 15v set $305 (5 and up)   **546**
1. Chemical elements
ISBN 0-7172-7572-8   LC 95-82222
Contents: v1 Hydrogen and the noble gases; v2 Sodium and potassium; v3 Calcium and magnesium; v4 Iron, chromium, and manganese; v5 Copper, silver, and gold; v6 Zinc, cadmium, and mercury v7 Aluminum; v8 Carbon; v9 Silicon; v10 Lead and tin; v11 Nitrogen and phosphorus; v12 Oxygen; v13 Sulfur; v14 Chlorine, fluorine, bromine, and iodine; v15 Uranium and other radioactive elements

This set "discusses each element's discovery, forms, extraction, industrial uses, and unique character. In a one-topic-per-spread format, text blocks surround several large, clear, full-color photos or, more rarely, schematics. . . . This resource will strengthen both school labs and library collections." SLJ

For a fuller review see: Booklist, January 15, 1997

The **Elements**. Benchmark Bks. (Tarrytown) 1999-2000 12v il lib bdg ea $22.79 (5 and up)
                                            546
1. Chemical elements

Contents: Aluminum, by J. Farndon; Calcium, by J. Farndon; Carbon, by G. Sparrow; Copper, by R. Beatty; Gold, by S. Angliss; Hydrogen, by J. Farndon; Iron, by G. Sparrow; Magnesium, by C. Uttley; Nitrogen, by J. Farndon; Oxygen, by J. Farndon; Phosphorus, by R. Beatty; Sulfur, by R. Beatty

These "titles cover where these substances are found, how they were discovered, their characteristics and reactions, and their importance in the human body and the environment. Each volume includes a double-page spread on the element's position in the periodic table. The captioned, full-color drawings, photographs, and diagrams clarify the text while boxed 'Did you Know?' items offer interesting extensions to it. . . . Informative, accessible science books that will be of interest for both general reading and report writing." SLJ

Includes glossaries

Fitzgerald, Karen

The story of oxygen. Watts 1996 63p il lib bdg $23 (4 and up)   **546**
1. Oxygen
ISBN 0-531-20225-9   LC 96-6202
"A First book"
Explores the history of the chemical element oxygen and explains its chemistry, how it works in the body, and its importance in our lives

"Colorful illustrations, photographs, diagrams, and charts support and enhance the text. All in all, this is a complete and informative overview." SLJ

Includes glossary and bibliographical references

548 Crystallography

Stangl, Jean, 1928-

Crystals and crystal gardens you can grow. Watts 1990 64p il lib bdg $23 (4 and up)   **548**
1. Crystals 2. Science—Experiments
ISBN 0-531-10889-9   LC 89-38999
"A First book"
The author discusses the nature and structure of crystals and presents experiments in crystal formation

With "clear explanatory background on crystal formations, and easy directions for experiments, this will meet a real need in every classroom and public library collection." Bull Cent Child Books

Includes bibliographical references

Symes, R. F.

Crystal & gem; written by R.F. Symes and R.R. Harding. Knopf 1991 63p il (Eyewitness books) (4 and up)   **548**
1. Crystals 2. Precious stones

LC 90-4930

Symes, R. F.—*Continued*

Also available Spanish language edition

Available DK Pub. edition $15.95; $19.99 lib bdg (ISBN 0-7894-5764-4; 0-7894-6574-4 lib bdg)

Describes how crystals form in nature, how crystals are grown artificially, and how crystals are used in industry. Numerous color photos with text identify the various gemstones

"The color photographs and drawings are dazzling and show care in selection and positioning. . . . The text is lucid, readable, and informative." Appraisal

549   Mineralogy

Symes, R. F.

Rocks & minerals; written by R.F. Symes and the staff of the Natural History Museum, London. Knopf 1988 63p il (Eyewitness books) (4 and up)
             549

1. Minerals 2. Rocks
             LC 87-26514

Also available Spanish language edition

Available DK Pub. edition $15.95; $19.99 lib bdg (ISBN 0-7894-5804-7; 0-7894-6551-5 lib bdg)

Text and photographs examine the creation, importance, erosion, mining, and uses of rocks and minerals

"The material presented is technically sound and well and appropriately condensed. This book is not a textbook, nor is it a field manual. As a general reference for the lay person, it provides, through the use of visual aids and associated text, useful information for individuals with no formal training in geology." Sci Books Films

550   Earth sciences

Gibbons, Gail

Planet earth/inside out. Morrow Junior Bks. 1995 unp il maps lib bdg $16.89; pa $4.95 (k-3)
             550

1. Earth 2. Geology

ISBN 0-688-09681-6 (lib bdg); 0-688-15849-8 (pa)
             LC 94-41926

"From Pangaea to recycling, Gibbons skims the surface of geology, touching on plate tectonics, volcanoes, earthquakes, and climates." SLJ

Gibbons' "explanations of the earth's interior are enlivened by comparisons . . . and her plentiful pictures, with their sharp outlines and broad blocks of color, will help clarify the concepts for the youngest learners." Booklist

Lauber, Patricia, 1924-

You're aboard Spaceship Earth; illustrated by Holly Keller. HarperCollins Pubs. 1996 32p il (Let's-read-and-find-out science) hardcover o.p. paperback available $4.95 (k-3)
             550

1. Earth sciences

ISBN 0-06-445159-3 (pa)
             LC 94-18704

In this book "life on our planet is compared with a manned shuttle mission that must take special care to in-

sure the health and safety of its crew. . . . Once that concept is established, youngsters learn interesting facts about the supplies needed to survive—food, air with oxygen, and water. Lauber is adept at writing for this audience, using simple vocabulary and straightforward sentences. . . . Keller's bright and colorful drawings further explain complicated concepts such as the water cycle." SLJ

Patent, Dorothy Hinshaw

Shaping the earth; photographs by William Muñoz. Clarion Bks. 2000 88p il maps $18 (4 and up)
             550

1. Geology

ISBN 0-395-85691-4
             LC 99-37093

Explains the forces that have created the geological features on the earth's surface

"This concise, attractive volume succeeds in a daunting task—to present the history of Earth in 88 pages of compelling, age-appropriate text. . . . William Muñoz's full-color photographs, well-chosen and reproduced, will draw young readers into the text. . . . A glossary and a list of further references, including Web sites, are appended." Booklist

Van Rose, Susanna

Earth; written by Susanna Van Rose. Dorling Kindersley 1994 64p il maps (Eyewitness science) $15.95; pa $19.99 (4 and up)
             550

1. Earth sciences

ISBN 0-7894-5575-7; 0-7894-6717-8 (pa)
             LC 93-33102

This "opens with ideas on the composition and formation of the planet; discusses properties of water and minerals (including the basic types of rock); covers oceanography, seismology, and the forces that build and destroy mountains; and ends with a mention of paleontology." SLJ

"Clear color photographs, maps, satellite images, and historical artwork are an integral part of a well-designed book." Horn Book Guide

The earth atlas; illustrated by Richard Bonson. Dorling Kindersley 1994 63p il maps $19.95 (5 and up)
             550

1. Geology

ISBN 1-56458-626-X
             LC 94-8765

"This very oversize volume looks at the geography of the earth, including the earth's crust, the ocean floor, and various kinds of rocks as well as the history of the earth." Booklist

"What is unique and fascinating about this book is its format: Each topic appears on a double page and consists of a brief introduction to major ideas, photographs, illustrations, maps, charts, and captions. The one-paragraph captions are crisp and informative. The full-color illustrations . . . are outstanding, and most portray geologic features in three-dimensional blocks." Sci Books Films

VanCleave, Janice Pratt
Janice VanCleave's earth science for every kid;
101 easy experiments that really work. Wiley 1991
231p il hardcover o.p. paperback available $12.95
(4 and up)   **550**
    1. Earth sciences—Experiments
    ISBN 0-471-53010-7 (pa)   LC 90-42724
Instructions for experiments, each introducing a different earth science concept
"An entertaining, educational, and nonthreatening aid
to understanding earth science. The easy experiments are
carefully organized." SLJ

The **Visual** dictionary of the earth. Dorling
    Kindersley 1993 64p il maps (Eyewitness visual
    dictionaries) $18.95 (4 and up)   **550**
    1. Earth sciences
    ISBN 1-56458-335-X   LC 93-18571
This volume provides an "overview of the Earth and
all its systems. Included among its 25 two-page topical
sections are coverage of geological time; the rock cycle;
mineral resources; and processes such as faulting and
folding, mountain building, and weathering and erosion.
In addition, the Earth's waters (rivers, lakes and ground-
water, coastlines, oceans, and seas) are addressed, as well
as the atmosphere and weather." Am Ref Books Annu,
1994
Includes glossary

551 Geology, hydrology, meteorology

Blobaum, Cindy, 1966-
Geology rocks! 50 hands-on activities to explore
the earth; illustrations by Michael Kline.
Williamson 1999 96p il pa $10.95 (4-6)   **551**
    1. Geology 2. Science—Experiments
    ISBN 1-88559-329-5   LC 98-53299
Presents fifty hands-on activities to introduce the science of geology and explain the formation and history of
the earth
"The text is witty but conveys much factual material.
The experiments can be done easily with household
items and include safety precautions. . . . The book is illustrated with red-and-purple tinted cartoons and photographs." SLJ
Includes bibliographical references

551.1 Gross structure and properties of the earth

Cole, Joanna
The magic school bus inside the Earth;
illustrated by Bruce Degen. Scholastic 1987 40p il
$15.95; pa $4.95 (2-4)   **551.1**
    1. Earth—Internal structure 2. Geology
    ISBN 0-590-40759-7; 0-590-40760-0 (pa)
                                              LC 87-4563
Also available Spanish language edition and CD-ROM
version

In this book Ms. Frizzle teaches "geology via a field
trip through the center of the earth. As her class learns
about fossils, rocks, and volcanoes, so will readers, absorbing information painlessly as they vicariously travel
through the caves, tunnels, and up through the cone of
a volcanic island shortly before it erupts. . . . Degen's
bright, colorful artwork includes many witty details to
delight observant children. Carried in cartoonlike balloons, the schoolmates' thoughts, banter, and asides add
spice to the geology lesson. Bright, sassy, and savvy, the
magic school bus books rate high in child appeal." Booklist

Gallant, Roy A.
Dance of the continents. Benchmark Bks.
(Tarrytown) 2000 80p il (Story of science) lib bdg
$19.95 (5 and up)   **551.1**
    1. Plate tectonics 2. Geology
    ISBN 0-7614-0962-9   LC 98-28046
Describes the development of geological theory from
the ancient Greek philosophers to the discovery of plate
tectonics, which explains the forming of geological struc-
tures
"This book is a good brief description of continental
drift as it is now perceived by most geologists." Sci
Books Films
Includes glossary and bibliographical references

Silverstein, Alvin
Plate tectonics; [by] Alvin Silverstein, Virginia
Silverstein [and] Laura Silverstein Nunn. 21st
Cent. Bks. (Brookfield) 1998 64p il maps (Science
concepts) lib bdg $24.90 (5 and up)   **551.1**
    1. Plate tectonics 2. Earthquakes 3. Volcanoes
    ISBN 0-7613-3225-1   LC 98-24934
Discusses plate tectonics, the theory that the surface of
the earth is always moving, and the connection of this
phenomenon to earthquakes and volcanoes
"The inviting layout includes many colorful photographs, maps, and diagrams, as well as some interesting
informational sidebars." Booklist
Includes glossary and bibliographical references

551.2 Volcanoes, earthquakes, thermal waters and gases

Lauber, Patricia, 1924-
Volcano: the eruption and healing of Mount St.
Helens. Bradbury Press 1986 60p il $17.99; pa
$8.99 (4 and up)   **551.2**
    1. Mount Saint Helens (Wash.) 2. Volcanoes
    ISBN 0-02-754500-8; 0-689-71679-6 (pa)
                                              LC 85-22442
    A Newbery Medal honor book, 1987
"A clearly written account of the volcano's 1980 eruption in Washington State, with handsome color photographs of every phase of the eruption and its aftermath.
Perhaps most interesting is the detailed description of the
healing process—what flora and fauna survived and
how." N Y Times Book Rev

Levy, Matthys

Earthquake games; earthquakes and volcanoes explained by 32 games and experiments; [by] Matthys Levy and Mario Salvadori; illustrated by Christina C. Blatt. Margaret K. McElderry Bks. 1997 116p il $16 (5 and up)   **551.2**

1. Earthquakes 2. Volcanoes
ISBN 0-689-81367-8   LC 96-48157

Uses numerous activities and experiments to explain the forces and phenomena connected with earthquakes and volcanoes

"An informative tool that effectively uses hands-on techniques to teach kids about geologic wonders." Booklist

Simon, Seymour, 1931-

Earthquakes. Morrow Junior Bks. 1991 unp il maps $16.95; pa $6.95 (3-6)   **551.2**

1. Earthquakes
ISBN 0-688-09633-6; 0-688-14022-X (pa)
     LC 90-19328

Examines the phenomenon of earthquakes, describing how and where they occur, how they can be predicted, and how much damage they can inflict

"This makes a lasting impression with its combination of direct text and sharp color photos and drawings. . . . This informational treasure will draw science enthusiasts and browsers alike." Booklist

Volcanoes. Morrow Junior Bks. 1988 unp il $15.95; lib bdg $15.88; pa $5.95 (3-6)   **551.2**

1. Volcanoes
ISBN 0-688-07411-1; 0-688-07412-X (lib bdg);
0-688-14029-7 (pa)   LC 87-33316

"Using examples like St. Helens and the volcanoes of Iceland and Hawaii, the author is able to address all aspects of his subject: the history, nature and causes of volcanoes." Publ Wkly

"The photographs are large, informative, and spectacular, reproduced in brilliant color. Aside from one confusing map of the earth's tectonic plates, this is a solid introduction." Bull Cent Child Books

Van Rose, Susanna

Volcano & earthquake; written by Susanna van Rose. Knopf 1992 61p il maps (Eyewitness books) (4 and up)   **551.2**

1. Volcanoes 2. Earthquakes
     LC 92-4710

Available DK Pub. edition $15.95; lib bdg $19.99 (ISBN 0-7894-5780-6; 0-7894-6587-6)

"A Dorling Kindersley book"

Photographs and text explain the causes and effects of volcanoes and earthquakes and examine specific occurrences throughout history

"Gorgeous graphics and outstanding design. . . . Coverage is primarily visual, with brief introductory text and informative captions. . . . This book will attract readers to an already popular topic, and will provide one of the most effective introductions available." SLJ

Walker, Sally M.

Earthquakes. Carolrhoda Bks. 1996 48p il (Carolrhoda earth watch book) lib bdg $21.27 (3-6)   **551.2**

1. Earthquakes
ISBN 0-87614-888-7   LC 94-36178

The author offers "explanations for how and where earthquakes occur, how scientists are working to predict them, and how to survive if one strikes. In addition to photographs, a number of informative charts and graphs extend the text. . . . This book is informative enough for reports, yet readable and visually appealing to browsers." SLJ

Includes glossary

551.3   Surface and exogenous processes and their agents

Simon, Seymour, 1931-

Icebergs and glaciers. Morrow 1987 unp il hardcover o.p. paperback available $5.95 (3-5)   **551.3**

1. Glaciers 2. Icebergs
ISBN 0-688-16705-5 (pa)   LC 86-18142

"After an explanation of the consistency of snowflakes, packed snow, and ice fields, the text describes the movement of glaciers by sliding or creeping, various processes of measurement, landscape alteration, geological effects of glacial movement, and the formation of icebergs." Bull Cent Child Books

The author "chronicles the development of glaciers and icebergs with a wonderfully clear, almost Spartan text that receives all of the support necessary from the magnificent color photographs which accompany it. . . . This book would be an excellent addition to any elementary school library or any personal juvenile collection." Appraisal

551.4   Geomorphology and hydrosphere

Kaplan, Elizabeth, 1956-

The tundra. Marshall Cavendish 1995 64p il (Biomes of the world) lib bdg $25.64 (4-6)   **551.4**

1. Tundra ecology 2. Arctic regions
ISBN 0-7614-0080-X   LC 95-2192

This book "concerns life in 'the earth's coldest biome,' including seasonal changes in the arctic tundra, the fragile ecosystem of the alpine tundra, wildlife from algae to musk oxen, and environmental hazards." Booklist

Includes bibliographical references

Kramer, Stephen

Caves; photographs by Kenrick L. Day. Carolrhoda Bks. 1995 48p il (Nature in action) lib bdg $21.27; pa $7.95 (4-6)   **551.4**

1. Caves
ISBN 0-87614-447-4 (lib bdg); 0-87614-896-8 (pa)
     LC 93-42136

Kramer, Stephen—*Continued*

The author "explains many aspects of speleology. He discusses various kinds of caves but focuses on limestone caves, describing the creation of stalactites, stalagmites, and other speleothems, giving an overview of cave flora and fauna, and offering guidelines for those interested in exploring caves themselves." Bull Cent Child Books

"Through an enticing introduction, full-color photographs of spectacular sites and features, and a generally accurate and useful text, this book provides readers with a glimpse of the alluring world of caving." SLJ

Includes glossary

Simon, Seymour, 1931-

Mountains. Morrow Junior Bks. 1994 unp il hardcover o.p. paperback available $6.95 (3-6)
551.4
1. Mountains
ISBN 0-688-15477-8 (pa)   LC 93-11398
Introduces various mountain ranges, how they are formed and shaped, and how they affect vegetation and animals, including humans

"The striking color photographs work well with the clear text to illustrate key points and highlight the diversity among the Earth's mountain ranges." Horn Book Guide

Zoehfeld, Kathleen Weidner

How mountains are made; illustrated by James Graham Hale. HarperCollins Pubs. 1995 29p il maps (Let's-read-and-find-out science) lib bdg $15.89; pa $4.95 (k-3)   **551.4**
1. Mountains 2. Geology
ISBN 0-06-024510-7 (lib bdg); 0-06-445128-3 (pa)
LC 93-45436
"Four children and a dog climbing a forest trail provide the framework for this discussion of mountains. Along the way, the knowledgeable characters explain the earth's structure and tectonic plates as well as the different types of mountains and how they are formed." Booklist

"The text and illustrations work together well in this sequential, well-organized book. Much credit goes to Hale's engaging watercolor illustrations done in cheery colors; they are simply drawn but add effective examples and diagrams." SLJ

551.46 Hydrosphere. Oceanography

Earle, Sylvia A., 1935-

Dive! my adventures in the deep frontier. National Geographic Soc. 1999 64p il map $18.95 (4-6)   **551.46**
1. Underwater exploration 2. Submarine diving
ISBN 0-7922-7144-0   LC 98-11480
The author relates some of her adventures studying and exploring the world's oceans, including tracking whales, living in an underwater laboratory, and helping to design a deep water submarine

"In this extraordinary photo-essay, an eminent marine biologist and ocean explorer combines personal adventure and scientific fact with glorious color action pictures." Booklist

Includes glossary

Gibbons, Gail

Exploring the deep, dark sea. Little, Brown 1999 unp il $14.95 (k-3)   **551.46**
1. Underwater exploration 2. Ocean bottom 3. Marine biology
ISBN 0-316-30945-1   LC 98-14443
"From the sunlight zone to the abyss, Gibbons follows the crew of a deep-diving submersible craft into the ocean depths, noting the changes in terrain and animal life at the various levels. Labels identify parts of the craft and the many animals, and explanations of the differing ecologies of the many levels are brief. Thoughtful attention to page design and narrative produce an account that is both spare and surprisingly rich." Horn Book Guide

Simon, Seymour, 1931-

Oceans. Morrow Junior Bks. 1990 unp il $16 (3-6)   **551.46**
1. Ocean
ISBN 0-688-09453-8   LC 89-28452
This book "covers the geography of the ocean floor, major currents, and El Nino (a shift in the prevailing currents that causes severe climactic changes). Tides, tsunami, waves, coastal erosion, and marine life are also touched upon." Booklist

"Simon presents clear, simplified explanations of natural phenomena with well-chosen full-color photographs that go beyond decoration. He includes good black-and-white diagrams of how tides work and how waves form and transfer energy. The endpapers are maps of the world showing how and where the major currents flow." SLJ

Stille, Darlene R.

Oceans. Children's Press 1999 47p il maps $22; pa $6.95 (2-4)   **551.46**
1. Ocean
ISBN 0-516-21510-8; 0-516-26768-X (pa)
LC 98-53857
"A True book"
An introduction to the ocean describing its physical characteristics, the plants and animals that live in or near it, and its importance to life on Earth

Includes bibliographical references

Sullivan, George

To the bottom of the sea; the exploration of exotic life, the Titanic, and other secrets of the oceans. 21st Cent. Bks. (Brookfield) 1999 80p il lib bdg $25.40 (5 and up)   **551.46**
1. Underwater exploration 2. Shipwrecks
ISBN 0-7613-0352-9   LC 98-41263
Examines different methods and technologies of undersea exploration, both past and present, the scientific discoveries that have been made, and the shipwrecks that have been explored

"Black-and-white and full-color photographs accompany the text. . . . Interesting and readable, this title is also useful for homework support." SLJ

Includes bibliographical references

VanCleave, Janice Pratt

Janice VanCleave's oceans for every kid; easy activities that make learning science fun. Wiley 1996 245p il maps (Science for every kid series) hardcover o.p. paperback available $12.95 (4 and up)   **551.46**

    1. Oceanography

    ISBN 0-471-12453-2 (pa)   LC 95-9201

Includes information on techniques and technologies of oceanography, the topology of the ocean floor, movement of the sea, properties of sea water, and life in the sea

"An engaging overview of marine sciences. Each chapter explores a topic in two to four pages, then poses questions accompanied by lucid explanations." SLJ

Includes glossary

551.48   Hydrology

Cole, Joanna

The magic school bus at the waterworks; illustrated by Bruce Degen. Scholastic 1986 39p il $15.95; pa $4.95 (2-4)   **551.48**

    1. Water 2. Water supply

    ISBN 0-590-43739-9; 0-590-40360-5 (pa)

                      LC 86-6672

Also available Spanish language edition and CD-ROM version

The author presents "specific facts about water and a memorable image of the water cycle process. The story involves a 'strange' teacher who takes her class on a magical trip: up to the clouds—down to earth in raindrops—down a stream into a reservoir where the water is purified—finally into the underground pipes leading back to school. The illustrations both enhance the humor and provide visual presentation of the water cycle." Appraisal

Dorros, Arthur

Follow the water from brook to ocean; written and illustrated by Arthur Dorros. HarperCollins Pubs. 1991 32p il (Let's-read-and-find-out science book) hardcover o.p. paperback available $4.95 (k-3)   **551.48**

    1. Water

    ISBN 0-06-445115-1 (pa)   LC 90-1438

Explains how water flows from brooks, to streams, to rivers, over waterfalls, through canyons and dams, to eventually reach the ocean

"An excellent presentation of introductory material about water. . . . The illustrations are simple, almost childlike, in soft colors." SLJ

Hiscock, Bruce, 1940-

The big rivers; the Missouri, the Mississippi, and the Ohio; written and illustrated by Bruce Hiscock. Atheneum Bks. for Young Readers 1997 unp il maps $16 (2-4)   **551.48**

    1. Floods 2. Mississippi River valley

    ISBN 0-689-80871-2   LC 96-2435

Describes the conditions that led up to the severe flooding in the Mississippi River Valley in 1993

"Hiscock's well-conceived and appealing watercolor paintings, some in double-page spreads, demonstrate clearly what is happening. His time line of rainfall and flood levels in 1993 is particularly effective. An excellent resource for an increasingly timely topic." Booklist

Lauber, Patricia, 1924-

Flood; wrestling with the Mississippi. National Geographic Soc. 1996 63p il maps $18.95 (4 and up)   **551.48**

    1. Floods 2. Mississippi River

    ISBN 0-7922-4141-X   LC 95-47338

This provides a "description of the Mississippi River: its modern history as a mighty natural force, as enemy and ally; and how it has impacted the lives of people who depend on it for better and for worse. Lauber looks at the 1927 and 1993 floods and highlights what has been learned about harnessing and controlling the Mississippi. Each page is well balanced with text and informative, well-chosen full-color photographs or drawings." SLJ

Rauzon, Mark J.

Water, water everywhere; [by] Mark J. Rauzon and Cynthia Overbeck Bix. Sierra Club Bks. for Children 1994 32p il $14.95; pa $6.95 (k-3)

                                551.48

    1. Water

    ISBN 0-87156-598-6; 0-87156-383-5 (pa)

                  LC 92-34521

Describes the forms water takes, how it has shaped Earth, and its importance to life

"Water's vital role in the life of our planet is vividly portrayed in a crisp, economical text that cultivates respect for the environment. . . . Striking, often full-page, color photographs will engage the imagination of young readers." Horn Book Guide

551.5   Meteorology

Branley, Franklyn Mansfield, 1915-

Air is all around you; by Franklyn M. Branley; illustrated by Holly Keller. rev ed. Crowell 1986 31p il (Let's-read-and-find-out science book) hardcover o.p. paperback available $4.95 (k-1)

                               551.5

    1. Air

    ISBN 0-06-445048-1 (pa)   LC 85-47884

    Also available Audiobook version

A revised and newly illustrated edition of the title first published 1962

Describes the various properties of air and shows how to prove that air takes up space and that there is air dissolved in water

"Illustrations in both bold and pastel colors are coordinated with the easy-to-read text and make this an eye-pleasing and informative book." SLJ

Kahl, Jonathan D.
National Audubon Society first field guide:
weather. Scholastic 1998 159p il $17.95; pa
$10.95 (4 and up)   **551.5**
1. Weather 2. Meteorology
ISBN 0-590-05469-4; 0-590-05488-0 (pa)
                                    LC 98-2938
Provides an overview of various weather conditions,
how they develop, and how they are studied
Includes glossary and bibliographical references

Simon, Seymour, 1931-
Weather. Morrow Junior Bks. 1993 unp il
$15.95; lib bdg $14.93; pa $6.95 (3-6)   **551.5**
1. Weather 2. Meteorology
ISBN 0-688-10546-7; 0-688-10547-5 (lib bdg);
0-688-17521-X (pa)   LC 92-31069
Explores the causes, changing patterns, and forecasting
of weather
"Gorgeous full-page color photos, helped by a few cogent diagrams, illustrate Simon's outline of how weather
works. . . . The organization is clear and logical." Bull
Cent Child Books

VanCleave, Janice Pratt
Janice VanCleave's weather; mind-boggling
experiments you can turn into science fair projects;
[by] Janice VanCleave. Wiley 1995 89p il
(Spectacular science projects series) pa $10.95 (4
and up)   **551.5**
1. Weather 2. Science projects 3. Science—Experiments
ISBN 0-471-03231-X   LC 94-25646
"Using everyday household items, the reading audience can demonstrate to itself such phenomena as differences in climate at different points on the Earth, lightning, wind direction and intensity, clouds, rain, fronts,
etc. Through excellent directions and adequate illustrations, the reader can do 20 simple experiments at little
or no cost that demonstrate many aspects of the weather." Sci Books Films
Includes glossary

551.51 Composition, regions, dynamics of atmosphere

Dorros, Arthur
Feel the wind; written and illustrated by Arthur
Dorros. Crowell 1989 32p il
(Let's-read-and-find-out science book) lib bdg
$15.89; pa $4.95 (k-3)   **551.51**
1. Winds
ISBN 0-690-04741-X (lib bdg); 0-06-445095-3 (pa)
                                    LC 88-18961
"The motion of air in the form of wind is discernible
in many ways. Simple text accompanied by bright illustrations explains the causes, power, effects, and uses of
wind. Encourages outdoor experimentation." Sci Child

551.55 Atmospheric disturbances and formations

Branley, Franklyn Mansfield, 1915-
Flash, crash, rumble, and roll; by Franklyn M.
Branley; illustrated by True Kelley. newly il ed.
HarperCollins Pubs. 1999 32p il
(Let's-read-and-find-out science) $15.95; lib bdg
$15.89; pa $4.95 (k-3)   **551.55**
1. Thunderstorms 2. Lightning
ISBN 0-06-027858-7; 0-06-027859-5 (lib bdg);
0-06-445179-8 (pa)   LC 97-43599
A revised and newly illustrated edition of the title first
published 1964 by Crowell
Explains how and why a thunderstorm occurs and
gives safety steps to follow when lightning is flashing
This offers "clear and informative explanations . . .
[and] colorful cartoonlike pictures." Horn Book Guide

Challoner, Jack
Hurricane & tornado; written by Jack Challoner.
Dorling Kindersley 2000 61p il maps (Eyewitness
books) $15.95; lib bdg $19.99 (4 and up) **551.55**
1. Weather 2. Natural disasters
ISBN 0-7894-5242-1; 0-7894-6804-2 (lib bdg)
                                    LC 99-44160
Describes dangerous and destructive weather conditions around the world, such as thunderstorms, tornadoes,
hurricanes, lightning, hail, and drought with photographs,
historical background, and legends

Cole, Joanna
The magic school bus inside a hurricane;
illustrated by Bruce Degen. Scholastic 1995 unp il
$15.95; pa $4.99 (2-4)   **551.55**
1. Hurricanes 2. Weather 3. Meteorology
ISBN 0-590-44686-X; 0-590-44687-8 (pa)
                                    LC 94-34703
Also available Spanish language edition and CD-ROM
version
"The magic school bus changes into a weather balloon
and then into an airplane as the class experiences the
hurricane and a spin-off tornado firsthand. As usual, Ms.
Frizzle's wardrobe is as changeable as the weather. The
familiar format features lots of weather information delivered via students' written reports and spoken comments." SLJ
"Cole presents the science in easy-to-understand terms,
with Degen clarifying the concepts and adding comic relief through double-page-spread pictures that brim with
details." Booklist

Lauber, Patricia, 1924-
Hurricanes; Earth's mightiest storms. Scholastic
1996 64p il maps $16.95 (4 and up)   **551.55**
1. Hurricanes
ISBN 0-590-47406-5   LC 95-25788
Tells how hurricanes form, how scientists study them,
and how they have affected the United States throughout
this century

Lauber, Patricia, 1924-—*Continued*

"The simple, dramatic prose communicates the rising tension and the terrifying facts. . . . Browsers will start with the clearly captioned photos of pounding seas, wrecked neighborhoods, and flattened trees. The spacious book design, with large type, thick paper, wide margins, and clear maps and diagrams, will keep them reading." Booklist

Includes bibliographical references

Simon, Seymour, 1931-

Storms. Morrow Junior Bks. 1989 unp il hardcover o.p. paperback available $5.95 (3-6)
551.55

1. Storms

ISBN 0-688-11708-2 (pa)　　　LC 88-22045

This book describes the atmospheric conditions which create thunderstorms, hailstorms, lightning, tornadoes, and hurricanes and how violent weather affects the environment and people

"The half- to full-page glossy color photographs are sure to attract young readers as will the subject. *Storms* is an excellent way to introduce the science of meteorology to children." Sci Books Films

Tornadoes. Morrow Junior Bks. 1999 unp il maps $16.95; lib bdg $16.89 (3-6)　　**551.55**

1. Tornadoes

ISBN 0-688-14646-5; 0-688-14647-3 (lib bdg)
LC 98-27953

Describes the location, nature, development, measurement, and destructive effects of tornadoes, as well as how to stay out of danger from them

"Incredible full-color photographs and diagrams, clearly portraying the different formations and devastating power of the windstorms, complement the text perfectly." Booklist

551.56　Atmospheric electricity and optics

Kramer, Stephen

Lightning; photographs by Warren Faidley. Carolrhoda Bks. 1992 48p il (Nature in action) lib bdg $21.27; pa $7.95 (4-6)　　**551.56**

1. Lightning

ISBN 0-87614-659-0 (lib bdg); 0-87614-617-5 (pa)
LC 91-21793

This introduction to lightning "explains how a thunderhead develops, how lightning results from negatively and positively charged electrons, kinds of lightning, and [includes] safety information." Bull Cent Child Books

"Diagrams supplement the well-written narrative in describing scientific concepts. Exceptionally fine, full-color photographs—each a work of art—perfectly illustrate the text, powerfully and spectacularly showing the majesty and might of this phenomenon." SLJ

Includes glossary

Simon, Seymour, 1931-

Lightning. Morrow Junior Bks. 1997 unp il $16; lib bdg $16.89; pa $5.95 (3-6)　　**551.56**

1. Lightning

ISBN 0-688-14638-4; 0-688-14639-2 (lib bdg); 0-688-16706-3 (pa)　　　LC 96-16962

Photographs and text explore the natural phenomenon of lightning

"The subject is exciting, the information is amazing, and the full-color photographs are riveting. . . . Simon's explanations are concise but thorough." Booklist

551.57　Hydrometeorology

Branley, Franklyn Mansfield, 1915-

Down comes the rain; by Franklyn M. Branley; illustrated by James Graham Hale. HarperCollins Pubs. 1997 31p il (Let's-read-and-find-out science) lib bdg $15.89; pa $4.95 (k-3)　　**551.57**

1. Rain 2. Clouds

ISBN 0-06-025338-X (lib bdg); 0-06-445166-6 (pa)
LC 96-3519

A revised and newly illustrated edition of Rain & hail published 1983 by Crowell

The author explains "how water is recycled, how clouds are formed, and why rain and hail occur. A few easy science activities are included. . . . The pen-and-ink with watercolor wash paintings clearly interpret the concepts presented on each page." SLJ

Snow is falling; by Franklyn M. Branley; illustrated by Holly Keller. HarperCollins Pubs. 2000 33p il (Let's-read-and-find-out science) $15.95; lib bdg $15.89; pa $4.95 (k-1)　　**551.57**

1. Snow

ISBN 0-06-027990-7; 0-06-027991-5 (lib bdg); 0-06-445186-0 (pa)　　　LC 98-23106

A revised and newly illustrated edition of the title first published 1963 by Crowell

Describes snow's physical qualities and how quantities of it can be fun as well as dangerous

"Keller's new illustrations are a good match for the spare, informative text. A few easy activities explore snow's different properties, and a list of websites is appended." Horn Book Guide

De Paola, Tomie, 1934-

The cloud book; words and pictures by Tomie de Paola. Holiday House 1975 30p il lib bdg $16.95; pa $6.95 (k-3)　　**551.57**

1. Clouds

ISBN 0-8234-0259-2 (lib bdg); 0-8234-0531-1 (pa)

The author instructs "young readers about the ten most common types of clouds, how they were named, and what they mean in terms of changing weather. Actually a very good text to use for early science instruction. Includes a scattering of traditional myths that have clouds as a basis." Adventuring with Books

Markle, Sandra, 1946-

A rainy day; illustrated by Cathy Johnson. Orchard Bks. 1993 unp il lib bdg $16.99 (k-2)
551.57

1. Rain

ISBN 0-531-08576-7　　　LC 91-17059

Markle, Sandra, 1946—*Continued*

Examines simple scientific concepts by observing the effect of raindrops on puddles, the sky, animals, and the surrounding landscape on a rainy day

"The text is straightforward and friendly, associating scientific concepts with familiar objects and examples. The visual narrative is supplied by watercolors that picture a young girl in a yellow slicker exploring her environment before, during, and after the rain." Booklist

McMillan, Bruce

The weather sky; photographed, illustrated, and written by Bruce McMillan. Farrar, Straus & Giroux 1991 40p il maps $16.95 (4 and up)

551.57

1. Weather 2. Clouds
ISBN 0-374-38261-1   LC 90-56151

A study of weather patterns and clouds that occur in the Earth's temperate zones

"The well-chosen black-and-white and color photographs . . . are as important in conveying the information as the text. . . . A clear and coherent introduction to meteorology that will certainly encourage readers to do some forecasting of their own." SLJ

Includes glossary

551.6   Climatology and weather

Arnold, Caroline, 1944-

El Niño; stormy weather for people and wildlife. Clarion Bks. 1998 48p il $16 (4 and up)   **551.6**
1. El Niño (Ocean current) 2. Climate
ISBN 0-395-77602-3   LC 98-4826

Explores the nature of the El Niño current and its effects on people and wildlife

This book has a "readable, informative text. . . . Full-color photos, a computer-image series, diagrams, and Internet sources bolster the narrative." SLJ

Includes glossary and bibliographical references

Gibbons, Gail

Weather words and what they mean. Holiday House 1990 unp il $16.95; pa $6.95 (k-3)   **551.6**
1. Weather
ISBN 0-8234-0805-1; 0-8234-0952-X (pa)
LC 89-39515

The author discusses the meaning of meteorological terms such as temperature, air pressure, thunderstorm and moisture

"Gibbons' easily identifiable artistic style works well with her explanations of sometimes misunderstood weather-related terms. Drawings are appealing, attractively arranged, and closely matched to the textual information. . . . An attractive introduction for weather units in the primary grades." SLJ

Seibert, Patricia

Discovering El Niño; how fable and fact together help explain the weather; illustrated by Jan Davey Ellis. Millbrook Press 1999 32p il lib bdg $22.90 (k-3)   **551.6**
1. El Niño (Ocean current) 2. Climate
ISBN 0-7613-1273-0   LC 99-13757

Traces the weather phenomenon known as El Niño from its first observation near Peruvian fishing villages to more recent appearances, discussing how scientists monitor it and how it affects other aspects of the weather

"Colorful illustrations accompany this well-written text." Horn Book

Singer, Marilyn, 1948-

On the same day in March; a tour of the world's weather; illustrated by Frané Lessac. HarperCollins Pubs. 2000 unp il $15.95; lib bdg $15.89 (k-3)   **551.6**
1. Weather
ISBN 0-06-028187-1; 0-06-028188-X (lib bdg)
LC 98-52797

Highlights a wide variety of weather conditions by taking a tour around the world and examining weather in different places on the same day in March

"For each setting, singer provides a few lines of lyrical text that vividly create the climate . . . as Lessac's single-and double-page spreads colorfully show us the way the weather and the world look. An appended author's note adds factual information to the mix, an endpaper map puts the places readers will visit in a global context. The book doubles as a delightfully agreeable introduction to both climatology and geography." Booklist

551.63   Weather forecasting and forecasts, reporting and reports

Gibbons, Gail

Weather forecasting. Four Winds Press 1987 unp il hardcover o.p. paperback available $5.99 (k-3)   **551.63**
1. Weather forecasting
ISBN 0-689-71683-4 (pa)   LC 86-7602

"The book is divided into four sections, one per season, which treat different kinds of weather as they're observed, recorded, and reported at a weather station." Bull Cent Child Books

"Any child can learn the basic concepts from the text at the bottom of each page, while the precocious can garner an impressive weather vocabulary by absorbing the terms labeled and defined within the artwork. Brightly illustrated with the artist's usual bold, flat colors, this book will serve as an appealing introduction to weather forecasting for young children." Booklist

Kahl, Jonathan D.

Weather watch; forecasting the weather; by Jonathan D.W. Kahl. Lerner Publs. 1996 72p il maps (How's the weather?) $21.27 (4-6)   **551.63**
1. Weather forecasting
ISBN 0-8225-2529-1   LC 95-9725

"Basic information on weather systems, maps, and forecasting tools used by the National Weather Service and other agencies worldwide is provided in a clear, simple text supplemented by good-quality, full-color photographs and diagrams." SLJ

Includes glossary

552 Petrology

Christian, Peggy
If you find a rock; written by Peggy Christian; photographs by Barbara Hirsch Lember. Harcourt 2000 unp il $16 (k-3)   **552**
  1. Rocks
  ISBN 0-15-239339-0   LC 98-48938
Celebrates the variety of rocks that can be found, including skipping rocks, chalk rocks, and splashing rocks
"Poetic text and thoughtfully composed, hand-tinted photographs combine to explore the variety and purposes of rocks. . . . Lember's intriguing artwork is especially suited to the quiet text. . . . A good story hour selection, especially for introducing primary geology units or setting the mood for creative writing." Booklist

De Paola, Tomie, 1934-
The quicksand book. Holiday House 1977 unp il lib bdg $16.95; pa $6.95 (k-3)   **552**
  1. Quicksand
  ISBN 0-8234-0291-6 (lib bdg); 0-8234-0532-X (pa)
                        LC 76-28762
Also available Spanish language edition
"Jungle Girl, swinging on a vine from her treehouse, falls into a patch of . . . [quicksand] but, fortunately, is observed by Jungle Boy. As she slowly sinks, her scholarly bespectacled young Tarzan delivers a long but interesting lecture on the properties of and useful means of rescue from quicksand." Horn Book
"De Paola "uses a picture-book format to present basic science information in an utterly appealing, humorous way. . . . Very funny and very sensible." SLJ

Gans, Roma, 1894-1996
Let's go rock collecting; illustrated by Holly Keller. newly il ed. HarperCollins Pubs. 1997 31p il (Let's-read-and-find-out science) $15.95; lib bdg $15.89 (k-2)   **552**
  1. Rocks—Collectors and collecting
  ISBN 0-06-027282-1; 0-06-027283-X (lib bdg)
                        LC 95-44999
A revised and newly illustrated edition of Rock collecting, published 1984 by Crowell
Describes the formation and characteristics of igneous, metamorphic, and sedimentary rocks and how to recognize and collect them
"The excellent diagrams, full-color photographs of specimens, and minor textual changes clarify the concepts (for example, Mohs' scale of hardness) and extend the presentation. . . . The pair of youngsters featured in Keller's brightly colored illustrations . . . convey the joys of being a rock hound." SLJ

Ricciuti, Edward R.
National Audubon Society first field guide: rocks and minerals; written by Edward Ricciuti, Margaret W. Carruthers. Scholastic 1998 159p il $17.95; pa $11.95 (4 and up)   **552**
  1. Rocks 2. Minerals
  ISBN 0-590-05463-5; 0-590-05484-8 (pa)
                        LC 97-17991

This aims to help beginning naturalists observe and understand over 150 types of rocks and minerals
This is "illustrated with vibrant, full-color photographs. . . . Attractive and useful." SLJ
Includes glossary and bibliographical references

VanCleave, Janice Pratt
Janice VanCleave's rocks and minerals; mind-boggling experiments you can turn into science fair projects. Wiley 1996 90p il (Spectacular science projects series) pa $10.95 (4 and up)   **552**
  1. Rocks 2. Minerals 3. Science projects 4. Science—Experiments
  ISBN 0-471-10269-5   LC 95-10324
"The experiments lead the investigator through a range of topics such as crystal shapes; mineral characteristics . . . magnetism in minerals; sedimentary, metamorphic, and igneous rock formation; rock weathering; fossil types and formation; and how to put together a mineral, rock, or fossil collection." Sci Books Films
"VanCleave presents stunningly clear, direct, and informative projects. They are generally simple enough for self-directed students to do on their own, but a teacher's guidance would be helpful." SLJ
Includes glossary

553.6 Other economic materials

Dewey, Jennifer
Mud matters; written and illustrated by Jennifer Owings Dewey; photographs by Stephen Trimble. Marshall Cavendish 1998 72p il $15.95 (4-6)
                              553.6
  1. Clay
  ISBN 0-7614-5014-9   LC 97-32929
A personal account describing various uses of mud in such activities as ritual dancing, making pottery, building villages, contructing nests, playing games, and celebrating customs
"Dewey's lively account includes rich descriptions of the mucky stuff, interesting information, and episodes from her own childhood. . . . The four chapters are accompanied by striking full-page photos and Dewey's own characteristically fine pencil drawings." Horn Book Guide
Includes glossary

Prager, Ellen J.
Sand; illustrated by Nancy Woodman. National Geographic Soc. 2000 29p il $15.95 (k-3) **553.6**
  1. Sand
  ISBN 0-7922-7104-1   LC 99-29943
Describes the formation of sand from materials such as coral, rock, or crystals and shows how it can be moved through water, wind, ice, and other erosion agents
"Prager's part science, part fun-and-games approach gives this book lots of appeal. A seagull disguised as a sleuth describes what sand is made of and how it is created. . . . Lively format, a 'digital collage' of pastels on sandpaper, bright watercolors, and sharp color photographs. A fun, fact-filled book." Booklist

553.7 Water

Hooper, Meredith
The drop in my drink; the story of water on our planet; illustrated by Chris Coady. Viking 1998 unp il $16.99 (3-5)   **553.7**
1. Water
ISBN 0-670-87618-6   LC 97-61733
This is the "story of water—where it comes from, how it behaves, why it matters—and the crucial role it has played throughout life on earth. The eye-catching illustrations are realistic and thought-provoking." Sci Child

Wick, Walter
A drop of water; a book of science and wonder; written and photographed by Walter Wick. Scholastic 1997 40p il $16.95 (4-6)   **553.7**
1. Water
ISBN 0-590-22197-3   LC 95-30068
The author "uses simple techniques to show water properties such as surface tension, adhesion, capillary attraction, molecular motion, freezing, evaporation, and condensation." Booklist
"This title is an elegant synthesis of science and art. . . . The close-up photographs are breathtakingly distinct; and the clarity provided by the combination of concept, text, and photography of this quality is noteworthy." Bull Cent Child Books

560 Paleontology. Paleozoology

Aliki
Fossils tell of long ago. rev ed. Crowell 1990 32p il (Let's-read-and-find-out science book) hardcover o.p. paperback available $4.95 (k-3)
560
1. Fossils
ISBN 0-06-445093-7 (pa)   LC 89-17247
Also available Spanish language edition
First published 1972
"Information about how fossils are formed and discovered is presented in simple text and an appealing variety of colorful illustrations. Includes directions for creating a fossil." Sci Child

Henderson, Douglas
Dinosaur tree. Bradbury Press 1994 31p il $16; pa $5.99 (2-4)   **560**
1. Fossil plants 2. Dinosaurs
ISBN 0-02-743547-4; 0-689-82943-4 (pa)
LC 93-34204
This book traces the hypothetical life cycle of a conifer tree not fossilized in the Petrified Forest National Park in Arizona. "Each full-page painting faces a page of text that explains the surrounding atmospheric, plant, and animal conditions as [the] tree grows in a Triassic forest. The tree's story starts 225 million years ago, and readers see it at 4 years, 50 years, 200 years, 300 years, 400 years, 500 years, and then . . . fossilization. Dinosaurs that lived at the time are pictured in their natural surroundings." SLJ
Includes glossary

Lessem, Don
Dinosaurs to dodos; an encyclopedia of extinct animals; illustrated by Jan Sovak. Scholastic 1999 112p il $16.95 (4 and up)   **560**
1. Prehistoric animals 2. Fossils 3. Extinct animals
ISBN 0-590-31684-2   LC 98-25863
Presents the names, physical characteristics, and places of origin of a variety of extinct animals, arranged chronologically into eras, periods, and epochs, and discusses times of mass extinction
This book is "good for browsing as well as for homework. The full-color illustrations are lively and realistic." SLJ
Includes bibliographical references

Lindsay, William, 1956-
Prehistoric life; photographed by Harry Taylor. Knopf 1994 63p il maps (Eyewitness books) (4 and up)   **560**
1. Fossils 2. Evolution
LC 93-32076
Also available Spanish language edition
Available DK Pub. edition $15.95; lib bdg $19.99 (ISBN 0-7894-5868-3; 0-7894-6601-5)
"A Dorling Kindersley book"
The author discusses "the fossil record and its evolutionary implications. . . . The information presented with the excellent photos of fossils and reconstructions is fact focused and generally accurate. In addition to presentations on various early life forms, there are pages devoted to the ice ages, fossil hunting, and extinctions." Sci Books Films

Taylor, Paul D., 1953-
Fossil. Knopf 1990 63p il (Eyewitness books) (4 and up)   **560**
1. Fossils
LC 89-36444
Also available Spanish language edition
Available DK Pub. edition $15.95; lib bdg $19.99 (ISBN 0-7894-5840-3; 0-7894-6568-X)
This book "details how fossils are formed and what man has learned about life on Earth from discovering them. The sections on early paleontology, fossil folklore, and the tools of paleontology are particularly well done." SLJ

Thompson, Sharon Elaine, 1952-
Death trap; the story of the La Brea Tar Pits. Lerner Publs. 1995 72p il lib bdg $23.95 (4 and up)   **560**
1. Fossils 2. California—Antiquities
ISBN 0-8225-2851-7   LC 93-39583
Thompson "begins at Hancock Park in Los Angeles, California, the site of the La Brea Tar Pits. She describes the unique conditions 25 million years ago that caused the formation of the asphalt pools where thousands of Ice Age animals were trapped, their bones preserved in the oily asphalt. . . . [She also] discusses how scientists use the fossil findings to learn more about Ice Age animal populations, migration patterns, climate, vegetarian and animal extinctions." Appraisal
"Excellent artist's re-creations of the prehistoric bring extra life to a fascinating story." Booklist
Includes glossary

The **Visual** dictionary of prehistoric life. Dorling
Kindersley 1995 64p il (Eyewitness visual
dictionaries) $15.95 (4 and up)　　　**560**
1. Prehistoric peoples 2. Fossils 3. Dinosaurs
ISBN 1-56458-859-9　　　　　　LC 94-30705
This volume presents a "history of the development of
life on earth through skillful integration of text, diagrams, and color photographs of fossils. Representations
of biological development are divided into sections on
plants and animals, introduced by text that sets the time
frame and evolutionary frame. Useful charts allow readers to compare population growth and extinction over
time." Horn Book Guide

567.9　Fossil reptiles. Dinosaurs

Arnold, Caroline, 1944-
Dinosaur mountain; graveyard of the past;
photographs by Richard Hewett. Clarion Bks. 1989
48p il $16 (4 and up)　　　　　　**567.9**
1. Dinosaurs 2. Dinosaur National Monument (Colo.
and Utah)
ISBN 0-89919-693-4　　　　　　LC 88-30218
This book describes the work of paleontologists in
learning about dinosaurs, especially the discoveries made
at Dinosaur National Monument
"Arnold seamlessly blends general information about
paleontology with facts about specific finds near the
Monument and additionally offers intriguing descriptions
of ongoing work. . . . Lively writing, a dramtic subject,
and a sure-fire hit with young readers." Horn Book

Dinosaurs all around; an artist's view of the
prehistoric world; photographs by Richard Hewett.
Clarion Bks. 1993 48p il $14.95; pa $7.95 (4 and
up)　　　　　　**567.9**
1. Dinosaurs
ISBN 0-395-62363-4; 0-395-86620-0 (pa)
LC 92-5726
On a visit to the workshop of Stephen and Sylvia
Czerkas where a life-size dinosaur model is being constructed, the reader learns much information about dinosaurs and how conclusions are made from fossil remains
"The meticulous work involved in creating the sculptures is pictured and described in clear photographs and
a direct, concise text." Horn Book

Bishop, Nic, 1955-
Digging for bird-dinosaurs; an expedition to
Madagascar. Houghton Mifflin 2000 48p il $16 (4
and up)　　　　　　**567.9**
1. Forster, Cathy 2. Dinosaurs 3. Birds 4. Fossils
5. Madagascar—Description
ISBN 0-395-96056-8　　　　　　LC 99-36145
The story of Cathy Forster's experiences as a member
of a team of paleontologists who went on an expedition
to the island of Madagascar in 1998 to search for fossil
birds
"Throughout the engaging, personal story, Bishop
presents a great deal of information in highly readable,
age-appropriate language, well matched by exceptional
full-color images of scientists at work and the Malagasy
landscape and people." Booklist
Includes bibliographical references

Cole, Joanna
The magic school bus: in the time of the
dinosaurs; illustrated by Bruce Degen. Scholastic
1994 unp il $15.95; pa $4.99 (2-4)　　　**567.9**
1. Dinosaurs
ISBN 0-590-44688-6; 0-590-44639-4 (pa)
LC 93-5753
Also available Spanish language edition and CD-ROM
version
"The fashionable Ms. Frizzle warps her students back
to the late Triassic period, where they begin a journey
forward through time in search of Maiasaura eggs for
Jeff, the Friz's paleontologist friend from high school."
Bull Cent Child Books
"An eye-catching, humorous book with bright, busy il-
lustrations . . . packed with information." Sci Books
Films

Dingus, Lowell
The tiniest giants; discovering dinosaur eggs;
[by] Lowell Dingus and Luis Chiappe. Doubleday
Bks. for Young Readers 1999 42p il $17.95 (4 and
up)　　　　　　**567.9**
1. Dinosaurs 2. Fossils
ISBN 0-385-32642-4　　　　　　LC 98-28886
"Two paleontologists recount their expedition to Patagonia, where they discovered a nesting ground that included eggs containing sauropod embryos. . . . The
book, illustrated with color photos, is a significant primary resource providing a firsthand description of how a dinosaur hunt is planned and performed and the post-
expedition lab research that must be done." Horn Book
Guide
Includes glossary and bibliographical references

Dinosaurs of the world; with an introduction by
Mark Norell; consultants, Michael Benton, Tom
Holtz; edited by Chris Marshall. Marshall
Cavendish 1998 11v il maps set $329.95 (4 and
up)　　　　　　**567.9**
1. Dinosaurs—Encyclopedias
ISBN 0-7614-7072-7　　　　　　LC 97-43365
"The first 10 volumes contain more than 200 articles
on dinosaurs and related topics. Volume 11 has been
designated the 'reference' volume, and features a brief
history of the earth, time lines, a list of famous fossil
sites and digs, dinosaur family trees, brief biographies of
24 dinosaur hunters, museums with pertinent collections,
and a section called 'Things to Do,' which lists resources
and activities." Booklist
"This superb set is current, well organized, and provides interesting and comprehensive coverage of life in
prehistoric times." SLJ

Dixon, Dougal, 1947-
Dougal Dixon's amazing dinosaurs; the fiercest,
the tallest, the smallest. Boyds Mills Press 2000
128p il lib bdg $17.95 (3-6)　　　　　　**567.9**
1. Dinosaurs
ISBN 1-563-97773-7
"Divided into four sections representing meat eaters,
long-necked plant eaters, armored dinosaurs, and two-
footed plant eaters, this book provides information on

Dixon, Dougal, 1947—*Continued*

these prehistoric creatures. Each double-page spread contains copious color illustrations and fact boxes that include helpful pronunciation guides." Horn Book Guide

"Dixon has compiled an impressive amount of information and organized it into an eye-catching, manageable format." Booklist

Includes bibliographical references

Dougal Dixon's dinosaurs. 2nd ed. Boyds Mills Press 1998 160p il $19.95 (4 and up)   **567.9**
1. Dinosaurs
ISBN 1-56397-722-2   LC 98-180620
First published 1993

The life and times of dinosaurs, from their evolution to the present-day discovery of their fossils

This "is a wonderful introduction to the most popular beasts of the ancient world. Loaded with full color illustrations and a wealth of dinosaur facts, it's sure to inspire young dinosaur enthusiasts to explore more fully this begone world." Appraisal

Dodson, Peter

An alphabet of dinosaurs; paintings by Wayne D. Barlowe; black-and-white illustrations by Michael Meaker. Scholastic 1995 unp il $16.95 (k-3)   **567.9**
1. Dinosaurs
ISBN 0-590-46486-8   LC 94-15522
"A Byron Preiss book"

"Using the alphabet as an arbitrary device, this book introduces 26 dinosaurs through brief informative text and two kinds of artwork. . . . Each right-hand page displays a full-color painting. On the left, a precise black-and-white ink drawing shows a full skeleton or a detail of bones, along with a few lines of text commenting on the dinosaur's physical features and habits." Booklist

"Barlowe's original artwork, more than the text . . . is what makes this alphabet book extraordinary. It shows how well illustration can work, by capturing a fine balance of realism, drama, and imagination." SLJ

Floca, Brian

Dinosaurs at the ends of the earth; the story of the Central Asiatic Expeditions. DK Ink 2000 unp il $15.95 (3-5)   **567.9**
1. Andrews, Roy Chapman, 1884-1960 2. Dinosaurs 3. Fossils
ISBN 0-7894-2539-4   LC 99-43071
"A Richard Jackson book"

Describes the expeditions led by Roy Chapman Andrews for New York's American Museum of Natural History to the Gobi Desert in Mongolia in an effort to uncover dinosaur fossils

"The upbeat dialogue feels historically appropriate, a tone that is reflected in the illustrations careful attention to period details, and the attention to scientific detail is also excellent." Horn Book Guide

Henderson, Douglas

Asteroid impact. Dial Bks. for Young Readers 2000 40p il map $16.99 (3-5)   **567.9**
1. Dinosaurs 2. Asteroids
ISBN 0-8037-2500-0   LC 99-38263

Text and illustrations explore the theory that the collision of an asteroid with the Earth ended the Cretaceous Period and caused the extinction of the dinosaurs

"Through vivid words and pictures, Henderson makes this lesson in Earth's history into a you-were-there experience that will captivate both children and adults. . . . Words and pictures work exceedingly well together. The illustrations, apparently acrylic paintings, are beautifully composed." Booklist

Lauber, Patricia, 1924-

Living with dinosaurs; illustrated by Douglas Henderson. Bradbury Press 1991 46p il maps hardcover o.p. paperback available $7.99 (3-6)   **567.9**
1. Dinosaurs
ISBN 0-689-82686-9 (pa)   LC 90-43265

This book "describes a stretch of sea and land in what is now Montana about 75 million years ago and depicts the dinosaurs, pterosaurs, mosasaurs, ammonites, and land and sea plants that lived in the area." Sci Books Films

Lessem, Don

Bigger than T. rex; the discovery of Giganotosaurus: the biggest meat-eating dinosaur ever found; illustrated by Robert F. Walters; scientific advisor, Rodolfo Coria. Crown 1997 32p il $16 (4 and up)   **567.9**
1. Dinosaurs 2. Fossils
ISBN 0-517-70930-9   LC 96-30562

Describes the discovery and reconstruction, in Patagonia, of the fossil remains of the largest carnivorous dinosaur yet known

This book "includes plenty of full-color photos from the actual dig. Brightly colored sketches make Giganotosaurus come to life. . . . This intriguing update to dinosaur collections will be both popular and useful." SLJ

Lindsay, William, 1956-

The great dinosaur atlas; written by William Lindsay; illustrated by Giuliano Fornari. DK Pub. 1999 64p il maps $19.95 (3-6)   **567.9**
1. Dinosaurs
ISBN 0-789-44728-2

A revised edition of the title first published 1991 by Messner

This book introduces "such subjects as the history of the shifting continents, archaeological excavations, and dinosaur characteristics. Information is clearly conveyed in the richly colored, incredibly detailed illustrations. . . . Lively prose effectively conveys the wealth of information by using comparisons kids can relate to; humor in text and subheads . . . will entertain as well as inform." Booklist

Norell, Mark

A nest of dinosaurs; the story of the Oviraptor; [by] Mark A. Norell and Lowell Dingus. Doubleday Bks. for Young Readers 1999 42p il $17.95 (5 and up)   **567.9**
1. Dinosaurs 2. Fossils
ISBN 0-385-32558-4   LC 98-7859

Norell, Mark—*Continued*

"Focusing on *Oviraptor,* a small, meat-eating dinosaur believed to steal eggs from other dinosaur nests, two paleontologists discuss their expeditions to a remote site in the Gobi Desert rich with Cretaceous Period fossils. In the process, the authors unearth not just dinosaur fossils, but the ways in which scientists develop and revise theories." Horn Book Guide

"A map of Mongolia and color and black-and-white photos and drawings are carefully placed to correspond with the text. . . . [This is a] veritable feast for the mind." SLJ

Includes glossary and bibliographical references

Parker, Steve

The age of the dinosaurs. Grolier Educ. 1999 12v il set $249 (5 and up)   **567.9**

1. Dinosaurs

ISBN 0-7172-9406-4   LC 98-44451

Contents: v1 Origins of the dinosaurs; v2 The early dinosaurs; v3 The carnosaurs; v4 The sauropods; v5 Dinosaurs and birds; v6 Dinosaur cousins; v7 The ornithopods; v8 Dinosaur pack-hunters; v9 The hadrosaurs; v10 The ceratopsians; v11 Horned dinosaurs; v12 Death of the dinosaurs

"Each slim volume features numerous diagrams and full-color illustrations with informative captions. . . . Coverage is thorough, and the text should be accessible for the intended audience." Booklist

Pringle, Laurence P.

Dinosaurs! strange and wonderful; illustrated by Carol Heyer. Boyds Mills Press 1995 unp il $15.95 (k-3)   **567.9**

1. Dinosaurs

ISBN 1-878093-16-9   LC 92-71273

Also available in paperback from Penguin Bks.

The author "introduces topics ranging from where the dinosaurs lived, what they ate, fossils, paleontologists, to how new discoveries lead to updated theories about dinosaurs' appearance, behavior and evolution." Appraisal

"Clearly written and well-suited to a younger audience, the book is meaty enough for slightly older readers too. Heyer's detailed acrylics, alternately realistic and stylized, offer an up-to-date representation of what the 'terrible lizards' may well have looked like." Publ Wkly

Tanaka, Shelley

Graveyards of the dinosaurs; what it's like to discover prehistoric creatures; paleontological consultation by Philip J. Currie, Mark Norell, and Paul Sereno; featuring illustrations by Alan Barnard. Hyperion Bks. for Children 1998 48p il maps $16.95; pa $7.99 (4-6)   **567.9**

1. Fossils 2. Dinosaurs

ISBN 0-7868-0375-4; 0-7868-1540-X (pa)

LC 97-31286

"An I Was There book"

"A Hyperion/Madison Press book"

Discusses the work of paleontologists who have found dinosaur bones and fossils in Canada, Argentina, and the Gobi Desert

"Full-color photos of the sites and of important finds and dramatic re-creations of dinosaurs in action enhance the readable text." Horn Book Guide

Includes glossary and bibliographical references

Zoehfeld, Kathleen Weidner

Dinosaur babies; illustrated by Lucia Washburn. HarperCollins Pubs. 1999 33p il (Let's-read-and-find-out science) $15.95; lib bdg $15.89; pa $4.95 (k-3)   **567.9**

1. Dinosaurs

ISBN 0-06-027141-8; 0-06-027142-6 (lib bdg); 0-06-445162-3 (pa)   LC 98-43594

Describes the parenting habits of the Maiasaura, a dinosaur whose way of raising children bore similarities to that of birds

"Washburn's beautifully shaded pastel illustrations, using glowing other-worldly colors, create eye-catching scenes. The title is catchy and the presentation is good; a fine book for dinosaur fans." Booklist

569   Fossil mammals

Aliki

Wild and woolly mammoths; written and illustrated by Aliki. rev ed. HarperCollins Pubs. 1996 32p il hardcover o.p. paperback available $6.95 (k-3)   **569**

1. Mammoths

ISBN 0-06-446179-3 (pa)   LC 94-48217

A revised and newly illustrated edition of the title first published 1977

An easy-to-read account of the woolly mammoth, a giant land mammal which has been extinct for over 11,000 years

"With concise text and informative art, Aliki illuminates the timeless appeal of these long-gone animals—and drops a gentle warning about the possible fate of tusked decendants." Publ Wkly

Giblin, James, 1933-

The mystery of the mammoth bones; and how it was solved. HarperCollins Pubs. 1999 97p il $15.95; lib bdg $15.89 (4 and up)   **569**

1. Peale, Charles Willson, 1741-1827 2. Mastodon 3. Fossil mammals

ISBN 0-06-027493-X; 0-06-027494-8 (lib bdg)

LC 98-6701

Describes the efforts of the artist, museum curator, and self-taught paleontologist, Charles Willson Peale, to excavate, study, and display the bones of a prehistoric creature that is later named "mastodon"

"Giblin's research is superb, and he turns to Peale's actual notes for details. He also includes recent information about the mammoth (and mastodon)." SLJ

Includes bibliographical references

570   Life sciences. Biology

Exploring life science. Marshall Cavendish 2000 11v set $329.95 (4-6)   **570**

1. Life sciences—Encyclopedias

ISBN 0-7614-7135-9   LC 98-52925

Exploring life science—*Continued*

Based on the high school level Encyclopedia of life sciences (1966)

"Arranged into a single alphabet, these more than 300 specific, easily digestible articles cover living things, the environment, and the life sciences themselves. Entries are enhanced by numerous crisply detailed photos, full-color drawings, and boxed closer looks at special issues or topics." SLJ

For a fuller review see: Booklist, Mar. 1, 2000

VanCleave, Janice Pratt

Janice VanCleave's play and find out about nature; easy experiments for young children. Wiley 1997 122p il $29.95; pa $12.95 (k-2)   **570**

1. Biology 2. Nature 3. Science—Experiments
ISBN 0-471-12939-9; 0-471-12940-2 (pa)

LC 96-2865

Provides instructions for fifty nature experiments and activities involving both plants and animals

"VanCleave's explanations are straightforward and concise. The book has a clear and uncluttered look." SLJ
Includes glossary

571.8   Reproduction, development, growth

Collard, Sneed B., III

Making animal babies; [by] Sneed B. Collard III; illustrated by Steve Jenkins. Houghton Mifflin 2000 unp il $16 (k-3)   **571.8**

1. Reproduction 2. Animal courtship
ISBN 0-395-95317-0   LC 99-35797

Describes the mating rituals and reproductive methods of a variety of animals, including flatworms, jellyfish, chameleons, and walruses

"On each page, Collard pairs a line or two of large-type text with a paragraph in smaller type that covers similar ground in more detail. . . . Jenkins creates beautiful, evocative, sometimes astonishingly realistic paper collages for this two-level survey of animal reproduction." Booklist
Includes glossary

Martin, Linda

Watch them grow; written by Linda Martin. Dorling Kindersley 1994 45p il $14.95 (k-2)

571.8

1. Growth
ISBN 1-56458-458-5   LC 93-25426

Explores the different stages in the life cycles of a variety of living things, including rabbits, frogs, puppies, and mushrooms

"Clearly numbered boxes contain uncluttered, full-color photographs and a simple sentence or two describing the specific changes that take place. . . . A visual treat for youngsters that teachers and parents will appreciate for its realistic presentation." SLJ

573.7   Musculoskeletal system

Llewellyn, Claire

The big book of bones; an introduction to skeletons. Bedrick Bks. 1998 48p il $17.95 (4-6)

573.7

1. Skeleton 2. Bones
ISBN 0-87226-546-3   LC 97-48329

"Each double-page spread focuses on a particular aspect of a working skeleton, such as how birds fly, fish swim, or humans dance or run. The clear, concise text is carefully integrated with the numerous illustrations." Booklist
Includes glossary

576.8   Evolution

Branley, Franklyn Mansfield, 1915-

Is there life in outer space? by Franklyn M. Branley; illustrated by Edward Miller. HarperCollins Pubs. 1999 31p il (Let's-read-and-find-out science) $15.95; lib bdg $15.89; pa $4.95 (k-3)   **576.8**

1. Life on other planets 2. Outer space—Exploration
ISBN 0-06-028146-4; 0-06-028145-6 (lib bdg); 0-06-445192-5 (pa)   LC 99-10904

A newly illustrated edition of the title first published 1984 by Crowell

Discusses some of the ideas and misconceptions about life in outer space and speculates on the existence of such life in light of recent space explorations

"Children curious about the possibility of life on distant planets will find much to think about in this speculative yet scientifically accurate text. The new illustrations, which incorporate photographs of planets, are bright and colorful." Horn Book Guide

Couper, Heather

Is anybody out there? [by] Heather Couper and Nigel Henbest; illustrated by Luciano Corbella. DK Pub. 1998 45p il $16.95 (4 and up)   **576.8**

1. Life on other planets
ISBN 0-7894-2798-2   LC 97-35398

Explores the possibility of life on other planets from both scientific and mythological perspectives

"The brief text is extended by the lengthy captions accompanying the many color photos and drawings. Despite the crowded format, readers will find solid discussions of astronomy and chemistry." Horn Book Guide
Includes glossary

Fradin, Dennis B.

Is there life on Mars? [by] Dennis Brindell Fradin; illustrated with full-color and black-and-white prints and photographs. Margaret K. McElderry Bks. 1999 136p il $19.95 (4 and up)

576.8

1. Mars (Planet) 2. Life on other planets
ISBN 0-689-82048-8   LC 98-38208

Fradin, Dennis B.—*Continued*

Examines the theories about life on Mars, providing both historical and current information about our exploration of the Red Planet

"Fradin's discussion is both cogent and thought-provoking." Bull Cent Child Books

Includes bibliographical references

Gamblin, Linda

Evolution; written by Linda Gamblin. Dorling Kindersley 1993 64p il map (Eyewitness science) $15.95; lib bdg $19.99 (4 and up)   **576.8**

1. Evolution

ISBN 0-7894-5579-X; 0-7894-6719-4 (lib bdg)

                             LC 92-54478

Text about and photography of experiments, animals, plants, bones, and fossils reveal the ideas and discoveries that have changed our understanding of the natural world and how life began

This offers "a wealth of outstanding color photographs and drawings and interesting information in a format that is particularly attractive for browsing." SLJ

577   Ecology

Allaby, Michael, 1933-

Biomes of the world. Grolier Educ. 1999 9v il maps lib bdg set $259 (5 and up)   **577**

1. Ecology

ISBN 0-7172-9341-6   LC 98-37524

Contents: v1 The Polar regions; v2 Deserts; v3 Oceans; v4 Wetlands; v5 Mountains; v6 Temperate forests; v7 Tropical forests; v8 Temperate grasslands; v9 Tropical grasslands

Explores each of the earth's major ecological regions, defining important features, animals, and environmental issues

This "is a well designed nine-volume set of books providing an excellent introduction to the principal biomes of planet Earth. The books are an outstanding resource for students and teachers." Sci Books Films

Lauber, Patricia, 1924-

Who eats what? food chains and food webs; illustrated by Holly Keller. HarperCollins Pubs. 1995 32p il (Let's-read-and-find-out science) $15.95; lib bdg $15.89; pa $4.95 (k-3)   **577**

1. Food chains (Ecology)

ISBN 0-06-022981-0; 0-06-022982-9 (lib bdg); 0-06-445130-5 (pa)   LC 93-10609

The author "demonstrates the interconnectedness of nature by showing how creatures form chains through the foods they eat. . . . Lauber gives several examples, from short chains (apple to child) to the web of connections between sea creatures. She uses sea otters to show how the disappearance of one link in the chain can disrupt the flow of food both up and down." Bull Cent Child Books

"Clear, simple ink-and-watercolor drawings illustrate the clear, simple text. Informative and intriguing, this basic science book leads children to think about the complex and interdependent web of life on Earth." Booklist

Orr, Richard

Nature cross-sections; illustrated by Richard Orr; written by Moira Butterfield. Dorling Kindersley 1995 30p il $17.95 (4 and up)   **577**

1. Habitat (Ecology) 2. Ecology

ISBN 0-7894-0147-9   LC 94-44798

"Orr's colorful paintings show cutaway views of ecosystems such as a rain forest, a tidal pool, and an American desert, as well as structures such as a beaver lodge and a beehive. . . . In addition to the brief introduction to each subject, short paragraphs identify and discuss portions of the illustrations." Booklist

"The large pages will captivate readers of all ages, kindling a long-lasting interest in the natural world." Sci Child

Pollock, Steve

Ecology; written by Steve Pollock. Dorling Kindersley 1993 64p il (Eyewitness science) $15.95; lib bdg $19.99 (4 and up)   **577**

1. Ecology

ISBN 0-7894-5581-1; 0-7894-6720-8 (lib bdg)

                             LC 93-10064

Illustrations and text provide information about ecology in general, specific ecosystems, and our changing understanding of life around us

"An appealing format, coupled with striking visual representations, provides an excellent view of ecosystems." Voice Youth Advocates

Scott, Michael M.

The young Oxford book of ecology; [by] Michael Scott. Oxford Univ. Press 1995 159p il (Young Oxford books) hardcover o.p. paperback available $16.95 (6 and up)   **577**

1. Ecology

ISBN 0-19-521428-5 (pa)   LC 95-7012

After explaining basic processes such as photosynthesis, food webs, and migration the author examines the earth's habitats and ecosystems. Extinction, conservation, pollution and habitat loss are also explored

This book is "not only lavishly illustrated with photographs, maps, diagrams, and drawings, but [it is] also packed with the kind of in-depth, interesting information students need for reports." Booklist

Includes glossary

Silver, Donald M., 1947-

Backyard; illustrated by Patricia J. Wynne. Scientific Am. Bks. for Young Readers 1993 47p il (One small square) o.p.; McGraw-Hill paperback available $7.95 (3-5)   **577**

1. Nature study 2. Ecology

ISBN 0-07-057930-X (pa)   LC 93-18353

Explains how to observe and explore plants, animals, and their interactions in your own backyard

VanCleave, Janice Pratt

Janice Vancleave's ecology for every kid; easy activities that make learning science fun. Wiley 1996 219p il maps (Science for every kid series) $29.95; pa $10.95 (4 and up) **577**

1. Ecology 2. Habitat (Ecology) 3. Science—Experiments

ISBN 0-471-10100-1; 0-471-10086-2 (pa)

LC 95-6112

This book of science activities covers "25 topics, ranging from plant and animal food chains to the effect of plastics on the environment. Subjects are introduced in a 'What You Need to Know' section that gives explanation of the scientific principles, plus plenty of everyday examples. A brief preparatory exercise follows, usually in the form of an imaginative game. . . . Simple black-line drawings are crisp, uncluttered, and well placed. . . . Solid information and a generous portion of fun are combined to elevate this selection above the standard collection of experiments." SLJ

Includes glossary

577.2 Specific factors affecting ecology

Cone, Patrick

Wildfire. Carolrhoda Bks. 1997 48p il (Nature in action) hardcover o.p. paperback available $7.95 (3-6) **577.2**

1. Forest fires 2. Forest ecology

ISBN 1-575-05027-7 (pa)

LC 95-40847

Briefly traces the history of wildfire before going on to discuss types, when and where they start, their behavior, ecological effects, fighting and preventing them

"Dramatic color photographs accompany Cone's focused look at the causes, types, and effects of wildfires. . . . [An] attractively presented, highly informative study." Booklist

Lauber, Patricia, 1924-

Summer of fire; Yellowstone 1988. Orchard Bks. 1991 64p il map $19.95 (4 and up) **577.2**

1. Forest fires 2. Yellowstone National Park 3. Forest ecology

ISBN 0-531-05943-X

LC 90-23032

Describes the season of fire that struck Yellowstone in 1988, and examines the complex ecology that returns plant and animal life to a seemingly barren, ash-covered expanse

"Interesting, action-filled writing plus a very detailed description of the fire and how it spread make for exciting reading. . . . The new, clear full-color photographs are outstanding." SLJ

Includes glossary and bibliographical references

Patent, Dorothy Hinshaw

Fire: friend or foe; photographs by William Muñoz. Clarion Bks. 1998 80p il $16 (4 and up) **577.2**

1. Forest fires 2. Forest ecology

ISBN 0-395-73081-3

LC 98-11754

Discusses forest fires and the effect that they have on both people and the natural world

"The text offers rich science support. . . . Muñoz's full-color photographs are a nice complement to the text." Booklist

Yellowstone fires; flames and rebirth; photos by William Muñoz and others. Holiday House 1990 40p il $14.95 (2-4) **577.2**

1. Forest fires 2. Yellowstone National Park 3. Forest ecology

ISBN 0-8234-0807-8

LC 89-24544

An account of the 1988 forest fire in Yellowstone National Park

"This is the only book which covers some financial issues, the media depiction of the fire, and the animals and birds disturbed or killed by firefighters. . . . Clear, colorful photos illustrate points covered in the text." SLJ

Simon, Seymour, 1931-

Wildfires. Morrow Junior Bks. 1996 unp il hardcover o.p. paperback available $6.95 (3-6)

577.2

1. Forest fires 2. Forest ecology

ISBN 0-688-17530-9 (pa)

LC 95-12653

"Exploring the place of fire in nature, Simon explains that . . . forest fires have important functions in the ecosystem. With a brilliantly clear and colorful photograph facing each page of text, the book describes the causes and the progression of the wildfires that burned areas of Yellowstone National Park in 1988, explains how the fires were beneficial in many ways. . . . Lucid writing and excellent book design." Booklist

577.3 Forest ecology

George, Jean Craighead, 1919-

One day in the tropical rain forest; illustrated by Gary Allen. Crowell 1990 56p il $15.95; lib bdg $15.89; pa $4.25 (4-6) **577.3**

1. Rain forest ecology 2. Natural history—Venezuela

ISBN 0-690-04767-3; 0-690-04769-X (lib bdg); 0-06-442016-7 (pa)

LC 89-36583

"The final day of a struggle between developers and conservationists over the Tropical Rain Forest of the Macaw as seen by a young Indian boy. A beautifully written story details the complexity, majesty, and interdependence of flora and fauna and teaches about indigenous people and scientists who inhabit a small part of Venezuela's rain forest." Sci Child

Includes bibliographical references

One day in the woods; illustrated by Gary Allen. Crowell 1988 42p il lib bdg $15.89; pa $4.25 (4-6) **577.3**

1. Forest ecology 2. Birds

ISBN 0-690-04724-X (lib bdg); 0-06-442017-5 (pa)

LC 87-21712

Rebecca discovers many things about plant and animal life when she spends the day in Teatown Woods in the Hudson Highlands of New York looking for the ovenbird

"Through naturalist George's precise descriptions,

George, Jean Craighead, 1919———*Continued*
readers follow Rebecca's progress through the day discovering the secrets of the spring foliage and learning much about the temperate forest and its inhabitants. Allen's refined pencil drawings of the skunk, wood ducks, flying squirrel, gypsy moth caterpillar, and other creatures that Rebecca encounters on her quest beautifully transcribe George's textual details." Booklist
Includes bibliographical references

Gibbons, Gail
Nature's green umbrella; tropical rain forests. Morrow Junior Bks. 1994 unp il maps $15.95; lib bdg $15.93; pa $5.95 (k-3)   **577.3**
  1. Rain forest ecology
  ISBN 0-688-12353-8; 0-688-12354-6 (lib bdg);
  0-688-15411-5 (pa)   LC 93-17569
Describes the climatic conditions of the rain forest as well as the different layers of plants and animals that comprise the ecosystem
The language is "simple, yet poetic and evocative. . . . Colorful maps pinpoint the locations of these global resources. Green vines entwine around the borders of each page and enclose the text and bright illustrations." Sci Books Films

Greenaway, Theresa, 1947-
Jungle; written by Theresa Greenaway; photographed by Geoff Dann. Knopf 1994 63p il (Eyewitness books) (4 and up)   **577.3**
  1. Rain forest ecology
           LC 94-7948
  Available DK Pub. edition $15.95; lib bdg $19.99
(ISBN 0-7894-5896-9; 0-7894-6603-1)
"A Dorling Kindersley book"
Color photographs, drawings, and brief text describe the animals, plants, and ecology of tropical forests of the world
The author "presents a clear understanding of the composition, similarities and differences among rain forests around the world. A good addition to the book lies in the explanation of the value of this type of ecosystem and, sadly, how jungles are being destroyed at a rapid rate on a daily basis." Appraisal

Grupper, Jonathan
Destination: rain forest. National Geographic Soc. 1997 31p il $16 (1-3)   **577.3**
  1. Rain forests 2. Rain forest ecology
  ISBN 0-7922-7018-5   LC 97-68
Describes the unique environment of and the varied animal and plant life found in the world's tropical rain forests
"Excellent photographs provide close-up views of the creatures, most from Central and South America and the rest from Southeast Asia and Africa. . . . Though too generalized for research, this still provides vivid glimpses of the rain forest and its inhabitants." Booklist

Jaspersohn, William
How the forest grew; illustrated by Chuck Eckart. Greenwillow Bks. 1989 55p il hardcover o.p. paperback available $4.95 (1-3)   **577.3**
  1. Forest ecology
  ISBN 0-688-11508-X (pa)   LC 79-16286

"A Greenwillow read-alone book"
A reissue of the title first published 1980
This "book traces the growth of a Massachusetts hardwood forest. . . . The book recounts each stage of the forest's growth and explains the reasons for the succession of different types of plant and animal life." Horn Book
"Many beautifully detailed black-and-white sketches thoroughly capture the atmosphere of the developing forest." Appraisal

Kaplan, Elizabeth, 1956-
Temperate forest. Marshall Cavendish 1996 64p il (Biomes of the world) lib bdg $25.64 (4-6)
           577.3
  1. Forest ecology
  ISBN 0-7614-0082-6   LC 95-4065
The author "discusses the four types of temperature forests, where they occur, and how they differ from one another as well as how they change through the seasons. Diagrams show the forest layers, the stages of primary succession, and a typical food web in the biome. The final chapter focuses on problems threatening temperature forests." Booklist
Includes bibliographical references

Lasky, Kathryn
The most beautiful roof in the world; exploring the rainforest canopy; photographs by Christopher G. Knight. Harcourt Brace & Co. 1997 unp il $18; pa $9 (4-6)   **577.3**
  1. Lowman, Margaret 2. Rain forest ecology
  ISBN 0-15-200893-4; 0-15-200897-7 (pa)
           LC 95-48193
"Gulliver Green"
Describes the work of Meg Lowman in the rainforest canopy, an area unexplored until the last ten years and home to previously unknown species of plants and animals
"Fresh in out-look and intriguing in details, this memorable book features colorful photographs that reflect the you-are-there quality of the text." Booklist
Includes glossary

Pfeffer, Wendy, 1929-
A log's life; illustrations by Robin Brickman. Simon & Schuster Bks. for Young Readers 1997 various paging il $16 (k-3)   **577.3**
  1. Oak 2. Forest ecology
  ISBN 0-689-80636-1   LC 95-30020
This is an "introduction to the life, death, and decay of an oak tree. The simple, informative text presents the complex cast of characters residing in or on the living tree as well as the decomposing log. . . . The verbal descriptions of this rich ecosystem are enhanced by striking illustrations of three-dimensional paper sculptures, often so realistic as to seem to be preserved natural specimens." SLJ

Silver, Donald M., 1947-

Woods; illustrated by Patricia J. Wynne. Scientific Am. Bks. for Young Readers 1995 48p il (One small square) o.p.; McGraw-Hill paperback available $7.95 (3-5)   **577.3**

1. Forest ecology

ISBN 0-07-057933-4 (pa)   LC 95-30815

Explains how to investigate the plant and animal life found in a small section of the woods

Staub, Frank J.

America's forests; written and photographed by Frank Staub. Carolrhoda Bks. 1998 48p il map (Carolrhoda earth watch book) lib bdg $21.27 (3-6)   **577.3**

1. Forests and forestry 2. Forest ecology

ISBN 1-57505-265-2   LC 98-7291

Examines the growth and changing nature of forests, the plants and animals living there, and the uses to which these lands are put

"Solid, accessible information presented in an attractive format. . . . Even students with little interest in nature will be drawn to the numerous full-color photographs that depict the beauty and variety of our country's woodlands." SLJ

Includes glossary

Stille, Darlene R.

Tropical rain forest. Children's Press 1999 47p il lib bdg $22 (2-4)   **577.3**

1. Rain forest ecology

ISBN 0-516-21511-6   LC 98-50753

"A True book"

Differentiates a tropical rain forest from all others, and describes its typical plant and animal life

"The plain style, accessible design, and beautiful photographs of landscapes and wildlife make this a good [title] for children's first research presentations." Booklist

Includes glossary and bibliographical references

577.4 Grassland ecology

Brandenburg, Jim

An American safari; adventures on the North American prairie; edited by JoAnn Bren Guernsey. Walker & Co. 1995 44p il hardcover o.p. paperback available $7.95 (4 and up)   **577.4**

1. Prairie ecology 2. Prairie animals

ISBN 0-8027-7502-0 (pa)   LC 94-24654

"Mingling facts with personal reflections, Brandenburg acquaints readers with the habitat that inspired him to become a nature photographer: the American prairie. Besides describing the experiences that led him to hunt with his camera rather than with traps and guns, he introduces various types of prairies, the animals that live there, what threatens their habitat, and how it can be saved." Booklist

"Exquisite photographs of the animals and the terrain, along with some astonishing figures, tell a dramatic story." Horn Book

Dunphy, Madeleine

Here is the African savanna; illustrated by Tom Leonard. Hyperion Bks. for Children 1999 unp il $14.99; lib bdg $15.99 (k-3)   **577.4**

1. Grassland ecology 2. Natural history—Africa

ISBN 0-7868-0162-X; 0-7868-2134-5 (lib bdg)

          LC 98-30007

Cumulative text describes the interdependence among the plants and animals of an African savanna

"The acrylic illustrations are rich with detail and gold-toned radiance. An endnote provides some additional information about conservation. This is an attractive, effective way to introduce ecology to young readers." Horn Book Guide

George, Jean Craighead, 1919-

One day in the prairie; illustrated by Bob Marstall. Crowell 1986 42p il hardcover o.p. paperback available $4.25 (4-6)   **577.4**

1. Prairie ecology 2. Tornadoes

ISBN 0-06-442039-6 (pa)   LC 85-48254

The animals on a prairie wildlife refuge sense an approaching tornado and seek protection before it touches down and destroys everything in its path

"Black-and-white pencil drawings expand the text and bring out the threat of the coming tornado. . . . George provides a brief but intense and detailed look at the North American prairie, equally suitable for a homework assignment or for browsing." SLJ

Includes bibliographical references

Patent, Dorothy Hinshaw

Prairies; photographs by William Muñoz. Holiday House 1996 40p il map $15.95 (4 and up)   **577.4**

1. Prairie ecology

ISBN 0-8234-1277-6   LC 96-14125

Describes the characteristics of the North American prairie, the plants and animals found there, and the efforts made to preserve and restore the landscape

"Large, clear, full-color photos on almost every page vividly capture the prairies and their natural wildlife. . . . *Prairies* provides a well-balanced amount of information that will give children a clear understanding of grassland regions." SLJ

Includes glossary

Silver, Donald M., 1947-

African savanna; illustrated by Patricia J. Wynne and Dianne Ettl. Scientific Am. Bks. for Young Readers 1994 48p il (One small square) o.p.; McGraw-Hill paperback available $7.95 (3-5)   **577.4**

1. Grassland ecology 2. Natural history—Africa

ISBN 0-07-057931-8 (pa)   LC 93-41285

Explores the grasslands which stretch across the continent of Africa below the Sahara and observes the animals living in that changing, endangered environment

Staub, Frank J.

America's prairies; written and photographed by Frank Staub. Carolrhoda Bks. 1994 47p il maps (Carolrhoda earth watch book) lib bdg $21.27 (3-6)   **577.4**

1. Prairie ecology

ISBN 0-87614-781-3   LC 93-7841

Describes the ecology and biology of the three different types of North American prairie—tallgrass, mixed-grass, and shortgrass

"A fact-filled trip from Indiana through the tallgrass prairie and the Great Plains to eastern Colorado. Discover ongoing changes through colorful photographs and informative text, and learn about plants that made travel difficult for previous generations." Sci Child

Includes glossary

Stille, Darlene R.

Grasslands. Children's Press 1999 47p il lib bdg $22; pa $6.95 (2-4)   **577.4**

1. Grassland ecology

ISBN 0-516-21509-4 (lib bdg); 0-516-26762-0 (pa)

LC 98-49728

"A True book"

Examines the different types of grasslands and the plant and animal life they support

Includes glossary and bibliographical references

577.5   Ecology of miscellaneous environments

Baylor, Byrd, 1924-

The desert is theirs; illustrated by Peter Parnall. Scribner 1975 unp il lib bdg $16; pa $5.95 (1-4)

577.5

1. Desert ecology 2. Papago Indians

ISBN 0-684-14266-X (lib bdg); 0-689-71105-X (pa)

LC 74-24417

"Poetic interpretations of Papago Indians' ecological and spiritual relationships with desert resources. . . . Illustrations add to the usefulness of this mood piece for sensitizing children to respect for nature, reading aloud, studying Indian cultures and techniques of using line, space and color." Read Teach

Bial, Raymond

A handful of dirt. Walker & Co. 2000 32p il $16.95; lib bdg $17.85 (3-6)   **577.5**

1. Soils 2. Soil ecology

ISBN 0-8027-8698-7; 0-8027-8699-5 (lib bdg)

LC 99-53632

The author "discusses how plant, animal, and mineral matter are broken down to create soil, as well as the vast amount of life forms soil supports, such as protozoa, earthworms, insects, moles, snakes, and prairie dogs. Tips on how to compost are included. The book is illustrated with crisp color photos, including several using an electron microscope." Horn Book Guide

Includes bibliographical references

Gibbons, Gail

Deserts. Holiday House 1996 unp il maps $16.95; pa $6.95 (k-3)   **577.5**

1. Deserts 2. Desert ecology

ISBN 0-8234-1276-8; 0-8234-1519-8 (pa)

LC 96-4086

"Gibbons briefly describes the formation and characteristics of deserts around the world. . . . Full-color illustrations depict the flora and fauna that thrive in this harsh environment." SLJ

"The illustrations make excellent use of detail and color. . . . This book is a good stepping stone on the subject. It contains just enough information to encourage further reading." Child Book Rev Serv

Lesser, Carolyn

Storm on the desert; written by Carolyn Lesser; illustrated by Ted Rand. Harcourt Brace & Co. 1997 unp il $16 (2-4)   **577.5**

1. Desert ecology 2. Thunderstorms

ISBN 0-15-272198-3   LC 95-44923

Describes the animal and plant life in a desert in the American Southwest and the effects of a short but violent thunderstorm

"The poetic prose is rich with terms and images of the plants and animals that have adapted to desert life. Illustrations done in pencil, pastel, chalk, and watercolor impart character to the animals and the storm itself." Horn Book Guide

Silver, Donald M., 1947-

Arctic tundra; illustrated by Patricia J. Wynne. Scientific Am. Bks. for Young Readers 1994 48p il (One small square) o.p.; McGraw-Hill paperback available $7.95 (3-5)   **577.5**

1. Tundra ecology

ISBN 0-07-057927-X (pa)   LC 94-4143

This book explores the ecology of the Arctic tundra and presents scientific activities and experiments

This book "is beautifully illustrated. Arctic tundra plants and animals in color are almost photographic in clarity and detail. . . . The experiments are valid and appropriate." Sci Books Films

Cactus desert; illustrated by Patricia J. Wynne. Scientific Am. Bks. for Young Readers 1995 48p il (One small square) o.p.; McGraw-Hill paperback available $7.95 (3-5)   **577.5**

1. Desert ecology

ISBN 0-07-057934-2 (pa)   LC 95-7096

This examines a few cubic meters of a desert habitat describing the plants and animal activities at various times of the day

"Colorful artwork. . . . Cautions about desert travel, a detailed catalog of desert residents, and prompts for recording observations make the book a fine companion for a desert trip." Horn Book Guide

Cave; illustrated by Patricia J. Wynne. Scientific Am. Bks. for Young Readers 1993 48p il (One small square) o.p.; McGraw-Hill paperback available $7.95 (3-5)   **577.5**

1. Caves

ISBN 0-07-057929-6 (pa)   LC 93-36570

Silver, Donald M., 1947-—*Continued*

This "introduction to caves and caving begins by instructing readers to explore a pictured square that depicts cave life. . . . Moving from the cave's entrance to the dark world inside, the author focuses on the abundant wildlife and geological formations, including bats, stalactites, and stalagmites. . . . Written with immediacy, the text is illustrated with colorful, detailed line drawings, and there are plenty of sidebars featuring worthwhile experiments." Booklist

Simon, Seymour, 1931-

Deserts. Morrow Junior Bks. 1990 unp il maps hardcover o.p. paperback available $6.95 (3-6)
577.5
1. Desert ecology
ISBN 0-688-15479-4 (pa)   LC 89-39738
Describes the nature and characteristics of deserts, where they are located, and how they are formed
"Spectacular photos of the deserts of the American southwest are used to show the various features from rippling sand, to wind-eroded rock formations, to the sparse vegetation characteristic of the area. There is a little information on how both plant and animal life have adapted to the harsh climate, and on the wonderful public lands such as Monument Valley, The Grand Canyon, etc." SLJ

Stille, Darlene R.

Deserts. Children's Press 1999 47p il lib bdg $22; pa $6.95 (2-4)
577.5
1. Desert ecology
ISBN 0-516-21508-6 (lib bdg); 0-516-26760-4 (pa)
LC 98-53856
"A True book"
Presents a general description of deserts and describes specific desert plants, animals, people, and activities
Includes glossary and bibliographical references

Wright-Frierson, Virginia, 1949-

A desert scrapbook; dawn to dusk in the Sonoran Desert. Simon & Schuster Bks. for Young Readers 1996 unp il $16 (3-5)
577.5
1. Desert ecology 2. Sonoran Desert
ISBN 0-689-80678-7   LC 95-19629
"Wright-Frierson invites readers to spend a day in her company, savoring the Sonoran Desert of the American Southwest. She presents a dawn to dusk panorama in a profusion of watercolor sketches and a brief, conversational text." SLJ

577.6 Aquatic ecology. Freshwater ecology

Gibbons, Gail

Marshes & swamps. Holiday House 1998 unp il $16.95; pa $6.95 (k-3)
577.6
1. Wetlands 2. Ecology
ISBN 0-8234-1347-0; 0-8234-1515-5 (pa)
LC 97-17995

Defines marshes and swamps, discusses how conditions in them may change, and examines the life found in and around them
"Gibbons balances a succinct, informative text with well-labeled watercolors." Horn Book Guide

Miller, Debbie S.

River of life; illustrated by Jon Van Zyle. Clarion Bks. 2000 32p il $15 (k-3)
577.6
1. River ecology 2. Natural history—Alaska
ISBN 0-395-96790-2   LC 99-38350
Describes a river in Alaska and the life that it supports, emphasizing how the living things around it are connected and dependent upon it for their survival
"Rich in word choice, this book develops strong images of the life cycle that unfolds along a river, as winter melts into spring and spring becomes the warm days of summer. Inviting illustrations help tell this story of a river ecosystem." Sci Child
Includes glossary

Silver, Donald M., 1947-

Pond; illustrated by Patricia J. Wynne. Scientific Am. Bks. for Young Readers 1994 48p il (One small square) o.p.; McGraw-Hill paperback available $10.95 (3-5)
577.6
1. Pond ecology
ISBN 0-07-057932-5 (pa)   LC 94-18044
Explores the richness and variety of life forms that can congregate in a peaceful, yet ever-changing, pond, from fish and fungi to mammals and monera

577.7 Marine ecology

Cerullo, Mary M.

Coral reef; a city that never sleeps; text by Mary M. Cerullo; photographs by Jeffrey L. Rotman. Cobblehill Bks. 1996 58p il $17.99 (4 and up)
577.7
1. Coral reefs and islands 2. Marine ecology
ISBN 0-525-65193-4   LC 95-6635
This describes the ecosystem of coral reefs and their inhabitants
"As fascinatingly fact-filled as the text is, it's even more outstanding because of Rotman's spectacular, full-color photographs." SLJ
Includes glossary and bibliographical references

Silver, Donald M., 1947-

Seashore; illustrated by Patricia J. Wynne. Scientific Am. Bks. for Young Readers 1993 48p il (One small square) o.p.; McGraw-Hill paperback available $10.95 (3-5)
577.7
1. Seashore ecology
ISBN 0-02-057928-8   LC 93-18354
Explores the richness and variety of life forms that congregate where the land meets the sea, from microscopic algae to the mighty manatee

578　Natural history of organisms and related subjects

Bernhard, Durga
Earth, sky, wet, dry; a book of nature opposites; written and illustrated by Durga Bernhard. Orchard Bks. 2000 unp il $16.95; lib bdg $17.99 (k-2)　　**578**
1. Animals 2. Plants 3. Opposites
ISBN 0-531-30213-X; 0-531-33213-6 (lib bdg)
LC 99-23084
Describes a variety of animals and plants, grouping them in such contrasting categories as spring and fall, inside and outside, and big and small
"The clearly delineated gouache paintings offer plenty of opportunities for observation and discussion. Six final pages illustrate, identify, and briefly discuss several dozen plants and animals that can be found in the paintings." Booklist

578.7　Organisms characteristic of specific kinds of environments

Arnold, Caroline, 1944-
A walk on the Great Barrier Reef; photographs by Arthur Arnold; with additional photographs by Marty Snyderman [et al.] Carolrhoda Bks. 1988 47p il (Carolrhoda nature watch book) lib bdg $23.93 (3-5)　　**578.7**
1. Coral reefs and islands 2. Marine animals 3. Great Barrier Reef (Australia)
ISBN 0-87614-285-4　　　　LC 87-27746
The author leads "the reader on a tour of discovery that explores the structure of the reef and the life cycles and habits of its various inhabitants. Following a discussion of how the reef was formed, the book includes diagrams of the three types of coral reef formations (fringing, barrier, and atoll)." Sci Child
"The fascinating plants and animals of Australia's Great Barrier Reef are described in a straightforward way and illustrated with stunning, clear full-color photographs." SLJ
Includes glossary

Pandell, Karen
Journey through the northern rainforest; photographs by Art Wolfe; illustrations by Denise Y. Takahashi. Dutton Children's Bks. 1999 unp il $17.99 (4 and up)　　**578.7**
1. Rain forest ecology 2. Pacific Northwest
ISBN 0-525-45804-2　　　　LC 99-31646
"The text combines discussion of the interdependence of plants, animals, and environments in the temperate rainforest ecosystem with a strong message against the irreversible devastation caused by logging. Color photographs and illustrations from an eagle's point of view accompany the informative text." Horn Book Guide

Simon, Seymour, 1931-
They swim the seas; the mystery of animal migration; illustrated by Elsa Warnick. Browndeer Press 1998 unp il $16 (3-6)　　**578.7**
1. Marine animals 2. Marine plants 3. Animals—Migration
ISBN 0-15-292888-X　　　　LC 97-4292
Companion volume to They walk the earth
Describes the migration of marine animals and plants as they journey through rivers, seas, and oceans
The author uses "spare, elegant language. . . . He has selected particularly intriguing creatures whose mysterious habits are certain to fascinate readers. . . . Warnick's fine watercolor illustrations are a perfect complement to Simon's fluid writing." Booklist

579　Microorganisms, fungi, algae

Maynard, Christopher
Micromonsters; life under the microscope; written by Chris Maynard. DK Pub. 1999 48p il (Eyewitness readers) $12.95; pa $3.95 (2-4)　**579**
1. Microorganisms
ISBN 0-7894-4757-6; 0-7894-4756-8 (pa)
LC 99-20401
Explores the hidden world of very small creatures that live around us and even inside us, including fleas, bedbugs, itch mites, and more
"Maynard supplies lots of interesting facts in this accessible, nicely designed Eyewitness Reader that is loaded with fairly good magnified photos and sidebars with related facts." Booklist

579.5　Fungi

Pascoe, Elaine
Slime, molds, and fungi; text by Elaine Pascoe; photographs by Dwight Kuhn. Blackbirch Press 1999 48p il (Nature close-up) lib bdg $18.95 (4 and up)　　**579.5**
1. Fungi
ISBN 1-56711-182-3　　　　LC 97-36751
Using hands-on natural science projects, explores and explains different types and characteristics of fungi
This is "clearly written and well organized, and the photographs are outstanding in their clarity and composition." SLJ
Includes glossary and bibliographical references

579.6　Mushrooms

Royston, Angela
Life cycle of a mushroom. Heinemann Lib. 2000 32p il lib bdg $13.95 (k-3)　　**579.6**
1. Mushrooms
ISBN 1-57572-210-0　　　　LC 99-46105
Introduces the life cycle of a mushroom, from formation of spores through underground growth of the mycelia to formation of mature mushrooms

Royston, Angela—*Continued*
This is an "excellent first book about mushrooms. . . . Photographs on each page are lovely and enhance the text, which is clear and contains a lot of factual information." Sci Books Films
Includes bibliographical references

580 Plants

Gibbons, Gail
From seed to plant. Holiday House 1991 unp il $16.95; pa $6.95 (k-3)   **580**
1. Seeds 2. Plants
ISBN 0-8234-0872-8; 0-8234-1025-0 (pa)
                                LC 90-47037
"Tracing the cycle of how seeds grow into plants and how flowering plants produce seeds, Gibbons creates a brightly illustrated picture book that includes a simple project . . . as well as information on the subject. . . . The basic facts are there, enhanced by illustrations that young children will find not only attractive, but also informative." Booklist

The **Visual** dictionary of plants. Dorling Kindersley 1992 64p il (Eyewitness visual dictionaries) $18.95 (4 and up)   **580**
1. Plants
ISBN 1-56458-016-4   LC 91-58208
Text and labeled illustrations depict a variety of plants and their parts, including woody, flowering, desert, and tropical plants
"Excellent photographs and clear illustrations depict a large sampling of plants. The text includes both scientific and common names and is filled with detailed labels and a brief, informative introduction for each ecosystem. This is an important reference for the classroom library or for the plant enthusiast." Sci Child

581 Specific topics in natural history of plants

VanCleave, Janice Pratt
Janice VanCleave's plants; mind-boggling experiments you can turn into science fair projects. Wiley 1997 90p il (Spectacular science projects series) pa $10.95 (4 and up)   **581**
1. Botany 2. Plants 3. Science projects 4. Science—Experiments
ISBN 0-471-14687-0   LC 96-2744
Presents facts about plants and includes experiments, projects, and activities related to each topic
This book "is inspiring without being flashy. . . . The black-and-white line drawings are sketchy but helpful. . . . This is a fine example of helpful information that is neither academically dry nor ingratiatingly slangy." SLJ
Includes glossary

582.13 Plants noted for their flowers

Hood, Susan
National Audubon Society first field guide: wildflowers. Scholastic 1998 159p il $17.95; pa $11.95 (4 and up)   **582.13**
1. Wild flowers
ISBN 0-590-05464-3; 0-590-05486-4 (pa)
                                LC 97-17992
Provides an overview of wildflowers and where they grow, with specific information about individual species
"Illustrated with vibrant, full-color photographs. . . . Attractive and useful." SLJ
Includes glossary and bibliographical references

582.16 Trees

Burnie, David
Tree; written by David Burnie. Knopf 1988 63p il (Eyewitness books) (4 and up)   **582.16**
1. Trees
                                LC 88-1572
Available DK Pub. edition $15.95; lib bdg $19.99 (ISBN: 0-7894-5820-9; 0-7894-6554-X lib bdg)
"Every imaginable aspect of the life of a tree is examined in a series of 2-page poster-format chapters, from 'The Birth of a Tree' to 'The Death of a Tree.' Anatomy, physiology, reproduction, growth and development are described using the best photographs I have seen in botanical literature and succinct, lively captions. Each page is a delight to the eye. . . . Of particular note is the coverage of tree diseases and pollution including acid rain, and the practical, amateur study of trees." Sci Books Films

Cassie, Brian, 1953-
National Audubon Society first field guide: trees; written by Brian Cassie. Scholastic 1999 159p il $17.95; pa $11.95 (4 and up)   **582.16**
1. Trees
ISBN 0-590-05472-4; 0-590-05490-2 (pa)
                                LC 98-21855
A visual guide to the natural science of trees as well as a field guide to the trees found in the United States and Canada
Includes glossary and bibliographical references

Dorros, Arthur
A tree is growing; illustrated by S.D. Schindler. Scholastic 1997 unp il $15.95 (2-4)   **582.16**
1. Trees
ISBN 0-590-45300-9   LC 96-10844
Tells about the structure of trees and how they grow, as well as their uses
"The text to this book . . . is spare, accurate and clear. The illustrations, colored etchings on parchment and pastel papers, are subtle and mysterious as well as accurate." N Y Times Book Rev

Ehlert, Lois, 1934-

Red leaf, yellow leaf. Harcourt Brace Jovanovich 1991 unp il $16 (k-3)   **582.16**

1. Trees

ISBN 0-15-266197-2   LC 90-21195

"In a quiet, first-person narrative, a young child details the life cycle of a sugar maple tree. . . . The story is quite brief, and the choice of a very large typeface makes the main portion of the book accessible to beginning readers. The concluding section offers more detailed and concrete botanical information and provides hints on selecting and planting one's own tree. . . . Ehlert has combined many media to create the book's dazzling illustrations." Horn Book

Gardner, Robert, 1929-

Science project ideas about trees. Enslow Pubs. 1997 96p il (Science project ideas) lib bdg $19.95 (5 and up)   **582.16**

1. Trees 2. Science projects 3. Science—Experiments

ISBN 0-89490-846-4   LC 97-6515

Contains many experiments introducing the processes that take place in plants and trees

The directions "dare easy to understand, and the vocabulary is fairly accessible. The accompanying diagrams are particularly sharp and clear." SLJ

Includes bibliographical references

Lauber, Patricia, 1924-

Be a friend to trees; illustrated by Holly Keller. HarperCollins Pubs. 1994 32p il (Let's-read-and-find-out science) lib bdg $15.89; pa $4.95 (k-3)   **582.16**

1. Trees

ISBN 0-06-021529-1 (lib bdg); 0-06-445120-8 (pa)   LC 92-24082

Also available Audiobook version

In this book "photosynthesis is explained, as well as the beauty and usefulness of trees. Easy conservation suggestions are also offered." Horn Book Guide

"This conveys a lot of information in a simple text with clear line-and-watercolor illustrations." Booklist

Maestro, Betsy, 1944-

Why do leaves change color? illustrated by Loretta Krupinski. HarperCollins Pubs. 1994 32p il (Let's-read-and-find-out science) lib bdg $15.89; pa $4.95 (k-3)   **582.16**

1. Leaves 2. Autumn

ISBN 0-06-022874-1 (lib bdg); 0-06-445126-7 (pa)   LC 93-9611

Also available Audiobook version

Explains how leaves change their colors in autumn and then separate from the tree as the tree prepares for winter

"This is an informative concept book. . . . Krupinski's bright gouache-and-colored pencil illustrations show a boy and a girl playing in a country landscape that changes with weather and light. There are also detailed pictures of leaves in different sizes, shapes, and colors. Maestro includes simple instructions for making a leaf rubbing and for pressing leaves, as well as suggestions for places to visit where the fall foliage is special." Booklist

Robbins, Ken

Autumn leaves. Scholastic Press 1998 39p il $15.95 (3-6)   **582.16**

1. Leaves 2. Autumn

ISBN 0-590-29879-8   LC 97-43895

Examines the characteristics of different types of leaves and explains how and why they change colors in the autumn

"Nicely produced, this attractive and instructive book employs full-color photos, most set against stark white backgrounds, to introduce children to a bounty of autumn leaves. . . . This is a sure bet for classroom use and will also be wonderful for parent-child and school outdoor expeditions." Booklist

583   Dicotyledons

Bash, Barbara

Desert giant; the world of the saguaro cactus. Sierra Club Bks.; Little, Brown 1989 unp il hardcover o.p. paperback available $6.95 (3-5)   **583**

1. Cactus 2. Desert ecology

ISBN 0-316-68307-0 (pa)   LC 88-4706

"Animals find food and shelter in the towering plant of the Sonoran desert, and the local Tohono O'odom Indians have multiple uses for it. The cactus's 200-year life cycle is depicted as part of the ecosystem with colorful illustrations and clear text." Sci Child

In the heart of the village; the world of the Indian Banyan tree. Sierra Club Bks. 1996 unp il $16.95 (3-5)   **583**

1. Banyan tree 2. India—Social life and customs

ISBN 0-87156-575-7   LC 95-51345

"In a small village in India, the sacred banyan tree is the center and heart of life, and it is protected and worshipped by the people. . . . This day in the life of a banyan is presented in lilting text that effectively captures the activities of a community and shows how its people revolve around this majestic tree. The rich, full-page watercolor illustrations make the book a natural for reading aloud." SLJ

Guiberson, Brenda Z.

Cactus hotel; illustrated by Megan Lloyd. Holt & Co. 1991 unp il $16.95; pa $6.95 (k-3)   **583**

1. Cactus 2. Desert ecology

ISBN 0-8050-1333-4; 0-8050-2960-5 (pa)   LC 90-41748

Describes the life cycle of the giant saguaro cactus, with an emphasis on its role as a home for other desert dwellers

"Guiberson's simple, understandable text gives an enjoyable lesson in desert ecology. Crisply attractive illustrations in color pencil and watercolor show the beauty of the desert landscape and its variety of wildlife." Booklist

Hughes, Meredith Sayles

Spill the beans and pass the peanuts: legumes. Lerner Publs. 1999 80p il lib bdg $26.60 (4 and up)   **583**

1. Legumes

ISBN 0-8225-2834-7   LC 98-29663

Hughes, Meredith Sayles—*Continued*

Presents information on the history, production, and uses of several popular members of the legume family: peanuts, lentils, peas, and beans, particularly soybeans. Includes recipes

"Chapters are illustrated with clear color and black-and-white photographs, reproductions, and drawings. Various cooking methods around the world are discussed and one recipe for each legume is provided. The tone is lively and the information is scientifically correct and thorough. . . . A rich presentation about these common but important foods." SLJ

Morrison, Gordon

Oak tree. Houghton Mifflin 2000 30p il $16 (3-6) **583**
1. Oak 2. Forest ecology
ISBN 0-395-95644-7 LC 98-55148
"Walter Lorraine books"
Describes the impact of the changing seasons on an old oak tree and the life that surrounds it
"Each phase of the tree's development is lovingly depicted in language and pictures that are scientific as well as colorful and accessible. . . . This book is equally engaging as reference or personal-interest reading for the science-minded child." Booklist

Royston, Angela

Life cycle of an oak tree. Heinemann Lib. 2000 32p il lib bdg $13.95 (k-3) **583**
1. Oak
ISBN 1-57572-211-9 LC 99-46855
Introduces the life cycle of an oak tree, from the sprouting of an acorn through its more than 100 years of growth
"Easy enough for primary-grade students, the book contains concepts appropriate for all elementary school students." Sci Books Films
Includes glossary and bibliographical references

Winner, Cherie

The sunflower family; photographs by Sherry Shahan. Carolrhoda Bks. 1996 48p il (Carolrhoda nature watch book) $23.93; pa $7.95 (3-6) **583**
1. Wild flowers
ISBN 1-57505-007-2; 1-57505-029-3 (pa)
LC 95-46110
The topic of this "book is the varied and adaptable Compositae family rather than just its namesake member, the sunflower. . . . This volume describes the distinct characteristics of the composites. . . . The making and dispersal of seeds is discussed and dazzlingly illustrated with full-color photos and diagrams. . . . The many uses of composites as food, lubricant, and pesticide are discussed. This is an excellent introduction to plant function and the concept of scientific grouping." SLJ
Includes glossary

585 Gymnosperms. Conifers

Bash, Barbara

Ancient ones; the world of the old-growth Douglas fir. Sierra Club Bks. for Children 1994 unp il (Tree tales) $16.95 (3-5) **585**
1. Douglas fir 2. Forest ecology
ISBN 0-87156-561-7 LC 93-45251
"Boxes of text set into double-page paintings sketch the activities of animals occupying a Pacific Northwest forest of mixed trees. Striking scenes of the skyward view, the lush canopy, dead and fallen trees, night and winter, and even a forest ablaze offer a broad view of life in this ecosystem, with special focus on the 'mighty Douglas fir.'" Horn Book Guide

590 Animals

Jenkins, Steve

Biggest, strongest, fastest. Ticknor & Fields Bks. for Young Readers 1995 unp il $16; pa $5.95 (k-2) **590**
1. Animals
ISBN 0-395-69701-8; 0-395-86136-5 (pa)
LC 94-21804
Companion volume to Hottest, coldest, highest, deepest
"Here are 14 creatures of distinction, including elephants, ants, jellyfish, cheetahs and fleas. The collage illustrations show them at work, and silhouette graphics with captions provide scientific information about comparative achievement." N Y Times Book Rev
"A helpful chart at the end contains further information about each creature, such as diet and habitat. An all-round superlative effort." SLJ

590.5 Zoology—Serial publications

Zoonooz. Zoological Soc. of San Diego $15 per year **590.5**
1. Zoos—Periodicals
ISSN 0044-5282
Monthly. First published 1926
This magazine describes the activities and exhibits of the San Diego Zoo. It includes illustrated articles written by members of the Zoo's staff

590.73 Collections and exhibits of living animals

Aliki

My visit to the zoo. HarperCollins Pubs. 1997 33p il $14.95; lib bdg $15.89; pa $6.95 (k-3) **590.73**
1. Zoos 2. Animals
ISBN 0-06-024939-0; 0-06-024943-9 (lib bdg); 0-06-446217-X (pa) LC 96-9897

Aliki—*Continued*

A day at the zoo introduces the different animals that exist in the world, where they come from, what their natural habitats are like, and whether or not they are endangered

"Aliki's accessible text and lush illustrations bring the animal world to life." SLJ

591.3   Genetics, evolution, young of animals

Bauer, Marion Dane, 1938-

If you were born a kitten; illustrated by JoEllen McAllister Stammen. Simon & Schuster Bks. for Young Readers 1997 unp il $16; pa $6.99 (k-1)   **591.3**

1. Animal babies 2. Childbirth
ISBN 0-689-80111-4; 0-689-84212-0 (pa)

LC 96-7408

Simply describes how various baby animals come into the world and what happens when a human baby is born

"Stammen's large pastel illustrations will be as good for small groups as for lap sharing, and Bauer's simple words are quiet and graceful, drawing intensity from references to the senses." Booklist

Simon, Seymour, 1931-

Wild babies. HarperCollins Pubs. 1997 unp il hardcover o.p. paperback available $7.95 (2-4)   **591.3**

1. Animal babies
ISBN 0-06-446206-4 (pa)   LC 96-14558

"Simon presents information on thirteen animals (mostly mammals, though a bird, amphibian, and reptile are included) and their birth and parenting practices." Horn Book Guide

"This volume combines appealing photos with intriguing details of animal life." Booklist

591.4   Physical adaptation

Burton, Robert, 1941-

Egg; photographed by Jane Burton and Kim Taylor; written by Robert Burton. Dorling Kindersley 1994 45p il hardcover o.p. paperback available $7.95 (3-5)   **591.4**

1. Embryology 2. Eggs
ISBN 0-7894-6069-6 (pa)   LC 93-28365

In this photographic story of hatching "introductory pages define an egg, name groups of animals that lay them, and show diagrams of one developing in a hen. Most examples presented are from the bird family, but amphibians, insects, snakes, and even a slug are represented. . . . Burton's book is one that children and teachers will reach for to further their understanding of the fascinating emergence of new life." SLJ

Includes glossary

Heller, Ruth

Chickens aren't the only ones. Grosset & Dunlap 1981 unp il $16.99; pa $6.99 (k-1)   **591.4**

1. Reproduction 2. Animal babies
ISBN 0-448-01872-1; 0-698-71778-6 (pa)

LC 80-85257

A pictorial introduction to the animals that lay eggs, including chickens as well as other birds, reptiles, amphibians, fishes, insects, and even a few mammals

The animals "are displayed in buoyant but realistic full-color drawings that sing out from the page. It's unusual to see a science lesson so festively done for such a young audience; in fact this has the fun of pure fiction, though it is straight fact." Booklist

Jenkins, Steve

Big & little. Houghton Mifflin 1996 unp il $14.95 (k-2)   **591.4**

1. Animals 2. Shape
ISBN 0-395-72664-6   LC 95-41162

Jenkins "points out the differences in size between animals who are similar in other ways. The artwork combines cuttings of colored, textured papers to form animals that stand out strikingly against white backgrounds. . . . One line of text comments on the two animals' sizes, habits, or habitats. The final pages include a presentation of the comparative sizes of all the animals, [and] a paragraph of additional information about each species." Booklist

Includes bibliographical references

The **Visual** dictionary of the skeleton. Dorling Kindersley 1995 64p il (Eyewitness visual dictionaries) $18.95 (4 and up)   **591.4**

1. Skeleton 2. Bones
ISBN 0-7894-0135-5   LC 95-11936

"This comprehensive and exquisitely illustrated treasure trove of anatomical terms provides clear and instant access to the skeletons of humans, trees, amphibians, sea mammals, and others." Sci Child

Zoehfeld, Kathleen Weidner

What lives in a shell? illustrated by Helen K. Davie. HarperCollins Pubs. 1994 32p il (Let's-read-and-find-out science) hardcover o.p. paperback available $4.95 (k-1)   **591.4**

1. Shells 2. Animal defenses
ISBN 0-06-445124-0 (pa)   LC 93-12428

Describes such animals as snails, turtles, and crabs, which live in shells and use these coverings as protection

This book uses "interesting and accurate illustrations and just the right words. . . . The science here is good, and the explanations should cause young readers to want to learn more." Sci Books Films

591.47   Protective and locomotor adaptations

Bishop, Nic, 1955-

The secrets of animal flight. Houghton Mifflin 1997 31p il $16 (3-6)   **591.47**

1. Flight 2. Animal behavior
ISBN 0-395-77848-4   LC 96-23131

Bishop, Nic, 1955-—*Continued*

"The mechanics of birds' flight are explored first; the author then turns his attention to bats, and, finally, to insects. In conclusion, he discusses unanswered questions that are still being researched." SLJ

"The many colorful photographs (bolstered by a few diagrams) expand the text with precision and beauty. . . . A good choice for curious browsers as well as information seekers." Booklist

Includes bibliographical references

Hickman, Pamela M.

Animals in motion; how animals swim, jump, slither and glide; written by Pamela Hickman; illustrations by Pat Stephens. Kids Can Press 2000 40p il $10.95; pa $5.95 (3-5)   **591.47**

1. Animal locomotion

ISBN 1-55074-573-5; 1-55074-575-1 (pa)

"The chapters are organized according to method of locomotion ('Swimmers and floaters,' 'Hoppers and jumpers,' 'Runners and walkers,' etc.). There's a lot of information to be found here, but what gives this book a different twist is that it encourages kids to think about the ways animals move and compare them to their own means of locomotion." SLJ

Jenkins, Steve

What do you do when something wants to eat you? Houghton Mifflin 1997 unp il $16 (k-3)   **591.47**

1. Animal defenses

ISBN 0-395-82514-8   LC 96-44993

Describes how various animals, including an octopus, a bombadier beetle, a puff adder, and a gliding frog, escape danger

"Jenkins achieves remarkable anatomical detail in his boldly textured cut-paper collages; simple backgrounds keep attention tightly focused on the animals and their survival strategies." Bull Cent Child Books

591.5 Behavior

Fraser, Mary Ann

Where are the night animals? HarperCollins Pubs. 1999 29p il (Let's-read-and-find-out science) $15.95; lib bdg $15.89; pa $4.95 (k-1)   **591.5**

1. Animal behavior

ISBN 0-06-027717-3; 0-06-027718-1 (lib bdg); 0-06-445176-3 (pa)   LC 97-34683

Describes various nocturnal animals and their nighttime activities, including the opossum, brown bat, and tree frog

"The narrative approach and affable, realistic paintings make this basic science lesson accessible and engaging to the preschool audience." Horn Book Guide

Selsam, Millicent Ellis, 1912-1996

Big tracks, little tracks; following animal prints; by Millicent E. Selsam; illustrated by Marlene Hill Donnelly. rev ed. HarperCollins Pubs. 1999 31p il (Let's-read-and-find-out science) lib bdg $15.89; pa $4.95 (k-3)   **591.5**

1. Animal tracks 2. Tracking and trailing

ISBN 0-06-028209-6 (lib bdg); 0-06-445194-1 (pa)   LC 98-18315

First published with this title 1995; originally published with title How to be a nature detective

This book "teaches young readers how to track animals by finding footprints and other clues. . . . Included is a new Find Out More page with lots of hands-on activites." Publisher's note

Settel, Joanne

Exploding ants; amazing facts about how animals adapt. Atheneum Bks. for Young Readers 1999 40p il $16 (4 and up)   **591.5**

1. Animal behavior

ISBN 0-689-81739-8   LC 97-35395

Describes examples of animal behavior that may strike humans as disgusting, including the "gross" ways animals find food, shelter, and safety in the natural world

"This attractive volume presents its material as wondrous science instead of sensational effect." Booklist

Includes glossary and bibliographical references

591.56 Behavior relating to life cycle

Bancroft, Henrietta

Animals in winter; by Henrietta Bancroft and Richard G. Van Gelder; illustrated by Helen K. Davie. rev ed, illustrated by Helen K. Davie. HarperCollins Pubs. 1997 32p il (Let's-read-and-find-out science) lib bdg $15.89; pa $4.95 (k-1)   **591.56**

1. Animal behavior 2. Winter

ISBN 0-06-027158-2 (lib bdg); 0-06-445165-8 (pa)   LC 95-36246

First published 1963

Describes the many different ways animals cope with winter, including migration, hibernation, and food storage

"The words are immediate . . . and the clear, active illustrations will draw new readers to a popular subject." Booklist

Collard, Sneed B., III

Animal dads; [by] Sneed B. Collard III; illustrated by Steve Jenkins. Houghton Mifflin 1997 unp il $15.95; pa $5.95 (k-3)   **591.56**

1. Animal behavior

ISBN 0-395-83621-2; 0-618-03299-1 (pa)   LC 96-22171

"The text highlights the roles and responsibilities of male parents in the wild, primarily the protection and care of their young." Horn Book Guide

"Each father and his offspring are presented on a single or double-page spread, illustrated with striking, cut-paper collage figures. The large, lifelike creatures are set against backgrounds that are true to each animal's natural habitat." SLJ

Simon, Seymour, 1931-

Ride the wind; airborne journeys of animals and plants; illustrated by Elsa Warnick. Browndeer Press 1997 unp il $15 (4-6)   **591.56**

1. Animals—Migration 2. Flight

ISBN 0-15-292887-1   LC 94-29052

"Simon concentrates on the travels of birds in these brief, factual nature stories, but also includes the migration of several insects, spiders, bats, and seeds. . . . The strength of this book is in the lovely paintings, which range from fairly detailed to suggestive, using shapes and colors to impart information." SLJ

They walk the earth; the extraordinary travels of animals on land; illustrated by Elsa Warnick. Browndeer Press 2000 unp il $17 (3-6)   **591.56**

1. Animals—Migration

ISBN 0-15-292889-8   LC 98-38732

Companion volume to They swim the seas

Describes the movement and migration of mammals and amphibians over varying conditions of land, covering such species as lemmings, elephants, caribou, and frogs

"This picture book for older readers joins Simon's dense, poetic text with quiet, detailed paintings." Booklist

Swinburne, Stephen R.

Safe, warm, and snug; illustrated by Jose Aruego and Ariane Dewey. Harcourt Brace & Co. 1999 unp il $16 (k-3)   **591.56**

1. Animal behavior 2. Animal babies

ISBN 0-15-201734-8   LC 98-9978

"Gulliver books"

Describes how a variety of animals, including kangaroos cockroaches, and pythons, protect their unhatched eggs and young offspring from predators

"Swinburne's informative verses combine with Aruego and Dewey's delightful artwork. . . . Appended with notes offering additional details for each species, this will be useful for primary science units and story hours." Booklist

591.68   Rare and endangered animals

Markle, Sandra, 1946-

Gone forever! an alphabet of extinct animals; [by] Sandra and William Markle; illustrated by Felipe Dávalos. Atheneum Bks. for Young Readers 1998 unp il $16 (k-3)   **591.68**

1. Extinct animals 2. Alphabet

ISBN 0-689-31961-4   LC 95-30805

Describes, for each letter of the alphabet, an animal which lived much more recently than dinosaurs and which is now extinct

"A picture of the letter and of the highlighted animal is accompanied by a succinct, clearly written paragraph that identifies characteristics of the beast and explains the reason behind its extinction. . . . An intriguing addition to natural history collections." Booklist

Includes bibliographical references

591.7   Animals characteristic of specific environments, animal ecology

Arnosky, Jim

Crinkleroot's guide to knowing animal habitats. Simon & Schuster Bks. for Young Readers 1997 unp il $14; pa $5.99 (k-3)   **591.7**

1. Habitat (Ecology) 2. Animals

ISBN 0-689-80583-7; 0-689-83538-8 (pa)

LC 96-19226

"The white-bearded Crinkleroot and his snake friend take a . . . tour of a series of wildlife habitats including wetlands, grasslands, and woodlands. For each habitat, numerous species of animals are portrayed." Horn Book Guide

"The facts are accurate, and the attractive pictures are clearly labeled." Booklist

Watching desert wildlife. National Geographic Soc. 1998 unp il $15.95 (3-6)   **591.7**

1. Desert animals

ISBN 0-7922-7304-4   LC 98-13189

Illustrations and text describe some of the animals the author encountered in the deserts of the American Southwest

"An informative and well-illustrated addition to science units on desert wildlife." Booklist

Cole, Joanna

The magic school bus on the ocean floor; illustrated by Bruce Degen. Scholastic 1992 unp il $15.95; pa $4.99 (2-4)   **591.7**

1. Ocean 2. Marine animals

ISBN 0-590-41430-5; 0-590-41431-5 (pa)

LC 91-17695

Also available Spanish language edition and CD-ROM version

On another special field trip on the magic school bus, Ms. Frizzle's class learns about the ocean and the different creatures that live there

"Cole's straightforward text explains the main action while energetic (but never hectic), colorful doublespread pictures supply a wealth of detail. . . . A perfect match of text and art, this is another first-class entry in a stellar series that makes science fascinating and fun." Booklist

Darling, Kathy

Desert babies; photographs by Tara Darling. Walker & Co. 1997 unp il map lib bdg $16.85 (k-3)   **591.7**

1. Desert animals 2. Animal babies

ISBN 0-8027-8480-1   LC 96-32912

This book "begins with a map showing the deserts of the world, indicating three types of terrain. Featured animals are the camel, caracal, gemsbok, mouse, quokka, coyote, emu, lemur, snake, tarantula, nilgai, tortoise, and vulture." Booklist

"Each animal rates a double-page spread with a few paragraphs highlighting its special tricks or traits, a sidebar of ready reference information, a small inset pho-

Darling, Kathy—*Continued*

to of an adult member of the species, a habitat code, and finally, a full-page close-up of the youngster itself. . . . The warmth and intimacy of the text suggests leisurely sharing between adults and non-readers, just as the researchable format suggests more studious perusal by beginning report-writers." Bull Cent Child Books

Seashore babies; photographs by Tara Darling. Walker & Co. 1997 unp il lib bdg $16.85 (k-3)

591.7

1. Animal babies 2. Seashore
ISBN 0-8027-8477-1   LC 96-26951

This book "explains the difference between coastal seas, tidal zones, and coastal shore habitats and then presents the gull, pelican, penguin, sea lion, seal, tern, turtle, horseshoe crab, sea star, crab, dolphin, manatee, sea horse, and otter." Booklist

"Most of the close-up color photos of these baby animals are big on charm, and the open, inviting layout and easy language will attract readers." Horn Book Guide

Johnson, Jinny

Simon & Schuster children's guide to sea creatures. Simon & Schuster Bks. for Young Readers 1998 80p il $19.95 (4 and up)   **591.7**
1. Marine animals
ISBN 0-689-81534-4   LC 97-8227

Describes the major groups of marine animals, including fish, birds, mammals, and crustaceans

"A beautifully illustrated guide, with a full-color drawing of each animal. . . . The book has enough information to be a useful research tool in the library. The organization, by habitat, is outstanding." Book Rep

Includes glossary

Lavies, Bianca

Compost critters; text and photographs by Bianca Lavies. Dutton Children's Bks. 1993 unp il $15.99 (4 and up)   **591.7**
1. Compost 2. Soil ecology
ISBN 0-525-44763-6   LC 92-35651

Examines how creatures, from bacteria and mites to millipedes and earthworms, aid in the process of turning compost into humus

"The author is to be commended for her excellent use of basic taxonomy in reference to animals. . . . The writing is very well done, and almost every page has a beautiful full-color photograph." Sci Books Films

591.9 Treatment of animals by continents, countries, localities

Arnold, Caroline, 1944-

African animals. Morrow Junior Bks. 1997 48p il $16.95 (k-3)   **591.9**
1. Animals—Africa
ISBN 0-688-14115-3   LC 96-16964

Describes animals of the African plains, forests, jungles, and deserts, and explains how each is able to adapt to its special environment

This offers "superb full-color photography, simple but intelligent language, and excellent organization." SLJ

South American animals. Morrow Junior Bks. 1999 48p il maps $16 (k-3)   **591.9**
1. Animals—South America
ISBN 0-688-15564-2   LC 98-7669

Discusses the variety of animals found in the rainforests, mountains, grasslands, and coastal regions of South America, including the birds, mammals, reptiles, and amphibians

"The photography is exceptional, with many wonderful close-ups, and the text is nicely written." Booklist

Darling, Kathy

Arctic babies; photographs by Tara Darling. Walker & Co. 1996 unp il map $15.95; lib bdg $16.85; pa $5.95 (k-3)   **591.9**
1. Animal babies 2. Animals—Arctic regions
ISBN 0-8027-8413-5; 0-8027-8414-3 (lib bdg); 0-8027-7504-7 (pa)   LC 95-37736

Photographs and text describe some of the young animals that are found in the frigid Arctic regions, including moose, foxes, walrus, porcupines, reindeer, and whales

"The full-color photos, including one full-page shot for each baby animal, allow easy identification, and the lively text and accompanying fact boxes deliver an age-appropriate amount of natural-science detail." Booklist

Rain forest babies; photographs by Tara Darling. Walker & Co. 1996 unp il map $15.95; pa $5.95 (k-3)   **591.9**
1. Animal babies 2. Rain forests
ISBN 0-8027-8411-9; 0-8027-7503-9 (pa)

LC 95-37738

Photographs and text describe some of the many unique young animals that live in the world's rain forests, including frogs, iguanas, macaws, orangutans, and tigers

592 Invertebrates

Lauber, Patricia, 1924-

Earthworms: underground farmers; illustrated by Todd Telander. Holt & Co. 1994 55p il hardcover o.p. paperback available $6.95 (3-5)   **592**
1. Worms
ISBN 0-8050-4897-9 (pa)   LC 93-79784

"A Redfeather book"

Based in part on the author's earlier work of the same title, published 1976 by Garrard

"Lauber introduces the anatomy, physiology, and life cycle of these easily recognizable invertebrates, exploring their preferred habitat (dark, cool, moist ground) and the role they play in aerating the soil and decomposing waste. Several chapters describe commercial worm production. . . . Short chapters, large print, and several full-color photos make for an attractive layout that will appeal to young readers." Booklist

593.4   Sponges

Esbensen, Barbara Juster

Sponges are skeletons; illustrated by Holly Keller. HarperCollins Pubs. 1993 32p il (Let's-read-and-find-out science book) $15.95; lib bdg $15.89; pa $4.95 (k-3)   **593.4**

1. Sponges

ISBN 0-06-021034-6; 0-06-021037-0 (lib bdg); 0-06-445184-4 (pa)   LC 92-9740

Explains how sponges are animals that live in the ocean and how they are harvested and used by humans

"The presentation is both lively and informative. . . . The text is simple and thought provoking, and the illustrations are bright and animated." Booklist

593.5   Coelenterates

George, Twig C., 1950-

Jellies; the life of jellyfish. Millbrook Press 2000 unp il lib bdg $21.90 (2-4)   **593.5**

1. Jellyfishes

ISBN 0-7613-1659-0   LC 99-48390

Describes the physical characteristics, habits, and natural environment of many species of jellyfish

"Gorgeous full-color underwater photos and a simple, readable text provide a fascinating introduction to some little-known and often unheralded marine organisms." SLJ

Landau, Elaine

Jellyfish. Children's Press 1999 47p il lib bdg $22; pa $6.95 (2-4)   **593.5**

1. Jellyfishes

ISBN 0-516-20676-1 (lib bdg); 0-516-26494-X (pa)   LC 98-16116

"A True book"

Introduces the size, shape, colors, and stinging tentacles of jellyfish and examines their survival in the world's waters since before the age of the dinosaurs

This "introduces younger children to the world of jellyfish in an interesting and easy-to-understand way. . . . The book is illustrated with color photos." Sci Books Films

Includes glossary and bibliographical references

593.9   Echinoderms and hemichordates

Fowler, Allan

Stars of the sea. Children's Press 2000 31p il (Rookie read-about science) $19; pa $4.95 (k-3)   **593.9**

1. Starfishes

ISBN 0-516-21214-1; 0-516-27057-5 (pa)   LC 98-52941

Describes the physical characteristics, habitats, and behavior of sea stars, also known as starfishes

"Large print, simple sentences, and one big colorful photo per page make this little book perfect for reading aloud or for early readers. . . . Beautifully illustrated." Sci Books Films

Includes glossary

Hurd, Edith Thacher, 1910-1997

Starfish; illustrated by Robin Brickman. HarperCollins Pubs. 2000 33p il (Let's-read-and-find-out science) $15.95; lib bdg $15.89; pa $4.95 (k-3)   **593.9**

1. Starfishes

ISBN 0-06-028356-4; 0-06-028357-2 (lib bdg); 0-06-445198-4 (pa)   LC 99-21063

A revised and newly illustrated edition of the title first published 1962 by Crowell

A simple introduction to the appearance, growth, habits, and behavior of starfish

"Lovely cut-paper collages placed on multicolored, watercolor ocean backgrounds make this easy-to-read title a treat for the eye." SLJ

594   Mollusks and mollusk-like animals

Fowler, Allan

A snail's pace. Children's Press 1999 31p il (Rookie read-about science) lib bdg $19; pa $4.95 (k-3)   **594**

1. Snails

ISBN 0-516-20812-8 (lib bdg); 0-516-26482-6 (pa)   LC 97-31280

Briefly describes the physical characteristics of snails and a few of the thousands of species of these creatures that exist

"Youngsters will immediately feel comfortable with the small size, large type, and numerous color photos." Booklist

Includes glossary

Wallace, Karen

Gentle giant octopus; illustrated by Mike Bostock. Candlewick Press 1998 29p il $15.99 (k-3)   **594**

1. Octopuses

ISBN 0-7636-0318-X   LC 98-9259

Describes the physical characteristics and behavior of a Giant Octopus and how she searches for a home at the bottom of the ocean, lays her eggs and protects them from predators until they can hatch

"Wallace and Bostock create ocean magic in their presentation of tantalizing information with simple elegance and beauty." Horn Book Guide

595.3   Crustaceans

Himmelman, John, 1959-

A pill bug's life; written and illustrated by John Himmelman. Children's Press 1999 unp il (Nature upclose) lib bdg $24; pa $6.95 (k-2)   **595.3**

1. Woodlice

ISBN 0-516-21165-X (lib bdg); 0-516-26798-1 (pa)   LC 99-30137

Describes the daily activities and life cycle of a pill bug or wood louse

"Each page offers a large, appealing illustration, drawing youngsters into the action." SLJ

Includes glossary

McDonald, Megan, 1959-
Is this a house for Hermit Crab? pictures by S.D. Schindler. Orchard Bks. 1990 unp il $15.95; pa $6.95 (k-2) **595.3**
1. Crabs
ISBN 0-531-05855-7; 0-531-07041-7 (pa)
LC 89-35653
"A Richard Jackson book"
"Hermit Crab has outgrown his house once again and prowls the beach looking for the right new domicile. Along the way he tries out a tin can, a bucket and a log, before he finds the right fit. The text has a read-aloud cadence and the illustrations are spacious and charming." N Y Times Book Rev

595.4 Chelicerates. Arachnids

Markle, Sandra, 1946-
Outside and inside spiders. Bradbury Press 1994 40p il $17; pa $5.99 (2-4) **595.4**
1. Spiders
ISBN 0-02-762314-9; 0-689-83120-X (pa)
LC 93-22643
"Magnified color photographs that provide remarkable views of spider bodies accompany a particularly intelligent essay. Both text and captions are informative and well spun with clear explanations and analogies." Horn Book Guide
Includes glossary

Parsons, Alexandra
Amazing spiders; written by Alexandra Parsons; photographed by Jerry Young. Knopf 1990 29p il (Eyewitness juniors) hardcover o.p. paperback available $9.99 (2-4) **595.4**
1. Spiders
ISBN 0-679-80226-6 (pa) LC 89-38833
Also available Spanish language edition
Text and photographs introduce some of the most amazing members of the spider family, such as bird-eating spiders, spitting spiders, and banana spiders
"The tone is lively and friendly, and each page is sprinkled with snappy subheads that catch the eye and imagination." Publ Wkly

Pringle, Laurence P.
Scorpion man; exploring the world of scorpions; photographs by Gary A. Polis. Scribner 1994 42p il $15.95 (4 and up) **595.4**
1. Polis, Gary A. 2. Scorpions
ISBN 0-684-19560-7 LC 93-34936
This "book discusses scorpions and profiles biologist Gary Polis, a worldwide authority on these animals. Polis' own vivid, close-up photographs illustrate the book, showing the scorpion in its natural habitat." Phelan. Sci Books for Young People
Includes bibliographical references

Ross, Michael Elsohn, 1952-
Spiderology; photographs by Brian Grogan; illustrations by Darren Erickson. Carolrhoda Bks. 2000 48p il (Backyard buddies) lib bdg $19.93; pa $6.95 (3-6) **595.4**
1. Spiders
ISBN 1-57505-387-X (lib bdg); 1-57505-438-8 (pa)
LC 98-51406
Describes the physical characteristics and habits of spiders and provides instructions for finding, collecting, and keeping spiders
"Clear color photographs and black-and-white diagrams enhance the text. . . . The experiments . . . are creative and easily replicable for a classroom demonstration or science fair project." Booklist
Includes glossary

595.6 Myriapods

Ross, Michael Elsohn, 1952-
Millipedeology; photographs by Brian Grogan; illustrations by Darren Erickson. Carolrhoda Bks. 2000 48p il (Backyard buddies) lib bdg $19.93; pa $6.95 (3-6) **595.6**
1. Millipedes
ISBN 1-57505-398-5 (lib bdg); 1-575505-436-1 (pa)
LC 99-35398
Describes the physical characteristics and behavior of the millipede and presents millipede-related activities
"Illustrated with diagrams, cartoons, and color photos." Horn Book Guide
Includes glossary

595.7 Insects

Arnosky, Jim
Crinkleroot's guide to knowing butterflies & moths. Simon & Schuster Bks. for Young Readers 1996 32p il $15 (k-3) **595.7**
1. Butterflies 2. Moths
ISBN 0-689-80587-X LC 95-9408
"After introducing some fundamentals of lepidopteran anatomy, Crinkleroot and his pet snake Sassafras go on a daytime walk to point out various butterflies and relate their life cycle and then on a night hike to observe and describe the ways of moths. Arnosky illustrates the book in lively fashion with bright, sunny watercolor paintings, showing all labeled butterflies and caterpillars in actual size." Booklist

Barner, Bob
Bugs! Bugs! Bugs! Chronicle Bks. 1999 unp il $12.95 (k-2) **595.7**
1. Insects
ISBN 0-8118-2238-9 LC 98-39604
A nonsense rhyme introduces children to familiar bugs. Includes a fun facts sections
"Bold colors and a lively rhyming text combine to make this eye-catching picture book a bug lover's delight." Booklist

Berger, Melvin, 1927-

Chirping crickets; illustrated by Megan Lloyd. HarperCollins Pubs. 1998 32p il (Let's-read-and-find-out science) $15.95; lib bdg $15.89; pa $4.95 (k-3)   **595.7**

1. Crickets

ISBN 0-06-024961-7; 0-06-024962-5 (lib bdg); 0-06-445180-1 (pa)   LC 96-51661

Describes the physical characteristics, behavior, and life cycle of crickets while giving particular emphasis to how they chirp

"Clear and detailed, the ink-and-watercolor artwork is often visually striking as well as educationally sound. . . . A well-rounded introduction." Booklist

How do flies walk upside down? questions and answers about insects; by Melvin and Gilda Berger; illustrated by Jim Effler. Scholastic Ref. 1999 48p il (Scholastic question and answer series) $12.95; pa $5.95 (3-5)   **595.7**

1. Insects

ISBN 0-590-13089-7; 0-439-08572-1 (pa)
LC 98-18457

A series of questions and answers provides information about the physical characteristics, senses, eating habits, life cycles, and behavior of different insects

"The colorful illustrations are detailed, vivid, and well conceived. . . . Attractive enough for browsers, yet solid enough to help support the curriculum." Booklist

Cole, Joanna

The magic school bus inside a beehive; illustrated by Bruce Degen. Scholastic 1996 47p il $15.95; pa $4.99 (2-4)   **595.7**

1. Bees

ISBN 0-590-44684-3; 0-590-025721-8 (pa)
LC 95-38288

Ms. Frizzle "introduces her class to the insect kingdom via an excursion through a honeybee hive. Garbed in bee costumes complete with antennae, and sprayed with the proper pheromones, the students are accepted by the workers and allowed to perform such chores as foraging for nectar and pollen, building honeycombs, making honey, and feeding larvae. . . . A plethora of pseudo school reports provide additional information on the topic. Degen's colorful and amusing cartoons heighten the adventures. Clearly written and well organized." SLJ

Demuth, Patricia, 1948-

Those amazing ants; by Patricia Brennan Demuth; illustrated by S.D. Schindler. Macmillan 1994 unp il $16 (k-2)   **595.7**

1. Ants

ISBN 0-02-728467-0   LC 93-1769

This describes the life cycle, job differentiation, and habitat of ants

"An excellent resource for young readers. . . . The language is simple, yet the portrayal of the complex life of these insects is accurate and informative." Sci Child

Dorros, Arthur

Ant cities; written and illustrated by Arthur Dorros. Crowell 1987 28p il (Let's-read-and-find-out science book) lib bdg $15.89; pa $4.95 (k-3)   **595.7**

1. Ants

ISBN 0-690-04570-0 (lib bdg); 0-06-445079-1 (pa)
LC 85-48244

"Using harvester ants as a basic example, Dorros shows how the insects build tunnels with rooms for different functions and how workers, queens, and males have distinct roles in the ant hill. Along the way, she works in details of food and reproduction, ending with descriptions of other kinds of ants and suggestions for ways to observe them (including instructions for making an ant farm). The text is simple without becoming choppy, the full-color illustrations are inviting as well as informative." Bull Cent Child Books

Dussling, Jennifer, 1970-

Bugs! bugs! bugs! written by Jennifer Dussling. DK Pub. 1998 32p il (Eyewitness readers) $12.95; pa $3.95 (1-3)   **595.7**

1. Insects

ISBN 0-7894-3762-7; 0-7894-3438-5 (pa)
LC 98-14975

Describes the hunting activities of various bugs, including the praying mantis, wood ant, and dragonfly

This offers "crisp, colorful shots to entice readers . . . [and] a chatty text that; while including such comfortable phrases as 'Yikes!' and 'That's a big turnoff!,' does present some thought-provoking information." SLJ

Facklam, Margery, 1927-

The big bug book; illustrated in actual size by Paul Facklam. Little, Brown 1994 32p il $16.95 (3-6)   **595.7**

1. Insects

ISBN 0-316-27389-9   LC 92-24517

Describes thirteen of the world's largest insects, including the birdwing butterfly and the Goliath beetle

"The full-color, airbrushed paintings are quite amazing. Their realistic, close-up views are certain to intrigue young audiences." Booklist

Includes glossary

Creepy, crawly caterpillars; illustrated by Paul Facklam. Little, Brown 1996 32p il hardcover o.p. paperback available $5.95 (3-6)   **595.7**

1. Caterpillars

ISBN 0-316-27342-2 (pa)   LC 93-41443

"After an introduction to basic caterpillar anatomy and behavior, Facklam presents a baker's dozen of common and decidedly uncommon species. . . . The clear, readable text is confined to most of one side of a double-page spread; the rest is taken up by an arresting, full-color, much magnified illustration of the caterpillar in question and a colorful base border depicting the four stages to flight—egg, caterpillar, chrysalis/cocoon, butterfly/moth." SLJ

Includes glossary

Feltwell, John
Butterflies and moths; written by John Feltwell. Dorling Kindersley 1993 61p il (Eyewitness explorers) hardcover o.p. paperback available $5.95 (3-5)　　　**595.7**
1. Butterflies 2. Moths
ISBN 0-7894-1680-8 (pa)　　　LC 92-54313
This guide "describes how butterflies fly, and how they see and smell. Also discussed is mating and laying eggs, and the birth of a caterpillar. Butterflies of the rain forest, the woodlands, the mountains, the desert and even the arctic are shown." Appraisal

Gibbons, Gail
The honey makers. Morrow Junior Bks. 1997 unp il $16.95; lib bdg $16.99; pa $5.95 (k-3)　　　**595.7**
1. Bees 2. Beekeeping 3. Honey
ISBN 0-688-11386-9; 0-688-11387-7 (lib bdg); 0-688-17531-7 (pa)　　　LC 95-42053
Covers the physical structure of honeybees and how they live in colonies, as well as how they produce honey and are managed by beekeepers
"Gibbons cheerfully distills a lot of useful information. . . . Honey-yellow borders serve to box in a user-friendly blend of text and bright watercolor and pencil renderings." Bull Cent Child Books

Monarch butterfly. Holiday House 1989 unp il $16.95; pa $6.95 (k-3)　　　**595.7**
1. Butterflies
ISBN 0-8234-0773-X; 0-8234-0909-0 (pa)　　　LC 89-1880
"Large-scale paintings, clearly detailed, and a simply written, sequential text describe the life cycle of the monarch butterfly and its migratory patterns. This is Gibbons at her best, providing information in a text that is cohesive and comprehensible." Bull Cent Child Books

Godkin, Celia, 1948-
What about ladybugs? Sierra Club Bks. for Children 1995 unp il $14.95 (k-3)　　　**595.7**
1. Garden ecology 2. Insect pests 3. Ladybugs
ISBN 0-87156-549-8　　　LC 93-4202
This book is about "a gardener and his attempt to rid his garden of pests. . . . He sprays with a chemical pesticide, which destroys both the good and bad insects. The garden falters, becomes infested with aphids and ants, and begins to die. The gardener realizes his mistake and turns to the natural way of doing things, allowing the ladybugs to keep the aphids in check." Appraisal
"A plea to children to value organic gardening, and a useful book for classes studying and protecting the environment." SLJ

Hawes, Judy
Fireflies in the night; illustrated by Ellen Alexander. rev ed. HarperCollins Pubs. 1991 32p il (Let's-read-and-find-out science book) hardcover o.p. paperback available $4.95 (k-1)　　　**595.7**
1. Fireflies
ISBN 0-06-445101-1 (pa)　　　LC 90-1587
A revised and newly illustrated edition of the title first published 1963

Describes how fireflies make their light, tells how to catch and handle them, and notes several uses for firefly light
"Alexander uses richly hued pastels for her illustrations of a young girl, her grandparents' farm, and the creatures of a summer night. . . . The colorful drawings and appealing cover represent the major changes in the book. . . . The brief, clearly written text is thorough enough to satisfy its intended audience." SLJ

Heiligman, Deborah
From caterpillar to butterfly; illustrated by Bari Weissman. HarperCollins Pubs. 1996 31p il (Let's-read-and-find-out science) $15.95; lib bdg $15.89; pa $4.95 (k-1)　　　**595.7**
1. Butterflies 2. Caterpillars
ISBN 0-06-024264-7; 0-06-024268-X (lib bdg); 0-06-445129-1 (pa)　　　LC 93-39055
Young children observe the metamorphosis of a caterpillar into a butterfly in a jar in their classroom
"Pen-and-ink and watercolor illustrations create a cheerful setting. . . . A small collection of butterflies commonly found in most parts of the U.S. and a list of addresses of butterfly centers are appended. An inviting book that young children can relate to and one that teachers will find valuable to support nature-study projects." SLJ

Johnson, Jinny
Simon & Schuster children's guide to insects and spiders. Simon & Schuster Bks. for Young Readers 1996 80p il $19.95 (4-6)　　　**595.7**
1. Insects 2. Spiders
ISBN 0-689-81163-2　　　LC 96-27600
Provides an introduction to more than 100 insects and arachnids, giving general information about family characteristics and habits, and more specific facts about some species
"Crisp and well-designed, this is an inviting visual introduction to insects and arachnids." Booklist
Includes glossary

Lasky, Kathryn
Monarchs; photographs by Christopher G. Knight. Harcourt Brace & Co. 1993 63p il hardcover o.p. paperback available $11 (4 and up)　　　**595.7**
1. Butterflies 2. Wildlife conservation
ISBN 0-15-255297-9 (pa)　　　LC 92-33972
"A Gulliver Green book"
Describes the life cycle and winter migrations of the eastern and western monarch butterflies and towns that protect their winter habitats including Pacific Grove, California and El Rosario, Mexico
"Vibrant description melds with fascinating full-color photographs in a book that strikes a perfect balance between science and humanity." SLJ

Latimer, Jonathan P.

Butterflies; [by] Jonathan P. Latimer, Karen Stray Nolting; illustrations by Amy Bartlett Wright; foreword by Virginia Marie Peterson. Houghton Mifflin 2000 48p il (Peterson field guides for young naturalists) $15; pa $5.95 (4 and up)   **595.7**

1. Butterflies
ISBN 0-395-97943-9; 0-395-97944-7 (pa)
                 LC 99-38605

A guide to help identify various butterflies, using the Peterson System of identification

Caterpillars; [by] Jonathan P. Latimer, Karen Stray Nolting; illustrations by Amy Bartlett Wright; foreword by Virginia Marie Peterson. Houghton Mifflin 2000 48p il (Peterson field guides for young naturalists) $15; pa $5.95 (4 and up)   **595.7**

1. Caterpillars
ISBN 0-395-97942-0; 0-395-97945-5 (pa)
                 LC 99-38944

Describes the physical characteristics, behavior, and habitat of a variety of caterpillars, arranged by the categories "Smooth," "Bumpy," "Sluglike," "Horned," "Hairy," "Bristly," and "Spiny"

Lavies, Bianca

Backyard hunter: the praying mantis; text and photographs by Bianca Lavies. Dutton 1990 unp il hardcover o.p. paperback available $5 (2-4) **595.7**

1. Praying mantis
ISBN 0-14-055494-7 (pa)   LC 89-37485

"Outstanding photographs document a thorough discussion of the behavior, life cycle, and development of an impressive insect that eats other insects alive. Insect observers will find the account stimulating and informative." Sci Child

Killer bees; text and photographs by Bianca Lavies. Dutton Children's Bks. 1994 unp il maps $15.99 (4 and up)   **595.7**

1. Bees
ISBN 0-525-45243-5   LC 94-18581

"Drawing on conversations with honey hunters, beekeepers, and scientists, this book explores life in the nests of killer bees, how climate has shaped their behavior, and the current breeding experiments to create a milder but equally productive bee." Publisher's note

"The many outstanding photographs help make this book feel very personal, as we get to see photographs of the scientist and people who work with or have been attacked by the bees." Sci Books Films

Monarch butterflies; mysterious travelers; text and photographs by Bianca Lavies. Dutton Children's Bks. 1992 unp il $15.99 (4 and up)   **595.7**

1. Butterflies 2. Natural history—Mexico
ISBN 0-525-44905-1   LC 92-28337

Text and photographs describe the physical characteristics, life cycle, migration, and study of monarch butterflies

"How butterflies are tagged and scientific data gathered leads to many interesting facts about their survival during dormancy. . . . The photo-documentary style with its open format and direct, clearly written text makes information accessible." SLJ

Micucci, Charles

The life and times of the honeybee. Ticknor & Fields Bks. for Young Readers 1995 32p il hardcover o.p. paperback available $5.95 (2-4)   **595.7**

1. Bees 2. Honey
ISBN 0-395-86139-X (pa)   LC 93-8135

The author "covers everything from distribution, reproduction, behavior, and honey manufacture to the honeybee's niche in history." Booklist

"The multitude of original watercolors bring the subject to life, provide a sense of scale and amplify the text. . . . A must acquisition for a library." Appraisal

Mound, L. A. (Laurence Alfred), 1934-

Insect; written by Laurence Mound. Knopf 1990 63p il (Eyewitness books) (4 and up)   **595.7**

1. Insects
                 LC 89-15603

Available DK Pub. edition $15.95; lib bdg $19.99 (ISBN 0-7894-45816-0; 0-7894-46566-3)

This volume covers "insect anatomy, particular insect species, and how insects survive and relate to other living things in an appealing, thorough presentation suitable for browsing or close study." Sci Child

Oppenheim, Joanne

Have you seen bugs? illustrated by Ron Broda. Scholastic 1998 c1996 31p il $15.95 (k-3) **595.7**

1. Insects
ISBN 0-590-05963-7   LC 96-46140

Describes in verse a variety of bugs and how they look, behave, and improve our lives

"The art-work, constructed of three-dimensional paper sculptures, consists of painted, molded, and sometimes embossed papers that are cut and combined into scenes of bugs in their habitats. . . . A pleasing and effective introduction to insects." Booklist

Pringle, Laurence P.

An extraordinary life; the story of a monarch butterfly; by Laurence Pringle; paintings by Bob Marstall. Orchard Bks. 1997 64p il $18.95; lib bdg $19.99; pa $7.95 (5 and up)   **595.7**

1. Butterflies
ISBN 0-531-30002-1; 0-531-33002-8 (lib bdg); 0-531-07169-3 (pa)   LC 96-31482

Introduces the life cycle, feeding habits, migration, predators, and mating of the monarch butterfly through the observation of one particular monarch named Danaus

"The narrative is scientifically sound and includes information from the most recent research. . . . The attractive, oversized book is lavished with realistic, full-color paintings." SLJ

Includes bibliographical references

Still, John
Amazing butterflies & moths; written by John Still; photographed by Jerry Young. Knopf 1991 29p il (Eyewitness juniors) lib bdg $11.99; pa $9.99 (2-4)   **595.7**
  1. Butterflies 2. Moths
  ISBN 0-679-91515-X (lib bdg); 0-679-81515-5 (pa)
                                        LC 90-19234
Photographic guide illustrates the life cycles and characteristics of various kinds of moths, butterflies, and caterpillars

VanCleave, Janice Pratt
Janice VanCleave's insects and spiders; mind-boggling experiments you can turn into science fair projects. Wiley 1998 92p il (Spectacular science projects series) pa $10.95 (4 and up)   **595.7**
  1. Insects 2. Spiders 3. Science projects 4. Science—Experiments
  ISBN 0-471-16396-1   LC 97-12595
Presents facts about insects and spiders and includes experiments, projects, and activities related to each topic
  "This title is chock-full of meaningful, but not difficult, projects. . . . Clear line drawings illustrate the text on almost every page. . . . The lucid text is well organized and liberally sprinkled with safety warnings." SLJ
  Includes glossary and bibliographical references

Janice VanCleave's play and find out about bugs; easy experiments for young children; [by] Janice VanCleave. Wiley 1999 121p il $29.95; pa $12.95 (k-2)   **595.7**
  1. Insects 2. Science—Experiments
  ISBN 0-471-17664-8; 0-471-17663-X (pa)
                                        LC 97-52088
Presents simple experiments answering such questions about insects as "Are spiders insects?" "Where do butterflies come from?" and "Why do fireflies light up?"
  "Each project leads seamlessly to the next with a child wondering about some aspect of these animals. . . . The black-and-white illustrations with purple highlights are flat and childlike, but clear and informative." SLJ
  Includes glossary

Whalley, Paul Ernest Sutton
Butterfly & moth; written by Paul Whalley. Knopf 1988 63p il (Eyewitness books) (4 and up)
                                        595.7
  1. Butterflies 2. Moths
                                        LC 88-1574
  Also available Spanish language edition
  Available DK Pub. edition $15.95; lib bdg $19.99 (ISBN 0-7894-5832-2; 0-7894-6556-6)
  This book "explores the changes that occur at each stage of the life cycles of these insects. Temperate, mountain, and exotic species are described as are shapes, camouflage, and mimicry." Sci Teach
  "This is an impressive, informative, and high-quality book." Sci Books Films

Wilsdon, Christina
National Audubon Society first field guide: insects; written by Christina Wilsdon. Scholastic 1998 159p il hardcover o.p. paperback available $8.95 (4 and up)   **595.7**
  1. Insects
  ISBN 0-590-05483-X (pa)   LC 97-17990
A visual guide to the natural science of insects which includes information on the ten most common orders, pollination, and life-cycles; also works as a field guide
  This offers "sharp, clear full-color photos. . . . inviting and easy-to-use." SLJ
  Includes glossary and bibliographical references

597 Cold-blooded vertebrates. Fishes

Berman, Ruth, 1958-
Sharks; photographs by Jeffrey L. Rotman. Carolrhoda Bks. 1995 47p il (Carolrhoda nature watch book) lib bdg $23.93; pa $7.95 (3-6) **597**
  1. Sharks
  ISBN 0-87614-870-4 (lib bdg); 0-87614-897-6 (pa)
                                        LC 94-21468
The author introduces shark physiology "through brief but detailed descriptions. Full-color photographs show the variety of sharks, and colorful diagrams amplify the easy-to-understand explanations of their behavior and anatomy. Unfamiliar terms are highlighted in bold print and defined in context; a photograph and caption further explicate them." SLJ
  Includes glossary

Cerullo, Mary M.
Sharks; challengers of the deep; text by Mary M. Cerullo; photographs by Jeffrey L. Rotman. Cobblehill Bks. 1993 57p il $17.99 (4 and up)
                                        597
  1. Sharks
  ISBN 0-525-65100-4   LC 92-14206
Describes the physical characteristics, behavior, and varieties of sharks and dispels common myths about them
  "This is an attractively designed volume, with clear type, quality paper, and outstanding full-color photographs. . . . The combination of excitement and straightforward fact is what makes this book compelling." Booklist
  Includes bibliographical references

The truth about great white sharks; written by Mary M. Cerullo; photographs by Jeffrey L. Rotman; illustrations by Michael Wertz. Chronicle Bks. 2000 48p il $14.95 (4 and up)   **597**
  1. Sharks
  ISBN 0-8118-2467-5   LC 00-31506
This provides information "about shark anatomy, senses, eating habits, and their relationships with humans. . . . The book also contains unusual information such as how these fish are measured and photographed and why they are not able to survive in an aquarium. The attractive layout blends line drawings, full-color photographs,

Cerullo, Mary M.—*Continued*

varied typefaces, and eye-catching graphics. Rotman's pictures are clear and informative. . . . This title will be accessible to reluctant readers and is a must for most collections." SLJ

Includes bibliographical references

Dubowski, Cathy East

Shark attack! written by Cathy East Dubowski. DK Pub. 1998 48p il (Eyewitness readers) $12.95; pa $3.95 (2-4)　　　　　　　　　　　　**597**

1. Sharks

ISBN 0-7894-3763-5; 0-7894-3440-7 (pa)

LC 98-14073

Describes the nearly disastrous encounter of a spear-fisherman with a shark off the coast of Australia

"The accurate text provides not only a lively history of several shark attacks, but also a look at scientific research, the wide variety of shark species, and the pressures on shark populations due to indiscriminate hunting and overfishing." SLJ

Includes glossary

Gibbons, Gail

Sharks. Holiday House 1992 unp il $16.95; pa $6.95 (k-3)　　　　　　　　　　　　　　　　**597**

1. Sharks

ISBN 0-8234-0960-0; 0-8234-1068-4 (pa)

LC 91-31524

Describes shark behavior and different kinds of sharks

The author's "bold, appealing illustrations (many of them labeled and explained) are the strength of the presentation. An excellent choice for even the youngest shark fan, this will be useful for simple reports as well." Booklist

Landau, Elaine

Electric fish. Children's Press 1999 47p il lib bdg $22; pa $6.95 (2-4)　　　　　　　　　**597**

1. Eels 2. Fishes

ISBN 0-516-20666-4 (lib bdg); 0-516-26491-5 (pa)

LC 98-16122

"A True book"

An introduction to various species of electric fish, particularly the electric eel, explaining how they generate and discharge electricity

Includes glossary and bibliographical references

Piranhas. Children's Press 1999 47p il lib bdg $22; pa $6.95 (2-4)　　　　　　　　　　**597**

1. Piranhas

ISBN 0-516-20673-7 (lib bdg); 0-516-26498-2 (pa)

LC 98-16117

"A True book"

An introduction to the various species of fish called piranhas, discussing their reputation as killers, their physical characteristics and habits, and their suitability as pets

"Clearly written, well-organized, and attractively fomatted." SLJ

Includes glossary and bibliographical references

Sea horses. Children's Press 1999 47p il lib bdg $22; pa $6.95 (2-4)　　　　　　　　　**597**

1. Sea horses

ISBN 0-516-20675-3 (lib bdg); 0-516-26503-2 (pa)

LC 98-16120

"A True book"

An introduction to sea horses, describing their physical characteristics and habits, as well as their suitability as pets

"Clear, full-color photographs appear on most pages. . . . Lucid text." SLJ

Includes glossary and bibliographical references

Ling, Mary

Amazing fish; written by Mary Ling; photographed by Jerry Young. Knopf 1991 29p il (Eyewitness juniors) lib bdg $11.99; pa $9.99 (2-4)　　　　　　　　　　　　　　　　**597**

1. Fishes

ISBN 0-679-91516-8 (lib bdg); 0-679-81516-3 (pa)

LC 90-49651

Also available Spanish language edition

Introduces memorable members of the fish world, explains what makes them unique, and describes important characteristics of the entire group

Macquitty, Miranda

Shark; written by Miranda MacQuitty. Knopf 1992 62p il maps (Eyewitness books) (4 and up)　　　　　　　　　　　　　　　　　　　　　**597**

1. Sharks

LC 92-4712

Available DK Pub. edition $15.95; lib bdg $19.99 (ISBN 0-7894-5778-4; 0-7894-6589-2); Spanish language edition also available

"A Dorling Kindersley book"

Describes, in text and photographs, the physical characteristics, behavior, and life cycle of various types of sharks

This "concentrates on the unusual, the strange, the odd, and the frightening with minimal text and clear, bright illustrations. . . . This is clearly a book for dipping in and out of, and not for reference." SLJ

Markle, Sandra, 1946-

Outside and inside sharks. Atheneum Bks. for Young Readers 1996 40p il $16; pa $5.99 (2-4)　　　　　　　　　　　　　　　　　　　**597**

1. Sharks

ISBN 0-689-80348-6; 0-689-82683-4 (pa)

LC 95-30245

"The book gives a basic overview of the physiology of the species (including the shark's senses, its digestive habits, and its reproduction), which is aided by photographs not only of sharks but also bits of shark interiors." Bull Cent Child Books

"The full-color photographs are striking, giving readers close-up looks at different species and body parts. Children fascinated by these creatures should be thrilled with Markle's offering." SLJ

Includes glossary

Parker, Steve

Fish; written by Steve Parker. Knopf 1990 63p il (Eyewitness books) (4 and up)　　　　**597**

1. Fishes

LC 89-36445

Parker, Steve—*Continued*
Also available Spanish language edition
Available DK Pub. edition $15.95; lib bdg $19.99
(ISBN 0-7894-5810-1; 0-7894-6569-8)
This illustrated guide to fish life discusses "color as camouflage, types of early fishes, oddities in the fish world, and fish physiology (feeding, breathing, reproducing, and defending themselves)." Booklist

Pfeffer, Wendy, 1929-
What's it like to be a fish? illustrated by Holly Keller. HarperCollins Pubs. 1996 32p il (Let's-read-and-find-out science) lib bdg $15.89; pa $4.95 (k-1)   **597**
1. Fishes
ISBN 0-06-024429-1 (lib bdg); 0-06-024429-1 (pa)
LC 94-6543
"By comparing goldfish to wild fish and human beings, this book describes the basic physiology of fish. The colorful illustrations are done in watercolors and pastels. . . . In a very accessible narrative that flows from point to point, the basic external anatomy of fish and such behaviors as movement, breathing, eating, and maintenance of temperature are defined in terms of caring for a goldfish in a bowl." Sci Books Films

Simon, Seymour, 1931-
Sharks. HarperCollins Pubs. 1995 unp il $16.95; pa $6.95 (2-4)   **597**
1. Sharks
ISBN 0-06-023029-0; 0-06-446187-4 (pa)
LC 95-1593
The author "explores the fascinating undersea life of sharks, examining the truths and myths about these amazing creatures. Astounding close-up photographs enhance the informative and exciting text." Sci Child

Smith, C. Lavett, 1927-
National Audubon Society first field guide: fishes; written by C. Lavett Smith. Scholastic 2000 159p il $17.95; pa $8.95 (4 and up)   **597**
1. Fishes
ISBN 0-590-64130-1; 0-590-64198-0 (pa)
LC 99-28106
Explores the world of fishes, discussing their classification, anatomy, behavior, and habitat, and providing photographs and detailed descriptions of individual taxonomic families
Includes bibliographical references

597.8 Amphibians

Cassie, Brian, 1953-
National Audubon Society first field guide: amphibians. Scholastic 1999 159p il $17.95; pa $8.95 (4 and up)   **597.8**
1. Amphibians
ISBN 0-590-63982-X; 0-590-64008-9 (pa)
LC 98-40931
Explores the world of amphibians, discussing their classification, anatomy, behavior, and habitat, and providing photographs and detailed descriptions of individual species
Includes glossary and bibliographical references

Clarke, Barry
Amazing frogs & toads; written by Barry Clarke; photographed by Jerry Young. Knopf 1990 29p il (Eyewitness juniors) lib bdg $11.99; pa $9.99 (2-4)   **597.8**
1. Frogs 2. Toads
ISBN 0-679-90688-6 (lib bdg); 0-679-80688-1 (pa)
LC 90-31882
Text and photographs introduce members of the frog and toad world and describe their unique characteristics
"Starting with a general statement . . . 11 intriguing topics are presented, with each double-spread dominated by a spectacular color photo." SLJ

Amphibian; written by Barry Clarke; photographed by Geoff Brightling and Frank Greenaway. Knopf 1993 63p il (Eyewitness books) (4 and up)   **597.8**
1. Amphibians
LC 92-1589
Available DK Pub. edition $15.95; lib bdg $19.99 (ISBN 0-7894-5754-7; 0-7894-6590-6)
"A Dorling Kindersley book"
Photographs and text examine the evolution, behavior, physical characteristics, and life cycle of all kinds of amphibians

Dewey, Jennifer
Poison dart frogs; [by] Jennifer Owings Dewey. Boyds Mills Press 1998 unp il $15.95; pa $8.95 (3-5)   **597.8**
1. Frogs
ISBN 1-56397-655-2; 1-56397-945-4 (pa)
LC 97-74194
A variety of colorful and tiny poison dart frogs living in the rain forests of Central and South America are pictured in their natural habitat. Topics covered include mating habits, natural predators, methods to extract the frog's poison, and their unique nurturing habits
"Dewey's straightforward text is clear and concise, providing enough fascinating details to interest young readers and listeners without overwhelming them." Booklist

French, Vivian
Growing frogs; illustrated by Alison Bartlett. Candlewick Press 2000 32p il $15.99 (k-3) **597.8**
1. Frogs
ISBN 0-7636-0317-1   LC 99-43695
A mother and child watch as tadpoles develop and grow into frogs
"The illustrations . . . are just right for a first encounter with tadpole mysteries. The text presents all of the essential tips in such a lively manner that readers will want to become involved." SLJ

Gibbons, Gail
Frogs. Holiday House 1993 unp il $16.95; pa $6.95 (k-3)   **597.8**
1. Frogs
ISBN 0-8234-1052-8; 0-8234-1134-6 (pa)
LC 93-269

Gibbons, Gail—*Continued*

An introduction to frogs, discussing their tadpole beginnings, noises they make, their hibernation, body parts, and how they differ from toads

"Gibbons' distinctive, labeled drawings identify the features described in the text, and her subjects float, swim, jump, and dive in colorful, lifelike illustrations. . . . This attractive book will appeal to prereaders, beginning readers, and the adults who read to those groups." Booklist

Patent, Dorothy Hinshaw

Flashy fantastic rain forest frogs; illustrations by Kendahl Jan Jubb. Walker & Co. 1997 31p il maps $15.95; pa $6.95 (k-3)   **597.8**

1. Frogs 2. Rain forests
ISBN 0-8027-8615-4; 0-8027-7536-5 (pa)
                                        LC 96-29060

Describes the physical characteristics, behavior, reproduction, and habitat of frogs that live in the rain forest

"The pictures are dense with color and line. . . . The book's well-written text is right on the mark for the age group." Booklist

Pfeffer, Wendy, 1929-

From tadpole to frog; illustrated by Holly Keller. HarperCollins Pubs. 1994 32p il (Let's-read-and-find-out science) $15.95; pa $4.95 (k-1)   **597.8**

1. Frogs
ISBN 0-06-023044-4; 0-06-445123-2 (pa)
                                        LC 93-3135

Also available Audiobook version

This "introduction sketches the most basic aspects of frog life - the laying and hatching of eggs, the stages of growth, eating and the danger of being eaten, and hibernation." Horn Book Guide

"The illustrations are simple, interesting, and just right for young children. The science is accurate and presented in a way to excite young readers to get outside and look for some frogs and tadpoles." Sci Books Films

Snedden, Robert

What is an amphibian? photographs by Oxford Scientific Films; illustrated by Adrian Lascom. Sierra Club Bks. for Children 1994 32p il $14.95 (3-6)   **597.8**

1. Amphibians
ISBN 0-87156-469-6   LC 93-11619

Defines amphibians and describes their lives, including their maturation, mating, sense perception, and feeding

"With stunning photographs and illustrations on each page [this book] can not help but be appealing to youngsters. In addition, the text is well written and simple without being condescending or cute." Appraisal

Includes glossary

Souza, D. M. (Dorothy M.)

Shy salamanders. Carolrhoda Bks. 1995 40p il (Creatures all around us) lib bdg $22.60 (4-6)   **597.8**

1. Salamanders
ISBN 0-87614-826-7   LC 94-9108

"There are many similarities and differences among the various families of salamanders found in the world. *Shy Salamanders* examines these traits, along with the life cycles and habits of these elusive creatures." Publisher's note

Includes glossary

Wallace, Karen

Tale of a tadpole. DK Pub. 1998 32p il (Eyewitness readers) $12.95; pa $3.95 (k-1)
                                        597.8

1. Frogs
ISBN 0-7894-3761-9; 0-7894-3437-7 (pa)
                                        LC 98-14976

Describes the development of a tadpole

This is "heavily illustrated with striking full-color photographs and insets that invite a close inspection of features that might normally be overlooked, such as the creature's delicate fingers, tiny nostrils, or long tongue. The photographs are well chosen to illustrate this lively, carefully written narrative." SLJ

597.9   Reptiles

Arnosky, Jim

All about turtles; written and illustrated by Jim Arnosky. Scholastic Press 2000 unp il $15.95 (k-3)
                                        597.9

1. Turtles
ISBN 0-590-48149-5   LC 99-29657

Describes the physical characteristics, behavior, and survival techniques of different kinds of land and sea turtles

"The realistic, colorful illustrations depict a wide variety of turtles. . . . This visual feast is accompanied by a simple text." SLJ

Behler, John L.

National Audubon Society first field guide: reptiles; written by John L. Behler. Scholastic 1999 160p il maps $17.95; pa $11.95 (4 and up)
                                        597.9

1. Reptiles
ISBN 0-590-05467-8; 0-590-05487-2 (pa)
                                        LC 98-8332

Explores the world of reptiles, discussing their subspecies and races, anatomy, behavior, and habitat, and providing photographs and detailed descriptions of individual species

"Clear, full-color photographs and short capsules of information make it easy to identify each animal and its relatives." SLJ

Includes glossary and bibliographical references

Berger, Melvin, 1927-

Look out for turtles! illustrated by Megan Lloyd. HarperCollins Pubs. 1992 32p il (Let's-read-and-find-out science book) lib bdg $15.89; pa $4.95 (k-3)   **597.9**

1. Turtles
ISBN 0-06-022540-8 (lib bdg); 0-06-445156-9 (pa)
                                        LC 90-36894

Berger, Melvin, 1927—*Continued*

"This simple introductory resource provides an overview of the different types of turtles and their characteristics and habits. It is a good resource for young children to use independently." Sci Child

Conant, Roger, 1909-

Peterson first guide to reptiles and amphibians; [by] Roger Conant, Robert C. Stebbins, Joseph T. Collins. Houghton Mifflin 1992 128p il pa $5.95 (6 and up) **597.9**

1. Reptiles 2. Amphibians

ISBN 0-395-62232-8   LC 91-33016

This is a guide to identification of reptile and amphibian species

This is "easy to use. The information is accurate and easy to understand. . . . Useful for browsing as well as for identification in the field." Voice Youth Advocates

Darling, Kathy

Komodo dragon on location; photographs by Tara Darling. Lothrop, Lee & Shepard Bks. 1997 40p il $16; lib bdg $15.93 (3-5) **597.9**

1. Komodo dragon

ISBN 0-688-13776-8; 0-688-13777-6 (lib bdg)

LC 96-3700

Describes the physical characteristics, habitat, and behavior of the giant lizards found only in Indonesia

"A thoughtfully written, strikingly photographed wildlife book." Horn Book Guide

Gibbons, Gail

Sea turtles. Holiday House 1995 unp il $16.95; pa $6.95 (k-3) **597.9**

1. Sea turtles

ISBN 0-8234-1191-5; 0-8234-1373-X (pa)

LC 94-48579

This book examines "the size, habitat, and diet of the eight kinds of sea turtles and efforts environmentalists are making to protect them." Sci Child

This is "a very appealing book. . . . The illustrations are lovely paintings, highlighted with black outlines and clear labels. Children should find the diagram that shows differences between sea turtles and other turtles fascinating because they are often familiar only with the latter." Sci Books Films

Gove, Doris

A water snake's year; illustrated by Beverly Duncan. Atheneum Pubs. 1991 31p il $13.95 (3-5) **597.9**

1. Snakes

ISBN 0-689-31597-X   LC 90-673

Presents a year in the life of a female water snake, resident of Great Smoky Mountains National Park

"Gore's elegant language and Duncan's handsome, naturalistic paintings make this a sure bet for group sharing and nature units." Booklist

Guiberson, Brenda Z.

Into the sea; illustrated by Alix Berenzy. Holt & Co. 1996 unp il $16.95; pa $6.95 (k-3) **597.9**

1. Sea turtles

ISBN 0-8050-2263-5; 0-8050-6481-8 (pa)

LC 95-46757

The author "recounts the life of a sea turtle from its days as a hatchling on a sandy beach through its return to the same island as an egg-laying adult many years later." Booklist

"Guiberson uses italicized sound words such as *tap, tap,* and *scritch* to draw readers into the story. Berenzy captures the essence of the text with her colored-pencil and gouache illustrations that alternate from dark to light, reflecting the various habitats." SLJ

Lauber, Patricia, 1924-

Snakes are hunters; illustrated by Holly Keller. Crowell 1988 32p il (Let's-read-and-find-out science book) hardcover o.p. paperback available $4.95 (k-3) **597.9**

1. Snakes

ISBN 0-06-445091-0 (pa)   LC 87-47695

Describes the physical characteristics of a variety of snakes and how they hunt, catch, and eat their prey

"Holly Keller's bright and cheerful drawings make a potentially frightening subject more approachable and add just enough detail to enhance the brief text. An upbeat, simple, and readable presentation of an inherently interesting subject." Horn Book

Markle, Sandra, 1946-

Outside and inside alligators. Atheneum Bks. for Young Readers 1998 40p il lib bdg $16 (2-4) **597.9**

1. Alligators

ISBN 0-689-81457-7   LC 97-39804

Describes the external and internal physical characteristics of alligators and how they find their food, mate, and raise their young

This is an "accessible and visually appealing introduction. . . . Large, full-color photographs abound, enhancing every page." SLJ

Includes glossary

Outside and inside snakes. Macmillan Bks. for Young Readers 1995 40p il $17; pa $5.99 (2-4) **597.9**

1. Snakes

ISBN 0-02-762315-7; 0-689-81998-6 (pa)

LC 94-20647

This volume "discusses how snakes capture their food, how they move, and how their sensory, digestive, musculo-skeletal, and reproductive systems function. The text is conversational, leading the young reader to each important question and its answer." Sci Books Films

"The photographs are particularly strong in this title, depicting unfamiliar snakes and showing close-ups of amazing snake activity. A fine addition to reptile collections." Horn Book

Includes glossary

McCarthy, Colin, 1951-

Reptile; written by Colin McCarthy. Knopf 1991 63p il (Eyewitness books) (4 and up)   **597.9**
1. Reptiles

LC 90-4890

Available DK Pub. edition $15.95; lib bdg $19.99 (ISBN 0-7894-5786-5; 0-7894-6575-2)

Photographs and text depict the many different kinds of reptiles, their similarities and differences, habitats, and behavior

This book "stands out because of the fascinating photographs, which are brilliantly lifelike and well-chosen to demonstrate concepts discussed. . . . The text is nicely balanced between straightforward factual data and intriguing bits of trivia." SLJ

Montgomery, Sy

The snake scientist; photographs by Nic Bishop. Houghton Mifflin 1999 48p il map $16; pa $4.95 (4 and up)   **597.9**
1. Mason, Bob 2. Snakes

ISBN 0-395-87169-7; 0-618-11119-0 (pa)

LC 98-6124

Discusses the work of Bob Mason and his efforts to study and protect snakes, particularly red-sided garter snakes

"The lively text communicates both the meticulous measurements required in this kind of work and the thrill of new discoveries. Large, full-color photos of the zoologist and young students at work, and lots of wriggly snakes, pull readers into the presentation." SLJ

Includes bibliographical references

Patent, Dorothy Hinshaw

The American alligator; photographs by William Muñoz. Clarion Bks. 1994 77p il $15.95 (4 and up)   **597.9**
1. Alligators

ISBN 0-395-63392-3   LC 93-37704

This "book offers an overview of the facts and folklore surrounding alligators and their family, the crocodilians. The informative text, which discusses the habits and life cycle of the cold-blooded animals, is complemented by the well-chosen full-color photographs that appear on almost every page." Booklist

Includes bibliographical references

Simon, Seymour, 1931-

Crocodiles & alligators. HarperCollins Pubs. 1999 unp il $15.95; lib bdg $15.89 (3-6)   **597.9**
1. Crocodiles 2. Alligators

ISBN 0-06-027473-5; 0-06-027474-3 (lib bdg)

LC 98-34705

Describes the physical characteristics and behavior of various members of the family of animals known as crocodilians

"The book is filled with interesting information, and the vivid, well-composed, full-color photographs and entertaining text will draw in browsers." SLJ

Snakes. HarperCollins Pubs. 1992 unp il $16.95; pa $6.95 (3-6)   **597.9**
1. Snakes

ISBN 0-06-022529-7; 0-06-446165-3 (pa)

LC 91-15948

Describes, in text and photographs, the physical characteristics, habits, and natural environment of various species of snakes

"Once again Simon demonstrates his skill in molding a lucid discussion and striking photographs into a compelling, informative overview." Horn Book

Smith, Trevor

Amazing lizards; written by Trevor Smith; photographed by Jerry Young. Knopf 1990 29p il (Eyewitness juniors) hardcover o.p. paperback available $9.99 (2-4)   **597.9**
1. Lizards

ISBN 0-679-80819-1 (pa)   LC 90-31884

Features some of the remarkable members of the lizard world, including the chameleon, flying gecko, and blue tongue skink, and describes important characteristics of the whole group

"This very attractive little book should delight younger readers with excellent color photographs of and interesting facts about selected lizards." Sci Books Films

The **Snake** book; photography by Frank Greenaway and Dave King. DK Pub. 1997 unp il $12.95; pa $7.95 (4-6)   **597.9**
1. Snakes

ISBN 0-7894-1526-7; 0-7894-6068-8 (pa)

LC 96-38294

Written and edited by Mary Ling and Mary Atkinson

The "creators of the book have used a stark white box as a background for some spectacular life-size photographs of 12 varieties of snakes. . . . Text containing very basic information about each snake sweeps around and inside the reptiles' coils, with the font varying in size from large to very small." Booklist

Staub, Frank J.

Sea turtles; written and photographed by Frank Staub. Lerner Publs. 1995 48p il (Early bird nature books) lib bdg $22.60 (2-4)   **597.9**
1. Sea turtles

ISBN 0-8225-3005-8   LC 94-4630

"Staub looks at the life cycles of the five types of sea turtles. Full-color photographs depict the animals in the ocean waters surrounding the U.S. and on the beaches where they lay their eggs. . . . Environmental dangers and attempts at protection are thoughtfully treated in a separate chapter." SLJ

Includes glossary

598 Birds

Arnold, Caroline, 1944-

Hawk highway in the sky; watching raptor migration; photographs by Robert Kruidenier. Harcourt Brace & Co. 1997 48p il $18 (4-6)

598

1. Hawks 2. Eagles 3. Falcons 4. Birds—Migration

ISBN 0-15-200868-3   LC 95-51213

"A Gulliver Green book"

Arnold, Caroline, 1944-—*Continued*

Provides information about hawks, eagles, and falcons and efforts to study them, especially the HawkWatch International Raptor Migration Project in the Goshute Mountains in Nevada

"Robert Kruidenier's sharply shot full-color photographs (many of them close-ups) work well with Arnold's clear, well-organized text, capturing the fierce beauty of the birds as well as the scientists' painstaking work." Booklist

Arnosky, Jim

All about owls. Scholastic 1995 unp il hardcover o.p. paperback available $5.99 (1-3)

598

1. Owls

ISBN 0-4390-5852-X (pa)   LC 94-44859

Text and illustrations show "where owls live, what they eat, how they care for their young, and how they see so well at night." Sci Child

"Arnosky writes with clarity and a sure sense of what will interest young children. With its well-composed watercolor paintings, this volume will appeal to science-book browsers as well as young students researching the topic." Booklist

All about turkeys. Scholastic 1998 unp il $15.95 (1-3)

598

1. Turkeys

ISBN 0-590-48147-9   LC 97-34716

Discusses turkeys, what they eat, where they sleep, and how they survive

"This will best serve the needs of children seeking information for reports, but the eye-catching art and informative text should draw its share of casual readers as well." SLJ

Crinkleroot's guide to knowing the birds. Bradbury Press 1992 32p il $15; pa $5.99 (k-3)

598

1. Birds

ISBN 0-02-705857-3; 0-689-81532-8 (pa)

LC 91-38234

An introduction to birds one might see in the woods

"Arnosky has created another wonderful nature guide featuring his lovable woodsman, Crinkleroot. . . . Arnosky's bright watercolors and precise renderings of different species make this an especially attractive book, and one that parents will enjoy using with their children. Teachers preparing nature units for primary grade students will also find this a useful resource." Booklist

Watching water birds. National Geographic Soc. 1997 unp il $16 (2-4)   **598**

1. Water birds

ISBN 0-7922-7073-8   LC 97-7594

Provides a personal look at various species of fresh- and saltwater birds, including loons and grebes, mergansers, mallards, wood ducks, Canada geese, gulls, and herons

Arnosky "weaves facts and many personal observations in the breezy conversational blocks of text and informative captions that surround the naturalistic, almost photoreal, watercolor paintings. . . . He offers marvelous anatomical detail and captures close-up views of that casual observers rarely get to see." SLJ

Bash, Barbara

Urban roosts: where birds nest in the city. Sierra Club Bks.; Little, Brown 1990 unp il hardcover o.p. paperback available $6.95 (1-4)   **598**

1. Birds—Nests

ISBN 0-316-08312-7 (pa)   LC 89-70187

"Excellent treatment of an unusual subject reveals that human-made places of steel, stone, and concrete are home to a variety of birds. Includes information on sparrows, finches, barn and snowy owls, swallows, swifts, nighthawks, killdeers, pigeons, wrens, crows, starlings, and falcons that have successfully adapted to city life." Sci Child

Bernhard, Emery

Eagles; lions of the sky; written by Emery Bernhard; illustrated by Durga Bernhard. Holiday House 1994 unp il $15.95 (k-3)   **598**

1. Eagles

ISBN 0-8234-1105-2   LC 93-1833

This "describes eagles' flying and hunting behavior; the physical characteristics of the four main groups of eagles; courtship, mating, and rearing of the young; their ecological value; and conservation problems." Horn Book Guide

"This dramatic picture book introduces a wealth of factual information. . . . The direct text is smoothly integrated with clear color illustrations that provide detail and connection." Booklist

Includes glossary

Brenner, Barbara

Chibi; a true story from Japan; by Barbara Brenner and Julia Takaya; illustrated by June Otani. Clarion Bks. 1996 63p il lib bdg $14.95; pa $5.95 (k-3)   **598**

1. Ducks 2. Japan—Social life and customs

ISBN 0-395-69623-2 (lib bdg); 0-395-72088-5 (pa)

LC 94-31082

This is a "true story about a duck who built her nest in a busy office park and then decided to take her brood across eight lanes of traffic to live in the moat of the Imperial Gardens. The ducks became an obsession of the Japanese in general and a photojournalist named Sato in particular, who made a media star out of the smallest and weakest duckling, Chibi, and who led the search when Chibi was lost in a typhoon." Bull Cent Child Books

The story "is told in a crisp, straightforward style and illustrated with uncluttered, realistic watercolor and ink artwork that has captured a sense of traditional Japanese painting." Horn Book Guide

Includes glossary

Burnie, David

Bird; written by David Burnie. Knopf 1988 63p il (Eyewitness books) (4 and up)   **598**

1. Birds

LC 87-26441

Available DK Pub. edition $15.95; lib bdg $19.99 (ISBN 0-7894-5800-4; 0-7894-6550-7)

A photo essay on the world of birds examining such topics as body construction, feathers and flight, the adaptation of beaks and feet, feeding habits, courtship, nests and eggs, and bird watching

Cherry, Lynne, 1952-

Flute's journey; the life of a wood thrush; written and illustrated by Lynne Cherry. Harcourt Brace & Co. 1997 unp il $15 (2-4)   **598**

1. Wood thrush

ISBN 0-15-292853-7   LC 96-17024

"A Gulliver green book"

A young wood thrush makes his first migration from his nesting ground in a forest preserve in Maryland to his winter home in Costa Rica and back again

This features "detailed watercolors. . . . The story and illustrations contain much useful information." Horn Book Guide

DuTemple, Lesley A., 1952-

North American cranes. Carolrhoda Bks. 1999 48p il (Carolrhoda nature watch book) $22.60 (3-6)   **598**

1. Cranes (Birds)

ISBN 1-57505-302-0   LC 98-4519

Describes the physical characteristics, diet, natural habitat, and life cycle of these large wading birds, and tells about the efforts of scientists to establish resident flocks

"Colorful and informative. . . . Illustrated with many excellent, full-color photos." Booklist

Esbensen, Barbara Juster

Tiger with wings; the great horned owl; illustrated by Mary Barrett Brown. Orchard Bks. 1991 unp il $16.95; lib bdg $17.99; pa $5.95 (2-4)   **598**

1. Owls

ISBN 0-531-05940-5; 0-531-08540-6 (lib bdg); 0-531-07071-9 (pa)   LC 90-23034

Describes the hunting technique, physical characteristics, mating ritual, and nesting and child-rearing practices of the great horned owl

"The watercolor paintings in mainly grays, brown, and blues beautifully convey information, mood, and sometimes humor. . . . The writing is clean and clear, with an occasional colorful simile or metaphor." SLJ

Gans, Roma, 1894-1996

How do birds find their way? illustrated by Paul Mirocha. HarperCollins Pubs. 1996 32p il (Let's-read-and-find-out science) lib bdg $15.89; pa $4.95 (k-3)   **598**

1. Birds—Migration

ISBN 0-06-020225-4 (lib bdg); 0-06-445150-X (pa)   LC 91-11918

The author "tells what ornithologists know about migration patterns and presents some of their theories about how birds know when to fly and their different means of navigation. Watercolor and colored-pencil illustrations show several species and their habitats, as well as a few maps and charts. The careful coloring and identification of specific birds add to the value of this attractive introductory text." SLJ

Gibbons, Gail

Gulls—gulls—gulls. Holiday House 1997 unp il $15.95 (k-3)   **598**

1. Gulls

ISBN 0-8234-1323-3   LC 97-1266

Describes the life cycle, behavior patterns, and habitat of various species of gulls, focusing on those found in North America

"Both illustration and text provide basic, easy-to-understand facts. . . . The format is attractive with framed, simply drawn watercolor illustrations showing the birds in the foreground against bright colorful seashore or seascape backgrounds of dominant blues and greens." SLJ

Penguins! Holiday House 1998 unp il maps $16.95; pa $6.95 (k-3)   **598**

1. Penguins

ISBN 0-8234-1388-8; 0-8234-1516-3 (pa)   LC 98-5194

Describes the habitat, physical characteristics, and behavior of different kinds of penguins

This book has "simply written, clear text. . . . The oversized format, brightly colored illustrations, and large type font result in an eye-catching appearance that will attract young researchers and the curious minded alike." SLJ

The puffins are back! HarperCollins Pubs. 1991 unp il $15.95 (k-3)   **598**

1. Puffins

ISBN 0-06-021603-4   LC 90-30525

A simple introduction to the physical characteristics, life cycle, and natural environment of the puffins living off the coast of Maine

"Gail Gibbons tells the story of the endangered puffin colony in a clear, direct text, weaving facts about puffin characteristics and behavior throughout her dramatic narrative. Her rich palette of blues and greens gives life and depth to the island setting and contrasts with the clean black and white of the puffins." Horn Book

Soaring with the wind; the bald eagle. Morrow Junior Bks. 1998 unp il $16.95; lib bdg $16.89 (k-3)   **598**

1. Bald eagle

ISBN 0-688-13730-X; 0-688-13731-8 (lib bdg)   LC 97-20497

Describes the characteristics, behavior, and life cycle of the bald eagle

"Appealing watercolor illustrations, labeled diagrams, definitions, and well-researched facts come together to form a perfect connection for teachers seeking to expand science units." SLJ

Goldin, Augusta R.

Ducks don't get wet; by Augusta Goldin; illustrated by Helen K. Davie. newly il ed. HarperCollins Pubs. 1999 32p il (Let's-read-and-find-out science) $15.95; lib bdg $15.89; pa $4.95 (k-3)   **598**

1. Ducks

ISBN 0-06-027881-1; 0-06-027882-X (lib bdg); 0-06-445187-9 (pa)   LC 97-43597

A newly illustrated edition of the title first published 1965 by Crowell

Goldin, Augusta R.—*Continued*

Describes the behavior of different kinds of ducks and, in particular, discusses how all ducks use preening to keep their feathers dry

"The text is well focused throughout. . . . Notable for its clarity, subtlety, and beauty, the artwork illustrates the text with precision and imagination." Booklist

Hickman, Pamela M.

Starting with nature bird book; written by Pamela Hickman; illustrated by Heather Collins. Kids Can Press 2000 c1996 32p il $12.95; pa $5.95 (4 and up)   598
1. Birds
ISBN 1-550-74471-2; 1-550-74810-6 (pa)
First published 1996 in Canada

"Two-page sections address general characteristics of birds, groupings, habitats, seasonal effects on birds, migration, songs, bird-watching, seabirds and prairie birds, the importance of birds, and some endangered species. Several activities, doable at home with simple materials, help maintain interest. . . . The volume clearly has been meticulously thought out, and the beautiful color drawings . . . mirror the text closely." Sci Books Films

Jenkins, Martin

The emperor's egg; illustrated by Jane Chapman. Candlewick Press 1999 29p il $16.99 (k-3)   598
1. Penguins
ISBN 0-7636-0557-3   LC 98-46839
Describes the parental behavior of Emperor penguins, focusing on how the male keeps the egg warm until it hatches and how the parents care for the chick after it is born

"Chapman's acrylics reflect the gleeful tone of the text without anthropomorphizing the subject, relying on the odd perspective and occasional close-up of the penguins' naturally comic visage to do the trick. . . . Beginning readers will get a charge out of something that's interesting, accurate, and theirs." Bull Cent Child Books

Jenkins, Priscilla Belz

A nest full of eggs; illustrated by Lizzy Rockwell. HarperCollins Pubs. 1995 32p il (Let's-read-and-find-out science) lib bdg $15.89; pa $5.95 (k-1)   598
1. Robins 2. Birds—Nests
ISBN 0-06-023442-3 (lib bdg); 0-06-445127-5 (pa)
LC 93-43804
This story features "a pair of robins that arrives in the spring, raises a family, and departs in the fall before winter arrives. . . . In addition to the robin family, several examples of the diversity of feathers and nests of other birds are included." Sci Books Films

This book "will catch children's interest, and the author's suggestions for materials to leave out to help robins build their nests are ones many children will want to follow." Bull Cent Child Books

Johnson, Sylvia A.

Inside an egg; photographs by Kiyoshi Shimizu. Lerner Publs. 1982 48p il (Lerner natural science book) lib bdg $22.60; pa $5.95 (4 and up)   598
1. Eggs 2. Chickens
ISBN 0-8225-1472-9 (lib bdg); 0-8225-9522-2 (pa)
LC 81-17235
Adapted from a work by Kiyoshi Shimizu published 1975 in Japan

Text and photographs trace the development of a chicken egg from the time it is laid until it is hatched

"New and difficult concept words are listed in bold type as they appear in the text. All color graphics are excellent; the close-up photographs are stunning. The format and general layout of text to photograph is without confusion and the [book is] loaded with facts." SLJ
Includes glossary

Latimer, Jonathan P.

Backyard birds; [by] Jonathan P. Latimer, Karen Stray Nolting; illustrations by Roger Tory Peterson; foreword by Virginia Marie Peterson. Houghton Mifflin 1999 48p il (Peterson field guides for young naturalists) $15; pa $5.95 (4 and up)   598
1. Birds
ISBN 0-395-95210-7; 0-395-92276-3 (pa)
LC 98-35509

Birds of prey; [by] Jonathan P. Latimer, Karen Stray Nolting; illustrations by Roger Tory Peterson; foreword by Virginia Marie Peterson. Houghton Mifflin 1999 48p il (Peterson field guides for young naturalists) $15; pa $5.95 (4 and up)   598
1. Birds of prey
ISBN 0-395-95211-5; 0-395-92277-1 (pa)
LC 98-35516

Bizarre birds; [by] Jonathan P. Latimer, Karen Stray Nolting; illustrations by Roger Tory Peterson; foreword by Virginia Marie Peterson. Houghton Mifflin 1999 48p il (Peterson field guides for young naturalists) $15; pa $5.95 (4 and up)   598
1. Birds
ISBN 0-395-95213-1; 0-395-92279-8 (pa)
LC 98-35512

Shorebirds; [by] Jonathan P. Latimer, Karen Stray Nolting; illustrations by Roger Tory Peterson; foreword by Virginia Marie Peterson. Houghton Mifflin 1999 48p il (Peterson field guides for young naturalists) $15; pa $5.95 (4 and up)   598
1. Birds
ISBN 0-395-95212-3; 0-395-92278-X (pa)
LC 98-35510
"Each guidebook includes a rather subjective selection of about 20 creatures. The organization of material is different in each title: the backyard birds are grouped by color, the raptors by size, and the bizarre birds by such characteristics as odd bills. The shorebirds are arranged

Latimer, Jonathan P.—*Continued*

by where they are likely to be seen—the air, water, ground, or grass. A two-page entry for each creature instructs readers on how to recognize it and provides a solid introduction to individual characteristics." SLJ

Songbirds; [by] Jonathan P. Latimer, Karen Stray Nolting; illustrations by Roger Tory Peterson; foreword by Virginia Marie Peterson. Houghton Mifflin 2000 48p il (Peterson field guides for young naturalists) $15; pa $5.95 (4 and up) **598**

1. Birds 2. Birdsongs

ISBN 0-395-97941-2; 0-395-97946-3 (pa)

LC 99-38293

Describes the physical characteristics, habitats, feeding habits, and voices of a variety of songbirds, arranged under the categories "Simple Songs," "Complex Songs," "Whistling Songs," "Warbling Songs," "Trilling Songs," "Name-sayers," and "Mimics"

Lerner, Carol, 1927-

Backyard birds of summer. Morrow Junior Bks. 1996 48p il lib bdg $15.93 (3-6) **598**

1. Birds

ISBN 0-688-13601-X   LC 95-12652

Companion volume to Backyard birds of winter (1994)

Describes primarily those species of birds which are tropical migrants visiting the North only during the nesting season. Includes suggestions for attracting birds to one's yard

"Lerner has created another lovely, informative title for budding ornithologists. . . . She combines beautiful watercolor illustrations with lucid prose." SLJ

Includes bibliographical references

Lynch, Wayne

Penguins! text and photographs by Wayne Lynch. Firefly Bks. (Willowdale) 1999 64p il map $19.95; pa $9.95 (4 and up) **598**

1. Penguins

ISBN 1-55209-421-9; 1-55209-424-3 (pa)

In a "first-person narrative, peppered with journal excerpts, personal observations, and anecdotes, Lynch discusses penguins' evolution, varied habitats, physical and behavioral adaptations, diet, predators, mating and nesting habits, and chick development." Horn Book Guide

This "is a delightful book. . . . The beautiful color photographs and the text tell a fascinating, exciting, and revealing story." Sci Books Films

Markle, Sandra, 1946-

Outside and inside birds. Bradbury Press 1994 40p il $17 (2-4) **598**

1. Birds

ISBN 0-02-762312-2   LC 93-38910

"Among the topics Markle tackles are feathers, flying, anatomy, eating habits, senses, birth, and growth. Other pictures examine in close detail the outsides of the winged wonders: their feathers, feet, preen glands, wings, beaks, and much more." SLJ

"Markle writes with verve, easily engaging her audience with questions, simple analogies, and comparisons. . . . The selection and display of photographs is masterful in demonstrating both the design features of bird bodies and the internal organs." Horn Book

Includes glossary

McMillan, Bruce

Nights of the pufflings; written and photo-illustrated by Bruce McMillan. Houghton Mifflin 1995 32p il $16; pa $5.95 (2-4) **598**

1. Puffins

ISBN 0-395-70810-9; 0-395-85693-0 (pa)

LC 94-14808

"For two weeks every year, the children of Heimaey Island, Iceland, stay out late rescuing hundreds of stranded pufflings. Many of the birds are confused by the village lights and need help flying toward the sea." Sci Child

"This fascinating story, combined with gorgeous color photographs, a simple, clear text, and handsome book design, makes an appealing package. McMillan includes the pronunciation of unfamiliar Icelandic names and words within the text and follows his story with an afterwood about the North Atlantic puffins." Horn Book

Includes bibliographical references

Penguins at home; gentoos of Antarctica; written and photo-illustrated by Bruce McMillan. Houghton Mifflin 1993 32p il $17 (2-4) **598**

1. Penguins

ISBN 0-395-66560-4   LC 92-34769

Describes the physical characteristics, behavior, and life cycle of the timid gentoo penguin

"First-rate photographs illustrate a text that supplies interesting information. . . . Large captions summarize important facts and detailed descriptions are provided to enrich the volume." Sci Child

Includes bibliographical references

Wild flamingos; written and photo-illustrated by Bruce McMillan. Houghton Mifflin 1997 32p il $17 (3-6) **598**

1. Flamingos

ISBN 0-395-84545-9   LC 97-1521

A photo essay describing the physical characteristics, natural habitat, and behavior of the flamingos of Bonaire, Netherlands Antilles

"Children can learn a great deal from the readable text. . . . The striking full-color photographs capture the birds in a variety of interesting poses." SLJ

Includes bibliographical references

Morrison, Gordon

Bald eagle. Houghton Mifflin 1998 30p il $16 (2-4) **598**

1. Bald eagle

ISBN 0-395-87328-2   LC 97-42007

"Walter Lorraine books"

"Large watercolor and black-ink drawings illustrate the life cycle of the American bald eagle." SLJ

This "works on several levels. . . . Without anthropomorphizing, Morrison offers an elegant, scientific look at the way eagles live in the wild." Booklist

National Audubon Society first field guide: birds. Scholastic 1998 159p il maps $17.95; pa $8.95 (4 and up) **598**
1. Birds
ISBN 0-590-05446-5; 0-590-05482-1 (pa)
LC 97-17989
A visual guide to the natural science of birds as well as a field guide to over 150 species found in North America
This offers "a great deal of information in a handy format . . . [and] large, beautifully colored photos of each bird." Booklist
Includes glossary and bibliographical references

Parry-Jones, Jemima
Amazing birds of prey; written by Jemima Parry-Jones; photographed by Mike Dunning. Knopf 1992 29p il (Eyewitness juniors) lib bdg $11.99; pa $9.99 (2-4) **598**
1. Birds of prey
ISBN 0-679-82771-9 (lib bdg); 0-679-82771-4 (pa)
LC 92-909
Introduces the physical characteristics and habits of birds of prey, including falcons, eagles, vultures, owls, and hawks

Patent, Dorothy Hinshaw
Eagles of America; photographs by William Muñoz. Holiday House 1995 40p il $15.95 (4 and up) **598**
1. Eagles
ISBN 0-8234-1198-2
LC 95-6083
"The only two native species of North American eagles, the bald and golden, are treated in this comparative presentation. Patent describes how their numbers declined dramatically during the 19th and 20th centuries. . . . She also discusses the work of wildlife rehabilitators and conservation efforts. Splendid full-color photographs illustrate the lively text and clarify descriptions." SLJ

Looking at penguins; photographs by Graham Robertson. Holiday House 1993 40p il $16.95 (3-5) **598**
1. Penguins
ISBN 0-8234-1037-4
LC 92-37673
Describes the different kinds of penguins, their habitat, behavior, and status as an endangered species
This features "good, clear photographs. . . . Intriguing information is scattered through the text." Booklist

Ospreys; photographs by William Muñoz. Clarion Bks. 1993 63p il $14.95 (4 and up) **598**
1. Ospreys 2. Wildlife conservation
ISBN 0-395-63391-5
LC 92-30103
Describes the physical characteristics and habits of ospreys, or fish hawks, as well as threats to their survival and efforts to protect them
"Clearly presented information and an attractive format (large print with numerous color photographs) will attract young readers." Booklist
Includes bibliographical references

Pigeons; photographs by William Muñoz. Clarion Bks. 1997 78p il $16 (4 and up) **598**
1. Pigeons
ISBN 0-395-69848-0
LC 96-42072

Describes the physical characteristics, behavior, and usefulness of these birds, which have lived with people since prehistoric times
"This informative book offers a well-researched and readable text illustrated with clear, full-color photographs." Booklist
Includes glossary

Peterson, Roger Tory, 1908-1996
A field guide to the birds; a completely new guide to all the birds of eastern and central North America; text and illustrations by Roger Tory Peterson; maps by Virginia Marie Peterson. 4th ed, completely rev and enl. Houghton Mifflin 1980 384p il maps 1998 reissue available $27; pa $18 **598**
1. Birds—North America
ISBN 0-395-91173-3; 0-395-91176-1 (pa)
LC 80-14304
Also available large format edition
"The Peterson field guide series"
First published 1934
Sponsored by the National Audubon Society and National Wildlife Federation
This guide to birds found east of the Rocky Mountains contains colored illustrations painted by the author, with description of each species on the facing page. Views of young birds and seasonal variations in plumage are included. Birds are arranged in eight major groups of body shape. There are also 390 colored maps showing summer and winter range

A field guide to western birds; text and illustrations by Roger Tory Peterson; maps by Virginia Marie Peterson. 3rd ed, completely rev and enl. Houghton Mifflin 1989 432p il maps 1998 reissue available $27; pa $18 **598**
1. Birds—West (U.S.)
ISBN 0-395-91174-5; 0-395-91173-7 (pa)
LC 89-31517
"The Peterson field guide series"
First published 1941
"A completely new guide to field marks of all species found in North America west of the 100th meridian and north of Mexico." Title page
Sponsored by the National Audubon Society, the National Wildlife Federation, and the Roger Tory Peterson Institute
This guide illustrates over 1,000 birds (700 species) on 165 color plates. In addition, over 400 distribution maps are included

Sattler, Helen Roney
The book of North American owls; illustrated by Jean Day Zallinger. Clarion Bks. 1995 64p il maps $17 (4 and up) **598**
1. Owls
ISBN 0-395-60524-5
LC 91-43626
This volume "includes owl classification and history, hunting and habitat, courtship and nesting, and the complex relationship between owls and humans. The comprehensive glossary includes all of the 21 North American species." Sci Child

Sattler, Helen Roney—*Continued*

This "is a superb ornithological primer. . . . The book is lavishly illustrated." Appraisal

Includes bibliographical references

Silverstein, Alvin

The California condor; [by] Alvin and Virginia Silverstein and Laura Silverstein Nunn. Millbrook Press 1998 64p il (Endangered in America) lib bdg $24.90 (4 and up)   **598**

1. Condors 2. Wildlife conservation

ISBN 0-7613-0264-6   LC 97-45025

Describes the physical characteristics and behavior of the California condor, its decline in numbers due to human population growth and activities, and the efforts being made to maintain its population

"Clearly reproduced color photographs enhance the readable text." Horn Book Guide

Includes bibliographical references

Stone, Lynn M.

Vultures. Carolrhoda Bks. 1993 48p il (Carolrhoda nature watch book) hardcover o.p. paperback available $7.95 (3-6)   **598**

1. Vultures

ISBN 0-8761-4950-6 (pa)   LC 92-26721

The author "describes the lives of raptors in general and specifically vultures. Often connected with death, these birds suffer from a negative image that Stone . . . disputes, discussing the important role of scavengers in cleaning up carrion and preventing the spread of disease. She also examines the different breeds, their nesting habits, modern-day threats to their existence, and the successful captive breeding program of the California Condor." SLJ

This book features "a readable text, accompanied by clear color photographs." Sci Child

Includes glossary and bibliographical references

599   Mammals

Bateman, Robert, 1930-

Safari; [by] Robert Bateman and Rick Archbold. Little, Brown 1998 unp il $17.95 (3-6)   **599**

1. Animals—Africa

ISBN 0-316-08265-1   LC 98-6139

"A Madison Press book"

Paintings and brief text present some of the animals found in Africa, including elephants, giraffes, cheetahs, wildebeests, lions, ostriches, and zebras

"At least one full page per spread is devoted to Bateman's spectacular oil paintings that are photographic in detail and perfectly capture the essence and beauty of their subjects. These illustrations combined with the text create a sort of travel diary that clearly conveys the artist's love of wildlife." SLJ

Grassy, John

National Audubon Society first field guide: mammals; written by John Grassy and Chuck Keene. Scholastic 1998 159p il maps $17.95; pa $8.95 (4 and up)   **599**

1. Mammals

ISBN 0-590-05471-6; 0-590-05489-9 (pa)

     LC 98-2939

Explores the world of mammals, identifying their characteristics and describing individual species

Includes glossary and bibliographical references

Parker, Steve

Mammal; written by Steve Parker. Knopf 1989 63p il (Eyewitness books) (4 and up)   **599**

1. Mammals

     LC 88-22656

Available DK Pub. edition $15.95; lib bdg $19.99 (ISBN 0-7894-5818-7; 0-7894-6560-4)

Photographs and text examine the world of mammals, depicting their development, feeding habits, courtship rituals, protective behavior, and physical adaptation to their various ways of life

This book takes a "comprehensive yet detailed look at members of the class that includes humans. Filled with color photographs keyed to the text, the book provides ample illustrations of a variety of mammals and their unique traits." Sci Books Films

599.2   Marsupials and monotremes

Burt, Denise

Kangaroos; photographs by Neil McLeod; edited by Sylvia A. Johnson. Carolrhoda Bks. 2000 48p il (Carolrhoda nature watch book) $23.93 (3-6)

    599.2

1. Kangaroos

ISBN 1-57505-388-8   LC 99-26680

"What makes a kangaroo distinct? What is a kangaroo, large or small? How does a kangaroo live, and what is its family life like? The book answers such questions superbly and concisely. Excellent photos support the text and vice versa." Sci Books Films

Includes glossary

Markle, Sandra, 1946-

Outside and inside kangaroos. Atheneum Bks. for Young Readers 1999 40p il $16 (2-4) **599.2**

1. Kangaroos

ISBN 0-689-81456-9   LC 98-45354

Describes the inner and outer workings of kangaroos, including their diet, anatomy, and life cycle

"The prose is engaging, incorporating direct address and well-chosen questions to encourage thought and participation. . . . Abundant full-color photos of kangaroos are fascinating and explicative." Booklist

Includes glossary

599.3 Miscellaneous orders of placental mammals

Bernhard, Emery
Prairie dogs; written by Emery Bernhard; illustrated by Durga Bernhard. Harcourt Brace & Co. 1997 unp il $15 (2-4)   **599.3**
1. Prairie dogs
ISBN 0-15-201286-9   LC 96-22849
"Gulliver books"
"Focusing on the black-tailed prairie dog . . . the book describes the animal's life cycle at length, including defense systems, mating cycles, and feeding habits, as well as its role in the ecosystem of the grasslands. Bernhard goes on to discuss how the prairie dog's reputation as a pest began, and what is being done to save it from extinction. This is a solid and well-written introduction, with added appeal in the gouache drawings." SLJ
Includes glossary

Gibbons, Gail
Rabbits, rabbits, & more rabbits! Holiday House 2000 unp il $16.95; pa $6.95 (k-3)   **599.3**
1. Rabbits
ISBN 0-8234-1486-8; 0-8234-1660-7 (pa)
LC 99-16765
Describes different kinds of rabbits, their physical characteristics, behavior, where they live, and how to care for them
"Colored washes and crayon shading enliven the clearly delineated ink drawings." Booklist

Patent, Dorothy Hinshaw
Prairie dogs; photographs by William Muñoz. Clarion Bks. 1993 63p il hardcover o.p. paperback available $6.95 (4 and up)   **599.3**
1. Prairie dogs 2. Prairie ecology
ISBN 0-395-52601-9 (pa)   LC 92-34724
Discusses the habits and life cycle of prairie dogs and examines their place in the ecology of their grassland environment
"The text and illustrations work together, each enlarging the other and both enlightening the reader. Appearing on nearly every page, the full-color photographs take readers out to the prairie to see its plants and animals clearly." Booklist
Includes bibliographical references

Powell, E. Sandy
Rats; photographs by Jerry Boucher. Lerner Publs. 1994 48p il (Early bird nature books) lib bdg $22.60 (2-4)   **599.3**
1. Rats
ISBN 0-8225-3003-1   LC 93-40925
This book contains "information about rat habits and habitats, different types of rats, their foods and burrows, and baby rats and their growing up." Sci Books Films
"Rats is a delightful book that gives a great boost to the reputation of these creatures. . . . It is loaded with beautiful color photographs." Sci Child
Includes glossary

Rounds, Glen, 1906-
Beaver. Holiday House 1999 unp il $16.95 (k-3)
599.3
1. Beavers
ISBN 0-8234-1440-X   LC 98-28803
Describes the physical characteristics, diet, and nighttime activities of the beaver, an expert swimmer and builder
"Round's rough, scribbly lines are especially suited to these evocative pictures of beavers at rest and at work. . . . The text, outlining the beaver's daily habits and modus vivendi, is a model of how to convey a wealth of information in just a few clear, well-phrased statements." Horn Book Guide

Tagholm, Sally
The rabbit; illustrated by Bert Kitchen; written by Sally Tagholm. Kingfisher (NY) 2000 32p il (Animal lives) $9.95 (2-4)   **599.3**
1. Rabbits
ISBN 0-7534-5214-6   LC 99-45787
Describes how the European rabbit, now found on every continent, burrows, breeds, feeds, plays, and lives
"Charming illustrations and an attractive layout support the lyrical and engaging text." Sci Child
Includes glossary

599.4 Bats

Ackerman, Diane
Bats; shadows in the night; photographs by Merlin Tuttle. Crown 1997 30p il $18; lib bdg $19.99 (4-6)   **599.4**
1. Bats
ISBN 0-517-70919-8; 0-517-70920-1 (lib bdg)
LC 96-6047
The author gets to see bats close up as she accompanies bat expert and founder of Bat Conservation International, Merlin Tuttle, on a trip to study these often misunderstood mammals
"Ackerman's personalized, poetic narrative is natural history writing at its best. . . . The profusion of Tuttle's crystal-clear full-color photos enhances and extends in text." Booklist

Bash, Barbara
Shadows of night; the hidden world of the little brown bat. Sierra Club Bks. for Children 1993 unp il hardcover o.p. paperback available $6.95 (1-3)
599.4
1. Bats
ISBN 0-87156-440-8 (pa)   LC 92-22713
Describes the life cycle, physical characteristics, and habits of the little brown bat
"The author's fascination with and unabashed affection for these nocturnal insect catchers comes through in her informative text and outstanding watercolors." SLJ

Earle, Ann

Zipping, zapping, zooming bats; illustrated by Henry Cole. HarperCollins Pubs. 1995 32p il (Let's-read-and-find-out science) lib bdg $15.89; pa $4.95 (k-3)   **599.4**

1. Bats

ISBN 0-06-023480-6 (lib bdg); 0-06-445133-X (pa)
LC 93-11052

"Brown bats are introduced as fliers, hunters, and contributors to good ecology in this simple discussion of the flying mammals' physical characteristics and behavior. The illustrations include realistic close-ups, informative diagrams, and scenes incorporating children. Instructions for building a bat house are included." Horn Book Guide

Gibbons, Gail

Bats. Holiday House 1999 unp il $16.95; pa $6.95 (k-3)   **599.4**

1. Bats

ISBN 0-8234-1457-4; 0-8234-1637-2 (pa)
LC 99-12051

Describes different kinds of bats, their physical characteristics, habits and behavior, and efforts to protect them

"The occasional splashes of color light up brilliantly against the dark backgrounds. Well suited for classroom use, this book makes a good case for bats as an admirable part of the natural world." Booklist

Markle, Sandra, 1946-

Outside and inside bats. Atheneum Bks. for Young Readers 1997 40p il $16 (2-4)   **599.4**

1. Bats

ISBN 0-689-81165-9   LC 96-48291

Describes the inner and outer workings of bats, discussing their diet, anatomy, and reproduction

"The photographs are excellent, clearly described and labeled. . . . The author presents a particularly felicitous accord of words and pictures in an outstanding science book." Horn Book

Includes glossary

Pringle, Laurence P.

Bats! strange and wonderful; by Laurence Pringle; illustrated by Meryl Henderson. Boyds Mills Press 2000 32p il $15.95 (3-5)   **599.4**

1. Bats

ISBN 1-56397-327-8

This "describes some general physical and behavioral characteristics common to all types of bats. The ways in which these flying mammals benefit world ecosystems . . . are emphasized. Vibrant, realistic watercolors of representative species extend the text on every page." SLJ

599.5   Cetaceans and sea cows

Berger, Melvin, 1927-

Do whales have belly buttons? questions and answers about whales and dolphins; [by] Melvin and Gilda Berger; illustrated by Higgins Bond. Scholastic Ref. 1999 48p (Scholastic question and answer series) lib bdg $12.95; pa $5.95 (2-4)   **599.5**

1. Whales 2. Dolphins

ISBN 0-590-13081-1 (lib bdg); 0-439-08571-3 (pa)
LC 98-13430

Provides answers to such questions as "Do all whales have teeth?", "How long do most whales live?", "Why do dolphins whistle?", and "Can dolphins save humans?"

"Basic up-to-date information presented in a chatty, readable style." SLJ

Davies, Nicola, 1958-

Big blue whale; illustrated by Nick Maland. Candlewick Press 1997 27p il $15.99 (k-3) **599.5**

1. Whales

ISBN 1-56402-895-X   LC 96-42327

Also available Big book edition

Examines the physical characteristics, habits, and habitats of the blue whale

"Davies's brief overview offers young readers exactly what they want to know about this magnificent animal, and her judicious use of comparison makes the abstract more understandable. . . . Maland's cross-hatched pen-and-ink drawings rest on blue watercolor wash backgrounds." Horn Book Guide

Dudzinski, Kathleen

Meeting dolphins; my adventures in the sea. National Geographic Soc. 2000 64p il $17.95 (4 and up)   **599.5**

1. Dolphins 2. Animal communication

ISBN 0-7922-7129-7   LC 99-39069

The author describes her work studying dolphin communication and her invention of a listening device that allows researchers to tell which of a group of dolphins is vocalizing underwater

"The lively, first-person narrative incorporates abundant facts and entertaining anecdotes, infused with Dudzinski's infectious enthusiasm for her subjects and her work. Beautiful, full-color photos are breathtaking and well chosen for explication." Booklist

Esbensen, Barbara Juster

Baby whales drink milk; illustrated by Lambert Davis. HarperCollins Pubs. 1994 32p il (Let's-read-and-find-out science) hardcover o.p. paperback available $4.95 (k-1)   **599.5**

1. Whales 2. Mammals

ISBN 0-06-445119-4 (pa)   LC 92-30375

Describes the behavior of the humpback whale, with an emphasis on the fact that it is a mammal and shares the characteristics of other mammals

"Full-color paintings, mainly in watery greens and

Esbensen, Barbara Juster—*Continued*

blues, show the animals in their habitat, along with a scene of a whale model in a museum and a map of migration. The book's strong point, though, is Esbensen's simple, informative text, which keeps its young audience clearly in view." Booklist

Jenkins, Priscilla Belz

A safe home for manatees; illustrated by Martin Classen. HarperCollins Pubs. 1997 32p il (Let's-read-and-find-out science) $15.95; lib bdg $14.89; pa $4.95 (k-2)   **599.5**

1. Manatees
ISBN 0-06-027149-3; 0-06-027150-7 (lib bdg); 0-06-445164-X (pa)   LC 96-3136

"A simple narrative follows a fictitious female manatee and her baby as she seeks a safe haven with sufficient food and warm, fresh water free from pollutants and human intrusion. Soft blue/green colored pencil and pastel illustrations provide visual reinforcement for young readers unfamiliar with these animals and their habitat and are perfectly matched with the text." SLJ

McNulty, Faith

How whales walked into the sea; illustrated by Ted Lewin. Scholastic Press 1999 unp il $16.95 (2-4)   **599.5**

1. Whales 2. Evolution
ISBN 0-590-89830-2   LC 98-38211

Explains how the earth's biggest mammal evolved from a land animal into a sea animal

"Readers will easily follow the almost poetic explanation of how modern whales came to be. Rand's illustrations, executed in acrylic, watercolor, and chalk, are appropriately watery." Horn Book Guide

599.63   Even-toed ungulates

Nicholson, Darrel

Wild boars; photographs by Craig Blacklock. Carolrhoda Bks. 1987 47p il (Carolrhoda nature watch book) lib bdg $23.93 (3-6)   **599.63**

1. Boars
ISBN 0-87614-308-7   LC 87-677

"Straightforward, informative text and fine, full-color photographs introduce the Eurasian wild boar, brought to North America for hunting and studied at a Minnesota farm. An excellent book about a hardy, adaptable animal." Sci Child

Walker, Sally M.

Hippos; photographs by Gerry Ellis. Carolrhoda Bks. 1998 48p il (Carolrhoda nature watch book) lib bdg $19.93 (3-6)   **599.63**

1. Hippopotamus
ISBN 1-57505-078-1   LC 96-38135

An introduction to the physical characteristics, habits, and natural environment of the common and the pygmy hippopotamus

This offers "a straightforward text and lots of excellent, well-chosen pictures of hippos in the wild." Booklist

Includes glossary

599.64   Bovids

Berman, Ruth, 1958-

American bison; photographs by Cheryl Walsh Bellville. Carolrhoda Bks. 1992 48p il map (Carolrhoda nature watch book) lib bdg $23.95 (3-6)   **599.64**

1. Bison
ISBN 0-87614-697-3   LC 91-25852

Discusses the life cycle of the bison, its role in the settlement of the American West, and its near extinction

"Readers will learn many interesting facts about this, the largest native American mammal. The book is replete with excellent color photos." Sci Books Films

Includes glossary

599.65   Deer

DuTemple, Lesley A., 1952-

North American moose. Carolrhoda Bks. 2000 48p il maps (Carolrhoda nature watch book) lib bdg $23.93 (3-6)   **599.65**

1. Moose
ISBN 1-57505-426-4   LC 99-37091

Describes the physical characteristics, life cycle, and behavior of North American moose

Miller, Debbie S.

A caribou journey; illustrated by Jon Van Zyle. Little, Brown 1994 unp il $15.95; pa $5.95 (2-4)   **599.65**

1. Caribou 2. Animals—Migration 3. Natural history—Alaska
ISBN 0-316-57380-9; 0-316-57174-1 (pa)   LC 93-9777

Surveys the migrations, habits, and habitat of a herd of caribou in Alaska

"Van Zyle's dramatic paintings that flow across each double-page spread are created with acrylics painted on untempered masonite panels, and vividly portray seasonal changes in the land and life cycle of the caribou. Both the words and pictures breathe life into the images of a cold and windy Arctic winter." SLJ

Patent, Dorothy Hinshaw

Deer and elk; photographs by William Muñoz. Clarion Bks. 1994 77p il maps $17 (4 and up)   **599.65**

1. Deer 2. Elk
ISBN 0-395-52003-7   LC 93-25894

"The text describes in detail the lives, enemies, and survival of North American whitetail deer, mule deer, and elk, among others. The color photographs of the shy, gentle creatures are effective, crisp, and clear." Horn Book Guide

"Numerous full-color photographs enhance the presentation; each includes a caption. A great addition to the animal science section of any library." SLJ

Includes bibliographical references

599.66   Odd-toed ungulates

Arnold, Caroline, 1944-

Rhino; photographs by Richard Hewett, with additional photographs by Arthur P. Arnold. Morrow Junior Bks. 1995 48p il $16; lib bdg $15.93 (3-5)   **599.66**

1. Rhinoceros

ISBN 0-688-12694-4; 0-688-12695-2 (lib bdg)

LC 94-23904

This volume "covers the life cycle, daily habits, problems, and efforts to save the five species of rhinoceroses in captivity and the wild." Sci Child

"The opening photos of Shimba, a three-week-old white rhino from the Edinburgh Zoo, quickly lure browsers into the accompanying text." SLJ

Ryden, Hope

Wild horses I have known. Clarion Bks. 1999 90p il $18 (4 and up)   **599.66**

1. Horses

ISBN 0-395-77520-5   LC 97-49021

Text and photographs depict mustang social behavior observed by the author, as well as an account of how the mustang established itself and adapted to being a wild horse in the American West

"A carefully crafted book that features abundant use of strikingly beautiful photographs. . . . A nice combination of elegance and sound information." Horn Book

Walker, Sally M.

Rhinos; photographs by Gerry Ellis. Carolrhoda Bks. 1996 48p il map (Carolrhoda nature watch book) lib bdg $23.93 (3-6)   **599.66**

1. Rhinoceros

ISBN 1-57505-008-0   LC 96-228

"There used to be 100 species of rhinos; now there are only 5, largely because they have been killed for their valuable horns. Walker begins her clear, accessible study with this sad history. She then moves on to physical traits and behaviors, diet, communication, procreation, and calf rearing of the remaining 13,000 animals. The attractive, candid color photos capture the strange physicality of the beasts." Booklist

Includes glossary

599.67   Elephants

Patent, Dorothy Hinshaw

African elephants; giants of the land; photographs by Oria Douglas-Hamilton. Holiday House 1991 40p il $14.95 (3-5)   **599.67**

1. Elephants

ISBN 0-8234-0911-2   LC 91-55028

Describes the physical characteristics, behavior, feeding, family life, and habitat of the African elephant

"Text and photographs successfully meld to create an informative book about the African elephant and its threatened survival in the wild." Booklist

Pringle, Laurence P.

Elephant woman; Cynthia Moss explores the world of elephants; [by] Laurence Pringle; photographs by Cynthia Moss. Atheneum Bks. for Young Readers 1997 42p il $16 (4 and up)   **599.67**

1. Moss, Cynthia 2. Elephants 3. Amboseli National Park (Kenya)

ISBN 0-689-80142-4   LC 96-40241

Pringle recounts the work of Cynthia Moss, world-renowned elephant researcher, in Kenya's Amboseli National Park

"Excellent photos, most in color, appear on nearly every page, providing an intriguing look at the elephants' world as they illustrate the well-written text." Booklist

Includes bibliographical references

599.7   Carnivores. Land carnivores

Arnosky, Jim

Otters under water. Putnam 1992 unp il hardcover o.p. paperback available $5.99 (k-2)   **599.7**

1. Otters

ISBN 0-698-11556-2 (pa)   LC 91-36792

This book offers a "glimpse of two young otters swimming, playing, and feeding in a sunlit pond under the watchful gaze of their mother. As always, this naturalist author/artist has enhanced the basic lesson through his inclusion of plants, creatures, and rock formations that form a part of the animals' natural habitat. His carefully executed colored-pencil and watercolor illustrations . . . reflect his keen observations of nature and his fine artistic talent. . . . The short, simple, oversized text, one sentence or phrase to a page, succinctly describes the pictured activity without detracting from the eye-catching view." SLJ

North, Sterling, 1906-1974

Rascal; illustrated by John Schoenherr. Dutton 1984 c1963 189p il $15.99; pa $5.99 (5 and up)   **599.7**

1. Raccoons

ISBN 0-525-18839-8; 0-14-034445-4 (pa)

LC 84-10292

Also available Spanish language edition

A Newbery Award honor book, 1964

First published 1963 with subtitle: A memoir of a better era

A book about Rascal "a young raccoon, Sterling North's pet the year he was eleven, in rural Wisconsin. . . . The book calls up a series of marvelous pictures; boy fishing in peaceful company of raccoon, boy riding on bike with raccoon (a demon for speed) standing up in the bike basket, raccoon with friend, a prize trotting horse, raccoon helping boy to win a pie-eating contest. A central episode is about an idyllic camping trip." Publ Wkly

Silverstein, Alvin
The sea otter; [by] Alvin, Virginia, and Robert Silverstein. Millbrook Press 1995 64p il map (Endangered in America) lib bdg $24.90; pa $6.95 (4 and up) **599.7**
1. Otters 2. Endangered species
ISBN 1-56294-418-5; 0-761-30165-8 (pa)
LC 94-17998
"The sea otter's behavior is described, including swimming, hunting, feeding, reproducing, and growing. Its main physical features are detailed, including those especially important to its lifestyle. . . . With color photographs, readng and organizations lists, a factual summary, and an index, this book is very suitable for use as a reference, in classrooms, and for general awareness." Sci Books Films
Includes bibliographical references

599.75   Cat family

Arnold, Caroline, 1944-
Cats: in from the wild; photographs by Richard R. Hewett. Carolrhoda Bks. 1993 48p il lib bdg $19.95 (3-5) **599.75**
1. Cats 2. Wild cats
ISBN 0-87614-692-2   LC 92-32986
"Arnold sets domestic cats next to their wilderness cousins to explore feline behaviors and the physical characteristics that allow cats to climb, hunt, and prowl so successfully. . . . Hewett . . . supplies an excellent variety of good-quality photographs." Booklist
Includes glossary

Clutton-Brock, Juliet
Cat; written by Juliet Clutton-Brock. Knopf 1991 63p il (Eyewitness books) (4 and up) **599.75**
1. Wild cats 2. Cats
LC 91-9399
Available DK Pub. edition $15.95; lib bdg $19.99 (ISBN 0-7894-5752-0; 0-7894-6578-7)
Text and photographs present the anatomy, behavior, habitats, and other aspects of wild and domestic cats
"The information is generally well written and well presented. . . . This is a browser's delight that will also appeal to the serious reader seeking facts about cats." Sci Books Films

Darling, Kathy
Lions; photographs by Tara Darling-Lyon. Carolrhoda Bks. 2000 48p il (Carolrhoda nature watch book) lib bdg $23.93 (3-6) **599.75**
1. Lions
ISBN 1-57505-404-3   LC 99-32632
Describes the physical characteristics and behavior of lions, as well as some of the threats they face
"Strong writing and animal photography work together to create [a book] that will be sought out for school assignments and recreational reading." Horn Book Guide
Includes glossary

Esbensen, Barbara Juster
Swift as the wind; the cheetah; illustrated by Jean Cassels. Orchard Bks. 1996 unp il $15.96; lib bdg $16.99 (2-4) **599.75**
1. Cheetahs
ISBN 0-531-09497-9; 0-531-08797-2 (lib bdg)
LC 95-666
Describes the physical characteristics and habits of the cheetah
"Elegantly and instructively illustrated with carefully detailed paintings this introduction to the fastest land animal includes sufficient information to provide a basic understanding of the cheetah and to differentiate it from other big cats. Esbensen also explains the factors that make cheetah survival difficult and contribute to its status as an endangered species." Horn Book Guide

MacMillan, Dianne M., 1943-
Cheetahs; photographs by Gerry Ellis. Carolrhoda Bks. 1997 48p il (Carolrhoda nature watch book) lib bdg $23.93; pa $7.95 (3-6) **599.75**
1. Cheetahs
ISBN 1-575-05044-7 (lib bdg); 1-575-05225-3 (pa)
LC 96-28554
Describes the physical characteristics, life cycle, behavior, and conservation of cheetahs
This is an "informative and attractively illustrated book. . . . Includes many clear full-color photographs of cheetahs in the wild." Booklist
Includes glossary

Morrison, Taylor, 1971-
Cheetah! Holt & Co. 1998 unp il $15.95 (k-3) **599.75**
1. Cheetahs
ISBN 0-8050-5121-X   LC 97-16683
Describes a day in the life of a cheetah family in the Seregeti National Park as the mother hunts to feed her cubs
"Realistic acrylic illustrations, many of which mimic stop-action photography, give a wonderful sense of the cheetah's agility and distinctive body language." Horn Book Guide

Parsons, Alexandra
Amazing cats; written by Alexandra Parsons; photographed by Jerry Young. Knopf 1990 29p il (Eyewitness juniors) pa $9.99 (2-4) **599.75**
1. Cats
ISBN 0-679-80690-3   LC 90-31885
Also available Spanish language edition
Features unusual members of the cat world, including the Turkish swimming cat, Scottish wildcat, and ocelot, and describes important characteristics of the whole group
"The text is generally interesting and accurate; the facts are presented in clear, simple language. The illustrations are detailed and engaging." Sci Books Films

Silverstein, Alvin

The Florida panther; [by] Alvin and Virginia Silverstein and Laura Silverstein Nunn. Millbrook Press 1997 64p il (Endangered in America) lib bdg $24.90 (4 and up) **599.75**

1. Pumas 2. Wildlife conservation

ISBN 0-7613-0049-X LC 96-42690

Describes the physical characteristics, behavior, and habitat of the Florida panther as well as the efforts being made to save it from extinction

"The full-color photos are clear and informative. . . . Thorough, clearly written." SLJ

Includes bibliographical references

Simon, Seymour, 1931-

Big cats. HarperCollins Pubs. 1991 unp il lib bdg $17.89; pa $6.95 (3-6) **599.75**

1. Wild cats

ISBN 0-06-021647-6 (lib bdg); 0-06-446119-X (pa)

LC 90-36374

Simon "begins with a general overview of the big cats, and then presents details on the tiger, lion, leopard, jaguar, puma, cheetah and snow leopard. . . . The author also discusses concerns about wildlife conservation." Appraisal

The author "offers a clear, succinct text illuminated with stunning, large color photographs." Booklist

Thapar, Valmik

Tiger; habitats, life cycles, food chains, threats. Raintree Steck-Vaughn Pubs. 2000 48p il (Natural world) $27.12; pa $9.95 (3-5) **599.75**

1. Tigers 2. Endangered species

ISBN 0-7398-1055-3; 0-7398-0946-6 (pa)

LC 98-53279

Explains the physical characteristics, life cycle, habits, habitat, and endangered status of the tiger

"The writing . . . is clear and lively. . . . The color photographs . . . demand attention." Booklist

Includes glossary and bibliographical references

Thompson, Sharon Elaine, 1952-

Built for speed; the extraordinary, enigmatic cheetah. Lerner Publs. 1998 88p il lib bdg $23.93 (5 and up) **599.75**

1. Cheetahs

ISBN 0-8225-2854-1 LC 96-51094

Describes the habitat, physical characteristics, and behavior of the cheetah, as well as efforts to ensure the continued existence of this fastest land mammal

This "includes and explains many fascinating details of the animals' lives in a comprehensive, well-organized, and attractive way." Sci Books Films

Includes glossary and bibliographical references

599.77 Dog family

Brandenburg, Jim

Scruffy; a wolf finds his place in the pack; edited by JoAnn Bren Guernsey. Walker & Co. 1996 unp il hardcover o.p. paperback available $7.95 (2-4) **599.77**

1. Wolves

ISBN 0-8027-7602-7 (pa) LC 96-5446

A professional photographer visits Ellesmere Island near the North Pole and observes the behavior of a pack of Arctic wolves, focusing on a timid male that becomes the pack's babysitter

"Brandenburg's photos are warm without being sentimental and the text direct and informative." Bull Cent Child Books

To the top of the world; adventures with Arctic wolves; edited by JoAnn Bren Guernsey. Walker & Co. 1993 44p il $16.95; pa $7.95 (4 and up) **599.77**

1. Wolves

ISBN 0-8027-8219-1; 0-8027-7462-8 (pa)

LC 93-12105

A wildlife photographer records in text and photographs two visits to Ellesmere Island, Northwest Territories, where he filmed a pack of Arctic wolves over several months

"Captivating pictures combine with an informal narrative to create a topnotch, firsthand view of a much-maligned animal." SLJ

George, Michael, 1964-

Wolves. Child's World 2000 32p il (Nature books) lib bdg $24.21 (1-3) **599.77**

1. Wolves

ISBN 1-56766-584-5 LC 98-36871

Describes the physical characteristics, behavior, habitat, and life cycle of wolves

"The gorgeous, full-color photographs are big, clear, and detailed." SLJ

Gibbons, Gail

Wolves. Holiday House 1994 unp il $16.95; pa $6.95 (k-3) **599.77**

1. Wolves

ISBN 0-8234-1127-3; 0-8234-1202-4 (pa)

LC 94-2108

"A simply written introduction that focuses on the gray, or timber, wolf. . . . Material covered includes physical characteristics, behavior within a pack, and communication by howling and body language. . . . The format is open and spacious, the print is large, and the realistic, watercolor illustrations are set against backgrounds of white and deep blues." SLJ

Silverstein, Alvin

The red wolf; [by] Alvin, Virginia, and Robert Silverstein. Millbrook Press 1994 64p il map (Endangered in America) lib bdg $24.90 (4 and up) **599.77**

1. Wolves 2. Endangered species

ISBN 1-56294-416-9 LC 93-42480

A look at the pros and cons of reintroducing the red wolf, thought to be threatened with extinction, to two sites in North Carolina

"The book is equally fair in discussing the opposition to the reintroduction of wolves to the wild by ranchers or other property owners adjacent to the release sites. Rarely has a book so dispassionately presented these areas of controversy. The illustrations are well chosen to complement the text." Sci Books Films

Includes bibliographical references

Simon, Seymour, 1931-

Wolves. HarperCollins Pubs. 1993 unp il hardcover o.p. paperback available $6.95 (3-6)

599.77

1. Wolves

ISBN 0-06-446176-9 (pa)   LC 92-25924

Text and photographs present the physical characteristics, habits, and natural environment of various species of wolves

"The text is well suited to the emerging naturalist—almost chatty in tone. The carefully credited photographs combine the beauty of the animal with action and the natural beauty of its habitat to effect a dramatic backdrop for the text." Horn Book

Smith, Roland, 1951-

Journey of the red wolf; photographs by the author. Cobblehill Bks. 1996 60p il $16.99 (4 and up)

599.77

1. Wolves 2. Wildlife conservation

ISBN 0-525-65162-4   LC 95-10641

In 1971, when red wolves were near extinction, seventeen of the wolves "were taken into captivity and became a part of the Red Wolf Captive Breeding Facility. *Journey of the Red Wolf* is the story of how this facility grew from 17 to almost 300 red wolves. . . . This is a well-written book, with many good color photographs illustrative of both the red wolf and the work of the captive breeding program." Sci Books Films

Swinburne, Stephen R.

Coyote; North America's dog. Boyds Mills Press 1999 32p il $15.95 (4-6)   **599.77**

1. Coyotes

ISBN 1-56397-765-6

The author describes the lifestyles of this "canine, its place in Native American folklore, the conflict between ranchers/farmers and this elusive predator, and the problems the animal faces as it struggles to thrive in pristine wilderness areas and in congested suburbs." SLJ

This book "packs a lot of information about North American coyotes into a small space. The author, a veteran park ranger, knows his subject well and succeeds in making it interesting to his audience. . . . The full-color photographs are clean and clear and enliven the text." Booklist

599.78   Bears

Markle, Sandra, 1946-

Growing up wild: bears. Atheneum Bks. for Young Readers 2000 30p il $16 (2-4)   **599.78**

1. Bears

ISBN 0-689-81888-2   LC 98-44693

Describes different kinds of bear cubs and the changes they go through in their appearance and behavior as they grow up and become successful adult bears

This offers "astounding views of northern bears captured in stellar photography. Accompanying these sharply focused, intimate shots is a text rich in facts about black, brown, grizzly, and polar bears. . . . With its engaging photos and detailed text, this selection . . . is a superlative addition to nature shelves." Booklist

Miller, Debbie S.

A polar bear journey; pictures by Jon Van Zyle. Little, Brown 1997 unp il $15.95 (2-4)   **599.78**

1. Polar bear

ISBN 0-316-57244-6   LC 96-42284

Details the life cycle of a mother polar bear and her two cubs, from their birth to their learning of survival lessons

"Lovely acrylic paintings accompany this informative and lyrical text." SLJ

Patent, Dorothy Hinshaw

Great ice bear; the polar bear and the Eskimo; illustrated by Anne Wertheim. Morrow Junior Bks. 1999 40p il map $16; lib bdg $15.93 (4 and up)

599.78

1. Polar bear 2. Inuit

ISBN 0-688-13767-9; 0-688-13768-7 (lib bdg)

LC 97-44820

Gives information about polar bears which inhabit the Arctic regions of Russia, Norway, Canada, the United States, Denmark, and Greenland and discusses their relationships with humans

"Cool blues and tawny yellows predominate in Wertheim's beautifully detailed illustrations. . . . Appealing and informative." Booklist

Includes bibliographical references

Looking at bears; photographs by William Muñoz. Holiday House 1994 40p il $15.95 (3-5)

599.78

1. Bears

ISBN 0-8234-1139-7   LC 94-1834

This introduction to bears of the world includes "the ancestry, physical characteristics, eating habits, intelligence, hibernation, senses, birth and growth, and interesting facts on each species of bear. What sets the book apart from others of its kind is Patent's elegant writing style as well as her small dazzling details. . . . Fine full-color photographs complement the text nicely." SLJ

Polar bears; photographs by William Munöz. Carolrhoda Bks. 2000 48p il map (Carolrhoda nature watch book) lib bdg $23.93 (3-6)   **599.78**

1. Polar bear

ISBN 1-57505-020-X   LC 99-29601

Describes the physical characteristics, diet, natural habitat, and life cycle of polar bears

"Each page includes a large, color photograph. . . . The lively writing style combined with many interesting facts make this a solid resource for reports and an excellent choice for young nature lovers." SLJ

Includes glossary

599.79   Marine carnivores

Cossi, Olga

Harp seals. Carolrhoda Bks. 1991 47p il map (Carolrhoda nature watch book) lib bdg $23.93; pa $6.95 (3-6)   **599.79**

1. Seals (Animals)

ISBN 0-87614-437-7 (lib bdg); 0-87614-567-5 (pa)

LC 90-2481

Cossi, Olga—*Continued*

Describes the life cycle, migratory patterns, behavior, and habitat of the harp seal

"The combination of text and photographs does a magnificent job of depicting the harp seal's world." Sci Books Films

Includes glossary

599.8   Primates

Darling, Kathy

Lemurs on location; photographs by Tara Darling. Lothrop, Lee & Shepard Bks. 1998 40p il $17; lib bdg $16.89 (3-5)   **599.8**
1. Lemurs
ISBN 0-688-12539-5; 0-688-12540-9 (lib bdg)
LC 97-36250

Describes the physical characteristics and behavior of different kinds of lemurs encountered on a trip to a forest in southeastern Madagascar

"Excellent, full-color photographs appear throughout the book, a precise, lively counterpoint to the discussion. The presentation is informative and well organized." Booklist

Goodall, Jane, 1934-

With love; illustrated by Alan Marks. North-South Bks. 1998 unp il $15.95; lib bdg $15.88 (4 and up)   **599.8**
1. Chimpanzees
ISBN 1-55858-911-2; 1-55858-912-0 (lib bdg)
LC 97-49948

First published 1994 by the Jane Goodall Institute

A collection of stories based on the author's experiences with chimpanzees in Gombe Stream National Park in Tanzania over a period of almost forty years

"Children will love these stories because they are sometimes silly or gross and because they are always tender, and young humans will recognize aspects of themselves in the younger chimps. . . . Marks' watercolor-and-ink paintings capture both action and stasis beautifully and without affectation or sentimentality." Booklist

Lewin, Ted, 1935-

Gorilla walk; [by] Ted & Betsy Lewin. Lothrop, Lee & Shepard Bks. 1999 48p il map $16; lib bdg $15.93 (4 and up)   **599.8**
1. Gorillas
ISBN 0-688-16509-5; 0-688-16510-9 (lib bdg)
LC 98-44727

Describes an expedition into the field in southern Uganda to observe mountain gorillas in their native habitat

"Briefly captioned, thumbnail watercolors picture the jungle trek, and magnificent double-page spreads replicate the exotic surroundings and show the animals close up." Booklist

Patterson, Francine

Koko-love! conversations with a signing gorilla; photographs by Ronald H. Cohn. Dutton Children's Bks. 1999 31p il $14.99 (1-4)   **599.8**
1. Gorillas 2. Animal communication
ISBN 0-525-46319-4

"More in the saga of Koko, the communicating gorilla who has pet kittens and continues to learn new language skills, is related by her surrogate mother, Dr. Patterson, and illustrated with good color photographs of various sizes showing Koko's activities and accomplishments in a lively format." SLJ

Redmond, Ian

Gorilla; written by Ian Redmond; photographed by Peter Anderson & Geoff Brightling. Knopf 1995 63p il maps (Eyewitness books) (4 and up)   **599.8**
1. Primates
LC 95-3241

Available DK Pub. edition $15.95; lib bdg $19.99 (ISBN 0-7894-6036-X; 0-7894-6613-9)

"A Dorling Kindersley book"

An illustrated look at primates, including lemurs, monkeys, and apes

This offers "the same fabulous layout, interesting photographs, and fascinating facts that have made the series so popular. . . . Fun to browse through." SLJ

599.93   Genetics, sex and age characteristics, evolution

Gallant, Roy A.

Early humans. Benchmark Bks. (Tarrytown) 1999 c2000 80p il maps (Story of science) lib bdg $19.95 (5 and up)   **599.93**
1. Fossil hominids 2. Human origins 3. Evolution
ISBN 0-7614-0960-2   LC 98-28037

Discusses human evolution and the search for the earliest forms of humans, examining the Neanderthals, Homo erectus, the variety of fossils found in Africa, and the early apelike hominids

"Richly illustrated with color photos, drawings, and charts. . . . Gallant writes clearly and provides readers with balanced, informative discussions." Booklist

Includes glossary and bibliographical references

600   TECHNOLOGY (APPLIED SCIENCES)

Biesty, Stephen

Stephen Biesty's incredible cross-sections; illustrated by Stephen Biesty; written by Richard Platt. Knopf 1992 48p il $20 (4 and up)   **600**
1. Technology 2. Architecture
ISBN 0-679-81411-6   LC 91-27439

"A Dorling Kindersley book"

Cross-sectional illustrations present an inside view of such structures as a medieval castle, factory, subway sta-

Biesty, Stephen—*Continued*

tion, coal mine, and oil rig

"Readers will be mesmerized by these intricately drawn illustrations. . . . The detailed drawings are fascinatingly realistic. But while the visuals can steal the show, the well-researched text should not be overlooked. . . . A sense of humor flavors both art and text in the striking oversize volume guaranteed to intrigue browsers and serious researchers alike." Booklist

Macaulay, David, 1946-

The new way things work; by David Macaulay with Neil Ardley. Houghton Mifflin 1998 400p il $35 (4 and up)   **600**

1. Technology 2. Machinery 3. Inventions

ISBN 0-395-93847-3   LC 98-14224

Also available CD-ROM version

First published 1988 with title: The way things work

Arranged in five sections this volume provides information on the "workings of hundreds of machines and devices—holograms, helicopters, airplanes, mobile phones, compact disks, hard disks, bits and bytes, cash machines. . . . Explanations [are also given] of the scientific principles behind each machine—how gears make work easier, why jumbo jets are able to fly, how computers actually compute." Publisher's note

608   Inventions and patents

Erlbach, Arlene

The kids' invention book. Lerner Publs. 1997 64p il lib bdg $22.60; pa $9.95 (4-6)   **608**

1. Inventions

ISBN 0-8225-2414-7 (lib bdg); 0-8225-9844-2 (pa)

LC 96-27105

Profiles eleven inventors between the ages of eight and fourteen, describes the steps involved in inventing a new product, and discusses contests, patents, lawyers, and clubs

"Readers will enjoy the stories behind such clever creations as an edible pet-food spoon, an adjustable jump-rope belt, and a portable wheelchair ramp; and the accounts serve as wonderful encouragement for kids who want to pursue ideas of their own." Booklist

Includes bibliographical references

609   Technology—Historical and geographic treatment

Bender, Lionel

Invention; written by Lionel Bender. Knopf 1991 63p il (Eyewitness books) (4 and up)   **609**

1. Inventions

LC 90-4888

Available DK Pub. edition $15.95; lib bdg $19.99 (ISBN 0-7894-5768-7; 0-7894-6576-0)

Photographs and text explore such inventions as the wheel, gears, levers, clocks, telephones, and rocket engines

"The photographs are . . . stunning, the information served up in tiny but fascinating bites." BAYA Book Rev

Inventions & inventors. Grolier Educ. 1999 10v il set $319   **609**

1. Inventors 2. Inventions

ISBN 0-7172-9384-X   LC 99-19310

Contents: v1 Air & space; v2 Buildings, homes & structures; v3 Communications; v4 Farming, food & biotechnology; v5 Instruments & measurement; v6 Land & water transportation; v7 Manufacturing & industry; v8 Medicine & health; v9 Military & security; v10 Power & energy

For a review see: Booklist, Feb. 15, 2000

Jones, Charlotte Foltz, 1945-

Mistakes that worked; illustrated by John O'Brien. Doubleday 1991 78p il hardcover o.p. paperback available $11.95 (4-6)   **609**

1. Inventions

ISBN 0-385-32043-4 (pa)   LC 89-37408

This book presents the stories behind forty things that were invented or named by accident, including aspirin, X-rays, frisbees, silly putty, and velcro

This is "a splendid book that is as informative as it is entertaining. . . . [O'Brien] contributes a wonderful assortment of quirky, colorful cartoons that add just the right touch of levity." Booklist

Includes bibliographical references

Tucker, Tom, 1944-

Brainstorm! the stories of twenty American kid inventors; with drawings by Richard Loehle. Farrar, Straus & Giroux 1995 148p il $15 (5 and up)   **609**

1. Inventors 2. Inventions

ISBN 0-374-30944-2   LC 94-38780

The author looks at inventions devised by children since the 18th century. Ear muffs, water skis, the popsicle, colored car wax and the electronic television are among the products discussed. Includes a discussion of how the Patent Office works

Includes glossary and bibliographical references

Wulffson, Don L., 1943-

The kid who invented the popsicle and other surprising stories about inventions. Cobblehill Bks. 1997 114p $13.99; pa $4.99 (4 and up)   **609**

1. Inventions

ISBN 0-525-65221-3; 0-14-130204-6 (pa)

LC 96-31148

"Beginning with animal crackers and ending with the zipper, this book alphabetically lists a number of 'inventions' and briefly describes how they came into being. Among the items noted are blue jeans, doughnuts, matches, miniature golf, and Scrabble." Booklist

This book is "very entertaining. . . . It would be a useful starting point for class projects." Sci Books Films

610.69   Medical personnel

Brazelton, T. Berry, 1918-

Going to the doctor; drawings by Alfred Womack; photographs by Sam Ogden. Addison Wesley Longman 1996 48p il $15 (k-3)   **610.69**

1. Medical care 2. Physicians

ISBN 0-201-40694-2   LC 96-9000

Brazelton, T. Berry, 1918-—*Continued*
"A Merloyd Lawrence book"
"Each double-page spread, framed by a colorful border, focuses on one aspect of the physical exam conducted by a doctor or a nurse-practitioner. The conversational, informative text . . . is presented with sketches revealing a child's (Brazelton's grandson's) point of view and with beautifully composed photos of 'Dr. B' talking with and examining his young patients." Booklist

610.9 Medical sciences—Historical and geographic treatment

Fisher, Leonard Everett, 1924-
The doctors; written & illustrated by Leonard Everett Fisher. Benchmark Bks. (Tarrytown) 1997 47p il (Colonial craftsmen) $21.36 (4 and up)
　　　　　　　　　　　　　　　　　　610.9
1. Medicine—History　2. Physicians　3. United States—History—1600-1775, Colonial period
ISBN 0-7614-0481-3　　　　　　LC 96-13081
A reissue of the title first published 1968 by Watts
Traces the early development of medicine in colonial America and discusses some of the methods and medications used at that time for treating illness

611 Human anatomy, cytology, histology

Balestrino, Philip
The skeleton inside you; illustrated by True Kelley. rev ed. Crowell 1989 32p il (Let's-read-and-find-out science book) hardcover o.p. paperback available $4.95 (k-3)　　　　**611**
1. Skeleton 2. Bones
ISBN 0-08-445087-2 (pa)　　　　LC 88-23672
A revised and newly illustrated edition of the title first published 1971
Balestrino seeks to "explain the human skeleton: what it is and what it does for us. He tells how the 206 different bones of the skeleton are joined together, how they grow, and how they help make blood for your whole body. He also describes what happens when bones break, and how they mend." Publisher's note
"Colorful, entertaining illustrations provide an excellent supplement to the clearly written text. . . . [This] is highly recommended as an introductory science book for young children." Sci Books Films

Barner, Bob
Dem bones; [illustrations and informational bone text by] Bob Barner. Chronicle Bks. 1996 unp il $14.95 (k-3)　　　　**611**
1. Skeleton 2. Bones
ISBN 0-8118-0827-0　　　　　　LC 95-29
An "introduction to the human skeleton, this picture book is based on the African American spiritual 'Dem bones.'. . . Each double-page spread illustrates one phrase from the song, which dances through the spread,

while in smaller letters Barner discusses one of the 10 bones named in the song in a few lines of simple, informative text." Booklist
"A rollicking read-aloud, sing-along treat for children as they learn anatomy, rhyme, and language. . . . Scientific facts and names combined with lyrics make this a fascinating book." Exploring Sci in the Libr

Biesty, Stephen
Stephen Biesty's incredible body; illustrated by Stephen Biesty; written by Richard Platt. DK Pub. 1998 32p il $19.95 (4 and up)　　　　**611**
1. Human anatomy
ISBN 0-7894-3424-5　　　　　　LC 98-16806
Uses the perspective of tiny people traveling through a man's body to present its various systems and organs and how they work
"The pen-and-ink and color drawings are nothing short of amazing." SLJ

Parker, Steve
The body atlas; illustrated by Giuliano Fornari. Dorling Kindersley 1993 63p il $19.95 (5 and up)
　　　　　　　　　　　　　　　　　　611
1. Human anatomy
ISBN 1-56458-224-8　　　　　　LC 92-54307
"The human body is mapped here in detail from head to toe, and in that order. Sections entitled 'Head and Neck,' 'Upper Torso,' 'Arm and Hand,' 'Lower Torso,' and 'Leg and Foot' neatly group a huge amount of information into meaningful, manageable units. Throughout, various organs are illustrated from both the outside and the inside. . . . In all sections, scientific photographs have been included to supplement Fornari's interesting medical illustrations." Booklist

Sweeney, Joan, 1930-
Me and my amazing body; illustrated by Annette Cable. Crown 1999 unp il $13; lib bdg $14.99; pa $6.99 (k-2)　　　　**611**
1. Human anatomy
ISBN 0-517-80053-5; 0-517-80054-3 (lib bdg); 0-375-80623-7 (pa)　　　　LC 98-34628
A girl describes how her skin, bones, muscles, brain, blood, heart, lungs, and stomach receive energy and function as parts of her body
With "lively text and simple, colorful illustrations, this picture book explains a lot of human anatomy and physiology." Booklist

The **Visual** dictionary of human anatomy. DK Pub. 1996 64p il (Eyewitness visual dictionaries) $18.95 (4 and up)　　　　**611**
1. Human anatomy
ISBN 0-7894-0445-1　　　　　　LC 95-52789
"This guide details the physical structure of the human body, naming its parts and providing basic information on how the systems function. The first section describes the skeletal, muscular, nervous, endocrine, circulatory, lymphatic, respiratory, digestive, urinary, and reproductive systems. . . . The second part of the book describes the detailed structure of body areas. . . . This organization clarifies the interrelationship of systems in each area. . . . Overall, it is a clear, informative reference source that should get heavy use." SLJ

The **Visual** dictionary of the human body. Dorling Kindersley 1991 64p il (Eyewitness visual dictionaries) $18.95 (4 and up) **611**
1. Human anatomy
ISBN 1-87943-118-1 LC 91-60899
This dictionary portrays and labels parts and systems of the human body, illustrated with hundreds of color photographs and drawings
"The colors of the illustrations are vibrant and seem true to life. . . . [This book] will provide enhancement and excitement to study activities." Booklist

612 Human physiology

Aliki
My feet. Crowell 1990 31p il (Let's-read-and-find-out science book) lib bdg $16.89; pa $5.95 (k-1) **612**
1. Foot
ISBN 0-690-04815-7 (lib bdg); 0-06-445106-2 (pa)
LC 89-49357
"An extensive discussion of feet, through simple text and playful illustration, demonstrates their parts, relative sizes, what they do, and what they wear in different seasons. Includes a handicapped child whose crutches supplement feet." Sci Child

My hands. rev ed. Crowell 1990 32p il (Let's-read-and-find-out science book) lib bdg $15.89; pa $4.95 (k-1) **612**
1. Hand
ISBN 0-690-04880-7 (lib bdg); 0-06-445096-1 (pa)
LC 89-49158
First published 1962
The author "calls attention to hand structure—fingers, nails, an opposable thumb—and the special ways we use our hands to carry on everyday activities. . . . The jaunty illustrations and simple but efficient text combine for a fresh take on some very basic information." Booklist

Berger, Melvin, 1927-
Why don't haircuts hurt? questions and answers about the human body; [by] Melvin and Gilda Berger; illustrated by Karen Barnes. Scholastic Ref. 1999 48p il (Scholastic question and answer series) $12.95; pa $5.95 (2-4) **612**
1. Human anatomy 2. Physiology
ISBN 0-590-13079-X; 0-439-08569-1 (pa)
LC 97-45874
Provides answers to a variety of questions about the human body including "Why do you blush?", "Why do you need two ears?", "How strong is hair?", and "What are goosebumps?"
"The student-friendly question-and-answer format is appealing, with simple and concise one or two paragraph answers and attractive, colorful illustrations." SLJ

Cole, Joanna
The magic school bus inside the human body; illustrated by Bruce Degen. Scholastic 1989 unp il lib bdg $15.95; pa $4.95 (2-4) **612**
1. Physiology 2. Human anatomy
ISBN 0-590-41426-7 (lib bdg); 0-590-41427-5 (pa)
LC 88-3070

Also available Spanish language edition
"Ms. Frizzle's class leaves on a trip to the science museum, but stops for a snack along the way. Arnold is left behind when his classmates reboard the bus. Meanwhile, Ms. Frizzle has miniaturized the bus and its riders. Unwittingly, Arnold swallows it. Traveling through Arnold's insides, the class visits his digestive system, arteries, lungs, heart, brain, and muscles, finally departing through his nostrils when he sneezes." Booklist
"This is an enjoyable look at factual material painlessly packaged with the ribbons and balloons of jokes and asides meant to appeal to kids. Degen's zany, busy, full-color drawings fill the pages with action and information far beyond the text." SLJ

VanCleave, Janice Pratt
Janice VanCleave's the human body for every kid; easy activities that make learning science fun. Wiley 1995 223p il $29.95; pa $12.95 (4 and up) **612**
1. Physiology 2. Human anatomy 3. Science—Experiments
ISBN 0-471-02413-9; 0-471-02408-2 (pa)
LC 94-20862
"The book's 23 chapters cover cells, skin, the brain, the senses, lungs, blood and the heart, the digestive system, bones, muscles, and genetics. Each chapter includes . . . background information, problem-solving strategies, and simple activities." Sci Child
"The activities described are easy to follow, are inexpensive, use readily obtainable supplies, and, most importantly, make the learning of human anatomy and physiology fun and exciting. Moreover, the material is presented in an organized, clear, and accurate manner." Sci Books Films

Walker, Richard
The Kingfisher first human body encyclopedia. Kingfisher (NY) 1999 112p il $16.95 (3-5) **612**
1. Human anatomy 2. Physiology
ISBN 0-7534-5177-8 LC 98-53275
An illustrated introduction to the different parts of the human body and how they work
"With stark white pages providing the backdrop for more than 500 vivid, full-color photographs, diagrams, and illustrations, *The Kingfisher First Human Body Encyclopedia* . . . is a visual delight for curious young minds." Booklist
Includes glossary

612.1 Blood and circulation

Ballard, Carol
The heart and circulatory system. Raintree Steck-Vaughn Pubs. 1997 48p il (Human body) lib bdg $25.68 (5 and up) **612.1**
1. Blood 2. Heart 3. Cardiovascular system
ISBN 0-8172-4800-5 LC 96-31764
Describes the parts of the circulatory system and how they function
"Organs and other components that contribute to the proper functioning of [the] system are illustrated with di-

Ballard, Carol—*Continued*

agrams, colored drawings, photographs, X rays, and electron micrographs, and are described in easy-to-read text."
Sci Books Films

Includes glossary and bibliographical references

Silverstein, Alvin

The circulatory system; [by] Alvin, Virginia and Robert Silverstein. 21st Cent. Bks. (Brookfeild) 1994 96p il (Human body systems) lib bdg $27.90 (5 and up)   **612.1**

1. Heart 2. Blood—Circulation

ISBN 0-8050-2833-1   LC 94-21426

This illustrated introduction to the circulatory system "briefly discusses related systems in plants and animals and the history of our knowledge of the human heart and blood vessels, then focuses on the various parts of the human circulatory system." Booklist

Includes glossary

Simon, Seymour, 1931-

The heart. Morrow Junior Bks. 1996 unp lib bdg $16; pa $6.95 (3-6)   **612.1**

1. Cardiovascular system 2. Heart

ISBN 0-688-11407-5 (lib bdg); 0-688-17059-5 (pa)
     LC 95-38021

This "introduces the human circulatory system: the heart, the blood, the arteries and veins, the transfer of oxygen and carbon dioxide, the functions of various blood cells, and heart problems and their solutions. The text is succinct and direct, making the details understandable without losing the sense that the whole process of circulation is 'strange and wonderful.' . . . The often striking pictures include many computer-enhanced photographs as well as diagrams and highly enlarged images made possible by electron microscopes. Handsome and well-conceived in every way." Booklist

612.2   Respiration

Parker, Steve

The lungs and respiratory system. Raintree Steck-Vaughn Pubs. 1997 48p il (Human body) lib bdg $27.12 (4 and up)   **612.2**

1. Lungs 2. Respiratory system

ISBN 0-8172-4803-X   LC 96-43516

Examines the different parts and functions of the lungs and respiratory system

The information in this book "is especially well organized and well coordinated with colorful illustrations and photographs." SLJ

Includes glossary and bibliographical references

612.3   Digestion

Showers, Paul, 1910-1999

How many teeth? illustrated by True Kelley. rev ed. HarperCollins Pubs. 1991 32p il (Let's-read-and-find-out science book) hardcover o.p. paperback available $4.95 (k-1)   **612.3**

1. Teeth

ISBN 0-06-445098-8 (pa)   LC 89-13995

A revised and newly illustrated edition of the title first published 1962 by Crowell

This introduction to teeth describes how many we have at various stages of life, why they fall out, and what they do

"Kelley's exuberant . . . pictures show a multiracial classroom and nonsexist family roles. . . . This text is unsurpassed in the clarity and wit with which it treats a subject of obsessive interest to young children." Booklist

What happens to a hamburger? illustrated by Edward Miller. HarperCollins Pubs. 2001 33p il (Let's-read-and-find-out-science) $15.95; lib bdg $15.89; pa $4.95 (k-3)   **612.3**

ISBN 0-06-027947-8; 0-06-027948-6 (lib bdg); 0-06-445183-6 (pa)   LC 97-39007

A newly illustrated edition of the title first published 1970

Explains the processes by which a hamburger and other foods are used to make energy, strong bones, and solid muscles as they pass through the digestive system

This edition offers "attractive new illustrations, enhanced in a few places with photos that show body parts such as the epiglottis and the stomach lining. . . . Miller's digital artwork has a jaunty, retro look." Booklist

Silverstein, Alvin

The digestive system; [by] Alvin, Virginia & Robert Silverstein. 21st Cent. Bks. (Brookfeild) 1994 96p il (Human body systems) lib bdg $27.90 (5 and up)   **612.3**

1. Digestion

ISBN 0-8050-2832-3   LC 94-19384

This illustrated overview of the physiology and anatomy of the digestive system also includes chapters on diet, eating habits and food poisoning

"The book has a clear, simple flow and primarily conversational style that make it easy to read." Sci Books Films

Includes glossary

612.4   Secretion, excretion, related functions

Silverstein, Alvin

The excretory system; [by] Alvin, Virginia and Robert Silverstein. 21st Cent. Bks. (Brookfeild) 1994 94p il (Human body systems) lib bdg $27.90 (5 and up)   **612.4**

1. Excretion

ISBN 0-8050-2834-X   LC 94-21425

This begins with a description of "excretion in animals, how wastes are formed, and a brief history. The urinary system and excretion through the skin, lungs, and digestive tract are all described, followed by sections on kidney dialysis, transplants, etc. [The text is] lucid, to the point, and highly readable. Photographs and simple diagrams are all in full color." SLJ

Includes glossary

612.6 Reproduction, development, maturation

Cole, Joanna
How you were born; photographs by Margaret Miller. rev & expanded ed. Morrow Junior Bks. 1993 48p il $15; pa $5.95 (k-2)   **612.6**
1. Pregnancy 2. Childbirth 3. Infants
ISBN 0-688-12059-8; 0-688-12061-X (pa)
LC 92-23970
A revised and newly illustrated edition of the title first published 1984
"Illustrated with photographs of culturally diverse families, Cole's text explains conception, the development of the fetus, and the birth process. A note to parents and a suggested reading list are included." J Youth Serv Libr

Gravelle, Karen
The period book; everything you don't want to ask (but need to know); by Karen Gravelle & Jennifer Gravelle; illustrations by Debbie Palen. Walker & Co. 1996 117p il $15.95; pa $8.95 (4 and up)   **612.6**
1. Menstruation
ISBN 0-8027-8420-8; 0-8027-7478-4 (pa)
LC 95-31101
"An aunt and her fifteen-year-old niece provide forthright information about tampon insertion, pelvic exams, body changes during puberty, and other topics adolescent girls might feel uncomfortable discussing with parents and friends. The cartoonlike illustrations and conversational tone make this a friendly, reassuring resource as well as a thorough one." Horn Book Guide

Harris, Robie H.
It's so amazing! a book about eggs, sperm, birth, babies, and families; illustrated by Michael Emberley. Candlewick Press 1999 81p il $21.99 (2-4)   **612.6**
1. Pregnancy 2. Childbirth 3. Sex education
ISBN 0-7636-0051-2   LC 98-33119
Uses bird and bee cartoon characters to present straightforward explanations of topics related to sexual development, love, reproduction, adoption, sexually transmitted diseases, and more
"While the illustrations are engaging and often hilarious, factual information is effectively presented in a clear, nonjudgmental tone that will inform and assure readers." SLJ

Jukes, Mavis
Growing up: it's a girl thing; straight talk about first bras, first periods, and your changing body; illustrations by Debbie Tilley. Knopf 1998 72p il lib bdg $16.99; pa $10 (4 and up)   **612.6**
1. Adolescence 2. Girls 3. Menstruation
ISBN 0-679-99027-5 (lib bdg); 0-679-89027-0 (pa)
LC 98-18113
This is a slightly revised version of chapters from the author's It's a girl thing

This "covers body hair and shaving, perspiration and deodorant, and how to buy your first bra. The second half of the book is devoted to what to expect and how to plan for your first period. . . . The narration has an easy, comfortable voice and imparts accurate and important information." SLJ

Parker, Steve
The reproductive system. Raintree Steck-Vaughn Pubs. 1998 48p il (Human body) lib bdg $25.68 (5 and up)   **612.6**
1. Reproduction 2. Growth
ISBN 0-8172-4806-4   LC 96-29685
Explains the parts of the reproductive system and their functions and provides an overview of human development from birth through adolescence
The text is "succinct but complete, and include[s] plenty of detail without being overwhelming." SLJ
Includes glossary and bibliographical references

Pringle, Laurence P.
Everybody has a bellybutton; your life before you were born; by Laurence Pringle; illustrated by Clare Wood. Boyds Mills Press 1997 unp il $14.95 (k-3)   **612.6**
1. Fetus 2. Pregnancy 3. Childbirth
ISBN 1-56397-009-0   LC 95-83168
This book describes fetal development from single cell to birth
Pringle "offers a gently phrased, solidly scientific look at the growth of a baby. . . . The narrative gives specific, sensorial details that will keep even young children engaged, and the description of childbirth is matter-of-fact and undisturbing. . . . Illustrations are softly realistic pencil drawings on pink and blue backgrounds." Booklist
Includes bibliographical references

Silverstein, Alvin
The reproductive system; [by] Alvin, Virginia, and Robert Silverstein. 21st Cent. Bks. (Brookfield) 1994 96p il (Human body systems) lib bdg $27.90 (5 and up)   **612.6**
1. Reproduction 2. Sex education
ISBN 0-8050-2838-2   LC 94-25912
This "describes male and female systems, hormones, fertilization, stages of pregnancy, STDs, and birth control. . . . Informative full-color photos, clear illustrations, and fact boxes appear throughout." SLJ
Includes glossary

612.7 Musculoskeletal system, integument

Ballard, Carol
The skeleton and muscular system. Raintree Steck-Vaughn Pubs. 1998 48p il (Human body) lib bdg $25.68 (5 and up)   **612.7**
1. Musculoskeletal system 2. Skeleton
ISBN 0-8172-4805-6   LC 96-29688

Ballard, Carol—*Continued*

Explains the various parts of the human skeleton and different types of muscles and their functions

The text is "well organized and well written. The full-color photos, diagrams, and illustrations are clear and complement the text." SLJ

Includes glossary and bibliographical references

Berger, Melvin, 1927-

Why I sneeze, shiver, hiccup, and yawn; illustrated by Paul Meisel. HarperCollins Pubs. 2000 unp il (Let's-read-and-find-out science) $15.95; lib bdg $15.89; pa $4.95 (k-3)   **612.7**
1. Reflexes 2. Nervous system
ISBN 0-06-028144-8; 0-06-028143-X (lib bdg); 0-06-445193-3 (pa)   LC 98-55542
A revised and newly illustrated edition of Why I cough, sneeze, shiver, hiccup & yawn, published 1983 by Crowell

An introduction to reflex acts that explains why we sneeze, shiver, hiccup, and yawn

"The writing is simple but effective, and the charming, colorful pen-and-ink and watercolors are [detailed]. . . . Attractive introductory nonfiction." SLJ

Showers, Paul, 1910-1999

Your skin and mine; illustrated by Kathleen Kuchera. rev ed. HarperCollins Pubs. 1991 32p il (Let's-read-and-find-out science book) hardcover o.p. paperback available $5.95 (k-3)   **612.7**
1. Skin
ISBN 0-06-445102-X (pa)   LC 90-37430
A revised and newly illustrated edition of the title first published 1965 by Crowell

Explains the basic properties of skin, how it protects the body, and how it can vary in color

"This book proves far superior to its predecessor. . . . Ink-and-watercolor illustrations are lively and vibrant." SLJ

Simon, Seymour, 1931-

Bones; our skeletal system. Morrow Junior Bks. 1998 unp il $16; lib bdg $15.93; pa $6.95 (3-6)   **612.7**
1. Bones 2. Skeleton
ISBN 0-688-14644-9; 0-688-14645-7 (lib bdg); 0-688-17721-2 (pa)   LC 97-44751
Describes the skeletal system and outlines the many important roles that bones play in the healthy functioning of the human body

"Simon once again proves his remarkable facility for making complicated science clear and understandable." Booklist

Muscles; our muscular system. Morrow Junior Bks. 1998 unp il $16; lib bdg $15.93; pa $6.95 (3-6)   **612.7**
1. Muscles
ISBN 0-688-14642-2; 0-688-14643-0 (lib bdg); 0-688-17720-4 (pa)   LC 97-44758
Describes the nature and work of muscles, the different kinds, and the effects of exercise and other activities

on them

"The full-paged illustrations are great and include full-color photographs, MRI scans, X rays, and excellent drawings." SLJ

612.8   Nervous functions. Sensory functions

Aliki

My five senses. rev ed. Crowell 1989 31p il (Let's-read-and-find-out science book) hardcover o.p. paperback available $4.95 (k-1)   **612.8**
1. Senses and sensation
ISBN 0-06-445083-X (pa)   LC 88-35350
First published 1962

The faculties of touch, hearing, sight, smelling and taste are introduced in relation to everyday experiences

"Each sense is used independently to observe common phenomena. Next, the author demonstrates more than one sense being used. . . . The book effectively introduced the five senses to young people." Appraisal

Cobb, Vicki, 1938-

Follow your nose; discover your sense of smell; illustrated by Cynthia C. Lewis. Millbrook Press 2000 unp il lib bdg $21.90 (3-6)   **612.8**
1. Smell
ISBN 0-7613-1521-7   LC 99-47872
Examines the sense of smell, how the nose detects different odors, and how we react to different smells. Includes simple experiments to test the sense of smell

An "entertaining and colorful book. . . . The science is accurate, and the pictorial and written anecdotes are cleverly directed toward advanced elementary school . . . students." Sci Books Films

Your tongue can tell; discover your sense of taste; ilustrations by Cynthia C. Lewis. Millbrook Press 2000 unp il lib bdg $21.90 (3-6)   **612.8**
1. Taste
ISBN 0-7613-1473-3   LC 99-47873
Text and suggested activities explore the sense of taste, how it works, and how it can help us detect which foods are sweet, sour, salty, or spicy

Cole, Joanna

The magic school bus explores the senses; illustrated by Bruce Degen. Scholastic Press 1999 47p il $15.95 (2-4)   **612.8**
1. Senses and sensation
ISBN 0-590-44697-5   LC 98-18662
Ms. Frizzle and her class explore the senses by traveling on the magic school bus in and out of an eye, ear, mouth, nose, and other parts of both human and animal bodies

"Along the margins are snippets of information in the form of Frizzle Facts and excerpts from kids' school reports. Degen's clever illustrations are both humorous and informative, acting as excellent visual aids for little learners." Booklist

Parker, Steve

The brain and the nervous system. Raintree Steck-Vaughn Pubs. 1997 48p il (Human body) lib bdg $27.12 (4 and up)   612.8

1. Brain 2. Nervous system

ISBN 0-8172-4802-1   LC 96-36804

Examines the different parts and functions of the brain and nervous system

In this volume each double-page spread covers "a particular subject—from brain waves to the main parts of the brain to sleep to memory. It's the artwork that really stands out. The well-captioned anatomical drawings are an excellent feature." Booklist

Includes bibliographical references

Pringle, Laurence P.

Explore your senses. Benchmark Bks. (Tarrytown) 2000 5v lib bdg ea $22.79 (3-6)   612.8

1. Senses and sensation

Contents: Hearing; Sight; Smell; Taste; Touch

Each title in this set describes a human sense organ, how it works and how to take care of it, compares it to animal senses, and includes a glossary

"Each large-format book includes several clear diagrams of body parts as well as many colorful photographs illustrating other aspects of the text. . . . Clearly written, this attractive series will be useful for elementary school units on the senses." Booklist

Rowan, Peter

Big head! illustrations by John Temperton. Knopf 1998 44p il $20 (4 and up)   612.8

1. Brain 2. Head

ISBN 0-679-89018-1   LC 97-39009

"Rowan briefly considers the function and structure of the eyes, ears, and neck, but she focuses mainly on the brain, providing humorous and intriguing asides and a few simple experiments. . . . The visuals, especially the large, easy-to-see cutaways of the parts of the brain, will be exceptionally useful, and the few judiciously placed overlays are used to good effect." Booklist

Showers, Paul, 1910-1999

Look at your eyes; illustrated by True Kelley. rev ed. HarperCollins Pubs. 1992 32p il (Let's-read-and-find-out science book) lib bdg $15.89 (k-1)   612.8

1. Eye

ISBN 0-06-020189-4   LC 91-10167

A revised and newly illustrated edition of the title first published 1962 by Crowell

Using a little boy's daily activities as a focal point, the author introduces some basic facts about the eyes

Sleep is for everyone; illustrated by Wendy Watson. HarperCollins Pubs. 1997 32p il (Let's read-and-find-out science) $14.95; pa $4.95 (k-2)   612.8

1. Sleep

ISBN 0-06-025392-4; 0-06-445141-0 (pa)

LC 96-49375

A newly illustrated edition of the title first published 1974 by Crowell

This volume examines "how different animals sleep, why we sleep, and what happens while we sleep and when we don't sleep enough. Colorful paper cut-out illustrations are simple and light-hearted with mottled paper as background creating a restful, gentle feeling." Horn Book Guide

Silverstein, Alvin

Sleep; [by] Alvin Silverstein, Virginia Silverstein, and Laura Silverstein Nunn. Watts 2000 48p il (My health) lib bdg $22.50; pa $6.95 (3-5)   612.8

1. Sleep

ISBN 0-531-11636-0 (lib bdg); 0-531-16452-7 (pa)

LC 98-53647

Discusses the activities of the body during sleep, the importance of sleep, common sleep disorders, and the phenomenon of dreams

Includes bibliographical references

Simon, Seymour, 1931-

The brain; our nervous system. Morrow Junior Bks. 1997 unp il $16.95; lib bdg $16.89; pa $6.95 (3-6)   612.8

1. Brain 2. Nervous system

ISBN 0-688-14640-6; 0-688-14641-4 (lib bdg); 0-688-17060-9 (pa)   LC 96-36801

Describes the various parts of the brain and the nervous system and how they function to enable us to think, feel, move, and remember

Simon's "clear, concise writing style is complemented by stunning color images taken with radiological scanners, such as CAT scans, MRIs, and SEMs (scanning electron microscopes.)" SLJ

613.2   Dietetics

Kalbacken, Joan

The food pyramid. Children's Press 1998 47p il hardcover o.p. paperback available $6.95 (2-4)   613.2

1. Nutrition 2. Health

ISBN 0-516-26376-5 (pa)   LC 97-8229

"A True book"

Introduces the food pyramid, describing each level in detail, and discusses nutrition, serving sizes, snacking, and the benefits of healthy eating

The text "delivers the information in a straightforward, clear form, accompanied by crisp photographs and highlighted captions that also serve as sidebars." Booklist

Includes glossary and bibliographical references

Vitamins and minerals. Children's Press 1998 47p il hardcover o.p. paperback available $6.95 (2-4)   613.2

1. Vitamins 2. Nutrition

ISBN 0-516-26387-0 (pa)   LC 97-8231

"A True book"

Kalbacken, Joan—*Continued*

Introduces the major vitamins and minerals found in various foods, and discusses them in relation to nutrition and healthy eating

This offers "large type, simple language, phonetic spellings for scientific words, and full-color photographs on each page." Horn Book Guide

Includes glossary and bibliographical references

Rockwell, Lizzy

Good enough to eat; a kid's guide to food and nutrition. HarperCollins Pubs. 1999 unp il $15.95 (k-3) **613.2**

1. Nutrition 2. Food

ISBN 0-06-027434-4   LC 97-32145

Describes the six categories of nutrients needed for good health, how they work in the body, and what foods provide each. Includes five recipes

"There's an amazing amount of information packed into this inviting, clear, and valuable book." SLJ

VanCleave, Janice Pratt

Janice VanCleave's food and nutrition for every kid; easy activities that make learning science fun. Wiley 1999 232p il (Science for every kid series) $29.95; pa $12.95 (4 and up) **613.2**

1. Nutrition 2. Food

ISBN 0-471-17666-4; 0-471-17665-6 (pa)

LC 98-53677

VanCleave instructs "about food groups, vitamins and minerals, the relationship between energy and food, how to read nutrition labels, and more. The text is straightforward, with good use of scientific terms. . . . The heart of this book is the array of activities that relate to real-life situations." SLJ

Includes glossary

613.6   Special topics of health and safety

Chaiet, Donna

The safe zone; a kid's guide to personal safety; by Donna Chaiet and Francine Russell; photographs by Lillian Gee. Beech Tree Bks. 1998 160p il $16; pa $4.95 (4 and up) **613.6**

1. Safety education

ISBN 0-688-15307-0; 0-688-15308-9 (pa)

LC 97-36309

Discusses various self-defense options which may be used when in an uncomfortable or unsafe situation and suggests what solutions might work in real life

"The frank discussions and on-target advice may go a long way toward making young people less vulnerable to those who prey upon them." SLJ

Includes bibliographical references

613.7   Physical fitness

Luby, Thia, 1954-

Children's book of yoga; games & exercises mimic plants & animals & objects. Clear Light Pubs. 1998 111p il $14.95 **613.7**

1. Yoga

ISBN 1-57416-003-6   LC 98-9712

Presents six complete yoga workouts designed for children from three to twelve years of age

"From the full-color cover, to the many interior glossy photographs of children in various yoga positions, this book is appealing to the eye. . . . The instructions and descriptions are brief but clear. . . . Both children and adults will appreciate this treasure." SLJ

613.9   Birth control, reproductive technology, sex hygiene

Brown, Laurene Krasny

What's the big secret? talking about sex with girls and boys; [by] Laurie Krasny Brown and Marc Brown. Little, Brown 1997 31p il $15.95; pa $5.95 (k-3) **613.9**

1. Sex education

ISBN 0-316-10915-0; 0-316-10183-4 (pa)

LC 96-15521

This "picture book's subject is sex and sexuality: not simply physical differences but also gender roles, the issue of privacy, and reproduction. . . . The Browns do an outstanding and very responsible job of introducing a wide variety of terms (everything from the expected, *umbilical cord,* to the unexpected, *masturbation,* which is handled with honesty but restraint), synthesizing a great deal of information kids want to know at this age, and presenting facts in a nonthreatening but forthright context. They even manage a good deal of humor along the way. . . . The words and illustrations work extremely well together, with the busy, bright cartoon art and balloon dialogue conveying as much of the information as the text." Booklist

Harris, Robie H.

It's perfectly normal; a book about changing bodies, growing up, sex, and sexual health; illustrated by Michael Emberley. Candlewick Press 1994 89p il $19.95; pa $10.99 (4 and up) **613.9**

1. Sex education

ISBN 1-56402-199-8; 1-56402-159-9 (pa)

LC 93-48365

The author "explains the physical, psychological, emotional and social changes that occur during puberty—and the implications of these changes." Publ Wkly

"This caring, conscientious, and well-crafted book will be a fine library resource as well as a marvelous adjunct to the middle-school sex-education curriculum. . . . The bold color cartoon drawings are very candid: a double-page spread of nudes, which beautifully demonstrates the varied shapes and sizes humans come in; a picture of a couple making love; one of a boy masturbating as he sits on his bed; another of a girl examining her genitals with

Harris, Robie H.—*Continued*
a mirror. . . . Harris' text, as forthright as Emberley's art, encompasses . . . (the structure of the reproductive system and puberty) . . . intercourse, birth, abortion, sexual health, abuse, and issues of responsibility and respect." Booklist

614 Forensic medicine, incidence & prevention of disease

Jackson, Donna, 1958-
The bone detectives; how forensic anthropologists solve crimes and uncover mysteries of the dead; by Donna M. Jackson; photographs by Charlie Fellenbaum. Little, Brown 1996 48p il lib bdg $16.95 (5 and up)   **614**
1. Forensic anthropology 2. Criminal investigation
ISBN 0-316-82935-8   LC 95-19051
"Jackson follows forensic anthropologist Dr. Michael Charney and his colleagues as they solve an actual case by developing a physical profile from bones and teeth, reconstructing the victim's skull, and using clues from fibers and other material to make further identification." Booklist
"Laced with eye-catching full-color photos, this readable book is a fine example of the application of scientific knowledge to the 'real' world." SLJ
Includes glossary

616.02 Domestic medicine and medical emergencies

Masoff, Joy, 1951-
Emergency! principal photography by Brian Michaud and Peter Escobedo. Scholastic Ref. 1999 48p il $16.95 (3-6)   **616.02**
1. Emergency medicine
ISBN 0-590-97898-5   LC 97-26995
Discusses all aspects of emergency medicine including the medical personnel and equipment needed to successfully help the patient
"A colorful, information-packed volume. Each double-page spread features lots of excellent full-color photographs, a large heading, and sidebars." SLJ
Includes bibliographical references

616.2 Diseases of the respiratory system

Silverstein, Alvin
Common colds; [by] Alvin Silverstein, Virginia Silverstein and Laura Silverstein Nunn. Watts 1999 48p il (My health) lib bdg $22.50; pa $6.95 (3-5)   **616.2**
1. Cold (Disease)
ISBN 0-531-11579-8 (lib bdg); 0-531-16410-1 (pa)
LC 98-22025

Explains how people catch colds, how the body fights the germs, how colds are spread, and what precautions people can take against them
This is "attractively designed, with plenty of sidebars containing fascinating facts and color photographs." Booklist
Includes glossary and bibliographical references

616.4 Diabetes

Pirner, Connie White
Even little kids get diabetes; pictures by Nadine Bernard Westcott. Whitman, A. 1991 unp il $13.95; pa $5.95 (k-1)   **616.4**
1. Diabetes
ISBN 0-8075-2158-2; 0-8075-2159-0 (pa)
LC 90-12738
A young girl who has had diabetes since she was two years old describes her adjustments to the disease
"Language is simple, age appropriate, and effectively gets the point across. The ink-and-watercolor drawings are lively and often upbeat. . . . Perhaps the most valuable part of the book is the 'note for parents,' which relates Pirner's personal experience over the last three years in caring for a diabetic child." SLJ

616.5 Diseases of integument, hair, nails

Caffey, Donna, 1954-
Yikes-lice! illustrations by Patrick Girouard. Whitman, A. 1998 unp il lib bdg $13.95 (k-3)
616.5
1. Lice
ISBN 0-8075-9374-5   LC 97-30679
Rhyming text describes what happens when a family discovers lice in the home and fights against them. Includes factual information about how lice live, spread, and can be eradicated

Silverstein, Alvin
Is that a rash? Watts 2000 48p il (My health) lib bdg $22.50; pa $6.95 (3-5)   **616.5**
1. Skin—Diseases
ISBN 0-531-11637-9 (lib bdg); 0-531-16451-9 (pa)
LC 98-53648
Describes various types of rashes with information on how they affect people, how they spread, and how to treat them, including some rashes associated with childhood diseases
Includes bibliographical references

616.8 Diseases of the nervous system and mental disorders

Gold, Susan Dudley
Alzheimer's disease; expert reviews by Paul R. Solomon and Jon C. Stuckey. rev ed. Enslow Pubs. 2000 48p il (Health watch) lib bdg $18.95 (4 and up)   **616.8**
1. Alzheimer's disease
ISBN 0-7660-1650-1   LC 00-8398

Gold, Susan Dudley—*Continued*
First published 1996 by Crestwood House
Discusses this degenerative disease of the nervous system, its effect on the patient's family members, and suggestions for coping and care
"Color photos and a concise, easy-to-read style will make this an attractive book for the middle schooler." Book Rep
Includes glossary and bibliographical references

616.85 Neuroses; speech and language disorders; disorders of personality, intellect, impulse control

Bode, Janet
Food fight; a guide to eating disorders for preteens and their parents. Simon & Schuster Bks. for Young Readers 1997 154p $16; pa $4.50 (5 and up)   **616.85**
1. Eating disorders
ISBN 0-689-80272-2; 0-689-81086-5 (pa)
         LC 96-29186
"This book defines eating disorders and discusses why they occur, who gets them, and what to do to help. Nutrition facts are also provided. A section for adults tells how to recognize eating disorders in children, how to get professional help, and what parents can do. . . . Bode includes numerous personal stories from preteens and adults. A list of organizations is appended." Horn Book Guide
"Bode's approach is highly readable and her tone is conversational. . . . Solid information is presented." SLJ
Includes bibliographical references

616.9 Other diseases

Berger, Melvin, 1927-
Germs make me sick! illustrated by Marylin Hafner. rev ed. HarperCollins Pubs. 1995 32p il (Let's-read-and-find-out science) $15.95; lib bdg $15.89; pa $4.95 (k-3)   **616.9**
1. Bacteria 2. Viruses
ISBN 0-06-024249-3; 0-06-024250-7 (lib bdg); 0-06-445154-2 (pa)   LC 93-27059
First published 1985
Explains how bacteria and viruses affect the human body and how the body fights them
This features "Hafner's lively color cartoon illustrations. . . . [It offers a] lively combination of fact and narrative that has made this a great title for easy reading and for sharing aloud." Booklist

616.97 Diseases of the immune system

McPhee, Andrew T.
AIDS. Watts 2000 63p il lib bdg $24; pa $8.95 (5 and up)   **616.97**
1. AIDS (Disease)
ISBN 0-531-11779-0 (lib bdg); 0-531-16528-0 (pa)
         LC 99-45288

"Watts library"
Discusses how AIDS is spread, diagnosed, and treated. Methods of protecting oneself from the disease are presented
Includes bibliographical references

Silverstein, Alvin
Allergies; [by] Alvin Silverstein, Virginia Silverstein and Laura Silverstein Nunn. Watts 1999 48p il (My health) lib bdg $22.50; pa $6.95 (3-5)   **616.97**
1. Allergy
ISBN 0-531-11581-X (lib bdg); 0-531-16409-8 (pa)
         LC 98-26033
Discusses the nature and effects of allergies, who gets them, how they develop, the different kinds, and how they are treated
This is "well written and complete, without being overly technical. The occasional cartoon illustrations are clear and informative, and the frequent close-up color photographs . . . are an added bonus." SLJ
Includes glossary and bibliographical references

617.1 Injuries and wounds. Sports medicine

Silverstein, Alvin
Cuts, scrapes, scabs, and scars; [by] Alvin Silverstein, Virginia Silverstein and Laura Silverstein Nunn. Watts 1999 48p il (My health) lib bdg $22.50; pa $6.95 (3-5)   **617.1**
1. Wounds and injuries 2. First aid
ISBN 0-531-11582-8 (lib bdg); 0-531-16411-X (pa)
         LC 98-36479
Describes how the body responds to wounds and heals itself when the skin is broken and discusses how to care for minor abrasions
Includes bibliographical references

617.6 Dentistry

Keller, Laurie
Open wide; Tooth School inside. Holt & Co. 2000 unp il lib bdg $16.95 (k-3)   **617.6**
1. Dentistry 2. Teeth
ISBN 0-8050-6192-4   LC 99-27965
Through a classroom setting in which teeth are the students, presents information about the structure and care of teeth and the services provided by dentists
"The sprawling comic art, featuring acrylics and collage, is busy with unruly figures riding on a 'molar coaster,' jumping rope made with floss, and engaging in food fights. . . . Consistently humorous, the book is instructive throughout." Horn Book

Silverstein, Alvin
Tooth decay and cavities; [by] Alvin Silverstein, Virginia Silverstein and Laura Silverstein Nunn. Watts 1999 48p il (My health) lib bdg $22; pa $6.95 (3-5)   **617.6**
1. Teeth
ISBN 0-531-11580-1 (lib bdg); 0-531-16412-8 (pa)
         LC 98-22024

Silverstein, Alvin—*Continued*
Describes the structure and function of teeth and discusses how cavities form and how to prevent them
Includes bibliographical references

621.3 Electrical engineering; superconductivity; electronics; communication engineering; computers

Cole, Joanna
The magic school bus and the electric field trip; illustrated by Bruce Degen. Scholastic 1997 48p il $15.95; pa $4.99 (2-4)   **621.3**
1. Electricity 2. Electric power
ISBN 0-590-44682-7; 0-590-44683-5 (pa)
LC 97-2080
Also available Spanish language edition
Ms. Frizzle takes her class on a field trip through the town's electrical wires so they can learn how electricity is generated and how it is used
"Spiced with plenty of puns and jokes, the writing and the colorful artwork continue the series' unbeatable combination of clearly presented information and plenty of fun." Booklist

621.32 Lighting

Wallace, Joseph, 1957-
The lightbulb; foldout illustration by Toby Welles. Atheneum Bks. for Young Readers 1999 80p il (Turning point inventions series) $17.95 (4 and up)   **621.32**
1. Edison, Thomas A. (Thomas Alva), 1847-1931
2. Electric lighting
ISBN 0-689-82816-0
This book "surveys the age-old search for a safe, clean light source, then concentrates on Thomas Alva Edison's work to invent and perfect the bulb. The many illustrations include black-and-white photographs, colorful diagrams, photos of artifacts, and period prints and paintings." Booklist
Includes bibliographical references

621.385 Telephony

Gearhart, Sarah
The telephone; foldout illustration by Toby Welles. Atheneum Bks. for Young Readers 1999 80p il (Turning point inventions series) $17.95 (4 and up)   **621.385**
1. Bell, Alexander Graham, 1847-1922 2. Telephone
ISBN 0-689-82815-2
This book "reflects on the history of long-distance communications, focusing on Alexander Graham Bell's life and achievements and culminating in his invention of the telephone." Booklist
"Well-written and interesting. . . . Attractive and easy to read, and a good mix of full-color and black-and-white photos and reproductions are well placed throughout." SLJ
Includes bibliographical references

621.8 Machine engineering

Bingham, Caroline, 1962-
Monster machines. DK Pub. 1998 32p il $14.95
                                                    621.8
1. Machinery
ISBN 0-7894-2796-6   LC 97-39624
Photographs and text examine the parts and functions of such large machines as trucks, jets, supertankers, tractors, bulldozers, and fire engines
"It is the sheer visual bigness (including two double-spread foldouts) of this oversized book that will captivate mechanically minded audiences." Horn Book Guide
Includes glossary

Hoban, Tana
Construction zone. Greenwillow Bks. 1997 unp il $15.95 (k-2)   **621.8**
1. Machinery
ISBN 0-688-12284-1   LC 96-5696
Hoban uses "full-color photographs to introduce construction equipment. Each of the 13 machines presented is given a two-page spread, one picture taken at middle distance, the other close up. The final two pages match thumbnail photos with explanatory text." SLJ
The "photos have extraordinary depth and detail." Booklist

621.9 Tools

Clements, Andrew, 1949-
Workshop; illustrated by David Wisniewski. Clarion Bks. 1998 unp il $16 (k-2)   **621.9**
1. Tools 2. Workshops
ISBN 0-395-85579-9   LC 97-48534
"From ruler to wrench, 13 basic tools are described in short text and bright, bold cut-paper illustrations. In each large-scale, double-page spread, a young apprentice watches a different craftsman at work with saw, chisel, grinder, or knife." SLJ
"Wisniewski's cut-paper illustrations and collage ably illustrate Clements' spare, poetic text. . . . A unique introduction to the world of wood and art for budding artisans." Bull Cent Child Books

623.8 Nautical engineering and seamanship

Fisher, Leonard Everett, 1924-
The shipbuilders; written & illustrated by Leonard Everett Fisher. Benchmark Bks. (Tarrytown) 1998 48p il (Colonial craftsmen) lib bdg $14.95 (4 and up)   **623.8**
1. Shipbuilding—History
ISBN 0-7614-0508-9   LC 96-36136
A reissue of the title first published 1971 by Watts
Traces the history of shipbuilding in the American colonies and describes each step in the building of an eighteenth-century ship
"Tools are described; technical terms defined; and the many clear illustrations and diagrams graphically detail every aspect of ship construction." SLJ

Kovacs, Deborah

Dive to the deep ocean; voyages of exploration and discovery. Raintree Steck-Vaughn Pubs. 2000 64p il maps (Turnstone ocean explorer book) lib bdg $28.55; pa $8.95 (4 and up)　　　**623.8**
　1. Alvin (Submersible) 2. Underwater exploration 3. Submersibles
　ISBN 0-7398-1234-3 (lib bdg); 0-7398-1235-1 (pa)
　　　　　　　　　　　　　　LC 99-17877

Relates the history of deep sea research, explaining how the development of submersibles, particularly the Alvin, has led to many fascinating discoveries
"The plentiful photographs and occasional diagram are well placed and present clear, concise information that reinforces what is read in the text." Sci Books Films
Includes glossary and bibliographical references

624　Civil engineering

Johmann, Carol, 1949-

Bridges! amazing structures to design, build & test; [by] Carol Johmann & Elizabeth Rieth; illustrations by Michael Kline. Williamson 1999 96p il pa $10.95 (4 and up)　　　**624**
　1. Bridges
　ISBN 1-88559-330-9　　　　LC 98-53272
"A Williamson Kaleidoscope Kids book"
Describes different kinds of bridges, their history, design, construction, and effects on populations, environmental dilemmas, safety, and more
"Eye-catching photographs and cartoon illustrations in blue and orange tones abound; clear organization of text and unifying page borders create an attractive graphic package. The volume includes a list of notable bridges by state and country." SLJ

Sturges, Philemon

Bridges are to cross; illustrated by Giles Laroche. Putnam 1998 unp il $15.99; pa $6.99 (2-4)　　　**624**
　1. Bridges
　ISBN 0-399-23174-9; 0-698-11874-X (pa)
　　　　　　　　　　　　　　LC 97-13775

Discusses different kinds of bridges, from train bridges to fortified castle bridges, and provides an example of each
"The pictures, a combination of paint and cut paper, show the bridges at their elegant best and reflect the surroundings, whether modern or ancient, beautifully. . . . This is guaranteed to make most readers look at bridges with new eyes." Booklist

624.1　Structural engineering and underground construction

Macaulay, David, 1946-

Underground. Houghton Mifflin 1976 109p il $18; pa $9.95 (4 and up)　　　**624.1**
　1. Civil engineering 2. Building 3. Public utilities
　ISBN 0-395-24739-X; 0-395-34065-9 (pa)

In this "examination of the intricate support systems that lie beneath the street levels of our cities, Macaulay explains the ways in which foundations for buildings are laid or reinforced, and how the various utilities or transportation services are constructed." Bull Cent Child Books
"Introduced by a visual index—a bird's eye view of a busy, hypothetical intersection with colored indicators marking the specific locations analyzed in subsequent pages—detailed illustrations are combined with a clear, precise narrative to make the subject comprehensible and fascinating." Horn Book
Includes glossary

625.1　Railroads

Barton, Byron

Trains. Crowell 1986 unp il lib bdg $15.89 (k-1)
　　　　　　　　　　　　　　625.1
　1. Railroads
　ISBN 0-690-04534-4　　　　LC 85-47898
Brief text and illustrations present a variety of trains and what they do
"The concepts are simple and Barton's illustrations are just enough, and no more." Publ Wkly

Big book of trains; [by] National Railway Museum, York, England. DK Pub. 1998 32p il $14.95 (4-6)　　　**625.1**
　1. Railroads
　ISBN 0-7894-3436-9　　　　LC 98-18830
Describes the locomotives, cars, tunnels, stations, and functions of such trains as freight trains, channel tunnel trains, bullet trains, mountain trains, and snow trains
Includes glossary

Coiley, John

Train; written by John Coiley. Knopf 1992 63p il (Eyewitness books) (4 and up)　　　**625.1**
　1. Railroads
　　　　　　　　　　　　　　LC 92-4711
Available DK Pub. edition $15.95; $19.99 lib bdg (ISBN 0-7894-5756-3; 0-7894-6588-4 lib bdg)
"A Dorling Kindersley book"
Traces the development of railways from the first Babylonian rutways to the electromagnetic, driverless trains of today and describes how trains are built and operated
"This book will appeal to those who enjoy trains and like to read about and look at a rich visual display of engines, cars, and other artifacts." Sci Books Films

625.7　Roads

Hennessy, B. G. (Barbara G.)

Road builders; pictures by Simms Taback. Viking 1994 unp il $14.99; pa $5.99 (k-2) **625.7**
　1. Roads 2. Trucks
　ISBN 0-670-83390-8; 0-14-054276-0 (pa)
　　　　　　　　　　　　　　LC 93-42248

Hennessy, B. G. (Barbara G.)—*Continued*

This book introduces "children to the process of building a road. The focus is on the vehicles involved, depicting them all together and then individually or in pairs as the project unfolds. Taback's cartoon illustration show the multiethnic crew at work and a flatbed truck carrying them to the next job when the highway is completed. This book is a good choice for both beginning readers and preschool construction buffs." SLJ

628.9   Fire-fighting technology

Beil, Karen Magnuson

Fire in their eyes; wildfires and the people who fight them. Harcourt Brace & Co. 1999 64p il $18; pa $10 (4 and up)   628.9
1. Fire fighters 2. Forest fires 3. Forest ecology
ISBN 0-15-201043-2; 0-15-201042-4 (pa)

LC 98-6378

Depicts in text and photographs the training, equipment, and real-life experiences of people who risk their lives to battle wildfires, as well as people who use fire for ecological reasons

"The ferocity of fire is forcefully depicted in both narrative and well-chosen photographs." Horn Book Guide
Includes glossary

Demarest, Chris L., 1951-

Firefighters A to Z. Margaret K. McElderry Bks. 2000 unp il lib bdg $16.95 (k-1)   628.9
1. Fire fighters 2. Alphabet
ISBN 0-689-83798-4   LC 99-56382

An alphabetical look at a firefighter's day

"There's nothing babyish or cute about the robust, action-oriented pastel artwork in *Firefighters A to Z*. . . . Permeated with intense primary colors, the images build on one another to convey the physical nature of this dramatic but serious job. The firefighters themselves, in their bulky yellow suits and oxygen masks, appear straight out of science fiction, but the smoothly rhyming text grounds their activities in reality." Horn Book

Gibbons, Gail

Fire! Fire! Crowell 1984 unp il lib bdg $15.89; pa $6.95 (k-3)   628.9
1. Fire fighting
ISBN 0-690-04416-X (lib bdg); 0-06-446058-4 (pa)

LC 83-46162

This book "depicts fire fighting in the city, country, forest, and on the water, and integrates some points on fire safety." Child Book Rev Serv

The author/illustrator "uses bright colors and simplified diagrams to convey the excitement and teamwork necessary in firefighting. There are details for children to pore over and the equipment in the illustrations is clearly labeled." SLJ

Kuklin, Susan

Fighting fires. Bradbury Press 1993 unp il hardcover o.p. paperback available $5.99 (k-3)
628.9
1. Fire fighters
ISBN 0-689-82434-3 (pa)   LC 92-38678

Text and photographs present the vehicles, equipment, and procedures used by fire fighters

The "full-color photographs vary in size from quarter to full page. Most of the action shots look a little staged, but are not stiff. Kuklin's prose reads easily and smoothly. . . . An excellent title to use with a community social-studies unit and during fire prevention week." SLJ

Marston, Hope Irvin, 1935-

Fire trucks; illustrated with photographs. rev and updated ed. Cobblehill Bks. 1996 48p il $16.99 (k-3)   628.9
1. Fire engines 2. Fire fighters
ISBN 0-525-65231-0   LC 95-47945

First published 1984 by Dodd, Mead

Describes different kinds of firefighting equipment, such as pumper trucks, fireboats, and the SuperScooper, an airplane used to fight forest fires, as well as the work of people who put out fires

This book "exhibits some state-of-the-art equipment. Crisp, clear, colorful photographs [are featured]." SLJ

Masoff, Joy, 1951-

Fire! principal photography by Jack Reznicki and Barry D. Smith. Scholastic Ref. 1998 48p il $16.95; pa $5.99 (3-6)   628.9
1. Fire fighters
ISBN 0-590-97872-1; 0-590-97585-4 (pa)

LC 97-10928

Presents the work done by fire fighters, including the equipment they use, the fires they fight, the rescues and investigations they perform, and the history and future of fire fighting

"Masoff's personal enthusiasm for her subject along with her attention to detail and clear, lively writing set this far above the common run of razzle-dazzle, photo-filled compendia." Horn Book Guide
Includes bibliographical references

629.13   Aeronautics

Brown, Don, 1949-

Ruth Law thrills a nation; story and pictures by Don Brown. Ticknor & Fields 1993 unp il $16; pa $5.95 (k-3)   629.13
1. Law, Ruth, b. 1887 2. Women air pilots
ISBN 0-395-66404-7; 0-395-73517-3 (pa)

LC 92-45701

Describes the record-breaking flight of a daring woman pilot, Ruth Law, from Chicago to New York in 1916

"Using a simple text and effective watercolors, Brown successfully re-creates the remarkable flying feat. He sets Law in her historical context with humor and precision." Booklist

Haskins, James, 1941-

Black eagles; African Americans in aviation. Scholastic 1995 196p il hardcover o.p. paperback available $4.50 (5 and up)   629.13
1. African American pilots
ISBN 0-590-45913-9 (pa)   LC 94-18623

Haskins, James, 1941-—*Continued*

"Haskins presents the . . . achievements of African-American aviators from the beginning of the twentieth century to the present." Horn Book Guide

"In addition to introducing the people involved, Haskins ably sets the background scene, revealing a social context of discrimination. . . . An excellent job of dealing with the particular and the more general aspects of 'what it was like.'" Booklist

Includes bibliographical references

Hunter, Ryan Ann, 1951-

Take off! illustrated by Edward Miller. Holiday House 2000 unp il lib bdg $15.95 (k-3)	**629.13**

1. Aeronautics 2. Airplanes

ISBN 0-8234-1466-3	LC 98-45423

"Traces flight from wing-flapping and balloons through Kitty Hawk and the twentieth-century flying boom, then examines the breadth of current aviation and some future possibilities." Bull Cent Child Books

"Bright, colorful illustrations offer youngsters plenty of airplanes and other flying machines to inspect. . . . Best perhaps are the endpapers showing 26 planes of different sizes from different periods in history, which offer children a chance to study the many variations in airplane shape and wing construction throughout the years." Booklist

629.133 Aircraft types

Nahum, Andrew

Flying machine; written by Andrew Nahum. Knopf 1990 62p il (Eyewitness books) (4 and up)	**629.133**

1. Aeronautics—History

LC 90-4007

Available DK Pub. edition $15.95; lib bdg $19.99 (ISBN 0-7894-5766-0; 0-7894-6571-X)

A photo essay tracing the history and development of aircraft from hot-air balloons to jetliners. Includes information on the principles of flight and the inner workings of various flying machines

"Strikingly clear images leap from a white background; numerous captions and brief text encourage browsing over methodical exploration. The whole effect is made orderly by careful layout and unobtrusive black outlines around each spread." SLJ

629.136 Airports

Maynard, Christopher

Airplane. Dorling Kindersley 1995 21p il (Mighty machines) $9.95; pa $5.95 (k-3) **629.136**

1. Airports 2. Airplanes 3. Machinery

ISBN 0-7894-0211-4; 0-7894-6075-0 (pa)

LC 95-19035

Explains how the airplanes and major pieces of equipment in an airport work and interact

"Each double-page spread focuses on one very large, clear, close-up photograph of a machine, with lots of visual and textual details all around it, including amazing facts of power and scale." Booklist

629.224 Trucks

Barton, Byron

Trucks. Crowell 1986 unp il lib bdg $15.89 (k-1)	**629.224**

1. Trucks

ISBN 0-690-04530-1	LC 85-47901

Also available Board book edition

Brief text and illustrations present a variety of trucks from cement trucks to ice-cream trucks, and what they do

"A tightly focused (book) . . . featuring Barton's trademark bright, blocky graphics and spare text." Publ Wkly

Llewellyn, Claire

Truck. Dorling Kindersley 1995 21p il (Mighty machines) $9.95; pa $5.95 (k-3)	**629.224**

1. Trucks 2. Machinery

ISBN 1-56458-516-6; 0-7894-6072-6 (pa)

LC 94-38034

Brief text accompanies labeled photographs and drawings describing large trucks and machinery used in construction including a giant dump truck, bulldozer, wheel loader, mass excavator, forklift, and paver

Robbins, Ken

Trucks; giants of the highway; text and pictures by Ken Robbins. Atheneum Bks. for Young Readers 1999 unp il $16 (k-2)	**629.224**

1. Trucks

ISBN 0-689-82664-8	LC 98-47640

Describes different kinds of tractor trailers, or big rigs, and the loads they haul

"Young truck enthusiasts will enjoy this well-written, attractive photo-essay." Booklist

Simon, Seymour, 1931-

Seymour Simon's book of trucks. HarperCollins Pubs. 2000 unp $15.95; lib bdg $15.89 (k-3)	**629.224**

1. Trucks

ISBN 0-06-028473-0; 0-06-028481-1 (lib bdg)

LC 99-14602

Describes various kinds of trucks and their functions, including a log truck, cement mixer truck, and sanitation truck

"The exciting photographs, many of them close-ups, will captivate youngsters. . . . The visual appeal of this book is very high and the information is clear and equally engaging." SLJ

Stille, Darlene R.

Trucks. Children's Press 1997 47p il lib bdg $22; pa $6.95 (2-4)	**629.224**

1. Trucks

ISBN 0-516-20343-6 (lib bdg); 0-516-26179-7 (pa)

LC 96-25727

"A True book"

Describes different kinds of trucks, including tractor trailers and tank trucks, pick-ups, tow trucks, fire trucks, garbage trucks, vans, and recreational vehicles

Includes bibliographical references

629.225 Work vehicles

Llewellyn, Claire
  Tractor. Dorling Kindersley 1995 21p il (Mighty machines) $9.95; pa $5.95 (k-3)   **629.225**
  1. Agricultural machinery
  ISBN 1-56458-515-8; 0-7894-6073-4 (pa)
                                          LC 94-24403
  Labeled photographs and drawings and brief text describe tractors, manure spreaders, plows, combine and forage harvesters, balers, and other agricultural machines

629.227 Cycles

Gibbons, Gail
  Bicycle book. Holiday House 1995 unp il $16.95; pa $6.95 (k-3)   **629.227**
  1. Bicycles 2. Cycling
  ISBN 0-8234-1199-0; 0-8234-1408-6 (pa)
                                          LC 95-5911
  "The history of bicycles, the science behind their design, descriptions of different types, their care, and safety rules are all clearly and simply presented in Gibbons's typical, inimitable style. Lots of color, accurate explanations, and interesting facts make this a winning choice." SLJ

629.228 Racing cars

Bingham, Caroline, 1962-
  Race car. DK Pub. 1996 21p il (Mighty machines) $9.95; pa $5.95 (k-3)   **629.228**
  1. Automobiles 2. Motorcycles 3. Racing
  ISBN 0-7894-0574-1; 0-7894-6074-2 (pa)
  Labeled photographs and drawings and brief text describe eight racing vehicles including a dragster, Le Mans race car, Grand Prix motorcycle, rally car, racing truck, motocross bike, Formula 1 car, and sidecar racer

Rex, Michael
  My race car. Holt & Co. 2000 unp il lib bdg $15.95 (k-1)   **629.228**
  1. Automobile racing 2. Automobiles
  ISBN 0-8050-6101-0   LC 99-31773
  "'I have a race car. I drive it all the time,' says a boy sitting on the floor with his toy cars. As the pages turn, the toy world becomes reality: the boy finds himself on the track with his crew, checking his car engine, and then driving his laps. . . . Short, simple sentences create excitement . . . and Rex's bright, thick-lined cartoon drawings are appealingly energetic and clear. A great choice for young race car enthusiasts who are beginning to read on their own." Booklist

629.4 Astronautics

Bredeson, Carmen
  John Glenn returns to orbit; life on the space shuttle. Enslow Pubs. 2000 48p il (Countdown to space) $18.95 (4 and up)   **629.4**
  1. Glenn, John, 1921- 2. Space flight 3. Space shuttles 4. Astronauts
  ISBN 0-7660-1304-9   LC 99-12490
  Describes the activities aboard the space shuttle Discovery during its historic flight in 1998 when John Glenn, at age seventy-seven, returned to space
  "The accessible [text is] accompanied by plenty of well-captioned photos and diagrams." Horn Book Guide
  Includes glossary and bibliographical references

Cole, Michael D.
  Moon base; first colony in space. Enslow Pubs. 1999 48p il (Countdown to space) lib bdg $18.95 (4 and up)   **629.4**
  1. Lunar bases 2. Moon—Exploration
  ISBN 0-7660-1118-6   LC 98-13126
  Describes the Apollo 11 mission to the moon, explains the need for establishing a moon base, and speculates about future situations in which the base would be used
  Includes glossary and bibliographical references

  Space launch disaster; when liftoff goes wrong. Enslow Pubs. 2000 48p il (Countdown to space) lib bdg $18.95 (4 and up)   **629.4**
  1. Space vehicle accidents
  ISBN 0-7660-1309-X   LC 99-32179
  Describes the dangers of launching spacecraft, covering the Russian Mars space probe explosion, the Apollo 1 fire, the Apollo 12 lightning strike, and the Challenger explosion
  Includes glossary and bibliographical references

629.44 Auxiliary spacecraft

Cole, Michael D.
  NASA space vehicles; capsules, shuttles, and space stations. Enslow Pubs. 2000 48p il (Countdown to space) lib bdg $18.95 (4 and up)   **629.44**
  1. Space vehicles 2. Outer space—Exploration
  ISBN 0-7660-1308-1   LC 99-35533
  Describes American space vehicles and their uses, including various space probes, the Mercury, Gemini, and Apollo capsules, Skylab, the space shuttles, and the International Space Station
  Includes glossary and bibliographical references

629.45 Manned space flight

Cole, Michael D.
  Astronauts; training for space. Enslow Pubs. 1999 48p il (Countdown to space) lib bdg $18.95 (4 and up)   **629.45**
  1. Astronauts
  ISBN 0-7660-1116-X   LC 98-3299

Cole, Michael D.—*Continued*

Describes the qualities needed to be part of the space program and various aspects of the training that astronaut candidates receive to prepare them for their first flight

This title should "be commended for presenting female as well as male role models for the budding astronaut." Sci Books Films

Includes glossary and bibliographical references

Space emergency; astronauts in danger. Enslow Pubs. 2000 48p il (Countdown to space) lib bdg $18.95 (4 and up)   **629.45**

1. Astronautics 2. Space vehicle accidents
ISBN 0-7660-1307-3   LC 99-26855

Describes emergencies that occurred during several space missions, including Apollo 13, Friendship 7, Gemini 8, and Mir

Includes glossary and bibliographical references

Dyson, Marianne J.

Space station science; life in free fall; foreword by Buzz Aldrin. Scholastic 1999 128p il $16.95 (4 and up)   **629.45**

1. Space stations 2. Astronautics
ISBN 0-590-05889-4   LC 98-45994

Describes space stations, the International Space Station, the training and activities of its crew, and the conditions that will exist on it, including weightlessness and the dangers of radiation and meteors. Includes experiments and activities simulating conditions in space

"The precisely written text, illustrated with many full-color photos, leads readers to imagine life in orbit. . . . A glossary and a list of organizations and Web sites conclude this inviting and informative volume." Booklist

Hehner, Barbara, 1947-

First on the moon; what it was like when man landed on the moon; illustrations by Greg Ruhl. Hyperion Bks. for Children 1999 48p il $16.99; pa $7.99 (4 and up)   **629.45**

1. Apollo 11 (Spacecraft) 2. Space flight to the moon
ISBN 0-7868-0489-0; 0-7868-1538-8 (pa)
LC 98-42651

"An I was there book"

An account of the first moon landing by Apollo 11 in 1969

"The informative and entertaining text is illustrated with an abundance of full-color and black-and-white photographs as well as paintings." SLJ

Includes glossary and bibliographical references

Vogt, Gregory

Apollo moonwalks; the amazing lunar missions. Enslow Pubs. 2000 48p il (Countdown to space) lib bdg $18.95 (4 and up)   **629.45**

1. Project Apollo 2. Space flight to the moon 3. Moon—Exploration
ISBN 0-7660-1306-5   LC 99-16921

Discusses the six Apollo missions that landed on the moon, describing the work performed there, what it is like to walk on the moon, and the collection of moon rocks

Includes glossary and bibliographical references

Spacewalks; the ultimate adventure in orbit; [by] Gregory L. Vogt. Enslow Pubs. 2000 48p il (Countdown to space) lib bdg $18.95 (4 and up)
629.45

1. Extravehicular activity (Space flight) 2. Space flight
ISBN 0-7660-1305-7   LC 99-37094

Describes the training and preparation for spacewalking, the hazards faced by astronauts, as well as the construction of spacesuits

Includes glossary and bibliographical references

629.47   Astronautical engineering

Branley, Franklyn Mansfield, 1915-

Floating in space; by Franklyn M. Branley; illustrated by True Kelley. HarperCollins Pubs. 1998 32p il (Let's-read-and-find-out science) lib bdg $15.89; pa $4.95 (k-3)   **629.47**

1. Astronauts 2. Space shuttles
ISBN 0-06-025433-5 (lib bdg); 0-06-445142-9 (pa)
LC 97-13052

Examines life aboard a space shuttle, describing how astronauts deal with weightlessness, how they eat and exercise, some of the work they do, and more

"This is a beautifully illustrated children's book. . . . The textual information is clearly written, easy to read, and well organized." Sci Books Films

629.8   Automatic control engineering

Sonenklar, Carol

Robots rising; with illustrations by John Kaufmann. Holt & Co. 1999 103p il $15.95 (3-5)
629.8

1. Robots
ISBN 0-8050-6096-0   LC 99-19717

Simple text and illustrations describe technological advancements in the field of robotics

"Short chapters, large print, and frequent black-and-white illustrations make the format appealing, and the lively text will attract browsers as well as young researchers." Booklist

Includes glossary and bibliographical references

630   Agriculture & related technologies

Splear, Elsie Lee, 1906-

Growing seasons; paintings by Ken Stark. Putnam 2000 unp il $15.99 (3-5)   **630**

1. Farm life 2. Seasons
ISBN 0-399-23460-8   LC 99-23586

Born into an Illinois farm family in 1906, Elsie Lee Splear describes how she, her parents, and her sisters lived in the early years of the twentieth century and how the changing seasons shaped their existence

"In this exceptionally well-designed book, life on a Midwestern farm at the turn of the century is exquisitely portrayed. . . . Stark's evocative paintings are filled with motion, life, and homey details." SLJ

630.1 Agriculture—Philosophy and theory. Country and farm life

Bial, Raymond
Portrait of a farm family. Houghton Mifflin 1995 48p il $15.95 (4 and up) **630.1**
1. Farm life 2. Agriculture
ISBN 0-395-69936-3   LC 94-38201
In this photo essay about the Steidinger family farm in Illinois "Bial explores the specifics of milking, raising feed-lot calves, and cutting silage and discusses the factors to be weighed before buying expensive equipment or choosing a particular kind of animal to raise. . . . Bial brings the Steidingers' everyday world to life, fitting it neatly into an excellent discussion of family-farm-based agriculture and the U.S. economy." Booklist
Includes bibliography

Peterson, Cris, 1952-
Century farm; one hundred years on a family farm; with photographs by Alvis Upitis. Boyds Mills Press 1999 unp il $16.95 (k-3) **630.1**
1. Farm life
ISBN 1-56397-710-9
"Peterson crafts a warmly personal look at their family farm, noting both constants and changes over the farm's hundred-year history. Family album photographs, reproduced in soft-edged sepia, give descriptions of the past a nostalgic yet immediate appeal and contrast well with the sharp-edged full-color contemporary shots." Horn Book Guide

633.1 Cereals

Aliki
Corn is maize; the gift of the Indians; written and illustrated by Aliki. Crowell 1976 33p il (Let's-read-and-find-out science book) lib bdg $15.89; pa $4.95 (k-3) **633.1**
1. Corn
ISBN 0-690-00975-5 (lib bdg); 0-06-445026-0 (pa)

In this book, the author provides a history of corn, or maize, and "also the life cycle of the plant itself, its growth and reproductive patterns, and its many uses. Excellent illustrations by the author help convey both cultural aspects and technological uses of corn." Sci Child

Landau, Elaine
Corn. Children's Press 1999 47p il lib bdg $22; pa $6.95 (2-4) **633.1**
1. Corn
ISBN 0-516-21026-2 (lib bdg); 0-516-26759-0 (pa)
LC 98-47332
"A True book"
Examines the history, cultivation, and uses of corn
"Landau does her usual fine job of explaining a topic so that it is understandable to kids." Booklist
Includes glossary and bibliographical references

Wheat. Children's Press 1999 47p il lib bdg $22; pa $6.95 (2-4) **633.1**
1. Wheat
ISBN 0-516-21029-7 (lib bdg); 0-516-26792-2 (pa)
LC 98-47333
"A True book"
Examines the history, cultivation, and uses of wheat
Includes glossary and bibliographical references

634 Orchards, fruits, forestry

Burns, Diane L.
Cranberries: fruit of the bogs; photographs by Cheryl Walsh Bellville. Carolrhoda Bks. 1994 48p il (Photo books) lib bdg $22.60; pa $7.95 (3-5) **634**
1. Cranberries
ISBN 0-87614-822-4 (lib bg); 0-87614-964-6 (pa)
LC 93-29620
"After a brief history of the cranberry in North America, the photo-essay focuses on the planting, growing, harvesting, and processing of the fruit known as the 'bog ruby.' An interesting account of a fruit with historical importance is accompanied by color photographs as clear as the autumn days needed for harvesting the cranberries." Horn Book Guide
Includes glossary

Gibbons, Gail
Apples. Holiday House 2000 unp il $16.95 (k-3) **634**
1. Apples
ISBN 0-8234-1497-3   LC 99-54246
Explains how apples were brought to America, how they grow, their traditional uses and cultural significance, and some of the varieties grown
"With its cheerful, bright illustrations and clear, simple presentation, this title will be the perfect pick for the perennial fall apple-book requests." SLJ

Hall, Zoe, 1957-
The apple pie tree; illustrated by Shari Halpern. Blue Sky Press (NY) 1996 unp il $15.95 (k-1) **634**
1. Apples
ISBN 0-590-62382-6   LC 95-31134
"From bud to fruit, two children follow the cycle of an apple tree as it is nurtured through the seasons. . . . The story ends with a nice, warm apple pie being taken from the oven. The large pictures and text are suitable for young children. The colorful, clear-cut illustrations use a paint and paper collage technique. An end note shows how bees pollinate the tree's flowers and offers a recipe for apple pie." SLJ

Hughes, Meredith Sayles
Yes, we have bananas; fruits from shrubs & vines. Lerner Publs. 1999 80p il lib bdg $26.60 (4 and up) **634**
1. Fruit 2. Fruit culture
ISBN 0-8225-2836-3   LC 98-45738

Hughes, Meredith Sayles—*Continued*

Describes the historical origins, domestication, uses, growing requirements, harvesting, and shipping of bananas, pineapples, berries, grapes, and melons

"In addition to the substantive text, many color illustrations depict the historical origins of each fruit, beautiful color photographs show the fruits themselves. Nutritional values and recipes are included for each fruit. A glossary of terms, a list of further readings, and an index are provided at the end of the text." Sci Books Films

Landau, Elaine

Apples. Children's Press 1999 47p il lib bdg $22; pa $6.95 (2-4)   **634**

1. Apples

ISBN 0-516-21024-6 (lib bdg); 0-516-26571-7 (pa)

LC 98-47327

"A True book"

Surveys the history, cultivation, and uses of apples and describes the different kinds

This "will fill a need for young report writers." Booklist

Includes glossary and bibliographical references

Bananas. Children's Press 1999 47p il lib bdg $22; pa $6.95 (2-4)   **634**

1. Banana

ISBN 0-516-21025-4 (lib bdg); 0-516-26574-1 (pa)

LC 98-47328

Examines the history, cultivation, and uses of bananas

Includes glossary and bibliographical references

Maestro, Betsy, 1944-

How do apples grow? illustrated by Giulio Maestro. HarperCollins Pubs. 1992 32p il (Let's-read-and-find-out science book) lib bdg $14.89; pa $4.95 (k-3)   **634**

1. Apples

ISBN 0-06-020056-1 (lib bdg); 0-06-445117-8 (pa)

LC 91-9468

Describes the life cycle of an apple from its initial appearance as a spring bud to that point in time when it becomes a fully ripe fruit

"Clear, complete. . . . Inquisitive children will find simple yet scientifically accurate answers to their questions about apple trees and their fruit. Large illustrations and limited text facilitate group-reading. The endearing, soft-toned drawings are clearly labelled, providing an excellent teaching tool or reference point for the science teacher." Sci Child

Micucci, Charles

The life and times of the apple. Orchard Bks. 1992 32p il $15.95; pa $6.95 (2-4)   **634**

1. Apples

ISBN 0-531-05939-1; 0-531-07067-0 (pa)

LC 90-22779

Presents a variety of facts about apples, including how they grow, crossbreeding and grafting techniques, harvesting practices, and the uses, varieties, and history of this popular fruit

"In covering so many aspects of the subject, the book

stretches across the curriculum, incorporating science, history, geography, and math. The format provides for interplay between the text and the many full-color illustrations, creating a most effective and attractive presentation of the subject." Booklist

634.9   Forestry

Appelbaum, Diana Karter

Giants in the land; [by] Diana Appelbaum; illustrated by Michael McCurdy. Houghton Mifflin 1993 unp il $17; pa $6.95 (2-4)   **634.9**

1. Trees 2. Lumber and lumbering 3. Shipbuilding—History

ISBN 0-395-64720-7; 0-618-03305-X (pa)

LC 92-26526

Describes how giant pine trees in New England were cut down during the colonial days to make massive wooden ships for the King's Navy

"The prose is restrained and lyrical. . . . McCurdy's dramatic black-and-white scratchboard drawings, many spread across two pages, capture the sweep and detail of the landscape." Booklist

635   Garden crops (Horticulture)

Björk, Christina

Linnea's windowsill garden; by Christina Björk and Lena Anderson; translated by Joan Sandin. R & S Bks. 1988 59p il $13 (3-6)   **635**

1. Gardening 2. Plants

ISBN 91-29-59064-7   LC 87-15016

Original Swedish edition, 1978

A "young plant lover gives information about every aspect of indoor gardening: choosing, planting, pruning, fertilizing, spraying, adjusting light and water." Bull Cent Child Books

Linnea's "zeal is infectious; readers will be looking around the house for seeds they can press into soil or coax into germination. Anderson's two-color illustrations explicate the projects cleanly and clearly, giving gardeners an excellent idea of when to look for shoots and when to run for the insecticide." Publ Wkly

Creasy, Rosalind

Blue potatoes, orange tomatoes; illustrations by Ruth Heller. Sierra Club Bks. for Children 1994 40p il $15.95; pa $6.95 (3-5)   **635**

1. Vegetable gardening 2. Vegetables

ISBN 0-87156-576-5; 0-87156-919-1 (pa)

LC 92-38800

Describes how to plant and grow a variety of colorful vegetables, including red corn, yellow watermelons, and multicolored radishes, and includes recipes

"With interesting and authentic information about gardening accompanied by brilliant, life-like illustrations, this book will not only promote the delight in growing plants but enhance the wonder in the natural world right in your own backyard." Appraisal

Gibbons, Gail

The pumpkin book. Holiday House 1999 unp il
$16.95; pa $6.95 (k-3)   **635**
   1. Pumpkin
   ISBN 0-8234-1465-5; 0-8234-1636-4 (pa)
                         LC 98-45267
Describes how pumpkins come in different shapes and
sizes, how they grow, and their traditional uses and cultural significance. Includes instructions for carving a
pumpkin and drying the seeds

"Bold, clear watercolor illustrations and a concise text
work together. . . . Gibbons succeeds once again at covering a topic in a useful way at just the right level for
beginning readers." SLJ

Lerner, Carol, 1927-

My backyard garden. Morrow Junior Bks. 1998
48p il $16 (4-6)   **635**
   1. Vegetable gardening
   ISBN 0-688-14755-0   LC 97-6460
   Companion volume to My indoor garden
Explains how to start your own vegetable garden and
how to cope with common problems, describing the
round of activities from month to month throughout the
year

"An elegant book design and Lerner's delicately detailed watercolors, complete with hand-lettered labels,
make this a pleasure to read as well as a solid source of
information." Booklist

Rockwell, Anne F., 1934-

One bean; pictures by Megan Halsey. Walker &
Co. 1998 unp il $14.95; pa $5.95 (k-2)   **635**
   1. Beans
   ISBN 0-8027-8648-0; 0-8027-7572-1 (pa)
                         LC 97-36249
"An easy-to-read text combines with lively illustrations to create the story of what happens to one small
bean when it interacts with some soil, just a little water,
a lot of sunlight, and a young child's tender care." Sci
Child

635.9   Flowers and ornamental plants

Lerner, Carol, 1927-

My indoor garden. Morrow Junior Bks. 1999
48p il $16; lib bdg $15.93 (4-6)   **635.9**
   1. Indoor gardening
   ISBN 0-688-14753-4; 0-688-14754-2 (lib bdg)
                         LC 98-18929
   Companion volume to My backyard garden
Discusses how to care for plants indoors, including
such aspects as light, temperature, humidity, pests, diseases, equipment, and how to choose and grow your own
plants

"Plentiful, detailed watercolor-and-pencil illustrations
work together with the book's step-by-step instruction to
inspire confidence in even the most timid indoor gardener." Horn Book Guide

Morris, Karyn

The Kids Can Press jumbo book of gardening;
written by Karyn Morris; illustrated by Jane
Kurisu. Kids Can Press 2000 240p il pa $14.95
(3-6)   **635.9**
   1. Gardening
   ISBN 1-55074-690-1
"Sections cover general information; fruit, vegetable,
and flower gardens; noninvasive native plants; gardens
that attract wildlife; and group projects. Projects range
from a few annuals in a container and thickets designed
with native wildlife in mind to community gardens. Directions are clear, with plenty of diagrams and illustrations." Booklist

636.1   Equines. Horses

Budiansky, Stephen

The world according to horses; how they run,
see, and think. Holt & Co. 2000 101p il $16.95 (4
and up)   **636.1**
   1. Horses
   ISBN 0-8050-6054-5   LC 99-31778
Discusses the interaction between people and horses,
the horse as a social animal, its intelligence, abilities to
communicate, athletic abilities, and physical evolution

"Intriguing premises are explained here in a straightforward and thought-provoking manner. . . . This title
also will serve as a valuable resource for a beginning basic science reasoning study." Voice Youth Advocates
   Includes glossary and bibliographical references

Clutton-Brock, Juliet

Horse; written by Juliet Clutton-Brock. Knopf
1992 63p il (Eyewitness books) (4 and up) **636.1**
   1. Horses
                         LC 91-53132
   Available DK Pub. edition $15.95; lib bdg $19.99
(ISBN 0-7894-5772-5; 0-7894-6582-5)
   "A Dorling Kindersley book"
A photo essay introducing members of the horse family, their evolution, behavior, importance, history, breeding, and training. Includes major international breeds of
domestic horses

"Browsers will find this smorgasbord of equine facts
fascinating." SLJ

Henderson, Carolyn

Horse & pony care. DK Pub. 1999 48p il (DK
riding club) hardcover o.p. paperback available
$7.95   **636.1**
   1. Horses 2. Ponies
   ISBN 0-7894-4269-8 (pa)   LC 98-49618
This book "provides an overview of the many facets
of caring for a horse or pony, including tips on handling,
health, and feeding. . . . Sure to be popular in areas
where youngsters have access to stables." Booklist
   Includes glossary

Isenbart, Hans-Heinrich, 1923-

Birth of a foal; photographs by Thomas David. Carolrhoda Bks. 1986 48p il (Carolrhoda nature watch book) lib bdg $22.60 (3-6)   **636.1**

    1. Horses

    ISBN 0-87614-239-0   LC 85-17406

Original German edition published 1983 in Switzerland

This book describes the birth and first few hours of a foal's life

"The text is quite detailed, containing many facts and figures about the developing fetus, how long it takes to be born, size and weight at birth, etc. . . . The illustrations are color photographs, varying somewhat in quality. Although most of the photographs are sharp and clear, a few are fuzzy or grainy. . . . All of the photographs are appropriate for even very young readers." Appraisal

Includes glossary

Lauber, Patricia, 1924-

The true-or-false book of horses; illustrated by Rosalyn Schanzer. HarperCollins Pubs. 2000 32p il $15.95; lib bdg $15.89 (2-4)   **636.1**

    1. Horses

    ISBN 0-688-16919-8; 0-688-16920-1 (lib bdg)

         LC 99-30763

Through a true-or-false format, presents statements about the history, uses, and behavior of horses

This "book combines a crowd-pleasing topic with generous measures of historical and behavioral information." Booklist

Meltzer, Milton, 1915-

Hold your horses; a feedbag full of fact and fable. HarperCollins Pubs. 1995 133p il lib bdg $15.89 (4 and up)   **636.1**

    1. Horses

    ISBN 0-06-024478-X   LC 95-2983

The author "examines equines' uses and contributions throughout history, starting with charioteers' steeds, through knights' chargers, military mounts, cowponies, farm horses, and racetrack Thoroughbreds." Bull Cent Child Books

"A well-researched, concisely written, and thought-provoking book that's as fascinating as the subject itself. Black-and-white reproductions and photographs appear throughout. An excellent choice for recreational reading or reports." SLJ

Includes bibliographical references

Patent, Dorothy Hinshaw

Horses; photos by William Muñoz. Carolrhoda Bks. 1994 48p il (Understanding animals) hardcover o.p. paperback available $7.95 (3-6)

         636.1

    1. Horses

    ISBN 0-87614-991-3 (pa)   LC 93-12329

Discusses the physical characteristics and behavior of horses and describes how domestic horses evolved from their wild relatives

This book features "accurate, accessible narrative, complemented by clear color photographs." Horn Book Guide

Includes glossary

Peterson, Cris, 1952-

Horsepower; the wonder of draft horses; photographs by Alvis Upitis. Boyds Mills Press 1997 unp il $16.95; pa $9.95 (k-3)   **636.1**

    1. Horses

    ISBN 1-56397-626-9; 1-56397-943-8 (pa)

         LC 96-84679

"This book focuses on three popular breeds of draft horses, commonly known as work horses: Belgians, Percherons, and Clydesdales. Peterson introduces the families who raise and care for the horses and discusses some horse-training procedures." Horn Book Guide

"Crisp, full-color photographs accompany the short, smoothly written text." SLJ

The **Visual** dictionary of the horse. Dorling Kindersley 1994 64p il (Eyewitness visual dictionaries) $18.95 (4 and up)   **636.1**

    1. Horses

    ISBN 1-56458-504-2   LC 93-20819

"Along with spreads detailing the animal's anatomy, there are two double-page spreads illustrated with full-color photographs of the various breeds, divided into light and heavy horses. Following this overview, the guide briefly focuses on the care and activities of equines today, including grooming, shoeing, racing, jumping, and equipment." SLJ

"In this visually spectacular introduction to horses and equine and equestrian terms, the information is complete and concise; color photographs and diagrams extend the text. The anatomical drawings, with detailed labeling, are particularly instructive and useful." Horn Book Guide

Includes glossary

636.4   Swine

Gibbons, Gail

Pigs. Holiday House 1999 unp il $16.95; pa $6.95 (k-3)   **636.4**

    1. Pigs

    ISBN 0-8234-1441-8; 0-8234-1554-6 (pa)

         LC 98-28807

Examines the basic characteristics, common breeds, intelligence, behavior, life cycle, and uses of pigs

"Bright with spring greens and yellows, this attractive book introduces pigs through simple sentences and many colorful pictures." Booklist

King-Smith, Dick, 1922-

All pigs are beautiful; illustrated by Anita Jeram. Candlewick Press 1993 unp il hardcover o.p. paperback available $5.99 (k-3)   **636.4**

    1. Pigs

    ISBN 1-56402-431-8 (pa)   LC 92-53136

"Read and wonder"

The author "interlards fond reminiscences of porkers he has known with interesting facts about them that are sure to keep children absorbed. His tone is affectionate, amusing, and informative. Jeram's pen-and-ink and watercolor illustrations, done in soft, earthy colors, are a warm match for the text." SLJ

636.6 Birds other than poultry

Mowat, Farley

Owls in the family; illustrated by Robert Frankenberg. Little, Brown 1961 103p il o.p.; Bantam Bks. paperback available $4.50 (4 and up)

636.6

1. Owls

ISBN 0-440-41361-3 (pa)

Also available in hardcover from Amereon

"An Atlantic Monthly Press book"

"Two owls, Wol and Weeps, who are found as babies at the beginning of this account, were the author's own pets during his boyhood in Saskatoon. The description of the owls' endearing and humorous traits, their intelligence and mischief in upsetting household and neighbors, is continuously absorbing and provocative of hearty laughter. Their personalities are vividly different. . . . Outstanding for reading aloud." Horn Book

636.7 Dogs

Calmenson, Stephanie

Rosie; a visiting dog's story; photographs by Justin Sutcliffe. Clarion Bks. 1994 47p il $15.95; pa $5.95 (k-3)

636.7

1. Dogs

ISBN 0-395-65477-7; 0-395-92722-6 (pa)

LC 93-21243

"Rosie is the true story of an endearing Tibetan terrier who works as a therapy dog with Delta Society's Pet Partners Program of New York City. Rosie's tenderness and enthusiasm come through in Sutcliffe's fantastic photos that chronicle Rosie's training and first visit to a children's hospital and a nursing home." Child Book Rev Serv

Cole, Joanna

My puppy is born; photographs by Margaret Miller. rev and expanded ed. Morrow Junior Bks. 1991 unp il hardcover o.p. paperback available $5.95 (k-3)

636.7

1. Dogs

ISBN 0-688-10198-4 (pa)

LC 90-42011

A revised and newly illustrated edition of the title first published 1973

"As a little girl anxiously awaits the birth of puppies by the Norfolk terrier next door, a story unfolds. The puppies' arrival and first few weeks of life and development are shown and described in a simple narrative." SLJ

"Exquisitely sharp, well-designed color photos capture the events, stage by stage. . . . As the puppy grows, the reader watches its first halting steps, messy eating habits, and snoozing poses. A gem for preschoolers and a sure bet for older youngsters." Booklist

The **Complete** dog book for kids; official publication of the American Kennel Club. Howell Bk. House; distributed by Hungry Minds 1996 274p il maps $34.95; pa $22.95 (4 and up)

636.7

1. Dogs

ISBN 0-87605-458-0; 0-87605-460-2 (pa)

LC 96-29228

This "begins with a general section that advises readers on buying a dog, responsibilities, rewards, and how to match a dog with one's situation. . . . More than 100 dogs are profiled, with information on history, appearance, health, and 'fun facts.' Crisp color photographs accompany each article. . . . A final section gives good advice about nutrition and health issues." Booklist

George, Jean Craighead, 1919-

How to talk to your dog; illustrated by Sue Truesdell. HarperCollins Pubs. 2000 26p il $9.95 (2-4)

636.7

1. Dogs

ISBN 0-06-027092-6

LC 98-41515

Describes how dogs communicate with people through their behavior and sounds and explains how to talk back to them using sounds, behavior, and body language

"The mixed photography (of George, representing the humans) and illustration (an endearingly scruffy yellow mutt is the main canine representative) is . . . effective. . . . This will be an accessible and perhaps paradigm-shifting introduction for young readers." Bull Cent Child Books

Gibbons, Gail

Dogs. Holiday House 1996 32p il $16.95; pa $6.95 (k-3)

636.7

1. Dogs

ISBN 0-8234-1226-1; 0-8234-1335-7 (pa)

LC 95-24966

An introduction to dogs including their history, types of breeds, senses, and ways of communication

Jones, Robert F., 1934-

Jake; a Labrador puppy at work and play; photographs by Bill Eppridge. Farrar, Straus & Giroux 1992 unp il $15; pa $6.95 (3-5)

636.7

1. Dogs—Training

ISBN 0-374-33655-5; 0-374-43713-0 (pa)

LC 92-8105

The author describes his new Labrador puppy's first year and how he trained the dog to sit, heel, fetch, and more

"An adorable puppy and a writer who understands dogs as deeply as he loves them are the subjects of this splendid photo essay. . . . Eppridge's photographs . . . cleanly capture Jake's brand of animal magnetism." Publ Wkly

Kehret, Peg

Shelter dogs; amazing stories of adopted strays. Whitman, A. 1999 unp il $14.95 (3-5)

636.7

1. Dogs

ISBN 0-8075-7334-5

LC 98-34760

Kehret, Peg—*Continued*

Tells the stories of eight stray dogs that were adopted from animal shelters and went on to become service dogs, actors, and heroes

"The writing is clear and straightforward, letting the drama and pathos of the dogs' triumphs, and the owners' dedication, carry the stories." SLJ

Kimmel, Elizabeth Cody

Balto and the great race; illustrated by Nora Koerber. Random House 1999 99p il map lib bdg $11.99; pa $3.99 (3-5)   **636.7**

1. Sled dog racing 2. Nome (Alaska) 3. Diphtheria
ISBN 0-679-99198-0 (lib bdg); 0-679-89198-6 (pa)
             LC 98-35753

"A Stepping Stone book"

Recounts how the sled dog Balto saved Nome, Alaska, in 1925 from a diphtheria epidemic by delivering medicine through a raging snowstorm

"Kimmel's writing deftly combines geography, sled racing, and historical background with the gripping adventure of Balto's race to save lives. In many ways, the book reads like fast-paced fiction. Koerber's serviceable black-and-white illustrations appear throughout and reflect the action. Sure to appeal to beginning chapter-book readers." SLJ

King-Smith, Dick, 1922-

Puppy love; illustrated by Anita Jeram. Candlewick Press 1997 unp il $15.99; pa $5.99 (k-3)   **636.7**

1. Dogs
ISBN 0-7636-0116-0; 0-7636-0698-7 (pa)
             LC 96-47423

The author describes some of the puppies of all sizes, from Dachshunds to Great Danes, that he and his family have loved over the years

"The book's first-person narrative has an avuncular tone that lends an appealing warmth and directness to the text. Jeram's . . . whimsical watercolors . . . capture the essence of puppy appeal." Publ Wkly

636.8   Cats

Cole, Joanna

My new kitten; photographs by Margaret Miller. Morrow Junior Bks. 1995 unp il lib bdg $14.93 (k-2)   **636.8**

1. Cats
ISBN 0-688-12902-1   LC 94-20295

"A brief, first-person text and full-page photographs follow the birth and growth of a litter of kittens in this simple, appealing documentary. A little girl watches her aunt's cat, Cleo, as she gives birth and cares for her kittens; eventually, the girl is allowed to choose a kitten for herself. The fine photographs of the luxuriant gray kittens have an inherent narrative." Horn Book

De Paola, Tomie, 1934-

The kids' cat book; written and illustrated by Tomie de Paola. Holiday House 1979 unp il o.p.; Owl Bks. (Toronto) paperback available $9.95 (2-4)   **636.8**

1. Cats
ISBN 0-920775-51-9 (pa)   LC 79-2090

Patrick goes to Granny Twinkle's for a free kitten and learns everything there is to know about cats—their different breeds, care, place in art and literature, and history

"The illustrations add great touches of humor and show cats being cats everywhere. All those who have new kittens will find useful information." Child Book Rev Serv

George, Jean Craighead, 1919-

How to talk to your cat; illustrated by Paul Meisel. HarperCollins Pubs. 2000 28p il $9.95 (2-4)   **636.8**

1. Cats
ISBN 0-06-027968-0   LC 98-41517

Describes how cats communicate with people through their behavior and sounds and explains how to talk back to them using sounds, behavior, and body language

"The writing style is breezy, conversational, and amusing, and is helped along by the many color illustrations. The photographs of the author are cleverly combined with humorous cartoon drawings of cats that display a great deal of intelligence and comedic personality. . . . A useful and readable addition to any pet collection." SLJ

Gibbons, Gail

Cats. Holiday House 1996 unp il $16.95; pa $6.95 (k-3)   **636.8**

1. Cats
ISBN 0-8234-1253-9; 0-8234-1410-8 (pa)
             LC 96-3953

Presents information about the physical characteristics, senses, and behavior of cats, as well as how to care for these animals and some general facts about them

"This easy-to-read picture book will appeal to lovers of the popular pet. Brightly colored illustrations identify different breeds, while the informative . . . text describes physical and behavioral traits of kittens and cats." Horn Book Guide

Lauber, Patricia, 1924-

The true-or-false book of cats; illustrated by Rosalyn Schanzer. National Geographic Soc. 1998 31p il $15.95 (k-3)   **636.8**

1. Cats
ISBN 0-7922-3440-5   LC 97-11144

Discusses the truth behind such beliefs as "Cats can see in total darkness," "Cats have nine lives," and "A cat signals its feelings with its tail"

The author "attends to each question in a lucid, nicely detailed yet concise fashion, with Rosalyn Schanzer's colorful, lively artwork adding humorous details that help the facts slide down easily. The illustrations make this look like a picture book for younger readers, but the text is keyed to older ones." Booklist

Tildes, Phyllis Limbacher
Calico's cousins; cats from around the world. Charlesbridge Pub. 1999 unp il lib bdg $15.95; pa $6.95 (k-3) **636.8**
1. Cats
ISBN 0-88106-648-6 (lib bdg); 0-88106-649-4 (pa)
LC 98-4011
"Calico, a domestic longhair cat, introduces various breeds by describing both their origin and common traits. Each double-page spread features realistic illustrations of several cats in an environment appropriate to their origin, and a map at the end provides geographical reference." Horn Book Guide

636.9 Other mammals

Hansen, Elvig
Guinea pigs. Carolrhoda Bks. 1992 48p il (Carolrhoda nature watch book) lib bdg $23.93; pa $6.95 (3-6) **636.9**
1. Guinea pigs
ISBN 0-87614-681-7; 0-87614-613-2 (pa)
LC 91-30694
Original German edition published 1988 in Switzerland
Describes the physical characteristics, habitat, and life cycle of the guinea pig
"Though uncaptioned, the pictures (featuring Hansen's own animals) are marvelous. . . . But the photos are more than simply bright, clear shots. They're informative and carefully keyed to the text. . . . It supplies plenty for both student researchers and prospective pet owners, all of whom will join browsers in eagerly thumbing through the wonderful pictures." Booklist
Includes glossary

King-Smith, Dick, 1922-
I love guinea pigs; illustrated by Anita Jeram. Candlewick Press 1995 c1994 unp il hardcover o.p. paperback available $5.99 (k-3) **636.9**
1. Guinea pigs
ISBN 0-7636-0150-0 (pa)
LC 94-4880
"Read and wonder"
First published 1994 in the United Kingdom
"King-Smith provides a bit of history and some general information about physical characteristics, concentrating most fully on the care of these responsive animals as pets. He mentions the rudiments of handling, housing, feeding, and watering, explaining that guinea pigs can live for several years and describing their repertoire of sounds. King-Smith's advice is interspersed with anecdotes about favorite guinea pigs he has owned." Horn Book
"Jeram's line-and-watercolor illustrations transform fuzzy lumps into curious, cuddly, thoroughly engaging creatures." SLJ

636.97 Fur farming

Johnson, Sylvia A.
Ferrets. Carolrhoda Bks. 1996 48p il (Carolrhoda nature watch book) lib bdg $23.95 (3-6) **636.97**
1. Ferrets
ISBN 1-57505-014-5
LC 96-7068
Presents information about the physical characteristics, behavior, and history of ferrets and discusses keeping and caring for these animals as pets
"In her coverage of both wild ferrets and their domesticated cousins, Johnson uses a nice balance of sharp photos and explanatory text." Booklist

637 Processing dairy and related products

Aliki
Milk from cow to carton. rev ed. HarperCollins Pubs. 1992 31p il (Let's-read-and-find-out science book) hardcover o.p. paperback available $5.95 (k-3) **637**
1. Dairying 2. Milk 3. Cattle
ISBN 0-06-445111-9 (pa)
LC 91-23807
First published 1974 by Crowell with title: Green grass and white milk
Briefly describes how a cow produces milk, how the milk is processed in a dairy, and how various other dairy products are made from milk
This features "full-color artwork. . . . An excellent primary-level introduction to dairy science." Booklist

Gibbons, Gail
The milk makers. Macmillan 1985 unp il $16; pa $5.99 (k-3) **637**
1. Dairying 2. Milk 3. Cattle
ISBN 0-02-736640-5; 0-689-71116-6 (pa)
LC 84-20081
Explains how cows produce milk and how it is processed before being delivered to stores
"Starting with dairy cows grazing at pasture, nothing is overlooked in the procedure, from the role of the calf to winter feed and shelter, the function of four stomachs, milking, milk handling, and the operation of a dairy. Diagrams of the cow stomachs as well as the machines used at farm and dairy leave no question unanswered, although city children will be unfamiliar with what it means to breed a cow. Finally, there is a pictorial list of the many other dairy products found in most homes." Sci Books Films

Peterson, Cris, 1952-
Extra cheese, please! mozzarella's journey from cow to pizza; photographs by Alvis Upitis. Boyds Mills Press 1994 unp il $15.95 (k-3) **637**
1. Dairying 2. Cheese
ISBN 1-56397-177-1
LC 93-70876

Peterson, Cris, 1952-—_Continued_

In photographs and text, this book introduces "dairying and cheese making. Using her own farm as an example, Peterson describes the care and feeding of dairy cattle, the milking process, and the steps involved in producing mozzarella cheese." Booklist

"Nicely balanced pages contain brief blocks of clearly written text and many full-color photographs." SLJ

Includes glossary and bibliographical references

639.2   Commercial fishing, whaling, sealing

Carrick, Carol

Whaling days; woodcuts by David Frampton. Clarion Bks. 1993 40p il $15.95; pa $6.95 (3-6)
      639.2

1. Whaling 2. Whales
ISBN 0-395-50948-3; 0-395-76480-7 (pa)
      LC 91-22483

Surveys the whaling industry, ranging from hunting in colonial America to modern whaling regulations and conservation efforts

"Frampton's strong woodcuts, tinted with muted tones of tan and blue, give the book a period look and a sense of drama. An informative and visually striking picture book for older children." Booklist

Includes glossary and bibliographical references

McKissack, Patricia C., 1944-

Black hands, white sails; the story of African-American whalers; [by] Patricia C. McKissack & Fredrick L. McKissack. Scholastic Press 1999 xxiv, 152p il $15.95 (5 and up)
      639.2

1. Whaling 2. African Americans
ISBN 0-590-48313-7
      LC 99-11439

A Coretta Scott King honor book for text, 2000

A history of African-American whalers between 1730 and 1880, describing their contributions to the whaling industry and their role in the abolitionist movement

"A well-researched and detailed book." SLJ

Includes bibliographical references

McMillan, Bruce

Salmon summer; written and photo-illustrated by Bruce McMillan. Houghton Mifflin 1998 32p il $16 (2-4)
      639.2

1. Salmon 2. Fishing 3. Alaska
ISBN 0-395-84544-0
      LC 97-29679

A photo essay describing a young native Alaskan boy fishing for salmon on Kodiak Island as his ancestors have done for generations

"McMillan documents the goings on with his trademark crystal-clear color photographs and an engaging text." Booklist

Includes glossary and bibliographical references

639.3   Fish culture

Cone, Molly, 1918-

Come back, salmon; how a group of dedicated kids adopted Pigeon Creek and brought it back to life; photographs by Sidnee Wheelwright. Sierra Club Bks. for Children 1992 48p il hardcover o.p. paperback available $7.95 (3-6)
      639.3

1. Salmon 2. Wildlife conservation
ISBN 0-87156-489-0 (pa)
      LC 91-29023

Describes the efforts of the Jackson Elementary School in Everett, Washington, to clean up a nearby stream, stock it with salmon, and preserve it as an unpolluted place where the salmon could return to spawn

"The photographs are superb. . . . Personal and inspiring, the text alternates between descriptions of the project, background information about pollution and renewal, and dialogue of the students recorded; additional scientific information is displayed in panels set off from the main text." Horn Book

Includes glossary

639.34   Aquariums

Aliki

My visit to the aquarium. HarperCollins Pubs. 1993 unp il $15.95; pa $6.95 (k-3)   **639.34**

1. Marine aquariums 2. Marine animals 3. Freshwater animals
ISBN 0-06-021458-9; 0-06-446186-6 (pa)
      LC 92-18678

During his visit to an aquarium, a boy finds out about the characteristics and environments of many different marine and freshwater creatures

"Fish facts, selected for their child-appeal and delivered in a brisk, conversational tone, are neatly organized by marine environment. . . . The dominant blues and greens of Aliki's watercolors are not only cool and inviting; they also provide visual continuity amid the riot of brightly colored fish." Booklist

Evans, Mark, 1962-

Fish. Dorling Kindersley 1993 45p il (ASPCA pet care guides for kids) $10.95; pa $5.95 (2-5)
      639.34

1. Aquariums 2. Fishes
ISBN 1-56458-222-1; 0-7894-7648-7 (pa)
      LC 92-53476

Describes how to set up and maintain an aquarium and how to care for fish as household pets

"Attractive, informative. . . . The bright full-color photos show multiethnic children caring for their animals. Lots of white space in the background make the step-by-step text easy to follow." SLJ

639.9 Conservation of biological resources

Fleming, Denise, 1950-
Where once there was a wood. Holt & Co. 1996
unp il $16.95; pa $6.95 (k-2)   639.9
1. Habitat (Ecology) 2. Wildlife conservation
ISBN 0-8050-3761-6; 0-8050-6482-6 (pa)
                                    LC 95-18906
"Fleming's brief text describes the many creatures
who once lived in a wild area but whose homes have
been destroyed by a new housing development. Fleming
includes an afterword that describes the things families
can do to create new backyard habitats for birds and animals." Horn Book Guide
"Lush, textured collage artwork features a stunning
combination and arrangement of colors with brilliant
hues juxtaposed against muted earth tones. . . . The gentle, poetic narration is never overpowered by the pictures." SLJ
Includes bibliographical references

Goodman, Susan, 1952-
Animal rescue; the best job there is; written by
Susan E. Goodman. Simon & Schuster 2000 48p
il maps (Ready-to-read) lib bdg $15; pa $3.99
(2-4)   639.9
1. Walsh, John 2. Wildlife conservation
ISBN 0-689-81794-0 (lib bdg); 0-689-81795-9 (pa)
                                    LC 98-32403
Describes the work of John Walsh as he travels the
world helping to save animals in Kuwait during the war
with Iraq, the Kobe earthqake, and floods in Surinam
"This is a great choice for booktalks or as a starting
point for discussions of geography, animals, or current
events." SLJ

Patent, Dorothy Hinshaw
Back to the wild; photos by William Muñoz.
Harcourt Brace & Co. 1997 69p il $18 (4-6)
                                            639.9
1. Wildlife conservation 2. Endangered species
ISBN 0-15-200280-4   LC 95-43254
"A Gulliver Green book"
"Examining the reintroduction of captive-bred endan-
gered species into the wild, Patent discusses the issue
generally and focuses specifically on reintroduction pro-
grams for the red wolf, the black-footed ferret, the gold-
en lion tamarin, and several species of lemur." Bull Cent
Child Books
This offers "striking color photos and an authoritative
text." Horn Book Guide

640 Home economics and family living

Fisher, Leonard Everett, 1924-
The homemakers; written & illustrated by
Leonard Everett Fisher. Benchmark Bks.
(Tarrytown) 1998 47p il (Colonial craftsmen)
$14.95 (4 and up)   640
1. Handicraft 2. United States—Social life and cus-
toms—1600-1775, Colonial period
ISBN 0-7614-0512-7   LC 96-38382
A reissue of the title first published 1973 by Watts
Describes how four staples—candles, soap, brooms,
and cider—were made in colonial times

641 Food and drink

Llewellyn, Claire
Oranges. Children's Press 1999 32p il (What's
for lunch?) lib bdg $20.50 (k-3)   641
1. Oranges
ISBN 0-516-21548-5   LC 99-28942
Presents facts about oranges, including how they are
grown, harvested, and marketed, as well as turned into
juice and flavoring for other foods
Includes glossary

641.3 Food

D'Amico, Joan, 1957-
The science chef; 100 fun food experiments and
recipes for kids; [by] Joan D'Amico, Karen Eich
Drummond; illustrations by Tina Cash-Walsh.
Wiley 1995 180p il $12.95 (5 and up)   641.3
1. Food 2. Cooking 3. Science—Experiments
ISBN 0-471-31045-X   LC 94-9045
This includes facts about food, recipes, and experi-
ments with food
"Attractively illustrated with black-and-white line
drawings, easy and interesting to read, and filled with
tidbits of information." SLJ
Includes glossary

De Paola, Tomie, 1934-
The popcorn book. Holiday House 1978 unp il
lib bdg $16.95; pa $6.95 (k-3)   641.3
1. Popcorn
ISBN 0-8234-0314-9 (lib bdg); 0-8234-0533-8 (pa)
                                    LC 77-21456
"While one twin prepares the treat, the other stays
close-by and reads aloud what popcorn is, how it's
cooked, stored, and made, how the Indians of the Americas discovered it, and who eats the most. . . . The best
thing about popcorn, the twins decide, is eating it. Two
recipes are included." Babbling Bookworm
The author-artist's "amusing soft-color pictures—each
bordered with a lavender frame—show action in the past
or the present while a few lines of text or balloon
speeches describe what is happening." Horn Book

Johnson, Sylvia A.

Tomatoes, potatoes, corn, and beans; how the foods of the Americas changed eating around the world. Atheneum Bks. for Young Readers 1997 138p $16 (6 and up)　　　　　**641.3**

1. Food 2. Vegetables

ISBN 0-689-80141-6　　　　　LC 96-7207

Describes many foods native to the Americas, including corn, peppers, peanuts, and chocolate, which were taken to Europe and used in new ways around the world

"This well-documented book is a treasure of information presented in a clear, interesting style. . . . There are b&w photos or drawings on nearly every page. The layout is attractive and well spaced for easy reading." Book Rep

Includes bibliographical references

Micucci, Charles

The life and times of the peanut. Houghton Mifflin 1997 31p il music $15.95; pa $5.95 (2-4)　　　　　**641.3**

1. Peanuts

ISBN 0-395-72289-6; 0-618-03314-9 (pa)

LC 96-1290

"The author presents information on how peanuts grow, how they are farmed, where they are produced . . . and how they are used worldwide. What sets this book apart is Micucci's amusing and creative techniques for bringing statistics to life. . . . The artwork is attractive . . . with great attention to line, movement, and color, all carefully placed on the pages." Booklist

Solheim, James

It's disgusting—and we ate it! true food facts from around the world—and throughout history! illustrated by Eric Brace. Simon & Schuster Bks. for Young Readers 1998 37p il $16 (4-6)　　　**641.3**

1. Food—History 2. Eating customs

ISBN 0-689-80675-2　　　　　LC 96-7406

This "look at culinary culture is divided into three sections, the first discussing the global breadth of tastes, the second describing some startling dishes of history, and the third revealing some of the colorful truths behind contemporary American favorites." Bull Cent Child Books

Includes bibliographical references

641.5　Cooking

Brady, April A.

Kwanzaa karamu; cooking and crafts for a Kwanzaa feast; illustrations by Barbara Knutson; photographs by Robert L. and Diane Wolfe; additional recipes by Cheryl Davidson Kaufman [et al.] Carolrhoda Bks. 1995 64p il lib bdg $21.27; pa $6.95 (4-6)　　　　　**641.5**

1. Cooking 2. Kwanzaa 3. African Americans—Social life and customs

ISBN 0-87614-842-9 (lib bdg); 0-87614-633-7 (pa)

LC 94-20871

This "introduction to the African American holiday of Kwanzaa not only clearly explains the origin and rituals of the holiday, but also introduces traditional foods and crafts. The 18 recipes included range from simple side and main dishes to salads and desserts. A 'Cooking Smart' section contains helpful hints and safety tips about handling raw food, hot pans, and knives." Booklist

Braman, Arlette N., 1952-

Kids around the world cook! the best foods and recipes from many lands. Wiley 2000 116p il pa $12.95 (4-6)　　　　　**641.5**

1. Cooking

ISBN 0-471-35251-9　　　　　LC 99-46110

Presents information on and recipes for a variety of foods from many countries, including Sweet Lassi from India, Challah from Israel, Strawberry Soup from Poland, Kushiyaki from Japan, and Prairie Berry Cake from Canada

D'Amico, Joan, 1957-

The healthy body cookbook; over 50 fun activities and delicious recipes for kids; [by] Joan D'Amico, Karen Eich Drummond; illustrations by Tina Cash-Walsh. Wiley 1999 184p il pa $12.95 (4-6)　　　　　**641.5**

1. Cooking 2. Nutrition

ISBN 0-471-18888-3　　　　　LC 98-2776

Discusses the various parts of the human body and what to eat to keep them healthy. Includes recipes that contain nutrients important for the heart, muscles, teeth, skin, nerves, and other parts of the body

"The line drawings are helpful and the writing is informal but straightforward. The recipes are clear, thoroughly explained, and tasty." SLJ

The math chef; over 60 math activities and recipes for kids; [by] Joan D'Amico, Karen Eich Drummond; illustrations by Tina Cash-Walsh. Wiley 1997 180p il pa $12.95 (4-6)　　　　　**641.5**

1. Cooking 2. Mathematics

ISBN 0-471-13813-4　　　　　LC 96-22143

Relates math and cookery by presenting math concepts and reinforcing them with recipes. Provides practice in converting from English to metric system, multiplying quantities, measuring area, estimating, and more

"The instructional value of this book is excellent. . . . The illustrations and content are accurate and very well depicted." Sci Books Films

Includes glossary

Easy menu ethnic cookbooks. Lerner Publs. 1982-1995 26v il maps lib bdg ea $19.93 (5 and up)　　　　　**641.5**

1. Cooking

Some titles also available in paperback

Available volumes in this series are: Cooking the African way, by C. R. Nabwire and B. V. Montgomery; Cooking the Australian way, by E. Germaine and A. Burckhardt; Cooking the Caribbean way, by C. D. Kaufman; Cooking the Chinese way, by L. Yu; Cooking the English way, by B. W. Hill; Cooking the French way, by

Easy menu ethnic cookbooks—*Continued*

L. M. Waldee; Cooking the German way, by H. Parnell; Cooking the Greek way, by L. W. Villios; Cooking the Irish way, by H. Hughes; Cooking the Israeli way, by J. Bacon; Cooking the Italian way, by A. Bisignano; Cooking the Japanese way, by R. Weston; Cooking the Korean way, by O. Chung and J. Monroe; Cooking the Lebanese way, by S. Amari; Cooking the Mexican way, by R. Coronado; Cooking the Russian way, by G. Plotkin and R. Plotkin; Cooking the South American way, by H. Parnell; Cooking the Spanish way, by R. Christian; Cooking the Swiss way, by H. Hughes; Cooking the Thai way, by S. Harrison and J. Monroe; Cooking the Vietnamese way, by C. T. Nguyen and J. Monroe; Desserts around the world; Ethnic cooking the microwave way, by N. Cappelloni; Holiday cooking around the world; How to cook a gooseberry fool, by M. Vaughan; Vegetarian cooking around the world

"Each of these attractive little cookbooks features workable and fairly authentic recipes that use readily available ingredients. Some basic facts about the geography, customs, and eating habits are given for each country. Cooking safety rules are included." Child Book Rev Serv

Gillies, Judi

The Kids Can Press jumbo cookbook; written by Judi Gillies and Jennifer Glossop; illustrated by Louise Phillips. Kids Can Press 2000 256p il pa $14.95 (4 and up)   **641.5**

1. Cooking

ISBN 1-55074-621-9

A "collection of over 100 recipes, arranged by categories such as 'Soups and Chilis'; 'Salads and Vegetables'; 'Pasta, Noodles, Rice and Grains'; etc. All have simple, step-by-step instructions, call for commonly available ingredients, and range in difficulty from boiled rice to sushi and shepherd's pie." SLJ

"The book's format is kid-friendly, with large print and cartoon art, but many of the numerous recipes are quite grown-up." Booklist

The **Good** Housekeeping illustrated children's cookbook; [edited by] Marianne Zanzarella; photographs by Tom Eckerle. Morrow Junior Bks. 1997 166p il (4-6)   **641.5**

1. Cooking

LC 96-18800

Available Hearst Bks. $20 (ISBN 1-588-16011-4)

General information on kitchen safety and food preparation accompanies recipes for meals from breakfast to dinner, as well as for snacks, drinks, and desserts

This book "places an emphasis on safety and cooking methods: a 22-page introduction gives thorough details about the dangers of sharp utensils, bacteria, and heat, followed by the importance of precise measurement, etc." SLJ

Includes glossary

Katzen, Mollie, 1950-

Honest pretzels; and 64 other amazing recipes for cooks ages 8 & up. Tricycle Press 1999 177p il $19.95 (4-6)   **641.5**

1. Vegetarian cooking

ISBN 1-88367-288-0

LC 99-20184

Provides step-by-step instructions for a variety of vegetarian recipes, arranged in such categories as "Breakfast Specials," "Soups, Sandwiches & Salads for Lunch or Supper," and "Desserts and a Few Baked Things"

"Small, colorful drawings illustrate most of the cooking instructions and brighten many of the other pages as well." Booklist

Kids' first cookbook; delicious-nutritious treats to make yourself. American Cancer Soc. 2000 88p il $13.95 (k-3)   **641.5**

1. Cooking

ISBN 0-944235-19-0

A collection of easy-to-make recipes for breakfast foods, snacks, main dishes, drinks, and desserts

"A cookbook with a contemporary look filled with nutrition information. . . . A solid effort that will encourage healthy eating habits." SLJ

Perl, Lila

Slumps, grunts, and snickerdoodles: what Colonial America ate and why; drawings by Richard Cuffari. Clarion Bks. 1975 125p il map $16 (4 and up)   **641.5**

1. Cooking 2. United States—Social life and customs—1600-1775, Colonial period

ISBN 0-395-28923-8

First published by Seabury Press

"In three major chapters dividing the pre-Revolutionary colonies into regions—New England, Middle Atlantic, Southern—the author explains ' . . . not only "what" the colonists ate and "why," but . . . the geographical and historical background as well as the intimate domestic surroundings.' . . . Emphasis is on foods grown in different areas and how traditional recipes developed from the materials available, but local manners and mores are also skillfully woven into the narrative." SLJ

Vezza, Diane Simone

Passport on a plate; a round-the-world cookbook for children; illustrated by Susan Greenstein. Simon & Schuster Bks. for Young Readers 1997 150p il $19.95 (5 and up)   **641.5**

1. Cooking

ISBN 0-689-80155-6

LC 96-50409

"This international cookbook contains 100 recipes from Africa, the Caribbean, China, France, Germany, India, Italy, Japan, Mexico, the Middle East, Russia, and Vietnam. Each place is introduced in a one-and-a-half-page explanation of the area's foods and eating habits. . . . They are clearly written and carefully chosen to represent the locale and the foods that are grown there." SLJ

Walker, Barbara Muhs, 1928-

The Little House cookbook; frontier foods from Laura Ingalls Wilder's classic stories; by Barbara M. Walker; illustrated by Garth Williams. Harper & Row 1979 240p il $16.95; pa $9.95 (5 and up)   **641.5**

1. Wilder, Laura Ingalls, 1867-1957 2. Cooking 3. Frontier and pioneer life

ISBN 0-06-026418-7; 0-06-446090-8 (pa)

LC 76-58733

Walker, Barbara Muhs, 1928——*Continued*

Recipes based on the pioneer food written about in the "Little House" books of Laura Ingalls Wilder, along with quotes from the books and descriptions of the food and cooking of pioneer times

"Illustrated by Williams's familiar warm drawings, the adaptations of menus from pioneer days include paragaphs describing the Wilder and Ingalls families working together, preparing holiday meals, individual foods, special treats and staple fare." Publ Wkly

Includes bibliographical references

Warshaw, Hallie

The sleepover cookbook; photography by Julie Brown; including healthy recipes by Diane Nepa. Sterling 2000 126p il $19.95 (4 and up)   **641.5**

1. Cooking

ISBN 0-8069-4497-8   LC 2001274608

A collection of kid-tested recipes, suitable for a sleepover or any time. Includes recipes, using readymade ingredients, for desserts, snacks, lunch, supper and breakfast dishes, soups, and salads

"The treats are easy to prepare. . . . Bold color photographs highlight almost every spread, with sleepovers pictured for boys and for girls." SLJ

Webb, Lois Sinaiko, 1922-

Holidays of the world cookbook for students. Oryx Press 1995 xxxiv, 297p il maps pa $29.50 (5 and up)   **641.5**

1. Cooking 2. Holidays

ISBN 0-89774-884-0   LC 95-26019

In this cookbook "more than 136 countries are represented, with 388 recipes. The U.S. is divided into six sections with 10 recipes for regional celebrations. History behind the holiday is included where possible, as is pertinent background information on the culture represented. . . . A discussion of different calendars used around the world is an interesting inclusion. The recipes' directions are clear and include equipment lists." SLJ

Includes glossary and bibliographical references

Zalben, Jane Breskin

To every season; a family holiday cookbook; written and illustrated by Jane Breskin Zalben. Simon & Schuster Bks. for Young Readers 1999 112p $19.95 (4 and up)   **641.5**

1. Cooking 2. Holidays

ISBN 0-689-81797-5   LC 98-35393

Gives brief histories and recipes for such holidays as Valentine's Day, Easter, Passover, the Fourth of July, and Kwanzaa

"A wonderful potpourri of recipes for many occasions. . . . Ingredients are easily obtainable and clearly listed. Illustrations have a soft delicacy that is both pleasing to the eye and well matched to the text." SLJ

Includes glossary

641.8 Cooking specific kinds of composite dishes

Jones, Judith

Knead it, punch it, bake it! the ultimate breadmaking book for parents and kids; [by] Judith and Evan Jones; illustrations by Mitra Modarressi. 2nd ed. Houghton Mifflin 1998 144p il spir $16 (3-6)   **641.8**

1. Bread

ISBN 0-395-89256-2   LC 98-27319

First published 1981 by Crowell

Presents more than forty recipes for baking all kinds and shapes of bread from French bread to peanut butter muffins to pizza

Morris, Ann

Bread, bread, bread; photographs by Ken Heyman. Lothrop, Lee & Shepard Bks. 1989 unp il $15.93; lib bdg $16; pa $5.95 (k-3)   **641.8**

1. Bread

ISBN 0-688-06335-7; 0-688-06334-9 (lib bdg); 0-688-12275-2 (pa)   LC 88-26677

Also available Big book edition

This photo essay shows different kinds of bread around the world from baguettes to challah

"Each picture offers a strong ethnic identity or a thought-provoking human interaction, with captions of only a few words in large print. An unusual index . . . gives background information about the pictures, citing the countries of origin and a few facts about each type of bread." SLJ

Paulsen, Gary

The tortilla factory; paintings by Ruth Wright Paulsen. Harcourt Brace & Co. 1995 unp il $16; pa $7 (k-3)   **641.8**

1. Tortillas

ISBN 0-15-292876-6; 0-15-201698-8 (pa)

LC 93-48590

Also available Spanish language edition

"Paulsen traces the journey of the corn, from harvest and grinding, to the tortilla factory, where people turn the corn flour into tortillas that, filled with beans, 'give strength to the brown hands that work the black earth to plant yellow seeds . . . '. Replete with the lush greens of healthy plants, the rich browns of adobe buildings and fertile soil, and the vibrant gold of ears of corn, the highly satisfying illustrations reinforce the reverential mood established by the spare poetic narrative." Horn Book

Zubrowski, Bernie, 1939-

Soda science; designing and testing soft drinks; illustrated by Roy Doty. Morrow Junior Bks. 1997 96p il (Boston Children's Museum activity book) lib bdg $14.95; pa $6.95 (4 and up)   **641.8**

1. Carbonated beverages 2. Science—Experiments

ISBN 0-688-13917-5 (lib bdg); 0-688-13983-3 (pa)

LC 96-23735

Zubrowski, Bernie, 1939—_Continued_

This "collection of experiments . . . explores the chemistry behind soda flavors, colors, and fizz, and also considers the marketing and statistical work necessary to create a successful product." Horn Book Guide

"Clear instructions and easy-to-follow pen-and-ink illustrations, well marked for safety procedures, accompany each step of the activities." SLJ

659.1   Advertising

Hoban, Tana

I read signs. Greenwillow Bks. 1983 unp il $18; lib bdg $15.93; pa $4.95 (k-2)   **659.1**
1. Signs and signboards
ISBN 0-688-02317-7; 0-688-02318-5 (lib bdg); 0-688-07331-X (pa)   LC 83-1482

In this book "30 verbal and 27 symbolic street signs have been caught on location in close-ups with a minimum of background to give just a soupçon of milieu (city, sky or apple tree) or hint of meaning ('Beware of dog' on chain link fence). Design is bold; primary colors are emphasized. The familiar predominates; more unusual signs . . . add interest." SLJ

666   Ceramic and allied technologies

Fisher, Leonard Everett, 1924-

The glassmakers; written & illustrated by Leonard Everett Fisher. Benchmark Bks. (Tarrytown) 1997 43p il (Colonial craftsmen) lib bdg $21.36 (4 and up)   **666**
1. Glass manufacture 2. United States—Social life and customs—1600-1775, Colonial period
ISBN 0-7614-0477-5   LC 96-16608

A reissue of the title first published 1964 by Watts

The author presents the history of glass, the techniques in making it, and the way colonial glassmakers worked

"Useful for school assignments. . . . Well-written text and strong, vibrant illustrations." Libr J

The potters; written & illustrated by Leonard Everett Fisher. Marshall Cavendish 2001 48p il (Colonial craftsmen) lib bdg $21.36 (4 and up)   **666**
1. Pottery 2. United States—Social life and customs—1600-1775, Colonial period
ISBN 0-7614-1149-6   LC 00-45161

A reissue of the title first published 1969 by Watts

This explains the development of pottery craft in colonial America

"Fisher's striking black-and-white illustrations are more attractive and effective than most full-color pictures in today's nonfiction." Booklist

Includes bibliographical references

670   Manufacturing

Biesty, Stephen

Stephen Biesty's incredible everything; illustrated by Stephen Biesty; written by Richard Platt. DK Pub. 1997 32p il $19.95 (4 and up)   **670**
1. Manufactures
ISBN 0-7894-2049-X   LC 97-15426

Cut-away illustrations and explanatory captions explain how such diverse objects as chocolate bars and cathedrals, false teeth and tanks are made

Biesty "manages to combine simplicity and fine detail in his drawings. . . . The authors convey to the reader the awe-inspiring technology and attention to detail that go into many of the everyday products we take for granted." Voice Youth Advocates

CD's, superglue, and salsa [series 2]; how everyday products are made; edited by Kathleen L. Witman, Kyung Lim Kalasky, & Neil Schlager. U.X.L 1996 2v il set $60   **670**
1. Manufactures
ISBN 0-7876-0870-X   LC 96-12523

Also available CDs, super glue, and salsa [series 1] edited by Sharon Rose & Neil Schlager 2v set $60 (ISBN 0-8103-9719-9)

This book describes "30 household or high-interest products, including bungee cords, bicycles, chewing gum, perfume, sunscreen, violins and 24 others." Publisher's note

Includes bibliographical references

675   Leather and fur processing

Fisher, Leonard Everett, 1924-

The tanners; written & illustrated by Leonard Everett Fisher. Benchmark Bks. (Tarrytown) 2001 43p (Colonial craftsmen) $21.36 (4 and up)   **675**
1. Tanning 2. Leather work 3. United States—Social life and customs—1600-1775, Colonial period
ISBN 0-7614-1148-8   LC 00-45159

A reissue of the title first published 1966 by Watts

This describes the development of leather making in Colonial America

Includes glossary

677   Textiles

Fisher, Leonard Everett, 1924-

The weavers; written & illustrated by Leonard Everett Fisher. Marshall Cavendish 1998 45p il (Colonial craftsmen) $14.95 (4 and up)   **677**
1. Weaving 2. United States—Social life and customs—1600-1775, Colonial period
ISBN 0-7614-0509-7   LC 96-36135

A reissue of the title first published 1966 by Watts

Presents background information on cloth making in the colonies and describes the various techniques involved

Keeler, Patricia A.
Unraveling fibers; [by] Patricia A. Keeler and Francis X. McCall, Jr. Atheneum Bks. for Young Readers 1995 35p il $16 (3-5)   **677**
1. Fibers 2. Fabrics
ISBN 0-689-31777-8   LC 93-13906
This book "looks at the sources of plant, animal, and synthetic fibers; describes the processes used to extract them from their natural states; and provides examples of finished products." SLJ
"The authors combine thoughtful explanations with liberal sprinklings of photographs silhouetted against white space in an attractive page design. . . . A useful and inviting overview." Horn Book

680   Manufacture of products for specific uses

Tunis, Edwin, 1897-1973
Colonial craftsmen and the beginnings of American industry; written and illustrated by Edwin Tunis. Johns Hopkins Univ. Press 1999 159p pa $18.95 (4 and up)   **680**
1. Decorative arts 2. United States—Social life and customs—1600-1775, Colonial period 3. Handicraft
ISBN 0-8018-6228-0   LC 99-20398
A reprint of the edition published 1965 by World Pub. Co.
The author describes the working methods and products, houses and shops, town and country trades, individual and group enterprises by which the early Americans forged the economy of the New World. He discusses such trades as papermaking, glassmaking, shipbuilding, printing, and metalworking
"An oversize book that is impressively handsome and that should be tremendously useful; well-organized and superbly illustrated, the text is comprehensive, lucid, and detailed. . . . An extensive index is appended." Chicago. Children's Book Center

681.1   Instruments for measuring time

Duffy, Trent
The clock; fold out illustration by Toby Willes. Atheneum Bks. for Young Readers 2000 80p il (Turning point inventions series) lib bdg $17.95 (4 and up)   **681.1**
1. Clocks and watches 2. Time
ISBN 0-689-82814-4   LC 99-65242
A history of time measurement, including a short biography of John Harrison, inventor of the chronemetric clock, and the effect of the clock on the Industrial Revolution
"This accessible and thorough treatment should be welcomed by students in search of an unusual topic for the ubiquitous 'invention report.'" Bull Cent Child Books
Includes bibliographical references

682   Small forge work (Blacksmithing)

Fisher, Leonard Everett, 1924-
The blacksmiths; written & illustrated by Leonard Everett Fisher. Marshall Cavendish 1999 47p il (Colonial craftsmen) lib bdg $21.36 (4 and up)   **682**
1. Blacksmithing 2. United States—History—1600-1775, Colonial period
ISBN 0-7614-0930-0   LC 99-33360
A reissue of the title first published 1976 by Watts
Introduces the history of blacksmithing and discusses the techniques, products, well-known blacksmiths, and commercial importance of this trade in colonial America
Includes bibliographical references

683   Hardware and household appliances

Rubin, Susan Goldman, 1939-
Toilets, toasters & telephones; the how and why of everyday objects; illustrated with photographs and with illustrations by Elsa Warnick. Browndeer Press 1998 132p il $20 (5 and up)   **683**
1. Industrial design 2. Inventions 3. Household equipment and supplies
ISBN 0-15-201421-7   LC 97-28650
"In addition to the three objects mentioned in the title, the lively text discusses the history and development of many familiar conveniences from refrigerators to paper clips. The book is readable, with solid grounding in research, and the appeal of the amusing trivia is well supported by the historical underpinnings." Horn Book Guide
Includes bibliographical references

684.1   Furniture

Fisher, Leonard Everett, 1924-
The cabinetmakers; written and illustrated by Leonard Everett Fisher. Benchmark Bks. (Tarrytown) 1997 47p il (Colonial craftsmen) $21.36 (4 and up)   **684.1**
1. Cabinetwork 2. American furniture 3. United States—Social life and customs—1600-1775, Colonial period
ISBN 0-7614-0479-1   LC 96-16606
A reissue of the title first published 1966 by Watts
The author explains that colonial American furniture is a reflection of the social life of the times and of the history of the craftsmen who designed it. He also discusses how cabinetmakers worked, what tools they used, and what skills were employed to bring about the final product
"Partly because Mr. Fisher's distinctive illustrative style lends itself well to the graining of wood, the pictures seem unusually handsome. [Includes] two pages of photographs of colonial furniture." Bull Cent Child Books

685　Leather and fur goods, and related products

Fisher, Leonard Everett, 1924-

The shoemakers; written & illustrated by Leonard Everett Fisher. Benchmark Bks. (Tarrytown) 1998 44p il (Colonial craftsmen) $14.95 (4 and up)　　**685**

1. Shoemakers 2. United States—Social life and customs—1600-1775, Colonial period

ISBN 0-7614-0510-0　　LC 96-40975

A reissue of the title first published 1967 by Watts

The author tells the history of the American shoemakers and gives an account of how they went about their work

"Written in a 'lucid, graphic manner. . . . A glossary of terms is included and the book is illustrated with carefully drawn, detailed pictures on every other page." Booklist

686.2　Printing

Fisher, Leonard Everett, 1924-

The printers; written & illustrated by Leonard Everett Fisher. Marshall Cavendish 1999 46p il (Colonial craftsmen) lib bdg $21.36 (4 and up)　　**686.2**

1. Printing—History 2. United States—History—1600-1775, Colonial period

ISBN 0-7614-0929-7　　LC 99-33361

A reissue of the title first published 1965 by Watts

Surveys the history of printing in colonial America, describing the work of the early printers, the development of the free press, and the printer's craft and technique

Includes bibliographical references

688.7　Recreational equipment

Wulffson, Don L., 1943-

Toys! amazing stories behind some great inventions; [by] Don Wulffson; with illustrations by Laurie Keller. Holt & Co. 2000 137p il $15.95 (4 and up)　　**688.7**

1. Toys 2. Inventions

ISBN 0-8050-6196-7　　LC 99-58440

Describes the creation of a variety of toys and games, from seesaws to Silly Putty and toy soldiers to Trivial Pursuit

"Each of the 25 chapters is illustrated with small, humorous drawings and discusses a particular toy or game's origin and development. The book ends with a bibliography and a list of Web sites. Good, readable fare for browsing or light research." Booklist

690　Buildings

Barton, Byron

Building a house. Greenwillow Bks. 1981 unp il hardcover o.p. paperback available $5.95 (k-1)　　**690**

1. Building 2. Houses

ISBN 0-688-09356-6 (pa)

"In the simplest possible book on building a house, a step-by-step, one-line description is given of the major factors in construction. Such workers as bricklayers, carpenters, plumbers, electricians, and painters do their own jobs until the small, bright red-and-green house is completed and a family moves in. Flat drawings in brilliant primary colors enable the very young to visualize the methods of housebuilding." Horn Book

Machines at work. Crowell 1987 unp il $15.95; lib bdg $15.89; pa $6.95 (k-1)　　**690**

1. Building

ISBN 0-694-00190-2; 0-690-04573-5 (lib bdg); 0-694-01107-X (pa)　　LC 86-24221

"Double-page illustrations depict a busy day at a construction site as workers (with the positive inclusion of women) knock down a building and start a new one." SLJ

"The short, punchy narrative reinforces the dynamics of the illustrations. . . . This should be a popular read-aloud for preschoolers and satisfying read-alone for beginners." Publ Wkly

Gibbons, Gail

How a house is built. Holiday House 1990 unp il $16.95; pa $6.95 (k-3)　　**690**

1. Building 2. Houses

ISBN 0-8234-0841-8; 0-8234-1232-6 (pa)

LC 90-55107

This book describes how the surveyor, heavy machinery operators, carpenter crew, plumbers, and other workers build a house

"With her customary bright illustrations, Gibbons gives a fine introduction to the construction of a wood-frame house. . . . Construction machines and materials as well as parts of the house are identified, and each stage of construction logically follows the others. Workers are drawn in both sexes and several skin tones." Booklist

Macaulay, David, 1946-

Mill. Houghton Mifflin 1983 128p il $18; pa $8.95 (4 and up)　　**690**

1. Mills 2. Textile industry—History

ISBN 0-395-34830-7; 0-395-52019-3 (pa)

LC 83-10652

This is an "account of the development of four fictional 19th-Century Rhode Island cotton mills. In explaining the construction and operation of a simple water-wheel powered wooden mill, as well as the more complex stone, turbine and steam mills to follow, the author also describes the rise and decline of New England's textile industry." SLJ

Includes glossary

Macaulay, David, 1946-—*Continued*
Unbuilding. Houghton Mifflin 1980 78p il $18;
pa $8.95 (4 and up)　　　　　**690**
1. Empire State Building (New York, N.Y.) 2. Building 3. Skyscrapers
ISBN 0-395-29457-6; 0-395-45425-5 (pa)
　　　　　　　　　　　　LC 80-15491
This fictional account of the dismantling and removal
of the Empire State Building describes the structure of a
skyscraper and explains how such an edifice would be
demolished
"Save for the fact that one particularly stunning double-page spread is marred by tight binding, the book is
a joy: accurate, informative, handsome, and eminently
readable." Bull Cent Child Books

Wilkinson, Philip, 1955-
Building; written by Philip Wilkinson;
photographed by Dave King & Geoff Dann. Knopf
1995 61p il (Eyewitness books) (4 and up)　**690**
1. Structural engineering 2. House construction
3. Building materials
　　　　　　　　　　　　LC 94-37733
Available DK Pub. edition $15.95; lib bdg $19.99
(ISBN 0-7894-6026-2; 0-7894-6607-4)
"A Dorling Kindersley book"
Fist published 1994 in the United Kingdom
This covers "the history of building techniques, mate-
rials, and philosophy from earth-and-thatch houses to ca-
thedrals and skyscrapers." SLJ
An "extremely handsome volume. . . . This is an in-
formative book, fascinating for study or browsing." Sci
Books Films

693　Construction in specific types of materials and for specific purposes

Rounds, Glen, 1906-
Sod houses on the Great Plains; written and
illustrated by Glen Rounds. Holiday House 1995
unp il $16.95; pa $6.95 (k-3)　　　　　**693**
1. Houses 2. Frontier and pioneer life
ISBN 0-8234-1162-1; 0-8234-1263-6 (pa)
　　　　　　　　　　　　LC 94-27390
"The author explains plainly and clearly just how the
homesteaders built their warm, dry, fireproof, ecological-
ly sound sod dwellings on the prairies more than a
century ago. His spare but evocative crayon illustrations
detail the text and add sly wit." N Y Times Book Rev

694　Wood construction. Carpentry

Walker, Lester
Carpentry for children; preface by David
Macaulay. Overlook Press 1982 208p il hardcover
o.p. paperback available $14.95 (4 and up)　**694**
1. Carpentry 2. Handicraft
ISBN 0-87951-990-8 (pa)　　　　LC 82-3469
A step-by-step guide to carrying out such carpentry
projects as a birdhouse, candle chandelier, doll cradle,
puppet theater, and coaster car

700　THE ARTS. FINE & DECORATIVE ARTS

701　Art—Philosophy and theory

Micklethwait, Lucy
A child's book of art: discover great paintings.
DK Pub. 1999 31p il $16.95 (3-6)　　　**701**
1. Art appreciation
ISBN 0-7894-4283-3　　　　　LC 98-37537
Invites the reader to take a closer look at paintings by
such artists as Botticelli, Bruegel, Velasquez, Copley,
and Van Gogh, providing information about the artist,
subject, and medium of each work of art
"There are questions on the left-hand page to draw
kids in and hold their interest. . . . There's no intimidating jargon. Micklethwait includes lots of fascinating
facts. . . . With adult guidance, kids will pore over the
pictures and point and talk. And they will be ready for
a visit to an art museum." Booklist

A child's book of art: great pictures, first words;
selected by Lucy Micklethwait. Dorling Kindersley
1993 64p il $16.95 (k-2)　　　　　**701**
1. Art appreciation 2. Vocabulary
ISBN 1-56458-203-5　　　　　LC 92-54320
An introduction to art that uses well-known works of
art to illustrate familiar words
"Micklethwait wisely includes an abundance of paintings featuring children, action scenes and vibrant colors—all elements guaranteed to snare a youngster's attention. The thematic arrangement of the works of art
places them in contexts familiar to kids." Publ Wkly

A child's book of play in art; great pictures,
great fun; selected by Lucy Micklethwait. DK Pub.
1996 45p il $16.95 (k-3)　　　　　**701**
1. Art appreciation
ISBN 0-7894-1003-6　　　　　LC 96-13959
"Forty-one works ranging from an Aboriginal bark
painting to a slick Lichtenstein homage to Van Gogh's
Arles bedroom are skillfully arranged in two-page 'exhibits,' with brief suggestions on how to approach them.
. . . Readers are urged to imitate the sounds, interpret
the costumes, adapt the patterns, and act out the stories
of rich and exciting images. . . . Micklethwait teaches
basic art concepts and pre-reading skills such as prediction and discrimination, but more importantly, the joy of
interactive reading. . . . A final section lists pictures by
title, description, artist, date, country, medium, size, and
location of the original." SLJ

702.8　Art—Technique, procedures, apparatus, equipment, materials

Gibbons, Gail
The art box. Holiday House 1998 unp il $16.95;
pa $6.95 (k-1)　　　　　**702.8**
1. Artists' materials
ISBN 0-8234-1386-1; 0-8234-1556-2 (pa)
　　　　　　　　　　　　LC 97-44171

Gibbons, Gail—*Continued*

Describes the many different kinds of tools and supplies which artists use to produce their work

This offers "Illustrations with clean lines and bright colors set against textured handmade papers. . . . The straightforward text combines boldface headings, captions, and succinct descriptions." Booklist

708 Art—Galleries, museums private collections

Brown, Laurene Krasny

Visiting the art museum; [by] Laurene Krasny Brown and Marc Brown. Dutton 1986 32p il hardcover o.p. paperback available $6.99 (k-3)

708

1. Art museums 2. Art appreciation
ISBN 0-14-054820-3 (pa)   LC 85-32552

As a family wanders through an art museum, they see examples of various art styles from primitive through twentieth-century pop art

"A lively, fact-filled introduction to the art museum for the whole family, with animated drawings and full-color reproductions of art from all over the world. . . . All of the paintings are identified, both in the text and in the back, and all possible periods of art—from primitive to modern—are shown." Publ Wkly

Thomson, Peggy, 1922-

The nine-ton cat: behind the scenes at an art museum; by Peggy Thomson and Barbara Moore; edited by Carol Eron. Houghton Mifflin 1997 96p il $21.95; pa $14.95 (4 and up)   **708**

1. National Gallery of Art (U.S.) 2. Art museums
ISBN 0-395-82655-1; 0-395-82683-7 (pa)

LC 96-18809

A behind-the-scenes look at the National Gallery of Art including its private spaces, workshops, offices, and labs where visitors rarely enter

"This fascinating look at what goes on behind the scenes is as appealing to look at as it is informative. The unsung heroes of the institution—curators, conservators, gardeners, security personnel—get their due in short, intriguing chapters. . . . Photos, all nicely captioned, are a careful, very successful mix of color and black-and-white shots, including pictures of some of the museum's treasures." Booklist

709.01 Arts of nonliterate peoples, and earliest times to 499

Arnold, Caroline, 1944-

Stories in stone; rock art pictures by early Americans; photographs by Richard Hewett. Clarion Bks. 1996 48p il map $16 (4 and up)

709.01

1. Native Americans—Antiquities 2. Rock drawings, paintings, and engravings
ISBN 0-395-72092-3   LC 96-387

This focuses "on the rock art found in the Coso Range of eastern California. . . . Arnold describes the various methods that were used to create the designs. She also discusses climatic changes in the area, beginning with the last Ice Age, and surmises what life might have been like for those ancient people." Booklist

"This is a crisply written, richly photographed account of the oldest known art in the world. . . . Hewett's color photographs are finely detailed, clear, and well composed, and they enrich the text enormously." Bull Cent Child Books

Includes glossary

711 Area planning

Macaulay, David, 1946-

City: a story of Roman planning and construction. Houghton Mifflin 1974 112p il $18; pa $7.95 (4 and up)   **711**

1. City planning—Rome 2. Civil engineering 3. Roman architecture
ISBN 0-395-19492-X; 0-395-34922-2 (pa)

"By following the inception, construction, and development of an imaginary Roman city, the account traces the evolution of Verbonia from the selection of its site under religious auspices in 26 B.C. to its completion in 100 A.D." Horn Book

Includes glossary

720 Architecture

Fisher, Leonard Everett, 1924-

The architects; written & illustrated by Leonard Everett Fisher; with additional photographs. Benchmark Bks. (Tarrytown) 1999 48p il (Colonial craftsmen) lib bdg $24.36 (4 and up)

720

1. Architecture 2. United States—Social life and customs—1600-1775, Colonial period
ISBN 0-7614-0931-9   LC 99-33370

A reissue of the title first published 1970 by Watts

Traces the history of architecture in the American colonies, describing the influence of existing styles and the needs of environment

"Illustrated with strong, informative, distinctive scratchboard drawings." Horn Book Guide

Includes bibliographical references

The **Visual** dictionary of buildings. Dorling Kindersley 1992 64p il (Eyewitness visual dictionaries) $16.95 (4 and up)   **720**

1. Architecture
ISBN 1-56458-102-0   LC 92-7673

Also available Spanish language edition

Labeled illustrations with explanatory text depict historical and contemporary structures, architectural elements, and building components from ancient times to the present

"This visual dictionary easily stands tall as an art history source as well as a reference for the structures, forms, and components of buildings." Booklist

726 Buildings for religious and related purposes

Macaulay, David, 1946-
Building the book Cathedral. Houghton Mifflin 1999 112p il $29.95 (4 and up)   **726**
1. Cathedrals 2. Gothic architecture
ISBN 0-395-92147-3   LC 99-17975
"Walter Lorraine books"
"On its twenty-fifth anniversary, the author recounts the origins of his first book and suggests revisions he'd make in light of what he's learned. . . . Most of the original *Cathedral: the story of it's construction* is reproduced in this oversized celebratory volume, along with lots of preliminary sketches, new commentary, and revised, or newly deployed, art. . . . Touches of informal humor further enliven a book that's already mesmerizing for both its original content and its insights into this author-illustrator's incisive, ebulliently creative mind." Horn Book

Cathedral: the story of its construction. Houghton Mifflin 1973 77p il $18; pa $8.95 (4 and up)   **726**
1. Cathedrals 2. Gothic architecture
ISBN 0-395-17513-5; 0-395-31668-5 (pa)
A Caldecott Medal honor book, 1974
This is a description, illustrated with black-and-white line drawings, of the construction of an imagined representative Gothic cathedral "in southern France from its conception in 1252 to its completion in 1338. The spirit that motivated the people, the tools and materials they used, the steps and methods of constructions, all receive . . . attention." Booklist
Includes glossary

Pyramid. Houghton Mifflin 1975 80p il $18; pa $8.95 (4 and up)   **726**
1. Pyramids 2. Egypt—Civilization
ISBN 0-395-21407-6; 0-395-32121-2 (pa)
The construction of a pyramid in 25th century B.C. Egypt is described. "Information about selection of the site, drawing of the plans, calculating compass directions, clearing and leveling the ground, and quarrying and hauling the tremendous blocks of granite and limestone is conveyed as much by pictures as by text." Horn Book
Includes glossary

728 Residential and related buildings

Morris, Ann
Houses and homes; photographs by Ken Heyman. Lothrop, Lee & Shepard Bks. 1992 32p il map $17; lib bdg $16.93; pa $5.95 (k-3)   **728**
1. Houses
ISBN 0-688-10168-2; 0-688-10169-0 (lib bdg); 0-688-13578-1 (pa)   LC 92-1365
A simple discussion of different kinds of houses and what makes them homes
"A striking photographic survey of housing around the world that will be a real eyeopener for many children. The lush, full-color photos, one to two per page, tell the real story, conveying nearly as much about those who live in these homes as they do about the dwellings themselves. . . . This is a solid addition for collections that support social studies or multicultural units, but would be equally fascinating to browsers throughout the age group." SLJ

Steltzer, Ulli
Building an igloo; text and photographs by Ulli Steltzer. Holt & Co. 1995 c1981 unp il $15.95; pa $6.95 (3-6)   **728**
1. Inuit 2. Igloos
ISBN 0-8050-3753-5; 0-8050-6313-7 (pa)   LC 95-5893
First published 1981 in Canada
"Steltzer follows Tookillkee Kiguktak, an Inuit, as he builds an igloo to use while on a hunting trip. The brief, clear text, thorough introduction, and brilliant black-and-white photographs make the book an exceptionally fascinating and respectful glimpse of a traditional art." Horn Book Guide

Yue, Charlotte
The igloo; [by] Charlotte and David Yue. Houghton Mifflin 1988 117p il $16; pa $7.95 (3-6)   **728**
1. Igloos 2. Inuit
ISBN 0-395-44613-9; 0-395-62986-1 (pa)   LC 88-6154
Describes how an igloo is constructed and the role it plays in the lives of the Eskimo people. Also discusses many other aspects of Eskimo culture that have helped them adapt to life in the Arctic
"This book is a tidy source of reference information, curriculum support, and just plain compelling reading." SLJ
Includes bibliographical references

728.8 Large and elaborate private dwellings

Gravett, Christopher
Castle; written by Christopher Gravett; photographed by Geoff Dann. Knopf 1994 63p il (Eyewitness books) (4 and up)   **728.8**
1. Castles 2. Fortification   LC 93-32594
Available DK Pub. edition $15.95; lib bdg $19.99 (ISBN 0-789-45888-8; 0-789-46598-1)
"A Dorling Kindersley book"
"*Castle* looks at European fortifications, Byzantine and Muslim-influenced constructions of the Crusades, and Japanese strongholds and defense strategies through photographs of architectural features, designs, and weapons. Everyday life is also documented with pictures of artifacts and people in period costumes." SLJ
"This book offers page after page of excellent photographs. . . . Each photo is clearly described in language concise enough that the reader understands the functioning of obscure implements and features of castles. The information presented is generally accurate." Sci Books Films

Macaulay, David, 1946-

Castle. Houghton Mifflin 1977 74p il $18; pa $8.95 (4 and up) **728.8**

1. Castles 2. Fortification

ISBN 0-395-25784-0; 0-395-32920-5 (pa)

LC 77-7159

A Caldecott Medal honor book, 1978

Macaulay depicts "the history of an imaginary thirteenth-century castle—built to subdue the Welsh hordes—from the age of construction to the age of neglect, when the town of Aberwyfern no longer needs a fortified stronghold." Economist

"The line drawings are meticulous in detail, lucidly illustrating architectural features described in the text and injected with a refreshing humor. . . . The writing is clear, crisp, and informative, with a smooth narrative flow." Bull Cent Child Books

Includes glossary

Steele, Philip

Castles. Kingfisher (NY) 1995 63p il $16.95; pa $10.95 (4 and up) **728.8**

1. Castles

ISBN 1-85697-547-9; 0-7534-5258-8 (pa)

LC 94-29366

An "overview of medieval European (and a few Near Eastern) castles. The book's strengths are its well-organized format and careful balance of text and illustrations. Steele touches on almost every facet of castle construction, inhabitants, celebrations, and rituals, as well as more mundane topics such as sanitation and the kitchen." SLJ

Includes glossary

730.9 Sculpture—Historical and geographic treatment

Curlee, Lynn, 1947-

Rushmore. Scholastic Press 1999 48p il $17.95 (4 and up) **730.9**

1. Borglum, Gutzon, 1867-1941 2. Mount Rushmore National Memorial (S.D.)

ISBN 0-590-22573-1

LC 98-16891

Describes how this patriotic shrine and tourist attraction was conceived, designed, and created by the dedicated artist Gutzon Borglum

The text "is straightforward and readable, giving a sense of the creator and the difficult project. The layout is spacious and pleasing, as are the large, carefully executed paintings." Booklist

Includes bibliographical references

736 Carving and carvings. Paper cutting and folding

Diehn, Gwen, 1943-

Making books that fly, fold, wrap, hide, pop up, twist, and turn; books for kids to make. Lark Bks. 1998 96p il $19.95 (4 and up) **736**

1. Paper crafts 2. Handicraft

ISBN 1-57990-023-2

LC 97-41037

Presents instructions for making various kinds of books including those that carry messages across space and time as well as those that save words, ideas, and pictures

"Clear directions and diagrams and attractive full-color photographs of completed projects will make it easy for readers to duplicate 18 different folded, wrapped, and pop-up books." Booklist

Includes glossary

Garza, Carmen Lomas

Making magic windows; creating papel picado/cut-paper art with Carmen Lomas Garza. Children's Bk. Press 1999 61p il pa $9.95 (3-6) **736**

1. Paper crafts

ISBN 0-89239-159-6

LC 98-38518

Provides instructions for making paper banners and more intricate cut-outs. Includes diagrams for creating specific images

"Based on workshops conducted by the artist, the step-by-step instructions and illustrations have been fine-tuned and are clear and easy to follow. . . . Multiculturally authentic and a guaranteed kid-crowd pleaser, this workbook is enthusiastically recommended for all craft collections." Booklist

Irvine, Joan, 1951-

How to make holiday pop-ups; illustrated by Linda Hendry. Morrow Junior Bks. 1996 64p il hardcover o.p. paperback available $6.95 (3-6) **736**

1. Paper crafts 2. Handicraft 3. Holidays

ISBN 0-688-13610-9 (pa)

LC 95-35174

First published 1995 in Canada

This "craft book suggests designs and provides detailed instructions for making holiday cards with pop-up pictures. . . . The line-and-watercolor illustrations reinforce the directions and show the finished product. This attractive addition to craft collections will be useful throughout the year." Booklist

How to make super pop-ups; illustrated by Linda Hendry. Morrow Junior Bks. 1992 96p il hardcover o.p. paperback available $6.95 (3-6) **736**

1. Paper crafts 2. Handicraft

ISBN 0-688-11521-7 (pa)

LC 92-2637

Companion volume to the author's How to make pop-ups (1988)

Provides instructions for making a variety of paper pop-ups, including animals, boats, robots, and enormous pop-ups for the stage

"Explicit, step-by-step instructions, accompanied by helpful black-and-white line drawings, are easy to follow. Each project includes suggestions for variation that will encourage children to think creatively." SLJ

739.2   Work in precious metals

Fisher, Leonard Everett, 1924-
The silversmiths; written & illustrated by Leonard Everett Fisher. Benchmark Bks. (Tarrytown) 1997 46p il (Colonial craftsmen) lib bdg $21.36 (4 and up)   **739.2**
1. Silverwork 2. United States—Social life and customs—1600-1775, Colonial period
ISBN 0-7614-0478-3   LC 96-16607
A reissue of the title first published 1964 by Watts
This is a story of early colonial silversmiths and how they worked to create beautiful and useful objects of art
"Respect for . . . achievement is reflected in striking full-page scratchboard illustrations and in concise, informative text." Horn Book

741.2   Drawing—Techniques, equipment, materials

Emberley, Ed
Ed Emberley's big green drawing book. Little, Brown 1979 91p il hardcover o.p. paperback available $9.95 (2-5)   **741.2**
1. Drawing
ISBN 0-316-23596-2 (pa)   LC 79-16247
The author "combines basic shapes (circles, triangles, lines, squiggles) to create a variety of cartoon people and animals. The crisp green-and-black illustrations on a white background are large and well spaced. . . . As in his other drawing books, Emberley's wordless step-by-step method is easy to follow; even very young children can successfully reproduce the simple but appealing figures." SLJ

Ed Emberley's big red drawing book. Little, Brown 1987 unp il hardcover o.p. paperback available $10.95 (2-5)   **741.2**
1. Drawing
ISBN 0-316-23435-4 (pa)   LC 87-3091
The author explains "how to create objects and figures by building up a series of simple lines and squiggles into a more complicated and complete whole. The color red suggests most of the subjects, among them a U.S. flag, a fire engine, and assorted red-and-green Christmas items." Booklist

Ed Emberley's drawing book: make a world. Little, Brown 1972 unp il hardcover o.p. paperback available $6.95 (2-5)   **741.2**
1. Drawing
ISBN 0-316-23644-6 (pa)
"Emberley gives directions for drawing, among a myriad of other things, 10 different kinds of cars, 16 varieties of trucks, and animals of all species including anteaters and dinosaurs." Book World
"The final three pages, which supply suggestions for making comic strips, posters, mobiles and games, help make the volume particularly appealing. For all developing artists and even plain scribblers." Horn Book

741.5   Cartoons, caricatures, comics

Pellowski, Michael, 1949-
The art of making comic books; [by] Michael Morgan Pellowski; with illustrations by Howard Bender. Lerner Publs. 1995 80p il (Media workshop) $21.27; pa $8.95 (5 and up)   **741.5**
1. Comic books, strips, etc. 2. Cartoons and caricatures
ISBN 0-8225-2304-3; 0-8225-9672-5 (pa)
LC 94-27589
"After a brief overview of comic-book history, the text describes the making of a comic book, explaining the various jobs people hold and the various stages books must go through. . . . Serious comic fans will relish Pellowski's detail-oriented and knowledgeable pragmatism." Bull Cent Child Books
Includes glossary and bibliographical references

741.6   Graphic design, illustration and commercial art

Biesty, Stephen
Stephen Biesty's incredible explosions; illustrated by Stephen Biesty; written by Richard Platt. DK Pub. 1996 32p il $19.95 (4 and up)
741.6
1. Illustration of books
ISBN 0-7894-1024-9   LC 96-13948
This book includes cross-section and other inside-view illustrations of twelve diverse subjects, including the Grand Canyon, an airport, a city block, a space station, a windmill, the human body, and the Tower Bridge
"Painstakingly crafted and filled with mind-boggling detail, [Biesty's] artwork invites close, repeated viewing; combined with Platt's brisk text, it is guaranteed to both educate and entertain." Publ Wkly

Carle, Eric
The art of Eric Carle. Philomel Bks. 1996 125p il $35   **741.6**
1. Picture books for children 2. Illustration of books
ISBN 0-399-22937-X   LC 95-24940
This is "both a textual and visual anthology: in addition to Carle's autobiographical chapter and the text of his 1990 speech at the Library of Congress, chapters include accolades from Ann Beneduce (Carle's U.S. editor) and from Dr. Viktor Christen (Carle's German editor). A photoessay on the artist's collage technique rubs shoulders with a forty-page gallery of his illustrations over the last quarter of a century, which precedes a look at some of his quick sketches and an illustrated bibliography of his oeuvre. The book's inviting layout may appeal to artistic youngsters as well as grown Carle fans, and the information about his working process, particularly the technical details, is absorbing." Bull Cent Child Books

Christelow, Eileen, 1943-
What do illustrators do? written and illustrated by Eileen Christelow. Clarion Bks. 1999 40p il $15 (1-3)   **741.6**
1. Illustration of books
ISBN 0-395-90230-4   LC 98-8297

Christelow, Eileen, 1943-—*Continued*

Companion volume to What do author's do?

Shows two illustrators going through all the steps involved in creating new picture books of "Jack and the Beanstalk," including layout, scale, and point-of-view

"Christelow gives readers a great deal of insight into the creative process while entertaining them. . . . The pen-and-ink and watercolor drawings are expressive and engaging throughout." SLJ

Marcus, Leonard S., 1950-

A Caldecott celebration; six artists and their paths to the Caldecott medal. Walker & Co. 1998 49p il $18.95　　　**741.6**

1. Caldecott Medal 2. Illustrators 3. Illustration of books

ISBN 0-8027-8656-1　　　LC 98-6616

Profiles six Caldecott award winning books and their authors, including Robert McCloskey's "Make Way for Ducklings," Marcia Brown's "Cinderella," Maurice Sendak's "Where the Wild Things Are," William Steig's "Sylvester and the Magic Pebble," Chris Van Allsburg's "Jumanji," and David Wiesner's "Tuesday"

"Marcus, who interviewed each artist, provides a lively, informative introduction to each book and its maker. A beautifully made book, this will serve as a fine resource for children interested in illustration and for teachers researching author/illustrator studies." Booklist

Includes glossary

Stevens, Janet

From pictures to words; a book about making a book; written and illustrated by Janet Stevens. Holiday House 1995 unp il $16.95 (k-3)　**741.6**

1. Picture books for children 2. Authorship

ISBN 0-8234-1154-0　　　LC 94-18976

"Stevens, appearing as herself sketched in black-and-white, is the main character in her story. She's surrounded by . . . animal characters who encourage her to write a book starring them. With help from Cat, Koala Bear, and Rhino, she does, explaining as she goes along the basic elements of writing and illustrating—setting, plot, tension, and characterization." Booklist

"The straightforward text carefully presents information while maintaining the narrative flow. Dialogue balloons and funny asides from the characters keep the presentation lively." SLJ

Stewig, John W.

Looking at picture books; by John Warren Stewig. Highsmith Press 1995 269p il $49　**741.6**

1. Picture books for children 2. Illustration of books 3. Children's literature—History and criticism

ISBN 0-917846-29-X　　　LC 94-35026

This overview includes chapters on "pictorial elements, such as shape, line, color, or proportion, and on composition. . . . The chapter on book design considers such things as the book's shape, type of paper chosen, typefaces, and page layout. There is also information here about the various media used in picture books." J Youth Serv Libr

Includes bibliographical references

Talking with artists [I-III]; compiled and edited by Pat Cummings. Bradbury Press 1992-1999 3v il $22; $19.95; $20 (4 and up)　　　**741.6**

1. Illustrators 2. Illustration of books

ISBN 0-02-724245-5 (v1); 0-689-80310-9 (v2 Simon & Schuster); 0-395-89132-9 (v3 Clarion Bks.)

LC 91-9982

Volume two published by Simon & Schuster Bks. for Young Readers; volume three published by Clarion Bks.

Each volume presents interviews with illustrators, who discuss their lives and works. Among the 14 artists in the first volume are Victoria Chess, Leo and Diane Dillon, Amy Schwartz, Tom Feelings, and Steven Kellogg. The 13 artists represented in the second volume include Brian Pinkney, Denise Fleming, Floyd Cooper, Maira Kalman, and David Wisniewski. Among the 13 illustrators profiled in the third volume are Raul Colon, Lisa Desimini, G. Brian Karas, Peter Sis, and Paul Zelinsky. Samples of each illustrator's work are included

Wings of an artist; children's book illustrators talk about their art; introduction by Julie Cummins; activity guide by Barbara Kiefer. Abrams 1999 31p il $17.95　　　**741.6**

1. Illustrators 2. Illustration of books

ISBN 0-8109-4552-5　　　LC 99-25906

More than twenty illustrators of children's books, including James Ransome, Robert Sabuda, Maira Kalman, and Maurice Sendak, talk about their work

"Aspiring artists, young and old, will be drawn to this collection. . . . It will serve as a useful art-education tool and as a stepping stone to discussions of fine art. An introduction and an idea-rich activity guide are also included." SLJ

741.9　Collections of drawings

—**I** never saw another butterfly—; children's drawings and poems from Terezin concentration camp, 1942-1944; edited by Hana Volavková; foreword by Chaim Potok; afterword by Vaclav Havel. expanded 2nd ed, by U.S. Holocaust Memorial Mus. Schocken Bks. 1993 xxii, 106p il $27.50; pa $17.50　　　**741.9**

1. Child artists 2. Children's writings 3. Terezin (Czechoslovakia: Concentration camp)

ISBN 0-8052-4115-9; 0-8052-1015-6 (pa)

LC 92-50477

Original Czech edition, 1959; first American edition published 1964 by McGraw-Hill

"Of the 15,000 children who passed through Terezin before going to Auschwitz, only 100 lived. This book is a collection of poems and drawings by some of them. . . . This touching book adds another facet to library collections on the Holocaust." SLJ

743　Drawing and drawings by subject

Ames, Lee J., 1921-

[Draw 50 series] Doubleday 1974-2000 25v prices vary (4 and up)　　　**743**

1. Drawing

Ames, Lee J., 1921-—*Continued*

Most titles available only in paperback

Available titles are: Draw 50 animals (1974); Draw 50 boats, ships, trucks, & trains (1976); Draw 50 airplanes, aircraft, & spacecraft (1977); Draw 50 dinosaurs and other prehistoric animals (1977); Draw 50 famous faces (1978); Draw 50 vehicles (1978); Draw 50 famous cartoons (1979); Draw 50 buildings and other structures (1980); Draw 50 dogs (1981); Draw 50 monsters, creeps, superheroes, demons, dragons, nerds, dirts, ghouls, giants, vampires, zombies, and other curiosa (1983); Draw 50 horses (1984); Draw 50 athletes (1985); Draw 50 cats (1986); Draw 50 cars, trucks, and motorcycles (1986); Draw 50 holiday decorations (1987); Draw 50 beasties and yugglies and turnover uglies and things that go bump in the night (1988); Draw 50 sharks, whales, and other sea creatures (1989); Draw 50 creepy crawlies (1991); Draw 50 endangered animals (1992); Draw 50 people (1993); Draw 50 flowers, trees, and other plants (1994); Draw 50 people of the Bible (1995); Draw 50 birds (1996); Draw 50 aliens, UFO's galaxy ghouls, milky way marauders, and other extraterrestrial creatures (1998); Draw 50 animal 'toons (2000)

Each volume presents step-by-step instructions for drawing a variety of animals, people, or objects

Emberley, Ed

Ed Emberley's drawing book of faces. Little, Brown 1975 32p il hardcover o.p. paperback available $6.95 (2-5)   **743**

1. Drawing 2. Face in art

ISBN 0-316-23655-1 (pa)

Provides step-by-step instructions for drawing a wide variety of faces reflecting various emotions and professions

Ed Emberley's great thumbprint drawing book. Little, Brown 1977 37p il lib bdg $15.95; pa $6.95 (2-5)   **743**

1. Drawing

ISBN 0-316-23613-6 (lib bdg); 0-316-23668-3 (pa)
       LC 76-57346

"The artist shows how to combine thumbprints and simple lines to create a multitude of animals, people, birds, and flowers." Booklist

"There is little text; most of the book consists of illustrations, step-by-step, of making pictures out of thumbprints. A few Emberley embellishments and a page that suggests other ways of making prints (carrot or potato) are included." Bull Cent Child Books

745.5   Handicrafts

Cook, Deanna F., 1965-

Kids' pumpkin projects; planting & harvest fun; illustrated by Kate Flanagan. Williamson 1998 98p il pa $8.95 (2-4)   **745.5**

1. Handicraft 2. Pumpkin

ISBN 1-885593-21-X   LC 97-48366

"A Williamson good times! book"

Provides instructions for fifty projects and activities involving pumpkins, including growing them, using them in recipes, and making things out of them

Hauser, Jill Frankel

Kids' crazy concoctions; 50 mysterious mixtures for art & craft fun; illustrated by Loretta Trezzo Braren. Williamson 1995 156p il pa $12.95 (3-6)
       745.5

1. Handicraft

ISBN 0-913589-81-0   LC 94-4633

"A Williamson kids can! book"

"Hauser includes recipes for homemade papers, glues, paints, molding doughs and clay; they are followed by directions for making decorator boxes, stationery, books, bookmarks, gift tags, mobiles, sand paintings, ornaments, toys, stained-glass art, and jewelry. Illustrated with pen-and-ink sketches, each project begins with a 'What You Need' list and numbered steps of 'What You Do.'. . . An outstanding practical resource for classrooms." SLJ

Press, Judy, 1944-

The little hands big fun craft book; creative fun for 2- to 6-year-olds; illustrated by Loretta Trezzo Braren. Williamson 1996 142p il pa $12.95
       745.5

1. Handicraft

ISBN 0-913589-96-9   LC 95-17574

Companion volume to The little hands art book (1994)

"A Williamson little hands book"

This includes "seventy five simple arts-and-crafts projects. . . . In the introduction, the author explains the 'whole learning' concept on which the activities are based and gives safety tips for working with young children. The crafts are organized under general headings, such as 'Animals and Trees,' 'Friendship,' and 'Family Fun.' . . . Of special interest to teachers and childcare providers is the section called 'Big Fun in Special Places,' which includes great pre- or post field trip projects relating to the zoo, circus, museum, library, aquarium, etc. Black-and-white cartoon drawings make the directions even easier to understand." SLJ

Ross, Kathy, 1948-

Crafts for Kwanzaa; illustrated by Sharon Lane Holm. Millbrook Press 1994 47p il (Holiday crafts for kids) lib bdg $23.90 (1-3)   **745.5**

1. Kwanzaa 2. Handicraft

ISBN 1-56294-412-6   LC 93-36690

This introduction to the African American celebration explains holiday history and includes ideas for gifts as well as decorations

Sattler, Helen Roney

Recipes for art and craft materials; with new illustrations by Marti Shohet. rev ed. Lothrop, Lee & Shepard Bks. 1987 144p il hardcover o.p. paperback available $4.95 (4 and up)   **745.5**

1. Handicraft—Equipment and supplies 2. Artists' materials

ISBN 0-688-13199-9 (pa)   LC 86-34271

First published 1973

The author explains "how to make pastes and glues, modeling compounds, papier-mâché, casting compounds, paints, inks, flower preservatives, recycled paper, and more. Activities are studies in applied science that can provoke questions that invite investigations, encourage careful observation, and celebrate the cleverness of hands as well as brain." Sci Child

St. Pierre, Stephanie

The Muppets' big book of crafts; by The Muppet Workshop and Stephanie St. Pierre; illustrations by Stephanie Osser; photographs by John E. Barrett. Workman 1999 322p il pa $18.95 (2-5) **745.5**

1. Handicraft
ISBN 0-7611-0526-3   LC 99-38606

Includes instructions for creating all kinds of craft projects, including rugs, placemats, costumes, masks, jewelry, models, puppets, and more

"A fun-filled, delightful book. . . . The directions are clear and complete, yet children will feel free to improvise. A sense of joy prevails in the instructions for the wildly funny as well as the more useful activities. Witty illustrations are populated by Muppet characters." SLJ

Temko, Florence

Traditional crafts from Africa; with illustrations by Randall Gooch; and photographs by Robert L. and Diane Wolfe. Lerner Publs. 1996 64p il maps (Culture crafts) lib bdg $23.93 (4 and up) **745.5**

1. Handicraft
ISBN 0-8225-2936-X   LC 95-8109

"Each chapter focuses on one craft technique and includes a project from a specific African region. Vivid maps of each region show its climate and the culture of its people. . . . Bright, full-color photographs accompany descriptions of technique. Clear diagrams demonstrate how to make reproductions of the crafts with readily available materials." SLJ

Includes glossary and bibliographical references

Traditional crafts from Mexico and Central America; with illustrations by Randall Gooch and photographs by Robert L. and Diane Wolfe. Lerner Publs. 1996 63p il (Culture crafts) lib bdg $23.93 (4 and up) **745.5**

1. Handicraft
ISBN 0-8225-2935-1   LC 95-46583

Provides instructions on how to make traditional Mexican and Central American handicraft such as metal ornaments, tissue paper banners, and Guatemalan worry dolls

"The directions and pictures are clear and enticing; there are full-color photographs of the completed projects as well as of the original handiwork that inspired them." SLJ

Includes glossary and bibliographical references

Traditional crafts from native North America; with illustrations by Randall Gooch; and photographs by Robert L. and Diane Wolfe. Lerner Publs. 1997 64p il map (Culture crafts) lib bdg $23.93 (4 and up) **745.5**

1. Handicraft 2. Native American art
ISBN 0-8225-2934-3   LC 96-4973

Provides instructions for making such traditional North American Indian crafts as dreamcatchers, beadwork, and cornhusk dolls

Includes glossary and bibliographical references

745.54 Paper handicrafts

Henry, Sandi, 1951-

Cut-paper play! dazzling creations from construction paper; illustrations by Norma Jean Jourdenais. Williamson 1997 160p il pa $12.95 **745.54**

1. Paper crafts
ISBN 1-88559-305-8   LC 96-33183

"A Williamson kids can! book"

Contains instructions for more than eighty two- and three-dimensional construction paper creations, including a Matisse cut-out, a hanging snake mobile, and a personal desk top robot

"Black-line drawings accompany the easy-to-follow directions and most projects do not need more than construction paper, scissors, and glue to complete." SLJ

745.592 Toys, models, miniatures, related objects

Kelly, Emery J.

Paper airplanes; models to build and fly; illustrations by Darren Erickson; photographs by Richard Trombley. Lerner Publs. 1997 64p il lib bdg $23.93 (4 and up) **745.592**

1. Airplanes—Models 2. Paper crafts
ISBN 0-8225-2401-5   LC 96-10909

Presents information on aerodynamic principles and flying techniques along with instructions for making twelve different paper airplanes

"The photos of the finished planes will have kids itching to make and fly them. Fortunately, the materials (paper, paperclips, tape) are readily available, and the instructions and patterns are clear." Booklist

Simon, Seymour, 1931-

The paper airplane book; illustrated by Byron Barton. Viking 1971 48p il pa $6.99 (3-5) **745.592**

1. Airplanes—Models 2. Paper crafts
ISBN 0-14-030925-X

Step-by-step instructions for making paper airplanes with suggestions for experimenting with them

745.594 Decorative objects

Ancona, George, 1929-

The piñata maker: El piñatero. Harcourt Brace & Co. 1994 unp il $17; pa $9 (k-3) **745.594**

1. Paper crafts 2. Bilingual books—English-Spanish 3. Mexico—Social life and customs
ISBN 0-15-261875-9; 0-15-200060-7 (pa)
LC 93-2389

Describes how Don Ricardo, a craftsman from Ejutla de Crespo in southern Mexico, makes piñatas for all the village birthday parties and other fiestas

"Ancona tells his story in both English and Spanish, with both languages on every page. His clear, bright, full-color photographs complement the detailed text, giving the reader much additional information." Horn Book

746.44   Embroidery

Cobb, Mary, 1931-
A sampler view of colonial life; illustrated by
Jan Davey Ellis. Millbrook Press 1999 64p il lib
bdg $24.90; pa $8.95 (2-5)   **746.44**
1. Embroidery 2. United States—Social life and cus-
toms—1600-1775, Colonial period
ISBN 0-7613-0372-3 (lib bdg); 0-7613-0382-0 (pa)
LC 98-2873
Describes the samplers stitched by girls in colonial
America and explains what these samplers tell about the
lives of their makers. Includes simple projects
"Many decorative watercolor illustrations make this an
attractive choice." Booklist

746.46   Patchwork and quilting

Bial, Raymond
With needle and thread; a book about quilts.
Houghton Mifflin 1996 48p il $14.95 (4 and up)
     746.46
1. Quilting 2. Quilts
ISBN 0-395-73568-8   LC 95-16416
"With illustrated examples of traditional patchwork
patterns . . . Bial describes the processes of marking,
piecing, and quilting. An historical overview ranges from
the Colonial period to the famous AIDS Memorial Quilt.
Highlighting the multicultural scope of this art form, Bial
shows work by Amish, African-American, and Hmong
quilters. The narrative is accessibly simple, the photography is clear and colorful." Bull Cent Child Books
Includes bibliographical references

Cobb, Mary, 1931-
The quilt-block history of pioneer days; with
projects kids can make; illustrated by Jan Davey
Ellis. Millbrook Press 1995 64p il lib bdg $24.90;
pa $8.95 (2-5)   **746.46**
1. Quilts 2. Frontier and pioneer life 3. Handicraft
ISBN 1-56294-485-1 (lib bdg); 1-56294-692-7 (pa)
LC 94-9279
"Presenting the history of American pioneers through
the quilts they made, this appealing book links common
experiences of the period with various quilt patterns."
Booklist
Includes bibliographical references

758   Other subjects in painting

Minor, Wendell
Grand Canyon; exploring a natural wonder;
words and pictures by Wendell Minor. Blue Sky
Press (NY) 1998 unp il $16.95; pa $5.99 (4 and
up)   **758**
1. Landscape painting 2. Grand Canyon (Ariz.)
ISBN 0-590-47968-7; 0-439-19278-1 (pa)
LC 97-40185

In watercolor sketches accompanied by text, the author
records his impressions of the Grand Canyon
A "visual treat for young landscape painters and travelers to the Grand Canyon. . . . Because the chatty text
meanders, touching on history, weather, nature, science,
and art, it won't help report writers much. It will, however, provide armchair travelers with a pleasant trip."
Booklist

759.01   Painting of nonliterate peoples, and earliest times to 499

Lauber, Patricia, 1924-
Painters of the caves. National Geographic Soc.
1998 48p il map $17.95 (4 and up)   **759.01**
1. Prehistoric art 2. Prehistoric peoples
ISBN 0-7922-7095-9   LC 97-24172
Describes the 1994 discovery made in Chauvet,
France, of a cave with Stone Age rock paintings, and
discusses the significance of cave art to people living in
prehistoric as well as modern times
"This impressive work is rich in both its artwork and
its text." Booklist
Includes bibliographical references

Patent, Dorothy Hinshaw
Mystery of the Lascaux Cave. Benchmark Bks.
(Tarrytown) 1999 64p il (Frozen in time) $27.07
(5 and up)   **759.01**
1. Prehistoric art 2. Prehistoric peoples
ISBN 0-7614-0784-7   LC 97-48276
Discusses the paintings on the walls of Lascaux Cave
in France including the cave's discovery, its significance,
and the efforts to preserve the paintings themselves
This title will be welcomed for its "clear expository
style, accuracy, [and] informative sidebars. . . . [It is]
heavily illustrated with crisp full-color photos and a few
paintings." SLJ
Includes glossary and bibliographical references

759.13   American painting

Fisher, Leonard Everett, 1924-
The limners; America's earliest portrait painters;
written & illustrated by Leonard Everett Fisher.
Benchmark Bks. (Tarrytown) 1999 47p il
(Colonial craftsmen) lib bdg $21.36 (4 and up)
     759.13
1. Portrait painting 2. American art 3. United
States—Social life and customs—1600-1775, Colonial
period
ISBN 0-7614-0932-7   LC 99-33369
A reissue of the title first published 1969 by Watts
Discusses the motivation, materials, and techniques of
the first "artists" in colonial America—the sign painters
who expanded their profession to include portrait paint-
ing—and how their works contribute to a better understanding of early American history and society
Includes bibliographical references

Honoring our ancestors; stories and pictures by fourteen artists; edited by Harriet Rohmer. Children's Bk. Press 1999 31p il $15.95

759.13

1. Artists—United States
ISBN 0-89239-158-8   LC 98-38686

Fourteen artists and picture book illustrators present paintings with descriptions of ancestors or other sources of inspiration that have inspired them

This is "rewarding in its breadth and vivacity. The portraits are thematically rich yet accessible; generally, the texts are cheerful and resist sentimentality." Horn Book Guide

Lawrence, Jacob, 1917-2000

The great migration; an American story; paintings by Jacob Lawrence; with a poem in appreciation by Walter Dean Myers. HarperCollins Pubs. 1993 unp il hardcover o.p. paperback available $8.95

759.13

1. African Americans in art
ISBN 0-06-443428-1 (pa)   LC 93-16788

Published by The Museum of Modern Art, The Phillips Collection, and HarperCollins Pubs.

"A noted African-American artist chronicles the 1916-1919 migration of blacks from the South through a sequence of 60 paintings and accompanying narrative captions." SLJ

"Lawrence is a storyteller with words as well as pictures: his captions and his own 1992 introduction to this book are the best commentary on his work." Booklist

769.5 Forms of prints

Parker, Nancy Winslow

Money, money, money; the meaning of the art and symbols on United States paper currency. HarperCollins Pubs. 1995 32p il map $16.95; lib bdg $16.89 (3-5)

769.5

1. Paper money 2. Signs and symbols
ISBN 0-06-023411-3; 0-06-023412-1 (lib bdg)
LC 93-43534

"The text provides information regarding the graphics of our money. Brief snippets about the various U.S. presidents, the decorations, and other related facts are supplied. The illustrations of the bills in question are small and blurred, but pertinent details on the bills are shown enlarged." Horn Book Guide

770 Photography and photographs

Varriale, Jim

Take a look around; photography activities for young people. Millbrook Press 1999 30p il $24.90 (4 and up)

770

1. Photography
ISBN 0-7613-1265-X   LC 98-32431

Uses projects to introduce various photographic concepts, including shadow and light, camera angles, composition, action, and more

"The book gets high marks for its clear how-to instructions, for its creative concepts, and for its simple glossary. . . . Varriale makes photography fun, while adding a level of surprising sophistication." SLJ

Includes bibliographical references

770.9 Photography—Historical and geographic treatment

Czech, Kenneth P.

Snapshot; America discovers the camera. Lerner Pubs. 1996 88p il $22.60 (5 and up)

770.9

1. Photography—History
ISBN 0-8225-1736-1   LC 95-51136

"A history of photography from its inception to its many influences in American history. . . . The author explains complex photographic inventions and processes in easy-to-understand language. . . . A profusion of excellent black-and-white photographs are distributed throughout and complement the text. Well-placed quotes, historical diagrams, anecdotes, and advertisements enhance and accent topics discussed." SLJ

Includes bibliographical references

771 Photography—Techniques, equipment, materials

Gibbons, Gail

Click! a book about cameras and taking pictures. Little, Brown 1997 unp il $14.95 (k-3)

771

1. Cameras 2. Photography
ISBN 0-316-30976-1   LC 95-46410

This "photography guide offers information on how cameras work and photographs are developed, as well as helpful tips for taking both indoor and outdoor pictures. 'Fun Photo Facts' and a quick history of photography round out the book, while Gibbons's cheerful illustrations depict children happily clicking their cameras in nature and at friends and family." Horn Book Guide

Price, Susanna

Click! fun with photography; [by] Susanna Price & Tim Stephens. Sterling 1997 48p il $14.95; pa $7.95 (4 and up)

771

1. Photography 2. Cameras
ISBN 0-8069-9541-6; 0-8069-9652-8 (pa)
LC 96-37211

First published 1995 in the United Kingdom

Presents the basics of photography, from choosing a camera to making the most of the flash

"With numerous full-color photos and a brief, clearly written text, this book exposes more than just the basics. The authors include frequent checklists that summarize major points and an extensive glossary. . . . A multitude of activities complete this useful introduction." SLJ

778.7   Photography under specific conditions

Zubrowski, Bernie, 1939-
Shadow play; making pictures with light and lenses; illustrated by Roy Doty. Morrow Junior Bks. 1995 112p il $15.93; pa $7.95 (4 and up)
        778.7
1. Shades and shadows
ISBN 0-688-13210-3; 0-688-13211-1 (pa)
        LC 94-27425
"A Boston Children's Museum activity book"
The author explains "the basic properties of light and how the study of shadows led to the invention of the camera. The more than 50 experiments are grouped into three general sections: the first shows how shadows are made in natural and artificial light; the second describes how a shadow box is constructed and used in further activities; and the third tells how a box camera is made." SLJ
"Most of the experiments, illustrated with simple line drawings, are best accomplished by pairs or small groups. Zubrowski knows his audience: these are exactly the activities children will enjoy doing and demonstrating to family, friends, and classmates." Horn Book

778.9   Photography of specific subjects

Kramer, Stephen
Eye of the storm; chasing storms with Warren Faidley; [by] Stephen Kramer; photographs by Warren Faidley. Putnam 1997 48p il $18.95; pa $6.99 (4 and up)   **778.9**
1. Faidley, Warren 2. Photography—Scientific applications 3. Storms
ISBN 0-399-23029-7; 0-698-11766-2 (pa)
        LC 96-19296
Storm chaser Warren Faidley discusses the techniques, dangers, and difficulties of photographing lightning, tornadoes, and hurricanes
This book offers "dramatic full-color photos [and]. . . readable, exciting text. . . . This eye-catching book will undoubtedly be utilized by nonfiction lovers hungry for a good read." SLJ
Includes glossary and bibliographical references

780   Music

Ardley, Neil, 1937-
A young person's guide to music; with music by Poul Ruders. Dorling Kindersley 1995 80p il $24.95 (5 and up)   **780**
1. Music 2. Orchestra
ISBN 0-7894-0313-7   LC 95-19595
"In association with the BBC Symphony Orchestra conducted by Andrew Davis." Title page
This "interactive guide to the orchestra is a combination of book and compact disk. The CD features a new

work by the Dutch composer Poul Ruder. . . . The text itself has facts on the orchestra as a whole, the conductor, composer, and each instrument. . . . A history section features a timeline, names of musicians and composers, definitions of musical forms with examples, and a glossary." SLJ
"A rich resource for young people who want to understand orchestral music." Booklist

780.89   Music of racial, ethnic, national groups

Igus, Toyomi, 1953-
I see the rhythm; paintings by Michele Wood; text by Toyomi Igus. Children's Bk. Press 1998 32p il $15.95 (4 and up)   **780.89**
1. African American music
ISBN 0-89239-151-0   LC 97-29310
Coretta Scott King award for illustration, 1999
Chronicles and captures poetically the history, mood, and movement of African American music
"The text, made up of free verse and music lyrics, incorporates different font sizes, shapes, and colors to underline the mood of each genre. . . . The colors of each full-page scenario underline the mood. . . This book celebrates music with art and words and successfully blends all three." SLJ

781   Music—General principles and musical forms

Sabbeth, Alex, 1950-
Rubber-band banjos and a java jive bass; projects and activities on the science of music and sound; project illustrations by Laurel Aiello. Wiley 1997 102p il pa $12.95 (4 and up)   **781**
1. Music 2. Sound 3. Musical instruments
ISBN 0-471-15675-2   LC 96-22144
This "presentation explores the world of sound and provides instructions for making musical instruments. Along the way, readers will learn about famous scientists who had musical inclinations. . . . Numerous, clear, pen-and-ink drawings illustrate the construction of instruments from a glass harmonica, to a violin, drums, and a foot-powered organ. . . . The scientific principles behind the creation of all the wonderful noises are explained, as is basic music notation." SLJ
Includes glossary

782.25   Sacred songs

All night, all day; a child's first book of African-American spirituals; selected and illustrated by Ashley Bryan; musical arrangements by David Manning Thomas. Atheneum Pubs. 1991 48p il music $16 **782.25**
1. Spirituals (Songs)
ISBN 0-689-31662-3   LC 90-753145
This is a "selection of 20 well-known spirituals." SLJ
"An exuberance of warm color and great variety in pattern and design distinguish the illustrations. . . . Excellent piano accompaniments and guitar chords further enrich the beautiful, wholly gratifying book." Horn Book

What a morning! the Christmas story in black spirituals; selected and edited by John Langstaff; illustrated by Ashley Bryan; arrangements for singing and piano by John Andrew Ross. Margaret K. McElderry Bks. 1987 unp il music hardcover o.p. paperback available $4.99

782.25

1. Spirituals (Songs)
ISBN 0-689-80807-0 (pa)   LC 87-750130

This "volume presents five black spirituals that celebrate the Christmas story. Langstaff has chosen 'Mary Had a Baby,' 'My Lord, What a Morning,' 'Go Tell it on the Mountain,' 'Sister Mary Had One Child,' and 'Behold That Star.'" Booklist

"Bryan's illustrations tie into the African-American theme, showing a black Holy family and multiracial wise men and shepherds. Bold brush strokes line each landscape and every garment. . . . This collection of songs exhibits an intimacy and compassion that give these spirituals a stunning universality." Publ Wkly

782.28   Carols

On Christmas Day in the morning; a traditional carol; illustrated by Melissa Sweet; foreword by John Langstaff. Candlewick Press 1999 unp il $15.99 (k-3)   **782.28**
1. English folk songs 2. Carols
ISBN 0-7636-0634-0   LC 98-51122

"The song upon which this book is based is actually called 'There was a pig went out to dig.'" Foreword

"Using a combination of watercolor, gouache and collage, the artist depicts 'a pig went out to dig,' 'a crow went out to sow' and a menagerie of other animal farmers. . . . Each spread is framed with a festive, gilded border and features a diminutive illustration of a different plant, the history and symbolism of which Sweet identifies in endnotes. Jolly and inventive." Publ Wkly

The **Twelve** days of Christmas   **782.28**
1. Carols

Some editions are:
Boyds Mills Press $14.95 Illustrated by John O'Brien (ISBN 1-56397-142-9)
HarperCollins Pubs. $15.95; lib bdg $15.89 Illustrated by Vladir Vagan (ISBN 0-06-027652-5; 0-06-028399-8)
Putnam pa $6.99 Illustrated by Jan Brett (ISBN 0-698-11569-4)
Simon & Schuster $15 Illustrated by Linnea Asplind Riley (ISBN 0-689-80275-7)

Illustrated versions of The Christmas carol in which a young woman's true love sends her extravagant gifts on each of the twelve days of Christmas

782.42   Songs

All the pretty little horses; a traditional lullaby; illustrated by Linda Saport. Clarion Bks. 1999 32p il music $15 (k-2)   **782.42**
1. Lullabies
ISBN 0-395-93097-9   LC 98-32129

A traditional lullaby presented with music, a note on the origin of the song, and pastel illustrations which reflect its possible connection to slaves in the American South

The "dreamy pastel illustrations in gorgeous color show an African American woman rocking her baby on the porch in the rural South long ago. . . . The magical realism is glowing and gentle. . . . With the music on the back page, this is sure to become a favorite version of a beautiful song." Booklist

Arroz con leche; popular songs and rhymes from Latin America; selected and illustrated by Lulu Delacre; English lyrics by Elena Paz; musical arrangements by Ana-María Rosado. Scholastic 1989 32p il music hardcover o.p. paperback available $4.99 (k-3)   **782.42**
1. Folk songs 2. Folklore—Latin America 3. Bilingual books—English-Spanish
ISBN 0-590-41886-6 (pa)

This is a bilingual collection of twelve folk songs and rhymes from Puerto Rico, Mexico and Argentina. Instructions for fingerplays and games accompany some of the songs. Musical arrangements for nine of the entries are included at the end of the book

"Delacre has selected lilting verses that are pleasing to the ear—ones likely to encourage non-Spanish-speakers to join in the fun. . . . Fresh, springlike colors brighten the pictures. . . . An author's note explains that many of the scenes depict real places." Booklist

Carle, Eric
Today is Monday; pictures by Eric Carle. Philomel Bks. 1993 unp il music $16.99; pa $6.99 (k-3)   **782.42**
1. Songs
ISBN 0-399-21966-8; 0-698-11563-5 (pa)
        LC 91-45866

Each day of the week brings a new food, until on Sunday all the world's children can come and eat it up

This song "gets new life in a picture book bursting with food, animals, and lots of energy. Beginning with the grinning cat on the cover . . . a zooful of animals act out the lyrics: snakes get tangled in spaghetti, elephants use their trunks to slurp 'Zoooop,' and pelicans catch fish on Friday. With text at a minimum, Carle's always innovative artwork steps center stage in an oversize format that allows gloriously colored collages to spread over two pages." Booklist

The **Children's** song index, 1978-1993; compiled by Kay Laughlin, Pollyanne Frantz, Ann Branton. Libraries Unlimited 1996 153p $37.50
        782.42
1. Songs—Indexes
ISBN 1-56308-332-9   LC 95-40236

"This book indexes more than 2,500 songs from 77 song books listed in *Cumulative Book Index, 1977-1994.* . . . [Songs are indexed] by song title, first line, or subject. . . . A quick reference tool for those who need to locate in which songbook a particular song can be found, this index encompasses songs appealing to children pre-kindergarten through middle school." Booklist

De colores and other Latin-American folk songs for children; selected, arranged, and translated by José-Luis Orozco; illustrated by Elisa Kleven. Dutton Children's Bks. 1994 56p il music $17.99; pa $6.99 (k-3)   **782.42**
1. Folk songs 2. Bilingual books—English-Spanish
ISBN 0-525-45260-5; 0-14-056548-5 (pa)

"Each of the 27 songs is presented with background notes; lyrics in both Spanish and English; simple arrangements for the voice, piano, and guitar; and suggestions for group sing-alongs and musical games. . . . The book is a delight for the eyes as well as the ear. . . . Kleven provides bountiful illustrations—the endpapers are sunshine bright with a crisp quilt of yellow flowers, and playful borders that ripple with colorful patterns and miniature pictures line the edge of every page." Booklist

Diez deditos. Ten little fingers & other play rhymes and action songs from Latin America; selected, arranged, and translated by José-Luis Orozco; illustrated by Elisa Kleven. Dutton Children's Bks. 1997 56p il music $18.99 (k-3)   **782.42**
1. Songs 2. Folklore—Latin America 3. Finger play 4. Bilingual books—English-Spanish
ISBN 0-525-45736-4

"This collection of fingerplays and action songs in Spanish and English comes with clear instructions for physical movements and simple musical notation. A brief sentence or paragraph introduces each entry. . . . Orozco's selections, some traditional, some written by himself, include versifications on such child-appealing subjects as dancing, singing, animals, weather, and food. . . . Kleven's collage illustrations practically pop off the pages with flashy colors and rich details that make each bustling composition a viewer's delight." Bull Cent Child Books

The **Farmer** in the dell; illustrated by Alexandra Wallner. Holiday House 1998 unp il music $15.95 (k-1)   **782.42**
1. Folk songs—United States
ISBN 0-8234-1382-9   LC 97-44206

An illustrated version of the traditional game song accompanied by music

"Wallner's primitive folk art sparkles with life, action, and energy. The colored pen-and-ink illustrations are packed with details." SLJ

Fishing for a dream; ocean lullabies and night verses; collected and illustrated by Kate Kiesler. Clarion Bks. 1999 29p il $16   **782.42**
1. Lullabies 2. Sea poetry 3. Poetry—Collections
ISBN 0-395-94149-0   LC 99-11182

A collection of lullabies centered on a theme of the sea, ships, and fishes

"This enchanting collection includes traditional lullabies such as 'Dance to Your Daddy' and classic poems such as Robert Louis Stevenson's 'My Bed Is a Boat', as well as more recent playful creations by Eve Merriam and Dahlov Ipcar. The gentle, muted colors in Kiesler's illustrations reinforce the calm, restful mood of the verses." SLJ

The **Fox** went out on a chilly night   **782.42**
1. Folk songs—United States

Available edition illustrated by Peter Spier pa $6.95 (ISBN 0-440-40829-6)

Set in New England, this old song tells about the trip the fox father made to town to get some of the farmer's plump geese for his family's dinner, and how he manages to evade the farmer who tries to shoot him

Spier's version is "a true picture book in the Caldecott-Brooke tradition. Fine drawings, lovely colors, and pictures so full of amusing details that young viewers will make fresh discoveries every time they . . . scrutinize these beautiful, action-filled pages." Horn Book

Go in and out the window; an illustrated songbook for young people; music arranged and edited by Dan Fox; commentary by Claude Marks. Metropolitan Mus. of Art; Holt & Co. 1987 144p il music $25.95   **782.42**
1. Songs
ISBN 0-8050-0628-1 (Holt)   LC 87-752208

"Sixty-one favorite songs . . . are presented alphabetically and illustrated with treasures from the Metropolitan Museum of Art. . . . The songs . . . are traditional rather than contemporary and come primarily from America and England, while the pictures, jewelry, sculpture, photographs, and so forth span 5,000 years of worldwide art." Booklist

"Imaginative and luxurious, the volume should stimulate and challenge the adult to deepen the awareness and broaden the aesthetic horizons of the young." Horn Book

Gonna sing my head off! American folk songs for children; collected and arranged by Kathleen Krull; illustrated by Allen Garns; introductory note by Arlo Guthrie. Knopf 1992 145p il music hardcover o.p. paperback available $12 **782.42**
1. Folk songs—United States
ISBN 0-679-87232-9 (pa)   LC 89-49562

"Work songs, love songs, ballads and blues, lullabies, spirituals, protest songs, and sheer nonsense make up this entertaining collection of 62 traditional and contemporary favorites. For each song, Krull provides the simplest piano and guitar arrangements in a clear double-page spread design that includes the words to all the verses. . . . The exuberant illustrations, mostly in bright pastels, manage to be both familiar and dramatic. . . . Informal notes at the head of each song give something about history, origin, performance, and possibilities for variation." Booklist

Guthrie, Woody, 1912-1967
Howdi do; pictures by Vladimir Radunsky. Candlewick Press 2000 unp il $12.99 (k-2)   **782.42**
1. Songs
ISBN 0-7636-0768-1   LC 99-34258
Includes audio CD

An illustrated version of the song about shaking hands as a friendly way to greet "everybody that I meet"

This "is a bouncy choice to share with young children. . . . Radunsky's bright, blocky collages, showing gregarious people and animals meeting and greeting, are a winning match for Guthrie's lyrics." Horn Book Guide

Guthrie, Woody, 1912-1967—*Continued*

This land is your land; words and music by Woody Guthrie; paintings by Kathy Jakobsen; with a tribute by Pete Seeger. Little, Brown 1998 unp il music $15.95 (k-3)   **782.42**
1. Songs

ISBN 0-316-39215-4   LC 96-54628

"The song is a paean to America's beautiful geography and landscapes, the diversity of its inhabitants, and the indomitable spirit of the American people. Here the complete lyrics serve as the book's main text and are brought to life by stunning, vibrant folk-art illustrations of the people and places of America, coast to coast and past to present. . . . A complete musical notation is included, as is a tribute to Guthrie written by folksinger Pete Seeger. The biographical scrapbook at the book's end is both fascinating and informative." Booklist

Hillenbrand, Will

Down by the station. Harcourt Brace & Co. 1999 unp il music $15 (k-2)   **782.42**
1. Songs

ISBN 0-15-201804-2   LC 98-41770
"Gulliver books"

In this version of a familiar song, baby animals ride to the children's zoo on the zoo train

"This twist on an old favorite combines sunny illustrations, playful humor, and appealing animals." SLJ

Hoberman, Mary Ann, 1930-

The eensy-weensy spider; adapted by Mary Ann Hoberman; illustrated by Nadine Bernard Westcott. Little, Brown 2000 unp il music $12.95 (k-3)   **782.42**
1. Songs 2. Finger play

ISBN 0-316-36330-8   LC 99-25701
An expanded version of the familiar children's finger-play rhyme describing what the little spider does after being washed out of the water-spout

"Whimsical, watercolor cartoons capture the light-hearted tone of the verse. . . . This sprightly adaptation lends itself to singing aloud and is sure to be a hit." SLJ

Hort, Lenny

The seals on the bus; illustrated by G. Brian Karas. Holt & Co. 2000 unp il $15.95 (k-2)   **782.42**
1. Songs

ISBN 0-8050-5952-0   LC 99-33612
Different animals—including seals, tigers, geese, rabbits, monkeys, and more—make their own sounds as they ride all around the town on a bus

"Karas' artwork combines cut paper, gouache, acrylic, and pencil to create a series of pleasingly varied scenes of cheerful chaos. A good story hour choice." Booklist

How sweet the sound: African-American songs for children; selected by Wade and Cheryl Hudson; illustrated by Floyd Cooper. Scholastic 1995 48p il music $15.95 (k-3)   **782.42**
1. Songs 2. African American music

ISBN 0-590-48030-8   LC 95-2406

"The lyrics of twenty-three African-American songs are illustrated with pastel drawings that depict peaceful scenes with quiet, muted colors. Included are spirituals and traditional songs, as well as more recent compositions by Huddie Ledbetter, James Brown, and Stevie Wonder. The melodies and guitar chords are provided in the back, with a few sentences about each song's origins." Horn Book Guide

Includes bibliographical references

Hush, little baby; a folk song; with pictures by Mark Frazee. Harcourt Brace & Co. 1999 unp il music $15 (k-2)   **782.42**
1. Folk songs—United States 2. Lullabies

ISBN 0-15-201429-2   LC 98-9608
In an old lullaby a baby is promised an assortment of presents from its adoring parent

"True to the song's Appalachian roots, Frazee sets the traditional lullaby in the hills of West Virginia, with big, detailed pictures that add character and exaggerated sibling rivalry to the nonsense story. . . . The music is on the last page, and Frazee's clear narrative pictures in acrylics and pencil capture the rhythm of the words, the historic particulars of the place, the nighttime farce, and the universal family scenarios of jealousy and love." Booklist

Johnson, James Weldon, 1871-1938

Lift every voice and sing   **782.42**
1. African American music 2. Songs

Available edition illustrated by Elizabeth Catlett $14.95 (ISBN 0-8027-8250-7)
Illustrated version of the song that has come to be considered the African American national anthem

"Ms Catlett's woodcuts, done in the 1940's, are a perfect complement to the text and help make this a book to be treasured for generations to come." Child Book Rev Serv

Kellogg, Steven, 1941-

A-hunting we will go! Morrow Junior Bks. 1998 unp il music $16; lib bdg $16; pa $5.95 (k-2)   **782.42**
1. Songs

ISBN 0-688-14944-8; 0-688-14945-6 (lib bdg); 0-06-443747-7 (pa)   LC 97-47296
In this modern version of the children's song, preparations for bedtime include "A-reading we will go, Now to the bath we go! Now off to bed we go!" Printed music on lining papers

"Children will appreciate all of the clever details. The cheery rhyming text and funny dialogue balloons beg to be shared aloud. An author's note comments on the history and variations of the song. A sing-out-loud bedtime romp." SLJ

Key, Francis Scott, 1779-1843

The Star-Spangled Banner   **782.42**
1. Star spangled banner (Song) 2. National songs—United States

Key, Francis Scott, 1779-1843—*Continued*

Some editions are:

Applewood Bks. $14.95 Illustrated by Ingri and Edgar Parin D'Aulaire (ISBN 1-557-09390-3)

Dell pa $10.95 Illustrated by Peter Spier (ISBN 0-440-40697-8)

Illustrated versions of Frances Scott Key's text for our national anthem

Kovalski, Maryann, 1951-

The wheels on the bus. Little, Brown 1987 unp il music hardcover o.p. paperback available $4.95 (k-2)   **782.42**

1. Songs

ISBN 0-316-50259-6 (pa)   LC 87-3441

"Joy Street books"

In this adaptation of a traditional children's song, "a long wait at the bus stop precipitates a suggestion from a grandmother that she and her two grandchildren pass the time by singing 'The Wheels on the Bus.' . . . Kovalski expertly conveys the spirit with which people sing this song. . . . The action of the song is followed through in detail, flowing from page to page with a cast of assorted characters depicted in watercolor with pencil illustrations." SLJ

Kroll, Steven

By the dawn's early light; the story of the Star spangled banner; illustrated by Dan Andreasen. Scholastic 1994 40p il maps music hardcover o.p. paperback available $5.99 (3-5)   **782.42**

1. Key, Francis Scott, 1779-1843 2. Star spangled banner (Song) 3. War of 1812

ISBN 0-590-45055-7 (pa)   LC 92-27101

This is an account of the events that led Francis Scott Key to compose the United States national anthem, during the War of 1812

"Handsome full-page oil paintings in warm golden tones blend nineteenth-century romance with twentieth-century realism. . . . Kroll's details of this dramatic story match those told at Fort McHenry today; judicious use of dialogue moves the story along while remaining true to the facts." Bull Cent Child Books

Includes bibliographical references

Langstaff, John M., 1920-

Frog went a-courtin'; retold by John Langstaff; with pictures by Feodor Rojankovsky. Harcourt Brace Jovanovich 1955 unp il music $16; pa $7 (k-3)   **782.42**

1. Folk songs

ISBN 0-15-230214-X; 0-15-633900-5 (pa)

"Retelling of a merry old Scottish ballad with many-colored illustrations about the marriage between Mr. Frog and Miss Mouse. A composite American version set to Appalachian mountain music." Chicago Public Libr

Oh, a-hunting we will go; [by] John Langstaff; pictures by Nancy Winslow Parker. Atheneum Pubs. 1974 unp il music hardcover o.p. paperback available $5.99 (k-2)   **782.42**

1. Folk songs

ISBN 0-689-71503-X (pa)

"A Margaret K. McElderry book"

The nonsense verses of this folk song trace the hunt for such animals as an armadillo, a fox, and a snake, and describe the imagined treatment of each animal once it is caught

"The 12 stanzas are complemented by Parker's droll crayon illustrations (the fox caught in the box is watching TV), and a score for guitar and piano is appended. An amusing addition to 'song' picture books." SLJ

Over in the meadow; with pictures by Feodor Rojankovsky. Harcourt Brace & Co. 1957 unp il music $16; pa $7 (k-2)   **782.42**

1. Folk songs 2. Counting

ISBN 0-15-258854-X; 0-15-670500-1 (pa)

"This old counting rhyme tells of ten meadow families whose mothers advise them to dig, run, sing, play, hum, build, swim, wink, spin and hop. The illustrations, half in full color, show the combination of realism and imagination which little children like best. The tune, arranged simply, is on the last page, and children will have fun acting the whole thing out." Horn Book

Leodhas, Sorche Nic, 1898-1968

Always room for one more; illustrated by Nonny Hogrogian. Holt & Co. 1965 unp il music $14.95; pa $5.95 (k-3)   **782.42**

1. Folk songs

ISBN 0-8050-0331-2; 0-8050-0330-4 (pa)

Awarded the Caldecott Medal, 1966

"A picture book based on an old Scottish folk song about hospitable Lachie MacLachlan, who invited in so many guests that his little house finally burst. Rhymed text . . . a glossary of Scottish words, and music for the tune are combined into an effective whole." Hodges. Books for Elem Sch Libr

MacDonald, Margaret Read

The round book; rounds kids love to sing; by Margaret Read MacDonald and Winifred Jaeger; illustrated by Yvonne LeBrun Davis. Linnet Bks. 1999 121p il music $22.50; pa $16.50   **782.42**

1. Songs

ISBN 0-208-02441-7; 0-208-02472-7 (pa)

"Eighty rounds for choral singing from the sixteenth to twentieth centuries are presented in this easy-to-follow resource book. . . . If you can already read music this is a handy source, and even novice sight readers will have little difficulty with these selections. The musical notation is beginner-basic, with the times clearly marked." Bull Cent Child Books

Mallett, David

Inch by inch; the garden song; pictures by Ora Eitan. HarperCollins Pubs. 1995 unp il music hardcover o.p. paperback available $5.95 (k-2)   **782.42**

1. Songs 2. Gardens

ISBN 0-06-443481-8 (pa)   LC 93-38352

"In this picture-book version of the song first published in 1975 . . . a young child plants seeds . . . weeds and tends them, and finally, gleans a bountiful harvest. . . . Employing a variety of media including cut paper, Eitan uses color and space to create a striking effect." SLJ

Medearis, Angela Shelf, 1956-

The zebra-riding cowboy; a folk song from the Old West; collected by Angela Shelf Medearis; illustrated by María Cristina Brusca. Holt & Co. 1992 unp il music hardcover o.p. paperback available $5.95 (k-3)   **782.42**

    1. Cowhands—Songs

    ISBN 0-8050-5302-6 (pa)   LC 91-27941

In this Western folk song, an educated fellow mistaken for a greenhorn proves his cowboy ability by riding a wild horse. Includes a discussion of Afro-American and Hispanic cowboys in the nineteenth century

"Brusca's color drawings burst with energy as she portrays the tough cowboys—whites, Hispanics, and African Americans—in the Wild West setting. The angular quality of the drawings communicates the harsh life of these hardworking men." Booklist

Old MacDonald had a farm   **782.42**

    1. Folk songs—United States

Some editions are:

Houghton Mifflin $15; pa $5.95 Illustrated by Carol Jones (ISBN 0-395-49212-2; 0-395-90125-1)

North-South Bks. lib bdg $14.88; pa $6.95 Illustrated by Holly Berry (ISBN 0-55858-282-7; 1-55858-703-9)

Scholastic Press $15.95 Illustrated by Amy Schwartz (ISBN 0-590-46189-3) Has title: Old MacDonald

Illustrated versions of the American folk song in which the inhabitants of Old MacDonald's farm are described, verse by verse

Priceman, Marjorie

Froggie went a-courting. Little, Brown 2000 unp il $14.95 (k-3)   **782.42**

    1. Folk songs 2. New York (N.Y.)—Fiction

    ISBN 0-316-71227-2   LC 99-25703

An updated version of the familiar folk song about the courtship and wedding of Frog and Ms. Mouse, set in New York City

"The humor lies primarily in knowing how different this version of the folksong is from more traditional ones. Priceman's lively, colorful paintings spill off the pages and appropriately reflect the celebratory atmosphere of the rhyming text." Horn Book Guide

Raffi

Baby Beluga; illustrated by Ashley Wolff. Crown 1990 unp il music (Raffi songs to read) hardcover o.p. paperback available $5.99 (k-2)   **782.42**

    1. Songs

    ISBN 0-517-58362-3 (pa)   LC 89-49367

    Also available Board book edition

Presents the illustrated text to the song about the little white whale who swims wild and free

"Wolff's striking double-page spreads show the young whale among its fellow Arctic Sea inhabitants. Diversifying her views, the illustrator eyes Baby Beluga and mother swimming together underwater; takes an aerial angle, looking down on the whales from a puffin's perspective; and observes the icy yet welcoming formations where seals, polar bears, and an Eskimo find shelter. . . . An inviting approach to reading encouragement." Booklist

Down by the bay; illustrated by Nadine Bernard Westcott. Crown 1987 unp il music (Raffi songs to read) hardcover o.p. paperback available $6.99 (k-2)   **782.42**

    1. Songs

    ISBN 0-517-56645-1 (pa)   LC 87-750291

    Also available Board book edition

This illustrated version of one of Raffi's songs depicts a variety of unusual sights to be seen "down by the bay"

The "cheerful nonsense verses are illustrated with equal cheer. Westcott's scraggly lines and bright, clear colors humorously portray the busy children, jolly animals, and frantic mothers that populate the song." SLJ

Five little ducks; illustrated by Jose Aruego and Ariane Dewey. Crown 1989 unp il music (Raffi songs to read) hardcover o.p. paperback available $5.99 (k-2)   **782.42**

    1. Songs

    ISBN 0-517-58360-7 (pa)   LC 88-3752

    Also available Board book edition

"In bold colors and uncluttered spreads, Aruego and Dewey present Mother Duck and her five ducklings waddling 'over the hills and far away'. . . . But after each outing, one less duckling returns until all have left the nest. Come spring, however, Mother is greeted by all five youngsters returning with their own quacking broods." Booklist

One light, one sun; illustrated by Eugenie Fernandes. Crown 1988 unp il music (Raffi songs to read) hardcover o.p. paperback available $6.50 (k-2)   **782.42**

    1. Songs

    ISBN 0-517-57644-9 (pa)   LC 87-22256

This book "describes how some things are shared by everyone in the world. The illustrations capture this theme by showing three different families engaged in similar daily activities (playing, mealtime, bedtime, etc.). Brightly colored illustrations depict a single parent family, a handicapped child, and an extended family living under one roof. The words of the song are set apart from the pictures, making it easy to read or sing along as the pages are turned." SLJ

Reid, Rob

Children's jukebox; a subject guide to musical recordings and programming ideas for songsters ages one to twelve. American Lib. Assn. 1995 225p il pa $25   **782.42**

    1. Songs—Indexes 2. Sound recordings—Indexes 3. Children's libraries

    ISBN 0-8389-0650-8   LC 95-6163

"Arranging selections into 35 categories reflecting 'popular themes for story programs and classroom use,' Reid has assembled 300 recordings, graded (preschool, primary, intermediate, all) for children ages 2 through 12. An alphabetically arranged discography and a selection of Reid's 'top twenty' suggestions for a core collection precede the thematic listings. . . . The annotations, which are arranged by broad subject—for example, animals, bath time, growing up, imagination—are short, informal, and spunky." Booklist

Includes bibliographical references

Seeger, Ruth Crawford, 1901-1953

Animal folk songs for children; traditional American songs; illustrated by Barbara Cooney. Linnet Bks. 1993 80p il music hardcover o.p. paperback available $17.50   **782.42**

1. Folk songs—United States 2. Animals

ISBN 0-208-02365-8 (pa)   LC 92-767692

A reissue of the title first published 1950 by Doubleday

Illustrated with black and white drawings, this is a collection of forty-three traditional songs arranged for piano

Songs of the Wild West; commentary by Alan Axelrod; arrangements by Dan Fox. Metropolitan Mus. of Art; Simon & Schuster Bks. for Young Readers 1991 128p il music $19.95   **782.42**

1. Cowhands—Songs 2. Folk songs—United States

ISBN 0-671-74775-4 (Simon & Schuster)

At head of title: The Metropolitan Museum of Art, in association with the Buffalo Bill Historical Center

"Axelrod combines 45 songs of the Old West with works of art from the Metropolitan Museum of Art and the Buffalo Bill Historical Center to create a nostalgic picture of cowboys and western settlers. . . . Each score is lavishly illustrated with memorable western art and introduced by a brief essay linking the song with art and history. A beautifully designed book that will appeal to armchair browsers as well as students researching the westward movement through its music and art." Booklist

Staines, Bill

All God's critters got a place in the choir; words and music by Bill Staines; pictures by Margot Zemach. Dutton 1989 unp il music hardcover o.p. paperback available $6.99 (k-2)
                782.42

1. Songs 2. Animals

ISBN 0-14-054838-6 (pa)   LC 88-31696

Also available in paperback from Puffin Bks.

This is an illustrated version of the children's song about musical animals. The score is included at the end of the volume

"While the noise of the animals' brays, moos, and quacks will be more fun when led and encouraged by a skilled folk singer, the rollicking, good-natured illustrations provide plenty of amusement for those who just want to look." Horn Book

Taback, Simms, 1932-

There was an old lady who swallowed a fly. Viking 1997 unp il $15.99   **782.42**

1. Folk songs

ISBN 0-670-86939-2

Also available Little, Brown paperback edition by Nadine Bernard Westcott with title: I know an old lady who swallowed a fly

A Caldecott Medal honor book, 1998

Simms Taback's illustrated version of the folk song in which an old lady swallows a variety of progressively larger animals

"Each page is full of details and humorous asides.

. . . A die-cut hole allows readers to see inside [the old lady's] belly, first the critters already devoured and, with the turn of the page, the new animal that will join the crowd in her ever-expanding stomach. . . . The text is handwritten on vivid strips of paper that are loosely placed on the patterned page, thus creating a lively interplay between the meaning of the words and their visual power." SLJ

Whippo, Walt

Little white duck; lyrics by Walt Whippo; music by Bernard Zaritzky; illustrations by Joan Paley. Little, Brown 2000 unp il music $13.95 (k-2)
                782.42

1. Songs

ISBN 0-316-03227-1   LC 99-13661

Based on the song of the same title, a little white duck causes a commotion in its pond

This song "gets a modern update courtesy of vibrant collage illustrations. Each verse of the song is sung by a small, brown mouse troubadour. . . . The illustrations are done in bright and beautiful shades of red, blue, and green." Booklist

Ziefert, Harriet

When I first came to this land; retold by Harriet Ziefert; pictures by Simms Taback. Putnam 1998 unp il $15.99; pa $5.99 (k-2)   **782.42**

1. Folk songs—United States

ISBN 0-399-23044-0; 0-698-11838-3 (pa)

          LC 97-9612

Illustrations and words to a traditional song describe the adventures of a pioneer who buys a farm and builds life for himself and his family

"The cumulative rhyme is accompanied by folk-art-style paintings with black outlines and bright, glowing colors and patterns. The humorous characters fairly float across the pages." Horn Book Guide

784.19   Musical instruments

Ardley, Neil, 1937-

Music. Knopf 1989 63p il (Eyewitness books) (4 and up)   **784.19**

1. Musical instruments

          LC 88-13394

Available DK Pub. edition $15.95; $19.99 lib bdg (ISBN 0-7894-5828-4; 0-789-4-6561-2)

Text and pictures introduce musical instruments from early times to the present—from pipes and flutes to electronic synthesizers

"Interesting historical asides and highlights about famous musicians contrast with the precisely labeled parts of the numerous illustrated instruments." Booklist

784.2 Symphony orchestra

Ganeri, Anita, 1961-
The young person's guide to the orchestra; Benjamin Britten's composition on CD narrated by Ben Kingsley; book written by Anita Ganeri. Harcourt Brace & Co. 1996 56p il $25 (4-6)

784.2

1. Orchestra 2. Musical instruments 3. Music appreciation
ISBN 0-15-201304-0   LC 95-41478
"Accompanying this book on orchestral music is a CD featuring Britten's *A Young Person's Guide to the Orchestra . . .* as well as Dukas' *The Sorcerer's Apprentice.* The book begins with an overview of the orchestra and then centers around groups of instruments, explaining a bit of their history and their sound's distinctive quality. . . . The book also introduces eight famous composers, world music, Benjamin Britten, and the background of *The Young Person's Guide to the Orchestra.* . . . Handsome and useful." Booklist
Includes glossary

Hayes, Ann
Meet the orchestra; written by Ann Hayes; illustrated by Karmen Thompson. Harcourt Brace Jovanovich 1990 unp il $16; pa $6 (k-3) **784.2**
1. Orchestra 2. Musical instruments
ISBN 0-15-200526-9; 0-15-200222-7 (pa)
LC 89-32959
Also available Spanish language edition
"Gulliver books"
Describes the features, sounds, and role of each musical instrument in the orchestra
"Spacious watercolors depicting animal musicians in formal evening dress enhance this charming introduction to the orchestra. . . . The descriptive writing has immediacy . . . while the artwork has a subtle sense of color and humor that increases the fun." Booklist

Koscielniak, Bruce
The story of the incredible orchestra; an introduction to musical instruments and the symphony orchestra. Houghton Mifflin 2000 unp il $15 (2-4)   **784.2**
1. Orchestra 2. Musical instruments
ISBN 0-395-96052-5   LC 98-43933
Describes the orchestra, the families of instruments of which it is made, and the individual instruments in each family
"The illustrations are dense with gentle color and filled with scenes of musicians at play and pictures of instruments, with banner labels adding more information. . . . A lot of information about who invented what and how it's played is packed into these engaging pages." Booklist

790.1 Recreational activities

Drake, Jane
The kids' summer handbook; by Jane Drake & Ann Love; illustrated by Heather Collins. Ticknor & Fields Bks. for Young Readers 1994 c1993 207p il hardcover o.p. paperback available $10.95 (4 and up)   **790.1**
1. Recreation 2. Handicraft 3. Nature craft
ISBN 0-395-68709-8 (pa)   LC 93-2524
First published 1993 in Canada with title: The kids cottage book
"Beach games, water safety, hiking and camping, wild-animal watching, snacks, and crafts are among the many outdoor and indoor activities covered in the thick volume. Most topics are introduced in two-page entries, with detailed directions and plentiful, homely drawings. The practical volume will interest children, parents, and teachers." Horn Book Guide

Love, Ann, 1947-
Kids and grandparents: an activity book; written by Ann Love & Jane Drake; illustrated by Heather Collins. Kids Can Press 2000 160p il $17.95; pa $10.95 (3-6)   **790.1**
1. Amusements
ISBN 1-550-74784-3; 1-550-74492-5 (pa)
First published 1999 in Canada
"A collection of more than 90 games, crafts, recipes, and activities for children to do with their grandparents. . . . A good choice for old-fashioned fun." SLJ

Williamson, Susan, 1944-
Summer fun! 60 activities for a kid-perfect summer; illustrations by Michael Kline. Williamson 1999 138p il pa $12.95   **790.1**
1. Amusements 2. Games 3. Handicraft
ISBN 1-885593-33-3   LC 98-53269
"A Williamson kids can! book"
Suggests a variety of activities for summertime, including nature study, cooking, crafts, games, creative activities, and more
"The 60 activities promised in the title hark back to a slower, quieter time. . . . The black-and-white cartoons that appear on each page add to the fun." SLJ

791.3 Circuses

Granfield, Linda
Circus; an album. DK Ink 1998 96p il $19.95; pa $10.95 (4 and up)   **791.3**
1. Circus
ISBN 0-7894-2453-3; 0-7894-2661-7 (pa)
LC 97-33523
First published 1997 in Canada
Traces the history of circuses from the time of ancient Egypt and Greece through their evolution in eighteenth-century Europe to the spectacles created by P.T. Barnum and other modern-day showmen
"Each page is a colorful montage of old photographs, postcards, period illustrations, posters, ticket stubs, rhymes and the like. Difficult to put down." Publ Wkly

Perkins, Catherine

The most excellent book of how to be a clown. Copper Beech Bks. 1996 32p il lib bdg $21.90; pa $6.95 (4-6)   **791.3**

1. Clowns

ISBN 0-7613-0486-X (lib bdg); 0-7613-0499-1 (pa)
                                          LC 95-47142

Provides information on such topics as: designing costumes and makeup, preparing a routine, performing stunts, and interacting with the audience

"Costuming, makeup, props, and acting tips, illustrated with clear color photographs, will readily engage the novice entertainer." Horn Book Guide

Includes glossary

791.43   Motion pictures

Hamilton, Jake

Special effects in film and television; written by Jake Hamilton. DK Pub. 1998 63p il $17.95 (4 and up)   **791.43**

1. Cinematography 2. Animation (Cinematography)

ISBN 0-7894-2813-X   LC 97-43121

Presents a behind-the-scenes look at some of the magic of the movies including the puppetry techniques used in ET, the animation in Toy Story, and much more

"Packed with lots of great movie stills, this introduction is a dazzling, but cursory, look behind the scenes. . . . Readers will be informed and possibly inspired." SLJ

Reynolds, David West

Star wars: incredible cross sections; illustrated by Hans Jenssen & Richard Chasemore. DK Pub. 1998 32p il $19.95   **791.43**

1. Star Wars films

ISBN 0-7894-3480-6   LC 98-22878

This book "includes diagrams for the *Millennium Falcon,* T-65 X-wing, Blockade Runner, Tie Fighters, Sandcrawler, and BLT-A4 Y-wing, among others. An elaborate four-page fold-out analyzes the Death Star in minute detail. . . . AT-AT Walkers, AT-STs, snowspeeders, and speeder bikes are also included. Diagrams are surrounded by inserts of fascinating trivia, history, and technical notes." Voice Youth Advocates

Star wars: the visual dictionary; written by David West Reynolds; special fabrications by Don Bies and Nelson Hall; new photography by Alexander Ivanov. DK Pub. 1998 64p il $19.95
                                          791.43

1. Star Wars films

ISBN 0-7894-3481-4   LC 98-22877

"This oversized volume is packed with full-color photographs of the characters and costumes, equipment, weaponry, mechanical droids, and assorted creatures from the *Star Wars* universe. . . . 'Data Files' provide additional, often fascinating, and personal tidbits about the inhabitants of this fantasy world. . . . It is a visual treat." SLJ

791.45   Television

Bentley, Nancy

The young producer's video book; how to write, direct, and shoot your own video; by Nancy Bentley, and Donna W. Guthrie; illustrated by Katy Keck Arnsteen. Millbrook Press 1995 64p il lib bdg $21.90 (4-6)   **791.45**

1. Video recording

ISBN 1-56294-566-1 (lib bdg)   LC 94-48300

"How to make a video, from idea to finished product, is presented in short, precise text and clever cartoons. The authors have efficiently outlined the stages of development, including planning, production, and editing, giving step-by-step instructions for each level and providing sample storyboard forms and camera sheets." SLJ

791.5   Puppetry and toy theaters

Briggs, Diane

101 fingerplays, stories, and songs to use with finger puppets. American Lib. Assn. 1999 129p il pa $25   **791.5**

1. Finger play 2. Puppets and puppet plays

ISBN 0-8389-0749-0   LC 98-42136

"Briggs gathers fun fingerplays to use primarily with finger puppets, although they can easily be adapted for use with stick puppets or flannel-board stories. The author also provides simple, traceable patterns to make the puppets and relates them to more than 350 books." SLJ

Includes discography and bibliographical references

Minkel, Walter

How to do "The three bears" with two hands; performing with puppets. American Lib. Assn. 2000 154p il pa $28   **791.5**

1. Puppets and puppet plays 2. Children's libraries

ISBN 0-8389-0756-3   LC 99-28228

This guide to performing puppet plays in libraries offers advice on such topics as voice control and manipulation technique, script writing and adaptation, puppets, stages, scenery and props, and includes five puppet show scripts and stage-building plans

Includes bibliographical references

792   Stage presentations

Bentley, Nancy

Putting on a play; the young playwright's guide to scripting, directing, and performing; [by] Nancy Bentley and Donna Guthrie; illustrated by Katy Keck Arnsteen. Millbrook Press 1996 64p il $23.40 (4-6)   **792**

1. Theater—Production and direction 2. Authorship

ISBN 0-7613-0011-2   LC 95-47543

A step-by-step guide for the playwright including suggestions for finding a story, writing a script, producing a play, and performing it on stage. Includes sample plays

"Budding thespians will find a wealth of good ideas in this clear and concise step-by-step guide." SLJ

792.09 Theater—Historical and geographic treatment

Aliki

William Shakespeare & the Globe; written & illustrated by Aliki. HarperCollins Pubs. 1999 48p il $15.95; lib bdg $15.89; pa $6.95 (3-6) **792.09**

1. Shakespeare, William, 1564-1616 2. Globe Theatre (London, England) 3. Shakespeare's Globe (London, England)

ISBN 0-06-027820-X; 0-06-027821-8 (lib bdg); 0-06-443722-1 (pa) LC 98-7903

The "text describes Shakespeare's life, the Elizabethan world and entertainments, and the ups and downs of the theatrical industry . . . including tidbits such as the Burbage brothers' piece-by-piece theft of the original Globe Theatre. A fast-forward to the twentieth century then treats Sam Wanamaker's dream of making the Globe rise again." Bull Cent Child Books

"A logically organized and engaging text, plenty of detailed illustrations with informative captions, and a clean design provide a fine introduction to both bard and theater." Horn Book Guide

792.5 Opera

Price, Leontyne

Aïda; as told by Leontyne Price; illustrated by Leo and Diane Dillon. Harcourt Brace Jovanovich 1990 unp il $19; pa $8 (4 and up) **792.5**

1. Opera—Stories, plots, etc.

ISBN 0-15-200405-X; 0-15-200987-6 (pa) LC 89-36481

Coretta Scott King Award for illustration, 1990

"Gulliver books"

"Based on the opera by Giuseppi Verdi"

Tragedy results when an enslaved Ethiopian princess falls in love with an Egyptian general

"The text appears on the left surmounted by a friezelike series of figures which interpret the action; on the right, a full-page illustration focuses on a particular character or grouping. A worthy introduction to the opera for a varied audience." Horn Book Guide

Rosenberg, Jane, 1949-

Sing me a story; the Metropolitan Opera's book of opera stories for children; introduction by Luciano Pavarotti. Thames & Hudson 1989 158p il hardcover o.p. paperback available $15.95 (4-6) **792.5**

1. Opera—Stories, plots, etc.

ISBN 0-500-27873-3 (pa) LC 88-51929

"Alongside the so-called ABC's—*Aida, La Boheme* and *Carmen*—are less often performed works such as *L'Enfant et les Sortileges, Porgy and Bess* and *The Love for Three Oranges*. The author skillfully refers to specific musical passages and uses dialogue drawn from the libretto to link each story to an actual performance. . . . Although brief accounts in general cannot do justice to the deep emotion and psychological insight of *Pagliacci* or *The Magic Flute*, these failings are more than redeemed by Rosenberg's handsomely detailed watercolors, which convey the opulent sensuality of opera at its most sublime." Publ Wkly

792.8 Ballet and modern dance

Bussell, Darcey

Ballet. Dorling Kindersley 2000 45p il $9.95 (4 and up) **792.8**

1. Ballet

ISBN 0-7894-5429-7 LC 99-51700

"DK superguides"

Replaces The young dancer, published 1994

The author, a professional ballerina, introduces the art of ballet, from the basic positions, poses, jumps, and exercises to folk and character dancing, makeup, choreography, and performing on stage

Castle, Kate

My ballet book; written by Kate Castle. DK Pub. 1998 61p il $15.95 (4 and up) **792.8**

1. Ballet

ISBN 0-7894-3432-6 LC 98-22803

Introduces the world of ballet and presents its notable stories, dancers, techniques, and routines

"Young balletomanes will pore over every detail of this colorful volume. . . . This book is copiously illustrated with photographs reflecting all manner of details about the art form." SLJ

Includes glossary

Fonteyn, Dame Margot, 1919-1991

Coppélia; as told by Margot Fonteyn; paintings by Steve Johnson and Lou Fancher. Harcourt Brace & Co. 1998 unp il $17; lib bdg $25.69 (3-5) **792.8**

1. Coppélia (Ballet) 2. Fairy tales 3. Dolls—Fiction

ISBN 0-15-200428-9; 0-8172-5740-3 (lib bdg) LC 95-52468

"Gulliver books"

A dollmaker cleverly schemes to pass his most beautiful doll off as a real girl, but he is outwitted by the townspeople he tries to deceive

"Having danced the starring role many times, Fonteyn has developed a wonderful feel for the characters' personalities. . . . Historical notes at the end of the book are brief but highly interesting. The lovely paintings are full of depth and texture enhanced with pieces of richly patterned fabric." SLJ

Grau, Andrée

Dance; written by Andrée Grau. Knopf 1998 59p il (Eyewitness books) (4 and up) **792.8**

1. Dance

LC 98-17269

Available DK Pub. edition $15.95; $19.99 lib bdg (ISBN 0-7894-5876-4; 0-7894-6625-2)

Surveys all forms of dance throughout the world, discussing its cultural and social significance, its costume, its history, and noted dancers and choreographers

Jones, Bill T.

Dance; written by Bill T. Jones and Susan Kuklin; photographed by Susan Kuklin. Hyperion Bks. for Children 1998 unp il $14.95; lib bdg $15.49 (k-3)   **792.8**

1. Dance

ISBN 0-7868-0362-2; 0-7868-2307-0 (lib bdg)

LC 97-32375

Introduces basic concepts of dance through poetic text and photographs

"This celebration of dance combines Kuklin's luminous photography with Jones' spare but lyrical first-person narrative to create a sense of three-dimensional movement arrested in space." Bull Cent Child Books

McCaughrean, Geraldine, 1951-

The Random House book of stories from the ballet; retold by Geraldine McCaughrean; illustrated by Angela Barrett. Random House 1995 c1994 112p il $20 (4 and up)   **792.8**

1. Ballet—Stories, plots, etc.

ISBN 0-679-87125-X   LC 94-22640

First published 1994 in the United Kingdom with title: The Orchard book of stories from the ballet

Contents: Swan Lake; Coppelia; Giselle; Cinderella; La Sylphide; The nutcracker; Romeo and Juliet; The firebird; Petrouchka; The sleeping beauty

"Dramatic plots, unusual characters, and magical spells are interwoven into each of the well-written retellings. The essence of a ballet production is successfully captured by the full-color illustrations." Booklist

Newman, Barbara

The illustrated book of ballet stories; written by Barbara Newman; illustrated by Gill Tomblin; with an introduction by Darcy Bussell. DK Pub. 1997 64p il $19.95; pa $7.95 (4-6)   **792.8**

1. Ballet—Stories, plots, etc.

ISBN 0-7894-2024-4; 0-7894-5466-1 (pa)

LC 97-15462

Also available without CD for $15.95 (ISBN 0-7894-2225-5)

In story and illustrations, presents five classic ballets: Giselle, Coppelia, Sleeping Beauty, The Nutcracker, and Swan Lake. Includes photographs from Royal Ballet productions, and is accompanied by an audio CD

"The storytelling is lively, the comments are insightful. . . . Featuring 18 selections from the five ballets, the CD provides an excellent recording of the music." Booklist

Includes glossary

Varriale, Jim

Kids dance; the students of Ballet Tech; text and photographs by Jim Varriale; with a foreword by Eliot Feld. Dutton Children's Bks. 1999 unp il $15.99 (4 and up)   **792.8**

1. Ballet Tech School (New York, N.Y.) 2. Ballet

ISBN 0-525-45536-1   LC 98-55905

Explains the rules, admissions process, academic classes, training exercises, and performances of Ballet Tech, America's first public school offering free ballet

lessons for children

"The full-color and black-and-white photos depict ethnically and racially diverse groups of children and a broad range of ages. The young dancers are seen at practice, in performance, and at rest. Their enthusiasm for their art comes through clearly, in the pictures and in the lively prose." Horn Book

793   Indoor games and amusements

Cole, Joanna

Pin the tail on the donkey and other party games; compiled by Joanna Cole and Stephanie Calmenson; illustrated by Alan Tiegreen. Morrow Junior Bks. 1993 48p il lib bdg $14.93 (k-2)   **793**

1. Games 2. Parties

ISBN 0-688-11892-5 (lib bdg)   LC 92-29786

Provides instructions for 20 simple party games for young children such as Musical Chairs, Giant Steps, and Peanut Hunt

"The step-by-step directions and parenthetical advice will please older kids, teachers, and parents, while young children looking for birthday party games will find the appealing ink-and-watercolor illustrations a big help in choosing their personal favorites." Booklist

Includes bibliographical references

The rain or shine activity book; fun things to make and do; by Joanna Cole and Stephanie Calmenson; illustrated by Alan Tiegreen. Morrow Junior Bks. 1997 192p il hardcover o.p. paperback available $9.95 (3-5)   **793**

1. Amusements 2. Games

ISBN 0-688-12133-0 (pa)   LC 96-37756

"A compendium of over 90 amusements for children that includes card games, riddles, street and jump rope rhymes, paper tricks, crafts, brain-teasers, and more. . . . Careful, step-by-step instructions are accompanied by illustrations of the procedures. Lively cartoon characters play cards, mix up play dough, and generally enjoy themselves." SLJ

793.2   Parties and entertainments

Ross, Kathy, 1948-

The best birthday parties ever! a kid's do-it-yourself guide; art by Sharon Lane Holm. Millbrook Press 1999 78p il lib bdg $24.90; pa $9.95 (2-4)   **793.2**

1. Parties 2. Birthdays

ISBN 0-7613-1410-5 (lib bdg); 0-7613-0989-6 (pa)

LC 98-27503

Provides instructions for the invitations, games, crafts, table decorations, and cakes for a dozen birthday parties based on such themes as outer space, puppets, and dinosaurs

"The book is appealing. The illustrations are colorful and plentiful." SLJ

793.3 Social, folk, national dancing

Ancona, George, 1929-
Let's dance! Morrow Junior Bks. 1998 unp il lib bdg $15.93 (k-3)   **793.3**
1. Dance
ISBN 0-688-16212-6 (lib bdg)   LC 97-52022
Simple text and photographs describe various dances from all over the world
This book includes "colorful photographs and action shots on white backgrounds. . . . All of the movements are described through a simple text in a large-print format. Additional small boxes provide more information." Booklist

793.7 Games not characterized by action

Cole, Joanna
Fun on the run; travel games and songs; by Joanna Cole and Stephanie Calmenson with Michael Street; illustrated by Alan Tiegreen. Morrow Junior Bks. 1999 126p il music $17; pa $6.95 (3-5)   **793.7**
1. Games 2. Songs
ISBN 0-688-14660-0; 0-688-14662-7 (pa)
                                         LC 98-42245
A collection of games and songs to enjoy while traveling, including word games, memory games, license plate games, writing games, geography games, jokes, and riddles
"Each game is clearly described in large print with numbered steps and has a black-and-white line drawing." SLJ

Math for the very young; a handbook of activities for parents and teachers; [by] Lydia Plonsky [et al.]; illustrated by Marcia Miller. Wiley 1995 210p il $29.95; pa $14.95   **793.7**
1. Mathematical recreations
ISBN 0-471-01671-3; 0-471-01647-0 (pa)
                                         LC 94-20861
"This guide suggests ways to introduce math to children through everyday activities. Sections include making a record book about the child and the family as well as activities for each month of the year, geometric crafts, math games, counting rhymes and stories, and ways to use math in the home and on the road." Booklist
Includes bibliographical references

793.73 Puzzles and puzzle games

Adler, David A., 1947-
The carsick zebra and other animal riddles; illustrated by Tomie de Paola. Holiday House 1983 unp il $13.95 (1-3)   **793.73**
1. Riddles
ISBN 0-8234-0479-X   LC 82-48750
In this collection of riddles "the questions appear at the top of the page, Tomie dePaola's simple yet witty black-and-white drawings fill the middle, and the answer appears at the bottom." Booklist

Easy math puzzles; illustrated by Cynthia Fisher. Holiday House 1997 unp il $15.95 (2-4)
                                         793.73
1. Mathematical recreations 2. Riddles
ISBN 0-8234-1283-0   LC 96-30921
A collection of mathematical riddles involving people, animals, coins, or food
These problems "stimulate and challenge children to use critical thinking skills to determine solutions—and they're fun. Adler's puzzles require clear reasoning more than sophisticated mathematics know-how or scratch paper. . . . Fisher's cartoon-style illustrations are cheerful and lively." SLJ

Agee, Jon
Elvis lives! and other anagrams; collected and illustrated by Jon Agee. Farrar, Straus & Giroux 2000 unp il $15   **793.73**
1. Word games
ISBN 0-374-32127-2   LC 99-38139
Agee "demonstrates how letters can be rearranged to produce new meanings. . . . 'Astronomer' converts to 'moonstarer', and a pig pronounces a 'dormitory' chamber a 'dirty room.'" Publ Wkly
"Agee's cartoonlike drawings bring out the most in every phrase. . . . An entertaining introduction to anagrams." Booklist

Go hang a salami! I'm a lasagna hog! and other palindromes. Farrar, Straus & Giroux 1992 unp il $12.21; pa $6.95   **793.73**
1. Word games
ISBN 0-374-33473-0; 0-374-44473-0 (pa)
                                         LC 91-31319
A collection of palindromes, sentences that read the same forward and backward
"Agee offers a humorous look at the concept, using more than 50 wacky alphabetic examples. . . . Cartoon sketches extend and often clarify the meaning of the crazy phrases." Booklist

Sit on a potato pan, Otis! more palindromes. Farrar, Straus & Giroux 1999 unp il $14.41
                                         793.73
1. Word games
ISBN 0-374-31808-5   LC 98-31783
"This volume collects more than sixty palindromes and displays them in witty cartoon drawings, notable for their off-center deadpan humor. Most of the entries will have readers chuckling aloud and trying to concoct their own palindromes." Horn Book Guide

So many dynamos! and other palindromes. Farrar, Straus & Giroux 1994 80p il hardcover o.p. paperback available $6.96   **793.73**
1. Word games
ISBN 0-374-46905-9 (pa)   LC 94-73749
"This book features one palindromic phrase per page or spread. . . . Even children who have never heard of a palindrome will be drawn to the cartoons, while readers fascinated by concept may want to try writing (and illustrating) their own." Booklist

The **Brain** explorer; puzzles, riddles, illusions, and other mental adventures; [by] Pat Murphy ... [et al.]; illustrations by Jason Gorski. Holt & Co. 1999 144p il (Exploratorium science-at-home book) $15.95 (5 and up)   **793.73**
1. Puzzles 2. Riddles 3. Magic tricks
ISBN 0-8050-4538-4   LC 98-54605
"An Owl book"
A collection of puzzles and activities dealing with memory, math, verbal skills, and visual perception

Cerf, Bennett, 1898-1971
Bennett Cerf's book of riddles; illustrated by Roy McKie. Beginner Bks. 1960 62p il $7.99 (k-3)   **793.73**
1. Riddles
ISBN 0-394-80015-X
These thirty-one riddles are arranged with the riddles being asked on one page and answered on the next, to keep the element of surprise
"Simple cartoonlike drawings use strong colour for their effect." Ont Libr Rev

Riddles and more riddles! illustrated by Debbie Palen. Random House 1999 unp il $7.99; lib bdg $11.99   **793.73**
1. Riddles 2. Jokes
ISBN 0-679-88970-1; 0-679-98970-6 (lib bdg)
      LC 99-20133
"Beginner books"
This volume combines Book of riddles (1960) and More riddles (1961)
A collection of riddles, such as "When is a cook bad? When she beats an egg." and "What kind of coat should be put on when it is wet? A coat of paint"

Cole, Joanna
Why did the chicken cross the road? and other riddles, old and new; compiled by Joanna Cole and Stephanie Calmenson; illustrated by Alan Tiegreen. Morrow Junior Bks. 1994 64p il hardcover o.p. paperback available $7.95 (3-5)   **793.73**
1. Riddles
ISBN 0-688-12204-3 (pa)   LC 94-2582
The authors "begin with a brief explanation about the origin of riddles and proceed with a collection of over two hundred, classic and new. Though many of the riddles appear in other collections, the book, illustrated with black-and-white line drawings, will be useful for its short bibliography and subject index." Horn Book Guide

Hall, Katy, 1947-
Creepy riddles; [by] Katy Hall and Lisa Eisenberg; pictures by S.D. Schindler. Dial Bks. for Young Readers 1998 48p il $13.99; pa $3.99 (k-2)   **793.73**
1. Riddles
ISBN 0-8037-1684-2; 0-14-130988-1 (pa)
      LC 94-37524
"Dial easy-to-read"

"A collection of riddles about vampires, ghosts, ghouls, and assorted monsters. . . . The illustrations are a scream. Schindler uses a find-nibbed pen to include lots of subtle details before adding vivid watercolor washes. . . . A superior choice for most joke or beginning-to-read collections." SLJ

Mummy riddles; [by] Katy Hall and Lisa Eisenberg; pictures by Nicole Rubel. Dial Bks. for Young Readers 1997 48p il $13.99; pa $3.99 (k-2)   **793.73**
1. Riddles
ISBN 0-8037-1846-2; 0-14-130364-6 (pa)
      LC 94-37525
"Dial easy-to-read"
In this riddle book "the droll and grisly wordplay will appeal to new readers. . . . The bright, detailed illustrations are as deadpan and silly as the words." Booklist

Snakey riddles; by Katy Hall and Lisa Eisenberg; pictures by Simms Taback. Dial Bks. for Young Readers 1990 48p il o.p.; Puffin Bks. paperback available $3.99 (k-2)   **793.73**
1. Riddles
ISBN 0-14-054588-3 (pa)   LC 88-23687
"Dial easy-to-read"
An illustrated collection of riddles about snakes
"Riddle lovers will groan with delight at some of these riddles. . . . The best thing about the book is the cleverly drawn, lively cartoon illustrations. Long, colorful snakes form borders framing the text and picture for each riddle." SLJ

Kessler, Leonard P., 1920-
Old Turtle's 90 knock-knocks, jokes, and riddles; [by] Leonard Kessler. Greenwillow Bks. 1991 48p il $15.95 (1-3)   **793.73**
1. Jokes 2. Riddles
ISBN 0-688-09585-2   LC 89-77505
An illustrated collection of animal jokes and riddles
This book includes "a string of jokes and riddles silly enough to please kids this age and usually simple enough not to baffle them. . . . Kessler's cartoonlike drawings, bright with watercolor washes, give the book a fresh, funny look that makes the verbal humor twice as effective." Booklist

Maestro, Giulio, 1942-
Riddle roundup. Clarion Bks. 1989 64p il hardcover o.p. paperback available $6.95 (2-4)   **793.73**
1. Riddles 2. Word games
ISBN 0-89919-537-7 (pa)   LC 86-33403
A collection of sixty-one riddles based on different kinds of word play such as puns, homonyms, and homographs

Maestro, Marco
Geese find the missing piece; school time riddle rhymes; by Marco and Giulio Maestro; pictures by Giulio Maestro. HarperCollins Pubs. 1999 48p il $14.95; lib bdg $14.89; pa $3.95 (k-2)   **793.73**
1. Riddles
ISBN 0-06-026220-6; 0-06-026221-4 (lib bdg); 0-06-443707-8 (pa)   LC 98-41513

Maestro, Marco—*Continued*

"An I can read book"

Rhyming riddles answer questions about a variety of animals at school

"The simple text and structure of the riddles are just right for the target audience. The book is populated by a colorful assortment of birds and animals that provide visual clues." SLJ

What do you hear when cows sing? and other silly riddles; by Marco and Giulio Maestro; pictures by Giulio Maestro. HarperCollins Pubs. 1996 48p il hardcover o.p. paperback available $3.95 (k-2)   **793.73**

1. Riddles

ISBN 0-06-444227-6 (pa)   LC 94-18686

"An I can read book"

"The subjects of the riddles will be familiar to most readers—trains, bugs, mice, fish, boats. . . . Most of the selections involve plays on words, but some are relatively straightforward. . . . Children will love the silly pictures, laugh at the riddles, enjoy sharing them with others, and expand their vocabularies all at the same time." SLJ

Spires, Elizabeth

Riddle road; puzzles in poems and pictures; illustrated by Erik Blegvad. Margaret K. McElderry Bks. 1999 26p il $15 (2-4)   **793.73**

1. Riddles

ISBN 0-689-81783-5   LC 97-36592

"The riddles on each page are accompanied by small, anecdotal watercolors that hold clues to the answer, some of them purposely misleading. Several are written in rhyme, but rhyming or not, they all benefit from reading aloud and they all tweak the imagination." Horn Book Guide

Steig, William, 1907-

C D B. Simon & Schuster Bks. for Young Readers 2000 c1968 47p il $16.95; pa $3.95
          793.73

1. Word games

ISBN 0-689-83160-9; 0-671-66689-4 (pa)
          LC 99-32720

First published 1968 by Windmill Bks.

Letters and numbers are used to create the sounds of words and simple sentences 4 u 2 figure out with the aid of illustrations

Readers "will delight in puzzling out the letter-and-number messages, aided by the simple, thickly outlined drawings and an answer key." Booklist

C D C? Farrar, Straus & Giroux 1984 unp il hardcover o.p. paperback available $4.95   **793.73**

1. Word games

ISBN 0-374-41024-0 (pa)   LC 84-48515

"Steig has devised letter and number sequences, with a few figures like $ and ¢ thrown in for good measure, which, when pronounced aloud, translate roughly into captions for the accompanying cartoon drawings." Booklist

"Flawlessly executed, purely pleasurable, the book is definitely 'D Q-R' for doldrums at any season." Horn Book

Steiner, Joan, 1943-

Look-alikes; photography by Thomas Lindley. Little, Brown 1998 unp il $13.95   **793.73**

1. Puzzles

ISBN 0-316-81255-2   LC 97-32795

This "puzzle book introduces Look-Alike Land in eleven double-page spreads that feature three-dimensional representations of the town's general store, hotel, and amusement park, among other settings. Each scene is composed of over one hundred everyday objects cunningly crafted to depict their life-size counterparts: a vacuum cleaner is a disposable razor; seat cushions are fig bars; and lamps are made from peppermint candies, chess pieces, and plastic pencil sharpeners." Horn Book

"Bursting with creativity, this work of visual genius will set imaginations soaring." Publ Wkly

Look-alikes, jr.; photography by Thomas Lindley. Little, Brown 1999 unp il $13.95 **793.73**

1. Puzzles

ISBN 0-316-81307-9   LC 99-11683

Simple verses challenge readers to identify the everyday objects used to construct eleven three-dimensional scenes, including a house, kitchen, bedroom, school bus, train, farm, and rocket

"The design is both witty and cunning, offering lots of just-hard-enough opportunities for looking and finding." Horn Book

Terban, Marvin

The dove dove; funny homograph riddles; illustrated by Tom Huffman. Clarion Bks. 1988 64p il hardcover o.p. paperback available $7.95 (3-5)   **793.73**

1. Riddles 2. Word games

ISBN 0-89919-810-4 (pa)   LC 88-2611

"An introduction to the sometimes confusing world of homographs—words that are spelled alike, but are pronounced differently and have different meanings. Using the general pattern of riddle and accompanying illustration, Terban leads readers through a variety of homographs. . . . The book will prove of interest to those students who enjoy the challenge of, and appreciate, word play." SLJ

Funny you should ask; how to make up jokes and riddles with wordplay; illustrated by John O'Brien. Clarion Bks. 1992 64p il hardcover o.p. paperback available $7.95 (3-5)   **793.73**

1. Riddles 2. English language—Homonyms 3. Puns

ISBN 0-395-58113-3 (pa)   LC 91-19509

The author "introduces four kinds of wordplay—homonyms, 'almost-sound-alike words,' homographs, and idioms. In a laid-back fashion that won't put off readers, he shows clearly how each type of wordplay works, provides numerous examples to illustrate . . . and suggests some words to use when making up jokes and riddles of one's own. O'Brien's black-and-white cartoon sketches, liberally scattered throughout, add the perfect visual touch. Great for classroom use and for aspiring comedians—of any age." Booklist

Includes bibliographical references

Wick, Walter

I spy; a book of picture riddles; photographs by Walter Wick; riddles by Jean Marzollo; design by Carol Devine Carson. Scholastic 1992 33p il $13.95   **793.73**

1. Puzzles
ISBN 0-590-45087-5   LC 91-28268

I spy Christmas; a book of picture riddles; photographs by Walter Wick; riddles by Jean Marzollo. Scholastic 1992 33p il $13.95   **793.73**

1. Puzzles
ISBN 0-590-45846-9   LC 91-45732

I spy extreme challenger! a book of picture riddles; photographs by Walter Wick; riddles by Jean Marzollo. Scholastic 2000 31p il $13.95   **793.73**

1. Puzzles
ISBN 0-439-19900-X   LC 00-27910

I spy fantasy; a book of picture riddles; photographs by Walter Wick; riddles by Jean Marzollo. Scholastic 1994 37p il $13.95   **793.73**

1. Puzzles
ISBN 0-590-46295-4   LC 93-44814

I spy fun house; a book of picture riddles; photographs by Walter Wick; riddles by Jean Marzollo. Scholastic 1993 33p il $13.95   **793.73**

1. Puzzles
ISBN 0-590-46293-8   LC 92-16425

I spy gold challenger! a book of picture riddles; photographs by Walter Wick; riddles by Jean Marzollo. Scholastic 1998 31p il $13.95   **793.73**

1. Puzzles
ISBN 0-590-04296-3   LC 98-13982

I spy mystery; a book of picture riddles; photographs by Walter Wick; riddles by Jean Marzollo. Scholastic 1993 37p il $13.95   **793.73**

1. Puzzles
ISBN 0-590-46294-6   LC 92-40863

I spy school days; a book of picture riddles; photographs by Walter Wick; riddles by Jean Marzollo. Scholastic 1995 33p il $13.95   **793.73**

1. Puzzles
ISBN 0-590-48135-5   LC 94-43629

I spy spooky night; a book of picture riddles; photographs by Walter Wick; riddles by Jean Marzollo. Scholastic 1996 31p il $15.95   **793.73**

1. Puzzles
ISBN 0-590-48137-1   LC 95-50528

I spy super challenger! a book of picture riddles; photographs by Walter Wick; riddles by Jean Marzollo. Scholastic 1997 31p il $13.95   **793.73**

1. Puzzles
ISBN 0-590-34128-6   LC 97-6864

I spy treasure hunt; a book of picture riddles; photographs by Walter Wick; riddles by Jean Marzollo. Scholastic 1999 36p $13.95   **793.73**

1. Puzzles
ISBN 0-439-04244-5   LC 99-30581

Also available I spy board books for younger readers "Cartwheel books"

"On oversize pages, brightly colored photographs are crammed with small objects; each double-page spread is organized by theme. . . . The rhyming captions at the foot of each page suggest objects to be found. . . . While the pages are very busy, it's the sort of crowding many young children enjoy, and it certainly fosters observation of detail." Bull Cent Child Books

793.8   Magic and related activities

Besmehn, Bobby

Juggling step-by-step. Sterling 1995 79p hardcover o.p. paperback available $8.95 (4 and up)   **793.8**

1. Juggling
ISBN 0-8069-0815-7 (pa)   LC 94-12873
"A Sterling/Chapelle book"

"A basic introduction to juggling. Beginning with a tossing move using one scarf, the tricks progress to two-person passes with several balls. Other routines include juggling rings and clubs, a special 'neck catch' trick, and an 'eat-an-apple-while-juggling' move." SLJ

"Each exceptionally clear, full-color photograph features a close-up of a young person juggling. The simple clothes and black backgrounds in the photos allow readers to focus on the jugglers' action." Booklist

Includes glossary

Broekel, Ray, 1923-

Hocus pocus: magic you can do; [by] Ray Broekel and Laurence B. White, Jr; illustrated by Mary Thelen. Whitman, A. 1984 48p il $13.95 (3-5)   **793.8**

1. Magic tricks
ISBN 0-8075-3350-5   LC 83-26096

Step-by-step instructions for twenty simple magic tricks, together with tips on patter, timing, slight-of-hand, and misdirection for the beginning magician

"Most children, if they read carefully, will be able to figure out the tricks. The black-and-white illustrations dabbed with purple are clearly marked, and the jokes that accompany them add a spot of humor." Booklist

Cobb, Vicki, 1938-

Bet you can! science possibilities to fool you; [by] Vicki Cobb and Kathy Darling; illustrated by Stella Ormai. Lothrop, Lee & Shepard Bks. 1990 112p il hardcover o.p. paperback available $4.50 (4 and up)   **793.8**

1. Scientific recreations 2. Magic tricks
ISBN 0-380-82180-X (pa)   LC 90-6690

Provides instructions for more than sixty tricks based on scientific experiments described in the text

Cobb, Vicki, 1938-—*Continued*

Bet you can't! science impossibilities to fool you; by Vicki Cobb and Kathy Darling; illustrated by Martha Weston. Lothrop, Lee & Shepard Bks. 1980 128p il hardcover o.p. paperback available $4.95 (4 and up)   **793.8**

1. Scientific recreations 2. Magic tricks
ISBN 0-380-54502-0 (pa)   LC 79-9254

More than 60 tricks are contained in this book. "Explanations of the scientific principles that make the trick impossible to accomplish are included. Some explanations contain an example from a child's everyday life in which the same scientific principles apply." Sci Books Films

Magic—naturally! science entertainments & amusements; illustrated by Lionel Kalish. rev ed. HarperCollins Pubs. 1993 150p il lib bdg $16.89 (4 and up)   **793.8**

1. Scientific recreations 2. Magic tricks
ISBN 0-06-022475-4   LC 90-21829

First published 1976 by Lippincott

"Each of the 30 tricks/experiments . . . begins with a list of easy-to-find materials and is followed by a description of the set up. Cobb . . . clearly explains the scientific principles behind the demonstrations. She emphasizes proper cautions when using fire or poisonous substances. Kalish's pen-and-ink illustrations are simple, but attractive and detailed enough to enhance the text. Performance tips enable young magicians to select just the right activities for their acts." SLJ

Wanna bet! science challenges to fool you; [by] Vicki Cobb and Kathy Darling; illustrated by Meredith Johnson. Lothrop, Lee & Shepard Bks. 1993 128p il hardcover o.p. paperback available $4.50 (4 and up)   **793.8**

1. Scientific recreations 2. Magic tricks
ISBN 0-380-71722-0 (pa)   LC 92-8962

Provides instructions for a variety of scientific tricks or challenges, such as slicing an apple in midair with a hammer or tying a knot in a chicken bone

"The text is lively, and Johnson's black-and-white sketches are humorous and abundant." Booklist

Leyton, Lawrence

My first magic book. Dorling Kindersley 1993 48p il $12.95 (3-5)   **793.8**

1. Magic tricks
ISBN 1-56458-319-8   LC 93-22104

Presents instructions for performing magic tricks and putting on a magic show

"An appealing presentation. Full-color photographs show multiethnic children making life-sized props and doing tricks, with explanations of how they are done and bits of appropriate patter." SLJ

Mitchelson, Mitch, 1950-

The most excellent book of how to be a juggler; illustrated by Rob Shone and Peter Harper. Copper Beech Bks. 1997 32p il lib bdg $21.90; pa $6.95   **793.8**

1. Juggling
ISBN 0-7613-0618-8 (lib bdg); 0-7613-0632-3 (pa)
LC 97-8012

This is an illustrated guide to juggling techniques, routines, and performances

White, Laurence B.

Math-a-magic: number tricks for magicians; [by] Laurence B. White, Jr. and Ray Broekel; illustrated by Meyer Seltzer. Whitman, A. 1989 48p il hardcover o.p. paperback available $4.95 (3-6)   **793.8**

1. Mathematical recreations 2. Magic tricks
ISBN 0-8075-4995-9 (pa)   LC 89-35395

"Each of the 21 tricks is presented in three sections: 'The Trick,' 'How to do it,' and 'The Math-A-Magic Secret' of why the trick works. . . . The showmanship and production of the trick as magic is stressed, with the math in the background as the key to making the tricks work." SLJ

Shazam! simple science magic; [by] Laurence B. White, Jr., & Ray Broekel; illustrated by Meyer Seltzer. Whitman, A. 1990 48p il hardcover o.p. paperback available $4.95 (3-6)   **793.8**

1. Scientific recreations 2. Magic tricks
ISBN 0-8075-7333-7 (pa)   LC 90-42441

"Section titles such as 'How to Hypnotize a Potato' or 'The Uncanny Can That Can' will entice young readers to investigate nineteen simple science 'tricks.' Humorous illustrations in simple black line, highlighted with orange, add appeal and clarity. Directions are given in short paragraphs rather than prescriptive 'steps,' and each bit of magic is explained scientifically in a highly readable style." Adventuring with Books

Wyler, Rose

Magic secrets; by Rose Wyler and Gerald Ames; pictures by Arthur Dorros. rev ed. Harper & Row 1990 63p il hardcover o.p. paperback available $3.95 (k-2)   **793.8**

1. Magic tricks
ISBN 0-06-444153-9 (pa)   LC 89-35841

"An I can read book"

A revised and newly illustrated edition of the title first published 1967

Easy magic tricks for the aspiring young magician

Spooky tricks; by Rose Wyler and Gerald Ames; pictures by S. D. Schindler. rev & newly il ed. HarperCollins Pubs. 1994 63p il hardcover o.p. paperback available $3.95 (k-2)   **793.8**

1. Magic tricks
ISBN 0-06-444172-5 (pa)   LC 92-47501

"An I can read book"

First published 1967

Describes how to write invisible messages, make ghosts appear on walls, and many other tricks

793.9   Other indoor diversions

Gryski, Camilla, 1948-
Cat's cradle, owl's eyes; a book of string games; illustrated by Tom Sankey. Morrow 1984 c1983 78p il hardcover o.p. paperback available $6.95 (4-6)   **793.9**
   1. String figures
   ISBN 0-688-03941-3 (pa)   LC 84-9075
   First published 1983 in Canada
This "book contains readily grasped directions for tricky, entertaining play. Sankey illustrates cat's cradle and its variations with expert, well-defined drawings of each step in the games. Children should enjoy practising manual dexterity as they master the feats described by themselves or in groups." Publ Wkly
"Brief notes on the ethnic and historical background accompany each figure, adding to the pleasure of achievement." Horn Book

795.3   Games dependent on drawing numbers or counters

Lankford, Mary D., 1932-
Dominoes around the world; illustrated by Karen Dugan. Morrow Junior Bks. 1998 40p il $16; lib bdg $15.93 (3-5)   **795.3**
   1. Games
   ISBN 0-688-14051-3; 0-688-14052-1 (lib bdg)
                   LC 97-20975
Examines the history and basic rules of the game of dominoes and describes how it can vary from country to country
"While perhaps best used as a domino-instruction aid, the information may be useful for reports and the clean, attractive layout invites browsing." SLJ
Includes glossary and bibliographical references

795.4   Card games

Cole, Joanna
Crazy eights and other card games; by Joanna Cole and Stephanie Calmenson; illustrated by Alan Tiegreen. Morrow Junior Bks. 1994 76p il $15; lib bdg $14.93; pa $6.95 (3-5)   **795.4**
   1. Card games
   ISBN 0-688-12199-3; 0-688-12200-0 (lib bdg); 0-688-12201-9 (pa)   LC 93-5427
Introduces the different suits and face cards in a deck of cards, explains how to hold, shuffle, and deal them, and provides instructions for such games as Aces Up, Go Fish, and Spit
"A good introduction to cards and card playing. . . . The text is clear, with big print and lots of white space. Black, white, and red line drawings are often funny and complement the text well." SLJ
Includes bibliographical references

796   Athletic and outdoor sports and games

Ajmera, Maya
Let the games begin! [by] Maya Ajmera, Michael Regan; with a foreword by Bill Bradley. Charlesbridge Pub. 2000 unp il $16.95; pa $6.95 (3-5)   **796**
   1. Sports
   ISBN 0-88106-067-4; 0-88106-068-2 (pa)
                   LC 99-24032
Text and photographs of children from around the world focus on various aspects of sports, including physical benefits, the importance of practice, overcoming obstacles, teamwork, and more
"In addition to illustrating how children all over the world love sports, this book will inspire youngsters to get involved in athletics and teach them about sportsmanship." SLJ

Gibbons, Gail
Playgrounds. Holiday House 1985 unp il $16.95 (k-3)   **796**
   1. Playgrounds
   ISBN 0-8234-0553-2   LC 84-19285
"Gibbons' text offers opportunities for children to extend their vocabularies and compare differences in swings, slides, climbing apparatus and sandbox tools. . . . A colorful treatment of a subject familiar to young children but seldom discussed in picture book format." SLJ

Play like a girl; a celebration of women in sports; edited by Sue Macy and Jane Gottesman. Holt & Co. 1999 32p il $16.95 (5 and up)   **796**
   1. Women athletes
   ISBN 0-8050-6071-5   LC 98-47754
"This photographic celebration of women in sport captures professional, college, Olympic, and amateur athletes doing what they love best. Excellent-quality, full and double-page action photographs are accompanied by excerpts from magazine articles, short stories, and fiction and nonfiction books." SLJ

Sierra, Judy
Children's traditional games; games from 137 countries and cultures; by Judy Sierra, Robert Kaminski. Oryx Press 1995 232p il pa $35   **796**
   1. Games
   ISBN 0-89774-967-7   LC 95-35623
The authors "describe popular games from 137 countries and cultures, including over 20 games from Native American groups. Each game . . . can be played by small groups in the classroom or on the playground." Publisher's note
Includes bibliographical references

Sports Illustrated for Kids. Time $29.95 per year   **796**
   1. Sports—Periodicals
   ISSN 1042-394X
   Monthly. First published 1989

Sports Illustrated for Kids—*Continued*

This magazine features articles about young people in sports, biographies of pros, playing tips, stories and puzzles

"The excitement and tension of sports are captured in the action-filled full-color photographs and brisk writing. . . . The focus of the . . . magazine is on fun, but stories 'emphasize the importance of values such as hard work, teamwork, practice, fair play, and a positive attitude.'" Richardson. Mag for Child. 2d edition

796.1 Miscellaneous games

Brown, Marc Tolon

Finger rhymes; collected and illustrated by Marc Brown. Dutton 1980 32p il hardcover o.p. paperback available $5.99 **796.1**
1. Finger play 2. Nursery rhymes
ISBN 0-14-055815-2 (pa)   LC 80-11492
"A Unicorn book"
Presents 14 rhymes with instructions for accompanying finger plays

Hand rhymes; collected and illustrated by Marc Brown. Dutton 1985 31p il lib bdg $15.99; pa $5.99 **796.1**
1. Finger play 2. Nursery rhymes
ISBN 0-525-44201-4; 0-14-054939-0 (pa)
                                   LC 84-25918
This collection "contains several adaptations, some new and lively material, and a few old favorites. . . . Each double-page spread contains the rhyme, with small but carefully detailed diagrams of the accompanying finger action and warmly colorful, amusing illustrations of fat kittens, bemused ducks, and happy children. Cozy, useful, and a pleasure to look at, the book is for those who deal with a lap-sitter as well as for the storyteller." Horn Book

Play rhymes; collected and illustrated by Marc Brown. Dutton 1987 32p il music hardcover o.p. paperback available $5.99 **796.1**
1. Finger play 2. Nursery rhymes
ISBN 0-14-054936-6 (pa)   LC 87-13537
A collection of twelve play rhymes with illustrations to demonstrate the accompanying finger plays or physical activities. Includes music for the six rhymes which are also songs
"The illustrations are full-color pastels with many small details and humorous elements to appeal to children. This is a good choice for program planning or for a rainy afternoon with a favorite child." SLJ

The **Eentsy**, weentsy spider: fingerplays and action rhymes; compiled by Joanna Cole and Stephanie Calmenson; illustrated by Alan Tiegreen. Morrow Junior Bks. 1991 64p il music hardcover o.p. paperback available $6.95 **796.1**
1. Finger play 2. Songs
ISBN 0-688-10805-9 (pa)   LC 90-44594
"This collection of 38 fingerplays and action rhymes ranges from the familiar 'I'm a Little Teapot,' to the older 'Two Fat Gentlemen.' Simple musical arrangements

are included where appropriate." SLJ
"Tiegreen uses a few simple lines to create a cast of multicultural characters whose enthusiasm is infectious. . . . An attractive, upbeat addition to the finger-play collection." Booklist
Includes bibliographical references

Erlbach, Arlene

Sidewalk games around the world; illustrated by Sharon Lane Holm. Millbrook Press 1997 64p il map hardcover o.p. paperback available $8.95 (3-5) **796.1**
1. Games
ISBN 0-7613-0178-X (pa)   LC 96-8715
Describes various games played by children in 26 countries around the world
"Equipment needs are simple, varying from chalk to jump ropes to jacks or stones. Directions are clearly and succinctly written. Each double-page spread includes a brief note about the country of origin, a world map showing its location, and a description of the game with illustrations. An added treat is the occasional language boxes giving common phrases . . . in that nation's language." SLJ
Includes bibliographical references

Miss Mary Mack and other children's street rhymes; compiled by Joanna Cole and Stephanie Calmenson; illustrated by Alan Tiegreen. Morrow Junior Bks. 1990 64p hardcover o.p. paperback available $7.95 **796.1**
1. Games 2. Nursery rhymes
ISBN 0-688-09749-9 (pa)   LC 89-37266
This is a collection of over 100 traditional childhood hand-clapping and street rhymes
"Tiegreen's lighthearted pen-and-ink illustrations are sure to tickle the fancy of young readers. . . . A book that's sure to produce smiles in any story hour or program." SLJ

796.2 Active games requiring equipment

Cole, Joanna

Marbles; 101 ways to play; by Joanna Cole and Stephanie Calmenson with Michael Street; illustrated by Alan Tiegreen. Morrow Junior Bks. 1998 127p il lib bdg $16; pa $8.95 (3-5) **796.2**
1. Games
ISBN 0-688-12205-1 (lib bdg); 0-688-12207-8 (pa)
                                   LC 97-36251
Traces the history of marbles and marble making, gives instructions for playing various kinds of games, explains related terms, and suggests further activities
"Alan Tiegreen's line drawings give the pages an appealing look, while showing exactly how to do what the instructions describe. Children looking for directions on marble games will find the text informative and even entertaining." Booklist
Includes glossary

Lankford, Mary D., 1932-

Hopscotch around the world; illustrated by Karen Milone. Morrow Junior Bks. 1992 47p il map hardcover o.p. paperback available $6.95 (3-5)   **796.2**

1. Hopscotch

ISBN 0-688-14745-3 (pa)   LC 91-17152

The author "presents 19 variations of hopscotch played in 16 countries around the world. Each double-page spread contains a diagram of the pattern to be scratched or chalked on the ground, a description of the game, step-by-step directions, and a large illustration showing how it is played. Lankford's research, briefly described in the text, brings in history as well as geography, language, and cultural differences. . . . A handsomely designed book on an unusual topic." Booklist

Includes bibliographical references

Levine, Shar

Awesome yo-yo tricks; [by] Shar Levine & Bob Bowden. Sterling 2000 96p il pa $9.95 (4 and up)   **796.2**

1. Yo-yos

ISBN 0-8069-4468-4   LC 99-51642

Presents the history of the yo-yo and describes the basic techniques involve in simple, intermediate, and advanced tricks

"Thirty-five feats of increasing difficulty are illustrated in sharp, step-by-step photographs. . . . This is an excellent choice that illustrates the joys of mastering the yo-yo." SLJ

796.21   Roller skating

Irwin, Dawn

Inline skating; foreword by Chris Edwards. Dorling Kindersley 2000 45p $9.95 (4 and up)   **796.21**

1. In-line skating

ISBN 0-7894-6542-6   LC 00-23246

"DK superguides"

Replaces The young inline skater, by Chris Edwards, published 1996

The author, a world champion skater, introduces the sport of inline skating, from basic skills and safety to performing simple stunts and taking part in competitions

796.323   Basketball

Gibbons, Gail

My basketball book. HarperCollins Pubs. 2000 unp il $5.95 (k-2)   **796.323**

1. Basketball

ISBN 0-688-17140-0   LC 99-87902

Introduces the basics of the game of basketball, describing the players, court, techniques, and rules of play

Includes glossary

McKissack, Fredrick, 1939-

Black hoops; the history of African Americans in basketball; [by] Fredrick McKissack, Jr. Scholastic Press 1999 154p il $15.95 (5 and up)   **796.323**

1. Basketball 2. African American athletes

ISBN 0-590-48712-4   LC 98-14107

Surveys the history of African Americans in basketball, from the beginning of the sport to the present, discussing individual teams and players and the integration of the National Basketball Association

"This book makes a unique and important contribution for this age range and should not be missed." SLJ

Includes glossary and bibliographical references

796.325   Volleyball

Jensen, Julie, 1957-

Fundamental volleyball; photographs by Andy King. Lerner Publs. 1995 63p il (Fundamental sports) lib bdg $22.60 (5 and up)   **796.325**

1. Volleyball

ISBN 0-8225-3452-5   LC 94-5743

This book begins with a brief history of the sport. The following chapters describe how to play the game; the importance of conditioning and practicing; advanced moves; and variations on the game

Includes glossary and bibliographical references

796.332   American football

Buckley, James, Jr.

America's greatest game; the real story of football and the NFL; foreword by Jerry Rice. Hyperion Bks. for Children 1998 64p il $16.95 (4 and up)   **796.332**

1. National Football League 2. Football

ISBN 0-7868-0433-5   LC 97-47744

A historical overview of how the game of football has evolved through the years and how the National Football League began

"This book consists mainly of outstanding full-color photographs of players at various levels of proficiency from peewee to pro. . . . Certain to be a popular browsing item for young football fans." SLJ

Football; created by NFL Publishing; written by James Buckley, Jr. DK Pub. 1999 63p il (Eyewitness books) $15.95; lib bdg $19.99 (4 and up)   **796.332**

1. Football

ISBN 0-7894-4725-8; 0-7894-6991-X (lib bdg)

      LC 99-24169

Provides an illustrated look at many varied aspects of the popular sport of professional football, including the history of the game, evolution of equipment, the playing field and modern stadiums, players, fans, and more

Gibbons, Gail

My football book. HarperCollins Pubs. 2000 unp il $5.95 (k-2)   **796.332**

1. Football

ISBN 0-688-17139-7   LC 99-87202

Gibbons, Gail—*Continued*

Introduces the basics of the game of football, describing the players, field, and how the game is played

"What shines through [in this book] is Gibbons's dedication to presenting the game as fun. . . . The illustrations, especially those of the players, clearly reflect the action." SLJ

Includes glossary

796.334   Soccer

Baddiel, Ivor

Ultimate soccer. DK Pub. 1998 96p il $16.95; pa $12.95 (4 and up)   796.334
1. Soccer
ISBN 0-7894-2795-8; 0-7894-3071-1 (pa)
LC 97-36602
Cover title: Soccer: the ultimate World Cup companion

"Baddiel begins with a history of soccer and then moves on to rules and techniques. Great teams and players from the various countries competing are highlighted. The concluding chapters cover World Cup games from 1930 to the present." SLJ

"An excellent resource for young soccer enthusiasts eager to know more about this international sport." Booklist

Blackstone, Margaret

This is soccer; illustrated by John O'Brien. Holt & Co. 1999 unp il $15.95 (k-2)   796.334
1. Soccer
ISBN 0-8050-2801-3   LC 98-23474

A simple introduction to the game of soccer, covering its equipment, players, and basic plays and depicting a game in progress

"The humorous illustrations, in watercolor and pen, convey plenty of action, with swirling lines and jagged marks showing lots of movement and kicks. . . . The book provides an appropriate starting point for beginners." Booklist

Coleman, Lori

Fundamental soccer; photographs by Andy King. Lerner Publs. 1995 64p il (Fundamental sports) lib bdg $22.60 (5 and up)   796.334
1. Soccer
ISBN 0-8225-3451-7   LC 94-11907

This "book covers the history of the sport, positions, equipment, basic and more advanced moves, rules, the merits of practice, and variations in the game. . . . King's colorful, clear, informative photographs enhance the text." SLJ

Includes glossary and bibliographical references

Gibbons, Gail

My soccer book. HarperCollins Pubs. 2000 unp il $5.95 (k-2)   796.334
1. Soccer
ISBN 0-688-17138-9   LC 99-34514

Briefly describes the equipment, terminology, rules, positions, and plays of one of the world's most popular games

This "small, snappily designed book [is] attractive, accessible. . . . Diverse groups of children, drawn in Gibbons' typically bright colors and cheery style, demonstrate sports equipment and game plays." Booklist

Includes glossary

Hornby, Hugh

Soccer; written by Hugh Hornby; photographed by Andy Crawford. Dorling Kindersley 2000 61p il (Eyewitness books) $15.95; lib bdg $19.99 (4 and up)   796.334
1. Soccer
ISBN 0-7894-5245-6; 0-7894-6803-4 (lib bdg)
LC 99-52770
Examines all aspects of the game of soccer: its history, rules, techniques, tactics, equipment, playing fields, competitive play, and more

"The pages are jam-packed with trivia illustrated by numerous full-color photographs of players and memorabilia that will please fans. . . . Hornby vividly captures the legacy of the sport." SLJ

796.34   Racket games

Hoyt-Goldsmith, Diane

Lacrosse; the national game of the Iroquois; photographs by Lawrence Migdale. Holiday House 1998 31p il $16.95 (3-5)   796.34
1. Lacrosse 2. Iroquois Indians 3. Native American games
ISBN 0-8234-1360-8   LC 97-37742

"Focusing on 13-year-old Monte Lyons, a member of the Onondaga Nation and third-generation lacrosse player, this photo-essay presents an interesting blend of Iroquois Confederacy history and information about a sport that is growing in popularity. . . . Vivid, full-color photographs accurately illustrate the game and provide an interesting look at the Onondaga Nation Territory." SLJ

Includes glossary

796.342   Tennis

Miller, Marc, 1957-

Fundamental tennis; photographs by Andy King. Lerner Publs. 1995 64p il (Fundamental sports) lib bdg $22.60 (5 and up)   796.342
1. Tennis
ISBN 0-8225-3450-9   LC 94-21107

This book presents a brief history of the game, the basics (including rackets, clothes, strokes, grips, serves, and stance), rules for singles play and rules for doubles, practice drills, and advanced shots. Color photographs show young tennis players in action

Includes glossary and bibliographical references

796.352　Golf

Krause, Peter, 1954-
Fundamental golf; photographs by Andy King. Lerner Publs. 1995 64p il (Fundamental sports) lib bdg $22.60 (5 and up)　　**796.352**
1. Golf
ISBN 0-8225-3454-1　　LC 94-23166
This book presents a brief history of the game; the basics, including the function of each type of golf club; rules and etiquette; and skill shots. Photographs of young golfers illustrate proper stance and swing motion
Includes glossary and bibliographical references

Simmons, Richard
Golf; written by Richard Simmons; foreword by Nick Faldo. Dorling Kindersley 2001 48p il $9.95 (4 and up)　　**796.352**
1. Golf
ISBN 0-7894-7390-9　　LC 00-57060
"DK superguides"
Replaces The young golfer, published 1999
This "includes an introduction to golf with information about the history of the game, expert instruction on playing the game, golf course layouts, and steps for taking your game to the next level." Publisher's note

796.357　Baseball

Anderson, Joan
Batboy; an inside look at spring training; photographs by Matthew Cavanaugh. Lodestar Bks. 1996 unp il $16.99 (3-6)　　**796.357**
1. Baseball
ISBN 0-525-67511-6　　LC 95-11793
This focuses "on 13-year-old Kenny Garibaldi, batboy for the San Francisco Giants. Text and full-color pictures follow Kenny through a typical day. . . . A real gem, for baseball fans and aspiring players, who will delight in seeing someone their own age so intimately involved in professional ball." Booklist
Includes glossary

Brashler, William
The story of Negro league baseball. Ticknor & Fields 1994 166p il $15.95 (5 and up)　　**796.357**
1. Baseball 2. African American athletes
ISBN 0-395-67169-8　　LC 93-36547
"This book intersperses chapters on such black stars as Satchel Paige, Josh Gibson, and Jackie Robinson among the accounts of the various Negro Leagues. Archival and scrapbook black-and-white photographs . . . appear throughout. A list of Negro League all-star teams chosen by a variety of groups and individuals is appended." SLJ
"The author brings to life some of the finest players and most interesting men who ever chose the career of baseball." Horn Book
Includes bibliographical references

Geng, Don
Fundamental baseball; photographs by Andy King. Lerner Publs. 1995 80p il (Fundamental sports) lib bdg $22.60 (5 and up)　　**796.357**
1. Baseball
ISBN 0-8225-3455-X　　LC 95-2017
Uses photographs of young athletes to demonstrate techniques of the basic skills involved in fielding, throwing, hitting, and baserunning
"Illustrated by clear [text] and step-by-step color photographs." Horn Book Guide
Includes glossary and bibliographical references

Gibbons, Gail
My baseball book. HarperCollins Pubs. 2000 unp il $5.95 (k-2)　　**796.357**
1. Baseball
ISBN 0-688-17137-0　　LC 99-32945
An introduction to baseball, describing the equipment, playing field, rules, players, and process of the game
"The information is well augmented by clearly labeled, colorful drawings." SLJ
Includes glossary

Kreutzer, Peter
Little League's official how-to-play baseball book; [by] Peter Kreutzer and Ted Kerley; illustrated by Alexander Verbitsky. Doubleday 1990 210p il hardcover o.p. paperback available $11.95 (4 and up)　　**796.357**
1. Little League Baseball, Inc. 2. Baseball
ISBN 0-385-24700-1 (pa)　　LC 89-28097
The "contents include gripping, throwing, and catching the ball; hitting; bunting; base running; sliding; pitching; defensive positioning; fitness; and warm-ups. . . . An added bonus is the inclusion of the Official Little League playing rules." Voice Youth Advocates

McKissack, Patricia C., 1944-
Black diamond; the story of the Negro baseball leagues; [by] Patricia C. McKissack and Fredrick McKissack, Jr. Scholastic 1994 184p il hardcover o.p. paperback available $5.99 (6 and up)　　**796.357**
1. Baseball 2. African American athletes
ISBN 0-590-68213-X (pa)　　LC 93-22691
Traces the history of baseball in the Negro Leagues and its great heroes, including Monte Irwin, Buck Leonard, and Cool Papa Bell
This is "an engaging account. . . . It includes a chronology, player profiles and wonderful photographs from the Negro Leagues." N Y Times Book Rev
Includes bibliographical references

Ritter, Lawrence S.
Leagues apart; the men and times of the Negro baseball leagues; illustrations by Richard Merkin. Morrow Junior Bks. 1995 unp il hardcover o.p. paperback available $5.95 (2-4)　　**796.357**
1. Baseball 2. African American athletes
ISBN 0-688-16693-8 (pa)　　LC 94-17512

Ritter, Lawrence S.—*Continued*

"Beginning with a brief history of the Negro Leagues, the text provides short biographies of twenty-two baseball players of color, interspersed with information about segregation and the racism of the 1920s through the 1940s. . . . Most of the players' biographies are accompanied by large stylized portraits in oil pastel." Horn Book

This "is a fine melding of text and illustration that makes accessible an important part of baseball history." SLJ

The story of baseball; foreword by Ted Williams. 3rd rev & expanded ed. Morrow Junior Bks. 1999 205p il $16.96; pa $7.95 (5 and up)
796.357
1. Baseball
ISBN 0-688-16264-9; 0-688-16265-7 (pa)
LC 98-35456
First published 1983

Traces the history of baseball, which was first played in a form resembling the modern game in Hoboken, New Jersey, in 1846, and first played by professional players in 1869

"This edition of *the* classic baseball book covers quite recent events, including Cal Ripken, Jr.'s amazing 1995 breaking of Lou Gehrig's record for consecutive games played as well as the spectacular 1998 season (in which Mark McGwire hit seventy home runs to overtake Roger Maris's sixty-one in 1961)." Horn Book Guide

Smyth, Ian

The young baseball player; written by Ian Smyth; with a foreword by Eduardo Perez. DK Pub. 1998 37p il (Young enthusiast) $15.95 (4 and up)
796.357
1. Baseball
ISBN 0-7894-2825-3
LC 97-41728

Provides information on the offensive and defensive techniques of baseball as well as on the history and equipment of the game, with step-by-step instructions on individual positions

This is "filled with beautifully-reproduced full-color photos. . . . Smyth provides solid, basic information in an attractive format." SLJ

Includes glossary

Young, Robert, 1951-

Game day; behind the scenes at a ballpark; photographs by Jerry Wachter. Carolrhoda Bks. 1998 48p il lib bdg $22.60 (3-5)
796.357
1. Baseball
ISBN 1-57505-084-6
LC 97-33592

Describes the various activities that take place behind the scenes before, during, and after a baseball game, using a Baltimore Orioles game at Oriole Park at Camden Yards as an example

"This comprehensive look at everything involved in making a game go smoothly will fascinate baseball enthusiasts." Booklist

796.41 Weight lifting

Knotts, Bob

Weightlifting. Children's Press 2000 47p il lib bdg $22; pa $6.95 (2-4)
796.41
1. Weight lifting
ISBN 0-516-21067-X (lib bdg); 0-515-20732-X (pa)
LC 99-15089

"A True book"

Describes the history of the sport of weight lifting, as well as the training, equipment, rules, and techniques involved

Includes bibliographical references

796.42 Track and field

Knotts, Bob

Track and field. Children's Press 2000 47p il lib bdg $22; pa $6.95 (2-4)
796.42
1. Track athletics
ISBN 0-516-21066-1 (lib bdg); 0-516-27031-1 (pa)
LC 99-15088

"A True book"

Describes the history of track competitions, the various events involved, as well as several of the stars in this sport

Includes bibliographical references

796.44 Sports gymnastics

Bragg, Linda Wallenberg

Fundamental gymnastics; photographs by Andy King. Lerner Publs. 1995 80p il (Fundamental sports) lib bdg $22.60 (5 and up)
796.44
1. Gymnastics
ISBN 0-8225-3453-3
LC 94-40770

"Four chapters provide a brief history of gymnastics, descriptions of the six events for boys and the four events for girls, the basic moves, the general workout, and competition. The events and some of the skills are shown in excellent-quality full-color photographs on each page. Interesting facts in orange boxes appear throughout." SLJ

Includes glossary and bibliographical references

Feldman, Jane

I am a gymnast; as photographed by Jane Feldman. Random House 2000 unp il (Young dreamers) $14.99; lib bdg $16.99 (3-5)
796.44
1. Gymnastics
ISBN 0-375-80251-7; 0-375-90251-1 (lib bdg)
LC 00-26216

Seven-year-old McKenzie Foster describes her training, practice, and performance as a rhythmic gymnast

Jackman, Joan

Gymnastics. Dorling Kindersley 2000 45p il $9.95 (4 and up)
796.44
1. Gymnastics
ISBN 0-7894-5430-0
LC 99-50026

Jackman, Joan—*Continued*
"DK superguides"
Replaces The young gymnast, published 1995
Explores every aspect of gymnastics including clothing, warming up, apparatuses, balances, rolls and rolling, headstands and handstands, tumbling, and vaulting

796.48   Olympic games

Anderson, Dave
The story of the Olympics; foreword by Carl Lewis. Morrow 1996 160p il hardcover o.p. paperback available $9.95 (5 and up)   **796.48**
1. Olympic games
ISBN 0-688-17640-2 (pa)   LC 95-35067
Traces the history of the Olympics from its beginning in 776 B.C. to the present and relates stories of particular events such as track and field, gymnastics, and speed skating
"A thorough and detailed history of the Olympics is presented in spirited, readable prose." SLJ

Knotts, Bob
The Summer Olympics. Children's Press 2000 48p il lib bdg $22; pa $6.95 (2-4)   **796.48**
1. Olympic games
ISBN 0-516-21064-5 (lib bdg); 0-516-27029-X (pa)
LC 99-15090
"A True book"
Describes the history, ideals, events, and heroes of the Olympic Games, with an emphasis on the Summer Olympics
"Large print and informative texts are the hallmarks of the series. The color photographs are plentiful." Booklist
Includes bibliographical references

Woff, Richard, 1953-
The ancient Greek Olympics. Oxford Univ. Press 2000 c1999 32p il $16.95 (4 and up)
796.48
1. Olympic games
ISBN 0-19-521581-8   LC 99-87603
First published 1999 in the United Kingdom
Describes the history, traditions, and competitive events connected with the Olympic games held in ancient Greece
"The text brings to life the sights and sounds of the spectacle, Woff provides the sort of juicy information that students will find invaluable for research. Illustrations, including photographs of Greek art and statuary, are plentiful." Booklist
Includes bibliographical references

796.5   Outdoor life

Drake, Jane
The kids campfire book; [by] Jane Drake & Ann Love; illustrated by Heather Collins; songs arranged by Matthew Dewar. Kids Can Press 1998 128p il music $17.95 (4-6)   **796.5**
1. Outdoor life
ISBN 0-55074-539-5

First published 1996 in Canada
Topics include "how to select the right wood for the specific type of fire that is being built; recipes for food to cook over an open fire; games to play; songs, complete with the music and lyrics, to sing; ghost stories for spine-tingling telling; helpful hints for interacting—or not—with wildlife and insects; guides to viewing the night sky; and the appropriate gear for sleeping under the stars. Black-and-white illustrations are scattered throughout the lively, readable text." Booklist

796.52   Walking and exploring by kind of terrain

Jenkins, Steve
The top of the world; climbing Mount Everest. Houghton Mifflin 1999 unp il $16 (2-4)   **796.52**
1. Mountaineering 2. Mount Everest (China and Nepal)
ISBN 0-395-94218-7   LC 98-42748
Describes the conditions and terrain of Mount Everest, attempts that have been made to scale this peak, and general information about the equipment and techniques of mountain climbing
"Jenkins' papercut illustrations are extraordinary—feathery light to catch the effect of fog radiating off the mountains, mottled and striated to replicate rocky plateaus, pebbled to look like ice flowers. . . . A very attractive book, with plenty of substance for curious children." Booklist
Includes bibliographical references

796.8   Combat sports

Ditchfield, Christin
Wrestling. Children's Press 2000 47p il lib bdg $22; pa $6.95 (2-4)   **796.8**
1. Wrestling
ISBN 0-516-21611-2 (lib bdg); 0-516-27033-8 (pa)
LC 99-28191
"A True book"
Describes the history, rules, and styles of wrestling
Includes bibliographical references

Knotts, Bob
Martial arts. Children's Press 2000 47p il lib bdg $22; pa $6.95 (2-4)   **796.8**
1. Martial arts
ISBN 0-516-21609-0 (lib bdg); 0-516-27028-1 (pa)
LC 99-15091
"A True book"
Introduces judo, karate, and several other martial arts, highlighting safety and the mental discipline involved
Includes bibliographical references

Mitchell, David, 1944-
Martial arts. Dorling Kindersley 2000 64p il $9.95 (4 and up)   **796.8**
1. Martial arts
ISBN 0-7894-5431-9   LC 99-50020

Mitchell, David, 1944-—*Continued*
"DK superguides"
Replaces The young martial artist, published 1992
An illustrated guide to the history and techniques of a variety of martial arts including judo, tae kwon do, karate, and aikido
This includes "clear color photos against white backgrounds, lengthy captions, and numerous labels." Horn Book Guide
Includes glossary

796.9   Ice and snow sports

Sullivan, George
Snowboarding; a complete guide for beginners. Cobblehill Bks. 1997 48p il $15.99 (4 and up)
796.9
1. Snowboarding
ISBN 0-525-65235-3   LC 96-22756
Aspects covered include "choosing a board, traversing techniques, freestyle tricks, and safety tips. The clear design and easy-to-read instructions provide a solid and attractive resource for beginners." Horn Book Guide
Includes glossary

796.91   Ice skating

Boo, Michael
The story of figure skating. Morrow Junior Bks. 1998 224p il $16.95; pa $7.95 (5 and up) **796.91**
1. Ice skating
ISBN 0-688-15820-X; 0-688-15821-8 (pa)
LC 98-13569
Surveys the history of figure skating and examines some of its notable performers
"From axel to Zamboni, from Jackson Haines to Tara Lipinski—its's all here. Boo has done a superb job." SLJ
Includes bibliographical references

Gutman, Dan
Ice skating; from axels to Zambonis. Viking 1995 176p il $14.99; pa $6.99   **796.91**
1. Ice skating
ISBN 0-670-86013-1; 0-14-037501-5 (pa)
LC 95-14598
"This book is actually a narrative discussion of figure skating. The first chapter describes the sport's history, beginning with skating's prehistoric origins. Remaining chapters discuss the evolution of ice skating as a sport, stars of the past and present, a day in the life of a young skater, terminology, and trivia. A complete glossary and charts listing world, Olympic and U.S. skating champions make this a handy reference work as well." Voice Youth Advocates

Isadora, Rachel
Sophie skates. Putnam 1999 unp il $15.99 (k-3)
796.91
1. Ice skating
ISBN 0-399-23046-7   LC 98-21930

Uses a story about a young girl who loves to ice skate to introduce the sport: the parts and care of skates, the techniques of different skating moves, and ice skating competitions
"On the large, white pages are graceful watercolors depicting all sorts of specific details. . . . This provides an excellent balance between information (the pictures of equipment and moves are labeled) and a profile of a believable little Asian American girl." Booklist

Morrissey, Peter, 1953-
Ice skating. Dorling Kindersley 2000 45p il $9.95 (4 and up)   **796.91**
1. Ice skating
ISBN 0-7894-5427-0   LC 99-50019
"DK superguides"
Replaces The young ice skater, published 1998
Introduces basic ice skating techniques and steps, includes photographic sequences explaining advanced skills, and gives advice on choosing equipment and warming up safely

Wilkes, Debbi
The figure skating book; a young person's guide to figure skating. Firefly Bks. (Buffalo) 2000 116p il $19.95; pa $12.95 (4 and up)   **796.91**
1. Ice skating
ISBN 1-55209-444-8; 1-55209-445-6 (pa)
The author "gives specific advice on which skates to buy (expensive), how to find a skating club, and skating technique—from the most basic glide to complicated maneuvers." Booklist

796.962   Ice hockey

Foley, Mike
Fundamental hockey; photographs by Andy King. Lerner Publs. 1996 80p il (Fundamental sports) lib bdg $22.60 (5 and up)   **796.962**
1. Hockey
ISBN 0-8225-3456-8   LC 95-7077
"A brief history of the sport is followed by an explanation of what players do during hockey practice and what occurs during a game. Finally, readers see some of the drills and variations of the game, such as broomball and sledge hockey, which is played by players with lower-body disabilities. A substantial glossary and list of places to write for more information are appended." SLJ
Includes glossary and bibliographical references

Sullivan, George
All about hockey; illustrated with photographs and diagrams. Putnam 1998 159p il $15.99 (5 and up)   **796.962**
1. Hockey
ISBN 0-399-23172-2   LC 97-38125
An introduction to the sport of ice hockey, including its history, equipment, techniques, terminology, rules, and players
"This clearly written guide provides a good, solid introduction to the sport." Booklist
Includes glossary and bibliographical references

798.2   Horsemanship

Feldman, Jane
I am a rider. Random House 2000 unp il
(Young dreamers) $14.99; lib bdg $16.99 (3-5)
     798.2
1. Horsemanship
ISBN 0-679-88664-8; 0-679-98664-2 (lib bdg)
     LC 99-56689
Thirteen-year-old Eve, whose mother is a riding in-
structor, describes her life growing up with a horse of
her own, Lightning
"Feldman documents Eve's story with her own high-
quality black-and-white and color photos, and a few from
Eve's family's personal collection. A must for young rid-
ing enthusiasts." Booklist

798.8   Dog racing

Paulsen, Gary
Puppies, dogs, and blue northers; reflections on
being raised by a pack of sled dogs. Harcourt
Brace & Co. 1996 81p il $16; pa $9.95 (5 and up)
     798.8
1. Sled dog racing 2. Dogs
ISBN 0-15-292881-2; 0-385-32585-1 (pa)
     LC 95-18981
Illustrated by Ruth Wright Paulsen
"In seven vignettes, Paulsen recounts the story of his
lead dog, Cookie, as she mates and gives birth, and her
puppies mature toward their destiny—to race and pull
sleds. Readers are drawn into that special bond between
driver and lead dog through Paulsen's real-life experiences racing in Minnesota. . . . Ruth Wright Paulsen's
occasional paintings add warmth and charm to the book."
SLJ

Wood, Ted, 1965-
Iditarod dream; Dusty and his sled dogs
compete in Alaska's Jr. Iditarod. Walker & Co.
1996 48p il map $16.95; lib bdg $17.85 (4 and up)
     798.8
1. Sled dog racing
ISBN 0-8027-8406-2; 0-8027-8407-0 (lib bdg)
     LC 95-31084
This "photo essay follows 15-year-old Dusty Whitte-
more of Cantwell, AK, through the 1995 Jr. Iditarod Sled
Dog Race—158 miles from Lake Lucille to Yentna and
back." SLJ
"Clear, close-up color photographs portray every stage
of the event and offer interesting information about the
difficulties and hazards of this two-day competition."
Booklist

799.1   Fishing

Arnosky, Jim
Flies in the water, fish in the air; a personal
introduction to fly fishing. Lothrop, Lee &
Shepard Bks. 1986 96p il $13.95 (5 and up)
     799.1
1. Fly casting
ISBN 0-688-05834-5   LC 84-29684

An anecdotal account of the pleasures of fly fishing,
discussing the choice and use of tackle, kinds of flies,
walking in water, and watching for fish
"This book is a hybrid. Coupled with a how-to manual
on fly fishing is a naturalist's exploration of freshwater
streams and ponds and their inhabitants. . . . The author's delightful, intricately detailed black-and-white
drawings complement the clear, informative prose." Appraisal

Bailey, John
Fishing. Dorling Kindersley 2001 48p il $9.95
(4 and up)   **799.1**
1. Fishing
ISBN 0-7894-7389-5   LC 00-57095
"DK superguides"
Replaces The young fishing enthusiast, published 1999
This covers "practical information on the basics of
fishing . . . including choosing the right rod and tackle
for fresh or saltwater fishing, preparing bait, casting
lines, identifying fish and what they eat, and much
more." Publisher's note

800   LITERATURE & RHETORIC

803   Literature—Encyclopedias and dictionaries

Brewer's dictionary of phrase and fable.
HarperCollins Pubs. $50   **803**
1. Literature—Dictionaries 2. Allusions

First published 1870. (16th edition 1999) Periodically
revised
Current edition edited by Adrian Room
"Over 15,000 brief entries give the meanings and origins of a broad range of terms, expressions, and names
of real, fictitious and mythical characters from world history, science, the arts and literature." N Y Public Libr.
Ref Books for Child Collect. 2d edition

808   Rhetoric

Christelow, Eileen, 1943-
What do authors do? Clarion Bks. 1995 32p il
$15; pa $5.95 (1-3)   **808**
1. Authorship 2. Authors 3. Illustrators 4. Publishers
and publishing
ISBN 0-395-71124-X; 0-395-86621-9 (pa)
     LC 94-19725
Companion volume to What do illustrators do?
The author "follows two next-door neighbors as they
independently develop stories about their pets—the
scruffy sheepdog, Rufus; and Max, his energetic feline
adversary. Dialogue in cartoon balloons and brief text
describe the writing process and the mechanics of publishing." SLJ
"Christelow packs a great deal of humor as well as information into her attractive pages. Best of all, she infuses the whole with a sense of the zest and love that
writers feel for their work." Booklist

James, Elizabeth

How to write super school reports; [by] Elizabeth James and Carol Barkin. rev ed. Lothrop, Lee & Shepard Bks. 1998 90p (School survival guide) $15; pa $4.95 (4 and up)   **808**

1. Report writing 2. Research

ISBN 0-688-16132-4; 0-688-16141-3 (pa)

LC 98-13767

First published 1983 with title: How to write a great school report

This guide "offers suggestions for choosing a topic, finding facts, using the library, organizing notes, and, finally, putting the report together. . . . Advice on how to conduct searches, cite sources, and validate information found on the Internet." SLJ

How to write terrific book reports; [by] Elizabeth James and Carol Barkin. rev ed. Lothrop, Lee & Shepard Bks. 1998 80p (School survival guide) $15; pa $4.95 (4 and up)   **808**

1. Report writing 2. Books—Reviews

ISBN 0-688-16131-6; 0-688-16140-5 (pa)

LC 98-9198

First published 1986 with title: How to write your best book report

"The authors explore what a book report is, how to choose a title, writing preliminary and final drafts, giving an oral presentation, the importance of the library in finding material, and other aspects of this common assignment." SLJ

Leedy, Loreen, 1959-

Messages in the mailbox; how to write a letter; written and illustrated by Loreen Leedy. Holiday House 1991 unp il $16.95; pa $5.95 (k-3)   **808**

1. Letter writing

ISBN 0-8234-0889-2; 0-8234-1079-X (pa)

LC 91-8718

Discusses the different kinds of letters, the parts of a letter, and who can be a potential correspondent, and provides examples

"Leedy's softly colored realistic illustrations feature both animal characters and people from a variety of cultures. The partnership of text and illustration gives a lively and interesting perspective to an otherwise dull topic. . . . A superb book that shouldn't be missed." SLJ

Stevens, Carla

A book of your own; keeping a diary or journal. Clarion Bks. 1993 100p $16 (5 and up)   **808**

1. Authorship 2. Diaries

ISBN 0-89919-256-4

LC 92-33818

"The author offers advice on getting started, selecting tools to use, maintaining privacy, and overcoming writer's block. . . . Stevens includes excerpts from the diaries of personal friends and historical figures. Among the famous diarists quoted are Anne Frank, Anais Nin, Theodore Roosevelt, Beatrix Potter, and Louisa May Alcott." Voice Youth Advocates

"A very useful book; libraries where journal writing is in the curriculum may want more than one copy." Booklist

Includes bibliographical references

Young, Sue

Writing with style. Scholastic Ref. 1997 143p (Scholastic guides) hardcover o.p. paperback available $8.95 (5 and up)   **808**

1. Authorship 2. Creative writing

ISBN 0-590-25424-3 (pa)

LC 96-8772

Presents tips for writing interesting stories, passionate essays, and exciting reports, focusing on the elements of sentence structure, paragraph organization, grammar, usage, punctuation, and footnotes

"The book is easy to comprehend, upbeat, and relevant. A must for library shelves and classrooms." SLJ

Includes bibliographical references

808.06   Writing children's literature

Origins of story; on writing for children; edited by Barbara Harrison and Gregory Maguire. Margaret K. McElderry Bks. 1999 206p il $20   **808.06**

1. Children's literature—History and criticism 2. Authors 3. Illustrators

ISBN 0-689-82604-4

LC 98-45300

Collection of 17 lectures originally presented at programs and lectures sponsored by Children's Literature New England

Among the "authors included are Betty Levin, Virginia Hamilton, Tom Feelings, Katherine Paterson, and Jill Paton Walsh. Thought-provoking and immensely readable, this is professional reading that's fun." Booklist

808.1   Rhetoric of poetry

Janeczko, Paul B., 1945-

How to write poetry. Scholastic Ref. 1999 117p il (Scholastic guides) $12.95 (5 and up)   **808.1**

1. Poetics

ISBN 0-590-10077-7

LC 98-26866

Provides practical advice with checklists on the art of writing poetry

"A friendly, accessible, and highly usable primer." Horn Book Guide

Includes glossary and bibliographical references

Poetry from A to Z; a guide for young writers; compiled by Paul B. Janeczko; illustrated by Cathy Bobak. Bradbury Press 1994 131p il $16 (5 and up)   **808.1**

1. Poetics 2. American poetry—Collections

ISBN 0-02-747672-3

LC 94-10528

"In his guide, Janeczko gives many examples and ideas to get young writers started writing poetry. The book is organized alphabetically with seventy-two poems on almost any topic you could imagine. In addition, fourteen exercises labeled 'Try This' explain how to write different types of poems and help a young writer get started." Voice Youth Advocates

Includes bibliographical references

808.3   Rhetoric of fiction

Bauer, Marion Dane, 1938-
What's your story? a young person's guide to writing fiction. Clarion Bks. 1992 134p $15; pa $6.95 (5 and up)   **808.3**
1. Authorship 2. Creative writing
ISBN 0-395-57781-0; 0-395-57780-2 (pa)
                     LC 91-3816
Discusses how to write fiction, exploring such aspects as character, plot, point of view, dialogue, endings, and revising
"Bauer reveals the somber reality that writing can be hard work, though worth the effort for those who persevere. What follows is a clear, concise elucidation on the elements of fiction. . . . Bauer has taken a thorough, clear, and functional approach to this topic." Horn Book

808.5   Rhetoric of speech

Otfinoski, Steven, 1949-
Speaking up, speaking out; a kid's guide to making speeches, oral reports, and conversation; illustrated by Carol Nicklaus. Millbrook Press 1996 79p il lib bdg $24.90; pa $8.95 (5 and up)
                               808.5
1. Public speaking
ISBN 1-56294-345-6 (lib bdg); 0-7613-0138-0 (pa)
                     LC 96-509
Provides strategies and encouraging tips for speaking in social situations, reading aloud, presenting oral reports, and making speeches of all kinds
"This appealing handbook provides youngsters with just about everything they need to know about oral communication. . . . Nicklaus's cartoon illustrations are appropriately lighthearted, adding touches of humor to the text." SLJ
Includes glossary and bibliographical references

808.8   Literature—Collections

Bauer, Caroline Feller, 1935-
Celebrations; read-aloud holiday and theme book programs; drawings by Lynn Gates Bredeson. Wilson, H.W. 1985 301p il $55 **808.8**
1. Holidays 2. Literature—Collections 3. Books and reading 4. Children's libraries
ISBN 0-8242-0708-4   LC 85-714
"Aimed at librarians and other adults who work with middle-grade children, this book offers a potpourri of ideas and suggestions for planning holiday programs. Each chapter focuses on a holiday—some well known, some concocted by Bauer—and includes prose [and poetry] selections, activities, and a booklist." Booklist

The **Oxford** book of scary tales; [edited by] Dennis Pepper. Oxford Univ. Press 1992 155p il $25 (5 and up)   **808.8**
1. Literature—Collections 2. Supernatural—Fiction
ISBN 0-19-278131-6

"The 35 stories and poems (half of them written for this book) vary in scariness, eschew the gruesome, and some—like that of the gravedigging great-grandfather—share a laugh. Although mostly British, there are retellings from Africa, India, Japan, and the United States." SLJ
"The poems here are as good as the tales, direct in voice and domestic in detail. The whole collection is clearly meant for reading aloud and sharing." Booklist

The **Read-aloud** treasury; compiled by Joanna Cole and Stephanie Calmenson; illustrated by Ann Schweninger. Doubleday 1988 255p il $19.95   **808.8**
1. Literature—Collections
ISBN 0-385-18560-X   LC 86-24138
An illustrated collection of classic and modern nursery rhymes, poems, stories, and activity games
"A lively and surprisingly inclusive treasury. . . . Some of the most valuable items include five stories reprinted with their original illustrations: 'Little Bear Goes to the Moon' from *Little Bear, Sylvester and the Magic Pebble, Angus and the Cat, Corduroy* and 'The Very Tall Mouse and the Very Short Mouse' from *Mouse Tales*. . . . Schweninger's full-color illustrations complement and enhance the positive and inviting tone of this collection." Publ Wkly

Snowy day: stories and poems; edited by Caroline Feller Bauer; illustrated by Margot Tomes. Lippincott 1986 68p il lib bdg $16.89 (2-4)
                               808.8
1. Literature—Collections
ISBN 0-397-32177-5   LC 85-45858
This collection "features three short stories—Uchida's Japanese 'New Year's Hats for the Statues,' Singer's Jewish 'The Snow in Chelm,' and Bauer's adaptation of the Russian 'Marika the Snowmaiden.' The 28 poems include selections by X. J. Kennedy, Gwendolyn Brooks, David McCord, Lilian Moore, Dennis Lee, Kaye Starbird, John Ciardi, Myra Cohn Livingston, Karla Kuskin, and others." Bull Cent Child Books
"Margot Tomes's charming, evocative, black-and-white illustrations of snowflakes and leafless trees, sleds, and snowballs add the perfect touch to a wintry treat." Horn Book
Includes bibliographical references

808.81   Poetry—Collections

A. Nonny Mouse writes again! poems selected by Jack Prelutsky; illustrated by Marjorie Priceman. Knopf 1993 unp il $13; pa $6.99 (1-3) **808.81**
1. Poetry—Collections
ISBN 0-679-83715-9; 0-679-88087-9 (pa)
                     LC 92-5214
An illustrated collection of primarily traditional or anonymous verses, in such categories as "Wordplay," "Food," "Impossible Doings," and "Bad Kids"
"There's something here for every taste—all enlivened by Marjorie Priceman's fluid, inviting watercolors." Horn Book

The **Baby's** bedtime book; [compiled and illustrated by] Kay Chorao. Dutton 1984 64p il $16.99; pa $5.99 **808.81**
1. Poetry—Collections 2. Nursery rhymes 3. Lullabies
ISBN 0-525-44149-2; 0-14-055384-3 (pa)
LC 84-6067
This collection includes traditional rhymes, lullabies and prayers ("Now I lay me down to sleep") and poems by authors including Blake, Kipling, Tennyson, Rossetti and Robert Louis Stevenson
"Luminous cross-hatched illustrations create magic for the 27 poems collected here. Each poem is adorned with Chorao's softly-colored full-page illustrations, bordered in tranquil blue. The poems include a few selections that well deserve a place in childhood, such as 'Hush, Little Baby' and 'Rock-a-bye Baby'; the majority are less familiar, including a few very special selections, such as Naidu's 'Cradle Song.'" SLJ

Carle, Eric
Eric Carle's animals, animals; poems compiled by Laura Whipple. Philomel Bks. 1989 82p il $21.99; pa $7.99 **808.81**
1. Animals—Poetry 2. Poetry—Collections
ISBN 0-399-21744-4; 0-698-11855-3 (pa)
LC 88-31646
"Illustrations take center stage in *Eric Carle's Animals Animals* . . . compiled by Laura Whipple. The well-chosen poems are from a variety of sources—the Bible, Shakespeare, Japanese Haiku, Pawnee Indian, weather sayings and contemporary poets like Judith Viorst, Ogden Nash, and Jack Prelutsky. On many pages the poem may be only two or three lines but the pictures are full-page spreads in Mr. Carle's familiar vividly colored, collage style." Kobrin Letter

Eric Carle's dragons dragons and other creatures that never were; compiled by Laura Whipple. Philomel Bks. 1991 69p il $19.99; pa $8.99 **808.81**
1. Mythical animals—Poetry 2. Poetry—Collections
ISBN 0-399-22105-0; 0-399-22837-3 (pa)
LC 91-11986
An illustrated collection of poems about dragons and other fantastic creatures by a variety of authors
"The collection offers a sumptuous viewing of Carle's rich blend of tissue-paper and paint collages and a grand introduction to the imaginary beasts. Laura Whipple concludes this adroit compilation with a brief commentary on the fabulous animals as 'a magical part of our human heritage.'" Horn Book
Includes glossary

Christmas poems; selected by Myra Cohn Livingston; illustrated by Trina Schart Hyman. Holiday House 1984 32p il lib bdg $15.95 **808.81**
1. Christmas—Poetry 2. Poetry—Collections
ISBN 0-8234-0508-7
LC 83-18559
The selections "range from the Nativity to John Ciardi's speculations about how Santa gets down to Key West to a nice limerick applauding Mrs. S. Claus. The collection gets its unity from Trina Schart Hyman's drawings, placing all the figures in the vicinity of a Christmas tree supervised by the family cat." Read Teach

Climb into my lap; first poems to read together; selected by Lee Bennett Hopkins; illustrated by Kathryn Brown. Simon & Schuster Bks. for Young Readers 1998 79p il $19.95 (k-3) **808.81**
1. Poetry—Collections
ISBN 0-689-80715-5
LC 97-18670
A collection of poems chosen to be read aloud, by such authors as Edward Lear, Charlotte Zolotow, and Nancy Willard
"Each selection, accompanied by Brown's gentle watercolor illustrations, expresses a sense of the wonder in the everyday world." SLJ

Curious cats in art and poetry; edited by William Lach. Atheneum Bks. for Young Readers; Metropolitan Mus. of Art 1999 48p il $16 **808.81**
1. Cats—Poetry 2. Cats in art 3. Poetry—Collections
ISBN 0-689-83055-6
LC 99-11663
Poems about cats by such poets as Langston Hughes, Kate Greenaway, Pablo Neruda, and William Blake are matched with works of art from the collections of the Metropolitan Museum of Art
"This playful compendium of poetry and fine art is sure to tickle every feline fanatic's fancy. The collection contains something for everyone." SLJ

The **Earth** is painted green; a garden of poems about our planet; edited by Barbara Brenner; illustrated by S. D. Schindler. Scholastic 1994 81p il hardcover o.p. paperback available $5.99 (4-6) **808.81**
1. Nature—Poetry 2. Poetry—Collections 3. Earth—Poetry
ISBN 0-590-45135-9 (pa)
LC 93-21466
"A Byron Preiss book"
"Nearly one hundred poems from around the world extol the various aspects of our great, green Earth and all of its botanical beauty. The tone of the poems ranges from playful to thought provoking; profuse illustrations rendered in precise watercolor add visual lushness to a rich, poetic experience." Horn Book Guide

Index to children's poetry; a title, subject, author, and first line index to poetry in collections for children and youth; compiled by John E. and Sara W. Brewton. Wilson, H.W. 1942-1965 3v **808.81**
1. Poetry—Indexes

Basic volume published 1942 $80 (ISBN 0-8242-0021-7); first supplement published 1954 $50 (ISBN 0-8242-0022-5); second supplement published 1965 $50 (ISBN 0-8242-0023-3)
The main volume indexes 15,000 poems by 2,500 authors in 130 collections. The two supplements analyze another 15,000 poems by 2700 authors in 151 collections
"This tool is an invaluable reference source." Peterson. Ref Books for Child
Continued by: Index to poetry for children and young people

Index to poetry for children and young people; a title, subject, author, and first line index to poetry in collections for children and young people. Wilson, H.W. 1972-1999 6v   **808.81**
1. Poetry—Indexes

A continuation of: Index to children's poetry. The volume published 1972 covering 1964-1969 compiled by John E. and Sara W. Brewton and G. Meredith Blackburn III o.p.; 1970-1975 published 1978 compiled by John E. Brewton, G. Meredith Blackburn III and Lorraine A. Blackburn o.p.; 1976-1981 published 1984 compiled by John E. Brewton, G. Meredith Blackburn III and Lorraine A. Blackburn o.p.; 1982-1987 published 1989 compiled by G. Meredith Blackburn III and Lorraine A. Blackburn o.p.; 1988-1992 published 1994 compiled by G. Meredith Blackburn III o.p.; 1993-1997 compiled by G. Meredith Blackburn III $80 (ISBN 0-8242-0939-7)

"This series is the key to poetry in any youth collection. It indexes anthologies by author, title, subject and first line and is essential both for identifying the elusive poem and for adding poetry on specific subjects to whole-language units, booktalks, bibliographies and thematic celebrations. The anthologies indexed are important for collection analysis and collection management. The indexes and the volumes analyzed are not candidates for weeding. Essential for every collection at every level." Stafford. Guide to Ref Materials for Sch Libr Media Cent. 5th edition

My song is beautiful; poems and pictures in many voices; selected by Mary Ann Hoberman. Little, Brown 1994 32p il lib bdg $16.95 (k-3)
    808.81
1. Poetry—Collections
ISBN 0-316-36738-9   LC 93-24976
"This small anthology of 14 poems celebrates diversity, not only in culture, but also in mood and genre (from invocation to nonsense verse) and in illustrator, artistic medium, and style. . . . There are fine poems by Nikki Giovanni, Jack Prelutsky, A. A. Milne, and others, including a Brooklyn seventh-grader; and there are translations from Central Eskimo, ancient Mexico, Korea, and Chippewa Indian. Each poem is illustrated by a different artist, among them, Ashley Bryan, David Diaz, and Keiko Narahashi." Booklist

The **New** Oxford treasury of children's poems; [edited by] Michael Harrison and Christopher Stuart-Clark. Oxford Univ. Press 1997 165p il $25 (3-5)   **808.81**
1. Poetry—Collections
ISBN 0-19-276137-4
Companion volume to The Oxford treasury of children's poems (1988)
"This anthology features primarily English and American poets, from W. B. Yeats and William Blake to Eve Merriam and Nikki Giovanni. While the focus is on older rhyming poems with playful subjects, there is a smattering of modern poetry, free verse, and serious themes." SLJ
"Large-format anthology features excellent poems illustrated in full color. . . . Eleven artists contributed illustrations that interpret the poetry with wit, verve, and delicacy." Booklist

The **Oxford** book of animal poems; [edited by] Michael Harrison and Christopher Stuart-Clark. Oxford Univ. Press 1992 157p il $12.95 (5 and up)   **808.81**
1. Animals—Poetry 2. Poetry—Collections
ISBN 0-19-276105-6   LC 91-050050
"Arranged by continent and illustrated by several artists in a variety of styles, the poems in this large, well-designed anthology are about wild animals all over the world. . . . For browsing and for curricular support, this collection will have wide appeal." Booklist

The **Oxford** book of Christmas poems; edited by Michael Harrison and Christopher Stuart-Clark. Oxford Univ. Press 1983 160p il hardcover o.p. paperback available $12.95 (4 and up)   **808.81**
1. Christmas—Poetry 2. Poetry—Collections
ISBN 0-19-276214-1 (pa)   LC 85-120897
This "collection of 120 British and American poems is organized into four sections around the season of winter, the coming of Advent, the Nativity and celebration of Christmas, and the anticipation of a new year. The poets are both well and lesser known, carefully chosen for a balance of old and new." Booklist

Side by side; poems to read together; collected by Lee Bennett Hopkins; illustrated by Hilary Knight. Simon & Schuster Bks. for Young Readers 1988 80p il lib bdg $19.95; pa $9.95
    808.81
1. Poetry—Collections
ISBN 0-671-63579-4; 0-671-73622-1 (pa)
      LC 87-33025
A collection of poems especially chosen to be read aloud, by authors ranging from Lewis Carroll and Robert Louis Stevenson to Gwendolyn Brooks and David McCord
"With the rhythmic, sometimes narrative verses, and the joyful antics of the characters prancing across the pages, this collection offers visual as well as aural treats for children and adults to savor together." Booklist

Sing a song of popcorn; every child's book of poems; illustrated by nine Caldecott Medal artists, Marcia Brown [et al.]; selected by Beatrice Schenk de Regniers [et al.] Scholastic 1988 142p il lib bdg $18.95   **808.81**
1. Poetry—Collections
ISBN 0-590-40645-0   LC 87-4330
Revised edition of Poems children will sit still for, published 1969
A collection of 128 poems by a variety of well-known authors with illustrations by nine Caldecott medalists
"A pleasant book, still a useful if conservative anthology, this has title, author, and first line indexes, and brief notes on the illustrators." Bull Cent Child Books

Talking to the sun: an illustrated anthology of poems for young people; selected and introduced by Kenneth Koch and Kate Farrell. Metropolitan Mus. of Art; Holt & Co. 1985 112p il $35   **808.81**
1. Poetry—Collections
ISBN 0-8050-0144-1 (Holt & Co.)   LC 85-15428

Talking to the sun: an illustrated anthology of poems for young people—*Continued*

"Poems from a wide variety of times and cultures and reproductions from the Metropolitan Museum of Art are organized by themes that include spring, love, nonsense, animals, and the secrets beneath the ordinary." Booklist

Valentine poems; selected by Myra Cohn Livingston; illustrated by Patience Brewster. Holiday House 1987 32p il lib bdg $16.95
808.81
1. Valentine's Day—Poetry 2. Poetry—Collections
ISBN 0-8234-0587-7 LC 85-31723

"A short anthology of poems for Valentine's Day that combines first-rate humorous and romantic verses by both contemporary and traditional poets. Both young listeners and independent readers will find the selections appealing. Brewster's humorous red and blue pencil illustrations of animals suit each poem, such as the two rabbits who show Love's strength for Karla Kuskin's 'To You'. . . . A plus for both school and public libraries needing Valentine's Day material." SLJ

War and the pity of war; edited by Neil Philip; illustrated by Michael McCurdy. Clarion Bks. 1998 96p il $20 (5 and up) **808.81**
1. War—Poetry 2. Poetry—Collections
ISBN 0-395-84982-9 LC 97-32897

Presents an illustrated collection of poems about the waste, horror, and futility of war as well as the nobility, courage, and sacrifice of individuals in wartime

"The selections, covering conflicts from ancient Persia to modern-day Bosnia, are by a wide variety of poets, from the well known (Tennyson, Whitman, Sandburg, Auden), to the obscure (Anakreon from ancient Greece and 11th-century Chinese poet Bunno). . . . The stark and simple scratchboard drawings are reminiscent of the Ernie Pyle illustrations from World War II and are as memorable as the best propaganda." SLJ

Winter poems; selected by Barbara Rogasky; illustrated by Trina Schart Hyman. Scholastic 1994 40p il $15.95; pa $5.99 **808.81**
1. Winter—Poetry 2. Poetry—Collections
ISBN 0-590-42872-1; 0-590-42873-X (pa)
LC 91-24419

"Rogasky has selected a wide range of poems—25 in all—dating from 10th-century Japan to the contemporary U.S. The best of the ages is represented, with familiar favorites from Shakespeare, Thomas Hardy, Robert Frost, Emily Dickinson, Carl Sandburg, etc. . . . Hyman's illustrations perfectly capture the spirit of that season, with acrylics in deep, chilling shades. . . . A beautiful presentation of outstanding quality." SLJ

A **Zooful** of animals; selected by William Cole; illustrated by Lynn Munsinger. Houghton Mifflin 1992 88p il $17.95; pa $8.95 **808.81**
1. Animals—Poetry 2. Poetry—Collections
ISBN 0-395-52278-1; 0-395-77873-5 (pa)
LC 91-21885

A collection of animal poems by authors including Rachel Field, Shel Silverstein, and John Ciardi

"Not your usual zoo, this happy gathering of poetry and verse is broadly inclusive of its denizens, who live in unfettered joy within handsomely designed pages. . . . Lynn Munsinger's full-color illustrations contribute to making this book outstanding. She has a wonderfully expressive yet delicate line, the ability to be elegant and humorous at the same time." Horn Book

808.82 Drama—Collections

The **Big** book of Christmas plays; 21 modern and traditional one-act plays for the celebration of Christmas; edited by Sylvia E. Kamerman. Plays 1988 357p $18.95 **808.82**
1. Christmas—Drama 2. One act plays
ISBN 0-8238-0288-4 LC 88-15691

This collection includes "adaptations of scenes from *Little Women, Les Misérables,* and *A Christmas Carol* . . . [as well as] more modern offerings. . . . The table of contents, which seemingly includes something for everyone from lower grades through high school, is arranged by age group. Appended production notes lists characters, playing time, costumes, props, setting, lighting, and sound effects." Booklist

Play index. Wilson, H.W. 1953-1997 9v **808.82**
1. Drama—Indexes
ISSN 0554-3037

First published 1953, covering the years 1949-1952, and edited by Dorothy Herbert West and Dorothy Margaret Peake $55. Additional volumes: 1953-1960 $55 edited by Estelle A. Fidell and Dorothy Margaret Peake; 1961-1967 $55 edited by Estelle A. Fidell; 1968-1972 $55 edited by Estelle A. Fidell; 1973-1977 $55 edited by Estelle A. Fidell; 1978-1982 $55 edited by Juliette Yaakov; 1983-1987 $65 edited by Juliette Yaakov and John Greenfieldt; 1988-1992 $90 edited by Juliette Yaakov and John Greenfieldt; 1993-1997 edited by Juliette Yaakov and John Greenfieldt $155

Play index indexes plays in collections and single plays; one-act and full-length plays; radio, television, and Broadway plays; plays for amateur production; plays for children, young adults, and adults. It is divided into four parts. Part I is an author, title, and subject index; the author or main entry includes the title of the play, brief synopsis of the plot, number of acts and scenes, size of cast, number of sets, and bibliographic information. Part II is a list of collections indexed, and Part III, a cast analysis, lists plays by the type of cast and number of players required. Part IV is a directory of publishers and distributors

"This index is an excellent source for locating published plays." Nichols. Guide to Ref Books for Sch Media Cent. 4th edition

Plays: the drama magazine for young people. Plays $30 per year **808.82**
1. Drama—Periodicals 2. Children's plays—Periodicals
ISSN 0032-1540

Monthly October through May, except January/February combined. First published 1941

Each issue of this magazine "offers approximately three plays for junior and senior high school students and three or more for the middle and lower grades. In addition, there is a dramatized classic and either a skit, a

Plays: the drama magazine for young people—
Continued
puppet play, or a choral reading. Production notes and
stage directions accompany each play." Katz. Mag for
Libr. 10th edition

808.88 Collections of miscellaneous writings

Bartlett, John, 1820-1905
Familiar quotations. Little, Brown $47.50
808.88

1. Quotations

First published 1855. (16th edition 1992) Periodically
revised. Editors vary
"Comprehensive collection of quotations in chronological order with author and keyword indexes." N Y Public
Libr. Ref Books for Child Collect. 2d edition

Cole, Joanna
Six sick sheep; 101 tongue twisters; compiled
by Joanna Cole and Stephanie Calmenson;
illustrated by Alan Tiegreen. Morrow Junior Bks.
1993 64p il hardcover o.p. paperback available
$6.95 (3-6)
808.88
1. Tongue twisters
ISBN 0-688-11068-1 (pa)
LC 92-5715
A collection of all kinds of tongue twisters: some only
two or three words long, some that tell a story, and some
featuring a theme
Includes bibliographical references

Quotations for kids; compiled and edited by J.A.
Senn; illustrations by Steve Pica. Millbrook
Press 1999 256p il map $24.95; lib bdg $39.90
(4 and up)
808.88
1. Quotations
ISBN 0-7613-1296-X; 0-7613-0267-0 (lib bdg)
LC 98-40310
An illustrated reference work offering more than 2000
quotations ranging from the Bible to folklore to children's literature
"Lively cartoonlike illustrations by Steve Pica and excellent cross-references enhance the volume. . . . The
compendium will have enormous appeal to all ages: it
will be useful for reports, creative writing, and discussion, as well as being a delightfully entertaining book to
browse." Booklist
Includes bibliographical references

Scholastic treasury of quotations for children;
[compiled by] Adrienne Betz. Scholastic Ref.
1998 254p $16.95 (4 and up)
808.88
1. Quotations
ISBN 0-590-27146-6
LC 97-34153
Presents 1,200 quotations from ancient to modern
times on topics such as cooperation, growing up, nature,
success, and faith
"A comprehensive and accessible compendium. . . .
An excellent introduction explains how to use the book,
guides readers on including quotations in their own
speaking and writing, and discusses sources consulted."
SLJ

Schwartz, Alvin, 1927-1992
Busy buzzing bumblebees and other tongue
twisters; illustrated by Paul Meisel. HarperCollins
Pubs. 1992 61p il lib bdg $15.89; pa $4.50 (k-2)
808.88

1. Tongue twisters
ISBN 0-06-025269-3 (lib bdg); 0-06-444036-2 (pa)
LC 91-4799

"An I can read book"
First published 1982 with different illustrations
This book "contains 46 easy-to-read tongue twisters."
SLJ
"Illustrated in wild, cheerful watercolors and with a
multicultural cast, this . . . collection of tongue twisters
is perfect for beginning readers." Booklist

809 Literary history and criticism

Carpenter, Humphrey
The Oxford companion to children's literature;
[by] Humphrey Carpenter and Mari Prichard.
Oxford Univ. Press 1984 586p il hardcover o.p.
paperback available $24.95
809
1. Children's literature—Dictionaries
ISBN 0-19-860228-6 (pa)
LC 83-15130
"One volume work with brief critiques of authors, illustrators, books, characters, and radio and television programs. Largely British in coverage of materials but does
include most Newbery winners as well as well-known
American, Australian and Canadian authors. Contemporary and historical subjects related to children's literature
are examined." N Y Public Libr. Ref Books for Child
Collect. 2d edition

810.3 American literature— Encyclopedias and dictionaries

McElmeel, Sharron L.
100 most popular children's authors;
biographical sketches and bibliographies. Libraries
Unlimited 1999 xxxi, 493p il (Popular authors
series) $48
810.3
1. Children's literature—Bio-bibliography
ISBN 1-56308-646-8
LC 98-41942
"Based on a 1997 survey of both teachers and students, this volume includes such well-known authors as
Beverly Clearly (most recognized by the survey respon-
dents) and classic writers like Lewis Carroll and C. S.
Lewis. Each entry provides several pages about the author and his or her writings followed by a section called
'Books and Notes,' which has details about specific books
and their themes, including bibliographic information. A
list of additional material about or by the author completes each entry." Booklist

100 most popular picture book authors and
illustrators; biographical sketches and
bibliographies. Libraries Unlimited 2000 xxix,
579p (Popular authors series) $55
810.3
1. Children's literature—Bio-bibliography 2. Picture
books for children—Bibliography
ISBN 1-56308-647-6
LC 00-23181

McElmeel, Sharron L.—*Continued*

The 100 profiles "are accompanied by photographs, reading lists, and lists of related information sources (such as Web pages). Contemporary authors and illustrators whose works are still in print provide the focus." Publisher's note

810.8 American literature— Collections

From sea to shining sea; a treasury of American folklore and folk songs; illustrated by eleven Caldecott Medal and four Caldecott honor book artists: Molly Bang [et al.]; compiled by Amy L. Cohn. Scholastic 1993 399p il music $29.95 **810.8**
1. American literature—Collections 2. Folklore— United States 3. Folk songs—United States
ISBN 0-590-42868-3   LC 92-30598
A compilation of more than 140 folk songs, tales, poems, non-fiction, and stories telling the history of America and reflecting its multicultural society
This is "a treasure chest that will be dipped into year after year and generation after generation. The attention to detail and love that each illustrator brought to their section is evident as is the research Ms. Cohn did before making her choices. A masterpiece that is also a gorgeous piece of book making." Child Book Rev Serv
Includes glossary and bibliographical references

Ready, set, read—and laugh! a funny treasury for beginning readers; compiled by Joanna Cole and Stephanie Calmenson. Doubleday Bks. for Young Readers 1995 144p il music $17.95 (k-3) **810.8**
1. American literature—Collections
ISBN 0-385-32119-8   LC 94-32535
This collection includes "5 stories (including Nancy Shaw's *Sheep in a Shop* and an excerpt from James Marshall's *Fox on the Job*); 14 poems (by Karla Kuskin, Eve Merriam, Lee Bennett Hopkins, and others); and 7 assorted riddles, songs, and games. The illustrations are bright and cheerful. . . . Adding to the volume's appeal to fledgling readers is the fact that it looks more like a chapter book than a typical beginning reader." SLJ

Rising voices; writings of young Native Americans; selected by Arlene B. Hirschfelder and Beverly R. Singer. Scribner 1992 115p o.p.; Ballantine Bks. paperback available $6.50 (5 and up) **810.8**
1. American literature—Native American authors— Collections 2. Native Americans 3. Children's writings
ISBN 0-804-11167-7 (pa)   LC 91-32083
Also available in paperback from Ivy Bks.
A collection of poems and essays in which young Native Americans speak of their identity, their families and communities, rituals, and the harsh realities of their lives
"These 'rising voices' speak eloquently in this important collection. . . . Some pieces are over 100 years old; some are quite current. Some were written by elementary school students, and others by high schoolers. All are poignant and haunting." Voice Youth Advocates

Scared silly! a book for the brave; [compiled and illustrated by] Marc Brown. Little, Brown 1994 61p il music $18.95; pa $7.95 (k-3) **810.8**
1. American literature—Collections
ISBN 0-316-11360-3; 0-316-10372-1 (pa)
LC 93-13501
An illustrated collection of spooky stories, poems, and riddles including a humorous array of ghosts, monsters, ghouls, and witches
This is "shivery enough to awe a young audience, yet silly enough for them to giggle their apprehensions away. Selections by such well-known authors as Ogden Nash, Jack Prelutsky, and Judith Viorst are included, as well as several original pieces by Brown. . . . Brown scores again with his own brand of warm, engaging watercolor art. . . . Brilliant colors, attention to detail, and the excellent balance of text and art provide a feast for the eye." SLJ

Stone Soup; the magazine by young writers and artists. Children's Art Foundation $33 per year **810.8**
1. Children's writings—Periodicals 2. Child artists— Periodicals
ISSN 0094-579X
Six issues a year. First published 1973
This magazine "provides young writers and artists a wonderful opportunity to submit their work for publication. Each of the stories, poetry, book reviews and artwork found in *Stone Soup* is the original work of the young contributors. Contributors are encouraged to submit writing and artwork based on their experiences and observations. Photographs of the writers and artists are included with their creations. *Stone Soup* is also available in a Braille edition." Katz. Mag for Libr. 10th edition

Thanksgiving: stories and poems; edited by Caroline Feller Bauer; illustrated by Nadine Bernard Westcott. HarperCollins Pubs. 1994 86p il music $14 **810.8**
1. Thanksgiving Day 2. American literature—Collections
ISBN 0-06-023326-5   LC 93-18631
A collection of stories, poems, and songs about Thanksgiving Day, by such authors as Aileen Fisher, Jack Prelutsky, Eve Merriam, and Yoshiko Uchida
"An amiable collection. . . . Cartoon sketches with gray wash dance across the pages, and recipes for pumpkin pie and cranberry sauce as well as directions for making a turkey garland to decorate the table are included." Horn Book
Includes bibliographical references

Yolen, Jane
Here there be dragons; illustrated by David Wilgus. Harcourt Brace & Co. 1993 149p il hardcover o.p. paperback available $10 (5 and up) **810.8**
1. Dragons—Fiction 2. American literature—Collections
ISBN 0-15-201705-4 (pa)   LC 92-23194
"Yolen has compiled a collection of her poetry and prose about dragons of all sizes, shapes and dispositions. She introduces each piece with a brief description includ-

Yolen, Jane—*Continued*

ing the circumstances surrounding its writing. . . . The poetry, like the prose, varies in length but will enthrall readers. David Wilgus' pen and ink drawings further enhance the book." Book Rep

810.9 American literature—History and criticism

Wilkinson, Brenda Scott, 1946-

African American women writers; [by] Brenda Wilkinson. Wiley 2000 166p il (Black stars) $22.95 (4 and up)   **810.9**
    1. African American authors—Bio-bibliography
    2. American literature—Women authors—Bio-bibliography
    ISBN 0-471-17580-3   LC 99-25552
Discusses the lives and work of such notable African American women authors as: Phillis Wheatley, Ida B. Wells-Barnett, Zora Neale Hurston, Gwendolyn Brooks, Nikki Giovanni, and Terry McMillan
Includes bibliographical references

811 American poetry

Ada, Alma Flor, 1938-

Gathering the sun; an alphabet in Spanish and English; English translation by Rosa Zubizarreta; illustrated by Simón Silva. Lothrop, Lee & Shepard Bks. 1997 unp il $16.95 (2-4)   **811**
    1. Mexican Americans—Poetry 2. Agricultural laborers—Poetry 3. Alphabet 4. Bilingual books—English-Spanish
    ISBN 0-688-13903-5
"Using the Spanish alphabet as a template, Ada has written 27 poems that celebrate both the bounty of the harvest and the Mexican heritage of the farmworkers and their families. The poems, presented in both Spanish and English, are short and simple bursts of flavor. . . . Silva's sun-drenched gouache paintings are robust, with images sculpted in paint." Booklist

Adoff, Arnold, 1935-

The basket counts; illustrated by Michael Weaver. Simon & Schuster Bks. for Young Readers 2000 46p il $17 (4 and up)   **811**
    1. Basketball—Poetry
    ISBN 0-689-80108-4   LC 98-47941
Illustrations and poetic text describe the movement and feel of the game of basketball
"The insider perspective of these evocative shaped-speech poems is complemented by the dynamic but straightforward street-art-inspired illustrations." Bull Cent Child Books

In for winter, out for spring; illustrations by Jerry Pinkney. Harcourt Brace Jovanovich 1990 unp il $14.95; pa $7 (k-3)   **811**
    1. Seasons—Poetry 2. Family life—Poetry
    ISBN 0-15-238637-8; 0-15-201492-6 (pa)
                       LC 90-33185

This collection of poems, told from the perspective of a young black farm girl, celebrates family life throughout the yearly cycle of seasons
"With his variegated watercolor and pencil illustrations, Pinkney captures the mood or essence of each poem. . . . Because the uninhibited layout of the free verse poetry may be confusing to younger readers, this book would benefit from one-on-one sharing. It certainly invites repeated readings." Bull Cent Child Books

Love letters; illustrated by Lisa Desimini. Blue Sky Press (NY) 1997 unp il $15.95 (3-6)   **811**
    1. Love poetry
    ISBN 0-590-48478-8   LC 96-19982
"This collection of twenty poems, written in letter form, celebrates love (and occasionally not-quite-love) for friends, teachers, family, pets, and even oneself. Adoff blends everyday images with humor and pays special attention to the visual appearance of each poem. Desimini's intriguing illustrations use a variety of techniques, including collage, sculpture, photographs, and paintings." Horn Book Guide

Touch the poem; poems by Arnold Adoff; pictures by Lisa Desimini. Blue Sky Press (NY) 2000 unp il $16.95 (k-3)   **811**
    1. Touch—Poetry
    ISBN 0-590-47970-9
A collection of poems about the sense of touch including a baby's foot in one's palm, peach fuzz on the lip, and the forehead against a cold window
"The solid imagery of Adoff's poetry takes on a visual dimension when paired with Desimini's bold photographs." Booklist

Alarcón, Francisco X., 1954-

From the bellybutton of the moon and other summer poems; poems, Francisco X. Alarcón; illustrations, Maya Christina Gonzalez. Children's Bk. Press 1998 31p il $15.95 (2-4)   **811**
    1. Summer—Poetry 2. Mexico—Poetry 3. Bilingual books—English-Spanish
    ISBN 0-89239-153-7   LC 97-37457
A bilingual collection of poems in which the renowned Mexican American poet revisits and celebrates his childhood memories of summers, Mexico, and nature
"Responding to and expanding on the poetry, Gonzalez's happy paintings weave rich waves of color in an exuberant dance between text and design." Booklist

Laughing tomatoes and other spring poems; illustrations, Maya Christina Gonzalez. Children's Bk. Press 1997 32p il $15.95 (2-4)   **811**
    1. Spring—Poetry 2. Nature—Poetry 3. Bilingual books—English-Spanish
    ISBN 0-89239-139-1   LC 96-7459
Title page and text in English and Spanish
"This bilingual collection of poems by Chicano poet Alarcón celebrates spring and the fruits of family and sunshine. . . . The poems are short and simple imagistic reflections exuberantly expanded by Gonzalez in colorful double-page illustrations." Booklist

Begay, Shonto

Navajo; visions and voices across the Mesa. Scholastic 1995 48p il $17.95 (5 and up)   **811**

1. Navajo Indians—Poetry

ISBN 0-590-46153-2   LC 93-31610

The author "presents a very personal view of contemporary Navajo life in this picture-book collection for older readers. Pairing 20 of his paintings with original poetry, Begay moves from the spiritual aspects of Navajo life through personal childhood memories into striking present-day images, concluding with an affirmation of continuing life and rebirth." Booklist

Brown, Calef

Dutch sneakers and flea keepers; 14 more stories. Houghton Mifflin 2000 unp il $15 (2-4)   **811**

1. Humorous poetry

ISBN 0-618-05183-X   LC 99-53722

Also available companion volume Polkabats and octopus slacks: 14 stories (1998)

This "collection is more a gallery of odd characters and their bizarre worlds than it is a book of tales. In zany, ebullient verse and stylish, wildly angled paintings, Brown presents an irresistible roundup of eccentrics. . . . Brown's paintings combine elements of folk art with swirling, energetic designs and ultrahip colors and details that match the text's irreverent wit and fantastic scenarios." Booklist

Bruchac, Joseph, 1942-

Thirteen moons on a turtle's back; a Native American year of moons; by Joseph Bruchac and Jonathan London; illustrated by Thomas Locker. Philomel Bks. 1992 unp il $16.95; pa $5.99 **811**

1. Native Americans—Folklore 2. Native Americans—Poetry 3. Seasons—Poetry

ISBN 0-399-22141-7; 0-698-11584-8 (pa)

LC 91-3961

"Native American stories are retold as poems that capture the cycles of the moon. Months slip by as the oil paintings show each moon in the shell of the turtle's back." Child Book Rev Serv

"Locker . . . has created a dramatic oil painting for each short tale. His artwork portrays seasonal changes in the land as well as the specific seasonal activities of humans and animals. The large format with minimal text will appeal to younger children, while the alternative calendar, based on changes in nature, will interest middle readers. An unusual, easy-to-use resource for librarians, teachers, and others wishing to incorporate multicultural activites throughout the year." Booklist

Bryan, Ashley, 1923-

Sing to the sun; poems and pictures by Ashley Bryan. HarperCollins Pubs. 1992 unp il pa $6.95

811

ISBN 0-06-443437-0   LC 91-38359

A collection of poems and paintings celebrating the ups and downs of life

"With an energetic beat that's hard to resist, Bryan drums out poetry with a Caribbean sway. These short poems that sing the praises of everyday joys are further charged by the riotous primary colors Bryan splashes around." Booklist

Burleigh, Robert, 1936-

Hoops; illustrated by Stephen T. Johnson. Harcourt Brace & Co. 1997 unp il $16   **811**

1. Basketball—Poetry

ISBN 0-15-201450-0   LC 96-18440

"Silver Whistle"

Illustrations and poetic text describe the movement and feel of the game of basketball

"Burleigh's staccato text is well matched by Johnson's dynamic pastels. Muted colors and a strong sense of motion as bodies leap and lift, pounce and poke, aptly complement the words." SLJ

Carlstrom, Nancy White, 1948-

Thanksgiving Day at our house; Thanksgiving poems for the very young; written by Nancy White Carlstrom; illustrated by R.W. Alley. Simon & Schuster Bks. for Young Readers 1999 31p il $15 (k-2)   **811**

1. Thanksgiving Day—Poetry

ISBN 0-689-80360-5   LC 98-49254

A collection of poems about one family's activities on Thanksgiving Day, including pondering the history behind the holiday, welcoming visiting relatives, praying for others, enjoying the good food, and giving thanks at the end of the day

"Sometimes humorous, sometimes tender, the lively details in Alley's illustrations make each turn of the page a delight." Booklist

Who said boo? Halloween poems for the very young; written by Nancy White Carlstrom; illustrated by R.W. Alley. Simon & Schuster Bks. for Young Readers 1995 32p il hardcover o.p. paperback available $5.99 (k-3)   **811**

1. Halloween—Poetry

ISBN 0-689-83151-X (pa)   LC 94-33577

A collection of poems celebrating such Halloween phenomena as monsters, witches, haunted houses, and jack-o-lanterns

"The verse is simple, full of action, rhyme, and physicality that small kids will love. The watercolor pictures are very bright and very detailed." Booklist

Child, Lydia Maria Francis, 1802-1880

Over the river and through the wood (k-2)

811

1. Thanksgiving Day—Poetry 2. Songs

Some editions are:

Holt & Co. $16.95; pa $6.95 Illustrated by David Catrow (ISBN 0-805-03825-6; 0-805-06311-0)

North-South Bks. $6.95 Illustrated by Christopher Manson (ISBN 1-55858-959-7)

Text originally published in volume 2 of the author's Flowers for children, 1844, under title: A boy's Thanksgiving Day

Illustrated versions of a poem about a family's visit to their grandparents for Thanksgiving

Ciardi, John, 1916-1986

You read to me, I'll read to you; drawings by Edward Gorey. Lippincott 1962 64p il hardcover o.p. paperback available $7.95   **811**

1. Humorous poetry

ISBN 0-06-446060-6 (pa)

Thirty-five "imaginative and humorous poems for an adult and a child to read aloud together. Written in a basic first-grade vocabulary, the poems to be read by the child alternate with poems to be read by the adult." Booklist

Dickinson, Emily, 1830-1886

I'm nobody! who are you? poems of Emily Dickinson for children; illustrated by Rex Schneider; with an introduction by Richard B. Sewall. Stemmer House 1978 84p il $21.95 (3-6)   **811**

ISBN 0-916144-21-6   LC 78-6828

"A Barbara Holdridge book"

This collection of Emily Dickinson's poetry is illustrated with full color drawings depicting life in nineteenth century New England

Includes glossary

Dunbar, Paul Laurence, 1872-1906

Jump back, Honey; poems; selected and with an introduction by Andrea Davis Pinkney; illustrations by Ashley Bryan [et al.] Jump at the Sun 1999 unp il $16.99; lib bdg $17.49   **811**

1. African Americans—Poetry

ISBN 0-7868-0464-5; 0-7868-2406-9 (lib bdg)

           LC 98-54252

A collection of "14 of Dunbar's poems. Opening with the bright colors of Ashley Bryan and the poem 'Dawn,' the carefully selected verses depict the full range of Dunbar's craft. . . . The signature art by Carole Byard, Jan Spivey Gilchrist, Brian Pinkney, Jerry Pinkney, and Faith Ringgold also grace these pages." SLJ

Eliot, T. S. (Thomas Stearns), 1888-1965

Growltiger's last stand; with The pekes and the pollicles and The song of the Jellicles; with pictures by Errol Le Cain. Farrar, Straus & Giroux; Harcourt Brace Jovanovich 1987 c1986 unp il hardcover o.p. paperback available $4.95   **811**

1. Cats—Poetry

ISBN 0-374-42811-5 (pa)

An illustrated presentation of three cat poems taken from the author's Old Possum's book of practical cats, first published 1939. This edition first published 1986 in the United Kingdom

This book is "best suited to readers with enough sophistication to appreciate the poet's wide-ranging vocabulary, frequent syntactical inversions and sly humor. Others may not know how to respond to the outward fierceness of the title poem or to the more clearly playful but still bellicose [second poem]. . . . Le Cain's richly textured illustrations are often droll, occasionally rather fearsome and always striking, particularly in his use of symmetry and pattern." Publ Wkly

Evans, Lezlie

Rain song; illustrated by Cynthia Jabar. Houghton Mifflin 1995 unp il $16; pa $5.95 (k-1)   **811**

1. Rain—Poetry

ISBN 0-395-69865-0; 0-395-85077-0 (pa)

           LC 94-17368

"A playful rhyming poem and energetic, lighthearted illustrations show two girls relishing the delights of a rainstorm." Booklist

Fleischman, Paul

Big talk; poems for four voices; illustrated by Beppe Giacobbe. Candlewick Press 2000 44p il $14.99 (4 and up)   **811**

ISBN 0-7636-0636-7   LC 99-46882

A collection of poems to be read aloud by four people, with color-coded text to indicate which lines are read by which readers

"Each poem is more demanding, and more rewarding, than the last. Giacobbe highlights the humor in strips of vignettes that run along the bottom of the page. This is 'toe-tapping, tongue-flapping fun.'" Horn Book Guide

I am phoenix: poems for two voices; illustrated by Ken Nutt. Harper & Row 1985 51p il hardcover o.p. paperback available $5.95 (4 and up)   **811**

1. Birds—Poetry

ISBN 0-06-446092-4 (pa)   LC 85-42615

"A Charlotte Zolotow book"

A collection of poems about birds to be read aloud by two voices

"Devotés of the almost lost art of choral reading should be among the first to appreciate this collection. . . . Printed in script form, the selections . . . have a cadenced pace and dignified flow; their combination of imaginative imagery and realistic detail is echoed by the combination of stylized fantasy and representational drawings in the black and white pictures, all soft line and strong nuance." Bull Cent Child Books

Joyful noise: poems for two voices; illustrated by Eric Beddows. Harper & Row 1988 44p il $15.95; lib bdg $15.89; pa $5.95 (4 and up)   **811**

1. Insects—Poetry

ISBN 0-06-021852-5; 0-06-021853-3 (lib bdg); 0-06-446093-2 (pa)   LC 87-45280

Awarded the Newbery Medal, 1989

"A Charlotte Zolotow book"

"This collection of poems for two voices explores the lives of insects. Designed to be read aloud, the phrases of the poems are spaced vertically on the page in two columns, one for each reader. The voices sometimes alternate, sometimes speak in chorus, and sometimes echo each other." Booklist

"There are fourteen poems in the handsomely designed volume, with stylish endpapers and wonderfully interpretive black-and-white illustrations. Each selection is a gem, polished perfection." Horn Book

Fletcher, Ralph, 1953-

Ordinary things; poems from a walk in early spring; drawings by Walter Lyon Krudop. Atheneum Bks. for Young Readers 1997 48p il $16 (5 and up)   **811**
1. Nature—Poetry 2. Spring—Poetry
ISBN 0-689-81035-0   LC 96-3393
A collection of poems recall the sights and feelings experienced on a springtime walk—from home, through the woods, and back again
"Simple, well-chosen language and careful observations make his early spring walk fresh and vivid. The illustrations, emphasizing light and shadows, provide a nice accompaniment to the poems." Horn Book Guide

Relatively speaking; poems about family; drawings by Walter Lyon Krudop. Orchard Bks. 1999 42p il lib bdg $15.99 (4 and up)   **811**
1. Family life—Poetry
ISBN 0-531-33141-5   LC 98-30238
"These poems come together to form a picture of one family. Narrated by the youngest member, each poem highlights a different person or event. . . . The selections are striking in their simplicity, universal themes, and realistic voice. Pen-and-ink line drawings detail items ranging from a favorite quilt to a water bucket and sponge used to wash the car." SLJ

Florian, Douglas, 1950-

Beast feast; poems and paintings by Douglas Florian. Harcourt Brace & Co. 1994 48p il $16; pa $7   **811**
1. Animals—Poetry
ISBN 0-15-295178-4; 0-15-201737-2 (pa)
                                            LC 93-10720
A collection of humorous poems about such animals as the walrus, anteater, and boa
"Most verses are rhymed and employ standard poetic schemes, but clever wordplay, good rhythm, and liberal humor in word and illustrations make a fine poetic feast." Horn Book Guide

Bing bang boing; poems and drawings by Douglas Florian. Harcourt Brace & Co. 1994 144p il $16   **811**
1. Nonsense verses
ISBN 0-15-233770-9   LC 94-3894
Also available in paperback from Penguin Bks.
An illustrated collection of more than 150 nonsense verses
"The author's spare, pen-and-ink drawings, like the poems themselves, deftly explore the comic potential in each combination of words. With a few clean lines, he creates an original, funny vision." SLJ

In the swim; poems and paintings. Harcourt Brace & Co. 1997 unp il $16   **811**
1. Marine animals—Poetry 2. Humorous poetry
ISBN 0-15-201307-5   LC 95-52616
"This collection of 21 original short poems features fresh-and saltwater critters such as the piranha, manatee, and rainbow trout." Booklist
"These clipped verses splash with mischief and wit. The watercolor paintings, one per poem, also connect the silly and sublime." Horn Book Guide

Insectlopedia; poems and paintings by Douglas Florian. Harcourt Brace & Co. 1998 47p il $16
                                                811
1. Insects—Poetry
ISBN 0-15-201306-7   LC 96-23029
Presents twenty-one short poems about such insects as the inchworm, termite, cricket, and ladybug
"The artwork consists of collages of drawn and painted images and printed letters on paper that is cut and juxtaposed for effect. The clever artwork, deftly constructed, and the entertaining collection of insect and arachnid verse it illustrates will delight readers." Booklist

Laugh-eteria; poems and drawings by Douglas Florian. Harcourt Brace & Co. 1999 157p $17
                                                811
1. Humorous poetry
ISBN 0-15-202084-5   LC 98-20047
Also available in paperback from Puffin Bks.
A collection of more than 100 humorous poems on such topics as ogres, pizza, fear, school, dragons, trees, and hair
"Florian's pithy poems echo playground chants (and sometimes, better yet, jeers) in their rhythmic recitability . . . and his focus on orality and absurdity makes them thematically irresistible. The line drawings have a sophisticated quirkiness." Bull Cent Child Books

Mammalabilia; poems and paintings by Douglas Florian. Harcourt 2000 47p il $16   **811**
1. Mammals—Poetry
ISBN 0-15-202167-1   LC 99-10702
A collection of humorous poems about mammals such as the tiger, gorilla, and rhebok
"This collection of 21 short light verse brims with whimsy and fun. . . . The artwork taps into childlike qualities without being simplistic; the animal portraits are clever yet appropriate. An irresistible homage to mammal memorabilia." Publ Wkly

On the wing; bird poems and paintings. Harcourt Brace & Co. 1996 47p il $16; pa $6
                                                811
1. Birds—Poetry
ISBN 0-15-200497-1; 0-15-202366-6 (pa)
                                             LC 95-9976
This "collection features 21 poems about a variety of birds, from hummingbird to vulture, roadrunner to emperor penguin. The imagery in these short poems finds visual expression in the full-page, watercolor paintings, illustrating verse with high spirits and ingenuous charm." Booklist

Winter eyes; poems & paintings by Douglas Florian. Greenwillow Bks. 1999 48p il $16   **811**
1. Winter—Poetry
ISBN 0-688-16458-7   LC 98-19483
A collection of poems about winter, including "Sled," "Icicles," and "Ice Fishing"
"The short rhyming lines are clear and will be easy to read aloud, and the softly toned watercolor-and-colored-pencil pictures show snowy winter scenes, some realistic, some playful." Booklist

Frost, Robert, 1874-1963

Birches; illustrated by Ed Young. Holt & Co. 1988 unp il hardcover o.p. paperback available $5.35   **811**

1. Trees—Poetry
ISBN 0-8050-1316-4 (pa)   LC 86-4787

An illustrated version of the well-known poem written in 1916, about birch trees and the pleasures of climbing them

"The freedom called for in the sweep and depth of Frost's words should not be hemmed in by rigidly defined illustrations, and Young allows this license, giving the viewer ample opportunity to absorb and be absorbed by the imagery. The text is set two to three lines to a page, with the poem repeated in its entirety at the end." Booklist

Robert Frost; edited by Gary D. Schmidt; illustrated by Henri Sorensen. Sterling 1994 48p il (Poetry for young people) $14.95 (4 and up)   **811**

ISBN 0-8069-0633-2   LC 94-11161

"A Magnolia Editions book"

This volume "contains a three-page overview of the poet's life, 29 poems selected and arranged around the seasons of the year, brief and apt commentaries on each, and a useful index of titles and subject matter. The realistic watercolor illustrations capture the delicate beauty of a New England spring and the glory of fall while still suggesting the around-the-corner chill of winter, a disquiet echoing throughout much of Frost's poetry." SLJ

George, Kristine O'Connell

The great frog race and other poems; pictures by Kate Kiesler; with an introduction by Myra Cohn Livingston. Clarion Bks. 1997 40p il $15 (3-5)   **811**

ISBN 0-395-77607-4   LC 95-51090

A collection of poems about frogs and dragonflies, wind and rain, a visit to the tree farm, the garden hose, and other aspects of country life

"George's astute imagery pairs beautifully with Kiesler's rich, warm-toned oil paintings to impart a strong sense of the pleasures of rural landscape." Booklist

Little dog poems; illustrated by June Otani. Clarion Bks. 1999 40p il $12 (k-2)   **811**

1. Dogs—Poetry
ISBN 0-395-82266-1   LC 97-46678

"Thirty short poems about a lively terrier, narrated by the dog's young mistress." SLJ

"The language is simple and concrete enough for the youngest listeners. Otani's pen and watercolor illustrations make a fine complement to the verse." Horn Book Guide

Old Elm speaks; tree poems; illustrated by Kate Kiesler. Clarion Bks. 1998 48p il $15 (2-4)   **811**

1. Trees—Poetry
ISBN 0-395-87611-7   LC 97-49333

A collection of short, simple poems which present images relating to trees in various circumstances and throughout the seasons

"George conveys a deep understanding of nature, here particularly of trees, in a way that is readily accessible to children. Kiesler's warm oil paintings beautifully complement the poems." Booklist

Giovanni, Nikki

Ego-tripping and other poems for young people; illustrations by George Ford; foreword by Virginia Hamilton. 2nd ed. Hill Bks. 1993 52p il hardcover o.p. paperback available $10.95 (5 and up)   **811**

1. African Americans—Poetry
ISBN 1-55652-189-8 (pa)   LC 93-29578

First published 1974

Giovanni has added 10 new poems to her earlier "collection of 23 poems for young people. Ford's illustrations in sepia shades are bold and full of character and dreaming. As Virginia Hamilton says in her foreword, Giovanni's voice is personal and warm, she 'celebrates ordinary folks' and writes of struggle and liberation. She's upbeat and celebratory without minimizing hard times." Booklist

Spin a soft black song: poems for children; illustrated by George Martins. rev ed. Hill & Wang 1985 57p il hardcover o.p. paperback available $4.95 (3-6)   **811**

1. African Americans—Poetry
ISBN 0-374-46469-3 (pa)   LC 84-19287

First published 1971

A poetry collection which recounts the feelings of black children about their neighborhoods, American society, and themselves

"A beautifully illustrated book of poems about black children for children of all ages. . . . Simple in theme but a very moving collection nonetheless." Read Ladders for Hum Relat. 5th edition

The sun is so quiet; poems; illustrations by Ashley Bryan. Holt & Co. 1996 31p il $14.95 (k-3)   **811**

1. Nature—Poetry 2. Seasons—Poetry
ISBN 0-8050-4119-2   LC 95-39357

A collection of poems primarily about nature and the seasons but also concerned with chocolate and scary movies

"Of the 13 poems presented here, 12 appeared in books published between 1973 and 1993. The new poem, entitled 'Connie,' represents the best of Giovanni: a series of quicksilver images that capture a mood to perfection. Painted in Bryan's signature style, the illustrations fill the pages with sunny colors and bold patterns." Booklist

Godwin, Laura

Barnyard prayers; illustrated by Brian Selznick. Hyperion Bks. for Children 2000 unp il $14.99; lib bdg $15.49 (k-2)   **811**

1. Domestic animals—Poetry 2. Prayers
ISBN 0-7868-0355-X; 0-7868-2302-X (lib bdg)
     LC 99-40918

A boy's toy farm animals come to life and talk to God in a series of prayers

"Gentle humor lightens the reverence in Godwin's poetry and also in Selznick's peaceful, twilit paintings." Booklist

Graham, Joan Bransfield

Flicker flash; poems by Joan Bransfield Graham; illustrated by Nancy Davis. Houghton Mifflin 1999 unp il $15   **811**
1. Light—Poetry
ISBN 0-395-90501-X   LC 98-12956

A collection of poems celebrating light in its various forms, from candles and lamps to lightning and fireflies
"A vivid fusion of ingenious concrete poetry and boldly colored graphics." SLJ

Splish splash; illustrated by Steven M. Scott. Ticknor & Fields 1994 unp $16   **811**
1. Water—Poetry
ISBN 0-395-70128-7   LC 94-1237

A collection of poems celebrating water in its various forms, from ice cubes to the ocean
"The variety of text styles, colors and formats is fascinating for young and older readers, and invites aspiring writers to experiment with their own poetry. The graphics are bright, crisp and inviting." Child Book Rev Serv

Greenfield, Eloise, 1929-

Angels; drawings by Jan Spivey Gilchrist; poems by Eloise Greenfield. Jump at the Sun 1998 unp il $15.49; lib bdg $15.49   **811**
1. African Americans—Poetry 2. Angels—Poetry
ISBN 0-7868-2390-9; 0-7868-0442-4 (lib bdg)
    LC 98-19827

A collection of poems which show angels guiding, comforting, and protecting Afro-American children during milestones in their lives as well as in the course of everyday activities
These poems "offer warmth and inspiration without an overabundance of sentimentality. Gilchrist's gently sepia-toned illustrations capture with realism and sensitivity the features of African-American children and adults—and angels." Horn Book Guide

Honey, I love, and other love poems; pictures by Diane and Leo Dillon. Crowell 1978 unp il $14.95; pa $5.95 (2-4)   **811**
1. African Americans—Poetry 2. Love poetry
ISBN 0-690-01334-5; 0-06-443097-9 (pa)
    LC 77-2845

"These 16 poems explore facets of warm, loving relationships with family, friends and schoolmates as experienced by a young Black girl. Central to the theme of the book is the idea that the child loves herself and is very confident in expressing that love." Interracial Books Child Bull
"The Dillons transform this quiet book into magic with soft, grey charcoal renderings of the young girl and her friends, overlaid with child-like brown scratchboard pictures embodying the images in the poems." SLJ

Under the Sunday tree; paintings by Amos Ferguson; poems by Eloise Greenfield. Harper & Row 1988 38p il hardcover o.p. paperback available $10.95 (2-4)   **811**
1. Bahamas—Poetry
ISBN 0-06-443257-2 (pa)   LC 87-29373

"This collection of poems and paintings present a vivid picture of life in the Bahamas. The poems cover a variety of subjects and occasionally seem to have been written to go with a painting. The folk-art styled paintings are detailed, vibrant and certainly evoke a picture of island life." Child Book Rev Serv

Grimes, Nikki

Come Sunday; written by Nikki Grimes; illustrated by Michael Bryant. Eerdmans 1996 unp il $15; pa $7.50 (k-3)   **811**
1. African Americans—Poetry
ISBN 0-8028-5108-8; 0-8028-5134-7 (pa)
    LC 95-33067

"In fourteen poems, a young girl named LaTasha describes a typical Sunday of worship at the Paradise Baptist Church. From the joyful rhythms of singing and swaying and the spiritual plunge of baptism to church suppers and visiting preachers, the conversational verse evokes both solemn and joyous moods. Loose-lined watercolors burst with life, aptly conveying a community gathered in worship." Horn Book Guide

A dime a dozen; pictures by Angelo. Dial Bks. for Young Readers 1998 54p il $15.99 (5 and up)
    811
1. African Americans—Poetry
ISBN 0-8037-2227-3   LC 97-5798

A collection of poems about an African-American girl growing up in New York
"Free-flowing and very accessible, the poetry may inspire readers to distill their own life experiences into precise, imaginative words and phrases." Booklist

Hopscotch love; a family treasury of love poems; illustrated by Melodye Benson Rosales. Lothrop, Lee & Shepard Bks. 1999 39p il $14.95 (4 and up)   **811**
1. Love poetry 2. African Americans—Poetry
ISBN 0-688-15667-3   LC 98-21310

A collection of more than twenty poems speaking of different kinds of love
"All of the poetry is simple, written with everyday language in a straightforward style that needs no analysis or search for symbolism. . . . This small treasury will lift readers' spirits and touch their hearts." SLJ

Is it far to Zanzibar? poems about Tanzania; illustrated by Betsy Lewin. Lothrop, Lee & Shepard Bks. 2000 unp il map $15.95; lib bdg $15.85 (2-4)   **811**
1. Tanzania—Poetry
ISBN 0-688-13157-3; 0-688-13158-1 (lib. bdg)
    LC 96-2335

Over a dozen poems with some aspect of the African country of Tanzania as a theme
"The rhyming, sing-song verse is light and playful. . . . Lewin's active cartoon-style watercolors pick up the jaunty rhythms and the mix of animals, foods, and people." Booklist

Meet Danitra Brown; illustrated by Floyd Cooper. Lothrop, Lee & Shepard Bks. 1994 unp il $15.93; pa $5.95 (2-4)   **811**
1. African Americans—Poetry 2. Friendship—Poetry
ISBN 0-688-12073-3; 0-688-15471-9 (pa)
    LC 92-43707

Grimes, Nikki—*Continued*

"A collection of 13 original poems that stand individually and also blend together to tell a story of feelings and friendship between two African-American girls. . . . Cooper's distinguished illustrations in warm dusty tones convey the feeling of closeness. The poignant text and lovely pictures are an excellent collaboration." SLJ

My man Blue; poems by Nikki Grimes; pictures by Jerome Lagarrigue. Dial Bks. for Young Readers 1999 unp il $15.99 (2-5)   **811**
     1. African Americans—Poetry
     ISBN 0-8037-2326-1   LC 98-28229

"In fourteen poems, an African-American boy talks about his friend Blue—a man his mother grew up with, who has decided to take young fatherless Damon under his wing. The poems are accessible and filled with imagery, and the intergenerational friendship is believable. . . . The unsentimental acrylic paintings aptly reflect the poems." Horn Book Guide

Hale, Sarah Josepha

Mary had a little lamb (k-2)   **811**
     1. Nursery rhymes 2. Sheep—Poetry

Some editions are:
Charlesbridge Pub. lib bdg $15.95 told and illustrated by Iza Trapani (ISBN 1-580-89009-1)
Orchard Bks. $14.95; lib bdg $14.99; pa $5.95 illustrated by Salley Maver (ISBN 0-531-06875-7; 0-531-08725-5; 0-531-07165-0)
First published 1830 by Marsh, Capen & Lyon with title: Mary's lamb
The famous nineteenth-century nursery rhyme about the school-going lamb

Heide, Florence Parry, 1919-

Oh, grow up! poems to help you survive parents, chores, school and other afflictions; by Florence Parry Heide and Roxanne Heide Pierce; illustrated by Nadine Bernard Westcott. Orchard Bks. 1996 unp il $15.95; lib bdg $16.99 (k-3)   **811**

     1. Humorous poetry
     ISBN 0-531-09471-5; 0-531-08771-9 (lib bdg)
                         LC 95-23177
"A Melanie Kroupa book"
"Brothers, sisters, braces, hand-me-downs, fancy restaurants, parental advice, school cafeteria food, and other facets of growing up are viewed from a child's perspective. . . . Fresh, lively, and wildly colorful, Westcott's line-and-watercolor artwork illustrates the book with pictures as bright and buoyant as the verse." Booklist

Herrera, Juan Felipe, 1948-

Laughing out loud, I fly; poems in English and Spanish; drawings by Karen Barbour. HarperCollins Pubs. 1998 unp il $15.95   **811**
     1. Bilingual books—English-Spanish
     ISBN 0-06-027604-5   LC 96-45476
     "Joanna Cotler books"

A collection of poems in Spanish and English about childhood, place, and identity
"Barbour's black-and-white drawings accompany each poem, delicately underlining its images but allowing the strong sensuality of the words to seep into readers' minds." SLJ

Hoberman, Mary Ann, 1930-

The llama who had no pajama; 100 favorite poems; written by Mary Ann Hoberman; illustrated by Betty Fraser. Browndeer Press 1998 68p il $20 (k-3)   **811**
     ISBN 0-15-200111-5   LC 95-18491
An illustrated collection of poems about all sorts of subjects, including "Wishes," "Ducks," "When I Need a Real Baby," and "Growing"
"The poems—peppy verses immediately identifiable as Hoberman's by their use of alliteration and repeated words and lines—seem to cover every subject under the sun; all are dependably child-centered. Further bonuses are Fraser's delicate yet merry watercolors and the varied, imaginative page design." Horn Book Guide

Hopkins, Lee Bennett, 1938-

Been to yesterdays: poems of a life; illustrations by Charlene Rendeiro. Wordsong 1995 64p il $14.95; pa $8.95 (4 and up)   **811**
     ISBN 1-56397-467-3; 1-56397-808-3 (pa)
                         LC 94-73320
Autobiographical poems capture a thirteen-year old boy's feelings, experiences, and aspirations in one tumultuous year of his life

Good rhymes, good times; original poems; pictures by Frané Lessac. HarperCollins Pubs. 1995 unp $16.95; pa $5.95 (k-2)   **811**
     ISBN 0-06-023499-7; 0-06-443598-9 (pa)
                         LC 93-8159

"Hopkins has collected 21 of his own children's poems published over the years. Rooted in the small events of a child's day, from jiggling a loose tooth to cuddling a pet, the poems are very simple, usually no more than one or two words to a line, with some affectionate wordplay and 'good rhymes.' Lessac's brilliantly colored illustrations in folk-art style set the poems in a vital multicultural city neighborhood." Booklist

Hubbell, Patricia

Boo! Halloween poems and limericks; illustrated by Jeff Spackman. Marshall Cavendish 1998 40p il $15.95 (k-3)   **811**
     1. Halloween—Poetry
     ISBN 0-7614-5023-8   LC 97-25428
A collection of limericks and other poems about Halloween, including "Halloween Scarecrow," "There Once Was a Witch from North Dublin," and "Pumpkin Surprise"
"The lurid acrylic pictures will draw kids in, and the ghoulish subjects will make them shudder and shake." Booklist

Hughes, Langston, 1902-1967

Carol of the brown king; nativity poems; illustrated by Ashley Bryan. Atheneum Bks. for Young Readers 1998 unp il $16 **811**
1. Jesus Christ—Nativity—Poetry
ISBN 0-689-81877-7   LC 97-30814
"A Jean Karl book"
"Six poems, five by Hughes and one from a Puerto Rican Christmas card that he translated from the Spanish, have been appealingly illustrated in glowing colors." N Y Times Book Rev

The dream keeper and other poems; including seven additional poems; illustrated by Brian Pinkney. Knopf 1994 83p il $13; pa $7.99 (5 and up) **811**
1. African Americans—Poetry
ISBN 0-679-84421-X; 0-679-88347-9 (pa)
    LC 92-10240
First published 1932
"Langston Hughes's poems range from the romantic to the poignant, from the spiritual to the challenging. His lyrical voice asks for recognition of the Negro, offers encouragement, and reminds his African-American brothers of their glorious past. Although the pieces in *The Dream Keeper* were written over a half-century ago . . . the words have the same strength of meaning and power as if they had been written today." Horn Book

The sweet and sour animal book; illustrations by students of the Harlem School of the Arts; introduction by Ben Vereen; afterword by George P. Cunningham. Oxford Univ. Press 1994 unp il $17.95; pa $9.95 **811**
1. Animals—Poetry 2. Child artists
ISBN 0-19-509185-X; 0-19-512030-2 (pa)
    LC 94-8779
"The Iona and Peter Opie library of children's literature"
"Twenty-seven previously unpublished, alphabetically arranged verses about animals, written in 1936. . . . Children from The Harlem School of the Arts have created brightly painted, three-dimensional clay or paper creatures to accompany the poems; full-color photographs of these sculptures are placed next to the selections. . . . An inspired artistic collaboration." SLJ

Janeczko, Paul B., 1945-

That sweet diamond; baseball poems; illustrated by Carole Katchen. Atheneum Bks. for Young Readers 1998 unp il $16 (4-6) **811**
1. Baseball—Poetry
ISBN 0-689-80735-X   LC 97-5044
"Nineteen free-verse poems about baseball describe the game from many angles—bases covered include an elderly fan's devotion, how to spit, and a curse for the pitcher. . . . Janeczko's love of baseball is infectious, and Katchen's illustrations capture the taut energy of both players and fans in thick smears of pastels." Horn Book Guide

Johnson, Angela, 1961-

The other side; Shorter poems. Orchard Bks. 1998 44p il $15.95; lib bdg $16.99; pa $6.95 (5 and up) **811**
1. African Americans—Poetry
ISBN 0-531-30114-1; 0-531-33114-8 (lib bdg); 0-531-07167-7 (pa)   LC 98-13736
A Coretta Scott King honor book for text, 1999
A collection of poems reminiscent of growing up as an African-American girl in Shorter, Alabama
"Photographs of the author as a child emphasize the personal nature of this captivating narrative." Horn Book

Johnston, Tony

It's about dogs; poems by Tony Johnston; paintings by Ted Rand. Harcourt 2000 48p il $16 (2-4) **811**
1. Dogs—Poetry
ISBN 0-15-202022-5   LC 98-53783
Presents poems about dogs and their attributes, including their loyalty to people, their love of food and smells, and their varied appearances and personalities
"Rand's versatile paintings capture the dog denizens and the poetic moods with verve. . . . There are poignant moments as well as funny in this richly rendered tribute to be read and savored." SLJ

Joseph, Lynn

Coconut kind of day; island poems; illustrated by Sandra Speidel. Lothrop, Lee & Shepard Bks. 1990 unp il $13.95; lib bdg $13.88 **811**
1. Trinidad and Tobago—Poetry
ISBN 0-688-09119-9; 0-688-09120-2 (lib bdg)
    LC 90-6676
Also available in paperback from Puffin Bks.
"Joseph's 13 brief poems recall a day in the life of a family in Trinidad. . . . Joseph frequently incorporates island speech patterns into her work. Speidel's illustrations add enormously to the book's appeal. Double-page spreads in soft, muted shades of blue, rose, gold, and green show the poems superimposed on one side. . . . A gentle, nostalgic, loving recollection about growing up in another part of the world." SLJ

Kuskin, Karla

Soap soup and other verses. HarperCollins Pubs. 1992 63p il hardcover o.p. paperback available $4.95 (k-2) **811**
ISBN 0-06-444174-1 (pa)   LC 91-22947
"A Charlotte Zolotow book. An I can read book"
A collection of poems about discovering the world
The author "uses short words and simple reversals that are both surprising and fun to read aloud. . . . The many watercolor illustrations are closely cued to the poems, giving a figurative expression to the verbal imagery that will be helpful to beginning readers. . . . With most rhymes providing some version of a poetic punchline at the end, struggling decoders will quickly learn that reading provides its own rewards." Bull Cent Child Books

Lawrence, Jacob, 1917-2000

Harriet and the Promised Land. Simon & Schuster Bks. for Young Readers 1993 unp il $18; pa $6.99 **811**

1. Tubman, Harriet, 1815?-1913—Poetry 2. Underground railroad—Poetry

ISBN 0-671-86673-7; 0-689-80965-4 (pa)

LC 92-33740

A newly illustrated edition of the title first published 1968 by Windmill Books

"Simple rhymes tell the story of Harriet Tubman, the slave who led many of her people North to freedom." Adventuring with Books

"The strength of this volume is in the forceful, stylized paintings by the famous black artist, which capture the degradation of slavery." Brooklyn. Art Books for Child

Lessac, Frané

Caribbean canvas. Wordsong 1994 unp il $15.95 **811**

1. Poetry—Collections 2. Caribbean region in art

ISBN 1-56397-390-1   LC 93-61864

A reissue of the title first published 1987 in the United Kingdom; first United States edition published 1989 by Lippincott

"This is a collection of Lessac's paintings of island life in Antigua, Barbados, Grenada, St. Kitts, Nevis, Redonda, and the Grenadines. [It also contains] West Indian proverbs and poems from a dozen poets, including Edward Brathwaite, A. L. Hendricks, and Evan Jones." Publisher's note

"The poems and proverbs included seem almost an afterthought to the striking illustrations, which, through brown faces, neon colors, and assorted scenes of buildings, beaches, and people, suggest both the joy and the harsher realities of tropical life." Booklist

Levy, Constance, 1931-

A crack in the clouds and other poems; illustrations by Robin Bell Corfield. Margaret K. McElderry Bks. 1998 40p il $15 (3-5) **811**

1. Nature—Poetry

ISBN 0-689-82204-9   LC 98-10652

A collection of thirty-eight original poems about the natural world

Corfield's "small, sepia-wash natural scenes strike graceful visual notes. Levy displays a consistently distinct voice and a lively imagination . . . to go along with the sharply attuned senses that every good poet needs." Booklist

Lewis, J. Patrick

The bookworm's feast; a potluck of poems; pictures by John O'Brien. Dial Bks. for Young Readers 1999 unp il $16.99 **811**

ISBN 0-8037-1692-3   LC 94-31897

A collection of poems on a variety of topics organized according to the courses of a meal

"There are selections for fans of wordplay, of limerick form, and of valentinelike verse, each accompanied by O'Brien's exuberant pen-and-water-color drawings." SLJ

Doodle dandies; poems that take shape; J. Patrick Lewis, words; Lisa Desimini, images; with design and typography by Ann Bobco and Lisa Desimini. Atheneum Bks. for Young Readers 1998 unp il $16 **811**

ISBN 0-689-81075-X   LC 96-1920

"An Anne Schwartz book"

A collection of poems each of which appears on the page in the shape of its subject so that the poem looks like whatever it's about

"Every page of this book is well designed, creating words and images that work together in harmony. . . . *Doodle Dandies* captures the joy that wordplay can bring." SLJ

A hippopotamusn't and other animal verses; pictures by Victoria Chess. Dial Bks. for Young Readers 1990 unp il hardcover o.p. paperback available $6.99 **811**

1. Animals—Poetry 2. Humorous poetry

ISBN 0-14-055273-1 (pa)   LC 87-24579

This is a collection of light verse that "concentrates on an intriguing selection of birds and beasts. Varied poetic forms include, among others, lively quatrains, couplets, and limericks as well as a charming haiku. . . . The tone is light; the effect genuinely humorous rather than merely funny—a mood complemented by Victoria Chess's colorful, expressive, and at times oh-so-subtly wicked illustrations. Her delicate, agile use of line underscores the quick wit of the poet to perfection." Horn Book

Lillegard, Dee

Wake up house! rooms full of poems; illustrated by Don Carter. Knopf 2000 unp il $12.95; lib bdg $14.99 (k-2) **811**

1. Houses—Poetry

ISBN 0-679-88351-7; 0-679-98351-1 (lib bdg)

LC 99-33420

Short poems which personify household objects from the bedroom window that greets the sun's morning rays to the nightlight that watches over sleeping dreamers

"Carter's clear, beautiful three-dimensional illustrations use foam board, plaster, and bold acrylic paints to produce art as tactile and immediate as the words." Booklist

Lindbergh, Reeve

Johnny Appleseed; a poem; paintings by Kathy Jakobsen. Little, Brown 1990 unp il hardcover o.p. paperback available $5.95 (k-3) **811**

1. Appleseed, Johnny, 1774-1845—Poetry 2. Frontier and pioneer life—Poetry

ISBN 0-316-52634-7 (pa)   LC 89-35192

"Joy Street books"

Rhymed text and illustrations relate the life of John Chapman, whose distribution of appleseeds and trees across the Midwest made him a legend and left a legacy still enjoyed today

"The folk art paintings add a dimension that enhances the lyrical, moving poem. Together they combine to capture daily pioneer life and the legend." Child Book Rev Serv

Little, Jean, 1932-

Hey world, here I am! illustrations by Sue Truesdell. Harper & Row 1989 88p il hardcover o.p. paperback available $4.95 (4-6) **811**

   ISBN 0-06-440384-X (pa)   LC 88-10987

   Text first published 1986 in Canada

A collection of poems and brief vignettes from the perspective of a girl named Kate Bloomfield, reflecting her views on friendship, school, family life, and the world

"Engaging and often humorous, the vignettes are short enough to capture even the most reluctant reader yet deep enough to make the most sophisticated think. . . . Truesdell's gray line-and-wash illustrations are a fine, funny touch." Booklist

Livingston, Myra Cohn

Celebrations; Myra Cohn Livingston, poet; Leonard Everett Fisher, painter. Holiday House 1985 unp il lib bdg $16.95; pa $6.95 **811**

   1. Holidays—Poetry

   ISBN 0-8234-0550-8 (lib bdg); 0-8234-0654-7 (pa)

                    LC 84-19216

   Companion volume to Festivals

"Sixteen short, mainly rhymed verses celebrate major holidays beginning with New Year's and ending with Christmas. A final page recalls that special event, 'birthday.' The book exhibits a fine variety of moods; all the poems would work with the intended audience. . . . Visually dramatic, the illustrations pack a punch. All but three of the poems appear on double-page spreads with text on one side, the painting encompassing both. In addition, the large page size, lack of margins, brilliant colors and surprising compositions all add a great sense of excitement." SLJ

A circle of seasons; Myra Cohn Livingston, poet; Leonard Everett Fisher, painter. Holiday House 1982 unp il hardcover o.p. paperback available $5.95 **811**

   1. Seasons—Poetry

   ISBN 0-8234-0696-3 (pa)   LC 81-20305

"A cycle of 12 quatrains, each with its own brief refrain, celebrates the four seasons depicted in expressionistic oil paintings." Booklist

"The paintings are stunning, bold and stylized but with delicate details; there is variety in the brushwork and use of color, uniformity in the excellent use of space and shape to achieve effective compositions. Nice to read alone, or aloud, nice to look at." Bull Cent Child Books

Cricket never does; a collection of haiku and tanka; illustrations by Kees de Kiefte. Margaret K. McElderry Bks. 1997 42p il $15 (4 and up) **811**

   1. Seasons—Poetry 2. Haiku

   ISBN 0-689-81123-3   LC 96-30528

A collection of more than fifty original haiku and tanka verses about the four seasons

"Livingston's skillful use of simple language . . . creates fresh images of the everyday world. Small pen-and-ink illustrations open each section." Horn Book Guide

Festivals; Myra Cohn Livingston, poet; Leonard Everett Fisher, painter. Holiday House 1996 32p il $16.95 **811**

   1. Festivals—Poetry

   ISBN 0-8234-1217-2   LC 95-31055

   Companion volume to Celebrations

"An eclectic collection of 14 poems celebrating festivals from around the world. The book begins in January with the Chinese New Year, ends in December with Kwanzaa, and includes the Vietnamese *Tet Nguyen-Dan,* Iranian *Now-Ruz,* Jewish Purim, Muslim Ramadan and *Id-Ul-Fitr,* Hindu *Diwali,* and Mexican Day of the Dead. . . . What makes the volume special, . . . is the inspired paring of text and artwork. . . . The words plus the accompanying illustration—purple pumpkins, orange moon, black sky—elicit a shiver of mystery and delight." SLJ

   Includes glossary

Flights of fancy and other poems. Margaret K. McElderry Bks. 1994 40p il $13.95 (5 and up) **811**

   ISBN 0-689-50613-9   LC 94-14476

In those forty short poems "Livingston describes sights and insights in simple, direct language, sometimes with an adult's voice and sometimes with a child's, making private observations or addressing a companion. Though the theme of flight recurs, both literally and figuratively, the selections include some post-Christmas thoughts, several 'Highway Haiku,' and tributes to Margot Tomes and Jacques D'Amboise." SLJ

I never told and other poems. Margaret K. McElderry Bks. 1992 42p $12.95 (4-6) **811**

   ISBN 0-689-50544-2   LC 91-20475

"Forty-two poems, none more than a page long (and most considerably less) show a range of form (concrete poetry, haiku, cinquains, free verse, etc.) tone, and subject, but Livingston retains her usual sharp focus throughout. . . . Kids who are bored stiff by discussions of poetic form will unknowingly savor it here, and confirmed poetry fans will revel in the variety at hand." Bull Cent Child Books

Keep on singing; a ballad of Marian Anderson; illustrated by Samuel Byrd. Holiday House 1994 unp il $15.95 (k-3) **811**

   1. Anderson, Marian, 1897-1993—Poetry

   ISBN 0-8234-1098-6   LC 93-46909

"In this ballad, Myra Cohn Livingston narrates the story of Marian Anderson's life, from her humble beginnings in Philadelphia in the early 1900s to her triumphant career as a world-renowned singer, despite racial barriers." Publisher's note

"The large illustrations, often based on photographs, use details sparingly and employ sweeping backgrounds to lend a feeling of significance to a scene. Adults may want to review Livingston's closing biographical notes before reading the book to children, but the ballad itself still catches the inspiring outlines of Anderson's life and makes her story accessible to a young audience." Booklist

Sky songs; Myra Cohn Livingston, poet; Leonard Everett Fisher, painter. Holiday House 1984 31p il lib bdg $16.95 **811**

   1. Sky—Poetry

   ISBN 0-8234-0502-8   LC 83-12955

Livingston, Myra Cohn—*Continued*

"Fourteen poems consisting of three cinquains each address the heavenly bodies—the moon, stars, planets, and shooting stars—and the changing moods of the sky from dawn to sunset, through storms and smog." Horn Book

"The author and artist combine their talents to create a book that is a pleasure to see and to read. Livingston's poems . . . are honed and sensitive, while Fisher's paintings combine, in double-page spreads, vibrant colors, and effective use of space, and wonderful variation of mood in handsomely composed paintings." Bull Cent Child Books

Longfellow, Henry Wadsworth, 1807-1882

Hiawatha; pictures by Susan Jeffers. Dial Bks. for Young Readers 1983 unp il hardcover o.p. paperback available $6.99 **811**
1. Native Americans—Poetry 2. Native Americans—Folklore
ISBN 0-14-055882-9 (pa) LC 83-7225
Also available Spanish language edition
Verses excerpted from the poem first published 1855 with title: Song of Hiawatha

"Jeffers has captured the essence of this brief section from the classic poem. . . . The pale tints of the pictures are in complete harmony with nature and with the text and show in detail how Hiawatha might have seen his world. A fine first exposure to the poem for children and a beautiful artistic experience." SLJ

Paul Revere's ride **811**
1. Revere, Paul, 1735-1818—Poetry 2. Lexington (Mass.), Battle of, 1775—Poetry

Some editions are:

Dutton $16.99; pa $6.99 Illustrated by Ted Rand (ISBN 0-525-44610-9; 0-14-055612-5)
Greenwillow Bks. pa $4.95 Illustrated by Nancy Winslow Parker (ISBN 0-688-12387-2)
National Geographic Soc. $16.95 Illustrated by Jeffrey Thompson. Has title: The midnight ride of Paul Revere (ISBN 0-7922-7674-4)

The famous narrative poem recreating Paul Revere's midnight ride in 1775 to warn the people of the Boston countryside that the British were coming

Merriam, Eve, 1916-1992

Bam, bam, bam; illustrated by Dan Yaccarino. Holt & Co. 1995 unp il $14.95; pa $5.95 (k-2)
811
ISBN 0-8050-3527-3; 0-8050-5796-X (pa)
LC 94-20300
A Bill Martin book

In this noisy poem, a wrecking ball demolishes old houses and stores to make way for a skyscraper

"Merriam's rhymes are simple like a sledgehammer blow, with the same rhythmic swing, and Yaccarino's bulky, brightly colored workers make the process look like fun." Booklist

Halloween A B C; illustrations by Lane Smith. Macmillan 1987 unp il o.p.; Aladdin Paperbacks paperback available $5.99 (k-2) **811**
1. Halloween—Poetry 2. Alphabet
ISBN 0-689-80198-X (pa) LC 86-23772

"These 26 Halloween poems, one for each letter of the alphabet, are, like most of Merriam's work, imaginative, inventive, and playful. Her unusual rhythms, rhythmic schemes, and twists of word or image are often humorous as well as seasonally spooky. . . . Smith's dark oil paintings on ecru pages match both the mood and the wit of the poems. . . . This is not a book for young children to learn the alphabet, but it is a witty, whimsical, and happily shivery book for Halloween sharing." SLJ

You be good and I'll be night: jump-on-the-bed poems; pictures by Karen Lee Schmidt. Morrow Junior Bks. 1988 unp il hardcover o.p. paperback available $5.95 (k-2) **811**
ISBN 0-688-13984-1 (pa) LC 87-24859

This "collection of twenty-eight poems features mostly jump-rope rhythms and chanting rhymes. . . . Each poem is accompanied with bouncy watercolor scenes, often including comically incongruous animals. . . . A few are too jingly, but on the whole this is nonsense with flair." Bull Cent Child Books

Moore, Clement Clarke, 1779-1863

The night before Christmas (k-3) **811**
1. Santa Claus—Poetry 2. Christmas—Poetry

Available in hardcover and paperback from various publishers, including editions illustrated by Tasha Tudor, Jan Brett, Arthur Rackham, and others
Text first published 1823 with title: A visit from St. Nicholas

This popular Christmas poem has been a favorite with American children ever since the author wrote it for his children in 1822. It is from this poem that we get the names for the Christmas reindeer

Mora, Pat

This big sky; pictures by Steve Jenkins. Scholastic 1998 unp il lib bdg $15.95 **811**
1. Southwestern States—Poetry
ISBN 0-590-37120-7 LC 97-7285
Poems that describe the landscape, people, and animals of the American Southwest

"Mora's poetry resonates with lush images. . . . Jenkins's cut-paper collages extend the earthy yet mystical tone of the poems. A glossary of Spanish words is appended." Horn Book Guide

Myers, Walter Dean, 1937-

Brown angels; an album of pictures and verse. HarperCollins Pubs. 1993 unp il $16.95; pa $6.95
811
1. African Americans—Poetry
ISBN 0-06-022917-9; 0-06-443455-9 (pa)
LC 92-36792

A collection of poems, accompanied by antique photographs, about African American children living around the turn of the century

"Myers has created an exquisite album. The 42 superbly sepia prints radiate intensely with the personalities of their subjects. The author's 11 original poems are in various forms and range from humorous to elegiac. The language is simple and reads aloud well." SLJ

Myers, Walter Dean, 1937-—*Continued*

Harlem; a poem; pictures by Christopher Myers.
Scholastic 1997 unp il $16.95   **811**
    1. African Americans—Poetry 2. Harlem (New York,
N.Y.)—Poetry
    ISBN 0-590-54340-7   LC 96-8108
    A Caldecott Medal honor book, 1998
    A poem celebrating the people, sights, and sounds of
Harlem
    "Myers's paean to Harlem sings, dances, and swaggers
across the pages, conveying the myriad sounds on the
streets. . . . Christopher Myers's collages add an edge to
his father's words, vividly bringing to life the sights and
scenes of Lenox Avenue." Horn Book Guide

Nash, Ogden, 1902-1971

The adventures of Isabel; pictures by James
Marshall. Little, Brown 1991 unp il hardcover o.p.
paperback available $5.95 (k-3)   **811**
    1. Girls—Poetry
    ISBN 0-316-59883-6 (pa)   LC 90-13284
    "Joy Street books"
    The feisty Isabel defeats giants, witches, and other
threatening creatures with ease
    "The amusing details of the illustrations . . . add to
an engaging combination of humor and reassurance."
Horn Book

Custard the dragon and the wicked knight;
illustrated by Lynn Munsinger. Little, Brown 1996
unp il hardcover o.p. paperback available $5.95
(k-3)   **811**
    1. Dragons—Poetry
    ISBN 0-316-59905-0 (pa)   LC 95-9719
    A newly illustrated edition of the title first published
1961
    In this humorous poem, Custard the cowardly dragon
saves the fair maiden Belinda from the wicked Sir
Garagoyle
    "Munsinger's deft portrayal of the poem's action and
characters is a perfect match for Nash's clever wordplay." SLJ

The tale of Custard the Dragon; illustrated by
Lynn Munsinger. Little, Brown 1995 unp il
hardcover o.p. paperback available $5.95 (k-3)
          811
    1. Dragons—Poetry
    ISBN 0-316-59031-2 (pa)   LC 94-6594
    Text first published 1936
    In this humorous poem, Custard the cowardly dragon
saves the day when a pirate threatens Belinda and her
pet animals
    "Munsinger does an appealing job of catching the mix
of wry humor and affection that has made Ogden's
whimsical poem a favorite with audiences young and old
for 60 years." Booklist

Numeroff, Laura Joffe

Sometimes I wonder if poodles like noodles;
written by Laura Numeroff; illustrated by Tim
Bowers. Simon & Schuster Bks. for Young
Readers 1999 unp il $15 (k-3)   **811**
    1. Humorous poetry
    ISBN 0-689-80563-2   LC 96-44988

An illustrated collection of humorous verses about a
child's day-to-day experiences and other topics
    "A light, playful tone permeates these twenty-one
mostly brief rhyming poems told from an imaginative
young girl's point of view. . . . Oil paintings rendered
in a warm palette of colors capture the collection's affectionate humor." Horn Book Guide

O'Neill, Mary Le Duc, 1908-1990

Hailstones and halibut bones; adventures in
color; newly illustrated by John Wallner.
Doubleday 1989 unp il $15.95; pa $9.95 (k-3)
          811
    1. Color—Poetry
    ISBN 0-385-24484-3; 0-385-41078-6 (pa)
          LC 88-484
    A newly illustrated edition of the title first published
1961
    Twelve poems reflect the author's feelings about vari-
ous colors
    "Wallner has created montages of each poem's images
and colored them with various hues of the featured color.
The results do complement the moods of the poems."
SLJ

Otten, Charlotte F.

January rides the wind; a book of months;
illustrated by Todd L.W. Doney. Lothrop, Lee &
Shepard Bks. 1997 unp il $16; lib bdg $16.89
(k-3)   **811**
    1. Months—Poetry
    ISBN 0-688-12556-5; 0-688-12557-3 (lib bdg)
          LC 92-44159
    Twelve poems, one describing each month
    "Laden with vivid metaphors, short poems for each
month of the year pay homage to nature's cycle. . . . Oil
paintings featuring children enjoying seasonal activities
shimmer with light and shadow, lending additional richness to a handsome volume." Horn Book Guide

Pomerantz, Charlotte

If I had a paka; poems in eleven languages;
illustrated by Nancy Tafuri. Greenwillow Bks.
1993 unp il lib bdg $13.93; pa $4.95 (k-3)   **811**
    ISBN 0-688-11901-8 (lib bdg); 0-688-12510-7 (pa)
          LC 92-33088
    A reissue of the title first published 1982
    This "collection of 12 short poems is in English, but
each poem uses a few words from a different language."
SLJ
    The author "has written some charming poems. . . .
The foreign words are melodious and interesting, and
they can always be understood in the context of the poems. The illustrations by Nancy Tafuri are exquisite
combinations of design, color and feeling." N Y Times
Book Rev

Prelutsky, Jack

The baby Uggs are hatching; pictures by James
Stevenson. Greenwillow Bks. 1982 32p il
hardcover o.p. paperback available $5.95 (k-3)
          811
    1. Nonsense verses
    ISBN 0-688-09239-X (pa)   LC 81-7266

Prelutsky, Jack—*Continued*

This volume contains humorous poems about imaginary creatures with names like: Ugg, Quossible, Smasheroo, Flotterzott, and Grebbles

"The catchy rhythms, humorous drawings, and deliciously alarming subjects make a splendid book." Horn Book

Beneath a blue umbrella: rhymes; pictures by Garth Williams. Greenwillow Bks. 1990 64p il lib bdg $15.95 (k-3) **811**

1. Nonsense verses 2. Nursery rhymes
ISBN 0-688-06429-9   LC 86-19406

A collection of illustrated humorous poems in which a hungry hippo raids a melon stand, a butterfly tickles a girl's nose, and children frolic in a Mardi Gras parade

"Prelutsky has an unerring sense of popular appeal; these verses bounce as rhythmically as children do on a bed or jumping rope. They also feature plenty of reassurance and humor, staples for chanting. Garth Williams' homey pen drawing and luminous colors enliven each full-page illustration with a dramatic simplicity set off by spacious book design." Bull Cent Child Books

Dog days; rhymes around the year; illustrated by Dyanna Wolcott. Knopf 1999 unp il $15; lib bdg $17.99 (k-1) **811**

1. Dogs—Poetry 2. Months—Poetry
ISBN 0-375-80104-9; 0-375-90104-3 (lib bdg)
LC 98-32373

A spirited dog describes what he enjoys doing each month of the year

The poems are "simple and agreeable enough for young children, particularly when accompanied by Wolcott's stylized yet endearing pictures. . . . Sometimes Matisse-like, always vibrant in line and color, these paintings will engage the attention of children." Booklist

The dragons are singing tonight; pictures by Peter Sis. Greenwillow Bks. 1993 39p il $16; lib bdg $15.93; pa $6.95 (2-5) **811**

1. Dragons—Poetry
ISBN 0-688-09645-X; 0-688-12511-5 (lib bdg); 0-688-16162-6 (pa)   LC 92-29013

"Dragons are verbally and visually portrayed in this collection with wonder, whimsy, and a touch of wistfulness. . . . The oil and gouache paintings on a gesso background have marvelous details and unexpected bursts of humor." SLJ

The gargoyle on the roof; poems by Jack Prelutsky; pictures by Peter Sis. Greenwillow Bks. 1999 39p il $15.89; lib bdg $16 (2-5) **811**

1. Monsters—Poetry
ISBN 0-688-16553-2; 0-688-09643-3 (lib bdg)
LC 99-10578

Presents poems about gargoyles, vampires, the bogeyman, gremlins, and other monsters

"Prelutsky achieves a masterful range in tone here. He evokes the traditional attributes of the monsters but gives children insight into what it would be like to be a monster. . . . Sis' cross-hatched oil-and-gouache paintings extend the poems, working especially well to catch the sinister and frightening mood." Booklist

The Headless Horseman rides tonight; more poems to trouble your sleep; illustrated by Arnold Lobel. Greenwillow Bks. 1980 38p il hardcover o.p. paperback available $4.95 (2-5) **811**

1. Monsters—Poetry
ISBN 0-688-11705-8 (pa)   LC 80-10372

"In addition to the perambulating mummy, the author deals with, among others, a writhing specter on a misty moor, a zombie, a sorceress, a baleful banshee . . . the abominable snowman and a headless horseman." Horn Book

The author's "rhymes are as lethal, lithe, and literate as ever and Lobel wrings every atmospheric ounce out of them." SLJ

It's Christmas; pictures by Marylin Hafner. Greenwillow Bks. 1981 46p il hardcover o.p. paperback available $5.95 (1-3) **811**

1. Christmas—Poetry
ISBN 0-688-14393-8 (pa)   LC 81-1100

Also available in paperback from Scholastic

"A Greenwillow read-alone book"

"The poems cover subjects of interest to children—making a Christmas list, performing in the school assembly, cutting a Christmas tree . . . [and dealing] with the disappointments that sometimes occur: being sick on Christmas, getting underwear as a gift and having a new sled but no snow. Marilyn Hafner's cartoonlike drawings add to the fun." SLJ

It's snowing! It's snowing! pictures by Jeanne Titherington. Greenwillow Bks. 1984 47p il $18.89 (1-3) **811**

1. Winter—Poetry 2. Snow—Poetry
ISBN 0-688-01513-1   LC 83-16583

"Soft gray-and-white drawings washed with blue complement seventeen poems that celebrate a child's delight in snow. From 'One Last Little Leaf' to 'The Snowman's Lament' the course of a season is marked by the natural phenomena and human activities of winter. . . . An easy-to-read format and large print suit the facility of the rhyme and accessibility of the imagery. Where more challenging vocabulary is introduced, contextual clues help the beginning reader." Horn Book

It's Thanksgiving; pictures by Marylin Hafner. Greenwillow Bks. 1982 47p il lib bdg $16; pa $5.95 (1-3) **811**

1. Thanksgiving Day—Poetry
ISBN 0-688-00442-3 (lib bdg); 0-688-14729-1 (pa)
LC 81-1929

"A Greenwillow read-alone book"

This "collection of poems about Thanksgiving has rhyme, rhythm, and humor as well as a variety of topics: helping Grandma with the meal, watching Daddy watch a football game, seeing a Thanksgiving Day parade, working on school projects, not being able to eat any of the holiday treats because of braces, and the Pilgrim Thanksgiving. The poems are illustrated by brisk, often comic drawings, line and wash. This isn't great poetry, but it has a bouncy quality that's appealing." Bull Cent Child Books

Prelutsky, Jack—*Continued*

It's Valentine's Day; pictures by Yossi Abolafia. Greenwillow Bks. 1983 47p il hardcover o.p. paperback available $5.95 (1-3)   **811**
 1. Valentine's Day—Poetry
 ISBN 0-688-14652-X (pa)   LC 83-1449
"A Greenwillow read-alone book"
"The 14 poems here range from the genuine joy of 'It's Valentine's Day' . . . to the giddy goofiness of 'I love you more than applesauce' or 'Jelly Jill loves Weasel Will'. . . .The rhymes are generally simple but clever and the line drawings in red and blue, with their expressive faces and explanatory vignettes, add tremendously to the enjoyment of the poetry." SLJ

Monday's troll; poems by Jack Prelutsky; pictures by Peter Sis. Greenwillow Bks. 1996 39p il $16; lib bdg $15.93; pa $5.95 (2-5)   **811**
 1. Supernatural—Poetry
 ISBN 0-688-09644-1; 0-688-14373-3 (lib bdg); 0-688-17529-5 (pa)   LC 95-7085
A collection of seventeen poems about such unsavory characters as witches, ogres, wizards, trolls, giants, a yeti, and seven grubby goblins
This "collection overflows with energy, tongue-in-cheek wit, rich vocabulary, and rollicking rhyme and meter. The oil and gouache paintings on gesso backgrounds are equally playful, as each gold-bordered, double-page spread adds more layers of meaning to the words." SLJ

My parents think I'm sleeping: poems; pictures by Yossi Abolafia. Greenwillow Bks. 1985 47p il $16; lib bdg $14.93; pa $6.95 (2-4)   **811**
 1. Sleep—Poetry
 ISBN 0-688-04018-7; 0-688-04019-5 (lib bdg); 0-688-14028-9 (pa)   LC 84-13640
This is a collection of humorous poems about bedtime
"Sometimes humorous, sometimes thoughtfully quiet, the poems reflect an interesting range of reactions to the night. . . . Illustrations, done for the most part in appropriate shades of gray and blue with occasional glints of yellow light, extend the nuances of the poetry." Horn Book

The new kid on the block: poems; drawings by James Stevenson. Greenwillow Bks. 1984 159p il $17.95; lib bdg $17.93 (3-6)   **811**
 1. Humorous poetry
 ISBN 0-688-02271-5; 0-688-02272-3 (lib bdg)   LC 83-20621
"Most of the 100-plus poems here are mini-jokes, wordplay, and character sketches . . . with liberal doses of monsters and meanies as well as common, garden-variety child mischief." Booklist
"The author's rollicking, silly poems bounce and romp with fun; Stevenson's cartoon-like sketches capture the hilarity with equal skill. A book everyone will enjoy dipping into." Child Book Rev Serv

Nightmares: poems to trouble your sleep; illustrated by Arnold Lobel. Greenwillow Bks. 1976 38p il lib bdg $13.93 (2-5)   **811**
 1. Monsters—Poetry
 ISBN 0-688-84053-1   LC 76-4820

This "collection of poems is calculated to evoke icy apprehension, and the poems about wizards, bogeymen, ghouls, ogres (well, one poem apiece to each or to others of their ilk) are exaggerated just enough to bring simultaneous grins and shudders. Prelutsky uses words with relish and his rhyme and rhythm are, as usual, deft. Lobel's illustrations are equally adroit, macabre yet elegant." Bull Cent Child Books

A pizza the size of the sun; poems by Jack Prelutsky; drawings by James Stevenson. Greenwillow Bks. 1996 159p il $18; lib bdg $17.93 (3-6)   **811**
 1. Humorous poetry
 ISBN 0-688-13235-9; 0-688-13236-7 (lib bdg)   LC 95-35930
Also available Audiobook version
This collection of humorous poems is "filled with zany people, improbable creatures, and rhythm and rhyme galore, all combining to celebrate the unusual, the mundane, and the slightly gruesome. . . . Each page is brimming with Stevenson's complementary, droll watercolors, reproduced here in black and white." SLJ

Ride a purple pelican; pictures by Garth Williams. Greenwillow Bks. 1986 64p il $17.95; pa $7.95 (k-3)   **811**
 1. Nonsense verses 2. Nursery rhymes
 ISBN 0-688-04031-4; 0-688-15625-8 (pa)   LC 84-6024
A collection of short nonsense verses and nursery rhymes
"Prelutsky has caught the rhythm and spirit of nursery rhymes in 29 short poems about drum-beating bunnies, bullfrogs on parade, Chicago winds, giant sequoias and other wondrous things. Many of these easy-to-remember poems are filled with delicious sounding American and Canadian place names. Garth Williams' full-color, full-page illustrations are good complements to the poems. Highly recommended." Child Book Rev Serv

Rolling Harvey down the hill; illustrated by Victoria Chess. Greenwillow Bks. 1980 30p il $16; lib bdg $15.93; pa $4.95 (1-3)   **811**
 1. Friendship—Poetry 2. Humorous poetry
 ISBN 0-688-80258-3; 0-688-84258-5 (lib bdg); 0-688-12270-1 (pa)   LC 79-18236
Also available Audiobook version
"Fifteen contemporary poems describe the mischievous antics of five apartment-house buddies." Child Book Rev Serv
"'Chess' puckish black-and-white scenes cash in on all the text's mischief. The motley cast is suitably disheveled and just bizarre enough in expression. This is fresh, funny, and quite in tune with scampish concerns." Booklist

The sheriff of Rottenshot: poems; pictures by Victoria Chess. Greenwillow Bks. 1982 32p il lib bdg $14.93; pa $4.95 (2-5)   **811**
 1. Nonsense verses
 ISBN 0-688-00198-X (lib bdg); 0-688-13635-4 (pa)   LC 81-6420
A collection of sixteen humorous poems
"Macabre art with a silver lining, the often-gruesome

Prelutsky, Jack—*Continued*

Chess drawings have robust humor of their own, for almost every lumpish human or lurking beast has either enough exaggeration or enough of a twinkle to be funny. Thus the illustrations are admirably suited to the often-ghoulish and very funny poems that Prelutsky writes with a strong use of meter and some entertaining wordplay." Bull Cent Child Books

Something big has been here; drawings by James Stevenson. Greenwillow Bks. 1990 160p il $17.95 (3-5)   **811**

1. Humorous poetry
ISBN 0-688-06434-5   LC 89-34773

Also available Audiobook version

An illustrated collection of humorous poems on a variety of topics

"Puns and verbal surprises abound. Clever use of alliteration and abundant variety in the sound and texture of words add to the pleasure. . . . Stevenson's small cartoons of snaggle-toothed animals and deadpan children extend and expand the mad humor of the poems, supporting but never overwhelming their good-natured fun. A fine prescription against the blues at any time of year." Horn Book

Tyrannosaurus was a beast; illustrated by Arnold Lobel. Greenwillow Bks. 1988 31p il lib bdg $15.93; pa $4.95 (2-5)   **811**

1. Dinosaurs—Poetry
ISBN 0-688-06443-4 (lib bdg); 0-688-11569-1 (pa)
LC 87-25131

A collection of humorous poems about dinosaurs

"Fourteen dinosaurs meet their match in this outstanding author/illustrator team. While Prelutsky's short, pithy, often witty verses sum up their essential characters, Lobel's line and watercolor portraits bring the beasts to life, enormous yet endearingly vulnerable." Booklist

Sandburg, Carl, 1878-1967

Carl Sandburg; edited by Frances Schoonmaker Bolin; illustrated by Steve Arcella. Sterling 1995 48p il (Poetry for young people) $14.95 (4 and up)
811

ISBN 0-8069-0818-1   LC 94-30777

"A Magnolia Editions book"

"The 33 poems in *Sandburg* vary in length and theme, but most are the staples of anthologies, e.g., 'Fog,' 'Arithmetic,' and 'We Must Be Polite.' The surrealistic illustrations, which appear to be rendered in pastels, are appealing; the soft edges and warm tones work well with Sandburg's imagery." SLJ

Grassroots; poems by Carl Sandburg; paintings by Wendell Minor. Browndeer Press 1998 unp il $18   **811**

1. Middle West—Poetry
ISBN 0-15-200082-8   LC 95-46419

Fourteen poems with mid-western themes or settings

"Sandburg's images are both ordinary and mythic. Beautiful, precisely detailed watercolor paintings reveal Minor's affinity for American's heartland, which is as heartfelt as the poet's." Horn Book Guide

Rainbows are made: poems; selected by Lee Bennett Hopkins; wood engravings by Fritz Eichenberg. Harcourt Brace Jovanovich 1982 81p il hardcover o.p. paperback available $13 (5 and up)   **811**

ISBN 0-15-265481-X (pa)   LC 82-47934

This book "offers some 70 short poems by Carl Sandburg and groups them by theme: the seasons, the sea, the imaginative mind, etc. Each theme explores different aspects of poetic creativity as envisioned by Sandburg and illustrated by Fritz Eichenberg's wood engravings. Eichenberg has truly captured the power and vigorousness of Sandburg's verse." SLJ

Schertle, Alice, 1941-

How now, brown cow? poems by Alice Schertle; paintings by Amanda Schaffer. Browndeer Press 1994 unp il hardcover o.p. paperback available $6.50   **811**

1. Cattle—Poetry
ISBN 0-15-201706-2 (pa)   LC 93-24052

This "collection of poems about cows abounds with tongue-in-cheek spoofs, verbal acrobatics and lyrical songs that are aptly illustrated by debut artist Schaffer's wry cast of brown and purple cows." Publ Wkly

I am the cat; illustrated by Mark Buehner. Lothrop, Lee & Shepard Bks. 1999 unp il $16.95 (k-3)   **811**

1. Cats—Poetry
ISBN 0-688-13153-0   LC 98-21306

"Four longer poems alternate with haiku in this slim, bold collection that observes different cats in tones both affectionate and sardonic. . . . Perspective and shadow add interesting nuances to scenes that are sometimes cartoonlike and often a bit surreal." SLJ

A lucky thing; poems by Alice Schertle; paintings by Wendell Minor. Harcourt Brace & Co. 1999 unp il $17   **811**

1. Nature—Poetry
ISBN 0-15-200541-2   LC 97-43166

A collection of fourteen poems about nature, including "Calling the Sun," "Showing the Wind," and "Invitation from a Mole"

"A book that's filled with both rhyming and free verse to inspire children's senses of observation. . . . Minor's bright watercolor paintings fill the pages with warmth and humor." SLJ

Scieszka, Jon, 1954-

The book that Jack wrote; illustrated by Daniel Adel. Viking 1994 unp $14.99; pa $5.99 (2-4)
811

1. Nursery rhymes
ISBN 0-670-84330-X; 0-14-055385-1 (pa)
LC 94-10932

"An updated version of 'This Is the House That Jack Built,' this cumulative tale tells of a blind rat who falls into a picture in the book that Jack wrote, thus setting off a chain of events in which the players are done in one by one until nothing is left but the book itself. . . . The dark tones of Adel's full-page oil paintings are a fine match for the irreverent mood of the piece." SLJ

Service, Robert W., 1874-1958

The cremation of Sam McGee; paintings by Ted Harrison; introduction by Pierre Berton. Greenwillow Bks. 1987 c1986 unp il $17.95 (4 and up) **811**

    1. Yukon Territory—Poetry
    ISBN 0-688-06903-7   LC 86-14971

Text first published 1907. This newly illustrated edition first published 1986 in Canada

"In the tradition of tall tales, the story of Sam McGee is told here in Service's original rollicking verses. Pledged to cremate his friend Sam, the narrator tells how, after carting the frozen body for miles, he stuffs it into a ship's roaring furnace. To his surprise, when he later opens the door he discovers Sam alive . . . and warm for the first time 'since he left Tennessee.'" Publ Wkly

"A fine example of a 20th-Century regional ballad, one that tells of the profound cold of the Yukon and how it affected the lives of two gold miners." SLJ

The shooting of Dan McGrew; paintings by Ted Harrison. Godine 1988 unp il hardcover o.p. paperback available $10.95 (4 and up) **811**

    1. Yukon Territory—Poetry
    ISBN 0-567-92065-9 (pa)   LC 88-6124

Text first published 1907

A narrative poem set in the Yukon describing the shoot-out in a saloon between a trapper and the man who stole his girl

"While the action of the poem is intense and demanding, the painterly illustrations by Harrison are overwhelmingly powerful; they seem to take on a life of their own, drawing readers' attentions away from the text and toward the surrealistic interpretation of events. . . . Harrison creates a pulsating world of hate and destruction; it's a fascinating interpretation of a well-known poem." Publ Wkly

Shields, Carol Diggory

Lunch money and other poems about school; written by Carol Diggory Shields; illustrated by Paul Meisel. Dutton Children's Bks. 1995 40p il $15.99; pa $5.99 (2-4) **811**

    1. Schools—Poetry 2. Humorous poetry
    ISBN 0-525-45345-8; 0-14-055890-X (pa)
                    LC 95-7332

A "collection of 24 childlike perceptions of the zanier happenings during a school day. The poems' appeal relies on irreverent topics, robust action, sing-song rhythms, and rhyming couplets. The bright, expresssive cartoonstyle illustrations highlight the rollicking nature of most of the selections." SLJ

Siebert, Diane

Mojave; paintings by Wendell Minor. Crowell 1988 unp il hardcover o.p. paperback available $5.95 (1-3) **811**

    1. Deserts—Poetry
    ISBN 0-064-43283-1 (pa)   LC 86-24329

"Paintings of the desert and its creatures illustrate a first-person poem in the voice of the Mojave." Bull Cent Child Books

"Regular rhythms and clever rhymes propel us through space and the vagaries of time. Wendell Minor's artistic vision at times parallels that of Georgia O'Keeffe. . . . [This is] a beautifully orchestrated book of illustrated poems." Christ Sci Monit

Sierra; paintings by Wendell Minor. HarperCollins Pubs. 1991 unp il hardcover o.p. paperback available $6.95 (1-3) **811**

    1. Sierra Nevada Mountains—Poetry
    ISBN 0-06-443441-9 (pa)   LC 90-30522

"In Siebert's rhymed couplets, a mountain speaks of its birth and growth, of the forests and animals it shelters, and of the cycle of life and death it supports." Booklist

"The story of the Sierras is told in lyrical rhymes that are both wonderful to read and full of information. The vivid and beautiful pictures that accompany each page give one the feeling of being in the midst of these delightful mountains." Sci Books Films

Sierra, Judy

Antarctic antics; a book of penguin poems; written by Judy Sierra; illustrated by Jose Aruego & Ariane Dewey. Harcourt Brace & Co. 1998 unp il $16 (k-3) **811**

    1. Penguins—Poetry 2. Antarctica—Poetry
    ISBN 0-15-201006-8   LC 96-41041

"Gulliver books"

A collection of poems celebrating the habits and habitat of Emperor penguins

"Kids will love these high-energy, humorous poems, with some factual information about penguin life woven in. Aruego and Dewey do a nice job of giving readers a feel for the penguins' beautiful but chilly habitat." Booklist

Silverstein, Shel

Falling up; poems and drawings by Shel Silverstein. HarperCollins Pubs. 1996 171p il $17.95; lib bdg $17.89 **811**

    1. Humorous poetry 2. Nonsense verses
    ISBN 0-06-024802-5; 0-06-024803-3 (lib bdg)
                    LC 96-75736

Also available Spanish language edition

This "collection includes more than 150 poems. . . . As always, Silverstein has a direct line to what kids like, and he gives them poems celebrating the gross, the scary, the absurd, and the comical. The drawings are much more than decoration. They often extend a poem's meaning and, in many cases, add some great comedy." Booklist

A light in the attic. Harper & Row 1981 167p il $17.95; lib bdg $17.89 **811**

    1. Humorous poetry 2. Nonsense verses
    ISBN 0-06-025673-7; 0-06-025674-5 (lib bdg)
                    LC 80-8453

This collection of more than one hundred poems "will delight lovers of Silverstein's raucous, rollicking verse and his often tender, whimsical, philosophical advice. . . . The poems are tuned in to kids' most hidden feelings, dark wishes and enjoyment of the silly. . . . The witty line drawings are a full half of the treat of this wholly satisfying anthology by the modern successor to Edward Lear and Hilaire Belloc." SLJ

Silverstein, Shel—*Continued*

Where the sidewalk ends; the poems & drawings of Shel Silverstein. Harper & Row 1974 166p il $17.95; lib bdg $17.89   **811**

1. Humorous poetry 2. Nonsense verses

ISBN 0-06-025667-2; 0-06-025668-0 (lib bdg)

Also available Audiobook version

"There are skillful, sometimes grotesque line drawings with each of the 127 poems, which run in length from a few lines to a couple of pages. The poems are tender, funny, sentimental, philosophical, and ridiculous in turn, and they're for all ages." Saturday Rev

Singer, Marilyn, 1948-

Family reunion; illustrated by R.W. Alley. Macmillan 1994 unp il $14.95 (k-3)   **811**

1. Family life—Poetry

ISBN 0-02-782883-2   LC 92-40336

"Read in sequence, this collection of 14 free-verse poems tells the story of a great day at a family reunion. Read alone each selection stands on its own. Outrageous, silly fun is the theme; and this gathering is full of gregarious, entertaining types. . . . Alley 's watercolor and pen illustrations help to reinforce the free-spirited mood of the day." SLJ

Sky words; illustrated by Deborah Kogan Ray. Macmillan 1994 unp il $14.95 (k-3)   **811**

1. Sky—Poetry

ISBN 0-02-782882-4   LC 92-3765

"Singer finds boundless inspiration in the sky as she creates poems about skywriting and tornadoes, about the world at twilight, about clouds and fog and monarch butterflies filling the air like orange leaves. Subtle internal and end rhyme schemes and rich imagery create a sumptuous flow of words. Reflecting the text, the illustrations vary in tone from abstract expressionism to realism." Horn Book Guide

Smith, Charles R.

Rimshots; basketball pix, rolls, and rhythms; [by] Charles R. Smith, Jr. Dutton Children's Bks. 1999 31p il $15.99; pa $6.99   **811**

1. Basketball—Poetry

ISBN 0-525-46099-3; 0-14-056678-3 (pa)

LC 98-20578

Stories and poems about playing basketball

"A collection comprising rhythmical prose that has the flavor of rap, inspirational musings, and concrete poetry. Design is an integral part of the whole. Display type, boldface, italics, and small and large fonts make words leap from the pages." Booklist

Smith, William Jay, 1918-

Around my room; poems by William Jay Smith; illustrations by Erik Blegvad. Farrar, Straus & Giroux 2000 31p il $16 (k-3)   **811**

ISBN 0-374-30406-8   LC 99-23556

"Smith's collection is for children who are in the mood for silliness. While there is plenty of strong new material, many of the 29 poems previously appeared in

his 'Laughing Time: Nonsense Poems' (1955). 'Around My Room' successfully reaches out to a younger audience. Erik Blegvad's illustrations nicely ground the verbal shenanigans with his crisp, consistently lovely, whimsical watercolors." N Y Times Book Rev

Soto, Gary

Canto familiar; [illustrated by Annika Nelson] Harcourt Brace & Co. 1995 79p il $18 (4-6)
811

1. Mexican Americans—Poetry

ISBN 0-15-200067-4   LC 94-24218

"This collection of simple free verse captures common childhood moments at home, at school, and in the street. Many of the experiences are Mexican American . . . and occasional Spanish words are part of the easy, colloquial, short lines. . . . The occasional full-page, richly colored woodcuts by Annika Nelson capture the child's imaginative take on ordinary things." Booklist

Neighborhood odes; illustrated by David Diaz. Harcourt Brace Jovanovich 1992 68p il $15.95 (4-6)   **811**

1. Hispanic Americans—Poetry

ISBN 0-15-256879-4   LC 91-20710

Also available in paperback from Scholastic

"Twenty-one poems, all odes, celebrate life in a Hispanic neighborhood. Other than the small details of daily life—peoples' names or the foods they eat—these poems could be about any neighborhood. With humor, sensitivity, and insight, Soto explores the lives of children. . . . David Diaz's contemporary black-and-white illustrations, which often resemble cut paper, effortlessly capture the varied moods—happiness, fear, longing, shame, and greed—of this remarkable collection. With a glossary of thirty Spanish words and phrases." Horn Book

Stevenson, James, 1929-

Candy corn; poems. Greenwillow Bks. 1999 55p il $15   **811**

ISBN 0-688-15837-4   LC 98-2965

A collection of short poems with titles such as "The Morning After Halloween," "Dumpsters," and "What Frogs Say To Each Other"

"Stevenson's images range from junkyard jumble to fragile blossoms. With minute particulars of ordinary life, his casual words and wonderful, scribbly ink-and-watercolor pictures work together to make you feel love and longing, mystery and wonder." Booklist

Cornflakes; poems by James Stevenson; with illustrations by the author. Greenwillow Bks. 2000 47p il $14.95   **811**

ISBN 0-688-16718-7   LC 99-29846

A collection of short poems with such titles as "I Can't Move Mountains," "Junkyard," and "Greenhouse in March"

Stevenson "disarms readers with his choice of subjects, his offhand ink-and-watercolor art and his wryly comic verse offering sharp new takes on objects or actions so familiar that they usually escape notice altogether." Publ Wkly

Stevenson, James, 1929-—-*Continued*
Popcorn; poems by James Stevenson; with illustrations by the author. Greenwillow Bks. 1998 64p il $15 **811**
ISBN 0-688-15261-9   LC 97-6320
A collection of short poems with such titles as "Popcorn," "Driftwood," and "My new bird book"
"With a physical immediacy and a casual voice, Stevenson's poems capture quiet, intensely moving moments of daily life in a small seaside town, and his exquisite, understated watercolors extend the concrete particulars of the words." Booklist

Sweet corn. Greenwillow Bks. 1995 63p il $15; pa $5.95 **811**
ISBN 0-688-12647-2; 0-688-17304-7 (pa)
LC 94-4902
A collection of short poems with titles such as "Screen door," "Bike rental," and "Photo album"
"James Stevenson's watercolors give further depth to his poetry: a pensiveness to the boy using his lemonade stand as an umbrella. Other poems are a visual experience of typography and colored background. About everyday things and situations, these poems could be used in classrooms to encourage students to write their own poetry." Child Book Rev Serv

Swenson, May, 1919-1989
The complete poems to solve; illustrated by Christy Hale. Macmillan 1993 115p il $13.95 (5 and up) **811**
1. Nature poetry
ISBN 0-02-788725-1   LC 92-26183
Includes poems first published in Poems to solve, and More poems to solve, published 1966 and 1971 respectively by Scribner
A selection of the author's poetry, largely dealing with nature, which challenges the reader to guess the subject of each poem or a meaning not immediately obvious
"The variety in the collection of seventy-two poems . . . illustrates the scope of Swenson's imaginative powers and verbal skills." Horn Book Guide

Thayer, Ernest Lawrence, 1863-1940
Casey at the bat   **811**
1. Baseball—Poetry
LC 88-45290
Some editions are:
Atheneum Pubs. $15 Illustrated by Gerald Fitzgerald (ISBN 0-689-31945-2)
Godine pa $10.95 Illustrations by Barry Moser; afterword by Donald Hall (ISBN 1-56792-072-1)
Putnam pa $5.95 With additional text and illustrations by Patricia Polacco (ISBN 0-698-11557-0)
First published 1888
A narrative poem about the celebrated baseball player who strikes out at the crucial moment of a game

Thomas, Joyce Carol
Brown honey in broomwheat tea; poems by Joyce Carol Thomas; illustrated by Floyd Cooper. HarperCollins Pubs. 1993 unp il $16.95; pa $4.95 (k-3) **811**
1. African Americans—Poetry
ISBN 0-06-021087-7; 0-06-443439-7 (pa)
LC 91-46043

"A dozen poems rooted in home, family, and the African American experience combine with a series of warm and evocative watercolors in this highly readable and attractive picture book." Booklist

Gingerbread days; poems; illustrated by Floyd Cooper. HarperCollins Pubs. 1995 unp il $14.95; pa $5.95 (k-3) **811**
1. African Americans—Poetry 2. Family life—Poetry
ISBN 0-06-023469-5; 0-06-446188-2 (pa)
LC 94-19566
"Joanna Cotler books"
"Paying tribute to each month of the year, short poems celebrate a loving African-American family's sense of spirituality and of self. The warmth of a January day spent with Grandma, the freedom of summer months, the realization of lasting December gifts, and more are chronicled." Horn Book Guide
"Cooper's paintings glow with light and warmth, conveying a strong sense of joy in living. With its large pictures and simple (sometimes thought-provoking) poems, this will work well with groups." Booklist

Turner, Ann Warren, 1945-
Mississippi mud; three prairie journals; [by] Ann Turner; pictures by Robert J. Blake. HarperCollins Pubs. 1997 unp il $16.95; lib bdg $16.89 (4 and up) **811**
1. Frontier and pioneer life—Poetry 2. Overland journeys to the Pacific—Poetry
ISBN 0-06-024432-1; 0-06-024433-X (lib bdg)
LC 95-10850
Poems reflecting the points of view of three pioneer children describe their family's journey from Kentucky to Oregon
"The images Turner creates are stunning. . . . Blake's watercolor illustrations elegantly capture the scenery in warm earth tones with a delightful attention to detail." SLJ

Updike, John
A child's calendar; illustrations by Trina Schart Hyman. Holiday House 1999 unp il $16.95 **811**
1. Months—Poetry
ISBN 0-8234-1445-0   LC 98-46166
A Caldecott Medal honor book, 2000
A newly illustrated edition of the title first published 1965 by Knopf
A collection of twelve poems describing the activities in a child's life and the changes in the weather as the year moves from January to December
"Hyman's colorful illustrations portray a multiracial family living in rural New Hampshire. . . . Each evocative illustration has its own story to tell, celebrating the small moments in children's lives with clarity and sensitivity, with empathy and joy." Booklist

Viorst, Judith
If I were in charge of the world and other worries; poems for children and their parents; illustrated by Lynne Cherry. Atheneum Pubs. 1981 56p il lib bdg $16.95; pa $4.95 (3-6) **811**
ISBN 0-689-30863-9 (lib bdg); 0-689-70770-3 (pa)
LC 81-2342

Viorst, Judith—*Continued*

"Forty-one lively, funny poems written from a wry, self-deprecating point of view. Some poems verge on adult feelings—such as a broken heart or a lyrical appreciation of spring—but most of them deal with children's worries, to which the author seems to be specially attuned." Horn Book

Sad underwear and other complications; poems; illustrated by Richard Hull. Atheneum Pubs. 1995 78p $16; pa $4.99 (3-6)   **811**

1. Humorous poetry
ISBN 0-689-31929-0; 0-689-83376-8 (pa)
LC 94-3357

"From 'The Seventh Swimming Lesson,' in which Sally finally puts her face in the water, to a practical version of 'Sleeping Beauty,' this is an inspired book of verse guaranteed to tickle the humerus again and again. Yet, poignancy is present, too. . . . Both humorous and dreamlike pen-and-ink illustrations are scattered throughout." SLJ

Wilbur, Richard, 1921-

The disappearing alphabet; illustrated by David Diaz. Harcourt Brace & Co. 1998 unp il $16 (3-5)   **811**

1. Alphabet
ISBN 0-15-201470-5   LC 97-24617

A collection of twenty-six short poems pondering what the world would be like if any letters of the alphabet should disappear

"The poems presented here were first printed in *The Atlantic Monthly* magazine. A series of rhyming couplets of varying lengths, they range from the innocently whimsical to the cleverly sophisticated. Diaz uses computer-generated illustrations to add just the right touches to the verses; the images are lush and playful at the same time." SLJ

Willard, Nancy

Pish, posh, said Hieronymus Bosch; illustrations by the Dillons. Harcourt Brace Jovanovich 1991 unp il $22 (2-5)   **811**

1. Bosch, Hieronymus, d. 1516—Poetry
ISBN 0-15-262210-1   LC 86-3173

In this poem, the housekeeper for medieval Dutch artist Hieronymus Bosch complains about the weird creatures which inhabit his home

"Once again, the Dillons have tailored their style to perfectly suit—and here, lend waggish twists to—their subject. Rendered in the opulent tones and peculiar, wild spirit of Bosch's works, their parade of fantastical creatures would make the master proud: animate cucumbers, an armor-plated, two-headed dragon, a flying fish with wings of pickles. . . . This eccentric work may not be for youngest children, but anyone with unusual vision and an affinity for the quirkiest corners of the imagination will find it a source of endless fascination." Publ Wkly

The sorcerer's apprentice; illustrated by Leo and Diane Dillon. Blue Sky Press (NY) 1993 unp il $16.95 (2-5)   **811**

1. Magicians—Poetry
ISBN 0-590-47329-8   LC 93-19912

Sylvia, the new apprentice to the great magician Tottibo, steals one of his spells to complete an impossible task and accidentally creates chaos

"The dancing, varied rhythms and the alliterative imagery of the poetry make this a read-aloud treasure. The book is a visual prize as well. Preposterous creatures swarm over cream-colored, gilt-bordered pages while small vignettes outside the frames open up each spread and advance the story line." Horn Book

A visit to William Blake's inn; poems for innocent and experienced travelers; illustrated by Alice and Martin Provensen. Harcourt Brace Jovanovich 1981 44p il $16; pa $7 (2-5)   **811**

1. Nonsense verses
ISBN 0-15-293822-2; 0-15-293823-0 (pa)
LC 80-27403

Awarded the Newbery Medal, 1982 and also a Caldecott Medal honor book for the same year

This "collection of sixteen nonsense verses describes the lively goings-on among several incongruous travelers who put up at an imaginary inn run by the English poet William Blake." Child Book Rev Serv

"Nancy Willard's fantasy is pure pleasure, and her joy is expressed in the juxtaposition of sense and nonsense. . . . Done chiefly in glowing tawny colors, the pictures are highly decorative, and the whole book, printed on buff paper speckled to simulate an antique look, presents an elegant appearance." Horn Book

The voyage of the Ludgate Hill; travels with Robert Louis Stevenson; illustrated by Alice and Martin Provensen. Harcourt Brace Jovanovich 1987 unp il $14.95; pa $4.95 (2-5)   **811**

1. Stevenson, Robert Louis, 1850-1894—Poetry
ISBN 0-15-294464-8; 0-15-200119-0 (pa)
LC 86-19502

"Inspired by Stevenson's letters, Nancy Willard has written a poem, part fact part fantasy, about his stormy ocean voyage from London to New York on a cargo-carrying steamer in 1887. Stevenson and his wife, and a few other adventurous passengers, are joined in this journey by a bevy of assorted animals: apes and baboons, monkeys and stallions, not to mention the shipmaster's cat." N Y Times Book Rev

"The Provensens' paintings, brush stroked in buff, brown, and blue, are mannered, with a restrained humor based on a juxtaposition of the mundane with the unreal. A delight to read aloud, this will need some background explanation from adults." Bull Cent Child Books

Wise, William, 1923-

Dinosaurs forever; pictures by Lynn Munsinger. Dial Bks. for Young Readers 2000 unp il $15.99 (k-3)   **811**

1. Dinosaurs—Poetry
ISBN 0-8037-2114-5   LC 99-34702

A collection of humorous poems about dinosaurs

This book offers "zippy poems and hilarious art that together humanize the extinct yet undyingly popular creatures." Booklist

Wong, Janet S., 1962-

Night garden; poems from the world of dreams; illustrated by Julie Paschkis. Margaret K. McElderry Bks. 2000 28p il $16 (3-6)   **811**

1. Dreams—Poetry

ISBN 0-689-82617-6   LC 98-46302

A collection of poems describing a variety of dreams, some familiar, some strange, some beautiful, and some on the darker side

"The combination of the impressionistic and the prosaic in these vivid poems invites rereading just as the fabulous images of the illustrations and the dreamy monochromatic backgrounds invite re-viewing." Bull Cent Child Books

The rainbow hand; poems about mothers and children; illustrations by Jennifer Hewitson. Margaret K. McElderry Bks. 1999 22p il $15 (4-6)   **811**

1. Mothers—Poetry

ISBN 0-689-82148-4   LC 97-50554

"Eighteen free verse poems about mothers and the experience of motherhood are told from the perspectives of both parent and child. The author's mother inspired the poems, but they transcend any particular relationship to become an honest portrayal of mother/child universalities. Stylized scratchboard and watercolor illustrations complement the poems." Horn Book Guide

Worth, Valerie

All the small poems and fourteen more; pictures by Natalie Babbitt. Farrar, Straus & Giroux 1994 194p il hardcover o.p. paperback available $6.95   **811**

ISBN 0-374-40345-7 (pa)   LC 94-8810

"As the title implies, all the original collaborations between this poet and artist are collected in this volume, which includes ninety-nine poems and an additional fourteen new ones. The earlier works have been widely praised, for good reason, and the new verses are every bit as worthy as their predecessors." Horn Book

Yolen, Jane

The ballad of the pirate queens; illustrated by David Shannon. Harcourt Brace & Co. 1995 unp il $16; pa $6 (3-5)   **811**

1. Bonny, Anne, b. 1700—Poetry 2. Read, Mary, 1680-1721—Poetry 3. Pirates—Poetry

ISBN 0-15-200710-5; 0-15-201885-9 (pa)

LC 94-7874

"A poem about Anne Bonney and Mary Reade, who were real pirates and who sailed on the sloop Vanity and fought the man-of-war Albion. They were tried in Jamaica in 1720 but, some say, were released because they were pregnant. Dramatic seafaring illustrations." N Y Times Book Rev

How beastly! a menagerie of nonsense poems; pictures by James Marshall. Wordsong 1994 46p il $14.95 (3-5)   **811**

1. Mythical animals—Poetry 2. Nonsense verses

ISBN 1-56397-086-4   LC 92-85036

A reissue of the title first published 1980 by Collins

This is a collection of nonsense verses on such imaginary creatures as the alligate, the tuner fish and the canterpillar

"For each of the twenty-two verses, a full-page line drawing washed with gray illuminates and comments on the fanciful fauna." Horn Book

O Jerusalem; illustrated by John Thompson. Blue Sky Press (NY) 1996 unp il lib bdg $15.95 (4 and up)   **811**

1. Jerusalem—Poetry

ISBN 0-590-48426-5   LC 95-6013

A poetic tribute to Jerusalem, in honor of the 3000th anniversary of its founding, celebrating its history as a holy city for three major religions

"Yolen captures the feelings of Judaism, Christianity, and Islam toward Jerusalem in her poetry, and Thompson brings her words to life in exquisite paintings." Booklist

The three bears holiday rhyme book; written by Jane Yolen; illustrated by Jane Dyer. Harcourt Brace & Co. 1995 32p il $15 (k-2)   **811**

1. Holidays—Poetry 2. Bears—Poetry

ISBN 0-15-200932-9   LC 93-17252

"Baby Bear, joined by Mother, Father, or their friend Goldilocks, celebtrates 15 special days throughout the year. Each occasion is featured in a splendid two-page water-color illustration with a short poem honoring the event." SLJ

The three bears rhyme book; illustrated by Jane Dyer. Harcourt Brace Jovanovich 1987 32p il lib bdg $14.95 (k-2)   **811**

1. Bears—Poetry

ISBN 0-15-286386-9   LC 86-19514

"The 16 poems offered here assume that Goldilocks and the three bears maintain a close friendship in spite of their initial encounter, which is not mentioned. The verses describe familiar activities such as taking a walk, eating porridge, having a birthday party, and going out in the rain." SLJ

"The universality of the events will certainly appeal to young listeners who'll find the words mirroring their own everyday activities. As for the illustrations, there's just one word for them—delightful. Executed in soft watercolors and colored pencils, the pictures are charming without being cloying, the humor is amusing without being broad." Booklist

811.008 American poetry— Collections

The 20th century children's poetry treasury; selected by Jack Prelutsky; illustrated by Meilo So. Knopf 1999 87p il $19.95; lib bdg $21.99   **811.008**

1. American poetry—Collections

ISBN 0-679-89314-8; 0-679-99314-2 (lib bdg)

LC 99-23988

A collection of more than 200 poems by such modern poets as Nikki Grimes, John Ciardi, Karla Kuskin, Ted Hughes, e.e. cummings, Eve Merriam, Deborah Chandra, Arnold Adoff, and more than 100 others

"While all of these selections have been published

The 20th century children's poetry treasury—
Continued

elsewhere, the format and illustrations in this collection give them new life. . . . So's watercolor illustrations are, by turn, impressionistic, childlike, silly, and serious, as called for by the tone of the poems featured. . . . A splendid collection." SLJ

Ashley Bryan's ABC of African-American poetry. Atheneum Bks. for Young Readers 1997 unp il $16; pa $5.99 (k-3) **811.008**
1. African Americans—Poetry 2. American poetry—African American authors—Collections 3. Alphabet
ISBN 0-689-81209-4; 0-689-84045-4 (pa)
LC 96-25148
"A Jean Karl book"

Each letter of the alphabet is represented by a line from a poem by a different African American poet, describing an aspect of the black experience

This book is illustrated "by Bryan's vivid tempera and gouache paintings. . . . The selections . . . display a loving acquaintance with poets from James Weldon Johnson to Rita Dove. While there is a full range of emotions, joy and pride predominate." SLJ

The Beauty of the beast; poems from the animal kingdom; selected by Jack Prelutsky; illustrated by Meilo So; opening poems for each section especially written for this anthology by Jack Prelutsky. Knopf 1997 101p il $25 (4-6) **811.008**
1. Animals—Poetry 2. Poetry—Collections
ISBN 0-679-87058-X
LC 96-14423

This collection includes "more than 200 animal poems by twentieth-century writers, loosely arranged into five sections—insects and worms, fish, reptiles, birds, and mammals. . . . The poets include Hoberman, Lawrence, Worth, Jarrell, Roethke, and many more." Booklist

"Prelutsky has selected a remarkable array of poems full of movement and sound. . . . Each page has several poems and bright watercolors that writhe with texture." SLJ

Includes bibliographical references

Birthday rhymes, special times; selected by Bobbye S. Goldstein; pictures by Jose Aruego and Ariane Dewey. Doubleday Bks. for Young Readers 1993 48p hardcover o.p. paperback available $5.99 (k-3) **811.008**
1. Birthdays—Poetry 2. American poetry—Collections
ISBN 0-440-41018-5 (pa)
LC 90-21488

A collection of poems about birthdays, by such authors as Dr. Seuss, John Ciardi, and Jack Prelutsky

"The poems . . . are relatively short (just right for a young child's short attention span) and range from the semi-serious to the quirkily whimsical to the tickle-your-funny-bone silly. Artists Aruego and Dewey . . . offer amusing, cartoonlike illustrations in bright, eye-catching colors. The drawings are imaginative and witty." Booklist

Blast off! poems about space; selected by Lee Bennett Hopkins; pictures by Melissa Sweet. HarperCollins Pubs. 1995 48p il lib bdg $15.89 (k-2) **811.008**
1. American poetry—Collections 2. Outer space—Poetry
ISBN 0-06-024261-2
LC 93-24536
"An I can read book"

"Hopkins collects twenty poems by a variety of writers on the subject of space: moon, the sun, stars, planets and meteorites. Most, including his own two, are fairly contemporary, except for 'Star light, star bright,' and one by Sara Teasdale from the 1930s. . . . The poems are well chosen and on a topic many children favor, and Sweet's watercolors capture their mix of wonder and joy well." Bull Cent Child Books

Book poems; poems from National Children's Book Week, 1959-1998; introduction by Lee Bennett Hopkins; [ed., Mary Perrotta Rich] Children's Bk. Council 1998 95p il pa $20 **811.008**
1. American poetry—Collections 2. Books and reading—Poetry
ISBN 0-933633-05-X
LC 99-158017

This anthology contains four decades of poems about the importance of books and reading. Includes biographies and bibliographies of the contributing poets

Includes bibliographical references

Christmas in the stable; poems selected and illustrated by Beverly K. Duncan. Harcourt Brace Jovanovich 1990 32p il hardcover o.p. paperback available $5 (2-4) **811.008**
1. Jesus Christ—Nativity—Poetry 2. Poetry—Collections
ISBN 0-15-201385-7 (pa)
LC 88-37953

A collection of poems by Jane Yolen, Elizabeth Coatsworth, Norma Farber, and others, each from the point of view of an animal or about the animals in the stable where the Christ Child lay asleep

"Though suffused with a spirit of peace and wonder, the pieces are refreshingly unsentimental and free of cliche. . . . Each selection and the animal painting that illustrates it are framed together with thin colored borders and centered against a tapestrylike background that is detailed with plants appropriate to the season. The graceful designs were inspired by medieval manuscripts and possess a similar quality of serenity and grace." Booklist

Cool salsa; bilingual poems on growing up Latino in the United States; edited by Lori M. Carlson; introduction by Oscar Hijuelos. Holt & Co. 1994 xx, 123p il $16.95; pa $4.50 (5 and up) **811.008**
1. American poetry—Hispanic American authors—Collections 2. Bilingual books—English-Spanish
ISBN 0-8050-3135-9; 0-449-70436-X (pa)
LC 93-45798

"This collection presents poems by 29 Mexican-American, Cuban-American, Puerto Rican, and other Central and South American poets, including Sandra Cisneros, Luis J. Rodriguez, Pat Mora, Gary Soto, Ana Castillo, Oscar Hijuelos, Ed J. Vega, Judith Ortiz-Cofer, and other Latino writers both contemporary and histori-

Cool salsa—*Continued*

cal. Brief biographical notes on the authors are provided. All the poems deal with experiences of teenagers." Book Rep

Days like this; a collection of small poems; selected and illustrated by Simon James. Candlewick Press 2000 45p il $17.99 **811.008**
ISBN 0-7636-0812-2   LC 99-11363

First published 1999 in the United Kingdom

A collection of short poems by such authors as Eve Merriam, Ogden Nash, and Charlotte Zolotow

"Pen-and-ink and watercolor cartoons reflect the everyday world. . . . A lively variety of perspectives and flashes of humor make this book worth many returns." SLJ

Dinosaurs: poems; selected by Lee Bennett Hopkins; illustrated by Murray Tinkleman. Harcourt Brace Jovanovich 1987 46p il $12.95; pa $6 (3-5)   **811.008**
1. Dinosaurs—Poetry 2. American poetry—Collections
ISBN 0-15-223495-0; 0-15-223496-9 (pa)
                        LC 86-14818

"In this volume of 18 poems, Hopkins invites us to 'Reflect upon the dinosaur,/A giant that exists no more.' With poems by Myra Cohn Livingston, Lilian Moore, Valerie Worth and others, the collection explores fossils . . . and the museums that house [them]." Publ Wkly

"The collection will offer a spur to the imagination which more scientific material may lack. Minutely crosshatched, black-and-white illustrations effectively recreate the nubbly, grainy skins of the mysterious, ponderous creatures and the swamps and savannas of their remote and shadowy world." Horn Book

Dreams of glory; poems starring girls; selected by Isabel Joshlin Glaser; illustrated by Pat Lowery Collins. Atheneum Bks. for Young Readers 1995 47p il $16 (3-5)   **811.008**
1. Girls—Poetry 2. American poetry—Collections
ISBN 0-689-31891-X   LC 95-15302

"A Lucas/Evans book"

"Divided into three sections labeled 'Sports,' 'Power,' and 'Dreams of Glory,' the thirty poems in this collection reflect the hopes, fears, and aspirations of modern girls. A good number of poets are represented—Lillian Morrison, Gertrude Stein, John Ridland, May Swenson, and others—and Glaser includes a few verses of her own. The poems are brief and accessible; the tone, inspirational and quietly resonating." Horn Book Guide

Extra innings; baseball poems; selected by Lee Bennett Hopkins; illustrated by Scott Medlock. Harcourt Brace Jovanovich 1993 40p il $16 (4 and up)   **811.008**
1. Baseball—Poetry 2. American poetry—Collections
ISBN 0-15-226833-2   LC 92-13013

Companion volume to Opening days

"A collection of 19 poems about baseball, bolstered by vibrant oil-on-paper illustrations that are sure to attract attention, even from reluctant readers. Poets include May Swenson, Lillian Morrison, Ernest Thayer, and Lee Bennett Hopkins." Booklist

For laughing out loud; poems to tickle your funnybone; selected by Jack Prelutsky; illustrated by Marjorie Priceman. Knopf 1991 84p il $17   **811.008**
1. American poetry—Collections 2. Humorous poetry
ISBN 0-394-82144-0   LC 90-33010

A collection of humorous poems by writers including Ellen Raskin, Karla Kuskin, Ogden Nash, and Arnold Lobel

"These nonsense verses by a wide variety of poets combine the domestic and the gross, deadpan and slapstick, with a lilting rhythm and satisfying rhyme. . . . The design is ebullient, often with several poems appearing on a double-page spread surrounded by wildly energetic wash-and-line illustrations." Booklist

Good books, good times! selected by Lee Bennett Hopkins; pictures by Harvey Stevenson. Harper & Row 1990 31p il lib bdg $16.89; pa $5.95 (1-3)   **811.008**
1. Books and reading—Poetry 2. American poetry—Collections
ISBN 0-06-022528-9 (lib bdg); 0-06-446222-6 (pa)
                        LC 89-49108

"A Charlotte Zolotow book"

An anthology of poems about the joys of books and reading. Includes selections by David McCord, Karla Kuskin, Myra Cohn Livingston, and Jack Prelutsky

"The tone of the poems . . . ranges from exuberant to meditative. The collection will excite any parent, teacher, or librarian looking for brief, accessible poems on the subject of books and reading. Stevenson's lighthearted watercolors perfectly capture the jubilant mood of the book." Horn Book

Hand in hand; an American history through poetry; collected by Lee Bennett Hopkins; illustrated by Peter M. Fiore. Simon & Schuster Bks. for Young Readers 1994 144p il $20 (4 and up)   **811.008**
1. United States—History—Poetry 2. American poetry—Collections
ISBN 0-671-73315-X   LC 92-24230

"Hopkins divides the country's past into nine arbitrary eras and presents 5-10 selections as representative of each period or theme. He includes patriotic songs, speeches, and individual anthems by a veritable feast of American poets, such as Walt Whitman, Carl Sandburg, Langston Hughes, and Robert Frost. . . . Fiore's bold impressionistic oil paintings, in the form of expansive tableaus and cameo vignettes, provide vivid visuals to go along with the poetic imagery." SLJ

Happy birthday; poems; selected by Lee Bennett Hopkins; illustrated by Hilary Knight. Simon & Schuster Bks. for Young Readers 1991 unp il $11.95 (k-3)   **811.008**
1. Birthdays—Poetry 2. American poetry—Collections
ISBN 0-689-83877-8   LC 90-10086

"Hopkins has assembled a collection of birthday verses from popular children's poets such as Beatrice Schenk de Regniers, Aileen Fisher, Myra Cohn Livingston, and Nancy White Carlstrom. Through watercolor, pen-and-ink, and colored-pencil cartoons, Knight tells the story of a birthday party from preparing the invitations to the writing of thank-you cards." SLJ

I am the darker brother; an anthology of modern poems by African Americans; edited and with an afterword by Arnold Adoff; drawings by Benny Andrews; introduction by Rudine Sims Bishop; foreword by Nikki Giovanni. rev ed. Simon & Schuster Bks. for Young Readers 1997 208p il $16; pa $4.99 **811.008**
1. American poetry—African American authors—Collections
ISBN 0-689-81241-8; 0-689-80869-0 (pa)
LC 97-144181

First published 1968

This anthology presents "the African-American experience through poetry that speaks for itself. . . . Because of the historical context of many of the poems, the book will be much in demand during Black History Month, but it should be used and treasured as part of the larger canon of literature to be enjoyed by all Americans at all times of the year. An indispensable addition to library collections." SLJ

I, too, sing America; three centuries of African American poetry; [selected and annotated by] Catherine Clinton; illustrated by Stephen Alcorn. Houghton Mifflin 1998 128p il $20 (6 and up) **811.008**
1. African Americans—Poetry 2. American poetry—African American authors—Collections
ISBN 0-395-89599-5 LC 97-46137

Also available Audiobook version

A collection of poems by African-American writers, including Lucy Terry, Gwendolyn Bennett, and Alice Walker

"For each poet, Clinton provides a biography and a brief, insightful commentary on the poem(s) she has chosen, including a discussion of political as well as literary connections. Alcorn's dramatic, full-page, full-color illustrations opposite each poem evoke the quiltlike patterns and rhythmic figures of folk art." Booklist

If you ever meet a whale; poems selected by Myra Cohn Livingston; illustrated by Leonard Everett Fisher. Holiday House 1992 32p il $14.95 (3-5) **811.008**
1. Whales—Poetry 2. American poetry—Collections
ISBN 0-8234-0940-6 LC 91-36265

A collection of poems about whales, by such authors as Jane Yolen, Theodore Roethke, and John Ciardi

"Fisher's majestic full-color paintings depict the underwater world in deep, cool hues shot with warmer or whiter highlights. . . . The spacious design, a necessity for displaying such mammoth creatures, is a fine counterpoint to the pithy poems." Booklist

Imagine that! poems of never-was; selected by Jack Perlutsky; illustrated by Kevin Hawkes. Knopf 1998 45p il $18; lib bdg $19.99 **811.008**
1. Nonsense verses 2. American poetry—Collections
ISBN 0-679-88206-5; 0-679-98206-X (lib bdg)
LC 96-45591

An illustrated collection of poems of fantasy and nonsense, by such authors as Jane Yolen, Conrad Aiken, and Karla Kuskin

"The sheer brio of the language is sure to amuse, and Prelutsky coaxes still more pleasure with his clever pairings and the volume's smooth flow. Equal credit goes to Hawkes . . . whose full-spread gouaches testify to an apparently tireless imagination." Publ Wkly

In daddy's arms I am tall; African Americans celebrating fathers; illustrated by Javaka Steptoe. Lee & Low Bks. 1997 unp il $15.95; pa $6.95 **811.008**
1. Fathers—Poetry 2. African Americans—Poetry 3. American poetry—Collections
ISBN 1-88000-031-8; 1-584-30016-7 (pa)
LC 97-7311

Coretta Scott King award for illustration, 1998

A collection of poems celebrating African-American fathers by Angela Johnson, E. Ethelbert Miller, Carole Boston Weatherford, and others

"Certain poems . . . elevate this collection above the mundane, but it is the illustrations that set this volume apart. Steptoe uses a variety of materials and techniques and art forms to enhance the language of the poems, including torn paper, collages, realia, paintings, and drawings." Horn Book

Jumpety-bumpety hop; a parade of animal poems; [compiled and illustrated by] Kay Chorao. Dutton Children's Bks. 1997 40p il $16.99; pa $6.99 **811.008**
1. Animals—Poetry 2. Poetry—Collections
ISBN 0-525-45825-5; 0-14-056671-6 (pa)
LC 97-10959

"Featuring the work of forty-eight poets, this warm and friendly collection contains poems that are diverse in tone and style, from elegant haiku to bouncy rhymes. The amicable animal characters are brought to life in jewel-toned pictures in which pigs dance jigs, monkeys jump on beds, and Kangaroos sleep in the sun." Horn Book Guide

Knock at a star; a child's introduction to poetry; [compiled by] X. J. Kennedy and Dorothy M. Kennedy; illustrated by Karen Lee Baker. rev ed. Little, Brown 1999 180p il $17.95; pa $10.95 **811.008**
1. American poetry—Collections 2. English poetry—Collections
ISBN 0-316-48436-9; 0-316-48800-3 (pa)
LC 98-21572

A revised and newly illustrated edition of the title first published 1982

An anthology of mostly very short poems by standard, contemporary, and anonymous poets, intended to stimulate interest in reading and writing poetry

"Karen Lee Baker's small, shaded-pencil drawings capture the many moods of the verse." Booklist

Lives: poems about famous Americans; selected by Lee Bennett Hopkins; illustrated by Leslie Staub. HarperCollins Pubs. 1999 31p il $15.95; lib bdg $15.89 (4 and up) **811.008**
1. United States—Biography—Poetry 2. American poetry—Collections
ISBN 0-06-027767-X; 0-06-027768-8 (lib bdg)
LC 98-29851

Lives: poems about famous Americans—*Continued*

A collection of poetic portraits of sixteen famous Americans from Paul Revere to Neil Armstrong, by such authors as Jane Yolen, Nikki Grimes, and X. J. Kennedy

"Hopkins's eloquent introduction praises the power of poetry. Concluding 'Notes on the Lives' give readers useful biographical information. Full-page portraits feature Staub's distinctive, flat, primitive style, and their backgrounds have details particular to the subject. . . . A winning combination of poems and illustrations." SLJ

Make a joyful sound; poems for children by African-American poets; illustrated by Cornelius Van Wright and Ying-Hwa Hu; edited by Deborah Slier. Scholastic 1996 107p il $13.95
811.008
1. African Americans—Poetry 2. American poetry—African American authors—Collections
ISBN 0-590-67432-3 LC 95-24413
A reissue of the title first published 1991 by Holiday House

A collection of traditional and contemporary poems covering a wide range of topics focusing on the African-American experience

"The illustrations . . . are as varied in style as the poems. Mediums include colored and graphite pencil, watercolor, and airbrush-applied dye. . . . Each poem forms a part of the pattern, not only of the black experience, but of universal human experience." SLJ

Marvelous math; a book of poems; selected by Lee Bennett Hopkins; illustrated by Karen Barbour. Simon & Schuster Bks. for Young Readers 1997 31p il $17 (3-5) **811.008**
1. Mathematics—Poetry 2. American poetry—Collections
ISBN 0-689-80658-2 LC 96-21597
Presents such poems as "Math Makes Me Feel Safe," "Fractions," "Pythagoras," and "Time Passes," by such writers as Janet S. Wong, Lee Bennett Hopkins, and Ilo Orleans

"Rhymed and open verse styles are represented, as are a variety of tones. . . . Barbour's lively illustrations dance and play around the poems. Her boldly outlined watercolor figures, often wearing ill-fitting hats, fill the pages with childlike whimsy." SLJ

My black me; a beginning book of black poetry; edited by Arnold Adoff. [rev. ed.] Dutton Children's Bks. 1994 83p $14.99; pa $5.99 (5 and up) **811.008**
1. American poetry—African American authors—Collections
ISBN 0-525-45216-8; 0-14-037443-4 (pa)
First published 1974

A compilation of poems reflecting thoughts on being black by such authors as Langston Hughes, Lucille Clifton, Nikki Giovanni, and Imamu Amiri Baraka

Never take a pig to lunch and other poems about the fun of eating; selected and illustrated by Nadine Bernard Westcott. Orchard Bks. 1994 64p il $18.95; pa $7.95 (k-3) **811.008**
1. Food—Poetry 2. American poetry—Collections
ISBN 0-531-08634-X; 0-531-07098-0 (pa)
LC 93-11801

"A Melanie Kroupa book"

"A food-oriented collection of limericks, free verse, and other styles of rhyme by such well-known poets and humorists as Ogden Nash, Eve Merriam, Florence Parry Heide, Jack Prelutsky, John Ciardi, David McCord, and others. Poems about popular treats, disgusting eating habits, and outrageous table manners are among the categories included. Westcott's rollicking cartoons, done in ink and acrylics, capture the fun." SLJ

Opening days; sports poems; selected by Lee Bennett Hopkins; illustrated by Scott Medlock. Harcourt Brace & Co. 1996 37p il $16 (4 and up) **811.008**
1. Sports—Poetry 2. American poetry—Collections
ISBN 0-15-200270-7 LC 94-43364
Companion volume to Extra innings

"A collection of eighteen poems focusing on a variety of athletic endeavors includes Jane Yolen's 'Karate Kid,' Arnold Adoff's 'I Am the Running Girl,' and Gary Soto's 'Ode to Weight Lifting.' . . . Enhanced by oil paintings with lustrous color." Horn Book Guide

The **Oxford** book of children's verse in America; edited by Donald Hall. Oxford Univ. Press 1985 xxxviii, 319p $35; pa $15.95 **811.008**
1. American poetry—Collections
ISBN 0-19-503539-9; 0-19-506761-4 (pa)
LC 84-20755

"Hall's intention, expressed in the introduction, is to create an anthology of American poetry actually written for or adopted by children during a particular historical period. The emphasis is on authenticity rather than personal taste." SLJ

"A fine and carefully winnowed collection of American poetry is gathered in a book that will interest students of children's literature and young people who simply enjoy browsing." Horn Book

The **Oxford** illustrated book of American children's poems; edited by Donald Hall. Oxford Univ. Press 1998 96p il $19.95
811.008
1. American poetry—Collections
ISBN 0-19-512373-5 LC 99-34419
The poems in this anthology "date back to Native American cradle songs and an alphabet from a 1727 primer, and include contemporary works by Gary Soto, Sandra Cisneros and Janet S. Wong. The wide-ranging selections include both fresh and familiar poems, many of which are set off by period artwork, some from early children's magazines." Publ Wkly

The **Palm** of my heart; poetry by African American children; edited by Davida Adedjouma; illustrated by Gregory Christie; introduction by Lucille Clifton. Lee & Low Bks. 1996 unp il $15.95; pa $6.95 **811.008**
1. American poetry—African American authors—Collections 2. African Americans—Poetry 3. Children's writings
ISBN 1-880000-41-5; 1-880000-76-8 (pa)
LC 96-13426
A Coretta Scott King honor book for illustration, 1997

The Palm of my heart—*Continued*

"Twenty short poems by African-American students are gathered in this picture-book-sized collection that celebrates being black. Stunning acrylic and colored-pencil illustrations enhance brief moodpieces. . . . Exaggerated and elongated human figures stand against blocks of color and suggested shapes, reflecting the energy and passion of the text." Bull Cent Child Books

Pass it on; African-American poetry for children; selected by Wade Hudson; illustrated by Floyd Cooper. Scholastic 1993 32p il $15.95 (k-3)
811.008

1. American poetry—African American authors—Collections

ISBN 0-590-45770-5   LC 92-16034

An illustrated collection of poetry by such Afro-American poets as Langston Hughes, Nikki Giovanni, Eloise Greenfield, and Lucille Clifton

"Cooper's beautifully individualized oil-wash portraits express the energy, the yearning, and the heartfelt emotion of this fine anthology." Booklist

The Place my words are looking for; what poets say about and through their work; selected by Paul B. Janeczko. Bradbury Press 1990 150p il $16 (4 and up)   **811.008**

1. American poetry—Collections 2. Poetics

ISBN 0-02-747671-5   LC 89-39331

"More than forty contemporary poets are included: Eve Merriam, X. J. Kennedy, Felice Holman, Gary Soto, Mark Vinz, Karla Kuskin, and John Updike, among others. Their contributions vary widely in theme and mood and style, though the preponderance of the pieces are written in modern idiom and unrhymed meter. The accompanying comments frequently are as insightful and eloquent as the poems themselves." Horn Book

Poem stew; poems selected by William Cole; pictures by Karen Ann Weinhaus. Lippincott 1981 84p il o.p.; HarperCollins Pubs. paperback available $4.95 (3-6)   **811.008**

1. Food—Poetry 2. Dining—Poetry 3. American poetry—Collections

ISBN 0-06-440136-7 (pa)   LC 81-47106

"Drawn from anonymous and traditional sources as well as from the works of such poets as Ogden Nash, John Ciardi, Jack Prelutsky, Myra Cohn Livingston, and the selector himself, the poems celebrate the subject of food. But they haven't been chosen for their appeal to gourmet palates; rather they comment on occasions when particular items of food become the impetus for a humorous narrative, lyric, or epigram. . . . With indexes of authors and titles." Horn Book

Poems for Jewish holidays; selected by Myra Cohn Livingston; illustrated by Lloyd Bloom. Holiday House 1986 32p il lib bdg $15.95 (k-3)
811.008

1. Jewish holidays—Poetry 2. American poetry—Collections

ISBN 0-8234-0606-7   LC 85-27179

"Sixteen poems celebrate 12 Jewish holidays. The poems vary from the traditional 'Had Gadya' taken from the Passover Haggadah, to the more playful, contemporary 'First Night of Hanukkah' by Ruth Rosten and the more sensitive and moving 'Tisha B'Av,' which commemorates a Jewish day of mourning, by Meyer Hahn. . . . Images effectively convey the moods of different holidays. However, it is Bloom's black-and-white illustrations that make this a truly distinguished book. Each of the ten full-page charcoal paintings captures the different aspects of the Jewish experience while keeping with the spirit of the poem." SLJ

Reflections on a gift of watermelon pickle . . . and other modern verse; [compiled by] Stephen Dunning, Edward Lueders, Hugh Smith. Lothrop, Lee & Shepard Bks. 1967 c1966 139p il $20 (6 and up)   **811.008**

1. American poetry—Collections

ISBN 0-688-41231-9   LC 67-29527

First published 1966 by Scott, Foresman in a text edition

"Although some of the [114] selections are by recognized modern writers, many are by minor or unknown poets, and few will be familiar to the reader. Nearly all are fresh in approach and contemporary in expression. . . . Striking photographs complementing or illuminating many of the poems enhance the attractiveness of the volume." Booklist

Salting the ocean; 100 poems by young poets; selected by Naomi Shihab Nye; pictures by Ashley Bryan. Greenwillow Bks. 2000 111p il $16.95 (4 and up)   **811.008**

1. Children's writings 2. American poetry—Collections

ISBN 0-688-16193-6   LC 99-30590

"These poems are divided into four topics: The Self and the Inner World, Where We Live, Anybody's Family, and the Wide Imagination." Horn Book Guide

"Nye presents the exceptional work of students in grades 1 through 12. . . . Illustrated with Ashley Bryan's signature bright-hued, bold-lined paintings and multicultural imagery, the poems are varied in both sophistication and subject." Booklist

Includes bibliographical references

Small talk; a book of short poems; selected by Lee Bennett Hopkins; illustrated by Susan Gaber. Harcourt Brace & Co. 1995 48p il $14 (2-4)   **811.008**

1. American poetry—Collections

ISBN 0-15-276577-8   LC 94-7601

"Hopkins collects thirty-three poems that together constitute no more than one hundred lines of poetry: these are very short poems, indeed. Twenty-seven authors are represented, ranging from Mother Goose to Carl Sandburg to several of today's poets for children. . . . Gaber illustrates each entry with a watercolor or colored-pencil drawing, each image carefully chosen to extend the poem's meaning." Bull Cent Child Books

Song and dance; poems selected by Lee Bennett Hopkins; illustrated by Cheryl Munro Taylor. Simon & Schuster Bks. for Young Readers 1997 32p il $16 (k-3)   **811.008**

1. Music—Poetry 2. Dance—Poetry 3. American poetry—Collections

ISBN 0-689-80159-9   LC 95-44841

Song and dance—*Continued*

A collection of poems about music and dance by such poets as Carl Sandburg, Charlotte Zolotow, Langston Hughes, and Eve Merriam

"Illustrated with bright collages. . . . Today's young readers will enjoy hearing these selections again and again—for the rhyme, for the rhythm, for the pleasure in the imagery." Booklist

Soul looks back in wonder; [illustrated by] Tom Feelings. Dial Bks. 1993 unp il $16.99; pa $6.99 (3-6) **811.008**
1. American poetry—African American authors—Collections
ISBN 0-8037-1001-1; 0-14-056501-9 (pa)
LC 93-824
Coretta Scott King award for illustration, 1994
Artwork and poems by such writers as Maya Angelou, Langston Hughes, and Askia Toure portray the creativity, strength, and beauty of their African American heritage

"This thoughtful collection of poetry is unique. . . . Feelings selected sketches done while he was in West Africa, South America, and at home in America. The original drawings were enhanced with colored pencils, colored papers, stencil cut-outs, and other techniques to give a collage effect. Marbled textures bring vibrancy to the work." Horn Book

Spectacular science; a book of poems; selected by Lee Bennett Hopkins; illustrated by Virginia Halstead. Simon & Schuster Bks. for Young Readers 1999 37p il $17 (2-4) **811.008**
1. Science—Poetry 2. American poetry—Collections
ISBN 0-689-81283-3
LC 97-46695
A collection of poems about science by a variety of poets, including Carl Sandburg, Valerie Worth, and David McCord

"Enticing double-spread pictures, large, imaginative, and blooming with color, will work well with small groups; and Hopkins . . . has rounded up a satisfying variety of works." Booklist

Sports! sports! sports! a poetry collection; selected by Lee Bennett Hopkins; pictures by Brian Floca. HarperCollins Pubs. 1999 48p il lib bdg $14.89; pa $3.95 (k-2) **811.008**
1. Sports—Poetry 2. American poetry—Collections
ISBN 0-06-027801-3 (lib bdg); 0-06-443713-2 (pa)
LC 98-8509
"An I can read book"

"Ice skating, baseball, and scuba diving are but three of the activities showcased in this collection of sports poetry, which includes work by editor Hopkins, Myra Cohn Livingston, Nikki Grimes, and others. The excitement, the sweet success, the thrill of competition are all here in the brief, lively poems, accompanied by equally lively cartoon-style artwork that bursts with action." Booklist

Stone bench in an empty park; selected by Paul Janeczko; with photographs by Henri Silberman. Orchard Bks. 2000 unp il $15.95; lib bdg $16.99 (4 and up) **811.008**
1. City and town life—Poetry 2. Haiku 3. Poetry—Collections
ISBN 0-531-30259-8; 0-531-33259-4 (lib bdg)
LC 99-44282

"The poets, ranging from Buson to James Berry, capture urban sights and scenes in haiku that, while including city images of icicles, cats, and spring winds, also celebrate newsstands, car washes, traffic, and stickball." Horn Book

Silberman's black-and-white photographs "were taken in response to the selected haikus, and they offer visuals that are sometimes elucidation, sometimes illustration, and sometimes counterpoint." Bull Cent Child Books

Surprises; selected by Lee Bennett Hopkins; illustrated by Megan Lloyd. Harper & Row 1984 64p il hardcover o.p. paperback available $3.95 (k-2) **811.008**
1. American poetry—Collections
ISBN 0-06-444105-9 (pa)
LC 83-47712
"An I can read book. A Charlotte Zolotow book"
Hopkins has put together a "collection of poems from the proverbial star-studded cast: X. J. Kennedy, Myra Cohn Livingston, Nikki Giovanni, Russell Hoban, Eve Merriam, Langston Hughes, Christina Rossetti, Carl Sandburg and on and on. These 38 poems, most previously published elsewhere, employ short words and simple language to tell their tale or paint their picture and often make good read-alouds as well as smart choices for beginning readers." SLJ

Until I saw the sea and other poems; a collection of seashore poems; [selected and illustrated by] Alison Shaw. Holt & Co. 1995 32p il hardcover o.p. paperback available $6.95 (k-2) **811.008**
1. Sea poetry 2. Poetry—Collections
ISBN 0-8050-5794-3 (pa)
LC 94-28810
"Authors John Masefield, e. e. cummings, and Myra Cohn Livingston, among others, explore sand castles, fog, seaweed, shells, and the ineffable lure of the ocean. The 19 poems range in complexity from brief and evocative to longer and more thoughtful verses. Shaw's expansive photographs dominate the page with their size and glowing colors." Booklist

Weather; poems selected by Lee Bennett Hopkins; pictures by Melanie Hall. HarperCollins Pubs. 1994 63p il hardcover o.p. paperback available $4.95 (k-2) **811.008**
1. Weather—Poetry 2. American poetry—Collections
ISBN 0-06-444191-1 (pa)
LC 92-14913
"An I can read book"
A collection of poems describing various weather conditions, by such authors as Christina G. Rossetti, Myra Cohn Livingston, and Aileen Fisher

"Hopkins' excellent choices are easily accessible in large type with a spacious design and brightly colored illustrations." Booklist

When the rain sings; poems by young Native Americans; [by] National Museum of the American Indian, Smithsonian Institution. Simon & Schuster Bks. for Young Readers 1999 76p il $16 (4 and up) **811.008**
1. Native Americans—Poetry 2. American poetry—Collections 3. Children's writings
ISBN 0-689-82283-9
LC 98-31784
A collection of poems written by young Native Americans, inspired by or matched with photographs of arti-

When the rain sings—_Continued_

facts and people from the National Museum of the American Indian

"The poems vary in intensity, mood, and complexity, but the poets' voices are unwavering in their sincerity and passion." Booklist

Yummy!; eating through a day; poems selected by Lee Bennett Hopkins; illustrated by Renée Flower. Simon & Schuster Bks. for Young Readers 2000 32p il $17 (k-3)   **811.008**
1. Food—Poetry 2. Poetry—Collections
ISBN 0-689-81755-X   LC 98-38507

A collection of brief poems about all different kinds of foods—from cereal and oranges to pasta, potato chips, and peas

"Flower's brilliant colored-pencil, water-color, and gouache paintings enliven each page. . . . Hopkins's mastery of the art of creating a delectable anthology is quite clear." SLJ

812 American drama

Bruchac, Joseph, 1942-

Pushing up the sky: seven native American plays for children; illustrated by Teresa Flavin. Dial Bks. for Young Readers 2000 94p il $18.99; pa $8.99 (3-5)   **812**
1. Native Americans—Drama
ISBN 0-8037-2168-4; 0-8037-2535-3 (pa)
LC 98-20483

Uses drama to tell seven different stories from Native American traditions including the Abenaki, Ojibway, Cherokee, Cheyenne, Snohomish, Tlingit, and Zuni

"The short, simple scripts are accessible to young, in-experienced actors. . . . Suggestions are given for easy-to-make costumes, props, and scenery. A variety of pen-and-ink drawings illustrate the plays, as well as one live-ly gouache illustration per selection." SLJ

Includes bibliographical references

812.008 American drama— Collections

You're on!: seven plays in English and Spanish; selected by Lori Marie Carlson. Morrow Junior Bks. 1999 139p $17 (4 and up)   **812.008**
1. Hispanic Americans—Drama 2. American drama—Collections 3. Bilingual books—English-Spanish
ISBN 0-688-16237-1   LC 99-17222

This includes plays by Gary Soto, Pura Belpré, Denise Ruiz, Federico García Lorca, Elena Castedo, Alfonsina Storni, and Oscar Hijuelos

"Each play is presented in both English and Spanish. Although the selections are short (anywhere from 3 to 10 pages), they vary greatly in complexity and style. . . . This unique resource will enrich any library's performing arts collection and be especially useful for those libraries serving Latino communities." Booklist

818 American miscellany

Sandburg, Carl, 1878-1967

The Sandburg treasury; prose and poetry for young people; introduction by Paula Sandburg; illustrated by Paul Bacon. Harcourt Brace Jovanovich 1970 480p il hardcover o.p. paperback available $24 (5 and up)   **818**
ISBN 0-15-202678-9 (pa)

"Including, 'Rootabaga stories,' 'Early moon,' 'Wind song,' 'Abe Lincoln grows up,' 'Prairie-town boy.'" Title page

This volume brings together all of Sandburg's books for young people; his whimsical stories, two books of poetry, a version of his biography of Abraham Lincoln, and portions of his autobiography specially edited for children

821 English poetry

Berry, James

Celebration song; a poem; illustrated by Louise Brierley. Simon & Schuster Bks. for Young Readers 1994 unp il $14 (k-3)   **821**
1. Jesus Christ—Nativity—Poetry 2. Caribbean region—Poetry
ISBN 0-671-86446-3   LC 93-87671

"Jamaican-born writer Berry sets his nativity poem in the West Indies. Baby Jesus is a year old, and his mother sings him a celebratory lullaby about his birth. Brierley's expressive double-spreads watercolors in folk-art style capture the warm brown shades of the people against the sunlit landscape." Booklist

Browning, Robert, 1812-1889

The Pied Piper of Hamelin; with illustrations by Kate Greenaway. Knopf 1993 104p il $12.95
821
ISBN 0-679-42812-7   LC 93-11265

Also available in paperback from Dover Publs.

A reissue of the edition first published 1880 in the United Kingdom; first United States edition 1882 by Lyman & Curtis

The Pied Piper pipes the village free of rats, and when the villagers refuse to pay him for the service he exacts a terrible revenge

Includes bibliographical references

Cohen, Barbara, 1932-1992

Canterbury tales; [by] Geoffrey Chaucer; selected, translated, and adapted by Barbara Cohen; illustrated by Trina Schart Hyman. Lothrop, Lee & Shepard Bks. 1988 87p il $17.95 (4 and up)   **821**
ISBN 0-688-06201-6   LC 86-21045

Contents: The nun's priest's tale; The pardoner's tale; The wife of Bath's tale; The franklin's tale

"Cohen's evident love and respect for Chaucer's writing keep her close to the text. Her writing retains the fla-

Cohen, Barbara, 1932-1992—*Continued*
vor of the times and the spirit of Chaucer's words while her prose retelling, enriched by Hyman's lively full-color paintings, enhances the book's appeal to young people. . . . An excellent introduction to *The Canterbury Tales* for young readers." Booklist

Farjeon, Eleanor, 1881-1965
Cats sleep anywhere; illustrated by Anne Mortimer. HarperCollins Pubs. 1996 unp il $14.95; pa $5.95   **821**
  1. Cats—Poetry
  ISBN 0-06-027334-8; 0-06-443554-7 (pa)
                  LC 95-50371
A newly illustrated edition of the title first published 1990 by Lippincott
Cats sleep on tables, chairs, sofas, in closets, in shoeboxes—all around the house
"Farjeon's short simple poem . . . is enhanced by a strong design and Mortimer's rich illustrations." Horn Book Guide

Hughes, Shirley
Rhymes for Annie Rose. Lothrop, Lee & Shepard Bks. 1995 unp il $16 (k-2)   **821**
  ISBN 0-688-14220-6   LC 94-37544
A collection of more than twenty poems about young Annie Rose and the daily activities of a child
"Annie Rose and her brother, Alfie, play and dream and discover the world. With wonderful domestic detail, Hughes' line-and-watercolor pictures capture the toddler's joy and mischief, fear and affection. . . . The words have a physicalness and a beat that children will love." Booklist

Lear, Edward, 1812-1888
The complete nonsense of Edward Lear; edited and introduced by Holbrook Jackson. Dover Publs. 1951 288p il pa $7.95   **821**
  1. Nonsense verses
  ISBN 0-486-20167-8
Also available in hardcover from Amereon and P. Smith
A reprint of the 1947 Faber edition published in the United Kingdom
"This is a choice contribution to the literature of laughter. Limericks, verses of all kinds, alphabets and botanics are as daft and amusing as the pictures." Adventuring With Books

The owl and the pussycat   **821**
  1. Nonsense verses
               LC 84-24897
Some editions are:
HarperCollins Pubs. $15.95 Illustrated by James Marshall (ISBN 0-06-205010-9)
Putnam $14.95; pa $6.95 Illustrated by Jan Brett (ISBN 0-399-21925-0; 0-698-11367-5)
First published 1871
After a courtship voyage of a year and a day, Owl and Pussy finally buy a ring from Piggy and are blissfully wed

The pelican chorus and other nonsense; illustrated by Fred Marcellino. HarperCollins Pubs. 1995 unp il $14.95   **821**
  1. Nonsense verses
  ISBN 0-06-205062-1   LC 94-78570
"Michael di Capua books"
"Three great nonsense rhymes by the inimitable Edward Lear—'The Pelican Chorus,' 'The Owl and the Pussycat,' and 'The New Vestments'—are presented with wildly comic illustrations, uniquely suited to their era and content. . . : Fred Marcellino's bouncy, humorous, and expressive illustrations enlarge and expand the narratives of all three verses. A great treat for lovers of Lear." Horn Book

McCaughrean, Geraldine, 1951-
The Canterbury tales; [retold by] Geraldine McCaughrean ; illustrated by Victor G. Ambrus. Oxford Univ. Press c1984 116p il hardcover o.p. paperback available $12.95 (4 and up)   **821**
  ISBN 0-19-274181-0 (pa)   LC 95-234683
An illustrated retelling of Geoffrey Chaucer's famous work in which a group of pilgrims in fourteenth-century England tell each other stories as they travel on a pilgrimage to the cathedral at Canterbury
"McCaughrean's accomplished prose version of the medieval classic retains the basic plot and humor of Chaucer's original poem. Colorful detailed illustrations accompany an accessible introduction to the medieval masterpiece." Horn Book Guide

Milne, A. A. (Alan Alexander), 1882-1956
Now we are six; with decorations by Ernest H. Shepard. Dutton 1961 c1927 104p il $22.99; pa $4.99 (k-3)   **821**
  ISBN 0-525-44960-4; 0-14-0361234-3 (pa)
First published 1927. "Reprinted September 1961 in this completely new format designed by Warren Chappell." Verso of title page
"The boy or girl who has liked 'When were were very young' and 'Winnie-the-Pooh' will enjoy reading about Alexander Beetle who was mistaken for a match, the knight whose armor didn't squeak, and the old sailor who had so many things which he wanted to do. There are other entertaining poems, also, and many pictures as delightful as the verses." Pittsburgh

When we were very young; with decorations by Ernest H. Shepard. Dutton 1961 c1924 102p il $10.99; pa $4.99 (k-3)   **821**
  ISBN 0-525-44445-9; 0-14-036123-5 (pa)
Also available Audiobook version
First published 1924. "Reprinted September 1961 in this completely new format designed by Warren Chappell." Verso of title page
Verse "written for Milne's small son Christopher Robin, which for its bubbling nonsense, its whimsy, and the unexpected surprises of its rhymes and rhythms, furnishes immeasurable joy to children." Right Book for the Right Child
"Mr. Milne's gay jingles have found a worthy accompaniment in the charming illustrations of Mr. Shepard." Saturday Rev

Milne, A. A. (Alan Alexander), 1882-1956—*Continued*

The world of Christopher Robin; the complete When we were very young and Now we are six; with decorations and new illustrations in full color, by E. H. Shepard. Dutton 1958 234p il $21.99 (k-3)　　**821**

ISBN 0-525-44448-3

Also available as part of a boxed set together with: The world of Pooh for $29.95 (ISBN 0-525-43348-1)

In this combined edition of the two titles entered separately "the black-and-white illustrations of the original book have been retained and in addition the artist has created end papers and eight full-page illustrations in color." Booklist

Simon, Francesca

Toddler time; illustrated by Susan Winter. Orchard Bks. 2000 36p il $15.95 (k-1)　　**821**

ISBN 0-531-30251-2　　　LC 99-32942

"This collection of nursery-type rhymes and poems is about everyday activities and occurrences. . . . The verses . . . are action packed and colorfully illustrated. The watercolor paintings reflect the joy of discovery, natural curiosity, and energy that toddlers possess." SLJ

Stevenson, Robert Louis, 1850-1894

A child's garden of verses (k-4)　　**821**

Some editions are:
Abrams $17.95 Illustrated by Joanna Isles (ISBN 0-8109-3196-6; LC 93-74829)
Knopf (Everyman's library children's classics) $13.95 Illustrated by Charles Robinson (ISBN 0-679-41799-0; LC 92-53175)
Oxford Univ. Press pa $14.95 Illustrated by Brian Wildsmith (ISBN 0-19-276065-3)

First published 1885 in the United Kingdom with title: Penny whistles

"Verses known and loved by one generation after another. Among the simpler ones for pre-school children are: Rain; At the Seaside; and Singing." Right Book for the Right Child

My shadow (k-3)　　**821**
1. Shades and shadows—Poetry

Some editions are:
Candlewick Press $12.99 Illustrated by Penny Dale (ISBN 0-7636-0923-4)
Godine $17.95; pa $9.95 Illustrations by Glenna Lang (ISBN 0-87923-788-0; 1-567-92108-6)

Illustrated versions of Stevenson's popular poem in which a child tells about her relationship with her shadow

821.008　English poetry—Collections

Call down the moon; poems of music; selected by Myra Cohn Livingston. Margaret K. McElderry Bks. 1995 170p $16 (6 and up)　　**821.008**
1. Music—Poetry 2. Poetry—Collections
ISBN 0-689-80416-4　　　LC 95-8283

"Divided into twelve subject sections ranging from poems about singing to poems about percussion, woodwinds, fiddles, and guitars, this collection demonstrates Livingston's skill as an anthologist. Poets included are diverse, with stylistic influences of the classics (Plato, Shakespeare and Herrick), China, Spain (Garcia Lorca), folk America (Edgar Lee Masters), and Ireland among others." Voice Youth Advocates

Ghost poems; edited by Daisy Wallace; illustrated by Tomie de Paola. Holiday House 1979 30p il lib bdg $14.95; pa $4.95 (1-4)　　**821.008**
1. Ghosts—Poetry 2. English poetry—Collections 3. American poetry—Collections
ISBN 0-8234-0344-0 (lib bdg); 0-8234-0849-3 (pa)
LC 78-11028

"Mostly inducing titters rather than terrors—is this collection by rhymsters with an active sense of the absurd. . . . Among the 17 entertainers are the old Scottish prayers ('Ghosties and Ghoulies'), two American Indian songs and contributions from conjurers of the past and present: Nancy Willard, Lilian Moore. X. J. Kennedy, Jack Prelutsky, et al., as well as anonymous selections from legends." Publ Wkly

"Illustrated with a quick and fearsome flourish by Tomie de Paola. . . . Here are wonderful poems to frighten young children with—but not really." N Y Times Book Rev

Here is my heart; love poems; compiled by William Jay Smith; illustrated by Jane Dyer. Little, Brown 1999 47p il $12.95　　**821.008**
1. Love poetry 2. English poetry—Collections 3. American poetry—Collections
ISBN 0-316-19765-3　　　LC 97-26665

"The mostly one-page selections are by William Shakespeare, Robert Louis Stevenson, Langston Hughes, Robert Frost, and Jack Prelutsky, among others, and also include old rhymes and folk songs. What really brings these verses alive are the soft and appealing color-pencil illustrations and exquisite book design." SLJ

Monster poems; edited by Daisy Wallace; illustrated by Kay Chorao. Holiday House 1976 29p il lib bdg $14.95 (1-4)　　**821.008**
1. Monsters—Poetry 2. English poetry—Collections 3. American poetry—Collections
ISBN 0-8234-0268-1

"These poems, collected from several sources, feature a Griggle who giggles while eating lunch, a nine-foot Ugstabuggle with hairy, grasping hands, a spangled pandemonium who is missing from the zoo, an Ombley-Gombley who sits upon a train track, and a Slithergadee who crawls out of the sea. Chorao's orange-and-blue creatures swarm over and around the rhymes, which are set off in white blocks, and lurk in corners and margins to add humor and eye-catching novelty for the reader." Booklist

The Oxford book of children's verse; chosen and edited with notes by Iona and Peter Opie. Oxford Univ. Press 1973 xxxi, 407p il hardcover o.p. paperback available $15.85
821.008
1. English poetry—Collections 2. American poetry—Collections
ISBN 0-19-282349-3 (pa)

The Oxford book of children's verse—*Continued*
Arranged chronologically, these 332 selections from British and American children's poetry include works by such poets as Chaucer, Charles and Mary Lamb, Kipling, Farjeon, Milne, Eliot and Nash

Poems for the very young; selected by Michael Rosen; illustrated by Bob Graham. Kingfisher (NY) 1993 77p il $17.95 (k-3) **821.008**
1. Poetry—Collections
ISBN 1-85697-908-3 LC 92-45574
This "is a mix of traditional rhymes, verse by poets, and pieces written by children that ranges over time and cultures, united by a sure sense of the richness of well-chosen words. The obvious care behind each poem's selection is matched by Graham's humorous watercolor cartoons that extend, interpret, and celebrate their subjects." SLJ

The **Random** House book of poetry for children; selected and introduced by Jack Prelutsky; illustrated by Arnold Lobel. Random House 1983 248p il $19.95 **821.008**
1. American poetry—Collections 2. English poetry—Collections
ISBN 0-394-85010-6 LC 83-2990
Opening poems for each section especially written for this anthology by Jack Prelutsky
In this anthology emphasis "is placed on humor and light verse; but serious and thoughtful poems are also included. . . . Approximately two thirds of the selections were written within the past forty years—the splendid contributions of such writers as John Ciardi, Aileen Fisher, Dennis Lee, Myra Cohn Livingston, David McCord, Eve Merriam, and Lilian Moore. [There are] . . . samplings of earlier poets from Shakespeare and Blake to Emily Dickinson and Walter de la Mare." Horn Book

Read-aloud rhymes for the very young; selected by Jack Prelutsky; illustrated by Marc Brown; with an introduction by Jim Trelease. Knopf 1986 98p il $19.95; lib bdg $21.99 (k-2)
821.008
1. English poetry—Collections 2. American poetry—Collections 3. Nursery rhymes
ISBN 0-394-87218-5; 0-394-97218-X (lib bdg)
LC 86-7147
"Prelutsky has selected and combined joyous, sensitive poems . . . by such traditional poets as Dorothy Aldis and A. A. Milne, as well as by more contemporary poets such as Karla Kuskin, Dennis Lee, and Prelutsky himself. All are lively, rhythmic poems that young children will enjoy. . . . Brown's bright pastel illustrations effectively use framing, action, and cheerful creatures to echo the light tone of the book. The poems are arranged with others of the same topic and include popular concerns of small children such as animals, bath time, dragons, and play. Teachers and librarians will appreciate poems about seasons, months, holidays, and special events that can be easily incorporated into story hours and classroom life." SLJ

Talking like the rain; a first book of poems; selected by X. J. Kennedy and Dorothy Kennedy; illustrated by Jane Dyer. Little, Brown 1992 96p il $19.95 (k-3) **821.008**
1. English poetry—Collections 2. American poetry—Collections
ISBN 0-316-48889-5 LC 89-13504
This is an "assortment of classic and contemporary verse for children. From Robert Louis Stevenson to Dennis Lee, with samples of most of the best children's poets ranging among the 123 selections, there's a sense of rolling rhyme that carries the reader from one singing page to another. And there are many pages, each designed to surround the poetry or set it into neat, discreet illustrations that project graphic images from verbal ones. . . . In selection, scope, and visual format, this is likely to be a volume many times revisited." Bull Cent Child Books

Witch poems; edited by Daisy Wallace; illustrated by Trina Schart Hyman. Holiday House 1976 30p il lib bdg $14.95; pa $4.95 **821.008**
1. Witches—Poetry 2. English poetry—Collections 3. American poetry—Collections
ISBN 0-8234-0281-9 (lib bdg); 0-8234-0850-7 (pa)

"A collection of 20 short witch poems, most by contemporary authors (X. J. Kennedy, Karla Kuskin, and company) but also including four traditional chants." SLJ
"All the poems are rich in the rhymes, refrains and wordplay of which good incantations are made." N Y Times Book Rev

822.3 William Shakespeare

Beneduce, Ann
The tempest; by William Shakespeare; retold by Ann Keay Beneduce; illustrated by Gennady Spirin. Philomel Bks. 1996 32p il $16.99 **822.3**
1. Shakespeare, William, 1564-1616—Adaptations
ISBN 0-399-22764-4 LC 94-33357
This is a retelling of Shakespeare's tale of "Prospero, a rich and respected Duke, who is cast out of Milan with his daughter, Miranda. Set adrift, they land on a strange, enchanted island. They are immediately surrounded by magical spirits—among them the helpful Ariel and the evil Caliban." Publisher's note
"Beneduce has captured the essence of Shakespeare's culminating work in a flowing prose retelling that incorporates some of the more famous passages, such as Prospero's speech and Ariel's songs. Spirin's illustrations, with emphasis on curvilinear compositions and carefully modeled figures, echo paintings of the Italian Renaissance and work well with the text." Horn Book Guide

Coville, Bruce
William Shakespeare's A midsummer night's dream; retold by Bruce Coville; pictures by Dennis Nolan. Dial Bks. 1996 unp il $16.99 **822.3**
1. Shakespeare, William, 1564-1616—Adaptations
ISBN 0-8037-1784-9 LC 94-12600
Also available Audiobook version

Coville, Bruce—*Continued*

A simplified prose retelling of Shakespeare's play about the strange events that take place in a forest inhabited by fairies who magically transform the romantic fate of two young couples

"Coville introduces the story and also conveys something of the poetry and drama. Nolan's framed graphite and watercolor paintings express the dreaminess and absurdity of the play, and the pictures have a theatrical flair." Booklist

William Shakespeare's Macbeth; retold by Bruce Coville; pictures by Gary Kelley. Dial Bks. 1997 unp il $16.99; lib bdg $16.89   **822.3**
1. Shakespeare, William, 1564-1616—Adaptations
ISBN 0-8037-1899-3; 0-8037-1900-0 (lib bdg)
              LC 97-7582

Also available Audiobook version

A simplified prose retelling of Shakespeare's play about a man who kills his king after hearing the prophesies of three witches

"Kelley's framed pastel illustrations of the hideous hags will hold kids from the start, and Coville's dramatic narrative will keep them reading. . . . Words and pictures are true to the dark, brooding spirit of the play." Booklist

William Shakespeare's Romeo and Juliet; retold by Bruce Coville; pictures by Dennis Nolan. Dial Bks. 1999 unp il $16.99   **822.3**
1. Shakespeare, William, 1564-1616—Adaptations
ISBN 0-8037-2462-4   LC 98-36178

A simplified prose retelling of Shakespeare's play about two young people who defy their warring families' prejudices and dare to fall in love

"Coville's treatment is generally faithful to the original and is nicely enhanced by Dennis Nolan's lushly romantic illustrations. . . . This is an accessible and enticing introduction to one of Shakespeare's most popular works." Booklist

Lamb, Charles, 1775-1834

Tales from Shakespeare; by Charles & Mary Lamb   **822.3**
1. Shakespeare, William, 1564-1616—Adaptations

Hardcover and paperback editions available from various publishers; Spanish language edition also available
First published 1807

"The *Tales* were the first version of 'Shakespeare' to be published specifically for children. They are written in a clear, vigorous style, not often encumbered by the attempt to make the language resemble that of the original. A lot is left out. . . . But the literary quality of the *Tales* makes them outshine almost every other English children's book of this period, and they proved an immediate and lasting success." Oxford Companion to Child Lit

McCaughrean, Geraldine, 1951-

Stories from Shakespeare; illustrated by Antony Maitland. Margaret K. McElderry Bks. 1995 143p il $19.95   **822.3**
1. Shakespeare, William, 1564-1616—Adaptations
ISBN 0-689-80037-1   LC 94-78244

"McCaughrean provides a cast of characters for each play and a brief statement that sets the work in context. Her rendition of 'Macbeth' is crisp, swiftly paced and properly horripilating—the best of the 10 plays she examines. While the dramas are much condensed, excerpts from the best-known speeches are provided as sidebars on many pages, and at the end of each play a portion of the actual text is attractively set, much as a poem might be." N Y Times Book Rev

Nesbit, E. (Edith), 1858-1924

The best of Shakespeare; introduction by Iona Opie; afterword by Peter Hunt. Oxford Univ. Press 1997 110p il (Iona and Peter Opie library of children's literature) $18.95; pa $9.95 (4 and up)
              822.3
1. Shakespeare, William, 1564-1616—Adaptations
ISBN 0-19-511689-5; 0-19-513213-0 (pa)
              LC 97-15223

Simplified prose retellings of Romeo and Juliet, Hamlet, The Merchant of Venice, Othello, The Tempest, King Lear, Macbeth, As You Like It, Twelfth Night, and The Winter's Tale

"These stories don't recapitulate every subplot but capture the essential events and retain a little of the original wording. . . . This volume features photographs from productions by the Royal Shakespeare Company in Stratford-upon-Avon, as well as several North American companies." Booklist

828   English miscellany

Carroll, Lewis, 1832-1898

The complete works of Lewis Carroll; with an introduction by Alexander Woollcott; and the illustrations by John Tenniel. Nonesuch Press; distributed by Viking 1990 c1989 1165p il hardcover o.p. paperback available $22.95   **828**
ISBN 0-14-010542-5 (pa)   LC 89-60108
This edition first published 1939 in the United Kingdom

In addition to Alice's adventures in Wonderland, Through the looking glass, Sylvie and Bruno, Sylvie and Bruno concluded, The hunting of the snark, Phantasmagoria and other poems, and Three sunsets and other poems, this volume collects Carroll's shorter prose, verse, stories, games, puzzles, problems, acrostics and a selection from Symbolic logic

Thomas, Dylan, 1914-1953

A child's Christmas in Wales   **828**
1. Christmas—Wales

Hardcover and paperback editions available from various publishers
First published 1954

A portrait of Christmas Day in a small Welsh town and of the author's childhood there

For any season of the year "the language is enchanting and the poetry shines with an unearthly radiance." NY Times Book Rev

841 French poetry

Bernos de Gasztold, Carmen

Prayers from the ark; selected poems by Carmen Bernos de Gasztold; translated from the French by Rumer Godden; illustrated by Barry Moser. Viking 1992 unp il hardcover o.p. paperback available $11.95 **841**

1. Noah's ark—Poetry 2. Animals—Poetry 3. Prayers 4. French poetry

ISBN 0-14-058677-6 (pa) LC 92-77

Poems selected from the 1962 Viking edition of the same title which was illustrated by Jean Primrose; the French originals appeared in two books published 1947 and 1955

An illustrated collection of poems, each a prayer by one of the animals in Noah's ark

"These 'prayers' of a selection of animals are poetic reflections on their natures, their functions, and their fates. Each creature is vividly self-characterized, wittily and concisely; at the same time, each unmistakably mirrors human feelings and foibles. . . . Moser contributes a brilliant portrait of every animal, subtly suggesting the very qualities revealed in each one's words. These splendid illustrations exactly suit the wide range of the text." SLJ

Cendrars, Blaise, 1887-1961

Shadow; translated and illustrated by Marcia Brown from the French of Blaise Cendrars. Scribner 1982 unp il $17; pa $6.99 (1-3) **841**

ISBN 0-684-17226-7; 0-689-71875-6 (pa)

LC 81-9424

Awarded the Caldecott Medal, 1983

Original text first published in France

This is the French poet's "version of a West African folk tale about a spirit that is at once elusive and multiform." N Y Times Book Rev

"Inspired by the exotic atmosphere and the dramatic possibilities of the text, Brown has choreographed a sequence of almost theatrical illustrations, placing human and animal figures—and their shadows—against brilliant, contrasting, always changing settings. Resplendent—yet controlled—in color, texture, and form, the work is an impressive, sophisticated example of the art of the picture book." Horn Book

883 Classical Greek epic poetry and fiction

Colum, Padraic, 1881-1972

The Trojan War and the adventures of Odysseus; illustrated by Barry Moser; afterword by Peter Glassman. Morrow 1997 177p $22 (4 and up) **883**

1. Homer—Adaptations 2. Odysseus (Greek mythology) 3. Trojan War

ISBN 0-688-14588-4 LC 96-34415

"Books of Wonder"

First published 1918 by Macmillan with title: The adventures of Odysseus and the tale of Troy. Variant title: The children's Homer

A retelling of the events of the Trojan War and the wanderings of Odysseus based on Homer's Iliad and Odyssey

"Several of the twelve watercolors that illustrate this version of the classic tale are expressive portraits of important characters, while other illustrations show battle scenes or depict the gods and creatures Odysseus encounters during his voyage. The formal language of the text may give some readers difficulty, but these stories are worth the effort." Horn Book

Philip, Neil

The adventures of Odysseus; retold by Neil Philip; illustrated by Peter Malone. Orchard Bks. 1997 72p il $17.95 (4-6) **883**

1. Homer—Adaptations 2. Odysseus (Greek mythology)

ISBN 0-531-30000-5 LC 96-28365

Retells the adventures of the hero Odysseus as he encounters many monsters and other obstacles on his journey home from the Trojan War

"This version of the Homeric tale is both faithful to the original story and accessible to a young audience. Philip's descriptive prose retains an epic feel. . . . Malone's painterly artwork complements the lengthy text. The deep blue, green, gold, and orange palette appropriately reflects the Mediterranean setting." Horn Book Guide

Sutcliff, Rosemary, 1920-1992

Black ships before Troy; the story of the Iliad; illustrated by Alan Lee. Delacorte Press 1993 128p il $24.95 (5 and up) **883**

1. Homer—Adaptations 2. Trojan War

ISBN 0-385-31069-2 LC 92-38782

Also available Audiobook version

Retells the story of the Trojan War, from the quarrel for the golden apple, and the flight of Helen with Paris, to the destruction of Troy

"Sutcliff's strong rhythms and Lee's misty watercolors in shades of brown, blue, and silvergray make this large-size volume great for reading aloud." Booklist

Includes bibliographical references

The wanderings of Odysseus; the story of the Odyssey; illustrated by Alan Lee. Delacorte Press 1996 119p il map $22.50 (5 and up) **883**

1. Homer—Adaptations 2. Odysseus (Greek mythology)

ISBN 0-385-32205-4 LC 95-15518

A retelling of the adventures of Odysseus on his long voyage home from the Trojan War

"Poetic without being self-conscious, cadenced without seeming artificial, this prose retelling of Homer's great work retains the epic grandeur of the original, yet addresses the comprehension of contemporary listeners. Spectacular watercolors incorporate motifs from Greek art in this handsome volume." Horn Book Guide

895.1   Chinese literature

Maples in the mist; children's poems from the
Tang dynasty; translated by Minfong Ho;
illustrated by Jean & Mou-sien Tseng. Lothrop,
Lee & Shepard Bks. 1996 unp il $16   **895.1**
1. Chinese poetry
ISBN 0-688-12044-X   LC 95-17357
A collection of short poems written over 1000 years
ago by such poets of the Tang Dynasty as Li Po, Yin
Luan, and Du Mu
"The book is an exquisite blending of Chinese thought
as expressed through the concise wording of Tang poetry
and the beauty of Chinese-style brushwork in 16 resplendent watercolors." Booklist

895.6   Japanese literature

Demi, 1942-
In the eyes of the cat; Japanese poetry for all
seasons; selected and illustrated by Demi;
translated by Tze-si Huang. Holt & Co. 1992 unp
il pa $6.95   **895.6**
1. Animals—Poetry 2. Japanese poetry—Collections
ISBN 0-8050-3383-1   LC 91-27728
"The poems were selected from the works of the Japanese masters and organized according to the seasons.
Each depicts an animal, from the familiar kittens to the
less familiar heron and egret. The poems evoke multi-
sensory images because of the carefully selected words
and the deceptively simplistic, brilliant illustrations. A
book to read, re-read and treasure." Child Book Rev Serv

Mado, Michio
The magic pocket; selected poems; decorations
by Mitsumasa Anno; translated by the Empress
Michiko of Japan. Margaret K. McElderry Bks.
1998 31p il $16 (k-3)   **895.6**
1. Japanese poetry—Collections 2. Bilingual books—
English-Japanese
ISBN 0-689-82137-9
"The Japanese and English versions of each of the 14
poems here appear on opposing pages." Publ Wkly
"The poems "are about childlike things and will appeal even to the very young. Fanciful and delicate, they
evoke simple images, images that Anno has realized with
playful hand-painted paper collages in shades of soft
mauve and gray." SLJ

897   North American native literatures

Dancing teepees: poems of American Indian
youth; selected by Virginia Driving Hawk
Sneve, with art by Stephen Gammell. Holiday
House 1989 32p il $16.95; pa $8.95 (3-5) **897**
1. Native Americans—Poetry
ISBN 0-8234-0724-1; 0-8234-0879-5 (pa)
LC 88-11075

An illustrated collection of poems from the oral tradition of Native Americans
This is an "eclectic collection, drawn from a variety
of tribal traditions. Printed on heavy paper, the book is
illustrated with a catalogue of marvelously rendered designs and motifs, ranging from those of the Northwest
Coast to the intricate beadwork patterns of the Great
Lakes and the zigzag geometric borders of Southwestern
pottery." N Y Times Book Rev

In the trail of the wind; American Indian poems
and ritual orations; edited by John Bierhorst.
Farrar, Straus & Giroux 1971 201p il hardcover
o.p. paperback available $4.95 (5 and up) **897**
1. Native Americans—Poetry
ISBN 0-374-43576-6 (pa)
This "collection of poetry, taken from the oral literature of more than 30 tribes of Indians of North, Central,
and South America and the Eskimos, is arranged topical-
ly under such headings as The beginning, Of rain and
birth, The words of war, and Death. . . . Background information on certain aspects of Indian thought and the
problems of translation are discussed in the introduction.
Appended are notes on each poem including translator
and source; a glossary of tribes, cultures, and languages;
and suggestions for further reading." Booklist
"A fascinating book to read, and to reread. . . . Its illustrations, selected from period engravings, makes it a
distinguished book to look at as well." Publ Wkly

Songs are thoughts; poems of the Inuit; edited
with an introduction by Neil Philip; illustrated
by Maryclare Foa. Orchard Bks. 1995 unp il
$15.95 (1-3)   **897**
1. Inuit—Poetry
ISBN 0-531-06893-5   LC 94-27866
"Collected largely by Danish ethnologist Knud Ras-
mussen during an Arctic expedition, these poems reflect
every aspect of Inuit life. Despite their brevity, they
project strong visual and emotional images that stay with
the listener or reader. Each double-page spread comprises
a poem set opposite a full-page oil painting. The strong,
colorful paintings, which reflect the mood of the poetry,
will intrigue children as much as the poetry itself."
Booklist

900   GEOGRAPHY & HISTORY

905   History—Serial publications

Calliope; exploring world history. Cobblestone
Pub. $29.95 per year   **905**
1. History—Periodicals
ISSN 1050-7086
Monthly except June, July and August. First published
1981 with title: Classical Calliope
A world history magazine for elementary and junior
high school students. "Content includes age-appropriate
research articles often written by academics in the field.
Readers will find photographs and drawings, maps,
timelines, and activities in each issue. . . . Calliope publishes original short poems, essays, and artwork submitted by readers. A helpful feature is the review section
where books, reference materials, magazines, and videos
are noted." Katz. Mag for Libr. 10th edition

909 World history. Civilization

Haskins, James, 1941-
Count your way through the Arab world; by Jim Haskins; illustrations by Dana Gustafson. Carolrhoda Bks. 1987 unp il lib bdg $19.95; pa $5.95 (2-4) **909**
1. Arab countries
ISBN 0-87614-304-4 (lib bdg); 0-87614-487-3 (pa)
LC 87-6391
Uses Arabic numerals from one to ten to introduce concepts about Arab countries and Arab culture

Knight, Margy Burns
Talking walls; illustrated by Anne Sibley O'Brien. Tilbury House 1992 unp il maps $17.95; pa $8.95 (3-5) **909**
1. Walls 2. World history
ISBN 0-88448-102-6; 0-88448-154-9 (pa)
LC 91-67867
Also available Spanish language edition
An illustrated description of walls around the world and their significance
"A praiseworthy celebration of similarities and differences among the world's peoples. . . . Young readers will recognize such landmarks as the Great Wall of China, the cave walls of Lascaux, the Wailing Wall and the Vietnam Memorial. More surprising selections feature the work of Australian aborigines, Indian Hindus, Islamic Egyptians, Native Americans and Africans. The narrative is respectful and egalitarian, with the clear intent of valuing no one people over another. O'Brien's . . . well-designed and affecting pastels cover each spread." Publ Wkly

Talking walls: the stories continue; illustrated by Anne Sibley O'Brien. Tilbury House 1996 unp il $17.95; pa $8.95 (3-5) **909**
1. Walls 2. World history
ISBN 0-88448-164-6; 0-88448-165-4 (pa)
LC 96-15123
Also available Spanish language edition
Introduces different cultures around the world by telling the stories of walls, from the Maya murals in Bonampak, Mexico, to dikes in the Netherlands
"Warm watercolors create just the right mood for the text. Some of the stories are sad, some are inspiring, and some mysterious, but each one says something unique about the people who constructed these structures." SLJ

Putnam, James
Pyramid; written by James Putnam; photographed by Geoff Brightling & Peter Hayman. Knopf 1994 63p il (Eyewitness books) (4 and up) **909**
1. Pyramids
LC 94-8804
Available DK Pub. edition $15.95; lib bdg $19.99 (ISBN 0-7894-5898-5; 0-7894-6602-3)
"A Dorling Kindersley book"
This introduction to pyramids of the world features "full-color photographs. The best coverage is given to Egyptian tombs, but pyramids in Nubia, Mexico, and Central America are also described. In addition to sharing information on what is known about the Egyptian pyramids, Putnam also mentions unsolved riddles about them, such as how many workers built them, how the stones were moved, etc." SLJ

909.81 World history—19th century, 1800-1899

Industrial revolution; John D. Clare, editor. Harcourt Brace & Co. 1994 64p il maps (Living history) $16.95 (5 and up) **909.81**
1. Industrial revolution
ISBN 0-15-200514-5
LC 93-2554
"Gulliver books"
Describes the dramatic technological, industrial, and social changes brought about by the Industrial Revolution in America and Europe
"The combination of dramatic photography and a clear, well-written text makes this period truly come to life." SLJ

909.82 World history—20th century, 1900-1999

Jennings, Peter, 1938-
The century for young people; [by] Peter Jennings, Todd Brewster; adapted by Jennifer Armstrong; photographs edited by Katherine Bourbeau. Random House 1999 245p il $29.95 **909.82**
1. World history—20th century
ISBN 0-385-32708-0
An adaptation of the authors' The century published 1998 by Doubleday
The "authors use primary sources throughout the narrative to highlight the events and people of the 1900s. . . . Excellent-quality, archival photos capture the moments on almost every page. This is a unique and valuable book." SLJ

910 Geography and travel

Jenkins, Steve
Hottest, coldest, highest, deepest. Houghton Mifflin 1998 unp il $16 (k-2) **910**
1. Geography
ISBN 0-395-89999-0
LC 97-53080
Companion volume to Biggest, strongest, fastest
Describes some of the remarkable places on earth, including the hottest, coldest, windiest, snowiest, highest, and deepest
This book "uses striking colorful paper collage illustrations. . . . This eye-catching introduction to geography will find a lot of use in libraries and classrooms." SLJ

Rockwell, Anne F., 1934-
Our earth; written and illustrated by Anne
Rockwell. Harcourt Brace & Co. 1998 unp il $13;
pa $6 (k-2)   **910**
   1. Geography
   ISBN 0-15-201679-1; 0-15-202383-6 (pa)
                            LC 97-1247
A simple introduction to geography which explains
such things as how the earth was shaped, how islands are
born from volcanoes, and how gushing springs affect rivers
"The watercolor-and-gouache illustrations are very accessible. The pictures should provoke questions; parents
and teachers can use the answers to provide kids with
more information." Booklist

910.3   Geography—Dictionaries, encyclopedias, gazetteers

The **World** Book encyclopedia of people and
places. World Bk. 6v il maps set $287   **910.3**
   1. Geography—Dictionaries

First published 1992. Revised annually
This set profiles more than 200 countries. Coverage of
each country includes an overview of its history, geography, economy, people, culture and government; a physi-
cal/political map; a locator map; and fact box

Worldmark encyclopedia of the nations. Gale
Res. 6v il maps set $395   **910.3**
   1. Geography—Dictionaries 2. World history—Dictionaries 3. World politics—Dictionaries

First published 1960 by Worldmark Press. (10th edition 2000) Periodically revised
The first volume of this set is devoted to the United
Nations, covering its structure, history, organization and
agencies. The remaining volumes, divided by geographic
area, consist of alphabetically arranged profiles of more
than 200 countries

910.4   Accounts of travel. Seafaring life. Buried treasure

Ballard, Robert D.
Exploring the Titanic; edited by Patrick Crean;
illustrations by Ken Marschall. Scholastic 1988
64p il maps (Time quest book) hardcover o.p.
paperback available $6.95 (4 and up)   **910.4**
   1. Titanic (Steamship) 2. Shipwrecks 3. Underwater
exploration
   ISBN 0-590-41952-8 (pa)   LC 88-6478
   "A Scholastic/Madison Press book"
A narrative for young readers based on the author's
The discovery of the Titanic
"The technically accurate and lucid explanations are
greatly enhanced by Marshall's stunning paintings, as
well as by diagrams and current and period photographs." SLJ
   Includes glossary and bibliographical references

Ghost liners; exploring the world's greatest lost
ships; by Robert D. Ballard and Rick Archbold;
illustrations by Ken Marschall. Little, Brown 1998
64p il $18.95 (4 and up)   **910.4**
   1. Shipwrecks
   ISBN 0-316-08020-9   LC 98-3412
   "A Madison Press book"
Depicts five famous ships that have been lost at sea
in modern times, the Empress of Ireland, the Lusitania,
the Andrea Doria, the Brittanic, and the Titanic
"The large, attractive format and informative text combine to make this an appealing book on a subject that
continues to fascinate young people." Booklist
   Includes glossary and bibliographical references

Fritz, Jean
Around the world in a hundred years; from
Henry the Navigator to Magellan; illustrated by
Anthony Bacon Venti. Putnam 1994 128p il maps
$18.99; pa $6.99 (4-6)   **910.4**
   1. Explorers
   ISBN 0-399-22527-7; 0-698-11638-0 (pa)
                          LC 92-27042
"Fritz examines the voyages of ten explorers, acknowledging that their contributions, though deserving of
recognition, were dearly bought. Opening and closing
chapters summarize the fourteenth-century world view
and indicate later expansion of geographic understanding.
As always, Fritz tempers scholarship with humor in this
brief volume—illustrated with drawings in pencil—which
reads like an adventure story." Horn Book Guide
   Includes bibliographical references

Gibbons, Gail
Sunken treasure. Crowell 1988 32p il lib bdg
$15.89; pa $6.95 (k-3)   **910.4**
   1. Nuestra Señora de Atocha (Ship) 2. Buried treasure
3. Shipwrecks
   ISBN 0-690-04736-3 (lib bdg); 0-06-446097-5 (pa)
                          LC 87-30114
"Gibbons concentrates on the ancient Spanish galleon,
the *Atocha*, which sank off the coast of Florida in 1662,
describing under labeled headings the sinking, the search,
the find, recording, salvage, restoration and preservation,
cataloguing, and eventual distribution of the treasure.
. . . A handsomely designed book, well organized, and
easily accessible to younger readers." Horn Book

Marschall, Ken
Inside the Titanic; illustrated by Ken Marschall;
text by Hugh Brewster. Little, Brown 1997 32p il
$18.95 (4 and up)   **910.4**
   1. Titanic (Steamship) 2. Shipwrecks
   ISBN 0-316-55716-1   LC 97-382
   "A Madison Press book"
"Color cutaway paintings of the *Titanic* in this oversize book allow readers to view every deck as they follow two 12-year-old boys exploring the vessel, and to
see how the liner struck the iceberg and sank." Booklist
   Includes glossary and bibliographical references

Spedden, Daisy Corning Stone, 1872-1950
Polar, the Titanic bear; illustrations by Laurie McGaw; introduction by Leighton H. Coleman. Little, Brown 1994 64p il $17.95 (3-6)   **910.4**
1. Titanic (Steamship)
ISBN 0-316-80625-0   LC 94-75240
"Written in 1913 as a gift to the author's son, this is the story of their true adventures as passengers and survivors of the Titanic. Told through the eyes of Polar, the son's stuffed bear, the book is illustrated with watercolors and actual photographs. An epilogue includes background on the society of the times, facts about the Titanic, and what became of the family." Child Book Rev Serv
"Well designed and thoughtfully researched, the book offers entertainment, history, and a glimpse of a vanished world." SLJ

910.5 Geography—Serial publications

National Geographic World. National Geographic Soc. $17.95 per year (3-6)   **910.5**
1. Geography—Periodicals
ISSN 0361-5499
Monthly. First published 1975
A publication for children 6 to 12 years old. "Topics covered in this magazine include science, travel, wildlife, exploration, history, anthropology, careers, biography, and just-for-fun articles. A regular feature, 'Kids Did It,' relates accomplishments of children and includes a photo of the child." Katz. Mag for Libr. 10th edition

911 Historical geography

Haywood, John, 1956-
World atlas of the past. Oxford Univ. Press 1999 4v il maps $100   **911**
1. World history 2. Historical geography
ISBN 0-19-521443-9   LC 99-215627
"An Andromeda book"
Contents: v1 The ancient world: earliest times to 1 BC; v2 The medieval world: AD 1 to 1492; v3 The age of discovery: 1492 to 1815; v4 Modern times: 1815 to the present
The "narrative text focuses on political and economic history, and in separate chapters singles out civilizations and political leaders. . . . Each of these chapters includes maps, timetables, fascinating photos and illustrations, and sidebars on topics such as the Koran, Cleopatra, and the Holocaust." Voice Youth Advocates
For a fuller review see: Booklist, Dec. 1, 1999
Includes bibliographical references

912 Atlases. Maps

DK student atlas. DK Pub. 1998 160p il maps $19.95   **912**
1. Atlases
ISBN 0-7894-2399-5   LC 97-45730

This atlas features "multi-colored maps, scenic photos, and topographical keys. . . . For school reports, the elevation maps, climate details, industry, farming, and land use charts, and landscape discussions will be invaluable. . . . An exciting, non-intimidating, yet factual resource for teaching basic world geography and map/chart reading skills." Sci Books Films

Goode's world atlas; editor, Edward B. Espenshade, Jr. Rand McNally il maps $34.95   **912**
1. Atlases

First published 1922 with title: Goode's school atlas. (20th edition 1999) Periodically revised
"Contains thematic maps and tables showing distribution of population, minerals, manufacturing, and other subjects. Also included are metropolitan-area maps, physical-political maps of regions, geographic tables, and ocean-floor maps showing earth movement. Pronouncing index included." N Y Public Libr. Book of How & Where to Look It Up

Johnson, Sylvia A.
Mapping the world. Atheneum Bks. for Young Readers 1999 32p il maps $16 (4 and up)   **912**
1. Maps
ISBN 0-689-81813-0   LC 98-7858
"Johnson traces the history of cartography from an early Babylonian image scratched into a clay tablet to maps developed with satellite and computer technology. . . . The slender book contains a number of clear full-color reproductions that suitably illustrate Johnson's descriptions. The writing is smooth and lucid and the material is well organized." SLJ
Includes bibliographical references

Millennium world atlas. DK Pub. 1999 xxxvi, 492p il maps $125   **912**
1. Atlases
ISBN 0-7894-4604-9
Accompanied by CD-ROM featuring satellite images of earth
This atlas features eight gatefold maps, an 80,000-place-name index, 200 terrain models, over 300 satellite maps, and over 750 photographs. Accompanying text describes regional economies, cultures, and politics
"Enormous and enormously informative . . . the awesome book affords an extraordinary view of our planet at the end of the century." Publ Wkly

National Geographic atlas of the world. National Geographic Soc. il maps $125   **912**
1. Atlases

First published 1963. (7th edition, 1999) Periodically revised
"Well balanced in coverage between the U.S. and the rest of the world, with maps by area rather than by state or country. While some maps have a crowded appearance, they are legible and generally up-to-date. Includes a fold-out map of the world using the recently adopted Robinson projection, and a number of spacecraft images of the earth and the planets. Indexes more than 150,000 place names." Guide to Ref Books. 11th edition [entry for 6th edition]

National Geographic world atlas for young explorers; photographs from Tony Stone Images. National Geographic Soc. 1998 176p il maps $24.95 (3-6)   **912**

1. Atlases

ISBN 0-7922-7341-9

Replaces National Geographic picture atlas of our world

This atlas includes photographs taken from space, political and physical maps, flags, and statistics

"Well designed for their target audience, the maps are mostly large, uncluttered, attractive, and easy to read. . . . Stunning full-color photographs appear throughout." SLJ

Includes glossary

Rand McNally children's atlas of the United States. Rand McNally il maps $14.95; pa $7.95 (4-6)   **912**

1. United States—Maps 2. Atlases

First published 1989. (1998 edition) Frequently revised

Maps and text present information about the topography, population, emblems, and other aspects of the different states in the United States

Rand McNally children's world atlas. Rand McNally il maps $14.95; pa $7.95 (4-6)   **912**

1. Atlases

First published 1989. (1998 edition) Frequently revised. Variant title Rand McNally children's atlas of the world

Presents maps showing the world's terrain, climate, major economic activities, and populations

Wright, David, 1939-

The Facts on File children's atlas; [by] David and Jill Wright. Facts on File il maps $18.95
   912

1. Atlases

First published 1987. (2000 edition) Frequently revised

This "atlas for the elementary-through junior-high-age student goes from a global perspective to the various continents and then to specific countries or regions within the continent. . . . The level of detail in the maps provides more information that can be found in some other atlases for children. Additional material includes statistics; quiz or puzzle questions; representations of flags, postage stamps, and coinage; and sidebars highlighting aspects of history or culture." Booklist

920   Biography

Books of biography are arranged as follows: 1. Biographical collections (920) 2. Biographies of individuals alphabetically by name of biographee (92)

Altman, Susan

Extraordinary black Americans; from colonial to contemporary times. Children's Press 1988 208p il lib bdg $37; pa $16.95 (5 and up)   **920**

1. African Americans—Biography

ISBN 0-516-00581-2 (lib bdg); 0-516-40581-0 (pa)
   LC 88-11977

A "collection of 85 short biographies interspersed with explanations of key historical (particularly civil rights) events. The scope is wide ranging: Altman's subjects are men and women recognized for their achievements in exploration, invention, literature, theater, the military, education, politics, science, medicine, music, and sports. . . . A priority choice for black-studies collections." Booklist

Armstrong, Carole

Lives and legends of the saints; with paintings from the great art museums of the world. Simon & Schuster 1995 45p il $17 (4 and up)   **920**

1. Christian saints

ISBN 0-689-80277-3   LC 94-43009

"The 20 saints and martyrs gathered here are, with few exceptions, either biblical figures central to the Christian story (John the Baptist, Joseph, Peter, Paul, Mary Magdalene) or heroes of the early church. The biographies are brief—two or three paragraphs at most. . . . The emphasis, both in text and in the artistic renderings, is on legend and miracle; the stories are drawn from church tradition and hagiology. The volume concludes with an index of the paintings and a complete calendar of the saints venerated on each day of the year." SLJ

Barber, James, 1952-

Presidents; written by James Barber; in association with the Smithsonian Institution. Dorling Kindersley 2000 64p il (DK eyewitness books) $15.95; lib bdg $19.95 (3-5)   **920**

1. Presidents—United States

ISBN 0-7894-5243-X; 0-7894-6992-8 (lib bdg)
   LC 99-43281

"A look at each president in the context of his times: political campaigns, family, speeches, national and world events, scandals, and general facts. . . . Black-and-white and color drawings and reproductions, including portraits and artifacts from the National Portrait Gallery, the National Museum of American History, and the Smithsonian Institution, appear throughout." SLJ

Blassingame, Wyatt

The look-it-up book of presidents. Random House il $12.99 (5 and up)   **920**

1. Presidents—United States

First published 1968 and periodically revised to include new Presidents and administrations

Blassingame, Wyatt—*Continued*

"Each president is (allotted) several pages of readable text that cover his politics and policies and touch upon his personal life. The good-sized print and well-chosen illustrations (black-and-white photographs, lithographs, and cartoons) combine in an easy-to-peruse layout." Booklist

Burns, Khephra

Black stars in orbit; NASA's African-American astronauts; [by] Khephra Burns and William Miles. Harcourt Brace & Co. 1995 72p il $20; pa $10 (4 and up)   **920**

1. Astronauts 2. African Americans—Biography
ISBN 0-15-200432-7; 0-15-200276-6 (pa)

LC 93-44624

"Gulliver books"

Based on a 1990 television documentary, this book begins "with a chapter on the African American pilots of World War II, the Tuskegee Airmen, and [continues] with the experience of Ed Dwight, a Korean War era pilot who was recommended for the Astronaut Training Program by President Kennedy. . . . The contributions of African American scientists and physicians who worked behind the scenes are documented, as is NASA's campaign, with the advent of the Space Shuttle Program, to recruit minority trainees. The authors use quotations from the television documentary to tell the compelling and at times horrifying story in a full and lively manner." SLJ

Calvert, Patricia, 1931-

Great lives: the American frontier. Atheneum Bks. for Young Readers 1997 388p il $25 (5 and up)   **920**

1. West (U.S.)—Biography 2. Frontier and pioneer life—West (U.S.)
ISBN 0-689-80640-X   LC 96-48519

A collective biography of great figures in the history of the American frontier

"Calvert's writing style is consistently readable and succinct. . . . In addition, the author maintains a balanced treatment of ethnic roles within their proper historical context. The brutality of both white men and Indians during this era is honestly depicted. This fascinating array of individuals will inspire and educate readers." SLJ

Includes bibliographical references

Faber, Doris, 1924-

Great lives: American literature; [by] Doris Faber and Harold Faber. Atheneum Bks. for Young Readers 1995 313p il $24 (5 and up)

920

1. Authors, American
ISBN 0-684-19448-1   LC 94-10866

"The lives of thirty American literary figures whose major work was completed by 1960 are covered in this collection. Novelists, poets and playwrights are included. . . . The 1960 parameter for inclusion limits the coverage of many women and minority writers but as a collective biography of major American literary figures, this does a more than adequate job of gathering the type of information needed by middle and junior high students." Voice Youth Advocates

Includes bibliographical references

Freedman, Russell

Indian chiefs. Holiday House 1987 151p il map lib bdg $19.95; pa $12.95 (6 and up)   **920**

1. Native Americans—Biography
ISBN 0-8234-0625-3 (lib bdg); 0-8234-0971-6 (pa)

LC 86-46198

This "book chronicles the lives of six renowned Indian chiefs, each of whom served as a leader during a critical period in his tribe's history. . . . The text relates information about the lives of each chief and aspects of Indian/white relationships that illuminate his actions. . . . The illustrations and photographs and an especially clear map augment the text well and add to the overall appeal of the book." Horn Book

Greenberg, Jan, 1942-

The American eye; eleven artists of the twentieth century; [by] Jan Greenberg and Sandra Jordan. Delacorte Press 1995 120p il $22.50 (6 and up)   **920**

1. Artists—United States
ISBN 0-385-32173-2   LC 94-30625

"This book examines American impulses in twentieth-century art by giving a chapter to each of eleven American artists. Figures included range from the ubiquitous (Georgia O'Keeffe, Jackson Pollock, Edward Hopper) to the less popularized (Arthur Dove, Eva Hesse, Romare Bearden), and their works (four or five pictured per artist) include a variety of painting and sculpture styles with a broad range of influences (kids will particularly enjoy the pop-culture homages of Stuart Davis and Andy Warhol)." Bull Cent Child Books

"The writing is insightful and the prose accessible and authoritative without being mired in pedantic scholarship." SLJ

Includes bibliographical references

Greenfield, Eloise, 1929-

Childtimes: a three-generation memoir; by Eloise Greenfield and Lessie Jones Little; with material by Pattie Ridley Jones; drawings by Jerry Pinkney and photographs from the authors' family albums. Crowell 1979 175p il lib bdg $15.89; pa $8.95 (4 and up)   **920**

1. African American women
ISBN 0-690-03875-5 (lib bdg); 0-06-446134-3 (pa)

LC 77-26581

Childhood memoirs of three African American women—grandmother, mother, and daughter—who grew up between the 1880's and the 1950's

"A carefully considered and thoughtful book, moving deliberately, constructed with loving care. The authors respect their child-readers (or listeners) and honor them with candor and honesty, tragedy and tears, providing chuckles and smiles as well." Interracial Books Child Bull

Hansen, Joyce

Women of hope; African Americans who made a difference; foreword by Moe Foner. Scholastic 1998 31p il $16.95 (4 and up)   **920**

1. African American women
ISBN 0-590-93973-4   LC 96-32117

Hansen, Joyce—*Continued*

Features photographs and biographies of thirteen African-American women, including Maya Angelou, Ruby Dee, and Alice Walker

"The book developed from a series of posters issued by the Bread and Roses Cultural Project of the National Health and Human Service Employees Union. . . . Hansen has added a clear, readable, and informative single-page commentary for each of the striking black-and-white portraits." SLJ

Includes bibliographical references

Haskins, James, 1941-

One more river to cross; the stories of twelve black Americans; by Jim Haskins. Scholastic 1992 204p il hardcover o.p. paperback available $4.50 (4 and up)   **920**

1. African Americans—Biography

ISBN 0-590-42897-7 (pa)   LC 91-8817

This book presents biographical sketches of twelve African Americans who courageously fought against racism to become leaders in their fields, including Marian Anderson, Ralph Bunche, Fannie Lou Hamer, and Malcolm X

"Through clear and dramatic writing, Haskins helps readers to understand the impact of institutional racism. . . . A valuable compilation for reading aloud, for independent recreational reading, and for reports." SLJ

Includes bibliographical references

Jacobs, William Jay

They shaped the game; Ty Cobb, Babe Ruth, Jackie Robinson. Scribner 1994 85p il $15.95 (4 and up)   **920**

1. Cobb, Ty, 1886-1961 2. Ruth, Babe, 1895-1948 3. Robinson, Jackie, 1919-1972 4. Baseball—Biography

ISBN 0-684-19734-0   LC 94-14007

"Jacobs does a commendable job of presenting accurate, interesting information in the 20-plus pages he devotes to each subject. While the majority of the text describes the outstanding athletic careers of the three men, Jacobs pulls no punches when covering the volatile off-field activities of Cobb and Ruth." SLJ

Includes bibliographical references

Just like me; stories and self-portraits by fourteen artists; edited by Harriet Rohmer. Children's Bk. Press 1997 31p il $15.95   **920**

1. Artists

ISBN 0-89239-149-9   LC 97-4467

Fourteen artists and picture book illustrators present self-portraits and brief descriptions that explore their varied ethnic origins, their work, and their feelings about themselves. Mira Reisberg, Stephen Von Mason, Carmen Lomas Garza, and George Littlechild are among the artists included

"This is a wonderful browsing item as well as an excellent teaching tool." SLJ

Knapp, Ron, 1952-

Top 10 American men's Olympic gold medalists. Enslow Pubs. 2000 48p il (Sports top 10) $18.95 (4 and up)   **920**

1. Athletes 2. Olympic games

ISBN 0-7660-1274-3   LC 99-40389

Profiles the lives and careers of Greg Barton, Dick Button, Eddie Eagan, Eric Heiden, Greg Louganis, Billy Mills, Edwin Moses, Dan O'Brien, Jesse Owens, and Mark Spitz

Includes bibliographical references

Krull, Kathleen, 1952-

Lives of the artists; masterpieces, messes (and what the neighbors thought); written by Kathleen Krull; illustrated by Kathryn Hewitt. Harcourt Brace & Co. 1995 96p il $20 (4 and up)   **920**

1. Artists

ISBN 0-15-200103-4   LC 94-35357

Also available from Raintree Steck-Vaughn Pubs.

"Krull's brief biographies provide basic facts as well as intriguing details. The subjects chosen range from the famous (Michelangelo Buonarroti) to the infamous (Andy Warhol) to the less well known. Hewitt's caricaturelike illustrations reflect and extend the lively text." Horn Book Guide

Includes glossary and bibliographical references

Lives of the athletes; thrills, spills (and what the neighbors thought); written by Kathleen Krull; illustrated by Kathryn Hewitt. Harcourt Brace & Co. 1997 96p il $20 (4 and up)   **920**

1. Athletes

ISBN 0-15-200806-3   LC 95-50702

Also available from Raintree Steck-Vaughn Pubs.

"Krull profiles twenty legendary athletes of the twentieth century who broke new ground in their sports and often broke through racial or gender barriers as well. . . . The brief biographies are enhanced by unusual details of personality and Hewitt's lively caricatures of the subjects." Horn Book

Includes bibliographical references

Lives of the musicians; good times, bad times (and what the neighbors thought); written by Kathleen Krull; illustrated by Kathryn Hewitt. Harcourt Brace Jovanovich 1993 96p il $20 (4 and up)   **920**

1. Composers

ISBN 0-15-248010-2   LC 91-33497

Also available from Raintree Steck-Vaughn Pubs.

"Twenty (including both Gilbert and Sullivan) composers, from Vivaldi to Gershwin, are here profiled in a series of irreverent, anecdotal vignettes, each stylishly illustrated with an elegant caricature." Bull Cent Child Books

Includes glossary and bibliographical references

Lives of the presidents; fame, shame (and what the neighbors thought); written by Kathleen Krull; illustrated by Kathryn Hewitt. Harcourt Brace & Co. 1998 96p il $20 (4 and up)   **920**

1. Presidents—United States

ISBN 0-8172-4049-7   LC 97-33069

Krull, Kathleen, 1952-—*Continued*

Also available from Raintree Steck-Vaughn Pubs.

Focuses on the lives of presidents as parents, husbands, pet-owners, and neighbors while also including humorous anecdotes about hairstyles, attitudes, diets, fears, and sleep patterns

"Packed with enough detail for brief reports, these articles are also just plain entertaining. . . . Hewitt's spirited watercolor cartoons add to the presentation immensely." SLJ

Includes bibliographical references

Lives of the writers; comedies, tragedies (and what the neighbors thought); written by Kathleen Krull; illustrated by Kathryn Hewitt. Harcourt Brace & Co. 1994 96p il $20 (4 and up)   **920**
1. Authors
ISBN 0-15-248009-9   LC 93-32436

Also available from Raintree Steck-Vaughn Pubs.

This offers "views of twenty writers . . . from various countries and historical periods. Included are William Shakespeare, Edgar Allan Poe, Mark Twain, Zora Neale Hurston, Isaac Bashevis Singer, and many others." Publisher's note

The "authors profiled are cleverly chosen. . . . Hewitt provides a full-page color portrait, part caricature, part realistic, for each, and Krull's text includes hard facts as well as enough lively anecdotes to make clear that the writers are human." Booklist

Includes glossary and bibliographical references

Littlefield, Bill

Champions; stories of ten remarkable athletes; paintings by Bernie Fuchs; with a foreword by Frank Deford. Little, Brown 1993 132p il $22.95; pa $10.95 (5 and up)   **920**
1. Athletes
ISBN 0-316-52805-6; 0-316-55849-4 (pa)
                                           LC 92-31390

A collection of sports biographies exploring athletes who have made extraordinary achievements, grown beyond their successes, and given something back to their sports. Satchel Paige, Julie Krone, Nate Archibald and Billy Jean King are among the ten athletes profiled

The author's "engrossing prose style makes each entry read like a story. Fuch's paintings are dramatic, depicting the excitement of each sport while offering accurate portraits." SLJ

Includes bibliographical references

McKissack, Patricia C., 1944-

African-American inventors; by Patricia and Fredrick McKissack. Millbrook Press 1994 96p il (Proud heritage) lib bdg $27.90 (5 and up)   **920**
1. African American inventors 2. Inventions
ISBN 1-56294-468-1   LC 93-42625

"After presenting a brief history of the patent process and the law, the McKissacks provide an overview of African American inventors throughout the 19th and 20th centuries, including those who were free born and those who were slaves. . . . Good-quality black-and-white photographs and reproductions, along with the drawings that accompanied the original patent applications, appear

throughout. This title fills a real need; its readable text gives information not often found in books on inventions or on U.S. history." SLJ

Includes bibliographical references

African-American scientists; by Patricia and Fredrick McKissack. Millbrook Press 1994 96p il (Proud heritage) lib bdg $27.90 (5 and up)   **920**
1. Scientists 2. African Americans—Biography
ISBN 1-56294-372-3   LC 93-11226

Examines the lives and achievements of African-American scientists from colonial days to the present

"Not only do the McKissacks provide documented, fascinating portraits of well-known figures such as Benjamin Banneker and George Washington Carver, but they also consider the remarkable contributions of persons rarely written about, including outstanding women scientists. Black-and-white photographs and artwork illustrate the text." Horn Book Guide

Includes bibliographical references

Meltzer, Milton, 1915-

Ten queens; portraits of women of power; illustrated by Bethanne Andersen. Dutton Children's Bks. 1998 134p il maps $24.99 (5 and up)   **920**
1. Queens
ISBN 0-525-45643-0   LC 97-36428

"The 10 women Meltzer showcases are Esther, Cleopatra, Boudicca, Zenobia, Eleanor of Aquitaine, Isabella of Spain, Elizabeth I, Christine of Sweden, Maria Theresa, and Catherine the Great." Booklist

Meltzer "has a storyteller's flair and an eye for the small details and anecdotes that bring these queens to life. . . . Colorful expressionistic paintings, boldly stroked onto unframed panels, enrich the pages." SLJ

Includes bibliographical references

Mulvihill, Margaret

The treasury of saints and martyrs. Viking 1999 80p il $19.99 (5 and up)   **920**
1. Christian saints
ISBN 0-670-88789-7   LC 99-70893

"Oversize and illustrated with museum art, the book introduces more than 40 saints, from the beginning of Christianity to the modern day. The life of each saint is discussed in a page or two of straightforward text that also features several illustrations. . . . A pleasure to look at and often inspiring. A calendar of saints and glossary are appended." Booklist

Sills, Leslie

Visions; stories about women artists: Mary Cassatt, Betye Saar, Leonora Carrington, Mary Frank. Whitman, A. 1993 58p il lib bdg $18.95 (5 and up)   **920**
1. Women artists
ISBN 0-8075-8491-6   LC 92-32909

Presents the lives and works of four pioneering women artists

"Written with clarity, simplicity, and insight. . . . Full-color reproductions of each artist's work are includ-

Sills, Leslie—*Continued*
ed. The text is further broken up by black-and-white photos of the subjects. Design and layout are carefully planned, resulting in a beautiful book worth sharing with many readers." SLJ

Includes bibliographical references

Sullivan, George
Quarterbacks! eighteen of football's greatest. Atheneum Bks. for Young Readers 1998 60p il $18 (5 and up)   **920**
1. Football—Biography
ISBN 0-689-81334-1   LC 97-34167
Profiles some of the top-rated quarterbacks of all time, including Sammy Baugh, Bart Starr, Fran Tarkenton, Dan Marino, Steve Young, and Troy Aikman
"Each athlete is described in a two-to-four page entry complete with action photographs, many in full color. The excellent introduction includes a good description of the quarterback's importance to the game and the qualities and skills required for the job." SLJ

Sullivan, Otha Richard, 1941-
African American inventors; Jim Haskins, general editor. Wiley 1998 164p il (Black stars) $22.95 (5 and up)   **920**
1. African American inventors
ISBN 0-471-14804-0   LC 97-46932
Profiles the lives of twenty-five African American inventors who made significant scientific contributions from the eighteenth century to modern times
This is "a particularly engaging book to read; Sullivan highlights those aspects of the subjects' lives that will interest readers the most and writes about them with insight. The book is attractive, too, with lots of historical engravings and photographs." Booklist

Includes bibliographical references

Talking with adventurers; conversations with Christina M. Allen [et al.]; compiled and edited by Pat Cummings and Linda Cummings. National Geographic Soc. 1998 95p il maps $19.95 (4-6)   **920**
1. Scientists
ISBN 0-7922-7068-1   LC 98-11457
Twelve men and women who work in the field of science discuss and explain their occupations, including what they might do in a day and the scariest thing that ever happened to them
"This well-organized book, with spectacular, well-placed, captioned photos, is sure to enhance classroom science studies and please the ever curious reader." Booklist

Includes glossary

Thimmesh, Catherine
Girls think of everything; illustrated by Melissa Sweet. Houghton Mifflin 2000 57p $16 (5 and up)   **920**
1. Women inventors 2. Inventions
ISBN 0-395-93744-2   LC 99-36270

"Ten women and two girls are given a few pages each. Included are Mary Anderson, who invented the windshield wiper (after she was told it wouldn't work); Ruth Wakefield, who, by throwing chunks of chocolate in her cookie batter, gave Toll House cookies to the world; and young Becky Schroeder, who invented Glo-paper because she wanted to write in the dark. The text is written in a fresh, breezy manner, but it is the artwork that is really outstanding." Booklist

Vare, Ethlie Ann
Women inventors & their discoveries; [by] Ethlie Ann Vare and Greg Ptacek; foreword by Ruth Handler. Oliver Press (Minneapolis) 1993 160p il (Profiles) lib bdg $16.95 (5 and up)   **920**
1. Women inventors 2. Inventions
ISBN 1-881508-06-4   LC 92-38268
Surveys the lives and work of such innovative women as Grace Hopper, Fannie Farmer, C. J. Walker, and Stephanie Kwolek
"Interesting facts about 10 obscure American women who invented famous things fill the pages of this very readable book." Booklist

Includes bibliographical references

920.003   Biographical reference works

Children's authors and illustrators: an index to biographical dictionaries. Gale Res. (Gale biographical index series) $175   **920.003**
1. Authors—Dictionaries—Indexes 2. Illustrators—Dictionaries—Indexes

First published 1976. (5th edition 1995) Periodically revised
Provides over 200,000 citations to biographical sketches for some 30,000 authors and illustrators in more than 650 reference sources

Eighth book of junior authors and illustrators; edited by Connie C. Rockman. Wilson, H.W. 2000 592p il $85   **920.003**
1. Authors—Dictionaries 2. Illustrators—Dictionaries 3. Children's literature—Bio-bibliography
ISBN 0-8242-0968-0   LC 99-86615
Previous volumes in Junior authors and illustrators series available in print and electronic editions
This addition to the series contains "information about 202 current authors and illustrators of books for children and young adults. In addition to the many fresh voices, the book contains revised entries on 15 artists and writers, such as Tom Feelings, Beverly Cleary, and Charlotte Zolotow, whose works continue to have an impact." SLJ
For a fuller review see: Booklist, Oct. 15, 2000

Explorers; from ancient times to the space age; consulting editors, John Logan Allen, E. Julius Dasch, Barry M. Gough. Macmillan Ref. USA 1999 3v il maps set $295 (5 and up) **920.003**
1. Explorers—Dictionaries
ISBN 0-02-864893-5   LC 98-8809

Explorers—*Continued*

"This set profiles 333 world explorers, including cartographers, merchants, navigators, botanists, archaeologists, treasure hunters, and astronauts. . . . Well-selected, high-quality black-and-white portraits and maps abound. . . . This is a solid resource with considerable browsing appeal." SLJ

For a fuller review see: Booklist, March 15, 1999

Explorers & discoverers; from Alexander the Great to Sally Ride; [edited by] Peggy Saari, Daniel B. Baker. U.X.L 1995-1999 7v il maps v1-4 set $99; v5-7 ea $45   **920.003**
1. Explorers—Dictionaries 2. Adventure and adventurers
ISBN 0-8103-9787-8; 0-7876-1990-6 (v5); 0-7876-2946-4 (v6); 0-7876-3681-9 (v7)
                      LC 95-166826
V5-7 edited by Nancy Pear and Daniel B. Baker

Profiles men and women explorers from ancient Greek scholars and travelers to contemporary astronauts and oceanographers

Keenan, Sheila, 1953-
Scholastic encyclopedia of women in the United States. Scholastic Ref. 1996 206p il $17.95 (5 and up)   **920.003**
1. Women—Biography—Dictionaries
ISBN 0-590-22792-0   LC 95-26236
"Keenan includes 217 biographical entries and brief cameos of 43 more subjects in sidebars. Each of the six chronological chapters begins with an essay, and more sidebars provide further cultural context, plus quotations and definitions for words like 'suffrage' and 'bra-burners.'" Publ Wkly

Kranz, Rachel
The biographical dictionary of African Americans; [by] Rachel Kranz and Philip Jo Koslow. Facts on File 1999 310p il $35; pa $18.95   **920.003**
1. African Americans—Biography—Dictionaries
ISBN 0-8160-3903-8; 0-8160-3904-6 (pa)
                 LC 98-12355
First published 1992 with title: The biographical dictionary of black Americans

This work "covers 230 individuals and ranges chronologically from Colonial times to the present and represents many fields of endeavor. . . . The black-and-white photographs and drawings are well chosen. All entries include books for further reading, and an extensive list of recommended resources is appended. Indexes organize the listings by area of activity, year of birth, and subject. A worthwhile purchase." SLJ

Merriam-Webster's biographical dictionary. Merriam-Webster 1995 1170p $27.95   **920.003**
1. Biography—Dictionaries

Replaces Webster's new biographical dictionary
This work "chronicles the lives of more than 34,000 celebrated, important, and notorious men and women from all parts of the world, all eras, and all fields of en-

deavor. . . . [Arranged alphabetically, the] entries provide birth and death dates, nationality or ethnic origin, pronunciations, pseudonyms, variant spellings, pertinent information about the individual's career, and more." Publisher's note

Murphy, Barbara Thrash
Black authors and illustrators of books for children and young adults; a biographical dictionary; foreword by E.J. Josey. 3rd ed. Garland 1999 xxiii,513p il $70   **920.003**
1. Children's literature—Bio-bibliography 2. African American authors—Bio-bibliography 3. Illustrators
ISBN 0-8153-2004-3   LC 98-42690
First published 1988 under the authorship of Barbara Rollock with title: Black authors and illustrators of children's books

This volume offers 274 biographical sketches. "Each entry ranges in length from a paragraph to two pages and includes such information as year and place of birth, influences, approaches to writing and or illustrating, achievements, awards, and a selected bibliography of works. Photographs of the authors or illustrators are included when available. An appendix of sample book covers and jackets is included, followed by an appendix listing books that have received awards or honors." Booklist

Something about the author; facts and pictures about authors and illustrators of books for young people. Gale Res. il ea $116   **920.003**
1. Authors—Dictionaries 2. Illustrators—Dictionaries 3. Children's literature—Bio-bibliography
ISSN 0276-816X

First published 1971. Frequency varies
Editors vary
"This important series gives comprehensive coverage of the individuals who write and illustrate for children. Each new volume adds about 100 profiles. Entries include career and personal data, a bibliography of the author's works, information on works in progress and references to further information." Safford. Guide to Ref Materials for Sch Libr Media Cent. 5th edition

Something about the author: autobiography series. Gale Res. il ea $116   **920.003**
1. Authors—Dictionaries 2. Illustrators—Dictionaries 3. Children's literature—Bio-bibliography
ISSN 0885-6842

First published 1986
Editors vary
An "ongoing series in which juvenile authors discuss their lives, careers, and published works. Each volume contains essays by 20 established writers or illustrators (e.g., Evaline Ness, Nonny Hogrogian, Betsy Byars, Jean Fritz) who represent all types of literature, preschool to young adult. . . . Some articles focus on biographical information, while others emphasize the writing career. Most, however, address young readers and provide family background, discuss the writing experience, and cite some factors that influenced it. Illustrations include portraits of the authors as children and more recent action pictures and portraits. There are cumulative indexes by authors, important published works, and geographical locations mentioned in the essays." Safford. Guide to Ref Books for Sch Libr Media Cent. 5th edition

92   Individual biography

Lives of individuals are arranged alphabetically under the name of the person written about. A number of subject headings have been added to the entries in this section to aid in curriculum work. It is not necessarily recommended that these subjects be used in the library catalog.

Ada, Alma Flor, 1938-

Ada, Alma Flor. Under the royal palms; a childhood in Cuba. Atheneum Bks. for Young Readers 1998 85p il $15 (4 and up)   **92**
   1. Authors, American 2. Women authors 3. Cuba—Social life and customs
   ISBN 0-689-80631-0   LC 97-48887
Companion volume to Where the flame trees bloom (1994)
   The author recalls her life and impressions growing up in Cuba
   "The attention paid to small daily things as well as the occasional awareness of historical events will encourage readers to look for their own family stories." Booklist

Adams, John Quincy, 1767-1848

Kent, Zachary. John Quincy Adams, sixth president of the United States. Children's Press 1987 98p il (Encyclopedia of presidents) lib bdg $25.50 (4 and up)   **92**
   1. Presidents—United States
   ISBN 0-516-01386-6   LC 86-31022
   A biography of the president who continued the family dedication to public service begun by his father, John Adams
   "Frequent illustrations include reproductions of historical art, photos, letters, newspapers, and documents, all of which add interest and authenticity to the text. The writing style is easy to read, marked by short declarative sentences." SLJ

Adams, Samuel, 1722-1803

Fradin, Dennis B. Samuel Adams; the father of American Independence; [by] Dennis Brindell Fradin. Clarion Bks. 1998 182p il $18 (6 and up)   **92**
   1. United States—History—1775-1783, Revolution
   ISBN 0-395-82510-5   LC 97-20027
Presents the life and accomplishments of the colonist and patriot who was involved in virtually every major event that resulted in the birth of the United States
   "Archival reproductions effectively complement a descriptive and accurate narrative that imaginatively integrates details of Adams's life with the social and political milieu of the time." Horn Book Guide
   Includes bibliographical references

Fritz, Jean. Why don't you get a horse, Sam Adams? illustrated by Trina Schart Hyman. Coward, McCann & Geoghegan; distributed by Putnam Pub. Group 1974 47p il $15.99; pa $5.99 (2-4)   **92**
   1. United States—History—1775-1783, Revolution
   ISBN 0-399-23401-2; 0-698-11416-7 (pa)

A brief biography of Samuel Adams describing his activities in stirring up the revolt against the British and how he was finally persuaded to learn to ride a horse
   "A piece of history far more entertaining and readable than most fiction. . . . The author has humanized a figure of the Revolution: Adams emerges a marvelously funny and believable man. The illustrations play upon his foibles; they are, in fact, even more outrageously mocking than the text. A tour de force, for both author and illustrator." Horn Book

Adler, David A., 1947-

Adler, David A. My writing day; photographs by Nina Crews. Owen, R.C. 1999 32p il (Meet the author) lib bdg $14.95 (1-3)   **92**
   1. Authors, American
   ISBN 1-57274-326-3   LC 99-11049
The author of many works of both fiction and nonfiction describes his life, his daily activities, and his creative process, showing how all are intertwined
   This is "filled with wonderful insights into the qualities that make a good writer. Engaging black-and-white and full-color photographs that have a 'you-are-there' immediacy are thoughtfully placed throughout." SLJ

Ailey, Alvin

Pinkney, Andrea Davis. Alvin Ailey; illustrated by Brian Pinkney. Hyperion Bks. for Children 1993 unp il $13.95; pa $4.95 (k-3)   **92**
   1. African American dancers
   ISBN 1-56282-413-9; 0-7868-1077-7 (pa)
              LC 92-54865
Describes the life, dancing, and choreography of Alvin Ailey, who created his own modern dance company to explore the black experience
   "Brian Pinkney's marvelously detailed scratchboard drawings are tinted with pastels to show the sweep and flow of dancers caught in the act of leaping, twirling, and soaring through the air. . . . The book is both informative and inspiring." SLJ

Anastasíа̃ Nikolaevna, Grand Duchess, daughter of Nicholas II, Emperor of Russia, 1901-1918

Brewster, Hugh. Anastasia's album. Hyperion Bks. for Children 1996 64p il $17.95 (5 and up)   **92**
   1. Russia—Kings and rulers
   ISBN 0-7868-0292-8   LC 96-18417
   "The book spans the tragically brief life of Grand Duchess Anastasia Romanov, the youngest daughter of Tsar Nicholas II, from her birth in 1901 to the execution of her entire family in 1918. Many of Anastasia's own black-and-white photographs, often hand-colored, along with other family photos, depict a close-knit family at home and at play. . . . Designed like a keepsake album, the book includes decorative drawings and a reproduction of the endpapers from Anastasia's own album. The excerpts from letters and diaries reveal Anastasia's impish sense of humor. . . . These materials, only recently recovered from Soviet archives, compose a sympathetic picture of the Romanov family, affording an intimate glimpse of the last days of imperial Russia." Horn Book
   Includes glossary and bibliographical references

Andersen, Hans Christian, 1805-1875

Langley, Andrew. Hans Christian Andersen; the dreamer of fairy tales; illustrated by Tony Morris. Oxford Univ. Press 1998 31p il (What's their story?) $12.95 (2-4)   **92**

1. Authors, Danish

ISBN 0-19-521435-8   LC 97-41960

This biography of the Danish author emphasizes the factors that led him to become a writer

"The vivid watercolor illustrations are attractive and entertaining. . . . [The book] will appeal to children." SLJ

Anderson, Marian, 1897-1993

Ferris, Jeri. What I had was singing: the story of Marian Anderson. Carolrhoda Bks. 1994 96p il lib bdg $23.93; pa $6.95 (4 and up)   **92**

1. African American singers 2. African American women

ISBN 0-87614-818-6 (lib bdg); 0-87614-634-5 (pa)
                    LC 93-28502

The author "tracks Anderson's life and career as a singer, from her youth in Philadelphia to her debut at the Metropolitan Opera. Warm and informative, the biography shows how the accomplished contralto, who at first received more recognition in Europe than in her own country because of racism, paved the way for the careers of future African-American singers." Horn Book Guide

Includes bibliographical references

Andrews, Roy Chapman, 1884-1960

Bausum, Ann. Dragon bones and dinosaur eggs: a photobiography of Roy Chapman Andrews. National Geographic Soc. 2000 64p il map $17.95 (5 and up)   **92**

1. Naturalists 2. Fossils 3. Dinosaurs

ISBN 0-7922-7123-8   LC 99-38363

A biography of the great explorer-adventurer, who discovered huge finds of dinosaur bones in Mongolia, pioneered modern paleontology field research, and became the director of the American Museum of Natural History

"Bausum's account reads smoothly, and a layout dense with captioned sepia photographs and quotes from Andrews provides plenty of oases for readers as they follow him through the desert." Bull Cent Child Books

Includes bibliographical references

Anning, Mary, 1799-1847

Anholt, Laurence. Stone girl, bone girl: the story of Mary Anning; illustrated by Sheila Moxley. Orchard Bks. 1999 c1998 unp il $15.95 (k-3)
                    92

1. Fossils

ISBN 0-531-30148-6   LC 98-36608

First published 1998 in the United Kingdom

A brief biography of the English girl whose discovery of an Ichthyosaurus skeleton in 1811 when she was twelve led to a life-long interest in fossils and other important discoveries

"The marvelously inventive artwork, drenched in the colors of the sea, is an exceptionally attractive backdrop for this story. . . . A book that exemplifies both well-crafted biography and good storytelling." Booklist

Atkins, Jeannine. Mary Anning and the sea dragon; pictures by Michael Dooling. Farrar, Straus & Giroux 1999 unp il $16 (k-3)   **92**

1. Fossils

ISBN 0-374-34840-5   LC 97-47547

An account of the finding of the first entire skeleton of an ichthyosaur, an extinct sea reptile, by a twelve-year-old English girl who went on to become a paleontologist

Anning's "patience and persistence, are emphasized in a smoothly crafted narrative. . . . Dooling's watercolors on textured paper employ a predominantly blue, gray, and brown palette." SLJ

Brown, Don. Rare treasure: Mary Anning and her remarkable discoveries; written and illustrated by Don Brown. Houghton Mifflin 1999 unp il $15 (k-3)   **92**

1. Fossils

ISBN 0-395-92286-0   LC 98-32372

Describes the life of the English girl whose discovery of an Ichthyosaurus fossil led to a lasting interest in other prehistoric animals

"Brown dwells on Mary's self-determination, focusing on her adventurous spirit . . . and lifelong quest for knowledge in her chosen field of study. . . . The understated watercolors suit the mood. Their subdued palette (ocean blues, sand browns) and simple compositions are undistracting." Bull Cent Child Books

Antin, Mary, 1881-1949

Wells, Rosemary. Streets of gold; pictures by Dan Andreasen. Dial Bks. for Young Readers 1999 39p il $15.99 (3-6)   **92**

1. Jews—Biography 2. United States—Immigration and emigration

ISBN 0-8037-2149-8   LC 97-50377

"This picture-book biography is based upon the life of Masha (Mary) Antin, who emigrated from Russia in 1894. This account has been adapted from her memoir, *The Promised Land*. . . . This beautiful story of hope and inspiration captures the spirit of those who gave up everything for a chance at a better life. The oil paintings provide an evocative accent to the narrative." SLJ

Appleseed, Johnny, 1774-1845

Aliki. The story of Johnny Appleseed; written and illustrated by Aliki. Prentice-Hall 1963 unp il o.p.; Simon & Schuster Bks. for Young Readers paperback available $5.95 (k-3)   **92**

1. Frontier and pioneer life

ISBN 0-671-66746-7 (pa)

Also available Spanish language edition

This is a picture-story of "Johnny Appleseed, the New Englander who wandered through the Middle West in the early days distributing seeds of apple trees for planting, and remaining to share his love for wild creatures, pioneer folk, and nature." Christ Sci Monit

Hodges, Margaret. The true tale of Johnny Appleseed; illustrated by Kimberly Bulcken Root. Holiday House 1997 unp il $16.95; pa $6.95 (k-3)
                    92

1. Frontier and pioneer life

ISBN 0-8234-1282-2; 0-8234-1509-0 (pa)
                    LC 96-30939

Appleseed, Johnny, 1774-1845—Continued

"This picture-book biography of an American folk hero recounts John Chapman's adventures as he treks from Pennsylvania to Indiana, planting apple seeds, telling stories, and sharing books with frontier families." Horn Book Guide

"Red apples glow as bright as rubies against the gentler shades of blue, green, and tan that dominate the line-and-watercolor illustrations. . . . The text has a fine, seamless quality, and the readers will find it a most appealing choice." Booklist

Kellogg, Steven. Johnny Appleseed; a tall tale retold and illustrated by Steven Kellogg. Morrow Junior Bks. 1988 unp il $16.95; lib bdg $16.89 (k-3)   92
    1. Frontier and pioneer life
    ISBN 0-688-06417-5; 0-688-06418-3 (lib bdg)
                                              LC 87-27317

Also available Big book edition
"Oversize pages have given Kellogg a fine opportunity for pictures that are on a large scale, colorful and animated if often busy with details. His version of Chapman's life is more substantial than the subtitle (*A Tall Tale*) would indicate, since the text makes clear the difference between what Chapman really did and what myths grew up about his work, his life, his personality, and his achievements. There's some exaggeration, but on the whole the biography is factual and written with clarity." Bull Cent Child Books

Armstrong, Lance

Stewart, Mark. Sweet victory: Lance Armstrong's incredible journey; the amazing story of the greatest comeback in sports. Millbrook Press 2000 64p il lib bdg $23.90; pa $7.95 (4 and up)   92
    1. Bicycle racing
    ISBN 0-7613-1861-5 (lib bdg); 0-7613-1387-7 (pa)
                                              LC 99-53173

The story of the bicyclist who, having won the battle against cancer, went on to win the world's most grueling bicycle race, the Tour de France
"This easy-to-read title is as inspirational as it is informational." SLJ

Armstrong, Neil, 1930-

Brown, Don. One giant leap: the story of Neil Armstrong. Houghton Mifflin 1998 unp il $16 (k-3)   92
    1. Astronauts
    ISBN 0-395-88401-2   LC 97-42152

Discusses the life and accomplishments of astronaut Neil Armstrong, from his childhood in Ohio to his famous moon landing
"The sense of Armstrong as a boy growing into his childhood dream is strong in the well-constructed text, and that feeling is extended through watercolors with an airy sense of lightness that suits the emotional tone." Bull Cent Child Books

Arthur, Chester Alan, 1829-1886

Simon, Charnan. Chester A. Arthur: twenty-first president of the United States. Children's Press 1989 98p il (Encyclopedia of presidents) lib bdg $25.50 (4 and up)   92
    1. Presidents—United States
    ISBN 0-516-01369-6   LC 89-35386

This book traces the early life, influences, and career of the president "in a straightforward manner with black-and-white photographs or drawings on nearly every page. . . . Includes a chronology of American history." Booklist

Asch, Frank

Asch, Frank. One man show; photographs by Jan Asch. Owen, R.C. 1997 32p il (Meet the author) lib bdg $14.95 (1-3)   92
    1. Authors, American
    ISBN 1-572-74095-7   LC 97-7626

In this autobiographical account an author and illustrator of children's books shares his life, daily activities, and creative process, and shows how all are intertwined
"Asch pays homage to his boyhood hero, Roy Rogers, and shares a wonderful picture of himself with Roy in later years. . . . The format is ideal for the intended audience. . . . Excellent, recent, full-color photos and/or old black-and-white pictures appear on every page." SLJ

Bach, Johann Sebastian, 1685-1750

Winter, Jeanette. Sebastian: a book about Bach. Harcourt Brace & Co. 1999 unp il $16 (k-3)
                                                      92
    1. Composers
    ISBN 0-15-200629-X   LC 98-5543

Describes how Johann Sebastian Bach survived the sorrows of his childhood and composed the music the world has come to love
"Winter's spare poetic text is beautiful. . . . In brilliant colors, with lots of blue and purple, the framed acrylic quiltlike paintings have depth and clear detail." Booklist

Ballard, Robert D.

Archbold, Rick. Deep-sea explorer: the story of Robert Ballard, discoverer of the Titanic. Scholastic 1994 144p il maps o.p.; Houghton Mifflin paperback available $9.60 (6 and up)
                                                      92
    1. Oceanography—Biography
    ISBN 0-395-73272-7 (pa)   LC 93-1983

This is a biography "of the scientist/explorer who discovered the *Titanic*, the *Bismarck*, and shipwrecks from the Battle of Guadalcanal." Booklist
"This is an engaging narrative of a sometimes controversial figure, providing a glimpse of the public frustrations and personal disappointments that pioneers often face." SLJ
Includes glossary and bibliographical references

Hill, Christine M. Robert Ballard; oceanographer who discovered the Titanic. Enslow Pubs. 1999 128p il (People to know) lib bdg $20.95 (5 and up)   92
    1. Oceanography—Biography
    ISBN 0-7660-1147-X   LC 98-54437

Ballard, Robert D.—*Continued*

A biography which covers the life and professional work of the man whose numerous missions to study the ocean floor led to the discovery of the wreck of the Titanic

"A valuable source. . . . A chronology, glossary, and meticulous endnotes add to the strength of this fine work." Booklist

Banneker, Benjamin, 1731-1806

Ferris, Jeri. What are you figuring now? a story about Benjamin Banneker; illustrations by Amy Johnson. Carolrhoda Bks. 1988 64p il (Carolrhoda creative minds book) lib bdg $21.27; pa $5.95 (3-5)   92
1. Astronomers 2. African Americans—Biography
ISBN 0-87614-331-1 (lib bdg); 0-87614-521-7 (pa)
LC 88-7267
A biography of the African American farmer and self-taught mathematician, astronomer, and surveyor for the new capital city of the United States in 1791, who also calculated a successful almanac notable for its preciseness

"Ferris' judicious use of dialogue and Johnson's full-page gray washes enhance this smooth, engaging biographical story; the mature style and succinct text make this a good choice for reluctant readers." Booklist

Hinman, Bonnie. Benjamin Banneker; American mathematician and astronomer; Arthur M. Schlesinger, senior consulting editor. Chelsea House 2000 79p il (Colonial leaders) lib bdg $18.95; pa $8.95 (4 and up)   92
1. Astronomers 2. African Americans—Biography
ISBN 0-7910-5348-2 (lib bdg); 0-7910-5691-0 (pa)
LC 99-24118
A biography of the eighteenth-century African American who taught himself mathematics and astronomy and helped survey what would become Washington, D.C

Banneker's "life, efforts, and achievements are described in a most engaging manner." Sci Books Films
Includes bibliographical references

Pinkney, Andrea Davis. Dear Benjamin Banneker; illustrated by Brian Pinkney. Harcourt Brace & Co. 1994 unp il $16; pa $6 (2-4)   92
1. Astronomers 2. African Americans—Biography
ISBN 0-15-200417-3; 0-15-201892-1 (pa)
LC 93-31162
"Gulliver books"
"The Pinkneys chronicle Banneker's work on his almanac and, most particularly, his letter to Thomas Jefferson, then secretary of state, protesting the country's—and Jefferson's—involvement in slavery." Bull Cent Child Books
This offers "lucid text and striking illustrations, rendered on scratchboard and colored with oil paint." Publ Wkly

Bates, Katharine Lee, 1859-1929

Younger, Barbara. Purple mountain majesties: the story of Katharine Lee Bates and "America the beautiful"; illustrated by Stacey Schuett. Dutton Children's Bks. 1998 unp il $16.99 (2-4)   92
1. America the beautiful (Song) 2. Women authors 3. Authors, American
ISBN 0-525-45653-8   LC 98-12884
A brief biography of the author and college professor whose travels across the United States inspired her to write the poem which became the song "America the Beautiful"

This book "has much to recommend it, from its concise but engagingly informative text to its single and double-page spreads illustrating the panorama of Bates' America." Bull Cent Child Books

Bell, Alexander Graham, 1847-1922

Fisher, Leonard Everett. Alexander Graham Bell. Atheneum Pubs. 1999 unp il $16 (4 and up)   92
1. Inventors
ISBN 0-689-81607-3   LC 97-32217
A biography of the prolific inventor who had a keen interest in voice and sound and who worked tirelessly on behalf of deaf people

"Well-composed acrylic paintings in black, white, and many shades of gray include scenes from the inventor's life as well as a full-page portrait. . . . Written with dignity and without concessions to limited vocabulary, this clear, concise biography will appeal to readers of any age." Booklist

Matthews, Tom L. Always inventing: a photobiography of Alexander Graham Bell. National Geographic Soc. 1999 64p il $17.95 (4 and up)   92
1. Inventors
ISBN 0-7922-7391-5   LC 98-27209
A biography, with photographs and quotes from Bell himself, which follows this well known inventor from his childhood in Scotland through his life-long efforts to come up with ideas that would improve people's lives

"Succinct, lively, and readable, the text is illustrated with many well-captioned period photographs of Bell, his family, his associate, and his inventions as well as a host of diagrams." Booklist

Includes bibliographical references

St. George, Judith. Dear Dr. Bell—your friend, Helen Keller. See entry under Keller, Helen, 1880-1968

Bemelmans, Ludwig, 1898-1962

Marciano, John. Bemelmans; the life & art of Madeline's creator; by John Bemelmans Marciano. Viking 1999 151p il $40   92
1. Authors, American 2. Illustrators
ISBN 0-670-88460-X   LC 99-25646
"The grandson of Ludwig Bemelmans writes an entirely affectionate biography, 'one with obvious and unapologetic bias,' of the *bon vivant* grandfather whose range of talent extended far beyond his signature Madeline books. . . . Marciano's attractive portrait of his

Bemelmans, Ludwig, 1898-1962—*Continued*
grandfather is done 'with loving care,' the very words inscribed on the Madeline sketch that ends this enchanting tale of talent." Horn Book
Includes bibliographical references

Bentley, Wilson Alwyn, 1865-1931
Martin, Jacqueline Briggs. Snowflake Bentley; illustrated by Mary Azarian. Houghton Mifflin 1998 unp il $16 (k-3)   **92**
1. Snow 2. Scientists
ISBN 0-395-86162-4   LC 97-12458
Awarded the Caldecott Medal, 1999
A biography of a self-taught scientist who photographed thousands of individual snowflakes in order to study their unique formations
"Azarian's woodblock illustrations, hand tinted with watercolors, blend perfectly with the text and recall the rural Vermont of Bentley's time. . . . The story of this man's life is written with graceful simplicity." SLJ

Blériot, Louis, 1872-1936
Provensen, Alice. The glorious flight: across the Channel with Louis Blériot, July 25, 1909; [by] Alice and Martin Provensen. Viking 1983 39p il hardcover o.p. paperback available $6.99 (1-4)   **92**
1. Air pilots 2. Airplanes—Design and construction
ISBN 0-14-050729-9 (pa)   LC 82-7034
Awarded the Caldecott Medal, 1984
This book "recounts the persistence of a Frenchman, Louis Blériot, to build a flying machine to cross the English Channel. For eight years (1901-1909) he tries and tries again to create a kind of contraption light enough to lift him off the ground and yet strong enough to keep from falling apart." SLJ
"A pleasing text recounts Bleriot's adventures with gentle humor and admiration for his earnest, if accident-prone, determination. Best of all, the pictures shine with the illustrator's delight in the wondrous flying machines themselves." Horn Book

Bloomer, Amelia Jenks, 1818-1894
Corey, Shana. You forgot your skirt, Amelia Bloomer; a very improper story; illustrated by Chesley McLaren. Scholastic Press 2000 unp il lib bdg $16.95 (k-2)   **92**
1. Feminism 2. Clothing and dress 3. Women's rights
ISBN 0-439-07819-9   LC 99-27181
This is a "biography of the woman who briefly rocked the nineteenth-century American fashion world with her liberating, eccentric pantaloon-styled garb." Bull Cent Child Books
"With an irresistible blend of humor, history and panache, this tale demonstrates how one woman's fashion statement reflected the changing role of women in society." Publ Wkly

Bonetta, Sarah Forbes, b. 1843?
Myers, Walter Dean. At her majesty's request; an African princess in Victorian England. Scholastic Press 1999 146p il maps $15.95 (5 and up)   **92**
ISBN 0-590-48669-1   LC 98-7217

Biography of the African princess saved from execution and taken to England where Queen Victoria oversaw her upbringing and where she lived for a time before marrying an African missionary
"Myers tells an extraordinary tale which will intrigue young readers. . . . A fascinating narrative of a little-known facet of Victorian history, this book is rich with illustrations, including photographs, sketches, portraits, and maps." ALAN
Includes bibliographical references

Bowie, James, 1799?-1836
Gaines, Ann. Jim Bowie; hero of the Alamo; [by] Ann Graham Gaines. Enslow Pubs. 2000 128p il (Historical American biographies) lib bdg $20.95 (5 and up)   **92**
1. West (U.S.)—Biography 2. Alamo (San Antonio, Tex.)
ISBN 0-7660-1253-0   LC 99-14239
Traces the life of the frontier settler and Texas defender who died in the attack on the Alamo, including information on his early days and his effect on American frontier culture
"Black-and white photos and reproductions appear throughout, and a helpful map of troop movements is also included. Useful for reports." SLJ
Includes glossary and bibliographical references

Braille, Louis, 1809-1852
Adler, David A. A picture book of Louis Braille; illustrated by John & Alexandra Wallner. Holiday House 1997 unp il $16.95; pa $6.95 (1-3)   **92**
1. Blind
ISBN 0-8234-1291-1; 0-8234-1413-2 (pa)
       LC 96-38453
Presents the life of the nineteenth-century Frenchman, accidentally blinded as a child, who originated the raised dot system of reading and writing used by the blind throughout the world
"The text is simple yet informative. . . . Adler sprinkles in interesting facts about early 19th-century France that help readers better grasp Braille's world. . . . Softly colored illustrations in line and watercolor add visual clues for younger children." SLJ

Freedman, Russell. Out of darkness: the story of Louis Braille; illustrated by Kate Kiesler. Clarion Bks. 1997 81p il $16.95; pa $7.95 (4 and up)   **92**
1. Blind
ISBN 0-395-77516-7; 0-395-96888-7 (pa)
       LC 95-52353
This biography "tells about Braille's life and the development of his alphabet system for the blind." SLJ
"Without melodrama, Freedman tells the momentous story in quiet chapters in his best plain style, making the facts immediate and personal. . . . A diagram explains how the Braille alphabet works, and Kate Kessler's full-page shaded pencil illustrations are part of the understated poignant drama." Booklist

Breckinridge, Mary, 1881-1965

Wells, Rosemary. Mary on horseback; three mountain stories; pictures by Peter McCarty. Dial Bks. for Young Readers 1998 53p il $17 (4 and up)   92

1. Nurses

ISBN 0-670-88923-7   LC 97-43409

Tells the stories of three families who were helped by the work of Mary Breckinridge, the first nurse to go into the Appalachian Mountains and give medical care to the isolated inhabitants. Includes an afterword with facts about Breckinridge and the Frontier Nursing Service she founded

"These beautifully written stories will remain with the reader long after the book is closed." Booklist

Bridges, Ruby

Bridges, Ruby. Through my eyes: the autobiography of Ruby Bridges; articles and interviews compiled and edited by Margo Lundell. Scholastic Press 1999 63p il $16.95 (4 and up)   92

1. African Americans—Civil rights 2. New Orleans (La.)—Race relations

ISBN 0-590-18923-9   LC 98-49242

Ruby Bridges recounts the story of her involvement, as a six-year-old, in the integration of her school in New Orleans in 1960

"Profusely illustrated with sepia photos—including many gritty journalistic reproductions—this memoir brings some of the raw emotions of a tumultuous period into sharp focus. . . . A powerful personal narrative that every collection will want to own." SLJ

Brown, Clara, 1800-1885

Lowery, Linda. Aunt Clara Brown; official pioneer; illustrations by Janice Lee Porter. Carolrhoda Bks. 1999 48p il (On my own biography) lib bdg $19.93; pa $5.95 (2-4)   92

1. African American women 2. Frontier and pioneer life

ISBN 1-57505-045-5 (lib bdg); 1-57505-416-7 (pa)
                                       LC 98-24259

A biography of the freed slave who made her fortune in Colorado and used her money to bring other former slaves there to begin new lives

"The well-defined primitivist shapes, canvas-y textures, and muted earth tones of the illustrations perfectly evoke the roughness of the terrain and the historical period, as well as the powerful basic emotions motivating the characters. The straightforward text allows the facts speak for themselves. . . . A good story and a solid resource." Bull Cent Child Books

Brown, Molly, 1867-1932

Blos, Joan W. The heroine of the Titanic: a tale both true and otherwise of the life of Molly Brown; illustrated by Tennessee Dixon. Morrow Junior Bks. 1991 unp il $16 (k-3)   92

1. Titanic (Steamship)

ISBN 0-688-07546-0   LC 90-35369

An anecdotal account of some of the adventurous activities of Molly Brown, with an emphasis on her survival of the sinking of the Titanic

"Illustrated with lavish and vigorous watercolors that sprawl across large double-page spreads, this talltaleish—and occasionally rhyming—rendition of the Molly Brown saga has the feel and appeal of a folk epic." Bull Cent Child Books

Bunting, Eve, 1928-

Bunting, Eve. Once upon a time; photographs by John Pezaris. Owen, R.C. 1995 32p il (Meet the author) $14.95 (1-3)   92

1. Authors, American 2. Women authors

ISBN 1-878450-59-X   LC 94-47220

"Bunting talks about her childhood in Ireland, immigration to the U.S., and her writing career, including how she came to write *The Wall* (1990) and *Smoky Night* (1994). . . . For classes discussing writers and their books, here's the next best thing to meeting Bunting." Booklist

Burns, Anthony, 1834-1862

Hamilton, Virginia. Anthony Burns: the defeat and triumph of a fugitive slave. Knopf 1988 193p hardcover o.p. paperback available $4.99 (5 and up)   92

1. Slavery—United States 2. African Americans—Biography

ISBN 0-679-83997-6 (pa)   LC 87-38063

A biography of the slave who escaped to Boston in 1854, was arrested at the instigation of his owner, and whose trial caused a furor between abolitionists and those determined to enforce the Fugitive Slave Act

"This book does exactly what good biography for children ought to do: takes readers directly into the life of the subject and makes them feel what it was like to be that person in those times." Horn Book

Includes bibliographical references

Byars, Betsy Cromer, 1928-

Byars, Betsy Cromer. The moon and I; [by] Betsy Byars. Messner 1991 96p il o.p.; Beech Tree Bks. paperback available $4.95 (4 and up)   92

1. Authors, American 2. Women authors

ISBN 0-688-13704-0 (pa)   LC 91-15000

A "personal narrative that gives readers some info about snakes, a fair amount of insight into how writers do what they do, and the unmistakable impression that autobiographies are great entertainment. Byars's genuine, humorous outlook on life shines through on every page." SLJ

Carson, Rachel, 1907-1964

Ransom, Candice F. Listening to crickets: a story about Rachel Carson; illustrations by Shelly O. Haas. Carolrhoda Bks. 1993 64p il (Carolrhoda creative minds book) lib bdg $21.27; pa $5.95 (3-5)   92

1. Women scientists

ISBN 0-87614-727-9 (lib bdg); 0-87614-615-9 (pa)
                                       LC 92-3470

Carson, Rachel, 1907-1964—*Continued*
This book traces "the course of Carson's life, her work, and her influence on ecological awareness." Booklist

This is "well written, and nicely illustrated with black-and-white drawings." Sci Books Films
Includes bibliographical references

Carter, Jimmy, 1924-
Wade, Linda R. James Carter: thirty-ninth president of the United States. Children's Press 1989 100p il (Encyclopedia of presidents) lib bdg $25.50 (4 and up)   **92**
1. Presidents—United States
ISBN 0-516-01372-6   LC 89-33754
Describes the life and achievements of the relatively unknown governor from Georgia who became president of the United States in 1977

Carver, George Washington, 1864?-1943
Adler, David A. A picture book of George Washington Carver; illustrated by Dan Brown. Holiday House 1999 unp il $16.95; pa $6.95 (1-3)
                                                      92
1. Scientists 2. African Americans—Biography
ISBN 0-8234-1429-9; 0-8234-1633-X (pa)
                                      LC 98-20261
A brief biography of the African American scientist who overcame tremendous hardship to make unusual and important discoveries in the field of agriculture
"The colorful illustrations complement the simple, but informative text to give children a solid introduction to one of America's most important scientists." SLJ
Includes bibliographical references

Aliki. A weed is a flower: the life of George Washington Carver; written and illustrated by Aliki. Simon & Schuster Bks. for Young Readers 1988 32p il hardcover o.p. paperback available $5.95 (k-3)   **92**
1. Scientists 2. African Americans—Biography
ISBN 0-671-66490-5 (pa)   LC 87-22864
First published 1965 by Prentice-Hall
Text and pictures present the life of the man, born a slave, who became a scientist and devoted his entire life to helping the South improve its agriculture

Mitchell, Barbara. A pocketful of goobers: a story about George Washington Carver; illustrations by Peter E. Hanson. Carolrhoda Bks. 1986 64p il (Carolrhoda creative minds book) lib bdg $21.27; pa $5.95 (3-5)   **92**
1. Scientists 2. African Americans—Biography
ISBN 0-87614-292-7 (lib bdg); 0-87614-474-1 (pa)
                                      LC 86-2690
Relates the scientific efforts of George Washington Carver, especially his production of more than 300 uses for the peanut
"This book tells his remarkable story accurately, sympathetically, and felicitously." Sci Books Films

Chaka, Zulu Chief, 1787?-1828
Stanley, Diane. Shaka, king of the Zulus; [by] Diane Stanley and Peter Vennema; illustrated by Diane Stanley. Morrow Junior Bks. 1988 unp il hardcover o.p. paperback available $5.95 (4 and up)   **92**
1. Zulu (African people)
ISBN 0-688-13114-X (pa)   LC 87-27376
A biography of the nineteenth-century military genius and Zulu chief
"Diane Stanley and Peter Vennema have culled the massive amount of historical material that exists about this strange and fascinating figure. Their text is lucid; the incidents are tactfully within the scope and decorum of a children's book but representative and true to the facts. . . . The rhythm of the illustrations . . . makes each page not only a realistic representation but also an artistic composition." N Y Times Book Rev
Includes bibliographical references

Champollion, Jean François, 1790-1832
Rumford, James. Seeker of knowledge; the man who deciphered Egyptian hieroglyphs. Houghton Mifflin 2000 unp il $15 (3-5)   **92**
1. Hieroglyphics
ISBN 0-395-97934-X   LC 99-37254
A biography of the French scholar whose decipherment of the Egyptian hieroglyphic language made the study of ancient Egypt possible
"Despite the book's traditional picture-book appearance, with a short text and nicely rendered watercolor art, the topic requires and gets sturdy treatment. . . . Those intrigued by hieroglyphs . . . will find this a useful introduction." Booklist

Churchill, Sir Winston, 1874-1965
Severance, John B. Winston Churchill; soldier, statesman, artist. Clarion Bks. 1996 144p il map $17.95 (5 and up)   **92**
1. Great Britain—Politics and government—20th century
ISBN 0-395-69853-7   LC 94-25129
This "biography presents an affectionate portrait of Britain's renowned Prime Minister. Although Severance focuses on Churchill's contributions during World War II, he also describes the statesman's boyhood, Boer War adventures, and political ascendancy." SLJ
"This fair, balanced, and duly appreciative biography is handsomely produced and illustrated with a fine collection of photographs." Horn Book Guide
Includes bibliographical references

Clark, Eugenie
Butts, Ellen. Eugenie Clark; adventures of a shark scientist; by Ellen R. Butts and Joyce R. Schwartz. Linnet Bks. 2000 107p il lib bdg $19.50 (5 and up)   **92**
1. Women scientists 2. Fishes
ISBN 0-208-02440-9   LC 99-44957
A biography of the American ichthyologist and diver known for her research with sharks and poisonous fish
"A welcome biography of a contemporary scientist." Booklist
Includes glossary and bibliographical references

Clark, Eugenie—*Continued*

Ross, Michael Elsohn. Fish watching with Eugenie Clark; illustrations by Wendy Smith. Carolrhoda Bks. 2000 48p il (Naturalist's apprentice) $19.93 (4 and up)   **92**

1. Women scientists 2. Fishes

ISBN 1-575-05384-5   LC 99-19963

Describes the life and career of ichthyologist Eugenie Clark, who began her research observing fresh-water aquarium fishes and moved on to the underwater study of sharks and other marine animals. Includes observation tips and and related activities

"Ross presents a bright, readable, up-to-the-minute biography. . . . The well-organized text is illustrated with a number of somewhat unpretentious black-and-white and full-color photos, but they are almost eclipsed by Smith's colorful drawings of a wide variety of fish mentioned in Clark's studies." SLJ

Includes bibliographical references

Cleopatra, Queen of Egypt, d. 30 B.C.

Stanley, Diane. Cleopatra; [by] Diane Stanley, Peter Vennema; illustrated by Diane Stanley. Morrow Junior Bks. 1994 unp il maps $16.95; pa $6.95 (4 and up)   **92**

1. Queens 2. Egypt—History

ISBN 0-688-10413-4; 0-688-15480-8 (pa)

LC 93-27032

This is a biography of the ancient Egyptian queen

"Lucid writing combines with carefully selected anecdotes, often attributed to the Greek historian Plutarch to create an engaging narrative. . . . Stanley's stunning, full-color gouache artwork is arresting in its large, well-composed images executed in flat Greek style." SLJ

Includes bibliographical references

Close, Chuck, 1940-

Greenberg, Jan. Chuck Close, up close; [by] Jan Greenberg and Sandra Jordan. DK Ink 1998 48p il $19.95; pa $10.95 (4 and up)   **92**

1. Artists—United States

ISBN 0-7894-2486-X; 0-7894-2658-7 (pa)

LC 97-31076

A biography of the revisionist artist who achieved prominence in the late 1960s for enormous, photographically realistic, black and white portraits of himself and his friends

"In this moving account of the acclaimed portraitist's triumph over a severe learning disorder and physical disabilities, handsome reproductions, photos and Close's own observations illuminate the sources of his innovative artistic approach." Publ Wkly

Includes glossary and bibliographical references

Cole, Joanna

Cole, Joanna. On the bus with Joanna Cole; a creative autobiography; by Joanna Cole, with Wendy Saul. Heinemann (Portsmouth) 1996 56p il (Creative sparks) $16.95 (2-4)   **92**

1. Authors, American 2. Women authors

ISBN 0-435-08131-4   LC 95-40133

The author discusses her life, how she came to be a writer, where she gets her ideas from, and what is involved in producing a book

"This attractive title is chock-full of colorful pictures, by various artists, from Cole's many books, as well as photographs of family and colleagues." SLJ

Columbus, Christopher

Fritz, Jean. Where do you think you're going, Christopher Columbus? pictures by Margot Tomes. Putnam 1980 80p il maps $15.99; pa $5.99 (2-4)   **92**

1. Explorers 2. America—Exploration

ISBN 0-399-20723-6; 0-698-11580-5 (pa)

LC 80-11377

Discusses the voyages of Christopher Columbus who was determined to beat everyone in the race to the Indies

"Reducing a life as well-documented as Columbus's to 80 pages must result in some simplifications of fact or context, but in this case they are not readily apparent. Mrs. Fritz's breezy narrative gives us a highly individual Columbus. . . . Margot Tomes's three-color illustrations are attractive, amusing and informative." N Y Times Book Rev

Sis, Peter. Follow the dream. Knopf 1991 unp il map hardcover o.p. paperback available $6.99 (k-3)   **92**

1. Explorers 2. America—Exploration

ISBN 0-679-88088-7 (pa)   LC 90-45276

Cover title: Follow the dream: the story of Christopher Columbus

In a pictorial retelling, Christopher Columbus overcomes a number of obstacles to fulfill his dream of sailing west to find a new route to the Orient

"The text is smoothly written and informative. Yet it is Sis's illustrations that make *Follow the Dream* so distinctive; his pictures, executed in oil, ink and watercolor, and gouache, complement and extend the narrative, adding additional facts and capturing young readers' interest by humanizing Columbus and vividly rendering his vision of a new world." Horn Book

Coubertin, Pierre de, baron, 1863-1937

Kristy, Davida. Coubertin's Olympics; how the games began. Lerner Publs. 1995 128p il lib bdg $26.60; pa $10.95 (5 and up)   **92**

1. Olympic games

ISBN 0-8225-3327-8 (lib bdg); 0-8225-9713-6 (pa)

LC 94-12889

This biography of Baron Pierre de Coubertin chronicles his efforts to revive "the Greek Olympic Games to an international level." SLJ

This is a "complex, interesting story. . . . A rewarding text for the patient reader." Booklist

Includes bibliographical references

Crazy Horse, Sioux Chief, ca. 1842-1877

Freedman, Russell. The life and death of Crazy Horse; drawings by Amos Bad Heart Bull. Holiday House 1996 166p il maps $21.95 (5 and up)   **92**

1. Oglala Indians

ISBN 0-8234-1219-9   LC 95-33303

Crazy Horse, Sioux Chief, ca. 1842-1877—*Continued*

A biography of the Oglala leader who relentlessly resisted the white man's attempt to take over Indian lands

This is "a compelling biography that is based on primary source documents and illustrated with pictographs by a Sioux band historian." Voice Youth Advocates

Includes bibliographical references

Crews, Donald

Crews, Donald. Bigmama's. Greenwillow Bks. 1991 unp il $16; lib bdg $15.93; pa $5.95 (k-3)
92

1. Authors, American 2. African Americans—Biography 3. Country life

ISBN 0-688-09950-5; 0-688-09951-3 (lib bdg); 0-688-15842-0 (pa)   LC 90-33142

Visiting Bigmama's house in the country, young Donald Crews finds his relatives full of news and the old place and its surroundings just the same as the year before

"This is an evocative celebration of the joy and wonder of childhood; would that every child had such a summer. The last page is a hauntingly lovely remembrance. The illustrations are perfect and make this a truly beautiful book." Child Book Rev Serv

Curie, Marie, 1867-1934

Parker, Steve. Marie Curie and radium. Chelsea House 1995 c1992 32p il (Science discoveries) lib bdg $15.95 (4 and up)   92

1. Chemists 2. Women scientists

ISBN 0-7910-3011-3   LC 94-20657

First published 1992 by HarperCollins Pubs.

Details the life and work of Marie Curie from early childhood to the discovery of radium and her two Nobel Prizes

Includes glossary

Poynter, Margaret. Marie Curie: discoverer of radium. Enslow Pubs. 1994 128p il maps (Great minds of science) lib bdg $17.95 (4 and up)
92

1. Chemists 2. Women scientists

ISBN 0-89490-477-9   LC 93-21224

This "biography emphasizes Marie Curie's early life of poverty, desire to study, and contributions to the fields of chemistry, physics, and medicine." Horn Book Guide

"The writing style is straightforward, with a combination of personal detail and scientific explanation. . . . Sure to be in demand for those middle-grade biography and science assignments." Booklist

Includes glossary and bibliographical references

Dalai Lama XIV, 1935-

Demi. The Dalai Lama; a biography of the Tibetan spiritual and political leader. Holt & Co. 1998 unp il $17.95 (3-6)   92

1. Buddhism 2. Tibet (China)

ISBN 0-8050-5443-X   LC 97-30654

In this biography of the Buddhist spiritual leader, Demi "uses straightforward prose and fluid, eastern-

influenced art—small pen-and-ink and watercolor images with fine, intricate detail. . . . Told with respect and devotion, this is an inspirational picture-book biography." Horn Book

Darwin, Charles, 1809-1882

Parker, Steve. Charles Darwin and evolution. Chelsea House 1995 c1992 32p il (Science discoveries) lib bdg $13.95 (4 and up)   92

1. Evolution 2. Naturalists

ISBN 0-7910-3007-5   LC 94-20656

Also available Spanish language edition

First published 1992 by HarperCollins Pubs.

Traces the life of the English naturalist from his early years through his expedition aboard the H.M.S. Beagle and the development of his theory of evolution by natural selection

Includes glossary and bibliographical references

De Paola, Tomie, 1934-

De Paola, Tomie. 26 Fairmount Avenue; written and illustrated by Tomie dePaola. Putnam 1999 56p il $13.99 (2-4)   92

1. Authors, American 2. Illustrators

ISBN 0-399-23246-X   LC 98-12918

A Newbery Medal honor book, 2000

Children's author-illustrator Tomie De Paola describes his experiences at home and in school when he was a boy

"A disarmingly unselfconscious reminiscence. . . . The immediacy of detail resists nostalgia, and dePaola is wise to what recent graduates of his picture books will find interesting. Neat sketches and silhouettes will draw browsers in to this satisfying easy chapter book." Horn Book Guide

Followed by Here we all are

De Paola, Tomie. Here we all are; a 26 Fairmount Avenue book; written and illustrated by Tomie DePaola. Putnam 2000 26p il $13.99 (2-4)   92

1. Authors, American 2. Illustrators

ISBN 0-399-23496-9   LC 99-46747

"Continuing the memoir begun in dePaola's Newbery Honor Book *26 Fairmount Avenue* (1999), this short chapter book shows young Tomie as he takes tap dancing lessons, finds his way in kindergarten, and waits a seemingly interminable 10 days for his mother and new baby sister to come home from the hospital. . . . Another satisfying book in a warm episodic family story that makes writing autobiography look easy." Booklist

Elleman, Barbara. Tomie de Paola; his art & his stories. Putnam 1999 218p il $35   92

1. Authors, American 2. Illustrators 3. Children's literature—History and criticism

ISBN 0-399-23129-3   LC 98-19821

"After summarizing dePaola's life, with particular reference to events most significant to his work in children's books, Elleman presents these books by category: autobiographical, religious, Christmas, folktales, Strega Nona, informational, etc." Horn Book

"Well-chosen examples of dePaola's art effectively il-

De Paola, Tomie, 1934-—_Continued_

lustrate Elleman's critical insights, photographs and illustrations on nearly every page create an appealing presentation. While children will enjoy poring over the collected illustrations, they are not the primary audience for this scholarly text." SLJ

Includes bibliographical references

Dickens, Charles, 1812-1870

Stanley, Diane. Charles Dickens; the man who had great expectations; [by] Diane Stanley & Peter Vennema; illustrated by Diane Stanley. Morrow Junior Bks. 1993 unp il $15; lib bdg $14.93 (4 and up)   **92**
1. Authors, English
ISBN 0-688-09110-5; 0-688-09111-3 (lib bdg)
LC 91-41552
"This picture-book biography of the great English novelist is attractive and appealing. Stanley's full-color, full-page gouache paintings are expressive and inviting; the abbreviated text covers all of the major events in Dickens's life." SLJ

Includes bibliographical references

Douglass, Frederick, 1817?-1895

Miller, William. Frederick Douglass; the last day of slavery; illustrated by Cedric Lucas. Lee & Low Bks. 1995 unp il $14.95; pa $6.95 (1-3)
92
1. Abolitionists 2. African Americans—Biography
ISBN 1-880000-17-2; 1-880000-42-3 (pa)
LC 94-26542
"This picture-book biography focuses on a crucial episode in the life of the great abolitionist Frederick Douglass: the day he stood up to a vicious overseer and fought back. As the tension builds to that confrontation, Miller tells the story of Douglass' life under slavery." Booklist

"This plain rendering is a powerful introduction to the man and to the tragedy of slavery. Cedric [Lucas's] vigorous figures set against richly colored and textured backgrounds effectively illuminate this thought-provoking biographical tale." Horn Book

Drake, Sir Francis, 1540?-1596

Marrin, Albert. The sea king: Sir Francis Drake and his times. Atheneum Bks. for Young Readers 1995 168p il maps $20 (6 and up)   **92**
1. Explorers
ISBN 0-689-31887-1   LC 95-60386
"Sir Francis Drake is seen variously as explorer, naval military genius, and pirate; Marrin paints a picture including all those characteristics and more, tracing Drake's life from his early days on the sea, through his unsuccessful and successful quests for Central American gold and his global circumnavigation, to his unofficial spearheading of the defeat of the Spanish Armada." Bull Cent Child Books

"Marrin does an exemplary job of defining words in context, incorporating quotations, explaining both sides of a conflict, all while retaining the essential drama of Britain's most famous sailor. Marrin's Drake is not just a swashbuckling hero, but a complex character." Voice Youth Advocates

Includes bibliographical references

Dunham, Katherine

O'Connor, Barbara. Katherine Dunham; pioneer of black dance. Carolrhoda Bks. 1999 104p il (Trailblazer biography) lib bdg $23.93 (5 and up)
92
1. African American dancers 2. African American women
ISBN 1-57505-353-5   LC 98-50426
A biography of Katherine Dunham, emphasizing her childhood, her love of anthropology and dance, and the creation of her unique dance style

"Throughout the accessible text, the performer's contributions and struggles are clearly portrayed. Attractive black-and-white photographs appear on almost every page." SLJ

Includes bibliographical references

Earhart, Amelia, 1898-1937

Adler, David A. A picture book of Amelia Earhart; illustrated by Jeff Fisher. Holiday House 1998 unp il $16.95; pa $6.95 (1-3)   **92**
1. Women air pilots
ISBN 0-8234-1315-2; 0-8234-1517-1 (pa)
LC 96-54854
Discusses the life of the pilot who was the first woman to cross the Atlantic by herself in a plane

This offers "a straightforward, informative text full of detail. The illustrations ably reflect both the humorous and more serious moments in the narrative." Horn Book Guide

Includes bibliographical references

Lauber, Patricia. Lost star: the story of Amelia Earhart. Scholastic 1988 106p il maps hardcover o.p. paperback available $4.50 (5 and up)   **92**
1. Women air pilots
ISBN 0-590-41159-4 (pa)   LC 88-3043
"Earhart's early life is covered succinctly, including the family problems that resulted from her father's alcoholism. Close to half of the book is concerned with the details of the last flight around the world and the mysterious disappearance, sure to hold the attention of readers. Small but very clear black-and-white photographs are included." SLJ

Includes bibliographical references

Szabo, Corinne. Sky pioneer: a photobiography of Amelia Earhart. National Geographic Soc. 1997 63p il maps $16 (4 and up)   **92**
1. Women air pilots
ISBN 0-7922-3737-4   LC 96-32763
A biography, with numerous photographs and quotes from Earhart herself, tracing this determined woman's life and interest in flying

"Readers will find the anecdotal text, captioned black-and-white photographs, and philosophical quotes from Earhart engrossing and motivating." SLJ

Includes bibliographical references

Eastman, George, 1854-1932

Mitchell, Barbara. CLICK!: a story about George Eastman; illustrations by Jan Hosking Smith. Carolrhoda Bks. 1986 56p il (Carolrhoda creative minds book) lib bdg $21.27; pa $5.95 (3-5)   **92**
1. Inventors 2. Photography—History
ISBN 0-87614-289-7 (lib bdg); 0-87614-472-5 (pa)
LC 86-2672
Follows the life and career of the man who revolutionized photography by developing a camera simple enough for anyone to use

Edelman, Marian Wright

Siegel, Beatrice. Marian Wright Edelman; the making of a crusader. Simon & Schuster Bks. for Young Readers 1995 159p il $15 (5 and up)
92
1. African American women 2. Children—Law and legislation
ISBN 0-02-782629-5   LC 94-41245
This is a biography of the "advocate for children and civil rights. . . . Siegel focuses mainly on Edelman's political work and her involvement in the civil rights movement." Voice Youth Advocates
This book "has the advantage of using primary sources, including an interview with the subject herself. . . . An unusually good example of contemporary biography." Booklist
Includes bibliographical references

Ederle, Gertrude, 1906-

Adler, David A. America's champion swimmer: Gertrude Ederle; written by David A. Adler; illustrated by Terry Widener. Harcourt 2000 unp il $16 (2-4)   **92**
1. Swimming—Biography 2. Women athletes
ISBN 0-15-201969-3   LC 98-54954
"Gulliver books"
Describes the life and accomplishments of Gertrude Ederle, the first woman to swim the English Channel and a figure in the early women's rights movement
This book "illustrated with richly colored acrylic paintings . . . captures the highlights of Ederle's life in evocative images and telling details that will appeal to children." N Y Times Book Rev

Edison, Thomas A. (Thomas Alva), 1847-1931

Nirgiotis, Nicholas. Thomas Edison. Children's Press 1994 32p il (Cornerstones of freedom) lib bdg $20.50 (4-6)   **92**
1. Inventors
ISBN 0-516-06676-5   LC 93-37028
"The author has focused on only a few of those among Edison's inventions of which the general public is aware: the electric light bulb, the phonograph, the motion picture system, and improvements to the telegraph and telephone. The book stresses the importance of learning, even without the benefit of good schooling, and dedication to one's work." Sci Books Films

Parker, Steve. Thomas Edison and electricity. Chelsea House 1995 32p il (Science discoveries) lib bdg $15.95 (4 and up)   **92**
1. Inventors
ISBN 0-7910-3012-1   LC 94-20658
First published 1992 by HarperCollins
Details the life and work of Thomas Edison, who developed such inventions as the stock ticker, the lightbulb, and the phonograph
Includes glossary

Edmonds, S. Emma E. (Sarah Emma Evelyn), 1841-1898

Reit, Seymour. Behind rebel lines: the incredible story of Emma Edmonds, Civil War spy. Harcourt Brace Jovanovich 1988 102p hardcover o.p. paperback available $6 (4 and up)   **92**
1. United States—History—1861-1865, Civil War 2. Spies
ISBN 0-15-200424-6 (pa)   LC 87-28079
"Gulliver books"
This biography tells of a Canadian-born woman who assumed male dress and served in the Union Army, first in a tent hospital, and then as a spy behind Confederate lines under various disguises
"Working from Emma's memoirs, U.S. Army records, and National Archives files, Reit has woven a suspense-filled account of a brave and loyal feminist." Booklist
Includes bibliographical references

Einstein, Albert, 1879-1955

Parker, Steve. Albert Einstein and relativity. Chelsea House 1995 c1994 32p il (Science discoveries) lib bdg $14.95 (4 and up)   **92**
1. Scientists
ISBN 0-7910-3003-2   LC 94-43924
First published 1994 in the United Kingdom
Discusses the life and times of the German-American scientist who revolutionized the study of modern physics
Includes glossary

Severance, John B. Einstein; visionary scientist. Clarion Bks. 1999 144p il $15 (5 and up)   **92**
1. Scientists
ISBN 0-395-93100-2   LC 98-51396
"Severance opens with a chapter designed to establish Einstein's place in and contribution to history in which he outlines how Einstein's theories sparked advances in many scientific fields. The succeeding chapters deal with Einstein's life chronologically, from his childhood, when he was thought to be learning disabled, to his later years, when his genius became apparent." Bull Cent Child Books
The author "does a commendable job of conveying both the complicated ideas that revolutionized the study of physics and the life of the thinker behind them." Publ Wkly
Includes bibliographical references

El Chino

Say, Allen. El Chino. Houghton Mifflin 1990 32p il $16; pa $6.95 (2-5)   **92**
1. Bullfights—Biography
ISBN 0-395-52023-1; 0-395-77875-1 (pa)
LC 90-35026

El Chino—*Continued*

A biography of Bill Wong, a Chinese American who became a famous bullfighter in Spain

"Say's text renders Billy's complex story with simplicity and grace, presenting Billy as an endearing, determined hero; Say's watercolors are luminous, filled with harmonious detail. The first several pages of the book are reproduced in sepia tones, but when Billy attends his first bullfight, the pictures burst into full color." Publ Wkly

Eleanor, of Aquitaine, Queen, consort of Henry II, King of England, 1122?-1204

Brooks, Polly Schoyer. Queen Eleanor: independent spirit of the medieval world; a biography of Eleanor of Aquitaine. Lippincott 1983 183p il map o.p.; Houghton Mifflin paperback available $8.95 (6 and up)   **92**
1. Great Britain—Kings and rulers 2. France—Kings and rulers
ISBN 0-395-98139-5 (pa)   LC 82-48776

A biography of the twelfth-century queen, first of France, then of England, who was the very lively wife of Henry II and mother of several notable sons, including Richard the Lionhearted

"The biographer has captured the subject's personality in a narrative as elegant and vivacious as Eleanor herself. And while obviously enthusiastic, the author nevertheless presents a balanced portrait: legend is separated from known facts; gossip from evidence." Horn Book

Includes bibliographical references

Ellington, Duke, 1899-1974

Pinkney, Andrea Davis. Duke Ellington; the piano prince and his orchestra; illustrated by Brian Pinkney. Hyperion Bks. for Children 1998 unp il $15.95; lib bdg $16.49 (2-4)   **92**
1. Jazz musicians 2. African Americans—Biography
ISBN 0-7868-0178-6; 0-7868-2150-7 (lib bdg)
LC 96-46031

A Caldecott Medal honor book, 1999; Coretta Scott King honor book for illustration, 1999

A brief recounting of the career of this jazz musician and composer who, along with his orchestra, created music that was beyond category

This is "written in a folksy, colloquial style. . . . The warmly colored, exquisitely designed scratchboard illustrations have a grand time evoking the sounds of Ellington's music." Horn Book Guide

Includes bibliographical references

Equiano, Olaudah, b. 1745

Cameron, Ann. The kidnapped prince: the life of Olaudah Equiano; by Olaudah Equiano; adapted by Ann Cameron; with an introduction by Henry Louis Gates, Jr. Knopf 1995 133p il hardcover o.p. paperback available $4.99 (4 and up)   **92**
1. Slavery 2. Blacks—Biography
ISBN 0-375-80346-7 (pa)   LC 93-29914

Adaptation of The interesting narrative of the life of Olaudah Equiano

This is an "adaptation of an influential slave narrative by an African prince who was kidnapped as a child and later freed from slavery; first published in 1789." N Y Times Book Rev

"The inspired simplicity of Cameron's adaptation quickly allows Equiano's gifted voice to establish a compelling relationship between himself and young readers. Well sculpted with detail." SLJ

Includes glossary and bibliographical references

Eratosthenes, 3rd cent. B.C.

Lasky, Kathryn. The librarian who measured the earth; illustrated by Kevin Hawkes. Little, Brown 1994 48p il $16.95 (2-5)   **92**
1. Astronomers
ISBN 0-316-51526-4   LC 92-42656

Describes the life and work of Eratosthenes, the Greek geographer and astronomer who accurately measured the circumference of the Earth

"Illustrating the text with warmth and humor, Hawkes' acrylic paintings capture the period details of the setting and clarify the geometric concepts used in the measurement. The often dramatic compositions vary from page to page, while the sunlit reds, oranges, and yellows glow brightly against the cooler blues and greens. . . . Entertaining as well as instructional." Booklist

Includes bibliographical references

Fleischman, Sid, 1920-

Fleischman, Sid. The abracadabra kid; a writer's life. Greenwillow Bks. 1996 198p il $16; pa $4.95 (5 and up)   **92**
1. Authors, American
ISBN 0-688-14859-X; 0-688-15855-2 (pa)
LC 95-47382

This autobiography, "turns real life into a story complete with cliffhangers. And it's a classic *boy's* story, from card tricks and traveling magic shows to World War II naval experiences and screen-writing gigs for John Wayne movies. En route, we learn how Fleischman learned the craft of writing." Bull Cent Child Books

Includes bibliographical references

Flipper, Henry O., 1856-1940

Pfeifer, Kathryn. Henry O. Flipper; [by] Kathryn Browne Pfeifer. 21st Cent. Bks. (Brookfield) 1993 80p il (African-American soldiers) lib bdg $23.90 (5 and up)   **92**
1. African American soldiers
ISBN 0-8050-2351-8   LC 93-10631

The author "chronicles the life of the first African American to graduate from West Point. Born a slave, Flipper had loving parents who wanted their son to receive a good education. His years of loneliness mixed with the insults he received at West Point are well detailed, and the circumstances that led to his dishonorable discharge from the army in 1881 are clearly explained. The almost 100-year attempt to have this discharge changed to an honorable one is discussed." SLJ

Includes bibliographical references

Ford, Henry, 1863-1947

Mitchell, Barbara. We'll race you, Henry: a story about Henry Ford; illustrations by Kathy Haubrich. Carolrhoda Bks. 1986 56p il (Carolrhoda creative minds book) lib bdg $21.27; pa $5.95 (3-5)   **92**
  1. Automobile industry 2. Inventors
  ISBN 0-87614-291-9 (lib bdg); 0-87614-471-7 (pa)
                LC 86-2691
A brief biography of Henry Ford with emphasis on how he came to develop fast, sturdy, and reliable racing cars that eventually gave him the idea for his Model T
"This book stands out from the general run of biographies for children because of the successful integration of a goodly amount of technological information with accurate and interesting biographical information." Appraisal

Fortune, Amos, 1709 or 10-1801

Yates, Elizabeth. Amos Fortune, free man; illustrations by Nora S. Unwin. Dutton 1950 181p il $15.99; pa $4.99 (4 and up)   **92**
  1. African Americans—Biography 2. Slavery—United States
  ISBN 0-525-25570-2; 0-140-34158-7 (pa)
  Awarded the Newbery Medal, 1951
"Born free in Africa, Amos Fortune was sold into slavery in America in 1725. After more than 40 years of servitude Amos was able to purchase his freedom and, in time, that of several others. He died a tanner of enviable reputation, a landowner, and a respected citizen of his community. Based on fact, this is a . . . story of a life dedicated to the fight for freedom and service to others." Booklist

Fossey, Dian

Matthews, Tom L. Light shining through the mist: a photobiography of Dian Fossey. National Geographic Soc. 1998 64p il $17.95 (4 and up)
                      92
  1. Gorillas 2. Women scientists
  ISBN 0-7922-7300-1   LC 97-34084
Traces the adventurous life of the American woman who worked as a zoologist among the mountain gorillas of the Virunga area of central Africa
"Gorgeous color photographs will be the main draw to this biography of the controversial primatologist, but Matthews's text also does a fine job." Horn Book
Includes bibliographical references

Francis, of Assisi, Saint, 1182-1226

Mayo, Margaret. Brother sun, sister moon: the life and stories of St. Francis; illustrated by Peter Malone. Little, Brown 2000 70p il $16.95 (3-6)
                      92
  1. Christian saints
  ISBN 0-316-56466-4   LC 99-33140
This "book opens with a section that concentrates on the essential facts of St. Francis's life. The biography is followed by engaging retellings of familiar legends such as that of St. Francis taming the wolf of Gubbio, and introducing the first Christmas crèche. Malone's illustrations employ the rich palette of medieval illumination reminiscent of books of hours." Horn Book Guide

Frank, Anne, 1929-1945

Adler, David A. A picture book of Anne Frank; illustrated by Karen Ritz. Holiday House 1993 unp il lib bdg $16.95; pa $6.95 (1-3)   **92**
  1. Jews—Netherlands 2. Holocaust, 1933-1945
  ISBN 0-8234-1003-X (lib bdg); 0-8234-1078-1 (pa)
                LC 92-17283
"Adler introduces Anne Frank and her family to primary grade readers. . . . Ritz's illustrations, some based on actual photographs, allow Anne's lively personality to emerge, and yet never appear undignified. . . . Adler's presentation is both sensitive and appropriate for the age group." Booklist

Frank, Anne. The diary of a young girl; translated from the Dutch by B. M. Mooyaart-Doubleday (6 and up)   **92**
  1. Jews—Netherlands 2. Holocaust, 1933-1945—Personal narratives
Available in various bindings and editions including Spanish language edition; Audiobook version also available
This is the diary of a "German-Jewish girl who hid from the Nazis with her parents, their friends, and some other fugitives in an Amsterdam warehouse from 1942 to 1944. Her diary, covering the years of hiding, was found by friends and published as *Het achterhus* (1947); it was later published in English as *The Diary of a Young Girl* (1952). . . . Written with humor as well as insight, it shows a growing girl with all the preoccupations of adolescence and first love. The diary ends three days before the Franks and their group were discovered by the Nazis." Reader's Ency. 3d edition

Frank, Anne. The diary of a young girl: the definitive edition; edited by Otto H. Frank and Mirjam Pressler; translated by Susan Massotty. Doubleday 1995 340p il $26; pa $5.99 (6 and up)
                      92
  1. Jews—Netherlands 2. Holocaust, 1933-1945—Personal narratives
  ISBN 0-385-47378-8; 0-553-57712-3 (pa)
                LC 94-41379
Also available Audiobook version
"This new translation of Frank's famous diary includes material about her emerging sexuality and her relationship with her mother that was originally excised by Frank's father, the only family member to survive the Holocaust." Libr J

Gold, Alison Leslie. Memories of Anne Frank; reflections of a childhood friend. Scholastic 1997 135p il hardcover o.p. paperback available $5.99 (5 and up)   **92**
  1. Pick-Goslar, Hannah   2. Jews—Netherlands 3. Holocaust, 1933-1945
  ISBN 0-590-90723-9 (pa)   LC 96-41185
This "story of Anne Frank's neighbor and friend, Hannah Elizabeth Pick-Goslar, recounts the tragedy of World War II through a young girl's eyes. . . . The account traces the childhood friendship of the two girls from the time Anne disappeared to the removal of Hannah and her family to concentration camps. The narrative also tells of the brief meeting between Anne and Hannah at Bergen-Belsen shortly before Anne's death." SLJ

Frank, Anne, 1929-1945—*Continued*

"Gold uses carefully chosen details and specific incidents to communicate the horrors of the Holocaust. . . . Readers drawn to Anne Frank's diary will be grateful for the fuller picture rendered here." Publ Wkly

Hurwitz, Johanna. Anne Frank: life in hiding; illustrated by Vera Rosenberry. Jewish Publ. Soc. 1988 62p il map $13.95 (3-5)   **92**
1. Jews—Netherlands 2. Holocaust, 1933-1945
ISBN 0-8276-0311-8   LC 87-35263
Also available in paperback from HarperCollins
The author "gives a concise explanation of the political and economic background to the Holocaust and provides a map of Europe and a chronology. She ably covers the events of Anne's life before, during, and after the period covered by the 'Diary of Anne Frank,' explaining the significance and importance of the 'Diary' throughout the world." SLJ

Rol, Ruud van der. Anne Frank, beyond the diary; a photographic remembrance; by Ruud van der Rol and Rian Verhoeven; in association with the Anne Frank House; translated by Tony Langham and Plym Peters; with an introduction by Anna Quindlen. Viking 1993 113p il maps $18.99; pa $9.99 (5 and up)   **92**
1. Jews—Netherlands 2. Holocaust, 1933-1945
ISBN 0-670-84932-4; 0-14-036926-0 (pa)
LC 92-41528
Original Dutch edition, 1992
Photographs, illustrations, and maps accompany historical essays, diary excerpts, and interviews, providing an insight to Anne Frank and the massive upheaval which tore apart her world
"Readers will become absorbed in the richness of the detail and careful explanation which revisit and expand the familiar, well-loved story." Horn Book

Franklin, Benjamin, 1706-1790

Adler, David A. A picture book of Benjamin Franklin; illustrated by John & Alexandra Wallner. Holiday House 1990 unp il lib bdg $16.95; pa $6.95 (1-3)   **92**
ISBN 0-8234-0792-6 (lib bdg); 0-8234-0882-5 (pa)
LC 89-20059
Surveys the life of Benjamin Franklin, highlighting his work as an inventor and statesman
"The Wallners' full-color, softly painted illustrations are well executed and add informative details to the text. None of Franklin's life is dealt with in detail. . . . Adler's book will provide an excellent resource for primary readers." SLJ

Fritz, Jean. What's the big idea, Ben Franklin? illustrated by Margot Tomes. Coward, McCann & Geoghegan; distributed by Putnam Pub. Group 1976 46p il $15.99; pa $5.99 (2-4)   **92**
ISBN 0-399-23487-X; 0-698-11372-1 (pa)
The text "focuses on Franklin's multifaceted career but also gives personal details and quotes some of his pithy sayings. Enough background information about colonial affairs is given to enable readers to understand the

importance of Franklin's contributions to the public good but not so much that it obtrudes on his life story. Although the text is not punctuated by references or footnotes, a page of notes (with numbers for pages referred to) is appended." Bull Cent Child Books

Giblin, James. The amazing life of Benjamin Franklin; by James Cross Giblin; illustrated by Michael Dooling. Scholastic Press 2000 48p il $17.95 (4-6)   **92**
ISBN 0-590-48534-2   LC 98-44738
A biography of the eighteenth-century printer, inventor, and statesman who played an influential role in the early history of the United States
"Giblin's writing is lively. . . . Dooling provides both expertly executed paintings and simple line drawings to bring Franklin's story close to today's readers. . . . More than enough material for report writers but an intriguing offering for biography lovers as well." Booklist
Includes bibliographical references

Fritz, Jean

Fritz, Jean. Homesick: my own story; illustrated with drawings by Margot Tomes and photographs. Putnam 1982 163p il $15.95; pa $5.99 (5 and up)   **92**
1. China
ISBN 0-399-20933-6; 0-698-11782-4 (pa)
LC 82-7646
A Newbery Medal honor book, 1983
Companion volume to China homecoming
This is a somewhat fictionalized memoir of the author's childhood in China. "Born in Hankow, where her father was director of the YMCA, Jean loved the city. . . . But she knew she 'belonged on the other side of the world'—in Pennsylvania with her grandmother and her other relations." Horn Book
"The descriptions of places and the times are vivid in a book that brings to the reader, with sharp clarity and candor, the yearnings and fears and ambivalent loyalties of a young girl." Bull Cent Child Books

Galilei, Galileo, 1564-1642

Fisher, Leonard Everett. Galileo. Macmillan 1992 unp il $17 (4 and up)   **92**
1. Astronomers
ISBN 0-02-735235-8   LC 91-31146
Examines the life and discoveries of the noted mathematician, physicist, and astronomer, whose work changed the course of science
"The fact-filled yet graceful narrative places Galileo within the continuum of scientific inquiry even as it reveals considerable information about his valuable discoveries. . . . The characteristic black-and-gray pages throughout—coupled with textured, chiaroscuro acrylic paintings—give the book a distinctive look while emphasizing the story's dramatic elements." Publ Wkly

Sis, Peter. Starry messenger; a book depicting the life of a famous scientist, mathematician, astronomer, philosopher, physicist, Galileo Galilei; created and illustrated by Peter Sis. Farrar, Straus & Giroux 1996 unp il $16; pa $5.95   **92**
1. Astronomers
ISBN 0-374-37191-1; 0-374-47027-8 (pa)
LC 95-44986

Galilei, Galileo, 1564-1642—*Continued*

A Caldecott Medal honor book, 1997

"Frances Foster books"

Describes the life and work of the man who changed the way people saw the galaxy, by offering objective evidence that the earth was not the fixed center of the universe

"Large, beautiful drawings reflect the ideas, events, books, maps, world view, and symbolism of the times. These intricate ink drawings, idiosyncratic in concept and beautifully tinted with delicate watercolor washes, are complemented by smaller drawings and prints that illustrate a side-text of significant dates, time lines, quotations, comments, and explanations. . . . Those drawn to the book will find that it works on many levels, offering not just facts but intuitive visions of another world." Booklist

Gandhi, Mahatma, 1869-1948

Fisher, Leonard Everett. Gandhi. Atheneum Bks. for Young Readers 1995 unp il map $16 (4 and up)   **92**

1. India—Politics and government 2. Passive resistance

ISBN 0-689-80337-0   LC 95-77023

"A brief overview of the social and political climate of India under British rule sets the stage for the narrative, which flows comfortably as the story traces Gandhi's arranged marriage at 13, his education, his move to South Africa, and how he came to be called Mahatma (Great Soul). . . . Gandhi's firm, enduring belief in nonviolent resistance, is clearly explained and demonstrated. . . . Fisher's hallmark, stark black-and-white paintings complement the narrative and give texture and character to the work." SLJ

Severance, John B. Gandhi, great soul. Clarion Bks. 1997 143p il map $16 (5 and up)   **92**

1. India—Politics and government 2. Passive resistance

ISBN 0-395-77179-X   LC 95-20887

Severance "begins with an introduction to Gandhi's message and gives a brief overview of the mahatma's personal evolution as well as India's external and internal struggles. He then chronicles Gandhi's life. . . . Severance details Gandhi's philosophy of *satyagraha*, or peaceful resistance." Booklist

"It is not only Gandhi who comes alive in this considered, well-documented biography but the multifarious personalities and politics of his world." Horn Book Guide

Includes bibliographical references

Gannett, Deborah Sampson, 1760-1827

McGovern, Ann. The secret soldier: the story of Deborah Sampson; illustrated by Ann Grifalconi. Four Winds Press 1987 c1975 62p il o.p.; Scholastic paperback available $4.50 (3-5)   **92**

1. United States—History—1775-1783, Revolution 2. Soldiers—United States 3. Women soldiers

ISBN 0-590-43052-1 (pa)

A reissue of the title first published 1975

A "biography of Deborah Sampson who, disguised as a boy, fought for one and a half years in the Continental army until her true identity was discovered (Deborah then became a wife and mother but still continued to defy convention by traveling and lecturing). History and biography from childhood to young adulthood, paralleling the young nation's fight for freedom with Deborah's own desire for independence and selfhood." SLJ

Gehrig, Lou, 1903-1941

Adler, David A. Lou Gehrig; the luckiest man; illustrated by Terry Widener. Harcourt Brace & Co. 1997 unp il $16 (2-4)   **92**

1. Baseball—Biography

ISBN 0-15-200523-4   LC 95-7997

"Gulliver books"

Traces the life of the Yankees' star ballplayer, focusing on his character and his struggle with the terminal disease amyotrophic lateral sclerosis

"Adler's restrained tone makes his description of Gehrig's stoic and uncomplaining struggle all the more moving. The illustrations, meticulously detailed . . . also pack an emotional wallop." Horn Book Guide

George III, King of Great Britain, 1738-1820

Fritz, Jean. Can't you make them behave, King George? pictures by Tomie de Paola. Coward, McCann & Geoghegan; distributed by Putnam Pub. Group 1977 45p il $15.99; pa $6.99 (2-4)   **92**

1. Great Britain—Kings and rulers

ISBN 0-698-20315-1; 0-698-20542-1 (pa)

    LC 75-33722

"As a boy, George is seen to have had struggles in deportment; as King George III, he is mystified that the colonists refuse to be taught. Bits of history, a sense of George's personality, and the loneliness of being king are all conveyed with good humor. The artist's drawings evoke more chuckles." LC. Child Books, 1977

George, Jean Craighead, 1919-

George, Jean Craighead. A tarantula in my purse; and 172 other wild pets; written and illustrated by Jean Craighead George. HarperCollins Pubs. 1996 134p il $14.95; pa $4.95 (4-6)   **92**

1. Women authors 2. Authors, American 3. Naturalists 4. Pets

ISBN 0-06-023626-4; 0-06-446201-3 (pa)

    LC 95-54151

"George tells of the many wild pets that lived with her family, particularly while her children were growing up. Each chapter describes a different animal or incident." Booklist

"Told in a casual and thoroughly engaging manner, the stories will enchant all animal lovers and even those who aren't." SLJ

Glover, Savion

Glover, Savion. Savion!: my life in tap; by Savion Glover and Bruce Weber. Morrow 2000 79p il $19.95 (5 and up) **92**

1. African American dancers 2. Choreographers 3. Tap dancing

ISBN 0-688-15629-0 LC 98-31517

Examines the life and career of the young tap dancer who speaks with his feet and who choreographed the Tony Award-winning Broadway show "Bring in da Noise, Bring in da Funk"

"Glover comes across in this vibrant book as confident but not arrogant. The black, white, and red text dances around the pages in a style and format that complement the subject matter." Voice Youth Advocates

Goble, Paul

Goble, Paul. Hau kola: hello friend; photographs by Gerry Perrin. Owen, R.C. 1994 32p il (Meet the author) $14.95 (1-3) **92**

1. Authors, American

ISBN 1-878450-44-1 LC 93-48167

"Goble's autobiography provides fascinating insight about this English transplant to Nebraska who has written and illustrated many award-winning books about Native Americans. . . . Clear, color photos on almost every page convey the artistry of one of our most prominent children's book authors and illustrators." Booklist

Goddard, Robert Hutchings, 1882-1945

Streissguth, Thomas. Rocket man: the story of Robert Goddard; [by] Tom Streissguth. Carolrhoda Bks. 1995 88p il lib bdg $23.93 (4 and up) **92**

1. Scientists

ISBN 0-87614-863-1 LC 94-22836

The author "describes Goddard's pioneering efforts to build rockets capable of leaving Earth's atmosphere that would become the basis of modern astronautical engineering. Explaining potentially difficult scientific principles clearly, he paints a vivid portrait of a brilliant but secretive scientist who refused to share his research and persevered in spite of repeated failures." Booklist

Includes glossary and bibliographical references

Goodall, Jane, 1934-

Goodall, Jane. My life with the chimpanzees. rev ed. Pocket Bks. 1996 156p il hardcover o.p. paperback available $4.99 (3-6) **92**

1. Chimpanzees 2. Women scientists

ISBN 0-671-56271-1 (pa) LC 97-122051

Also available Audiobook version

"A Byron Preiss book. A Minstrel book"

First published 1988

The well-known English zoologist describes her early interest in animals and how this led to her study of chimpanzees at the Gombe Stream Reserve in Tanzania

"Family snapshots add to the special feeling of being let into Goodall's circle of friends as the famous scientist recounts her adventures with the chimps and illustrates many of her subjects' distinctive personalities. . . . This outstanding autobiography will be a noteworthy choice for school and public libraries." Booklist

Grant, Ulysses S. (Ulysses Simpson), 1822-1885

Archer, Jules. A house divided: the lives of Ulysses S. Grant and Robert E. Lee. Scholastic 1995 184p il $14.95; pa $4.50 (5 and up) **92**

1. Lee, Robert E. (Robert Edward), 1807-1870 2. Generals 3. United States—History—1861-1865, Civil War

ISBN 0-590-48325-0; 0-590-46102-8 (pa)

LC 93-38886

"In alternating chapters, Archer looks at Grant and Lee's formative years and early careers. He then highlights their roles in the war, occasionally stopping at particular battles to demonstrate each man's character through his actions. The final two chapters tell of the subjects' postwar lives." SLJ

"This book is a great comparison of two men who lived at the same time in history. Each achieved fame through different routes. Students could use this book as the resource for a comparison and contrast assignment. Further, those with an interest in the Civil War will find the work fascinating." Voice Youth Advocates

Includes bibliographical references

Gutenberg, Johann, 1397?-1468

Fisher, Leonard Everett. Gutenberg. Macmillan 1993 unp il $14.95 (4 and up) **92**

1. Printing—History

ISBN 0-02-735238-2 LC 92-26991

"Fisher's biography of Johann Gutenberg, the creator of movable type, is marked by careful research, clear writing, and striking illustrations." Horn Book

Hamilton, Alice

McPherson, Stephanie Sammartino. The workers' detective: a story about Dr. Alice Hamilton; illustrations by Janet Schulz. Carolrhoda Bks. 1992 64p il (Carolrhoda creative minds book) lib bdg $21.27 (3-5) **92**

1. Women physicians

ISBN 0-87614-699-X LC 91-23634

A biography of Dr. Alice Hamilton, social worker and doctor, whose work brought attention to the health risks associated with particular jobs

"McPherson has researched her subject thoroughly and does an effective, concise job of combining historical information on the industrial revolution with Hamilton's life and interests. . . . Realistic black-and-white pencil drawings enhance the highly readable text that is stimulating enough for older reluctant readers." SLJ

Includes bibliographical references

Hancock, John, 1737-1793

Fritz, Jean. Will you sign here, John Hancock? pictures by Trina Schart Hyman. Coward, McCann & Geoghegan; distributed by Putnam Pub. Group 1976 47p il $14.99; pa $5.99 (2-4) **92**

1. United States—History—1775-1783, Revolution

ISBN 0-399-23306-7; 0-698-11440-X (pa)

"A straightforward biography of the rich Boston dandy with the gigantic signature. When he signed the Declaration of Independence he quipped, 'There! George the Third can read "that" without his spectacles. Now he can

Hancock, John, 1737-1793—*Continued*
double his reward for my head.'" Saturday Rev
"An affectionate look at a flamboyant, egocentric, but kindly, patriot, the book is a most enjoyable view of history. . . . The delightful illustrations exactly suit the times and the extraordinary character of John Hancock." Horn Book

Handel, George Frideric, 1685-1759
Venezia, Mike. George Handel; written and illustrated by Mike Venezia. Children's Press 1995 32p il (Getting to know the world's greatest composers) lib bdg $22.50; pa $6.95 (k-3)   **92**
1. Composers
ISBN 0-516-04539-3 (lib bdg); 0-516-44539-1 (pa)
LC 94-36345
Examines the life, career and influence of the German composer Handel through brief text, photographs, and cartoon drawings

Hansberry, Lorraine, 1930-1965
McKissack, Patricia C. Young, black, and determined: a biography of Lorraine Hansberry; by Patricia C. McKissack and Fredrick L. McKissack. Holiday House 1998 152p il $18.95 (6 and up)
92
1. Dramatists, American 2. African American women
ISBN 0-8234-1300-4   LC 97-2084
A biography of the black playwright who received great recognition for her work at an early age
"The McKissacks' biography sparkles with the energy and passion that characterize their subject." Booklist
Includes bibliographical references

Henry, Patrick, 1736-1799
Fritz, Jean. Where was Patrick Henry on the 29th of May? illustrated by Margot Tomes. Coward, McCann & Geoghegan; distributed by Putnam Pub. Group 1975 47p il $15.99; pa $6.99 (2-4)   **92**
1. United States—History—1600-1775, Colonial period
ISBN 0-399-23305-9; 0-698-11439-6 (pa)
A "portrait of a founding father. Patrick Henry was born on May 29, and the author uses this date to focus on significant periods in his life. Henry's skill at oratory is shown in development as well as his anger at English laws, until they peak in his famous speech." Child Book Rev Serv
"The color pictures are artful evocations of the [18th] century in America and the text presents Patrick Henry as a human being—not a sterilized historic 'figure.'" Publ Wkly

Hensel, Fanny Cécile Mendelssohn, 1805-1847
Kamen, Gloria. Hidden music; the life of Fanny Mendelssohn. Atheneum Bks. for Young Readers 1996 82p il $15 (4 and up)   **92**
1. Women composers
ISBN 0-689-31714-X   LC 95-15215

This biography offers a portrait of Fanny Mendelssohn Hensel, "a talented pianist and composer who was never accorded the recognition given her brother, Felix. Kamen describes the social milieu into which Fanny was born, conveying a feeling of frustration bordering on tragedy. An epilogue relates Fanny's story to the larger question of women's place in the world of music by outlining the accomplishments of later pioneers such as Nadia Boulanger, Sarah Caldwell, and Wanda Landowska." Horn Book Guide
Includes glossary and bibliographical references

Henson, Matthew Alexander, 1866-1955
Ferris, Jeri. Arctic explorer: the story of Matthew Henson. Carolrhoda Bks. 1989 80p il maps lib bdg $24.50; pa $6.25 (3-6)   **92**
1. Explorers 2. North Pole 3. African Americans—Biography
ISBN 0-87614-370-2 (lib bdg); 0-87614-507-1 (pa)
LC 88-34449
"A high adventure biography of Matthew Henson, the black explorer who accompanied Robert Peary on six expeditions to the North Pole. Henson's great courage, determination, and adaptability were crucial elements in the success of the expeditions. Black-and-white photographs supplement well-written text." Sci Child
Includes bibliographical references

Herrera, Juan Felipe, 1948-
Herrera, Juan Felipe. The upside down boy; story by Juan Felipe Herrera; illustrations by Elizabeth Gómez. Children's Bk. Press 2000 31p il $15.95 (k-3)   **92**
1. Poets 2. Mexican Americans—Biography 3. Bilingual books—English-Spanish
ISBN 0-89239-162-6   LC 99-49113
Title page and text in English and Spanish
The author recalls the year when his farm worker parents settled down in the city so that he could go to school for the first time
"Herrera's poetic prose sings with a unique voice in both languages, and Gómez's illustrations are colorful and ethereal." Horn book guide

Hiawatha, 15th cent.
Fradin, Dennis B. Hiawatha: messenger of peace; [by] Dennis Brindell Fradin. Margaret K. McElderry Bks. 1992 40p il map $16 (3-5)   **92**
1. Iroquois Indians
ISBN 0-689-50519-1   LC 90-26312
Recounts the life of the fifteenth-century Iroquois Indian who brought five tribes together to form the long-lasting Iroquois Federation
"The book is copiously illustrated with both black-and-white and full-color photographs of Indian artifacts and of paintings and sculpture by Native American artists, all relevant to the text. This attractive volume helps fill the need for good, readable biographies for this age group." SLJ
Includes bibliographical references

Hopkins, Lee Bennett, 1938-

Hopkins, Lee Bennett. The writing bug; photographs by Diane Rubinger. Owen, R.C. 1993 32p il (Meet the author) $14.95 (1-3)   92
1. Authors, American
ISBN 1-878450-38-7   LC 93-11994
"While showing readers his study and his gardens, Hopkins talks about the sights, sounds, memories, and experiences that inspire him to write." Booklist
This book is "ideally suited for younger students seeking to fulfill school assignments." Horn Book Guide

Houdini, Harry, 1874-1926

Matthews, Tom L. Spellbinder: the life of Harry Houdini. Holiday House 2000 88p il $18.95 (5 and up)   92
1. Magicians
ISBN 0-8234-1499-X   LC 99-45629
This biography "weaves together information about the magician's personal life and his public exploits. . . . An appealing, accessible introduction to a consummate artist." SLJ
Includes bibliographical references

Houston, Samuel, 1793-1863

Fritz, Jean. Make way for Sam Houston; illustrations by Elise Primavera. Putnam 1986 109p il map $15.99; pa $5.99 (4 and up)   92
ISBN 0-399-21303-1; 0-698-11646-1 (pa)
                                      LC 85-25601
This is a biography of the "lawyer, governor of Tennessee, general in the wars against Santa Anna, president of the Republic of Texas, and finally U.S. senator and governor of the state of Texas." Horn Book
"Artfully weaving the threads of fact, Fritz creates a biography that is both interesting and informative. Developing Houston as a human character that readers can identify with as well as admire, and drawing him against the scene of America's own political turmoil, Fritz gives us a book to be read and to be felt." Voice Youth Advocates
Includes bibliographical references

Howe, James, 1946-

Howe, James. Playing with words; photographs by Michael Craine. Owen, R.C. 1994 32p il (Meet the author) $14.95 (1-3)   92
1. Authors, American
ISBN 1-878450-40-9   LC 93-48166
This is an "easy-to-read, thoughtful autobiography. . . . Sharp color photos on almost every page document Howe's story and provide insight into the behind-the-scenes life of a popular wordsmith." Booklist

Hughes, Langston, 1902-1967

Cooper, Floyd. Coming home: from the life of Langston Hughes. Philomel Bks. 1994 unp il lib bdg $16.95; pa $6.99 (2-4)   92
1. Poets, American 2. African American authors
ISBN 0-399-22682-6 (lib bdg); 0-698-11612-7 (pa)
                                      LC 93-36332

This "biography highlights pivotal events in Hughes's life, emphasizing his loneliness as a child and his development as a poet. . . . Cooper's hazy illustrations in gold, brown, and sepia tones reveal keen observations of people and neighborhood. The text and art combine to create a fine tribute and introduction to the writer's life." Horn Book
Includes bibliographical references

Meltzer, Milton. Langston Hughes; illustrated by Stephen Alcorn. Millbrook Press 1997 239p il lib bdg $40.90; pa $20.95 (6 and up)   92
1. Poets, American 2. African American authors
ISBN 0-7613-0205-0 (lib bdg); 0-7613-0372-8 (pa)
                                      LC 97-1403
A revised and newly illustrated edition of the title first published 1968 by Crowell
Tells the story of a leading poet of the Harlem Renaissance during the 1920s who devoted his life to writing about the black experience in America
"Alcorn's stylized, two-toned prints pique excitement and interest and invite repeated viewings. . . . Only slight, subtle changes have been made in the well-written text. . . . An author's note precedes the text. The bibliography has been updated and includes audio and video recordings. The compelling artistry of this edition makes it a first-purchase consideration even for libraries that own the older title." SLJ

Hurston, Zora Neale, 1891-1960

Miller, William. Zora Hurston and the chinaberry tree; illustrated by Cornelius Van Wright and Ying-hwa Hu. Lee & Low Bks. 1994 unp il $15.95; pa $6.95 (k-3)   92
1. African American authors 2. Women authors
ISBN 1-880000-14-8; 1-880000-33-4 (pa)
                                      LC 94-1291
"This biography, which covers a brief period in Zora Neale Hurston's childhood, ends with the young girl grieving over her mother's death but finding inner power and strength from her mother's life." Horn Book
"Conveying the changing expressions on the face of the young Hurston as easily as they show the grandeur of the sky at nightfall, the versatile artists neatly capture the emotions in this lucidly told story." Publ Wkly

Porter, A. P. Jump at de sun: the story of Zora Neale Hurston; foreword by Lucy Ann Hurston. Carolrhoda Bks. 1992 95p il hardcover o.p. paperback available $6.95 (4 and up)   92
1. African American authors 2. Women authors
ISBN 0-87614-546-2 (pa)   LC 91-37241
Follows the life of the African American writer known for her novels, plays, articles, and collections of folklore
This is "written in engagingly fresh prose and attractively laid out in a large, clear type. . . . The well-chosen and appropriately placed black-and-white photographs serve not only to extend the text, but also to put faces on the many names that crop up in the story of Hurston's eventful life." SLJ
Includes bibliographical references

Huynh, Quang Nhuong

Huynh, Quang Nhuong. The land I lost: adventures of a boy in Vietnam; with pictures by Vo-Dinh Mai. Harper & Row 1982 115p il lib bdg $15.89; pa $4.95 (4 and up)   **92**

  1. Vietnam—Social life and customs

ISBN 0-397-32448-0 (lib bdg); 0-06-440183-9 (pa)
                       LC 80-8437

"Each chapter in this book of reminiscence about the author's boyhood in a hamlet in the Vietnamese highlands, is a separate episode, although the same characters appear in many of the episodes. . . . The writing has an ingenuous quality that adds to the appeal of the strong sense of familial and communal ties that pervades the story." Bull Cent Child Books

Huynh, Quang Nhuong. Water buffalo days; growing up in Vietnam; pictures by Jean and Mou-sien Tseng. HarperCollins Pubs. 1997 116p il $13.95; pa $4.95 (3-5)   **92**

  1. Vietnam—Social life and customs 2. Water buffalo

ISBN 0-06-024957-9; 0-06-446211-0 (pa)
                      LC 96-35058

The author describes his close relationship to his water buffalo, Tank, when he was growing up in a village in the central highlands of Vietnam

"Most of the incidents described are entertaining and readers will learn fascinating information about the importance of these animals in this culture. . . . The Tsengs' soft sketches show Tank, his young master, and the various villagers mentioned in the text." SLJ

Ishi

Kroeber, Theodora. Ishi, last of his tribe; drawings by Ruth Robbins. Parnassus Press 1964 209p il maps $14.95 (5 and up)   **92**

  1. Yana Indians

ISBN 0-395-27644-6

Also available in paperback from Bantam Bks.

"The true story of a California Yahi Indian [discovered in 1911 by anthropologists] who survives the invasion by the white man, while the rest of his tribe die off." Notable Books, 1964

Written "with a grave simplicity . . . utterly right for the subject. The cultural details are quite unobtrusive: they are simply there, an evidence of the author's knowledge and empathy." Bull Cent Child Books

Includes glossary

Jackson, Stonewall, 1824-1863

Fritz, Jean. Stonewall; with drawings by Stephen Gammell. Putnam 1979 152p il map $16.99; pa $5.99 (4 and up)   **92**

  1. Generals 2. United States—History—1861-1865, Civil War

ISBN 0-399-20698-1; 0-698-11552-X (pa)
                      LC 79-12506

A biography of the brilliant southern general who gained the nickname Stonewall by his stand at Bull Run during the Civil War

"Fritz's trenchant, compassionate life of General Thomas Jonathan Jackson grips the reader and makes one understand why Stonewall is an honored legend in American history. . . . The tragic irony of his death at age 39 is movingly described." Publ Wkly

Includes bibliographical references

Jacobs, Barron, 1843-1936

Stanley, Jerry. Frontier merchants. See entry under Jacobs, Lionel, 1841-1922

Jacobs, Harriet A. (Harriet Ann), 1813-1896 or 7

Fleischner, Jennifer. I was born a slave: the story of Harriet Jacobs; with illustrations by Melanie K. Reim. Millbrook Press 1997 93p il lib bdg $25.90; pa $12.95 (5 and up)   **92**

  1. Slavery—United States

ISBN 0-7613-0111-9 (lib bdg); 0-7613-3016-6 (pa)
                      LC 96-44350

Traces the life of a slave who suffered mistreatment from her master, spent years as a fugitive from slavery in North Carolina, and was eventually released to freedom with her children

"Basing her account on Jacobs's autobiography written in 1861, Fleischner presents a moving and readable record of one woman's experiences. . . . Reim's powerful, full-page woodcut prints illustrate incidents from Jacobs's life." SLJ

Includes bibliographical references

Jacobs, Lionel, 1841-1922

Stanley, Jerry. Frontier merchants; Lionel and Barron Jacobs and the Jewish pioneers who settled the West. Crown 1998 100p il $19 (4-6)   **92**

  1. Jacobs, Barron, 1843-1936 2. Frontier and pioneer life—West (U.S.) 3. Jews—Biography

ISBN 0-517-80019-5   LC 97-51160

Tells the story of Lionel and Barron Jacobs, Jewish merchants who started with a general store in Tucson in 1867 and went on to found Arizona's first bank

"In a narrative that is brisk yet rich in detail and theme, Stanley creates a vivid sense of place as he introduces an aspect of the American frontier seldom presented to children and adolescents." Horn Book Guide

Includes bibliographical references

Jefferson, Thomas, 1743-1826

Adler, David A. A picture book of Thomas Jefferson; illustrated by John & Alexandra Wallner. Holiday House 1990 unp il lib bdg $16.95; pa $6.95 (1-3)   **92**

  1. Presidents—United States

ISBN 0-8234-0791-8 (lib bdg); 0-8234-0881-7 (pa)
                      LC 89-20076

Traces the life and achievements of the architect, bibliophile, president, and author of the Declaration of Independence

"The book includes an amazing amount of material. An appealing package with simple language and detailed drawings." Horn Book

Giblin, James. Thomas Jefferson; a picture book biography; by James Cross Giblin; illustrated by Michael Dooling. Scholastic 1994 48p il $16.95 (2-4)   **92**

  1. Presidents—United States

ISBN 0-590-44838-2   LC 93-23340

Jefferson, Thomas, 1743-1826—*Continued*

"Giblin records the significant events in Jefferson's long and varied career with enough personal incidents and sidelights to give readers some sense of the man himself, as well as his place in history. . . . Dooling's dramatic oil paintings stretch across each double-page spread. . . . Historically accurate and visually handsome." Booklist

Joan, of Arc, Saint, 1412-1431

Hodges, Margaret. Joan of Arc; the Lily Maid; illustrated by Robert Rayevsky. Holiday House 1999 unp il $16.95 (2-4)   92
1. Christian saints 2. France—History—1328-1589, House of Valois
ISBN 0-8234-1424-8   LC 98-24260
A biography of the fifteenth-century peasant girl who led a French army to victory against the English, witnessed the crowning of King Charles VII, and was later burned at the stake for witchcraft
"Hodges tells Joan's story with simplicity, distilling the myriad events of bravery and betrayal down to their essence. . . . The pictures are full of action and naive charm, and they have the same strong simplicity as the text. Rayevsky incorporates medieval styles and techniques into his artwork, using two printmaking techniques: dry point and etching." Booklist

Poole, Josephine. Joan of Arc; illustrated by Angela Barrett, research by Vincent Helyas. Knopf 1998 unp il $18; pa $6.99 (2-4)   92
1. Christian saints 2. France—History—1328-1589, House of Valois
ISBN 0-679-89041-6; 0-375-80355-6 (pa)
                    LC 97-46667
This is a "biography of Saint Joan, the 15th-century farmer's daughter who heard voices from heaven directing her to lead the French in battle during the Hundred Years' War." Publ Wkly
"The text mixes the high adventure of Joan's crusade with the maiden's most personal reactions to the dramatic events engulfing her life. . . . Barrett's lovely illustrations are alternately pastoral, celestial, and spirited. The spreads sweep along and will gather younger readers with their zeal." Booklist

Stanley, Diane. Joan of Arc. Morrow Junior Bks. 1998 unp il $16 (4 and up)   92
1. Christian saints 2. France—History—1328-1589, House of Valois
ISBN 0-688-14329-6   LC 97-45652
A biography of the fifteenth-century peasant girl who led a French army to victory against the English and was burned at the stake for witchcraft
Stanley "orchestrates the complexities of history into a gripping, unusually challenging story in this exemplary biography. . . . Judiciously chosen details build atmosphere in both the text and the artwork—painstakingly wrought, gilded paintings modeled after the illuminated manuscripts of Joan's day." Publ Wkly
Includes bibliographical references

Jones, Mother, 1830-1930

Kraft, Betsy Harvey. Mother Jones; one woman's fight for labor. Clarion Bks. 1995 116p il $16.95 (4 and up)   92
1. Reformers 2. Labor—United States
ISBN 0-395-67163-9   LC 94-19715
"This biography of union organizer Mary Harris Jones, more popularly known as Mother Jones, is as much a history of the American labor movement from the 1870s-1930s as it is the story of one woman's life. Kraft tells about Jones's childhood in Ireland; the tragic death of her husband and children from yellow fever in Memphis; and her defiant commitment to bringing about changes." SLJ
"This scintillating, well-illustrated biography achieves the formidable task of doing justice to its redoubtable subject." Publ Wkly
Includes bibliographical references

Joyce, William

Joyce, William. The world of William Joyce scrapbook; text and art by William Joyce; photographs by Philip Gould; designed by Christine Kettner. HarperCollins Pubs. 1997 48p il $16.95 (2-5)   92
1. Illustrators 2. Authors, American
ISBN 0-06-027432-8   LC 97-71688
"A Laura Geringer book"
"Joyce offers tidbits of information about his childhood, his working life, and his family. He also provides brief summaries of and background information about his picture books." SLJ
"Given Joyce's manic approach to story, art, and apparently, to life, the busy melange of snapshots, photo vignettes, and drawings is completely appropriate." Bull Cent Child Books

Kaiulani, Princess of Hawaii, 1875-1899

Stanley, Fay. The last princess: the story of Princess Ka'iulani of Hawai'i; illustrated by Diane Stanley. HarperCollins Pubs. 2001 40p il maps $15.95; lib bdg $15.89 (4 and up)   92
1. Princesses 2. Hawaii—History
ISBN 0-688-18020-5; 0-06-029215-6 (lib bdg)
                    LC 00-32048
A reissue of the title first published 1991 by Four Winds Press
Recounts the story of Hawaii's last heir to the throne, who was denied her right to rule when the monarchy was abolished
"The princesses's story sheds new light on long-forgotten history; the vibrant, handsome gouache illustrations establish the lush Hawaiian background and provide historic detail." Horn Book
Includes bibliographical references

Keats, Ezra Jack, 1916-1983

Engel, Dean. Ezra Jack Keats; a biography with illustrations; [by] Dean Engel and Florence B. Freedman. Silver Moon Press 1995 81p il $24.95 (3-5)   92
1. Authors, American 2. Illustrators
ISBN 1-881889-65-3   LC 94-34960

Keats, Ezra Jack, 1916-1983—Continued

A "profile of a significant creator of twentieth-century children's books, this study of Ezra Jack Keats for young readers is based on reminiscences of conversations with and autobiographical essays by the subject. . . . The illustrations, most from published works, integrate Keats's persona with that of his characters." Horn Book

"This attractive, oversized volume is a must read for Keats's many fans and a marvelous way to introduce (or reintroduce) children to his work." SLJ

Kehret, Peg

Kehret, Peg. Small steps: the year I got polio. Whitman, A. 1996 179p il $14.95; pa $5.95 (4-6) **92**

1. Poliomyelitis
ISBN 0-8075-7457-0; 0-8075-7458-9 (pa)
LC 95-52641

This "memoir takes readers back to 1949 when the author, at age 12, contracted polio. . . . She describes her seven-month ordeal—her diagnosis and quarantine, her terrifying paralysis, her slow and difficult recuperation—and the people she encountered along the way." Booklist

Kehret "writes in an approachable, familiar way, and readers will be hooked from the first page on." SLJ

Keita, Soundiata, d. 1255

Wisniewski, David. Sundiata; lion king of Mali; story and pictures by David Wisniewski. Clarion Bks. 1992 unp il $17; pa $5.95 (1-4) **92**

1. Mali—History
ISBN 0-395-61302-7; 0-395-76481-5 (pa)
LC 91-27951

The story of Sundiata, who overcame physical handicaps, social disgrace, and strong opposition to rule Mali in the thirteenth century

"Passed down through oral tradition, this historical account has the drama and depth of a folktale. The illustrations—elaborate collages inspired by the artifacts and culture of the Malinke—create a series of dramatic images. The intricacy of the paper-cuts and the richness of the colors and patterns give the artwork visual as well as narrative strength." Booklist

Keller, Helen, 1880-1968

Adler, David A. A picture book of Helen Keller; illustrated by John & Alexandra Wallner. Holiday House 1990 unp il lib bdg $16.95; pa $6.95 (1-3) **92**

1. Blind 2. Deaf
ISBN 0-8234-0818-3 (lib bdg); 0-8234-0950-3 (pa)
LC 89-77510

A brief biography of the woman who overcame her handicaps of being both blind and deaf

"The Wallners' line and watercolor cartoons match the simple text and are appropriate to the book's tone." SLJ

St. George, Judith. Dear Dr. Bell—your friend, Helen Keller. Putnam 1992 95p il o.p.; Beech Tree Bks. paperback available $4.95 (5 and up) **92**

1. Bell, Alexander Graham, 1847-1922 2. Blind 3. Deaf
ISBN 0-688-12814-9 (pa)
LC 91-37327

Also available in paperback from Morrow

Follows the parallel lives of Helen Keller and Alexander Graham Bell, who continued to encounter and support each other from that eventful meeting when he recommended she be given a teacher and thus led her to Annie Sullivan

"A lively style and plenty of quotes from each person's writing and letters show the feelings and thoughts behind the friendship. Black-and-white photographs show scenes from both of their lives as well as of their times together." SLJ

Includes bibliographical references

Kennedy, John F. (John Fitzgerald), 1917-1963

Adler, David A. A picture book of John F. Kennedy; illustrated by Robert Casilla. Holiday House 1991 unp il lib bdg $16.95; pa $6.95 (1-3) **92**

1. Presidents—United States
ISBN 0-8234-0884-1 (lib bdg); 0-8234-0976-7 (pa)
LC 90-23589

Depicts the life and career of John F. Kennedy

"Adler presents a brief, clearly written text that provides basic information about his subject in an appealing format. . . . Casilla's watercolors are full-color copies of famous photographs." SLJ

Kennedy, Robert F., 1925-1968

Harrison, Barbara. A ripple of hope: the life of Robert F. Kennedy; [by] Barbara Harrison and Daniel Terris. Lodestar Bks. 1997 133p il $16.99 (6 and up) **92**

1. Politicians
ISBN 0-525-67506-X
LC 96-42447

This book focuses on the life of Robert F. Kennedy, from his childhood with the Kennedy clan to his assassination in 1968, with an emphasis on his commitment to social issues

"The writing is crisp, often focusing on the unexpected. . . . There is also a wealth of small details that illuminate the man." Booklist

Includes bibliographical references

Kenny, Elizabeth, 1886-1952

Crofford, Emily. Healing warrior: a story about Sister Elizabeth Kenny; illustrations by Steve Michaels. Carolrhoda Bks. 1989 64p il (Carolrhoda creative minds book) lib bdg $21.27 (3-5) **92**

1. Nurses
ISBN 0-87614-382-6
LC 89-33474

"This biography traces Sister Kenny's life from childhood, through her nursing career, to her death at age 72 in 1952. Known as the founder of modern physical rehabilitation, the Australian nurse was instrumental in improving treatment of polio patients." Sci Child

This book is "well written and, while a bit of dialogue may have been invented, on the whole, [it] seems to be authoritative and objective. . . . [A] good introduction to [an] admirable medical pioneer that will attract recreational readers and be useful for reports." SLJ

Includes bibliographical references

Kherdian, Veron, 1907-

Kherdian, David. The road from home; the story of an Armenian girl. Greenwillow Bks. 1979 238p il map lib bdg $15.93; pa $5.95 (6 and up) **92**

1. Armenians—Turkey 2. Armenian massacres, 1915-1923

ISBN 0-688-84205-4 (lib bdg); 0-688-14425-X (pa)

LC 78-72511

A Newbery Medal honor book, 1980

The author presents a "biography of his mother's early life as a young Armenian girl. Veron Dumehjian was part of a prosperous Armenian family in Turkey, but the Armenian minority undergoes a holocaust when the Turkish government persecutes its Christian minorities. In 1915 Veron and her family are deported and, as refugees, live through hardships of disease, starvation, bombing, and fire until, at sixteen, Veron is able to go to America as a 'mail-order' bride." Babbling Bookworm

King, Coretta Scott, 1927-

Medearis, Angela Shelf. Dare to dream: Coretta Scott King and the civil rights movement; illustrated by Anna Rich. Lodestar Bks. 1994 60p il (Rainbow biography) $13.99; pa $4.99 (3-5) **92**

1. King, Martin Luther, 1929-1968 2. African American women 3. African Americans—Civil rights

ISBN 0-525-67426-8; 0-14-130202-X (pa)

LC 93-33573

This biography "charts the milestones in King's life from her early ambitions to be an opera singer through her marriage, her involvement in the civil rights movement, and her continuation of her husband's work after his death. . . . Illustrated with soft pencil drawings as well as numerous black-and-white photographs." Booklist

Includes bibliographical references

King, Martin Luther, 1929-1968

Adler, David A. Martin Luther King, Jr.; free at last; illustrated by Robert Casilla. Holiday House 1986 48p il lib bdg $15.95 (2-4) **92**

1. African Americans—Biography 2. African Americans—Civil rights

ISBN 0-8234-0618-0 LC 86-4670

"A short, chronological account of the life and major activities of this Civil Rights leader. . . . Preceded by a chronology of the major dates in King's life, the text is divided into four chapters and illustrated very fully with black-and-white paintings. . . . The book is pleasing in appearance, and the didactic thrust of explaining background issues and the value of King's beliefs and actions is well modulated." Horn Book

Adler, David A. A picture book of Martin Luther King, Jr.; illustrated by Robert Casilla. Holiday House 1989 unp il lib bdg $16.95; pa $6.95 (1-3) **92**

1. African Americans—Biography 2. African Americans—Civil rights

ISBN 0-8234-0770-5 (lib bdg); 0-8234-0847-7 (pa)

LC 89-1930

Also available with Audiobook

This "biography takes a look at the life, leadership, and ideals of Dr. Martin Luther King, Jr. Adler examines King's family background, leadership of the Montgomery bus boycott, and the 1963 march on Washington, D.C. By focusing primarily on these events, Adler provides young readers with enough basic information to form a well-rounded picture of King and his ideals. However, the outstanding feature of this book is the vivid watercolor illustrations, which are sure to capture readers' attention. Casilla dramatically reveals the mood and feelings of the era." SLJ

Bray, Rosemary L. Martin Luther King; paintings by Malcah Zeldis. Greenwillow Bks. 1995 47p il hardcover o.p. paperback available $6.95 (2-4) **92**

1. African Americans—Biography 2. African Americans—Civil rights

ISBN 0-688-15219-8 (pa) LC 93-41002

"Vivid full-page paintings in a folk art style give special strength to a straightforward biography of the civil rights leader." N Y Times Book Rev

Haskins, James. I have a dream: the life and words of Martin Luther King, Jr.; by Jim Haskins. Millbrook Press 1992 111p il lib bdg $20.40; pa $12.95 (5 and up) **92**

1. African Americans—Biography 2. African Americans—Civil rights

ISBN 1-56294-087-2 (lib bdg); 1-56294-837-7 (pa)

LC 91-42528

Presents the life, words, and principles of the noted civil rights worker through extensive quotations from his speeches and writings

"All quotations are sourced, and Haskins includes a time line of important events in King's life as well as suggestions for further reading. A serviceable, practical biography, this will be a good addition to any size collection." Booklist

Marzollo, Jean. Happy birthday, Martin Luther King; illustrated by J. Brian Pinkney. Scholastic 1993 unp il $15.95 (k-3) **92**

1. African Americans—Biography 2. African Americans—Civil rights

ISBN 0-590-44065-9 LC 91-42137

Also available Big book edition

"This very easy biography of Martin Luther King is distinguished by its succinct explanations of King's achievements. . . . The narrative of King's life is smooth and accessible. Pinkney's scratchboard paintings are fluidly drawn, warm, and dignified." Bull Cent Child Books

Kobayashi, Issa, 1763-1827

Gollub, Matthew. Cool melons—turn to frogs!: the life and poems of Issa; story and Haiku translations by Matthew Gollub; illustrations by Kazuko G. Stone; calligraphy by Keiko Smith. Lee & Low Bks. 1998 unp il $16.95 (3-6) **92**

1. Poets

ISBN 1-88000-071-7 LC 98-13087

A biography and introduction to the work of the Japanese haiku poet whose love for nature finds expression in the more than thirty poems included in this book

Kobayashi, Issa, 1763-1827—*Continued*

This contains the life of the poet "told in simple language; lots of his exquisite and accessible haiku; limpid watercolor and colored pencil illustrations reminiscent of Japanese prints and drawings; and beautiful Japanese calligraphy." Booklist

Kuskin, Karla

Kuskin, Karla. Thoughts, pictures, and words; photographs by Nicholas Kuskin. Owen, R.C. 1995 32p il (Meet the author) $14.95 (1-3)   **92**

1. Authors, American 2. Women authors
ISBN 1-878450-41-7   LC 95-1290

In this book "Kuskin discusses poetry and prose, writing and illustration. Her account is studded with memories, anecdotes, poems, and thoughts of family." Booklist

Lafayette, Marie Joseph Paul Yves Roch Gilbert du Motier, marquis de, 1757-1834

Fritz, Jean. Why not, Lafayette? illustrated by Ronald Himler. Putnam 1999 87p il $16.99 (5 and up)   **92**

1. United States—History—1775-1783, Revolution
ISBN 0-399-23411-X   LC 98-31417

Traces the life of the French nobleman who fought for democracy in revolutions in both the United States and France

This biography is "chock-full of quotes, anecdotes, and wry humor." Booklist

Includes bibliographical references

Lange, Dorothea, 1895-1965

Partridge, Elizabeth. Restless spirit: the life and work of Dorothea Lange. Viking 1998 122p il $21.99 (6 and up)   **92**

1. Women photographers
ISBN 0-670-87888-X   LC 98-9807

A biography of Dorothea Lange, whose photographs of migrant workers, Japanese American internees, and rural poverty helped bring about important social reforms

"Generously placed throughout this accessibly written biography are the photographic images that make Lange a pre-eminent artist of the century. The book is elegantly designed and the photographic reproductions are excellent." Bull Cent Child Books

Lawrence, Jacob, 1917-2000

Duggleby, John. Story painter: the life of Jacob Lawrence. Chronicle Bks. 1998 55p il $16.95 (4 and up)   **92**

1. African American artists
ISBN 0-8118-2082-3   LC 98-4513

A biography of the African American artist who grew up in the midst of the Harlem Renaissance and became one of the most renowned painters of the life of his people

"Lawrence's expressionistic, stark paintings, in excellent full-page color reproduction . . . nicely complement Duggleby's measured account of a materially poor but culturally rich childhood and Lawrence's subsequent struggles and successes." Publ Wkly

Includes bibliographical references

Leathers, Blanche

Gilliland, Judith Heide. Steamboat!: the story of Captain Blanche Leathers; pictures by Holly Meade. DK Pub. 2000 unp il $16.95 (2-4)   **92**

1. Steamboats
ISBN 0-7894-2585-8   LC 99-14811

Describes how Blanche Douglas Leathers studied the Mississippi River and passed the test to become a steamboat captain in 1894

"Exuberantly colored cut-paper art effectively realizes the three central characters of the story: Blanche, the river, and the romantic steamboat itself." Horn Book Guide

Lee, Robert E. (Robert Edward), 1807-1870

Archer, Jules. A house divided: the lives of Ulysses S. Grant and Robert E. Lee. See entry under Grant, Ulysses S. (Ulysses Simpson), 1822-1885

Leonardo, da Vinci, 1452-1519

Stanley, Diane. Leonardo da Vinci. Morrow Junior Bks. 1996 unp il $16.95; lib bdg $15.93; pa $6.95 (4 and up)   **92**

1. Artists, Italian
ISBN 0-688-10437-1; 0-688-10438-X (lib bdg); 0-688-16155-3 (pa)   LC 95-35227

"Stanley begins with a brief introduction to the Italian Renaissance and then looks at the life of the artist. The text pages feature a series of sketches from Leonardo's notebooks. These vivid drawings, chosen to reflect ideas and events in the story, juxtapose well with the large illustrations created with colored pencil, gouache, and watercolors on the facing pages. . . . The craftsmanship that makes this biography so solid in concept, appealing in design, and accessible in presentation extends to the scholarship behind it, as glimpsed in the appended postscript and bibliographies." Booklist

Lester, Helen

Lester, Helen. Author; a true story. Houghton Mifflin 1997 32p il $11 (k-3)   **92**

1. Women authors
ISBN 0-395-82744-2   LC 96-9645

An "autobiographical look at the evolution of a writer describes Lester's experiences—including her earliest three-year-old scribbles and the acceptance of her first manuscript (on the seventh try). Illustrated with Lester's own rather childlike illustrations, this lighthearted but realistic (and helpful) guide for the writer has lots of fresh tips for young authors-in-the-making." Horn Book Guide

Lincoln, Abraham, 1809-1865

Adler, David A. A picture book of Abraham Lincoln; illustrated by John & Alexandra Wallner. Holiday House 1989 unp il lib bdg $16.95; pa $6.95 (1-3)   **92**

1. Presidents—United States
ISBN 0-8234-0731-4 (lib bdg); 0-8234-0801-9 (pa)   LC 88-16393

Follows the life of the popular president, from his childhood on the frontier to his assassination after the

Lincoln, Abraham, 1809-1865—*Continued*
end of the Civil War

"While the author does include details that make the narratives more specific or realistic, he avoids fictionalizing. The Wallners' attractive line-and-watercolor illustrations evoke the past with the narrative quality of American naive painting and a certain gentle charm all their own." Booklist

Freedman, Russell. Lincoln: a photobiography. Clarion Bks. 1987 150p il $16.95; pa $7.95 (4 and up)   **92**
1. Presidents—United States
ISBN 0-89919-380-3; 0-395-51848-2 (pa)
LC 86-33379
Awarded the Newbery Medal, 1988

The author "begins by contrasting the Lincoln of legend to the Lincoln of fact. His childhood, self-education, early business ventures, and entry into politics comprise the first half of the book, with the rest of the text covering his presidency and assassination." SLJ

This is "a balanced work, elegantly designed and enhanced by dozens of period photographs and drawings, some familiar, some refreshingly unfamiliar." Publ Wkly
Includes bibliographical references

Harness, Cheryl. Abe Lincoln goes to Washington, 1837-1865; written and illustrated by Cheryl Harness. National Geographic Soc. 1997 unp il maps $18 (2-4)   **92**
1. Presidents—United States
ISBN 0-7922-3736-6   LC 96-9587
Companion volume to Young Abe Lincoln: the frontier days, 1809-1837 (1996)

Portrays Lincoln's life as a lawyer in Springfield, a devoted husband and father, and president during the Civil War years

"The text gallops through years of history, with sudden stops for surprisingly vivid little scenes. . . . Filled with color and action, Harness' paintings and maps dominate the pages and provide a wealth of historical detail as well as a humanizing view of the Lincolns." Booklist
Includes bibliographical references

Lincoln, in his own words; edited by Milton Meltzer; illustrated by Stephen Alcorn. Harcourt Brace & Co. 1993 226p il $22.95 (6 and up)
92
1. United States—History—1861-1865, Civil War
2. Presidents—United States
ISBN 0-15-245437-3   LC 92-17431
Combines background commentary with quotes from Lincoln's letters, speeches, and public papers to provide a personal view of his life, thoughts, and actions

"Meltzer gives Lincoln's words rich historical context by framing them with the facts of his life. Alcorn's powerful black-and-white and color linoleum block prints have impact and majesty." Booklist
Includes bibliographical references

Lincoln, Mary Todd, 1818-1882
Santow, Dan. Mary Todd Lincoln, 1818-1882. Children's Press 1999 111p il (Encyclopedia of first ladies) $33 (4 and up)   **92**
1. Presidents' spouses—United States
ISBN 0-516-20481-5   LC 98-45254

A biography of the wife of the sixteenth president of the United States, discussing her upbringing, marriage, and the tragedies that marred her life
Includes bibliographical references

Lindbergh, Charles, 1902-1974
Burleigh, Robert. Flight: the journey of Charles Lindbergh; illustrated by Mike Wimmer; introduction by Jean Fritz. Philomel Bks. 1991 unp il $16.99; pa $5.99 (2-4)   **92**
1. Aeronautics—Flights 2. Air pilots
ISBN 0-399-22272-3; 0-698-11425-6 (pa)
LC 90-35401
Describes how Charles Lindbergh achieved the remarkable feat of flying nonstop and solo from New York to Paris in 1927

"Using Charles Lindbergh's autobiography, *The Spirit of St. Louis*, as the basis for his text, Burleigh vividly creates that first solo flight in words, while Wimmer fashions exhilarating pictures that are, above all else, emotional. . . . This artistic emotion . . . works terrifically with the terseness of the near-poetic text." Booklist

Lowry, Lois
Lowry, Lois. Looking back; a book of memories. Houghton Mifflin 1998 181p il $16 (5 and up)   **92**
1. Authors, American 2. Women authors
ISBN 0-395-89543-X   LC 98-11376
Also available in paperback from Delacorte Press
"A Walter Lorraine book"

Using family photographs and quotes from her books, the author provides glimpses into her life

"A compelling and inspirational portrait of the author emerges from these vivid snapshots of life's joyful, sad and surprising moments." Publ Wkly

Madison, James, 1751-1836
Fritz, Jean. The great little Madison. Putnam 1989 159p il $15.95; pa $5.99 (5 and up)   **92**
1. Presidents—United States
ISBN 0-399-21768-1; 0-698-11621-6 (pa)
LC 88-31584
"Small, soft-spoken, and by nature diffident, James Madison found it difficult to speak in the midst of controversy, but his zeal and his convictions in the struggle between Republicans and Federalists gave him confidence, and his successes brought him to the presidency. Fritz has given a vivid picture of the man and an equally vivid picture of the problems—especially the internal dissension—that faced the leaders of the new nation. . . . Notes by the author and a bibliography are appended." Bull Cent Child Books

Mahy, Margaret
Mahy, Margaret. My mysterious world; photographs by David Alexander. Owen, R.C. 1995 32p il (Meet the author) $14.95 (1-3)   **92**
1. Women authors
ISBN 1-878450-58-1   LC 95-1291

Mahy, Margaret—*Continued*

"Mahy introduces her New Zealand home 'in the shell of an old volcano' and takes readers along as she writes, plants trees, plays with her dog, answers children's letters, and reads aloud to a school class." Booklist

"Mahy's story is unique because of setting (rural New Zealand), and because of the high quality of the accompanying photographs showing the author at work and play." SLJ

Malcolm X, 1925-1965

Myers, Walter Dean. Malcolm X; a fire burning brightly; illustrated by Leonard Jenkins. HarperCollins Pubs. 2000 unp il $15.95 (3-6)
                                                        92

1. African Americans—Biography
ISBN 0-06-027707-6   LC 99-21527

This biography of the civil rights activist "combines quotes from interviews and speeches." Bull Cent Child Books

"Myers's spare and eloquent narrative makes the complexities of Malcolm X's story accessible without compromising its integrity. The book has appeal for reluctant teen readers as well as younger readers. The sophisticated paintings blend realism with abstraction to heighten the underlying emotional drama of scenes." Horn Book Guide

Mandela, Nelson

Cooper, Floyd. Mandela; from the life of the South African statesman; written and illustrated by Floyd Cooper. Philomel Bks. 1996 unp il $15.95; pa $6.99 (2-4)   **92**

1. South Africa—Race relations 2. South Africa—Politics and government
ISBN 0-399-22942-6; 0-698-11816-2 (pa)
                                      LC 95-19639

In this biography "the author focuses more closely on Mandela's boyhood and schooling than on his adulthood as an anti-apartheid activist or his ascension to the presidency of South Africa." Publ Wkly

"Cooper's oil paintings are infused with golden light. Elegant composition and subtle shifts in perspective add emotional value to the carefully focused account." SLJ

Includes bibliographical references

Marshall, Thurgood

Adler, David A. A picture book of Thurgood Marshall; illustrated by Robert Casilla. Holiday House 1997 unp il $16.95; pa $6.95 (1-3)   **92**

1. United States. Supreme Court 2. African Americans—Biography 3. Judges
ISBN 0-8234-1308-X; 0-823-41506-6 (pa)
                                      LC 96-37248

Follows the life of the first African-American to serve as a judge on the United States Supreme Court

"Adler presents the high points of Marshall's life with enough detail to humanize the man. . . . Sensitive line-and-watercolor illustrations on every page add warmth to the story as they define people and settings." Booklist

Matzeliger, Jan, 1852-1889

Mitchell, Barbara. Shoes for everyone: a story about Jan Matzeliger; illustrations by Hetty Mitchell. Carolrhoda Bks. 1986 63p il (Carolrhoda creative minds book) lib bdg $21.27; pa $5.95 (3-5)   **92**

1. Shoe industry 2. African American inventors
ISBN 0-87614-290-0 (lib bdg); 0-87614-473-3 (pa)
                                      LC 86-4157

A biography of the half-Dutch half-black Surinamese man who, despite the hardships and prejudice he found in his new Massachusetts home, invented a shoe-lasting machine that revolutionized the shoe industry in the late nineteenth century

This is "a compelling story of human endeavor. A clear text blessedly allows the extraordinary individual in focus, Jan Matzeliger, . . . to emerge without undue exclamatory adulation." Bull Cent Child Books

Mays, Osceola, 1909-

Mays, Osceola. Osceola; memories of a sharecropper's daughter; collected and edited by Alan Govenar; illustrated by Shane W. Evans. Hyperion Bks. for Children 2000 63p il $15.99 (3-6)   **92**

1. African American women
ISBN 0-7868-2357-7   LC 98-40411

"Jump at the Sun"

A sharecropper's daughter describes her childhood in Texas in the early years of the twentieth century

"Shane W. Evan's strong paintings of Mays and her daily life suggest both folk art and subversive modern art with their flat, broad strokes and slightly skewed perspectives. This is a valuable, deeply affecting addition to the history of this period, and it will give young readers insight into the roots of contemporary racism." Booklist

McCarty, Oseola

Coleman, Evelyn. The riches of Oseola McCarty; illustrated by Daniel Minter. Whitman, A. 1998 48p il $14.95 (3-5)   **92**

1. African American women
ISBN 0-8075-6961-5   LC 98-11570

A brief biography of Oseola McCarty, a hard-working washer woman who, without a formal education herself, donated a portion of her life savings to the University of Southern Mississippi to endow a scholarship fund for needy students

"Coleman conducted interviews with McCarty, her friends, and family, and this original research shows in the solid text. . . . Daniel Minter's wonderful woodcuts enliven the text and add depth to the story." Booklist

Includes bibliographical references

McPhail, David M.

McPhail, David M. In flight with David McPhail; a creative autobiography; written and illustrated by David McPhail. Heinemann (Portsmouth) 1996 41p il (Creative sparks) pa $15.95 (2-4)   **92**

1. Authors, American 2. Illustrators
ISBN 0-435-08132-2   LC 95-40132

McPhail, David M.—*Continued*

In this autobiography "McPhail explains his need to write in some place other than home, how he and his editors negotiate ideas, and the steps involved in illustrating a book. A page from his drawing book, a dummy from *The Magical Adventures of Moony B. Finch* and thumbnail sketches show children, his thought processes and preparation for a book. Many original black-line, watercolor pictures of his familiar bears and pigs decorate the pages as well." SLJ

Michelangelo Buonarroti, 1475-1564

Stanley, Diane. Michelangelo. HarperCollins Pubs. 2000 unp il $15.95 (4 and up)   **92**
1. Artists, Italian
ISBN 0-688-15085-3

A biography of the Renaissance sculptor, painter, architect, and poet, well known for his work on the Sistine Chapel in Rome's St. Peter's Cathedral

This is "as readable as it is useful. . . . Integrating Michelangelo's art with Stanley's watercolor, gouache, and colored-pencil figures and settings has the desired effect: readers will be dazzled with the master's ability, while at the same time pulled into his daily life and struggles." SLJ

Includes bibliographical references

Morgan, Ann Haven, 1882-1966

Ross, Michael Elsohn. Pond watching with Ann Morgan; illustrations by Wendy Smith. Carolrhoda Bks. 2000 48p il $19.93 (4 and up)   **92**
1. Women scientists
ISBN 1-57505-385-3   LC 99-24953

Describes the life and work of Ann Haven Morgan, who studied, taught, and wrote about the animals of ponds and streams and the importance of an ecological approach to conservation. Includes related activities

"A unique combination of biography and natural history. . . . The photographs and full-color illustrations amplify the text." SLJ

Includes glossary and bibliographical references

Moses, Grandma, 1860-1961

Oneal, Zibby. Grandma Moses: painter of rural America; illustrated by Donna Ruff; paintings by Grandma Moses. Viking Kestrel 1986 58p il (Women of our time) hardcover o.p. paperback available $4.99 (4 and up)   **92**
1. Artists—United States 2. Women artists
ISBN 0-14-032220-5 (pa)   LC 86-4071

A biography focusing on the early years of Grandma Moses, who was known for her paintings of rural America

"Though short, this biographical sketch brims with the energy of both the woman and the artist. . . . Oneal does an exemplary job of interpreting the artist's work, giving a semblance of the style and flavor in a brisk, evocative narrative. Recommended not only as a biography of a woman who succeeded in her craft but also as an inspirational source for fledgling artists." Booklist

Mozart, Wolfgang Amadeus, 1756-1791

Isadora, Rachel. Young Mozart. Viking 1997 unp il $15.99; pa $5.99 (2-4)   **92**
1. Composers
ISBN 0-670-87120-6; 0-14-056478-0 (pa)
          LC 96-5948

This "introduction to Mozart's life concentrates on his childhood but also touches on his brief adult life, his successes, and his flaws." Horn Book Guide

Isadora "demonstrates both a simplicity of focus and an artist's eye for detail, selecting scenes and elements in Mozart's life of most interest to children. . . . Serene watercolors provide an almost impressionistic backdrop to the unfolding events. . . . They serve to give readers a strongly rooted sense of place." Publ Wkly

Obata, Chiura, 1888-1975

Ross, Michael Elsohn. Nature art with Chiura Obata; illustrations by Wendy Smith. Carolrhoda Bks. 2000 48p il (Naturalist's apprentice) $19.93 (4 and up)   **92**
1. Artists 2. Japanese Americans
ISBN 1-57505-378-0   LC 98-49073

Describes the life and work of nature artist and Japanese American Chiura Obata. Includes tips on how readers can make their own nature art

"This well-written, historically illuminating biography will inspire appreciation of the beauty and wonder in nature, and teachers will appreciate the art exercises that are included." Booklist

Includes glossary and bibliographical references

O'Keeffe, Georgia, 1887-1986

Turner, Robyn Montana. Georgia O'Keeffe. Little, Brown 1991 32p il (Portraits of women artists for children) hardcover o.p. paperback available $9.95 (4-6)   **92**
1. Artists—United States 2. Women artists
ISBN 0-316-85654-1 (pa)   LC 90-19352

A biography of a prominent American artist renowned for her images of gigantic flowers, cityscapes, and distinctive desert scenes

This is "a rich, colorful biography. The reproductions chosen to illustrate her life are excellent. . . . Throughout, the succinct, clear prose stresses O'Keeffe's art, her search for ways to express her feelings, her love for nature, and her total subjection of all else to the study and the demands of a creative life." SLJ

Venezia, Mike. Georgia O'Keeffe; written and illustrated by Mike Venezia. Children's Press 1993 31p il (Getting to know the world's greatest artists) lib bdg $22.50; pa $6.95 (k-3)   **92**
1. Artists—United States 2. Women artists
ISBN 0-516-02297-0 (lib bdg); 0-516-42297-9 (pa)
          LC 93-13004

Briefly examines the life and work of the twentieth-century American artist known for her paintings of flowers and presents examples of her art

Winter, Jeanette. My name is Georgia; a portrait. Harcourt Brace & Co. 1998 unp il $16 (k-3)   **92**
1. Artists—United States 2. Women artists
ISBN 0-15-201649-X   LC 97-7087

O'Keeffe, Georgia, 1887-1986—_Continued_

Presents, in brief text and illustrations, the life of the painter who drew much of her inspiration from nature

"Winter mirrors the artist's stark imagery and strong personality in spare, poetic text and folk art—inspired illustrations." Publ Wkly

O'Malley, Grace, 1530?-1603?

McCully, Emily Arnold. The pirate queen; written and illustrated by Emily Arnold McCully. Putnam 1995 unp il $16.95; pa $6.99 (k-3)   **92**
    1. Pirates 2. Ireland—History
    ISBN 0-399-22657-5; 0-698-11629-1 (pa)
                           LC 94-5389

This "book introduces a colorful figure in Irish history. Born in 1530, Grania O'Malley took to the sea as a child, learning her father's trade of seafaring (and piracy) and saving his life in a battle with English buccaneers. She later married, had children, led her own ships, and built her own kingdom in Clew Bay. . . . Rich with color and the effects of light on seascapes, landscapes, and people, the artwork makes the most of the story's dramatic content." Booklist

Owens, Jesse, 1913-1980

Adler, David A. A picture book of Jesse Owens; [by] David Adler; illustrated by Robert Casilla. Holiday House 1992 unp il lib bdg $16.95; pa $6.95 (1-3)   **92**
    1. African American athletes 2. Track athletics—Biography
    ISBN 0-8234-0966-X (lib bdg); 0-8234-1066-8 (pa)
                          LC 91-44735

A simple biography of the noted black track star who competed in the 1936 Berlin Olympics

Paige, Satchel, 1906-1982

Cline-Ransome, Lesa. Satchel Paige; paintings by James E. Ransome. Simon & Schuster Bks. for Young Readers 2000 unp il $16 (2-4)   **92**
    1. Baseball—Biography 2. African American athletes
    ISBN 0-689-81151-9   LC 97-13790

Examines the life of the legendary baseball player, who was the first African-American to pitch in a Major League World Series

"Cline-Ransome plays up the mythic elements of the Paige story in her rollicking narrative, while Ransome's paintings jump off the page with bright colors and startling contrasts." Booklist

    Includes bibliographical references

Parks, Rosa, 1913-

Adler, David A. A picture book of Rosa Parks; illustrated by Robert Casilla. Holiday House 1993 unp il lib bdg $16.95; pa $6.95 (1-3)   **92**
    1. African American women 2. African Americans—Civil rights
    ISBN 0-8234-1041-2 (lib bdg); 0-8234-1177-X (pa)
                          LC 92-41826

A biography of the Alabama black woman whose refusal to give up her seat on a bus helped establish the civil rights movement

This features "simple narrative text and the dramatic color illustrations." Booklist

Greenfield, Eloise. Rosa Parks; illustrated by Gil Ashby. HarperCollins Pubs. 1995 41p il lib bdg $14.89; pa $4.25 (2-4)   **92**
    1. African American women 2. African Americans—Civil rights
    ISBN 0-06-027110-8 (lib bdg); 0-06-442025-6 (pa)
                          LC 95-35497

A newly illustrated edition of the title first published 1973

A biography of the black woman whose acts of civil disobedience led to the 1956 Supreme Court order to desegregate buses in Montgomery, Alabama

Parks, Rosa. I am Rosa Parks; by Rosa Parks with Jim Haskins; pictures by Wil Clay. Dial Bks. for Young Readers 1997 48p il $13.99; lib bdg $13.89 (1-3)   **92**
    1. African American women 2. African Americans—Civil rights
    ISBN 0-8037-1206-5; 0-8037-1207-3 (lib bdg)
                          LC 96-896

"Dial easy-to-read"

The black woman whose acts of civil disobedience led to the 1956 Supreme Court order to desegregate buses in Montgomery, Alabama, explains what she did and why

"The famous civil rights activist has simplified her YA autobiography, _Rosa Parks: My Story_, and made it accessible to beginning readers. . . . The style is clear and direct. . . . The design is spacious, with big type, and Clay's paintings, some of them based on famous photographs, capture the segregation scene and the fight to end it." Booklist

Parks, Rosa. Rosa Parks: my story; by Rosa Parks with Jim Haskins. Dial Bks. 1992 192p il $17.99; pa $5.99 (5 and up)   **92**
    1. African American women 2. African Americans—Civil rights
    ISBN 0-8037-0673-1; 0-14-130120-7 (pa)
                          LC 89-1124

Rosa Parks describes her early life and experiences with race discrimination, and her participation in the Montgomery bus boycott and the civil rights movement

"A remarkable story, a record of quiet bravery and modesty, a document of social significance, a taut drama told with candor." Bull Cent Child Books

Patrick, Saint, 373?-463?

De Paola, Tomie. Patrick: patron saint of Ireland. Holiday House 1992 unp il lib bdg $16.95; pa $6.95 (k-3)   **92**
    1. Christian saints
    ISBN 0-8234-0924-4; 0-8234-1077-3 (pa)
                          LC 91-19417

Relates the life and legends of Patrick, the patron saint of Ireland

"The combination of book design, text, and illustration is suitably reverent but never saccharine; the whole is a well-executed treatment of an appealing subject." Horn Book

Tompert, Ann. Saint Patrick; illustrated by Michael Garland. Boyds Mills Press 1998 unp il $15.95 (k-3)   **92**
    1. Christian saints
    ISBN 1-56397-659-5   LC 97-72774

Patrick, Saint, 373?-463?—*Continued*

A picture book biography of the patron saint of Ireland

"Tompert concentrates on facts rather than legend for her text. . . . Garland's art-work—a full painting facing every gilt-edged page of text—does a good job with detail and texture; there is also a folk-art feel to the pictures." Booklist

Paulsen, Gary

Paulsen, Gary. My life in dog years; with drawings by Ruth Wright Paulsen. Delacorte Press 1998 137p il $15.95; pa $4.95 (4 and up)   92
1. Authors, American 2. Dogs
ISBN 0-385-32570-3; 0-440-41471-7 (pa)
LC 97-40254
Also available Thorndike Press large print edition
The author describes some of the dogs that have had special places in his life, including his first dog, Snowball, in the Philippines; Dirk, who protected him from bullies; and Cookie, who saved his life
"Paulsen differentiates his canine friends beautifully, as only a keen observer and lover of dogs can. At the same time, he presents an intimate glimpse of himself, a lonely child of alcoholic parents, who drew strength and solace from his four-legged companions and a love of the great outdoors. Poignant but never saccharine, honest, and open." Booklist

Peale, Charles Willson, 1741-1827

Wilson, Janet. The ingenious Mr. Peale; painter, patriot, and man of science; illustrated with paintings by Charles Willson Peale. Atheneum Bks. for Young Readers 1996 122p il $16 (4 and up)   92
1. Artists—United States
ISBN 0-689-31884-7   LC 95-30818
Narrates the life of the early American portrait painter who established the first public picture gallery in America and who pursued numerous other interests including natural history
"Quotations from Peale's diary and letters offer a sense of the man's personality. Reproductions of his paintings and sketches appear throughout the book. This readable biography offers an intriguing portrait of Peale as well as a fresh perspective on a significant period in American history." Booklist
Includes bibliographical references

Peet, Bill

Peet, Bill. Bill Peet: an autobiography. Houghton Mifflin 1989 190p il $20; pa $12 (4 and up)   92
1. Walt Disney Productions 2. Authors, American 3. Illustrators
ISBN 0-395-50932-7; 0-395-68982-1 (pa)
LC 88-37067
A Caldecott Medal honor book, 1990
This memoir "describes the life of the well-known children's book author who worked as an illustrator for Walt Disney from the making of 'Dumbo' until 'Mary Poppins.'" N Y Times Book Rev

"Every page of this oversized book is illustrated with Peet's unmistakable black-and-white drawings of himself and the people, places, and events described in the text. Familiar characters from his books and movies appear often." SLJ

Penn, William, 1644-1718

Kroll, Steven. William Penn; founder of Pennsylvania; illustrated by Ronald Himler. Holiday House 2000 unp il $16.95 (3-5)   92
1. Society of Friends 2. Pennsylvania—History
ISBN 0-8234-1439-6   LC 98-18932
A biography of William Penn, founder of the Quaker colony of Pennsylvania, who struggled throughout his life for the freedom to practice his religion
"The watercolor, pencil, and gouache paintings light up the book with their mix of dramatic scenes and sensitive portraits. . . . This biographical picture book will be a useful and certainly a handsome addition to library collections." Booklist

Peter I, the Great, Emperor of Russia, 1672-1725

Stanley, Diane. Peter the Great. Morrow Junior Bks. 1999 32p il $16 (4 and up)   92
1. Russia—Kings and rulers
ISBN 0-688-16708-X   LC 98-45250
A reissue of the title first published 1986 by Four Winds Press
A biography of the tsar who began the transformation of Russia into a modern state in the late seventeenth-early eighteenth centuries
The author's "material is presented with a modicum of oversimplification and a plethora of details that are sure to fascinate children. But what really makes this biography shine are its breathtaking illustrations. The meticulously researched, vivid scenes of Russian life during Peter's reign—courts, countryside, architecture, costumes—are beautifully rendered." Publ Wkly

Pick-Goslar, Hannah

Gold, Alison Leslie. Memories of Anne Frank. See entry under Frank, Anne, 1929-1945

Pickett, Bill, ca. 1860-1932

Pinkney, Andrea Davis. Bill Pickett, rodeo ridin' cowboy; written by Andrea D. Pinkney; illustrated by Brian Pinkney. Harcourt Brace & Co. 1996 unp il $16; pa $6 (k-3)   92
1. Cowhands 2. African Americans—Biography 3. Rodeos
ISBN 0-15-200100-X; 0-15-202103-5 (pa)
LC 95-35920
"Gulliver books"
Describes the life and accomplishments of the son of a former slave whose unusual bulldogging style made him a rodeo star
"The story is told with verve, relish, and just enough of a cowboy twang, with Pinkney giving an excellent overview of the history of rodeos and black cowboys in a closing note. Husband Brian Pinkney's pictures, in his typical scratchboard technique, are well suited to the story, their lines and colors swirling with movement and excitement on the deep black surface." Booklist
Includes bibliographical references

Pinkerton, Allan, 1819-1884

Wormser, Richard. Pinkerton: America's first private eye. Walker & Co. 1990 119p il $19.95; lib bdg $19.85 (5 and up)   **92**

1. Detectives
ISBN 0-8027-6964-0; 0-8027-6965-9 (lib bdg)

LC 90-12362

Examines the life of the detective who founded his own agency and introduced a system to help track criminals down and tie them to crimes

"An intriguing subject, lively prose, and in-depth analysis combine to make this a first-rate biography. . . . Wormser never tries to paper over the contradictions or erase Pinkerton's warts. He makes abundant anecdotal use of Pinkerton's detective cases, and the result is fresh and thought provoking, engrossing despite a high ratio of text to illustration." Booklist

Includes bibliographical references

Pocahontas, d. 1617

Fritz, Jean. The double life of Pocahontas; with illustrations by Ed Young. Putnam 1983 96p il $14.99; pa $3.99 (4 and up)   **92**

1. Powhatan Indians 2. Jamestown (Va.)—History
ISBN 0-399-21016-4; 0-14-032257-4 (pa)

LC 83-9662

"Pocahontas, the daughter of the seventeenth century Indian chief Powhatan, . . . saved the life of Captain John Smith and later married John Rolfe. In tracing the girl's life, the author has explored the history of the Jamestown colony from 1607 to 1622 and has given [an] . . . account of the often unhappy relationship between the colonists and the Indians." Horn Book

Includes bibliographical references

Polacco, Patricia

Polacco, Patricia. Firetalking; photographs by Lawrence Migdale. Owen, R.C. 1994 32p il (Meet the author) $14.95 (1-3)   **92**

1. Women authors 2. Authors, American
ISBN 1-878450-55-7   LC 93-48162

"Polacco explains how childhood evenings of 'firetalking' with her Russian and Irish grandparents formed the basis of many of her stories. The black-and-white and full-color photographs add to the intimacy of the [text]." SLJ

Potter, Beatrix, 1866-1943

Johnson, Jane. My dear Noel: the story of a letter from Beatrix Potter. Dial Bks. for Young Readers 1999 unp il $15.99; lib bdg $15.89 (k-3)   **92**

1. Authors, English 2. Women authors 3. Women artists
ISBN 0-8037-2050-5; 0-8037-2051-3 (lib bdg)

LC 96-11074

"When young Noel Moore becomes sick while his friend Miss Potter is away on holiday, she writes him an illustrated letter—the story that will eventually become *The Tale of Peter Rabbit*. In this book based on actual events, text and illustrations remain true to the known facts, using watercolor with pen outlines to depict subtly colored but lively scenes reminiscent of the period." Horn Book Guide

Ramsey, Alice Huyler, d. 1983

Brown, Don. Alice Ramsey's grand adventure; written and illustrated by Don Brown. Houghton Mifflin 1997 32p il $16; pa $5.95 (k-3)   **92**

1. Automobile travel 2. United States—Description
ISBN 0-395-70127-9; 0-618-07316-7 (pa)

LC 96-31783

Describes the difficulties faced by the first woman to make a cross-country journey from New York to San Francisco in an automobile in 1909

"Brown tells the tale in dramatic fashion, choosing entertaining details with a sure hand. His ink-and-watercolor sketches depict an intrepid-looking figure in heavy duster and goggles, steering a ramshackle Maxwell through a succession of rough, lonely landscapes." SLJ

Reiss, Johanna

Reiss, Johanna. The upstairs room. Crowell 1972 196p $15.95; pa $5.95 (4 and up)   **92**

1. Jews—Netherlands 2. Holocaust, 1933-1945—Personal narratives
ISBN 0-690-85127-8; 0-06-440370-X (pa)

Also available Spanish language edition

A Newbery Medal honor book, 1973

"In a vital, moving account the author recalls her experiences as a Jewish child hiding from the Germans occupying her native Holland during World War II. . . . Ten-year-old Annie and her twenty-year-old sister Sini, . . . are taken in by a Dutch farmer, his wife, and mother who hide the girls in an upstairs room of the farm house. Written from the perspective of a child the story affords a child's-eye-view of the war." Booklist

Followed by The journey back (1976)

Revere, Paul, 1735-1818

Fritz, Jean. And then what happened, Paul Revere? pictures by Margot Tomes. Coward, McCann & Geoghegan; distributed by Putnam Pub. Group 1973 45p il $15.99; pa $5.99 (2-4)   **92**

1. United States—History—1775-1783, Revolution
ISBN 0-399-23337-7; 0-698-11351-9 (pa)

This "description of Paul Revere's ride to Lexington is funny, fast-paced, and historically accurate; it is given added interest by the establishment of Revere's character: busy, bustling, versatile, and patriotic, a man who loved people and excitement. The account of his ride is preceded by a description of his life and the political situation in Boston, and it concludes with Revere's adventures after reaching Lexington." Bull Cent Child Books

Ripken, Cal, Jr.

Herman, Gail. Cal Ripken, Jr.; play ball! by Cal Ripken, Jr. and Mike Bryan; adapted by Gail Herman; illustrated by Stan Silver. Dial Bks. for Young Readers 1999 48p il $13.99; pa $3.99 (1-3)   **92**

1. Baltimore Orioles (Baseball team) 2. Baseball—Biography
ISBN 0-8037-2415-2; 0-14-130184-8 (pa)

LC 98-26366

"Dial easy-to-read"

Adaptation of The only way I know, by Cal Ripken, Jr. and Mike Bryan (1997)

Ripken, Cal, Jr.—_Continued_

A simple biography of the highly honored player for the Baltimore Orioles, who in 1995 broke the record for playing the most games in a row

This "is sure to be a hit with young baseball fans, but its appeal will not be limited to them. . . . The text is nicely balanced with portrayals of both slumps and streaks, anecdotes and statistics. The combination of first-person narration with full-color photographs and realistic paintings . . . will pull kids into the life and thoughts of this hardworking player." SLJ

Rivera, Diego, 1886-1957

Winter, Jonah. Diego; [illustrated] by Jeanette Winter; text by Jonah Winter; translated from the English by Amy Prince. Knopf 1991 unp il hardcover o.p. paperback available $6.99 (k-3)
92
1. Artists, Mexican 2. Bilingual books—English-Spanish
ISBN 0-679-85617-X (pa)   LC 90-25923
This book "in both Spanish and English, chronicles the life of Mexican muralist Diego Rivera. . . . Jonah Winter's crisp text and Jeanette Winter's elaborately bordered, dynamic illustrations successfully convey the spirit of the man and his work." Publ Wkly

Robinson, Jackie, 1919-1972

Adler, David A. A picture book of Jackie Robinson; illustrated by Robert Casilla. Holiday House 1994 unp il $16.95; pa $6.95 (1-3)   92
1. Baseball—Biography 2. African American athletes
ISBN 0-8234-1122-2; 0-8234-1304-7 (pa)
LC 93-27224
"A brief look at the life of baseball great Jackie Robinson. The subject's childhood, sporting accomplishments, and later endeavors are touched upon, as are the bigotry and prejudice he faced as the first African American to play in the major leagues. . . . Casilla's full-and double-page watercolors provide attractive backgrounds for the text. A sound introduction to a significant figure." SLJ

Dingle, Derek T. First in the field: baseball hero Jackie Robinson. Hyperion Bks. for Children 1998 48p il $16.95 (3-6)   92
1. Baseball—Biography 2. African American athletes
ISBN 0-7868-0348-7   LC 97-41333
A biography which discusses the discrimination faced by Jackie Robinson, the baseball legend who became the first African American to play Major League baseball for the Brooklyn Dodgers

"The narrative is written in a clear, matter-of-fact style. The archival black-and-white photographs are well chosen and of excellent quality." SLJ
Includes bibliographical references

Golenbock, Peter. Teammates; written by Peter Golenbock; designed and illustrated by Paul Bacon. Harcourt Brace Jovanovich 1990 unp il $16; pa $7 (1-4)   92
1. Reese, Pee Wee, 1919-1999 2. Brooklyn Dodgers (Baseball team) 3. Baseball—Biography 4. African American athletes
ISBN 0-15-200603-6; 0-15-284286-1 (pa)
LC 89-38166

"Gulliver books"

Describes the racial prejudice experienced by Jackie Robinson when he joined the Brooklyn Dodgers and became the first black player in Major League baseball and depicts the acceptance and support he received from his white teammate Pee Wee Reese

"Golenbock's bold and lucid style distills this difficult issue, and brings a dramatic tale vividly to life. Bacon's spare, nostalgic watercolors, in addition to providing fond glimpses of baseball lore, present a haunting portrait of one man's isolation. Historic photographs of the major characters add interest and a touch of stark reality to an unusual story, beautifully rendered." Publ Wkly

Rockwell, Norman, 1894-1978

Gherman, Beverly. Norman Rockwell; storyteller with a brush. Atheneum Bks. for Young Readers 2000 57p il $19.95 (4 and up)   92
1. Artists—United States
ISBN 0-689-82001-1   LC 98-36546
Describes the life and work of the popular American artist who depicted both traditional and contemporary subjects, including children, family scenes, astronauts, and the poor

"The format of the biography is appealing and attractive. The pages are replete with color reproductions of Rockwell's paintings as well as photographs of the man and his family. The text is well researched and authentic; the writing style is free-flowing and the words capture the naturalness of Rockwell's paintings." SLJ
Includes bibliographical references

Röntgen, Wilhelm Conrad, 1845-1923

Gherman, Beverly. The mysterious rays of Dr. Röntgen; illustrated by Stephen Marchesi. Atheneum Pubs. 1994 24p il lib bdg $14.95 (2-4)
92
1. Scientists 2. X-rays
ISBN 0-689-31839-1   LC 92-38966
Describes the work of Wilhelm Röntgen, the German physicist who won the first Nobel Prize in Physics in 1901 for his discovery of X rays

This book "combines the excitement of scientific discovery with an accessible explanation of how the rays work. . . . The handsome period color oil illustrations on every page help to personalize the drama." Booklist
Includes bibliographical references

Roosevelt, Eleanor, 1884-1962

Adler, David A. A picture book of Eleanor Roosevelt; illustrated by Robert Casilla. Holiday House 1991 unp il lib bdg $16.95; pa $6.95 (1-3)
92
1. Presidents' spouses—United States
ISBN 0-8234-0856-6 (lib bdg); 0-8234-1157-5 (pa)
LC 90-39212
A brief account of the life and accomplishments of Eleanor Roosevelt

"A crisply written biography enhanced by realistic watercolors." SLJ

Roosevelt, Eleanor, 1884-1962—_Continued_
Cooney, Barbara. Eleanor. Viking 1996 unp il $15.99; pa $6.99 (k-3)   **92**
   1. Presidents' spouses—United States
   ISBN 0-670-86159-6; 0-14-055583-8 (pa)
                    LC 96-7723
"Beginning the story with Eleanor Roosevelt's mother's disappointment at her birth, the author emphasizes the girl's lonely and often fearful childhood. . . . The book ends with Eleanor's public role still to come. A brief afterword provides information about her worldwide influence in her later life." SLJ
"There are many biographies of Eleanor Roosevelt but this one is special. Not only does it boast Cooney's artwork, but it also gets to the heart of a young girl, which in many ways is as interesting as Roosevelt's later, well-known accomplishments." Booklist

Freedman, Russell. Eleanor Roosevelt; a life of discovery. Clarion Bks. 1993 198p il $17.95; pa $10.95 (5 and up)   **92**
   1. Presidents' spouses—United States
   ISBN 0-89919-862-7; 0-395-84520-3 (pa)
                  LC 92-25024
A Newbery Medal honor book, 1994
"Readers are made privy to the telling details of a full life through numerous quotes from Roosevelt and her wide inner circle in this frank, well-documented portrait of the 'First Lady of the World.' A superlative biography." SLJ
Includes bibliographical references

Roosevelt, Franklin D. (Franklin Delano), 1882-1945
Freedman, Russell. Franklin Delano Roosevelt. Clarion Bks. 1990 200p il $18; pa $8.95 (5 and up)   **92**
   1. Presidents—United States
   ISBN 0-89919-379-X; 0-395-62978-0 (pa)
                  LC 89-34986
Photographs and text trace the life of Franklin Delano Roosevelt
"The carefully researched, highly readable text and extremely effective coordination of black-and-white photographs chronicle Roosevelt's priviledged youth, his early influences, and his maturation. . . . Even students with little or no background in American history will find this an intriguing and inspirational human portrait." SLJ
Includes bibliographical references

Roosevelt, Theodore, 1858-1919
Fritz, Jean. Bully for you, Teddy Roosevelt! illustrations by Mike Wimmer. Putnam 1991 127p il $15.95; pa $5.99 (5 and up)   **92**
   1. Presidents—United States
   ISBN 0-399-21769-X; 0-698-11609-7 (pa)
                  LC 90-8142
Follows the life of the twenty-sixth president, discussing his conservation work, hunting expeditions, family life, and political career
"Jean Fritz gives a rounded picture of her subject and deftly blends the story of a person and a picture of an era." Bull Cent Child Books
Includes bibliographical references

Ross, Betsy, 1752-1836
Wallner, Alexandra. Betsy Ross; written and illustrated by Alexandra Wallner. Holiday House 1994 unp il $16.95; pa $6.95 (k-2)   **92**
   1. United States—History—1775-1783, Revolution
   2. Flags—United States
   ISBN 0-8234-1071-4; 0-8234-1355-1 (pa)
                  LC 93-3559
An introduction to the life of the Philadelphia seamstress credited with sewing the first American flag
"More inviting than most young biographies, this is a good book for taking Ms. Ross from a cameo role to a starring part and using her to explain early American urban life." Bull Cent Child Books

Rudolph, Wilma, 1940-1994
Krull, Kathleen. Wilma unlimited: how Wilma Rudolph became the world's fastest woman; illustrated by David Diaz. Harcourt Brace & Co. 1996 unp il $16; pa $6 (2-4)   **92**
   1. African American athletes 2. Women athletes
   3. Track athletics—Biography
   ISBN 0-15-201267-2; 0-15-202098-5 (pa)
                  LC 95-32105
A biography of the African-American woman who overcame crippling polio as a child to become the first woman to win three gold medals in track in a single Olympics
"Brightly colored paintings contrast with sepia-toned photographic backgrounds, creating juxtapositions that extend both the text and the pictures in the foreground. Krull's understated conversational style is perfectly suited to Rudolph's remarkable and inspiring story." Horn Book Guide

Russell, Charles M. (Charles Marion), 1864-1926
Winter, Jeanette. Cowboy Charlie: the story of Charles M. Russell. Harcourt Brace & Co. 1995 unp il $15 (k-3)   **92**
   1. Artists—United States 2. West (U.S.) in art
   ISBN 0-15-200857-8   LC 94-48480
This biography tells the "story of Charles Marion Russell, a renowned artist of the Old West, who as a child growing up in St. Louis dreamed of a life in the West and becoming a cowboy. . . . [Winter's] muted acrylic palette is dominated by mauve, rust, purple, and varied greens. Among the many scenes of wildlife, cattle, and cowboys is a fold-out page in the center of the book showing the majestic western terrain. . . . The simple telling works well as an adventure story, a brief view of frontier life, and an introduction to the artist." Horn Book

Rustin, Bayard, 1910-1987
Haskins, James. Bayard Rustin: behind the scenes of the civil rights movement. Hyperion Bks. for Children 1997 121p il $14.95; lib bdg $15.49 (5 and up)   **92**
   1. African Americans—Biography 2. African Americans—Civil rights
   ISBN 0-7868-0168-9; 0-7868-2140-X (lib bdg)
                  LC 96-1256

Rustin, Bayard, 1910-1987—*Continued*

A biography of Bayard Rustin, a skillful organizer behind the scenes of the American civil rights movement whose ideas strongly influenced Martin Luther King, Jr

"Haskins not only gives enough personal information to flesh out his subject . . . but also presents each historical event with nuance, fairness, and clarity. Obviously an excellent resource for reports, this is also a moving, inspirational story." Booklist

Includes bibliographical references

Rylant, Cynthia

Rylant, Cynthia. Best wishes; photographs by Carlo Ontal. Owen, R.C. 1992 32p il map (Meet the author) $14.95 (1-3)   **92**

1. Authors, American 2. Women authors
ISBN 1-87845-020-4   LC 92-7796

Children's author Cynthia Rylant describes her life and writing process and how they are interwoven

"The color photos . . . have a candid snapshot quality that contributes to the friendly informality of the text." Bull Cent Child Books

Sacagawea, b. 1786

Adler, David A. A picture book of Sacagawea; illustrated by Dan Brown. Holiday House 2000 unp il $16.95; pa $6.95 (1-3)   **92**

1. Lewis and Clark Expedition (1804-1806) (1804-1806) 2. Shoshoni Indians
ISBN 0-8234-1485-X; 0-8234-1665-8 (pa)
                    LC 99-37135

A biography of the Shoshone woman who joined the Lewis and Clark Expedition

"The narrative is clear, direct, and never fictionalized. . . . The soft watercolor art is more successful in depicting landscapes than human figures." Booklist

Includes bibliographical references

St. George, Judith. Sacagawea. Putnam 1997 115p maps $16.95 (4-6)   **92**

1. Lewis and Clark Expedition (1804-1806) 2. Shoshoni Indians
ISBN 0-399-23161-7   LC 96-49311

Tells the story of the Shoshoni Indian girl who served as interpreter, peacemaker, and guide for the Lewis and Clark Expedition to the Northwest in 1805-1806

"In a well-written and well-researched account, St. George humanizes her subject. . . . Adventure lovers will find much to like in the book." Booklist

Includes bibliographical references

Sandburg, Carl, 1878-1967

Meltzer, Milton. Carl Sandburg; a biography. 21st Cent. Bks. (Brookfield) 1999 144p il lib bdg $31.40 (5 and up)   **92**

1. Poets, American
ISBN 0-7613-1364-8   LC 98-46373

A biography of the poet who became known for his ability to speak to the common people, by shaping out of the plain English of ordinary Americans the voice of their vast experience

"In this attractively designed biography, extremely short chapters and photographs highlight the most interesting elements of Sandburg's life." Booklist

Includes bibliographical references

Sasaki, Sadako, 1943-1955

Coerr, Eleanor. Sadako; illustrated by Ed Young. Putnam 1993 unp il $17.95; pa $6.99 (1-4)   **92**

1. Leukemia 2. Atomic bomb—Physiological effect 3. Hiroshima (Japan)—Bombardment, 1945
ISBN 0-399-21771-1; 0-698-11588-0 (pa)
                    LC 92-41483

"This is the same story as the author's *Sadako and the Thousand Paper Cranes*, told through an entirely new text. In this abbreviated version, the beautiful, limpid prose and crisp dialogue further telescope Sadako's fight with leukemia. . . . Young's pastels vividly capture all the moods of the narrative, place, and characters. . . . A masterful collaboration." SLJ

Coerr, Eleanor. Sadako and the thousand paper cranes; paintings by Ronald Himler. Putnam 1977 64p il $16.99; pa $4.99 (3-6)   **92**

1. Leukemia 2. Atomic bomb—Physiological effect 3. Hiroshima (Japan)—Bombardment, 1945
ISBN 0-399-20520-9; 0-698-11802-2 (pa)
                    LC 76-9872

Also available Spanish language edition and Audiobook version

"A story about a young girl of Hiroshima who died from leukemia ten years after the dropping of the atom bomb. Her dreams of being an outstanding runner are dimmed when she learns she has the fatal disease. But her spunk and bravery, symbolized in her efforts to have faith in the story of the golden crane, are beautifully portrayed by the author." Babbling Bookworm

Schumann, Clara, 1819-1896

Reich, Susanna. Clara Schumann; piano virtuoso. Clarion Bks. 1999 118p il $18 (5 and up)   **92**

1. Pianists
ISBN 0-395-89119-1   LC 98-24510

Describes the life of the German pianist and composer who made her professional debut at age nine and who devoted her life to music and to her family

"This thoroughly researched book draws on primary sources, both Clara's own diaries and her voluminous correspondence with her husband. . . . Reich's lucid, quietly passionate biography is liberally illustrated with photographs and reproductions." Horn Book Guide

Sequoyah, 1770?-1843

Klausner, Janet. Sequoyah's gift; a portrait of the Cherokee leader; with an afterword by Duane H. King. HarperCollins Pubs. 1993 111p il lib bdg $15.89 (4 and up)   **92**

1. Cherokee Indians
ISBN 0-06-021236-5   LC 92-24939

"Sequoyah is best remembered for his remarkable feat of creating a Cherokee syllabary that allowed his people to read and write their own language. Klausner's detailed account includes discussion of Sequoyah's role during the Trail of Tears journey, the forced removal in 1838 of the Cherokee nation from Georgia to what became Oklahoma. . . . This is a solid work with many applications for study." Booklist

Includes bibliographical references

Seuss, Dr.

Weidt, Maryann N. Oh, the places he went; a story about Dr. Seuss—Theodore Seuss Geisel; illustrations by Kerry Maguire. Carolrhoda Bks. 1994 64p il (Carolrhoda creative minds book) lib bdg $21.27; pa $5.95 (3-5)   **92**

1. Authors, American 2. Illustrators
ISBN 0-87614-823-2 (lib bdg); 0-87614-627-2 (pa)
LC 93-41370

This is a biography of the popular author and illustrator of children's picture books

"A lively, straightforward overview of Theodor Geisel's life and work. . . . Maguire's full-page pencil sketches capture the subject's appearance and personality." SLJ

Includes bibliographical references

Shackleton, Sir Ernest Henry, 1874-1922

Kostyal, K. M. Trial by ice: a photobiography of Sir Ernest Shackleton. National Geographic Soc. 1999 64p il map $17.95 (4 and up)   **92**

1. Explorers 2. Antarctica—Exploration
ISBN 0-7922-7393-1   LC 99-20980

Traces the adventurous life of the South Pole explorer whose ship, the Endurance, was frozen in ice and crushed, leaving the captain and crew to fight for survival

"The stunning, archival black-and-white photographs are this book's strength." SLJ

Includes bibliographical references

Shakespeare, William, 1564-1616

Stanley, Diane. Bard of Avon: the story of William Shakespeare; by Diane Stanley and Peter Vennema; illustrated by Diane Stanley. Morrow Junior Bks. 1992 unp il $16.95; pa $5.95 (4 and up)   **92**

1. Dramatists
ISBN 0-688-09108-3; 0-688-16294-0 (pa)
LC 90-46564

A brief biography of the world's most famous playwright, using only historically correct information

"A remarkably rounded picture of Shakespeare's life and the period in which he lived is presented . . . together with a thoughtful attempt to relate circumstances in his personal life to the content of his plays. . . . The text is splendidly supported by the illustrations, which are stylized, yet recognizable, and present a clear view of life in the late sixteenth century. A discerning, knowledgeable biography, rising far above the ordinary." Horn Book

Includes bibliographical references

Simmons, Philip

Lyons, Mary E. Catching the fire: Philip Simmons, blacksmith; with photographs by Mannie Garcia. Houghton Mifflin 1997 47p il $16 (4 and up)   **92**

1. African American artists
ISBN 0-395-72033-8   LC 96-38643

Tells the story of this African American artist, the great-grandson of slaves, who has achieved fame and admiration for his ornamental wrought-iron creations

"The narrative, based on Simmons' memories and words, involves readers through its lively presentation of an intriguing subject. . . . Photographs appear on every spread, with black-and-white pictures of Simmons' early days and beautifully lit and composed color shots of the man today." Booklist

Includes bibliographical references

Simon, Seymour, 1931-

Simon, Seymour. From paper airplanes to outer space; photographs by Nina Crews. Owen, R.C. 2000 32p il (Meet the author) $14.95 (1-3)   **92**

1. Authors, American
ISBN 1-57274-374-3   LC 99-45224

The children's book author describes his life, his daily activities, and his creative process, showing how all are intertwined

Sitting Bull, Dakota Chief, 1831-1890

Bruchac, Joseph. A boy called Slow: the true story of Sitting Bull; illustrated by Rocco Baviera. Philomel Bks. 1994 unp il $15.95; pa $6.99 (1-3)   **92**

1. Dakota Indians
ISBN 0-399-22692-3; 0-698-11616-X (pa)
LC 93-21233

The author "recounts the early years of the young Lakota boy who grows from an unprepossessing child named 'Slow,' to a youth whose careful and deliberate actions bring honor to the name, to a young warrior whose courage in defeating the Crow earns him his father's vision name Tatan'ka Iyota'ke—Sitting Bull." Bull Cent Child Books

"Baviera's darkly atmospheric, dramatic paintings frequently feature startling bits of bright color, as in the setting sun or a piece of sky visible through the smoke hole of a family's tipi. The pictures evoke a sense of timelessness and distance, possessing an almost mythic quality that befits this glimpse into history." Horn Book

Spinelli, Jerry, 1941-

Spinelli, Jerry. Knots in my yo-yo string; the autobiography of a kid. Knopf 1998 148p il lib bdg $16.99; pa $10.95 (4 and up)   **92**

1. Authors, American
ISBN 0-679-98791-6 (lib bdg); 0-679-88791-1 (pa)
LC 97-30827

Also available Thorndike Press large print edition

This Italian-American Newbery Medalist presents a humorous account of his childhood and youth in Norristown, Pennsylvania

"There is an 'everyboy' universality to Spinelli's experiences, but his keen powers of observation and recall turn the story into a richly rewarding personal history." Horn Book Guide

Stanton, Elizabeth Cady, 1815-1902

Fritz, Jean. You want women to vote, Lizzie Stanton? illustrated by DyAnne DiSalvo-Ryan. Putnam 1995 88p il $16.99; pa $5.99 (2-4)   **92**

1. Feminism 2. Women—Suffrage
ISBN 0-399-22786-5; 0-698-11764-6 (pa)
LC 94-30018

Stanton, Elizabeth Cady, 1815-1902—*Continued*
This is a biography of the 19th century feminist and advocate of women's suffrage
"With remarkable clarity, sensitivity, and momentum, Fritz has captured—but never imprisoned [Stanton's] spirit in an accessible, fascinating portrait." Horn Book
Includes bibliographical references

Stetson, John Batterson, 1830-1906
Carlson, Laurie M. Boss of the plains; the hat that won the West; by Laurie Carlson; pictures by Holly Meade. DK Pub. 1998 unp il $16.95; pa $5.95 (k-3)   **92**
1. Hats
ISBN 0-7894-2479-7; 0-7894-2657-9 (pa)
LC 97-30995
"A Melanie Kroupa book"
The story of John Stetson and how he came to create the most popular hat west of the Mississippi
"Carlson's storytelling prose sets the scene and tells the tale concisely and enticingly, and Meade's mixed-media illustrations have an appropriately rough-and-ready feel." Horn Book Guide
Includes bibliographical references

Stevenson, Robert Louis, 1850-1894
Gherman, Beverly. Robert Louis Stevenson, teller of tales. Atheneum Bks. for Young Readers 1996 136p il $16 (5 and up)   **92**
1. Authors, Scottish
ISBN 0-689-31985-1   LC 95-52448
This biography of the Scottish author of Treasure Island and The strange case of Dr. Jekyll and Mr. Hyde recounts "his childhood, marriage, and . . . travels. There are occasional black-and-white photos, unobtrusive chapter notes at the back, and a bibliography. A wonderful extra bonus is the brief stanza of Stevenson's singing poetry at the head of each chapter." Booklist

Murphy, Jim. Across America on an emigrant train. Clarion Bks. 1993 150p il $17 (5 and up)
92
1. Authors, Scottish 2. Railroads—History 3. United States—Description
ISBN 0-395-63390-7   LC 92-38650
"Murphy presents a forthright and thoroughly engrossing history of the transcontinental railway, with entries from Robert Louis Stevenson's 1879 journal as he rode cross country. It's also an inviting introduction to Stevenson, with a romance in the bargain." SLJ
Includes bibliographical references

Stowe, Harriet Beecher, 1811-1896
Fritz, Jean. Harriet Beecher Stowe and the Beecher preachers. Putnam 1994 144p il $15.95; pa $5.99 (5 and up)   **92**
1. Beecher family 2. Women authors 3. Authors, American 4. Abolitionists
ISBN 0-399-22666-4; 0-698-11660-7 (pa)
LC 93-6408
This is a biography of the abolitionist author of "Uncle Tom's Cabin," with an emphasis on the influence of

her preacher father and her family on her life and work
"Written with vivacity and insight, this readable and engrossing biography is an important contribution to women's history as well as to the history of American letters." Horn Book
Includes bibliographical references

Tallchief, Maria
Tallchief, Maria. Tallchief; America's prima ballerina; by Maria Tallchief with Rosemary Wells; illustrations by Gary Kelley. Viking 1999 unp il $15.99 (3-5)   **92**
1. Dancers 2. Native American women
ISBN 0-670-88756-0   LC 98-35783
Ballerina Maria Tallchief describes her childhood on an Osage reservation, the development of her love of dance, and her rise to success in that field
"Through eloquent words, readers are immediately drawn into the first-person narrative. . . . As beautiful as the text is, so too are Kelley's pictures. The large illustrations, several covering double-page spreads, are rendered in soft pastels." SLJ

Tillage, Leon, 1936-
Tillage, Leon. Leon's story; [by] Leon Walter Tillage; collage art by Susan L. Roth. Farrar, Straus & Giroux 1997 107p il $14; pa $4.95 (4 and up)   **92**
1. African Americans 2. North Carolina—Race relations
ISBN 0-374-34379-9; 0-374-44330-0 (pa)
LC 96-43544
The son of a North Carolina sharecropper recalls the hard times faced by his family and other African Americans in the first half of the twentieth century and the changes that the civil rights movement helped bring about
The author's "voice is direct, the words are simple. There is no rhetoric, no commentary, no bitterness. . . . This quiet drama will move readers of all ages . . . and may encourage them to record their own family stories." Booklist

Truth, Sojourner, d. 1883
Adler, David A. A picture book of Sojourner Truth; illustrated by Gershom Griffith. Holiday House 1994 unp il $16.95; pa $6.95 (1-3)   **92**
1. African American women 2. Abolitionists 3. Feminism
ISBN 0-8234-1072-2; 0-8234-1262-8 (pa)
LC 93-7478
An introduction to the life of the woman born into slavery who became a well-known abolitionist and crusader for the rights of African Americans in the United States
The author "portrays his subject in a realistic manner, discussing slavery and other issues in an easy-to-read style. The quotes, while undocumented, are simple enough for the target audience and help to place events in context. Excellent-quality watercolor illustrations capture the action and provide effective representations and details of the time period." SLJ

Truth, Sojourner, d. 1883—*Continued*

Ferris, Jeri. Walking the road to freedom: a story about Sojourner Truth; illustrations by Peter E. Hanson. Carolrhoda Bks. 1988 64p il (Carolrhoda creative minds book) lib bdg $21.27; pa $5.95 (3-5)   **92**

1. African American women 2. Feminism 3. Abolitionists

ISBN 0-87614-318-4 (lib bdg); 0-87614-505-5 (pa)

LC 87-18277

"Truth, born into slavery in New York in about 1797, survived several wrenching sales as a child. Securing her freedom, she determined to 'walk up and down the land, telling others about God's goodness.' She sang and spoke out against slavery and in support of women's rights throughout the Midwest, becoming well known and widely respected. . . . Hanson's [illustrations] are more impressionistic, with muted backgrounds." Booklist

McKissack, Patricia C. Sojourner Truth; a voice for freedom; [by] Patricia and Fredrick McKissack; illustrated by Michael Bryant. Enslow Pubs. 1992 32p il (Great African Americans) lib bdg $14.95 (1-3)   **92**

1. African American women 2. Feminism 3. Abolitionists

ISBN 0-89490-313-6   LC 92-6190

Also available in paperback from Scholastic

Describes the life of the anti-slavery and women's rights activist, from her beginnings in slavery to her tireless campaign for the rights and welfare of the freedmen

"Short sentences, large, well-spaced text, and a blend of black-and-white photographs and sketches. . . . [This] will give an overview of that great woman's achievements." SLJ

Includes glossary

Tubman, Harriet, 1815?-1913

Adler, David A. A picture book of Harriet Tubman; illustrated by Samuel Byrd. Holiday House 1992 unp il $16.95; pa $6.95 (1-3)   **92**

1. African American women 2. Underground railroad

ISBN 0-8234-0926-0; 0-8234-1065-X (pa)

LC 91-19628

Biography of the black woman who escaped from slavery to become famous as a conductor on the Underground Railroad

This book features "brief, easy-to-read text. . . . Byrd's appealing, colorful illustrations convey the quiet dignity of a brave heroine." Booklist

Ferris, Jeri. Go free or die: a story about Harriet Tubman; illustrations by Karen Ritz. Carolrhoda Bks. 1988 63p il (Carolrhoda creative minds book) $21.27; pa $5.95 (3-5)   **92**

1. African American women 2. Underground railroad

ISBN 0-87614-317-6; 0-87614-504-7 (pa)

LC 87-18279

This is "the story of Harriet Tubman, born a slave in Maryland in 1820. Fiercely determined to 'go free or die,' Tubman, aided by the Quakers, mastered the intricate maneuvering of the Underground Railroad, and from 1850 to 1861 made 19 trips leading more than 300 slaves to freedom, never losing one. Using a clear direct

style, Ferris does not dwell on the brutal injustices . . . but rather on [her] against-all-odds perseverance to fight for equal rights. Ritz' illustrations have a haunting antique-photo quality." Booklist

Tutankhamen, King of Egypt

Sabuda, Robert. Tutankhamen's gift; written and illustrated by Robert Sabuda. Atheneum Pubs. 1994 unp il $17; pa $6.99 (k-3)   **92**

1. Egypt—Antiquities

ISBN 0-689-31818-9; 0-689-81730-4 (pa)

LC 93-5401

"His tutor foresees that little Tutankhamen's 'gift for the gods' will someday be revealed. That day comes sooner than expected, when the young boy becomes pharaoh after his brother's death and rebuilds the beautiful temples created by his father and destroyed by his brother. Bold pictures outlined in black against a background of painted, handmade Egyptian papyrus illustrate the book, and an afterword provides historical details." Horn Book Guide

Twain, Mark, 1835-1910

Harness, Cheryl. Mark Twain and the queens of the Mississippi. Simon & Schuster Bks. for Young Readers 1998 unp il $16 (3-5)   **92**

1. Authors, American 2. Mississippi River 3. Steamboats

ISBN 0-689-81542-5   LC 97-40799

Focuses on this American author's connection with steamboats on the Mississippi River while also presenting a history of the craft

"Full of action and color, the watercolor-and-colored-pencil illustrations give readers many vivid images of the river, the people who traveled it, the events that marked Twain's times, and the man himself. . . . An unusually lively picture-book biography and an accessible, informative introduction to the life of Mark Twain." Booklist

Includes bibliographical references

Lasky, Kathryn. A brilliant streak: the making of Mark Twain; illustrated by Barry Moser. Harcourt Brace & Co. 1998 41p il $18 (4 and up)
                                 92

1. Authors, American

ISBN 0-15-252110-0   LC 95-18479

An illustrated biography of young Samuel Clemens, who grew up to be the writer known as Mark Twain

"An obvious delight in her subject makes Lasky's biography an appealing choice, and a similar enthusiasm invests Moser's illustrations." Horn Book Guide

Includes bibliographical references

Uchida, Yoshiko, 1921-1992

Uchida, Yoshiko. The invisible thread. Messner 1991 136p il (In my own words) o.p.; Beech Tree Bks. paperback available $4.95 (5 and up)   **92**

1. Authors, American 2. Japanese Americans 3. Women authors

ISBN 0-688-13703-2 (pa)   LC 91-12398

Children's author, Yoshiko Uchida, describes growing up in Berkeley, California, as a Nisei, second generation

Uchida, Yoshiko, 1921-1992—*Continued*
Japanese American, and her family's internment in a Nevada concentration camp during World War II
The author "writes with mastery of style and an implicit respect for her readers." Bull Cent Child Books
Includes bibliographical references

Valentine, Saint
Sabuda, Robert. Saint Valentine; retold and illustrated by Robert Sabuda. Atheneum Pubs. 1992 unp il $16.95; pa $5.99 (1-3) **92**
1. Christian saints
ISBN 0-689-31762-X; 0-689-82429-7 (pa)
LC 91-25012
Recounts an incident in the life of St. Valentine, a physician who lived some 200 years after Christ, in which he treated a small child for blindness
"The fluid, straightforward retelling of the legend is accompanied by evocative, mosaiclike illustrations created from colored cut paper. Varying sizes of illustrations, careful page placement, and effective use of white space create the impression of the large-scale period mosaics. A fine melding of text and art." SLJ

Villa, Pancho, 1878-1923
O'Brien, Steven. Pancho Villa. Chelsea House 1994 111p il (Hispanics of achievement) lib bdg $19.95; pa $9.95 (5 and up) **92**
1. Mexico—History
ISBN 0-7910-1257-3 (lib bdg); 0-7910-3114-4 (pa)
LC 93-37890
The author "handles the life and lifestyle of Villa, one of Mexico's controversial, legendary heroes, in a candid and unbiased manner. Illustrated with black-and-white photographs, the biography of this revolutionary is an enjoyable, readable, welcome addition." Horn Book Guide
Includes bibliographical references

Walker, C. J., Madame, 1867-1919
Lasky, Kathryn. Vision of beauty: the story of Sarah Breedlove Walker; illustrated by Nneka Bennett. Candlewick Press 2000 unp il $16.99 (3-5) **92**
1. African American businesspeople 2. African American women
ISBN 0-7636-0253-1 LC 99-19594
A biography of Sarah Breedlove Walker who, though born in poverty, pioneered in hair and beauty care products for black women, and became a great financial success
"Lasky's engaging account moves smoothly through events in Walker's life. . . . The illustrations . . . are attractive and rich in historical detail." Booklist

McKissack, Patricia C. Madam C.J. Walker; self-made millionaire; [by] Patricia and Fredrick McKissack; series consultant: Russell L. Adams; illustrations by Michael Bryant. Enslow Pubs. 1992 32p il (Great African Americans) $14.95 (1-3) **92**
1. African American businesspeople 2. African American women
ISBN 0-89490-311-X LC 92-6189

Describes the life of the black laundress who founded a cosmetics company and became the first female self-made millionaire in the United States

Washington, Booker T., 1856-1915
McKissack, Patricia C. Booker T. Washington; leader and educator; [by] Patricia and Fredrick McKissack; illustrated by Michael Bryant. Enslow Pubs. 1992 32p il (Great African Americans) lib bdg $14.95 (1-3) **92**
1. Tuskegee Institute 2. African American educators
ISBN 0-89490-314-4 LC 92-5356
A biography of the former slave who founded Tuskegee University and later became the most powerful African American leader at the turn of the century

Washington, George, 1732-1799
Harness, Cheryl. George Washington. National Geographic Soc. 2000 48p il $17.95 (3-5) **92**
1. Presidents—United States
ISBN 0-7922-7096-7 LC 99-29920
Presents the life of George Washington, focusing on the Revolutionary War years and his presidency
"Detailed paintings, full of action and rich with color, portray Washington as well as important moments in American history. . . . This heavily illustrated biography serves as a good introduction to Washington." Booklist
Includes bibliographical references

Washington, Mary Ball, 1708-1789
Fritz, Jean. George Washington's mother; illustrated by DyAnne DiSalvo-Ryan. Grosset & Dunlap 1992 48p il $7.99; pa $3.99 (1-3) **92**
1. Washington, George, 1732-1799 2. Presidents—United States—Mothers
ISBN 0-448-40385-4; 0-448-40384-6 (pa)
LC 91-34247
"All aboard reading"
Describes the life of the mother of our first president and her relationship with her children
"Fritz brings the excitement of history to newly independent readers. . . . Using factual data and funny incidents, the author humorously depicts Mary Ball Washington as a manipulative and stubborn worrywart. The numerous, half- and full-page, pencil-and-watercolor illustrations . . . complement the text and extend the humor." SLJ

Wells-Barnett, Ida B., 1862-1931
Fradin, Dennis B. Ida B. Wells; mother of the civil rights movement; [by] Dennis Brindell Fradin and Judith Bloom Fradin. Clarion Bks. 2000 178p il $18 (5 and up) **92**
1. African American women 2. African Americans—Civil rights
ISBN 0-395-89898-6 LC 99-37038
This "biography chronicles the life of teacher, writer, publisher and civil rights champion, Ida B. Wells." ALAN
"This stellar biography of one of history's most inspiring women offers an excellent overview of Wells's life and contributions. . . . Black-and-white photographs and reproductions enhance the clear, well-written text." SLJ
Includes bibliographical references

West, Benjamin, 1738-1820

Brenner, Barbara. The boy who loved to draw: Benjamin West; illustrated by Olivier Dunrea. Houghton Mifflin 1999 unp il $15 (k-3)   **92**

1. Artists—United States

ISBN 0-395-85080-0   LC 97-5183

Recounts the life story of the Pennsylvania artist who began drawing as a boy and eventually became well known on both sides of the Atlantic

"Naive in style and reminiscent of some colonial art, the illustrations present clear visual expressions of the activities and emotions related in the story. . . . A fascinating look at art in colonial times, and a likable portrait of the artist as a young boy." Booklist

Wild Boy of Aveyron, d. 1828

Gerstein, Mordicai. The wild boy; based on the true story of the Wild Boy of Aveyron. Foster Bks. 1998 39p il $16 (k-3)   **92**

1. Wild children

ISBN 0-374-38431-2   LC 97-37246

Relates the story of a boy who grew up wild in the forests of France and was captured in 1800, studied and cared for and named Victor, but who never learned to speak

"Gerstein's prose finds power in its simplicity and emotional resonance in its declarative understatement. . . . The narrative strength and energy of the illustrations expand the inherent drama of Victor's situation. Together, Gerstein's text and pictures work to create an unforgettable story." Booklist

Wilder, Laura Ingalls, 1867-1957

Anderson, William T. Pioneer girl: the story of Laura Ingalls Wilder; by William Anderson; illustrated by Dan Andreasen. HarperCollins Pubs. 1998 unp il $15.95; lib bdg $15.89; pa $5.35 (2-4)   **92**

1. Authors, American 2. Women authors 3. Frontier and pioneer life

ISBN 0-06-027243-0; 0-06-027244-9 (lib bdg); 0-06-446234-X (pa)   LC 96-31203

Recounts the life story of the author of the "Little House" books, from her childhood in Wisconsin to her old age at Rocky Ridge Farm

"Laura Ingalls Wilder's many fans will delight in this inviting biographical overview in a picture-book format, graced by Andreasen's dreamy landscapes, glowing prairie skies and warm character portraits." Publ Wkly

Wilder, Laura Ingalls. West from home; letters of Laura Ingalls Wilder to Almanzo Wilder, San Francisco, 1915; edited by Roger Lea MacBride; historical setting by Margot Patterson Doss. Harper & Row 1974 124p il $16.95; pa $5.95 (6 and up)   **92**

1. San Francisco (Calif.)—Description 2. Authors, American 3. Women authors

ISBN 0-06-024110-1; 0-06-440081-6 (pa)

LC 73-14342

This collection is "edited from letters sent to her beloved husband while Laura spent two months in late 1915 visiting their daughter and immersing herself in the sights of bustling San Francisco and the exciting Panama-Pacific Exposition. Wilder readers of all ages will lose themselves in this trip—the adults with nostalgia and wholesome pleasure, the youth with wonder and awe over the sights vividly described in her inimitable combination of homespun literary and journalistic styles." Child Book Rev Serv

Williams, Roger, 1604?-1683

Avi. Finding Providence: the story of Roger Williams; story by Avi; illustrations by James Watling. HarperCollins Pubs. 1997 46p il $14.95; lib bdg $15.89 (2-4)   **92**

1. United States—History—1600-1775, Colonial period 2. Rhode Island—History

ISBN 0-06-025179-4; 0-06-025294-4 (lib bdg)

LC 95-46360

"An I can read chapter book"

After being forced to leave the Massachusetts Bay Colony, Roger Williams travels south and, with the help of the Narragansett Indians, founds Providence, Rhode Island

"Plentiful dialogue speeds the action along, and even the philosophical issues are cogently presented for young readers in the form of Williams' interrogation at the trial. Watling's watercolors have a rough-hewn quality appropiate to the early colonies, and his grave figures are charged with tension." Bull Cent Child Books

Wood, Grant, 1892-1942

Duggleby, John. Artist in overalls: the life of Grant Wood. Chronicle Bks. 1996 56p il map $15.95 (4 and up)   **92**

1. Artists—United States

ISBN 0-8118-1242-1   LC 95-34070

Follows the life of the Iowa farm boy who struggled to realize his talents and who painted in Paris but returned home to focus on the land and people he knew best

"The text provides a good, basic introduction to Wood's work and his life as an artist. Throughout the book, reproductions (most in full color) of the paintings and black-and-white photographs of the artist add greatly to the book's usefulness and visual appeal." Booklist

Woodson, Carter Godwin, 1875-1950

Haskins, James. Carter G. Woodson; the man who put "Black" in American history; by Jim Haskins and Kathleen Benson; illustrated by Melanie Reim. Millbrook Press 2000 48p il $24 (4 and up)   **92**

1. African Americans—Biography

ISBN 0-7613-1264-1   LC 98-53912

A biography of the son of former slaves who received a Ph.D. in history from Harvard and devoted his life to bringing the achievements of his race to the world's attention

"Simple, accessible prose paints a dimensional portrait, aptly accompanied by abstract, evocative black-and-white artwork." Booklist

Includes bibliographical references

Wright, Orville, 1871-1948

Freedman, Russell. The Wright brothers: how they invented the airplane; with original photographs by Wilbur and Orville Wright. Holiday House 1991 129p il $19.95; pa $12.95 (5 and up) **92**

1. Wright, Wilbur, 1867-1912 2. Aeronautics—History

ISBN 0-8234-0875-2; 0-8234-1082-X (pa)

LC 90-48440

A Newbery Medal honor book, 1992

In this "combination of photography and text, Freedman reveals the frustrating, exciting, and ultimately successful journey of these two brothers from their bicycle shop in Dayton, Ohio, to their Kitty Hawk flights and beyond. . . . An essential purchase for younger YAs." Voice Youth Advocates

Includes bibliographical references

Wright, Wilbur, 1867-1912

Freedman, Russell. The Wright brothers: how they invented the airplane. See entry under Wright, Orville, 1871-1948

Yep, Laurence

Yep, Laurence. The lost garden. Messner 1991 117p il (In my own words) o.p.; HarperCollins Pubs. paperback available $4.95 (5 and up) **92**

1. Authors, American 2. Chinese Americans

ISBN 0-688-13701-6 (pa)   LC 90-40647

The author describes how he grew up as a Chinese American in San Francisco and how he came to use his writing to celebrate his family and his ethnic heritage

"The writing is warm, wry, and humorous. . . . *The Lost Garden* will be welcomed as a literary autobiography for children and, more, a thoughtful probing into what it means to be an American." SLJ

Zaharias, Babe Didrikson, 1911-1956

Freedman, Russell. Babe Didrikson Zaharias; the making of a champion. Clarion Bks. 1999 192p il $18 (5 and up) **92**

1. Women athletes

ISBN 0-395-63367-2   LC 98-50208

A biography of Babe Didrikson, who broke records in golf, track and field, and other sports, at a time when there were few opportunities for female athletes

"Freedman's measured yet lively style captures the spirit of the great athlete. . . . Plenty of black-and-white photos capture Babe's spirit and dashing good looks; the documentation . . . is impeccable." Horn Book

Includes bibliographical references

Zhang, Song Nan

Zhang, Song Nan. A little tiger in the Chinese night; an autobiography in art. Tundra Bks. 1993 48p il $19.95; pa $9.95 **92**

1. Artists, Chinese

ISBN 0-88776-320-0; 0-88776-356-1 (pa)

"Song Nan Zhang traces his life in China, describing an idyllic childhood after World War II; his youthful idealism during the 'Great Leap Forward,' which entailed years of hard work under harsh conditions; and the even more horrible Cultural Revolution." SLJ

"The writing is so vivid and the story so involving that it is hard to put down. Best of all, colorful, well-composed illustrations appear on nearly every spread, bringing Zhang's experiences more sharply into focus." Booklist

929 Genealogy, names, insignia

Taylor, Maureen, 1955-

Through the eyes of your ancestors. Houghton Mifflin 1999 86p il $16; pa $8.95 (4 and up) **929**

1. Genealogy

ISBN 0-395-86980-3; 0-395-86982-X (pa)

LC 98-8776

Discusses genealogy, the study of one's family, examining how such an interest develops, how to get started, how to use family stories and keepsakes, where to get help, and the positive effects of such study

"Motivated young researchers with adult help will find the book a good starting place." SLJ

Includes bibliographical references

929.9 Flags

Brandt, Sue R., 1916-

State flags; including the Commonwealth of Puerto Rico. Watts 1992 63p il lib bdg $25 (5 and up) **929.9**

1. Flags—United States

ISBN 0-531-20001-9   LC 92-8948

Describes the history, design, and significance of the fifty state flags

Includes bibliographical references

Crampton, W. G. (William G.)

Flag; written by William Crampton. Knopf 1989 63p il (Eyewitness books) $19.99; lib bdg $16.99 (4 and up) **929.9**

1. Flags

ISBN 0-394-82255-2; 0-394-92255-7 (lib bdg)

LC 88-27174

A photographic essay about flags from countries all over the world and such special flags as signal flags for ships and boats, flags for special festivals and sports, political flags and coats of arms. Also includes information about the meaning of shapes and colors on flags

Haban, Rita D.

How proudly they wave; flags of the fifty states. Lerner Publs. 1989 111p il lib bdg $23.95 (4 and up) **929.9**

1. Flags—United States

ISBN 0-8225-1799-X   LC 89-2302

Haban, Rita D.—*Continued*

"Haban presents full-color pictures of the 50 state flags. . . . Two-page descriptions explain who designed the flag, what the design means, and when each flag was officially adopted. . . . A glossary lists flag-related terms, and an accompanying diagram shows the parts of a flag. An enormously useful reference source for both school and public librarians." Booklist

930　History of ancient world to ca.499

Ancient civilizations. Grolier Educ. 2000 10v il maps $319 (5 and up)　　　　　　　**930**
1. Ancient civilization 2. Archeology—Encyclopedias
ISBN 0-7172-9471-4　　　　　　LC 99-28387

This encyclopedia incorporates "three types of alphabetical entries. The first describes in selective detail an ancient civilization or people. The second chronicles the discovery of noteworthy and unique archeological sites and examines the evidence that provides solid clues as to their former inhabitants. The third type of entry is a discussion of specific subjects such as medicine and surgery and their role in various cultures. . . . The profuse illustrations include clearly captioned color photos and drawings and lucid maps." SLJ
For a fuller review see: Booklist, Sept. 1, 2000

The **Visual** dictionary of ancient civilizations. Dorling Kindersley 1994 64p il map (Eyewitness visual dictionaries) $18.95 (4 and up)　　　　　　　**930**
1. Ancient civilization
ISBN 1-56458-701-0　　　　　　LC 94-8395

Labeled illustrations and text briefly describe ancient artifacts and civilizations of the world. Timelines are included

930.1　Archaeology

Deem, James M.

Bodies from the bog. Houghton Mifflin 1998 42p il $16 (4 and up)　　　　　　**930.1**
1. Mummies 2. Prehistoric peoples 3. Archeology
ISBN 0-395-85784-8　　　　　　LC 97-12010

Describes the discovery of bog bodies in northern Europe and the evidence which their remains reveal about themselves and the civilizations in which they lived

"The text is engaging and accessible, and the starkly dramatic photos are given dignity by the spacious and understated page design." Horn Book Guide

Early humans. Knopf 1989 63p il maps (Eyewitness books) (4 and up)　　　　**930.1**
1. Prehistoric peoples 2. Ancient civilization
LC 88-13431

Available DK Pub. edition $15.95; lib bdg $19.99 (ISBN 0-7894-5806-3; 0-7894-6559-0)

Text and photographs present a description of early humans: their origins; their tools and weapons; how they hunted and foraged for food; and the role of family life, money, religion, and magic

"The book is beautifully illustrated, with a paragraph of text at the beginning of each two-page section and an explanatory caption for each artifact pictured. The 25 sections range in topic from the toolmakers to the first artists to bronzeworking." Sci Books Films

Getz, David, 1957-

Frozen girl; illustrations by Peter McCarty. Holt & Co. 1998 72p il $14.95 (5 and up)　　　**930.1**
1. Archeology 2. Mummies 3. Peru—Antiquities 4. Incas
ISBN 0-8050-5153-8　　　　　　LC 97-40643

"A Redfeather book"

Discussses the discovery, history, and significance of an Incan mummy found frozen in the mountains of Peru
Includes bibliographical references

Frozen man; illustrated by Peter McCarty. Holt & Co. 1994 68p il maps $14.95; pa $7.95 (5 and up)　　　　　　　**930.1**
1. Archeology 2. Prehistoric peoples 3. Mummies
ISBN 0-8050-3261-4; 0-8050-4645-3 (pa)
LC 94-9109

"A Redfeather book"

"This is an account of the mummified stone-age corpse who was found in Austria in 1991. . . . Getz's generally well-organized information and smooth exposition makes the effort to understand the Iceman, as this book calls him, into an intriguing detective story. This could well stimulate the interest of kids who didn't think they liked science or archeology. Black-and-white drawings include useful maps and diagrams." Bull Cent Child Books
Includes glossary and bibliographical references

Goodman, Susan, 1952-

Stones, bones, and petroglyphs; digging into Southwest archaeology; by Susan E. Goodman; photographs by Michael J. Doolittle. Atheneum Bks. for Young Readers 1998 48p il (Ultimate field trip 2) $17 (4 and up)　　　　**930.1**
1. Pueblo Indians—Antiquities 2. Excavations (Archeology)
ISBN 0-689-81121-7　　　　　　LC 97-6501

"Modern eighth graders experience the long-ago habitations of the Pueblo people as they work side-by-side with archaeologists in this account of a week-long field trip to Crow Canyon Archaeological Center in Colorado and Mesa Verde National Park." Horn Book Guide

The author and illustrator "have combined clear, informative, color photographs with simply stated, easy-to-comprehend prose." SLJ
Includes glossary and bibliographical references

McIntosh, Jane

Archeology; written by Jane McIntosh. Knopf 1994 63p il (Eyewitness books) (4 and up) **930.1**
1. Archeology
LC 94-9378

Available DK Pub. edition $15.95; lib bdg $19.99 (ISBN 0-7894-5864-0; 0-7894-6605-8)

"A Dorling Kindersley book"

McIntosh, Jane—*Continued*

This volume "touches on aspects of archaeology in many locations around the world. Each double-page spread examines one or two concepts: preservation and decay, excavation, clues to the past, human remains, fakes and forgeries, etc. . . . Readers are not likely to use this book for research, but will want to make repeated short visits." SLJ

Patent, Dorothy Hinshaw

Secrets of the ice man. Benchmark Bks. (Tarrytown) 1999 72p il (Frozen in time) $27.07 (5 and up)   **930.1**
1. Archeology 2. Prehistoric peoples 3. Mummies
ISBN 0-7614-0782-0   LC 97-49512
Describes the examination of the Ice Man, his clothing and equipment, found in the Alps near the Austrian-Italian border in September 1991 and thought to be more than 4000 years old

This book is "well researched." Book Rep
Includes glossary and bibliographical references

Reinhard, Johan

Discovering the Inca Ice Maiden; my adventures on Ampato. National Geographic Soc. 1998 48p il $19.95 (5 and up)   **930.1**
1. Archeology 2. Mummies 3. Peru—Antiquities 4. Incas
ISBN 0-7922-7142-4   LC 97-31291
A first-person account of the 1995 discovery of the over 500-year-old Peruvian ice mummy on Mount Ampato and a description of the subsequent retrieval and scientific study

"Vibrant color photographs of the mummy and Incan artifacts found on the expedition illustrate the engrossing text." Horn Book Guide
Includes glossary

931   China to 420 A.D.

Cotterell, Arthur

Ancient China; written by Arthur Cotterell; photographed by Alan Hills & Geoff Brightling. Knopf 1994 63p il maps (Eyewitness books) (4 and up)   **931**
1. China—Civilization
                                       LC 94-9319
Available DK Pub. edition $15.95; lib bdg $19.99 (ISBN 0-7894-5866-7; 0-7894-6604-X)

"A Dorling Kindersley book"

"This volume touches upon such topics as Chinese history, the first emperor, inventions, health and medicine, waterways, food and drink, clothing, the Silk Road, and arts and crafts. . . . The book will . . . be popular for browsing." SLJ

Patent, Dorothy Hinshaw

The incredible story of China's buried warriors. Benchmark Bks. (Tarrytown) 2000 64p il maps (Frozen in time) $18.95 (5 and up)   **931**
1. Ch'in Shih-huang, Emperor of China, 259-210 B.C. 2. China—Antiquities
ISBN 0-7614-0783-9   LC 99-34971

Describes the archaeological find of thousands of life-sized terra cotta warrior statues discovered in China, and discusses the emperor who had them created and placed in his tomb

The "attractive magazine-type design will encourage browsing: full-page color illustrations, both archival and contemporary, appear opposite almost every page of detailed text." Booklist

Includes glossary and bibliographical references

933   Palestine to 70 A.D.

Waldman, Neil, 1947-

Masada; written and illustrated by Neil Waldman. Morrow Junior Bks. 1998 64p il maps $16 (4 and up)   **933**
1. Jews—History 2. Excavations (Archeology) 3. Masada Site (Israel)
ISBN 0-688-14481-0   LC 97-32912
Discusses the history of Masada, from the building of Herod's Temple through its use by Zealots as a refuge from the Romans to its rediscovery in the mid-20th century

"Dramatic illustrations and two large maps, all in charcoal shades of acrylic and India ink, show realistic scenes, many of them painted from photos, relief sculptures, and artifacts found during the excavation of Masada." SLJ

Includes glossary and bibliographical references

936   Europe north and west of Italian peninsula to ca. 499 A.D.

Martell, Hazel Mary

The Celts. Viking 1996 c1994 48p il maps (See through history) $19.99 (4 and up)   **936**
1. Celtic civilization 2. Celts
ISBN 0-670-86558-3   LC 95-61265
First published 1994 in the United Kingdom

This volume examines the customs and daily lives of the Celtic people in "see-through cutaways of a Celtic house, a stone tower, a Celtic Christian monastery, and the tombs of a noblewoman and a prince." Publisher's note

"Martell has assembled a fact-filled, visually attractive look at the history and customs of the Celtic people. . . . It fulfills its purpose of providing easily acquired, visual and textual material for reports." SLJ

Includes glossary

936.1   Scotland to 410 A.D.

Arnold, Caroline, 1944-

Stone Age farmers beside the sea; Scotland's prehistoric village of Skara Brae; photographs by Arthur P. Arnold. Clarion Bks. 1997 48p il map $15.95 (4 and up)   **936.1**
1. Scotland—Antiquities 2. Prehistoric peoples
ISBN 0-395-77601-5   LC 96-20021

Arnold, Caroline, 1944-—*Continued*

Describes the Stone Age settlement preserved in the sand dunes on one of Scotland's Orkney Islands, telling how it was discovered and what it reveals about life in prehistoric times

Arnold "carefully distinguishes between what is known and what is surmised about the people who lived at Skara Brae. . . . The photos' clear images, subtle colors, and pleasing compositions give the book its pervasive sense of beauty." Booklist

Includes glossary

937   Roman Empire

Caselli, Giovanni

In search of Pompeii; uncovering a buried Roman city; written and illustrated by Giovanni Caselli. Bedrick Bks. 1999 44p il (In search of) $18.95 (3-5)   937

1. Pompeii (Extinct city)
ISBN 0-87226-545-5   LC 99-21352

Describes the discovery and excavation of the ruins of the ancient city of Pompeii, buried by the eruption of Mount Vesuvius in 79 A.D., and what has been learned about life there

Corbishley, Mike

Ancient Rome; [by] Michael Corbishley. Facts on File 1989 96p il maps (Cultural atlas for young people) $19.95 (5 and up)   937

1. Rome—Antiquities 2. Rome—Civilization
ISBN 0-8160-1970-3   LC 88-31687
"An Equinox book"

This topical atlas "begins with a 'Table of Dates,' a chronology of the history, arts, and literature of [Roman] culture. The remainder of [the] book is made up of double-page spreads, each covering a different subject." Booklist

Includes glossary and bibliographical references

James, Simon, 1957-

Ancient Rome. Viking 1992 48p il map (See through history) $19.99 (4 and up)   937

1. Rome—Antiquities 2. Rome—Civilization
ISBN 0-670-84493-4   LC 91-68543

Describing the Roman Empire during the Augustan era, this book combines "fine illustrations, both photographs and drawings, with a clearly written text. . . . Clear acetate pages interspersed throughout [the book] . . . may be lifted to reveal the inner workings of the structures depicted. Even more useful is the fact that the captions are fully indexed with the rest of the text." SLJ

Includes glossary

Patent, Dorothy Hinshaw

Lost city of Pompeii. Benchmark Bks. (Tarrytown) 1999 64p il (Frozen in time) lib bdg $27.07 (5 and up)   937

1. Pompeii (Extinct city)
ISBN 0-7614-0785-5   LC 99-34980

Describes the destruction of Pompeii by the eruption of Mount Vesuvius in 79 A.D. and how its rediscovery nearly 1700 years later provided information about life in the Roman Empire

This combines "dramatic history with fascinating information. . . . Attractive magazine-type design will encourage browsing: full-page color illustrations, both archival and contemporary, appear opposite almost every page of detailed text." Booklist

Includes glossary and bibliographical references

Watkins, Richard Ross

Gladiator; by Richard Watkins. Houghton Mifflin 1997 80p il map $17; pa $7.95 (4 and up)   937

1. Gladiators 2. Rome—Social life and customs
ISBN 0-395-82656-X; 0-618-07032-X (pa)
          LC 96-21107

Describes the history of gladiators, including types of armor, use of animals, amphitheaters, and how the practice fit into Roman society for almost 700 years

"In a balanced treatment of a potentially sensational topic, Watkins provides colorfully written, detailed accounts of the fights as well as pithy discussions of what gladiators meant to the Romans and what they tell us about Roman society. . . . The solid gray-and-white drawings illustrate the text effectively." Booklist

Includes glossary and bibliographical references

938   Greece to 323 A.D.

Hart, Avery

Ancient Greece! 40 hands-on activities to experience this wondrous age; [by] Avery Hart & Paul Mantell; illustrations by Michael Kline. Williamson 1999 104p il pa $10.95 (4 and up)   938

1. Greece—Civilization 2. Handicraft
ISBN 1-885593-25-2   LC 98-35762
"A Kaleidoscope Kids book"

Introduces the places, people, historical events, myths, culture, and philosophy of ancient Greece. Includes forty hands-on activities, such as making an early Greek theater, building an Ionic temple, and pressing olives for oil

This is "a clever title that encourages learning and creativity." SLJ

Includes bibliographical references

Pearson, Anne

Ancient Greece; written by Anne Pearson. Knopf 1992 63p il (Eyewitness books) (4 and up)   938

1. Greece—Civilization
          LC 92-4713
Available DK Pub. edition $15.95; lib bdg $19.99 (ISBN 0-7894-5750-4; 0-7894-6586-0)
"A Dorling Kindersley book"

Describes the land, history, and civilization of ancient Greece

"One will enjoy this book just for its multitude of visual images. . . . This is a great pictorial presentation of the ancient Greeks and their civilization—their politics, games, dining, clothing, art, and science." Sci Books Films

940.1 Europe—Early history to 1453

Biesty, Stephen
Stephen Biesty's cross-sections: Castle; illustrated by Stephen Biesty; written by Richard Platt. Dorling Kindersley 1994 27p il $16.95 (4 and up) **940.1**
  1. Castles 2. Medieval civilization
  ISBN 1-56458-467-4   LC 93-30158
This "volume displays pictures of a cutaway medieval castle, revealing how the castle was constructed for protection and showing the way of life shared by those inside its walls." Horn Book Guide
"The duo's trademark humor is evident throughout. . . . Not only is the book guaranteed to attract browsers, but it will also make fun and fruitful work of report research." Booklist

Corbishley, Mike
The Middle Ages. Facts on File 1989 96p il maps (Cultural atlas for young people) $19.95 (5 and up) **940.1**
  1. Medieval civilization 2. Middle Ages
  ISBN 0-8160-1973-8   LC 88-31692
"An Equinox book"
Maps, charts, illustrations, and text explore the history and culture of the Middle Ages
"Corbishley gives fair and equal coverage to all areas of medieval Europe, including Russia and Scandinavia, which some books omit. The maps are excellent, precise, clear, and easy to read and understand, and the illustrations, particularly those of works of art, are wonderful." Includes bibliographical references

Gravett, Christopher
Knight; written by Christopher Gravett; photographed by Geoff Dann. Knopf 1993 63p il (Eyewitness books) (4 and up) **940.1**
  1. Knights and knighthood 2. Medieval civilization
    LC 92-1590
Available DK Pub. edition $15.95; lib bdg $19.99 (ISBN 0-7894-5874-8; 0-7894-6592-2)
"A Dorling Kindersley book"
Discusses the age of knighthood, covering such aspects as arms, armor, training, ceremonies, tournaments, the code of chivalry, and the Crusades
"The strength of the 'Eyewitness' title is, of course, the wonderful full-color photographs." SLJ

Hart, Avery
Knights & castles; 50 hands-on activities to experience the Middle Ages; [by] Avery Hart & Paul Mantell. Williamson 1998 96p il pa $10.95 (4 and up) **940.1**
  1. Medieval civilization 2. Middle Ages 3. Knights and knighthood 4. Handicraft
  ISBN 1-885593-17-1   LC 97-32863
"A Kaleidoscope Kids book"

Introduces the Middle Ages, including activities and crafts that are representative of medieval life, for example creating an hour glass, a catapult, a coat of arms, and a code of honor
"The text is written in a breezy tone and illustrated with a combination of line drawings and blue-or-purple-ink reproductions of medieval art and woodcuts." SLJ
Includes bibliographical references

940.2 Europe—1453-

Langley, Andrew
Renaissance. Knopf 1999 59p il (Eyewitness books) $19; lib bdg $20.99 (4 and up) **940.2**
  1. Renaissance
  ISBN 0-375-80136-7; 0-375-90136-1 (lib bdg)
    LC 98-49766
"A Dorling Kindersley book"
An overview of the philosophy, inventions, art, government, religion, and daily life of the Renaissance
"Langley has combined in-depth research with the arresting, trademark photographs of the series to showcase a complex period in European history." SLJ

Wood, Tim
The Renaissance. Viking 1993 48p il maps (See through history) $19.99 (4 and up) **940.2**
  1. Renaissance
  ISBN 0-670-85149-3   LC 93-60028
Drawings, photographs, and text describe 15th and 16th century European civilization. Four see-through acetate pages lift to reveal the inner structures of three buildings and Columbus' ship, the Santa Maria
Includes glossary

940.3 World War I, 1914-1918

Dolan, Edward F., 1924-
America in World War I. Millbrook Press 1996 96p il maps lib bdg $28.90 (5 and up) **940.3**
  1. World War, 1914-1918—United States
  ISBN 1-56294-522-X   LC 95-35487
Explains the roots of World War I and shows how the United States was drawn in despite strong sentiment for remaining uninvolved. Actions of U.S. troops "over there," new weapons such as the tank and airplane, the home front, and the peace that ended the war are covered
"The author's prose is taut and seemingly effortless, but he wisely never overwhelms or dazzles young readers with extraneous facts and figures. . . . Maps and black-and-white reproductions of period photographs and graphics with informative captions augment the volume's general attractiveness and usefulness." SLJ
Includes bibliographical references

Gay, Kathlyn
World War I; [by] Kathlyn Gay, Martin Gay. 21st Cent. Bks. (NY) 1995 64p il maps (Voices from the past) lib bdg $23.90 (5 and up) **940.3**
  1. World War, 1914-1918
  ISBN 0-8050-2848-X   LC 95-12300

Gay, Kathlyn—*Continued*
An illustrated look at America's role in World War I on the battlefield and on the home front. Includes excerpts from letters, diaries and newspaper accounts
Includes bibliographical references

940.53 World War II, 1939-1945

Abells, Chana Byers
The children we remember; photographs from the Archives of Yad Vashem, the Holocaust Martyrs' and Heroes' Remembrance Authority, Jerusalem, Israel. Greenwillow Bks. 1986 unp il $16 (3-6) **940.53**
    1. Holocaust, 1933-1945
    ISBN 0-688-06371-3   LC 85-24876
Text and photographs briefly describe the fate of Jewish children before, during, and after the Holocaust
"This is a book of few words, assuming some background knowledge of World War II and the Holocaust. And in this case, less is more, for the carefully selected photos dominate the unobtrusive statements describing scenes of children helping each other, children dying, children surviving. In acknowledging, along with the book jacket, that this is 'a story that must be told to all of today's children,' one also hopes there is an adult nearby to help share the shock of scenes like the one in which a soldier is shooting a mother and her baby." Bull Cent Child Books

Adler, David A., 1947-
Child of the Warsaw ghetto; illustrated by Karen Ritz. Holiday House 1995 unp il $15.95 (3-5) **940.53**
    1. Baum, Froim, 1936- 2. Holocaust, 1933-1945 3. Jews—Poland
    ISBN 0-8234-1160-5   LC 94-27779
This "is the story of life in the Warsaw ghetto as seen through the eyes of fourteen-year-old Froim Baum." J Youth Serv Libr
"Adler relates his subject's story in a direct, simple style. . . . It's an impressive tale of courage and survival. The effect of Adler's text is heightened by the large pastel drawings on each gray-toned page." SLJ

Hiding from the Nazis; illustrated by Karen Ritz. Holiday House 1997 unp il $15.95; pa $6.95 (2-4) **940.53**
    1. Baer, Lore, 1938- 2. Holocaust, 1933-1945 3. World War, 1939-1945—Jews 4. Jews—Netherlands
    ISBN 0-8234-1288-1; 0-8234-1666-6 (pa)
                                        LC 96-38451
The true story of Lore Baer who as a four-year-old Jewish child was placed with a Christian family in the Dutch farm country to avoid persecution by the Nazis
"Adler includes a lot of factual information about the history of the time and about the people in the story, before and after the war. Ritz's realistic watercolors in warm shades of brown focus on the small girl whose childhood games of hide-and-seek become a terrifying reality." Booklist

Hilde and Eli, children of the Holocaust; illustrated by Karen Ritz. Holiday House 1994 unp il $16.95 (3-5) **940.53**
    1. Rosenzweig, Hilde, 1923-1941 2. Lax, Eli, 1932-1944 3. Holocaust, 1933-1945
    ISBN 0-8234-1091-9   LC 93-38229
"Through the biographies of two Jewish children, this picture book for older readers will bring home to gradeschoolers what the Holocaust meant to kids like them. Nothing is sensationalized, but the facts are terrifying. . . . The SS murdered Hilde in a freight train filled with poisonous gas. Eli died in the gas chambers in Auschwitz. The text is quiet, the particulars inexorable, drawn from Adler's interviews with the surviving relatives. The illustrations are powerfully realistic." Booklist

Bachrach, Susan D., 1948-
Tell them we remember; the story of the Holocaust. Little, Brown 1994 109p il maps $21.95; pa $14.95 (5 and up) **940.53**
    1. United States Holocaust Memorial Museum 2. Holocaust, 1933-1945
    ISBN 0-316-69264-6; 0-316-07484-5 (pa)
                                        LC 93-40090
"Intended to extend the experience of the United States Holocaust Memorial Museum beyond its walls, this book reproduces some of its artifacts, photographs, maps, and taped oral and video histories. . . . Bachrach makes the victims of Hitler's cruelty immediate to readers, showing that, like readers, they were individuals with hobbies and desires, friends and families. . . . This is a very personal approach to Holocaust history and a very effective one." SLJ
Includes glossary and bibliographical references

Gold, Alison Leslie
A special fate; Chiune Sugihara, hero of the Holocaust. Scholastic Press 2000 176p $15.95 (5 and up) **940.53**
    1. Sugihara, Sempo, 1900-1986 2. Holocaust, 1933-1945 3. World War, 1939-1945—Jews—Rescue
    ISBN 0-590-39525-4   LC 99-24298
A biography of Chiune Sugihara, a Japanese consul in Lithuania, who saved the lives of thousands of Jews during World War II by issuing visas against the orders of his superiors
"This is one of the great Holocaust rescue stories. . . . [Gold] draws on interviews with Sugihara's wife and other witnesses." Booklist

Greenfeld, Howard
The hidden children. Ticknor & Fields Bks. for Young Readers 1993 118p il $17; pa $7.95 (4 and up) **940.53**
    1. Holocaust, 1933-1945—Personal narratives 2. Jews—Europe
    ISBN 0-395-66074-2; 0-395-86138-1 (pa)
                                        LC 93-20326
Describes the experiences of those Jewish children who were forced to go into hiding during the Holocaust and survived to tell about it
"Illustrated with black-and-white photographs, the

Greenfeld, Howard—*Continued*

moving stories and dramatic facts make inspiring, and often troubling, reading. A lovely, important book about heroism and survival." Horn Book Guide

Includes bibliographical references

Leapman, Michael, 1938-

Witnesses to war; eight true-life stories of Nazi persecution. Viking 1998 127p il maps $16.99; pa $7.99 (5 and up)   **940.53**

1. Holocaust, 1933-1945 2. World War, 1939-1945—Children

ISBN 0-670-87386-1; 0-14-130841-9 (pa)

LC 98-208868

The author "suggests the far reaches of Nazi terror by focusing on the experiences of eight children, each victimized during WWII." Publ Wkly

"Leapman presents an authoritative, informative, and attractive work. . . . The narrative is riveting." Voice Youth Advocates

Meltzer, Milton, 1915-

Never to forget: the Jews of the Holocaust. Harper & Row 1976 217p maps hardcover o.p. paperback available $6.95 (6 and up)   **940.53**

1. Holocaust, 1933-1945

ISBN 0-06-446118-1 (pa)   LC 75-25409

"The mass murder of six million Jews by the Nazis during World War II is the subject of this compelling history. Interweaving background information, chilling statistics, individual accounts and newspaper reports, it provides an excellent introduction to its subject." Interracial Books Child Bull

Includes bibliographical references

Rescue: the story of how Gentiles saved Jews in the Holocaust. Harper & Row 1988 168p maps lib bdg $16.89; pa $7.95 (6 and up)   **940.53**

1. Holocaust, 1933-1945 2. World War, 1939-1945—Jews—Rescue

ISBN 0-06-024210-8 (lib bdg); 0-06-446117-3 (pa)

LC 87-47816

A recounting drawn from historic source material of the many individual acts of heroism performed by righteous gentiles who sought to thwart the extermination of the Jews during the Holocaust

"This is an excellent portrayal of a difficult topic. Meltzer manages to both explain without accusing, and to laud without glorifying. . . . The discussion of the complicated relations between countries are clear, but not simplistic. An impressive aspect of this book is its lack of didacticism." Voice Youth Advocates

Includes bibliographical references

Mochizuki, Ken, 1954-

Passage to freedom; the Sugihara story; written by Ken Mochizuki; illustrated by Dom Lee; afterword by Hiroki Sugihara. Lee & Low Bks. 1997 unp il $15.95 (3-6)   **940.53**

1. Sugihara, Sempo, 1900-1986 2. Holocaust, 1933-1945 3. World War, 1939-1945—Jews—Rescue

ISBN 1-88000-049-0   LC 96-35359

"The story of a Japanese diplomat who saved thousands of Jewish refugees in defiance of official government orders." SLJ

"Lee's stirring mixed-media illustrations in sepia shades are humane and beautiful. . . . The immediacy of the narrative will grab kids' interest and make them think." Booklist

Perl, Lila

Four perfect pebbles; a Holocaust story; by Lila Perl and Marion Blumenthal Lazan. Greenwillow Bks. 1996 130p il $16; pa $4.95 (6 and up)
940.53

1. Holocaust, 1933-1945—Personal narratives 2. Jews—Germany

ISBN 0-688-14294-X; 0-380-73188-6 (pa)

LC 95-9752

"Starting with a description of one of the days that Marion Blumenthal Lazan survived in Bergen-Belsen, this chronicle of her experiences during the Holocaust then goes further back for a look at her family's secure prewar life in Germany." Bull Cent Child Books

"This book warrants attention both for the uncommon experiences it records and for the fullness of that record. . . . Quotes from Lazan's 87-year-old mother are invaluable—her memories of the family's experiences afford Marion's story a precision and wholeness rarely available to child survivors." Publ Wkly

Includes bibliographical references

Rosenberg, Maxine B., 1939-

Hiding to survive; stories of Jewish children rescued from the Holocaust. Clarion Bks. 1994 166p il $15.95; pa $6.95 (5 and up)   **940.53**

1. Holocaust, 1933-1945—Personal narratives 2. Jews—Europe

ISBN 0-395-65014-3; 0-395-90020-4 (pa)

LC 93-28328

First person accounts of fourteen Holocaust survivors who as children were hidden from the Nazis by non-Jews

"Told in the plain, unvarnished language of childhood memories, these harrowing first-person accounts are particularly moving in their straightforward simplicity, and all are accompanied by photos of the survivors as children and as they are today." Voice Youth Advocates

Includes glossary and bibliographical references

Toll, Nelly S., 1935-

Behind the secret window; a memoir of a hidden childhood during Word War Two. Dial Bks. 1993 161p il $17.99 (6 and up)   **940.53**

1. Jews—Poland 2. Holocaust, 1933-1945—Personal narratives

ISBN 0-8037-1362-2   LC 92-21831

The author recalls her experiences when she and her mother were hidden from the Nazis by a Gentile couple in Lwów, Poland, during World War II

"Toll writes of her experiences in an emotionally controlled, thoughtful manner that only serves to emphasize the horrors she experienced. She relies extensively on a diary she began when she entered hiding at the age of eight, and her story is illustrated with full-color paintings she made during the same period." Booklist

Tunnell, Michael O.

The children of Topaz; the story of a Japanese-American internment camp; based on a classroom diary; by Michael O. Tunnell and George W. Chilcoat. Holiday House 1996 74p il $18.95 (5 and up)   **940.53**

1. Central Utah Relocation Center 2. Japanese Americans—Evacuation and relocation, 1942-1945 3. World War, 1939-1945—Children

ISBN 0-8234-1239-3   LC 95-49360

"Interned behind barbed wire in a desert relocation camp in Topaz, Utah, Japanese American teacher Lillian 'Anne' Yamauchi Hori kept a classroom diary with her third-grade class from May to August 1943. . . . Twenty of the small diary entries appear in this book, together with several black-and-white archival photos of the camps. Tunnell and Chilcoat provide a long historical introduction and then detailed commentary that puts each diary entry in the context of what was happening in the camp and in the country at war. . . . The primary sources have a stark authority; it's the very ordinariness of the children's concerns that grabs you." Booklist

Includes bibliographical references

940.54 World War II, 1939-1945 (Military conduct of the war)

Kuhn, Betsy

Angels of mercy; the Army nurses of World War II. Atheneum Bks. for Young Readers 1999 114p il maps $18 (5 and up)   **940.54**

1. United States. Army Nurse Corps 2. World War, 1939-1945—Women 3. Women in the armed forces

ISBN 0-689-82044-5   LC 98-36610

Relates the experiences of World War II Army nurses, who brought medical skills, courage, and cheer to hospitals throughout Europe, North Africa, and the Pacific

"Excellent reproductions, maps and a time line accompany the clear, well-written text." SLJ

Includes bibliographical references

Maruki, Toshi, 1912-

Hiroshima no pika; words and pictures by Toshi Maruki. Lothrop, Lee & Shepard Bks. 1982 c1980 unp il $16.95   **940.54**

1. Hiroshima (Japan)—Bombardment, 1945 2. World War, 1939-1945—Japan

ISBN 0-688-01297-3   LC 82-15365

First published 1980 in Japan

Focusing on the experiences of a real family "the horrifying story of the atomic bombing or 'flash' of Hiroshima is told here with a remarkable eloquence, including many poignant details. The story is terribly disturbing and painful to read, but the narrative is at the same time so spare and compelling one must go on. . . . Young people twelve and over, as well as adults, should know this terrible story. This superb book can begin to tell it to them." Appraisal

McGowen, Tom

Germany's lightning war; Panzer divisions of World War II. 21st Cent. Bks. (Brookfield) 1999 64p il (Military might) lib bdg $24.90 (5 and up)   **940.54**

1. World War, 1939-1945—Germany 2. Military tanks

ISBN 0-7613-1511-X   LC 98-44009

Discusses the development and actions of German tank units in World War II, covering specific battles and the changes that tanks brought to warfare in general

This book "should inspire youngsters to pursue their interest in the subject." SLJ

Sink the Bismarck; Germany's super-battleship of World War II. 21st Cent. Bks. (Brookfield) 1999 64p il (Military might) lib bdg $24.90 (5 and up)   **940.54**

1. Bismarck (Battleship) 2. World War, 1939-1945—Naval operations

ISBN 0-7613-1510-1   LC 98-48500

Describes the actions of the German battleship "Bismarck" during World War II and the operations of the British navy to destroy this ship

The presentation is "straightforward, simple. . . . The writing is . . . easy to follow." SLJ

941.5 Ireland

January, Brendan, 1972-

Ireland. Children's Press 1999 47p il map lib bdg $22; pa $6.95 (2-4)   **941.5**

1. Ireland

ISBN 0-516-21186-2; 0-516-26493-1 (pa)

      LC 98-15762

"A True book"

Presents an overview of the history, geography, climate, and culture of Ireland

"Almost all of the pages include a glossy, full-color photograph or a historical reproduction with highlighted, easy-to-read captions. . . . The information is sufficient for basic reports." SLJ

Includes bibliographical references

942 England and Wales

Blashfield, Jean F.

England. Children's Press 1997 143p il maps (Enchantment of the world, second series) $33 (4 and up)   **942**

1. England

ISBN 0-516-20471-8   LC 97-5662

Describes the geography, history, economy, language, religions, culture, people, plants, and animals of England

Includes bibliographical references

942.01 England—Early history to 1066

Crossley-Holland, Kevin
The world of King Arthur and his court; people, places, legend, and lore; illustrated by Peter Malone. Dutton Children's Bks. 1999 c1998 125p il $25 (5 and up) **942.01**
1. Arthur, King 2. Great Britain—History—0-1066 3. Middle Ages
ISBN 0-525-46167-1 LC 98-37698
First published 1998 in the United Kingdom
Surveys the known history of King Arthur, the legends and lore surrounding him, his treatment in literature, and the possible historical background of his associates and stories
An "eminently browsable, stylishly written trove of Arthuriana. . . . Lavishly detailed, both the full-spread paintings and spot illustrations are ripe with mystery and romance." Publ Wkly

942.02 England—Norman period, 1066-1154

Nikola-Lisa, W.
Till year's good end; a calendar of medieval labors; illustrated by Christopher Manson. Atheneum Bks. for Young Readers 1997 unp il $16 (2-4) **942.02**
1. Farm life—England 2. England—Social life and customs 3. Middle Ages
ISBN 0-689-80020-7 LC 95-45822
"This is a pictorial of the monthly labors done by medieval peasants. Rhyming couplet banners unfurl across each double-page spread, announcing the month and its accompanying labor . . . while further textual details can be found below the illustrations." Bull Cent Child Books
"Handsome artwork rendered in pen-and-ink and watercolor lend solidity and grace to this almanac of the medieval agricultural year. . . . Nikola-Lisa's . . . succinct but informative prose provides an excellent introduction to rural life in the Middle Ages." Publ Wkly

943 Central Europe. Germany

Ayer, Eleanor H.
Germany; in the heartland of Europe. Benchmark Bks. (Tarrytown) 1996 64p il maps (Exploring cultures of the world) lib bdg $27.07 (4 and up) **943**
1. Germany
ISBN 0-7614-0189-X LC 95-15341
This introductory survey of Germany discusses "geography, people, and history. Also covered are customs, school, recreation, and the arts. . . . [The text contains] engaging details about everyday life and customs. The accompanying color photographs are generally high in quality." Horn Book Guide
Includes glossary and bibliographical references

Stein, R. Conrad, 1937-
Berlin. Children's Press 1997 64p il maps (Cities of the world) lib bdg $26.50 (5 and up) **943**
1. Berlin (Germany)
ISBN 0-516-20582-X LC 96-50147
Describes the history, culture, people, daily life, and points of interest of Germany's major city
Includes bibliographical references

943.7 Czech Republic and Slovakia

Sioras, Efstathia
Czech Republic. Marshall Cavendish 1999 128p il maps (Cultures of the world) lib bdg $35.64 (5 and up) **943.7**
1. Czech Republic
ISBN 0-7614-0870-3 LC 98-30290
Describes the geography, history, government, economy, people, lifestyle, religion, language, arts, leisure, festivals, and food of the Czech Republic
Includes glossary and bibliographical references

943.8 Poland

Hintz, Martin, 1945-
Poland. Children's Press 1998 144p il (Enchantment of the world, second series) lib bdg $33 (4 and up) **943.8**
1. Poland
ISBN 0-516-20605-2 LC 97-25559
Describes the history, geography, economy, plants and animals, language, religion, sports, arts, and people of this central European country which has ties to both East and West
Includes bibliographical references

943.9 Hungary

Steins, Richard
Hungary; crossroads of Europe. Benchmark Bks. (Tarrytown) 1997 64p il (Exploring cultures of the world) lib bdg $18.95 (4 and up) **943.9**
1. Hungary
ISBN 0-7614-0141-5 LC 96-51582
Describes the geography, history, culture, and people of Hungary
"Color photographs and easy-to-read [text makes the book] accessible and appealing." Horn Book
Includes glossary and bibliographical references

944 France and Monaco

Landau, Elaine
France. Children's Press 2000 47p il lib bdg $22; pa $6.95 (2-4) **944**
1. France
ISBN 0-516-21173-0 (lib bdg); 0-516-27023-0 (pa)
LC 99-14956

Landau, Elaine—*Continued*
"A True book"
Describes the geography, history, culture, and people of France, the largest country in Western Europe
Includes bibliographical references

Nardo, Don, 1947-
France. Children's Press 2000 144p il (Enchantment of the world, Second series) lib bdg $33 (4 and up)　　　　　**944**
1. France
ISBN 0-516-21052-1　　　　　LC 99-12685
Describes the geography, plants, animals, history, economy, language, sports, arts, religions, culture, and people of France
Includes bibliographical references

NgCheong-Lum, Roseline, 1962-
France. Stevens, G. 1999 96p il (Countries of the world) lib bdg $26.60 (4 and up)　　　**944**
1. France
ISBN 0-8368-2260-9　　　　　LC 98-33770
An overview of France, discussing its history, geography, government, economy, culture, and relations with North America
"The full-color photos on every page are outstanding and the style of writing is graceful." SLJ
Includes glossary and bibliographical references

945　Italian Peninsula and adjacent islands. Italy

King, David C.
Italy; gem of the Mediterranean. Benchmark Bks. (Tarrytown) 1998 64p il maps (Exploring cultures of the world) lib bdg $18.95 (4 and up)　　　　　**945**
1. Italy
ISBN 0-7614-0394-9　　　　　LC 97-6452
Discusses the geography, history, economy, culture, and people of Italy
"The accessible text . . . include[s] engaging topics about everyday life, such as school, sports, entertainment, and food." Horn Book Guide
Includes glossary and bibliographical references

Macaulay, David, 1946-
Rome antics. Houghton Mifflin 1997 79p il $18 (4 and up)　　　　　**945**
1. Rome (Italy)—Description
ISBN 0-395-82279-3　　　　　LC 97-20941
"Modern Rome is seen through the skewed perspective of a homing pigeon's erratic flight through the city streets as she delivers a message to an artist in a garret. . . . Macaulay adds sly touches of humor to the pen-and-ink sketches. . . . The book includes a map of the city 'As the pigeon flies' with each structure numbered, and an addendum shows the 22 featured buildings with a paragraph or two of interesting facts about each one." SLJ

Sheehan, Sean, 1951-
Malta. Marshall Cavendish 2000 128p il maps (Cultures of the world) lib bdg $35.64 (5 and up)　　　　　**945**
1. Malta
ISBN 0-7614-0993-9　　　　　LC 99-53436
The text covers Malta's "government, economy, people, lifestyles, religion, language, arts and leisure, festivals, and food. . . . Copious colorful photographs and reproductions complement and reinforce the facts presented." SLJ
Includes glossary and bibliographical references

946　Iberian Peninsula and adjacent islands. Spain

Chicoine, Stephen
Spain; bridge between continents. Benchmark Bks. (Tarrytown) 1997 64p il maps (Exploring cultures of the world) lib bdg $18.95 (4 and up)　　　　　**946**
1. Spain
ISBN 0-7614-0143-1　　　　　LC 96-45498
Examines the geography, people, customs, and history of one of the largest countries on the continent of Europe
"Color photographs and easy-to-read text make the book . . . accessible and appealing, as do the inclusion of traditional recipes and lists of common Spanish . . . phrases. Chapters devoted to festivals, foods, and the arts are especially entertaining." Horn Book Guide
Includes glossary and bibliographical references

947　Eastern Europe. Russia

Harvey, Miles
The fall of the Soviet Union. Children's Press 1995 30p il maps (Cornerstones of freedom) lib bdg $20.50; pa $5.95 (4-6)　　　　　**947**
1. Soviet Union—History 2. Former Soviet republics—History
ISBN 0-516-06694-3; 0-516-46694-1 (pa)
　　　　　LC 94-24371
Beginning with the revolution in 1917, the author traces events through the fall of the former Soviet Union
"An enormous amount of complex history is broken down into a highly readable text enhanced by full-color and black-and-white photographs of Russian life past and present." SLJ

Kent, Deborah, 1948-
Moscow. Children's Press 2000 64p il (Cities of the world) $26.50 (5 and up)　　　　　**947**
1. Moscow (Russia)
ISBN 0-516-21193-5　　　　　LC 99-33909
Describes the history, culture, daily life, food, sports, people, and points of interest in the capital of Russia
Includes bibliographical references

947.5 Caucasus

Dhilawala, Sakina, 1964-
Armenia. Marshall Cavendish 1997 128p il
maps (Cultures of the world) lib bdg $35.64 (5
and up)   **947.5**
1. Armenia
ISBN 0-7614-0683-2   LC 96-30046
Discusses the geography, history, government, economy, culture, and religion of the republic atop the Armenian Plateau in the Caucausus Mountains
Includes glossary and bibliographical references

Spilling, Michael
Georgia. Marshall Cavendish 1998 128p il maps
(Cultures of the world) lib bdg $35.64 (5 and up)
947.5
1. Georgia (Republic)
ISBN 0-7614-0691-3   LC 97-16570
Describes the geography, history, government, economy, people, lifestyle, religion, language, arts, leisure, festivals, and food of a Caucasian republic with a turbulent
past
Includes glossary and bibliographical references

947.6 Moldova

Sheehan, Patricia, 1954-
Moldova. Marshall Cavendish 2000 128p il
maps (Cultures of the world) lib bdg $35.64 (5
and up)   **947.6**
1. Moldova
ISBN 0-7614-0997-1   LC 99-53433
An illustrated look at the history and culture of the
small landlocked country between Russia and the
Ukraine that proclaimed its independence in August,
1991
Includes glossary and bibliographical references

947.7 Ukraine

Bassis, Volodymyr
Ukraine. Marshall Cavendish 1997 128p il maps
(Cultures of the world) lib bdg $35.64 (5 and up)
947.7
1. Ukraine
ISBN 0-7614-0684-0   LC 96-40207
Examines the geography, history, government, econo-
my, and customs of Ukraine, formerly part of the Union
of Soviet Socialist Republics
Includes glossary and bibliographical references

947.8 Belarus

Levy, Patricia Marjorie, 1951-
Belarus. Marshall Cavendish 1998 128p il maps
(Cultures of the world) lib bdg $35.64 (5 and up)
947.8
1. Belarus
ISBN 0-7614-0811-8   LC 97-48562

This describes the geography, history, government,
economy, people, lifestyle, religion, language, arts, leisure, festivals, and food of Belarus
Includes glossary and bibliographical references

947.9 Lithuania, Latvia, Estonia

Barlas, Robert
Latvia. Marshall Cavendish 2000 128p il map
(Cultures of the world) lib bdg $35.64 (5 and up)
947.9
1. Latvia
ISBN 0-7614-0977-7   LC 99-30168
Describes the geography, history, government, econo-
my, people, religion, language, arts, leisure, festivals, and
food of Latvia
Includes glossary and bibliographical references

Kagda, Sakina, 1939-
Lithuania. Marshall Cavendish 1997 128p il
maps (Cultures of the world) lib bdg $35.64 (5
and up)   **947.9**
1. Lithuania
ISBN 0-7614-0681-6   LC 96-29460
Examines the geography, history, government, economy, and customs of the Baltic state
"Kagda manages to tell an interesting story in *Lithuania*, by writing gracefully and eschewing the use of too
much detail." SLJ
Includes glossary and bibliographical references

Spilling, Michael
Estonia. Marshall Cavendish 1999 128p il maps
(Cultures of the world) lib bdg $35.64 (5 and up)
947.9
1. Estonia
ISBN 0-7614-0951-3   LC 98-43682
Introduces the geography, history, government, econo-
my, culture, and people of Estonia, the northernmost and
least populated of the three Baltic states
Includes glossary and bibliographical references

948 Scandinavia

Margeson, Susan M.
Viking; written by Susan M. Margeso;
photographed by Peter Anderson. Knopf 1994 63p
il maps (Eyewitness books) (4 and up)   **948**
1. Vikings
LC 93-32593
Available DK Pub. edition $15.95; lib bdg $19.99
(ISBN 0-7894-5894-2; 0-7894-6599-X)
"A Dorling Kindersley book"
This overview of Viking culture ranges from domestic
life and social structure "to the more violent aspects of
their explorations and expansions into new territories."
SLJ
"This book is a very fine supplement to texts dealing
with the history of Europe and with the Vikings." Sci
Books Films

948.97   Finland

Lee, Tan Chung, 1949-
Finland. Marshall Cavendish 1996 128p il maps (Cultures of the world) lib bdg $35.64 (5 and up)
948.97

1. Finland
ISBN 0-7614-0280-2   LC 95-44860
Describes the geography, history, government, people, and culture of this isolated country, which gained its independence from Russia in 1917
Includes glossary and bibliographical references

Lewin, Ted, 1935-
The reindeer people; written and illustrated by Ted Lewin. Macmillan 1994 unp il $14.95 (3-5)
948.97

1. Sami (European people) 2. Lapland
ISBN 0-02-757390-7   LC 93-19252
Lewin "introduces the Sami people who live north of the Arctic Circle. . . . Six vignettes portray a blue, frozen land teeming with activity. . . . The author's highly descriptive prose is as luxurious as a reindeer coat, and his finely detailed, snapshot-style watercolors will engage readers of any age." Publ Wkly

McNair, Sylvia, 1924-
Finland. Children's Press 1997 143p il (Enchantment of the world, second series) $33 (4 and up)
948.97

1. Finland
ISBN 0-516-20472-6   LC 97-4972
Describes the geography, plants, animals, history, economy, language, religions, culture, sports, arts, and people of Finland
Includes bibliographical references

949.12   Iceland

Wilcox, Jonathan, 1960-
Iceland. Marshall Cavendish 1996 128p il maps (Cultures of the world) lib bdg $35.64 (5 and up)
949.12

1. Iceland
ISBN 0-7614-0279-9   LC 95-30016
Describes this island of fire and ice which is located in the North Atlantic and which is today populated sparsely by descendants of Viking settlers
Includes glossary and bibliographical references

949.3   Southern Low Countries. Belgium

Burgan, Michael
Belgium. Children's Press 2000 144p il (Enchantment of the world, second series) $33 (4 and up)
949.3

1. Belgium
ISBN 0-516-21006-8   LC 99-21338

Describes the geography, plants and animals, history, economy, language, religions, culture, sports and arts, and people of Belgium
Includes bibliographical references

Pateman, Robert, 1954-
Belgium. Marshall Cavendish 1995 128p il maps (Cultures of the world) lib bdg $35.64 (5 and up)
949.3

1. Belgium
ISBN 0-7614-0176-8   LC 95-14900
Introduces the geography, history, government, economy, culture, and people of the small European country of Belgium
"Organization is clear and user friendly. Fine-quality, full-color photographs and reproductions draw readers in and help to hold their interest." SLJ
Includes glossary and bibliographical references

949.35   Luxembourg

Sheehan, Patricia, 1954-
Luxembourg. Marshall Cavendish 1997 128p il maps (Cultures of the world) lib bdg $35.64 (5 and up)
949.35

1. Luxembourg
ISBN 0-7614-0685-9   LC 96-53367
Discusses the geography, history, government, economy, and customs of the smallest of the Benelux countries
This is "lucidly written. . . . Informative chapters include discussion about body language, religion, education, and women." Horn Book Guide
Includes glossary and bibliographical references

949.65   Albania

Wright, David K., 1943-
Albania. Children's Press 1997 143p il maps (Enchantment of the world, second series) $33 (4 and up)
949.65

1. Albania
ISBN 0-516-20468-8   LC 97-4973
Describes the geography, plants, animals, history, economy, language, religions, culture, sports, arts, and people of Albania
Includes bibliographical references

949.7   Yugoslavia, Croatia, Slovenia, Bosnia and Hercegovina, Macedonia

Marx, Trish, 1948-
One boy from Kosovo; photographs by Cindy Karp. Lothrop, Lee & Shepard Bks. 2000 24p il $15.95; lib bdg $15.89 (3-6)
949.7

1. Kosovo (Serbia) 2. Refugees
ISBN 0-688-17732-8; 0-688-17733-6 (lib bdg)
LC 99-51793

Marx, Trish, 1948-—*Continued*

Tells the story of Edi Fejzullahu and his family, Albanians who fled their home in Kosovo to live in a Macedonian refugee camp when the Serbs adopted a policy of ethnic cleansing against Albanians

"The color photographs maintain the intimacy of snapshots, but are framed by the discerning eye of a professional; the writing is steady and understated, allowing the facts of Edi's life to speak for themselves." Horn Book

Milivojevic, JoAnn

Serbia. Children's Press 1999 144p il maps (Enchantment of the world, Second series) $33 (4 and up) **949.7**

1. Serbia

ISBN 0-516-21196-X   LC 98-19256

An introduction to the geography, history, natural resources, economy, culture, and people of Serbia, the larger of the two republics that make up the country of Yugoslavia

"An accessible, well-illustrated overview." SLJ

Includes bibliographical references

951 China and adjacent areas

Dramer, Kim

People's Republic of China. Children's Press 1999 144p il maps (Enchantment of the world, second series) lib bdg $33 (4 and up) **951**

1. China

ISBN 0-516-21077-7   LC 98-17643

Describes the geography, plants and animals, history, economy, language, religions, culture, and people of the People's Republic of China, home of one of the world's oldest continuous civilizations

"An attractive, insightful book with a broad scope." SLJ

Includes glossary and bibliographical references

Sis, Peter

Tibet; through the red box. Farrar, Straus & Giroux 1998 unp il maps $25 **951**

1. Tibet (China)

ISBN 0-374-37552-6   LC 97-50175

A Caldecott Medal honor book, 1999

"Frances Foster books"

"When Sis opens the red lacquered box that has sat on his father's table for decades, he finds the diary his father kept when he was lost in Tibet in the mid-1950s. The text replicates the diary's spidery handwriting, while the illustrations depict elaborate mazes and mandalas, along with dreamlike spreads that are filled with fragmented details of the father's and son's lives. . . . Impeccably designed and beautifully made, the book has a dreamlike quality that will keep readers of many ages coming back to find more in its pages." Booklist

951.04 China—Period of Republic, 1912-1949

Fritz, Jean

China's Long March; 6,000 miles of danger; with illustrations by Yang Zhr Cheng. Putnam 1988 124p il maps $16.95 (6 and up) **951.04**

1. China—History—1912-1949

ISBN 0-399-21512-3   LC 87-31171

Describes the events of the 6,000 mile march undertaken by Mao Zedong and his Communist followers as they retreated before the forces of Chiang Kai-shek

"Because Fritz is adept at gauging her intended audience, and because most of her material is based on interviews with survivors, the writing has an easy flow and an immediacy that make the ordeal vivid and personal." Bull Cent Child Books

Includes bibliographical references

951.05 China—Period of People's Republic, 1949-

Fritz, Jean

China homecoming; with photographs by Michael Fritz. Putnam 1985 143p il $18.99 (6 and up) **951.05**

1. China

ISBN 0-399-21182-9   LC 84-24775

Companion volume to Homesick: my own story

This account of the author's return to Hankow after four decades "is intended for a slightly older readership than 'Homesick' . . . as it is not only an autobiography, but also a glimpse of Chinese history and a social commentary. It is, however, a book to be read and reread." SLJ

Includes bibliographical references

Jiang, Ji-li

Red scarf girl; a memoir of the Cultural Revolution; foreword by David Henry Hwang. HarperCollins Pubs. 1997 285p $15.95; pa $5.95 (6 and up) **951.05**

1. China—History—1949-1976—Personal narratives

ISBN 0-06-027585-5; 0-06-446208-0 (pa)

LC 97-5089

"This is an autobiographical account of growing up during Mao's Cultural Revolution in China in 1966. . . . Jiang describes in terrifying detail the ordeals of her family and those like them, including unauthorized search and seizure, persecution, arrest and torture, hunger, and public humiliation. . . . Her voice is that of an intelligent, confused adolescent, and her focus on the effects of the revolution on herself, her family, and her friends provides an emotional focal point for the book, and will allow even those with limited knowledge of Chinese history to access the text." Bull Cent Child Books

951.25 Hong Kong

Kagda, Falaq
Hong Kong. ref ed. Marshall Cavendish 1998
128p il maps (Cultures of the world) lib bdg
$35.64 (5 and up) **951.25**
1. Hong Kong (China)
ISBN 0-7614-0692-1 LC 97-15885
Surveys the geography, history, government, economy,
and culture of this territory on China's southeastern
coast, made up of a section of the mainland and 235 islands of various sizes
Includes glossary and bibliographical references

951.7 Mongolia

Cheng, Pang Guek, 1950-
Mongolia. Marshall Cavendish 1999 128p il
maps (Cultures of the world) lib bdg $35.64 (5
and up) **951.7**
1. Mongolia
ISBN 0-7614-0954-8 LC 98-31897
Describes the geography, history, government, economy, people, lifestyle, religion, language, arts, leisure, festivals, and food of Mongolia
"High-quality, full-color photography combines with
clearly written text and meaningful sidebars." SLJ
Includes glossary and bibliographical references

952 Japan

Blumberg, Rhoda, 1917-
Commodore Perry in the land of the Shogun.
Lothrop, Lee & Shepard Bks. 1985 144p il map
$18.95 (5 and up) **952**
1. Perry, Matthew Calbraith, 1794-1858 2. United
States Naval Expedition to Japan (1852-1854) 3. Unit-
ed States—Foreign relations—Japan 4. Japan—For-
eign relations—United States
ISBN 0-688-03723-2 LC 84-21800
A Newbery Medal honor book, 1986
"The diplomatic expeditions of Commodore Matthew
C. Perry to secure a treaty to provide for U.S. trade with
Japan are described. The black-and-white period illustra-
tions and informative text provide an in-depth and inti-
mate view of nineteenth century Japan, Japanese and
U.S. values and attitudes, and treaty negotiations." Soc
Educ
Includes bibliographical references

Haskins, James, 1941-
Count your way through Japan; by Jim Haskins;
illustrations by Martin Skoro. Carolrhoda Bks.
1987 unp il lib bdg $19.93; pa $5.95 (2-4) **952**
1. Japan
ISBN 0-87614-301-X (lib bdg); 0-87614-485-7 (pa)
LC 87-6398
Presents the numbers one to ten in Japanese, using
each number to introduce concepts about Japan and its
culture

Heinrichs, Ann
Japan. Children's Press 1998 143p il
(Enchantment of the world, second series) lib bdg
$33 (4 and up) **952**
1. Japan
ISBN 0-516-20649-4 LC 97-38771
Describes the history, geography, plants and animals,
economy, language, people and culture of the island nation of Japan
"The writing is clear . . . the topics covered are broad
in scope and will be suitable for assignments. Good-
quality, full-color photographs, reproductions, and maps
are interspersed throughout." SLJ
Includes bibliographical references

953 Arabian Peninsula and adjacent areas

Foster, Leila Merrell
Oman. Children's Press 1999 144p il maps
(Enchantment of the world, second series) lib bdg
$33 (4 and up) **953**
1. Oman
ISBN 0-516-20964-7 LC 98-19572
Describes the geography, plants and animals, history,
economy, language, religions, culture, and people of
Oman, a small nation strategically located on the eastern
part of the Arabian peninsula
Includes bibliographical references

953.3 Yemen

Hestler, Anna
Yemen. Marshall Cavendish 1999 128p il maps
(Cultures of the world) lib bdg $35.64 (5 and up)
953.3
1. Yemen
ISBN 0-7614-0956-4 LC 98-53993
Presents information about the geography, history,
government, and economy of this country located on the
southwestern tip of the Arabian Peninsula and describes
many aspects of the lifestyle of its people
Includes glossary and bibliographical references

953.67 Kuwait

Foster, Leila Merrell
Kuwait. Children's Press 1998 143p il
(Enchantment of the world, second series) lib bdg
$33 (4 and up) **953.67**
1. Kuwait
ISBN 0-516-20604-4 LC 97-23845
Describes the history, geography, economy, language,
religion, sports, arts, and people of this oil-rich country
located on the northwestern shore of the Persian Gulf
Includes bibliographical references

O'Shea, Maria
Kuwait. Marshall Cavendish 1999 128p il maps (Cultures of the world) lib bdg $35.64 (5 and up)
953.67
1. Kuwait
ISBN 0-7614-0871-1   LC 98-25833
Introduces the geography, history, religious beliefs, government, and people of Kuwait, a small country on the Persian Gulf
Includes glossary and bibliographical references

953.8   Saudi Arabia

Fazio, Wende
Saudi Arabia. Children's Press 1999 47p il lib bdg $22; pa $6.95 (2-4)   **953.8**
1. Saudi Arabia
ISBN 0-516-21190-0 (lib bdg); 0-516-26502-4 (pa)
LC 98-12273
"A True book"
Provides an overview of the geography, history, and culture of the Kingdom of Saudi Arabia
"An informative text is coupled with crisp photographs." Horn Book Guide
Includes glossary and bibliographical references

956.7   Iraq

Foster, Leila Merrell
Iraq. Children's Press 1997 144p il (Enchantment of the world, second series) lib bdg $33 (4 and up)   **956.7**
1. Iraq
ISBN 0-516-20584-6   LC 97-2005
Describes the geography, history, culture, industry, and people of Iraq, formerly known as Mesopotamia
Includes bibliographical references

956.92   Lebanon

Sheehan, Sean, 1951-
Lebanon. ref ed. Marshall Cavendish 1997 128p il maps (Cultures of the world) lib bdg $35.64 (5 and up)   **956.92**
1. Lebanon
ISBN 0-7614-0283-7   LC 96-22480
This describes the geography, history, government, economy and culture of Lebanon
Includes glossary and bibliographical references

956.93   Cyprus

Spilling, Michael
Cyprus. Marshall Cavendish 2000 128p il maps (Cultures of the world) lib bdg $35.64 (5 and up)
956.93
1. Cyprus
ISBN 0-7614-0978-5   LC 99-31942

Discusses the geography, history, government, economy, people, and culture of Cyprus
Includes glossary and bibliographical references

956.94   Palestine. Israel

Haskins, James, 1941-
Count your way through Israel; illustrations by Rick Hanson. Carolrhoda Bks. 1990 unp il lib bdg $19.93; pa $5.95 (2-4)   **956.94**
1. Israel
ISBN 0-87614-415-6 (lib bdg); 0-87614-558-6 (pa)
LC 90-1594
An introduction to the land and people of Israel accompanied by instructions on how to read and pronounce the numbers one through ten in Hebrew

Hintz, Martin, 1945-
Israel; by Martin Hintz and Stephen Hintz. Children's Press 1999 144p il (Enchantment of the world, second series) lib bdg $33 (4 and up)
956.94
1. Israel
ISBN 0-516-21108-0   LC 98-17642
Describes the geography, plants and animals, history, economy, language, religions, culture, and people of Israel
Includes bibliographical references

956.95   West Bank and Jordan

South, Coleman
Jordan. Marshall Cavendish 1997 128p il maps (Cultures of the world) lib bdg $35.64 (5 and up)
956.95
1. Jordan
ISBN 0-7614-0287-X   LC 96-18307
Examines the geography, history, government, economy, and culture of Jordan
Includes glossary and bibliographical references

959.3   Thailand

McNair, Sylvia, 1924-
Thailand. Children's Press 1998 144p (Enchantment of the world, second series) $33 (4 and up)   **959.3**
1. Thailand
ISBN 0-516-21100-5   LC 98-16319
Explores the geography, history, arts, religion, and everyday life of Thailand
Includes bibliographical references

959.4   Laos

Mansfield, Stephen
Laos. Marshall Cavendish 1998 128p il maps (Cultures of the world) lib bdg $35.64 (5 and up)
959.4
1. Laos
ISBN 0-7614-0689-1   LC 97-16568

Mansfield, Stephen—*Continued*
Introduces the geography, history, religious beliefs,
government, and people of Laos
Includes glossary and bibliographical references

959.7   Vietnam

Skelton, Olivia
Vietnam; still struggling, still spirited.
Benchmark Bks. (Tarrytown) 1998 64p il maps
(Exploring cultures of the world) lib bdg $18.95 (4
and up)   **959.7**
1. Vietnam
ISBN 0-7614-0395-7   LC 97-8802
Describes the geography, history, climate, government,
people, and culture of this small country in the southeastern corner of Asia
"An accessible introduction to Vietnam is especially
good at exploring the human side of the country—including work and school customs, cultural traditions, food,
and celebrations." Horn Book Guide
Includes glossary and bibliographical references

959.704   Vietnam—1949-

Ashabranner, Brent K., 1921-
Their names to live; what the Vietnam Veterans
Memorial means to America; [by] Brent
Ashabranner; photographs by Jennifer
Ashabranner. Millbrook Press 1998 64p il $24.90
(6 and up)   **959.704**
1. Vietnam Veterans Memorial (Washington, D.C.)
ISBN 0-7613-3235-9   LC 98-21004
Describes the planning and creation of the Vietnam
Veterans Memorial and how it came to be a symbol for
the dead of all American wars
"A simple, often-moving book of information, photo-
graphs, and reflections on the Memorial." Booklist
Includes bibliographical references

Kilborne, Sarah S.
Leaving Vietnam; the journey of Tuan Ngo, a
boat boy; illustrated by Melissa Sweet. Simon &
Schuster Bks. for Young Readers 1999 48p il map
$15; pa $3.99 (1-4)   **959.704**
1. Political refugees 2. Vietnam
ISBN 0-689-80798-8; 0-689-80797-X (pa)
LC 97-15061
"Ready-to-read"
Tells the story of a boy and his father who endure
danger and difficulties when they escape by boat from
Vietnam, spend days at sea, and then months in refugee
camps before making their way to the United States
This "will intrigue readers while giving them a
glimpse of recent history. The seven chapters are complemented by watercolor illustrations and a simple map
of the country." SLJ

Schmidt, Jeremy, 1949-
Two lands, one heart; an American boy's
journey to his mother's Vietnam; [by] Jeremy
Schmidt, Ted Wood; photographs by Ted Wood.
Walker & Co. 1995 44p il maps $15.95; lib bdg
$18.85 (3-5)   **959.704**
1. Sharp, Timothy James 2. Vietnam—Description
ISBN 0-8027-8357-0; 0-8027-8358-9 (lib bdg)
LC 94-33648
"After years of hearing stories and seeing pictures of
his mother's homeland, young TJ travels to Vietnam to
visit the family his mother left behind as a child during
the Vietnam War. A narrative rich in detail and striking,
full-color photographs capture TJ's adventure and in the
process, introduce readers to the Vietnamese culture and
landscape." Booklist

960   Africa

Haskins, James, 1941-
African beginnings; [by] James Haskins &
Kathleen Benson; paintings by Floyd Cooper.
Lothrop, Lee & Shepard Bks. 1998 48p il map
$18; lib bdg $17.93 (4-6)   **960**
1. Africa—History
ISBN 0-688-10256-5; 0-688-10257-3 (lib bdg)
LC 94-9848
This is an "overview of the great African kingdoms
between 3800 B.C. and A.D. 1800. Sections on the king-
doms of Nubia, Egypt, Jenne-Jeno, Ghana, Mao,
Songhay, etc., briefly discuss trade, education, art, agri-
culture, and other practices." Bull Cent Child Books
Cooper "fills in the geographical and cultural details
with soft-edged, luminous oil paintings." Publ Wkly
Includes bibliographical references

From Afar to Zulu; a dictionary of African
cultures; [by] Jim Haskins, and Joann Biondi.
Walker & Co. 1995 212p il maps $18.95; lib bdg
$17.85; pa $10.95 (4 and up)   **960**
1. Africa—Social life and customs—Dictionaries
ISBN 0-8027-8290-6; 0-8027-8291-4 (lib bdg);
0-8027-7550-0 (pa)   LC 94-11545
This volume describes "more than 30 major and 200
smaller ethnic groups on the African continent. History,
social customs, religions, political issues and contemporary events are discussed in each entry." BAYA Book
Rev
Includes bibliographical references

Musgrove, Margaret, 1943-
Ashanti to Zulu: African traditions; pictures by
Leo and Diane Dillon. Dial Bks. for Young
Readers 1976 unp il $15.99; pa $5.99 (3-6)   **960**
1. Africa—Social life and customs 2. Ethnology—Af-
rica
ISBN 0-8037-0357-0; 0-14-054604-9 (pa)
Awarded the Caldecott Medal, 1977
"In brief texts arranged in alphabetical order, each ac-
companied by a large framed illustration, the author in-
troduces 'the reader to twenty-six African peoples by de-
picting a custom important to each.' . . . In most of the

Musgrove, Margaret, 1943- —*Continued*
paintings the artists 'have included a man, a woman, a
child, their living quarters, an artifact, and a local animal' and have, in this way, stressed the human and the
natural ambience of the various peoples depicted." Horn
Book
   "The writing is dignified and the material informative,
but it is the illustrations that make the book outstanding."
Bull Cent Child Books

961.1   Tunisia

Brown, Roslind Varghese
   Tunisia. Marshall Cavendish 1998 128p il maps
(Cultures of the world) lib bdg $35.64 (5 and up)
                                                      961.1
   1. Tunisia
   ISBN 0-7614-0690-5   LC 97-15883
   Examines the history, economy, people, lifestyles, and
culture of this Arab country in northern Africa
   Includes glossary and bibliographical references

961.2   Libya

Willis, Terri
   Libya. Children's Press 1999 144p il
(Enchantment of the world, second series) lib bdg
$33 (4 and up)   **961.2**
   1. Libya
   ISBN 0-516-21008-4   LC 98-28174
   Describes the history, geography, economy, culture,
people, and religion of the North African country of Lib-
ya
   Includes bibliographical references

962   Egypt and Sudan

Heinrichs, Ann
   Egypt. Children's Press 1997 143p il maps
(Enchantment of the world, second series) $33 (4
and up)   **962**
   1. Egypt
   ISBN 0-516-20470-X   LC 97-2438
   Describes the geography, plants, animals, history,
economy, language, religions, culture, sports, arts, and
people of Egypt
   Includes bibliographical references

King, David C.
   Egypt; ancient traditions, modern hopes.
Benchmark Bks. (Tarrytown) 1997 64p il map
(Exploring cultures of the world) lib bdg $18.95 (4
and up)   **962**
   1. Egypt
   ISBN 0-7614-0142-3   LC 96-49588
   Discusses the geography, history, culture, daily life,
and people of the North African country of Egypt
   "Illustrated with color photographs. . . . A sampling
of Arabic phrases and a traditional recipe add to the
book's appeal." Horn Book
   Includes glossary and bibliographical references

962.4   Sudan

Levy, Patricia Marjorie, 1951-
   Sudan. Marshall Cavendish 1997 128p il maps
(Cultures of the world) $35.64 (5 and up)   **962.4**
   1. Sudan
   ISBN 0-7614-0284-5   LC 96-20493
   Examines the geography, history, government, econo-
my, and culture of the war-torn country where the
African and Arab worlds mingle
   Includes glossary and bibliographical references

965   Algeria

Kagda, Falaq
   Algeria. Marshall Cavendish 1997 128p il maps
(Cultures of the world) lib bdg $35.64 (5 and up)
                                                      965
   1. Algeria
   ISBN 0-7614-0680-8   LC 96-40373
   Examines the geography, history, government, econo-
my, people, and culture of Algeria
   Includes glossary and bibliographical references

966.2   Mali, Burkina Faso, Niger

McKissack, Patricia C., 1944-
   The royal kingdoms of Ghana, Mali, and
Songhay; life in medieval Africa; [by] Patricia and
Fredrick McKissack. Holt & Co. 1993 142p il
maps hardcover o.p. paperback available $8.95 (5
and up)   **966.2**
   1. Ghana   Empire—History   2. Mali—History
   3. Songhai Empire
   ISBN 0-8050-4259-8 (pa)   LC 93-4838
   Examines the civilizations of the Western Sudan
which flourished from 700 to 1700 A.D., acquiring such
vast wealth that they became centers of trade and culture
for a continent
   "The McKissacks are careful to distinguish what is
known from what is surmised; they draw on the oral tradition, eyewitness accounts, and contemporary scholarship; and chapter source notes discuss various conflicting
views of events." Booklist
   Includes bibliographical references

966.23   Mali

Brook, Larry
   Daily life in ancient and modern Timbuktu;
illustrations by Ray Webb. Runestone Press 1999
64p il (Cities through time) lib bdg $25.26 (4 and
up)   **966.23**
   1. Tombouctou (Mali)
   ISBN 0-8225-3215-8   LC 98-18314
   Examines the history of the city of Timbuktu, or Tombouctou, from its time as a camping site for nomadic

Brook, Larry—*Continued*
Tuaregs through its prominence in the sixteenth century to the current decline it faces

"Brook presents the political and social history of the city known as the 'Pearl of Africa' in clean, engaging prose." Horn Book Guide

Includes bibliographical references

966.26   Niger

Seffal, Rabah
Niger. Marshall Cavendish 2001 128p il maps (Cultures of the world) lib bdg $35.64 (5 and up)
      966.26
1. Niger
ISBN 0-7614-0995-5   LC 99-55064
A history and geography as well as a description of the government, economy, people, lifestyle, religion, language, arts, leisure time activities, festivals, and food of this landlocked West African country

Includes glossary and bibliographical references

966.3   Senegal

Berg, Elizabeth, 1953-
Senegal; [by] Elizabeth L. Berg. Marshall Cavendish 1999 128p il maps (Cultures of the world) lib bdg $35.64 (5 and up)   **966.3**
1. Senegal
ISBN 0-7614-0872-X   LC 98-7790
Describes the geography, history, economy, lifestyle, and religion of Senegal, as well as its people, languages, and festivals

Includes glossary and bibliographical references

966.62   Liberia

Levy, Patricia Marjorie, 1951-
Liberia; [by] Patricia Levy. Marshall Cavendish 1998 128p il maps (Cultures of the world) lib bdg $35.64 (5 and up)   **966.62**
1. Liberia
ISBN 0-7614-0810-X   LC 97-43613
Describes the geography, history, government, economy, people, lifestyle, religion, language, arts, leisure, festivals, and food of the West African nation of Liberia

Includes glossary and bibliographical references

966.68   Ivory Coast

Sheehan, Patricia, 1954-
Côte d'Ivoire. Marshall Cavendish 2000 128p il maps (Cultures of the world) lib bdg $35.64 (5 and up)   **966.68**
1. Ivory Coast
ISBN 0-7614-0980-7   LC 99-27250
Surveys the geography, history, government, economy, and culture of Côte d'Ivoire, formerly known as the Ivory Coast

Includes glossary and bibliographical references

966.7   Ghana

Levy, Patricia Marjorie, 1951-
Ghana. Marshall Cavendish 1999 128p il maps (Cultures of the world) lib bdg $35.64 (5 and up)
      966.7
1. Ghana
ISBN 0-7614-0952-1   LC 98-49004
Describes the geography, history, government, economy, people, lifestyle, religion, language, arts, leisure, festivals, and food of Ghana

This offers "a readable text along with plenty of clear color photos." Horn Book Guide

Includes glossary and bibliographical references

966.9   Nigeria

Onyefulu, Ifeoma, 1959-
Ogbo; sharing life in an African village. Gulliver Bks. 1996 unp il $15 (2-4)   **966.9**
1. Igbo (African people) 2. Nigeria—Social life and customs
ISBN 0-15-200498-X   LC 95-8882
"This photo-essay describes daily life in [an Igbo village in] eastern Nigeria by focusing on social relationships. A child explains that everyone born within a five-year period belongs to an *ogbo*, or age group, and the members have a lifelong responsibility for each other and for working together in the community." Booklist

"Onyefulu's vibrant full-color photography and clear, direct language communicate images of African village life that are aesthetically appealing and also real." SLJ

967.51   Zaire

Heale, Jay
Democratic Republic of the Congo. Marshall Cavendish 1999 128p il maps (Cultures of the world) lib bdg $35.64 (5 and up)   **967.51**
1. Congo (Republic)
ISBN 0-7614-0874-6   LC 98-28538
Describes the geography, history, government, economy, people, lifestyle, religion, languages, arts, leisure, festivals, and food of the third largest country in Africa, a former colony of Belgium

Includes glossary and bibliographical references

967.6   Uganda and Kenya

Barlas, Robert
Uganda. Marshall Cavendish 2000 128p il maps (Cultures of the world) lib bdg $35.64 (5 and up)
      967.6
1. Uganda
ISBN 0-7614-0981-5   LC 99-27577
Discusses the geography, history, government, economy, people, and culture of the African nation of Uganda

Includes glossary and bibliographical references

967.62 Kenya

King, David C.
Kenya; let's all pull together! Benchmark Bks. (Tarrytown) 1998 64p il maps (Exploring cultures of the world) lib bdg $18.95 (4 and up)   **967.62**
1. Kenya
ISBN 0-7614-0393-0   LC 97-14448
Describes the geography, history, language, people, and culture of this country on the east coast of Africa
Includes glossary and bibliographical references

967.73 Somalia

Hassig, Susan M., 1969-
Somalia. Marshall Cavendish 1997 128p il maps (Cultures of the world) lib bdg $35.64 (5 and up)
967.73
1. Somalia
ISBN 0-7614-0288-8   LC 96-20492
Discusses the geography, history, government, economy, people, and culture of this peninsular African nation on the Indian Ocean
Includes glossary and bibliographical references

967.8 Tanzania

Heale, Jay
Tanzania. Marshall Cavendish 1998 128p il maps (Cultures of the world) lib bdg $35.64 (5 and up)   **967.8**
1. Tanzania
ISBN 0-7614-0809-6   LC 97-42180
Describes the geography, history, government, economy, ethnic groups, lifestyle, religion, language, arts, leisure, festivals, and food of this Eastern African nation
This offers "a clear and informative text [and] . . . captioned color photographs." Horn Book Guide
Includes glossary and bibliographical references

968 Southern Africa. Republic of South Africa

Blauer, Ettagale
South Africa; by Ettagale Blauer and Jason Lauré. Children's Press 1998 144p il (Enchantment of the world, second series) lib bdg $33 (4 and up)
968
1. South Africa
ISBN 0-516-20606-0   LC 97-26014
Describes the geography, plants, animals, history, economy, languages, religions, sports, arts, and people of a country that shares land borders with six nations and surrounds one of them
Includes bibliographical references

968.8 Namibia, Botswana, Lesotho, Swaziland

Brandenburg, Jim
Sand and fog; adventures in Southern Africa; edited by JoAnn Bren Guernsey. Walker & Co. 1994 44p il map hardcover o.p. paperback available $6.95 (4 and up)   **968.8**
1. Namibia 2. Desert ecology 3. Photography of animals
ISBN 0-8027-7476-8 (pa)   LC 93-30425
This is a "collection of images of life—both human and animal—in the desert realms of Namibia." Publ Wkly
The author "combines exquisite color pictures with a first-person narrative to produce a book noteworthy for its craftsmanship, artistry, and perspective." Horn Book Guide

968.94 Zambia

Holmes, Timothy
Zambia. Marshall Cavendish 1998 128p il maps (Cultures of the world) lib bdg $35.64 (5 and up)
968.94
1. Zambia
ISBN 0-7614-0694-8   LC 97-22298
Describes the geography, history, government, economy, people, lifestyle, religion, language, arts, leisure, festivals, and food of this high plateau country in the interior of Africa
Includes glossary and bibliographical references

969.1 Madagascar

Heale, Jay
Madagascar. Marshall Cavendish 1998 128p il maps (Cultures of the world) lib bdg $35.64 (5 and up)   **969.1**
1. Madagascar
ISBN 0-7614-0693-X   LC 97-16569
Introduces the geography, history, religious beliefs, government, and people of Madagascar
This offers a "lucidly written text. . . . Informative chapters include discussion about ethnic groups, rites of passage, family life, sports, etiquette, and human rights." Horn Book Guide
Includes glossary and bibliographical references

970 North America

Peoples of the Americas. Marshall Cavendish 1999 11v set $329.95   **970**
1. Ethnology—America
ISBN 0-7614-7050-6   LC 98-2801
Contents: v1 Anguilla-Belize; v2 Bermuda-Brazil; v3 Canada-Cayman Islands; v4 Chile-Costa Rica; v5 Cuba-French Guiana; v6 Greenland-Jamaica; v7 Martinique-Paraguay; v8 Peru-Turks and Caicos Islands; v9 United States of America; v10 United States of America-Virgin Islands

Peoples of the Americas—*Continued*

"The 50 entries, arranged alphabetically by country, vary in length from 2 to 74 pages and focus on native, ethnic, and immigrant groups in these nations. Discussions center on their way of life; on their contributions, both cultural and political; and often, on their struggle for survival." SLJ

"The amount of information, logical organization, multiple access points, and attractive layout combine to create a reference tool that most school and public libraries will want in their collections." Booklist

970.004 North American native peoples

Ancona, George, 1929-
Powwow; photographs and text by George Ancona. Harcourt Brace Jovanovich 1993 unp il $17; pa $9 (3-6)   **970.004**
1. Crow Fair (Crow Agency, Mont.) 2. Native Americans—Rites and ceremonies
ISBN 0-15-263268-9; 0-15-263269-7 (pa)
LC 92-15912
A photo essay on the pan-Indian celebration called a powwow, this particular one being held on the Crow Reservation in Montana
The book is "illustrated with well-placed, full-color photos that clearly reflect the text. . . . An exquisite kaleidoscope of Native American music, customs, and crafts." SLJ

Andryszewski, Tricia, 1956-
The Seminoles; people of the Southeast. Millbrook Press 1995 64p il map (Native Americans) lib bdg $22.90 (4-6)   **970.004**
1. Seminole Indians
ISBN 1-56294-530-0   LC 94-21819
This book describes the history and culture of the Seminoles of Florida. A traditional recipe, game and story are included
Includes glossary and bibliographical references

Arnold, Caroline, 1944-
The ancient cliff dwellers of Mesa Verde; photographs by Richard Hewett. Clarion Bks. 1992 64p il $15.95; pa $6.95 (4 and up)   **970.004**
1. Pueblo Indians
ISBN 0-395-56241-4; 0-618-05149-X (pa)
LC 91-8145
Discusses the native Americans known as the Anasazi, who migrated to southwestern Colorado in the first century A.D. and mysteriously disappeared in 1300 A.D. after constructing extensive dwellings in the cliffs of the steep canyon walls
"A thorough and attractive introduction to the Anasazi people with outstanding photographs of the dramatic vistas and ceremonial chambers within this national park." SLJ
Includes glossary

Baylor, Byrd, 1924-
When clay sings; illustrated by Tom Bahti. Scribner 1972 unp il $16 (1-4)   **970.004**
1. Native American art 2. Native Americans—Southwestern States 3. Pottery
ISBN 0-684-18829-5
Also available in paperback from Aladdin paperbacks
A Caldecott Medal honor book, 1973
"A lyrical tribute to an almost forgotten time of the prehistoric Indian of the desert West presents broken bits of pottery from this ancient time. The designs and drawings, done in rich earth tones, are derived from prehistoric pottery found in the American Southwest." Read Ladders for Hum Relat. 6th edition

Bealer, Alex W.
Only the names remain; the Cherokees and the Trail of Tears; illustrated by Kristina Rodanas. Little, Brown 1996 79p il hardcover o.p. paperback available $4.95 (4-6)   **970.004**
1. Cherokee Indians
ISBN 0-316-08519-7 (pa)
A reissue with new illustrations of the title first published 1972
The author describes "the rise of the Cherokee Nation, with its written language, constitution, and republican form of government, and its tragic betrayal in the 1830s." Chicago Public Libr

Bonvillain, Nancy
The Navajos; people of the Southwest. Millbrook Press 1995 64p il (Native Americans) lib bdg $21.90 (4-6)   **970.004**
1. Navajo Indians
ISBN 1-56294-495-9   LC 94-21818
An illustrated overview of the history and culture of the largest Native American tribe in contemporary America. A traditional song and recipe are included
Includes bibliographical references

Braine, Susan
Drumbeat—heartbeat; a celebration of the powwow; text and photographs by Susan Braine. Lerner Publs. 1995 48p il (We are still here: Native Americans today) lib bdg $21.27; pa $6.95 (3-6)   **970.004**
1. Native Americans—Rites and ceremonies
ISBN 0-8225-2656-5 (lib bdg); 0-8225-9711-X (pa)
LC 94-42594
The author explains how powwows "started, when and where they are held, and what one can expect to see there. Detailed descriptions of the various dance styles for both men and women are given, followed by information on the singing and drumming, a special plus. . . . Informative full-color photographs are well placed throughout." SLJ
Includes glossary and bibliographical references

Brill, Marlene Targ

The Trail of Tears; the Cherokee journey from home. Millbrook Press 1995 64p il maps (Spotlight on American history) lib bdg $24.90 (5 and up) **970.004**

1. Cherokee Indians

ISBN 1-56294-486-X LC 94-16988

This is an "account of the history of the Cherokee Nation's conflicts with white colonizers of its tribal lands; the U.S. government's removal of the people from their ancestral homes in 1838; and their forced migration West to Oklahoma. The text is sparingly, but appropriately, illustrated with full-color and black-and-white reproductions and photographs. Solid and useful appendixes are included." SLJ

Includes bibliographical references

Bruchac, Joseph, 1942-

The Trail of Tears; illustrated by Diana Magnuson. Random House 1999 46p il lib bdg $11.99; pa $3.99 (2-4) **970.004**

1. Cherokee Indians

ISBN 0-679-99052-6 (lib bdg); 0-679-89052-1 (pa) LC 98-36199

"Step into reading"

Recounts how the Cherokees, after fighting to keep their land in the nineteenth century, were forced to leave and travel 1200 miles to a new settlement in Oklahoma, a terrible journey known as the Trail of Tears

"Magnuson's colorful pictures, packed with people and action, are a little bright for the subject, but strong new readers will find that nonfiction can tell a powerful story." Booklist

Ciment, James

Scholastic encyclopedia of the American Indian; [by] James Ciment with Ronald LaFrance. Scholastic Ref. 1996 224p il maps $18.95 (4 and up) **970.004**

1. Native Americans—Encyclopedias

ISBN 0-590-22790-4 LC 95-26171

This is an "introduction to the history and cultures of nearly 150 tribes and groups, from Inuit to Maya. . . . Each entry contains a fact box and map, followed by a simply written narrative adorned with a plethora of cross references and plenty of small, sepia-toned photos." SLJ

Ehrlich, Amy, 1942-

Wounded Knee: an Indian history of the American West; adapted for young readers by Amy Ehrlich from Dee Brown's Bury my heart at Wounded Knee. Holt & Co. 1974 202p il maps hardcover o.p. paperback available $10.95 (6 and up) **970.004**

1. Native Americans—West (U.S.) 2. Native Americans—Wars 3. West (U.S.)—History

ISBN 0-8050-2700-9 (pa)

This book traces the plight of the Navaho, Apache, Cheyenne and Sioux Indians in their struggles against the white man in the West between 1860 and 1890. It recounts battles and their causes, participants, and consequences during this era

"Some chapters [of the original] have been deleted, others condensed, and in some instances sentence structure and language have been simplified. The editing is good, and this version is interesting, readable, and smooth. " SLJ

Includes bibliographical references

Fisher, Leonard Everett, 1924-

Anasazi. Atheneum Bks. for Young Readers 1997 unp il map $16 (4 and up) **970.004**

1. Pueblo Indians—Antiquities

ISBN 0-689-80737-6 LC 96-26642

"The Anasazi, a tribe known as 'the ancient ones,' lived in the Four Corners area of Utah, Colorado, New Mexico and Arizona. . . . Fisher combines a compressed text with dramatic art . . . to tell the Anasazi's story. The book is attractive and in many ways informative about Anasazi life: their homes, agriculture, artwork." Booklist

Flanagan, Alice K.

The Pueblos. Children's Press 1998 47p il maps $22 (2-4) **970.004**

1. Pueblo Indians

ISBN 0-516-20626-5 LC 97-12683

"A True book"

Examines the culture, history, and society of the Pueblos

Includes bibliographical references

Freedman, Russell

Buffalo hunt. Holiday House 1988 52p il lib bdg $21.95; pa $8.95 (4 and up) **970.004**

1. Native Americans—Great Plains 2. Bison

ISBN 0-8234-0702-0 (lib bdg); 0-8234-1159-1 (pa) LC 87-35303

The author discusses the importance of the buffalo in the lore and day-to-day life of the Indian tribes of the Great Plains. He describes hunting methods, the uses found for each part of the animal, and the near disappearance of the buffalo as white hunters, traders and settlers moved west

"Freedman has hit his stride in terms of selection, style, and illustration: the color reproductions of historical art work form a stunning complement to the carefully researched, graceful presentation of information." Bull Cent Child Books

Griffin-Pierce, Trudy

The encyclopedia of Native America. Viking 1995 192p il $27.99 **970.004**

1. Native Americans—Encyclopedias

ISBN 0-670-85104-3 LC 94-61491

"Each chapter covers a specific geographical area of the United States, such as The Great Plains or the Southwest, and the tribes that resided there. Topics include languages of tribes with a map showing where each language group lived, descriptions of each tribe and its way of life, and European contact with the tribes and the results. Along with historical information about the tribes, Griffin-Pierce has included information on the present-day status of Native Americans." Book Rep

Hirschfelder, Arlene B.

American Indian stereotypes in the world of children; a reader and bibliography. 2nd ed, by Arlene Hirschfelder, Paulette Fairbanks Molin, Yvonne Wakim. Scarecrow Press 1999 343p il $45; pa $32.50   **970.004**

1. Native Americans 2. Race awareness
ISBN 0-8108-3612-2; 0-8108-3613-0 (pa)
                 LC 98-49654

First published 1982

"This volume presents a collection of . . . articles detailing uses and abuses of Native American symbols, images, ideas, and stories that are directed at youth in the mass media. Toys, cartoons, textbooks, general reading, media portrayals, sports, logos, nicknames and more are discussed in stand-alone articles." Voice Youth Advocates

Includes bibliographical references

Native Americans today; resources and activities for educators, grades 4-8; [by] Arlene Hirschfelder, Yvonne Beamer. Teacher Ideas Press 1999 243p il pa $25   **970.004**

1. Native Americans—Study and teaching
ISBN 1-56308-694-8   LC 99-16299

"Focusing on contemporary Native Americans, Hirschfelder and Beamer have created a comprehensive guide for teaching about American Indians. From the first chapter, which addresses terminology (*American Indians* verses *Native Americans*), stereotypes, and some things to avoid (using masks and headdresses), the authors provide clear guidance about topics of study and activities." Booklist

Includes bibliographical references

Hoyt-Goldsmith, Diane

Apache rodeo; photographs by Lawrence Migdale. Holiday House 1995 32p il $15.95 (3-5)
     970.004

1. Apache Indians 2. Rodeos
ISBN 0-8234-1164-8   LC 94-26583

This is an introduction to "the Apache of the Fort Apache Indian Reservation in Whiteriver, Arizona. Using ten-year-old Felecita La Rose as its focus and narrator, the book summarizes Apache history, customs, and daily life, and then goes on to its feature event: the rodeo." Bull Cent Child Books

"The many full-color photographs that appear throughout make it easy for other children to see how Felicita's life is like and unlike their own. An appealing introduction to Apache life today." Booklist

Includes glossary

Arctic hunter; photographs by Lawrence Migdale. Holiday House 1992 30p il $16.95; pa $6.95 (3-5)   **970.004**

1. Inuit
ISBN 0-8234-0972-4; 0-8234-1124-9 (pa)
                 LC 92-2563

"Hoyt-Goldsmith follows 10-year-old Reggie Joule and his family as they journey to their spring hunting and fishing camp north of the Arctic Circle. . . . Readers will share in Reggie's excitement as he accompanies the men on a seal hunt and makes his first kill. Hoyt-

Goldsmith treats the Iñupiaq culture with great respect. . . . Migdale's photographs illustrate the text beautifully." Booklist

Includes glossary

Buffalo days; photographs by Lawrence Migdale. Holiday House 1997 30p il maps $16.95 (3-5)   **970.004**

1. Crow Indians 2. Bison
ISBN 0-8234-1327-6   LC 97-13209

Describes life on a Crow Indian reservation in Montana, and the importance these tribes place on buffalo, which are once again thriving in areas where the Crow live

"Hoyt-Goldsmith's text is interesting and simple enough for younger readers, but it may be Migdale's attractive photographs that will draw most children to this book. Colorful, crisp, and informative, they clearly present the lives of both the people and the animals." SLJ

Includes glossary

Pueblo storyteller; photographs by Lawrence Migdale. Holiday House 1991 26p il $16.95; pa $6.95 (3-5)   **970.004**

1. Pueblo Indians
ISBN 0-8234-0864-7; 0-8234-1080-3 (pa)
                 LC 90-46405

A young Cochiti Indian girl living with her grandparents in the Cochiti Pueblo near Santa Fe, New Mexico, describes her home and family and the day-to-day life and customs of her people

"The bright, crisp, almost shadowless photographs smoothly integrate additional details into the lively text." Publ Wkly

Includes glossary

Totem pole; photographs by Lawrence Migdale. Holiday House 1990 30p il lib bdg $16.95 (3-5)
     970.004

1. Native Americans—Northwest Coast of North America 2. Totems and totemism
ISBN 0-8234-0809-4   LC 89-26720

A Tsimshian Indian boy proudly describes how his father carved a totem pole for the Klallam tribe and the subsequent ceremonial celebration

"The writing is simple and direct, the tone of pride is strong, the information is not often found in books for children, and the book is imbued with cultural dignity and a sense of the value of the extended family and community." Bull Cent Child Books

Includes glossary

Keegan, Marcia

Pueblo boy; growing up in two worlds. Cobblehill Bks. 1991 unp il $15.99 (3-5)
     970.004

1. Pueblo Indians
ISBN 0-525-65060-1   LC 90-45187

Also available from Clear Light Pubs.

Text and photographs depict the home, school, and cultural life of a young Indian boy named Timmy growing up on the San Ildefonso Pueblo in New Mexico

"The clear, colorful photographs in this respectful photo essay will attract an enthusiastic audience, and Keegan's text is interesting and readable." Horn Book

King, Sandra

Shannon: an Ojibway dancer; photographs by Catherine Whipple; with a foreword by Michael Dorris. Lerner Publs. 1993 48p il map (We are still here: Native Americans today) hardcover o.p. paperback available $6.95 (3-6)   **970.004**
1. Ojibwa Indians
ISBN 0-8225-9643-1 (pa)   LC 92-27261
Shannon, a twelve-year-old Ojibwa Indian living in Minneapolis, Minnesota, learns about her tribe's traditional costumes from her grandmother and gets ready to dance at a powwow
"Numerous, colorful photographs show Shannon's daily activities as well as the costumes and dances at the powwow. The photos combine with a contemporary focus and straightforward text to make the book an excellent choice for middle readers." Booklist
Includes glossary and bibliographical references

Left Hand Bull, Jacqueline

Lakota hoop dancer; text by Jacqueline Left Hand Bull and Suzanne Haldane; with photographs by Suzanne Haldane. Dutton Children's Bks. 1999 unp il $15.99 (3-6)   **970.004**
1. Teton Indians 2. Native American dance
ISBN 0-525-45413-6   LC 98-21905
Follows the activities of Kevin Locke, a Hunkpapa Indian, as he prepares for and performs the traditional Lakota hoop dance
"The well-written narrative is nicely matched with large full-color photos showing Locke's costumes, various dance designs, homeland, and family." Booklist
Includes glossary and bibliographical references

Native Americans. Grolier Educ. 1999 10v apply to publisher for price (4 and up)   **970.004**
1. Native Americans—Encyclopedias
LC 99-28319
"Entries on tribal groups from the Arctic to Central America, individuals, and aspects of Native life are included in this alphabetically arranged set. . . . Full-color and black-and-white photographs, reproductions, and a number of maps appear throughout the set." SLJ
For a fuller review see: Booklist, Jan. 1-15, 2000

Patterson, Lotsee

Indian terms of the Americas; [by] Lotsee Patterson, Mary Ellen Snodgrass; original illustrations by Dan Timmons. Libraries Unlimited 1994 275p il maps $35   **970.004**
1. Native Americans—Dictionaries
ISBN 1-56308-133-4   LC 93-47170
"Each of the approximate 850 entries provides a pronunciation guide for the term, an alternate form or spelling, a definition of Indian vocabulary, people, places, and events, boldface words that refer to other listings in the book, and other related terms for more information. . . . Drawings and photos greatly enhance the meaning of the terms." Book Rep

Peters, Russell M.

Clambake; a Wampanoag tradition; photographs by John Madama; with a foreword by Michael Dorris. Lerner Publs. 1992 48p il (We are still here: Native Americans today) lib bdg $21.27; pa $6.95 (3-6)   **970.004**
1. Wampanoag Indians
ISBN 0-8225-2651-4 (lib bdg); 0-8225-9621-0 (pa)
LC 92-8423
"The traditional clambake, or Apponaug, of the Wampanoag Indians of the Northeastern American coast holds important spiritual and cultural meaning for the people of the tribe. This is the story of how young Steven, a Mashpee Wampanoag, celebrates his first Apponaug with friends and relatives on tribal lands of Cape Cod, Massachusetts." Publisher's note
"The full-color photographs illustrate the clearly written text and portray real people who are part of the contemporary world, passing on old traditions to their children." SLJ
Includes glossary and bibliographical references

Powell, Suzanne I.

The Pueblos; [by] Suzanne Powell. Watts 1993 64p il lib bdg $22.50; pa $6.95 (4 and up)
970.004
1. Pueblo Indians
ISBN 0-531-20068-X (lib bdg); 0-531-15703-2 (pa)
LC 93-18368
"A First book"
Discusses the traditional and modern way of life of the Pueblos, examining their history, culture, religion, and ability to survive and thrive in difficult conditions
Includes glossary and bibliographical references

Roessel, Monty

Kinaaldá: a Navajo girl grows up; text and photographs by Monty Roessel; with a foreword by Michael Dorris. Lerner Publs. 1993 48p il map (We are still here: Native Americans today) hardcover o.p. paperback available $6.95 (3-6)
970.004
1. Navajo Indians
ISBN 0-8225-9641-5 (pa)   LC 92-35204
Celinda McKelvey, a Navajo girl, participates in the Kinaalda, the traditional coming-of-age ceremony of her people
"The text is spare but clear, with sufficient detail to inform general readers; the color photographs are crisp and well composed." Horn Book Guide
Includes glossary and bibliographical references

Songs from the loom; a Navajo girl learns to weave; text and photographs by Monty Roessel. Lerner Publs. 1995 48p il (We are still here: Native Americans today) lib bdg $21.27; pa $6.95 (3-6)   **970.004**
1. Navajo Indians 2. Weaving
ISBN 0-8225-2657-3 (lib bdg); 0-8225-9711-X (pa)
LC 94-48765
"Ten-year-old Jaclyn's grandmother teaches her the art of traditional Navajo rug-weaving. Jaclyn learns the

Roessel, Monty—*Continued*

songs and stories that invest the weaving with meaning, as well as the use of the proper tools and techniques. The color photographs of contemporary Navajo life are clear and engrossing, enhancing the solid text." Horn Book Guide

Includes glossary and bibliographical references

Sneve, Virginia Driving Hawk

The Apaches; illustrated by Ronald Himler. Holiday House 1997 32p il (First Americans book) $16.95 (3-5)   **970.004**
     1. Apache Indians
     ISBN 0-8234-1287-3   LC 96-41358

Describes the social structure, daily life, religion, government relations, and history of the Apache people

"Sneve's text is not exhaustive, but it does provide some detailed information. Himler's atmospheric oil paintings expand on the words to give readers a fuller appreciation of the subject." SLJ

The Cherokees; illustrated by Ronald Himler. Holiday House 1996 32p il maps (First Americans book) $16.95 (3-5)   **970.004**
     1. Cherokee Indians
     ISBN 0-8234-1214-8   LC 95-24099

"This brief description of the Cherokee nation begins with a creation myth and includes some traditions, history, and contemporary socio-cultural information." Bull Cent Child Books

This "is a sound treatment of the Cherokee people that will encourage youngsters to read further. . . . Himler's nicely executed paintings add detail, clarify the text, and contribute to the reader's understanding of history." Horn Book Guide

The Cheyennes; illustrated by Ronald Himler. Holiday House 1996 32p il maps (First Americans book) $16.95 (3-5)   **970.004**
     1. Cheyenne Indians
     ISBN 0-8234-1250-4   LC 95-50696

The author describes "Cheyenne creation stories, westward migration, culture, history, and conditions for the tribe today. . . . The tragic heritage of Cheyenne-white violence takes up the bulk of the text. Himler's watercolors take the form of clear maps and marvelously rendered characters. . . . A worthy addition that brings to life these people and their culture." SLJ

The Hopis; illustrated by Ronald Himler. Holiday House 1995 32p il maps (First Americans book) $16.95 (3-5)   **970.004**
     1. Hopi Indians
     ISBN 0-8234-1194-X   LC 95-1259

"After opening with a retelling of the creation myth, Sneve goes on to provide a fair amount of detail about the religion, social structure, and general way of life of the Hopi. . . . Sneve's prose is simple and straightforward, with short, clear sentences. Himler's appealing oil paintings lend a rich atmosphere to the book." SLJ

The Iroquois; illustrated by Ronald Himler. Holiday House 1995 32p il map (First Americans book) $16.95 (3-5)   **970.004**
     1. Iroquois Indians
     ISBN 0-8234-1163-X   LC 94-03748

In this illustrated overview of the Six Nations of the Iroquois the author "includes a highly abridged creation story; an account of the traditional government of the people; descriptions of men's, women's, and children's roles; food; spiritual beliefs; the use of wampum; and the people today." SLJ

The Navajos; illustrated by Ronald Himler. Holiday House 1993 32p il (First Americans book) hardcover o.p. paperback available $6.95 (3-5)   **970.004**
     1. Navajo Indians
     ISBN 0-8234-1168-0 (pa)   LC 92-40330

Provides an overview of the history, culture, and way of life of the Navajo Indians

"Himler's paintings enliven the matter-of-fact text." Booklist

The Nez Percé; illustrated by Ronald Himler. Holiday House 1994 32p il map (First Americans book) $16.95 (3-5)   **970.004**
     1. Nez Percé Indians
     ISBN 0-8234-1090-0   LC 93-38598

This discussion of the Nez Percé Indians "begins with a Chopunnish creation story, followed by descriptions of daily life and an abbreviated history. Himler's paintings beautifully enhance the text." Booklist

The Seminoles; illustrated by Ronald Himler. Holiday House 1994 32p il map (First Americans book) $16.95 (3-5)   **970.004**
     1. Seminole Indians
     ISBN 0-8234-1112-5   LC 93-14316

Discusses the history, lifestyle, customs, and current situation of the Seminoles

"The writing is smooth, if necessarily generalized, and Himler's watercolors are especially suited to the swampy backdrops and dramatic action that characterized the Seminoles' struggle to survive." Bull Cent Child Books

The Sioux; illustrated by Ronald Himler. Holiday House 1993 32p il (First Americans book) $16.95; pa $6.95 (3-5)   **970.004**
     1. Dakota Indians
     ISBN 0-8234-1017-X; 0-8234-1171-0 (pa)
         LC 92-23946

Identifies the different tribes of the Sioux Indians and discusses their beliefs and traditional way of life

"Himler's art work balances the aesthetic with the instructive, the past with the present, in compositions that are steeped in plains . . . hues and are vibrant with action." Bull Cent Child Books

Terry, Michael Bad Hand

Daily life in a Plains Indian village, 1868. Clarion Bks. 1999 48p il maps $20; pa $9.95 (4 and up)   **970.004**
     1. Native Americans—Great Plains
     ISBN 0-395-94542-9; 0-395-97499-2 (pa)
         LC 98-32382

Depicts the historical background, social organization, and daily life of a Plains Indian village in 1868, presenting interiors, landscapes, clothing, and everyday objects

"The author presents short paragraphs of fascinating information accompanied by visuals that explain even more than the text." SLJ

Includes glossary

970.01 North America—Early history to 1599

Brenner, Barbara
If you were there in 1492. Bradbury Press 1991 106p il maps hardcover o.p. paperback available $5.99 (4-6) **970.01**
1. Columbus, Christopher 2. World history—15th century 3. America—Exploration
ISBN 0-689-82241-3 (pa)   LC 90-24099
Readers take a trip back in time to learn about the culture and civilization of 15th century Europe and Spain, and the discovery of America by Columbus
"Fascinating details keep company with a style that may strike some readers as cutesy but that gives a wealth of interesting facts about life in late 15th-century Spain. . . . The numerous black-and-white reproductions of woodcuts, maps, and period paintings are informative as well as decorative." SLJ
Includes bibliographical references

Maestro, Betsy, 1944-
The discovery of the Americas; by Betsy and Giulio Maestro. Lothrop, Lee & Shepard Bks. 1990 48p il maps $16.95; pa $6.95 (2-4) **970.01**
1. America—Exploration
ISBN 0-688-06837-5; 0-688-11512-8 (pa)
            LC 89-32375
Also available Spanish language edition
Discusses both hypothetical and historical voyages of discovery to America by the Phoenicians, Saint Brendan of Ireland, the Vikings, and such later European navigators as Columbus, Cabot, and Magellan
"The dazzlingly clean and accurate prose and the exhilarating beauty of the pictures combine for an extraordinary achievement in both history and art." SLJ

Exploration and conquest; the Americas after Columbus, 1500-1620; [by] Betsy & Giulio Maestro. Lothrop, Lee & Shepard Bks. 1994 48p il maps lib bdg $15.93; pa $6.95 (2-4) **970.01**
1. America—Exploration
ISBN 0-688-09268-3 (lib bdg); 0-688-15474-3 (pa)
            LC 93-48618
This is a "discussion of the European exploration and conquest of the 'New World.' The author carefully explains that, 'The great gain of one people was the great loss of another' and traces the disastrous effects that the Portuguese, Spanish, English, French, and Dutch had on the native peoples of the Americas, while acknowledging the benefits the Europeans enjoyed." SLJ
"The book's most outstanding feature is its full-color artwork. Large, double-page spreads give scope to dramatic landscapes, while smaller pictures on every page show events, places, and maps pertinent to the text. . . . This book provides a useful overview of the period." Booklist

Marzollo, Jean
In 1492; illustrated by Steve Björkman. Scholastic 1991 unp il (k-2) **970.01**
1. Columbus, Christopher 2. America—Exploration 3. Explorers
            LC 91-100

Available Big book edition $19.95 (ISBN 0-590-72737-0)
Rhyming text describes Christopher Columbus's first voyage to the New World
"The tale is surprisingly clear and complete, despite the brief and simple text. . . . Björkman's light-hearted illustrations are top-notch—his oceanscapes are suitably sweeping, his ships imposing, his characters endearing in their naïveté." Publ Wkly

Sattler, Helen Roney
The earliest Americans; illustrated by Jean Day Zallinger. Clarion Bks. 1993 125p il maps $19 (5 and up) **970.01**
1. Native Americans—Antiquities 2. Prehistoric peoples 3. America—Antiquities
ISBN 0-395-54996-5   LC 91-9463
Covers the history of early man in America from the earliest known sites to approximately 1492 A.D
"A readable archaeologically based account of pre-Columbian history, profusely illustrated in meticulous detail." SLJ
Includes bibliographical references

Steins, Richard
Exploration and settlement. Raintree Steck-Vaughn Pubs. 2000 96p il maps (Making of America) $28.55 (5 and up) **970.01**
1. America—Exploration 2. Native Americans
ISBN 0-8172-5700-4   LC 99-46961
Recounts the stories of the French, English, and Dutch in the New World, their reasons for settlement, and their relations with the native Americans
"Back matter includes glossaries, bibliographies, time lines, and Web sites. Colorfully illustrated with maps as well as period prints, paintings, and drawings." Booklist

971 Canada

Sateren, Shelley Swanson
Canada; star of the north. Benchmark Bks. (Tarrytown) 1996 64p il maps (Exploring cultures of the world) $27.07 (4 and up) **971**
1. Canada
ISBN 0-7614-0199-7   LC 95-25703
Describes the geography, history, people, and culture of the second largest country in the world
Includes bibliographical references

971.27 Manitoba

Kurelek, William, 1927-1977
A prairie boy's summer; paintings and story by William Kurelek. Houghton Mifflin 1975 unp il o.p.; Tundra Bks. paperback available $10.95 (3-5)
            971.27
1. Children—Canada 2. Farm life—Canada 3. Summer
ISBN 0-88776-116-X (pa)

Kurelek, William, 1927-1977—_Continued_

This book shows "many details of the artist's life when he was a boy growing up on a farm in Western Canada." Horn Book

"It is, of course, the pictures by this distinguished Canadian artist that give the book its distinction; each full-color page glows with life and vigor, and the paintings have both a felicity of small details and a remarkable evocation of the breadth and sweep of the Manitoba prairie." Bull Cent Child Books

A prairie boy's winter; paintings and story by William Kurelek. Houghton Mifflin 1973 unp il hardcover o.p. paperback available $8.95 (3-5)
971.27
1. Children—Canada 2. Farm life—Canada 3. Winter
ISBN 0-395-36609-7 (pa)
The author depicts the rigors and pleasures of boyhood winters on a Manitoba farm in the 1930's including hauling hay, playing hockey, and surviving a blizzard

971.3   Ontario

Fisher, Leonard Everett, 1924-
Niagara Falls; nature's wonder. Holiday House 1996 63p il $16.95 (4 and up)   **971.3**
1. Niagara Falls (N.Y. and Ont.)
ISBN 0-8234-1240-7   LC 95-42740
"This book focuses on Niagara Falls more as a cultural and historical institution than as a natural phenomenon. . . . Among the topics covered are the Maid of the Mist ferry, the construction of suspension bridges over the Niagara River, the impact of the Falls on painters and writers, and the persistent attempt to conquer them via tightrope, raft, and barrel. The many black-and-white illustrations include nineteenth-century paintings, engravings, and broadsides as well as nineteenth- and twentieth-century photographs." Booklist

Greenwood, Barbara
A pioneer sampler; the daily life of a pioneer family in 1840; illustrated by Heather Collins. Ticknor & Fields Bks. for Young Readers 1995 240p il $18.95; pa $10.95 (4 and up)   **971.3**
1. Frontier and pioneer life
ISBN 0-395-71540-7; 0-395-88393-8 (pa)
                   LC 94-12829
First published 1994 in Canada with title: A pioneer story
"Using a combination of fiction and fact-filled supplementary commentary, with illustrations inspired by Garth Williams, the author tells the story of the Robertsons, a large, hardworking farm family. Good projects for school or home." N Y Times Book Rev

971.9   Northern territories of Canada

Jones, Charlotte Foltz, 1945-
Yukon gold; the story of the Klondike Gold Rush. Holiday House 1999 99p il $18.95 (4 and up)   **971.9**
1. Klondike River valley (Yukon)—Gold discoveries
ISBN 0-8234-1403-5   LC 98-20977

Recounts the quest for gold that took place in the late 1890s in the Klondike region of the Yukon Territory of northwestern Canada and Alaska

"Historical photographs, posters and newspaper headlines give readers a flavor of the times. This is a solid resource for information about the period." Publ Wkly
Includes glossary and bibliographical references

Walsh Shepherd, Donna, 1948-
The Klondike gold rush. Watts 1998 64p il maps lib bdg $23 (4 and up)   **971.9**
1. Klondike River valley (Yukon)—Gold discoveries
ISBN 0-531-20360-3   LC 97-38340
"A First book"
Describes the adventures of those who flocked to the Klondike after gold was discovered there in 1896
"Short enough to appeal to reluctant researchers and long enough to provide a basic grasp of the events, the book succeeds admirably." SLJ
Includes bibliographical references

972   Middle America. Mexico

Ancona, George, 1929-
Charro; the Mexican cowboy. Harcourt Brace & Co. 1999 unp il $18; pa $9 (3-6)   **972**
1. Cowhands 2. Mexico—Social life and customs
ISBN 0-15-201047-5; 0-15-201046-7 (pa)
                  LC 98-13396
Text and photographs present the traditions and the annual celebration of the charro, the Mexican cowboy
"Ancona's pictures just keep getting better and better, moving readers forward with motion, color, and excitement. A 'don't miss' from a master." SLJ
Includes glossary

Mayeros; a Yucatec Maya family. Lothrop, Lee & Shepard Bks. 1997 40p il $16 (3-6)   **972**
1. Mayas
ISBN 0-688-13465-3   LC 96-2309
Text and photographs present the life and customs of the descendants of the Maya now living in the Yucatan Peninsula area of Mexico
"In an involving text, the activities of three generations of men, women, and children are described. In addition, information about the geography and history of the region is seamlessly interspersed throughout the narrative. . . . Crisp, full-color photographs amplify the actions described in the text." SLJ
Includes glossary

Arnold, Caroline, 1944-
City of the Gods; Mexico's ancient city of Teotihuacán; photographs by Richard Hewitt. Clarion Bks. 1994 48p il map $14.95 (4 and up)
                       972
1. Native Americans—Mexico 2. Teotihuacán site (San Juan Teotihuacán, Mexico)
ISBN 0-395-66584-1   LC 93-40811
In text and photographs, this book examines the ancient city of Teotihuacán in Mexico
"Students doing reports will find this a good resource, but the arresting photographs will draw browsers in as well." Booklist
Includes glossary

Hewitt, Sally
The Aztecs. Children's Press 1996 24p il maps
(Footsteps in time) $18 (1-3)   **972**
1. Aztecs
ISBN 0-516-08071-7   LC 95-25252
An illustrated introduction to Aztec geography, history
and culture. Includes ideas and step-by-step instructions
for several related projects and activities

Kent, Deborah, 1948-
Mexico. Benchmark Bks. (Tarrytown) 1996 64p
il maps (Exploring cultures of the world) lib bdg
$27.07 (4 and up)   **972**
1. Mexico
ISBN 0-7614-0187-3   LC 95-15339
Covers the geography, history, people, customs, and
the arts of Mexico
Includes bibliographical references

Kimmel, Eric A.
Montezuma and the fall of the Aztecs;
illustrated by Daniel San Souci. Holiday House
2000 unp il $16.95 (3-5)   **972**
1. Montezuma II, Emperor of Mexico, ca. 1480-1520
2. Aztecs 3. Mexico—History
ISBN 0-8234-1452-3   LC 99-37134
"Hernán Cortés and his small force of Spanish soldiers
arrived on the coast of Mexico in 1519. Within three
years . . . the Aztec empire had collapsed. Kimmel prefaces his account of these events with a few pages of
background information on the empire and Montezuma's
rule. The story of Cortés's marches inland, his capture of
the native leader, and the siege on Tenochtitlan is simply
but dramatically told. San Souci's light-filled, detailed
watercolors paint a vivid picture of these adversaries."
SLJ
Includes bibliographical references

Milord, Susan, 1954-
Mexico! 40 activities to experience Mexico past
& present; illustrations by Michael Kline.
Williamson 1998 96p il maps pa $10.95   **972**
1. Mexico
ISBN 1-88559-322-8   LC 98-34153
"A Kaleidoscope kids book"
"Milord provides an amazing amount of information
about Mexico, ranging from ancient history through the
Spanish conquest to contemporary life. Activities include
such standards as making an *Ojo de Dios* and a *piñata*,
but there are also directions for creating marzipan skulls
for the Day of the Dead celebration, as well as recipes
for salsa, tortillas, and hot chocolate. . . . This is an excellent starting point for students investigating this culture." SLJ
Includes bibliographical references

Staub, Frank J.
Children of Yucatán; written and photographed
by Frank Staub. Carolrhoda Bks. 1996 47p il
(World's children) lib bdg $23.93 (3-5)   **972**
1. Children—Mexico 2. Mayas 3. Yucatán (Mexico)—Social life and customs
ISBN 0-87614-984-0   LC 95-35027

Describes life in Yucatán, Mexico, focusing on the
daily activities and cultural history of some modern Mayan children
"Along with providing historical and geographic background, [this] photo-essay creates a vital sense of immediacy by interweaving the names of the children who are
pictured with descriptions of their daily activiites." Booklist

Stein, R. Conrad, 1937-
The Aztec empire. Benchmark Bks. (Tarrytown)
1996 80p il (Cultures of the past) $28.50 (4 and
up)   **972**
1. Aztecs
ISBN 0-7614-0072-9   LC 95-7333
An illustrated look at Aztec art, architecture, religion,
mythology, government and society
Includes glossary and bibliographical references

Mexico. Children's Press 1998 144p il maps
(Enchantment of the world, second series) lib bdg
$33 (4 and up)   **972**
1. Mexico
ISBN 0-516-20650-8   LC 97-40708
This describes the geography, history, government,
economy and culture of Mexico
"For the most part, the writing and presentation of in-
formation are of high quality." SLJ
Includes bibliographical references

Tanaka, Shelley
Lost temple of the Aztecs; what it was like
when the Spaniards invaded Mexico; illustrations
by Greg Ruhl; diagrams and maps by Jack
McMaster; historical consultation by Eduardo
Matos Moctezuma. Hyperion Bks. for Children;
Madison Press Bks. 1998 48p il maps (I was there
books) $16.95; pa $7.99 (4 and up)   **972**
1. Aztecs 2. Mexico—History
ISBN 0-7868-0441-6; 0-7868-1542-6 (pa)
          LC 98-10986
"A Hyperion/Madison Press book"
Uses the discovery of the temple in Mexico City, what
was the Aztec city of Tenochtitlan, to introduce the story
of the Spanish conquest of Moctezuma and his empire in
the sixteenth century
"Lavishly illustrated with full-color photos, period artwork, and dramatic full-page paintings, the book is handsome and eye-catching." SLJ
Includes glossary and bibliographical references

Wood, Tim
The Aztecs. Viking 1992 48p il maps (See
through history) $19.99 (4 and up)   **972**
1. Aztecs
ISBN 0-670-84492-6   LC 91-68542
This book describes Aztec civilization
This is "particularly readable and well-designed. Topics are covered adequately and are sensibly arranged, and
the better-than-average color illustrations are bolstered by
photos of artifacts." Booklist
Includes glossary

972.81　Guatemala

Out of the dump: writings and photographs by children from Guatemala; edited by Kristine L. Franklin & Nancy McGirr; translated from the Spanish by Kristine L. Franklin. Lothrop, Lee & Shepard Bks. 1995 unp il lib bdg $18.93

972.81

1. Children—Guatemala 2. Children's writings
ISBN 0-688-13924-8　　　　　LC 95-9782

"Nancy McGirr initiated a project to provide a group of children living in a Guatemala City garbage dump with cameras and encouragement; this book consists of examples of their photographs and essays. The poignant black-and-white photos clearly depict the abject poverty that surrounds these young people. . . . Both children and adults will find this title refreshing in its honesty and insight." SLJ

Sheehan, Sean, 1951-
Guatemala. Marshall Cavendish 1998 128p il maps (Cultures of the world) lib bdg $35.64 (5 and up)　　　　　972.81

1. Guatemala
ISBN 0-7614-0812-6　　　　　LC 97-44619

Introduces the geography, history, religion, government, economy, and culture of one of the poorest countries in the western hemisphere

"A good-quality full-color photograph, reproduction, or map appears on most pages. This [is a] solid volume." SLJ

Includes glossary and bibliographical references

972.83　Honduras

McGaffey, Leta
Honduras. Marshall Cavendish 1999 128p il maps (Cultures of the world) lib bdg $35.64 (5 and up)　　　　　972.83

1. Honduras
ISBN 0-7614-0955-6　　　　　LC 98-54908

This is a look at the Central American nation. "Following introductory chapters on the geography, history, and government, the clearly written book focuses on contemporary life. The economy, population, religion, leisure activities, holidays, indigenous and ethnic groups, and rural and urban lifestyles are all covered. . . . A quality, full-color photograph appears on almost every page." SLJ

Includes glossary and bibliographical references

972.84　El Salvador

Foley, Erin, 1967-
El Salvador. Marshall Cavendish 1994 128p il maps (Cultures of the world) $35.64 (5 and up)
972.84

1. El Salvador
ISBN 1-85435-696-8　　　　　LC 94-22567

This book "traces the history of the Spanish Conquest and the influences of Indian languages and liberation theology on the people. The political role of the United States in recent history should prove helpful to anyone trying to understand the country's recent and devastating struggle against abuse and injustice." SLJ

Includes glossary and bibliographical references

972.85　Nicaragua

Kott, Jennifer, 1971-
Nicaragua. Marshall Cavendish 1994 128p il maps (Cultures of the world) $35.64 (5 and up)
972.85

1. Nicaragua
ISBN 1-85435-695-X　　　　　LC 94-28809

An illustrated overview of the geography, economy, history, government, politics, and culture of Nicaragua

Includes glossary and bibliographical references

972.86　Costa Rica

Foley, Erin, 1967-
Costa Rica. Marshall Cavendish 1997 128p il maps (Cultures of the world) lib bdg $35.64 (5 and up)　　　　　972.86

1. Costa Rica
ISBN 0-7614-0285-3　　　　　LC 96-17309

Surveys the geography, history, government, and culture of the oldest democracy in Latin America

Includes glossary and bibliographical references

Morrison, Marion
Costa Rica. Children's Press 1998 144p il maps (Enchantment of the world, second series) lib bdg $33 (4 and up)　　　　　972.86

1. Costa Rica
ISBN 0-516-20469-6　　　　　LC 97-40665

Describes the geography, history, culture, religion, and people of the small Central American nation of Costa Rica

Includes bibliographical references

972.87　Panama

Hassig, Susan M., 1969-
Panama; [by] Susan Hassig. Marshall Cavendish 1996 128p il (Cultures of the world) lib bdg $35.64 (5 and up)　　　　　972.87

1. Panama
ISBN 0-7614-0278-0　　　　　LC 95-44491

This is an introduction to the geography, history, people, and culture of Panama

This offers "simple prose, color photographs, and an attractive layout that features information boxes and sidebars. . . . A solid introduction." Horn Book Guide

Includes glossary and bibliographical references

972.91 Cuba

Sheehan, Sean, 1951-
Cuba. Marshall Cavendish 1994 128p il maps (Cultures of the world) $35.64 (5 and up) **972.91**
1. Cuba
ISBN 1-85435-691-7   LC 94-22574
This introduction to Cuba "covers geography, history, government, economy, population, lifestyle, religion, language, arts, leisure, festivals, and food. . . . The material is well organized in easily readable sections, accurately illustrated with well-placed, full-color photographs on every page." SLJ
Includes glossary and bibliographical references

Wolf, Bernard, 1930-
Cuba: after the revolution; written and photographed by Bernard Wolf. Dutton Children's Bks. 1999 unp il $16.99 (4 and up)   **972.91**
1. Cuba—Social life and customs
ISBN 0-525-46058-6   LC 99-26223
In words and pictures, describes the daily life of Ana Moreira, the daughter of two Havana artists, as she goes to school, takes ballet lessons, and plays in the park
"While not a completely balanced view, this is a beautiful photo-essay. . . . This book will serve to demystify and familiarize children with a population that may largely have been unknown to them until now." SLJ

972.94 Haiti

Hintz, Martin, 1945-
Haiti. Children's Press 1998 143p il maps (Enchantment of the world, second series) lib bdg $33 (4 and up)   **972.94**
1. Haiti
ISBN 0-516-20603-6   LC 97-25518
Describes the geography, history, government, people, and culture of the second oldest republic in the Western Hemisphere
Includes bibliographical references

972.96 Bahama Islands

Barlas, Robert
Bahamas. Marshall Cavendish 2000 128p il maps (Cultures of the world) lib bdg $35.64 (5 and up)   **972.96**
1. Bahamas
ISBN 0-7614-0992-0   LC 99-88028
Introduces the geography, history, government, economy, religion, language, arts, leisure activities, festivals, food, and people of this archipelago lying in the Atlantic Ocean off the coast of Florida
Includes bibliographical references

Hintz, Martin, 1945-
The Bahamas; by Martin & Stephen Hintz. Children's Press 1997 143p il maps (Enchantment of the world, second series) $33 (4 and up)
972.96
1. Bahamas
ISBN 0-516-20583-8   LC 97-596
Describes the geography, plants, animals, history, economy, language, religions, culture, sports, arts, and people of the Bahamas
Includes bibliographical references

972.98 Windward and other southern islands

Elias, Marie Louise
Barbados. Marshall Cavendish 2000 128p il maps (Cultures of the world) lib bdg $35.64 (5 and up)   **972.98**
1. Barbados
ISBN 0-7614-0976-9   LC 99-27594
Discusses the geography, history, government, economy, people, and culture of Barbados, a small island nation in the Caribbean
Includes glossary and bibliographical references

973 United States

America the beautiful, second series. Children's Press 1998-2000 47v il maps lib bdg ea $33 (4 and up)   **973**
1. United States
Replaces titles in the original series published 1987-1992
Volumes available are: Alabama, by L. Davis; Alaska, by D. Walsh Shepherd; Arizona, by J. F. Blashfield; California, by A. Heinrichs; Colorado, by J. F. Blashfield; Connecticut, by S. McNair; Delaware, by J. F. Blashfield; Florida, by A. Heinrichs; Georgia, by N. Robinson Masters; Hawaii, by M. Hintz; Idaho, by C. George; Illinois, by A. Santella; Indiana, by A. Heinrichs; Iowa, by M. Hintz; Kansas, by N. Robinson Masters; Kentucky, by R. C. Stein; Louisiana, by M. Hintz; Maine, by D. Kent; Maryland, by M. Burgan; Massachusetts, by S. McNair; Michigan, by M. Hintz; Minnesota, by M. Hintz; Mississippi, by C. George; Missouri, by M. Hintz; Montana, by C. George; Nebraska, by S. McNair; Nevada, by R. C. Stein; New Hampshire, by R. C. Stein; New Jersey, by R. C. Stein; New Mexico, by D. Kent; New York, by A. Heinrichs; North Carolina, by M. Hintz; North Dakota, by M. Hintz; Ohio, by A. Heinrichs; Oklahoma, by J. Reedy; Oregon, by S. Ingram; Pennsylvania, by A. Heinrichs; Puerto Rico, by L. Davis; Rhode Island, by S. McNair; South Carolina, by R. C. Stein; Texas, by A. Heinrichs; Utah, by D. Kent; Virginia, by J. F. Blashfield; Washington, D.C., by R. C. Stein; West Virginia, by W. Fazio; Wisconsin, by J. F. Blashfield; Wyoming, by D. Kent
"Several chapters on the history of the state begin each book; sections on geography, government and politics, the economy, diversity of the population, education, arts and leisure, famous citizens, and museums and his-

America the beautiful, second series—*Continued*
torical sites follow." SLJ

These books "are solid purchases for many libraries. They feature clear, lively writing with considerable amounts of information. . . . Maps are a particularly strong feature." Booklist

Celebrate the states. Benchmark Bks. (Tarrytown) 1996-2001 48v il maps music lib bdg ea $35.64 (4 and up)   **973**

1. United States

Volumes available are: Alabama, by D. Shirley; Alaska, by R. Stefoff; Arkansas, by L. Altman; Arizona, by M. McDaniel; California, by L. Altman; Colorado, by E. H. Ayer; Connecticut, by V. Sherrow; Delaware, by M. Schuman; Florida, by P. Chang; Georgia, by S. Otfinoski; Hawaii, by J. Goldberg; Idaho, by R. Steffof; Illinois, by M. T. Brill; Indiana, by M. T. Brill; Iowa, by P. Morice; Kansas, by R. Bjorkland; Kentucky, by T. Barrett; Louisiana, by S. LeVert; Maine, by M. Dornfeld; Maryland, by L. Pietrzyk; Massachusetts, by S. LeVert; Michigan, by M. T. Brill; Minnesota, by M. Schwabacher; Mississippi, by D. Shirley; Missouri, by M. Bennett; Nevada by R. Stefoff; New Hampshire, by S. Otfinoski; New Jersey, by W. Moragne; New Mexico, by M. McDaniel; New York, by V. Schomp; North Carolina, by D. Shirley; Ohio, by V. Sherrow; Oklahoma, by G. Baldwin; Oregon, by R. Stefoff; Pennsylvania, by S. Peters; Rhode Island, by T. Klein; South Carolina, by N. Hoffman; South Dakota, by M. McDaniel; Tennessee, by T. Barrett; Texas, by C. Bredeson; Utah, by R. Steffof; Vermont, by D. Elish; Virginia, by T. Barrett; Washington, by R. Steffof; Washington, D.C., by D. Elish; West Virginia, by N. Hoffman; Wisconsin, by K. Zeinert; Wyoming by G. Baldwin

"These books each contain six chapters devoted to the state's geography, history, government and economy, people, achievements, and landmarks. A section of reference facts and figures is also included. Competently written, the books serve as attractive and accessible introductions to the . . . states." Horn Book Guide

Hakim, Joy

A history of US. 2nd ed. Oxford Univ. Press 1999 11v il maps set $219.45; pa $153.45 (5 and up)   **973**

1. United States—History
ISBN 0-19-512773-0; 0-19-512774-9 (pa)
     LC 98-180015

First published 1993-1995

Contents: bk 1 The first Americans; bk 2 Making thirteen colonies; bk 3 From colonies to country; bk 4 The new nation; bk 5 Liberty for all?; bk 6 War, terrible war; bk 7 Reconstruction and reform; bk 8 An age of extremes; bk 9 War, peace, and all that jazz; bk 10 All the people; bk 11 Sourcebook and index

Presents the history of America from the earliest times of the Native Americans to the Clinton administration

This is an "inviting American history series that has proved useful in the circulating collection as well as on the reference shelf." Booklist

Includes bibliographical references

Leedy, Loreen, 1959-

Celebrate the 50 states; written and illustrated by Loreen Leedy. Holiday House 1999 32p il maps $16.95; pa $6.95 (k-3)   **973**

1. United States
ISBN 0-8234-1431-0; 0-8234-1631-3 (pa)
     LC 99-10986

Introduces statistics, emblems, notable cities, products, and other facts about the fifty states, United States territories, and Washington, D.C

"Brightly colored and amusingly designed, this is a simple yet winning introduction to the U.S." Booklist

St. George, Judith, 1931-

So you want to be president; illustrated by David Small. Philomel Bks. 2000 52p il $17.99 (3-6)   **973**

1. Presidents—United States
ISBN 0-399-23407-1   LC 98-40002

Awarded the Caldecott Medal, 2001

Presents an assortment of facts about the qualifications and characteristics of U.S. presidents, from George Washington to Bill Clinton

This book "is easy enough to read even for children in the lower grades, but like many such books it is ideally enjoyed by a child with an adult. That way, its rich anecdotes provoke questions, answers, definitions, recollections and more anecdotes." N Y Times Book Rev

Includes bibliographical references

973.03   United States—History— Encyclopedias and dictionaries

Bock, Judy

Scholastic encyclopedia of the United States; [by] Judy Bock, Rachel Kranz; [pub. in assn. with] Bascom Communications. Scholastic Ref. 1997 140p il maps $17.95 (4 and up)   **973.03**

1. United States—Encyclopedias
ISBN 0-590-94747-8   LC 96-39774

Presents historical, geographical, and miscellaneous information about each of the fifty states

Junior Worldmark encyclopedia of the states. 2nd ed. U.X.L 1999 4v il maps set $115 (4 and up)   **973.03**

1. United States—Dictionaries
ISBN 0-7876-3796-3   LC 99-20448

First published 1996; based on Worldmark encyclopedia of the states

This resource provides coverage of every state in the U.S., including the District of Columbia and U.S. dependencies. Among the subject areas addressed are: history, geography, local government, industry, ethnic groups, religion, migration and education. Famous natives of each state are noted

This "is a well-organized, clearly written presentation of basic information." Am Ref Books Annu, 2001

973.05   United States—History— Serial publications

Cobblestone; discover American history. Cobblestone Pub. $26.95 per year   **973.05**
1. United States—History—Periodicals
ISSN 0199-5197

Monthly except June, July and August. First published 1980

"*Cobblestone* is a history magazine written for upper elementary and junior high age students. Each issue focuses in-depth on a single topic. Unfamiliar words are highlighted in the text and defined in sidebars throughout the magazine. The illustrations are meaningful and interesting. Book, media, and web site reviews provide additional information for readers and teachers." Katz. Mag for Libr. 10th edition

973.2   United States—Colonial period, 1607-1775

King, David C.
Colonial days; discover the past with fun projects, games, activities, and recipes. Wiley 1998 118p il (American kids in history) pa $12.95 (3-6)
973.2
1. United States—Social life and customs—1600-1775, Colonial period
ISBN 0-471-16168-3   LC 97-16083
"A Roundtable Press book"
Illustrations by Bobbie Moore
Discusses colonial life in America, depicts a year in the life of a fictional colonial family, and presents projects and activities, such as butter churning, candle dipping, baking bread, and playing colonial games
"Explanatory text alternates with instructions and other sidebars that provide brief history lessons. The materials needed are readily accessible in grocery, hobby, or craft stores. The line drawings are clear and helpful." SLJ
Includes glossary and bibliographical references

Maestro, Betsy, 1944-
The new Americans; colonial times, 1620-1689; illustrated by Giulio Maestro. Lothrop, Lee & Shepard Bks. 1998 48p il maps $16.95; lib bdg $16.89 (2-4)   **973.2**
1. United States—History—1600-1775, Colonial period 2. Canada—History—0-1763 (New France)
ISBN 0-688-13448-3; 0-688-13449-1 (lib bdg)
LC 95-19636
Traces the competition among the American Indians, French, English, Spanish, and Dutch for land, furs, timber, and other resources of North America
This is "accessibly written and meticulously illustrated. . . . Giulio Maestro's carefully detailed watercolor and color-pencil art includes maps, closely focused spot illustrations and dramatic spreads, which together provide a vivid picture of the century's pivotal events." Publ Wkly

Tunis, Edwin, 1897-1973
Colonial living; written and illustrated by Edwin Tunis. Johns Hopkins paperbacks ed. Johns Hopkins Univ. Press 1999 155p il pa $18.95
973.2
1. United States—Social life and customs—1600-1775, Colonial period
ISBN 0-8018-6227-2   LC 99-22591
A reprint of the title first published 1957 by World Pub. Co.
"Common everyday aspects of colonial living from 1564-1770 are highlighted by the detailed descriptions and numerous black and white illustrations of items such as tools, home furnishings, clothing, etc." N Y Public Libr. Ref Books for Child Collect

973.3   United States—Periods of Revolution and Confederation, 1775-1789

The **American** revolutionaries: a history in their own words, 1750-1800; edited by Milton Meltzer. Crowell 1987 210p il hardcover o.p. paperback available $6.95 (6 and up)   **973.3**
1. United States—History—1775-1783, Revolution 2. United States—History—1755-1763, French and Indian War
ISBN 0-06-446145-9 (pa)   LC 86-47846
"Meltzer has assembled a collage of eyewitness accounts, speech and diary excerpts, letters, and other documents for a chronological account of the half century that included the American Revolution. . . . The voices of women who accompanied the troops and of blacks who fought with the army are both represented." Bull Cent Child Books

Brenner, Barbara
If you were there in 1776. Bradbury Press 1994 136p il $17 (4-6)   **973.3**
1. United States. Declaration of Independence 2. United States—Social life and customs
ISBN 0-02-712322-7   LC 93-24060
Demonstrates how the concepts and principles expressed in the Declaration of Independence were drawn from the experiences of living in America in the late eighteenth century, with emphasis given to how children lived on a New England farm, a Southern plantation, and the frontier
"The author's inclusion of details of how peoples' lives began to change as a result of the Revolution and her accessible style are the selling points here. Both budding historians and report writers will find this title worth their time." SLJ
Includes bibliographical references

Cox, Clinton
Come all you brave soldiers; blacks in the Revolutionary War. Scholastic 1999 182p il $15.95 (6 and up)   **973.3**
1. African American soldiers 2. United States—History—1775-1783, Revolution
ISBN 0-590-47576-2   LC 97-44198

Cox, Clinton—*Continued*

Tells the story of the thousands of black men who served as soldiers fighting for independence from England during the American Revolutionary War

"An interesting and informative survey. . . . Black-and-white reproductions of period prints, documents, and paintings are included." SLJ

Includes bibliographical references

Ferrie, Richard

The world turned upside down; George Washington and the Battle of Yorktown. Holiday House 1999 168p il maps $18.95 (5 and up)
973.3

1. Yorktown (Va.)—History—Siege, 1781
ISBN 0-8234-1402-7   LC 98-19574

This examination of the events surrounding the pivotal Revolutionary War battle that led to the defeat of the British forces at Yorktown, Virginia, focuses on the central role of General George Washington

An "exemplary and readable history. . . . The text is engrossing, the format inviting, the facts accurate, and the illustrative material—maps, photographs, and reproductions—informative." Horn Book

Includes bibliographical references

Kroll, Steven

The Boston Tea Party; illustrated by Peter Fiore. Holiday House 1998 unp il $16.95; pa $6.95 (3-5)
973.3

1. Boston Tea Party, 1773 2. United States—History—1775-1783, Revolution
ISBN 0-8234-1316-0; 0-8234-1557-0 (pa)
LC 96-54855

Describes the events preceding, during, and following the event which helped precipitate the American Revolutionary War

This book offers a "brief text written in a matter-of-fact style. . . . Presented in the format of a long picture book and illustrated with full-page watercolor art, the story unfolds step by step." SLJ

Murphy, Jim, 1947-

A young patriot; the American Revolution as experienced by one boy. Clarion Bks. 1996 101p il maps $15.95; pa $7.95 (5 and up)   **973.3**

1. Martin, Joseph Plumb, 1760-1850 2. United States—History—1775-1783, Revolution
ISBN 0-395-60523-7; 0-395-90019-0 (pa)
LC 93-38789

"Using Joseph Plumb Martin's first person account of his participation in the Revolutionary War as primary source material, Murphy intertwines this story of one teenager's life as a soldier with broader information about the Revolution, to put Martin's story in context. The handsome, informative, and fascinating look at American history is illustrated with many period reproductions." Horn Book Guide

Includes bibliographical references

Stein, R. Conrad, 1937-

Valley Forge. Children's Press 1994 28p il (Cornerstones of freedom) lib bdg $20.50; pa $5.95 (4-6)   **973.3**

1. Washington, George, 1732-1799 2. United States—History—1775-1783, Revolution
ISBN 0-516-06683-8 (lib bdg); 0-516-46683-6 (pa)
LC 94-9490

First published 1985 with title: The story of Valley Forge

The author "describes how, routed at the Battle of Brandywine, Washington's forces retreated to Valley Forge. Quotations personalize their suffering, their resolve, and their loyalty to Washington. The addition of full-color and black-and-white photos, period paintings, and reproductions adds enormously to the book's appeal." SLJ

973.4   United States—Constitutional period, 1789-1809

Sakurai, Gail, 1952-

The Louisiana Purchase. Children's Press 1998 30p il maps (Cornerstones of freedom) lib bdg $20.50; pa $5.95 (4-6)   **973.4**

1. Louisiana Purchase
ISBN 0-516-20791-1 (lib bdg); 0-516-26336-6 (pa)
LC 97-12015

Chronicles the historical background and political maneuvers that led to the Louisiana Purchase by President Thomas Jefferson in 1803

973.5   United States—1809-1845

Goodman, Susan, 1952-

Ultimate field trip 4: a week in the 1800s; by Susan E. Goodman; photographs by Michael J. Doolittle. Atheneum Bks. for Young Readers 2000 50p il $17 (5 and up)   **973.5**

1. Kings Landing Historical Settlement (N.B.)
2. United States—Social life and customs
ISBN 0-689-83045-9   LC 99-19156

Describes the experiences of a group of middle school students who spend a week at Kings Landing Historical Settlement, learning what life was like for young people in the nineteenth century

"Well written and beautifully photographed, this book offers a vicarious experience that teachers may want to share with their classes." Booklist

Includes bibliographical references

973.7   United States— Administration of Abraham Lincoln, 1861-1865. Civil War

Beller, Susan Provost, 1949-

To hold this ground; a desperate battle at Gettysburg. Margaret K. McElderry Bks. 1995 95p il maps $14.95 (5 and up)   **973.7**

1. Gettysburg (Pa.), Battle of, 1863
ISBN 0-689-50621-X   LC 94-12775

Beller, Susan Provost, 1949-—Continued

"Beller examines the battle for Little Round Top and the two colonels who faced each other on that fateful July day. William Calvin Oates fought for the confederacy, and Joshua Lawrence Chamberlain commanded the 20th Maine. While this book tells the story of the battle that day, it focuses on the two men and the role they played not only in this battle but in the history of this country after the war was over." Book Rep

Includes bibliographical references

Clinton, Catherine, 1952-

Scholastic encyclopedia of the Civil War. Scholastic Ref. 1999 112p il maps $18.95 (4 and up)   **973.7**

    1. United States—History—1861-1865, Civil War— Encyclopedias

    ISBN 0-590-37227-0   LC 98-45492

"A Fair Street Productions book"

Traces the course of the Civil War, year by year, using profiles of important people, eyewitness accounts, and period art

This "provides a cogent introduction to the Civil War. Fully illustrated with black-and-white reproductions of period photos, paintings, drawings, and engravings. . . . Well-chosen features and sidebars offer interesting supplementary information, first-person accounts, and fast facts about the conflict." Booklist

Cox, Clinton

Undying glory; the story of the Massachusetts 54th Regiment. Scholastic 1991 167p il hardcover o.p. paperback available $4.50 (6 and up)   **973.7**

    1. United States. Army. Massachusetts Infantry Regiment, 54th (1863-1865) 2. United States—History— 1861-1865, Civil War 3. African American soldiers

    ISBN 0-590-44171-X (pa)   LC 90-22303

"This book discusses the history of the formation of the African-American Fifty-fourth Massachusetts Regiment and its battles from 1863 to 1865. The regiment's unsung heroes found an enemy in both the Confederate army and the Union government, both of which treated them as second-class soldiers." Soc Educ

Includes bibliographical references

Fraser, Mary Ann

Vicksburg—the battle that won the Civil War. Holt & Co. 1999 104p il maps $16.95 (4 and up)   **973.7**

    1. Vicksburg (Miss.)—Siege, 1863

    ISBN 0-8050-6106-1   LC 99-19701

Describes the events preceding and during the key Civil War battle of Vicksburg, its significance, and its aftermath

"Bringing the history to life, quotations from diaries, memoirs, and other sources give voices to the participants. Illustrations . . . include black-and-white photographs, maps, and engravings. Source notes, a glossary, and lists of books and Internet sites are appended." Booklist

Haskins, James, 1941-

Black, blue, & gray; African Americans in the Civil War. Simon & Schuster Bks. for Young Readers 1998 154p $17 (5 and up)   **973.7**

    1. United States—History—1861-1865, Civil War 2. African American soldiers

    ISBN 0-689-80655-8   LC 97-25414

An historical account of the role of African-American soldiers in the Civil War

"This tightly organized book is packed with facts and meticulously footnoted, yet it reads like a novel, thanks to the author's stylistic skills." SLJ

Includes bibliographical references

January, Brendan, 1972-

John Brown's raid on Harpers Ferry. Children's Press 2000 30p il (Cornerstones of freedom) $20.50; pa $5.95 (4-6)   **973.7**

    1. Brown, John, 1800-1859 2. Harpers Ferry (W. Va.)—History—John Brown's Raid, 1859

    ISBN 0-516-21144-7; 0-516-27037-0 (pa)

                          LC 99-14965

Recounts the story of John Brown's rebellion in Harpers Ferry in 1859, intended to start a massive slave uprising in the South and the establishment of a state in the Allegheny Mountains for freed slaves

Murphy, Jim, 1947-

The boys' war; Confederate and Union soldiers talk about the Civil War. Clarion Bks. 1990 110p il $18; pa $7.95 (5 and up)   **973.7**

    1. United States—History—1861-1865, Civil War

    ISBN 0-89919-893-7; 0-395-66412-8 (pa)

                          LC 89-23959

This book includes diary entries, personal letters, and archival photographs to describe the experiences of boys, sixteen years old or younger, who fought in the Civil War

"An excellent selection of more than 45 sepia-toned contemporary photographs augment the text of this informative, moving work." SLJ

Includes bibliographical references

The long road to Gettysburg. Clarion Bks. 1992 116p il maps $17; pa $7.95 (5 and up)   **973.7**

    1. Gettysburg (Pa.), Battle of, 1863

    ISBN 0-395-55965-0; 0-618-05157-0 (pa)

                          LC 90-21881

Describes the events of the Battle of Gettysburg in 1863 as seen through the eyes of two actual participants, nineteen-year-old Confederate lieutenant John Dooley and seventeen-year-old Union soldier Thomas Galway. Also discusses Lincoln's famous speech delivered at the dedication of the National Cemetery at Gettysburg

The author "uses all of his fine skills as an information writer—clarity of detail, conciseness, understanding of his age group, and ability to find the drama appealing to readers—to frame a well-crafted account of a single battle in the war." Horn Book

Includes bibliographical references

973.8   United States—Reconstruction period, 1865-1901

Mettger, Zak

Reconstruction; America after the Civil War. Lodestar Bks. 1994 122p il (Young readers' history of the Civil War) $16.99 (5 and up)

973.8

1. Reconstruction (1865-1876) 2. United States—Politics and government—1865-1898
ISBN 0-525-67490-X   LC 93-44665

The author explains the "post-Civil War era, a time she defines as 'a period of great hope and crushing disappointment.' She accomplishes her goal with a clearly written, well-explained history. Unflinching in the details about lynchings, the Ku Klux Klan, and corrupt governments, she manages to put a human face on the times." SLJ

Includes glossary and bibliographical references

Viola, Herman J.

It is a good day to die; Indian eyewitnesses tell the story of the Battle of the Little Bighorn. Crown 1998 101p il maps lib bdg $19.99 (5 and up)

973.8

1. Custer, George Armstrong, 1839-1876 2. Little Bighorn, Battle of the, 1876 3. Dakota Indians—Wars 4. Cheyenne Indians
ISBN 0-517-70913-9   LC 98-16477

A series of eyewitness accounts of the 1876 Battle of Little Bighorn and the defeat of General Custer as told by Native American participants in the war

"This is a thought-provoking, accessible compilation that will give new insight to the study of American history." Bull Cent Child Books

Includes bibliographical references

973.922   United States—Administration of John F. Kennedy, 1961-1963

Hampton, Wilborn

Kennedy assassinated! the world mourns: a reporter's story. Candlewick Press 1997 96p il $17.99 (5 and up)

973.922

1. Kennedy, John F. (John Fitzgerald), 1917-1963—Assassination 2. Journalism
ISBN 1-56402-811-9   LC 96-25801

This is the author's "account of November 22, 1963, when, as a cub reporter for UPI in Dallas, he was drafted to cover JFK's assassination. His personal response to the tragedy is fluidly juxtaposed with the nuts and bolts of scooping the story in this insider's view of one of the most pivotal events of our nation's recent history." Publ Wkly

Includes bibliographical references

974   Northeastern United States

Bial, Raymond

Mist over the mountains; Appalachia and its people. Houghton Mifflin 1997 unp il $14.95 (4 and up)

974

1. Appalachian region 2. Mountain life
ISBN 0-395-73569-6   LC 96-7466

This is an "account of Appalachian history, farming methods, religion, storytelling, folk arts, moonshine, resources, and traditions. The heart of the book lies not in the text but in the photographs. . . . Some of the photos, particularly the historical ones, come from other sources, but most are Bial's and reflect his signature style, strong on color, clarity, and human interest." Booklist

Includes bibliographical references

Rylant, Cynthia

Appalachia; the voices of sleeping birds; illustrated by Barry Moser. Harcourt Brace Jovanovich 1991 21p il $17; pa $6

974

1. Appalachian region
ISBN 0-15-201605-8; 0-15-201893-X (pa)

LC 90-36798

"This is a running narrative description of the dogs, people, houses, seasons, and lifestyles of Appalachia." Bull Cent Child Books

"Taking her subtitle from a passage by James Agee, the author conveys with a marvelous economy of words the essence of the very special part of America where she was raised. A poetic text projects emotion as well as information. . . . Moser's watercolors capture the scene perfectly. . . . The book is a treasure—simply a beautiful combination of text and art." Horn Book

974.1   Maine

Dean, Julia

A year on Monhegan Island. Ticknor & Fields Bks. for Young Readers 1995 46p il $14.95 (4-6)

974.1

1. Monhegan Island (Me.)
ISBN 0-395-66476-4   LC 93-24534

The author "chronicles the seasons on Monhegan Island, a small community off the coast of central Maine. Beginning with late fall, she describes how the few permanent inhabitants deal with their isolated life. . . . Crisp, clear photos on nearly every page show many of the island's residents at work and play, as well as the natural beauty of Monhegan's craggy beaches and ancient forests. . . . Useful for geography units and fascinating for would-be visitors." Booklist

974.4 Massachusetts

Bowen, Gary

Stranded at Plimoth Plantation, 1626; words and woodcuts by Gary Bowen; introduction by David Freeman Hawke. HarperCollins Pubs. 1994 81p il map $19.95; pa $10.95 (3-5) **974.4**

1. Pilgrims (New England colonists) 2. Massachusetts—History—1600-1775, Colonial period

ISBN 0-06-022541-6; 0-06-440719-5 (pa)

LC 93-31016

The author "gives an account of the year 1626 at the by-then-well-established Pilgrim colony, rendered in the form of a journal kept by an orphaned 13-year-old. Shipwrecked on the way to Jamestown, taken in by the settlers at Plimoth, Christopher Sears observes their customs, planting, harvesting, home tutoring, the eight-hour Sabbath meeting, court day, the use of the stocks, etc." Publ Wkly

"The youthful voice and observations, in language that is a remarkable blend of clarity and period flavor, provide a more intimate and involving picture of the period than more straightforward factual accounts." SLJ

Fritz, Jean

Who's that stepping on Plymouth Rock? illustrated by J. B. Handelsman. Coward, McCann & Geoghegan 1975 30p il $15.99; pa $6.99 (2-4) **974.4**

1. Plymouth Rock

ISBN 0-698-20325-9; 0-698-11681-X (pa)

An "account of the Rock which is visited yearly by about one and a half million people. It stands now under a monument on the waterfront of Plymouth, Massachusetts, sacred to the memory of the First Comers (Pilgrims) but it has figured in many adventures since the Pilgrims did—or did not—step upon it in 1620." Publ Wkly

"Both a delightful story and a perceptive commentary on how the mythmaking process works in American history." N Y Times Book Rev

Sewall, Marcia, 1935-

The pilgrims of Plimoth; written and illustrated by Marcia Sewall. Atheneum Pubs. 1986 48p il $16.95; pa $5.99 (3-6) **974.4**

1. Pilgrims (New England colonists) 2. Massachusetts—History—1600-1775, Colonial period

ISBN 0-689-31250-4; 0-689-80861-5 (pa)

LC 86-3362

The author provides a "first-person narrative account of the Mayflower voyage of 1620 and the early years of the Plymouth colony. This is not the personal diary of an individual, but rather a journal of the community." Booklist

"Translating narrative and descriptive details into visual images, the illustrations accompany every page of text, occasionally overspreading double pages for panoramic effects. Combining subtle, modulating color with a spiritual as well as an actual luminosity, the paintings—done in gouache—are vibrant with the daily pulse of life among an energetic, enterprising people." Horn Book

Waters, Kate

On the Mayflower; voyage of the ship's apprentice & a passenger girl; photographs by Russ Kendall. Scholastic 1996 40p il $16.95; pa $5.99 (2-4) **974.4**

1. Mayflower (Ship) 2. Pilgrims (New England colonists) 3. Massachusetts—History—1600-1775, Colonial period

ISBN 0-590-67308-4; 0-439-09941-2 (pa)

LC 95-43980

"Waters tells a story of the *Mayflower's* passage to America through the characters of William Small, the apprentice to the master of the ship, and Ellen Moore, an eight-year-old passenger. The text is based on historical documents. . . . Kendall's clear, full-color photographs, shot on the *Mayflower II*, complement the story. This book is well written, designed, and photographed." SLJ

Includes glossary

Samuel Eaton's day; a day in the life of a Pilgrim boy; photographs by Russ Kendall. Scholastic 1993 40p il $16.95; pa $5.99 (2-4) **974.4**

1. Pilgrims (New England colonists) 2. Massachusetts—History—1600-1775, Colonial period

ISBN 0-590-46311-X; 0-590-48053-7 (pa)

LC 92-32325

Text and photographs follow a six-year-old Pilgrim boy through a busy day during the spring harvest in 1627

"The photographs, taken at Plimoth Plantation, an outdoor living history museum, entice the reader back into the seventeenth century with their authenticity and detail. A vivid description of the hardships endured as well as the pride felt by these English colonists in their new American community." Horn Book

Includes glossary

Sarah Morton's day; a day in the life of a pilgrim girl; photographs by Russell Kendall. Scholastic 1989 32p il $16.95; pa $5.99 (2-4) **974.4**

1. Pilgrims (New England colonists) 2. Massachusetts—History—1600-1775, Colonial period

ISBN 0-590-42634-6; 0-590-44871-4 (pa)

LC 88-35581

Text and photographs of Plimouth Plantation follow a pilgrim girl through a typical day as she milks the goats, cooks and serves meals, learns her letters, and adjusts to her new stepfather

This "is a highly accessible account of pilgrim life. Attractive color photographs invigorate the text."

Includes glossary

974.7 New York

Curlee, Lynn, 1947-

Liberty. Atheneum Bks. for Young Readers 2000 41p $18 (3-5) **974.7**

1. Bartholdi, Frédéric Auguste, 1834-1904 2. Statue of Liberty (New York, N.Y.)

ISBN 0-689-82823-3

LC 98-44732

Curlee, Lynn, 1947-—*Continued*

The author narrates the "story of Liberty's creation, from its conception by French professor Édouard de Laboulaye (who proposed the idea at a dinner party attended by young sculptor Frédéric-Auguste Bartholdi) to the fulfillment of Bartholdi's obsession to create a monument to liberty that would rival the Colossus of Rhodes." Horn Book

"Curlee's illustrations—bold, bright full-page acrylic paintings, most dramatically composed—are helpful in conveying technical details and in portraying the various stages in the creation of the statue. But they are also quite beautiful, for they communicate not just information but also excitement and sentiment." N Y Times Book Rev

Fradin, Dennis B.

The New York Colony. Children's Press 1988 159p il lib bdg $32 (4 and up)   **974.7**
1. New York (State)—History
ISBN 0-516-00389-5   LC 87-35803

"Beginning with the 1300s, when the Algonquian and Iroquois Indians were the dominant tribes, Fradin traces the development of New York state. . . . Fradin's lively word pictures chronicle everyday life as the colony moves from Dutch to English domination, and his account ends in 1790 with the relocation of the nation's capital from New York to Philadelphia. Biographical sketches of historical state figures are interspersed, and the crisply designed book includes a liberal use of portraits and engravings. A colonial America time line is a handy reference; overall, a competent, attractive offering." Booklist

Maestro, Betsy, 1944-

The story of the Statue of Liberty; [by] Betsy & Giulio Maestro. Lothrop, Lee & Shepard Bks. 1986 39p il hardcover o.p. paperback available $5.95 (k-3)   **974.7**
1. Bartholdi, Frédéric Auguste, 1834-1904 2. Statue of Liberty (New York, N.Y.)
ISBN 0-688-08746-9 (pa)   LC 85-11324

"Although Maestro simplifies the story—including only the most important people's names, for example—she still presents an accurate account of what happened. The exceptional drawings are visually delightful—primarily in the blue-green range, although they are in full color—and cover most of every page. Human figures—workers, tourists—are included in many drawings, indicating the statue's tremendous scale. Further, the drawings involve viewers through the use of unusual perspectives and angles and by placing the statue in scenes of city life." SLJ
Includes bibliographical references

974.8 Pennsylvania

Fradin, Dennis B.

The Pennsylvania colony. Children's Press 1988 160p il maps lib bdg $32 (4 and up)   **974.8**
1. Pennsylvania—History
ISBN 0-516-00390-9   LC 88-11975

A history of the colony of Pennsylvania, from the time of the earliest European settlers to the aftermath of the battle for independence that resulted in statehood. Includes biographical sketches of some individuals prominent in Pennsylvania history

975 Southeastern United States. Southern States

Erickson, Paul, 1976-

Daily life on a Southern plantation, 1853. Lodestar Bks. 1998 c1997 48p il $16.99; pa $7.99 (4-6)   **975**
1. Plantation life 2. Slavery—United States
ISBN 0-525-67547-7; 0-14-056668-6 (pa)
          LC 97-22540
First published 1997 in the United Kingdom

Recreates a southern plantation of 1853 and describes the daily lives of its owners and of the slaves who worked there

"Erickson uses a family to make the information in the text accessible. This book follows two families . . . one living in the 'Big House'; and the other a slave family, through a typical day—a technique that provides a personal, well-informed view of slavery." Horn Book Guide

Includes glossary

975.3 District of Columbia (Washington)

Fisher, Leonard Everett, 1924-

The White House. Holiday House 1989 96p il $16.95 (4 and up)   **975.3**
1. White House (Washington, D.C.)
ISBN 0-8234-0774-8   LC 89-1990

"A fresh, captivating commentary of the conception and evolution of America's most famous residence. Through anecdotal prose and wonderful historical photos, Fisher demystifies the prestigious monument by showing it to be a home—complete with its foibles, quirks, and inconveniences." SLJ

Fradin, Dennis B.

Washington, D.C; by Dennis Brindell Fradin. Children's Press 1992 64p il map lib bdg $27 (3-5)   **975.3**
1. Washington (D.C.)
ISBN 0-516-03851-6   LC 91-32919

"An introduction to our culturally and ethnically diverse capitol, highlighting its history, economy, and historic sites of interest. A timeline, map, glossary, and index make the information easily accessible, while the full-color photographs keep interest high." SLJ

975.5 Virginia

Fisher, Leonard Everett, 1924-
Monticello. Holiday House 1988 64p il $18.95;
pa $8.95 (4 and up)   **975.5**
1. Jefferson, Thomas, 1743-1826—Homes and haunts
ISBN 0-8234-0688-1; 0-8234-1406-X (pa)
                                    LC 87-25219
"The text opens with summary background on the development of English and American architecture, the specific buildings that influenced Jefferson, and his early
planning. Various stages of construction and modification
demonstrate Jefferson's ingenuity and wide-ranging intelligence as he adapted classical structures to local landscape. The decay of the property after Jefferson's death
and its eventual renovation give as much sense of history
as the building's conception. The photographs, reproductions, diagrams, and drawings are a masterly mix of
graphic information." Bull Cent Child Books

Richards, Norman, 1932-
Monticello. Children's Press 1995 30p il
(Cornerstones of freedom) lib bdg $20.50; pa
$5.95 (4-6)   **975.5**
1. Jefferson, Thomas, 1743-1826—Homes and haunts
ISBN 0-516-06695-1 (lib bdg); 0-516-46695-X (pa)
                                    LC 94-35654
A revised and newly illustrated edition of The story of
Monticello, published 1970
The construction and furnishing of the home of Thom-
as Jefferson "are described as they relate to the events of
Jefferson's life and to the founding of our country. The
well-written text is handsomely enhanced by full-color
and black-and-white photographs and illustrations of the
house, gardens, and Jefferson's inventions. His beliefs
and feelings about slavery are briefly discussed." SLJ

975.7 South Carolina

Fradin, Dennis B.
The South Carolina Colony; by Dennis Brindell
Fradin; consultant, Stephen Hoffius. Children's
Press 1992 160p il maps lib bdg $32 (4 and up)
                                        975.7
1. South Carolina
ISBN 0-516-00397-6   LC 91-32330
Describes the history and people of South Carolina
from its earliest settlements to statehood in 1788

975.8 Georgia

Fradin, Dennis B.
The Georgia colony; by Dennis Brindell Fradin.
Children's Press 1990 143p il lib bdg $32 (4 and
up)   **975.8**
1. Georgia
ISBN 0-516-00392-5   LC 89-34954
A historical account of Georgia's early days, from its
creation as a colony for debtors in the 1700's until its
admission as the fourth state in 1788
"The format features large print, wide margins, and a
liberal use of portraits, photos, and engravings. Biographical sketches, set off from the main text, will be a boon
to report writers. Because the text reads easily, it will be
a good choice for reluctant researchers." Booklist

975.9 Florida

George, Jean Craighead, 1919-
Everglades; paintings by Wendell Minor.
HarperCollins Pubs. 1995 unp il $15.95; lib bdg
$16.89; pa $6.95 (2-4)   **975.9**
1. Everglades (Fla.)
ISBN 0-06-021228-4; 0-06-021229-2 (lib bdg);
0-06-446194-7 (pa)   LC 92-9517
"Though structured as a tale told to five children
whom a storyteller has poled into the Everglades, the
narrative focuses on the history of that unusual
ecosystem. The narrator tells how the Everglades became
'a living kaleidoscope of color and beauty,' filled with
plants and animals, and how human involvement has
changed the ecology, devastating the area. . . . When the
children ask about what happened to the orchids, egrets,
and alligators, the storyteller suggests that they can make
a happy ending to the story when they grow up." Booklist
"The story and the art create a mystical tale that flows
from a serene start to a powerful conclusion." SLJ

976.4 Texas

Garland, Sherry, 1948-
Voices of the Alamo; written by Sherry
Garland; illustrated by Ronald Himler. Scholastic
Press 2000 unp il $16.95 (3-6)   **976.4**
1. Alamo (San Antonio, Tex.) 2. Texas—History
ISBN 0-590-98833-6   LC 99-18274
From the 1500s to the present, different voices and
perspectives of men and women—Indian, Mexican, Span-
ish, Texan, and American—recount the history of the Al-
amo and its region
"Himler's outstanding double-page watercolors depict
characters, sweeping landscapes, battle scenes, and the
Alamo throughout its history and fill the pages with
bright colors." SLJ
Includes glossary and bibliographical references

Lourie, Peter
Rio Grande; from the Rocky Mountains to the
Gulf of Mexico. Boyds Mills Press 1999 46p il
$17.95; pa $9.95 (4 and up)   **976.4**
1. Rio Grande valley
ISBN 1-56397-706-0; 1-56397-896-2 (pa)
                                    LC 97-77907
The author "reports on his 1,900-mile journey down
the Rio Grande, from its headwaters near a former silver
town in Colorado to its inconspicuous outlet into the
Gulf. In dramatic prose . . . he not only describes the
passing scenery but also evokes some of its colorful history. . . . Unusually well-chosen photographs enhance
the connections between the river's past and present with
a mix of historical shots, new portraits, and landscapes
in sharp color, and even a satellite picture." Booklist

Turner, Robyn Montana
Texas traditions; the culture of the Lone Star state. Little, Brown 1996 96p il $19.95; pa $12.95 (4 and up)　　　　　　　**976.4**
1. Texas
ISBN 0-316-85675-4; 0-316-85639-8 (pa)
LC 95-34360
Discusses the history, geography, industry, and arts of Texas and includes such topics as folk medicine, home schooling, cowboy poets, the original rodeo, and contributions of Texas women
"Diversity is the theme of this carefully written, intelligent, and timely study. . . . The book is handsomely illustrated with full-color reproductions of paintings, photographs, posters, and maps, many from archival sources." Booklist
Includes bibliographical references

977.3　Illinois

Murphy, Jim, 1947-
The great fire. Scholastic 1995 144p il maps $16.95 (5 and up)　　　　　　　**977.3**
1. Fires—Chicago (Ill.)
ISBN 0-590-47267-4　　　　　LC 94-9963
Newbery honor book, 1996
"Firsthand descriptions by persons who lived through the 1871 Chicago fire are woven into a gripping account of this famous disaster. Murphy also examines the origins of the fire, the errors of judgment that delayed the effective response, the organizational problems of the city's firefighters, and the postfire efforts to rebuild the city. Newspaper lithographs and a few historical photographs convey the magnitude of human suffering and confusion." Horn Book Guide
Includes bibliographical references

978　Western United States

Blumberg, Rhoda, 1917-
The incredible journey of Lewis and Clark. Lothrop, Lee & Shepard Bks. 1987 143p il maps $18; pa $9.95 (5 and up)　　　　　　　**978**
1. Lewis, Meriwether, 1774-1809 2. Clark, William, 1770-1838 3. Lewis and Clark Expedition (1804-1806) 4. West (U.S.)—Exploration
ISBN 0-688-06512-0; 0-688-14421-7 (pa)
LC 87-4235
Describes the expedition led by Lewis and Clark to explore the unknown western regions of America at the beginning of the nineteenth century
"Blumberg's writing is dignified but never dry, and her sense of narrative makes familiar history an exciting story." Bull Cent Child Books
Includes bibliographical references

Calabro, Marian
The perilous journey of the Donner Party. Clarion Bks. 1999 192p il maps $20 (5 and up)　　　　　　　**978**
1. Donner party 2. Frontier and pioneer life—West (U.S.) 3. Overland journeys to the Pacific
ISBN 0-395-86610-3　　　　　LC 98-29610

Uses materials from letters and diaries written by survivors of the Donner Party to relate the experiences of that ill-fated group as they endured horrific circumstances on their way to California in 1846-47
"Calabro's offering is a fine addition to the Donner Party canon and particularly well suited to its young audience, for whom the story of hardship and survival will be nothing short of riveting. . . . From the haunting cover with its lonely campfire to the recounting of a survivors' reunion, this is a page-turner." Booklist
Includes bibliographical references

Flanagan, Alice K.
The Zunis. Children's Press 1998 47p il $22 (4 and up)　　　　　　　**978**
1. Zuni Indians
ISBN 0-516-20630-3　　　　　LC 97-6712
Examines the history, culture, and society of the Zuni Indians, one of the groups of Pueblo Indians living in New Mexico
Includes bibliographical references

Freedman, Russell
Children of the wild West. Clarion Bks. 1983 104p il map $18; pa $6.95 (4 and up)　　　　**978**
1. Children—West (U.S.) 2. Frontier and pioneer life—West (U.S.) 3. West (U.S.)—History
ISBN 0-89919-143-6; 0-395-54785-7 (pa)
LC 83-5133
"A smooth narrative and numerous historical photographs combine for an intriguing backward look at how children fared in pioneer times." Booklist

Cowboys of the wild West. Clarion Bks. 1985 103p il map lib bdg $17.95; pa $9.95 (4 and up)　　　　　　　**978**
1. Cowhands 2. Frontier and pioneer life—West (U.S.) 3. West (U.S.)—History
ISBN 0-89919-301-3 (lib bdg); 0-395-54800-4 (pa)
LC 85-4200
"Freedman describes the herders' duties on the open range roundups and trail rides, their ranch and line-camp life, the clothes and equipment dictated by their work, and the economic necessities that defined the job in its heyday, from the 1860s to the 1890s." Bull Cent Child Books
"The author does a fine job of presenting us with information without belittling the real place the cowboy has in both history and fiction. Bibliography and index." Horn Book

An Indian winter; paintings and drawings by Karl Bodmer. Holiday House 1992 88p il $21.95; pa $12.95 (6 and up)　　　　　　　**978**
1. Wied, Maximilian, Prinz von, 1782-1867 2. Native Americans—Missouri River valley 3. Missouri River valley—Description
ISBN 0-8234-0930-9; 0-8234-1158-3 (pa)
LC 91-24205
Relates the experiences of a German prince, his servant, and a young Swiss artist as they traveled through the Missouri River Valley in 1833 learning about the territory and its inhabitants and recording their impressions in words and pictures

Freedman, Russell—*Continued*
"The pictures are particularly effective in presenting rich details of village life, clothing, ceremonies, and customs. Both the book's specific information about native peoples and its use of primary-source material make it a valuable creation." Horn Book
Includes bibliographical references

Granfield, Linda
Cowboy: an album. Ticknor & Fields 1994 96p il $18.95 (5 and up)   **978**
1. Cowhands 2. West (U.S.)
ISBN 0-395-68430-7   LC 93-11027
An introduction to cowboys, their history, their daily life, famous cowboys and cowgirls, and portrayals of cowboys in modern films
"Offering a broad vision of the subject, yet full of intriguing details, this compendium of cowboy history and lore will satisfy browsers and researchers alike." Booklist
Includes bibliographical references

Katz, William Loren
Black women of the Old West. Atheneum Bks. for Young Readers 1995 84p il $18 (5 and up)   **978**
1. African American women 2. Frontier and pioneer life—West (U.S.) 3. West (U.S.)—History
ISBN 0-689-31944-4   LC 95-9969
This work contains "vignettes and photographs of dozens of women, some famous, others unknown outside their own family circles, who lived across the West in the 19th and early 20th centuries." N Y Times Book Rev
"Katz succeeds in establishing that women of color were an important, if unsung, presence on the westward-shifting frontier." Bull Cent Child Books

King, David C.
Pioneer days; discover the past with fun projects, games, activities, and recipes. Wiley 1997 118p il (American kids in history) pa $12.95 (3-6)   **978**
1. Frontier and pioneer life—West (U.S.) 2. West (U.S.)—Social life and customs
ISBN 0-471-16169-1   LC 96-37495
This book is an "assortment of history, culture, crafts, and stories to teach about the daily life of the pioneers. . . . [Crafts and recipes include] air-dried flowers, toys and games, homemade soda pop, johnny-cakes, and various holiday ornaments. The author's research is evident, and the presentation of the activities and recipes is so engaging that the book will appeal to a wide audience." SLJ
Includes glossary and bibliographical references

Wild West days; discover the past with fun projects, games, activities, and recipes. Wiley 1998 118p il (American kids in history) pa $12.95 (3-6)   **978**
1. Ranch life 2. West (U.S.)—Social life and customs
ISBN 0-471-23919-4   LC 97-48557
Discusses what life was like for the people who settled the West between 1870 and 1900, follows a year in

the life of a fictional family of that time, and presents projects and activities, such as designing a brand stamp and making a yarn picture
Includes glossary and bibliographical references

Lavender, David Sievert, 1910-
The Santa Fe Trail; [by] David Lavender. Holiday House 1995 64p il $15.95 (4 and up)   **978**
1. Santa Fe Trail
ISBN 0-8234-1153-2   LC 94-16638
This is a "history of the route that, for some sixty years, serviced the commerical and military wagon trade between Missouri and New Mexico. Lavender traces the Trail's expansion from William Becknell's 1821 gamble on open trade with Mexico to the road's demise at the advent of the steam locomotive in 1879." Bull Cent Child Books
"Well-placed, black-and-white reproductions, including historical photographs, complement the text. . . . This is a carefully written and worthwhile purchase." SLJ

Snowbound; the tragic story of the Donner Party; by David Lavender. Holiday House 1996 87p il maps $18.95 (4 and up)   **978**
1. Donner party 2. Frontier and pioneer life—West (U.S.) 3. Overland journeys to the Pacific
ISBN 0-8234-1231-8   LC 95-41266
Relates the ordeals faced by a group of pioneers on their journey from Illinois to California in 1846
The author "draws on authentic primary documents, combining a vivid narrative with his analysis of what happened and why. His handsomely designed, slightly oversize volume has lots of photos of the places and people." Booklist
Includes bibliographical references

Meltzer, Milton, 1915-
Driven from the land; the story of the Dust Bowl. Benchmark Bks. (Tarrytown) 2000 111p il (Great journeys) lib bdg $31.36 (4 and up)   **978**
1. Great Plains—History 2. Dust storms 3. Great Depression, 1929-1939
ISBN 0-7614-0968-8   LC 98-47501
Describes the economic and environmental conditions that led to the Great Depression and the horrific dust storms that drove people from their homes westward during the 1930s
"Well-reproduced photographs by Dorothea Lange and others of the time greatly enhance the text." Booklist
Includes bibliographical references

Miller, Brandon Marie
Buffalo gals; women of the old West. Lerner Publs. 1995 88p il (People's history series) lib bdg $22.60; pa $8.95 (5 and up)   **978**
1. Women—West (U.S.) 2. Frontier and pioneer life—West (U.S.) 3. West (U.S.)—History
ISBN 0-8225-1730-2 (lib bdg); 0-8225-9772-1 (pa)
LC 94-5063
"Westward migration, housekeeping difficulties, professions, forms of entertainment, and intercultural rela-

Miller, Brandon Marie—*Continued*

tions are some of the topics discussed in this . . . overview of women's experiences in getting to and surviving in the West." Bull Cent Child Books

The author "catches both the bone-wearying labor and the excitement that sometimes made living in the West worthwhile. She deftly augments her text with excerpts from journals and memoirs as well as photographs from regional archives, which are especially effective because the images are not familiar ones." Booklist

Includes bibliographical references

Patent, Dorothy Hinshaw

Homesteading; settling America's heartland; photographs by William Muñoz. Walker & Co. 1998 32p il maps $16.95 (3-6)   **978**
1. Frontier and pioneer life—West (U.S.) 2. West (U.S.)—Social life and customs
ISBN 0-8027-8664-2   LC 98-12463

Chronicles the activities of the homesteaders who settled the vast American prairies during the late nineteenth and early twentieth centuries

"An attractive, informative, and well-written guide." Booklist

West by covered wagon; retracing the pioneer trails; photographs by William Muñoz. Walker & Co. 1995 31p il maps $15.95 (3-6)   **978**
1. Overland journeys to the Pacific 2. West (U.S.)
ISBN 0-8027-8377-5   LC 94-48233

"Patent contrasts the Westmont Wagoneers' annual modern-day wagon ride in Montana with the experiences of pioneers traveling the Oregon trail during the 1800s. Color photographs of the Wagoneers' expedition accompany the informative text." Horn Book Guide

Rounds, Glen, 1906-

Cowboys. Holiday House 1991 unp il lib bdg $16.95; pa $5.95 (k-2)   **978**
1. Cowhands
ISBN 0-8234-0867-1 (lib blg); 0-8234-1061-7 (pa)
          LC 90-46501

Follows a cowboy from sunup to bedtime as he rounds up cattle, kills a rattlesnake, and plays cards in the bunkhouse after dinner

The author "conveys a surprising amount of information in his deceptively simple narrative, appropriate for even the youngest story-hour audience. His blackline illustrations, shaded in golds, browns, and blues, depict the barren landscape of the Great Plains as well as many details of ranch life." Booklist

Sakurai, Gail, 1952-

Asian-Americans in the old West. Children's Press 2000 30p il (Cornerstones of freedom) $20.50; pa $5.95 (4-6)   **978**
1. West (U.S.)—History 2. Asian Americans
ISBN 0-516-21152-8; 0-516-27035-4 (pa)
          LC 99-24463

Describes the important role of the Chinese, Japanese, and other Asians in the settlement of the American West

Schanzer, Rosalyn

How we crossed the West; the adventures of Lewis & Clark. National Geographic Soc. 1997 unp il $18 (3-5)   **978**
1. Lewis, Meriwether, 1774-1809 2. Clark, William, 1770-1838 3. Lewis and Clark Expedition (1804-1806)
ISBN 0-7922-3738-2   LC 96-6585

This "account of the 1804-1805 journey [has] . . . a text composed of brief excerpts drawn from the actual journals and letters written by Lewis and Clark and members of the expedition." SLJ

"Pithy and sometimes humorous, the text tells of contacts with Native Americans, encounters with wildlife . . . and the hardships of the trail. Warm in color and accessible in style, the acrylic paintings have a folk-art inspiration." Booklist

Scott, Ann Herbert, 1926-

Cowboy country; pictures by Ted Lewin. Clarion Bks. 1993 unp il $16; pa $6.95 (k-3)   **978**
1. Cowhands 2. West (U.S.)
ISBN 0-395-57561-3; 0-395-76482-3 (pa)
          LC 92-24499

An "old buckaroo" tells how he became a cowboy, what the work was like in the past, and how this life has changed

The author "succinctly captures the laconic speaking rhythms and distinctive jargon of her subject. . . . Lewin's . . . well-lit watercolors suggest the affability of the weathered narrator and the awe of the boy with him." Publ Wkly

979.4   California

Jaskol, Julie

City of angels; in and around Los Angeles; by Julie Jaskol & Brian Lewis; illustrated by Elisa Kleven. Dutton Children's Bks. 1999 47p il $16.99 (2-4)   **979.4**
1. Los Angeles (Calif.)
ISBN 0-525-46214-7   LC 99-35233

Surveys the history, historic sites, ethnic neighborhoods, festivals, and culture of the Los Angeles area

This offers "bright, exuberant collages filled with fascinating, minute details and a few paragraphs of text equally jam-packed with tidbits of information." SLJ

Krensky, Stephen, 1953-

Striking it rich; the story of the California gold rush; illustrated by Anna DiVito. Simon & Schuster Bks. for Young Readers 1996 48p il maps $15; pa $3.99 (2-4)   **979.4**
1. California—Gold discoveries 2. Overland journeys to the Pacific 3. Frontier and pioneer life—California
ISBN 0-689-80804-6; 0-689-80803-8 (pa)
          LC 95-52432

"Ready-to-read"

This account "includes the 1848 discovery of gold, the spread of gold fever, the land and sea routes to Califor-

Krensky, Stephen, 1953-—Continued
nia, the life of the miners, the injustices to immigrants, the population growth, and the economic development of Northern California." SLJ

"The story of the gold rush is told with verve, excitement, and wry wit. . . . DiVito's colorful line illustrations express the energy, naïveté, and lawlessness of the men who rushed to make a fortune." Booklist

Murrow, Liza Ketchum, 1946-
The gold rush; [by] Liza Ketchum; based upon the Public Television series; with an introduction by Ken Burns and Stephen Ives. Little, Brown 1996 118p il hardcover o.p. paperback available $12.95 (5 and up)   **979.4**
1. California—Gold discoveries 2. Frontier and pioneer life—California
ISBN 0-316-49047-4 (pa)   LC 95-43210
Illustrates the event which drew thousands of people to California and its effect on the gold seekers, the Spanish settlers, and the native Indian tribes who lived there
Includes bibliographical references

Stanley, Jerry, 1941-
Hurry freedom; African Americans in Gold Rush California. Crown 2000 85p il $18.95; lib bdg $20.99 (5 and up)   **979.4**
1. Gibbs, Mifflin Wistar, 1823-1915 2. California—Gold discoveries 3. African Americans
ISBN 0-517-80094-2; 0-517-80096-9 (lib bdg)
                                 LC 99-57818
Recounts the history of African Americans in California during the Gold Rush while focusing on the life and work of Mifflin Gibbs
"Good-quality, archival photos fill the pages. Some of them portray blacks and whites working side by side, others exemplify the time and culture discussed throughout the book. As the title suggests, the focus remains on African Americans, yet Stanley does note that Asian Americans and other minority groups also endured mistreatment at this time." SLJ
Includes bibliographical references

979.5 Oregon. Pacific Northwest

Fisher, Leonard Everett, 1924-
The Oregon Trail. Holiday House 1990 64p il maps $18.95 (4 and up)   **979.5**
1. Overland journeys to the Pacific 2. Oregon Trail 3. West (U.S.)—History
ISBN 0-8234-0833-7   LC 90-55103
Charts the journey of those who followed the Oregon Trail in the first half of the nineteenth century
"Fisher brings this migration to life with a clear, readable text that makes generous use of the emigrants' own journal entries. . . . The illustrations are many and varied, including maps, photographs, drawings, documents, and paintings." Booklist

979.8 Alaska

Meyer, Carolyn
In a different light; growing up in a Yup'ik Eskimo village in Alaska; [by] Carolyn Meyer with research assistance by Bernadine Bainton; contemporary photographs by John McDonald; archival photographs courtesy of the University of Alaska Fairbanks. Margaret K. McElderry Bks. 1996 181p il $17 (4 and up)   **979.8**
1. Inuit 2. Alaska—Social life and customs
ISBN 0-689-80146-7   LC 95-31140
A study of the contemporary Yupik culture in an Alaskan village as seen through the eyes of a typical family
"Meyer's story approach becomes a skillfully crafted vehicle for conveying cultural detail. . . . The month-by-month account of school, work, celebration, and leave taking is empathetic and probing. Poverty, alcohol abuse, and shifting sexual mores are explained honestly as are the personal respect and responsibilities binding extended families." Horn Book
Includes bibliographical references

981 Brazil

Galvin, Irene Flum
Brazil; many voices, many faces. Benchmark Bks. (Tarrytown) 1996 64p il maps (Exploring cultures of the world) lib bdg $27.07 (4 and up)
                                 981
1. Brazil
ISBN 0-7614-0200-4   LC 95-44087
An illustrated look at the geography, history, people and culture of the largest country in South America
Includes bibliographical references

Heinrichs, Ann
Brazil. Children's Press 1997 144p il maps (Enchantment of the world, second series) $33 (4 and up)   **981**
1. Brazil
ISBN 0-516-20602-8   LC 97-14376
Describes the geography, plants, animals, history, economy, culture, and people of Brazil
Includes bibliographical references

982 Argentina

Hintz, Martin, 1945-
Argentina. Children's Press 1998 144p il (Enchantment of the world, second series) $33 (4 and up)   **982**
1. Argentina
ISBN 0-516-20647-8   LC 97-40666
Describes the geography, history, culture, religion, and people of the environmentally diverse South American country of Argentina
Includes bibliographical references

983   Chile

Pickering, Marianne

Chile; where the land ends. Benchmark Bks. (Tarrytown) 1997 63p il maps (Exploring cultures of the world) lib bdg $27.07 (4 and up)   **983**

1. Chile

ISBN 0-7614-0333-7   LC 96-19989

Discusses the geography, history, people, and culture of this land of contrasts

Includes glossary and bibliographical references

984   Bolivia

Hermes, Jules, 1962-

The children of Bolivia. Carolrhoda Bks. 1995 47p il (World's children) $23.93 (3-5)   **984**

1. Children—Bolivia 2. Bolivia—Social life and customs

ISBN 0-87614-935-2   LC 94-44092

Introduces the history and culture of Bolivia through the daily lives of children who live there

Pateman, Robert, 1954-

Bolivia. Marshall Cavendish 1996 128p il maps (Cultures of the world) lib bdg $35.64 (5 and up)   **984**

1. Bolivia

ISBN 0-7614-0178-4   LC 95-14899

Presents information on the history, geography, religion, language, festivals, and other aspects of this landbound country of South America

Includes bibliographical references

985   Peru

Falconer, Kieran, 1970-

Peru. Marshall Cavendish 1996 128p il maps (Cultures of the world) lib bdg $35.64 (5 and up)   **985**

1. Peru

ISBN 0-7614-0179-2   LC 95-14898

Full-color photographs accompany information on many aspects of this South American country beginning with its geography and history and including government, religion, arts, and food

Includes glossary and bibliographical references

King, David C.

Peru; lost cities, found hopes. Benchmark Bks. (Tarrytown) 1998 64p il maps (Exploring cultures of the world) lib bdg $34.21 (4 and up)   **985**

1. Peru

ISBN 0-7614-0396-5   LC 97-2722

Examines the geography, history, government, people, and culture of Peru

"An accessible introduction to the South American country. . . . Kid-friendly topics such as school, holidays, and food are also discussed." Horn Book Guide

Includes glossary and bibliographical references

986.1   Colombia

Markham, Lois

Colombia; the gateway to South America. Benchmark Bks. (Tarrytown) 1997 64p il (Exploring cultures of the world) lib bdg $27.07 (4 and up)   **986.1**

1. Colombia

ISBN 0-7614-0140-7   LC 96-51580

Introduces the geography, history, people, and culture of the country known as the Gateway to South America

"Although Colombia's poverty, civil unrest, and drug trafficking are briefly mentioned, the volume concentrates on sunnier topics, such as family relationships, festivals, and the arts. . . . The clear text is accessible and readable." Horn Book Guide

Includes glossary and bibliographical references

Morrison, Marion

Colombia. Children's Press 1999 144p il (Enchantment of the world, second series) lib bdg $33 (4 and up)   **986.1**

1. Colombia

ISBN 0-516-21106-4   LC 98-19307

Describes the geography, history, economy, natural resources, culture, religion, and people of the South American country of Colombia

Includes bibliographical references

986.6   Ecuador

Foley, Erin, 1967-

Ecuador; [by] Erin L. Foley. Marshall Cavendish 1995 128p il maps (Cultures of the world) $35.64 (5 and up)   **986.6**

1. Ecuador

ISBN 0-7614-0173-3   LC 94-45266

This introduction to the history and culture of Ecuador "is especially successful in explaining social and economic hierarchies within the country. The cultures of the indigenous populations, blacks, mestizos, Hispanics, and other immigrants are discussed. The author describes how members within each group relate to one another and how these diverse cultures create the 'hierarchical pyramid' that is Ecuadorian society." SLJ

Includes glossary and bibliographical references

Lourie, Peter

Lost treasure of the Inca. Boyds Mills Press 1999 48p il maps $18.95 (4 and up)   **986.6**

1. Incas 2. Ecuador—Description 3. Buried treasure

ISBN 1-56397-743-5

The author describes his search in the mountains of Ecuador for gold hidden by the Incas

Lourie "succumbed to altitude sickness and had to descend without discovering a glimmer of the gold. But he did return with a ripping good yarn to tell . . . and some breathtaking photographs of the mistshrouded volcanic peaks. This should be a hot pick for armchair travelers." Bull Cent Child Books

Includes glossary

988.1 Guyana

Jermyn, Leslie
Guyana. Marshall Cavendish 2000 128p il maps (Cultures of the world) lib bdg $35.64 (5 and up)
988.1
1. Guyana
ISBN 0-7614-0994-7   LC 99-55063
Examines the geography, history, government, economy, people, and culture of Guyana
Includes glossary and bibliographical references

989.2 Paraguay

Jermyn, Leslie
Paraguay. Marshall Cavendish 2000 128p il maps (Cultures of the world) lib bdg $35.64 (5 and up)
989.2
1. Paraguay
ISBN 0-7614-0979-3   LC 99-27257
Describes the geography, history, government, economy, people, lifestyle, religion, language, arts, leisure, festivals, and food of Paraguay
Includes glossary and bibliographical references

989.5 Uruguay

Jermyn, Leslie
Uruguay. Marshall Cavendish 1999 128p il maps (Cultures of the world) lib bdg $35.64 (5 and up)
989.5
1. Uruguay
ISBN 0-7614-0873-8   LC 98-27375
Describes the geography, history, government, economy, people, lifestyle, religion, language, arts, leisure, festivals, and food of the smallest country in South America
Includes glossary and bibliographical references

993 New Zealand

Smelt, Roselynn
New Zealand. Marshall Cavendish 1998 128p il maps (Cultures of the world) lib bdg $35.64 (5 and up)
993
1. New Zealand
ISBN 0-7614-0808-8   LC 97-42179
Introduces the geography, history, religion, government, economy, and culture of a Pacific-island country first populated by the Maori, to whom it was the "Land of the Long White Cloud"
Includes glossary and bibliographical references

994 Australia

Heinrichs, Ann
Australia. Children's Press 1998 144p il (Enchantment of the world, second series) $33 (4 and up)
994
1. Australia
ISBN 0-516-20648-6   LC 98-15780
Explores the geography, history, arts, religions, and everyday life of the Land Down Under, also called the Lucky Country
Includes bibliographical references

Meisel, Jacqueline Drobis
Australia; the land down under. Benchmark Bks. (Tarrytown) 1997 64p il (Exploring cultures of the world) lib bdg $27.07 (4 and up)
994
1. Australia
ISBN 0-7614-0139-3   LC 96-45293
Discusses the geography, history, people, and culture of this country, which is also a continent in the Southern Hemisphere
This is a "brief, but information-packed, survey. . . . Details about holiday celebrations, sports, and the unusual schooling-by-radio that some outback children receive add to the interest and accessibility of the volume." Horn Book Guide
Includes glossary and bibliographical references

Petersen, David, 1946-
Australia. Children's Press 1998 47p il maps $22 (2-4)
994
1. Australia
ISBN 0-516-20765-2   LC 97-33041
"A True book"
An illustrated intoduction to the geography, history, wildlife, and people of Australia
Includes bibliographical references

995.3 Papua New Guinea. New Guinea region

Gascoigne, Ingrid
Papua New Guinea. Marshall Cavendish 1998 128p il maps (Cultures of the world) lib bdg $35.64 (5 and up)
995.3
1. Papua New Guinea
ISBN 0-7614-0813-4   LC 97-43611
Discusses the geography, history, economy, government, varied culture and peoples of the country made up of more than 600 islands and archipelagos
Includes glossary and bibliographical references

996 Polynesia and Micronesia

Arnold, Caroline, 1944-
Easter Island; giant stone statues tell of a rich and tragic past; text and photographs by Caroline Arnold. Clarion Bks. 2000 48p il map $15 (4 and up)
996
1. Easter Island
ISBN 0-395-87609-5   LC 99-27189
"Images of the large statues, or *moai*, on Easter Island are highly recognizable, and have fostered many romanticized popular accounts of their mysterious origins. Caroline Arnold avoids theatrical speculation in this straightforward account of what archaeologists have determined

Arnold, Caroline, 1944---_Continued_
about the history of the Rapanui people and their monuments. The clearly written text is accompanied by breathtaking color photographs that show the beauty of the island and its rich collection of archaeological features." Horn Book

Includes bibliographical references

NgCheong-Lum, Roseline, 1962-
Fiji. Marshall Cavendish 2000 128p il maps (Cultures of the world) lib bdg $35.64 (5 and up)   **996**
1. Fiji
ISBN 0-7614-0996-3   LC 99-54120
Describes the geography, history, government, economy, people, lifestyle, religion, language, arts, leisure, festivals, and food of South Pacific island of Fiji
Includes glossary and bibliographical references

Tahiti. Marshall Cavendish 1997 128p il maps (Cultures of the world) $35.64 (5 and up)   **996**
1. Tahiti (French Polynesia)
ISBN 0-7614-0682-4   LC 96-40213
Discusses the geography, history, government, economy, people, and culture of the largest island in French Polynesia
This offers "lucidly written text. . . . Chapters include discussion of nuclear testing in the Pacific, the Tahitian language, and nationalism in the French territory. Maps and a page of basic facts about Tahiti round out the useful book." Horn Book Guide

Includes glossary and bibliographical references

998   Arctic islands and Antarctica

Beattie, Owen
Buried in ice; by Owen Beattie and John Geiger with Shelley Tanaka. Scholastic 1992 64p il maps (Time quest book) hardcover o.p. paperback available $6.95 (4 and up)   **998**
1. Franklin, Sir John, 1786-1847 2. Arctic regions
ISBN 0-590-43849-2 (pa)   LC 91-23897
"A Scholastic/Madison Press book"
Probes the tragic and mysterious fate of Sir John Franklin's failed expedition to the Arctic to find the Northwest Passage in 1845
"The narrative is interspersed with an imaginative section that relates the story of the expedition from the point of view of 19-year-old Luke, a member of the crew. While the text is exciting, the book's greatest strength is its superb illustrations: drawings, paintings, and historic and present day photographs are used to enrich each page." SLJ
Includes glossary and bibliographical references

Burleigh, Robert, 1936-
Black whiteness; Admiral Byrd alone in the Antarctic; illustrated by Walter Lyon Krudop. Atheneum Bks. for Young Readers 1998 36p il $16 (3-5)   **998**
1. Byrd, Richard Evelyn, 1888-1957 2. Antarctica—Exploration
ISBN 0-689-81299-X   LC 96-21999

"Byrd's solitary sojourn at Little America during the unimaginably cold, dark Antarctic winter of 1934 is captured in a lyrical text strengthened by dramatic, impressive paintings." SLJ

Kimmel, Elizabeth Cody
Ice story; Shackleton's lost expedition. Clarion Bks. 1999 120p il maps $18 (4 and up)   **998**
1. Shackleton, Sir Ernest Henry, 1874-1922 2. Endurance (Ship) 3. Imperial Trans-Antarctic Expedition (1914-1917) 4. Antarctica—Exploration
ISBN 0-395-91524-4   LC 98-29956
Describes the events of the 1914 Shackleton Antarctic expedition, when the ship the Endurance was crushed in a frozen sea and the men made the perilous journey across ice and stormy seas to reach inhabited land
"The amazing story is well served in this account, which includes photos by expedition photographer Frank Hurley." Horn Book Guide
Includes bibliographical references

Steger, Will
Over the top of the world; explorer Will Steger's trek across the Arctic; [by] Will Steger and Jon Bowermaster; sidebars by Barbara Horlbeck. Scholastic 1997 63p il $17.95; pa $5.99 (4 and up)   **998**
1. Arctic regions 2. North Pole
ISBN 0-590-84860-7; 0-590-84861-5 (pa)
     LC 96-6913
An account of explorer Will Steger's expedition from Russia to Canada by way of the North Pole, traveling by dog sled and canoe
"Written with a crispness and an immediacy, the narrative reads like an adventure story, with dramatic, compelling photographs." Booklist

Taylor, Barbara, 1954-
Arctic & Antarctic; written by Barbara Taylor; photographed by Geoff Brightling. Knopf 1995 63p il (Eyewitness books) (4 and up)   **998**
1. Polar regions
     LC 94-37730
Available DK Pub. edition $15.95; lib bdg $19.99 (ISBN 0-7894-5850-0; 0-7894-6606-6)
"A Dorling Kindersley book"
This overview "features a series of two-page spreads focusing on the history, geology, plant life, wildlife and ecology of the polar regions. Each two-page topic is given a paragraph of explanatory text surrounded by diagrams, maps, charts and photographs with lengthy captions." Appraisal

Wheeler, Sara
Greetings from Antarctica. Bedrick Bks. 1999 45p il $15.95   **998**
1. Antarctica
ISBN 0-87226-295-2   LC 98-37203
The author tells the story of her experiences living and working in Antarctica
"The book includes brief descriptions of scientific re-

Wheeler, Sara—*Continued*

search, wildlife, life on the bases, and historical expeditions. Each colorful . . . double-page layout features a letter from the author describing her visit to the continent." Horn Book

Includes bibliographical references

Fic FICTION

A number of subject headings have been added to the books in this section to aid in curriculum work. It is not necessarily recommended that these subjects be used in the library catalog.

Ackerman, Karen, 1951-

The night crossing; illustrated by Elizabeth Sayles. Knopf 1994 56p il hardcover o.p. paperback available $4.50 (3-5)   **Fic**

1. Holocaust, 1933-1945—Fiction 2. Jews—Austria—Fiction

ISBN 0-679-87040-7 (pa)   LC 94-10805

In 1938, having begun to feel the persecution that all Jews are experiencing in their Austrian city, Clara and her family escape over the mountains into Switzerland

"Ackerman's writing is clear and direct; despite its simplicity, it is never banal. This is an excellent fictional introduction to the Holocaust." SLJ

Adams, Richard, 1920-

Watership Down. Scribner Classics c1972 429p $27.50 (6 and up)   **Fic**

1. Rabbits—Fiction 2. Allegories

ISBN 0-684-83605-4

Also available in paperback from Avon Bks. and Audiobook version

First published 1972 in the United Kingdom; first United States edition 1974 by Macmillan

"Faced with the annihilation of its warren, a small group of male rabbits sets out across the English downs in search of a new home. Internal struggles for power surface in this intricately woven, realistically told adult adventure when the protagonists must coordinate tactics in order to defeat an enemy rabbit fortress. It is clear that the author has done research on rabbit behavior, for this tale is truly authentic." Shapiro. Fic for Youth. 3d edition

Adler, David A., 1947-

Cam Jansen and the mystery of the stolen diamonds; illustrated by Susanna Natti. Viking 1980 58p il $13.99; pa $3.99 (2-4)   **Fic**

1. Mystery fiction

ISBN 0-670-20039-5; 0-14-034670-8 (pa)

LC 79-20695

Easy-to-read titles about Cam Jansen are also available

Cam Jansen, a fifth-grader with a photographic memory, and her friend Eric help solve the mystery of the stolen diamonds

This is a "fast-action uncomplicated adventure . . . [with] a touch of humor, a breezy writing style, and some very enjoyable pen-and-ink drawings." Booklist

Other available titles about Cam Jansen are:

Cam Jansen and the barking treasure mystery (1999)

Cam Jansen and the birthday mystery (2000)
Cam Jansen and the catnapping mystery (1998)
Cam Jansen and the chocolate fudge mystery (1993)
Cam Jansen and the ghostly mystery (1996)
Cam Jansen and the mystery at the haunted house (1992)
Cam Jansen and the mystery at the monkey house (1985)
Cam Jansen and the mystery of Flight 54 (1989)
Cam Jansen and the mystery of the Babe Ruth baseball (1982)
Cam Jansen and the mystery of the carnival prize (1984)
Cam Jansen and the mystery of the circus clown (1983)
Cam Jansen and the mystery of the dinosaur bones (1981)
Cam Jansen and the mystery of the gold coins (1982)
Cam Jansen and the mystery of the monster movie (1984)
Cam Jansen and the mystery of the stolen corn popper (1986)
Cam Jansen and the mystery of the television dog (1981)
Cam Jansen and the mystery of the UFO (1980)
Cam Jansen and the scary snake mystery (1997)
Cam Jansen and the Triceratops Pops mystery (1995)

Aiken, Joan, 1924-

The wolves of Willoughby Chase; illustrated by Pat Marriott. Delacorte Press 2000 c1962 181p $16.95; pa $4.99 (5 and up)   **Fic**

1. Great Britain—Fiction

ISBN 0-385-32790-0; 0-440-49603-9 (pa)

First published 1962 in the United Kingdom; first United States edition 1963 by Doubleday

"In this burlesque of a Victorian melodrama, two London children are sent to a country estate while their parents are away. Here they outwit a wicked governess, escape from packs of hungry wolves, and restore the estate to its rightful owner." Hodges. Books for Elem Sch Libr

"Plot, characterization, and background blend perfectly into an amazing whole. . . . Highly recommended." SLJ

Other available titles in this series are:

Black hearts in Battersea (1964)
Cold Shoulder Road (1996)
The cuckoo tree (1971)
Dangerous games (1999)
Is underground (1993)
The stolen lake (1981)

Alcock, Vivien, 1924-

The cuckoo sister. Delacorte Press 1986 c1985 160p o.p.; Houghton Mifflin paperback available $4.95 (6 and up)   **Fic**

1. Sisters—Fiction 2. London (England)—Fiction

ISBN 0-395-81651-3 (pa)   LC 85-20648

First published 1985 in the United Kingdom

"Eleven year old Kate Seton becomes very upset when an underfed 13-year-old shows up at her parents' home with a letter stating that she is Kate's sister—stolen from a pram outside a store where Mrs. Seton had been shopping. Rosie doesn't believe the story that she is Emma Seton and frantically tries to find her mother who has left with no trace. Kate eventually comes to love Rosie and tries to provide a clue that will enable her to stay. Characterizations are very vivid and although it definitely has a British flavor, students will empathize with Kate and Rosie." Voice Youth Advocates

Alcock, Vivien, 1924-—*Continued*

The monster garden. Delacorte Press 1988 134p
o.p.; Houghton Mifflin paperback available $4.95
(4 and up)   **Fic**
1. Monsters—Fiction 2. Father-daughter relationship—Fiction 3. Science fiction
ISBN 0-618-00337-1 (pa)

"The story of a young girl who unexpectedly finds
herself nurturing a creature of unknown origin. Frankie
Stein is the daughter of a scientist whose preoccupation
with his work drives a wedge among the family members. When Frankie obtains some unknown genetic 'material,' she finds herself having to cope with a growing
'monster.'" SLJ

"*The Monster Garden* is a deft fantasy; it is also a
story of compassionate love and growing self-reliance."
Bull Cent Child Books

Alcott, Louisa May, 1832-1888

Little women; or Meg, Jo, Beth and Amy (5 and
up)   **Fic**
1. Family life—Fiction 2. New England—Fiction

Available from various publishers
First published 1868

The story of the New England home life of the four
March sisters. Each 'little woman's' personality differs:
Jo's quick temper and restless desire for the freedom of
a boy's life; Meg's hatred of poverty and her longing for
pretty clothes; Amy's all-engulfing self-interest; and gentle Beth's love of home and family

The tale is "related with sympathy, humour, and sin-
cerity. This lively natural narrative of family experience
is as well-loved today as when it first appeared." Toronto
Public Libr. Books for Boys & Girls
Other available titles about members of the March fami-
ly are:
Eight cousins (1875)
Jo's boys (1886)
Little men (1871)
Rose in bloom (1876)

An old-fashioned Thanksgiving (3-5)   **Fic**
1. Family life—Fiction 2. Thanksgiving Day—Fiction
3. New England—Fiction

Various editions available

"In this story, which first appeared in 'St. Nicholas'
magazine in 1881, Alcott recounts the escapades of a
New Hampshire farm family in the 1820s. When the parents are unexpectedly called away on Thanksgiving Day,
the children pitch in to make their version of the traditional holiday feast and, with little knowledge and less
caution, bumble along toward a culinary catastrophe reminiscent of Meg and Jo's dinner in 'Little Women.'"
Booklist

Alexander, Lloyd

The Arkadians. Dutton Children's Bks. 1995
272p $16.99; pa $5.99 (5 and up)   **Fic**
1. Fantasy fiction
ISBN 0-525-45415-2; 0-14-038073-6 (pa)
                                      LC 94-35025
Also available Audiobook version

To escape the wrath of the king and his wicked sooth-
sayers, Lucian joins with Fronto, a poet-turned-jackass,
and Joy-in-the-Dance, a young girl with mystical powers,
on a series of epic adventures

"On one level, this is a rousing adventure complete
with cliffhangers and do-or-die situations. On another,
readers familiar with Greek mythology will find clever
hints at the myths' purpose and genesis." SLJ

The Beggar Queen. Dutton 1984 221p o.p.; Dell
paperback available $4.99 (5 and up)   **Fic**
1. Adventure fiction
ISBN 0-440-90548-6 (pa)   LC 83-25502

The concluding volume in the author's Westmark trilogy, begun with Westmark and The Kestrel (1982)

"Since the end of the war with Regia, Theo has become a consul to Mickle, now Queen Augusta. However,
peace lasts only two years, when Cabbarus invades the
country to wrest the kingdom back from Mickle. Theo is
forced to take up arms again to help his beloved queen
and country." Roman. Sequences

The book of three. rev ed. Holt & Co. 1999
190p (Chronicles of Prydain, 1) $18.95 (5 and up)
                                           Fic
1. Fantasy fiction
ISBN 0-8050-6132-0   LC 98-40901
Also available in paperback from Dell
First published 1964

"The first of five books about the mythical land of
Prydain finds Taran, an assistant pig keeper, fighting
with Prince Gwydion against the evil which theatens the
kingdom." Hodges. Books for Elem Sch Libr

"Related in a simple, direct style, this fast-paced tale
of high adventure has a well-balanced blend of fantasy,
realism, and humor." SLJ
Other available titles about the mythical land of Prydain
are:
The black cauldron (1965)
The castle of Llyr (1966)
The foundling and other tales of Prydain
The high king, entered separately
Taran Wanderer (1967)

The cat who wished to be a man. Dutton 1973
107p hardcover o.p. paperback available $4.99
(4-6)   **Fic**
1. Cats—Fiction
ISBN 0-14-130704-8 (pa)   LC 73-77447
Also available Audiobook version

When he begins dealing with humanity, Lionel the cat
begins to understand why his wizard master was reluctant to change him into a man

This is "a comic and ebullient fantasy; just right for
reading aloud." Horn Book

Gypsy Rizka. Dutton Children's Bks. 1999 195p
$16.99; pa $4.99 (5 and up)   **Fic**
1. Gypsies—Fiction 2. Fantasy fiction
ISBN 0-525-46121-3; 0-14-130980-6 (pa)
                                      LC 98-41399

Living alone in her wagon on the outskirts of a Greater Dunitsa while waiting for her father's return, Rizka,
a Gypsy and a trickster, exposes the ridiculous foibles of
some of the townspeople

Alexander, Lloyd—*Continued*

"Scenes of broad slapstick effervesce with mind-tickling repartee in this book that is . . . lively, satirical, and with a core of pure gold." Horn Book Guide

The high king. Holt & Co. 1999 c1968 253p rev ed (Chronicles of Prydain) $18.95 (5 and up)

Fic

1. Fantasy fiction
ISBN 0-8050-6135-5   LC 98-40900
Also available in paperback from Dell
Awarded The Newbery Medal, 1969
Concluding title in the chronicles of Prydain which include: The book of three, The black cauldron, The castle of Llyr, and Taran Wanderer
First published 1968
This edition includes a pronunciation guide
In this final volume Taran, the assistant pig-keeper "becomes High King of Prydain, Princess Eilonwy becomes his queen, the predictions of Taran's wizard guardian Dallben are fulfilled, and the forces of black magic led by Arawn, Lord of Annuvin, Land of the Dead, are vanquished forever." SLJ
"The fantasy has the depth and richness of a medieval tapestry, infinitely detailed and imaginative." Saturday Rev

The Illyrian adventure. Dutton 1986 132p o.p.; Dell paperback available $3.99 (5 and up)   Fic
1. Adventure fiction
ISBN 0-440-40297-2 (pa)   LC 85-30762
"Sixteen-year-old Vesper Holly drags her long-suffering guardian, Brinnie, off to Illyria to vindicate her late father's reputation as a scholar. With humor, beguiling charm, and intelligence she manages to find a treasure, thwart a conspiracy to murder Illyria's King Osman, and guide two rival factions to the peace table." Wilson Libr Bull
"Alexander's archeological mystery has intricate plotting and witty wording." Bull Cent Child Books
Other available adventure titles featuring Vesper Holly are:
The Drackenberg adventure (1988)
The El Dorado adventure (1987)
The Jedera adventure (1989)
The Philadelphia adventure (1990)

The iron ring. Dutton Children's Bks. 1997 283p $16.99; pa $4.99 (5 and up)   Fic
1. Adventure fiction 2. India—Fiction
ISBN 0-525-45597-3; 0-14-130348-4 (pa)
          LC 96-29730
"Young Tamar, ruler of a small Indian kingdom, wagers with a visiting king and loses his kingdom and his freedom. Traveling to the king's land to make good on his debt, he collects quite an entourage and eventually overcomes his enemies with his friends' help. This tale offers delightful characters, a philosophical interest in the meaning of life, a thoughtful look at the caste system, and a clever use of Indian animal folktales." Horn Book Guide

The marvelous misadventures of Sebastian; grand extravaganza, including a performance by the entire cast of the Gallimaufry-Theatricus. Dutton 1970 204p hardcover o.p. paperback available $5.99 (4 and up)   Fic
1. Adventure fiction 2. Musicians—Fiction
ISBN 0-14-130816-8 (pa)   LC 70-116879
"Sebastian, a teenage fiddler, gets involved in court intrigue and muddles his way to eventual success in ousting a cruel usurper from the throne." Natl Counc of Teach of Engl. Adventuring with Books
"The intricacy of plot, the humor and allusiveness of the writing, the exaggerated characterization, and the derring-do of romantic adventures are knit into a lively and elaborate tale that can be enjoyed for its action and appreciated for its subtler significance." Sutherland. The Best in Child Books

The remarkable journey of Prince Jen. Dutton Children's Bks. 1991 273p $16.99 (5 and up)

Fic

1. Adventure fiction 2. China—Fiction
ISBN 0-525-44826-8   LC 91-13720
Also available in paperback from Dell
Bearing six unusual gifts, young Prince Jen in Tang Dynasty China embarks on a perilous quest and emerges triumphantly into manhood
"Alexander satisfies the taste for excitement, but his vivid characters and the food for thought he offers will nourish long after the last page is turned." SLJ

Westmark. Dutton 1981 184p o.p.; Laurel-Leaf Bks. paperback available $4.50 (5 and up)   Fic
1. Adventure fiction
ISBN 0-440-99731-3 (pa)
A boy fleeing from criminal charges falls in with a charlatan, his dwarf attendant, and an urchin girl, travels with them about the kingdom of Westmark, and ultimately arrives at the palace where the king is grieving over the loss of his daughter
The author "peoples his tale with a marvelous cast of individuals, and weaves an intricate story of high adventure that climaxes in a superbly conceived conclusion, which, though predictable, is reached through carefully built tension and subtly added comic relief." Booklist
Followed by The Kestrel (1982), and The Beggar Queen

Almond, David, 1951-

Kit's wilderness. Delacorte Press 1999 229p $15.95 (5 and up)   Fic
1. Coal mines and mining—Fiction 2. Ghost stories 3. Great Britain—Fiction
ISBN 0-385-32665-3   LC 99-34332
Also available Thorndike Press large print edition and Audiobook version
Thirteen-year-old Kit goes to live with his grandfather in the decaying coal mining town of Stoneygate, England, and finds both the old man and the town haunted by ghosts of the past
The author "explores the power of friendship and family, the importance of memory, and the role of magic in our lives. This is a highly satisfying literary experience." SLJ

Almond, David, 1951——*Continued*

Skellig. Delacorte Press 1999 c1998 182p
$15.95; pa $4.99 (5 and up)   **Fic**
1. Fantasy fiction
ISBN 0-385-32653-X; 0-440-41602-7 (pa)
           LC 98-23121
Also available Thorndike Press large print edition and
Audiobook version
First published 1998 in the United Kingdom
Unhappy about his baby sister's illness and the chaos
of moving into a dilapidated old house, Michael retreats
to the garage and finds a mysterious stranger who is
something like a bird and something like an angel
"The plot is beautifully paced and the characters are
drawn with a graceful, careful hand. . . . A lovingly
done, thought-provoking novel." SLJ

Andersen, Hans Christian, 1805-1875

The little match girl; illustrated by Rachel
Isadora. Putnam 1987 30p il $16.99 (3-5)   **Fic**
ISBN 0-399-21336-8   LC 85-30082
The wares of the poor little match girl illuminate her
cold world, bringing some beauty to her brief, tragic life
"Isadora follows Andersen's lead, neither
sensationalizing nor apologizing for the tale's potentially
sentimental plot. . . . A moving, original picture-book
interpretation of the classic tale." Booklist

The nightingale; [illustrated by] Lisbeth
Zwerger; translated from the Danish by Anthea
Bell. North-South Bks. 1999 unp il $15.95; pa
$6.95 (2-5)   **Fic**
1. Fairy tales 2. Nightingales—Fiction
ISBN 0-7358-1118-0; 0-7358-1120-2 (pa)
           LC 98-45563
"A Michael Neugebauer book"
A reissue of the edition published 1984 by Picture
Book Studio
Though the emperor banishes the nightingale in pref-
erence for a jeweled mechanical imitation, the little bird
remains faithful and returns years later when the emperor
is near death and no one else can help him
"A faithful rendering of the famous narrative into
well-cadenced storytelling prose. . . . The paintings are
understated and . . . emphasize characterization more
than action or setting." Horn Book Guide

The princess and the pea; illustrated by
Dorothée Duntze. Holt, Rinehart & Winston 1985
unp il $16.95 (k-3)   **Fic**
1. Fairy tales
ISBN 0-03-005738-8   LC 85-7199
A young girl feels a pea through twenty mattresses
and twenty featherbeds and proves she is a real princess
"This classic Andersen fairy tale is presented in simple text and with elaborate illustrations. . . . Duntze appears to set the story during the Renaissance, and her illustrations are precise, intricate and detailed." SLJ

The swineherd; [illustrated by] Lisbeth Zwerger;
translated from the Danish by Anthea Bell.
North-South Bks. 1995 c1982 unp il $14.95 (1-4)
          Fic
1. Fairy tales
ISBN 1-55858-428-5   LC 94-32153

"A Michael Neugebauer book"
A reissue of the 1982 Morrow edition
A prince disguises himself as a swineherd and learns
the true character of the princess he desires
The story "is given a comic and earthy tone by
Zwerger's expressive line." SLJ

Thumbelina; unabridged translation by Erik
Haugaard; illustrated by Arlene Graston. Delacorte
Press 1997 unp il $16.95 (3-5)   **Fic**
1. Fairy tales
ISBN 0-385-32251-8   LC 95-53284
After being kidnapped by an ugly toad, a beautiful girl
no bigger than a thumb has a series of dreadful experiences before meeting a fairy prince just her size
"The narrative is smooth, spare, and rich in descriptive
language that is never ornate. . . . Graston's watercolor
illustrations . . . are beautifully textured, with a tiled impression in the background and carefully distinguished
details." SLJ

Armstrong, Jennifer, 1961-

Black-eyed Susan; a novel; illustrated by Emily
Martindale. Crown 1995 120p il $15 (3-5)   **Fic**
1. Frontier and pioneer life—Fiction 2. Parent-child
relationship—Fiction 3. South Dakota—Fiction
ISBN 0-517-70107-3   LC 95-2276
Also available in paperback from Random House
Ten-year-old Susie and her father love living on the
South Dakota prairie with its vast, uninterrupted views of
land and sky, but Susie's mother greatly misses their old
life in Ohio
"Armstrong's elegant, spare prose is readable and
evocatively re-creates the time and place." SLJ

Steal away. Orchard Bks. 1992 206p o.p.;
Scholastic paperback available $3.99 (5 and up)
          Fic
1. Slavery—Fiction 2. African Americans—Fiction
3. Underground railroad—Fiction
ISBN 0-590-46921-5 (pa)   LC 91-18504
"A Richard Jackson book"
In 1855 two thirteen-year-old girls, one white and one
black, run away from a southern farm and make the difficult journey north to freedom, living to recount their
story forty-one years later to two similar young girls
"Armstrong's novel has pace and suspense, characterization that is solid and consistent, and a crescendo that
builds to a logical yet dramatic climax." Bull Cent Child
Books

Armstrong, William Howard, 1914-1999

Sounder; [by] William H. Armstrong;
illustrations by James Barkley. Harper & Row
1969 116p il $15.95; pa $6 (5 and up)   **Fic**
1. Dogs—Fiction 2. African Americans—Fiction
3. Family life—Fiction
ISBN 0-06-020143-6; 0-06-080975-2 (pa)
Also available Audiobook version
Awarded the Newbery Medal, 1970
"Set in the South in the era of sharecropping and segregation, this succinctly told tale poignantly describes the
courage of a father who steals a ham in order to feed his

Armstrong, William Howard, 1914-1999—Continued

undernourished family; the determination of the eldest son, who searches for his father despite the apathy of prison authorities; and the devotion of a coon dog named Sounder." Shapiro. Fic for Youth. 3d edition

Arrington, Frances

Bluestem. Philomel Bks. 2000 140p $16.99 (4-6)
Fic
1. Sisters—Fiction 2. Frontier and pioneer life—Fiction
ISBN 0-399-23564-7   LC 99-53726
With their father away and their mother traumatized by some unknown event, eleven-year-old Polly and her younger sister are left to take care of themselves and their prairie homestead
"Arrington uses poetic language and deep description to provide her audience with a clear vision of the open prairie. Her characters are realistic and their struggle evident." ALAN

Atwater, Richard Tupper, 1892-1948

Mr. Popper's penguins; [by] Richard and Florence Atwater; illustrated by Robert Lawson. Little, Brown 1938 138p il $16.95; pa $4.95 (3-5)
Fic
1. Penguins—Fiction
ISBN 0-316-05842-4; 0-316-05843-2 (pa)
A Newbery Medal honor book, 1939
When Mr. Popper, a mild little painter and decorator with a taste for books and movies on polar explorations, was presented with a penguin, he named it Captain Cook. From that moment on life was changed for the Popper family
"To the depiction of the penguins in all conceivable moods Robert Lawson [the] artist has brought not only his skill but his individual humor, and his portrayal of the wistful Mr. Popper is memorable." N Y Times Book Rev

Auch, Mary Jane

Frozen summer. Holt & Co. 1998 202p $16.95 (4 and up)
Fic
1. Frontier and pioneer life—Fiction 2. Mentally ill—Fiction 3. New York (State)—Fiction
ISBN 0-8050-4923-1   LC 98-23485
Also available in paperback from Dell
Sequel to Journey to nowhere
In this second title in the Genesee trilogy, twelve-year-old Mem's new home in the wilderness of western New York is disrupted when the birth of another baby sends her mother into "spells" that disconnect her from reality
"A thoughtful novel for readers ready to move beyond stories of idealized pioneers." Booklist
Followed by The road to home

I was a third grade science project; illustrated by Herm Auch. Holiday House 1998 96p il $15.95 (2-4)
Fic
1. School stories 2. Hypnotism—Fiction
ISBN 0-8234-1357-8   LC 97-41996

Also available in paperback from Bantam Bks.
While trying to hypnotize his dog for the third grade science fair, Brian accidentally makes his best friend Josh think he's a cat
"Auch's wisecracking third-graders and superb comic timing will have readers rolling on the floor." Booklist

Journey to nowhere. Holt & Co. 1997 202p $15.95 (4 and up)
Fic
1. Frontier and pioneer life—Fiction 2. New York (State)—Fiction
ISBN 0-8050-4922-3   LC 96-42249
Also available in paperback from Bantam Bks.
This is the first title in the Genesee trilogy. In 1815, while traveling by covered wagon to settle in the wilderness of western New York, eleven-year-old Mem experiences a flood and separation from her family
"A well-written, realistic, and thoroughly researched novel." Booklist
Followed by Frozen summer

The road to home. Holt & Co. 2000 216p $16.95 (4 and up)
Fic
1. Frontier and pioneer life—Fiction 2. New York (State)—Fiction
ISBN 0-8050-4921-5   LC 99-49230
This is the concluding volume in the Genesee trilogy. In 1817, after her mother has died and her father abandoned his children, thirteen-year-old Mem searches for a new home for Joshua, herself, and their little sister
"Filled with action, adventure, and lots of solid historical detail." SLJ

Avi, 1937-

Abigail takes the wheel; story by Avi; pictures by Don Bolognese. HarperCollins Pubs. 1999 54p il $14.95; lib bdg $14.89; pa $3.95 (2-4)
Fic
1. Ships—Fiction 2. New York (N.Y.)—Fiction
ISBN 0-06-027662-2; 0-06-027663-0 (lib bdg); 0-06-444281-0 (pa)   LC 98-36887
"An I can read chapter book"
When the first mate of the freight boat Neptune falls ill, it is up to Abigail, the captain's daughter, to steer the ship up the Hudson River from New Jersey to New York City
"Avi's generous dose of adventure and suspense, combined with his straightforward yet compelling storytelling style, custom-fit this tale for new chapter-book readers. Bolognese's subdued watercolors create a turn-of-the-century nautical atmosphere." Horn Book Guide

The barn. Orchard Bks. 1994 106p $14.95 (4-6)
Fic
1. Farm life—Fiction 2. Frontier and pioneer life—Fiction
ISBN 0-531-06861-7   LC 94-6920
Also available in paperback from Avon Bks.
"A Richard Jackson book"
In an effort to fulfill their dying father's last request, nine-year-old Ben and his brother and sister construct a barn on their land in the Oregon Territory in the 1850s
"While focusing mainly on his characters, Avi presents a vivid picture of the time and place, including fairly involved details about how the barn is constructed. This novel . . . is a thought-provoking and engaging piece of historical fiction." SLJ

Avi, 1937-—*Continued*

Blue heron. Bradbury Press 1992 186p $15 (5 and up)   **Fic**
1. Family life—Fiction 2. Herons—Fiction
ISBN 0-02-707751-9   LC 91-4308
Also available in paperback from Avon Bks.

While spending the month of August on the Massachusetts shore with her father, stepmother, and their new baby, almost thirteen-year-old Maggie finds beauty in and draws strength from a great blue heron, even as the family around her unravels

"Maggie emerges as a sensitive heroine whose perceptions are genuine as well as compelling. Reflecting the complexity of people and their emotions, this novel explores rather than solves the conflicts introduced." Publ Wkly

Encounter at Easton. Pantheon Bks. 1980 o.p.; Avon Bks. paperback available $4.99 (5 and up)   **Fic**
1. Runaway children—Fiction 2. Contract labor—Fiction 3. Pennsylvania—Fiction 4. United States—History—1600-1775, Colonial period—Fiction
ISBN 0-380-73241-6 (pa)   LC 79-9439
"Robert and Elizabeth, two indentured servants who fled their master in *Night Journeys*, are floundering toward Easton, Pennsylvania, and hoped-for safety. Elizabeth is gravely ill, however, and Robert is forced to leave her with Mad Moll, an outcast who wanders the hills. Thinking he has met a friend, Robert enters the employ of Nathaniel Hill, a man paid to hunt down the children, and is caught up in a disastrous climax of events." Booklist

"The tale is told through alternating testimonies of the major parties involved. . . . In his terse style, Avi manipulates these narratives with skill, sustaining suspense." SLJ

The fighting ground. Lippincott 1984 157p hardcover o.p. paperback available $4.95 (5 and up)   **Fic**
1. United States—History—1775-1783, Revolution—Fiction
ISBN 0-06-440185-5 (pa)   LC 82-47719
"It's April 1776, and the fighting ground is both the farm country of Pennsylvania and the heart of a boy which is 'wonderful ripe for war.' Twenty-four hours transform Jonathan from a cocky 13-year-old, eager to take on the British, into a young man who now knows the horror, the pathos, the ambiguities of war." Voice Youth Advocates

The author "has written a taut, fast-paced novel that builds to a shattering climax. His protagonist's painful, inner struggle to understand the intense and conflicting emotions brought on by a war that spares no one is central to this finely crafted novel." ALAN

Midnight magic. Scholastic Press 1999 249p $15.99 (5 and up)   **Fic**
1. Magicians—Fiction 2. Renaissance—Fiction 3. Italy—Fiction
ISBN 0-590-36035-3   LC 98-50192
In Italy in 1491, Mangus the magician and his apprentice are summoned to the castle of Duke Claudio to determine if his daughter is indeed being haunted by a ghost

An "entertaining tale of mystery and intrigue." SLJ

Night journeys. Pantheon Bks. 1979 143p o.p.; Avon Bks. paperback available $4.99 (5 and up)   **Fic**
1. Society of Friends—Fiction 2. Contract labor—Fiction 3. Pennsylvania—Fiction 4. United States—History—1600-1775, Colonial period—Fiction 5. Orphans—Fiction
ISBN 0-380-73242-4 (pa)   LC 78-10151
Set in 1768 on the Pennsylvania-New Jersey border, this story "concerns 12-year-old Peter York and his guardian, Everett Shinn, a devout Quaker. . . . News that two runaway indentured servants are in the area prompts Mr. Shinn . . . to organize a search. Peter assumes that the runaways are swarthy ruffians and . . . he joins the hunt. His discovery that they are mistreated children sets up a different scenario in which he and then his guardian are emotionally and physically involved." Christ Sci Monit

This is a "fast-paced, suspenseful tale. . . . The tightly constructed, disaster-laden scenes . . . zestfully carry along the plot to its satisfying conclusion." Booklist

Followed by Encounter at Easton

Perloo the bold. Scholastic 1998 225p $16.95; pa $4.99 (5 and up)   **Fic**
1. Fantasy fiction
ISBN 0-590-11002-0; 0-590-11003-9 (pa)
                                       LC 97-10681
Perloo, a peaceful scholar who has been chosen to succeed Jolaine as leader of the furry underground people called the Montmers, finds himself in danger when Jolaine dies and her evil son seizes control of the burrow

"Avi has brought these creatures and their world to life in a fast-paced, compelling read."

Poppy; illustrated by Brian Floca. Orchard Bks. 1995 147p il $15.95; lib bdg $16.99 (3-5)   **Fic**
1. Animals—Fiction 2. Allegories
ISBN 0-531-09483-9; 0-531-08783-2 (lib bdg)
                                       LC 95-6040
Also available in paperback from Avon Bks.
"A Richard Jackson book"

"As ruler of Dimwood Forest, Ocax the hoot owl has promised to protect the mice occupying an abandoned farmhouse as long as they ask permission before 'moving about.' Poppy, a timid dormouse, is a loyal, obedient subject—until she sees Ocax devour her fiancé and hears the owl deny her father's request to seek new living quarters. To prove that the intimidating ruler is really a phony, Poppy embarks on a dangerous and eye-opening quest, which ends with her one-on-one battle with Ocax. . . . An engaging blend of romance, suspense and parody." Publ Wkly

Other available titles about Dimwood Forest are:
Ereth's birthday (2000)
Poppy and Rye (1998)
Ragweed (1999)

S.O.R. losers. Bradbury Press 1984 90p $15 (5 and up)   **Fic**
1. Soccer—Fiction 2. School stories
ISBN 0-02-793410-1   LC 84-11022
Also available in paperback from Avon Bks.

Each member of the South Orange River eighth-grade soccer team has qualities of excellence, but not on the

Avi, 1937——*Continued*
soccer field

"Short, pithy chapters highlighting key events maintain the pace necessary for successful comedy. . . . The style is vivid, believably articulate, for the narrator and his teammates may be deficient athletically but not intellectually. Certainly, the team manifesto 'People have a right to be losers' is as refreshing as it is iconoclastic." Horn Book

Something upstairs; a tale of ghosts. Orchard Bks. 1988 120p $15.95; lib bdg $16.99 (5 and up)

Fic

1. Ghost stories
ISBN 0-531-05782-8; 0-531-08382-9 (lib bdg)
LC 88-60094

Also available in paperback from Avon Bks.
"A Richard Jackson book"

"When 12-year-old Kenny Huldorf moves with his family to Providence, Rhode Island, he finds himself embroiled in the century-old murder of a teenage slave named Caleb. Not only is Kenny haunted by the injustice of the murder, but also by the ghost of Caleb himself, who summons Kenny back in time to the early 19th Century, where the boy must solve Caleb's murder to return to his own century." SLJ

"This ghostly tale is exciting and well-written." Child Book Rev Serv

The true confessions of Charlotte Doyle; decorations by Ruth E. Murray. Orchard Bks. 1990 215p $18.95; lib bdg $17.99 (6 and up)   Fic
1. Sea stories
ISBN 0-531-05893-X; 0-531-08493-0 (lib bdg)
LC 90-30624

Also available in paperback from Avon Bks.
A Newbery Medal honor book, 1991
"A Richard Jackson book"

This is a "seafaring adventure, set in 1832. Charlotte Doyle, 13, returning from school in England to join her family in Rhode Island, is deposited on a seedy ship with a ruthless, mad captain and a mutinous crew. Refusing to heed warnings about Captain Jaggery's brutality, Charlotte seeks his guidance and approval only to become his victim, a pariah to the entire crew, and a convicted felon for the murder of the first mate." SLJ

The author has "fashioned an intriguing, suspenseful, carefully crafted tale, with nonstop action on the high seas." Booklist

Babbitt, Natalie
The eyes of the Amaryllis. Farrar, Straus & Giroux 1977 127p hardcover o.p. paperback available $4.95 (5 and up)   Fic
1. Sea stories 2. Grandmothers—Fiction
ISBN 0-374-42238-9 (pa)   LC 77-11862

"The sea holds countless mysteries and gives up very few secrets; when she does, it is truly a remarkable event, an event that eleven-year-old Geneva Reade experiences when she visits her grandmother who lives in a house by the water's edge. Sent for to tend her Gran through a broken leg, Jenny is put to work, at once, combing the beach for a sign from her grandfather, a captain lost at sea with his ship and crew thirty years

ago." Child Book Rev Serv

"The book succeeds as a well-wrought narrative in which a complex philosophical theme is developed through the balanced, subtle use of symbol and imagery. It is a rare story." Horn Book

Kneeknock Rise; story and pictures by Natalie Babbitt. Farrar, Straus & Giroux 1970 117p il hardcover o.p. paperback available $4.95 (4-6)

Fic

1. Allegories 2. Superstition—Fiction
ISBN 0-374-44260-6 (pa)

Also available Audiobook version
A Newbery Medal honor book, 1971

"Did you ever meet a Megrimum? There is one in KneeKnock Rise, and on stormy nights the villagers of Instep tremble in delicious delight as its howls echo over the Mammoth Mountains. Egan learns a lesson when he climbs to meet and conquer the Megrimum." Best Sellers

"An enchanting tale imbued with a folk flavor, enlivened with piquant imagery and satiric wit." Booklist

The search for delicious. Farrar, Straus & Giroux 1969 167p il $16; pa $4.95 (5 and up)

Fic

ISBN 0-374-36534-2; 0-374-46536-3 (pa)
Also available Audiobook version
"An Ariel book"

The Prime Minister is compiling a dictionary and when no one at court can agree on the meaning of delicious, the King sends his twelve-year-old messenger to poll the country

"The theme, foolish arguments can lead to great conflict, may not be clear to all children who will enjoy this fantasy." Best Sellers

Tuck everlasting. Farrar, Straus & Giroux 1975 139p $16; pa $4.95 (5 and up)   Fic
1. Fantasy fiction
ISBN 0-374-37848-7; 0-374-48009-5 (pa)
Also available Audiobook version

The Tuck family is confronted with an agonizing situation when they discover that a ten-year-old girl and a malicious stranger now share their secret about a spring whose water prevents one from ever growing any older

"The story is macabre and moral, exciting and excellently written." N Y Times Book Rev

Bagnold, Enid
National Velvet (5 and up)   Fic
1. Horses—Fiction 2. Great Britain—Fiction

Available from Buccaneer Bks. and in paperback from Avon Bks.
First published 1935

An English girl, Velvet Brown, wins a magnificent piebald horse in a lottery and determines to enter and win the Grand National Steeplechase even though girls are not allowed to ride in that race

Baker, Olaf
Where the buffaloes begin; illustrated by Stephen Gammell. Puffin Bks. 1985 c1981 unp il pa $6.99 (2-4)   Fic
1. Native Americans—Fiction 2. Bison—Fiction
ISBN 0-14-050560-1   LC 85-5682

Baker, Olaf—*Continued*

A Caldecott Medal honor book, 1982

First published in book form 1981 by Warne

"Originally published in 1915 in 'St. Nicholas Magazine,' the story tells in four short chapters of the adventure of Little Wolf, a ten-year-old Indian boy. He was fascinated by a tribal legend about a lake to the south, a sacred spot where the buffaloes were said to originate. . . . Narrated in cadenced prose rich in images, the story evokes the Plains Indians' feelings of reverence for the buffalo. Magnificent full- and double-page pencil drawings . . . capture the immensity of the prairie and the mighty strength of the awesome beasts." Horn Book

Banks, Lynne Reid, 1929-

The Indian in the cupboard. Doubleday 1980 181p il $16.95 (5 and up)   **Fic**

1. Native Americans—Fiction 2. Fantasy fiction

ISBN 0-385-17051-3   LC 79-6533

Also available in paperback from Avon Bks. and Audiobook version

Illustrated by Brock Cole

A nine-year-old boy receives a plastic Indian, a cupboard, and a little key for his birthday and finds himself involved in adventure when the Indian comes to life in the cupboard and befriends him

Other available titles in this series are:

The mystery of the cupboard (1993)

The return of the Indian (1986)

The secret of the Indian (1989)

Barrie, J. M. (James Matthew), 1860-1937

Peter Pan (3-5)   **Fic**

1. Fairy tales

Also available Audiobook version

Some editions are:

Everyman's Lib. Children's Classics $12.95 Illustrated by F. D. Bedford (ISBN 0-679-41792-3)

Pavilion Bks. $24.95 Illustrated by Michael Foreman (ISBN 1-851-45179-X) Has title: Peter Pan and Wendy

Simon & Schuster $25 Illustrated by Raquel Jaramillo (ISBN 0-743-21449-8)

Viking $22.99 Illustrated by Scott Gustafson (ISBN 0-670-84180-3)

First published 1911 by Scribner with title: Peter and Wendy

This is the story of "how Wendy, John, and Michael flew with Peter Pan, the boy who never grows up, to adventures in the Never-Never Land with pirates, redskins, and the fairy Tinker Bell. [It is] in Barrie's inimitable style, pleasing the child with delightful absurdities and the adult with good-humored satire." Right Book for the Right Child

Barron, T. A.

The lost years of Merlin. Philomel Bks. 1996 326p $19.99 (6 and up)   **Fic**

1. Merlin (Legendary character)—Fiction 2. Fantasy fiction

ISBN 0-399-23018-1   LC 96-33920

Also available in paperback from Berkley Pub. Group and Audiobook version

"A boy, hurled on the rocks by the sea, regains consciousness unable to remember anything—not his parents, not his own name. He is sure that the secretive Branwen is not his mother, despite her claims, and that Emrys is not his real name. The two soon find themselves feared because of Branwen's healing abilities and Emrys' growing powers. . . . Barron has created not only a magical land populated by remarkable beings but also a completely magical tale, filled with ancient Celtic and Druidic lore, that will enchant readers." Booklist

Other available titles in this series are:

The fires of Merlin (1998)

The mirror of Merlin (1999)

The seven songs of Merlin (1997)

The wings of Merlin (2000)

Bartoletti, Susan Campbell, 1958-

A coal miner's bride; the diary of Anetka Kaminska. Scholastic 2000 219p il (Dear America) $10.95 (4 and up)   **Fic**

1. Polish Americans—Fiction 2. Coal mines and mining—Fiction 3. Immigrants—Fiction

ISBN 0-439-05386-2   LC 99-29864

A diary account of thirteen-year-old Anetka's life in Poland in 1896, immigration to America, marriage to a coal miner, widowhood, and happiness in finally finding her true love

"Bartoletti paints an accessible and evocative picture of life in a harsh era." SLJ

Bauer, Marion Dane, 1938-

On my honor. Clarion Bks. 1986 90p $15 (4 and up)   **Fic**

1. Accidents—Fiction

ISBN 0-89919-439-7   LC 86-2679

Also available in paperback from Dell and Audiobook version

A Newbery Medal honor book, 1987

When his best friend drowns while they are both swimming in a treacherous river that they had promised never to go near, Joel is devastated and terrified at having to tell both sets of parents the terrible consequences of their disobedience

"Bauer's association of Joel's guilt with the smell of the polluted river on his skin is particularly noteworthy. Its miasma almost rises off the pages. Descriptions are vivid, characterization and dialogue natural, and the style taut but unforced. A powerful, moving book." SLJ

Baum, L. Frank (Lyman Frank), 1856-1919

The Wizard of Oz (3-6)   **Fic**

1. Fantasy fiction

Also available Audiobook version. Simon & Schuster Commemorative Pop-Up edition for younger readers illustrated by Robert Sabuda also available

Some editions are:

Books of Wonder $21.95 Illustrated by William Wallace Denslow (ISBN 0-688-06944-4)

Holt & Co. $29.95 Illustrated by Michael Hague (ISBN 0-805-06430-3)

North-South Bks. $19.95 Illustrated by Lisbeth Zwerger (ISBN 1-55858-638-5)

Pavilion Bks. $24.95 Illustrated by Michael Foreman (ISBN 1-862-05343-X)

Baum, L. Frank (Lyman Frank), 1856-1919—
Continued

First published 1900 with title: The wonderful Wizard of Oz

Here are the adventures of Dorothy who, in her dreams, escapes from her bed in Kansas to visit the Emerald City and to meet the wonderful Wizard of Oz, the Scarecrow, the Tin Woodman, and the Cowardly Lion

Other available titles about the land of Oz are:
Dorothy and the Wizard in Oz (1908)
The land of Oz (1904)
Little Wizard stories of Oz (1985)
The magic of Oz (1919)
The marvelous land of Oz (1904)
Ozma of Oz (1907)
The patchwork girl of Oz (1913)
The tin woodsman of Oz (1918)

Bawden, Nina, 1925-

Granny the Pag. Clarion Bks. 1996 184p $15 (4 and up) **Fic**
1. Grandmothers—Fiction
ISBN 0-395-77604-X   LC 95-38191
Also available in paperback from Puffin Bks.
First published 1995 in the United Kingdom
Originally abandoned by her actor parents who later attempt to gain custody, Cat wages a spirited campaign to decide her own fate and remain with her grandmother
"Bawden has created some enormously appealing characters in this funny and very touching novel." SLJ

Humbug. Clarion Bks. 1992 133p $13.95 (4 and up) **Fic**
1. Truthfulness and falsehood—Fiction
ISBN 0-395-62149-6   LC 91-33900
Also available in paperback from Puffin Bks.
When eight-year-old Cora is sent to stay next door with the seemingly pleasant woman called Aunt Sunday, she is tormented by Aunt Sunday's mean-spirited, deceitful daughter, but finds an ally in Aunt Sunday's elderly mother
"Characters are beautifully and intricately drawn. . . . Bawden deals forthrightly with harsh truths; she acknowledges that children can hate, and she shatters a host of childhood notions about grown-ups, honesty, and fairness. Along with that, she delivers a riveting plot and a totally credible Cora." Booklist

Beatty, Patricia, 1922-1991

Charley Skedaddle. Morrow 1987 186p o.p.; Troll Assocs. paperback available $4.95 (5 and up) **Fic**
1. United States—History—1861-1865, Civil War—Fiction 2. Farm life—Fiction 3. Virginia—Fiction
ISBN 0-816-71317-0 (pa)   LC 87-12270
"12-year-old Charley Quinn, a cocky boy from the Bowery, runs away and finagles a job as a drummer in the Union army. In his first battle he meets the horrors of war face to face and, without thought to an injured friend, 'skedaddles' into the Virginia mountains." Booklist
"The author notes that she has based Charley's fictional adventures on actual accounts, and her reading and research lend authenticity to her story. . . . Charley's Civil

War adventures . . . move at a lively pace and offer an entertaining account of a young city slicker's growing respect for his new surroundings." Horn Book

Jayhawker. Morrow Junior Bks. 1991 214p hardcover o.p. paperback available $5.95 (5 and up) **Fic**
1. United States—History—1861-1865, Civil War—Fiction 2. Underground railroad—Fiction 3. Spies—Fiction
ISBN 0-688-14422-5 (pa)   LC 91-17890
In the early years of the Civil War, teenage Kansan farm boy Lije Tulley becomes a Jayhawker, an abolitionist raider freeing slaves from the neighboring state of Missouri, and then goes undercover there as a spy
"Peppered with fascinating historical figures, vivid with drama and action, Beatty's story has an accuracy and a realism that are both addictive and illuminating." Booklist

Turn homeward, Hannalee. Morrow 1984 193p $16; pa $5.95 (5 and up) **Fic**
1. United States—History—1861-1865, Civil War—Fiction 2. Georgia—Fiction 3. Child labor—Fiction
ISBN 0-688-03871-9; 0-688-16676-8 (pa)
LC 84-8960
This "historical fiction shows how the Civil War affected one segment of the population—the southern mill workers—and is based on fact. . . . The protagonists are Hannalee and Jem, twelve and ten, who are shipped from their Georgia town (and their recently widowed, pregnant mother) to Indiana, where they are offered as workers to anyone who wants them." Bull Cent Child Books
"The story is vintage Beatty, with a forthright, plain-spoken heroine who has gumption to spare. As a period piece, it is a vivid, seemingly authentic picture of what times might have been like for a hardworking, white, Southern family." Booklist

Bell, Anthea

The nutcracker; [by] E.T.A. Hoffmann; retold by Anthea Bell; illustrated by Lisbeth Zwerger. Picture Bk. Studio 1987 unp il $16; pa $4.95 (2-4) **Fic**
1. Fairy tales 2. Christmas—Fiction
ISBN 0-88708-051-0; 0-88708-156-8 (pa)
LC 87-15249
"A Michael Neugebauer book"
First published 1983 by Neugebauer Press with a longer text with title: The nutcracker and the mouse-king
After hearing how her toy nutcracker got his ugly face, a little girl helps break the spell and changes him into a handsome prince
This book "features full pages of text alternating with Lisbeth Zwerger's beautiful full-page, full-color illustrations, including one double-page spread. . . . Anthea Bell's translation for this book is a slightly condensed version of the original story, which, of course, differs substantially from the ballet version." Horn Book

Bellairs, John

The curse of the blue figurine. Dial Bks. for Young Readers 1983 200p hardcover o.p. paperback available $4.99 (5 and up) **Fic**
1. Mystery fiction
ISBN 0-14-038005-1 (pa)   LC 82-73217

Bellairs, John—*Continued*

Also available Brad Strickland's titles based on John Bellairs characters

"The terror for young Johnny Dixon begins when cranky eccentric Professor Childermass tells him that St. Michael's Church is haunted by Father Baart, an evil sorcerer who mysteriously disappeared years ago. When Johnny finds a blue Egyptian figurine hidden in the church basement, he takes it home in spite of the warning note from Father Baart threatening harm to anyone who removes it from the church." SLJ

The author "intertwines real concerns with sorcery in a seamless fashion, bringing dimension to his characters and events with expert timing and sharply honed atmosphere." Booklist

Other available titles about Johnny Dixon and Professor Childermass are:

The chessmen of doom (1989)
The eyes of the killer robot (1986)
The mummy, the will and the crypt (1983)
The revenge of the wizard's ghost (1985)
The secret of the underground room (1990)
The spell of the sorcerer's skull (1984)
The trolley to yesterday (1989)

The house with a clock in its walls; pictures by Edward Gorey. Dial Bks. for Young Readers 1973 179p il o.p.; Puffin Bks. paperback available $4.99 (5 and up)   **Fic**

1. Witchcraft—Fiction

ISBN 0-14-036336-X (pa)

Also available Brad Strickland's titles based on John Bellair's characters

In 1948, Lewis, a ten-year-old orphan, goes to New Zebedee, Michigan with his warlock Uncle Jonathan, who lives in a big mysterious house and practices white magic. Together with their neighbor, Mrs. Zimmerman, a witch, they search to find a clock that is programmed to end the world and has been hidden in the walls of the house by the evil Isaac Izard

"Bellairs's story and Edward Gorey's pictures are satisfyingly frightening." Publ Wkly

Other available titles about Lewis are:

The doom of the haunted opera (1995)
The figure in the shadows (1975)
The ghost in the mirror (1993)
The letter, the witch, and the ring (1976)
The vengeance of the witch-finder (1993)

Berends, Polly Berrien

The case of the elevator duck; illustrated by Diane Allison. Random House 1989 60p il hardcover o.p. paperback available $3.99 (3-5)   **Fic**

1. Ducks—Fiction 2. Apartment houses—Fiction 3. Mystery fiction

ISBN 0-394-82646-9 (pa)   LC 88-23971

"A Stepping Stone book"

A newly illustrated edition of the title first published 1973

Gilbert finds a lost duck in the elevator of his apartment building, and must do some secret detective work to find its owner, since no pets are allowed in the housing project

A "light mystery for begining readers. The action is

humorously illustrated by Washburn's line sketches; and Berends' first-person, short-sentence story is personable, plausible, and useful for librarians needing simple, satisfying material for their easy mystery shelves." Booklist

Betancourt, Jeanne, 1941-

My name is brain Brian. Scholastic 1993 128p hardcover o.p. paperback available $4.50 (4-6)   **Fic**

1. Dyslexia—Fiction 2. School stories 3. Friendship—Fiction

ISBN 0-590-44922-2 (pa)   LC 92-16513

On title page the word "brain" appears with an "X" through it

Although he is helped by his new sixth grade teacher after being diagnosed as dyslexic, Brian still has some problems with school and with people he thought were his friends

"Betancourt's depiction of Brian's emotional and psychological growth is believable and involving." Booklist

Bianco, Margery Williams, 1880-1944

The velveteen rabbit; or, How toys become real; by Margery Williams (2-4)   **Fic**

1. Toys—Fiction 2. Rabbits—Fiction 3. Fairy tales

Some editions are:

Doubleday $13.95 illustrated by William Nicholson (ISBN 0-385-07725-4)

Holt & Co. $16.95 Illustrated by Michael Hague (ISBN 0-8050-0209-X)

Hyperion Bks. for Children $12.95 Illustrated by Loretta Krupinski (ISBN 0-7868-0319-3)

First published 1922 by Doran

"The story of a toy rabbit that becomes real through the love of a child and the intervention of a fairy." Bull Cent Child Books

Billingsley, Franny, 1954-

The Folk Keeper. Atheneum Bks. for Young Readers 1999 162p $16 (5 and up)   **Fic**

1. Fantasy fiction

ISBN 0-689-82876-4   LC 98-48778

Also available Thorndike Press large print edition and Audiobook version

"A Jean Karl book"

Orphan Corinna disguises herself as a boy to pose as a Folk Keeper, one who keeps the Evil Folk at bay, and discovers her heritage as a seal maiden when she is taken to live with a wealthy family in their manor by the sea

"The intricate plot, vibrant characters, dangerous intrigue, and fantastical elements combine into a truly remarkable novel steeped in atmosphere." Horn Book

Well wished. Atheneum Bks. for Young Readers 1997 170p $16; pa $4.99 (4-6)   **Fic**

1. Wishes—Fiction 2. Magic—Fiction 3. Fantasy fiction

ISBN 0-689-81210-8; 0-689-83255-9 (pa)

     LC 96-24511

"A Jean Karl book"

Billingsley, Franny, 1954——*Continued*

"In Nuria's town, a magical wishing well grants individuals one wish per lifetime, but if possible, twists the requests to produce a ruinous outcome. When Nuria wishes that her crippled friend 'had a body just like mine,' the girls switch bodies. Fantasy elements play a pivotal role in the plot, but keen character development leaves the strongest impression in this well-constructed, thought-provoking first novel." Horn Book Guide

Björk, Christina

Linnea in Monet's garden; text, Christina Björk; drawings, Lena Anderson. R & S Bks. 1987 52p il $13 (3-5) **Fic**
1. Monet, Claude, 1840-1926—Fiction 2. Paris (France)—Fiction
ISBN 91-29-58314-4 LC 87-45163
Original Swedish edition, 1985
"Linnea and her elderly friend Mr. Bloom travel to Paris, visit Monet's home in Giverny, picnic in the artist's garden, and admire the waterlilies and the Japanese bridge which he often painted. In Paris, the two companions stop at a museum to see Impressionist paintings, view the sunlight over the Seine, and chatter about the life and times of the artist. The book ends with a page of information about things to do and see in Paris." SLJ
"In addition to the long but smooth text peppered with dialogue are photographs of Monet's paintings, house, and family as well as colorful drawings of the little girl's excursion. . . . A splendid way to introduce children to impressionism and to the man behind the masterpieces." Booklist

Vendela in Venice; pictures by Inga-Karin Eriksson; translated by Patricia Crampton. R & S Bks. 1999 93p il $18 (4 and up) **Fic**
1. Venice (Italy)—Fiction
ISBN 91-296-4559-X LC 98-49243
Originally published in Sweden
On a visit to Venice with her father, Vendela experiences the richness and beauty of the city and its palaces, gondolas, and statues
"The illustrations comprise Inga-Karin Eriksson's beautifully composed paintings, photographs, maps, and sketches. Asides and appendixes add to the book's value as source and, since they are all written in the same winsome style, will increase the reader's delight." Booklist

Blackwood, Gary L.

The Shakespeare stealer; [by] Gary Blackwood. Dutton Children's Bks. 1998 216p $15.99 (5 and up) **Fic**
1. Shakespeare, William, 1564-1616—Fiction 2. Theater—Fiction 3. Orphans—Fiction 4. Great Britain—History—1485-1603, Tudors—Fiction
ISBN 0-525-45863-8 LC 97-42987
A young orphan boy is ordered by his master to infiltrate Shakespeare's acting troupe in order to steal the script of "Hamlet," but he discovers instead the meaning of friendship and loyalty
"Wry humor, cliffhanger chapter endings, and a plucky protagonist make this a fitting introduction to Shakespeare's world." Horn Book

Blos, Joan W., 1928-

A gathering of days: a New England girl's journal, 1830-32; a novel. Scribner 1979 144p $15; pa $4.99 (6 and up) **Fic**
1. New Hampshire—Fiction
ISBN 0-684-16340-3; 0-689-71419-X (pa)
LC 79-16898
Awarded the Newbery Medal, 1980
The journal of a 14-year-old girl, kept the last year she lived on the family farm, records daily events in her small New Hampshire town, her father's remarriage, and the death of her best friend
"The 'simple' life on the farm is not facilely idealized, the larger issues of the day are felt . . . but it is the small moments between parent and child, friend and friend that are at the fore, and the core, of this low-key, intense, and reflective book." SLJ

Blume, Judy

Are you there God? it's me, Margaret. Twentieth anniversary ed. Bradbury Press 1990 c1970 149p $16 (5 and up) **Fic**
1. Adolescence—Fiction 2. Religions—Fiction
ISBN 0-02-710991-7 LC 90-44484
Also available in paperback from Dell and Audiobook version
First published 1970
"A perceptive story about the emotional, physical, and spiritual ups and downs experienced by 12-year-old Margaret, child of a Jewish-Protestant union." Natl Counc of Teach of Engl. Adventuring with Books. 2d edition
"The writing style is lively, the concerns natural, and the problems are treated with both humor and sympathy, but the story is intense in its emphasis on the four girls' absorption in, and discussions of, menstruation and brassieres." Bull Cent Child Books

Freckle juice; illustrated by Sonia O. Lisker. Four Winds Press 1971 40p il lib bdg $16 (2-4) **Fic**
ISBN 0-02-711690-5
Also available in paperback from Dell
"A gullible second-grader pays 50¢ for a recipe to grow freckles." Best Books for Child
"Spontaneous humor, sure to appeal to the youngest reader." Horn Book

It's not the end of the world. Bradbury Press 1972 169p o.p.; Dell paperback available $4.99 (4-6) **Fic**
1. Divorce—Fiction 2. Parent-child relationship—Fiction
ISBN 0-440-44158-7 (pa)
Unwilling to adjust to her parents' impending divorce, twelve-year-old Karen Newman attempts a last ditch effort at arranging a reconciliation. This story tells how her scheme goes awry when an unplanned confrontation between her parents sharply illuminates for Karen the reality of the situation
"A believable first-person story with good characterization, particularly of twelve-year-old Karen, and realistic treatment of the situation." Booklist

Blume, Judy—*Continued*

Otherwise known as Sheila the Great. Dutton 1972 188p lib bdg $15.99; pa $4.99 (4-6) **Fic**

1. Fear—Fiction

ISBN 0-525-36455-2 (lib bdg); 0-440-46701-2 (pa)

Also available Audiobook version

Ten-year-old Sheila is secretly afraid of dogs, spiders, bees, ghosts and the dark. When she and her family leave New York for their summer home, she has to face up to her problems

"An unusual and merry treatment of the fears of a young girl. . . . This is a truly appealing book in which the author makes her points without a single preachy word." Publ Wkly

Tales of a fourth grade nothing; illustrated by Roy Doty. Dutton 1972 120p il hardcover o.p. paperback available $4.99 (3-6) **Fic**

1. Brothers—Fiction 2. Family life—Fiction

ISBN 0-440-48474-X (pa)

Also available Audiobook version

This story describes the trials and tribulations of nine-year-old Peter Hatcher who is saddled with a pesky two-year-old brother named Fudge who is constantly creating trouble, messing things up, and monopolizing their parents' attention. Things come to a climax when Fudge gets at Peter's pet turtle

"The episode structure makes the book a good choice for reading aloud." Saturday Rev

Other available titles about Peter and Fudge are:

Fudge-a-mania (1990)

Superfudge (1980)

Bond, Michael, 1926-

A bear called Paddington; with drawings by Peggy Fortnum. Houghton Mifflin 1998 c1958 128p il $15 (2-5) **Fic**

1. Bears—Fiction 2. Great Britain—Fiction

ISBN 0-395-92951-2

Also available in paperback from Dell; Spanish language edition also available; picture books about Paddington for younger readers are also available

First published 1958 in the United Kingdom; first United States edition 1960

"Mr. and Mrs. Brown first met Paddington on a railway platform in London. Noticing the sign on his neck reading 'Please look after this bear. Thank you,' they decided to do just that. From there on home was never the same though the Brown children were delighted." Publ Wkly

Other available titles about Paddington Bear are:

More about Paddington

Paddington abroad

Paddington at large

Paddington at work

Paddington goes to town

Paddington helps out

Paddington marches on

Paddington on screen

Paddington on stage

Paddington on top

Paddington takes the air

Paddington takes the test

Paddington takes to TV

Paddington's storybook

Bond, Nancy, 1945-

A string in the harp. Atheneum Pubs. 1976 370p il $19; pa $5.99 (6 and up) **Fic**

1. Taliesin—Fiction 2. Fantasy fiction 3. Wales—Fiction

ISBN 0-689-50036-X; 0-689-80445-8 (pa)

LC 75-28181

"A Margaret K. McElderry book"

"Present-day realism and the fantasy world of sixth-century Taliesin meet in an absorbing novel set in Wales. The story centers around the Morgans—Jen, Peter, Becky, and their father—their adjustment to another country, their mother's death, and especially, Peter's bitter despair, which threatens them all." LC. Child Books, 1976

Boston, L. M. (Lucy Maria), 1892-1990

The children of Green Knowe; with illustrations by Peter Boston. Harcourt Brace & Co. 1955 157p il hardcover o.p. paperback available $6 (4-6) **Fic**

1. Fantasy fiction 2. Great Britain—Fiction

ISBN 0-15-217151-7 (pa)

First published 1954 in the United Kingdom

"Tolly comes to live with his great-grandmother at Green Knowe, her ancestral mansion in the English countryside. Here the present blends with the past, and the children of another era become his playmates and help him to break the curse put upon the house by a gypsy." Hodges. Books for Elem Sch Libr

"A special book for the imaginative child, in which mood predominates and fantasy and realism are skillfully blended; not the least of the book's charm is the rapport that exists between the lonely little boy and the understanding old woman who lives with her memories." Booklist

Other available titles about Green Knowe are:

The river at Green Knowe (1959)

A stranger at Green Knowe (1961)

Bowdish, Lynea

Brooklyn, Bugsy, and me; pictures by Nancy Carpenter. Farrar, Straus & Giroux 2000 83p il $15 (3-5) **Fic**

1. Grandfathers—Fiction 2. Moving—Fiction 3. Brooklyn (New York, N.Y.)—Fiction

ISBN 0-374-30993-0 LC 99-36267

In 1953 nine-year-old Sam moves with his mother from West Virginia to Brooklyn and finds that his grandfather, a well-liked neighborhood character nicknamed Bugsy, does not seem to want him in his life

"Short, easy reading that is both well developed and satisfying." Horn Book Guide

Boyd, Candy Dawson, 1946-

Charlie Pippin. Macmillan 1987 182p o.p.; Viking paperback available $4.99 (4-6) **Fic**

1. Father-daughter relationship—Fiction 2. Vietnam War, 1961-1975—Fiction 3. African Americans—Fiction

ISBN 0-14-032587-5 (pa) LC 86-23780

Boyd, Candy Dawson, 1946—— *Continued*
"Charlie (Chartreuse) Pippin is eleven, jealous of her older sister Sienna, baffled by her father's stern intransigence. She's black and bright; she's often in trouble at school (and that makes even more trouble at home) because she sets up businesses in school. Charlie wonders why her father is so angry, why he is irked by her school project, which entails a study of the Vietnam War in which he served." Bull Cent Child Books
"Boyd's story probes sensitive issues with remarkable balance. . . . The story's impact won't quickly fade." Booklist

Bradley, Kimberly Brubaker
Ruthie's gift; illustrated by Dave Kramer. Delacorte Press 1998 150p il $14.95; pa $4.50 (3-5)   **Fic**
1. Farm life—Fiction 2. Family life—Fiction 3. Siblings—Fiction 4. Indiana—Fiction
ISBN 0-385-32525-8; 0-440-41405-9 (pa)
                                                              LC 97-19396
Just before the beginning of World War I, eight-year-old Ruthie, who lives with her parents and six brothers on a farm in Indiana, wishes for a sister and tries to behave like the lady her mother wants her to be
"Brisk pacing, affectionate humor and an unforgettable heroine." Publ Wkly

Branford, Henrietta, 1946-
Fire, bed, & bone. Candlewick Press 1998 122p $15.99 (5 and up)   **Fic**
1. Dogs—Fiction 2. Middle Ages—Fiction 3. Great Britain—History—1154-1399, Plantagenets—Fiction
ISBN 0-7636-0338-4   LC 97-17491
Also available Audiobook version
In 1381 in England, a hunting dog recounts what happens to his beloved master Rufus and his family when they are arrested on suspicion of being part of the peasants' rebellion led by Wat Tyler and the preacher John Ball
"The dog's observant eye, sympathetic personality, and courageous acts hook the reader into what is both irresistible adventure and educational historical fiction." Booklist

Brink, Carol Ryrie, 1895-1981
Caddie Woodlawn; illustrated by Trina Schart Hyman. Macmillan 1973 275p il $17; pa $4.99 (4-6)   **Fic**
1. Frontier and pioneer life—Fiction 2. Wisconsin—Fiction
ISBN 0-02-713670-1; 0-689-71370-3 (pa)
Awarded the Newbery Medal, 1936
First published 1935
Caddie Woodlawn was eleven in 1864. Because she was frail, she had been allowed to grow up a tomboy. Her capacity for adventure was practically limitless, and there was plenty of adventure on the Wisconsin frontier in those days. The story covers one year of life on the pioneer farm, closing with the news that Mr. Woodlawn had inherited an estate in England, and the unanimous decision of the family to stay in Wisconsin. Based upon the reminiscences of the author's grandmother
The typeface "is eminently clear and readable, and the illustrations in black and white . . . are attractive and expressive." Wis Libr Bull

Brisson, Pat
Sky memories; paintings by Wendell Minor. Delacorte Press 1999 71p il $14.95 (3-5)   **Fic**
1. Mother-daughter relationship—Fiction 2. Cancer—Fiction 3. Death—Fiction
ISBN 0-385-32606-8   LC 98-38962
When ten-year-old Emily learns that her mother has cancer, the two of them begin a ritual that will help Emily remember her mother after she is dead
"A quiet, moving story." Booklist

Brittain, Bill
Shape-changer. HarperCollins Pubs. 1994 108p hardcover o.p. paperback available $4.95 (4 and up)   **Fic**
1. Science fiction 2. Extraterrestrial beings—Fiction
ISBN 0-06-440514-1 (pa)   LC 93-27268
Two seventh-grade friends help a shape-changing policeman from the planet Rodinam as he tries to recapture an alien master criminal who can also change form
"Funny scenes abound in the fast-paced, enthralling adventure." Horn Book Guide

Brooks, Bruce, 1950-
Everywhere. Harper & Row 1990 70p lib bdg $13.89 (4 and up)   **Fic**
1. Grandfathers—Fiction 2. Death—Fiction
ISBN 0-06-020729-9   LC 90-4073
Afraid that his beloved grandfather will die after suffering a heart attack, a nine-year-old boy agrees to join ten-year-old Dooley in performing a mysterious ritual called soul switching
"Echoes of the great Southern writers with their themes of loneliness and faith can be heard in this masterly novella. . . . Brooks's precise use of language is a tour de force." Horn Book

Brooks, Walter R., 1886-1958
Freddy the detective; illustrated by Kurt Wiese. Overlook Press 1997 256p il $23.95 (3-5)   **Fic**
1. Pigs—Fiction 2. Mystery fiction
ISBN 0-87951-809-X   LC 97-10214
A reissue of the title first published 1932 by Knopf
Freddy the pig does some detective work in order to solve the mystery of a missing toy train
"This book will be great fun for all who have not outgrown the gift of fitting becoming personalities to our animal friends." N Y Her Trib Books
Other available titles about Freddy are:
Freddy and Mr. Camphor (1944)
Freddy and the baseball team from Mars (1955)
Freddy and the bean home news (1943)
Freddy and the dragon (1958)
Freddy and the ignormus (1941)
Freddy and the space ship (1953)
Freddy goes to Florida (1949) First published 1927 with title: To and again
Freddy goes to the North Pole (1951) First published 1930 with title: More to and again
Freddy the pilot (1952)
Freddy the politician (1948) First published 1939 with title: Wiggins for President

Bruchac, Joseph, 1942-

The arrow over the door; pictures by James Watling. Dial Bks. for Young Readers 1998 89p il $15.99 (4-6)   **Fic**

1. Native Americans—Fiction 2. Society of Friends—Fiction 3. United States—History—1775-1783, Revolution—Fiction

ISBN 0-8037-2078-5   LC 96-36701

"In this fictionalized account of a Quaker assembly's encounter with a band of Indian scouts in service to King George's Loyalists, Bruchac alternates the viewpoints of fourteen-year-old Samuel Russell and his Abenaki counterpart, Stands Straight." Bull Cent Child Books

"Bruchac's elegant and powerful writing fills in much of the fascinating detail of this serendipitous wartime friendship. . . . Watling's rugged, textured pen-and-ink drawings provide an atmospheric backdrop." Publ Wkly

Children of the longhouse. Dial Bks. for Young Readers 1996 150p $14.99; pa $4.99 (4 and up)
                                          Fic

1. Mohawk Indians—Fiction 2. Siblings—Fiction 3. Twins—Fiction

ISBN 0-8037-1793-8; 0-14-038504-5 (pa)
                                          LC 95-11344

Eleven-year-old Ohkwa'ri and his twin sister Otsi:stia must make peace with a hostile gang of older boys in their Mohawk village during the late 1400s

"This is a fascinating story that will leave the middle-grade reader with an appreciation for Mohawk culture." Book Rep

Sacajawea; the story of Bird Woman and the Lewis and Clark Expedition. Silver Whistle Bks. 2000 199p $17 (6 and up)   **Fic**

1. Sacagawea, b. 1786—Fiction 2. Clark, William, 1770-1838—Fiction 3. Lewis and Clark Expedition (1804-1806) (1804-1806)—Fiction 4. Native Americans—Fiction

ISBN 0-15-202234-1   LC 99-47653

Sacajawea, a Shoshoni Indian interpreter, peacemaker, and guide, and William Clark alternate in describing their experiences on the Lewis and Clark Expedition to the Northwest

This is an "intelligent, elegantly written novel." SLJ

Buchholz, Quint, 1957-

The collector of moments; translated from the German by Peter F. Neumeyer. Farrar, Straus & Giroux 1999 unp il $18 (3-6)   **Fic**

1. Artists—Fiction

ISBN 0-374-31520-5   LC 99-10202

When Max, an artist, departs for a long journey, the boy who is his friend and neighbor visits his apartment and discovers an exhibition of pictures created just for him

"There's a beautiful stillness in this picture book for older readers, in the exquisite timbre and tempo of the language and in the radiant purity of the images." Booklist

Bulla, Clyde Robert, 1914-

The Paint Brush Kid; illustrated by Ellen Beier. Random House 1999 64p il lib bdg $11.99; pa $3.99 (2-4)   **Fic**

1. Artists—Fiction 2. Mexican Americans—Fiction

ISBN 0-679-99282-0 (lib bdg); 0-679-89282-6 (pa)
                                          LC 97-51153

"A Stepping Stone book"

Nine-year-old Gregory paints pictures representing the life of the Mexican American old man known as Uncle Pancho and attempts to save him from losing his house

"The conclusion is realistic—satisfying, yet containing some unresolved conflict." Horn Book Guide

The sword in the tree; illustrated by Paul Galdone. Crowell 1956 113p il lib bdg $15.89; pa $4.25 (3-5)   **Fic**

1. Arthur, King—Fiction 2. Knights and knighthood—Fiction

ISBN 0-690-79909-8 (lib bdg); 0-064-42132-5 (pa)

A story of England in King Arthur's days. Shan, the son of Lord Weldon, takes on the duties of a knight and seeks redress against his uncle, who had usurped his father's rights. A picture of the Knights of the Round Table and King Arthur develops

"A good story for beginning readers, this is also excellent for the older child who is a slow reader, because of the stimulating combination of exciting adventure, short sentences, and easy vocabulary." N Y Times Book Rev

Bunting, Eve, 1928-

Blackwater. HarperCollins Pubs. 1999 146p $15.95; lib bdg $15.89; pa $4.95 (5 and up)
                                          Fic

1. Death—Fiction 2. Guilt—Fiction

ISBN 0-06-027838-2; 0-06-027843-9 (lib bdg); 0-06-440890-6 (pa)   LC 99-24895

"Joanna Cotler books"

When a boy and girl are drowned in the Blackwater River, thirteen-year-old Brodie must decide whether to confess that he may have caused the accident

"Bunting's thought-provoking theme, solid characterization and skillful juggling of suspense and pathos make this a top-notch choice." Publ Wkly

Nasty, stinky sneakers. HarperCollins Pubs. 1994 105p $15.95; lib bdg $14.89; pa $4.95 (4-6)
                                          Fic

ISBN 0-06-024236-1; 0-06-024237-X (lib bdg); 0-06-440507-9 (pa)   LC 93-34641

Will ten-year-old Colin find his missing stinky sneakers in time to enter The Stinkiest Sneakers in the World contest?

"A fast-paced, funny book that should elicit some delighted groans." Horn Book Guide

Some frog! illustrated by Scott Medlock. Harcourt Brace & Co. 1998 unp il $15 (2-4)
                                          Fic

1. Father-son relationship—Fiction 2. Divorce—Fiction

ISBN 0-15-277082-8   LC 96-24844

Bunting, Eve, 1928-—*Continued*

Billy is disappointed when his father doesn't show up to help him catch a frog for the frog-jumping competition at school, but the one he and his mother catch wins the championship and Billy begins to accept his father's absence

"The author does an excellent job of presenting a realistic situation and its resolution in straightforward yet eloquent prose. Medlock's bright oil illustrations appear on almost every page, adroitly mirroring the child's emotions and the contest events." SLJ

Spying on Miss Müller. Clarion Bks. 1995 179p $15 (5 and up)   **Fic**
1. World War, 1939-1945—Fiction 2. School stories 3. Ireland—Fiction
ISBN 0-395-69172-9   LC 94-15003
Also available in paperback from Bantam Bks.

At Alveara boarding school in Belfast at the start of World War II, thirteen-year-old Jessie must deal with her suspicions about a teacher whose father was German and with her worries about her own father's drinking problem

"A thoughtful, moving coming-of-age novel. Jessie and her world . . . are portrayed with page-turning immediacy." Horn Book

Burch, Robert, 1925-

Ida Early comes over the mountain. Viking 1980 145p hardcover o.p. paperback available $4.99 (4 and up)   **Fic**
1. Great Depression, 1929-1939—Fiction 2. Country life—Fiction 3. Georgia—Fiction
ISBN 0-14-034534-5 (pa)   LC 79-20532
"Set in the mountains of rural Georgia during the Depression. Ida Early arrives one day to the motherless Sutton family of four children. Mr. Sutton agrees to hire her as a temporary housekeeper." Interracial Books Child Bull

"The book works on two levels—the hilarious account of Ida Early's exotic housekeeping in which real cleverness and skill is as effective and amazing as any fantasy magic, and the gentle, touching story of an ungainly woman's longing for beauty and femininity. . . . [A] fine book." SLJ

Another available title about Ida Early is:
Christmas with Ida Early (1983)

Queenie Peavy; illustrated by Jerry Lazare. Viking 1966 159p il hardcover o.p. paperback available $4.99 (5 and up)   **Fic**
1. Georgia—Fiction
ISBN 0-14-032305-8 (pa)
Also available Audiobook version
"Defiant, independent and intelligent, 13-year-old Queenie idolized her father who was in jail and was neglected by her mother who had to work all the time. Growing up in the [Depression] 1930's in Georgia, Queenie eventually understands her father's real character, herself and her relationships to those about her." Wis Libr Bull

"Queenie is so real that the reader becomes deeply involved in everything that concerns her." Horn Book

Burgess, Melvin

Kite. Farrar, Straus & Giroux 2000 c1997 181p $16 (5 and up)   **Fic**
1. Birds—Fiction 2. Endangered species—Fiction 3. Great Britain—Fiction
ISBN 0-374-34228-8   LC 99-46872
First published 1997 in the United Kingdom
Although the landowner for whom his father works as a gamekeeper hates all birds of prey, Taylor and his friend raise an endangered red kite in secret

"Burgess offers a compellingly detailed view of a way of life and ways of thinking that may attract young naturalists." Bull Cent Child Books

Burnett, Frances Hodgson, 1849-1924

A little princess (4-6)   **Fic**
1. School stories 2. Great Britain—Fiction

Available from various publishers, including a HarperCollins paperback edition illustrated by Tasha Tudor; also available Audiobook version

First American edition published 1892 by Scribner in shorter form with title: Sara Crewe

The story of Sara Crewe, a girl who is sent from India to a boarding school in London, left in poverty by her father's death, and rescued by a mysterious benefactor

"The story is inevitably adorned with sentimental curlicues but the reader will hardly notice them since the story itself is such a satisfying one. Tasha Tudor's gentle, appropriate illustrations make this a lovely edition." Publ Wkly

The secret garden (4-6)   **Fic**

Also available Audiobook version
Some editions are:
Books of Wonder $21.95 Illustrated by Saelig Gallagher (ISBN 0-688-14582-5)
HarperCollins Pubs. lib bdg $14.89; pa $3.50 Illustrated by Tasha Tudor; 0-397-32162-7; 0-06-440-188-X)
First published 1909 by Stokes
"Neglected by his father because of his mother's death at his birth, Colin lives the life of a spoilt and incurable invalid until, on the arrival of an orphaned cousin, the two children secretly combine to restore his mother's locked garden and Colin to health and his father's affection." Four to Fourteen

Burnford, Sheila, 1918-1984

The incredible journey. Little, Brown 1961 145p o.p.; Amereon reprint available $18.95 (4 and up)
                                                    Fic
1. Cats—Fiction 2. Dogs—Fiction 3. Canada—Fiction
ISBN 0-88410-099-0
Also available in paperback from Bantam Bks.
"A half-blind English bull terrier, a sprightly yellow Labrador retriever, and a feisty Siamese cat have resided for eight months with a friend of their owners, who are away on a trip. Then their temporary caretaker leaves them behind in order to take a short vacation. The lonely trio decides to tackle the harsh 250-mile hike across the Canadian wilderness in search of home, despite the human and wild obstacles the group will encounter." Shapiro. Fic for Youth. 3d edition

Butterworth, Oliver, 1915-1990

The enormous egg; illustrated by Louis Darling. Little, Brown 1956 187p il hardcover o.p. paperback available $4.95 (4 and up)   **Fic**

1. Dinosaurs—Fiction

ISBN 0-316-11920-2 (pa)

"Up in Freedom, New Hampshire, one of the Twitchell's hens laid a remarkable egg. . . . Six weeks later when a live dinosaur hatched from the egg, the hen was dazed and upset, the Twitchells dumbfounded, and the scientific world went crazy. Twelve-year-old Nate who had taken care of the egg and made a pet out of the triceratops tells of the hullabaloo." Booklist

This story is "great fun . . . . And if you have any trouble visualizing a Triceratops moving placidly through the twentieth-century world you need only turn to Louis Darling's illustrations to believe." NY Times Book Rev

Byars, Betsy Cromer, 1928-

The burning questions of Bingo Brown; [by] Betsy Byars. Viking 1988 166p hardcover o.p. paperback available $4.99 (4 and up)   **Fic**

1. School stories

ISBN 0-14-032479-8 (pa)   LC 87-21022

Also available Spanish language edition

A boy is puzzled by the comic and confusing questions of youth and worried by disturbing insights into adult conflicts

"A fully worked out novel. . . . Readers will recognize the pitfalls, agonies, and joys of elementary school life in this book. . . . The short chapters and comic style are designed to appeal to young readers and to move them right into other books." Christ Sci Monit

Other available titles about Bingo Brown are:

Bingo Brown and the language of love (1989)

Bingo Brown, gypsy lover (1990)

Bingo Brown's guide to romance (1992)

Cracker Jackson; [by] Betsy Byars. Viking Kestrel 1985 147p $15.99; pa $4.99 (5 and up)   **Fic**

1. Wife abuse—Fiction 2. Child abuse—Fiction

ISBN 0-670-80546-7; 0-14-031881-X (pa)   LC 84-24684

"Young Jackson discovers that his ex-baby sitter has been beaten by her husband; and, spurred by affection for her, the boy enlists his friend Goat to help drive her to a home for battered women. The pathetic story of Alma, with her adored baby, tidy home, and treasured collection of Barbie dolls, is relieved by flashbacks to the two boys' antics at school and by their hilarious, if potentially lethal, attempt to drive her to safety." Horn Book

"Suspense, danger, near-tragedy, heartbreak and tension-relieving, unwittingly comic efforts at seriously heroic action mark this as the best of middle-grade fiction to highlight the problems of wife-battering and child abuse." SLJ

The Cybil war; [by] Betsy Byars; illustrated by Gail Owens. Viking 1981 126p il hardcover o.p. paperback available $4.99 (4-6)   **Fic**

1. Friendship—Fiction

ISBN 0-14-034356-3 (pa)   LC 80-26912

"Simon is deeply smitten by Cybil, a fourth-grade classmate, and just as deeply angered by his once-closest friend Tony, a blithely inventive liar who persists in telling fibs to and about Cybil to strengthen his cause: Tony is also smitten by Cybil." Bull Cent Child Books

"In her gently comic style, Byars presents Simon and the other people in her . . . story (even nasty Tony) as subteens who are people dealing with real problems. . . . Owens has illustrated sympathetically, making up a book that readers will take to their hearts." Publ Wkly

The house of wings; [by] Betsy Byars; illustrated by Daniel Schwartz. Viking 1972 142p il hardcover o.p. paperback available $4.99 (4-6)   **Fic**

1. Cranes (Birds)—Fiction 2. Grandfathers—Fiction

ISBN 0-14-031523-3 (pa)

"A young boy reeling from the pain of temporary parental abandonment forges a relationship with an eccentric grandfather whom he despises. In attempting to rescue and mend a wounded crane, they come to respect each other for what they are, and as men." Book World

This story "has an unsentimental and potent message about wildlife and draws a telling portrait of a human relationship. Save for the brief appearance of the parents, Sammy and his grandfather are the only characters. The book's spare construction makes it strong." Saturday Rev

Me Tarzan; by Betsy Byars; illustrations by Bill Cigliano. HarperCollins Pubs. 2000 86p il $14.95; lib bdg $14.89 (3-5)   **Fic**

1. School stories 2. Acting—Fiction 3. Animals—Fiction

ISBN 0-06-028706-3; 0-06-028707-1 (lib bdg)   LC 99-34512

When Dorothy gets the part of Tarzan in the class play, her tremendous yell attracts the attention of increasingly larger and wilder animals

"This very funny story, peppered with likable characters and on-target dialogue, will delight readers." SLJ

The midnight fox; [by] Betsy Byars; illustrated by Ann Grifalconi. Viking 1968 157p il hardcover o.p. paperback available $4.99 (4-6)   **Fic**

1. Foxes—Fiction

ISBN 0-14-031450-4 (pa)

"City-bred Tommy hates the idea of spending the summer on Aunt Millie's farm while his parents bicycle through Europe. Once he is there, however, a black fox shatters his conviction that he and animals share a mutual antipathy; fascinated, he stalks and watches the wild creature for two months—until it steals some of Aunt Millie's poultry and has to be hunted down." Booklist

"What distinguishes the story from many others on the same theme is the simplicity and beauty of the writing and the depth of the characterization." Horn Book

The night swimmers; by Betsy Byars; illustrated by Troy Howell. Delacorte Press 1980 131p il hardcover o.p. paperback available $4.50 (5 and up)   **Fic**

1. Single parent family—Fiction 2. Siblings—Fiction

ISBN 0-440-45857-9 (pa)   LC 79-53597

With their mother dead and their father working nights, Retta tries to be mother to her two younger broth-

Byars, Betsy Cromer, 1928-—*Continued*
ers but somehow things just don't seem to be working
right

"The plot moves a little slowly but characterization is
good." Voice Youth Advocates

The not-just-anybody family; [by] Betsy Byars;
illustrated by Jacqueline Rogers. Delacorte Press
1986 149p il hardcover o.p. paperback available
$4.50 (5 and up) **Fic**
1. Siblings—Fiction 2. Family life—Fiction
ISBN 0-440-45951-6 (pa) LC 85-16184

"It's an ordinary day in the Blossom family: Junior,
with Maggie and Vernon watching, is poised to fly off
the barn in homemade wings; Mom's on the rodeo circuit; and Pap and his dog, Mud, are in town. By evening, Pap's in jail; Junior's in the hospital; Mud is gone;
and Maggie helps Vernon break into jail to be with their
grandfather." Publisher's note

"The story of the pathetically self-reliant, eccentric,
but deeply loving family makes a book that is funny and
sad, warm and wonderful." Horn Book
Other available titles about the Blossom family are:
A Blossom promise (1987)
The Blossoms and the Green Phantom (1987)
The Blossoms meet the Vulture Lady (1986)
Wanted—Mud Blossom (1991)

The pinballs; [by] Betsy Byars. Harper & Row
1977 136p lib bdg $15.89; pa $4.95 (5 and up)
Fic
1. Foster home care—Fiction 2. Friendship—Fiction
ISBN 0-06-020918-6 (lib bdg); 0-06-440198-7 (pa)

Also available Audiobook version

"Pinballs go where they're pushed—and life's 'tilts'
have thrown together three misfits. Suddenly finding
themselves in a warm, loving foster home are Thomas J.,
eight, who is homeless now that his octogenarian twin
guardians are hospitalized; Harvey, 13, whose mother ran
off to a commune and whose hard-drinking father ran
over him in a car; and Carlie, 15, who cannot get along
with a succession of stepfathers—or the rest of the
world, for that matter." SLJ

"A deceptively simple, eloquent story, its pain and ac-
rimony constantly mitigated by the author's light, offhand style and by Carlie's wryly comic view of life."
Horn Book

The summer of the swans; [by] Betsy Byars;
illustrated by Ted CoConis. Viking 1970 142p il
$15.99; pa $4.99 (5 and up) **Fic**
1. Mentally handicapped children—Fiction 2. Siblings—Fiction
ISBN 0-670-68190-3; 0-14-031420-2 (pa)
Also available Audiobook version
Awarded the Newbery Medal, 1971

"The thoughts and feelings of a young girl troubled by
a sense of inner discontent which she cannot explain are
tellingly portrayed in the story of two summer days in
the life of fourteen-year-old Sara Godfrey. Sara is jolted
out of her self-pitying absorption with her own inadequa-
cies by the disappearance of her ten-year-old retarded
brother who gets lost while trying to find the swans he
had previously seen on a nearby lake. Her agonizing, al-

beit ultimately successful, search for Charlie and the reactions of others to this traumatic event help Sara gain
a new perspective on herself and life." Booklist

Tornado; by Betsy Byars; illustrations by Doron
Ben-Ami. HarperCollins Pubs. 1996 49p il $14.95;
lib bdg $14.89; pa $4.25 (2-4) **Fic**
1. Dogs—Fiction 2. Tornadoes—Fiction
ISBN 0-06-026449-7; 0-06-026452-7 (lib bdg);
0-06-442063-9 (pa) LC 95-41584

As they wait out a tornado in their storm cellar, a
family listens to their farmhand tell stories about the dog
that was blown into his life by another tornado when he
was a boy

"The handsome illustrations by Doron Ben-Ami give
the volume a more distinguished, less juvenile look than
the typical chapter book and convey the story's drama,
warmth, and occasional humor. Parents and teachers will
find this an excellent book to read aloud, and dog lovers
of any age will find it irresistible." Booklist

Trouble River; [by] Betsy Byars; illustrated by
Rocco Negri. Viking 1969 158p il hardcover o.p.
paperback available $4.99 (4-6) **Fic**
1. Frontier and pioneer life—Fiction 2. Rivers—Fiction
ISBN 0-14-034243-5 (pa)

Dewey Martin and his grandmother must make their
way down the Trouble River on a home-made raft to escape the danger of hostile Indians. They find the raft
hard to navigate on the river, but they persevere and
eventually reach Hunter City and safety

"A philosophy of not giving up amid hardships and a
sense of real love and family solidarity predominate."
Read Ladders for Hum Relat. 6th edition

Calmenson, Stephanie
Get well, Gators! by Stephanie Calmenson and
Joanna Cole; illustrated by Lynn Munsinger.
Morrow Junior Bks. 1998 63p il lib bdg $15.93
(1-3) **Fic**
1. Alligators—Fiction 2. Sick—Fiction 3. Fairs—Fic-
tion
ISBN 0-688-14787-9 LC 97-15756

When Allie Gator comes down with swamp flu, she
worries that she will miss going to the street fair with
her best friend Amy Gator

"Munsinger's expressive illustrations bring the gators
to life. . . . Fans of the earlier 'Gator Girls' books will
be happy to follow this new adventure, and newcomers
will be inspired to go back and read the others." SLJ
Other available titles about The Gator Girls are:
The Gator Girls (1995)
Gator Halloween (1999)
Rockin' reptiles (1997)

Cameron, Ann, 1943-
Gloria's way; pictures by Lis Toft. Farrar,
Straus & Giroux 2000 96p il $15 (2-4) **Fic**
1. Friendship—Fiction 2. Family life—Fiction
3. African Americans—Fiction
ISBN 0-374-32670-3 LC 99-12104
"Frances Foster books"

Cameron, Ann, 1943-—*Continued*

This companion volume to the series featuring Julian and Huey centers on their friend Gloria. Gloria shares special times with her mother and father and with her friends

"Lis Toft's shaded pencil drawings portray these African American characters and their predicaments with warmth and humor." Booklist

The stories Julian tells; illustrated by Ann Strugnell. Pantheon Bks. 1981 71p il lib bdg $15.99; pa $4.99 (2-4)   **Fic**
1. Family life—Fiction 2. African Americans—Fiction

ISBN 0-394-94301-5 (lib bdg); 0-394-82892-5 (pa)
LC 80-18023

"When seven-year-old Julian tells his little brother, Huey, that cats come from catalogues, Huey believes him. But when he flips the pages of the catalogue and doesn't find any cats, he begins to cry and Julian has some fast explaining to do. . . . A loving family is the center for six happy stories about catalog cats, strange teeth, a garden, a birthday fig tree and a new friend." West Coast Rev Books

"Strugnell's delightful drawings depict Julian, his little brother Huey and their parents as black, but they could be members of any family with a stern but loving and understanding father." Publ Wkly

Other available titles about Julian and his family are:
Julian, dream doctor (1990)
Julian, secret agent (1988)
Julian's glorious summer (1987)
More stories Huey tells (1997)
More stories Julian tells (1986)
The stories Huey tells (1995)

Cameron, Eleanor, 1912-1996

The court of the stone children. Dutton 1973 191p hardcover o.p. paperback available $4.99 (5 and up)   **Fic**
1. Museums—Fiction 2. Mystery fiction
ISBN 0-14-034289-3 (pa)
Also available in hardcover from P. Smith
In a San Francisco museum of French art and furniture, Nina encounters the ghost of Dominique, a girl who lived in the nineteenth-century. Spurred on by the appearance of the ghost, Nina sets out to untangle a murder mystery which had remained unsolved since Napoleon's day

"A nice concoction of mystery, fantasy, and realism adroitly blended in a contemporary story. . . . The characters are interesting, the plot threads nicely integrated." Bull Cent Child Books

The wonderful flight to the Mushroom Planet; with illustrations by Robert Henneberger. Little, Brown 1954 214p il hardcover o.p. paperback available $7.95 (4-6)   **Fic**
1. Science fiction
ISBN 0-316-12540-7 (pa)
"An Atlantic Monthly Press book"
Two boys help a neighbor build a space ship in answer to an ad and take off for the dying planet of Basidium. There they help the inhabitants to restore an essential food to their diets and thereby save the life of the planet

"Scientific facts are emphasized in this well-built story. Since they are necessary to the development of the story the reader absorbs them naturally as he soars with the boys on the mission." N Y Times Book Rev

Carlson, Natalie Savage, 1906-

The family under the bridge; pictures by Garth Williams. Harper & Row 1958 99p il lib bdg $15.89; pa $5.95 (3-5)   **Fic**
1. Tramps—Fiction 2. Christmas—Fiction 3. Paris (France)—Fiction
ISBN 0-06-020991-7 (lib bdg); 0-06-440250-9 (pa)

A Newbery Medal honor book, 1959
"Old Armand, a Parisian hobo, enjoyed his solitary, carefree life. . . . Then came a day just before Christmas when Armand, who wanted nothing to do with children because they spelled homes, responsibility, and regular work, found that three homeless children and their working mother had claimed his shelter under the bridge. How the hobo's heart and life become more and more deeply entangled with the little family and their quest for a home is told." Booklist

"Garth Williams' illustrations are perfect for this thoroughly delightful story of humor and sentiment." Libr J

Carroll, Lewis, 1832-1898

Alice's adventures in Wonderland (4 and up)
    Fic

1. Fantasy fiction

Also available Audiobook version
Some editions are:
Books of Wonder $16.95 Illustrated by John Tenniel (ISBN 0-688-11087-8)
Candlewick Press $24.99 Illustrated by Helen Oxenbury (ISBN 0-763-60804-1)
Dutton $19.99 Illustrated by Abelardo Morell (ISBN 0-525-46094-2)
North-South Bks. $19.95 Illustrated by Lisbeth Zwerger (ISBN 0-7358-1166-0)
St. Martin's Press $14.95 Illustrated by John Tenniel (ISBN 0-312-01821-5)
"First told in 1862 to the little Liddell girls. Written out for Alice Liddell, published, and first copy given to her in 1865." Arnold
Variant title: Alice in Wonderland
"A rabbit who took a watch out of his waistcoat pocket seemed well-worth following to Alice so she hurried after him across the field, down the rabbit hole, and into a series of adventures with a group of famous and most unusual characters." Let's Read Together
This fantasy "is one of the most quoted books in the English language. Every child should be introduced to Alice, though its appeal will not be universal." Natl Counc of Teach of Engl. Adventuring with Books
Followed by Through the looking glass, and what Alice found there

Alice's adventures in Wonderland, and Through the looking glass (4 and up)   **Fic**
1. Fantasy fiction

Carroll, Lewis, 1832-1898—*Continued*

Available from various publishers including a Dell paperback edition illustrated by John Tenniel

A combined edition of the two titles first published 1865 and 1872 respectively. Through the looking glass, the sequel to Alice's adventures in Wonderland, "tells of Alice's experiences when, curious about the world behind the mirror, she climbs over the mantel through the glass. In looking-glass country, everything is reversed, just as reflections are reversed in a mirror. Brooks and hedges divide the land into a checkerboard, and Alice finds herself a white pawn in the whimsical and fantastic game of chess that constitutes the bulk of the story. . . . The ballad 'Jabberwocky' is found in the tale." Reader's Ency. 4th edition

Cassedy, Sylvia, 1930-1989

Behind the attic wall. Crowell 1983 315p lib bdg $15.89 (5 and up) **Fic**
1. Uncles—Fiction 2. Orphans—Fiction 3. Ghost stories 4. Dolls—Fiction
ISBN 0-690-04337-6　　　　　　　LC 82-45922
Also available in paperback from Avon Bks.

Maggie, a rebellious twelve-year-old orphan "is sent to stay with two elderly great-aunts; like other guardians they are horrified by the behavior of the . . . hostile child. . . . That is the realistic matrix for a fantasy world behind the attic wall, where Maggie finds two dolls who are articulate and who draw her into their world so that she becomes engaged and protective." Bull Cent Child Books

"The gradual merging of the story into fantasy, detail by telling detail, demands patience and attention on the part of the reader, but the wonderfully strange denouement will reward perseverance." Horn Book

Caudill, Rebecca, 1899-1985

A certain small shepherd; with illustrations by William Pène Du Bois. Holt & Co. 1965 48p il hardcover o.p. paperback available $6.95 (4 and up) **Fic**
1. Physically handicapped children—Fiction 2. Christmas—Fiction 3. Appalachian region—Fiction
ISBN 0-8050-5392-1 (pa)

The author tells of "the singleminded enthusiasm of [Jamie], a little mute boy, who is given the part of one of the shepherds in a church celebration. . . . The pageant never takes place as a blizzard immobilizes the poor mountain community where the child lives, but the small shepherd is so deeply committed to his part that he acts it out impulsively [and speaks] when a baby is born to a family of travelers, caught by the storm and obliged to take refuge in the church." Book Week

"Set in the mountains of Appalachia, the tender, moving story, illustrated with poignantly interpretive drawings, expresses anew the age-old Christmas message of love and wonder." Booklist

Did you carry the flag today, Charley? illustrated by Nancy Grossman. Holt & Co. 1966 94p il lib bdg $16.95; pa $4.50 (2-4) **Fic**
1. School stories 2. Appalachian region—Fiction
ISBN 0-8050-1201-X (lib bdg); 0-03-086620-0 (pa)

A "story about a small and lively boy, just turned five, who has his first encounter with the necessary strictures of the classroom at a summer school in Appalachia. Charley, obstreperous youngest in a family of ten, is given a full picture of the joys and the responsibilities he will encounter; his brothers and sisters tell him that one child 'who has been specially good that day' has the honor of carrying the flag at the head of the line to the bus. . . . This is a realistic and low-keyed story with good dialogue." Bull Cent Child Books

Choi, Sook Nyul

Year of impossible goodbyes. Houghton Mifflin 1991 171p $16 (5 and up) **Fic**
1. Korea—Fiction
ISBN 0-395-57419-6　　　　　　　LC 91-10502
Also available in paperback from Dell

A young Korean girl named Sookan survives the oppressive Japanese and Russian occupation of North Korea during the 1940s, to later escape to freedom in South Korea

"Tragedies are not masked here, but neither are they overdramatized. . . . The observations are honest, the details authentic, the characterizations vividly developed." Bull Cent Child Books

Other available titles about Sookan are:
Echoes of the white giraffe (1993)
Gathering of pearls (1994)

Christopher, John, 1922-

The White Mountains. Macmillan 1967 184p $17; pa $4.99 (5 and up) **Fic**
1. Science fiction
ISBN 0-02-718360-2; 0-02-042711-5 (pa)
Also available Spanish language edition

"The world of the future is ruled by huge and powerful machine-creatures, the Tripods, who control mankind by implanting metal caps in their skulls when they reach the age of fourteen. Three boys . . . see that the people about them are mindless conformists [and] decide to flee to the White Mountains (Switzerland), where there is a colony of free men." Saturday Rev

This "remarkable story . . . belongs to the school of science-fiction which puts philosophy before technology and is not afraid of telling an exciting story." Times Lit Suppl

Other available titles about the Tripods are:
The city of gold and lead (1967)
The pool of fire (1968)
When the Tripods came (1988)

Christopher, Matt, 1917-1997

The dog that called the pitch; illustrated by Daniel Vasconcellos. Little, Brown 1998 34p il $14.95 (2-4) **Fic**
1. Dogs—Fiction 2. Extrasensory perception—Fiction 3. Baseball—Fiction
ISBN 0-316-14207-7　　　　　　　LC 97-28224

Mike and his dog Harry, the Airedale with ESP, are shocked to discover that the new umpire for Mike's baseball games can hear their mental conversations

"With plenty of illustrations, the text tells a fast-paced story, just right for newly independent readers." Horn Book Guide

Christopher, Matt, 1917-1997—*Continued*

The hit-away kid; illustrated by George Ulrich. Little, Brown 1988 60p il lib bdg $12.95; pa $4.50 (2-4)   **Fic**
1. Baseball—Fiction
ISBN 0-316-13995-5 (lib bdg); 0-316-14007-4 (pa)
LC 87-24406
Barry McGee, star batter for the Peach Street Mudders, enjoys winning so much that he has a tendency to bend the rules; then the dirty tactics of the pitcher on a rival team give him a new perspective on sports ethics
"This is predictable in theme if not in plot (Barry's team loses), but kids will get the reading practice they need on a subject that's palatable and popular." Bull Cent Child Books

Tackle without a team; illustrated by Margaret Sanfilippo. Little, Brown 1989 145p il $15.95 (4-6)   **Fic**
1. Football—Fiction 2. Drugs—Fiction 3. Mystery fiction
ISBN 0-316-14067-8   LC 88-22644
Unjustly dismissed from the football team for drug possession, Scott learns that only by finding out who planted the marijuana in his duffel bag can he clear himself with his parents
"Christopher's message—that smoking cigarettes or pot is a bummer—comes through loud and clear. Lots of action and enough suspense hold the plot together." Booklist

Tennis ace. Little, Brown 2000 116p $15.95; pa $3.95 (3-6)   **Fic**
1. Tennis—Fiction 2. Parent-child relationship—Fiction 3. Siblings—Fiction
ISBN 0-316-13519-4; 0-316-13491-0 (pa)
LC 99-48067
Steve and Ginny are frustrated because their father ignores her talent as a tennis player while pushing him harder and harder to win at the sport
"The plot is transparent but the lively action throughout will keep young players intrigued." SLJ

Clapp, Patricia, 1912-
Constance: a story of early Plymouth. Lothrop, Lee & Shepard Bks. 1968 255p o.p.; Morrow paperback available $5.95 (5 and up)   **Fic**
1. Pilgrims (New England colonists)—Fiction 2. Massachusetts—History—1600-1775, Colonial period—Fiction
ISBN 0-688-10976-4 (pa)
Also available in hardcover from P. Smith
The imaginary "journal kept by Constance Hopkins, daughter of Stephen Hopkins and ancestress of Patricia Clapp. Constance began jotting down her impressions and intimate thoughts at the age of fifteen on the eve of the 'Mayflower's' arrival and continued up to the day of her wedding five years later." Horn Book
"The characters come alive, the writing style is excellent, and the historical background is smoothly integrated." Bull Cent Child Books

Cleary, Beverly
Dear Mr. Henshaw; illustrated by Paul O. Zelinsky. Morrow 1983 133p il $16; lib bdg $15.89 (4-6)   **Fic**
1. Divorce—Fiction 2. Parent-child relationship—Fiction 3. School stories
ISBN 0-688-02405-X; 0-688-02406-8 (lib bdg)
LC 83-5372
Also available in paperback from Avon Bks.; Spanish language edition also available
Awarded the Newbery Medal, 1984
"Leigh Botts started writing letters to his favorite author, Boyd Henshaw, in the second grade. Now, Leigh is in the sixth grade, in a new school, and his parents are recently divorced. This year he writes many letters to Mr. Henshaw, and also keeps a journal. Through these the reader learns how Leigh adjusts to new situations, and of his triumphs." Child Book Rev Serv
"The story is by no means one of unrelieved gloom, for there are deft touches of humor in the sentient, subtly wrought account of the small triumphs and tragedies in the life of an ordinary boy." Horn Book
Followed by Strider

Ellen Tebbits; illustrated by Louis Darling. Morrow 1951 160p il $16; lib bdg $15.93 (3-5)   **Fic**
1. School stories
ISBN 0-688-21264-6; 0-688-31264-0 (lib bdg)
Also available in paperback from Avon Bks.
"Ellen Tebbits is eight years old, takes ballet lessons, wears bands on her teeth, and has a secret—she wears woolen underwear. But she finds a friend in Austine, a new girl in school, who also wears woolen underwear. They have the usual troubles that beset 'best friends' in grade school plus some that are unusual." Carnegie Libr of Pittsburgh
"Their experiences in the third grade are comical and very appealing to children in the middle grades." Hodges. Books for Elem Sch Libr

Henry Huggins; illustrated by Louis Darling. HarperCollins Pubs. 2000 155p il $15.95; lib bdg $15.93; pa $4.95 (3-5)   **Fic**
ISBN 0-688-21385-5; 0-688-31385-X (lib bdg); 0-380-70912-0 (pa)   LC 00-27567
Also available Spanish language edition
A reissue of the title first published 1950 by Morrow
"Henry Huggins is a typical small boy who, quite innocently, gets himself into all sorts of predicaments—often with the very apt thought, 'Won't Mom be surprised.' There is not a dull moment but some hilariously funny ones in the telling of Henry's adventures at home and at school." Booklist
Other available titles about Henry Huggins are:
Henry and Beezus (1952)
Henry and Ribsy (1954)
Henry and the clubhouse (1962)
Henry and the paper route (1957)
Ribsy (1964)

Mitch and Amy; illustrated by Bob Marstall. Morrow Junior Bks. 1991 222p il $15 (3-5)   **Fic**
1. Twins—Fiction 2. School stories
ISBN 0-688-10806-7   LC 91-25657
Also available in paperback from Avon Bks.

Cleary, Beverly—*Continued*

A newly illustrated edition of the title first published 1967

"The twins Mitch and Amy are in the fourth grade. Mitch is plagued by a bully and by reading difficulties, Amy struggles with multiplication tables, and their patient mother mediates their squabbles." SLJ

"The writing style and dialogue, the familial and peer group relationships, the motivations and characterizations all have the ring of truth. Written with ease and vitality, lightened with humor, the story is perhaps most appealing because it is clear that the author respects children." Bull Cent Child Books

The mouse and the motorcycle; illustrated by Louis Darling. Morrow 1965 158p il $16 (3-5)
Fic
1. Mice—Fiction
ISBN 0-688-21698-6
Also available in paperback from Avon Bks. and Audiobook version

"A fantasy about Ralph, a mouse, who learns to ride a toy motorcycle and goes on wild rides through the corridors of the hotel where he lives. Keith, the boy to whom the motorcycle belongs, becomes fast friends with Ralph and defends him when danger threatens." Hodges. Books for Elem Sch Libr

"The author shows much insight into the thoughts of children. She carries the reader into an imaginative world that contains many realistic emotions." Wis Libr Bull

Other available titles about Ralph are:
Ralph S. Mouse (1982)
Runaway Ralph (1970)

Muggie Maggie; illustrated by Kay Life. Morrow Junior Bks. 1990 70p il $16; lib bdg $15.93 (2-4)
Fic
1. Handwriting—Fiction 2. School stories
ISBN 0-688-08553-9; 0-688-08554-7 (lib bdg)
LC 89-38959
Also available in paperback from Avon Bks.; Spanish language edition also available

Maggie resists learning cursive writing in the third grade, until she discovers that knowing how to read and write cursive promises to open up an entirely new world of knowledge for her

"This deceptively simple story is accessible to primary-grade readers able to read longhand, as some of the text is in script. . . . Everything in this book rings true, and Cleary has created a likable, funny heroine about whom readers will want to know more." SLJ

Otis Spofford; illustrated by Louis Darling. Morrow 1953 191p il $16; lib bdg $14.93 (3-5)
Fic
1. School stories
ISBN 0-688-21720-6; 0-688-31720-0 (lib bdg)
Also available in paperback from Avon Bks.

"Otis, a mischievous, fun loving boy, is always getting in and out of trouble. His mother, a dancing teacher, is busy and often leaves Otis on his own. This book tells of several episodes in Otis's life—from his sneaking vitamins to a white rat to 'disprove' a diet experiment, to getting his final 'come-uppance' when a trick on Ellen Tebbits backfires." Read Ladders for Hum Relat. 6th edition

"This writer has her elementary school down pat, and manages to report her growing boys, teachers, and P.T.A. meetings so that parents chuckle and boys laugh out loud." N Y Her Trib Books

Ramona the pest; illustrated by Louis Darling. Morrow 1968 192p il $16; lib bdg $15.93 (3-5)
Fic
1. Kindergarten—Fiction 2. School stories
ISBN 0-688-21721-4; 0-688-31721-9 (lib bdg)
Also available in paperback from Avon Bks.; Spanish language edition also available; Audiobook version also available

"Ramona Quimby comes into her own. Beezus keeps telling her to stop acting like a pest, but Ramona is five now, and she is convinced that she is 'not' a pest; she feels very mature, having entered kindergarten, and she immediately becomes enamoured of her teacher. Ramona's insistence on having just the right kind of boots, her matter-of-fact interest in how Mike Mulligan got to a bathroom, her determination to kiss one of the boys in her class, and her refusal to go back to kindergarten because Miss Binney didn't love her any more—all of these incidents or situations are completely believable and are told in a light, humorous, zesty style." Bull Cent Child Books

Other available titles about Ramona are:
Beezus and Ramona (1955)
Ramona and her father (1977)
Ramona and her mother (1979)
Ramona, forever (1984)
Ramona Quimby, age 8 (1981)
Ramona the brave (1975)
Ramona's world (1999)

Socks; illustrated by Beatrice Darwin. Morrow 1973 156p il $15.95; lib bdg $15.93 (3-5)
Fic
1. Cats—Fiction 2. Infants—Fiction
ISBN 0-688-20067-2; 0-688-30067-7 (lib bdg)
Also available in paperback from Avon Bks.

"The Brickers' kitten, Socks, is jealous when they bring a baby home from the hospital. How he copes with this rivalry makes an amusing story true to cat nature." Cleveland Public Libr

"Not being child-centered, this may have a smaller audience than earlier Cleary books, but it is written with the same easy grace, the same felicitous humor and sharply observant eye." Bull Cent Child Books

Strider; illustrated by Paul O. Zelinsky. Morrow Junior Bks. 1991 179p il $16; lib bdg $15.89 (4 and up)
Fic
1. Dogs—Fiction 2. Divorce—Fiction
ISBN 0-688-09900-9; 0-688-09901-7 (lib bdg)
LC 90-6608
Also available in paperback from Avon Bks.; Spanish language edition also available
Sequel to Dear Mr. Henshaw

In a series of diary entries, Leigh Botts, now fourteen and beginning high school, tells how he comes to terms with his parents' divorce, acquires joint custody of an abandoned dog, and joins the track team at school

"The development of the narrative is vintage Beverly Cleary, an inimitable blend of comic and poignant moments." Horn Book

Cleaver, Vera

Where the lillies bloom; [by] Vera & Bill Cleaver; illustrated by Jim Spanfeller. Lippincott 1969 174p il $15.95; pa $4.95 (5 and up)   **Fic**

1. Orphans—Fiction 2. Siblings—Fiction 3. Appalachian region—Fiction

ISBN 0-397-31111-7; 0-064-47005-9 (pa)

Mary Call Luther is "fourteen years old and made of granite. When her sharecropper father dies, Mary Call becomes head of the household, responsible for a boy of ten and a retarded, gentle older sister. Mary and her brother secretly bury their father so they can retain their home [in the Appalachian hills]; tenaciously she fights to keep the family afloat by selling medicinal plants and to keep them together by fending off [Kiser Pease, their landlord], who wants to marry her sister." Saturday Rev

"The setting is fascinating, the characterization good, and the style of the first-person story distinctive." Bull Cent Child Books

Followed by Trial Valley (1977)

Clements, Andrew, 1949-

Frindle; pictures by Brian Selznick. Simon & Schuster Bks. for Young Readers 1996 105p il $15; pa $4.50 (4-6)   **Fic**

1. School stories

ISBN 0-689-80669-8; 0-689-81876-9 (pa)

LC 95-26671

Also available Audiobook version

When he decides to turn his fifth grade teacher's love of the dictionary around on her, clever Nick Allen invents a new word and begins a chain of events that quickly moves beyond his control

"Sure to be popular with a wide range of readers, this will make a great read-aloud as well." Booklist

The janitor's boy; a novel; by the best-selling author of Frindle. Simon & Schuster Bks. for Young Readers 2000 140p $15 (4-6)   **Fic**

1. Father-son relationship—Fiction 2. School stories

ISBN 0-689-81818-1   LC 99-47457

Also available Thorndike Press large print edition and Audiobook version

Fifth grader Jack finds himself the target of ridicule at school when it becomes known that his father is one of the janitors, and he turns his anger onto his father

"Clements' strength is his realistic depiction of public schools. . . . Jack's antics and those of his classmates ring true, as do the behaviors of the teachers and administrators." Booklist

The Landry News; illustrations by Salvatore Murdocca. Simon & Schuster Bks. for Young Readers 1999 123p il $15; pa $4.99 (4-6)   **Fic**

1. Newspapers—Fiction 2. Teachers—Fiction 3. School stories

ISBN 0-689-81817-3; 0-689-82868-3 (pa)

LC 98-34376

Also available Thorndike Press large print edition

A fifth-grader starts a newspaper with an editorial that prompts her burnt-out classroom teacher to really begin teaching again, but he is later threatened with disciplinary action as a result

"The text flows effortlessly yet explores thought-provoking issues such as intellectual freedom that are likely to engender further exploration." Horn Book Guide

Clifford, Eth, 1915-

Help! I'm a prisoner in the library; illustrated by George Hughes. Houghton Mifflin 1979 105p il $16 (3-5)   **Fic**

1. Libraries—Fiction 2. Blizzards—Fiction

ISBN 0-395-28478-3   LC 79-14447

Also available in paperback from Scholastic

"Caught in a blinding snowstorm with their car out of gas, Mary Rose and Jo-Beth are told to stay put while their father finds fuel for the stalled vehicle. Jo-Beth, however, develops 'an emergency' and Mary Rose takes her to a nearby library to find a restroom. . . . Without warning the girls find themselves locked in when the building closes early. As the storm worsens, the lights and telephone go out and a series of flying objects, creaking noises, and moaning sounds thoroughly frighten the girls. . . . Clifford uses a light touch while evoking a pleasingly scary atmosphere that children will enjoy. Spirited dialogue and swift pace are an additional plus." Booklist

The remembering box; illustrated by Donna Diamond. Houghton Mifflin 1985 70p il $16 (3-5)   **Fic**

1. Grandmothers—Fiction 2. Jews—Fiction 3. Death—Fiction

ISBN 0-395-38476-1   LC 85-10851

Also available in paperback from Beech Tree Bks.

Nine-year-old Joshua's weekly visits to his beloved grandmother on the Jewish Sabbath give him an understanding of love, family, and tradition which helps him accept her death

"This warm and loving relationship between a boy and his grandmother is beautifully depicted. . . . Diamond's silhouettes, used for the stories that Grandma tells Joshua, are dramatic, and her meticulously detailed black-and-white illustrations of Joshua and his grandmother are both expressive and moving." SLJ

Clifton, Lucille, 1936-

The lucky stone; illustrated by Dale Payson. Delacorte Press 1979 64p il hardcover o.p. paperback available $3.99 (3-5)   **Fic**

1. African Americans—Fiction 2. Charms—Fiction

ISBN 0-440-45110-8 (pa)   LC 78-72862

"Four short stories about four generations of Black women and their dealings with a lucky stone. . . . Clifton uses as a frame device a grandmother telling the history of the stone to her granddaughter; by the end the granddaughter has inherited the stone herself. . . . The story is written in Black dialect." SLJ

"This book contains information on various aspects of Black culture—slavery, religion and extended family—all conveyed in a way that is both positive and accurate." Interracial Books Child Bull

Coatsworth, Elizabeth Jane, 1893-1986

The cat who went to heaven; [by] Elizabeth Coatsworth; illustrated by Lynd Ward. Macmillan 1958 62p il $17; pa $4.99 (4 and up)   **Fic**

1. Cats—Fiction 2. Japan—Fiction

ISBN 0-02-719710-7; 0-689-71433-5 (pa)

LC 58-10917

Also available Audiobook version

Coatsworth, Elizabeth Jane, 1893-1986—Continued

First published 1930. The 1958 edition is a reprint with new illustrations of the book which won the Newbery Medal award in 1931

"Watched by his little cat, Good Fortune, a Japanese artist paints a picture of the Buddha receiving homage from the animals. By tradition the cat should not be among them, but the artist risks his reputation by adding Good Fortune and is vindicated by a miracle." Hodges. Books for Elem Sch Libr

"Into this lovely and imaginative story the author has put something of the serenity and beauty of the East and of the gentleness of a religion that has a place even for the humblest of living creatures." N Y Times Book Rev

Coerr, Eleanor, 1922-

Mieko and the fifth treasure; calligraphy by Cecil H. Uyehara. Putnam 1993 77p $14.99 (3-5)

Fic

1. Artists—Fiction 2. Nagasaki (Japan)—Bombardment, 1945—Fiction 3. Japan—Fiction
ISBN 0-399-22434-3   LC 92-14660
Also available in paperback from Dell

Staying with her grandparents after the atomic bomb has been dropped on Nagasaki, ten-year-old Mieko feels that the happiness in her heart has departed forever and she will no longer be able to produce a beautiful drawing for the contest at school

"The story conveys a wonderfully delicate sense of Japanese people, customs, and beliefs. Coerr has created an intriguing and beautifully told tale whose strong message about friendship, self-confidence, and hope is inspiring." Booklist

Cohen, Barbara, 1932-1992

The carp in the bathtub; illustrated by Joan Halpern. Lothrop, Lee & Shepard Bks. 1972 48p il o.p.; Kar-Ben Copies paperback available $5.95 (2-4)

Fic

1. Jews—Fiction 2. Fishes—Fiction
ISBN 0-930-49467-9 (pa)
Also available Audiobook version

Set in New York City. "Leah and Harry have made friends of Joe, the appealing carp their mother has swimming in the bathtub, awaiting its execution on the Feast of Seder. Joe will make marvelous 'gefilte' fish but the children are determined to save him. They sneak him into the tub of a neighbor, but alas; his change of scene is only a reprieve, not a pardon. A delightfully warm book with pictures equally appealing." Publ Wkly

Thank you, Jackie Robinson; drawings by Richard Cuffari. Lothrop, Lee & Shepard Bks. 1974 125p il hardcover o.p. paperback available $4.95 (4-6)

Fic

1. Baseball—Fiction   2. Friendship—Fiction
3. African Americans—Fiction
ISBN 0-688-15293-7 (pa)

"When 60-year-old Davey (Black) comes to work at the inn for Sam's mother, Sam (Jewish and fatherless) gains a friend. Davey takes Sam to see the Brooklyn Dodgers (circa 1945), and an avid, statistic-spouting Dodger fan is born. When Davey becomes ill, Sam gets Jackie Robinson and his teammates to autograph a ball for Davey." Child Book Rev Serv

"Cohen's characters have unusual depth and her story succeeds as a warm, understanding consideration of friendship and, finally, death." Booklist

Collier, James Lincoln, 1928-

Jump ship to freedom; [by] James Lincoln Collier, Christopher Collier. Delacorte Press 1981 198p hardcover o.p. paperback available $5.50 (6 and up)

Fic

1. United States—History—1783-1809—Fiction
2. Slavery—Fiction 3. African Americans—Fiction
ISBN 0-440-44323-7 (pa)   LC 81-65492
Companion volume to War comes to Willie Freeman and Who is Carrie?

In 1787 Dan Arabus, a fourteen-year-old slave, anxious to buy freedom for himself and his mother, escapes from his dishonest master and tries to find help in cashing the soldier's notes received by his father, Jack Arabus, for fighting in the Revolution

"The period seems well researched, and the speech has an authentic ring without trying to imitate a dialect." SLJ

My brother Sam is dead; by James Lincoln Collier and Christopher Collier. Four Winds Press 1985 c1974 216p $17 (6 and up)

Fic

1. United States—History—1775-1783, Revolution—Fiction
ISBN 0-02-722980-7   LC 84-28787
Also available in paperback from Scholastic and Audiobook version

A reissue of the title first published 1974

"In 1775 the Meeker family lived in Redding, Connecticut, a Tory community. Sam, the eldest son, allied himself with the Patriots. The youngest son, Tim, watched a rift in the family grow because of his brother's decision. Before the war was over the Meeker family had suffered at the hands of both the British and the Patriots." Shapiro. Fic for Youth. 3d edition

War comes to Willy Freeman; [by] James Lincoln Collier, Christopher Collier. Delacorte Press 1983 178p hardcover o.p. paperback available $4.99 (6 and up)

Fic

1. United States—History—1775-1783, Revolution—Fiction 2. African Americans—Fiction 3. Slavery—Fiction
ISBN 0-440-49504-0 (pa)   LC 82-70317

This deals with events prior to those in Jump ship to freedom, and involves members of the same family. "Willy is thirteen when she begins her story, which takes place during the last two years of the Revolutionary War; her father, a free man, has been killed fighting against the British, her mother has disappeared. Willy makes her danger-fraught way to Fraunces Tavern in New York, her uncle, Jack Arabus, having told her that Mr. Fraunces may be able to help her. She works at the tavern until the war is over, goes to the Arabus home to find her mother dying, and participates in the trial (historically accurate save for the fictional addition of Willy) in which her uncle sues for his freedom and wins." Bull Cent Child Books

Collier, James Lincoln, 1928——_Continued_

Who is Carrie? [by] James Lincoln Collier, Christopher Collier. Delacorte Press 1984 158p hardcover o.p. paperback available $4.99 (6 and up)   **Fic**
   1. United States—History—1783-1809—Fiction 2. Slavery—Fiction 3. African Americans—Fiction
   ISBN 0-440-49536-9 (pa)   LC 83-23947
Companion volume to Jump ship to freedom, and War comes to Willy Freeman

Carrie "is a kitchen slave in Samuel Fraunces Tavern. . . . She keeps in touch with her special friend, Dan Arabus, and he enlists Carrie's help in finding out if the new government will honor the notes with which Dan hopes to purchase his mother's freedom. In so doing, Carrie finds out the truth about herself." Child Book Rev Serv

"This is historical fiction at its best. The Collier's familiar 'How Much of This Book is True' addendum fills readers in on the essentials concerning fictional and factual elements of the plot, as well as the research involved in its composition." SLJ

Collodi, Carlo, 1826-1890
The adventures of Pinocchio (3-6)   **Fic**
   1. Puppets and puppet plays—Fiction 2. Fairy tales

Various editions available including Spanish language edition
An Italian classic for children, written late in the 19th century. Variant title: Pinocchio
"When Geppetto discovered a piece of wood which talked, he carved it into a marionette and named him Pinocchio. Although he is a wooden boy, Pinocchio has a lively and nimble mind and an ardent curiosity which lead to unexpected and extraordinary results. A light-hearted and original fantasy in which children can identify themselves with Pinocchio and grasp the simple and practical morality which underlies the story." Toronto Public Libr. Books for Boys & Girls

Coman, Carolyn
What Jamie saw. Front St. 1995 126p $13.95 (5 and up)   **Fic**
   1. Child abuse—Fiction
   ISBN 1-886910-02-2   LC 95-23545
Also available in paperback from Puffin Bks. and Audiobook version
A Newbery Medal honor book, 1996
Having fled to a family friend's hillside trailer after his mother's boyfriend tried to throw his baby sister against a wall, nine-year-old Jamie finds himself living an existence full of uncertainty and fear
"Shocking in its simple narration and child's-eye view, _What Jamie Saw_ is a bittersweet miracle in understated language and forthright hopefulness." SLJ

Conford, Ellen
Annabel the actress starring in "Gorilla my dreams"; illustrated by Renee Williams-Andriani. Simon & Schuster Bks. for Young Readers 1999 64p il $14; pa $3.99 (2-4)   **Fic**
   1. Actors—Fiction 2. Parties—Fiction
   ISBN 0-689-81404-6; 0-689-83883-2 (pa)
                     LC 97-39449
Though a little disappointed that her first acting part is to be a gorilla at a birthday party, Annabel determines to really get into the role
"The vocabulary is appropriate for those graduating from easy-readers, but the language is never stilted. Amusing pen-and-ink illustrations appear on almost every page." SLJ
Another available title about Annabel is:
Annabel the actress starring in "Just a little extra" (2000)

A case for Jenny Archer; illustrated by Diane Palmisciano. Little, Brown 1988 61p il hardcover o.p. paperback available $4.50 (2-4)   **Fic**
   ISBN 0-316-15352-4 (pa)   LC 88-14169
"A Springboard book"
After reading three mysteries in a row, Jenny becomes convinced that the neighbors across the street are up to no good and decides to investigate
Other available titles about Jenny Archer are:
Can do, Jenny Archer (1991)
Get the picture, Jenny Archer (1994)
Jenny Archer, author (1989)
Jenny Archer to the rescue (1990)
A job for Jenny Archer (1988)
Nibble, nibble, Jenny Archer (1993)
What's cooking, Jenny Archer? (1989)

Conly, Jane Leslie
Crazy lady! HarperCollins Pubs. 1993 180p lib bdg $15.89; pa $5.95 (5 and up)   **Fic**
   1. Prejudices—Fiction 2. Death—Fiction 3. Alcoholics—Fiction 4. Mentally handicapped—Fiction
   ISBN 0-06-021360-4 (lib bdg); 0-06-440571-0 (pa)
                     LC 92-18348
Also available Audiobook version
A Newbery Medal honor book, 1994
"A Laura Geringer book"
As he tries to come to terms with his mother's death, Vernon finds solace in his growing relationship with the neighborhood outcasts, an alcoholic and her retarded son
The narration "is fast and blunt, and the conversations are lively and true." Bull Cent Child Books

Racso and the rats of NIMH; illustrations by Leonard Lubin. Harper & Row 1986 278p il $15.95; lib bdg $16.89; pa $4.95 (4 and up)   **Fic**
   1. Mice—Fiction 2. Rats—Fiction
   ISBN 0-06-021361-2; 0-06-021362-0 (lib bdg); 0-06-440245-2 (pa)   LC 85-42634
Sequel to Mrs. Frisby and the rats of NIMH by Robert C. O'Brien
This book "continues the NIMH saga with a focus on the second rodent generation: Timothy, Mrs. Frisby's son, and Racso, son of the rebel rat Jenner. On his way to classes at Thorn Valley, Timothy saves Racso's life

Conly, Jane Leslie—*Continued*

but is himself severely injured. Both reach the Utopian colony only to discover that the valley and surrounding farms are to be turned into a tourist lake and campgrounds." SLJ

"The book is cleverly and gracefully built upon both the philosophy of self-sufficiency and the details of the plot of its predecessor. Given the difficulty of writing good sequels, *Racso and the Rats of NIMH* is an outstanding success." Horn Book

Another available title about the rats of NIMH is:
RT, Margaret, and the rats of NIMH (1990)

While no one was watching. Holt & Co. 1998 233p $16.95 (5 and up)   **Fic**
1. Poverty—Fiction
ISBN 0-8050-3934-1   LC 97-48718
Also available in paperback from HarperCollins and Audiobook version

This "story is told from the point of view of five characters: siblings Earl, Frankie, and Angela (on their own after their aunt disappears on a drinking binge) and, from a very different part of the city, Maynard and Addie (whose pet rabbit has been stolen by affection-starved, seven-year-old Frankie). Conly writes convincingly and unsentimentally about the working class poor in an urban setting." Horn Book Guide

Conrad, Pam, 1947-1996

My Daniel. Harper & Row 1989 137p lib bdg $15.89; pa $4.95 (5 and up)   **Fic**
1. Nebraska—Fiction
ISBN 0-06-021314-0 (lib bdg); 0-06-440309-2 (pa)
LC 88-19850
"When she's 80 years old, Julia Summerwaithe decides to visit her grandchildren, Ellie and Stevie, in New York City, for the first time. She has something important to show them; in the Natural History Museum is the dinosaur she and her brother discovered on their farm in Nebraska when they were young. But even more important to Julia than seeing the dinosaur is sharing her memories of the discovery and excavation with her grandchildren." SLJ

"Rendering scenes from both the past and the present with equal skill, Conrad is at the peak of her storytelling powers." Publ Wkly

Prairie songs; illustrations by Darryl S. Zudeck. Harper & Row 1985 167p il lib bdg $15.89; pa $4.95 (5 and up)   **Fic**
1. Frontier and pioneer life—Fiction 2. Nebraska—Fiction
ISBN 0-06-021337-X (lib bdg); 0-06-440206-1 (pa)
LC 85-42633
"The deterioration of the frail, young wife of a doctor who is unable to adapt to the harshness of prairie life is made more vivid because the reader views it through the eyes of an adolescent girl who lives nearby. Set in Nebraska at the turn of the century, this story is rich with detail about the beauty and hardships of pioneer life in the American West." Soc Educ

Stonewords; a ghost story. Harper & Row 1990 130p hardcover o.p. paperback available $4.95 (5 and up)   **Fic**
1. Ghost stories 2. Space and time—Fiction
ISBN 0-06-440354-8 (pa)   LC 89-36382

Zoe discovers that her house is occupied by the ghost of an eleven-year-old girl, who carries her back to the day of her death in 1870 to try to alter that tragic event

"The supernatural and time-travel elements of the book are viscerally convincing, and the desperate neediness of both girls is fierce and real. The disquieting ending is in the richest gothic tradition, resolving one mystery only to reveal another even more frightening. This is a very scary book." Bull Cent Child Books

Zoe rising. HarperCollins Pubs. 1996 131p hardcover o.p. paperback available $4.95 (5 and up)   **Fic**
1. Space and time—Fiction 2. Mother-daughter relationship—Fiction
ISBN 0-06-440687-3 (pa)   LC 95-42663
Companion volume to Stonewords
"A Laura Geringer book"

Zoe, traveling back to the time when her mother was a child, intervenes in the past in order to save the future

"The writing is splendidly atmospheric, with Conrad beautifully guiding readers through Zoe's misty corporeal changes and into a riveting, terrifying climax." Booklist

Cooper, Susan, 1935-

The Boggart. Margaret K. McElderry Bks. 1993 196p $15; pa $4.99 (4-6)   **Fic**
1. Supernatural—Fiction 2. Scotland—Fiction 3. Canada—Fiction
ISBN 0-689-50576-0; 0-689-80173-4 (pa)
LC 92-15527
After visiting the castle in Scotland which her family has inherited and returning home to Canada, twelve-year-old Emily finds that she has accidentally brought back with her a boggart, an invisible and mischievous spirit with a fondness for practical jokes

"Using both electronics and theater as metaphors for magic, Cooper has extended the world of high fantasy into contemporary children's lives through scenes superimposing the ordinary and the extraordinary." Bull Cent Child Books

Another available title about the Boggart is:
The Boggart and the monster (1997)

Dawn of fear; illustrated by Margery Gill. Harcourt Brace Jovanovich 1970 157p il o.p.; Aladdin Bks. (NY) paperback available $4.99 (5 and up)   **Fic**
1. Great Britain—Fiction 2. World War, 1939-1945—Fiction
ISBN 0-689-71327-4 (pa)
During World War II, three English boys' fearless unconcern with the enemy planes that flew daily on their way to bomb London, gradually underwent a change as the night raids grew more severe. This is the story of how, through the destruction—not by bombs—of the secret camp they were building, the boys came face-to-face with grown-up hatred, and then they knew the meaning of fear

"The characterization [is] deft and the dialogue natural, [and] the relationship between the boys and a young man who is about to enter the Merchant Navy [is] particularly perceptive." Sutherland. The Best in Child Books

Cooper, Susan, 1935——_Continued_

The grey king; illustrated by Michael Heslop. Atheneum Pubs. 1975 208p il $17; pa $4.99 (5 and up)   **Fic**
1. Good and evil—Fiction 2. Fantasy fiction 3. Wales—Fiction
ISBN 0-689-50029-7; 0-689-82984-1 (pa)
Awarded the Newbery Medal, 1976
"A Margaret K. McElderry book"
"In the fourth of Cooper's Arthurian fantasies, Will Stanton, last and youngest of the Old Ones, the strange Welsh boy, Bran, and the sheep dogs and ghostly gray foxes of the mountains are drawn into the epic struggles of a world beyond time." SLJ
"So well-crafted that it stands as an entity in itself, the novel . . . is nevertheless strengthened by its relationship to the preceding volumes—as the individual legends within the Arthurian cycles take on deeper significance in the context of the whole. A spellbinding tour de force." Horn Book

King of shadows. Margaret K. McElderry Bks. 1999 186p $16 (5 and up)   **Fic**
1. Shakespeare, William, 1564-1616—Fiction 2. Actors—Fiction
ISBN 0-689-82817-9   LC 98-51127
Also available Audiobook version
While in London as part of an all-boy acting company preparing to perform in a replica of the famous Globe Theatre, Nat Field suddenly finds himself transported back to 1599 and performing in the original theater under the tutelage of Shakespeare himself
"Cleverly explicating old and new acting and performance techniques, Susan Cooper entertains her contemporary readers while giving them a first-rate theatrical education." N Y Times Book Rev

Over sea, under stone; illustrated by Margery Gill. Harcourt Brace Jovanovich 1966 c1965 252p il $17 (5 and up)   **Fic**
1. Fantasy fiction 2. Good and evil—Fiction 3. Great Britain—Fiction
ISBN 0-15-259034-X
Also available in paperback from Macmillan
First published 1965 in the United Kingdom
In this series about the "conflict between the good of the Servants of Light and the evil of the Powers of Dark, Cooper has created an intricate fantasy. Ancient lore and mythology are believably interwoven into a modern setting. Ostensibly, the three Drew children, on a holiday in Cornwall, find an old map and, aided by their uncle, they begin a search for an ancient treasure linked with King Arthur. With each book, more reliance is placed on folklore and legend. There is much action and excitement included in the carefully wrought stories." Roman. Sequences
Other available titles in The dark is rising series are:
The dark is rising (1973)
Greenwitch (1974)
The grey king
Silver on the tree (1977)

Seaward. Atheneum Pubs. 1983 167p hardcover o.p. paperback available $4.99 (6 and up)   **Fic**
1. Fantasy fiction
ISBN 0-02-042190-9 (pa)   LC 83-7055

"A Margaret K. McElderry book"
"Fleeing from unhappiness, two young people are cast into a different reality. . . . Cally and West are the two young people. Cally's ancestors may have been seals; West's were probably Shamana. Having nothing better to do, the two set off for the sea, where they expect to find their parents. As they travel, they are hounded by strange creatures. However, they survive and reach the sea where they learn that Life and Death are related by necessity and where they learn to embrace the reality from which they once fled." ALAN
"This metaphysical adventure has appeal for beginning fantasy readers." SLJ

Corbett, Scott, 1913-

The lemonade trick; illustrated by Paul Galdone. Little, Brown 1960 103p il o.p.; Scholastic paperback available $4.50 (3-5)   **Fic**
1. Fantasy fiction
ISBN 0-590-32197-8 (pa)
"An Atlantic Monthly Press book"
A brew from his Feats O'Magic chemistry set, given to him by the mysterious Mrs. Graymalkin, changes Kerby into a perfect gentleman; unfortunately, it has the opposite effect on good boys
"An ingenious bit of magic has been mixed by [the author] and dashingly illustrated . . . to please eight-year-old readers . . . and even some a bit older who like a fairly simple story that doesn't take too long to read." N Y Her Trib Books

Couloumbis, Audrey

Getting near to baby. Putnam 1999 211p $17.99 (5 and up)   **Fic**
1. Sisters—Fiction 2. Death—Fiction 3. Aunts—Fiction
ISBN 0-399-23389-X   LC 99-18191
Also available Thorndike Press large print edition
A Newbery Medal honor book, 2000
Although thirteen-year-old Willa Jo and her Aunt Patty seem to be constantly at odds, staying with her and Uncle Hob helps Willa Jo and her younger sister come to terms with the death of their family's baby
"Couloumbis's writing is strong; she captures wonderfully the Southern voices of her characters and conveys with great depth powerful emotions. . . . A compelling novel." SLJ

Coville, Bruce

Jennifer Murdley's toad; a magic shop book; illustrated by Gary A. Lippincott. Harcourt Brace Jovanovich 1992 156p il $16.95 (4-6)   **Fic**
1. Toads—Fiction 2. Fantasy fiction
ISBN 0-15-200745-8   LC 91-33811
Also available in paperback from Pocket Bks. and Audiobook version
"Jane Yolen books"
When an ordinary looking fifth grader purchases a talking toad, she embarks on a series of extraordinary adventures
"This light, fast-paced fantasy has touches of humor (at times low comedy), an implicit moral, and a hint that Jennifer may be in for more adventures." Booklist

Coville, Bruce—*Continued*

Jeremy Thatcher, dragon hatcher; a magic shop book; illustrated by Gary A. Lippincott. Jane Yolen Bks. 1991 148p il $16.95 (4-6)   **Fic**
1. Dragons—Fiction 2. Fantasy fiction
ISBN 0-15-200748-2   LC 90-5101
Also available in paperback from Pocket Bks. and Audiobook version

Small for his age but artistically talented, twelve-year-old Jeremy Thatcher unknowingly buys a dragon's egg

This is "right on target. Not only is the story involving but the reader can really get a feeling for Jeremy as a person. Coville's technique of combining the real world with a fantasy one works well in this story." Voice Youth Advocates

The skull of truth; a magic shop book; illustrated by Gary A. Lippincott. Harcourt Brace & Co. 1997 195p il $17 (4-6)   **Fic**
1. Truthfulness and falsehood—Fiction 2. Fantasy fiction
ISBN 0-15-275457-1   LC 97-9264
Also available in paperback from Pocket Bks.

Charlie, a sixth-grader with a compulsion to tell lies, acquires a mysterious skull that forces its owner to tell only the truth, causing some awkward moments before he understands its power

"Coville has structured the story very carefully, with a great deal of sensitivity to children's thought processes and emotions. The mood shifts from scary to funny to serious are fused with understandable language and sentence structures." SLJ

Cox, Judy, 1954-

Weird stories from the Lonesome Café; illustrated by Diane Kidd. Harcourt 2000 72p il $15 (2-4)   **Fic**
1. Restaurants—Fiction 2. Uncles—Fiction 3. Nevada—Fiction
ISBN 0-15-202134-5   LC 98-56016
"Browndeer Press"

Sam moves to Nevada with his uncle to run a café in the middle of nowhere, and although Uncle Clem insists that nothing ever happens there, his clientele consists of a number of strange characters, including Dorothy and Toto, Elvis, and Bigfoot

This "will satiate kids with an appetite for shenanigans, and Kidd's black-and-white cartoon art dishes out an extra dollop of fun." Publ Wkly

Creech, Sharon

Absolutely normal chaos. HarperCollins Pubs. 1995 c1990 230p $15.95; lib bdg $15.89; pa $5.95 (5 and up)   **Fic**
1. Family life—Fiction
ISBN 0-06-026989-8; 0-06-026992-8 (lib bdg); 0-06-440632-6 (pa)   LC 95-22448
First published 1990 in the United Kingdom

"Mary Lou Finney's summer journal describes family life in a high-spirited household in Ohio that includes five children." N Y Times Book Rev

"Those in search of a light, humorous read will find it; those in search of something a little deeper will also be rewarded." SLJ

Bloomability. HarperCollins Pubs. 1998 273p $15.95; lib bdg $15.89; pa $5.95 (5 and up)   **Fic**
1. School stories 2. Switzerland—Fiction
ISBN 0-06-026993-6; 0-06-026994-4 (lib bdg); 0-06-440823-X (pa)   LC 98-14601
"Joanna Cotler books"

When her aunt and uncle take her from New Mexico to Lugano, Switzerland, to attend an international school, thirteen-year-old Dinnie discovers her world expanding

"As if fresh, smart characters in a picturesque setting weren't engaging enough, Creech also poses an array of knotty questions, both personal and philosophical. . . . A story to stimulate both head and heart." Booklist

Chasing Redbird. HarperCollins Pubs. 1997 261p $15.95; lib bdg $15.89; pa $5.95 (5 and up)   **Fic**
1. Family life—Fiction 2. Kentucky—Fiction
ISBN 0-06-026987-1; 0-06-026988-X (lib bdg); 0-06-440696-2 (pa)   LC 96-44128
"Joanna Cotler books"

Thirteen-year-old Zinnia Taylor uncovers family secrets and self truths while clearing a mysterious settler trail that begins on her family's farm in Kentucky

"With frequent flashbacks, the narrative makes clear the complexities of the story, while the unsolved puzzles lead the reader on to the end. The writing is laced with figurative language and folksy comments that intensify both atmosphere and emotion." Horn Book Guide

Walk two moons. HarperCollins Pubs. 1994 280p $15.95; lib bdg $15.89; pa $5.95 (6 and up)   **Fic**
1. Death—Fiction 2. Grandparents—Fiction 3. Family life—Fiction 4. Friendship—Fiction
ISBN 0-06-023334-6; 0-06-023337-0 (lib bdg); 0-06-440517-6 (pa)   LC 93-31277
Also available Audiobook version
Awarded the Newbery Medal, 1995

After her mother leaves home suddenly, thirteen-year-old Sal and her grandparents take a car trip retracing her mother's route. Along the way, Sal recounts the story of her friend Phoebe, whose mother also left

"An engaging story of love and loss, told with humor and suspense. . . . A richly layered novel about real and metaphorical journeys." SLJ

The Wanderer; drawings by David Diaz. HarperCollins Pubs. 2000 305p $15.95; lib bdg $15.89 (5 and up)   **Fic**
1. Sailing—Fiction 2. Family life—Fiction 3. Sea stories
ISBN 0-06-027730-0; 0-06-027731-9 (lib bdg)   LC 99-42699
A Newbery Medal honor book, 2001
"Joanna Cotler books"

Thirteen-year-old Sophie and her cousin Cody record their transatlantic crossing aboard the Wanderer, a forty-five foot sailboat, which, along with uncles and another cousin, is en route to visit their grandfather in England

"The story is exciting, funny, and brimming with life. . . . This is a beautifully written and imaginatively constructed novel." SLJ

Cresswell, Helen

Ordinary Jack. Macmillan 1977 195p o.p. (5 and up) **Fic**

1. Family life—Fiction

LC 77-5146

Eleven-year-old Jack, the only "ordinary" member of the talented and eccentric Bagthorpe family, concocts a scheme to distinguish himself as a modern-day prophet

Titles in the series: Absolute zero (1978); Bagthorpes abroad (1984); Bagthorpes haunted (1985); Bagthorpes liberated (1989); Bagthorpes unlimited (1978); Bagthorpes v. the world (1979) o.p.

Cruise, Robin, 1951-

Fiona's private pages. Harcourt 2000 195p $15 (5 and up) **Fic**

1. Diaries—Fiction

ISBN 0-15-202210-4 LC 99-50559

Eleven-year-old Fiona "and her younger brother, Sam, are adjusting to life in two households after their parents' divorce. . . . Her favorite teacher moves away, her parents are both involved in new relationships, and her grandmother develops Alzheimer's. . . . Her biggest challenge, though, is deciding what to do when she discovers that a friend has anorexia." SLJ

"The writing style is energetic and highly believable, with a voice that sounds just like a bright, reasonably sensitive sixth-grade girl." Booklist

Another available title about Fiona is:

The top-secret journal of Fiona Clare Jardin (1998)

Curry, Jane Louise, 1932-

A stolen life. Margaret K. McElderry Bks. 1999 198p $16 (5 and up) **Fic**

1. Scotland—Fiction 2. Virginia—Fiction 3. United States—History—1600-1775, Colonial period—Fiction

ISBN 0-689-82932-9 LC 98-51103

In 1758 in Scotland, teenaged Jamesina MacKenzie finds her courage and resolution severely tested when she is abducted by "spiriters" and, after a harrowing voyage across the Atlantic, sold as a bond slave to a Virginia planter

"This is a solid piece of exciting prerevolutionary historical fiction with a courageous heroine." SLJ

Curtis, Christopher Paul

Bud, not Buddy. Delacorte Press 1999 245p $16.95 (4 and up) **Fic**

1. Orphans—Fiction 2. African Americans—Fiction 3. Great Depression, 1929-1939—Fiction

ISBN 0-385-32306-9 LC 99-10614

Also available Thorndike Press large print edition and Audiobook version

Awarded the Newbery Medal, 2000; Coretta Scott King Award for text, 2000

Ten-year-old Bud, a motherless boy living in Flint, Michigan, during the Great Depression, escapes a bad foster home and sets out in search of the man he believes to be his father—the renowned bandleader, H. E. Calloway of Grand Rapids

"Curtis says in a afterword that some of the characters are based on real people, including his own grandfathers, so it's not surprising that the rich blend of tall tale, slapstick, sorrow, and sweetness has the wry, teasing warmth of family folklore." Booklist

The Watsons go to Birmingham—1963; a novel. Delacorte Press 1995 210p $16.95 (4 and up) **Fic**

1. African Americans—Fiction 2. Family life—Fiction 3. Prejudices—Fiction

ISBN 0-385-32175-9 LC 95-7091

Also available in paperback from Bantam Bks. and Audiobook version

A Newbery Medal honor book, 1996

The ordinary interactions and everyday routines of the Watsons, an African American family living in Flint, Michigan, are drastically changed after they go to visit Grandma in Alabama in the summer of 1963

"Curtis's ability to switch from fun and funky to pinpoint-accurate psychological imagery works unusually well. . . . Ribald humor, sly sibling digs, and a totally believable child's view of the world will make this book an instant hit." SLJ

Cushman, Karen

The ballad of Lucy Whipple. Clarion Bks. 1996 195p $13.95 (5 and up) **Fic**

1. Frontier and pioneer life—Fiction 2. Family life—Fiction 3. California—Gold discoveries—Fiction

ISBN 0-395-72806-1 LC 95-45257

Also available in paperback from HarperCollins

In 1849, twelve-year-old California Morning Whipple, who renames herself Lucy, is distraught when her mother moves the family from Massachusetts to a rough California mining town

"Cushman's heroine is a delightful character, and the historical setting is authentically portrayed." SLJ

Catherine, called Birdy. Clarion Bks. 1994 169p $14.95 (6 and up) **Fic**

1. Middle Ages—Fiction 2. Great Britain—Fiction

ISBN 0-395-68186-3 LC 93-23333

Also available in paperback from HarperCollins and Audiobook version

A Newbery Medal honor book, 1995

The fourteen-year-old daughter of an English country knight keeps a journal in which she records the events of her life, particularly her longing for adventures beyond the usual role of women and her efforts to avoid being married off

"In the process of telling the routines of her young life, Birdy lays before readers a feast of details about medieval England. . . . Superb historical fiction." SLJ

The midwife's apprentice. Clarion Bks. 1995 122p $10.95 (6 and up) **Fic**

1. Middle Ages—Fiction 2. Midwives—Fiction 3. Great Britain—Fiction

ISBN 0-395-69229-6 LC 94-13792

Also available in paperback from HarperCollins and Audiobook version

Awarded the Newbery Medal, 1996

In medieval England, a nameless, homeless girl is taken in by a sharp-tempered midwife, and in spite of obstacles and hardship, eventually gains the three things she most wants: a full belly, a contented heart, and a place in this world

"Earthy humor, the foibles of humans both high and low, and a fascinating mix of superstition and genuinely

Cushman, Karen—*Continued*
helpful herbal remedies attached to childbirth make this
a truly delightful introduction to a world seldom seen in
children's literature." SLJ

Cutler, Jane
Rats! pictures by Tracey Campbell Pearson.
Farrar, Straus & Giroux 1996 114p il $14; pa
$4.95 (3-5)   **Fic**
1. Brothers—Fiction 2. Family life—Fiction
ISBN 0-374-36181-9; 0-374-46203-8 (pa)
                                          LC 95-22953
Fourth-grader Jason and his younger brother Edward
shop for school clothes, get ready for Halloween, acquire
a couple of pet rats, and deal with not-birthday presents
from Aunt Bea
"The brothers, alternately squabbling and supporting
each other, are convincing in this lighthearted episodic
novel." Horn Book Guide
Other available titles about Jason and Edward are:
'Gator aid (1999)
No dogs allowed (1992)

Dahl, Roald
The BFG; pictures by Quentin Blake. Farrar,
Straus & Giroux 1982 219p il $16 (4-6)   **Fic**
1. Giants—Fiction 2. Orphans—Fiction
ISBN 0-374-30469-6   LC 82-15548
Also available in paperback from Penguin Bks.
Kidsnatched from her orphanage by a BFG (Big
Friendly Giant), who spends his life blowing happy
dreams to children, Sophie concocts with him a plan to
save the world from nine other man-gobbling cannybull
giants
This "is a book not all adults will like, but most kids
will. . . . Highly unusual, often hilarious, and occasionally vulgar, even grisly." Booklist

The enormous crocodile; illustrated by Quentin
Blake. Knopf 2000 c1978 unp il $15.95; lib bdg
$16.99 (2-4)   **Fic**
1. Crocodiles—Fiction 2. Animals—Fiction
ISBN 0-375-81046-3; 0-375-91046-8 (lib bdg)
Also available in paperback from Puffin Bks.
A reissue of the title first published 1978
"'For my lunch today,' says the crocodile, 'I would
like a nice juicy little child.' To this end, he sets off
from the muddy river to go to town. On his way he
meets Humpy Rumpy the hippo, Trunky the elephant,
Muggle-Wump the monkey, and the Roly-Poly bird, all
of whom are horrified by his quest. Each in turn manages to foil one of his attempts on unsuspecting children." SLJ
"Mr. Dahl's gift for sonorous and inventive language
carries the story along merrily . . . and Quentin Blake's
squidgy jungle and scaly villain, colorful crowds and
righteous elephant couldn't be improved upon." N Y
Times Book Rev

James and the giant peach; a children's story;
illustrated by Lane Smith. Knopf 1996 126p il
$16; lib bdg $17.99 (4-6)   **Fic**
1. Fantasy fiction
ISBN 0-679-88090-9; 0-679-98090-3 (lib bdg)
                                          LC 91-33489

Also available in paperback from Penguin Bks.; Spanish language edition also available; Audiobook version
also available
A newly illustrated edition of the title first published
1961
After the death of his parents, little James is forced to
live with Aunt Sponge and Aunt Spike, two cruel old
harpies. A magic potion causes the growing of a giant-
sized peach on a puny peach tree. James sneaks inside
the peach and finds a new world of insects. With his
new family, James heads for many adventures
"A 'juicy' fantasy, 'dripping' with humor and imagination." Commonweal

The magic finger; illustrated by Quentin Blake.
Viking 1995 62p il $16.99; pa $4.99 (2-4)   **Fic**
1. Hunting—Fiction 2. Magic—Fiction
ISBN 0-670-85252-X; 0-14-130229-1 (pa)
                                          LC 92-31443
A newly illustrated edition of the title first published
1966 by Harper & Row
Angered by a neighboring family's sport hunting, an
eight-year-old girl turns her magic finger on them
This is an "original and intriguing fantasy." Booklist

Matilda; illustrations by Quentin Blake. Viking
Kestrel 1988 240p il $15.99; pa $5.99 (4-6)   **Fic**
1. School stories
ISBN 0-670-82439-9; 0-14-034294-X (pa)
                                          LC 88-40312
Also available Spanish language edition and
Audiobook version
"Matilda knows how to be extremely and creatively
naughty—lining her father's hat with super glue, putting
her mother's hair bleach in her father's hair tonic bottle,
for example. This streak of imaginative wickedness not
only allows her to make a loyal friend, Lavender, but
also to wreak revenge on her unloving parents, defeat the
fiendish headmistress, Miss Turnbull, and return her victimized teacher, the enchanting Miss Honey, to her rightful place in the world." N Y Times Book Rev
"Dahl has written another fun and funny book with a
child's perspective on an adult world. As usual, Blake's
comical sketches are the perfect complement to the satirical humor." SLJ

Dalgliesh, Alice, 1893-1979
The bears on Hemlock Mountain; illustrated by
Helen Sewell. Scribner c1952 unp il hardcover o.p.
paperback available $4.99 (1-4)   **Fic**
1. Bears—Fiction
ISBN 0-689-71604-4 (pa)
Also available Audiobook version
A Newbery Medal honor book, 1953
"This is the story of a little boy sent by his mother to
borrow an iron from an aunt who lived on the other side
of Hemlock Mountain—really only a hill. Jonathan's
mother did not believe that there were bears on Hemlock
Mountain but Jonathan did. . . . The two-color, some-
what stylized illustrations seem right for the story."
Booklist
"Jonathan's adventure is a tall tale passed down in
Pennsylvania, which might have happened to a pioneer
boy almost anywhere. Full of suspense and humor, it will
make good reading aloud." N Y Her Trib Books

Dalgliesh, Alice, 1893-1979—*Continued*
The courage of Sarah Noble; illustrations by
Leonard Weisgard. Scribner 1986 c1954 52p il
$15.99 (2-4) **Fic**
1. Frontier and pioneer life—Fiction 2. Native Americans—Fiction 3. Connecticut—Fiction
ISBN 0-684-18830-9 LC 86-26191
A Newbery Medal honor book, 1955
A reissue of the title first published 1954
"Sarah, though only eight, cooked for her father while
he made a new home for the family in the Connecticut
wilderness of 1707. When Mr. Noble returned to Massachusetts for the rest of the family, leaving Sarah with a
friendly Indian, her courage was sorely tested." Hodges.
Books for Elem Sch Libr
"Based on a true incident in Connecticut history—the
founding of New Milford—this story is one to be long
remembered for its beautiful simplicity and dignity.
Leonard Weisgard's pictures add just the right sense of
background." N Y Times Book Rev

Danziger, Paula, 1944-
Amber Brown is not a crayon; illustrated by
Tony Ross. Putnam 1994 80p il $14.99 (2-4)
Fic
1. Friendship—Fiction 2. Moving—Fiction 3. School
stories
ISBN 0-399-22509-9 LC 92-34678
Also available in paperback from Scholastic
The year she is in the third grade is a sad time for
Amber because her best friend Justin is getting ready to
move to a distant state
"Ross's black-and-white sketches throughout add humor and keep the pages turning swiftly. Danziger reaches
out to a younger audience in this funny, touching slice
of third-grade life, told in the voice of a feisty, lovable
heroine." SLJ
Other available titles about Amber Brown are:
Amber Brown goes fourth (1995)
Amber Brown is feeling blue (1998)
Amber Brown sees red (1997)
Amber Brown wants extra credit (1996)
Forever Amber Brown (1996)
I, Amber Brown (1999)
You can't eat your chicken pox, Amber Brown (1995)

P.S. Longer letter later; [by] Paula Danziger &
Ann M. Martin. Scholastic 1998 234p $15.95; pa
$4.99 (5 and up) **Fic**
1. Friendship—Fiction 2. Letters—Fiction
ISBN 0-590-21310-5; 0-590-21311-3 (pa)
LC 97-19120
Also available Audiobook version
Companion volume to Snail mail no more
Twelve-year-old best friends Elizabeth and Tara-Starr
continue their friendship through letter-writing after Tara-Starr's family moves to another state
"The authenticity of the well-drawn characters gives
life and vitality to the story. . . . Readers will thoroughly enjoy this fast-paced read." SLJ

Snail mail no more; [by] Paula Danziger & Ann
M. Martin. Scholastic Press 2000 307p $16.95 (5
and up) **Fic**
1. Friendship—Fiction 2. Letters—Fiction
ISBN 0-439-06335-3 LC 99-33593

Also available Audiobook version
Companion volume to P.S. Longer letter later
Now that they live in different cities, thirteen-year-old
Tara and Elizabeth use e-mail to "talk" about everything
that is occurring in their lives and to try to maintain their
closeness as they face big changes
"A funny, thought-provoking page-turner that will delight readers and leave them ready for more messages."
Booklist

De Angeli, Marguerite Lofft, 1889-1987
The door in the wall; by Marguerite de Angeli.
Doubleday 1989 c1949 120p il $16.95 (4-6) **Fic**
1. Physically handicapped children—Fiction 2. Great
Britain—Fiction 3. Middle Ages—Fiction
ISBN 0-385-07283-X
Also available in paperback from Dell and Audiobook
version
Awarded the Newbery Medal, 1950
First published 1949
Robin, a crippled boy in fourteenth-century England,
proves his courage and earns recognition from the King
"An enthralling and inspiring tale of triumph over
handicap. Unusually beautiful illustrations, full of authentic detail, combine with the text to make life in England
during the Middle Ages come alive." N Y Times Book
Rev

Thee, Hannah! written and illustrated by
Marguerite de Angeli. Herald Press 2000 99p il pa
$15.99 (3-5) **Fic**
1. Society of Friends—Fiction 2. Philadelphia (Pa.)—
Fiction
ISBN 0-8361-9106-4 LC 99-52422
A reissue of the title first published 1940 by
Doubleday
Nine-year-old Hannah, a Quaker living in Philadelphia
just before the Civil War, longs to have some fashionable dresses like other girls but comes to appreciate her
heritage and its plain dressing when her family saves the
life of a runaway slave
"Hannah and the other children are very real and, in
addition to the [author's] lovely pictures that follow the
story, the street cries of old Philadelphia are effectively
introduced and illustrated at the beginning of each chapter." Libr J

DeFelice, Cynthia C.
The apprenticeship of Lucas Whitaker; [by]
Cynthia DeFelice. Farrar, Straus & Giroux 1996
151p $15 (4 and up) **Fic**
1. Apprentices—Fiction 2. Orphans—Fiction 3. Physicians—Fiction
ISBN 0-374-34669-0 LC 95-26728
Also available in paperback from Avon Bks.
"Orphaned Lucas Whitaker has lost all his family to
consumption, the scourge of the mid-nineteenth century.
His grief leads him away from the family's marginal hill
farm, and he stumbles into an apprenticeship with Doc
Beecher, a rare college-trained physician. The pace of
this fine piece of historical fiction is brisk in spite of a
wealth of detail that not only establishes the setting but
exposes beliefs and attitudes of the day regarding health,
hygiene, and witchcraft." Horn Book

DeFelice, Cynthia C.—_Continued_

The ghost of Fossil Glen; [by] Cynthia DeFelice. Farrar, Straus & Giroux 1998 167p $16 (4-6) **Fic**
1. Ghost stories
ISBN 0-374-31787-9　　　　　　LC 97-33230
Also available in paperback from Avon Bks. and Thorndike Press large print edition
"Sixth-grader Allie Nichols encounters the ghost of Lucy Stiles and becomes involved with Lucy's unsolved death, eventually finding proof that Lucy was murdered." Horn Book Guide
"A supernatural cliff-hanger with breathless chases and riveting suspense." SLJ

Weasel; [by] Cynthia DeFelice. Macmillan 1990 119p $15 (4 and up) **Fic**
1. Frontier and pioneer life—Fiction 2. Ohio—Fiction
ISBN 0-02-726457-2　　　　　　LC 89-37794
Also available in paperback from Avon Bks.
Alone in the Ohio frontier wilderness in the winter of 1839 while his father is recovering from an injury, eleven-year-old Nathan runs afoul of the renegade killer known as Weasel and makes a surprising discovery about the concept of revenge
"Despite its clear point of view, the book is ideal for discussion and debate—a fine choice as a novel to teach in a literature-based curriculum, where children can be stimulated to think about moral choices and about some of the unhappy truths of frontier settlement." Booklist

DeJong, Meindert, 1906-1991

The house of sixty fathers; pictures by Maurice Sendak. Harper & Row 1956 189p il lib bdg $15.89; pa $5.95 (4-6) **Fic**
1. Sino-Japanese Conflict, 1937-1945—Fiction 2. China—Fiction
ISBN 0-06-021481-3 (lib bdg); 0-06-440200-2 (pa)

A Newbery Medal honor book, 1957
This story is set in "China during the early days of the Japanese invasion. Tien Pao, a small Chinese boy, and his family fled inland on a sampan when the Japanese attacked their coastal village, but Tien Pao was separated from his parents during a storm and swept back down the river on the sampan. . . . [The author paints] starkly realistic word pictures that give the reader the full impact of the terror, pain, hunger and finally the joy that Tien Pao knew during his search for his family." Bull Cent Child Books

The wheel on the school; pictures by Maurice Sendak. Harper & Row 1954 298p il $15.95; lib bdg $15.89; pa $5.95 (4-6) **Fic**
1. Storks—Fiction 2. School stories 3. Netherlands—Fiction
ISBN 0-06-021585-2; 0-06-021586-0 (lib bdg); 0-06-440021-2 (pa)
Also available Spanish language edition
Awarded the Newbery Medal, 1955
"Six Dutch children encouraged by a sensitive schoolmaster search for a wheel to place on the schoolhouse roof as a nesting place for storks. Their efforts and ultimate success lead to better understanding among the children and closer ties to older members of the community." Read Ladders for Hum Relat
"This author goes deeply into the heart of childhood and has written a moving story, filled with suspense and distinguished for the quality of its writing." Child Books Too Good To Miss

Delton, Judy

Angel's mother's wedding; illustrated by Margot Apple. Houghton Mifflin 1987 166p il $16 (3-5) **Fic**
1. Weddings—Fiction 2. Family life—Fiction
ISBN 0-395-44470-5　　　　　　LC 87-16937
"Angel's capacity for worry, added to her friend Edna's knowledge of how a wedding should be properly organized, leads to confusions and misunderstandings that reach almost epic proportions. . . . Humor, affection, and action narrowly skirting disaster mark each chapter in the progress from bridal shower to wedding march. Angel, her family, and friends are all pleasantly ordinary folk with a singular capacity to bring near-chaos into the normally quiet routines and celebrations of their daily life." Horn Book
Other available titles about Angel are:
Angel bites the bullet (2000)
Angel in charge (1985)
Angel spreads her wings (1999)
Angel's mother's baby (1989)
Angel's mother's boyfriend (1986)
Back yard Angel (1983)

Demas, Corinne, 1947-

If ever I return again. HarperCollins Pubs. 2000 197p $15.95; lib bdg $15.89 (5 and up) **Fic**
1. Whaling—Fiction 2. Voyages and travels—Fiction 3. Sea stories 4. Letters—Fiction
ISBN 0-06-028717-9; 0-06-028718-7 (lib bdg)
　　　　　　LC 99-40586
In 1856, twelve-year-old Celia Snow sets sail with her parents on her father's whaling ship and chronicles her subsequent adventures on the more than two-year voyage in a series of letters written to her cousin Abigail
"The girl's fresh, bright perspective is starkly juxtaposed with the harshness of whaling life and a conniving crew. Her effervescent personality . . . makes this a highly accessible work of historical fiction." SLJ

DiCamillo, Kate

Because of Winn-Dixie. Candlewick Press 2000 182p $15.99 (4-6) **Fic**
1. Dogs—Fiction 2. Florida—Fiction
ISBN 0-7636-0776-2　　　　　　LC 99-34260
A Newbery honor book, 2001
Ten-year-old India Opal Buloni describes her first summer in the town of Naomi, Florida, and all the good things that happen to her because of her big ugly dog Winn-Dixie
"This well-crafted, realistic, and heartwarming story will be read and reread as a new favorite deserving a long-term place on library shelves." SLJ

Dickens, Charles, 1812-1870

A Christmas carol (4 and up)   **Fic**
1. Christmas—Fiction 2. Ghost stories 3. Great Britain—Fiction

Some editions are:
Holiday House $18.95 Illustrated by Trina Schart Hyman (ISBN 0-8234-0486-2)
Margaret K. McElderry Bks. $19.95 Illustrated by Quentin Blake (ISBN 0-689-80213-7)
North-South Bks. $19.95 Illustrated by Lisbeth Zwerger (ISBN 0-7358-1259-4)
Written in 1843
In this Christmas story of nineteenth century England "a miser, Scrooge, through a series of dreams, finds the true Christmas spirit. . . . The story ends with the much-quoted cry of Tiny Tim, the crippled son of Bob Cratchit, whom Scrooge now aids: 'God bless us, every one!'" Haydn. Thesaurus of Book Dig
"There is perhaps no story in English literature better known and loved, or one that carries a more potent appeal to the Christmas sentiment." Springfield Repub

Dodge, Mary Mapes, 1830-1905

Hans Brinker; or, The silver skates (4 and up)
Fic
1. Ice skating—Fiction 2. Netherlands—Fiction

Various editions available
First published 1865
A new friend gives Hans and his sister Gretel enough money for one pair of ice skates, so Hans insists that Gretel enter the grand competition for silver skates, while he seeks the great Doctor who consents to try to restore their father's memory

Dorris, Michael

Morning Girl. Hyperion Bks. for Children 1992 74p hardcover o.p. paperback available $4.99 (4-6)
Fic
1. Taino Indians—Fiction 2. America—Exploration—Fiction
ISBN 0-78681-358-X (pa)   LC 92-52989
Also available Spanish language edition
Twelve year old Morning Girl, a Taino Indian who loves the day, and her younger brother Star Boy, who loves the night, take turns describing their life on a Bahamian island in 1492; in Morning Girl's last narrative, she witnesses the arrival of the first Europeans to her world
"The author uses a lyrical, yet easy-to-follow, style to place these compelling characters in historical context. . . . Dorris does a superb job of showing that family dynamics are complicated, regardless of time and place. . . . A touching glimpse into the humanity that connects us all." Horn Book

Sees Behind Trees. Hyperion Bks. for Children 1996 104p $14.95; pa $4.99 (4 and up)   **Fic**
1. Native Americans—Fiction 2. Vision disorders—Fiction
ISBN 0-7868-0224-3; 0-7868-1357-1 (pa)
LC 96-15859

"For the partially sighted Walnut, it is impossible to prove his right to a grown-up name by hitting a target with his bow and arrow. With his highly developed senses, however, he demonstrates that he can do something even better: he can see 'what cannot be seen,' which earns him the name Sees Behind Trees. . . . Set in sixteenth-century America, this richly imagined and gorgeously written rite-of-passage story has the gravity of legend. Moreover, it has buoyant humor and the immediacy of a compelling story that is peopled with multidimensional characters." Booklist

The window. Hyperion 1997 106p lib bdg $17.49; pa $4.99 (4 and up)   **Fic**
1. Family life—Fiction 2. Interracial marriage—Fiction 3. Racially mixed people—Fiction
ISBN 0-7868-2240-6 (lib bdg); 0-7868-1373-3 (pa)
LC 97-2822
When Rayona's Native American mother enters an alcoholic treatment facility, her estranged father, a Black man, finally introduces her to his side of the family, who are not at all what she expected
"Rayona, the heroine of Dorris' adult novels *Yellow Raft in Blue Water and Cloud Chamber*, is eleven years old in this prequel. . . . Rayona is beautifully realized, her emotional complexity combining with her self-awareness and generosity of heart to make her a three-dimensional character that reaches out from the page." Bull Cent Child Books

Dowell, Frances O'Roark

Dovey Coe. Atheneum Bks. for Young Readers 2000 181p $16 (4 and up)   **Fic**
1. Mountain life—Fiction 2. North Carolina—Fiction
ISBN 0-689-83174-9   LC 99-46870
When accused of murder in her North Carolina mountain town in 1928, Dovey Coe, a stronged-willed twelve-year-old girl, comes to a new understanding of others, including her deaf brother
"Dowell has created a memorable character in Dovey, quick-witted and honest to a fault. . . . This is a delightful book, thoughtful and full of substance." Booklist

Draanen, Wendelin van

Sammy Keyes and the hotel thief. Knopf 1998 163p il $15; lib bdg $16.99; pa $4.99 (4-6) **Fic**
1. Mystery fiction
ISBN 0-679-88839-X; 0-679-98839-4 (lib bdg); 0-679-89264-8 (pa)   LC 97-40776
Thirteen-year-old Sammy's penchant for speaking her mind gets her in trouble when she involves herself in the investigation of a robbery at the "seedy" hotel across the street from the seniors' building where she is living with her grandmother
"This is a breezy novel with vivid characters." Bull Cent Child Books
Other available titles about Sammy Keyes are:
Sammy Keyes and the curse of Moustache Mary (2000)
Sammy Keyes and the Hollywood mummy (2001)
Sammy Keyes and the runaway elf (1999)
Sammy Keyes and the Sisters of Mercy (1999)
Sammy Keyes and the skeleton man (1998)

Du Bois, William Pène, 1916-1993

The twenty-one balloons; written and illustrated by William Pène Du Bois. Viking 1947 179p il $16.99; pa $5.99 (5 and up)   Fic

1. Balloons—Fiction
ISBN 0-670-73441-1; 0-14-032097-0 (pa)
Also available Audiobook version
Awarded the Newbery Medal, 1948

"Professor Sherman set off on a flight across the Pacific in a giant balloon, but three weeks later the headlines read 'Professor Sherman in wrong ocean with too many balloons.' This book is concerned with the professor's explanation of this phenomenon. His account of his one stopover on the island of Krakatoa which blew up with barely a minute to spare to allow time for his escape, is the highlight of this hilarious narrative." Ont Libr Rev

Duffey, Betsy

Spotlight on Cody; illustrated by Ellen Thompson. Viking 1998 74p il $14.99; pa $4.99 (2-4)   Fic

1. School stories
ISBN 0-670-88077-9; 0-14-130987-3 (pa)
LC 98-17461

Nine-year-old Cody Michaels is bound for stardom in the third grade talent show just as soon as he figures out his talent

"Truly funny scenes juxtaposed with Cody's distress at his situation and lively pacing combine to make this a very appealing chapter book." Booklist

Other available titles about Cody are:
Cody unplugged (1999)
Cody's secret admirer (1998)
Hey, new kid! (1996)
Virtual Cody (1997)

Durbin, William, 1951-

The journal of Sean Sullivan; a Transcontinental Railroad worker. Scholastic 1999 188p il (My name is America) $10.95 (5 and up)   Fic

1. West (U.S.)—Fiction 2. Railroads—Fiction
ISBN 0-439-04994-6   LC 98-47705

In 1867, fifteen-year-old Sean experiences both hardships and rewards when he joins his father in working on the building of the Transcontinental Railroad

This "focuses on historic details to bring the Old West vibrantly alive. . . . Durbin expertly handles racial issues and also does a good job of being authentic to the time and place, yet sensitive to modern sensibilities." Booklist

Durrant, Lynda, 1956-

The beaded moccasins; the story of Mary Campbell. Clarion Bks. 1998 183p $15 (5 and up)   Fic

1. Campbell, Mary, fl. 1764—Fiction 2. Delaware Indians—Fiction
ISBN 0-395-85398-2   LC 97-16288
Also available in paperback from Dell

After being captured by a group of Delaware Indians and given to their leader as a replacement for his dead granddaughter, twelve-year-old Mary Campbell is forced to travel west with them to Ohio

"Based on a 1759 historical incident. . . . Thoughtful characterizations, a strong sense of place, and an involving present tense narration make this a solid historical novel." Horn Book Guide

Eager, Edward, 1911-1964

Half magic; illustrated by N.M. Bodecker. Harcourt Brace & Co. 1999 192p il $17; pa $6 (4-6)   Fic

1. Fantasy fiction
ISBN 0-15-202069-1; 0-15-202068-3 (pa)
LC 99-24558

Also available Audiobook version
"An Odyssey/Harcourt Brace young classic"
A reissue of the title first published 1954

Faced with a dull summer in the city, Jane, Mark, Katharine, and Martha suddenly find themselves involved in a series of extraordinary adventures after Jane discovers an ordinary-looking coin that seems to grant wishes

"Entertaining and suspenseful fare for readers of make-believe." Booklist

Other available titles in this series are:
Knight's castle (1956)
Magic by the lake (1957)
The time garden (1958)

Magic or not? illustrated by N. M. Bodecker. Harcourt Brace & Co. 1999 197p il $17; pa $6 (4-6)   Fic

1. Fantasy fiction
ISBN 0-15-202081-0; 0-15-202080-2 (pa)
LC 99-22566

"An Odyssey/Harcourt Brace young classic"
A reissue of the title first published 1959

When the family moves to Connecticut, twins James and Laura make new friends and begin a series of unusual adventures after discovering an old well that seems to be magic in their backyard

"The children are lifelike and likable, their doings are entertaining." Booklist

Another available title in this series is:
The well-wishers (1960)

Seven-day magic; illustrated by N.M. Bodecker. Harcourt Brace & Co. 1999 190p il $17; pa $6 (4-6)   Fic

1. Fantasy fiction
ISBN 0-15-202079-9; 0-15-202078-0 (pa)
LC 99-22563

A reissue of the title first published 1962

"Five children find a magic book that describes themselves, and realize that they can create their own magic by wishing with the book. . . . The children are lively and a bit precocious. . . . [The book has] humor, and some fresh and imaginative situations." Bull Cent Child Books

Eckert, Allan W., 1931-

Incident at Hawk's Hill; with illustrations by John Schoenherr. Little, Brown 1998 173p il $15.95; pa $5.95 (6 and up)   Fic

1. Badgers—Fiction 2. Wilderness survival—Fiction 3. Saskatchewan—Fiction
ISBN 0-316-21905-3; 0-316-20948-1 (pa)

Eckert, Allan W., 1931-—_Continued_

A Newbery Medal honor book, 1972

First published 1971

This account of an actual incident in Saskatchewan at the turn of the century tells of six-year-old Ben Macdonald, more attuned to animals than to people, who gets lost on the prairie and is nurtured by a female badger for two months before being found. Although a strange bond continues between the boy and the badger, the parents' understanding of their son and his communication with them improve as a result of the bizarre experience

"A very deeply moving, well written book." Jr Bookshelf

Followed by Return to Hawk's Hill (1998)

Ellis, Sarah, 1952-

Next-door neighbors. Margaret K. McElderry Bks. 1990 154p $16 (4 and up)   **Fic**

1. Friendship—Fiction 2. Family life—Fiction 3. Canada—Fiction

ISBN 0-689-50495-0   LC 89-37923

Her family's move to a new town in Canada leaves shy twelve-year-old Peggy feeling lonely and uncomfortable, until she befriends the unconventional George and the Chinese servant of her imperious neighbor Mrs. Manning

"The theme of prejudicial scapegoating is confidently woven into an essentially optimistic school-and-family story, with neither characterization nor plot succumbing to didacticism." Bull Cent Child Books

English, Karen

Francie. Farrar, Straus & Giroux 1999 199p $16 (5 and up)   **Fic**

1. African Americans—Fiction 2. Race relations—Fiction 3. Alabama—Fiction

ISBN 0-374-32456-5   LC 98-53047

Coretta Scott King honor book for text, 2000

"The best student in her small, all-black school in preintegration Alabama, 12-year-old Francie hopes for a better life. . . . When Jessie, an older school friend who is without family, is forced on the run by a racist employer, Francie leaves her mother's labeled canned food for him in the woods. Only when the sheriff begins searching their woods . . . does she realize the depth of the danger she may have brought to her family. Francie's smooth-flowing, well-paced narration is gently assisted by just the right touch of the vernacular. Characterization is evenhanded and believable, while place and time envelop readers." SLJ

Enright, Elizabeth, 1909-1968

Gone-Away Lake; illustrated by Beth and Joe Krush. Harcourt 2000 c1957 256p il $17; pa $6 (4-6)   **Fic**

ISBN 0-15-202274-0; 0-15-202272-4 (pa)

       LC 99-55281

A Newbery Medal honor book, 1958

"An Odyssey/Harcourt young classic"

A reissue of the title first published 1957

Portia and her cousin Julian discover adventure in a hidden colony of forgotten summer houses on the shores of a swampy lake

"Excellent writing, clear in setting of scene and details of nature, and strong in appeal for children." Horn Book

Another available title about Gone-Away Lake is:
Return to Gone-Away Lake (1961)

Erdrich, Louise

The birchbark house. Hyperion Bks. for Children 1999 244p il $17.99; lib bdg $18.49 (4 and up)   **Fic**

1. Ojibwa Indians—Fiction

ISBN 0-7868-0300-2; 0-7868-2241-4 (lib bdg)

       LC 98-46366

Also available Thorndike Press large print edition

Omakayas, a seven-year-old Native American girl of the Ojibwa tribe, lives through the joys of summer and the perils of winter on an island in Lake Superior in 1847

"Erdrich crafts images of tender beauty while weaving Ojibwa words seamlessly into the text. Her gentle spot art throughout complements this first of several projected stories that will 'attempt to retrace [her] own family's history.'" Horn Book Guide

Estes, Eleanor, 1906-1988

Ginger Pye; with illustrations by the author. Harcourt 2000 306p il $17; pa $6 (4-6)   **Fic**

1. Dogs—Fiction

ISBN 0-15-202499-9; 0-15-202505-7 (pa)

       LC 00-26700

Awarded the Newbery Medal, 1952

"An Odyssey/Harcourt young classic"

A reissue of the title first published 1951

The disappearance of a new puppy named Ginger and the appearance of a mysterious man in a mustard yellow hat bring excitement into the lives of the Pye children

Estes' drawings are "vivid, amusing sketches that point up and confirm the atmosphere of the story. It is a book to read and reread." Saturday Rev

Another available title about the Pye family is:
Pinky Pye (1958)

The hundred dresses; illustrated by Louis Slobodkin. Harcourt Brace & Co. 1944 80p il $16; pa $6 (4-6)   **Fic**

ISBN 0-15-237374-8; 0-15-642350-2 (pa)

A Newbery Medal honor book, 1945

"The 100 dresses are just dream dresses, pictures Wanda Petronski has drawn, but she describes them in self-defense as she appears daily in the same faded blue dress. Not until Wanda, snubbed and unhappy, moves away leaving her pictures at school for an art contest, do her classmates realize their cruelty." Books for Deaf Child

"Written with great simplicity it reveals, in a measure, the pathos of human relationships and the suffering of those who are different. Mr. Slobodkin's water-colors interpret the mood of the story and fulfill the quality of the text." N Y Public Libr

The Moffats; illustrated by Louis Slobodkin. Harcourt 2001 290p il $17; pa $6 (4-6)   **Fic**

1. Family life—Fiction

ISBN 0-15-202535-9; 0-15-202541-3 (pa)

       LC 00-39726

A reissue of the title first published 1941

Estes, Eleanor, 1906-1988—*Continued*

Relates the adventures and misadventures of the four Moffat children living with their widowed mother in a yellow house on New Dollar Street in the small town of Cranbury, Connecticut

"A captivating family story with highly individual characters. Each chapter is a separate episode, suitable for reading aloud." Hodges. Books for Elem Sch Libr

Other available titles about the Moffats are:

The middle Moffat (1942)
The Moffat Museum (1983)
Rufus M. (1943)

The witch family; illustrated by Edward Ardizzone. Harcourt 2000 223p il $17; pa $6 (4-6)   **Fic**

1. Witches—Fiction

ISBN 0-15-202604-5; 0-15-202610-X (pa)

LC 99-89152

"An Odyssey/Harcourt young classic"

A reissue of the title first published 1960

"The Old Witch, the Little Witch Girl and Witch Baby are all the creations of crayons wielded by Amy and Clarissa. . . . As their imaginations run riot, the witches take on an independent life of their own, and the two groups mix and mingle." Libr J

"A very special book that is certain to give boundless pleasure." Horn Book

Etchemendy, Nancy, 1952-

The power of Un. Front St./Cricket Bks. 2000 148p $14.95 (4 and up)   **Fic**

1. Fantasy fiction

ISBN 0-8126-2850-0   LC 99-58281

When he is given a device that will allow him to "undo" what has happened in the past, Gib Finney is not sure what event from the worst day in his life he should change in order to keep his sister from being hit by a truck

The author has a "knack for writing hilarious dialogue that perfectly paints the funny, poignant, and altogether unpredictable world of eleven and twelve year olds. . . . A unique, thought-provoking book." Voice Youth Advocates

Evans, Douglas, 1953-

The elevator family. Delacorte Press 2000 87p $14.95 (3-5)   **Fic**

1. Hotels and motels—Fiction 2. San Francisco (Calif.)—Fiction

ISBN 0-385-32723-4   LC 99-49610

The four members of the Wilson family decide to spend their holiday in one of the elevators at the San Francisco Hotel

"Evans' lighthearted story is just the sort of realistic fantasy that will appeal to beginning chapter-book readers." Booklist

Farley, Walter, 1915-1989

The Black Stallion; illustrated by Domenick D'Andrea; with a new foreword. Golden anniversary ed. Random House 1991 196p il $17; pa $5.50 (4 and up)   **Fic**

1. Horses—Fiction

ISBN 0-679-81349-7; 0-679-81343-8 (pa)

LC 90-53670

A newly illustrated edition of the title first published 1941

Young Alec Ramsay is shipwrecked on a desert island with a horse destined to play an important part in his life. Following their rescue their adventure continues in America

This story "continues to please. Each energetic black-and-white pencil drawing done by D'Andrea . . . shows the glossy Black in action." Horn Book Guide

Other available titles about the Black Stallion are:

The Black Stallion and Flame (1960)
The Black Stallion returns (1945)
The Black Stallion's ghost (1969)
Son of the Black Stallion (1947)
The young Black Stallion (1989)

Farmer, Nancy, 1941-

The Ear, the Eye, and the Arm; a novel. Orchard Bks. 1994 311p $18.95; lib bdg $19.99 (6 and up)   **Fic**

1. Science fiction 2. Zimbabwe—Fiction

ISBN 0-531-06829-3; 0-531-08679-8 (lib bdg)

LC 93-11814

Also available in paperback from Puffin Bks.

A Newbery Medal honor book, 1995

"A Richard Jackson book"

In 2194 in Zimbabwe, General Matsika's three children Tendai, Rita, and Kuda, are kidnapped and put to work in a plastic mine, while three mutant detectives named The Ear, the Eye and the Arm use their special powers to search for them

"Throughout the story, it's the thrilling adventure that will grab readers, who will also like the comic, tender characterizations." Booklist

A girl named Disaster. Orchard Bks. 1996 309p $19.95; lib bdg $20.99 (6 and up)   **Fic**

1. Supernatural—Fiction 2. Adventure fiction 3. Mozambique—Fiction 4. Zimbabwe—Fiction

ISBN 0-531-09539-8; 0-531-08889-8 (lib bdg)

LC 96-15141

Also available in paperback from Penguin Bks. and Audiobook version

A Newbery Medal honor book, 1997

"A Richard Jackson book"

While journeying from Mozambique to Zimbabwe to escape an arranged marriage, eleven-year-old Nhamo struggles to escape drowning and starvation and in so doing comes close to the luminous world of the African spirits

"This story is humorous and heartwrenching, complex and multilayered." SLJ

Feiffer, Jules

The man in the ceiling; entirely written and illustrated by Jules Feiffer. HarperCollins Pubs. 1993 185p il $15; pa $6.95 (4-6) **Fic**

1. Artists—Fiction

ISBN 0-06-205035-4; 0-06-205907-6 (pa)

LC 92-59953

"Michael di Capua books"

"With his quest to invent the best-ever superhero, 10-year-old cartoonist Jimmy Jiggett bids for immortality—or at least some attention from his type-A father." Publ Wkly

"Feiffer's deft depiction of moments of family dysfunction are wickedly funny. His rough-drawn, signature cartoon illustrations are charged with an energy that matches the briskly paced text." Booklist

Fenner, Carol

The king of dragons. Margaret K. McElderry Bks. 1998 216p $17; pa $4.99 (5 and up) **Fic**

1. Homeless persons—Fiction

ISBN 0-689-82217-0; 0-689-83540-X (pa)

LC 98-15434

Also available Audiobook version

Having lost access to the old railroad station where they had been staying, homeless Ian and his father move into an unused city courthouse and try to avoid being discovered by the authorities

"The characters are sharply etched, and the narrative moves swiftly, with moments of poignancy and suspense." Horn Book Guide

Yolonda's genius. Margaret K. McElderry Bks. 1995 211p hardcover o.p. paperback available $5.99 (4-6) **Fic**

1. Siblings—Fiction 2. Musicians—Fiction 3. African Americans—Fiction

ISBN 0-689-81327-9 (pa)

LC 94-46962

Also available Audiobook version

A Newbery Medal honor book, 1996

After moving from Chicago to Grand River, Michigan, fifth grader Yolonda, big and strong for her age, determines to prove that her younger brother is not a slow learner but a true musical genius

"In this brisk and appealing narrative, readers are introduced to a close-knit, middle-class African-American family. . . . [This novel] is suffused with humor and spirit." Horn Book

Field, Rachel, 1894-1942

Hitty: her first hundred years; with illustrations by Dorothy P. Lathrop. Macmillan 1929 207p il $17; pa $5.50 (4 and up) **Fic**

1. Dolls—Fiction

ISBN 0-02-734840-7; 0-689-82284-7 (pa)

Awarded the Newbery Medal, 1930

"Hitty, a doll of real character carved from a block of mountain ash, writes a story of her eventful life from the security of an antique-shop window which she shares with Theobold, a rather over-bearing cat. . . . The illustrations by Dorothy P. Lathrop are the happiest extension of the text." Cleveland Public Libr

Fine, Anne

Bad dreams. Delacorte Press 2000 133p $15.95 (4-6) **Fic**

1. Books and reading—Fiction 2. Friendship—Fiction 3. Magic—Fiction 4. School stories

ISBN 0-385-32757-9

LC 99-47788

Despite her preference for books over friends, Melanie gradually becomes involved with a new classmate and determined to find the reason for her strange behavior

This "will hook readers until the last page. . . . A subtle and absorbing tale." Publ Wkly

Flour babies. Little, Brown 1994 c1992 178p o.p.; Dell paperback available $4.50 (6 and up) **Fic**

1. School stories

ISBN 0-440-21941-8 (pa)

LC 93-35698

First published 1992 in the United Kingdom

When his class of underachievers is assigned to spend three torturous weeks taking care of their own "babies" in the form of bags of flour, Simon makes amazing discoveries about himself while coming to terms with his long-absent father

"There's no mistaking Fine's underlying theme (she's not a bit subtle), but it's couched in such splendid, trenchant humor—spiffy one-liners, funny, well-devised characters, and hilarious situations—that the story simply flies along." Booklist

Step by wicked step; a novel. Little, Brown 1996 138p $15.95 (4-6) **Fic**

1. Divorce—Fiction 2. Stepfamilies—Fiction

ISBN 0-316-28345-2

LC 95-43251

Also available in paperback from Bantam Bks.

"Five children, all part of stepfamilies, spend the night in an old mansion as part of a class trip and read a journal they discover, written generations earlier by a boy their age. The diary inspires them to tell their own stories about struggling with change and shifting family conditions. The stories are wise and powerful, together composing an affecting and honest novel." Horn Book Guide

The Tulip touch; a novel. Little, Brown 1997 149p $15.95 (6 and up) **Fic**

1. Friendship—Fiction

ISBN 0-316-28325-8

LC 96-47185

Also available in paperback from Dell and Audiobook version

Natalie, who lives in the large hotel managed by her father, has a dangerous friendship with Tulip, the wildly uncontrollable girl on a neighboring farm

"A provocative, disturbing novel. . . . This deeply felt, convincingly described examination of a complicated relationship leaves many issues properly unresolved. It would be a wonderful springboard for discussions. . . . It is also a very good read." SLJ

Fisher, Dorothy Canfield, 1879-1958

Understood Betsy; with new illustrations by Kimberly Bulcken Root. Holt & Co. 1999 229p il $17.95 (4-6) **Fic**

1. Farm life—Fiction 2. Vermont—Fiction

ISBN 0-8050-6073-1

LC 99-25265

A newly illustrated edition of the title first published 1917

Fisher, Dorothy Canfield, 1879-1958—*Continued*

Timid and small for her age, nine-year-old Elizabeth Ann discovers her own abilities and gains a new perception of the world around her when she goes to live with relatives on a farm in Vermont

"Kimberly Bulcken Root's inviting, unaffected pencil drawings have a cozy feel to them. . . . 'Understood Betsy' is sure to delight a new generation." N Y Times Book Rev

Fitzgerald, John D., 1907-1988

The Great Brain; illustrated by Mercer Mayer. Dial Bks. for Young Readers 1967 175p $6.99 (4 and up) **Fic**

1. Utah—Fiction

ISBN 0-8037-2590-6

Also available in paperback from Dell

"The Great Brain was Tom Dennis ('T.D.') Fitzgerald, age ten, of Adenville, Utah; the time, 1896. . . . This autobiographical yarn is spun by his brother John Dennis ('J.D.'), age seven . . . who can tell stories about himself and his family with enough tall-tale exaggeration to catch the imagination." Horn Book

Other available titles about the Great Brain are:
The Great Brain at the academy (1972)
The Great Brain does it again (1975)
The Great Brain is back (1995)
The Great Brain reforms (1973)
Me and my little brain (1971)
More adventures of the Great Brain (1969)
The return of the Great Brain (1974)

Fitzhugh, Louise, 1928-1974

Harriet the spy; written and illustrated by Louise Fitzhugh. Harper & Row 1964 298p il $15.95; lib bdg $15.89; pa $5.95 (4 and up) **Fic**

1. School stories

ISBN 0-06-021910-6; 0-06-021911-4 (lib bdg); 0-06-440331-9 (pa)

Also available Audiobook version

"Harriet roams her Manhattan neighborhood spying on everyone who interests her and writing down her opinions in a notebook. When fellow sixth-graders find her notes and read her caustic remarks about them, she is ostracized until she finds a way to make a place for herself in the school." Hodges. Books for Elem Sch Libr

"A very, very funny and a very, very affective story; the characterizations are marvelously shrewd, the pictures of urban life and of the power structure of the sixth grade class are realistic." Bull Cent Child Books

Another available title about Harriet is:
The long secret (1965)

Fleischman, Paul

The borning room. HarperCollins Pubs. 1991 101p hardcover o.p. paperback available $4.95 (6 and up) **Fic**

1. Frontier and pioneer life—Fiction 2. Ohio—Fiction

ISBN 0-06-447099-7 (pa)   LC 91-4432

"A Charlotte Zolotow book"

Lying at the end of her life in the room where she was born in 1851, Georgina remembers what it was like to grow up on the Ohio frontier

"Fleischman successfully tackles many important themes and once again gifts readers with writing lush with similes, metaphors, and allusions, so subtly woven into the mesh of the narrative that they enrich without distracting. A memorable novel, rich and resonant in familial love and the strength of connection and tradition." SLJ

Bull Run; woodcuts by David Frampton. HarperCollins Pubs. 1993 104p il lib bdg $15.89; pa $4.95 (6 and up)   **Fic**

1. Bull Run, 1st Battle of, 1861—Fiction 2. United States—History—1861-1865, Civil War—Fiction

ISBN 0-06-021447-3 (lib bdg); 0-06-440588-5 (pa)

LC 92-14745

Also available Audiobook version

"A Laura Geringer book"

"In a sequence of sixty one- to two-page narratives, fifteen fictional characters (and one real general) recount their experiences during the Civil War. A few encounter each other, most meet unawares or not at all, but they have in common a battle, Bull Run, that affects—and sometimes ends—their lives." Bull Cent Child Books

"Abandoning the conventions of narrative fiction, Fleischman tells a vivid, many-sided story in this original and moving book. An excellent choice for readers' theater in the classroom or on stage." Booklist

The Half-a-Moon Inn; illustrated by Kathy Jacobi. Harper & Row 1980 88p il hardcover o.p. paperback available $4.95 (4-6)   **Fic**

1. Kidnapping—Fiction 2. Physically handicapped children—Fiction 3. Hotels and motels—Fiction

ISBN 0-06-440364-5 (pa)   LC 79-2010

"A mute boy, Aaron, leaves the cottage he shares with his mother to search for her when she is days late returning from market. Lost in a blizzard, he seeks shelter at the Half-A-Moon Inn. Here the evil crone Miss Grackle, who owns the place, forces Aaron to abet her thieving. The boy tries to warn guests against Miss Grackle but none of them can read his hastily written notes. . . . The ending is a terrific twist." Publ Wkly

"Despite the grimness of Aaron's predicament, accentuated by dark scratch drawings of figures in grotesque proportion, the story's tone is hopeful and its style concrete and brisk. Elements of folklore exist in the story's characterization, structure, and narration." SLJ

Lost! a story in string; illustrated by C.B. Mordan. Holt & Co. 2000 unp il $15.95   **Fic**

1. Wilderness survival—Fiction 2. Grandmothers—Fiction 3. String figures—Fiction

ISBN 0-8050-5583-5   LC 99-27997

A grandmother tells a story about a young girl who uses her wits and what is available to her to help her survive when she is lost in the snow. Includes instructions for creating a number of string figures mentioned in the story

"Mordan depicts the unfolding action in elegant ink drawings that have the look of woodcuts. . . . This story celebrates the power of the imagination while providing an interactive opportunity for children to participate." Booklist

Fleischman, Paul—*Continued*

Saturnalia. Harper & Row 1990 113p hardcover
o.p. paperback available $4.95 (6 and up)   **Fic**
1. Narraganset Indians—Fiction 2. Apprentices—Fiction 3. Prejudices—Fiction 4. Boston (Mass.)—Fiction
ISBN 0-06-447089-X (pa)   LC 89-36380

"A Charlotte Zolotow book"

This novel is set in Boston in 1681. Fourteen-year-old
William, a Narraganset Indian captured six years earlier
in a raid, is apprenticed to Mr. Currie, a printer. "William's accomplishments enrage Mr. Baggot, the tithing-
man whose grandsons were killed by Indians. . . . William often wanders the streets after curfew playing an Indian melody on a small bone flute in the hope of finding
his lost brother. One night, the melody does bring him
to an uncle and young cousin, now servants of a cruel
eyeglass maker. When the eyeglass maker is found murdered, . . . [Mr. Baggot] accuses William of the crime."
Horn Book

"While William is the main focus of the story, there
are several bubbling subplots that illuminate the texture
of Puritan colonial life. . . . Especially welcome as a
support for history units, this absorbing story exemplifies
Fleischman's graceful, finely honed use of the English
language." Booklist

Seedfolks; illustrations by Judy Pedersen.
HarperCollins Pubs. 1997 69p $14.95; lib bdg
$14.89; pa $4.95 (4 and up)   **Fic**
1. Gardens—Fiction 2. City and town life—Fiction
ISBN 0-06-027471-9; 0-06-027472-7 (lib bdg);
0-06-447207-8 (pa)   LC 96-26696

"Joanna Cotler books"

This "novel tells about an urban garden started by a
child and nurtured by people of all ages and ethnic and
economic backgrounds. Each of the thirteen chapters is
narrated by a different character, allowing the reader to
watch as a community develops out of disconnected lives
and prior suspicions." Horn Book Guide

"The characters' vitality and the sharply delineated details of the neighborhood make this not merely an exercise in craftsmanship or morality but an engaging, entertaining novel as well." Booklist

Fleischman, Sid, 1920-

The 13th floor; a ghost story; illustrations by
Peter Sís. Greenwillow Bks. 1995 134p il $15
(4-6)   **Fic**
1. Fantasy fiction 2. Pirates—Fiction
ISBN 0-688-14216-8   LC 94-42806

Also available in paperback from Dell

When his older sister disappears, twelve-year-old Buddy Stebbins follows her back in time and finds himself
aboard a seventeenth-century pirate ship captained by a
distant relative

"Liberally laced with dry wit and thoroughly satisfying; . . . readers could hardly ask for more." Publ Wkly

Bandit's moon; illustrations by Jos. A. Smith.
Greenwillow Bks. 1998 136p $15 (4-6)   **Fic**
1. Murieta, Joaquín, d. 1853—Fiction 2. Thieves—
Fiction 3. California—Gold discoveries—Fiction
4. Adventure fiction
ISBN 0-688-15830-7   LC 97-36197

Also available in paperback from Dell

Twelve-year-old Annyrose relates her adventures with
Joaquín Murieta and his band of outlaws in the California gold-mining region during the mid-1800s

"A quick read, with lots of twists, wonderful phrasing,
historical integrity, and a bit of the tall tale thrown in."
SLJ

By the Great Horn Spoon! illustrated by Eric
von Schmidt. Little, Brown 1963 193p il $16.95;
pa $5.95 (4-6)   **Fic**
1. California—Gold discoveries—Fiction
ISBN 0-316-28577-3; 0-316-28612-5 (pa)

"An Atlantic Monthly Press book"

"Jack and his aunt's butler, Praiseworthy, stow away
on a ship bound for California. Here are their adventures
aboard ship and in the Gold Rush of '49." Publ Wkly

Chancy and the grand rascal; illustrated by Eric
von Schmidt. Little, Brown 1966 179p il $15; pa
$4.95 (4-6)   **Fic**
1. Frontier and pioneer life—Fiction
ISBN 0-316-28575-7; 0-316-26012-6 (pa)

"An Atlantic Monthly Press book"

"A young boy sets out to find his brothers and sisters,
separated by the death of their parents in the Civil War,
and meets a 'Grand Rascal' who leads him through many
adventures in the battle of wits and colorful tall-talking."
Bruno. Books for Sch Libr, 1968

"This is one of those rare children's books where language and story are one. It is a world of hyperbole and
homely detail, an ebullient, frontier, Bunyanesque
world." Christ Sci Monit

The ghost on Saturday night; illustrated by
Laura Cornell. Greenwillow Bks. 1997 53p il $15;
pa $4.95 (3-5)   **Fic**
1. Ghost stories 2. West (U.S.)—Fiction 3. Thieves—
Fiction
ISBN 0-688-14919-7; 0-688-14920-0 (pa)
LC 96-43551

A newly illustrated edition of the title first published
1974 by Little, Brown

When Professor Pepper gives Opie tickets to a ghost-
raising instead of a nickel in payment for being guided
through the dense fog, Opie manages to make money
anyway by helping to thwart a bank robbery

"This story is filled with the hyperbole, piquant phrasing, and bravura that make Fleischman's books so much
fun to read." Horn Book Guide

Here comes McBroom! three more tall tales;
illustrated by Quentin Blake. Greenwillow Bks.
1992 79p il hardcover o.p. paperback available
$4.95 (3-5)   **Fic**
1. Farm life—Fiction 2. Tall tales
ISBN 0-688-16364-5   LC 91-32689

Also available in hardcover from P. Smith

The stories were originally published separately by
Grosset and Dunlap

Contents: McBroom the rainmaker (c1973);
McBroom's ghost (c1971); McBroom's zoo (c1972)

The tall tale adventures of a farm family

Fleischman's "humor is still as fresh as ever, and
Quentin Blake's illustrations continue to delight." Booklist

Fleischman, Sid, 1920-—*Continued*

Other available titles about McBroom are:

McBroom tells a lie (1976)

McBroom tells the truth (1981)

McBroom's wonderful one-acre farm: three tall tales (1992)

Jim Ugly; illustrations by Jos. A. Smith. Greenwillow Bks. 1992 130p il $16 (4 and up)

Fic

1. Dogs—Fiction 2. West (U.S.)—Fiction

ISBN 0-688-10886-5   LC 91-14392

Also available in paperback from Dell and Audiobook version

The adventures of twelve-year-old Jake and Jim Ugly, his father's part-mongrel, part-wolf dog, as they travel through the Old West trying to find out what really happened to Jake's actor father

"Fleischman wields his magic pen once again in a fast-moving, picaresque adventure with memorable characters, a well-honed descriptive style—perfectly suited to tone, time, and place—and a sure sense of story." Horn Book

The midnight horse; illustrations by Peter Sis. Greenwillow Bks. 1990 84p il $16 (3-6)   **Fic**

1. Magicians—Fiction 2. Ghost stories 3. Orphans—Fiction

ISBN 0-688-09441-4   LC 89-23441

Also available in paperback from Dell

Touch enlists the help of The Great Chaffalo, a ghostly magician, to thwart his great-uncle's plans to put Touch into the orphan house and swindle The Red Raven Inn away from Miss Sally

"The prose is colorful and earthy. . . . Good and bad are clearly defined, a happy ending is never in doubt, and the reader must accept in good faith the capricious appearances of a deceased but still-practicing magician." Horn Book

Mr. Mysterious & Company; illustrated by Eric von Schmidt. Greenwillow Bks. 1997 153p il $15; pa $4.95 (5 and up)   **Fic**

1. Magic—Fiction 2. Overland journeys to the Pacific—Fiction

ISBN 0-688-14921-9; 0-688-14922-7 (pa)

LC 96-41225

Also available Spanish language edition

A reissue of the title first published 1962 by Little, Brown

Story of a covered wagon family who traveled across the country to California in 1884, giving magic shows to earn their living

"A lighthearted and delightful family story." Booklist

The whipping boy; illustrations by Peter Sis. Greenwillow Bks. 1986 90p il $16.95 (5 and up)

Fic

1. Thieves—Fiction 2. Adventure fiction

ISBN 0-688-06216-4   LC 85-17555

Also available in paperback from Troll and Audiobook version

Awarded the Newbery Medal, 1987

"A round tale of adventure and humor, this follows the fortunes of Prince Roland (better known as Prince

Brat) and his whipping boy, Jemmy, who has received all the hard knocks for the prince's mischief. . . . There's not a moment's lag in pace, and the stock characters, from Hold-Your-Nose Billy to Betsy's dancing bear Petunia, have enough inventive twists to project a lively air to it all." Bull Cent Child Books

Fleming, Ian, 1908-1964

Chitty-Chitty-Bang-Bang; the magical car; illustrated by John Burningham. Random House 1964 111p il hardcover o.p. paperback available $3.99 (4-6)   **Fic**

1. Automobiles—Fiction

ISBN 0-394-81948-9 (pa)

Also available in hardcover from Amereon and Buccaneer Bks.; Spanish language edition also available

"An ingenious nonsense tale about an English family and their remarkable old car. Gifted with the ability to navigate land, sea, and air, Chitty-Chitty-Bang-Bang rescues the family from floods, traffic jams, and gangsters." Hodges. Books for Elem Sch Libr

Fletcher, Ralph, 1953-

Fig pudding. Clarion Bks. 1995 136p $15 (4 and up)   **Fic**

1. Family life—Fiction 2. Death—Fiction

ISBN 0-395-71125-8   LC 94-3654

Also available in paperback from Dell

"Twelve-year-old Cliff, the oldest of six children . . . recalls the past year in episodes focusing on his brothers and his sister. . . . There were good times, but there were also ones he'd like to forget—among them, the death of one brother." Booklist

"Written with humor, perception, and clarity of language, the book resonates with laughter and sorrow." SLJ

Flying solo. Clarion Bks. 1998 138p $15 (5 and up)   **Fic**

1. School stories 2. Death—Fiction

ISBN 0-395-87323-1   LC 98-10775

Also available in paperback from Dell

Rachel, having chosen to be mute following the sudden death of a classmate, shares responsibility with the other sixth-graders who decide not to report that the substitute teacher failed to show up

"Fletcher expertly balances a wide variety of emotions, giving readers a story that is by turns sad, poignant, and funny." Booklist

Fletcher, Susan, 1951-

Shadow spinner. Atheneum Bks. for Young Readers 1998 219p $17; pa $4.99 (6 and up)

Fic

1. Storytelling—Fiction 2. Physically handicapped—Fiction 3. Iran—Fiction

ISBN 0-689-81852-1; 0-689-83051-3 (pa)

LC 97-37346

"A Jean Karl book"

When Marjan, a thirteen-year-old crippled girl, joins the Sultan's harem in ancient Persia, she gathers for Shahrazad the stories which will save the queen's life

"An elegantly written novel that will delight and entertain even as it teaches." SLJ

Forbes, Esther, 1891-1967

Johnny Tremain; illustrated by Michael McCurdy. Houghton Mifflin 1998 293p il $20 (5 and up)   **Fic**

1. Boston (Mass.)—Fiction 2. United States—History—1775-1783, Revolution—Fiction

ISBN 0-395-90011-5   LC 98-228478

Also available in paperback from Dell

Awarded the Newbery Medal, 1944

A newly illustrated edition of the title first published 1943

After injuring his hand, a silversmith's apprentice in Boston becomes a messenger for the Sons of Liberty in the days before the American Revolution

"This sumptuous new gift edition is illustrated with vigorous woodcuts." Horn Book Guide

Fox, Paula

The eagle kite; a novel. Orchard Bks. 1995 127p $15.95; lib bdg $14.99 (6 and up)   **Fic**

1. Homosexuality—Fiction 2. Father-son relationship—Fiction 3. AIDS (Disease)—Fiction 4. Death—Fiction

ISBN 0-531-06892-7; 0-531-08742-5 (lib bdg)
LC 94-26415

"A Richard Jackson book"

Liam's father has AIDS, and his family cannot talk about it until Liam reveals a secret that he has tried to deny ever since he saw his father embracing another man at the beach

"The author's refusal to diminish the tangled emotional issues that underlie her story quietly challenges all preconceptions, and readers cannot help but be deeply affected." Publ Wkly

A likely place; illustrated by Edward Ardizzone. Macmillan 1967 57p il hardcover o.p. paperback available $3.99 (3-5)   **Fic**

1. Babysitters—Fiction

ISBN 0-689-81402-X (pa)

Both at home and at school, nine-year-old "Lewis suffers from the over-solicitude of hovering parents and concerned teachers. The big change comes when his parents go off on a trip, leaving him in the care of Miss Fitchlow, who practices yoga, eats yoghurt, and allows him to go to the park alone." Libr J

"Paula Fox knows how children talk, think and act. Edward Ardizzone's illustrations convey in masterly fashion the oddities of character and situation that bring perplexity, purpose and wonder into an imaginative child's daily life." N Y Times Book Rev

One-eyed cat; a novel. Bradbury Press 1984 216p $14.95 (5 and up)   **Fic**

1. Firearms—Fiction 2. Cats—Fiction

ISBN 0-02-735540-3   LC 84-10964

Also available in paperback from Dell; Spanish language edition also available

A Newbery Medal honor book, 1985

"Told by his father that he's too young for the air rifle an uncle gives him as a birthday present, Ned sneaks the gun out one night and takes a shot at a shadowy creature. He is subsequently smitten with guilt when he sees a one-eyed feral cat, and the knowledge that he may

have been responsible as well as [having disobeyed] his father colors all his days." Bull Cent Child Books

The author's "writing is sure. Her characterization is outstanding, and she creates a strong sense of place and mood." SLJ

The slave dancer; a novel; with illustrations by Eros Keith. Bradbury Press 1973 176p il $16.95 (5 and up)   **Fic**

1. Slave trade—Fiction 2. Sea stories

ISBN 0-02-735560-8   LC 73-80642

Also available in paperback from Dell; Spanish language edition and Audiobook version also available

Awarded the Newbery Medal, 1974

"Thirteen-year-old Jessie Bollier is kidnapped from New Orleans and taken aboard a slave ship. Cruelly tyrannized by the ship's captain, Jessie is made to play his fife for the slaves during the exercise period into which they are forced in order to keep them fit for sale. When a hurricane destroys the ship, Jessie and Ras, a young slave, survive. They are helped by an old black man who finds them, spirits Ras north to freedom, and assists Jessie to return to his family." Shapiro. Fic for Youth. 3d edition

The stone-faced boy; illustrated by Donald A. Mackay. Bradbury Press 1968 106p il hardcover o.p. paperback available $3.95 (4-6)   **Fic**

1. Siblings—Fiction 2. Family life—Fiction

ISBN 0-689-71127-1 (pa)

Also available Spanish language edition

"The story is a perceptive character study of a lonely, timid middle child in a family of five self-possessed, individualistic children. To save himself from teasing by classmates and siblings, Gus Oliver has learned to mask his feelings so well that he has lost all ability to show emotion. Even the startling and unexpected arrival of an eccentric, outspoken great-aunt appears to leave Gus unmoved but the night his sister inveigles him into going out in the dark and the cold to rescue a stray dog, he gains a new-found confidence in himself." Booklist

The village by the sea. Orchard Bks. 1988 147p $16.95 (5 and up)   **Fic**

1. Aunts—Fiction

ISBN 0-531-05788-7   LC 88-60099

Also available in paperback from Dell

"A Richard Jackson book"

"Emma is sent to stay with her fractious aunt and eccentric uncle, where she experiences the devastating effects of envy and the power of love and forgiveness." SLJ

"Although the emotional layering is sophisticated, the viewpoint is unfalteringly that of the child. The novel is easy to read and complex to consider, an encounter that moves the reader from Gothic narrative suspense to compassionate illumination of the dark in human nature." Bull Cent Child Books

Franklin, Kristine L.

Lone wolf. Candlewick Press 1997 220p hardcover o.p. paperback available $4.99 (4 and up)   **Fic**

1. Friendship—Fiction 2. Family life—Fiction

ISBN 0-763-60480-1 (pa)   LC 96-33287

Franklin, Kristine L.—*Continued*

"Perry and his father live in the woods of northern Minnesota, where they moved three years ago after his mother left them. The arrival of a big, warm family next door weakens his resolve to ignore the past and be a loner like his dad." Horn Book Guide

"Strong characters, a plot that works on many levels, and an engaging background make this . . . a standout." SLJ

Freeman, Martha, 1956-

The trouble with cats; illustrated by Cat Bowman Smith. Holiday House 2000 77p il $15.95 (2-4) **Fic**
1. School stories 2. Stepfathers—Fiction 3. Cats—Fiction 4. San Francisco (Calif.)—Fiction
ISBN 0-8234-1479-5   LC 99-29291
After a difficult first week of third grade, Holly begins to adjust to her new school and living in her new stepfather's tiny apartment with his four cats

"Bowman contributes pen-and-ink drawings with lines that quiver with energy. . . . Freeman has a knack for wholesome, undemanding fiction . . . with enough action and humor to carry the plot." Bull Cent Child Books

Freeman, Suzanne T.

The cuckoo's child; by Suzanne Freeman. Greenwillow Bks. 1996 249p $15 (5 and up)
          Fic
ISBN 0-688-14290-7   LC 95-8385
Also available in paperback from Disney Press and Audiobook version

"Mia, who has grown up in Beirut but longs to be a 'normal' American, gets her wish under tragic circumstances when her parents are apparently lost at sea. Transported with disoriented suddenness to live with her aunt in . . . America, Mia struggles to fit into her new world. . . . This novel is emotionally intense and very real." Horn Book Guide

Fritz, Jean

The cabin faced west; illustrated by Feodor Rojankovsky. Coward-McCann; distributed by Putnam Pub. Group 1958 124p il $15.99; pa $5.99 (3-6)   **Fic**
1. Scott, Ann Hamilton—Fiction 2. Frontier and pioneer life—Fiction 3. Pennsylvania—Fiction
ISBN 0-698-20016-0; 0-14-032256-6 (pa)
Also available in paperback from Puffin Bks.

"Ann is unhappy when her family moves from Gettysburg to the Pennsylvania frontier, but she soon finds friends and begins to see that there is much to enjoy about her new home—including a visit from General Washington." Hodges. Books for Elem Sch Libr

Early thunder; illustrated by Lynd Ward. Coward-McCann 1967 255p il o.p.; Puffin Bks. paperback available $5.99 (6 and up) **Fic**
1. United States—History—1600-1775, Colonial period—Fiction 2. Salem (Mass.)—Fiction
ISBN 0-14-032259-0 (pa)

"The political conflict in Salem, Mass., 1774-75, is realized in the agony of David, the 14-year-old son of a Tory doctor, who struggles to determine where his own allegiance lies." Coughlan. Creating Independence, 1763-1789

"The period details and the historical background are excellent, both in themselves and in the easy way they are incorporated into the story." Bull Cent Child Books

George Washington's breakfast; Paul Galdone drew the pictures. Coward-McCann 1969 unp il hardcover o.p. paperback available $5.99 (2-4)
          Fic
1. Washington, George, 1732-1799—Fiction
ISBN 0-698-11611-9 (pa)
Having the same birthday as George Washington, George W. Allen wants everything else in his life just as Washington had it, but he can not find out what Washington ate for breakfast

"Paul Galdone's red, white, and blue illustrations . . . are appropriate to the story and, like it, are not overstated. Younger and reluctant readers may enjoy this." SLJ

Gannett, Ruth Stiles, 1923-

My father's dragon; illustrated by Ruth Chrisman Gannett. Random House 1948 86p il hardcover o.p. paperback available $4.99 (1-4)
          Fic
1. Dragons—Fiction 2. Fantasy fiction 3. Animals—Fiction
ISBN 0-394-89048-5 (pa)
A Newbery Medal honor book, 1949

This is a combination of fantasy, sense, and nonsense. It describes the adventures of a small boy, Elmer Elevator, who befriended an old alley cat and in return heard the story of the captive baby dragon on Wild Island. Right away Elmer decided to free the dragon. The tale of Elmer's voyage to Tangerina and his arrival on Wild Island, his encounters with various wild animals, and his subsequent rescue of the dragon follows

Other available titles in this series are:
The dragons of Blueland (1951)
Elmer and the dragon (1950)

Gantos, Jack

Heads or tails; stories from the sixth grade. Farrar Straus Giroux 1994 151p il $16; pa $4.95 (5 and up)   **Fic**
1. Diaries—Fiction 2. Family life—Fiction 3. School stories
ISBN 0-374-32909-5; 0-374-42923-5 (pa)
          LC 93-43117
"Jack is trying to survive his sixth-grade year, and he narrates, through a series of short-stories-cum-chapters, his difficulties in dodging the obstacles life throws in his path. . . . The writing is zingy and specific, with snappily authentic dialogue and a vivid sense of juvenile experience. . . . Jack and his family have a recognizably thorny relationship. This is a distinctive and lively sequence of everyday-life stories." Bull Cent Child Books

Other available titles about Jack are:
Jack on the tracks (1999)
Jack's black book (1997)
Jack's new power (1995)

Gantos, Jack—*Continued*

Joey Pigza swallowed the key. Farrar, Straus & Giroux 1998 153p $16 (5 and up)   **Fic**

1. Attention deficit disorder—Fiction 2. School stories

ISBN 0-374-33664-4   LC 98-24264

Also available in paperback from HarperCollins and Audiobook version

To the constant disappointment of his mother and his teachers, Joey has trouble paying attention or controlling his mood swings when his prescription meds wear off and he starts getting worked up and acting wired

This "frenetic narrative pulls at heartstrings and tickles funny bones." SLJ

Another available title about Joey Pigza is:
Joey Pigza loses control (2000)

Gardiner, John Reynolds, 1944-

Stone Fox; illustrated by Marcia Sewall. Crowell 1980 81p il $15.95; lib bdg $15.89; pa $4.95 (2-5)   **Fic**

1. Sled dog racing—Fiction 2. Dogs—Fiction

ISBN 0-690-03983-2; 0-690-03984-0 (lib bdg); 0-06-440132-4 (pa)   LC 79-7895

Also available Spanish language edition

"When his usually spry grandfather won't get out of bed Willy searches for a remedy. Back taxes are the problem and the only way to get the money is to win the dogsled race. Stone Fox, a towering Indian who has never lost a race, is primary competition. Both want the prize money for the government—Willy for taxes and Stone Fox to buy his native land back." SLJ

This story "is rooted in a Rocky Mountain legend, a locale faithfully represented in Sewall's wonderful drawings. . . . In Gardiner's bardic chronicle, the tension is teeth rattling, with the tale flying to a conclusion that is almost unbearably moving, one readers won't soon forget." Publ Wkly

Garfield, Leon, 1921-1996

Black Jack. Farrar, Straus & Giroux 2000 197p $18; pa $6.95 (6 and up)   **Fic**

1. Apprentices—Fiction 2. Adventure fiction 3. London (England)—Fiction

ISBN 0-374-30827-6; 0-374-40696-0 (pa)

       LC 99-57836

A reissue of the title first published 1968 in the United Kingdom; first United States edition 1969 by Pantheon

A young apprentice in eighteenth-century London begins a strange adventure when he inadvertently becomes involved with a wanted criminal and a girl who is reputedly mad

"The cast of characters is intriguing and the atmosphere of the times zestfully portrayed." Booklist

Smith. Farrar, Straus & Giroux 2000 195p $18; pa $6.95 (6 and up)   **Fic**

1. Thieves—Fiction 2. Adventure fiction 3. London (England)—Fiction

ISBN 0-374-37082-6; 0-374-46762-5 (pa)

       LC 99-57837

A reissue of the title first published 1967 by Pantheon

Moments after he steals a document from a man's pocket, an illiterate young pickpocket in eighteenth-century London witnesses the man's murder by two men who want the document

"A lusty, flavorsome tale of adventure." Booklist

Gates, Doris, 1901-1987

Blue willow; illustrated by Paul Lantz. Viking 1940 172p il hardcover o.p. paperback available $5.99 (4 and up)   **Fic**

1. Migrant labor—Fiction 2. California—Fiction

ISBN 0-14-030924-1 (pa)

Also available in hardcover from P. Smith and Audiobook version

"Having to move from one migrant camp to another intensifies Janey Larkin's desire for a permanent home, friends, and school. The only beautiful possession the family has is a blue willow plate handed down from generation to generation. It is a reminder of happier days in Texas and represents dreams and promises for a better future. Reading about this itinerant family's ways of life, often filled with despair and yet always hopeful, leaves little room for the reader's indifference." Read Ladders for Hum Relat. 6th edition

Gauch, Patricia Lee

This time, Tempe Wick? [illustrated by] Margot Tomes. Putnam 1992 43p il $15.99 (3-5)   **Fic**

1. United States—History—1775-1783, Revolution—Fiction

ISBN 0-399-21880-7   LC 91-30894

A reissue of the title first published 1974 by Coward, McCann & Geoghegan

Based on a Revolutionary War legend about a real girl, this story tells how Tempe Wick helped feed and clothe the thousands of American soldiers who spent the winters of 1780 and 1781 in Jockey Hollow, New Jersey. When the soldiers mutinied, Tempe had to use her wits and courage to prevent two of them from stealing her horse

"The book presents a realistic and humane view of the war and of the people who fought it. . . . The writing is the perfect vehicle for the illustrations—in the artist's inimitable style—which capture the down-to-earth, unpretentious, and humorous quality of the storytelling." Horn Book

Thunder at Gettysburg; drawings by Stephen Gammell. Putnam 1990 c1975 46p il map $17.95 (3-5)   **Fic**

1. Gettysburg (Pa.), Battle of, 1863—Fiction

ISBN 0-399-22201-4   LC 89-70047

Also available in paperback from Dell

A reissue of the title first published 1975 by Coward, McCann & Geoghegan

Fourteen-year-old Tillie becomes involved in the tragic battle of July 1-3, 1863

"Gauch has drawn on the experiences of a real person, in this case Tillie Pierce Alleman, whose 1889 book 'At Gettysburg' provided the basis of the story. Gammell's thorough pencilled scenes are full of atmosphere and acute emotion, their escalating drama effectively congruent with that of the story." Booklist

Gauthier, Gail, 1953-

A year with Butch and Spike. Putnam 1998 216p $16.99; pa $5.99 (4-6)   **Fic**
1. School stories
ISBN 0-399-23216-8; 0-698-11827-8 (pa)
LC 97-13823

Upon entering the sixth grade, straight-A student Jasper falls under the spell of the dreaded, irrepressible Cootch cousins

"Gauthier demonstrates a real talent here for humorous hyperbole and episodic classroom comedy." Booklist

George, Jean Craighead, 1919-

Frightful's mountain; written and illustrated by Jean Craighead George; with a foreword by Robert F. Kennedy, Jr. Dutton Children's Bks. 1999 258p il $15.99 (5 and up)   **Fic**
1. Falcons—Fiction 2. Wildlife conservation—Fiction 3. New York (State)—Fiction
ISBN 0-525-46166-3   LC 99-32932
Sequel to On the far side of the mountain

The life of Frightful the peregrine falcon "now depends on breaking the imprinting bond she has formed with Sam Gribley and learning to live as a wild bird. . . . The writing is lyrical and the author's obvious love and respect for her subject come through. Frightful's story is filled with excitement and adventure." SLJ

Julie; illustrated by Wendell Minor. HarperCollins Pubs. 1994 226p il $15.95; lib bdg $14.89; pa $4.95 (6 and up)   **Fic**
1. Inuit—Fiction 2. Arctic regions—Fiction 3. Wolves—Fiction
ISBN 0-06-023528-4; 0-06-023529-2 (lib bdg); 0-06-440573-7 (pa)   LC 93-27738

This sequel to Julie of the wolves "details Julie's adjustment to family and modernization after returning home. Her father's musk oxen enterprise depicts the problems inherent to environment-versus-economics issues as Julie struggles to save her wolf friends." Sci Child

Followed by Julie's wolf pack

Julie of the wolves; pictures by John Schoenherr. Harper & Row 1972 170p il $15.95; lib bdg $15.89; pa $5.95 (6 and up)   **Fic**
1. Inuit—Fiction 2. Wolves—Fiction 3. Arctic regions—Fiction 4. Wilderness survival—Fiction
ISBN 0-06-021943-2; 0-06-021944-0 (lib bdg); 0-06-440058-1 (pa)

Also available Spanish language edition and Audiobook version

Awarded the Newbery Medal, 1973

"Lost in the Alaskan wilderness, thirteen-year old Miyax [Julie in English], an Eskimo girl, is gradually accepted by a pack of Arctic wolves that she comes to love." Booklist

"The superb narration includes authentic descriptions and details of the Eskimo way-of-life and of Eskimo rituals. . . . The whole book has a rare, intense reality which the artist enhances beautifully with animated drawings." Horn Book

Followed by Julie

Julie's wolf pack; illustrated by Wendell Minor. HarperCollins Pubs. 1997 192p il $15.95; lib bdg $15.89; pa $5.95 (6 and up)   **Fic**
1. Wolves—Fiction 2. Arctic regions—Fiction
ISBN 0-06-027406-9; 0-06-027407-7 (lib bdg); 0-06-440721-7 (pa)   LC 96-54858

Follows the story begun in Julie of the wolves and continued in Julie

This focuses "primarily on the wolf pack led by Kapu, son of Amaroq, hero of *Julie of the Wolves*. Kapu's leadership is not as absolute as his father's and he must constantly fight off challenges from a new member of the pack, and the appearance of rabies in the territory means that his leadership is all that stands between the pack and destruction. . . . Though Julie appears occasionally, what's really absorbing here are the pack dramas and adventures, and kids will relish slipping into the four-footed world." Bull Cent Child Books

My side of the mountain; written and illustrated by Jean Craighead George. Dutton 1988 177p il $15.99; pa $5.99 (5 and up)   **Fic**
1. Outdoor life—Fiction 2. Catskill Mountains (N.Y.)—Fiction
ISBN 0-525-44392-4; 0-525-44395-9 (pa)
LC 87-27556

A reissue of the title first published 1959

"Sam Gribley feels closed in by the city and his large family so he runs away to the Catskills and the land that had belonged to his grandfather. He tells the story of his year in the wilderness—the loneliness, the struggle to survive, and the need for companionship." Read Ladders for Hum Relat. 6th edition

"The book is all the more convincing for the excellence of style, the subtlety of humor, aptness of phrases, and touches of poetry." Horn Book

Followed by On the far side of the mountain

On the far side of the mountain; written and illustrated by Jean Craighead George. Dutton Children's Bks. 1990 170p il $15.99; pa $4.99 (5 and up)   **Fic**
1. Outdoor life—Fiction 2. Catskill Mountains (N.Y.)—Fiction
ISBN 0-525-44563-3; 0-140-34248-6 (pa)
LC 89-25988

In this sequel To my side of the mountain, Sam's peaceful existence in his wilderness home is disrupted when his sister runs away and his pet falcon is confiscated by a conservation officer

"A tense, believable plot; likable characters; and a strong, positive message about the joys and beauty of the mountains . . . combine to make this story a jewel." Booklist

Followed by Frightful's mountain

There's an owl in the shower; illustrated by Christine Herman Merrill. HarperCollins Pubs. 1995 133p il $14.95; lib bdg $14.89; pa $4.95 (3-5)   **Fic**
1. Owls—Fiction 2. Endangered species—Fiction
ISBN 0-06-024891-2; 0-06-024892-0 (lib bdg); 0-06-442062-0 (pa)   LC 94-38893

Because protecting spotted owls has cost Borden's father his job as a logger in the old growth forest of north-

George, Jean Craighead, 1919-—_Continued_
ern California, Borden intends to kill any spotted owl he sees, until he and his father find themselves taking care of a young owlet

"George's writing skill and knowledge of animal behavior turn what could have been nothing but a message into an absorbing story that shows both sides of the controversy. . . . Merrill's drawings perfectly capture the engaging bird and the family's affection for it." SLJ

Giff, Patricia Reilly
Kidnap at the Catfish Cafe; illustrated by Lynne Cravath. Viking 1998 73p il lib bdg $13.99; pa $3.99 (3-5)   **Fic**
1. Mystery fiction
ISBN 0-670-88180-5 (lib bdg); 0-14-130821-4 (pa)
LC 98-5711
Assisted by her cat Max, sixth grader Minnie starts up her new detective agency by investigating a kidnapping and a thief who will steal anything, even a hot stove

"Young mystery lovers will enjoy the witty story with its standout characters." Booklist
Another available title about Minnie and Max is:
Mary Moon is missing (1998)

Lily's crossing. Delacorte Press 1997 180p $15.95; pa $5.50 (4 and up)   **Fic**
1. World War, 1939-1945—Fiction 2. Friendship—Fiction
ISBN 0-385-32142-2; 0-440-41453-9 (pa)
LC 96-23021
Also available Thorndike Press large print edition and Audiobook version

A Newbery honor book, 1998

During a summer spent at Rockaway Beach in 1944, Lily's friendship with a young Hungarian refugee causes her to see the war and her own world differently

"Gentle elements of danger and suspense . . . keep the plot moving forward, while the delicate balance of characters and setting gently coalesces into an emotional whole that is fully satisfying." Bull Cent Child Books

Gilson, Jamie, 1933-
4B goes wild; illustrated by Linda Strauss Edwards. Lothrop, Lee & Shepard Bks. 1983 160p il lib bdg $16 (4-6)   **Fic**
1. Camping—Fiction 2. School stories
ISBN 0-688-02236-7   LC 83-948
"Hobie Hanson, a sensitive fourth grader, tells of the time two fourth grade classes went on a three day camping trip. Along with learning about the country, they learned how to work together, and developed new relationships with each other and the adults with them." Child Book Rev Serv

"There are sustaining threads, but the plot is episodic; the writing style is breezy and comic, occasionally a bit cute; the characters are drawn with variable depth and some exaggeration; the dialogue is natural, one of the strong points of Gilson's writing." Bull Cent Child Books

Other available titles about Hobie Hanson are:
Double dog dare (1988)
Hobie Hanson, you're weird (1987)
Thirteen ways to sink a sub (1982)

Bug in a rug; illustrated by Diane deGroat. Clarion Bks. 1998 69p il $15 (2-4)   **Fic**
1. School stories 2. Clothing and dress—Fiction 3. Uncles—Fiction
ISBN 0-395-86616-2   LC 97-16437
Seven-year-old Richard is self-conscious when he receives a pair of purple pants from his aunt and uncle and has to wear them to school, but he is even more worried when his uncle shows up for a visit to his classroom

"Gilson captures the thoughts and fears of second graders through authentic dialogue and solid characterization." SLJ

Do bananas chew gum? Lothrop, Lee & Shepard Bks. 1980 158p hardcover o.p. paperback available $4.95 (4-6)   **Fic**
1. Reading—Fiction 2. Learning disabilities—Fiction
ISBN 0-688-15294-5 (pa)   LC 80-11414
Able to read and write at only a second grade level, sixth-grader Sam Mott considers himself dumb until he is prompted to cooperate with those who think something can be done about his problem

"This is a wonderfully written story, with real situations and a main character for whom the reader feels anguish at his fear of his learning disability being discovered, but also exultation when he correctly reads a long and difficult word. . . . This is a story that leaves you feeling good." Voice Youth Advocates

Hello, my name is Scrambled Eggs; illustrated by John Wallner. Lothrop, Lee & Shepard Bks. 1985 159p il $16 (4 and up)   **Fic**
1. Vietnamese—United States—Fiction
ISBN 0-688-04095-0   LC 84-10075
Also available in paperback from Pocket Bks.

"A humorous account of what happens when a Vietnamese family, sponsored by the church, moves into Harvey's home temporarily. To make himself feel more important, Harvey decides to make educating and Americanizing the 12-year-old boy his project. By the end of the book, Tuan is not the only one who has received an education." SLJ

"Entertaining and also thought-provoking, this is a popular-reading item that has nice substance." Booklist

Gipson, Frederick Benjamin, 1903-1973
Old Yeller; [by] Fred Gipson; drawings by Carl Burger. Harper & Row 1956 158p il $23; pa $4.95 (6 and up)   **Fic**
1. Dogs—Fiction 2. Texas—Fiction 3. Frontier and pioneer life—Fiction
ISBN 0-06-011545-9; 0-06-440-382-3 (pa)
LC 56-8780
Also available Audiobook version
A Newbery Medal honor book, 1957
"Travis at fourteen was the man of the family during the hard summer of 1860 when his father drove his herd of cattle from Texas to the Kansas market. It was the summer when an old yellow dog attached himself to the family and won Travis' reluctant friendship. Before the summer was over, Old Yeller proved more than a match for thieving raccoons, fighting bulls, grizzly bears, and mad wolves. This is a skillful tale of a boy's love for a dog as well as a description of a pioneer boyhood and it can't miss with any dog lover." Horn Book

Goble, Paul

Beyond the ridge; story and illustrations by Paul Goble. Bradbury Press 1989 unp il hardcover o.p. paperback available $5.99 (2-4) **Fic**

1. Native Americans—Fiction

ISBN 0-689-71731-8 (pa) LC 87-33113

At her death an elderly Plains Indian woman experiences the afterlife believed in by her people, while the surviving family members prepare her body according to their custom

"Goble's illustrations—in a double spread of gray rocks, smoothly surfaced in a skyscape of flying vultures—make a dignified context for a moving, direct discussion of death." Bull Cent Child Books

Godden, Rumer, 1907-1998

The doll's house; illustrated by Tasha Tudor. Viking 1962 c1947 136p il hardcover o.p. paperback available $4.99 (2-4) **Fic**

1. Dollhouses—Fiction 2. Dolls—Fiction

ISBN 0-14-030942-X (pa)

First published 1947 in the United Kingdom; first United States edition illustrated by Dana Saintsbury published 1948

Adventures of a brave little hundred-year-old Dutch farthing doll, her family, their Victorian dollhouse home and the two little English girls to whom they all belonged. Tottie's great adventure was when she went to the exhibition, Dolls through the ages, and was singled out for notice by the Queen who opened the exhibition

"Each doll has a firmly drawn, recognizably true character; the children think and behave convincingly. . . . The story is enthralling, and complete in every detail." Spectator

Goodman, Joan E., 1950-

Hope's crossing; [by] Joan Elizabeth Goodman. Houghton Mifflin 1998 212p $15 (5 and up) **Fic**

1. United States—History—1775-1783, Revolution—Fiction

ISBN 0-395-86195-0 LC 97-2796

Also available in paperback from Puffin Bks.

When kidnapped by English Loyalists during the Revolutionary War, thirteen-year-old Hope draws on every ounce of courage within her to respond to the ordeal

A "gripping historical novel." Booklist

Gorman, Carol

Dork in disguise. HarperCollins Pubs. 1999 164p $15.95; lib. bdg $15.89; pa $4.95 (4 and up) **Fic**

1. School stories

ISBN 0-06-024866-1; 0-06-024867-X (lib bdg); 0-06-440891-4 (pa) LC 99-27898

Starting middle school in a new town, brainy Jerry Flack changes his image from "dork" to "cool kid," only to discover that he'd rather be himself

"Humor keeps the plot jumping, and the novel's resolution is admirably restrained." Horn Book Guide

Grahame, Kenneth, 1859-1932

The reluctant dragon (3-5) **Fic**

1. Dragons—Fiction 2. Fairy tales

Some editions are:

Holiday House $14.95; pa $6.95 Illustrated by Ernest H. Shepard (ISBN 0-8234-0093-X; 0-8234-0755-1)

Holt & Co. pa $6.95 Illustrated by Michael Hague (ISBN 0-8050-0802-0)

This chapter from Dream days was first published 1938 by Holiday House

This "is the droll tale of a peace-loving dragon who is forced to fight St. George. The dragon's friend, called simply the Boy, arranges a meeting between St. George and the dragon, and a mock fight is planned. St. George is the hero of the day, the dragon is highly entertained at a banquet, and the Boy is pleased to have saved both the dragon and St. George." Huck. Child Lit in the Elem Sch. 3d edition

The wind in the willows (4-6) **Fic**

1. Animals—Fiction

Some editions are:

Holt & Co. $25.95 Illustrated by Michael Hague (ISBN 0-8050-0213-8)

St. Martin's Press $19.95 Illustrated by Patrick Benson (ISBN 0-312-13624-2)

First published 1908 by Scribner

In this fantasy "the characters are Mole, Water Rat, Mr. Toad, and other small animals, who live and talk like humans but have charming individual animal characters. The book is a tender portrait of the English countryside." Reader's Ency

Gray, Luli, 1945-

Falcon's egg. Houghton Mifflin 1995 133p $16 (3-5) **Fic**

1. Dragons—Fiction 2. New York (N.Y.)—Fiction

ISBN 0-395-71128-2 LC 94-16731

Also available in paperback from Bantam Bks.

"Falcon is an 11-year-old girl in New York City and the egg is red, hot, and discovered in Central Park. Falcon enlists the help of an older friend and neighbor to hide it until it hatches, fearing that her mother won't let her keep it. Soon elderly Aunt Emily; her ornithologist friend, Fernando Maldonado; and Falcon's younger brother join the cozy group that gathers to ponder the egg. When Egg hatches, she is a dragon. . . . Each of the characters is rich in wit, wisdom, and human foibles. . . . The real world blends well with the fantasy elements as tidbits of lore and locale are woven seamlessly." SLJ

Greene, Bette, 1934-

Philip Hall likes me, I reckon maybe; pictures by Charles Lilly. Dial Bks. for Young Readers 1974 135p il hardcover o.p. paperback available $4.99 (4-6) **Fic**

1. Friendship—Fiction 2. African Americans—Fiction 3. Arkansas—Fiction

ISBN 0-14-130312-3 (pa)

Also available Audiobook version

A Newbery Medal honor book, 1975

Eleven-year-old Beth, an African American girl from Arkansas, thinks that Philip Hall likes her, but their on-again, off-again relationship sometimes makes her wonder

"The action is sustained; . . . the illustrations are excellent black-and-white pencil sketches." Read Teach

Followed by Get on out of here, Philip Hall (1981)

Greene, Bette, 1934-—*Continued*

Summer of my German soldier. Dial Bks. for Young Readers 1973 230p hardcover o.p. paperback available $5.99 (6 and up)   **Fic**

1. World War, 1939-1945—Fiction 2. German prisoners of war—Fiction 3. Arkansas—Fiction

ISBN 0-14-130636-X (pa)

"Patty knows the pain of loneliness, rejection, and beatings in a family where she is the ugly duckling, unable to gain her parents' love. This is in contrast to the affection shown to her beautiful and submissive sister. Anton Reiker is a German prisoner-of-war in a camp outside of Jenkinsville, Arkansas, and when he escapes, Patty helps him. Because her family is Jewish, she pays dearly for this intervention." Shapiro. Fic for Youth. 3d edition

Followed by Morning is a long time coming (1978)

Greene, Constance C.

Beat the turtle drum; illustrated by Donna Diamond. Viking 1976 119p il hardcover o.p. paperback available $4.99 (5 and up)   **Fic**

1. Sisters—Fiction 2. Death—Fiction

ISBN 0-14-036850-7 (pa)

Also available Audiobook version

"Joss saves money for her 11th birthday so that she can rent a horse for a week. She and her older sister, who narrates the story, have the happiest week of their lives until Joss falls from the apple tree and breaks her neck. Joss's death stuns the family." SLJ

"Written with an eloquent and moving simplicity." NY Times Book Rev

A girl called Al; illustrated by Byron Barton. Viking 1969 127p il hardcover o.p. paperback available $5.99 (5 and up)   **Fic**

1. Friendship—Fiction

ISBN 0-14-034786-0 (pa)

Also available Audiobook version

"Written in an amusing first-person style, this is the story of a friendship between two seventh grade girls. Al (short for Alexandra) and the unnamed narrator of the story learn much from Mr. Richards, the elderly assistant superintendent of their apartment house, as he helps build their self-confidence and reveals his own ability to accept life's problems as well as its joys." Read Ladders for Hum Relat. 6th edition

Greene, Stephanie

Owen Foote, frontiersman; illustrated by Martha Weston. Clarion Bks. 1999 88p il $14 (2-4)   **Fic**

1. Outdoor life—Fiction

ISBN 0-395-61578-X   LC 98-44843

Second grader Owen Foote is looking forward to spending seventh grade with his friend Joseph in their tree fort, until some bullies visiting his neighbor, Mrs. Gold, threaten to wreck the fort

"Real-boy characters with an appealingly loyal friendship, a good balance of narrative and dialogue, and an honestly childlike sense of the way the world works." Horn Book

Other available titles about Owen Foote are:
Owen Foote, money man (2000)
Owen Foote, second grade strongman (1997)
Owen Foote, soccer star (1998)

Greenfield, Eloise, 1929-

Easter parade; illustrated by Jan Spivey Gilchrist. Hyperion Bks. for Children 1998 41p il lib bdg $14.49 (2-4)   **Fic**

1. Easter—Fiction 2. Cousins—Fiction 3. African Americans—Fiction

ISBN 0-7868-2271-6   LC 97-14279

Although the young cousins live many miles apart, Leanna in Chicago and Elizabeth in Washington, D.C., both prepare for an Easter parade against the backdrop of the Second World War

"Greenfield's lyrical prose evokes a warm tone and depth of character and circumstance. Expressive sepia-colored illustrations in oval frames become cameo photographs from the family album." Horn Book Guide

Sister; drawings by Moneta Barnett. Crowell 1974 83p il $15.95; pa $4.95 (4 and up)   **Fic**

1. Sisters—Fiction 2. Single parent family—Fiction 3. African Americans—Fiction

ISBN 0-690-00497-4; 0-06-440199-5 (pa)

A 13-year-old black girl whose father is dead watches her 16-year-old sister drifting away from her and her mother and fears she may fall into the same self-destructive behavior herself. While waiting for her sister's return home, she leafs through her diary, reliving both happy and unhappy experiences while gradually recognizing her own individuality

"The book is strong . . . strong in perception, in its sensitivity, in its realism." Bull Cent Child Books

Greenwald, Sheila

Rosy Cole: she grows and graduates. Orchard Bks. 1997 92p il $15.95 (3-5)   **Fic**

1. School stories

ISBN 0-531-30022-6   LC 97-9899

" Rosy decides to set her sights on the most exclusive high school in town. . . . Even her well-known talent in art suffers as she pushes onward. Disasters ensue. It is Donald who finally gets Rosy to see that she should be true to herself and seek acceptance into a public school that specializes in art." SLJ

"With a liberal sprinkling of black-and-white sketches of the characters, this sunny, gently comic story may not probe deeply, but it still brings the point home." Booklist

Griffin, Adele

The other Shepards. Hyperion Bks. for Children 1998 218p $14.95; lib bdg $15.49; pa $5.99 (6 and up)   **Fic**

1. Sisters—Fiction 2. New York (N.Y.)—Fiction

ISBN 0-7868-0423-8; 0-7868-2370-4 (lib bdg); 0-7868-1333-4 (pa)   LC 98-12609

Teenage Holland and her younger sister Geneva, having always lived under the shadow of siblings who died before they were born, struggle to establish separate identities and escape from the oppressive weight of their parents' continuing grief

"This is a stunning, quietly moving novel." SLJ

Griffin, Peni R.

Switching well. Margaret K. McElderry Bks. 1993 218p $17 (5 and up) **Fic**
1. Space and time—Fiction 2. Texas—Fiction
ISBN 0-689-50581-7 LC 92-38442
Also available in paperback from Puffin Bks.

Two twelve-year-old girls in San Antonio, Texas, Ada in 1891 and Amber in 1991, switch places through a magic well and try desperately to return to their own times

"A fine blend of time travel and friendship, laced with insight into social history and attitudes." SLJ

Griffith, Helen V.

Alex and the cat; pictures by Sonja Lamut. Greenwillow Bks. 1997 50p il $15 (1-3) **Fic**
1. Dogs—Fiction 2. Cats—Fiction
ISBN 0-688-15241-4 LC 96-43627
This compilation includes three stories first published separately: Alex and the cat (1982), More Alex and the cat (1983), and Alex remembers (1983)

The adventures of Alex the dog, who wants to be treated like the family cat, tries to restore a baby bird to a robin's nest, and attempts to migrate to avoid the winter snow

"Griffith cleverly keeps the language pared down and repetitive without making it terse or boring. Oversized type and a comfortable helping of white space on every page will reassure timid readers; softly hued two-color illustrations with real character appear one or two to a spread." Bull Cent Child Books

Grove, Vicki

Destiny. Putnam 2000 169p $16.99 (5 and up) **Fic**
1. Family life—Fiction 2. Artists—Fiction
ISBN 0-399-23449-7 LC 99-27778
Twelve-year-old Destiny tries to find meaning in her art in a life complicated by three younger siblings, a mother who dreams of winning the lottery, and her mother's unscrupulous boyfriend

"The vivid details and snappy dialogue in each of the characters' interactions keep this story grounded and valuable." Publ Wkly

Reaching Dustin. Putnam 1998 199p $16.99 (5 and up) **Fic**
1. School stories
ISBN 0-399-23008-4 LC 97-8181
"An interview assignment forces Carly to get to know Dustin Groat, the most unpopular member of her sixth-grade class. Dustin's unsociable behavior began at school in third grade, just after his mother died, and Carly and her friends have looked down upon him ever since. . . . Carly's inner development is convincingly painful as she realizes the part she played in creating Dustin's problems." SLJ

Gutman, Dan

Babe and me; a baseball card adventure. Avon Bks. 2000 161p il $15 (4 and up) **Fic**
1. Ruth, Babe, 1895-1948—Fiction 2. Baseball—Fiction
ISBN 0-380-97739-7 LC 99-36778

With their ability to travel through time using vintage baseball cards, Joe and his father have the opportunity to find out whether Babe Ruth really did call his shot when he hit that homerun in the third game of the 1932 World Series against the Chicago Cubs

"Readers will enjoy the action, the rich baseball lore, and the sense of adventure." Booklist
Other available titles in this series are:
Honus and me (1997)
Jackie and me (1999)

Haas, Jessie

Beware the mare; pictures by Martha Haas. Greenwillow Bks. 1993 64p il $15; pa $4.95 (3-5) **Fic**
1. Horses—Fiction 2. Grandfathers—Fiction
ISBN 0-688-11762-7; 0-688-814981-2 (pa)
LC 92-14505
Gramps gets a good bargain on an apparently perfect bay mare for Lily, but because the horse is named Beware he suspects that there may be something wrong with her

"The book will capture young horse lovers with its believable characters and realistic dialogue." SLJ
Other available titles about Beware are:
Be well, Beware (1996)
Beware and Stogie (1998)
A blue for Beware (1995)

Unbroken. Greenwillow Bks. 1999 185p $14.95 (5 and up) **Fic**
1. Death—Fiction 2. Orphans—Fiction 3. Horses—Fiction
ISBN 0-688-16260-6 LC 98-10485
Also available Thorndike Press large print edition

Following her mother's death in the early 1900s, thirteen-year-old Harry lives on Aunt Sarah's farm where an accident with her spirited colt leaves her a changed young woman

"The quiet novel moves quickly and is enriched by genuine dialogue, realistic portrayals of grief, and careful observations in the first-person narrative." Horn Book Guide

Hahn, Mary Downing, 1937-

Anna all year round; illustrated by Diane deGroat. Clarion Bks. 1999 133p il $15 (3-5) **Fic**
1. Family life—Fiction 2. Baltimore (Md.)—Fiction
ISBN 0-395-86975-7 LC 98-19985
Eight-year-old Anna experiences a series of episodes, some that are funny, others sad, involving friends and family during a year in Baltimore just before World War I

"Based on the childhood of the author's mother. . . . Hahn's use of the present tense helps keep nostalgia at bay, as does the energetic, just-dashed-off quality of deGroat's rough pencil sketches." Horn Book Guide
Another available title about Anna is:
Anna on the farm (2001)

As ever, Gordy. Clarion Bks. 1998 184p $15 (5 and up) **Fic**
1. Siblings—Fiction
ISBN 0-395-83627-1 LC 97-18913

Hahn, Mary Downing, 1937——*Continued*

Also available in paperback from Avon Bks.

A sequel to Following my own footsteps

When he and his younger sister move in with their older brother after their grandmother dies, thirteen-year-old Gordy finds himself caught between the boy he was when he lived with his abusive father and the boy his grandmother was helping him become

"Played against a well-rendered post-World War II setting, Gordy's recidivism into his previously wild ways is presented with emotional complexity, as is his love/hate relationship with a female classmate." Horn Book Guide

Daphne's book. Clarion Bks. 1983 177p $15 (5 and up)   **Fic**
1. School stories 2. Friendship—Fiction 3. Authorship—Fiction 4. Family life—Fiction
ISBN 0-89919-183-5   LC 83-7348

Also available in paperback from Avon Bks.

As author Jessica and artist Daphne collaborate on a picture book for a seventh-grade English class contest, Jessica becomes aware of conditions in Daphne's home life that seem to threaten her health and safety

"The story is compelling in its portrayal of peer group cruelty and the disturbing dilemma Daphne faces. Jessica's own conflict about how long to shield Daphne will provoke its share of thought too. Characterizations are strong and the situations pressing." Booklist

The dead man in Indian Creek. Clarion Bks. 1990 130p $15 (5 and up)   **Fic**
1. Mystery fiction
ISBN 0-395-52397-4   LC 89-22162

Also available in paperback from Avon Bks.

When Matt and Parker learn the body they found in Indian Creek is a drug-related death, they fear Parker's mother may be involved

"Though readers will respond viscerally to the action, what sets the book apart are Hahn's insightful character sketches, especially her portrayal of Matt, whose first-person musings will both entertain and give pause." Booklist

The doll in the garden; a ghost story. Clarion Bks. 1989 128p $15 (4-6)   **Fic**
1. Space and time—Fiction 2. Ghost stories
ISBN 0-89919-848-1   LC 88-20365

Also available in paperback from Avon Bks.

After Ashley and Kristi find an antique doll buried in old Miss Cooper's garden, they discover that they can enter a ghostly turn-of-the-century world by going through a hole in the hedge

"Hahn's elegant use of language, as well as her ability to probe complex emotions at a child's level, elevates this above-the-ordinary ghost tale into a story with universal themes." Booklist

Following my own footsteps. Clarion Bks. 1996 186p $15 (5 and up)   **Fic**
1. Domestic violence—Fiction 2. Grandmothers—Fiction 3. World War, 1939-1945—Fiction
ISBN 0-395-76477-7   LC 95-50144

Also available in paperback from Avon Bks.

In 1945, Gordy's grandmother takes him and his family into her North Carolina home after his abusive father is arrested, and he just begins to respond to his grandmother's loving discipline when his father returns

"Hahn gets us inside her character so quickly and skillfully that she maintains our sympathy for William without ever resorting to the sentimental. . . . Sometimes heartrending, sometimes funny, Gordy Smith will prove memorable to all who meet him." Booklist

Followed by As ever, Gordy

The Gentleman Outlaw and me—Eli; a story of the Old West. Clarion Bks. 1996 212p $15 (5 and up)   **Fic**
1. Frontier and pioneer life—Fiction 2. West (U.S.)—Fiction
ISBN 0-395-73083-X   LC 95-18802

Also available in paperback from Avon Bks.

In 1887 twelve-year-old Eliza, disguised as a boy and traveling towards Colorado in search of her missing father, falls in with Calvin Featherbone, a "Gentleman Outlaw" and joins him in his illegal schemes

Hahn "succeeds in bringing the ambiance of the Old West to her novel. The result is a fast, funny, and entertaining adventure." SLJ

Promises to the dead. Clarion Bks. 2000 202p $15 (5 and up)   **Fic**
1. Slavery—Fiction 2. United States—History—1861-1865, Civil War—Fiction 3. Maryland—Fiction
ISBN 0-395-96394-X   LC 99-48525

Twelve-year-old Jesse leaves his home on Maryland's Eastern Shore to help a young runaway slave find a safe haven in the early days of the Civil War

"Hahn skillfully blends the language and customs of the Civil War era with an exciting plot." Voice Youth Advocates

Stepping on the cracks. Clarion Bks. 1991 216p $16 (5 and up)   **Fic**
1. World War, 1939-1945—Fiction
ISBN 0-395-58507-4   LC 91-7706

Also available in paperback from Avon Bks.

In 1944, while her brother is overseas fighting in World War II, eleven-year-old Margaret gets a new view of the school bully Gordy when she finds him hiding his own brother, an army deserter, and decides to help him

"Well-drawn characters and a satisfying plot. . . . There is plenty of action and page-turning suspense to please those who want a quick read, but there is much to ponder and reflect on as well." SLJ

Time for Andrew; a ghost story. Clarion Bks. 1994 165p $15 (5 and up)   **Fic**
1. Ghost stories 2. Space and time—Fiction
ISBN 0-395-66556-6   LC 93-2877

Also available in paperback from Avon Bks.

When he goes to spend the summer with his great-aunt in the family's old house, eleven-year-old Drew is drawn eighty years into the past to trade places with his great-great-uncle who is dying of diphtheria

"There's plenty to enjoy in this delightful time-slip fantasy: a fascinating premise, a dastardly cousin, some good suspense, and a roundup of characters to care about." Booklist

Hahn, Mary Downing, 1937-——*Continued*
Wait till Helen comes; a ghost story. Clarion
Bks. 1986 184p $15 (4-6)   **Fic**
1. Ghost stories 2. Stepchildren—Fiction
ISBN 0-89919-453-2   LC 86-2648
Also available in paperback from Avon Bks.

Molly and Michael dislike their spooky new stepsister
Heather but realize that they must try to save her when
she seems ready to follow a ghost child to her doom

"Intertwined with the ghost story is the question of
Molly's moral imperative to save a child she truly dislikes. Though the emotional turnaround may be a bit
quick for some, this still scores as a first-rate thriller."
Booklist

Hamilton, Virginia, 1936-
The bells of Christmas; illustrations by Lambert
Davis. Harcourt Brace Jovanovich 1989 59p $19;
pa $8 (4-6)   **Fic**
1. Christmas—Fiction 2. Family life—Fiction
3. African Americans—Fiction 4. Ohio—Fiction
ISBN 0-15-206450-8; 0-15-201550-7 (pa)
                                          LC 89-7468
"On Christmas Day, 1890, in Ohio, the Bell family
comes along the National Road to spend the holiday with
Jason and his family. The gentle story is stuffed like a
proper plum pudding with specific details of rural life almost a century ago." N Y Times Book Rev

Cousins. Philomel Bks. 1990 125p $16.99 (5
and up)   **Fic**
1. Death—Fiction 2. Cousins—Fiction 3. Grandmothers—Fiction 4. African Americans—Fiction
ISBN 0-399-22164-6   LC 90-31451
Also available in paperback from Scholastic; Spanish
language edition also available

Concerned that her grandmother may die, Cammy is
unprepared for the accidental death of her cousin Patty
Ann

"The book deals essentially with emotions and sensa-
tions, and the writing reverberates with honesty and
truth. Virginia Hamilton encases the story in family tradition, which offsets the instabilities of contemporary
life, and she beautifully counterposes superstition and ra-
tionality, separation and reconciliation, love and death."
Horn Book

Followed by Second Cousins

Drylongso; written by Virginia Hamilton;
illustrated by Jerry Pinkney. Harcourt Brace
Jovanovich 1992 54p il hardcover o.p. paperback
available $9 (3-5)   **Fic**
1. Droughts—Fiction 2. Farm life—Fiction 3. African
Americans—Fiction
ISBN 0-15-201587-6 (pa)   LC 91-25575
As a great wall of dust moves across their drought-
stricken farm, a family's distress is relieved by a young
man called Drylongso, who literally blows into their
lives with the storm

"In an understated story of drought and hard times
and longing for rain, a great writer and a great artist
have pared down their rich, exuberant styles to something quieter but no less intense. . . . The characters are
vital and lovingly individualized, set against a landscape
washed in thick drifts of pale red dust. Pinkney's paintings in watercolor, pastel, and pencil have a flowing softness, like snow." Booklist

The house of Dies Drear; illustrated by Eros
Keith. Macmillan 1968 246p il $17; pa $4.99 (5
and up)   **Fic**
1. African Americans—Fiction 2. Mystery fiction
3. Ohio—Fiction
ISBN 0-02-742500-2; 0-02-043520-7 (pa)
"A hundred years ago, Dies Drear and two slaves he
was hiding in his house, an Underground Railroad station
in Ohio, had been murdered. The house, huge and isolated, was fascinating, Thomas thought, but he wasn't sure
he was glad Papa had bought it—funny things kept happening, frightening things." Bull Cent Child Books

"The answer to the mystery comes in a startling dramatic dénouement that is pure theater. This is gifted
writing; the characterization is unforgettable, the plot imbued with mounting tension." Saturday Rev

Followed by The mystery of Drear House

M. C. Higgins the great. Macmillan 1974 278p
$18; pa $4.99 (6 and up)   **Fic**
1. African Americans—Fiction 2. Family life—Fiction 3. Appalachian region—Fiction
ISBN 0-02-742480-4; 0-02-043490-1 (pa)
Awarded the Newbery Medal, 1975
M.C. Higgins, a 13-year-old black boy "dreams of
saving his family's house from an Ohio strip mining slag
heap and finds that the answer to his dreams lies in coming to terms with his family heritage and his own identity." Publisher's note

"This is a deeply involving story possessing a folklor-
ish quality. Superstition and magic are deeply rooted in
its telling. Characterizations are highly original. The unusual setting and uniqueness of story line make this outstanding juvenile literature." Child Book Rev Serv

The mystery of Drear House; the conclusion of
the Dies Drear chronicle. Greenwillow Bks. 1987
217p $16.95 (5 and up)   **Fic**
1. African Americans—Fiction 2. Buried treasure—
Fiction 3. Mystery fiction
ISBN 0-688-04026-8   LC 86-9829
Also available in paperback from Scholastic
"Professor Small, Thomas' father, is engaged in cataloging a treasure house of antiques which have been hidden in one of the caverns on the property, which is a
maze of tunnels and caves. He must protect these treasures from discovery by a neighboring family who are
searching for them in order to sell them." Voice Youth
Advocates

"Ingredients such as secret rooms and passages, moving walls, and awesome treasure will play well to a popular audience; yet substantive portrayals of characters
and relationships provide the depth one associates with
Hamilton. This solid tale displays a sensitivity toward
feelings, emotions, and conflicting values—all in the
context of a fantastic mystery laid to rest." Booklist

Plain City. Blue Sky Press (NY) 1993 194p
$13.95; pa $4.99 (5 and up)   **Fic**
1. Racially mixed people—Fiction 2. African Americans—Fiction
ISBN 0-590-47364-6; 0-590-47365-4 (pa)
                                         LC 93-19910
Twelve-year-old Buhlaire, a "mixed" child who feels
out of place in her community, struggles to unearth her

Hamilton, Virginia, 1936-—*Continued*
past and her family history as she gradually discovers
more and more about her long-missing father

"Richly textured with a cast of unforgettable characters, this extraordinary novel offers a rare glimpse of unconditional love, family loyalty and compassion." Publ
Wkly

The planet of Junior Brown. Macmillan 1971
210p $18; pa $4.99 (6 and up)   **Fic**
1. Friendship—Fiction 2. African Americans—Fiction
ISBN 0-02-742510-X; 0-02-043540-1 (pa)
"This is the story of a crucial week in the lives of two
black, eighth-grade dropouts who have been spending
their time with the school janitor. Each boy is presented
as a distinct individual. Jr. is a three-hundred pound musical prodigy as neurotic as his overprotective mother.
Buddy has learned to live by his wits in a world of
homeless children. Buddy becomes Jr. Brown's protector
and says to the other boys, 'We are together because we
have to learn to live for each other.'" Read Ladders for
Hum Relat. 6th edition

Second cousins. Blue Sky Press (NY) 1998
168p $14.95 (5 and up)   **Fic**
1. Cousins—Fiction 2. African Americans—Fiction
ISBN 0-590-47368-9   LC 98-12859
Also available in paperback from Scholastic
Sequel to Cousins
The friendship of twelve-year-old cousins Cammy and
Elodie is threatened when the family reunion includes
two other cousins near their age and Elodie is tempted
to drop Cammy for a new companion
"The author's on-target dialogue and skillfully drawn
characterizations compensate for the book's uneven pac-
ing." Publ Wkly

Zeely; illustrated by Symeon Shimin. Macmillan
1967 122p il $17; pa $4.99 (4 and up)   **Fic**
1. African Americans—Fiction
ISBN 0-02-742470-7; 0-689-71695-8 (pa)
"Imaginative eleven-year-old Geeder is stirred when
she sees Zeely Tayber, who is dignified, stately, and six-
and-a-half feet tall. Geeder thinks Zeely looks like the
magazine picture of the Watusi queen. Through meeting
Zeely personally and getting to know her, Geeder finally
returns to reality." Read Ladders for Hum Relat. 5th edition

Hansen, Brooks, 1965-
Caesar's antlers; with drawings by the author.
Farrar, Straus & Giroux 1997 217p il $16 (5 and
up)   **Fic**
1. Reindeer—Fiction 2. Sparrows—Fiction
ISBN 0-374-31024-6   LC 96-53148
Bette, a mother sparrow separated by accident from
her mate, takes her chicks on a long search when a faith-
ful reindeer permits her to make a nest in his antlers
"Simply written, yet full of wonder and magic, the
story builds to a satisfying, if tragic conclusion. . . .
Spare ink drawings add to the quiet mood." SLJ

Hansen, Joyce
The captive. Scholastic 1994 195p $13.95; pa
$4.50 (5 and up)   **Fic**
1. Slavery—Fiction
ISBN 0-590-41625-1; 0-590-41624-3 (pa)
"Modeled after an actual slave narrative, this moving
first-person tale follows twelve-year-old Kofi from his
kidnapping in West Africa to his cruel enslavement in
Massachusetts and his subsequent freedom and career as
a sailor. The well-crafted and compelling survival story
juxtaposes two cultures and gives a unique account of
slavery from the sufferer's perspective." Horn Book
Guide

Which way freedom? Walker & Co. 1986 120p
o.p.; Avon Bks. paperback available $4.99 (5 and
up)   **Fic**
1. African Americans—Fiction 2. United States—History—1861-1865, Civil War—Fiction
ISBN 0-380-71408-6 (pa)   LC 85-29547
"Walker's American history series for young readers"
The author "describes the way in which one young
black man, Obi, struggles over a period of three years
(1861-1864) politically and ideologically toward the goal
of being a free man. . . . [He] eventually joins a Union
regiment and is one of the few to escape from the
bloody battle at Fort Pillow, Tennessee." Bull Cent Child
Books
"There is sufficient action to sustain readers' interest,
but it is in the book's characterization that the chief
strength lies. . . . A sensitive, thought-provoking historical novel." SLJ
Followed by Out from this place (1988)

Harlow, Joan Hiatt
Star in the storm. Margaret K. McElderry Bks.
2000 150p $16   **Fic**
1. Dogs—Fiction 2. Newfoundland—Fiction
ISBN 0-689-82905-1   LC 99-20416
In 1912, fearing for the safety of her beloved Newfoundland dog Sirius because of a new law outlawing
non-sheepherding dogs in her Newfoundland village,
twelve-year-old Maggie tries to save him by keeping him
hidden
"Containing many authentic details of life in a remote
region in days gone by, this story is educational as well
as exciting." Booklist

Harrison, Barbara
Theo. Clarion Bks. 1999 166p $15 (5 and up)
                                             Fic
1. World War, 1939-1945—Fiction 2. Greece—Fiction 3. Puppets and puppet plays—Fiction 4. Orphans—Fiction
ISBN 0-89919-959-3   LC 98-45823
Theo, an orphaned puppeteer performs bravely on and
off the stage after joining the Greek resistance movement
during World War II
"A story full of intensity that resonates with humor,
hope, and—above all—goodness." Horn Book

Härtling, Peter, 1933-
Crutches; translated from the German by Elizabeth D. Crawford. Lothrop, Lee & Shepard Bks. 1988 163p $12.95 (5 and up)   **Fic**
1. Friendship—Fiction 2. Austria—Fiction
ISBN 0-688-07991-1   LC 88-80400
Original German edition, 1986
A young boy, searching vainly for his mother in postwar Vienna, is befriended by a man on crutches, a former German officer, and together they find hope for the future
"Because of its pacing, the book, while re-creating a specific time in history, has the intensity of an adventure story; it is equally remarkable for its development of theme without sacrificing believability or sense of story. . . . The bittersweet ending is poignant but not manipulative." Horn Book

Harvey, Brett
Cassie's journey; going West in the 1860s; illustrated by Deborah Kogan Ray. Holiday House 1988 unp il lib bdg $14.35; pa $6.95 (2-4)   **Fic**
1. Overland journeys to the Pacific—Fiction 2. Frontier and pioneer life—Fiction 3. West (U.S.)—Fiction
ISBN 0-8234-0684-9 (lib bdg); 0-8234-1172-9 (pa)
LC 87-23599
A young girl relates the hardships and dangers of traveling with her family in a covered wagon from Illinois to California during the 1860's
"Harvey has based this story of westward migration on the diaries of pioneer women. . . . [This is] a fascinating piece of historical fiction. . . . Ray's soft charcoal drawings carry a solemnity that gives the account a serious edge while evoking the loneliness and breadth of the landscape." Booklist

My prairie Christmas; illustrations by Deborah Kogan Ray. Holiday House 1990 unp il $16.95; pa $5.95 (2-4)   **Fic**
1. Christmas—Fiction 2. Frontier and pioneer life—Fiction 3. West (U.S.)—Fiction
ISBN 0-8234-0827-2; 0-8234-1064-1 (pa)
LC 90-55104
On the first Christmas after Eleanor's family moves to a house on the prairie, everyone becomes worried when Papa goes out to cut down a Christmas tree and does not come back
"Ray's soft-edged illustrations capture the prairie vistas and the warm family interactions well. The narrative is flowing and comfortable." Booklist

Hautzig, Esther Rudomin, 1930-
A gift for Mama; [by] Esther Hautzig; illustrated by Donna Diamond. Viking 1981 56p il hardcover o.p. paperback available $3.99 (3-6)
Fic
1. Gifts—Fiction 2. Jews—Poland—Fiction 3. Poland—Fiction
ISBN 0-14-038551-7 (pa)   LC 80-24973
"Sara, an only child, determines to buy her mother a gift for Mother's Day rather than make one as she has in the past. . . . She manages to earn the nine zlotys for the satin slippers with blue leather trim by mending and repairing the clothes of her aunt's friends at the university." Child Book Rev Serv
"The book is set in Poland, the author's homeland [in the 1930s] and the reader learns much about Jewish customs and Polish lifestyle. The illustrations are beautiful, high-quality monoprints, which are pictures painted on glass and then transferred to paper by using an etching press." Interracial Books Child Bull

Heide, Florence Parry, 1919-
The shrinking of Treehorn; drawings by Edward Gorey. Holiday House 1971 unp il lib bdg $16.95; pa $6.95 (2-5)   **Fic**
ISBN 0-8234-0189-8 (lib bdg); 0-8234-0975-9 (pa)

Treehorn spends an unhappy day and night shrinking. Yet when he tells his mother, father, teacher and principal of his problem they're all too busy to do anything about it. To Treehorn's great relief he finally discovers a magical game that restores him to his natural size, but then he starts turning green!
This "is an imaginative little whimsy, whose sly humor and macabre touches are perfectly matched in Edward Gorey's illustrations." Book World

Henkes, Kevin, 1960-
The birthday room. Greenwillow Bks. 1999 152p $16 (5 and up)   **Fic**
1. Family life—Fiction 2. Uncles—Fiction
ISBN 0-688-16733-0   LC 98-39887
Also available in paperback from Puffin Bks. and Audiobook version
"For his twelfth birthday, Ben Hunter receives a room that he can use as an art studio and a letter from his uncle—the one responsible for the loss of Ben's little finger when Ben was a toddler. . . . Mrs. Hunter, who has been angry at her brother since the accident, reluctantly agrees to go to Oregon with Ben." Booklist
"Told in spare, unobtrusive prose, a story that helps us see our own chances for benefiting from mutual tolerance, creative conflict resolution, and other forms of good will." Horn Book

Protecting Marie. Greenwillow Bks. 1995 195p $15.95 (5 and up)   **Fic**
1. Father-daughter relationship—Fiction 2. Dogs—Fiction
ISBN 0-688-13958-2   LC 94-16387
Also available in paperback from Puffin Bks.
Relates twelve-year-old Fanny's love-hate relationship with her father, a temperamental artist, who has given Fanny a new dog
"The characters ring heartbreakingly true in this quiet, wise story; they are complex and difficult—like all of us—and worthy of our attention." Horn Book

Sun & Spoon. Greenwillow Bks. 1997 135p $15 (4 and up)   **Fic**
1. Grandmothers—Fiction 2. Death—Fiction
ISBN 0-688-15232-5   LC 96-46259
Also available in paperback from Puffin Bks.
"Spoon, 10, spends his summer trying to reconfigure his world, which seems strangely out of kilter since his

Henkes, Kevin, 1960-—*Continued*
grandmother's death." SLJ

"Sensitively placed metaphors enrich the narrative, embuing its perceptive depictions of grief with a powerful message of affirmation." Publ Wkly

Words of stone. Greenwillow Bks. 1992 152p
$16 (5 and up) **Fic**
1. Friendship—Fiction
ISBN 0-688-11356-7 LC 91-28543

Also available in paperback Puffin Bks.; Spanish language edition also available

Busy trying to deal with his many fears and his troubled feelings for his dead mother, ten-year-old Blaze has his life changed when he meets the boisterous and irresistible Joselle

"A story rich in characterization, dramatic subplots, and some very creepy moments." SLJ

Henry, Marguerite, 1902-1997
Brighty of the Grand Canyon; illustrated by Wesley Dennis. Rand McNally 1953 222p il o.p.; Aladdin Bks. (NY) paperback available $4.99 (4 and up) **Fic**
1. Donkeys—Fiction 2. Grand Canyon (Ariz.)—Fiction
ISBN 0-689-71485-8 (pa) LC 53-7233

Drawn from a real-life incident, this is the story of "Brighty, the shaggy little burro who roamed the canyons of the Colorado River [and] had a will of his own. He liked the old prospector and Uncle Jim and he helped solve a mystery, but chiefly he was the freedom-loving burro." Chicago Public Libr

"Only those who are unfamiliar with the West would say it is too packed with drama to be true. And the author's understanding warmth for all of God's creatures still shines through, her superb ability as a story teller making this a vivid tale." Christ Sci Monit

Justin Morgan had a horse; illustrated by Wesley Dennis. Rand McNally 1954 169p il o.p.; Aladdin Bks. (NY) paperback available $4.99 (4 and up) **Fic**
1. Horses—Fiction 2. Vermont—Fiction
ISBN 0-689-71534-X (pa) LC 54-8903

A Newbery Medal honor book, 1946

An expanded version of the book first published 1945 by Wilcox & Follett

Story of the brave little Vermont work horse from which came the famous American breed of Morgan horses. Justin Morgan first owned the horse, but it was the boy Joel Goss who loved 'Little Bub,' later called 'Justin Morgan,' followed him through his career, rescued him from a cruel master, and finally had the pleasure of having him ridden by James Monroe when he was President of the United States

A horse story "in a book that is rich in human values—the sort of book that makes you proud and sometimes brings a lump to your throat." Book Week

King of the wind; illustrated by Wesley Dennis. Macmillan 1991 172p il $16.95; pa $4.99 (4 and up) **Fic**
1. Horses—Fiction
ISBN 0-02-743629-2; 0-689-71486-6 (pa)
LC 91-13474

Also available Audiobook version

Awarded the Newbery Medal, 1949

A reissue of the title first published 1948 by Rand McNally

"A beautiful, sympathetic story of the famous [ancestor of a line of great thoroughbred horses] . . . and the little mute Arabian stable boy who accompanies him on his journey across the seas to France and England [in the eighteenth century]. The lad's fierce devotion to his horse and his great faith and loyalty are skillfully woven into an enthralling tale which children will long remember. The moving quality of the writing is reflected in the handsome illustrations." Wis Libr Bull

Misty of Chincoteague; illustrated by Wesley Dennis. Macmillan 1991 173p il $16.95; pa $4.99 (4 and up) **Fic**
1. Horses—Fiction 2. Chincoteague Island (Va.)—Fiction 3. Assateague Island National Seashore (Md. and Va.)—Fiction
ISBN 0-02-743622-5; 0-689-71492-0 (pa)
LC 90-27237

Also available Spanish language edition and Audiobook version

A Newbery Medal honor book, 1948

First published 1947 by Rand McNally

"The islands of Chincoteague and Assateague, just off the coast of Virginia, are the setting. . . . Two children have their hearts set on owning a wild pony and her colt, descendants, so legend says, of the Moorish ponies who were survivors of a Spanish galleon wrecked there long ago." Booklist

"The beauty and pride of the wild horses is the highpoint in the story, and skillful drawings of them reveal their grace and swiftness." Ont Libr Rev

Other available titles about the ponies of Chincoteague Island are:
Sea star, orphan of Chincoteague (1949)
Stormy, Misty's foal (1963)

Henry, O., 1862-1910
The gift of the Magi (5 and up) **Fic**
1. Christmas—Fiction

Available from various publishers

"The tale of a poor young couple who sacrifice their dearest possessions to buy each other Christmas gifts." Bull Cent Child Books

Hermes, Patricia, 1936-
Our strange new land; Elizabeth's diary, Jamestown, Virginia, 1609. Scholastic 2000 109p (My America) $8.95 (3-5) **Fic**
1. Jamestown (Va.)—Fiction 2. United States—History—1600-1775, Colonial period—Fiction
ISBN 0-439-11208-7 LC 99-56356

Nine-year-old Elizabeth keeps a journal of her experiences in 1609 in Jamestown, Virginia, as she encounters Indians, suffers hunger and the death of friends, and helps her father build their first home

"This is a quick, easy read. Hermes has created a sensitive main character and readers will empathize with her fears and emotions." SLJ

Hesse, Karen

Just Juice; pictures by Robert Andrew Parker. Scholastic 1998 138p il $14.95; pa $4.99 (3-5)

Fic

1. Literacy—Fiction 2. Family life—Fiction 3. Poverty—Fiction

ISBN 0-590-03382-4; 0-590-03383-2 (pa)

LC 98-13375

Realizing that her father's lack of work has endangered her family, nine-year-old Juice decides that she must return to school and learn to read in order to help their chances of surviving and keeping their house

"Hesse's plain, beautiful words tell of the harsh dailiness of poverty through the eyes of a child." Booklist

Letters from Rifka. Holt & Co. 1992 148p $16.95 (5 and up)

Fic

1. Immigration and emigration—Fiction 2. Jews—Fiction 3. Letters—Fiction

ISBN 0-8050-1964-2   LC 91-48007

Also available in paperback from Puffin Bks.

In letters to her cousin, Rifka, a young Jewish girl, chronicles her family's flight from Russia in 1919 and her own experiences when she must be left in Belgium for a while when the others emigrate to America

"Based on the true story of the author's great-aunt, the moving account of a brave young girl's story brings to life the day-to-day trials and horrors experienced by many immigrants as well as the resourcefulness and strength they found within themselves." Horn Book

A light in the storm; the Civil War diary of Amelia Martin. Scholastic 1999 169p (Dear America) $10.95 (4 and up)

Fic

1. United States—History—1861-1865, Civil War—Fiction 2. Delaware—Fiction

ISBN 0-590-56733-0   LC 98-49204

In 1860 and 1861, while working in her father's lighthouse on an island off the coast of Delaware, fifteen-year-old Amelia records in her diary how the Civil War is beginning to devastate her divided state

"This well-paced story features a seamless combination of history, sociology, drama, and romance."

The music of dolphins. Scholastic 1996 181p $14.95; pa $4.99 (6 and up)

Fic

1. Wild children—Fiction 2. Dolphins—Fiction

ISBN 0-590-89797-7; 0-590-89798-5 (pa)

LC 96-3494

Using sophisticated computer technology, Mila, a fifteen-year-old girl who has been raised by dolphins, records her thoughts about her reintroduction to the human world

"Deceptively easy in format, this is a complex and demanding book. . . . This powerful exploration of how we become human and how the soul endures is a song of beauty and sorrow, haunting and unforgettable." SLJ

Out of the dust. Scholastic 1997 227p $15.95; pa $4.99 (5 and up)

Fic

1. Dust storms—Fiction 2. Farm life—Fiction 3. Great Depression, 1929-1939—Fiction 4. Oklahoma—Fiction

ISBN 0-590-36080-9; 0-590-37125-8 (pa)

LC 96-40344

Also available Spanish language edition and Audiobook version

Awarded the Newbery Medal, 1998

"After facing loss after loss during the Oklahoma Dust Bowl, Billie Jo begins to reconstruct her life." SLJ

"Hesse's writing transcends the gloom and transforms it into a powerfully compelling tale of a girl with enormous strength, courage, and love. The entire novel is written in very readable blank verse." Booklist

Sable; illustrated by Marcia Sewall. Holt & Co. 1994 81p il $15.95; pa $7.95 (2-4)

Fic

1. Dogs—Fiction

ISBN 0-8050-2416-6; 0-8050-5772-2 (pa)

LC 93-33646

"A Redfeather book"

Tate Marshall is delighted when a stray dog turns up in the yard one day, but Sable, named for her dark, silky fur, causes trouble with the neighbors and has to go

"The early chapter book relates a dog tale sweet and scary enough for any budding pet lover." Horn Book Guide

Hickman, Janet

Jericho; a novel. Greenwillow Bks. 1994 135p $15 (5 and up)

Fic

1. Grandmothers—Fiction 2. Family life—Fiction 3. Old age—Fiction

ISBN 0-688-13398-3   LC 93-37309

An account of twelve-year-old Angela's visit to help take care of her great-grandmother alternates with the story of the old woman's life

"The author's unsentimental narrative reveals a sharp eye for detail, a profound understanding of the aging process and a deep love for humanity." Publ Wkly

Hill, Elizabeth Starr

Bird Boy; pictures by Lesley Liu. Farrar, Straus & Giroux 1999 55p il $15 (2-4)

Fic

1. Birds—Fiction 2. Fishing—Fiction 3. Physically handicapped—Fiction 4. China—Fiction

ISBN 0-374-30723-7   LC 98-51942

Chang, a mute Chinese boy whose father uses cormorants to fish, is pleased when he is finally old enough to help with the Big Catch and the raising of a new bird

"Youngsters, especially those with disabilities, will strongly identify with Chang, and Lesley Liu's detailed drawings capture the flavor of the Chinese landscape." Booklist

Hobbs, Will

Jason's gold. Morrow Junior Bks. 1999 221p $15.95; pa $4.95 (5 and up)

Fic

1. Klondike River Valley (Yukon)—Gold discoveries—Fiction 2. Voyages and travels—Fiction 3. Orphans—Fiction

ISBN 0-688-15093-4; 0-380-72914-8 (pa)

LC 99-17973

Also available Audiobook version

When news of the discovery of gold in Canada's Yukon Territory in 1897 reaches fifteen-year-old Jason, he embarks on a 10,000-mile journey to strike it rich

"The successful presentation of a fascinating era, coupled with plenty of action, makes this a good historical fiction choice." SLJ

Hobbs, Will—*Continued*

Kokopelli's flute. Atheneum Bks. for Young Readers 1995 148p $16 (5 and up)   **Fic**
1. Flutes—Fiction 2. Magic—Fiction 3. Native Americans—Fiction 4. New Mexico—Fiction
ISBN 0-689-31974-6   LC 95-8422
Also available in paperback from Avon Bks.

Thirteen-year-old Tepary discovers an old flute in a cliff dwelling in New Mexico, and through its power he learns about ancient Native American magic
"Outstanding characters, plot, mood, and setting combine in this satisfying and memorable book." SLJ

Hodges, Margaret

Gulliver in Lilliput; retold by Margaret Hodges from Gulliver's travels by Jonathan Swift; illustrated by Kimberly Bulcken Root. Holiday House 1995 unp il $16.95; pa $6.95 (3-6)   **Fic**
1. Fantasy fiction
ISBN 0-8234-1147-8; 0-8234-1303-9 (pa)
               LC 94-15037
On a voyage in the South Seas, an Englishman finds himself shipwrecked in Lilliput, a land of people only six inches high
"Hodges's adaptation of Part I of *Gulliver's Travels* is a masterful retelling of the 18th-century classic. While condensing the story considerably, she has retained not only the important details of the involved plot, but also the flavor of Swift's rich, descriptive language. . . . Root's stunning pen-and-watercolor illustrations do much to bring the fanciful tale to life." SLJ

Hoffmann, E. T. A. (Ernst Theodor Amadeus), 1776-1822

Nutcracker; pictures by Maurice Sendak; translated by Ralph Manheim. Crown 1984 102p il $20 (4 and up)   **Fic**
1. Fairy tales 2. Christmas—Fiction
ISBN 0-517-58659-2   LC 83-25266
This "book stems from Sendak's costume and set designs for the Pacific Northwest Ballet's 1981 production. That production, and this volume, differ from the traditional ballet as they are based on Hoffmann's original 1816 long short story, rather than a French version of Hoffmann's tale." SLJ
"The smooth, elegant, new translation re-creates the flavor of the period and does justice to the story. . . . The occasional quirkiness of the pictures . . . eerily reflect the mysterious story. Altogether a magnificent, splendid combination of talents." Horn Book

Holling, Holling C., 1900-1973

Paddle-to-the-sea; written and illustrated by Holling Clancy Holling. Houghton Mifflin 1941 unp il lib bdg $20; pa $10 (4-6)   **Fic**
1. Great Lakes region—Fiction
ISBN 0-395-15082-5 (lib bdg); 0-395-29203-4 (pa)

A Caldecott Medal honor book, 1942
A toy canoe with a seated Indian figure is launched in Lake Nipigon by the Indian boy who carved it and in four years travels through all the Great Lakes and the St. Lawrence River to the Atlantic. An interesting picture of the shore life of the lakes and the river with striking full page pictures in bright colors and marginal pencil drawings
"The canoe's journey is used to show the flow of currents and of traffic, and each occurrence is made to seem plausible. . . . There are also diagrams of a sawmill, a freighter, the canal locks at the Soo, and Niagara Falls." Libr J

Holm, Anne, 1922-

North to freedom; translated from the Danish by L. W. Kingsland. Harcourt Brace 1965 190p hardcover o.p. paperback available $6 (6 and up)   **Fic**
1. Refugees—Fiction
ISBN 0-15-257553-7 (pa)
First published 1963 in Denmark; first United States edition published 1965
"Twelve-year-old David, whose only memory is of life in a prison camp, escapes and makes his way across Europe alone. Before he is reunited with his mother, his prison-bred fear of people has gradually faded, and he has learned that goodness as well as evil exists in the world." Hodges. Books for Elem Sch Libr

Holm, Jennifer L.

Our only May Amelia. HarperCollins Pubs. 1999 253p il $15.95; lib bdg $15.89 (5 and up)   **Fic**
1. Frontier and pioneer life—Fiction 2. Family life—Fiction 3. Finnish Americans—Fiction 4. Washington (State)—Fiction
ISBN 0-06-027822-6; 0-06-028354-8 (lib bdg)
               LC 98-47504
Also available Thorndike Press large print edition and Audiobook version
A Newbery Medal honor book, 2000
As the only girl in a Finnish American family of seven brothers, May Amelia Jackson resents being expected to act like a lady while growing up in Washington State in 1899
"The voice of the colloquial first-person narrative rings true and provides a vivid picture of frontier and pioneer life. . . . An afterword discusses Holm's research into her own family's history and that of other Finnish immigrants." Horn Book Guide

Holman, Felice

Slake's limbo. Scribner 1974 117p hardcover o.p. paperback available $4.99 (6 and up)   **Fic**
1. Runaway children—Fiction 2. Subways—Fiction 3. New York (N.Y.)—Fiction
ISBN 0-689-71066-6 (pa)
Aremis Slake, at the age of thirteen, takes to the New York City subways as a refuge from an abusive home life and oppressive school system
"The economically told chronicle of Slake's adventures is more than a survival saga: it is also an eloquent study of poverty, of fear, and finally of hope." Horn Book

Holt, Kimberly Willis

Mister and me; with illustrations by Leonard Jenkins. Putnam 1998 74p $13.99; pa $4.99 (3-5)

Fic

1. Remarriage—Fiction 2. African Americans—Fiction 3. Louisiana—Fiction

ISBN 0-399-23215-X; 0-698-11869-3 (pa)

LC 97-40329

In a small Louisiana mill town in 1940, Jolene does not want her Momma to marry the logger who is courting her, but it seems that even her most defiantly bad behavior cannot make him go away

"This heartfelt story is filled with richly developed characters who deal with all-too-real problems." Booklist

My Louisiana sky. Holt & Co. 1998 200p $16.95 (6 and up)

Fic

1. Mentally handicapped—Fiction 2. Louisiana—Fiction

ISBN 0-8050-5251-8

LC 98-12345

Also available in paperback from Dell and Audiobook version

Growing up in Saitter, Louisiana, in the 1950s, twelve-year-old Tiger Ann struggles with her feelings about her stern, but loving grandmother, her mentally slow parents, and her good friend and neighbor, Jesse

"Holt never resorts to over-dramatization or sentimentality in developing her uncannily credible characters." Horn Book Guide

When Zachary Beaver came to town. Holt & Co. 1999 227p $16.95 (5 and up)

Fic

1. Friendship—Fiction 2. Obesity—Fiction 3. Texas—Fiction

ISBN 0-8050-6116-9

LC 99-27998

Also available Audiobook version

During the summer of 1971 in a small Texas town, thirteen-year-old Toby and his best friend Cal meet the star of a sideshow act, 600-pound Zachary, the fattest boy in the world

"Holt writes with a subtle sense of humor and sensitivity, and reading her work is a delightful experience." Voice Youth Advocates

Holub, Josef, 1926-

The robber and me; translated from the German by Elizabeth D. Crawford. Holt & Co. 1997 213p $16.95 (5 and up)

Fic

1. Orphans—Fiction 2. Germany—Fiction

ISBN 0-8050-5599-1

LC 97-19106

Also available in paperback from Dell

Because he knows that the man accused of robbery is innocent, Boniface, an eleven-year-old orphan, struggles to find the courage to reveal the truth to his uncle in their small German village in 1867

"While the core of this wonderfully readable story is a somewhat serious one, the telling is full of humor and good spirit. . . . Crawford's translation is fluid and accessible." SLJ

Includes glossary

Honey, Elizabeth, 1947-

Don't pat the wombat! Knopf 2000 c1996 142p il $14.95; lib bdg $16.99 (4-6)

Fic

1. Camps—Fiction 2. School stories 3. Australia—Fiction

ISBN 0-375-80578-8; 0-375-90578-2 (lib bdg)

LC 99-87237

First published 1996 in Australia

Illustrated by William Clarke

Wormz, Nicko, and their friends fear that their experience at a school camp in the Australian bush will be ruined by the presence of the dreaded Mr. Cromwell as a substitute chaperon

"The humorous short chapters, informal tone, and camaraderie among the boys are sure to make [this book] a hit, even with reluctant readers." SLJ

Hooks, William H.

Freedom's fruit; paintings by James Ransome. Knopf 1996 unp il $16 (3-5)

Fic

1. Slavery—Fiction 2. African Americans—Fiction 3. Magic—Fiction

ISBN 0-679-82438-3

LC 93-235

Mama Marina, a slave woman and conjurer in the Old South, casts a spell on her master's grapes as part of her plan to win freedom for her daughter Sheba and the man Sheba loves

"Hooks weaves a hopeful, poetic story about the ability of the oppressed to outwit those with power. Ransome's full-page paintings are lush and vivid." Horn Book

Hopkinson, Deborah

Birdie's lighthouse; written by Deborah Hopkinson; illustrated by Kimberly Bulcken Root. Atheneum Bks. for Young Readers 1997 unp il $16; pa $5.99 (1-3)

Fic

1. Lighthouses—Fiction 2. Maine—Fiction

ISBN 0-689-81052-0; 0-689-83529-9 (pa)

LC 94-24097

"An Anne Schwartz book"

Written in diary form, this "book tells the story of Birdie Holland, daughter of a lighthouse keeper on a tiny island off the Maine coast in 1855. Her brother helps their father in the lighthouse until he becomes a fisherman and leaves the island. Then Birdie must take his place. When her father becomes ill during a severe northeaster, she must carry out the duties alone." SLJ

"With an exemplary assemblage of genre paintings perfectly attuned to the flow of the text, the whole is restrained yet charged with emotion." Horn Book

Horowitz, Anthony, 1955-

The Devil and his boy. Philomel Bks. 2000 c1998 182p $16.99 (5 and up)

Fic

1. Theater—Fiction 2. Adventure fiction 3. London (England)—Fiction

ISBN 0-399-23432-2

LC 99-39791

First published 1998 in the United Kingdom

In 1593, thirteen-year-old Tom travels through the English countryside to London, where he falls in with a troupe of actors and finds himself in great danger from

Horowitz, Anthony, 1955-—*Continued*

several sources

"In this delightful and inventive mixture of historical fact and grand storytelling, Horowitz has conjured a fabulous, fast-paced tale of humor, intrigue, magic, and adventure." Voice Youth Advocates

Horvath, Polly

The trolls. Farrar, Straus & Giroux 1999 135p $16 (3-6)   **Fic**
1. Aunts—Fiction 2. Family life—Fiction 3. Siblings—Fiction
ISBN 0-374-37787-1   LC 98-34375
Also available Audiobook version

Eccentric Aunt Sally comes from Canada to babysit the Anderson children while their parents are on a trip to Paris and every night the bedtime story adds another piece to a very suspect family history

"A surprisingly poignant undercurrent adds even greater depth to this skillfully written comic novel." Horn Book Guide

When the circus came to town. Farrar, Straus & Giroux 1996 138p $15; pa $4.95 (4-6)   **Fic**
1. Circus—Fiction 2. Prejudices—Fiction 3. Friendship—Fiction 4. Family life—Fiction
ISBN 0-374-38308-1; 0-374-48367-1 (pa)
        LC 96-11591

Although Ivy and her family welcome the Halibuts, and their son Alfred becomes her best friend, not all the townspeople are pleased to have circus people as neighbors, especially as other circus families move in

"With snappy dialogue and a witty text, Horvath makes a point about discrimination and tolerance, yet keeps the tone animated and humorous." SLJ

Houston, James A., 1921-

Frozen fire; a tale of courage; by James Houston; drawings by the author. Atheneum Pubs. 1977 149p il $16.99; pa $4.95 (6 and up)   **Fic**
1. Wilderness survival—Fiction 2. Arctic regions—Fiction 3. Inuit—Fiction
ISBN 0-689-50083-1; 0-689-71612-5 (pa)
        LC 77-6366
"A Margaret K. McElderry book"

"Based on the true and dramatic ordeal of an Eskimo boy in the 1960's, this adventure story is set . . . in the far north. Kayak, a classmate of Matthew Morgan's in their Baffin Island school, suggests to his new friend Mattoosie (Matthew) that they take a snowmobile and go to the rescue of Mattoosie's father when the latter, a prospector, disappears. The spare can of gasoline leaks, and the two boys face a homeward trek through seventy-five miles of whirling snow and bitter cold." Bull Cent Child Books

"Convincing dialogue, good pace, and lean style mark this as first-class adventure with a partial basis in fact." SLJ

Followed by Black diamonds (1982)

Howard, Ellen

The gate in the wall. Atheneum Bks. for Young Readers 1999 148p il $16 (5 and up)   **Fic**
1. Canals—Fiction 2. Child labor—Fiction 3. Orphans—Fiction 4. Great Britain—Fiction
ISBN 0-689-82295-2   LC 98-22250

"A Jean Karl book"

In nineteenth-century England, ten-year-old Emma, accustomed to long working hours at the silk mill and the poverty and hunger of her sister's house, finds her life completely changed when she inadvertently gets a job on a canal boat carrying cargoes between several northern towns

"Howard has given her story a highly interesting venue and has created a cast of characters who are fully dimensional and engaging." Horn Book Guide

Howe, Deborah, 1946-1978

Bunnicula; a rabbit-tale of mystery; by Deborah and James Howe; illustrated by Alan Daniel. Atheneum Bks. for Young Readers 1999 98p il $16; pa $3.99 (4-6)   **Fic**
1. Animals—Fiction 2. Mystery fiction
ISBN 0-689-83219-2; 0-689-80659-0 (pa)
        LC 99-28790
Also available Audiobook version
A reissue of the title first published 1979

"When the Monroes add a new pet to their household and vegetables are drained of their juices and turn white overnight, all the clues point to the little bunny they found in the theater the night they went to see a Dracula movie. The Monroes do not suspect Bunnicula, but their bookish cat, Chester, does. . . . He enlists the help of Harold, the dog, in getting to the bottom of the mystery." Child Book Rev Serv

This book is "blithe, sophisticated, and distinguished for the wit and humor of the dialogue." Bull Cent Child Books

Howe, James, 1946-

The celery stalks at midnight; illustrated by Leslie Morrill. Atheneum Pubs. 1983 111p il $16 (4-6)   **Fic**
1. Animals—Fiction 2. Mystery fiction
ISBN 0-689-30987-2   LC 83-2665
Also available in paperback from Avon Bks. and Audiobook version

"Convinced that Bunnicula, the Monroe family's pet rabbit, is a kind of vegetarian vampire, Chester becomes alarmed when the object of his suspicions mysteriously disappears. His overworked imagination begins to envision the possible consequences of Bunnicula's appetite for vegetable juices. . . . With his two canine companions—Harold, the narrator, and Howie, a naïve dachshund—Chester sets forth to locate Bunnicula and to save the victims." Horn Book

"The amusing and skillful black-and-white sketches capture the animals' antics and expressions of alternating doubt, skepticism, disgust and worry in this clever tale abounding with puns, wild chases and slapstick humor." SLJ

Other available titles about Harold and Chester are:
Bunnicula strikes again! (1999)
Howliday Inn (1982)
Nighty-nightmare (1987)
Return to Howliday Inn (1992)

Howe, James, 1946-—*Continued*

Dew drop dead; a Sebastian Barth mystery. Atheneum Pubs. 1990 156p $16; pa $4.50 (4-6)

Fic

1. Mystery fiction 2. Homeless persons—Fiction
ISBN 0-689-31425-6; 0-689-80760-0 (pa)

LC 89-34697

"A Jean Karl book"

"Sebastian Barth and his friends Corrie and David discover what appears to be a dead body in the long-abandoned Dew Drop Inn. But when they return with the police, the body has vanished. Police theory—that the 'body' was a homeless man passed-out drunk—is refuted when the kids find the body again in the woods, undeniably dead and possibly murdered." SLJ

"The story is well crafted and has substance beyond escapist fare as a result of Howe's inclusion of secondary storylines involving the homeless and Sebastian's own worries about his father's pending job loss." Booklist

Other available titles about Sebastian Barth are:

Eat your poison, dear (1986)

Stage fright (1986)

What Eric knew (1985)

Hughes, Ted, 1930-1998

The iron giant; a story in five nights; illustrated by Andrew Davidson. Knopf 1999 79p il $16; lib bdg $17.99; pa $4.99 (4-6)

Fic

1. Science fiction
ISBN 0-375-80167-7; 0-375-90167-1 (lib bdg); 0-375-80153-7 (pa)

LC 98-41368

A newly illustrated edition of the title first published 1968 by Harper & Row; published in the United Kingdom with title: The iron man

This is the story of an Iron Giant "who appears from nowhere and stalks the earth, devouring tractors and barbed wire for his supper. . . . But in the end he has to save the world from a creature from Outer Space." NY Times Book Rev

Hunt, Irene, 1907-

Across five Aprils. Follett 1964 223p o.p.; Berkley Bks. paperback available $4.99 (5 and up)

Fic

1. United States—History—1861-1865, Civil War—Fiction 2. Illinois—Fiction 3. Farm life—Fiction
ISBN 0-425-10241-6 (pa)

LC 64-17209

A Newbery Medal honor book, 1965

"Jethro Creighton, a boy of nine when the story begins, watches five Aprils come and go while his southern Illinois family is caught up emotionally and physically in the terrible conflict of the Civil War. Authentic background, a feeling for the people of that time, and a story that never loses the reader's interest." Wilson Libr Bull

Hunter, Mollie, 1922-

The mermaid summer. Harper & Row 1988 118p lib bdg $15.89; pa $4.95 (4 and up) **Fic**

1. Mermaids and mermen—Fiction 2. Grandfathers—Fiction
ISBN 0-06-022628-5 (lib bdg); 0-06-440344-0 (pa)

LC 87-45984

"A Charlotte Zolotow book"

With the help of her brother, Jon, nine-year-old Anna daringly seeks to discover the secret means to undo a mermaid's curse upon their grandfather

"Hunter's atmospherically rich story, set about a century ago, unfolds against a tapestry of local color. The delicately intertwining plot skeins reveal both tightly controlled suspense and an intriguing puzzle. Characters are well realized and fit the time and setting as well as the folkloric mold that Hunter once again uses to thoroughly enchant her readers." Booklist

A stranger came ashore; a story of suspense. Harper & Row 1975 163p hardcover o.p.; paperback available $4.95 (6 and up) **Fic**

1. Mythical animals—Fiction 2. Shetland (Scotland)—Fiction
ISBN 0-06-440082-4 (pa)

The author "mingles the reality of the lives of fishermen-crofters and the legends of the Selkies, the seal-folk of the Shetland Islands. A young man, Finn Learson, appears during a fierce storm. Is he the lone survivor of a shipwreck or is he—as young Rob suspects—a seal-man who plans to take Rob's sister to his ocean home? The folklore of the Selkies and the customs of the islands are woven throughout the tale, which culminates in a suspense-filled struggle between the forces of good and evil." Bull Cent Child Books

Hurwitz, Johanna

The adventures of Ali Baba Bernstein; illustrated by Gail Owens. Morrow 1985 82p il $17 (2-4) **Fic**

1. Personal names—Fiction
ISBN 0-688-04161-2

LC 84-27387

Also available in paperback from Avon Bks.

"Tired of his ordinary name, David Bernstein, age eight, decides he wants to be called Ali Baba, and he has a series of . . . adventures, culminating in a birthday party to which he invites every David Bernstein in the Manhattan telephone directory. That's when he realizes how different people with the same name can be, and he decides that some day he might go back to calling himself David." Bull Cent Child Books

"Hurwitz' characters, as always, are believable, the situations realistic and the plot well developed." SLJ

Another available title about Ali Baba Bernstein is:
Hurray for Ali Baba Bernstein (1989)

Baseball fever; illustrated by Ray Cruz. Morrow 1981 128p il o.p.; Avon Bks. paperback available $4.50 (3-5) **Fic**

1. Baseball—Fiction 2. Father-son relationship—Fiction
ISBN 0-380-73255-6 (pa)

LC 81-5633

"Ten-year-old Ezra suffers from 'Baseball Fever' and a father who has no interest in the sport. Mr. Feldman is constantly nagging Ezra to show an interest in chess. A weekend trip that takes the pair to Cooperstown and the Hall of Fame sets the stage for father-and-son rapprochement." SLJ

"A brisk, breezy story about a believable family is told with warmth and humor." Bull Cent Child Books

Class clown; illustrated by Sheila Hamanaka. Morrow 1987 98p il $15.95 (2-4) **Fic**

1. School stories
ISBN 0-688-06723-9

LC 86-23624

Hurwitz, Johanna—_Continued_

Also available in paperback from Scholastic

Lucas Cott "is the problem child in class; although extremely bright, he acts out involuntarily at the most inopportune moments. Even when he is trying his best to do assignments properly, things go wrong." Horn Book

"There are some very funny moments here, as well as some gentle and touching ones. . . . Realistic dialogue, short sentences in large print, and commonplace situations that sparkle with humor combine to make this a fine choice for children just beginning chapter books." SLJ

Other available titles in this series are:

Class president (1990)
School spirit (1994)
School's out (1990)
Spring break (1997)
Teacher's pet (1988)

Faraway summer; illustrated by Mary Azarian. Morrow Junior Bks. 1998 155p lib bdg $14.95; pa $4.95 (4-6)   **Fic**

1. Farm life—Fiction 2. Jews—Fiction 3. Vermont—Fiction

ISBN 0-688-15334-8 (lib bdg); 0-380-73256-4 (pa)
                                        LC 97-36363

"It's the summer of 1910, and Hadassah Rabinowitz, called Dossi, a Russian Jewish immigrant girl living in New York City, sets off for a Fresh Air Fund holiday on a farm in Vermont." N Y Times Book Rev

"Mary Azarian's occasional small woodcuts in black and white help create a sense of the period. . . . The warm characterization will keep readers interested in a story that shows how the hosts as well as the visitor benefit from the encounter with the stranger." Booklist

The hot & cold summer; illustrated by Gail Owens. Morrow 1984 160p il lib bdg $16 (3-5)
                                        Fic

1. Friendship—Fiction
ISBN 0-688-02746-6   LC 83-19336
Also available in paperback from Scholastic

"Ten-year-olds Rory and Derek are best friends—a unit that does not need outsiders. So when their neighbor tells them that her niece is coming for the summer and that she expects they'll be great chums, Rory decides that the best attack is to ignore the girl from the start. But Bolivia . . . is not to be shunted aside. With the help of her talking parrot, she knows how to get attention and, once gotten, how to keep it. . . . This episodic novel is cheerful and perceptive—right on target for both boys and girls." Booklist

Other available titles about Rory, Derek, and Bolivia are:

The cold & hot winter (1988)
The down & up fall (1996)
The up & down spring (1993)

Much ado about Aldo; pictures by John Wallner. Morrow 1978 95p il lib bdg $15.89 (3-5)
                                        Fic

1. Vegetarianism—Fiction
ISBN 0-688-32160-7   LC 78-5434
Also available in paperback from Puffin Bks.

"Aldo ponders on the meanings of everything in his orbit, especially relationships. He enters enthusiastically into a class project, a terrarium with crickets. When the teacher adds chameleons to the tank, however, Aldo realizes the purpose of the project: to teach how living things feed on each other. In shock and horror, Aldo becomes a vegetarian and gets into a fix when he stealthily rescues the crickets." Publ Wkly

"Aldo is an earnest and likeable character in a convincing family story with a pleasant urban setting. The author has a remarkable ability to project the amusements and worries of childhood, conveying them in a deceptively simple style." Horn Book

Other available titles about Aldo are:

Aldo Applesauce (1979)
Aldo Ice Cream (1981)
Aldo Peanut Butter (1990)

New neighbors for Nora; illustrated by Lillian Hoban. Morrow Junior Bks. 1991 78p il lib bdg $12.88 (2-4)   **Fic**

1. Apartment houses—Fiction 2. City and town life—Fiction

ISBN 0-688-09948-3   LC 90-47882

A newly illustrated edition of the title first published 1979

Describes the adventures of an inquisitive seven-year-old and her neighbors in a New York City apartment building

"Hurwitz's prose is effortless and affecting." Publ Wkly

Another available title about Nora is:
Busybody Nora (1976)

Rip-roaring Russell; illustrated by Lillian Hoban. Morrow 1983 80p il hardcover o.p. paperback available $4.95 (2-4)   **Fic**

1. Family life—Fiction 2. School stories
ISBN 0-688-16664-4 (pa)   LC 83-1019

Russell the four-year-old neighbor of Nora in New neighbors for Nora "faces the challenges of growing up in his own inimitable way. . . . Being a big brother disturbs him because baby Elisa takes altogether too much of his mother's time, but by the book's end, he decides that it isn't so bad." SLJ

"The action is low-keyed. . . . This is both realistic and sunny, with good adult-child relationships, the appeal of everyday life experiences, and a light, humorous treatment." Bull Cent Child Books

Other available titles about Russell and Elisa are:

E is for Elisa (1991)
Elisa in the middle (1995)
Ever clever Elisa (1997)
Make room for Elisa (1993)
Russell and Elisa (1989)
Russell rides again (1985)
Russell sprouts (1987)
Summer with Elisa (2000)

Starting school; illustrated by Karen Dugan. Morrow Junior Bks. 1998 102p il $15 (2-4)   **Fic**

1. Twins—Fiction 2. Brothers—Fiction 3. School stories

ISBN 0-688-15685-1   LC 97-47298

Marius and Marcus, the "younger twin brothers of Lucas Cott, star of the Class Clown series, devise antics of

Hurwitz, Johanna—*Continued*

their own when they head off to separate kindergartens in the same school." Horn Book

"Hurwitz incorporates lots of true-to-age details and jokes to give an authentic picture of how little ones tend to see the world, interact with others, and view themselves." Booklist

Ibbotson, Eva

The secret of platform 13; illustrated by Sue Porter. Dutton Children's Bks. 1998 c1994 231p il $15.99; $5.99 (5 and up) **Fic**

1. Fantasy fiction

ISBN 0-525-45929-4; 0-141-30286-0 (pa)

LC 97-44601

Also available Audiobook version

First published 1994 in the United Kingdom

Odge Gribble, a young hag, accompanies an old wizard, a gentle fey, and a giant ogre on their mission through a magical tunnel from their Island to London to rescue their King and Queen's son who had been stolen as an infant

"Lively, funny fantasy with a case of mistaken identity and a cast of eccentric characters." SLJ

Which witch? illustrated by Annabel Large. Dutton Children's Bks. 1999 c1979 231p il $15.99; pa $4.99 (4 and up) **Fic**

1. Witchcraft—Fiction 2. Magic—Fiction 3. Fantasy fiction

ISBN 0-525-46164-7; 0-14-130427-8 (pa)

LC 99-10199

First published 1979 in the United Kingdom

Deciding that he must sire a child to carry on his tradition of Loathing Light and Blighting the Beautiful, the Great Wizard Arriman announces a competition among the witches of Todcaster, one of whom will marry him

"The story's strength lies in its witty, satirical twists on beauty pageants and the Cinderella story, and its di-mensional, generally comedic characters. . . . However, the Roald Dahl-esque humor is overshadowed by a par-ticularly macabre scenario involving rats. . . . This one is not for the faint of heart or stomach." Booklist

Irving, Washington, 1783-1859

Rip Van Winkle (5 and up) **Fic**

1. New York (State)—Fiction

Some editions are:

Dial Bks. $19.95 Illustrated by Arthur Rackham (ISBN 0-8037-1264-2)

Morrow (Books of Wonder) $21.95 Illustrated by N. C. Wyeth (ISBN 0-688-07459-6)

Originally appeared 1819 in Irving's The sketch book of Geoffrey Crayon, Gent.

Rip Van Winkle "is based on a folk tale. Henpecked Rip and his dog Wolf wander into the Catskill mountains before the Revolutionary War. There they meet a dwarf, whom Rip helps to carry a keg. They join a group of dwarfs playing ninepins. When Rip drinks from the keg, he falls asleep and wakes 20 years later, an old man. Re-turning to his town, he discovers his termagant wife dead, his daughter married, and the portrait of King George replaced by one of George Washington. Irving uses the folk tale to present the contrast between the new and old societies." Reader's Ency. 3d edition

Irwin, Hadley

Jim-Dandy. Margaret K. McElderry Bks. 1994 135p $15 (5 and up) **Fic**

1. Custer, George Armstrong, 1839-1876—Fiction 2. Frontier and pioneer life—Fiction 3. Kansas—Fic-tion 4. Horses—Fiction

ISBN 0-689-50594-9 LC 93-22611

Also available in paperback from Troll

Living after the Civil War on a Kansas homestead with his stern stepfather, thirteen-year-old Caleb raises a beloved colt and becomes involved in General Custer's raids on the Cheyenne

"A thought-provoking read that's sure to promote dis-cussion." SLJ

The original Freddie Ackerman. Margaret K. McElderry Bks. 1992 183p $15; pa $3.99 (5 and up) **Fic**

1. Aunts—Fiction 2. Islands—Fiction 3. Maine—Fic-tion

ISBN 0-689-50562-0; 0-689-80389-3 (pa)

LC 91-43145

Twelve-year-old Trevor Frederick Ackerman refuses to spend another summer with his extended family of di-vorced parents, step-parents, and step-brothers and step-sisters, so he is sent up to Maine to stay with two eccen-tric great aunts and there gets involved in a series of ad-ventures

"This is a beautiful coming-of-age story with wonder-ful characterizations. Trevor's loneliness and low self-esteem are palpable as he escapes painful realities through a series of fantasies of himself as a war hero. . . . A fine book with a winning combination of humor and poignancy." SLJ

Isaacs, Anne, 1949-

Treehouse tales; illustrations by Lloyd Bloom. Dutton Children's Bks. 1997 85p il $14.99; pa $4.99 (3-5) **Fic**

1. Farm life—Fiction 2. Pennsylvania—Fiction

ISBN 0-525-45611-2; 0-14-038738-2 (pa)

LC 96-24549

Three interconnected stories relate the experiences and adventures of three 1880s Pennsylvania farm children in their family tree house, which serves as a refuge, a source of adventure, a lookout post, and a frightening dragon's lair

"Isaac's lighthearted tales sparkle with warmth and humor." Booklist

Jacques, Brian

Redwall; illustrated by Troy Howell. anniversary ed. Philomel Bks. 1997 351p il $22.95; pa $12.95 (6 and up) **Fic**

1. Mice—Fiction 2. Animals—Fiction 3. Fantasy fic-tion

ISBN 0-399-23160-9; 0-399-23629-5 (pa)

LC 97-226680

Also available Audiobook version

First published 1986

When the peaceful life of ancient Redwall Abbey is shattered by the arrival of the evil rat Cluny and his vil-lainous hordes, Matthias, a young mouse, determines to

Jacques, Brian—*Continued*

find the legendary sword of Martin the Warrior which, he is convinced, will help Redwall's inhabitants destroy the enemy

"Thoroughly engrossing . . . despite its length. . . . The theme will linger long after the story is finished." Booklist

Other available titles about Redwall Abbey are:
The Bellmaker (1995)
The legend of Luke (1999)
The long patrol (1998)
Lord Brocktree (2000)
Mariel of Redwall (1992)
Marlfox (1998)
Martin the Warrior (1994)
Mattimeo (1990)
Mossflower (1988)
The outcast of Redwall (1996)
Pearls of Lutra (1997)
Salamandastron (1993)

James, Mary, 1927-

Shoebag. Scholastic 1990 135p hardcover o.p. paperback available $4.50 (5 and up) **Fic**
1. Cockroaches—Fiction 2. Fantasy fiction
ISBN 0-590-43030-0 (pa) LC 89-10828
Shoebag, a happy young cockroach who finds himself suddenly changed into a little boy, changes the lives of those around him before returning to his former life as an insect

"Fans of the improbable will find this cockroach fantasy holds appeal, while the combination of humor and possible discussion topics offers opportunities for interchange." Booklist

Another available title about Shoebag is:
Shoebag returns (1996)

Jansson, Tove, 1914-2001

Moominsummer madness; translated by Thomas Warburton. Farrar, Straus & Giroux 1991 c1955 159p il $13.95; pa $5.95 (4-6) **Fic**
1. Fantasy fiction
ISBN 0-374-35039-6; 0-374-45310-1 (pa)
LC 90-56150
Original Swedish edition 1954; this translation first published 1955 in the United Kingdom; first United States edition 1961 by Henry Z. Walck

A flood hits Moomin Valley and triggers a series of adventures for the Moomins

"Newcomers to the long-established Moominvalley series might first glance at the simple, playfully illustrated appendix—'Moomin Gallery'—to acquaint themselves with the host of Moomin-species that adorn the plot. Once initiated, it's difficult not to be drawn in by the inventive adventures of Moomintroll and his family." Publ Wkly

Other available titles about the Moomintrolls are:
Comet in Moominland (1968)
Finn Family Moomintroll (1965)
Moominland midwinter(1967)
Moominpapa at sea (1967)
Moominpapa's memoirs (1994)
Tales from Moominvalley (1964)

Jarrell, Randall, 1914-1965

The animal family; decorations by Maurice Sendak. HarperCollins Pubs. 1996 179p il $15.95; pa $6.95 (4 and up) **Fic**
1. Animals—Fiction 2. Fantasy fiction
ISBN 0-06-205088-5; 0-06-205904-1 (pa)
LC 94-76270
"Michael di Capua books"

A reissue of the title first published 1965 by Pantheon Bks.

A lonely hunter living in the wilderness beside the sea gains a family made up of a mermaid, a bear, a lynx, and a boy

This story is "sensitively related with touches of humor and wisdom. A delight for the imaginative reader." Booklist

The bat-poet; pictures by Maurice Sendak. HarperCollins Pubs. 1996 42p il $13.95; pa $6.95 (2-4) **Fic**
1. Bats—Fiction 2. Poetry—Fiction
ISBN 0-06-205084-2; 0-06-205905-X (pa)
LC 94-76271
"Michael di Capua books"

A reissue of the title first published 1964 by MacMillan

A bat who can't sleep days makes up poems about the woodland creatures he now perceives for the first time

"A lovely book, perfectly illustrated—one well worth a child's attention and affection." Publ Wkly

Jarvis, Robin

The dark portal; book one of the Deptford mice trilogy. SeaStar Bks. 2000 243p il $17.95 (5 and up) **Fic**
1. Mice—Fiction 2. Rats—Fiction 3. Fantasy fiction
ISBN 1-58717-021-3 LC 00-26517
"Books of wonder"

First published 1989 in the United Kingdom

The first title in a projected trilogy. While on a rescue mission, a few daring mice journey below to the sewers to an evil world populated by rats who peel mice before eating them and worship the Dark Lord

This "is a spooky and enthralling animal fantasy. . . . Jarvis provides counterpoint to the heart-racing adventure with scenes of haunting beauty." Publ Wkly

Jennings, Richard W.

Orwell's luck; [by] Richard Jennings. Houghton Mifflin 2000 146p $15 (5 and up) **Fic**
1. Rabbits—Fiction 2. Magic—Fiction
ISBN 0-618-03628-8 LC 99-33501
"Walter Lorraine books"

While caring for an injured rabbit which becomes her confidant, horoscope writer, and source of good luck, a thoughtful seventh grade girl learns to see things in more than one way

"This absolutely captivating tale is about everyday magic . . . filled with quiet humor and seamless invention. The characters . . . are the sort that readers fall in love with." Booklist

Jeppson, Ann-Sofie

Here comes Pontus! illustrated by Catarina Kruusval; translated by Frances Corry. R & S Bks. 2000 29p il $14 (2-4)   **Fic**
1. Horses—Fiction
ISBN 91-29-64561-1   LC 99-52908
Original Swedish edition, 1998

Pontus the pony tells his story as he is sold and moves to a new farm where he belongs to a little girl with a yellow mane. Includes factual information about the care of horses

"This combination of factual information and slight story line works because the pony is believable and his reactions to many of the incidents . . . capture the behavior and reactions of real horses. Kruusval's art mirrors the action in the text, and the pictures are filled with realistic details of the stables." SLJ

Johnson, Angela, 1961-

Heaven. Simon & Schuster Bks. for Young Readers 1998 138p $16; pa $4.99 (6 and up)   **Fic**
1. Adoption—Fiction 2. African Americans—Fiction
ISBN 0-689-82229-4; 0-689-82290-1 (pa)
                                                LC 98-3291
Also available Thorndike Press large print edition
Coretta Scott King Award for text, 1999

Fourteen-year-old Marley's seemingly perfect life in the small town of Heaven is disrupted when she discovers that her father and mother are not her real parents

"In spare, often poetic prose . . . Johnson relates Marley's insightful quest into what makes a family." SLJ

Songs of faith. Orchard Bks. 1998 103p $15.95; lib bdg $16.99 (5 and up)   **Fic**
1. Divorce—Fiction 2. African Americans—Fiction
ISBN 0-531-30023-4; 0-531-33023-0 (lib bdg)
                                                LC 97-40216
Also available in paperback from Knopf

Living in a small town in Ohio in 1975 and desperately missing her divorced father, thirteen-year-old Doreen comes to terms with disturbing changes in her family life

"Johnson has set attractive and realistic African-American characters in situations in which race is not the focus. This short, sensitive book will appeal most to reflective readers." SLJ

Jones, Diana Wynne

Castle in the air. Greenwillow Bks. 1991 199p $15.95 (6 and up)   **Fic**
1. Fantasy fiction
ISBN 0-688-09686-7   LC 90-30266

In this "follow-up to Howl's Moving Castle, . . . the protagonist is a young carpet merchant called Abdullah, who spends much of his time creating a richly developed daydream in which he is the long-lost son of a great prince, kidnapped as a child by a villainous bandit. . . . Feisty Sophie and the Wizard Howl (from Howl's Moving Castle) do not become apparent till late in the story, but their fortunes do link up with those of Abdullah and his love. Jones maintains both suspense and wit throughout, demonstrating once again that frequently nothing is what it seems to be." Booklist

Howl's moving castle. Greenwillow Bks. 1986 212p $15.95 (6 and up)   **Fic**
1. Fantasy fiction
ISBN 0-688-06233-4   LC 85-21981

"When the wicked Witch of the Waste turns Sophie Hatter into an ugly crone, the girl seeks refuge in Wizard Howl's moving castle. To her surprise and dismay, she finds herself embroiled in a contest between the witch and the wizard, in the tangled love affairs of the wizard, and in a perplexing mystery." Child Book Rev Serv

"Satisfyingly, Sophie meets a fate far exceeding her dreary expectations. This novel is an exciting, multifaceted puzzle, peopled with vibrant, captivating characters. A generous sprinkling of humor adds potency to this skillful author's spell." Voice Youth Advocates

Jukes, Mavis

Blackberries in the dark; pictures by Thomas B. Allen. Knopf 1985 unp il hardcover o.p. paperback available $3.99 (2-4)   **Fic**
1. Grandmothers—Fiction 2. Death—Fiction
ISBN 0-679-86570-5 (pa)   LC 85-4259

Nine-year-old Austin visits his grandmother the summer after his grandfather dies and together they try to come to terms with their loss

"This spare story vividly captures the emotions of painful times and shows how they ease with sharing and remembering. . . . Poignant and perceptive, this has impressive resonance for so brief a story, and readers won't easily shed its warm afterglow. Heavily shaped pencil drawings are scattered throughout." Booklist

Like Jake and me; pictures by Lloyd Bloom. Knopf 1984 unp il hardcover o.p. paperback available $7.99 (2-4)   **Fic**
1. Stepfathers—Fiction 2. Spiders—Fiction
ISBN 0-394-89263-1 (pa)   LC 83-8380
A Newbery Medal honor book, 1985

In this book "timid Alex strives to be like his rugged cowboy stepfather, and the two find a common bond when Alex demonstrates his bravery by 'rescuing' Jake from a wolf spider that is crawling on his clothes." SLJ

"The humorous short story is illustrated picture-book fashion with a series of misty, soft-edged paintings. . . . The story might be an excellent springboard for discussion of relationships and emotions; at the very least it's a satisfying vignette of the tender spots left when families take new shapes." Booklist

Juster, Norton, 1929-

The phantom tollbooth; illustrated by Jules Feiffer. Random House 1961 255p il $19.95; pa $5.50 (5 and up)   **Fic**
1. Fantasy fiction
ISBN 0-394-81500-9; 0-394-82037-1 (pa)

"Milo, a boy who receives a surprise package which, when put together, is a toll-booth, goes off in a toy automobile on a tour of an imaginary country." Bull Cent Child Books

"It's all very clever. The author plays most ingeniously on words and phrases . . . and on concepts of averages and infinity and such . . . while the pictures are even more diverting than the text, for they add interesting details." N Y Her Trib Books

Karr, Kathleen

The great turkey walk. Farrar, Straus & Giroux 1998 197p $16; pa $4.95 (5 and up) **Fic**
  1. Turkeys—Fiction 2. West (U.S.)—Fiction
ISBN 0-374-32773-4; 0-374-42798-4 (pa)
                            LC 97-38859

Also available Audiobook version
In 1860, a somewhat simple-minded fifteen-year-old boy attempts to herd one thousand turkeys from Missouri to Denver, Colorado, in hopes of selling them at a profit
"Based on an actual event, this is a lively and entertaining story." Horn Book Guide

Man of the family. Farrar, Straus & Giroux 1999 178p $16 (4 and up) **Fic**
  1. Hungarian Americans—Fiction 2. Family life—Fiction 3. New Jersey—Fiction
ISBN 0-374-34764-6   LC 99-26051
During the 1920s, life for Istvan, the eldest child of a Hungarian-American family, holds both joy and sadness
"The episodes are amusing and sometimes fascinating, but the warm relationship between father and son lies at the heart of this excellent novel." SLJ

Skullduggery. Hyperion Bks. for Children 2000 227p lib bdg $16.49; pa $15.99 (5 and up) **Fic**
  1. Phrenology—Fiction 2. Orphans—Fiction 3. Adventure fiction
ISBN 0-7868-0506-4 (lib bdg); 0-7868-2439-5 (pa)
                            LC 99-39426
In 1839, twelve-year-old Matthew's job as assistant to the phrenologist Dr. Cornwall takes him up and down the Eastern Seaboard and to Europe, as they rob graves and try to find out who is following them and why
"The narrative's somewhat formal style contains glints of dark humor and quietly reveals the characters of the smart, deferential boy and his imperfect but sincere partner." Horn Book Guide

Kehret, Peg

Don't tell anyone. Dutton Children's Bks. 2000 137p $15.99 (4 and up) **Fic**
  1. Cats—Fiction 2. Criminals—Fiction
ISBN 0-525-46388-7   LC 99-89605
Twelve-year-old Megan does not realize that feeding a group of feral cats living in a field near her house will involve her as a witness to a traffic accident and in the dangerous plan of an unstable criminal
"There are subplots galore in this quick read . . . but they all hang together, and thanks to Kehret's even tone, the scary aspects won't frighten younger readers." Booklist

Earthquake terror. Cobblehill Bks. 1996 132p $14.99; pa $4.99 (4-6) **Fic**
  1. Earthquakes—Fiction 2. Siblings—Fiction 3. Physically handicapped—Fiction
ISBN 0-525-65226-4; 0-14-038343-3 (pa)
                            LC 95-20462
When an earthquake hits the isolated island in northern California where his family had been camping, twelve-year-old Jonathan Palmer must find a way to keep himself, his partially paralyzed younger sister, and their dog alive until help arrives

"The accessible, dramatic survival story explores themes of responsibility and bravery, and the fast pace will keep readers turning the pages." Horn Book Guide

Keith, Harold, 1903-

Rifles for Watie. Crowell 1957 332p lib bdg $15.89; pa $5.95 (6 and up) **Fic**
  1. Watie, Stand, 1806-1871—Fiction 2. United States—History—1861-1865, Civil War—Fiction
ISBN 0-690-04907-2 (lib bdg); 0-06-447030-X (pa)

Awarded the Newbery Medal, 1958
"Young Jeff Bussey longs for the life of a Union soldier during the Civil War, but before long he realizes the cruelty and savagery of some men in the army situation. The war loses its glamor as he sees his very young friends die. When he is made a scout, his duties take him into the ranks of Stand Watie, leader of the rebel troops of the Cherokee Indian Nation, as a spy." Stensland. Lit By & About the Am Indian

Kendall, Carol

The Gammage Cup; a novel of the Minnipins; illustrated by Erik Blegvad. Harcourt 2000 283p il $17; pa $6 **Fic**
  1. Fantasy fiction
ISBN 0-15-202487-5; 0-15-202493-X (pa)
                            LC 99-55279

A Newbery Medal honor book, 1960
"An Odyssey/Harcourt young classic"
A reissue of the title first published 1959
A handful of Minnipins, a sober and sedate people, rise up against the Periods, the leading family of an isolated mountain valley, and are exiled to a mountain where they discover that the ancient enemies of their people are preparing to attack
"An original and wholly delightful tale." Booklist
Another available title about the Minnipins is:
The whisper of Glocken (1965)

Kerr, Judith

When Hitler stole Pink Rabbit; illustrated by the author. Coward-McCann 1972 c1971 191p il hardcover o.p. paperback available $4.99 (4 and up) **Fic**
  1. Jewish refugees—Fiction
ISBN 0-698-11589-9 (pa)
First published 1971 in the United Kingdom
"Anna, aged nine, finds that her family suddenly has to leave Berlin for Switzerland because the Nazis have won an election. In packing, she has to choose between two stuffed animals—an old beloved pink rabbit and a new dog. She chooses the dog, assuming that their exile will be temporary. Only gradually as her family moves from Switzerland to France to England in search of a meager living does she realize that she will never return to Germany and that she will never see the rabbit again." Economist
"This tale of a refugee family is based on the author's childhood experience and, although anti-Semitism in Germany and financial depression everywhere are a somber backdrop, the book is warm and cozy, filled with the small, homely details of events that are important in a child's life." Saturday Rev
Followed by The other way around (1975)

Kimmel, Elizabeth Cody

In the stone circle. Scholastic 1998 225p $15.95
(5 and up)   **Fic**

1. Ghost stories 2. Wales—Fiction
ISBN 0-590-21308-3   LC 97-14737

While spending the summer in an old stone house in
Wales, fourteen-year-old Cristyn comes to terms with the
death of her mother while satisfying the request of a thirteenth-century princess

"Kimmel handles the history and the ghost of the girl
Carwen with a deft naturalness that keeps both vivid, and
the resolution of all the plots strands is satisfying without
being overly pat." Booklist

Visiting Miss Caples. Dial Bks. 2000 168p
$16.99 (6 and up)   **Fic**

1. Old age—Fiction 2. Friendship—Fiction
ISBN 0-8037-2502-7   LC 99-27899

The elderly shut-in she visits once a week becomes an
unexpected source of friendship and strength for thirteen-
year-old Jenna, and they help each other face and overcome painful aspects of their lives

"Young readers coping with difficult changes at
school and at home will respond to this thoughtful story." Booklist

King-Smith, Dick, 1922-

Ace, the very important pig; illustrations by
Lynette Hemmant. Crown 1990 134p il hardcover
o.p. paperback available $4.99 (3-5)   **Fic**

1. Pigs—Fiction
ISBN 0-679-81931-2 (pa)   LC 90-1447

Also available in paperback from P. Smith

Farmer Tubbs' amazing pig, Ace of Clubs, eventually
winds up on television for his cleverness

"The author exploits his joyful sense of the absurd to
the hilt, combining a gentle ribbing of country folk and
their animal counterparts with a genuine affection." Horn
Book

Babe: the gallant pig; written by Dick
King-Smith, illustrated by Mary Rayner. Crown
1985 c1983 118p il $15; pa $4.99 (3-5)   **Fic**

1. Pigs—Fiction
ISBN 0-517-55556-5; 0-679-87393-7 (pa)
                                       LC 84-11429

Also available Spanish language edition

First published 1983 in the United Kingdom with title:
The sheep-pig

A piglet destined for eventual butchering arrives at the
farmyard, is adopted by an old sheep dog, and discovers
a special secret to success

"Mary Rayner's engaging black-and-white drawings
capture the essence of Babe and the skittishness of sheep
and enhance this splendid book—which should once and
for all establish the intelligence and nobility of pigs."
Horn Book

The cuckoo child; illustrated by Leslie W.
Bowman. Hyperion Bks. for Children 1993 127p
il hardcover o.p. paperback available $4.99 (3-5)
                                              Fic

1. Ostriches—Fiction 2. Geese—Fiction 3. Farm
life—Fiction
ISBN 0-7868-1351-2 (pa)   LC 92-72029

"Eight-year-old Jack steals a huge ostrich egg that is
about to be fed to a snake in Wildlife Park. Jack sets the
egg under the farmyard goose; it hatches, and Jack raises
Oliver, the ostrich chick, until he's two years old. . . .
King-Smith has a lot of fun with the way humans and
animals resemble each other. He characterizes the farmyard with comedy and warmth, and Bowman's illustrations capture the cackles and chaos." Booklist

Jenius: the amazing guinea pig; illustrated by
Brian Floca. Hyperion Bks. for Children 1996 52p
il $13.95; pa $3.95 (2-4)   **Fic**

1. Guinea pigs—Fiction 2. School stories
ISBN 0-7868-0243-X; 0-7868-1135-8 (pa)
                                       LC 95-50633

"Hyperion chapters"

Eight-year-old Judy tries to convince her parents and
classmates that her brilliant guinea pig can do all the
tricks which she says it can

"There is both humor and suspense in the short novel.
. . . The format, with large type, plenty of white space
and Floca's cheerful line drawings, makes this brief novel well-suited to young readers just moving into chapter
books." Horn Book

A mouse called Wolf; illustrated by Jon
Goodell. Crown 1997 98p il $16; lib bdg $17.99;
pa $4.99 (2-4)   **Fic**

1. Mice—Fiction 2. Music—Fiction
ISBN 0-517-70973-2; 0-517-70974-0 (lib bdg);
0-375-80066-2 (pa)   LC 97-1526

A mouse with an unusual name shares his musical gift
with a widowed concert pianist

This book "succeeds not because of its action or clever premise but because of its determined main character,
its gentle wit, and its positive message." Booklist

Pigs might fly; a novel; drawings by Mary
Rayner. Viking 1982 158p il hardcover o.p.
paperback available $4.99 (3-5)   **Fic**

1. Pigs—Fiction 2. Farm life—Fiction 3. Physically
handicapped—Fiction 4. Great Britain—Fiction
ISBN 0-14-034537-X (pa)   LC 81-11525

First published 1980 in the United Kingdom with title:
Daggie Dogfoot

"Daggie Dogfoot (his front trotters are formed like
paws) is the nickname bestowed on the runt of a litter
born on a pig farm in England. Daggie overhears, out of
its ironic context, the comment that 'pigs might fly' and
this becomes his goal. His attempts to fly lead to his
learning how to swim, with the help of a Muscovy duck
and a happy-go-lucky otter. After a fierce rainstorm
bursts the dam upstream, flooding most of the farm and
carrying the food-storage shed downstream, it is Daggie
who must swim to get help." SLJ

"Written with wit and controlled ebullience, this has
excellent characterization, pithy dialogue, good pace, and
admirable line drawings." Bull Cent Child Books

King-Smith, Dick, 1922-—*Continued*

The school mouse; illustrated by Cynthia Fisher. Hyperion Bks. for Children 1995 123p il hardcover o.p. paperback available $4.99 (3-5)

Fic

1. Mice—Fiction 2. Books and reading—Fiction
ISBN 0-7868-1156-0 (pa)   LC 94-48443

"By reading a warning on the package, pretty school mouse Flora prevents her illiterate parents from eating the little blue pellets that have been placed throughout the school by an exterminator. . . . With his usual blend of wit, humor, and lively dialogue, King-Smith spins another endearing, vital animal tale." Booklist

Sophie's Tom; illustrated by David Parkins. Candlewick Press 1991 110p il hardcover o.p. paperback available $4.99 (3-5)   Fic

1. Cats—Fiction 2. Great Britain—Fiction
ISBN 1-56402-373-7 (pa)   LC 91-58756

Sophie "finds a stray cat and tries to talk her parents into letting her keep it. Set against the backdrop of this story are Sophie's first experiences with school. . . . A good readaloud for Sophie's contemporaries, this is a funny chronicle of a rugged and interesting little girl." Bull Cent Child Books

Other available titles about Sophie are:
Sophie hits six (1993)
Sophie in the saddle (1994)
Sophie is seven (1995)
Sophie's Lucky (1996)
Sophie's snail (1989)

Spider Sparrow; illustrated by Peter Bailey. Crown 2000 163p $16.95; lib bdg $18.99 (4-6)

Fic

1. Mentally handicapped—Fiction 2. Farm life—Fiction 3. World War, 1939-1945—Fiction 4. Great Britain—Fiction
ISBN 0-517-80043-8; 0-517-80044-6 (lib bdg)
          LC 99-30707

Also available Audiobook version

Spider, a baby abandoned on an English farm, grows up to be mentally slower than other children but manifests a remarkable talent for communicating with animals as he comes of age during World War II

"Poignant and wise, this deeply moving tale is not to be missed." Publ Wkly

Three terrible trins; illustrated by Mark Teague. Crown 1994 105p il $15; pa $4.99 (3-5)   Fic

1. Mice—Fiction 2. Cats—Fiction
ISBN 0-517-59828-0; 0-679-88552-8 (pa)
          LC 93-44157

Three mice brothers, ignoring the class system separating the four clans of rodents in their farmhouse, befriend a lower class mouse and form a team to fight cats

"King-Smith excels in creating vivid characters and a fast-paced plot. . . . All in all, a delightful romp, illustrated with humorous black-and-white drawings, that will appeal to readers who enjoy fantastic animal stories." SLJ

The water horse; illustrated by David Parkins. Crown 1998 c1990 118p il $16; pa $4.99 (3-5)

Fic

1. Sea monsters—Fiction 2. Scotland—Fiction
ISBN 0-517-80026-8; 0-375-80352-1 (pa)
          LC 98-2972

First published 1990 in the United Kingdom

In 1930, on the coast of Scotland, eight-year-old Kirstie finds a large egg which hatches into an unusual sea creature, and as he grows her family must decide what to do with him

"This well-written, fast-paced fantasy combines a popular subject with appealing, distinctive characters, humor, and drama." Booklist

Kingsley, Charles, 1819-1875

The water babies (4-6)   Fic
1. Fairy tales

Also available Audiobook version
Some editions are:
Millbrook Press $23.40 Illustrated by Jan Ormerod (ISBN 0-761-30411-8)
Morrow Junior Bks. $22 Illustrated by Jessie Willcox Smith (ISBN 0-688-14831-X)
First published 1863

"A Victorian fairy story about Tom, a runaway chimney-sweep, whom fairies change into a water-baby. . . . Tom's adventurous experiences with stream and sea dwellers are told with fine imagination and simple sincerity." Books for Boys & Girls

Kinsey-Warnock, Natalie

The Canada geese quilt; illustrated by Leslie W. Bowman. Dutton 1989 60p il $14.99 (3-5)   Fic

1. Quilts—Fiction 2. Grandmothers—Fiction 3. Family life—Fiction 4. Vermont—Fiction
ISBN 0-525-65004-0   LC 88-32661

Also available in paperback from Dell

Worried that the coming of a new baby and her grandmother's serious illness will change the warm familiar life on her family's Vermont farm, ten-year-old Ariel combines her artistic talent with her grandmother's knowledge to make a very special quilt

"Written in simple language, this intergenerational love story succeeds in touching the heart through its rare combination of sensitivity and grit. Bowman's softly shaded pencil drawings subtly suggest the 1940s Vermont setting, characters, and mood." Booklist

Kipling, Rudyard, 1865-1936

The beginning of the armadilloes   Fic
1. Armadillos—Fiction

Some editions are:
Harcourt $14.95 Illustrated by Lorinda Bryan Cauley (ISBN 0-15-206380-3)
North-South Bks. lib bdg $15.88 Illustrated by John A. Rowe (ISBN 1-55858-483-8)
Story originally published 1902 as part of Kipling's Just so stories

A tortoise and a hedgehog combine their natural assets and transform themselves into armadillos to escape the hungry attention of a young jaguar

Kipling, Rudyard, 1865-1936—*Continued*

The elephant's child   **Fic**
1. Elephants—Fiction

Some editions are:
Crocodile Bks. USA pa $6 Illustrated by Jan Mogensen
(ISBN 0-940793-77-6)
Harcourt pa $6 Illustrated by Lorinda Bryan Cauley
(ISBN 0-15-225386-6)
Originally published 1902 as part of Kipling's Just so
stories
"This well-known whimsical fantasy that explains how
the insatiably curious elephant child got his trunk is a
fine example of one of Kipling's greatest classics." Adventuring with Books

Klause, Annette Curtis

Alien secrets. Delacorte Press 1993 227p
$15.95; pa $4.99 (5 and up)   **Fic**
1. Science fiction 2. Mystery fiction
ISBN 0-385-30928-7; 0-440-41061-4 (pa)
                                          LC 92-31326
On her journey to the distant planet where her parents
are working, twelve-year-old Puck befriends a troubled
alien and becomes involved in a dangerous mystery involving a precious artifact
"This fast-paced adventure novel features a smart heroine, an appealing alien, plenty of intrigue, and a noble
mission that readers won't be able to resist." SLJ

Kline, Suzy, 1943-

Herbie Jones; illustrated by Richard Williams.
Putnam 1985 95p il $13.99; pa $4.99 (3-5)   **Fic**
1. School stories
ISBN 0-399-21183-7; 0-14-032071-7 (pa)
                                          LC 84-24915
Herbie's experiences in the third grade include finding
bones in the boy's bathroom, wandering away from his
class on their field trip, and being promoted to a higher
reading group
This is "filled with light humor in its accounts of
classroom incidents." Bull Cent Child Books
Other available titles about Herbie Jones are:
Herbie Jones and Hamburger Head (1989)
Herbie Jones and the birthday showdown (1993)
Herbie Jones the the class gift (1987)
Herbie Jones and the dark attic (1992)
Herbie Jones and the monster ball (1988)
What's the matter with Herbie Jones? (1986)

Horrible Harry in room 2B; pictures by Frank
Remkiewicz. Viking Kestrel 1988 56p il hardcover
o.p. paperback available $3.99 (2-4)   **Fic**
1. School stories
ISBN 0-14-038552-5 (pa)   LC 88-14204
Harry "is the devilish second grader who plays pranks
and gets into mischief but can still end up a good friend.
In a series of brief scenes, children meet Harry as he
shows a garter snake to Song Lee and later ends up being a snake himself for Halloween. His trick to make
scary people out of pencil stubs backfires when no one
is scared, and his budding romance with Song Lee goes
nowhere on the trip to the aquarium. . . . This story
should prove to be popular with those just starting chapter books." SLJ

Other available titles about Horrible Harry and Song
Lee are:
Horrible Harry and the ant invasion (1989)
Horrible Harry and the Christmas surprise (1991)
Horrible Harry and the Drop of Doom (1998)
Horrible Harry and the dungeon (1996)
Horrible Harry and the green slime (1989)
Horrible Harry and the kickball wedding (1992)
Horrible Harry and the purple people (1997)
Horrible Harry at Halloween (2000)
Horrible Harry goes to the moon (2000)
Horrible Harry moves up to third grade (1998)
Horrible Harry's secret (1990)
Song Lee and Leech Man (1995)
Song Lee and the hamster hunt (1994)
Song Lee and the "I hate you" notes (1999)
Song Lee in room 2B (1993)

Mary Marony, mummy girl; illustrations by
Blanche Sims. Putnam 1994 78p il $13.99 (2-4)
                                                  Fic
1. Halloween—Fiction 2. School stories 3. Speech
disorders—Fiction
ISBN 0-399-22609-5   LC 93-14348
Second-grader Mary Marony wants to be something
scary for Halloween so she can get back at Marvin, who
makes fun of Mary's stuttering
"Kline's characters deal with real problems in upbeat,
yet believable ways. . . . A fine addition to the burgeoning easy-chapter-book genre as well as a popular offering
for Halloween." Booklist
Other available titles about Mary Marony and Marvin
are:
Marvin and the mean words (1997)
Marvin and the meanest girl (2000)
Mary Marony and the chocolate surprise (1995)
Mary Marony and the snake (1992)
Mary Marony hides out (1993)

Orp and the FBI. Putnam 1995 94p il $14.99
(4-6)   **Fic**
1. Mystery fiction
ISBN 0-399-22664-8   LC 94-24552
"When Orp and his friend Derrick start a detective
agency, Famous Bathtub Investigators (FBI), Orp's little
sister, Chloe, starts a rival one, Chloe's Investigation
Agency (CIA). So when the children notice strange lights
and sounds coming from the next-door neighbor's house,
both the FBI . . . and CIA turn out to investigate."
Booklist
"The plot develops smoothly and believably with
many amusing turns along the way, and the level of suspense is well maintained." SLJ
Other available titles about Orp are:
Orp (1989)
Orp and the chop suey burgers (1990)
Orp goes to the hoop (1991)

Knight, Joan

Charlotte in Giverny; by Joan MacPhail Knight;
watercolor illustrations by Melissa Sweet.
Chronicle Bks. 2000 unp il $15.95 (3-6)   **Fic**
1. Artists—Fiction 2. France—Fiction
ISBN 0-8118-2383-0   LC 99-6878

Knight, Joan—*Continued*

While living in France in 1892, Charlotte, a young American girl, writes a journal of her experiences including those among the Impressionist painters at the artist colony of Giverny. Includes profiles of artists who appear in the journal and a glossary of French words

"The profuse illustrations, a mix of 1890s postcards and other memorabilia, reproductions of (mostly) impressionistic paintings by the mentioned artists, and Melissa Sweet's delicately drawn vignettes of vegetables and other items, lay an air of sunny, well-bred tranquility over the scene." Booklist

Koertge, Ronald

Tiger, tiger, burning bright; a novel. Orchard Bks. 1994 179p $17.95; lib bdg $18.99 (6 and up)   **Fic**

1. Grandfathers—Fiction 2. Old age—Fiction 3. California—Fiction

ISBN 0-531-06840-4; 0-531-08690-9 (lib bdg)

            LC 93-37758

"A Melanie Kroupa book"

Worried that his mother will send his beloved grandfather to a nursing home "for his own good," Jesse and some of his eighth-grade classmates accompany Pappy into the mountains near their small California town to look for the tiger tracks he claims to have seen

"Koertge has created a quirky, often hilarious, cast of characters in a small central California town. . . . The dialogue, whether between Jesse and his family members or between Jesse and his cronies, sounds exactly right." Book Rep

Konigsburg, E. L.

About the B'nai Bagels; written and illustrated by E. L. Konigsburg. Atheneum Pubs. 1969 172p il o.p.; Dell paperback available $4.50 (4-6)   **Fic**

1. Jews—Fiction 2. Baseball—Fiction

ISBN 0-440-40034-1 (pa)

A "story of a Jewish Little League team. Twelve-year-old Mark Stezer has problems: his mother is manager of the team; his brother is coach. This makes some sticky situations and 'overlaps' in his life. And he has worries about losing his best friend. Mark matures, having to make some difficult decisions on his own." Read Ladders for Hum Relat. 5th edition

"Penetrating characterizations emerge by implication; and the author's unfailing humor and her deep understanding of human nature are as noticeable as ever." Horn Book

From the mixed-up files of Mrs. Basil E. Frankweiler; written and illustrated by E. L. Konigsburg. Atheneum Pubs. 1967 162p il $16; pa $5.50 (4-6)   **Fic**

1. Metropolitan Museum of Art (New York, N.Y.)—Fiction

ISBN 0-689-20586-4; 0-689-71181-6 (pa)

Also available in paperback from Dell and Audiobook version

Awarded the Newbery Medal, 1968

"Claudia, feeling misunderstood at home, takes her younger brother and runs away to New York where she sets up housekeeping in the Metropolitan Museum of Art, making ingenious arrangements for sleeping, bathing, and laundering. She and James also look for clues to the authenticity of an alleged Michelangelo statue, the true story of which is locked in the files of Mrs. Frankweiler, its former owner. Claudia's progress toward maturity is also a unique introduction to the Metropolitan Museum." Moorachian. What is a City?

Jennifer, Hecate, Macbeth, William McKinley, and me, Elizabeth; written and illustrated by E. L. Konigsburg. Atheneum Pubs. 1967 117p il $16 (4-6)   **Fic**

1. Friendship—Fiction 2. Witchcraft—Fiction 3. African Americans—Fiction

ISBN 0-689-30007-7

Also available in paperback from Dell

A Newbery Medal honor book, 1968

"Two fifth grade girls, one of whom is the first black child in a middle-income suburb, play at being apprentice witches in this amusing and perceptive story." NY Public Libr. Black Exper in Child Books

A proud taste for scarlet and miniver; written and illustrated by E. L. Konigsburg. Atheneum Pubs. 1973 201p il $17 (5 and up)   **Fic**

1. Eleanor, of Aquitaine, Queen, consort of Henry II, King of England, 1122?-1204—Fiction

ISBN 0-689-30111-1

Also available in paperback from Dell

This is an historical novel about the 12th century queen, Eleanor of Aquitaine, wife of kings of France and England and mother of King Richard the Lion Hearted and King John. Impatiently awaiting the arrival of her second husband, King Henry II, in heaven, she recalls her life with the aid of some contemporaries

The author "has succeeded in making history amusing as well as interesting. . . . The characterization is superb. . . . The black-and-white drawings are skillfully as well as appropriately modeled upon medieval manuscript illuminations and add their share of joy to the book." Horn Book

Up from Jericho Tel. Atheneum Pubs. 1986 178p $17; pa $4.99 (5 and up)   **Fic**

1. Actors—Fiction 2. Mystery fiction

ISBN 0-689-31194-X; 0-689-82332-0 (pa)

            LC 85-20061

"Jeanmarie and Malcolm are both unpopular, both bossy, both latchkey children; both live in a trailer park, and both want to be famous. Jeanmarie knows that she will be a famous actress and that Malcolm will one day be a famous scientist. These two friends embark on a series of adventures encouraged by the spirit of the long dead actress, Tallulah. Yes, presumably 'the' Tallulah! Tallulah, as a ghost, has the ability to make them invisible, and in that state the kids are sent to find the missing Regina Stone." Voice Youth Advocates

"Konigsburg always provides fresh ideas, tart wit and humor, and memorable characters. As for style, she is a natural and gifted storyteller. . . . This is a lively, clever, and very funny book." Bull Cent Child Books

Konigsburg, E. L.—*Continued*

The view from Saturday. Atheneum Bks. for Young Readers 1996 163p $16; pa $4.99 (4-6)

Fic

1. School stories 2. Friendship—Fiction 3. Physically handicapped—Fiction

ISBN 0-689-80993-X; 0-689-81721-5 (pa)

LC 95-52624

Awarded the Newbery Medal, 1997

"A Jean Karl book"

Four students, with their own individual stories, develop a special bond and attract the attention of their teacher, a paraplegic, who choses them to represent their sixth-grade class in the Academic Bowl competition

"Glowing with humor and dusted with magic. . . . Wrought with deep compassion and a keen sense of balance." Publ Wkly

Korman, Gordon, 1963-

The sixth grade nickname game. Hyperion Bks. for Children 1998 154p $14.95; lib bdg $15.49; pa $4.99 (4-6) **Fic**

1. Nicknames—Fiction 2. School stories

ISBN 0-7868-0432-7; 0-7868-2382-8 (lib bdg); 0-7868-1335-0 (pa) LC 98-12343

Also available Thorndike Press large print edition

Eleven-year-old best friends Jeff and Wiley, who like to give nicknames to their classmates, try to find the right one for the new girl Cassandra, while adjusting to the football coach who has become their new teacher

"This is a funny, fast-paced grade-school romp." Bull Cent Child Books

Koss, Amy Goldman, 1954-

The Ashwater experiment. Dial Bks. for Young Readers 1999 153p $16.99; pa $5.99 (4 and up)

Fic

1. Moving—Fiction 2. Friendship—Fiction 3. California—Fiction

ISBN 0-8037-2391-1; 0-14-131092-8 (pa)

LC 98-23995

Also available Thorndike Press large print edition

Twelve-year-old Hillary, who has traveled across the country all her life with her parents who sell crafts, finds herself facing a stay of nine whole months in Ashwater, California

"Koss artfully sidesteps the predictable and crafts a truly original piece of fiction brimming with humor and insight." Horn Book Guide

The girls. Dial Bks. for Young Readers 2000 121p $16 (5 and up) **Fic**

1. Friendship—Fiction

ISBN 0-8037-2494-2 LC 99-19318

Also available Thorndike Press large print edition

"One Saturday morning a girl finds out that her group of friends, for reasons unknown, has decided to exclude her. As the short novel moves over the course of the weekend, five girls narrate in turns, each moving the story forward as well as providing sometimes unwitting commentary on her friends' versions of events." Horn Book Guide

"This provocative page-turner will be passed from one girl to the next." SLJ

How I saved Hanukkah; pictures by Diane deGroat. Dial Bks. for Young Readers 1998 88p il $15.99; pa $4.99 (3-5) **Fic**

1. Hanukkah—Fiction 2. Jews—Fiction

ISBN 0-8037-2241-9; 0-14-130982-2 (pa)

LC 96-52715

Marla, the only Jewish student in her fourth-grade class, wishes she celebrated Christmas like her best friend Lucy, until one year when she decides to learn all about Hanukkah and to teach her family about it too

"Koss keeps this hoary-sounding plot fresh and believable by talking up, not down, to readers and by virtue of a witty, warmly realized cast." Publ Wkly

Krumgold, Joseph, 1908-1980

Onion John; illustrated by Symeon Shimin. Crowell 1959 248p il lib bdg $15.89; pa $5.95 (5 and up) **Fic**

1. Friendship—Fiction

ISBN 0-690-04698-7 (lib bdg); 0-06-440144-8 (pa)

Awarded the Newbery Medal, 1960

The story "of Andy Rusch, twelve, and European-born Onion John, the town's odd-jobs man and vegetable peddler who lives in a stone hut and frequents the dump. Andy . . . tells of their . . . friendship and of how he and his father, as well as Onion John, are affected when the Rotary Club, at his father's instigation, attempts to transform Onion John's way of life." Booklist

"The writing has dignity and strength. There is conflict, drama, and excellent character portrayal." SLJ

Kurtz, Jane

The storyteller's beads. Harcourt Brace & Co. 1998 154p $15 (5 and up) **Fic**

1. Friendship—Fiction 2. Prejudices—Fiction 3. Blind—Fiction 4. Ethiopia—Fiction

ISBN 0-15-201074-2 LC 97-42312

"Gulliver books"

During the political strife and famine of the 1980's, two Ethiopian girls, one Christian and the other Jewish and blind, struggle to overcome many difficulties, including their prejudices about each other, as they make the dangerous journey out of Ethiopia

"The novel presents an involving portrait of Ethiopian culture through the eyes of two well-defined characters." Horn Book Guide

Langton, Jane

The fledgling. Harper & Row 1980 182p il lib bdg $15.89; pa $5.95 (5 and up) **Fic**

1. Geese—Fiction 2. Fantasy fiction

ISBN 0-06-023679-5 (lib bdg); 0-06-440121-9 (pa)

LC 79-2008

Also available Audiobook version

A Newbery Medal honor book, 1981

"An Ursula Nordstrom book"

"Quiet, introspective Georgie . . . yearns to fly. An encounter with a large, old Canadian goose, which stops at Walden Pond on its migratory journey south, brings her that chance. . . . Then neighboring Mr. Preek, who tries to save Georgie from what he thinks is an attacking

Langton, Jane—*Continued*

predator, and Miss Prawn, who sees the girl's feat as a saintly sign, interfere." Booklist

The writing is alternately solemn and funny, elevated and colloquial. It is mythic, almost sacred, in passages involving Georgie and the goose; it is satiric, almost irreverent, when it relates to Mr. Preek and Miss Prawn." Horn Book

Lasky, Kathryn

Dreams in the golden country; the diary of Zipporah Feldman, a Jewish immigrant girl. Scholastic 1998 188p il (Dear America) $9.95 (4 and up)   **Fic**
1. Jews—Fiction 2. Immigration and emigration—Fiction 3. New York (N.Y.)—Fiction
ISBN 0-590-02973-8   LC 97-26213
Twelve-year-old Zippy, a Jewish immigrant from Russia, keeps a diary account of the first eighteen months of her family's life on the Lower East Side of New York City in 1903-1904

"The hopes and dreams of a young girl are beautifully portrayed through Lasky's eloquent and engaging narrative." SLJ

Elizabeth I; red rose of the House of Tudor. Scholastic 1999 237p il (Royal diaries) $10.95 (4 and up)   **Fic**
1. Elizabeth I, Queen of England, 1533-1603—Fiction 2. Great Britain—History—1485-1603, Tudors—Fiction
ISBN 0-590-68484-1   LC 99-11178
In a series of diary entries, Princess Elizabeth, the eleven-year-old daughter of King Henry VIII, celebrates holidays and birthdays, relives her mother's execution, revels in her studies, and agonizes over her father's health

"Well written and captivating." Voice Youth Advocates

Marie Antoinette; princess of Versailles. Scholastic 2000 236p il (Royal diaries) $10.95 (4 and up)   **Fic**
1. Marie Antoinette, Queen, consort of Louis XVI, King of France, 1755-1793—Fiction
ISBN 0-439-07666-8   LC 99-16804
In 1769, thirteen-year-old Maria Antonia Josepha Johanna, daughter of Empress Maria Theresa, begins a journal chronicling her life at the Austrian court and her preparations for her future role as queen of France

"Quality writing, lively characterizations, and abundant historical detail." Booklist

The night journey; with drawings by Trina Schart Hyman. Warne 1981 149p il o.p.; Penguin Bks. paperback available $4.99 (4 and up)   **Fic**
1. Jews—Fiction 2. Russia—Fiction
ISBN 0-14-032048-2 (pa)   LC 81-2225
Also available Spanish language edition

This novel "describes the escape of a Jewish family from the persecutions and pogroms of Tsarist Russia. . . . It is told as a story-within-a-story, as thirteen-year-old Rachel learns, bit by bit, what her great-grandmother went through as a child." Bull Cent Child Books

"The novel shifts back and forth from the dangerous journey out of Russia to Rachel's own casual, secure life at home and school. These transitions are handled with a smoothness that doesn't break the intrinsic tension of the story, and the contrast between the two lives demonstrates with poignant clarity the real meaning of freedom. The portrayal of warm, supportive families in both stories becomes a link between past and present." SLJ

True north; a novel of the underground railroad. Blue Sky Press (NY) 1996 267p $14.95; pa $4.99 (6 and up)   **Fic**
1. Abolitionists—Fiction 2. Underground railroad—Fiction 3. Slavery—Fiction
ISBN 0-590-20523-4; 0-590-20524-2 (pa)
LC 95-2922
"Fourteen-year-old Lucy is the youngest daughter of a proper, upper-middle-class family living in Boston in 1858. Afrika, a young slave, doesn't know how old she is, but she knows it's time to make a run for freedom via the Underground Railroad. The girls' lives collide when Lucy discovers Afrika hiding in her grandfather's house. . . . Rich imagery and detail add to the suspenseful plot, and the characters, revealed in alternating perspectives, are vivid and believable." Booklist

Lawrence, Iain, 1955-

The smugglers. Delacorte Press 1999 183p $15.95; pa $4.99 (5 and up)   **Fic**
1. Smuggling—Fiction 2. Adventure fiction 3. Great Britain—History—1714-1837—Fiction
ISBN 0-385-32663-7; 0-440-41596-9 (pa)
LC 98-41582
Sequel to The wreckers

As the nineteenth century begins, sixteen-year-old John Spencer sets out to sail his father's schooner, The Dragon, from Kent to London and becomes involved in smuggling and danger

"The book's nonstop action, fast-paced plot, and picturesque characters make for a real page-turner." SLJ

The wreckers. Delacorte Press 1998 196p $15.95; pa $4.99 (5 and up)   **Fic**
1. Shipwrecks—Fiction 2. Adventure fiction 3. Great Britain—History—1714-1837—Fiction
ISBN 0-385-32535-5; 0-440-41545-4 (pa)
LC 97-31625
Also available Thorndike Press large print edition

"In 1799 fourteen-year-old John Spencer survives a shipwreck on the coast of Cornwall. To his horror, he soon learns that the villagers are not rescuers, but pirates who lure ships ashore in order to plunder their cargoes. . . . Lawrence creates an edge-of-the-chair survival/mystery story. Fast-moving, mesmerizing." Horn Book Guide

Followed by The smugglers

Lawson, Robert, 1892-1957

Ben and me; a new and astonishing life of Benjamin Franklin, as written by his good mouse Amos; lately discovered, edited and illustrated by Robert Lawson. Little, Brown 1939 113p il $16.95; pa $5.95 (5 and up)   **Fic**
1. Franklin, Benjamin, 1706-1790—Fiction 2. Mice—Fiction
ISBN 0-316-51732-1; 0-316-51730-5 (pa)

Lawson, Robert, 1892-1957—*Continued*

"How Amos, a poor church mouse, oldest son of a large family, went forth into the world to make his living, and established himself in Benjamin Franklin's old fur cap, 'a rough frontier-cabin type of residence,' and made himself indispensable to Ben with his advice and information, and incidentally let himself in for some very strange experiences is related here in a merry compound of fact and fancy." Bookmark

"The sophisticated and clever story is illustrated by even more sophisticated and clever line drawings." Roundabout of Books

Mr. Revere and I; set down and embellished with numerous drawings by Robert Lawson. Little, Brown 1953 152p il hardcover o.p. paperback available $5.95 (5 and up) **Fic**
    1. Revere, Paul, 1735-1818—Fiction 2. Horses—Fiction 3. United States—History—1775-1783, Revolution—Fiction
    ISBN 0-316-51729-1 (pa)

"Being an account of certain episodes in the career of Paul Revere, Esq., as recently revealed by his horse, Scheherazade, late pride of His Royal Majesty's 14th Regiment of Foot." Subtitle

"A delightful tale which is perfect for reading aloud to the whole family. The make-up is excellent, illustrations are wonderful, and the reader will get a very interesting picture of the American Revolution." Libr J

Rabbit Hill. Viking 1944 127p il lib bdg $16.99; pa $4.99 (3-6) **Fic**
    1. Rabbits—Fiction 2. Animals—Fiction
    ISBN 0-670-58675-7 (lib bdg); 0-14-031010-X (pa)

Also available Audiobook version

Awarded the Newbery Medal, 1945

"Story of the great rejoicing among the wild creatures when the news goes round that new people are coming to live in the big house. For people in the big house will mean a garden and a garden means food. Their hopes are rewarded. The new people are 'planting folks' and the garden is big enough to provide for all." Wis Libr Bull

"Robert Lawson, because he loves the Connecticut country and the little animals of field and wood and looks at them with the eye of an artist, a poet and a child, has created for the boy and girl, indeed for the sensitive reader of any age, a whole, fresh, lively, amusing world." N Y Times Book Rev

Followed by The tough winter (1954)

Le Guin, Ursula K., 1929-

Catwings; illustrations by S. D. Schindler. Orchard Bks. 1988 39p il hardcover o.p. paperback available $3.95 (2-4) **Fic**
    1. Cats—Fiction 2. Fantasy fiction
    ISBN 0-531-07110-3 (pa)   LC 87-33104
Also available in paperback from Scholastic
"A Richard Jackson book"
"When four kittens with wings are born in a rough city neighborhood, their mother nurtures and protects them as they grow and learn to fly. At her urging they soon escape the dangerous streets and alleys, flying to a forest where they find more enemies but, finally, new

friends." Booklist

"Le Guin's adroit writing style, the well-observed feline detail, the thematic concern for natural victims of human environment, and the gentle humor make this a prime choice for reading aloud, although one would not want children to miss the fine-line hatch drawings that further project the satisfying sense of reality." Bull Cent Child Books

Other available titles about Catwings are:
Catwings return (1989)
Jane on her own (1999)
Wonderful Alexander and the Catwings (1994)

A wizard of Earthsea. Atheneum Pubs. 1991 197p $18 (6 and up) **Fic**
    1. Fantasy fiction
    ISBN 0-689-31720-4   LC 90-23884
Also available in paperback from Bantam Bks.
"A Parnassus Press book"
A reissue of the title first published 1968 by Parnassus Press

"An imaginary archipelago is the setting for . . . [this] fantasy. . . . In a willful misuse of his limited powers, the novice wizard unleashes a shadowy, malevolent creature that endangers his life and the world of Earthsea." Booklist

A "powerful fantasy-allegory. Though set as prose, the rhythms of the langauge are truly and consistently poetical." Read Ladders for Hum Relat. 5th edition

Other available titles about Earthsea are:
The farthest shore (1984)
Tehanu (1990)
The tombs of Atuan (1988)

L'Engle, Madeleine, 1918-

Meet the Austins. Farrar, Straus & Giroux 1997 216p $16 (5 and up) **Fic**
    1. Family life—Fiction 2. Orphans—Fiction
    ISBN 0-374-34929-0   LC 96-27655
Also available in paperback from Dell
A revised edition of the title first published 1960 by Vanguard Press
This edition includes a "chapter titled 'The Anti-Muffins,' which deals with being concerned for others and true to oneself." Book Rep

A "story of the family of a country doctor, told by the twelve-year-old daughter, during a year in which a spoiled young orphan, Maggy, comes to live with them. . . . [This is an] account of the family's adjustment to Maggy and hers to them." Horn Book

Other available titles about the Austins are:
The moon by night (1963)
A ring of endless light (1980)
Troubling a star (1994)

A wrinkle in time. Farrar, Straus & Giroux 1962 211p $17 (5 and up) **Fic**
    1. Fantasy fiction
    ISBN 0-374-38613-7
Also available in paperback from Dell and Audiobook version

Awarded the Newbery Medal, 1963

"A brother and sister, together with a friend, go in search of their scientist father who was lost while engaged in secret work for the government on the tesseract

L'Engle, Madeleine, 1918-—*Continued*
problem. A tesseract is a wrinkle in time. The father is a prisoner on a forbidding planet, and after awesome and terrifying experiences, he is rescued, and the little group returns safely to Earth and home." Child Books Too Good To Miss

"It makes unusual demands on the imagination and consequently gives great rewards." Horn Book

Other available titles in this series are:
Many waters (1986)
A swiftly tilting planet (1978)
A wind in the door (1973)

Levin, Betty, 1927-
Shadow-catcher. Greenwillow Bks. 2000 152p $15.95 (4 and up)   **Fic**
1. Grandfathers—Fiction 2. Photography—Fiction 3. Mystery fiction
ISBN 0-688-17862-6   LC 99-45087
Although he often fancied himself a detective, Jonathan must become a real sleuth when he attempts to solve a mystery while accompanying his grandfather, a Civil War veteran and traveling photographer in Maine

"The well-crafted, engaging mystery . . . neatly frames a story of character growth and development." Booklist

Levine, Gail Carson, 1947-
Dave at night. HarperCollins Pubs. 1999 281p $15.95; lib bdg $15.89; pa $5.95 (5 and up)
     Fic
1. Orphans—Fiction 2. Jews—Fiction 3. African Americans—Fiction 4. New York (N.Y.)—Fiction
ISBN 0-06-028153-7; 0-06-028154-5 (lib bdg); 0-06-440747-0 (pa)   LC 98-50069
Also available Audiobook version

When orphaned Dave is sent to the Hebrew Home for Boys where he is treated cruelly, he sneaks out at night and is welcomed into the music- and culture-filled world of the Harlem Renaissance

"The magic comes from Levine's language and characterization. This novel will provide inspiration for all children while offering a unique view of a culturally diverse New York City." SLJ

Ella enchanted. HarperCollins Pubs. 1997 232p $15.95; lib bdg $15.89; pa $5.95 (5 and up)
     Fic
1. Fantasy fiction
ISBN 0-06-027510-3; 0-06-027511-1 (lib bdg); 0-06-440705-5 (pa)   LC 96-30734
Also available Thorndike Press large print edition and Audiobook version

A Newberry Medal honor book, 1998

In this novel based on the story of Cinderella, Ella struggles against the childhood curse that forces her to obey any order given to her

"As finely designed as a tapestry, Ella's story both neatly incorporates elements of the original tale and mightily expands them." Booklist

The princess test; illustrated by Mark Elliott. HarperCollins Pubs. 1999 91p il (Princess tales) $9.95; lib bdg $9.89 (4 and up)   **Fic**
1. Fairy tales
ISBN 0-06-028062-X; 0-06-028063-8 (lib bdg)
     LC 98-27960
In this humorous retelling of Hans Christian Andersen's "The Princess and the Pea," Lorelei must pass many difficult tests in order to prove that she is a true princess and win the hand of Prince Nicholas

"Breezily told, with a wealth of comic detail, slyly contemporary dialogue, and genuine affection for the genre that inspired [it]." Bull Cent Child Books

Other available titles in the Princess tales series are:
Cinderellis and the glass hill (2000)
The fairy's mistake (1999)
Princess Sonora and the long sleep (1999)

Levitin, Sonia, 1934-
Journey to America; illustrated by Charles Robinson. Atheneum Pubs. 1993 c1970 150p il $16; pa $4.99 (4 and up)   **Fic**
1. World War, 1939-1945—Fiction 2. Jewish refugees—Fiction 3. Family life—Fiction
ISBN 0-689-31829-4; 0-689-71130-1 (pa)
     LC 93-163980
A reissue of the title first published 1970

"In a strong immigration story, Lisa Platt, the middle daughter, tells how her family is forced to leave Nazi Germany and make a new life in the United States. First their father leaves, then the others escape to Switzerland, where they endure harsh conditions. After months of separation, the family is reunited in New York." Rochman Against borders

Followed by Silver days (1989)

The return. Atheneum Pubs. 1987 213p map o.p.; Fawcett Bks. paperback available $4.50 (6 and up)   **Fic**
1. Jews—Ethiopia—Fiction 2. Antisemitism—Fiction
ISBN 0-449-70280-4 (pa)   LC 86-25891
"In a docunovel of a Jewish Ethiopian family's flight to Israel, Levitin focuses on an orphan, Desta, whose older brother, Joas, persuades her to leave the village where hunger and political recriminations constantly threaten their lives." Bull Cent Child Books

"A vivid and compelling book. . . . Levitin's tour de force is sensitively written; her command of the language is impressive and she uses Ethiopian terms effectively, interspersing them in ways readers will understand." Booklist

Levoy, Myron
Alan and Naomi. Harper & Row 1977 192p hardcover o.p. paperback available $4.95 (6 and up)   **Fic**
1. Friendship—Fiction 2. Jews—Fiction 3. Mentally ill—Fiction 4. World War, 1939-1945—Fiction
ISBN 0-06-440209-6 (pa)
"After reluctantly agreeing to befriend Naomi, a disturbed war refugee who has crumbled under the memory of seeing her father beaten to death by Nazis, Alan breaks through her defenses and begins truly to like

Levoy, Myron—*Continued*
her—only to lose her when a violent incident shatters her fragile sanity." Booklist
"This warming story with its ethnic humor, its compassionate families, and its heart-wrenching ending is one of the more honest approaches to the repercussions of W.W.II." SLJ

Levy, Elizabeth, 1942-
My life as a fifth-grade comedian. HarperCollins Pubs. 1997 184p $15.95; pa $4.95 (4-6)   **Fic**
1. School stories
ISBN 0-06-026602-3; 0-06-440723-3 (pa)
LC 97-3842
Also available Audiobook version
"Bobby loves to joke around, but his constant misbehavior in class is about to land him in the School for Intervention. That's where his older brother went before he got kicked out of school and out of the house. Bobby's last chance to prove himself to his teacher, the principal, and his sarcastic father is to organize a school-wide stand-up comedy contest." Publisher's note
"Levy incorporates a cornucopia of jokes and a wealth of subtle advice on becoming a comic. There is great pleasure in seeing Bobby and his father's earlier sarcasm and angry dialogue transformed by a turn of attitude into universal, and really funny comedy." SLJ

Seventh grade tango. Hyperion Bks. for Children 2000 153p $15.99; lib bdg $16.49 (5 and up)   **Fic**
1. Dancers—Fiction 2. Friendship—Fiction 3. School stories
ISBN 0-7868-0498-X; 0-7868-2427-1 (lib bdg)
LC 99-53124
When Rebecca, a seventh-grader, is paired up with her friend Scott for a dance class at school, she learns a lot about who her real friends are
"Descriptive prose, snappy dialogue, and diverse characters enhance the story, which notably portrays ballroom dance as a hip, fun activity." Booklist

Lewis, C. S. (Clive Staples), 1898-1963
The lion, the witch, and the wardrobe; illustrated by Pauline Baynes. HarperCollins Pubs. 1994 189p il $16.95; lib bdg $16.89; pa $6.95 (4 and up)   **Fic**
1. Fantasy fiction
ISBN 0-06-023481-4; 0-06-023482-2 (lib bdg); 0-06-440499-4 (pa)   LC 93-8889
Also available Thorndike Press large print edition, and Audiobook version; Spanish language edition also available
A reissue of the title first published 1950 by Macmillan
Four English schoolchildren find their way through the back of a wardrobe into the magic land of Narnia and assist Aslan, the golden lion, to triumph over the White Witch, who has cursed the land with eternal winter
This begins "the 'Narnia' stories, outstanding modern fairy tales with an underlying theme of good overcoming evil." Child Books Too Good to Miss
Other available titles about Narnia are:
The horse and his boy (1954)

The last battle (1956)
The magician's nephew (1956)
Prince Caspian (1951)
The silver chair (1953)
The voyage of the Dawn Treader (1952)

Lewis, Maggie
Morgy makes his move; illustrated by Michael Chesworth. Houghton Mifflin 1999 74p il $15 (2-4)   **Fic**
1. Moving—Fiction 2. School stories 3. Massachusetts—Fiction
ISBN 0-395-92284-4   LC 98-43245
When third-grader Morgy MacDougal-MacDuff moves from California to Massachusetts with his parents, he has a lot of new things to get used to before he feels comfortable
"Heavy issues are handled lightly; language is simple and straightforward; Michael Chesworth's illustrations are funny and exaggerated." Booklist

Lindgren, Astrid, 1907-
Pippi Longstocking; translated from the Swedish by Florence Lamborn; illustrated by Louis S. Glanzman. Viking 1950 158p il lib bdg $15.99; pa $4.99 (3-6)   **Fic**
1. Sweden—Fiction
ISBN 0-670-55745-5 (lib bdg); 0-14-032772-4 (pa)

Also available Audiobook version; The adventures of Pippi Longstocking, omnibus volume of the three titles about Pippi, is also available
Original Swedish edition, 1945
"There were no more dull days for Tommy and Annika after they made the acquaintance of Pippi Longstocking. Pippi was nine years old, her strength—and her imagination—was prodigious, and except for her monkey and horse, she lived alone unrestrained by adults." Booklist
Other available titles about Pippi Longstocking are:
Pippi goes on board (1957)
Pippi in the South Seas (1959)

Ronia, the robber's daughter; translated by Patricia Crampton. Viking 1983 176p il hardcover o.p. paperback available $4.99 (4-6)   **Fic**
1. Thieves—Fiction 2. Middle Ages—Fiction
ISBN 0-14-031720-1 (pa)   LC 82-60081
Also available in hardcover from P. Smith
Original Swedish edition, 1981
"Ronia, the robber's daughter, meets Birk, son of her father's rival, and the result is a benefit to all in both camps. Thanks to a shrewd older friend, the young people bring about the union of their parents' forces and, even better, learn to make a living legally." Publ Wkly
"The book is full of high adventure, hairsbreadth escapes, droll earthy humor, and passionate emotional energy; and cast over the whole narrative is a primitive, ecstatic response to the changing seasons and the wonders of nature." Horn Book

Lisle, Janet Taylor, 1947-

Afternoon of the elves. Orchard Bks. 1989 122p $15.95; lib bdg $16.99 (4-6)   **Fic**
  1. Friendship—Fiction 2. Mentally ill—Fiction
  ISBN 0-531-05837-9; 0-531-08437-X (lib bdg)
                                          LC 88-35099
Also available in paperback from Scholastic
A Newbery Medal honor book, 1990
"Nine-year-old Hillary has a happy home, all the material possessions she wants, and plenty of friends at school. Eleven-year-old Sara-Kate is an outcast, thin, poorly dressed, with failing grades, a decrepit house, and a weedy yard adjoining Hillary's neat garden. But Sara-Kate has an elf village, and with it she hooks Hillary into a friendship that thrives on elf stories but suffers from Sara-Kate's stormy moods and prickly pride. It is for Hillary to discover that Sara-Kate alone is caring for a mother who is mentally ill, penniless, and unable to provide the most basic physical or emotional necessities." Bull Cent Child Books
"'Afternoon of the elves' is a distinctive portrayal of the way children figure out ways to inhabit the world when there aren't any adults around." N Y Times Book Rev

Forest. Orchard Bks. 1993 150p $16.95 (5 and up)   **Fic**
  1. Squirrels—Fiction 2. Fantasy fiction
  ISBN 0-531-06803-X   LC 93-9630
"A Richard Jackson book"
Twelve-year-old Amber's invasion of an organized forest community of squirrels starts a war between humans and beasts, despite the protests of an unconventional and imaginative squirrel named Woodbine
"Lisle has created a world of innocence marked with heartache, truth infused with absurdity, and wisdom relinquished to recklessness—all in the guise of animal fantasy." Bull Cent Child Books

The lost flower children; illustrated by Satomi Ichikawa. Philomel Bks. 1999 122p il $16.99; pa $4.99 (4-6)   **Fic**
  1. Sisters—Fiction 2. Aunts—Fiction 3. Gardens—Fiction
  ISBN 0-399-23393-8; 0-698-11880-4 (pa)
                                          LC 98-34912
After their mother's death, Olivia and Nellie go to live with their Great Aunt Minty where they discover a tiny tea cup in the garden and a storybook about children turned into flowers by a fairy spell
"Humorous, poignant, and magical, this story has a fantastical, creative story-within-a-story, characters of depth and appeal, and an irresistible mystery resulting in personal transformation." Booklist

Little, Jean, 1932-

From Anna; pictures by Joan Sandin. Harper & Row 1972 201p il hardcover o.p. paperback available $4.95 (4-6)   **Fic**
  1. Vision disorders—Fiction 2. Family life—Fiction 3. Germans—Canada—Fiction
  ISBN 0-06-440044-1 (pa)
"Often ridiculed by her older brothers and sisters and chided by her mother for her awkwardness and lack of ability, nine-year-old Anna is prickly and uncommunica-

tive, but when her family moves to Canada in 1933 to get away from the growing oppression in their native Germany a doctor discovers that Anna has an acute vision problem. Fitted with glasses and sent to a special school for visually handicapped children Anna is slowly drawn out of her shell by an understanding teacher and new friends. . . . This is an engaging story of Anna's adjustment to life and her family's to a new homeland." Booklist
Followed by Listen for the singing (1977)

Lobel, Arnold

Fables; written and illustrated by Arnold Lobel. Harper & Row 1980 40p il $15.95; lib bdg $15.89; pa $6.95 (3-5)   **Fic**
  1. Animals—Fiction
  ISBN 0-06-023973-5; 0-06-023974-3 (lib bdg); 0-06-443046-4 (pa)   LC 79-2004
Awarded the Caldecott Medal, 1981
"Short, original fables, complete with moral, poke subtle fun at human foibles through the antics of 20 memorable animal characters. . . . Despite the large picture-book format, the best audience will be older readers who can understand the innuendos and underlying messages. Children of all ages, however, will appreciate and be intrigued by the artist's fine, full-color illustrations. Tones are deftly blended to luminescent shadings, and the pictorial simplicity of ideas, droll expressions, and caricature of behavior work in many instances as complete and humorous stories in themselves." Booklist

London, Jack, 1876-1916

The call of the wild (5 and up)   **Fic**
  1. Dogs—Fiction 2. Alaska—Fiction

Hardcover and paperback editions available from various publishers, including editions illustrated by Barry Moser and Philippe Munch
First published 1903 by Macmillan
"The dog hero, Buck, is stolen from his comfortable home and pressed into service as a sledge dog in the Klondike. At first he is abused by both men and dogs, but he learns to fight ruthlessly and finally finds in John Thornton a master whom he can respect and love. When Thornton is murdered, he breaks away to the wilds and becomes the leader of a pack of wolves." Reader's Ency

White Fang (5 and up)   **Fic**
  1. Dogs—Fiction 2. Alaska—Fiction

Hardcover and paperback editions available from various publishers, including editions illustrated by Ed Young and Philippe Munch
First published 1906
White Fang "is about a dog, a cross-breed, sold to Beauty Smith. This owner tortures the dog to increase his ferocity and value as a fighter. A new owner, Weedom Scott, brings the dog to California, and, by kind treatment, domesticates him. White Fang later sacrifices his life to save Scott." Haydn. Thesaurus of Book Dig

Lord, Bette Bao

In the Year of the Boar and Jackie Robinson; illustrations by Marc Simont. Harper & Row 1984 169p il lib bdg $15.89; pa $4.95 (4-6)　　**Fic**
　1. Chinese Americans—Fiction 2. School stories
　ISBN 0-06-024004-0 (lib bdg); 0-06-440175-8 (pa)
　　　　　　　　　　　　　　　　　LC 83-48440
"In a story based in part on the author's experience as an immigrant, Shirley Temple Wong . . . arrives in Brooklyn and spends her first year in public school." Bull Cent Child Books

"Warm-hearted, fresh, and dappled with humor, the episodic book, which successfully encompasses both Chinese dragons and the Brooklyn Dodgers, stands out in the bevy of contemporary problem novels. And the unusual flavor of the text infiltrates the striking illustrations picturing the pert, pigtailed heroine making her way in 'Mei Guo'—her new 'Beautiful Country.'" Horn Book

Love, D. Anne

A year without rain. Holiday House 2000 118p $15.95 (4 and up)　　**Fic**
　1. Family life—Fiction 2. Frontier and pioneer life—Fiction 3. Remarriage—Fiction 4. South Dakota—Fiction
　ISBN 0-8234-1488-4　　　　　　　　LC 99-35825
Her mother's death and a year-long drought has made life difficult for twelve-year-old Rachel and her family on their farm in the Dakotas, but when she learns that her father plans to get married again, it is almost more than Rachel can bear

This "is simply yet artfully told with characters both realistic and endearing." SLJ

Lovelace, Maud Hart, 1892-1980

Betsy-Tacy; illustrated by Lois Lenski. HarperCollins Pubs. 1994 c1940 112p il $13.95; pa $5.95 (2-4)　　**Fic**
　1. Friendship—Fiction 2. Minnesota—Fiction
　ISBN 0-06-024415-1; 0-06-440096-4 (pa)
A reissue of the title first published 1940 by Crowell
Betsy and Tacy (short for Anastacia) were two little five-year-olds, such inseparable friends that they were regarded almost as one person. This is the story of their friendship in a little Minnesota town in the early 1900's

The author "has written a story of real literary merit as well as one with good story interest." Libr J
　Other available titles about Betsy through adolescence and young womanhood with reading levels to grade 5 and up are:
Betsy and Joe (1948)
Betsy and Tacy go downtown (1943)
Betsy and Tacy go over the big hill (1942)
Betsy and the great world (1952)
Betsy in spite of herself (1946)
Betsy, Tacy and Tib (1941)
Betsy was a junior (1947)
Betsy's wedding (1955)
Heavens to Betsy (1945)

Lowry, Lois

Anastasia Krupnik. Houghton Mifflin 1979 113p $16 (4-6)　　**Fic**
　1. Family life—Fiction
　ISBN 0-395-28629-8

Also available in paperback from Dell
This book describes the tenth year in the life of fourth-grader Anastasia. As she "experiences rejection of a long labored-over poem, fights acceptance of the coming arrival of a baby sibling, deliberates about becoming Catholic (in order to change her name), has a crush on Washburn Cummings who constantly dribbles an imaginary basketball, and learns to understand her senile grandmother's inward eye, she grows and matures." Booklist

"Anastasia's father and mother—an English professor and an artist—are among the most humorous, sensible, and understanding parents to be found in . . . children's fiction, and Anastasia herself is an amusing and engaging heroine." Horn Book
　Other available titles about Anastasia Krupnik and her family are:
All about Sam (1988)
Anastasia, absolutely (1995)
Anastasia again! (1981)
Anastasia, ask your analyst (1984)
Anastasia at this address (1991)
Anastasia at your service (1982)
Anastasia has the answers (1986)
Anastasia on her own (1985)
Anastasia's chosen career (1987)
Attaboy Sam! (1992)
See you around Sam! (1996)
Zooman Sam (1999)

Autumn Street. Houghton Mifflin 1980 188p $16 (4 and up)　　**Fic**
　1. World War, 1939-1945—Fiction 2. Friendship—Fiction
　ISBN 0-395-27812-0　　　　　　　　LC 80-376
Also available in paperback from Dell
"Elizabeth, the teller of the story, feels danger around her when her father goes to fight in World War II. She, her older sister, and her pregnant mother go to live with her grandparents on Autumn Street. Tatie, the black cook-housekeeper, and her street-wise grandson Charley love Elizabeth and reassure her during this difficult time." Child Book Rev Serv

"Characters, dialogue, believable plot combine in this well written story to capture the mind and heart of all who read this memorable and touching book." Voice Youth Advocates

Gathering blue. Houghton Mifflin 2000 215p $15 (5 and up)　　**Fic**
　1. Science fiction
　ISBN 0-618-05581-9　　　　　　　　LC 00-24359
"Walter Lorraine books"
Lame and suddenly orphaned, Kira is mysteriously removed from her squalid village to live in the palatial Council Edifice, where she is expected to use her gifts as a weaver to do the bidding of the all-powerful Guardians

"Lowry has once again created a fully realized world full of drama, suspense, and even humor." SLJ

The giver. Houghton Mifflin 1993 180p $15 (6 and up)　　**Fic**
　1. Science fiction
　ISBN 0-395-64566-2　　　　　　　　LC 92-15034
Also available in paperback from Bantam Bks. and Audiobook version

Lowry, Lois—*Continued*

Awarded the Newbery Medal, 1994

Given his lifetime assignment at the Ceremony of Twelve, Jonas becomes the receiver of memories shared by only one other in his community and discovers the terrible truth about the society in which he lives

"A riveting, chilling story that inspires a new appreciation for diversity, love, and even pain. Truly memorable." SLJ

Number the stars. Houghton Mifflin 1989 137p $16 (4 and up)   **Fic**

1. World War, 1939-1945—Fiction 2. Jews—Fiction 3. Friendship—Fiction 4. Denmark—Fiction

ISBN 0-395-51060-0   LC 88-37134

Also available in paperback from Dell

Awarded the Newbery Medal, 1990

"Best friends Annemarie Johansen and Ellen Rosen must suddenly pretend to be sisters one night when Ellen's parents go into hiding to escape a Nazi roundup in wartime Copenhagen. With the help of a young resistance fighter, the Johansens smuggle the Rosens aboard Annemarie's uncle's fishing boat bound for freedom in Sweden. But it is Annemarie who actually saves all their lives by transporting a handkerchief coated with blood and cocaine to deaden the search dogs' sense of smell." Bull Cent Child Books

"The appended author's note details the historical incidents upon which Lowry bases her plot. . . . The whole work is seamless, compelling, and memorable." Horn Book

The one hundredth thing about Caroline. Houghton Mifflin 1983 150p $16 (5 and up)   **Fic**

1. Single parent family—Fiction

ISBN 0-395-34829-3   LC 83-12629

Also available in paperback from Dell

"Caroline, fascinated by dinosaurs, spends much of her free time prowling New York's Museum of Natural History; her best friend, Stacy, practices being an investigative reporter. The combination proves disastrous when Caroline's mother becomes interested in Frederick Fiske, the mysterious man in the fifth-floor apartment who looks, Caroline is convinced, like the evil 'Tyrannosaurus rex' and who seemingly wants to eliminate Caroline and her brother, J.P." Booklist

"Lowry's style is bright, fast-paced and funny, with skillfully-drawn, believable characters." SLJ

Followed by Switcharound

Rabble Starkey. Houghton Mifflin 1987 192p $16 (5 and up)   **Fic**

1. Friendship—Fiction

ISBN 0-395-43607-9   LC 86-27542

Also available in paperback from Dell

"Parable Starkey and her mother, Sweet Hosanna, move into the Bigelows' house to take charge of the children after Mrs. Bigelow's hospitalization for mental illness. . . . [This is] a smooth first-person narrative that quietly takes on class as well as individual differences. In the end, Lowry has managed to portray a large, diverse cast by carefully and consistently focusing the point of view as one of a maturing observer." Bull Cent Child Books

Stay! Keeper's story. Houghton Mifflin 1997 127p il $15 (5 and up)   **Fic**

1. Dogs—Fiction

ISBN 0-395-87048-8   LC 97-1569

Also available in paperback from Dell

"The canine narrator is a mongrel with class, a poetically inclined, refined animal of good upbringing if not bloodlines. He leaves the relative safety of his first home (an alley outside a French restaurant) for the perils of the wide world in search of a human friend." Bull Cent Child Books

"The author proves she is as well versed in animal behavior as in human sensibilities. Her warm sense of humor and vivid imagination . . . accentuate Keeper's unorthodox perceptions of the world." Publ Wkly

A summer to die; illustrated by Jenni Oliver. Houghton Mifflin 1977 154p il $16 (5 and up)   **Fic**

1. Sisters—Fiction 2. Death—Fiction

ISBN 0-395-25338-1   LC 77-83

Also available in paperback from Bantam Bks.

"Meg, 13, envies her older sister's popularity and prettiness and finds it difficult to cope with Molly's degenerating illness and eventual death." Booklist

"As told by Meg, the chronicle of this experience is a sensitive exploration of the complex emotions underlying the adolescent's first confrontation with human mortality; the author suggests nuances of contemporary conversation and situations without sacrificing the finesse with which she limns her characters." Horn Book

Switcharound. Houghton Mifflin 1985 118p il $16 (5 and up)   **Fic**

1. Siblings—Fiction 2. Family life—Fiction

ISBN 0-395-39536-4   LC 85-14576

Also available in paperback from Dell

Sequel to The one hundredth thing about Caroline

Forced to spend a summer with their father and his "new" family, Caroline, age eleven, and J.P., age thirteen, are given unpleasant responsibilities for which they are determined to get revenge

"There is a bit too convenient an all-ends-tied final chapter, but the strong characterization, the humorous style and yeasty dialogue, and the change and development (including some shaking of stereotypical sex roles) in the two main characters give the story both substance and appeal." Bull Cent Child Books

Your move, J.P.! Houghton Mifflin 1990 122p $16 (5 and up)   **Fic**

1. School stories

ISBN 0-395-53639-1   LC 89-24707

Also available in paperback from Dell

Caroline's older brother, twelve-year-old J.P. Tate, who appeared in The one hundredth thing about Caroline and Switcharound, has a "crush on Angela Galsworthy, newly arrived at his private school from London, England. . . . Anxious to sustain Angela's interest, J.P. tells her that he is suffering from triple framosis, a rare but fatal disease. Angela believes him and J.P. is stuck with his lie." Bull Cent Child Books

"The author makes the most of the humor in J.P.'s antics but maintains a rueful sympathy throughout for his plight and for his eventual admission of truth." Horn Book

Lunn, Janet Louise Swoboda, 1928-

The root cellar; [by] Janet Lunn. Scribner 1983 c1981 229p o.p.; Puffin Bks. paperback available $5.99 (5 and up) **Fic**
1. Space and time—Fiction 2. Orphans—Fiction 3. Farm life—Fiction 4. United States—History—1861-1865, Civil War—Fiction
ISBN 0-14-038036-1 (pa) LC 83-3246
First published 1981 in Canada
"Rose, a twelve-year-old orphan, is unhappy in her new home. When she goes down into the root cellar she finds herself back in Civil War days. She makes friends with the former tenants of the old house and becomes involved in their war-torn lives. She finally decides she belongs in modern times and returns with a better spirit." Child Book Rev Serv
"It's hard not to feel for Rose as she learns, for the first time in her life, how to be part of a family and have companions her own age. The descriptions of the physical surroundings and conditions in the post-Civil War time period are particularly vivid, and the pieces fit together well in this fast-paced, readable novel." SLJ

Lyons, Mary E.

Letters from a slave girl; the story of Harriet Jacobs. Scribner 1992 146p il $16; pa $4.99 (6 and up) **Fic**
1. Jacobs, Harriet A. (Harriet Ann), 1813-1896 or 7—Fiction 2. Slavery—Fiction 3. African Americans—Fiction 4. Letters—Fiction
ISBN 0-684-19446-5; 0-689-80015-0 (pa)
LC 91-45778
A fictionalized version of the life of Harriet Jacobs, told in the form of letters that she might have written during her slavery in North Carolina and as she prepared for escape to the North in 1842
This "is historical fiction at its best. . . . Mary Lyons has remained faithful to Jacobs's actual autobiography throughout her readable, compelling novel. . . . Her observations of the horrors of slavery are concise and lucid. The letters are written in dialect, based on Jacobs's own writing and on other slave narrations of the period." Horn Book

MacDonald, Betty, 1908-1958

Mrs. Piggle-Wiggle; illustrated by Hilary Knight. Lippincott 1957 c1947 118p il $15.95; pa $4.95 (2-4) **Fic**
ISBN 0-397-31712-3; 0-06-440148-0 (pa)
First published 1947
Chapters follow "the amazing versatility of Mrs. Piggle-Wiggle who loves children good or bad, who never scolds but who has positive cures for 'Answer-Backers,' 'Never-Want-To-Go-To-Bedders,' and other children with special problems." Books for Deaf Child
The author "mixes a little psychology with a lot of common sense, and seasons with nonsense, to produce the most palatable type of lecture on good behavior. Hilary Knight's illustrations catch the mood of the whole delightful business." Chicago Sunday Trib
Other available titles about Mrs. Piggle-Wiggle are:
Hello, Mrs. Piggle-Wiggle (1957)
Mrs. Piggle-Wiggle's farm (1954)
Mrs. Piggle-Wiggle's magic (1949)

MacDonald, George, 1824-1905

At the back of the North Wind (4-6) **Fic**
1. Fairy tales

Available from various publishers, including a Morrow hardcover edition illustrated by Jessie Willcox Smith
First published 1871
"There is a rare quality in Macdonald's lovely fairy tales which relates spiritual ideals with the everyday things of life. This one tells of Diamond, the little son of a coachman, and his friendship with the North Wind who appears to him in various guises." Toronto Public Libr. Books for Boys & Girls

The light princess; with pictures by Maurice Sendak. Farrar, Straus & Giroux 1969 110p il hardcover o.p. paperback available $5.95 (3-6) **Fic**
1. Fairy tales
ISBN 0-374-44458-7 (pa)
This fairy story originally appeared 1864 in the author's novel Adela Cathcart and was reprinted in his 1867 story collection Dealings with the fairies
"The problems of the princess who had been deprived, as an infant, of her gravity and whose life hung in the balance when she grew up are amusing as ever and the sweet capitulation to love that brings her (literally) to her feet, just as touching. All of the best of Macdonald is reflected in the Sendak illustrations: the humor and wit, the sweetness and tenderness, and the sophistication—and they are beautiful." Sutherland. The Best in Child Books

The princess and the goblin (3-6) **Fic**
1. Fairy tales

Some editions are:
Knopf (Everyman's library children's classics) $12.95 Illustrated by Arthur Hughes (ISBN 0-679-42810-0)
Morrow (Books of Wonder) $22.95 Illustrated by Jessie Willcox Smith (ISBN 0-688-06604-6)
First published 1872
"Living in a great house on the side of a mountain in a country where hideous spiteful goblins inhabit the dark caverns below the mines, little Princess Irene and Curdie the miner's son have many strange adventures. . . . To adults Macdonald's stories have an allegorical significance, to each succeeding generation of children they are wonderful fairytale adventures." Four to Fourteen
Followed by The princess and Curdie

MacLachlan, Patricia

Arthur, for the very first time; illustrated by Lloyd Bloom. Harper & Row 1980 117p il lib bdg $15.89; pa $4.95 (4-6) **Fic**
ISBN 0-06-024047-4 (lib bdg); 0-06-440288-6 (pa)
LC 79-2007
A "recounting of ten-year-old Arthur's activities and introspections during a summer spent with a great-uncle and a great-aunt. The offbeat relatives cultivate equally offbeat friends, climb trees, and speak French to their pet chicken. Arthur also enjoys the companionship of a veterinarian's granddaughter." Horn Book
"Good-hearted good humor. . . . The colorfulness of the characters is unrelenting; each is more exaggerated unique and zany than the other." SLJ

MacLachlan, Patricia—*Continued*

Baby. Delacorte Press 1993 132p $15.95 (5 and up)   **Fic**
1. Infants—Fiction 2. Death—Fiction 3. Islands—Fiction
ISBN 0-385-31133-8   LC 93-22117
Also available in paperback from Dell

Taking care of a baby left with them at the end of the tourist season helps a family come to terms with the death of their own infant son

"Short, spare, powerful, this is a story which touches deep emotions and lingers in the heart." Horn Book

The facts and fictions of Minna Pratt. Harper & Row 1988 136p lib bdg $14.89; pa $4.95 (4 and up)   **Fic**
1. Musicians—Fiction
ISBN 0-06-024117-9 (lib bdg); 0-06-440265-7 (pa)
LC 85-45388

"A Charlotte Zolotow book"

"Minna Pratt plays the cello and wishes she would get her vibrato. She wishes someone would answer her questions about herself and life and love. . . . Then she meets Lucas Ellerby. His life seems so perfect and he has a vibrato. As their friendship develops Minna finds that life is not always as it seems and even when you think you know someone or something there may be a hidden side that will surprise you." Voice Youth Advocates

"Ms. MacLachlan's skillful handling of her subject, and above all her vivid characterization . . . place her story in the ranks of outstanding middle-grade fiction." N Y Times Book Rev

Journey. Delacorte Press 1991 83p $14.95; pa $4.99 (4 and up)   **Fic**
1. Family life—Fiction
ISBN 0-385-30427-7; 0-440-40809-1 (pa)
LC 90-21052

When their mother goes off, leaving her two children with their grandparents, they feel as if their past has been erased until Grandfather finds a way to restore it to them

"This is a spellbinding tale, lean only in its length. The author's clipped dialogue and meticulously pared-down descriptions convey a deceptive simplicity—there are deep, intricate rumblings beneath the surface calm of MacLachlan's words." Publ Wkly

Sarah, plain and tall. Harper & Row 1985 58p $14.95; lib bdg $14.89; pa $4.95 (3-5)   **Fic**
1. Stepmothers—Fiction 2. Frontier and pioneer life—Fiction
ISBN 0-06-024101-2; 0-06-024102-0 (lib bdg); 0-06-440205-3 (pa)   LC 83-49481
Also available Spanish language edition and Audiobook version

Awarded the Newbery Medal, 1986

"A Charlotte Zolotow book"

When their father invites a mail-order bride to come live with them in their prairie home, Caleb and Anna are captivated by their new mother and hope that she will stay

"It is the simplest of love stories expressed in the simplest of prose. Embedded in these unadorned declarative sentences about ordinary people, actions, animals, facts, objects and colors are evocations of the deepest feelings of loss and fear, love and hope." N Y Times Book Rev

Followed by Skylark

Seven kisses in a row; pictures by Maria Pia Marrella. Harper & Row 1983 56p il lib bdg $15.89; pa $4.95 (2-4)   **Fic**
1. Aunts—Fiction 2. Uncles—Fiction 3. Family life—Fiction
ISBN 0-06-024084-9 (lib bdg); 0-06-440231-2 (pa)
LC 82-47718

"A Charlotte Zolotow book"

"How different life is for Emma and Zachary when Aunt Evelyn and Uncle Elliott babysit for them while their parents attend an 'eyeball meeting'! No seven kisses before breakfast or divided grapefruit with cherry. Nevertheless both learn from the others—Emma learns to eat broccoli and her aunt and uncle learn about babies and what they do." Child Book Rev Serv

"The brief understated story makes few demands on the reader, but it is full of humor and the warmth of family caring and mutual affection. Informal, offhand pen-and-ink drawings reflect the tone of both story and style." Horn Book

Skylark. HarperCollins Pubs. 1994 86p $12.95; lib bdg $12.89; pa $4.95 (3-5)   **Fic**
1. Stepmothers—Fiction   2. Droughts—Fiction
3. Frontier and pioneer life—Fiction
ISBN 0-06-023328-1; 0-06-023333-8 (lib bdg); 0-06-440622-9 (pa)   LC 93-33211

Sequel to Sarah, plain and tall

"Sarah and the two children travel to Maine to visit her aunts—leaving Jacob behind. Only letters connect them—until, just before school starts, Jacob reappears, and the old bonds are strengthened with the promise of a new baby in the spring. . . . The book is suffused with joy and, ultimately, hope." Horn Book Guide

Magorian, Michelle, 1947-

Good night, Mr. Tom. Harper & Row 1981 318p lib bdg $16.89; pa $4.95 (6 and up)   **Fic**
1. Child abuse—Fiction 2. Adoption—Fiction
3. Great Britain—Fiction
ISBN 0-06-024079-2 (lib bdg); 0-06-440174-X (pa)
LC 80-8444

"When children are evacuated from London during World War II, Tom Oakley, a taciturn near-recluse who has never recovered from the deaths of his wife and child, takes in and forms a mutually healing relationship with eight-year-old Willie, a sickly, quiet boy who bears the marks of brutal beatings." Booklist

"The ending is tense, dramatic, believable, and satisfying. . . . Magorian uses dialogue and dialect well, giving local color as well as using them to establish character." Bull Cent Child Books

Maguire, Gregory

The good liar. Clarion Bks. 1999 129p $15 (4 and up)   **Fic**
1. World War, 1939-1945—Fiction 2. France—Fiction
ISBN 0-395-90697-0   LC 98-19981

Maguire, Gregory—*Continued*
First published 1995 in Ireland
Now an old man living in the United States, Marcel recalls his childhood in German-occupied France, especially the summer that he and his older brother Rene befriended a young German soldier
"At once poignant, thoughtful, and laced with humor, the book offers readers an unusual perspective on history." Horn Book Guide

Seven spiders spinning; illustrated by Dirk Zimmer. Clarion Bks. 1994 132p il $15 (4-6)
Fic
1. Spiders—Fiction 2. School stories
ISBN 0-395-68965-1   LC 93-30478
Also available in paperback from HarperCollins
Seven prehistoric spiders that had been trapped in ice for thousands of years bring excitement to rural Vermont and briefly unite two rival clubs at a local elementary school
"There is quite a bit of tongue-in-cheek humor here. . . . Characters are almost caricatures. . . . Yet, somehow it all comes together to create a funny, shivery story." SLJ
Other available titles in this series are:
Five alien elves (1998)
Four stupid Cupids (2000)
Six haunted hairdos (1997)

Mahy, Margaret
The other side of silence. Viking 1995 170p $14.99 (6 and up)
Fic
1. Family life—Fiction 2. New Zealand—Fiction
ISBN 0-670-86455-2   LC 95-8615
"Speechless Hero (labelled an 'elective mute' by those who think they know) sees her life in two parts: real life ('what everyone agreed about') and true life ('what you somehow know inside yourself'). She finds these lives entwining, at first seductively and then insidiously, when she is taken up by an eccentric woman who lives in a spooky old mansion surrounded by thick woods." Bull Cent Child Books
"Mahy's exceptional imagination and storytelling prowess will make it difficult for readers to leave this book behind them—hers is a tale with staying power." Publ Wkly

Tingleberries, tuckertubs and telephones; a tale of love and ice-cream; illustrated by Robert Staermose. Viking 1996 c1995 95p il $12.99; pa $4.99 (3-5)
Fic
1. Orphans—Fiction 2. Pirates—Fiction 3. Grandmothers—Fiction
ISBN 0-670-86331-9; 0-14-038973-3 (pa)
LC 96-138455
First published 1995 in the United Kingdom
"Saracen Hobday is a painfully shy orphan who has lived all his life on a secluded island with his granny, a retired detective. When the villainous pirate Grudge-Gallows escapes from prison, Granny is suddenly called back to active duty. Left on his own, bashful Saracen falls in love, makes a fortune marketing tingleberries, and single-handedly . . . brings down a dastardly gang of pirates." Booklist
"Combining farce and fantasy with a strong dose of technology, Mahy creates a glorious frolic that is brought to a fun-filled end." Horn Book Guide

Martin, Ann M., 1955-
The doll people; by Ann M. Martin and Laura Godwin; with pictures by Brian Selznick. Hyperion Bks. for Children 2000 256p il $15.99; lib bdg $16.49 (3-5)
Fic
1. Dolls—Fiction
ISBN 0-7868-0361-4; 0-7868-2372-0 (lib bdg)
LC 98-12344
A family of porcelain dolls that has lived in the same house for one hundred years is taken aback when a new family of plastic dolls arrives and doesn't follow The Doll Code of Honor
"A lighthearted touch and a dash of drama make this a satisfying read." SLJ

Mathis, Sharon Bell, 1937-
Sidewalk story; illustrated by Leo Carty. Viking 1971 71p il hardcover o.p. paperback available $4.99 (3-5)
Fic
1. Friendship—Fiction 2. African Americans—Fiction
ISBN 0-14-032165-9 (pa)   LC 86-4075
"Upset because her best friend Tanya and her family are being evicted and their belongings piled on the sidewalk and frustrated by her own mother's unwillingness to become involved, Lilly Etta phones first the police and then the newspaper for help and in the night creeps out to cover the things with sheets and blankets—and herself—to protect them from the wind and rain. Enhanced by several sensitive double-spread paintings in black and white." Booklist

Matthews, Mary, 1928-
Magid fasts for Ramadan; illustrated by E. B. Lewis. Clarion Bks. 1996 48p il $16; pa $6.95 (2-4)
Fic
1. Ramadan—Fiction 2. Cairo (Egypt)—Fiction
ISBN 0-395-66589-2; 0-618-04035-8 (pa)
LC 95-10452
Magid, an eight-year-old Muslim boy in Cairo, is determined to celebrate Ramadan by fasting, despite the opposition of family members who feel that he is not yet old enough to fast
"An informative afterword about the Islamic faith, a glossary and a pronunciation guide make it a good tool for teaching children about Islam." Publ Wkly

Mayne, William, 1928-
Hob and the goblins; illustrated by Norman Messenger. Dorling Kindersley 1994 c1993 140p il $15.95 (4 and up)
Fic
1. Fairies—Fiction 2. Fantasy fiction
ISBN 1-56458-713-4   LC 94-7029
First published 1993 in the United Kingdom
Hob, the friendly spirit who lives under the stairs and protects the house, must do battle with a variety of evil beings trying to take control of his family's home
"Mayne's writing style is deceptively simple, presenting a complex, fanciful world in a matter-of-fact manner. His quiet humor enhances the book's appeal, as do the cleverly illustrated initials at the start of each chapter." SLJ

Mazer, Harry, 1925-

The wild kid. Simon & Schuster Bks. for Young Readers 1998 103p $15; pa $4.99 (4 and up) **Fic**

1. Mentally handicapped—Fiction 2. Wild children—Fiction 3. Runaway children—Fiction
ISBN 0-689-80751-1; 0-689-82289-8 (pa)
LC 97-42578
Twelve-year-old Sammy, who is mildly retarded, runs away from home and becomes a prisoner of Kevin, a wild kid living in the woods
"A gripping survival story with flesh-and-blood characters." SLJ

Mazer, Norma Fox, 1931-

Good night, Maman. Harcourt Brace & Co. 1999 185p $16 (5 and up) **Fic**
1. Holocaust, 1933-1945—Fiction 2. World War, 1939-1945—Fiction 3. Jewish refugees—Fiction
ISBN 0-15-201468-3   LC 98-49220
Also available in paperback from HarperCollins
After spending years fleeing from the Nazis in war-torn Europe, twelve-year-old Karin Levi and her older brother Marc find a new home in a refugee camp in Oswego, New York
"Mazer convincingly constructs a fictional yet moving memoir of one girl's forever-altered life, and in Karin she gives readers a memorable heroine." Bull Cent Child Books

McCaffrey, Anne

Dragonsong. Atheneum Pubs. 1976 202p o.p.; Bantam Bks. paperback available $6.99 (6 and up) **Fic**

1. Fantasy fiction
ISBN 0-553-25852-4 (pa)   LC 75-30530
Also available G.K. Hall large print edition
"Forbidden by her stern father to make the music she loves, Menolly runs away from Half-Circle Sea Hold on the Planet Pern, takes shelter with fire lizards, and finds a new life opening up for her." LC. Child Books, 1976
"The author explores the ideas of alienation, rebellion, love of beauty, the role of women and the role of the individual in society with some sensitivity in a generally well-structured plot with sound characterizations." SLJ
Others available titles in the Harper Hall series are:
Dragondrums (1979)
Dragonsinger (1977)

McCaughrean, Geraldine, 1951-

The stones are hatching. HarperCollins Pubs. 2000 c1999 130p $15.95; lib bdg $15.89; pa $5.95 (5 and up) **Fic**
1. Fantasy fiction
ISBN 0-06-028765-9; 0-06-028766-7 (lib bdg); 0-06-447218-3 (pa)   LC 99-39895
First published 1999 in the United Kingdom
Eleven-year-old Phelim and his companions, a Maiden, a Fool, and a strange black Horse, journey to the Stoor Worm's lair to destroy the long-forgotten Worm and its Hatchlings, who have been roused from their slumber by the sounds of war
"With lyrical language, pieces of old songs and poetry, and wondrous imagery, McCaughrean has created a story of amazing depth and breadth." Horn Book Guide

McCloskey, Robert, 1914-

Homer Price. Viking 1943 149p il $15.99; pa $4.99 (4-6)   **Fic**
ISBN 0-670-37729-5; 0-14-030927-6 (pa)
Six "stories about the exploits of young Homer Price, who divides his time between school and doing odd jobs at his father's filling station and in his mother's tourist lunchroom two miles outside of Centerburg." Bookmark
"Text and pictures are pure Americana, hilarious and convincing in their portrayal of midwestern small-town life." Child Books Too Good to Miss
Another available title about Homer Price is:
Centerburg tales (1951)

McCully, Emily Arnold

The bobbin girl. Dial Bks. for Young Readers 1996 unp il $15.99 (3-5)   **Fic**
1. Strikes—Fiction 2. Factories—Fiction 3. United States—History—1815-1861—Fiction 4. Massachusetts—Fiction
ISBN 0-8037-1827-6   LC 95-6997
Rebecca, a ten-year-old bobbin girl working in a textile mill in Lowell, Massachusetts, in the 1830s, must make a difficult decision—will she participate in the first workers' strike in Lowell?
"McCully weaves historical facts and fictional characters into an intriguing story. The author's note details the background, incidents, and people who inspired the book. Beautifully composed watercolor paintings give a vivid impression of America in the 1830s and bring the period to life." Booklist

Hurry! illustrated by Emily Arnold McCully, adapted from Farewell to the Farivox by Harry Hartwick. Harcourt 2000 unp il $16 (2-4) **Fic**
1. Wildlife conservation—Fiction
ISBN 0-15-201579-5   LC 97-45564
"Browndeer Press"
In 1916, a young boy named Tom Elson living in Iowa meets a stranger who has an unusual animal called a Farivox, maybe the last of its kind, and Tom becomes determined to buy it
"The tale gently but firmly makes its point and provides an excellent springboard for discussion. . . . The illustrations are vintage McCully, perfectly capturing the time period and its ambience with brightly colored but soft-edged watercolors." SLJ

McDonald, Megan, 1959-

Judy Moody; illustrated by Peter Reynolds. Candlewick Press 2000 160p il $15.99 (2-4) **Fic**
1. School stories
ISBN 0-7636-0685-5   LC 99-13464
Third grader Judy Moody is in a first day of school bad mood until she gets an assignment to create a collage all about herself and begins creating her masterpiece, the Me collage
"This beginning chapter book features large type; simple, expressive prose and dialogue; and plenty of child-appealing humor." Booklist

McGill, Alice

Miles' song. Houghton Mifflin 2000 213p $15 (6 and up) **Fic**

1. Slavery—Fiction 2. African Americans—Fiction
ISBN 0-395-97938-2

In 1851 in South Carolina, Miles, a twelve-year-old slave, is sent to a "breaking ground" to have his spirit broken but endures the experience by secretly taking reading lessons from another slave

"Strong characterizations and a driving sense of action carry the plot." Bull Cent Child Books

McGraw, Eloise Jarvis, 1915-2000

The moorchild; [by] Eloise McGraw. Margaret K. McElderry Bks. 1996 241p $17 (4 and up) **Fic**

1. Fantasy fiction 2. Fairies—Fiction
ISBN 0-689-80654-X   LC 95-34107

Newbery Medal honor book, 1997

"Saaski, a half-human, half-Moorfolk child, is banished from the Mound and placed as a changeling in a human village, where she is regarded with suspicion and treated with scorn." Horn Book Guide

"Incorporating some classic fantasy motifs and icons, McGraw . . . conjures up an appreciably familiar world that, as evidence of her storytelling power, still strikes an original chord." Publ Wkly

McKay, Hilary

Dog Friday. Margaret K. McElderry Bks. 1995 135p $15; pa $4.50 (4-6) **Fic**

1. Dogs—Fiction 2. Great Britain—Fiction
ISBN 0-689-80383-4; 0-689-81765-7 (pa)
                                LC 95-4446

First published 1994 in the United Kingdom

Ten-year-old Robin Brogan is determined to keep the dog he finds abandoned on the beach from being impounded by the police

"The sharply realized characters, fast-paced story, and witty dialogue make this English novel both distinctive and refreshing." Booklist

Other available titles about the Brogan family and their friends are:

The amber cat (1997)
Dolphin luck (1999)

The exiles. Margaret K. McElderry Bks. 1992 217p hardcover o.p. paperback available $4.50 (5 and up) **Fic**

1. Sisters—Fiction 2. Grandmothers—Fiction
ISBN 0-689-80592-6 (pa)   LC 91-38220

The four Conroy sisters spend a wild summer at the seaside with Big Grandma, who tries to break them of their reading habit by substituting fresh air and hard work for books and gets unexpected results

This is an "extremely and continuously funny book." Bull Cent Child Books

Other available titles about The exiles are:

The exiles at home (1994)
The exiles in love (1998)

McKinley, Robin

Beauty: a retelling of the story of Beauty & the beast. Harper & Row 1978 247p $15.95; pa $5.95 (6 and up) **Fic**

1. Fairy tales
ISBN 0-06-024149-7; 0-06-440477-3 (pa)
                                LC 77-25636

"McKinley's version of this folktale is embellished with rich descriptions and settings and detailed characterizations. The author has not modernized the story but varied the traditional version to attract modern readers. The values of love, honor, and beauty are placed in a magical setting that will please the reader of fantasy." Shapiro. Fic for Youth. 3d edition

The hero and the crown. Greenwillow Bks. 1985 246p lib bdg $16.95 (6 and up) **Fic**

1. Fantasy fiction
ISBN 0-688-02593-5   LC 84-4074

Also available in paperback from Ace Bks.

Awarded the Newbery Medal, 1985

"A prequel rather than sequel to 'The Blue Sword' [1982], McKinley's second novel set in the . . . mythical kingdom of Damar centers on Aerin, daughter of a Damarian king and his second wife, a witchwoman from the feared, demon-ridden North. The narrative follows Aerin as she seeks her birthright, becoming first a dragon killer and eventually the savior of the kingdom." Booklist

The author "has in this suspenseful prequel . . . created an utterly engrossing fantasy, replete with a fairly mature romantic subplot as well as adventure." N Y Times Book Rev

McKissack, Patricia C., 1944-

Color me dark; the diary of Nellie Lee Love, the great migration North. Scholastic 2000 218p (Dear America) $10.95 (4 and up) **Fic**

1. African Americans—Fiction 2. Chicago (Ill.)—Fiction
ISBN 0-590-51159-9   LC 99-16459

Eleven-year-old Nellie Lee Love records in her diary the events of 1919, when her family moves from Tennessee to Chicago, hoping to leave the racism and hatred of the South behind

"The strong narrative will keep children involved and give them a great deal of social history to absorb along the way." Booklist

A picture of Freedom; the diary of Clotee, a slave girl. Scholastic 1997 192p il maps (Dear America) $10.95 (4 and up) **Fic**

1. Slavery—Fiction 2. Underground railroad—Fiction 3. Books and reading—Fiction 4. African Americans—Fiction
ISBN 0-590-25988-1   LC 96-25673

In 1859 twelve-year-old Clotee, a house slave who must conceal the fact that she can read and write, records in her diary her experiences and her struggle to decide whether to escape to freedom

"McKissack brings Clotee alive through touching and sobering details of slave life." SLJ

McKissack, Patricia C., 1944-—*Continued*
Run away home. Scholastic 1997 160p $14.95
(5 and up)   **Fic**
1. African Americans—Fiction 2. Apache Indians—
Fiction 3. Alabama—Fiction
ISBN 0-590-46751-4   LC 96-43673
"This story of the young Apache who escaped from
the train transporting Geronimo and his companions-in-
exile from Florida to Alabama is rooted in the author's
family history. The narrator is eleven-year-old Sarah Jane
Crossman, who first befriends Sky when, sick and friend-
less, he seeks shelter in her family's barn." Horn Book
"Grabbing readers with wonderful characters, an engaging plot, and vital themes, McKissack weaves a compelling story of cultural clash, tragedy, accommodation,
and ultimate triumph." SLJ

Mead, Alice
Crossing the Starlight Bridge. Bradbury Press
1994 122p il $15; pa $4.50 (3-5)   **Fic**
1. Penobscot Indians—Fiction
ISBN 0-02-765950-X; 0-689-80105-X (pa)
                                      LC 93-40978
Nine-year-old Rayanne's life turns upside down when
her father leaves and she has to move off the Penobscot
reservation and go to live with her grandmother
"Mead deftly establishes a child's point of view with
simple and unpretentious language. . . . This is a gentle
and understanding story of a young girl's adjustment to
change." Bull Cent Child Books

Junebug. Farrar, Straus & Giroux 1995 101p
$15 (3-5)   **Fic**
1. African Americans—Fiction 2. Sailing—Fiction
ISBN 0-374-33964-3   LC 95-5421
Also available in paperback from Dell
"Junebug approaches his tenth birthday with fear because he knows he'll be forced by the older boys in his
housing project to join a gang. On his birthday, with
luck and persistence, Junebug realizes his secret dream
of one day sailing a boat. The novel contains vivid descriptions of the grim realities of inner-city life but also
demonstrates that strong convictions and warm hearts can
bring about change." Horn Book Guide
Another available title about Junebug is:
Junebug and the Reverend (1998)

Menotti, Gian Carlo, 1911-
Amahl and the night visitors; illustrated by
Michèle Lemieux. Morrow 1986 64p il $21 (2-4)
                                              Fic
1. Jesus Christ—Nativity—Fiction 2. Magi—Fiction
ISBN 0-688-05426-9   LC 84-27196
Relates how a crippled young shepherd comes to accompany the three Kings on their way to pay hommage
to the newborn Jesus
"Some of the pictures, which are dominated by red-
dish brown, have rich tension and composition, as in the
one of Amahl's mother contemplating theft, or in the
portrait of Melchior describing the Christ child. . . .
There is a great deal to look at, and the story, popular
since the opera's 1951 debut, has sentimental appeal, humor, and some commanding moments." Bull Cent Child
Books

Merrill, Jean, 1923-
The pushcart war; with illustrations by Ronni
Solbert. HarperCollins Pubs. 1992 c1964 222p il
o.p.; Dell paperback available $4.99 (5 and up)
                                              Fic
1. Trucks—Fiction 2. New York (N.Y.)—Fiction
ISBN 0-440-47147-8 (pa)
A reissue of the title first published 1964 by W.R.
Scott
"Arrogant, mammoth trucks threaten to crowd people,
small cars, pushcarts, and peddlers off the streets of New
York. When a truck contemptuously runs down a pushcart, the peddlers rebel and wage a guerrilla war against
the trucks, using a primitive, but effective, secret weapon. Funny, dramatic, tongue-in-cheek satire on the sheer
bigness which is overwhelming urban life but which is
here, for once, defeated by the little people who 'are' the
city." Moorachian. What is a City?

The toothpaste millionaire; prepared by the
Bank Street College of Education. Houghton
Mifflin 1974 c1972 90p il hardcover o.p.
paperback available $4.95 (4-6)   **Fic**
1. Business—Fiction
ISBN 0-395-96063-0 (pa)
First copyright 1972
Illustrated by Jan Palmer
The author recounts the adventures of twelve-year-old
Rufus Mayflower who starts manufacturing and selling
toothpaste when he is in the sixth grade. By the time he
is an eighth grader, he is a millionaire and ready to retire
This story "is laden rather heavily with arithmetic and
business details, but rises above it. . . . The illustrations
are engaging, the style is light, the project interesting
(with more than a few swipes taken at advertising and
business practices in our society) and Rufus a believable
genius." Bull Cent Child Books

Meyer, Carolyn
Isabel; jewel of Castilla. Scholastic 2000 204p
(Royal diaries) $10.95 (4 and up)   **Fic**
1. Isabella I, Queen of Spain, 1451-1504—Fiction
2. Spain—Fiction
ISBN 0-439-07805-9   LC 99-16805
While waiting anxiously for others to choose a husband for her, Isabella, the future Queen of Spain, keeps
a diary account of her life as a member of the royal family
"The writing flows well and is age appropriate, and
Meyer makes a distinction between history and fiction in
the appended historical notes. A family tree and glossary
of characters are included." Horn Book Guide

Mikaelsen, Ben, 1952-
Petey. Hyperion Bks. for Children 1998 280p
$15.95; pa $5.99 (5 and up)   **Fic**
1. Cerebral palsy—Fiction 2. Physically handicapped—Fiction 3. Old age—Fiction
ISBN 0-7868-0426-2; 0-7868-1336-9 (pa)
                                      LC 98-10183
In 1922 Petey, who has cerebral palsy, is
misdiagnosed as an idiot and institutionalized; sixty years
later, still in the institution, he befriends a boy and

Mikaelsen, Ben, 1952-—*Continued*
shares with him the joy of life

"Mikaelsen successfully conveys Petey's strangled attempts to communicate. He captures the slow passage of time, the historical landscape encompassed. He brings emotions to the surface and tears to readers' eyes." SLJ

Miles, Miska, 1899-1986
Annie and the Old One; illustrated by Peter Parnall. Little, Brown 1971 44p il lib bdg $16.95; pa $7.95 (1-4) **Fic**
1. Navajo Indians—Fiction 2. Death—Fiction
ISBN 0-316-57117-2 (lib bdg); 0-316-57120-2 (pa)

A Newbery Medal honor book, 1972
"An Atlantic Monthy Press book"
"Annie, a young Navajo girl, struggles with the realization that her grandmother, the Old One, must die. Slowly and painfully, she accepts the fact that she cannot change the cyclic rhythms of the earth to which the Old One has been so sensitively attuned." Wis Libr Bull

This is "a poignant, understated, rather brave story of a very real child, set against a background of Navajo traditions and contemporary Indian life. Fine expressive drawings match the simplicity of the story." Horn Book

Mills, Claudia, 1954-
You're a brave man, Julius Zimmerman. Farrar, Straus & Giroux 1999 152p $16 (5 and up) **Fic**
1. Mother-son relationship—Fiction 2. Babysitting—Fiction 3. School stories
ISBN 0-374-38708-7 LC 98-50799
Sequel to Losers, Inc. (1997)
Twelve-year-old Julius has his hands full over the summer when his mother attempts to improve his grades and teach him responsibility by signing him up for a French class and getting him a job babysitting

The author's "humorously constructed scenes . . . are both touching and peppered with laugh-out-loud aperçus. . . . Although the ending is a little bit neat, this novel as a whole rings satisfyingly true." Publ Wkly

Milne, A. A. (Alan Alexander), 1882-1956
The complete tales of Winnie-the-Pooh; with decorations by Ernest H. Shepard. Dutton Children's Bks. 1996 344p il $35 (1-4) **Fic**
1. Bears—Fiction 2. Animals—Fiction 3. Toys—Fiction
ISBN 0-525-45723-2
A combined edition of Winnie-the-Pooh and The house at Pooh Corner

The house at Pooh Corner; with decorations by Ernest H. Shepard. Dutton c1928 180p il $9.95; pa $4.99 (1-4) **Fic**
1. Bears—Fiction 2. Animals—Fiction 3. Toys—Fiction
ISBN 0-525-32302-3; 0-14-036122-7 (pa)
First published 1928
"Pooh and Piglet built a house for Eeyore at Pooh Corner. They called it that because it was shorter and sounded better than did Poohanpiglet Corner. Christopher

Robin, Rabbit, and other old acquaintances of 'Winnie-the-Pooh' appear, and a new friend, Tigger, is introduced." Carnegie Libr of Pittsburgh

"It is hard to tell what Pooh Bear and his friends would have been without the able assistance of Ernest H. Shepard to see them and picture them so cleverly. . . . They are, and should be, classics." N Y Times Book Rev

The Pooh story book; with decorations and illustrations in full color by E. H. Shepard. Dutton 1965 77p il $14.99; pa $5.99 (1-4) **Fic**
1. Bears—Fiction 2. Animals—Fiction 3. Toys—Fiction
ISBN 0-525-37546-5; 0-14-038168-6 (pa)
Excerpts from: The house at Pooh Corner and Winnie-the-Pooh
Contents: In which a house is built at Pooh Corner for Eeyore; In which Piglet is entirely surrounded by water; In which Pooh invents a new game and Eeyore joins in

Winnie-the-Pooh; illustrated by Ernest H. Shepard, colored by Hilda Scott. Dutton 1974 c1926 161p il $10.99; pa $4.99 (1-4) **Fic**
1. Bears—Fiction 2. Animals—Fiction 3. Toys—Fiction
ISBN 0-525-44443-2; 0-14-036121-9 (pa)
Also available Audiobook version
First published 1926
"The kindly, lovable Pooh is one of an imaginative cast of animal characters which includes Eeyore, the wistfully gloomy donkey, Tigger, Piglet, Kanga, and Roo, all living in a fantasy world presided over by Milne's young son, Christopher Robin. Many of the animals are drawn from figures in Milne's life, though each emerges as a universally recognizable type." Reader's Ency

The world of Pooh; the complete Winnie-the-Pooh and The House at Pooh Corner; with decorations and new illustrations in full color by E. H. Shepard. Dutton 1957 314p il $21.99 (1-4) **Fic**
1. Bears—Fiction 2. Animals—Fiction 3. Toys—Fiction
ISBN 0-525-44447-5
This combined edition of the two titles entered separately contains the original black and white "illustrations and eight delightful new full-page pictures printed in lovely soft colors." Publ Wkly

Moeri, Louise
Save Queen of Sheba. Dutton 1981 116p hardcover o.p. paperback available $4.99 (4 and up) **Fic**
1. Survival after airplane accidents, shipwrecks, etc.—Fiction 2. Siblings—Fiction 3. West (U.S.)—Fiction
ISBN 0-14-037148-6 (pa) LC 80-23019
"A marauding band of Sioux have botched the job of scalping twelve-year-old King David. He awakes with a massive head wound to find that he is alone amidst the wreckage of the wagon train and the bodies of the other travelers. Searching desperately, he finds his six-year-old sister, Queen of Sheba, unharmed but mightily unhappy. Collecting scant food supplies, a rifle, and a plow horse

Moeri, Louise—*Continued*

who has returned, the two children set off across the prairie to seek the remnants of a wagon train that might be a few days ahead." Child Book Rev Serv

"Vivid scenes are held taut by a continuity of background. . . . Memorable for reading aloud, with discussion, or alone." Booklist

Mohr, Nicholasa, 1935-

Going home. Dial Bks. for Young Readers 1986 192p hardcover o.p. paperback available $4.99 (4-6)   **Fic**
1. Puerto Ricans—New York (N.Y.)—Fiction 2. Puerto Rico—Fiction
ISBN 0-14-130644-0 (pa)   LC 85-20621

Feeling like an outsider when she visits her relatives in Puerto Rico for the first time, eleven-year-old Felita tries to come to terms with the heritage she always took for granted

"This is a convincing story that captures the universality of preteen relationships." Rochman. Against borders

Another available title about Felita is:
Felita (1979)

Montgomery, L. M. (Lucy Maud), 1874-1942

Anne of Green Gables (5 and up)   **Fic**
1. Adoption—Fiction 2. Prince Edward Island—Fiction

Available from various publishers, including a Grosset & Dunlap edition illustrated by Jody Lee; also available Audiobook version

First published 1908 by Page

"Daily doings and dreams from her 10th to 17th year of a lively, imaginative child, adopted by an elderly brother and sister on a Prince Edward Island farm." N Y State Libr

Other available titles about Anne are:
Anne of Avonlea (1909)
Anne of Ingleside (1939)
Anne of the island (1915)
Anne of Windy Poplars (1936)
Anne's house of dreams (1917)

Morey, Walt, 1907-1992

Gentle Ben; illustrated by John Schoenherr. Dutton 1965 191p il hardcover o.p. paperback available $4.99 (5 and up)   **Fic**
1. Bears—Fiction 2. Alaska—Fiction
ISBN 0-14-036035-2 (pa)

Set in Alaska before statehood, this is the story of 13-year-old Mark Anderson who befriends a huge brown bear which has been chained in a shed since it was a cub. Finally Mark's father buys the bear, but Orca City's inhabitants eventually insist that the animal, named Ben, be shipped to an uninhabited island. However, the friendship of Mark and Ben endures

The author "has written a vivid chronicle of Alaska, its people and places, challenges and beauties. Told with a simplicity and dignity which befits its characters, human and animal, [it] is a memorable reading experience." SLJ

Morpurgo, Michael

Arthur, high king of Britain; illustrated by Michael Foreman. Harcourt Brace & Co. 1995 137p il $22 (4 and up)   **Fic**
1. Arthur, King—Fiction 2. Arthurian romances
ISBN 0-15-200080-1   LC 93-33620

First published 1994 in the United Kingdom

A twelve-year-old boy comes across Arthur Pendragon, who has just awakened from his long sleep beneath the earth, and hears from him some of the exciting stories of his past

"The sweep of this version encompasses a rich array of beloved stories . . . as well as some of their noteworthy yet lesser-known kin. . . . Although he offers no source notes, Morpurgo has clearly done wide research. . . . He follows in a time-honored tradition of adaptation and abridgment, but he never neglects the integrity and authenticity of the stories he tells. . . . [Foreman's] soft watercolor scenes are pricked with a cool freshness; blues, greens, golds, and purples shimmer together into variances of seasonal changes, windswept hilltops, and shadowed castles." Bull Cent Child Books

Waiting for Anya. Viking 1991 c1990 172p $14.99; pa $4.99 (5 and up)   **Fic**
1. World War, 1939-1945—Fiction 2. Jews—France—Fiction 3. France—History—1940-1945, German occupation—Fiction
ISBN 0-670-83735-0; 0-14-038431-6 (pa)
LC 90-50560

First published 1990 in the United Kingdom

"A World War II adventure story set in Vichy, France, this centers on a young shepherd, Jo, who becomes involved in smuggling Jewish children across the border from his mountain village to Spain. Morpurgo has injected the basic conventions of heroism and villainy with some complexities of character. . . . Independent readers will appreciate the simple, clear style and fast-paced plot of the book, which will also hold up well in group read-alouds, commanding attention to ethics as well as action." Bull Cent Child Books

Murrow, Liza Ketchum, 1946-

Orphan journey home; by Liza Ketchum; illustrated by C.B. Mordan. Avon Bks. 2000 162p $15 (4-6)   **Fic**
1. Frontier and pioneer life—Fiction 2. Voyages and travels—Fiction 3. Orphans—Fiction
ISBN 0-380-97811-3   LC 99-42649

In 1828, while traveling from Illinois to Kentucky, twelve-year-old Jesse and her two brothers and sister lose their parents to the milk sickness and must try to finish the dangerous journey by themselves

"Originally published as a newspaper serial, the fast-paced, present-tense narrative is written in short, cliffhanger chapters, each accompanied by an effective illustration." Horn Book Guide

Myers, Walter Dean, 1937-

Fast Sam, Cool Clyde, and Stuff. Viking 1975 190p hardcover o.p. paperback available $4.99 (6 and up)   **Fic**
1. Friendship—Fiction 2. African Americans—Fiction 3. Harlem (New York, N.Y.)—Fiction
ISBN 0-14-032613-8 (pa)

Myers, Walter Dean, 1937——*Continued*

"In an affectionate, colloquial narrative, Stuff, now 18, recalls the time when he was 13, hanging out on 116th Street, and enjoying being part of a circle of dependable friends, the best of whom were Fast Sam and Cool Clyde." Booklist

"A funny, fast-paced story of teenagers in the ghetto. The characters are memorable." Read Teach

The journal of Joshua Loper; a black cowboy. Scholastic 1999 158p il (My name is America) $10.95 (5 and up)   **Fic**
1. Cowhands—Fiction 2. African Americans—Fiction 3. West (U.S.)—Fiction
ISBN 0-590-02691-7   LC 98-18661

In 1871 Joshua Loper, a sixteen-year-old black cowboy, records in his journal his experiences while making his first cattle drive under an unsympathetic trail boss

"With characteristic research, sensitivity, and insight, Myers offers a lively, youthful portrait of the life and times of this black cowboy." SLJ

The journal of Scott Pendleton Collins; a World War II soldier. Scholastic 1999 140p il (My name is America) $10.95 (5 and up)   **Fic**
1. World War, 1939-1945—Fiction
ISBN 0-439-05013-8   LC 99-13615

A seventeen-year-old soldier from central Virginia records his experiences in a journal as his regiment takes part in the D-Day invasion of Normandy and subsequent battles to liberate France

"This brief novel presents an accurate depiction of the horror of battle. The narrative voice is engaging and believable." SLJ

Me, Mop, and the Moondance Kid; illustrated by Rodney Pate. Delacorte Press 1988 154p il hardcover o.p. paperback available $4.99 (4-6)
                    Fic
1. Baseball—Fiction 2. Adoption—Fiction 3. Friendship—Fiction
ISBN 0-440-40396-0 (pa)   LC 88-6503

"Eleven-year-old T. J. and his younger brother Billy, a.k.a. the Moondance Kid, have been living with their adoptive parents for about six months, and are settling in well. They are worried that their friend Mop, a girl who has not yet been adopted, may be transferred to an orphanage some distance away. Mop decides to join T. J.'s little league team in order to get close to the coach and his wife, whom she suspects are interested in adopting her." SLJ

"Myers's keen sense of humor, quick, natural dialogue and irresistible protagonists make this novel a winner." Publ Wkly

Naidoo, Beverley

Chain of fire; illustrations by Eric Velasquez. Lippincott 1990 c1989 245p il hardcover o.p. paperback available $4.95 (5 and up)   **Fic**
1. South Africa—Race relations—Fiction
ISBN 0-06-440468-4 (pa)   LC 89-27551
First published 1989 in the United Kingdom

"The political awakening of fifteen-year-old Naledi, who first appeared in *Journey to Jo'burg*, is recounted

with passion and eloquence as the author describes the resettling of Black villagers to their new and barren 'homeland'—the result of South Africa's policy of apartheid." Horn Book Guide

Journey to Jo'burg; a South African story; illustrations by Eric Velasquez. Lippincott 1986 80p il lib bdg $15.89; pa $4.95 (5 and up)   **Fic**
1. South Africa—Race relations—Fiction
ISBN 0-397-32169-4 (lib bdg); 0-06-440237-1 (pa)
                    LC 85-45508

"This touching novel graphically depicts the plight of Africans living in the horror of South Africa. Thirteen-year-old Maledi and her 9-year-old brother leave their small village, take the perilous journey to the city, and encounter, firsthand, the painful struggle for justice, freedom, and dignity in the 'City of Gold.' A provocative story with a message readers will long remember." Soc Educ

Followed by Chain of fire

No turning back; a novel of South Africa. HarperCollins Pubs. 1997 c1995 189p lib bdg $15.89; pa $4.95 (5 and up)   **Fic**
1. Runaway children—Fiction 2. South Africa—Fiction
ISBN 0-06-027506-5 (lib bdg); 0-06-440749-7 (pa)
                    LC 96-28980
First published 1995 in the United Kingdom

When the abuse at home becomes too much for twelve-year-old Sipho, he runs away to the streets of Johannesburg and learns to survive in the post-apartheid world

"Charged with a rhythm that begins beating on the first page and carries through until the last, Naidoo's novel is a can't-put-it-down account." Horn Book

Namioka, Lensey

Ties that bind, ties that break; a novel. Delacorte Press 1999 154p $15.95; pa $4.99 (5 and up)   **Fic**
1. Sex role—Fiction 2. China—Fiction
ISBN 0-385-32666-1; 0-440-41599-3 (pa)
                    LC 98-27877

"In early twentieth-century China, Ailin's liberal father allows her to avoid the tradition of foot-binding, but a broken engagement makes her family fear for her future. Ailin's intelligence and hard work—and a lot of luck—lead her to a new life in America." Horn Book Guide

"In lyrical, descriptive prose, Namioka compassionately portrays a young girl's coming-of-age in a repressive, challenging time." Booklist

Yang the youngest and his terrible ear; illustrated by Kees de Kiefte. Little, Brown 1992 134p il o.p.; Dell paperback available $4.50 (4-6)
                    Fic
1. Chinese—United States—Fiction 2. Family life—Fiction
ISBN 0-440-40917-9 (pa)   LC 91-30345
"Joy Steet books"

Recently arrived in Seattle from China, musically untalented Yingtao is faced with giving a violin performance to attract new students for his father when he

Namioka, Lensey—*Continued*
would rather be working on friendships and playing baseball

"Namioka explores issues of diversity, self-realization, friendship, and duty with sensitivity and a great deal of humor." Horn Book

Other available titles about the Yang family are:
Yang the eldest and his odd jobs (2000)
Yang the second and her secret admirers (1998)
Yang the third and her impossible family (1995)

Napoli, Donna Jo, 1948-
The prince of the pond; otherwise known as De Fawg Pin; illustrated by Judy Schachner. Dutton Children's Bks. 1992 151p il $15.99; pa $4.99 (4-6) **Fic**
   1. Frogs—Fiction
   ISBN 0-525-44976-0; 0-14-037151-6 (pa)
                 LC 91-40340

This story based on the frog prince motif is "told from the point of view of Jade, a female frog. . . . Pin (as the Prince calls himself, hampered in his speech by a long, fat tongue attached at the front of his mouth) is handsome, but strangely ignorant of everything . . . so Jade must teach him the ropes. . . . Eventually, when the opportunity of kissing a princess represents itself, Pin leaps at it and disappears from Jade's life forever." Booklist

"Point of view is all here, and Napoli uses it to involve the reader in a touching story. . . . The consistency and mini-drama of a frog's-eye view (one at a time), coupled with a poignant ending that doesn't shy away from loss, makes this an animal fantasy that fairy tale readers will relish. . . . Schachner's numerous ink-and-wash drawings go far in supporting the characterization." Bull Cent Child Books

Stones in water. Dutton Children's Bks. 1997 209p $16.99; pa $4.99 (5 and up) **Fic**
   1. World War, 1939-1945—Fiction
   ISBN 0-525-45842-5; 0-14-130600-9 (pa)
                 LC 97-14253

After being taken by German soldiers from a local movie theater along with other Italian boys including his Jewish friend, Roberto is forced to work in Germany, escapes into the Ukrainian winter, before desperately trying to make his way back home to Venice

This is a "gripping, meticulously researched story (loosely based on the life of an actual survivor)." Publ Wkly

Naylor, Phyllis Reynolds, 1933-
The agony of Alice. Atheneum Pubs. 1985 131p $16; pa $4.99 (5 and up) **Fic**
   1. Teachers—Fiction 2. School stories
   ISBN 0-689-31143-5; 0-689-81672-3 (pa)
                 LC 85-7957

Eleven-year-old, motherless Alice decides she needs a gorgeous role model who does everything right; and when placed in homely Mrs. Plotkin's class she is greatly disappointed until she discovers it's what people are inside that counts

"The lively style exhibits a deft touch at capturing the essence of an endearing heroine growing up without a mother." SLJ

Other available titles about Alice are:
Achingly Alice (1998)
Alice in April (1993)
Alice in lace (1996)
Alice in rapture, sort of (1989)
Alice in-between (1994)
Alice on the outside (1999)
Alice the brave (1995)
All but Alice (1992)
The grooming of Alice (2000)
Outrageously Alice (1997)
Reluctantly Alice (1991)

The fear place. Atheneum Pubs. 1994 118p $16.95; pa $4.50 (5 and up) **Fic**
   1. Brothers—Fiction 2. Pumas—Fiction 3. Camping—Fiction
   ISBN 0-689-31866-9; 0-689-80442-3 (pa)
                 LC 93-38891

When he and his older brother Gordon are left camping alone in the Rocky Mountains, twelve-year-old Doug faces his fear of heights and his feelings about Gordon—with the help of a cougar

This is "a solid action story, tense and involving. . . . A satisfying wilderness adventure." Publ Wkly

The grand escape; illustrated by Alan Daniel. Atheneum Pubs. 1993 148p il o.p.; Dell paperback available $4.99 (4-6) **Fic**
   1. Cats—Fiction 2. Adventure fiction
   ISBN 0-440-40968-3 (pa)   LC 91-40816

After years of being strictly house cats, Marco and Polo escape into the wonderful, but dangerous outside world and are sent on three challenging adventures by a group of cats known as the Club of Mysteries

"While Naylor's feline explorers are amusing and lovable, their behavior is always catlike, and their interpretation of human foibles is often hilarious." Booklist

Peril in the Bessledorf Parachute Factory. Atheneum Bks. for Young Readers 2000 c1999 148p $16 (4-6) **Fic**
   ISBN 0-689-82539-0   LC 98-36606

"A Jean Karl book"

Bernie's attempt to marry off his sister Delores results in mystery and near-disaster at the Bessledorf Parachute Factory

"The humor is right on target for middle-graders." Booklist

Other available titles in the Bessledorf series are:
The bomb in the Bessledorf bus depot (1996)
The face in the Bessledorf funeral parlor (1993)
The treasure of Bessledorf Hill (1997)

Shiloh. Atheneum Pubs. 1991 144p $15; pa $5.50 (4-6) **Fic**
   1. Dogs—Fiction 2. West Virginia—Fiction
   ISBN 0-689-31614-3; 0-689-83583-3 (pa)
                 LC 90-603

Also available Shiloh trilogy as a boxed set $35; pa $14.99 (ISBN 0-689-82327-4; 0-689-01525-9) Audiobook version of trilogy also available

Awarded the Newbery Medal, 1992

When he finds a lost beagle in the hills behind his West Virginia home, Marty tries to hide it from his fami-

Naylor, Phyllis Reynolds, 1933-—*Continued*
ly and the dog's real owner, a mean-spirited man known to shoot deer out of season and to mistreat his dogs

"A credible plot and characters, a well-drawn setting, and nicely paced narration combine in a story that leaves the reader feeling good." Horn Book

Other available titles about Shiloh are:
Saving Shiloh (1997)
Shiloh season (1996)

Nelson, Theresa, 1948-
And one for all. Orchard Bks. 1989 182p $16.95 (5 and up) **Fic**
1. Vietnam War, 1961-1975—Fiction 2. Siblings—Fiction
ISBN 0-531-05804-2 LC 88-22490
Also available in paperback from Dell
"A Richard Jackson book"
Geraldine's close relationship with her older brother Wing and his friend Sam changes when Wing joins the Marines and Sam leaves for Washington to join a peace march

"Plot, dialogue, and setting are effortlessly authentic and never overwhelmed by the theme. . . . Smoothly written and easily read, this also manages to challenge assumptions in a thought-provoking probe of the past." Bull Cent Child Books

Earthshine; a novel. Orchard Bks. 1994 182p $16.95; lib bdg $17.99 (5 and up) **Fic**
1. AIDS (Disease)—Fiction 2. Father-daughter relationship—Fiction 3. Homosexuality—Fiction
ISBN 0-531-06867-6; 0-531-08717-4 (lib bdg)
LC 94-8793
Also available in paperback from Laurel-Leaf Bks.
"A Richard Jackson book"
"Slim—real name Margery—is twelve, living with her actor father and her father's lover, Larry; her father is dying of AIDS, and Slim participates in a church youth group for kids close to people with the disease." Bull Cent Child Books
"Major and minor characters are real people and never case studies. And the author's use of language expresses both the action and underlying feelings while remaining true to the voice of the narrator. . . . This special book should find a wide audience." SLJ

Nesbit, E. (Edith), 1858-1924
The enchanted castle; illustrated by Paul O. Zelinsky; afterword by Peter Glassman. Morrow Junior Bks. 1992 292p il lib bdg $22.95 (4-6)
Fic
1. Fantasy fiction 2. Great Britain—Fiction
ISBN 0-688-05435-8 LC 91-46267
First published 1907 in the United Kingdom; first United States edition 1908 by Harper & Brothers
Four English children find a wonderful world of magic through an enchanted wishing ring
"With fine, cross-hatched lines tinted in luminous colors, Zelinsky's artwork is as lively as the story and very much of the period." Booklist

Five children and it; illustrated by Paul O. Zelinsky. Morrow 1999 242p il $22 (4-6) **Fic**
1. Fantasy fiction 2. Great Britain—Fiction
ISBN 0-688-13545-5 LC 98-50391

Also available Audiobook version
"Books of Wonder"
First published 1902 in the United Kingdom; first United States edition 1905 by Dodd, Mead & Co.

When four brothers and sisters discover a Psammead, or sand-fairy, in the gravel pit near the country house where they are staying, they have no way of knowing all the adventures its wish-granting will bring them
This "features twelve appropriately Edwardian watercolor paintings by Zelinsky." Horn Book

Other available titles in this series are:
The Phoenix and the carpet (1904)
The story of the amulet (1907)

The railway children; with illustrations by C. E. Brock. Knopf 1993 294p il $12.95 (4-6) **Fic**
1. Family life—Fiction 2. Railroads—Fiction 3. Great Britain—Fiction
ISBN 0-679-42534-9 LC 92-55074
Also available in paperback from various publishers
"An Everyman's Library Children's Classic"
A reissue of the title first published 1906 by Macmillan

When their father is sent away to prison, three London children move to the country where they keep busy preventing accidents on the nearby railway, making many new friends, and generally learning a good deal about themselves

Neufeld, John, 1938-
Almost a hero. Atheneum Bks. for Young Readers 1995 147p $15; pa $3.99 (5 and up)
Fic
1. Child abuse—Fiction 2. Homeless persons—Fiction 3. Death—Fiction
ISBN 0-689-31971-1; 0-689-80740-6 (pa)
LC 94-12785
"Ben Derby is a 12-year-old whose teacher has assigned to him a week of charitable work during spring break. Ben works at a day care center for homeless children, one of whom Ben thinks he sees being abused in the grocery store. When 'the system' is too cautious in its response, Ben and his friends plan a bold rescue of the child." Booklist
"Ben ponders some difficult questions in ways that young readers, who may face similar moral challenges themselves, will relate to." Bull Cent Child Books

Neville, Emily Cheney, 1919-
It's like this, Cat; [by] Emily Neville; pictures by Emil Weiss. Harper & Row 1963 180p il lib bdg $15.89; pa $3.95 (5 and up) **Fic**
1. Cats—Fiction 2. New York (N.Y.)—Fiction
ISBN 0-06-024391-0 (lib bdg); 0-06-440073-5 (pa)

Awarded the Newbery Medal, 1964
This is the "story of a fourteen-year-old growing up in the neighborhood of Gramercy Park in New York City. He tells of life in the city and his relationships with his parents, neighbors, and friends. It is his pet, a stray tom cat whom he adopts, that brings him two new friends, one a troubled boy and the other his first girl." Wis Libr Bull

Neville, Emily Cheney, 1919——*Continued*

"A story told with a great amount of insight into human relationships. . . . This all provides a wonderfully real picture of a city boy's outlets and of one likable adolescent's inner feelings. An exceedingly fresh, honest, and well-rounded piece of writing." Horn Book

Newman, Robert, 1909-1988

The case of the Baker Street Irregular; a Sherlock Holmes story. Atheneum Pubs. 1978 216p hardcover o.p. paperback available $4.95 (5 and up)   **Fic**

1. Mystery fiction 2. London (England)—Fiction
ISBN 0-689-70766-5 (pa)   LC 77-15463

Brought to London under mysterious circumstances by his tutor, young Andrew Tillett seeks the help of Sherlock Holmes when his tutor is kidnapped and he himself is threatened with the same fate

"The author is as urbane and fluent as the legendary Mr. Holmes; he seems thoroughly comfortable with the characters, the atmosphere, and the turn-of-the-century London setting; and the story moves along with unflagging energy." Horn Book

Nichol, Barbara

Beethoven lives upstairs; illustrated by Scott Cameron. Orchard Bks. 1994 c1993 unp il $15.95; pa $5.95 (3-5)   **Fic**

1. Beethoven, Ludwig van, 1770-1827—Fiction
2. Uncles—Fiction 3. Letters—Fiction
ISBN 0-531-06828-5; 0-531-7118-9 (pa)
                                          LC 93-5774

First published 1993 in Canada

The letters that ten-year-old Christoph and his uncle exchange show how Christoph's feelings for Mr. Beethoven, the eccentric boarder that shares his house, change from anger and embarrassment to compassion and admiration

"The oil pictures are rich and dark, with glowing, candlelit interiors; they define the period while giving a strong sense of character. But it's the story that holds you, as tension builds until the triumphant first performance of the Ninth." Booklist

Nixon, Joan Lowery, 1927-

Aggie's home. Delacorte Press 1998 116p il (Orphan train children) $9.95; pa $4.50 (3-5)
                                          Fic

1. Orphans—Fiction 2. Women—Suffrage—Fiction
ISBN 0-385-32295-X; 0-440-41312-5 (pa)
                                          LC 97-47760

A clumsy and unattractive twelve-year-old, Aggie is sure no one will want to adopt her when she rides the orphan train out west, but when she meets the eccentric Bradon family she begins to have some hope. Includes historical information about orphan trains and the woman's suffrage movement

"Readers will enjoy watching this spirited child stick up for herself despite the consequences." SLJ

Other available titles in the Orphan train children series are:

David's search (1998)
Lucy's wish (1998)
Will's choice

A family apart. Stevens, G. 2000 162p il $21.27 (5 and up)   **Fic**

1. Foster home care—Fiction 2. Siblings—Fiction
3. United States—History—1783-1865—Fiction
ISBN 0-8368-2638-8   LC 99-55932

Also available in paperback from Bantam Bks.

A reissue of the title first published 1987 by Bantam Bks.

The first volume in the "Orphan train" series is set in 1860. When their widowed mother can no longer support them, Frances Kelley and her five brothers and sisters are sent on the orphan train by the Children's Aid Society of New York City to live with farm families in Missouri

"The plot is rational and well paced; the characters are real and believable; the time setting important to U.S. history, and the values all that anyone could ask for." Voice Youth Advocates

Other available titles in the Orphan train series are:
Caught in the act (1988)
Circle of love (1997)
A dangerous promise (1994)
In the face of danger (1988)
Keeping secrets (1995)
A place to belong (1989)

Nordstrom, Ursula, 1910-1988

The secret language; pictures by Mary Chalmers. Harper & Row 1960 167p il hardcover o.p. paperback available $4.95 (3-5)   **Fic**

1. School stories
ISBN 0-06-440022-0 (pa)

A "story about two eight-year-old girls at boarding school. None of the experiences that Vicky and Martha have are unusual; none dramatic; yet all of the details of their year make absorbing reading. Vicky is homesick and Martha is a rebel; as they adjust to each other and as they adapt themselves to the pattern of school life, both girls find satisfactions and both grow up a little. The writing style has a gentle humor, a warm understanding, and an easy narrative flow that seems effortless." Bull Cent Child Books

Norton, Mary, 1903-1992

Bed-knob and broomstick; illustrated by Erik Blegvad. Harcourt 2000 227p il $17; pa $6 (3-6)
                                          Fic

1. Fantasy fiction 2. Witchcraft—Fiction
ISBN 0-15-202450-6; 0-15-202456-5 (pa)
                                          LC 99-89153

"An Odyssey/Harcourt young classic"

A combined edition of The magic bed-knob (1943) and Bonfires and broomsticks (1947); present title is a reissue of the 1957 edition

With the powers they acquire from a spinster who is studying to be a witch, three English children have a series of exciting and perilous adventures traveling on a flying bed that takes them to a London police station, a tropical island, and back in time to the seventeenth century

The Borrowers; illustrated by Beth and Joe Krush. Harcourt Brace 1953 180p il $17; pa $6 (3-6)   **Fic**

1. Fairy tales
ISBN 0-15-209987-5; 0-15-209990-5 (pa)

Norton, Mary, 1903-1992—*Continued*

First published 1952 in the United Kingdom

A "fascinating fantasy about a tiny family that lived beneath the kitchen floor of an old English country house and 'borrowed' from the larger human residents to fill their modest needs. Their sudden discovery by a small boy visitor almost proves to be their undoing. The imaginative details about the activities of the miniature people have tremendous appeal for children." Child Books Too Good to Miss

Other available titles about the Borrowers are:
The Borrowers afield (1955)
The Borrowers afloat (1959)
The Borrowers aloft (1961)
The Borrowers avenged (1982)

O'Brien, Robert C., 1918-1973

Mrs. Frisby and the rats of NIMH; illustrated by Zena Bernstein. Atheneum Pubs. 1971 223p il lib bdg $17; pa $5.50 (4 and up)   **Fic**
1. Mice—Fiction 2. Rats—Fiction
ISBN 0-689-20651-8 (lib bdg); 0-689-71068-2 (pa)

Awarded the Newbery Medal, 1972

"Mrs. Frisby, a widowed mouse, is directed by an owl to consult with the rats that live under the rosebush about her problem of moving her sick son from the family's endangered home. Upon entering the rats' quarters, Mrs. Frisby discovers to her astonishment that the rats are not ordinary rodents, but highly intelligent creatures that escaped from an NIMH laboratory after being taught to read." Booklist

"The story is fresh and ingenious, the style witty, and the plot both hilarious and convincing." Saturday Rev

Followed by Racso and the rats of NIMH by Jane Leslie Conly

O'Connor, Barbara

Me and Rupert Goody. Foster Bks. 1999 105p $15 (4-6)   **Fic**
1. Mentally handicapped—Fiction 2. Racially mixed people—Fiction 3. Mountain life—Fiction
ISBN 0-374-34904-5   LC 98-30235
Also available Thorndike Press large print edition

Eleven-year-old Jennalee is jealous when Rupert Goody, a slow-thinking black man, arrives in her Smoky Mountains community and claims to be the son of Uncle Beau, the owner of the general store and Jennalee's only friend

"An absorbing story peopled with carefully drawn and memorable characters." SLJ

O'Dell, Scott, 1898-1989

The black pearl; illustrated by Milton Johnson. Houghton Mifflin 1967 140p il $17 (6 and up)
          Fic
1. Pearl fisheries—Fiction 2. Baja California (Mexico: Peninsula)—Fiction
ISBN 0-395-06961-0
Also available in paperback from Dell; Spanish language edition also available
A Newbery Medal honor book, 1968

"The people of Baja California feared a demon creature, a giant ray—El Manta Diablo. He was believed to live in a cave at the end of a lagoon. . . . Yet Ramón Salazar, goaded by the taunts of the greatest pearl diver of his father's fleet, dared to enter the cave to dive for a pearl even more wonderful than the one El Sevillano had boasted of. And he found it—the Paragon of Pearls, the Pearl of Heaven. Then came the encounter with the Manta." Horn Book

"The stark simplicity of the story and the deeper significance it holds in the triumph of good over evil add importance to the book, but even without that the book would be enjoyable as a rousing adventure tale with supernatural overtones and beautifully maintained tempo and suspense." Bull Cent Child Books

The captive. Houghton Mifflin 1979 210p $16 (6 and up)   **Fic**
1. Mayas—Fiction 2. Mexico—Fiction
ISBN 0-395-27811-2   LC 79-15809
This story set in the 16th century "centers on the adventures of a young Jesuit seminarian who goes to the New World as part of a Spanish expedition. Full of Christian idealism, Julián Escobar believes his role is to convert the savages. Instead, he succumbs to the temptation to pose as the reincarnated Mayan deity [Kukulcán]." Child Book Rev Serv

"Characterizations are all finely drawn, and Julián's transformation from insecure, humane seminarian to pretend god is remarkable in its honest development." SLJ

Island of the Blue Dolphins; illustrated by Ted Lewin. Houghton Mifflin 1990 181p il $20 (5 and up)   **Fic**
1. Native Americans—Fiction 2. Wilderness survival—Fiction 3. San Nicolas Island (Calif.)—Fiction
ISBN 0-395-53680-4   LC 90-35331
Also available in paperback from Dell; Spanish language edition also available; Audiobook version also available
Awarded the Newbery Medal, 1961
A reissue with new illustrations of the title first published 1960

"Unintentionally left behind by members of her California Native American tribe who fled a tragedy-ridden island, young Karana must construct a life for herself. Without bitterness or self-pity, she is able to extract joy and challenge from her eighteen years of solitude." Shapiro. Fic for Youth. 2d edition

Followed by Zia

The King's fifth; decorations and maps by Samuel Bryant. Houghton Mifflin 1966 264p $17 (5 and up)   **Fic**
1. Estevan, d. 1539—Fiction 2. Mexico—Fiction
ISBN 0-395-06963-7
A Newbery Medal honor book, 1967
"Fifteen-year-old Esteban sailed with Admiral Alarcon as a cartographer; carrying supplies for Coronado, the expedition went astray and a small group was put ashore to find Coronado's camp. Thus begins a harrowing story of the exciting and dangerous journey in search of the fabled gold of Cibola." Sutherland. The Best in Child Books

O'Dell, Scott, 1898-1989—*Continued*

Sarah Bishop. Houghton Mifflin 1980 184p $16
(6 and up)   **Fic**
  1. United States—History—1775-1783, Revolution—
Fiction 2. American loyalists—Fiction 3. New York
(State)—Fiction
  ISBN 0-395-29185-2   LC 79-28394
  Also available in paperback from Scholastic
  "Surrounded by war, prejudice, and fear, fifteen-year-
old Sarah Bishop quietly determines to live her own kind
of life in the wilderness that was Westchester County,
New York, during the Revolution. Orphaned Sarah
plucks up her courage when she is wrongfully dealt with
by both the American and British forces, and she creates
a home for herself and her animal friends in the forest
near Long Pond." Child Book Rev Serv
  "Despite a series of highly dramatic incidents, the story line is basically sharp and clear; O'Dell's messages
about the bitterness and folly of war, the dangers of superstition, and the courage of the human spirit are
smoothly woven into the story, as are the telling details
of period and place." Bull Cent Child Books

Sing down the moon. Houghton Mifflin 1970
137p $17 (5 and up)   **Fic**
  1. Navajo Indians—Fiction
  ISBN 0-395-10919-1
  Also available in paperback from Dell
  A Newbery Medal honor book, 1971
  This story is told "through the eyes of a young Nava-
ho girl as she sees the rich harvest in the Canyon de
Chelly in 1864 destroyed by Spanish slavers and the sub-
sequent destruction by white soldiers which forces the
Navahos on a march to Fort Sumner." Publ Wkly
  "There is a poetic sonority of style, a sense of identifi-
cation, and a note of indomitable courage and stoicism
that is touching and impressive." Saturday Rev

Streams to the river, river to the sea; a novel of
Sacagawea. Houghton Mifflin 1986 191p $16 (5
and up)   **Fic**
  1. Sacagawea, b. 1786—Fiction 2. Lewis and Clark
Expedition (1804-1806)—Fiction 3. Native Ameri-
cans—Fiction
  ISBN 0-395-40430-4   LC 86-936
  Also available in paperback from Fawcett Bks.
  This novel "tells the story of the Lewis and Clark ex-
pedition through the eyes of the young Shoshone woman
who served as interpreter and, often, guide." Soc Educ
  "An informative and involving choice for American
history students and pioneer-adventure readers." Bull
Cent Child Books

Zia. Houghton Mifflin 1976 179p $18 (5 and
up)   **Fic**
  1. Native Americans—Fiction 2. Christian missions—
Fiction
  ISBN 0-395-24393-9   LC 75-44156
  Also available in paperback from Dell
  In this sequel to Island of the Blue Dolphins, the author invents a niece for Karana "in the character of Zia,
a young Indian who lives at the Santa Barbara Mission
and who dreams of sailing to the island to rescue her
aunt. After one thwarted attempt to get there, and impris-
onment for helping some fellow Indians flee the Mission,

Zia finds her dream realized." N Y Times Book Rev
  "Zia is an excellent story in its own right, written in
a clear, quiet, and reflective style which is in harmony
with the plot and characterization." SLJ

Oppel, Kenneth

Silverwing. Simon & Schuster Bks. for Young
Readers 1997 217p $17; pa $4.99 (5 and up)
                                                Fic
  1. Bats—Fiction
  ISBN 0-689-81529-8; 0-689-82558-7 (pa)
                                    LC 97-10977
  When a newborn bat named Shade but sometimes
called "Runt" becomes separated from his colony during
migration, he grows in ways that prepare him for even
greater journeys
  "Oppel's bats are fully developed characters who, if
not quite cuddly, will certainly earn readers' sympathy
and respect. In *Silverwing* the author has created an intriguing microcosm of rival species, factions, and religions." Horn Book
  Followed by Sunwing

Sunwing. Simon & Schuster Bks. for Young
Readers 2000 266p $17 (5 and up)   **Fic**
  1. Bats—Fiction
  ISBN 0-689-82674-5   LC 99-25322
  In this sequel to Silverwing, Shade, a young bat,
searches for his father and struggles to prevent the evil
jungle bat Goth from wiping out the sun
  "The intertwining story lines, evil villain, and intense
action will keep readers enthralled." Horn Book Guide

Orgel, Doris

The devil in Vienna. Dial Bks. for Young
Readers 1978 246p o.p.; Puffin Bks. paperback
available $5.99 (6 and up)   **Fic**
  1. Austria—Fiction   2. Jews—Austria—Fiction
3. Holocaust, 1933-1945—Fiction 4. Friendship—Fiction
  ISBN 0-14-032500-X (pa)   LC 78-51319
  "Although fictional, the events in this story about the
Nazi occupation of Austria are based on the author's experiences as a child in Vienna. Inge is Jewish, her best
friend Lieselotte is the daughter of a Nazi officer so devoted to Hitler that he had moved his family to Germany, returning only after the Anschluss. Although the
girls have been forbidden to meet by both sets of parents, Inge knows her friend is loyal; when her parents
are having difficulty in leaving the country, Inge turns to
Lieselotte's uncle, a Catholic priest, for help. The story
ends with the refugees' safe arrival in Yugoslavia." Bull
Cent Child Books
  "The book arouses in its readers anguish, fury, admiration, scorn—it couldn't be a more effective story or a
more powerful illustration of the reason 'never to forget.'" Publ Wkly

Orlev, Uri, 1931-

The island on Bird Street; translated by Hillel Halkin. Houghton Mifflin 1984 162p $16; pa $5.95 (5 and up)　　　　　　　　　　**Fic**
1. Holocaust, 1933-1945—Fiction 2. Jews—Poland—Fiction 3. World War, 1939-1945—Fiction 4. Poland—Fiction
ISBN 0-395-33887-5; 0-395-61623-9 (pa)
　　　　　　　　　　　　　　　LC 83-26524
Original Hebrew edition, copyright 1981
This is the "story of an 11-year-old boy's life during the Holocaust. Alex, entirely on his own in an empty Polish ghetto, is sustained by his father's admonition to wait for him. Over rooftops, through attics and basements he traverses the deserted sector in his struggle for life." SLJ
"The author has written a book that offers on one level a first-rate survival story and on another a haunting glimpse of the war's effects on individual people. . . . Although the tone of the book reflects the boy's cheerful, logical disposition, the loneliness and utter desperation of his situation come through with a piercing clarity." Horn Book

The man from the other side; translated from the Hebrew by Hillel Halkin. Houghton Mifflin 1991 186p $16 (6 and up)　　　　　　　**Fic**
1. World War, 1939-1945—Fiction 2. Holocaust, 1933-1945—Fiction
ISBN 0-395-53808-4　　　　　　　LC 90-47898
Also available in paperback from Puffin Bks.
Living on the outskirts of the Warsaw Ghetto during World War II, fourteen-year-old Marek and his grandparents shelter a Jewish man in the days before the Jewish uprising
"Strong emotions and swift actions bombard the reader in this fact-based book. The well-done translation projects the book's intensity." Child Book Rev Serv

Osborne, Mary Pope, 1949-

Adaline Falling Star. Scholastic Press 2000 170p $16.95 (4 and up)　　　　　　　　　　**Fic**
1. Carson, Kit, 1809-1868—Fiction 2. Arapaho Indians—Fiction 3. Racially mixed people—Fiction
ISBN 0-439-05947-X　　　　　　　LC 99-30689
Feeling abandoned by her deceased Arapaho mother and Kit Carson, her explorer father, Adaline Falling Star runs away from the prejudiced cousins with whom she is staying and comes close to death in the wilderness, with only a mongrel dog for company
"Told in the girl's colorful frontier voice, this is an engaging tale of true grit and self-discovery." Booklist

My brother's keeper; Virginia's diary. Scholastic 2000 109p (My America) $8.95 (3-5)　　　**Fic**
1. Gettysburg (Pa.), Battle of, 1863—Fiction 2. United States—History—1861-1865, Civil War—Fiction
ISBN 0-439-15307-7　　　　　　　LC 00-20200
In 1863, as the Civil War approaches her quiet town of Gettysburg, Pennsylvania, nine-year-old Virginia records in a journal the horrible things she witnesses before, during, and after the Battle of Gettysburg
"Osborne successfully creates individual characters, and she poses difficult questions about war and the waste of human life." SLJ

Park, Barbara, 1947-

Junie B. Jones and her big fat mouth; illustrated by Denise Brunkus. Random House 1993 69p il lib bdg $11.99; pa $3.99 (2-4)　　　　　**Fic**
1. Kindergarten—Fiction 2. School stories
ISBN 0-679-94407-9 (lib bdg); 0-679-84407-4 (pa)
　　　　　　　　　　　　　　　LC 92-50957
"A First stepping stone book"
When her kindergarten class has Job Day, Junie B. goes through much confusion and excitement before deciding on the "bestest" job of all
"Brunkus' energetic drawings pick up the slapstick action and the spunky comic hero." Booklist
Other available titles about Junie B. Jones are:
Junie B. Jones and a little monkey business (1993)
Junie B. Jones and some sneaky peeky spying (1994)
Junie B. Jones and that meanie Jim's birthday (1996)
Junie B. Jones and the mushy gushy valentine (1999)
Junie B. Jones and the stupid smelly bus (1992)
Junie B. Jones and the yucky blucky fruitcake (1995)
Junie B. Jones has a monster under her bed (1997)
Junie B. Jones has a peep in her pocket (2000)
Junie B. Jones is a beauty shop guy (1998)
Junie B. Jones is a graduation girl (2001)
Junie B. Jones is a party animal (1997)
Junie B. Jones is (almost) a flower girl (1999)
Junie B. Jones is Captain Field Day (2000)
Junie B. Jones is not a crook (1997)
Junie B. Jones loves handsome Warren (1996)
Junie B. Jones smells something fishy (1998)

Mick Harte was here. Apple Soup Bks. 1995 89p $15; pa $4.99 (4-6)　　　　　　　**Fic**
1. Siblings—Fiction 2. Death—Fiction
ISBN 0-679-87088-1; 0-679-88203-0 (pa)
　　　　　　　　　　　　　　　LC 94-27272
Thirteen-year-old Phoebe recalls her younger brother Mick and his death in a bicycle accident
"The author is adept at portraying the stages of grief and the effects of this sudden tragedy on the family. The book's tone of sadness is mitigated by humor, reassurance, and hope." SLJ

My mother got married (and other disasters). Knopf 1989 138p hardcover o.p. paperback available $4.99 (4-6)　　　　　　　　　**Fic**
1. Stepfamilies—Fiction
ISBN 0-394-85059-9 (pa)　　　　　LC 88-27257
Twelve-year-old Charles experiences many difficulties in adjusting to a new stepfather, stepsister, and stepbrother
"Stories about divorce are nothing new, but Parks does a superb job of giving this one a fresh feel. Charlie's first-person dialogue is humorous but also realistically bitter. . . . A story of surprising depth." Booklist

Skinnybones. Knopf 1982 112p hardcover o.p. paperback available $3.99 (4-6)　　　　　**Fic**
1. School stories 2. Baseball—Fiction
ISBN 0-679-88792-X (pa)　　　　　LC 81-20791
The novel's hero "Alex Frankovitch (short, thin 'Skinnybones'), is a realist who knows that winning the Most Improved Player awards for six years only means that each year he has started out 'stink-o' and gone to 'smelly.' His particular nemesis this year is T.J. Stoner;

Park, Barbara, 1947—*Continued*

T.J.'s brother plays for the Chicago Cubs, and T.J.'s so good he could be suiting up with them momentarily himself. At least that's the way it seems to Alex, who always manages to be on T.J.'s wrong side and in the middle of a disaster because of it. Alex finally comes into his own when he wins the Kitty Fritters TV Contest and thus gets his own taste of what being a celebrity is like." Booklist

Another available title about Skinnybones is:
Almost starring Skinnybones (1988)

Park, Linda Sue

The kite fighters; decorations by Eung Won Park. Clarion Bks. 2000 136p $15 (4-6)   **Fic**
    1. Kites—Fiction 2. Brothers—Fiction 3. Korea—Fiction
ISBN 0-395-94041-9   LC 99-36936

In Korea in 1473, eleven-year-old Young-sup overcomes his rivalry with his older brother Kee-sup, who as the first-born son receives special treatment from their father, and combines his kite-flying skill with Kee-sup's kite-making skill in an attempt to win the New Year kite-fighting competition

"Besides catching the excitement of the ancient sport, the novel deals with intense sibling rivalry. . . . [The story feels] consistently well-grounded in its time and place." Booklist

Paterson, Katherine

Bridge to Terabithia; illustrated by Donna Diamond. Crowell 1977 128p il $15.95; pa $5.95 (4 and up)   **Fic**
    1. Friendship—Fiction 2. Death—Fiction 3. Virginia—Fiction
ISBN 0-690-01359-0; 0-06-440184-7 (pa)
       LC 77-2221

Also available Audiobook version
Awarded the Newbery Medal, 1978

The life of Jess, a ten-year-old boy in rural Virginia expands when he becomes friends with a newcomer who subsequently meets an untimely death trying to reach their hideaway, Terabithia, during a storm

"Jess and his family are magnificently characterized; the book abounds in descriptive vignettes, humorous sidelights on the clash of cultures, and realistic depictions of rural school life." Horn Book

Come sing, Jimmy Jo. Lodestar Bks. 1985 193p $15.99; pa $5.99 (5 and up)   **Fic**
    1. Country music—Fiction 2. Family life—Fiction
ISBN 0-525-67167-6; 0-14-037397-7 (pa)
       LC 84-21123

Also available Spanish language edition

When his family becomes a successful country music group and makes him a featured singer, eleven-year-old James has to deal with big changes in all aspects of his life, even his name

"What Katherine Paterson does so well is catch the cadence of the locale without sounding fake. There isn't a false note in her diction. She has created a West Virginian world that is entirely believable: homely, honest, goodhearted. . . . This book is James's personal inward journey, and it is deeply felt." Christ Sci Monit

The great Gilly Hopkins. Crowell 1978 148p $14.95; lib bdg $15.89; pa $5.95 (5 and up)
            Fic

    1. Foster home care—Fiction
ISBN 0-690-03837-2; 0-690-03838-0 (lib bdg);
0-06-440201-0 (pa)   LC 77-27075

"Cool, scheming, and deliberately obstreperous, 11-year-old Gilly is ready to be her usual obnoxious self when she arrives at her new foster home. . . . But Gilly's old tricks don't work against the all-encompassing love of the huge, half-illiterate Mrs. Trotter. . . . Determined not to care she writes a letter full of wild exaggerations to her real mother that brings, in return, a surprising visit from an unknown grandmother." Booklist

"A well-structured story, [this] has vitality of writing style, natural dialogue, deep insight in characterization, and a keen sense of the fluid dynamics in human relationships." Bull Cent Child Books

Jip; his story. Lodestar Bks. 1996 181p $15.99; pa $5.99 (5 and up)   **Fic**
    1. Slavery—Fiction 2. African Americans—Fiction 3. Vermont—Fiction 4. Racially mixed people—Fiction
ISBN 0-525-67543-4; 0-14-038674-2 (pa)
       LC 96-2680

While living on a Vermont poor farm during 1855 and 1856, Jip learns that his mother was a runaway slave, and that his father, the plantation owner, plans to reclaim him as property

"This historically accurate story is full of revelations and surprises, one of which is the return appearance of the heroine of *Lyddie*. . . . The taut, extremely readable narrative and its tender depictions of friendship and loyalty provide first-rate entertainment." Publ Wkly

Lyddie. Lodestar Bks. 1991 182p $15.95; pa $5.99 (5 and up)   **Fic**
    1. United States—History—1815-1861—Fiction 2. Massachusetts—Fiction 3. Factories—Fiction
ISBN 0-525-67338-5; 0-14-037389-6 (pa)
       LC 90-42944

Also available Spanish language edition

Impoverished Vermont farm girl Lyddie Worthen is determined to gain her independence by becoming a factory worker in Lowell, Massachusetts, in the 1840s

"Not only does the book contain a riveting plot, engaging characters, and a splendid setting, but the language—graceful, evocative, and rhythmic—incorporates the rural speech patterns of Lyddie's folk, the simple Quaker expressions of the farm neighbors, and the lilt of fellow mill girl Bridget's Irish brogue. . . . A superb story of grit, determination, and personal growth." Horn Book

The master puppeteer; illustrated by Haru Wells. Crowell 1976 c1975 179p il hardcover o.p. paperback available $4.95 (6 and up)   **Fic**
    1. Puppets and puppet plays—Fiction 2. Japan—Fiction
ISBN 0-06-440281-9 (pa)

"In 18th-century Osaka, Japan, Jiro, son of a starving puppetmaker, runs away from home to apprentice himself to Yoshida, the ill-tempered master of the Hanaza puppet theater. As Jiro works to learn the art of the puppeteer and travels among the savage, hunger-crazed bands of

Paterson, Katherine—*Continued*

night rovers in search of his parents, he becomes aware of a mysterious connection between Saboro, a Robin Hood-like figure, and the Hanaza theater itself." SLJ

"The make-believe world of the Japanese puppet theatre merges excitingly with the hungry, desperate realities of 18th century Osaka in this better-than-average junior novel." Bull Cent Child Books

Of nightingales that weep; illustrated by Haru Wells. Crowell 1974 170p il hardcover o.p. paperback available $4.95 (6 and up)   **Fic**
    1. Japan—Fiction
    ISBN 0-06-440282-7 (pa)

"Takiko, daughter of a famous samurai killed in the wars, is taken into the court of the boy emperor Antoku as a musician and personal servant. Takiko's conflicting loyalties to the Heike-supported court, a dashing Genji warrior, and her physically grotesque but goodhearted peasant stepfather form the impetus for her internal development while the war rages around her." Booklist

Park's quest. Lodestar Bks. 1988 148p hardcover o.p. paperback available $4.99 (5 and up)   **Fic**
    1. Farm life—Fiction 2. Vietnamese Americans—Fiction
    ISBN 0-14-034262-1 (pa)   LC 87-32422
    Also available Spanish language edition

Eleven-year-old Park makes some startling discoveries when he travels to his grandfather's farm in Virginia to learn about his father who died in the Vietnam War and meets a Vietnamese-American girl named Thanh

The author "confronts the complexity, the ambiguity, of the war and the emotions of those it involved with an honesty that young readers are sure to recognize and appreciate." N Y Times Book Rev

Preacher's boy. Clarion Bks. 1999 168p $15 (5 and up)   **Fic**
    1. Family life—Fiction 2. Christian life—Fiction
    3. Vermont—Fiction
    ISBN 0-395-83897-5   LC 98-50083
    Also available Thorndike Press large print edition

In 1899, ten-year-old Robbie, son of a preacher in a small Vermont town, gets himself into all kinds of trouble when he decides to give up being Christian in order to make the most of his life before the end of the world

"With warmth, humor, and her powerful yet plain style, Paterson draws empathetic and memorable characters." SLJ

Paton Walsh, Jill, 1937-

Fireweed. Farrar, Straus & Giroux 1970 c1969 133p hardcover o.p. paperback available $4.95 (5 and up)   **Fic**
    1. World War, 1939-1945—Fiction 2. London (England)—Fiction
    ISBN 0-374-42316-4 (pa)
    First published 1969 in the United Kingdom

During World War II, "Bill and Julie had found each other by chance, each of them lurking around London after having started off with a group of children being evacuated. Julie had money, Bill could cope, and togeth-

er the two made a clandestine home in the rubble of a building. Only when Julie was caught by a raid did Bill, staring in anguish at the fresh ruins, realize how important she had become to him." Saturday Rev

"The development of a relationship . . . is one of the two main achievements of this book. . . . The second achievement is the setting, the picture given without squeamishness or apparent over-emphasis of London in the blitz—the humour, the fear, the misery, the sometimes uncanny normality." Times Lit Suppl

Patron, Susan

Maybe yes, maybe no, maybe maybe; pictures by Dorothy Donahue. Orchard Bks. 1993 87p il $15.95 (3-5)   **Fic**
    1. Moving—Fiction 2. Sisters—Fiction
    ISBN 0-531-05482-9   LC 92-34067
    "A Richard Jackson book"

When her hardworking mother decides to move, eight-year-old PK uses her imagination and storytelling to help her older and younger sisters adjust

"The author's distinctive voice and characters drive this engaging novel, with its easy vocabulary, large type, and scattered, full-page wash paintings." Horn Book Guide

Paulsen, Gary

Alida's song. Delacorte Press 1999 88p $15.95 (5 and up)   **Fic**
    1. Grandmothers—Fiction 2. Farm life—Fiction
    ISBN 0-385-32586-X   LC 98-37015

In this sequel to The cookcamp, "Grandma Alida once again steps in at a troubled time in her grandson's life. Now the boy is 14; living with violent, drunken parents. . . . [A] letter arrives from his grandmother offering him a summer job as a hired hand on a farm. . . . He accepts the offer and experiences a season of hard work, music, dancing, and hearty meals served up with warmth, love, and understanding. . . . This beautifully written novella is a quiet tribute to a loving relative." SLJ

The cookcamp. Orchard Bks. 1991 115p $15.95 (5 and up)   **Fic**
    1. Grandmothers—Fiction 2. World War, 1939-1945—Fiction
    ISBN 0-531-05927-8   LC 90-7734
    Also available in paperback from Dell
    "A Richard Jackson book"

During World War II, a little boy is sent to live with his grandma, a cook in a camp for workers building a road through the wilderness

"Paulsen's simply told story strikes extraordinary emotional chords. . . . Those hungry for adventure stories, as well as more introspective readers, will be spellbound by this stirring novel." Publ Wkly
    Followed by Alida's song

Dogsong. Bradbury Press 1985 177p (6 and up)   **Fic**
    1. Inuit—Fiction 2. Arctic regions—Fiction
          LC 84-20443
    Available in hardcover and paperback from Atheneum
    A Newbery Medal honor book, 1986

Paulsen, Gary—*Continued*

A fourteen-year-old Eskimo boy who feels assailed by the modernity of his life takes a 1400-mile journey by dog sled across ice, tundra, and mountains seeking his own "song" of himself

The author's "mystical tone and blunt prose style are well suited to the spare landscape of his story, and his depictions of Russell's icebound existence add both authenticity and color to a slick rendition of the vision-quest plot, which incorporates human tragedy as well as promise." Booklist

The haymeadow; illustrated by Ruth Wright Paulsen. Delacorte Press 1992 195p il hardcover o.p. paperback available $4.99 (6 and up) **Fic**

1. Ranch life—Fiction 2. Sheep—Fiction 3. Wyoming—Fiction

ISBN 0-440-40923-3 (pa) LC 91-36666

Also available Audiobook version

Fourteen-year-old John comes of age and gains self-reliance during the summer he spends up in the Wyoming mountains tending his father's herd of sheep

"The protagonist is clearly imagined; the style is both consciously simple and dramatic. . . . There's even a touch of humor." Bull Cent Child Books

Mr. Tucket. Delacorte Press 1994 166p $15.95; pa $4.50 (5 and up) **Fic**

1. Frontier and pioneer life—Fiction 2. West (U.S.)—Fiction

ISBN 0-385-31169-9; 0-440-41133-5 (pa) LC 93-31180

In 1848, while on a wagon train headed for Oregon, fourteen-year-old Francis Tucket is kidnapped by Pawnee Indians and then falls in with a one-armed trapper who teaches him how to live in the wild

"Superb characterizations, splendidly evoked setting and thrill-a-minute plot make this book a joy to gallop through." Publ Wkly

Other available titles about Francis Tucket are:

Call me Francis Tucket (1995)

Tucket's gold (1999)

Tucket's home (2000)

Tucket's ride (1997)

The winter room. Orchard Bks. 1989 103p $15.95; lib bdg $16.99 (5 and up) **Fic**

1. Farm life—Fiction 2. Minnesota—Fiction

ISBN 0-531-05839-5; 0-531-08439-6 (lib bdg) LC 89-42541

Also available in paperback from Dell

A Newbery Medal honor book, 1990

"A Richard Jackson book"

A young boy growing up on a northern Minnesota farm describes the scenes around him and recounts his old Norwegian uncle's tales of an almost mythological logging past

"While this seems at first to be a collection of anecdotes organized around the progression of the farm calendar, Paulsen subtly builds a conflict that becomes apparent in the last brief chapters, forceful and well-prepared. . . . Lyrical and only occasionally sentimental, the prose is clean, clear, and deceptively simple." Bull Cent Child Books

Pearce, Philippa, 1920-

Tom's midnight garden; illustrated by Susan Einzig. Lippincott 1959 c1958 229p il lib bdg $15.89; pa $5.95 (4 and up) **Fic**

1. Fantasy fiction 2. Space and time—Fiction

ISBN 0-397-30477-3 (lib bdg); 0-06-440445-5 (pa)

First published 1958 in the United Kingdom

"Daytime life for Tom at his aunt's home in England is dull, but each night he participates through fantasy in the lives of the former inhabitants of the interesting old house in which he is spending an enforced vacation. The book is British in setting and atmosphere. The element of mystery is well sustained, and the reader is left to make his own interpretation of the reality of the story." Adventuring with Books

Peck, Richard, 1934-

The ghost belonged to me; a novel. Viking 1975 183p hardcover o.p. paperback available $4.99 (5 and up) **Fic**

1. Ghost stories

ISBN 0-14-038671-8 (pa)

"Although he tries to avoid her, thirteen-year-old Alexander Armsworth relates how his classmate and neighbor, Blossom Culp, involves him in a ghost mystery. Later, Blossom relates her own stories with a most convincing air. Humor and excitement play a big role in the stories, which are set in 1913. The characters are unusual and unforgettable. Peck writes with a flair for the dramatic." Roman. Sequences

Other available titles about Blossom Culp are:

The dreadful future of Blossom Culp (1983)

Ghosts I have been (1977)

A long way from Chicago; a novel in stories. Dial Bks. for Young Readers 1998 148p $15.99; pa $4.99 (5 and up) **Fic**

1. Grandmothers—Fiction 2. Great Depression, 1929-1939—Fiction

ISBN 0-8037-2290-7; 0-14-1303522 (pa) LC 98-10953

Also available Audiobook version

A Newbery Medal honor book, 1999

Joe recounts his annual summer trips to rural Illinois with his sister during the Great Depression to visit their larger-than-life grandmother

"The novel reveals a strong sense of place, a depth of characterization, and a rich sense of humor." Horn Book

Followed by A year down yonder

Lost in cyberspace. Dial Bks. for Young Readers 1995 151p $15.99; pa $4.99 (5 and up) **Fic**

1. Space and time—Fiction 2. School stories

ISBN 0-8037-1931-0; 0-14-037856-1 (pa) LC 94-48330

While dealing with changes at home, sixth-grader Josh and his friend Aaron use the computer at their New York prep school to travel through time, learning some secrets from the school's past and improving Josh's home situation

This "will appeal to today's computer-literate generation while allowing their imaginations to soar. A time-traveling journey that will keep the reader on the edge of his seat—or computer." Child Book Rev Serv

Peck, Richard, 1934——*Continued*

A year down yonder. Dial Bks. for Young Readers 2000 130p $16.99 (5 and up)   **Fic**
1. Grandmothers—Fiction 2. Great Depression, 1929-1939—Fiction
ISBN 0-8037-2518-3   LC 99-43159
Awarded the Newbery Medal, 2001
This sequel to A long way from Chicago "tells the story of Joey's younger sister, Mary Alice, 15, who spends the year of 1937 back with Grandma Dowdel in a small town in Illinois." Booklist
"Peck has created a delightful, insightful tale that resounds with a storyteller's wit, humor, and vivid description." SLJ

Peck, Robert Newton, 1928-
A day no pigs would die. Knopf 1973 c1972 150p $24; pa $5.50 (6 and up)   **Fic**
1. Shakers—Fiction 2. Farm life—Fiction 3. Vermont—Fiction
ISBN 0-394-48235-2; 0-679-85306-5 (pa)
Also available in hardcover from P. Smith and Audiobook version
"Rob lives a rigorous life on a Shaker farm in Vermont in the 1920s. Since farm life is earthy, this book is filled with Yankee humor and explicit descriptions of animals mating. A painful incident that involves the slaughter of Rob's beloved pet pig is instrumental in urging him toward adulthood. The death of his father completes the process of his accepting responsibility." Shapiro. Fic for Youth. 3d edition

Soup; illustrated by Charles C. Gehm. Knopf 1974 96p il hardcover o.p. paperback available $5.50 (5 and up)   **Fic**
1. Friendship—Fiction 2. Vermont—Fiction
ISBN 0-679-89261-3 (pa)
Also available Audiobook version
"Soup was Robert Peck's best friend during his boyhood, and this is an episodic account of some of the ploys and scrapes the two shared when they were in elementary school." Bull Cent Child Books
"Rural Vermont during the 1920's is the setting for this nostalgic account. . . . In a laconic and wryly humorous style, the author relates the activities of the mischievous twosome. . . . The black-and-white pencil drawings, artistically executed in the manner of Norman Rockwell, reflect the understated story." SLJ
Other available titles about the author and his friend Soup are:
Soup 1776 (1995)
Soup ahoy (1994)
Soup for president (1978)
Soup in love (1992)
Soup on wheels (1981)
Soup's hoop (1990)

Perkins, Lynne Rae
All alone in the universe. Greenwillow Bks. 1999 140p il $15.95 (5 and up)   **Fic**
1. Friendship—Fiction
ISBN 0-688-16881-7   LC 98-50093
Also available Audiobook version

Debbie is dismayed when her best friend Maureen starts spending time with ordinary, boring Glenna
"A poignant story written with sensitivity and tenderness." SLJ

Petersen, P. J., 1941-
I hate weddings; illustrated by Lynne Cravath. Dutton Children's Bks. 2000 104p il $15.99 (3-5)   **Fic**
1. Weddings—Fiction   2. Remarriage—Fiction 3. Stepfamilies—Fiction
ISBN 0-525-46327-5   LC 99-48165
When Dan has to meet his new stepfamily and take part in his father's wedding, he finds that all sorts of horrible and embarrassing things happen to him
"Petersen's breezy, exaggerated style brings out the humor and absurdity in even the most difficult moments of blending a family. This is a short, cheery novel." Horn Book Guide
Other available titles about Dan are:
I hate camping (1991)
I hate company (1994)

Petry, Ann Lane
Tituba of Salem Village; [by] Ann Petry. Crowell 1964 254p hardcover o.p. paperback available $4.95 (6 and up)   **Fic**
1. Tituba—Fiction   2. Salem   (Mass.)—Fiction 3. Witchcraft—Fiction 4. African Americans—Fiction
ISBN 0-694-40403-X (pa)
"From the beauty of the island of Barbados, Tituba is uprooted to the dreary, gray cold of Boston. As the slave in the household of the minister, Samuel Parris, Tituba cooks, nurses, and attends to his sickly wife, daughter, and niece. When the minister moves to a new post in Salem Village, Tituba becomes the central figure in a witchcraft trial." Shapiro. Fic for Youth. 3d edition

Philbrick, W. R. (W. Rodman)
REM world; [by] Rodman Philbrick. Blue Sky Press (NY) 2000 192p $16.95 (4 and up)   **Fic**
1. Fantasy fiction
ISBN 0-439-08362-1   LC 99-54843
Eleven-year-old Arthur Woodbury's attempt to lose weight fast and escape his nickname of Biscuit Butt takes him to an endangered dream world where he faces fantastic adventures and learns the true meaning of courage
"Imaginative characters and a string of cliffhangers make [this] . . . novel a fun and fast-paced read." Publ Wkly

Pierce, Tamora, 1954-
Magic steps; book one of the Circle opens quartet. Scholastic Press 2000 264p $16.95 (5 and up)   **Fic**
1. Fantasy fiction
ISBN 0-590-39588-2   LC 99-31943
Based on characters in the author's Circle of Magic quartet

Pierce, Tamora, 1954-—_Continued_

Sandry "is a 'stitch witch' who can weave magic as well as cloth. She reluctantly takes on twelve-year-old Pasco as a student, and the plot revolves around her struggles as a first-time teacher and her involvement in investigating a series of vicious murders." Horn Book Guide

"Using descriptive, personable prose, Pierce combines dimensional characters, intricate details, plot twists, and alternating story lines for a gripping read. . . . There is some vivid violence." Booklist

Pinkwater, Daniel Manus, 1941-

Fat men from space; written and illustrated by Daniel Manus Pinkwater. Dodd, Mead 1977 57p il o.p.; Dell paperback available $3.99 (3-6)   **Fic**
1. Food—Fiction 2. Science fiction
ISBN 0-440-44542-6 (pa)   LC 77-6091

"Young William goes to the dentist and comes out with a filling that receives radio programs. Exploring the infinite possibilities of a tooth radio, he attaches a wire to a chainlink fence, touches it to his molar, and tunes in on an invading 'spaceburger' from the planet Spiegel. Before he can warn anyone of earth's peril, he is captured and 'floated' up to the spaceburger where he meets the invaders—fat men with glasses, wearing plaid sport jackets. Their raid is successful—Earth is stripped of all its junk food." SLJ

"Message books aren't usually this much fun, but Pinkwater makes his a polished romp." Bull Cent Child Books

The Hoboken chicken emergency; illustrated by Jill Pinkwater. Atheneum Pubs. 1999 108p il lib bdg $15; pa $4.99 (3-6)   **Fic**
1. Chickens—Fiction
ISBN 0-689-83060-2 (lib bdg); 0-689-82889-6 (pa)
LC 00-268579

A newly illustrated edition of the title first published 1977 by Prentice-Hall

Arthur goes to pick up the turkey for Thanksgiving dinner but comes back with a 260-pound chicken

"A contemporary tall tale that will stretch middle graders' imagination, sense of humor, and enthusiasm for reading." Booklist

Lizard music; written and illustrated by D. Manus Pinkwater. Dodd, Mead 1976 157p il o.p.; Bantam Bks. paperback available $4.99 (4 and up)
Fic
1. Science fiction
ISBN 0-440-41319-2 (pa)

"Left alone when his parents go on a vaction, Victor discovers, through late-night TV, a community of intelligent lizards and the Chicken Man. The succeeding adventures take Victor through some strange but thought-provoking escapades. Children associate with the ending—a return to normal but dull life when the rest of the family returns. A good read-aloud book." Read Teach

Platt, Richard, 1953-

Castle diary; the journal of Tobias Burgess, page; transcribed by Richard Platt; illuminated by Chris Riddell. Candlewick Press 1999 64p il $21.99 (4 and up)   **Fic**
1. Castles—Fiction 2. Middle Ages—Fiction
ISBN 0-7636-0489-5   LC 98-42779

As a page in his uncle's castle in thirteenth-century England, eleven-year-old Tobias records in his journal his experiences learning how to hunt, play games of skill, and behave in noble society. Includes notes on noblemen, castles, and feudalism

"Rewarding observant viewers with dramatic or humorous details of gesture and expression, Chris Riddell's deftly drawn ink-and-watercolor illustrations brighten the pages and complement the lively tone of the text." Booklist

Polacco, Patricia

The butterfly. Philomel Bks. 2000 unp il $16.99 (2-4)   **Fic**
1. Jews—France—Fiction 2. World War, 1939-1945—Fiction 3. France—Fiction
ISBN 0-399-23170-6   LC 99-30038

During the Nazi occupation of France, Monique's mother hides a Jewish family in her basement and tries to help them escape to freedom

"Polacco's use of color has never been more effective. . . . The bold pattern and heightened color of the insect provides a counterpoint to the equally dynamic black-on-red swastikas. Convincing in its portrayal of both the disturbing and humanitarian forces of the time." SLJ

Polikoff, Barbara Garland

Life's a funny proposition, Horatio. Holt & Co. 1992 103p $14.95 (5 and up)   **Fic**
1. Death—Fiction 2. Grandfathers—Fiction
ISBN 0-8050-1972-3   LC 91-46724

Also available in paperback from Puffin Bks.

As Horatio tries to adjust to the death of his father from lung cancer, O.P., Horatio's grandfather, mourns the loss of his dog Mollie

"While capable of great tenderness, the understated writing style is both bracing and poignantly funny." Bull Cent Child Books

Pope, Elizabeth Marie, 1917-

The Perilous Gard; illustrated by Richard Cuffari. Houghton Mifflin 1974 280p il o.p.; Puffin Bks. paperback available $5.99 (6 and up)
Fic
1. Great Britain—Fiction 2. Druids and Druidism—Fiction 3. Fantasy fiction
ISBN 0-14-034912-X (pa)

A Newbery Medal Honor book, 1975

In 1558 while imprisoned in a remote castle, a young girl becomes involved in a series of events that leads to an underground labyrinth peopled by the last practitioners of Druidic magic.

"The description of the Fairy Folk's life and customs is fascinating and the plot is mystical and exciting enough for all fantasy lovers." SLJ

Porte, Barbara Ann

If you ever get lost; the adventures of Julia and Evan; pictures by Nancy Carpenter. Greenwillow Bks. 2000 80p il $15.95 (2-4)   **Fic**
1. Siblings—Fiction
ISBN 0-688-16947-3   LC 98-32133

Julia and her younger brother Eric share several adventures, including getting lost at a marathon race, going grocery shopping, helping to catch two thieves at a pet store, and learning to speak Spanish

"The book has a sweet, old-fashioned air. Nancy Carpenter's lively line drawings with gray washes balance that feeling with an appealing, modern look." Booklist

Propp, Vera W.

When the soldiers were gone. Putnam 1999 101p $14.99 (3-5)   **Fic**
1. Jews—Netherlands—Fiction 2. Netherlands—Fiction
ISBN 0-399-23325-3   LC 97-50169

After the German occupation of the Netherlands, Benjamin leaves the Christian family with whom he had been living and reunites with his real parents who returned from hiding

"The miracle of this tale, based on an actual wartime story, is the constancy of Henk's voice; we see his world entirely through his eyes." Horn Book Guide

Pullman, Philip, 1946-

Clockwork; or, All wound up; with illustrations by Leonid Gore. Levine Bks. 1998 c1996 112p il $14.95; pa $4.99 (4 and up)   **Fic**
1. Supernatural—Fiction
ISBN 0-590-12999-6; 0-590-12998-8 (pa)
          LC 97-27458

First published 1996 in the United Kingdom

Long ago in Germany, a storyteller's story and an apprentice clockwork-maker's nightmare meet in a menacing, lifelike figure created by the strange Dr. Kalmenius

"Pullman laces his tale with subtle humor while maintaining the suspense until the end. Misty, moody, and atmospheric black-and-white drawings by Leonid Gore make a perfect fit for this gothic gem." Voice Youth Advocates

The firework-maker's daughter; illustrations by S. Saelig Gallagher. Levine Bks. 1999 97p il $15.95 (4 and up)   **Fic**
1. Fireworks—Fiction 2. Magic—Fiction 3. Elephants—Fiction 4. Adventure fiction
ISBN 0-590-18719-8   LC 98-41048

In a country far to the east, Chulak and his talking white elephant Hamlet help Lila seek the Royal Sulphur from the sacred volcano so that she can become a master maker of fireworks like her father

"This story is abundantly good natured and rich with humorous scenes and philosophical underpinings." Booklist

I was a rat! illustrated by Kevin Hawkes. Knopf 2000 164p $15.95; lib bdg $17.99 (4 and up)
          Fic
1. Fantasy fiction
ISBN 0-375-80176-6; 0-375-90176-0 (lib bdg)
          LC 99-31806

First published 1999 in the United Kingdom with illustrations by Peter Bailey

"Pullman tells what happens to Cinderella's rat-turned-pageboy, who, busily sliding down banisters at the palace, misses the pumpkin-coach ride home and gets trapped in boy form. Young readers will find the story completely entertaining, whether or not they appreciate the playful spoofing of sensational news stories, mob mentality, and the royal family." Horn Book Guide

Radin, Ruth Yaffe, 1938-

Escape to the forest; based on a true story of the Holocaust; illustrated by Janet Hamlin. HarperCollins Pubs. 2000 90p il $13.95; lib bdg $13.89 (3-6)   **Fic**
1. Holocaust, 1933-1945—Fiction 2. Jews—Poland—Fiction
ISBN 0-06-028520-6; 0-06-028521-4 (lib bdg)
          LC 99-26426

Sarah, a young Jewish girl living with her family in Poland at the beginning of World War II, recalls the horrors of life under first the Russians then the Nazis, before fleeing to join Tuvia Bielski, a partisan who tried to save as many Jews as possible. Based on a true story

"Stylistically simple but strongly plotted, the narrative makes good use of suspense and contrast." Bull Cent Child Books

Raskin, Ellen, 1928-1984

The mysterious disappearance of Leon (I mean Noel). Dutton 1971 149p il hardcover o.p. paperback available $5.99 (4 and up)   **Fic**
1. New York (N.Y.)—Fiction 2. Mystery fiction
ISBN 0-14-032945-5 (pa)

"Wed at the age of five to a seven-year-old husband (it solved a business difficulty for their two families), the very young Mrs. Leon Carillon immediately loses her spouse, who is sent off to boarding school. This is the hilarious account of her search for Leon, aided by adopted twins, when she is older. With clever clues to stimulate the reader's participation, the story is a bouquet of wordplay garnished with jokes, sly pokes at our society, daft characters, and soupcon of slapstick. Fresh and funny, it's the kind of book that passes from child to child." Saturday Rev

The Westing game. Dutton 1978 185p lib bdg $15.99; pa $5.99 (5 and up)   **Fic**
1. Mystery fiction
ISBN 0-525-42320-6 (lib bdg); 0-14-038664-5 (ps)
          LC 77-18866

Awarded the Newbery Medal, 1979

"This mystery puzzle . . . centers on the challenge set forth in the will of eccentric multimillionaire Samuel Westing. Sixteen heirs of diverse backgrounds and ages are assembled in the old 'Westing house,' paired off, and given clues to a puzzle they must solve—apparently in order to inherit." SLJ

"The rules of the game make eight pairs of the players; each oddly matched couple is given a ten thousand dollar check and a set of clues. The result is a fascinating medley of word games, disguises, multiple aliases and subterfuges—in a demanding but rewarding book." Horn Book

Rawlings, Marjorie Kinnan, 1896-1953

The yearling; with pictures by N. C. Wyeth. Scribner 1985 c1938 400p il $28; pa $5.95 (6 and up)   **Fic**
    1. Deer—Fiction 2. Florida—Fiction
ISBN 0-684-18461-3; 0-02-044931-3 (pa)
                  LC 85-40301
First published 1938; this is a reissue of the 1939 edition

"Young Jody Baxter lives a lonely life in the scrub forest of Florida until his parents unwillingly consent to his adopting an orphan fawn. The two become inseparable until the fawn destroys the meager crops. Then Jody realizes that this situation offers no compromise. In the sacrifice of what he loves best, he leaves his own yearling days behind." Read Ladders for Hum Relat. 5th edition

Rawls, Wilson, 1913-

Where the red fern grows; the story of two dogs and a boy. Doubleday c1961 212p $16.95; pa $5.99   **Fic**
    1. Dogs—Fiction 2. Ozark Mountains—Fiction
ISBN 0-385-32330-1; 0-440-41267-6 (pa)
Also available Audiobook version
First published 1961

"Looking back more than 50 years to his boyhood in the Ozarks, the narrator recalls how he achieved his heart's desire in the ownership of two redbone hounds, how he taught them all the tricks of hunting, and how they won the championship coon hunt before Old Dan was killed by a mountain lion and Little Ann died of grief. Although some readers may find this novel hackneyed and entirely too sentimental, others will enjoy the fine coon-hunting episodes and appreciate the author's feelings for nature." Booklist

Reaver, Chap, 1935-1993

Bill. Delacorte Press 1994 216p hardcover o.p. paperback available $3.99 (5 and up)   **Fic**
    1. Dogs—Fiction 2. Father-daughter relationship—Fiction 3. Prohibition—Fiction
ISBN 0-440-41153-X (pa)   LC 93-35491
With the help of her faithful dog Bill and the officer responsible for putting her father in jail, thirteen-year-old Jessica faces changes in her life when she realizes that her father will not stop drinking and making moonshine

"The story contains everything a reader could want— spunky, intriguing characters; a smart, loyal dog; hidden treasure; a raft trip; and a happy ending. Never lapsing into melodrama, the gripping novel depicts a girl and her dog who never give up and never let go of each other." Horn Book Guide

Recorvits, Helen

Goodbye, Walter Malinski; pictures by Lloyd Bloom. Foster Bks. 1999 85p il $15 (3-6)   **Fic**
    1. Great Depression, 1929-1939—Fiction 2. Family life—Fiction 3. Death—Fiction 4. Polish Americans—Fiction
ISBN 0-374-32747-5   LC 97-35451

"Fifth-grader Wanda narrates a quiet portrait of Polish immigrants struggling to make ends meet in 1934. Out-of-work Pa takes out his frustrations on Wanda's older brother Walter. When Walter dies in an accident, the shock is great, but the family . . . is brought together with new affection. Beautifully composed illustrations add to the period atmosphere conveyed in the accessible, simply phrased narrative." Horn Book Guide

Reeder, Carolyn, 1937-

Across the lines. Atheneum Bks. for Young Readers 1997 220p $17 (5 and up)   **Fic**
    1. United States—History—1861-1865, Civil War—Fiction 2. African Americans—Fiction 3. Race relations—Fiction
ISBN 0-689-81133-0   LC 96-31068
Also available in paperback from Avon Bks.

Edward, the son of a white plantation owner, and his black house servant and friend Simon witness the siege of Petersburg during the Civil War

"Twelve-year-old Edward and his family flee to Petersburg just before the Yankees capture their Virginia plantation; Simon, Edward's former slave and companion, performs various jobs for Union troops advancing on the same city. During the span of a year, the boys make parallel journeys toward a deeper understanding of the complex nature of freedom and friendship. Told in the alternating voices of Edward and Simon, this thoughtful Civil War story resonates with authenticity." Horn Book Guide

Shades of gray. Macmillan 1989 152p $16 (4 and up)   **Fic**
    1. Orphans—Fiction 2. Uncles—Fiction 3. United States—History—1861-1865, Civil War—Fiction
ISBN 0-02-775810-9   LC 89-31976
Also available in paperback from Avon Bks.

At the end of the Civil War, twelve-year-old Will, having lost all his immediate family, reluctantly leaves his city home to live in the Virginia countryside with his aunt and the uncle he considers a "traitor" because he refused to take part in the war

"Minor plot threads (Will's adjustment to rural life, his relationships with the local boys and his affection for his cousin Meg) provide changes of tone and tempo in a novel that has, despite an uneven pace, both momentum and nuance." Bull Cent Child Books

Rinaldi, Ann, 1934-

The journal of Jasper Jonathan Pierce, a pilgrim boy. Scholastic Press 2000 155p il (My name is America) $10.95 (4 and up)   **Fic**
    1. Pilgrims (New England colonists)—Fiction 2. Massachusetts—Fiction
ISBN 0-590-51078-9   LC 99-26028
A fourteen-year-old indentured servant keeps a journal of his experiences on the Mayflower and during the building of Plimoth Plantation in 1620 and 1621

"Written in a believable voice, the novel offers an interesting perspective on life aboard the ship and among the first colonists." Horn Book Guide

Riskind, Mary, 1944-

Apple is my sign. Houghton Mifflin 1981 146p
$14.95; pa $5.95 (5 and up)   **Fic**
  1. Deaf—Fiction
  ISBN 0-395-30852-6; 0-395-65747-4 (pa)

"The story is set in Pennsylvania at the time of the
first horseless carriages . . . in a school for the deaf.
Ten-year-old Harry is at first homesick, but he soon
makes friends, becomes excited about learning to draw
and learning to talk. Aware that his father is ashamed of
his own deafness (both parents are deaf) and that his
mother is not, Harry learns to accept his situation." Bull
Cent Child Books

"In a lengthy note the author explains that she had
deaf parents and learned sign language before she
learned to speak. She also explores some characteristics
of sign language, which has been translated into print via
sentence syntax and spelling. A warm, unpretentious story." Booklist

Ritter, John H., 1951-

Over the wall. Philomel Bks. 2000 312p $17.99
(6 and up)   **Fic**
  1. Baseball—Fiction 2. New York (N.Y.)—Fiction
  ISBN 0-399-23489-6   LC 99-49911

Thirteen-year-old Tyler, who has trouble controlling
his anger, spends an important summer with his cousins
in New York City, playing baseball and sorting out how
he feels about violence, war, and in particular the Vietnamese conflict that took his grandfather's life

"Sports are just a part of this ambitious work that
presents a compelling, multilayered story." SLJ

Roberts, Willo Davis

The girl with the silver eyes. Atheneum Pubs.
1980 181p o.p.; Scholastic paperback available
$4.50 (4-6)   **Fic**
  1. Psychokinesis—Fiction
  ISBN 0-590-44248-1 (pa)   LC 80-12391

"Silver eyes are not all that set ten-year-old Katie
apart from her peers—she's able to move things by
thinking about them and talk to animals. Living with her
mother for the first time since she was three, Katie tries
to adjust to the other adults in the building, to her
mom's male friend, and to her own strange situation."
SLJ

"Much of the book's first half relies on diverting readers with examples of Katie's powers . . . while the second section builds more suspensefully around her efforts
to track down the source of her problem, other children
who might share it, and someone who will help her deal
with it. . . . Roberts' smooth writing will lure them right
to the end." Booklist

The kidnappers. Atheneum Bks. for Young
Readers 1998 137p $15; pa $3.99 (4 and up)
                                                Fic
  1. Kidnapping—Fiction 2. Wealth—Fiction 3. New
  York (N.Y.)—Fiction
  ISBN 0-689-81394-5; 0-689-81393-7 (pa)
                      LC 96-53677
  "A Jean Karl book"

No one believes eleven-year-old Joey, who has a reputation for telling tall tales, when he claims to have witnessed the kidnapping of the class bully outside their expensive New York City private school

"The combination of a witty narrative and a suspenseful plot makes this a good page-turner that will leave
even the most reluctant readers glued to their seats."
Booklist

Scared stiff. Atheneum Pubs. 1991 188p $16 (5
and up)   **Fic**
  1. Mystery fiction 2. Amusement parks—Fiction
  3. Brothers—Fiction
  ISBN 0-689-31692-5   LC 90-37732
  "A Jean Karl book"

When their mother disappears, two brothers go to stay
with a great uncle in a mobile home park next to an
abandoned amusement park and begin a search which
puts themselves in danger

"The brisk pace, fluid style, and excitement of the
novel are sure to entertain readers, while the sensitive
handling of such issues as separation and alcoholism, and
the not-perfect ending make the book a cut above the
general fare." SLJ

The view from the cherry tree. Atheneum Pubs.
1975 181p $16; pa $4.99 (5 and up)   **Fic**
  1. Mystery fiction
  ISBN 0-689-30483-8; 0-689-71131-X (pa)

"Thoroughly disgruntled by the furor which accompanies his sister's wedding, eleven-year-old Rob Mallory
retires to his favorite perch in the cherry tree. There, he
is a horrified witness to the murder of an unpleasant
neighborhood recluse. Because of the wedding preparations and the arrival of hordes of relatives, no adult will
believe Rob's story. Soon, he finds that someone
knows—and is trying to kill him, too." Child Book Rev
Serv

"Although written in a direct and unpretentious style,
this is essentially a sophisticated story, solidly constructed, imbued with suspense, evenly paced, and effective in
conveying the atmosphere of a household coping with
the last-minute problems and pressures of a family wedding." Bull Cent Child Books

Robertson, Keith, 1914-1991

Henry Reed, Inc.; illustrated by Robert
McCloskey. Viking 1958 239p il hardcover o.p.
paperback available $4.99 (4-6)   **Fic**
  ISBN 0-14-034144-7 (pa)

"Henry Reed, on vacation from the American School
in Naples, keeps a record of his research into the
American free-enterprise system, to be used as a school
report on his return. With a neighbor, Midge Glass, he
starts a business in pure and applied research, which results in some very free and widely enterprising experiences, all recorded deadpan in his journal. Very funny
and original escapades." Hodges. Books for Elem Sch
Libr

Another available title about Henry Reed is:
Henry Reed's babysitting service (1966)

Robinet, Harriette Gillem, 1931-

Forty acres and maybe a mule. Atheneum Bks. for Young Readers 1998 132p $16; pa $4.99 (4 and up)   **Fic**

1. African Americans—Fiction 2. Reconstruction (1865-1876)—Fiction 3. United States—History—1865-1898—Fiction

ISBN 0-689-82078-X; 0-689-83317-2 (pa)

LC 97-39169

Also available Thorndike Press large print edition

"A Jean Karl book"

Born with a withered leg and hand, Pascal, who is about twelve years old, joins other former slaves in a search for a farm and the freedom which it promises

"Robinet skillfully balances her in-depth historical knowledge with the feelings of her characters, creating a story that moves along rapidly and comes to a bittersweet conclusion." Booklist

Walking to the bus-rider blues. Atheneum Bks. for Young Readers 2000 146p $16 (5 and up)

Fic

1. African Americans—Fiction 2. Race relations—Fiction

ISBN 0-689-83191-9   LC 99-29054

"A Jean Karl book"

Twelve-year-old Alfa Merryfield, his older sister, and their grandmother struggle for rent money, food, and their dignity as they participate in the Montgomery, Alabama bus boycott in the summer of 1956

"Ingredients of mystery, suspense, and humor enhance and personalize this well-constructed story that offers insight into a troubled era." SLJ

Robinson, Barbara

The best Christmas pageant ever; pictures by Judith Gwyn Brown. Harper & Row 1972 80p il $15.95; lib bdg $15.89; pa $4.95 (4-6)   **Fic**

1. Christmas—Fiction 2. Pageants—Fiction

ISBN 0-06-025043-7; 0-06-025044-5 (lib bdg); 0-06-447044-X (pa)

Also available Audiobook version

In this story the six Herdmans, "absolutely the worst kids in the history of the world," discover the meaning of Christmas when they bully their way into the leading roles of the local church nativity play

"Although there is a touch of sentiment at the end . . . the story otherwise romps through the festive preparations with comic relish, and if the Herdmans are so gauche as to seem exaggerated, they are still enjoyable, as are the not-so-subtle pokes at pageant-planning in general." Bull Cent Child Books

Another available title about the Herdmans is:

The best school year ever (1994)

Rocklin, Joanne

Strudel stories. Delacorte Press 1999 131p $14.95; pa $4.50 (4 and up)   **Fic**

1. Jews—Fiction 2. Family life—Fiction 3. Storytelling—Fiction

ISBN 0-385-32602-5; 0-440-41509-8 (pa)

LC 98-23141

Also available Thorndike Press large print edition

"Members of a Jewish family tell their stories across generations while baking strudel in kitchens from Odessa to New York's lower east side to Los Angeles. . . . Rocklin based her fiction on 'the memoirs of ordinary people,' and each of her narrators has an individual, personal voice that rings true." Bull Cent Child Books

Rockwell, Thomas, 1933-

How to eat fried worms; pictures by Emily McCully. Watts 1973 115p il lib bdg $25 (3-6)

Fic

1. Worms—Fiction

ISBN 0-531-02631-0

Also available in paperback from Dell and Audiobook version

"The stakes are high when Alan bets $50 that his friend Billy can't eat 15 worms (one per day). . . . Billy's mother, instead of upchucking, comes to her son's aid by devising gourmet recipes like Alsatian Smothered Worm. Alan wants to win as desperately as Billy, who is itching to buy a used minibike, and few holds are barred in the contest." SLJ

"A hilarious story that will revolt and delight bumptious, unreachable, intermediate-grade boys and any other less particular mortals that read or listen to it. . . . The characters and their families and activities are natural to a T, and this juxtaposed against the uncommon plot, makes for some colorful, original writing in a much-needed comic vein." Booklist

Rodgers, Mary, 1931-

Freaky Friday. Harper & Row 1972 145p $15.95; lib bdg $15.89; pa $4.95 (4 and up)

Fic

ISBN 0-06-025048-8; 0-06-025049-6 (lib bdg); 0-06-440046-8 (pa)

Also available Audiobook version

"'When I woke up this morning, I found I'd turned into my mother.' So begins the most bizarre day in the life of 13-year-old Annabel Andrews, who discovers one Friday morning she has taken on her mother's physical characteristics while retaining her own personality. Readers will giggle in anticipation as Annabel plunges madly from one disaster to another trying to cope with various adult situations." Publ Wkly

"A fresh, imaginative, and entertaining story." Bull Cent Child Books

Rodowsky, Colby F., 1932-

Hannah in between; [by] Colby Rodowsky. Farrar, Straus & Giroux 1994 151p $15 (5 and up)

Fic

1. Alcoholism—Fiction 2. Mother-daughter relationship—Fiction

ISBN 0-374-32837-4   LC 93-35478

Also available in paperback from Troll

As she starts seventh grade, twelve-year-old Hannah can no longer ignore her mother's increasingly erratic behavior caused by drinking

"This heartrending novel offers a frank, sensitive depiction of alcoholism and its effects." Publ Wkly

Rodowsky, Colby F., 1932-—*Continued*

Not my dog; pictures by Thomas F. Yezerski. Farrar, Straus & Giroux 1999 69p il $15 (2-4)

Fic

1. Dogs—Fiction
ISBN 0-374-35531-2   LC 98-26126

Eight-year-old Ellie has to give up her life-long dream of getting a puppy after her parents agree to take in the dog that Great-aunt Margaret can no longer keep

"The author writes a genuine, gently humorous and uncomplicated story about compromise and love." Publ Wkly

Spindrift; [by] Colby Rodowsky. Farrar, Straus & Giroux 2000 136p $16 (5 and up)   Fic

1. Sisters—Fiction 2. Divorce—Fiction
ISBN 0-374-37155-5   LC 99-36263

During the summer after seventh grade, Cassie sees her close-knit family life in Bethany Beach, Delaware, changing drastically as her older sister has a baby, reveals the true nature of her husband, and announces the breakup of her marriage

"Readers drawn more to emotional drama than to action plots will find much to satisfy them in this realistic family story." Booklist

The Turnabout Shop; [by] Colby Rodowsky. Farrar, Straus & Giroux 1998 135p $16 (4-6)

Fic

1. Death—Fiction 2. Orphans—Fiction
ISBN 0-374-37889-4   LC 97-33229

Also available in paperback from HarperCollins

In "conversations" with her dead mother, fifth-grader Livvy records her adjustment to living in Baltimore with a woman she had never met, and as she comes to see the wisdom of her mother's choice as she gets to know the woman's large, loving family

"The characters are all well developed and the situations are entirely believable. What stands out most here, though, is Livvy's voice. Its blend of humor and heartbreak makes this a very real and unforgettable novel." SLJ

Rosen, Michael J., 1954-

Elijah's angel; a story for Chanukah and Christmas; illustrated by Aminah Brenda Lynn Robinson. Harcourt Brace Jovanovich 1992 unp il $16; pa $6   Fic

1. Pierce, Elijah, 1892-1984—Fiction 2. Artists—Fiction 3. Jews—Fiction 4. Christmas—Fiction 5. Hanukkah—Fiction
ISBN 0-15-225394-7; 0-15-201558-2 (pa)
LC 91-37552

At Christmas-Hanukkah time, Elijah Pierce, a black Christian woodcarver gives a carved angel to Michael, a young Jewish friend, who struggles with accepting the Christmas gift until he realizes that friendship means the same thing in any religion

"Perhaps because it's based on reality, Michael and Elijah's relationship rings sweetly true. The naive-style paintings, done in house paint on scrap rags, boldly simulate woodcuts, and though the artwork is not pretty, it, too, has the feel of reality." Booklist

A school for Pompey Walker; illustrated by Aminah Brenda Lynn Robinson. Harcourt Brace & Co. 1995 unp il $16   Fic

1. Slavery—Fiction 2. African Americans—Fiction
ISBN 0-15-200114-X   LC 94-6240

This "story is based on the life of Gussie West, a slave who sold himself into slavery again and again, escaped each time with the help of his white friend, and used the money to build a school for freed black children. . . . Drawing on slave memoirs, Rosen imagines Pompey Walker telling his story, an elderly man remembering and talking to the children in his school." Booklist

"The narrator's voice is startlingly clear and natural. . . . Using dyes and bold, sinuous lines to suggest the rich, transparent coloring and stylized figures of stained glass, Robinson's full- and half-page illustrations convey strong feelings through facial expressions and gnarled, slightly oversized hands." SLJ

Ross, Adrienne

In the quiet. Delacorte Press 2000 148p $14.95 (5 and up)   Fic

1. Aunts—Fiction 2. Death—Fiction
ISBN 0-385-32678-5   LC 99-35219

Eleven-year-old Sammy must deal with the death of her mother and the arrival of her mother's long-lost sister, who has a special gift

"The introspective first-person narrative effectively conveys Sammy's struggle and the story's hopeful resolution." Horn Book Guide

Rowling, J. K.

Harry Potter and the sorcerer's stone; illustrations by Mary Grandpré. Levine Bks. 1998 c1997 309p il $19.95; pa $6.99 (4 and up)   Fic

1. Fantasy fiction 2. Witchcraft—Fiction
ISBN 0-590-35340-3; 0-590-35342-X (pa)
LC 97-39059

Also available Thorndike Press large print edition and Audiobook version; Spanish language edition also available

First published 1997 in the United Kingdom with title: Harry Potter and the philosopher's stone

Rescued from the outrageous neglect of his aunt and uncle, Harry, a young boy with a great destiny, proves his worth while attending Hogwarts School for Wizards and Witches

This "is a brilliantly imagined and beautifully written fantasy." Booklist

Other available titles about Harry Potter are:
Harry Potter and the Chamber of Secrets (1999)
Harry Potter and the Goblet of Fire (2000)
Harry Potter and the prisoner of Azkaban (1999)

Ruckman, Ivy, 1931-

Night of the twisters. Crowell 1984 153p lib bdg $15.89; pa $4.95 (3-6)   Fic

1. Tornadoes—Fiction 2. Nebraska—Fiction
ISBN 0-690-04409-7 (lib bdg); 0-06-440176-6 (pa)
LC 83-46168

"Twelve-year-old Dan describes the events leading up to the hour that his town was struck seven times by tor-

Ruckman, Ivy, 1931——_Continued_

nadoes. Alone at home, [in Grand Island, Nebraska] Dan, his baby brother, and his best friend Arthur ride out the storm huddled in the shower stall in Dan's basement and then begin the search for their parents." Sci Child

"Ruckman does a good job of creating and maintaining suspense, produces dialogue that sounds appropriate for a stress situation, and gives her characters some depth and differentiation." Bull Cent Child Books

Ruskin, John, 1819-1900

The king of the Golden River   **Fic**
1. Fairy tales

Available Candlewick Press edition illustrated by Juan Wijngaard
Written 1841
After Gluck's cruel and greedy older brothers refuse hospitality to a mysterious visitor, their prosperous farm fails and one by one each brother makes the perilous journey to find treasure in the nearby Golden River
"As a piece of literature it is excellent, with its charming descriptions full of color and sound." Johnson. Anthology of Children's Literature

Rylant, Cynthia

A blue-eyed daisy. Bradbury Press 1985 99p $15 (5 and up)   **Fic**
1. Family life—Fiction 2. West Virginia—Fiction
ISBN 0-02-777960-2   LC 84-21554
This story "describes a year in a child's life. . . . Ellie is eleven, youngest of five girls. She wishes her father didn't drink but understands his frustration. . . . It is a bond between them when they acquire a hunting dog. . . . She also acquires a best friend during the year, gets her first kiss (and is surprised to see that she enjoys it) and adjusts to the fact that some of the events in her life will be sad ones." Bull Cent Child Books
"Episodic in nature, the story captures, as if in a frozen frame, the brief moments between childhood and adolescence." Horn Book

A fine white dust. Bradbury Press 1986 106p $16; pa $4.99 (5 and up)   **Fic**
1. Religion—Fiction 2. Friendship—Fiction 3. Family life—Fiction
ISBN 0-02-777240-3; 0-689-80462-8 (pa)
LC 86-1003
Also available Audiobook version
A Newbery Medal honor book, 1987
The visit of the traveling Preacher Man to his small North Carolina town gives new impetus to thirteen-year-old Peter's struggle to reconcile his own deeply felt religious belief with the beliefs and non-beliefs of his family and friends
"Blending humor and intense emotion with a poetic use of language, Cynthia Rylant has created a taut, finely drawn portrait of a boy's growth from seeking for belief, through seduction and betrayal, to a spiritual acceptance and a readiness 'for something whole.'" Horn Book

Missing May. Orchard Bks. 1992 89p $14.99; lib bdg $15.99 (5 and up)   **Fic**
1. Death—Fiction 2. West Virginia—Fiction
ISBN 0-531-05996-0; 0-531-08596-1 (lib bdg)
LC 91-23303

Also available in paperback from Dell and Audiobook version
Awarded the Newbery Medal, 1993
"A Richard Jackson book"
After the death of the beloved aunt who has raised her, twelve-year-old Summer and her uncle Ob leave their West Virginia trailer in search of the strength to go on living
"There is much to ponder here, from the meaning of life and death to the power of love. That it all succeeds is a tribute to a fine writer who brings to the task a natural grace of language, an earthly sense of humor, and a well-grounded sense of the spiritual." SLJ

Sachar, Louis, 1954-

Holes. Farrar, Straus & Giroux 1998 233p $16 (5 and up)   **Fic**
1. Juvenile delinquency—Fiction 2. Friendship—Fiction 3. Buried treasure—Fiction
ISBN 0-374-33265-7   LC 97-45011
Also available in paperback from Dell and Audiobook version
Awarded the Newbery Medal, 1999
"Frances Foster books"
As further evidence of his family's bad fortune which they attribute to a curse on a distant relative, Stanley Yelnats is sent to a hellish correctional camp in the Texas desert where he finds his first real friend, a treasure, and a new sense of himself
"This delightfully clever story is well-crafted and thought-provoking, with a bit of a folklore thrown in for good measure." Voice Youth Advocates

Marvin Redpost, kidnapped at birth? illustrated by Neal Hughes. Random House 1992 68p il hardcover o.p. paperback available $3.99 (2-4)
Fic
ISBN 0-679-81946-0 (pa)   LC 91-51105
"A First Stepping Stone book"
Red-haired Marvin is convinced that the reason he looks different from the rest of his family is that he is really the lost prince of Shampoon
"Written almost completely in dialogue, the story is fast paced, easy to read, and full of humor." SLJ
Other available titles about Marvin Redpost are:
Marvin Redpost, a flying birthday cake (1999)
Marvin Redpost, a magic crystal (2000)
Marvin Redpost, alone in his teacher's house (1994)
Marvin Redpost, class president (1999)
Marvin Redpost, is he a girl? (1993)
Marvin Redpost, superfast, out of control (2000)
Marvin Redpost, why pick on me? (1993)

Wayside School gets a little stranger; illustrated by Joel Schick. Morrow Junior Bks. 1995 168p il $16; pa $4.95 (3-6)   **Fic**
1. School stories
ISBN 0-688-13694-X; 0-380-72381-6 (pa)
LC 94-25448

Also available Audiobook version
This is "about the zany goings-on in [an] unorthodox 30-story-tall school. . . . The narrative revolves around the wacky substitute teachers who take Mrs. Jewls's place when she is on maternity leave." Publ Wkly

Sachar, Louis, 1954-—*Continued*

"Sachar's offering contains hilarity, malevolence, romance, relentless punning, goofiness, inspiration, revenge, and poignancy." SLJ

Other available titles about Wayside School are:
Sideways stories from Wayside School (1978)
Wayside School is falling down (1989)

Sachs, Marilyn, 1927-

The bears' house. Dutton 1987 c1971 67p o.p.; Avon Bks. paperback available $4.99 (4-6)   **Fic**
1. Family life—Fiction 2. Dollhouses—Fiction
ISBN 0-380-70582-6 (pa)   LC 86-29267
First published 1971 by Doubleday in an illustrated edition

"Life is grim for nine-year-old Fran Ellen. Father has deserted the family, mother has retreated into apathy and tears, and the five children shift for themselves. Fran Ellen's only joy is Baby Flora. Rejected at home and taunted at school, Fran Ellen adopts as her own the classroom doll house, compensating for her unhappiness with . . . fantasies in which its tenants, the three bears, adore her." Saturday Rev

"Superb characterizations and uncommonly skilled writing draw the reader completely into the realities and fantasies of Fran Ellen's world." Libr J

Saint-Exupéry, Antoine de, 1900-1944

The little prince; written and illustrated by Antoine de Saint-Exupery; translated from the French by Richard Howard. Harcourt 2000 83p il $18; pa $8   **Fic**
ISBN 0-15-202398-4; 0-15-601219-7 (pa)
     LC 99-50439
A new translation of the title first published 1943 by Reynal & Hitchcock

"This many-dimensional fable of an airplane pilot who has crashed in the desert is for readers of all ages. The pilot comes upon the little prince soon after the crash. The prince tells of his adventures on different planets and on Earth as he attempts to learn about the universe in order to live peacefully on his own small planet. A spiritual quality enhances the seemingly simple observations of the little prince." Shapiro. Fic for Youth. 3d edition

Salten, Felix, 1869-1945

Bambi; a life in the woods il (4-6)   **Fic**
1. Deer—Fiction

Various editions available
Original German edition, 1923; first United States edition published 1928 by Simon & Schuster

"Bambi is a young deer, growing up in a forest, at first a curious child playing about his mother in glade and meadow, conversing with grasshoppers, squirrels and his own little cousins, Faline and Gobo." N Y Libr

"Felix Stalten's story of deer life in the woods that fringe the Danube is neither sentimental nor used to point a moral. It derives its dramatic value, legitimately, from the animals' fear and terror of their historic enemy—man. . . . In his absorption with details that author has brought his whole forest to life, yet these details are selected with a poet's intuition for delicacy of effect." NY Her Trib Books

Sawyer, Ruth, 1880-1970

Roller skates; written by Ruth Sawyer and illustrated by Valenti Angelo. Viking 1995 c1936 186p il $15.99; pa $5.99 (4-6)   **Fic**
1. New York (N.Y.)—Fiction
ISBN 0-670-60310-4; 0-14-030358-8 (pa)
     LC 85-43418
Also available in hardcover from P. Smith
Awarded the Newbery Medal, 1937
A reissue of the title first published 1936

"For one never-to-be forgotten year Lucinda Wyman (ten years old) was free to explore New York on roller skates. She made friends with Patrick Gilligan and his hansom cab, with Policeman M'Gonegal, with the fruit vendor, Vittore Coppicco and his son Tony, and with many others. All Lucinda's adventures are true and happened to the author herself as is borne out by the occasional pages of Lucinda's diary which are a part of the story." Horn Book

Schmidt, Gary D.

Anson's way. Clarion Bks. 1999 213p $15 (5 and up)   **Fic**
1. Ireland—Fiction
ISBN 0-395-91529-5   LC 98-29220
While serving as a British Fencible to maintain the peace in Ireland, Anson finds that his sympathy for a hedge master places him in conflict with the law of King George II

"Wonderfully descriptive, captivating prose and well-defined characters draw readers into eighteenth-century Ireland." Booklist

Schnur, Steven

The shadow children; illustrated by Herbert Tauss. Morrow Junior Bks. 1994 86p il $16; lib bdg $15.95 (5 and up)   **Fic**
1. Holocaust, 1933-1945—Fiction 2. Ghost stories 3. France—Fiction
ISBN 0-688-13281-2; 0-688-13831-4 (lib bdg)
     LC 94-5098
While spending the summer on his grandfather's farm in the French countryside, eleven-year-old Etienne discovers a secret dating back to World War II and encounters the ghosts of Jewish children who suffered a dreadful fate under the Nazis

"The prose is spare and beautiful, and the expressive charcoal illustrations move from the warm affection of the present to the shadowy horror that won't go away." Booklist

Schulman, Janet

The nutcracker; [by] E.T.A. Hoffmann; adapted by Janet Schulman; illustrated by Renée Graef; audio CD narrated by Claire Bloom with music by Peter Ilyich Tchaikovsky. HarperCollins Pubs. 1999 34p il $19.95 (4 and up)   **Fic**
1. Fairy tales 2. Christmas—Fiction
ISBN 0-06-027814-5   LC 97-22346
Also available Audiobook version
This adaptation of the Nutcracker with illustrations by Kay Chorao was published 1979 by Dutton

Schulman, Janet—*Continued*

One Christmas after hearing how the toy nutcracker made by her godfather got his ugly face, a little girl helps break the spell and watches him change into a handsome prince

"Graef's illustrations are floridly old-fashioned, with careful attention to period detail." Booklist

Schur, Maxine, 1948-

The circlemaker; by Maxine Rose Schur. Dial Bks. for Young Readers 1994 179p hardcover o.p. paperback available $4.99 (5 and up) **Fic**

1. Jews—Russia—Fiction 2. Russia—Fiction
ISBN 0-14-037997-5 (pa) LC 93-17983

In mid-nineteenth century Russia, Mendel Cholinsky, a twelve-year-old Jewish boy tries to escape to America to avoid being taken into the Czar's army for twenty-five years of military service

"The action and suspense will draw readers to a book that could also be used by teachers and librarians for units on Russia, Judaism, multiculturalism, and prejudice." Book Rep

Scieszka, Jon, 1954-

Knights of the kitchen table; illustrated by Lane Smith. Viking 1991 55p il (Time Warp Trio) $14.99; pa $4.99 (3-5) **Fic**

1. Fantasy fiction
ISBN 0-670-83622-2; 0-14-034603-1 (pa)
LC 90-51009

"Transported to the Middle Ages, three friends save themselves from a dragon and a giant through quick thinking. The tongue-in-cheek narrative makes for laugh-out-loud enjoyment, and the easy-to-read sentences and zany dialogue perfectly suit the breathless pace." SLJ

Other available titles about The Time Warp Trio are:
2095 (1995)
The good, the bad, and the goofy (1992)
It's all Greek to me (1999)
The not-so-jolly Roger (1991)
See you later, gladiator (2000)
Summer reading is killing me! (1998)
Tut, tut (1996)
Your mother was a Neanderthal (1993)

Sebestyen, Ouida, 1924-

Out of nowhere; a novel. Orchard Bks. 1994 183p lib bdg $17.99 (5 and up) **Fic**

1. Dogs—Fiction 2. Foster home care—Fiction
ISBN 0-531-08689-5 LC 93-37759

Also available in paperback from Puffin Bks.

"A Melanie Kroupa book"

When he no longer fits into his vagabond mother's life, thirteen-year-old Harley adopts an abandoned dog and falls in with an outspoken old woman, a cantankerous junk collector, and an energetic and loving teenage girl

"This poignant story is beautifully written, and readers will delight in it." SLJ

Words by heart. Little, Brown 1979 162p o.p.; Bantam Bks. paperback available $4.99 (5 and up) **Fic**

1. African Americans—Fiction 2. Race relations—Fiction 3. Family life—Fiction
ISBN 0-440-22688-0 (pa) LC 78-27847

"An Atlantic Monthly Press book"

"It is 1910, and Lena's family is the only black family in her small Southwestern town. When Lena wins a scripture reciting contest that a white boy is supposed to win, her family is threatened. Lena's father tries to make her understand that by hating the people who did this, the problems that cause their behavior are not solved. Only more hatred and violence cause Lena and the village to understand the words of her father." ALAN

Followed by On fire (1985)

Seidler, Tor, 1952-

Mean Margaret; pictures by Jon Agee. Michael Di Capua Bks. 1997 165p il $15.95 (3-6) **Fic**

1. Marmots—Fiction
ISBN 0-06-205090-7

This is the "story of a newly wed woodchuck couple who find a willful, wailing human toddler and take her into their home and into their hearts." SLJ

"Both hilarious and heartwarming, *Mean Margaret* is a delightful fantasy filled with memorably offbeat characters and situations. . . . Agee's black-and-white drawings match the text in wit and boundless good humor." Booklist

The steadfast tin soldier; [by] Hans Christian Andersen; illustrated by Fred Marcellino; retold by Tor Seidler. HarperCollins Pubs. 1992 28p il $14.95; pa $6.95 (1-4) **Fic**

1. Toys—Fiction 2. Fairy tales
ISBN 0-06-205000-1; 0-06-205900-9 (pa)
LC 92-52690

"Michael di Capua books"

This is a retelling of Andersen's fairy tale in which the one-legged tin soldier falls in love with a paper ballerina

The text is "lively and readable. . . . Marcellino . . . creates an exceptionally handsome version of the tale. Set in the nineteenth century, presumably in Denmark, the book includes impressive outdoor scenes under a pewter gray winter sky and domestic indoor scenes golden with the diffuse light of candles. Softly delineated forms and figures appear in a series of formally composed scenes sometimes reminiscent of dramatic tableaux. Designed with a sense of quiet elegance." Booklist

The Wainscott weasel; illustrated by Fred Marcellino. HarperCollins Pubs. 1993 193p il lib bdg $19.89; pa $11.95 (4-6) **Fic**

1. Weasels—Fiction 2. Animals—Fiction
ISBN 0-06-205033-8 (lib bdg); 0-06-205911-4 (pa)
LC 92-54526

"The weasels' summer begins with the visiting Wendy being charmed by both Zeke and Bagley Jr. . . . But Bagley pines for Bridget, a beautiful fish who lives in the nearby brook. . . . When Bridget's life is in danger, Bagley learns he can be a hero." Child Book Rev Serv

"Seidler's pacing is superb; he builds a solid structure within each chapter. A dry wit inspires his characterizations. . . . Marcellino enhances and even extends the beguiling ambiance with his exceptionally expressive art." Publ Wkly

Selden, George, 1929-1989

The cricket in Times Square; illustrated by Garth Williams. Farrar, Straus & Giroux 1960 151p il $16 (3-6)   **Fic**

1. Cats—Fiction 2. Crickets—Fiction 3. Mice—Fiction 4. New York (N.Y.)—Fiction

ISBN 0-374-31650-3

Also available in paperback from Dell and Audiobook version; Spanish language edition also available

A Newbery Medal honor book, 1961

"An Ariel book"

"A touch of magic comes to Times Square subway station with Chester, a cricket from rural Connecticut. He is introduced to the distinctive character of city life by three friends: Mario Bellini, whose parents operate a newsstand; Tucker, a glib Broadway mouse; and Harry, a sagacious cat. Chester saves the Bellinis' business by giving concerts from the newsstand, bringing to rushing commuters moments of beauty and repose. This modern fantasy shows that, in New York, anything can happen." Moorachian. What is a City?

Other available titles about Chester and his friends are:
Chester Cricket's new home (1983)
Chester Cricket's pigeon ride (1981)
Harry Cat's pet puppy (1974)
Harry Kitten and Tucker Mouse (1986)
The old meadow (1987)
Tucker's countryside (1969)

The genie of Sutton Place. Farrar, Straus & Giroux 1973 175p hardcover o.p. paperback available $4.95 (4 and up)   **Fic**

ISBN 0-374-42530-2 (pa)

Also available in hardcover from P. Smith

Adapted from the television play written by the author and Kenneth Heuer

"Tim turns to his dead father's diaries for some occult wisdom to help him keep Sam, a beloved mongrel his aunt has banished from their apartment. What he finds is a spell that summons the genie Abdullah from a thousand years' captivity in a woven carpet." Booklist

"The speedy action and clever dialogue in this witty book are sure to entice readers." SLJ

Sendak, Maurice

Higglety pigglety pop! or, There must be more to life; story and pictures by Maurice Sendak. HarperCollins Pubs. c1967 69p il $14.95; pa $8.95 (2-4)   **Fic**

1. Dogs—Fiction

ISBN 0-06-028479-X; 0-06-443021-9 (pa)

Copyright renewed 1995

In this modern fairy tale "Jennie, the Sealyham terrier, leaves home because 'there must be more to life than having everything.' When she applies for a job as the leading lady of the World Mother Goose Theater, she discovers that what she lacks is experience. What follows are her adventures and her gaining of experience; finally Jennie becomes the leading lady of the play." Wis Libr Bull

"The story has elements of tenderness and humor; it also has . . . typically macabre Sendak touches. . . . The illustrations are beautiful, amusing, and distinctive." Sutherland. The Best in Child Books

Seredy, Kate, 1899-1975

The Good Master; written and illustrated by Kate Seredy. Viking 1935 210p il hardcover o.p. paperback available $4.99 (4-6)   **Fic**

1. Farm life—Fiction 2. Hungary—Fiction

ISBN 0-14-030133-X (pa)

A Newbery Medal honor book, 1936

Into this story of Jancsi, a ten-year-old Hungarian farm boy and his little hoyden of a cousin Kate from Budapest, is woven a description of Hungarian farm life, fairs, festivals, and folk tales. Under the tutelage of Jancsi's kind father, called by the neighbors The Good Master, Kate calms down and becomes a more docile young person

"The steady warm understanding of the wise father, the Good Master, is a shining quality throughout." Horn Book

Followed by The singing tree (1939)

The white stag; written and illustrated by Kate Seredy. Viking 1937 94p il hardcover o.p. paperback available $4.99 (4-6)   **Fic**

1. Hungary—Fiction

ISBN 0-14-031258-7 (pa)

Awarded the Newbery Medal, 1938

"Striking illustrations interpret this hero tale of the legendary founding of Hungary, when a white stag and a red eagle led the people to their promised land." Hodges. Books for Elem Sch Libr

Serraillier, Ian, 1912-1994

The silver sword; illustrated by C. Walter Hodges. Phillips 1959 c1956 187p il $31.95 (5 and up)   **Fic**

1. World War, 1939-1945—Fiction 2. Polish refugees—Fiction

ISBN 0-87599-104-1

First published 1956 in the United Kingdom; first United States edition published 1959 by Criterion Books

"As a result of World War II, the Balicki family of Warsaw are separated from one another. Living in bombed-out cellars or the countryside the children are helped by Edek until his arrest for smuggling and from then on by Jan, a sullen orphan. The privations of each member of the family, especially the children, are graphically described as each works toward their rendezvous, Switzerland, and freedom. A suspense-filled, exciting story." Read Ladders for Hum Relat. 5th edition

Service, Pamela F.

Stinker from space. Scribner 1988 83p o.p.; Fawcett Bks. paperback available $5.99 (4-6)   **Fic**

1. Science fiction

ISBN 0-449-70330-4 (pa)   LC 87-25266

An agent of the Sylon Confederacy, fleeing from enemy ships, crash lands on Earth, transfers his mind to the body of a skunk, and enlists the aid of two children in getting back to his home planet

"A first-class, funny science fantasy that will hook middle-grade readers right from the first scene. . . . The situation is gratifyingly absurd, the development satisfyingly natural." Bull Cent Child Books

Sewell, Anna, 1820-1878

Black Beauty (4-6)   **Fic**
1. Horses—Fiction 2. Great Britain—Fiction

Some editions are:
Grosset & Dunlap (Illustrated junior library) $14.95 Illustrated by Fritz Eichenberg (ISBN 0-448-40942-9)
Knopf (Everyman's library children's classics) $13.95 Illustrated by Lucy Kemp-Welch (ISBN 0-679-42811-9)
First published 1877 in the United Kingdom; first United States edition, 1891
This is "the most celebrated 'Animal Story' of the 19th cent., an account of a horse's experiences at the hands of many owners, ranging from the worthy Squire Gordon to a cruel cab-owner." Oxford Companion to Child Lit

Shalant, Phyllis

Bartleby of the mighty Mississippi; with illustrations by Anna Vojtech. Dutton Children's Bks. 2000 164p il $15.99 (3-6)   **Fic**
1. Turtles—Fiction
ISBN 0-525-46033-0   LC 99-89893
After being abandoned in a pond, Bartleby, a pet turtle, meets many other creatures, learns to survive in the wild, and decides to go in search of his birthplace
"Shalant's novel is a sweet, warm allegory about the pains of growing up." SLJ

Beware of kissing Lizard Lips. Dutton Children's Bks. 1995 183p $14.99 (4-6)   **Fic**
1. School stories 2. Martial arts—Fiction 3. Korean Americans—Fiction
ISBN 0-525-45199-4   LC 94-44389
"Zach wants to stop being Mouseboy, the smallest in the sixth grade, and at the mercy of Lizard Lips, the tallest girl. He finds some hope, physically and spiritually, from learning tae kwon do and becomes interested in a girl in his class." SLJ
"This is a laugh-out-loud story about growing up male, written without a trace of condescension." Booklist

Shreve, Susan Richards

The flunking of Joshua T. Bates; [by] Susan Shreve; illustrated by Diane de Groat. Knopf 1984 82p il hardcover o.p. paperback available $4.99 (3-5)   **Fic**
1. School stories 2. Teachers—Fiction 3. Family life—Fiction
ISBN 0-679-84187-3 (pa)   LC 83-19636
"Sometimes children, especially boys, are held back in school even if they are smart. To his dismay, Joshua T. Bates was supposed to repeat the whole third grade, but he was lucky enough to have a very sympathetic teacher." N Y Times Book Rev
"In addition to the warm depiction of a teacher-pupil relationship, the story has other relationships, astutely drawn: Joshua's parents, the former classmate who teases Joshua, the best friend who stoutly defends him. The dialogue is particularly good, often contributing to characterization, just as often crisply humorous." Bull Cent Child Books
Other available titles about Joshua are:
Joshua T. Bates in trouble again (1997)
Joshua T. Bates takes charge (1993)

Shyer, Marlene Fanta

Welcome home, Jellybean. Scribner 1978 152p hardcover o.p. paperback available $4.99 (5 and up)   **Fic**
1. Mentally handicapped—Fiction 2. Siblings—Fiction
ISBN 0-689-71213-8 (pa)   LC 77-17970
"'When my sister turned thirteen the school where she lived got her toilet-trained and my mother decided she ought to come home to live, once and for all.' So begins Neil Oxley's story of how it was to have his profoundly retarded sister re-enter the family circle." Booklist
"Painful, honest, and convincing, this is quietly written and very effective in evoking sympathy and understanding for retarded children and for their families." Bull Cent Child Books

Singer, Isaac Bashevis, 1904-1991

The fools of Chelm and their history; pictures by Uri Shulevitz; translated by the author and Elizabeth Shub. Farrar, Straus & Giroux 1973 57p il $14; pa $4.95 (4 and up)   **Fic**
1. Jews—Fiction
ISBN 0-374-32444-1; 0-374-42429-2 (pa)
The "town of Chelm is just like every place else, only worse, as numerous shortages, foolish citizens, and inept leaders combine to make life thoroughly miserable. . . . Singer mocks the 'advantages'—such as war, crime, and revolution—that civilization brings to Chelm, as the leadership changes but never improves." Booklist
"An amusing story, well-told. The pen-and-ink illustrations embellish the text, adding droll touches of their own." Horn Book

Skurzynski, Gloria

The virtual war. Simon & Schuster Bks. for Young Readers 1997 152p $16; pa $4.99 (6 and up)   **Fic**
1. Science fiction 2. Virtual reality—Fiction
ISBN 0-689-81374-0; 0-689-82425-4 (pa)
LC 96-35346
In a future world where global contamination has necessitated limited human contact, three young people with unique genetically engineered abilities are teamed up to wage a war in virtual reality
"Skurzynski's anti-war message is clear yet never didactic; her characters are complex and fully realized, the pacing brisk, and the story compelling." Bull Cent Child Books

Sleator, William

The beasties. Dutton Children's Bks. 1997 198p $15.99; pa $5.99 (6 and up)   **Fic**
1. Ecology—Fiction 2. Horror fiction
ISBN 0-525-45598-1; 0-14-130639-4 (pa)
LC 97-6147
"In this horror tale, Doug and his sister are captured by the beasties who live in tunnels underneath the forest. Threatened and genetically mutated by the destruction of the wilderness, the beasties have taken to kidnapping people and amputating body parts they need. Sleator handles the ickier aspects of the story with aplomb, and the menacing atmosphere and suspense-serving pace are all they should be." Horn Book Guide

Sleator, William—*Continued*

The boxes. Dutton Children's Bks. 1998 196p
$15.99; pa $4.99 (6 and up)   **Fic**
1. Science fiction
ISBN 0-525-46012-8; 0-14-130810-9 (pa)
                                          LC 98-9285
When she opens two strange boxes left in her care by
her mysterious uncle, fifteen-year-old Annie discovers a
swarm of telepathic creatures and unleashes a power capable of slowing down time
"Sleator has written a page-turner. . . . His writing is
crisp and clean, letting the story speak for itself." Voice
Youth Advocates

Interstellar pig. Dutton 1984 197p hardcover
o.p. paperback available $4.99 (5 and up)   **Fic**
1. Science fiction
ISBN 0-14-037595-3 (pa)   LC 84-4132
"Solitary and bored, Barney is quickly attracted by the
exotic appearance and protean personalities of Zena,
Manny, and Joe, who have rented the summer house next
door. The interest of the sophisticated adults in sixteen-
year-old Barney at first flatters, then intrigues, and finally terrifies him as he becomes absorbed in their compulsion to possess 'The Piggy.' When he realizes that the
talisman has power, the game expands in significance."
Horn Book
The author "draws the reader in with intimations of
danger and horror, but the climactic battle is more slapstick than horrific, and the victor's prize could scarcely
be more ironic. Problematic as straight science fiction
but great fun as a spoof on human-alien contact." Booklist

Into the dream; illustrated by Ruth Sanderson.
Dutton 1979 137p il hardcover o.p. paperback
available $4.99 (5 and up)   **Fic**
1. Extrasensory perception—Fiction 2. Psychokinesis—Fiction 3. Unidentified flying objects—Fiction
ISBN 0-14-130814-1 (pa)   LC 78-11825
When two youngsters realize they are having the same
frightening dream, they begin searching for an explanation for this mysterious coincidence
"Tightly woven suspense and an ingenious, totally involving plot line . . . make this a thriller of top-notch
quality." Booklist

Rewind. Dutton Children's Bks. 1999 120p
$15.99; pa $4.99 (4 and up)   **Fic**
1. Science fiction 2. Death—Fiction
ISBN 0-525-46130-2; 0-14-131101-0 (pa)
                                          LC 99-12260
"When Peter is mowed down by a car and killed after
running into the street following a fight with his parents,
he learns, in the 'great white light,' that he has another
chance. In fact, he gets three chances to go back and
change the events of his life so that the accident never
occurs. . . . The premise is irresistible, and the suspense
crackles." Horn Book

Slepian, Jan, 1921-
The Broccoli tapes. Philomel Bks. 1989 157p
$15.99 (5 and up)   **Fic**
1. Cats—Fiction 2. Death—Fiction 3. Hawaii—Fiction
ISBN 0-399-21712-6   LC 88-25490

"Both 12-year-old Sara and her 13-year-old brother,
Sam, have trouble adjusting to Hawaii during the five
months that their family is living there. . . . When Sara
and Sam rescue a wild cat (who is later named Broccoli),
they meet Eddie Nutt. At first Eddie is as suspicious and
untrusting as Broccoli until the bonds of friendship gradually develop. The story unfolds through Sara's cassette
tapes sent to her teacher and classmates back home." SLJ
"Slepian is a fine writer, and the elements of her story
are smoothly meshed, the action and characterization mutually affective. The message that love is worth the
chance of pain is given by the people in her story, not
didactically imposed by the author." Bull Cent Child
Books

Slote, Alfred
Finding Buck McHenry. HarperCollins Pubs.
1991 250p lib bdg $15.89; pa $4.95 (4-6)   **Fic**
1. Baseball—Fiction 2. African Americans—Fiction
ISBN 0-06-021653-0 (lib bdg); 0-06-440469-2 (pa)
                                          LC 90-39190
Eleven-year-old Jason, believing the school custodian
Mack Henry to be Buck McHenry, a famous pitcher
from the old Negro League, tries to enlist him as a coach
for his Little League team by revealing his identity to the
world
"Slote skillfully blends comedy, suspense and baseball
in a highly entertaining tale." Publ Wkly

Hang tough, Paul Mather. Lippincott 1973 156p
hardcover o.p. paperback available $4.95 (4-6)
                                              Fic
1. Leukemia—Fiction 2. Baseball—Fiction
ISBN 0-06-440153-7 (pa)
"Paul Mather, a Little League star pitcher before he
contracted leukemia, is unable to resist the temptation to
demonstrate his skill when his family moves to Michigan
and he ends up in the hospital." Booklist
"The story of Paul's candor and courage is convincing, sad but never morbid, in a book that has depth and
integrity." Bull Cent Child Books

The trading game. Lippincott 1990 200p
hardcover o.p. paperback available $4.95 (4-6)
                                              Fic
1. Baseball cards—Fiction 2. Grandfathers—Fiction
ISBN 0-06-440438-2 (pa)   LC 89-12851
"Andy Harris' baseball-card collection, inherited from
his recently deceased father, contains some valuable
items, including a 1952 Mickey Mantle card worth
$2500. He's willing, however, to trade Mantle for a 25-
cent card that pictures his grandfather, Jim 'Ace 459'
Harris, whom Andy idolizes. . . . It's not until Grampa
coaches Andy that he learns why the relationship between his father and grandfather was strained." SLJ
"Slote does a masterful job grounding the moral dilemmas of growing up within the rigorously measured
world of the baseball diamond. Friendship, father-son intimacy, and the rough edges of adult life are all examined and filtered through the eyes of a boy who instinc-
tively understands more than he knows." Booklist

Smith, Doris Buchanan

A taste of blackberries; illustrated by Charles Robinson. Crowell 1973 58p il lib bdg $14.89; pa $4.95 (4-6)   **Fic**
1. Death—Fiction 2. Friendship—Fiction
ISBN 0-690-80512-8 (lib bdg); 0-06-440238-4 (pa)

A "portrayal of the death of a close friend. While gathering Japanese beetles to help a neighbor, Jamie is stung by a bee and falls screaming and writhing to the ground. His best friend (never named) disgustedly stalks off, only to find later that Jamie is dead of the bee sting. The boy feels guilty because he thought Jamie was clowning and didn't try to help. The boy is very withdrawn the week of the funeral, but comes to grips with the tragedy and learns to manage his grief." SLJ

"A difficult and sensitive subject, treated with taste and honesty, is woven into a moving story about a believable little boy. The black-and-white illustrations are honest, affective, and sensitive." Horn Book

Smith, Janice Lee, 1949-

The kid next door and other headaches; stories about Adam Joshua; drawings by Dick Gackenbach. Harper & Row 1984 143p il lib bdg $14.89 (2-4)   **Fic**
1. Friendship—Fiction
ISBN 0-06-025793-8   LC 83-47689

"Adam Joshua and Nelson, who are best friends as well as next-door neighbors, play and battle as best friends do. Their finest hour is coping with a visit from Nelson's truly horrid cousin Cynthia." N Y Times Book Rev

"This book has all the ingredients necessary for the often reluctant transition from easy readers to chapter books: large print and an ample supply of dialogue, humor and wonderfully funny black-and-white illustrations." SLJ

Other available titles about Adam Joshua are:
The monster in the third dresser drawer and other stories about Adam Joshua (1981)
The show-and-tell war and other stories about Adam Joshua (1988)

Smith, Robert Kimmel, 1930-

Bobby Baseball; illustrated by Alan Tiegreen. Delacorte Press 1989 165p il hardcover o.p. paperback available $4.50 (4-6)   **Fic**
1. Father-son relationship—Fiction 2. Baseball—Fiction
ISBN 0-440-40417-7 (pa)   LC 89-1175

Ten-year-old Bobby is passionate about baseball and convinced that he is a great player. The only problem is to get a chance to prove his skill, especially to his father

"Baseball fans who share Bobby's fantasies will admire his determination and empathize with his stinging realization. Smith's crisp dialogue vivifies the book's appealing characters, and Tiegreen's illustrations lend an antic touch to Bobby's predicaments. This is an upbeat, refreshing celebration of the spirit of our national pastime." Publ Wkly

Chocolate fever; illustrated by Gioia Fiammenghi. Putnam 1989 c1972 93p il $13.89 (4-6)   **Fic**
ISBN 0-399-61224-6   LC 88-23508

Also available in paperback from Dell and Audiobook version

A reissue of the title first published 1972 by Coward-McCann

"You've heard of too much of a good thing? You've never heard of it the way it happens to Henry Green. Henry's a chocolate maven, first class. No, that's too mild. Henry's absolutely freaky over chocolate, loco over cocoa. He can't get enough, until—aaarrrfh! Brown spots, brown bumps all over Henry. It's (gulp) 'Chocolate Fever.'" N Y Times Book Rev

"It's all quite preposterous and lots of laughs, and so are the cartoon illustrations." Publ Wkly

The war with Grandpa; illustrated by Richard Lauter. Delacorte Press 1984 141p il hardcover o.p. paperback available $4.99 (4-6)   **Fic**
1. Grandfathers—Fiction 2. Family life—Fiction
ISBN 0-440-49276-9 (pa)   LC 83-14366

"Pete's Grandpa comes to live with the family and bumps Pete out of the room he's had 'forever.' Egged on by his buddies, Pete starts a war of notes and practical jokes. To his surprise, Grandpa enjoys the skirmishes and the two carry on a quiet campaign for a while. In the final episode, Pete realizes just how wrong he has been and Grandpa comes up with a happy solution. This should be a winner with the middle grade set." Child Book Rev Serv

Sneve, Virginia Driving Hawk

High Elk's treasure; illustrated by Oren Lyons. Holiday House 1995 c1972 96p il $15.95   **Fic**
1. Dakota Indians—Fiction
ISBN 0-8234-0212-6

A reissue of the title first published 1972

"When Joe High Elk and his sister take refuge from a storm in a cave used by their revered ancestor Steps High Like an Elk, Joe finds a mysterious package that may shed light on the true story of the Battle of the Little Big Horn. . . . [This] paints an authentic portrait of modern Sioux life and culture." Horn Book Guide

Snicket, Lemony

The bad beginning; illustrations by Brett Helquist. HarperCollins Pubs. 1999 162p il (Series of unfortunate events) $8.95; lib bdg $14.89 (4 and up)   **Fic**
1. Orphans—Fiction
ISBN 0-06-440766-7; 0-06-028312-2 (lib bdg)
    LC 99-14750

After the sudden death of their parents, the three Baudelaire children must depend on each other and their wits when it turns out that the distant relative who is appointed their guardian is determined to use any means necessary to get their fortune

"While the misfortunes hover on the edge of being ridiculous, Snicket's energetic blend of humor, dramatic irony, and literary flair makes it all perfectly believable. . . . Excellent for reading aloud." SLJ

Other available titles about the Baudelaire children are:
The austere academy (2000)
The ersatz elevator (2000)
The miserable mill (2000)
The reptile room (1999)
The vile village (2001)
The wide window (2000)

Snyder, Zilpha Keatley

Cat running. Delacorte Press 1994 168p $15.95; pa $4.99 (4 and up)   **Fic**
1. Great Depression, 1929-1939—Fiction 2. Running—Fiction
ISBN 0-385-31056-0; 0-440-41152-1 (pa)
                                              LC 94-447

"Sixth grader Cat Kinsey is sure she is the fastest runner in Brownwood School until Zane Perkins arrives barefoot and clothed in ragged overalls. He's an 'Okie,' and to most Californians during the Great Depression, that automatically translates to 'lazy, dirty, and shiftless.' When Cat's father forbids her to wear slacks because he feels they are unseemly, she ignores Zane's challenge and refuses to race during the school's annual Play Day. . . . This story is both appealing and informative. The characters are well drawn and beautifully motivated." SLJ

The Egypt game; drawings by Alton Raible. Atheneum Pubs. 1967 215p il $17 (5 and up)
                                              Fic
ISBN 0-689-30006-9
Also available in paperback from Dell
A Newbery Medal honor book, 1968

"Six children of different ethnic backgrounds secretly play a game invented by a white girl and a [black] girl who are fascinated by their own imaginations and by ancient Egypt. The Egypt game helps solve one girl's personal problems and it leads to the capture of a mentally ill murderer who attacks one of the girls." Wis Libr Bull

This book "is strong in characterization, the dialogue is superb, the plot is original, and the sequences in which the children are engaged in sustained imaginative play are fascinating, and often very funny." Saturday Rev

The headless cupid; illustrated by Alton Raible. Atheneum Pubs. 1971 203p il $17 (5 and up)
                                              Fic
1. Occultism—Fiction
ISBN 0-689-20687-9
Also available in paperback from Dell
A Newbery Medal honor book, 1972

"Story of an unhappy adolescent's preoccupation with the occult, her relationships with her step-siblings, and her eventual acceptance of the tangible world. Set in present-day California." Publisher's note

"The author portrays children with acute understanding, evident both in her delineation of Amanda and David and of the distinctively different younger children. Good style, good characterization, good dialogue, good story." Sutherland. The Best in Child Books

Libby on Wednesdays. Delacorte Press 1990 196p hardcover o.p. paperback available $4.99 (5 and up)   **Fic**
1. Authorship—Fiction   2. Friendship—Fiction
3. School stories
ISBN 0-440-40498-3 (pa)   LC 89-34959

"Libby, age eleven, very bright and the only child in an unconventional but strong household, has heretofore been home-educated. She is enrolled in public school for 'socialization' but soon finds that her peers tease her and mock her enormous wealth of knowledge. Only when she is selected for a writer's group does she forge ties

to some equally gifted students." Child Book Rev Serv

"Vivid descriptions and clear portraits of the characters give an honest, forthright picture of these classmate-turned-friends who come to accept their difficulties and to care about each other. It's an absorbing story, filled with real young people and genuine concerns." SLJ

The runaways. Delacorte Press 1999 245p $15.95; pa $4.99 (4 and up)   **Fic**
1. Runaway children—Fiction 2. Nevada—Fiction
ISBN 0-385-32599-1; 0-440-41512-8 (pa)
                                              LC 98-22258

Twelve-year-old Dani hates living in the small desert town of Rattler Springs, Nevada, but her plans to run away get complicated when nine-year-old Stormy and an imaginative new girl named Pixie decide they want to go along

"The book is set in the 1950s, and the dying town and desperate people are very real and touching. The plight of these creative and neglected children will keep readers turning the pages." SLJ

The witches of Worm; illustrated by Alton Raible. Atheneum Pubs. 1972 183p il $17 (5 and up)   **Fic**
1. Witchcraft—Fiction 2. Cats—Fiction
ISBN 0-689-30066-2
Also available in paperback from Dell
A Newbery Medal honor book, 1973

Jessica, the neglected child of a divorcee, "finds a deserted, new-born kitten which she calls 'Worm' since it is virtually hairless and blind. When this Worm turns—daily becoming more dominant over its mistress—Jessica is convinced she is in the grip of a hellish force that makes her play harmful tricks on her mother and on her few friends." Publ Wkly

"This is a haunting story of the power of mind and ritual, as well as of misunderstanding, anger, loneliness and friendship. It is written with humor, pace, a sure feeling for conversation and a warm understanding of human nature." Commonweal

Sobol, Donald J., 1924-

Encyclopedia Brown, boy detective; illustrated by Leonard Shortall. Dutton Children's Bks. 1963 88p il o.p.; Bantam Bks. paperback available $4.50 (3-5)   **Fic**
1. Mystery fiction
ISBN 0-553-15724-8 (pa)
First published by Thomas Nelson

"Leroy Brown earns his nickname by applying his encyclopedic learning to community mysteries. The reader is asked to anticipate solutions before checking them in the back of the book." Natl Counc of Teach of Engl. Adventuring with Books. 2d edition

"The answers are logical; some are tricky, but there are no trick questions, and readers who like puzzles should enjoy the . . . challenge. The episodes are lightly humorous, brief, and simply written." Bull Cent Child Books

Other available titles about Encyclopedia Brown are:
Encyclopedia Brown and the case of the dead eagles (1975)
Encyclopedia Brown and the case of the disgusting sneakers (1990)

Sobol, Donald J., 1924-—*Continued*
Encyclopedia Brown and the case of the midnight visitor (1977)
Encyclopedia Brown and the case of the mysterious handprints (1985)
Encyclopedia Brown and the case of Pablo's nose (1996)
Encyclopedia Brown and the case of the secret pitch (1965)
Encyclopedia Brown and the case of the sleeping dog (1998)
Encyclopedia Brown and the case of the slippery salamander (1999)
Encyclopedia Brown and the case of the treasure hunt (1988)
Encyclopedia Brown and the case of the two spies (1994)
Encyclopedia Brown finds the clues (1966)
Encyclopedia Brown gets his man (1967)
Encyclopedia Brown keeps the peace (1969)
Encyclopedia Brown lends a hand (1974)
Encyclopedia Brown saves the day (1970)
Encyclopedia Brown sets the pace (1982)
Encyclopedia Brown shows the way (1972)
Encyclopedia Brown solves them all (1968)
Encyclopedia Brown takes the cake! (1983)
Encyclopedia Brown takes the case (1973)
Encyclopedia Brown tracks them down (1971)

Soto, Gary
Taking sides. Harcourt Brace Jovanovich 1991 138p $17; pa $8 (5 and up)   **Fic**
1. Hispanic Americans—Fiction 2. Basketball—Fiction
ISBN 0-15-284076-1; 0-15-284077-X (pa)
LC 91-11082
Fourteen-year-old Lincoln Mendoza, an aspiring basketball player, must come to terms with his divided loyalties when he moves from the Hispanic inner city to a white suburban neighborhood
This is a "light but appealing story. . . . Because of its subject matter and its clear, straightforward prose, it will be especially good for reluctant readers." SLJ
Includes glossary

Speare, Elizabeth George, 1908-1994
The bronze bow. Houghton Mifflin 1961 255p $16; pa $6.95 (6 and up)   **Fic**
1. Jesus Christ—Fiction 2. Christianity—Fiction 3. Palestine—Fiction
ISBN 0-395-07113-5; 0-395-13719-5 (pa)
Awarded the Newbery Medal, 1962
"A book about the days of the early Christians. A vividly written story of a young Jewish rebel who was won over to the gentle teachings of Jesus. Daniel had sworn vengence against the Romans who had killed his parents, and he had become one of a band of outlaws. Forced to return to the village to care for his sister, Daniel found ways—dangerous ways—to work against the Roman soldiers. Each time he saw the Rabbi Jesus, the youth was drawn to his cause; at last he resolved his own conflict by giving up his hatred and, as a follower of the Master, accepting his enemies. The story has drama and pace, fine characterization, and colorful background detail; the theme of conflict and conversion is handled with restraint and perception." Bull Cent Child Books

The sign of the beaver. Houghton Mifflin 1983 135p $16 (5 and up)   **Fic**
1. Frontier and pioneer life—Fiction 2. Native Americans—Fiction 3. Friendship—Fiction
ISBN 0-395-33890-5   LC 83-118
Also available in paperback from Dell and Audiobook version
A Newbery Medal honor book, 1984
Left alone to guard the family's wilderness home in eighteenth-century Maine, Matt is hard-pressed to survive until local Indians teach him their skills
Matt "begins to understand the Indians' ingenuity and respect for nature and the devastating impact of the encroachment of the white man. In a quiet but not unsuspenseful story . . . the author articulates historical facts along with the adventures and the thoughts, emotions, and developing insights of a young adolescent." Horn Book

The witch of Blackbird Pond. Houghton Mifflin 1958 249p $16 (6 and up)   **Fic**
1. Connecticut—History—1600-1775, Colonial period—Fiction 2. Witchcraft—Fiction 3. Puritans—Fiction
ISBN 0-395-07114-3   LC 58-11063
Also available in paperback from Dell
Awarded the Newbery Medal, 1959
"Headstrong and undisciplined, Barbados-bred Kit Tyler is an embarrassment to her Puritan relatives, and her sincere attempts to aid a reputed witch soon bring her to trial as a suspect." Child Books Too Good to Miss

Sperry, Armstrong, 1897-1976
Call it courage; illustrations by the author. Macmillan 1940 95p il $16; pa $4.99 (5 and up)   **Fic**
1. Polynesia—Fiction
ISBN 0-02-786030-2; 0-689-71391-6 (pa)
Also available Audiobook version; Spanish language edition also available
Awarded the Newbery Medal, 1941
"Because he fears the ocean, a Polynesian boy is scorned by his people and must redeem himself by an act of courage. His lone journey to a sacred island and the dangers he faces there earn him the name Mafatu, 'Stout Heart.' Dramatic illustrations add atmosphere and mystery." Hodges. Books for Elem Sch Libr

Spinelli, Jerry, 1941-
Crash. Knopf 1996 162p $16; pa $4.99 (5 and up)   **Fic**
1. Football—Fiction 2. Grandfathers—Fiction 3. Friendship—Fiction
ISBN 0-679-87957-9; 0-679-88550-1 (pa)
LC 95-30942
"Crash is a star football player. He torments Penn, a classmate who is everything Crash is not—friendly, small, and a pacifist. When his beloved grandfather comes to live with his family and suffers a debilitating stroke, Crash begins to see value in many of the things he has scorned." Horn Book Guide
"Readers will devour this humorous glimpse at what jocks are made of while learning that life does not require crashing helmet-headed through it." SLJ

Spinelli, Jerry, 1941——*Continued*

Maniac Magee; a novel. Little, Brown 1990 184p $14.95; pa $5.95 (5 and up)   **Fic**
1. Orphans—Fiction 2. Homeless persons—Fiction 3. Race relations—Fiction
ISBN 0-316-80722-2; 0-316-80906-3 (pa)
LC 89-27144
Awarded the Newbery Medal, 1991
"Orphaned at three, Jeffery Lionel Magee, after eight unhappy years with relatives, one day takes off running. A year later, he ends up 200 miles away in Two Mills, a highly segregated community. Part tall tale and part contemporary realistic fiction, this unusual novel magically weaves timely issues of homelessness, racial prejudice, and illiteracy into an energetic story that bursts with creativity, enthusiasm, and hope for the future. In short, it's a celebration of life." Booklist

There's a girl in my hammerlock. Simon & Schuster Bks. for Young Readers 1991 199p hardcover o.p. paperback available $4.99 (5 and up)   **Fic**
1. Wrestling—Fiction 2. Sex role—Fiction 3. School stories
ISBN 0-671-86695-8 (pa)   LC 91-8765
Thirteen-year-old Maisie joins her school's formerly all-male wrestling team and tries to last through the season, despite opposition from other students, her best friend, and her own teammates
The author "tackles a meaty subject—traditional gender roles—with his usual humor and finesse. The result, written in a breezy, first-person style, is a rattling good sports story that is clever, witty and tightly written." Publ Wkly

Wringer. HarperCollins Pubs. 1997 228p $15.95; lib bdg $15.89; pa $5.95 (4 and up)   **Fic**
1. Courage—Fiction 2. Violence—Fiction 3. Pigeons—Fiction
ISBN 0-06-024913-7; 0-06-024914-5 (lib bdg); 0-06-440578-8 (pa)   LC 96-37897
A Newbery Medal honor book, 1998
"Joanna Cotler books"
"During the annual pigeon shoot, it is a town tradition for 10-year-old boys to break the necks of wounded birds. In this riveting story told with verve and suspense, Palmer rebels." SLJ

Spinner, Stephanie, 1943-
Be first in the universe; [by] Stephanie Spinner and Terry Bisson. Delacorte Press 2000 133p $14.95 (4-6)   **Fic**
1. Twins—Fiction 2. Extraterrestrial beings—Fiction 3. Science fiction
ISBN 0-385-32687-4   LC 99-39933
While staying with their hippie grandparents, ten-year-old twins, Tod and Tessa, discover an unusual shop at the nearby mall, where they find a lie-detecting electronic pet, a Do-Right machine, and other alien gadgets which help them foil their nemeses, the evil Gneiss twins
"Spinner and Bisson . . . write with verve and wit, and a good time will be had by all." Booklist

Spyri, Johanna, 1827-1901
Heidi (4 and up)   **Fic**
1. Alps—Fiction 2. Switzerland—Fiction

Also available Audiobook version
Some editions are:
Grosset & Dunlap (Illustrated junior library) $15.99 Illustrated by William Sharp (ISBN 0-448-40563-6)
Morrow Junior Bks. (Books of Wonder) $24.95 Illustrated by Jessie W. Smith (ISBN 0-688-14519-1)
First published 1880
"The story of Heidi is the story of the greatness of her affection for her pet goats, for Peter and her grandfather, and for her mountain home. Permeating the whole tale is the play of sunshine and shadow on the slopes of the jagged peaks of the great, glittering, snow-capped mountains of Heidi's [Swiss] Alpine home. A book which finds a responsive chord in every young heart." Toronto Public Libr

Stanek, Muriel
I speak English for my mom; illustrations by Judith Friedman. Whitman, A. 1989 unp il lib bdg $13.95 (2-4)   **Fic**
1. Mexican Americans—Fiction 2. Mother-daughter relationship—Fiction
ISBN 0-8075-3659-8   LC 88-20546
Lupe, a young Mexican American, must translate for her mother who speaks only Spanish until Mrs. Gomez decides to learn English in order to get a better job
"Stanek provides a nicely rounded look at a situation common to immigrant families." Booklist

Stanley, Diane, 1943-
Roughing it on the Oregon Trail; illustrated by Holly Berry. HarperCollins Pubs. 2000 unp (Time-traveling twins) $15.95; lib bdg $15.89 (2-4)   **Fic**
1. Oregon Trail—Fiction 2. Overland journeys to the Pacific—Fiction 3. Frontier and pioneer life—Fiction
ISBN 0-06-027065-9; 0-06-027066-7 (lib bdg)
LC 98-41711
"Joanna Cotler Books"
Twins Liz and Lenny, along with their time-traveling grandmother, join a group of pioneers journeying west on the Oregon Trail in 1843
"An engaging trip and a painless history lesson." SLJ

Steig, William, 1907-
Abel's island. Farrar, Straus & Giroux 1976 117p il $15; pa $4.95 (3-5)   **Fic**
1. Mice—Fiction 2. Survival after airplane accidents, shipwrecks, etc.—Fiction
ISBN 0-374-30010-0; 0-374-40016-4 (pa)
"Abel is a mouse who lives in cultured comfort on an inherited income and dotes on his bride Amanda. Ever gentlemanly, Abel leaves the safety of a cave (they've taken shelter while on a picnic) to rescue Amanda's gauzy scarf. He is swept off by wind and rain, catapulted into a torrent of water, and lands on an island. This is really sort of a Robinson Crusoe Tale, as the heretofore pampered and indolent Abel learns to cope with solitude,

Steig, William, 1907-—*Continued*

find food and shelter, avoid a predatory owl, and eventually find his way back—a year later—to his loving wife and luxurious home." Bull Cent Child Books

"The line drawings washed with gray faithfully and delightfully record not only the rigors of Abel's experiences but the refinement of his domestic existence." Horn Book

Dominic; story and pictures by William Steig. Farrar, Straus & Giroux 1972 145p il hardcover o.p. paperback available $4.95 (3-5)   **Fic**

1. Dogs—Fiction

ISBN 0-374-41826-8 (pa)

Dominic, a gregarious dog, sets out on the high road one day, going no place in particular, but moving along to find whatever he can. And that turns out to be plenty, including an invalid pig who leaves Dominic his fortune; a variety of friends and adventures; and even—in the end—his life's companion

"A singular blend of naïveté and sophistication, comic commentary and philosophizing, the narrative handles situation clichés with humor and flair—perhaps because of the author's felicitous turn of phrase, his verbal cartooning, and his integration of text and illustrations. A chivalrous and optimistic tribute to gallantry and romance." Horn Book

The real thief; story and pictures by William Steig. Farrar, Straus & Giroux 1973 58p il hardcover o.p. paperback available $3.95 (3-5)   **Fic**

1. Animals—Fiction 2. Thieves—Fiction

ISBN 0-374-46208-9 (pa)

"Proud of his job as guard to the Royal Treasury, loyal to his king (Basil the bear) Gawain the goose is baffled by the repeated theft of gold and jewels from the massive building to which only Gawain and Basil have keys. He is heartsick when the king dismisses him publicly and calls him a disgrace to the kingdom. Sentenced to prison, the goose flies off to isolation. The true thief, a mouse, is penitent and decides that he will go on stealing so that the king will know Gawain is innocent." Bull Cent Child Books

"Steig's gray line-and-wash drawings provide a charming accompaniment to a wholly winning story." SLJ

Stevenson, Robert Louis, 1850-1894

The strange case of Dr. Jekyll and Mr. Hyde; illustrations by François Place. Viking 2000 105p il (Whole story) $25.99 (5 and up)   **Fic**

ISBN 0-670-88865-6   LC 99-75659

First published 1886; this illustrated edition published 1999 in France

"The story follows Dr. Jekyll, by day a respectable doctor, who by night roams the back alleys of London as a monstrous criminal." Publisher's note

"This edition of Stevenson's classic tale gives the flavor of late Victorian England through its lively ink-and-watercolor illustrations and plentiful reproductions of period photos, sketches, engravings, and paintings. Marginal notes comment on Stevenson and on aspects of the story and of Victorian culture that might be obscure to modern readers." Booklist

Treasure Island (6 and up)   **Fic**

1. Buried treasure—Fiction 2. Pirates—Fiction

Also available Spanish language edition
Some editions are:

Grosset & Dunlap (Illustrated junior library) $15.99 Illustrated by Norman Price (ISBN 0-448-06025-6)

Knopf (Everyman's library children's classics) $14.95 Illustrated by Mervyn Peake (ISBN 0-679-41800-8)

Scribner $28 Illustrated by N. C. Wyeth (ISBN 0-684-17160-0)

First published 1882

Young Jim Hawkins discovers a treasure map in the chest of an old sailor who dies under mysterious circumstances at his mother's inn. He shows it to Dr. Livesey and Squire Trelawney who agree to outfit a ship and sail to Treasure Island. Among the crew are the pirate Long John Silver and his followers who are in pursuit of the treasure

"A masterpiece among romances. . . . Pew, Black Dog, and Long John Silver are a villainous trio, strongly individualized, shedding an atmosphere of malignancy and terror. The scenery of isle and ocean contrasts vividly with the savagery of the action." Baker. Guide to the Best Fic

Stolz, Mary, 1920-

A dog on Barkham Street; pictures by Leonard Shortall. Harper & Row 1960 184p il lib bdg $15.89; pa $4.95 (4-6)   **Fic**

1. Dogs—Fiction

ISBN 0-06-025841-1 (lib bdg); 0-06-440160-X (pa)

"Fifth-grader Edward Frost has two seemingly insurmountable problems—to rid himself of the constant tormenting by the bully who lives next door and to convince his parents that he is responsible enough to have a dog. It is the coming of his irresponsible vagabond uncle with a beautiful young collie that precipitates the solution of Edward's problems." Booklist

"Simple, everyday events and very familiar people make up this story, but there is nothing ordinary about the way those ingredients are assembled. . . . This author has a remarkable ability to get inside her characters, whether they are young boys, adolescent girls, parents or hobos, and the result in this book is a reading experience as sharp as reality." Horn Book

Another available title about Edward Frost and Martin Hastings is:

The bully of Barkham Street (1963)

Go fish; illustrated by Pat Cummings. HarperCollins Pubs. 1991 69p il lib bdg $14.89; pa $4.50 (2-4)   **Fic**

1. Grandfathers—Fiction   2. Fishing—Fiction
3. African Americans—Fiction

ISBN 0-06-025822-5 (lib bdg); 0-06-440466-8 (pa)
                    LC 90-4860

Companion volume to Storm in the night

After spending the day fishing in the Gulf of Mexico with Grandfather, eight-year-old Thomas has a quiet evening on the porch hearing more about his African heritage

"The text is easy to read, laced with gentle humor, and designed with rounded, black-and-white pictures in

Stolz, Mary, 1920-—*Continued*

a pop-art style. . . . A book that's all the more effective for its low-key, companionable tone." Bull Cent Child Books

Another available title about Thomas and his grandfather is:
Stealing home (1992)

Strickland, Brad

The hand of the necromancer; frontispiece by Edward Gorey. Dial Bks. for Young Readers 1996 168p lib bdg $14.89; pa $4.99 (5 and up)   Fic
1. Mystery fiction
ISBN 0-8037-1830-6 (lib bdg); 0-14-038695-5 (pa)
LC 95-47222
Continues John Bellairs' series about Johnny Dixon and Professor Childermass
Thirteen-year-old Johnny Dixon and his friend Professor Childermass battle an evil wizard for possession of a bewitched hand which can be used to rule the world
Other available titles about Johnny Dixon and Professor Childermass by Brad Strickland are:
The bell, the book and the spellbinder (1997)
The wrath of the grinning ghost (1999)

John Bellairs's Lewis Barnavelt in The specter from the magician's museum; frontispiece by Edward Gorey. Dial Bks. for Young Readers 1998 149p $15.99; pa $5.99 (5 and up)   Fic
1. Witchcraft—Fiction
ISBN 0-8037-2202-8; 0-14-038652-1 (pa)
LC 97-47167
Continues John Bellairs' series about Lewis Barnavelt
When the evil sorceress Belle Frisson ensnares Rose Rita Pottinger in a magic web in order to steal her life force, Lewis Barnavelt must risk his own life to save his friend
Other available titles about Lewis Barnavelt by Brad Strickland are:
The beast under the wizard's bridge (2000)
The tower at the end of the world (2001)

Tate, Eleanora E., 1948-

Thank you, Dr. Martin Luther King, Jr.! Watts 1990 237p o.p.; Bantam Bks. paperback available $4.99 (4 and up)   Fic
1. African Americans—Fiction
ISBN 0-553-15886-4 (pa)   LC 89-70665
"Fourth grader Mary Elouise Avery struggles with a low self-image in this consciousness-raising story of black pride. When Gumbo Grove Elementary School prepares for its annual Presidents' Month play, Mary Elouise is selected as narrator for the new black history segment. . . . By story's end, her part in the play has given Mary Elouise a better understanding of her heritage." SLJ
"Tate tackles a sensitive issue, taking pains to keep characters multidimensional and human. . . . Clear-eyed and accessible." Booklist
Another available title about Gumbo Grove is:
The secret of Gumbo Grove (1967)

Taylor, Mildred D.

The friendship; pictures by Max Ginsburg. Dial Bks. for Young Readers 1987 53p il $15.99; pa $4.99 (4 and up)   Fic
1. African Americans—Fiction 2. Race relations—Fiction 3. Mississippi—Fiction
ISBN 0-8037-0417-8; 0-14-038964-4 (pa)
LC 86-29309
Coretta Scott King Award for text, 1988
This "story about race relations in rural Mississippi during the Depression focuses on an incident between an old Black man, Mr. Tom Bee, and a white storekeeper, Mr. John Wallace. Indebted to Tom for saving his life as a young man, John had promised they would always be friends. But now, years later, John insists that Tom call him 'Mister' and shoots the old man for defiantly—and publicly—calling him by his first name. Narrator Cassie Logan and her brothers . . . are verbally abused by Wallace's villainous sons before witnessing the encounter." Bull Cent Child Books

The gold Cadillac; pictures by Michael Hays. Dial Bks. for Young Readers 1987 43p il $15.99; pa $4.99 (4 and up)   Fic
1. African Americans—Fiction 2. Prejudices—Fiction 3. Race relations—Fiction
ISBN 0-8037-0342-2; 0-14-038963-6 (pa)
LC 86-11526
"The shiny gold Cadillac that Daddy brings home one summer evening marks a stepping stone in the lives of Wilma and 'lois, two black sisters growing up in Ohio during the fifties. At first neighbors and relatives shower them with attention. But when the family begins the long journey to the South to show off the car to their Mississippi relatives, the girls, for the first time, encounter the undisguised ugliness of racial prejudice." Horn Book
"Full-page sepia paintings effectively portray the characters, setting, and mood of the story events as Hays ably demonstrates his understanding of the social and emotional environments which existed for blacks during this period." SLJ

Let the circle be unbroken. Dial Bks. for Young Readers 1981 394p $16.99; pa $4.99 (4 and up)   Fic
1. African Americans—Fiction 2. Mississippi—Fiction 3. Great Depression, 1929-1939—Fiction
ISBN 0-8037-4748-9; 0-14-034892-1 (pa)
LC 81-65854
This novel featuring the Logans covers "a series of tangential events so that it is a family record, a picture of the depression years in rural Mississippi, and an indictment of black-white relations in the Deep South. A young friend is convicted of a murder of which he is innocent, a pretty cousin is insulted by some white boys and her father taunted because he married a white woman, an elderly neighbor tries to vote, the government pays farmers to plow their crops under, etc." Bull Cent Child Books
The author "provides her readers with a literal sense of witnessing important American history. . . . Moreover, [she] never neglects the details of her volatile 9-year-old heroine's interior life. The daydreams, the jealousy, the incredible ardor of that age come alive." N Y Times Book Rev

Taylor, Mildred D.—*Continued*

Mississippi bridge; by Mildred Taylor; pictures by Max Ginsburg. Dial Bks. for Young Readers 1990 62p il hardcover o.p. paperback available $4.99 (4 and up)   **Fic**
  1. Race relations—Fiction 2. African Americans—Fiction 3. Prejudices—Fiction 4. Mississippi—Fiction
ISBN 0-14-130817-6 (pa)   LC 89-27898
In this story featuring the children of Mississippi's Logan family, "Jeremy Simms, a 10-year-old white neighbor, describes a harrowing incident after the Logans and other blacks are ordered off the weekly bus in a foggy rainstorm." N Y Times Book Rev
"Taylor has shaped this episode into a haunting meditation that will leave readers vividly informed about segregation practices and the unequal rights that prevailed in that era. . . . The incident and its context constitute a telling piece of social history." Booklist

The road to Memphis; by Mildred Taylor. Dial Bks. 1989 290p $15; pa $5.99 (4 and up)   **Fic**
  1. Race relations—Fiction 2. African Americans—Fiction 3. Mississippi—Fiction
ISBN 0-8037-0340-6; 0-14-036077-8 (pa)
LC 88-33654
Coretta Scott King award for text, 1989
Sadistically teased by two white boys in 1940's rural Mississippi, Cassie Logan's friend, Moe, severely injures one of the boys with a tire iron and enlists Cassie's help in trying to flee the state
"Taylor's continued smooth, easy language provides readability for all ages, with a focus on universal human pride, worthy values, and individual responsibility. This action-packed drama is highly recommended." Voice Youth Advocates

Roll of thunder, hear my cry; frontispiece by Jerry Pinkney. Dial Bks. for Young Readers 1976 276p $16.99; pa $5.99 (4 and up)   **Fic**
  1. African Americans—Fiction 2. Great Depression, 1929-1939—Fiction 3. Mississippi—Fiction
ISBN 0-8037-7473-7; 0-14-038451-0 (pa)
Awarded the Newbery Medal, 1977
"The time is 1933. The place is Spokane, Mississippi where the Logans, the only black family who own their own land, wage a courageous struggle to remain independent, displeasing a white plantation owner bent on taking their land. But this suspenseful tale is also about the story's young narrator, Cassie, and her three brothers who decide to wage their own personal battles to maintain the self-dignity and pride with which they were raised. . . . Ms. Taylor's richly textured novel shows a strong, proud black family . . . resisting rather than succumbing to oppression." Child Book Rev Serv

Song of the trees; pictures by Jerry Pinkney. Dial Bks. for Young Readers 1975 48p il $15.99; pa $3.99 (4 and up)   **Fic**
  1. African Americans—Fiction 2. Great Depression, 1929-1939—Fiction 3. Mississippi—Fiction
ISBN 0-8037-5452-3; 0-440-41396-6 (pa)
Eight-year-old Cassie Logan tells how her family "leaving Mississippi during the Depression was cheated into selling for practically nothing valuable and beautiful giant old pines and hickories, beeches and walnuts in the forest surrounding their house." Adventuring with Books

The well; David's story. Dial Bks. for Young Readers 1995 92p $14.99; pa $4.99 (4 and up)
Fic
  1. African Americans—Fiction 2. Race relations—Fiction 3. Mississippi—Fiction
ISBN 0-8037-1802-0; 0-14-038642-4 (pa)
LC 94-25360
"David Logan (Cassie's father) tells this story from his childhood. . . . There's a drought, and the Logans possess the only well in the area that has not gone dry. Black and white alike come for water freely given by the family, but the Simms boys can't seem to stand the necessary charity, and their resentment explodes when David's big brother Hammer beats Charlie Simms after Charlie hits David." Bull Cent Child Books
This story "delivers an emotional wallop in a concentrated span of time and action. . . . This story reverberates in the heart long after the final paragraph is read." Horn Book

Taylor, Sydney, 1904-1978

All-of-a-kind family; illustrated by Helen John. Follett 1951 192p il o.p.; Dell paperback available $4.995 (4-6)   **Fic**
  1. Jews—Fiction 2. New York (N.Y.)—Fiction
ISBN 0-440-40059-4 (pa)
Also available Audiobook version
"Five little Jewish girls grow up in New York's lower east side in a happy home atmosphere before the first World War." Carnegie Libr of Pittsburgh
"A genuine and delightful picture of a Jewish family . . . with an understanding mother and father, rich in kindness and fun though poor in money. The important part the public library played in the lives of these children is happily evident; and the Jewish holiday celebrations are particularly well described." Horn Book
  Other available titles about this family are:
All-of-a-kind family downtown (1957)
All-of-a-kind family uptown (1957)
Ella of all-of-a-kind family (1978)
More all-of-a-kind family (1954)

Taylor, Theodore, 1921-

The cay. Delacorte Press c1969 137p $16.95 (5 and up)   **Fic**
  1. Race relations—Fiction 2. Caribbean region—Fiction 3. Survival after airplane accidents, shipwrecks, etc.—Fiction 4. Blind—Fiction
ISBN 0-385-07906-0
Also available in paperback from HarperCollins and Audiobook version
"When the freighter which was to take Phillip and his mother from wartime Curacao to the United States is torpedoed, Phillip finds himself afloat on a small raft with a huge, old, very black West Indian man. Phillip becomes blind from injuries and resents his dependence upon old Timothy. Through exciting adventures on a very small cay (coral island), Phillip learns to overcome his prejudice toward Timothy and to see him as a man and a friend. Following the aftermath of a fierce tropical storm, Timothy dies. Phillip survives to live a more complete life because of his friend and because he has grown with the changes that occurred in his life." Read Ladders for Hum Relat. 5th edition
Followed by Timothy of the cay

Taylor, Theodore, 1921-—*Continued*

Timothy of the cay. Harcourt Brace & Co. 1993
161p $13.95 (5 and up)   **Fic**
  1. Race relations—Fiction 2. Caribbean region—Fiction 3. Survival after airplane accidents, shipwrecks,
etc.—Fiction 4. Blind—Fiction
  ISBN 0-15-288358-4   LC 93-7898
Also available in paperback from HarperCollins
Sequel to The cay
Having survived being blinded and shipwrecked on a
tiny Caribbean island with the old black man Timothy,
twelve-year-old white Phillip is rescued and hopes to regain his sight with an operation. Alternate chapters follow the life of Timothy from his days as a young cabin
boy
  "Somewhat more thoughtful than its well-loved ante-
cedent, this boldly drawn novel is no less commanding."
Publ Wkly

The trouble with Tuck. Doubleday 1981 110p
$15.95; pa $4.50 (5 and up)   **Fic**
  1. Dogs—Fiction 2. Blind—Fiction
  ISBN 0-385-17774-7; 0-440-41696-5 (pa)
                                            LC 81-43139
Helen trains her blind dog Tuck to follow and trust a
seeing-eye companion dog
This is "a touching dog story, written with good flow,
pace, and structure." Bull Cent Child Books
  Another available title about Helen and Tuck is:
Tuck triumphant (1991)

Temple, Frances, 1945-1995

Grab hands and run. Orchard Bks. 1993 165p
$15.95; lib bdg $16.99 (6 and up)   **Fic**
  1. El Salvador—Fiction 2. Refugees—Fiction 3. Canada—Fiction
  ISBN 0-531-05480-2; 0-531-08630-5 (lib bdg)
                                           LC 92-34063
Also available in paperback from HarperCollins
"A Richard Jackson book"
After his father disappears, twelve-year-old Felipe, his
mother, and his younger sister set out on a difficult and
dangerous journey, trying to make their way from their
home in El Salvador to Canada
  "The taut and absorbing escape is made all the more
real by the fully fleshed out characters and heart-stopping
situations." SLJ

The Ramsay scallop; a novel. Orchard Bks.
1994 310p $18.95; lib bdg $19.99 (6 and up)
                                                Fic
  1. Middle Ages—Fiction 2. Pilgrims and pilgrim-
ages—Fiction
  ISBN 0-531-06836-6; 0-531-08686-0 (lib bdg)
                                           LC 93-29697
Also available in paperback from HarperCollins
"A Richard Jackson book"
At the turn of the fourteenth century in England, fourteen-year-old Elenor finds her betrothal to an ambitious
lord's son launching her on a memorable pilgrimage to
far-off Spain
  "With a nod to *The Canterbury Tales*, the book high-

lights the stories that their fellow pilgrims share with
Elenor and Thomas; the stories are sad, romantic, and instructive, and all help shape the journey into the special
thing it becomes for the duo. . . . The leisurely pace of
the pilgrimage allows the author to introduce a large cast
of characters and to decorate her story with historical details that enlighten and intrigue." Booklist

Tonight, by sea; a novel. Orchard Bks. 1995
152p $15.95; lib bdg $16.99 (6 and up)   **Fic**
  1. Haiti—Fiction 2. Refugees—Fiction
  ISBN 0-531-06899-4; 0-531-08749-2 (lib bdg)
                                           LC 94-32167
Also available in paperback from HarperCollins
"A Richard Jackson book"
As governmental brutality and poverty become unbearable, Paulie joins with others in her small Haitian
village to help her uncle secretly build a boat they will
use to try to escape to the United States
  "In an elegant prose style [the author] captures the
lyrical cadence of Creole speech and paints an affecting
portrait of a proud, resourceful people trying to survive
in the face of lawlessness and tyranny." SLJ

Thomas, Jane Resh, 1936-

The comeback dog; drawings by Troy Howell.
Clarion Bks. 1981 62p il $16 (3-5)   **Fic**
  1. Dogs—Fiction 2. Farm life—Fiction
  ISBN 0-395-29432-0   LC 80-12886
Also available in paperback from Bantam Bks.
  "Grieving over the loss of his dog, Daniel claims he
doesn't want another dog, but when he finds one that is
near death, he takes her home and gives her loving care.
The dog, Lady, gets well but seems fearful and hostile;
irritated, Daniel lets her off the leash to run away. When
she comes back, some weeks later, her face bristling with
porcupine quills, he's again irritated but quickly decides
to help Lady and is then gratified when she shows trust
and affection." Bull Cent Child Books
  "The matter-of-fact, life-must-go-on attitude of Daniel's concerned parents is particularly well communicat-
ed. . . . Numerous soft pencil drawings greatly enhance
the exceptionally gentle, poignant story." Horn Book

Thompson, Kate

Switchers. Hyperion Bks. for Children 1998
219p $14.95; pa $5.99 (6 and up)   **Fic**
  1. Weather—Fiction 2. Supernatural—Fiction 3. Arctic regions—Fiction
  ISBN 0-7868-0380-0; 0-7868-1396-2 (pa)
                                           LC 97-33056
Also available Audiobook version
When freakish weather grips the Arctic regions and
moves southward Tess and Kevin save the world from
disaster through their ability to switch into animal forms
  "A terrific read that's sure to keep youngsters turning
pages. . . . This tale will incite imaginations and provide
a launching pad for discussion." SLJ
Followed by Midnight's choice (1999)

Thurber, James, 1894-1961

Many moons; illustrated by Louis Slobodkin.
Harcourt Brace 1943 unp il $16; pa $7 (1-4)
                                                Fic
  1. Fairy tales
  ISBN 0-15-251873-8; 0-15-251877-9 (pa)

Thurber, James, 1894-1961—*Continued*
Also available with illustrations by Marc Simont for $14.95 (ISBN 0-15-251872-X); pa $7 (ISBN 0-15-201895-6)

Awarded the Caldecott Medal, 1944

This is "the story of a little princess who fell ill of a surfeit of raspberry tarts and would get well only if she could have the moon. The solving of this baffling court problem, how to get the moon, results in an original and entertaining picture-storybook." Booklist

"Louis Slobodkin's pictures float on the pages in four colors: black and white cannot represent them. They are the substance of dreams . . . the long thoughts little children, and some adults wise as they, have about life." N Y Her Trib Books

Tolan, Stephanie S., 1942-
Save Halloween! Morrow Junior Bks. 1993 168p $16; pa $4.95 (5 and up)   **Fic**
1. Halloween—Fiction 2. Christian life—Fiction 3. School stories
ISBN 0-688-12168-3; 0-688-15497-2 (pa)
                     LC 93-10635

Eleven-year-old Johnna, who is deeply involved in the sixth grade Halloween pageant although her family views it as a celebration of an un-Christian holiday, decides that she must follow her own beliefs

"Thoughtful, pithy, and entertaining, this will intrigue readers from cover to cover." Booklist

Tolkien, J. R. R. (John Ronald Reuel), 1892-1973
The hobbit; or, There and back again; illustrated by the author. Houghton Mifflin 1938 310p il $16; pa $12 (4 and up)   **Fic**
1. Fantasy fiction
ISBN 0-395-07122-4; 0-618-00221-9 (pa)

Also available from Houghton Mifflin in an edition with illustrations by Michael Hague for $29.95 (ISBN 0-395-36290-3); pa $17.95 (ISBN 0-395-52021-5); Audiobook version also available

First published 1937 in the United Kingdom

"This fantasy features the adventures of hobbit Bilbo Baggins, who joins a band of dwarfs led by Gandalf the Wizard. Together they seek to recover the stolen treasure that is hidden in Lonely Mountain and guarded by Smaug the Dragon." Shapiro. Fic for Youth. 2d edition

Followed by The lord of the rings, a trilogy intended for older readers

Tomlinson, Theresa
The Forestwife. Orchard Bks. 1995 170p $16.95; lib bdg $17.99 (6 and up)   **Fic**
1. Maid Marian (Legendary character)—Fiction 2. Robin Hood (Legendary character)—Fiction 3. Great Britain—Fiction
ISBN 0-531-09450-2; 0-531-08750-6 (lib bdg)
                     LC 94-33007

In England during the reign of King Richard I, fifteen-year-old Marian escapes from an arranged marriage to live with a community of forest folk that includes a daring young outlaw named Robert

"This exciting book is based on Medieval folk tales of the Green Lady and Green Man and Robin Hood. . . . The book is full of strong, memorable characters, action, and vivid descriptions with an underlying love story." Voice Youth Advocates

Travers, P. L. (Pamela L.), 1899-1996
Mary Poppins; illustrated by Mary Shepard. rev ed. Harcourt Brace & Co. 1997 c1981 202p il $18; pa $6 (4-6)   **Fic**
1. Fantasy fiction
ISBN 0-15-252595-5; 0-15-201717-8 (pa)
                     LC 97-223987

Also available in hardcover from Buccaneer Bks. and Audiobook version

First published 1934; this is a reissue of the 1981 revised edition

An extraordinary English nanny blows in on the East Wind with her parrot-headed umbrella and magic carpet-bag and introduces her charges, Jane and Michael Banks, to some delightful people and experiences

"The chapter 'Bad Tuesday,' in which Mary and the Banks children travel to the four corners of the earth and meet the inhabitants, has been criticized for portraying minorities in an unfavorable light. . . . [In] the revised edition . . . the entourage meet up with a polar bear, macaw, panda, and dolphin instead of Eskimos, Africans, Chinese, and American Indians." Booklist

Other available titles about Mary Poppins are:
Mary Poppins comes back (1935)
Mary Poppins in the park (1952)
Mary Poppins opens the door (1943)

Treviño, Elizabeth Borton de, 1904-
I, Juan de Pareja. Farrar, Straus & Giroux 1993 c1965 180p hardcover o.p. paperback available $4.95 (6 and up)   **Fic**
1. Juan, de Pareja—Fiction 2. Velázquez, Diego, 1599-1660—Fiction
ISBN 0-374-43525-1 (pa)

Also available Audiobook version

Awarded the Newbery Medal, 1966

First published 1965

The black slave boy, Juan de Pareja, "began a new life when he was taken into the household of the Spanish painter, Velázquez. As he worked beside the great artist learning how to grind and mix colors and prepare canvases, there grew between them a warm friendship based on mutual respect and love of art. Created from meager but authentic facts, the story, told by Juan, depicts the life and character of Velázquez and the loyalty of the talented seventeenth-century slave who eventually won his freedom and the right to be an artist." Booklist

Tunis, John R., 1889-1975
The Kid from Tomkinsville; illustrated by Jay Hyde Barnum. Harcourt 1940 355p il hardcover o.p. paperback available $6 (5 and up)   **Fic**
1. Baseball—Fiction
ISBN 0-15-242567-5 (pa)

As the newest addition to the Brooklyn Dodgers, young Roy Tucker's pitching helps pull the team out of a slump; but, when a freak accident ends his career as a pitcher, he must try to find another place for himself on the team

Tunis, John R., 1889-1975—*Continued*
Other available titles about Roy Tucker and the Brooklyn Dodgers are:
Keystone kids (1943)
The kid comes back (1946)
Rookie of the year (1944)
World Series (1941)

Turner, Ann Warren, 1945-
Grasshopper summer. Macmillan 1989 166p hardcover o.p. paperback available $4.99 (4-6)
Fic
1. Frontier and pioneer life—Fiction 2. South Dakota—Fiction
ISBN 0-689-83522-1 (pa)   LC 88-13847
In 1874 eleven-year-old Sam and his family move from Kentucky to the southern Dakota Territory, where harsh conditions and a plague of hungry grasshoppers threaten their chances for survival
"Carefully selected details, skillfully woven into the story line, evoke a sense of place and time. . . . Both a family story and an account of pioneer living, the book is accessible as well as informative." Horn Book

Nettie's trip South; [by] Ann Turner; illustrated by Ronald Himler. Macmillan 1987 unp il $16; pa $5.99 (3-5)
Fic
1. Slavery—Fiction
ISBN 0-02-789240-9; 0-689-80117-3 (pa)
LC 86-18135
"In 1859 Nettie is allowed to accompany her brother, who has been assigned his first newspaper story, and an older sister on the trip from Albany, New York, to Richmond. The text appears in the form of a letter Nettie writes to a friend, and . . . the story recounts her poignantly felt reactions to the viewing of slave quarters and an auction of black men and women." Horn Book
"Himler's charcoal drawings fashion scenes rich with character and emotion. . . . A vivid piece of history for early elementary students or older picture-book audiences." Booklist

Turner, Megan Whalen, 1965-
The Queen of Attolia. Greenwillow Bks. 2000 279p $15.95 (6 and up)
Fic
1. Adventure fiction 2. Thieves—Fiction
ISBN 0-688-17423-X   LC 99-26916
In this sequel to The thief, Eugenides, Royal Thief of Eddis, summons all his wit and wiles in an attempt to conquer the rival Queen of Attolia
"The intense read is thoroughly involving and wholly satisfying on all fronts." Horn Book

The thief. Greenwillow Bks. 1996 219p $15.95 (6 and up)
Fic
1. Adventure fiction 2. Thieves—Fiction
ISBN 0-688-14627-9   LC 95-41040
Also available in paperback from Puffin Bks. and Audiobook version
A Newbery Medal honor book, 1997
"Gen languishes in prison for boasting of his skill as a thief. The magus—the king's powerful advisor—needing a clever thief to find an ancient ring that gives the

owner the right to rule a neighboring country, bails Gen out. Their journey toward the treasure is marked by danger and political intrigue, and features a motley cast, tales of old gods, and the revelation of Gen's true identity." Publisher's note
"A tantalizing, suspenseful, exceptionally clever novel. . . . The author's characterization of Gen is simply superb." Horn Book
Followed by The Queen of Attolia

Twain, Mark, 1835-1910
The adventures of Huckleberry Finn (5 and up)
Fic
1. Mississippi River—Fiction 2. Missouri—Fiction

Available from various publishers including a Morrow Junior Bks./Books of Wonder edition illustrated by Steven Kellogg; Audiobook version is also available
First published in 1885
"Huck, escaping from his blackguardly father, who had imprisoned him in a lonely cabin, meets Jim, a runaway slave, on Jackson's Island in the Mississippi River. Together they float on a raft down the mighty stream. . . . Two confidence men join them and they drift into many extraordinary adventures, in the course of which Tom Sawyer reappears. Tom's Aunt Sally wants to adopt Huck, who decides he had better disappear again, lest he be 'sivilized'. . . . The struggle in Huck's soul between his 'respectable' Southern prejudices and his growing appreciation of Jim's value and dignity as a human being is an ironic and powerful indictment of the moral blindness of a slaveholding society." Herzberg. Reader's Ency of Am Lit

The adventures of Tom Sawyer (5 and up)
Fic
1. Mississippi River—Fiction 2. Missouri—Fiction

Available from various publishers including a Morrow Junior Bks./Books of Wonder edition illustrated by Barry Moser; Audiobook version is also available
First published 1876
The plot "is episodic, dealing in part with Tom's pranks in school, Sunday school, and the respectable world of his Aunt Polly, and in part with his adventures with Huck Finn, the outcast son of the local ne'er-do-well. . . . Tom and Huck witness a murder and, in terror of the murderer, Injun Joe, secretly flee to Jackson's island. They are searched for, are finally mourned for dead, and return to town in time to attend their own funeral. Tom and his sweetheart, Becky Thatcher get lost in a cave in which Injun Joe is hiding. . . . The story closely follows incidents involving Twain and his friends that occured in Hannibal, Mo." Herzberg. Reader's Ency of Am Lit
Followed by Tom Sawyer abroad (1894) and Tom Sawyer, detective (1896)

Uchida, Yoshiko, 1921-1992
A jar of dreams. Atheneum Pubs. 1981 131p $16; pa $4.99 (5 and up)
Fic
1. Japanese Americans—Fiction 2. Family life—Fiction 3. Prejudices—Fiction 4. California—Fiction
ISBN 0-689-50210-9; 0-689-71672-9 (pa)
LC 81-3480

Uchida, Yoshiko, 1921-1992—*Continued*

"A Margaret K. McElderry book"

"A story of the Depression Era is told by eleven-year-old Rinko, the only girl in a Japanese-American family living in Oakland and suffering under the double burden of financial pressure and the prejudice that had increased with the tension of economic competition. Into the household comes a visitor who is a catalyst for change." Bull Cent Child Books

"Rinko in her guilelessness is genuine and refreshing, and her worries and concerns seem wholly natural, honest, and convincing." Horn Book

Another available title about Rinko Tsujimura and her family is:

The best bad thing (1983)

Journey home; illustrated by Charles Robinson. Atheneum Pubs. 1978 131p il $16; pa $4.99 (5 and up)   **Fic**

1. Japanese Americans—Fiction 2. Prejudices—Fiction 3. Family life—Fiction
ISBN 0-689-50126-9; 0-689-70755-X (pa)
LC 78-8792

Sequel to Journey to Topaz

"A Margaret K. McElderry book"

After their release from an American concentration camp, Yuki and her family try to reconstruct their lives amidst strong anti-Japanese feelings which breed fear, distrust, and violence

Journey to Topaz; a story of the Japanese-American evacuation; illustrated by Donald Carrick. Scribner 1971 149p il o.p.; Creative Art Pubs. paperback available $9.95 (5 and up)   **Fic**

1. Japanese Americans—Evacuation and relocation, 1942-1945—Fiction
ISBN 0-916870-85-5 (pa)

This is the story of eleven-year-old Yuki, her eighteen-year-old brother and her mother, who were uprooted, evacuated and interned in Topaz, the War Relocation Center in Utah during World War II

"This tragic herding of innocent people is described with dignity and a sorrowful sense of injustice that never becomes bitter." Saturday Rev

Followed by Journey home

Vail, Rachel

Daring to be Abigail; a novel. Orchard Bks. 1996 128p $15.95; lib bdg $16.99 (4-6)   **Fic**

1. Camps—Fiction
ISBN 0-531-09517-7; 0-531-08867-7 (lib bdg)
LC 95-33531

Also available in paperback from Puffin Bks.

"A Richard Jackson book"

"Eleven-year-old Abigail plans to 'reinvent herself' at summer camp. Instead, torn between her newfound popularity and her empathy for the camp outcast, she learns more about who she really is." Horn Book Guide

"The dialogue is fresh and genuine. Readers will be drawn to the novel's authenticity and will find themselves empathizing with Abby, yet laughing at her escapades." SLJ

Van Leeuwen, Jean

Bound for Oregon; pictures by James Watling. Dial Bks. for Young Readers 1994 167p il map hardcover o.p. paperback available $5.99 (4-6)   **Fic**

1. Todd, Mary Ellen, 1843-1924—Fiction 2. Overland journeys to the Pacific—Fiction 3. Oregon Trail—Fiction
ISBN 0-14-038319-0 (pa)
LC 93-26709

A fictionalized account of the journey made by nine-year-old Mary Ellen Todd and her family from their home in Arkansas westward over the Oregon Trail in 1852

"The appealing narrator, the forthright telling, and the concrete details of life along the Oregon Trail will draw readers into the story." Booklist

Vande Velde, Vivian, 1951-

Smart dog. Harcourt Brace & Co. 1998 145p $16 (4-6)   **Fic**

1. Dogs—Fiction
ISBN 0-15-201847-6
LC 98-4771

Also available in paperback from Dell

Fifth grader Amy finds her life growing complicated when she meets and tries to hide an intelligent, talking dog who has escaped from a university lab

"The accessible vocabulary, quick-moving plot, and humor make the novel appealing for reluctant readers as well as a good choice for reading aloud." Horn Book

There's a dead person following my sister around. Harcourt Brace & Co. 1999 143p $16 (4 and up)   **Fic**

1. Ghost stories 2. Slavery—Fiction 3. Underground railroad—Fiction
ISBN 0-15-202100-0
LC 99-11462

Ted becomes concerned and intrigued when his five-year-old sister Vicki begins receiving visits from the ghosts of two runaway slaves

"There is sufficient humor, action, and scariness to keep readers engaged." SLJ

Verne, Jules, 1828-1905

20,000 leagues under the sea; illustrated by the Dillons; translated by Anthony Bonner. HarperCollins Pubs. 2000 394p il $21.95 (5 and up)   **Fic**

1. Science fiction 2. Submarines—Fiction
ISBN 0-688-10535-1
LC 00-24336

Also available other translations from various publishers and Audiobook version

"Books of Wonder"

Original French edition, 1870

Retells the adventures of a French professor and his two companions as they sail above and below the world's oceans as prisoners on the fabulous electric submarine of the deranged Captain Nemo

Vining, Elizabeth Gray, 1902-1999

Adam of the road; illustrated by Robert Lawson. Viking 1942 317p il hardcover o.p. paperback available $5.99 (5 and up)   **Fic**

1. Minstrels—Fiction 2. Middle Ages—Fiction 3. Great Britain—Fiction
ISBN 0-14-032464-X (pa)

Vining, Elizabeth Gray, 1902-1999—*Continued*

Awarded the Newbery Medal, 1943

Tale of a minstrel and his son Adam, who wandered through southeastern England in the thirteenth century. Adam's adventures in search of his lost dog and his beloved father led him from St. Alban's Abbey to London, and thence to Winchester, back to London, and then to Oxford where the three were at last reunited

Voigt, Cynthia

Come a stranger. Atheneum Pubs. 1986 190p hardcover o.p. paperback available $4.99 (6 and up) **Fic**

1. African Americans—Fiction 2. Race relations—Fiction

ISBN 0-689-804444-X (pa)   LC 86-3610

"Mina Smiths, the assertive, intelligent young black girl whom readers caught a glimpse of in 'Dicey's Song' is the central figure in this thoughtful coming-of-age novel. Mina is young, only 11 at the story's beginning, and thoroughly involved in ballet. She attends a special ballet camp on a scholarship but is bounced out the following year; in the midst of puberty she has become ungainly—but she wonders if the real reason is that she is black. The shock of rejection and the resulting preoccupation with her identity as a young black woman shadow Mina as her life proceeds on a new course centered on family and friends; there is also her quiet, intense but hopeless love for Tamer Shipp, the summer replacement minister who understands her heart in a way no one else can." Booklist

Dicey's song. Atheneum Pubs. 1982 196p $17 (6 and up) **Fic**

1. Grandmothers—Fiction 2. Siblings—Fiction

ISBN 0-689-30944-9   LC 82-3882

Also available in paperback from Fawcett Bks. and Audiobook version

Awarded the Newbery Medal, 1983

Sequel to Homecoming

Dicey "had brought her siblings to the grandmother they'd never seen when their mother (now in a mental institution) had been unable to cope. This is the story of the children's adjustment to Gram (and hers to them) and to a new school and a new life—but with some of the old problems. Dicey, in particular, has a hard time since she must abandon her role of surrogate mother and share the responsibility with Gram." Bull Cent Child Books

"The vividness of Dicey is striking; Voigt has plumbed and probed her character inside out to fashion a memorable protagonist. Unlike most sequels, this outdoes its predecessor by being more fully realized and consequently more resonant." Booklist

Homecoming. Atheneum Pubs. 1981 312p $18 (6 and up) **Fic**

1. Siblings—Fiction 2. Abandoned children—Fiction

ISBN 0-689-30833-7   LC 80-36723

Also available in paperback from Fawcett Bks.

"When their momma abandons them in a shopping center, Dicey Tillerman and her three younger brothers and sisters set out on foot for where momma was ostensibly taking them—to Great-Aunt Cilla's in Bridgeport, Connecticut. They arrive to find only Cousin Eunice; Priscilla has died. Eunice, mindlessly religious and insen-

sitive to their needs, agrees to look after them. But Dicey knows she has to take another chance and another journey, this time to Crisfield, Maryland, where she hopes their unknown grandmother might provide a better home." Booklist

"The characterizations of the children are original and intriguing, and there are a number of interesting minor characters encountered in their travels." SLJ

Followed by Dicey's song

Vos, Ida, 1931-

Anna is still here; translated by Terese Edelstein and Inez Smidt. Houghton Mifflin 1993 139p $15 (4 and up) **Fic**

1. Holocaust, 1933-1945—Fiction 2. Jews—Netherlands—Fiction 3. Netherlands—Fiction

ISBN 0-395-65368-1   LC 92-1618

Also available in paperback from Puffin Bks.

Original Dutch edition, 1986

In this sequel to Hide and seek, Anna now thirteen "has been reunited with her parents, who are loving but still unable to speak of their own time in hiding or of the loss of family and friends. . . . The story mainly concerns the rebuilding of her relationship with her parents and a tenuous friendship with Mrs. Neumann, a woman who is searching for her little daughter, lost in the tides of war. . . . A striking, and ultimately hopeful, account of how the human spirit survives and recovers." Horn Book

Hide and seek; translated by Terese Edelstein and Inez Smidt. Houghton Mifflin 1991 132p $15 (4 and up) **Fic**

1. Holocaust, 1933-1945—Fiction 2. Jews—Netherlands—Fiction 3. Netherlands—Fiction

ISBN 0-395-56470-0   LC 90-4980

Also available in paperback from Puffin Bks.

Original Dutch edition, 1981

Anna, a young Jewish girl living in Holland, tells of her experiences during the Nazi occupation, her years in hiding, and the after shock when the war finally ends

"Drawing on her own experiences during WW II, Vos fills the narrative with understated but painfully realistic moments. . . . Vos's novel deserves special attention for its sensitive and deeply affecting consideration of life after liberation." Publ Wkly

Followed by Anna is still here

The key is lost; translated by Terese Edelstein. HarperCollins Pubs. 2000 272p (4 and up) **Fic**

1. Holocaust, 1933-1945—Fiction 2. Jews—Netherlands—Fiction 3. Netherlands—Fiction

Original Dutch edition, 1996

When the Germans occupy Holland in 1940 and begin to persecute the Jews there, twelve-year-old Eva and her sister, Lisa, assume false names and move from one hiding place to another

"This simply told, understated story is based on the author's own experiences. . . . [It offers] clearly etched and believably developed characters." SLJ

Wallace, Barbara Brooks, 1922-

Cousins in the castle. Atheneum Bks. for Young Readers 1996 152p $16; pa $3.99 (4-6) **Fic**

1. Orphans—Fiction 2. Mystery fiction

ISBN 0-689-80637-X; 0-689-80778-3 (pa)

LC 95-23484

"A Jean Karl book"

"When the recently orphaned Amelia sails from Victorian England to her guardian in America, she finds herself the target of a plan to steal her fortune. It's a close call for Amelia, but the scheme fails, and all ends well. Wallace weaves long-lost relatives, goodhearted helpers, and despicable kidnappers—not to mention improbable plot twists—into an enjoyable story fraught with Gothic atmosphere." Horn Book Guide

Ghosts in the gallery. Atheneum Bks. for Young Readers 2000 136p $16 (5 and up) **Fic**

1. Orphans—Fiction 2. Grandfathers—Fiction

ISBN 0-689-83175-7

LC 99-29055

"A Jean Karl book"

When eleven-year-old Jenny arrives at her grandfather's house but is not recognized as one of the family because of a servant's intrigue, the young orphan endures a difficult fate

"Guaranteed thrills and chills." Horn Book Guide

The twin in the tavern. Atheneum Pubs. 1993 179p $15; pa $4.99 (4-6) **Fic**

1. Orphans—Fiction 2. Twins—Fiction 3. Mystery fiction

ISBN 0-689-31846-4; 0-689-80167-X (pa)

LC 92-36429

"A Jean Karl book"

Taddy, a young orphan, afraid of being sent to the workhouse, finds himself at the mercy of the unsavory owner of a tavern in Alexandria, Virginia, while he tries to solve the mystery surrounding his past and a missing twin

"With a fine hand for Gothic embroidery and a nifty surprise conclusion that ties up all the loose ends, Wallace has delivered [a] . . . very satisfying read." SLJ

Wallace, Bill, 1947-

Beauty. Holiday House 1988 177p $16.95 (4-6) **Fic**

1. Horses—Fiction 2. Farm life—Fiction

ISBN 0-8234-0715-2

LC 88-6422

Also available in paperback from Pocket Bks.

Unhappy about his parents splitting up and moving with his mother to Grandpa's farm, eleven-year-old Luke finds comfort in riding and caring for a horse named Beauty

"Wallace's horse story is strong on sentiment, and its tear-jerker finale packs a wallop. . . . The story will stir up genuine emotion." Booklist

A dog called Kitty. Holiday House 1980 153p $15.95 (4-6) **Fic**

1. Dogs—Fiction 2. Farm life—Fiction

ISBN 0-8234-0376-9

LC 80-16293

Also available in paperback from Minstrel Bks.

Afraid of dogs since he was attacked by a mad one as a baby, Ricky resists taking in a homeless pup that shows up at the farm

"Some minor plot elements are contrived enough to strain credibility, but Ricky is real, as are his family and friends, and there is no lack of action. Recommended also for older reluctant readers for its fast pace, popular appeal, and second-to-third-grade reading level." Booklist

Walter, Mildred Pitts, 1922-

Justin and the best biscuits in the world; with illustrations by Catherine Stock. Lothrop, Lee & Shepard Bks. 1986 122p il $16 (3-6) **Fic**

1. Sex role—Fiction 2. Grandfathers—Fiction 3. Family life—Fiction 4. African Americans—Fiction

ISBN 0-688-06645-3

LC 86-7148

Also available in paperback from Knopf

Coretta Scott King Award for text, 1987

"Justin can't seem to do anything right at home. His sisters berate his dishwashing and his mother despairs of his ever properly tidying his room. As for Justin, he angrily rejects the tasks as 'women's work.' Enter now Justin's widowed grandfather, who sizes up the situation, invites Justin for a visit to his ranch, and through daily routines quietly shows Justin that 'it doesn't matter who does the work, man or woman, when it needs to be done.'" Booklist

"The strong, well-developed characters and humorous situations in this warm family story will appeal to intermediate readers; the large print will draw slow or reluctant readers." SLJ

Suitcase; illustrated by Teresa Flavin. Lothrop, Lee & Shepard Bks. 1999 107p il $13.50 (3-6) **Fic**

1. Artists—Fiction 2. African Americans—Fiction

ISBN 0-688-16547-8

LC 99-11488

Despite his love of drawing and his feelings of inadequacy as an athlete, sixth-grader Xander "Suitcase" Bingham works to become a baseball player to win the approval of his father

"The book is reassuring in its honest portrayal of his insecurities and his willingness to persevere." Horn Book Guide

Ward, Lynd Kendall, 1905-1985

The silver pony; a story in pictures; by Lynd Ward. Houghton Mifflin 1973 174p il $18; pa $6.95 (2-4) **Fic**

1. Horses—Fiction 2. Stories without words

ISBN 0-395-14753-0; 0-395-64377-5 (pa)

"Eighty pictures in shades of gray, black, and white tell the story of a lonely farm boy whose dreams of his adventures on a winged horse become confused with reality. One night the boy leans out his window fantasizing that the horse is carrying him to the moon; but the dream turns into a nightmare as rockets and missiles fill the air around them, then explode, killing the horse and sending the boy hurtling through space—really out the window to his own yard below. The boy recovers physically and, with the help of his parents, doctor, and a real colt, emotionally. This is a complex story subtly conveyed without words—a unique experience for readers and nonreaders alike." Booklist

Warner, Sally

Totally confidential. HarperCollins Pubs. 2000 195p $15.95; lib bdg $15.89 (4 and up)   **Fic**
1. Family life—Fiction 2. Friendship—Fiction
ISBN 0-06-028261-4; 0-06-028262-2 (lib bdg)
LC 99-36101

After dispensing good advice to her clients, professional listener Quinney finds herself in need of advice for dealing with her weird family and changing relationships with her best friends

"This lively, engaging novel sympathetically portrays some familiar themes." Booklist

Waters, Fiona

Oscar Wilde's The selfish giant; retold by Fiona Waters; illustrated by Fabian Negrin. Knopf 2000 c1999 il $16.95; lib bdg $18.99 (2-5)   **Fic**
1. Fairy tales 2. Giants—Fiction
ISBN 0-375-80319-X; 0-375-90319-4 (lib bdg)
LC 99-32495

This retelling first published 1999 in the United Kingdom

A once selfish giant welcomes the children to his previously forbidden garden and is eventually rewarded by an unusual little child

"Water's retelling of Wilde's allegorical fairy tale stays close to the original, and Negrin's lavish, theatrical illustrations express the dramatic contrasts at the heart of the story." Booklist

Watkins, Yoko Kawashima

My brother, my sister, and I. Bradbury Press 1994 275p hardcover o.p. paperback available $4.99 (6 and up)   **Fic**
1. World War, 1939-1945—Fiction 2. Japan—Fiction
ISBN 0-689-80656-6 (pa)   LC 93-23535

"The author continues her autobiographical account begun in *So Far from the Bamboo Grove* with the story of how the two sisters, Ko and Yoko, now reunited with their brother Hideyo, try to survive in postwar Japan." Horn Book

"Watkins's first-person narrative is beautifully direct and emotionally honest." Publ Wkly

So far from the bamboo grove. Lothrop, Lee & Shepard Bks. 1986 183p map hardcover o.p. paperback available $4.95 (6 and up)   **Fic**
1. World War, 1939-1945—Fiction 2. Korea—Fiction 3. Japan—Fiction
ISBN 0-688-13115-8 (pa)   LC 85-15939

A fictionalized autobiography in which eight-year-old Yoko escapes from Korea to Japan with her mother and sister at the end of World War II

"An admirably told and absorbing novel." Horn Book

Followed by My brother, my sister and I

Waugh, Sylvia

The Mennyms. Greenwillow Bks. 1994 c1993 212p $16 (5 and up)   **Fic**
1. Dolls—Fiction 2. Family life—Fiction 3. Great Britain—Fiction
ISBN 0-688-13070-4   LC 93-15901

Also available in paperback from Avon Bks.

First published 1993 in the United Kingdom

The Mennyms, a family of life-size rag dolls living in a house in England and pretending to be human, see their peaceful existence threatened when the house's owner announces he is coming from Australia for a visit

"The suspenseful, seamless fantasy is rich in detail and imagination." Horn Book Guide

Other available titles about the Mennyms are:
Mennyms alive (1997)
Mennyms alone (1996)
Mennyms in the wilderness (1995)
Mennyms under siege (1996)

Weeks, Sarah

Regular Guy. HarperCollins Pubs. 1999 120p $14.95; lib bdg $14.89; pa $4.95 (4-6)   **Fic**
1. Parent-child relationship—Fiction
ISBN 0-06-028367-X; 0-06-028368-8 (lib bdg); 0-06-440782-9 (pa)   LC 99-12118

"A Laura Geringer book"

Because he is so different from his eccentric parents, twelve-year-old Guy is convinced he has been switched at birth with a classmate whose parents seem more normal

"Weeks treats the situation with wild exaggeration, a farcical plot, and just a touch of tenderness. . . . Many middle-graders will enjoy the gross humor (lots of snot and clatter and fishy smells) as much as the view of embarrassing adults who love you even though they drive you nuts." Booklist

Other available titles about Guy are:
Guy time (2000)
My Guy (2001)

Westall, Robert, 1929-1993

The machine gunners. Greenwillow Bks. 1976 c1975 186p hardcover o.p. paperback available $4.95 (6 and up)   **Fic**
1. World War, 1939-1945—Fiction 2. Great Britain—Fiction
ISBN 0-688-15498-0 (pa)

First published 1975 in the United Kingdom

"Garmouth, England, is under constant bombing attack by the Germans in World War II. Charles McGill finds a machine gun in a downed German plane and, with that weapon as protection, he and his friends construct a fortress in preparation for an enemy attack. They capture a German soldier who becomes their friend. Instead of the expected Nazis, other gangs and their families become the enemy. An attack mistakenly thought to be by Nazis leaves their only ally, the German soldier, dead." Shapiro. Fic for Youth. 2d edition

Followed by Fathom five (1980)

Weston, Carol

The diary of Melanie Martin; or, How I survived Matt the Brat, Michelangelo, and the Leaning Tower of Pizza. Knopf 2000 144p $15.95; lib bdg $17.99 (3-6)   **Fic**
1. Voyages and travels—Fiction 2. Family life—Fiction 3. Italy—Fiction
ISBN 0-375-80509-5; 0-375-90509-X (lib bdg)
LC 99-53384

Weston, Carol—*Continued*

Fourth-grader Melanie Martin writes in her diary, describing her family's trip to Italy and all that she learned

"Sections of the book are laugh-out-loud funny and Weston's descriptions will have readers wanting to see the country for themselves. An enjoyable read." SLJ

Whelan, Gloria

Goodbye, Vietnam. Knopf 1992 135p hardcover o.p. paperback available $3.99 (4 and up)   **Fic**
1. Refugees—Fiction 2. Vietnamese—Fiction
ISBN 0-679-82376-X (pa)   LC 91-3660

Thirteen-year-old Mai and her family embark on a dangerous sea voyage from Vietnam to Hong Kong to escape the unpredictable and often brutal Vietnamese government

"While the book has the suspense and appeal of any good escape story, Whelan is neither melodramatic nor sentimental, and the sometimes horrific details of the scary voyage are plain but understated." Bull Cent Child Books

Homeless bird. HarperCollins Pubs. 2000 216p $15.95; lib bdg $15.89; pa $4.95 (6 and up)
       Fic
1. Women—India—Fiction 2. India—Fiction
ISBN 0-06-028454-4; 0-06-028452-8 (lib bdg); 0-06-440819-1 (pa)   LC 99-33241

When thirteen-year-old Koly enters into an ill-fated arranged marriage, she must either suffer a destiny dictated by India's tradition or find the courage to oppose it

"This beautifully told, inspiring story takes readers on a fascinating journey through modern India and the universal intricacies of a young woman's heart." Booklist

White, E. B. (Elwyn Brooks), 1899-1985

Charlotte's web; pictures by Garth Williams. Harper & Row 1952 184p il $16.95; lib bdg $16.89; pa $5.95 (3-6)   **Fic**
1. Pigs—Fiction 2. Spiders—Fiction
ISBN 0-06-026385-7; 0-06-026386-5 (lib bdg); 0-06-440055-7 (pa)

Also available Spanish language edition and Audiobook version

A Newbery Medal honor book, 1953

The story of a little girl who could talk to animals, but especially the story of the pig, Wilbur, and his friendship with Charlotte, the spider, who could not only talk but write as well

"Illustrated with amusing sketches . . . [this] story is a fable for adults as well as children and can be recommended to older children and parents as an amusing story and a gentle essay on friendship." Libr J

Stuart Little; pictures by Garth Williams. Harper & Row 1945 131p il $16.95; lib bdg $16.89; pa $5.95 (3-6)   **Fic**
1. Mice—Fiction
ISBN 0-06-026395-4; 0-06-026396-2 (lib bdg); 0-06-440056-5 (pa)

Also available Spanish language edition and Audiobook version

This is "the story of a 'Tom Thumb'-like child born to a New York couple who is to all intents and purposes a mouse. . . . The first part of the book explores, with dead-pan humour, the advantages and disadvantages of having a mouse in one's family circle. Then Stuart sets out on a quest in search of his inamorata, a bird named Margalo, and the story ends in mid-air. The book is outstandingly funny and sometimes touching." Oxford Companion to Child Lit

The trumpet of the swan; illustrated by Fred Marcellino. HarperCollins Pubs. 2000 251p il $16.95; lib bdg $16.89; pa $5.95 (3-6)   **Fic**
ISBN 0-06-028935-X; 0-06-028936-8 (lib bdg); 0-06-440867-1 (pa)   LC 99-44250

Also available Spanish language edition and Audiobook version

A newly illustrated edition of the title first published 1970

Louis, a voiceless Trumpeter swan, finds himself far from his wilderness home when he determines to communicate by learning to play a stolen trumpet

The author "deftly blends true birdlore with fanciful adventures in a witty, captivating fantasy." Booklist

White, Ruth

Belle Prater's boy. Farrar, Straus & Giroux 1996 196p $16 (5 and up)   **Fic**
1. Cousins—Fiction 2. Virginia—Fiction 3. Appalachian region—Fiction
ISBN 0-374-30668-0   LC 94-43625

Also available in paperback from Dell and Audiobook version

A Newbery Medal honor book, 1997

"Gypsy and her cousin Woodrow become close friends after Woodrow's mother disappears. Both sixthgraders feel deserted by their parents—Gypsy discovers that her father committed suicide—and need to define themselves apart from these tragedies. White's prose evokes the coal mining region of Virginia and the emotional quality of her characters' transformations." Horn Book Guide

White, T. H. (Terence Hanbury), 1906-1964

The sword in the stone; with illustrations by Dennis Nolan. Putnam 1993 256p il $22.99 (4 and up)   **Fic**
1. Arthur, King—Fiction 2. Merlin (Legendary character)—Fiction
ISBN 0-399-22502-1   LC 92-24808

Also available in paperback from Dell

A newly illustrated edition of the title first published 1938 in the United Kingdom; first United States edition 1939 by G.P Putnam's Sons

"In White's classic story about the boyhood of King Arthur, Wart—unaware of his true identity—is tutored by Merlyn, who occasionally transform the young boy into various animals as part of his schooling. Contemporary children will still enjoy the text, which is both fantastical and down-to-earth." Horn Book Guide

Wiggin, Kate Douglas Smith, 1856-1923

The Bird's Christmas Carol; by Kate Douglas Wiggin; illustrated by Jessie Gillespie. Memorial ed. Houghton Mifflin 1941 84p il $9.95; pa $4.95 (3-5) **Fic**
  1. Christmas—Fiction
ISBN 0-395-07205-0; 0-395-89110-8 (pa)
First published 1888
"The story of Carol Bird, an invalid girl so named because she was born at Christmas." Oxford Companion to Child Lit

Rebecca of Sunnybrook Farm; with illustrations by Helen Mason Grose; afterword by Peter Glassman. Morrow 1994 291p il $12.95 (4 and up) **Fic**
  1. Aunts—Fiction 2. New England—Fiction
ISBN 0-688-13481-5   LC 94-9899
Also available various hardcover reprint and paperback editions
A reissue of the title first published 1903 by Houghton, Mifflin
Talkative, ten-year-old Rebecca goes to live with her spinster aunts, one harsh and demanding, the other soft and sentimental, with whom she spends seven difficult but rewarding years growing up
"Six full-color illustrations and numerous pen-and-ink drawings attractively depict the familiar characters and old-time setting of the classic novel. Wiggin's story . . . continues to hold appeal." Horn Book Guide

Wilde, Oscar, 1854-1900

The selfish giant (2-5) **Fic**
  1. Fairy tales 2. Giants—Fiction

Available Putnam & Grosset Group edition illustrated by Saelig Gallagher
This is the "story of a giant whose garden is wrapped in winter until he shares it with the children who live nearby." Booklist

Wilder, Laura Ingalls, 1867-1957

Little house in the big woods; illustrated by Garth Williams. newly illustrated, uniform ed. Harper & Row 1953 237p il $16.95; lib bdg $16.89; pa $3.50 (4-6) **Fic**
  1. Frontier and pioneer life—Fiction 2. Wisconsin—Fiction
ISBN 0-06-026430-6; 0-06-026431-4 (lib bdg); 0-06-107005-X (pa)
First published 1932
This book "tells the story of the author's earliest days 'in the Big Woods of Wisconsin, in a little grey house made of logs.' The style of narrative is simple, almost naive, but the pioneer life is described unsqueamishly, with attention to such details as the butchering of the family hog. As in later books, the author refers to herself in the third person as 'Laura.' The record of daily life far from any town is punctuated with stories told in the evenings by Pa, who is also a great singer of folk-songs." Oxford Companion to Child Lit
  Other available titles in the Little House series are:
By the shores of Silver Lake (1939)

Farmer boy (1933)
The first four years (1971)
Little house on the prairie (1935)
Little town on the prairie (1941)
The long winter (1940)
On the banks of Plum Creek (1937)
These happy golden years (1943)

Williams, Laura E.

The executioner's daughter. Holt & Co. 2000 134p $15.95 (6 and up) **Fic**
  1. Middle Ages—Fiction
ISBN 0-8050-6234-3   LC 99-49259
Thirteen-year-old Lily, daughter of the town's executioner living in fifteenth-century Europe, decides whether to fight against her destiny or to rise above her fate
" This well-written story is an excellent vehicle for demonstrating the harsh realities of life in the Middle Ages." SLJ

Williams, Vera B.

Scooter. Greenwillow Bks. 1993 147p il $15; lib bdg $14.93 (3-5) **Fic**
  1. Moving—Fiction 2. Divorce—Fiction 3. Friendship—Fiction
ISBN 0-688-09376-0; 0-688-09377-9 (lib bdg)
    LC 90-38489
After her parent's divorce "Elana Rose Rosen and her mother relocate to an apartment in a big city housing project where 'Lanny' spends the summer making friends and practicing her favorite scooter tricks." Publ Wkly
"The voice is totally authentic, and Williams peppers the pages with ink drawings that have an equally authentic childlike zest." Bull Cent Child Books

Willis, Patricia

The barn burner. Clarion Bks. 2000 196p $15 (5 and up) **Fic**
  1. Great Depression, 1929-1939—Fiction 2. Runaway children—Fiction 3. Family life—Fiction
ISBN 0-395-98409-2   LC 99-42223
In 1933 while running from a bad situation at home and suspected of having set fire to a barn, fourteen-year-old Ross finds haven with a loving family which helps him make an important decision
"By tying an unsentimental look at the era together with a mystery, the author has created a story that is both appealing and of literary merit." SLJ

Willner-Pardo, Gina

Daphne Eloise Slater, who's tall for her age; illustrated by Glo Coalson. Clarion Bks. 1997 39p il $15 (2-4) **Fic**
  1. School stories
ISBN 0-395-73080-5   LC 95-44050
Daphne didn't mind being the tallest girl in her class until third grade, when a classmate begins teasing her about her height and she must decide whether to retaliate
"The situations are realistic, and Willner-Pardo captures the importance of the small events that make up life in the elementary school. Coalson's light watercolors . . . are warm and lively." Horn Book Guide

Willner-Pardo, Gina—*Continued*

Figuring out Frances. Clarion Bks. 1999 134p
$14 (4-6)   **Fic**
   1. Friendship—Fiction 2. Grandmothers—Fiction
3. Alzheimer's disease—Fiction
   ISBN 0-395-91510-4   LC 98-50082
Ten-year-old Abigail's neighbor Travis, her best friend
although he is at a different school, upsets her when he
transfers to her school, ignores her, and laughs at her
grandmother's Alzheimer's along with his new friends
   "The writing is witty, sincere, and insightful. This is
a gem of a book." SLJ

Wilson, Diane L.

I rode a horse of milk white jade; [by] Diane
Lee Wilson. Orchard Bks. 1998 232p $18.95 (6
and up)   **Fic**
   ISBN 0-531-30024-2   LC 97-23838
   Also available in paperback from HarperCollins
Oyuna tells her granddaughter the story of how love
for her horse enabled her to win a race and bring good
luck to her family living in Mongolia in 1339
   This "story is an exciting one that will reward dili-
gent, proficient readers." SLJ

Winthrop, Elizabeth

The castle in the attic; frontispiece and chapter
title decorations by Trina Schart Hyman. Holiday
House 1985 179p il $15.95 (4-6)   **Fic**
   1. Fantasy fiction
   ISBN 0-8234-0579-6   LC 85-5607
   Also available in paperback from Dell and Audiobook
version
   "William is ten, both of his parents work, and he has
always been taken care of by Mrs. Phillips; when she
tells him she is going home to England, he is distraught,
even though her farewell gift is a large replica of a castle, a toy that has been in her family for generations.
There's one little figurine, Sir Simon, and a tale that he
will some day come to life. For William, he does, and
the boy becomes completely involved with Sir Simon
and then with a Mrs. Phillips that William has caused to
shrink, by a magic token, to Sir Simon's size. The only
way that he can show repentance and rescue her is to
shrink himself." Bull Cent Child Books
   "Well-crafted, easy to follow, this excursion into
knightly times and affairs is further enhanced by the cover art, chapter decorations, and, most important of all, a
thoughtful floor plan of the castle." Horn Book
   Another available title about William and Sir Simon is:
The battle for the castle (1993)

Wiseman, David, 1916-

Jeremy Visick. Houghton Mifflin 1981 170p
hardcover o.p. paperback available $7.95 (5 and
up)   **Fic**
   1. Space and time—Fiction 2. Supernatural—Fiction
3. Miners—Fiction 4. Great Britain—Fiction
   ISBN 0-395-56153-1 (pa)   LC 80-28116
   "Sent by his teacher to explore some local grave-
stones, Matthew is inexorably drawn to the message on

the 1852 Visick family marker, with its tragic tag line,
'And to Jeremy Visick, . . . aged 12 years, whose body
still lies in Wheal Maid.' Numerous nocturnal ramblings
find Matthew firmly entrenched in the long-dead family's
affairs and their work in the Wheal Maid mine. One
night, Matthew compulsively follows young Jeremy into
the mine, where he learns how the boy died and, though
barely escaping death himself, finally brings peace to the
boys restless ghost." Booklist
   "This story blends the mystery and awe of the supernatural with the real terror and peril of descending the
shaft of an 1850 Cornish copper mine." SLJ

Wisler, G. Clifton, 1950-

Mr. Lincoln's drummer. Lodestar Bks. 1995
131p $15.99; pa $4.99 (4 and up)   **Fic**
   1. Johnston, William J., b. 1850—Fiction 2. United
States—History—1861-1865, Civil War—Fiction
   ISBN 0-525-67463-2; 0-14-038542-8 (pa)
                         LC 94-20328
Recounts the courageous exploits of Willie Johnston,
an eleven-year-old Civil War drummer, who became the
youngest recipient of the Congressional Medal of Honor
   "Lively dialogue, vivid battle scenes,
unsentimentalized heroism, and a fair amount of wry humor make this an especially good choice for history-shy
readers." Bull Cent Child Books

Red Cap. Lodestar Bks. 1991 160p hardcover
o.p. paperback available $4.99 (4 and up)   **Fic**
   1. Powell, Ransom J., 1849-1899—Fiction
2. Andersonville Prison—Fiction 3. United States—
History—1861-1865, Civil War—Fiction
   ISBN 0-14-036936 (pa)   LC 90-21944
A young Yankee drummer boy displays great courage
when he's captured and sent to Andersonville Prison
   The author "presents a well-researched view of the
war. He effectively interweaves the known facts of Powell's life with first-person accounts of other soldiers and
prisoners to create an exciting story." SLJ

Wojciechowska, Maia, 1927-

Shadow of a bull; drawings by Alvin Smith.
Atheneum Pubs. 1964 165p il $16; pa $4.99 (6
and up)   **Fic**
   1. Bullfights—Fiction 2. Spain—Fiction
   ISBN 0-689-30042-5; 0-689-71567-6 (pa)
   Awarded the Newbery Medal, 1965
   "Manolo was the son of the great bullfighter Juan
Olivar. Ever since his father's death the town of
Arcangel [Spain] has waited for [the time] when Manolo
would be twelve and face his first bull. From the time
he was nine and felt in his heart that he was a coward,
Manolo worked and prayed that he might at least face
this moment with honor, knowing it could well bring his
death." Publ Wkly
   "In spare, economical prose [the author] makes one
feel, see, smell the heat, endure the hot Andalusian sun
and shows one the sand and glare of the bullring. Above
all, she lifts the veil and gives glimpses of the terrible
loneliness in the soul of a boy. . . . Superbly illustrated." N Y Times Book Rev

Wolff, Virginia Euwer

Bat 6. Scholastic 1998 230p $16.95; pa $4.99 (5 and up) **Fic**
1. Softball—Fiction 2. Japanese Americans—Fiction 3. Prejudices—Fiction
ISBN 0-590-89799-3; 0-590-89800-0 (pa)
LC 97-14742
Also available Audiobook version
"During a sixth-grade girls' softball game in 1949, a deeply troubled girl whose father was killed at Pearl Harbor attacks a Japanese-American girl whose family was interned. . . . Wolff's evocation of period and place is masterful, and the questions she raises about war, race, and cherished beliefs are difficult and honest." Horn Book Guide

The Mozart season. Holt & Co. 1991 249p o.p.; Scholastic paperback available $4.99 (6 and up)
Fic
1. Violinists—Fiction
ISBN 0-439-16309-9 (pa)
LC 90-23635
Allegra spends her twelfth summer practicing a Mozart concerto for a violin competition and finding many significant connections in her world
"With a clear, fresh voice that never falters, Wolff gives readers a delightful heroine, a fully realized setting, and a slowly building tension that reaches a stunning climax." SLJ

Woodruff, Elvira

Dear Levi; letters from the Overland Trail; illustrated by Beth Peck. Knopf 1994 119p il hardcover o.p. paperback available $4.99 (4-6)
Fic
1. Overland journeys to the Pacific—Fiction 2. Frontier and pioneer life—Fiction 3. Letters—Fiction
ISBN 0-679-88558-7 (pa)
LC 93-5315
Twelve-year-old Austin Ives writes letters to his younger brother describing his three-thousand-mile journey from their home in Pennsylvania to Oregon in 1851
"Atmospheric black-and-white pencil sketches illustrate a few of the story's major events, and a clearly drawn map traces the wagon's route on the Overland Trail. The well-paced story is a page turner." Horn Book Guide

Woodson, Jacqueline

I hadn't meant to tell you this. Delacorte Press 1994 115p $15.95; pa $4.50 (6 and up) **Fic**
1. African Americans—Fiction 2. Friendship—Fiction 3. Incest—Fiction 4. Child sexual abuse—Fiction
ISBN 0-385-32031-0; 0-440-021960-4 (pa)
LC 93-8733
Marie, the only black girl in the eighth grade willing to befriend her white classmate Lena, discovers that Lena's father is doing horrible things to her in private
"Woodson's characters are deftly drawn, whole individuals; her spare prose and crystal images create a haunting, poetic novel." Horn Book Guide
Followed by Lena

Lena. Delacorte Press 1999 115p $15.95; pa $4.99 (6 and up) **Fic**
1. Runaway teenagers—Fiction 2. Sisters—Fiction
ISBN 0-385-32308-5; 0-440-22669-4 (pa)
LC 98-24317

Sequel to I hadn't meant to tell you this
Thirteen-year-old Lena and her younger sister Dion mourn the death of their mother as they hitchhike from Ohio to Kentucky while running away from their abusive father
"Soulful, wise and sometimes wrenching, this taut story never loses its grip on the reader." Publ Wkly

Wrede, Patricia C., 1953-

Dealing with dragons. Harcourt Brace Jovanovich 1990 212p $17 (6 and up) **Fic**
1. Fairy tales 2. Dragons—Fiction
ISBN 0-15-222900-0
LC 89-24599
Also available in paperback from Scholastic
"Jane Yolen books"
Bored with traditional palace life, a princess goes off to live with a group of dragons and soon becomes involved with fighting against some disreputable wizards who want to steal away the dragons' kingdom
"A decidedly diverting novel with plenty of action and many slightly skewed fairy-tale conventions that add to the laugh-out-loud reading pleasure and give the story a wide appeal. The good news is that this is book one in the Enchanted Forest Chronicles." Booklist
Other available titles in the Enchanted Forest Chronicles are:
Calling on dragons (1993)
Searching for dragons (1991)
Talking to dragons (1993)

Wright, Betty Ren

The dollhouse murders. Holiday House 1983 149p $15.95 (4 and up) **Fic**
1. Mystery fiction
ISBN 0-8234-0497-8
LC 83-6147
Also available in paperback from Scholastic and Audiobook version
A dollhouse filled with a ghostly light in the middle of the night and dolls that have moved from where she last left them lead Amy and her retarded sister to unravel the mystery surrounding grisly murders that took place years ago
"More than just a mystery, this offers keen insight into the relationship between handicapped and nonhandicapped siblings and glimpses into the darker adult emotions of guilt and anger. A successful, full-bodied work." Booklist

The ghost in Room 11; illustrated by Jacqueline Rogers. Holiday House 1998 112p il $15.95 (3-5)
Fic
1. Ghost stories 2. School stories
ISBN 0-8234-1318-7
LC 96-53696
When his family moves to a small town near Milwaukee, Matt's efforts to fit into his new fourth-grade class are complicated by his poor spelling and his encounter with the ghost of one of the school's former teachers
"Wright offers another intriguing variation on the classic ghost narrative, one that focuses on emotions and maturity instead of fear." Booklist

Wright, Betty Ren—*Continued*

The ghosts of Mercy Manor. Scholastic 1993 172p hardcover o.p. paperback available $3.99 (4 and up)   **Fic**
1. Ghost stories 2. Orphans—Fiction 3. Mystery fiction
ISBN 0-590-43602-3 (pa)   LC 92-21557

Twelve-year-old Gwen, an orphan who comes to live with the Mercy family, discovers that the house is haunted by the ghost of a sad-looking young girl and is determined to solve the mystery behind her appearances

"Superbly written and suspenseful throughout." Voice Youth Advocates

The moonlight man. Scholastic Press 2000 181p $15.95 (5 and up)   **Fic**
1. Ghost stories
ISBN 0-590-25237-2   LC 99-27016

When their father moves them for the seventh time in the five years since their mother's death, Jenny and her younger sister hope to stay in this latest house and try to find out about the malevolent ghost who seems bent on getting revenge on their elderly neighbors

"Sympathetic characters and spooky happenings make this eerie tale perfect for dark winter nights." Booklist

Nothing but trouble; drawings by Jacqueline Rogers. Holiday House 1995 119p il $15.95 (4 and up)   **Fic**
1. Aunts—Fiction 2. Dogs—Fiction 3. Mystery fiction
ISBN 0-8234-1175-3   LC 94-34285
Also available in paperback from Scholastic

"When Vannie Kirkland is dropped off with an aged aunt she's never met while her parents search for work in California, things don't look great. For one, aunt Bert thinks Vannie's diminutive dog, Muffy, is a noisy, destructive little bundle. But Aunt Bert's less prickly side is revealed when mysterious prowlers start vandalizing her farm." Booklist

"The plot is cleanly structured and should hold readers' interest. . . . Overall, a satisfying story for a wide range of mystery fans." SLJ

Wyss, Johann David, 1743-1818

The Swiss family Robinson (5 and up)   **Fic**
1. Survival after airplane accidents, shipwrecks, etc.—Fiction

Some editions are:
Grosset & Dunlap (Illustrated junior library) $16.99 Illustrated by Lynd Kendall Ward (ISBN 0-448-06022-1)
Knopf (Everyman's library children's classics) $14.95 Illustrated by Louis Rhead (ISBN 0-679-43640-5)
Originally published 1812-1813 in Switzerland

"A Swiss family—a pastor, his wife, and four boys—are shipwrecked on an uninhabited island. They gradually establish an attractive way of life for themselves, and their many adventures are used by their father to form the basis of lessons in natural history and the physical sciences." Oxford Companion to Child Lit

Yarbrough, Camille, 1938-

The shimmershine queens. Putnam 1988 142p hardcover o.p. paperback available $4.99 (4-6)
                                              Fic
1. African Americans—Fiction 2. School stories 3. Prejudices—Fiction
ISBN 0-698-811369-1 (pa)   LC 88-11539

"Angie and her friend Michelle are in fifth grade, where Angie is taunted because her skin is so dark. It's an elderly visiting relative . . . who makes Angie feel her own worth and who explains 'shimmershine' as the glow you get when you feel good about yourself." Bull Cent Child Books

"This story carries a clear message about the dire need for students to respect themselves, each other, and education. The dialogue (rendered in black English) rings true, and the characterizations have depth." Booklist

Yep, Laurence

The amah. Putnam 1999 181p $15.99; pa $5.99 (5 and up)   **Fic**
1. Family life—Fiction 2. Chinese Americans—Fiction
ISBN 0-399-23040-8; 0-698-11878-2 (pa)
                                        LC 98-49046

"When her mother becomes the amah (Chinese governess) for a wealthy white girl, twelve-year-old Amy must skip her ballet classes—in which she is preparing for the role of Cinderella's mean stepsister—to baby-sit her siblings." Horn Book Guide

"An enjoyable book about friendship, family, and traditions." Voice Youth Advocates

Child of the owl. Harper & Row 1977 217p lib bdg $15.89; pa $4.95 (5 and up)   **Fic**
1. Chinese Americans—Fiction 2. Grandmothers—Fiction 3. San Francisco (Calif.)—Fiction
ISBN 0-06-026743-7 (lib bdg); 0-06-440336-X (pa)
                                        LC 76-24314

"Casey, a 12-year-old Chinese American girl, is more American than Chinese. When her father, a compulsive gambler, is hospitalized after a severe beating, Casey moves in with her grandmother in San Francisco's Chinatown. Although she is a street-smart child, Casey finds that she is an outsider in this community. Her grandmother teaches her something of her heritage and what it means to be 'a child of the owl.'" Shapiro. Fic for Youth. 3d edition

The cook's family. Putnam 1998 184p $15.99; pa $4.99 (5 and up)   **Fic**
1. Chinese Americans—Fiction 2. Grandmothers—Fiction
ISBN 0-03-992907-8; 0-698-11804-9 (pa)
                                        LC 97-23892

Sequel to Ribbons (1996)

As her parents' arguments become more frequent, Robin looks forward to the visits that she and her grandmother make to Chinatown, where they pretend to be an elderly cook's family, giving Robin new insights into her Chinese heritage

"The sense of place is immediate. . . . This is a fun story . . . and a unique one that will appeal to readers on several levels." SLJ

Yep, Laurence—*Continued*

Dragon's gate. HarperCollins Pubs. 1993 273p
$15.95; pa $5.95 (6 and up)   **Fic**
1. Chinese—United States—Fiction 2. Railroads—
Fiction
ISBN 0-06-022971-3; 0-06-440489-7 (pa)
        LC 92-43649
Sequel to The serpent's children (1984) and Mountain
light (1985)

A Newbery Medal honor book, 1994

When he accidentally kills a Manchu, a fifteen-year-
old Chinese boy is sent to America to join his father, an
uncle, and other Chinese working to build a tunnel for
the transcontinental railroad through the Sierra Nevada
mountains in 1867

"Yep has succeeded in realizing the primary characters
and the irrepressibly dramatic story. . . . The carefully
researched details will move students to thought and discussion." Bull Cent Child Books

Dragonwings. Harper & Row 1975 248p lib bdg
$15.89; pa $5.95 (5 and up)   **Fic**
1. Chinese Americans—Fiction 2. San Francisco
(Calif.)—Fiction
ISBN 0-06-026738-0 (lib bdg); 0-06-440085-9 (pa)

"In 1903 Moon Shadow, eight years old, leaves China
for the 'Land of the Golden Mountains,' San Francisco,
to be with his father, Windrider, a father he has never
seen. There, beset by the trials experienced by most for-
eigners in America, Moonrider shares his father's
dream—to fly. This dream enables Windrider to endure
the mockery of the other Chinese, the poverty he suffers
in this hostile place—the land of the white demons—and
his loneliness for his wife and his own country." Shapiro.
Fic for Youth. 3d edition

Hiroshima; a novella. Scholastic 1995 56p
$9.95; pa $4.50 (4 and up)   **Fic**
1. Hiroshima (Japan)—Bombardment, 1945—Fiction
ISBN 0-590-20832-2; 0-590-20833-0 (pa)
        LC 94-18195
"This moving and detailed narrative chronicles the
dropping of the atomic bomb on Hiroshima and its effects on its citizens, especially on twelve-year-old Sachi.
Based on true accounts, this book describes the horrors
and sadness as well as the courage and hope that result
from war." Soc Educ

The journal of Wong Ming-Chung; a Chinese
miner. Scholastic 2000 219p il (My name is
America) $10.95 (4 and up)   **Fic**
1. California—Gold discoveries—Fiction 2. Chinese—United States—Fiction
ISBN 0-590-38607-7   LC 99-28405
A young Chinese boy nicknamed Runt records his experiences in a journal as he travels from southern China
to California in 1852 to join his uncle during the Gold
Rush

"The engrossing story involves readers from start to
finish. . . . An engaging book with strong characters that
successfully weaves fact with fiction." SLJ

Later, gator. Hyperion Bks. for Children 1995
122p lib bdg $14.49; pa $4.50 (4-6)   **Fic**
1. Chinese Americans—Fiction 2. Brothers—Fiction
3. Alligators—Fiction
ISBN 0-7868-2083-7 (lib bdg); 0-7868-1160-9 (pa)
        LC 94-11254
"Teddy resents his goody-goody brother, Bobby.
Urged to get Bobby a suitable pet for his eighth birthday,
Teddy buys an alligator instead. Bobby unexpectedly
adores Oscar—sharp teeth, voracious appetite, and all.
The challenge of feeding Oscar unites the boys, but also
gets Teddy in trouble . . . again." Publisher's note

"The characterizations of the family and portrayal of
the culture of San Francisco's Chinatown are plausible
and likable. Yep acknowledges the peril and cruelty of
exotic pet ownership in a brief afterword." Horn Book

Another available title about Teddy and Bobby is:
Cockroach cooties (2000)

The magic paintbrush; drawings by Suling
Wang. HarperCollins Pubs. 2000 89p il $13.95; lib
bdg $13.89 (3-5)   **Fic**
1. Chinese Americans—Fiction 2. Magic—Fiction
ISBN 0-06-028199-5; 0-06-028200-2 (lib bdg)
        LC 99-34959
A magic paintbrush transports Steve and his elderly
caretakers from their drab apartment in Chinatown to a
world of adventures

"Yep's crisp style keeps the pages turning, and he
leavens his story with snappy dialogue, realistic characters and plenty of wise humor." Publ Wkly

The star fisher. Morrow Junior Bks. 1991 150p
$16 (6 and up)   **Fic**
1. Chinese Americans—Fiction 2. Moving—Fiction
3. Prejudices—Fiction
ISBN 0-688-09365-5   LC 90-23785
Also available in paperback from Puffin Bks.

Fifteen-year-old Joan Lee and her family find the adjustment hard when they move from Ohio to West Virginia in the 1920s

"Based on experiences from Laurence Yep's own family history, the story offers unique insight into the plight
of ethnic minorities. It is disturbing but never depressing,
poignant but not melancholy. . . . The book is a pleasure
to read, entertaining its audience even as it educates their
hearts." Horn Book

Thief of hearts. HarperCollins Pubs. 1995 197p
lib bdg $14.89; pa $5.95 (5 and up)   **Fic**
1. Chinese Americans—Fiction 2. Friendship—Fiction
3. San Francisco (Calif.)—Fiction
ISBN 0-06-025342-8 (lib bdg); 0-06-440591-5 (pa)
        LC 94-18703
"Stacy is not pleased that she's been elected by her
parents to show a new girl from China around school,
particularly when it turns out that Hong Ch'un is snotty
and difficult, even calling Stacy *t'ung chung*, 'mixed
seed.' Stacy's mother (whose story was told in *Child of
the Owl*) . . . is of Chinese descent, and her father Caucasian, and when Hong Ch'un is accused by the other
kids of stealing, Stacy feels torn between parental instruction, ethnic loyalty, and peer acceptance." Bull Cent
Child Books

"Told with candor and controlled emotion, this first-
person narrative presents a difficult topic in a manner accessible to a wide audience." Horn Book

Yolen, Jane

Commander Toad and the voyage home; pictures by Bruce Degen. Putnam 1998 64p il $15.99; pa $4.99 (1-3)   **Fic**
1. Toads—Fiction 2. Science fiction
ISBN 0-399-23122-6; 0-698-11602-X (pa)
LC 96-21739
Commander Toad leads the lean green space machine "Star Warts" to find new worlds but runs into trouble when he sets course for home
"Yolen captures the high drama of space fiction in a delightful story that never loses sight of developing readers, who will be old enough to get the jokes but still young enough to relish the goofiness." Booklist
Other available titles about Commander Toad are:
Commander Toad and the big black hole (1996)
Commander Toad and the dis-asteroid (1996)
Commander Toad and the intergalactic spy (1997)
Commander Toad and the Planet of the Grapes (1996)
Commander Toad and the space pirates (1997)
Commander Toad in space (1996)

The devil's arithmetic. Viking Kestrel 1988 170p hardcover o.p. paperback available $4.99 (4 and up)   **Fic**
1. Jews—Fiction 2. Holocaust, 1933-1945—Fiction
ISBN 0-14-034535-3 (pa)   LC 88-14235
"During a Passover Seder, 12-year-old Hannah finds herself transported from America in 1988 to Poland in 1942, where she assumes the life of young Chaya. Within days the Nazis take Chaya and her neighbors off to a concentration camp, mere components in the death factory. As days pass, Hannah's own memory of her past, and the prisoners' future, fades until she is Chaya completely." Publ Wkly
"Through Hannah, with her memories of the present and the past, Yolen does a fine job of illustrating the importance of remembering. She adds much to children's understanding of the effects of the Holocaust." SLJ

The dragon's boy. Harper & Row 1990 120p $14.95 (5 and up)   **Fic**
1. Arthur, King—Fiction 2. Merlin (Legendary character)—Fiction
ISBN 0-06-026789-5   LC 89-24642
"This is a retelling of the education and coming of age of 13-year-old Artos (Arthur). Old Linn (Merlin) is to be his teacher, but, doubting he can command the boy's attention, he constructs a fire-breathing dragon as a façade." SLJ
"Scattered throughout the book are broad hints of Artos's identity, but even children unfamiliar with the legendary King Arthur should find the crisply told story accessible and entertaining." Horn Book

Young, Ed

Pinocchio; adaptation from C. Collodi's [by] Ed. Young. Philomel Bks. 1995 44p il $18.95 (3-6)
Fic
1. Puppets and puppet plays—Fiction 2. Fairy tales
ISBN 0-399-22941-8   LC 95-10127
"Adapted from the original version of The adventures of Pinocchio, translated by M. A. Murray and published in the United Kingdom in 1892." Verso of title page

"Ed Young presents an illustrated edition of this famous Italian fantasy. Although his version of the story is considerably shorter than Collodi's text, it retains a sense of the adventure, humor, and pathos that made the original *Pinocchio* a classic. In the full-color, collage artwork, Young builds scenes from deftly cut and composed materials that include cloth as well as textured, painted, and printed papers highlighted with pastels." Booklist

Yumoto, Kazumi

The friends; translated by Cathy Hirano. Farrar, Straus & Giroux 1996 169p $15 (5 and up)   **Fic**
1. Friendship—Fiction   2. Old   age—Fiction
3. Death—Fiction 4. Japan—Fiction
ISBN 0-374-32460-3   LC 96-11134
Also available in paperback from Dell
Original Japanese edition, 1992
Curious about death, three sixth-grade boys named Kiyama, Kawabe, and Yamashita decide to spy on an old man waiting for him to die, but they end up becoming his friends
"The translation from the Japanese is immediate, both lyrical and casual. The characters . . . are subtly drawn. Readers will be moved by the terror of death, the bond across generations, and the struggle of those whom society labels losers." Booklist

Zalben, Jane Breskin

Unfinished dreams; a novel. Simon & Schuster Bks. for Young Readers 1996 160p $16 (5 and up)
Fic
1. Jews—Fiction 2. Violinists—Fiction 3. AIDS (Disease)—Fiction 4. School stories
ISBN 0-689-80033-9   LC 95-44424
In this "story about Jason, a twelve-year-old Jewish fledgling violinist who must suffer the slings of the class bully, AIDS becomes the background thread as a beloved principal enters the final stages of the disease. The naturalness of the dialogue, the richness of emotion, and the views expressed about valuing individual strengths, talents, and differences make this book a recommended read." Horn Book Guide

Zemser, Amy Bronwen

Beyond the mango tree. Greenwillow Bks. 1998 166p $15; pa $4.95 (5 and up)   **Fic**
1. Diabetes—Fiction 2. Liberia—Fiction
ISBN 0-688-16005-0; 0-06-440786-1 (pa)
LC 97-32268
While living in Liberia with her possessive, diabetic mother and often-absent father, twelve-year-old Sarina longs for a friend with whom to experience the world beyond her yard
"Zemser's poetic, wrenching narrative transports readers to a foreign land, but the truths they uncover will surely hit home." Publ Wkly

S C STORY COLLECTIONS

Books in this class include collections of short stories by one author and collections by more than one author. Folk tales are entered in class 398.2. Collections of general literature, American literature, English literature, etc.—which may include but are not limited to short stories—are entered in classes 808.8, 810.8, 820.8, etc.

Alexander, Lloyd
The foundling and other tales of Prydain. rev & expanded ed. Holt & Co. 1999 98p $17.95 (5 and up) **S C**
1. Fantasy fiction 2. Short stories
ISBN 0-8050-6130-4   LC 98-42807
First published 1973; this revised and expanded edition includes two additional stories Coll and his white pig and The truthful harp, first published separately 1965 and 1967 respectively
Eight short stories dealing with events that preceded the birth of Taran, the Assistant Pig-Keeper and key figure in the author's five works on the Kingdom of Prydain which began with The book of three
"The stories are written with vivid grace and humor." Chicago. Children's Book Center [review of 1973 edition]

American fairy tales; from Rip Van Winkle to the Rootabaga stories; compiled by Neil Philip; illustrated by Michael McCurdy; preface by Alison Lurie. Hyperion 1996 160p il lib bdg $23.49; pa $12.95 (6 and up) **S C**
1. Fairy tales 2. Short stories
ISBN 0-7868-2171-X (lib bdg); 0-7868-1093-9 (pa)
LC 95-49143
Among the authors represented in this story collection are Nathaniel Hawthorne, Frank Stockton, Howard Pyle, and Louisa May Alcott
"Brief, carefully honed introductions set each selection in context and analyze its peculiarly American aspects. . . . With appended source notes and selective bibliography, this collection will serve as a fine resource for American literary study and as a springboard for further exploration." Horn Book

Andersen, Hans Christian, 1805-1875
The little mermaid and other fairy tales; collected and with an introduction by Neil Philip; illustrated by Isabelle Brent. Viking 1998 137p il $21.99 (4-6) **S C**
1. Fairy tales 2. Short stories
ISBN 0-670-87840-5   LC 98-60069
Includes seventeen fairy tales including the well known, such as The tinderbox and The emperor's new clothes, as well as the lesser known, such as Little Ida's flowers and The beetle
"This volume combines an informal storytelling voice and a glamorous design with lots of gold leaf and lavishly colored illustrations." Booklist

The swan's stories; selected and translated by Brian Alderson; illustrated by Chris Riddell. Candlewick Press 1997 143p il $22.99 **S C**
1. Fairy tales 2. Short stories
ISBN 1-56402-894-1   LC 96-47197

A collection of Andersen's stories, including "The Steadfast Tin Soldier," "The Fir Tree," and "The Money Pig"
These are "excellent translations that flow smoothly with a casual and comfortable feel. The illustrations are superb." Horn Book Guide

Avi, 1937-
What do fish have to do with anything? and other stories; illustrated by Tracy Mitchell. Candlewick Press 1997 202p il $16.99; pa $5.99 (4 and up) **S C**
1. Short stories
ISBN 0-7636-0329-5; 0-7636-0412-7 (pa)
LC 97-1354
"Willie believes a homeless man possesses a cure for unhappiness. A minister dares his devilish son to be good. Pet-obsessed Eve receives visitations from two deceased cats. . . . These are among seven . . . stories dealing with communication in troubled relationships." Publisher's note
"While Avi's endings are not tidy, they are effective: each story brings its protagonist beyond childhood self-absorption to the realization that one is an integral part of a bigger picture." Horn Book

Babbitt, Natalie
The Devil's other storybook; stories and pictures by Natalie Babbitt. Farrar, Straus & Giroux 1987 81p il hardcover o.p. paperback available $4.95 (4-6) **S C**
1. Devil—Fiction 2. Short stories
ISBN 0-374-41704-0 (pa)   LC 86-32760
"Michael di Capua books"
Featuring the same creature as in The Devil's storybook, this companion volume contains 10 additional tales

The Devil's storybook; stories and pictures by Natalie Babbitt. Farrar, Straus & Giroux 1974 101p il hardcover o.p. paperback available $3.95 (4-6) **S C**
1. Devil—Fiction 2. Short stories
ISBN 0-374-41708-3 (pa)
Ten "stories about the machinations of the Devil to increase the population of his realm. He is not always successful and, despite his clever ruses, meets frustration as often as his intended victims do." Horn Book
"Twists of plot within traditional themes and a briskly witty style distinguish this book, illustrated amusingly with black-and-white line drawings." Booklist

Bond, Michael, 1926-
Paddington's storybook; illustrated in color and black and white by Peggy Fortnum. Houghton Mifflin 1984 c1983 159p il $25 (2-5) **S C**
1. Bears—Fiction 2. Great Britain—Fiction 3. Short stories
ISBN 0-395-36667-4   LC 84-12900
First published 1983 in the United Kingdom
"A selection of some of the very best stories about a very fine bear published over the past 25 years. Watercolor has been added to the original line drawings." N Y Times Book Rev

Conrad, Pam, 1947-1996

Our house; the stories of Levittown; illustrations by Brian Selznick. Scholastic 1995 65p il $14.95 (4-6) **S C**

1. Short stories 2. Levittown (N.Y.)—Fiction

ISBN 0-590-46523-6   LC 94-42126

Six stories, one from each decade from the 1940s to the 1990s, about children growing up in Levittown, New York

"Vivid descriptions and poignant observations leave indelible impressions. . . . Conrad's fresh, imaginative approach to the concept of 'home' makes this an ideal starting point for discussion, creative writing, and other class activities." Booklist

Coville, Bruce

Oddly enough; stories by Bruce Coville; illustrations by Michael Hussar. Harcourt Brace & Co. 1994 122p $15.95 (6 and up) **S C**

1. Horror fiction 2. Short stories

ISBN 0-15-200093-3   LC 94-16286

Also available in paperback from Archway

"Jane Yolen books"

A collection of nine short stories featuring an angel, unicorn, vampire, werewolf, and other unusual creatures

"The stories are well written. . . . The plots . . . are always clear and characterizations deftly drawn. . . . A worthwhile purchase, particularly for classroom discussions." SLJ

Delacre, Lulu, 1957-

Salsa stories; stories and linocuts by Lulu Delacre. Scholastic Press 2000 105p il $15.95 (4-6) **S C**

1. Latin America—Fiction 2. Family life—Fiction 3. Short stories

ISBN 0-590-63118-7   LC 99-25534

A collection of stories within the story of a family celebration where the guests relate their memories of growing up in various Latin American countries. Also contains recipes

"Kids will respond to both the warmth and the anxiety of the family life described in the vivid writing, and in Delacre's nicely composed linocuts." Booklist

Don't read this! and other tales of the unnatural; [by] Margaret Mahy [et al.]; illustrations by The Tjong Khing. Front St. 1998 213p il $15.95 (6 and up) **S C**

1. Ghost stories 2. Short stories

ISBN 1-886910-22-7   LC 98-3215

Published in the United Kingdom with title: Fingers on the back of the neck and other ghost stories

An international collection of ghost stories and spooky tales by such authors as Susan Cooper, Roberto Piumini, and Bjarne Reuter

"These are enjoyable, unsettling tales sans sex and gore—refreshing and recommended." Voice Youth Advocates

Ellis, Sarah, 1952-

Back of beyond; stories of the supernatural. Margaret K. McElderry Bks. 1997 136p $15 (6 and up) **S C**

1. Supernatural—Fiction 2. Short stories

ISBN 0-689-81484-4   LC 97-6844

A collection of twelve otherworldly stories which blend reality and unreality

"The stories are consistently well written, and Ellis seems to have had a wonderful time creating 12 intriguing, completely different views of the supernatural—from the playfully weird to the truly eerie." Booklist

Fleischman, Paul

Graven images; 3 stories; illustrations by Andrew Glass. Harper & Row 1982 85p il hardcover o.p. paperback available $4.95 (6 and up) **S C**

1. Supernatural—Fiction 2. Short stories

ISBN 0-06-440186-3 (pa)   LC 81-48649

A Newbery Medal honor book, 1983

"A Charlotte Zolotow book"

Three stories about people whose lives are influenced by sculptured figures. In Saint Crispin's follower, "Nicholas, an apprentice cobbler, believes the statue of St. Crispin in his village square is guiding him to a successful courtship with a comely lass. . . . The other two tales are grim examples of retribution. A wooden figurehead, 'The Binnacle Boy,' unmasks a killer in an old whaling port, and a statue commissioned by a ghost proves that a father has murdered his son in 'The Man of Influence.'" Publ Wkly

A **Glory** of unicorns; compiled by Bruce Coville; illustrated by Alix Berenzy. Scholastic 1998 198p il $16.95; pa $4.50 (5 and up) **S C**

1. Unicorns—Fiction 2. Short stories

ISBN 0-590-95943-3; 0-449-06628-X (pa)

LC 97-13689

Eleven stories and one poem, by such authors as Nancy Varian Berberick, Gregory Maguire, and Margaret Bechard, about unicorns in both mythical and contemporary settings

"Exciting and thought-provoking. Even readers who shy away from the science fiction/fantasy genres will enjoy these short tales and their special messages." Voice Youth Adovates

Jiménez, Francisco, 1943-

The circuit: stories from the life of a migrant child. University of N.M. Press 1997 134p pa $10.95 (5 and up) **S C**

1. Mexican Americans—Fiction 2. Migrant labor—Fiction 3. Short stories

ISBN 0-8263-1797-9   LC 97-4844

Also available in hardcover from Houghton Mifflin and Audiobook version

A collection of twelve short stories about Mexican American migrant farmworkers

"Each of these short stories builds quietly to a surprise that reveals the truth, and together the stories lead to the tearing climax." Booklist

Kimmel, Eric A.

The jar of fools: eight Hanukkah stories from Chelm; illustrated by Mordicai Gerstein. Holiday House 2000 56p il $18.95 (3-5)   **S C**
1. Hanukkah—Fiction 2. Jews—Fiction 3. Short stories
ISBN 0-8234-1463-9   LC 99-57823
Drawing on traditional Jewish folklore, these Hanukkah stories relate the antics of the people of Chelm, thought--perhaps incorrectly--to be a town of fools
"Kimmel gets the shtetl setting, the humanity, and the farce. . . . Gerstein's detailed ink-on-oil paint artwork, one full-page picture per story, captures the intricate silliness and slapstick." Booklist

Sword of the samurai; adventure stories from Japan. Harcourt Brace & Co. 1999 114p $15 (4 and up)   **S C**
1. Japan—Fiction 2. Adventure fiction 3. Short stories
ISBN 0-15-201985-5   LC 98-16633
Also available in paperback from HarperCollins
"Browndeer Press"
Eleven short stories about samurai warriors, their way of life, courage, wit, and foolishness
"These selections offer something for everyone: humor, wisdom and adventure along with a gentle and graceful introduction to the code of ethics that continues to shape Japan today." Publ Wkly

Kipling, Rudyard, 1865-1936

The jungle book: the Mowgli stories; illustrated by Jerry Pinkney; afterword by Peter Glassman. Morrow 1995 258p il $22.95 (4 and up)   **S C**
1. Animals—Fiction 2. India—Fiction 3. Short stories
ISBN 0-688-09979-3   LC 92-1415
Selected stories from Kipling's two "Jungle Books" chronicle the adventures of Mowgli, the boy reared by a pack of wolves in an Indian jungle. Also includes "Rikki-Tikki-Tavi"
The handsome illustrations in dappled watercolors show to admiration the lush jungle growth, the watchful animals, and Mowgli himself. A glorious pairing of text and illustration." Horn Book

Just so stories; illustrated by Barry Moser; afterword by Peter Glassman. Morrow 1996 148p il $21.95 (3-6)   **S C**
1. Animals—Fiction 2. India—Fiction 3. Short stories
ISBN 0-688-13957-4 (Morrow)   LC 95-13714
Also available Audiobook version
First published 1902
A set of tales that "give far-fetched humorous explanations of the chief physical characteristics of certain animals." Oxford Companion to Child Lit

Konigsburg, E. L.

Altogether, one at a time; illustrated by Gail E. Haley [et al.] Atheneum Pubs. 1971 79p il hardcover o.p. paperback available $4.99 (4-6)   **S C**
1. Short stories
ISBN 0-689-71290-1 (pa)

"Compelled to invite a child he doesn't want to his birthday party in 'Inviting Jason,' Stanley likes the boy even less afterwards, but for a different reason. A 10-year-old boy learns something about old age in 'The Night of the Leonids' when he realizes his grandmother has lost her chance to see a shower of stars that occurs only once every 33½ years. The spirit of a long dead camp counselor helps an obese girl make up her mind that she will never have to attend Camp Fat again. In 'Momma at the Pearly Gates,' Momma tells the story of how, as a girl, she was called a 'dirty nigger' by a white classmate." Libr J

Marshall, James, 1942-1992

Rats on the range and other stories. Dial Bks. for Young Readers 1993 80p $13.99; pa $3.99 (2-4)   **S C**
1. Animals—Fiction 2. Short stories
ISBN 0-8037-1384-3; 0-14-038645-9 (pa)
    LC 92-28918
In eight animal stories the reader meets a rat family that vacations at a dude ranch, a pig who takes lessons in table manners, a mouse who keeps house for a tomcat, and a buzzard who leaves his money to the Society for Stray Cats—or does he?
"In this collection, which brilliantly demonstrates Marshall's gift for humor, there are eight gems." Horn Book Guide

Rats on the roof, and other stories. Dial Bks. for Young Readers 1991 79p il lib bdg $12.89; pa $4.99 (2-4)   **S C**
1. Animals—Fiction 2. Short stories
ISBN 0-8037-0835-1 (lib bdg); 0-14-038646-7 (pa)
    LC 90-44084
An illustrated collection of seven stories about various animals, including a frog with magnificent legs, a hungry brontosaurus, and a mouse who gets married
"Marshall's fertile imagination gets lots of exercise here as does his sardonic wit, and he's included plenty of expressive illustrations, all done in his signature style." Booklist

McKissack, Patricia C., 1944-

The dark-thirty; Southern tales of the supernatural; illustrated by Brian Pinkney. Knopf 1992 122p il lib bdg $17.99; pa $12 (4 and up)   **S C**
1. Ghost stories 2. African Americans—Fiction 3. Short stories
ISBN 0-679-91863-9 (lib bdg); 0-679-88335-5 (pa)
    LC 92-3021
Also available in paperback from Dell
A Newbery Medal honor book, 1993; Coretta Scott King Award for text, 1993
A collection of ghost stories with African American themes, designed to be told during the Dark Thirty—the half hour before sunset—when ghosts seem all too believable
"Strong characterizations are superbly drawn in a few words. The atmosphere of each selection is skillfully developed and sustained to the very end. Pinkney's stark scratchboard illustrations evoke an eerie mood, which heightens the suspense of each tale." SLJ

Medearis, Angela Shelf, 1956-

Haunts; five hair-raising tales; drawings by Trina Schart Hyman. Holiday House 1996 37p il $15.95 (4 and up)   S C

1. Ghost stories 2. Short stories

ISBN 0-8234-1280-6   LC 96-17336

This includes "five short stories about creepy, crawly horrors, spooky ghosts, and things that go bump in the night." Publisher's note

These stories are "accessibly short, gleefully scary, and blessed with terrifically horrific cover and interior art by Trina Schart Hyman." Bull Cent Child Books

The Oxford treasury of children's stories;

[compiled by] Michael Harrison and Christopher Stuart-Clark. Oxford Univ. Press 1994 159p il hardcover o.p. paperback available $12.95 (3-5)   S C

ISBN 0-19-278112-X (pa)

This anthology includes twenty-six stories by such authors as Julius Lester, James Berry, Joan Aiken, and Margaret Mahy

"The selections are suitable for reading aloud and are mostly fantastic, with a generous sprinkling of dragons, giants, and other magical beings, and the tone is predominantly humorous. Six different illustrators contribute full-page and smaller watercolors." SLJ

Paterson, Katherine

Angels & other strangers: family Christmas stories. Crowell 1979 118p hardcover o.p. paperback available $4.95 (5 and up)   S C

1. Christmas—Fiction 2. Short stories

ISBN 0-06-440283-5 (pa)   LC 79-63797

"The author weaves stories about miracles of the Christmas season—miracles that take place on a truly human level. Each story is based on the Christian message of the birth of Christ and the significance that message takes on for the characters. She writes of the poor, the desolate, and the lonely as well as of the arrogant, the complacent, and the proud." Horn Book

Rylant, Cynthia

Children of Christmas; stories for the season; drawings by S. D. Schindler. Orchard Bks. 1987 38p il hardcover o.p. paperback available $6.95 (4 and up)   S C

1. Christmas—Fiction 2. Short stories

ISBN 0-531-07012-5 (pa)   LC 87-1690

These Christmas stories are "about lost things: a stray cat, a stray bachelor, a grandfather who has lost the connection to the youngest generation, a misunderstood boy who receives a cowboy set instead of a doctor kit and who tries to hold onto a lost dream." Read Teach

"Rylant's Christmas is a sad and lonely one, but her ability to summon the joys of the season through her writing is extraordinary. Schindler's illustrations, appropriately, are both reserved and inciting." Publ Wkly

Every living thing; stories; decorations by S. D. Schindler. Bradbury Press 1985 81p hardcover o.p. paperback available $4.99 (5 and up)   S C

1. Animals—Fiction 2. Short stories

ISBN 0-689-71263-4 (pa)   LC 85-7701

"This book tells twelve stories about lonely people whose lives have been changed for the better by an association with an animal. Many of the stories are heartwarming and meant to be read aloud. Through a parrot, a twelve-year-old boy learns how much his father loves him; a retired schoolteacher and an old collie renew their life by becoming friends with young children. While some of the stories are overly sentimental, the majority realistically show the importance of animals in our lives." Okla State Dept of Educ

Sandburg, Carl, 1878-1967

Rootabaga stories; illustrated by Michael Hague. Harcourt Brace Jovanovich 1988-1989 2v il ea $19.95; pa $7   S C

1. Fairy tales 2. Short stories

ISBN 0-15-269061-1 (v1); 0-15-269065-4 (v1 pa); 0-15-269062-X (v2); 0-15-269063-8 (v2 pa)

       LC 88-935

First published 1922

"These fanciful tales reflect Sandburg's interest in folk ballads and nonsense verse. He modeled his expansive fictional land on the American Midwest. The lighthearted stories, referred to as moral tales by Sandburg, feature such silly characters as Hot Dog the Tiger, Gimme the Ax, White Horse Girl, Blue Wind Boy, and Jason Squiff the Cistern Cleaner." Merriam Webster's Ency of Lit

Rootabaga stories; illustrated by Michael Hague. Harcourt Brace Jovanovich 1988-1989 2v il ea $19.95; pa $4.95   S C

1. Fairy tales 2. Short stories

ISBN 0-15-269061-1 (v1); 0-15-269065-4 (v1 pa); 0-15-269062-X (v2); 0-15-269063-8 (v2 pa)

       LC 88-935

A newly illustrated combined edition of Rootabaga stories and Rootabaga pigeons, first published separately 1922 and 1923 respectively

The stories combine "the realism of the American middle West with a great deal of fancy and symbolism. A certain amount of repetition and the use of mouth-filling words create a rhythm and a singing quality which make the stories particularly suitable for reading aloud." Right Book for the Right Child

"The illustrations are a good match to the lively prose of these highly imaginative tales." SLJ

Singer, Isaac Bashevis, 1904-1991

The power of light; eight stories for Hanukkah; with illustrations by Irene Lieblich. Farrar, Straus & Giroux 1980 86p il $15; pa $8.95 (4 and up)   S C

1. Hanukkah—Fiction 2. Jews—Fiction 3. Short stories

ISBN 0-374-36099-5; 0-374-45984-3 (pa)

       LC 80-20263

"The stories, bound together by recurring Hanukkah motifs—the lamp, the dreidel, and the pancakes, tell chiefly of events affecting the lives of Eastern European Jews. Ranging from such somber happenings as the drafting of small Jewish boys to serve in the Russian army during the nineteenth century through the bombing and burning of the Warsaw ghetto, the harrowing events are seen in the context of the celebration of Hanukkah." Horn Book

Singer, Isaac Bashevis, 1904-1991—*Continued*

"The stories vary from realism to incorporation of the miraculous . . . but are united in their strong piety as they are in the polished craftsmanship and warmth with which they are written." Bull Cent Child Books

Stories for children. Farrar, Straus & Giroux 1984 337p $22.95; pa $14 (4 and up) S C
1. Jews—Fiction 2. Short stories
ISBN 0-374-37266-7; 0-374-46489-8 (pa)

LC 84-13612

This collection of thirty-six stories includes "parables, beast fables, allegories and reminiscences. Some stories are silly and charming, while others are wildly fantastic, dealing with savagery and miracles in mythical, medieval Poland. Frequently they are about scary situations, but all tend to end happily, with an edifying idea. Most appealing is the Nobel Prize winner's sheer story-telling power. In this respect, he has no equal among contemporaries." N Y Times Book Rev

Soto, Gary

Baseball in April, and other stories. 10th anniversary ed. Harcourt Brace Jovanovich 2000 c1990 111p $16; pa $6 (5 and up) S C
1. Mexican Americans—Fiction 2. California—Fiction 3. Short stories
ISBN 0-15-202573-1; 0-15-205721-8 (pa)
Also available Spanish language edition and Audiobook version
A reissue of the title first published 1990
A collection of eleven short stories focusing on the everyday adventures of Hispanic young people growing up in Fresno, California
Each story "gets at the heart of some aspect of growing up. The insecurities, the embarrassments, the triumphs, the inequities of it all are chronicled with wit and charm. Soto's characters ring true and his knowledge of, and affection for, their shared Mexican-American heritage is obvious and infectious." Voice Youth Advocates

Petty crimes. Harcourt Brace & Co. 1998 157p $16 (5 and up) S C
1. Mexican Americans—Fiction 2. California—Fiction 3. Short stories
ISBN 0-15-201658-9

LC 97-37114

A collection of short stories about Mexican American youth growing up in California's Central Valley
"A sense of family strength relieves the under-current of sadness in these raw stories." Horn Book Guide

Spinelli, Jerry, 1941-

The library card. Scholastic 1997 148p $15.95; pa $4.99 (4 and up) S C
1. Books and reading—Fiction 2. Short stories
ISBN 0-590-46731-X; 0-590-38633-6 (pa)

LC 96-18412

"A library card is the magical object common to each of these four stories in which a budding street thug, a television addict, a homeless orphan, and a lonely girl are all transformed by the power and the possibilities that await them within the walls of the public library. Spinelli's characters . . . are unusual and memorable; his writing both humorous and convincing." Horn Book Guide

Wilde, Oscar, 1854-1900

The fairy tales of Oscar Wilde; illustrated by Isabelle Brent; edited with an introduction by Neil Philip. Viking 1994 141p il $19.99 (3-6) S C
1. Fairy tales 2. Short stories
ISBN 0-670-85585-5
"The stories were originally published as 'The Happy Prince and other Tales' (1888) and 'A House of Pomegranates' (1891)." Verso of title page

Wrede, Patricia C., 1953-

Book of enchantments. Harcourt Brace & Co. 1996 234p $17 (6 and up) S C
1. Magic—Fiction 2. Short stories
ISBN 0-15-201255-9

LC 95-41036

Also available in paperback from Scholastic
"Jane Yolen books"
"This collection of original short stories uses archetypal fairy- and folktale motifs that feature strong female protagonists. Wrede's forte in firmly establishing characterization allows the reader to care about the outcome of each of the ten stories. Fine examples of new twists on ancient tales, the stories range in tone from witty to sad." Horn Book Guide

Wynne-Jones, Tim

The book of changes; stories. Orchard Bks. 1995 c1994 143p $15.95 (4 and up) S C
1. Short stories
ISBN 0-531-09489-8

LC 95-6034

"A Melanie Kroupa book"
First published 1994 in Canada
The stories "focus on what seem to be ordinary events: a frantic search for inspiration for a class project, a chance to appear a hero to a younger child, the tyranny of a class bully. Yet with his prowess for crafting each tale so that it neatly comes full circle, Wynne-Jones makes the quotidian well worth reading about. . . . The characters' on-target thoughts and banter attest to the author's familiarity with—and compassion for—today's kids." Publ Wkly

Lord of the Fries and other stories. DK Pub. 1999 214p $17.95 (5 and up) S C
1. Canada—Fiction 2. Short stories
ISBN 0-7894-2623-4

LC 98-41581

"'Lord of the Fries' features a pair of friends who try to penetrate the mysterious past of a legendarily cranky fast-food entrepreneur; 'The Fallen Angel' features a choirboy bedeviled by a new and problematic arrival in the choir loft; 'The Chinese Babies' bring together a Welsh-speaking English Canadian, a van full of French Canadians, several generations of moody family, and some important games of chess." Bull Cent Child Books
"Fresh dialogue, sympathetic and idiosyncratic protagonists, and surprises around every corner." Publ Wkly

Some of the kinder planets: stories. Orchard Bks. 1995 c1993 130p $15.95; lib bdg $16.99 (4 and up) S C
1. Short stories
ISBN 0-531-09451-0; 0-531-08751-4 (lib bdg)

LC 94-33009

Also available in paperback from Puffin Bks.

Wynne-Jones, Tim—*Continued*

First published 1993 in Canada

"This collection of nine short stories offers offbeat vignettes of contemporary life as well as tales of ghosts, aliens, and historical figures. Clear writing combines with clever concepts and varied subject matter to make the book accessible and enjoyable to a wide audience." SLJ

E EASY BOOKS

This section consists chiefly of fiction books that would interest children from pre-school through third grade. Easy books that have a definite nonfiction subject content are usually classified with other nonfiction books. Easy books listed here include:

1. Picture books, whether fiction or nonfiction, that the young child can use independently

2. Fiction books with very little or scattered text, with large print and with vocabulary suitable for children with reading levels of grades 1-3

3. Picture storybooks with a larger amount of text to be used primarily by or with children in pre-school through grade 3

Ackerman, Karen, 1951-

By the dawn's early light; illustrated by Catherine Stock. Atheneum Pubs. 1994 unp il hardcover o.p. paperback available $5.99   **E**

1. Mothers—Fiction 2. Factories—Fiction 3. Grandmothers—Fiction

ISBN 0-689-82481-5 (pa)   LC 92-35633

Rachel and Josh stay with their grandmother while their mother works at night in a factory

"Told from the eight or nine-year-old daughter's perspective, the text is honest without being maudlin or bitter. . . . Warm, often impressionistic watercolor illustrations accurately convey the misty, wee-small hour setting as well as the glow of family relationships. Characters are predominantly African-American females." SLJ

Song and dance man; illustrated by Stephen Gammell. Knopf 1988 unp il lib bdg $16.99; pa $6.99   **E**

1. Entertainers—Fiction 2. Grandfathers—Fiction

ISBN 0-394-99330-6 (lib bdg); 0-679-81995-9 (pa)

LC 87-3200

Awarded the Caldecott Medal, 1989

"Grandpa takes three grandchildren up to the attic, where he arranges lights and gives a performance that enchants his audience. They tell him they wish they could have seen him dance in 'the good old days' but he says he wouldn't trade a million good old days for the time he spends with the narrators." Bull Cent Child Books

The illustrator "captures all the story's inherent joie de vivre with color pencil renderings that fairly leap off the pages." Booklist

Adams, Adrienne

The Easter egg artists. Scribner 1976 unp il hardcover o.p. paperback available $5.99   **E**

1. Rabbits—Fiction 2. Easter—Fiction 3. Egg decoration—Fiction

ISBN 0-689-71481-5 (pa)

"The Abbotts, rabbits who design Easter Eggs, are worried that son Orson will not follow the family trade. On a winter vacation Orson and the family paint a car, a house, an airplane, a bridge, and Orson becomes a committed Easter Egg Artist. Children rated this charming story with its lovely illustrations one of the most beautiful picture books of the year." Read Teach

Adler, David A., 1947-

The Babe & I; written by David A. Adler; illustrated by Terry Widener. Harcourt Brace & Co. 1999 unp il $16   **E**

1. Ruth, Babe, 1895-1948—Fiction 2. Great Depression, 1929-1939—Fiction

ISBN 0-15-201378-4   LC 97-37580

"Gulliver books"

While helping his family make ends meet during the Depression by selling newspapers, a boy meets Babe Ruth

"Widener's illustrations evoke the ambiance of the period in this book that is carefully paced and remarkable for its unified focus." Horn Book Guide

Young Cam Jansen and the dinosaur game; illustrated by Susanna Natti. Viking 1996 32p il $13.99; pa $3.99   **E**

1. Mystery fiction

ISBN 0-670-86399-8; 0-14-037779-4 (pa)

LC 95-46463

Titles about Cam Jansen for older readers are also available

"A Viking easy-to-read"

"At Jane's birthday party, everyone guesses the number of toy dinosaurs in a big jar. Jennifer 'the Camera' Jansen's photographic memory helps her nab Robert, who has cheated in order to win all the dinosaurs. Observant readers can follow Cam's reasoning and solve the mystery, too." Horn Book Guide

Other available easy-to-read titles about Cam Jansen are:

Young Cam Jansen and the baseball mystery (1999)

Young Cam Jansen and the ice skate mystery (1998)

Young Cam Jansen and the library mystery (2001)

Young Cam Jansen and the lost tooth (1997)

Young Cam Jansen and the missing cookie (1996)

Young Cam Jansen and the pizza shop mystery (2000)

Adoff, Arnold, 1935-

Black is brown is tan; pictures by Emily Arnold McCully. Harper & Row 1973 31p il $15.95; pa $5.95   **E**

1. Stories in rhyme 2. Family life—Fiction 3. Race relations—Fiction

ISBN 0-06-020083-9; 0-06-443269-6 (pa)

This story in rhyme describes "a warm, racially-mixed family who reads, cuts wood, plays, and eats together." Booklist

"Arnold Adoff's spare free verse combines familiar images in a startling original way . . . and Emily McCully's beautiful watercolors are radiant with feeling and life." SLJ

Agee, Jon

The incredible painting of Felix Clousseau. Farrar, Straus & Giroux 1988 unp il hardcover o.p. paperback available $4.95   **E**

ISBN 0-374-43582-0 (pa)   LC 87-046072

"When the Royal Palace holds a competition, Clousseau . . . is ridiculed for his simple painting of a duck—until it goes 'QUACK!' and walks out of the frame. . . . Suddenly Paris is agog, all of the man's paintings are coming alive." Booklist

"A well-defined drawing style is enhanced by dark, rich colors, thickly and boldly applied. Agee provides much food for the spirit with his spare storytelling and distinctive artwork." Publ Wkly

Ahlberg, Allan

Bravest ever bear; illustrated by Paul Howard. Candlewick Press 1999 unp il $15.99   **E**

1. Fairy tales

ISBN 0-7636-0783-5   LC 98-51833

Fairy tale characters tell their stories from their own perspective, with new endings, and find themselves encountering each other as their stories overlap

"This whimsical, charming book is filled with hilarious nonsequiturs and inventive plot twists with much kid appeal. . . . Brightly colored, detailed illustrations provide apt accompaniment, placing the disparate characters in lively, chaotic scenarios with witty results." Booklist

Ahlberg, Janet

The baby's catalogue; [by] Janet and Allan Ahlberg. Little, Brown 1982 unp il hardcover o.p. paperback available $6.95   **E**

1. Infants—Fiction 2. Vocabulary

ISBN 0-316-02038-9 (pa)   LC 82-9928

"An Atlantic Monthly press book"

"Titles and labels are the only print on the pages of a book that begins with a page headed 'Babies' and goes through the objects and activities and people that most babies see on a typical day. There are Moms, Dads, brothers and sisters, toys, high chairs, diapers, meals, books, baths, bedtimes, etc. The softly colored paintings are cheerful and amusing, the format is clean and uncluttered, and the whole should provide hours of pointing, identification, and naming." Bull Cent Child Books

Each peach pear plum; an 'I spy' story; [by] Janet and Allan Ahlberg. Viking 1979 c1978 unp il $14.99; pa $4.99   **E**

1. Stories in rhyme

ISBN 0-670-28705-9; 0-14-050639-X (pa)

LC 78-16726

Also available Board book edition

First published 1978 in the United Kingdom

This book "invites children to play 'I spy' and point out nursery rhyme and story characters such as Jack and Jill, the Three Bears, Cinderella, etc. who are semi-hidden within . . . [the] illustrations." SLJ

The characters hide "in a pleasant, rural, watercolor world that's decorative but never precious or self-regarding. This is a lovely small book, well-conceived and very well drawn, gentle, humorous, unsentimental." N Y Times Book Rev

Peek-a-boo! by Janet & Allan Ahlberg. Viking 1981 unp il hardcover o.p. paperback available $5.99   **E**

1. Infants—Fiction 2. Family life—Fiction 3. Stories in rhyme

ISBN 0-14-050107-X (pa)

Also available Board book edition

Published in the United Kingdom with title: Peepo!

Brief rhyming clues invite the reader to look through holes in the pages for a baby's view of the world from breakfast to bedtime

"Perfectly tuned for a first-book experience. . . . The full-color paintings reveal a reassuringly disorganized but loving family in pastel-framed scenes that feature tiny familiar objects as part of the border." Booklist

Alborough, Jez

Duck in the truck. HarperCollins Pubs. 2000 unp il $14.95   **E**

ISBN 0-06-028685-7   LC 99-60934

"A rhyming text relates the troubles of a duck whose truck gets stuck in the muck. . . . The art makes the most of the story's physical comedy, with exaggerated humor and an engaging animal cast, including a frog, a sheep, and a goat who all come to help out." Horn Book Guide

My friend Bear. Candlewick Press 1998 unp il $16.99; pa $5.99   **E**

1. Bears—Fiction 2. Teddy bears—Fiction 3. Stories in rhyme

ISBN 0-7636-0583-2; 0-7636-1414-9 (pa)

LC 97-32557

Eddie and his teddy bear meet a very big bear in the woods, and Eddie and the big bear become good friends

"Young children will find plenty to like in this straightforward story about loneliness and friendship. The large-scale artwork, created with watercolor, crayon, and pencil, dramatizes every emotion suggested in the rhymed verses." Booklist

Other available titles about Eddie are:

It's the bear (1994)

Where's my teddy? (1992)

Watch out! Big Bro's coming! Candlewick Press 1997 unp il hardcover o.p. paperback available $6.99   **E**

1. Animals—Fiction

ISBN 0-7636-0584-0 (pa)   LC 96-30318

"A young mouse alerts frog that 'Big Bro' is on the way, stretching his arms wide to show Big Bro's immensity. Frog in turn tells parrot, who tells chimpanzee, who tells elephant, each animal imagining the worst—which gets bigger and bigger. In the watercolor and ink illustrations that fill each page, bright colors and slightly goofy expressions help the reader smile knowingly from a safe distance." Horn Book Guide

Alda, Arlene, 1933-

Arlene Alda's 1 2 3. Tricycle Press 1998 unp il $12.95   **E**

1. Counting

ISBN 1-883672-71-6   LC 98-5966

Alda, Arlene, 1933-—*Continued*

"The numerals 1 through 10 and back again are portrayed with great imagination in fine, full-color photographs. The examples reflect the shapes of the numbers themselves: four is formed by the crossed legs of a flamingo, eight is two bagels frosted with cream cheese lying on a plate. . . . A unique, challenging concept book." SLJ

Alexander, Lloyd

The fortune-tellers; illustrated by Trina Schart Hyman. Dutton Children's Bks. 1992 unp il $15.99; pa $5.99   E
    1. Fortune telling—Fiction 2. Cameroon—Fiction
    ISBN 0-525-44849-7; 0-14-056233-8 (pa)
                                 LC 91-30684

A carpenter goes to a fortune teller and finds the predictions about his future coming true in an unusual way

"Alexander's rags-to-riches story combines universal elements of the trickster character and the cumulative disaster tale. Hyman's pictures set it all in a vibrant community in Cameroon, West Africa. . . . The energetic, brilliantly colored paintings are packed with people and objects that swirl around the main characters. . . . With its ups and downs, this is a funny, playful story that evokes the irony of the human condition." Booklist

The House Gobbaleen; illustrated by Diane Goode. Dutton Children's Bks. 1995 unp il hardcover o.p. paperback available $5.99   E
    1. Fairy tales 2. Cats—Fiction
    ISBN 0-14-056504-3 (pa)   LC 94-23300

Unhappy over what he considers his bad luck, Tooley ignores his cat's warnings and invites a greedy little man into his home in the mistaken hope of improving his fortunes

"Alexander's rolling, lilting language is a joy to read aloud, and the seamlessly written story with its wry undertone will engage both young listeners and older readers. . . . Goode's bright, cheery paintings and distinctive style capture the spirit of the tale." SLJ

Alexander, Martha G.

Blackboard Bear; [by] Martha Alexander. 2nd ed. Candlewick Press 1999 unp il $12.99   E
    1. Bears—Fiction
    ISBN 0-7636-0667-7   LC 98-53913

First published 1969 by Dial Press

When a little boy is not allowed to play with the older children, he creates an imaginary friend by drawing a giant bear on his blackboard

This edition "has been full-colored, gently, and given a larger trim size for a new lease on life." Horn Book Guide

Other available titles about Blackboard Bear are:

And my mean old mother will be sorry, Blackboard Bear (1972)

I sure am glad to see you, Blackboard Bear (1976)

You're a genius, Blackboard Bear (1995)

How my library grew, by Dinah; story and pictures by Martha Alexander. Wilson, H.W. 1983 unp il $25   E
    1. Libraries—Fiction
    ISBN 0-8242-0679-7   LC 82-20204

"Told through the eyes of a young girl talking to her stuffed friend, Teddy, this softly colored, child-like story describes a library being built across the street. Through the seasons, Dinah and Teddy watch a hole being dug and the building going up; they wonder about its use and delight in designing a surprise for opening day. . . . Small vignettes, often grouped two or three to a page, enticingly depict the library's construction and open-for-business scenes, making the library a very inviting and stimulating place to be." Booklist

When the new baby comes, I'm moving out; story and pictures by Martha Alexander. Dial Bks. for Young Readers 1979 unp il hardcover o.p. paperback available $4.99   E
    1. Siblings—Fiction 2. Infants—Fiction
    ISBN 0-1405-4723-1 (pa)   LC 79-4275

"Although this is a companion to 'Nobody asked me if I wanted a baby sister,' the action precedes the first book in that the object of Oliver's sibling jealousy hasn't been born yet. Mom is due any day and Oliver is feeling hostile. So hostile in fact, that he fantasizes stuffing his pregnant mother into a garbage can and taking it to the dump." SLJ

"The clean, small-scale pictures echo the warmth and humor of the story." Bull Cent Child Books

Aliki

Best friends together again. Greenwillow Bks. 1995 unp il lib bdg $14.89   E
    1. Friendship—Fiction
    ISBN 0-688-13754-7   LC 94-12989

Companion volume to We are best friends

"Robert can't wait for Peter's visit. Even though Peter has moved away, the two consider themselves best friends. The boys soon learn that although some things have changed, their friendship remains intact. The child-like pleasure and joy of reunion are captured by the straightforward text and enhanced by bright illustrations." Horn Book Guide

Painted words: Marianthe's story one. Greenwillow Bks. 1998 unp il $16; lib bdg $15.89   E
    1. School stories 2. Immigration and emigration—Fiction
    ISBN 0-688-15663-0; 0-688-15664-9 (lib bdg)
                               LC 97-34653

Bound back to back with: Spoken memories: Marianthe's story two

Two separate stories, the first telling of Mari's starting school in a new land, and the second describing village life in her country before she and her family left in search of a better life

"In simple, understated language, Aliki has captured the emotions and experiences of many of today's children. Colored-pencil and crayon illustrations in soft primary and secondary colors reinforce the mood of the text." SLJ

The two of them; written and illustrated by Aliki. Greenwillow Bks. 1979 unp il hardcover o.p. paperback available $5.95   E
    1. Grandfathers—Fiction 2. Death—Fiction
    ISBN 0-688-07337-9 (pa)   LC 79-10161

Aliki—*Continued*

Describes the relationship of a grandfather and his granddaughter from her birth to his death

"The eloquent illustrations in muted full color and the smaller soft-pencil drawings show the life the two shared as well as the tenderness and pure pleasure implicit in their relationship. . . . The book transcends the labored introductions to geriatrics which have proliferated in contemporary children's literature and describes with sensitivity and truth the changing seasons of human life." Horn Book

We are best friends. Greenwillow Bks. 1982 unp il $17; pa $5.95　　　　　　　　　　　　　E
1. Friendship—Fiction
ISBN 0-688-00822-4; 0-688-07037-X (pa)
LC 81-6549

Companion volume to Best friends together again

When Robert's best friend Peter moves away, both are unhappy, but they learn that they can make new friends and still remain best friends

"Brightly lit pictures in cheerful primary colors portray with just a stroke of the pen the misery of losing a friend who must move away and the tentative beginnings of a new companionship. . . . Details of school and home abound in the lively pictures." Horn Book

Welcome, little baby. Greenwillow Bks. 1987 unp il $16　　　　　　　　　　　　　　　　E
1. Infants—Fiction 2. Mothers—Fiction
ISBN 0-688-06810-3
LC 86-7648

A mother welcomes her newborn infant, and tells what life will be like as the child grows older

"Tender pictures in pastel colors are appropriate for a minimal text, not substantial but effective in its message of love." Bull Cent Child Books

Allard, Harry, 1928-

Bumps in the night; pictures by James Marshall. Delacorte Press 1996 48p il $13.95; pa $3.99
　　　　　　　　　　　　　　　　　　　　E
1. Ghost stories 2. Animals—Fiction
ISBN 0-385-32282-8; 0-440-41286-2 (pa)
LC 96-3687

"A Yearling first choice chapter book"

A reissue of the title first published 1979 by Doubleday

"Dudley the Stork hears noises in his house at night and encounters a ghost. In order to find out what the ghost wants, Dudley and his friends have Madam Kreepy hold a seance. The story is humorous and spooky. The illustrations show us an unusual assortment of characters and add to the story line." Children's Bk Rev Serv

Miss Nelson is missing! [by] Harry Allard, James Marshall. Houghton Mifflin 1977 32p il $16; pa $5.95　　　　　　　　　　　　　　E
1. School stories 2. Teachers—Fiction
ISBN 0-395-25296-2; 0-395-40146-1 (pa)
LC 76-55918

Also available Spanish language edition and in paperback with Audiobook

Illustrated by James Marshall

"The kids in room 207 were so fresh and naughty that they lost their sweet-natured teacher, the blonde Miss Nelson, and got in her place the sour-souled Miss Swamp." N Y Times Book Rev

"Humor and suspense fill the pages of [this book]." Christ Sci Monit

Other available titles about Miss Nelson are:
Miss Nelson has a field day (1985)
Miss Nelson is back (1982)

Anaya, Rudolfo A.

Farolitos for Abuelo; [by] Rudolfo Anaya; illustrated by Edward Gonzales. Hyperion Bks. for Children 1998 unp il $15.99; lib bdg $16.49
　　　　　　　　　　　　　　　　　　　　E
1. Grandfathers—Fiction 2. Death—Fiction 3. Mexican Americans—Fiction 4. Christmas—Fiction
ISBN 0-7868-0237-5; 0-7868-2186-8 (lib bdg)
LC 97-46710

When Luz's beloved grandfather dies, she places luminaria around his grave on Christmas Eve as a way of remembering him

"Spare and sturdy in both its art and text." Publ Wkly

The farolitos of Christmas; [by] Rudolfo Anaya; illustrated by Edward Gonzales. Hyperion Bks. for Children 1995 unp il $16.95; lib bdg $16.49
　　　　　　　　　　　　　　　　　　　　E
1. Christmas—Fiction 2. Mexican Americans—Fiction
ISBN 0-7868-0060-7; 0-7868-2047-0 (lib bdg)
LC 94-48073

With her father away fighting in World War II and her grandfather too sick to create the traditional luminaria, Luz helps create farolitos, little lanterns, for their Christmas celebration instead

"The narrative provides a satisfying explanation for the Mexican tradition of *farolitos*. Paintings complement the text of this warm family story, which naturally incorporates Spanish words." Horn Book Guide

Andersen, Hans Christian, 1805-1875

The emperor's new clothes; translated and introduced by Naomi Lewis; illustrated by Angela Barrett. Candlewick Press 1997 unp il $15.99; pa $5.99　　　　　　　　　　　　　　　E
1. Fairy tales
ISBN 0-7636-0119-5; 0-7636-1281-2 (pa)
LC 96-45004

Two rascally weavers convince the emperor they are making him beautiful new clothes, visible only to those fit for their posts, but when he wears them during a royal procession, a child recognizes that the emperor has nothing on

This book "introduces the Emperor and his problems in a sophisticated setting that looks much like pre-World War I Monaco. Lewis's . . . translation is smooth and contemporary and easily transmits the wry humor that distinguishes the story. The illustrations, incorporated into a design of exceptional cleverness and wit, are spectacular." Horn Book

Andersen, Hans Christian, 1805-1875—*Continued*

Thumbeline; illustrated by Lisbeth Zwerger; translated by Anthea Bell. North-South Bks. 2000 unp il $15.95; pa $6.95   E

ISBN 0-7358-1213-6; 0-7358-1210-1 (pa)

LC 99-57073

"A Michael Neugebauer book"

A reissue of 1985 edition published by Picture Book Studio

The adventures of a tiny girl no bigger than a thumb and her many animal friends

"The book's squarish design . . . draws the reader's attention to the exceptional art. Lovely, lean, lithe lines combine with a palette of tawny earth tones to create a minimalist world redolent with grace and rich with imagination." Horn Book Guide

Anderson, Lena

Tea for ten; translated by Elisabeth Kallick Dyssegaard. R & S Bks. 2000 unp il $14   E

1. Counting

ISBN 91-29-64557-3   LC 99-52906

Original Swedish edition, 1998

Hedgehog is lonely until nine of her friends arrive, introducing the numbers from one to ten

"The text is simply written and complemented by gentle, childlike watercolor illustrations." SLJ

Anholt, Catherine

Harry's home; [by] Catherine and Laurence Anholt. Farrar, Straus & Giroux 2000 c1999 unp il $16   E

1. Farm life—Fiction 2. Grandfathers—Fiction 3. Home—Fiction

ISBN 0-374-32870-6   LC 99-16597

First published 1999 in the United Kingdom

Harry enjoys visiting his grandfather's farm and seeing the homes of all the animals, but in the end he is happy to return to his own home in the city

"The many details in this simple story will appeal to any young listeners who have ever wondered what it's like to live somewhere different. The warm illustrations are full of movement and charm." Horn Book Guide

Anno, Mitsumasa, 1926-

Anno's counting book. Crowell 1977 c1975 unp il $16.95; lib bdg $16.89; pa $5.95   E

1. Counting 2. Seasons—Fiction 3. Stories without words

ISBN 0-690-01287-X; 0-690-01288-8 (lib bdg); 0-06-443123-1 (pa)   LC 76-28977

Also available Big book edition

Original Japanese edition, 1975

"A distinctive, beautifully conceived counting book in which twelve full-color doublespreads show the same village and surrounding countryside during different hours (by the church clock) and months. Both the seasons and community changes are studied, as such components of the scene as flowers, trees, animals, people, and buildings increase from one to twelve." LC. Child Books, 1977

Appelbaum, Diana Karter

Cocoa ice; by Diana Appelbaum; pictures by Holly Meade. Orchard Bks. 1997 unp il $16.95; lib bdg $17.99   E

1. Ice—Fiction 2. Dominican Republic—Fiction 3. Maine—Fiction

ISBN 0-531-30040-4; 0-531-33040-0 (lib bdg)

LC 96-40365

A girl in Santo Domingo tells how cocoa is harvested during the late 1800s while at the same time her counterpart in Maine tells about the harvesting of ice

"Meade's vibrant cut-paper and gouache illustrations capture the action, industry, and natural beauty of each locale. Filled with fascinating, child-centered details and engaging artwork." SLJ

Appelt, Kathi, 1954-

Bats around the clock; illustrated by Melissa Sweet. HarperCollins Pubs. 2000 unp il $15.95; lib bdg $15.89   E

1. Bats—Fiction 2. Rock music—Fiction 3. Stories in rhyme

ISBN 0-688-16469-2; 0-688-16470-6 (lib bdg)

LC 99-15502

Click Dark hosts a special twelve-hour program of American Bat Stand where the bats rock and roll until the midnight hour ends

"The rhymes are delightful and the narrative jives right along." SLJ

Other available titles about the bats are:

The bat jamboree (1996)

Bats on parade (1999)

Bayou lullaby; pictures by Neil Waldman. Morrow Junior Bks. 1995 unp il $16   E

1. Lullabies 2. Stories in rhyme

ISBN 0-688-12856-4   LC 94-16639

This is "a rhythmic, soothing lullaby for a little girl who lives in a house by the banks of the bayou. . . . The verse is evocative and lovely, but the true merit of the book lies in Waldman's double-page acrylic paintings. Each scene is a self-contained work of art and a visual feast. He has set the swamp's luminous flora and fauna against a velvety black background, and richly fluorescent shades of greens, purples, blues, and teals decorate the pages." SLJ

Cowboy dreams; illustrated by Barry Root. HarperCollins Pubs. 1999 unp il $14.95; lib bdg $14.89   E

1. Cowhands—Fiction 2. Dreams—Fiction 3. West (U.S.)—Fiction 4. Stories in rhyme

ISBN 0-06-027763-7; 0-06-027764-5 (lib bdg)

LC 98-18316

A little cowpoke is lulled to sleep by dreams of the sights and sounds of the Western landscape at night

"Rhythmic rhymes and imaginative artwork combine in a cozy bedtime tale." SLJ

Oh my baby, little one; pictures by Jane Dyer. Harcourt Brace & Co. 2000 unp il $16   E

1. Mother-child relationship—Fiction 2. Stories in rhyme

ISBN 0-15-200041-0   LC 99-6363

Appelt, Kathi, 1954——*Continued*

"An exploration of the love that exists between mother and child, even when Mama Bird must leave her baby at nursery school. Told in rhyming verse, each four-line stanza is a reassurance that mama's love will permeate all areas of Baby Bird's day." SLJ

"The light, bright pictures will charm young listeners, who will find this book best enjoyed while cuddled up next to Mama." Booklist

Apple, Margot

Brave Martha; written and illustrated by Margot Apple. Houghton Mifflin 1999 unp il $15　　E
1. Cats—Fiction 2. Bedtime—Fiction
ISBN 0-395-59422-7　　LC 97-42616

One night when she has to go to bed without her cat Sophie, Martha worries about all the things she sees and hears in the dark

"The pencil-and-watercolor illustrations meld with the spare text, accurately reflecting the book's tone in their various shadings." SLJ

Ardizzone, Edward, 1900-1979

Little Tim and the brave sea captain. Lothrop, Lee & Shepard Bks. 2000 c1936 unp il $16　　E
ISBN 0-688-17678-X　　LC 99-33894

A reissue of the title first published 1936 by Oxford University Press

Follows the adventures of a stowaway boy, including his friendship with captain and crew and near shipwreck during a violent storm

"The pictures are rapid wash drawings full of swing, salt and slap, the sea scenes especially good, full of action." N Y Her Trib Books

Other available titles about Tim are:
Tim and Charlotte (1951)
Tim and Ginger (1965)
Tim in danger (1953)
Tim to the rescue (1949)
Tim's friend Towser (1962)

Armstrong, Jennifer, 1961-

Chin Yu Min and the ginger cat; illustrated by Mary Grandpré. Crown 1993 unp il hardcover o.p. paperback available $6.99　　E
1. China—Fiction 2. Cats—Fiction
ISBN 0-517-88549-2 (pa)　　LC 92-8658

Through her friendship with a ginger cat, a haughty Chinese widow learns to be humble and to provide for herself

"The rich, graceful text is complemented by Grandpré's stylish, cinematic illustrations. The use of dramatic lighting and unusual perspective lends an animated look to the characters, who act in a vibrant landscape saturated with brilliant colors." Booklist

Arnold, Katya

Me too! two small stories about small animals; retold and illustrated by Katya Arnold; based on stories by V. Suteev. Holiday House 2000 unp il $15.95　　E
1. Animals—Fiction
ISBN 0-8234-1483-3　　LC 99-16696

"In 'Me Too,' Chick copies all of Duckling's actions, until his friend goes swimming, whereupon Chick learns that following suit is not always a good idea. In 'Three Kittens,' a black, a gray, and a white kitten all turn white when they jump into a canister of flour while chasing a mouse." SLJ

"The simple, light-hearted tellings . . . are well matched by Arnold's distinctive illustrations, drawn with playful, energetic black line and colored with bright acrylics." Horn Book

Arnold, Marsha Diane, 1948-

Heart of a tiger; pictures by Jamichael Henterly. Dial Bks. for Young Readers 1995 unp il $14.99
E
1. Cats—Fiction 2. Tigers—Fiction 3. India—Fiction
ISBN 0-8037-1695-8　　LC 94-17126

"Small kitten Number Four must find a name for himself for his naming day. Not wanting to be called Smallest of All, he searches out Bengal, the beautiful tiger whose ways he greatly admires. He learns much from the big cat, and when he saves the tiger's life, he earns the name Heart of a Tiger. Arnold's original story has the feel of an oft-told tale, and Henterly's watercolors reward a lingering look." Horn Book Guide

The pumpkin runner; pictures by Brad Sneed. Dial Bks. for Young Readers 1998 unp il $15.99; lib bdg $15.89　　E
1. Running—Fiction 2. Pumpkin—Fiction 3. Australia—Fiction
ISBN 0-8037-2124-2; 0-8037-2125-0 (lib bdg)
LC 97-26666

An Australian sheep rancher who eats pumpkins for energy enters a race from Melbourne to Sydney, despite people laughing at his eccentricities

"Sneed's cleverly skewed perspectives and Arnold's engaging style make this book, like its star, an easy winner." Publ Wkly

Arnosky, Jim

Every autumn comes the bear. Putnam 1993 unp il hardcover o.p. paperback available $5.99　　E
1. Bears
ISBN 0-698-11405-1 (pa)　　LC 92-30515

Every autumn a bear shows up behind the farm, and goes through a series of routines before finding a den among the hilltop boulders where he sleeps all winter long

"The lean, powerful text uses an intimate, conversational tone. . . . Each of the full-page watercolors is vibrant, translucent and strikingly composed." Publ Wkly

Little lions. Putnam 1998 unp il $15.99　　E
1. Pumas—Fiction
ISBN 0-399-22944-2　　LC 96-49837

On a rocky ledge, two baby mountain lions play and purr and meow under the protection of their mother

"Like the text, the sunny, sensitive watercolor paintings are entertaining and reassuring without falling into sentimentality." Booklist

Mouse letters; a very first alphabet book. Clarion Bks. 1999 unp il $4.95　　E
1. Mice—Fiction 2. Alphabet 3. Stories without words
ISBN 0-395-55386-5　　LC 98-19334

Arnosky, Jim—*Continued*

A whimsical mouse experiences many mishaps while using sticks to form the letters of the alphabet

"Color-cued outlining and highlighting make the letters (in gold) . . . in each illustration easy to identify, and there's just enough suggestion of a plot to engage pre-readers in supplying the narrative. Sturdy stock assures [this] will stand up to the constant thumbing [it deserves]." Bull Cent Child Books

Mouse numbers; a very first counting book. Clarion Bks. 1999 unp il $4.95   E
1. Mice—Fiction 2. Counting 3. Stories without words
ISBN 0-395-55006-8   LC 98-19347
A mouse counts objects from one to ten on the way to the beach and back again

Raccoons and ripe corn. Lothrop, Lee & Shepard Bks. 1987 unp il hardcover o.p. paperback available $5.95   E
1. Raccoons
ISBN 0-688-10489-4 (pa)   LC 87-4243
"A mother raccoon and two older kits come in autumn dusk to a farmer's field, enjoy a star-lit romp and feed, then skulk off at dawn. A trail of fall leaves across the title pages leads to 11 double-spreads of open pencil sketches and color washes of woods and farm." SLJ

"Arnosky's pictures have a way of making nature larger than life. His raccoons are a strong focus of attention, and the hushed nighttime mood is almost palpable. The nature lesson implicit in the depicted episode is not romantic; these raccoons are greedy and somewhat destructive." Booklist

Rattlesnake dance. Putnam 2000 unp il music $15.99   E
1. Rattlesnakes—Fiction
ISBN 0-399-22755-5   LC 99-21634
A rattlesnake slithers into a cave and shakes and wriggles in a rattlesnake dance of pure bliss, while other hissing snakes join the underground ball

Aruego, Jose

Look what I can do. Scribner 1971 unp il hardcover o.p. paperback available $5.99   E
1. Water buffalo—Fiction
ISBN 0-689-71205-7 (pa)
"The story of two carabaos who get carried away trying to outdo each other and almost come to a sad end." Booklist

"There are just fifteen words in this story . . . whose valuable message should be intelligible to the young non-reader. . . . Sprightly, cartoon-like drawings are the focal point." Book World

We hide, you seek; by Jose Aruego and Ariane Dewey. Greenwillow Bks. 1979 unp il $16; lib bdg $15.93   E
1. Camouflage (Biology)—Fiction
ISBN 0-688-80201-X; 0-688-84201-1 (lib bdg)
     LC 78-13638
"An oafishly good-natured rhino, invited into a jungle-wide game of hide and seek, bumbles from one scene to the next, accidentally exposing would-be hiders (leopards, crocodiles, lions) at every stop; then turning the tables on his playmates, cleverly hides himself. Readers are served up a wealth of information in 27 words (plus end-papers that give a page-by-page identification of the species pictured) and droll scenes drenched in the vibrant tones of an East African palette." SLJ

Asch, Frank

Baby Bird's first nest. Harcourt Brace & Co. 1999 unp il $15   E
1. Birds—Fiction 2. Frogs—Fiction
ISBN 0-15-201726-7   LC 97-32653
"Gulliver books"
When Baby Bird takes a tumble from her mama's nest in the middle of the night, she finds a friend in Little Frog

"A satisfying read-aloud with just enough adventure, wit, and common sense to engage listeners and vocabulary easy enough for beginning readers. . . . Asch's trademark pen-and-ink drawings have been 'colorized' in Adobe Photoshop. The technique is very effective with deep, rich color fading to lighter shades." SLJ

Barnyard lullaby. Simon & Schuster Bks. for Young Readers 1998 unp il music $15   E
1. Domestic animals—Fiction 2. Lullabies 3. Bedtime—Fiction
ISBN 0-689-81363-5   LC 96-44987
Although the farmer only hears animal noises, when the different barnyard animals sing lullabies to their respective children, the babies understand the words. Includes music

"Soothing lullabies combine with the deep evening palette of Asch's trademark illustrations to make this a comforting bedtime read." Horn Book Guide

Moonbear's dream. Simon & Schuster Bks. for Young Readers 1999 unp il $15   E
1. Bears—Fiction 2. Birds—Fiction 3. Dreams—Fiction
ISBN 0-689-82244-8   LC 98-24133
When Moonbear and his friend Little Bird see a kangaroo in the backyard, they think they must be dreaming, so they do things they would not do if they were awake

"Asch's familiar restrained illustrations . . . neatly reflect the story's understated humor and the beloved silliness of Moonbear's world." Booklist

Other available titles in this series are:
Good night Baby Bear (1998)
Goodbye house (1985)
Happy birthday, Moon (1982)
Just like Daddy (1981)
Moonbear's pet (1997)
Mooncake (1983)
Moondance (1993)
Moongame (1984)

Atwell, Debby, 1953-

Barn; written and illustrated by Debby Atwell. Houghton Mifflin 1996 unp il $15.95   E
ISBN 0-395-78568-5   LC 96-11044
Follows the life of a country barn from the late eighteenth-century to the present day

Atwell, Debby, 1953-—*Continued*

"The charming folk-art-style paintings complement the text perfectly and give added meaning to this unusual and warm story about the rhythms of time and our own haunting continuity with the past." Booklist

Auch, Mary Jane

Bantam of the opera; written and illustrated by Mary Jane Auch. Holiday House 1997 unp il $16.95

E

1. Singers—Fiction 2. Opera—Fiction 3. Roosters—Fiction

ISBN 0-8234-1312-8   LC 96-40169

Luigi the rooster wins fame and fortune when the star of the Cosmopolitan Opera Company and his understudy both come down with chicken pox on the same night

"The brightly colored illustrations capture the exaggerated humor of the text." Booklist

Peeping Beauty; written and illustrated by Mary Jane Auch. Holiday House 1993 unp il $16.95; pa $6.95

E

1. Chickens—Fiction 2. Foxes—Fiction 3. Ballet—Fiction

ISBN 0-8234-1001-3; 0-8234-1170-2 (pa)

LC 92-16374

Poulette the dancing hen falls into the clutches of a hungry fox, who exploits her desire to become a great ballerina

"The language is lively, and filled with witty phrases and ballet references. Using bright colors and just enough detail, Auch sets her cast of characters against a simple backdrop." SLJ

Another available title about Poulette is:
Hen Lake (1995)

Aylesworth, Jim, 1943-

Country crossing; illustrated by Ted Rand. Atheneum Pubs. 1991 unp il $16.95; pa $5.99

E

1. Railroads—Fiction 2. Night—Fiction

ISBN 0-689-31580-5; 0-689-71895-0 (pa)

LC 89-78184

Recreates the sights and sounds at a country crossing one summer night, as an old car patiently awaits the passing of a long and noisy freight train

"Times past are evoked in a combination of onomatopoeic text and richly hued illustrations. . . . The effect of text and pictures is powerful—as close as one can come to total sensory involvement through the pages of a book." Horn Book

The full belly bowl; illustrated by Wendy Halperin. Atheneum Bks. for Young Readers 1998 unp il $16

E

1. Fairy tales

ISBN 0-689-81033-4   LC 98-14052

In return for the kindness he showed a wee small man, a very old man is given a magical bowl that causes problems when it is not used properly

"From the dainty pictures on the endpapers to the stunning artwork inside, this book is a feast for the eyes. The story . . . is just as good, smoothly blending folktale conventions with touches of magic and a dusting of comedy." Booklist

My son John; woodcuts by David Frampton. Holt & Co. 1994 unp il hardcover o.p. paperback available $5.95

E

1. Nursery rhymes

ISBN 0-8050-5517-7 (pa)   LC 92-27192

"In the tradition of 'Diddle Diddle Dumpling, My Son John.' Aylesworth offers 14 new verses." Booklist

"This book is a feast for the eyes and ears. Aylesworth amplifies the simple nursery classic with a rainbow of rich, descriptive verses on additional names, evoking all of the five senses in the process. The rhymes are enhanced by an exceptional layout using brilliant woodcuts done with brightly colored oils." SLJ

Old black fly; illustrations by by Stephen Gammell. Holt & Co. 1992 unp il $16.95; pa $6.95

E

1. Flies—Fiction 2. Alphabet 3. Stories in rhyme

ISBN 0-8050-1401-2; 0-8050-3924-4 (pa)

LC 91-26825

Also available Board book edition

Rhyming text and illustrations follow a mischievous old black fly through the alphabet as he has a very busy bad day landing where he should not be

Aylesworth's "snappy couplets constitute a waggish presentation of a basic concept. . . . Gammell's paintings are exuberant splashes of mayhem—rainbows of splattered hues from which truly memorable characters emerge. His appropriately bug-eyed (and cross-eyed) fly and gap-toothed humans sporting crazy hairdos provide a level of dementia that children will relish." Publ Wkly

Azarian, Mary

A farmer's alphabet. Godine 1981 61p il $19.95; pa $14.95

E

1. Alphabet 2. Farm life

ISBN 0-87923-394-X; 0-87923-397-4 (pa)

LC 80-84938

"Large, bold woodcuts make up an album of farming scenes obviously from New England—for example, 'M' is for maple sugar. A few scenes look cold and stern—showing winter and icicles—but there are children jumping in hay and flying a kite as well as . . . 'N' for neighbor and 'G' for a garden bursting with vegetables." Horn Book

A gardener's alphabet. Houghton Mifflin 2000 unp il $16

E

1. Alphabet 2. Gardening

ISBN 0-618-03380-7   LC 99-44242

An alphabet book featuring words associated with gardening, including bulbs, compost, digging, insects, and weeds

"The stunning black wood-cuts, hand tinted with strong watercolors, are full of action and detail." SLJ

Baker, Barbara, 1947-

Digby and Kate and the beautiful day; pictures by Marsha Winborn. Dutton Children's Bks. 1998 48p il $13.99

E

1. Dogs—Fiction 2. Cats—Fiction

ISBN 0-525-45855-7

Baker, Barbara, 1947-—*Continued*

Digby the dog and Kate the cat disagree about many things but they remain best friends

"The artwork . . . together with the cheerful stories make up good, light fare for beginning readers." Horn Book Guide

Other available titles about Digby and Kate are:
Digby and Kate (1988)
Digby and Kate again (1989)

One Saturday afternoon; pictures by Kate Duke. Dutton Children's Bks. 1999 47p il $13.99   **E**
1. Family life—Fiction 2. Bears—Fiction
ISBN 0-525-45882-4   LC 98-41605

Also available One Saturday morning pa $3.50 (ISBN 0-14-038605-X)

"Dutton easy reader"

"Each bear in a family of six finds a satisfying way to enjoy Saturday afternoon: reading, coloring, playing school, baking and eating bread, going for a solitary walk, and for the youngest, drawing on the wall. Devoting a chapter to each bear, Baker writes with humor and understanding, and Duke is an expert at capturing the right gestures and expressions." Horn Book Guide

Baker, Jeannie

The hidden forest. Greenwillow Bks. 2000 unp il $16.95; lib bdg $16.89   **E**
1. Kelps—Fiction 2. Underwater exploration—Fiction 3. Australia—Fiction
ISBN 0-688-15760-2; 0-688-15761-0 (lib bdg)
     LC 99-23175

When a friend helps him retrieve the fishtrap he lost while trying to fish just off the coast of eastern Tasmania, Ben comes to see the Giant Kelp forest where he lost his fishtrap in a new light

"The stunning mixed media collages are creatively constructed to reproduce the diving experience." Horn Book Guide

Where the forest meets the sea; story and pictures by Jeannie Baker. Greenwillow Bks. 1988 c1987 unp il $16; lib bdg $16.89   **E**
1. Australia—Fiction 2. Rain forests—Fiction
ISBN 0-688-06363-2; 0-688-06364-0 (lib bdg)
     LC 87-7551

First published 1987 in the United Kingdom

On a camping trip in an Australian rain forest with his father, a young boy thinks about the history of the plant and animal life around him and wonders about their future

The illustrations "are relief collages 'constructed from a multitude of materials, including modeling clay, papers, textured materials, preserved natural materials, and paints.' Integrated by the artist's vision, the collages create three-dimensional effects on two-dimensional pages drawing the reader into each scene as willing observer and explorer." Horn Book

Window. Greenwillow Bks. 1991 unp il lib bdg $16.89   **E**
1. Stories without words 2. Human ecology—Fiction 3. Australia—Fiction
ISBN 0-688-08918-6   LC 90-3922

"The story in this wordless book is told through the outdoor scene viewed over time from one child's bedroom window. Initially, a mother holding her infant son gazes out at the lush Australian bush; as the boy gets older, civilization swallows up the wilderness." Horn Book Guide

"Filled with marvelous detail, the textured collages make an affecting statement about the erosion of the planet Earth." SLJ

Baker, Keith, 1953-

The magic fan; written and illustrated by Keith Baker. Harcourt Brace Jovanovich 1989 unp il $14.95; pa $7   **E**
1. Japan—Fiction
ISBN 0-15-250750-7; 0-15-200983-3 (pa)
     LC 88-18727

Despite the laughter of his fellow villagers, Yoshi uses his building skills to make a boat to catch the moon, a kite to reach the clouds, and a bridge that mimics the rainbow

"The artwork, acrylics on illustration board, is framed within the outline of an open fan. The text appears outside this frame, and fan-shaped die-cuts allow the reader to turn the inner page and see a second picture on each double-page spread. . . . An entertaining tale as well as an elegant addition to the picture-book shelf." Booklist

Quack and count. Harcourt Brace & Co. 1999 unp il $14   **E**
1. Addition 2. Ducks 3. Counting
ISBN 0-15-292858-8   LC 98-7924

"Seven uniquely marked ducklings slide, chase bees, and play peekaboo as they group on double-spread pages to illustrate ways to add up to their sum. . . . Jaunty scenes in cut-paper collage with a gracious array of colors offer plenty of extras." SLJ

Balian, Lorna

Humbug witch. Abingdon Press 1965 unp il o.p.; Humbug Bks. reprint available $14.95   **E**
1. Witches—Fiction
ISBN 1-881772-24-1

This book is about "a little witch and her unsuccessful attempts at witchcraft. One evening she wearily takes off piece after piece of comical attire—the last of which proves to be a mask, revealing a hilarious little girl underneath! Too good to miss." Adventuring with Books. 2d edition

Bang, Molly, 1943-

Goose; written and illustrated by Molly Bang. Blue Sky Press (NY) 1996 unp il $10.95   **E**
1. Geese—Fiction
ISBN 0-590-89005-0   LC 95-47616

Adopted by woodchucks at birth, a baby goose never feels she truly belongs—until the day she discovers she can fly

"The telling is simple and lovely, not one word too many. . . . Bang's animals are exquisitely drawn, both fragile and sturdy." Booklist

Bang, Molly, 1943—*Continued*

The Grey Lady and the Strawberry Snatcher. Four Winds Press 1980 unp il $16; pa $5.99

E

1. Strawberries—Fiction 2. Stories without words
ISBN 0-02-708140-0; 0-689-80381-8 (pa)

LC 79-21243

A Caldecott Medal honor book, 1981

The strawberry snatcher tries to wrest the strawberries from the grey lady but as he follows her through shops and woods he discovers some delicious blackberries instead

"Bang's illustrations are unparalleled in effects, full-color paintings and collages in which the surrealistic and the representational combine to tell a story without words." Publ Wkly

The paper crane. Greenwillow Bks. 1985 unp il $16; pa $5.95

E

ISBN 0-688-04108-6; 0-688-07333-6 (pa)

LC 84-13546

"Bang gives a modern setting and details to the consoling story of a good man, deprived by unlucky fate of his livelihood, whose act of kindness and generosity is repaid by the restoration of his fortunes, through the bringing to life of a magical animal—the paper crane." SLJ

"Every detail of the restaurant interior, from the strawberries on the cake to the floral centerpieces, is a delight to the eye and imagination. . . . The book successfully blends Asian folklore themes with contemporary Western characterization." Horn Book

Ten, nine, eight. Greenwillow Bks. 1983 unp il $16; lib bdg $15.89; pa $5.95

E

1. Lullabies 2. Counting
ISBN 0-688-00906-9; 0-688-00907-7 (lib bdg); 0-688-10480-0 (pa)

LC 81-20106

Also available Board book edition

A Caldecott Medal honor book, 1984

"In countdown style, the text of this counting book begins with '10 small toes all washed and warm,' and ends with '1 big girl all ready for bed.' The captions rhyme . . . and the pictures—warm, bright paintings—show a black father and child snuggling in a chair, the child yawning, and the child hugging her toy bear after some loving good night kisses." Bull Cent Child Books

When Sophie gets angry—really, really angry. Blue Sky Press (NY) 1999 unp il $15.95

E

ISBN 0-590-18979-4

LC 97-42209

A Caldecott Medal honor book, 2000

"Sophie loses a tug-of-war altercation with her sister over a stuffed monkey, and her anger propels her out of the house and into an anger-reducing run. After running, crying, climbing a tree, and being soothed by the breeze, Sophie feels better and goes home, where everyone is happy to see her." Bull Cent Child Books

"The text is appropriately brief, for it is Bang's double-page illustrations, vibrating with saturated colors, that reveal the drama of the child's emotions." SLJ

Banks, Kate, 1960-

And if the moon could talk; pictures by Georg Hallensleben. Foster Bks. 1998 unp il $15

E

1. Bedtime—Fiction 2. Night—Fiction 3. Moon—Fiction
ISBN 0-374-30299-5

LC 97-29770

As evening progresses into nighttime, the moon looks down on a variety of nocturnal scenes, including a child getting ready for bed

"The deeply saturated tones of the lovely; impressionistic oil paintings perfectly match the somnolent feeling of the text." SLJ

Baboon; pictures by Georg Hallensleben. Farrar, Straus & Giroux 1997 unp il $14

E

1. Baboons—Fiction
ISBN 0-374-30474-2

LC 96-20888

"Frances Foster books"

Original French edition, 1994

"A baby baboon sees a forest and concludes that the world is green, but then his mother takes him farther afield. . . . Everything he encounters expands his understanding, and when night falls, he has seen with his own eyes that the world is a big and varied place." Publisher's note

"Visible brush-strokes give texture to the impressionistic paintings, and adept lighting evokes sunlight and shadow. The simple, eloquent text is as subtly understated." Horn Book Guide

The night worker; pictures by Georg Hallensleben. Farrar, Straus & Giroux 2000 unp il $16

E

1. Night—Fiction 2. Work—Fiction 3. Building—Fiction
ISBN 0-374-35520-7

LC 99-27595

"Frances Foster books"

Alex wants to be a "night worker" like his father who goes to work at a construction site after Alex goes to bed

"Banks' elegant, simple words and poetic images and rhythms evoke the book's exciting activity and the secure comfort Alex feels with his father. With thick brush strokes and deep, satisfying primary and earth colors, Hallensleben's paintings extend the story's balance of exhilarating intensity and reassuring calm." Booklist

Bannerman, Helen, 1862 or 3-1946

The story of Little Babaji; illustrated by Fred Marcellino. HarperCollins Pubs. 1996 unp il $14.95; lib bdg $14.89

E

1. India—Fiction 2. Tigers—Fiction
ISBN 0-06-205064-8; 0-06-205065-6 (lib bdg)

"Michael di Capua books"

In this edition of the Story of Little Black Sambo, originally published 1899, the characters have been given Indian names

Babaji gives his new clothing to tigers who threaten to eat him, but they chase one another around a tree until they turn to butter

"Marcellino has set the story of Little Black Sambo in India. . . . Except for a change of names . . . Bannerman's text is essentially unaltered, retaining the narrative rhythm that has always paced a tightly patterned plot. Marcellino's watercolor paintings project a toy-like quality that emphasizes humor over suspense." Bull Cent Child Books

Bányai, István, 1949-
Re-zoom. Viking 1995 unp il $15.99; pa $5.99
E

1. Stories without words
ISBN 0-670-86392-0; 0-14-055694-X (pa)
LC 95-14265

A wordless picture book presents a series of scenes, each one from farther away, showing, for example, a boat which becomes the image on a magazine, which is held in a hand, which belongs to a boy, and so on

This book offers "originality, an assured sense of design and composition, and an avant-garde sensibility that children, especially older ones, will love." SLJ

Zoom. Viking 1995 unp il $15.99; pa $6.99
E

1. Stories without words
ISBN 0-670-85804-8; 0-14-055774-1 (pa)
LC 94-33181

A wordless picture book presents a series of scenes, each one from farther away, showing, for example, a girl playing with toys which is actually a picture on a magazine cover, which is part of a sign on a bus, and so on

"If the concept is not wholly new, the execution is superior. Readers are in for a perpetually surprising—and even philosophical—adventure." Publ Wkly

Barasch, Lynne
Radio rescue. Farrar, Straus & Giroux 2000 unp il $16
E

1. Amateur radio stations—Fiction 2. Cipher and telegraph codes—Fiction
ISBN 0-374-36166-5
LC 99-22384

"Frances Foster books"

In 1923, after learning Morse code and setting up his own amateur radio station, a twelve-year-old boy sends a message that leads to the rescue of a family stranded by a hurricane in Florida. Based on experiences of the author's father

"In a well-designed mix of insets, brief sketches, and full-page drawings, the author's uncluttered color cartoons do an excellent job of illustrating the technology and the code, at the same time creating likeable, expressive characters." Booklist

Barber, Antonia, 1932-
The Mousehole cat; illustrated by Nicola Bayley. Macmillan 1990 unp il hardcover o.p. paperback available $5.99
E

1. Cats—Fiction 2. Sea stories
ISBN 0-689-80837-2 (pa)
LC 90-31533

Also available Spanish language edition

"In the village of Mowzel lives a proud, determined cat named Mowzer. Her 'pet' is an old fisherman who provides her with succulent fresh fish. When the Storm Cat blocks the village, Tom and Mowzer venture forth anyhow. Mowzer's eloquent purring tames the ferocious giant and enables Tom to pull in a boat-load of fish." Child Book Rev Serv

"This delicate, charming tale and the exquisite illustrations of stormy seas, gleaming fish, and delightful cats and townspeople make an extremely handsome book, splendid for reading aloud." Horn Book

Barner, Bob
Fish wish. Holiday House 2000 unp il $16.95
E

1. Coral reefs and islands—Fiction
ISBN 0-8234-1482-5
LC 99-44491

A young boy's dream sends him on an underwater journey through a coral reef. Includes factual information on coral reefs and the animals that live in them

"The impressive collage illustrations combine pieces of torn, cut, and sometimes painted papers with found objects and bits of fabric. Bold forms and striking color combinations give the double-page spreads a vibrant sense of place and motion." Booklist

Barracca, Debra
The adventures of Taxi Dog; by Debra and Sal Barracca; pictures by Mark Buehner. Dial Bks. for Young Readers 1990 30p il $15.99; pa $5.99
E

1. Dogs—Fiction 2. Stories in rhyme
ISBN 0-8037-0671-5; 0-14-056665-1 (pa)
LC 89-1056

"In snappy, rhymed lines, Maxi recalls his days as a stray and his adoption by taxi-driving Jim. Applying oil paint over acrylics, Buehner creates color with lush character. The hues' intense depth, coupled with the artist's finesse with perspective, will draw readers into the action." Booklist

Other available titles about Maxi, the Taxi Dog are:
Maxi, the hero (1991)
Maxi, the star (1993)
A Taxi Dog Christmas (1994)

Barron, T. A.
Where is Grandpa? illustrated by Chris K. Soentpiet. Philomel Bks. 2000 unp il $15.99 E

1. Grandfathers—Fiction 2. Death—Fiction
ISBN 0-399-23037-8
LC 97-29549

As his family reminisces after his beloved grandfather's death, a boy realizes that his grandfather is still with him in all the special places they shared

"The reassuring message is fitting, and the realistic watercolors are suitably expressive and luminous." Horn Book Guide

Barton, Byron
Bones, bones, dinosaur bones. Crowell 1990 unp il $15.95; lib bdg $15.89
E

1. Dinosaurs
ISBN 0-690-04825-4; 0-690-04827-0 (lib bdg)
LC 89-71306

"From the field search for dinosaur bones to reconstructed skeletons for museum display, paleontology as process is revealed in simple text, bold print, and flat illustrations with heavy, black outlines. Includes labeled illustrations of eight dinosaurs." Sci Child

Dinosaurs, dinosaurs. Crowell 1989 unp il $15.95; lib bdg $15.89; pa $5.95
E

1. Dinosaurs
ISBN 0-694-00269-0; 0-690-04768-1 (lib bdg); 0-06-443298-X (pa)
LC 88-22938

Also available Big book edition and Board book edition

Barton, Byron—*Continued*

This book examines the many different kinds of dinosaurs, big and small, those with spikes and those with long, sharp teeth

"Barton conveys the primordial sense of excitement that draws children to these beasts. Despite the illustrations' simplicity, Barton's dinosaurs' expressions are not mammalian smiles; they have a saurian quality all their own. The endpapers identify the creatures by scientific name and pronunciation. Barton wisely keeps his text simple, describing dinosaurs only by size and physical features." SLJ

I want to be an astronaut. Crowell 1988 unp il lib bdg $15.89; pa $6.95   E
  1. Astronautics
ISBN 0-690-04744-4 (lib bdg); 0-06-443280-7 (pa)
           LC 87-24311
Also available Board book edition
"First-person text describes the experiences the speaker might have on a space mission. Simple text and bold, full-color illustrations are a delightful introduction to an astronaut's activities." Sci Child

The wee little woman. HarperCollins Pubs. 1995 unp il $14.95; lib bdg $14.89   E
  1. Cats—Fiction 2. Milk—Fiction
ISBN 0-06-023387-7; 0-06-023388-5 (lib bdg)
           LC 94-18683
When a wee little woman milks her wee little cow and leaves the bowl of milk on her wee little table, the situation proves too tempting for a mischievous wee little cat

"This reassuring story is told in simple words with lots of repetition. The large paper cuts are done in primary colors against vivid green and yellow backgrounds in designs that are simple yet humorous and expressive. A satisfying and attractive choice for the very young." Booklist

Bartone, Elisa

American too; [illustrated by] Ted Lewin. Lothrop, Lee & Shepard Bks. 1996 unp il $16; lib bdg $15.93   E
  1. Italian Americans—Fiction 2. New York (N.Y.)—Fiction
ISBN 0-688-13278-2; 0-688-13279-0 (lib bdg)
"Rosina, an Italian immigrant, wants to be a modern American girl. Questioning the characteristics and traditions of her family, she reacts with anger instead of pride when told she will be the queen of the San Gennaro feast. The Statue of Liberty provides inspiration and when the festival procession begins, Rosina appears, not in the white taffeta dress made by her mother, but dressed as Lady Liberty. . . . Lewin is a skilled watercolorist. His familiar, realistic illustrations capture the expressions and emotions of the characters. Set in New York City shortly after World War I, the pictures give a general feel for the interiors and dress of the time." SLJ

Peppe the lamplighter; illustrations by Ted Lewin. Lothrop, Lee & Shepard Bks. 1993 unp il $16.95; lib bdg $15.89; pa $5.95   E
  1. Italian Americans—Fiction 2. New York (N.Y.)—Fiction
ISBN 0-688-10268-9; 0-688-10269-7 (lib bdg); 0-688-15469-7 (pa)   LC 92-1397

A Caldecott Medal honor book, 1994

Peppe's father is upset when he learns that Peppe has taken a job lighting the gas street lamps in his New York City neighborhood

"Peppe's quiet quest for familial respect and pleasure in his work is touching and rhythmically written. The early-American city scenes are dark but have a nice period luminescence in the myriad street and table lamps, and the earth-toned watercolors lend the bustling streets and interiors of Little Italy an air both somber and lively." Bull Cent Child Books

Battle-Lavert, Gwendolyn, 1951-

The shaking bag; written by Gwendolyn Battle-Lavert; illustrated by Aminah Brenda Lynn Robinson. Whitman, A. 2000 unp il $15.95   E
ISBN 0-8075-7328-0   LC 99-16974
"Miss Annie Mae always feeds the birds in her yard, even when she has little to eat herself. One night a young stranger named Raven Reed appears on her doorstep and, shaking her empty birdseed sack, provides her with all she needs. Strong, earthy, and with touches of humor, the art is a good match for a well-honed narrative." Horn Book Guide

Bauer, Marion Dane, 1938-

Jason's bears; illustrated by Kevin Hawkes. Hyperion Bks. for Children 2000 unp il $14.99
                         E
  1. Bears—Fiction
ISBN 0-7868-0356-8   LC 98-52968
Jason's enthusiasm for bears is dampened when his big brother tells him that they are going to eat him up

"Richly colored, humorous acrylic paintings show Jason overcoming his fears with his own bravery in this good read-aloud choice." Horn Book Guide

Bayer, Jane, d. 1985

A my name is Alice; pictures by Steven Kellogg. Dial Bks. for Young Readers 1984 unp il $16.99; pa $6.99   E
  1. Stories in rhyme 2. Alphabet
ISBN 0-8037-0123-3; 0-14-054668-5 (pa)
           LC 84-7059
"Each page contains (in the border above the illustration) the name of an animal ('A my name is Alice') and its spouse ('and my husband's name is Alex.'), their locale ('We come from Alaska') and occupation ('and we sell ants.'). Two sentences appear beneath the illustrations on each page identifying the kind of animals in the verse ('Alice is an 'Ape.' Alex is an 'Anteater.')." SLJ

"It is a superlative blend of visual and textual nonsense because the visual surprises keep the repetitive pattern in the text from becoming tedious. The verbal parts gradually expand in their ludicrousness, in their cataloging of zany characters and occupations." Wilson Libr Bull

Baylor, Byrd, 1924-

Hawk, I'm your brother; illustrated by Peter Parnall. Scribner 1976 unp il lib bdg $16; pa $5.99
                         E
  1. Hawks—Fiction
ISBN 0-684-14571-5 (lib bdg); 0-689-71102-6 (pa)

Baylor, Byrd, 1924—*Continued*

A Caldecott Medal honor book, 1977

"Driven by the desire to fly, Rudy Soto steals a baby hawk from its nest in the hope that having a hawk as his 'brother' will somehow enable him to take flight. Seeing the hawk's frustration in confinement, the boy finally releases it." Interracial Books Child Bull

"In the poetic simplicity of the writing, Baylor echoes the quietness of the desert and she captures the essence of the desert people's affinity for natural things. Both are reflected in Parnall's spacious illustrations, as clean and poetic as is the writing." Bull Cent Child Books

Beard, Darleen Bailey, 1961-

Twister; pictures by Nancy Carpenter. Farrar, Straus & Giroux 1999 unp il $16   E

1. Tornadoes—Fiction 2. Siblings—Fiction

ISBN 0-374-37977-7   LC 95-13862

"Lucille and her little brother, Natt, are partaking in the idle pleasures of summer when a storm blows up; when the storm throws a funnel cloud, Mama commands her brood out of their mobile home to safety in the storm cellar . . . while she goes in search of an elderly neighbor. . . . Lucille's present-tense first-person narration is unforcedly full of telling details that make the account immediate. . . . Carpenter's thick, smudgy pastels deftly convey the viscousness of summer air before a storm and the weight of the threatening skies and the inky cellar dark." Bull Cent Child Books

Bell, Anthea

The Snow Queen; a fairy tale; by Hans Christian Andersen; translated and adapted by Anthea Bell; illustrated by Bernadette Watts. North-South Bks. 1987 unp il $15.95; pa $7.95   E

1. Fairy tales

ISBN 1-558-58053-0; 1-558-58779-9 (pa)

           LC 87-1518

After the Snow Queen abducts her friend Kai, Gerda sets out on a perilous and magical journey to find him

"The story is written with clarity and simplicity. Watts' paintings are full of atmosphere, thoughtfully composed, and likely to appeal to children." Booklist

Bemelmans, Ludwig, 1898-1962

Madeline; story and pictures by Ludwig Bemelmans. Viking 1985 c1939 unp il $16.99; pa $6.99   E

1. Paris (France)—Fiction 2. Stories in rhyme

ISBN 0-670-44580-0; 0-14-056439-X (pa)

Also available Big book edition and Audiobook version

A Caldecott Medal honor book, 1940

A reissue of the title first published 1939 by Simon & Schuster

"Madeline is a nonconformist in a regimented world—a Paris convent school. This rhymed story tells how she made an adventure out of having appendicitis." Hodges. Books for Elem Sch Libr

Other available titles about Madeline are:

Madeline and the bad hat (1957)

Madeline and the gypsies (1959)

Madeline in London (1961)

Madeline's Christmas (1985)

Madeline's rescue; story and pictures by Ludwig Bemelmans. Viking 1985 c1953 unp il $16.99; pa $6.99   E

1. Dogs—Fiction 2. Paris (France)—Fiction 3. Stories in rhyme

ISBN 0-670-44716-1; 0-14-056651-1 (pa)

Also available with Audiobook

Awarded the Caldecott Medal, 1954

First published 1953

A picture-story book with rhymed text about little Madeline in Paris. This time she falls into the Seine and is rescued by 'a dog that kept its head.' The dog, named Genevieve, was promptly adopted by Madeline's boarding school mistress and her twelve pupils. When Genevieve was turned out by snobbish trustees the little girls were inconsolable, until Genevieve solved their problem

Benchley, Nathaniel, 1915-1981

A ghost named Fred; pictures by Ben Shecter. Harper & Row 1968 unp il lib bdg $15.89   E

1. Ghost stories

ISBN 0-06-020474-5

"An I can read mystery"

"George, an imaginative child used to playing alone, went into an empty house to get out of the rain; there he met an absent-minded ghost named Fred, who knew there was a treasure but had forgotten where. Only when Fred opened an umbrella for George's homeward journey did the treasure materialize." Bull Cent Child Books

"More humorous than scary . . . this is a pleasing and acceptable ghost story for beginning readers." Booklist

Small Wolf; story by Nathaniel Benchley; pictures by Joan Sandin. HarperCollins Pubs. 1994 64p il hardcover o.p. paperback available $3.95

           E

1. Native Americans—Fiction 2. United States—History—1600-1775, Colonial period—Fiction

ISBN 0-06-444180-6 (pa)   LC 93-26717

"An I can read book"

A newly illustrated edition of the title first published 1972

A young Native American boy sets out to hunt on Manhattan Island and discovers some strange people with white faces and very different ideas about land

"Simply written but not stilted, the book has dramatic and humanitarian interest as well as historical use, and the illustrations have the same dramatic simplicity." Bull Cent Child Books

Berenstain, Stan, 1923-

Bears on wheels; by Stan and Jan Berenstain. Random House 1969 unp il $7.99   E

1. Bears—Fiction 2. Counting

ISBN 0-394-80967-X

Titles about the bears are available in various series on different reading levels. For complete listing see publisher's catalog

"A Bright & early book"

The authors' illustrations are used with numbers in this counting book which tells the story of a small bear who goes out for a ride on one small wheel. As the bear rides on, traffic and unwanted passengers accumulate

Berenzy, Alix, 1957-

A Frog Prince; written and illustrated by Alix Berenzy. Holt & Co. 1989 unp il $16.95; pa $6.95
E

1. Fairy tales 2. Frogs—Fiction
ISBN 0-8050-0426-2; 0-8050-1848-4 (pa)
LC 88-29628

"Based on the original story: Der Froschkönig." Verso of title page

"Beginning like Grimm's fairy tale 'The Frog Prince,' this story takes an unusual twist, leading to new adventures and a surprise ending. Told from the frog's point of view." Booklist

"Berenzy's palette of deep rich color, alternately gilded with light and cloaked in darkness, displays a magnificent utilization of light and shadow. A wonderful book—wry, touching, funny, and completely satisfying." SLJ

Berger, Barbara, 1945-

Grandfather Twilight. Philomel Bks. 1984 unp il $16.99; pa $6.99
E
1. Night—Fiction
ISBN 0-399-20996-4; 0-698-11394-2 (pa)
LC 83-19490

Also available Board book edition

"The coming of night is fancifully explained via the glowing figure of Grandfather Twilight, a benign, mysterious figure who walks shimmering through the woods to the seaside to release an incandescent pearl that becomes the moon. The slight story gets a lift from the attractive illustrations, which are full-color paintings with soft textures, and deep, rich color." Booklist

Beskow, Elsa, 1874-1953

Pelle's new suit; picture book by Elsa Beskow; translated by Marion Letcher Woodburn. Harper & Row 1929 unp il o.p.; Gryphon House reprint available $16.95
E
1. Sweden—Fiction
ISBN 0-86315-092-6

"Charming pictures tell the story of how Pelle earned his new suit. He is shown raking hay, bringing in wood, feeding pigs, going on errands and at the same time, each process in the making of the suit is followed, beginning with the shearing of the lamb. The coloring of the pictures (which show both Swedish peasant house interiors and out-of-door scenes) is quite lovely." N Y Public Libr

Best, Cari

Red light, green light, mama and me; pictures by Niki Daly. Orchard Bks. 1995 unp il $15.95; lib bdg $16.99
E
1. Mother-daughter relationship—Fiction 2. Libraries—Fiction 3. African Americans—Fiction
ISBN 0-531-09452-9; 0-531-08752-2 (lib bdg)
LC 94-33010

"A Melanie Kroupa book"

After taking the train downtown, Lizzie spends the day at the public library, helping her mother who is a children's librarian

"An excellent match for Best's text, Daly's gentle watercolors follow this African-American mother and daughter through their day and bring a small city library to life." Horn Book Guide

Three cheers for Catherine the Great; illustrated by Giselle Potter. DK Pub. 1999 unp il $16.95
E
1. Grandmothers—Fiction 2. Birthdays—Fiction 3. Gifts—Fiction 4. Russian Americans—Fiction
ISBN 0-7894-2622-6
LC 98-41153

"A Melanie Kroupa book"

Sara's Russian grandmother has requested that there be no presents at her seventy-eighth birthday party so Sara must think of a gift from her heart

"In lively, lyrical prose, Best celebrates a special family relationship, and conveys the unique challenges and joys of an immigrant's new life. . . . Potter's festive, whimsical artwork is an irresistible play of vibrant colors and patterns, filled with rich detail and diverse, expressive characters." Booklist

Blake, Quentin, 1932-

Mrs. Armitage and the big wave. Harcourt Brace & Co. 1998 c1997 unp il $15
E
1. Surfing—Fiction 2. Dogs—Fiction
ISBN 0-15-201642-2
LC 97-15420

First published 1997 in the United Kingdom

Mrs. Armitage and her dog Breakspear head out surfing, but each time they paddle out they think of another outlandish thing they need

"Spunky pen-and-ink and watercolor illustrations sketch a lively beach scene and an intrepid elderly heroine, who flamboyantly saves a drowning young girl." Horn Book Guide

Blake, Robert J.

Akiak; a tale from the Iditarod. Philomel Bks. 1997 unp il lib bdg $16.99
E
1. Dogs—Fiction 2. Iditarod Trail Sled Dog Race, Alaska—Fiction 3. Alaska—Fiction
ISBN 0-399-22798-9
LC 97-2251

Akiak the sled dog refuses to give up after being injured during the Iditarod sled dog race

"The story is stirring and involving. . . . Blake's oils are snow-blown and vivid, with varying perpectives but an emphasis on dog-level views. . . . An endpaper map depicts Iditarod routes and makes it easy to follow Akiak's journey; an author's note gives a little more background about the race and the relevant details." Bull Cent Child Books

Blegvad, Lenore

Anna Banana and me; illustrated by Erik Blegvad. Atheneum Pubs. 1985 unp il hardcover o.p. paperback available $5.99
E
1. Fear—Fiction
ISBN 0-689-71114-X (pa)
LC 84-457

Also available Spanish language edition

"A Margaret K. McElderry book"

"Anna Banana is fearless; she thrives on adventure and eagerly explores new situations. When this free spirit meets a cautious, timid male playmate in a city park, he is drawn into her exciting yet scary world. . . . Erik Blegvad's pen-and-ink and watercolor illustrations complement the simple, poetic text." SLJ

Blegvad, Lenore—*Continued*

First friends; pictures by Erik Blegvad.
HarperFestival 2000 unp il $9.95   **E**
    1. Friendship—Fiction 2. School stories 3. Stories in
rhyme
    ISBN 0-694-01273-4
    "Harper growing tree"
    "The young narrator invites readers to come inside a
classroom. Detailed pen-and-ink illustrations, set against
a white background, picture young children comfortably
engaged in preschool activities. Simple word repetition in
the rhymed text provides a quiet introduction to the no-
tion of school and its attendant possibilities." Horn Book
Guide

Blood, Charles L., 1929-

The goat in the rug; as told to Charles L. Blood
& Martin Link by Geraldine; illustrated by Nancy
Winslow Parker. Parents Mag. Press 1976 unp il
o.p.; Aladdin Bks. (NY) paperback available $5.99
                                                 E
    1. Goats—Fiction 2. Navajo Indians—Fiction 3. Rugs
and carpets—Fiction
    ISBN 0-689-71418-1 (pa)
    "A goat's-eye view of how a Navajo rug is made,
from the shearing of our supposed narrator ('Geraldine')
to the dyeing and weaving. By the time the rug is finished, Geraldine has grown enough wool to start another
one." Saturday Rev
    "Parker's vivid primary colored illustrations are as en-
joyable and humorous as the instructive text." SLJ

Blos, Joan W., 1928-

Old Henry; illustrated by Stephen Gammell.
Morrow 1987 unp il $16; lib bdg $15.93; pa $6.95
                                                 E
    1. Stories in rhyme
    ISBN 0-688-06399-3; 0-688-06400-0 (lib bdg);
0-688-09935-1 (pa)   LC 86-21745
    A "poem-portrait of an old man who offends the
neighbors with his raggedy house and renegade ways.
When Old Henry moves in, people expect him 'to fix
things up a bit. He did not think of it.' Instead, he
spreads his paraphernalia over the uncut grass, rejects offers of help shoveling snow, and finally moves out.
Amazingly, he and the community come to miss each
other." Bull Cent Child Books
    "This very lightly told story about social tolerance and
the merits of diversity is deftly illustrated in soft, colored-pencil drawings that capture the characters perfectly." N Y Times Book Rev

Blume, Judy

The one in the middle is the green kangaroo;
illustrated by Irene Trivas. rev American ed.
Bradbury Press 1991 unp il $16   **E**
    1. Family life—Fiction 2. Siblings—Fiction
    ISBN 0-02-711055-9   LC 91-154236
    Also available in paperback from Dell
    Original edition illustrated by Lois Axeman published
1969 by Reilly & Lee; this is a newly illustrated reissue
of the 1981 edition

Freddy hates being the middle one in the family until
he gets a part in the school play
    "Trivas' bouncy, good-natured illustrations seem des-
tined to charm even the most critical viewers. . . . This
edition seems better designed for reading aloud to children." Booklist

The Pain and the Great One; illustrations by
Irene Trivas. Bradbury Press 1984 unp il lib bdg
$17   **E**
    1. Siblings—Fiction
    ISBN 0-02-711100-8   LC 84-11009
    Also available in paperback from Dell
    A six-year-old (The Pain) and his eight-year-old sister
(The Great One) see each other as troublemakers and the
best-loved in the family
    "Young readers, depending on their position within
the family, will readily identify with either character and
may learn empathy for the other. Used in a group, this
will provide much healthy discussion. . . . Trivas' vibrant colors add depth and humor to a valuable book on
sibling relationships." SLJ

Bodnar, Judit Z.

Tale of a tail; illustrated by John Sandford.
Lothrop, Lee & Shepard Bks. 1998 unp il $15.95;
lib bdg $15.89   **E**
    1. Bears—Fiction 2. Foxes—Fiction 3. Fishing—Fic-
tion
    ISBN 0-688-12174-8; 0-688-12175-6 (lib bdg)
                                             LC 93-19046
    Not wishing to share his fish with Bear, Fox slyly di-
rects him how to catch his own, not realizing the extraordinary event that would result
    "The earth tones in Sandford's oil paintings give an
air of coziness to the brisk winter setting and bring out
the lighthearted fun of the friendly trickery." SLJ

Bogacki, Tomek

My first garden. Farrar, Straus & Giroux 2000
unp il $16   **E**
    1. Gardens—Fiction
    ISBN 0-374-32518-9   LC 99-24503
    "Frances Foster books"
    "A train ride triggers memories of childhood for the
adult narrator, who then journeys back in his mind to his
boyhood home, where, among others things, he planted
a flower garden that brought his neighbors together."
Horn Book Guide
    "The illustrations are softly colored and fuzzily im-
pressionistic, just right for the quiet text." SLJ

Bonners, Susan, 1947-

The wooden doll. Lothrop, Lee & Shepard Bks.
1991 unp il $13.95   **E**
    1. Dolls—Fiction 2. Grandparents—Fiction
    ISBN 0-688-08280-7   LC 90-33647
    "Stephanie feels excited but strange staying with her
grandparents by herself and hopes that her uncommuni-
cative grandfather will understand when she secretly
plays with his treasured Polish doll. Well-delineated
emotions and believable characters come to life in a pensive intergenerational story, with evocative, full-color
paintings." Horn Book Guide

Bonsall, Crosby Newell, 1921-1995

The case of the hungry stranger; by Crosby Bonsall. HarperCollins Pubs. 1992 64p lib bdg $15.89; pa $3.95   **E**
  1. Mystery fiction
  ISBN 0-06-020571-7 (lib bdg); 0-06-444026-5 (pa)
                        LC 91-13345
Also available with Audiobook; Spanish language edition also available
"An I can read book"
A reissue of the title first published 1963. This edition has full color illustrations
Wizard and his friends are clueless when they are sent on the trail of a blueberry pie thief, until Wizard hits on a plan that is sure to nab the sweet-toothed pilferer
  This offers "suspense and humor." Horn Book
Other available titles in this series are:
The case of the cat's meow (1965)
The case of the double cross (1980)
The case of the dumb bells (1966)
The case of the scaredy cats (1971)

The day I had to play with my sister; story and pictures by Crosby Bonsall. newly il ed. HarperCollins Pubs. 1999 32p il lib bdg $12.89; pa $3.95   **E**
  1. Siblings—Fiction
  ISBN 0-06-028181-2 (lib bdg); 0-06-444253-5 (pa)
                        LC 98-20342
"My first I can read book"
A newly illustrated edition of the title first published 1972
A young boy becomes very frustrated when he tries to teach his little sister to play hide-and-seek
"The extremely simple text . . . is one with which children can readily identify. . . . The realistic atmosphere makes Bonsall's book an excellent addition to the very early reading shelves." SLJ

Mine's the best. newly il ed. HarperCollins Pubs. 1996 32p il lib bdg $15.89; pa $3.95   **E**
  ISBN 0-06-027091-8 (lib bdg); 0-06-444213-6 (pa)
                        LC 95-12405
"My first I can read book"
A newly illustrated edition of the title first published 1973
Two little boys meet at the beach, each sure that his balloon is better
"The playful illustrations tell their own story; the extremely brief text (not to mention the head start provided by the two initial wordless spreads) will give new readers a sense of accomplishment." Horn Book Guide

Who's a pest? Harper & Row 1962 64p il lib bdg $15.89; pa $3.95   **E**
  ISBN 0-06-020621-7 (lib bdg); 0-06-444099-0 (pa)

"An I can read book"
"In this truly funny . . . book a small boy named Homer proves that he is not a pest as his four sisters, a rabbit, chipmunk, and lizard claim. The drawings are as laughable as the text and the tongue-twisting dialog begs to be read aloud." Booklist
Another available title about Homer is:
Piggle (1973)

Who's afraid of the dark? by Crosby Bonsall. Harper & Row 1980 32p il lib bdg $15.89; pa $3.95   **E**
  1. Night—Fiction 2. Fear—Fiction
  ISBN 0-06-020599-7 (lib bdg); 0-06-444071-0 (pa)
                        LC 79-2700
"An Early I can read book"
"A little boy describes to a friend the nighttime fears of his dog Stella. Stella shivers in the dark, he claims; she sees shapes and hears scary sounds. The doubting but sympathetic friend offers a suggestion—hug Stella in the night and comfort her until her fears go away. . . . The illustrations in shades of light blue and brown are filled with as much life and warmth as ever." Horn Book

Borden, Louise, 1949-

A. Lincoln and me; illustrated by Ted Lewin. Scholastic 1999 unp il $15.95; pa $5.99   **E**
  1. Lincoln, Abraham, 1809-1865—Fiction
  ISBN 0-590-45714-4; 0-590-45715-2 (pa)
                        LC 98-51921
With the help of his teacher, a young boy realizes that he not only shares his birthday and similar physical appearance with Abraham Lincoln, but that he is like him in other ways as well
"Borden's text flows nicely, creating imagery of the physical presence of the man. Lewin's distinctive watercolors lend style and substance to the book, producing a treat for the eyes." SLJ

Caps, hats, socks, and mittens; a book about the four seasons; illustrated by Lillian Hoban. Scholastic 1989 unp il hardcover o.p. paperback available $5.99   **E**
  1. Seasons—Fiction
  ISBN 0-590-44872-2 (pa)   LC 87-28776
Also available Big book edition
"Borden takes children around the calendar and introduces them to the uniqueness of each season. . . . The simple prose is illustrated by Hoban's distinctive drawings, featuring groups of round-cheeked children. . . . Cheery colors add to the book's ebullient feel." Booklist

Good luck, Mrs. K! written by Louise Borden; illustrated by Adam Gustavson. Margaret K. McElderry Bks. 1999 unp il $15   **E**
  1. Teachers—Fiction 2. Cancer—Fiction 3. School stories
  ISBN 0-689-82147-6   LC 97-50553
"Ann loves her third-grade teacher, who makes every child feel special and who introduces subjects with great zest. When Mrs. K. has cancer surgery the students are sad, but they (and their teacher) survive the year to return in the fall." Horn Book Guide
"A truly endearing story. Gustavson's watercolor illustrations exude all of the warmth and vibrancy of Borden's words." SLJ

The little ships; the heroic rescue at Dunkirk in World War II; illustrated by Michael Foreman. Margaret K. McElderry Bks. 1997 unp il $15
                              E
  1. Dunkerque (France), Battle of, 1940—Fiction
  2. World War, 1939-1945—Fiction
  ISBN 0-689-80827-5   LC 95-52557

Borden, Louise, 1949---*Continued*

A young English girl and her father take their sturdy fishing boat and join the scores of other civilian vessels crossing the English Channel in a daring attempt to rescue Allied and British troops trapped by Nazi soldiers at Dunkirk

"Borden's descriptive style is potent, and Foreman's watercolors perfectly express the dulled and watery scenes of devastation, the exhausted and hopeful soldiers awaiting rescue." Horn Book Guide

Bottner, Barbara, 1943-

Bootsie Barker bites; illustrated by Peggy Rathmann. Putnam 1992 unp il $15.99; pa $5.99 **E**

ISBN 0-399-22125-5; 0-698-11427-2 (pa)

LC 91-12182

"When Bootsie comes to play, she casts herself as a dinosaur, and the intimidated narrator as a turtle or salamander to be eaten. The girl dreams that her enemy will go away on her own, but faced with a possible sleepover, she uses her wits to make Bootsie-the-dinosaur a thing of the past." Publisher's note

"Bottner's tone is a model of simplicity and matter-of-factness, sometimes droll but never coy. Rathmann's neon-bright, full-color artwork extends the emotional tenor and the humor of the text." Booklist

Boulton, Jane

Only Opal; the diary of a young girl; by Opal Whiteley; selected [and adapted] by Jane Boulton; illustrations by Barbara Cooney. Philomel Bks. 1994 unp il $15.95; pa $5.99 **E**

1. Whiteley, Opal Stanley 2. Frontier and pioneer life 3. Oregon

ISBN 0-399-21990-0; 0-698-11564-3 (pa)

LC 91-38581

"Opal Whiteley's diary was first published in 1920 by the Atlantic Monthly Press and is available in a longer form, *Opal: The Journal of an Understanding Heart*, published by Tioga Publishing Company, adapted by Jane Boulton"

"Orphaned at five, Opal was taken in by an Oregon family who gave her shelter but little else. Transcribed into a lyrical text with luminous watercolors, the account captures the life of a turn-of-the-century child who, despite the odds, remains true to herself and the memories of her 'Angel Mother and Angel Father.'" Horn Book Guide

Bowen, Betsy

Antler, bear, canoe; a northwoods alphabet year. Little, Brown 1991 unp il hardcover o.p. paperback available $5.95 **E**

1. Alphabet 2. Nature 3. Seasons

ISBN 0-316-10315-2 (pa)

LC 90-33754

"Joy Street books"

Introduces the letters of the alphabet in woodcut illustrations and brief text depicting the changing seasons in the northern woods

"From its memorable, unusually fine woodcuts, to the telling glimpse it offers of a life that is close to the rhythms of nature, this debut is no garden variety ABC book." Publ Wkly

Bradby, Marie

Momma, where are you from? illustrated by Chris K. Soentpiet. Orchard Bks. 2000 unp il $16.95; lib bdg $17.99 **E**

1. African Americans—Fiction 2. Mother-daughter relationship—Fiction

ISBN 0-531-30105-2; 0-531-33105-9 (lib bdg)

LC 99-23068

Momma describes the special people and surroundings of her childhood, in a place where the edge of town met the countryside, in a time when all the children at school were brown

"Soentpiet's detailed, beautifully lit paintings freeze the mother's vivid memories, culminating in a dreamy, gray-toned montage of all the previous scenes. Children will be inspired by the mother's eloquent, proud answer to her daughter's essential question." Booklist

More than anything else; story by Marie Bradby; pictures by Chris K. Soentpiet. Orchard Bks. 1995 unp il $15.95; lib bdg $16.99 **E**

1. Washington, Booker T., 1856-1915—Fiction 2. African Americans—Fiction 3. Books and reading—Fiction

ISBN 0-531-09464-2; 0-531-08764-6 (lib bdg)

LC 94-48804

"A Richard Jackson book"

Nine-year-old Booker works with his father and brother at the saltworks but dreams of the day when he'll be able to read

"An evocative text combines with well-crafted, dramatic watercolors to provide a stirring, fictionalized account of the early life of Booker T. Washington." Horn Book

Braun, Trudi

My goose Betsy; illustrated by John Bendall-Brunello. Candlewick Press 1999 unp il $16.99 **E**

1. Geese—Fiction

ISBN 0-7636-0449-6

LC 98-3456

Betsy the goose makes a cozy nest, lays her eggs, and tends to them until her little goslings are hatched. Includes a section with facts about geese

"Down-to-earth language, a minimum of detail, and an abundance of large yet cozy illustrations make this just right for the intended audience." Horn Book Guide

Brenner, Barbara

Wagon wheels; story by Barbara Brenner; pictures by Don Bolognese. Newly il ed. HarperCollins Pubs. 1993 64p il $15.95; lib bdg $15.89; pa $3.95 **E**

1. Frontier and pioneer life—Fiction 2. African Americans—Fiction

ISBN 0-06-020668-3; 0-06-020669-1 (lib bdg); 0-06-444052-4 (pa)

LC 92-18780

"An I can read book"

A newly illustrated edition of the title first published 1978

Shortly after the Civil War a black family travels to Kansas to take advantage of the free land offered through the Homestead Act

Brenner, Barbara—*Continued*
"The based-on-fact story . . . is as fascinating as ever. Beautifully narrated with sensitivity, compassion, and just the right amount of suspense, and featuring new full-color illustrations." Horn Book Guide

Brett, Jan, 1949-
Annie and the wild animals; written and illustrated by Jan Brett. Houghton Mifflin 1985 unp il lib bdg $15; pa $5.95   E
    1. Animals—Fiction 2. Cats—Fiction
    ISBN 0-395-37800-1 (lib bdg); 0-395-51006-6 (pa)
                         LC 84-19818
Also available with Audiobook
When Annie's cat disappears, she attempts friendship with a variety of unsuitable woodland animals, but with the emergence of Spring, everything comes right
"Miss Brett uses colorful borders filled with detail to provide miniature previews of the narrative action and a story around a story, so that the reader instantly becomes an insider. The small glimpses of the world outside Annie's cottage move the tale forward and embellish the pages with grace and skill." N Y Times Book Rev

The hat. Putnam 1997 unp il $16.95   E
    1. Hedgehogs—Fiction 2. Animals—Fiction 3. Clothing and dress—Fiction
    ISBN 0-399-23101-3   LC 96-54015
When Lisa hangs her woolen clothes in the sun to air them out for winter, the hedgehog, to the amusement of the other animals, ends up wearing a stocking on his head
This story "has charm and humor. . . . The setting is the Danish countryside (detailed down to the moss on a tree) on a day when the first snow begins to fall, and Brett conveys the season with such loving spirit that children will almost wish for winter." Booklist

Trouble with trolls. Putnam 1992 unp il $16.99; pa $5.99   E
    1. Fairy tales
    ISBN 0-399-22336-3; 0-698-11791-3 (pa)
                         LC 91-41061
While climbing Mt. Baldy, Treva outwits some trolls who want to steal her dog
"Bursting with energy and fine detail, the double-page spreads, which escape their cross-stitch borders, depict a beautiful mountain landscape, dotted with trees and rocks that make excellent hiding places for the pesky trolls. Cutaway scenes beneath the spreads tell a concurrent story, picturing the trolls readying their home for Tuffi while an uninvited guest works its way down the chimney, then inside. Playful and funny, with a valiant female protagonist, this is a first-rate read." Booklist

The wild Christmas reindeer; written and illustrated by Jan Brett. Putnam 1990 unp il $16.99; pa $6.99   E
    1. Reindeer—Fiction 2. Christmas—Fiction
    ISBN 0-399-22192-1; 0-698-11652-6 (pa)
                         LC 89-36095
"The story's heroine is Teeka, who is asked by Santa to get the reindeer ready to fly. . . . Only when she realizes that hugging works better than bossing, do the reindeer unite into the working team that Santa needs to bring Christmas to the world. . . . Brett provides ornamental pictures, heavily detailed and decoratively bordered. . . . Beautifully conceived and finely wrought." Booklist

Briggs, Raymond, 1934-
Father Christmas. Random House 1997 c1973 unp il $18.99   E
    1. Santa Claus—Fiction 2. Christmas—Fiction
    ISBN 0-679-88776-8   LC 97-5667
A reissue of the title first published 1973 by Coward-McCann
A rather grumpy Father Christmas delivers gifts on Christmas Eve
"Each small picture is precisely detailed, convincingly well-drawn, and alive with action; the longer and larger frames—including some full-page spreads—offer a lot of visual contrast in size, color, and contents." Booklist

The snowman. Random House 1978 unp il $17; pa $7.99   E
    1. Stories without words 2. Dreams—Fiction 3. Snow—Fiction
    ISBN 0-394-83973-0; 0-394-88466-3 (pa)
                         LC 78-55904
Also available Board book edition
A "wordless picture book about a small boy who expertly fashions a snowman and then dreams that his splendid creation comes alive. Affably greeting the child, the snowman enters the house and is introduced to the delights and dangers of gadgetry. . . . Finally, no longer earthbound, the two friends go soaring over city and countryside, magical in their snowy beauty." Horn Book
"The pastel-toned pencil-and-crayon pictures in their neat rectangular frames will hold the attention of primary 'readers.'" SLJ

Brisson, Pat
The summer my father was ten; illustrated by Andrea Shine. Boyds Mills Press 1998 unp il $15.95; pa $7.95   E
    ISBN 1-56397-435-5; 1-56397-829-6 (pa)
                         LC 97-72769
A father tells his daughter the story of how he damaged a neighbor's garden when he was a boy and what he did to make amends
"The personal narrative voice, the heartfelt characters, and the daily gardening work . . . are celebrated in the gorgeously detailed pictures that show how a garden transforms a vacant lot." Booklist

Brown, Jeff, 1926-
Flat Stanley; pictures by Tomi Ungerer. Harper & Row 1964 unp il lib bdg $15.89   E
    ISBN 0-06-020681-0
"When an enormous bulletin board fell on him as he lay in bed Stanley Lambchop emerged as flat as a pancake. Once he got used to his half-inch thickness Stanley came to enjoy it and so did his parents— he could be lowered through sidewalk gratings, mailed to California, rolled up like wallpaper and tied with a string for carrying, and disguised as a framed picture to help catch art thieves in the museum. Comical colored pictures accentuate the humor of this rib-tickling story." Booklist

Brown, Laurene Krasny

Rex and Lilly family time; stories by Laurie Krasny Brown; pictures by Marc Brown. Little, Brown 1995 32p il lib bdg $12.95; pa $3.95

E

1. Dinosaurs—Fiction 2. Siblings—Fiction
ISBN 0-316-11385-9 (lib bdg); 0-316-11109-0 (pa)
LC 93-24162

"A Dino easy reader"

This book includes three adventures of a dinosaur brother and sister, Rex and Lilly "making a birthday surprise for mom, getting a housekeeping robot that goes wild, choosing the best pet. . . . [The text is] straightforward, often using repetitive sentence structure and phrases, and [lays] the groundwork for the humorous (and sometimes silly) watercolor-and-ink illustrations." SLJ

Other available titles about Rex and Lilly are:
Rex and Lilly playtime (1995)
Rex and Lilly schooltime (1997)

Brown, Marc Tolon

Arthur's nose; by Marc Brown. Little, Brown 1976 32p il $15.95; pa $5.95   E
1. Nose—Fiction 2. Aardvark—Fiction
ISBN 0-316-11193-7; 0-316-11070-1 (pa)

Books about Arthur are also available in other formats including board books, easy-to-read books, and chapter books

"An Atlantic Monthly Press book"

"Arthur the aardvark is unhappy with his long nose. When he finally decides to visit a rhinologist to have it changed, he discovers that he can't come up with a different kind of nose that suits him. No alterations are done, for Arthur comes to realize that 'I'm just not me without my nose.' The overworked lesson is pleasantly conveyed with surprisingly little text and large and colorful illustrations so that independent readers may be tempted to pick this up." SLJ

Other available titles about Arthur are:
Arthur babysits (1992)
Arthur goes to camp (1982)
Arthur lost and found (1998)
Arthur meets the president (1991)
Arthur writes a story (1996)
Arthur's April Fool (1983)
Arthur's baby (1987)
Arthur's birthday (1989)
Arthur's chicken pox (1994)
Arthur's Christmas (1985)
Arthur's computer disaster (1997)
Arthur's eyes (1979)
Arthur's family vacation (1993)
Arthur's first sleepover (1994)
Arthur's Halloween (1982)
Arthur's new puppy (1993)
Arthur's perfect Christmas (2000)
Arthur's pet business (1990)
Arthur's teacher trouble (1986)
Arthur's Thanksgiving (1983)
Arthur's tooth (1985)
Arthur's TV trouble (1995)
Arthur's underwear (1999)
Arthur's valentine (1980)

D.W. all wet; [by] Marc Brown. Little, Brown 1988 unp il $15.95; pa $5.95   E
1. Beaches—Fiction 2. Siblings—Fiction 3. Aardvark—Fiction
ISBN 0-316-11077-9; 0-316-11268-2 (pa)
LC 87-15752

Also available Board book edition
"Joy Street books"

Arthur the Aardvark's little sister D.W. "announces 'I don't like the beach, and I don't like to get wet.' She asks to leave the minute she arrives, she won't play and she's afraid of getting sunburned. It's Arthur who helps change D.W.'s mind about the beach by unexpectedly tossing her into very shallow water." Publ Wkly

"A simple, even predictable vignette, but entertaining nonetheless because of Brown's warm pictures." Booklist

Other available titles about D.W. are:
D.W. flips (1987)
D.W. go to your room! (1999)
D.W. rides again (1993)
D.W. the picky eater (1995)
D.W. thinks big (1993)
D.W.'s library card (2001)
D.W.'s lost blankie (1998)

Brown, Margaret Wise, 1910-1952

Another important book; pictures by Chris Raschka. HarperCollins Pubs. 1999 unp il $15.95; lib bdg $15.89   E
1. Growth—Fiction 2. Counting 3. Stories in rhyme
ISBN 0-06-026282-6; 0-06-026283-4 (lib bdg)
LC 98-7212

Also available The important book $15.95; lib bdg $14.89 (ISBN 0-06-020720-5; 0-06-020721-3)

"Joanna Cotler books"

Illustrations and simple rhyming text describe how a child grows from ages one through six

"Raschka assigns each age group a geometric shape: a simple circle represents age one, pairs of stacked squares indicate two, a five-pointed star signifies five and so on. . . . It's a pleasure to hear the organic rhythms of Brown's prose . . . and Raschka paints in boisterous surprises." Publ Wkly

Big red barn; pictures by Felicia Bond. Newly illustrated ed. Harper & Row 1989 unp il $15.95; lib bdg $15.89   E
1. Animals—Fiction 2. Farm life—Fiction 3. Stories in rhyme
ISBN 0-06-020748-5; 0-06-020749-3 (lib bdg)
LC 85-45814

Also available Board book edition, Big book edition, and with Audiobook; Spanish language edition also available

A newly illustrated edition of the title first published 1956

Rhymed text and illustrations introduce the many different animals that live in the big red barn

"The large illustrations are somewhat stylized, but still have a strong sense of detail and reality. The bright colors will attract young readers. The short text on each page is superimposed on the picture, but always in a way that is easy to read. Children will enjoy studying each of the pages as the day progresses from early morning to night." SLJ

Brown, Margaret Wise, 1910-1952—*Continued*

Bunny's noisy book; pictures by Lisa McCue. Hyperion 2000 unp il $14.99   E

1. Rabbits—Fiction 2. Sound—Fiction

ISBN 0-7868-0472-6   LC 99-19024

A little bunny listens to noises all around him and then makes some of his own

"McCue's brightly colored, detailed illustrations depicting a warm spring day from sunup to sundown are eye-catching and engaging. . . . This joyful adventure will work well as a lap-sit or storytime selection." SLJ

A child's good night book; pictures by Jean Charlot. HarperCollins Pubs. 1992 unp il $12.95
E

1. Night—Fiction 2. Bedtime—Fiction

ISBN 0-06-021028-1   LC 91-45340

Also available Board book edition

A Caldecott Medal honor book, 1944

A reissue of the title first published 1943 by W. R. Scott

As an invitation to sleepiness the author writes of birds and animals, sailboats, automobiles and little children as they settle down for the night

"Soft, colored-crayon drawings show night coming on. . . . A quiet, tender, bedtime book, gently, but not prosaically, illustrated." Horn Book

Four fur feet; illustrated by Woodleigh Marx Hubbard. Hyperion Bks. for Children 1994 unp il $12.95   E

1. Animals—Fiction

ISBN 0-7868-0002-X   LC 93-31523

A newly illustrated edition of the title first published 1961 by W. R. Scott

Poetic text and illustrations describe an animal's journey around the world on his four fur feet

This is "a simple, repetitive tale with the sort of serious whimsy Brown wrote so well. . . . Hubbard's new artwork depicts the creature itself—and a magnificent beast it is, too—with bright squiggles of red adorning its yellow coat and luxurious curly black whiskers." SLJ

Goodnight moon; pictures by Clement Hurd. Harper & Row 1947 unp il $14.95; lib bdg $14.89; pa $5.95   E

1. Rabbits—Fiction 2. Night—Fiction 3. Stories in rhyme

ISBN 0-06-020705-1; 0-06-020706-X (lib bdg); 0-06-443017-0 (pa)

Also available Board book edition, Big book edition, and with Audiobook

"The coming of night is shown in pictures which change from bright to dark as a small rabbit says good night to the familiar things in his nest." Hodges. Books for Elem Sch Libr

"A clever goodnight book in which pages are progressively darker as the leaves are turned. There are many objects to identify and children enjoy picking out familiar words." Books for Deaf Child

Little Fur family; illustrated by Garth Williams. HarperCollins Pubs. 1991 unp il $15.95   E

ISBN 0-06-020745-0

First published 1946; this is a reissue of the 1951 edition

"This story of a little fur child's day in the woods ends when his parents sing him to sleep with a lovely bedtime song." Publisher's note

This "book will still charm readers. . . . Williams's softly lit illustrations are enchanting." Horn Book

The little scarecrow boy; pictures by David Diaz. newly il ed. HarperCollins Pubs. 1998 unp il $15.95; lib bdg $15.89   E

1. Scarecrows—Fiction

ISBN 0-06-026284-2; 0-06-026290-7 (lib bdg)
LC 97-32558

"Joanna Cotler books"

Early one morning, a little scarecrow whose father warns him that he is not fierce enough to frighten a crow goes out into the cornfield alone

"Diaz provides wonderful illustrations for a story Brown wrote in the 1940s. . . . Brown's masterful use of repetition and rhythm creates a fine read-aloud story. The warm watercolor illustrations incorporate straw and patchwork." SLJ

On Christmas Eve; illustrated by Nancy Edwards Calder. HarperCollins Pubs. 1996 unp il $16.95; pa $5.95   E

1. Christmas—Fiction

ISBN 0-06-023648-5; 0-06-443670-5 (pa)
LC 93-43636

A newly illustrated edition of the title first published 1961 by W.R. Scott

Unable to sleep on Christmas Eve, four children creep downstairs to see the tree, their stockings, their wrapped gifts, and to hear the singing of the carolers

"Calder depicts the idyllic Christmas experience with a Victorian house in full array, snow falling outside, and a soft glow suffusing the children's thrilled faces." Booklist

The runaway bunny; pictures by Clement Hurd. Harper & Row 1972 c1942 unp il $14.95; lib bdg $14.89; pa $5.95   E

1. Rabbits—Fiction

ISBN 0-06-020765-5; 0-06-020766-3 (lib bdg); 0-06-443018-9 (pa)

Also available with Audiobook and Board book edition

A reissue, with some illustrations redrawn, of the title first published 1942

"Within a framework of mutual love, a bunny tells his mother how he will run away and she answers his challenge by indicating how she will catch him." SLJ

"The text has the simplicity of a folk tale and the illustrations are black and white or double page drawings in startling colour." Ont Libr Rev

Brown, Ruth

A dark, dark tale; story and pictures by Ruth Brown. Dial Bks. for Young Readers 1981 unp il hardcover o.p. paperback available $6   E

1. Cats—Fiction

ISBN 0-14-054621-9 (pa)

In a "style used by storytellers of ghostly tales, Brown begins 'Once upon a time there was a dark, dark moor' and goes on to describe the 'dark, dark wood' on the

Brown, Ruth—*Continued*

moor, the 'dark, dark house' in the wood and the stygian rooms in the huge place. A nimble black cat accompanies explorers of the mansion and leaps with them in gleeful terror when the final 'dark, dark thing' is discovered." Publ Wkly

"The book's mysterious power is engendered by the illustrations of weed-choked gardens and abandoned, echoing halls, of mullioned windows and blowing curtains." Time

The picnic. Dutton Children's Bks. 1993 unp il $15.99   E
  1. Animals—Fiction
  ISBN 0-525-45012-2   LC 92-5718
"A picnic in a meadow as seen by the resident creatures who run for cover—rabbits, moles and mice." NY Times Book Rev
"Brown makes use of unusual perspectives in her energetic, earth-toned watercolors. The economically told story has a gentle message just right for sharing with young animal lovers." Horn Book Guide

Toad. Dutton Children's Bks. 1997 c1996 unp il $15.99; pa $5.99   E
  1. Toads—Fiction
  ISBN 0-525-45757-7; 0-14-056550-7 (pa)
  First published 1996 in the United Kingdom
"The text tells of an 'odorous, oozing, foul and filthy' toad, a greedy predator who crunches bugs, munches flies, and slurps worms. Paintings in bilious, septic hues of green unfold another narrative: toad himself is being stalked and eyed as prey by a lizardlike monster, deftly camouflaged in the background. The rhythmic text, humorous climax, and slimy protagonist make the book a fine read aloud." Horn Book Guide

Browne, Anthony

Piggybook. Knopf 1986 unp il hardcover o.p. paperback available $7.99   E
  1. Mothers—Fiction 2. Family life—Fiction
  ISBN 0-679-80837-X (pa)   LC 86-3008
When Mrs. Piggott unexpectedly leaves one day, her demanding family begins to realize just how much she did for them
"As in most of Browne's art, there is more than a touch of irony and visual humor here, bringing off the didactic with a light touch and turning the lesson into satire." Bull Cent Child Books

Voices in the park. DK Ink 1998 unp il $15.95   E
  1. Gorillas—Fiction 2. Parks—Fiction
  ISBN 0-7894-2522-X   LC 97-48730
"A simple outing is described by two parents and two children, each with a different point of view and emotional outlook. Intriguing illustrations of the gorilla characters and surreal touches add layers of visual humor." SLJ

Willy the dreamer. Candlewick Press 1998 unp il $16.99   E
  1. Chimpanzees—Fiction 2. Dreams—Fiction
  ISBN 0-7636-0378-3   LC 97-2135
  Also available Spanish language edition

Willy the chimp dreams of being a movie star, a singer, a sumo wrestler, an artist, a giant, and other exciting figures

"Whether readers are wholly untutored or art history experts, the closer they look, the more jokes they will find. Fresh, funny and full of surprises." Publ Wkly
Other available titles about Willy are:
Willy and Hugh (1991)
Willy the champ (1986)
Willy the wizard (1995)
Willy's pictures (2000)

Bruchac, Joseph, 1942-

Crazy Horse's vision; illustrated by S.D. Nelson. Lee & Low Bks. 2000 unp il $16.95   E
  1. Crazy Horse, Sioux Chief, ca. 1842-1877—Fiction
  2. Oglala Indians—Fiction
  ISBN 1-88000-094-6   LC 99-47451
A story based on the life of the dedicated young Lakota boy who grew up to be one of the bravest defenders of his people
"Bruchac has created a memorable tale about Crazy Horse's childhood. . . . In beautiful illustrations inspired by the ledger book style of the Plains Indians, Sioux artist Nelson fills the pages with both action and quiet drama." Booklist

Brunhoff, Jean de, 1899-1937

The story of Babar, the little elephant; translated from the French by Merle S. Haas. Random House 1937 c1933 47p il $14; lib bdg $13.99   E
  1. Elephants—Fiction
  ISBN 0-394-80575-5; 0-394-90575-X (lib bdg)
  Original French edition, 1931; this is a reduced format version of the 1933 United States edition
"Babar runs away from the jungle and goes to live with an old lady in Paris, where he adapts quickly to French amenities. Later he returns to the jungle and becomes king. Much of the charm of the story is contributed by the author's gay pictures." Hodges. Books for Elem Sch Libr
Other available titles about Babar by Jean de Brunhoff are:
Babar and Father Christmas (1940)
Babar and his children (1938)
Babar the king (1935)
Bonjour, Babar! (2000)
Travels of Babar (1934)
Other available titles about Babar by Laurent de Brunhoff are:
Babar and the ghost (1981)
Babar and the succotash bird (2000)
Babar learns to cook (1978)
Babar saves the day (1976)
Babar's ABC (1983)
Babar's book of color (1984)
Babar's little girl (1987)
Meet Babar and his family (1973)

Brusca, María Cristina

Three friends. Tres amigos; a counting book; [by] María Cristina Brusca and Toña Wilson; illustrated by María Cristina Brusca. Holt & Co. 1995 unp il $15.95   E
  1. Counting 2. Bilingual books—English-Spanish
  ISBN 0-8050-3707-1   LC 94-44648

Brusca, María Cristina—*Continued*

This "bilingual text teaches the numbers one to ten by incorporating a Southwestern flavor. Brief sentences count objects, while the illustrations show the adventures of two cowboys. The artwork is amusing, and a picture glossary contains terms for objects that are in the illustrations but not mentioned in the text." Horn Book Guide

Buckley, Helen E. (Helen Elizabeth), 1918-

Grandfather and I; [illustrated by] Jan Ormerod. Lothrop, Lee & Shepard Bks. 1994 unp il $16; lib bdg $15.93; pa $5.95　　　　　　　　　　E

1. Grandfathers—Fiction

ISBN 0-688-12533-6; 0-688-12534-4 (lib bdg); 0-688-17526-0 (pa)　　　　　　　　LC 93-22936

A newly illustrated edition of the title first published 1959

A child considers how Grandfather is the perfect person to spend time with because he is never in a hurry

"Ormerod's full-color paintings teem with the warmth of a loving intergenerational family and fairly burst from the pages." SLJ

Grandmother and I; [illustrated by] Jan Ormerod. Lothrop, Lee & Shepard Bks. 1994 unp il $16.95; pa $5.95　　　　　　　　　　E

1. Grandmothers—Fiction

ISBN 0-688-12531-X; 0-688-17525-2 (pa)　　　　　　　　LC 93-22937

A newly illustrated edition of the title first published 1961

A child considers how Grandmother's lap is just right for those times when lightning is coming in the window or the cat is missing

"The watercolor art, done mostly in earth tones, varies from soft to sassy, but most of all, it is honest. Any child who has shared the unconditional love of a grandparent will see that love reflected here." Booklist

Buehner, Caralyn

Fanny's dream; pictures by Mark Buehner. Dial Bks. for Young Readers 1996 unp il $15.99　　　E

1. Marriage—Fiction 2. Farm life—Fiction

ISBN 0-8037-1496-3　　　　　　　　LC 94-31910

Fanny Agnes is a sturdy farm girl who dreams of marrying a prince, but when her fairy godmother doesn't show up, she decides on a local farmer instead

"Fanny Agnes is a delight: a feminist with a wry sense of humor, she balances her dreams with common sense and a loving heart. What's more, there's plenty for youngsters to enjoy in the robust, bucolic pictures, which seem almost to jump off the page." Booklist

I did it, I'm sorry; pictures by Mark Buehner. Dial Bks. for Young Readers 1998 unp il $15.99; lib bdg $15.89; pa $5.99　　　　　　　　E

1. Animals—Fiction

ISBN 0-8037-2010-6; 0-8037-2011-4 (lib bdg); 0-14-056722-4 (pa)　　　　　　　　LC 97-10216

Ollie Octopus, Bucky Beaver, Howie Hogg, and other animal characters encounter moral dilemmas involving such virtues as honesty, thoughtfulness, and trustworthiness. The reader is invited to select the appropriate behavior from a series of choices, and the letter for the correct answer is hidden in the pictures

"The artist has "concealed bumblebees, cats, rabbits and dinosaurs, among other things, in each of his lush and expressive oil-and-acrylic paintings. . . . Caralyn Buehner's snappy, alliterative text makes for an exuberant read-aloud." Publ Wkly

Bulla, Clyde Robert, 1914-

The chalk box kid; illustrated by Thomas B. Allen. Random House 1987 unp il $11.99; pa $3.99　　　　　　　　E

ISBN 0-394-99102-8; 0-394-89102-3 (pa)　　　　　　　　LC 87-4683

"Gregory's family moves to a smaller house in a poorer part of town; the father has lost his factory job. There is no yard at the new house in which to play, but Gregory explores a nearly burnt-out building that formerly was a chalk factory. Gregory finds plenty of chalk in the debris as he cleans up, and the artist in him soars." Publ Wkly

"As usual, Bulla manages a poignant depth within the confines of simple style and narrative. Understated and easy to read, this nevertheless tackles problems that are not easy to solve without exercising the imagination." Bull Cent Child Books

Daniel's duck; pictures by Joan Sandin. Harper & Row 1979 60p il lib bdg $15.89; pa $3.95　　　　　　　　E

1. Wood carving—Fiction

ISBN 0-06-020909-7 (lib bdg); 0-06-444031-1 (pa)　　　　　　　　LC 77-25647

"An I can read book"

"Daniel, who lived in 'a cabin on a mountain in Tennessee,' wanted 'to make something for the spring fair,' as the rest of the family were doing. Using the block of wood and the knife his father gave him, the boy carved a duck with its head looking backward. At the fair, people laughed when they saw the carving, and Daniel thought his work was being ridiculed: but he was more than consoled by a famous local wood-carver, who not only praised Daniel's duck but offered to buy it. The easy-to-read story and the simple format are excellently served by the subdued three-color illustrations, which round out the account of a traditional Appalachian family." Horn Book

Bunting, Eve, 1928-

Butterfly house; illustrated by Greg Shed. Scholastic Press 1999 unp il $15.95　　　　　　　　E

1. Butterflies—Fiction 2. Grandfathers—Fiction 3. Stories in rhyme

ISBN 0-590-84884-4　　　　　　　　LC 98-16349

With the help of her grandfather, a little girl makes a house for a larva and watches it develop before setting it free, and every summer after that butterflies come to visit her

"Shed's gouache-on-canvas paintings evoke feelings of warmth and nostalgia suited to the quiet story. Earth tones predominate, especially the browns and oranges found in this species. Appended with directions for raising a butterfly." Booklist

Bunting, Eve, 1928-—*Continued*

Can you do this, Old Badger? written by Eve
Bunting; illustrated by LeUyen Pham. Harcourt
Brace & Co. 2000 c1999 unp il $15   E
    1. Badgers—Fiction 2. Old age—Fiction
    ISBN 0-15-201654-6   LC 98-39809
Although Old Badger cannot do some things as easily
as he used to, he can still teach Little Badger the many
things he knows about finding good things to eat and
staying safe and happy
  "Cozy woodland scenes, rendered in dusky forest
greens, royal blue, and earth tones, illustrate a satisfying
yarn that hints at the natural life cycle." Horn Book
Guide
Another available title about Little Badger is:
Little Badger, terror of the seven seas (2001)

Cheyenne again; illustrated by Irving Toddy.
Clarion Bks. 1995 unp il $16   E
    1. Cheyenne Indians—Fiction 2. School stories
    ISBN 0-395-70364-6   LC 94-43287
Young Bull, "a young Cheyenne boy tells how he's
taken from his parents on the reservation in the late
1880s and sent to a boarding school, where he's forced
to learn white ways. . . . This is a picture book for older
readers, a grim story of painful separation and forced as-
similation. . . . The short, spare lines of free verse are
illustrated by double-page-spread oil and acrylic paintings
that contrast the open landscape with the stiffness of figures forced into uniform and regimentation." Booklist

Dandelions; illustrated by Greg Shed. Harcourt
Brace & Co. 1995 unp $16   E
    1. Frontier and pioneer life—Fiction 2. Family life—
    Fiction 3. Nebraska—Fiction
    ISBN 0-15-200050-X   LC 94-27104
"Like the dandelions she plants on the roof of their
Nebraska soddie, Zoe believes that the transplanting of
her family will 'take,' despite the difficult transition.
Young Zoe's narration conveys both youthful confidence
and fear as the family work to adjust to their new life.
Gouache illustrations effectively portray the vast, sun-
drenched prairie and complement the text." Horn Book
Guide

December; illustrated by David Diaz. Harcourt
Brace & Co. 1997 unp il $16; pa $6   E
    1. Christmas—Fiction 2. Homeless persons—Fiction
    ISBN 0-15-201434-9; 0-15-202422-0 (pa)
                            LC 96-21148
A homeless family's luck changes after they help an
old woman who has even less than they do at Christmas
  "Using elements of traditional folktales, Bunting provides a simply told story that is infused with the miraculous. . . . The artwork . . . is top-notch, intricate collages created from scraps of newspaper and images from
the story make an arresting backdrop for the bold acryl-
ic-and-watercolor pictures." Booklist

Dreaming of America; an Ellis Island story;
illustrated by Ben Stahl. BridgeWater Bks. 1999
unp il lib bdg $15.95   E
    1. Immigration and emigration—Fiction 2. Irish
    Americans—Fiction
    ISBN 0-8167-6520-0   LC 99-25708

Based on a true story this is a "portrayal of the voyage of Annie Moore, an Irish girl who, on her 15th birthday on the first day of 1892, was the first immigrant to
be processed at Ellis Island." Publ Wkly
  "The realistic illustrations are effective and rich in vibrant blues and browns. . . . On several occasions, they
are paired with reproductions of archival photographs
and records. . . . A solid account of a journey that many
immigrants made at the turn of the century." SLJ

Flower garden; written by Eve Bunting;
illustrated by Kathryn Hewitt. Harcourt Brace &
Co. 1994 unp il $16; pa $6   E
    1. Flowers—Fiction 2. Birthdays—Fiction 3. Stories
    in rhyme
    ISBN 0-15-228776-0; 0-15-202372-0 (pa)
                            LC 92-25766

Also available Big book edition
  "The young narrator has, with the help of her father,
assembled a 'garden in a shopping cart' to take home
and plant in a window box high above the city as a
birthday gift for her mother." Horn Book Guide
  "The simple rhymed verse, which skips along in pace
with the child's anticipation, is smoothly integrated with
the vibrant, lifelike paintings." Booklist

Fly away home; illustrated by Ronald Himler.
Clarion Bks. 1991 32p il $16; pa $5.95   E
    1. Homeless persons—Fiction 2. Airports—Fiction
    ISBN 0-395-55962-6; 0-395-66415-2 (pa)
                            LC 90-42353
A homeless boy who lives in an airport with his father, moving from terminal to terminal and trying not to
be noticed, is given hope when he sees a trapped bird
find its freedom
  "Himler's quiet paintings echo the economy and the
touching quality of the story, which is all the more effective in depicting the plight of the homeless because it is
so low-keyed." Bull Cent Child Books

Ghost's hour, spook's hour; illustrated by
Donald Carrick. Clarion Bks. 1987 unp il lib bdg
$16; pa $6.95   E
    1. Night—Fiction 2. Fear—Fiction
    ISBN 0-89919-484-2 (lib bdg); 0-395-56244-9 (pa)
                            LC 86-31674

Also available with Audiobook
  "A little boy, frightened by a howling wind and by a
bedside lamp that doesn't turn on, creeps down to his
parents' room only to find their bed empty and to hear
more strange slitherings and thumpings on their window." Horn Book
  "Bunting masterfully paces her story, with each fear
of the child climaxing in his discovery of the basis for
the sound. . . . The text is extended by Carrick's paintings, most of which brood with the darkness and . . .
change completely when the boy, with his parents, is no
longer afraid: warm, comforting gold tones then enrobe
the family. A book that provides the perfect blend of
chills and comfort." SLJ

How many days to America? a Thanksgiving
story; illustrated by Beth Peck. Clarion Bks. 1988
unp il lib bdg $16; pa $5.95   E
    1. Refugees—Fiction 2. Thanksgiving Day—Fiction
    ISBN 0-89919-521-0 (lib bdg); 0-395-54777-6 (pa)
                            LC 88-2590

Bunting, Eve, 1928—*Continued*

Also available with Audiobook

Refugees from an unnamed Caribbean island embark on a dangerous boat trip to America where they have a special reason to celebrate Thanksgiving

"Bunting's simple tale focuses on the hardships of the journey and on the American ideals of freedom and safety. She wisely leaves aside the issues of politics in the homeland or in this country. Her prose is poetically spare. . . . Peck's richly colored crayon drawings yield added enjoyment. . . . A poignant story and a thought-provoking discussion starter." SLJ

Market Day; pictures by Holly Berry. HarperCollins Pubs. 1996 unp il lib bdg $15.89; pa $5.95   E
1. Markets—Fiction 2. Fairs—Fiction 3. Ireland—Fiction
ISBN 0-06-025368-1 (lib bdg); 0-06-443517-2 (pa)
           LC 95-5604
"Joanna Cotler book"

Tess and Wee Boy observe the farm animals, wonder at the sword-swallower, hear playing of pipes, and experience all the excitement of a country fair in Ireland

"Bunting draws from her own childhood in Ireland, and the writing she offers is pure and totally evocative. . . . There couldn't be a better match for Bunting's words than Berry's enthusiastic, jam-packed pictures. There's so much to see, so much life swirling around, that kids will hardly know where to look first." Booklist

The Mother's Day mice; illustrated by Jan Brett. Clarion Bks. 1986 unp il lib bdg $15; pa $5.95
           E
1. Gifts—Fiction 2. Mice—Fiction
ISBN 0-89919-387-0 (lib bdg); 0-89919-702-7 (pa)
           LC 85-13991
Also available with Audiobook

"Three little mice go out on a spring morning in search of Mother's Day presents. After suitable adventures they return with a dandelion, a strawberry and a song." N Y Times Book Rev

"The story is a sweet one, saved from being too sugary by Brett's wonderful full-color illustrations." Booklist

Night tree; illustrated by Ted Rand. Harcourt Brace Jovanovich 1991 unp il $16; pa $6   E
1. Trees—Fiction 2. Christmas—Fiction
ISBN 0-15-257425-5; 0-15-200121-2 (pa)
           LC 90-36178
A family makes its annual pilgrimage to decorate an evergreen tree with food for the forest animals at Christmastime

"Bunting's quiet text and Rand's watercolors have just the right nighttime mood, capturing the mystery of the woods where there are 'secrets all around us.'" Bull Cent Child Books

A perfect Father's Day; illustrated by Susan Meddaugh. Clarion Bks. 1991 unp il hardcover o.p. paperback available $5.95   E
1. Father's Day—Fiction 2. Father-daughter relationship—Fiction
ISBN 0-395-66416-0 (pa)   LC 90-42355
Also available with Audiobook

When four-year-old Susie treats her father to a series of special activities for Father's Day, they just happen to be all of her own favorite things

"Bunting's simple, witty text sketches a warm father-daughter relationship and affectionately glances at the four-year-old mind at work. Meddaugh's bright watercolor and pencil illustrations add to the humor." Booklist

A picnic in October; illustrated by Nancy Carpenter. Harcourt Brace & Co. 1999 unp il $16
           E
1. Statue of Liberty (New York, N.Y.)—Fiction 2. Immigration and emigration—Fiction 3. Italian Americans—Fiction
ISBN 0-15-201656-2   LC 98-20044
A boy finally comes to understand why his grandmother insists that the family come to Ellis Island each year to celebrate Lady Liberty's birthday

"The talented Bunting makes this into a real story with characters that ring true. Carpenter's art, vibrant with sea and sky blues, has the same realistic feel." Booklist

Scary, scary Halloween; pictures by Jan Brett. Clarion Bks. 1986 unp il $15; pa $5.95   E
1. Halloween—Fiction 2. Cats—Fiction 3. Stories in rhyme
ISBN 0-89919-414-1; 0-89919-799-X (pa)
           LC 86-2642
Also available with Audiobook

A band of trick-or-treaters and a mother cat and her kittens spend a very scary Halloween

"Tailored for nursery and pre-school holiday read-aloud sessions, this is a slightly spooky picturebook with bright graphics on a black background showing costumed creepies prancing through the night, all watched by four pairs of green eyes hiding under a porch. . . . The faces on the creatures, the pumpkins, and even the trees will inspire shivers of delight in any darkened room." Bull Cent Child Books

Secret place; illustrated by Ted Rand. Clarion Bks. 1996 26p il $15   E
1. City and town life—Fiction 2. Nature—Fiction
ISBN 0-395-64367-8   LC 95-20466
"A little boy learns that the city, with all its grime and smoke and noise, can also be home for wildlife, when he discovers a 'secret place' in a river flowing between concrete walls. . . . Bunting's prose is evocative . . . and Rand's paintings vividly convey both the grayness of the city and the colors of the graceful wild creatures." Booklist

Smoky night; written by Eve Bunting; illustrated by David Diaz. Harcourt Brace & Co. 1994 unp il $16; pa $6   E
1. Riots—Fiction 2. Los Angeles (Calif.)—Fiction 3. African Americans—Fiction 4. Korean Americans—Fiction
ISBN 0-15-269954-6; 0-15-201884-0 (pa)
           LC 93-14885
Awarded the Caldecott Medal, 1995

When the Los Angeles riots break out in the streets of their neighborhood, Daniel and his mother, African Americans, make friends with Mrs. Kim, a Korean grocer from across the street

Bunting, Eve, 1928-—*Continued*

"Diaz's bold artwork is a perfect match for the intensity of the story. Thick black lines border vibrant acrylic paintings. . . . Diaz places these dynamic paintings on collages of real objects that, for the most part, reinforce the narrative action. . . . Both author and illustrator insist on a headlong confrontation with the issue of rapport between different races, and the result is a memorable, thought-provoking book." Horn Book

So far from the sea; illustrated by Chris K. Soentpiet. Clarion Bks. 1998 30p il $16   **E**
  1. Japanese Americans—Evacuation and relocation, 1942-1945—Fiction
  ISBN 0-395-72095-8   LC 97-28176

When seven-year-old Laura and her family visit Grandfather's grave at the Manzanar War Relocation Center, the Japanese American child leaves behind a special symbol

"Soentpiet's impressionistic watercolors perfectly complement Bunting's evocative text." SLJ

Someday a tree; illustrated by Ronald Himler. Clarion Bks. 1993 unp il $15; pa $5.95   **E**
  1. Trees—Fiction 2. Pollution—Fiction
  ISBN 0-395-61309-4; 0-395-76478-5 (pa)
                    LC 92-24074

Alice, her parents, and their neighbors try to save an old oak tree that has been poisoned by pollution

"Himler's soft, realistic watercolors spread over double pages and complement the sensitive, poetic mood of the story." SLJ

Train to Somewhere; illustrated by Ronald Himler. Clarion Bks. 1996 32p il $16; pa $5.95   **E**
  1. Orphans—Fiction 2. Adoption—Fiction 3. Abandoned children—Fiction
  ISBN 0-395-71325-0; 0-618-04031-5 (pa)
                    LC 95-6787

"Traveling on an Orphan Train in the late 1800s, Marianne tells herself that her mother, who went west some time ago, will surely come to meet her. At the last stop in Somewhere, Iowa, she finds not her mother, but an unlikely-looking older couple who just may be the family she needs. The illustrations convey the poignancy and historical setting of Marianne's journey." Horn Book Guide

The Wall; illustrated by Ronald Himler. Clarion Bks. 1990 unp il $15; pa $5.95   **E**
  1. Vietnam Veterans Memorial (Washington, D.C.)—Fiction
  ISBN 0-395-51588-2; 0-395-62977-2 (pa)
                    LC 89-17429

"A father and his young son come to the Vietnam Veterans Memorial to find the name of the grandfather the boy never knew. This moving account is beautifully told from a young child's point of view; the watercolors capture the impressive mass of the wall of names as well as the poignant reactions of the people who visit there." Horn Book Guide

The Wednesday surprise; illustrated by Donald Carrick. Clarion Bks. 1989 unp il lib bdg $16; pa $5.95   **E**
  1. Grandmothers—Fiction 2. Reading—Fiction
  ISBN 0-89919-721-3 (lib bdg); 0-395-54776-8 (pa)
                    LC 88-12117

This "first-person account tells of the special gift that seven-year-old Anna and her grandmother have planned for her dad's birthday: secretly, the two read books together until finally, the grandmother has learned to read." SLJ

"Bunting's writing is simple and warm and direct, showing rather than telling the book's audience that reading is both a skill and a joy. Carrick's pictures echo the warmth, especially in the faces of the family, painted in realistically detailed watercolors with a careful attention to familial resemblance. A gentle charmer." Bull Cent Child Books

Burleigh, Robert, 1936-

Home run; the story of Babe Ruth; illustrated by Mike Wimmer. Harcourt Brace & Co. 1998 unp il $16   **E**
  1. Ruth, Babe, 1895-1948—Fiction 2. Baseball—Fiction
  ISBN 0-15-200970-1   LC 95-10038

"A Silver Whistle book"

A poetic account of the legendary Babe Ruth as he prepares to make a home run

"With a flowing minimal text, Burleigh brings the Babe to life through the moment of one at bat. . . . Wimmer's sprawling, photorealistic oil paintings depict the larger-than-life figure and his surroundings with folksy Norman Rockwell-like charm." SLJ

Messenger, messenger; illustrated by Barry Root. Atheneum Bks. for Young Readers 2000 unp il $16   **E**
  1. City and town life—Fiction 2. Cycling—Fiction 3. Stories in rhyme
  ISBN 0-689-82103-4   LC 98-20566

Calvin Curbhopper, a bicycle messenger, makes his way through the city in all kinds of conditions to make sure that his messages get delivered on time

"The brightly colored gouache spreads extend the kinetic rhythms in the rhyming text. In realistic detail, they convey the city's buzzing workday activity." Booklist

Burningham, John, 1936-

John Burningham's ABC. Crown 1993 unp il   **E**
  1. Alphabet
                    LC 92-42765

Only available Board book edition

A reissue of the title first published 1964 in the United Kingdom; first United States edition 1967 by Bobbs-Merrill

Upper and lower case letters and labeled pictures depict dogs, flowers, umbrellas, a wasp, and other animals and objects from A to Z

"Lively, vigorous, glowing, John Burningham's alphabet book demands attention. . . . In addition to the brilliance of color and boldness of form, there are also touches of the unexpected." Horn Book

Burningham, John, 1936-—*Continued*

Mr. Gumpy's outing. Holt & Co. 1971 c1970
unp il $16.95; pa $6.95   **E**
1. Animals—Fiction
ISBN 0-8050-0708-3; 0-8050-1315-6 (pa)
Also available Big book edition
First published 1970 in the United Kingdom
"Mr. Gumpy is about to go off for a boat ride and is
asked by two children, a rabbit, a cat, a dog, and other
animals if they may come. To each Mr. Gumpy says yes,
if—if the children don't squabble, if the rabbit won't
hop, if the cat won't chase the rabbit or the dog tease the
cat, and so on. Of course each does exactly what Mr.
Gumpy forbade, the boat tips over, and they all slog
home for tea in friendly fashion." Sutherland. The Best
in Child Books
Another available title about Mr. Gumpy is:
Mr. Gumpy's motor car (1976)

Burton, Virginia Lee, 1909-1968
Katy and the big snow; story and pictures by
Virginia Lee Burton. Houghton Mifflin 1943 32p
il $15; pa $6.95   **E**
1. Tractors—Fiction 2. Snow—Fiction
ISBN 0-395-18155-0; 0-395-18562-9 (pa)
Also available with Audiobook
"Katy was a beautiful red crawler tractor. In summer
she wore a bulldozer to push dirt with. In winter she
wore a snowplow. She was big and strong and the harder
the job the better she liked it. When the Big Snow covered the city of Geoppolis like a thick blanket, Katy
cleared the city from North to South and East to West."
Ont Libr Rev

The little house; story and pictures by Virginia
Lee Burton. Houghton Mifflin 1942 40p il $14.95;
pa $5.95   **E**
1. Houses—Fiction 2. City and town life—Fiction
ISBN 0-395-18156-9; 0-395-25938-X (pa)
Also available with Audiobook
Awarded the Caldecott Medal, 1943
"The little house was very happy as she sat on the
quiet hillside watching the changing seasons. As the
years passed, however, tall buildings grew up around her,
and the noise of city traffic disturbed her. She became
sad and lonely until one day someone who understood
her need for twinkling stars overhead and dancing apple
blossoms moved her back to just the right little hill."
Child Books Too Good to Miss

Maybelle, the cable car; written and illustrated
by Virginia Lee Burton. Houghton Mifflin 1996
42p il $16; pa $5.95   **E**
1. Cable railroads—Fiction 2. San Francisco
(Calif.)—Fiction
ISBN 0-395-82847-3; 0-395-84003-1 (pa)
                                                  LC 96-9845
A reissue of the title first published 1952
Maybelle loves to carry people up and down the hilly
streets of San Francisco, until the City Fathers decide
that she should be taken out of service in the name of
progress
"The brightly colored line drawings [by the author]

are baroque in flavor, in keeping with the whimsey of
the story, which is done in a loose-jointed blank verse,
fine for reading aloud." N Y Times Book Rev

Mike Mulligan and his steam shovel; story and
pictures by Virginia Lee Burton. Houghton Mifflin
1939 unp il $14.95; pa $5.95   **E**
1. Steam-shovels—Fiction
ISBN 0-395-16961-5; 0-395-25939-8 (pa)
Also available Spanish language edition
"Mike Mulligan remains faithful to his steam shovel,
Mary Anne, against the threat of the new gas and Diesel-
engine contraptions and digs his way to a surprising and
happy ending." New Yorker
"One of the most convincing personifications of a machine ever written. Lively pictures, dramatic action, and
a satisfying conclusion." Adventuring with Books. 2d
edition

Butler, Dorothy, 1925-
My brown bear Barney; illustrated by Elizabeth
Fuller. Greenwillow Bks. 1989 unp il $15.95
                                                            E
1. Teddy bears—Fiction
ISBN 0-688-08567-9   LC 88-21199
First published 1988 in New Zealand
"As a wide-eyed, straight-haired little girl enumerates
all the places she takes her brown bear, Barney, her
faithful teddy is spied amid the weeds in the wheelbar-
row, sunning at the beach, and—of course—tucked into
bed. . . . But when the youngster itemizes the things
she'll carry to school, the omnipresent Barney is conspic-
uously absent." Booklist
"Every item on the little girl's checklists is first pictured clearly for easy identification and then imaginatively placed in its proper narrative context in an inviting,
bright full-page illustration with just enough detail to fascinate but not overwhelm." Horn Book
Another available title about Barney is:
My brown bear Barney at the party (2000)

Byars, Betsy Cromer, 1928-
The Golly sisters go West; by Betsy Byars;
pictures by Sue Truesdell. Harper & Row 1986
c1985 64p il lib bdg $15.89; pa $3.95   **E**
1. Entertainers—Fiction 2. Frontier and pioneer life—
Fiction 3. West (U.S.)—Fiction
ISBN 0-06-020884-8 (lib bdg); 0-06-444132-6 (pa)
                                                  LC 84-48474
Also available with Audiobook
"An I can read book"
May-May and Rose, the singing, dancing Golly sisters, travel west by covered wagon, entertaining people
along the way
"In the first story, they learn the hard way how to
make a horse move forward; in the second, they give
their first road show to an audience of two dogs; in the
third, they get lost; in the fourth, try to inncorporate the
horse into their act; in the fifth, make up after one of
their constant arguments; in the sixth, talk themselves out
of a nighttime scare. The dialogue and antics are convincingly like those of rivalrous young siblings anywhere
on the block. The story lines are cleverer than much
easy-to-read fare, and the old-West setting adds flair. The
accompanying watercolors, too, add a generous dollop of
humor." Bull Cent Child Books

Byars, Betsy Cromer, 1928-—Continued
Other available titles about the Golly sisters are:
The Golly sisters ride again (1994)
Hooray for the Golly sisters! (1990)

My brother, Ant; by Betsy Byars; illustrations
by Marc Simont. Viking 1996 31p il $13.99; pa
$3.99   E
1. Brothers—Fiction
ISBN 0-670-86664-4; 0-14-038345-X (pa)
LC 95-23725
Also available Audiobook version
"A Viking easy-to-read"
In four separate stories, Ant's older brother gets rid of
the monster under Ant's bed, forgives Ant for drawing
on his homework, tries to read a story, and helps Ant
write a letter to Santa
"The affectionate relationship between the boys under-
scores all the stories. Simont's lively, realistic watercol-
ors enhance the understated humor." SLJ
Another available title about Ant is:
Ant plays Bear (1997)

Bynum, Janie
Otis. Harcourt 2000 unp il $14   E
1. Pigs—Fiction 2. Friendship—Fiction
ISBN 0-15-202153-1   LC 99-6087
Because Otis likes to stay clean, he is different from
the other pigs and has trouble finding friends who hate
the mud as much as he does
"The cartoonlike pen-and-ink and watercolor illustrations show a comfortable family enjoying all the pastoral
pleasures of pig life. This simple story about self-
acceptance is nicely embellished with repetition and humor." Horn Book Guide

Cabrera, Jane, 1968-
Dog's day. Orchard Bks. 2000 c1999 unp il
$12.95   E
1. Dogs—Fiction
ISBN 0-531-30262-8   LC 99-42662
First published 1999 in the United Kingdom
Dog has a very busy day with his animal friends,
swinging from the trees with Monkey, flying through the
clouds with Bird, hopping and jumping with Rabbit, and
more
"Cabrera uses a bold art style executed in thickly applied gouache that gives the impression of finger painting. . . . This is an excellent choice for story hours."
Booklist

Over in the meadow. Holiday House 2000
c1999 unp il $16.95   E
1. Counting 2. Animals—Fiction 3. Stories in rhyme
ISBN 0-8234-1490-6   LC 99-22683
First published 1999 in the United Kingdom
A variation of the counting rhyme that introduces a
variety of animals and their activities
"The acrylics with heavy obvious brush strokes have
the look of finger painting. The movement and energy
conveyed in the illustrations enhance the rhyme, and listeners may be inspired to act out the animal actions or
chime in." SLJ

Caines, Jeannette Franklin, 1938-
Abby; pictures by Steven Kellogg. Harper &
Row 1973 32p il hardcover o.p. paperback
available $5.95   E
1. Adoption—Fiction 2. Siblings—Fiction 3. African
Americans—Fiction
ISBN 0-06-443049-9 (pa)
Abby, an adopted pre-schooler, "loves to look at her
baby book, even more, to listen to stories told by her
mother and by her brother, Kevin, about the day she became part of the family. . . . A crisis arises when Kevin
announces he can't be bothered with her because she's
a girl. But the clouds roll by when big brother says he
was only fooling and that he loves her." Publ Wkly
This "story of a warm and loving black family living
in a city apartment could be used to introduce the subject
of adoption. . . . Shaded drawings showing the family at
home perfectly complement the story." SLJ

Just us women; by Jeannette Caines; illustrated
by Pat Cummings. Harper & Row 1982 32p il
hardcover o.p. paperback available $5.95   E
1. Aunts—Fiction 2. Travelers—Fiction 3. African
Americans—Fiction
ISBN 0-06-443056-1 (pa)   LC 81-48655
This is the "story of a Black little girl planning a long
car trip with her favorite aunt. Enjoying being together,
'no boys and no men, just us women,' they pack carefully and buy two road maps (because last year Aunt Martha forgot their lunch and the map on the kitchen table)."
SLJ
"The pleasure of that trip and the warm relationship
it represents shine through in realistic, sometimes photo-
graph-like pictures." Booklist

Calhoun, Mary, 1926-
Cross-country cat; illustrated by Erick Ingraham.
Morrow 1979 unp il $17; lib bdg $16.93; pa $4.95
E
1. Cats—Fiction
ISBN 0-688-22186-6; 0-688-32186-0 (lib bdg);
0-698-06519-8 (pa)   LC 78-31718
Also available with Audiobook
When he becomes lost in the mountains, Henry, a cat
with the unusual ability of walking on two legs finds his
way home on cross-country skis
"Only the careful blending of skills by a talented au-
thor and illustrator could turn such a farfetched plot into
a warm, rich, and rewarding story. The realistic illustra-
tions seem to be enveloped in a glowing light and invite
the reader to step right into the story." Child Book Rev
Serv
Other available titles about Henry are:
Blue-ribbon Henry (1999)
Henry the sailor cat (1994)
High-wire Henry (1991)
Hot-air Henry (1981)

Flood; illustrated by Erick Ingraham. Morrow
Junior Bks. 1997 unp il $16   E
1. Floods—Fiction
ISBN 0-688-13919-1   LC 96-14836
One fictional Midwestern family is forced to leave
their home during the flooding of the Mississippi River
in 1993

Calhoun, Mary, 1926-—*Continued*

"Powerful in its understatement. . . . The storytelling is quiet, but it is tightly paced as it moves inexorably to the climax. . . . Ingraham's pastel pencil and watercolor illustrations are extraordinary, both the sweeping views of the stormy midwestern landscape and the interior close-up scenes of the family facing their loss together." Booklist

Cannon, Janell, 1957-

Crickwing; written and illustrated by Janell Cannon. Harcourt 2000 unp il $16   E
1. Cockroaches—Fiction 2. Ants—Fiction
ISBN 0-15-201790-9   LC 99-50456
A lonely cockroach named Crickwing has a creative idea that saves the day for the leaf-cutter ants when their fierce forest enemies attack them
"An amusing tale lightly rooted in natural history. . . . Cannon's illustrations skillfully blur the line between fact and fancy." Publ Wkly

Stellaluna. Harcourt Brace Jovanovich 1993 unp il $16   E
1. Bats—Fiction 2. Birds—Fiction
ISBN 0-15-280217-7   LC 92-16439
Also available Audiobook version
After she falls headfirst into a bird's nest, a baby bat is raised like a bird until she is reunited with her mother
"Cannon's delightful story is full of gentle humor. . . . [She] provides good information about bats in the story, amplifying it in two pages of notes at the end of the book. Her full-page colored-pencil-and-acrylic paintings fairly glow." Booklist

Verdi. Harcourt Brace & Co. 1997 unp il $16   E
1. Snakes—Fiction 2. Old age—Fiction
ISBN 0-15-201028-9   LC 96-18442
A young python does not want to grow slow and boring like the older snakes he sees in the tropical jungle where he lives
"Cannon's acrylic-and pencil illustrations look almost three-dimensional with the blend of plain gray pencil and brightly colored paints. . . . Cannon blends natural science with story, providing a double-page spread of added information on snakes." Booklist

Caple, Kathy

The friendship tree. Holiday House 2000 48p il lib bdg $14.95   E
1. Sheep—Fiction 2. Trees—Fiction 3. Friendship—Fiction
ISBN 0-8234-1376-4   LC 98-39043
"A Holiday House reader"
This book "includes four little stories about trees. Best friends Blanche and Otis are sheep who live next door to each other and share their sorrows and joys. . . . The line-and-watercolor illustrations reflect the sweet, gentle tone of the text with the soft, pastel shades." Booklist

Capucilli, Alyssa, 1957-

Biscuit's new trick; story by Alyssa Capucilli; pictures by Pat Schories. HarperCollins Pubs. 2000 unp il $12.95; lib bdg $12.89   E
1. Dogs—Fiction
ISBN 0-06-028067-0; 0-06-028068-9 (lib bdg)
            LC 99-23004
"My first I can read book"
"While his owner tries to teach him to fetch a ball, Biscuit the dog chews his bone or chases the cat—that is, until the ball lands in a mud puddle. . . . The simple language . . . and playful watercolor illustrations make this an appealing choice for beginning readers." Horn Book Guide
Other available titles about Biscuit are:
Bathtime for Biscuit (1998)
Biscuit (1996)
Biscuit finds a friend (1997)
Biscuit wants to play (2001)
Biscuit's picnic (1998)
Happy birthday, Biscuit! (1999)
Hello, Biscuit! (1998)

Carle, Eric

Do you want to be my friend? Crowell 1971 unp il $15.95; lib bdg $15.89; pa $6.95   E
1. Mice—Fiction 2. Stories without words
ISBN 0-690-24276-X; 0-690-01137-7 (lib bdg); 0-06-443127-4 (pa)
Also available Board book edition
"The only text is the title question at the start and a shy 'Yes' at the close. The pictures do the rest, as the hopeful mouse overtakes one large creature after another. With each encounter, the mouse sees (on the right-hand page) an interesting tail. Turn the page, and there is a huge lion, or a malevolent fox, or a peacock, and then, at last another wee mouse." Saturday Rev
"Good material for discussion and guessing games. . . . The pictures tell an amusing story and they are good to look at as well." Times Lit Suppl

Does a kangaroo have a mother, too? HarperCollins Pubs. 2000 unp il $16.95; lib bdg $16.89   E
1. Animals
ISBN 0-06-028768-3; 0-06-028767-5 (lib bdg)
            LC 99-36147
"The repetitious text is perfect for the toddler set. 'Does a lion have a mother, too? Yes! A LION has a mother. Just like me and you.' The text is repeated on every spread as the author showcases a dozen different animal mothers and their babies. . . . The vibrant artwork is classic Carle and should delight its audience." SLJ

From head to toe. HarperCollins Pubs. 1997 unp il $16.95; lib bdg $16.89; pa $6.95   E
1. Exercise 2. Animals
ISBN 0-06-023515-2; 0-06-023516-0 (lib bdg); 0-06-443596-2 (pa)   LC 95-53141
Also available Board book edition
"A giraffe bends its neck, a monkey waves its arms, etc. The repetitive text has the animal stating the movement and asking, 'Can you do it?' Each child responds, 'I can do it!' Carle's vivid cut-paper collages are striking and invite sharing individually or with a group." SLJ

Carle, Eric—*Continued*

The grouchy ladybug. HarperCollins Pubs. 1996
unp il $16.95; lib bdg $16.89; pa $6.95   E
1. Ladybugs—Fiction
ISBN 0-06-027087-X; 0-06-027088-8 (lib bdg);
0-06-443450-8 (pa)   LC 95-26581
Also available Board book edition

A reissue of the title first published 1977 by Crowell

A grouchy ladybug, looking for a fight, challenges everyone she meets regardless of their size or strength

"The finger paint and collage illustrations—as bold as the feisty hero—are satisfyingly placed on pages sized to suit the successive animals that appear. . . . Tiny clocks show the time of each enjoyable encounter, with the sun rising and setting as the action proceeds." SLJ

A house for Hermit Crab. Picture Bk. Studio
1988 c1987 unp il $16   E
1. Crabs—Fiction
ISBN 0-88708-056-1   LC 87-29261
Also available Miniature editon

"Hermit Crab, having outgrown his old shell, sets out to find a new one. He's a bit frightened at first, but over the course of the next year acquires not only a shell, but also an array of sea creatures to decorate, clean, and protect his new home. The story ends with him once again outgrowing his shell." SLJ

"The bright illustrations in Carle's familiar style, which seems particularly suited to undersea scenes, and the cumulative story are splendid, and one of the book's greatest strengths is the encouraging, hopeful view that the outside world is full of exciting possibilities." Horn Book

The mixed-up chameleon; by Eric Carle.
Crowell 1984 unp il $15.95; lib bdg $15.89; pa
$6.95   E
1. Chameleons—Fiction
ISBN 0-690-04396-1; 0-690-04397-X (lib bdg);
0-06-443162-2 (pa)   LC 83-45950
Also available Board book edition

A revised and newly illustrated edition of the title first published 1975

"A chameleon goes to a zoo where it wishes it could become like the different animals it sees. It does, but then isn't happy until it wishes it could be itself again." Child Book Rev Serv

The author "has replaced the heavy-lined, childlike, scrawled colors with crisp, appealing collages and has streamlined the text. The cutaway pages have been retained, and none of the humor has been lost. The simpler text results in a smoother flow, and children will enjoy the resulting repetition." Booklist

The very busy spider. Philomel Bks. 1984 unp
il $19.99; pa $6.95   E
1. Spiders—Fiction
ISBN 0-399-21166-7; 0-399-21592-1 (pa)
      LC 84-5907
Also available Board book edition

"Blown by the wind across the book's first pages and onto a fence post near a farm yard, a spider begins to spin a web. Her task allows her no time to answer barnyard animals, each of whom invites her to join in a fa-vorite activity. Finally, her web completed, she snags the pesty fly that's been annoying all of the animals and, exhausted, falls asleep." SLJ

This book "has a disarming ingenuousness and a repetitive structure that will capture the response of preschool audiences. Of special note is the book's use of raised lines for the spider, its web, and an unsuspecting fly. Both sighted and blind children will be able to follow the action with ease." Booklist

The very clumsy click beetle. Philomel Bks.
1999 unp il $21.99   E
1. Beetles—Fiction 2. Animals—Fiction
ISBN 0-399-23201-X   LC 97-33417

A clumsy young click beetle learns to land on its feet with encouragement from various animals and a wise old beetle. An electronic chip with a built-in battery creates clicking sounds to accompany the story

"Done in colored tissue-paper collage, the illustrations burst from the pages and are charmingly rendered. . . . A well-crafted story, joyfully illustrated." SLJ

The very hungry caterpillar. Philomel Bks. 1981
c1970 unp il $19.99   E
1. Caterpillars—Fiction
ISBN 0-399-20853-4
Also available Board book edition and Miniature edition

First published 1970 by World Publishing Company

"This caterpillar is so hungry he eats right through the pictures on the pages of the book—and after leaving many holes emerges as a beautiful butterfly on the last page." Best Books for Child, 1972

The very lonely firefly. Philomel Bks. 1995 unp
il $22.99   E
1. Fireflies—Fiction
ISBN 0-399-22774-1   LC 94-27827
Also available Board book edition

A lonely firefly goes out into the night searching for other fireflies

"The illustrations are painted cut-paper collages, designed to draw the eye to the page. This is a compelling accomplishment." SLJ

The very quiet cricket. Philomel Bks. 1990 unp
il $21.99   E
1. Crickets—Fiction
ISBN 0-399-21885-8   LC 89-78317
Also available Board book edition

A very quiet cricket who wants to rub his wings together and make a sound as do so many other animals finally achieves his wish

"The text is skillfully shaped; the illustrations convey energy and immediacy; and, in a surprise ending, a microchip inserted in the last page replicates the cricket's chirp." Horn Book Guide

Carlson, Nancy L., 1953-
I like me! [by] Nancy Carlson. Viking Kestrel
1988 unp il lib bdg $15.99; pa $5.99   E
1. Pigs—Fiction
ISBN 0-670-82062-8 (lib bdg); 0-14-050819-8 (pa)
      LC 87-32616
Also available Big book edition and with Audiobook

Carlson, Nancy L., 1953-—_Continued_

By admiring her finer points and showing that she can take care of herself and have fun even when there's no one else around, a charming pig proves the best friend you can have is yourself

This book is "visually interesting, with sturdy animals drawn in a deliberately artless style. Simple shapes, strong lines, and clear colors, with lots of pattern mixing, show what is not described in the minimal text. The text is hand-lettered." SLJ

Another available title in this series is:
ABC I like me! (1997)

Carlstrom, Nancy White, 1948-

Jesse Bear, what will you wear? illustrations by Bruce Degen. Macmillan 1986 unp il $16; pa $5.99　　　　　　　　　　　　　　　　E

1. Bears—Fiction 2. Stories in rhyme
ISBN 0-02-717350-X; 0-689-80623-X (pa)
　　　　　　　　　　　　　　LC 85-10610

Also available Board book edition
"The happy, singsong verse of the title follows Jesse Bear through the changes of clothes and activities of his day, even to bath and bed." N Y Times Book Rev

"The big, cheerful watercolor paintings show the baby bear in loving relation to his family and world. Without crossing the line into sentimentality, this offers a happy, humorous soundfest that will associate reading aloud with a sense of play." Bull Cent Child Books

Other available titles about Jesse Bear are:
Better not get wet, Jesse Bear (1988)
Guess who's coming, Jesse Bear (1998)
Happy birthday, Jesse Bear (1994)
How do you say it today, Jesse Bear? (1992)
It's about time, Jesse Bear, and other rhymes (1990)
Let's count it out, Jesse Bear (1996)
What a scare, Jesse Bear! (1999)
Where is Christmas, Jesse Bear? (2000)

Carrick, Carol

The accident; pictures by Donald Carrick. Seabury Press 1976 unp il o.p.; Houghton Mifflin paperback available $6.95　　　　　　　E

1. Death—Fiction 2. Dogs—Fiction
ISBN 0-89919-041-3 (pa)　　　　LC 76-3532
"A Clarion book"

After his dog, Bodger, is hit by a truck and killed, Christopher must deal with his own feelings of depression and guilt

"The story strikes home for anyone who has experienced the loss of a pet. . . . The artist's characteristically literal watercolors are overlaid with mustard and light brown hues, and . . . succeed in pinning down the story's sober mood." Booklist

Other available titles about Christopher are:
Ben and the porcupine (1981)
Left behind (1988)
Lost in the storm (1974)
Sleep out (1973)

Big old bones; a dinosaur tale; illustrated by Donald Carrick. Clarion Bks. 1989 unp il hardcover o.p. paperback available $6.95　　E

1. Fossils—Fiction
ISBN 0-395-61582-8 (pa)　　　　LC 88-16967

"In this tale the learned professor Potts and his family are traveling out West when he finds a fascinating site with quantities of very large, very old bones. He takes them home and tries different ways of assembling them, but the resulting skeletons are too absurd to be believed. . . . The book is a gentle spoof of early paleontologists who were a little unsure of exactly what they had found. It will be a treat for almost every child over the age of three, who will have an enjoyable feeling of superiority as the professor bungles about, making ridiculous mistakes." Horn Book

Mothers are like that; illustrated by Paul Carrick. Clarion Bks. 2000 unp il $15　　E

1. Mothers 2. Animals
ISBN 0-395-88351-2　　　　　　LC 99-16587

A simple description of animal and human mothers caring for their young

"The text in this gentle, lulling bedtime story of maternal love is brief but complete. The acrylic paintings . . . brim with child-appealing, close-up portraits of mother animals and their babies. Everything about this small and cozy book—topic, tone, format—is just right for the intended audience." Horn Book Guide

Patrick's dinosaurs; pictures by Donald Carrick. Clarion Bks. 1983 unp il lib bdg $15; pa $5.95
　　　　　　　　　　　　　　　　　　E

1. Dinosaurs—Fiction 2. Brothers—Fiction
ISBN 0-89919-189-4 (lib bdg); 0-89919-402-8 (pa)
　　　　　　　　　　　　　　　LC 83-2049

"During a zoo visit, Patrick's older brother Hank compares the size, habits, and ferocity of dinosaurs to the animals in the zoo, blithely unaware that Patrick is becoming increasingly afraid. . . . Only at home over peanut-butter-and-jelly sandwiches, when Hank assures him that 'dinosaurs have been gone for sixty million years,' can Patrick relax." Booklist

"The Carricks do a particularly good job of creating an impressive array of creatures both in text and illustrations—realistic pencil drawings washed in muted greens, browns and oranges." SLJ

Other available titles about Patrick's dinosaurs are:
Patrick's dinosaurs on the Internet (1999)
What happened to Patrick's dinosaurs? (1986)

Carson, Jo, 1946-

You hold me and I'll hold you; story by Jo Carson; pictures by Annie Cannon. Orchard Bks. 1992 unp il $15.95; lib bdg $16.99; pa $6.95
　　　　　　　　　　　　　　　　　　E

1. Death—Fiction
ISBN 0-531-05895-6; 0-531-08495-7 (lib bdg);
0-531-07088-3 (pa)　　　　　　　LC 91-16370
"A Richard Jackson book"

When a great-aunt dies, a young girl finds comfort in being held by her father and in holding, too

The author "has created an engaging and straightforward heroine to dramatize the impact of death on a child—this girl thinks, reacts and talks in a remarkably believable fashion, making her narration all the more touching. . . . Lightly tinted watercolors with collaged-in materials provide an unthreatening setting, and Cannon . . . paints a family of reassuringly lovable people. . . . A moving and sensitive exploration of a difficult topic." Publ Wkly

Caseley, Judith, 1951-

Dear Annie. Greenwillow Bks. 1991 unp il hardcover o.p. paperback available $5.95   **E**
    1. Grandfathers—Fiction 2. Letters—Fiction
    ISBN 0-688-13575-7 (pa)   LC 90-39793
Presents a series of postcards and letters Annie sends to or receives from her loving grandfather from the time she is born

"The line-and-watercolor illustrations of the letters and the cozy details of Grandpa's and Annie's lives are bright vignettes set within lots of white space, giving the book an open and friendly tone. The affection between a grandparent and child is rarely captured with such easygoing warmth." Bull Cent Child Books

Mama, coming and going. Greenwillow Bks. 1994 unp il $15.95   **E**
    1. Infants—Fiction 2. Mothers—Fiction 3. Siblings—Fiction
    ISBN 0-688-11441-5   LC 92-29402
Big sister Jenna recalls the funny things that Mama forgot to do after baby Mickey was born

"The cheerful watercolor-and-pencil drawings are filled with bright yellows, blues, and reds. . . . A light-hearted glance at a loving family during a topsy-turvy time." SLJ

Mr. Green Peas. Greenwillow Bks. 1995 unp il lib bdg $14.93; pa $4.95   **E**
    1. Iguanas—Fiction 2. Pets—Fiction 3. School stories
    ISBN 0-688-12860-2 (lib bdg); 0-688-16092-1 (pa)
    LC 93-24183
Norman is sad because he's the only one in his nursery school class who doesn't have a pet, until he gets a pet iguana

"Everything about this book is charming: the tantalizing subject, the large text in bold print, the decorative borders, and the colorful illustrations, which brim with interesting details to hold children's attention." Booklist

Castañeda, Omar S., 1954-1997

Abuela's weave; illustrated by Enrique O. Sanchez. Lee & Low Bks. 1993 unp il $15.95; pa $6.95   **E**
    1. Grandmothers—Fiction 2. Guatemala—Fiction 3. Weaving—Fiction
    ISBN 1-880000-00-8; 1-880000-20-2 (pa)
    LC 92-71927
Also available Spanish language edition
A young Guatemalan girl and her grandmother grow closer as they weave some special creations and then make a trip to the market in hopes of selling them

"Castañeda affectingly portrays the loving rapport between a child and her grandmother, as well as the beauty of his homeland's cultural traditions. Sanchez's bright, richly grained acrylic-on-canvas paintings bring dimension to the characters and authenticity to the setting." Publ Wkly

Catalanotto, Peter

The painter. Orchard Bks. 1995 unp il $15.95; lib bdg $16.99; pa $5.95   **E**
    1. Artists—Fiction 2. Father-daughter relationship—Fiction
    ISBN 0-531-09465-0; 0-531-08765-4 (lib bdg); 0-531-07116-2 (pa)   LC 94-48808

"A Richard Jackson book"
"Throughout the day a child asks her father to play with her, but except for brief breaks for silly games, he has to work in his studio, where he is painting a picture of a blue car. Finally, after dinner, they have time to paint together. The simple text, told in the first person by the young girl, is enhanced by soft yet realistic watercolors of a warm family life." Horn Book Guide

Cauley, Lorinda Bryan, 1951-

Clap your hands. Putnam 1992 unp il $16.99; pa $5.99   **E**
    1. Animals—Fiction 2. Stories in rhyme
    ISBN 0-399-22118-2; 0-698-11428-0 (pa)
    LC 91-12863
Rhyming text instructs the listener to find something yellow, roar like a lion, give a kiss, tell a secret, spin in a circle, and perform other playful activities along with the human and animal characters pictured

"In a series of lively double-page spreads, the illustrations feature glowing colors and make good use of Cauley's gift for characterization. . . . Some parts of the book would be fun as action rhymes for preschool story time. . . . Parent-child sharing would also be fun, though not at bedtime: this book's bugle call is not taps, but reveille." Booklist

Chambers, Veronica

Amistad rising; a story of freedom; illustrated by Paul Lee. Harcourt Brace & Co. 1998 unp il $16   **E**
    1. Cinque, 1811?-1879—Fiction 2. Amistad (Schooner)—Fiction 3. Slavery—Fiction
    ISBN 0-15-201803-4   LC 97-27987
A fictional account of the 1839 revolt of Africans aboard the slave ship Amistad and the subsequent legal case argued before the Supreme Court in 1841 by former president John Quincy Adams

"Cinqué's bravery and inspirational leadership are the heart of the book. . . . The figures of the man and his followers are heroic in size in Lee's action-filled acrylic paintings. . . . The brevity of facts and the poetic quality of emotional description make the book a fine read-aloud choice." SLJ

Charlip, Remy

Hooray for me! by Remy Charlip & Lilian Moore; paintings by Vera B. Williams. Tricycle Press 1996 unp il $14.95   **E**
    ISBN 1-88367-243-0   LC 96-2449
A reissue of the title first published 1975 by Parents' Magazine Press

"Two kids realize they are both 'me' and then continue the discussion with a whole crowd, discovering that 'me' can be an aunt, a nephew, a second cousin, a great-grandfather. Bright, dreamlike watercolors enhance this joyful look at self-discovery." Horn Book Guide

Sleepytime rhyme. Greenwillow Bks. 1999 unp il $16.95; lib bdg $15.89   **E**
    1. Mothers—Fiction 2. Stories in rhyme
    ISBN 0-688-16271-1; 0-688-16272-X (lib bdg)
    LC 98-41040

Charlip, Remy—*Continued*

Illustrations and rhyming text convey a mother's love for her child

"The artwork is crisp, simple, and bright. The equally simple rhyming text chronicles all the parts of the baby its mother loves." Booklist

Cherry, Lynne, 1952-

The great kapok tree; a tale of the Amazon rainforest. Harcourt Brace Jovanovich 1990 unp il $16; pa $7   E

1. Rain forests—Fiction 2. Conservation of natural resources—Fiction

ISBN 0-15-200520-X; 0-15-202614-2 (pa)

LC 89-2208

Also available Big book edition

"Gulliver books"

The many different animals that live in a great kapok tree in the Brazilian rainforest try to convince a man with an ax of the importance of not cutting down their home

"A carefully researched picture book about the Brazilian rain forest is strikingly illustrated and presented in a large format. Cherry captures the Amazonian proportions of the plants and animals that live there by using vibrant colors, intricate details, and dramatic perspectives. . . . The writing is simple and clear, yet makes a serious point about humans' destructive ways." Booklist

Chinn, Karen, 1959-

Sam and the lucky money; illustrated by Cornelius Van Wright, and Ying-Hwa Hu. Lee & Low Bks. 1995 unp $15.95; pa $6.95   E

1. Chinese New Year—Fiction 2. Chinese Americans—Fiction

ISBN 1-880000-13-X; 1-880000-53-9 (pa)

LC 94-11766

This is a "tale of a young boy eager to spend his 'lucky money' on Chinese New Year day. As Sam searches the streets of Chinatown for ways to spend his four dollars, he stumbles upon a stranger in need. After he decides to give, rather than spend, his money, Sam realizes that he's 'the lucky one.'" Horn Book Guide

"The illustrators masterfully combine Chinatown's exotic setting with the universal emotions of childhood through expressive portraits of the characters." SLJ

Chocolate, Debbi, 1954-

The piano man; [by] Debbi Chocolate; illustrations by Eric Velasquez. Walker & Co. 1998 unp il lib bdg $16.95; pa $7.95   E

1. Grandfathers—Fiction   2. Pianists—Fiction 3. African Americans—Fiction

ISBN 0-8027-8647-2 (lib bdg); 0-8027-7578-0 (pa)

LC 97-22668

A young Afro-American girl recalls the life story of her grandfather who performed in vaudeville and played piano for the silent movies

"Velasquez's exuberant, realistic paintings follow the thread of family life. . . . This vivid picture of America's past may well prompt discussions of the nation's history as well as family roots." Publ Wkly

Choi, Sook Nyul

Halmoni and the picnic; illustrated by Karen Milone. Houghton Mifflin 1993 31p il $16   E

1. Korean Americans—Fiction 2. Grandmothers—Fiction

ISBN 0-395-61626-3

LC 91-34121

A third grade class helps Halmoni, Yunmi's newly arrived Korean grandmother, feel more comfortable with her life in the United States

"Choi's text, sentimental but never saccharine, captures a jumble of emotions. . . . With a light hand Choi delivers a happy ending. Dugan's serviceable pencil and watercolor illustrations are warm in spirit and accurate in their detail." Publ Wkly

Another available title about Yunmi and Halmoni is: Yunmi and Halmoni's trip (1997)

Chorao, Kay, 1936-

Pig and Crow. Holt & Co. 2000 unp il $16.95   E

1. Pigs—Fiction 2. Crows—Fiction

ISBN 0-8050-5863-X

LC 99-31776

"Crow trades a series of three 'magic' items for lonely Pig's baked goods. Magic seeds grow into nonmagic pumpkins. A magic worm changes into a butterfly and, heartbreakingly for Pig, flies away. Finally, Crow brings a magic egg, which hatches into a companionable goose." Horn Book Guide

"Chorao's gouache-and-ink illustrations are so wonderfully expressive that the joy on Pig's face when the butterfly hatches and the horror as it flies away tell the story as effectively as the words." Booklist

Christelow, Eileen, 1943-

Five little monkeys jumping on the bed; retold and illustrated by Eileen Christelow. Clarion Bks. 1989 unp il $15; pa $5.95   E

1. Monkeys—Fiction 2. Counting

ISBN 0-89919-769-8; 0-395-55701-1 (pa)

LC 88-22839

Also available Board book edition and with Audiobook

A counting book in which one by one the five little monkeys jump on the bed only to fall off and bump their heads

"Squiggling, swirling lines of color capture the sense of unbridled motion as the monkeys bounce and, one by one, topple from the bed. After all five bandaged youngsters finally fall asleep, a relaxed mama gratefully retires to her room . . . to bounce on 'her' bed. An amusingly presented counting exercise." Booklist

Other available titles about the five little monkeys are:

Don't wake up Mama! (1992)

Five little monkeys sitting in a tree (1991)

Five little monkeys wash the car (2000)

Five little monkeys with nothing to do (1996)

Cleary, Beverly

The hullabaloo ABC; illustrated by Ted Rand. rev ed. Morrow Junior Bks. 1998 unp il $16; lib bdg $15.93   E

1. Noise—Fiction 2. Farm life—Fiction 3. Stories in rhyme 4. Alphabet

ISBN 0-688-15182-5; 0-688-15183-3 (lib bdg)

LC 97-6457

Cleary, Beverly—*Continued*

A revised and newly illustrated edition of the title first published 1960 by Parnassus Press

An alphabet book in which two children demonstrate all the fun that is to be had by making and hearing every kind of noise as they dash about on the farm

"Rand's expert watercolor illustrations on crisp white backgrounds bring the action to life with just the slightest touch of nostalgia." SLJ

Clements, Andrew, 1949-

Circus family dog; illustrated by Sue Truesdell. Clarion Bks. 2000 32p il $15   E

1. Dogs—Fiction 2. Circus—Fiction

ISBN 0-395-78648-7   LC 99-52657

Grumps is content to do his one trick in the center ring at the circus, until a new dog shows up and steals the show—temporarily

"The combination of Clements's impeccable storyteller pacing and Truesdell's creative and whimsical cartoons create a reading and visual experience second only to actually being at the circus. The illustrator uses a mixture of watercolors with pen and ink to bring the action to life in vibrant colors." SLJ

Temple cat; illustrated by Kate Kiesler. Clarion Bks. 1996 31p il $16   E

1. Cats—Fiction 2. Egypt—Fiction

ISBN 0-395-69842-1   LC 94-44082

A temple cat in ancient Egypt grows tired of being worshipped and cared for in a reverent fashion and travels to the seaside, where she finds genuine affection with a fisherman and his children

"Kiesler's warm paintings in shades of brown and gleaming gold capture both the splendor of the temple setting and the physicalness of the furry adventurer." Booklist

Clifton, Lucille, 1936-

Everett Anderson's 1-2-3; illustrations by Ann Grifalconi. Holt & Co. 1992 unp il $14.95   E

1. Remarriage—Fiction 2. African Americans—Fiction 3. Stories in rhyme

ISBN 0-8050-2310-0   LC 92-8031

A reissue of the title first published 1977 by Holt, Rinehart & Winston

As a small boy's mother considers remarriage, he considers the numbers one, two, and three--sometimes they're lonely, sometimes crowded, but sometimes just right

"The illustrations, strongly drawn with bold, broken lines, are large in scale, almost all pictures of the three characters with only minimal background details. The text is tender, artful in the simplicity and brevity with which it gets to the gist of the matter." Bull Cent Child Books

Other available titles about Everett Anderson are:

Everett Anderson's Christmas coming (c1971)

Everett Anderson's friend (c1976)

Everett Anderson's goodbye (c1983)

Everett Anderson's nine month long (c1978)

Everett Anderson's year (c1974)

Some of the days of Everett Anderson (c1970)

Climo, Shirley, 1928-

The cobweb Christmas; illustrated by Joe Lasker. Crowell 1982 unp il hardcover o.p. paperback available $5.95   E

1. Christmas—Fiction 2. Spiders—Fiction

ISBN 0-06-443110-X (pa)   LC 81-43879

"Every year Tante shooed the animals and spiders from her cottage so that she could prepare for Christmas. But every year . . . she would ask the animals back to her cottage, for she had heard that on Christmas Eve they might speak. . . . This year, as always, the old woman . . . fell asleep. She never heard 'the rusty, squeaky voices' of the neglected spiders, hoping to be let in. But Christkindel . . . opened the door for the spiders, who covered the tree with sticky webs; then . . . Christkindel transformed the webs into strands of gold and silver." Horn Book

"Lasker's watercolor paintings fill each page they occupy with glowing color. The scenes he sets are contained but full, with sparely composed rustic interiors and appropriate touches of glory when Christkindel works his magic. A good-looking, involving story for the Christmas shelf." Booklist

Coerr, Eleanor, 1922-

The big balloon race; pictures by Carolyn Croll. Harper & Row 1981 62p il lib bdg $15.89; pa $3.95   E

1. Balloons—Fiction

ISBN 0-06-021353-1 (lib bdg); 0-06-444053-2 (pa)   LC 80-8368

Also available with Audiobook

"An I can read book"

The author "recounts the winning of a hydrogen balloon race by Carlotta Myers, a famous aeronaut, and her stowaway daughter Ariel. Balloon facts are slipped naturally and painlessly into the story, which moves cogently along. The novel subject matter, straightforward mother-daughter relationship, and clear composition of the orange, blue and gray illustrations . . . make for a high-flying new look at a piece of the past." SLJ

Chang's paper pony; pictures by Deborah Kogan Ray. Harper & Row 1988 64p il lib bdg $15.89; pa $3.95   E

1. Chinese Americans—Fiction 2. Horses—Fiction 3. Gold mines and mining—Fiction

ISBN 0-06-021329-9 (lib bdg); 0-06-444163-6 (pa)   LC 87-45679

"An I can read book"

This story is "set at the time of California's Gold Rush. Chang and his grandfather work in the kitchen of a mining camp. As a result of hard work and honesty, not to mention fair play by one of the miners, Chang gets the pony of his dreams. But the story does not prettify the ugly way many immigrant Chinese were treated." N Y Times Book Rev

"Ray's forceful drawings support the text well and firmly establish the dusty mining-town environment. She is particularly adept at showing the vulnerability of children, as well as the ways in which large and small joys affect them." Publ Wkly

Coerr, Eleanor, 1922——_Continued_

The Josefina story quilt; pictures by Bruce Degen. Harper & Row 1986 64p il $15.95; lib bdg $15.89; pa $3.95   **E**

1. Quilts—Fiction 2. Overland journeys to the Pacific—Fiction

ISBN 0-06-021348-5; 0-06-021349-3 (lib bdg); 0-06-444129-6 (pa)   LC 85-45260

Also available with Audiobook

"An I can read book"

While traveling west with her family in 1850, a young girl makes a patchwork quilt chronicling the experiences of the journey and reserves a special patch for her pet hen Josefina

"The story makes the history go down easily, and an author's note at the end fills in facts about the western trip and the place of quilts as pioneer diaries. The charcoal and blue/yellow wash illustrations are clear and natural . . . a good introduction to historical fiction that children can read for themselves." SLJ

Cohen, Barbara, 1932-1992

Molly's pilgrim; illustrated by Daniel Mark Duffy. Lothrop, Lee & Shepard Bks. 1998 unp il $15; pa $3.95   **E**

1. Jews—Fiction 2. School stories 3. Thanksgiving Day—Fiction 4. Immigration and emigration—Fiction

ISBN 0-688-16279-7; 0-688-16280-0 (pa)

LC 98-9227

A newly illustrated edition of the title first published 1983

Told to make a Pilgrim doll for the Thanksgiving display at school, Molly is embarassed when her mother tries to help her out by creating a doll dressed as she herself was dressed before leaving Russia to seek religious freedom

Cohen, Miriam, 1926-

It's George! story by Miriam Cohen; illustrations by Lillian Hoban. Greenwillow Bks. 1988 unp il o.p.; Dell paperback available $4.99   **E**

1. School stories

ISBN 0-440-411645 (pa)   LC 86-19384

"Classmates in a multi-ethnic schoolroom learn to appreciate the special quality of George, who is far from the best student in first grade, but who wins deserved media publicity for being quick-witted enough to telephone an emergency number when an elderly friend, on whom he calls every day, collapses." Bull Cent Child Books

"The satisfying plot, coupled with Hoban's cheerful watercolor paintings . . . will be enjoyed for its positive message." Horn Book

Other available titles in this series are:

"Bee my valentine!" (1978)

Best friends (1971)

Don't eat too much turkey! (1987)

Jim meets the thing (1981)

No good in art (1980)

See you tomorrow, Charles (1983)

So what? (1982)

Starring first grade (1985)

When will I read? (1977)

Will I have a friend? (1967)

Cole, Brock, 1938-

Buttons. Farrar, Straus & Giroux 2000 unp il $16   **E**

ISBN 0-374-31001-7   LC 99-27162

When their father eats so much that he pops the buttons off his britches, each of his three daughters tries a different plan to find replacements

"A delectable tall tale. . . . Cole's narrative has a humorous lilt that's as much fun as his rollicking illustrations." Horn Book Guide

Cole, Henry

I took a walk. Greenwillow Bks. 1998 unp il lib bdg $15   **E**

1. Animals—Fiction 2. Nature—Fiction

ISBN 0-688-15115-9   LC 97-6692

A visit to woods, pasture, and pond brings encounters with various birds, insects, and other creatures of nature. Flaps fold out to reveal the animals hidden on each two-page spread

"Executed in acrylic paint, the realistic nature scenes invite close and careful inspection." Horn Book Guide

Collier, Bryan

Uptown. Holt & Co. 2000 unp il $15.95   **E**

1. African Americans—Fiction 2. Harlem (New York, N.Y.)—Fiction

ISBN 0-805-05721-8   LC 99-31774

Coretta Scott King award for illustration, 2001

A tour of the sights of Harlem, including the Metro-North Train, brownstones, shopping on 125th Street, a barber shop, summer basketball, the Boy's Choir, and sunset over the Harlem River

"Collier's evocative watercolor-and-collage illustrations create a unique sense of mood and place. Bold color choices for text as well as background pages complement engagingly detailed pictures of city life." SLJ

Collington, Peter

Clever cat. Knopf 2000 unp il $15.95; lib bdg $17.99   **E**

1. Cats—Fiction

ISBN 0-375-80477-3; 0-375-90477-8 (lib bdg)

LC 99-40373

When Mr. and Mrs. Ford discover that Tibbs the cat can get his own food they give him a house key and a credit card, but when they make him get a job, do the shopping, and pay rent, he begins to wonder if he is really that clever after all

"Detailed, expressive paintings, grouped several to a page, extend the pointed comedy in this layered story." Booklist

Cooney, Barbara, 1917-2000

Chanticleer and the fox; adapted and illustrated by Barbara Cooney. Crowell 1958 unp il $16.95; lib bdg $16.89; pa $6.95   **E**

1. Fables 2. Foxes—Fiction 3. Roosters—Fiction

ISBN 0-690-18561-8; 0-690-18562-6 (lib bdg); 0-690-04318-X (pa)

Awarded the Caldecott Medal, 1959

"Adaptation of the 'Nun's Priest's Tale' from the Canterbury Tales." Verso of title page

Cooney, Barbara, 1917-2000—_Continued_

"Chanticleer, the rooster, learns the pitfalls of vanity, while the fox who captures, then loses him, learns the value of self-control." Books for Deaf Child

This adaptation "retains the spirit of the original in its telling and in the beautiful, strongly colored illustrations softened by detailed lines. . . . [It] will be excellent for reading aloud to children." Libr J

Island boy; story and pictures by Barbara Cooney. Viking Kestrel 1988 unp il lib bdg $16.99; pa $5.99   E
1. Islands—Fiction 2. Growth—Fiction 3. Family life—Fiction
ISBN 0-670-81749-X (lib bdg); 0-14-050756-6 (pa)
LC 88-175

"This book, based on a historical account, tells 'the story of Matthais Tibbetts, the youngest of the twelve children of pioneering parents who settled in the early nineteenth century on an uninhabited Maine island. . . . Matthais in time returned to his beloved island to establish his roots, to marry, and to raise a family." Horn Book

"Lyrical in its telling and flawless in its visualization, Cooney's book shows the interdependence of three generations of life off the New England coast. This island is a treasure." SLJ

Miss Rumphius; story and pictures by Barbara Cooney. Viking 1982 unp il $15.99   E
ISBN 0-670-47958-6   LC 82-2837
Also available with Audiobook; Spanish language edition also available

As a child Great-aunt Alice Rumphius resolved that when she grew up she would go to faraway places, live by the sea in her old age, and do something to make the world more beautiful—and she does all those things, the last being the most difficult of all

"The idea of offering beauty as one's heritage is appealing, the story is nicely told, and the illustrations are quite lovely, especially the closing scenes of a hill covered with flowers being gathered by children." Bull Cent Child Books

Cooper, Elisha
Ballpark. Greenwillow Bks. 1998 unp il $15   E
1. Baseball—Fiction
ISBN 0-688-15755-6   LC 97-18756
Describes the activities that go on in all areas of a baseball stadium both before and during a game

"The text is compact, child-centered free verse, and the loose watercolor and pencil sketches convey character and emotion gesturally and with remarkable economy." Horn Book Guide

Cooper, Helen, 1963-
Pumpkin soup. Farrar, Straus & Giroux 1999 c1998 unp il $15   E
1. Cats—Fiction 2. Squirrels—Fiction 3. Ducks—Fiction
ISBN 0-374-36164-9   LC 98-18677
First published 1998 in the United Kingdom

The Cat and the Squirrel come to blows with the Duck in arguing about who will perform what duty in preparing their pumpkin soup, and they almost lose the Duck's friendship when he decides to leave them

"Cooper serves up a well-rounded tale told with storyteller's cadences. . . . Rich autumn colors and enchanting details on large spreads and spot illustrations embellish characterizations and setting." SLJ

Cowcher, Helen
Jaguar. Scholastic 1997 32p il $15.95   E
1. Jaguars—Fiction 2. Venezuela—Fiction
ISBN 0-590-29937-9   LC 96-52956
"The story begins with a jaguar looking out over a lagoon, then shifts to a herder hunting the jaguar to protect his cattle. . . . Finally, the man sees the cat and raises his rifle. Suddenly engulfed by a vision of the jaguar as 'an ancestral guardian protecting his own,' the man drops his rifle . . . and vows to find another way of safeguarding his herd. . . . The books setting—Venezuela's Orinoco flood-plain—is not often seen, and the wildlife paintings are striking. An unusual, thought-provoking addition to collections." Booklist

Tigress. Farrar, Straus & Giroux 1991 unp il $14.95; pa $5.95   E
1. Tigers—Fiction 2. Wildlife refuges—Fiction
ISBN 0-374-37567-4; 0-374-47781-7 (pa)
LC 91-12513
Herdsmen work with a wildlife sanctuary ranger to keep their animals safe from a marauding tigress

"Stunning illustrations of magnificent beasts and a substantive story line reinforce the importance of maintaining nature's delicate balance." SLJ

Cowley, Joy
Gracias, the Thanksgiving turkey; illustrated by Joe Cepeda. Scholastic 1996 unp il $15.95; pa $5.99   E
1. Turkeys—Fiction 2. Thanksgiving Day—Fiction 3. Puerto Ricans—Fiction 4. New York (N.Y.)—Fiction
ISBN 0-590-46976-2; 0-590-46977-0 (pa)
LC 95-25063
Also available Spanish language edition

"Little Miguel lives in a New York City apartment with his grandparents and his aunt, while his truck-driving father is on the road. Papa sends Miguel a turkey to fatten for Thanksgiving, but the boy names the bird Gracias and loves him as a pet. . . . The inclusion of Spanish words within the text is handled well, with most meanings evident from the context, but a short glossary also appears on the last page. Cepeda's oil paintings . . . vividly create Miguel's colorful, sympathetic community as well as individual characters." Booklist

Red-eyed tree frog; story by Joy Cowley; illustrated with photographs by Nic Bishop. Scholastic Press 1999 unp il $16.95   E
1. Frogs
ISBN 0-590-87175-7   LC 98-15674
This frog found in the rain forest of Central America spends the night searching for food while also being careful not to become dinner for some other animal

"Stunning color photographs and a gripping interactive text." Booklist

Coy, John

Strong to the hoop; illustrations by Leslie Jean-Bart. Lee & Low Bks. 1999 unp il $16.95
E

1. Basketball—Fiction
ISBN 1-88000-080-6   LC 98-33264

Ten-year-old James tries to hold his own and prove himself on the basketball court when the older boys finally ask him to join them in a game

"Coy's text moves with all the free-wheeling speed of playground ball. . . . Best of all, though, are Jean-Bart's collage-style illustrations, produced by combining Polaroid photographs and scratchboard drawings." Booklist

Crews, Donald

Carousel. Greenwillow Bks. 1982 unp il lib bdg $15.93
E

ISBN 0-688-00909-3   LC 82-3062

"Crews uses both color photography of words and paintings in Art Deco style of the carousel; a brief text describes the ride, from the horses waiting, silent and still, to the end of a whirling ride. The speeded, blurred pictures of the carousel in motion and of the words (boom, too) that signify the calliope sounds are very effective. Despite the lack of story line, this should appeal to children because of the brilliant color, the impression of speed, and the carousel itself." Bull Cent Child Books

Freight train. Greenwillow Bks. 1978 unp il $15.95; lib bdg $15.89; pa $5.95
E

1. Railroads 2. Color
ISBN 0-688-80165-X; 0-688-84165-1 (lib bdg); 0-688-11701-5 (pa)   LC 78-2303

Also available Board book edition and Big book edition

A Caldecott Medal honor book, 1979

"Crews, with a minimum of descriptive words, has drawn a stylized freight train passing by, slowly at first, then in a blur of black and bright color." Babbling Bookworm

"The young child can learn to identify the engine, the caboose and the different cars. . . . A delightful introduction to railroad transportation and to the colors in the spectrum." America

Harbor. Greenwillow Bks. 1982 unp il lib bdg $15.93; pa $4.95
E

1. Harbors 2. Ships
ISBN 0-688-00862-3 (lib bdg); 0-688-07332-8 (pa)   LC 81-6607

"Liners, tankers, barges, and freighters move in and out. Ferryboats shuttle from shore to shore. Busiest of all are the tugboats as they push and tow the big ships to their docks. The New York harbor is full of action." Publisher's note

This book "is an exciting, educational and beautiful show-and-tell. . . . The full-page, full-color paintings will delight children. . . . Crew's outstanding feat here . . . is demonstrating the widely different sizes of the boats in pictures matching and contrasting them with trucks and other land vehicles." Publ Wkly

Night at the fair; pictures and words by Donald Crews. Greenwillow Bks. 1998 unp il $15; lib bdg $14.93
E

1. Fairs—Fiction
ISBN 0-688-11483-0; 0-688-11484-9 (lib bdg)
          LC 96-48780

Nighttime is a wonderful time to enjoy the lights, the games, and the rides at a fair

"Each borderless double-page spread bursts with color and light and action and noise. . . . A minimal text acts for the most part as captioning or clues us in to what's coming next in this truly spectacular visual experience." Horn Book Guide

Parade. Greenwillow Bks. 1983 unp il lib bdg $15.93; pa $4.95
E

1. Parades
ISBN 0-688-01996-X (lib bdg); 0-688-06520-1 (pa)
          LC 82-20927

"Full-color illustrations and a brief text combine to present the various elements of a city parade. Beginning with an early morning empty street and then readying street vendors, excitement mounts as crowds swell to greet a parade of bright images; flags, floats, a marching band, baton twirlers, antique cars and bicycles and a new fire engine. The parade ends and crowds thin; a street cleaning machine sweeps up the remains." SLJ

The author/illustrator's "refined poster-art approach to evoking an event works again here. . . . A polished assembly of crisp shapes, effective compositions, and pure, bright color." Booklist

Sail away. Greenwillow Bks. 1995 unp il $15.95; lib bdg $15.93; pa $5.95
E

1. Sailing—Fiction
ISBN 0-688-11053-3; 0-688-11054-1 (lib bdg); 0-688-17517-1 (pa)   LC 94-6004

"A family rows a small dinghy out to a sailboat to spend the day on the water, only to have the bright sky turn dark as high winds churn up an angry sea. Calm finally returns, and the sail ends with light from the setting sun and a lighthouse leading the boat to a safe mooring." Booklist

"To read any Crews book is to be immersed in sights and sounds vividly rendered and perfectly phrased, and this book proves no exception. The paintings move and swell; the words are haiku-like in their efficiency and implication." Horn Book

School bus. Greenwillow Bks. 1984 unp il $16; lib bdg $15.89; pa $5.95
E

1. School stories 2. Buses—Fiction
ISBN 0-688-02807-1; 0-688-02808-X (lib bdg); 0-688-12267-1 (pa)   LC 83-18681

"The book takes readers through the morning hours, when the buses roll to collect children from their parents and deposit them at different schools, to the end of the day, when they return to gather their riders together again and bring them back to the corners where mothers and fathers are awaiting the homeward-bound scholars." Publ Wkly

"The author-artist cleverly avoids monotony in his subject matter by using different size buses and a pleasing variety of background, perspectives, and the directions in which they travel. Even the potentially tiresome yellow of the buses provides both a unifying element and a contrast for the cheerful colors of the children's clothing and for the bustle of city streets." Horn Book

Crews, Donald—*Continued*

Shortcut. Greenwillow Bks. 1992 unp il $16; lib bdg $15.93; pa $5.95   E
  1. Railroads—Fiction 2. African Americans—Fiction
  ISBN 0-688-06436-1; 0-688-06437-X (lib bdg); 0-688-813576-5 (pa)   LC 91-36312
  Children taking a shortcut by walking along a railroad track find excitement and danger when a train approaches
  "The story . . . is a perfect foil for the artist's masterful renderings of trains. . . . Scenes portraying the frightened children are equally effective in this out of the ordinary drama set forth with uncommon artistry." Publ Wkly

Truck. Greenwillow Bks. 1980 unp il $15.95; lib bdg $15.89; pa $4.95   E
  1. Trucks
  ISBN 0-688-80244-3; 0-688-84244-5 (lib bdg); 0-688-10481-9 (pa)   LC 79-19031
  Also available Board book edition and Big book edition
  A Caldecott Medal honor book, 1981
  A bright red tractor-trailer truck "sporting a chalk-white 'Trucking' label affixed to its side . . . pushes its way across the United States to deliver its prized cargo of tricycles." Christ Sci Monit
  "Although there is no text, the story is far from wordless; trucks, buses, and vans are emblazoned with letters and emblems, the streets are lined with familiar traffic signs, and a truck stop is festooned with advertisements in neon lights. The artist depicts no people; the silent red truck is the main character of an imaginative, almost pop-art view of mobile America." Horn Book

Crews, Nina

A high, low, near, far, loud, quiet story. Greenwillow Bks. 1999 unp il $16; lib bdg $15.93   E
  1. English language—Synonyms and antonyms
  ISBN 0-688-16794-2; 0-688-16795-0 (lib bdg)   LC 98-33273
  Labeled photographs present opposites such as fast and slow, large and small, and rough and smooth
  "With expressive faces and body language, each active picture suggests a story, and preschoolers will enjoy talking about the feelings and dynamics in each scenario." Booklist

You are here. Greenwillow Bks. 1998 unp il $16; lib bdg $15.93   E
  1. African Americans—Fiction
  ISBN 0-688-15753-X; 0-688-15754-8 (lib bdg)   LC 97-36312
  When the rain keeps Mariah and Joy confined to the indoors, they create a magic map and go on a fantastic imaginary voyage
  "The smoothly pitched text builds in excitement as the images and action begin to fully take shape in readers' minds. . . . Crews creates photographic compositions with inventive shifts in proportion and perspective." Publ Wkly

Cronin, Doreen

Click, clack, moo; cows that type; pictures by Betsy Lewin. Simon & Schuster Bks. for Young Readers 2000 unp il $15   E
  1. Cattle—Fiction 2. Domestic animals—Fiction 3. Typewriters—Fiction
  ISBN 0-689-83213-3   LC 97-29718
  A Caldecott Medal honor book, 2001
  When Farmer Brown's cows find a typewriter in the barn they start making demands, and go on strike when the farmer refuses to give them what they want
  "A laugh-out-loud look at life on a very funny farm. . . . Lewin's hilarious cartoons deftly capture the farmer's exasperation and the animals' sheer determination." SLJ

Crowe, Robert L.

Clyde monster; illustrated by Kay Chorao. Dutton 1976 unp il hardcover o.p. paperback available $5.99   E
  1. Monsters—Fiction 2. Night—Fiction 3. Fear—Fiction
  ISBN 0-14-054743-6 (pa)
  "In an amusing reversal of roles, a young monster is afraid of the dark because he believes that a person may be lurking under the bed or in a corner." LC. Child Books, 1976
  "The now familiar table-turning theme for children afraid of monsters takes on effective, rational proportions in a very amusing tale. . . . Chorao's softly grotesque portraits add character without chill." Booklist

Cummings, Pat, 1950-

Angel baby. Lothrop, Lee & Shepard Bks. 2000 unp il $15.95; lib bdg $18.89   E
  1. Infants—Fiction 2. Siblings—Fiction 3. African Americans—Fiction 4. Stories in rhyme
  ISBN 0-688-14821-2; 0-688-14822-0 (lib bdg)   LC 99-11502
  In her mother's eyes, Amanda Lynne's baby brother is a perfect angel, but to Amanda the baby doesn't always seem so angelic
  "Cummings captures the lot of the older sister in a readable rhyme, while her artwork shows the mischievousness of the little 'angel'. . . . The two-page spreads are brightly colored and full of nuance." Booklist

Clean your room, Harvey Moon! Bradbury Press 1991 unp il $16.95; pa $5.99   E
  1. African Americans—Fiction 2. Stories in rhyme
  ISBN 0-02-725511-5; 0-689-71798-9 (pa)   LC 89-23863
  Harvey tackles a big job: cleaning his room
  "Cummings's art is a boisterous clutter of color, providing just the right mood for her bouncy, rhyming text." Publ Wkly

Curtis, Gavin, 1965-

The bat boy & his violin; illustrated by E.B. Lewis. Simon & Schuster Bks. for Young Readers 1998 unp il $16   E
  1. Violinists—Fiction 2. Baseball—Fiction 3. Father-son relationship—Fiction 4. African Americans—Fiction
  ISBN 0-689-80099-1   LC 97-25417

Curtis, Gavin, 1965-—Continued

Coretta Scott King honor book for illustration

Reginald is more interested in practicing his violin than in his father's job managing the worst team in the Negro Leagues, but when Papa makes him the bat boy and his music begins to lead the team to victory, Papa realizes the value of his son's passion

"Lewis's soft watercolor illustrations portray the characters with depth and beauty, resulting in a very special book." SLJ

Curtis, Jamie Lee

Tell me again about the night I was born; illustrated by Laura Cornell. HarperCollins Pubs. 1996 unp il $16.95; lib bdg $15.89; pa $5.95

E

1. Adoption—Fiction 2. Infants—Fiction

ISBN 0-06-024528-X; 0-06-024529-8 (lib bdg); 0-06-443581-4 (pa)   LC 95-5412

Also available Board book edition and with Audiobook

"Joanna Cotler books"

"The young female narrator asks her adoptive parents to 'tell me again' the story of her birth and introduction into the family she is now a part of. . . . The humorous, cartoon-style pictures by Laura Cornell . . . are a perfect visual counterpart to the text." Horn Book

Cushman, Doug

Inspector Hopper; story and pictures by Doug Cushman. HarperCollins Pubs. 2000 64p il $14.95; lib bdg $14.89   E

1. Insects—Fiction 2. Mystery fiction

ISBN 0-06-028382-3; 0-06-028383-1 (lib bdg)

LC 99-30878

"An I can read book"

Inspector Hopper and his perpetually hungry assistant McBugg solve three mysteries for their insect friends

"Beginning readers will find a familiar structure, natural language, compelling plot, supporting illustrations, and engaging characters. . . . The light watercolors define the characters as soft-boiled while slyly playing on stereotypes out of film noir." Horn Book Guide

Cutler, Jane

The cello of Mr. O; illustrated by Greg Couch. Dutton Children's Bks. 1999 unp il $15.99   E

1. Violoncellos—Fiction 2. War—Fiction 3. Musicians—Fiction

ISBN 0-525-46119-1   LC 98-42692

When a concert cellist plays in the square for his neighbors in a war-besieged city, his priceless instrument is destroyed by a mortar shell, but he finds the courage to return the next day to perform with a harmonica

Couch's "soft-focus watercolors in burnished shades of gold, copper and fiery red have a dreamlike quality that effectively contrast with the unsentimental narration." Publ Wkly

Cuyler, Margery

100th day worries; illustrated by Arthur Howard. Simon & Schuster Bks. for Young Readers 2000 unp il $16   E

1. School stories 2. Counting

ISBN 0-689-82979-5   LC 98-52887

Jessica worries about collecting 100 objects to take to class for the 100th day of school

"Energetic pen-and-ink squiggles and bright watercolors fill the pages with round-eyed figures and striped, dotted, and floral patterns as the groups of objects are described and counted." Booklist

Daly, Niki, 1946-

Jamela's dress; story & pictures by Niki Daly. Farrar, Straus & Giroux 1999 unp il $16   E

1. Clothing and dress—Fiction 2. Blacks—Fiction 3. South Africa—Fiction

ISBN 0-374-33667-9   LC 98-42048

Jamela gets in trouble when she takes the expensive material intended for a new dress for Mama, parades it in the street, and allows it to become dirty and torn

"The watercolors are a happy combination of color and movement that bring to life the sights and scenes of the busy streets of Jamela's town. The characters are lively and emotive. . . . Nguni words and phrases, spoken within the text, are artfully explained in context. . . . With its rising pace and strong narrative, Jamela's story is a joyful evocation of community and family." Bull Cent Child Books

My dad; story and pictures by Niki Daly. Margaret K. McElderry Bks. 1995 unp il $16

E

1. Alcoholism—Fiction 2. Fathers—Fiction

ISBN 0-689-50620-1   LC 94-14455

"Though the brother and sister featured here dearly love their father, they are embarrassed and increasingly anxious about his drinking. . . . A Friday-night school concert becomes the turning point; Dad shows up drunk and humiliates his children. . . . The tale ends on a hopeful note, however, with Dad persuaded to join Alcoholics Anonymous. Daly's gentle touch extends to both words and pictures: her sensitive, graceful prose is coupled with soft-focus watercolors that underscore the poignancy of her characters' struggles." Publ Wkly

Not so fast, Songololo; written & illustrated by Niki Daly. Atheneum Pubs. 1986 c1985 unp il hardcover o.p. paperback available $4.95   E

1. Blacks—Fiction   2. Grandmothers—Fiction 3. South Africa—Fiction

ISBN 0-689-80154-8 (pa)   LC 85-71034

"A Margaret K. McElderry book"

First published 1985 in the United Kingdom

"The setting is South Africa and the names of the people are like poetry: Uzuti, Mongi, Mr. Motiki. Malusi is now old enough to accompany his grandmother, Gogo, into the city to shop. She is an old woman—ample, proud, not quite in step with modern technology, and she no longer moves quickly. Malusi (Songololo to his grandmother) helps her with her shopping." Publ Wkly

"The watercolor illustrations are splendidly evocative of the affection between the generations and of the South African city scene, which, surprisingly, is hardly distinguishable from an American city. The beautiful, gentle book about the ordinary occurrences of daily life has an extraordinary effect." Horn Book

Daugherty, James Henry, 1889-1974

Andy and the lion; by James Daugherty. Viking 1938 unp il hardcover o.p. paperback available $5.99   E

1. Lions—Fiction

ISBN 0-14-050277-7 (pa)

A Caldecott Medal honor book, 1939

A modern picture story of Androcles and the lion in which Andy, who read a book about lions, was almost immediately plunged into action. The next day he met a circus lion with a thorn in his paw. Andy removed the thorn and earned the lion's undying gratitude

"This is a tall tale for little children. It is typically American in its setting and its fun. The large full page illustrations are in yellow, black and white and the brief, hand-lettered text on the opposite page is clear and readable." Libr J

De Groat, Diane

Trick or treat, smell my feet. Morrow Junior Bks. 1998 unp il $15; lib bdg $14.93; pa $4.95   E

1. Halloween—Fiction 2. Siblings—Fiction

ISBN 0-688-15766-1; 0-688-15767-X (lib bdg); 0-688-17061-7 (pa)   LC 97-32916

"When Gilbert and his sister accidentally bring each other's costumes to school for the annual Halloween parade, Gilbert ends up donning a ballerina outfit." Publ Wkly

"De Groat's funny watercolor pictures capture the various animal creatures' very human expressions and body language." Booklist

Other available titles about Gilbert are:

Happy birthday to you, you belong in the zoo (1999)

Jingle, bells, homework smells (2000)

Roses are pink, your feet really stink (1996)

De Paola, Tomie, 1934-

The baby sister; written and illustrated by Tomie dePaola. Putnam 1996 unp il $16.99; pa $5.99   E

1. Infants—Fiction 2. Siblings—Fiction 3. Grandmothers—Fiction

ISBN 0-399-22908-6; 0-698-11773-5 (pa)   LC 94-37218

"Tommy's mother is expecting a baby. Tommy helps get the baby's room ready and longs for a sister with a red ribbon in her hair. He's thrilled when the baby is a girl, but while his mother is away in the hospital, his Italian grandmother comes to stay, and he finds it hard to get along with her. . . . Simple lines and warm colors convey the affection in the extended family and the special closeness between Tommy and his parents." Booklist

Bill and Pete; story and pictures by Tomie de Paola. Putnam 1978 unp il hardcover o.p. paperback available $5.99   E

1. Crocodiles—Fiction 2. Birds—Fiction

ISBN 0-698-11400-0 (pa)

"Near the Nile River, long ago, William Everett Crocodile chooses Pete the plover for his toothbrush, and they become friends as well. When the reptile scholar despairs of writing all the letters in his name, Pete has an idea and William passes the test by penning 'Bill.' Then, the Bad Guy (a human trapper) captures Bill and plans to make a suitcase of him. The solution to that problem is heady fun." Publ Wkly

"De Paola has again created an imaginative, humorous tale which he illustrates in happy pinks, greens, yellows, and blues." SLJ

Other available titles about Bill and Pete are:

Bill and Pete go down the Nile (1987)

Bill and Pete to the rescue (1998)

An early American Christmas; written and illustrated by Tomie dePaola. Holiday House 1987 unp il lib bdg $16.95; pa $6.95   E

1. Christmas—Fiction 2. German Americans

ISBN 0-8234-0617-2 (lib bdg); 0-8234-0979-1 (pa)   LC 86-3102

"A German family moves from the old country to a small New England town in the 1800's. The town doesn't celebrate Christmas, but the family forges ahead with bayberry candles, evergreen decorations, a Christmas tree in the parlor, and carols on the night air. Gradually, all the households become 'Christmas families'." Child Book Rev Serv

"This provides a fascinating look at Christmas as it once was: a holiday whose customs were entwined with the season's natural bounty. . . . This is a warm and beautifully realized tribute to the spirit and traditions of the season." Publ Wkly

Jamie O'Rourke and the pooka. Putnam 2000 unp il $16.99   E

1. Ireland—Fiction

ISBN 0-399-23467-5   LC 99-22469

While his wife is away, lazy Jamie O'Rourke relies on a pooka to clean up the messes that he and his friends make

"DePaola's cozy, colorful illustrations are a good match for the lighthearted, rhythmic text." Horn Book Guide

The knight and the dragon; story and pictures by Tomie de Paola. Putnam 1980 unp il $16.99; pa $5.99   E

1. Knights and knighthood—Fiction 2. Dragons—Fiction

ISBN 0-399-20707-4; 0-698-11623-2 (pa)   LC 79-18131

"A boy knight feels he really ought to fight a dragon and, in a cave far away, a dragon begins to feel he ought to defend his species' honor by a duel with a knight. . . . When the foes finally meet, the encounter becomes something else." Publ Wkly

"Very few words and typical de Paola illustrations make this lighthearted jest. . . . There's a chuckle on every page, especially for librarians, as the castle librarian saves both warriors from disgrace with the right books from her horse-drawn bookmobile!" Child Book Rev Serv

Nana Upstairs & Nana Downstairs; written and illustrated by Tomie dePaola. Putnam 1998 unp il $16.99; pa $5.99   E

1. Grandmothers—Fiction 2. Death—Fiction

ISBN 0-399-23108-0; 0-698-11836-7 (pa)   LC 96-31908

A newly illustrated edition of the title first published 1973

De Paola, Tomie, 1934—*Continued*

"Every Sunday four-year-old Tommy's family goes to visit his grandparents. His grandmother is always busy downstairs, but his great-grandmother is always to be found in bed upstairs, because she is 94 years old. . . . [Tommy] is desolate when his upstairs nana dies, but his mother comforts him by explaining that 'she will come back in your memory whenever you think about her'." Booklist

"The illustrations are vintage dePaola, and the warm palette conveys the boy's love for his elderly relatives." Horn Book Guide

The night of Las Posadas; written and illustrated by Tomie dePaola. Putnam 1999 unp il $15.99

E

1. Mary, Blessed Virgin, Saint—Fiction 2. Joseph, Saint—Fiction 3. Christmas—Fiction 4. Santa Fe (N.M.)—Fiction
ISBN 0-399-23400-4   LC 98-36405

At the annual celebration of Las Posadas in old Santa Fe, the husband and wife slated to play Mary and Joseph are delayed by car trouble, but a mysterious couple appear who seem perfect for the part

"DePaola's talent for crafting folktales is honed to near-perfection, and his pages glow with the soft sun-washed hues of the Southwest." Publ Wkly

Now one foot, now the other; story and pictures by Tomie de Paola. Putnam 1981 unp il $15.99; pa $7.99

E

1. Grandfathers—Fiction
ISBN 0-399-20774-0; 0-399-20775-9 (pa)
LC 80-22239

"Bobby's much loved grandfather has had a stroke. After a long hospitalization, the man returns home unable to speak, walk or care for himself. . . . Their roles reversed, the youngster helps his grandfather learn to walk again 'now one foot, now the other.'" SLJ

"De Paola sensitively provides an understanding portrayal about grandparents' illness. . . . Soft blues and tans, textured with pencil shadings, provide a tranquil backdrop for the emotion-filled faces that expressively suggest the changing relationship of the old man and the boy." Booklist

Strega Nona: an old tale; retold and illustrated by Tomie de Paola. Simon & Schuster 1988 c1975 unp il $16; pa $6.95

E

1. Witches—Fiction 2. Italy—Fiction
ISBN 0-671-66283-X; 0-671-66606-1 (pa)
LC 88-11438

Also available Board book edition; Spanish language edition also available

A Caldecott Medal honor book, 1976

A reissue of the title first published 1975 by Prentice-Hall

In this Italian folk-tale set in Calabria, "Strega Nona, 'Grandma Witch,' leaves Big Anthony alone with her magic pasta pot. He decides to give the townspeople a treat. . . . Big Anthony doesn't know how to make the pot stop. The town is practically buried in spaghetti before Strega Nona returns to save the day." SLJ

"Tomie de Paola has used simple colors, simple line, and medieval costume and architecture in his spaciously composed humorous pictures." Bull Cent Child Books

Other available titles about Strega Nona and Big Anthony are:
Big Anthony and the magic ring (1979)
Big Anthony: his story (1998)
Merry Christmas, Strega Nona (1986)
Strega Nona: her story (1996)
Strega Nona meets her match (1993)
Strega Nona takes a vacation (2000)
Strega Nona's magic lessons (1982)

Tom; written and illustrated by Tomie dePaola. Putnam 1993 unp il $15.99; pa $5.99   E

1. Grandfathers—Fiction
ISBN 0-399-22417-3; 0-698-11448-5 (pa)
LC 92-1022

"In a story based on his own childhood, Tomie de-Paola tells about little Tommy's regular Sunday visits with his grandfather, Tom. . . . With gentle humor and his usual mastery of line and composition, dePaola conveys the strong bond of affection between Tom and little Tommy." Horn Book Guide

De Regniers, Beatrice Schenk

May I bring a friend? illustrated by Beni Montresor. Atheneum Pubs. 1964 unp il hardcover o.p. paperback available $5.99   E

1. Animals—Fiction
ISBN 0-689-71353-3 (pa)

Awarded the Caldecott Medal, 1965

"Each time the little boy in this picture book is invited to take tea or dine with the King and Queen, he brings along a somewhat difficult animal friend. Their Highnesses always cope and are wonderfully rewarded in the end." Publ Wkly

"Rich color and profuse embellishment adorn an opulent setting. Absurdities and contrasts are so imaginatively combined in a hilarious comedy of manners that the merriment can be enjoyed on several levels." Horn Book

What can you do with a shoe? pictures by Maurice Sendak. Margaret K. McElderry Bks. 1997 unp il $15   E

1. Stories in rhyme
ISBN 0-689-81231-0   LC 96-20871

First published 1955 by Harper

A boy and girl playing dress up ask the reader for imaginative and real uses of a shoe, a chair, a hat, a cup, a broom, and finally a bed

"Together the author and illustrator have produced a book which will charm children old enough to see the humor in incongruities." N Y Times Book Rev

DeFelice, Cynthia C.

Clever crow; [by] Cynthia DeFelice; illustrated by S.D. Schindler. Atheneum Bks. for Young Readers 1998 unp il $16   E

1. Crows—Fiction 2. Stories in rhyme
ISBN 0-689-80671-X   LC 97-10697

Angry at Crow for flying off with her mother's keys, Emma tries to trick the wily bird

"Schindler's fetching colored-pencil illustrations on parchment paper achieve a subtle texture. A lively read-aloud, the rhymed story with its simple refrain holds a witty element of surprise at story's end." Horn Book Guide

Degen, Bruce, 1945-

Jamberry; story and pictures by Bruce Degen. Harper & Row 1983 unp il $15.95; lib bdg $15.89; pa $5.95 **E**

1. Stories in rhyme 2. Berries—Fiction
ISBN 0-06-021416-3; 0-06-021417-1 (lib bdg); 0-06-443068-5 (pa) LC 82-47708
Also available Board book edition and with Audiobook

"Boy meets bear, and together they go berry-picking by canoe, through fields and by pony and 'Boys-in-Berries' train, all the way to Berryland." Child Book Rev Serv

"Berries and jam are roundly celebrated in a lilting rhyme that, coupled with the jaunty colored pictures, makes it . . . a good pick for sharing one on one, or fun to read aloud as a poetry introduction." Booklist

Del Negro, Janice

Lucy Dove; illustrated by Leonid Gore. DK Pub. 1998 unp il $16.95 **E**

1. Monsters—Fiction 2. Scotland—Fiction
ISBN 0-7894-2514-9 LC 97-43607
"A Melanie Kroupa book"

While sewing the laird's trews by moonlight in a haunted churchyard in return for a sackful of gold, an aging seamstress outwits a terrible monster

"This deliciously shivery tale has pitch-perfect prose, matched by ethereal illustrations that seem imbued with mist and moonlight." Publ Wkly

Demi, 1942-

The emperor's new clothes; a tale set in China. Margaret K. McElderry Bks. 2000 unp il $19.95 **E**

1. Fairy tales 2. China—Fiction
ISBN 0-689-83068-8 LC 99-24883

In this retelling of Hans Christian Andersen's tale, two rascals sell a vain Chinese emperor an invisible suit of clothes

"Demi's retelling is lucid, graceful, and true to the original. . . . Figures are delicately outlined; they are painted with flat, jewel-like colors and metallic gold and set against subtly patterned grounds that resemble silk damask. . . . A lovely and meticulously wrought rendition." Horn Book Guide

Kites; magic wishes that fly up to the sky. Crown 1999 unp il $17; lib bdg $18.99 **E**

1. Kites—Fiction 2. China—Fiction
ISBN 0-517-80049-7; 0-517-80050-0 (lib bdg) LC 98-41372

"In long-ago China, a woman commissioned an artist to paint a special dragon kite for her son. . . . Word of the artist's talent traveled, and he was soon asked to create a wide variety of flyers for other villagers. The small, intricate, colorful kites illustrated in Demi's signature style and set against blues and greens are lovely to look at and will encourage readers to appreciate their beauty. Captions offer brief explanations of the different emblematic figures, creatures, and symbols. . . . There is also mention of a Chinese festival devoted to kites, as well as detailed instructions for making a kite." SLJ

DiSalvo-Ryan, DyAnne, 1954-

A dog like Jack. Holiday House 1999 unp il $15.95 **E**

1. Dogs—Fiction 2. Death—Fiction
ISBN 0-8234-1369-1 LC 97-41949

After a long life of chasing squirrels, licking ice cream cones, and loving his adoptive family, an old dog comes to the end of his days

"Thoughtful words and tender pictures beautifully convey the special relationship between a young boy and his dog." Booklist

Grandpa's corner store. HarperCollins Pubs. 2000 unp il $15.95; lib bdg $15.89 **E**

1. Grocery trade—Fiction 2. Grandfathers—Fiction
ISBN 0-688-16716-0; 0-688-16717-9 (lib bdg) LC 99-15504

Grandfather's corner grocery business is threatened by a new supermarket, but his granddaughter, Lucy, organizes the neighbors to convince him to stay

"The characterizations are strong, the illustrations deft and affecting, the story complex and uplifting." Horn Book Guide

Uncle Willie and the soup kitchen. Morrow Junior Bks. 1991 unp il hardcover o.p. paperback available $5.95 **E**

1. Uncles—Fiction 2. Poverty—Fiction
ISBN 0-688-15285-6 (pa) LC 90-6375

A boy spends the day with Uncle Willie in the soup kitchen where he works preparing and serving food for the hungry

"The color-pencil and wash illustrations observe . . . [a] balance between attracting the viewer with softly blended colors and avoiding the sentimentality of glamorizing an essentially sad situation. Without sacrifice of story, the total effect leaves young listeners with new considerations of society and social service, a theme too often neglected in picture books." Bull Cent Child Books

Dorros, Arthur

Abuela; illustrated by Elisa Kleven. Dutton Children's Bks. 1991 unp il $16.99; pa $5.99 **E**

1. Hispanic Americans—Fiction 2. Grandmothers—Fiction
ISBN 0-525-44750-4; 0-14-056225-7 (pa) LC 90-21459

Also available Spanish language edition

While riding on a bus with her Hispanic grandmother, a little girl named Rosalba imagines that they are carried up into the sky and fly over the sights of New York City

"Each illustration is a masterpiece of color, line, and form that will mesmerize youngsters. . . . The smooth text, interspersed with Spanish words and phrases, provides ample context clues, so the glossary, while helpful, is not absolutely necessary." Booklist

Another available title about Rosalba and her grandmother is:
Isla (1995)

Dorros, Arthur—*Continued*

Radio Man. Don Radio; a story in English and Spanish; Spanish translation by Sandra Marulanda Dorros. HarperCollins Pubs. 1993 unp il hardcover o.p. paperback available $6.95   E

1. Migrant labor—Fiction 2. Mexican Americans—Fiction 3. Bilingual books—English-Spanish

ISBN 0-06-443482-6 (pa)   LC 92-28369

As he travels with his family of migrant farmworkers, Diego relies on his radio to provide him with companionship and help connect him to all the different places in which he lives

"Spot art separates English and Spanish on text pages that alternate with affecting, primitive-like acrylic paintings." Publ Wkly

Tonight is Carnaval; illustrated with arpilleras sewn by the Club de Madres Virgen del Carmen of Lima, Peru. Dutton Children's Bks. 1991 unp il hardcover o.p. paperback available $6.99   E

1. Festivals—Fiction 2. Peru—Fiction

ISBN 0-14-055467-X (pa)   LC 90-32391

A family in South America eagerly prepares for the excitement of Carnaval

"Dorros' text is appealing and informative, emphasizing the strong communal life of the village. However, the real star of this book is its illustration. The action is shown in *arpilleras*, the distinctive South American wall hangings made from cut-and-sewn pieces of cloth. The Club de Madres Virgen del Carmen of Lima, Peru, has created about a dozen of these cheerful fabric pictures in bright primary colors. . . . Appended are a short glossary of foreign-language terms and an illustrated explanation of how *arpilleras* are made." Booklist

Dragonwagon, Crescent

Half a moon and one whole star; illustrations by Jerry Pinkney. Macmillan 1986 unp il hardcover o.p. paperback available $5.99   E

1. Night—Fiction 2. Sleep—Fiction 3. Stories in rhyme

ISBN 0-689-71415-7 (pa)   LC 85-13818

The summer night is full of wonderful sounds and scents as Susan falls asleep

"The poem has some lilting phrases and some sharp images; occasionally the rhyme or meter falters, but the concept of night activity and the sleeping household should appeal to the read-aloud audience." Bull Cent Child Books

Drescher, Henrik, 1955-

Simon's book. Lothrop, Lee & Shepard Bks. 1983 unp il hardcover o.p. paperback available $6.95   E

1. Drawing—Fiction 2. Monsters—Fiction

ISBN 0-688-10484-3 (pa)   LC 82-24931

"A frightening yet humorous-looking monster . . . chases young Simon through the pages of his drawing pad. A finished book—'Simon's Book'—is left upon the table for the real Simon to discover when he wakes in the morning." SLJ

"Using the story-within-a-story format, the author-artist embarks on an exhilarating exploration, in a child-like yet sophisticated manner, of the elusive border separating dream and reality. . . . Original, fresh, and engaging, the book is deliciously thrilling." Horn Book

Drucker, Malka, 1945-

Grandma's latkes; written by Malka Drucker; illustrated by Eve Chwast. Harcourt Brace Jovanovich 1992 unp il hardcover o.p. paperback available $6   E

1. Hanukkah—Fiction 2. Jews—Fiction

ISBN 0-15-201388-1 (pa)   LC 91-30086

"Gulliver books"

Grandma explains the meaning of Hanukkah while showing Molly how to cook latkes for the holiday. Recipe included

"The dark lines of the woodcut illustrations, painted with pale watercolors, have a warm, old-fashioned quality that enhances the idea of passing a people's history from one generation to the next." Horn Book

Dugan, Barbara

Loop the loop; pictures by James Stevenson. Greenwillow Bks. 1992 unp il $16.95   E

1. Old age—Fiction 2. Friendship—Fiction

ISBN 0-688-09647-6   LC 90-21727

Annie and old Mrs. Simpson form a friendship that lasts even after the woman enters a nursing home

"Dugan develops her story line with a sure and light touch, which is echoed in Stevenson's simple, congenial cartoon sketches, roughly shaded in light watercolors. The dénouement is both poignant and upbeat." Horn Book

Duke, Kate

One guinea pig is not enough. Dutton Children's Bks. 1998 unp il $15.99   E

1. Guinea pigs 2. Counting

ISBN 0-525-45918-9   LC 97-21367

Also available other guinea pig titles in Board book editions

A little guinea pig is quite lonely until, one by one, nine others, plus ten of their moms or dads, add to the general excitement

"With mixed media drawings that bubble with energy from beginning to end, this is an exuberant and clever introduction to math." Publ Wkly

Another available title about the guinea pigs is: Twenty is too many (2000)

Duncan, Lois, 1934-

I walk at night; paintings by Steve Johnson and Lou Fancher. Viking 2000 unp il $15.99   E

1. Cats—Fiction

ISBN 0-670-87513-9   LC 99-32057

This is a "description of a cat's multifaceted personality—docile pet by day, untamed beast in dreams, adventurer by night." SLJ

"The paintings rely on the contrast between cobalt shadows and subtle light sources for emphasis, and the night-blue palette gives an air of mystery to the wanderings of the midnight cat." Bull Cent Child Books

Dunrea, Olivier, 1953-

Bear Noel. Farrar, Straus & Giroux 2000 unp il $16   E

1. Bears—Fiction 2. Animals—Fiction 3. Christmas—Fiction

ISBN 0-374-39990-5   LC 99-27600

Dunrea, Olivier, 1953——*Continued*

The animals of the North Woods react with excitement as they hear Bear Noel coming to bring them Christmas

"Dunrea beautifully creates the effect of falling snow throughout the pictures and uses a limited palette of browns, grays, and greens with flashes of fox red to lend a celebratory feel." Booklist

Durán, Cheli

Hildilid's night; illustrated by Arnold Lobel. Macmillan 1971 unp il hardcover o.p. paperback available $4.99 **E**

1. Night—Fiction

ISBN 0-689-80538-1 (pa)

A Caldecott Medal honor book, 1972

"Hating the night, [an old woman named] Hildilid tries to sweep it away with a broom, spanks it, digs a grave for it, tries to stuff it into a sack, and so on. Exhausted by her vain endeavors, she falls asleep just as the sun comes up and the detested darkness is gone." Bull Cent Child Books

"The black-and-white line drawings, into which yellow is occasionally but strategically inserted, perfectly illustrate the rhythmically narrative lines." Horn Book

Eastman, P. D. (Philip D.), 1909-1986

Are you my mother? written and illustrated by P. D. Eastman. Beginner Bks. 1960 63p il $7.99; lib bdg $13.99 **E**

1. Birds—Fiction 2. Bilingual books—English-Spanish

ISBN 0-394-80018-4; 0-394-90018-9 (lib bdg)

Also available Board book edition; Spanish-English edition also available

"A small bird falls from his nest and searches for his mother. He asks a kitten, a hen, a dog, a cow, a boat, [and] a plane . . . 'Are you my mother?' Repetition of words and phrases and funny pictures are just right for beginning readers." Chicago. Public Libr

Edwards, Pamela Duncan

Honk! illustrated by Henry Cole. Hyperion Bks. for Children 1998 unp il $14.95; lib bdg $15.49; pa $5.99 **E**

1. Ballet—Fiction 2. Swans—Fiction

ISBN 0-7868-0435-1; 0-7868-2384-4 (lib bdg); 0-7868-1298-2 (pa) LC 97-44260

A ballet-loving swan wins acclaim when she manages to join the other dancers in a performance of Swan Lake

"A lighthearted, winning tale. . . . Mimi's character, so devoted and so innocent, is an appealing one, and the humor in both text and illustrations carries the day." Horn Book Guide

Some smug slug; illustrated by Henry Cole. HarperCollins Pubs. 1996 32p il $15.95; lib bdg $15.89; pa $5.95 **E**

1. Slugs (Mollusks)—Fiction 2. Animals—Fiction

ISBN 0-06-024789-4; 0-06-024792-4 (lib bdg); 0-06-443502-4 (pa) LC 94-18682

"A slug senses a slope and saunters on up, against the advice of a sparrow, a spider, and a skink, among others, and meets with a sudden, spontaneous demise. Such is the life of a slug told with a multitude of common and not so common 'S' words (shantung). . . . Realistically detailed, earth-toned illustrations focus attention on each scene. . . . This slug is so appealing and full of personality that it will certainly garner sympathy." SLJ

Egan, Tim

Metropolitan cow; written and illustrated by Tim Egan. Houghton Mifflin 1996 unp il $15; pa $5.95 **E**

1. Cattle—Fiction 2. Pigs—Fiction 3. Friendship—Fiction

ISBN 0-395-73096-1; 0-395-96059-2 (pa) LC 95-23382

Although his parents, very cosmopolitan cows, are uncomfortable with the idea, Bennett becomes good friends with Webster, a young pig who moves in next door

"The splendid romp through bovine and porcine prejudice is made more pointed by the extremely urban and sophisticated setting, portrayed in richly colored watercolor and ink illustrations." Horn Book Guide

Egielski, Richard

Jazper. HarperCollins Pubs. 1998 unp il $15.95; lib bdg $15.89 **E**

1. Insects—Fiction 2. Magic—Fiction

ISBN 0-06-027817-X; 0-06-027999-0 (lib bdg) LC 97-32556

"A Laura Geringer book"

While watching a house for five menacing moths, Jaz, an industrious young bug, teaches himself how to transform into various other things and then must use this talent to save himself

"Evoking animated cartoons of the thirties [Egielski's] energetic, drolly imaginative pictures are filled with details that delight the eye and tickle the rib." Booklist

Ehlert, Lois, 1934-

Circus. HarperCollins Pubs. 1992 unp il $15.95 **E**

1. Circus—Fiction 2. Animals—Fiction

ISBN 0-06-020252-1 LC 91-12067

Leaping lizards, marching snakes, a bear on the high wire, and others perform in a somewhat unusual circus

"The book approximates a light show in visual intensity, with neon-bright illustrations set against black or bold backgrounds. The figures . . . are a hodgepodge of geometric shapes. . . . The use of complementary colors and interlocking shapes also gives the illustrations energy. . . . The sprightly rhythm of Ms. Ehlert's text complements her Day-Glo palette. Echoing a ringmaster's speech, she's afraid of neither alliteration . . . nor hyperbole." N Y Times Book Rev

Color farm. Lippincott 1990 unp il $15.95; lib bdg $15.89 **E**

1. Color 2. Shape

ISBN 0-397-32440-5; 0-397-32441-3 (lib bdg) LC 89-13561

Ehlert, Lois, 1934—*Continued*

"A delightful die-cut exploration of how shapes and colors can be layered and overlapped to create the faces of farm animals. Includes geometric pictures of a rooster, a chicken, a goose, a duck, a cat, a dog, a sheep, a pig, and a cow." Sci Child

Color zoo. Lippincott 1989 unp il $16.95; lib bdg $16.89 **E**
1. Color 2. Shape
ISBN 0-397-32259-3; 0-397-32260-7 (lib bdg)
LC 87-17065
Also available Board book edition
A Caldecott Medal honor book, 1990

This "book features a series of cutouts stacked so that with each page turn, a layer is removed to reveal yet another picture. Each configuration is an animal: a tiger's face (a circle shape) and two ears disappear with a page turn to leave viewers with a square within which is a mouse. . . . There are three such series, and each ends with a small round-up of the shapes used so far. . . . On the reverse of the turned page is the shape cutout previously removed with the shape's printed name." SLJ

"Not only an effective method for teaching basic concepts, the book is also a means for sharpening visual perception, which encourages children to see these shapes in other contexts." Horn Book

Eating the alphabet; fruits and vegetables from A to Z. Harcourt Brace Jovanovich 1989 unp il $16; pa $7 **E**
1. Alphabet 2. Fruit 3. Vegetables
ISBN 0-15-224435-2; 0-15-224436-0 (pa)
LC 88-10906
Also available Board book edition
An alphabetical tour of the world of fruits and vegetables, from apricot and artichoke to yam and zucchini

"The objects depicted, shown against a white ground, are easily identifiable for the most part, and represent the more common sounds of the letter shown. . . . Both upper- and lower-case letters are printed in large, black type. A nice added touch is the glossary which includes the pronunciation and interesting facts about the origin of each fruit and vegetable, how it grows, and its uses. An exuberant, eye-catching alphabet book." SLJ

Feathers for lunch. Harcourt Brace Jovanovich 1990 unp il $16; pa $7 **E**
1. Cats—Fiction 2. Birds—Fiction 3. Stories in rhyme
ISBN 0-15-230550-5; 0-15-200986-8 (pa)
LC 89-29459
Also available Big book edition
This "book is both a story and a beginning nature guide. A pet cat wants to vary his diet with wild birds, but each attempt gains him only feathers. Twelve different bird species are . . . illustrated. . . . On each page, the bird's typical call is printed and plants pictured are named." SLJ

"Ehlert has attempted many things in these pages—for instance, the birds are all drawn life-size—and has succeeded in all of them; her lavish use of bold color against generous amounts of white space is graphically appealing, and the large type, nearly one-half-inch tall, invites attempts by those just beginning to read. An engaging, entertaining, and recognizably realistic story." Horn Book

Growing vegetable soup; written and illustrated by Lois Ehlert. Harcourt Brace Jovanovich 1987 unp il $15; pa $6 **E**
1. Vegetable gardening—Fiction
ISBN 0-15-232575-1; 0-15-232580-8 (pa)
LC 86-22812
Also available Big book edition and Spanish language edition

"Brightly-colored large illustrations and a boldly-worded text show how to plant and grow vegetables for Dad's soup. Shocking pinks, reds and greens give the illustrations an almost three-dimensional quality and will be good for large audiences of preschoolers." Child Book Rev Serv

Hands. Harcourt Brace & Co. 1997 unp il $13 **E**
ISBN 0-15-201506-X
LC 96-8871
When a child works alongside her parents doing carpentry, sewing, and gardening, she thinks of being an artist as well when she grows up

"The imaginatively designed book, featuring a diecut cover in the shape of a pair of bright yellow work gloves, opens to reveal smaller, rectangular pages interspersed with spreads of unusual size and shape (e.g., resembling handprints, scissors, even a paintbox that opens). Striking photographs of fabric, ribbon, tools, wood and seed packets give the book an appropriately tactile quality." Publ Wkly

Market day; a story told with folk art; written and designed by Lois Ehlert. Harcourt 2000 unp il $16 **E**
1. Markets—Fiction 2. Farm life—Fiction 3. Stories in rhyme
ISBN 0-15-202158-2
LC 99-6252
On market day, a farm family experiences all the fun and excitement of going to and from the farmers' market

"The very young will enjoy the spare, simple rhymes. . . . All ages will appreciate the illustrations, comprising images of folk art, primitive art, and textiles from around the world. An annotated inventory of the featured items is included." Horn Book Guide

Mole's hill; a woodland tale. Harcourt Brace & Co. 1994 unp il $15; pa $7 **E**
1. Moles (Animals)—Fiction
ISBN 0-15-255116-6; 0-15-201890-5 (pa)
LC 93-31151
When Fox tells Mole she must move out of her tunnel to make way for a new path, Mole finds an ingenious way to save her home

"Ehlert's language is compact and telling. . . . The art . . . is dark-hued, appropriately nocturnal without losing spirit or contrast, and the beads stippled across the cutout cloth shapes lend interesting texture to the planes of color. . . . The story (which Ehlert says she based on a fragment of a Seneca tale, with source completely cited in the book) has charm and vigor." Bull Cent Child Books

Nuts to you! Harcourt Brace Jovanovich 1993 unp il $16 **E**
1. Squirrels—Fiction 2. Stories in rhyme
ISBN 0-15-257647-9
LC 92-19441

Ehlert, Lois, 1934—*Continued*

"A frisky squirrel digs up bulbs and steals birdseed from a nearby feeder; in his boldest act, he enters the young narrator's apartment through a tear in the window screen. The quick-thinking child entices the mischievous squirrel back outside with some peanuts. . . . The story, told in brisk rhyme, is a fast-paced romp, and the large, dramatically styled collages will dazzle even the largest audiences. . . . The four concluding pages offer basic information about squirrels." Horn Book

Planting a rainbow; written and illustrated by Lois Ehlert. Harcourt Brace Jovanovich 1988 unp il lib bdg $16; pa $6   E

1. Gardening—Fiction 2. Flowers—Fiction
ISBN 0-15-262609-3 (lib bdg); 0-15-262610-7 (pa)
LC 87-8528

Also available Big book edition and Spanish language edition

A mother and daughter plant a rainbow of flowers in the family garden

"The stylized forms of the plants are clearly and beautifully designed, and the primary, blazing colors of the blossoms dazzle in their resplendence. The minimal text, in very large print, is exactly right to set off the glorious illustrations, making a splendid beginning book of colors and flowers cleverly arranged for young readers." Horn Book

Snowballs. Harcourt Brace & Co. 1995 unp il $16; pa $7   E

1. Snow—Fiction
ISBN 0-15-200074-7; 0-15-202095-0 (pa)
LC 94-47183

"Using 'good stuff' like seeds, nuts, corn kernels, and colorful yarn kids create a wonderful snow family. Placed on vertical page spreads, the snow characters extend the full length of the book, a perspective that enhances the drama of their inevitable demise when the sun comes out. Large, well-designed illustrations effectively blend open space, colorful paper cutouts, and real objects." Horn Book Guide

Top cat. Harcourt Brace & Co. 1998 unp il $16   E

1. Cats—Fiction 2. Stories in rhyme
ISBN 0-15-201739-9   LC 97-8818

The top cat in a household is reluctant to accept the arrival of a new kitten but decides to share various survival secrets with it

"Ehlert creates a memorable cat duo in her trademark cut-paper collage style. . . . Children and other feline fans will quickly warm to this spunky story of rivalry and acceptance." Publ Wkly

Ehrlich, Amy, 1942-

Leo, Zack, and Emmie together again; pictures by Steven Kellogg. Dial Bks. for Young Readers 1987 56p il hardcover o.p. paperback available $3.99   E

1. Friendship—Fiction
ISBN 0-14-037946-0 (pa)   LC 86-16810
"An Easy-to-read book"

In this title "three second graders are involved . . . in four loosely connected episodes that take place in the winter: they play in the snow, meet Santa Claus, suffer through chicken pox . . . and make Valentine cards. . . . Ehrlich's writing is direct and uncluttered. There is just enough conflict in the plot to create interest. Kellogg's full-color illustrations consistently add humor to the text and make this book hard to put down." SLJ

Another available title about Leo, Zack, and Emmie is: Leo, Zack, and Emmie (1981)

Parents in the pigpen, pigs in the tub; pictures by Steven Kellogg. Dial Bks. for Young Readers 1993 unp il hardcover o.p. paperback available $5.99   E

1. Animals—Fiction 2. Farm life—Fiction
ISBN 0-14-056297-4 (pa)   LC 91-15601

Tired of their usual routine, the farm animals insist on moving into the house, so the family decides to move into barn, but eventually everyone tires of this new arrangement

"Ehrlich's text begs to be read aloud in an exaggerated country twang, while Kellogg's watercolor illustrations are rambling and full of humorous details." SLJ

Eichenberg, Fritz, 1901-1990

Ape in a cape; an alphabet of odd animals. Harcourt Brace & Co. 1952 unp il hardcover o.p. paperback available $7   E

1. Animals 2. Alphabet
ISBN 0-15-607830-9 (pa)
A Caldecott Medal honor book, 1953

"Each letter of the alphabet from A for ape to Z for zoo is represented by a full-page picture of an animal with a brief nonsense rhyme caption explaining it. For example: mouse in a blouse, pig in a wig, toad on the road, whale in a gale." Publ Wkly

"The skill of a craftsman distinguishes this picture book illustrated with bold and lively drawings printed in three colors." N Y Public Libr

Eilenberg, Max

Cowboy Kid; illustrated by Sue Heap. Candlewick Press 2000 unp il $15.99   E

1. Bedtime—Fiction 2. Toys—Fiction
ISBN 0-7636-1058-5   LC 99-54076

Also available companion volume Cowboy Baby by Sue Heap

A young boy has difficulty getting to sleep because his toys seem to need so many hugs and kisses at bedtime

"Heap's bright acrylic and watercolor paintings feature striking yet simple figures in uncluttered compositions that are just right for the book's intended audience." Booklist

Emberley, Ed

Go away, big green monster! Little, Brown 1992 unp il $15.95   E

1. Monsters—Fiction 2. Fear—Fiction 3. Bedtime—Fiction
ISBN 0-316-23653-5   LC 92-6231

Emberley, Ed—*Continued*

"In the first half of this fear-dispelling book, graphically distinctive die-cut pages reveal, bit by bit, a monster with 'sharp white teeth' and 'scraggly purple hair.' The process is then reversed as the text commands each scary feature to 'go away,' until there is nothing at all left of the monster but a black page instructing 'Don't Come Back! Until I say so.' Entertaining and empowering for young children." Horn Book Guide

Ernst, Lisa Campbell, 1957-

Goldilocks returns. Simon & Schuster Bks. for Young Readers 2000 unp il $16   E
  1. Bears—Fiction 2. Fairy tales
  ISBN 0-689-82537-4   LC 98-30099
Fifty years after Goldilocks first met the three bears, she returns to fix up their cottage and soothe her guilty conscience
  "The spirited illustrations, featuring a stout, bespectacled Goldi, enchance the humor of this clever sequel to the familiar tale." Horn Book Guide

Sam Johnson and the blue ribbon quilt. Lothrop, Lee & Shepard Bks. 1983 32p il lib bdg $15.89; pa $4.95   E
  1. Quilts—Fiction
  ISBN 0-688-01517-4 (lib bdg); 0-688-11505-5 (pa)
        LC 82-9980
While mending the awning over the pig pen, Sam discovers that he enjoys sewing the various patches together but meets with scorn and ridicule when he asks his wife if he could join her quilting club
  The illustrations "bring an old-timey, bucolic scene to life and show steps in an equal-rights issue." Publ Wkly

When Bluebell sang. Bradbury Press 1989 unp il hardcover o.p. paperback available $5.99   E
  1. Cattle—Fiction
  ISBN 0-689-71584-6 (pa)   LC 88-22262
Bluebell the cow's talent for singing brings her stardom but she soon longs to be back at the farm—if she can get away from her greedy manager
  "An amusing, lighthearted tale ideal for early grades' story hours, and also an enjoyable read-alone for third and fourth graders. The pastel-hued, cartoon-like illustrations are humorous without being silly. The text, which appears opposite the illustrations, is decorated with drawings of Bluebell's mementos—photos, tickets and posters—which add to the fun." SLJ

Zinnia and Dot. Viking 1992 unp il $15.99; pa $5.99   E
  1. Chickens—Fiction
  ISBN 0-670-83091-7; 0-14-054199-3 (pa)
        LC 91-36178
Zinnia and Dot, self-satisfied hens who bicker constantly about who lays better eggs, put aside their differences to protect a prime specimen from a marauding weasel
  "Ernst has an easy storytelling style and a flair for grouchy dialogue that clucks to be read aloud, and her line-and-wash paintings, lighted with gentle yellow tones, warm the comedy." Bull Cent Child Books

Ets, Marie Hall, 1893-1984

Gilberto and the Wind. Viking 1963 32p il $15.99; pa $5.99   E
  1. Winds—Fiction
  ISBN 0-670-34025-1; 0-14-050276-9 (pa)
  Also available Spanish language edition
  "I am Gilberto and this is the story of me and the Wind." Title page
  "A little Mexican boy thinks aloud about all the things his playmate the wind does with him, for him, and against him. The wind calls him to play, floats his balloon, refuses to fly his kite, blows his soap bubble into the air, races with him, and rests with him under a tree." SLJ
  "In brown, black, and white against soft gray pages, this author-artist has caught in a very appealing book . . . the emotions and attitudes of childhood." Horn Book

Just me; written and illustrated by Marie Hall Ets. Viking 1965 32p il $15.99; pa $5.99   E
  ISBN 0-670-41109-4; 0-14-050325-0 (pa)
  A Caldecott Medal honor book, 1966
  "A little boy plays a game commonly enjoyed by small children for its imaginative as well as muscular demands. He goes from one animal to another, mimicking its ambulation, moving 'just like' it. When there is a chance to take a boat ride with Dad, the game ends abruptly, and another kind of imitation begins—emulation of father." Horn Book
  "Strong, simply designed illustrations and brief, rhythmic text." LC. Child Books, 1965

Play with me; story and pictures by Marie Hall Ets. Viking 1955 31p il hardcover o.p. paperback available $5.99   E
  1. Animals—Fiction
  ISBN 0-14-050178-9 (pa)
  A Caldecott Medal honor book, 1956
  On a sunny morning in the meadow an excited little girl tries to catch the meadow creatures and play with them. But, one by one, they all run away. Finally, when she learns to sit quietly and wait, there is a happy ending
  The "pictures done in muted tones of brown, gray and yellow . . . accurately reflect the little girl's rapidly changing moods of eagerness, bafflement, disappointment and final happiness." N Y Times Book Rev

Everitt, Betsy

Mean soup. Harcourt Brace Jovanovich 1992 unp il $16; pa $7   E
  ISBN 0-15-253146-7; 0-15-200227-8 (pa)
        LC 91-15244
Horace feels really mean at the end of a bad day, until he helps his mother make Mean Soup
  "The text features short sentences and easy but effective vocabulary, so the story bubbles with a building excitement. Everitt's . . . stylized paintings and bold palette—hot pinks, purples and black predominate—convey all of the feisty emotion of a frustrated youngster." Publ Wkly

Falconer, Ian

Olivia; written and illustrated by Ian Falconer. Atheneum Bks. for Young Readers 2000 unp il $16 E

1. Pigs—Fiction
ISBN 0-689-82953-1   LC 99-24003
A Caldecott Medal honor book, 2001
"An Anne Schwartz book"
Whether at home getting ready for the day, enjoying the beach, or at bedtime, Olivia is a feisty pig who has too much energy for her own good
"The spacious design of the book; the appeal of the strong, clever art; and the humor that permeates every page make this a standout. . . . Falconer . . . renders Olivia's world in charcoal with dollops of red brightening the pages." Booklist

Falls, C. B. (Charles Buckles), 1874-1960

ABC book; designed and cut on wood by C.B. Falls. Books of Wonder 1998 unp il $15; lib bdg $14.93 E

1. Alphabet
ISBN 0-688-14712-7; 0-688-16263-0 (lib bdg)
LC 97-47301
A reissue of the title first published 1923 by Doubleday
Presents an animal for each letter of the alphabet, from antelope and bear to yak and zebra
"The bold, blocky woodcuts and screens of flat color in bright hues have an appealing simplicity." Horn Book

Faulkner, Matt

Black belt. Knopf 2000 unp il $16.95; lib bdg $18.99 E

1. Karate—Fiction 2. Japan—Fiction
ISBN 0-375-80157-X; 0-375-90157-4 (lib bdg)
LC 99-88442
After hiding in a karate school to escape a bully, Bushi wakes up in another time and learns from a karate master that intelligence can be more powerful than mere strength
"The full-color, glossy pictures, packed with action and extraordinary detail, will appeal to fans of the graphic novel." Booklist

Fearnley, Jan

Mr. Wolf's pancakes. Little Tiger Press 2000 c1999 unp il $14.95 E

ISBN 1-888-44476-2   LC 2001-834
Available from Janex International, Inc. and M.E. Media
First published 1999 in the United Kingdom
"Mr. Wolf seeks assistance from his neighbors, but Chicken Little, Wee Willy Winkle, the Gingerbread Man, Little Red Riding Hood and the Three Little Pigs all nastily refuse. Of course, when Mr. Wolf eventually whips up the pancakes all by himself, they demand a share of his culinary creation. Mr. Wolf . . . lets the marauders into the kitchen—and then gobbles them all up. . . . Chipper watercolors depict a sunny storybook town. . . . A gleeful twist on a nursery staple." Publ Wkly

Feelings, Muriel, 1938-

Jambo means hello; Swahili alphabet book; pictures by Tom Feelings. Dial Bks. for Young Readers 1981 unp il hardcover o.p. paperback available $6.99 E

1. Alphabet 2. Swahili language 3. East Africa
ISBN 0-14-054652-9 (pa)
A Caldecott Medal honor book, 1975
This book "gives a word for each letter of the alphabet (the Swahili alphabet has 24 letters) save for 'q' and 'x', and a sentence or two provides additional information. A double-page spread of soft black and white drawings illustrates each word. . . . The text gives a considerable amount of information about traditional East African life as well as some acquaintance with the language that is used by approximately 45 million people." Bull Cent Child Books
"Integrated totally in feeling and mood, the book has been engendered by an intense personal vision of Africa—one that is warm, all-enveloping, quietly strong and filled with love." Horn Book

Moja means one; Swahili counting book; pictures by Tom Feelings. Dial Bks. for Young Readers 1971 unp il hardcover o.p. paperback available $5.99 E

1. Counting 2. Swahili language 3. East Africa
ISBN 0-14-054662-6 (pa)
A Caldecott Medal honor book, 1972
The book "uses double-page spreads for each number, one to ten, with beautiful illustrations that depict aspects of East African culture as well as numbers of objects in relation to the various numbers." Publ Wkly
"A short introduction explaining the importance of Swahili and providing a map of the areas in which it is spoken expands the book's use beyond the preschool level of the text into the first three school grades." SLJ

Feiffer, Jules

Bark, George. HarperCollins Pubs. 1999 unp il $14.95; lib bdg $14.98 E

1. Dogs—Fiction
ISBN 0-06-205185-7; 0-06-205186-5 (lib bdg)
"Michael di Capua books"
"George the puppy has a problem — he just can't bark. He can meow, quack, oink, moo; but not bark." NY Times Book Rev
"Feiffer's characters are unforgettable, the text is brief and easy to follow, and the pictures burst with the sort of broad physical comedy that a lot of children just love." Booklist

I lost my bear. Morrow Junior Bks. 1998 unp il $16; lib bdg $15.93; pa $5.95 E

ISBN 0-688-15147-7; 0-688-15148-5 (lib bdg); 0-688-17722-0 (pa)   LC 97-34475
"When a young girl loses her best toy, she plays detective to find it. After consulting other family members to no avail, she follows her sister's suggestion to throw another stuffed animal on the chance that it will land in the same place." SLJ
"Feiffer tells his story through cartoon panels and dialogue balloons, and the energetic illustrations suit the vibrant text." Bull Cent Child Books

Fisher, Leonard Everett, 1924-

The ABC exhibit. Macmillan 1991 unp il $15.95 **E**

1. Alphabet

ISBN 0-02-735251-X LC 90-6639

Introduces the letters of the alphabet in paintings of subjects from Acrobat to Zinnia

"The intensity of color and precision of detail invite readers to linger, to identify, and to observe. The alphabet is merely the framework; the lesson is in the appreciation of art." SLJ

Flack, Marjorie, 1897-1958

Ask Mr. Bear. Macmillan 1958 c1932 unp il $15; pa $5.99 **E**

1. Animals—Fiction 2. Birthdays—Fiction

ISBN 0-02-735390-7; 0-02-043090-6 (pa)

First published 1932

Danny did not know what to give his mother for a birthday present, so he set out to ask various animals—the hen, the duck, the goose, the lamb, the cow and others, but he met with very little success until he met Mr. Bear

This "will have a strong appeal to very young children because of its repetition, its use of the most familiar animals, its gay pictures and the cumulative effect of the story." N Y Times Book Rev

Fleischman, Paul

Time train; illustrations by Claire Ewart. HarperCollins Pubs. 1991 unp il hardcover o.p. paperback available $6.95 **E**

1. Dinosaurs—Fiction 2. Fantasy fiction

ISBN 0-06-443351-X (pa) LC 90-27357

"A Charlotte Zolotow book"

A class takes a field trip back through time to observe living dinosaurs in their natural habitat

"The deadpan humor and gloriously animated watercolors provide unlimited entertainment." SLJ

Weslandia; illustrated by Kevin Hawkes. Candlewick Press 1999 unp il $15.99 **E**

1. Plants—Fiction 2. Gardening—Fiction

ISBN 0-7636-0006-7 LC 98-30240

Wesley's garden produces a crop of huge, strange plants which provide him with clothing, shelter, food, and drink, thus helping him create his own civilization and changing his life

"This story about a nonconformist creating his own reality resonates with imagination and humor. . . . His natural creativity is reflected in Hawkes' vivid recreations of Wesley's altered environment, lush illustrations that have a realistic whimsy." Bull Cent Child Books

Fleischman, Sid, 1920-

The scarebird; pictures by Peter Sis. Greenwillow Bks. 1988 unp il lib bdg $15.89; pa $4.95 **E**

1. Friendship—Fiction 2. Farm life—Fiction

ISBN 0-688-07318-2 (lib bdg); 0-688-13105-0 (pa)

LC 87-4099

A lonely old farmer realizes the value of human friendship when a young man comes to help him and his scarecrow with their farm

"The oil paintings by Peter Sis are wonderfully evocative. They capture the quiet dignity of the sturdy old farmer and of the farm set in a vast expanse of field and sky. Together, words and pictures create a memorable portrait of a loving human being." Horn Book

Fleming, Candace

A big cheese for the White House; the true tale of a tremendous cheddar; illustrated by S.D. Schindler. DK Pub. 1999 unp il $16.95 **E**

1. Jefferson, Thomas, 1743-1826—Fiction 2. Cheese—Fiction

ISBN 0-7894-2573-4 LC 98-41152

In 1801, in Chesire, Massachusetts, Elder John Leland organizes his fellow townspeople to make a 1,235 pound cheddar cheese for President Jefferson

"Fleming says in her historical note that the events are true but that some of the characters are not. . . . Schindler's lively period illustrations, in pen and watercolor with delicate cross-hatching, express the wry characterizations and triumphant larger-than-life action." Booklist

Gabriella's song; illustrated by Giselle Potter. Atheneum Bks. for Young Readers 1997 unp il $16 **E**

1. Music—Fiction 2. Venice (Italy)—Fiction

ISBN 0-689-80973-5 LC 96-2459

"An Anne Schwartz book"

Gabriella finds music all around her as she walks about the city of Venice, Italy, and she shares her song with everyone she meets

"The author conveys a love for music and for Venice, giving children an idea of where music begins and what it can mean to people. The illustrations, in rich terracotta and turquoise, are luscious." Booklist

The hatmaker's sign; a story; by Benjamin Franklin; retold by Candace Fleming; illustrated by Robert Andrew Parker. Orchard Bks. 1998 unp il $16.95; lib bdg $17.99; pa $6.95 **E**

1. Jefferson, Thomas, 1743-1826—Fiction 2. Franklin, Benjamin, 1706-1790—Fiction

ISBN 0-531-30075-7; 0-531-33075-3 (lib bdg); 0-531-07174-X (pa) LC 97-27596

To heal the hurt pride of Thomas Jefferson as Congress makes changes to his Declaration of Independence, Benjamin Franklin tells his friend the story of a hatmaker and his sign

"Based on an anecdote in *The Papers of Thomas Jefferson*, the story has a folktale-like quality that lends itself to being read aloud. The illustrations give dimension to the characters and a sense of times past." Horn Book Guide

When Agnes caws; written by Candice Fleming; illustrated by Giselle Potter. Atheneum Bks. for Young Readers 1999 unp il $16 **E**

1. Birds—Fiction

ISBN 0-689-81471-2 LC 97-32921

"An Anne Schwartz book"

Fleming, Candace—*Continued*

When eight-year-old Agnes Peregrine, an accomplished birdcaller, travels with her parents to the Himalayas in search of the elusive pink-headed duck, she encounters a dastardly foe

"Gently distorted perspectives in the expressive illustrations add to the melodramatic spoofiness of this flibbertigibbet tale." Horn Book Guide

Fleming, Denise, 1950-

Barnyard banter. Holt & Co. 1994 unp il $16.95; pa $6.95　　E
 1. Animals—Fiction 2. Stories in rhyme
 ISBN 0-8050-1957-X; 0-8050-5581-9 (pa)
           LC 93-11032

All the farm animals are where they should be, clucking and mucking, mewing and cooing, except for the missing goose

"Strong rhythm and rhyme, plus fun onomatopoetic animal sounds, demand reading aloud. But even more delightful than the engaging text are Fleming's spectacular illustrations. . . . They create realistically textured, bold, bright settings for the whimsical critters to romp through." SLJ

Count! Holt & Co. 1992 unp il $16.95; pa $6.95　　E
 1. Counting 2. Animals
 ISBN 0-8050-1595-7; 0-8050-4252-0 (pa)
           LC 91-25686

Also available Board book edition

The antics of lively and colorful animals present the numbers one to ten, twenty, thirty, forty, and fifty

"A fresh, upbeat concept book. Lizards, giraffes, toucans, butterflies are available for counting—if only they'll hold still long enough! Fuchsias and oranges, teals and purples, roll over the pages blending into each other in Fleming's beautiful couched paper with hand cut-stencil illustrations. Her explosions of color and motion are captivating and energizing." SLJ

The everything book. Holt & Co. 2000 64p il $18.95　　E
 ISBN 0-8050-6292-0　　　　　　LC 99-53626

A collection of simple works which introduce colors, shapes, numbers, animals, food, and nursery rhymes

"The book includes everything needed to make it an anthology of preschool interests and concerns. . . . The very attractive illustrations, done in Fleming's characteristic bold and energetic style, were produced by pouring cotton pulp through hand-cut stencils, the result being simple forms that are attractively textured, with edges that are just fuzzy enough to look soft and friendly." SLJ

In the small, small pond. Holt & Co. 1993 unp il $16.95; pa $6.95　　E
 1. Pond ecology—Fiction 2. Stories in rhyme
 ISBN 0-8050-2264-3; 0-8050-5983-0 (pa)
           LC 92-25770

A Caldecott Medal honor book, 1994

Illustrations and rhyming text describe the activities of animals living in and near a small pond as spring progresses to autumn

"The brilliant, primitive illustrations were made by pouring colored cotton pulp through hand-cut stencils.

Against the eye-catching colors, the four-word rhymes in bold black print dance, each double-page spread picturing and describing a different creature. Text, pictures, layout, and design are all beautifully done." SLJ

In the tall, tall grass. Holt & Co. 1991 unp il $16.95; pa $6.95　　E
 1. Animals—Fiction 2. Stories in rhyme
 ISBN 0-8050-1635-X; 0-8050-3941-4 (pa)
           LC 90-26444

Also available Big book edition

Rhymed text (crunch, munch, caterpillars lunch) presents a toddler's view of creatures found in the grass from lunchtime till nightfall, such as bees, ants, and moles

"Boldly colored in grassy greens, sunny yellows, and evening blues, the impressionistic illustrations make this a real treat for eyes as well as ears." Booklist

Lunch. Holt & Co. 1993 unp il $16.95; pa $6.95　　E
 1. Mice—Fiction 2. Color
 ISBN 0-8050-1636-8; 0-8050-4646-1 (pa)
           LC 92-178

Also available Board book edition

"A very hungry mouse nibbles and crunches his way through the various components of a vegetarian repast, while the text introduces readers to the individual foods and their respective colors." Publ Wkly

"Fleming continues to work in the medium of handmade paper built from layers of colored pulp that has been forced through a stencil. A huge typeface and the judicious use of large blocks of bold, solid color give this book a fresh look. Delectable fun, and, with its simple yet engaging plot, sure to be requested over and over by the youngest readers." Horn Book

Mama cat has three kittens. Holt & Co. 1998 unp il $16.95　　E
 1. Cats—Fiction
 ISBN 0-8050-5745-5　　　　　　LC 98-12249

While two kittens copy everything their mother does, their brother naps

"Fleming's kittens, created by pouring colored cotton pulp through hand-cut stencils, are large and bold and set against colorful backdrops. An excellent choice for reading aloud to groups." SLJ

Time to sleep. Holt & Co. 1997 unp il $16.95　　E
 1. Winter—Fiction 2. Animals—Fiction 3. Hibernation—Fiction
 ISBN 0-8050-3762-4　　　　　　LC 96-37553

When Bear notices that winter is nearly here he hurries to tell Snail, after which each animal tells another until finally the already sleeping Bear is awakened in his den with the news

"Fleming's simple text is ripe with astute observations of the natural world and animal behavior. . . . Fleming's 'pulp painting' style results in lushly textured handmade paper compositions saturated with earthy browns, reds and golds." Publ Wkly

Floca, Brian

Five trucks. DK Ink 1999 unp il $15.95　　E
 1. Trucks—Fiction 2. Airports—Fiction
 ISBN 0-7894-2561-0　　　　　　LC 98-19834

Floca, Brian—*Continued*

Five different trucks do five different jobs to get an airplane ready for takeoff

"Floca offers a book that's simple enough for a two-year-old (prime age for the young truck enthusiast), without being boring or simple-minded. The artwork, ink line with watercolor washes, uses every spread to good advantage." Booklist

Florian, Douglas, 1950-

Turtle day. Crowell 1989 unp il lib bdg $15.89

E

1. Turtles—Fiction

ISBN 0-690-04745-2   LC 88-30321

"A turtle's typical day is recounted in simple, predictable text and childlike, full-color drawings. Format invites readers to anticipate what the turtle will do next." Sci Child

Flournoy, Valerie, 1952-

The patchwork quilt; pictures by Jerry Pinkney. Dial Bks. for Young Readers 1985 unp il $16.99

E

1. Quilts—Fiction 2. Family life—Fiction 3. African Americans—Fiction

ISBN 0-8037-0097-0   LC 84-1711

Coretta Scott King Award for illustrations, 1986

Using scraps cut from the family's old clothing, Tanya helps her grandmother and mother make a beautiful quilt that tells the story of her Afro-American family's life

"Plentiful full-page and double-page paintings in pencil, graphite and watercolor are vivid yet delicately detailed, bespeaking the warm physical bonds among members of this family. Giving a sense of dramatization to the text, which is longer than most picture books, the illustrations provide just the right style and mood for the story and are well placed within the text." SLJ

Fox, Mem, 1946-

Hattie and the fox; illustrated by Patricia Mullins. Bradbury Press 1987 c1986 unp il $16; pa $5.99

E

1. Chickens—Fiction 2. Foxes—Fiction

ISBN 0-02-735470-9; 0-689-71611-7 (pa)

LC 86-18849

First published 1986 in Australia

"Hattie is a fine, portly, and observant hen, and she knows there is something wrong when she spies a sharp foxy nose in the bushes. Her alarmist and ever escalating announcements, however, bring nothing but bored and languid replies." Horn Book

"Bright, whimsical tissue collage and crayon illustrations add zest to this simple cumulative tale, and reveal more action than is expressed by the text alone." SLJ

Koala Lou; illustrated by Pamela Lofts. Harcourt Brace Jovanovich 1989 c1988 unp il $15; pa $6

E

1. Koalas—Fiction

ISBN 0-15-200502-1; 0-15-200076-3 (pa)

LC 88-26810

"Gulliver books"

First published 1988 in Australia

This story is "set in the Australian bush. Koala Lou feels bereft when her mother becomes preoccupied with a growing brood of younger koala children. In her desire to recapture her mother's attention and affection, the enterprising Koala Lou decides to become a contestant in the Bush Olympics." Horn Book

"A reassuring story for the child who feels neglected when siblings arrive." Child Book Rev Serv

Night noises; written by Mem Fox; illustrated by Terry Denton. Harcourt Brace Jovanovich 1989 unp il $16; pa $4.95

E

1. Night—Fiction 2. Sleep—Fiction

ISBN 0-15-200543-9; 0-15-257421-2 (pa)

LC 89-2162

"Gulliver books"

Old Lily Laceby dozes by the fire with her faithful dog Butch Aggie at her feet as strange night noises herald a surprising awakening

"With an almost joltingly bright palette . . . Denton has divided up many of the double-page spreads into three scenes: the main one depicting Lily Laceby and Butch Aggie in various stages of alertness, another showing the chronology of Lily's life, and the third cleverly revealing clues to the mysterious activity outdoors. The text, in Mem Fox's Houdini-like hands, reads beautifully—the language, pacing, tension, and sparks of excitement absolutely at one with the artwork." Horn Book

Sleepy bears; illustrated by Kerry Argent. Harcourt Brace & Co. 1999 unp il $16

E

1. Bears—Fiction 2. Bedtime—Fiction 3. Stories in rhyme

ISBN 0-15-202016-0   LC 98-42640

"Mother Bear tucks in her six cubs, sending them off on dreamy adventures. Baxter dreams of pirates, Bella of the circus, Winifred of the jungle, Tosca of kingdoms, Ali of divine foods, and Baby Bear of moonbeams. . . . The rhymes are well written, and the charming pictures, done in gouache, watercolor, and colored pencil, are full of funny details." SLJ

Sophie; illustrated by Aminah Brenda Lynn Robinson. Harcourt Brace & Co. 1994 c1989 unp il $13.95; pa $6

E

1. Grandfathers—Fiction 2. African Americans—Fiction

ISBN 0-15-277160-3; 0-15-201598-1 (pa)

LC 94-1976

First published 1989 in Australia

"In this cyclical tale, Grandpa welcomes infant Sophie into the world; much later, Sophie is saddened when 'there was no Grandpa.' The birth of Sophie's own child completes the circle." Publ Wkly

"The artwork is rich, expressionist, heavily lined oil. . . . The oversized hands depicted in many drawings exemplify the handholding theme, and the sunny hues of earth and garden convey with warmth a loving and extended African-American family." Bull Cent Child Books

Tough Boris; illustrated by Kathryn Brown. Harcourt Brace & Co. 1994 unp il $16; pa $6

E

1. Pirates—Fiction 2. Parrots—Fiction

ISBN 0-15-289612-0; 0-15-201891-3 (pa)

LC 92-8015

Fox, Mem, 1946——_Continued_

Boris von der Borch is a tough pirate but he weeps when his parrot dies

"The text is deceptively simple, but the observant child will quickly fill in the details, aptly provided in the illustrations. The reassuring message, although understated, is clear and effective." Horn Book Guide

Wombat divine; illustrated by Kerry Argent. Harcourt Brace & Co. 1996 unp il $15; pa $6

E

1. Christmas—Fiction 2. Wombats—Fiction 3. Animals—Fiction

ISBN 0-15-201416-0; 0-15-202096-9 (pa)

LC 96-5480

Wombat auditions for the Nativity play, but has trouble finding the right part

"Fox spiffily combines a witty text with her wonderful art. Here the fun comes with seeing all sorts of Australian animals (emu, bilby, kangaroo) decked out in their Christmas-play garb." Booklist

Frasier, Debra, 1953-

On the day you were born. Harcourt Brace Jovanovich 1991 unp il $16 E

1. Earth 2. Childbirth

ISBN 0-15-257995-8 LC 90-36816

Also available Big book edition and Audiobook version

This combination of text and paper-collage graphics depicts the earth's preparation for, and celebration of, the birth of a newborn baby

"The text reads like unrhymed poetry, and both parents and educators will find themselves wanting to share this book over and over with individuals and with groups. A three-page appendix that includes miniature versions of each spread elaborates on natural phenomena for older readers—migrating animals, spinning Earth, rising tide, falling rain, growing trees, and more." SLJ

Freeman, Don, 1908-1978

Corduroy; story and pictures by Don Freeman. Viking 1968 32p il lib bdg $14.99; pa $5.99

E

1. Teddy bears—Fiction

ISBN 0-670-24133-4 (lib bdg); 0-14-050173-8 (pa)

Also available Big book edition and Spanish language edition

"One day Corduroy, a toy bear who lives in a big department store, discovers he has lost a button. That night he goes to look for it and in his search he sees many strange and wonderful things. He does not find his button, but the following morning he finds what he has always wanted—a friend, Lisa." Read Ladders for Hum Relat. 6th edition

"The art and story are direct and just right for the very young who like bears and escalators." Book World

Another available title about Corduroy is:

A pocket for Corduroy (1978)

Dandelion; story and pictures by Don Freeman. Viking 1964 48p il hardcover o.p. paperback available $5.99 E

1. Lions—Fiction

ISBN 0-14-050218-1 (pa)

"Dandelion, properly invited by note to Jennifer Giraffe's tea-and-taffy party, pays no heed to the words, 'Come as you are.' At his regular haircut appointment he allows Lou Kangaroo and helper to do him up properly, according to the new fashions for lions. But pride goeth before a fall—and it is not surprising that Jennifer's tall door is closed on the unrecognizable stranger; nor that after being restored by a heavy rainfall to something nearer his usual state, he makes the party, after all. Mr. Freeman cleverly depicts an assortment of personalities in his many animal characters. The party scenes and the barber shop are wonderfully amusing." Horn Book

Freymann, Saxton

How are you peeling? foods with moods; [by] Saxton Freymann and Joost Elffers. Scholastic 1999 unp il $15.95 E

1. Emotions

ISBN 0-439-10431-9 LC 99-18162

"Arthur A. Levine books"

Brief text and photographs of carvings made from vegetables introduce the world of emotions by presenting leading questions such as "Are you feeling angry?"

"Kids will find the inherent silliness irresistible and be drawn in by the book's visual appeal: the colors are strong, the photography is excellent, and the expressions . . . are surprisingly masterful." Booklist

One lonely sea horse; [by Saxton Freymann and Joost Elffers] Scholastic 2000 unp il $15.95 E

1. Counting 2. Friendship—Fiction 3. Marine animals—Fiction 4. Stories in rhyme

ISBN 0-439-11014-9 LC 99-33396

"Arthur A. Levine books"

One lonely sea horse learns that she has a lot of friends—friends she can really "count" on

"In beautifully photographed dioramas, fruits and vegetables are transformed into sea flora and fauna. . . . The edible characters are wonderfully expressive, with a wide range of emotions captured through the use of a few simple slits and seeds." Booklist

Friedman, Ina R.

How my parents learned to eat; illustrated by Allen Say. Houghton Mifflin 1984 30p il $15; pa $5.95 E

1. Dining—Fiction 2. Japan—Fiction

ISBN 0-395-35379-3; 0-395-44235-4 (pa)

LC 83-18553

Also available with Audiobook

An American sailor courts a Japanese girl and each tries, in secret, to learn the other's way of eating

"The illustrations have precise use of line and soft colors, and the composition is economical. A warm and gentle story of an interracial family." Bull Cent Child Books

Friedrich, Elizabeth, 1949-

Leah's pony; illustrated by Michael Garland. Boyds Mills Press 1996 unp il $14.95; pa $8.95

E

1. Farm life—Fiction 2. Great Depression, 1929-1939—Fiction

ISBN 1-56397-189-5; 1-56397-828-8 (pa)

LC 95-79657

Friedrich, Elizabeth, 1949-—*Continued*

"When drought in the 1930s turns their farm land into dust, Leah's papa has to put everything they own up for auction. Knowing how much he needs his tractor, Leah makes the decision to sell her beloved pony and bids all her money for the tractor—one dollar. Neighbors follow her example, placing penny bids and returning things to Leah's parents." Horn Book Guide

Gackenbach, Dick, 1927-

What's Claude doing? Clarion Bks. 1984 unp il hardcover o.p. paperback available $5.95　　**E**
1. Dogs—Fiction
ISBN 0-89919-464-8 (pa)　　　　　LC 83-14983
"Claude, a 'do-good' hound, can't be persuaded by his friends to come outside and join their fun. Suspense builds as the animals (and children) wonder just what Claude is doing." SLJ

"Large three-color pictures featuring a perky cast of animal characters and a pared-down text make this cozy, mildly suspenseful winter story a prime read-aloud choice for the toddler set." Booklist
Another available title about Claude is:
Claude the dog (1974)

Gág, Wanda, 1893-1946

Millions of cats. Coward-McCann 1928 unp il hardcover o.p. paperback available $5.99　　**E**
1. Cats—Fiction
ISBN 0-698-11363-2 (pa)
A Newbery Medal honor book, 1929
A "story-picture book about a very old man and a very old woman who wanted one little cat and who found themselves with 'millions and billions and trillions of cats.'" St Louis Public Libr
It is "a perennial favorite among children and takes a place of its own, both for the originality and strength of its pictures and the living folktale quality of its text." NY Her Trib Books

Gammell, Stephen, 1943-

Is that you, winter? a story. Silver Whistle Bks.; Harcourt Brace & Co. 1997 unp il $16; pa $7
　　　　　　　　　　　　　　　　　　　　　　E
1. Winter—Fiction
ISBN 0-15-201415-2; 0-15-202434-4 (pa)
　　　　　　　　　　　　　　　　　LC 96-24319
Though Old Man Winter starts off the day feeling grumpy, his mood improves when he is reminded of how special he really is
"In full-bleed, double-page spreads, the artist's trademark rainbow of gauzy lines, splatters and swirls of paint create a dreamy, winter wonderland backdrop for his spunky and memorable starring character." Publ Wkly

Once upon MacDonald's farm. rev format ed. Simon & Schuster Bks. for Young Readers 2000 c1981 unp il $15　　**E**
1. Farm life—Fiction 2. Animals—Fiction
ISBN 0-689-82885-3　　　　　LC 99-30691
First published 1981 by Four Winds Press

MacDonald tries farming with exotic circus animals, but has better luck with his neighbor's cow, horse, and chicken—or does he?
"The accomplished, shaded pencil drawings are well suited to this slyly humorous tale with an unexpected twist." Horn Book Guide

Gantos, Jack

Rotten Ralph; written by Jack B. Gantos; illustrated by Nicole Rubel. Houghton Mifflin 1976 unp il lib bdg $16; pa $6.95　　**E**
1. Cats—Fiction
ISBN 0-395-24276-2 (lib bdg); 0-395-29202-6 (pa)

"The protagonist of this story is a mean and nasty cat, Ralph. As his young owner, Sarah, and her family say, he is very difficult to love. Finally on a trip to the circus his behavior becomes unforgivable and they leave him. There he is treated as miserably as he has treated everyone else and he comes home a week later a wiser, more benevolent cat—well, almost." Child Book Rev Serv
The "bright watercolor scenes . . . capturing Ralph's demonic meanness and his family's chagrin are a perfect complement to the text." SLJ
Other available titles about Ralph the cat are:
Back to school for Rotten Ralph (1998)
Happy birthday Rotten Ralph (1990)
Not so Rotten Ralph (1994)
Rotten Ralph's rotten Christmas (1984)
Rotten Ralph's rotten romance (1997)
Rotten Ralph's show and tell (1989)
Rotten Ralph's trick or treat! (1986)
Wedding bells for Rotten Ralph (1999)
Worse than rotten, Ralph (1978)

Garland, Sherry, 1948-

My father's boat; illustrated by Ted Rand. Scholastic 1998 unp il $15.95　　**E**
1. Father-son relationship—Fiction 2. Vietnamese Americans—Fiction 3. Fishing—Fiction
ISBN 0-590-47867-2　　　　　LC 97-19021
A Vietnamese-American boy spends a day with his father on his shrimp boat, listening as he describes how his own father fishes on the South China Sea
"The text flows effortlessly. The spectacular double-page watercolor and acrylic spreads are filled with the colors and moods of the ocean." SLJ

Garza, Carmen Lomas

Family pictures; paintings by Carmen Lomas Garza; stories by Carmen Lomas Garza; as told to Harriet Rohmer; version in Spanish, Rosalma Zubizarreta. Children's Bk. Press 1990 30p il lib bdg $19.95; pa $7.95　　**E**
1. Hispanic Americans—Fiction 2. Bilingual books—English-Spanish
ISBN 0-89239-050-6 (lib. bdg.); 0-89239-108-1 (pa)
　　　　　　　　　　　　　　　　　LC 89-27845
Text and title page in English and Spanish
The author describes her experiences growing up in a Hispanic community in Texas
"An inspired celebration of American cultural diversity. . . . The English text is simple and reads smoothly,

Garza, Carmen Lomas—*Continued*

but it is Zubizarreta's Spanish rendition that has real verve and style. From the exquisite cut-paper images on the text pages, to the brilliant paintings, to the strong family bonds expressed in the text, Family Pictures/Cuadros de familia is a visual feast, and an aural delight." SLJ

Gauch, Patricia Lee

Christina Katerina and the time she quit the family; illustrated by Elise Primavera. Putnam 1987 unp il hardcover o.p. paperback available $5.99   E
1. Family life—Fiction
ISBN 0-698-11762-X (pa)   LC 86-18658

"It all begins on a 'perfectly good' Saturday morning when Christina Katerina, who has been unjustly accused of just about everything, changes her name to Agnes and quits on the spot. 'You go your way. We'll go ours,' announces Mildred (a k a Mother)." N Y Times Book Rev

"Primavera's spiffy watercolors pulse with reality, and although the scenarios are at times inevitably exaggerated, no one should mind the dramatic license when the situation, in words and pictures, comes right from the heart." Booklist

Other available titles about Christina Katerina are:
Christina Katerina & the box (1971)
Christina Katerina and Fats and the Great Neighborhood War (1997)

Dance, Tanya; [illustrations by] Satomi Ichikawa; story by Patricia Lee Gauch. Philomel Bks. 1989 unp il $16.99; pa $5.99   E
1. Ballet—Fiction
ISBN 0-399-21521-2; 0-698-11378-0 (pa)
LC 88-9935

Tanya loves ballet dancing, repeating the moves she sees her older sister using when practicing for class or a recital, and soon Tanya is big enough to go to ballet class herself

"Gauch's sweet story gains strength from Ichikawa's soft watercolor paintings, which celebrate Tanya's enthusiasm with a sharp sense of how small children move. . . . A gentle, knowing book." Booklist

Other available titles about Tanya are:
Bravo Tanya (1992)
Presenting Tanya the Ugly Duckling (1999)
Tanya and Emily in a dance for two (1994)
Tanya and the magic wardrobe (1997)

Geisert, Arthur

After the flood. Houghton Mifflin 1994 32p il $16.95   E
1. Noah's ark—Fiction
ISBN 0-395-66611-2   LC 93-758

After surviving the Flood, Noah and his family settle in a sheltered valley with the animals they have saved and begin the glorious experience of repopulating the Earth

"The minimalist statements are extended in marvelously intricate, sensitively rendered, full-color etchings." Horn Book Guide

Oink. Houghton Mifflin 1991 unp il $15; pa $5.95   E
1. Pigs—Fiction 2. Stories without words
ISBN 0-395-55329-6; 0-395-74516-0 (pa)
LC 90-46123

"The only word in this book is OINK! Mother pig takes her piglets exploring but always makes certain they return with her. But one day, as she sleeps, they romp away and find themselves stranded in a tree. When mother finds them, her one OINK brings them down and they are marched back, safe but subdued." Child Book Rev Serv

"Children of all ages will love this porcine family, so appealingly etched in pale pink and black and white. The droll illustrations exude an understated hilarity." Publ Wkly

Another available title about mother pig and her piglets is:
Oink, oink (1993)

Pigs from 1 to 10. Houghton Mifflin 1992 32p il $16   E
1. Counting 2. Pigs—Fiction
ISBN 0-395-58519-8   LC 92-5097

Ten pigs go on an adventurous quest. The reader is asked to find all ten of them, and the numerals from zero to nine, in each picture

"Geisert's inventiveness knows no bounds, and his illustrations both inspire the imagination and convey a homey charm. The final page, a triumphant aggregation of pigs and numbers, is especially endearing." Publ Wkly

Pigs from A to Z. Houghton Mifflin 1986 unp il $17.95; pa $7.95   E
1. Alphabet 2. Pigs—Fiction
ISBN 0-395-38509-1; 0-395-77874-3 (pa)
LC 86-18542

Seven piglets cavort through a landscape of hidden letters as they build a tree house

"At the back of the book is a key that shows where the artist has secreted all the letters in each illustration; some are plain, some are subtle and every picture has, in addition to its principal letter, one or two from the alphabetical surroundings. . . . So 'Pigs From A to Z' succeeds as narrative, alphabet book, counting book (are all seven piglets in each etching?), puzzle book and as art." N Y Times Book Rev

Geisert, Bonnie, 1943-

Mountain town; [by] Bonnie and Arthur Geisert. Houghton Mifflin 2000 32p il $16   E
1. Mountain life 2. Cities and towns 3. West (U.S.) 4. Seasons
ISBN 0-395-95390-1   LC 99-29856

Describes a year in the present-day life of a mountain town that was founded when prospectors searching for gold arrived in the Rocky Mountains in the mid-nineteenth century

"Etchings enhanced with watercolors provide sweeping panoramas. . . . Perspectives include bird's-eye views as well as above and belowground cross sections. The present-tense text occasionally provides helpful explanations for the already-informative pictures." SLJ

Geisert, Bonnie, 1943-—*Continued*

Prairie town; [by] Bonnie and Arthur Geisert. Houghton Mifflin 1998 32p il $16　　　　**E**

1. Cities and towns 2. Middle West 3. Seasons

ISBN 0-395-85907-7　　　　LC 97-40049

Describes a year in the life of a prairie town including the effect of seasons and of economics on the ebb and flow of this agricultural community

"The text is clear and uncondescending. . . . A pleasure as social history, as Americana, and as an unusually creative use of fine illustration to convey information." Horn Book Guide

River town; [by] Bonnie and Arthur Geisert. Houghton Mifflin 1999 32p il $16　　　　**E**

1. Cities and towns 2. Rivers 3. Seasons

ISBN 0-395-90891-4　　　　LC 98-17249

Describes, in brief text and illustrations, a year in the life of a river bank town and the many changes that occur throughout the seasons

"Through a spare text and panoramic double-page spreads rich in small details, life across four seasons unfolds. . . . The full-color illustrations are exquisitely drawn in ink so that even the smallest figure is recognizable." SLJ

George, Jean Craighead, 1919-

Look to the North; a wolf pup diary; illustrated by Lucia Washburn. HarperCollins Pubs. 1997 unp il $14.95; lib bdg $15.89; pa $5.95　　　　**E**

1. Wolves—Fiction

ISBN 0-06-023641-8; 0-06-023640-X (lib bdg); 0-06-443510-5 (pa)　　　　LC 95-39162

Brief diary entries that mark the passage of the seasons introduce the events in the lives of three wolves as they grow from helpless pups to participants in their small pack's hunt

"The delicately textured acrylic paintings offer lively yet loving views of the wolves, perfectly complementing George's appealing text." Booklist

Morning, noon, and night; paintings by Wendell Minor. HarperCollins Pubs. 1999 unp il $15.95; lib bdg $15.89　　　　**E**

1. Day—Fiction 2. Animals—Fiction

ISBN 0-06-023628-0; 0-06-023629-9 (lib bdg)

LC 97-28796

Each day as the sun makes its dawn-to-dusk journey from the Eastern seaboard to the Pacific coast, the animals perform their daily activities

This offers "rhythmic, lyrical text. . . . Minor's lushly detailed paintings capture the beauty of both animals and landscape, elucidating the subtle journey the book makes from east coast to west." Horn Book Guide

Snow Bear; illustrated by Wendell Minor. Hyperion Bks. for Children 1999 unp il $15.99; lib bdg $16.99　　　　**E**

1. Polar bear—Fiction 2. Inuit—Fiction 3. Arctic regions—Fiction

ISBN 0-7868-0456-4; 0-7868-2398-4 (lib bdg)

LC 98-46388

Bessie and a polar bear cub named Snow Bear play on the ice, while her older brother and the mother bear watch to make sure that everyone is safe

"The simple, pleasing text is accompanied by luminous watercolors that faithfully record this charming (if improbable) chance meeting." SLJ

George, Lindsay Barrett

In the woods: who's been here? Greenwillow Bks. 1995 unp il $16; lib bdg $15.93; pa $4.95　　　　**E**

1. Forest animals

ISBN 0-688-12318-X; 0-688-12319-8 (lib bdg); 0-688-16163-4 (pa)　　　　LC 93-16244

A boy and girl in the autumn woods find an empty nest, a cocoon, gnawed bark, and other signs of unseen animals and their activities

"Children will be drawn to George's vivid gouache paintings, especially those depicting the animals in their natural surroundings. . . . For most childen this will be an excellent introduction to classroom nature units and the perfect prelude to a walk in the woods." Booklist

Other available titles in this series are:

Around the pond: who's been here? (1996)

Around the world: who's been here? (1999)

In the snow: who's been here? (1995)

George, William T.

Box Turtle at Long Pond; pictures by Lindsay Barrett George. Greenwillow Bks. 1989 unp il $16; lib bdg $15.89　　　　**E**

1. Turtles—Fiction

ISBN 0-688-08184-3; 0-688-08185-1 (lib bdg)

LC 88-18787

On a busy day at Long Pond, Box Turtle searches for food, basks in the sun, and escapes a raccoon

"A beautifully illustrated book that introduces a pond environment. . . . The reader learns of other plants, animals, and insects that inhabit the pond." Sci Child

Other available titles about Long Pond are:

Beaver at Long Pond (1988)

Christmas at Long Pond (1992)

Geringer, Laura

A three hat day; pictures by Arnold Lobel. Harper & Row 1985 30p il lib bdg $15.89; pa $5.95　　　　**E**

1. Hats—Fiction

ISBN 0-06-021989-0 (lib bdg); 0-06-443157-6 (pa)

LC 85-42640

This "is about R.R. Pottle the Third, an inveterate collector of hats. Wearing one at a time usually suits him, but on days when he is depressed, he wears three all at once. It is on such a day that he meets Ida, the shop clerk, and not long after, R.R. Pottle the Fourth is born—an inveterate collector of shoes." Wilson Libr Bull

"Lobel's energetic line drawings with warm, full-color washes contribute their own dignity and humor to the characters. . . . With its light touch, good pacing, and satisfying symmetry, this is a pleasing choice to read aloud." Booklist

Gershator, David

Bread is for eating; [by] David and Phillis Gershator; illustrated by Emma Shaw-Smith. Holt & Co. 1995 unp il music $15.95; pa $6.95   E
1. Bread—Fiction 2. Songs 3. Hispanic Americans—Fiction
ISBN 0-8050-3173-1; 0-8050-5798-6 (pa)

LC 94-28811

A mother "explains, poetically, how wheat is planted, grown, harvested, milled, and baked to loaves of life-giving bread. A little song, *El pan es para comer* (music included) accompanies each step in the process. Spanish and English are blended seamlessly with the graceful narrative. Shaw-Smith's heroic-style pictures, filled with rich, glowing reds and yellows, are crammed with disparate details." SLJ

Gerstein, Mordicai, 1935-

The mountains of Tibet. Harper & Row 1987 unp il hardcover o.p. paperback available $6.95

E

1. Reincarnation—Fiction 2. Tibet (China)—Fiction
ISBN 0-06-443211-4 (pa)   LC 85-45684

The author "has created a tale of reincarnation inspired by his reading of the *Tibetan Book of the Dead*. A little boy is born in a valley high in the mountains of Tibet. . . . Looking at the stars, he dreams of visiting other worlds and seeing other countries and peoples. . . . After his death a voice offers him a chance to live another life; he chooses from the galaxies, star systems, planets, and life forms." Horn Book

"As the illustrator of his own spare text, Mr. Gerstein . . . makes tasteful allusions to Tibetan art, creating a colorful, well-balanced picture book in the classic mold. Every element complements the story or, indeed, adds to it." N Y Times Book Rev

Gibbons, Faye, 1938-

Mama and me and the Model-T; illustrations by Ted Rand. Morrow Junior Bks. 1999 unp il $16; lib bdg $15.93   E
1. Automobiles—Fiction 2. Sex role—Fiction 3. Mountain life—Fiction 4. Family life—Fiction
ISBN 0-688-15298-8; 0-688-15299-6 (lib bdg)

LC 98-31518

When Mama gets behind the wheel of the new Model-T which her husband just drove into the yard of their Georgia mountain home, she proves that she can drive a car as well as the men of the family

"Rand's delightful watercolors display the heartfelt warmth and humor of the noisy blended family." Booklist

Mountain wedding; illustrated by Ted Rand. Morrow Junior Bks. 1996 unp il $16; lib bdg $16.89   E
1. Weddings—Fiction 2. Mountain life—Fiction 3. Family life—Fiction
ISBN 0-688-11348-6; 0-688-11349-4 (lib bdg)

LC 95-18197

"Ma Searcy and Mr. Long stand before the preacher as the children, seven Longs and five Searcys, who clearly take exception to the marriage and to each other, stand in two opposing lines, prepared for battle. The children join forces, however, when a swarm of honeybees brings on a crisis. Gibbon's unassuming story of family solidarity unexpectedly achieved is splendidly augmented by Rand's funny and appealing watercolors." Horn Book Guide

Gibbons, Gail

The seasons of Arnold's apple tree. Harcourt Brace Jovanovich 1984 unp il $15; pa $6   E
1. Seasons—Fiction 2. Trees—Fiction
ISBN 0-15-271246-1; 0-15-271245-3 (pa)

LC 84-4484

Arnold enjoys his apple tree through the changing year: its springtime blossoms, the swing and tree-house it supports, its summer shade, its autumn harvest; in the winter, the tree's branches hold strings of popcorn and berries for the birds

"Two major concepts emerge here, the first being the passage of the seasons, the second the valuable resource Arnold has in his apple tree. . . . Gibbons' crisp pictures ensure that the multifaceted lesson is explicit, bright and cheery." Booklist

Giff, Patricia Reilly

Watch out, Ronald Morgan! illustrated by Susanna Natti. Viking Kestrel 1985 24p il hardcover o.p. paperback available $5.99   E
1. Eyeglasses—Fiction 2. School stories
ISBN 0-14-050638-1 (pa)   LC 84-19623

Ronald has many humorous mishaps until he gets a pair of eyeglasses. Includes a note for adults about children's eye problems

"Told in a forthright manner but with appreciation for children's candor, the book's dialogue rings true with catchy humor. . . . Natti's illustrations show the characters to be bright, colorful informal figures who move with the text." SLJ

Other available titles about Ronald Morgan are:
Good luck, Ronald Morgan (1996)
Happy birthday, Ronald Morgan! (1986)
Ronald Morgan goes to bat (1988)
Ronald Morgan goes to camp (1995)
Today was a terrible day (1980)

Giganti, Paul, Jr.

Each orange had 8 slices; a counting book; by Paul Giganti, Jr.; pictures by Donald Crews. Greenwillow Bks. 1992 unp il $15.95; pa $5.95

E

1. Counting 2. Mathematics
ISBN 0-688-10428-2; 0-688-13985-X (pa)

LC 90-24167

This volume presents a series of statements about the illustrations: "'On my way to Grandma's I saw 2 fat cows. Each cow had 2 calves. Each calf had 4 skinny legs,' and the questions follow: 'How many fat cows . . . calves . . . legs were there in all?'" SLJ

"This bright, well-designed book challenges young children to think analytically about what's on its pages. . . . Since the objects are organized into sets and subsets, this could be used to introduce the concept of multiplication as well as counting and addition." Booklist

Giganti, Paul, Jr.—*Continued*

How many snails? a counting book; by Paul Giganti, Jr.; pictures by Donald Crews. Greenwillow Bks. 1988 unp il $15.95; lib bdg $15.89; pa $5.95   **E**
   1. Counting
   ISBN 0-688-06369-1; 0-688-06370-5 (lib bdg); 0-688-13639-7 (pa)   LC 87-26281

"Instead of inviting children to count static objects, Mr. Giganti poses a series of simple, direct questions designed to encourage youngsters to determine the often subtle differences between those objects. Donald Crews . . . concentrates here on decorating each page with objects that supply the necessary links to the text. Some of the pages—depicting a collection of motley dogs at the park or beautiful toy boats and trucks, cars and airplanes at a toy store—are a joy to look at." N Y Times Book Rev

Ginsburg, Mirra

The chick and the duckling; translated [and adapted] from the Russian of V. Suteyev; pictures by Jose & Ariane Aruego. Macmillan 1972 unp il hardcover o.p. paperback available $4.95   **E**
   1. Ducks—Fiction 2. Chickens—Fiction
   ISBN 0-689-71226-X (pa)

"The adventures of a duckling who is a leader and a chick who follows suit. When the chick decides that an aquatic life is not for him, this brief selection for reading aloud comes to a humorous conclusion." Wis Libr Bull

"The sunny simplicity of the illustrations is just right for a slight but engaging text, and they add a note of humor that is a nice foil for the bland directness of the story." Bull Cent Child Books

Good morning, chick; by Mirra Ginsburg, adapted from a story by Korney Chukovsky; pictures by Byron Barton. Greenwillow Bks. 1980 unp il lib bdg $15.89; pa $5.95   **E**
   1. Chickens—Fiction
   ISBN 0-688-84284-4 (lib bdg); 0-688-08741-8 (pa)
                   LC 80-11352

"In this simple preschool tale . . . a chick hatches out of an egg ('like this'), learns to eat worms ('like this'), is scared by a cat ('like this'), falls in a pond ('like this'), and is coddled back to fluffiness by Mom ('like this')." SLJ

"Based upon a tale by the great Russian poet and storyteller, the totally childlike picture book for the very young employs an engaging device: The text, illustrated with a bright vignette, appears on each of the left-hand pages; then, after pausing briefly and leading the eye to the right, a sentence runs to completion on the opposite page with two words contained in a large storytelling picture done in bold, brilliant color." Horn Book

Glass, Andrew

Folks call me Appleseed John. Doubleday Bks. for Young Readers 1995 unp il hardcover o.p. paperback available $6.95   **E**
   1. Appleseed, Johnny, 1774-1845—Fiction 2. Frontier and pioneer life—Fiction 3. Brothers—Fiction
   ISBN 0-440-41466-0 (pa)   LC 93-41046

A fictionalized account describing how John Chapman (Johnny Appleseed) was joined in the western Pennsylvania wilderness by his half-brother Nathaniel, who was unprepared for John's spartan lifestyle and unusual ways

"Full of understated humor, the text is readable yet retains the flavor of rural pioneer speech." Horn Book Guide

Gliori, Debi

Mr. Bear's new baby. Orchard Bks. 1999 unp il $15.95   **E**
   1. Bears—Fiction 2. Infants—Fiction
   ISBN 0-531-30152-4   LC 98-30530

Mr. and Mrs. Bear and the other forest animals despair of ever getting Baby Bear to stop crying and go to sleep, but Small Bear knows just how to solve the problem

"Watercolor illustrations with pen-and-ink details depict interesting characters with expressive faces and a house agreeably cluttered with baby paraphernalia." Horn Book Guide
Other available titles about the Bear family are:
Mr. Bear says "Are you there, Baby Bear?" (1999)
Mr. Bear to the rescue (2000)
Mr. Bear's vacation (2000)

No matter what. Harcourt Brace & Co. 1999 unp il $16   **E**
   1. Parent-child relationship—Fiction 2. Foxes—Fiction 3. Stories in rhyme
   ISBN 0-15-202061-6   LC 98-47277

Small, a little fox, seeks reassurance that Large will always provide love, no matter what

"Gliori's whimsical illustrations use warm, inviting color to invoke the same sense of emotional security as the rhyming text." Booklist

Goble, Paul

Death of the iron horse; story and illustrations by Paul Goble. Bradbury Press 1987 unp il hardcover o.p. paperback available $5.99   **E**
   1. Cheyenne Indians—Fiction 2. Railroads—Fiction
   ISBN 0-689-71686-9 (pa)   LC 85-28011

The author "has taken several accounts of the 1867 Cheyenne attack of a Union Pacific freight train . . . and combined them into a story from the Indians' viewpoint. As the Cheyenne Prophet Sweet Medicine had foretold, strange hairy people were invading the land, killing women and children and driving off the horses. Descriptions of the iron horse inspired curiosity and fear in the young braves who decided to go out and protect their village from this new menace. Keeping fairly close to actual Indian accounts, Goble presents the braves' bold attack on the train, glossing over the deaths of the train crew." SLJ

Dream wolf; story and illustrations by Paul Goble. Bradbury Press 1990 unp il $14.95; pa $5.99   **E**
   1. Native Americans—Fiction 2. Wolves—Fiction
   ISBN 0-02-736585-9; 0-689-81506-9 (pa)
                   LC 89-687

Revised edition of The friendly wolf, published 1974

Goble, Paul—*Continued*

When two Plains Indian children become lost, they are cared for and guided safely home by a friendly wolf

"*Dream Wolf* is filled with glowing imagery—the illustrations showing nightfall, the children's search for shelter and the wolf's first, dreamlike appearance are particularly riveting. Once again, Goble has captured the lives and legends of this tribe in a magnificent picture book." Publ Wkly

Godard, Alex

Mama, across the sea; adapted from the French by George Wen. Holt & Co. 2000 unp il $16.95

         E

1. Mothers—Fiction 2. Caribbean region—Fiction

ISBN 0-8050-6161-4   LC 99-10098

Although she loves the sunny island where she lives with her grandparents, Cecile longs to see her mother again

"The lives of many children whose parents must leave their homes to find economic opportunity is reflected in this tale. The rich paintings are full of details, and a folktale about a mermaid is interwoven in the story." Horn Book Guide

Godwin, Laura

Little white dog; illustrated by Dan Yaccarino. Hyperion Bks. for Children 1998 unp il $14.95; pa $5.99

         E

1. Animals—Fiction 2. Color—Fiction 3. Stories in rhyme

ISBN 0-7868-0297-9; 0-7868-1515-9 (pa)

       LC 97-21261

One by one, a series of animals disappears into the background, until, with the lights turned on, each animal searches for the next in line

"Young children can sharpen their pattern recognition skills on this virtuoso essay in graphic design." Booklist

Goldin, Barbara Diamond

The world's birthday; a Rosh Hashanah story; pictures by Jeanette Winter. Harcourt Brace Jovanovich 1990 unp il hardcover o.p. paperback available $5

         E

1. Rosh ha-Shanah—Fiction 2. Jews—Fiction

ISBN 0-15-200045-3 (pa)   LC 89-29208

"To celebrate Rosh Hashanah, the Jewish holiday commemorating the birth of the world, young Daniel wants to host a birthday party and invite the world as guest of honor." Booklist

"This is a delightful holiday story about a young child making his own personal connection to belief and ritual. Each full-page watercolor illustration is juxtaposed to a full page of text; the gentle colors and earnest, wide-eyed expressions add greatly to the strength of the text." SLJ

Golding, Kim

Counting kids. Dorling Kindersley 2000 unp il $9.95

         E

1. Counting

ISBN 0-7894-2678-1   LC 99-47084

"A rhyming text and computer-enhanced photographs of children reinforce counting from 1 to 10. . . . An enjoyable counting book for both beginning counters and the more confident." Booklist

Goodall, John S., 1908-1996

Creepy castle. Margaret K. McElderry Bks. 1998 c1975 unp il $8.95   E

1. Stories without words 2. Mice—Fiction

ISBN 0-689-82205-7   LC 97-76364

A reissue of the title first published 1975 by Atheneum

In this wordless picture book, a mouse and his lady overcome danger and escape from a deserted castle

"The story is clear, the plot sturdy, the pictures exciting and romantic. Great fun." Bull Cent Child Books

Shrewbettina's birthday. Margaret K. McElderry Bks. 1998 c1970 unp il $8.95   E

1. Stories without words 2. Shrews—Fiction 3. Mice—Fiction

ISBN 0-689-822-6-5   LC 97-76363

A reissue of the title first published 1970 in the United Kingdom; first United States edition 1971 by Harcourt

In this wordless picture book, "Shrewbettina goes marketing for her birthday party [and] her purse is snatched by a thief. A dashing young friend apprehends the villain and restores her money; and the day ends happily with a gala evening of feasting and dancing." Horn Book

"The Victorian dress and the English village setting give a quaint and pastoral flavor to the story. . . . Soft, sentimental drawings have a pastel charm, telling the tale very clearly." Bull Cent Child Books

The surprise picnic. Margaret K. McElderry Bks. 1999 c1977 unp il $8.95   E

1. Stories without words 2. Cats—Fiction

ISBN 0-689-82359-2

A reissue of the title first published 1977 by Atheneum

In this wordless picture book, a mother cat and her kittens find unexpected adventures when they picnic on a small island

"Full of charming detail." Horn Book Guide

Goode, Diane

Mama's perfect present. Dutton Children's Bks. 1996 unp il $15.99; pa $5.99   E

1. Dogs—Fiction 2. Birthdays—Fiction 3. Gifts—Fiction 4. Paris (France)—Fiction

ISBN 0-525-45493-4; 0-14-056549-3 (pa)

       LC 96-7776

As two children search the streets of Paris for the right gift for their mother's birthday, their dachshund, Zaza, creates chaos at each shop

"This is a true picture story, with the understated text serving as a straight-faced, innocent commentary on the action, which is visualized through careful manipulation of line, deft shading, and delicate hatching." Horn Book

Gramatky, Hardie, 1907-1979

Little Toot; pictures and story by Hardie Gramatky. Putnam c1939 unp il $16.99; pa $6.99

         E

1. Tugboats—Fiction

ISBN 0-399-22419-X; 0-698-11576-7 (pa)

Also available Board book edition

Gramatky, Hardie, 1907-1979—*Continued*

Story and pictures describe the early career of a saucy little tug-boat too pleased with himself to do any real work until one day when he found himself out on the ocean in a storm. Then Little Toot earned the right to be called a hero

"Mr. Gramatky tells his story with humor and enjoyment, giving, too, a genuine sense of the water front in both pictures and story." Horn Book

Gray, Libba Moore

My mama had a dancing heart; illustrated by Raúl Colón. Orchard Bks. 1995 unp il $15.95; lib bdg $16.99; pa $5.95   E
1. Dance—Fiction 2. Mother-daughter relationship—Fiction 3. Seasons—Fiction
ISBN 0-531-09470-7; 0-531-08770-0 (lib bdg); 0-531-07142-1 (pa)   LC 94-48802
"A Melanie Kroupa book"
"In spring, summer, fall and winter, a mother leads her young daughter in dancing a celebratory ballet, a hymn to the season. When the girl is older, she is a ballerina and remembers that her mother gave her a dancing heart. . . . Colón's etched watercolors in earth and muted jewel tones give the book an old-fashioned ambiance. . . . Gray's writing lends itself to reading aloud, but independent readers will also enjoy it." SLJ

Small Green Snake; pictures by Holly Meade. Orchard Bks. 1994 unp il $15.95; lib bdg $16.99; pa $5.95   E
1. Snakes—Fiction
ISBN 0-531-06844-7; 0-531-08694-1 (lib bdg); 0-531-07090-5 (pa)   LC 93-49396
Despite his mother's warning not to wander, Small Green Snake wiggles away to investigate the new sound from across the garden wall
"This is a romping, rhyming delight of a story that must be read aloud so that the many S's and the great words and catchy phrases can be fully enjoyed. The fresh and funny tornpaper collages are a perfect complement to the spirited text." SLJ

Greenberg, David

Bugs! by David T. Greenberg; illustrated by Lynn Munsinger. Little, Brown 1997 unp il $14.95   E
1. Insects—Fiction 2. Stories in rhyme
ISBN 0-316-32574-0   LC 96-23023
Celebrates the disgusting and horrible things you can do with a bunch of bugs
"These rhymes are ardently subversive. . . . Munsinger's pictures are sweetly colored, conferring a winsome giddiness on the proceedings." Horn Book Guide

Greene, Rhonda Gowler, 1955-

Barnyard song; illustrated by Robert Bender. Atheneum Bks. for Young Readers 1997 unp il $14   E
1. Domestic animals—Fiction 2. Sick—Fiction 3. Stories in rhyme
ISBN 0-689-80758-9   LC 96-1923

When the barnyard animals catch the flu, the farmer takes care of them until their usual voices return

"A playful read-aloud with a square-dance cadence and deeply saturated, warm-and-fuzzy colors." SLJ

Greenfield, Eloise, 1929-

Africa dream; illustrated by Carole Byard. Crowell 1977 unp il lib bdg $15.89; pa $5.95   E
1. Africa—Fiction
ISBN 0-690-04776-2 (lib bdg); 0-06-443277-7 (pa)   LC 77-5080
Coretta Scott King Award, 1978
"As ethereal as the title implies, this sparsely worded prose-poem relates the benign dream experience of a young child who transports her mind to 'Long-ago Africa.'" Booklist

Grandmama's joy; illustrated by Carole Byard. Philomel Bks. c1980 unp il $16.99; pa $5.99   E
1. African Americans—Fiction 2. Grandmothers—Fiction
ISBN 0-399-21064-4; 0-698-11754-9 (pa)   LC 79-11403
First published 1980 by Collins
This is the story of the relationship between Grandmama and Rhondy. Rhondy has lived with Grandmama since she "was a baby and her parents died in a car accident. Rhondy's attempts to cheer the sad woman fail, and Rhondy learns why; they must move to a cheaper home. But the girl is persistent and cheers her by reminding her of the love they share." SLJ
"This extremely gifted and sensitive writer consistently . . . illuminates key aspects of the Black experience in a way that underlines both its uniqueness and universality. . . . Carole Byard's beautiful expressive drawings match the tone of the story." Interracial Books Child Bull

Grandpa's face; illustrated by Floyd Cooper. Philomel Bks. 1988 unp il lib bdg $16.99; pa $6.99   E
1. Grandfathers—Fiction 2. Actors—Fiction
ISBN 0-399-21525-5 (lib bdg); 0-399-22106-9 (pa)   LC 87-16729
"Tamika fears that her grandfather, an actor, is incapable of loving her when she sees him practicing a cruel expression. The young girl's turmoil and its resolution are keenly felt through evocative text and striking pictures." SLJ

She come bringing me that little baby girl; illustrated by John Steptoe. Lippincott 1974 unp il hardcover o.p. paperback available $6.95   E
1. Siblings—Fiction 2. Infants—Fiction 3. African Americans—Fiction
ISBN 0-06-443296-3 (pa)
"For Kevin, who had wanted a baby brother, the arrival of his pink-shawled baby sister proved a bitter disappointment. Not only was she the wrong sex, she also cried too much, had too many wrinkles to look new, and most provoking of all she occupied everyone's attention. How he changed his opinion about his sister is developed

Greenfield, Eloise, 1929——*Continued*
in a sensitive first-person text, complemented and extended by the poignant, darkly brilliant, three-color illustrations. A familiar situation handled with rare charm, culminating in a visual and verbal paean to familial love." Horn Book

Greenstein, Elaine, 1959-
Dreaming; a countdown to sleep. Scholastic 2000 unp il $15.95   **E**
  1. Bedtime—Fiction 2. Counting
ISBN 0-439-06302-7   LC 99-25125
"Arthur A. Levine books"
A child counts down to sleep by observing the world around, from ten silent houses to one lone swan
"The illustrations—richly textured gouache overpainting of monotype prints—sit framed in the midnight blue of the text pages they face. Gentle to read aloud, pretty to look upon." Booklist

Gregory, Nan
How Smudge came; story by Nan Gregory; pictures by Ron Lightburn. Red Deer College Press; distributed by Orca Bk. Pubs. 1995 unp il o.p.; Walker & Co. paperback available $6.95   **E**
  1. Dogs—Fiction 2. Mentally handicapped—Fiction
ISBN 0-8027-7522-5 (pa)
"Northern lights books for children"
"Cindy finds a stray puppy in a snowstorm, sneaks it up to her room, and snuggles up to it in bed. . . . You respond to the universal pet story before the illustrations show that Cindy is a young woman with Down syndrome. The initial empathy is never lost. Cindy lives in a group home; it's a comfortable place, but there's no privacy and no place for her puppy. . . . Lightburn's realistic pictures in soft-tone colored pencil have the same beautiful sense of fragility, steadfastness, and connection." Booklist

Grifalconi, Ann
Tiny's hat. HarperCollins Pubs. 1999 unp il $14.95; lib bdg $14.89   **E**
  1. Blues music—Fiction 2. Father-daughter relationship—Fiction 3. African Americans—Fiction
ISBN 0-06-027654-1; 0-06-027655-X (lib bdg)
        LC 96-42555
A young girl who misses her father, a traveling blues musician, lifts her own spirits by wearing his hat and singing his songs
"Dedicated to singer Billie Holiday and containing a note about the origin of 'the blues,' this story rings with the beat and cadence of that soulful music. Grifalconi uses thick, dense background colors, overlaying them with chalky lines that give texture and dimension." SLJ

Griffith, Helen V.
Grandaddy's place; pictures by James Stevenson. Greenwillow Bks. 1987 unp il lib bdg $15.89; pa $4.95   **E**
  1. Farm life—Fiction 2. Grandfathers—Fiction
ISBN 0-688-06254-7 (lib bdg); 0-688-10491-6 (pa)
        LC 86-19573

"Janetta accompanies her mother to the country to meet her grandfather for the first time. . . . This vacation in the country seems doomed until her grandfather tells of some absolutely incredible incidents that happened to him on this very farm. . . . Imaginative, talltale humor abounds throughout the smooth, well-paced text. . . . Watercolor illustrations, executed in warm pastels, lend visual clarity, exuding warmth and satisfaction." SLJ
Other available titles about Janetta and her grandfather are:
Georgia music (1986)
Grandaddy and Janetta (1993)
Grandaddy's stars (1995)

Grossman, Bill
My little sister ate one hare; illustrated by Kevin Hawkes. Crown 1996 unp il lib bdg $18.99   **E**
  1. Counting 2. Stories in rhyme
ISBN 0-517-59601-6   LC 95-7539
"The narrator's omnivorous younger sister sucks down nine lizards, eight worms, seven polliwogs, six mice, five bats, four shrews, three ants, two snakes, and one hare ('We thought she'd throw up then and there./But she didn't') Eventually ten peas prove to be her undoing. . . . The grossness is restrained but still kid-appealing, with touches that will provoke giggles. . . . Hawkes' art sets all this dietary derring-do in a darkened theater, with Sis chowing down on stage as a wide-eyed audience looks on in horror and amazement." Bull Cent Child Books

Guarino, Deborah, 1954-
Is your mama a llama? illustrated by Steven Kellogg. Scholastic 1989 unp il $15.95; pa $5.99   **E**
  1. Llamas—Fiction 2. Animals—Fiction 3. Stories in rhyme
ISBN 0-590-41387-2; 0-590-44725-4 (pa)
        LC 87-32315
Also available Board book edition and Big book edition; Spanish language edition also available
A young llama asks his friends if their mamas are llamas and finds out, in rhyme, that their mothers are other types of animals
"The lines are clean as well as exuberant, the colors well-blended as well as bright, and the compositions uncluttered as well as appealing. An ingenious page design invites choral participation, and the ending will encourage a cozy hiatus for bed/nap time." Bull Cent Child Books

Guback, Georgia
Luka's quilt. Greenwillow Bks. 1994 unp il $14.95; lib bdg $15   **E**
  1. Quilts—Fiction 2. Grandmothers—Fiction 3. Hawaii—Fiction
ISBN 0-688-12154-3; 0-688-12155-1 (lib bdg)
        LC 93-12241
When Luka's grandmother makes a traditional Hawaiian quilt for her, she and Luka disagree over the colors it should include
"Eye-catching collages of brightly painted papers, the

Guback, Georgia—*Continued*

illustrations express the characters' emotions and show a delight in the Hawaiian landscape and traditions. . . . An involving story that's all the more satisfying because the ending offers no mere emotional patch up but a real solution." Booklist

Guy, Ginger Foglesong

Fiesta! pictures by Rene King Moreno. Greenwillow Bks. 1996 unp il $15.95   **E**
1. Parties—Fiction 2. Counting 3. Bilingual books—English-Spanish
ISBN 0-688-14331-8   LC 95-35848
"Three children begin with *una canasta* (one basket) and proceed to fill it with scrumptious candies, trinkets, and toys in preparation for a Mexican fiesta. . . . A simple bilingual text provides numbers in English and Spanish. The soft-edged full-color illustrations done in pencils, pastels, and watercolors have a subtle folkloric quality." SLJ

Haas, Jessie

Hurry! pictures by Jos. A. Smith. Greenwillow Bks. 2000 unp il $15.95   **E**
1. Grandparents—Fiction 2. Farm life—Fiction
ISBN 0-688-16889-2   LC 99-30706
Nora helps her grandparents get the hay in before a rainstorm ruins the crop
"The text is filled with rich, sensory descriptions and brief, lyrical sentences that convey the smells, sounds, and rhythms of the task." Booklist

Sugaring; pictures by Jos. A. Smith. Greenwillow Bks. 1996 unp il $15.95   **E**
1. Maple sugar—Fiction 2. Grandfathers—Fiction 3. Horses—Fiction
ISBN 0-688-14200-1   LC 95-38139
Nora wants to find a way to give the horses a special treat for helping her grandfather and her gather sap to make maple syrup
"The realistic watercolor illustrations effectively capture the scenes; color and texture are skillfully used to depict the cold, hard job of gathering the sap and the hot steamy atmosphere of the sugar house."

Hader, Berta, 1891-1976

The big snow. Macmillan 1948 unp il $17; pa $6.95   **E**
1. Animals 2. Winter
ISBN 0-02-737910-8; 0-02-043300-X (pa)
Awarded the Caldecott Medal, 1949
This book shows "the birds and animals which come for the food put out by an old couple after a big snow." Hodges. Books for Elem Sch Libr

Hall, Donald, 1928-

Lucy's Christmas; written by Donald Hall; illustrated by Michael McCurdy. Browndeer Press; Harcourt Brace Jovanovich 1994 unp il $14.95; pa $7   **E**
1. Christmas—Fiction 2. Gifts—Fiction
ISBN 0-15-276870-X; 0-15-201943-X (pa)
LC 92-46292

"A charming look back at an early-twentieth-century Christmas, when gifts were handmade. The story follows Lucy and her family through the snowy days of paper chain and calendar construction, jars of homemade applesauce, and the popcorn and ribbon candy gifts to be distributed at the church. The colored scratchboard illustrations imbue the scenes with warmth and lively family activity." Horn Book Guide

Ox-cart man; pictures by Barbara Cooney. Viking 1979 unp il $16.99; pa $6.99   **E**
1. New England—Fiction
ISBN 0-670-53328-9; 0-14-050441-9 (pa)
LC 79-14466
Awarded the Caldecott Medal, 1980
"It is fall and a farmer loads a cart with the year's produce, journeys to market, sells, buys, and returns to his family to begin the year's work anew. The journey, and the ensuing year, unfold at a stately pace against the rich 19th-century New England backdrop alive with the subtly changing colors and activities of the succeeding seasons." SLJ
"The stunning combination of text and illustrations, suggesting early American paintings on wood, depict the countryside through which [the farmer] travels, the jostle of the marketplace, and the homely warmth of family life." Horn Book

Hall, Jacque

What does the rabbit say? illustrated by Reg Cartwright. Doubleday Bks. for Young Readers 2000 unp il $15.95   **E**
1. Animals—Fiction 2. Rabbits—Fiction 3. Stories in rhyme
ISBN 0-385-32552-5   LC 98-44375
Rhyming text presents the sounds made by various animals, from quacking ducks to buzzing bees, and wonders what the rabbit says
"Children will enjoy quacking with the ducks, growling with the bear, and hissing with the snake. Cartwright's stylized illustrations done in deeply saturated colors add interest and action to the merry text." SLJ

Hall, Zoe, 1957-

It's pumpkin time! illustrated by Shari Halpern. Blue Sky Press (NY) 1994 unp il $14.95   **E**
1. Pumpkin—Fiction 2. Halloween—Fiction 3. Gardening—Fiction
ISBN 0-590-47833-8   LC 93-35909
A sister and brother plant and tend their own pumpkin patch so they will have jack-o-lanterns for Halloween
"Painted paper collages accompany a simple, but effective, story." Child Book Rev Serv

The surprise garden; illustrated by Shari Halpern. Blue Sky Press (NY) 1998 unp il $15.95   **E**
1. Gardens—Fiction 2. Seeds—Fiction 3. Vegetables—Fiction
ISBN 0-590-10075-0   LC 97-9735
After sowing unmarked seeds, three youngsters wait expectantly for their garden to grow
This is a "charming picture book, which is as informa-

Hall, Zoe, 1957——*Continued*
tive as it is appealing. . . . Halpern's collages are a true delight: the cut-paper shapes are crisp and bright, and the clever use of perspective makes every page different." Booklist

Hamanaka, Sheila
All the colors of the earth. Morrow Junior Bks. 1994 unp il $16; lib bdg $15.89; pa $4.95   **E**
ISBN 0-688-11131-9; 0-688-11132-7 (lib bdg); 0-688-17062-5 (pa)   LC 93-27118
Reveals in verse that despite outward differences children everywhere are essentially the same and all are lovable
"A poetic picture book and an exemplary work of art. . . . Hamanaka's oil paintings are all double-page spreads filled with the colors of earth, sky, and water, and the texture of the artist's canvas shines through. The text is arranged in undulant waves across each painting." SLJ

I look like a girl. Morrow Junior Bks. 1999 unp il $16; lib bdg $15.93   **E**
1. Animals—Fiction 2. Stories in rhyme
ISBN 0-688-14625-2; 0-688-14626-0 (lib bdg)   LC 98-44723
In her imagination, a young girl assumes many shapes and forms, from dolphin and condor to wolf and jaguar
"The lush watercolor illustrations are so vibrant they'll draw children right into the fantasy game." Booklist

Harper, Dan, 1963-
Telling time with Big Mama Cat; illustrated by Barry Moser and Cara Moser. Harcourt Brace & Co. 1998 unp il $15   **E**
1. Time—Fiction 2. Clocks and watches—Fiction 3. Cats—Fiction
ISBN 0-15-201738-0   LC 97-18952
A cat describes her activities at various times throughout the day from morning to night. Features a clock with movable hands
"The simple, consistent arrangement of text and pictures on each page gently frames the humor and perfectly captures the everyday dramas of naptime and tea parties." SLJ

Harper, Isabelle
Our new puppy; illustrated by Barry Moser. Blue Sky Press (NY) 1996 unp il $14.95   **E**
1. Dogs—Fiction
ISBN 0-590-56926-0   LC 95-26168
When the puppy Floyd joins the family, Eliza and Isabelle see how Rosie the family dog reacts and learn what it is like having and being a younger sibling
"Slyly humorous, well-crafted, and well-placed watercolors from unique perspectives complement the understated, highly recognizable personalities presented in the straightforward text." SLJ

Harris, Robie H.
Happy birth day! illustrated by Michael Emberley. Candlewick Press 1996 unp il $17.99   **E**
1. Childbirth—Fiction 2. Infants—Fiction
ISBN 1-56402-424-5   LC 95-34547

A mother tells her child about its first day of life from the moment of birth through the end of the birth day
"The description of the infant's first sounds and actions is gentle and poetic. Emberley's illustrations in pencil and pastels fill the oversized pages with soft-focused, cozy colors and true-to-life detail." SLJ

Hartman, Gail
As the crow flies; a first book of maps; illustrated by Harvey Stevenson. Bradbury Press 1991 32p il maps hardcover o.p. paperback available $5.99   **E**
1. Animals—Fiction 2. Maps—Fiction
ISBN 0-689-71762-8 (pa)   LC 90-33982
"Simple words and pictures describe the travels of an eagle, a rabbit, a crow, a police horse, a seagull, and the moon. A pictorial map for each animal is given; all maps are joined in 'The Big Map' at the end." SLJ
"Stevenson's bright pen-and-ink with watercolor illustrations contain many interesting details, yet never seem overcluttered. . . . This is an attractive picture book that should find a niche in story hours and classrooms." Booklist

Hautzig, Deborah, 1956-
The nutcracker ballet; retold by Deborah Hautzig; illustrated by Carolyn Ewing. Random House 1992 48p il hardcover o.p. paperback available $3.99   **E**
1. Fairy tales
ISBN 0-679-82385-9 (pa)   LC 92-3320
"Step into reading"
A little girl helps break the spell on her toy nutcracker and changes him into a handsome prince
"Hautzig retells the story of *The Nutcracker,* concentrating on the narrative content of the first act. . . . The simple vocabulary makes this edition accessible to beginning readers; bright watercolor artwork adds an immediate appeal." Booklist

Havill, Juanita
Jamaica's find; illustrations by Anne Sibley O'Brien. Houghton Mifflin 1986 32p il $16; pa $5.95   **E**
1. African Americans—Fiction 2. Toys—Fiction
ISBN 0-395-39376-0; 0-395-45357-7 (pa)   LC 85-14542
Also available with Audiobook; Spanish language edition also available
"When Jamaica discovers a raggedy stuffed dog at the park, she decides to take it home. Her family's reaction is lukewarm at best . . . and she broods over her mother's suggestion that she return it to the park desk. Reluctantly, she does. Just after that, Jamaica encounters a little girl named Kristin, who has come to search for her missing toy dog." Booklist
"This is a pleasant picture book with warm, expressive pictures and an appealing story line that encourages values clarification." Interracial Books Child Bull
Other available titles about Jamaica are:
Jamaica and Brianna (1993)
Jamaica and the substitute teacher (1999)
Jamaica tag-along (1989)
Jamaica's blue marker (1995)

Hayes, Joe, 1945-

A spoon for every bite; illustrated by Rebecca Leer. Orchard Bks. 1996 unp il $16.95; lib bdg $17.99; pa $5.95   E

1. Wealth—Fiction 2. Hispanic Americans—Fiction

ISBN 0-531-09499-5; 0-531-08799-9 (lib bdg); 0-531-07143-X (pa)   LC 95-22019

"Hayes combines two themes from Southwestern Hispanic tradition—rich and poor *compadres*, and the tortilla as an eating utensil—into a humorous tale in which a poor couple teaches their boastful neighbor a lesson. . . . Leer complements the lively text with pastel illustrations in rich and lustrous tones reminiscent of oil paintings." Bull Cent Child Books

Hayes, Sarah

Eat up, Gemma; written by Sarah Hayes; illustrated by Jan Ormerod. Lothrop, Lee & Shepard Bks. 1988 unp il lib bdg $16; pa $5.95   E

1. Infants—Fiction 2. African Americans—Fiction

ISBN 0-688-08149-5 (lib bdg); 0-688-13638-9 (pa)   LC 87-36205

Baby Gemma refuses to eat, throwing her breakfast on the floor and squashing her grapes, until her brother gets an inspired idea

"Narrated from the perspective of an adoring older brother, the story is indeed one that rings familiar to most families. . . . Ormerod's bold and vibrant watercolors present a warm and loving portrait of a black family." Horn Book

Hazen, Barbara Shook, 1930-

Digby; story by Barbara Shook Hazen; pictures by Barbara J. Phillips-Duke. HarperCollins Pubs. 1996 32p il $14.95; lib bdg $15.89; pa $3.95   E

1. Dogs—Fiction 2. Old age—Fiction

ISBN 0-06-026253-2; 0-06-026254-0 (lib bdg); 0-06-444239-X (pa)   LC 95-1689

"An I can read book"

"A boy wants the family dog to play ball, but his big sister explains that Digby is too old now to run and catch. . . . The story of aging and of time passing is told in very simple conversation . . . and the bright contemporary pictures show the bond between the African American brother and sister and their beloved pet." Booklist

Hearne, Betsy Gould

Seven brave women; illustrated by Bethanne Andersen. Greenwillow Bks. 1997 unp il $15; lib bdg $14.93   E

1. Genealogy—Fiction 2. Courage—Fiction 3. Women—Fiction

ISBN 0-688-14502-7; 0-688-14503-5 (lib bdg)   LC 96-10414

"In this picture book divided into eight brief chapters, a young girl narrates the history of seven generations of brave women in her family, ending with her resolve to make history in her own way." Bull Cent Child Books

"Hearne's smooth writing style is suited to the succinct narrative; her carefully selected details help bring the past to life. . . . Andersen . . . has created oil paintings full of color, light, and movement." SLJ

Heide, Florence Parry, 1919-

The day of Ahmed's secret; [by] Florence Parry Heide & Judith Heide Gilliland; illustrated by Ted Lewin. Lothrop, Lee & Shepard Bks. 1990 unp il hardcover o.p. paperback available $5.95   E

1. Cairo (Egypt)—Fiction

ISBN 0-688-14023-8 (pa)   LC 90-52694

"Ahmed has monumental news to share with his family, but first he must complete the age-old duties of a butagaz boy, delivering cooking gas to customers all over Cairo. The juxtaposition of old and new is a repeated theme in Heide and Gilliland's thoughtful story of a young boy living in the bustling metropolis surrounded by thousand-year-old walls and buildings. . . . Enhanced by Lewin's distinguished photorealistic watercolors, the sights, sounds, and smells of the exotic setting come to life. . . . At home at last, surrounded by his loving family, Ahmed demostrates his newly acquired facility, proudly writing his name in Arabic." SLJ

Sami and the time of the troubles; [by] Florence Parry Heide & Judith Heide Gilliland; illustrated by Ted Lewin. Clarion Bks. 1992 unp il $16; pa $6.95   E

1. Family life—Fiction 2. Lebanon—Fiction

ISBN 0-395-55964-2; 0-395-72085-0 (pa)   LC 91-14343

A ten-year-old Lebanese boy in Beirut goes to school, helps his mother with chores, plays with his friends, and lives with his family in a basement shelter when bombings occur and fighting begins on his street

"Three marvelously talented collaborators offer a powerful, poignant book. Heide and Gilliland's lyrically written, haunting story makes clear that war threatens not only physical existence but affects the human spirit as well. Lewin's watercolor illustrations capture contemporary Beirut with stunning clarity and drama." SLJ

Heine, Helme

Friends; written and illustrated by Helme Heine. Atheneum Pubs. 1982 unp il lib bdg $16; pa $5.99   E

1. Friendship—Fiction 2. Animals—Fiction

ISBN 0-689-50256-7 (lib bdg); 0-689-71083-6 (pa)   LC 82-45313

"A Margaret K. McElderry book"

This is an "account of the friendship between three animals, a mouse, a cock and a pig. . . . They do everything together like true friends should, but at bedtime, having all tried in turn the mousehole, the pigsty and the perch, they decide that they are after all quite different, and each sets off to his own bed to dream happy dreams of one another." Times Lit Suppl

"Heine's visual imagination makes the images extraordinary. . . . Watercolors take full advantage of the white page. The double-page scene at dusk with silhouetted cottage and tree is a fine restful transition from the frenetic daytime fun to the final funny efforts to bed down." SLJ

Another available title about the friends is:

Friends go adventuring (1995)

Heine, Helme—Continued

The most wonderful egg in the world; written and illustrated by Helme Heine. Atheneum Pubs. 1983 unp il hardcover o.p. paperback available $5.99   E
1. Chickens—Fiction
ISBN 0-689-71117-4 (pa)   LC 82-49350
"A Margaret K. McElderry book"

"Three proud hens—Dotty, with the most beautiful feathers; Stalky, with the most beautiful legs; and Plumy, with the most beautiful crest—quarrel about which one of them is the most beautiful." Horn Book

"The message here—'What you can do is more important than what you look like'—is conveyed simply but effectively, with the theme of uniqueness and individuality nicely underplayed. The watercolor illustrations, mostly in pale tones with much open white space, are full of fun. . . . Children will be rewarded with new, humorous details on each rereading." SLJ

Helldorfer, Mary Claire, 1954-

Hog music; by M. C. Helldorfer; illustrated by S. D. Schindler. Viking 2000 unp il $15.99   E
1. Frontier and pioneer life—Fiction 2. Voyages and travels—Fiction 3. Gifts—Fiction
ISBN 0-670-87182-6   LC 99-42059
Travelers along the National Road help make sure that the birthday gift that Lucy's great aunt has sent makes it all the way from Maryland to her family's farm in Illinois

"The period story gives a sense of nineteenth-century life—from its curious conveyances to the sense of adventure. While simplistic at times, the folk-art-like illustrations provide a homey, comfortable atmosphere." Horn Book Guide

Phoebe and the River Flute; by M. C. Helldorfer; illustrated by Paul Hess. Doubleday Bks. for Young Readers 2000 unp il $15.95   E
1. Fairy tales
ISBN 0-385-32338-7   LC 00-699574
"When Phoebe, keeper of the royal birds, is sent to capture the rare River Flute, she catches the bird but then releases it so it's free to return. Likewise, when she returns empty-handed, the kind prince, though he loves Phoebe, gives her the same choice." Horn Book Guide
"This modern fairy tale is a charming fantasy. The text is both crisp and dreamy. . . . Hess's stunning, deeply colored stylized drawings are a fine counterpoint to this symbolic story." SLJ

Henderson, Kathy

The baby dances; illustrated by Tony Kerins. Candlewick Press 1999 unp il $15.99   E
1. Infants—Fiction 2. Growth—Fiction
ISBN 0-7636-0374-0   LC 98-23596
Recounts the development of a baby, from birth to rolling over, crawling, standing, and finally walking
"Henderson's well-crafted text is rhythmic and full of evocative images. . . . Kerins's full-page pastel illustrations are remarkably realistic and glow with warmth and tenderness." SLJ

Henkes, Kevin, 1960-

Chester's way. Greenwillow Bks. 1988 unp il $15.95; lib bdg $15.89; pa $5.95   E
1. Mice—Fiction
ISBN 0-688-07607-6; 0-688-07608-4 (lib bdg);
0-688-15472-7 (pa)   LC 87-14882
The mice Chester and Wilson share the exact way of doing things, until Lilly moves into the neighborhood and shows them that new ways can be just as good
"Henkes' charming cartoons are drawn with pen-and-ink, washed over with cheerful watercolors. They give witty expressions to his characters." SLJ

Chrysanthemum. Greenwillow Bks. 1991 unp il $15.95; lib bdg $15.89; pa $5.95   E
1. Personal names—Fiction 2. School stories 3. Mice—Fiction
ISBN 0-688-09699-9; 0-688-09700-6 (lib bdg);
0-688-814732-1 (pa)   LC 90-39803
Also available Spanish language edition
Chrysanthemum, a mouse, loves her name, until she starts going to school and the other children make fun of it
"The text, precise and evocative, uses contrast and repetition to achieve rhythm and balance; the illustrations are forthright yet delicately colored, remarkable for the agility of the fine line which creates setting and characters." Horn Book

Circle dogs; illustrated by Dan Yaccarino. Greenwillow Bks. 1998 unp il $15; lib bdg $14.93; pa $5.95   E
1. Dogs—Fiction 2. Shape—Fiction
ISBN 0-688-15446-8; 0-688-15447-6 (lib bdg);
0-06-443757-4 (pa)   LC 97-33037
Circle dogs live in a square house with a square yard, eat circle snacks, and dig circle holes
"The text is simple, almost primer-like, with lots of onomatopoeic words. . . . The lively gouache paintings in large flat areas of color have a retro look." SLJ

Jessica. Greenwillow Bks. 1989 unp il $15.95; lib bdg $15.89; pa $5.95   E
1. Imaginary playmates—Fiction
ISBN 0-688-07829-X; 0-688-07830-3 (lib bdg);
0-688-15847-1 (pa)   LC 87-38087
"A shy preschooler insists that her friend Jessica is not imaginary—and, in the end, she's absolutely correct. Henkes' depiction of play-alone and play-together time brims with buoyant camaraderie in this upbeat story of friendship fulfilled." SLJ

Julius, the baby of the world. Greenwillow Bks. 1990 unp il $15.95; lib bdg $15.89; pa $5.95
E
1. Mice—Fiction
ISBN 0-688-08943-7; 0-688-08944-5 (lib bdg);
0-688-14388-1 (pa)   LC 88-34904
Also available Spanish language edition
Lilly, the girl mouse who debuted in Chester's way "may still be the queen of the world, but her new brother 'Julius is the baby of the world.' Suffering from a severe case of sibling-itis, she warns pregnant strangers: 'You will live to regret that bump under your dress.' While her understanding parents shower her with 'compliments

Henkes, Kevin, 1960——*Continued*
and praise and niceties of all shapes and sizes,' nothing
works until snooty Cousin Garland comes for a visit."
Booklist

"Magically, Henkes conveys a world of expressions
and a wide range of complex emotions with a mere line
or two upon the engaging mousey faces of Lilly and her
family. A reassuring, funny book for all young children
who suffer from new-sibling syndrome." SLJ

Lilly's purple plastic purse. Greenwillow Bks.
1996 unp il $14.95; lib bdg $14.89   E
1. Mice—Fiction 2. School stories
ISBN 0-688-12897-1; 0-688-12898-X (lib bdg)
                                      LC 95-25085
"Lilly loves everything about school. . . . But most of
all, she loves her teacher, Mr. Slinger. . . . The little
mouse will do anything for him—until he refuses to allow her to interrupt lessons to show the class her new
movie-star sunglasses, three shiny quarters, and purple
plastic purse. Seething with anger, she writes a mean story about him and places it in his book bag at the end of
the day. . . . Rich vocabulary and just the right amount
of repetition fuse perfectly with the watercolor and
black-pen illustrations. . . . Clever dialogue and other
funny details will keep readers looking and laughing."
SLJ

Oh! words by Kevin Henkes; pictures by Laura
Dronzek. Greenwillow Bks. 1999 unp il $15; lib
bdg $14.89   E
1. Snow—Fiction 2. Animals—Fiction
ISBN 0-688-17053-6; 0-688-17054-4 (lib bdg)
                                      LC 98-51890
The morning after a snowfall finds animals and children playing
"Imbued with a soft, fuzzy quality, the full-color
acrylic illustrations evoke the haziness of falling snow,
and the illustrator's choice of blue and white as dominant
colors is gently soothing. A winter book that's sure to
please." SLJ

Owen. Greenwillow Bks. 1993 unp il $15.96;
lib bdg $15.89   E
1. Blankets—Fiction
ISBN 0-688-11449-0; 0-688-11450-4 (lib bdg)
                                      LC 92-30084
Also available Spanish language edition
A Caldecott Medal honor book, 1994
Owen's parents try to get him to give up his favorite
blanket before he starts school, but when their efforts
fail, they come up with a solution that makes everyone
happy
This is "imbued with Henkes's characteristically understated humor, spry text and brightly hued watercolor-
and-ink pictures." Publ Wkly

Sheila Rae, the brave. Greenwillow Bks. 1987
unp il $16; lib bdg $15.89; pa $5.95   E
1. Mice—Fiction
ISBN 0-688-07155-4; 0-688-07156-2 (lib bdg);
0-688-14738-0 (pa)   LC 86-25761
"A mouse both boastful and fearless, Sheila Rae decides to go home from school by taking a new route. She
walks backwards with her eyes closed, growls at dogs
and cats, climbs trees, turns new corners and crosses dif-

ferent streets—and ends up in the middle of unfamiliar
territory." Publ Wkly
"Bouncy watercolors in spring-like colors with some
pen-and-ink detailing highlight Sheila Rae's bravado in
an engaging and amusing way, and Henkes provides
Sheila Rae, Louise, and their school friends with highly
expressive faces." SLJ

Wemberly worried. Greenwillow Bks. 2000 unp
il $15.95; lib bdg $15.89   E
1. School stories 2. Mice—Fiction
ISBN 0-688-17027-7; 0-688-17028-5 (lib bdg)
                                      LC 99-34341
A mouse named Wemberly, who worries about everything, finds that she has a whole list of things to worry
about when she faces the first day of nursery school
The author combines "good storytelling, careful characterization, and wonderfully expressive artwork to create
an entertaining and reassuring picture book that addresses
a common concern." SLJ

Herman, Charlotte
How Yussel caught the gefilte fish; a Shabbos
story; illustrated by Katya Krenina. Dutton
Children's Bks. 1999 unp il $16.99   E
1. Jews—Fiction 2. Sabbath—Fiction 3. Family
life—Fiction
ISBN 0-525-45449-7   LC 97-3792
When he goes fishing with his father for the first time,
Yussel hopes to catch the gefilte fish for his family's
Shabbos dinner, but instead he catches a carp, a trout,
and a pike
"The deep glowing colors . . . evoke a sense of
warmth that perfectly matches the feeling of the story."
Booklist

Herold, Maggie Rugg
A very important day; illustrated by Catherine
Stock. Morrow Junior Bks. 1995 unp il $16.95; lib
bdg $15.93   E
1. Naturalization—Fiction 2. Immigration and emigration—Fiction 3. New York (N.Y.)—Fiction
ISBN 0-688-13065-8; 0-688-13066-6 (lib bdg)
                                      LC 94-16647
Two-hundred nineteen people from thirty-two different
countries make their way to downtown New York in a
snowstorm to be sworn in as citizens of the United
States
"After the first quiet, gray-tone painting, which pictures a solitary face staring out at a city dawn dotted
with snowflakes, this book bursts forth in a riot of color
and activity. . . . A glossary supplies guidance for pronouncing names, and a clear, nicely detailed overview of
the process of naturalization rounds things out. Pictures
and story combine to make the joy of the day conta-
gious." Booklist

Herriot, James
Moses the kitten; illustrated by Peter Barrett. St.
Martin's Press 1984 unp il hardcover o.p.
paperback available $6.95   E
1. Cats—Fiction 2. Farm life—Fiction
ISBN 0-312-06419-5 (pa)   LC 84-50930

Herriot, James—*Continued*

"Found by Herriot among the frozen rushes, the kitten was quickly adopted by a farm family, warmed back to liveliness in an [open] oven, and named Moses. What the veterinarian-author found, on his next visit, was that Moses had inserted himself into a litter of piglets and been accepted as one of the family, both at feeding times and at sleep-in-a-heap naptime." Bull Cent Child Books

"Patience, kindness and caring are the dominant themes here, and the storyline and characterizations never deviate from this. The text is complemented throughout with appropriate, well-placed soft pastel watercolors [depicting] in detail the northern English countryside." SLJ

Hesse, Karen

Come on, rain! pictures by Jon J. Muth. Scholastic Press 1999 unp il $15.95   E
1. Rain—Fiction 2. Summer—Fiction
ISBN 0-590-33125-6   LC 98-11575
A young girl eagerly awaits a coming rainstorm to bring relief from the oppressive summer heat

"Beautifully drafted watercolor paintings illustrate the lyrical text, creating a wonderful sense of atmosphere." Horn Book Guide

Lester's dog; illustrated by Nancy Carpenter. Crown 1993 unp il $16   E
1. Dogs—Fiction 2. Friendship—Fiction 3. Cats—Fiction
ISBN 0-517-58357-7   LC 92-27674
This is a "story about a boy who, with the help of a deaf friend, conquers his fear of a neighbor's dog that bit him years earlier. In the process, he saves a kitten and befriends an elderly, recently widowed man. Carpenter's pictures give vivid life to Hesse's gripping story, set in a 1940s neighborhood. The prose reverberates with powerful words." SLJ

Hest, Amy

Gabby growing up; illustrated by Amy Schwartz. Simon & Schuster Bks. for Young Readers 1998 unp il $16   E
1. Grandfathers—Fiction 2. Birthdays—Fiction
ISBN 0-689-80573-X   LC 96-53145
On her way to meet Grandpa in Central Park to go ice skating on his birthday, Gabby gets a new grown-up looking haircut

"Schwartz's artwork, done in gouache and colored pencil, beautifully captures the alternating boldness and shyness of a young girl coming into her own." Booklist

In the rain with Baby Duck; illustrated by Jill Barton. Candlewick Press 1995 unp il $16.99; pa $5.99   E
1. Rain—Fiction 2. Ducks—Fiction
ISBN 1-56402-532-2; 0-7636-0697-9 (pa)
      LC 94-48929
"Mr. and Mrs. Duck can't understand why Baby Duck doesn't like walking in the rain. Grandpa Duck understands though and gets out an umbrella and a pair of red boots just Baby Duck's size, that once belonged to Mrs. Duck." Child Book Rev Serv

"Hest's delightful text exudes charm, and beginning readers will find the large type and simple vocabulary a helpful bonus. Perfect for a rainy-day story time." Booklist

Other titles about Baby Duck are:
Baby Duck and the bad eyeglasses (1996)
Off to school, Baby Duck (1999)
You're the boss, Baby Duck (1997)

Mabel dancing; illustrated by Christine Davenier. Candlewick Press 2000 unp il $15.99
      E
1. Bedtime—Fiction 2. Dance—Fiction 3. Parties—Fiction
ISBN 0-7636-0746-0   LC 99-34807
Mabel doesn't want to go to sleep while Mama and Papa are having a dance party downstairs

"Calm, rhythmic prose combined with swirly, muted watercolor and ink illustrations establish the story's mood and capture Mabel's lively spirit." Horn Book Guide

Nana's birthday party; pictures by Amy Schwartz. Morrow Junior Bks. 1993 unp il $15.95; lib bdg $14.93   E
1. Grandmothers—Fiction 2. Birthdays—Fiction 3. Cousins—Fiction
ISBN 0-688-07497-9; 0-688-07498-7 (lib bdg)
      LC 92-10260
Maggie who writes stories, and her cousin Brette, who paints pictures, combine their talents to create the grandest present ever for their grandmother Nana's birthday.

"Schwartz's fluid yet exuberant watercolors perfectly capture the cousins—as friends and as competitors—in all their differences and make a beautiful show of Nana's cozy apartment, busy with color and pattern. . . . A warm, wise story about cousins that captures continuity and affection across generations." Booklist

The purple coat; pictures by Amy Schwartz. Four Winds Press 1986 unp il $14.95; pa $5.99
      E
1. Coats—Fiction 2. Grandfathers—Fiction
ISBN 0-02-743640-3; 0-689-71634-6 (pa)
      LC 85-29186
"Gabrielle has always gotten a navy coat in the fall, but, this year, to Mama's dismay, she yearns for a purple one. Grandpa, their favorite tailor, discovers a solution to please all." Child Book Rev Serv

"The artwork is full color, and the deep shades and vibrant colors (especially that purple) are arresting. The numerous details and patternings catch the eye and make for pictures that can be looked at over and over; each time the story's satisfying conclusion rings sweetly true." Booklist

When Jessie came across the sea; illustrated by P.J. Lynch. Candlewick Press 1997 unp il $16.99
      E
1. Immigration and emigration—Fiction 2. Jews—Fiction 3. Grandmothers—Fiction
ISBN 0-7636-0094-6   LC 97-6250
A thirteen-year-old Jewish orphan reluctantly leaves her grandmother and immigrates to New York City, where she works for three years sewing lace and earning money to bring Grandmother to the United States, too

"The elements of the plot fall neatly into place, and Hest communicates the heroine's courage and maturity convincingly and without fanfare. The subtle, emotional exposition is enriched by Lynch's . . . dramatically charged watercolor and gouache illustrations." Publ Wkly

Heyward, DuBose, 1885-1940

The country bunny and the little gold shoes; as told to Jenifer; pictures by Marjorie Flack. Houghton Mifflin 1939 unp il lib bdg $15; pa $5.95   E

1. Rabbits—Fiction 2. Easter—Fiction
ISBN 0-395-15990-3 (lib bdg); 0-395-18557-2 (pa)

Also available with Audiobook
This is an Easter story for young readers which grew out of a story the author has told and retold to his young daughter. It is of the little country rabbit who wanted to become one of the five Easter bunnies, and how she managed to realize her ambition
"It is really imaginative and well written. . . . The colored pictures are just right too." New Yorker

High, Linda Oatman

Barn savers; illustrated by Ted Lewin. Boyds Mills Press 1999 unp il $15.95   E
1. Barns—Fiction
ISBN 1-56397-403-7
"Waking before dawn, a boy accompanies his father to an old barn. Their job is to save the barn from the bulldozers, taking it apart board by board so that the parts can be sold. . . . The illustrations, whether moonlit or washed by brilliant sunshine, reflect the dignity of the plain-spoken, first-person text." Booklist

Hill, Elizabeth Starr

Evan's corner; story by Elizabeth Starr Hill; pictures by Sandra Speidel. Viking 1991 unp il hardcover o.p. paperback available $5.99   E
1. Family life—Fiction 2. African Americans—Fiction
ISBN 0-14-054406-2 (pa)   LC 89-24839
A revised and newly illustrated edition of the title first published 1967 by Holt, Rinehart and Winston
Needing a place to call his own, Evan is thrilled when his mother points out that their crowded apartment has eight corners, one for each family member
"The new illustrations are bright and suit the text." Horn Book

Hindley, Judy

The big red bus; illustrated by William Benedict. Candlewick Press 1995 unp il hardcover o.p. paperback available $5.99   E
1. Vehicles—Fiction 2. Roads—Fiction
ISBN 0-7636-1250-2 (pa)   LC 94-48928
"A traffic jam starts when a bus hits a huge pothole, holding up a long series of vehicles . . . until the bus is pulled out and the steamroller plugs the hole." Child Book Rev Serv
"The action is simple, sequential, and quick paced. Benedict's jaunty ink lines, flat gouache colors, and bold sense of design, including a clever fold-out section, create an energetic array of agreeable characters and vehicles." SLJ

Eyes, nose, fingers and toes; a first book about you; illustrated by Brita Granström. Candlewick Press 1999 unp il $15.99   E
1. Stories in rhyme
ISBN 0-7636-0440-2   LC 98-23597

A group of toddlers demonstrate all the fun things that they can do with their eyes, ears, mouths, hands, legs, feet—and everything in between
"With an exuberant rhyme and cheerful art . . . this should be an immediate hit both at story hours and on the home front." Booklist

Hines, Anna Grossnickle, 1946-

Daddy makes the best spaghetti. Clarion Bks. 1986 unp il   E
1. Father-son relationship—Fiction
                                   LC 85-13993
Available Board book edition and with Audiobook
"Corey and his father enjoy a close relationship that is aptly demonstrated in picture and story. He teases Corey and they spend time together doing things such as shopping for groceries and making a pot of spaghetti or being silly at bath time and getting ready for bed. Hines' simple but warm pencil drawings play out the scenes by capitalizing on the incidents described in the text; the strong sense of family (Mother is here too) is evident." Booklist

What can you do in the rain? pictures by Thea Kliros. Greenwillow Bks. 1999 unp il lib bdg $6.95   E
1. Rain—fiction
ISBN 0-688-16077-8   LC 98-13381
Cover title
The rain provides opportunities to feel it fall, hear it patter, and mix a mud pie
This "toddler-sized board [book] feature[s] watercolor paintings of multicultural children splashing in puddles. . . . The rhythm of the sentences . . . will appeal to young listeners. Both words and pictures allow them to experience the world through all of the senses." SLJ
Other available titles in this series are:
What can you do in the snow? (1999)
What can you do in the sun? (1999)
What can you do in the wind? (1999)

Ho, Minfong

Hush! a Thai lullaby; pictures by Holly Meade. Orchard Bks. 1996 unp il $15.95; lib bdg $16.99; pa $6.95 (k-3)   E
1. Thailand—Fiction 2. Lullabies
ISBN 0-531-09500-2; 0-531-08850-2 (lib bdg); 0-531-07166-9 (pa)   LC 95-23251
A Caldecott Medal honor book, 1997
"A mother goes to each animal, from lizard to water buffalo to elephant, trying to quiet noises that might wake her child. When the animals are silenced and the mother finally falls asleep, the baby lies awake, with wide eyes and a smile. Ho's rhythmic text is fine for reading aloud. . . . The setting, apparently a remote Thai village, is gently evoked in cut paper and ink pictures that are bold enough to be used with groups. . . . The comforting earth tones suit the quiet nature of the story." Booklist

Hoban, Lillian

Arthur's Christmas cookies; words and pictures by Lillian Hoban. Harper & Row 1972 63p il lib bdg $15.89; pa $3.95   E

1. Chimpanzees—Fiction 2. Christmas—Fiction 3. Baking—Fiction

ISBN 0-06-022368-5 (lib bdg); 0-06-444055-9 (pa)

Also available with Audiobook

"An I can read book"

When Arthur decides to make Christmas cookies for his parents, a "disastrous mistake in the ingredients makes the cookies inedible but the story ends happily when Arthur turns them into holiday decorations." Publ Wkly

The characters are chimpanzees but "are endearingly like human children. . . . The Christmas setting is appealing, the plot has problem, conflict, and solution yet is not too complex for the beginning independent reader, and the simplicity and humor make the book an appropriate one for reading aloud to preschool children also." Bull Cent Child Books

Other available titles about Arthur are:

Arthur's back to school day (1996)
Arthur's birthday party (1999)
Arthur's camp-out (1993)
Arthur's funny money (1981)
Arthur's great big valentine (1989)
Arthur's Halloween costume (1984)
Arthur's Honey Bear (1974)
Arthur's loose tooth (1985)
Arthur's pen pal (1976)
Arthur's prize reader (1978)

Silly Tilly's Thanksgiving dinner; story and pictures by Lillian Hoban. Harper & Row 1990 63p il lib bdg $15.89; pa $3.95   E

1. Thanksgiving Day—Fiction 2. Moles (Animals)—Fiction 3. Animals—Fiction

ISBN 0-06-022423-1 (lib bdg); 0-06-444154-7 (pa)
LC 89-29287

"An I can read book"

Forgetful Silly Tilly Mole nearly succeeds in ruining her Thanksgiving dinner, but her animal friends come to the rescue with tasty treats

"Watercolors in vibrant autumn hues accentuate this comedy of errors with quirky characterizations and fine brushwork." Booklist

Other available titles about Silly Tilly are:

Silly Tilly and the Easter Bunny (1987)
Silly Tilly's valentine (1998)

Hoban, Russell

Bedtime for Frances; pictures by Garth Williams. HarperCollins Pubs. 1995 c1960 31p il $15.95; lib bdg $15.89; pa $5.95   E

1. Badgers—Fiction 2. Bedtime—Fiction

ISBN 0-06-027106-X; 0-06-027107-8 (lib bdg); 0-06-443451-6 (pa)   LC 94-43809

Also available Spanish language edition

A reissue of the title first published 1960

"A little badger with a lively imagination comes up with one scheme after another to put off going to sleep but father badger proves himself as smart as his daughter." Bookmark

"The soft humorous pictures of these lovable animals in human predicaments are delightful." Horn Book

Other available titles about Frances are:

A baby sister for Frances (1964)
A bargain for Frances (1970)
Best friends for Frances (1969)
A birthday for Frances (1968)
Bread and jam for Frances (1964)

Hoban, Tana

26 letters and 99 cents. Greenwillow Bks. 1987 unp il $15.95; lib bdg $15.89; pa $5.95   E

1. Alphabet 2. Counting 3. Coins

ISBN 0-688-06361-6; 0-688-06362-4 (lib bdg); 0-688-14389-X (pa)   LC 86-11993

This concept book "is really two books in one. *26 Letters* is a delightful ABC handbook. Each page shows two letters (in both upper- and lowercase) paired with objects from airplane to zipper. Turning the book around reveals the even more creative *99 Cents*. Here Hoban clearly shows youngsters how to count by pairing photos of numbers with pennies, nickels, dimes and quarters in a variety of combinations. The book counts ones from 1¢ to 30¢, by fives from 30¢ to 50¢, by tens from 50¢ to 90¢, culminating in 99¢. . . . An extremely inventive approach that will be hailed by parents, teachers and librarians." Publ Wkly

Black on white. Greenwillow Bks. 1993 unp il $5.95   E

ISBN 0-688-11918-2   LC 92-18897

Black illustrations against a white background depict such objects as an elephant, butterfly, and leaf

This board book features "the stunning, sophisticated photography of Tana Hoban. . . . Simply the best for babies." Horn Book Guide

A children's zoo. Greenwillow Bks. 1985 unp il $14.93; lib bdg $17   E

1. Animals

ISBN 0-688-05202-9; 0-688-05204-5 (lib bdg)
LC 84-25318

This is a photographic "portfolio of zoo denizens. . . . Each species is matted with a narrow white line, framed in black, and placed opposite a black page against which . . . white sans serif letters list three of that species' characteristics as well as its name." Horn Book

"For the most part, the photographs are standard zoo fare, but a few are truly different and amusing." SLJ

Includes glossary

Colors everywhere. Greenwillow Bks. 1995 unp il $16.95; lib bdg $16.89   E

1. Color

ISBN 0-688-12762-2; 0-688-12763-0 (lib bdg)
LC 93-24847

"On each page of this wordless picture book is a color photograph accompanied by a bar graph that displays the spectrum of colors found in the photo." Booklist

"Very young children will enjoy naming the pictured objects, while older readers will be drawn into exploring the colors' varying tones. A book children will come back to over and over." Horn Book

Dig, drill, dump, fill. Greenwillow Bks. 1975 unp il $15.93   E

1. Machinery

ISBN 0-688-84016-7

Hoban, Tana—_Continued_

"This all-photographic presentation shows loaders, rollers, dump trucks, and other heavy construction machines at work. What they are and what they do are explained simply and concisely in a three-page picture glossary." Publisher's note

Dots, spots, speckles, and stripes. Greenwillow Bks. 1987 unp il $16; lib bdg $15.93   E
  ISBN 0-688-06862-6; 0-688-06863-4 (lib bdg)
                                        LC 86-22919
Photographs show dots, spots, speckles, and stripes as found on clothing, flowers, faces, animals, and other places
  "Not only are the photos in this title technically superb, but the composition and the subjects are imaginative yet clearly identifiable. . . . Going beyond a concept book on patterns, _Dots, Spots, Speckles, and Stripes_ becomes a thought-provoking photo essay that can be appreciated by older children." Horn Book

Exactly the opposite. Greenwillow Bks. 1990 unp il $16.95; lib bdg $14.93   E
  1. English language—Synonyms and antonyms
  ISBN 0-688-08861-9; 0-688-08862-7 (lib bdg)
                                        LC 89-27227
"Using a variety of people, animals, and objects found in outdoor settings of both the city and the country, [the author] introduces and expands on the concept of opposites in this wordless photographic book. The photographs are clear, bright, and enticing. Pairs of opposites are presented on facing pages." SLJ

Is it larger? Is it smaller? Greenwillow Bks. 1985 unp il $14.95; pa $4.95   E
  1. Size
  ISBN 0-688-04027-6; 0-688-15287-2 (pa)
                                        LC 84-13719
"In each full-color photograph of the wordless picture book Hoban juxtaposes similar objects of differing size. In the simplest pictures only one kind of object is shown, such as three bright plastic sand cups in graduated sizes or three maple leaves. More complex compositions group several related items: measuring cups, bowls, and utensils; fish, shells, and pebbles in an aquarium. Still others contrast dissimilar objects that have common features. . . . In the photographs, Hoban demonstrates once again her mastery of the elements of composition, such as color, texture, and balance." Horn Book

Is it red? Is it yellow? Is it blue? An adventure in color. Greenwillow Bks. 1978 unp il lib bdg $16; pa $4.95   E
  1. Color 2. Size 3. Shape
  ISBN 0-688-84171-6 (lib bdg); 0-688-07034-5 (pa)
                                        LC 78-2549
Illustrations and brief text introduce colors and the concepts of shape and size
  "The wordless book is simply designed and opens the eye to the marvelous world of color; each stark-white page contains one photograph which nearly fills it. In the bottom margin the predominant colors in the photograph are indicated by a row of corresponding circles." Horn Book

Is it rough? Is it smooth? Is it shiny? Greenwillow Bks. 1984 unp il $18; lib bdg $17.93   E
  ISBN 0-688-03823-9; 0-688-03824-7 (lib bdg)
                                        LC 83-25460
Color photographs without text introduce objects of many different textures, such as pretzels, foil, hay, mud, kitten, and bubbles
  "Extraordinarily crisp, clean color photographs allow Hoban to call attention to textures." Booklist

Let's count. Greenwillow Bks. 1999 unp il $16; lib bdg $15.89   E
  1. Counting
  ISBN 0-688-16008-5; 0-688-16009-3 (lib bdg)
                                        LC 98-44739
Photographs and dots introduce the numbers one to one hundred
  "Hoban brings us another dazzling picture book. . . . Her photos range from the simple—1 hen, 8 Dalmatian puppies—to the more sophisticated—6 twirling rings on the arms of a circus performer; 12 rolls of toilet paper unpacked and stored on a pantry shelf." Booklist

Look book. Greenwillow Bks. 1997 unp il $16   E
  ISBN 0-688-14971-5   LC 96-46268
"Viewers first encounter a piece of an image, viewed through a small, die-cut circle on a black page. The full-color object—be it a flower, a pigeon, or a hot pretzel—is revealed with the turn of a page. Another turn of the page provides a larger view." SLJ
  "Hoban presents a dazzling assortment of color photographs that celebrate the rich detail of everyday things." Booklist

Of colors and things. Greenwillow Bks. 1989 unp il $16; lib bdg $15.93; pa $4.95   E
  1. Color
  ISBN 0-688-07534-7; 0-688-07535-5 (lib bdg); 0-688-04585-5 (pa)   LC 88-11101
Photographs of toys, food, and other common objects are grouped on each page according to color
  "Hoban hits on a simple device to heighten a child's awareness, but what lifts this above the average concept book is the quality of its design and illustration." Booklist

Over, under & through, and other spatial concepts. Macmillan 1973 unp il $17   E
  1. Vocabulary
  ISBN 0-02-744820-7
  In brief text and photographs, the author depicts several spatial concepts—over, under, through, on, in, around, across, between, beside, below, against, and behind
  "Children who are confused by these concepts may need help understanding that many of the pictures illustrate more than one concept. However, both the photographs and the format, with the words printed large on broad yellow bands at the beginning of each section, are uncluttered and appealing." Booklist

Shadows and reflections. Greenwillow Bks. 1990 unp il $16; lib bdg $12.88   E
  1. Shades and shadows
  ISBN 0-688-07089-2; 0-688-07090-6 (lib bdg)
                                        LC 89-30461

Hoban, Tana—*Continued*

Photographs without text feature shadows and reflections of various objects, animals, and people

"This imaginative, wordless book of color photographs is a visual treat, offering witty and subtle sets of images for enriching the eyes of children and adults." SLJ

Shapes, shapes, shapes. Greenwillow Bks. 1986 unp il $15.95; lib bdg $15.89; pa $5.95   **E**
1. Shape
ISBN 0-688-05832-9; 0-688-05833-7 (lib bdg);
0-688-14740-2 (pa)   LC 85-17569

Photographs of familiar objects such as chair, barrettes, and manhole cover present a study of rounded and angular shapes

"Tana Hoban has created an excellent concept book that will encourage children to look for specific shapes in everyday urban scenes. . . . The photographs not only serve to teach shapes and colors but are works of art themselves. . . . This book not only succeeds in helping children learn shapes, but helps to instill in them observational instincts that are such an important, integral part of many disciplines, especially science." Appraisal

So many circles, so many squares. Greenwillow Bks. 1998 unp il $15; lib bdg $15.89   **E**
1. Shape
ISBN 0-688-15165-5; 0-688-15166-3 (lib bdg)
     LC 97-10110

The geometric concepts of circles and squares are shown in photographs of wheels, signs, pots, and other familiar objects

"Teachers and young children will find plenty to talk about as they look at the colorful, well-composed, and clearly defined images." Booklist

White on black. Greenwillow Bks. 1993 unp il $5.95   **E**
ISBN 0-688-11919-0   LC 92-20092

In this board book, white illustrations against a black background depict such objects as a horse, baby bottle, and sailboat

"Hoban's compositions are so supple and her layouts so well balanced that she casts a kind of spell." Publ Wkly

Hoberman, Mary Ann, 1930-

And to think that we thought that we'd never be friends; illustrated by Kevin Hawkes. Crown 1999 unp il $15.95   **E**
1. Friendship—Fiction 2. Siblings—Fiction 3. Stories in rhyme
ISBN 0-517-80068-3   LC 98-39419

A brother and sister learn that friendship is better than fighting and they soon spread their message all over the world

"Madcap illustrations, executed in acrylics, revel in absurdities while enhancing the colorful rhyme." Horn Book Guide

One of each; illustrated by Marjorie Priceman. Little, Brown 1997 unp il hardcover o.p. paperback available $5.95   **E**
1. Friendship—Fiction 2. Stories in rhyme 3. Dogs—Fiction
ISBN 0-316-36644-7 (pa)   LC 96-34831

Oliver Tolliver, a dog who lives alone in his little house with just one of everything, discovers that it is more fun to have two of everything and share with a friend

"Artwork with a Parisian flair and skewed perspectives endows the dog's house with every bit as much charm as the witty rhyming text conjures in this clever ode to friendship." Publ Wkly

Hoestlandt, Jo, 1948-

Star of fear, star of hope; illustrations by Johanna Kang; translated from the French by Mark Polizzotti. Walker & Co. 1995 unp il hardcover o.p. paperback available $8.95   **E**
1. Holocaust, 1933-1945—Fiction 2. Jews—Fiction 3. Paris (France)—Fiction
ISBN 0-8027-7588-8 (pa)   LC 94-32378

Nine-year-old Helen is confused by the disappearance of her Jewish friend during the German occupation of Paris

"The pastel pictures in sepia tones are understated, with an old-fashioned, almost childlike simplicity. . . . Without being maudlin or sensational, the story brings the genocide home." Booklist

Hoff, Syd, 1912-

Danny and the dinosaur; story and pictures by Syd Hoff. HarperFestival 1999 unp il $14.95
   E
1. Dinosaurs—Fiction
ISBN 0-694-01297-1   LC 98-47691

Also available original edition in hardcover and paperback as well as paperback with Audiobook

"An I can read picture book"

A reissue of the title first published 1958 as An I can read book

A little boy is surprised and pleased when one of the dinosaurs from the museum agrees to play with him

"The bold, humorous, colored pictures convey the imaginative story. . . . Because of the simple vocabulary and sentence structure, first-graders can actually read this story." Libr J

Other available titles about Danny and the dinosaur are:
Danny and the dinosaur go to camp (1996)
Happy birthday, Danny and the dinosaur (1995)

Oliver; story and pictures by Syd Hoff. HarperCollins Pubs. 2000 64p il $14.95; lib bdg $14.89; pa $3.95   **E**
1. Elephants—Fiction 2. Circus—Fiction
ISBN 0-06-028708-X; 0-06-028709-8 (lib bdg);
0-06-444272-1 (pa)   LC 99-25591

"An I can read book"

A newly illustrated edition of the title first published 1960

Oliver the elephant looks elsewhere for employment after learning that the circus already has enough elephants

"One of the most warm-hearted and appealing easy-to-read books available." SLJ

Hoff, Syd, 1912-—*Continued*

Sammy the seal; story and pictures by Syd Hoff. Newly illustrated ed. HarperCollins Pubs. 2000 64p il $14.95; lib bdg $14.89; pa $3.95　　E

1. Seals (Animals)—Fiction 2. Zoos—Fiction

ISBN 0-06-028545-1; 0-06-028546-X (lib bdg); 0-06-444270-5 (pa)　　LC 99-13805

"An I can read book"

A newly illustrated edition of the title first published 1959

Anxious to see what life is like outside the zoo, Sammy the seal explores the city, goes to school, and plays with the children but decides that there really is no place like home

"Happy adventures told in entertaining colored cartoonlike drawings and in simple vocabulary and short sentences which first graders can read with a minimum of help." Booklist

Hoffman, Mary, 1945-

Amazing Grace; pictures by Caroline Binch. Dial Bks. for Young Readers 1991 unp il $16.99　　　　　　　　　　　　　　　　　E

1. African Americans—Fiction 2. Theater—Fiction

ISBN 0-8037-1040-2　　LC 90-25108

Although her classmates say that she cannot play Peter Pan in the school play because she is black and a girl, Grace discovers that she can do anything she sets her mind to

"Gorgeous watercolor illustrations portraying a determined, talented child and her warm family enhance an excellent text and positive message of self-affirmation. Grace is an amazing girl and this is an amazing book." SLJ

Other available titles about Grace are:

Boundless Grace (1995)

Starring Grace (2000)

Holabird, Katharine

Angelina ballerina; story by Katharine Holabird; illustrations by Helen Craig. Pleasant 2000 unp il $9.95　　　　　　　　　　　　　　　　　　E

1. Mice—Fiction 2. Ballet—Fiction

ISBN 1-584-85135-X　　LC 00-22882

A reissue of the title first published 1983 by Potter

Angelina the mouse loves to dance and wants to become a ballerina more than anything else in the world

"Touches of humor, attention to detail, a feel for dance and truly anthropomorphic mice make the illustrations a major part of the book." Child Book Rev Serv

Other available titles about Angelina are:

Angelina and Alice (1987)

Angelina and the princess (1984)

Angelina at the fair (1985)

Angelina on stage (1986)

Angelina's baby sister (1991)

Angelina's Christmas (1985)

Angelina's Halloween (2000)

Hooper, Meredith

River story; written by Meredith Hooper; illustrated by Bee Willey. Candlewick Press 2000 29p il $15.99　　　　　　　　　　　　　E

1. Rivers—Fiction

ISBN 0-7636-0792-4　　LC 99-53730

Follows a river from its source as a mountain stream formed from melting snow, as it rushes over rocks and through valleys to the busy city, and finally to its end, where it joins the sea

"Hooper's rhythmic, sibilant text and Willey's luminous illustrations, dominated by vibrant yellows and greens, trace the course of a river." Horn Book Guide

Hopkinson, Deborah

A band of angels; a story inspired by the Jubilee Singers; illustrated by Raúl Colón. Atheneum Bks. for Young Readers 1999 unp il $16　　　　E

1. Moore, Ella Sheppard, 1851-1914—Fiction 2. Jubilee Singers (Musical group)—Fiction 3. African Americans—Fiction 4. Gospel music—Fiction

ISBN 0-689-81062-8　　LC 96-20011

"An Anne Schwartz book"

Based on the life of Ella Sheppard Moore. The daughter of a slave forms a gospel singing group and goes on tour to raise money to save Fisk University

"Lilting prose, poignant historical details and arresting portraits of trailblazing singers lost in song contribute to this triumphant tale." Publ Wkly

Maria's comet; written by Deborah Hopkinson; illustrated by Deborah Lanino. Atheneum Bks. for Young Readers 1999 unp il $16　　　　　E

1. Mitchell, Maria, 1818-1889—Fiction

ISBN 0-689-81501-8　　LC 97-46676

"An Anne Schwartz book"

As a young girl, budding astronomer Maria Mitchell dreams of searching the night sky and some day finding a new comet

"Warm, deep tones of brown and midnight blue suffuse the soft-edged, full-page acrylic views of the house, sky, and seaside town. . . . The well-structured story is fanciful and rich in poetic imagery that will work for reading aloud." SLJ

Sweet Clara and the freedom quilt; paintings by James Ransome. Knopf 1993 unp il $16; lib bdg $16.99; pa $6.99　　　　　　　　　　　E

1. Slavery—Fiction 2. Quilts—Fiction

ISBN 0-679-82311-5; 0-679-92311-X (lib bdg); 0-679-87472-0 (pa)　　LC 91-11601

Clara, a young slave, stitches a quilt with a map pattern which guides her to freedom in the North

"The smooth, optimistic, first-person vernacular of the story is ably accompanied by Ransome's brightly colored, full-page paintings." Horn Book Guide

Horenstein, Henry

A is for—? a photographer's alphabet of animals. Harcourt Brace & Co. 1999 unp il $16

　　　　　　　　　　　　　　　　　　E

1. Animals 2. Alphabet

ISBN 0-15-201582-5　　LC 98-31424

"Gulliver books"

"More visual puzzle than early concept book, the title presents each letter alongside a photograph of the relevant creature—if you can figure out what the relevant creature is. Some letters are easy . . . but some are more challenging. . . . Even when the answer is fairly guessable, the view is original. . . . Artistic and creative." Bull Cent Child Books

Hort, Lenny

How many stars in the sky? paintings by James E. Ransome. Tambourine Bks. 1991 unp il o.p.; HarperCollins Pubs. paperback available $5.95
E

1. Stars—Fiction 2. Father-son relationship—Fiction
ISBN 0-688-15218-X (pa)   LC 90-36044
One night when Mama is away, Daddy and child seek a good place to count the stars in the night sky

"Ransome uses thick, visible strokes in his dense oil paintings that completely fill each large-format page. In general they present a nice variety of scenes to match the flow of the text, and the closeness between the black father and son is warmly portrayed. A fresh look at an age-old concept." SLJ

Houston, Gloria

My great-aunt Arizona; illustrated by Susan Condie Lamb. HarperCollins Pubs. 1992 unp il $15.95; lib bdg $15.84; pa $5.95
E

1. Teachers 2. Appalachian region
ISBN 0-06-022606-4; 0-06-022607-2 (lib bdg); 0-06-443374-9 (pa)   LC 90-44112
The author tells the life story of "her great aunt Arizona who never traveled farther than the next town where she trained as a teacher before returning to her small Appalachian community's one-room schoolhouse. Though not well-traveled, Arizona encouraged her students to dream of faraway places and was always there to give them hugs and kisses." Child Book Rev Serv

"The pleasant, conversational rhythm of the prose, the unobtrusive use of repetition, and the ability to sum up the unique quality of a life in a few telling phrases give the writing its substance. . . . Sunny and lively, the watercolor paintings have a naive quality that suits the story well." Booklist

The year of the perfect Christmas tree; an Appalachian story; pictures by Barbara Cooney. Dial Bks. for Young Readers 1988 unp il $15.99
E

1. Christmas—Fiction 2. Appalachian region—Fiction
ISBN 0-8037-0299-X   LC 87-24551
"It's 1918 in the mountains of North Carolina, and the custom in the village is for one family to select and donate the Christmas tree each year. In the spring Ruthie and her father select a perfect balsam high on a rocky crag. Then Father goes to war. Still, on Christmas Eve the tree is in the church and Ruthie plays the angel. The winning illustrations perfectly match the tone of this affecting story, which comes from the author's family." NY Times Book Rev

Howard, Elizabeth Fitzgerald, 1927-

Aunt Flossie's hats (and crab cakes later); paintings by James Ransome. Clarion Bks. 1991 31p il $16; pa $6.95
E

1. Hats—Fiction 2. Aunts—Fiction 3. African Americans—Fiction
ISBN 0-395-54682-6; 0-395-72077-X (pa)
LC 90-33332
Also available with Audiobook

Sara and Susan share tea, cookies, crab cakes, and stories about hats when they visit their favorite relative, Aunt Flossie

"This is an affecting portrait of a black American family and of the ways in which shared memories can be a thread, invisible yet strong, that ties generations together. Howard's quiet, sure telling is well matched by Ransome's art—elegant, expressive oil paintings that convey warmth, joy, tenderness and love." Publ Wkly

Chita's Christmas tree; illustrated by Floyd Cooper. Bradbury Press 1989 unp il hardcover o.p. paperback available $5.99
E

1. Christmas—Fiction 2. Family life—Fiction 3. African Americans—Fiction
ISBN 0-689-71739-3 (pa)   LC 88-26250
"A turn-of-the-century story begins on the Saturday before Christmas, when Chita and her father go out of the city (Baltimore) to choose a tree. Papa marks it with Chita's name and assures her that Santa Claus will get it to their house. The story continues, quietly, with preparations for the holiday, a dinner for the black family and relatives on Christmas Eve, and Chita's happy discovery the next morning that the big, decorated tree does indeed have her name carved on it." Bull Cent Child Books

"The paintings that surround the almost-poetic text are softly unfocused and glow with a golden color that suffuses the scenes. Yet despite the dreamy feeling of the art, carefully delineated characters play their parts perfectly in the family scenes." Booklist

Another available title about Chita is:
Papa tells Chita a story (1995)

Virgie goes to school with us boys; illustrated by E.B. Lewis. Simon & Schuster Bks. for Young Readers 2000 unp il $16
E

1. African Americans—Fiction
ISBN 0-689-80076-2   LC 97-49406
In the post-Civil War South, a young African American girl is determined to prove that she can go to school just like her older brothers

"The story is a superb tribute to the author's great aunt, the inspiration for this book. . . . Lewis's watercolor illustrations capture the characters with warmth and dignity." SLJ

When will Sarah come? story by Elizabeth Fitzgerald Howard; pictures by Nina Crews. Greenwillow Bks. 1999 unp il $16; lib bdg $15.95
E

1. Siblings—Fiction
ISBN 0-688-16180-4; 0-688-16181-2 (lib bdg)
LC 98-42169
A little boy waits and listens all day for his older sister to come home from school

"An excellent book about how it feels to be left behind when an older sibling starts school. . . . The sharp, full-color photos and very simple text detail the African-American child's day." SLJ

Howe, James, 1946-

Horace and Morris but mostly Dolores; written by James Howe; illustrated by Amy Walrod. Atheneum Bks. for Young Readers 1999 unp il $16   **E**

    1. Mice—Fiction 2. Friendship—Fiction 3. Sex role—Fiction

    ISBN 0-689-31874-X   LC 96-17645

"Three adventure-loving mice are best friends until gender stereotypes separate them, driving Horace and Morris into a rowdy boys-only clubhouse while Dolores reluctantly goes off to join the ultra-ladylike Cheese Puffs. The bold artwork suits the book's lively protest against conformity." Horn Book Guide

Pinky and Rex; illustrated by Melissa Sweet. Atheneum Pubs. 1990 38p il $15; pa $3.99   **E**

    1. Museums—Fiction   2. Friendship—Fiction 3. Toys—Fiction

    ISBN 0-689-31454-X; 0-689-82348-7 (pa)

                          LC 89-30786

"Pinky, a boy named for his favorite color, and Rex, a girl whose name reflects her interest in dinosaurs, live next door to each other; they each have twenty-seven stuffed animals and are best friends. . . . They go to the museum and discover that even best friends can vie with each other for the last remaining pink dinosaur in the museum store." Horn Book

"Sweet's gently washed, jovial illustrations reflect the unpretentious sincerity of Rex and Pinky's relationship, while Howe's readable text blending natural dialogue with narrative, is divided into individual chapters." Booklist

Other available titles about Pinky and Rex are:
Pinky and Rex and the bully (1996)
Pinky and Rex and the double-dad weekend (1995)
Pinky and Rex and the just-right pet (2001)
Pinky and Rex and the mean old witch (1991)
Pinky and Rex and the new baby (1993)
Pinky and Rex and the new neighbors (1997)
Pinky and Rex and the perfect pumpkin (1998)
Pinky and Rex and the school play (1998)
Pinky and Rex and the spelling bee (1991)
Pinky and Rex get married (1990)
Pinky and Rex go to camp (1992)

Scared silly: a Halloween treat; illustrated by Leslie Morrill. Morrow Junior Bks. 1989 unp il hardcover o.p. paperback available $4.95   **E**

    1. Halloween—Fiction 2. Animals—Fiction

    ISBN 0-688-16322-X (pa)   LC 88-7837

Titles about Harold and Chester for older readers by Deborah Howe and James Howe are also available

At head of title: Harold & Chester in

The Monroes leave their cat, Chester, and two dogs, Harold and Howe, alone on Halloween night, unaware that their pets are about to be visited by a strange figure who might be a wicked witch

"Howe's pacing is perfect, and the ending is unexpected. But it is Morrill's artwork that really enhances the drama. Exciting watercolors capture the individuality of the animals and the creepiness of the setting as shadows gradually fall." Booklist

Other available picture books about Harold and Chester are:
Creepy-crawly birthday (1991)

The fright before Christmas (1988)
Hot fudge (1990)

There's a dragon in my sleeping bag; illustrated by David S. Rose. Atheneum Pubs. 1994 unp il $15; pa $5.99   **E**

    1. Brothers—Fiction 2. Imaginary playmates—Fiction

    ISBN 0-689-31873-1; 0-689-81922-6 (pa)

                          LC 93-26572

Also available Spanish language edition

Alex is intimidated by his older brother Simon's imaginary dragon, until he is able to create his own friend—a camel named Calvin

"The story is humorous and heartwarming without being overly cute, and Rose's acrylic illustrations are colorful and imaginative." Booklist

Another available title about Simon is:
There's a monster under my bed (1986)

Howland, Naomi

Latkes, latkes, good to eat; a Chanukah story. Clarion Bks. 1999 31p il $15   **E**

    1. Magic—Fiction 2. Hanukkah—Fiction 3. Jews—Russia—Fiction

    ISBN 0-395-89903-6   LC 97-50616

In an old Russian village, Sadie and her brothers are poor and hungry until an old woman gives Sadie a frying pan that will make potato pancakes until it hears the magic words that make it stop

"Howland effectively sets her story in a Russian shtetl, using words, intonation, and especially pictures. Working in gouache and colored pencil, she offers a snowy landscape peopled with Jewish villagers who work hard and celebrate harder." Booklist

Huck, Charlotte S.

A creepy countdown; by Charlotte Huck; pictures by Jos. A. Smith. Greenwillow Bks. 1998 unp il $15; lib bdg $14.93; pa $5.95   **E**

    1. Halloween—Fiction 2. Counting 3. Stories in rhyme

    ISBN 0-688-15460-3; 0-688-15461-1 (lib bdg); 0-688-17717-4 (pa)   LC 97-36283

Ten scary Halloween things, such as jack-o-lanterns, bats, and witches, count from one to ten and then back down again

"Huck's spirited counting rhyme . . . trips easily off the tongue, and Smith's black ink on scratchboard with watercolor overlays provide appropriate ghoulish harmony." SLJ

Hughes, Shirley

Alfie and the birthday surprise. Lothrop, Lee & Shepard Bks. 1998 c1997 unp il $16   **E**

    1. Cats—Fiction 2. Death—Fiction 3. Birthdays—Fiction

    ISBN 0-688-15187-6   LC 97-6472

First published 1997 in the United Kingdom

The death of Bob's cat prompts his friends and family to give him a surprise birthday party and a very special present

"In the deceptively simple story, the theme stresses compassion and concern for others; the soft palette and skillfully limned figures capture the essence of these emotions without undue sentimentality." Horn Book Guide

Hughes, Shirley—*Continued*

Other available titles about Alfie and his family are:

Alfie's 1 2 3 (2000)

Alfie's ABC (1998)

Dogger. Lothrop, Lee & Shepard Bks. 1988 c1977 unp il hardcover o.p. paperback available $6.95   E

1. Toys—Fiction

ISBN 0-688-11704-X (pa)   LC 87-33787

First published 1977 in the United Kingdom. First United States edition published 1978 by Prentice-Hall with title: David and Dog

A youngster is upset by the loss of his favorite stuffed dog

"Hughes' story . . . is warmly satisfying, due in part to the way the illustrations capture the comfortable disarray that seems to rule wherever children are present. . . . Hughes has a way of zeroing in on the foibles of childhood with remarkable accuracy; this doesn't miss its mark." Booklist

Out and about. Lothrop, Lee & Shepard Bks. 1988 unp il $16   E

1. Seasons—Fiction 2. Stories in rhyme

ISBN 0-688-07690-4   LC 87-17000

Rhyming text depicts the pleasures of the outdoors in all kinds of weather, through the four seasons

"The children who romp through these non-stop family scenes are rosy, cared-for, active, and enthusiastically messy. Hughes' drawing is always good, but the composition and coloration here mark some of her most cohesive book design and art work." Bull Cent Child Books

Stories by firelight. Lothrop, Lee & Shepard Bks. 1993 unp il $16   E

1. Winter—Fiction 2. Short stories

ISBN 0-688-04568-5   LC 92-38207

In a series of brief winter episodes, a child learns about a mythical sea creature, a boy and his grandfather build a bonfire, and Mrs. Toomly Stones pays a scary visit

"No one captures the real innocence and emotions of childhood with less sentimentality than Hughes. Designed with an appealing jacket and full-color illustrations on every page, this book will be in demand for reading aloud or reading alone." Booklist

Huneck, Stephen

Sally goes to the beach; written and illustrated by Stephen Huneck. Abrams 2000 unp il $17.95
E

1. Dogs—Fiction 2. Beaches—Fiction

ISBN 0-8109-4186-4   LC 99-28421

Sally, a black Labrador retriever, goes to the beach, where she enjoys various activities with other visiting dogs

"The playful pup's enjoyment is conveyed through a simple but engaging text and beautiful, full-page woodblock prints." SLJ

Hurd, Edith Thacher, 1910-1997

Johnny Lion's book; pictures by Clement Hurd. New ed. HarperCollins Pubs. 2001 63p il $14.95; lib bdg $14.89; pa $3.95   E

1. Lions—Fiction

ISBN 0-06-029333-0; 0-06-029334-9 (lib bdg); 0-06-444297-7 (pa)

"An I can read book"

A reissue of the title first published 1965

When his parents go out hunting, Johnny Lion stays home and experiences exciting adventures reading a book about a baby lion who goes out into the world and gets lost

"A subtle boost for the joys of reading in a story with engaging illustrations." Booklist

Other available titles about Johnny Lion are:

Johnny Lion's bad day (1970)

Johny Lion's rubber boots (1972)

Hurd, Thacher

Art dog. HarperCollins Pubs. 1996 unp il $14.95; lib bdg $15.89; pa $5.95   E

1. Dogs—Fiction 2. Artists—Fiction

ISBN 0-06-024424-0; 0-06-024425-9 (lib bdg); 0-06-443489-3 (pa)   LC 95-31092

When the Mona Woofa is stolen from the Dogopolis Museum of Art, a mysterious character who calls himself Art Dog tracks down and captures the thieves

"This is exuberantly drawn by Hurd, who has imbued Art Dog with the flash and dash every artist feels at times; but Hurd also captures the shyness that comes with displaying your art. Kids will respond not just to the pictures but also to a story that does as well with characters as with plot." Booklist

Little Mouse's big valentine. Harper & Row 1990 unp il hardcover o.p. paperback available $5.95   E

1. Mice—Fiction 2. Valentine's Day—Fiction

ISBN 0-06-443281-5 (pa)   LC 89-34515

After several unsuccessful attempts to give his special valentine to someone, Little Mouse finally finds just the right recipient

"The plot of boy mouse meets girl mouse may be simple, but it is offset by delightful characterizations. The book's small size gives it added appeal for its intended audience." Publ Wkly

Mama don't allow; starring Miles and the Swamp Band. Harper & Row 1984 unp il lib bdg $15.89; pa $5.95   E

1. Bands (Music)—Fiction 2. Alligators—Fiction

ISBN 0-06-022690-0 (lib bdg); 0-06-443078-2 (pa)
LC 83-47703

Miles and the Swamp Band have the time of their lives playing at the Alligator Ball, until they discover the menu includes Swamp Band soup

"The multi-colored full-spread watercolor illustrations are stunningly bright and full of movement, far outpacing the story line in energy and imagination." SLJ

Mystery on the docks. Harper & Row 1983 unp il hardcover o.p. paperback available $6.95   E

1. Mystery fiction 2. Rats—Fiction

ISBN 0-06-443058-8 (pa)   LC 82-48261

Hurd, Thacher—*Continued*

Ralph, a short order cook, rescues a kidnapped opera singer from Big Al and his gang of nasty rats

Hurd "creates real excitement (albeit tongue-in-cheek) with his colorful pictures and fast-paced plot. There's a mysterious aura to the docks, and the stereotyped good and bad guys are hilarious. The unabashed fun and excitement make it perfect for reading aloud." Child Book Rev Serv

Zoom City. HarperCollins Pubs. 1998 unp il $5.95　　　　　　　　　　　　　　　　　E
1. Automobiles—Fiction
ISBN 0-694-01057-X　　　　　　LC 96-49437
Cars honk, beep, stop, go, zoom, crash, and get repaired

"A fast-paced, zip-zapping board book that begs to be read with as much gusto as possible. . . . The bright and busy illustrations are packed with energy." SLJ

Hurwitz, Johanna

New shoes for Silvia; illustrated by Jerry Pinkney. Morrow Junior Bks. 1993 unp il $16; pa $4.95　　　　　　　　　　　　　　　　　E
1. Shoes—Fiction 2. Latin America—Fiction
ISBN 0-688-05286-X; 0-688-17115-X (pa)
　　　　　　　　　　　　　　LC 92-40868
Silvia receives a pair of beautiful red shoes from her Tia Rosita and finds different uses for them until she grows enough for them to fit

"This simple story, told in spare prose, speaks universally to the imagination and emotions. Pinkney's spirited watercolors animate the narrative and are large enough for group sharing." SLJ

Hutchins, Pat, 1942-

1 hunter. Greenwillow Bks. 1982 unp il $16.95; pa $4.95　　　　　　　　　　　　　　　　E
1. Counting 2. Animals—Fiction
ISBN 0-688-00614-0; 0-688-06522-8 (pa)
　　　　　　　　　　　　　　LC 81-6352
This is "a 1 to 10 and back again counting book. . . . Here, a Mr. Magoo-type hunter blunders through the jungle entirely missing the camouflaged elephants (2), giraffes (3), ostriches (4), etc." SLJ

"Humorous illustrations done in a flat, clear style make an outstanding counting book." Horn Book

Changes, changes. Macmillan 1971 unp il $16; pa $5.99　　　　　　　　　　　　　　　　E
1. Toys—Fiction 2. Dolls—Fiction 3. Stories without words
ISBN 0-02-745870-9; 0-689-71137-9 (pa)
This wordless book shows how two wooden dolls rearrange a child's building blocks to form various objects

"Another book for the very young child who delights in 'reading' by himself, the lack of text amply compensated for by the bright, bold pictures and the imaginative use of blocks and two stiff little dolls." Bull Cent Child Books

Clocks and more clocks. Macmillan 1970 unp il hardcover o.p. paperback available $5.99　　　E
1. Clocks and watches—Fiction
ISBN 0-689-71769-5 (pa)

"After buying four clocks, Mr. Higgins is still not sure which one is right because there is always a few minutes difference between them." Booklist

"A minimum of well-chosen words and bright colored pictures tell the droll tale." Horn Book

Don't forget the bacon! Greenwillow Bks. 1976 unp il hardcover o.p. paperback available $5.95
　　　　　　　　　　　　　　　　　　E
ISBN 0-688-08743-4 (pa)
Also available Big book edition

"Surely anyone could remember four items on a grocery list! A play on words, however, leads the shopper into interesting predicaments. Children gleefully follow the strange replacements that result. A great book for developing visual literacy and word play." Read Teach

The doorbell rang. Greenwillow Bks. 1986 unp il $15.95; lib bdg $15.89; pa $5.95　　　　E
ISBN 0-688-05251-7; 0-688-05252-5 (lib bdg); 0-688-09234-9 (pa)　　　　　　LC 85-12615
Also available Big book edition and Spanish language edition

"Victoria and Sam are delighted when Ma bakes a tray of a dozen cookies, even though Ma insists that her cookies aren't as good as Grandma's. They count them and find that each can have six. But the doorbell rings, friends arrive and the cookies must be re-divided. This happens again and again, and the number of cookies on each plate decreases as the visitors' pile of gear in the corner of the kitchen grows larger." SLJ

"Bright, joyous, dynamic, this wonderfully humorous piece of realism for the young is presented simply but with style and imagination." Horn Book

Good-night, Owl! Macmillan 1972 unp il $16; pa $5.99　　　　　　　　　　　　　　　E
1. Owls—Fiction
ISBN 0-02-745900-4; 0-689-71371-1 (pa)
Also available Big book edition

Owl takes revenge on the birds and the animals who have not let him sleep during the day

"The ending is perky, the pictures funny, and the simplicity and repetition of pattern in the text are encouraging for the pre-reader." Bull Cent Child Books

Happy birthday, Sam. Greenwillow Bks. 1978 unp il hardcover o.p. paperback available $5.95
　　　　　　　　　　　　　　　　　　E
1. Birthdays—Fiction
ISBN 0-688-10482-7 (pa)　　　　　LC 78-1295
Sam "wakes to find that being a year older hasn't changed the fact that he can't reach a light switch, or the clothes in his closet, or the tap above the sink where he'd like to play with the boat he's received as a present from his parents. Then Grandpa's present arrives; it's a small sturdy chair, and it enables Sam to reach everything." Bull Cent Child Books

"Sunny yellow and bright green predominate in this cheerfully stylized, full-color picture book." Booklist

Rosie's walk. Macmillan 1968 unp il $16; pa $5.99　　　　　　　　　　　　　　　　E
1. Chickens—Fiction 2. Foxes—Fiction
ISBN 0-02-745850-4; 0-02-043750-1 (pa)
Also available Spanish language edition

Hutchins, Pat, 1942-—*Continued*

"Rosie the hen goes for a walk around the farm and gets home in time for dinner, completely unaware that a fox has been hot on her heels every step of the way. The viewer knows, however, and is not only held in suspense but tickled by the ways in which the fox is foiled at every turn by the unwitting hen. A perfect choice for the youngest." Booklist

Ten red apples. Greenwillow Bks. 2000 $15.95; lib bdg $15.89   **E**
1. Domestic animals—Fiction 2. Apples—Fiction 3. Counting 4. Stories in rhyme
ISBN 0-688-16797-7; 0-688-16798-5 (lib bdg)
LC 99-25065

In rhyming verses, one animal after another neighs, moos, oinks, quacks and makes other appropriate sounds as each eats an apple from the farmer's tree

"A concept book that blends rhyming, counting, repetition, and animal sounds into a charming, folksy story. . . . The gouache paintings are bright and clear." SLJ

Titch. Macmillan 1971 unp il hardcover o.p. paperback available $5.99   **E**
1. Siblings—Fiction
ISBN 0-689-71688-5 (pa)

"How does it feel to be the youngest child in the family? To have an older brother and sister who lead a more exciting life? . . . [The author] has, with a minimum of well-chosen words and bright, engaging illustrations, triumphantly related the story of a small boy who surpasses his brother and sister with one simple action." Publ Wkly

Other available titles about Titch are:
Tidy Titch (1991)
You'll soon grow into them, Titch (1983)

Where's the baby? Greenwillow Bks. 1988 unp il $12.95; lib bdg $12.88; pa $4.95   **E**
1. Monsters—Fiction 2. Infants—Fiction 3. Cleanliness—Fiction
ISBN 0-688-05933-3; 0-688-05934-1 (lib bdg); 0-688-17063-3 (pa)   LC 86-33566

When Grandma, Ma, and Hazel Monster want to find Baby Monster, they follow the messy trail he has left

"Delightful. . . . Each brightly decked illustration is cluttered with everyday objects for the young reader to identify and the text is a loping doggerel entirely in keeping with the rough-and-ready storyline." Times Lit Suppl

Other available titles about the Monster family are:
It's my birthday (1999)
Silly Billy (1992)
The very worst monster (1985)

The wind blew. Macmillan 1974 unp il hardcover o.p. paperback available $5.99   **E**
1. Winds—Fiction 2. Stories in rhyme
ISBN 0-689-71744-X (pa)

"Full-color paintings illustrate a rhymed cumulative text depicting the frantic efforts of unwary pedestrians to recover possessions snatched away by a mischievous and unpredictable wind. . . . Although the brief text is a pleasant, rhythmic accompaniment to the pictures, the story can be 'read' from the doublespread illustrations. A humorous and imaginative treatment of a familiar situation." Horn Book

Isaacs, Anne, 1949-

Swamp Angel; illustrated by Paul O. Zelinsky. Dutton Children's Bks. 1994 unp il $15.99; pa $6.99   **E**
1. Tall tales 2. Frontier and pioneer life—Fiction 3. Tennessee—Fiction
ISBN 0-525-45271-0; 0-14-055908-6 (pa)
LC 93-43956

A Caldecott Medal honor book, 1995

Along with other amazing feats, Angelica Longrider, also known as Swamp Angel, wrestles a huge bear, known as Thundering Tarnation, to save the winter supplies of the settlers in Tennessee

"Isaacs tells her original story with the glorious exaggeration and uproarious farce of the traditional tall tale and with its typical laconic idiom—you just can't help reading it aloud. . . . Zelinsky's detailed oil paintings in folk-art style are exquisite, framed in cherry, maple, and birch wood grains. They are also hilarious, making brilliant use of perspective to extend the mischief and the droll understatement." Booklist

Isadora, Rachel

123 pop! Viking 2000 unp il $15.99   **E**
1. Counting
ISBN 0-670-88859-1   LC 99-56686

Numbers from one to twenty, and 500, 1000, and 10,000 are represented by illustrations in the pop art style

"Rendered in the bold graphic lines and clear, unshaded shapes, the objects are appealing and easily identified as they nearly explode off the page. . . . A sophisticated, playful introduction to numbers." Booklist

ABC pop! Viking 1999 unp il $15.99   **E**
1. Alphabet
ISBN 0-670-88329-8   LC 98-45690

Each letter of the alphabet is represented by illustrations in a pop art style

The "vividly colored images with their heavy black outlines evoke the graphic look of Roy Lichtenstein and, to a lesser degree, Andy Warhol. . . . Isadora's artfully energetic book will appeal to eyes of all ages." Booklist

At the crossroads. Greenwillow Bks. 1991 unp il lib bdg $15.93; pa $4.95   **E**
1. Fathers—Fiction 2. South Africa—Fiction
ISBN 0-688-05271-1 (lib bdg); 0-688-13103-4 (pa)
LC 90-30751

South African children gather to welcome home their fathers who have been away for ten months working in the mines

"The characters' anticipation, patience, and joy speak loudest here, both in text and in brilliantly lit watercolor paintings." Bull Cent Child Books

Ben's trumpet. Greenwillow Bks. 1979 unp il $16.95; pa $6.95   **E**
1. Musicians—Fiction 2. African Americans—Fiction
ISBN 0-688-80194-3; 0-688-10988-8 (pa)
LC 78-12885

A Caldecott Medal honor book, 1980

This is the story of Ben, a boy whose dream is to be a jazz trumpeter but who is too poor to own an instrument until a real musician, remembering his own dreams,

Isadora, Rachel—*Continued*
puts one into the boy's hands

"The art is astonishingly varied in its brilliant recreation—in the margins, in the urban backgrounds—of the commercial art of the 20's and 30's." N Y Times Book Rev

City seen from A to Z. Greenwillow Bks. 1983 unp il hardcover o.p. paperback available $3.95
E

1. City and town life 2. Alphabet
ISBN 0-688-12032-6 (pa)   LC 82-11966
Twenty-six black-and-white drawings of scenes of city life suggest words beginning with each letter of the alphabet

"The activities or objects or concepts in this urban alphabet book . . . reflect the multiethnic composition of a city, and they seldom include words that are not easily comprehensible. The first letter of each word (sometimes two words, like 'Roller skate') is in brown, the rest of the word in black, adequately distinguished from, but blending with the soft, soft illustrations that are highly textured, often stippled, dramatic in composition." Bull Cent Child Books

Lili at ballet. Putnam 1993 unp il $16.99; pa $6.99
E
1. Ballet—Fiction
ISBN 0-399-22423-8; 0-698-11408-6 (pa)
LC 92-8429
Lili dreams of becoming a ballerina and goes to her ballet lessons four afternoons a week

"Isadora uses pastel shades of purple, pink, green, and blue with bold splashes of black. This is a prettily illustrated book that captures the magic and hard work involved in ballet." SLJ

Other available titles about Lili are:
Lili backstage (1997)
Lili on stage (1995)

Listen to the city. Putnam 2000 unp il $15.99
E
1. City and town life 2. Sound
ISBN 0-399-23047-5   LC 98-20282
Illustrations and simple text describe the sights and sounds of a day in the city

"The vibrant pop-art illustrations . . . make this book distinctive. The use of rich primary colors, coupled with the unique design of the pages, sometimes juxtaposing images in oddly angled segments, captures the energy of urban life." SLJ

Max; story & pictures by Rachel Isadora. Macmillan 1976 unp il hardcover o.p. paperback availaible $4.99
E
1. Baseball—Fiction 2. Ballet—Fiction
ISBN 0-02-043800-1 (pa)   LC 76-9088
Max "is the star of his baseball team. On a Saturday morning, he has time to spare before his game and accepts (with some hidden disdain) the invitation of his sister, Lisa, to watch her ballet class in action. Max is surprised to find himself interested and happy to join the students at their teacher's suggestion. . . . The experience pays off at the ball park where Max hits a home run. Now he warms up for the game each week at Lisa's dancing class. The pictures are an ebullient combination

of grace and comedy, with the leggy students dipping and soaring, in contrast to Max in his uniform." Publ Wkly

Swan Lake; adapted and illustrated by Rachel Isadora. Putnam 1989 unp il hardcover o.p. paperback available $5.95
E
1. Ballet—Stories, plots, etc. 2. Fairy tales
ISBN 0-698-11370-5 (pa)   LC 88-29843
A prince's love for a swan queen overcomes an evil sorcerer's spell in this fairy tale adaptation of the classic ballet

"The illustrations and the text (which is clear and straightforward) effectively re-create the ballet, with all its mystery and romanticism." N Y Times Book Rev

Ivimey, John W. (John William), 1868-1961
The complete story of the three blind mice; illustrated by Paul Galdone. Clarion Bks. 1987 unp il lib bdg $13.95
E
1. Mice—Fiction 2. Stories in rhyme
ISBN 0-89919-481-8   LC 87-689
First published 1909 in the United Kingdom with title: Complete version of ye three blind mice

"Galdone found this story—Ivimey's tale of the three blind mice—in a collection of antique British children's stories and knew he wanted to reillustrate it. . . . The sprightly text is written in the same rhyme as the song (which is given with the music on the dust jacket), making this a perfect read-aloud for story hours. Galdone's familiar, jaunty artwork is done in rich colors and catches all the humorous nuances of a tale that will appeal greatly to young children." Booklist

Iwamatsu, Atushi Jun, 1908-1994
Crow Boy; [by] Taro Yashima. Viking 1955 37p il lib bdg $17.99; pa $5.99
E
1. School stories 2. Japan—Fiction
ISBN 0-670-24931-9 (lib bdg); 0-14-050172-X (pa)

Also available Spanish language edition
A Caldecott Medal honor book, 1956

"A young boy from the mountain area of Japan goes to school in a nearby village, where he is taunted by his classmates and feels rejected and isolated. Finally an understanding teacher helps the boy gain acceptance. The other students recognize how wrong they have been and nickname him 'Crow Boy' because he can imitate the crow's calls with such perfection." Adventuring with Books. 2d edition

"A moving story interpreted by the author's distinctive illustrations, valuable for human relations and for its picture of Japanese school life." Hodges. Books for Elem Sch Libr

Umbrella; [by] Taro Yashima. Viking 1958 30p il hardcover o.p. paperback available $5.99
E
1. Umbrellas and parasols—Fiction
ISBN 0-14-050240-8 (pa)
A Caldecott Medal honor book, 1959

"Momo, given an umbrella and a pair of red boots on her third birthday, is overjoyed when at last it rains and she can wear her new rain togs." Hodges. Books for

Iwamatsu, Atushi Jun, 1908-1994—*Continued*

Elem Sch Libr

In this simple tale, young children "will be carried along by their identification with the actions of this very real little girl. . . . The beauty of the book makes this worthwhile." Horn Book

Jackson, Ellen B., 1943-

Cinder Edna; by Ellen Jackson; illustrated by Kevin O'Malley. Lothrop, Lee & Shepard Bks. 1994 unp il $16; lib bdg $15.93; pa $5.95   E

1. Fairy tales

ISBN 0-688-12322-8; 0-688-12323-6 (lib bdg); 0-688-16295-9 (pa)   LC 92-44160

Cinderella and Cinder Edna, who live with cruel stepmothers and stepsisters, have different approaches to life; and, although each ends up with the prince of her dreams, one is a great deal happier than the other

"O'Malley's full-page, full-color illustrations are exuberant and funny. Ella is suitably bubble-headed and self-absorbed while Edna is plain, practical, and bound to enjoy life." SLJ

Jaffe, Nina

In the month of Kislev; a story for Hanukkah; illustrated by Louise August. Viking 1992 30p il $15   E

1. Hanukkah—Fiction 2. Jews—Fiction

ISBN 0-670-82863-7   LC 91-45804

A rich, arrogant merchant takes the family of a poor peddler to court and learns a lesson about the meaning of Hanukkah

"A story rich in folkloric tradition, crisply told and firmly placed in an old-world setting. . . . The illustrations, prepared as woodcuts painted in oils on paper with warm browns, soft blues, and lots of black shading, have the rich look of rubbed wood." SLJ

James, Betsy

Mary Ann. Dutton Children's Bks. 1994 unp il $14.99   E

1. Praying mantis—Fiction 2. Friendship—Fiction

ISBN 0-525-45077-7   LC 93-13364

"Amy is miserable when her best friend moves away and wishes she could have 'hundreds of Mary Anns'—so that if one moved away, she would still have more. Then Amy finds a praying mantis, whom she names Mary Ann, and, when her new friend's eggs hatch, she gets her wish: 'hundreds and hundreds of Mary Anns!'" Horn Book Guide

"A shining example of a science lesson couched within an evocative story. . . . The pleasantly warm tones of the watercolor-and-ink illustrations portray the full gamut of emotions from true sadness to unabated joy. . . . The book concludes with a valuable author's note that presents fascinating facts and hints for raising these intriguing creatures." SLJ

Tadpoles. Dutton Children's Bks. 1999 unp il $14.99   E

1. Frogs—Fiction 2. Siblings—Fiction 3. Growth—Fiction

ISBN 0-525-46197-3   LC 98-47055

Molly likes her tadpoles better than her baby brother Davey but admires Davey's growth over a period of several months and compares it to the development of her tadpoles. Includes instructions for caring for tadpoles

"Cheerful watercolor and colored pencil illustrations reflect the everyday events of the text, while circular inserts show the developing embryos and their metamorphosis into frogs. A springlike palette of sunny colors . . . and pleasing compositions give the expressive figures of Molly and Davey charm and appeal." Bull Cent Child Books

James, J. Alison

The drums of Noto Hanto; story by J. Alison James; illustrations by Tsukushi. DK Pub. 1999 unp il $16.95   E

1. Drums—Fiction 2. Japan—Fiction

ISBN 0-789-42574-2   LC 98-21075

"A Richard Jackson"

The people in a small village in ancient Japan manage to drive off the forces of a powerful warlord using only their ingenuity and the many different village drums

"A simply yet powerfully told tale. . . . Tsukushi's cut-paper illustrations capture the time, place, and mood of the story." SLJ

Jay, Alison

Picture this . . . Dutton 2000 c1999 unp il $15.99   E

ISBN 0-525-46380-1

First published 1999 in the United Kingdom

"Each page of this . . . book names one featured item in the picture ('ball / teddy bear / hat') and one hidden item that will be featured in the next picture. . . . Rendered in a folk-art style, the muted illustrations look as if the surface they were painted on has crackled with age. The repeated motifs and intriguing ambiance will encourage multiple readings." Horn Book Guide

Jocelyn, Marthe, 1956-

Hannah's collections. Dutton Children's Bks. 2000 unp il $14.99   E

1. Collectors and collecting—Fiction

ISBN 0-525-46442-5   LC 99-462104

Unable to decide which of her many collections to take to school, Hannah surveys her collections of buttons, shells, feathers, and other wonderful objects and comes up with a unique solution

"Spreads and individual scenes in this bright, boldly graphic picture book possess startling clarity. . . . The story framework presents ingenious opportunities for preschoolers to practice some important thinking skills: counting, mathematical grouping, naming objects, and creative problem solving are all seamlessly wrapped up in this fresh, visually vibrant display." Booklist

Another available title about Hannah is:

Hannah and the seven dresses (1999)

Johnson, Angela, 1961-

Do like Kyla; paintings by James E. Ransome. Orchard Bks. 1990 unp il $15.95; lib bdg $14.99; pa $6.95   E

1. Sisters—Fiction 2. African Americans—Fiction

ISBN 0-531-05852-2; 0-531-08452-3 (lib bdg); 0-531-07040-9 (pa)   LC 89-16229

Johnson, Angela, 1961-—*Continued*
"A Richard Jackson book"
A little girl imitates her big sister Kyla all day, until in the evening Kyla imitates her
"Ransome's solid oil paintings feature two lively black girls firmly placed in a loving home, with both father and mother, and a neighborhood that pulses with realism." Booklist

Down the winding road; story by Angela Johnson; illustrations by Shane Evans. DK Ink 2000 unp il $15.95   E
1. Country life—Fiction 2. Family life—Fiction 3. African Americans—Fiction
ISBN 0-7894-2596-3   LC 99-41102
"A Richard Jackson book"
The annual summer visit to the country home of the Old Ones, the uncles and aunts who raised Daddy, brings joy and good times
"Johnson's language and selection of scenes are artfully simple and harmonize beautifully with Evans' full- and double-page oil paintings." Booklist

Julius; story by Angela Johnson; pictures by Dav Pilkey. Orchard Bks. 1993 unp il $16.95; pa $6.95   E
1. Pigs—Fiction
ISBN 0-531-05465-9; 0-531-07102-2 (pa)
                                            LC 92-24175
"A Richard Jackson book"
"Young Maya receives a gift from her grandfather, which he believes will help her learn about fun and sharing—a playful pig named Julius. The multimedia collages contain many artistic references. . . . They feature large areas of bright color or pattern, juxtaposed to create a visually dazzling, childlike vision of the world. An exuberant, joyful collaboration." Horn Book Guide

Tell me a story, Mama; pictures by David Soman. Orchard Bks. 1989 unp il $15.95; lib bdg $14.99; pa $6.95   E
1. Mother-daughter relationship—Fiction 2. African Americans—Fiction
ISBN 0-531-05794-1; 0-531-08394-2 (lib bdg); 0-531-07032-8 (pa)   LC 88-17917
A young girl and her mother remember together all the girl's favorite stories about her mother's childhood
"Soman's vivid, lively watercolors capture the essence of the mood and message as they deftly portray the quotidian portraits of two generations of a black family. Both language and art are full of subtle wit and rich emotion, resulting in a beautifully realized evocation of treasured childhood and family moments." SLJ

When I am old with you; story by Angela Johnson; pictures by David Soman. Orchard Bks. 1990 unp il $15.95; lib bdg $16.99; pa $6.95
                                                    E
1. Grandfathers—Fiction 2. Old age—Fiction
ISBN 0-531-05884-0; 0-531-08484-1 (lib bdg); 0-531-07035-2 (pa)   LC 89-70928
"A Richard Jackson book"
A young black boy imagines being old with Grandaddy and joining him in such activities as playing cards all day, visiting the ocean, and eating bacon on the porch
"A warm, affectionate portrait of a special relationship with impressive watercolors that are full of life." Horn Book Guide

Johnson, Crockett, 1906-1975
Harold and the purple crayon. Harper & Row 1955 unp il $14.95; lib bdg $14.89; pa $5.95
                                                    E
ISBN 0-06-022935-7; 0-06-022936-5 (lib bdg); 0-06-443022-7 (pa)
Also available Spanish language edition
"As Harold goes for a moonlight walk, he uses his purple crayon to draw a path and the things he sees along the way, then draws himself back home." Hodges. Books for Elem Sch Libr
Other available titles about Harold are:
Harold's ABC (1963)
Harold's circus (1959)
Harold's fairy tale (1986)
Harold's trip to the sky (1957)
A picture for Harold's room (1960)

Johnson, Dinah
Quinnie Blue; paintings by James Ransome. Holt & Co. 2000 unp il $16.95   E
1. Grandmothers—Fiction 2. African Americans—Fiction
ISBN 0-8050-4378-0   LC 98-47830
Hattie wonders about the activities of her grandmother Quinnie Blue when she was little
"In the rich oil illustrations for this poetic, celebratory text, blue-bordered scenes of Grandma's childhood alternate with white-bordered scenes from the narrator's life." Horn Book Guide

Johnson, Donald B. (Donald Barton), 1933-
Henry hikes to Fitchburg; [by] D. B. Johnson. Houghton Mifflin 2000 unp il $15   E
1. Thoreau, Henry David, 1817-1862—Fiction 2. Nature—Fiction 3. Walking—Fiction 4. Bears—Fiction
ISBN 0-395-96867-4   LC 99-35302
While his friend works hard to earn the train fare to Fitchburg, Henry the bear walks the thirty miles through woods and fields, enjoying nature and the time to think great thoughts. Includes biographical information about Henry David Thoreau
"This splendid book works on several levels. Johnson's adaption of a paragraph taken from Thoreau's *Walden* (set down in an author's note) illuminates the contrast between materialistic and naturalistic views of life without ranting or preaching. His illustrations are breathtakingly rich and filled with lovingly rendered details." Booklist

Johnson, Paul Brett
The cow who wouldn't come down; story and pictures by Paul Brett Johnson. Orchard Bks. 1993 unp il $15.95; lib bdg $16.99; pa $6.95   E
1. Cattle—Fiction
ISBN 0-531-05481-0; 0-531-08631-3 (lib bdg); 0-531-07091-3 (pa)   LC 92-27592

Johnson, Paul Brett—*Continued*
"A Richard Jackson book"
Miss Rosemary tries everything to coax her flying cow Gertrude down from the sky
"A rib-tickling read-aloud about a cow who defies gravity and logic, complemented by comical, light-dappled illustrations." SLJ

Lost; by Paul Brett Johnson and Celeste Lewis; illustrated by Paul Brett Johnson. Orchard Bks. 1996 unp il $15.95; lib bdg $16.99   E
1. Dogs—Fiction 2. Deserts—Fiction
ISBN 0-531-09501-0; 0-531-08851-0 (lib bdg)
                                   LC 95-20846
"A Richard Jackson book"
"During a camp-out in Arizona's Tonto National Forest, a girl and her father realize that their dog, Flag, has run off. Unable to find him, they post notices and return to the desert on weekends to search again and again. An old prospector tells them that there's not much hope, but later he finds the dog and takes him home to the girl. . . . Acrylic paintings on the left-hand pages show readers what's happening to Flag. . . . On the opposite page of the spread, sketchy colored-pencil drawings show what Flag's owner is doing as she waits for his return. A satisfying picture book portraying love, separation, and reunion." Booklist

Johnson, Stephen, 1964-
Alphabet city; [by] Stephen T. Johnson. Viking 1995 unp il $15.99; pa $6.99   E
1. Alphabet
ISBN 0-670-85631-2; 0-14-055904-3 (pa)
                                   LC 95-12335
A Caldecott Medal honor book, 1995
"Beginning with the *A* formed by a construction site's sawhorse and ending with the *Z* found in the angle of a fire escape, Johnson draws viewers' eyes to tiny details within everyday objects to find letters." SLJ
"Only after careful scrutiny will viewers realize that these arresting images aren't photographs but compositions of pastels, watercolors, gouache and charcoal. A visual tour de force, Johnson's ingenious alphabet book transcends the genre by demanding close inspection of not just letters, but the world." Publ Wkly

City by numbers. Viking 1998 unp il $15.99
                                            E
1. Counting
ISBN 0-670-87251-2   LC 98-20391
Paintings of various sites around New York City—from a shadow on a building to a wrought iron-gate to the Brooklyn Bridge—depict the numbers from one to twenty-one
"The numbers are more difficult to read than the letters of 'Alphabet City,' but perhaps the stretching of vision for this companion book makes it a grander and more complex achievement." N Y Times Book Rev

Johnston, Tony
Alice Nizzy Nazzy, the Witch of Santa Fe; illustrated by Tomie dePaola. Putnam 1995 unp il hardcover o.p. paperback available $5.99   E
1. Witches—Fiction 2. New Mexico—Fiction
ISBN 0-698-11650-X (pa)   LC 93-44375

Johnson and dePaola "transport Baba Yaga, one of Russia's great folklore figures, to the American Southwest. Incarnated here as Alice Nizzy Nazzy, the child-eating witch lives in an adobe hut perched on 'skinny roadrunner feet' and surrounded by a fence of prickly pear cactus. When Manuela wanders by in search of her lost sheep, she ends up in Alice's soup caldron." Publ Wkly
"Johnson's writing snaps with life. . . . dePaola has filled the book with the bright colors of the Southwest, using brick red borders and lots of teal, purple, and orange. Alice is a satisfying blend of spookiness and silliness." Bull Cent Child Books

The barn owls; illustrated by Deborah Kogan Ray. Charlesbridge Pub. 2000 unp il $15.95   E
1. Owls—Fiction
ISBN 0-88106-981-7   LC 99-18763
"A Talewinds book"
For at least one hundred years, generations of barn owls have slept, hunted, called, raised their young, and glided silently above the wheat fields around an old barn
"A few words of simple, poetic text accompany each picture, stressing the ebb and flow of life in and around the barn. . . . The pictures match the text's simplicity and understated tone, making this a quietly eloquent nature book." Booklist

The cowboy and the black-eyed pea; illustrated by Warren Ludwig. Putnam 1992 unp il $15.99; pa $4.95   E
1. Fairy tales 2. Cowhands—Fiction 3. West (U.S.)—Fiction
ISBN 0-399-22330-4; 0-698-11356-X (pa)
                                   LC 91-21606
In this adaptation of "The Princess and the Pea," the wealthy daughter of a Texas rancher devises a plan to find a real cowboy among her many suitors
"Rich with the language and details of the Wild West. Ludwig's colorful illustrations heighten the story's exaggerated humor (especially in facial expressions) and contrast nicely with the deadpan text. A great choice for a read-aloud." Booklist

Day of the Dead; illustrated by Jeanette Winter. Harcourt Brace & Co. 1997 unp il $14; pa $6
                                            E
1. All Souls' Day—Fiction 2. Mexico—Fiction
ISBN 0-15-222863-2; 0-15-202446-8 (pa)
                                   LC 96-2276
Describes a Mexican family preparing for and celebrating the Day of the Dead
"Spanish phrases are a natural part of the storytelling as the children ask questions about the cooking and preparations. . . . Winter's brilliantly colored, acrylic illustratons in folk-art style express the magic realism that is part of the ceremony under the stars." Booklist

The ghost of Nicholas Greebe; pictures by S.D. Schindler. Dial Bks. for Young Readers 1996 unp il $15.99; lib bdg $14.89; pa $5.99   E
1. Ghost stories 2. Bones—Fiction 3. Dogs—Fiction
ISBN 0-8037-1648-6; 0-8037-1649-4 (lib bdg); 0-14-056267-2 (pa)
                                   LC 95-35324
In Colonial Massachusetts, the ghost of a recently-buried farmer haunts his widow's house after a dog takes

Johnston, Tony—*Continued*

one of his bones on a long journey

"Johnston's rather sophisticated language suits the story, as does the artwork, which is loaded with delicate crosshatched details. Somber without being depressing, the pictures are suitably eerie." Booklist

The quilt story; pictures by Tomie dePaola. Putnam 1985 unp il $16.99; pa $5.95   E

1. Quilts—Fiction 2. Mother-daughter relationship—Fiction

ISBN 0-399-21009-1; 0-399-21008-3 (pa)

LC 84-18212

A pioneer mother lovingly stitches a beautiful quilt which warms and comforts her daughter Abigail; many years later another mother mends and patches it for her little girl

"DePaola's full-color tempera illustrations add much to the story—the folk-art style matches the text perfectly and will grab the attention of young 'book browsers.'" SLJ

The soup bone; illustrated by Margot Tomes. Harcourt Brace Jovanovich 1990 unp il $12.95; pa $4.95   E

1. Skeleton—Fiction 2. Halloween—Fiction

ISBN 0-15-277255-3; 0-15-277256-1 (pa)

LC 89-19900

Looking for a soup bone on Halloween, a little old lady finds a hungry skeleton instead

"The folkloric quality of the text, with its repetitive alliterative phrases, is ably complemented by Margot Tomes's superb illustrations. The two principals come alive against richly textured backgrounds in the interplay of light and shadow which creates dimension and defines space." Horn Book

Jonas, Ann

The 13th clue. Greenwillow Bks. 1992 unp il $16.95   E

1. Puzzles 2. Birthdays—Fiction 3. Parties—Fiction

ISBN 0-688-09742-1   LC 91-34586

A young girl follows thirteen clues to a surprise birthday party

"Puzzles the girl and the reader must decipher include a rebus, words formed by clothes hanging on a clothesline, letters that spell out different words upside down and right side up, and words with their letters scrambled. . . . The full-color artwork, with its delightful changes of perspective, shows a sure sense of design. While the book looks 'young,' it will appeal most to those early and middle elementary school children who are fascinated by wordplay." Booklist

Aardvarks, disembark! Greenwillow Bks. 1990 unp il lib bdg $17.89   E

1. Noah's ark 2. Rare animals 3. Alphabet

ISBN 0-688-07207-0   LC 89-27225

After the flood, Noah calls out of the ark a variety of little-known animals, many of which are now endangered

"The book concludes with a list of the 132 species pictured, and one line of information about each. Those now extinct or endangered are indicated. Realistic, accurate watercolors; an impressive, special book." Horn Book Guide

The quilt. Greenwillow Bks. 1984 unp il $16; lib bdg $15.93   E

1. Quilts—Fiction

ISBN 0-688-03825-5; 0-688-03826-3 (lib bdg)

LC 83-25385

Also available in paperback from Puffin Bks.

"A little girl is given a new patchwork quilt, and at bedtime she amuses herself by identifying the materials used in its making. Later, she has a colorful dream in which she almost loses her stuffed dog, Sally (a piece of Sally is in the quilt, too)." Child Book Rev Serv

"The intricate illustrations in Jonas's book can be described only in superlatives. Backed by a length of golden-yellow calico imprinted with small red flowers, a quilt fashioned from squares in a variety of colors is the prize shown to readers by a dear little girl." Publ Wkly

Reflections. Greenwillow Bks. 1987 unp il $16; lib bdg $15.93   E

1. Seashore—Fiction

ISBN 0-688-06140-0; 0-688-06141-9 (lib bdg)

LC 86-33545

"Imaginative book about a day at the seashore. At what is the end in most books, this book is reversed and read from back to front with re-interpreted artwork and new captions. Clever idea executed with skill, flare, and appealing, full-color illustrations. Excellent for encouraging observation and making predictions." Sci Child

Round trip. Greenwillow Bks. 1983 unp il $15.95; pa $4.95   E

1. City and town life—Fiction

ISBN 0-688-01772-X; 0-688-09986-6 (pa)

LC 82-12026

Black and white illustrations and text record the sights on a day trip to the city and back home again to the country. The trip to the city is read from front to back and the return trip, from back to front, upside down

"Although one or two pictures too easily suggest their upside-down images and the device is occasionally strained, the author-artist displays a fine sense of graphic design and balance, and pictorial beauty is never sacrificed for mere cleverness." Horn Book

Splash! Greenwillow Bks. 1995 unp il $16; lib bdg $16.89; pa $5.95   E

1. Counting 2. Animals—Fiction

ISBN 0-688-11051-7; 0-688-11052-5 (lib bdg); 0-688-15284-8 (pa)   LC 94-4110

A little girl's turtle, fish, frogs, dog, and cat jump in and out of a backyard pond, constantly changing the answer to the question "How many are in my pond?"

"A clever concept book with physical humor and exciting acrylic paintings that capture the heat and drama of a sunny summer day." Booklist

The trek. Greenwillow Bks. 1985 unp il hardcover o.p. paperback available $4.95   E

ISBN 0-688-08742-6 (pa)   LC 84-25962

Also available Spanish language edition

The author-illustrator presents the story of a young girl's daydream on her way to school. Familiar objects are transformed by her imagination as the walk turns into a jungle journey where exotic animals lie in wait

"It's up to the reader to find and identify all the ani-

Jonas, Ann—*Continued*

mals [the girl] sees lurking on a lawn, along a fence, in a grove of trees, or popping out of a fruit stand. The last two pages picture and identify all the creatures camouflaged in the illustrations, and many a viewer will be forced to flip back for further investigation of a hiding place." Bull Cent Child Books

Two bear cubs. Greenwillow Bks. 1982 unp il lib bdg $15.93   E
1. Bears—Fiction
ISBN 0-688-01408-9   LC 82-2860

"Two bear cubs, bent on exploration, stray from their mother in pursuit of adventure (a skunk) and wind up lost. They try their luck getting honey from a bee tree and fish from a stream, and the text repeats, 'Where is their mother?' Mother, meanwhile, appears in the background of each illustration, keeping a watchful eye on the proceedings and revealing herself in the end for a joyful reunion." SLJ

"The illustrations in Jonas's story demonstrate her unerring sense of how to use boldly contrasting colors and uncluttered shapes for maximum effect." Publ Wkly

Watch William walk. Greenwillow Bks. 1997 unp il $15; lib bdg $14.89   E
1. Walking—Fiction 2. Dogs—Fiction 3. Ducks—Fiction
ISBN 0-688-14172-2; 0-688-14175-7 (lib bdg)
LC 96-7467

"Every word in this alliterative story begins with 'W': the boy, William; his friend Wilma; the dog, Wally; the duck, Wanda. They walk, waddle [and] wade." N Y Times Book Rev

"If there isn't quite a story, Jonas does manage to spin out quite a lot of action. The clear pen-and-watercolor pictures are dramatic, all seen from above, the figures simple and bright, their shadows and footprints in silhouettes of widening circles." Booklist

Jonell, Lynne, 1956-

It's my birthday, too! written by Lynne Jonell; illustrated by Petra Mathers. Putnam 1999 unp il $12.99   E
1. Brothers—Fiction 2. Parties—Fiction 3. Birthdays—Fiction
ISBN 0-399-23323-7   LC 97-49635

Christopher would rather have a dog than a little brother who ruins his birthday parties, but when his brother begins to act like a puppy Christopher has a change of heart

"Mathers's kindergarten-crayon drawings capture all the emotional drama between the brothers and add unremarked-upon details of the birthday-party setting." Horn Book Guide

Let's play rough; pictures by Ted Rand. Putnam 2000 unp il $13.99   E
1. Father-son relationship—Fiction
ISBN 0-399-23039-4   LC 99-10624

A father and son have fun playing rough on the couch, grabbing, tossing, and tickling

"Wavy lines of type reflect the rambunctious mood, which is further enhanced by uncluttered illustrations." Horn Book Guide

Joosse, Barbara M., 1949-

Mama, do you love me? illustrated by Barbara Lavallee. Chronicle Bks. 1991 unp il $14.95   E
1. Mother-daughter relationship—Fiction 2. Inuit—Fiction
ISBN 0-87701-759-X   LC 90-1863

Also available Board book edition

"A young girl asks how much her mother loves her, even when she is naughty, and receives warm, reassuring answers. The twist on this familiar theme is that the two are Inuits, and the text and pictures draw on their unique culture. . . . Two pages of back matter define and explain the functions of various terms in Inuit life past and present. Charming, vibrant watercolor illustrations expand the simple rhythmic text, adding to the characters' personalities and to the cultural information." SLJ

Joyce, William

Bently & egg; story and pictures by William Joyce. HarperCollins Pubs. 1992 unp il $15.95; pa $5.95   E
1. Frogs—Fiction 2. Ducks—Fiction 3. Eggs—Fiction
ISBN 0-06-020385-4; 0-06-443352-8 (pa)
LC 91-55499

Also available Board book edition

"A Laura Geringer book"

"Bently Hopperton, a singing frog, baby-sits a duck egg for his friend Kack Kack. The egg is kidnapped, and in the process of rescuing it, Bently and the egg have a series of adventures." Child Book Rev Serv

"The illustrations, painted in the palest of springtime palettes, feature animals that are large on the page and comically expressive but rendered with a softness that is not typical of Joyce's previous work. The playful language, full-bodied and musical, is a pleasure to read aloud and will fall deliciously on the ears of eager young listeners." Horn Book

A day with Wilbur Robinson. Harper & Row 1990 unp il hardcover o.p. paperback available $6.95   E
ISBN 0-06-443339-0 (pa)   LC 90-4066

"A young narrator, going to see his best friend Wilbur, remarks, 'His house is the greatest place to visit.' Readers soon see why. Wilbur's large household includes an aunt whose train set is life-sized, an uncle who shares his 'deep thoughts' . . . and a grandfather who trains a dancing frog band. There's not much in the way of formal plot here—save a slight mystery involving Grandfather's missing false teeth—but Joyce's wonderfully strange paintings abound with hilarious, surprising details and leave the impression that a lot has happened." Publ Wkly

Dinosaur Bob and his adventures with the family Lazardo. new ed. HarperCollins Pubs. 1995 unp il music $16.95; lib bdg $16.89   E
1. Dinosaurs—Fiction
ISBN 0-06-021074-5; 0-06-021075-3 (lib bdg)
LC 94-19100

"A Laura Geringer book"

A revised and enlarged edition of the title first published 1988

Joyce, William—*Continued*
"The Lazardo family goes on safari to Africa where they find a dinosaur. They name him Bob and take him back to Pimlico Hills. . . . Bob soon becomes famous because he can play the trumpet, dance, and most importantly play baseball." Child Book Rev Serv [review of 1988 edition]

George shrinks; story and pictures by William Joyce. Harper & Row 1985 unp il $15.95; pa $5.95   **E**
1. Size—Fiction 2. Fantasy fiction
ISBN 0-06-023070-3; 0-06-443129-0 (pa)
    LC 83-47697
Also available Miniature edition
"A young boy named George awakes from his nap to discover he has become as small as a mouse. . . . Resting against the alarm clock is a piece of poster-size paper on which parental instructions are written telling George all that he should do after getting up. . . . Most of the book's text consists of this note's contents." N Y Times Book Rev
"The colorful illustrations, executed with painstaking attention to detail, create a surreal landscape from an ordinary breakfast-cereal world, as familiar objects become monumental structures through which the diminutive George moves with panache." Horn Book

Kalan, Robert
Blue sea; illustrated by Donald Crews. Greenwillow Bks. 1979 unp il hardcover o.p. paperback available $5.95   **E**
1. Size—Fiction 2. Fishes—Fiction
ISBN 0-688-11509-8 (pa)   LC 78-18396
Several fishes of varying size introduce space relationships and size differences
"On a deep-blue background, the words 'blue sea' appear in a paler shade and then the first of Crews's eye-filling paintings, 'little fish,' in bright yellow. While Kalan keeps his text to an irreducible minimum, the pictures increase in color and complexity." Publ Wkly

Jump, frog, jump! pictures by Byron Barton. Greenwillow Bks. 1981 unp il hardcover o.p. paperback available $5.95   **E**
1. Frogs—Fiction 2. Stories in rhyme
ISBN 0-688-09241-1 (pa)   LC 81-1401
Also available Big book edition; Spanish language edition also available
"For the frog, life in the swampy pond was hazardous in the extreme. Everyone, it seemed was out to get him—first a fish; then a snake, a turtle, a net, and finally some boys. The resourceful frog, however, had one big advantage—he was a champion jumper." Horn Book
"The excitement generated by the tale is matched by the humor in Barton's pictures. They resemble naive art but demonstrate superior skill in vibrant juxtaposition of colors and in the masterful composition that intensifies the story's momentum." SLJ

Rain; illustrated by Donald Crews. Greenwillow Bks. 1978 unp il lib. bdg $16.89; pa $5.95   **E**
1. Rain
ISBN 0-688-84139-2 (lib bdg); 0-688-10479-7 (pa)
    LC 77-25312

Brief text and illustrations describe a rainstorm, beginning with a blue sky, yellow sun and white clouds being replaced by gray sky and rain and ending with a bright rainbow-spanned scene

Kalman, Maira
Next stop, Grand Central. Putnam 1999 unp il $15.99   **E**
1. Grand Central Terminal (New York, N.Y.)
ISBN 0-399-22926-4   LC 98-25135
A simple introduction to the thousands of activities going on everyday in Grand Central, a train station in New York City
"Capturing all the hustle, bustle, and throbbing life of Grand Central Station, Kalman maintains an appropriately frenetic pace, parading the nonstop activity across the pages in a conglomeration of colorful vignettes. Kalman's odd-ball humor is in full evidence here." Horn Book Guide

Kaplan, Howard, 1950-
Waiting to sing; story by Howard Kaplan; illustrated by Hervé Blondon. DK Ink 2000 unp il $15.95   **E**
1. Mothers—Fiction 2. Music—Fiction 3. Death—Fiction
ISBN 0-7894-2615-3   LC 99-41081
"A Richard Jackson book"
A family that loves music and spends many hours at the piano is devastated by the death of the mother, but those still living find consolation in the beautiful music that also remains
"Illustrator Blondon's pastel pictures, in muted earth tones of brown, taupe, ocher, and tan, create a twilight world of light and shadow that beautifully captures the haunting, elegiac tone and atmosphere of the text." Booklist

Karas, G. Brian
The windy day. Simon & Schuster Bks. for Young Readers 1998 unp il $16   **E**
1. Winds—Fiction
ISBN 0-689-81449-6   LC 97-25427
One day the wind blows into a tidy little town, giving a tidy little boy named Bernard a hint of how wonderful and exciting the world is
"Karas's quiet, simple text is carried by his whimsical and exuberant illustrations. Scenes of the tidy town begin in neat, straight pencil drawings on beige paper. The wind brings in color (gouache and acrylic paints), movement, tilting perspective, and general excitement." SLJ

Karim, Roberta
Kindle me a riddle; a pioneer story; pictures by Bethanne Andersen. Greenwillow Bks. 1999 34p il $16; lib bdg $15.93   **E**
1. Frontier and pioneer life—Fiction 2. Family life—Fiction 3. Riddles—Fiction
ISBN 0-688-16203-7; 0-688-16204-5 (lib bdg)
    LC 98-18955

Karim, Roberta—*Continued*

The riddles that a pioneer family share explain the origin of such things in their lives as their log cabin, johnnycakes, the broom, a cloak, candles, and more

"Andersen matches Karim's homespun, image-rich language with vibrant, airy scenes of a cozy, well-appointed log cabin and rolling countryside amply dotted with trees." Publ Wkly

Kasza, Keiko

Dorothy & Mikey. Putnam 2000 unp il $12.99
                           E
1. Friendship—Fiction 2. Hippopotamus—Fiction
ISBN 0-399-23356-3   LC 98-18318
Three stories featuring Mikey and Dorothy, two hippo friends who play and compete with one another

"Kasza's illustrations, filled with action and humor, show her genius at using negative space and varied page designs." Horn Book Guide

The wolf's chicken stew. Putnam 1987 unp il $16.99; pa $5.99   E
1. Wolves—Fiction 2. Chickens—Fiction
ISBN 0-399-21400-3; 0-399-22000-9 (pa)
                           LC 86-12303
"An old plot takes a new turn after the wolf, determined to fatten a chicken for his stew, bakes goodies for her every day only to find them consumed by a horde of baby chicks who shame 'Uncle Wolf' with their adoring gratitude." Bull Cent Child Books

"Kasza combines quivery line and shaded color to turn Wolf and Chicken into scuptural forms. Landscape images are treated similarly, and produce an open, expansive feeling when placed asymmetrically. Wolf is comically and suspensefully visualized, making the flimflamming refrains sound just right for such a charismatic rascal." Wilson Libr Bull

Kay, Verla, 1946-

Gold fever; illustrations by S.D. Schindler. Putnam 1999 unp il $15.99   E
1. California—Gold discoveries—Fiction 2. West (U.S.)—Fiction
ISBN 0-399-23027-0   LC 97-49634
In this brief rhyming story set during the gold rush, Jasper leaves his family and farm to pursue his dream of finding gold

"Schindler's colored pencil drawings convey the rugged scenery and the gritty enterprise of digging and sluicing for gold. Kay's tongue-in-cheek economy beautifully encapsulates this brief, colorful moment in history." Horn Book Guide

Keats, Ezra Jack, 1916-1983

Apt. 3. Viking 1999 unp il $15.99; pa $5.99
                           E
1. City and town life—Fiction 2. Brothers—Fiction 3. Blind—Fiction
ISBN 0-670-88342-5; 0-14-056507-8 (pa)
                           LC 98-41043
A reissue of the title first published 1971 by Macmillan

On a rainy day two brothers try to discover who is playing the harmonica they hear in their apartment building

"The well-paced text is illustrated with shadowy paintings that capably convey both the dingy surroundings and the brothers' affection." Horn Book Guide

Clementina's cactus. Viking 1999 c1982 unp il $13.99   E
1. Cactus—Fiction 2. Deserts—Fiction 3. Stories without words
ISBN 0-670-88545-2   LC 98-47506
A reissue of the title first published 1982

"Little Clementina, a pioneer girl, examines an ugly cactus near her small shack. The next day after a storm, the cactus is abloom with brilliant yellow flowers. Showing both the sun-bleached vastness of a desert country as well as its brilliance, the wordless double-page spreads tell the story without a text." Horn Book Guide

Hi, cat! Viking 1999 unp il $15.99   E
1. Cats—Fiction 2. African Americans—FIction
ISBN 0-670-88546-0   LC 98-37764
A reissue of the title first published 1970 by Macmillan

This book "tells the story of Peter's friend Archie and the inquisitive, nondescript, half-grown alley cat that tags after him and manages to make a shambles out of the boys' street carnival. The text provides an adequate framework for Keats's bold bright paintings of a lively city neighborhood." Horn Book Guide

Another available title about Archie is:
Pet show! (1972)

Louie. Greenwillow Bks. 1983 c1975 unp il lib bdg $14.89   E
1. Puppets and puppet plays—Fiction
ISBN 0-688-02383-5
First published 1975

A shy, withdrawn boy loses his heart to a puppet

"This story is illustrated with the same glowing colors . . . and with some of the postercollage that is the artist's trademark. The aura is touching without being maudlin, the writing simple and informal. . . . The elements of kindness to others, imaginative play, and a fervent wish granted should have a strong appeal to the picture book audience." Sutherland. The Best in Child Books

Other available titles about Louie are:
Louie's search (1980)
Regards to the man in the moon (1981)
The trip (1978)

My dog is lost! [by] Ezra Jack Keats and Pat Cherr. Viking 1999 unp il $15.99; pa $5.99   E
1. Puerto Ricans—Fiction 2. Dogs—Fiction 3. New York (N.Y.)—Fiction
ISBN 0-670-88550-9; 0-14-056569-8 (pa)
                           LC 98-37755
A reissue of the title first published 1960 by Crowell
"Juanito, who speaks only Spanish, has just arrived in New York from Puerto Rico—and he's lost his dog. Searching through the city, he meets children from Chinatown, Little Italy, Park Avenue, and Harlem and manages to make his problem clear to all of them in spite of language difficulties. Lively pictures in brilliant red and black illustrate the entertaining [book]." Horn Book Guide

Keats, Ezra Jack, 1916-1983—*Continued*

Over in the meadow; [written and] illustrated by Ezra Jack Keats. Viking 1999 unp il $15.99; pa $5.99　　　　　　　　　　　　　　　　　E
1. Nursery rhymes 2. Animals—Poetry 3. Counting
ISBN 0-670-88344-1; 0-14-056508-6 (pa)
　　　　　　　　　　　　　　　　LC 98-47037
A reissue of the title first published 1971 by Four Winds Press
Based on Southern Appalachian counting rhyme from late 1800's attributed to Olive A. Wadsworth
An old nursery poem introduces animals and their young and the numbers one through ten
"The book features Keats's illustrations that show animals in lively characteristic activity." Horn Book Guide

The snowy day. Viking 1962 31p il lib bdg $15.99; pa $5.99　　　　　　　　　　　　　　E
1. Snow—Fiction
ISBN 0-670-65400-0 (lib bdg); 0-14-050182-7 (pa)

Also available Board book edition and Big book edition; Spanish language edition also available
Awarded the Caldecott Medal, 1963
A small "boy's ecstatic enjoyment of snow in the city is shown in vibrant pictures. Peter listens to the snow crunch under his feet, makes the first tracks in a clean patch of snow, makes angels and a snowman. At night in his warm bed he thinks over his adventures, and in the morning wakens to the promise of another lovely snowy day." Moorachian. What is a City?
　Other available titles about Peter are:
Goggles (1969)
A letter to Amy (1968)
Peter's chair (1967)
Whistle for Willie (1964)

Keller, Holly
Geraldine's blanket. Greenwillow Bks. 1984 unp il hardcover o.p. paperback available $5.95　　E
1. Blankets—Fiction
ISBN 0-688-07810-9 (pa)　　　　　LC 83-14062
"Geraldine's pink blanket was a baby present from Aunt Bessie. It's worn now and patched, and when Aunt Bessie sends her a doll, Geraldine preserves and transfers her affections simultaneously by using the scraps for a doll dress." N Y Times Book Rev
"Simply but wonderfully expressive line drawings washed with pastel colors capture the gentleness and humor of the story." SLJ
　Other available titles about Geraldine are:
Geraldine and Mrs. Duffy (2000)
Geraldine first (1996)
Geraldine's baby brother (1994)
Geraldine's big snow (1988)
Merry Christmas, Geraldine (1997)

Grandfather's dream. Greenwillow Bks. 1994 unp il $15.95　　　　　　　　　　　　　　E
1. Cranes (Birds)—Fiction 2. Grandfathers—Fiction 3. Vietnam—Fiction
ISBN 0-688-12339-2　　　　　　　LC 93-18186

After the end of the war in Vietnam, a young boy's grandfather dreams of restoring the wetlands of the Mekong delta, hoping that the large cranes that once lived there will return
"Keller uses simple, direct storytelling and vivid watercolor and ink illustrations to present a complex theme in a story of hope and rebirth." Horn Book Guide

Horace. Greenwillow Bks. 1991 unp il $16; pa $4.95　　　　　　　　　　　　　　　　　E
1. Adoption—Fiction
ISBN 0-688-09831-2; 0-688-11844-5 (pa)
　　　　　　　　　　　　　　　　LC 90-30750
"Horace is adopted. He is also spotted, and he is loved and cared for by his new mother and father—who are striped. But . . . Horace feels the need to search out his roots. And although he does find a brood that resembles him physically, it is not a family that truly loves him. . . . Keller . . . deals with a sensitive subject in a way that is perceptive but not sentimental. . . . The bright, boldly colored illustrations feature a lively animal cast and numerous amusing details." Publ Wkly
　Other available titles about Horace are:
Brave Horace (1998)
That's mine, Horace (2000)

Jacob's tree. Greenwillow Bks. 1999 unp il $15; lib bdg $14.89　　　　　　　　　　　　E
1. Size—Fiction 2. Growth—Fiction 3. Family life—Fiction
ISBN 0-688-15995-8; 0-688-15996-6 (lib bdg)
　　　　　　　　　　　　　　　　LC 98-2978
Jacob is the smallest one in his family and although everyone tells him he will grow, he finds it hard to wait
"The warmly drawn domestic scenes have simple charm, and the economical text perfectly encapsulates this universal predicament." Horn Book Guide

Kelley, True, 1946-
I've got chicken pox; written and illustrated by True Kelley. Dutton Children's Bks. 1994 unp il $14.99　　　　　　　　　　　　　　　　E
1. Chickenpox—Fiction 2. Sick—Fiction
ISBN 0-525-45185-4　　　　　　　LC 93-11685
When Jess gets chicken pox it seems glamorous at first, but soon she gets tired of being stuck at home
"The text very realistically portrays the various emotional stages of chicken pox. . . . The illustrations are rendered in bright, engaging watercolors—many have charming details. . . . Each of the illustrations has a border that reflects the stage of Jess's progressing chicken pox. Another welcome feature is the inclusion of a 'pox fact' at the bottom of each page, many of which answer the most commonly asked questions of patients or parents regarding chicken pox." Sci Books Films

Kellogg, Steven, 1941-
Aster Aardvark's alphabet adventures. Morrow 1987 unp il $16; lib bdg $14.93; pa $3.95　　E
1. Alphabet 2. Animals—Fiction
ISBN 0-688-07256-9; 0-688-07257-7 (lib bdg); 0-688-11571-3 (pa)　　　　　　　LC 87-5715
Alliterative text and pictures present adventures of animals from A to Z

Kellogg, Steven, 1941-—*Continued*

"Glowing with bright, harmonious hues, the lively, if sometimes crowded, watercolor scenes display plots, subplots, and myriad details. . . . Children will delight in this zany celebration of the sound and sense of words and will savor the sight of so many silly situations so clearly out of hand." Booklist

Best friends; story and pictures by Steven Kellogg. Dial Bks. for Young Readers 1986 unp il $16.99; pa $6.99   E

1. Friendship—Fiction

ISBN 0-8037-0099-7; 0-14-054607-3 (pa)

LC 85-15971

Kathy feels lonely and betrayed when her best friend Louise goes away for the summer and has a wonderful time

"The watercolor and ink illustrations are appealingly bright and magical. Kathy and Louise's daydreams are vividly and flamboyantly portrayed, with 'reality' just as attractively pictured." SLJ

I was born about 10,000 years ago; a tall tale; retold and illustrated by Steven Kellogg. Morrow Junior Bks. 1996 unp il music $16; pa $5.95   E

1. Tall tales 2. Stories in rhyme

ISBN 0-688-13411-4; 0-688-16156-1 (pa)

LC 95-35079

"A tall tale based on a traditional folk song. . . . Children spin their yarns weaving outrageous tales of what they have witnessed. Everything from seeing Pharaoh's daughter fish Moses out of the water and Columbus's discovery of the New World, to driving cattle with Pecos Bill and playing hopscotch on the moon are a part of these kids' whoppers. . . . Humor abounds in the vivid illustrations and the text. . . . The book ends on a good note with the catchy score for the book's title song." SLJ

The missing mitten mystery; story and pictures by Steven Kellogg. Dial Bks. for Young Readers 2000 unp il $15.99   E

ISBN 0-8037-2566-3   LC 99-54777

First published 1974 with title: The mystery of the missing red mitten

Annie searches the neighborhood for her red mitten, the fifth she's lost this winter

"Kellog really outdoes himself with pictures that are filled with good cheer, warm spirits, and happy daydreams. . . . A book that's upbeat and touching by turns." Booklist

Much bigger than Martin; story and pictures by Steven Kellogg. Dial Bks. for Young Readers 1976 unp il hardcover o.p. paperback available $6.99   E

1. Brothers—Fiction

ISBN 0-14-054666-9 (pa)

"Henry doesn't like being Martin's little brother when he's victim in games, gets the smallest piece of cake, or finds the basketball loop too high for his shots. . . . The imagination scenes, where Henry perceives himself as a giant towering over Martin, are where Kellogg's touches of subtle humor and whimiscal detail are most effective. The black line drawings are washed in hues of gold, green, and blue." Booklist

The mysterious tadpole. Dial Bks. for Young Readers 1977 unp il hardcover o.p. paperback available $6.99   E

1. Pets—Fiction

ISBN 0-14-054870-X (pa)   LC 77-71517

"Lively details in the author's full-color illustrations portray the fantastic growth and lovable behavior of a tadpole sent Louis from Loch Ness, Scotland, for his birthday." LC. Child Books, 1977

Pinkerton, behave! story and pictures by Steven Kellogg. Dial Bks. for Young Readers 1979 unp il $16.99; pa $6.99   E

1. Dogs—Fiction

ISBN 0-8037-6573-8; 0-14-054687-1 (pa)

LC 78-31794

"Pinkerton is a large dog modeled after the author-artist's harlequin Great Dane. He appears to be untrainable, both at home and at obedience school. Actually, he responds consistently to commands, but when he is told to fetch, he tears the newspaper to shreds; and when he is told to get the burglar, he licks the face of the dummy he is expected to destroy. One day, when a real burglar appears, Pinkerton's small owner remembers the dog's idiosyncrasies, commands him to fetch, and all ends well." SLJ

"Kellogg wittily captures expressions and movements of animal and human, wisely allowing the focal humor to emanate through the faces and action and forgoing the background detail usually found in his work." Booklist

Other available titles about Pinkerton are:

Prehistoric Pinkerton (1987)

A Rose for Pinkerton (1981)

Tallyho, Pinkerton! (1982)

Kesselman, Wendy Ann

Emma; illustrated by Barbara Cooney. Doubleday 1980 unp il o.p.; Dell paperback available $6.99   E

1. Painting—Fiction 2. Old age—Fiction

ISBN 0-440-40847-4 (pa)   LC 77-15161

This book is "about a lonely grandmother named Emma, who, after her 72d birthday, began to paint pictures, starting with images of the village where she had lived as a girl. The illustrations capture Emma's personal and artistic style with charm." N Y Times Book Rev

Kessler, Leonard P., 1920-

Here comes the strikeout. newly il ed. HarperCollins Pubs. 1992 64p il lib bdg $15.89; pa $3.95   E

1. Baseball—Fiction

ISBN 0-06-023156-4 (lib bdg); 0-06-444011-7 (pa)

LC 91-14717

Also available with Audiobook

"An I can read book"

A revised and newly illustrated edition of the title first published 1965

This "concerns a boy who can't hit a baseball until he follows the advice of a friend. 'Lucky helmets won't do it. Lucky bats won't do it. Only hard work will do it.' . . . A winner." Booklist

Kessler, Leonard P., 1920-—*Continued*

Kick, pass, and run; story and pictures by Leonard Kessler. newly il ed. HarperCollins Pubs. 1996 64p il lib bdg $15.89; pa $3.95   E
  1. Football—Fiction
ISBN 0-06-027105-1 (lib bdg); 0-06-444210-1 (pa)
                  LC 95-6185
"An I can read book"
A newly illustrated edition of the title first published 1966
"After a group of animal friends watches a boys' football team play, they are eager to have their own game. An apple serves as a ball until Frog eats it; a paper-bag football works until Duck kicks and pops it. The game is kept alive when a real football from the boys' game sails into the animals' midst. [A] simply told story with plenty of sports action." Horn Book Guide

Last one in is a rotten egg. newly il ed. HarperCollins Pubs. 1999 64p $14.95; lib bdg $14.89; pa $3.95   E
  1. Swimming—Fiction
ISBN 0-06-028484-6; 0-06-028485-4 (lib bdg); 0-06-444262-4 (pa)   LC 98-50882
"An I can read book"
A newly illustrated edition of the title first published 1969
After Freddy is pushed into deep water by a couple of toughs, he decides to learn to swim
"This lively . . . sports story has been newly illustrated with a multicultural cast in a New York City neighborhood." Booklist

Khalsa, Dayal Kaur

Cowboy dreams. Potter 1990 unp il hardcover o.p. paperback available $5.99   E
  1. Cowhands—Fiction
ISBN 0-517-88744-4 (pa)   LC 89-22782
"A young city girl dreams of being a cowgirl and riding horses in the Wild West. Unable to do so, the basement banister, pieces of clothesline and an old blanket become her horse and its trappings." Child Book Rev Serv
"Humorous touches are many. . . . 'Cowboy Dreams' showcases the author-illustrator's special gift for discerning and communicating what is important to children, and since this book is as much about the power of dreams and imagination as it is about the West, it will fascinate young people from coast to coast." Horn Book

How pizza came to Queens. Potter 1989 unp il $15; pa $5.99   E
  1. New York (N.Y.)—Fiction
ISBN 0-517-57126-9; 0-517-88538-7 (pa)
                LC 88-22452
May, of My family vacation (1988) is visiting her good friends the Penny sisters. An Italian visitor to their Queens home bemoans the unavailability of pizza until the thoughtful girls enable her to make some
"It is a straightforward little story, with bright, bold, naïve paintings. Any young pizza lover will relish it." N Y Times Book Rev

Kimmel, Eric A.

The Chanukkah guest; illustrated by Giora Carmi. Holiday House 1990 unp il $16.95; pa $6.95   E
  1. Hanukkah—Fiction 2. Bears—Fiction
ISBN 0-8234-0788-8; 0-8234-0978-3 (pa)
                LC 89-20073
On the first night of Chanukkah, Old Bear wanders into Bubba Brayna's house and receives a delicious helping of potato latkes when she mistakes him for the rabbi
"In this comical story, Kimmel captures the kindness of an old woman and the innocence of a hungry bear in an unusual visit. Carmi's airy pastel illustrations shade the tale with a golden glow appropriate for the Festival of Lights." Publ Wkly

Four dollars and fifty cents; illustrated by Glen Rounds. Holiday House 1990 unp il lib bdg $16.95; pa $5.95   E
  1. Cowhands—Fiction 2. West (U.S.)—Fiction
ISBN 0-8234-0817-5 (lib bdg); 0-8234-1024-2 (pa)
                LC 89-77515
Originally published in Cricket
To avoid paying the Widow Macrae the four dollars and fifty cents he owes her, deadbeat cowboy Shorty Long plays dead and almost gets buried alive
"Rounds's outrageous, bold, line-and-crayon drawings perfectly suit the tale's Western flavor. A fast-paced, funny story." Horn Book

Grizz! illustrated by Andrew Glass. Holiday House 2000 unp il $16.95   E
  1. Devil—Fiction 2. Cowhands—Fiction
ISBN 0-8234-1469-8   LC 98-43332
Cowboy Lucky Doolin makes a deal with the Devil, agreeing not to wash, shave, or change his clothes for seven years, thus earning a fortune and the hand of his true love
"This outwit-the-devil tale gets a wild west twist, enhanced by folksy prose and lively oil-and-watercolor illustrations." Booklist

Hershel and the Hanukkah goblins; written by Eric A. Kimmel; illustrated by Trina Schart Hyman. Holiday House 1989 unp il $16.95; pa $6.95   E
  1. Hanukkah—Fiction 2. Fairies—Fiction 3. Jews—Fiction
ISBN 0-8234-0769-1; 0-8234-1131-1 (pa)
                LC 89-1954
A Caldecott Medal honor book, 1990
"The setting is an Eastern European village, and the plot is a little like Halloween Hanukkah—it seems that goblins are occupying the synagogue on the hill. Along comes plucky Hershel of Ostropol, and he cleverly outwits the demons." N Y Times Book Rev
This "will fit companionably with haunted castle variants. Hyman is at her best with windswept landscapes, dark interiors, close portraiture, and imaginatively wicked creatures. Both art and history are charged with energy." Bull Cent Child Books

I took my frog to the library; pictures by Blanche Sims. Viking Penguin 1990 unp il hardcover o.p. paperback available $5.99   E
  1. Pets—Fiction 2. Libraries—Fiction
ISBN 0-14-050916-X (pa)   LC 89-37866

Kimmel, Eric A.—*Continued*

"Havoc reigns when Bridgett's animal friends accompany her to the library." SLJ

"Sims plays with the inherent humor of Kimmel's brief story, painting young patrons' horror at a python shedding her skin all over the picture books or their uneasy amusement as a giraffe reads over their shoulders. Finally young Bridgett agrees to the librarian's suggestion that she come alone to the library, leaving her animal friends content at home with the elephant reading to them. A hilariously enjoyable introduction to library manners for young patrons." Booklist

The magic dreidels; a Hanukkah story; illustrated by Katya Krenina. Holiday House 1996 unp il $16.95; pa $6.95   E

1. Hanukkah—Fiction 2. Jews—Fiction 3. Fairy tales
ISBN 0-8234-1256-3; 0-8234-1274-1 (pa)
LC 96-2405

"When Jacob drops his dreidel down the well, the goblin who lives under the water gives the boy a magic dreidel that spins out delicious latkes (potato pancakes) with sour cream and applesauce. But Fruma Sarah, the neighborhood busybody, tricks him out of the goblin's gift. . . . The brightly colored pictures by Ukrainian American artist Krenina combine magic realism with a cheerful magazine illustration style. At the end are notes on the Hanukkah traditions, including details on the dreidel game. Kids will enjoy the story of the trickster out-tricked." Booklist

Kitamura, Satoshi

Me and my cat? Farrar, Straus & Giroux 2000 unp il $16   E

1. Cats—Fiction 2. Magic—Fiction
ISBN 0-374-34906-1   LC 99-16598

A young boy spends an unusual day after awakening to find that he and his cat have switched bodies

"Kitamura's oddball sense of humor finds a perfect outlet here, and readers will find a fresh and lively diversion in this uncommon adventure." Horn Book Guide

Sheep in wolves' clothing. Farrar, Straus & Giroux 1996 c1995 unp il $15; pa $5.95   E

1. Sheep—Fiction 2. Wolves—Fiction
ISBN 0-374-36780-9; 0-374-46456-1 (pa)
LC 95-18199

First published 1995 in the United Kingdom

When wolves steal their fluffy coats, two sheep turn to Detective Baa for help

"Kitamura's lively, comical drawings, tinted with dusky washes, give the picture book enough adventure and comedy to appeal to young children who like books where something *happens*." Booklist

Kitchen, Bert

Animal alphabet. Dial Bks. for Young Readers 1984 unp il $13.95; pa $6.99   E

1. Alphabet 2. Animals
ISBN 0-8037-0117-9; 0-14-054601-4 (pa)
LC 83-23929

The reader is invited to guess the identity of twenty-six unusual animals illustrating the letter of the alphabet

"Color and line are masterfully manipulated to produce a three-dimensional effect so that each animal seems to have been arrested in motion. Skillful rendering of textures provides effective contrast with the stark, glossy paper, adds visual excitement, and imbues each species with vitality, while the oversized format, allowing for generous expanses of white, is particularly suited to the elegance of the concept." Horn Book

Kleven, Elisa

Hooray, a piñata! Dutton Children's Bks. 1996 unp il $16.99; pa $5.99   E

1. Birthdays—Fiction 2. Parties—Fiction 3. Toys—Fiction
ISBN 0-525-45605-8; 0-14-056764-X (pa)
LC 95-45750

After she chooses a cute dog piñata for her birthday party, Clara pretends it is her pet and she doesn't want it to get broken

"The bright watercolor and cut-paper illustrations are a visual fiesta. Tiny details abound in the full- and double-page scenes. . . . Both the affectionate story and vibrant artwork are sure to please children." SLJ

The paper princess. Dutton Children's Bks. 1994 unp il $16.99; pa $6.99   E

1. Drawing—Fiction
ISBN 0-525-45231-1; 0-14-056424-1 (pa)
LC 93-32612

A little girl makes a picture of a princess that comes to life and is carried off by the wind

"The jubilant, communicative collage art captivates the reader, as the winning text beguiles. A delightful reading experience." Horn Book Guide

Koide, Tan, 1938-1986

May we sleep here tonight? illustrated by Yasuko Koide. Margaret K. McElderry Bks. 2001 unp il $12.95   E

1. Animals—Fiction
ISBN 0-689-83288-5   LC 99-34963

Original Japanese edition 1981; first United States edition published 1982 by Atheneum Pubs.

Several lost animals find a cozy house in the woods, settle down for the night, and are startled when the house's very big owner arrives

" The cozy interiors, appealingly drawn animals, and familiar themes transcend cultural borders." Booklist

Koller, Jackie French

One monkey too many; illustrated by Lynn Munsinger. Harcourt Brace & Co. 1999 unp il $16   E

1. Monkeys—Fiction 2. Stories in rhyme
ISBN 0-15-200006-2   LC 96-50350

"Seven mischievous monkeys wreak havoc as 'one monkey too many' climbs first onto a bike made for one, then into a golf cart for two, then into a canoe for three, and so on." Horn Book Guide

"The joke is delightful, and Munsinger's boisterous illustrations, with animal characters galore . . . are full of expression, movement, and wacky comedy." Booklist

Kopper, Lisa, 1950-

Daisy knows best. Dutton Children's Bks. 1999 unp il $12.99　　　　　　　　　　　　　E
1. Dogs—Fiction 2. Infants—Fiction
ISBN 0-525-45915-4　　　　　　LC 98-28178
"Daisy teaches her puppies—and the baby—important things: how to open the mail (with their teeth), set the table (or un-set it), and dig in the garden. But it turns out that Mother, not Daisy, knows best." Horn Book Guide
"The story reads aloud well, and the text is simple and repetitive enough for beginning readers. The soft, pencil illustrations reflect the lively humor and chaotic events described in the narrative." SLJ
　Other available titles about Daisy are:
Daisy is a mommy (1997)
Daisy's babies (2000)

Kraus, Robert, 1925-

Little Louie the baby bloomer; pictures by Jose Aruego & Ariane Dewey. HarperCollins Pubs. 1998 unp il $15.95; lib bdg $15.89; pa $5.95
　　　　　　　　　　　　　　　　　E
1. Tigers—Fiction 2. Brothers—Fiction
ISBN 0-06-026293-1; 0-06-026294-X (lib bdg); 0-06-443656-X (pa)　　　　LC 96-42434
Companion volume to Leo the late bloomer (1971)
Leo the tiger worries and wonders why his little brother Louie can't do anything right, but his parents encourage Leo to be patient
"Young readers will appreciate the engaging visual humor." SLJ

Mort the sport; illustrated by John Himmelman. Orchard Bks. 2000 unp il $15.95; lib bdg $16.99
　　　　　　　　　　　　　　　　　E
1. Baseball—Fiction 2. Violinists—Fiction
ISBN 0-531-30247-4; 0-531-33247-0 (lib bdg)
　　　　　　　　　　　　LC 99-28574
Mort's attempts to excel at playing both baseball and the violin make him so confused that he decides to take up chess instead
"With the moral couched in laugh-out-loud humor, this story will delight young readers and story-time listeners." Booklist

Whose mouse are you? pictures by José Aruego. Macmillan 1970 unp il　　　　　　　　E
1. Mice—Fiction 2. Stories in rhyme

Available from Simon & Schuster
A lonely little mouse has to be resourceful in order to bring his family back together
"This is an absolute charmer of a picture book, original, tender, and childlike. The rhyming text is so brief, so catchy, and so right that a child will remember the words after one or two readings, and the large, uncluttered illustrations are gay and appealing." Booklist
　Other available titles about the mouse and his family are:
Come out and play, little mouse (1987)
Mouse in love (2000)
Where are you going, little mouse? (1986)

Krauss, Ruth, 1911-1993

The carrot seed; pictures by Crockett Johnson. Harper & Row 1945 unp il $14.95; pa $5.95
　　　　　　　　　　　　　　　　　E
ISBN 0-06-023350-8; 0-06-443210-6 (pa)
Also available Board book edition; Spanish language edition also available
Simple text and picture show how the faith of a small boy, who planted a carrot seed, was rewarded
"Crockett Johnson's pictures are perfect and the brief text is just right." Book Week

A very special house; pictures by Maurice Sendak. Harper & Row 1953 unp il $17.89　　E
ISBN 0-06-023456-3
A Caldecott Medal honor book, 1954
"The very special house is a house which exists in the imagination of a small boy—a house where the chairs are for climbing, the walls for writing on, and the beds for jumping on; a house where a lion, a giant, or a dead mouse is welcome, and where nobody ever says stop. Told in a chanting rhythm that demands participation by the reader; the imaginary characters, objects, and doings are pictured in line drawings almost as a child would scribble them while the real little boy stands out boldly in bright blue overalls." Booklist

Krensky, Stephen, 1953-

How Santa got his job; illustrated by S.D. Schindler. Simon & Schuster Bks. for Young Readers 1998 unp il $15　　　　　　　　E
1. Santa Claus—Fiction
ISBN 0-689-80697-3　　　　　　LC 97-23474
This "peek at Santa's resumé reveals how various odd jobs, like chimney sweep and mail carrier, helped prepare him for his world-famous career. . . . [Schindler's] intricate pen-and-watercolor illustrations make Santa's evolution from boyish redhead to the familiar heavy-set, snowy-bearded character a joy to watch." Publ Wkly

Lionel at large; pictures by Susanna Natti. Dial Bks. for Young Readers 1986 56p il hardcover o.p. paperback available $3.99　　　　　　E
1. Family life—Fiction
ISBN 0-8037-0556-5 (pa)　　　　LC 85-15930
"Dial easy-to-read"
"Five simply written stories for the beginning independent reader are illustrated by full-color drawings, line-and-wash, that have a cheerful vitality and humor. Each story is a modest anecdote about Lionel: a visit to the doctor, a confrontation with the necessity of eating vegetables, a nervous hunt for an older sister's pet snake . . . in other words, experiences similar to those most children have. There's a quiet humor in the writing, so that readers can enjoy the joke while they are empathizing with Lionel's problems and with his success in overcoming or tolerating them." Bull Cent Child Books
　Other available titles about Lionel are:
Lionel and his friends (1996)
Lionel and Louise (1992)
Lionel at school (2000)
Lionel in the fall (1987)
Lionel in the spring (1990)
Lionel in the summer (1998)
Lionel in the winter (1994)

Kroeger, Mary Kay, 1950-

Paperboy; by Mary Kay Kroeger and Louise Borden; illustrated by Ted Lewin. Clarion Bks. 1996 31p il $16.95   **E**

1. Newspaper carriers—Fiction 2. Boxing—Fiction 3. Cincinnati (Ohio)—Fiction

ISBN 0-395-64482-8   LC 94-34246

In Cincinnati in 1927, paperboy Willie Brinkman tries to sell extras on the Dempsey-Tunney boxing match in his workingman's neighborhood

"Lewin's watercolors bring Willie's Cincinnati to life. . . . Black-and-white 'stills' of Dempsey and Tunney share some pages with vivid, animated full-color scenes of the Brinkman family. An engaging work that will bring home, through well-chosen details and a well-told story, the intimate connections one can make with 'famous facts' when the personal perspective is added." SLJ

Kroll, Steven

The biggest pumpkin ever; illustrated by Jeni Bassett. Holiday House 1984 unp il $16.95   **E**

1. Pumpkin—Fiction   2. Halloween—Fiction 3. Mice—Fiction

ISBN 0-8234-0505-2   LC 83-18492

Also available in paperback from Scholastic

"A village mouse and a field mouse fall in love with the same pumpkin. Clayton feeds and waters it by day, while Desmond tends it at night. What a surprise when the two finally bump into each other! Whose pumpkin is it—Clayton's for the pumpkin contest, or Desmond's for a jack-o'-lantern?" Publisher's note

"The cheerful, bright watercolor illustrations are as captivating as the text. Children will delight in reading or hearing this story at any time of the year." Child Book Rev Serv

Kroll, Virginia L.

Faraway drums; by Virginia Kroll; illustrated by Floyd Cooper. Little, Brown 1998 unp il $14.95   **E**

1. African Americans—Fiction 2. Sisters—Fiction 3. Africa—Fiction

ISBN 0-316-50449-1   LC 95-14517

Jamila and her little sister are frightened by the loud city noises at their new apartment, but they find comfort in recalling the stories their great-grandma used to tell about life in Africa

"The hazy sepia-toned illustrations conjure up scenes from the girl's imagination without downplaying the reality of her situation." Horn Book Guide

Masai and I; by Virginia Kroll; illustrations by Nancy Carpenter. Four Winds Press 1992 unp il hardcover o.p. paperback available $5.99   **E**

1. Masai (African people)—Fiction 2. African Americans—Fiction

ISBN 0-689-80454-7 (pa)   LC 91-24561

Linda, a little girl who lives in the city, learns about East Africa and the Masai in school, and imagines what her life might be like if she were Masai

"The book's creative design—a Western scene on one page of each spread faces a typical Masai scene on the other—seamlessly blends corroborative colors and details." Publ Wkly

Krudop, Walter, 1966-

The man who caught fish; [by] Walter Lyon Krudop. Farrar, Straus & Giroux 2000 unp il $16   **E**

1. Thailand—Fiction 2. Fairy tales

ISBN 0-374-34786-7   LC 98-49493

A stranger with a bamboo pole magically catches fish and hands them out to villagers, saying "One person, one fish," but the king will not be content until he receives a whole basket of fish

"Impressionistic pastel colors re-create a Thailand of long ago. . . . The tale speaks pointedly to the folly of pride; its lessons of generosity, peaceful resistance, and the temptations of privilege are universal." Horn Book Guide

Kurtz, Jane

Faraway home; illustrated by E.B. Lewis. Harcourt Brace & Co. 2000 unp il $16   **E**

1. Father-daughter relationship—Fiction 2. African Americans—Fiction 3. Ethiopia—Fiction

ISBN 0-15-200036-4   LC 96-47664

"Gulliver books"

Desta's father, who needs to return briefly to his Ethiopian homeland, describes what it was like for him to grow up there

"Lewis captures the lyricism and rich imagery of the text with his evocative, realistic watercolors." SLJ

Only a pigeon; [by] Jane and Christopher Kurtz; illustrated by E.B. Lewis. Simon & Schuster Bks. for Young Readers 1997 unp il $16   **E**

1. Pigeons—Fiction 2. Ethiopia—Fiction

ISBN 0-689-80077-0   LC 95-44056

Ondu-ahlem carefully trains his pigeons and prepares them for the day when he and other Ethiopian boys test the homing instinct and loyalty of their precious birds

"There is gentleness in the words and light-filled watercolors of this picture book. . . . Kids will be caught by the pet story of pigeon raising . . . as much as by the account of one boy and the place where he lives." Booklist

Kuskin, Karla

City dog; written and illustrated by Karla Kuskin. Clarion Bks. 1994 30p il $14.95; pa $5.95   **E**

1. Dogs—Fiction 2. Stories in rhyme

ISBN 0-395-66138-2; 0-395-90016-6 (pa)

    LC 93-8252

A rhyming tale of a city dog's first outing in the country

"Kuskin's soft-edged, sun-dappled watercolors make a spacious setting for the verses, which appear in one piece for a cohesive reading at the book's end. Words and pictures that at first glance appear naive accrue a rhythmic warmth that deepens with each runthrough." Bull Cent Child Books

I am me; illustrated by Dyanna Wolcott. Simon & Schuster Bks. for Young Readers 2000 unp il $14   **E**

1. Family life—Fiction

ISBN 0-689-81473-9   LC 98-7911

Kuskin, Karla—*Continued*

After being told how she resembles other members of her family, a young girl states positively and absolutely that she is "NO ONE ELSE BUT ME"

"The illustrations set the story during a family trip to the beach, and in Wolcott's brightly colored double-page spreads, all the rhythmic curves . . . show the natural connections around us, the loving family embrace across generations, and the child's exuberant energy as her own individual self." Booklist

The Philharmonic gets dressed; by Karla Kuskin; illustrations by Marc Simont. Harper & Row 1982 unp il hardcover o.p. paperback available $5.95   E
    1. Clothing and dress 2. Orchestra
    ISBN 0-06-443124-4 (pa)   LC 81-48658
"A Charlotte Zolotow book"
"The 105 members of the orchestra (92 men and 13 women) are shown showering, dressing, traveling and setting themselves up on stage for an evening's concert." SLJ
"The vigor and humor of Simont's illustrations add vitality to a direct, simple text." Bull Cent Child Books

Kvasnosky, Laura McGee

Zelda and Ivy. Candlewick Press 1998 unp il $15.99   E
    1. Foxes—Fiction 2. Sisters—Fiction
    ISBN 0-7636-0469-0   LC 97-28179
In three brief stories, Ivy, the younger of two fox sisters, goes along with her older sister's schemes, even when they seem a bit daring

"Kvasnosky's illustrations of the two young fox siblings are as spirited and full of life as her very funny text." Horn Book Guide
Other available titles about Zelda and Ivy are:
Zelda and Ivy and the boy next door (1999)
Zelda and Ivy at Christmas (2000)

LaMarche, Jim

The raft. Lothrop, Lee & Shepard Bks. 2000 unp il $15.95; lib bdg $15.89   E
    1. Grandmothers—Fiction 2. Rafting (Sports)—Fiction 3. Rivers—Fiction 4. Animals—Fiction
    ISBN 0-688-13977-9; 0-688-13978-7 (lib bdg)
     LC 99-35546
Reluctuant Nicky spends a wonderful summer with Grandma who introduces him to the joy of rafting down the river near her home and watching the animals along the banks

"LaMarche introduces young readers to a visually resplendent, magical world. . . . Nicky's descriptive first-person narration supports the radiant, expressive illustrations." SLJ

Lamorisse, Albert, 1922-1970

The red balloon. Doubleday 1957 c1956 unp il $16.95; pa $12.95   E
    1. Balloons—Fiction 2. Paris (France)—Fiction
    ISBN 0-385-00343-9; 0-385-14297-8 (pa)
    Original French edition, 1956

"The chief feature of this book is the stunning photographs, many in color, which were taken during the filming of the French movie of the same name. A little French schoolboy Pascal catches a red balloon which turns out to be magic. The streets of Paris form a backdrop for a charming story and superb photographs." Libr J

Lasky, Kathryn

Marven of the Great North Woods; written by Kathryn Lasky; illustrated by Kevin Hawkes. Harcourt Brace & Co. 1997 unp il $16   E
    1. Lumber and lumbering—Fiction 2. Minnesota—Fiction 3. Jews—Fiction
    ISBN 0-15-200104-2   LC 96-2334
When his Jewish parents send him to a Minnesota logging camp to escape the influenza epidemic of 1918, ten-year-old Marven finds a special friend

"Inspired by her father's childhood, Lasky's handsomely crafted picture book is also a captivating survival story. . . . Contributing to the book's vivid sense of time and place are Hawkes' graphically accomplished paintings." Booklist

Pond year; illustrated by Mike Bostock. Candlewick Press 1995 unp il $13.99; pa $5.99   E
    1. Ponds—Fiction 2. Friendship—Fiction
    ISBN 1-56402-187-4; 0-7636-0112-8 (pa)
     LC 94-14834
Two young girls enjoy playing and exploring in the nearby pond where they discover tadpoles, insects, wildflowers in the summer, and a place to ice skate in the winter

"Laced with informative facts and brimming with Bostock's . . . at once exuberant and delicate watercolors, this book is both a comical salute to friendship and a field guide." Publ Wkly

She's wearing a dead bird on her head! illustrated by David Catrow. Hyperion Bks. for Children 1995 unp il $14.95; lib bdg $14.89; pa $5.95   E
    1. Hemenway, Harriet, d. 1960—Fiction 2. Hall, Minna—Fiction
    ISBN 0-7868-0065-8; 0-7868-2052-7 (lib bdg); 0-7868-1164-1 (pa)   LC 94-18204
"Lasky tells the story of two strong-willed women who started the Audubon Society in Massachusetts around the turn of the century. When wearing dead birds as hat decorations became a raging fashion, Harriet Hemenway and her cousin Minna Hall were outraged. They contacted other ladies of fashion to start a club, named it after John James Audubon and began the Bird Hat Campaign. . . . Most, but not all, of the incidents are based on actual events." SLJ
"Reflecting humorous touches in the text, the colorful ink-and-watercolor artwork pokes fun at the extremes of fashion and the haughty pretensions of society. Based on exaggeration and caricature, the broad humor is carried off in a good-natured way." Booklist

Lasky, Kathryn—*Continued*

Show and Tell bunnies; illustrated by Marylin Hafner. Candlewick Press 1998 unp il $15.99

              E

1. Rabbits—Fiction 2. School stories 3. Spiders—Fiction

ISBN 0-7636-0396-1   LC 98-17484

Clyde the bunny is nervous about what he should take for show and tell, but he ends up sharing a wonderful surprise with his class which hatches into hundreds of spiders

"Lasky's whimsical story and Hafner's colorful, lively illustrations, which provide the sort of details children love to notice, make a winning combination." Booklist

Other available titles about Clyde are:

Lunch bunnies (1996)

Science fair bunnies (2000)

Leaf, Munro, 1905-1976

The story of Ferdinand; illustrated by Robert Lawson. Viking 1936 unp il $16.99; pa $6.99

              E

1. Bulls—Fiction 2. Bullfights—Fiction 3. Spain—Fiction

ISBN 0-670-67424-9; 0-14-050234-3 (pa)

Also available with Audiobook; Spanish language edition also available

"Ferdinand was a peace-loving little bull who preferred smelling flowers to making a reputation for himself in the bull ring. His story is told irresistbly in pictures and few words." Wis Libr Bull

"The drawings picture not only Ferdinand but Spanish scenes and characters as well." N Y Public Libr

Lee, Jeanne M.

Silent Lotus. Farrar, Straus & Giroux 1991 unp il $14.95; pa $5.95

              E

1. Dance—Fiction 2. Deaf—Fiction 3. Cambodia—Fiction

ISBN 0-374-36911-9; 0-374-46646-7 (pa)

            LC 90-55141

Although she cannot speak or hear, Lotus, a young Cambodian girl, trains as a Khmer court dancer and becomes eloquent in dancing out the legends of the gods

"Lee tells her story with simple, undecorated prose, carefully balancing all the story elements. Her flat, stylized paintings are reminiscent of Far-Eastern art and do much to capture the ambiance of the ancient setting." Horn Book

Lee, Milly

Nim and the war effort; pictures by Yangsook Choi. Farrar, Straus & Giroux 1997 unp il $16

              E

1. World War, 1939-1945—Fiction 2. Chinese Americans—Fiction

ISBN 0-374-35523-1   LC 96-11595

"Frances Foster books"

"It's the last day of the newspaper drive and Nim, a Chinese-American girl in San Francisco during World War II, is determined to win. . . . Nim's sweet seriousness and ingenuity are captured in the text and in the luminous, grave illustrations." N Y Times Book Rev

Leighton, Maxinne Rhea

An Ellis Island Christmas; illustrated by Dennis Nolan. Viking 1992 31p il hardcover o.p. paperback available $6.99

              E

1. Immigration and emigration—Fiction 2. Polish Americans—Fiction 3. Christmas—Fiction

ISBN 0-14-055344-4 (pa)   LC 91-47731

Having left Poland and braved ocean storms to join her father in America, Krysia arrives at Ellis Island on Christmas Eve

"Nolan's soft-textured watercolors express Krysia's bewilderment and hope. . . . Leighton's language is quiet, and the incidents are general enough for children and those who read to them to fill in the details of their own family journeys." Booklist

Lesser, Carolyn

Dig hole, soft mole; illustrated by Laura Regan. Harcourt Brace & Co. 1996 unp il $15 E

1. Moles (Animals)—Fiction 2. Stories in rhyme

ISBN 0-15-223491-8   LC 95-11697

A star-nosed mole travels underground and underwater, exploring marsh and pond

"The lyrical, rhyming verse is filled with wonderful imagery, descriptive language, and delightful action words. . . . Regan's oil-and-gouache paintings, nicely rendered in muted earth tones, depict in detail the plethora of creatures that inhabit the marshland." Booklist

Lester, Helen

Hooway for Wodney Wat; illustrated by Lynn Munsinger. Houghton Mifflin 1999 32p il $15

              E

1. Speech disorders—Fiction 2. School stories

ISBN 0-395-92392-1   LC 98-46149

"Walter Lorraine books"

All his classmates make fun of Rodney because he can't pronounce his name, but it is Rodney's speech impediment that drives away the class bully

"Munsinger's watercolor with pen-and-ink illustrations positively bristle with humor and each rat, mouse, hamster, and capybara is fully realized as both rodent and child." SLJ

Three cheers for Tacky; illustrated by Lynn Munsinger. Houghton Mifflin 1994 32p il $15; pa $5.95

              E

1. Penguins—Fiction   2. Contests—Fiction 3. Cheerleading—Fiction

ISBN 0-395-66841-7; 0-395-82-740-X (pa)

            LC 93-14342

"Practicing with his classmates for a cheerleading contest, Tacky the penguin falls over his own feet, can't remember the right words, and looks simply slovenly. He finally gets it right, but, on the big day, he reverts to his usual form." Horn Book Guide

This "is a smooth, fun read. Munsinger's full-color illustrations are charming and subtle." SLJ

Other available titles about Tacky are:

Tacky and the emperor (2000)

Tacky in trouble (1998)

Tacky the penguin (1988)

Lester, Julius

Black cowboy, wild horses; a true story; [by] Julius Lester, Jerry Pinkney. Dial Bks. 1998 unp il $16.99; lib bdg $16.89   E
1. Lemmons, Bob—Fiction 2. Horses—Fiction
3. Cowhands—Fiction 4. African Americans—Fiction
ISBN 0-8037-1787-3; 0-8037-1788-1 (lib bdg)
LC 97-25210
A black cowboy is so in tune with wild mustangs that they accept him into the herd, thus enabling him single-handedly to take them to the corral
This story is told in "vivid, poetic prose. . . . Pinkney's magnificent earth-toned paintings bring to life the wild beauty of the horses and the western plains." Horn Book Guide

Sam and the tigers; a new telling of Little Black Sambo; pictures by Jerry Pinkney. Dial Bks. for Young Readers 1996 unp il $15.99; pa $6.99
E
1. Tigers—Fiction
ISBN 0-8037-2028-9; 0-14-056288-5 (pa)
LC 95-43080
A boy named Sam, who lives in the land of Sam-sam-sa-mara, gives his new school clothes to tigers who threaten to eat him, but he re-claims them when the tigers chase one another until they turn into butter
"The rolling, lilting narrative is a model of harmony, clarity, and meticulously chosen detail. . . . Pinkney's lively pencil-and-watercolor illustrations sprawl extravagantly across double spreads and are smoothly integrated with the narrative." SLJ

What a truly cool world! illustrated by Joe Cepeda. Scholastic 1999 unp il $15.95   E
1. Creation—Fiction 2. God—Fiction 3. Angels—Fiction
ISBN 0-590-86468-8   LC 96-31438
Discovering that making a world takes a lot of work, God calls on his secretary Bruce and the angel Shaniqua to help him create bushes, grass, flowers, and butterflies
"The language is contemporary, colloquial, and humorous, and Cepeda's colorful, stylized illustrations capture the spirit of what Lester calls a 'black storytelling voice.'" Horn Book Guide

Lester, Mike

A is for salad. Putnam & Grosset 2000 unp il $9.99   E
1. Alphabet
ISBN 0-399-23388-1   LC 99-20900
Each letter of the alphabet is presented in an unusual way, such as: "A is for salad" showing an alligator eating a bowl of greens
The author "makes parody into a hilarious farce that both mocks the original and creates its own wonderful silliness. Each wicked picture, in bright acrylics with thick, black lines, is an animal scenario that tells an outlandish story. . . . This isn't for very young children just learning their letters . . . it's for grade-schoolers who will get the jokes and love the irreverent nonsense." Booklist

Levinson, Nancy Smiler, 1938-

Snowshoe Thompson; pictures by Joan Sandin. HarperCollins Pubs. 1992 64p il map lib bdg $15.89; pa $3.95   E
1. Thompson, Snowshoe, 1827-1876—Fiction 2. Postal service—Fiction 3. Frontier and pioneer life—Fiction 4. Skiing—Fiction
ISBN 0-06-023802-X (lib bdg); 0-06-444206-3 (pa)
LC 90-37401
"An I can read book"
One winter John Thompson skis across the Sierra Nevada Mountains and creates a path upon which mail and people may travel, thus earning his nickname "Snowshoe Thompson"
"Based on a real Gold Rush hero, Levinson's story is a satisfying blend of heartache . . . and action. . . . Sandin's paintings amplify the contrasts between the warm browns of cozy, wood-stove interiors and the gray-white sweep of snow and mountains." Bull Cent Child Books

Levinson, Riki

Watch the stars come out; illustrated by Diane Goode. Dutton 1985 unp il hardcover o.p. paperback available $6.99   E
1. Immigration and emigration—Fiction
ISBN 0-14-055506-4 (pa)   LC 84-28672
Grandma tells about her mama's journey to America by boat, years ago
"Because the story doesn't actually pinpoint the nationality or religion of its characters, it could be read as a portrait of any number of immigrant groups that streamed into this country between the 1880's and 1920's. . . . Diane Goode's beautiful, dreamlike paintings with their charmingly expressive figures manage to capture—even for the very young—the depth and emotion of the immigrant experience." N Y Times Book Rev

Levitin, Sonia, 1934-

Nine for California; illustrated by Cat Bowman Smith. Orchard Bks. 1996 unp il $16.95; lib bdg $16.99; pa $6.95   E
1. Frontier and pioneer life—Fiction 2. Overland journeys to the Pacific—Fiction
ISBN 0-531-09527-4; 0-531-08877-4 (lib bdg); 0-531-07176-6 (pa)   LC 96-1958
"Mama and her five kids, including narrator Amanda and Baby Betsy, leave Missouri to meet Pa in far-off 'Californ-y,' where he's been working in the gold fields. . . . The group groans as Mama insists on bringing a huge, bulging sack that makes the coach all the more cramped. But when her bag of tricks saves the passengers from Indians, a buffalo stampede, robbers and even boredom, everyone stops complaining." Publ Wkly
"The bright, colorful cartoons lend an amused, tongue-in-cheek tone to the story, making this exaggerated, composite narrative almost believable." SLJ
Other available titles about Amanda and her family are:
Boomtown (1998)
Taking charge (1999)

Lewin, Betsy, 1937-

Booby hatch. Clarion Bks. 1995 32p il $14.95; pa $4.95   **E**

1. Birds—Fiction 2. Galapagos Islands—Fiction

ISBN 0-395-68703-9; 0-395-84516-5 (pa)

LC 94-19309

Pépe, a young blue-footed booby, is born on a tiny island and grows until he is old enough to mate and help create a new little booby

"Although the tone is more leisurely than dramatic, the narrative is totally satisfying. . . . Lewin's watercolor landscapes are spare and evocative." SLJ

Lewin, Hugh, 1939-

Jafta; story by Hugh Lewin; pictures by Lisa Kopper. Carolrhoda Bks. 1983 c1981 unp il lib bdg $18.60; pa $4.95   **E**

1. Animals—Fiction 2. South Africa—Fiction

ISBN 0-87614-207-2 (lib bdg); 0-87614-494-6 (pa)

LC 82-12847

First published 1981 in the United Kingdom

"A small boy in South Africa, Jafta, says 'When I'm happy I purr like a lion cub, or skip like a spider, or laugh like a hyena. And sometimes I want to jump like an impala, and dance like a zebra . . .' and so on. . . . The illustrations have no background clutter, showing only the attractive brown child and the appealing animals." Bull Cent Child Books

Other available titles about Jafta are:

Jafta and the wedding (1983)

Jafta—the journey (1984)

Jafta—the town (1984)

Jafta's father (1983)

Jafta's mother (1983)

Lewin, Ted, 1935-

The storytellers. Lothrop, Lee & Shepard Bks. 1998 unp il $16; lib bdg $15.89   **E**

1. Storytelling—Fiction 2. Grandfathers—Fiction 3. Morocco—Fiction

ISBN 0-688-15178-7; 0-688-15179-5 (lib bdg)

LC 97-15744

Abdul and Grandfather pass through the streets of Fez, Morocco, and stop at an old gate, where Grandfather performs as a storyteller

"Lewin has created striking acrylic paintings that capture the colors and the sights of Fez. . . . The story flows easily, using a few Arabic terms (italicized and explained either in the accompanying glossary or in context) to enhance the flavor of the tale." SLJ

Lewis, Kim

Just like Floss. Candlewick Press 1998 unp il $15.99; pa $5.99   **E**

1. Dogs—Fiction

ISBN 0-7636-0684-7; 0-7636-1079-8 (pa)

LC 98-4954

Floss the sheep dog has a litter of puppies and Floss's owners want to keep the one that is just like Floss

"From the endpapers, with their soft colored-pencil illustration of a snowy grassland landscape, to the appealing portrayal of the dogs and the children, Lewis has created [a] . . . heartwarming book." SLJ

Another available title about Floss is:

Floss (1992)

Little calf. Candlewick Press 2000 unp il $9.99   **E**

1. Cattle—Fiction

ISBN 0-7636-0899-8   LC 99-28784

Katie watches as the newborn calf on her farm takes its first wobbly steps and then skitters back to its mother to drink her milk

"The language generates a sense of comfort and warmth, while simultaneously including enough tactile detail to engage youngsters. Lewis's trademark soft, yet realistic colored-pencil illustrations perfectly reflect the scenes described in the [text]." SLJ

Other available titles about Katie are:

Little lamb (2000)

Little puppy (2000)

Lexau, Joan M.

Don't be my valentine; a classroom mystery; story by Joan M. Lexau; pictures by Syd Hoff. HarperCollins Pubs. 1999 64p il $14.95; lib bdg $14.89; pa $3.95   **E**

1. Valentine's Day—Fiction 2. Mystery fiction

ISBN 0-06-028239-8; 0-06-028240-1 (lib bdg); 0-06-444254-3 (pa)   LC 85-42621

"An I can read book"

A reissue of the title first published 1985

"When Amy Lou bugs Sam by helping him whether he needs it or not, he makes her a mean Valentine card. Then he loses it before the school party, and it ends up in his teacher's pile instead. Sam must find out who put it there. Hoff's cartoon illustrations capture the mood of this amusing story that portrays real emotions and squabbles." Horn Book Guide

Go away, dog; story by Joan L. Nodset; pictures by Paul Meisel. HarperCollins Pubs. 1997 32p il $12.95; lib bdg $14.89; pa $3.95   **E**

1. Dogs—Fiction

ISBN 0-06-027502-2; 0-06-027503-0 (lib bdg); 0-06-444231-4 (pa)   LC 96-27272

"My first I can read book"

A newly illustrated edition of the title first published 1963

An old dog's friendly persistence slowly convinces a young boy to take him home.

"Engaging, watercolor illustrations. . . . With its controlled vocabulary, this will be a sure-fire hit with emergent readers." SLJ

Who took the farmer's [hat]? [by] Joan L. Nodset; pictures by Fritz Siebel. Harper & Row 1963 unp il lib bdg $15.89; pa $6.95   **E**

1. Animals—Fiction

ISBN 0-06-024566-2 (lib bdg); 0-06-443174-6 (pa)

"Away flew the farmer's hat. In his search for it he found that his hat could be many things to many animals including, most permanently, a bird's nest." Publ Wkly

Lied, Kate

Potato; a tale from the Great Depression; written by Kate Lied; illustrated by Lisa Campbell Ernst. National Geographic Soc. 1997 unp il $16   **E**

1. Great Depression, 1929-1939—Fiction 2. Potatoes—Fiction

ISBN 0-7922-3521-5   LC 96-11926

Lied, Kate—*Continued*

"A family whose home has been repossessed find work picking potatoes and parlay this chance into survival. Based on an incident in the lives of the author's grandparents, the book, with its forthright, elegant text and deceptively simple illustrations, offers a true child's perspective on the Great Depression." Horn Book Guide

Lindbergh, Reeve

Nobody owns the sky; the story of "Brave Bessie" Coleman; illustrated by Pamela Paparone. Candlewick Press 1996 unp il hardcover o.p. paperback available $5.99   E
    1. Coleman, Bessie, 1896?-1926—Fiction 2. Women air pilots—Fiction 3. African Americans—Fiction 4. Stories in rhyme
    ISBN 0-7636-0361-9 (pa)   LC 96-6901
A rhymed telling of the life of the first African American aviator, who dreamed of flying as a child in the cotton fields of Texas, and persevered until she made that dream come true
The text "creates a cadence of bold rhythms that young children will want to hear again and again. Paparone's superb folk-art illustrations, rendered in brilliantly colorful acrylic paintings, provide accurate visual details." SLJ

Lindgren, Astrid, 1907-

The Tomten; adapted by Astrid Lindgren from a poem by Viktor Rydberg; illustrated by Harald Wiberg. Coward-McCann 1961 unp il hardcover o.p. paperback available $5.99   E
    1. Winter—Fiction 2. Fairy tales
    ISBN 0-6981-1591-0 (pa)
"Snowy farm pictures and warm scenes inside barn, sheds, and house show the Tomten, a little Swedish troll, going quietly about to the animals on cold winter nights comforting them with the promise that spring will come. The text was adapted from a nineteenth-century poem by Viktor Rydberg, and the pictures are by an outstanding Swedish painter of animals and nature. An unusual and beautiful picture book." Horn Book
Another available title about the Tomten is:
The Tomten and the fox (1966)

Lionni, Leo, 1910-1999

Alexander and the wind-up mouse. Pantheon Bks. 1970 c1969 unp il hardcover o.p. paperback available $5.99   E
    1. Mice—Fiction
    ISBN 0-394-82911-5 (pa)
A Caldecott Medal honor book, 1970
"Alexander wants to be a wind-up mouse like Willie, who is the little girl's favorite toy. A magic lizard can change him, but then he learns that Willie's key is broken and decides to turn Willie into a real mouse like himself." Adventuring With Books. 2d edition
The author's "collage illustrations are dazzling in their color and bold design and contribute to a beautiful and appealing picture book." Booklist

The biggest house in the world. Pantheon Bks. 1968 unp il hardcover o.p. paperback available $5.99   E
    1. Snails—Fiction
    ISBN 0-394-82740-6 (pa)
"In this picture book a small snail has a very large wish. He wants the largest house in the world. But by telling the youngster a story, his wise father helps him to see the impracticality of being encased in a magnificent monstrosity too big to move." Book Week

A color of his own. Pantheon Bks. 1975 unp hardcover o.p. paperback available $6.99   E
    1. Chameleons—Fiction 2. Color—Fiction
    ISBN 0-679-88785-7 (pa)
Also available Board book edition
"When a young chameleon grows tired of constantly changing color, he decides to sit on a leaf and stay green forever. But even the leaf changes color in the fall. After he meets another chameleon and makes a friend, he learns to accept himself. Lionni's simple print illustrations work well with the short text to achieve a satisfying whole." Horn Book Guide

An extraordinary egg. Knopf 1994 unp il $16; lib bdg $16.99; pa $5.99   E
    1. Frogs—Fiction 2. Alligators—Fiction 3. Friendship—Fiction
    ISBN 0-679-85840-7; 0-679-95840-1 (lib bdg); 0-679-89385-7 (pa)   LC 93-28565
Also available Spanish language edition
Jessica the frog befriends an alligator that hatches from an egg she brought home, thinking it is a chicken
"Lionni's understated text perfectly complements his signature illustrations, which are a skillful combination of collage, crayon, and watercolors." SLJ

Fish is fish. Pantheon Bks. 1970 unp il hardcover o.p. paperback available $5.99   E
    1. Frogs—Fiction 2. Fishes—Fiction
    ISBN 0-394-82799-6 (pa)
The frog tells the fish all about the world above the sea. The fish, however, can only visualize it in terms of fish-people, fish-birds and fish-cows
"The story is slight but pleasantly and simply told, the illustrations are page-filling, deft, colorful, and amusing." Bull Cent Child Books

Frederick. Pantheon Bks. 1967 unp il $17.95; lib bdg $18.99; pa $5.99   E
    1. Mice—Fiction
    ISBN 0-394-81040-6; 0-394-91040-0 (lib bdg); 0-394-82614-0 (pa)
Also available Spanish language edition
A Caldecott Medal honor book, 1968
"While other mice are gathering food for the winter, Frederick seems to daydream the summer away. When dreary winter comes, it is Frederick the poet-mouse who warms his friends and cheers them with his words." Wis Libr Bull
"This captivating book . . . sings a hymn of praise to poets in a gentle story that is illustrated with gaiety and charm." Saturday Rev

Lionni, Leo, 1910-1999—*Continued*

Inch by inch. Astor-Honor 1960 unp il o.p.; HarperCollins Pubs. paperback available $5.95
E

1. Worms—Fiction 2. Birds—Fiction
ISBN 0-688-13283-9 (pa)

A Caldecott Medal honor book, 1961

This is a "small tale about an inchworm who liked to measure the robin's tail, the flamingo's neck, the whole of a hummingbird but not a nightingale's song." Christ Sci Monit

"This is a book to look at again and again. The semi-abstract forms are sharply defined, clean and strong, the colors subtle and glowing, and the grassy world of the inchworm is a special place of enchantment." N Y Times Book Rev

It's mine! Knopf 1986 c1985 unp il hardcover o.p. paperback available $5.99
E
1. Frogs—Fiction
ISBN 0-679-88084-4 (pa)   LC 85-190

Original German edition, 1985

"Three childlike frogs spend their days bickering and baiting each other: It's mine, claims one about the water. Another purports ownership of the earth—or a worm—or a butterfly—or whatever. It isn't until disaster almost strikes and they are saved by a toad that Milton, Rupert and Lydia realize that private ownership isn't that important. . . . Collages of marbled-textured paper, all in cool, crisp, spring-like colors against a stark white background, are a perfect match for this story of selfishness on the pond." SLJ

Little blue and little yellow; a story for Pippo and Ann and other children. Astor-Honor 1959 unp il o.p.; HarperCollins Pubs. paperback available $5.95
E
1. Color—Fiction
ISBN 0-688-13285-5 (pa)

The author uses "splashes of color and abstract forms to tell the story of little blue and his friend little yellow who hugged and hugged each other until they were green—and unrecognizable to their parents." Booklist

"So well are the dots handled on the pages that little blue and little yellow and their parents seem to have real personalities. It should inspire interesting color play and is a very original picture book by an artist." N Y Her Trib Books

Matthew's dream. Knopf 1991 unp il hardcover o.p. paperback available $5.99
E
1. Mice—Fiction 2. Artists—Fiction
ISBN 0-679-87318-X (pa)   LC 90-34242

Also available Spanish language edition

A visit to an art museum inspires a young mouse named Matthew to become a painter

"Lionni brings his own joyful shapes and colors into play here. . . . The text is direct yet abundantly meaningful—poetic without becoming sappy." Publ Wkly

Swimmy. Pantheon Bks. c1963 unp il $16; pa $5.99
E
1. Fishes—Fiction
ISBN 0-394-81713-3; 0-394-82620-5 (pa)

A Caldecott Medal honor book, 1964

"Swimmy, an insignificant fish, escapes when a whole school of small fish are swallowed by a larger one. As he swims away from danger he meets many wonderful, colorful creatures and later saves another school of fish from the jaws of the enemy." Ont Libr Rev

"To illustrate his clever, but very brief story, Leo Lionni has made a book of astonishingly beautiful pictures, full of undulating, watery nuances of shape, pattern, and color." Horn Book

Little, Mimi Otey

Yoshiko and the foreigner. Farrar, Straus & Giroux 1996 unp il $16
E
1. Prejudices—Fiction 2. Japan—Fiction
ISBN 0-374-32448-4   LC 95-33512

"Frances Foster books"

"Yoshiko aids a confused and inadvertently hilarious gaijin, or foreigner, on a Tokyo train. Yoshiko continues to see the pleasant African American soldier Flem but knows her family would never approve. Flem asks about them and sends them gifts through Yoshiko, who continues to hide his identity. After Flem's return to the States, she receives two letters, one for her father and one asking her to marry him." Booklist

"The large full-page watercolors provide immediacy by pulling readers into the world of a Japanese woman in the 1950s. . . . On the final spread, the fictional story is given factual surprise with the inclusion of a black-and-white wedding photograph of Little's parents, Yoshiko Sasagawa and Flem Otey." Horn Book

Lobel, Anita, 1934-

Alison's zinnia. Greenwillow Bks. 1990 unp il $16; pa $5.95
E
1. Flowers—Fiction 2. Alphabet
ISBN 0-688-08865-1; 0-688-14737-2 (pa)
    LC 89-23700

"More than two dozen little girls, a full alphabet of them, pick flowers for their friends: 'Alison acquired an Amaryllis for Beryl' and 'Nancy noticed a Narcissus for Olga' and so on till 'Zena zeroed in on a Zinnia for Alison.' Underneath each large handsome floral illustration is a smaller picture of the named child and her flower. Charming." N Y Times Book Rev

One lighthouse, one moon. Greenwillow Bks. 2000 40p il $15.95; lib bdg $15.89
E
1. Days—Fiction 2. Months—Fiction 3. Counting
ISBN 0-688-15539-1; 0-688-15540-5 (lib bdg)
    LC 98-50790

This is a "three-part introduction to days, seasons, colors, counting, and other basics. The first section pictures a little girl's feet as they journey through a week, with a different colored shoe marking each day's activity. . . . The second section shows Nini the cat in postcard-size images that reflect those from the 12 months of the year. The title section presents the numbers 1 through 10 in serene images of shoreline activity. . . . The simple phrases are lyrical in places, and Lobel's beautiful paintings, with their rich patterns and textures, luxurious detail, and sophisticated palette, will inspire children to linger over the pages and connect new words with images." Booklist

Lobel, Arnold

Frog and Toad are friends. Harper & Row 1970 64p il $15.95; lib bdg $15.89; pa $3.95　　**E**
1. Frogs—Fiction 2. Toads—Fiction
ISBN 0-06-023957-3; 0-06-023958-1 (lib bdg); 0-06-444020-6 (pa)
Also available with Audiobook; Spanish language edition also available
A Caldecott Medal honor book, 1971
"An I can read book"
Here are five stories . . . which recount the adventures of two best friends—Toad and Frog. The stories are: Spring; The story; A lost button; A swim; The letter
The stories are told "with humor and perception. Illustrations in soft green and brown enhance the smooth flowing and sensitive story." SLJ
Other available titles about Frog and Toad are:
Days with Frog and Toad (1979)
Frog and Toad all year (1976)
Frog and Toad together (1972)

Grasshopper on the road. Harper & Row 1978 62p il lib bdg $15.89; pa $3.95　　**E**
1. Locusts—Fiction 2. Animals—Fiction
ISBN 0-06-023962-X (lib bdg); 0-06-444094-X (pa)
LC 77-25653
Also available Audiobook version
"An I can read book"
"Grasshopper's journey is divided into six chapters. In each chapter he meets a different animal or animals attending to a spectrum of tasks. The chapters weave a tale of habit—doing without questioning. Grasshopper gives his need-for-change reaction to each one, but only a worm in his apple home is open to change." Child Book Rev Serv
"The contemporary version of the fable of the ant and the grasshopper is told in a repetitive I-Can-Read text and extended in three-color illustrations which delicately capture the grasshopper's microcosmic world view." Horn Book

Ming Lo moves the mountain; written and illustrated by Arnold Lobel. Greenwillow Bks. 1982 unp il hardcover o.p. paperback available $5.95　　**E**
1. Mountains—Fiction 2. Houses—Fiction
ISBN 0-688-10995-0 (pa)
LC 81-13327
"Ming Lo and his wife love their house, but not the mountain that overshadows it. So, at his wife's bidding, Ming Lo undertakes to move the mountain by following the advice of a wise man." Child Book Rev Serv
"An original tale utilizing folkloric motifs, the book is Chinese-like rather than Chinese, for the artist has created an imagined landscape. The setting, shown in flowing lines and tones of delicate watercolors, provides a source of inspiration drawn from an ancient artistic tradition; particularly effective in conveying a sense of distance are the panoramic double-page spreads." Horn Book

Mouse soup. Harper & Row 1977 63p il $15.95; lib bdg $15.89; pa $3.95　　**E**
1. Mice—Fiction
ISBN 0-06-023967-0; 0-06-023968-9 (lib bdg); 0-06-444041-9 (pa)
LC 76-41517
Also available with Audiobook
"An I can read book"

"In an effort to save himself from a weasel's stew pot, a little mouse tells the weasel four separate stories." West Coast Rev Books
"An artistic triumph with enough suspense, humor and wisdom to hold any reader who has a trace of curiosity and compassion. . . . The little one triumphs over the big one, and every child will rejoice. The exquisite wash drawings in mousey shades of grays, blues, greens and golds, have enough humor and pathos to exact repeated scrutiny. Like the stories, they improve with each reading." N Y Times Book Rev

Mouse tales. Harper & Row 1972 61p il $15.95; lib bdg $15.89; pa $3.95　　**E**
1. Mice—Fiction
ISBN 0-06-023941-7; 0-06-023942-5 (lib bdg); 0-06-444013-3 (pa)
Also available with Audiobook
"An I can read book"
Papa Mouse tells seven bedtime stories, one for each of his sons
Contents: The wishing well; Clouds; Very tall mouse and very short mouse; The mouse and the winds; The journey; The odd mouse; The bath
"The illustrations have soft colors and precise, lively little drawings of the imaginative and humorous events in the stories. The themes are familiar to children: cloud shapes, wishing, a tall and a short friend who observe—and greet—natural phenomena on a walk, taking a bath, et cetera." Bull Cent Child Books

On Market Street; pictures by Anita Lobel; words by Arnold Lobel. Greenwillow Bks. 1981 c1980 unp il $17; lib bdg $16.93; pa $6.95　　**E**
1. Shopping—Fiction 2. Alphabet 3. Stories in rhyme
ISBN 0-688-80309-1; 0-688-84309-3 (lib bdg); 0-688-08745-0 (pa)
LC 80-21418
A Caldecott Medal honor book, 1982
In this "alphabet book, a boy trots down Market Street buying presents for a friend, each one starting with a letter of the alphabet. Every letter is illustrated by a figure . . . composed of, for instance, apples or wigs or quilts or Xmas trees." Horn Book
"The artist has adapted the style of old French trade engravings, infusing it with a wonderful sense of color and detail. . . . Arnold Lobel's words ring of old rhymes, but it is these intricate, lovely drawings that take the day, and truly make it brighter." N Y Times Book Rev

Owl at home. Harper & Row 1982 64p il lib bdg $15.89; pa $3.95　　**E**
1. Owls—Fiction
ISBN 0-06-023949-2 (lib bdg); 0-06-444034-6 (pa)

Also available with Audiobook
"An I can read book"
Five stories describe the adventures of a lovably foolish owl
"A child reader or listener in a kind of one-upmanship over wide-eyed tufted Owl will bristle with anxiety to have him perceive what causes two bewildering bumps under the blanket at the foot of his bed. The best scope for Lobel's inventiveness in drawing is, however, the opening episode where 'poor old' Winter makes a pushy

Lobel, Arnold—_Continued_

entry into Owl's home. Muted browns and greys are countered by an animation that fully reveals Owl's distresses and contentments." Wash Post Child Book World

The rose in my garden; pictures by Anita Lobel. Greenwillow Bks. 1984 unp il hardcover o.p. paperback available $6.95   **E**

1. Flowers—Fiction 2. Stories in rhyme

ISBN 0-688-12265-5 (pa)   LC 83-14097

"A cumulative poem tells of a lovely garden, starting with 'this is the rose in my garden,' continuing through the lilies, bluebells, daisies, and other flowers, and culminating with a cat chasing a field mouse. A bee on the rose awakens and stings the cat, thus allowing the mouse to escape, and the text ends with the opening lines." Horn Book

"Lovely to look at, and enjoyable for reading aloud." Bull Cent Child Books

Small pig; story and pictures by Arnold Lobel. Harper & Row 1969 63p il lib bdg $15.89; pa $3.95   **E**

1. Pigs—Fiction

ISBN 0-06-023932-8 (lib bdg); 0-06-444120-2 (pa)

"An I can read book"

This "is the story of a pig who, finding the clean farm unbearable, runs away to look for mud—and ends up stuck in cement. His facial expressions alone are worth the price of the book; the illustrations, in blue, green, and gold, are a perfect complement to the story. Humor, adventure, and short, simple sentences provide a real treat for beginning readers." SLJ

A treeful of pigs; pictures by Anita Lobel. Greenwillow Bks. 1979 unp il lib bdg $16.89

    E

1. Pigs—Fiction 2. Farm life—Fiction

ISBN 0-688-84177-5   LC 78-1810

A "story about a farmer's wife who tries everything to pry her lazy husband out of bed. He says he'll come to help her when the pigs grow on trees, fall from the sky, or 'bloom in the garden like flowers.' His wife knows how to work magic, and she makes each one of them happen with the help of a cooperative brood of piglets." Child Book Rev Serv

"The framed, full-color illustrations, characterized by intricately detailed designs in costumes and setting, are as elaborate as the diction is simple. The total effect, however, is one of unity, for the two are combined into a true picture book in which words and illustrations are interdependent." Horn Book

Uncle Elephant. Harper & Row 1981 62p il lib bdg $15.89; pa $3.95   **E**

1. Elephants—Fiction 2. Uncles—Fiction

ISBN 0-06-023980-8 (lib bdg); 0-06-444104-0 (pa)

     LC 80-8944

"An I can read book"

Uncle Elephant takes care of his nephew whose parents are lost at sea. This book describes the way they lived together until the parents are rescued and little elephant rejoins them

"Nine gentle stories for the beginning independent

reader; the soft grey, peach, and green tones of the deft pictures are an appropriate echo of the mood." Bull Cent Child Books

Locker, Thomas, 1937-

The mare on the hill. Dial Bks. for Young Readers 1985 unp il hardcover o.p. paperback available $6.99   **E**

1. Horses—Fiction

ISBN 0-14-055339-8 (pa)   LC 85-1684

Grandfather brings home a fearful mare to breed, hoping that his grandsons can teach her to trust people again

"Locker tells a solid story, in a minimum of well-chosen words. . . . Each event is printed on the reader's mind by Locker's ineffable paintings of the matchless terrain of the Hudson River Valley. The artist's rich colors emphasize changes wrought by the four seasons in the country, largely undisturbed by 'progress,' where people live in harmony with nature." Publ Wkly

Where the river begins. Dial Bks. for Young Readers 1984 unp il $17.99; pa $6.99   **E**

1. Grandfathers—Fiction 2. Camping—Fiction 3. Rivers—Fiction

ISBN 0-8037-0089-X; 0-14-054595-6 (pa)

     LC 84-1709

"Two young boys journey with their grandfather to find the beginning of the river that flows by their house. In full-page landscape paintings and simple prose, Thomas Locker follows the journey." Sci Child

"Admittedly, the simple narrative text is overshadowed by the magnificence of its illustrations. But their limpid beauty and exquisite detail are—to paraphrase Emerson—their own excuse for being. Reminiscent of the work of great landscape painters like Turner, Constable, and the American George Inness, the paintings follow not only the course of the river but the nearly three-day journey of the old man and the boys." Horn Book

Loh, Morag Jeanette, 1935-

Tucking Mommy in; by Morag Loh; illustrated by Donna Rawlins. Orchard Bks. 1988 c1987 unp il hardcover o.p. paperback available $5.95   **E**

1. Sisters—Fiction 2. Mother-daughter relationship—Fiction 3. Sleep—Fiction

ISBN 0-531-07025-5 (pa)   LC 87-16740

First published 1987 in Australia

Two sisters tuck their mother into bed one evening when she is especially tired

"The amusing turnabout on standard bedtime routines is a sweet reflection of the spontaneous love and generosity children sometimes show. Rawlins' pictures depict a raven-haired family at ease with each other's company. Her scenes show an eye for the dishevelment that follows children's footsteps, and the warm, sunny colors that dominate add to the story's good vibrations." Booklist

London, Jonathan, 1947-

Ali, child of the desert; illustrated by Ted Lewin. Lothrop, Lee & Shepard Bks. 1997 unp il $16; lib bdg $15.93   **E**

1. Sahara Desert—Fiction 2. Nomads—Fiction

ISBN 0-688-12560-3; 0-688-12561-1 (lib bdg)

     LC 92-44164

London, Jonathan, 1947-—*Continued*

On a trip to market across the Sahara Desert, Ali becomes separated from his father during a sandstorm and finds shelter with a goatherd

Author and artist "tell the story of sizzling sun and lonely darkness in realistic detail. Lewin's watercolor paintings are rich with story."

Baby whale's journey; illustrated by Jon Van Zyle. Chronicle Bks. 1999 unp il $14.95   E

1. Whales—Fiction

ISBN 0-8118-2496-9   LC 99-13020

Off the Pacific coast of Mexico, a baby sperm whale is born, feeds, speaks to her mother in clicks, and spends her days diving, spy-hopping, lob-tailing, and rolling as she grows and learns the ways of the sea

This book offers "London's lyrical text and Van Zyle's dramatic paintings dominated by blues and purples. . . . An informative afterword supplies additional facts about sperm whales, and a reader's guide offers thoughtful ideas for discussion of both the scientific and poetic aspects of the text." Horn Book Guide

Froggy learns to swim; illustrated by Frank Remkiewicz. Viking 1995 unp il $15.99; pa $5.99   E

1. Swimming—Fiction 2. Frogs—Fiction

ISBN 0-670-85551-0; 0-14-055312-6 (pa)

LC 94-43077

Froggy is afraid of the water until his mother, along with his flippers, snorkle, and mask, help him learn to swim

"Vivid watercolor cartoons add the humor, showing the comical facial expressions and hilarious beachwear. Froggy's childlike dialogue and the sound words—'zook! zik!'; 'flop flop . . . splash!'—make this story a wonderful read-aloud." SLJ

Other available titles about Froggy are:
Froggy bakes a cake (2000)
Froggy gets dressed (1992)
Froggy goes to bed (2000)
Froggy goes to school (1996)
Froggy plays soccer (1999)
Froggy's best Christmas (2000)
Froggy's first kiss (1998)
Froggy's Halloween (1999)
Let's go, Froggy! (1994)

Red wolf country; illustrated by Daniel San Souci. Dutton Children's Bks. 1996 unp il $15.99; pa $5.99   E

1. Wolves—Fiction

ISBN 0-525-45191-9; 0-14-056450-0 (pa)

LC 95-10384

The "text, written in free verse, follows a pair of red wolves as they hunt for food in the snow, survive an encounter with a gun-toting farmer, and settle into a den to have their pups. From shadowy winter through sun-drenched summer, San Souci's realistic paintings strikingly portray the wolves and the setting, identified in an afterword and map on the back cover as the southeastern United States." Horn Book Guide

Shawn and Keeper: show-and-tell; illustrated by Renée Williams-Andriani. Dutton Children's Bks. 2000 unp il $13.99; pa $3.99   E

1. Dogs—Fiction

ISBN 0-525-46114-0; 0-14-130367-0 (pa)

LC 99-23500

"Dutton easy reader"

Shawn and his dog Keeper remain the best of friends even after the show-and-tell where Keeper trips the teacher, spills glue, knocks over the fish tank, and doesn't perform a single trick

"The repetitive text and visual clues will help new readers gain confidence in their skills. The lively illustrations add greatly to the book's charm and are filled with humor." SLJ

Another available title about Shawn and Keeper is: Shawn and Keeper and the birthday party (1999)

Snuggle wuggle; illustrations by Michael Rex. Harcourt Brace & Co. 2000 unp il $13   E

1. Animals—Fiction 2. Hugging—Fiction

ISBN 0-15-202159-0   LC 98-41769

"Silver Whistle"

Text and illustrations describe how various animal mothers cuddle their babies

"The large-scale, shaded pencil drawings are tinted with solid colors to create strong, clear images of animals and their young. . . . A comforting book for bedtime reading." Booklist

Look, Lenore

Love as strong as ginger; illustrated by Stephen T. Johnson. Atheneum Pubs. 1999 unp il $15   E

1. Chinese Americans—Fiction 2. Grandmothers—Fiction 3. Work—Fiction

ISBN 0-689-81248-5   LC 96-43459

"An Anne Schwartz book"

A Chinese American girl comes to realize how hard her grandmother works to fulfill her dreams when they spend a day together at the grandmother's job cracking crabs

"Inspired by the author's memories of her grandmother, this gentle story is carefully and precisely told. . . . Johnson's expressive pastel-and-watercolor illustrations are rendered in muted colors and set within wide, softly colored margins." SLJ

Loomis, Christine

Cowboy bunnies; pictures by Ora Eitan. Putnam 1997 unp il $15.99; pa $5.99   E

1. Cowhands—Fiction 2. Rabbits—Fiction 3. Stories in rhyme

ISBN 0-399-22625-7; 0-698-11831-6 (pa)

LC 96-43057

Little bunnies spend their day pretending to be cowboys: riding their ponies, mending fences, counting cows, eating chow, and singing cowboy tunes until it is time for bed

"The gouache paintings are done on plywood slats juxtaposed in an almost cinematic way that provides an effective and inventive counterpoint to the steadiness of the verse; the paint is thinly applied to allow the texture of the wood to become part of the pictures. This is cozy adventure." Horn Book

Loomis, Christine—*Continued*

Another available title about the little bunnies is:
Astro bunnies (2001)

Lorbiecki, Marybeth

Sister Anne's hands; illustrated by K. Wendy Popp. Dial Bks. for Young Readers 1998 unp il $15.99; $15.89   **E**

1. Race relations—Fiction 2. School stories 3. African Americans—Fiction 4. Nuns—Fiction
ISBN 0-8037-2038-6; 0-8037-2039-4 (lib bdg)
LC 97-26671

Seven-year-old Anna has her first encounter with racism in the 1960s when an African American nun comes to teach at her parochial school

"The story has honesty and integrity and the two main characters are well crafted. The velvety pastel illustrations have the soft focus and pale palette of a distant memory coupled with exquisite detail." SLJ

Lord, John Vernon, 1939-

The giant jam sandwich; story and pictures by John Vernon Lord, with verses by Janet Burroway. Houghton Mifflin 1973 c1972 32p il lib bdg $17; pa $5.95   **E**

1. Wasps—Fiction 2. Stories in rhyme
ISBN 0-395-16033-2 (lib bdg); 0-395-44237-0 (pa)

Also available with Audiobook

First published 1972 in the United Kingdom

This is a story in rhymed verse "about the citizens of Itching Down, who, attacked by four million wasps, make a giant jam sandwich to attract and trap the insects. With dump truck, spades, and hoes the people spread butter and strawberry jam across an enormous slice of bread; then, when the wasps settle, they drop the other slice from five helicopters and a flying tractor." Booklist

"Highly amusing in the details of John Vernon Lord's illustrations. . . . The figures are deliciously grotesque, their expressions wickedly accurate and the colours cheerfully vivid." Jr Bookshelf

Lotu, Denize, 1946-

Running the road to ABC; by Denizé Lauture; illustrated by Reynold Ruffins. Simon & Schuster Bks. for Young Readers 1996 unp il $16; pa $5.99   **E**

1. Haiti—Fiction 2. School stories
ISBN 0-689-80507-1; 0-689-83165-X (pa)
LC 95-38290

A Coretta Scott King honor book for illustration, 1997

Long before the sun even thinks of rising the Haitian children run to school where they learn the letters, sounds, and words of their beautiful books

"The rich lyrical language used by the author, a Haitian poet, creates a strong sense of place. . . . The lush, green country and sense of hope are reflected and enhanced by stylized, warmly detailed gouache paintings." Horn Book

Low, Joseph, 1911-

Mice twice; story & pictures by Joseph Low. Atheneum Pubs. 1980 unp il hardcover o.p. paperback available $5.99   **E**

1. Animals—Fiction
ISBN 0-689-71060-7 (pa)   LC 79-23274

A Caldecott Medal honor book, 1981

"A Margaret K. McElderry book"

"Mouse asks to bring a friend when Cat invites her to dinner, and while Cat licks his whiskers at the thought of more than one mouse, Mouse has in mind her friend Dog. And so begins a round of very hospitable and polite dinners with a slightly more outrageous friend brought along every night." SLJ

"Wit triumphant is the motif of an original tale which combines an elegantly crafted text with colorful illustrations." Horn Book

Lowery, Linda

Twist with a burger, jitter with a bug; illustrated by Pat Dypold. Houghton Mifflin 1994 unp il $16   **E**

1. Dance 2. Stories in rhyme
ISBN 0-395-67022-5   LC 93-38236

"Bold, brash cut-paper collages in bright neon colors illustrate an exuberant rhyme about music and dance—all kinds of dance, from polka and mambo to jitterbug, waltz, and ballet. The pages bounce with play and movement." Booklist

Luciani, Brigitte

How will we get to the beach? illustrated by Eve Tharlet; translated by Rosemary Lanning. North-South Bks. 2000 unp il $14.95; lib bdg $14.88   **E**

1. Beaches—Fiction 2. Transportation—Fiction
ISBN 0-7358-1268-3; 0-7358-1269-1 (lib bdg)
LC 99-57086

"A Michael Neugebauer book"

The reader is asked to guess what Roxanne must leave behind (ball, umbrella, book, turtle, or baby) as she tries various means of transportation to get to the beach

"The writing is spare, yet the story flows seamlessly. . . . Though on the surface the colorful pictures appear simple, details abound. . . . This book also introduces the concepts of color . . . and counting." SLJ

Luenn, Nancy, 1954-

Nessa's fish; illustrated by Neil Waldman. Atheneum Pubs. 1990 unp il hardcover o.p. paperback available $5.99   **E**

1. Inuit—Fiction 2. Grandmothers—Fiction
ISBN 0-689-81465-8 (pa)   LC 89-15048

Also available Spanish language edition

"Nessa, an Inuit girl, and her grandmother go on an ice-fishing expedition. When Grandmother falls ill, Nessa uses her wits, her courage, and the remembered advice of her father and her grandfather to defend their catch from a fox, a pack of wolves, and a bear. Luminous watercolor paintings set the action within a remarkable variety of land- and snowscapes seen in the same place at different times of the day and night. . . . Well designed, the book invites readers to linger over its many striking visual images." Booklist

Lum, Kate

What! cried Granny; an almost bedtime story; pictures by Adrian Johnson. Dial Bks. for Young Readers 1999 unp il $15.99   **E**

1. Bedtime—Fiction 2. Grandmothers—Fiction

ISBN 0-8037-2382-2   LC 98-19642

First published 1998 in the United Kingdom with title: What!

"Sleeping over at Granny's for the first time, Patrick delays the inevitable, saying he can't go to bed because he doesn't even have a bed; or a blanket; or a teddy bear. In response to each legitimate complaint, Granny springs into action, chopping down a tree to build a bed, and so on." Horn Book Guide

This "combines the deadpan and the surreal in wild words and neon-colored acrylic illustrations." Booklist

Lyon, George Ella, 1949-

Cecil's story; paintings by Peter Catalanotto. Orchard Bks. 1991 unp il $15.99; lib bdg $16.99; pa $5.95   **E**

1. United States—History—1861-1865, Civil War—Fiction

ISBN 0-531-05912-X; 0-531-08512-0 (lib bdg); 0-531-07063-8 (pa)   LC 90-7775

"A Richard Jackson book"

A boy thinks about the possible scenarios that exist for him at home if his father goes off to fight in the Civil War

"The trauma of separation is sensitively explored . . . in this evocative picture book. . . . Each page has a simple line or two of text, complemented dramatically by double-page watercolor paintings of extraordinary quality." SLJ

Come a tide; story by George Ella Lyon; pictures by Stephen Gammell. Orchard Bks. 1990 unp il lib bdg $21.95; pa $6.95   **E**

1. Floods—Fiction 2. Country life—Fiction

ISBN 0-531-08454-X (lib bdg); 0-531-07036-0 (pa)   LC 89-35650

"A Richard Jackson book"

"'It'll come a tide,' says Grandma after a four-day deluge. She's right: as the streams and creeks rush down the hill to the river, the water rises, sending residents of the hollows packing. The narrator's family hightails it up the hill to Grandma's house." Booklist

"Capturing the diction and homely imagery of a down-to-earth rural community, the first-person text richly evokes the sturdy qualities of folks who, beset by spring floods, respond to nature's challenges with common sense and wry humor. . . . In combination with Stephen Gammell's energetic illustrations, remarkable for their expressive lines and elegant use of watercolor, it becomes an exemplary picture story book, regional in setting but universal in appeal." Horn Book

Dreamplace; paintings by Peter Catalanotto. Orchard Bks. 1993 unp il $15.95; pa $6.95   **E**

1. Pueblo Indians—Fiction

ISBN 0-531-05466-7; 0-531-07101-4 (pa)   LC 92-25102

"A Richard Jackson book"

Present-day visitors describe what they see when they visit the pueblos where the Anasazi lived long ago

"Simple and direct, Lyon's poetic text sketches the main ideas, while the illustrations define and defy places, people, and times. . . . Rich with atmosphere, delicate with sensitivity, and dreamlike in its evocation of dual realities, this would be an imaginative choice to read before a class trip to any historic site." Booklist

Mama is a miner; story by George Ella Lyon; paintings by Peter Catalanotto. Orchard Bks. 1994 unp il lib bdg $16.99   **E**

1. Mother-daughter relationship—Fiction 2. Miners—Fiction

ISBN 0-531-08703-4   LC 93-49398

"A Richard Jackson book"

"Mama is a coal miner in Appalachia. From the warmth of the family kitchen, a child thinks about her mother's job, and words and pictures set the worlds of home and work side by side. . . . Children will hear the poetry that leaps from the particulars of the workplace, both in the child's simple narrative and in the miners' rhymes. . . . Catalanotto's double-page-spread watercolors focus on the loving bond between the child and her mother, when they're together in the light-filled house, and when they're thinking of each other above and below ground." Booklist

One lucky girl; illustrated by Irene Trivas. DK Pub. 2000 unp il $15.95   **E**

1. Tornadoes—Fiction 2. Family life—Fiction

ISBN 0-7894-2613-7   LC 98-41149

Even though their trailer is destroyed by a tornado, a young boy's family is grateful because they find his baby sister alive

"Lyon's telling—based, apparently, on a true story—has the spareness and vividness of poetry. The watercolors portray a family and neighborhood united by calamity and joy." Horn Book Guide

Who came down that road? story by George Ella Lyon; paintings by Peter Catalanotto. Orchard Bks. 1992 unp il hardcover o.p. paperback available $5.95   **E**

1. Roads—Fiction

ISBN 0-531-07073-5 (pa)   LC 91-20742

"A Richard Jackson book"

Mother and child ponder the past in discussing who might have traveled down an old, old road, looking backwards from pioneer settlers all the way to prehistoric animals

"The spare and elegant text creates a poetic yet childlike mood. . . . Catalanotto's double-page watercolor paintings, which make extensive use of light and shadow for dramatic effect, are dreamy, romanticized representations of each scenario." SLJ

Macaulay, David, 1946-

Black and white. Houghton Mifflin 1990 unp il $17   **E**

ISBN 0-395-52151-3   LC 89-28888

Awarded the Caldecott Medal, 1990

Four brief "stories" about parents, trains, and cows, or is it really all one story? The author recommends careful

Macaulay, David, 1946—_Continued_
inspection of words and pictures to both minimize and enhance confusion

"The magic of _Black and White_ comes not from each story, . . . but from the mysterious interactions between them that creates a fifth story. . . . Eventually, the stories begin to merge into a surrealistic tale spanning several levels of reality. . . . _Black and White_ challenges the reader to use text and pictures in unexpected ways." Publ Wkly

Shortcut. Houghton Mifflin 1995 unp il $15.95; pa $7.95   **E**
ISBN 0-395-52436-9; 0-618-00607-9 (pa)
LC 95-2542

"This picture book concerns six humans whose paths cross and recross in the eight chapters of brief text and distinctive artwork. Albert and his horse, June, take their wagon of melons to market, sell them, and go home. . . . Patty's pet pig, Pearl, wanders onto an abandoned railroad line. . . . Professor Tweet is studying birds when suddenly his hot air balloon breaks free and heads toward a nearby cathedral spire. . . . Seemingly inconsequential details in one story become the moving forces in another." Booklist

"Because _Shortcut_ is not linear in its progression but rather an exploration of simultaneity and concepts of time and space, it is a picture book for sophisticated readers who enjoy puzzles and unraveling clues. . . . David Macaulay deserves applause for challenging his readers as well as entertaining them through boldly conceived illustrations with a cast of wonderfully caricatured characters." Horn Book

Why the chicken crossed the road. Houghton Mifflin 1987 31p il lib bdg $16; pa $6.95   **E**
ISBN 0-395-44241-9 (lib bdg); 0-395-58411-6 (pa)
LC 87-2908

"A ridiculous chicken sets off a circular story involving a herd of cows, a bridge, a train, a robber, the fire department and some hydrangeas. Chaos. The illustrations are suitably wild—painted with brilliant color and almost palpable energy." N Y Times Book Rev

Macdonald, Suse, 1940-
Alphabatics. Bradbury Press 1986 unp il $17.95; pa $6.95   **E**
1. Alphabet
ISBN 0-02-761520-0; 0-689-71625-7 (pa)
LC 85-31429

A Caldecott Medal honor book, 1987
MacDonald "maneuvers each letter to create a visual image as well as an object that begins with that letter." Child Book Rev Serv

The "_A_ tilts, flops over, and literally becomes an ark as it turns itself around. An _N_ turns over, glides up a tree trunk, and becomes a nest for three young birds. Crisp, fresh, and totally effective, it's a unique way of looking at the alphabet. This is a book for creative thinking and sheer enjoyment of MacDonald's precise graphics, rather than for object identification among the very young." SLJ

Peck, slither and slide. Gulliver Bks. 1997 unp il $15   **E**
1. Animals
ISBN 0-15-200079-8
LC 96-18439

"A book of hidden-animal guessing games. Each double-page spread provides visual clues to an animal's identity, together with a verb that might be associated with that creature's behavior. . . . In design and typography, the verbs cleverly imitate the actions they depict. . . . MacDonald's illustrations are nicely textured collages of tissue paper colored with acrylic paint." SLJ

Sea shapes. Harcourt Brace & Co. 1994 unp il $13.95; pa $6   **E**
1. Shape 2. Marine animals
ISBN 0-15-200027-5; 0-15-201700-3 (pa)
LC 93-27957

"Gulliver books"
"Each double-page spread is devoted to a different shape. On each left-hand page, a sequence of simple pictures shows a basic shape evolving into the shape of a marine animal. The opposite page pictures the animal in the sea. The brightly colored paper collages make it easy to follow along as the sea animal develops. The shapes chosen go beyond the ordinary to include, for example, a fan shape, a diamond, a crescent, and a hexagon. MacDonald uses the three final pages to present some information about each animal." Booklist

MacLachlan, Patricia
All the places to love; paintings by Mike Wimmer. HarperCollins Pubs. 1994 unp il $16.95; lib bdg $16.89   **E**
1. Farm life—Fiction 2. Family life—Fiction
ISBN 0-06-021098-2; 0-06-021099-0 (lib bdg)
LC 92-794

A young boy describes the favorite places that he shares with his family on his grandparents' farm and in the nearby countryside

Wimmer's "paintings beautifully convey the splendor of nature, as well as the deep affection binding three generations. This inspired pairing of words and art is a timeless, uplifting portrait of rural family life." Publ Wkly

Mama One, Mama Two; pictures by Ruth Lercher Bornstein. Harper & Row 1982 unp il lib bdg $16.89   **E**
1. Foster home care—Fiction 2. Mother-daughter relationship—Fiction 3. Mental illness—Fiction
ISBN 0-06-024082-2
LC 81-47795

"When Maudie is awakened by the baby's crying, her foster mother tells her the story of how she came to live in this temporary home. Together they describe the girl's mother's increasingly withdrawn behavior that led to the institutionalization of the girl's 'Mama One' and her subsequent placement with Katherine, whom she calls 'Mama Two.' They discuss Maudie's feelings and her hopes for her mother's quick recovery. This articulation of her fears calms the troubled child." SLJ

"Softly-crayoned pastel pictures, simply and tenderly composed and nicely fitting the mood of the story, show the love that is the mortar of the text." Bull Cent Child Books

MacLachlan, Patricia—*Continued*

Three Names; pictures by Alexander Pertzoff. Harper & Row 1991 31p il lib bdg $16.89; pa $5.95   **E**

1. Grandfathers—Fiction 2. Dogs—Fiction 3. Frontier and pioneer life—Fiction

ISBN 0-06-024036-9 (lib bdg); 0-06-443360-9 (pa)

LC 90-4444

"A Charlotte Zolotow book"

Great-grandfather reminisces about going to school on the prairie with his dog Three Names

"A rhythmic text, remarkable for subtle, exact imagery and complemented by luminous, impressionistic water-colors." Horn Book

Madrigal, Antonio Hernandez

Erandi's braids; written by Antonio Hernandez Madrigal; illustrated by Tomie dePaola. Putnam 1999 unp il $15.99   **E**

1. Hair—Fiction 2. Mother-daughter relationship—Fiction 3. Mexico—Fiction

ISBN 0-399-23212-5   LC 97-49631

In a poor Mexican village, Erandi surprises her mother by offering to sell her long, beautiful hair in order to raise enough money to buy a new fishing net

"This tale of love and sacrifice is based on an actual Mexican practice in the 1940s and 50s. The facial expressions in dePaola's warm illustrations add to the poignancy of the story." Horn Book Guide

Maestro, Betsy, 1944-

Ferryboat; by Betsy and Giulio Maestro. Crowell 1986 unp il map lib bdg $15.89   **E**

1. Boats and boating—Fiction

ISBN 0-690-04520-4   LC 85-47887

A family crosses the Connecticut River on a ferryboat and observes how the ferry operates

Illustrated with "sunny watercolor paintings in realistically detailed double-page spreads. . . . Children who are familiar with the procedure should enjoy this recreation of their experience, and others may be intrigued. . . . An appended note gives historical information about the ferry on which the book is based, the Chester-Hadlyme Ferry, which began operating in 1769." Bull Cent Child Books

Taxi; a book of city words; by Betsy & Giulio Maestro. Clarion Bks. 1989 unp il lib bdg $14.95; pa $6.95   **E**

1. Vocabulary 2. City and town life

ISBN 0-89919-528-8 (lib bdg); 0-395-54811-X (pa)

LC 88-22867

"A taxi moves through a city in the course of an ordinary day. The text describes what happens in the action-oriented pictures. The best illustrations strive to capture a quality of urban motion and lively urban streets." N Y Times Book Rev

Mahy, Margaret

17 kings and 42 elephants; pictures by Patricia MacCarthy. Dial Bks. for Young Readers 1987 26p il $16.99; pa $6.99   **E**

1. Animals—Fiction 2. Stories in rhyme

ISBN 0-8037-0458-5; 0-8037-0781-9 (pa)

LC 87-5311

A newly illustrated edition of the title first published 1972 in the United Kingdom

Seventeen kings and forty-two elephants romp with a variety of jungle animals during their mysterious journey through a wild, wet night

"This book takes you on a jungle journey you will never forget. . . . The text is lyrical, humorous, and full of nonsense and fantasy. Children and adults will be charmed by the melodic use of language and the beautiful batik illustrations." Child Book Rev Serv

Boom, baby, boom, boom! illustrated by Patricia MacCarthy. Viking 1997 c1996 unp il $15.99   **E**

1. Drums—Fiction 2. Infants—Fiction 3. Animals—Fiction

ISBN 0-670-87314-4   LC 96-60725

First published 1996 in the United Kingdom

"A group of animals watches through the window as Mama puts her little one in the high chair and piles the tray full of food. . . . Mama sits down at her drum set, closes her eyes, and blissfully beats away, while one by one, the animals come in and share the cheerful toddler's feast." Booklist

"This crackerjack charmer . . . will delight toddlers with its silliness, animal sounds, and 'boom!boom!boom!' . . . MacCarthy's whimsical illustrations are a perfect blend of pastel hues and intense colors." SLJ

The boy who was followed home; pictures by Steven Kellogg. Watts 1975 unp il o.p.   **E**

1. Hippopotamus—Fiction 2. Witches—Fiction

A witch's pill is supposed to cure Robert of the hippopotami who daily follow him home from school

"An amusing, nonsensical story is told in a bland, direct style, and the illustrations echo both qualities; Kellogg's softly-tinted pictures have delightful details." Bull Cent Child Books

The great white man-eating shark; a cautionary tale; pictures by Jonathan Allen. Dial Bks. for Young Readers 1990 unp il hardcover o.p. paperback available $5.99   **E**

1. Sharks—Fiction

ISBN 0-14-055745-8 (pa)   LC 89-1514

Greedy to have the cove where he swims all to himself, Norvin, who looks a bit like a shark, pretends to be one, scaring off the other swimmers and leaving him in happy aquatic solitude—until he is discovered by an amorous female shark

"Mahy's amusing tongue-in-cheek tale meets its match in Allen's droll drawings. Norvin's wonderfully shifty eyes and the vivid expressions on the faces of his victims are certain to tickle funnybones." Publ Wkly

The rattlebang picnic; pictures by Steven Kellogg. Dial Bks. for Young Readers 1994 unp il $14.99; pa $5.99   **E**

1. Family life—Fiction 2. Automobiles—Fiction

ISBN 0-8037-1318-5; 0-14-055579-X (pa)

LC 93-36294

The McTavishes, their seven children, and Granny McTavish take their old rattlebang of a car on a picnic

Mahy, Margaret—_Continued_

up Mt. Fogg and have an exciting adventure

"An original tall tale with an outrageously bizarre plot. . . . Only Mahy could concoct a story about an overcooked pizza saving a family from rivers of hot lava. Her writing is vivid, funny, and full of details that will be dear to a child's heart. And Kellogg's watercolors are a perfect match, adding to the air of deadpan chaos." SLJ

Simply delicious! drawings by Jonathan Allen. Orchard Bks. 1999 unp il $15.95   E
1. Animals—Fiction 2. Ice cream, ices, etc.—Fiction
ISBN 0-531-30181-8   LC 98-46185

A resourceful father engages in all kinds of acrobatic moves to keep an assortment of jungle creatures from getting the double-dip-chocolate-chip-and-cherry ice cream cone he is taking home to his son

"The tongue-twisting text and comical illustrations swiftly propel the silly story forward." Horn Book Guide

A summery Saturday morning; illustrated by Selina Young. Viking 1998 unp il $15.99; pa $5.99   E
1. Stories in rhyme 2. Summer—Fiction
ISBN 0-670-87943-6; 0-14-05720-8 (pa)
LC 97-61542

"A Vanessa Hamilton book"

A woman and "a group of children take the dogs out, chase cats and boys on bikes . . . and get chased themselves by a stern-looking goose and her seven goslings. . . . The rhythm and repetition in the verse and the clear summer hues of the paintings make this a book that virtually begs to be read aloud and shared." Booklist

Manushkin, Fran

Latkes and applesauce; a Hanukkah story; illustrated by Robin Spowart. Scholastic 1990 unp il hardcover o.p. paperback available $4.99   E
1. Hanukkah—Fiction 2. Jews—Fiction
ISBN 0-590-42265-0 (pa)   LC 88-38916

When a blizzard leaves a family housebound one Hanukkah, they share what little food they have with a stray kitten and dog

"To their surprise and delight, the dog digs in the snow and unearths some potatoes, and the kitten has to be rescued from a tree that still has apples on its branches. . . . The two new pets are named Latke and Applesauce. The dark, slightly impressionistic illustrations in warm tones capture the feeling of a time past and of a family that has an abundance of affection. The story of the holiday, a recipe for latkes, instructions for the dreidel game, and the names of a few other books about the holiday are appended." Horn Book

The matzah that Papa brought home; illustrated by Ned Bittinger. Scholastic 1995 unp il $14.95   E
1. Jews—Fiction 2. Passover—Fiction 3. Stories in rhyme
ISBN 0-590-47146-5   LC 94-9952

A cumulative rhyme in the style of "The House That Jack Built" describes the traditions connected to a family's celebration of the Passover seder

"While the text is well done and great fun, the illustrations, rendered in oils, are stellar. Each masterful painting has a subtext. The family members are constantly moving or gesturing. . . . Three pages at the end tell the story of Passover. A unique, lively offering." SLJ

Marcellino, Fred, 1939-2001

I, crocodile. HarperCollins Pubs. 1999 unp il $15.95; pa $15.89   E
1. Napoleon I, Emperor of the French, 1769-1821—Fiction 2. Crocodiles—Fiction
ISBN 0-06-205168-7; 0-06-205199-7 (pa)

"Michael di Capua books"

"The tale, inspired by a 19th-century French satire by an unknown author, centers on a crocodile captured in Egypt and transported to Paris by Napoleon, who decides to cook and eat the animal. But the crocodile . . . escapes into the sewers and makes his own dinner out of a lady of Napoleon's court." N Y Times Book Rev

"The text is reportorial in tone, a perfect complement to the extravagant, expressive illustrations. . . . A sophisticated picture book, this is one publication with appeal to many different audiences." Horn Book

Marshall, Edward, 1942-1992

Fox and his friends; pictures by James Marshall. Dial Bks. for Young Readers 1982 56p il hardcover o.p. paperback available $3.99   E
1. Foxes—Fiction
ISBN 0-14-037007-2 (pa)   LC 81-68769

"Dial easy-to-read"

"Fox has one objective—having fun with his motley group of friends. Unfortunately, his desires regularly conflict with his mother's insistence that he care for his younger sister Louise or with his responsibilities when assigned to traffic patrol." Horn Book

"The sibling exchanges and situations are comically true to life, as is Fox's duty/pleasure conflict. The red, green and black illustrations, showing a defiant Louise, a beleaguered Fox, a wonderful assortment of creature friends and a hilariously feeble group of old hounds pick the story up and add character embellishment and humor." SLJ

Other available titles about Fox are:
Fox all week (1984)
Fox at school (1983)
Fox in love (1982)
Fox on wheels (1983)
Other available titles about Fox written by the author using the name James Marshall are:
Fox be nimble (1990)
Fox on stage (1993)
Fox on the job (1988)
Fox outfoxed (1992)

Space case; pictures by James Marshall. Dial Bks. for Young Readers 1980 unp il $16.99; lib bdg $6.99   E
1. Science fiction 2. Halloween—Fiction
ISBN 0-8037-8005-2; 0-14-054704-5 (lib bdg)
LC 80-13369

Also available with Audiobook

"The 'thing'—a neon yellow robot-like creature from space—arrives on Halloween for a look around and is

Marshall, Edward, 1942-1992—*Continued*

promptly mistaken for a costumed trick-or-treater. It spends the night with a friendly child . . . visits at school (the teacher takes it for a science project) and leaves promising to return for the next fun holiday, Christmas." SLJ

"The open ending of the brief story is as satisfying as it is original, for the small space traveler is thoroughly childlike in its insouciance, curiosity, and concern for self-gratification. The text is an economical, tongue-in-cheek accompaniment to the various levels of humor depicted in the illustrations." Horn Book

Three by the sea; pictures by James Marshall. Dial Bks. for Young Readers 1981 48p il hardcover o.p. paperback available $3.99   E
  ISBN 0-14-037004-8 (pa)
  Also available with Audiobook
  "Dial easy-to-read"
  "When Lolly, on a beach picnic with friends Sam and Spider, reads a story ('The rat saw the cat and the dog.') aloud, it is rated dull. So Sam uses the same rat and cat characters to tell one of his own, and Spider tops Sam's managing to scare the other two with his tale of a monster that passes by the rat and cat to find some tasty kids." SLJ
  "The mild lunacy of the illustrations (an almost vertical hill, a neatly striped cat) with their ungainly, comical figures is nicely matched with the bland directness of the writing. This is good-humored and amusing." Bull Cent Child Books
  Another available title about Spider, Sam, and Lolly is:
Four on the shore (1985)
  Another available title about Spider, Sam, and Lolly written by the author using the name James Marshall is:
Three up a tree (1986)

Marshall, James, 1942-1992

The cut-ups. Viking Kestrel 1984 unp il hardcover o.p. paperback available $5.99   E
  ISBN 0-14-050637-3 (pa)   LC 84-40256
  Practical jokers Spud and Joe get away with every trick in the book until the day they meet a little girl named Mary Frances Hooley
  "This book may not show the subtle wit of Marshall at his best . . . but it is good-humored fun that will certainly entice readers and listeners." SLJ
  Other available titles about Spud and Joe are:
The cut-ups at Camp Custer (1989)
The cut-ups carry on (1990)
The cut-ups crack up (1992)

George and Martha; written and illustrated by James Marshall. Houghton Mifflin 1972 46p il lib bdg $16; pa $6.95   E
  1. Hippopotamus—Fiction 2. Friendship—Fiction
  ISBN 0-395-16619-5 (lib bdg); 0-395-19972-7 (pa)

  Also available with Audiobook; Spanish language edition also available
  In these five short episodes which include a misunderstanding about split pea soup, invasion of privacy and a crisis over a missing tooth, two not very delicate hippopotamuses reveal various aspects of friendship
  "The pale pictures of these creatures and their adventures—in yellows, pinks, greens, and grays—capture the directness and humor of the stories." Horn Book
  Other available titles about George and Martha are:
George and Martha back in town (1984)
George and Martha encore (1973)
George and Martha, one fine day (1978)
George and Martha rise and shine (1976)
George and Martha round and round (1988)
George and Martha, tons of fun (1980)

Swine Lake; [pictures by] Maurice Sendak. HarperCollins Pubs. 1999 unp il $15.95; pa $15.89   E
  1. Ballet—Fiction 2. Wolves—Fiction 3. Pigs—Fiction
  ISBN 0-06-205171-7; 0-06-205172-5 (pa)
        LC 98-73253
  "Michael di Capua books"
  A hungry wolf attends a performance of Swine Lake, performed by the Boarshoi Ballet, intending to eat the performers, but he is so entranced by the story unfolding that he forgets about his meal
  "Both Marshall and Sendak are cleverly comic here . . . the text shines. Sendak's art captures the nuance as well as all the humor of the story." Booklist

Yummers! Houghton Mifflin 1973 30p il lib bdg $16; pa $5.95   E
  1. Pigs—Fiction 2. Turtles—Fiction 3. Weight loss—Fiction
  ISBN 0-395-14757-3 (lib bdg); 0-395-39590-9 (pa)

  Worried about her weight, Emily Pig "jumps rope; her friend Eugene [Turtle] suggests a walk as better exercise, but the walk is interrupted by a series of snacks. Emily, who has said 'Yummers,' to everything, finally has a tummy ache. She thinks it must have been due to all the walking, and agrees with Eugene when he suggests that she stay in bed and eat plenty of good food." Bull Cent Child Books
  "Corpulent, amiable Emily moves with monumental charm in the humorous, bright pastel pictures." Horn Book
  Other available titles about Emily Pig and Eugene Turtle are:
Taking care of Carruthers (1981)
What's the matter with Carruthers? (1972)
Yummers too: the second course (1986)

Marshall, Janet Perry, 1938-

A honey of a day; by Janet Marshall. Greenwillow Bks. 2000 unp il $15.95   E
  1. Wild flowers—Fiction 2. Animals—Fiction 3. Weddings—Fiction
  ISBN 0-688-16917-1   LC 98-32207
  The names and illustrations of many wildflowers are interwoven into a story about a bears' Woodland wedding
  "This book offers a lot: a pleasant story, bright and well-designed illustrations, and a lesson in flower identification that will not soon fade." Booklist

Martin, Ann M., 1955-

Rachel Parker, kindergarten show-off; by Ann Martin; illustrated by Nancy Poydar. Holiday House 1992 unp il $16.95; pa $6.95   E
    1. Friendship—Fiction 2. School stories
    ISBN 0-8234-0935-X; 0-8234-1067-6 (pa)
                           LC 91-25793

Five-year-old Olivia's new neighbor Rachel is in her kindergarten class, and they must overcome feelings of jealousy and competitiveness to be friends

"Olivia's first-person narrative, chatty and comic, imparts a breath of fresh air to a common situation. (Commendably, no point is made of the fact that Olivia is African American while her eventual pal is white.) Filled with entertaining touches, Poydar's true-to-life illustrations scattered throughout the text adroitly capture the girls' changeable emotions." Publ Wkly

Martin, Bill, 1916-

Barn dance! by Bill Martin, Jr. and John Archambault; illustrated by Ted Rand. Holt & Co. 1986 unp il $16.95; pa $6.95   E
    1. Stories in rhyme 2. Dance—Fiction 3. Country life—Fiction
    ISBN 0-8050-0089-5; 0-8050-0799-7 (pa)
                           LC 86-14225

Unable to sleep on the night of a full moon, a young boy follows the sound of music across the fields and finds an unusual barn dance in progress

"The bouncy rhyme will be a pleasure for listeners and tellers as they pick up the twang and the barn-dance beat. Rand's raucous two-page watercolor spreads are as spirited as the story poem." Booklist

A beasty story; [written by] Bill Martin, Jr. & [illustrated by] Steven Kellogg. Harcourt Brace & Co. 1999 unp il $16   E
    1. Mice—Fiction 2. Color—Fiction 3. Stories in rhyme
    ISBN 0-15-201683-X   LC 97-49519

A group of mice venture into a dark, dark woods where they find a dark brown house with a dark red stair leading past other dark colors to a spooky surprise

"A rhymed narrative tells the story along the top of the pages, with the mice commenting in rhymed conversation as they move through the adventure. The silly resolution will appeal to young children. . . . Kellogg's lively ink-and-watercolor art strikes just the right note for the gently suspenseful story." Booklist

Brown bear, brown bear what do you see? pictures by Eric Carle. Holt & Co. 1992 unp il $15.95   E
    1. Color—Fiction 2. Animals—Fiction 3. Stories in rhyme
    ISBN 0-8050-1744-5   LC 91-29115
    Also available Board book edition

A newly illustrated edition of the title first published 1967 by Holt, Rinehart & Winston

A chant in which a variety of animals, each one a different color, answers the question, "What do you see?"

"Carle's large, brilliantly colored animals set against a white background make the book perfect for sharing with a group of preschoolers, while Martin's repetitious text is eminently chantable—a boon for beginning readers." Horn Book

Chicka chicka boom boom; by Bill Martin, Jr. and John Archambault; illustrated by Lois Ehlert. Simon & Schuster Bks. for Young Readers 1989 unp il $15; pa $6.99   E
    1. Alphabet 2. Stories in rhyme
    ISBN 0-671-67949-X; 0-689-83568-X (pa)
                           LC 89-4315

Also available with Audiobook

An alphabet rhyme/chant that relates what happens when the whole alphabet tries to climb a coconut tree

"Ehlert's illustrations—bold, colorful shapes—are contained by broad polka-dotted borders, like a proscenium arch through which the action explodes. Tongue-tingling, visually stimulating, with an insistent repetitive chorus of 'chicka chicka boom boom,' the book demands to be read again and again and again." Horn Book

The ghost-eye tree; by Bill Martin, Jr. and John Archambault; illustrated by Ted Rand. Holt & Co. 1985 unp il $16.95; pa $6.95   E
    1. Ghost stories 2. Fear—Fiction
    ISBN 0-8050-0208-1; 0-8050-0947-7 (pa)
                           LC 85-8422

"On a dark and ghostly night a brother and sister are sent to fetch a pail of milk from the other end of town. They must pass the fearful ghost-eye tree, old and horribly twisted, looking like a monster, with a gap in the branches where the moon shines through like an eye. . . . The story is rhythmically told, sometimes rhyming, always moving ahead, sharp with the affectionate teasing of the brother and sister. The realistic watercolor illustrations are superb—strong, striking, very dark, with highlights of moonlight and lantern light that cast a spooky, scary spell. A splendidly theatrical book for storytelling and reading aloud." Horn Book

Knots on a counting rope; by Bill Martin, Jr. and John Archambault; illustrated by Ted Rand. Holt & Co. 1987 unp il $16.95; pa $6.95   E
    1. Native Americans—Fiction 2. Grandfathers—Fiction 3. Blind—Fiction
    ISBN 0-8050-0571-4; 0-8050-5479-0 (pa)
                           LC 87-14858

Also available paperback Big edition and with Audiobook

A different version of the title illustrated by Joe Smith was published in 1966

"Boy-Strength-of-Blue-Horses begs his grandfather to tell him again the story of the night he was born. In a question-and-answer litany, the boy and his grandfather share the telling of the events on that special night." SLJ

"The powerful spare poetic text is done full justice by Rand's fine full-color illustrations, which capture both the drama and brilliance of vast southwestern space and the intimacy of starlit camp-fire scenes. While classified as an Indian story the love, hope, and courage expressed are universal, meriting a wide audience." Booklist

The maestro plays; by Bill Martin, Jr.; pictures by Vladimir Radunsky. Holt & Co. 1994 unp il $15.95   E
    1. Musicians—Fiction
    ISBN 0-8050-1746-1   LC 94-1916

"At center stage is a clown-like creature, 'The Maestro,' who plays a progression of instruments. And how

Martin, Bill, 1916-—*Continued*
does he play? In an intriguing variety of ways, including some that are easy enough to understand ('flowingly, glowingly, knowingly, showingly, goingly') and some that will require youngsters to use their imaginations ('nippingly, drippingly, zippingly, clippingly, pippingly'." Publ Wkly
"Radunsky's wonderfully bizarre illustrations, created from hand-colored cut paper, are a visual delight. . . . An infectious rhythm builds, at times lapsing into nonsense, but resulting in an almost perfect coupling of text and illustration." SLJ

Polar bear, polar bear, what do you hear? by Bill Martin, Jr.; pictures by Eric Carle. Holt & Co. 1991 unp il $15.95 E
1. Animals—Fiction 2. Stories in rhyme
ISBN 0-8050-1759-3   LC 91-13322
Also available Board book edition and paperback Big edition; Spanish language edition also available
Zoo animals from polar bear to walrus make their distinctive sounds for each other, while children imitate the sounds for the zookeeper
"Carle's characteristically inventive, jewel-toned artwork forms a seamless succession of images that fairly leap off the pages." Publ Wkly

Martin, David, 1944-
Five little piggies; stories by David Martin; illustrated by Susan Meddaugh. Candlewick Press 1998 unp il $16.99; pa $6.99 E
1. Pigs—Fiction
ISBN 1-56402-918-2; 0-763-61081-X (pa)
                                        LC 97-14667
"Five short tales that elaborate on the adventures of each of the five pigs in the traditional nursery rhyme." SLJ
"Meddaugh's wonderfully expressive watercolor-and-ink cartoon drawings add hilarious details that combine the sloppy and the affectionate with the siblings' constant tantrums and rivalry." Booklist

Martin, Jacqueline Briggs
Grandmother Bryant's pocket; pictures by Petra Mathers. Houghton Mifflin 1996 48p il $14.95; pa $5.95 E
1. Fear—Fiction   2. Grandmothers—Fiction
3. Maine—Fiction
ISBN 0-395-68984-8; 0-618-03309-2 (pa)
                                        LC 94-31309
"In 1787, Sarah Bryant is eight years old and lives on a farm in Maine. She and her spotted dog Patches are inseparable companions until that spring, when the barn burns down and Patches is killed in the fire. Sarah begins to have bad dreams . . . and so she is sent to her grandparents, an herbalist and a woodworker, for solace and healing." Horn Book
"Appealingly structured in one-and two-page chapters, the book is illustrated with watercolor paintings. Executed in naive style, the artwork has an unassuming sweetness." Booklist

Martin, Rafe, 1946-
Will's mammoth; illustrated by Stephen Gammell. Putnam 1989 unp il $16.99 E
1. Mammoths—Fiction
ISBN 0-399-21627-8   LC 88-11651
"Will loves mammoths—huge, hairy, woolly mammoths. His parents explain that there are no mammoths left in the world, but Will knows better. Off he goes into an iridescent, snowbound world of his own creation, where he quickly finds all manner of woolly prehistoric beasts." SLJ
"Gammell's depiction of a child's rich imagination is illustrated in vivid colors. The fantasy spreads use winter whites and blues as background for subtly individualized animals who move energetically across the pages." Booklist

Marzollo, Jean
Home sweet home; illustrated by Ashley Wolff. HarperCollins Pubs. 1997 unp il $14.95; lib bdg $14.89; pa $5.95 E
1. Prayers
ISBN 0-06-027562-6; 0-06-027353-4 (lib bdg); 0-06-443501-6 (pa)   LC 96-35410
"Marzollo's simple prayerful poem begins 'Bless each bee/Each flower and tree' and goes on to introduce other animals and plants, including turtles and snakes, ducks and drakes, whales and snails, foals and tadpoles." Booklist
"Bold black lines define each detail of the striking illustrations. As soothing as a lullaby, the prayer celebrates life in all its diversity." Horn Book Guide

Pretend you're a cat; pictures by Jerry Pinkney. Dial Bks. for Young Readers 1990 unp il $15.99; pa $4.99 E
1. Animals—Fiction 2. Stories in rhyme
ISBN 0-8037-0773-8; 0-14-055993-0 (pa)
                                        LC 89-34546
"Each double spread consists of a large painting of an animal, a smaller painting—boxed—of children imitating the animal, and of a series of questions [in verse]. Sample 'Can you climb? Can you leap? Can you stretch? Can you sleep? Can you hiss? Can you scat? Can you purr like a cat? What else can you do like a cat?'" Bull Cent Child Books
"The rhymed verses are vivid and straightforward, and Pinkney's inventive watercolor and pencil drawings are as engaging as the characters and animals he portrays." Publ Wkly

Massie, Diane Redfield
The baby beebee bird; pictures by Steven Kellogg. Newly illustrated. HarperCollins Pubs. 2000 unp il $15.95; lib bdg $15.89 E
1. Animals—Fiction 2. Sleep—Fiction
ISBN 0-06-028083-2; 0-06-028084-0 (lib bdg)
                                        LC 99-33421
A newly illustrated edition of the title first published 1963
The zoo animals find a way to keep the baby beebee bird awake during the day so that they can get some sleep at night
"The facial expressions on Kellogg's animals loom large, extending . . . the simple story and giving visual voice to a story big on child appeal." Booklist

Mathers, Petra

Lottie's new beach towel. Atheneum Bks. for Young Readers 1998 unp il $15 **E**

1. Chickens—Fiction 2. Beaches—Fiction
ISBN 0-689-81606-5   LC 97-6689
"An Anne Schwartz book"

Lottie the chicken has a number of adventures at the beach, during which her new towel comes in handy

"Pure fun, with a resourceful, big-hearted main character; humor in both text and pictures; and a good story, elegantly shaped." Horn Book

Another available title about Lottie is:
Lottie's new friend (1999)

Mayer, Mercer, 1943-

A boy, a dog, and a frog. Dial Bks. for Young Readers 1967 unp il hardcover o.p. paperback available $4.99 **E**

1. Frogs—Fiction 2. Stories without words
ISBN 0-14-054611-1 (pa)

"Without the need for a single word, humorous, very engaging pictures tell the story of a little boy who sets forth with his dog and a net on a summer day to catch an enterprising and personable frog. Even very young preschoolers will 'read' the tiny book with the greatest satisfaction and pleasure." Horn Book

Other available titles in this series are:
A boy, a dog, a frog, and a friend (1971)
Frog goes to dinner (1974)
Frog on his own (1973)
Frog, where are you? (1969)
One frog too many (1975)

There's a nightmare in my closet. Dial Bks. for Young Readers 1968 unp il $15.99; pa $5.99 **E**

1. Fear—Fiction
ISBN 0-8037-8682-4; 0-14-054712-6 (pa)

A young boy confronts the frightening creature lurking in his closet

"Childhood fear of the dark and the resulting exercise in imaginative exaggeration are given that special Mercer Mayer treatment in this dryly humorous fantasy. Young children will easily empathize with the boy and can be comforted by his experience." SLJ

Another available title about this boy is:
There's an alligator under my bed (1987)

McBratney, Sam

Guess how much I love you; illustrated by Anita Jeram. Candlewick Press 1995 unp il $15.99 **E**

1. Rabbits—Fiction 2. Father-son relationship—Fiction
ISBN 1-56402-473-3   LC 94-1599

Also available Board book edition; Spanish language edition also available

During a bedtime game, every time Little Nutbrown Hare demonstrates how much he loves his father, Big Nutbrown Hare gently shows him that the love is returned even more

"Neither sugary nor too cartoonlike, the watercolors, in soft shades of brown and greens with delicate ink-line details, warmly capture the loving relationship between parent and child as well as the comedy that stems from little hare's awe of his wonderful dad." Booklist

Just you and me; illustrated by Ivan Bates. Candlewick Press 1998 unp il $15.99; pa $5.99 **E**

1. Geese—Fiction 2. Animals—Fiction 3. Storms—Fiction
ISBN 0-7636-0436-4; 0-7636-1078-X (pa)
LC 97-16456

As a storm approaches, Little Goosey and Big Gander Goose join other animals in searching for a place to hide

"McBratney's serene prose is as warm as a sheltering embrace. . . . In a series of pastoral scenes rendered in watercolor and colored pencil and laced with gentle humor, Bates echoes the story's quiet tone." Publ Wkly

McCloskey, Robert, 1914-

Blueberries for Sal. Viking 1948 54p il $16.99; pa $5.99 **E**

1. Bears—Fiction 2. Maine—Fiction
ISBN 0-670-17591-9; 0-14-050169-X (pa)

Also available with Audiobook
A Caldecott Medal honor book, 1949

"The author-artist tells what happens on a summer day in Maine when a little girl and a bear cub, wandering away from their blueberry-picking mothers, each mistakes the other's mother for its own. The Maine hillside and meadows are real and lovely, the quiet humor is entirely childlike, and there is just exactly the right amount of suspense for small children." Wis Libr Bull

Another available title about Sal is: One morning in Maine, entered separately

Lentil. Viking 1940 unp il $16.99; pa $5.99 **E**

1. Harmonicas—Fiction 2. Ohio—Fiction
ISBN 0-670-42357-2; 0-14-050287-4 (pa)

Picture-story book about a small boy who could not sing, but who could work wonders on a simple harmonica, especially on the day when the great Colonel Carter returned to his home town

"Big, vigorous, amusing pictures in black-and-white, with an Ohio small-town background." New Yorker

Make way for ducklings. Viking 1941 unp $15.99; pa $6.99 **E**

1. Ducks—Fiction 2. Boston (Mass.)—Fiction
ISBN 0-670-45149-5; 0-14-056434-9 (pa)

Also available with Audiobook; Spanish language edition also available

Awarded the Caldecott Medal, 1942

"A family of baby ducks was born on the Charles River near Boston. When they were old enough to follow, Mother Duck, with some help from a friendly policeman, trailed them through Boston traffic to the pond in the Public Garden." Bookmark

"There are some very beautiful drawings in this book." Horn Book

One morning in Maine. Viking 1952 64p il $17.99; pa $5.99 **E**

1. Maine—Fiction
ISBN 0-670-52627-4; 0-14-050174-6 (pa)

A Caldecott Medal honor book, 1953

The events of this "story—Sal's discovery of her first loose tooth, the loss of the tooth while digging clams,

McCloskey, Robert, 1914--- *Continued*

the consequent wish on a gull's feather, and the wish come true—occur in the course of one morning in Maine. The lovely Maine seacoast scenes and the doings of Sal with her family and friends are drawn with enticing detail in beautiful, big double-spread lithographs printed in dark blue." Booklist

Time of wonder. Viking 1957 63p il $18.99; pa $6.99   **E**
1. Maine—Fiction
ISBN 0-670-71512-3; 0-14-050201-7 (pa)
Awarded the Caldecott Medal, 1958
"A summer on an island in Maine is described through the simple everyday experiences of children, but also reveals the author's deep awareness of an attachment to all the shifting moods of season and weather, and the salty, downright character of the New England people." Top News

McCully, Emily Arnold

The ballot box battle. Knopf 1996 unp il $17; lib bdg $18.99; pa $6.99   **E**
1. Stanton, Elizabeth Cady, 1815-1902—Fiction 2. Feminism—Fiction 3. Women—Suffrage—Fiction
ISBN 0-679-87938-2; 0-679-97938-7 (lib bdg); 0-679-89312-1 (pa)   LC 95-38095
The author "creates a fictional neighbor for Elizabeth Cady Stanton in the person of young Cordelia. . . . Mrs. Stanton, who is age 65, tells Cordelia about her childhood and how she sought to assuage her father's grief over her brother Eleazur's death by learning and accomplishing as much as any boy. . . . Stanton then prods a reluctant Cordelia into accompanying her as she unsuccessfully tries to cast a ballot." Booklist
"McCully's richly hued, softly textured paintings beautifully evoke the late 19th-century era and the small-town world of Tenafly, NJ, where the widowed Stanton spent her last years. Skillfully weaving fact and story, *The Ballot Box Battle* offers a history lesson pleasingly framed in a story about an independent young girl." SLJ

Beautiful warrior; the legend of the nun's kung fu. Levine Bks. 1998 unp il $16.95   **E**
1. Martial arts—Fiction 2. China—Fiction
ISBN 0-590-37487-7   LC 97-3823
"Born near the end of the Ming Dynasty, a girl grows up to become a fighting nun, renowned for her martial arts. Later, when a timid village girl asks for help in deterring her loutish husband-to-be, the nun teaches her kung fu so she can save herself. The story is intriguing, and the watercolors . . . are filled with dramatic motion." Horn Book Guide

The grandma mix-up; story and pictures by Emily Arnold McCully. Harper & Row 1988 63p il lib bdg $15.89; pa $3.95   **E**
1. Grandmothers—Fiction
ISBN 0-06-024202-7 (lib bdg); 0-06-444150-4 (pa)   LC 87-29378
"An I can read book"
Young Pip doesn't know what to do when two very different grandmothers come to baby sit, each with her own way of doing things

"McCully's two-color, line-and-wash drawings emphasize the personality differences by consciously flouting stereotypes: Pip's laid-back Grandma Sal has white hair and glasses, while his strict Grandma Nan dresses like a teenager. Choice of words and sentence length will make the sly humor easy for beginning readers to grasp." Booklist
Other available titles about Pip and his grandmothers are:
Grandmas at bat (1993)
Grandmas at the lake (1990)

Mirette on the high wire. Putnam 1992 unp il $16.99; pa $5.99   **E**
1. Tightrope walking—Fiction 2. Paris (France)—Fiction
ISBN 0-399-22130-1; 0-698-11443-4 (pa)   LC 91-36324
Awarded the Caldecott Medal, 1993
Mirette learns tightrope walking from Monsieur Bellini, a guest in her mother's boarding house, not knowing that he is a celebrated tightrope artist who has withdrawn from performing because of fear
"With a rich palette of deep colors, the artist immerses the reader in 19th-century Paris. Colorful theatrical personalities . . . fill the glowing interiors with robust life. And the exterior scenes . . . are filled with the magic of a Paris night when anything can happen. . . . An exuberant and uplifting picture book." N Y Times Book Rev
Other available titles about Mirette and Bellini are:
Mirette & Bellini cross Niagra Falls (2000)
Starring Mirette and Bellini (1997)

Monk camps out; story and pictures by Emily Arnold McCully. Levine Bks. 2000 unp il lib bdg $15.95   **E**
1. Mice—Fiction 2. Camping—Fiction
ISBN 0-439-09976-5   LC 99-23237
A young mouse named monk decides to spend the night camping out alone in his backyard, but his parents have other ideas
"McCully's simple, eloquent text and expressive, loosely rendered illustrations alternate between Monk's quiet adventure and his parents' protective watch." Horn Book Guide
Another available title about Monk is:
Mouse practice (1999)

An outlaw Thanksgiving. Dial Bks. for Young Readers 1998 unp il $15.99; pa $6.99   **E**
1. Cassidy, Butch, b. 1866 or 7—Fiction 2. Railroads—Fiction 3. West (U.S.)—Fiction 4. Thanksgiving Day—Fiction
ISBN 0-8037-2197-8; 0-14-056768-2 (pa)   LC 97-29553
While travelling with her mother cross-country by train in 1896, a young girl unexpectedly shares Thanksgiving dinner with the notorious outlaw, Butch Cassidy
"McCully's single- and double-page full-color spreads evocatively capture the ambiance of the early trains, the sweep of the landscape, and the excitement of the adventure; the artist also deftly individualizes her characters with aplomb." SLJ

McDermott, Gerald

Papagayo; the mischief maker; written and illustrated by Gerald McDermott. Harcourt Brace Jovanovich 1992 unp il $16.95; pa $8   E

1. Parrots—Fiction

ISBN 0-15-259465-5; 0-15-259464-7 (pa)

LC 91-40364

A reissue of the title first published 1980 by Windmill Bks.

Papagayo, the noisy parrot, helps the night animals save the moon from being eaten up by the moon dog

"McDermott's original story assumes folktale proportions. . . . Art for the story is striking; deep tropical colors seem intensified by glossy page surfaces, and they nearly vibrate against the intermittent deep-blue backdrop of a night sky." Booklist

Tim O'Toole and the wee folk; an Irish tale; told and illustrated by Gerald McDermott. Viking 1990 unp il hardcover o.p. paperback available $5.99   E

1. Fairy tales 2. Ireland—Fiction

ISBN 0-14-050675-6 (pa)   LC 89-8913

A very poor Irishman is provided with magical things by the "wee folk", but he must then keep his good fortune out of the hands of the greedy McGoons

"McDermott's characteristic illustrations are a perfect accompaniment to the cheery good humor of the story; flocks of tiny leprechauns resembling fields of shamrocks cavort over the bright green hillsides. The comical folk art and the economical use of language, as well as its slight hint of brogue, will make this book a pleasurable choice for story hour." Horn Book

McDonald, Megan, 1959-

The great pumpkin switch; story by Megan McDonald; pictures by Ted Lewin. Orchard Bks. 1992 unp il $15.95; pa $6.95   E

1. Pumpkin—Fiction 2. Siblings—Fiction

ISBN 0-531-05450-0; 0-531-07065-4 (pa)

LC 91-39660

"A Richard Jackson book"

An old man tells his grandchildren how he and a friend accidentally smashed the pumpkin his sister was growing and had to find a replacement

"The extraordinary watercolors depict the period with bold, sure strokes and add nuances and depth to the story; the portraits, especially that of a broadly smiling, youthful Grandpa, are unabashedly joyful. A book that cuts across generations with its sensitivity and gentle wit." Booklist

Insects are my life; story by Megan McDonald; pictures by Paul Brett Johnson. Orchard Bks. 1995 unp il $15.95; lib bdg $16.99; pa $6.95   E

1. Insects—Fiction

ISBN 0-531-06874-9; 0-531-08724-7 (lib bdg); 0-531-07093-X (pa)   LC 94-21960

"A Richard Jackson book"

No one at home or school understands Amanda Frankenstein's devotion to insects until she meets Maggie

"Factual tidbits slipped surreptitiously into the appealing text add information to this spirited tale. . . . Full-page and vignette illustrations rendered in soft-hued watercolors, colored pencils, and pastels complement and add humor to the story." SLJ

The potato man; story by Megan McDonald; pictures by Ted Lewin. Orchard Bks. 1991 unp il $15.95; lib bdg $16.99; pa $5.95   E

1. Peddlers and peddling—Fiction

ISBN 0-531-05914-6; 0-531-08514-7 (lib bdg); 0-531-07053-0 (pa)   LC 90-7758

"A Richard Jackson book"

Grandpa tells stories of the fruit and vegetable peddler in his childhood neighborhood, a man he learns to appreciate after a rocky start

"McDonald and Lewin have created a lovely, evocative period piece. The artist's horse-drawn wagons, rugged faces and turn-of-the-century kitchen are perfectly matched by the gentle homespun writing style." Publ Wkly

McGill, Alice

Molly Bannaky; written by Alice McGill; pictures by Chris K. Soentpiet. Houghton Mifflin 1999 unp il $16   E

1. Banneker, Benjamin, 1731-1806—Fiction 2. Farm life—Fiction 3. United States—History—1600-1775, Colonial period—Fiction

ISBN 0-395-72287-X   LC 96-3000

Relates how Benjamin Banneker's grandmother journeyed from England to Maryland in the late seventeenth century, worked as an indentured servant, began a farm of her own, and married a freed slave

"The writing is descriptive but spare, the implied emotions more resonant echoes than obvious pronouncements. Soentpiet's watercolors use the contrasting play of light and dark to cast the figures in this family drama in bold relief. The compositions . . . have a weighty, monumental feel to them." Bull Cent Child Books

McKissack, Patricia C., 1944-

Flossie & the fox; pictures by Rachel Isadora. Dial Bks. for Young Readers 1986 unp il $15.99   E

1. Foxes—Fiction 2. African Americans—Fiction

ISBN 0-8037-0250-7   LC 86-2024

A wily fox notorious for stealing eggs meets his match when he encounters a bold little girl in the woods who insists upon proof that he is a fox before she will be frightened

"The watercolor and ink illustrations, with realistic figures set on impressionistic backgrounds, enliven this humorous and well-structured story which is told in the black language of the rural south. The language is true, and the illustrations are marvelously complementary in their interpretation of the events. This spirited little girl will capture readers from the beginning, and they'll adore her by the end of this delightful story." SLJ

The honest-to-goodness truth; illustrated by Giselle Potter. Atheneum Pubs. 2000 unp il $16   E

1. Honesty—Fiction

ISBN 0-689-82668-0   LC 98-47070

"An Anne Schwartz book"

After promising never to lie, Libby learns that it's not always necessary to blurt out the whole truth either

"The pastel watercolor and ink illustrations capture the story's Southern milieu, warmth, and humor." Horn Book Guide

McKissack, Patricia C., 1944——*Continued*

Ma Dear's aprons; illustrations by Floyd Cooper. Atheneum Bks. for Young Readers 1997 unp il $16; pa $5.99   **E**
1. Mother-son relationship—Fiction 2. African Americans—Fiction
ISBN 0-689-81051-2; 0-689-83262-1 (pa)
LC 94-48450
"An Anne Schwartz book"
"In this tribute to her great-grandmother, McKissack tells the story of Ma Dear, African-American single mother and domestic worker in the turn of the century South. Her son David Earl always knows what day it is by the 'clean, snappy-fresh apron Ma Dear is wearing—a different one for every day of the week.'" Bull Cent Child Books
"The homely reminiscence is aptly illustrated with Cooper's soft oil wash paintings. . . . Text and illustrations together create a portrait of a family working hard to survive but also finding much to be joyful about." Horn Book

A million fish—more or less; illustrated by Dena Schutzer. Knopf 1992 unp il hardcover o.p. paperback available $6.99   **E**
1. Tall tales 2. Fishing—Fiction 3. Louisiana—Fiction 4. African Americans—Fiction
ISBN 0-679-88086-0 (pa)   LC 91-17323
"While Hugh Thomas is fishing, Papa-Daddy and Elder Abbajon row out of the fog swapping bayou tales. He doesn't believe their stories, but when he catches a million fish and has all but three taken by a giant gator, raccoon pirates, and a cat, he has his own whopping good story about the Bayou Clapateaux." Publisher's note
"The play between fantasy and reality is neatly handled, with action following exaggeration in an ambiguous way that leaves the ending open as to who's telling the truth and who believes what. The African-American characters and swamp setting swirl across the pages in thick, rounded strokes of brazen-hued paint, well-matched with the story's brassy flash." Bull Cent Child Books

Mirandy and Brother Wind; illustrated by Jerry Pinkney. Knopf 1988 unp il hardcover o.p. paperback available $6.99   **E**
1. Dance—Fiction 2. Winds—Fiction 3. African Americans—Fiction
ISBN 0-679-88333-9 (pa)   LC 87-349
A Caldecott Medal honor book, 1989; Coretta Scott King award for illustrations, 1989
"Mirandy is sure that she'll win the cake walk if she can catch Brother Wind for her partner, but he eludes all the tricks her friends advise. When she finally does catch him with her own quick wits, she ends up wishing instead for her boyfriend Ezel to overcome his clumsiness. Sure enough, the two children finish first in high style." Bull Cent Child Books
"Ms. McKissack and Mr. Pinkney's ebullient collaboration captures the texture of rural life and culture 40 years after the end of slavery. . . . Each page of 'Mirandy and Brother Wind' sparkles with life." N Y Times Book Rev

McLeod, Emilie, 1926-1982

The bear's bicycle; by Emilie Warren McLeod; illustrated by David McPhail. Little, Brown 1975 31p il hardcover o.p. paperback available $5.95
E
1. Bears—Fiction 2. Cycling—Fiction
ISBN 0-316-56206-8 (pa)
"An Atlantic Monthly Press book"
"Bicycle safety is demonstrated through colorful pictures leavened by a parallel set of humorous pictures of a teddy-bear-turned-real who takes the hazardous consequences of ignoring the safety rules." Read Teach

McLerran, Alice, 1933-

Roxaboxen; illustrated by Barbara Cooney. Lothrop, Lee & Shepard Bks. 1991 unp il $16; lib bdg $16.89   **E**
ISBN 0-688-07592-4; 0-688-07593-2 (lib bdg)
LC 89-8057
Also available in paperback from Puffin Bks.
A hill covered with rocks and wooden boxes in the desert becomes an imaginary town named Roxaboxen for Marian, her sisters, and their friends
"A celebration of the transforming magic of the imagination, the story was inspired by McLerran's mother's reminiscences of her childhood in Yuma, Arizona. . . . The story, told as though from the memory of a Roxaboxenite, brings their play to life through concrete details and a spare, understated style. Equally vivid, Cooney's full-color artwork evokes the striking variety of colors and moods found in the desert landscape." Booklist

McMillan, Bruce

Counting wildflowers. Lothrop, Lee & Shepard Bks. 1986 unp il lib bdg $15.93; pa $4.95   **E**
1. Counting 2. Wild flowers
ISBN 0-688-02860-8 (lib bdg); 0-688-14027-0 (pa)
LC 85-16607
A counting book with photographs of wildflowers illustrating the numbers one through twenty
"Dazzling photographs of twenty-three wildflowers are the major feature of this deftly constructed, multipurpose concept book. On the simplest level this is a counting book. . . . The book is also a simple identification guide, with the popular name of each variety appearing just above the photograph; all the flowers are listed again at the end along with the scientific name, months of blooming, and type of terrain where found." Horn Book

Growing colors. Lothrop, Lee & Shepard Bks. 1988 32p il $16; pa $4.95   **E**
1. Color 2. Vegetables 3. Fruit
ISBN 0-688-07844-3; 0-688-13112-3 (pa)
LC 88-2767
"A colors book using fruits and vegetables of every hue. Each double-page spread has a small photograph of the whole plant and a large close-up of the fruit or vegetable. The colors are announced in bold type tinted in the appropriate shade. . . . At the end of the book, there is a picture glossary of all the colors and plants used." Publ Wkly
"A luscious-looking book that will help children identify colors. . . . This is notably a treat for kids and an example of photography as an art form in picture books." Bull Cent Child Books

McMillan, Bruce—*Continued*

Mouse views; what the class pet saw; written and photo-illustrated by Bruce McMillan. Holiday House 1993 32p il $16.95; pa $6.95   **E**

1. Mice—Fiction

ISBN 0-8234-1008-0; 0-8234-1132-X (pa)

LC 92-25921

Photographic puzzles follow an escaped pet mouse through a school while depicting such common school items as scissors, paper, books, and chalk. Readers are challenged to identify the objects as seen from the mouse's point of view

"Children will see this brightly illustrated puzzle book, with its combination of story and game, as pure fun. Teachers will appreciate the chance to hone their students' observational skills and also to introduce mapping through the map at the book's conclusion." Booklist

Step by step. Lothrop, Lee & Shepard Bks. 1987 unp il $13.95; lib bdg $13.95   **E**

1. Infants—Fiction 2. Growth—Fiction

ISBN 0-688-07233-X; 0-688-07234-8 (lib bdg)

LC 87-4195

"A tiny infant sleeps, rolls over, stands up, walks and then, at 14 months, runs, in this photographic portrait of a child's first moves." Publ Wkly

"Families with one and two year olds will enjoy looking at these familiar moments, unposed and natural. This book works not so much of itself, but because of the response it will call from children looking at it and the opportunity for discussion that may follow." SLJ

McMullan, Kate, 1947-

Papa's song; pictures by Jim McMullan. Farrar, Straus & Giroux 2000 unp il $15   **E**

1. Bears—Fiction 2. Sleep—Fiction

ISBN 0-374-35732-3   LC 99-34556

"Granny Bear, Grandpa Bear, and Mama Bear each take a turn at singing Baby to sleep, but only Papa Bear knows the 'right song'; he takes Baby out on the river where the soothing river sounds quickly put Baby Bear to sleep. The watercolors are likewise soothing, depicting a cradle-like boat on the blue moonlit river and a cozy bear home, aglow with candlelight and love." Horn Book Guide

McPhail, David M.

The bear's toothache; written and illustrated by David McPhail. Little, Brown 1972 31p il hardcover o.p. paperback available $5.95   **E**

1. Bears—Fiction 2. Teeth—Fiction

ISBN 0-316-56325-0 (pa)

Also available with Audiobook

"An Atlantic Monthly Press book"

"In this delightful fantasy, a small boy receives a nocturnal visit from a bear with a sore tooth. Pulling on the tooth doesn't work, eating fails to loosen it, and hitting it with a pillow breaks a lamp and wakes up father. The boy's cowboy rope is securely fastened to tooth and bedpost and, as the bear jumps out the window, the tooth finally pops out. The grateful bear then gives it to the boy to put under his pillow. The simple text is accompanied by full-page pastel pictures which are filled with action and detail and are superbly suited to this imaginative bedtime tale." SLJ

Drawing lessons from a bear; [by] David McPhail. Little, Brown 2000 unp il $14.95   **E**

1. Bears—Fiction 2. Artists—Fiction

ISBN 0-316-56345-5   LC 98-54966

A bear explains how he became an artist, first experimenting with simple drawings, then continuing to draw both things around him and things in his imagination. Includes tips for drawing

"This gentle story combines a humorous tone with warm, cozy watercolors to create inspiration for budding artists." SLJ

Edward and the pirates; [by] David McPhail. Little, Brown 1997 unp il $15.95   **E**

1. Books and reading—Fiction 2. Pirates—Fiction

ISBN 0-316-56344-7   LC 95-38451

Companion volume to Santa's book of names (1993)

Once Edward has learned to read, books and his vivid imagination provide him with great adventures

"McPhail's rich acrylic paintings exude a dark and mysterious aura and feature many sinister-looking characters from Edward's books lurking around every corner." Booklist

Mole music; written and illustrated by David McPhail. Holt & Co. 1999 unp il $15.95   **E**

1. Moles (Animals)—Fiction 2. Violins—Fiction 3. Music—Fiction

ISBN 0-8050-2819-6   LC 98-21318

Feeling that something is missing in his simple life, Mole acquires a violin and learns to make beautiful, joyful music

"McPhail's delicate watercolor-and-ink illustrations work with the simple text to create a lyrical celebration of music and musicians." Booklist

Pig Pig grows up; by David McPhail. Dutton 1980 unp il hardcover o.p. paperback available $5.99   **E**

1. Pigs—Fiction

ISBN 0-525-44195-6 (pa)

"A Unicorn book"

Only when faced with a dire emergency does Pig Pig finally react like a grown-up and admit he is not a baby any more

"Large drawings in subdued full color are uncluttered and go straight to the point; full of humor and action, they virtually tell the story by themselves." Horn Book

Another available title about Pig Pig is:
Pig Pig gets a job (1990)

Pigs aplenty, pigs galore! [by] David McPhail. Dutton Children's Bks. 1993 unp il $15.99; pa $6.99   **E**

1. Pigs—Fiction 2. Stories in rhyme

ISBN 0-525-45079-3; 0-14-055313-4 (pa)

LC 92-27986

"As pigs of every size, shape, and dress (including Elvis) arrive at his house in every possible vehicle, a riotous party begins and lasts through the night as the perplexed narrator looks on." SLJ

"The rhyme is bouncy enough, but it's the pictures that will have parents and kids howling. Using deep watercolors set against a black background, McPhail presents a magnificent group of porkers, whose capacity for costumes and capers is truly wondrous." Booklist

McPhail, David M.—*Continued*

Other available titles about the pigs are:
Pigs ahoy! (1995)
Those can-do pigs (1996)

The puddle; [by] David McPhail. Farrar, Straus
& Giroux 1998 unp il $15; pa $4.95   E
1. Rain—Fiction 2. Animals—Fiction
ISBN 0-374-36148-7; 0-374-46030-2 (pa)
                                        LC 97-10872
A boy sets out to sail his boat in a puddle and is
joined by a frog, a turtle, an alligator, a pig, and an elephant
The pictures "add all sorts of subtle comedy to the
simple text, and whether McPhail is painting gloomy
skies, a muddy puddle, or one of his familiar-looking
pigs, he handles his medium with expert skill." Booklist

Meade, Holly

John Willy and Freddy McGee. Marshall
Cavendish 1998 unp il $15.95   E
1. Guinea pigs—Fiction
ISBN 0-7614-5033-5   LC 97-50362
Two guinea pigs escape from their safe but boring
cage and have an adventure in the tunnels of the family's
pool table
"Zesty cut-paper collages track all of the details of
this funny outing." SLJ

Meddaugh, Susan

The best place. Houghton Mifflin 1999 unp il
$15   E
1. Wolves—Fiction 2. Animals—Fiction
ISBN 0-395-97994-3   LC 98-50184
After traveling around the world to make sure that the
view from his screen porch is the best, an old wolf tries
drastic measures to get his house back from the rabbit
family that had bought it
"Meddaugh combines understated humor with her expressive watercolor illustratons to produce a delightful
book." SLJ

Cinderella's rat. Houghton Mifflin 1997 32p il
$15   E
1. Rats—Fiction 2. Fairy tales
ISBN 0-395-86833-5   LC 97-2156
One of the rats that was turned into a coachman by
Cinderella's fairy godmother saves his rat sister's life,
but an inept magician turns her into a girl who says
"woof."
"The telling is a perfect example of a successful frac-
tured fairy tale, with switched point of view. . . . The
buoyant line drawings capture the whimsy." SLJ

Hog-eye. Houghton Mifflin 1995 32p il $14.95;
pa $5.95   E
1. Pigs—Fiction 2. Wolves—Fiction
ISBN 0-395-74276-5; 0-395-93746-9 (pa)
                                        LC 95-3951
Meddaugh presents a "story within a story as a piglet
tells her family how she was caught by a wolf and nearly made into soup. Seeing that her captor is illiterate
. . . she reads him a recipe that sends him on a wild

wolf chase." SLJ
"The little pig's tale is fast-paced, funny, and creatively told. Clear typeface and conversation balloons combine with brightly animated, expressive illustrations that
propel readers to the satisfying conclusion of this fresh
cautionary tale." Horn Book Guide

Martha speaks. Houghton Mifflin 1992 unp il
$15; pa $5.95   E
1. Dogs—Fiction
ISBN 0-395-63313-3; 0-395-72024-9 (pa)
                                        LC 91-48455
Also available Spanish language edition
Problems arise when Martha, the family dog, learns to
speak after eating alphabet soup
"Good-natured and amusing, with cheerful illustrations
of the delightfully stocky Martha and her amazed fami-
ly." Horn Book
Other available titles about Martha are:
Martha and Skits (2000)
Martha blah blah (1996)
Martha calling (1994)
Martha walks the dog (1998)

Meggs, Libby Phillips

Go home! the true story of James the cat.
Whitman, A. 2000 unp il $15.95   E
1. Cats—Fiction
ISBN 0-8075-2975-3   LC 99-41372
A homeless cat spends several seasons trying to survive the elements until at last a suburban family adopts
him
"Meggs' lovely picture book, based on a true story,
teaches children about kindness. . . . [She] captures the
cat's lonely plight in watercolors that juxtapose the glow
of firelight inside with the harsh winter landscape outside." Booklist

Meister, Cari

Tiny's bath; illustrated by Rich Davis. Viking
1998 unp il $13.89; pa $3.99   E
1. Dogs—Fiction 2. Baths—Fiction
ISBN 0-670-87962-2; 0-14-130267-4 (pa)
                                        LC 98-3844
"A Viking easy-to-read"
Tiny is a very big dog who loves to dig, and when it
is time for his bath, his owner has trouble finding a place
to bathe him
"In this book for the least sophisticated beginning
readers, each sentence appears on a single line, and only
one sentence appears on a page. Illustrations mirror text,
providing clues that support readers as they decipher
both words and events. Add Tiny to the roll call of great
dogs in children's literature." Horn Book Guide
Other available titles about Tiny are:
Tiny goes to the library (2000)
When Tiny was tiny (1999)

Melmed, Laura Krauss

Little Oh; illustrated by Jim LaMarche. Lothrop,
Lee & Shepard Bks. 1996 unp il $15.95; lib bdg
$15.93   E
1. Origami—Fiction 2. Japan—Fiction
ISBN 0-688-14208-7; 0-688-14209-5 (lib bdg)
                                        LC 95-25427

Melmed, Laura Krauss—*Continued*

This is an "original folk tale (set in Japan) . . . about a little origami paper girl in a pink kimono who springs to life one morning and adopts her astonished maker as her mother." Bull Cent Child Books

"While the narrative echoes folktales told around the world, the realistic colored paintings establish setting and character with loving specificity." SLJ

Merrill, Jean, 1923-

The Girl Who Loved Caterpillars; a twelfth century tale from Japan; adapted by Jean Merrill; illustrated by Floyd Cooper. Philomel Bks. 1992 unp il $16.99; pa $5.99 **E**

1. Fairy tales 2. Japan—Fiction
ISBN 0-399-21871-8; 0-698-11393-4 (pa)
LC 91-29054

In this retelling of an anonymous twelfth-century Japanese story, the young woman Izumi resists social and family pressures as she befriends caterpillars and other socially unacceptable creatures

"This story of an independent girl has a surprisingly contemporary tone. . . . Merrill's adaptation is cleanly yet elegantly styled, as are Cooper's pastel double spreads, which elaborate on the many vivid images in the story." Bull Cent Child Books

Micklethwait, Lucy

I spy: an alphabet in art; devised & selected by Lucy Micklethwait. Greenwillow Bks. 1992 unp il $19.95; pa $9.95 **E**

1. Art appreciation 2. Alphabet
ISBN 0-688-11679-5; 0-688-14730-5 (pa)
LC 91-42212

Presents objects for the letters of the alphabet through paintings by such artists as Magritte, Picasso, Botticelli, and Vermeer

"The author's stated intention of introducing young children to fine art, her choice of paintings, the handsome book design, and the quality of paper and reproduction take this beyond the usual alphabet book." Booklist

Other available titles in this series are:
I spy a freight train: transportation in art (1996)
I spy a lion: animals in art (1994)
I spy two eyes: numbers in art (1993)

Milgrim, David

Cows can't fly; written and illustrated by David Milgrim. Viking 1998 unp il $15.99; pa $5.99 **E**

1. Cattle—Fiction 2. Stories in rhyme
ISBN 0-670-87475-2; 0-14-056721-6 (pa)
LC 97-25434

"The story tells of what happens when the young narrator's picture of flying cows is caught by the wind and eventually settles in a cow pasture. Obviously impressionable, The cows themselves lift off the ground and take flight. The child is delighted to see the bovine airships, but can not convince any adults to look upward to take in the amazing sight." SLJ

"In the deftly drawn illustrations, comic effects abound, and cartoon-style balloons allow the characters to comment outside the rhyming text." Booklist

Miller, Margaret, 1945-

Big and little. Greenwillow Bks. 1998 unp il $15; lib bdg $14.93 **E**

1. Size
ISBN 0-688-14748-8; 0-688-14749-6 (lib bdg)
LC 97-17242

Photographs and easy text introduce the concepts of size and opposites

"This book uses cheerful, clear color photos of active toddlers to teach basic concepts." Booklist

Guess who? Greenwillow Bks. 1994 unp il $16.95 **E**

1. Occupations
ISBN 0-688-12783-5
LC 93-26704

A child is asked who delivers the mail, gives haircuts, flies an airplane, and performs other important tasks. Each question has several different answers from which to choose

"Gender and ethnic representation are deftly handled. The author's sharp, clear full-color photographs are well composed, and her use of cropped photos and white space alternating with bled photos is an effective tool for involving youngsters." SLJ

My five senses. Simon & Schuster 1994 unp il hardcover o.p. paperback available $5.99 **E**

1. Senses and sensation
ISBN 0-689-82009-7 (pa)
LC 93-1956

"Five attractive preschoolers of different races narrate this simple photographic survey of sensory activities. In a succession of four-page sequences, each child engages in a variety of experiences that demonstrates each of the senses. The clear, uncluttered design is effective and inviting in this beautifully conceived and executed book." Horn Book Guide

Who uses this? Greenwillow Bks. 1990 unp il lib bdg $15.93; pa $5.95 **E**

1. Tools 2. Occupations
ISBN 0-688-08279-3 (lib bdg); 0-688-17057-9 (pa)
LC 89-30456

"Brilliant color photographs introducing common objects such as a hammer, a football, and a rolling pin are accompanied by the question, 'Who uses this?' The object is then pictured being used by an adult and by a child. This concept book—quietly nonsexist—is ideal for reading aloud to the youngest listeners." Horn Book Guide

Whose shoe? Greenwillow Bks. 1991 unp il $16 **E**

1. Shoes
ISBN 0-688-10008-2
LC 90-38491

Illustrates a variety of footwear and matches each wearer with the appropriate shoe

"Miller has consciously avoided stereotypes, picturing a male ballet dancer and children from many racial groups. She understands children's fascination with make-believe and dress-up, and this newest book should spark much imaginative play." Horn Book

Miller, Sara Swan

Three more stories you can read to your dog; illustrated by True Kelley. Houghton Mifflin 2000 unp il $14 **E**

1. Dogs—Fiction

ISBN 0-395-92293-3   LC 99-39880

Stories addressed to dogs and written from a dog's point of view, featuring such topics as going to the vet, making friends with a rocklike creature, and getting a bath

"The witty, believable portrayal of canine thoughts and behavior will amuse readers. . . . True Kelley's lively ink-and-watercolor illustrations brighten every page." Booklist

Other available titles in this series are:

Three stories you can read to your cat (1997)

Three stories you can read to your dog (1995)

Miller, William, 1959-

Night golf; illustrated by Cedric Lucas. Lee & Low Bks. 1999 unp il $15.95 **E**

1. African Americans—Fiction 2. Golf—Fiction 3. Prejudices—Fiction

ISBN 1-88000-079-2   LC 98-47168

Despite being told that only whites can play golf, James becomes a caddy and is befriended by an older African American man who teaches him to play on the course at night

"Gentle paste and pencil illustrations support this quietly powerful story." Horn Book Guide

The piano; illustrated by Susan Keeter. Lee & Low Bks. 2000 unp il $15.95 **E**

1. Pianos—Fiction 2. Old age—Fiction 3. African Americans—Fiction

ISBN 1-88000-098-9   LC 99-38004

Tia's love of music leads her to a job in the home of an older white woman who not only teaches her to play the piano but also about caring for others

"The characters are brought to life and Tia's warm, open innocence is evident in the expressive artwork. This is a gentle story depicting a friendship that crosses age and racial barriers." SLJ

Richard Wright and the library card; illustrated by Gregory Christie. Lee & Low Bks. 1997 unp il $15.95; pa $6.95 **E**

1. Wright, Richard, 1908-1960—Fiction 2. African Americans—Fiction 3. Books and reading—Fiction

ISBN 1-88000-057-1; 1-88000-088-1 (pa)

     LC 97-6847

Based on a scene from Wright's autobiography, Black boy, in which the seventeen-year-old African-American borrows a white man's library card and devours every book as a ticket to freedom

"Christie's powerful impressionistic paintings in acrylic and colored pencil show the harsh racism in the Jim Crow South. . . . Words and pictures express the young man's loneliness and confinement and, then, the power he found in books." Booklist

Millman, Isaac

Moses goes to school. Farrar, Straus & Giroux 2000 unp $16 **E**

1. Deaf—Fiction 2. Sign language—Fiction 3. School stories

ISBN 0-374-35069-8   LC 99-40582

"Frances Foster books"

Moses and his friends enjoy the first day of school at their special school for the deaf and hard of hearing, where they use sign language to talk to each other

"Child-friendly cartoon illustrations do a marvelous job of emphasizing the normalcy and charm of these youngsters. . . . The double-page layouts nicely accommodate the primary pictorial action along with written text and ASL inserts. . . . [This is a] great contribution to children's education about disabilities that also succeeds as effective storytelling in its own right." SLJ

Another available title about Moses is:

Moses goes to a concert (1998)

Mills, Claudia, 1954-

Gus and Grandpa and the two-wheeled bike; pictures by Catherine Stock. Farrar, Straus & Giroux 1999 47p il $13 **E**

1. Cycling—Fiction 2. Grandfathers—Fiction

ISBN 0-374-32821-8   LC 97-44203

Gus doesn't want to give up the training wheels on his bike, even for a new five-speed bicycle, until Grandpa helps him learn how to get along without them

"Mills conveys strong sentiment without a trace of mawkishness, and Stock's illustrations in loose line and watercolor augment the story of this childhood rite of passage expressively." Horn Book Guide

Other available titles about Gus and Grandpa are:

Gus and Grandpa (1997)

Gus and Grandpa and show-and-tell (2000)

Gus and Grandpa and the Christmas cookies (1997)

Gus and Grandpa at the hospital (1998)

Gus and Grandpa ride the train (1998)

Minarik, Else Holmelund

Little Bear; pictures by Maurice Sendak. Harper & Row 1957 63p il $15.95; lib bdg $15.89; pa $3.95 **E**

1. Bears—Fiction

ISBN 0-06-024240-X; 0-06-024241-8 (lib bdg); 0-06-444004-4 (pa)

Also available with Audiobook

"An I can read book"

Four episodes "about Little Bear . . . as he persuades his mother to make him a winter outfit—only to discover his fur coat is all he needs; makes himself some birthday soup—and then is surprised with a birthday cake; takes an imaginary trip to the moon, and finally goes happily off to sleep as his mother tells him a story about 'Little Bear.'" Bull Cent Child Books

The pictures "depict all the warmth of feeling and the special companionship that exists between a small child and his mother." Publ Wkly

Other available titles about Little Bear are:

Father Bear comes home (1959)

A kiss for Little Bear (1968)

Little Bear's friend (1960)

Little Bear's visit (1961)

Minarik, Else Holmelund—*Continued*
No fighting, no biting! pictures by Maurice
Sendak. Harper & Row 1958 62p il lib bdg
$15.89; pa $3.95   E
    1. Alligators—Fiction
    ISBN 0-06-024291-4 (lib bdg); 0-06-444015-X (pa)

"An I can read book"
"A young lady who is unable to read in peace because
of two children squabbling beside her tells them a story
about two little alligators whose fighting and biting almost lead to disastrous consequences with a big hungry
alligator. Children are sure to accept and enjoy the lesson
in this little adventure tale and be amused by the expressive old-fashioned drawings." Booklist

Miranda, Anne, 1954-
To market, to market; written by Anne Miranda;
illustrated by Janet Stevens. Harcourt Brace & Co.
1997 unp il $16   E
    1. Stories in rhyme 2. Animals—Fiction
    ISBN 0-15-200035-6   LC 95-26326
In this "riff on the old nursery rhyme, 'To market, to
market, to buy a fat pig,' a plump matron makes a series
of increasingly calamitous purchases of animals at the
supermarket. Hungry and cranky after the raucous menagerie turns her house topsy-turvy, the lady . . . wisely
decides to make vegetable soup instead." Publ Wkly
"Patterned, staccato verses tell the zany tale, but it is
Stevens's wonderfully wild illustrations that bring it to
life. The conventional home's interior is pictured in flat
gray charcoal tones. The woman and her animals are colorful, oversized figures that burst off the pages." SLJ

Mitchell, Margaree King, 1953-
Uncle Jed's barbershop; illustrated by James
Ransome. Simon & Schuster Bks. for Young
Readers 1993 unp il $16; pa $6.99   E
    1. Uncles—Fiction 2. Barbers and barbershops—Fic-
tion 3. African Americans—Fiction
    ISBN 0-671-76969-3; 0-689-81913-7 (pa)
    LC 91-44148
Despite serious obstacles and setbacks Sarah Jean's
Uncle Jed, the only black barber in the county, pursues
his dream of saving enough money to open his own bar-
bershop
"The author's convivial depictions of family life are
enhanced by Ransome's . . . spirited oil paintings, which
set the affectionate intergenerational cast against brightly
patterned walls and crisp, leaf-strewn landscapes." Publ
Wkly

Mitchell, Rita Phillips
Hue Boy; pictures by Caroline Binch. Dial Bks.
for Young Readers 1993 unp il hardcover o.p.
paperback available $9.95   E
    1. Caribbean region—Fiction 2. Growth—Fiction
    ISBN 0-14-056354-7 (pa)   LC 92-18560
Everyone in little Hue Boy's island village has suggestions on how to help him grow, but he learns to stand
tall in a way all his own
"Mitchell's sympathetic story and fluid, lilting prose
are a fitting springboard for Binch . . . whose supremely
expressive watercolors make the most of the tale's Caribbean setting." Publ Wkly

Mochizuki, Ken, 1954-
Baseball saved us; written by Ken Mochizuki;
illustrated by Dom Lee. Lee & Low Bks. 1993
unp il $15.95; pa $6.95   E
    1. Japanese Americans—Evacuation and relocation,
1942-1945—Fiction 2. World War, 1939-1945—Fiction 3. Baseball—Fiction 4. Prejudices—Fiction
    ISBN 1-880000-01-6; 0-880000-19-9 (pa)
    LC 92-73215
Also available Spanish language edition
A Japanese American boy learns to play baseball
when he and his family are forced to live in an internment camp during World War II, and his ability to play
helps him after the war is over
"Fences and watchtowers are in the background of
many of Lee's moving illustrations, some of which were
inspired by Ansel Adams' 1943 photographs of
Manzanar. . . . The baseball action will grab kids—and
so will the personal experience of bigotry." Booklist

Heroes; written by Ken Mochizuki; illustrated
by Dom Lee. Lee & Low Bks. 1995 unp il
$15.95; pa $6.95   E
    1. Japanese Americans—Fiction 2. Prejudices—Fic-
tion
    ISBN 1-880000-16-4; 1-880000-50-4 (pa)
    LC 94-26541
"In the 1960's Donnie Okada took a lot of razzing
from the other boys in the neighborhood; they insisted
that he had to be the enemy in their war games because
he looked like the enemy, and they did not believe his
father and uncle had served in the American military.
Dad and Uncle Yosh give those boys a dignified and effective lesson." N Y Times Book Rev
"The book is a powerful exploration of the cruelty
children can inflict upon one another and of the confusion and pain borne by the target of such unthinking racism." Horn Book

Modarressi, Mitra
Yard sale! DK Pub. 2000 unp il $15.95   E
    1. Garage sales—Fiction
    ISBN 0-7894-2651-X   LC 99-27592
"A DK ink book"
"After Mr. Flotsam's yard sale, Spudville's residents
are irritated to find that their unexpectedly magical purchases, such as a flying rug and a nonstop pasta maker,
are threatening to disrupt their orderly lives. . . . The
watercolor illustrations for this light, amusing tale show
a multicultural cast of round-faced townspeople." Horn
Book Guide

Modell, Frank
One zillion valentines. Greenwillow Bks. 1981
unp il lib bdg $14; pa $4.95   E
    1. Valentine's Day—Fiction
    ISBN 0-688-00569-1 (lib bdg); 0-688-07329-8 (pa)
    LC 81-2215
"Milton and Marvin decide that valentines are for everybody and proceed to distribute the simple hearts they
have drawn up to everyone in the neighborhood. The
leftovers they sell for a nickel and with the money
they've made, buy a giant box of candy to share." Booklist

Modell, Frank—*Continued*

"The plot is impeccably logical, and its execution—both in text and drawings—completely childlike. From the opening gambit to a thoroughly satisfying conclusion, the story moves briskly; the author-illustrator captures the essence of youthful optimism in the situation and a comic spirit in the exuberant, cartoonlike illustrations." Horn Book

Mollel, Tololwa M. (Tololwa Marti)

My rows and piles of coins; illustrated by E. B. Lewis. Clarion Bks. 1999 32p il $15   E
1. Money—Fiction 2. Bicycles—Fiction 3. Tanzania—Fiction
ISBN 0-395-75186-1   LC 98-21586
A Coretta Scott King honor book for illustration, 2000
A Tanzanian boy saves his coins to buy a bicycle so that he can help his parents carry goods to market, but then he discovers that in spite of all he has saved, he still does not have enough money

"The story is natural and never excessively moralistic. The fluid, light-splashed watercolor illustrations lend a sense of place and authenticity." SLJ

Monjo, F. N., 1924-1978

The drinking gourd; a story of the Underground Railroad; pictures by Fred Brenner. Newly illustrated ed. HarperCollins Pubs. 1993 62p il $15.95; lib bdg $15.89; pa $3.95   E
1. Underground railroad—Fiction
ISBN 0-06-024329-5; 0-06-024330-9 (lib bdg); 0-06-444042-7 (pa)   LC 92-10823
Also available with Audiobook
"An I can read book"
First published 1970
Set in New England in the decade before the Civil War. For mischievous behavior in church, Tommy is sent home to his room, but wanders instead into the barn. There he discovers that his father is helping runaway slaves escape to Canada

"The simplicity of dialogue and exposition, the level of concepts, and the length of the story [makes] it most suitable for the primary grades reader. The illustrations are deftly representational, the whole a fine addition to the needed body of historical books for the very young." Bull Cent Child Books

Mora, Pat

Tomás and the library lady; illustrated by Raúl Colón. Knopf 1997 unp il $17; lib bdg $18.99; pa $6.99   E
1. Rivera, Tomás—Fiction 2. Books and reading—Fiction 3. Libraries—Fiction 4. Migrant labor—Fiction 5. Mexican Americans—Fiction
ISBN 0-679-80401-3; 0-679-90401-8 (lib bdg); 0-375-80349-1 (pa)   LC 89-37490
While helping his family in their work as migrant laborers far from their home, Tomás finds an entire world to explore in the books at the local public library

"Mora's story is based on a true incident in the life of the famous writer Tomás Rivera, the son of migrant workers who became an education leader and university president. . . . Colón's beautiful scratchboard illustrations, in his textured, glowingly colored, rhythmic style, capture the warmth and the dreams that the boy finds in the world of books." Booklist

Uno, dos, tres: one, two, three; illustrated by Barbara Lavallee. Clarion Bks. 1996 43p il $15; pa $6.95   E
1. Mexico—Fiction 2. Counting 3. Stories in rhyme 4. Bilingual books—English-Spanish
ISBN 0-395-67294-5; 0-618-05468-5 (pa)
    LC 94-15337
"Two girls search a Mexican market for gifts for their mother's birthday in this counting book in both English and Spanish. . . . Cheerful stylized paintings in muted reds, blues, and yellows depict designs from Mexican art and use pattern to highlight the number sequence." Horn Book Guide

Morimoto, Junko

The two bullies; translated from an original Japanese story by Isao Morimoto. Crown 1999 c1997 unp il $17   E
1. China—Fiction 2. Japan—Fiction
ISBN 0-517-80061-6   LC 98-41774
First published 1997 in Australia
Two bullies, one from China and one from Japan, inadvertently intimidate one another before meeting face to face and never fight as a result

"Splendid watercolor illustrations enhance this story's humor and sense of place." SLJ

Morozumi, Atsuko

One gorilla; a counting book. Farrar, Straus & Giroux 1990 unp il hardcover o.p. paperback available $4.95   E
1. Gorillas—Fiction 2. Counting
ISBN 0-374-45646-1 (pa)
Published in the United Kingdom with title: And one gorilla

The author begins this counting book "with the words: 'Here is a list of things I love. One gorilla.' He goes on to accumulate a number of other things he loves: 'Two butterflies among the flowers and one gorilla. Three budgerigars in my house and one gorilla.'" Quill Quire

"The illustrations, delicately drawn but vividly colored, have a misty quality to them that adds to the air of fantasy. . . . The pictures delightfully capture the personality of each animal. Searching out the creatures in each two-page spread is enjoyable and moderately challenging." SLJ

Morpurgo, Michael

Wombat goes walkabout; illustrated by Christian Birmingham. Candlewick Press 2000 unp il $16.99   E
1. Wombats—Fiction 2. Animals—Fiction 3. Australia—Fiction
ISBN 0-7636-1168-9   LC 99-47082
While looking for his mother, Wombat meets many animals that are not impressed with his talent for digging and thinking, but when a fire approaches, they change their minds

"Morpurgo's prose is spare and poetic, with skillful repetition of words and sounds. Birmingham realistically depicts the animals against full-page impressionistic landscapes." Booklist

Moss, Lloyd

Zin! zin! zin! a violin; illustrated by Marjorie Priceman. Simon & Schuster Bks. for Young Readers 1995 unp il $16; pa $6.99   **E**

1. Musical instruments 2. Counting 3. Stories in rhyme

ISBN 0-671-88239-2; 0-689-83524-8 (pa)

LC 93-37902

A Caldecott Medal honor book, 1996

"Rhyming couplets present 10 instruments and their characteristics. . . . In the process of adding instruments, the book teaches the names of musical groups up to a chamber group of 10 as well as the categories into which the instruments fall: strings, reeds, and brasses. Amazingly, Moss conveys this encyclopedic information while keeping the poem streamlined and peppy. Priceman's sprightly, sunny hued gouache paintings should take a bow, too." Booklist

Most, Bernard, 1937-

ABC T-Rex. Harcourt Brace & Co. 2000 unp il $13   **E**

1. Dinosaurs—Fiction 2. Alphabet

ISBN 0-15-202007-1   LC 98-51128

A young T-Rex loves his ABCs so much that he eats them up, experiencing on each letter a word that begins with that letter

"Heavy black lines define the cartoonlike drawings, brightened with a colorful palette emphasizing shades of green, purple, and orange. Fun for alphabetically inclined preschoolers." Booklist

How big were the dinosaurs. Harcourt Brace & Co. 1994 unp il $16; pa $7   **E**

1. Dinosaurs

ISBN 0-15-236800-0; 0-15-200852-7 (pa)

LC 93-19152

Describes the size of different dinosaurs by comparing them to more familiar objects, such as a school bus, a trombone, or a bowling alley

"The colorful drawings, of children interacting with dinosaurs, will be attractive to children. The text is easy to read. This book will delight young dinosaur lovers." Sci Books Films

Whatever happened to the dinosaurs? written and illustrated by Bernard Most. Harcourt Brace Jovanovich 1984 unp il lib bdg $16; pa $4.95   **E**

1. Dinosaurs—Fiction

ISBN 0-15-295295-0 (lib bdg); 0-15-295296-9 (pa)

LC 84-3779

Also available miniature edition

The author "offers various fantastic explanations to answer his title question. 'Did the dinosaurs go to another planet? . . . did a magician make them disappear? . . . Are the dinosaurs in the hospital?'" SLJ

"A hilarious book, sure to be popular for individual reading or with groups." Child Book Rev Serv

Mullins, Patricia

V for vanishing; an alphabet of endangered animals. HarperCollins Pubs. 1994 c1993 unp il $15; pa $6.95   **E**

1. Endangered species 2. Extinct animals 3. Alphabet

ISBN 0-06-023556-X; 0-06-443471-0 (pa)

LC 93-8181

First published 1993 in Australia

An ABC book featuring illustrations of endangered and extinct animals from around the world

"Careful scholarship, intelligent presentation, and gorgeous artwork combine to make this a fascinating book for a wide audience." Horn Book

Murphy, Jill, 1949-

Peace at last. Dial Bks. for Young Readers 1980 unp il hardcover o.p. paperback available $5.99   **E**

1. Night—Fiction 2. Bears—Fiction

ISBN 0-8037-6964-4 (pa)   LC 80-15659

Mr. Bear spends the night searching for enough peace and quiet to go to sleep

"The story appears on the verso pages with line drawings; facing pages are in full color; the pictures have warmth and humor and the story is told in brisk, forthright style with an appealing refrain that will probably elicit listener-participation, 'Oh, NO! I can't stand THIS.'" Bull Cent Child Books

A quiet night in. Candlewick Press 1994 c1993 unp il $12.95; pa $4.99   **E**

1. Elephants—Fiction 2. Bedtime—Fiction

ISBN 1-56402-248-X; 1-56402-673-6 (pa)

LC 93-875

First published 1993 in the United Kingdom

Mr. and Mrs. Large's attempt to put the children to bed early and have a quiet night on their own has an unexpected ending

"The illustrations are first rate; especially priceless are the expressions on the elephants' faces. The text is full of humor and instantly recognizable as true to life." SLJ

Murphy, Stuart J., 1942-

Pepper's journal; a kitten's first year; illustrated by Marsha Winborn. HarperCollins Pubs. 2000 34p il (MathStart) $15.95; lib bdg $15.89; pa $4.95   **E**

1. Calendars—Fiction 2. Cats—Fiction

ISBN 0-06-027618-5; 0-06-446723-6 (lib bdg); 0-06-027619-3 (pa)   LC 98-47523

Lisa keeps a journal of her new kitten's first year

"This useful, appealing Math-Start book sets out to conquer calendar time, and as it does, it skillfully covers the care and development of kittens, too. . . . Winborn's illustrations of a loving, single-parent household are warm. . . . End papers contain activities for extending the concepts." Booklist

Myers, Christopher A.

Black cat. Scholastic Press 1999 unp il $16.95   **E**

1. Cats—Fiction 2. City and town life—Fiction

ISBN 0-590-03375-1   LC 98-28609

Myers, Christopher A.—*Continued*

A Coretta Scott King honor book for illustration, 2000

A black cat wanders through the streets of a city

"With striking photo-collages enhanced with gouache and ink, this book captures the gritty beauty of the city." Horn Book Guide

Wings. Scholastic Press 2000 unp il $16.95
E

ISBN 0-590-03377-8   LC 99-87389

"Myers retells the myth of Icarus through the story of Ikarus Jackson, the new boy on the block, who can fly above the rooftops and over the crowd. In this contemporary version, the winged kid nearly falls from the sky . . . because jeering kids in the schoolyard and repressive adults don't like his being different and try to break his soaring spirit. . . . Myers' beautiful cut-paper collages are eloquent and open." Booklist

Myers, Walter Dean, 1937-

The blues of Flats Brown; illustrated by Nina Laden. Holiday House 2000 unp il $16.95   E

1. Dogs—Fiction 2. Blues music—Fiction

ISBN 0-8234-1480-9   LC 99-16695

To escape an abusive master, a junkyard dog named Flats runs away and makes a name for himself from Mississippi to New York City playing blues on his guitar

"The narrator's vernacular, rhythmic and easy-rolling, has the feel of a timeless legend, and the vibrant, jewel-toned illustrations, dominated by moody, bittersweet, tonal variations of blue, are filled with rich detail, expressive characters, and fantastic landscapes." Booklist

Narahashi, Keiko

Two girls can! Margaret K. McElderry Bks. 2000 unp il $16   E

1. Friendship—Fiction

ISBN 0-689-82618-4   LC 98-45301

This "picture book considers things that two girls can do together: from climbing a wall to climbing a tree; from getting 'really, really mad' at a companion to making up; from sharing a treat to sharing a joke to sharing a friend." Booklist

"The peppy, loosely rendered watercolor illustrations aptly capture the action and mood." Horn Book Guide

Neitzel, Shirley

The bag I'm taking to Grandma's; pictures by Nancy Winslow Parker. Greenwillow Bks. 1995 unp il $16.95; pa $4.95   E

1. Stories in rhyme

ISBN 0-688-12960-9; 0-688-15840-4 (pa)

LC 94-4115

This story is presented in "simple cumulative verse and rebuses. A young boy is packing for a trip to visit his grandmother. He fills a shopping bag with his mitt, cars, space ship, wooden animals, his favorite stuffed rabbit, his pillow, a book, a flashlight. But then along comes mom with ideas of her own." SLJ

"Nancy Winslow Parker's spare, softly-colored sketches are comic and expressive, supplying the humor in deft conjunction with the text. . . . The rhyming rebus invites shared reading with individual children and groups." Horn Book

The dress I'll wear to the party; pictures by Nancy Winslow Parker. Greenwillow Bks. 1992 unp il hardcover o.p. paperback available $6.95
E

1. Clothing and dress—Fiction 2. Stories in rhyme

ISBN 0-688-14261-3 (pa)   LC 91-30906

In cumulative verses and rebuses a girl describes how she is dressing up in her mother's party things

"The perky, crisp cartoons executed in ink, watercolor, and colored-pencil, are exactly right for capturing the sprightly objects and events. The rollicking rhythm, vivid language, and appealing art make a handsome package." SLJ

The jacket I wear in the snow; pictures by Nancy Winslow Parker. Greenwillow Bks. 1989 unp il $15.95; pa $5.95   E

1. Clothing and dress—Fiction 2. Snow—Fiction 3. Stories in rhyme

ISBN 0-688-08028-6; 0-688-04587-1 (pa)

LC 88-18767

Also available Big book edition

A young girl names all the clothes that she must wear to play in the snow

"Written in cheerful, cumulative verse that recalls the well-known favorite nursery rhyme 'The House That Jack Built,' the text, with its easy-going rhythm, will be simple for children to recite from memory. . . . The artist's drawings are executed in her familiar style using watercolor, pencil, and pen; they combine with the large typeface and a generous amount of white space to create a tremendously appealing book." Horn Book

Ness, Evaline, 1911-1986

Sam, Bangs & Moonshine; written and illustrated by Evaline Ness. Holt & Co. 1966 unp il $15.95; pa $6.95   E

ISBN 0-8050-0314-2; 0-8050-0315-0 (pa)

Awarded the Caldecott Medal, 1967

Young Samantha, or Sam, "the fisherman's daughter, finally learns to draw the line between reality and the 'moonshine' [her fantasies] in which her mother is a mermaid, she owns a baby kangaroo, and can talk to her cat." Publisher's note

"In this unusually creative story the fantasy in which many, many children indulge is presented in a realistic and sympathetic context. The illustrations in ink and pale color wash (mustard, grayish-aqua) have a touching realism, too. This is an outstanding book." SLJ

Newberry, Clare Turlay, 1903-1970

April's kittens. HarperCollins Pubs. 1993 c1940 32p il $16.95   E

1. Cats—Fiction

ISBN 0-06-024400-3

A Caldecott Medal honor book, 1941

A reissue of the title first published 1940

"Though old-fashioned, the story of a small girl's yearning to keep both a mother cat and one of her kittens still speaks to pet owners young and old. Newberry's simple, charcoal drawings of the felines are as elegant and endearing as ever." Horn Book

Newcome, Zita, 1959-

Toddlerobics. Candlewick Press 1996 unp il hardcover o.p. paperback available $5.99   **E**

1. Exercise—Fiction 2. Stories in rhyme

ISBN 0-763-60113-6 (pa)   LC 95-21062

A group of toddlers has fun as they stretch high, bend low, clap their hands, bump bottoms, and generally enjoy exercising

"Young listeners will want to join the activity and practice small movements, such as pointing to eyes and noses, as well as participate in the various group activities. The cheery illustrations convey motion very well, and the multiethnic group of children . . . are vividly drawn." Booklist

Also available:

Toddlerobics animal fun (1999)

Noble, Trinka Hakes

The day Jimmy's boa ate the wash; pictures by Steven Kellogg. Dial Bks. for Young Readers 1980 unp il $15.99; pa $4.95   **E**

1. Farm life—Fiction 2. Snakes—Fiction 3. School stories

ISBN 0-8037-1723-7; 0-8037-0094-6 (pa)

   LC 80-15098

"One small girl, reporting to her mother after a class visit to a farm, nonchalantly describes the frenzied day; she works backward from effects to causes, beginning with the statement that the day was kind of dull and boring until the cow started crying. Why? A haystack fell on her. How? The farmer hit it with his tractor. Why? He was busy yelling at the pigs to get off the school bus . . . and she goes on to unfold the tale of how Jimmy's boa escaped, set the hens in a flurry, precipitated an egg-throwing match, and so on." Bull Cent Child Books

"The illustrations, which depict disgruntled chickens, expressive pigs, and smiling cats as well as other individualized animal and human characters, show the artist's flair for humorous detail." Horn Book

Other available titles about Jimmy's boa are:

Jimmy's boa and the big splash birthday bash (1989)

Jimmy's boa bounces back (1984)

Meanwhile back at the ranch; pictures by Tony Ross. Dial Bks. for Young Readers 1987 unp il hardcover o.p. paperback available $5.99   **E**

1. Ranch life—Fiction

ISBN 0-14-054564-6 (pa)   LC 86-11651

"Rancher Hicks leads a life so uneventful that he takes a trip to town just to see what is happening. Wife Elna stays home. While the rancher is amusing himself with the high life in Sleepy Gulch—getting his whiskers trimmed, having lunch at Millie Mildew's, and watching a turtle cross Main Street—Elna is home winning contests, inheriting fortunes, starring in movies, and entertaining the President." SLJ

"Noble's tongue-in-cheek story fits rollickingly into the tall-tale genre while Ross' exuberant full-color pictures wring every bit of humor from the already funny tale." Booklist

Nolen, Jerdine

Big Jabe; illustrations by Kadir Nelson. Lothrop Lee & Shepard Bks. 2000 unp il $15.95; lib bd; $15.89   ▮

1. Slavery—Fiction 2. African Americans—Fiction

ISBN 0-688-13662-1; 0-688-13663-X (lib bdg)

   LC 99-3800

Momma Mary tells stories about a special young ma who does wondrous things, especially for the slaves o the Plenty Plantation

"Nolen recounts her original tale with a light touc and lyrical voices that add depth and resonance to its im agery and serious overtones. The gouache and watercolc illustrations convey both the lush summer and the rigor ous life of the slaves. This powerful story will be partic ularly effective shared aloud." Horn Book Guide

Harvey Potter's balloon farm; [illustrated by Mark Buehner. Lothrop, Lee & Shepard Bks. 199 unp il $15.95; lib bdg $15.93; pa $5.95   ▮

1. Tall tales 2. Balloons—Fiction 3. Farm life—Fic tion

ISBN 0-688-07887-7; 0-688-07888-5 (lib bdg)
0-688-15845-5 (pa)   LC 91-3812

"Harvey Potter's unusual crop is balloons—whicl grow just like corn on long, sturdy stalks. Harvey Potte himself is not at all unusual, and his friend, a youn; African-American girl, is determined to uncover the se cret of his curious harvest. The story is lively, but o even greater attraction are the vivid, air-brushed illustra tions of balloons with expressive faces in every size, col or, and shape." Horn Book Guide

Raising dragons; illustrated by Elise Primavera Silver Whistle Bks. 1998 unp il $16   ▮

1. Dragons—Fiction 2. Farm life—Fiction

ISBN 0-15-201288-5   LC 95-4330

A farmer's young daughter shares numerous adven tures with the dragon that she raises from infancy

"Nolen's chimerical text meets its match i Primavera's imaginative and bold illustrations." Hor Book Guide

Novak, Matt, 1962-

Little Wolf, Big Wolf. HarperCollins Pubs. 200 46p il $14.95; lib bdg $14.89   ▮

1. Wolves—Fiction 2. Friendship—Fiction

ISBN 0-06-027486-7; 0-06-027487-5 (lib bdg)

   LC 99-1061

"An I can read book"

Although they are very different, two wolves discove that they can still be friends

"Illustrations provide appropriate visual clues for th simple language of the stories." Horn Book Guide

Numeroff, Laura Joffe

The Chicken sisters; by Laura Numeroff pictures by Sharleen Collicott. HarperCollins Pubs 1997 unp il $14.95; lib bdg $14.89; pa $5.95   ▮

1. Chickens—Fiction 2. Sisters—Fiction 3. Wolves—Fiction

ISBN 0-06-026679-1; 0-06-026680-5 (lib bdg)
0-06-443520-2 (pa)   LC 96-3029

Numeroff, Laura Joffe—*Continued*

"A Laura Geringer book"

"Violet, Poppy, and Babs, the chicken sisters, possess talents that annoy the neighbors until a threatening wolf moves into the neighborhood. The illustrations achieve a captivating sense of texture that adds immediacy to the humorous story." Horn Book Guide

If you give a mouse a cookie; by Laura Numeroff; illustrated by Felicia Bond. Harper & Row 1985 unp il $15.95; lib bdg $15.89   E

1. Mice—Fiction

ISBN 0-06-024586-7; 0-06-024587-5 (lib bdg)

LC 84-48343

Also available Big book edition and Spanish language edition

Relating the cycle of requests a mouse is likely to make after you give him a cookie takes the reader through a young child's day

"Children love to indulge in supposition or to ask 'what will happen if. . .?' and here there is a long, satisfying chain of linked and enjoyably nonsensical causes and effects. . . . The illustrations, neatly drawn, spaciously composed, and humorously detailed, extend the story just the way picture book illustrations should." Bull Cent Child Books

Other available titles in this series are:

If you give a moose a muffin (1991)

If you give a pig a pancake (1998)

If you take a mouse to the movies (2000)

What mommies do best; by Laura Numerott; illustrated by Lynn Munsinger. Simon & Schuster Bks. for Young Readers 1998 unp il $13   E

1. Mothers—Fiction 2. Fathers—Fiction 3. Sex role—Fiction

ISBN 0-689-80577-2

LC 96-44375

Bound back to back and inverted with: What daddies do best

"The first half shows a mother bear, pig, mouse, elephant, and porcupine engaging in everyday activities with her children. . . . Flip the book and read that Daddies can do the same thing. Munsinger's winsome water-color depictions of the animals are warm and humorous. A perfect cuddly bedtime or storytime read-aloud choice." SLJ

Oberman, Sheldon, 1949-

The always prayer shawl; illustrated by Ted Lewin. Boyds Mills Press 1994 unp il $15.95

E

1. Jews—Fiction 2. Immigration and emigration—Fiction

ISBN 1-878093-22-3

Also available in paperback from Puffin Bks.

This story "tells of the Jewish boy Adam, growing up in a shtetl, whose life drastically changes when famine and chaos in old Russia force his parents to immigrate to America. At parting, Adam's beloved grandfather gives the boy a gift, a prayer shawl ('my always prayer shawl'), which was presented to the grandfather by *his* grandfather, for whom Adam was named. . . . As good as any of Lewin's best work, the watercolors are abundantly detailed and wonderfully expressive. . . . The pic-

tures enrich the tranquil telling, which harks back to the biblical Adam, as it movingly depicts how memory and tradition add texture and richness to our lives—even as other things around us change." Booklist

O'Connor, Jane, 1947-

Super Cluck; by Jane O'Connor and Robert O'Connor; pictures by Megan Lloyd. HarperCollins Pubs. 1991 64p il hardcover o.p. paperback available $4.95   E

1. Chickens—Fiction

ISBN 0-06-444162-8 (pa)   LC 90-32832

"An I can read book"

Chuck Cluck, an alien chick living on Earth, earns the name Super Cluck when he uses his super strength to save baby chicks from a rat

"Bursting with energy, Lloyd's bright, detailed illustrations lend humor and verve to this I Can Read book." Publ Wkly

Olaleye, Isaac

Bitter bananas; illustrated by Ed Young. Boyds Mills Press 1994 unp il $14.95   E

1. Baboons—Fiction 2. Rain forests—Fiction 3. Africa—Fiction

ISBN 1-56397-039-2   LC 93-73306

Also available in paperback from Puffin Bks.

"Baboons are stealing the sweet palm sap that the young African boy Yusuf sells at market, and it takes patience, ingenuity, and several trials before Yusuf outwits his forest rivals with a lure of tempting sap and bananas—laced with wormwood." Bull Cent Child Books

"Olaleye's eminently readable text naturally calls for audience participation. Young renders the story beautifully in cut-paper collages of vibrant pink and lush green." Booklist

Onyefulu, Ifeoma, 1959-

Chidi only likes blue; an African book of colors. Cobblehill Bks. 1997 unp il $14.99   E

1. Nigeria—Social life and customs 2. Color

ISBN 0-525-65243-4

The author "uses colors to explore Nigerian culture by allowing the young narrator, Nneka, to explain why she likes each color: red is the color of the cap worn by the oldest and wisest chiefs; black is the color women paint on their houses during the dry season. The beautiful photographs vividly illustrate the unusual information presented in the straightforward text." Horn Book

Emeka's gift; an African counting story. Cobblehill Bks. 1995 unp il $13.55   E

1. Counting 2. Nigeria

ISBN 0-525-65205-1   LC 94-30700

This "counting book cum photoessay weaves into its narrative details of life among the Igala people of southern Nigeria. 'One boy'—Emeka— walks to the neighboring village to visit his grandmother, wondering about a suitable gift for her. He passes various possibilities along the way . . . and imagines how Granny might react to each one. . . . Onyefulu . . . sprinkles informative sidebars alongside her tale of Emeka's journey. . . . Lucid, attractively composed photographs of Igala people and their artifacts add to the book's multicultural import." Publ Wkly

Oppel, Kenneth

Peg and the whale; illustrated by Terry Widener. Simon & Schuster Bks. for Young Readers 2000 unp il $16.95   E

1. Whaling—Fiction 2. Tall tales
ISBN 0-689-82423-8   LC 98-42685

Peg, a big strapping seven-year-old lass who has caught everything else in the sea, joins the crew of the whaling ship Viper and sets out to catch herself a whale

"Children will like the way the illustrations splash across the pages, the tale's delightful humor, and the wonderful rhythm of the words." Booklist

Oppenheim, Shulamith Levey

The lily cupboard; illustrated by Ronald Himler. HarperCollins Pubs. 1992 unp il hardcover o.p. paperback available $6.95   E

1. World War, 1939-1945—Fiction 2. Netherlands—Fiction 3. Jews—Netherlands—Fiction
ISBN 0-06-443393-5 (pa)   LC 90-38592

"A Charlotte Zolotow book"

Miriam, a young Jewish girl, is forced to leave her parents and hide with strangers in the country during the German occupation of Holland

"The golden glow of the illustrations light both the painful scenes of the family parting and the wholesome scenes of the kindly, solid farm family and their home. This gentle story for young children is a welcome addition to the tales of heroism during World War II." Horn Book

Oram, Hiawyn

Princess Chamomile's garden; illustrated by Susan Varley. Dutton Children's Bks. 2000 unp il $16.99   E

1. Princesses—Fiction 2. Gardens—Fiction 3. Mice—Fiction
ISBN 0-525-46387-9   LC 99-87242

After working with the royal gardener, Princess Chamomile, a mouse, decides that she would really like to create a garden all her own

"The childlike sensibility of the text and the buoyant illustrations, complete with a foldout showing the garden in all its glory, make a winning combination." Horn Book Guide

Another available title about Princess Chamomile is: Princess Chamomile gets her way (1999)

The wrong overcoat; written by Hiawyn Oram; pictures by Mark Birchall. Carolrhoda Bks. 2000 unp il $15.95   E

1. Chimpanzees—Fiction 2. Coats—Fiction
ISBN 1-57505-453-1   LC 99-44222

Despite the insistence of his family and friends that his new overcoat suits him perfectly, Chimp dislikes it so much that he finds a way to get rid of it

"The story unfolds with economy and a sure sense of its audience. Just as pleasing are the ink drawings, washed with bright water-colors, which illustrate the tale with originality and wit." Booklist

Ormerod, Jan

Ms MacDonald has a class. Clarion Bks. 1996 unp il music $15.95   E

1. School stories 2. Stories in rhyme
ISBN 0-395-77611-2   LC 95-38192

"One day Ms. MacDonald takes her class to a farm. . . . On their return, they put together costumes, paint scenery, and come up with an impromptu performance for an audience of their family members." Booklist

"Ormerod's drawings capture the personalities and animated exuberance of her characters. . . . Musical scores separate vignettes of action, creating pages that flow with a plethora of details and escapades." SLJ

Osofsky, Audrey

Dreamcatcher; illustrated by Ed Young. Orchard Bks. 1992 unp il $15.95; lib bdg $16.99; pa $5.95   E

1. Ojibwa Indians—Fiction 2. Infants—Fiction 3. Family life—Fiction
ISBN 0-531-05988-X; 0-531-08588-0 (lib bdg); 0-531-07113-8 (pa)   LC 91-20029

"All day, an Ojibwa baby watches from a cradle as little boys play and Mother, big sister, Grandmother, and Father work nearby. At night, baby sleeps peacefully, for sister has made a dreamcatcher, a small willow hoop woven with a taut net of nettle fibers that catches bad dreams and holds them until the sun destroys their power, while letting good dreams slip through." Booklist

"Young's pastels are vibrantly colored but as tender as the text. . . . The artist's treatment emphasizes the universally human as well as the culturally particular in this empathic glimpse of Ojibway life." SLJ

Oxenbury, Helen, 1938-

It's my birthday. Candlewick Press 1994 c1993 unp il $9.99; pa $3.99   E

1. Cake—Fiction 2. Birthdays—Fiction 3. Animals—Fiction
ISBN 1-56402-412-1; 0-56402-602-7 (pa)   LC 93-39667

First published 1993 in the Netherlands

The birthday child's animal friends bring ingredients and help make a birthday cake

"Oxenbury tells a cumulative story for the very young child with clear watercolors and a simple, cheerful text. The telling has a satisfying rhythm and repetition." Booklist

Pippo gets lost. Aladdin Bks. (NY) 1989 unp il   E

1. Toys—Fiction
      LC 89-340

Available Board book edition

Tom is very worried when he searches the house and can't find his stuffed monkey Pippo

Other available titles about Tom and Pippo are:
Tom and Pippo and the bicycle (1994)
Tom and Pippo go for a walk (1988)
Tom and Pippo on the beach (1993)
Tom and Pippo read a story (1988)
Tom and Pippo's day (1989)

Pak, Soyung

Dear Juno; illustrated by Susan Kathleen Hartung. Viking 1999 unp il $15.99　　E
1. Grandmothers—Fiction 2. Letters—Fiction 3. Korean Americans—Fiction
ISBN 0-670-88252-6　　LC 98-43408
Although Juno, a Korean American boy, cannot read the letter he receives from his grandmother in Seoul, he understands what it means from the photograph and dried flower that are enclosed and decides to send a similar letter back to her
"The handsome layout, featuring ample white space and illustrations that cover anywhere from one page to an entire spread, perfectly suit the gentle, understated tone of the text." SLJ

Palatini, Margie

Piggie pie! illustrated by Howard Fine. Clarion Bks. 1995 unp il $15; pa $5.95　　E
1. Witchcraft—Fiction 2. Pigs—Fiction 3. Wolves—Fiction
ISBN 0-395-71691-8; 0-395-86618-9 (pa)
　　LC 94-19726
Also available with Audiobook
"Gritch the Witch sets out for Old MacDonald's Farm to get herself a meal of plump piggies. Alerted, however, . . . the swine hastily don sheep, cow, and other barnyard disguises and fool her. . . . The still-hungry Gritch is persuaded to give up by a Big Bad Wolf . . . and the two go off for lunch, each picturing the other made into a sandwich. . . . The exuberant illustrations are colorful and action-filled. Greedy (but not too bright) witch and wolf both get what they deserve in this thoroughly enjoyable romp." SLJ

Paraskevas, Betty

On the day the tall ships sailed; by Betty Paraskevas and Michael Paraskevas. Simon & Schuster Bks. for Young Readers 2000 unp il music $16　　E
1. Ships—Fiction 2. Eagles—Fiction 3. New York (N.Y.)—Fiction 4. Fourth of July—Fiction
ISBN 0-689-82864-0　　LC 99-22600
"The text is a patriotic song describing how a single eagle soars high above the tall ships sailing up the Hudson River on the Fourth of July. . . . The rich, acrylic illustrations feature a black, white, and yellow raptor set against a mostly blue background of sky and sea. . . . With music appended, this is a good choice for story hours, especially on Independence Day." Booklist

Parish, Peggy, 1927-1988

Amelia Bedelia; pictures by Fritz Siebel. HarperFestival 1999 unp il $14.95　　E
ISBN 0-694-01296-3　　LC 98-31782
Also available in paperback with Audiobook
"An I can read picture book"
First published 1963; reissued 1992 as an I can read book (still available in hardcover and paperback)
"Amelia Bedelia is a maid whose talent for interpreting instructions literally results in comical situations, such as dressing the chicken in fine clothes." Hodges. Books for Elem Sch Libr

Other available titles about Amelia Bedelia by Peggy Parish are:
Amelia Bedelia and the baby (1981)
Amelia Bedelia and the surprise shower (1996)
Amelia Bedelia goes camping (1985)
Amelia Bedelia helps out (1979)
Amelia Bedelia's family album (1988)
Come back, Amelia Bedelia (1971)
Good work, Amelia Bedelia (1976)
Merry Christmas, Amelia Bedelia (1986)
Play ball, Amelia Bedelia (1972)
Teach us, Amelia Bedelia (1977)
Thank you, Amelia Bedelia (1964)
Other available titles about Amelia Bedelia by Hermen Parish are:
Amelia Bedelia 4 mayor (1999)
Bravo, Amelia Bedelia (1997)
Good driving, Amelia Bedelia (1995)

Park, Frances

The royal bee; by Frances Park and Ginger Park; illustrations by Christopher Zhong-Yuan Zhang. Boyds Mills Press 2000 unp il $15.95; pa $8.95　　E
1. Korea—Fiction 2. Reading—Fiction
ISBN 1-56397-614-5; 1-56397-867-9 (pa)
　　LC 98-88234
"Song-ho is a poor peasant boy in Korea who eavesdrops outside a classroom that only admits privileged boys. The kindly teacher, however, allows him to attend, and so stellar is his academic performance that he represents the school in the Royal Bee—a yearly contest of knowledge." Horn Book Guide
"This simply and eloquently told tale is well paired with large, bold oil-paint-on-board illustrations." SLJ

Paterson, Katherine

Marvin's best Christmas present ever; story by Katherine Paterson; pictures by Jane Clark Brown. HarperCollins Pubs. 1997 48p il $14.95; pa $3.95　　E
1. Gifts—Fiction 2. Christmas—Fiction 3. Family life—Fiction
ISBN 0-06-027159-0; 0-06-444265-9 (pa)
　　LC 96-31692
"An I can read book"
"Marvin wants to make his parents a Christmas present that will last forever. His older sister helps him make a wreath, and they hang it on the outside of their trailer home. . . . Finally, the wreath is so dry and brown that the family decides it must come down, and Marvin is heartbroken—but then there is a great discovery: a bird has made a nest in the wreath, and there are six tiny eggs. The holiday message of rebirth and renewal is part of the story . . . which Paterson tells in simple words without condescension. Brown's pictures in Christmas colors on every page extend the family warmth and fun in the farm setting." Booklist

Paul, Ann Whitford

Eight hands round; a patchwork alphabet; illustrated by Jeanette Winter. HarperCollins Pubs. 1991 unp il $15.95; lib bdg $15.89; pa $5.95
E

1. Quilts 2. Alphabet 3. Frontier and pioneer life
ISBN 0-06-024689-8; 0-06-024704-5 (lib bdg); 0-06-443464-8 (pa)
LC 88-745

Introduces the letters of the alphabet with names of early American patchwork quilt patterns and explains the origins of the designs by describing the activity or occupation they derive from

"The slightly stylized pictures have a crayonlike texture, and throughout, colors are soft and fresh. Attractive and informative, this could easily perk up a unit on pioneer life." Booklist

Hello toes! Hello feet! illustrated by Nadine Bernard Westcott. DK Ink 1998 unp il $15.95; pa $5.95
E

1. Foot—Fiction 2. Stories in rhyme
ISBN 0-7894-2481-9; 0-7894-2664-1 (pa)
LC 97-31002

"A Melanie Kroupa book"

A girl takes delight in all the things she and her feet do throughout the day

"Colorful cartoon line-and-wash illustrations, featuring plenty of purple and pink, are an ideal match for the energetic rhyme." SLJ

Payne, Emmy, 1919-

Katy No-Pocket; pictures by H. A. Rey. Houghton Mifflin 1944 unp il lib bdg $17; pa $5.95
E

1. Kangaroos—Fiction 2. Animals—Fiction
ISBN 0-395-17104-0 (lib bdg); 0-395-13717-9 (pa)

Also available with Audiobook

Katy Kangaroo was most unfortunately unprovided with a pocket in which to carry her son Freddy. She asked other animals with no pockets how they carried their children but none of their answers seemed satisfactory. Finally a wise old owl advised her to try to find a pocket in the City, and so off she went and in the City she found just what she and Freddy needed

Peacock, Carol Antoinette

Mommy far, Mommy near; an adoption story; written by Carol Antoinette Peacock; illustrated by Shawn Brownell. Whitman, A. 2000 unp il
E

1. Adoption—Fiction 2. Mother-child relationship—Fiction 3. Chinese Americans—Fiction
LC 99-36108

Elizabeth, who was born in China, describes the family who has adopted her and tries to sort out her feelings for her mother back in China

"The situation is handled sensitively by the author, who writes from personal experience. . . . The faces deftly show the strong emotional bond between adoptive mother and daughter." Horn Book Guide

Pearson, Tracey Campbell

Where does Joe go? Farrar, Straus & Giroux 1999 unp il $16
E

1. Restaurants—Fiction 2. Santa Claus—Fiction
ISBN 0-374-38319-7
LC 98-37745

Because Joe's Snack Bar always closes for the season, the townspeople speculate about where Joe goes for the winter

"Cartoon illustrations chockablock with witty details. . . . Fresh and funny, this light-hearted romp concludes with a wordless surprise ending: Joe is none other than Santa." Publ Wkly

Peet, Bill

Big bad Bruce. Houghton Mifflin 1977 38p il $16; pa $7.95
E

1. Bears—Fiction 2. Witches—Fiction
ISBN 0-395-25150-8; 0-395-32922-1 (pa)
LC 76-62502

Also available with Audiobook

Bruce, a bear bully, never picks on anyone his own size until he is diminished in more ways than one by a small but very independent witch

"The language of the text is almost musical, with lots of words used for the sheer pleasure or appropriateness of their sounds. The illustrations are colorful and amusing." Child Book Rev Serv

Cowardly Clyde. Houghton Mifflin 1979 38p il hardcover o.p. paperback available $7.95
E

1. Horses—Fiction 2. Courage—Fiction
ISBN 0-395-36171-0 (pa)
LC 78-24343

"Brave Sir Galavant and his cowardly steed Clyde take up the challenge to rid the farmers of the terrible 'giant owl-eyed ox-footed ogre.' Clyde, who quivers at a scarecrow, is terrified, but finds that by acting brave, you become brave." Read Teach

"The writing is brisk and casual; the illustrations are colorful and vigorous." Bull Cent Child Books

Eli; illustrated by the author. Houghton Mifflin 1978 38p il hardcover o.p. paperback available $8.95
E

1. Lions—Fiction 2. Vultures—Fiction 3. Friendship—Fiction
ISBN 0-395-36611-9 (pa)
LC 77-17500

"The story of pathetic Eli, a 'king of the jungle' who's too old to fight. Feeding on leftovers one day, Eli is disgusted by hovering vultures, but 'noblesse oblige' compels him to rescue one bird, Vera, from a jackal who snatches her. Eli routs the jackal and earns the unwelcome friendship of the birds. . . . Comes the day when the hunters are closing in on him; Vera and the flock persuade Eli to play dead. . . . The hunters see no glory in hauling off a dead body, apparently the feast of vultures, and the old cat is saved." Publ Wkly

This offers "the author-artist's flair for exaggerated expressions, plentiful action, and bold use of color." Booklist

Huge Harold; written and illustrated by Bill Peet. Houghton Mifflin 1961 unp il lib bdg $16; pa $7.95
E

1. Rabbits—Fiction 2. Stories in rhyme
ISBN 0-395-18449-5 (lib bdg); 0-395-32923-X (pa)

Peet, Bill—*Continued*

"Harold the rabbit grows and grows—to dimensions which deprive him of normal hiding places but help him, after a bizarre chase, to an astonishing and wonderful achievement." Horn Book

This story, "told in rhyming couplets and colored drawings, is action filled and laughable." Booklist

The whingdingdilly; written and illustrated by Bill Peet. Houghton Mifflin 1970 60p il $16; pa $7.95   E

1. Dogs—Fiction 2. Witches—Fiction

ISBN 0-395-24729-2; 0-395-31381-3 (pa)

Also available with Audiobook

"Scamps, the dog, wants to be a horse, but a well-meaning witch turns him into a Whingdingdilly with the hump of a camel, zebra's tail, giraffe's neck, elephant's front legs and ears, rhinoceros' nose, and reindeer's horns." Adventuring With Books. 2d edition

Pelletier, David

The graphic alphabet. Orchard Bks. 1996 unp il $17.95   E

1. Alphabet

ISBN 0-531-36001-6   LC 96-4001

A Caldecott Medal honor book, 1997

In this alphabet book "a stylized letter Y, pink against a black background, is turned on its side and looks like a mouth open in a yawn. . . . The letter Q is repeated in squares, becoming a handsome quilt, and a three-dimensional golden H hovers over a darkened sky. Even for those who know their letters very well, some of the pictures demand a second look before the artist's view is clear. But that's the point; things can be more than or different from what they seem. An engaging book that will certainly have art-class relevance." Booklist

Penn, Malka

The miracle of the potato latkes; a Hanukkah story; illustrated by Giora Carmi. Holiday House 1994 unp il $15.95   E

1. Hanukkah—Fiction 2. Jews—Russia—Fiction

ISBN 0-8234-1118-4   LC 93-29921

"Every Hanukkah Tante Golda makes potato latkes for all her friends. One year, when all but one potato are gone, she makes latkes for a starving beggar. Trusting in God to provide, she finds one potato on the first day, two on the second and so on. Each day she invites an additional friend to share her meal. The crayon illustrations suit the Russian location and somewhat folktale quality of the story. A recipe for latkes is provided." Child Book Rev Serv

Pérez, Amada Irma

My very own room; story by Amada Irma P´erez; illustrations by Maya Christina Gonzalez. Children's Bk. Press 2000 30p il $15.95   E

1. Mexican Americans—Fiction 2. Family life—Fiction 3. Bilingual books—English-Spanish

ISBN 0-89239-164-2   LC 00-20769

Title page and text in English and Spanish

With the help of her family, a resourceful Mexican American girl realizes her dream of having a space of her own to read and to think

"Gonzalez' palette is replete with joyfully exuberant colors; rich magentas, purples, and blues contrast with the warm golds of faces and arms, and the dark eyes and hair offer further contrast with the backgrounds and skin colors. Pérez based this story on her own life . . . and the text . . . exudes a comfortably familiar, accessible voice." Bull Cent Child Books

Perkins, Lynne Rae

Home lovely. Greenwillow Bks. 1995 unp il $15; lib bdg $14.93   E

1. Gardening—Fiction

ISBN 0-688-13687-7; 0-688-13688-5 (lib bdg)

LC 94-21917

"When she and her mother move into a bare, raw-looking trailer, Tiffany plants some seedlings she finds and, with help from mail carrier Bob, grows a beautiful garden. The trailer's transformation into a place rich with color is captured in the illustrations. The book is especially welcome for its affirmation of working-class life." Horn Book Guide

Peters, Lisa Westberg

Cold little duck, duck, duck; pictures by Sam Williams. Greenwillow Bks. 2000 unp il $15.95; lib bdg $15.89   E

1. Ducks—Fiction 2. Spring—Fiction 3. Stories in rhyme

ISBN 0-688-16178-2; 0-688-16179-0 (lib bdg)

LC 99-29880

Early one spring a little duck arrives at her pond and finds it still frozen, but not for long

"The poetic text, well served by expressive watercolors, is set in a large black typeface (inviting letter and word recognition); colorful and playful typefaces are used for the rhythmic three-word refrains." Horn Book Guide

Pilkey, Dav, 1966-

The Hallo-wiener. Blue Sky Press (NY) 1995 unp il $14.95; pa $5.99   E

1. Dogs—Fiction 2. Halloween—Fiction

ISBN 0-590-41703-7; 0-439-07946-2 (pa)

LC 94-40949

All the other dogs make fun of Oscar the dachshund until one Halloween when, dressed as a hot dog, Oscar bravely rescues the others

"Pilkey's bold, colorful illustrations add life to his simple tale of courage and friendship." Horn Book Guide

The paperboy; story and paintings by Dav Pilkey. Orchard Bks. 1996 unp il $15.95; lib bdg $16.99; pa $6.95   E

1. Newspaper carriers—Fiction

ISBN 0-531-09506-1; 0-531-08856-1 (lib bdg); 0-531-07139-1 (pa)   LC 95-30641

A Caldecott Medal honor book, 1997

"A Richard Jackson book"

Pilkey, Dav, 1966—*Continued*

"In the quiet hour before dawn, a boy and his dog get out of their warm bed, eat their breakfasts, and deliver the newspapers. . . . Happy together before the rest of the world awakes, they finish the job and head back home to bed, where they dream of flying across the night sky." Booklist

"The palette of the artwork is rich and inviting, and an emphasis is put on balance and geometric form, giving solidity to this celebration of routine. A meditative evocation of the extraordinary aspects of ordinary living." Horn Book Guide

Pinczes, Elinor J.

One hundred hungry ants; illustrated by Bonnie MacKain. Houghton Mifflin 1993 unp il $16; pa $5.95   E
1. Ants—Fiction 2. Mathematics—Fiction 3. Stories in rhyme
ISBN 0-395-63116-5; 0-395-97123-3 (pa)
LC 91-45415
One hundred hungry ants head towards a picnic to get yummies for their tummies, but stop to change their line formation, illustrating the various ways one hundred may be divided

"Kids will enjoy the bouncy rhyme and the comical portrayal of the ants, while teachers will appreciate the entertaining demonstration of a math concept. The illustrations, which look like linocuts tinted with flat colors, have a distinctive style and a definite sense of humor." Booklist

Pinkney, Brian

The adventures of Sparrowboy. Simon & Schuster Bks. for Young Readers 1997 unp il $16; pa $5.99   E
1. Flight—Fiction 2. Comic books, strips, etc.—Fiction
ISBN 0-689-81071-7; 0-689-83534-5 (pa)
LC 96-19028
"Henry the paperboy accidentally collides with a sparrow and discovers that he can fly—just like Falconman, his favorite comic strip superhero." Booklist

"The plot unravels chiefly through Pinkney's . . . airy, motion-filled art, expertly rendered in scratchboard, transparent dyes and gouaches. . . . Clever quips and asides add humor and playful melodrama." Publ Wkly

Cosmo and the robot. Greenwillow Bks. 2000 unp il $15.95; lib bdg $15.89   E
1. Robots—Fiction 2. Mars (Planet)—Fiction 3. Science fiction
ISBN 0-688-15940-0; 0-688-15941-9 (lib bdg)
LC 98-32209
Cosmo, a boy living on Mars, must come up with a quick solution when his malfunctioning robot Rex threatens his sister Jewel

Pinkney's "trademark art, created on scratchboard with dyes and acrylic paints, presents a barren planet in the slightly kitschy tradition of '50s science fiction. Even with the outlandish plot and extraterrestrial setting, the author/artist lets ordinary family dynamics shine brightly." Publ Wkly

Pinkney, Gloria Jean, 1941-

Back home; pictures by Jerry Pinkney. Dial Bks. for Young Readers 1992 unp il $16.99; pa $6.99   E
1. Farm life—Fiction 2. North Carolina—Fiction 3. African Americans—Fiction
ISBN 0-8037-1168-9; 0-14-056547-7 (pa)
LC 91-22610
Eight-year-old Ernestine returns to visit relatives on the North Carolina farm where she was born

"Gloria Pinkney's text has a relaxed pace that is perfectly suited to the summer setting. Her characterizations are particularly well drawn, and her dialogue thoroughly convincing. In some of Jerry Pinkney's finest work, sunlight filters through his pencil and watercolor illustrations, imbuing them with a feathery soft glow." Publ Wkly

Pinkney, Jerry, 1939-

The little match girl; [by] Hans Christian Andersen; adapted and illustrated by Jerry Pinkney. Phyllis Fogelman Bks. 1999 unp il $16.99   E
ISBN 0-8037-2314-8   LC 99-13814
The wares of the poor little match girl illuminate her cold world, bringing some beauty to her brief, tragic life

"A faithful retelling of a classic tale. . . . The story's haunting death imagery . . . may disturb the very young, but ultimately Pinkney's vision proves as transcendent as Andersen's." Publ Wkly

Rikki-tikki-tavi; by Rudyard Kipling; adapted and illustrated by Jerry Pinkney. Morrow Junior Bks. 1997 unp il $16.95; lib bdg $15.93   E
1. Mongooses—Fiction 2. Cobras—Fiction 3. India—Fiction
ISBN 0-688-14320-2; 0-688-14321-0 (lib bdg)
LC 96-51194
This is a retelling of the story from Rudyard Kipling's The jungle book in which a mongoose saves an English boy and his family from cobras in their garden in India

"Dramatic in content, sensitive in line, and rich with color, the illustrations in this picture book make full use of the broad, double-page spreads. Children who are not familiar with the story will be captivated; those who have had the story read to them before will find new things to shiver over." Booklist

The ugly duckling; [by] Hans Christian Andersen; adapted and illustrated by Jerry Pinkney. Morrow Junior Bks. 1999 unp il $15.95; lib bdg $15.89   E
1. Swans—Fiction
ISBN 0-688-15932-X; 0-688-15933-8 (lib bdg)
LC 98-23604
A Caldecott Medal honor book, 2000
An ugly duckling spends an unhappy year ostracized by the other animals before he grows into a beautiful swan

"This is an elegantly accessible retelling, with illustrations full of lively, emotive animals and the kind of vigorous movement that young children are bound to find appealing." Bull Cent Child Books

Pinkwater, Daniel Manus, 1941-

Young Larry; [by] Daniel Pinkwater; illustrated by Jill Pinkwater. Marshall Cavendish 1997 unp il $14.95   E

1. Polar bear—Fiction
ISBN 0-7614-5004-1   LC 96-41670

After being hit on the head by his mother and told to fend for himself, Larry the polar bear floats from Baffin Bay to New Jersey where he gets a job as a lifeguard

"Pen-and-ink and marker illustrations in vivid tones extend Larry's character through expression, posture, and pose. . . . At once both simple and sophisticated [this book has] a fabulously quirky, memorable character." SLJ

Other titles about Larry are:
At the Hotel Larry (1998)
Bongo Larry (1998)
Ice cream Larry (1999)

Piper, Watty

The little engine that could; retold by Watty Piper; illustrated by George & Doris Hauman. 60th anniversary edition. Platt & Munk Pubs. 1990 c1930 unp il $16.99; pa $7.99   E

1. Railroads—Fiction
ISBN 0-448-40041-3; 0-448-40520-2 (pa)   LC 89-81287

Also available Board book edition and Big book edition

First published 1930

"When a train carrying good things to children breaks down, the little blue engine proves his courage and determination. The rhythmic, repetitive text encourages children to help tell the story." Hodges. Books for Elem Sch Libr

Plourde, Lynn

Pigs in the mud in the middle of the rud; illustrated by John Schoenherr. Blue Sky Press (NY) 1997 unp il $15.95   E

1. Automobiles—Fiction 2. Domestic animals—Fiction 3. Grandmothers—Fiction 4. Stories in rhyme
ISBN 0-590-56863-9   LC 96-23098

A feisty grandmother and her family struggle to get an assortment of farm animals out of the road so the family can pass in their T-Model Ford

"The rollicking rhyming text and bustling watercolors make a noisy, uproarious reading experience." Horn Book Guide

Polacco, Patricia

Babushka's doll. Simon & Schuster Bks. for Young Readers 1990 unp il $16.95; pa $6.95   E

1. Dolls—Fiction
ISBN 0-671-68343-8; 0-689-80255-2 (pa)   LC 89-6122

"When Natasha wants something, she wants it now—not after her grandmother, Babushka, has finished her chores. Babushka gets tired of this attitude, and finally goes off to the market, leaving Natasha to play with a special doll that she keeps on a high shelf. The doll comes to life and subjects Natasha to the same sort of insistent whining that Natasha used on Babushka." SLJ

"Polacco's distinctive artwork interprets the story with style and verve. Using pencil, marker, and paint, she creates a series of varied compositions, highlighting muted shades with an occasional flare of bright colors and strong patterns. . . . A good, original story, illustrated with panache." Booklist

The bee tree. Philomel Bks. 1993 unp il $16.99; pa $6.99   E

1. Books and reading—Fiction 2. Bees—Fiction
ISBN 0-399-21965-X; 0-698-11696-8 (pa)   LC 92-8660

To teach his daughter the value of books, a father leads a growing crowd in search of the tree where the bees keep all their honey

"With a lively plot and a beautifully depicted backdrop of a rural Michigan community early in the twentieth century, this book delivers its lovely sentiment with originality and verve." Booklist

Chicken Sunday. Philomel Bks. 1992 unp il $16.99; pa $6.99   E

1. Easter—Fiction 2. Friendship—Fiction
ISBN 0-399-22133-6; 0-698-11615-1 (pa)   LC 91-16030

Also available Spanish language edition

To thank old Eula for her wonderful Sunday chicken dinners, her two grandsons and their friend, a girl who has "adopted" her since her own "babushka" died, sell decorated eggs and buy her a beautiful Easter hat

"Without being heavy-handed, Polacco's text conveys a tremendous pride of heritage as it brims with rich images from her characters' African American and Russian Jewish cultures. Her vibrant pencil-and-wash illustrations glow—actual family photographs have been worked into several spreads." Publ Wkly

Just plain Fancy. Bantam Bks. 1990 unp il hardcover o.p. paperback available $6.99   E

1. Amish—Fiction 2. Peacocks—Fiction
ISBN 0-440-40937-3 (pa)   LC 89-27856

"In Naomi's Amish community, plainness is a way of life; still, Naomi would like just once to have something fancy. So when a peacock is mysteriously hatched among her chickens, Naomi's feelings are mixed. Delighted with Fancy's plumage, she also worries that her colorful bird will be shunned." Booklist

"The author-illustrator offers a lively story in a nontraditional setting that is depicted faithfully in both text and illustration." Horn Book

The keeping quilt. rev format ed. Simon & Schuster Bks. for Young Readers 1998 unp il $16   E

1. Quilts—Fiction 2. Jews—Fiction
ISBN 0-689-82090-9   LC 97-47690

A reissue of the title first published 1988

A homemade quilt ties together the lives of four generations of an immigrant Jewish family, remaining a symbol of their enduring love and faith

"Jewish customs and the way they've shifted through the years are portrayed unobtrusively in the story, which is illustrated in sepia pencil, except for the quilt, which sparks every page with its strong colors." Booklist

Polacco, Patricia—*Continued*

Mrs. Katz and Tush. Bantam Bks. 1992 unp hardcover o.p. paperback available $6.99   **E**
1. Friendship—Fiction 2. Jews—Fiction 3. African Americans—Fiction
ISBN 0-440-40936-5 (pa)   LC 91-18710
"A Bantam little rooster book"

A long-lasting friendship develops between Larnel, a young African-American, and Mrs. Katz, a lonely, Jewish widow, when Larnel presents Mrs. Katz with a scrawny kitten without a tail

"Polacco has used loving details in both words and art work to craft a moving and heartfelt story of a friendship that reaches across racial and generational differences." Horn Book

Mrs. Mack. Philomel Bks. 1998 38p il $16.99   **E**
1. Horses—Fiction 2. Michigan—Fiction
ISBN 0-399-23167-6   LC 97-52946
The author remembers the summer when she was ten years old and staying with her father in Michigan where she took riding lessons and became best friends with a perfect horse

"Polacco uses her characteristic pencil sketches filled in with warm colors to depict her characters, who come across with down-to-earth realism suffused with tenderness." Booklist

My rotten redheaded older brother. Simon & Schuster Bks. for Young Readers 1994 unp il $16; pa $5.99   **E**
1. Siblings—Fiction
ISBN 0-671-72751-6; 0-689-82036-4 (pa)
LC 93-13980
"Featuring an obnoxious, freckle-faced, bespectacled boy and a comforting, tale-telling grandmother, this autobiographical story is as satisfying as a warm slice of apple pie. Patricia can't quite understand how anyone could possibly like her older brother Richard. Whether picking blackberries or eating raw rhubarb, he always manages to outdo her, rubbing it in with one of his 'extra-rotten, weasel-eyed, greeny-toothed grins.' When their Bubbie teaches Patricia to wish on a falling star, she knows just what to ask for." SLJ

Pink and Say. Philomel Bks. 1994 unp il $16.99   **E**
1. Friendship—Fiction 2. United States—History—1861-1865, Civil War—Fiction
ISBN 0-399-22671-0   LC 93-36340
Also available Spanish language edition

Say Curtis describes his meeting with Pinkus Aylee, a black soldier, during the Civil War, and their capture by Southern troops

"Polacco pulls out all the stops in this heart-wrenching tale of Civil War valor which has been passed through several generations of the author's family. . . . Say's narration rings true, incorporating rough-edged grammar and idiomatic vocabulary. Polacco's signature line-and-watercolor paintings epitomize heroism, tenderness, and terror. . . . Unglamorized details of the conventions and atrocities of the Civil War target readers well beyond customary picture book age." Horn Book

Rechenka's eggs; written and illustrated by Patricia Polacco. Philomel Bks. 1988 unp il lib bdg $16.99; pa $6.99   **E**
1. Geese—Fiction 2. Easter—Fiction 3. Eggs—Fiction 4. Russia—Fiction
ISBN 0-399-21501-8 (lib bdg); 0-698-11385-3 (pa)
LC 87-1658
An injured goose rescued by Babushka, having broken the painted eggs intended for the Easter Festival in Moscva, lays thirteen marvelously colored eggs to replace them, then leaves behind one final miracle in egg form before returning to her own kind

"Polacco achieves optimal dramatic contrast by using bold shapes against uncluttered white space and by contrasting rich colors and design details with faces in black and white." Bull Cent Child Books

Thank you, Mr. Falker. Philomel Bks. 1998 unp il $16.99   **E**
1. Reading—Fiction 2. Teachers—Fiction 3. Learning disabilities—Fiction
ISBN 0-399-23166-8   LC 97-18685
At first, Trisha loves school, but her difficulty learning to read makes her feel dumb, until, in the fifth grade, a new teacher helps her understand and overcome her problem

"Young readers struggling with learning difficulties will identify with Trisha's situation and find reassurance in her success. Polacco's gouache-and-pencil compositions deftly capture the emotional stages—frustration, pain, elation—of Trisha's journey." Publ Wkly

Thunder cake. Philomel Bks. 1990 unp il hardcover o.p. paperback available $6.99   **E**
1. Thunderstorms—Fiction 2. Fear—Fiction 3. Grandmothers—Fiction
ISBN 0-698-11581-3 (pa)   LC 89-33405
"Polacco illustrates a first-person narrative about a little girl's experience on her grandmother's farm in Michigan. A Russian immigrant, Babushka placates her granddaughter's fears by baking a 'Thunder Cake' that requires the two of them to gather ingredients to the count of the approaching booms." Bull Cent Child Books

"Polacco succeeds with both words and art. . . . The carefully drawn faces, done in pencil, contrast with the rest of the colorful folk art." Booklist

Tikvah means hope; written and illustrated by Patricia Polacco. Doubleday Bks. for Young Readers 1994 unp il hardcover o.p. paperback available $5.99   **E**
1. Jews—Fiction 2. Fires—Fiction 3. Sukkoth—Fiction 4. Cats—Fiction
ISBN 0-440-41229-3 (pa)   LC 93-32311
"Justine's neighbor, elderly Mr. Roth, is preparing for the Jewish harvest holiday Sukkoth. Justine and her friend Duane help Mr. Roth build his Sukkah in the yard. . . . They see the orange glow and realize that the hills of Oakland, where they live, are on fire. They stay in a school gym while the fire burns for two days, and when they return to their neighborhood, they find it completely devastated. Miraculously, the Sukkah has survived untouched, as has Mr. Roth's cat, Tikvah, whose name in Hebrew means 'hope.'" Bull Cent Child Books

"Polacco's vibrantly colored illustrations pulse with energy and emotion. . . . Good Sukkoth stories are rare; rooted in an actual event as well as in ages-old tradition, this one is a priceless gem." Booklist

Polacco, Patricia—*Continued*

The trees of the dancing goats. Simon & Schuster Bks. for Young Readers 1996 unp il $16; pa $6.99   **E**
1. Hanukkah—Fiction   2. Christmas—Fiction 3. Jews—Fiction
ISBN 0-689-80862-3; 0-689-83857-3 (pa)
    LC 95-26670
Also available with Audiobook
"On the family farm in Michigan, Trisha and Richard watch as Babushka and Grampa prepare for Hanukkah in their native Russian way. . . . When scarlet fever debilitates their neighbors, Trisha's whole family pitches in to make and deliver holiday dinners and Christmas trees." Publ Wkly

Welcome Comfort. Philomel Bks. 1999 unp il $16.99   **E**
1. Santa Claus—Fiction   2. Christmas—Fiction 3. Foster home care—Fiction
ISBN 0-399-23169-2   LC 98-29558
Welcome Comfort, a lonely foster child, is assured by his friend the school custodian that there is a Santa Claus, but he does not discover the truth until one wondrous and surprising Christmas Eve
"This warm blend of fantasy and reality delivers a satisfying surprise ending. . . . Polacco's artwork is even more vibrant than usual, and her Santa scenes are sure-fire crowd-pleasers." Publ Wkly

Politi, Leo, 1908-1996
Song of the swallows. Scribner 1987 c1949 unp il music $16; pa $5.99   **E**
1. Swallows—Fiction 2. California—Fiction 3. Missions—Fiction
ISBN 0-684-18831-7; 0-689-71140-9 (pa)
Awarded the Caldecott Medal, 1950
A reissue of title first published 1949
"The swallows always appeared at the old Mission of Capistrano on St. Joseph's Day and Juan who lived nearby wondered how they could tell that from all others. This tender poetic story of the coming of springtime is touched by the kindliness of the good Fathers of the Mission as a little boy knew it. Lovely pictures in soft colors bring out the charm of the southern California landscape and the melody of the swallow song adds to the feeling of Spring." Horn Book

Pomerantz, Charlotte
The chalk doll; pictures by Frané Lessac. Lippincott 1989 30p il hardcover o.p. paperback available $6.95   **E**
1. Dolls—Fiction 2. Mother-daughter relationship—Fiction 3. Jamaica—Fiction
ISBN 0-06-443333-1 (pa)   LC 88-872
"Rose has a cold and must stay in bed. Before she settles in for a nap, she coaxes her mother to tell stories of her Jamaican childhood. The scene shifts from Rose's colorful room filled with toys to a simple little house in the village where her mother grew up. The stories are touching for the contrast between the poverty and yearning of these childhood memories and the obvious com-

fort of their present lives." Horn Book
"The stylized illustrations by the West Indian artists Frané Lessac are primitive in bright, oscillating colors, evoking poverty in a tropical paradise as well as mother-daughter affection in a well-appointed home." N Y Times Book Rev

The outside dog; story by Charlotte Pomerantz; pictures by Jennifer Plecas. HarperCollins Pubs. 1993 62p il lib bdg $15.89; pa $3.95   **E**
1. Dogs—Fiction 2. Grandfathers—Fiction 3. Puerto Rico—Fiction
ISBN 0-06-024783-5 (lib bdg); 0-06-444187-3 (pa)
    LC 91-6351
Also available with Audiobook
"An I can read book"
Marisol, who lives in Puerto Rico, wants a dog very much but her grandfather will not let her have one, until a skinny mutt wins him over
"Unlike most easy readers, not everything is spelled out in the story, and kids will have to make connections, the very thing that will increase their reading ability. Some Spanish words and phrases (defined at the beginning of the book) also deepen the story. But most importantly, this is lively, fun, and filled with pen-and-watercolor art that captures the affection that binds this new family." Booklist

The piggy in the puddle; pictures by James Marshall. Macmillan 1974 unp il $15; pa $5.99
    E
1. Pigs—Fiction 2. Stories in rhyme
ISBN 0-02-774900-2; 0-689-71293-6 (pa)
The "rhythmic tale of a small pig that scorns soap and refuses to leave her puddle. Her pleasure is infectious and finally mother, father, and brother join her in 'the very merry middle' of the 'muddy little puddle.'" Booklist
"The soft pastel drawings add just the right touch to the humorous bedtime story which demands to be read aloud." Child Book Rev Serv

You're not my best friend anymore; pictures by David Soman. Dial Bks. for Young Readers 1998 unp il lib bdg $15.89   **E**
1. Friendship—Fiction
ISBN 0-8037-1560-9   LC 93-42595
Molly and Ben are best friends and share everything until they have a fight
"The realistic watercolor portraits are intense with feeling and connection. . . . The pictures show that Molly is white and Ben is black and their double birthday party is in a comfortable multiracial neighborhood." Booklist

Pomeroy, Diana
One potato; a counting book of potato prints. Harcourt Brace & Co. 1996 unp il $16; pa $6
    E
1. Counting 2. Prints
ISBN 0-15-200300-2; 0-15-202330-5 (pa)
    LC 95-10986
A counting book which uses images of fruits and vegetables to illustrate numbers from one to one hundred

Pomeroy, Diana—*Continued*

and which also includes an explanation of how to do potato printing

"The counting is clear and progressively more challenging, and the botanical prints, made with potatoes, are luscious and lovely." Booklist

Wildflower ABC; an alphabet of potato prints. Harcourt Brace & Co. 1997 unp il $16   E

1. Wild flowers 2. Alphabet

ISBN 0-15-201041-6   LC 96-19748

This is a "picture book illustrating wildflowers from A to Z. Each bordered page features one plant; intricate potato cuts are printed on cloth. . . . Two pages of appended notes in small type offer a few lines of information about each plant, including its scientific name, common names, plant family, myths, legends, and lore." Booklist

The fine detail that Pomeroy "includes, her exceptional blends and shadings of color, and the rainbow palette of the borders result in a stunning presentation." SLJ

Porte, Barbara Ann

Harry in trouble; pictures by Yossi Abolafia. Greenwillow Bks. 1989 47p il lib bdg $15.93; pa $4.99   E

1. Lost and found possessions—Fiction

ISBN 0-688-07722-6 (lib bdg); 0-440-80210-5 (pa)
      LC 87-21253

Harry is upset about losing his library card three times in a row, but feels better when he learns that his father and his friend Dorcas sometimes lose things

"Porte's story has an easy-to-read format which nicely fits the present tense childlike first-person narration. Abolafia's expressive cartoon style illustrations ably convey characters' emotions." SLJ

Tale of a tadpole; illustrated by Annie Cannon. Orchard Bks. 1997 unp il $15.95; lib bdg $16.99
      E

1. Toads—Fiction

ISBN 0-531-30049-8; 0-531-33049-4 (lib bdg)
      LC 96-53890

"A Richard Jackson book"

Francine and her family watch as their pet tadpole Fred gradually changes into what they think is a frog until Grandpa tells them Fred is a toad that should be living in the backyard

"Cannon's soft watercolor illustrations not only capture the warmth of the family but also accurately depict the evolution of the toad. Solid science is packed into a lovely story." Booklist

Potter, Beatrix, 1866-1943

The story of Miss Moppet. Warne il $6.99
      E

1. Cats—Fiction 2. Mice—Fiction

ISBN 0-7232-3480-9

First published 1906

Miss Moppet is a kitten who uses her wiles to capture a curious mouse. But her trickery amounts to naught when she herself is outwitted

Other available titles about Moppet's brother Tom and sister Mittens are:

The complete adventures of Tom Kitten and his friends (1984)

The roly-poly pudding (1908)

The tale of Tom Kitten (1935)

The tailor of Gloucester. Warne il $6.99   E

1. Tailoring—Fiction 2. Mice—Fiction 3. Christmas—Fiction

ISBN 0-7232-3462-0

Also available Simon & Schuster edition illustrated by David Jorgensen, which is also available with Audiobook

First published in 1903

"The cat Simpkin looked after his master when he was ill, but it was the nimble-fingered mice who used snippets of cherry-coloured twist and so finished the embroidered waist coat for the worried tailor. A Christmastime story set in old Gloucester." Four to Fourteen

"A read-aloud classic in polished style, perfectly complemented by the author's exquisite watercolor illustrations." Hodges. Books for Elem Sch Libr

The tale of Jemima Puddle-duck. Warne $6.99
      E

1. Ducks—Fiction

ISBN 0-7232-3468-X

Also available French language and Spanish language editions

First published 1908

"Jemima Puddle-duck's obstinate determination to hatch her own eggs, makes a story of suspense and sly humor." Toronto Public Libr. Books for Boys & Girls

The tale of Mr. Jeremy Fisher. Warne $6.99; pa $2.25   E

1. Frogs—Fiction

ISBN 0-7232-3466-3; 0-7232-3491-4 (pa)

First published 1906

A frog fishing from his lilly pad boat doesn't catch any fish, but one catches him

The tale of Mrs. Tiggy-Winkle. Warne il $6.99
      E

1. Hedgehogs—Fiction

ISBN 0-7232-3465-5

First published 1905

Lucie visits the laundry of Mrs. Tiggy-Winkle, a hedgehog, and finds her lost handerchiefs

The tale of Mrs. Tittlemouse. Warne il $6.99; pa $2.25   E

1. Mice—Fiction

ISBN 0-7232-3470-1; 0-7232-3495-7 (pa)

First published 1910

The story of a little mouse's funny house, the visitors she has there, and how she finally rids herself of the untidy, messy ones

The tale of Peter Rabbit. Warne il $6.99   E

1. Rabbits—Fiction

ISBN 0-7232-3460-4

Also available French language and Spanish language editions

First published 1903

Potter, Beatrix, 1866-1943—*Continued*

All about the famous rabbit family consisting of Flopsy, Mopsy, Cotton-tail and especially Peter Rabbit who disobeys Mother Rabbit's admonishment not to go into Mr. McGregor's garden

"Distinctive writing and a strong appeal to a small child's sense of justice and his sympathies make this an outstanding story. The water color illustrations add charm to the narrative by their simplicity of detail and delicacy of color." Child Books Too Good to Miss

Other available titles about Peter Rabbit and his family are:

The tale of Benjamin Bunny (1904)
The tale of Mr. Tod (1912)
The tale of the flopsy bunnies (1909)

The tale of Pigling Bland. Warne il $6.99; pa $2.25 **E**
1. Pigs—Fiction
ISBN 0-7232-3474-4; 0-7232-3499-X (pa)
First published 1913

"Pigling's story ends happily with a perfectly lovely little black Berkshire pig called Pigwig." Toronto Public Libr. Books for Boys & Girls

The tale of Squirrel Nutkin. Warne il $6.99
E
1. Squirrels—Fiction
ISBN 0-7232-3461-2
First published 1903

Each day the squirrels gather nuts, Nutkin propounds a riddle to Mr. Brown, the owl, until impertinent Nutkin, over-estimating Mr. Brown's patience, gets his due

The tale of Timmy Tiptoes. Warne il $6.99; pa $2.25 **E**
1. Squirrels—Fiction
ISBN 0-7232-3471-X; 0-7232-3496-5 (pa)
First published 1911

An innocent squirrel accused of stealing nuts is forced down a hole in a tree, where he meets a friendly chipmunk

The tale of two bad mice. Warne il $6.99; pa $2.25 **E**
1. Mice—Fiction
ISBN 0-7232-3464-7; 0-7232-3489-2 (pa)
First published 1904

"Two mischievous little mice pilfer a doll's house to equip their own. They are caught and finally make amends for what they have done. Perfectly charming illustrations and a most enticing tale." Adventuring With Books. 2d edition

Priceman, Marjorie

Emeline at the circus. Knopf 1999 unp il $15; lib bdg $16.99 **E**
1. Circus—Fiction 2. Teachers—Fiction
ISBN 0-679-87685-5; 0-679-97685-X (lib bdg)
LC 98-28873

While her teacher Miss Splinter is lecturing her second-grade class about the exotic animals, clowns, and other performers they are watching at the circus, Emeline accidentally becomes part of the show

"Priceman captures the show's frenzied grace in freely painted forms that dance and swirl in a richly saturated palette." Horn Book Guide

How to make an apple pie and see the world. Knopf 1994 unp il $16; pa $6.99 **E**
1. Baking—Fiction 2. Voyages and travels—Fiction
ISBN 0-679-83705-1; 0-679-88083-6 (pa)
LC 93-12341

Since the market is closed, the reader is led around the world to gather the ingredients for making an apple pie

"The perfect blend of whimsical illustrations and tongue-in-cheek humor makes this an irresistable offering. The recipe is included." Child Book Rev Serv

Prigger, Mary Skillings

Aunt Minnie McGranahan; illustrated by Betsy Lewin. Clarion Bks. 1999 31p il $15 **E**
1. Aunts—Fiction 2. Orphans—Fiction
ISBN 0-395-82270-X
LC 98-33501

The townspeople in St. Clere, Kansas, are sure it will never work out when the neat and orderly spinster, Minnie McGranahan, takes her nine orphaned nieces and nephews into her home in 1920

"In a dexterous style, Prigger employs repetitive elements to establish and maintain a spry tempo in clipped, spruce sentences. . . . The black outlines of Lewin's . . . witty, loose watercolors punctuate the pages in a flurry of scribbles, suggesting the kind of bursting-at-the-seams activity." Publ Wkly

Prokofiev, Sergey, 1891-1953

Peter and the wolf; translated by Maria Carlson; illustrated by Charles Mikolaycak. Viking 1982 unp il hardcover o.p. paperback available $5.99
E
1. Wolves—Fiction 2. Fairy tales
ISBN 0-14-050633-0 (pa)
LC 81-70402

This book retells the orchestral fairy tale of the boy who, ignoring his grandfather's warnings, proceeds to capture a wolf

"Prokofiev's classic, designed to teach children the instruments of an orchestra, has been published in picture book form before, but never better illustrated. The translation is smooth. . . . The paintings are rich in color, dramatic in details of costume or architecture, strong in composition, with distinctive individuality in the faces of people and of the wolf." Bull Cent Child Books

Pyle, Howard, 1853-1911

Bearskin; illustrated by Trina Schart Hyman; afterword by Peter Glassman. Morrow Junior Bks. 1997 unp il $16; lib bdg $15.93 **E**
1. Fairy tales
ISBN 0-688-09837-1; 0-688-09838-X (lib bdg)
LC 96-32451

A brave young man who has been raised by a bear with unusual powers rescues a princess from a menacing dragon and fulfills a long-ago prophecy that he would marry the king's daughter

"Using india ink and acrylic paints, Hyman has made a series of pictures as spirited and good-hearted as the tale. The line is fluid and graceful, the content is dramatic and sometimes humorous." Booklist

Rael, Elsa Okon

What Zeesie saw on Delancey Street; illustrated by Marjorie Priceman. Simon & Schuster Bks. for Young Readers 1996 unp il $16; pa $5.99   **E**
1. Jews—Fiction 2. New York (N.Y.)—Fiction 3. Immigration and emigration—Fiction
ISBN 0-689-80549-7; 0-689-83838-3 (pa)
LC 95-11321
"The setting is a Jewish American community on Manhattan's Lower East Side in the early 1900s. On her seventh birthday, Zeesie is excited to attend her first 'package party' with her parents; it's a fund-raising party where families and friends who emigrated from the same village abroad get together and organize to bring new immigrants to America." Booklist
"The text has the intimacy of a family chronicle. Its understated tone serves as an effective foil for exuberant illustrations, steeped in a rosy glow, that employ varied perspectives. . . . Recipes for *tsimmes* and *leykach* (honey cake) round out a generous presentation." Horn Book

Rappaport, Doreen

Dirt on their skirts; the story of the young women who won the world championship; [by] Doreen Rappaport, Lyndall Callan; pictures by E.B. Lewis. Dial Bks. for Young Readers 1999 unp il $16.99   **E**
1. All-American Girls Professional Baseball League—Fiction 2. Baseball—Fiction
ISBN 0-8037-2042-4   LC 98-47080
Margaret experiences the excitement of watching the 1946 championship game of the All-American Girls Professional Baseball League as it goes into extra innings
"With its economy of language and telling period details, this book provides an exciting slice of sports history and an appealing bit of Americana. . . . Lewis's finely wrought watercolor paintings deftly capture the crowd and the action on the field." SLJ

Raschka, Christopher

Like likes like; [by] Chris Raschka. DK Pub. 1998 unp il $15.95   **E**
1. Cats—Fiction
ISBN 0-7894-2564-5   LC 98-3659
"A Richard Jackson book"
Two cats fall in love in a rose garden
"Raschka's text has a distinct rhythm that will carry readers along, and the energy of his pastel and watercolor illustrations is nearly palpable." Bull Cent Child Books

Mysterious Thelonious; [by] Chris Raschka. Orchard Bks. 1997 unp il $13.95; lib bdg $14.99   **E**
1. Monk, Thelonious, 1917-1982 2. Jazz musicians
ISBN 0-531-30057-9; 0-531-33057-5 (lib bdg)
LC 97-6994
Raschka "has created an unusual portrait of Thelonious Monk and 'Misterioso.' By matching the tones of the color wheel to the chromatic musical scale and then translating the notes of the piece into colors, Raschka captures its whimsical, lyrical and startling contours. . . . Raschka's truly remarkable watercolors . . . capture with intense poignancy Monk's idiosyncratic postures." N Y Times Book Rev

Yo! Yes? by Chris Raschka. Orchard Bks. 1993 unp il $15.95; lib bdg $16.99; pa $6.95   **E**
1. Friendship—Fiction 2. Race relations—Fiction 3. African Americans—Fiction
ISBN 0-531-05469-1; 0-531-08619-4 (lib bdg); 0-531-07108-1 (pa)   LC 92-25644
A Caldecott Medal honor book, 1994
"A Richard Jackson book"
Two lonely characters, one black and one white, meet on the street and become friends
"The design and drawing are bold, spare and expressive; the language has the strength and rhythm of a playground chant." Bull Cent Child Books
Another available title about these characters is: Ring! Yo? (2000)

Rathmann, Peggy

10 minutes till bedtime. Putnam 1998 unp il $16.99   **E**
1. Hamsters—Fiction 2. Bedtime—Fiction
ISBN 0-399-23103-X   LC 97-51295
A boy's hamster leads an increasingly large group of hamsters on a tour of the boy's house, while his father counts down the minutes to bedtime
"Children will pore over the comical details and follow closely the antics of the numbered hamsters, each one with a personality of its own." SLJ

Good night, Gorilla. Putnam 1994 unp il $14.99; pa $5.99   **E**
1. Zoos—Fiction
ISBN 0-399-22445-9; 0-698-11649-6 (pa)
LC 92-29020
Also available Board book edition
An unobservant zookeeper is followed home by all the animals he thinks he has left behind in the zoo
"In a book economical in text and simple in illustration, the many amusing, small details, as well as the tranquil tone of the story, make this an outstanding picture book." Horn Book Guide

Officer Buckle and Gloria. Putnam 1995 unp il $16.99   **E**
1. School stories 2. Dogs—Fiction 3. Safety education—Fiction
ISBN 0-399-22616-8   LC 93-43887
Awarded the Caldecott Medal, 1996
"When rotund, good-natured officer Buckle visits school assemblies to read off his sensible safety tips, the children listen, bored and polite, dozing off one by one. But when the new police dog, Gloria, stands behind him, secretly miming the dire consequences of acting imprudently, the children suddenly become attentive, laughing uproariously and applauding loudly. . . . The deadpan humor of the text and slapstick wit of the illustrations make this a terrific combination. Large, expressive line drawings illustrate the characters with finesse, and the Kool-Aid-bright washes add energy and pizzazz." Booklist

Rattigan, Jama Kim

Dumpling soup; illustrated by Lillian Hsu-Flanders. Little, Brown 1993 unp il $16.95; pa $5.95　　　　E

　　1. Family life—Fiction 2. New Year—Fiction 3. Hawaii—Fiction

　　ISBN 0-316-73445-4; 0-316-73047-5 (pa)

　　　　　　　　　　　　　　LC 91-42949

"Marisa, a seven-year-old Asian-American girl who lives in Hawaii, explains the traditions that exist in her family to celebrate the New Year. Her family . . . consists of people who are Japanese, Chinese, Korean, Hawaiian, and *haole* (Hawaiian for white person). . . . A glossary of English, Hawaiian, Japanese, and Korean words provides pronunciations and definitions for many of the possibly unfamiliar terms that weave in and out of the text. A thoroughly enjoyable celebration of family warmth and diverse traditions, illustrated with cheery watercolors." Horn Book

Ray, Mary Lyn

Basket moon; illustrated by Barbara Cooney. Little, Brown 1999 unp il $15.95　　　　E

　　ISBN 0-316-73521-3　　　　LC 96-49013

After hearing some men call his father and him hillbillies on his first trip into the nearby town of Hudson, a young boy is not so sure he still wants to become a basket maker

"The story is told by the boy in lyrical prose, and is graced by Cooney's soft-hued oil-and-acrylic paintings." SLJ

Red rubber boot day; illustrated by Lauren Stringer. Harcourt 2000 unp il $16　　　　E

　　1. Rain—Fiction

　　ISBN 0-15-213756-4　　　　LC 97-25676

A child describes all the things there are to do on a rainy day

"The short text and appealing subject make this picture book accessible to young children. Stringer's acrylic paintings are as vivid as the text." Booklist

Reiser, Lynn

Cherry pies and lullabies. Greenwillow Bks. 1998 39p il music $16; lib bdg $15.93　　　　E

　　1. Mother-daughter relationship—Fiction 2. Grandmothers—Fiction

　　ISBN 0-688-13391-6; 0-688-13392-4 (lib bdg)

　　　　　　　　　　　　　　LC 95-2259

Companion volume to Tortillas and lullabies

This book "describes how traditions of baking, flowerwreathing, quilting, and lullaby singing are passed down from mother to daughter in one family." Horn Book Guide

"The well-executed watercolor-and-ink illustrations convey how the traditions alter through the years. . . . An ingenious family tree at the back of the book helps make the concept of generations enjoyable and clear." Booklist

The surprise family. Greenwillow Bks. 1994 unp il $16　　　　E

　　1. Chickens—Fiction 2. Ducks—Fiction

　　ISBN 0-688-11671-X　　　　LC 93-16249

A baby chicken accepts a young boy as her mother and later becomes a surrogate mother for some ducklings that she has hatched

"Complemented by amusing watercolor and ink illustrations, the story promotes unconditional love within families without sounding didactic." Horn Book Guide

Tortillas and lullabies. Tortillas y cancioncitas; pictures by "Corazones Valientes"; coordinated and translated by Rebecca Hart. Greenwillow Bks. 1998 40p il $16; lib bdg $15.93　　　　E

　　1. Mother-daughter relationship—Fiction 2. Grandmothers—Fiction 3. Bilingual books—English-Spanish

　　ISBN 0-688-14628-7; 0-688-14629-5 (lib bdg)

　　　　　　　　　　　　　　LC 97-7096

Companion volume to Cherry pies and lullabies

In this "picture book, four everyday activities are depicted—making tortillas, gathering flowers, washing clothes, and singing a lullaby—as they are repeated by the women of a family over the last four generations. . . . Six Costa Rican women worked together to produce the striking acrylic folk-art paintings. With deeply saturated, glowing tones and a decidedly Central American style, the pictures enhance and extend the lyrical narrative, which is printed in English and in Spanish." SLJ

Rey, H. A. (Hans Augusto), 1898-1977

Curious George. Houghton Mifflin 1941 unp il $14.95; pa $5.95　　　　E

　　1. Monkeys—Fiction

　　ISBN 0-395-15993-8; 0-395-15023-X (pa)

Also available Big book edition and with Audiobook; Spanish language edition also available

Also available book form adaptations from the Curious George film series, edited by Margret Rey and Alan J. Shalleck

Curious George goes to the hospital was written by Margret Rey and H. A. Rey in collaboration with the Children's Hospital Medical Center; and Curious George flies a kite was written by Margret Rey with pictures by H. A. Rey

Colored picture book, with simple text, describing the adventures of a curious small monkey, and the difficulties he had in getting used to city life, before he went to live in the zoo

"The bright lithographs in red, yellow, and blue, are gay and lighthearted, following the story closely with the same speed and animated humour." Ont Libr Rev

Other available titles about Curious George are:

Curious George flies a kite (1958)

Curious George gets a medal (1957)

Curious George goes to the hospital (1966)

Curious George learns the alphabet (1963)

Curious George rides a bike (1952)

Curious George takes a job (1947)

Rey, Margret

Whiteblack the penguin sees the world; [by] Margret & H. A. Rey. Houghton Mifflin 2000 unp il $15　　　　E

　　1. Penguins—Fiction

　　ISBN 0-618-07389-2　　　　LC 00-23196

In search of new stories for his radio program, Whiteblack the penguin sets out on a journey and has

Rey, Margret—*Continued*

some interesting adventures

"The plot is very well crafted, and Whiteblack's adventures are appealingly silly, almost slapstick. H. A. Rey's watercolors make great use of the white paper, contrasting it with deep hues of yellow, red, and ultramarine blue and thick black outlines." Booklist

Rice, Eve, 1951-

Benny bakes a cake; story and pictures by Eve Rice. Greenwillow Bks. 1993 c1981 unp il $14

E

1. Birthdays—Fiction 2. Cake—Fiction

ISBN 0-688-11579-9

A reissue of the title first published 1981

"It is Benny's birthday, and Mama lets him help bake the cake. But when Benny's cake is done, Ralph, the dog, helps himself to the biggest piece. Luckily Papa saves the day." SLJ

"A reassuring domestic story spiced with Ralph's mischief; a perennial favorite just right for its preschool audience." Horn Book

City night; pictures by Peter Sis. Greenwillow Bks. 1987 unp il lib bdg $12.93   E

1. City and town life—Fiction 2. Night—Fiction 3. Stories in rhyme

ISBN 0-688-06857-X   LC 86-12021

The rhyming text follows a family as they set out for a nighttime jaunt through city streets

"Urban life after dark shines and glows in this book, with a texture and depth to the rough-hewn illustrations that will charm city-dwellers and country kids alike." Publ Wkly

Sam who never forgets. Greenwillow Bks. 1977 unp il hardcover o.p. paperback available $5.95

E

1. Zoos—Fiction 2. Animals—Fiction

ISBN 0-688-07335-2 (pa)   LC 76-30370

Sam is "a zoo keeper who 'never, never forgets' to feed the animals promptly at three o'clock. The beasts have their doubts when it looks like Sam has neglected to feed poor Elephant who is both hungry and crestfallen. Happily, Sam returns with a whole wagon of hay." SLJ

"A simple, unpretentious story with child appeal that lies in the naive, straightforward telling and elemental emotional interactions of the characters. . . . Rice has forsaken her pen drawings for bright, unlined colored shapes. The figures are pleasantly stylized, the scenes evenly composed." Booklist

Riley, Linnea Asplind

Mouse mess; [by] Linnea Riley. Blue Sky Press (NY) 1997 unp il $15.95   E

1. Mice—Fiction 2. Food—Fiction 3. Stories in rhyme

ISBN 0-590-10048-3   LC 96-49499

A hungry mouse leaves a huge mess when it goes in search of a snack

"Cut-paper collages, set against black backgrounds, depict a chubby-cheeked mouse spilling, cutting, and eating a variety of colorful foods. . . . The rhyming text, filled with crunching and munching sounds, is rhythmic and fun to read aloud." SLJ

Ringgold, Faith

Aunt Harriet's Underground Railroad in the sky. Crown 1992 unp il lib bdg $17.99; pa $6.99

E

1. Tubman, Harriet, 1815?-1913—Fiction 2. Slavery—Fiction 3. Underground railroad—Fiction

ISBN 0-517-58768-8 (lib bdg); 0-517-88543-3 (pa)

LC 92-20072

With Harriet Tubman as her guide, Cassie [featured in Tar Beach] retraces the steps escaping slaves took on the Underground Railroad in order to reunite with her younger brother

"Ringgold's dynamic paintings combine historical fact with strongly realized emotions. . . . Two pages of historical notes on Tubman and the Underground Railroad, including a map and bibliography, round out the volume." Booklist

Tar Beach. Crown 1991 unp il $18; pa $6.99

E

1. African Americans—Fiction 2. Dreams—Fiction 3. Harlem (New York, N.Y.)—Fiction

ISBN 0-517-58030-6; 0-517-58984-2 (pa)

LC 90-40410

A Caldecott Medal honor book, 1992; Coretta Scott King Award for illustration, 1992

Eight-year-old Cassie dreams of flying above her Harlem home, claiming all she sees for herself and her family. Based on the author's quilt painting of the same name

"Part autobiographical, part fictional, this allegorical tale sparkles with symbolic and historical references central to African-American culture. The spectacular artwork, a combination of primitive naive figures in a flattened perspective against a boldly patterned cityscape, resonates with color and texture." Horn Book

Robins, Joan

Addie meets Max; pictures by Sue Truesdell. Harper & Row 1985 31p il lib bdg $15.89; pa $3.95   E

1. Friendship—Fiction

ISBN 0-06-025064-X (lib bdg); 0-06-444116-4 (pa)

LC 84-48329

"An Early I can read book"

Addie discovers that the new boy next door, Max, and his dog are not so terrible when she helps him bury his newly lost tooth

"A realistic, mildly funny story is pleasant for reading aloud as well as for the beginning independent reader. The illustrations, line and wash, have vigor and humor." Bull Cent Child Books

Another available title about Addie and Max is: Addie's bad day (1993)

Rockwell, Anne F., 1934-

At the beach; [by] Anne & Harlow Rockwell. Macmillan 1987 unp il hardcover o.p. paperback available $4.95   E

1. Beaches

ISBN 0-689-71494-7 (pa)   LC 86-2943

"A young preschooler accompanies her mother to the beach and in a first-person narrative describes familiar beach activities such as putting on sunscreen and chasing

Rockwell, Anne F., 1934-—*Continued*

sandpipers." SLJ

"Harlow Rockwell is at his best with the deceptively naive arrangements of pleasing shapes and strong primary colors, but the more crowded beach scenes afford a welcome contrast in their busy, if controlled, activity." Horn Book

Career day; story by Anne Rockwell; pictures by Lizzy Rockwell. HarperCollins Pubs. 2000 unp il $14.95; lib bdg $14.89　　　　　　E
1. School stories 2. Occupations—Fiction
ISBN 0-06-027565-0; 0-06-027566-9 (lib bdg)
　　　　　　　　　　　　　　LC 97-20999
Each child in Mrs. Madoff's class brings a visitor who tells the group about his or her job
"Clearly laid out and cheerfully presented, this picture book strikes just the right tone for its intended audience." Booklist

The first snowfall; [by] Anne & Harlow Rockwell. Macmillan 1987 unp il $13.95; pa $5.99
　　　　　　　　　　　　　　　　　E
1. Snow—Fiction
ISBN 0-02-777770-7; 0-689-71614-1 (pa)
　　　　　　　　　　　　　　LC 86-23712
A child enjoys the special sights and activities of a snow-covered world with her father
"Children will vicariously enjoy the fragrance and warmth of the steaming hot cocoa the young girl drinks upon her return home. Only the illustration of her mother in an incorrect and awkward skiing position mars this otherwise inviting and useful introduction to the joys of the season." Horn Book

Thanksgiving Day; story by Anne Rockwell; pictures by Lizzy Rockwell. HarperCollins Pubs. 1999 unp il $14.95; lib bdg $14.89　　　　E
1. Thanksgiving Day—Fiction 2. School stories
ISBN 0-06-027795-5; 0-06-028388-2 (lib bdg)
　　　　　　　　　　　　　　LC 97-39290
Mrs. Madoff's preschool class learns about Thanksgiving and puts on a play about the origins of the holiday
"Rockwell's cartoon illustrations of dewy-eyed preschoolers in their various roles combine with the simple text to create an excellent example of a holiday concept book for inquisitive young readers." SLJ

Rohmann, Eric

Time flies. Crown 1994 unp il $17; lib bdg $17.99; pa $6.99　　　　　　　　　　E
1. Stories without words 2. Birds—Fiction 3. Dinosaurs—Fiction
ISBN 0-517-59598-2; 0-517-59599-0 (lib bdg); 0-517-88555-7 (pa)　　　　　LC 93-28200
A Caldecott Medal honor book, 1995
A wordless tale in which a bird flying around the dinosaur exhibit in a natural history museum has an unsettling experience when the dinosaur seems to come alive and view the bird as a potential meal
"The handsome, atmospheric paintings heighten the drama as they tell their simple, somewhat mysterious, and quite short story." Booklist

Rollings, Susan

New shoes, red shoes. Orchard Bks. 2000 unp il $15.95　　　　　　　　　　　　E
1. Shoes—Fiction 2. Stories in rhyme
ISBN 0-531-30268-7　　　　　LC 99-48058
A little girl delights in a world full of all different kinds of shoes—especially the new shoes she gets to wear to a party
"A bouncy, rhyming text captures a little girl's delight at getting new shoes. . . . The vibrant, childlike gouache illustrations reflect the little girl's excitement and the very young tone of the text." SLJ

Root, Phyllis, 1949-

Aunt Nancy and Cousin Lazybones; illustrated by David Parkins. Candlewick Press 1998 unp il $16.99　　　　　　　　　　　　　E
1. Cousins—Fiction
ISBN 1-56402-425-3　　　　　LC 97-51157
When Cousin Lazybones comes to visit Aunt Nancy but refuses to help with any of the work around the house, she must figure out a scheme to get rid of him
"Peppered with homespun Midwestern colloquialisms and rhythmic repetitions, Root's text begs to be read aloud. Parkins's paintings show small, wiry Aunt Nancy and big, bleary Cousin Lazybones with humorously exaggerated but realistically recognizable facial expressions." Horn Book Guide
Another available title about Aunt Nancy is:
Aunt Nancy and Old Man Trouble (1996)

Grandmother Winter; pictures by Beth Krommes. Houghton Mifflin 1999 unp il $15
　　　　　　　　　　　　　　　　　E
1. Winter—Fiction 2. Snow—Fiction 3. Animals—Fiction
ISBN 0-395-88399-7　　　　　LC 98-50515
When Grandmother Winter shakes out her feather quilt birds, bats, bears, and other creatures prepare themselves for the cold
"Root's cadenced text, lyrical and sweet, is nicely matched by Krommes's handsome stylized art rendered in scratchboard and watercolor." Horn Book Guide

Rosen, Michael, 1946-

We're going on a bear hunt; retold by Michael Rosen; illustrated by Helen Oxenbury. Margaret K. McElderry Bks. 1989 unp il $17　　　E
1. Bears—Fiction 2. Hunting—Fiction
ISBN 0-689-50476-4　　　　　LC 88-13338
Also available Board book edition and Big book edition; Spanish language edition also available
"Glorious puddles of watercolor alternate with impish charcoal sketches in this refreshing interpretation of an old hand rhyme in which a man, four children, and a dog stalk the furry beast through mud and muck, high and low. A book with a genuine atmosphere of togetherness and boundless enthusiasm for the hunt." SLJ

Rosenberg, Liz

Monster mama; story by Liz Rosenberg; illustrations by Stephen Gammell. Philomel Bks. 1993 unp il $15.95; pa $6.99   E

1. Mother-son relationship—Fiction 2. Monsters—Fiction

ISBN 0-399-21989-7; 0-698-11429-9 (pa)

LC 91-46825

"Patrick loves his strange and powerful mother, and when the local bullies insult her, his anger transforms him, and he chases them with glowing eyes and 'truly monstrous' laughter. Gammell's splattered paintings in brilliant watercolors and frenetic lines express all the mad energy and transformation of the story." Booklist

Rosenberry, Vera

Vera's first day of school. Holt & Co. 1999 unp il $15.95   E

1. School stories

ISBN 0-8050-5936-9   LC 98-43347

Vera cannot wait for the day when she starts school, but the first day does not go exactly as she has anticipated

"Rosenberry's playful, brightly colored gouache illustrations capture Vera's jubilation-turned-dismay." Horn Book Guide

Other available titles about Vera are:

Vera runs away (2000)

When Vera was sick (1998)

Ross, Pat

Meet M and M; pictures by Marylin Hafner. Pantheon Bks. 1980 41p il o.p.; Puffin Bks. paperback available $3.99   E

1. Friendship—Fiction

ISBN 0-14-038731-5 (pa)   LC 79-190

"An I am reading book"

"Because they look so much alike, Mandy and Mimi like to pretend they're twins; they share everything, including bubble baths and toys. . . . Total amity. Then, 'one crabby day,' they have a squabble, it takes several miserable days more before they make up, and there is a happy reunion as they meet on the stairs halfway between their apartments." Bull Cent Child Books

"Beginning readers will have no difficulty with the humorously told, very real incidents, and the way in which the impasse is breached and friendship restored is particularly childlike. The many black-and-white pencil drawings capture the girls' facial expressions especially well." Horn Book

Other available titles about M and M (Mandy and Mimi) are:

M and M and the bad news babies (1983)

M and M and the Halloween monster (1991)

M and M and the haunted house game (1980)

M and M and the mummy mess (1986)

Roth, Susan L.

Cinnamon's day out; a gerbil adventure. Dial Bks. for Young Readers 1998 unp il $15.99; lib bdg $15.89   E

1. Gerbils—Fiction

ISBN 0-8037-2322-9; 0-8037-2323-7 (lib bdg)

LC 97-24620

A gerbil escapes from his cage and enjoys a day on his own before being happily returned

"In the whimsical multi-media collages, Cinnamon appears almost life-size. . . . With a gentle sense of humor, Roth convincingly narrates from Cinnamon's point of view." Publ Wkly

Rotner, Shelley

The body book; [by] Shelley Rotner & Steve Calcagnino. Orchard Bks. 2000 unp il $15.95; lib bdg $16.99   E

ISBN 0-531-30256-3; 0-531-33256-X (lib bdg)

LC 99-34866

Simple text and photographs present some of the parts of the human body, including eyes, nose, hands, legs, and toes

"The joyful, spontaneous photos, one to eight per spread, burst with enthusiasm." Publ Wkly

Rounds, Glen, 1906-

Once we had a horse. [new ed] Holiday House 1996 unp il $15.95   E

1. Horses—Fiction

ISBN 0-8234-1241-5   LC 95-25939

A revised and newly illustrated edition of the title first published 1971

Several children who live on a ranch in Montana spend the summer playing with a gentle old horse which had been left in their yard

This "is a delightful blend of Rounds's dry, witty storytelling with illustrations that capture the humor of the horse/child antics." SLJ

Washday on Noah's ark; a story of Noah's ark. Holiday House 1985 unp il hardcover o.p. paperback available $5.95   E

1. Noah's ark 2. Tall tales

ISBN 0-8234-0880-9 (pa)   LC 84-22380

When the forty-first day on the ark dawns bright and clear, Mrs. Noah decides to do the wash, and having no rope long enough, devises an ingenious clothesline

"This goes far afield from the original; Noah gets his information on the impending storm from weather reports, not God. And, as in many tall tales, animals are not given the best of treatment . . . but the simple shapes and softly textured colors make a nice combination. The art radiates a sense of movement and fun that young children will find appealing." Booklist

Ruelle, Karen Gray, 1957-

The Thanksgiving beast feast. Holiday House 1999 32p il $14.95   E

1. Thanksgiving Day—Fiction 2. Cats—Fiction 3. Animals—Fiction

ISBN 0-8234-1511-2   LC 98-51339

"A Holiday House reader"

Harry the cat and his sister Emily celebrate Thanksgiving by making a holiday feast for the animals in their yard

"Simple and child-centered, the story reads well and uses repetition in ways that sound natural, while reinforcing word recognition. Pleasantly childlike, the naive ink drawings are tinted with gentle washes." Booklist

Ruelle, Karen Gray, 1957——_Continued_

Other available titles about Harry and Emily are:
The monster in Harry's backyard (1999)
Snow valentines (2000)

Russo, Marisabina

The big brown box. Greenwillow Bks. 2000 unp
il $15.95   **E**
1. Boxes—Fiction 2. Brothers—Fiction
ISBN 0-688-17096-X   LC 99-14871

As he plays in a very large box in his room and turns
it into a house, then a cave, then a boat, Sam is reluctant
to let his little brother Ben join him, but then he finds
the perfect way for them to share

"The well-paced, child-centered text is complemented
by Russo's trademark two-dimensional gouache illustrations that realistically capture the creative play of children." SLJ

Hannah's baby sister. Greenwillow Bks. 1998
unp il $15   **E**
1. Infants—Fiction 2. Siblings—Fiction
ISBN 0-688-15831-5   LC 97-31412

Hannah, who is sure that the new baby in her family
is going to be a girl, is disappointed at first when it turns
out to be a boy

"This loving family is warmly portrayed in both the
text and in the cheerful, childlike paintings with Russo's
signature use of flat areas of color and pattern." SLJ

Mama talks too much. Greenwillow Bks. 1999
unp il $16   **E**
1. City and town life—Fiction 2. Mother-daughter relationship—Fiction
ISBN 0-688-16411-0   LC 98-17695

On the way to the store, Celeste is frustrated when her
mother constantly stops to talk with neighborhood
friends, until Celeste finds a reason of her own for stopping

"Warm, tactile shapes defined by strong gouache colors fill the pages, as Celeste and Mama walk the city
sidewalks and cross at the light. Winsome and utterly
recognizable." Booklist

Ryan, Pam Muñoz

Amelia and Eleanor go for a ride; based on a
true story; story by Pam Muñoz Ryan; pictures by
Brian Selznick. Scholastic Press 1999 unp il
$16.95   **E**
1. Earhart, Amelia, 1898-1937—Fiction 2. Roosevelt,
Eleanor, 1884-1962—Fiction
ISBN 0-590-96075-X   LC 98-31788

A fictionalized account of the night Amelia Earhart
flew Eleanor Roosevelt over Washington, D.C. in an airplane

"Hewing closely to documented accounts, Ryan's inviting text adds drama and draws parallels between the
two protagonists with fictional touches. . . . Selznick's
illustrations, black-and-white graphite accented with
touches of purple pencil, both capture the vibrancy of his
subjects and evoke the feel of a more glamorous era."
Publ Wkly

Ryder, Joanne

Each living thing; illustrations by Ashley Wolff.
Harcourt 2000 unp il $16   **E**
1. Animals—Fiction 2. Stories in rhyme
ISBN 0-15-201898-0   LC 98-51832
"Gulliver Books"

Celebrates the creatures of the earth, from spiders dan-
gling in their webs to owls hooting and hunting out of
sight, and asks that we respect and care for them

"Wolff's intense gouache paintings, outlined in black,
are as lyrical as the text, with just the right balance of
simplicity and subtle detail." Booklist

My father's hands; illustrated by Mark Graham.
Morrow Junior Bks. 1994 unp il $16.95   **E**
1. Father-daughter relationship—Fiction 2. Gardening—Fiction
ISBN 0-688-09189-X   LC 93-27116

"A little girl and her father share the wonders of nature as they examine several small creatures in the garden—a pink worm, a golden beetle, a sliding snail, and
a praying mantis. Graham's lovely double-page, impressionistic oil paintings clearly focus on the man and his
daughter, with closeups of faces and hands in nearly every illustration. The garden in the background, lush with
flowers and vegetable plants, provides a picturesque setting for this simple, straightforward description of a special parent/child outing." SLJ

Rylant, Cynthia

All I see; story by Cynthia Rylant; pictures by
Peter Catalanotto. Orchard Bks. 1988 unp il
$17.95; pa $6.95   **E**
1. Artists—Fiction 2. Painting—Fiction
ISBN 0-531-05777-1; 0-531-07048-4 (pa)
                                            LC 88-42547
"A Richard Jackson book"

"The story of a shy boy, Charlie, who, while summer-
ing by a lake, becomes fascinated with the work of a
painter named Gregory. Secretly watching Gregory paint
and hum Beethoven's Fifth symphony to his white cat,
Charlie eventually communicates by canvas, leaving first
a picture and then messages before coming out into the
open for lessons, a gift of paints, and friendship." Bull
Cent Child Books

"Soft-focus, soft-color illustrations—double-page watercolors—are full of sun and shadow, leaves and water,
and gentle peace punctuated by bursts of energy, as
when Gregory's cat springs while geese take flight. The
pictures carry a sense of the mystery of art. This is romantic, but not sentimental." Libr J

Henry and Mudge; the first book of their
adventures; story by Cynthia Rylant; pictures by
Suçie Stevenson. Bradbury Press 1987 39p il $15;
pa $3.99   **E**
1. Dogs—Fiction
ISBN 0-689-81004-0; 0-689-71399-1 (pa)
                                            LC 86-13615

Also available Spanish language edition

This book tells "about a boy named Henry and his
dog, Mudge. . . . Henry yearns for a dog and convinces
his parents to get one. Mudge is small at first, but soon
grows 'out of seven collars in a row' to become enor-

Rylant, Cynthia—*Continued*

mous, and Henry's best friend. Then comes a day when Mudge is lost, and boy and dog realize what they mean to each other." N Y Times Book Rev

"The stories are lighthearted and affectionate. Backed by line-and-wash cartoon drawings, they celebrate the familiar in a down-to-earth way that will please young readers." Booklist

Other available titles about Henry and Mudge are:
Henry and Mudge and Annie's good move (1998)
Henry and Mudge and Annie's perfect pet (2000)
Henry and Mudge and the bedtime thumps (1991)
Henry and Mudge and the best day of all (1995)
Henry and Mudge and the careful cousin (1994)
Henry and Mudge and the forever sea (1989)
Henry and Mudge and the happy cat (1990)
Henry and Mudge and the long weekend (1992)
Henry and Mudge and the sneaky crackers (1998)
Henry and Mudge and the Snowman plan (1999)
Henry and Mudge and the starry night (1998)
Henry and Mudge and the wild wind (1993)
Henry and Mudge get the cold shivers (1989)
Henry and Mudge in puddle trouble (1987)
Henry and Mudge in the family trees (1997)
Henry and Mudge in the green time (1987)
Henry and Mudge in the sparkle days (1988)
Henry and Mudge take the big test (1991)
Henry and Mudge under the yellow moon (1987)

Mr. Griggs' work; illustrated by Julie Downing. Orchard Bks. 1989 unp il hardcover o.p. paperback available $6.95   E
1. Postal service—Fiction
ISBN 0-531-07037-9 (pa)   LC 88-1484
Mr. Griggs so loves his work at the post office that he thinks of it all the time and everything reminds him of it

"Line drawings and the controlled brightness of restrained crayon work are the media for pictures that have clean composition and that are nicely synchronized with the text. . . . Nice to have a story about someone who enjoys a job that is not glamorous." Bull Cent Child Books

Mr. Putter and Tabby pour the tea; illustrated by Arthur Howard. Harcourt Brace & Co. 1994 unp il $13; pa $5.95   E
1. Cats—Fiction 2. Old age—Fiction
ISBN 0-15-256255-9; 0-15-200901-9 (pa)
     LC 93-21470
"Mr. Putter, a lonely old man, finds a friend in Tabby, an elderly cat he gets from the pound." Booklist

"Rylant's charming story of two elderly characters is complemented and enhanced by Howard's delightful illustrations, done in pencil, watercolor, and gouache." SLJ

Other available titles about Mr. Putter and Tabby are:
Mr. Putter and Tabby bake the cake (1994)
Mr. Putter and Tabby feed the fish (2001)
Mr. Putter and Tabby fly the plane (1997)
Mr. Putter and Tabby paint the porch (2000)
Mr. Putter and Tabby pick the pears (1995)
Mr. Putter and Tabby row the boat (1997)
Mr. Putter and Tabby take the train (1998)
Mr. Putter and Tabby toot the horn (1998)
Mr. Putter and Tabby walk the dog (1994)

Night in the country; pictures by Mary Szilagyi. Bradbury Press 1986 unp il hardcover o.p. paperback available $5.99   E
1. Night—Fiction 2. Country life—Fiction
ISBN 0-689-71473-4 (pa)   LC 85-70963
Text and illustrations describe the sights and sounds of nighttime in the country

"Rich with nuances, the images and sounds evoked by the text have brought forth deeply shadowed drawings by the artist; likewise, the text will conjure up vivid imaginings in the minds of young children. The journey through nighttime fittingly concludes that night animals 'will spend a day in the country listening to you.' Each page invites children to look, listen and explore." SLJ

The old woman who named things; illustrated by Kathryn Brown. Harcourt Brace & Co. 1996 unp il $16; pa $6   E
1. Old age—Fiction 2. Dogs—Fiction
ISBN 0-15-257809-9; 0-15-202102-7 (pa)
     LC 93-40537
"A feisty old woman who has outlived all her friends resorts to naming inanimate objects as a creative alternative to solitude. She feeds a shy, homeless pup at her gate but refuses any closer ties, fearful that the dog won't last as long as her car, house, or chair. But love triumphs over reason." Horn Book Guide

"Brown's watercolors vividly picture an unconventional old woman. . . . Rylant and Brown together create with affection and lovingly humorous touches a glimpse of old age lived with relish." Booklist

Poppleton; book one; illustrated by Mark Teague. Blue Sky Press (NY) 1997 48p il $15.95; pa $3.99   E
1. Pigs—Fiction 2. Friendship—Fiction
ISBN 0-590-84782-1; 0-590-84783-X (pa)
     LC 96-3365
"City pig Poppleton adjusts to small-town life in this . . . chapter book. In 'Neighbors,' the polite Poppleton tries to think up a polite way to say 'no thanks' to Cherry Sue, a friendly llama who invites him to breakfast, lunch and dinner every single day. . . . The second vignette, 'The Library,' details Poppleton's reading ritual, which demands solitude. Finally, 'The Pill' introduces Fillmore, a sick goat who refuses to take his pill unless Poppleton hides it in a cake. . . . [Rylant's] concise sentences mimic the characters' good manners and wryly point up the failures of etiquette. Teague contributes fetching watercolor-and-pencil images of the pudgy pig, slender llama and dignified goat." Publ Wkly

Other available titles about Poppleton are:
Poppleton and friends (1997)
Poppleton everyday (1998)
Poppleton forever (1998)
Poppleton has fun (2000)
Poppleton in Fall (1999)
Poppleton in Spring (1999)
Poppleton through and through (2000)

The relatives came; story by Cynthia Rylant; illustrated by Stephen Gammell. Bradbury Press 1985 unp il lib bdg $16; pa $5.99   E
1. Family life—Fiction
ISBN 0-02-777220-9 (lib bdg); 0-689-71738-5 (pa)
     LC 85-10929

A Caldecott Medal honor book, 1986

Rylant, Cynthia—*Continued*

"The relatives have come—in an old station wagon that smells 'like a real car'—bringing with them hugs and laughs, quiet talk, and, at night when all are asleep hither and yon, 'all that new breathing.'" Booklist

"If there's anything more charming than the tone of voice in this story, it's the drawings that go with it. Stephen Gammell . . . fills the pages with bright, crayony pictures teeming with details that children should enjoy poring over for hours." N Y Times Book Rev

Silver packages; an Appalachian Christmas story; paintings by Chris K. Soentpiet. Orchard Bks. 1997 unp il $16.95; lib bdg $17.99   E
1. Christmas—Fiction 2. Railroads—Fiction 3. Appalachian region—Fiction
ISBN 0-531-30051-X; 0-531-33051-6 (lib bdg)
LC 96-53876
"A Richard Jackson book"

Every year at Christmas a rich man rides a train through Appalachia and throws gifts to the poor children who are waiting, in order to repay a debt he owes the people who live there

"With restraint and an economy of words, Rylant's emotionally rich story . . . speaks eloquently of gratitude and social responsibility. Soentpiet's handsome, realistic paintings capture the drama, rural landscape, and full range of human emotion." Booklist

This year's garden; pictures by Mary Szilagyi. Bradbury Press 1984 unp il hardcover o.p. paperback available $4.95   E
1. Gardens—Fiction 2. Seasons—Fiction
ISBN 0-689-71122-0 (pa)   LC 84-10974
This book tells "about a family's planning of its summer vegetable garden, the seeding and harvesting, and the enjoyment of the preserved crop through the summer and fall—and then the planning again, as the bare brown garden patch waits, like the family, for next year's garden." Bull Cent Child Books

"Rylant's words are set against Szilagyi's richly colored pictures. Deep hues from a multicolored palette make the visual landscape as fertile as the story. Even city-bred readers will come away with a sense of what it's all about." Booklist

When I was young in the mountains; illustrated by Diane Goode. Dutton 1982 unp il $15.99; pa $6.99   E
1. Appalachian region—Fiction
ISBN 0-525-42525-X; 0-525-44198-0 (pa)
LC 81-5359
A Caldecott Medal honor book, 1983

"Based on the author's memories of an Appalachian childhood, this is a nostalgic piece. . . . There is no story line, but a series of memories, each beginning, 'When I was young in the mountains . . .' as the author reminisces about the busy, peaceful life of an extended family and their community." Bull Cent Child Books

"The people in the story are poor in material things, but rich in family pleasures. The title becomes a pleasing refrain that is used to herald a change in topic. Illustrations and text are placed on a bed of white space, without borders, which makes them look uncrowded and imparts a great feeling of freedom." SLJ

Samuels, Barbara

Duncan & Dolores. Bradbury Press 1986 unp il hardcover o.p. paperback available $4.99   E
1. Cats—Fiction
ISBN 0-689-71294-4 (pa)   LC 85-17119
This is "the story of a small girl's adjustment to a newly-acquired cat. And vice versa. Duncan avoids her noisy roughness; she feels rebuffed and is jealous because the cat clearly prefers her older sister. However, Dolores gets the point, and the longed-for rapport ensues." Bull Cent Child Books

"The cheerful, childlike illustrations are remarkably expressive, clearly showing the rapidly alternating feelings of Duncan and the pleasant, sisterly relationship of sensible Faye and bouncy Dolores. The whole book is a charming illustration of the old aphorism that in getting to know cats, less is more." Horn Book

Another available title about Duncan and Dolores is: Aloha Dolores (2000)

Sandburg, Carl, 1878-1967

The Huckabuck family and how they raised popcorn in Nebraska and quit and came back; pictures by David Small. Farrar, Straus & Giroux 1999 unp il $16   E
1. Farm life—Fiction
ISBN 0-374-33511-7   LC 98-6676
The text was originally published in 1923 by Harcourt, Brace & Company in the book Rootabaga stories

After the popcorn the Huckabucks had raised explodes in a fire and Pony Pony Huckabuck finds a silver buckle inside a squash, the family decides it is time for a change

"Small's watercolors have a translucent, airy quality that suits the fantastical elements of Sandburg's story. . . . Sandburg's language is as bracing as a tonic, and the inherent humor and rhythms of his tale are as invigorating today as when it was first written." Bull Cent Child Books

Sanders, Scott R. (Scott Russell), 1945-

Aurora means dawn; illustrated by Jill Kastner. Bradbury Press 1989 unp il $16; pa $5.99   E
1. Frontier and pioneer life—Fiction 2. Ohio—Fiction
ISBN 0-02-778270-0; 0-689-81907-2 (pa)
LC 88-24127

"Mr. and Mrs. Sheldon, traveling from Connecticut by covered wagon, arrive in Aurora, Ohio in 1800; they have been told that Aurora is a village with homes, a mill, and a store. What they find, using the land-company's map, is a surveyor's post. Trapped by debris from a storm, the family is able to reach their site when settlers from a nearby village help clear the road." Bull Cent Child Books

"The use of detail is engaging, yet it never slows the pace. Sentences are placed so that the action corresponds to that depicted in the luminous, vital, and well-composed watercolor paintings." Horn Book

Warm as wool; by Scott Russell Sanders; illustrated by Helen Cogancherry. Bradbury Press 1992 unp il hardcover o.p. paperback available $5.99   E
1. Frontier and pioneer life—Fiction 2. Ohio—Fiction
ISBN 0-689-82242-1 (pa)   LC 91-34987

Sanders, Scott R. (Scott Russell), 1945-—Continued

When Betsy Ward's family moves to Ohio from Connecticut in 1803, she brings along a sockful of coins to buy sheep so that she can gather wool, spin cloth, and make clothes to keep her children warm

"Cogancherry's watercolors, done in earth tones that reflect natural colors and lighting, convey a sure sense of pioneer life. This is a warm book about the struggle to stay warm, and a strong heroine is captured in both story and pictures." Booklist

Sandin, Joan, 1942-

The long way westward. Harper & Row 1989 63p il hardcover o.p. paperback available $3.95   E

1. Immigration and emigration—Fiction 2. Swedish Americans—Fiction
ISBN 0-06-444198-9 (pa)   LC 89-2024

Also available prior volume The long way to a new land (1981)

"An I can read book"

Relates the experiences of two young brothers and their family, immigrants from Sweden, from their arrival in New York through the journey to their new home in Minnesota

"The text does a nice job of evoking the mix of excitement and apprehension that gripped newcomers to the U.S. Details of the long train ride from New York pace the book and inform readers unobtrusively as the nicely detailed pen-and-wash drawings bring the story to life. A fine bit of historical fiction for beginning readers." Booklist

Saul, Carol P., 1947-

Barn cat; a counting book; illustrated by Mary Azarian. Little, Brown 1998 unp il lib bdg $15.95; pa $5.95   E

1. Cats—Fiction 2. Counting 3. Stories in rhyme
ISBN 0-316-76113-3; 0-316-71140-3 (pa)
      LC 97-7052

Because she's looking for something special, the great barn cat notices but shows no interest in the activities of the animals which can be counted around her

"Azarian's exceedingly handsome woodcuts tether Saul's lyrical counting book to a pastoral setting." Publ Wkly

Say, Allen, 1937-

Allison. Houghton Mifflin 1997 32p il $17   E

1. Interracial adoption—Fiction 2. Japanese Americans—Fiction
ISBN 0-395-85895-X   LC 97-7528

When Allison realizes that she looks more like her Japanese doll than like her parents, she comes to terms with this unwelcomed discovery through the help of a stray cat

"A subtle, sensitive probing of interracial adoption, this exquisitely illustrated story will encourage thoughtful adult-child dialogue on a potentially difficult issue." Publ Wkly

The bicycle man. Parnassus Press 1982 unp il lib bdg $16; pa $5.95   E

1. Cycling—Fiction 2. Japan—Fiction
ISBN 0-395-32254-5 (lib bdg); 0-395-50652-2 (pa)
      LC 82-2980

The amazing tricks two American soldiers do on a borrowed bicycle are a fitting finale for the school sports day festivities in a small village in occupied Japan

"The kindly, openhearted story is beautifully pictured in a profusion of delicate pen-and-ink drawings washed in gentle colors. Meticulously hatched and cross-hatched, they reflect the guileless joy and exuberance of adults and children alike in a book that celebrates human friendship." Horn Book

Emma's rug. Houghton Mifflin 1996 32p il $16.95   E

1. Artists—Fiction 2. Rugs and carpets—Fiction
ISBN 0-395-74294-3   LC 96-14189

"Walter Lorraine books"

"From infancy, Emma has loved her rug. . . . When Emma begins to draw and paint, she amazes everyone. At school, she wins medals for her art, . . . Then disaster strikes: Mother dumps the 'dirty' rug in the washing-machine. All of Emma's quiet explodes in a picture of violent anguish. . . . She gives up, dumps all the art stuff—until one day she glimpses something wild and beautiful on the wall of her room. . . . She starts to draw again." Booklist

Say's "deftly understated tale leaves ample room for readers' own interpretations. Yet it is his superb visual images, which have the semblance of faultlessly composed photographs, that make the most indelible mark here. . . . An impressive creation, to be appreciated on many levels." Publ Wkly

Grandfather's journey; written and illustrated by Allen Say. Houghton Mifflin 1993 32p il $16.95   E

1. Japanese Americans—Fiction 2. Grandfathers—Fiction 3. Voyages and travels—Fiction 4. Japan—Fiction
ISBN 0-395-57035-2   LC 93-18836

Awarded the Caldecott Medal, 1994

A Japanese American man recounts his grandfather's journey to America which he later also undertakes, and the feelings of being torn by a love for two different countries

"The brief text is simple and unaffected, but the emotions expressed are deeply complex. The paintings are astonishingly still, like the captured moments found in a family photo album. Each translucent watercolor is suffused with light. . . . Flawless in his execution, Say has chronicled three generations of a family whose hearts have been divided between two nations." SLJ

The lost lake. Houghton Mifflin 1989 32p il $16; pa $6.95   E

1. Father-son relationship—Fiction 2. Camping—Fiction
ISBN 0-395-50933-5; 0-395-63036-3 (pa)
      LC 89-11026

"Luke is disappointed in his relationship with his taciturn, work-absorbed father, with whom he is spending the summer. Early one morning his father awakens him with exciting news of a camping trip: they are going to

Say, Allen, 1937—*Continued*

find the Lost Lake, a very special and secret place Luke's father used to visit with his own father. But their arduous hike brings them to a lake that has since been discovered by many people; they agree to blaze a new trail and find their own private place." Horn Book

"Using colors as crisp and clean as the outdoors, Say effectively alternates between scenes where father and son are the focus and those where the landscape predominates. Both in story and art, a substantial piece." Booklist

Tea with milk. Houghton Mifflin 1999 32p il $17   E
1. Japanese Americans—Fiction 2. Japan—Fiction
ISBN 0-395-90495-1   LC 98-11667
"Walter Lorraine books"

After growing up near San Francisco, Masako (or May) returns with her parents to their native Japan, but she feels foreign and out of place until she finds a job in Osaka and marries a man with a similarly mixed background

"Say's masterfully executed watercolors tell as much of this story . . . as his eloquent prose." Publ Wkly

Tree of cranes; written and illustrated by Allen Say. Houghton Mifflin 1991 32p il $17.95   E
1. Christmas—Fiction 2. Mother-son relationship—Fiction 3. Japan—Fiction
ISBN 0-395-52024-X   LC 91-14107

A Japanese boy learns of Christmas when his mother decorates a pine tree with paper cranes

"The quiet, graciously told picture book is a perfect blend of text and art. Fine-lined and handsome, Say's watercolors not only capture fascinating details of the boy's far away home . . . but also depict, with simple grace, the rich and complex bond between mother and child that underlies the story." Booklist

Schachner, Judith Byron

The Grannyman. Dutton Children's Bks. 1999 unp il $15.99   E
1. Cats—Fiction 2. Old age—Fiction
ISBN 0-525-46122-1   LC 98-52964

Simon the cat is so old that most of his parts have stopped working, but just when he is ready to breathe his last breath, his family brings home a new kitten for him to raise

"Schachner's expressive watercolor-and-mixed-media artwork mirrors the affection, humor, and warmth of her finely crafted text." Booklist

Schaefer, Carole Lexa

The squiggle; illustrated by Pierr Morgan. Crown 1996 unp il $17; lib bdg $18.99; pa $6.99   E
ISBN 0-517-70047-6; 0-517-70048-4 (lib bdg); 0-517-88579-4 (pa)   LC 95-2299

As she walks to the park with her school class, a young Chinese girl finds a piece of string which her imagination turns into a dragon's tail, an acrobat, fireworks, a storm cloud, and more

"A distinctly Asian look is conveyed through the ver-

tical calligraphy of the title on the cover and through the clothing and facial expressions of the chunky children in the gouache-and-marker illustrations. . . . The very easy text effectively uses onomatopoeia to capture the crackle of fireworks and the stillness of a deep pool." SLJ

Schaefer, Lola M., 1950-

This is the sunflower; pictures by Donald Crews. Greenwillow Bks. 2000 unp $15.95; lib bdg $15.89   E
1. Sunflowers—Fiction 2. Birds—Fiction 3. Stories in rhyme
ISBN 0-688-16413-7; 0-688-16414-5 (lib bdg)   LC 98-46682

A cumulative verse describing how a sunflower in a garden blossoms and, with the help of the birds, spreads its seeds to create an entire patch of sunflowers

"A beautiful, noteworthy title. The velvety watercolors are clearly defined and saturated with color. . . . This is perfect for story hours; also recommend it to budding ornithologists, who will appreciate the illustrated key identifying the birds pictured in the text." Booklist

Scheer, Julian

Rain makes applesauce; by Julian Scheer & Marvin Bileck. Holiday House 1964 unp il $16.95   E
ISBN 0-8234-0091-3

A Caldecott Medal honor book, 1965

"A book of original nonsense, illustrated with intricate drawings. Small children live the refrains, 'Rain makes applesauce' and 'You're just talking silly talk,' and enjoy the fantastic details in the pictures." Hodges. Books for Elem Sch Libr

Schertle, Alice, 1941-

Down the road; illustrated by E.B. Lewis. Browndeer Press 1995 unp il $16; pa $6   E
1. Eggs—Fiction 2. Country life—Fiction
ISBN 0-15-276622-7; 0-15-202471-9 (pa)   LC 94-9901

Hetty "makes her first solo jaunt to Mr. Birdie's store for fresh eggs, determined to prove how responsible she is. On the way home, temptation beckons in the guise of an apple tree; Hetty breaks the eggs while picking fruit, then hides among the branches in shame. Papa and Mama take her failure better than she expects and, instead of scolding, join her in the tree and share apple pie for breakfast." Bull Cent Child Books

"The story is remarkable for its evocative imagery, and the loving interchange between the characters set a charming tone. The words are perfectly complemented by Lewis' dazzling, impressionistic watercolors." Booklist

Schick, Eleanor, 1942-

Mama. Marshall Cavendish 2000 unp il $15.95   E
1. Mothers—Fiction 2. Death—Fiction
ISBN 0-7614-5060-2   LC 99-16373

A girl remembers special moments with Mama and starts to feel better after grieving over her death

Schick, Eleanor, 1942-—_Continued_

"In keeping with the book's rich tone, Schick's watercolors have a softness broken only by occasional bare branches of the trees. The author offers no glib solutions to loss; rather, she paints an honest portrait of one girl's grief that should resonate with children who have themselves experienced the death of a parent." Booklist

Schnur, Steven

Night lights; pictures by Stacey Schuett. Foster Bks. 2000 unp il $16   **E**
1. Counting 2. Night—Fiction 3. Bedtime—Fiction 4. Stories in rhyme
ISBN 0-374-35522-3   LC 99-22386
Each night before going to bed, Melinda counts the lights, from one seashell on the nursery wall to a million twinkling stars
"This lovely picture book has much to offer. . . . Schuett's beautiful illustrations are exceptionally well executed and appealing. . . . The idea of a youngster thinking about the ever-widening parameters of her world is intriguing and well captured." SLJ

Spring; an alphabet acrostic; illustrated by Leslie Evans. Clarion Bks. 1999 unp il $15   **E**
1. Spring 2. Alphabet
ISBN 0-395-82269-6   LC 98-22704
Describes spring, with its animals, green smells, and renewed outside activities. When read vertically, the first letters of the lines of text spell related words arranged alphabetically, from "April" to "zenith"
"The evocative free verse captures the season's promise, as do the colorful block-print illustrations." Horn Book Guide

Spring thaw; illustrated by Stacey Schuett. Viking 2000 unp il $15.99   **E**
1. Spring—Fiction 2. Farm life—Fiction
ISBN 0-670-87961-4   LC 99-22543
"Schnur describes a rural landscape emerging from winter. From sun up till sun down on the small farm, the first signs of spring appear: a warm wind in the trees, the creaking of the old house, dripping icicles, and overflowing sap buckets. The soft edges and thick brush strokes of Schuett's paintings aptly capture the turning of the season." Horn Book Guide

The tie man's miracle; a Chanukah tale; illustrated by Stephen T. Johnson. Morrow Junior Bks. 1995 unp il $16   **E**
1. Hanukkah—Fiction 2. Jews—Fiction
ISBN 0-688-13463-7   LC 94-39854
On the last night of Chanukah, after hearing how an old man lost his family in the Holocaust, a young boy makes a wish that is carried to God as the menorah candles burn down
"This touching tale links remembrance of the Holocaust with the Jewish celebration of Hanukkah in a sensitive and accessible way. The watercolor illustrations are especially moving." Horn Book

Schoenherr, John, 1935-

Rebel. Philomel Bks. 1995 unp il $15.95; pa $5.99   **E**
1. Geese—Fiction
ISBN 0-399-22727-X; 0-698-11619-4 (pa)
LC 94-15568
"The illustrations portray an individualistic gosling going his own way, while the narrative tells the parents' story of protecting their young from predators. Although almost abandoned, Rebel is reunited with his family as they prepare to join other geese at the brooding ground." Horn Book Guide
"The action in the artwork creates a lively counterpoint to the low-key text, setting up a tension that gives resonance to the story. The artwork offers views of the pond ecosystem lit by sun and moon and suffused with subtle colors." Booklist

Schotter, Roni

Captain Snap and the children of Vinegar Lane; illustrations by Marcia Sewall. Orchard Bks. 1989 unp il $14.95; pa $5.95   **E**
1. Friendship—Fiction
ISBN 0-531-05797-6; 0-531-07038-7 (pa)
LC 88-22489
The children of Vinegar Lane discover that bad-tempered old Captain Snap has a wonderful secret
"The twitchy, wiggly children of Vinegar Lane scamper through Sewall's woodcutesque paintings in this crackling good story of pint-sized neighbors who melt the Captain's hard heart with a couple of good deeds and a whole lot of high spirits." SLJ

Nothing ever happens on 90th Street; illustrated by Kyrsten Brooker. Orchard Bks. 1996 unp il $16.95; lib bdg $17.99; pa $5.95   **E**
1. Authorship—Fiction 2. New York (N.Y.)—Fiction
ISBN 0-531-09536-3; 0-531-08886-3 (lib bdg); 0-531-07136-7 (pa)   LC 96-4000
"A Melanie Kroupa book"
When Eva sits on her stoop in New York City trying to complete a school assignment by writing about what happens in her neighborhood, she gets a great deal of advice and action
"Brooker incorporates pieces of newspaper, scraps of patterned cloth, and small objects into her paintings. . . . She poses her characters in appropriately theatrical stances; their wide gestures and exaggerated expressions suit this lively, fluently told tale perfectly." SLJ

Schroeder, Alan, 1961-

Minty: a story of young Harriet Tubman; pictures by Jerry Pinkney. Dial Bks. for Young Readers 1996 unp il $16.99; lib bdg $16.89   **E**
1. Tubman, Harriet, 1815?-1913—Fiction 2. Slavery—Fiction
ISBN 0-8037-1888-8; 0-8037-1889-6 (lib bdg)
LC 95-23499
Coretta Scott King Award for illustration, 1997
"Young Araminta, or 'Minty,' who will later in life be known as Harriet Tubman, proves too clumsy and defiant to be a house slave and is sent by Mistress Brodas to work in the fields. . . . The child purposely frees the

Schroeder, Alan, 1961-—*Continued*
muskrats from the traps she has been ordered to empty and is cruelly whipped and threatened to be sold 'downriver.' Certain that his headstrong daughter will one day attempt to run away, Minty's father begins to instruct her in outdoor survival and navigation." Bull Cent Child Books

Pinkney's "paintings, done in pencil, colored-pencils, and watercolor, use light and shadow to great effect. . . . This is a dramatic story that will hold listeners' interest and may lead them to biographical material." SLJ

Ragtime Tumpie; paintings by Bernie Fuchs. Little, Brown 1989 unp il hardcover o.p. paperback available $5.95   E
1. Baker, Josephine, 1906-1975—Fiction 2. African Americans—Fiction 3. Dance—Fiction
ISBN 0-316-77504-5 (pa)   LC 87-37221
"Joy Street books"
A fictionalized account of "the childhood of Josephine Baker, the St. Louis girl who became the toast of Paris and, for many, epitomized the Jazz Age." Bull Cent Child Books
"This book evokes the magic of ragtime St. Louis, its down-and-out places and its joys. Both the prose and paintings are bursts of color." N Y Times Book Rev

Satchmo's blues; illustrated by Floyd Cooper. Doubleday Bks. for Young Readers 1996 unp il $15.95; pa $6.99   E
1. Armstrong, Louis, 1900-1971—Fiction 2. African American musicians—Fiction 3. New Orleans (La.)—Fiction
ISBN 0-385-32046-9; 0-440-41472-5 (pa)
                                       LC 93-41082
A fictional recreation of the youth of trumpeter Louis Armstrong in New Orleans
"This book is full of gorgeous writing, accompanied by Cooper's atmospheric paintings." SLJ

Smoky Mountain Rose; an Appalachian Cinderella; pictures by Brad Sneed. Dial Bks. for Young Readers 1997 unp il $16.99; pa $5.99
                                                   E
1. Fairy tales 2. Appalachian region—Fiction
ISBN 0-8037-1733-4; 0-14-056673-2 (pa)
                                       LC 92-1250
"Schroeder offers his own variant of the Cinderella story, using enough dialect to make an enjoyable read-aloud. In his version, a hog plays the role of the fairy godmother, and Rose falls in love not with a prince, but with a wealthy man who 'made his fortune in sowbellies and grits.' The dynamic artwork features elongated figures in pleasing compositions." Horn Book Guide

Schuch, Steve
A symphony of whales; illustrated by Peter Sylvada. Harcourt Brace & Co. 1999 unp il $16
                                                   E
1. Whales—Fiction 2. Music—Fiction 3. Siberia (Russia)—Fiction
ISBN 0-15-201670-8   LC 98-17248
Young Glashka's dream of the singing of whales, accompanied by a special kind of music, leads to the res-

cue of thousands of whales stranded in a freezing Siberian bay
"This is a quiet, powerful story, beautifully extended by Sylvada's paintings of ghostly whale shapes and glowing, fin-shaped skies." Booklist

Schumaker, Ward
In my garden; a counting book. Chronicle Bks. 2000 unp il $13.95   E
1. Gardens—Fiction 2. Counting
ISBN 0-8118-2689-9   LC 99-6880
In this garden the reader learns to count from one watering can to ten snails, from twenty weepy onions to fifty cherry pies and even to 233 peas
"The whimsical cartoons with soft, flat colors and outlined in black were rendered in Adobe Photoshop. The objects to be counted all have faces . . . and the 7 birds are singing from sheet music by Bach. This is a clever, enjoyable addition to the rich variety of counting books available." SLJ

Schur, Maxine, 1948-
The peddler's gift; [by] Maxine Rose Schur; pictures by Kimberly Bulcken Root. Dial Bks. for Young Readers 1999 unp il $15.99   E
1. Peddlers and peddling—Fiction 2. Jews—Russia—Fiction
ISBN 0-8037-1978-7   LC 98-36171
"Originally published in different form as Shnook the peddler by Dillon Press Inc." Verso of title page
A young boy in turn-of-the-century rural Russia learns that appearances are often deceiving after he steals and then tries to return a dreidel to the traveling peddler Shnook
"The fine storytelling, rhythmic and controlled, is complemented by well-composed illustrations noteworthy for their willowy line and subdued palette." Horn Book Guide

Schwartz, Amy, 1954-
Annabelle Swift, kindergartner; story and pictures by Amy Schwartz. Orchard Bks. 1988 unp il hardcover o.p. paperback available $6.95   E
1. School stories 2. Sisters—Fiction
ISBN 0-531-07027-1 (pa)   LC 87-15403
"Annabelle is starting school and her older sister Lucy prepares Annabelle for kindergarten, but some of her training backfires. In spite of some embarrassment in the classroom, Annabelle makes a hit with her fellow classmates." Child Book Rev Serv
"In illustrations that carefully evoke the naive and awkward drawings of children, Schwartz captures the essence of childhood. . . . Line and wash illustrations in crayon-bright colors reveal a classroom that is cheerful, warm, and inviting." SLJ

Bea and Mr. Jones; story and pictures by Amy Schwartz. Bradbury Press 1982 unp il hardcover o.p. paperback available $4.99   E
1. Fathers—Fiction 2. School stories 3. Business—Fiction
ISBN 0-689-71796-2 (pa)   LC 81-18031

Schwartz, Amy, 1954-—*Continued*

"Bea is tired of kindergarten, and Mr. Jones is fed up with being chained to a desk all day. So the two decide to change places, a pleasure for both." Booklist

"A nice treatment of role reversal, this junior tall tale is told with simplicity and humor, and is illustrated with soft pencil drawings that have pudgy people, nice textural quality, and some funny details, such as Mr. Jones, lying on the floor and using blocks to spell out 'antidisestablishmentarianism.'" Bull Cent Child Books

Oma and Bobo; story and pictures by Amy Schwartz. Bradbury Press 1987 unp il hardcover o.p. paperback available $5.99   E

1. Dogs—Fiction 2. Grandmothers—Fiction
ISBN 0-689-82115-8 (pa)   LC 86-10665

"When Alice is told she can have a dog for her birthday, she hurries down to the pound and picks out an old black-and-white mutt she names Bobo. Oma, Alice's grandmother, is not keen on the idea of a dog." Booklist

"This is a fresh portrait of an unlikely friendship that allows room for both humor and dignity. Schwartz's eccentric illustrations have a 50's mood colored by an 80's sensibility, and are filled with witty details and patterns . . . exactly suiting the dry tone of the text." Bull Cent Child Books

A teeny, tiny baby. Orchard Bks. 1994 unp il $16.95; lib bdg $17.99; pa $6.95   E

1. Infants—Fiction 2. City and town life—Fiction
ISBN 0-531-06818-8; 0-531-08668-2 (lib bdg); 0-531-07177-4 (pa)   LC 93-4876

"A Richard Jackson book"

"'I'm a teeny tiny baby and I know how to get anything I want.' So begins an infant's hilarious narration of his many needs and pleasures. . . . Everyone who has had a baby in the family will respond to the gentle humor in Schwartz's gouache paintings." SLJ

Schwartz, David M., 1951-

How much is a million? pictures by Steven Kellogg. Lothrop, Lee & Shepard Bks. 1985 unp il $17; lib bdg $16.89; pa $5.95   E

1. Million (The number) 2. Billion (The number) 3. Trillion (The number)
ISBN 0-688-04049-7; 0-688-04050-0 (lib bdg); 0-688-09933-5 (pa)   LC 84-5736

Also available paperback Big edition

"Marvelosissimo the Mathematical Magician leads the reader through Steven Kellogg's scenes of fantasy to express the concepts of a million, a billion and a trillion. The text is all printed in capital letters to point out the expanding scenes portrayed in the fabulous illustrations. The idea is to make possible to children the awesome concept of large numbers. It is a delightful fantasy as a picture book, but it is even more compelling as a first reader." Okla State Dept of Educ

If you made a million; pictures by Steven Kellogg. Lothrop, Lee & Shepard Bks. 1989 unp il $17; lib bdg $16.89; pa $5.95   E

1. Personal finance
ISBN 0-688-07017-5; 0-688-07018-3 (lib bdg); 0-688-13634-6 (pa)   LC 88-12819

The author examines "how one earns money, how checks are used instead of cash, why banks pay interest on money deposited, [and] why interest is charged on loans." Booklist

"The concepts of banks and banking . . . are all explained with absurd and humorous examples involving Ferris wheels, ogres, and rhinoceroses. . . . The best advice of all is 'Enjoying your work is more important than money.' Steven Kellogg's splendidly funny illustrations contain a troupe of two cats, one dog, numerous kids, a unicorn, and the wonderful magician Marvelosissimo." Horn Book

Schwartz, Henry

Albert goes Hollywood; story by Henry Schwartz; pictures by Amy Schwartz. Orchard Bks. 1992 unp il $15.95; lib bdg $16.99   E

1. Dinosaurs—Fiction 2. Motion pictures—Fiction
ISBN 0-531-05980-4; 0-531-08580-5 (lib bdg)   LC 91-18495

"A Richard Jackson book"

Liz gets to keep her pet dinosaur Albert when she finds him a job in the movies

"Amy Schwartz's fresh and funny illustrations are a perfect complement for her father's wry and understated text." SLJ

Another available title about Liz and Albert is:
How I captured a dinosaur (1989)

Scieszka, Jon, 1954-

The Frog Prince continued; story by Jon Scieszka; paintings by Steve Johnson. Viking 1991 unp il $14.95; pa $6.99   E

1. Fairy tales 2. Frogs—Fiction
ISBN 0-670-83421-1; 0-14-054285-X (pa)   LC 90-26537

After the frog turns into a prince, he and the Princess do not live happily ever after and the Prince decides to look for a witch to help him turn back into a frog

"The dialogue is witty; the plot, as logical as it is offbeat. Steve Johnson's paintings, executed in a rich and somber palette, are like stage settings; his depiction of the various characters is inspired." Horn Book

Math curse; illustrated by Lane Smith. Viking 1995 unp il $16.99   E

1. Mathematics—Fiction
ISBN 0-670-86194-4   LC 95-12341

When the teacher tells her class that they can think of almost everything as a math problem, one student acquires a math anxiety which becomes a real curse

"Bold in design and often bizarre in expression, Smith's paintings clearly express the child's feelings of bemusement, frustration, and panic as well as her eventual joy when she overcomes the math curse. . . . A child-centered, witty picture book." Booklist

Squids will be squids; fresh morals, beastly fables; by Jon Scieszka & Lane Smith; designed by Molly Leach. Viking 1998 unp il $17.99   E

1. Fables
ISBN 0-670-88135-X   LC 98-5710

Scieszka, Jon, 1954——*Continued*

Contemporary fables with tongue-in-cheek morals address such topics as homework, curfews, and television commercials

"Smith ardently keeps pace with Scieszka's leaps of fancy, lending credence to a talking piece of toast, a walrus with a phone and a spiny, spiteful blowfish. . . . Beneath this duo's playful eccentricity readers will discover some powerful insights into human nature." Publ Wkly

The Stinky Cheese Man and other fairly stupid tales; [by Jon Scieszka & Lane Smith] Viking 1992 unp il $16.99　　　　E

ISBN 0-670-84487-X　　　　　LC 91-48194

A Caldecott Medal honor book, 1993

"Cinderumpelstiltskin and The Really Ugly Duckling are among the tales that Jack the narrator tries to present. But the Dedication is upside down; the Table of Contents is late; and Little Red Running Shorts and the wolf quit." Publisher's note

"The picture-book set will probably recognize the stories enough to know that what's going on isn't what's 'supposed' to happen. But *The Stinky Cheese Man* isn't a book for little ones. It will take older children (that's teens along with 10s) to follow the disordered story lines and appreciate the narrative's dry wit, wordplay, and wacky, sophomoric jokes. . . . Smith's New Wave art is an intricate part of the whole, extending as well as reinforcing the narrative; the pictures are every bit as comically insolent and deliberately clever as the words." Booklist

The true story of the 3 little pigs; by A. Wolf; as told to Jon Scieszka; illustrated by Lane Smith. Viking 1999 unp il $16.99　　　　E

1. Wolves—Fiction 2. Pigs—Fiction

ISBN 0-670-88844-3　　　　　LC 00-266873

A reissue of the title first published 1989

The wolf gives his own outlandish version of what really happened when he tangled with the three little pigs

"This tenth anniversary edition . . . includes an introduction by the imprisoned wolf himself, still claiming his innocence and professing to be a model prisoner (with no knowledge of how that saw got in the cake his granny sent him)." Horn Book Guide

Scott, Ann Herbert, 1926-

Brave as a mountain lion; illustrated by Glo Coalson. Clarion Bks. 1996 31p il $14.95　　　E

1. School stories 2. Shoshoni Indians—Fiction

ISBN 0-395-66760-7　　　　　LC 94-42906

Spider is afraid to get up on stage in front of everybody in the school spelling bee, but after listening to his father's advice, decides that he too will try to be as brave as his Shoshoni ancestors

"This story is well shaped and rhythmically told. Coalson's subdued watercolor and pastel illustrations depict the wintry landscapes and interiors with sensitivity and detail." SLJ

Hi; illustrated by Glo Coalson. Philomel Bks. 1994 unp il $15.95　　　　　E

1. Postal service—Fiction

ISBN 0-399-21964-1

　　　　　　　　　　LC 91-42978

"Margarita calls an exuberant 'Hi' to each person in line at the post office, but no one responds. With each failed attempt, the toddler's greeting becomes softer and more hesitant, but when her whispered 'Hi' elicits a big smile and a warm greeting from the 'post-office lady,' Margarita cheerfully calls, 'Bye!' all the way out the door. A perfect meld of a childhood incident with tender and expressive watercolors." Horn Book Guide

On Mother's lap; illustrated by Glo Coalson. Clarion Bks. 1992 32p il $15; pa $6.95　　　E

1. Inuit—Fiction 2. Mother-child relationship—Fiction

ISBN 0-395-58920-7; 0-395-62976-4 (pa)

　　　　　　　　　　LC 91-17765

Also available Board book edition and with Audiobook

A newly illustrated edition of the title first published 1972 by McGraw-Hill

"Sitting on his mother's lap, a young Eskimo boy gathers his belongings until he, some toys, his puppy, and a blanket are all crowded together in the rocking chair. When his baby sister cries, the boy claims there is no room for her, but Mother proves him wrong, and the threesome settle comfortably in the chair. Soft illustrations depict a cozy scene and a loving family." Horn Book

Segal, Lore Groszmann

Tell me a Mitzi; [by] Lore Segal; pictures by Harriet Pincus. Farrar, Straus & Giroux 1970 unp il hardcover o.p. paperback available $5.95　　　E

1. Family life—Fiction

ISBN 0-374-47502-4 (pa)

The author injects an element of fantasy into these three stories of family life, the first of which deals with Mitzi's safari to grandma's and grandpa's house, the second with a confrontation with the common cold, and the third with her brother Jacob's encounter with a Presidential motorcade

"The illustrations, while they do not boast attractive children, are full of vitality and humor, the busy urban neighborhood and homely people having a rueful charm." Sutherland. The Best in Child Books

Seibold, J. Otto

Olive the other reindeer; by J. Otto Seibold and Vivian Walsh. Chronicle Bks. 1997 unp il $12.95

　　　　　　　　　　　　　　　E

1. Reindeer—Fiction 2. Dogs—Fiction 3. Christmas—Fiction 4. Santa Claus—Fiction

ISBN 0-8118-1807-1　　　　　LC 97-9876

Thinking that "all of the other reindeer" she hears people singing about include her, Olive the dog reports to the North Pole to help Santa Claus on Christmas Eve

"Seibold has developed a signature style with computer digitized art, and his playful skewed lines and warm shades of ochre, pimento and olive green are user-friendly." Publ Wkly

Sendak, Maurice

Alligators all around; an alphabet. Harper & Row 1962 unp il lib bdg $15.89; pa $4.95　　　E

1. Alphabet

ISBN 0-06-025530-7 (lib bdg); 0-06-443254-8 (pa)

Sendak, Maurice—*Continued*

Originally published in smaller format as volume one of the "Nutshell library"

An alphabet book of alligators doing dishes, juggling jelly beans, throwing tantrums and wearing wigs, all from A to Z

Chicken soup with rice; a book of months. Harper & Row 1962 30p il lib bdg $15.89; pa $4.95   E

1. Seasons—Fiction 2. Stories in rhyme

ISBN 0-06-025535-8 (lib bdg); 0-06-443253-X (pa)

Also available Big book edition

Originally published in smaller format as volume two of the "Nutshell library"

Pictures and verse illustrate the delight of eating chicken soup with rice in every season of the year

In the night kitchen. 25th anniversary ed. HarperCollins Pubs. 1996 c1970 unp il $16.95; lib bdg $16.89; pa $6.95   E

1. Fantasy fiction

ISBN 0-06-026668-6; 0-06-026669-4 (lib bdg); 0-06-443436-2 (pa)

A Caldecott Medal honor book, 1971

First published 1970

"A small boy falls through the dark, out of his clothes, and into the bright, night kitchen where he is stirred into the cake batter and almost baked, jumps into the bread dough, kneads and shapes it into an airplane, and flies up over the top of the Milky Way to get milk for the bakers." Booklist

"A perfect midnight fantasy. The feelings, smells, sights, and comforting emotions which young children experience are here in lovely dream colors." Brooklyn. Art Books for Child

One was Johnny; a counting book. Harper & Row 1962 unp il lib bdg $15.89; pa $4.95   E

1. Counting

ISBN 0-06-025540-4 (lib bdg); 0-06-443251-3 (pa)

Originally published in smaller format as volume three of the "Nutshell library"

Counting from one to ten and back again to one, Johnny, who starts off alone, acquires too many numbered visitors for his own comfort, until they disappear one by one

Outside over there. Harper & Row 1981 unp il $20; pa $8.95   E

1. Fairy tales 2. Sisters—Fiction

ISBN 0-06-025523-4; 0-06-443185-1 (pa)

LC 79-2682

A Caldecott Medal honor book, 1982

"An Ursula Nordstrom book"

With Papa off to sea and Mama despondent, Ida must go outside over there to rescue her baby sister from goblins who steal her to be a goblin's bride

"A gentle yet powerful story in the romantic tradition. . . . Soft in tones, rich in the use of light and color . . . the pictures are particularly distinctive for the tenderness with which the children's faces are drawn, the classic handling of texture, the imaginative juxtaposition of in-fant faces and the baroque landscape details that might have come from Renaissance paintings." Bull Cent Child Books

Pierre; a cautionary tale in five chapters and a prologue. Harper & Row 1962 48p il lib bdg $15.89; pa $4.95   E

1. Stories in rhyme

ISBN 0-06-025965-5 (lib bdg); 0-06-443252-1 (pa)

Originally published in smaller format as volume four of the "Nutshell library"

A story in verse about a little boy called Pierre who insisted upon saying 'I don't care' until he said it once too often and learned a well needed lesson

The sign on Rosie's door; story and pictures by Maurice Sendak. Harper & Row 1960 46p il $17.95   E

ISBN 0-06-025505-6

The sign on imaginative Rosie's door read, 'If you want to know a secret, knock three times.' The secret was that Rosie was now Alinda. With her friends Kathy, Sol, Pudgy, Dolly, and Lenny, and with the help of the Music Man, Alinda has a Fourth of July celebration. Then Alinda the lady singer leaves as Rosie becomes someone else

Where the wild things are; story and pictures by Maurice Sendak. Harper & Row 1963 unp il $16.95; lib bdg $16.89; pa $6.95   E

1. Fantasy fiction

ISBN 0-06-025492-0; 0-06-025493-9 (lib bdg); 0-06-443178-9 (pa)

Also available Spanish language edition

Awarded the Caldecott Medal, 1964

"A tale of very few words about Max, sent to his room for cavorting around in his wolf suit, who dreamed of going where the wild things are, to rule them and share their rumpus. Then a longing to be 'where someone loved him best of all' swept over him." Book Week

"This vibrant picture book in luminous, understated full color has proved utterly engrossing to children with whom it has been shared. . . . A sincere, preceptive contribution which bears repeated examination." Horn Book

Serfozo, Mary

What's what? a guessing game; illustrated by Keiko Narahashi. Margaret K. McElderry Bks. 1996 unp il $15; pa $5.99   E

1. English language—Synonyms and antonyms

ISBN 0-689-80653-1; 0-689-83322-9 (pa)

LC 95-40098

Illustrations and rhyming text provide examples of what is soft and hard, warm and cold, wet and dry, long and short, and light and dark and describe how a puppy is all these things at once

"Narahashi's splendid watercolors . . . capture all of the joy and sense of wonder of the childhood investigations Serfozo names and celebrates." SLJ

Who said red? illustrated by Keiko Narahashi. Margaret K. McElderry Bks. 1988 unp il $16; pa $5.99   E

1. Color

ISBN 0-689-50455-1; 0-689-71592-7 (pa)

LC 88-9345

Serfozo, Mary—*Continued*

This "picture book about colors also has a storyline as an extra treat for its preschool audience. The jaunty, rhyming text is a conversation between two playmates, a little boy searching for his lost red kite and his older sister." Booklist

This book has "very little text, and the door is wide open to the imagination. For the smallest child, familiar objects can be labeled and identified. Keiko Narahashi's watercolors are misty and delicate, but so accurate when looked at closely that children can identify not only types of leaves but a woodpecker, a monarch butterfly and a tiger lily. In several cases, finding the creatures becomes a hide-and-seek game that playfully builds a child's powers of observation." N Y Times Book Rev

Seuss, Dr.

The 500 hats of Bartholomew Cubbins. Random House 1990 c1938 unp il $14.95 E
1. Hats—Fiction
ISBN 0-394-84484-X LC 88-38412
Also available Spanish language edition
"A Vanguard Press book"
A reissue of the title first published 1938 by Vanguard Press

"A read-aloud story telling what happened to Bartholomew Cubbins when he couldn't take his hat off before the King." Hodges. Books for Elem Sch Libr

"It is a lovely bit of tomfoolery which keeps up the suspense and surprise until the last page, and of the same ingenious and humorous imagination are the author's black and white illustrations in which a red cap and then an infinite number of red caps titillate the eye." N Y Times Book Rev

And to think that I saw it on Mulberry Street. Random House 1989 c1937 unp il $14.95; lib bdg $15.99 E
1. Nonsense verses 2. Stories in rhyme
ISBN 0-394-84494-7; 0-394-94494-1 (lib bdg)
LC 88-38411
"A Vanguard Press book"
A reissue of the title first published 1937 by Vanguard Press

This book tells in rhyme accompanied by pictures how little Marco saw a horse and wagon on Mulberry Street. Then "how that horse became a zebra, then a reindeer, then an elephant, and how the cart turned into a band wagon with a retinue of police to guide it through the traffic on Mulberry Street, only the book can properly explain." Christ Sci Monit

"A fresh, inspiring picture-story book in bright colors. . . . As convincing to a child as to the psychologist in quest of a book with an appeal to the child's imaginations." Horn Book

Bartholomew and the oobleck; written and illustrated by Dr. Seuss. Random House 1949 unp il $14.95 E
ISBN 0-394-80075-3
A Caldecott Medal honor book, 1950
"Bored with the same old kinds of weather, the King of Didd commanded his magicians to stir up something new and different. What they produced was a gooey, gummy green stuff which might have wrecked the kingdom had it not been for Bartholomew Cubbins, the page boy." Booklist

The cat in the hat. Random House 1957 61p il $7.99; lib bdg $11.99 E
1. Cats—Fiction 2. Nonsense verses 3. Stories in rhyme 4. Bilingual books—English-Spanish
ISBN 0-394-80001-X; 0-394-90001-4 (lib bdg)
Also available in a bilingual Spanish-English edition and with Audiobook

A nonsense story in verse illustrated by the author about an unusual cat and his tricks which he displayed for the children one rainy day

Another available title about The cat in the hat is: The cat in the hat comes back! (1958)

Green eggs and ham. Beginner Bks. 1960 62p il $7.99; lib bdg $11.99; pa $7.95 E
1. Food—Fiction 2. Nonsense verses 3. Stories in rhyme
ISBN 0-394-80016-8; 0-394-90016-2 (lib bdg); 0-394-89220-8 (pa)
Also available with Audiobook; Spanish language edition also available

This book is about "Sam-I-Am who wins a determined campaign to make another Seuss character eat a plate of green eggs and ham." Libr J

"The happy theme of refusal-to-eat changing to relish will be doubly enjoyable to the child who finds many common edibles as nauseating as the title repast. The pacing throughout is magnificent, and the opening five pages, on which the focal character introduces himself with a placard: 'I am Sam,' are unsurpassed in the controlled-vocabulary literature." Saturday Rev

Hooray for Diffendoofer Day! [by] Dr. Seuss with some help from Jack Prelutsky & Lane Smith. Knopf 1998 unp il $17; lib bdg $18.99 E
1. School stories 2. Stories in rhyme
ISBN 0-679-89008-4; 0-679-99008-9 (lib bdg)
LC 97-39725
The students of Diffendoofer School celebrate their unusual teachers and curriculum, including Miss Fribble who teaches laughing, Miss Bonkers who teaches frogs to dance, and Mr. Katz who builds robotic rats

"Given an unfinished manuscript (some sketches, snippets of verse, and jottings of names—but no plot) retrieved after Seuss's death, Prelutsky and Smith have brought this fragment to fruition in a style that does credit to all three artists." Horn Book Guide

Horton hatches the egg. Random House 1940 unp il $14.95; lib bdg $15.99 E
1. Elephants—Fiction 2. Nonsense verses 3. Stories in rhyme
ISBN 0-394-80077-X; 0-394-90077-4 (lib bdg)
"Horton, the elephant, is faithful one hundred percent as he carries out his promise to watch a bird's egg while she takes a rest. Hilarious illustrations and a surprise ending." Adventuring with Books. 2d edition

Horton hears a Who! Random House 1954 unp il $14.95; lib bdg $16.99 E
1. Elephants—Fiction 2. Nonsense verses 3. Stories in rhyme
ISBN 0-394-80078-8; 0-394-90078-2 (lib bdg)

Seuss, Dr.—*Continued*

"Although considered the biggest blame fool in the Jungle of Nool, the faithful and kindhearted elephant of 'Horton hatches the egg' believing that a person's a person no matter how small, stanchly defends the Whos, too-small-to-be-seen inhabitants of Whoville, a town which exists on a dust speck." Booklist

"The verses are full of the usual lively, informal language and amazing rhymes that have delighted such a world-wide audience in the good 'doctor's' other books." N Y Her Trib Books

How the Grinch stole Christmas. Random House 1957 unp il $14   E
1. Christmas—Fiction 2. Nonsense verses 3. Stories in rhyme
ISBN 0-394-80079-6

Also available Audiobook version; Spanish language edition also available

"The Grinch lived on a mountain where it was able to ignore the people of the valley except at Christmas time when it had to endure the sound of their singing. One year it decided to steal all the presents so there would be no Christmas, but much to its amazement discovered that people did not need presents to enjoy Christmas. It thereupon reformed, returned the presents and joined in the festivities." Bull Cent Child Books

"The verse is as lively and the pages are as bright and colorful as anyone could wish." Saturday Rev

If I ran the circus. Random House 1956 unp il $14.95   E
1. Circus—Fiction 2. Nonsense verses 3. Stories in rhyme
ISBN 0-394-80080-X

The author-illustrator "presents the fabulous Circus McGurkus with its highly imaginative young owner, Morris McGurk and its intrepid performer, Sneelock, behind whose store the circus is to be housed. There are the expected number of strange creatures with nonsensical names, but the real humor lies in the situations, and especially those involving Mr. Sneelock. There is fun for the entire family here." Bull Cent Child Books

If I ran the zoo. Random House 1950 unp il $14.95; lib bdg $16.99   E
1. Zoos—Fiction 2. Nonsense verses 3. Stories in rhyme
ISBN 0-394-80081-8; 0-394-90081-2 (lib bdg)

A Caldecott Medal honor book, 1951

"Assembled here are the rare and wonderful creatures which young Gerald McGrew collects from far and unusual places for the 'gol-darndest zoo on the face of the earth." Booklist

"As you turn the pages, the imaginings get wilder and funnier, the rhymes more hilarious. There will be no age limits for this book, because families will be forced to share rereading and quotation, for a long long time." NY Her Trib Books

McElligot's pool; written and illustrated by Dr. Seuss. Random House 1947 unp il $14.95   E
1. Fishing—Fiction 2. Nonsense verses 3. Stories in rhyme
ISBN 0-394-80083-4

A Caldecott Medal honor book, 1948

"In spite of warnings that there are no fish in McElligot's Pool, a boy continues to fish and to imagine the rare and wonderful denizens of the deep which he just 'might' catch." Hodges. Books for Elem Sch Libr

"Fine color surrounding a host of strange creatures enlivens this amazing fish story for all ages." Horn Book

Oh, the places you'll go! Random House 1990 unp il $17   E
1. Stories in rhyme
ISBN 0-679-80527-3   LC 89-36892

Also available Spanish language edition

Advice in rhyme for proceeding in life; weathering fear, loneliness, and confusion; and being in charge of your actions

"The combination of the lively text and wacky, offbeat pictures will delight both children and their parents." Child Book Rev Serv

Seymour, Tres

Hunting the white cow; story by Tres Seymour; pictures by Wendy Anderson Halperin. Orchard Bks. 1993 unp il $16.95; lib bdg $17.99; pa $6.95   E
1. Cattle—Fiction 2. Farm life—Fiction
ISBN 0-531-05496-9; 0-531-08646-1 (lib bdg); 0-531-07085-9 (pa)   LC 92-43757

"A Richard Jackson book"

A child watches as more and more people join in the attempts to catch the family cow that has gotten loose, each remarking on how special the cow is

"Wendy Halperin's soft colored-pencil drawings of fields and woods that drift far back into the distant hills add to the mythic aura. A unique and imaginative book." Horn Book

Shannon, David, 1959-

A bad case of stripes. Blue Sky Press (NY) 1998 unp il $15.95   E
ISBN 0-590-92997-6   LC 96-54643

In order to ensure her popularity, Camilla Cream always does what is expected, until the day arrives when she no longer recognizes herself

"Shannon's exaggerated, surreal, full-color illustrations take advantage of shadow, light, and shifting perspective to show the girl's plight. . . . This very funny tale speaks to the challenge many kids face in choosing to act independently." SLJ

No, David! Blue Sky Press (NY) 1998 unp il $14.95   E
ISBN 0-590-93002-8   LC 97-35125

Also available Spanish language edition

A Caldecott Medal honor book, 1999

"All little David hears from his mother as he writes on the wall, runs naked down the road, lets water pour over the side of the tub, sticks his finger far, far up his nose, and the like is 'No, David!.'" Booklist

"The vigorous and wacky full-color acrylic paintings portray a lively and imaginative boy whose stick-figure body conveys every nuance of anger, exuberance, defiance, and best of all, the reassurance of his mother's love." SLJ

Another available title about David is:
David goes to school (1999)

Shannon, George, 1952-

Dance away! illustrated by Jose Aruego and Ariane Dewey. Greenwillow Bks. 1982 unp il hardcover o.p. paperback available $4.95   E
1. Rabbits—Fiction 2. Foxes—Fiction 3. Dance—Fiction
ISBN 0-688-10483-5 (pa)   LC 81-6391
"One day Rabbit discovers his friends in the paws of a hungry fox but through his dance is able to outwit the rascal and save them all." Booklist
"The synthesis of well-defined, identifiable characters with the text is irresistible. The brevity of the plot, the perceivable conflict, and the humor of the illustrations suggest a special appeal to preschoolers." Horn Book

Lizard's home; illustrated by Jose Aruego and Ariane Dewey. Greenwillow Bks. 1999 unp il $16; lib bdg $15.93   E
1. Lizards—Fiction 2. Snakes—Fiction
ISBN 0-688-16002-6; 0-688-16003-4 (lib bdg)   LC 98-41055
Companion volume to Lizard's song (1981)
When Snake starts sleeping on the rock where Lizard lives, Lizard must figure out how to get his home back
"Shannon's bouncy text is echoed in Aruego and Dewey's ebullient watercolors of flower-filled landscapes and colorful critters." SLJ

Tomorrow's alphabet; pictures by Donald Crews. Greenwillow Bks. 1996 unp il $16; pa $5.95   E
1. Alphabet
ISBN 0-688-13504-8; 0-688-16424-2 (pa)   LC 94-19484
"In 26 double-page spreads, the letters of the alphabet are used to demonstrate where things come from. 'A is for seed' is followed on the next page with 'tomorrow's APPLE.' 'D is for puppy—tomorrow's DOG.'. . . All of the combinations are clever, well chosen, and well within youngsters' experience. . . . Each two-page spread offers brightly colored, large and realistic depictions of the objects named." SLJ

Sharmat, Marjorie Weinman, 1928-

Gila monsters meet you at the airport; pictures by Byron Barton. Macmillan 1980 unp il $16.95; pa $4.95   E
1. Moving—Fiction 2. West (U.S.)—Fiction
ISBN 0-02-782450-0; 0-689-71383-5 (pa)   LC 80-12264
A New York City boy's preconceived ideas of life in the West make him very apprehensive about the family's move there
"The exaggeration is amusing, the style yeasty, with a nice final touch; the illustrations are comic and awkward, but add little that's not inherent in the story." Bull Cent Child Books

Mitchell is moving; pictures by Jose Aruego & Ariane Dewey. Macmillan 1978 47p il hardcover o.p. paperback available $3.99   E
1. Dinosaurs—Fiction 2. Friendship—Fiction 3. Moving—Fiction
ISBN 0-02-782410-1; 0-689-80876-3 (pa)
Also available with Audiobook

"Ready-to-read"
"Mitchell is a dinosaur who decides to move, despite the efforts of Margo, his neighbor and best friend. The three-color art is simple, breezy, and right on target." Horn Book Guide

Nate the Great; illustrated by Marc Simont. Coward, McCann & Geoghegan 1972 60p il o.p.; Dell paperback available $4.50   E
1. Mystery fiction
ISBN 0-440-46126-X (pa)
"A Break-of-day book"
Nate the Great, a junior detective who has found missing balloons, books, slippers, chickens and even a goldfish, is now in search of a painting of a dog by Annie, the girl down the street
"The illustrations capture the exaggerated, tongue-in-cheek humor of the story." Booklist
Other available titles about Nate the Great are:
Nate the Great and me: the case of the fleeing fang (1998)
Nate the Great and the boring beach bag (1987)
Nate the Great and the crunchy Christmas (1996)
Nate the Great and the fishy prize (1985)
Nate the Great and the Halloween hunt (1989)
Nate the Great and the lost list (1975)
Nate the Great and the missing key (1981)
Nate the Great and the monster mess (1999)
Nate the Great and the mushy valentine (1994)
Nate the Great and the musical note (1990)
Nate the Great and the phony clue (1977)
Nate the Great and the pillowcase (1993)
Nate the Great and the snowy trail (1982)
Nate the Great and the sticky case (1978)
Nate the Great and the stolen base (1992)
Nate the Great and the tardy tortoise (1995)
Nate the Great goes down in the dumps (1989)
Nate the Great goes undercover (1974)
Nate the Great, San Francisco detective (2000)
Nate the Great saves the King of Sweden (1997)
Nate the Great stalks stupidweed (1986)

Sharmat, Mitchell, 1927-

Gregory, the terrible eater; illustrated by Jose Aruego and Ariane Dewey. Four Winds Press 1985 c1980 unp il $16   E
1. Goats—Fiction 2. Diet—Fiction
ISBN 0-02-782250-8   LC 85-29290
Also available in paperback from Scholastic
A reissue of the title first published 1980
"Gregory is not your average goat. In fact, he's the original goat gourmet, abandoning bottle caps in favor of bananas and trading last year's boots for bread and butter." SLJ
"Aruego and Dewey's illustrations are highly amusing, thanks to their goats' dot-eyed facial expressions. . . . There is energy in the pictures; they are beguiling and help to carry the humor." Booklist

Shaw, Charles, 1892-1974

It looked like spilt milk. Harper & Row 1947 unp il $14.95; lib bdg $14.89; pa $5.95   E
ISBN 0-06-025566-8; 0-06-025565-X (lib bdg); 0-06-443159-2 (pa)
Also available Board book edition and Big book edition

Shaw, Charles, 1892-1974—*Continued*

White silhouettes on a blue background with simple captions: "sometimes it looked like a tree," "Sometimes it looked like a bird," etc. lead to a surprise ending "sometimes it looked like split milk, but what it was was—"

"What one thing could look like all of these? On the last page you are told, and I could no more tell you now than I could spoil an adult mystery by a review that gives away its solution." N Y Her Trib Books

Shaw, Nancy

Sheep in a jeep; illustrated by Margot Apple. Houghton Mifflin 1986 32p il lib bdg $14; pa $4.95   **E**
1. Sheep—Fiction 2. Stories in rhyme
ISBN 0-395-41105-X (lib bdg); 0-395-47030-7 (pa)
LC 86-3101
Also available Board book edition and with Audiobook

"When five sheep pile into one little jeep, there is trouble . . . [as] the poor woolly travelers push, shove, and attempt to drive their way from one calamity to another." Horn Book

"Shaw demonstrates a promising capacity for creating nonsense rhymes. . . . Veteran illustrator Apple's whimsical portraits of the sheep bring the story to life. Pleasing and lighthearted, this has much appeal for young readers." Publ Wkly
Other available titles about the sheep are:
Sheep in a shop (1991)
Sheep on a ship (1989)
Sheep out to eat (1992)
Sheep take a hike (1994)
Sheep trick or treat (1997)

Shelby, Anne

Homeplace; illustrations by Wendy Anderson Halperin. Orchard Bks. 1995 unp il $16.95; lib bdg $17.99; pa $6.95   **E**
1. Farm life—Fiction 2. Family life—Fiction
ISBN 0-531-06882-X; 0-531-08732-8 (lib bdg); 0-531-07178-2 (pa)   LC 94-24856
"A Richard Jackson book"
"A grandmother is able to trace her family back to 1810 when her homestead was built by her great-great-great-grandpa. She shares this legacy with her granddaughter as she describes the way each generation lived." Child Book Rev Serv

"The text is brief, but poetic—a fitting accompaniment to the rhythm of life presented in the earth-toned watercolors." SLJ

Shetterly, Susan Hand, 1942-

Shelterwood; illustrated by Rebecca Haley McCall. Tilbury House 1999 unp il $16.95   **E**
1. Trees—Fiction 2. Forests and forestry—Fiction 3. Grandfathers—Fiction
ISBN 0-88448-210-3   LC 99-12470
While staying with her grandfather in his house in the woods, Sophie learns about the different kinds of trees and enjoys the beauties of the natural world

"Matching the quiet simplicity of the words are

McCall's oil paint illustrations. Painted with a soft, impressionistic quality, they evoke not only the changing light and moods of the woods, but also the feel of distant and cherished memories. . . . A striking and effective natural history." Booklist

Shields, Carol Diggory

Martian rock; illustrated by Scott Nash. Candlewick Press 2000 unp il $15.99   **E**
1. Life on other planets—Fiction 2. Planets—Fiction 3. Penguins—Fiction 4. Stories in rhyme
ISBN 0-7636-0598-0   LC 98-51123
A group of Martians looking for life on the different planets in the solar system make a surprising discovery just as they are about to give up

"Shields' bouncy, rhyimg text is hilarious, and Nash's cartoon illustrations . . . are inspired." Booklist

Showers, Paul, 1910-1999

The listening walk; illustrated by Aliki. new ed. HarperCollins Pubs. 1991 unp il lib bdg $15.89; pa $5.95   **E**
1. Father-daughter relationship—Fiction
ISBN 0-06-021638-7 (lib bdg); 0-06-443322-6 (pa)
LC 90-30526
Also available Spanish language edition
A revised and newly illustrated edition of the title first published 1961 by Crowell

A little girl and her father take a quiet walk and identify the sounds around them

Aliki's "artwork features active scenes, all created with an array of spring colors. A fine resource for preschool and primary grades studying the senses and worth reading just for fun." Booklist

Shub, Elizabeth

The white stallion; illustrated by Rachel Isadora. Greenwillow Bks. 1982 56p il o.p.; Bantam Bks. paperback available $3.99   **E**
1. Horses—Fiction 2. West (U.S.)—Fiction
ISBN 0-440-41292-7 (pa)   LC 81-20308
"A Greenwillow read-alone book"
Retold from James Frank Dobie's Tales of the mustang

Carried away from her wagon train in Texas in 1845 by the old mare she is riding, a little girl is befriended by a white stallion

"The quietly compelling story, framed by the grandmother's opening and closing lines to her granddaughter, is riveting without ever sensationalizing or anthropomorphizing. Elizabeth Shub's straightforward, lean text is part of the book's quality and appeal, but even more credit goes to the superb ink drawings." SLJ

Shulevitz, Uri, 1935-

Dawn; words and pictures by Uri Shulevitz. Farrar, Straus & Giroux 1974 unp il hardcover o.p. paperback available $5.95   **E**
ISBN 0-374-41689-3 (pa)
"Drawn from a Chinese poem, the spare text tells of an old man and his grandson asleep by the shore of a

Shulevitz, Uri, 1935——_Continued_

mountain lake. With the approach of daylight, the water-color illustrations, which start out small, dark, and blurred, slowly become more focused and detailed: the moon casts a soft glow; a breeze riffles the water; mists rise. As the old man and the boy push out on to the lake in their boat, a hint of color suffuses the scene; and finally . . . the sun rises over the mountain and they are bathed in full color." SLJ

"The purity of the hues, well-produced on ample spreads, the subtle graphic development from scene to scene, and the sharply focused simplicity of the few words make this a true art experience." Horn Book

Rain, rain, rivers; words and pictures by Uri Shulevitz. Farrar, Straus & Giroux 1969 unp il $16

E

1. Rain
ISBN 0-374-36171-1

A child indoors watches the rain on the window and in the streets and tells how it falls on the fields, hills, and seas

"There is no story line but interest is captured and held by the beauty of the striking illustrations and the strong, pervasive mood they evoke." Booklist

Snow. Farrar, Straus & Giroux 1998 unp il $16

E

1. Snow—Fiction
ISBN 0-374-37092-3   LC 97-37257
Also available Audiobook version
A Caldecott Medal honor book, 1999

As snowflakes slowly come down, one by one, people in the city ignore them, and only a boy and his dog think that the snowfall will amount to anything

"Passersby are caricatured into humorous figures bent into impossible postures, their tall hats, parasols, and funny shoes giving them an almost circus-clown appearance. . . . The elegantly stark text suits the elegant architectural lines of the cityscape." Bull Cent Child Books

Siebert, Diane

Plane song; paintings by Vincent Nasta. HarperCollins Pubs. 1993 unp il hardcover o.p. paperback available $6.95

E

1. Airplanes—Fiction 2. Stories in rhyme
ISBN 0-06-443367-6 (pa)   LC 92-17359
Rhymed text and illustrations describe different kinds of planes and their unique abilities

"Using words that rise and fall in the rhythm of flight, the poet conjures up images of different aircraft. Nasta's stunning illustrations realize these images beautifully in oil paintings of planes soaring through the clouds, highlighted against the changing colors of the sky." SLJ

Train song; paintings by Mike Wimmer. Crowell 1990 unp il hardcover o.p. paperback available $6.95

E

1. Railroads—Fiction 2. Stories in rhyme
ISBN 0-06-443340-4 (pa)   LC 88-389
Rhymed text and illustrations describe the journey of a transcontinental train

"Wimmer's luminous, nostalgic paintings will enable readers to grasp the beauty and power of the trains and the landscape across which they travel." Publ Wkly

Truck song; pictures by Byron Barton. Crowell 1984 unp il lib bdg $15.89; pa $6.95

E

1. Trucks—Fiction 2. Stories in rhyme
ISBN 0-690-04411-9 (lib bdg); 0-06-443134-7 (pa)

LC 83-46173

"Vivid illustrations and a rhythmic text describe the transcontinental journey of a truck driver. Readers/listeners get a sense of overland travel and the diverse American landscape it provides." Soc Educ

Siegelson, Kim L., 1962-

In the time of the drums; illustrated by Brian Pinkney. Hyperion Bks. for Children 1999 unp il $15.99; lib bdg $16.49

E

1. Slavery—Fiction 2. Gullahs—Fiction 3. Igbo (African people)—Fiction 4. Grandmothers—Fiction
ISBN 0-7868-0436-X; 0-7868-2386-0 (lib bdg)

LC 98-30347

"Jump at the sun"

Mentu, an American-born slave boy, watches his beloved grandmother, Twi, lead the insurrection at Teakettle Creek of Ibo people arriving from Africa on a slave ship

The "finely etched art dramatically captures the story's simultaneous sadness and hope. . . . At once magical yet chillingly real, this is a thought-provoking and memorable work." Publ Wkly

Silverman, Erica

Don't fidget a feather; illustrated by S.D. Schindler. Macmillan 1994 unp il $16; pa $5.99

E

1. Contests—Fiction 2. Ducks—Fiction 3. Geese—Fiction 4. Friendship—Fiction
ISBN 0-02-782685-6; 0-689-81967-6 (pa)

LC 93-8707

"After they compete at swimming and flying, a duck and a gander hold a freeze-in-place contest. Bees, rabbits, and crows pester them and a fox drags them off to his cave; still neither moves. But when Gander's life is in danger, Duck shows that she's the 'true and forever champion of champions.'" Publisher's note

"Schindler's delicate pastel illustrations lend a soft quality to the humor and warmth of Silverman's tale of friendship." Booklist

Simmons, Jane

Come along, Daisy! Little, Brown 1998 c1997 unp il $13.95

E

1. Ducks—Fiction
ISBN 0-316-79790-1   LC 97-26682
Also available Board book editions featuring Daisy the duck

First published 1997 in the United Kingdom

Daisy the duckling becomes so engrossed in playing with dragonflies and lily pads that she temporarily loses her mother

"The inquisitive duckling is an expressive splash of yellow in Simmons's blue-green pondscapes; the story unfolds in a series of watery panoramas amid bold forms and broad strokes of color. . . . This is a gem of a story and a masterful piece of picture-book artistry." SLJ

Other available titles about Daisy are:
Daisy and the Beastie (2000)
Daisy and the egg (1998)

Simms, Laura, 1947-

Rotten teeth; illustrated by David Catrow. Houghton Mifflin 1998 unp il $15   E
1. School stories 2. Teeth—Fiction
ISBN 0-395-82850-3   LC 97-2528

When Melissa takes a big glass bottle of authentic pulled teeth from her father's dental office for a show-and-tell presentation, she becomes a first-grade celebrity

"Catrow's watercolors are a suitably twisted complement to Simms' somewhat warped sense of humor (actually, it's perfect for this audience)." Bull Cent Child Books

Sis, Peter

Dinosaur! Greenwillow Bks. 2000 unp il $14.95   E
1. Dinosaurs 2. Stories without words
ISBN 0-688-17049-8   LC 99-32923

While taking a bath, a young boy is joined by all sorts of dinosaurs

"A wordless picture book that takes readers on a wild adventure of the imagination. . . . This imaginative story with wonderful end-papers naming the creatures should appeal to all young dinosaur lovers. Sis's barely fleshed-out, cookie-cutter cartoons tell the story." SLJ

Fire truck. Greenwillow Bks. 1998 unp il $15.95   E
1. Fire engines—Fiction
ISBN 0-688-15878-1   LC 97-29320

Matt, who loves fire trucks, wakes up one morning to find that he has become a fire truck, with one driver, two ladders, three hoses, and ten boots. Features a gate-fold illustration that opens into a three-page spread

"Sís blends simple text with bold pictures to give insight into one boy's vivid imagination." SLJ

Komodo! Greenwillow Bks. 1993 unp il $16; lib bdg $15.89; pa $5.95   E
1. Komodo dragon—Fiction 2. Indonesia—Fiction
ISBN 0-688-11583-7; 0-688-11584-5 (lib bdg); 0-688-16695-4 (pa)   LC 92-25811

A young boy who loves dragons goes with his parents to the Indonesian island of Komodo in hopes of seeing a real dragon. Includes factual information about the Komodo dragon

"The story, assisted by the art in its moodily surreal tone, is simply written but implies worlds." Bull Cent Child Books

Madlenka. Farrar, Straus & Giroux 2000 unp il $17   E
ISBN 0-374-39969-7   LC 99-57730
"Frances Foster books"

Madlenka, whose New York City neighbors include the French baker, the Indian news vendor, the Italian ice-cream man, the South American grocer, and the Chinese shopkeeper, goes around the block to show her friends her loose tooth and finds that it is like taking a trip around the world

"The real magic comes in the cleverly cut-away windows in each storefront through which children glimpse complex, global dreamscapes. Madlenka journeys through these mystical places, too, and it is these surreal, wordless stories-within-the-story that will excite a wide range of children, launching them in their own imagined departures." Booklist

Ship ahoy! Greenwillow Bks. 1999 unp il $14.95   E
1. Ships 2. Stories without words
ISBN 0-688-16644-X   LC 98-46673

A child on a sofa imagines it turning into a succession of ships, culminating in an encounter with a sea monster

This is a "wordless picture book. . . . The drawings are limned in shades of blue and green encircled by lots of clean, white space. The result is a charmingly simple, entrancing book." SLJ

Trucks, trucks, trucks. Greenwillow Bks. 1999 unp il $14.95   E
1. Trucks
ISBN 0-688-16276-2   LC 98-4482

A little boy cleans up his room using a variety of trucks and gives a one word description of their work such as hauling, plowing, and loading. Features a gate-fold illustration that opens into a three-page spread

"Sís creates a simple, bold look. . . . Gouache paints in yellow, black, and gray are set off by plenty of white space. The single verbs on each page are rendered in shades of blue, purple, green, and orange. This cheery romp is perfect for toddlers." SLJ

Sisulu, Elinor Batezat

The day Gogo went to vote; South Africa, April 1994; illustrated by Sharon Wilson. Little, Brown 1996 unp il $15.95; pa $5.95   E
1. Blacks—Fiction 2. Elections—Fiction 3. South Africa—Fiction
ISBN 0-316-70267-6; 0-316-70271-4 (pa)   LC 95-5300

Thembi and her beloved great-grandmother, who has not left the house for many years, go together to vote on the momentous day when black South Africans are allowed to vote for the first time

"The full-page pastel illustrations are powerful, alternating the dark interiors of a Soweto township home with sun-filled outdoor scenes. . . . A unique, inspiring story about passionate attachment to freedom and hope for democracy." SLJ

Skolsky, Mindy Warshaw

Hannah and the whistling tea kettle; story by Mindy Warshaw Skolsky; pictures by Diane Palmisciano. DK Ink 2000 unp il $15.95   E
1. Grandparents—Fiction 2. Gifts—Fiction 3. New York (N.Y.)—Fiction
ISBN 0-7894-2602-1   LC 99-41079
"A Richard Jackson book"

Picture book adaptation of a story in The whistling teakettle and other stories about Hannah, published 1977 by Harper & Row

Other titles about Hannah designed for older readers include: Love from your friend Hannah (1998); Welcome to the Grand View, Hannah (2000); You're the best, Hannah (2000)

When she goes to visit her grandparents in the Bronx, Hannah wonders if her grandmother will consider the whistling tea kettle Hannah is bringing a necessity worth keeping when it helps to foil a robbery

"This sweet, warm-hearted story of family life in 1930s New York is charmingly illustrated by Palmisciano in bright colors, with characters and settings having a fun, comic strip feel to them." Booklist

Skorpen, Liesel Moak

We were tired of living in a house; [by] Liesel Moak Skorpen; [illustrated by] Joe Cepeda. Putnam 1999 unp il $15.99   **E**

ISBN 0-399-23016-5   LC 97-14529

A newly illustrated edition of the title first published 1969 by Coward-McCann

Four children, a cat, and a dog move to a tree, a raft, a cave, and finally the seashore, enjoying each new dwelling until they discover its drawbacks

The text "is delightfully lyrical, patterned, and filled with alliteration. . . . Cepeda's brilliantly colored oil paintings are filled with humor." SLJ

Slate, Joseph, 1928-

Miss Bindergarten celebrates the 100th day of kindergarten; illustrated by Ashley Wolff. Dutton Children's Bks. 1998 unp il $16.99   **E**

1. Kindergarten—Fiction 2. Animals—Fiction 3. Stories in rhyme

ISBN 0-525-46000-4   LC 98-10486

To celebrate one hundred days in Miss Bindergarten's kindergarten class, all her students bring one hundred of something to school, including a one hundred-year-old relative, one hundred candy hearts, and one hundred polka dots

"Wolff's sturdy, genially observed illustrations prove a perfect match for Slate's rhyming text." Publ Wkly

Other available titles about Miss Bindergarten are:

Miss Bindergarten gets ready for kindergarten (1996)
Miss Bindergarten stays home from kindergarten (2000)
Miss Bindergarten's craft center (1999)

Sloat, Teri

Farmer Brown goes round and round; illustrated by Nadine Bernard Westcott. DK Ink 1999 unp il $15.95   **E**

1. Farm life—Fiction 2. Domestic animals—Fiction 3. Tornadoes—Fiction 4. Stories in rhyme

ISBN 0-7894-2512-2   LC 98-14272

"A Melanie Kroupa book"

A twister strikes Farmer Brown's farm and mixes the animals all up, so that the cows oinked, sheep clucked, hens brayed, and his hound neighed

"Westcott's sunny, frantic cartoons and Sloat's bouncy verse work together hand in glove to crank up the comedy." Booklist

Other available titles about Farmer Brown are:

Farmer Brown shears his sheep (2000)
The thing that bothered Farmer Brown (1995)

There was an old lady who swallowed a trout; illustrated by Reynold Ruffins. Holt & Co. 1998 unp il $15.95   **E**

1. Stories in rhyme 2. Pacific Northwest—Fiction

ISBN 0-8050-4294-6   LC 98-11607

Set on the coast of the Pacific Northwest, this variation on the traditional cumulative rhyme describes the silly consequences of an old woman's fishy diet

"Ruffins's colorful illustrations reflect both the zaniness of the rhyme and the coastal locale." SLJ

Slobodkina, Esphyr, 1908-

Caps for sale; a tale of a peddler, some monkeys & their monkey business; told and illustrated by Esphyr Slobodkina. Addison Wesley Longman 1947 unp il $15.95; pa $5.95   **E**

1. Monkeys—Fiction 2. Peddlers and peddling—Fiction

ISBN 0-201-09147-X; 0-06-443143-6 (pa)

Also available Big book edition and with Audiobook; Spanish language edition also available

A picture book story which "provides hilarious confusion. A cap peddler takes a nap under a tree. When he wakes up, his caps have disappeared. He looks up in the tree and sees countless monkeys, each wearing a cap and grinning." Parent's Guide To Child Read

Small, David, 1945-

George Washington's cows. Farrar Straus Giroux 1994 unp il $15; pa $4.95   **E**

1. Washington, George, 1732-1799—Fiction 2. Animals—Fiction 3. Stories in rhyme

ISBN 0-374-32535-9; 0-374-42534-5 (pa)

LC 93-39989

Humorous rhymes about George Washington's farm where the cows wear dresses, the pigs wear wigs, and the sheep are scholars

"Small's watercolors immeasurably extend his zany poem and make maximum use of the double-page spreads. Cleverly designed and well-executed scenes are filled with silly details that children will love." Booklist

Imogene's antlers; written and illustrated by David Small. Crown 2000 c1985 unp il $15.95; lib bdg $17.99; pa $6.99   **E**

ISBN 0-375-81048-X; 0-375-91048-4 (lib bdg); 0-517-56242-1 (pa)

First published 1985

One Thursday Imogene wakes up with a pair of antlers growing out of her head and causes a sensation wherever she goes

The author "maximizes the inherent humor of the absurd situation by allowing the imaginative possibilities of Imogene's predicament to run rampant. The brief text is supported by Small's expansive watercolors. They brim with humorous details." SLJ

Smith, Cynthia Leitich

Jingle dancer; illustrated by Cornelius Van Wright and Ying-Hwa Hu. Morrow Junior Bks. 2000 unp il $15.95; lib bdg $15.89   **E**

1. Creek Indians—Fiction 2. Native American dance—Fiction

ISBN 0-688-16241-X; 0-688-16242-8 (lib bdg)

LC 99-15503

Jenna, a member of the Muscogee, or Creek, Nation, borrows jingles from the dresses of several friends and relatives so that she can perform the jingle dance at the powwow. Includes a note about the jingle dance tradition and its regalia

"The colorful, well-executed watercolor illustrations lend warmth to the story." Booklist

Smith, Lane
Glasses: who needs 'em? Viking 1991 unp il
$15.99; pa $5.99   **E**
1. Eyeglasses—Fiction
ISBN 0-670-84160-9; 0-14-054484-4 (pa)
LC 91-9827

Also available Spanish language edition
"When a young patient states, 'I'm worried about
looking like a dork,' the optometrist lists others who
wear spectacles—'monster-movie' stuntpeople, famous
inventors, entire planets. Just when he decides the doctor
is crazy, the boy looks through the glasses and sees what
he's been missing (almost everyone and everything in the
world wearing glasses)." SLJ
The author's "outlandish, surreal illustrations combine
with a loopy layout and fanciful type design to provide
an abundance of laughter." Publ Wkly

Soto, Gary
Chato's kitchen; illustrated by Susan Guevara.
Putnam 1995 unp il $16.99; pa $6.99   **E**
1. Cats—Fiction 2. Mice—Fiction
ISBN 0-399-22658-3; 0-698-11600-3 (pa)
LC 93-43503

Also available Spanish language edition
To get the "ratoncitos," little mice, who have moved
into the barrio to come to his house, Chato the cat prepares all kinds of good food: fajitas, frijoles, salsa, enchi-
ladas, and more
"Soto adeptly captures the flavor of life in *el barrio*
in this amusing tale. The animal characters have distinct
personalities, and their language, sprinkled with Spanish
phrases and expressions, credibly brings them to life.
Best of all, though, are Guevara's striking illustrations
that enrich the text with delightful, witty details. Each
page exudes 'East L.A. culture,' creating vivid scenes in
which bold colors and shapes combine to increase the
humor and tension in the narrative." SLJ
Another available title about Chato is:
Chato and the party animals (2000)

Snapshots from the wedding; illustrated by
Stephanie Garcia. Putnam 1997 unp il $15.99; pa
$5.99   **E**
1. Weddings—Fiction 2. Mexican Americans—Fic-
tion
ISBN 0-399-22808-X; 0-698-11752-2 (pa)
LC 95-5793

Maya, the flower girl, describes a Mexican American
wedding through snapshots of the day's events, beginning with the procession to the altar and ending with her
sleeping after the dance
"Garcia's three-dimensional found-object and clay-
sculpture sets, framed like Mexican altar scenes in
opensided wooden boxes set against bridal lace, are a delightful confection of expressive faces and cunning details. . . . This is an unusually engaging book that will
have broad appeal." Bull Cent Child Books

Too many tamales; illustrated by Ed Martinez.
Putnam 1992 unp il $16.99; pa $6.99   **E**
1. Christmas—Fiction 2. Mexican Americans—Fic-
tion
ISBN 0-399-22146-8; 0-698-11412-4 (pa)
LC 91-19229

Maria tries on her mother's wedding ring while helping make tamales for a Christmas family get together,
but panic ensues when hours later, she realizes the ring
is missing
This is "a very funny story, full of delicious surprise.
The handsome, realistic oil paintings, in rich shades of
brown, red, and purple, are filled with light, evoking the
togetherness of an extended family." Booklist

Speed, Toby
Brave potatoes; illustrated by Barry Root.
Putnam 2000 unp il $15.99   **E**
1. Potatoes—Fiction   2. Vegetables—Fiction
3. Fairs—Fiction
ISBN 0-399-23158-7   LC 98-16345
Potatoes set off across the darkened fair grounds to
enjoy the rides, but Hackemup the chef has other plans
for them
"Root's cartoons in shaded hues of red, orange, purple, and green vivify the veggies. An exciting story full
of fun, complemented by delightful illustrations." SLJ

Spier, Peter, 1927-
Peter Spier's circus! Doubleday 1992 unp il
hardcover o.p. paperback available $7.50   **E**
1. Circus—Fiction
ISBN 0-440-40935-7 (pa)   LC 90-23282
A traveling circus arrives, sets up its village of tents,
performs for the crowd, and then moves on again
"Peter Spier fills every bit of the volume with busy
scenes. . . . The reader is shown a multitude of trucks,
house trailers, railroad cars, cages, animals, people, and
paraphernalia. . . . Peter Spier's characteristic sketches,
lightly tinted in watercolor, are an energetic tour de
force. . . . The book is masterful in capturing the amazing complexity of the circus world." Horn Book

Spinelli, Eileen, 1942-
Night shift daddy; illustrated by Melissa Iwai.
Hyperion Bks. for Children 2000 unp il $14.99; lib
bdg $15.49   **E**
1. Father-daughter relationship—Fiction 2. Bedtime—
Fiction 3. Stories in rhyme
ISBN 0-7868-0495-5; 0-7868-2424-7 (lib bdg)
LC 98-52499

A father shares dinner and bedtime rituals with his
daughter before going out to work the night shift
"The rhyming text manages to convey many feelings—love, loneliness, anticipation—in few words; the
mood is reinforced beautifully by the rich, detailed illustrations, especially those depicting a child's room at
night." Horn Book Guide

Thanksgiving at the Tappletons'; illustrated by
Maryann Cocca-Leffler. newly il ed. HarperCollins
Pubs. 1992 c1982 unp il lib bdg $16.89; pa $5.95
E
1. Thanksgiving Day—Fiction
ISBN 0-06-020872-4 (lib bdg); 0-06-443204-1 (pa)
LC 91-33250

A newly illustrated edition of the title first published
1982 by Addison-Wesley

Spinelli, Eileen, 1942-—*Continued*

"'Thanksgiving at the Tappletons' was always a big day. But one year, when each member of the family is unable to contribute his usual part of the meal—the turkey falls in a pond; the salad makings are fed to pet rabbits—they make do with liverwurst and cheese sandwiches and are thankful for being together. The light, humorous illustrations are a match for the droll text." Horn Book Guide

Stanley, Diane, 1943-

Rumpelstiltskin's daughter. Morrow Junior Bks. 1997 unp il $16; lib bdg $15.93　　　　E
　1. Fairy tales
　ISBN 0-688-14327-X; 0-688-14328-8 (lib bdg)
　　　　　　　　　　　　　　　LC 96-14834
"Rumpelstiltskin's daughter relies on her cleverness instead of magic. When the king orders her to spin straw into gold, she tricks him out of his greedy ways and becomes prime minister of his kingdom. The illustrations provide splendid, detailed palace interiors and endow the characters, especially the king and his minions, with comically exaggerated features." Horn Book Guide

Saving Sweetness; illustrated by G. Brian Karas. Putnam 1996 unp il $16.99　　　　E
　1. Orphans—Fiction 2. West (U.S.)—Fiction
　ISBN 0-399-22645-1　　　　LC 95-10621
The sheriff of a dusty western town rescues Sweetness, an unusually resourceful orphan, from nasty old Mrs. Sump and her terrible orphanage

"Telling the tale from the sheriff's point of view, Stanley packs this fast-paced adventure full of language that begs to be read aloud. . . . Combining gouache, acrylic, and pencil drawings with cyanotype photographs, Karas's illustrations evoke the arid landscape of the West yet remain wonderfully original." SLJ

　Another available title about Sweetness is:
Raising Sweetness (1999)

Steig, William, 1907-

The amazing bone. Farrar, Straus & Giroux 1976 unp il $17; pa $5.95　　　　E
　1. Pigs—Fiction 2. Bones—Fiction
　ISBN 0-374-30248-0; 0-374-40358-9 (pa)
A Caldecott Medal honor book, 1977
On her way home from school, Pearl finds an unusual bone that has unexpected powers

"Steig's marvelously straightfaced telling comes with a panoply of ultra-spring landscapes for pink-dressed Pearl to tiptoe through. And there's no holding back the chortles at the wonderfully expressive faces the artist delights in. This is a tight mesh of witty storytelling and art bound to please any audience." Booklist

Brave Irene. Farrar, Straus & Giroux 1986 unp il $17; pa $5.95　　　　E
　ISBN 0-374-30947-7; 0-374-40927-7 (pa)
　　　　　　　　　　　　　　　LC 86-80957
Also available Spanish language edition
"Hardworking Mrs. Bobbin has just finished a beautiful ballgown for the duchess, but she has a headache and can't deliver it. Brave and devoted daughter Irene takes

charge, tucking her mother snugly into bed and determinedly marching out into a raging snowstorm with the dress. Howling 'GO HO-WO-WOME' at poor Irene, the fierce wind rips the box open and the gown sails out, 'waltzing through the powdered air with tissue-paper attendants.'" Publ Wkly

"With sure writing and well-composed, riveting art, Steig keeps readers with Irene every step of the long way. The pictures, which take up about two-thirds of each page, are done in winter blues, purples, and grays that gradually get darker as Irene trudges on. An overlay of swirling white snow adds appropriate atmosphere." Booklist

Caleb & Kate. Farrar, Straus & Giroux 1977 unp il hardcover o.p. paperback available $5.95
　　　　　　　　　　　　　　　　E
　1. Dogs—Fiction 2. Witches—Fiction
　ISBN 0-374-41038-0 (pa)　　　LC 77-4947
"Though Caleb the carpenter loves Kate the weaver very much, he leaves her one day because of a quarrel. In the deep woods where he is resting Yedida the witch turns him into a dog. The tale of his faithfulness and love for his wife, even though he is a dog, is . . . told. Their love is shared to the end, when a remarkable turn of events enables him to return to his former self." Child Book Rev Serv

"The well-cadenced storytelling has a certain old-fashioned elegance of language, and the humor is emphasized by an atmosphere of mock-pathos. William Steig is a superb artist with the literary ingenuity to produce durable, energetic stories." Horn Book

Doctor De Soto. Farrar, Straus & Giroux 1982 unp il $16; pa $4.95　　　　E
　1. Dentists—Fiction 2. Mice—Fiction 3. Animals—Fiction
　ISBN 0-374-31803-4; 0-374-41810-1 (pa)
　　　　　　　　　　　　　　　LC 82-15701
Also available Spanish language edition
A Newbery Medal honor book, 1983
"Dr. De Soto is a mouse dentist who, with his assistant Mrs. De Soto, treats all creatures large and small but none that are injurious to mice. When Fox begs for help, the couple face a dilemma. He is in pain and professional ethics demand that they pull his aching tooth and replace it with a sound one." Publ Wkly

This "book goes beyond the usual tale of wit versus might; the story achieves comic heights partly through the delightful irony of the situation. . . . Watercolor paintings, with the artist's firm line and luscious color, depict with aplomb the eminently dentistlike mouse as he goes about his business." Horn Book

　Another available title about Doctor De Soto is:
Doctor De Soto goes to Africa (1992)

Pete's a pizza. HarperCollins Pubs. 1998 unp il $14.95; lib bdg $14.89　　　　E
　1. Father-son relationship—Fiction
　ISBN 0-06-205157-1; 0-06-205158-X (lib bdg)
　　　　　　　　　　　　　　　LC 97-78384
"Michael di Capua books"
Pete "moodily contemplates a rain-drenched landscape when his understanding father decides to cheer him up by transforming him into a pizza. The recipe: plenty of kneading, stretching, twirling, and decorating with delica-

Steig, William, 1907-—*Continued*
cies such as cheese (in reality pieces of paper) and tomatoes (checkers), plus tickling and obviously lots of love."
Horn Book

"The watercolor illustrations are executed in a clean palette with precise lines in tightly controlled compositions, the semi-formality of which only add to the hilarity. . . . This is a jolly, affectionate story." Bull Cent Child Books

Sylvester and the magic pebble. Simon & Schuster 1969 unp il $16; pa $5.99   E
1. Donkeys—Fiction
ISBN 0-671-66154-X; 0-671-66269-4 (pa)
LC 80-12314

Also available Spanish language edition
Awarded the Caldecott Medal, 1970
"Sylvester the young donkey was a pebble collector; one day he found a flaming red stone, shiny and round—and quite unaccountably able to grant wishes. Overjoyed, Sylvester was planning to share his magic with his family when 'a mean, hungry lion' appeared. Startled and panicky, Sylvester wished himself transformed into a rock. In vain his grieving parents searched for their beloved child; all worried animals took up the hunt. Then, after months of sorrow and mourning, poor Sylvester was fortuitously but logically restored. A remarkable atmosphere of childlike innocence pervades the book; beautiful pictures in full, natural color show daily and seasonal changes in the lush countryside and greatly extend the kindly humor and the warm, unselfconscious tenderness." Horn Book

Stenmark, Victoria
The singing chick; illustrated by Randy Cecil. Holt & Co. 1999 unp il $15.95   E
1. Animals—Fiction 2. Singing—Fiction
ISBN 0-8050-5255-0   LC 98-6609
A newly hatched, happily singing chick is eaten by a fox, who then starts singing before being eaten by a wolf, and so begins a chain of eating and singing for a series of animals
"Jaunty, lushy colored paintings wring every possible bit of humor out of the goofy situation in this hugely amusing read-aloud." Horn Book Guide

Steptoe, John, 1950-1989
Baby says. Lothrop, Lee & Shepard Bks. 1988 unp il $15; lib bdg $15.89   E
1. Brothers—Fiction 2. Infants—Fiction
ISBN 0-688-07423-5; 0-688-07424-3 (lib bdg)
LC 87-17296
"Little brother keeps throwing his Teddy bear until he finally topples the block city Big Brother is building. All ends well when understanding Big Brother realizes that Little Brother only wants to help. After hugs and kisses, the project is started over again—together." Child Book Rev Serv

"With simplicity of style and soft, pastel colored pencil drawings the author-artist depicts the tender, caring relationship of an older brother for his baby brother." Horn Book

Stevie. Harper & Row 1969 unp il hardcover o.p. paperback available $6.95   E
1. African Americans—Fiction
ISBN 0-06-443122-3 (pa)
A small black boy, Robert "tells the story of the intruder, Stevie, who comes to stay at his house because both parents are working. Stevie is a pest. He tags along after Robert, he messes up toys, he wants everything he sees. Worst of all, 'my momma never said nothin' to him.' But Robert is an only child, and after Stevie goes, the house is still. He remembers the games they played, the way Stevie looked up to him." Saturday Rev

"Warm and touching, the first-person story is effectively told in idiomatic language and is illustrated with expressive lifelike paintings in dark and brilliant colors." Booklist

Stevens, Janet
Cook-a-doodle-doo! [by] Janet Stevens and Susan Stevens Crummel; illustrated by Janet Stevens. Harcourt Brace & Co. 1999 unp il $17   E
1. Cooking—Fiction 2. Roosters—Fiction 3. Animals—Fiction
ISBN 0-15-201924-3   LC 98-8853
With the questionable help of his friends, Big Brown Rooster manages to bake a strawberry shortcake which would have pleased his great-grandmother, Little Red Hen

"With the main story and each hilarious, mouthwatering double-page picture of pandemonium, there is a quiet sidebar in small type that explains what recipes are, what ingredients are, what measuring and baking means, and how to make a strawberry shortcake, step by step. The luscious illustrations on hand-made paper are beautifully drawn and deliciously textured. . . . The full recipe is printed on the last page." Booklist

Stevenson, James, 1929-
"Could be worse!". Greenwillow Bks. 1977 unp il hardcover o.p. paperback available $5.95   E
1. Grandfathers—Fiction 2. Dreams—Fiction
ISBN 0-688-07035-3 (pa)   LC 76-28534
Also available with Audiobook
MaryAnn and Louie "comment on the fact that their grandfather . . . goes through the same routine every morning. . . . But one day Grandpa fools them and tells a long, involved story of a dream-fantasy in which he went from one peril to another." Bull Cent Child Books

"Stevenson's sketchy watercolors, arranged in panels, trace Grandpa's adventures. . . . A read-aloud picture story guaranteed to tickle young funny bones." Booklist

Don't make me laugh. Farrar, Straus & Giroux 1999 unp il $16   E
1. Animals—Fiction
ISBN 0-374-31827-1   LC 98-41780
"Frances Foster books"
"Mr. Frimdimpny, a heavy, bossy, gloomy alligator, lays down the rules for reading this book: Do not laugh! Do not smile! If you do, you have to go back to the front of the book. Then various slapstick scenarios show animal characters in mess and mayhem—caused by the

Stevenson, James, 1929-—_Continued_

reader." Booklist

"The book is a surefire winner at storytime as well as for family reading time. The large cartoons and short text keep everyone's attention focused on the zany action." SLJ

Don't you know there's a war on? Greenwillow Bks. 1992 unp il lib bdg $15.93   E
1. World War, 1939-1945—United States 2. Authors, American 3. Illustrators
ISBN 0-688-11384-2   LC 91-31461
The author recalls his efforts to win the Second World War, including planting a victory garden, collecting tin foil, and looking for spies
The author's "combination of casual, poetic text and small, blurry watercolor sketches, several to a page, creates an exquisite memoir that also communicates what it's like to remember." Booklist

The most amazing dinosaur. Greenwillow Bks. 2000 unp il $15.95; lib bdg $15.89   E
1. Museums—Fiction 2. Rats—Fiction 3. Animals—Fiction
ISBN 0-688-16432-3; 0-688-16433-1 (lib bdg)
    LC 99-25347
Wilfred the rat takes shelter in a natural history museum, where he befriends the animals living there and accidentally collapses a dinosaur skeleton, reassembling it in a creative way
"The humor and pacing of this story is absolutely perfect, with the matter-of-fact tone of the text heightened and expanded by Stevenson's quirky watercolor-and-pen illustrations." SLJ

The Mud Flat Olympics. Greenwillow Bks. 1994 56p il $15; lib bdg $14.93   E
1. Animals—Fiction 2. Games—Fiction
ISBN 0-688-12923-4; 0-688-12924-2 (lib bdg)
    LC 93-28118
At the Mud Flat Olympics if the animals don't win the Deepest Hole Contest, the All-Snail High Hurdles, or the River-Cross Freestyle, they can still come to the picnic after the games and have ice cream for dessert
"This is a great example of the author-artist's mischievous verbal wit. It also shows off Stevenson's remarkable ability to turn splashes of watercolor and a few freewheeling ink lines into expressive cartoon characters." Booklist
Other available titles about Mud Flat are:
Christmas at Mud Flat (2000)
Heat wave at Mud Flat (1997)
Mud Flat April Fool (1998)
The Mud Flat mystery (1997)
Mud Flat spring (1999)
Yard sale (1996)

The Sea View Hotel. Greenwillow Bks. 1994 unp il lib bdg $14.93   E
1. Mice—Fiction 2. Vacations—Fiction 3. Animals—Fiction
ISBN 0-688-13470-X
A newly illustrated edition of the title first published 1978
As the only child at the Sea View Hotel, Hubert the mouse is having a miserable two-week vacation until he

encounters the hotel handyman
"A story with simplicity, harmony, and ease in the telling. . . . The characters, whose bodies in their turn-of-the-century clothing seem human, have heads of birds, turtles, dogs, or whatever suits their personality or Stevenson's whimsy." SLJ

A village full of valentines. Greenwillow Bks. 1995 39p il $16; pa $4.95   E
1. Valentine's Day—Fiction 2. Animals—Fiction
ISBN 0-688-13602-8; 0-688-15839-0 (pa)
    LC 94-624
"A series of simple vignettes all center around Valentine's Day. Clifford, the turtle, doesn't believe in sending a valentine until he gets one. As a result, he's been waiting for fifty-six years. On the other hand, Mona, Tina, and Mary Lou are all so anxious to make valentines, they quarrel about how to divide the work fairly. . . . Though the first six chapters seem to tell unrelated stories about making, giving, and receiving valentines, the last chapter ties all the stories together when everyone in the village gathers at Sidney's barn for a party." Horn Book
"Stevenson has done a masterful job of creating stories easy enough for new readers to read alone, each with a twist or joke based on a character's personality." Bull Cent Child Books

Stewart, Sarah

The gardener; pictures by David Small. Farrar, Straus & Giroux 1997 unp il $16; pa $5.95   E
1. Gardening—Fiction 2. Letters—Fiction 3. Great Depression, 1929-1939—Fiction
ISBN 0-374-32517-0; 0-374-42518-3 (pa)
    LC 96-30894
Also available with Audiobook
A Caldecott Medal honor book, 1998
"In the depth of the Depression, Lydia Grace Finch is sent to the big city to live with her dour Uncle Jim and cultivates an urban garden." N Y Times Book Rev
"Stewart's quiet story, relayed in the form of letters written by a little girl, focuses on a child who literally makes joy blossom. Small's illustrations . . . [offer] wonderfully expressive characters, ink-line details, and patches of pastel." Booklist

The library; pictures by David Small. Farrar, Straus & Giroux 1995 unp il $16; pa $5.95   E
1. Books and reading—Fiction 2. Stories in rhyme
ISBN 0-374-34388-8; 0-374-44394-7 (pa)
    LC 94-30320
Elizabeth Brown loves to read more than anything else, but when her collection of books grows and grows, she must make a change in her life
"Framed watercolors give the book an old-fashioned, scrapbooklike appearance. . . . Small black-ink line drawings decorate the verses below and often add an additional touch of humor. This is a funny, heartwarming story about a quirky woman with a not-so-peculiar obsession." SLJ

Stoeke, Janet Morgan

A hat for Minerva Louise. Dutton Children's Bks. 1994 unp il $13.99; pa $5.99   E
1. Chickens—Fiction 2. Hats—Fiction
ISBN 0-525-45328-8; 0-14-055666-4 (pa)
    LC 94-2139

Stoeke, Janet Morgan—*Continued*

Also available Minerva Louise Board books

Minerva Louise, a snow-loving chicken, mistakes a pair of mittens for two hats to keep both ends warm

This "is a rare find: a picture book exactly on target for preschoolers that sacrifices none of the essential elements of plot, character, and humor. . . . The pictures, in large rectangles of bright primary colors, are easy for preschoolers to 'read' and contain most of the book's considerable humor." Horn Book

Other available titles about Minerva Louise are:

A friend for Minerva Louise (1997)

Minerva Louise (1988)

Minerva Louise at school (1996)

Minerva Louise at the fair (2000)

Stojic, Manya

Rain; written and illustrated by Manya Stojic. Crown 2000 unp il $15.95; lib bdg $17.99   **E**

1. Rain—Fiction 2. Animals—Fiction 3. Africa—Fiction

ISBN 0-517-80085-3; 0-517-80086-1 (lib bdg)

LC 99-35298

The animals of the African savanna use their senses to predict and then enjoy the rain

"The brilliant double-page spreads, the play on the five senses, and a text that invites participation make this one trip to Africa you can't afford to miss!" SLJ

Stolz, Mary, 1920-

Storm in the night; illustrated by Pat Cummings. Harper & Row 1988 unp il lib bdg $15.89; pa $5.95   **E**

1. Thunderstorms—Fiction 2. Grandfathers—Fiction 3. Fear—Fiction

ISBN 0-06-025913-2 (lib bdg); 0-06-443256-4 (pa)

LC 85-45838

After a power failure during a thunderstorm, Thomas, his grandfather and Ringo the cat go out on the porch. Grandfather tells Thomas a story of his own childhood fear of storms and how concern for his equally frightened pet helped him to overcome it

"Presenting a glorified portrayal of a white cat, a beautiful black child, and a gentle old man, the dark, shadowy paintings are made luminous by 'the carrot-colored flames in the wood stove' or by lightning slashing across the navy-blue sky; every illustration is imbued with the boy's sensory awareness during a night of wonder and discovery." Horn Book

Stuve-Bodeen, Stephanie, 1965-

Elizabeti's doll; illustrated by Christy Hale. Lee & Low Bks. 1998 unp il $15.95   **E**

1. Siblings—Fiction 2. Tanzania—Fiction

ISBN 1-88000-070-9   LC 98-13086

When a young Tanzanian girl gets a new baby brother, she finds a rock, which she names Eva, and makes it her baby doll

"Vibrant patterns and soft watercolor backgrounds evoke a sense of place and familial love." SLJ

Another available title about Elizabeti is:

Mama Elizabeti (2000)

Suen, Anastasia

Delivery; illustrated by Wade Zahares. Viking 1999 unp il $15.99   **E**

1. Stories in rhyme

ISBN 0-670-88455-3   LC 99-25077

A rhyming look at a number of deliveries that take place in a day, from a morning newspaper delivery to people being transported by airplanes

"This book has a nice, understated tone. The text doesn't overwhelm Zahares's stylized artwork. Bold and angular, the illustrations have an almost impressionistic feel." SLJ

Window music; illustrated by Wade Zahares. Viking 1998 unp il $15.99; pa $6.99   **E**

1. Railroads—Fiction 2. Stories in rhyme

ISBN 0-670-87287-3; 0-14-056093-9 (pa)

LC 97-27306

Describes the trip taken by a train as it travels over hills, through valleys, past horses and orange trees until it arrives at the next station

"The illustrations jump off the page with intense colors and dynamic design, and the short text underscores the actions and ambiance of each spread." Horn Book Guide

Swift, Hildegarde Hoyt, d. 1977

The little red lighthouse and the great gray bridge; by Hildegarde H. Swift and Lynd Ward. Harcourt Brace Jovanovich 1942 unp il $17; pa $8   **E**

1. George Washington Bridge (N.Y. and N.J.)—Fiction 2. Lighthouses—Fiction

ISBN 0-15-247040-9; 0-15-652840-1 (pa)

"After the great beacon atop the . . . George Washington Bridge was installed, the little red lighthouse feared he would no longer be useful, but when an emergency arose, the little lighthouse proved that he was still important." Hodges. Books for Elem Sch Libr

"The story is written with imagination and a gift for bringing alive this little lighthouse and its troubles. . . . [Lynd Ward's] illustrations have some distinction and one in particular, the fog creeping over the river clutching at the river boats, has atmosphere, rhythm and good colour." Ont Libr Rev

Swope, Sam

Gotta go! Gotta go! pictures by Sue Riddle. Farrar, Straus & Giroux 2000 unp il $12   **E**

1. Butterflies—Fiction 2. Caterpillars—Fiction

ISBN 0-374-32757-2   LC 99-28503

Although she does not know why or how, a caterpillar who becomes a monarch butterfly is certain that she must make her way to Mexico

"The rhythm and repetition are infectious; and the pen-and-ink and watercolor illustrations, set against expanses of white space, enlarge the book remarkably." Horn Book Guide

Taback, Simms, 1932-

Joseph had a little overcoat. Viking 1999 unp il music $15.99   **E**

1. Clothing and dress—Fiction 2. Jews—Fiction

ISBN 0-670-87855-3   LC 98-47721

Taback, Simms, 1932-—*Continued*
Awarded the Caldecott Medal, 2000
A newly illustrated edition of the title first published
1977 by Random House
A very old overcoat is recycled numerous times into
a variety of garments. Based on a Yiddish folk song,
which is included
"Taback's inventive use of die-cut pages shows off his
signature artwork. . . . This diverting, sequential story
unravels as swiftly as the threads of Joseph's well-loved,
patch-covered plaid coat." Publ Wkly

Tafuri, Nancy
Counting to Christmas. Scholastic 1998 unp il
$15.95   E
  1. Christmas—Fiction 2. Counting
  ISBN 0-590-27143-1   LC 97-32059
A child counts the days to Christmas, from one to
twenty-five, preparing a surprise for the woodland animals as she waits
"The large scale of the illustrations relative to the size
of the page and the bright colors used throughout make
this an excellent choice for story hours. The book ends
with a few pages of suggested activities: making holiday
cards, popcorn-cranberry garlands, gingerbread cookies,
and decorations that can be eaten by animals." Booklist

Have you seen my duckling? Greenwillow Bks.
1984 unp il $16.95; lib bdg $16.89; pa $5.95
                                                  E
  1. Ducks—Fiction
  ISBN 0-688-02797-0; 0-688-02798-9 (lib bdg);
  0-688-10994-2 (pa)   LC 83-17196
Also available Board book edition
A Caldecott Medal honor book, 1985
"In a picture book virtually wordless except for the repeated question of the title, seven ducklings obediently
cluster in their nest, while the eighth—more daring and
more curious—scrambles after an errant butterfly." Horn
Book
"Tafuri's artwork . . . features clean lines, generous
figures, and clear, cool colors. She also adds nice detail—feathers, for instance, that you can almost feel under your hands." Booklist

Snowy flowy blowy; a twelve months rhyme;
based on an old poem by Gregory Gander.
Scholastic Press 1999 unp il $15.95   E
  1. Months—Fiction 2. Seasons—Fiction 3. Stories in
  rhyme
  ISBN 0-590-18973-5   LC 98-47509
Rhyming text provides a descriptive word for each
month of the year and takes a country family through the
changes and surprises of the year's cycle
"The large, clear pictures make a perfect presentation
for sharing with a group, which will join in chanting the
rhyme a second time around." SLJ

Spots, feathers, and curly tails. Greenwillow
Bks. 1988 unp il $16.95; lib bdg $16.89   E
  1. Domestic animals
  ISBN 0-688-07536-3; 0-688-07537-1 (lib bdg)
                                    LC 87-15638

Questions and answers highlight some outstanding
characteristics of farm animals, such as a chicken's
feathers and a horse's mane
"In the watercolor illustrations with black pen outline,
Nancy Tafuri manages in the simplest style to give energy and personality to the animals through the angle of a
head or the set of a snout. The story will provide a successful experience for both child and adult reader and is
an ideal book for the beginning reader to entertain a
younger sibling in a game they'll both enjoy." Horn
Book

This is the farmer. Greenwillow Bks. 1994 unp
il $16.95   E
  1. Farm life—Fiction
  ISBN 0-688-09468-6   LC 92-30082
A farmer's kiss causes an amusing chain of events on
the farm
"The well-defined, watercolor-and-ink double-spread
illustrations are . . . of the highest quality. The brief story is rhythmic, predictable, and printed in extra-large
type." SLJ

What the sun sees. Greenwillow Bks. 1997 unp
il $16   E
  1. Day—Fiction 2. Night—Fiction 3. Sun—Fiction
  4. Moon—Fiction
  ISBN 0-688-14493-4   LC 96-20976
Bound back to back and inverted with What the moon
sees
"Tafuri uses a 'flip-book' technique to show readers
similar settings first from the point of view of the sun,
and then from that of the moon (or vice versa). She provides a pleasant introduction to many opposites in scenes
that will be familiar to a young audience—busy/restful
city and country scenes, awake/sleeping animals and children. . . . A spare and repetitious text reinforces the
continuity and contrast of daytime and nightime experiences. A detached perspective and a panoramic distancing of colored-pencil and watercolor illustrations allow
viewers to feel as though they are indeed looking down
on the cycles on time." SLJ

Talbott, Hudson
O'Sullivan stew; a tale cooked up in Ireland.
Putnam 1999 unp il $15.99   E
  1. Fairy tales 2. Ireland—Fiction
  ISBN 0-399-23162-5   LC 98-5721
When the witch of Crookhaven, a village on the zig-
zagging coast of Ireland, has her horse stolen by the
King and strikes back with famine and disaster, Kate de-
cides to save the day by getting the horse back for her
"Energetic humorous illustrations, rich in kelly green,
are a perfect match for this tale's Irish blarney." Horn
Book Guide

Tapahonso, Luci, 1953-
Navajo ABC; a Diné alphabet book; written by
Luci Tapahonso and Eleanor Schick; illustrations
by Eleanor Schick. Macmillan Bks. for Young
Readers 1995 unp il $16; pa $5.99   E
  1. Navajo Indians 2. Alphabet
  ISBN 0-689-80316-8; 0-689-82685-0 (pa)
                                    LC 94-46881

Tapahonso, Luci, 1953—*Continued*

"The authors present a Diné alphabet book using objects and words familiar to the Navajo culture. Four letters appear with Diné words, but the remaining 22 are associated with English ones—belt, grandma, yucca, etc. Each pairing is illustrated by a colored-pencil picture of the object, plant, or person named. A glossary, which includes pronunciation guidance, provides translations and a cultural context for each item." Booklist

"Tapahonso has created a wonderful introduction to her people and their language, and Schick's pastel pencil drawings are a perfect complement." SLJ

Taulbert, Clifton L.

Little Cliff and the porch people; paintings by E.B. Lewis. Dial Bks. for Young Readers 1999 unp il $15.99; lib bdg $15.89   E
1. African Americans—Fiction 2. Mississippi—Fiction
ISBN 0-8037-2174-9; 0-8037-2175-7 (lib bdg)
                                                   LC 98-5503
Sent to buy special butter for Mama Pearl's candied sweet potatoes and told to get back lickety-split, Little Cliff is delayed by all his neighbors when they want to contribute their own ingredients

"The old Mississippi setting is authentic, the intergenerational relationships are realistic, and Lewis's illustrations add warmth to the simply told story." Horn Book Guide

Teague, Mark, 1963-

How I spent my summer vacation; written and illustrated by Mark Teague. Crown 1995 unp il $16; lib bdg $17.99; pa $6.99   E
1. Cowhands—Fiction 2. West (U.S.)—Fiction
ISBN 0-517-59998-8; 0-517-59999-6 (lib bdg); 0-517-88556-5 (pa)   LC 94-13019
"Wallace Bleff recounts to a teacher his rip-roaring vacation rustling cattle and stoking campfires. Captured by boisterous cowpokes, Wallace learns to sling rope and even averts a threatening cattle stampede. Told as a story-within-a-story, the rhymed, evenly paced text with acrylic illustrations will be an ice-breaking read-aloud for students returning to school." Horn Book Guide

One Halloween night. Scholastic Press 1999 unp il $14.95   E
1. Halloween—Fiction
ISBN 0-590-63803-3   LC 98-47719
"One Halloween, when nothing seems to go right, Wendell, Floyd, and Mona find themselves chased by the class bully and her nasty friends, dressed as witches. But, as Wendell says, 'Anything can happen on Halloween.'" Horn Book Guide

"This witty tale gets a boost from hyperbolic, rough-and tumble acrylics." Publ Wkly

Pigsty. Scholastic 1994 unp il $14.95   E
1. Pigs—Fiction 2. Cleanliness—Fiction
ISBN 0-590-45915-5   LC 93-21179
When Wendell doesn't clean up his room, a whole herd of pigs comes to live with him

"Much of the tale's fun resides in Teague's quirky acrylic art. . . . Whether Wendell and his friends are jumping on the bed or playing Monopoly on the rug, their antics are rendered in the bold palette of a gleefully inventive imagination. Highly recommended for neat-freaks and mess-makers alike." Publ Wkly

Testa, Fulvio, 1947-

If you take a paintbrush; a book of colors. Dial Bks. for Young Readers 1983 unp il hardcover o.p. paperback available $5.99   E
1. Color
ISBN 0-14-054646-4 (pa)   LC 82-45512
Also available Spanish language edition
"The book begins with endpapers that have tubes of paint, rulers, compasses, and other art supplies scattered in delightful disarray. Following this are short but clear statements about a color—'yellow is the color of the sun.' This faces a bordered picture that features the sun beating down on the sands of the desert as two children atop a camel ride by. 'Brown is the color of chocolate' is illustrated by two young bakers watching as a third oozes frosting down the side of a cake." Booklist

"Simple, yet imaginative, the book deals with the concept of color in an attractive, appealing manner." Child Book Rev Serv

Thayer, Jane, 1904-

The popcorn dragon; written by Jane Thayer; illustrated by Lisa McCue. Morrow Junior Bks. 1989 unp il $16.95   E
1. Dragons—Fiction
ISBN 0-688-08340-4   LC 88-39855
A newly illustrated edition of the title first published 1953

Though his hot breath is the envy of all the other animals, a young dragon learns that showing off does not make friends

"McCue's new full-color illustrations capture the whimsical mood of the fable. The animals, although too coy, have appealing humanlike expressions which convey their envy and contempt." SLJ

The puppy who wanted a boy; illustrated by Lisa McCue. Morrow 1986 unp il lib bdg $13.93; pa $5.95   E
1. Dogs—Fiction 2. Christmas—Fiction
ISBN 0-688-05945-7 (lib bdg); 0-688-08293-9 (pa)
                                                   LC 85-15465
Also available with Audiobook
A newly illustrated edition of the title first published 1958

"More than anything in the world, Petey, a puppy, wanted a boy for Christmas. Nothing else his mother suggested would do, and none of the other dogs would give him their boys. Dejected, Petey passes the Home for Boys where a lonely newcomer sits on the steps. Petey has found not one boy, but 50 boys full of love." SLJ

"It is the same, somewhat sentimental but certainly appealing tale that Thayer fashioned in 1958, when this was originally published; however, McCue's affectionately drawn, warmly colored illustrations go a long way toward perking up the story." Booklist

Thomas, Jane Resh, 1936-

Saying good-bye to Grandma; illustrated by Marcia Sewall. Clarion Bks. 1988 48p il hardcover o.p. paperback available $7.95   E
  1. Death—Fiction 2. Grandmothers—Fiction
  ISBN 0-395-54779-2 (pa)   LC 87-20826
"An anecdotal account of seven-year-old Suzie's trip to her grandparent's house to attend her grandmother's funeral. Activities with her cousins, her feelings about her grandmother, and relating to her grieving grandfather are all conveyed." Child Book Rev Serv
"Marcia Sewall's colorful, loose, almost faceless illustrations are just sketchy enough to contribute to the book's universality; a child could picture himself or herself in any of these scenes." N Y Times Book Rev

Thomas, Joyce Carol

I have heard of a land; illustrated by Floyd Cooper. HarperCollins Pubs. 1998 unp il $14.95; lib bdg $14.89; pa $5.95   E
  1. Oklahoma—Fiction 2. Frontier and pioneer life—Fiction 3. African Americans—Fiction
  ISBN 0-06-023477-6; 0-06-023478-4 (lib bdg); 0-06-443617-9 (pa)   LC 95-48791
A Coretta Scott King honor book for illustration, 1999
"Joanna Cotler books"
Describes the joys and hardships experienced by an African-American pioneer woman who staked a claim for free land in the Oklahoma territory
"The strength and tenderness of Thomas' text are matched by Cooper's always evocative artwork." Booklist

Thomas, Shelley Moore

Good night, Good Knight; pictures by Jennifer Plecas. Dutton Children's Bks. 2000 47p il $13.99   E
  1. Knights and knighthood—Fiction 2. Dragons—Fiction 3. Bedtime—Fiction
  ISBN 0-525-46326-7   LC 99-28415
"Dutton easy reader"
A Good Knight helps three little dragons who are having trouble getting to sleep
"The short, simple, repetitive phrases are sure to capture the imaginations of young children. . . . With a palette dominated by the blues, grays, and purples of the nightime setting, Plecas's illustrations are a wonderful complement to this endearing tale." SLJ

Thomassie, Tynia

Feliciana Feydra LeRoux; a Cajun tall tale; illustrated by Cat Bowman Smith. Little, Brown 1995 unp il hardcover o.p. paperback available $4.95   E
  1. Alligators—Fiction 2. Cajuns—Fiction 3. Louisiana—Fiction
  ISBN 0-316-84459-4 (pa)   LC 93-30347
"Feliciana's grandpa won't let her go alligator hunting in the Louisiana Cajun bajou. When she sneaks out, Feliciana causes fun and excitement, and even becomes a heroine." Soc Educ
This "combines breezy watercolors and a swinging text that's perfect for reading aloud. A note on Cajun culture, a glossary, and a pronunciation guide are included." Booklist

Another available title about Feliciana is:
Feliciana meets d'Loup Garou (1998)

Thompson, Kay, d. 1998

Kay Thompson's Eloise; a book for precocious grown ups; drawings by Hilary Knight. Simon & Schuster 1995 c1955 65p il $17   E
  1. Hotels and motels—Fiction 2. New York (N.Y.)—Fiction
  ISBN 0-671-22350-X   LC 96-103190
Also available Ultimate edition which includes the original Eloise story, Eloise in Moscow, Eloise in Paris, Eloise at Christmastime, and a scrapbook of photographs, memorabilia, and drawings
A reissue of the title first published 1955
This is the "tale of the little girl who makes merry mayhem from her digs on the top floor of New York's Plaza Hotel." Horn Book
Other available titles about Eloise are:
Eloise at Christmastime (1958)
Eloise in Paris (1957)
Eloise in Moscow (1959)
Eloise's guide to life (2000)

Thurber, James, 1894-1961

The great Quillow; illustrated by Steven Kellogg. Harcourt Brace Jovanovich 1994 56p il $17.95   E
  1. Fairy tales
  ISBN 0-15-232544-1   LC 91-20586
"An HBJ contemporary classic"
A newly illustrated edition of the title first published 1944
Quillow, a tiny toymaker, defeats a ferocious giant named Hunder and saves his town from destruction
"The lively full-color illustrations are pure Kellogg: energetic line, sunlit color, broad humor, subtle detail, and exuberant spirit. . . . The artwork captures the bustle and the bickering of the story as well as the terror and the wonder." Booklist

Titherington, Jeanne, 1951-

Pumpkin, pumpkin. Greenwillow Bks. 1986 23p il $16.95; lib bdg $16.89; pa $5.95   E
  ISBN 0-688-05695-4; 0-688-05696-2 (lib bdg); 0-688-09930-0 (pa)   LC 84-25334
"Softly colored pencil illustrations in a realistic style effectively communicate Jamie's pride as a very young gardener. He plants a seed, then grows and harvests a pumpkin from which he saves seeds for next year. The large, detailed drawings capture Jamie's anticipation and pleasure just right. The garden creatures appearing on every page and grandpa, whom we catch sight of now and then, are a delightful supporting cast. Nonreaders can easily follow the story in pictures alone. Very large, clear print on facing pages makes the simple narrative inviting for beginning readers, too." SLJ

Tompert, Ann, 1918-

Grandfather Tang's story; illustrated by Robert Andrew Parker. Crown 1990 unp il $16; lib bdg $17.99; pa $6.99   E
  1. Foxes—Fiction
  ISBN 0-517-57487-X; 0-517-57272-9 (lib bdg); 0-517-88558-1 (pa)   LC 89-22205

Tompert, Ann, 1918-—*Continued*

"An old Chinese man sits beneath a tree with his granddaughter, telling her the tale of two foxes who change themselves into ever-fiercer animals as they compete for dominance. As he speaks, he rearranges two tangram puzzles to form the shapes of the animals. . . . Directions for making tangrams, described as ancient Chinese puzzles, appear on the book's last page." Booklist

"Parker's watercolor washes complement the text, adding energy and tension, as well as evoking oriental brushwork technique. However, the text is strong enough to stand on its own, and will be valued by storytellers and listeners alike." SLJ

Torres, Leyla

Subway sparrow. Farrar, Straus & Giroux 1993 unp il $15; pa $6.95   E
1. Subways—Fiction 2. Birds—Fiction 3. New York (N.Y.)—Fiction
ISBN 0-374-37285-3; 0-374-47129-0 (pa)
LC 92-55104
Also available Spanish language edition
Although the passengers of a New York City subway train speak different languages, they work together to rescue a frightened bird
"Colorful watercolor paintings illustrate this multicultural story. . . . The brief text, which includes phrases in Spanish and Polish, advances the plot while allowing the double-spread illustrations to convey the action. . . . The expressive pictures and the caring tone transcend any particular place or time." SLJ

Tresselt, Alvin R., 1916-2000

Hide and seek fog; by Alvin Tresselt; illustrated by Roger Duvoisin. Lothrop, Lee & Shepard Bks. 1965 unp il lib bdg $15.93; pa $5.95   E
1. Fog
ISBN 0-688-51169-4 (lib bdg); 0-688-07813-3 (pa)

Also available with Audiobook
A Caldecott Medal honor book, 1966
"This is not a plotted story but rather a mood picture book . . . describing a fog which rolls in from the sea to veil an Atlantic seacoast village for three days. The beautiful paintings, most of them double-spreads, and the brief, poetic text sensitively and effectively evoke the atmosphere of the 'worst fog in twenty years' and depict the reactions of children and grown-ups to it." Booklist

Wake up, city! [by] Alvin Tresselt; pictures by Carolyn Ewing. Lothrop, Lee & Shepard Bks. 1990 unp il $13.95; lib bdg $13.88   E
1. City and town life—Fiction
ISBN 0-688-08652-7; 0-688-08653-5 (lib bdg)
LC 89-45901
A revised and newly illustrated edition of the title first published 1957
"Tresselt's description of some of the things that happen when the day starts in a large city are just as applicable now as then; Ewing's paintings add some touches that will please feminists (a policewoman, a woman bus driver—at least, a bus driver who could be a woman) and some that relect the architectural variety, the bustle of various activities, and the multiracial composition of the urban scene." Bull Cent Child Books

White snow, bright snow; by Alvin Tresselt; illustrated by Roger Duvoisin. Lothrop, Lee & Shepard Bks. 1988 c1947 unp il $16.95; lib bdg $15.89; pa $5.95   E
1. Snow—Fiction
ISBN 0-688-41161-4; 0-688-51161-9 (lib bdg); 0-688-08294-7 (pa)   LC 88-10018
Awarded the Caldecott Medal, 1948
A reissue of the title first published 1947
When it begins to look, feel, and smell like snow, everyone prepares for a winter blizzard

Trivizas, Eugene, 1946-

The three little wolves and the big bad pig; illustrated by Helen Oxenbury. Margaret K. McElderry Bks. 1993 unp il $17; pa $6.99   E
1. Pigs—Fiction 2. Wolves—Fiction
ISBN 0-689-50569-8; 0-689-81528-X (pa)
LC 92-24829
Also available Spanish language edition
"In this reverse of 'The Three Little Pigs' the wolves build with cement, barbed wire and reinforced chains. In response, the 'big bad pig' uses a sledgehammer, pneumatic drill and dynamite." Child Book Rev Serv
"Trivizas laces the text with funny, clever touches. . . . Oxenbury's watercolors capture the story's broad humor and add a wealth of supplementary details, with exquisite renderings of the wolves' comic temerity and the pig's bellicose stances." Publ Wkly

Tryon, Leslie

Albert's birthday; written and illustrated by Leslie Tryon. Atheneum Bks. for Young Readers 1999 unp il $16   E
1. Birthdays—Fiction 2. Parties—Fiction 3. Animals—Fiction
ISBN 0-689-82296-0   LC 98-36621
Patsy Pig plans a surprise birthday party for her friend Albert, giving careful instructions to all their friends, but she forgets to invite the guest of honor
"The prose is personable and engaging, and colorful, exquisitely detailed illustrations portray the animal cast in such familiar human settings as a classroom and a town." Booklist
Other available titles about Albert are:
Albert's alphabet (1991)
Albert's ballgame (1996)
Albert's Christmas (1997)
Albert's field trip (1993)
Albert's Halloween (1998)
Albert's play (1992)
Albert's Thanksgiving (1994)

Tsubakiyama, Margaret

Mei-Mei loves the morning; written by Margaret Holloway Tsubakiyama; paintings by Cornelius Van Wright & Ying-Hwa Hu. Whitman, A. 1999 unp il $15.95   E
1. Grandfathers—Fiction 2. China—Fiction
ISBN 0-8075-5039-6   LC 97-26675
A young Chinese girl and her grandfather enjoy a typical morning riding on grandpa's bicycle to do errands

Tsubakiyama, Margaret—*Continued*
and meet friends in the park

"The gentle prose is accompanied by expressive, luminous watercolor paintings, detailing the people, places, and activities that are characteristic of China." Booklist

Tudor, Tasha, 1915-
1 is one. Simon & Schuster Bks. for Young Readers 2000 unp il $16   **E**
1. Counting
ISBN 0-689-82843-8   LC 99-31290
A Caldecott Medal honor book, 1957
A reissue of the title first published 1956 by Oxford University Press

"The author-artist has with characteristic charming quaintness written and illustrated a counting book. Delicately tinted, decoratively bordered pictures and rhyming lines of text count from one to twenty." Booklist

Tunnell, Michael O.
Mailing May; illustrated by Ted Rand. Greenwillow Bks. 1997 unp il $16; lib bdg $15.89; pa $5.95   **E**
1. Postal service—Fiction 2. Railroads—Fiction 3. Grandmothers—Fiction
ISBN 0-688-12878-5; 0-688-12879-3 (lib bdg); 0-06-443742-8 (pa)   LC 96-35259
"A Tambourine book"

In 1914, because her family cannot afford a train ticket to her grandmother's town, May gets mailed and rides the mail car on the train to see her grandmother

"Children will delight in the fantasy aspects of the tale even after they discover that the story is true. . . . Rand's watercolor illustrations are masterful, as is the design of the book as a whole." SLJ

Turkle, Brinton Cassaday, 1915-
Do not open; by Brinton Turkle. Dutton 1981 unp il hardcover o.p. paperback available $5.99   **E**
1. Seashore—Fiction 2. Cats—Fiction 3. Magic—Fiction
ISBN 0-14-054747-9 (pa)

"Elderly Miss Moody and her cat, Captain Kidde, find a bottle on the seashore. Miss Moody ignores the label warning 'DO NOT OPEN' and liberates a horror. But the spunky woman tells the thing only mice scare her so it becomes a mouse that Kidde takes care of 'tout de suite.'" Publ Wkly

"The strong, simple composition that is typical of Turkle is especially well suited to the still isolation of deserted beaches, and the combination of rich color used with restraint and the framed squares of clear print adds to the visual appeal of the pages. The story is a nice blend of realism and fantasy." Bull Cent Child Books

Turner, Ann Warren, 1945-
Dust for dinner; story by Ann Turner; pictures by Robert Barrett. HarperCollins Pubs. 1995 64p il lib bdg $15.89; pa $3.95   **E**
1. Great Depression, 1929-1939—Fiction 2. Family life—Fiction 3. Farm life—Fiction
ISBN 0-06-023377-X (lib bdg); 0-06-444225-X (pa)   LC 93-34634

"An I can read book"

Jake narrates the story of his family's life in the Oklahoma dust bowl and the journey from their ravaged farm to California during the Great Depression

"Turner takes a sad episode in history and fashions it into a story that has some depth as well as some drama. . . . Realistic, nicely executed illustrations decorate every page." Booklist

Katie's trunk; by Ann Turner; illustrations by Ron Himler. Macmillan 1992 unp il $15; pa $5.99   **E**
1. United States—History—1775-1783, Revolution—Fiction
ISBN 0-02-789512-2; 0-689-81054-7 (pa)   LC 91-20409

Katie, whose family is not sympathetic to the rebel soldiers during the American Revolution, hides under the clothes in her mother's wedding trunk when they invade her home

"Based on a true incident, this bit of historical fiction . . . is unusual because the perspective is from a Tory family's point of view. . . . The illustrations are lovely period paintings that complement, but never overpower, the story." Horn Book

Through moon and stars and night skies; by Ann Turner; pictures by James Graham Hale. Harper & Row 1989 unp il lib bdg $15.89; pa $6.95   **E**
1. Adoption—Fiction
ISBN 0-06-026190-0 (lib bdg); 0-06-443308-0 (pa)   LC 87-35044

Also available with Audiobook
"A Charlotte Zolotow book"

A boy who came from Southeast Asia to be adopted by a couple in this country remembers how unfamiliar and frightening some of the things were in his new home, before he accepted the love to be found there

"This touching, memorable tale is illustrated in warm watercolor-and-ink pictures that gently contrast the narrator's Asian home with his new life in America. It will serve as a meaningful introduction to adoption as well as a starting point for a discussion on cultural transitions." SLJ

Uchida, Yoshiko, 1921-1992
The bracelet; story by Yoshiko Uchida; illustrated by Joanna Yardley. Philomel Bks. 1993 unp il $16.99; pa $5.95   **E**
1. Japanese Americans—Evacuation and relocation, 1942-1945—Fiction 2. World War, 1939-1945—Fiction 3. Friendship—Fiction
ISBN 0-399-22503-X; 0-698-11390-X (pa)   LC 92-26196

Emi, a Japanese American in the second grade, is sent with her family to an internment camp during World War II, but the loss of the bracelet her best friend has given her proves that she does not need a physical reminder of that friendship

"The book (previously published as a short story) is a gentle, honest introduction to the treatment of the Japanese-Americans during the war, and Yardley's delicate pencil-and-watercolor paintings are cleanly drawn and richly colored, with scant pencil lines softly framing the sad scenes. A brief afterword gives a context for the story." Bull Cent Child Books

Udry, Janice May

A tree is nice; pictures by Marc Simont. Harper & Row 1956 unp il $15.95; lib bdg $15.89; pa $5.95   E
1. Trees—Fiction
ISBN 0-06-026155-2; 0-06-026156-0 (lib bdg); 0-06-443147-9 (pa)
Also available Spanish language edition
Awarded the Caldecott Medal, 1957
"In childlike terms and in enticing pictures, colored and black and white, author and artist set forth reasons why trees are nice to have around—trees fill up the sky, they make everything beautiful, cats get away from dogs in them, leaves come down and can be played in, and trees are nice to climb in, to hang a swing in, or to plant. A picture book sure to please young children." Booklist

What Mary Jo shared; pictures: Eleanor Mill. Whitman, A. 1966 unp il lib bdg $14.95   E
1. African Americans—Fiction 2. School stories
ISBN 0-8075-8842-3
Also available in paperback from Scholastic
"Whenever Mary Jo selected something to 'show and tell', her classmates had already chosen it. Finally she brought a very special person to share with the class—her father." N Y Public Libr. Black Exper in Child Books
"The writing is smooth and natural, and the illustrations, done in soft colors and black and white, are charming." We Build Together

Uff, Caroline

Lulu's busy day. Walker & Co. 2000 unp il $14.95   E
ISBN 0-8027-8716-9   LC 99-36100
Lulu enjoys many activities during the day, including drawing a picture, visiting the park, and reading a bedtime story
"The simple illustrations in a muted primary palette contain soft, round figures, and the spare text encourages children to point out favorite objects from their own busy days." Horn Book Guide
Other available titles about Lulu are:
Happy birthday, Lulu! (2000)
Hello, Lulu (1999)

Ungerer, Tomi, 1931-

Crictor. Harper & Row 1958 32p il $15.95; pa $5.95   E
1. Snakes—Fiction
ISBN 0-06-026180-3; 0-06-443044-8 (pa)
A story "about the boa constrictor that was sent to Madame Bodot, who lived and taught school in a little French town. She called the snake Crictor and he became a great pet, learned, debonair and brave. The boys used him for a slide and the girls for a jump-rope. When Crictor captured a burglar by coiling around him until the police came, he was awarded impressive tokens of esteem and affection of the townspeople. Engaging line drawings echo the restrained and elegant absurdities of the text." Bull Cent Child Books

The three robbers. Atheneum Pubs. 1962 unp il o.p.; Roberts Rinehart Pubs. paperback available $6.95   E
1. Thieves—Fiction
ISBN 1-570-98206-6 (pa)
Three robbers who roam the countryside are subdued by the charm of a little girl named Tiffany
"With vigorous, sweeping design and stained glass colors on black and midnight blue Tomi Ungerer presents three of the most charming fierce robbers." Christ Sci Monit

Van Allsburg, Chris

Bad day at Riverbend. Houghton Mifflin 1995 unp il $17.95   E
ISBN 0-395-67347-X   LC 95-4154
When Sheriff Hardy investigates the source of a brilliant light and shiny slime afflicting Riverbend, he finds that the village is becoming part of a child's coloring book streaked with greasy crayons
"Van Allsburg cuts loose with this inventive spoof that will keep readers guessing right up to the end. . . . Van Allsburg clearly had fun with his one, and readers likely will too." Publ Wkly

Ben's dream; story and pictures by Chris Van Allsburg. Houghton Mifflin 1982 31p il lib bdg $16.95; pa $4.95   E
1. Dreams—Fiction
ISBN 0-395-32084-4; 0-395-87470-X (pa)
    LC 81-20029
"When rain spoils Ben's ball game with Margaret, he returns to an empty house, falls asleep in his father's chair, and embarks on a dream. In a marvelous series of double-page black-and-white pictures meticulously textured with hatching, one shares Ben's voyage past such sights as the Statue of Liberty, the Sphinx, and the Mount Rushmore presidents, all with flood waters lapping about their respective chins and waists. Dramatic angles, closeups from above and below, and careful architectural details which recall the work of David Macaulay dazzle the eye and the imagination as Ben's little house floats upon the waters on its splendid excursion. . . . A visual tour de force." Horn Book

The garden of Abdul Gasazi; written and illustrated by Chris Van Allsburg. Houghton Mifflin 1979 unp il lib bdg $17.95   E
1. Magic—Fiction 2. Dogs—Fiction
ISBN 0-395-27804-X
Also available with Audiobook
A Caldecott Medal honor book, 1980
"When Fritz, the naughty dog, ran into the garden of Abdul Gasazi, a retired magician, Alan was terrified, for he knew that dogs were not allowed beyond the vine-covered wall. Fritz eluded Alan, who ultimately came to the magician's imposing house and politely requested the return of the dog. His request was granted, but Fritz, who had been turned into a duck, compounded his original naughtiness by flying away with Alan's cap." Horn Book
The full page "lithographlike drawings are astonishing—eerie, monumental, surreal and witty all at once—and the effect of the whole is original and unforgettable." Books of the Times

Van Allsburg, Chris—*Continued*

Jumanji; written and illustrated by Chris Van Allsburg. Houghton Mifflin 1981 unp il $17.95
E

1. Games—Fiction

ISBN 0-395-30448-2   LC 80-29632

Also available with Audiobook; Spanish language edition also available

Awarded the Caldecott Medal, 1982

"Two children, alone at home while their parents are gone for the afternoon, play a game they have found lying under a tree. Judy reads the rules for the game, 'Jumanji,' and realizes that it must be played to the end; not until they begin play do she and Peter know why that's true. With each roll of the dice, there's a new hazard: a menacing lion, a troop of destructive monkeys, a torrential monsoon, a herd of rhinos, etc." Bull Cent Child Books

"Through the masterly use of light and shadow, the interplay of design elements, and audacious changes in perspective and composition, the artist conveys an impression of color without losing the dramatic contrast of black and white." Horn Book

Just a dream. Houghton Mifflin 1990 unp il $17.95
E

1. Environmental protection—Fiction 2. Pollution—Fiction 3. Dreams—Fiction

ISBN 0-395-53308-2   LC 90-41343

"Walter, an environmental ignoramus of a 10-year-old, is careless or scornful of such elementary actions as recycling or tree planting. One nightmarish evening, however, he visits a future where his daydreams of technological paradise are demolished. Instead, there is merely a horrifically exacerbated continuation of today's eco-problems: landfills, expressways, smog, lifeless oceans, and vanished wilderness. Walter awakens reformed, and is rewarded with another dream: the future redeemed." SLJ

"Once again Van Allsburg demonstrates his unique artistic magic in combining foresight, wisdom and striking artwork to deliver an ecological message concerning conservation and renewal. . . . The full-color, striking paintings evoke the intense revelations of Walter's dreams." Child Book Rev Serv

The mysteries of Harris Burdick. Houghton Mifflin 1984 unp il lib bdg $17.95
E

ISBN 0-395-35393-9   LC 84-9006

Also available Spanish language edition

Presents a series of loosely related drawings each accompanied by a title and a caption which the reader may use to make up his or her own story

Rendered in the author's "signature velvet black and white . . . the pictures are nothing short of spectacular. . . . While some may find this just an excuse for handsome artwork, others will see its great potential for stretching a child's imagination. Although the book could be used in countless ways, primarily it will make storytellers of children. They will need little prompting once they set their eyes on Van Allsburg's provocative scenes. An inventive, useful concoction." Booklist

The Polar Express; written and illustrated by Chris Van Allsburg. Houghton Mifflin 1985 unp il $18.95
E

1. North Pole—Fiction 2. Santa Claus—Fiction 3. Christmas—Fiction

ISBN 0-395-38949-6   LC 85-10907

Also available Audiobook version and Spanish language edition

Awarded the Caldecott Medal, 1986

A magical train ride on Christmas Eve takes a boy to the North Pole to receive a special gift from Santa Claus

This offers "stunning paintings in which Van Allsburg uses dark, rich colors and misty shapes in contrast with touches of bright white-gold light to create scenes, interior and exterior, that have a quality of mystery that imbues the strong composition to achieve a soft, evocative mood." Bull Cent Child Books

The stranger. Houghton Mifflin 1986 unp il lib bdg $18
E

ISBN 0-395-42331-7   LC 86-15235

"A mysterious figure, accidentally struck down by a farmer's truck, stays with the farmer's family until he recovers his memory, participating in the life of the farm. The man—it seems—is Jack Frost, or the spirit of winter; the weather cannot continue its change without him, and when he recalls his function, he takes his leave of his human friends with tears in his eyes." N Y Times Book Rev

"The full-color illustrations, framed in white, evoke an old-fashioned New England landscape at the end of summer; some are remarkably peaceful in tone, others slightly spooky by virtue of brooding colors, unexpected perspectives, or the stranger's peculiar expressions." Bull Cent Child Books

The sweetest fig. Houghton Mifflin 1993 unp il $17.95
E

1. Dreams—Fiction 2. Magic—Fiction 3. Dogs—Fiction

ISBN 0-395-67346-1   LC 93-12692

Also available Spanish language edition

After being given two magical figs that make his dreams come true, Monsieur Bibot sees his plans for future wealth upset by his long-suffering dog

"The full-color, expressive illustrations are filled with nuance, detail and mystery. Once again, Van Allsburg weaves a spell with ultimate skill and creativity." Child Book Rev Serv

The widow's broom. Houghton Mifflin 1992 unp il $17.95
E

1. Magic—Fiction 2. Witchcraft—Fiction

ISBN 0-395-64051-2   LC 92-7110

Also available Spanish language edition

A witch's worn-out broom serves a widow well, until her neighbors decide the thing is wicked and dangerous

"In addition to being a neatly understated piece of storytelling, this fuels Van Allsburg's best kind of illustration—darkly rounded, speckle-textured art with eerie effects. . . . The doubling of the unexpectedly beautiful young witch and the sensible heroine delivers a healthy dose of female power, which kids can subconsciously digest while enjoying the slightly scary images tempered with a text given to straight-faced humor." Bull Cent Child Books

Van Allsburg, Chris—*Continued*

The wreck of the Zephyr; written and illustrated by Chris Van Allsburg. Houghton Mifflin 1983 unp il lib bdg $17.95 **E**
ISBN 0-395-33075-0   LC 82-23371
"The story-within-a-story is a fantasy told by an old man, a tale of a boy who sees flying boats and is determined that he, too, will learn to make his boat, the Zephyr, fly. He succeeds, but the boat is wrecked, and he suffers a broken leg. The tale over, the old man limps away." Bull Cent Child Books
This "displays recognizable hallmarks of the artist's work: beauty of composition, striking contrasts of light and shadow, and especially the fascinating ambiguity of illusion and reality." Horn Book

The wretched stone. Houghton Mifflin 1991 unp il $17.95 **E**
1. Sea stories
ISBN 0-395-53307-4   LC 91-11525
A strange glowing stone picked up on a sea voyage captivates a ship's crew and has a terrible transforming effect on them
"Although Van Allsburg clearly has a message to convey, he has added to the book an enjoyable and necessary dollop of humor. The story has a quiet, understated, yet suspenseful tone; most of the plot's considerable drama is conveyed in the impressive illustrations." Horn Book

The Z was zapped; a play in twenty-six acts; performed by the Caslon Players; written and directed by Chris Van Allsburg. Houghton Mifflin 1987 unp il $17.95; pa $7.95 **E**
1. Alphabet
ISBN 0-395-44612-0; 0-395-93748-5 (pa)
    LC 87-14988
At head of title: The Alphabet Theatre proudly presents
This book presents a "series of beautifully executed full-page black-and-white illustrations showing letters undergoing varieties of existential *Angst* on a tasteful little stage, each with an explanatory line of copy printed on its backside." N Y Times Book Rev
"Children can try to guess what action has occured, thereby increasing their vocabulary and the fun, or they can turn the page and read the text, or better yet—do both. This clever romp resembles old vaudeville theater, with one curious act following the next." SLJ

Van Laan, Nancy

Moose tales; illustrated by Amy Rusch. Houghton Mifflin 1999 unp il $15; pa $5.95 **E**
1. Moose—Fiction 2. Animals—Fiction
ISBN 0-395-90863-9; 0-618-11128-X (pa)
    LC 97-41273
Moose takes a walk, takes a nap under a tree that Beaver is gnawing, and finally joins all his friends in making an almost perfect snow creature with antlers
"The text is well paced, and the stories work either as read-alouds or independent reads. Rusch's illustrations feature the toothy, winsome forest dwellers. . . . Most children will enjoy their cheerful camaraderie and appreciate rthe gentle humor." SLJ

Possum come a-knockin'; illustrated by George Booth. Knopf 1990 unp il lib bdg $14.99; pa $6.99 **E**
1. Opossums—Fiction 2. Stories in rhyme
ISBN 0-394-92206-9 (lib bdg); 0-679-83468-0 (pa)
    LC 88-12751
The narrator "sees a possum a-knockin' at the door. While Granny is a-rockin' and a-knittin', and Ma's a-cookin' and Pa's a-fixin', . . . [the boy] unsuccessfully tries to tell them about the possum." Booklist
The author has produced a wonderfully rhythmic and funny trickster tale told in a controlled dialect that is consistent throughout. Booth's critters—possum, cat, and dog—are priceless. Friend possum is the wiliest and slyest varmint one could imagine. The humans are pretty funny, too, while the stage set is appropriately countrified. The story is a raucous romp." Horn Book

A tree for me; illustrated by Sheila White Samton. Knopf 2000 unp il $14.95; lib bdg $17.99 **E**
1. Trees 2. Animals 3. Counting 4. Stories in rhyme
ISBN 0-679-89384-9; 0-679-99384-3 (lib bdg)
    LC 99-47440
A child climbs five different trees, looking for a place to hide and finding an increasing number of animals already in residence, until finally the perfect tree is found
"The simple rhyming text is fun to read aloud, and although it's highly repetitive, its spirited rhythm keeps it from becoming boring. Bright collages show the variety of woodland creatures in the trees." Horn Book Guide

Van Leeuwen, Jean

Going West; pictures by Thomas B. Allen. Dial Bks. for Young Readers 1991 unp il $17.99; pa $5.99 **E**
1. Frontier and pioneer life—Fiction 2. Family life—Fiction
ISBN 0-8037-1027-5; 0-14-056096-3 (pa)
    LC 90-20694
Follows a family's emigration by prairie schooner from the East, across the plains to Kansas
"Into a gentle text brimming with family warmth and love, Van Leeuwen . . . packs a wealth of emotional moments. . . . Allen's . . . scumbled, subdued pastel drawings, on sepia stock, masterfully conjure up the expanse of land and feelings." Publ Wkly

Nothing here but trees; pictures by Phil Boatwright. Dial Bks. for Young Readers 1998 unp il $15.99 **E**
1. Frontier and pioneer life—Fiction 2. Ohio—Fiction
ISBN 0-8037-2178-1   LC 97-34318
A close-knit pioneer family carves out a new home amidst the densely forested land of Ohio in the early nineteenth century
"Boatwright's handsome oil-and-acrylic paintings show the close-knit family in a wilderness that is lonely, scary, and exciting." Booklist

Tales of Oliver Pig; pictures by Arnold Lobel. Dial Bks. for Young Readers 1979 64p il hardcover o.p. paperback available $3.99 **E**
1. Pigs—Fiction 2. Family life—Fiction
ISBN 0-14-036549-4 (pa)   LC 79-4276

Van Leeuwen, Jean—*Continued*

Also available Spanish language edition

"Dial easy-to-read"

"Oliver encounters many true-to-life situations and decides how to cope with them: what to do on a rainy day, how to make a bad day into a good one, what to do when Grandma comes, how to dress for the snow, and most confusing, what to do when Mother cries." Child Book Rev Serv

The book is "filled with the warmth of the commonplace, the jostling joys and sorrows of siblings and the love of a pig family. . . . Arnold Lobel's illustrations, often in miniature, carry on the tender, yet never sentimental tone." SLJ

Other available titles about the Pig family are:

Amanda Pig and her best friend Lollipop (1998)
Amanda Pig and her big brother Oliver (1982)
Amanda Pig on her own (1991)
Amanda Pig, school girl (1997)
More tales of Amanda Pig (1985)
More tales of Oliver Pig (1981)
Oliver, Amanda, and Grandmother Pig (1987)
Oliver and Albert, friends forever (2000)
Oliver and Amanda and the big snow (1995)
Oliver and Amanda's Christmas (1989)
Oliver and Amanda's Halloween (1992)
Oliver Pig at school (1990)
Tales of Amanda Pig (1983)

Vaughan, Marcia, 1951-

Snap! written by Marcia Vaughan; illustrated by Sascha Hutchinson. Scholastic 1996 c1994 unp il $14.95 **E**

1. Kangaroos—Fiction 2. Animals—Fiction 3. Australia—Fiction

ISBN 0-590-60377-9 LC 95-11773

Joey the kangaroo plays games with Twisker the bush mouse, Slider the snake, Prickler the echidna, Flatso the platypus, and Sly-tooth the crocodile

"Lilting rhythm and wordplay give new zip to an old story, and Hutchinson's torn-paper collage illustrations, lively and intensely colored against a white background, seem almost three-dimensional." Booklist

Whistling Dixie; illustrated by Barry Moser. HarperCollins Pubs. 1995 31p il $15.95 **E**

1. Animals—Fiction 2. Marshes—Fiction 3. Supernatural—Fiction

ISBN 0-06-021030-3 LC 91-45831

Dixie Lee brings home an alligator, a snake, and an owl as pets to protect her family from such spooky creatures as the churn-turners, the bogeyman, and the mist-sisters

"Spiced with Cajun dialect and sayings that conjure up vivid images and a wonderful look at Southern life, this read-aloud combines realism and fantasy in a humorous way that will delight youngsters. The pictures are bright and colorful." Child Book Rev Serv

Viorst, Judith

Alexander and the terrible, horrible, no good, very bad day; illustrated by Ray Cruz. Atheneum Pubs. 1972 unp il $14; pa $4.99 **E**

ISBN 0-689-30072-7; 0-689-71173-5 (pa)

Also available Spanish language edition

The author "describes the plight of a boy for whom everything goes wrong from the moment he steps out of bed and discovers he has gum stuck in his hair to his return to bed that night when he has to wear his hated railroad-train pajamas and the cat decides to sleep with one of his brothers instead of with him. His mother consoles him by remarking that some days are like that." Booklist

"Small listeners can enjoy the litany of disaster, and perhaps be stimulated to discuss the possibility that one contributes by expectation. The illustrations capture the grumpy dolor of the story, ruefully funny." Sutherland. The Best In Child Books

Other available titles about Alexander are:

Alexander, who is not (do you hear me?) going (I mean it) to move (1995)
Alexander, who used to be rich last Sunday (1978)

Earrings! illustrated by Nola Langner Malone. Atheneum Pubs. 1990 unp il $16.95; pa $5.99 **E**

ISBN 0-689-31615-1; 0-689-71669-9 (pa)

LC 89-17846

"The curly-haired protagonist pleads, cajoles and bargains to get pierced ears; she points out that she is the only girl in 'her class, the world or the solar system' without them. She promises to walk the dog, clean her room, read a book a week for a year and be nice to her little brother if she is only granted her wish." Publ Wkly

"Viorst homes in on minor childhood crises with the perfect blend of humor and insight, and Malone's expressive and comic figures are miniature character studies in themselves." Horn Book

My mama says there aren't any zombies, ghosts, vampires, creatures, demons, monsters, fiends, goblins, or things. Atheneum Pubs. 1973 unp il $16; pa $5.99 **E**

1. Monsters—Fiction 2. Mothers—Fiction

ISBN 0-689-30102-2; 0-689-71204-9 (pa)

This book deals humorously with the childhood sense of being threatened by "imaginary monsters and a mother's reassurances that they don't exist. While wanting to believe his mother, Nick is also aware that she often makes mistakes . . . like the time she made Nick wear his boots on a sunny day." SLJ

The tenth good thing about Barney; illustrated by Erik Blegvad. Atheneum Pubs. 1971 25p il $14; pa $4.99 **E**

1. Death—Fiction 2. Cats—Fiction

ISBN 0-689-20688-7; 0-689-71203-0 (pa)

"A little boy saddened by the death of his cat thinks of nine good things about Barney to say at his funeral. Later his father helps him discover a tenth good thing: Barney is in the ground helping grow flowers and trees and grass and 'that's a pretty nice job for a cat.'" Booklist

"The author succinctly and honestly handles both the emotions stemming from the loss of a beloved pet and the questions about the finality of death which naturally arise in such a situation. . . . An unusually good book that handles a difficult subject straightforwardly and with no trace of the macabre." Horn Book

Voake, Charlotte

Ginger. Candlewick Press 1997 unp il $16.99;
pa $6.99   E
1. Cats—Fiction
ISBN 0-7636-0108-X; 0-7636-0788-6 (pa)
                         LC 96-20890
When Ginger the cat gets fed up with dealing with her
owner's new kitten, it takes drastic measures to make the
two of them friends
"The warm, expressive watercolor illustrations are a
perfect compliment to the winsome, enchanting text."
Child Book Rev Serv

Here comes the train. Candlewick Press 1998
unp il $15.99   E
1. Railroads—Fiction 2. Family life—Fiction
ISBN 0-7636-0438-0   LC 97-39312
Every Saturday, Chloe, her little brother William, and
their father bicycle to a footbridge over the railroad
tracks and wait for the trains to come thundering under
them
"Voake's clear, casual watercolor-and-ink illustrations
make great use of perspective. . . . Kids will recognize
the excitement and also the magic of the last page, when
the child in bed at night can hear the sound of the train
in the distance." Booklist

Waber, Bernard

A firefly named Torchy. Houghton Mifflin 1999
46p il $15; pa $5.95   E
1. Fireflies
ISBN 0-395-90496-X; 0-395-90497-8 (pa)
A reissue of the title first published 1970
A little firefly is unhappy because his light is so
bright all the plants and animals think it is daytime
"The brilliant nonsense is cleverly shown in scenes
that switch from darkness to a white daytime kind of illumination. The fine, funny answer to the problem unfolds with a fantastic and unexpected display of lights."
Horn Book Guide

Ira sleeps over. Houghton Mifflin 1972 48p il
lib bdg $15; pa $5.95   E
ISBN 0-395-13893-0 (lib bdg); 0-395-20503-4 (pa)

Also available with Audiobook; Spanish language edition also available
"A small boy's joy in being asked to spend the night
with a friend who lives next door is unrestrained until
his sister raises the question of whether or not he should
take his teddy bear. Torn between fear of being considered babyish and fear of what it may be like to sleep
without his bear, Ira has a hard time deciding what to
do. His dilemma is resolved happily, however, when he
discovers that his friend Reggie also has a nighttime bear
companion. An appealing picture book which depicts
common childhood qualms with empathy and humor in
brief text and colorful illustrations." Booklist
Another available title about Ira is:
Ira says goodbye (1988)

A lion named Shirley Williamson. Houghton
Mifflin 1996 40p il $15.95; pa $6.95   E
1. Lions—Fiction 2. Zoos—Fiction
ISBN 0-395-80979-7; 0-618-05580-0 (pa)
                         LC 96-11187

This is a story of the "mishaps that befall a lion
named Shirley Williamson. Because of her unusual
name, Seymour, the zookeeper, indulges her with beautiful roses; admiring fans send her flattering letters. . . .
The other lions, Goobah, Poobah, and Aroobah, growl in
jealous rage over Shirley's exceptional status. Then, one
ill-fated day . . . Shirley is stripped of her name and
simply becomes Bongo. Miserable and homesick for Africa, she escapes from her cage and hunts down Seymour
in Brooklyn. In the end, she regains her special name
and accepts the fact that the zoo is her home." SLJ
This is "a story that is both hysterical and poignant.
It succeeds at every level, offering a plot that prances
along, characters that show the inevitable tangle of emotions life elicits, and artwork that is so funny yet sly that
adults and children can both relish it." Booklist

Lyle, Lyle, crocodile. Houghton Mifflin 1965
48p il $15; pa $5.95   E
1. Crocodiles—Fiction 2. New York (N.Y.)—Fiction
ISBN 0-395-16995-X; 0-395-13720-9 (pa)
Also available with Audiobook
Lyle the crocodile who lives in New York City
"wants desperately to win the friendship of the cat Loret-
ta two doors away but every time Loretta catches a
glimpse of him she flings herself into a nervous fit."
Booklist
"The illustrations are cartoon-like, lively, and colorful.
. . . The situation is nicely exploited with a bland
daffiness." Bull Cent Child Books
Other available titles about Lyle are:
Funny, funny Lyle (1987)
The house on East 88th Street (1962)
Lovable Lyle (1969)
Lyle and the birthday party (1966)
Lyle at Christmas (1998)
Lyle at the office (1994)
Lyle finds his mother (1974)

Waddell, Martin

Can't you sleep, Little Bear? illustrated by
Barbara Firth. 2nd U.S. ed. Candlewick Press 1992
unp il $15.99; pa $5.99   E
1. Bears—Fiction 2. Bedtime—Fiction
ISBN 1-56402-007-X; 1-56402-262-5 (pa)
                         LC 91-71858
Also available Big book edition and Spanish language
edition
First published 1988 in the United Kingdom
When bedtime comes Little Bear is afraid of the dark,
until Big Bear brings him lights and love
"Firth's brightly lit watercolor and soft pencil illustra-
tions, framed in the dark blue of the night, capture the
cozy, physical affection of the story, the playfulness of
Little Bear, . . . the shadowy mystery of the moonlit
landscape, and the huge comforting presence of a parent
who is always there when you call." Booklist
Other available titles about Little Bear are:
Good job, Little Bear! (1999)
Let's go home, Little Bear (1993)
Little Bear's baby book (2000)
You and me, Little Bear (1996)

Waddell, Martin—*Continued*
Farmer duck; illustrated by Helen Oxenbury. Candlewick Press 1992 c1991 unp il $15.99; pa $4.99　　　　　　　　　　　　　　　　　　E
　1. Ducks—Fiction 2. Farm life—Fiction
　ISBN 1-56402-009-6; 1-56402-596-9 (pa)
　　　　　　　　　　　　　　　　LC 91-71855
Also available Big book edition
First published 1991 in the United Kingdom
When a kind and hardworking duck nearly collapses from overwork, while taking care of a farm because the owner is too lazy to do so, the rest of the animals get together and chase the farmer out of town
"Hilarious art masterfully captures the expressions of the put-upon duck, the supportive cast, and the slovenly ergophobic who reads the newspaper and chomps on bonbons in bed. . . . With its lilting, large-print text and satisfying resolution, it's as perfect for beginning readers as it is for story hours." SLJ

Owl babies; illustrated by Patrick Benson. Candlewick Press 1992 unp il $15.99　　　　E
　1. Owls—Fiction
　ISBN 1-56402-101-7　　　　　　LC 91-58750
Also available Board book edition and Spanish language edition
Three owl babies whose mother has gone out in the night try to stay calm while she is gone
"The illustrations, executed in black ink and watercolor, capture in every feather and expression the little owls' worry and watchfulness as well as their complete joy when Owl Mother returns." Horn Book

Rosie's babies; written by Martin Waddell; illustrated by Penny Dale. Candlewick Press 1999 unp il $15.99　　　　　　　　　　　E
　1. Infants—Fiction 2. Mother-child relationship—Fiction 3. Toys—Fiction
　ISBN 0-7636-0718-5　　　　　　LC 98-36166
As her mother gets her baby brother ready for bed, a young girl describes how she takes care of her own babies—stuffed animals—doing the same things that her mother does
"Soft watercolors in cozy blue and brown tones set a homey scene and lovingly portray both the family relationships and the imaginary adventures."

Who do you love? illustrated by Camilla Ashforth. Candlewick Press 1999 unp il $12.99　　　　　　　　　　　　　　　　　　　E
　1. Cats—Fiction 2. Bedtime—Fiction
　ISBN 0-7636-0586-7　　　　　　LC 98-3455
At bedtime a mother cat and her kitten Holly play the game "Who Do You Love?" and Holly describes everyone she loves and her reasons for doing so
"Ashforth's soft, dreamy watercolors portray homey scenes. . . . Both art and story capture how a young child thinks." Booklist

Walker, Sally M.
The 18 penny goose; story by Sally M. Walker; pictures by Ellen Beier. HarperCollins Pubs. 1998 61p il lib bdg $15.89; pa $3.95　　　　　E
　1. Geese—Fiction 2. New Jersey—Fiction 3. United States—History—1775-1783, Revolution—Fiction
　ISBN 0-06-027557-X (lib bdg); 0-06-444250-0 (pa)
　　　　　　　　　　　　　　　LC 96-46229

"An I can read book"
Eight-year-old Letty attempts to save her pet goose from marauding British soldiers in New Jersey during the Revolutionary War
"Based on a true event, Walker's retelling includes strong details and plenty of drama. Watercolors convey the period setting in somber muted tones." Horn Book Guide

Wallace, Karen
Scarlette Beane; illustrated by Jon Berkeley. Dial Bks. for Young Readers 2000 c1999 unp il $15.99　　　　　　　　　　　　　　　E
　1. Gardening—Fiction 2. Vegetables—Fiction
　ISBN 0-8037-2475-6　　　　　　LC 98-47173
First published 1999 in the United Kingdom
When family members give five-year-old Scarlette a garden, she succeeds in growing gigantic vegetables and creating something wonderful
"The optimistic text matches the glowing paintings of vegetables and rich earth, and the rough acrylic illustrations on textured paper give enough small details of the Deane family homestead to reward close observation." Horn Book Guide

Walsh, Ellen Stoll, 1942-
For Pete's sake. Harcourt Brace & Co. 1998 unp il $15　　　　　　　　　　　　　　　E
　1. Alligators—Fiction 2. Flamingos—Fiction
　ISBN 0-15-200324-X　　　　　　LC 97-25677
Pete, an alligator who thinks that he is a flamingo, worries when he begins to notice the differences between him and his flamingo friends
"Walsh's precise paper-cut collages are just right. Subtly textured and with spacious, stark white backgrounds, they are pleasingly simple, giving the comedy and the message plenty of unencumbered opportunity to sink in." Booklist

Mouse count. Harcourt Brace Jovanovich 1991 unp il lib bdg $13; pa $5.50　　　　　　E
　1. Mice—Fiction 2. Snakes—Fiction 3. Counting
　ISBN 0-15-256023-8 (lib bdg); 0-15-200223-5 (pa)
　　　　　　　　　　　　　　　LC 90-35915
Also available Board book edition
Ten mice outsmart a hungry snake
"Children will delight in this counting game that is couched in an exciting, original story. . . . The torn paper collage and tempra illustrations are lively and depict the story's unerring drama through an uncluttered form and line." SLJ
Another available title about the mice is:
Mouse paint (1989)

Walter, Mildred Pitts, 1922-
Brother to the wind; pictures by Diane and Leo Dillon. Lothrop, Lee & Shepard Bks. 1985 unp il lib bdg $15.89　　　　　　　　　　　　E
　1. Flight—Fiction 2. Africa—Fiction
　ISBN 0-688-03812-3　　　　　　LC 83-26800
With the help of Good Snake, Emeke, a young African boy gets his dearest wish

Walter, Mildred Pitts, 1922-—*Continued*

"Elements of folk legend—such as the wise woman, the oracular snake and its magic talismans, talking animals—contribute a timeless power to Emeke's lessons of faith and self-reliance. The illustrations emphasize the coalition of dream and necessity, which fuels Emeke's ingenuity. Vibrantly colored scenes of Emeke's daily life in the village are superimposed against personifications of the surreal forces which inspire his imagination." Horn Book

Walter, Virginia A.

"Hi, pizza man!"; by Virginia Walter; pictures by Ponder Goembel. Orchard Bks. 1995 unp il lib bdg $16.99; pa $6.95   **E**

1. Animals—Fiction
ISBN 0-531-08735-2 (lib bdg); 0-531-07107-3 (pa)
LC 94-24855

"A Richard Jackson book"
While a young girl waits for the delivery of a hot pizza, she provides the appropriate animal sounds for a variety of pretend animal pizza deliverers

"Each two-page spread features ink-and-acrylic wash artwork that boldly introduces a marvelous menagerie. . . . On target for the age-group, who will enjoy the noisy fun alone or in groups." Booklist

Walters, Virginia

Are we there yet, Daddy? illustrated by S. D. Schindler. Viking 1999 unp il $15.99   **E**

1. Automobile travel—Fiction 2. Maps—Fiction
3. Stories in rhyme
ISBN 0-670-87402-7   LC 97-18220

A young boy describes the trip he and his father make to Grandma's house, measuring how many miles are left at various points on the trip

"This unique picture book combines maps and counting skills with a bouncy refrain that invites kids to join in. . . . The flat, pastel pictures add enlivening details to the repetitive text." SLJ

Walton, Rick

One more bunny; adding from one to ten; illustrated by Paige Miglio. Lothrop, Lee & Shepard Bks. 2000 unp il $15.95; lib bdg $15.89
E

1. Counting 2. Addition 3. Rabbits 4. Stories in rhyme
ISBN 0-688-16847-7; 0-688-16848-5 (lib bdg)
LC 99-27642

Bunnies frolicking at the playground introduce the numbers one through ten and the principles of simple addition

"Fun predominates, both in Miglio's spring-like colored-pencil-and-watercolor pictures . . . and in Walton's refrain: 'Here comes one more bunny.'" Booklist

Ward, Lynd Kendall, 1905-1985

The biggest bear; by Lynd Ward. Houghton Mifflin 1988 84p il lib bdg $16; pa $6.95   **E**

1. Bears—Fiction
ISBN 0-395-14806-5 (lib bdg); 0-395-15024-8 (pa)
LC 88-176366

Also available with Audiobook
Awarded the Caldecott Medal, 1953
A reissue of the title first published 1952

"Johnny Orchard never did acquire the bearskin for which he boldly went hunting. Instead, he brought home a cuddly bear cub, which grew in size and appetite to mammoth proportions and worried his family and neighbors half to death." Child Books Too Good to Miss

Watson, Wendy

Thanksgiving at our house. Clarion Bks. 1991 unp il hardcover o.p. paperback available $6.95
E

1. Thanksgiving Day—Fiction 2. Family life—Fiction
ISBN 0-395-69944-4 (pa)   LC 90-26138

The family busily prepares for Thanksgiving and has a grand feast with visiting relatives. Includes Thanksgiving poems

"The homey details are told in an easy-to-read narrative and pictured in Watson's usual crisp, lively ink-and-watercolor quasi-comic-strip illustrations in warm, muted tones. The rounded, robust, active figures of the children and adults of all ages express the happiness and comfort of a close, loving family." SLJ

Watts, Bernadette, 1942-

The ugly duckling; by Hans Christian Andersen; adapted and illustrated by Bernadette Watts. North-South Bks. 2000 unp il $15.95; lib bdg $15.88   **E**

1. Fairy tales
ISBN 0-7358-1388-4; 0-7358-1389-2 (lib bdg)
LC 00-35125

An ugly duckling spends an unhappy year ostracized by the other animals before he grows into a beautiful swan

The "detailed double-paged spreads are beautiful. . . . Watts' active pastoral landscapes, filled with light and movement, capture the changing seasons and the sturdy, unwanted outsider's search for home." Booklist

Weiss, Nicki, 1954-

Where does the brown bear go? Greenwillow Bks. 1989 unp il $17   **E**

1. Animals—Fiction 2. Night—Fiction
ISBN 0-688-07862-1   LC 87-36980

Also available Board book edition
When the lights go down on the city street and the sun sinks far behind the seas, the animals of the world are on their way home for the night

"The rich, dark colors of a velvet night sky, polka dotted with stars, form the background for this enchanting lullaby. . . . Repetition and alliteration are skillfully employed in the verses; the rhythm and rhymes are so perfect that it takes only a reading or two before the poem is committed to memory. . . . Altogether, an exquisite book to end a young one's day." Horn Book

Weitzman, Jacqueline Preiss

You can't take a balloon into the Metropolitan Museum; story by Jacqueline Preiss Weitzman; pictures by Robin Preiss Glasser. Dial Bks. for Young Readers 1998 37p il $16.99　　E
1. Metropolitan Museum of Art (New York, N.Y.)—Fiction 2. New York (N.Y.)—Fiction 3. Stories without words

ISBN 0-8037-2301-6　　　　LC 97-31629

In this wordless story, a young girl and her grandmother view works inside the Metropolitan Museum of Art, while the balloon she has been forced to leave outside floats around New York City causing a series of mishaps that mirror scenes in the museum's artworks

"Lively, squiggly ink sketches with characters picked out in watercolor and gouache for accent, along with reproductions of art from the Met . . . tell a vivid, happy tale." Booklist

You can't take a balloon into the National Gallery; story by Jacqueline Preiss Weitzman; pictures by Robin Preiss Glasser. Dial Bks. for Young Readers 2000 36p il $16.99　　E
1. National Gallery of Art (U.S.)—Fiction 2. Washington (D.C.)—Fiction 3. Stories without words

ISBN 0-8037-2303-2　　　　LC 99-36367

While a brother and sister, along with their grandmother, visit the National Gallery of Art, the balloon they were not allowed to bring into the museum floats around Washington, D.C., causing a series of mishaps at various tourist sites. Images of thirty-two famous Americans appear among the illustrations

"The illustrations are exuberantly splashed with color. . . . Lots of fun, either as preparation for a visit to Washington, D.C., or as a way to encourage children to take the time to really examine the pictures in a book." Booklist

Wells, Rosemary, 1943-

Edward unready for school. Dial Bks. for Young Readers 1995 unp il $7.99　　E
1. Bears—Fiction 2. School stories

ISBN 0-8037-1884-5　　　　LC 95-7890

"Edward's first week of playschool is so painful for him that his teacher sends for his parents, announcing, 'Not everyone is ready for the same things at the same time.'" Publ Wkly

"The simple text is enhanced by the humor of the ink and watercolor art; together they work perfectly to capture this facet of childhood experience." Horn Book

Other available titles about Edward the unready are:
Edward in deep water (1995)
Edward's overwhelming overnight (1995)

Emily's first 100 days of school. Hyperion Bks. for Children 2000 unp il $16.99　　E
1. School stories 2. Rabbits—Fiction 3. Counting

ISBN 0-7868-0507-2　　　　LC 99-27021

Starting with number one for the first day of school, Emily the rabbit learns the numbers to one hundred in many different ways

"Wells manages to find fresh, engaging presentations for that many numbers. Alive with color and thematically relevant decoration, the oversized pages are sometimes divided into several panels, but never feel too busy." Horn Book Guide

Fritz and the Mess Fairy. Dial Bks. for Young Readers 1991 unp il $14　　E
1. Fairies—Fiction 2. Skunks—Fiction

ISBN 0-8037-0981-1　　　　LC 90-26671

Fritz, a skunk and a master at creating terrible messes, meets his match when his science project goes wrong and the Mess Fairy emerges

"An unexpected twist caps this spirited tale, illustrated with Wells's distinctive watercolors that brim with droll details. As ever, her childlike sensibilities and zany sense of humor are perfectly on target." Publ Wkly

Hazel's amazing mother. Dial Bks. for Young Readers 1985 unp il hardcover o.p. paperback available $5.99　　E
1. Mothers—Fiction

ISBN 0-14-054911-0 (pa)　　　　LC 85-1447

When Hazel and her beloved doll Eleanor are set upon by bullies, Hazel's mother comes to the rescue in a surprising way

"The power of maternal love may be exaggerated here, but the lap audience will understand that mothers are their defenders and will do extraordinary things for their young. As is true of other books by Wells, the characters are small animals in appearance; in behavior they are people. . . . Breezy and funny, but also touching, this should appeal to children's sense of justice as well as their faith in parental omnipotence." Bull Cent Child Books

Max's first word. Dial Bks. for Young Readers 1979 unp il　　E
1. Vocabulary—Fiction 2. Siblings—Fiction 3. Rabbits—Fiction

　　　　LC 79-59745

Available Board book edition
"Very first books"

The book depicts "the trials of put-upon Ruby and her infant brother, Max. . . . Ruby puts a cup on Max's high-chair tray and orders him to say 'cup.' Slamming the cup firmly down, Max shouts 'Bang!' And 'Bang!' is what he responds to all Ruby's teaching as she points out things in the kitchen. . . . When she hands Max an apple, she says 'yum-yum,' whereupon the tricky baby hollers 'Delicious!'" Publ Wkly

Other available titles about Max and Ruby are:
Bunny cakes (1997)
Goodnight Max (2000)
Max and Ruby's first Greek myth: Pandora's box (1993)
Max and Ruby's Midas: another Greek myth (1995)
Max cleans up (2000)
Max's bath (1985)
Max's bedtime (1985)
Max's birthday (1985)
Max's breakfast (1985)
Max's chocolate chicken (1989)
Max's Christmas (1986)
Max's dragon shirt (1991)
Max's new suit (1979)
Max's ride (1979)
Max's toys (1979)

McDuff moves in; pictures by Susan Jeffers. Hyperion Bks. for Children 1997 unp il $12.95　　E
1. Dogs—Fiction

ISBN 0-7868-0318-5　　　　LC 96-38221

Wells, Rosemary, 1943-—*Continued*

Also available The McDuff stories, which includes McDuff moves in, McDuff comes home, McDuff and the baby, and McDuff's new friend. Spanish language edition also available

A white terrier "is rejected at several doors before finding a loving home, complete with an herbal bath and vanilla rice pudding." SLJ

"This collaboration by Wells and Jeffers is as sweet, substantial, and comforting as that bowl of rice pudding and will suit the many children who like stories with simple words, clear story lines, and happily-ever-after endings." Booklist

Other available titles about McDuff are:

McDuff and the baby (1997)
McDuff comes home (1997)
McDuff's new friend (1998)

Morris's disappearing bag. Viking 1999 unp il
$15.99   E
 1. Christmas—Fiction 2. Rabbits—Fiction
ISBN 0-670-88721-8   LC 00-267633
First published 1975 by Dial Bks. for Young Readers

Morris is so disappointed with his Christmas present that he invents a disappearing bag, which gives him a chance to share his brother's and sister's gifts

In this version "Morris re-appears in a full-color, full-size edition of the Christmas day story." Horn Book Guide

Moss pillows; a voyage to The Bunny Planet. Dial Bks. for Young Readers 1992 unp il E
 1. Rabbits—Fiction
          LC 91-41600
Only available as part of miniature boxed set Voyage to the Bunny Planet that includes First tomato (1992) and The island light (1992)

Robert's visit to relatives is disastrous, but a visit to the Bunny Planet cheers him up as he experiences the day that should have been

"As always, Wells shows her empathy for children's feelings of helplessness and their dreams of escape. . . . The bad day is described in a weary impersonal voice. . . . In contrast, the idyllic planet visit is recounted in an upbeat first-person narrative in rhyme. . . . Not many books could make both the shame and the happiness so entertaining. Wells evokes the embarrassment and pain with touching comedy and without a trace of condescension." Booklist

Noisy Nora; with all new illustrations. Dial Bks. for Young Readers 1997 unp il $15.99; pa $5.99
              E
 1. Mice—Fiction 2. Stories in rhyme
ISBN 0-670-88722-6; 0-14-056728-3 (pa)
Also available Audiobook version

A newly illustrated edition of the title first published 1973

Little Nora, tired of being ignored, tries to gain her family's attention by being noisy. When this doesn't work Nora disappears but returns when she is sure she has been missed

"All new illustrations infuse this much-loved picture book . . . with energy. Vibrant colors and a larger format make the characters seem to jump out at readers." SLJ

Read to your bunny. Scholastic 1998 c1997 unp
il $7.95; pa $2.99   E
 1. Rabbits—Fiction 2. Books and reading—Fiction
3. Stories in rhyme
ISBN 0-590-30284-1; 0-439-08717-1 (pa)
          LC 97-17704

Brief rhyming text and colorful illustrations tell what happens when parents and children share twenty minutes a day reading

"Each line of text gets one of Wells' delightful bordered pictures of parents and children at all sorts of activities, from bathing to skating, but always with a book in hand." Booklist

Shy Charles; written and illustrated by Rosemary Wells. Dial Bks. for Young Readers 1988 unp il hardcover o.p. paperback available $5.99   E
 1. Mice—Fiction 2. Stories in rhyme
ISBN 0-14-054537-9 (pa)   LC 87-27247

"Charles, a young mouse, is perfectly happy playing by himself, and social contacts are an endless ordeal. He can't or won't say 'thank you' in public places, can't or won't cope with dancing lessons or football. But when the baby sitter falls down the stairs, Charles is able to comfort her and call for help, before resuming his shy silence." N Y Times Book Rev

"Wells' illustrations . . . show the plump, large-eared cast to be full of charm and cleverness. Facial expressions, posture, and background details substantially extend the humor of the story. The simple rhythm of the rhyming text is subtle and playful." SLJ

Yoko. Hyperion Bks. for Children 1998 unp il
$14.95; lib bdg $15.49   E
 1. Food—Fiction 2. School stories
ISBN 0-7868-0395-9; 0-7868-2345-3 (lib bdg)
          LC 98-12342

When Yoko brings sushi to school for lunch, her classmates make fun of what she eats—until one of them tries it for himself

"Wells sets the story in an active preschool classroom, and her clear ink-and-watercolor pictures have never been more expressive and tender, with a range of animal characters that are endearingly human in body language and expression." Booklist

We're going on a lion hunt; [illustrated by] David Axtell. Holt & Co. 2000 c1999 unp il $15.95
              E
 1. Lions—Fiction 2. Africa—Fiction
ISBN 0-8050-6159-2   LC 98-47507
First published 1999 in the United Kingdom

Two girls set out bravely in search of a lion, going through long grass, a swamp, and a cave before they find what they're looking for

"Axtell takes a storytime classic to the African savanna. . . . [His] sun-soaked, impressionistic oil paintings offer beautiful landscapes and engaging details. . . . Large figures on the page make this a good choice for storytimes as well as lap times." SLJ

Westcott, Nadine Bernard, 1949-

The lady with the alligator purse; adapted and illustrated by Nadine Bernard Westcott. Little, Brown 1988 unp il hardcover o.p. paperback available $4.95   E
1. Nonsense verses
ISBN 0-316-93136-5 (pa)   LC 87-21368
Also available Board book edition
"Joy Street books"
"Westcott adapts a jump rope rhyme about the misadventures of Tiny Tim to create a zany book of nonsense that demands reading aloud. After the mischievous baby drinks his bathwater, eats the soap, and tries to stuff the bathtub down his throat, his mother calls the doctor, the nurse, and the lady with the alligator purse. When medical cures fail, the lady produces pizza. The colorful illustrations filled with frenzied activities sustain the silliness and the absurdity of the story." SLJ

Weston, Martha, 1947-

Space guys! Holiday House 2000 32p il $14.95
                                             E
1. Extraterrestrial beings—Fiction 2. Stories in rhyme
ISBN 0-8234-1487-6   LC 99-34267
"A Holiday House reader"
A boy is visited by beings that look like robots that arrive in a flying saucer from outer space
"The rhyming text gallops through the silly, appealing story with spare, well-chosen beginner's vocabulary printed in large type. But it's Weston's illustrations that give the story its exuberant energy." Booklist

Whybrow, Ian

Sammy and the dinosaurs; illustrated by Adrian Reynolds. Orchard Bks. 1999 unp il $15.95   E
1. Dinosaurs—Fiction 2. Toys—Fiction
ISBN 0-531-30207-5   LC 99-22387
Sammy finds toy dinosaurs in the attic that come to life when he names each one
"Big oversized shapes, simple but expressive features (on humans and dinosaurs), and unusual perspectives combine in compositions easily large enough for group viewing; with a coziness that never falls into the saccharine, text and art bring the story home." Bull Cent Child Books

Wiesner, David

Free fall. Lothrop, Lee & Shepard Bks. 1988 unp il lib bdg $16.93; pa $6.95   E
1. Dreams—Fiction 2. Stories without words
ISBN 0-688-05584-2 (lib bdg); 0-688-10990-X (pa)
                                   LC 87-22834
A Caldecott Medal honor book, 1989
A young boy dreams of daring adventures in the company of imaginary creatures inspired by the things surrounding his bed
"Technical virtuosity is the trademark of the double-page watercolor spreads. Especially notable is the solidity of forms and architectural details." SLJ

Hurricane. Clarion Bks. 1990 unp il $16; pa $5.95   E
1. Hurricanes—Fiction 2. Brothers—Fiction
ISBN 0-395-54382-7; 0-395-62974-8 (pa)
                                   LC 90-30070

Also available with Audiobook
"A family weathers a hurricane; the next day, in the post-hurricane yard, the two boys in the family play on a great fallen elm, imagining it to be a jungle, a pirate ship, and a space ship. A handsome book, affording opportunities for sharing fears and dreams of adventure." Horn Book Guide

June 29, 1999. Clarion Bks. 1992 unp il $15.95; pa $5.95   E
1. Vegetables—Fiction
ISBN 0-395-59762-5; 0-395-72767-7 (pa)
                                   LC 91-34854
"Either Holly Evans's science project that sent vegetable seedlings into the ionosphere is enormously successful—or else something unearthly is going on." SLJ
"Here an understated, fairly straightforward text is a perfect foil for the outrageous scenes of vegetables run amok. Realistic watercolors reveal red peppers that need to be roped down, beans with bemused Arizona sheep clambering over them, and gargantuan peas floating down the Mississippi like logs to the sawmill. Fans of Wiesner's offbeat sense of humor will be delighted." Horn Book

Sector 7. Clarion Bks. 1999 unp il $16   E
1. Empire State Building (New York, N.Y.)—Fiction
2. Clouds—Fiction 3. Stories without words
ISBN 0-395-74656-6   LC 96-40343
A Caldecott Medal honor book, 2000
While on a school trip to the Empire State Building, a boy is taken by a friendly cloud to visit Sector 7, where he discovers how clouds are shaped and channeled throughout the country
"Wiesner's lofty watercolors render words superfluous as he transforms the sky into magical scenes of marine life, reminding children of the innate power of their own imagination." Publ Wkly

Tuesday. Clarion Bks. 1991 unp il $17; pa $5.95   E
1. Frogs—Fiction
ISBN 0-395-55113-7; 0-395-87082-8 (pa)
                                   LC 90-39358
Awarded the Caldecott Medal, 1992
Frogs rise on their lily pads, float through the air, and explore the nearby houses while their inhabitants sleep
"Wiesner offers a fantasy watercolor journey accomplished with soft-edged realism. Studded with bits of humor, the narrative artwork tells a simple, pleasant story with a consistency and authenticity that makes the fantasy convincing." Booklist

Wild, Margaret, 1948-

Our granny; story by Margaret Wild; pictures by Julie Vivas. Ticknor & Fields 1994 c1993 unp il $16; pa $5.95   E
1. Grandmothers—Fiction
ISBN 0-395-67023-3; 0-395-88395-4 (pa)
                                   LC 93-11950
First published 1993 in Australia
"Two young children present a catalog of all the varying sizes, shapes, and types of grandmothers, interspersed with loving comments about their own granny, who has 'a wobbly bottom' and wears a funny bathing suit. . . . Vivas's lively illustrations capture the grandmothers in their most comic moments." Horn Book Guide

Wild, Margaret, 1948-—*Continued*

Tom goes to kindergarten; [illustrated by] David Legge. Whitman, A. 2000 unp il $15.95   E
1. Giant panda—Fiction 2. School stories
ISBN 0-8075-8012-0   LC 99-50420
When Tom, a young panda, goes to his very first day of kindergarten, his whole family stays and plays and wishes they could be in kindergarten too
"Large, bright, whimsical watercolors make this a perfect book both for group storytelling and for one-on-one sharing." SLJ

Wildsmith, Brian, 1930-
ABC. Watts 1963 c1962 unp il   E
1. Alphabet

Available Board book edition; Spanish language Board book also available
First published 1962 in the United Kingdom
An alphabet book which illustrates animals and objects, identifying each on a facing page in capital and lower case letters, setting off the first letter with special emphasis." N Y Times Book Rev
"Bold, original pictures drawn in the individual style of an artist provide an excellent beginning for a child's education." N Y Her Trib Books

Brian Wildsmith's birds. Watts 1967 unp il o.p.; Oxford Univ. Press paperback available $9.95   E
1. Birds
ISBN 0-19-272117-8 (pa)
Paperback edition has title: Birds
"Mr. Wildsmith has tied a series of pictures of birds . . . to their group names: a watch of nightingales, a nye of pheasants, a congregation of plover, et cetera. There is no other text." Saturday Rev
"Birds—how well the subject lends itself to this artist's exquisite use of color!. . . The child will have fun with the terms while absorbing truly beautiful illustrations." Horn Book

Brian Wildsmith's fishes. Watts 1968 unp il o.p.; Oxford Univ. Press paperback available $11.95   E
1. Fishes
ISBN 0-19-272151-8 (pa)
Paperback edition has title: Fishes
The author "presents groups of fishes. A cluster of porcupine fish, a hover of trout, a spread of sticklebacks, and flocks, schools, and streams of other fish swim across the pages in a riot of color." Booklist

Brian Wildsmith's wild animals. Watts 1967 unp il o.p.; Oxford Univ. Press paperback available $11.95   E
1. Mammals
ISBN 0-19-272103-8 (pa)
Paperback edition has title: Wild animals
"A pride of lions, a lepe of leopards, a skulk of foxes, and a cete of badgers are among the cleverly captured groups of wild beasts that stalk the vivid, glowing pages of this fascinating picture book. A splendid, eyecatching . . . volume." Booklist

A Christmas story. Eerdmans Bks. for Young Readers 1998 unp il $17   E
1. Jesus Christ—Nativity—Fiction 2. Donkeys—Fiction
ISBN 0-8028-5173-8   LC 98-18067
A reissue of the title first published 1989 by Knopf
Rebecca, a young girl living in Nazareth, accompanies a small donkey searching for his mother to a stable in Bethlehem where they both witness a special event
"The story is very simple but incorporates details from the biblical account. Both homey and glorious, Wildsmith's paintings use muted browns and greens for the shepherds and their surroundings and bright gold for the star pointing them toward Bethlehem." Horn Book Guide

Wilkes, Angela
My first word book. DK Pub. 1999 64p il $16.95   E
1. Vocabulary
ISBN 0-7894-3977-8   LC 99-206690
Also available Board book edition
A slightly revised edition of the title first published 1991
"Common, familiar objects, animals, and activities—featured in clear, bright photos set against a white background or in small drawings—are grouped together on double-page spreads with such headings as 'On the farm' and 'Colors, shapes, and numbers.' Children will be drawn to the bright, cheerful pages of this first vocabulary lesson." Horn Book Guide

Williams, Karen Lynn
Galimoto; illustrated by Catherine Stock. Lothrop, Lee & Shepard Bks. 1990 unp il $16.95; pa $5.95   E
1. Toys—Fiction 2. Malawi—Fiction
ISBN 0-688-08789-2; 0-688-10991-8 (pa)
LC 89-2258
"In Malawi, Africa, according to the author's note, *galimoto* are intricate and popular push toys crafted by children. Williams tells the story of seven-year-old Kondi's quest to find ample scrap material to fashion his own toy pickup truck. Visits to his uncle's shop, the miller, and the trash heap yield enough wire to allow him to create a plaything which he proudly uses to lead his friends in their evening game. Kondi's perseverance and the pleasure he takes in his accomplishment are just two of the delights of this appealing story. Stock's graceful watercolors portray life in a bustling village and include enough detail . . . to give readers the flavor of a day in this southern African nation." Horn Book

Painted dreams; pictures by Catherine Stock. Lothrop, Lee & Shepard Bks. 1998 unp il $16; lib bdg $15.93   E
1. Haiti—Fiction 2. Artists—Fiction
ISBN 0-688-13901-9; 0-688-13902-7 (lib bdg)
LC 97-32920
Because her Haitian family is too poor to be able to buy paints for her, eight-year-old Ti Marie finds her own way to create pictures that make the heart sing
"Beautifully composed and full of life, Stock's watercolors suggest the personalities of the characters through their expressions and gestures." Booklist

Williams, Karen Lynn—_Continued_

When Africa was home; pictures by Floyd Cooper. Orchard Bks. 1991 unp il lib bdg $16.99; pa $6.95   E
   1. Africa—Fiction
   ISBN 0-531-08525-2 (lib bdg); 0-531-07043-3 (pa)
                                        LC 90-7684
"A Richard Jackson book"
After returning to the United States, Peter's whole family misses the warmth and friendliness of their life in Africa; so Peter's father looks for another job there
"The joyful text and Cooper's boldly drawn, glowing oil-wash pictures evoke the intensely physical experience of the small child, his delight in the place and culture, what it feels like to belong there." Booklist

Williams, Laura E.

ABC kids; [by] Laura Ellen Williams. Philomel Bks. 2000 unp il $15.99   E
   1. Alphabet
   ISBN 0-399-23370-9   LC 98-37179
Presents one object, person, or animal for each letter of the alphabet, from an apple to a zipper
"Stunning close-up photography shows preschoolers having fun. . . . The key words, presented in lowercase, are commonplace and easily identifiable within each page. The crystal-clear photos are brimming with child-like energy and the poses are inventive." SLJ

Williams, Linda

The little old lady who was not afraid of anything; illustrated by Megan Lloyd. Crowell 1986 unp il $15.95; lib bdg $15.89; pa $5.95
                                               E
   ISBN 0-690-04584-0; 0-690-04586-7 (lib bdg); 0-06-443183-5 (pa)   LC 85-48250
Also available with Audiobook; Spanish language edition also available
A little old lady who is not afraid of anything must deal with a pumpkin head, a tall black hat, and other spooky objects that follow her through the dark woods trying to scare her
"A delightful picture book, perfect for both independent reading pleasure and for telling aloud." SLJ

Williams, Sherley Anne, 1944-1999

Working cotton; written by Sherley Anne Williams; illustrated by Carole Byard. Harcourt Brace Jovanovich 1992 unp il $14.95; pa $7
                                               E
   1. Migrant labor—Fiction 2. Cotton—Fiction
   3. African Americans—Fiction
   ISBN 0-15-299624-9; 0-15-201482-9 (pa)
                                        LC 91-21586
A Caldecott Medal honor book, 1993
A young black girl relates the daily events of her family's migrant life in the cotton fields of central California
"Byard's acrylic paintings contribute weight and emotion to Williams's spare text. The fields and family members fill each full-page spread, drawing the reader very close to the action of the story. The mural-like

paintings glow with blue and brown tones, recreating the textures and hues of the cotton fields. Williams's text, based on her poems, has a lyrical, rhythmic quality." Horn Book

Williams, Sue, 1948-

Let's go visiting; written by Sue Williams; illustrated by Julie Vivas. Harcourt Brace & Co. 1998 unp il $15; pa $7   E
   1. Domestic animals—Fiction 2. Counting 3. Stories in rhyme
   ISBN 0-15-201823-9; 0-15-202410-7 (pa)
                                        LC 97-34398
"Gulliver books"
A counting story in which a boy visits his farmyard friends, from one brown foal to six yellow puppies
"The bold illustrations, simple yet full of motion, combine with a lively text to make this perfect for toddler story hours." Booklist

Williams, Suzanne

Library Lil; illustrated by Steven Kellogg. Dial Bks. for Young Readers 1997 unp il $15.99; lib bdg $14.89   E
   1. Librarians—Fiction 2. Books and reading—Fiction
   3. Tall tales
   ISBN 0-8037-1698-2; 0-8037-1699-0 (lib bdg)
                                        LC 95-23490
A formidable librarian makes readers not only out of the once resistant residents of her small town, but out of a tough-talking, television-watching motorcycle gang as well
"The silliness of both story and pictures are perfectly matched. Kellogg's distinctive toothy kids and laughing cats crowd the pages, fitting right in with the baby-faced biker banditos." SLJ

Williams, Vera B.

A chair for my mother. Greenwillow Bks. 1982 unp il $15.95; lib bdg $15.93; pa $5.95   E
   1. Family life—Fiction 2. Saving and investment—Fiction 3. Chairs—Fiction
   ISBN 0-688-00914-X; 0-688-00915-8 (lib bdg); 0-688-04074-8 (pa)   LC 81-7010
Also available Big book edition and Spanish language edition
A Caldecott Medal honor book, 1983
Rosa, her waitress mother, and her grandmother save dimes to buy a comfortable armchair after all their furniture is lost in a fire
"The cheerful paintings take up the full left-hand page and face, in most cases, a small chunk of the text set against a modulated wash of a complementing color; a border containing a pertinent motif surrounds the two pages, further unifying the design. The result is a superbly conceived picture book expressing the joyful spirit of a loving family." Horn Book
Other available titles about Rosa and her family are:
Music, music for everyone (1984)
Something special for me (1983)

Cherries and cherry pits. Greenwillow Bks. 1986 unp il lib bdg $16.93; pa $5.95   E
   1. African Americans—Fiction 2. Drawing—Fiction
   ISBN 0-688-05146-4 (lib bdg); 0-688-10478-9 (pa)
                                        LC 85-17156

Williams, Vera B.—*Continued*

"Bidemmi, a young black child, draws splendid pictures. 'As she draws, she tells the story of what she is drawing,' always starting with the word 'this.' . . . Finally, Bidemmi tells her story, revealing her wish for her neighborhood and her world. Each story involves cherries—buying, sharing, and enjoying them." SLJ

"Williams' portraits of Bidemmi drawing are done in watercolor; the drawings Bidemmi makes are done with bright markers, some being simple sketches, others filling the page with color, looking like naive, but glorious icons. The interior stories are well integrated with each other, and the whole adds up to a study of child as artist that is fresh, vibrant, and exciting." Bull Cent Child Books

Lucky song. Greenwillow Bks. 1997 unp il $15; lib bdg $14.93 E
1. Day—Fiction 2. Kites—Fiction 3. Songs—Fiction
ISBN 0-688-14459-4; 0-688-14460-8 (lib bdg)
LC 96-7151

"Evie flies the kite made by her grandfather until it's time to go home for supper all tired and ready for bed. This patterned story, showing a little girl surrounded by a loving family, ends by circling back to the beginning. It is illustrated using brilliantly colored watercolors." Child Book Rev Serv

"More more more" said the baby; 3 love stories. Greenwillow Bks. 1990 unp il $15.95; lib bdg $15.89; pa $5.95 E
1. Infants—Fiction 2. Family life—Fiction
ISBN 0-688-09173-3; 0-688-09174-1 (lib bdg); 0-688-814736-4 (pa)
LC 89-2023
Also available Board book edition
A Caldecott Medal honor book, 1991

Three babies are caught up in the air and given loving attention by a father, grandmother, and mother

"The pages reverberate with bright colors and vigorous forms, and the rhythmic language begs to be read aloud." Horn Book Guide

Stringbean's trip to the shining sea; greetings from Vera B. Williams, story and pictures; and Jennifer Williams, more pictures. Greenwillow Bks. 1987 unp il $15.95; lib bdg $15.89; pa $4.95 E
1. West (U.S.)—Fiction
ISBN 0-688-07161-9; 0-688-07162-7 (lib bdg); 0-688-16701-2 (pa)
LC 86-29502

"Stringbean and big brother Fred (joined en route by Potato, Stringbean's dog) take a car trip from their home in Kansas to the Pacific Ocean, and their pilgrimage is recorded herein in the form of a mock photo and postcard album." Bull Cent Child Books

"The use of mixed media—watercolors, Magic Markers, and colored pencils—is as aesthetically pleasing as it is skillful. Nothing has been forgotten; nothing more needs to be added. Not for the usual picture-book set, this travelogue storybook will appeal to slightly older audiences." Horn Book

Three days on a river in a red canoe. Greenwillow Bks. 1984 unp il lib bdg $16.89; pa $5.95 E
1. Canoes and canoeing—Fiction 2. Camping—Fiction
ISBN 0-688-84307-7 (lib bdg); 0-688-04072-1 (pa)
LC 80-23893

In this book, a "canoe trip for two children and two adults is recorded with all its interesting detail in a spontaneous first-person account and engaging full-color drawings on carefully designed pages. Driving to a river site, making camp, paddling the craft, negotiating a waterfall, swimming, fishing, dealing with a sudden storm, and even rescuing one overboard child are all described as important incidents in a summertime adventure." Horn Book

Willis, Jeanne

Earthlets, as explained by Professor Xargle; illustrated by Tony Ross. Dutton 1989 unp il $15.99 E
1. Extraterrestrial beings—Fiction 2. Infants—Fiction
ISBN 0-525-44465-3
LC 88-23692
Professor Xargle's class of extraterrestrials learns about the physical characteristics and behavior of the human baby

"This funny view of babies is fraught with Professor Xargle's well-meaning, zany misinterpretations. Willis's clever and original text will particularly delight older siblings who may also find that babies are a separate species. Ross's inspired paintings bristle with out-of-this-world color and imagination." Publ Wkly

Wilner, Isabel

B is for Bethlehem; a Christmas alphabet; illustrated by Elisa Kleven. Dutton Children's Bks. 1990 unp il $14.99; pa $5.99 E
1. Jesus Christ—Nativity—Poetry 2. Alphabet
ISBN 0-525-44622-2; 0-14-055610-9 (pa)
LC 89-49481
Rhyming verses introduce the letters of the alphabet and the events surrounding the birth of Jesus

This book includes "unique and appealing pictures. Kleven offers mixed-media collage using watercolor, cut paper, and drawings, giving her artwork a radiant, folkloric look. . . . Wilner first wrote the piece for second graders to perform. Though it certainly could be used in this manner, the book seems a natural in its present, lovely form." Booklist

Winch, John, 1944-

The old woman who loved to read. Holiday House 1997 c1996 unp il $16.95; pa $6.95 E
1. Books and reading—Fiction 2. Country life—Fiction 3. Australia—Fiction
ISBN 0-8234-1281-4; 0-8234-1348-9 (pa)
LC 96-19665
First published 1996 in Australia

"An old woman moves to the country to have time to read quietly but is besieged by the needs of garden, house, orchard, and animals throughout the year. The large, detailed paintings, revealing the many Australian animals that co-exist with the woman, have an earthy, country feel and expand the scope of the text." Horn Book Guide

Winter, Jeanette

Follow the drinking gourd; story and pictures by Jeanette Winter. Knopf 1988 unp il music hardcover o.p. paperback available $7.99　　　E
1. Slavery—Fiction 2. Underground railroad—Fiction 3. African Americans—Fiction
ISBN 0-679-81997-5 (pa)　　　LC 88-9661
By following directions in a song, taught them by an old sailor, runaway slaves journey north along the Underground Railroad to freedom in Canada
"Complementing the few lines of text per page are dark-hued illustrations horizontally framed with a fine black line and plenty of white space. . . . The art carries the weight of introducing children to a riveting piece of U.S. history, and the music included at the end of the book will fix it in their minds." Bull Cent Child Books

Josefina. Harcourt Brace & Co. 1996 unp il $15
　　　E
1. Women artists—Fiction 2. Mexico—Fiction 3. Counting
ISBN 0-15-201091-2　　　LC 95-34110
"In a sunny patio in Mexico, there is one rising sun in a sky where two angels keep watch over three houses. . . . Throughout her life—from her childhood through the deaths of her parents, her marriage to José, and the birth of their nine children, Josefina works the soft clay into figures to create this world. . . . Inspired by the painted clay figures decorating Josefina Aguilar's patio in Ocotlán, Mexico, Winter has crafted a picture-book vision of the folk artist's life that cleverly turns into a bilingual counting story. . . . Paired with a simple prose narrative, the artwork creates an effect that is both elegant and soothing." Booklist

Winthrop, Elizabeth

Promises; illustrated by Betsy Lewin. Clarion Bks. 2000 32p il $16　　　E
1. Cancer—Fiction 2. Mother-daughter relationship—Fiction
ISBN 0-395-82272-6　　　LC 99-27186
"Sarah's mother is very sick, presumably with cancer, and has lost all her energy and her hair. Sarah is alternately scared, angry, and sad until her mother begins her gradual recovery. The characters are well developed, and the sensitive, calm story offers realistic reassurances and hope for children with a sick parent. Lewin's cartoon-style pen-and-ink and watercolor illustrations help lighten an otherwise serious book." Horn Book Guide

Shoes; illustrated by William Joyce. Harper & Row 1986 19p il lib bdg $16.89; pa $5.95　　　E
1. Shoes—Fiction 2. Stories in rhyme
ISBN 0-06-026592-2 (lib bdg); 0-06-443171-1 (pa)
　　　LC 85-45841
Also available Board book edition and with Audiobook
"A jaunty rhyme about shoes of all kinds—'shoes for fishing, shoes for wishing, shoes for muddy squishing.' The roly-poly figures are drawn from a child's perspective." N Y Times Book Rev
"This lilting rhyme about shoes and feet easily pleases. . . . Backing the verses are full-color drawings of children busily involved with one kind of shoe or another. Joyce's pictures are animated, energetic, and warmly colored." Booklist

Wise, William, 1923-

Ten sly piranhas; a counting story in reverse (a tale of wickedness—and worse!); pictures by Victoria Chess. Dial Bks. for Young Readers 1993 unp il $15.99　　　E
1. Fishes—Fiction 2. Counting 3. Stories in rhyme
ISBN 0-8037-1200-6　　　LC 91-33704
A school of ten sly piranhas gradually dwindles as they waylay and eat each other, and the last is eaten by a crocodile
"The combination of a jaunty, rhymed text and gleefully fiendish illustrations demonstrates with delicious derring-do that the wicked frequently receive their just deserts." Horn Book

Wiseman, Bernard

Morris and Boris at the circus; by B. Wiseman. Harper & Row 1988 64p il lib bdg $15.89; pa $3.95　　　E
1. Moose—Fiction 2. Bears—Fiction 3. Circus—Fiction
ISBN 0-06-026478-0 (lib bdg); 0-06-444143-1 (pa)
　　　LC 87-45682
"An I can read book"
"Morris the Moose and his friend Boris the Bear . . . take a trip to the circus. Morris has never gone before, so he doesn't quite have the big picture. He thinks the clown's nose is red because he has a cold, and when they join the performers in the ring, Morris rides 'bearback' on Boris, instead of on a horse." Booklist
"The cartoon illustrations with bold colors provide ample context clues for beginning readers. This delightful combination of text and illustrations will entice children to read and re-read this book." SLJ

Wisniewski, David

Rain player; story and pictures by David Wisniewski. Clarion Bks. 1991 unp il $17; pa $6.95　　　E
1. Mayas—Fiction 2. Games—Fiction
ISBN 0-395-55112-9; 0-395-72083-4 (pa)
　　　LC 90-44101
Also available with Audiobook
To bring rain to his thirsty village, Pik challenges the rain god to a game of pok-a-tok
"This original tale combines research on Mayan history and legend with a suspenseful sports story. . . . Intricate and dramatic cut-paper illustrations powerfully recreate the foliage, landscape, architecture, and clothing of the Mayan classical period. . . . An author's note provides fascinating background information on Mayan civilization and gives in-depth explanations of some of the words and phrases used in the text." Horn Book

The warrior and the wise man; story and pictures by David Wisniewski. Lothrop, Lee & Shepard Bks. 1989 unp il $16; lib bdg $15.93; pa $5.95　　　E
1. Fairy tales 2. Japan—Fiction
ISBN 0-688-07889-3; 0-688-07890-7 (lib bdg); 0-688-16159-6 (pa)　　　LC 88-21678
This original fairy tale "describes the quests of the twin sons of the emperor of Japan for five magical ele-

Wisniewski, David—*Continued*

ments of the world: earth, water, fire, wind, and cloud. The brother who returns first will inherit the throne." Booklist

"The striking cut-paper illustrations, executed and reproduced with virtuosity, make use of black silhouettes against emotionally charged colors that modulate and change from page to page and create a dynamic, almost cinematographic effect. In a detailed end note Wisniewski explicates the visual references to be seen in the costumes, decorations, and artifacts and thus establishes the historical, religious, and artistic authenticity of his work." Horn Book

The wave of the Sea-Wolf; story and pictures by David Wisniewski. Clarion Bks. 1994 unp il $17; pa $5.95   E
1. Tlingit Indians—Fiction
ISBN 0-395-66478-0; 0-395-96892-5 (pa)
LC 93-18265

Kchokeen, a Tlingit princess, is rescued from drowning by a guardian spirit that later enables Kchokeen to summon a great wave and save her people from hostile strangers

"Vivid storytelling is complemented by textured cut-paper illustrations that paint the forest landscape in lacy layers. . . . Wisniewski's ability to convey both high drama and simple emotion lends a sense of authenticity to this original tale." Publ Wkly

Wojciechowski, Susan

The Christmas miracle of Jonathan Toomey; illustrated by P.J. Lynch. Candlewick Press 1995 unp il $18.99   E
1. Wood carving—Fiction 2. Christmas—Fiction 3. Friendship—Fiction
ISBN 1-56402-320-6   LC 94-48917
Also available with Audiobook

The widow McDowell and her seven-year-old son Thomas ask the gruff Jonathan Toomey, the best woodcarver in the valley, to carve the figures for a Christmas creche

"The story verges on the sentimental, but it's told with feeling and lyricism. . . . Lynch's sweeping illustrations, in shades of wood grain, are both realistic and gloriously romantic, focusing on faces and hands at work before the fire and in the lamplight." Booklist

Wolff, Ashley, 1956-

Stella & Roy. Dutton Children's Bks. 1993 unp il $13.99; pa $5.99   E
1. Cycling—Fiction
ISBN 0-525-45081-5; 0-14-055884-5 (pa)
LC 92-27005

"In true 'Hare and Tortoise' fashion, older, overconfident Stella takes her time pedalling round a lake, stopping to check out the flora and fauna, while toddler Roy repeatedly rolls 'right on by.' The luminously tinted linoleum prints perfectly capture the thrill of the race." SLJ
Another available title about Stella & Roy is:
Stella & Roy go camping (1999)

Wolff, Patricia Rae

The toll-bridge troll; illustrated by Kimberly Bulcken Root. Harcourt Brace & Co.; Browndeer Press 1995 unp il $15; pa $6   E
1. Fairy tales
ISBN 0-15-277665-6; 0-15-202105-1 (pa)
LC 93-32298

A troll tries to prevent Trigg from crossing the bridge on the way to school only to be outwitted by the boy's riddles

"While the humor of the text lies partly in the slyly matter-of-fact tone, the illustrations ground the whimsy in a wealth of detail—like the troll's knobby, skinned knees and his petulant expression." Horn Book

Wong, Janet S., 1962-

Buzz; illustrated by Margaret Chodos-Irvine. Harcourt 2000 unp il $15   E
ISBN 0-15-201923-5   LC 99-6148

"A young child relates the simple morning events that happen in his house, all of which seem to make a buzz." Booklist

"Chodos-Irvine's use of various print-making techniques results in illustrations that are strongly geometric and graphically clean, in springtime colors that suit the cheerful tone of the text. The humor in both text and pictures contributes to the light-hearted atmosphere." Bull Cent Child Books

This next New Year; pictures by Yangsook Choi. Foster Bks. 2000 unp il $16   E
1. Chinese New Year—Fiction
ISBN 0-374-35503-7   LC 99-22377

"A Chinese-Korean boy reflects on what Chinese New Year means to him. By sweeping last year's mistakes and bad luck out of the house, he hopes to make room for 'a fresh start, my second chance.'" Horn Book Guide

"Choi's smooth, brightly colored paintings . . . ably illustrate the optimistic activity and the yearning in the accessible, rhythmic text." Booklist

Wood, Audrey

The Bunyans; illustrated by David Shannon. Blue Sky Press (NY) 1996 unp il $15.95   E
1. Bunyan, Paul (Legendary character) 2. Tall tales
ISBN 0-590-48089-8   LC 95-26170

Paul Bunyan "meets a gigantic woman, and he and Carrie are soon married. Two oversize children arrive and play a important role in the formation of many of America's natural wonders: Niagara Falls, Bryce Canyon, and Big Sur, among others. . . . Wood captures the tongue-in-cheek tone and the exaggeration bordering on the ridiculous that characterize American tall tales. . . . Shannon's realistic, full-color paintings provide a counterpoint to the text, serving to make it seem almost believable. The artist's figures are large and solid." SLJ

Elbert's bad word; illustrated by Audrey and Don Wood. Harcourt Brace Jovanovich 1988 unp il $15; pa $6   E
1. Parties—Fiction
ISBN 0-15-225320-3; 0-15-201367-9 (pa)
LC 86-7557

Wood, Audrey—*Continued*

"A bad word, spoken by a small boy at a fashionable garden party, creates havoc, and the child, Elbert, gets his mouth scrubbed out with soap. The bad word, in the shape of a long-tailed furry monster, will not go away until a wizard-gardener cooks up some really delicious, super-long words that everyone at the party applauds. This single-idea cautionary tale has lively, absurdist pictures of tiara-crowned, formally dressed adults recoiling in horror or cavorting with glee when Elbert, the only child at the party, speaks a word." SLJ

Heckedy Peg; illustrated by Don Wood. Harcourt Brace Jovanovich 1987 unp il lib bdg $16; pa $7   E
1. Fairy tales 2. Witches—Fiction
ISBN 0-15-233678-8 (lib bdg); 0-15-233679-6 (pa)
LC 86-33639

"The poor mother of seven children, each named for a day of the week, goes off to market promising to return with individual gifts that each child has requested and admonishing them to lock the door to strangers and not to touch the fire. The gullible children are tricked into disobeying their mother by the witch, Heckedy Peg, who turns them all into various kinds of food. The mother can rescue her children only by guessing which child is the fish, the roast rib, the bread. . . . This story, deep and rich with folk wisdom, is stunningly illustrated with Don Wood's luminous paintings. . . . With variety of color and line he enhances every nuance of the text, from the individuality of the children and the stalwart mother to the unrelenting evil of the witch. A tour de force in every way." SLJ

King Bidgood's in the bathtub; written by Audrey Wood; illustrated by Don Wood. Harcourt Brace Jovanovich 1985 unp il lib bdg $16   E
1. Kings and rulers—Fiction 2. Baths—Fiction
ISBN 0-15-242730-9   LC 85-5472
Also available Big book edition
A Caldecott Medal honor book, 1986
Despite pleas from his court, a fun-loving king refuses to get out of his bathtub to rule his kingdom
"The few simple words of text per large, well-designed page invite story-telling—but keep the group very small, so the children can be close enough to pore over the brilliant, robust illustrations." SLJ

The napping house; illustrated by Don Wood. Harcourt Brace Jovanovich 1984 unp il lib bdg $16   E
1. Sleep—Fiction
ISBN 0-15-256708-9   LC 83-13035
Also available Big book edition, Board book edition, and with Audiobook; Spanish language edition also available
"In this sleepytime cumulative tale, all are pleasantly napping until a pesky flea starts the clamor that wakes up the whole family—mouse, cat, dog, child, and granny." Child Book Rev Serv
"The cool blues and greens are superseded by warm colors and bursts of action as each sleeper wakes, ending in an eruption of color and energy as naptime ends. A deft matching of text and pictures adds to the appeal of cumulation, and to the silliness of the mound of sleepers—just the right kind of humor for the lap audience." Bull Cent Child Books

Sweet dream pie; pictures by Mark Teague. Blue Sky Press (NY) 1998 unp il $15.95   E
1. Tall tales 2. Baking—Fiction 3. Dreams—Fiction
ISBN 0-590-96204-3   LC 96-54644
"Ma Brindle, against her better judgment, prepares her enormous Sweet Dream Pie, filled with every sugary thing imaginable. Expansive, slightly off-kilter paintings detail the unusual occurrences, from a chocolate whirlwind to frolicking dream creatures, that visit the neighborhood once it succumbs to pie frenzy." Horn Book Guide

Wood, Don, 1945-

Piggies; written by Don and Audrey Wood; illustrated by Don Wood. Harcourt Brace Jovanovich 1991 unp il $16; pa $7   E
1. Bedtime—Fiction 2. Pigs—Fiction
ISBN 0-15-256341-5; 0-15-200217-0 (pa)
LC 89-24598
Also available Board book edition
Ten little piggies dance on a young child's fingers and toes before finally going to sleep
"A happy text and luxuriant, witty pictures make this a book to pore over again and again." Booklist

Wood, Douglas, 1951-

What dads can't do; pictures by Doug Cushman. Simon & Schuster Bks. for Young Readers 2000 unp il $14   E
1. Fathers—Fiction
ISBN 0-689-82620-6   LC 98-41773
"The young, green, reptilian narrator enumerates all the things dads—and especially the green reptilian one pictured—can never do. Dads 'can't cross the street without holding hands,' they 'lose at checkers and cards,' and 'Dads can push, but they can't swing.'" Horn Book Guide
"This amusing picture book will tickle youngsters' funny bones and make every parent and child smile with recognition. . . . Cushman's large, delightful, pen-and-ink and watercolor cartoons . . . capture perfectly the father-and-son interactions." SLJ

Woodruff, Elvira

The memory coat; story by Elvira Woodruff; illustrations by Michael Dooling. Scholastic Press 1999 unp il $15.95   E
1. Ellis Island Immigration Station—Fiction 2. Immigration and emigration—Fiction 3. Jews—Fiction
ISBN 0-590-67717-9   LC 95-30048
In the early 1900s, cousins Rachel and Grisha leave their Russian shtetl with the rest of their family to come to America, hopeful that they will all pass the dreaded inspection at Ellis Island
This offers "warm, realistic period paintings, some in color, some in sepia shades. . . . In a long, interesting author's note, Woodruff discusses the shtetl and immigrant history." Booklist

Woodson, Jacqueline

We had a picnic this Sunday past; illustrated by Diane Greenseid. Hyperion Bks. for Children 1998 c1997 unp il lib bdg $15.49   **E**
1. Family life—Fiction 2. African Americans—Fiction
ISBN 0-7868-2192-2   LC 96-16312
Teeka describes her various relatives and the foods they bring to the annual family picnic
"If this is more character sketch than actual story, the solid acrylic paintings help bring all the people in this African American family to life." Booklist

Wormell, Mary

Why not? Farrar, Straus & Giroux 2000 unp il $15   **E**
1. Cats—Fiction 2. Domestic animals—Fiction
ISBN 0-374-38422-3   LC 99-27163
When his mother repeatedly tells him not to bother the other animals, Barnaby the kitten always asks: "Why?"
"Patterned language will promote expectation and recognition; uncluttered woodblock pictures pair well with the rustic farm setting, and the book's large print will facilitate group sharing." Horn Book Guide

Yaccarino, Dan

Deep in the jungle; written and illustrated by Dan Yaccarino. Atheneum Bks. for Young Readers 2000 unp il $16   **E**
1. Lions—Fiction 2. Animals—Fiction 3. Circus—Fiction
ISBN 0-689-82235-9   LC 98-24088
"An Anne Schwartz book"
After being tricked into joining the circus, an arrogant lion escapes and returns to the jungle where he lives peacefully with the animals he used to terrorize
"The dryly humorous story is illustrated with cheerful, retro-style art." Horn Book Guide

Yacowitz, Caryn

Pumpkin fiesta; illustrated by Joe Cepeda. HarperCollins Pubs. 1998 unp il $15.95   **E**
1. Pumpkin—Fiction 2. Mexico—Fiction
ISBN 0-06-027658-4   LC 96-48580
Hoping to win a prize for the best pumpkin at the fiesta, Foolish Fernando tries to copy Old Juana's successful gardening techniques, but without really watching to see how much effort and love she puts into her work. Includes a recipe for pumpkin soup
"The warm-toned oil paintings contain flat but expressive figures. The book is both amusing and satisfying, competently executed, and good for read-aloud sharing." Horn Book Guide

Yarbrough, Camille, 1938-

Cornrows; illustrated by Carole Byard. Coward, McCann & Geoghegan 1979 unp il hardcover o.p. paperback available $5.99   **E**
1. African Americans—Fiction 2. Hair—Fiction
ISBN 0-698-11436-1 (pa)   LC 78-24010
Coretta Scott King Award for illustration, 1980

This story illustrates how the hair style of cornrows, a symbol in Africa since ancient times, can today in this country symbolize the courage of Afro-Americans
"Dialect is used but not overused. Byard's black-and-white drawings . . . are attractive and welcome." SLJ

Yolen, Jane

How do dinosaurs say goodnight? illustrated by Mark Teague. Blue Sky Press (NY) 2000 unp il $15.95   **E**
1. Bedtime—Fiction 2. Dinosaurs—Fiction 3. Stories in rhyme
ISBN 0-590-31681-8   LC 98-56134
Mother and child ponder the different ways a dinosaur can say goodnight, from slamming his tail and pouting to giving a big hug and kiss
"The text is sweet and simple—just right for the wonderful pictures that really make this picture book special. . . . Endpapers introduce the critter cast in all their gorgeous glory: tyrannosaurus rex, dimetrodon, and more, in vivid, yet still earthbound colors." Booklist

King Long Shanks; illustrated by Victoria Chess. Harcourt Brace & Co. 1998 unp il $15   **E**
1. Fairy tales 2. Frogs—Fiction
ISBN 0-15-200013-5   LC 94-48359
In this adaptation of Hans Christian Andersen's The emperor's new clothes, a frog king agrees to let two flattering scoundrels create an outfit for him that will show off his fine, long, strong legs and test the loyalty of his subjects
"Lots of amphibian details ('Eat your flies') and humorous pen-and-ink and watercolor illustrations (dominated by shades of green) make this a lighthearted, satisfying retelling." Horn Book Guide

Letting Swift River go; illustrated by Barbara Cooney. Little, Brown 1992 unp il hardcover o.p. paperback available $4.95   **E**
1. Country life—Fiction 2. Massachusetts—Fiction
ISBN 0-316-96860-9 (pa)   LC 90-47909
Relates Sally Jane's experience of changing times in rural America, as she lives through the drowning of the Swift River towns in western Massachusetts to form the Quabbin Reservoir
"Yolen's descriptions of life in rural western Massachusetts are redolent with the sights and sounds of a childhood spent outdoors. . . . The watercolor, pencil, and pastel paintings by Barbara Cooney lovingly proclaim the pleasures of each season and capture the joys of a rural way of life many children can no longer experience firsthand." Horn Book

Off we go! illustrated by Laurel Molk. Little, Brown 2000 unp il lib bdg $12.95   **E**
1. Animals—Fiction   2. Grandmothers—Fiction 3. Stories in rhyme
ISBN 0-316-90228-4   LC 98-6893
One by one, baby woodland creatures leave home and sing their way to visit grandma
"Rhyme, repetition, and the playful, onomatopoeic language make this especially appealing for read-alouds. Large watercolors in earthy tones of gray, green, and brown are soft and fluid." Horn Book Guide

Yolen, Jane—*Continued*

Owl moon; illustrated by John Schoenherr. Philomel Bks. 1987 unp il lib bdg $16.99   **E**
1. Owls—Fiction 2. Father-daughter relationship—Fiction
ISBN 0-399-21457-7   LC 87-2300
Awarded the Caldecott Medal, 1988
"The poetic narrative is told from the point of view of a child who 'has been waiting to go owling with Pa for a long, long time.' The father and child venture forth on a cold winter night not to capture, but to commune with, the great horned owl." SLJ
This book "conveys the scary majesty of winter woods at night in language that seldom overreaches either character or subject. . . . Jane Yolen and John Schoenherr, who are both prolific, have done excellent work in the past, but this book has a magic that is extremely rare in books for any age." N Y Times Book Rev

Piggins and the royal wedding; illustrated by Jane Dyer. Harcourt Brace Jovanovich 1989 c1988 unp il hardcover o.p. paperback available $4.95
   E
1. Mystery fiction 2. Pigs—Fiction
ISBN 0-15-20078-X (pa)   LC 88-5399
"Piggins, the imperturbable butler, is summoned to solve the mystery of a missing wedding ring. The royal family, the well-dressed Reynard family, and their cozy Edwardian period home are all amusingly depicted in the busy and colorful illustrations." Horn Book
Other available titles about Piggins are:
Picnic with Piggins (1988)
Piggins (1987)

Raising Yoder's barn; paintings by Bernie Fuchs. Little, Brown 1998 unp il lib bdg $15.95
   E
1. Amish—Fiction 2. Farm life—Fiction
ISBN 0-316-96887-0   LC 97-13101
Eight-year-old Matthew tells what happens when fire destroys the barn on his family's farm and all the Amish neighbors come to rebuild it in one day
"Luminous, impressionistic-style oil paintings reveal images of Amish life. . . . Poetic language and stunning art-work pay tribute to a close-knit lifestyle and a commitment to family and community" SLJ

Sleeping ugly; by Jane Yolen; pictures by Diane Stanley. Coward, McCann & Geoghegan 1981 64p il hardcover o.p. paperback available $5.99   **E**
1. Fairy tales
ISBN 0-698-11560-0 (pa)
"A Break-of-day book"
When beautiful Princess Miserella, Plain Jane, and a fairy fall under a sleeping spell, a prince undoes the spell in a surprising way
"Diane Stanley's expressive illustrations, jumping from once upon a time to right now, add an intriguing perspective to the tale's witty text and humorous play with fairy tale conventions." SLJ

Yorinks, Arthur, 1953-

Company's coming; illustrated by David Small. Hyperion Bks. for Children 2000 unp il $15.99; lib bdg $16.49   **E**
1. Extraterrestrial beings—Fiction
ISBN 0-7868-0500-5; 0-7868-2433-6 (lib bdg)
     LC 99-56159
A reissue of the title first published 1988 by Crown
Chaos erupts when Moe and Shirley invite some visitors from outer space to stay for dinner with the relatives
"The hilarious dialogue in this storybook 'is as well timed as the best comedy act,' and pen-and-ink illustrations capture the mayhem perfectly." N Y Times Book Rev

Harry and Lulu; illustrated by Martin Matje. Hyperion Bks. for Children 1999 unp il $15.99; lib bdg $16.49   **E**
1. Dogs—Fiction   2. Toys—Fiction   3. Paris (France)—Fiction 4. France—Fiction
ISBN 0-7868-0335-5; 0-7868-2276-7 (lib bdg)
     LC 97-28205
Lulu, who has always wanted a dog, instead gets a very unusual stuffed animal that takes her on a trip to France
"The artwork, executed in watercolor and gouache, suits the tale perfectly. . . . An insouciant yet sweet story." Booklist

Hey, Al; story by Arthur Yorinks; pictures by Richard Egielski. Farrar, Straus & Giroux 1986 unp il $17; pa $5.95   **E**
1. Fantasy fiction
ISBN 0-374-33060-3; 0-374-42985-5 (pa)
     LC 86-80955
Awarded the Caldecott Medal, 1987
"Al, a janitor, and his faithful dog, Eddie, live in a single room on the West Side. . . . Their tiny home is crowded and cramped; their life is an endless struggle. Al and Eddie are totally miserable until a large and mysterious bird offers them a change of fortune." Publisher's note
"Egielski's solid naturalism provides just the visual foil needed to establish the surreal character of this fantasy. The muted earth tones of the one-room flat contrast symbolically with the bright hues of the birds' plumage and the foliage of the floating paradise. The anatomical appropriateness of Al and Eddie plays neatly against the flamboyant depiction of the plants. Text and pictures work together to challenge readers' concept of reality." SLJ

Young, Ruth

Golden Bear; illustrations by Rachel Isadora. Viking 1992 unp il $15.99; pa $6.99   **E**
1. Bears—Fiction 2. Stories in rhyme
ISBN 0-670-82577-8; 0-14-050959-3 (pa)
     LC 89-24843
"Golden Bear and his friend (an unnamed African-American child) do many things together—rocking in the rocking chair, ice-skating and playing the violin." Child Book Rev Serv
"While the rhyming text is agreeable, Isadora's winsome artwork steals the show. Her chalk drawings fill

Young, Ruth—*Continued*

the pages with simple shapes and deep-toned colors. . . .
A good bedtime book and, for those who can read the
music on the endpapers, a bedtime song as well." Booklist

Who says moo? illustrated by Lisa Campbell
Ernst. Viking 1994 unp il $13.99   E
1. Animals
ISBN 0-670-85162-0   LC 94-11878
Simple questions in rhyme invite young children to
identify animals by sound, color, or other description
"It is Ernst's lively art that places this above the usual
riddle books. Using large, rounded shapes and a layout
that has the air of action (monkeys swinging and horses
galloping across spreads), Ernst provides delightful pictures that will work especially well for groups. A key at
the end identifies all the creatures. Fun for little ones."
Booklist

Zamorano, Ana

Let's eat! illustrated by Julie Vivas. Scholastic
1997 unp il $15.95; pa $5.99   E
1. Family life—Fiction 2. Spain—Fiction
ISBN 0-590-13444-2; 0-439-06758-8 (pa)
            LC 96-25928
Each day Antonio's Mamá tries to get everyone to sit
down together to eat, but someone is always busy elsewhere, until the family celebrates a new arrival
"Children will delight in Antonio's grown-up responsibilities and enjoy the comfortable but unique predictability of the text. . . . The vibrant watercolor illustrations
are accentuated by a crisp white background." SLJ

Zemach, Harve

The judge; an untrue tale; with pictures by
Margot Zemach. Farrar, Straus & Giroux 1969 unp
il $17; pa $6.95   E
1. Judges—Fiction 2. Stories in rhyme
ISBN 0-374-33960-0; 0-374-43962-1 (pa)
A Caldecott Medal honor book, 1970
"Enthroned on his bench, a curmudgeon of a judge
hears a prisoner plead that he didn't know that what he
did was against the law, but that he had seen a horrible
beast. 'This man has told an untrue tale. Throw him in
jail!' Each additional prisoner adds to the story; each in-
furiates the judge." Sutherland. The Best in Child Books

Mommy, buy me a china doll; pictures by
Margot Zemach. Farrar, Straus & Giroux 1975
c1966 unp il hardcover o.p. paperback available
$4.95   E
1. Folk songs—United States
ISBN 0-374-45286-5 (pa)
A reprint of the title first published 1966 by Follett
A "picture book version of the cumulative folk song
that has the appeals of repetition, of a chain of mildly
nonsensical actions, and of a warmly satisfying ending.
Eliza Lou's request for a china doll leads to proposals
that it be bought with Daddy's feather bed, so Daddy
would have to sleep in the horsey's bed, and the horsey
would have to sleep in Sister's bed, and so on, and so
on. Each page of print is faced by a full-page illustration
in color, humorous in mood." Bull Cent Child Books

Ziefert, Harriet

April Fool! illustrated by Chris Demarest.
Viking 2000 unp il $13.89; pa $3.99   E
1. April Fools' Day—Fiction 2. Elephants—Fiction
3. Stories in rhyme
ISBN 0-670-88762-5; 0-14-130582-7 (pa)
            LC 99-26014
"A Viking easy-to-read"
On April 1, Will tells his friends how he once saw a
bike-riding elephant who sang through his trunk while
juggling six bags of junk
"Jaunty ink drawings tinted with bright washes give
this Viking Easy-to-Read title a cheerful look. . . . Upbeat fare for beginning readers and a possible read-aloud
choice for younger children." Booklist

First He made the sun; paintings by Todd
McKie. Putnam 2000 unp il $15.99   E
1. Creation 2. Stories in rhyme
ISBN 0-399-23199-4   LC 99-27020
Presents a rhyming rendition of the six days in which
God made the seas, the skies, and the creatures and of
the seventh day on which He rested to admire them
"McKie's exuberant illustrations work delightfully
with the bouncy text. [With] flat perspective, bright col-
ors, and simple shapes." SLJ

Hats off for the Fourth of July! illustrated by
Gus Miller. Viking 2000 unp il $15.99   E
1. Parades 2. Fourth of July 3. Stories in rhyme
ISBN 0-670-89118-5   LC 99-42057
Spectators wait to see what will come next as they
watch the town's Fourth of July parade
"Ziefert records the events in rhyme as Miller supplies
colorful illustrations of each new attraction as it passes.
. . . A good addition to any holiday collection and ex-
cellent for reading aloud." Booklist

A new coat for Anna; pictures by Anita Lobel.
Knopf 1986 unp il hardcover o.p. paperback
available $6.99   E
1. Coats—Fiction
ISBN 0-394-89861-3 (pa)   LC 86-2722
Set in a war-torn town in post-World War II Eastern
Europe. Even though there is no money, Anna's mother
finds a way to make Anna a badly needed winter coat
"Ziefert's writing is clear and succinct, but it is in
Lobel's brightly colored paintings that the story truly unfolds. . . . The expressiveness of the faces in Lobel's
paintings brings life to the story. Ziefert's tale, based on
a true story, carries a simple lesson that will be understood and cherished by all ages." SLJ

Pushkin meets the bundle; [by] Harriet M.
Ziefert; paintings by Donald Saaf. Atheneum Bks.
for Young Readers 1998 unp il $16   E
1. Dogs—Fiction 2. Infants—Fiction
ISBN 0-689-81413-5   LC 96-37748
"An Anne Schwartz book"
Pushkin the dog, once the apple of his owners' eyes,
tries to cope with the arrival of a new baby to the house
"The text is simple, clear, and perfect for reading
alone or with a group. Saaf's lively and expressive
gouache illustrations effectively draw readers into the ac-
tion and emotion." SLJ
Another available title about Pushkin is:
Pushkin minds the bundle (2000)

Ziefert, Harriet—*Continued*

Train song; paintings by Donald Saaf. Orchard
Bks. 2000 unp il $14.95   **E**
1. Railroads 2. Stories in rhyme
ISBN 0-531-30204-0   LC 99-32219
A young boy watches a freight train go by on its daily
run
A "steady rhythm chugs through the book, telling the
story in rhymed couplets. Large in scale and naive in
style, Saaf's gouache paintings illustrate the text with becoming directness and simplicity." Booklist

Zimmerman, Andrea Griffing

My dog Toby; [by] Andrea Zimmerman and
David Clemesha; illustrated by True Kelley.
Harcourt 2000 unp il $15   **E**
1. Dogs—Fiction
ISBN 0-15-202014-4   LC 98-35246
"Silver Whistle"
Toby the dog is a beloved pet, but he doesn't seem
to be able to do any tricks
"The understated humor of the text is amplified by the
buoyant spirits of Kelley's amusing illustrations. Black-
ink drawings, vividly tinted with watercolors and acrylics, bring humor even to the most deadpan lines in the
narration." Booklist

Trashy town; [by] Andrea Zimmerman and
David Clemesha; illustrated by Dan Yaccarino.
HarperCollins Pubs. 1999 unp il $14.95; lib bdg
$14.89   **E**
1. Refuse and refuse disposal—Fiction
ISBN 0-06-027139-6; 0-06-027140-X (lib bdg)
LC 98-27495
Little by little, can by can, Mr. Gillie, the trash man,
cleans up his town
"Short energetic sentences propel the tale. . . . Em-
ploying primary colors dominated by bold blues,
Yaccarino's vibrant art has a retro look." Booklist

Zion, Gene

Harry the dirty dog; pictures by Margaret Bloy
Graham. Harper & Row 1956 unp il $15.95; lib
bdg $15.89; pa $6.95   **E**
1. Dogs—Fiction
ISBN 0-06-026865-4; 0-06-026866-2 (lib bdg);
0-06-443009-X (pa)
Also available Spanish language edition
"A runaway dog becomes so dirty his family almost
doesn't recognize him. Harry's flight from scrubbing
brush and bath water takes him on a tour of the city.
Road repairs, railroad yards, construction sites, and coal
deliveries contribute to his grimy appearance and show
aspects of city life that contrast with the tidy suburb that
is 'home.'" Moorachian. What is a City?
"Harry's fun and troubles are told simply, and the
drawings are full of action and humor. The combination
will have great appeal for the very young." Horn Book
Other available titles about Harry are:
Harry and the lady next door (1960)
Harry by the sea (1965)
No roses for Harry! (1958)

Zolotow, Charlotte, 1915-

The beautiful Christmas tree; illustrated by Yan
Nacimbene. Houghton Mifflin 1999 32p il $15
E
1. City and town life—Fiction 2. Trees—Fiction
3. Christmas—Fiction
ISBN 0-395-91365-9   LC 98-50006
A newly illustrated edition of the title first published
1972 by Parnassus Press
Although his elegant neighbors do not appreciate his
efforts, a kind old man transforms his rundown house
and a small neglected pine tree into the best on the street
"In handsome depictions of the urban setting,
Nascimbene's delicate watercolors convey the emotional
warmth of Zolotow's testament to a simple man's faith
and love." Horn Book Guide

The bunny who found Easter; illustrated by
Helen Craig. Houghton Mifflin 1998 unp il $15
E
1. Rabbits—Fiction 2. Easter—Fiction
ISBN 0-395-86265-5   LC 97-36827
A newly illustrated edition of the title first published
1959 by Parnassus Press
A lonely rabbit searches for others of his kind from
summer through winter until spring arrives and he finds
one special bunny
"Zolotow's stylistic trademarks—tender lyricism, poetic prose, and a compassionate tone—continue to satisfy
children. Craig's charming pastel paintings in ink, watercolor, and colored pencil bring the bunny to life." SLJ

The hating book; pictures by Ben Shecter.
Harper & Row 1969 32p il hardcover o.p.
paperback available $5.95   **E**
1. Friendship—Fiction
ISBN 0-06-443197-5 (pa)
"A little girl tells of several instances of being rebuffed by her friend, ending with the comment, 'I hated
my friend.' Finally, at the urging of her mother, she goes
to see the friend and asks her why she's been so 'rotten.'
The answer is that 'Sue said Jane said you said I looked
like a freak.' The actual remark had been that she looked
'neat.' The point of the book is clear as the two friends
make plans to play together the following day." Read
Ladders for Hum Relat. 6th edition

Mr. Rabbit and the lovely present; pictures by
Maurice Sendak. Harper & Row 1962 unp il
$15.95; pa $5.95   **E**
1. Birthdays—Fiction 2. Color—Fiction 3. Rabbits—
Fiction
ISBN 0-06-026945-6; 0-06-443020-0 (pa)
Also available Spanish language edition
A Caldecott Medal honor book, 1963
"A serious little girl and a tall, other-worldly white
rabbit converse about a present for her mother. 'But
what?' said the little girl. 'Yes, what?' said Mr. Rabbit.'
It requires a day of searching—for red, yellow, green,
and blue, all things the mother likes, to make a basket
of fruit for the present." Horn Book
"The quiet story, told in dialogue, is illustrated in
richly colored pictures which exactly fit the fanciful
mood." Hodges. Books for Elem Sch Libr

Zolotow, Charlotte, 1915-—_Continued_

My friend John; illustrated by Amanda Harvey. Doubleday Bks. for Young Readers 2000 unp il $14.95   E

1. Friendship—Fiction

ISBN 0-385-32651-3   LC 98-54582

A newly illustrated edition of the title first published 1968 by Harper & Row

John's best friend tells everything he knows about John, the secrets they share, their likes and dislikes, and the fun they have as friends

"Harvey illustrates the brief text with large watercolor paintings bordered in white. . . . These pals are full of fun and mischief and young readers will enjoy their antics." SLJ

The old dog; paintings by James Ransome. rev and newly illustrated ed. HarperCollins Pubs. 1995 unp il $15.95   E

1. Dogs—Fiction 2. Death—Fiction

ISBN 0-06-024409-7   LC 93-41081

A revised and newly illustrated edition of the title first published 1972 by Coward, McCann & Geoghegan under the author's pseudonym Sarah Abbott

When Ben finds his old dog dead one morning, he spends the rest of the day thinking about all the good times they had together

"Zolotow's elemental story . . . is newly illustrated here with rich oil paintings. . . . An unsentimental story about connection and loss and renewal." Booklist

The quarreling book; pictures by Arnold Lobel. Harper & Row 1963 unp il hardcover o.p. paperback available $5.95   E

ISBN 0-06-443034-0 (pa)

"Father forgets to kiss Mother goodbye when starting to work one morning, so Mother is unhappy and becomes cross with Jonathan James who takes out his feelings on his sister, and the chain continues until reversed by the dog who thinks being shoved off the bed is just a game and lots of fun. The sequence, then starts in happy reverse until at five, with the rain ending, Mr. James comes home and kisses Mrs. James." SLJ

It is "a worthwhile book which clearly demonstrates the far-reaching effects one's actions have on others. Even the youngest child will grasp its lesson easily. The illustrations are whimsical, detailed and expressive." NY Times Book Rev

The seashore book; paintings by Wendell Minor. HarperCollins Pubs. 1992 unp il $16.95; pa $6.95   E

1. Seashore—Fiction 2. Mother-son relationship—Fiction

ISBN 0-06-020213-0; 0-06-443364-1 (pa)

LC 91-22783

A mother's words help a little boy imagine the sights and sounds of the seashore, even though he's never seen the ocean

"Minor's crisply detailed watercolors evoke place with imaginative accuracy and visual grace, and Zolotow's . . . spare, poetic text provides a lyrical and nostalgic paean to the wonders of seaside life." Publ Wkly

Some things go together; pictures by Ashley Wolff. newly il ed. HarperFestival 1999 unp il $9.95   E

ISBN 0-694-01197-5   LC 98-70966

"Harper growing tree"

A newly illustrated edition of the title first published 1969 by Crowell

"Pairs of related images, such as 'Peace with dove/Home with love' and 'Mountains with high/Birds with fly,' are sweetly depicted in Wolff's sturdy, old-fashioned-looking illustrations." Horn Book Guide

When the wind stops; illustrated by Stefano Vitale. rev and newly illustrated ed. HarperCollins Pubs. 1995 unp il $15.95; pa $6.95   E

1. Nature—Fiction

ISBN 0-06-025425-4; 0-06-443472-9 (pa)

LC 94-14477

A revised and newly illustrated edition of the title first published 1962 by Abelard-Schuman

A mother explains to her son that in nature an end is also a beginning as day gives way to night, winter ends and spring begins, and, after it stops falling, rain makes clouds for other storms

"The full-color scenes, painted on wood, gloriously depict heaven and earth and give concrete meaning to abstract concepts. Not only wonderful for lap sharing, this beautiful book will also be a rich supplement for a science unit on the elements or the seasons." Booklist

William's doll; pictures by William Pène Du Bois. Harper & Row 1972 30p il $15.95; lib bdg $15.89; pa $5.95   E

1. Dolls—Fiction 2. Sex role—Fiction

ISBN 0-06-027047-0; 0-06-027048-9 (lib bdg); 0-06-443067-7 (pa)

When little William asks for a doll, the other boys scorn him and his father tries to interest him in conventional boys' playthings such as a basketball and a train. His sympathetic grandmother buys him the doll, explaining his need to have it to love and care for so that he can practice being a father

"Very, very special. The strong, yet delicate pictures . . . convey a gentleness of spirit and longing most effectively, as William pantomimes his craving." N Y Times Book Rev

PART 2

LIST OF RECOMMENDED WEB RESOURCES

LIST OF RECOMMENDED WEB RESOURCES

700+ great sites. American Library Association
Free

http://www.ala.org/parentspage/greatsites/
amazing.html

Lists children's sites selected for clear statement of authorship and sponsorship, clearly defined purpose, good design, stability, and use of sound information to inform, educate, or entertain. Subjects include arts and entertainment, literature and language, people, geography, and science and technology.

A. Pintura: art detective. Educational Web
Adventures   Free (4 and up)

http://www.eduweb.com/pintura

An online game about art history and composition, in which players attempt to discover a painting's artist by examining paintings by famous artists from Gaugin to Van Gogh for composition, style, and subject.

Absurd math. Learningwave   Free (5 and up)

http://www.hrmvideo.com/abmath

In this online interactive game, players work to overthrow a tyranny which punishes all thought, and mathematical thought in particular. They are presented with a series of pre-algebra problems which increase in difficulty as they approach success. The mathematics is surprisingly demanding, despite requiring only arithmetic up to decimal fractions, but hints and e-mail help are available.

Access excellence activities exchange. National
Health Museum   Free (6 and up)

http://www.accessexcellence.org/AE/mspot

Interactive, online scientific mysteries teach problem-solving and inquiry. In one, players must decide whether an outbreak of sickness on a racing yacht is dangerous enough to require to breaking off the race.

Alien empire. PBS   Free (3-6)

http://www.wnet.org/nature/alienempire/
metropolis.html

Provides pictures, sounds, animation, and videos on insects. Articles discuss insect reproduction, societies, migration, and survival strategies. Includes animated presentations on monarch butterflies, mayflies, and bees and a list of insect information resources.

Amazon Interactive. Educational Web Adventures
Free (3-6)

http://www.eduweb.com/amazon.html

Explains the geography of the Ecuadorian Amazon and the culture of the Quichua people through online games and activities. In one interactive game, players try to set up and manage a sustainable, community-based ecotourism project along the Río Napo.

America the beautiful online. Grolier Educational
From $335/yr. (4 and up)

http:www.go.grolier.com

By subscription only. Tel. 888-326-6546

A reference source on the U.S., the states, and territories, with 1,000 new articles covering the following topics: history, economy, government, cities and capitals, rivers and lakes, geography, and landforms. Articles are enchanced with photos, maps, narrated slide shows, and pre-selected Web links on the Grolier Internet Index. Profiles of famous Americans include every president. Information is also included on national parks, natural wonders, monuments, museums, zoos, and historic places. Both key word searches and advanced searches can be limited to article titles or to full text. The site also includes an almanac and a dictionary. Lesson plans and activities are provided for teachers.

American government. ABC-CLIO $499/yr. (6 and up)

http://www.abc-clio.com/schools/

By subscription only. Tel. 800-368-6868

This comprehensive resource on all aspects of American government includes topic overviews, essays, court cases, biographies, speeches, and historical documents. Students can explore pre-designed topics such as Congressional Powers, the Presidency, Civil Rights, and Political Parties by key words. Advanced searches can be limited by topic and category (movements, organizations, statistics, quotes, etc.). The Home page provides changing news articles and feature stories linked to related articles in the database. Teachers can customize the site by adding announcements, syllabi, calendar of assignments, tests, etc. Teachers also have access to professional articles and links to additional resources. Includes the *Merriam-Webster's Collegiate Dictionary.*

"Well designed, with good content and strategically placed links. Students will enjoy digging deep into this source. Highly recommended for school and public libraries." (Library Journal)

American history. ABC-Clio $499/yr. (6 and up)

http://www.abc-clio.com/schools/

By subscription only. Tel. 800-368-6868

This site provides coverage and resources on American history from 1350 to the present. The Home page includes ever-changing feature stories and current events with links to related articles. Information can be searched by key word or phrase as well as through advanced searches by category, including documents, quotes, timelines, and types of multimedia. Teachers can customize the site by adding announcements, syllabi, calendar of assignments, tests, etc. Teachers also have access to professional articles and links to additional resources. Includes the *Merriam-Webster's Collegiate Dictionary.*

"An easily navigable, appealing and comprehensive resource that would be extremely useful for the study of United States history." (Evalutech Web site)

America's story. Library of Congress   Free (5 and up)

http://www.americaslibrary.gov/cgi-bin/page.cgi

America's story—*Continued*

This site sets out to "put the story back in history" for children, using letters, diaries, records and tapes, films, sheet music, maps, prints, and photographs from the Library of Congress collections. Includes sections on famous Americans, on each historical period, and on popular culture.

Animals A to Z. Oakland Zoo   Free (3-6)

http://www.oaklandzoo.org/atoz/atoz.html

A database of text, pictures, sound, and video on approximately one hundred zoo animals.

ArtEdventures. Sanford   Free (3-6)

http://www.sanford-artedventures.com/play/play.html

Six interactive online games teach about art history and technique. In one, players must learn about landscape painting techniques from great American landscape painters or face a lifetime of working in a bank. In another they are called upon to design furniture and household appliances for a diplomatic delegation of aliens.

Become a historical detective. Library of Congress   Free (6 and up)

http://memory.loc.gov/ammem/ndlpedu/activity/detectiv.html

Teaches research by posing a question about a historical mystery and giving hints on finding the answer. Includes links to the American Memory collection of primary historical source materials.

Biointeractive. Howard Hughes Medical Institute   Free (5 and up)

http://www.biointeractive.org

In four virtual laboratories children can diagnose cardiac diseases, identify pathogens by DNA sequencing, dissect out a leech's nervous system, and diagnose diseases by assaying antibodies.

Black belt for kids. Black Belt Magazine   Free (4 and up)

http://www.blackbeltmag.com/bbkids

Articles on martial arts for children, written with an effort to emphasize self-control and personal development. Includes biographical profiles of famous martial artists.

BLS Career Information. U.S. Bureau of Labor Statistics   Free (5 and up)

http://stats.bls.gov/k12/html/edu_over.htm

Provides vocational guidance for children interested in the arts, mathematics, science, physical activities, the outdoors, social science, or reading.

Born in slavery. Library of Congress   Free (5 and up)

http://memory.loc.gov/ammem/snhtml/snhome.html

Contains more than 2,300 first-person oral histories of slavery and 500 photographs of former slaves collected in the 1930s as part of the Federal Writer's Project. Some narratives contain descriptions of shocking cruelty while others convey an almost nostalgic view of plantation life. Many narratives contain a word commonly used by African Americans in the 1930s South when speaking of themselves that some children may find horrifying.

Build a prairie. Bell Museum of Natural History   Free (3-6)

http://www1.umn.edu/bellmuse/mnideals/prairie/build/index.html

In this interactive game, players restore a prairie to its native state. They reintroduce native grasses, wildflowers, birds, animals, and insects, taking care not to introduce exotic, invasive species. Upon successfully completing each stage, they are shown an animation of their prairie's progress.

C.E.R.F. (Curriculum and education resource finder). Media Flex   From $500/yr. (K and up)

http://www.cerfinfo.com/search/

By subscription only. Tel. 877-331-1022

A directory of weekly updated Web sites that have been pre-screened and selected for use in the instructional setting. Users can search for sites by key word (with Boolean operators), by topic lists, or by grade level range (including professional). Information about each site includes the title, hyperlinked URL, relevant subject areas, correlations to McRel (Mid-continent Research for Education and Learning) standards, and cross references to related topics. Sites can also be saved to a bibliography with an option to e-mail results.

"A big plus for C.E.R.F. is the extensive use of links from outside the United States, giving a more global perspective to inquiry." (Book Report)

Cats: plans for perfection. National Geographic   Free (3-6)

http://www.nationalgeographic.com/features/97/cats

This site is organized around the conceit that all feline species were designed by a team of engineers, who faced engineers' usual difficulties with budgets and schedules. As it tells the story of the design project's progress, the site teaches the relationship between feline structure and function.

Children's butterfly site. U.S. Geological Survey   Free (4-6)

http://www.mesc.nbs.gov/butterfly/Butterfly.html

An expert on butterflies answers children's questions and a gallery exhibits photographs of butterflies from around the world. Children may submit questions if they are not already answered on the site.

Children's literature comprehensive database. bigchalk.com $325/yr

http://www.bigchalk.com

By subscription only. Tel. 800-860-9228

The database contains more than 500,000 MARC records and 35,000 reviews from baby board books to young adult novels drawn from sources such as *Children's Literature Newsletter, Kirkus, Science Books and Films,* and *VOYA.* Reviews can be searched by key word with options to limit by category (fiction or nonfiction), genre, age, language, author/illustrator, publisher, publication date, and search term qualifiers such as exact phrase and singular or plural forms. Search results are ranked in relevancy order and each record provides a one-sentence annotation, text of reviews, as well as hyperlinks to related subject terms and other works by the author and reviewers. Also provided are the call number, LCCN, Dewey classification, ISBN/ISSN, and a link to the MARC record.

"This is a great resource for librarians, media specialists, teachers, and parents." (School Library Journal)

Classroom today. Classroom connect $249/yr. (3 and up)

http://www.classroom.com

By subscription only. Tel. 800-638-1639

Links topics in Science, Social Studies, Math, Reading and Language Arts with Internet resources aligned with McREL (Mid-continent Research for Education and Learning) and state standards. The site offers choices of grade-level range and up to four sub-topic levels of major subject areas. Each topical section provides guiding questions, a lesson plan, links to related Web resources, quizzes, field trips, and other activities. There is also a searchable library of Web-based resources for teaching and professional development organized by broad topics. Teachers can set up their own class pages of assignments and assess student work with individual student notebooks, portfolios, and auto-scored, multiple-choice quizzes.

"A well-planned site with rich and current resources for teachers to use in their classrooms. The site takes the searching out of planning individual units and presents resources in a very organized and easy-to-follow manner." (MultiMedia Schools)

Connected university. Classroom Connect $349/yr.

http://cu.classroom.com

By subscription only. Tel. 800-638-1639

Connected University offers educators 24-hour-a-day access to instructor-led courses, self-paced courses, technology "how to" tips, and software tutorials. Courses are available on a broad range of topics from teaching reading standards to how to build a Web page. Graduate credits and continuing education units can be obtained from partner universities. Thousands of pre-screened, educator-friendly Web sites are provided in the CU Library.

Curriculum resource center. Facts on File From $299/yr. (4 and up)

http://www.fofweb.com

By subscription only. Tel. 800-322-8755

Database of copyright-free, reproducible, black-and-white and color maps, historical maps, graphs, charts, timelines, illustrations, and other hand-out materials with visual content and text. Subjects dealt with are environment, geography, health and fitness, general science, United States history and government, and world history. The materials in this database display in *Adobe Acrobat* (link to free download provided).

Digital learning center for microbial ecology: the microbe zoo. Michigan State University Free (3-6)

http://commtechlab.msu.edu/sites/dlc-me/zoo

Includes pictures and descriptions of microbes and explanations of how they interact with their environment and with each other.

Discover the history of life. University of California Museum of Paleontology Free (5 and up)

http://www.ucmp.berkeley.edu/historyoflife/histoflife.html

Exhibits explain how the theories of phylogeny, geology, and evolution fit together in paleontology. Also includes pages on special exhibits and a mystery fossil identification game.

Dragonfly. University of Miami Free (3-5)

http://www.muohio.edu/Dragonfly

Clicking on parts of a picture or on a list of topics moves one to articles, pictures, and interactive educational games on such topics as animal flight, ecosystems, trees, skeletons, animal communication, navigation, and genetics.

Earth science explorer. NASA Free (4 and up)

http://www.cotf.edu/ete/modules/msese/explorer.htm

This site is organized around a museum floor plan, with one floor devoted to earth sciences and the other devoted to paleontology. The earth sciences section contains tutorials on geologic time, plate tectonics, geological cycles, and biomes. The paleontological section presents contending theories of dinosaur extinction with the evidence for each.

eLibrary elementary. bigchalk.com $475/yr. (K-6)

http://www.bigchalk.com

By subscription only. Tel. 800-860-9228

Age-appropriate online research of 100 full-text magazine, newspaper, book, and transcript resources, plus thousands of maps and pictures. Searches can be entered by key word with Boolean operators. There are options to limit searches by format: newspapers, magazine articles, reference books (*World Book, World Almanac for Kids, Webster's New World Dictionary*), pictures, maps, and radio and television transcripts. Search results are listed with the reading level by grade and icons to designate the type of resource. Results can be sorted in relevancy order or by date, reading level, or media type. Includes a dictionary and a thesaurus.

eNature.com. Audubon Society Free (4 and up)

http://www.enature.com

Audubon field guides online and searchable, with descriptions and color photographs of over 4,800 North American plants and animals. If given a zip code, the site will provide descriptions and pictures of birds native to that region.

Encyclopedia Smithsonian. Smithsonian Institution Free

http://www.si.edu/resource/faq/start.htm

This very large site provides an alphabetical list of links to Smithsonian resources. Not all of the material is written for children, but almost all of the subjects covered will be of interest to them.

Exploring Leonardo. Boston Museum of Science Free (5 and up)

http://www.mos.org/sln/Leonardo/LeoHomePage.html

Interactive site describes some of Leonardo's inventions, and gives a chance to analyze them and design others. Explains his system of perspective, provides a brief biography, and discusses his habit of writing in reverse.

Exploring the planets. National Air and Space Museum Free (4 and up)

http://www.nasm.edu/ceps/etp

Exploring the planets—*Continued*

Explains how the planets of the solar system have been explored from Earth and by spacecraft. Includes information on and photographs of each planet, of asteroids, and of comets. In an activity, one describes satellite photographs and compares one's descriptions to those of an astronomer.

Fake out. Houghton Mifflin   Free (3-6)

http://www.eduplace.com/fakeout

In this variation of a classic word game, players are given an unlikely, but actual, word and a set of plausible definitions to select among. Players are also invited to invent plausible definitions for upcoming words.

Federal resources for educational excellence. Federal Resources for Educational Excellence Free

http://www.ed.gov/free

Lists hundreds of educational Web sites supported by U.S. government agencies. Subjects include arts, educational technology, foreign languages, health and safety, language arts, mathematics, physical education, science, social studies, and vocational education.

Geo mysteries. Children's Museum of Indianapolis   Free (3-6)

http://www.childrensmuseum.org/geomysteries/index2.html

Three interactive mystery-solving games teach basic geological principles. In each, players use a combination of theory and experiment to identify a mysterious mineral.

Ghosts in the castle. National Geographic   Free (3-6)

http://www.nationalgeographic.com/castles/enter.html

As one tours a virtual castle, ghosts reminisce about their lives there.

Grammar gorillas. Learning Network   Free (3-6)

http://www.funbrain.com/grammar

In this game, players identify parts of speech in sentences. The more correct answers they get, the more bananas the gorillas get.

Great athletes of the twentieth century. EBSCO nd $595/yr. (5 and up)

http://www.web4classroom.com

By subscription only. Tel. 800-653-2726

Part of EBSCO's 20th Century Series. Database of over 900 sports personalities, covering more than 60 sports categories. Athletes covered are from the United States and more than 40 other countries. Entry for each athlete includes a biography and links to related magazine and newspaper articles, charts, graphs, and photos. There are also Web links organized by sports categories and a note-taking feature. Supports key word and natural language searching.

Great events of the twentieth century. EBSCO $595/yr. (6 and up)

http://www.web4classroom.com

By subscription only. Tel. 800-653-2726

Part of EBSCO's 20th Century Series. The database covers over 550 significant events of the twentieth century from the United States as well as from over 125 other geographic locations. The article for each event includes a description of the event, information about the people involved, pertinent dates and places, and the historical context. There are links to over 7,000 newspaper and journal articles as well as related images, maps, flags, and Web sites. Users can search by category, name, decade, country, Web links, and key word.

Great scientific achievements of the twentieth century. EBSCO $595/yr. (6 and up)

http://www.web4classroom.com

By subscription only. Tel. 800-653-2726

Part of EBSCO's 20th Century Series. Database of over 500 scientific milestones of the twentieth century, ranging from the identification of neuron cells to the first cloning of an animal. Articles include background information on the achievement and the scientific advancement represented, information on the people involved, and a description of the subsequent impact on modern life. There are also links to over 4,000 related newspaper and magazine articles as well as images and Web links. Users can search by scientific category, scientists' names, decade, key terms, Web links, and key word.

Grolier multimedia encyclopedia online. Grolier Educational   From $335/yr. (5 and up)

http:www.go.grolier.com

By subscription only. Tel. 888-326-6546

General encyclopedia covering all subjects with multimedia and current events features. Information can be located by browsing categories such as U.S. history, language and literature, life sciences, and technology, or by key words. Both key word searches and advanced searches can be limited to article titles or to full text. Articles include hyperlinked cross references, related Web links, and bibliographies. There are also links to related magazine articles provided by EBSCO. The Brain Jam feature changes frequently and explores a topic in more depth, enhanced with Web links, activities, and teacher resources.

"A wonderfully easy-to-use title that provides good overviews to large topics, good definitions and brief biographies, and highly useful cross-referencing....Highly recommended for public and school libraries." (Library Journal)

A **guided** tour of the visible human. MadSci Network   Free (5 and up)

http://www.madsci.org/%7Elynn/VH/tour.html

The Visible Human Project has taken over 18,000 sections of a human body, scanned them, and made the images available over the Internet. This site uses some of the scanned images in an anatomy tutorial. Animations are used to show how to visualize transverse, coronal, and sagittal sections in three dimensions.

The **hero's** adventure. Maricopa Center for Learning and Instruction   Free (5 and up)

http://www.mcli.dist.maricopa.edu/smc/journey

In The Hero With a Thousand Faces, Joseph Campbell writes that hero myths follow a general formula. This site provides an interactive form based on this formula, with which writers can construct mythic, heroic stories.

How things work. University of Virginia   Free (6 and up)

http://rabi.phys.virginia.edu/HTW//

How things work—*Continued*

A professor of physics answers e-mail questions about how things—machines, everyday processes, toys and games, among others—work. The explanations are as complete as they can be without mathematics, but the language is not needlessly technical. Includes an archive of answered questions.

Hunkin's experiments. Pelham Projects Ltd.   Free (4 and up)

http://www.HunkinsExperiments.com

A cartoonist with an engineering degree shows how to do hundreds of demonstrations, illusions, and tricks. Examples include how to move a cup of water by balloon, to peel bananas automatically, to photograph the path of a pendulum, to prove that 1=2, to prove that there is no black in a television picture, to pull a string through your neck, and to push a cube through a cube of the same size.

Illusionworks. Illusionworks   Free (4 and up)

http://illusionworks.com/index.shtml

A collection of optical illusions, along with scientific explanations, interactive demonstrations, school projects, illusion artwork, puzzles, and three-dimensional graphics.

InfoTrac junior edition. Gale Group   From $835/yr. (5-8)

http://www.galegroup.com

By subscription only. Tel. 800-877-4253

InfoTrac Junior Edition features full-text articles from periodical titles relevant to the interests and curriculum needs of upper elementary, junior high, and middle school students. Broad search term results offer suggested narrower terms with related subdivisions and types of source documents. An optional child-friendly interface is available that includes a Toolbox with tips for doing research and writing reports. Newspapers and magazines are updated daily. Includes a dictionary feature and maps.

InfoTrac kid's edition. Gale Group   From $395/yr. (K-6)

http://www.galegroup.com

By subscription only. Tel. 800-877-4253

InfoTrac Kid's Edition introduces young students to the research process by providing access to magazines, reference books, and newspaper articles selected for the age group. The database supports simple key word and advanced searching. Broad search term results offer suggested narrower terms with related subdivisions and types of source documents. An optional child-friendly interface is available that includes a Toolbox with tips for doing research and writing reports. Includes a dictionary feature and maps.

Inside art. Educational Web Adventures   Free (4 and up)

http://www.eduweb.com/insideart/index.html

An online game which explores a painting from the inside out. During an art museum tour, players are sucked into a vortex and find themselves inside Van Gogh's Bank of the Oise at Auvers. Their only hope of escape is, with the help of a fish named Trish, to place the painting in its artistic and historical context.

Interactive online exhibits. London Natural History Museum   Free (3-6)

http://www.nhm.ac.uk/interactive/index.html

Current exhibits include a video feed from a leafcutter ant colony, a database of dinosaur pictures, a multimedia presentation on eclipses, and an online game in which players use various instruments to identify objects from the museum's collection.

Junior reference collection. Gale Group   From $525/yr. (4-8)

http://www.galegroup.com

By subscription only. Tel. 800-877-4253

Online version of the Gale Group's U·X·L electronic resources for students and librarians that combines the information from U·X·L Biographies 2.0, U·X·L Science, U·X·L Junior DISCovering Authors 2.0, U·X·L Junior Worldmark and U·X·L Multicultural, with entries written at an appropriate reading level. The combined database provides a single query interface that permits searching by people, places, subjects, authors, books, and timeline. Custom searches can be limited by Boolean operators and by data types. Includes the *Merriam-Webster's Collegiate*, *Biographical*, and *Geographical* dictionaries.

Keiko's corner. Ocean Futures Society   Free (3-5)

http://www.oceanfutures.org/keiko_corner.html

Reports on the process by which Keiko, the orca that starred in the movie Free Willy, is being prepared for reintroduction to the wild in Iceland. Includes pictures and recent news updates.

Kid territory. San Diego Zoo   Free (3-6)

http://204.216.178.162/wildideas/kids

Includes biographical profiles of zoo animals, job descriptions of zoo workers, articles on zookeeping, and games.

Kids space connection. Kids Space   Free (3-6)

http://www.ks-connection.org

Children may post messages or stories on bulletin boards, search for pen pals, and post links to their Web pages. Postings are screened to protect children's privacy and safety.

KidsClick!. Ramapo Catskill Library System   Free

http://sunsite.berkeley.edu/KidsClick!

List sites selected to inform or entertain children from kindergarten to seventh grade in Dewey Decimal System order. Includes a child's search engine and a child's tutorial on Internet searching.

Kinetic City cyber club. American Association for the Advancement of Science   Free (3-6)

http://www.kineticcity.com/newindex.html

This compendium of science teaching games is based on the fictional premise that a virtual, computer-simulated world inhabited by artificial intelligences is endangered by a computer virus that is deleting the laws of nature. To save the world, players must first learn scientific laws and then re-establish them by answering test questions.

Lands and peoples online. Grolier Educational   From $335/yr. (4 and up)

http://www.go.grolier.com

By subscription only. Tel. 888-326-6546

Lands and peoples online—*Continued*

An international geography reference based on the print version. Articles have hyperlinked outlines and cross references and include photos, maps, flags, facts and figures, and Internet links. A Culture Cross feature enables users to compare two countries, continents, or states/provinces from the persepctive of land, people, economy, history, or facts and figures. Also included are highlights of current events around the world, an atlas, an almanac, and games and quizzes for students. Both key work seaches and advances searches can be limited to titles or to full text.

"The ease of navigation and the multiple access points make it easy for beginning researchers to find what they need. The ability to create specific searches and locate precise elements of information make Lands and Peoples Online attractive for more sophisticated assignments as well." (Booklist)

Life in ancient Egypt. Carnegie Museum of Natural History   Free (5 and up)

http://www.clpgh.org/cmnh/exhibits/egypt/index.html

Presents a picture of ancient Egyptian society, technology, and beliefs by displaying and explaining several thematic groups of artifacts.

Living in space. Children's Museum of Indianapolis   Free (5 and up)

http://www.childrensmuseum.org/cosmicquest/ spacestation/index2.html

In this online game, players design space stations of increasing size and complexity.

Math forum problems. Swarthmore College Free (4 and up)

http://forum.swarthmore.edu/library/problems

An archive of elementary, middle school, geometry, algebra, discrete mathematics, trigonometry, and calculus word problems, each with a variety of solutions.

Mind over matter. National Institute on Drug Abuse   Free (5 and up)

http://www.nida.nih.gov/mom/momindex.html

Describes drugs' effects on brain anatomy and physiology and the way in which these effects affect emotion and behavior.

Museum of ancient inventions. Smith College Free (4 and up)

http://www.smith.edu/hsc/museum/ancient_inventions /hsclist.htm

Pictures and descriptions of replicas of forty-six ancient devices, with explanations of how they work and why they were important. Devices range from a distaff and a hoe, to toys and cosmetics, to a lighthouse and a ship breaker.

NASA explores. NASA   Free (4 and up)

http://NASAexplores.com/cgi-bin/index.pl

This site contains articles discussing recent scientific research at NASA. Each article is available at reading levels suitable for elementary school students, middle school students, and high school students.

The NASA Qwhiz. NASA   Free (2-6)

http://prime.jsc.nasa.gov/Qwhiz/

A real-time, multi-player Web game in which players study for and take quizzes on math, science, space exploration and other topics. Players can play aginst each other or against a computer.

NASA's why files. NASA   Free (3-5)

http://whyfiles.larc.nasa.gov/treehouse.html

This site contains four interactive games in which players use research and logic to design an airplane, to hold electrical expenditures within a defined limit, to solve a city's noise problem, and to identify the source of an unpleasant odor. Also includes instructions for home science investigations.

Natural history notebooks. Canadian Museum of Nature   Free (3-6)

http://www.nature.ca/notebooks/english

Provides short descriptions and sketches of 246 animal species. The text is from the museum's book series of the same title and the sketches are by a former chief illustrator.

The New book of knowledge online. Grolier Educational   From $335/yr. (3 and up)

http://www.go.grolier.com

By subscription only. Tel. 888-326-6546

A general encyclopedia covering all subjects and selected current events for younger children. Articles have hyperlinked outlines and links that include photos, maps, profiles of famous people, magazine articles from EBSCO, and related pre-selected Internet sites. Both key word searches and advanced searches can be limited to article titles or to full text. The NBK News feature highlights current topics of interest to children with links to related articles in the database as well as Internet sites and lesson plans for teachers. Includes a dictionary and thesaurus.

The New book of popular science online. Grolier Educational   From $335/yr. (5 and up)

http://www.go.grolier.com

By subscription only. Tel. 888-326-6546

A science and technology reference site with articles found in the print version along with science in the news. Articles are organized by broad topics and feature hyperlinked outlines and links to related topics. Both key word searches and advanced searches can be limited to article titles or to full text. Sidebars have options for selected readings, Web links, careers, etc. Current news stories are frequently updated with one story featuring related classroom activities and worksheets. A Skywatch section is also updated on a regular basis to provide a current map of the heavens and accompanying text of what stargazers can expect to see. There are puzzles and games for students and an option to communicate with a science expert via e-mail.

"The quantity and quality of graphics and features such as NewsBytes and SciZone are appealing to students, teachers, parents, and librarians. Recommended for school and public libraries." (Library Journal)

New view almanac. EBSCO $595/yr. (6 and up)

http://www.web4classroom.com

By subscription only. Tel. 800-653-2726

New view almanac—*Continued*

Part of EBSCO's Visual Reference Series. Information is organized by 12 broad categories (agricultural resources, health and nutrition, transportation and energy, etc.) that branch to several levels of sub-topics. Results lists provide links to a brief main article, related articles and Web sites, graphics, and charts. Searches can also be conducted by key word, title, and Web link categories. There are links to resources for educators and students. Includes a note-taking feature.

"A good selection for those interested in providing research tools that offer a visually appealing interface....should spark student interest in research." (Library Talk)

NGAKids. National Gallery of Art   Free (3-6)

http://www.nga.gov/kids/kids.htm

Offers multimedia tours of famous paintings from the National Gallery. The paintings have been selected to appeal to children and the tours use animations and embedded links to discuss their subjects and composition. Also includes an animated tour of the museum's sculpture garden.

NMAI conexus. National Museum of the American Indian   Free (5 and up)

http://www.conexus.si.edu/main.htm

This site offers a virtual tour of the museum's New York annex in which images can be enlarged and rotated in three dimensions. Also includes an online exhibit on the theft, sale, and loss of North American Indian culture.

NoveList. EBSCO   From $250/yr.

http://www.epnet.com/

By subscription only. Tel. 800-653-2726

An online readers' advisory service designed to assist users in locating new fiction books based on books they have read or topics in which they are interested. Books can be located by title, genre, setting, time period, character name, theme, author, or by describing a book's plot. The database includes subject and key word access to more than 100,000 fiction titles. There are 32,000 subject headings for fiction, based on the Hennepin County Public Library's cataloging system. Included are 1,200 theme-oriented book lists and 160 award lists. There are also 56,000 full-text book reviews and descriptions from *Library Journal, Publishers Weekly, Booklist* and *School Library Journal*, as well as links to author Home pages and other fiction-related Web sites.

"NoveList is a reader's paradise and a reference librarian's dream....Public, academic, special librarians everywhere—just do yourselves a favor and subscribe." (Library Journal)

Ology. American Museum of Natural History   Free (4-6)

http://ology.amnh.org

Children are rewarded for working through science tutorials with electronic picture cards, which they can then arrange on their own pages. Tutorials on astronomy, genetics, and paleontology, as well as opportunities to submit questions to museum scientists by e-mail, are available.

Online exhibits. Field Museum   Free (3-6)

http://www.fmnh.org/exhibits/online_exhib.htm

Collection of exhibits shows such things as photographs of a 19th-century hunt for two lions who had eaten 128 workers building a Ugandan railway bridge, an animated, insect's-eye view of underground life, and paintings of stages in life's evolution.

Online reader. EBSCO   From $1295/yr. (4-12)

http://www.epnet.com/

By subscription only. Tel. 800-653-2726

Designed to improve reading comprehension, this site is a collection of periodical article and comprehension tests available in the complete version (3,000 articles and tests) or as separate programs for elementary, middle school, or secondary levels. Most articles are nonfiction, but tone or content may be humorous, scholarly, consumer-oriented, or scientific. Test questions present multiple-choice, analogy, sequence, web classification, and missing step formats. Through the Administrative function, teachers can assign specific passages to any or all students in a class, or students can work through articles in a self-paced mode progressing through Lexile levels based on reading sucess. The curriculum management tool allows teachers to save and share lessons, units, and assignments. Teachers can also search state-level curricula and the McREL (Mid-continent Research for Education and Learning) benchmarks.

"An outstanding, valuable resource. Teachers can use it to improve student comprehension of informational material, provide background information, improve student test-taking skills, and much more. The program can be an important tool to help students prepare for state-administered tests nationwide." (MultiMedia Schools)

Primary search. EBSCO $549/yr. (3 and up)

http://www.web4classroom.com

By subscription only. Tel. 800-653-2726

This is a children's periodical reference database for elementary schools and children's reading rooms. It provides cover-to-cover, cumulative indexing and abstracts for 78 titles dating from 1984 and full-text coverage for 52 titles as early as 1990. The database also features: 18 student reference books (including the *American Heritage Children's Dictionary*), full-text historical documents, full-text student pamphlets, the *Encyclopedia of Animals*, images and maps, and Lexile reading level indicators. It uses a child-friendly *Searchosaurus* interface for locating information by key word or by subject.

The Quest channel. Classroom Connect $249/yr. (K-6)

http://quest.classroom.com/

By subscription only. Tel. 800-638-1639

The Quest Channel uses the Internet to direct a team of experts to discover answers to important historical and scientific questions throughout the world. A one-year subscription provides access to two live Quests as well as archived journeys: AfricaQuest, AmericaQuest, AsiaQuest, AutraliaQuest, GalapagosQuest, IslandQuest, and MayaQuest. Current Quests feature live interaction with a real expedition team via e-mail. Students are provided information about the geography of the area, its plants and animals, and the history and culture of the people. Each live Quest comes with a Curriculum Guide with teaching tips, over a hundred McREL (Mid-continent Research for Education and Learning) standards-based classroom activities, printable documents, and a four-color map poster.

Ranger Ricks's kids' zone. National Wildlife Federation   Free (3-5)

http://www.nwf.org/kids

Ranger Ricks's kids' zone—*Continued*

Includes games and tutorials teaching about wilderness, wildlife, and conservation.

Readers' guide for young people. H. W. Wilson From $995/yr. (4-8)

http://www.hwwilson.com

By subscription only. Tel. 800-367-6770

Provides full-text articles, article abstracts, and indexing of select periodicals for young people, along with coverage of select journals for educators. Of the 77 titles indexed and abstracted, 54 also have full text, going back to 1994. The children's materials cover both homework topics and hobbies, including biographical stories, reviews of books and performances, experiments, recipes, speeches, and how-to instructions. Topics of interest to educators and librarians include children's librarianship, curriculum development, and children's literature. Reviews of some 4,000 books, CD-ROMs, and Web and video resources are cited each year. The database is searchable through a controlled vocabulary and key words. Codes for different types of authors, titles, subject headings, article contents, and physical descriptions are used.

"[This product] moves students from the familiar thick green or red print versions [of "Readers' Guide to Periodical Literature"] to a fast electronic format for locating information....As more magazines are added in full-text version, this database will continue to be an essential in research for students." (School Library Media Activities Monthly)

Riverdeep.net. Riverdeep, Inc. From $600/yr. (4 and up)

http://www.riverdeep.net

By subscription only. Tel. 800-564-2587

A curriculum resource with a variety of programs, activities, and reference tools. The Destination Math program for grades four and up uses animation and natural language narration to provide self-paced tutorials and activities related to concepts such as numbers, fractions, decimals, and percents. For grades six and up the site offers the Logal Middle School Science Gateways and Explorer simulations and an EarthPulse Center for the middle school earth science curriculum. A Living Library section offers searchable reference materials such as the *World Book International,* Time.com for Kids, *Bartlett's Quotations,* almanacs, dictionaries, etc.

Robotics: sensing, thinking, acting. Tech Museum of Innovation Free (4 and up)

http://www.thetech.org/robotics

This online exhibition explains what robots are, what they do, how they work, and who builds them. Includes video clips of researchers explaining how they design robots, ethicists discussing potential moral problems with a successful artificial intelligence program, and artists discussing robots as art. Also includes an activity in which one tries to control an exploratory device with a lag between command and response, as there would be over a great distance.

Science experiments on-line. Facts on File From $299/yr. (3 and up)

http://www.fofweb.com

By subscription only. Tel. 800-322-8755

A database of hundreds of science experiments covering a broad range of subject matter and skill levels. The categories of experiments provided are biology, chemistry, earth science, nature, physics, space, and weather, as well as "Historical Experiments," based on the work of well-known scientists, and "Historical Inventions." Search results provide the hyperlinked title of each experiment, grade range, a one-sentence summary, time required (less or greater than an hour), participation (individual or group), adult supervision (optional or required) setting (home or school), and relevant key terms/topics/principles. Experiments display in *Adobe Acrobat* (link to free download provided), and include diagrams, safety information, and detailed instructions.

"A superb collection of useful and fun science experiments that could serve students from elementary school through college freshmen....Highly recommended for school and public libraries." (Library Journal)

SimScience. National Science Foundation Free (5 and up)

http://www.simscience.org/

Provides tutorials on four areas of scientific research that depend on supercomputer simulations: membranes, fluid flow, dam cracking, and crackling noise. Tutorials are offered at elementary, secondary, and college reading levels.

SIRS discoverer deluxe on the web. SIRS Mandarin $600/yr. (3-8)

http://www.sirs.com/products/database.htm

By subscription only. Tel. 800-232-7477

Reference database of full-text articles searchable by key words (options for Boolean operators, truncation, phrases, and natural language); subject tree (15 broad categories with sub-topics); and subject headings (primarily Library of Congress). Advanced search options are also available. Articles are drawn from newspapers, magazines, and U.S. government documents, as well as contributions by the SIRS staff. Articles are color-coded by reading level: easy (grades 1-4), moderate (grades 5-7), and challenging (grade 8 and above). Results can be viewed in order of relevance or by date, and include icons to denote graphics and related activities, biographies, and fictional articles. The site includes Current Events articles updated daily, *The World Almanac for Kids, Funk and Wagnalls New Encyclopedia,* maps, a dictionary, and a thesaurus. Country Facts articles cover more than 100 countries, each of the fifty states and territories, and the Canadian provinces. A monthly Spotlight of the Month feature draws articles together centered on a theme.

"SIRS Discoverer on the Web offers well-organized information and simplified search capabilites for student research." (Evalutech Web site)

Smithsonian expeditions. Smithsonian Institution Free (5 and up)

http://www.mnh.si.edu//anthro/laexped

Tells the story of the North and Latin American naturalists who collaborated on anthropological, botanical, and zoological expeditions in South America in the 19th and early 20th centuries.

SOS math. Math Medics, L.L.C. Free (4 and up)

http://www.sosmath.com/index.html

Provides tutorials and practice exams on elementary to college-level mathematics.

Sports science. Exploratorium   Free (4-6)

http://www.exploratorium.edu/sports/index.html

Multimedia presentations teach about the physics and biomechanics of baseball, mountain biking, skateboarding, and hockey. Includes an article by a rock-climbing physicist on hands and the force of friction.

Star journey. National Geographic   Free (4 and up)

http://www.nationalgeographic.com/features/97/stars

This site provides a star chart with embedded links to thirty-nine Hubble space telescope photographs of the corresponding heavenly bodies. Also includes articles on the Hubble space telescope and on constellations.

StarChild. NASA   Free (4 and up)

http://starchild.gsfc.nasa.gov/docs/StarChild

Contains descriptions and photographs of the solar system, more distant heavenly bodies, and space probes. All writing is available at both elementary and secondary reading levels.

State geography. ABC-CLIO $499/yr. (4 and up)

http://www.abc-clio.com/schools/

By subscription only. Tel. 800-368-6868

Covers the people, places, events, trends, statistics, news, attractions, politics, culture, environment, government, and history of all 50 states in the U.S. The site also includes biographies and primary source documents. Searchable by key word and advanced search options that allow filtering by categories. Teachers can customize the site by setting up classes and posting information such as announcements, syllabi, discussion questions, handouts, and tests. The Home page has frequently updated news articles and feature stories that are linked to related articles in the database. Includes the *Merriam-Webster's Collegiate Dictionary.*

"The site's entries are authoritative and well linked. This online reference would be a boon to busy teachers who want to use the Internet in the instruction of geography. Highly recommended." (The Book Report)

Stories from the Web. Birmingham Library and Information Services   Free (3-5)

http://hosted.ukoln.ac.uk/stories/index.htm

Recommends books by genre, presents information about and interviews with children's authors, and offers chances to finish stories begun by professional authors or to review favorite books. Children's stories and reviews are posted on the site.

Student resource center junior. Gale Group   From $1,550/yr. (4-8)

http://www.galegroup.com

By subscription only. Tel. 800-877-4253

Student Resource Center Junior provides content based on national curriculum standards, including literature, science, geography, and multicultural studies, as well as biographical information. The database has original reference material in the form of overviews and critical essays, primary source documents from the American Journey series, and articles from periodicals and newspapers updated daily. Search results are returned by document type. The site includes periodical back files from 1986; more than 16,000 timeline event descriptions; more than 15,000 photographs, maps, and graphics; and more than 41,000 primary source documents (diaries, letters, recordings, etc.). There are also full-text articles from encyclopedias and almanacs, as well as hundreds of audio and video clips. Includes *Merriam-Webster's Collegiate, Biographical,* and *Geographical* dictionaries.

Tiger on the loose. Tiger Information Center   Free (4 and up)

http://www.5tigers.org/adventures/adventxt/a1.htm

In this online game, players use a tiger information handbook to find the species of an escaped tiger, check the authenticity of reports of its location, and find and rescue it. In the process they learn about tiger species, behavior, and management.

Treasure Island. UK Office for Library and Information Networking   Free (4 and up)

http://www.ukoln.ac.uk/services/treasure

Includes information and links on Robert Louis Stevenson, a link to the book's complete text, opportunities to have reviews of the book or designs for the perfect pirate posted on the site, and an Internet treasure hunt.

TryScience. IBM   Free (5 and up)

http://www.tryscience.org

A compendium of interactive games from science museums. In "Starfleet Academy," players answer questions and adjust controls to advance in rank within a Star Trek scenario. In "Animal Attraction," players determine what traits attract various pollinators to plants by observing their behavior. In "Catch the Spirit of COSI," players solve a code as they explore a maze-like building.

Unforgettable letters. U.S. Postal Service   Free (5 and up)

http://www.usps.gov/letters/fr_ul.html

A collection of famous letters. Includes a letter from a Union soldier to the parents of a Confederate soldier whom he found dying on the battlefield, a letter from Leonardo da Vinci presenting his resume to a prospective employer, and Amelia Earhart's last letter to her mother.

Virtual Renaissance. Twin Groves Junior High School   Free (6 and up)

http://renaissance.district96.k12.il.us

This tutorial on Renaissance history is presented as a trip back through time to various sites in Europe and England. Local people explain their lives and Renaissance art, science, exploration, trade, politics, war, religion, and society.

The **watershed** game. Bell Museum of Natural History   Free (3-6)

http://www1.umn.edu/bellmuse/mnideals/watershed/watershed2.html

The watershed game—*Continued*

In this game, players make decisions about recreation, agriculture, and transportation to ensure a watershed's health. They set water policy in a national park, an agricultural area, a neighborhood, and a city and are informed of their decisions' effects on water quality.

The Ways of Knowing Trail. Brookfield Zoo Free (3-5)

http://www.brookfieldzoo.org/
0.asp?nSection=9&PageID=248&nLinkID=22

In this online game, players find their way through an African rain forest with the help of the children of a farmer, a ranger, a scientist, and a forest dweller. They learn that there are different ways of knowing and experiencing a forest, none of which are complete without the others.

Who's out there? SETI Institute Free (5 and up)

http://www.seti.org/game/index.html

In this online game, players design a research project to search for extraterrestrial intelligent life. Upon successful completion, they are given an opportunity to decode a possible signal from such a species, and to post a suggestion for a message to send in return.

The why files. University of Wisconsin Free (5 and up)

http://whyfiles.org

Each week this site posts new articles on the science behind recent news stories. Previous stories are archived under subject headings and are searchable.

World atlas on-line. Facts on File From $299/yr. (6 and up)

http://www.fofweb.com

By subscription only. Tel. 800-322-8755

An interactive database of maps and information related to geographic regions and countries of the world, as well as states and Canadian provinces. The site provides full-color political, elevation, and outline maps of each geographic entity, as well as multiple maps depicting information ranging from political and economic data to energy and natural resources. "Fact Files" have information on countries such as vital statistics, government, history, and chronologies. Links to related Web sites are included.

"Allows for easy access to current information in lieu of hard copy versions that become outdated quickly. This is a worthwhile purchase for classroom and media center use for research." (Evalutech Web site)

World book online. World Book Publishing From $395/yr. (4 and up)

http://www.worldbookonline.com

By subscription only. Tel. 800-975-3250

General reference encyclopedia with all articles from the print version of World Book Encyclopedia along with multimedia elements and updated articles and information. (750 new articles, 550 new Back in Time articles, 60 special reports, and 4500 revised articles were added in a single year.) This online reference also has links to full-text articles in over 250 magazines and newspapers, as well as links to more than 10,000 editor-approved Web sites. Back in Time articles, taken from World Book Yearbooks, dating back to 1922, provide in-depth coverage of people and events from the perspective of the times. A Surf the Millennium feature introduces the major political, cultural, and scientific events of the last 10 centuries. Includes a fully integrated dictionary.

"This flexible, easy-to-use, online resource is an excellent tool for student research. By integrating historical background and current information, it makes history more relevant to events of the day. Highly recommended." (The Book Report)

World geography. ABC-CLIO $499/yr. (6 and up)

http://www.abc-clio.com/schools/

By subscription only. Tel. 800-368-6868

Provides in-depth, current information for a comprehensive catalog of countries and regions. Each country page provides an overview of the nation, historical and governmental information, fact and figures, important events, biographies, primary source documents, lists of organizations, and maps. Articles are extensively cross-referenced through hyperlinks. In addition to key word searches, there are advanced search options to limit by categories of information. Teachers can customize the site by adding discussion questions, handouts, tests, etc. The site also features daily news articles and feature stories with links to related articles. Includes *Merriam-Webster's Collegiate Dictionary* and *Merriam-Webster's Collegiate Thesaurus*.

"An excellent reference tool...that also can be used as a daily organizational resource for students logging on to find their assignments for the day." (Evalutech Web site)

The yuckiest site on the Internet. Discovery Channel Free (3-5)

http://yucky.kids.discovery.com

Covers the coarser aspects of biology. Includes scientifically sound discussions of such topics as regurgitation, flatulence, cockroaches, and worms. Includes recordings of vulgar noises and a whack-a-roach game.

PART 3

AUTHOR, TITLE, SUBJECT, AND ANALYTICAL INDEX

This index to the books in the Classified Catalog includes author, title, subject, and analytical entries; added entries for publishers' series, illustrators, joint authors, and editors of works entered under title; and name and subject cross-references, all arranged in one alphabet.

　　The number or symbol in bold-face type at the end of each entry refers to the Dewey Decimal Classification or to the Fiction (Fic), Story Collection (SC), or Easy Books (E) section where the main entry for the book will be found. Works classed in 92 are entered under the name of the person written about. The parenthetical notation following the title of a work indicates the grade level at which the item is most likely to be of interest.

　　For further directions for the use of this index and for examples of entries, see How to Use Children's Catalog.

1 2 3, Arlene Alda's. Alda, A.	**E**
1 hunter. Hutchins, P.	**E**
1 is one. Tudor, T.	**E**
2 x 2 = boo!. Leedy, L.	**513**
3-2-1 Contact. See Contact Kids	**505**
4B goes wild. Gilson, J.	**Fic**
4th of July See Fourth of July	
10 minutes till bedtime. Rathmann, P.	**E**
The **11:59**. McKissack, P. C.	
In McKissack, P. C. The dark-thirty p35-42	**S C**
12 ways to get to 11. Merriam, E.	**510**
The **13th** clue. Jonas, A.	**E**
The **13th** floor. Fleischman, S.	**Fic**
17 kings and 42 elephants. Mahy, M.	**E**
The **18** penny goose. Walker, S. M.	**E**
The **20th** century children's poetry treasury	**811.008**
26 Fairmount Avenue. De Paola, T.	**92**
26 letters and 99 cents. Hoban, T.	**E**
52 programs for preschoolers. Briggs, D.	**027.62**
100 most popular children's authors. McElmeel, S. L.	**810.3**
100 most popular picture book authors and illustrators. McElmeel, S. L.	**810.3**
100th day worries. Cuyler, M.	**E**
101 fingerplays, stories, and songs to use with finger puppets. Briggs, D.	**791.5**
123 pop!. Isadora, R.	**E**
201 awesome, magical, bizarre & incredible experiments, Janice VanCleave's. VanCleave, J. P.	**507.8**
202 oozing, bubbling, dripping & bouncing experiments, Janice VanCleave's. VanCleave, J. P.	**507.8**
203 icy, freezing, frosty, cool & wild experiments, Janice Van Cleave's. VanCleave, J. P.	**507.8**
The **500** hats of Bartholomew Cubbins. Seuss, Dr.	**E**
700+ great sites. See entry in Part 2: Web Resources	

2095. Scieszka, J. See note under Scieszka, J.	
Knights of the kitchen table	**Fic**
20,000 leagues under the sea. Verne, J.	**Fic**

A

A.B.C.'s See Alphabet	
A-hunting we will go!. Kellogg, S.	**782.42**
A-hunting we will go. See Langstaff, J. M. Oh, a-hunting we will go	**782.42**
A.I.D.S. (Disease) See AIDS (Disease)	
A is for—? Horenstein, H.	**E**
A is for salad. Lester, M.	**E**
A. Lincoln and me. Borden, L.	**E**
A my name is Alice. Bayer, J.	**E**
A. Nonny Mouse writes again! (1-3)	**808.81**
A. Pintura: art detective. (4 and up) See entry in Part 2: Web Resources	
A to Zen. Wells, R.	**495.6**
A to Zoo. Lima, C. W.	**011.6**
AAAS See American Association for the Advancement of Science	
AACR See Anglo-American cataloguing rules	

Aardema, Verna

Anansi does the impossible! (k-3)	**398.2**
Bimwili & the Zimwi (k-3)	**398.2**
Borreguita and the coyote (k-3)	**398.2**
Bringing the rain to Kapiti Plain (k-3)	**398.2**
Koi and the kola nuts (k-3)	**398.2**
The lonely lioness and the ostrich chicks (k-3)	**398.2**
Misoso (3-5)	**398.2**

Contents: Leelee Goro; Anansi and the phantom food; The Boogey Man's wife; Half-a-Ball-of-Kenki; The hen and the dove; The Sloogey Dog and the stolen aroma; The cock and the jackal; No, Boconono!; Toad's trick; Goso the teacher; Hapendeki and Binti the Bibi; Kindai and the ape

Oh, Kojo! How could you! (k-3)	**398.2**
Rabbit makes a monkey of lion (k-3)	**398.2**
This for that (k-3)	**398.2**
Traveling to Tondo (k-3)	**398.2**
Who's in Rabbit's house? (k-3)	**398.2**

Aardema, Verna—*Continued*
Why mosquitoes buzz in people's ears (k-3)
398.2

Aardvark
Fiction
Brown, M. T. Arthur's nose   **E**
Brown, M. T. D.W. all wet   **E**

Aardvarks, disembark!. Jonas, A.   **E**

AASL *See* American Association of School Librarians

Aayoga with many excuses. MacDonald, M. R.
In MacDonald, M. R. The storyteller's start-up book p161-64   **372.6**

Abandoned children
Warren, A. Orphan train rider (4 and up)
362.7
Fiction
Bunting, E. Train to Somewhere   **E**
Voigt, C. Homecoming (6 and up)   **Fic**

The **abandoned** girl. Bruchac, J.
In Bruchac, J. The girl who married the Moon p21-28   **398.2**

Abby. Caines, J. F.   **E**

ABC. Wildsmith, B.   **E**

ABC book. Falls, C. B.   **E**

The **ABC** exhibit. Fisher, L. E.   **E**

ABC I like me!. Carlson, N. L. See note under Carlson, N. L. I like me!   **E**

ABC, John Burningham's. Burningham, J.   **E**

ABC kids. Williams, L. E.   **E**

ABC pop!. Isadora, R.   **E**

ABC T-Rex. Most, B.   **E**

ABCs *See* Alphabet

Abe Lincoln goes to Washington, 1837-1865. Harness, C.   **92**

Abe Lincoln grows up. Sandburg, C.
In Sandburg, C. The Sandburg treasury p383-477   **818**

Abells, Chana Byers
The children we remember (3-6)   **940.53**

Abel's island. Steig, W.   **Fic**

Abernathy, Alexia
See/See also pages in the following book(s):
Thimmesh, C. Girls think of everything (5 and up)   **920**

Abigail takes the wheel. Avi   **Fic**

Abnaki Indians
See also Penobscot Indians
Folklore
Bruchac, J. Gluskabe and the four wishes (k-3)
398.2

Abolafia, Yossi, 1944-
(il) Porte, B. A. Harry in trouble   **E**
(il) Prelutsky, J. It's Valentine's Day   **811**
(il) Prelutsky, J. My parents think I'm sleeping: poems   **811**

Abolitionists
January, B. John Brown's raid on Harpers Ferry
973.7
Adler, D. A. A picture book of Sojourner Truth (1-3)   **92**
Ferris, J. Walking the road to freedom: a story about Sojourner Truth (3-5)   **92**

Fritz, J. Harriet Beecher Stowe and the Beecher preachers (5 and up)   **92**
McKissack, P. C. Sojourner Truth (1-3)   **92**
Miller, W. Frederick Douglass (1-3)   **92**
See/See also pages in the following book(s):
McKissack, P. C. Black hands, white sails (5 and up)   **639.2**
Fiction
Lasky, K. True north (6 and up)   **Fic**

About the B'nai Bagels. Konigsburg, E. L.
Fic

About twins. Rotner, S.   **306.8**

The **abracadabra** kid. Fleischman, S.   **92**

Abridged Dewey decimal classification and relative index. Dewey, M.   **025.4**

Absolutely normal chaos. Creech, S.   **Fic**

Absurd math. (5 and up) See entry in Part 2: Web Resources

Abuela. Dorros, A.   **E**

Abuela's weave. Castañeda, O. S.   **E**

Abuse of children *See* Child abuse

Abuse of wives *See* Wife abuse

Accadians (Sumerians) *See* Sumerians

Access excellence activities exchange. (6 and up) See entry in Part 2: Web Resources

The **accident.** Carrick, C.   **E**

Accidents
See also types of accidents, e.g. Aircraft accidents; and subjects with the subdivision *Accidents*
Fiction
Bauer, M. D. On my honor (4 and up)   **Fic**
Prevention
See also Safety education

The **accursed** house. San Souci, R.
In San Souci, R. More short & shivery p121-26   **398.2**

Ace, the very important pig. King-Smith, D.
Fic

Achingly Alice. Naylor, P. R. See note under Naylor, P. R. The agony of Alice   **Fic**

Ackerman, Diane
Bats (4-6)   **599.4**

Ackerman, Karen, 1951-
By the dawn's early light   **E**
The night crossing (3-5)   **Fic**
Song and dance man   **E**

Acoustics *See* Sound

Acquired immune deficiency syndrome *See* AIDS (Disease)

Across America on an emigrant train. Murphy, J.
92

Across five Aprils. Hunt, I.   **Fic**

Across the lines. Reeder, C.   **Fic**

Acting
Costume
See Costume
Fiction
Byars, B. C. Me Tarzan (3-5)   **Fic**

Activism, Social *See* Social action

Adler, David A., 1947——Continued
Cam Jansen and the Triceratops Pops mystery.
See note under Adler, D. A. Cam Jansen and
the mystery of the stolen diamonds   **Fic**
The carsick zebra and other animal riddles (1-3)
   793.73
Chanukah in Chelm (k-3)   **398.2**
Child of the Warsaw ghetto (3-5)   **940.53**
Easy math puzzles (2-4)   **793.73**
Fraction fun (2-4)   **513**
Lou Gehrig (2-4)   **92**
Hiding from the Nazis (2-4)   **940.53**
Hilde and Eli, children of the Holocaust (3-5)
   940.53
How tall, how short, how faraway (k-3)
   530.8
Martin Luther King, Jr. (2-4)   **92**
My writing day (1-3)   **92**
A picture book of Abraham Lincoln (1-3)
   92
A picture book of Amelia Earhart (1-3)   **92**
A picture book of Anne Frank (1-3)   **92**
A picture book of Benjamin Franklin (1-3)
   92
A picture book of Eleanor Roosevelt (1-3)
   92
A picture book of George Washington Carver
(1-3)   **92**
A picture book of Harriet Tubman (1-3)
   92
A picture book of Helen Keller (1-3)   **92**
A picture book of Jackie Robinson (1-3)
   92
A picture book of Jesse Owens (1-3)   **92**
A picture book of John F. Kennedy (1-3)
   92
A picture book of Louis Braille (1-3)   **92**
A picture book of Martin Luther King, Jr. (1-3)
   92
A picture book of Rosa Parks (1-3)   **92**
A picture book of Sacagawea (1-3)   **92**
A picture book of Sojourner Truth (1-3)
   92
A picture book of Thomas Jefferson (1-3)
   92
A picture book of Thurgood Marshall (1-3)
   92
Roman numerals (2-4)   **513**
Shape up! (2-4)   **516**
Young Cam Jansen and the baseball mystery.
See note under Adler, D. A. Young Cam Jan-
sen and the dinosaur game   **E**
Young Cam Jansen and the dinosaur game
   E
Young Cam Jansen and the ice skate mystery.
See note under Adler, D. A. Young Cam Jan-
sen and the dinosaur game   **E**
Young Cam Jansen and the library mystery. See
note under Adler, D. A. Young Cam Jansen
and the dinosaur game   **E**
Young Cam Jansen and the lost tooth. See note
under Adler, D. A. Young Cam Jansen and
the dinosaur game   **E**
Young Cam Jansen and the missing cookie. See
note under Adler, D. A. Young Cam Jansen
and the dinosaur game   **E**

Young Cam Jansen and the pizza shop mystery.
See note under Adler, D. A. Young Cam Jan-
sen and the dinosaur game   **E**
Admirable hare. McCaughrean, G.
In McCaughrean, G. The golden hoard: myths
and legends of the world p49-51
   398.2
Adoff, Arnold, 1935-
The basket counts (4 and up)   **811**
Black is brown is tan   **E**
In for winter, out for spring (k-3)   **811**
Love letters (3-6)   **811**
Touch the poem (k-3)   **811**
(ed) I am the darker brother. See I am the
darker brother   **811.008**
(ed) My black me. See My black me
   811.008
Adolescence
Jukes, M. Growing up: it's a girl thing (4 and
up)   **612.6**
Jukes, M. It's a girl thing (5 and up)
   305.23
Fiction
Blume, J. Are you there God? it's me, Margaret
(5 and up)   **Fic**
Adolescents *See* Teenagers
Adopted by the eagles. Goble, P.   **398.2**
Adoption
Krementz, J. How it feels to be adopted (4 and
up)   **362.7**
See/See also pages in the following book(s):
Warren, A. Orphan train rider (4 and up)
   362.7
Fiction
Bunting, E. Train to Somewhere   **E**
Caines, J. F. Abby   **E**
Curtis, J. L. Tell me again about the night I was
born   **E**
Johnson, A. Heaven (6 and up)   **Fic**
Keller, H. Horace   **E**
Magorian, M. Good night, Mr. Tom (6 and up)
   Fic
Montgomery, L. M. Anne of Green Gables (5
and up)   **Fic**
Myers, W. D. Me, Mop, and the Moondance
Kid (4-6)   **Fic**
Peacock, C. A. Mommy far, Mommy near
   E
Turner, A. W. Through moon and stars and
night skies   **E**
Adoption, Interracial *See* Interracial adoption
Adventure and adventurers
Explorers & discoverers   **920.003**
Fiction
See Adventure fiction
Adventure fiction
See also Science fiction; Sea stories
Alexander, L. The Beggar Queen (5 and up)
   Fic
Alexander, L. The Illyrian adventure (5 and up)
   Fic
Alexander, L. The iron ring (5 and up)   **Fic**
Alexander, L. The marvelous misadventures of
Sebastian (4 and up)   **Fic**

Afanas´ev, A. N. (Aleksandr Nikolaevich), 1826-1871—*Continued*

and the lobster; Nikita the Tanner; The wolf; The goat shedding on one side; The bold knight, the apples of youth, and the water of life; Two out of the sack; The man who did not know fear; The merchant's daughter and the maidservant; The priest's laborer; The peasant and the corpse; The arrant fool; Lutoniushka; Barter; The grumbling old woman; The white duck; If you don't like it don't listen; The magic swan geese; Prince Danila Govorila; The wicked sisters; The princess who never smiled; Baba Yaga; Jack Frost; Husband and wife; Little Sister Fox and the wolf; The three kingdoms, copper, silver, and golden; The cock and the hand mill; Tereschichka; King Bear; Magic; The one-eyed evil; Sister Alionushka, brother Ivanushka; The seven Semyons; The merchant's daughter and the slanderer; The robbers; The lazy maiden; The miraculous pipe; The Sea King and Vasilisa the Wise; The fox as mourner; Vasilisa the Beautiful; The bun; The foolish wolf; The bear, the dog, and the cat; The bear and the cock; Dawn, Evening, and Midnight; Two Ivans, soldier's sons; Prince Ivan and Byely Polyanin; The crystal mountain; Koshchey the Deathless; The Firebird and Princess Vasilisa; Beasts in a pit; The dog and the woodpecker; Two kinds of luck; Go I know not whither—fetch I know not what; The wise wife; The goldfish; The golden-bristled pig, the golden-feathered duck, and the golden-maned mare; The duck with golden eggs; Elena the Wise; Treasure-trove; Maria Morevna; The soldier and the king; The sorceress; Ilya Muromets and the dragon; The devil who was a potter; Clever answers; Dividing the goose; The feather of Finist, the Bright Falcon; The Sun, the Moon, and the Raven; The bladder, the straw, and the shoe; The thief; The vampire; The beggar's plan; Woman's way; The foolish German; The enchanted princess; The raven and the lobster; Prince Ivan, the firebird, and the gray wolf; Shemiaka the judge

Afanas´ev, Aleksandr Nikolaevich *See* Afanas´ev, A. N. (Aleksandr Nikolaevich), 1826-1871

Africa

Fiction

Greenfield, E. Africa dream	**E**
Kroll, V. L. Faraway drums	**E**
Olaleye, I. Bitter bananas	**E**
Stojic, M. Rain	**E**
Walter, M. P. Brother to the wind	**E**
We're going on a lion hunt	**E**
Williams, K. L. When Africa was home	**E**

Folklore

See Folklore—Africa

History

Haskins, J. African beginnings (4-6)   **960**

Natural history

See Natural history—Africa

Social life and customs

Musgrove, M. Ashanti to Zulu: African traditions (3-6)   **960**

See/See also pages in the following book(s):
Temko, F. Traditional crafts from Africa (4 and up)   **745.5**

Social life and customs—Dictionaries

Haskins, J. From Afar to Zulu (4 and up)   **960**

Africa, East *See* East Africa

Africa, South *See* South Africa

Africa dream. Greenfield, E.   **E**

African American artists

Duggleby, J. Story painter: the life of Jacob Lawrence (4 and up)   **92**

Lyons, M. E. Catching the fire: Philip Simmons, blacksmith (4 and up)   **92**

African American athletes

Adler, D. A. A picture book of Jackie Robinson (1-3)   **92**

Adler, D. A. A picture book of Jesse Owens (1-3)   **92**

Brashler, W. The story of Negro league baseball (5 and up)   **796.357**

Cline-Ransome, L. Satchel Paige (2-4)   **92**

Dingle, D. T. First in the field: baseball hero Jackie Robinson (3-6)   **92**

Golenbock, P. Teamates [biography of Jackie Robinson] (1-4)   **92**

Krull, K. Wilma unlimited: how Wilma Rudolph became the world's fastest woman (2-4)   **92**

McKissack, F. Black hoops (5 and up)   **796.323**

McKissack, P. C. Black diamond (6 and up)   **796.357**

Ritter, L. S. Leagues apart (2-4)   **796.357**

African American authors

Cooper, F. Coming home: from the life of Langston Hughes (2-4)   **92**

Meltzer, M. Langston Hughes (6 and up)   **92**

Miller, W. Zora Hurston and the chinaberry tree (k-3)   **92**

Porter, A. P. Jump at de sun: the story of Zora Neale Hurston (4 and up)   **92**

Bio-bibliography

Murphy, B. T. Black authors and illustrators of books for children and young adults   **920.003**

Wilkinson, B. S. African American women writers (4 and up)   **810.9**

African American businesspeople

Lasky, K. Vision of beauty: the story of Sarah Breedlove Walker (3-5)   **92**

McKissack, P. C. Madam C.J. Walker (1-3)   **92**

African American dancers

Glover, S. Savion!: my life in tap (5 and up)   **92**

O'Connor, B. Katherine Dunham (5 and up)   **92**

Pinkney, A. D. Alvin Ailey (k-3)   **92**

African American educators

McKissack, P. C. Booker T. Washington (1-3)   **92**

The **African** American family album. Hoobler, D.   **305.8**

African American folklore *See* African Americans—Folklore

African American inventors

McKissack, P. C. African-American inventors (5 and up)   **920**

Mitchell, B. Shoes for everyone: a story about Jan Matzeliger (3-5)   **92**

Sullivan, O. R. African American inventors (5 and up)   **920**

African American literature *See* American literature—African American authors

African American music

See also Gospel music

How sweet the sound: African-American songs for children (k-3)   **782.42**

Igus, T. I see the rhythm (4 and up)   **780.89**

African Americans—Biography—*Continued*

Miller, W. Frederick Douglass (1-3)   **92**

Mitchell, B. A pocketful of goobers: a story about George Washington Carver (3-5)   **92**

Myers, W. D. Malcolm X (3-6)   **92**

Pinkney, A. D. Bill Pickett, rodeo ridin' cowboy (k-3)   **92**

Pinkney, A. D. Dear Benjamin Banneker (2-4)   **92**

Pinkney, A. D. Duke Ellington (2-4)   **92**

Yates, E. Amos Fortune, free man (4 and up)   **92**

Biography—Dictionaries

Kranz, R. The biographical dictionary of African Americans   **920.003**

Civil rights

Adler, D. A. Martin Luther King, Jr. (2-4)   **92**

Adler, D. A. A picture book of Martin Luther King, Jr. (1-3)   **92**

Adler, D. A. A picture book of Rosa Parks (1-3)   **92**

Bray, R. L. Martin Luther King (2-4)   **92**

Bridges, R. Through my eyes: the autobiography of Ruby Bridges (4 and up)   **92**

Duncan, A. F. The National Civil Rights Museum celebrates everyday people (3-6)   **323.1**

Fradin, D. B. Ida B. Wells (5 and up)   **92**

Greenfield, E. Rosa Parks (2-4)   **92**

Haskins, J. Bayard Rustin: behind the scenes of the civil rights movement (5 and up)   **92**

Haskins, J. Freedom Rides (5 and up)   **323.1**

Haskins, J. I have a dream: the life and words of Martin Luther King, Jr. (5 and up)   **92**

King, C. Oh, freedom! (5 and up)   **323.1**

King, M. L. I have a dream   **323.1**

Marzollo, J. Happy birthday, Martin Luther King (k-3)   **92**

Medearis, A. S. Dare to dream: Coretta Scott King and the civil rights movement (3-5)   **92**

O'Neill, L. Little Rock (5 and up)   **370**

Parks, R. I am Rosa Parks (1-3)   **92**

Parks, R. Rosa Parks: my story (5 and up)   **92**

Education

Haskins, J. Separate, but not equal (5 and up)   **379**

Employment

See also African American businesspeople

Fiction

Armstrong, J. Steal away (5 and up)   **Fic**

Armstrong, W. H. Sounder (5 and up)   **Fic**

Best, C. Red light, green light, mama and me   **E**

Boyd, C. D. Charlie Pippin (4-6)   **Fic**

Bradby, M. Momma, where are you from?   **E**

Bradby, M. More than anything else   **E**

Brenner, B. Wagon wheels   **E**

Bunting, E. Smoky night   **E**

Caines, J. F. Abby   **E**

Caines, J. F. Just us women   **E**

Cameron, A. Gloria's way (2-4)   **Fic**

Cameron, A. The stories Julian tells (2-4)   **Fic**

Chocolate, D. The piano man   **E**

Clifton, L. Everett Anderson's 1-2-3   **E**

Clifton, L. The lucky stone (3-5)   **Fic**

Cohen, B. Thank you, Jackie Robinson (4-6)   **Fic**

Collier, B. Uptown   **E**

Collier, J. L. Jump ship to freedom (6 and up)   **Fic**

Collier, J. L. War comes to Willy Freeman (6 and up)   **Fic**

Collier, J. L. Who is Carrie? (6 and up)   **Fic**

Crews, D. Shortcut   **E**

Crews, N. You are here   **E**

Cummings, P. Angel baby   **E**

Cummings, P. Clean your room, Harvey Moon!   **E**

Curtis, C. P. Bud, not Buddy (4 and up)   **Fic**

Curtis, C. P. The Watsons go to Birmingham—1963 (4 and up)   **Fic**

Curtis, G. The bat boy & his violin   **E**

English, K. Francie (5 and up)   **Fic**

Fenner, C. Yolonda's genius (4-6)   **Fic**

Flournoy, V. The patchwork quilt   **E**

Fox, M. Sophie   **E**

Greene, B. Philip Hall likes me, I reckon maybe (4-6)   **Fic**

Greenfield, E. Easter parade (2-4)   **Fic**

Greenfield, E. Grandmama's joy   **E**

Greenfield, E. She come bringing me that little baby girl   **E**

Greenfield, E. Sister (4 and up)   **Fic**

Grifalconi, A. Tiny's hat   **E**

Hamilton, V. The bells of Christmas (4-6)   **Fic**

Hamilton, V. Cousins (5 and up)   **Fic**

Hamilton, V. Drylongso (3-5)   **Fic**

Hamilton, V. The house of Dies Drear (5 and up)   **Fic**

Hamilton, V. M. C. Higgins the great (6 and up)   **Fic**

Hamilton, V. The mystery of Drear House (5 and up)   **Fic**

Hamilton, V. Plain City (5 and up)   **Fic**

Hamilton, V. The planet of Junior Brown (6 and up)   **Fic**

Hamilton, V. Second cousins (5 and up)   **Fic**

Hamilton, V. Zeely (4 and up)   **Fic**

Hansen, J. Which way freedom? (5 and up)   **Fic**

Havill, J. Jamaica's find   **E**

Hayes, S. Eat up, Gemma   **E**

Hill, E. S. Evan's corner   **E**

Hoffman, M. Amazing Grace   **E**

Holt, K. W. Mister and me (3-5)   **Fic**

Hooks, W. H. Freedom's fruit (3-5)   **Fic**

Hopkinson, D. A band of angels   **E**

Howard, E. F. Aunt Flossie's hats (and crab cakes later)   **E**

Howard, E. F. Chita's Christmas tree   **E**

African Americans—Fiction—*Continued*

Howard, E. F. Virgie goes to school with us boys   E

Isadora, R. Ben's trumpet   E

Johnson, A. Do like Kyla   E

Johnson, A. Down the winding road   E

Johnson, A. Heaven (6 and up)   Fic

Johnson, A. Songs of faith (5 and up)   Fic

Johnson, A. Tell me a story, Mama   E

Johnson, D. Quinnie Blue   E

Keats, E. J. Hi, cat!   E

Konigsburg, E. L. Jennifer, Hecate, Macbeth, William McKinley, and me, Elizabeth (4-6)   Fic

Kroll, V. L. Faraway drums   E

Kroll, V. L. Masai and I   E

Kurtz, J. Faraway home   E

Lester, J. Black cowboy, wild horses   E

Levine, G. C. Dave at night (5 and up)   Fic

Lindbergh, R. Nobody owns the sky   E

Lorbiecki, M. Sister Anne's hands   E

Lyons, M. E. Letters from a slave girl (6 and up)   Fic

Mathis, S. B. Sidewalk story (3-5)   Fic

McGill, A. Miles' song (6 and up)   Fic

McKissack, P. C. Color me dark (4 and up)   Fic

McKissack, P. C. The dark-thirty (4 and up)   S C

McKissack, P. C. Flossie & the fox   E

McKissack, P. C. Let my people go (4 and up)   221.9

McKissack, P. C. Ma Dear's aprons   E

McKissack, P. C. A million fish—more or less   E

McKissack, P. C. Mirandy and Brother Wind   E

McKissack, P. C. A picture of Freedom (4 and up)   Fic

McKissack, P. C. Run away home (5 and up)   Fic

Mead, A. Junebug (3-5)   Fic

Miller, W. Night golf   E

Miller, W. The piano   E

Miller, W. Richard Wright and the library card   E

Mitchell, M. K. Uncle Jed's barbershop   E

Myers, W. D. Fast Sam, Cool Clyde, and Stuff (6 and up)   Fic

Myers, W. D. The journal of Joshua Loper (5 and up)   Fic

Nolen, J. Big Jabe   E

Paterson, K. Jip (5 and up)   Fic

Petry, A. L. Tituba of Salem Village (6 and up)   Fic

Pinkney, G. J. Back home   E

Polacco, P. Mrs. Katz and Tush   E

Raschka, C. Yo! Yes?   E

Reeder, C. Across the lines (5 and up)   Fic

Ringgold, F. Tar Beach   E

Robinet, H. G. Forty acres and maybe a mule (4 and up)   Fic

Robinet, H. G. Walking to the bus-rider blues (5 and up)   Fic

Rosen, M. J. A school for Pompey Walker   Fic

Schroeder, A. Ragtime Tumpie   E

Sebestyen, O. Words by heart (5 and up)   Fic

Slote, A. Finding Buck McHenry (4-6)   Fic

Steptoe, J. Stevie   E

Stolz, M. Go fish (2-4)   Fic

Tate, E. E. Thank you, Dr. Martin Luther King, Jr.! (4 and up)   Fic

Taulbert, C. L. Little Cliff and the porch people   E

Taylor, M. D. The friendship (4 and up)   Fic

Taylor, M. D. The gold Cadillac (4 and up)   Fic

Taylor, M. D. Let the circle be unbroken (4 and up)   Fic

Taylor, M. D. Mississippi bridge (4 and up)   Fic

Taylor, M. D. The road to Memphis (4 and up)   Fic

Taylor, M. D. Roll of thunder, hear my cry (4 and up)   Fic

Taylor, M. D. Song of the trees (4 and up)   Fic

Taylor, M. D. The well (4 and up)   Fic

Thomas, J. C. I have heard of a land   E

Udry, J. M. What Mary Jo shared   E

Voigt, C. Come a stranger (6 and up)   Fic

Walter, M. P. Justin and the best biscuits in the world (3-6)   Fic

Walter, M. P. Suitcase (3-6)   Fic

Williams, S. A. Working cotton   E

Williams, V. B. Cherries and cherry pits   E

Winter, J. Follow the drinking gourd   E

Woodson, J. I hadn't meant to tell you this (6 and up)   Fic

Woodson, J. We had a picnic this Sunday past   E

Yarbrough, C. Cornrows   E

Yarbrough, C. The shimmershine queens (4-6)   Fic

Folklore

Bang, M. Wiley and the Hairy Man (1-4)   398.2

Hamilton, V. The people could fly: American black folktales (4 and up)   398.2

Hamilton, V. When birds could talk & bats could sing (3-5)   398.2

Keats, E. J. John Henry (k-3)   398.2

Lester, J. John Henry (k-3)   398.2

Lester, J. The knee-high man, and other tales (k-3)   398.2

Lester, J. The last tales of Uncle Remus (4-6)   398.2

Raw Head, bloody bones (4-6)   398.2

San Souci, R. The hired hand (2-4)   398.2

San Souci, R. The secret of the stones (k-3)   398.2

San Souci, R. Sukey and the mermaid (1-4)   398.2

Sanfield, S. The adventures of High John the Conqueror (4 and up)   398.2

Stevens, J. Tops and bottoms (k-3)   398.2

See/See also pages in the following book(s):

Hamilton, V. A ring of tricksters p13-43   398.2

African Americans—*Continued*
History
Branch, M. M. Juneteenth (5 and up)
394.26
Haskins, J. Out of the darkness (5 and up)
305.8
Myers, W. D. Now is your time! (6 and up)
305.8
Patrick, D. The New York Public Library amazing African American history (5 and up)
305.8
History—Sources
The Black Americans: a history in their own words, 1619-1983 (6 and up)   **305.8**
Music
See African American music
Poetry
Ashley Bryan's ABC of African-American poetry (k-3)   **811.008**
Dunbar, P. L. Jump back, Honey   **811**
Giovanni, N. Ego-tripping and other poems for young people (5 and up)   **811**
Giovanni, N. Spin a soft black song: poems for children (3-6)   **811**
Greenfield, E. Angels   **811**
Greenfield, E. Honey, I love, and other love poems (2-4)   **811**
Grimes, N. Come Sunday (k-3)   **811**
Grimes, N. A dime a dozen (5 and up)
811
Grimes, N. Hopscotch love (4 and up)   **811**
Grimes, N. Meet Danitra Brown (2-4)   **811**
Grimes, N. My man Blue (2-5)   **811**
Hughes, L. The dream keeper and other poems (5 and up)   **811**
I, too, sing America (6 and up)   **811.008**
In daddy's arms I am tall   **811.008**
Johnson, A. The other side (5 and up)   **811**
Make a joyful sound   **811.008**
Myers, W. D. Brown angels   **811**
Myers, W. D. Harlem   **811**
The Palm of my heart   **811.008**
Thomas, J. C. Brown honey in broomwheat tea (k-3)   **811**
Thomas, J. C. Gingerbread days (k-3)   **811**
Social life and customs
Bial, R. The strength of these arms (4 and up)
326
Brady, A. A. Kwanzaa karamu (4-6)   **641.5**
Chocolate, D. Kwanzaa (3-5)   **394.26**
Chocolate, D. My first Kwanzaa book (k-2)
394.26
Pinkney, A. D. Seven candles for Kwanzaa (k-3)   **394.26**
Walter, M. P. Kwanzaa: a family affair (4 and up)   **394.26**

African Americans in art
Lawrence, J. The great migration   **759.13**

African Americans in literature
Christmas gif' (3-6)   **394.26**
The Coretta Scott King Awards book, 1970-1999   **028.5**
Stephens, C. G. Coretta Scott King Award books   **028.5**

African animals. Arnold, C.   **591.9**

African art
Finley, C. The art of African masks (5 and up)
391
African beginnings. Haskins, J.   **960**
African elephants. Patent, D. H.   **599.67**
African savanna. Silver, D. M.   **577.4**
African tales, uh-huh, Ashley Bryan's. Bryan, A.
398.2

Africans
United States
Ashabranner, B. K. The new African Americans (4 and up)   **305.8**
After the flood. Geisert, A.   **E**
After the spill. Markle, S.   **363.7**
Afternoon of the elves. Lisle, J. T.   **Fic**
Against borders. Rochman, H.   **011.6**
Age *See* Old age
The **age** of chivalry. Bulfinch, T.
In Bulfinch, T. Bulfinch's Mythology
291
The **age** of fable. Bulfinch, T.
In Bulfinch, T. Bulfinch's Mythology
291
The **age** of the dinosaurs. Parker, S.   **567.9**

Agee, Jon
Elvis lives! and other anagrams   **793.73**
Go hang a salami! I'm a lasagna hog! and other palindromes   **793.73**
The incredible painting of Felix Clousseau
E
Sit on a potato pan, Otis!   **793.73**
So many dynamos! and other palindromes
793.73
(il) Seidler, T. Mean Margaret   **Fic**

Aggie's home. Nixon, J. L.   **Fic**

Aglebemu. Bruchac, J.
In Bruchac, J. When the Chenoo howls
398.2

Agnes, Michael
(ed) Webster's New World children's dictionary. See Webster's New World children's dictionary   **423**

The **agony** of Alice. Naylor, P. R.   **Fic**

Agricultural laborers
Atkin, S. B. Voices from the fields (5 and up)
331.5
Hoyt-Goldsmith, D. Migrant worker (3-5)
331.5
Poetry
Ada, A. F. Gathering the sun (2-4)   **811**

Agricultural machinery
Llewellyn, C. Tractor (k-3)   **629.225**

Agricultural pests
See also Insect pests

Agriculture
Bial, R. Portrait of a farm family (4 and up)
630.1

Aguinaldo. Delacre, L.
In Delacre, L. Salsa stories p62-70   **S C**

Ahlberg, Allan
Bravest ever bear   **E**
(jt. auth) Ahlberg, J. The baby's catalogue
E

Ahlberg, Allan—*Continued*
(jt. auth) Ahlberg, J. Each peach pear plum
          E
(jt. auth) Ahlberg, J. Peek-a-boo! **E**
Ahlberg, Janet
The baby's catalogue **E**
Each peach pear plum **E**
Peek-a-boo! **E**
Aïda. Price, L. **792.5**
AIDS (Disease)
McPhee, A. T. AIDS (5 and up) **616.97**
See/See also pages in the following book(s):
Fry, V. L. Part of me died, too p133-58 (5 and up) **155.9**
        Fiction
Fox, P. The eagle kite (6 and up) **Fic**
Nelson, T. Earthshine (5 and up) **Fic**
Zalben, J. B. Unfinished dreams (5 and up) **Fic**
Aiello, Laurel
(il) Sabbeth, A. Rubber-band banjos and a java jive bass **781**
Aiken, Joan, 1924-
Black hearts in Battersea. See note under Aiken, J. The wolves of Willoughby Chase **Fic**
Cold Shoulder Road. See note under Aiken, J. The wolves of Willoughby Chase **Fic**
The cuckoo tree. See note under Aiken, J. The wolves of Willoughby Chase **Fic**
Dangerous games. See note under Aiken, J. The wolves of Willoughby Chase **Fic**
Is underground. See note under Aiken, J. The wolves of Willoughby Chase **Fic**
The stolen lake. See note under Aiken, J. The wolves of Willoughby Chase **Fic**
Think of a word
In The Oxford treasury of children's stories p82-90 **S C**
The wolves of Willoughby Chase (5 and up) **Fic**
Aikman, Troy
See/See also pages in the following book(s):
Sullivan, G. Quarterbacks! p9-11 (5 and up) **920**
Ailey, Alvin
        About
Pinkney, A. D. Alvin Ailey (k-3) **92**
Air
Branley, F. M. Air is all around you (k-1) **551.5**
        Experiments
Ardley, N. The science book of air (3-5) **507.8**
Air is all around you. Branley, F. M. **551.5**
Air pilots
See also African American pilots; Women air pilots
Burleigh, R. Flight: the journey of Charles Lindbergh (2-4) **92**
Provensen, A. The glorious flight: across the Channel with Louis Blériot, July 25, 1909 (1-4) **92**
Airplanes
Barton, B. Airplanes (k-1) **387.7**
Barton, B. Airport (k-1) **387.7**

Hunter, R. A. Take off! (k-3) **629.13**
Maynard, C. Airplane (k-3) **629.136**
   Design and construction
Provensen, A. The glorious flight: across the Channel with Louis Blériot, July 25, 1909 (1-4) **92**
        Fiction
Siebert, D. Plane song **E**
        Models
Kelly, E. J. Paper airplanes (4 and up) **745.592**
Simon, S. The paper airplane book (3-5) **745.592**
Airports
Barton, B. Airport (k-1) **387.7**
Maynard, C. Airplane (k-3) **629.136**
        Fiction
Bunting, E. Fly away home **E**
Floca, B. Five trucks **E**
Ajmera, Maya
Let the games begin! (3-5) **796**
Akiak. Blake, R. J. **E**
Akkadians (Sumerians) *See* Sumerians
Akron-Summit County Public Library (Ohio). Science and Technology Division
Science fair project index, 1973-1980/1985-1989. See Science fair project index, 1973-1980/1985-1989 **507.8**
ALA filing rules **025.3**
Alabama
Davis, L. Alabama
In America the beautiful, second series **973**
Shirley, D. Alabama
In Celebrate the states **973**
        Fiction
English, K. Francie (5 and up) **Fic**
McKissack, P. C. Run away home (5 and up) **Fic**
Aladdin. Philip, N.
In Philip, N. The Arabian nights p79-98 **398.2**
Aladdin and the slave of the lamp, The story of. Alderson, B.
In Alderson, B. The Arabian nights p142-82 **398.2**
Aladdin and the wonderful lamp
In The Arabian nights entertainments p295-315 **398.2**
In The Blue fairy book p72-85 **398.2**
Alamo (San Antonio, Tex.)
Gaines, A. Jim Bowie (5 and up) **92**
Garland, S. Voices of the Alamo (3-6) **976.4**
Alan and Naomi. Levoy, M. **Fic**
Alarcón, Francisco X., 1954-
From the bellybutton of the moon and other summer poems (2-4) **811**
Laughing tomatoes and other spring poems (2-4) **811**
Alaska
McMillan, B. Salmon summer (2-4) **639.2**
Stefoff, R. Alaska
In Celebrate the states **973**

Alaska—*Continued*

Walsh Shepherd, D. Alaska

In America the beautiful, second series **973**

Fiction

Blake, R. J. Akiak **E**

London, J. The call of the wild (5 and up) **Fic**

London, J. White Fang (5 and up) **Fic**

Morey, W. Gentle Ben (5 and up) **Fic**

Natural history

See Natural history—Alaska

Social life and customs

Meyer, C. In a different light (4 and up) **979.8**

Nome

See Nome (Alaska)

Albania

Wright, D. K. Albania (4 and up) **949.65**

Albert Einstein and relativity. Parker, S. **92**

Albert goes Hollywood. Schwartz, H. **E**

Albert's alphabet. Tryon, L. See note under Tryon, L. Albert's birthday **E**

Albert's ballgame. Tryon, L. See note under Tryon, L. Albert's birthday **E**

Albert's birthday. Tryon, L. **E**

Albert's Christmas. Tryon, L. See note under Tryon, L. Albert's birthday **E**

Albert's field trip. Tryon, L. See note under Tryon, L. Albert's birthday **E**

Albert's Hallowween. Tryon, L. See note under Tryon, L. Albert's birthday **E**

Albert's play. Tryon, L. See note under Tryon, L. Albert's birthday **E**

Albert's Thanksgiving. Tryon, L. See note under Tryon, L. Albert's birthday **E**

Alborough, Jez

Duck in the truck **E**

It's the bear! See note under Alborough, J. My friend Bear **E**

My friend Bear **E**

Watch out! Big Bro's coming! **E**

Where's my teddy? See note under Alborough, J. My friend Bear **E**

The **alchemist**. McCaughrean, G.

In McCaughrean, G. The crystal pool: myths and legends of the world p41-44 **398.2**

Alcock, Vivien, 1924-

A change of aunts

In The Oxford book of scary tales p24-35 **808.8**

The cuckoo sister (6 and up) **Fic**

The monster garden (4 and up) **Fic**

Alcoholics

Fiction

Conly, J. L. Crazy lady! (5 and up) **Fic**

Alcoholism

Pringle, L. P. Drinking (5 and up) **362.292**

Fiction

Daly, N. My dad **E**

Rodowsky, C. F. Hannah in between (5 and up) **Fic**

Alcorn, Stephen, 1958-

(il) I, too, sing America. See I, too, sing America **811.008**

(il) Lincoln, in his own words. See Lincoln, in his own words **92**

(il) Meltzer, M. Langston Hughes **92**

Alcott, Louisa May, 1832-1888

Eight cousins. See note under Alcott, L. M. Little women **Fic**

Jo's boys. See note under Alcott, L. M. Little women **Fic**

Little men. See note under Alcott, L. M. Little women **Fic**

Little women (5 and up) **Fic**

Little women; dramatization. See Hackett, W. A merry Christmas

An old-fashioned Thanksgiving (3-5) **Fic**

Rose in bloom. See note under Alcott, L. M. Little women **Fic**

Rosy's journey

In American fairy tales p92-104 **S C**

See/See also pages in the following book(s):

Faber, D. Great lives: American literature p91-99 (5 and up) **920**

Krull, K. Lives of the writers p52-55 (4 and up) **920**

Alda, Arlene, 1933-

Arlene Alda's 1 2 3 **E**

Alderson, Brian

The Arabian nights (6 and up) **398.2**

Contents: The two kings, Shah Shahryar and Shah Zaman, and the Wazir's daughter Sheherezade; The tale of the fisherman and the Jinni; The tale of the porter of Baghdad; The tale of the hunchback; The fable of the birds and the beasts and the carpenter; The fable of the wolf and the fox; The fable of the mongoose and the mouse; The tale of the ebony horse; The tale which Ali the Persian told to amuse Harun al-Rashid; Ma'an bin-Zaidah, the donkey and the cucumbers; The story of Sindbad the Porter and Sindbad the Sailor; The tale of the City of Brass; The tale of the man who stole the dog's golden dish; The tale of the ruined man and his dream; The tale of the simpleton and his donkey; The tale of Ja'afar the barmecide and the ailing Bedouin; The story of Ali Baba and the forty thieves; The story of Aladdin and the slave of the lamp

The tale of the turnip (k-3) **398.2**

(comp) Andersen, H. C. The swan's stories **S C**

Aldo Applesauce. Hurwitz, J. See note under Hurwitz, J. Much ado about Aldo **Fic**

Aldo Ice Cream. Hurwitz, J. See note under Hurwitz, J. Much ado about Aldo **Fic**

Aldo Peanut Butter. Hurwitz, J. See note under Hurwitz, J. Much ado about Aldo **Fic**

Alex and the cat. Griffith, H. V. **Fic**

Alex remembers. Griffith, H. V.

In Griffith, H. V. Alex and the cat **Fic**

Alexander, David, 1956-

(il) Mahy, M. My mysterious world **92**

Alexander, Ellen

(il) Hawes, J. Fireflies in the night **595.7**

Alexander, Lloyd

The Arkadians (5 and up) **Fic**

The Beggar Queen (5 and up) **Fic**

The black cauldron. See note under Alexander, L. The book of three **Fic**

The book of three (5 and up) **Fic**

The castle of Llyr. See note under Alexander, L. The book of three **Fic**

Alexander, Lloyd—*Continued*
The cat who wished to be a man (4-6) **Fic**
The Drackenberg adventure. See note under Alexander, L. The Illyrian adventure **Fic**
The El Dorado adventure. See note under Alexander, L. The Illyrian adventure **Fic**
The fortune-tellers **E**
The foundling and other tales of Prydain (5 and up) **S C**
Contents: The foundling; The stone; The true enchanter; The rascal crow; The sword; The smith, the weaver, and the harper; Coll and his white pig; The truthful harp
Gypsy Rizka (5 and up) **Fic**
The high king (5 and up) **Fic**
The House Gobbaleen **E**
The Illyrian adventure (5 and up) **Fic**
The iron ring (5 and up) **Fic**
The Jedera adventure. See note under Alexander, L. The Illyrian adventure **Fic**
The marvelous misadventures of Sebastian (4 and up) **Fic**
The Philadelphia adventure. See note under Alexander, L. The Illyrian adventure **Fic**
The remarkable journey of Prince Jen (5 and up) **Fic**
Taran Wanderer. See note under Alexander, L. The book of three **Fic**
Westmark (5 and up) **Fic**
See/See also pages in the following book(s):
Newbery and Caldecott Medal books, 1966-1975 p48-55 **028.5**

Alexander, Martha G.
And my mean old mother will be sorry, Blackboard Bear. See note under Alexander, M. G. Blackboard Bear **E**
Blackboard Bear **E**
How my library grew, by Dinah **E**
I sure am glad to see you, Blackboard Bear. See note under Alexander, M. G. Blackboard Bear **E**
When the new baby comes, I'm moving out **E**
You're a genius, Blackboard Bear. See note under Alexander, M. G. Blackboard Bear **E**

Alexander, Sally Hobart
Do you remember the color blue? (4 and up) **362.4**

Alexander and the terrible, horrible, no good, very bad day. Viorst, J. **E**

Alexander and the wind-up mouse. Lionni, L. **E**

Alexander, who is not (do you hear me?) going (I mean it) to move. Viorst, J. See note under Viorst, J. Alexander and the terrible, horrible, no good, very bad day **E**

Alexander, who used to be rich last Sunday. Viorst, J. See note under Viorst, J. Alexander and the terrible, horrible, no good, very bad day **E**

Alexeieff, Alexander, 1901-1982
(il) Afanas′ev, A. N. Russian fairy tales **398.2**

Alfie and the birthday surprise. Hughes, S. **E**

Alfie's 1 2 3. Hughes, S. See note under Hughes, S. Alfie and the birthday surprise **E**

Alger, Leclaire *See* Leodhas, Sorche Nic, 1898-1968

Algeria
Kagda, F. Algeria (5 and up) **965**

Algonquian Indians
See also Delaware Indians
Folklore
Curry, J. L. Turtle Island: tales of the Algonquian nations (4-6) **398.2**
Norman, H. Trickster and the fainting birds (4 and up) **398.2**

Ali, Muhammad, 1942-
See/See also pages in the following book(s):
Littlefield, B. Champions p81-92 (5 and up) **920**

Ali Baba and the forty thieves. Philip, N.
In Philip, N. The Arabian nights p131-42 **398.2**

Ali Baba and the forty thieves, The story of. Alderson, B.
In Alderson, B. The Arabian nights p120-42 **398.2**

Ali, child of the desert. London, J. **E**

Alice in April. Naylor, P. R. See note under Naylor, P. R. The agony of Alice **Fic**

Alice in-between. Naylor, P. R. See note under Naylor. P. R. The agony of Alice **Fic**

Alice in lace. Naylor, P. R. See note under Naylor, P. R. The agony of Alice **Fic**

Alice in rapture, sort of. Naylor, P. R. See note under Naylor, P. R. The agony of Alice **Fic**

Alice in Wonderland. See Carroll, L. Alice's adventures in Wonderland **Fic**

Alice Nizzy Nazzy, the Witch of Santa Fe. Johnston, T. **E**

Alice on the outside. Naylor, P. R. See note under Naylor, P. R. The agony of Alice **Fic**

Alice Ramsey's grand adventure. Brown, D. **92**

Alice the brave. Naylor, P. R. See note under Naylor, P. R. The agony of Alice **Fic**

Alice's adventures in Wonderland. Carroll, L. **Fic**
also in Carroll, L. The complete works of Lewis Carroll p9-120 **828**

Alice's adventures in Wonderland, and Through the looking glass. Carroll, L. **Fic**

Alida's song. Paulsen, G. **Fic**

Alien empire. (3-6) See entry in Part 2: Web Resources

Alien encounters. Campbell, P. A. **001.9**

Alien secrets. Klause, A. C. **Fic**

Aliens
See also Immigrants
United States
See also United States—Immigration and emigration

Aliens from outer space *See* Extraterrestrial beings

Aliki
Best friends together again **E**

Aliki—*Continued*

Communication (k-3)   **302.2**
Corn is maize (k-3)   **633.1**
Feelings (k-3)   **152.4**
Fossils tell of long ago (k-3)   **560**
The gods and goddesses of Olympus (2-5)   **292**
Hello! good-bye! (k-3)   **395**
Manners (k-3)   **395**
A medieval feast (2-5)   **394.1**
Milk from cow to carton (k-3)   **637**
My feet (k-1)   **612**
My five senses (k-1)   **612.8**
My hands (k-1)   **612**
My visit to the aquarium (k-3)   **639.34**
My visit to the zoo (k-3)   **590.73**
Painted words: Marianthe's story one   **E**
The story of Johnny Appleseed (k-3)   **92**
The two of them   **E**
We are best friends   **E**
A weed is a flower: the life of George Washington Carver (k-3)   **92**
Welcome, little baby   **E**
Wild and woolly mammoths (k-3)   **569**
William Shakespeare & the Globe (3-6)   **792.09**
(il) Showers, P. The listening walk   **E**

Aliosha Popovich. Afanas´ev, A. N.
In Afanas´ev, A. N. Russian fairy tales p67-71   **398.2**

Aliquipiso. Mayer, M.
In Mayer, M. Women warriors p71-74   **398**

Alison's zinnia. Lobel, A.   **E**

All aboard reading [series]
Fritz, J. George Washington's mother   **92**

All about hockey. Sullivan, G.   **796.962**

All about owls. Arnosky, J.   **598**

All about Sam. Lowry, L. See note under Lowry, L. Anastasia Krupnik   **Fic**

All about turkeys. Arnosky, J.   **598**

All about turtles. Arnosky, J.   **597.9**

All alone in the universe. Perkins, L. R.   **Fic**

All-American Girls Professional Baseball League
Fiction
Rappaport, D. Dirt on their skirts   **E**

All but Alice. Naylor, P. R. See note under Naylor. P. R. The agony of Alice   **Fic**

All God's children (k-3)   **242**

All God's critters got a place in the choir. Staines, B.   **782.42**

All Hallows' Eve *See* Halloween

All I see. Rylant, C.   **E**

All night, all day   **782.25**

All-of-a-kind family. Taylor, S.   **Fic**

All-of-a-kind family downtown. Taylor, S. See note under Taylor, S. All-of-a-kind family   **Fic**

All-of-a-kind family uptown. Taylor, S. See note under Taylor, S. All-of-a-kind family   **Fic**

All of our noses are here. Schwartz, A.
In Schwartz, A. All of our noses are here, and other noodle tales p22-37   **398.2**

All of our noses are here, and other noodle tales. Schwartz, A.   **398.2**

All pigs are beautiful. King-Smith, D.   **636.4**

All roads lead to Wales. McCaughrean, G.
In McCaughrean, G. The golden hoard: myths and legends of the world p52-59   **398.2**

All Souls' Day
Ancona, G. Pablo remembers (k-3)   **394.26**
Hoyt-Goldsmith, D. Day of the Dead (3-5)   **394.26**
Lasky, K. Days of the Dead (4-6)   **394.26**
Fiction
Johnston, T. Day of the Dead   **E**

All the colors of the earth. Hamanaka, S.   **E**

All the places to love. MacLachlan, P.   **E**

All the pretty little horses (k-2)   **782.42**

All the small poems and fourteen more. Worth, V.   **811**

All the stars in the sky. Rylant, C.
In Rylant, C. Children of Christmas p32-38   **S C**

Allaby, Michael, 1933-
Biomes of the world (5 and up)   **577**

Allard, Harry, 1928-
Bumps in the night   **E**
Miss Nelson has a field day. See note under Allard, H. Miss Nelson is missing!   **E**
Miss Nelson is back. See note under Allard, H. Miss Nelson is missing!   **E**
Miss Nelson is missing!   **E**

Allegories
See also Fables
Adams, R. Watership Down (6 and up)   **Fic**
Avi. Poppy (3-5)   **Fic**
Babbitt, N. Kneeknock Rise (4-6)   **Fic**

Allen, Christina M.
See/See also pages in the following book(s):
Talking with adventurers p8-15 (4-6)   **920**

Allen, Gary
(il) George, J. C. One day in the tropical rain forest   **577.3**
(il) George, J. C. One day in the woods   **577.3**

Allen, John Logan, 1941-
(ed) Explorers. See Explorers   **920.003**

Allen, Jonathan, 1957-
(il) Mahy, M. The great white man-eating shark   **E**
(il) Mahy, M. Simply delicious!   **E**

Allen, Thomas B., 1928-
(il) Bulla, C. R. The chalk box kid   **E**
(il) Jukes, M. Blackberries in the dark   **Fic**
(il) Van Leeuwen, J. Going West   **E**

Allergy
Silverstein, A. Allergies (3-5)   **616.97**

Allerleirauh. Grimm, J.
In The Green fairy book p276-81   **398.2**

Alley, R. W. (Robert W.)
(il) Carlstrom, N. W. Thanksgiving Day at our house   **811**

Alvin (Submersible)
Kovacs, D. Dive to the deep ocean (4 and up)
623.8

Always inventing: a photobiography of Alexander Graham Bell. Matthews, T. L. **92**

The **always** prayer shawl. Oberman, S. **E**

Always room for one more. Leodhas, S. N.
782.42

Alzheimer's disease
Gold, S. D. Alzheimer's disease (4 and up)
616.8
Fiction
Willner-Pardo, G. Figuring out Frances (4-6)
Fic

The **amah**. Yep, L. **Fic**

Amahl and the night visitors. Menotti, G. C.
Fic

Amanda Pig and her best friend Lollipop. Van Leeuwen, J. See note under Van Leeuwen, J. Tales of Oliver Pig **E**

Amanda Pig and her big brother Oliver. Van Leeuwen, J. See note under Van Leeuwen, J. Tales of Oliver Pig **E**

Amanda Pig on her own. Van Leeuwen, J. See note under Van Leeuwen, J. Tales of Oliver Pig **E**

Amanda Pig, school girl. Van Leeuwen, J. See note under Van Leeuwen, J. Tales of Oliver Pig **E**

Amankamek. Bruchac, J.
In Bruchac, J. When the Chenno howls
398.2

Amari, Suad
Cooking the Lebanese way
In Easy menu ethnic cookbooks **641.5**

Amateur radio stations
Fiction
Barasch, L. Radio rescue **E**

Amazing birds of prey. Parry-Jones, J. **598**

The **amazing** bone. Steig, W. **E**

Amazing butterflies & moths. Still, J. **595.7**

Amazing cats. Parsons, A. **599.75**

Amazing fish. Ling, M. **597**

Amazing frogs & toads. Clarke, B. **597.8**

Amazing Grace. Hoffman, M. **E**

The **amazing** impossible Erie Canal. Harness, C.
386

The **amazing** life of Benjamin Franklin. Giblin, J.
92

Amazing lizards. Smith, T. **597.9**

Amazing spiders. Parsons, A. **595.4**

Amazon Interactive. (3-6) See entry in Part 2: Web Resources

Amber Brown goes fourth. Danziger, P. See note under Danziger, P. Amber Brown is not a crayon **Fic**

Amber Brown is feeling blue. Danziger, P. See note under Danziger, P. Amber Brown is not a crayon **Fic**

Amber Brown is not a crayon. Danziger, P.
Fic

Amber Brown sees red. Danziger, P. See note under Danziger, P. Amber Brown is not a crayon **Fic**

Amber Brown wants extra credit. Danziger, P. See note under Danziger, P. Amber Brown is not a crayon **Fic**

The **amber** cat. McKay, H. See note under McKay, H. Dog Friday **Fic**

Amboseli National Park (Kenya)
Pringle, L. P. Elephant woman (4 and up)
599.67

Ambrus, Victor G., 1935-
(il) McCaughrean, G. The Canterbury tales
821
(il) Riordan, J. King Arthur **398.2**

Amelia and Eleanor go for a ride. Ryan, P. M.
E

Amelia Bedelia. Parish, P. **E**

Amelia Bedelia 4 mayor. Parish, H. See note under Parish, P. Amelia Bedelia **E**

Amelia Bedelia and the baby. Parish, P. See note under Parish, P. Amelia Bedelia **E**

Amelia Bedelia and the surprise shower. Parish, P. See note under Parish, P. Amelia Bedelia
E

Amelia Bedelia goes camping. Parish, P. See note under Parish, P. Amelia Bedelia **E**

Amelia Bedelia helps out. Parish, P. See note under Parish, P. Amelia Bedelia **E**

Amelia Bedelia's family album. Parish, P. See note under Parish, P. Amelia Bedelia **E**

America
See also Latin America
Antiquities
Sattler, H. R. The earliest Americans (5 and up)
970.01
Exploration
Brenner, B. If you were there in 1492 (4-6)
970.01
Fritz, J. Brendan the Navigator (3-5) **398.2**
Fritz, J. Where do you think you're going, Christopher Columbus? (2-4) **92**
Maestro, B. The discovery of the Americas (2-4) **970.01**
Maestro, B. Exploration and conquest (2-4)
970.01
Marzollo, J. In 1492 (k-2) **970.01**
Sis, P. Follow the dream [biography of Christopher Columbus] (k-3) **92**
Steins, R. Exploration and settlement (5 and up)
970.01

Exploration—Fiction
Dorris, M. Morning Girl (4-6) **Fic**

America in World War I. Dolan, E. F. **940.3**

America the beautiful (Song)
Younger, B. Purple mountain majesties: the story of Katharine Lee Bates and "America the beautiful" (2-4) **92**

America the beautiful online. (4 and up) See entry in Part 2: Web Resources

America the beautiful, second series (4 and up)
973

The **American** alligator. Patent, D. H. **597.9**

American art
Fisher, L. E. The limners (4 and up)
759.13

American artists *See* Artists—United States

American Association for the Advancement of Science
Science Books & Films. See Science Books & Films **016.5**

American Association of School Librarians
Information power **027.8**

American bison *See* Bison

American bison. Berman, R. **599.64**

The **American** book of days **394.26**

American colonies *See* United States—History—1600-1775, Colonial period

American cooking *See* Cooking

American drama
Collections
You're on!: seven plays in English and Spanish (4 and up) **812.008**

The **American** eye. Greenberg, J. **920**

American fairy tales (6 and up) **S C**

American family albums [series]
Hoobler, D. The African American family album **305.8**
Hoobler, D. The Chinese American family album **305.8**
Hoobler, D. The Cuban American family album **305.8**
Hoobler, D. The German American family album **305.8**
Hoobler, D. The Irish American family album **305.8**
Hoobler, D. The Italian American family album **305.8**
Hoobler, D. The Japanese American family album **305.8**
Hoobler, D. The Jewish American family album **305.8**
Hoobler, D. The Mexican American family album **305.8**
Hoobler, D. The Scandinavian American family album **305.8**

American furniture
Fisher, L. E. The cabinetmakers (4 and up) **684.1**

American government. (6 and up) See entry in Part 2: Web Resources

The **American** Heritage children's dictionary **423**

The **American** Heritage picture dictionary (k-1) **423**

American history. (6 and up) See entry in Part 2: Web Resources

American Indians *See* Native Americans

American kids in history [series]
King, D. C. Colonial days **973.2**
King, D. C. Pioneer days **978**
King, D. C. Wild West days **978**

American Library Association
See also American Association of School Librarians; Association for Library Service to Children

American Library Association. Children's Services Division *See* Association for Library Service to Children

American Library Association publications
ALA filing rules **025.3**
American Association of School Librarians. Information power **027.8**
Bauer, C. F. Caroline Feller Bauer's new handbook for storytellers **372.6**
Bauer, C. F. Leading kids to books through magic **027.62**
Bauer, C. F. Leading kids to books through puppets **027.62**
Benne, M. Principles of children's services in public libraries **027.62**
Berger, P. Internet for active learners **004.6**
Book Links **028.505**
Booklist **028.1**
Briggs, D. 52 programs for preschoolers **027.62**
Briggs, D. 101 fingerplays, stories, and songs to use with finger puppets **791.5**
Building a special collection of children's literature in your library **025.2**
Carlson, A. D. Flannelboard stories for infants and toddlers **372.6**
Cataloging correctly for kids **025.3**
Champlin, C. Storytelling with puppets **372.6**
Cianciolo, P. J. Informational picture books for children **028.1**
The Coretta Scott King Awards book, 1970-1999 **028.5**
Exploring science in the library **027.8**
Gorman, M. The concise AACR2, 1998 revision **025.3**
Hit list: frequently challenged books for children **016.8**
Intellectual freedom manual **323.44**
Jeffery, D. A. Literate beginnings **027.62**
Journal of Youth Services in Libraries **027.6205**
Minkel, W. Delivering Web reference services to young people **025.04**
Minkel, W. How to do "The three bears" with two hands **791.5**
Murray, L. K. Basic Internet for busy librarians **004.6**
The Newbery & Caldecott medal books, 1986-2000 **028.5**
The Newbery and Caldecott awards **028.5**
Nichols, J. Storytimes for two-year-olds **027.62**
Reid, R. Children's jukebox **782.42**
Rochman, H. Against borders **011.6**
Ross, C. The frugal youth cybrarian **025.2**
Scheps, S. G. The librarian's guide to homeschooling resources **021.2**
Trawicky, B. Anniversaries and holidays **394.26**
Walter, V. A. Output measures for public library service to children **027.62**

American literature
See also various forms of American literature, e.g. American poetry

An **Amish** wedding. Ammon, R.   **289.7**

An **Amish** year. Ammon, R.   **289.7**

Amistad (Schooner)
>Jurmain, S. Freedom's sons (4 and up)   **326**
>Myers, W. D. Amistad: a long road to freedom (5 and up)   **326**

>**Fiction**

>Chambers, V. Amistad rising   **E**

Amistad rising. Chambers, V.   **E**

Ammon, Bette D.
>Worth a thousand words   **011.6**

Ammon, Richard
>An Amish wedding (k-3)   **289.7**
>An Amish year (k-3)   **289.7**
>Conestoga wagons   **388.3**

Amphibians
>*See also* Frogs; Salamanders
>Cassie, B. National Audubon Society first field guide: amphibians (4 and up)   **597.8**
>Clarke, B. Amphibian (4 and up)   **597.8**
>Conant, R. Peterson first guide to reptiles and amphibians (6 and up)   **597.9**
>Snedden, R. What is an amphibian? (3-6)   **597.8**

Amsha the giant. Schwartz, H.
>*In* Schwartz, H. A coat for the moon and other Jewish tales p42-45   **398.2**

Amusement parks
>**Fiction**
>Roberts, W. D. Scared stiff (5 and up)   **Fic**

Amusements
>*See also* Juggling
>Cole, A. I saw a purple cow, and 100 other recipes for learning   **372**
>Cole, J. The rain or shine activity book (3-5)   **793**
>Love, A. Kids and grandparents: an activity book (3-6)   **790.1**
>Williamson, S. Summer fun!   **790.1**

Amzat and his brothers. Fox, P.
>*In* Fox, P. Amzat and his brothers: three Italian tales p1-25   **398.2**

Amzat and his brothers: three Italian tales. Fox, P.   **398.2**

Ananse the Spider in search of a fool. Bryan, A.
>*In* Bryan, A. Ashley Bryan's African tales, uh-huh p1-8   **398.2**

Ananse's feast. Mollel, T. M.   **398.2**

Anansi (Legendary character)
>Aardema, V. Anansi does the impossible! (k-3)   **398.2**
>Aardema, V. Oh, Kojo! How could you! (k-3)   **398.2**
>Haley, G. E. A story, a story (k-3)   **398.2**
>Kimmel, E. A. Anansi and the talking melon (k-3)   **398.2**
>Kimmel, E. A. Anansi goes fishing (k-3)   **398.2**
>McDermott, G. Anansi the spider (k-3)   **398.2**
>Mollel, T. M. Ananse's feast (k-3)   **398.2**
>Temple, F. Tiger soup (k-3)   **398.2**

See/See also pages in the following book(s):
>Hamilton, V. A ring of tricksters p47-71   **398.2**

Anansi and Candlefly. Sherlock, Sir P. M.
>*In* Sherlock, Sir P. M. West Indian folk-tales p97-104   **398.2**

Anansi and Nothing go hunting for wives. Courlander, H.
>*In* Courlander, H. Cow-tail switch, and other West African stories p95-102   **398.2**

Anansi and Snake the postman. Sherlock, Sir P. M.
>*In* Sherlock, Sir P. M. West Indian folk-tales p71-76   **398.2**

Anansi and the mind of god. McCaughrean, G.
>*In* McCaughrean, G. The golden hoard: myths and legends of the world p110-13   **398.2**

Anansi and the phantom food. Aardema, V.
>*In* Aardema, V. Misoso p9-13   **398.2**

Anansi and the pig. Sierra, J.
>*In* Sierra, J. Nursery tales around the world p65-67   **398.2**

Anansi and the talking melon. Kimmel, E. A.   **398.2**

Anansi does the impossible!. Aardema, V.   **398.2**

Anansi goes fishing. Kimmel, E. A.   **398.2**

Anansi hunts with Tiger. Sherlock, Sir P. M.
>*In* Sherlock, Sir P. M. West Indian Folk-tales p118-24   **398.2**

Anansi the spider. McDermott, G.   **398.2**

Anansi's fishing expedition. Courlander, H.
>*In* Courlander, H. Cow-tail switch, and other West African stories p47-58   **398.2**

Anansi's old riding-horse. Sherlock, Sir P. M.
>*In* Sherlock, Sir P. M. West Indian folk-tales p105-11   **398.2**

Anasazi. Fisher, L. E.   **970.004**

Anasazi culture *See* Pueblo Indians

Anastasia *See* Anastasîâ Nikolaevna, Grand Duchess, daughter of Nicholas II, Emperor of Russia, 1901-1918

Anastasia, absolutely. Lowry, L. See note under Lowry, L. Anastasia Krupnik   **Fic**

Anastasia again!. Lowry, L. See note under Lowry, L. Anastasia Krupnik   **Fic**

Anastasia, ask your analyst. Lowry, L. See note under Lowry, L. Anastasia Krupnik   **Fic**

Anastasia at this address. Lowry, L. See note under Lowry, L. Anastasia Krupnik   **Fic**

Anastasia at your service. Lowry, L. See note under Lowry, L. Anastasia Krupnik   **Fic**

Anastasia has the answers. Lowry, L. See note under Lowry, L. Anastasia Krupnik   **Fic**

Anastasia Krupnik. Lowry, L.   **Fic**

Anastasia on her own. Lowry, L. See note under Lowry, L. Anastasia Krupnik   **Fic**

Anastasia's album. Brewster, H.   **92**

Anastasia's chosen career. Lowry, L. See note under Lowry, L. Anastasia Krupnik   **Fic**

Angels. Greenfield, E.   **811**

Angels & other strangers: family Christmas stories. Paterson, K.   **S C**

Angels and other strangers. Paterson, K.
In Paterson, K. Angels & other strangers: family Christmas stories p1-16   **S C**

The **angel's** mistake. Prose, F.   **398.2**

Angel's mother's baby. Delton, J. See note under Delton, J. Angel's mother's wedding   **Fic**

Angel's mother's boyfriend. Delton, J. See note under Delton, J. Angel's mother's wedding   **Fic**

Angel's mother's wedding. Delton, J.   **Fic**

Angels of mercy. Kuhn, B.   **940.54**

The **angel's** wings. Schwartz, H.
In Schwartz, H. The diamond tree p107-13   **398.2**

Angliss, Sarah
Gold
In The Elements [Benchmark Bks.]   **546**

Anglo-American cataloguing rules
Gorman, M. The concise AACR2, 1998 revision   **025.3**

The **angry** woman. Lester, J.
In Lester, J. The last tales of Uncle Remus p56-61   **398.2**

Angus and the cat. Flack, M.
In The Read-aloud treasury p156-78   **808.8**

Anholt, Catherine
Harry's home   **E**

Anholt, Laurence
Stone girl, bone girl: the story of Mary Anning (k-3)   **92**
(jt. auth) Anholt, C. Harry's home   **E**

Animal alphabet. Kitchen, B.   **E**

Animal babies
Bauer, M. D. If you were born a kitten (k-1)   **591.3**
Darling, K. Arctic babies (k-3)   **591.9**
Darling, K. Desert babies (k-3)   **591.7**
Darling, K. Rain forest babies (k-3)   **591.9**
Darling, K. Seashore babies (k-3)   **591.7**
Heller, R. Chickens aren't the only ones (k-1)   **591.4**
Simon, S. Wild babies (2-4)   **591.3**
Swinburne, S. R. Safe, warm, and snug (k-3)   **591.56**

Animal behavior
See also Animal defenses
Bancroft, H. Animals in winter (k-1)   **591.56**
Bishop, N. The secrets of animal flight (3-6)   **591.47**
Collard, S. B., III. Animal dads (k-3)   **591.56**
Fraser, M. A. Where are the night animals? (k-1)   **591.5**
Settel, J. Exploding ants (4 and up)   **591.5**
Swinburne, S. R. Safe, warm, and snug (k-3)   **591.56**

Animal communication
Dudzinski, K. Meeting dolphins (4 and up)   **599.5**

Patterson, F. Koko-love! (1-4)   **599.8**

Animal courtship
Collard, S. B., III. Making animal babies (k-3)   **571.8**

Animal dads. Collard, S. B., III   **591.56**

Animal defenses
See also Camouflage (Biology)
Jenkins, S. What do you do when something wants to eat you? (k-3)   **591.47**
Zoehfeld, K. W. What lives in a shell? (k-1)   **591.4**

Animal fables from Aesop. McClintock, B.   **398.2**

The **animal** family. Jarrell, R.   **Fic**

Animal folk songs for children. Seeger, R. C.   **782.42**

Animal lives [series]
Tagholm, S. The rabbit   **599.3**

Animal locomotion
Hickman, P. M. Animals in motion (3-5)   **591.47**

Animal migration *See* Animals—Migration

Animal rescue. Goodman, S.   **639.9**

Animal stories *See* Animals—Fiction

Animal tracks
Selsam, M. E. Big tracks, little tracks (k-3)   **591.5**

Animals
See also Pets; Prehistoric animals; Rare animals; names of orders and classes of the animal kingdom; kinds of animals characterized by their environments; and names of individual species
Aliki. My visit to the zoo (k-3)   **590.73**
Arnosky, J. Crinkleroot's guide to knowing animal habitats (k-3)   **591.7**
Arnosky, J. Crinkleroot's nature almanac (k-3)   **508**
Bernhard, D. Earth, sky, wet, dry (k-2)   **578**
Bible. Selections. Animals of the Bible (1-4)   **220.8**
Carle, E. Does a kangaroo have a mother, too?   **E**
Carle, E. From head to toe   **E**
Carrick, C. Mothers are like that   **E**
Eichenberg, F. Ape in a cape   **E**
Fleming, D. Count!   **E**
Hader, B. The big snow   **E**
Hoban, T. A children's zoo   **E**
Horenstein, H. A is for—?   **E**
Jenkins, S. Big & little (k-2)   **591.4**
Jenkins, S. Biggest, strongest, fastest (k-2)   **590**
Kitchen, B. Animal alphabet   **E**
Macdonald, S. Peck, slither and slide   **E**
Seeger, R. C. Animal folk songs for children   **782.42**
Staines, B. All God's critters got a place in the choir (k-2)   **782.42**
Van Laan, N. A tree for me   **E**
Young, R. Who says moo?   **E**

Animals—*Continued*

Camouflage

See Camouflage (Biology)

Courtship

See Animal courtship

Fiction

Aardema, V. Rabbit makes a monkey of lion (k-3)   **398.2**

Aardema, V. Traveling to Tondo (k-3)   **398.2**

Aardema, V. Who's in Rabbit's house? (k-3)   **398.2**

Aardema, V. Why mosquitoes buzz in people's ears (k-3)   **398.2**

Alborough, J. Watch out! Big Bro's coming!   E

Allard, H. Bumps in the night   E

Arnold, K. Me too!   E

Avi. Poppy (3-5)   Fic

Brett, J. Annie and the wild animals   E

Brett, J. The hat   E

Brett, J. The mitten (k-2)   **398.2**

Brown, M. W. Big red barn   E

Brown, M. W. Four fur feet   E

Brown, R. The picnic   E

Bruchac, J. The great ball game (k-3)   **398.2**

Brusca, M. C. When jaguars ate the moon and other stories about animals and plants of the Americas (2-4)   **398.2**

Buehner, C. I did it, I'm sorry   E

Burningham, J. Mr. Gumpy's outing   E

Byars, B. C. Me Tarzan (3-5)   Fic

Cabrera, J. Over in the meadow   E

Carle, E. The very clumsy click beetle   E

Cauley, L. B. Clap your hands   E

Cole, H. I took a walk   E

Dahl, R. The enormous crocodile (2-4)   Fic

De Regniers, B. S. May I bring a friend?   E

Dunrea, O. Bear Noel   E

Edwards, P. D. Some smug slug   E

Ehlert, L. Circus   E

Ehrlich, A. Parents in the pigpen, pigs in the tub   E

Ets, M. H. Play with me   E

Flack, M. Ask Mr. Bear   E

Fleming, D. Barnyard banter   E

Fleming, D. In the tall, tall grass   E

Fleming, D. Time to sleep   E

Fox, M. Wombat divine   E

Galdone, P. Henny Penny (k-2)   **398.2**

Galdone, P. The monkey and the crocodile (k-2)   **398.2**

Gammell, S. Once upon MacDonald's farm   E

Gannett, R. S. My father's dragon (1-4)   Fic

George, J. C. Morning, noon, and night   E

Godwin, L. Little white dog   E

Grahame, K. The wind in the willows (4-6)   Fic

Guarino, D. Is your mama a llama?   E

Hall, J. What does the rabbit say?   E

Hamanaka, S. I look like a girl   E

Hamilton, V. A ring of tricksters   **398.2**

Hartman, G. As the crow flies   E

Heine, H. Friends   E

Henkes, K. Oh!   E

Hoban, L. Silly Tilly's Thanksgiving dinner   E

Howe, D. Bunnicula (4-6)   Fic

Howe, J. The celery stalks at midnight (4-6)   Fic

Howe, J. Scared silly: a Halloween treat   E

Hutchins, P. 1 hunter   E

Jacques, B. Redwall (6 and up)   Fic

Jarrell, R. The animal family (4 and up)   Fic

Jonas, A. Splash!   E

Kellogg, S. Aster Aardvark's alphabet adventures   E

Kellogg, S. Chicken Little (k-3)   **398.2**

Kipling, R. The jungle book: the Mowgli stories (4 and up)   S C

Kipling, R. Just so stories (3-6)   S C

Koide, T. May we sleep here tonight?   E

LaMarche, J. The raft   E

Lawson, R. Rabbit Hill (3-6)   Fic

Lester, J. The knee-high man, and other tales (k-3)   **398.2**

Lester, J. The last tales of Uncle Remus (4-6)   **398.2**

Lewin, H. Jafta   E

Lexau, J. M. Who took the farmer's [hat]?   E

Lobel, A. Fables (3-5)   Fic

Lobel, A. Grasshopper on the road   E

London, J. Snuggle wuggle   E

Low, J. Mice twice   E

Mahy, M. 17 kings and 42 elephants   E

Mahy, M. Boom, baby, boom, boom!   E

Mahy, M. Simply delicious!   E

Marshall, J. Rats on the range and other stories (2-4)   S C

Marshall, J. Rats on the roof, and other stories (2-4)   S C

Marshall, J. P. A honey of a day   E

Martin, B. Brown bear, brown bear what do you see?   E

Martin, B. Polar bear, polar bear, what do you hear?   E

Marzollo, J. Pretend you're a cat   E

Massie, D. R. The baby beebee bird   E

Mayo, M. Mythical birds & beasts from many lands (3-6)   **398.2**

McBratney, S. Just you and me   E

McClintock, B. Animal fables from Aesop (1-4)   **398.2**

McPhail, D. M. The puddle   E

Meddaugh, S. The best place   E

Milne, A. A. The complete tales of Winnie-the-Pooh (1-4)   Fic

Milne, A. A. The house at Pooh Corner (1-4)   Fic

Milne, A. A. The Pooh story book (1-4)   Fic

Milne, A. A. Winnie-the-Pooh (1-4)   Fic

Milne, A. A. The world of Pooh (1-4)   Fic

Miranda, A. To market, to market   E

Morpurgo, M. Wombat goes walkabout   E

Oxenbury, H. It's my birthday   E

Payne, E. Katy No-Pocket   E

Animals—Fiction—*Continued*

Rice, E. Sam who never forgets   E

Root, P. Grandmother Winter   E

Ruelle, K. G. The Thanksgiving beast feast   E

Ryder, J. Each living thing   E

Rylant, C. Every living thing (5 and up)   S C

Seidler, T. The Wainscott weasel (4-6)   Fic

Slate, J. Miss Bindergarten celebrates the 100th day of kindergarten   E

Small, D. George Washington's cows   E

Steig, W. Doctor De Soto   E

Steig, W. The real thief (3-5)   Fic

Stenmark, V. The singing chick   E

Stevens, J. Cook-a-doodle-doo!   E

Stevenson, J. Don't make me laugh   E

Stevenson, J. The most amazing dinosaur   E

Stevenson, J. The Mud Flat Olympics   E

Stevenson, J. The Sea View Hotel   E

Stevenson, J. A village full of valentines   E

Stojic, M. Rain   E

Tresselt, A. R. The mitten (k-2)   398.2

Tryon, L. Albert's birthday   E

Van Laan, N. Moose tales   E

Vaughan, M. Snap!   E

Vaughan, M. Whistling Dixie   E

Walter, V. A. "Hi, pizza man!"   E

Weiss, N. Where does the brown bear go?   E

Yaccarino, D. Deep in the jungle   E

Yolen, J. Off we go!   E

Folklore

See also Dragons; Monsters; Mythical animals

Hibernation

See Hibernation

Infancy

See Animal babies

Migration

Miller, D. S. A caribou journey (2-4)   599.65

Simon, S. Ride the wind (4-6)   591.56

Simon, S. They swim the seas (3-6)   578.7

Simon, S. They walk the earth (3-6)   591.56

Photography

See Photography of animals

Poetry

The Beauty of the beast (4-6)   811.008

Bernos de Gasztold, C. Prayers from the ark   841

Carle, E. Eric Carle's animals, animals   808.81

Demi. In the eyes of the cat   895.6

Florian, D. Beast feast   811

Hughes, L. The sweet and sour animal book   811

Jumpety-bumpety hop   811.008

Keats, E. J. Over in the meadow   E

Lewis, J. P. A hippopotamusn't and other animal verses   811

The Oxford book of animal poems (5 and up)   808.81

A Zooful of animals   808.81

Africa

Arnold, C. African animals (k-3)   591.9

Bateman, R. Safari (3-6)   599

Arctic regions

Darling, K. Arctic babies (k-3)   591.9

South America

Arnold, C. South American animals (k-3)   591.9

Animals, Domestic *See* Domestic animals

Animals, Extinct *See* Extinct animals

Animals, Fossil *See* Fossils

Animals, Habits and behavior of *See* Animal behavior

Animals, Mythical *See* Mythical animals

Animals A to Z. (3-6) See entry in Part 2: Web Resources

Animals, animals, Eric Carle's. Carle, E.   808.81

Animals in motion. Hickman, P. M.   591.47

Animals in winter. Bancroft, H.   591.56

Animals of the Bible. Bible. Selections   220.8

The **animals** share. Hamilton, V.
    In Hamilton, V. A ring of tricksters p97-103   398.2

Animation (Cinematography)

Hamilton, J. Special effects in film and television (4 and up)   791.43

The **anklet.** Philip, N.
    In Philip, N. The Arabian nights p33-37   398.2

Anna all year round. Hahn, M. D.   Fic

Anna Banana: 101 jump-rope rhymes   398.8

Anna Banana and me. Blegvad, L.   E

Anna is still here. Vos, I.   Fic

Anna on the farm. Hahn, M. D. See note under Hahn, M. D. Anna all year round   Fic

Annabel the actress starring in "Gorilla my dreams". Conford, E.   Fic

Annabel the actress starring in "Just a little extra". Conford, E. See note under Conford, E. Annabel the actress starring in "Gorilla my dreams"   Fic

Annabelle Swift, kindergartner. Schwartz, A.   E

Anne of Avonlea. Montgomery, L. M. See note under Montgomery, L. M. Anne of Green Gables   Fic

Anne of Green Gables. Montgomery, L. M.   Fic

Anne of Ingleside. Montgomery, L. M. See note under Montgomery, L. M. Anne of Green Gables   Fic

Anne of the island. Montgomery, L. M. See note under Montgomery, L. M. Anne of Green Gables   Fic

Anne of Windy Poplars. Montgomery, L. M. See note under Montgomery, L. M. Anne of Green Gables   Fic

The **Anne** rehearsals. Wynne-Jones, T.
    In Wynne-Jones, T. Lord of the Fries and other stories p91-115   S C

Anne's house of dreams. Montgomery, L. M. See note under Montgomery, L. M. Anne of Green Gables   **Fic**

Annie and the Old One. Miles, M.   **Fic**

Annie and the wild animals. Brett, J.   **E**

Annie Christmas. Hamilton, V.
In Hamilton, V. Her stories p84-89   **398.2**

Annie Christmas. San Souci, R.
In San Souci, R. Cut from the same cloth p35-40   **398.2**

Anning, Mary, 1799-1847
About
Anholt, L. Stone girl, bone girl: the story of Mary Anning (k-3)   **92**
Atkins, J. Mary Anning and the sea dragon (k-3)   **92**
Brown, D. Rare treasure: Mary Anning and her remarkable discoveries (k-3)   **92**

Anniversaries and holidays. Trawicky, B.   **394.26**

Anno, Masaichiro
Anno's mysterious multiplying jar (2-5)   **512**

Anno, Mitsumasa, 1926-
Anno's counting book   **E**
Anno's magic seeds (k-3)   **513**
Anno's math games (k-3)   **513**
Anno's math games II (k-3)   **513**
Anno's math games III (k-3)   **513**
(jt. auth) Anno, M. Anno's mysterious multiplying jar   **512**
(il) Mado, M. The magic pocket   **895.6**

Anno's counting book. Anno, M.   **E**
Anno's magic seeds. Anno, M.   **513**
Anno's math games. Anno, M.   **513**
Anno's math games II. Anno, M.   **513**
Anno's math games III. Anno, M.   **513**
Anno's mysterious multiplying jar. Anno, M.   **512**

Another important book. Brown, M. W.   **E**

Ansige Karamba, the glutton. Courlander, H.
In Courlander, H. cow-tail switch, and other West African stories p119-28   **398.2**

Anson's way. Schmidt, G. D.   **Fic**

The ant and the bear. Lelooska
In Lelooska. Spirit of the cedar people p8-11   **398.2**

The ant and the grasshopper. Poole, A. L.   **398.2**

Ant cities. Dorros, A.   **595.7**

Ant plays Bear. Byars, B. C. See note under Byars, B. C. My brother, Ant   **E**

Antarctic antics. Sierra, J.   **811**

Antarctica
McMillan, B. Summer ice (3-6)   **508**
Wheeler, S. Greetings from Antarctica   **998**
Exploration
Burleigh, R. Black whiteness (3-5)   **998**
Kimmel, E. C. Ice story (4 and up)   **998**
Kostyal, K. M. Trial by ice: a photobiography of Sir Ernest Shackleton (4 and up)   **92**

Natural history
See Natural history—Antarctica
Poetry
Sierra, J. Antarctic antics (k-3)   **811**

Anthony Burns: the defeat and triumph of a fugitive slave. Hamilton, V.   **92**

Anthropogeography *See* Human geography
Anthropology
See also Forensic anthropology
Periodicals
Faces   **306.05**

Antin, Mary, 1881-1949
About
Wells, R. Streets of gold (3-6)   **92**

Antiquities
See also Archeology
Wilcox, C. Mummies & their mysteries (4-6)   **393**

Antiquity of man *See* Human origins
Antisemitism
Fiction
Levitin, S. The return (6 and up)   **Fic**

Antler, bear, canoe. Bowen, B.   **E**

Antonyms *See* Opposites
Ants
Demuth, P. Those amazing ants (k-2)   **595.7**
Dorros, A. Ant cities (k-3)   **595.7**
Fiction
Cannon, J. Crickwing   **E**
Pinczes, E. J. One hundred hungry ants   **E**

Anzovin, Steven, 1954-
(jt. auth) Kane, J. N. Famous first facts   **031.02**

Apache Indians
Hoyt-Goldsmith, D. Apache rodeo (3-5)   **970.004**
Sneve, V. D. H. The Apaches (3-5)   **970.004**
See/See also pages in the following book(s):
Ehrlich, A. Wounded Knee: an Indian history of the American West (6 and up)   **970.004**
Fiction
McKissack, P. C. Run away home (5 and up)   **Fic**

Apache rodeo. Hoyt-Goldsmith, D.   **970.004**

Apartment houses
Fiction
Berends, P. B. The case of the elevator duck (3-5)   **Fic**
Hurwitz, J. New neighbors for Nora (2-4)   **Fic**

Ape in a cape. Eichenberg, F.   **E**

Apes
See also Chimpanzees; Gorillas

Apfel, Necia H., 1930-
Orion, the Hunter (4 and up)   **523.8**

Apiculture *See* Beekeeping; Bees
Apollo 11 (Spacecraft)
Hehner, B. First on the moon (4 and up)   **629.45**

Apollo moonwalks. Vogt, G.   **629.45**

Apollo Project *See* Project Apollo

Appalachia. Rylant, C.   974

Appalachian Mountain region *See* Appalachian region

Appalachian region
Bial, R. Mist over the mountains (4 and up)   974

Houston, G. My great-aunt Arizona   E
Rylant, C. Appalachia   974
Fiction
Caudill, R. A certain small shepherd (4 and up)   Fic

Caudill, R. Did you carry the flag today, Charley? (2-4)   Fic

Cleaver, V. Where the lillies bloom (5 and up)   Fic

Hamilton, V. M. C. Higgins the great (6 and up)   Fic

Houston, G. The year of the perfect Christmas tree   E
Rylant, C. Silver packages   E
Rylant, C. When I was young in the mountains   E

Schroeder, A. Smoky Mountain Rose   E
White, R. Belle Prater's boy (5 and up)   Fic

Apparitions. San Souci, R.
In San Souci, R. A terrifying taste of short & shivery p30-34   398.2

Appelbaum, Diana Karter
Cocoa ice   E
Giants in the land (2-4)   634.9

Appelt, Kathi, 1954-
The bat jamboree. See note under Appelt, K. Bats around the clock   E
Bats around the clock   E
Bats on parade. See note under Appelt, K. Bats around the clock   E
Bayou lullaby   E
Cowboy dreams   E
Oh my baby, little one   E

Appetite disorders *See* Eating disorders

Apple, Margot
Brave Martha   E
(il) Delton, J. Angel's mother's wedding   Fic
(il) Shaw, N. Sheep in a jeep   E

An **apple** from The Tree of Life. Schwartz, H.
In Schwartz, H. A journey to paradise and other Jewish tales p6-11   398.2

Apple is my sign. Riskind, M.   Fic

The **apple** of contentment. Pyle, H.
In American fairy tales p81-91   S C

The **apple** pie tree. Hall, Z.   634

Apples
Gibbons, G. Apples (k-3)   634
Hall, Z. The apple pie tree (k-1)   634
Landau, E. Apples (2-4)   634
Maestro, B. How do apples grow? (k-3)   634

Micucci, C. The life and times of the apple (2-4)   634
Fiction
Hutchins, P. Ten red apples   E

Appleseed, Johnny, 1774-1845
About
Aliki. The story of Johnny Appleseed (k-3)   92

Hodges, M. The true tale of Johnny Appleseed (k-3)   92
Kellogg, S. Johnny Appleseed (k-3)   92
See/See also pages in the following book(s):
Calvert, P. Great lives: the American frontier p81-92 (5 and up)   920
Fiction
Glass, A. Folks call me Appleseed John   E
Poetry
Lindbergh, R. Johnny Appleseed (k-3)   811

Applied arts *See* Decorative arts

Appointment in Samarra. San Souci, R.
In San Souci, R. Even more short & shivery p1-4   398.2

Appraisal   016.5

Apprentices
Fiction
DeFelice, C. C. The apprenticeship of Lucas Whitaker (4 and up)   Fic
Fleischman, P. Saturnalia (6 and up)   Fic
Garfield, L. Black Jack (6 and up)   Fic

The **apprenticeship** of Lucas Whitaker. DeFelice, C. C.   Fic

Approximate computation
Murphy, S. J. Betcha! (1-3)   519.5

April Fool!. Ziefert, H.   E

April Fools' Day
Fiction
Ziefert, H. April Fool!   E

April Mendez. Spinelli, J.
In Spinelli, J. The library card   S C

April's kittens. Newberry, C. T.   E

Apt. 3. Keats, E. J.   E

Aquanauts *See* Underwater exploration

Aquariums
See also Marine aquariums
Evans, M. Fish (2-5)   639.34
Murphy, S. J. Room for Ripley (1-3)   530.8

Aquatic animals *See* Marine animals

Aquatic birds *See* Water birds

Aquatic plants *See* Marine plants

Arab countries
Haskins, J. Count your way through the Arab world (2-4)   909
The **Arabian** nights. Alderson, B.   398.2
The **Arabian** nights. Philip, N.   398.2
The **Arabian** nights entertainments (5 and up)   398.2

Arabian Peninsula
See also Oman

Arabs
Folklore
Alderson, B. The Arabian nights (6 and up)   398.2

The Arabian nights entertainments (5 and up)   398.2

Ben-'Ezer, E. Hosni the dreamer (2-4)   398.2

Argent, Kerry, 1960-
(il) Fox, M. Sleepy bears   **E**
(il) Fox, M. Wombat divine   **E**
Argentina
Hintz, M. Argentina (4 and up)   **982**
Folklore
See Folklore—Argentina
Argonauts (Greek mythology)
Colum, P. The Golden Fleece and the heroes who lived before Achilles (5 and up)
    292
See/See also pages in the following book(s):
Hamilton, E. Mythology p159-79 (6 and up)
    292
Arid regions
See also Deserts
Arion and the dolphins. McCaughrean, G.
In McCaughrean, G. The crystal pool: myths and legends of the world p67-70
    398.2
Arithmetic
See also Addition; Fractions; Multiplication; Subtraction
McMillan, B. Jelly beans for sale (k-2)
    332.4
Murphy, S. J. Betcha! (1-3)   **519.5**
Estimation
See Approximate computation
Study and teaching—Periodicals
Teaching Children Mathematics   **510.7**
Arithmetic Teacher. See Teaching Children Mathematics   **510.7**
Arizona
Blashfield, J. F. Arizona
In America the beautiful, second series
    973
McDaniel, M. Arizona
In Celebrate the states   **973**
The **ark**. Geisert, A.   **222**
The **Arkadians**. Alexander, L.   **Fic**
Arkansas
Altman, L. J. Arkansas
In Celebrate the states   **973**
Fiction
Greene, B. Philip Hall likes me, I reckon maybe (4-6)   **Fic**
Greene, B. Summer of my German soldier (6 and up)   **Fic**
Race relations
O'Neill, L. Little Rock (5 and up)   **370**
Arlene Alda's 1 2 3. Alda, A.   **E**
Armadillos
Fiction
Kipling, R. The beginning of the armadilloes
    Fic
The **armchair** traveler. McCaughrean, G.
In McCaughrean, G. The bronze cauldron: myths and legends of the world p26-30
    398.2
Armenia
Dhilawala, S. Armenia (5 and up)   **947.5**
Folklore
See Folklore—Armenia

Armenian massacres, 1915-1923
Kherdian, D. The road from home [biography of Veron Kherdian] (6 and up)   **92**
Armenians
Turkey
Kherdian, D. The road from home [biography of Veron Kherdian] (6 and up)   **92**
Armer, Laura Adams, 1874-1963
See/See also pages in the following book(s):
Newbery Medal books, 1922-1955 p101-06
    028.5
The **armless** maiden. Afanas'ev, A. N.
In Afanas'ev, A. N. Russian fairy tales p294-99   **398.2**
Armor
Byam, M. Arms & armor (4 and up)
    355.8
Yue, C. Armor (4 and up)   **355.8**
Armored cars (Tanks) *See* Military tanks
Arms and armor *See* Armor; Weapons
Armstrong, Carole
Lives and legends of the saints (4 and up)
    920
Women of the Bible (5 and up)   **220.9**
Armstrong, Jennifer, 1961-
Black-eyed Susan (3-5)   **Fic**
Chin Yu Min and the ginger cat   **E**
Steal away (5 and up)   **Fic**
Jennings, P. The century for young people
    909.82
Armstrong, Lance
About
Stewart, M. Sweet victory: Lance Armstrong's incredible journey (4 and up)   **92**
Armstrong, Louis, 1900-1971
Fiction
Schroeder, A. Satchmo's blues   **E**
Armstrong, Neil, 1930-
About
Brown, D. One giant leap: the story of Neil Armstrong (k-3)   **92**
Armstrong, William Howard, 1914-1999
Sounder (5 and up)   **Fic**
See/See also pages in the following book(s):
Newbery and Caldecott Medal books, 1966-1975 p58-65   **028.5**
Army life *See* Soldiers
Army Nurse Corps *See* United States. Army Nurse Corps
Arndt, Ursula
(il) Barth, E. Hearts, cupids, and red roses
    394.26
(il) Barth, E. Holly, reindeer, and colored lights
    394.26
(il) Barth, E. Lilies, rabbits, and painted eggs
    394.26
(il) Barth, E. Shamrocks, harps, and shillelaghs
    394.26
(il) Barth, E. Turkeys, Pilgrims, and Indian corn
    394.26
(il) Barth, E. Witches, pumpkins, and grinning ghosts   **394.26**
(il) Giblin, J. Fireworks, picnics, and flags
    394.26

Arno, Enrico, 1913-1981
  (il) Fritz, J. Brendan the Navigator   **398.2**
Arnold, Arthur
  (il) Arnold, C. Rhino   **599.66**
  (il) Arnold, C. Stone Age farmers beside the sea
    936.1
  (il) Arnold, C. A walk on the Great Barrier Reef
    578.7

Arnold, Caroline, 1944-
  African animals (k-3)   **591.9**
  The ancient cliff dwellers of Mesa Verde (4 and
    up)   **970.004**
  Cats: in from the wild (3-5)   **599.75**
  City of the Gods (4 and up)   **972**
  Dinosaur mountain (4 and up)   **567.9**
  Dinosaurs all around (4 and up)   **567.9**
  Easter Island (4 and up)   **996**
  El Niño (4 and up)   **551.6**
  Hawk highway in the sky (4-6)   **598**
  Rhino (3-5)   **599.66**
  South American animals (k-3)   **591.9**
  Stone Age farmers beside the sea (4 and up)
    936.1
  Stories in stone (4 and up)   **709.01**
  A walk on the Great Barrier Reef (3-5)
    578.7

Arnold, Katya
  Me too!   **E**

Arnold, Marsha Diane, 1948-
  Heart of a tiger   **E**
  The pumpkin runner   **E**
The **Arnold** Lobel book of Mother Goose (k-2)
    398.8

Arnosky, Jim
  All about owls (1-3)   **598**
  All about turkeys (1-3)   **598**
  All about turtles (k-3)   **597.9**
  Crinkleroot's guide to knowing animal habitats
    (k-3)   **591.7**
  Crinkleroot's guide to knowing butterflies &
    moths (k-3)   **595.7**
  Crinkleroot's guide to knowing the birds (k-3)
    598
  Crinkleroot's nature almanac (k-3)   **508**
  Every autumn comes the bear   **E**
  Flies in the water, fish in the air (5 and up)
    799.1
  Little lions   **E**
  Mouse letters   **E**
  Mouse numbers   **E**
  Otters under water (k-2)   **599.7**
  Raccoons and ripe corn   **E**
  Rattlesnake dance   **E**
  Watching desert wildlife (3-6)   **591.7**
  Watching water birds (2-4)   **598**
Arnott, Kathleen
  Unanana and the elephant
    In Womenfolk and fairy tales p127-34
    398.2

Arnsteen, Katy Keck, 1934-
  (il) Bentley, N. Putting on a play   **792**
  (il) Bentley, N. The young journalist's book
    070.1
  (il) Bentley, N. The young producer's video
    book   **791.45**

Aronson, Billy
  Meteors (4 and up)   **523.5**
Around my room. Smith, W. J.   **811**
Around-the-house history [series]
  Lauber, P. What you never knew about fingers,
    forks, & chopsticks   **394.1**
Around the pond: who's been here? George, L. B.
  See note under George, L. B. In the woods:
  who's been here?   **E**
Around the world in a hundred years. Fritz, J.
    910.4
Around the world: who's been here? George, L.
  B. See note under George, L. B. In the
  woods: who's been here?   **E**
The **arrant** fool. Afanas'ev, A. N.
  In Afanas'ev, A. N. Russian fairy tales p334-
  36   **398.2**
Arrington, Frances
  Bluestem (4-6)   **Fic**
The **arrow** over the door. Bruchac, J.   **Fic**
Arrow to the sun. McDermott, G.   **398.2**
Arrowhead Finger. Bruchac, J.
  In Bruchac, J. The girl who married the
  Moon p13-20   **398.2**
Arroz con leche (k-3)   **782.42**
Art
  See/See also pages in the following book(s):
  Bauer, C. F. Celebrations p1-24   **808.8**
      Museums
    See Art museums
Art, African *See* African art
Art, American *See* American art
Art, Indian *See* Native American art
Art, Jewish *See* Jewish art and symbolism
Art, Prehistoric *See* Prehistoric art
Art appreciation
  Beckett, W. A child's book of prayer in art
    (3-6)   **242**
  Brown, L. K. Visiting the art museum (k-3)
    708
  Micklethwait, L. A child's book of art: discover
    great paintings (3-6)   **701**
  Micklethwait, L. A child's book of art: great
    pictures, first words (k-2)   **701**
  Micklethwait, L. A child's book of play in art
    (k-3)   **701**
  Micklethwait, L. I spy: an alphabet in art
    E
Art around the world [series]
  Finley, C. The art of African masks   **391**
The **art** box. Gibbons, G.   **702.8**
Art dog. Hurd, T.   **E**
Art industries and trade *See* Decorative arts
Art museums
    See also names of individual art museums
  Brown, L. K. Visiting the art museum (k-3)
    708
  Thomson, P. The nine-ton cat: behind the scenes
    at an art museum (4 and up)   **708**
The **art** of African masks. Finley, C.   **391**
The **art** of Eric Carle. Carle, E.   **741.6**

The **art** of making comic books. Pellowski, M.
741.5

The **art** of the story-teller. Shedlock, M. L.
372.6

ArtEdventures. (3-6) See entry in Part 2: Web Resources

Arthur, King
About
Crossley-Holland, K. The world of King Arthur and his court (5 and up) **942.01**

Giblin, J. The dwarf, the giant, and the unicorn (3-5) **398.2**

Green, R. L. King Arthur and his Knights of the Round Table (5 and up) **398.2**

Riordan, J. King Arthur (5 and up) **398.2**

Sabuda, R. Arthur and the sword (k-3)
398.2

Sutcliff, R. The light beyond the forest (4 and up) **398.2**

Sutcliff, R. The road to Camlann (4 and up)
398.2

Sutcliff, R. The sword and the circle (4 and up)
398.2

Talbott, H. Excalibur (3-5) **398.2**

Talbott, H. King Arthur and the Round Table (3-5) **398.2**

See/See also pages in the following book(s):
Shedlock, M. L. The art of the story-teller p173-78 **372.6**
Fiction
Bulla, C. R. The sword in the tree (3-5)
Fic

Morpurgo, M. Arthur, high king of Britain (4 and up) **Fic**

White, T. H. The sword in the stone (4 and up)
Fic

Yolen, J. The dragon's boy (5 and up) **Fic**

Arthur, Chester Alan, 1829-1886
About
Simon, C. Chester A. Arthur: twenty-first president of the United States (4 and up) **92**

Arthur and the sword. Sabuda, R. **398.2**

Arthur babysits. Brown, M. T. See note under Brown, M. T. Arthur's nose **E**

Arthur, for the very first time. MacLachlan, P.
Fic

Arthur goes to camp. Brown, M. T. See note under Brown, M. T. Arthur's nose **E**

Arthur, high king of Britain. Morpurgo, M.
Fic

Arthur in the cave. Thomas, W. J.
In Shedlock, M. L. The art of the story-teller p173-78 **372.6**

Arthur lost and found. Brown, M. T. See note under Brown, M. T. Arthur's nose **E**

Arthur meets the president. Brown, M. T. See note under Brown, M. T. Arthur's nose
E

Arthur writes a story. Brown, M. T. See note under Brown, M. T. Arthur's nose **E**

Arthurian romances
See also Grail
Giblin, J. The dwarf, the giant, and the unicorn (3-5) **398.2**

Green, R. L. King Arthur and his Knights of the Round Table (5 and up) **398.2**

Hastings, S. Sir Gawain and the loathly lady (3 and up) **398.2**

Hodges, M. The kitchen knight (3 and up)
398.2

Morpurgo, M. Arthur, high king of Britain (4 and up) **Fic**

Paterson, K. Parzival (5 and up) **398.2**

Riordan, J. King Arthur (5 and up) **398.2**

Sabuda, R. Arthur and the sword (k-3)
398.2

Sutcliff, R. The light beyond the forest (4 and up) **398.2**

Sutcliff, R. The road to Camlann (4 and up)
398.2

Sutcliff, R. The sword and the circle (4 and up)
398.2

Talbott, H. Excalibur (3-5) **398.2**

Talbott, H. King Arthur and the Round Table (3-5) **398.2**

Arthur's April Fool. Brown, M. T. See note under Brown, M. T. Arthur's nose **E**

Arthur's baby. Brown, M. T. See note under Brown, M. T. Arthur's nose **E**

Arthur's back to school day. Hoban, L. See note under Hoban, L. Arthur's Christmas cookies
E

Arthur's birthday. Brown, M. T. See note under Brown, M. T. Arthur's nose **E**

Arthur's birthday party. Hoban, L. See note under Hoban, L. Arthur's Christmas cookies **E**

Arthur's camp-out. Hoban, L. See note under Hoban, L. Arthur's Christmas cookies **E**

Arthur's chicken pox. Brown, M. T. See note under Brown, M. T. Arthur's nose **E**

Arthur's Christmas. Brown, M. T. See note under Brown, M. T. Arthur's nose **E**

Arthur's Christmas cookies. Hoban, L. **E**

Arthur's computer disaster. Brown, M. T. See note under Brown, M. T. Arthur's nose
E

Arthur's eyes. Brown, M. T. See note under Brown, M. T. Arthur's nose **E**

Arthur's family vacation. Brown, M. T. See note under Brown, M. T. Arthur's nose **E**

Arthur's first sleepover. Brown, M. T. See note under Brown, M. T. Arthur's nose **E**

Arthur's funny money. Hoban, L. See note under Hoban, L. Arthur's Christmas cookies **E**

Arthur's great big valentine. Hoban, L. See note under Hoban, L. Arthur's Christmas cookies
E

Arthur's Halloween. Brown, M. T. See note under Brown, M. T. Arthur's nose **E**

Arthur's Halloween costume. Hoban, L. See note under Hoban, L. Arthur's Christmas cookies
E

Arthur's Honey Bear. Hoban, L. See note under Hoban, L. Arthur's Christmas cookies **E**

Arthur's loose tooth. Hoban, L. See note under Hoban, L. Arthur's Christmas cookies **E**

Arthur's new puppy. Brown, M. T. See note under Brown, M. T. Arthur's nose **E**

Asbjornsen, Peter Christen, 1812-1885—*Continued*

The three billy goats gruff
In Tomie dePaola's favorite nursery tales p42-45   **398.2**

The three sisters who were entrapped into a mountain
In Womenfolk and fairy tales p156-63   **398.2**

Why the sea is salt
In The Blue fairy book p136-40   **398.2**

Asch, Frank

Baby Bird's first nest   **E**

Barnyard lullaby   **E**

Good night Baby Bear. See note under Asch, F. Moonbear's dream   **E**

Goodbye house. See note under Asch, F. Moonbear's dream   **E**

Happy birthday, Moon. See note under Asch, F. Moonbear's dream   **E**

Just like Daddy. See note under Asch, F. Moonbear's dream   **E**

Moonbear's dream   **E**

Moonbear's pet. See note under Asch, F. Moonbear's dream   **E**

Mooncake. See note under Asch, F. Moonbear's dream   **E**

Moondance. See note under Asch, F. Moonbear's dream   **E**

Moongame. See note under Asch, F. Moonbear's dream   **E**

One man show (1-3)   **92**

Asch, Jan

(il) Asch, F. One man show   **92**

Ash, Russell

Incredible comparisons (4 and up)   **031.02**

Ash. McCaughrean, G.
In McCaughrean, G. The silver treasure: myths and legends of the world p42-50   **398.2**

Ashabranner, Brent K., 1921-

The new African Americans (4 and up)   **305.8**

Their names to live (6 and up)   **959.704**

Ashabranner, Jennifer

(il) Ashabranner, B. K. The new African Americans   **305.8**

(il) Ashabranner, B. K. Their names to live   **959.704**

Ashanti (African people)
Folklore

Aardema, V. Oh, Kojo! How could you! (k-3)   **398.2**

Courlander, H. Cow-tail switch, and other West African stories (4-6)   **398.2**

McDermott, G. Anansi the spider (k-3)   **398.2**

Mollel, T. M. Ananse's feast (k-3)   **398.2**

Ashanti to Zulu: African traditions. Musgrove, M.   **960**

Ashby, Gil

(il) Greenfield, E. Rosa Parks   **92**

Ashe, Arthur

See/See also pages in the following book(s):

Krull, K. Lives of the athletes p75-77 (4 and up)   **920**

Ashes. Babbitt, N.
In Babbitt, N. The Devil's storybook p63-71   **S C**

Ashforth, Camilla

(il) Waddell, M. Who do you love?   **E**

Ashley Bryan's ABC of African-American poetry (k-3)   **811.008**

Ashley Bryan's African tales, uh-huh. Bryan, A.   **398.2**

Ashpet
In Grandfather tales p115-23   **398.2**

The **Ashwater** experiment. Koss, A. G.   **Fic**

Asian Americans

Sakurai, G. Asian-Americans in the old West (4-6)   **978**

Asian-Americans in the old West. Sakurai, G.   **978**

Ask Mr. Bear. Flack, M.   **E**

Ask the bones. Olson, A. N.
In Olson, A. N. Ask the bones: scary stories from around the world p30-36   **398.2**

Ask the bones: scary stories from around the world. Olson, A. N.   **398.2**

ASPCA pet care guides for kids [series]

Evans, M. Fish   **639.34**

The **ass.** Philip, N.
In Philip, N. The Arabian nights p77-78   **398.2**

The **ass,** the table and the stick. Jacobs, J.
In Jacobs, J. English fairy tales p203-07   **398.2**

Assateague Island National Seashore (Md. and Va.)
Fiction

Henry, M. Misty of Chincoteague (4 and up)   **Fic**

Association for Educational Communications and Technology

American Association of School Librarians. Information power   **027.8**

Association for Library Service to Children

The Newbery and Caldecott awards. See The Newbery and Caldecott awards   **028.5**

Aster Aardvark's alphabet adventures. Kellogg, S.   **E**

Asteroid impact. Henderson, D.   **567.9**

Asteroids

Henderson, D. Asteroid impact (3-5)   **567.9**

Kraske, R. Asteroids (5 and up)   **523.4**

Marsh, C. S. Asteroids, comets, and meteors (4-6)   **523.6**

Simon, S. Comets, meteors, and asteroids (3-6)   **523.6**

Vogt, G. Asteroids, comets, and meteors (2-4)   **523.6**

Asteroids, comets, and meteors. Marsh, C. S.   **523.6**

Asteroids, comets, and meteors. Vogt, G.   **523.6**

Astro bunnies. Loomis, C. See note under Loomis, C. Cowboy bunnies   **E**

Astronautics

   See also Space flight

   Barton, B. I want to be an astronaut   **E**

   Cole, M. D. Hubble Space Telescope (4 and up)   **522**

   Cole, M. D. Space emergency (4 and up)   **629.45**

   Dyson, M. J. Space station science (4 and up)   **629.45**

Accidents

   See Space vehicle accidents

Astronauts

   Branley, F. M. Floating in space (k-3)   **629.47**

   Bredeson, C. John Glenn returns to orbit (4 and up)   **629.4**

   Brown, D. One giant leap: the story of Neil Armstrong (k-3)   **92**

   Burns, K. Black stars in orbit (4 and up)   **920**

   Cole, M. D. Astronauts (4 and up)   **629.45**

   See/See also pages in the following book(s):

   Haskins, J. Black eagles p138-71 (5 and up)   **629.13**

Astronomers

   Ferris, J. What are you figuring now? a story about Benjamin Banneker (3-5)   **92**

   Fisher, L. E. Galileo (4 and up)   **92**

   Fradin, D. B. The planet hunters (5 and up)   **523.4**

   Hinman, B. Benjamin Banneker (4 and up)   **92**

   Lasky, K. The librarian who measured the earth [biography of Eratosthenes] (2-5)   **92**

   Pinkney, A. D. Dear Benjamin Banneker (2-4)   **92**

   Sis, P. Starry messenger [biography of Galileo Galilei]   **92**

Fiction

   Hopkinson, D. Maria's comet   **E**

Astronomy

   See also Constellations; Sky; Stars

   Berger, M. Do stars have points? (2-4)   **523**

   Bond, P. DK guide to space (4 and up)   **520**

   Campbell, A. The New York Public Library amazing space (5 and up)   **520**

   Cole, J. The magic school bus, lost in the solar system (2-4)   **523**

   Cole, M. D. Hubble Space Telescope (4 and up)   **522**

   Ford, H. The young astronomer (4 and up)   **520**

   Fradin, D. B. The planet hunters (5 and up)   **523.4**

   Hirst, R. My place in space (2-4)   **520**

   Mechler, G. National Audubon Society first field guide: night sky (4 and up)   **520**

   Mitton, J. The Scholastic encyclopedia of space   **520**

   Stott, C. Night sky (3-5)   **520**

   VanCleave, J. P. Janice VanCleave's constellations for every kid (4 and up)   **523.8**

   The Visual dictionary of the universe (4 and up)   **520**

   Wilsdon, C. The solar system: an A-Z guide   **520.3**

Periodicals

   Odyssey   **520.5**

At her majesty's request [biography of Sarah Forbes Bonetta] Myers, W. D.   **92**

At the back of the North Wind. MacDonald, G.   **Fic**

At the beach. Delacre, L.

   In Delacre, L. Salsa stories p18-27   **S C**

At the beach. Lee, H. V.   **495.1**

At the beach. Rockwell, A. F.   **E**

At the crossroads. Isadora, R.   **E**

At the Hotel Larry. Pinkwater, D. M. See note under Pinkwater, D. M. Young Larry   **E**

At the wish of the fish. Lewis, J. P.   **398.2**

Ata, Te, 1895-1995

   Moroney, L. Baby rattlesnake   **398.2**

Atalanta the huntress. Yolen, J.

   In Yolen, J. Not one damsel in distress p1-10   **398.2**

Athletes

   See also African American athletes; Women athletes

   Knapp, R. Top 10 American men's Olympic gold medalists (4 and up)   **920**

   Krull, K. Lives of the athletes (4 and up)   **920**

   Littlefield, B. Champions (5 and up)   **920**

Athletics

   See also Sports; Track athletics

Atkin, S. Beth

   Voices from the fields (5 and up)   **331.5**

Atkins, Jeannine, 1953-

   Mary Anning and the sea dragon (k-3)   **92**

Atkinson, Mary, 1938-

   The Snake book. See The Snake book   **597.9**

Atlantis

   Balit, C. Atlantis (2-4)   **398.2**

Atlases

   DK student atlas   **912**

   Goode's world atlas   **912**

   Millennium world atlas   **912**

   National Geographic atlas of the world   **912**

   National Geographic world atlas for young explorers (3-6)   **912**

   Rand McNally children's atlas of the United States (4-6)   **912**

   Rand McNally children's world atlas (4-6)   **912**

   Wright, D. The Facts on File children's atlas   **912**

Atmosphere

   See also Air; Sky

Atocha (Ship) *See* Nuestra Señora de Atocha (Ship)

Atomic bomb

Physiological effect

   Coerr, E. Sadako [biography of Sadako Sasaki] (1-4)   **92**

Atomic bomb—Physiological effect—*Continued*
Coerr, E. Sadako and the thousand paper cranes [biography of Sadako Sasaki] (3-6) **92**

Atomic energy *See* Nuclear energy

Atomic theory
Gallant, R. A. The ever changing atom (5 and up) **539.7**

Atoms
Gallant, R. A. The ever changing atom (5 and up) **539.7**

Atonement, Day of *See* Yom Kippur

Attaboy, Sam!. Lowry, L. See note under Lowry, L. Anastasia Krupnik **Fic**

Attention deficit disorder
Fiction
Gantos, J. Joey Pigza swallowed the key (5 and up) **Fic**

Attucks, Crispus, d. 1770
See/See also pages in the following book(s):
Haskins, J. One more river to cross (4 and up) **920**

Atwater, Florence Carroll, 1896-1979
(jt. auth) Atwater, R. T. Mr. Popper's penguins **Fic**

Atwater, Richard Tupper, 1892-1948
Mr. Popper's penguins (3-5) **Fic**

Atwell, Debby, 1953-
Barn **E**

Auch, Herm
(il) Auch, M. J. I was a third grade science project **Fic**

Auch, Mary Jane
Bantam of the opera **E**
Frozen summer (4 and up) **Fic**
Hen Lake. See note under Auch, M. J. Peeping Beauty **E**
I was a third grade science project (2-4) **Fic**
Journey to nowhere (4 and up) **Fic**
Peeping Beauty **E**
The road to home (4 and up) **Fic**

Audio video market place. See AV market place **371.3025**

Audiobooks
Following titles have audiobook versions:
Aardema, V. Bringing the rain to Kapiti Plain **398.2**
Adams, R. Watership Down **Fic**
Adler, D. A. A picture book of Martin Luther King, Jr. **92**
Alexander, L. The Arkadians **Fic**
Alexander, L. The cat who wished to be a man **Fic**
Allard, H. Miss Nelson is missing! **E**
Almond, D. Kit's wilderness **Fic**
Almond, D. Skellig **Fic**
Armstrong, W. H. Sounder **Fic**
Babbitt, N. Kneeknock Rise **Fic**
Babbitt, N. The search for delicious **Fic**
Babbitt, N. Tuck everlasting **Fic**
Bang, M. Wiley and the Hairy Man **398.2**
Banks, L. R. The Indian in the cupboard **Fic**
Barrie, J. M. Peter Pan **Fic**

Bauer, M. D. On my honor **Fic**
Baum, L. F. The Wizard of Oz **Fic**
Bemelmans, L. Madeline **E**
Bemelmans, L. See Bemelmans, L. Madeline's rescue **E**
Billingsley, F. The Folk Keeper **Fic**
Blume, J. Are you there God? it's me, Margaret **Fic**
Blume, J. Otherwise known as Sheila the Great **Fic**
Blume, J. Tales of a fourth grade nothing **Fic**
Bonsall, C. N. The case of the hungry stranger **E**
Branford, H. Fire, bed, & bone **Fic**
Branley, F. M. Air is all around you **551.5**
Brett, J. Annie and the wild animals **E**
Brown, M. Stone soup **398.2**
Brown, M. W. Big red barn **E**
Brown, M. W. Goodnight moon **E**
Brown, M. W. The runaway bunny **E**
Bunting, E. Ghost's hour, spook's hour **E**
Bunting, E. How many days to America? **E**
Bunting, E. The Mother's Day mice **E**
Bunting, E. A perfect Father's Day **E**
Bunting, E. Scary, scary Halloween **E**
Burch, R. Queenie Peavy **Fic**
Burnett, F. H. A little princess **Fic**
Burnett, F. H. The secret garden **Fic**
Burton, V. L. Katy and the big snow **E**
Burton, V. L. See Burton, V. L. The little house **E**
Byars, B. C. The Golly sisters go West **E**
Byars, B. C. My brother, Ant **E**
Byars, B. C. The pinballs **Fic**
Byars, B. C. The summer of the swans **Fic**
Calhoun, M. Cross-country cat **E**
Cannon, J. Stellaluna **E**
Carlson, N. L. I like me! **E**
Carroll, L. Alice's adventures in Wonderland **Fic**
Christelow, E. Five little monkeys jumping on the bed **E**
Cleary, B. The mouse and the motorcycle **Fic**
Cleary, B. Ramona the pest **Fic**
Clements, A. Frindle **Fic**
Clements, A. The janitor's boy **Fic**
Coatsworth, E. J. The cat who went to heaven **Fic**
Coerr, E. The big balloon race **E**
Coerr, E. The Josefina story quilt **E**
Coerr, E. Sadako and the thousand paper cranes **92**
Cohen, B. The carp in the bathtub **Fic**
Collier, J. L. My brother Sam is dead **Fic**
Coman, C. What Jamie saw **Fic**
Conly, J. L. Crazy lady! **Fic**
Conly, J. L. While no one was watching **Fic**
Cooney, B. Miss Rumphius **E**
Cooper, S. King of shadows **Fic**
Coville, B. Jennifer Murdley's toad **Fic**
Coville, B. Jeremy Thatcher, dragon hatcher **Fic**

Audiobooks—*Continued*

McDermott, G. See McDermott, G. Arrow to the sun **398.2**
McPhail, D. M. The bear's toothache **E**
Milne, A. A. When we were very young **821**
Milne, A. A. Winnie-the-Pooh **Fic**
Minarik, E. H. Little Bear **E**
Monjo, F. N. The drinking gourd **E**
Montgomery, L. M. Anne of Green Gables **Fic**
Naylor, P. R. Shiloh **Fic**
Nesbit, E. Five children and it **Fic**
O'Dell, S. Island of the Blue Dolphins **Fic**
Palatini, M. Piggie pie! **E**
Parish, P. Amelia Bedelia **E**
Paterson, K. Bridge to Terabithia **Fic**
Paulsen, G. The haymeadow **Fic**
Payne, E. Katy No-Pocket **E**
Peck, R. A long way from Chicago **Fic**
Peck, R. N. A day no pigs would die **Fic**
Peck, R. N. Soup **Fic**
Peet, B. Big bad Bruce **E**
Peet, B. The whingdingdilly **E**
Perkins, L. R. All alone in the universe **Fic**
Pfeffer, W. From tadpole to frog **597.8**
Polacco, P. The trees of the dancing goats **E**
Pomerantz, C. The outside dog **E**
Potter, B. The tailor of Gloucester **E**
Prelutsky, J. A pizza the size of the sun **811**
Prelutsky, J. Rolling Harvey down the hill **811**
Prelutsky, J. Something big has been here **811**
Rawls, W. Where the red fern grows **Fic**
Rey, H. A. Curious George **E**
Robinson, B. The best Christmas pageant ever **Fic**
Rockwell, T. How to eat fried worms **Fic**
Rodgers, M. Freaky Friday **Fic**
Rowling, J. K. Harry Potter and the sorcerer's stone **Fic**
Rylant, C. A fine white dust **Fic**
Rylant, C. Missing May **Fic**
Sachar, L. Holes **Fic**
Sachar, L. Wayside School gets a little stranger **Fic**
Schulman, J. The nutcracker **Fic**
Schwartz, A. Ghosts! **398.2**
Schwartz, A. More scary stories to tell in the dark **398.2**
Scott, A. H. On Mother's lap **E**
Selden, G. The cricket in Times Square **Fic**
Seuss, Dr. The cat in the hat **E**
Seuss, Dr. Green eggs and ham **E**
Seuss, Dr. How the Grinch stole Christmas **E**
Sharmat, M. W. Mitchell is moving **E**
Shaw, N. Sheep in a jeep **E**
Shulevitz, U. Snow **E**
Silverstein, S. Where the sidewalk ends **811**
Slobodkina, E. Caps for sale **E**

Smith, R. K. Chocolate fever **Fic**
Soto, G. Baseball in April, and other stories **S C**
Speare, E. G. The sign of the beaver **Fic**
Sperry, A. Call it courage **Fic**
Spyri, J. Heidi **Fic**
Stevenson, J. "Could be worse!" **E**
Stewart, S. The gardener **E**
Sutcliff, R. Black ships before Troy **883**
Taylor, S. All-of-a-kind family **Fic**
Taylor, T. The cay **Fic**
Thayer, J. The puppy who wanted a boy **E**
Thompson, K. Switchers **Fic**
Tolkien, J. R. R. The hobbit **Fic**
Travers, P. L. Mary Poppins **Fic**
Tresselt, A. R. Hide and seek fog **E**
Treviño, E. B. de. I, Juan de Pareja **Fic**
Turner, A. W. Through moon and stars and night skies **E**
Turner, M. W. The thief **Fic**
Twain, M. The adventures of Huckleberry Finn **Fic**
Twain, M. The adventures of Tom Sawyer **Fic**
Van Allsburg, C. The garden of Abdul Gasazi **E**
Van Allsburg, C. See Van Allsburg, C. Jumanji **E**
Van Allsburg, C. See Van Allsburg, C. The Polar Express **E**
Verne, J. 20,000 leagues under the sea **Fic**
Voigt, C. Dicey's song **Fic**
Waber, B. Ira sleeps over **E**
Waber, B. Lyle, Lyle, crocodile **E**
Ward, L. K. See Ward, L. K. The biggest bear **E**
Wells, R. Noisy Nora **E**
White, E. B. Charlotte's web **Fic**
White, E. B. Stuart Little **Fic**
White, E. B. The trumpet of the swan **Fic**
White, R. Belle Prater's boy **Fic**
Wiesner, D. Hurricane **E**
Williams, L. The little old lady who was not afraid of anything **E**
Winthrop, E. The castle in the attic **Fic**
Winthrop, E. Shoes **E**
Wisniewski, D. Rain player **E**
Wojciechowski, S. The Christmas miracle of Jonathan Toomey **E**
Wolff, V. E. Bat 6 **Fic**
Wood, A. The napping house **E**
Wright, B. R. The dollhouse murders **Fic**

Reviews

AudioFile **028.1**
AudioFile **028.1**
Audiovisual materials

Catalogs

Adamson, L. G. Literature connections to American history, K-6 **016.973**
Adamson, L. G. Literature connections to world history, K-6 **016.9**
The Elementary school library collection **011.6**

Directories

AV market place **371.3025**

Audiovisual materials—*Continued*
Reviews
Science Books & Films   **016.5**

August, Louise
  (il) Jaffe, N. In the month of Kislev   **E**
  (il) Jaffe, N. The way meat loves salt
    398.2
  (il) Musleah, R. Why on this night?   **296.4**

Aulnoy, Madame d', 1650 or 51-1705
  The Blue Bird
    In The Green fairy book p1-26   **398.2**
  Felicia and the pot of pinks
    In The Blue fairy book p148-56   **398.2**
  The story of Pretty Goldilocks
    In The Blue fairy book p193-205   **398.2**
  The White Cat
    In The Blue fairy book p157-73   **398.2**
  The wonderful sheep
    In The Blue fairy book p214-30   **398.2**
  The yellow dwarf
    In The Blue fairy book p30-50   **398.2**
    In The Classic fairy tales p68-80   **398.2**
  San Souci, R. The white cat   **398.2**

Aunt Clara Brown. Lowery, L.   **92**

Aunt Flossie's hats (and crab cakes later). How-
ard, E. F.   **E**

Aunt Harriet's Underground Railroad in the sky.
Ringgold, F.   **E**

Aunt Minnie McGranahan. Prigger, M. S.   **E**

Aunt Nancy and Cousin Lazybones. Root, P.
    E

Aunt Nancy and old man trouble. Root, P. See
note under Root, P. Aunt Nancy and Cousin
Lazybones   **E**

Aunt Pitty Patty's piggy. Aylesworth, J.
    398.2

Aunts
Fiction
Caines, J. F. Just us women   **E**
Couloumbis, A. Getting near to baby (5 and up)
    Fic
Fox, P. The village by the sea (5 and up)
    Fic
Horvath, P. The trolls (3-6)   **Fic**
Howard, E. F. Aunt Flossie's hats (and crab
cakes later)   **E**
Irwin, H. The original Freddie Ackerman (5 and
up)   **Fic**
Lisle, J. T. The lost flower children (4-6)
    Fic
MacLachlan, P. Seven kisses in a row (2-4)
    Fic
Prigger, M. S. Aunt Minnie McGranahan   **E**
Ross, A. In the quiet (5 and up)   **Fic**
Wiggin, K. D. S. Rebecca of Sunnybrook Farm
(4 and up)   **Fic**
Wright, B. R. Nothing but trouble (4 and up)
    Fic

Aurora means dawn. Sanders, S. R.   **E**
Auroras
Souza, D. M. Northern lights (4-6)   **538**
Austen, Jane, 1775-1817
See/See also pages in the following book(s):
  Krull, K. Lives of the writers p24-27 (4 and up)
    920

The **austere** academy. Snicket, L. See note under
Snicket, L. The bad beginning   **Fic**
Australia
Heinrichs, A. Australia (4 and up)   **994**
Meisel, J. D. Australia (4 and up)   **994**
Petersen, D. Australia (2-4)   **994**
Fiction
Arnold, M. D. The pumpkin runner   **E**
Baker, J. The hidden forest   **E**
Baker, J. Where the forest meets the sea   **E**
Baker, J. Window   **E**
Honey, E. Don't pat the wombat! (4-6)   **Fic**
Morpurgo, M. Wombat goes walkabout   **E**
Vaughan, M. Snap!   **E**
Winch, J. The old woman who loved to read
    E

Austria
Fiction
Härtling, P. Crutches (5 and up)   **Fic**
Orgel, D. The devil in Vienna (6 and up)
    Fic
Author. Lester, H.   **92**
Author talk (4 and up)   **028.5**
Authors
    See also Women authors
Author talk (4 and up)   **028.5**
Christelow, E. What do authors do? (1-3)
    808
Gillespie, J. T. The Newbery companion
    028.5
Hey! listen to this   **028.5**
Krull, K. Lives of the writers (4 and up)
    920
The Newbery & Caldecott medal books, 1986-
2000   **028.5**
Newbery and Caldecott Medal books, 1966-1975
    028.5
Newbery and Caldecott Medal books, 1976-1985
    028.5
Newbery Medal books, 1922-1955   **028.5**
Origins of story   **808.06**
Dictionaries
Eighth book of junior authors and illustrators
    920.003
Something about the author   **920.003**
Something about the author: autobiography se-
ries   **920.003**
Dictionaries—Indexes
Children's authors and illustrators: an index to
biographical dictionaries   **920.003**
Authors, African American See African
American authors
Authors, American
Ada, A. F. Under the royal palms (4 and up)
    92
Adler, D. A. My writing day (1-3)   **92**
Anderson, W. T. Pioneer girl: the story of Laura
Ingalls Wilder (2-4)   **92**
Asch, F. One man show (1-3)   **92**
Bunting, E. Once upon a time (1-3)   **92**
Byars, B. C. The moon and I (4 and up)
    92
Cole, J. On the bus with Joanna Cole (2-4)
    92
Crews, D. Bigmama's (k-3)   **92**

Avi, 1937-—*Continued*

Night journeys (5 and up)   Fic

Perloo the bold (5 and up)   Fic

Poppy (3-5)   Fic

Poppy and Rye. See note under Avi. Poppy   Fic

Ragweed. See note under Avi. Poppy   Fic

S.O.R. losers (5 and up)   Fic

Something upstairs (5 and up)   Fic

The true confessions of Charlotte Doyle (6 and up)   Fic

What do fish have to do with anything? and other stories (4 and up)   S C

    Contents: What do fish have to do with anything?; The goodness of Matt Kaizer; Talk to me; Teacher tamer; Pets; What's inside; Fortune cookie

Aviation *See* Aeronautics

Aviators *See* Air pilots

Awani Indians *See* Miwok Indians

Awards, Literary *See* Literary prizes

Awesome experiments in electricity & magnetism. Dispezio, M. A.   537

Awesome yo-yo tricks. Levine, S.   796.2

Axelrod, Alan, 1952-

Songs of the Wild West. See Songs of the Wild West   782.42

Axtell, David

(il) We're going on a lion hunt. See We're going on a lion hunt   E

Ayer, Eleanor H.

Colorado

    In Celebrate the states   973

Germany (4 and up)   943

Aylesworth, Jim, 1943-

Aunt Pitty Patty's piggy (k-3)   398.2

The completed hickory dickory dock   398.8

Country crossing   E

The full belly bowl   E

The Gingerbread man (k-3)   398.2

My son John   E

Old black fly   E

Ayres, Becky *See* Hickox, Rebecca

Azarian, Mary

A farmer's alphabet   E

A gardener's alphabet   E

(il) Hurwitz, J. Faraway summer   Fic

(il) Martin, J. B. Snowflake Bentley [biography of Wilson Alwyn Bentley]   92

(il) Saul, C. P. Barn cat   E

See/See also pages in the following book(s):

The Newbery & Caldecott medal books, 1986-2000 p306-16   028.5

The **Aztec** empire. Stein, R. C.   972

Aztecs

Hewitt, S. The Aztecs (1-3)   972

Kimmel, E. A. Montezuma and the fall of the Aztecs (3-5)   972

Stein, R. C. The Aztec empire (4 and up)   972

Tanaka, S. Lost temple of the Aztecs (4 and up)   972

Wood, T. The Aztecs (4 and up)   972

Folklore

Bierhorst, J. Doctor Coyote (1-4)   398.2

Kimmel, E. A. The two mountains (3-5)   398.2

B

B is for Bethlehem. Wilner, I.   E

Baba Yaga & the wise doll. Oram, H.   398.2

Baba Yaga. Afanas'ev, A. N.

    In Afanas'ev, A. N. Russian fairy tales p194-95   398.2

Baba Yaga [another story]. Afanas'ev, A. N.

    In Afanas'ev, A. N. Russian fairy tales p363-65   398.2

Baba Yaga and the brave youth. Afanas'ev, A. N.

    In Afanas'ev, A. N. Russian fairy tales p76-79   398.2

Baba Yaga and Vasilisa the brave. Mayer, M.   398.2

Baba Yaga Bony-Legs. Mayo, M.

    In Mayo, M. Magical tales from many lands p105-15   398.2

Babar and Father Christmas. Brunhoff, J. de See note under Brunhoff, J. de. The story of Babar, the little elephant   E

Babar and his children. Brunhoff, J. de See note under Brunhoff, J. de. The story of Babar, the little elephant   E

Babar and the ghost. Brunhoff, L. de See note under Brunhoff, J. de. The story of Babar, the little elephant   E

Babar and the succotash bird. Brunhoff, L. de See note Brunhoff, J. de. The story of Babar, the little elephant   E

Babar learns to cook. Brunhoff, L. de See note under Brunhoff, J. de. The story of Babar, the little elephant   E

Babar saves the day. Brunhoff, L. de See note under Brunhoff, J. de. The story of Babar, the little elephant   E

Babar the king. Brunhoff, J. de See note under Brunhoff, J. de. The story of Babar, the little elephant   E

Babar's ABC. Brunhoff, L. de See note under Brunhoff, J. de. The story of Babar, the little elephant   E

Babar's book of color. Brunhoff, L. de See note under Brunhoff, J. de. The story of Babar, the little elephant   E

Babar's little girl. Brunhoff, L. de See note under Brunhoff, J. de. The story of Babar, the little elephant   E

Babbitt, Natalie

The Devil's other storybook (4-6)   S C

    Contents: The fortunes of Madame Organza; Justice; The soldier; Boating; How Akbar went to Bethlehem; The signpost; Lessons; The fall and rise of Bathbone; Simple sentences; The ear

The Devil's storybook (4-6)   S C

    Contents: Wishes; The very pretty lady; The harps of Heaven; The imp in the basket; Nuts; A palindrome; Ashes; Perfection; The rose and the minor demon; The power of speech

The eyes of the Amaryllis (5 and up)   Fic

Kneeknock Rise (4-6)   Fic

Ouch! (k-3)   398.2

Babbitt, Natalie—*Continued*

The search for delicious (5 and up)   **Fic**

Tuck everlasting (5 and up)   **Fic**

(il) Worth, V. All the small poems and fourteen more   **811**

The **Babe** & I. Adler, D. A.   **E**

Babe and me. Gutman, D.   **Fic**

Babe: the gallant pig. King-Smith, D.   **Fic**

Babies *See* Infants

Baboons

Fiction

Banks, K. Baboon   **E**

Olaleye, I. Bitter bananas   **E**

Baboushka and the three kings. Robbins, R.   **398.2**

Babushka. McCaughrean, G.

In McCaughrean, G. The silver treasure: myths and legends of the world p75-80   **398.2**

Babushka and the three wise men. Montgomerie, N. M.

In Christmas fairy tales p89-90   **398.2**

Babushka's doll. Polacco, P.   **E**

Babushka's Mother Goose. Polacco, P.   **398.8**

Baby. MacLachlan, P.   **Fic**

The **baby** beebee bird. Massie, D. R.   **E**

Baby Beluga. Raffi   **782.42**

Baby Bird's first nest. Asch, F.   **E**

The **baby** dances. Henderson, K.   **E**

Baby Duck and the bad eyeglasses. Hest, A. See note under Hest, A. In the rain with Baby Duck   **E**

Baby rattlesnake. Moroney, L.   **398.2**

Baby says. Steptoe, J.   **E**

The **baby** sister. De Paola, T.   **E**

A **baby** sister for Frances. Hoban, R. See note under Hoban, R. Bedtime for Frances   **E**

The **baby** Uggs are hatching. Prelutsky, J.   **811**

Baby whales drink milk. Esbensen, B. J.   **599.5**

Baby whale's journey. London, J.   **E**

The **baby** who loved pumpkins. Lester, J.

In Lester, J. The last tales of Uncle Remus p46-48   **398.2**

The **Baby's** bedtime book   **808.81**

The **baby's** catalogue. Ahlberg, J.   **E**

The **baby's** game book. Wilner, I.   **398.8**

The **Baby's** lap book   **398.8**

Babysitters

Fiction

Fox, P. A likely place (3-5)   **Fic**

Babysitting

Fiction

Mills, C. You're a brave man, Julius Zimmerman (5 and up)   **Fic**

Bach, Johann Sebastian, 1685-1750

About

Winter, J. Sebastian: a book about Bach (k-3)   **92**

See/See also pages in the following book(s):

Krull, K. Lives of the musicians p14-17 (4 and up)   **920**

Bachrach, Susan D., 1948-

Tell them we remember (5 and up)   **940.53**

Back home. Pinkney, G. J.   **E**

Back in the beforetime. Curry, J. L.   **398.2**

Back in the spaceship again. Sands, K.   **016.8**

Back of beyond. Ellis, S.   **S C**

Back to school for Rotten Ralph. Gantos, J. See note under Gantos, J. Rotten Ralph   **E**

Back to the wild. Patent, D. H.   **639.9**

Back yard Angel. Delton, J. See note under Delton, J. Angel's mother's wedding   **Fic**

Backyard. Silver, D. M.   **577**

Backyard birds. Latimer, J. P.   **598**

Backyard birds of summer. Lerner, C.   **598**

Backyard buddies [series]

Ross, M. E. Millipedeology   **595.6**

Ross, M. E. Spiderology   **595.4**

Backyard hunter: the praying mantis. Lavies, B.   **595.7**

Bacon, Joan Chase *See* Bowden, Joan Chase, 1925-

Bacon, Josephine, 1942-

Cooking the Israeli way

In Easy menu ethnic cookbooks   **641.5**

Bacon, Paul, 1923-

(il) Golenbock, P. Teammates [biography of Jackie Robinson]   **92**

(il) Sandburg, C. The Sandburg treasury   **818**

Bacteria

Berger, M. Germs make me sick! (k-3)   **616.9**

The **bad** beginning. Snicket, L.   **Fic**

A **bad** case of stripes. Shannon, D.   **E**

Bad day at Riverbend. Van Allsburg, C.   **E**

Bad dreams. Fine, A.   **Fic**

Bad Heart Buffalo, Amos, ca. 1869-1913

(il) Freedman, R. The life and death of Crazy Horse   **92**

Bad Heart Bull, Amos *See* Bad Heart Buffalo, Amos, ca. 1869-1913

The **bad** news. Schwartz, A.

In From sea to shining sea p311   **810.8**

A **bad** road for cats. Rylant, C.

In Rylant, C. Every living thing p56-65   **S C**

The **bad** wife. Afanas'ev, A. N.

In Afanas'ev, A. N. Russian fairy tales p56-57   **398.2**

Baddiel, Ivor

Ultimate soccer (4 and up)   **796.334**

Badgers

Fiction

Bunting, E. Can you do this, Old Badger?   **E**

Eckert, A. W. Incident at Hawk's Hill (6 and up)   **Fic**

Hoban, R. Bedtime for Frances   **E**

Baer, Lore, 1938-
About
Adler, D. A. Hiding from the Nazis (2-4)
940.53
The **bag** I'm taking to Grandma's. Neitzel, S.
E
Bagnold, Enid
National Velvet (5 and up)   Fic
Bahamas
Barlas, R. Bahamas (5 and up)   972.96
Hintz, M. The Bahamas (4 and up)   972.96
Poetry
Greenfield, E. Under the Sunday tree (2-4)
811
Bahti, Tom, 1926-1972
(il) Baylor, B. When clay sings   970.004
Bailey, Carolyn Sherwin, 1875-1961
See/See also pages in the following book(s):
Newbery Medal books, 1922-1955 p290-99
028.5
Bailey, John
Fishing (4 and up)   799.1
Bailey, Peter, 1946-
(il) King-Smith, D. Spider Sparrow   Fic
Baja California (Mexico: Peninsula)
Fiction
O'Dell, S. The black pearl (6 and up)   Fic
Baker, Augusta, 1911-1998
(jt. auth) Greene, E. Storytelling   372.6
Baker, Barbara, 1947-
Digby and Kate. See note under Baker, B. Digby and Kate and the beautiful day   E
Digby and Kate again. See note under Baker, B. Digby and Kate and the beautiful day   E
Digby and Kate and the beautiful day   E
One Saturday afternoon   E
Baker, Charles
The Christmas doubters
In The Big book of Christmas plays p265-74
808.82
Baker, Christopher W., 1956-
Scientific visualization (5 and up)   006
Virtual reality (5 and up)   006
Baker, Daniel B.
(ed) Explorers & discoverers. See Explorers & discoverers   920.003
Baker, Ella, 1903-1986
See/See also pages in the following book(s):
Hansen, J. Women of hope p12-13 (4 and up)
920
Baker, Jeannie
The hidden forest   E
Where the forest meets the sea   E
Window   E
Baker, Josephine, 1906-1975
Fiction
Schroeder, A. Ragtime Tumpie   E
Baker, Karen, 1965-
(il) Knock at a star. See Knock at a star
811.008
Baker, Keith, 1953-
Big fat hen   398.8
The magic fan   E

Quack and count   E
Baker, Olaf
Where the buffaloes begin (2-4)   Fic
Baker, Pamela J., 1947-
My first book of sign (k-3)   419
Baker, Sara Josephine, 1873-1945
See/See also pages in the following book(s):
Vare, E. A. Women inventors & their discoveries p67-81 (5 and up)   920
The **baker's** dozen. Forest, H.   398.2
Baking
See also Bread; Cake
Fiction
Hoban, L. Arthur's Christmas cookies   E
Priceman, M. How to make an apple pie and see the world   E
Wood, A. Sweet dream pie   E
Balaam (Biblical figure)
About
Paterson, K. The angel and the donkey (3-5)
222
Balboa, Vasco Núñez de, 1475-1519
See/See also pages in the following book(s):
Fritz, J. Around the world in a hundred years p83-93 (4-6)   910.4
Bald eagle
Gibbons, G. Soaring with the wind (k-3)
598
Morrison, G. Bald eagle (2-4)   598
Baldak Borisievich. Afanas'ev, A. N.
In Afanas'ev, A. N. Russian fairy tales p90-96   398.2
Balder and the mistletoe. McCaughrean, G.
In McCaughrean, G. The crystal pool: myths and legends of the world p102-06
398.2
Baldwin, Guy
Oklahoma
In Celebrate the states   973
Wyoming
In Celebrate the states   973
Balestrino, Philip
The skeleton inside you (k-3)   611
Balian, Lorna
Humbug witch   E
Balit, Christina
Atlantis (2-4)   398.2
Ball, Mary *See* Washington, Mary Ball, 1708-1789
The **ballad** of Lucy Whipple. Cushman, K.
Fic
The **ballad** of the pirate queens. Yolen, J.
811
Ballard, Carol
The heart and circulatory system (5 and up)
612.1
The skeleton and muscular system (5 and up)
612.7
Ballard, Robert D.
Exploring the Titanic (4 and up)   910.4
Ghost liners (4 and up)   910.4

The **banza**. Wolkstein, D.   398.2

Baptists

     See also Mennonites

Bar mitzvah

     Kimmel, E. A. Bar mitzvah (5 and up)
         296.4

Barasch, Lynne

     Radio rescue   E

Barbados

     Elias, M. L. Barbados (5 and up)   972.98

Barber, Antonia, 1932-

     The Mousehole cat   E

Barber, Daniel Wynn

     Tiger in the snow

     In The Oxford book of scary tales p36-43
         808.8

Barber, James, 1952-

     Presidents (3-5)   920

Barbers and barbershops

         Fiction

     Mitchell, M. K. Uncle Jed's barbershop   E

Barbie. Soto, G.

     In Soto, G. Baseball in April, and other stories p33-42   S C

Barbour, Karen

     (il) Herrera, J. F. Laughing out loud, I fly
         811

     (il) Marvelous math. See Marvelous math
         811.008

Bard of Avon: the story of William Shakespeare. Stanley, D.   92

The **Barefoot** book of Buddhist tales. See Chödzin, S. The wisdom of the crows and other Buddhist tales   294.3

A **bargain** for Frances. Hoban, R. See note under Hoban, R. Bedtime for Frances   E

Baring, Maurice, 1874-1945

     The blue rose

     In Shedlock, M. L. The art of the story-teller p204-12   372.6

Bark, George. Feiffer, J.   E

Barkin, Carol, 1944-

     (jt. auth) James, E. How to write super school reports   808

     (jt. auth) James, E. How to write terrific book reports   808

Barkley, James

     (il) Armstrong, W. H. Sounder   Fic

Barlas, Robert

     Bahamas (5 and up)   972.96

     Latvia (5 and up)   947.9

     Uganda (5 and up)   967.6

Barlowe, Wayne Douglas

     (il) Dodson, P. An alphabet of dinosaurs
         567.9

Barn. Atwell, D.   E

The **barn**. Avi   Fic

The **barn** burner. Willis, P.   Fic

Barn cat. Saul, C. P.   E

Barn dance!. Martin, B.   E

The **barn** owls. Johnston, T.   E

Barn savers. High, L. O.   E

Barnard, Alan

     (il) Tanaka, S. Graveyards of the dinosaurs
         567.9

Barner, Bob

     Bugs! Bugs! Bugs! (k-2)   595.7

     Dem bones (k-3)   611

     Fish wish   E

Barnes, Harold

     The proud cock

     In Shedlock, M. L. The art of the story-teller p191-94   372.6

Barnes, Karen

     (il) Berger, M. Why don't haircuts hurt?
         612

Barnes-Svarney, Patricia

     The New York Public Library science desk reference (5 and up)   500

Barnett, Ida B. Wells- See Wells-Barnett, Ida B., 1862-1931

Barnett, Moneta, 1922-1976

     (il) Greenfield, E. Sister   Fic

Barns

         Fiction

     High, L. O. Barn savers   E

Barnum, Jay Hyde, d. 1962

     (il) Tunis, J. R. The Kid from Tomkinsville
         Fic

Barnyard banter. Fleming, D.   E

Barnyard lullaby. Asch, F.   E

Barnyard prayers. Godwin, L.   811

Barnyard song. Greene, R. G.   E

Barr, Catherine

     (ed) From biography to history. See From biography to history   016.8

Barracca, Debra

     The adventures of Taxi Dog   E

     Maxi, the hero. See note under Barracca, D. The adventures of Taxi Dog   E

     Maxi, the star. See note under Barracca, D. The adventures of Taxi Dog   E

     A Taxi Dog Christmas. See note under Barracca, D. The adventures of Taxi Dog
         E

Barracca, Sal

     (jt. auth) Barracca, D. The adventures of Taxi Dog   E

Barrera, Rosalinda B.

     (ed) Kaleidoscope. See Kaleidoscope   011.6

Barrett, Angela

     (il) Andersen, H. C. The emperor's new clothes
         E

     (il) McCaughrean, G. The Random House book of stories from the ballet   792.8

     (il) Poole, J. Joan of Arc   92

     (il) Poole, J. Snow White   398.2

Barrett, John E.

     (il) St. Pierre, S. The Muppets' big book of crafts   745.5

Barrett, Peter, 1935-

     (il) Herriot, J. Moses the kitten   E

Barrett, Robert, 1949-

     (il) Turner, A. W. Dust for dinner   E

The **battle** of birds. Philip, N.
In Philip, N. Celtic fairy tales p15-26
    398.2

The **battle** of Chihaya Castle. Kimmel, E. A.
In Kimmel, E. A. Sword of the samurai p53-62   **Fic**

The **battle** of the drums. McCaughrean, G.
In McCaughrean, G. The bronze cauldron: myths and legends of the world p63-67
    398.2

Bauer, Caroline Feller, 1935-
Caroline Feller Bauer's new handbook for storytellers   **372.6**
Celebrations   **808.8**
Leading kids to books through crafts
    027.62
Leading kids to books through magic
    027.62
Leading kids to books through puppets
    027.62
Marika the snowmaiden
In Snowy day: stories and poems p45-49
    808.8
The poetry break   **372.6**
Read for the fun of it   **027.62**
Supermarket Thanksgiving
In Thanksgiving: stories and poems p57-68
    810.8
This way to books   **028.5**
(ed) Snowy day: stories and poems. See Snowy day: stories and poems   **808.8**
(ed) Thanksgiving: stories and poems. See Thanksgiving: stories and poems   **810.8**

Bauer, Marion Dane, 1938-
If you were born a kitten (k-1)   **591.3**
Jason's bears   **E**
On my honor (4 and up)   **Fic**
What's your story? (5 and up)   **808.3**

Bauermeister, Erica
Let's hear it for the girls   **028.1**

Baugh, Sammy, 1914-
See/See also pages in the following book(s):
Sullivan, G. Quarterbacks! p54-56 (5 and up)
    920

Baum, Froim, 1936-
About
Adler, D. A. Child of the Warsaw ghetto (3-5)
    940.53

Baum, L. Frank (Lyman Frank), 1856-1919
Dorothy and the Wizard in Oz. See note under Baum, L. F. The Wizard of Oz   **Fic**
The glass dog
In American fairy tales p105-15   **S C**
The land of Oz. See note under Baum, L. F. The Wizard of Oz   **Fic**
Little Wizard stories of Oz. See note under Baum, L. F. The Wizard of Oz   **Fic**
The magic of Oz. See note under Baum, L. F. The Wizard of Oz   **Fic**
The marvelous land of Oz. See note under Baum, L. F. The Wizard of Oz   **Fic**
Ozma of Oz. See note under Baum, L. F. The Wizard of Oz   **Fic**
The patchwork girl of Oz. See note under Baum, L. F. The Wizard of Oz   **Fic**

The tin woodsman of Oz. See note under Baum, L. F. The Wizard of Oz   **Fic**
The Wizard of Oz (3-6)   **Fic**

Baum, Lyman Frank *See* Baum, L. Frank (Lyman Frank), 1856-1919

Baumfree, Isabella *See* Truth, Sojourner, d. 1883

Bausum, Ann
Dragon bones and dinosaur eggs: a photobiography of Roy Chapman Andrews (5 and up)   **92**

Baviera, Rocco
(il) Bruchac, J. A boy called Slow: the true story of Sitting Bull   **92**

Bavin (Clark R.) National Fish and Wildlife Forensics Laboratory *See* National Fish and Wildlife Forensics Laboratory

Bawden, Nina, 1925-
Granny the Pag (4 and up)   **Fic**
Humbug (4 and up)   **Fic**

Baxter, Kathleen A.
Gotcha!   **028.1**

Bayard Rustin: behind the scenes of the civil rights movement. Haskins, J.   **92**

Bayer, Jane, d. 1985
A my name is Alice   **E**

Bayley, Nicola, 1949-
(il) Barber, A. The Mousehole cat   **E**

Baylor, Byrd, 1924-
The desert is theirs (1-4)   **577.5**
Hawk, I'm your brother   **E**
The way to start a day (1-4)   **291.4**
When clay sings (1-4)   **970.004**

Baynes, Pauline, 1922-
(il) Lewis, C. S. The lion, the witch, and the wardrobe   **Fic**

Bayou lullaby. Appelt, K.   **E**

Bazler, Judith A.
(ed) Science experiments on file. See Science experiments on file   **507.8**

Be a friend to trees. Lauber, P.   **582.16**

Be first in the universe. Spinner, S.   **Fic**

Be not far from me. Kimmel, E. A.   **221.9**

Be well, Beware. Haas, J. See note under Haas, J. Beware the mare   **Fic**

Bea and Mr. Jones. Schwartz, A.   **E**

Beaches
Rockwell, A. F. At the beach   **E**
Fiction
Brown, M. T. D.W. all wet   **E**
Huneck, S. Sally goes to the beach   **E**
Luciani, B. How will we get to the beach?
    E
Mathers, P. Lottie's new beach towel   **E**

Beacons of light: lighthouses. Gibbons, G.
    387.1

The **beaded** moccasins. Durrant, L.   **Fic**

Bealer, Alex W.
Only the names remain (4-6)   **970.004**

Beamer, Yvonne
(jt. auth) Hirschfelder, A. B. Native Americans today   **970.004**

Beans
Rockwell, A. F. One bean (k-2)   **635**

Beans—*Continued*
See/See also pages in the following book(s):
Johnson, S. A. Tomatoes, potatoes, corn, and beans p26-37 (6 and up) **641.3**

The **bear**. Afanas'ev, A. N.
In Afanas'ev, A. N. Russian fairy tales p74-75 **398.2**

The **bear** and the children. Schwartz, H.
In Schwartz, H. The diamond tree p93-96 **398.2**

The **bear** and the cock. Afanas'ev, A. N.
In Afanas'ev, A. N. Russian fairy tales p455-56 **398.2**

The **bear** boy. Bruchac, J.
In Bruchac, J. Flying with the eagle, racing with the great bear p78-82 **398.2**

A **bear** called Paddington. Bond, M. **Fic**

The **bear-child**. MacDonald, M. R.
In MacDonald, M. R. Look back and see p107-14 **372.6**

The **bear** in the forest. Jaffe, N.
In Jaffe, N. The mysterious visitor p63-75 **398.2**

The **bear** maiden. Curry, J. L.
In Curry, J. L. Turtle Island: tales of the Algonquian nations p103-10 **398.2**

Bear Noel. Dunrea, O. **E**

The **bear**, the dog, and the cat. Afanas'ev, A. N.
In Afanas'ev, A. N. Russian fairy tales p453-55 **398.2**

The **Bear** Woman. Bruchac, J.
In Bruchac, J. The girl who married the Moon p75-83 **398.2**

Beard, Darleen Bailey, 1961-
Twister **E**

Bearden, Romare, 1914-1988
See/See also pages in the following book(s):
Greenberg, J. The American eye p51-59 (6 and up) **920**
Haskins, J. One more river to cross (4 and up) **920**

Beardsley, Aubrey, 1872-1898
(il) Green, R. L. King Arthur and his Knights of the Round Table **398.2**

Bearhead. Kimmel, E. A. **398.2**

Bears
See also Polar bear
Arnosky, J. Every autumn comes the bear **E**
Markle, S. Growing up wild: bears (2-4) **599.78**
Patent, D. H. Looking at bears (3-5) **599.78**

Fiction
Alborough, J. My friend Bear **E**
Alexander, M. G. Blackboard Bear **E**
Asch, F. Moonbear's dream **E**
Baker, B. One Saturday afternoon **E**
Barton, B. The three bears (k-1) **398.2**
Bauer, M. D. Jason's bears **E**
Berenstain, S. Bears on wheels **E**
Bodnar, J. Z. Tale of a tail **E**
Bond, M. A bear called Paddington (2-5) **Fic**

Bond, M. Paddington's storybook (2-5) **S C**
Carlstrom, N. W. Jesse Bear, what will you wear? **E**
Dalgliesh, A. The bears on Hemlock Mountain (1-4) **Fic**
Dunrea, O. Bear Noel **E**
Ernst, L. C. Goldilocks returns **E**
Fox, M. Sleepy bears **E**
Galdone, P. The three bears (k-2) **398.2**
Gliori, D. Mr. Bear's new baby **E**
Johnson, D. B. Henry hikes to Fitchburg **E**
Jonas, A. Two bear cubs **E**
Kimmel, E. A. The Chanukkah guest **E**
Marshall, J. Goldilocks and the three bears (k-2) **398.2**
McCloskey, R. Blueberries for Sal **E**
McLeod, E. The bear's bicycle **E**
McMullan, K. Papa's song **E**
McPhail, D. M. The bear's toothache **E**
McPhail, D. M. Drawing lessons from a bear **E**
Milne, A. A. The complete tales of Winnie-the-Pooh (1-4) **Fic**
Milne, A. A. The house at Pooh Corner (1-4) **Fic**
Milne, A. A. The Pooh story book (1-4) **Fic**
Milne, A. A. Winnie-the-Pooh (1-4) **Fic**
Milne, A. A. The world of Pooh (1-4) **Fic**
Minarik, E. H. Little Bear **E**
Morey, W. Gentle Ben (5 and up) **Fic**
Murphy, J. Peace at last **E**
Peet, B. Big bad Bruce **E**
Rosen, M. We're going on a bear hunt **E**
Stevens, J. Tops and bottoms (k-3) **398.2**
Taylor, H. P. When Bear stole the chinook (k-3) **398.2**
Waddell, M. Can't you sleep, Little Bear? **E**
Ward, L. K. The biggest bear **E**
Wells, R. Edward unready for school **E**
Wiseman, B. Morris and Boris at the circus **E**
Young, R. Golden Bear **E**
Poetry
Yolen, J. The three bears holiday rhyme book (k-2) **811**
Yolen, J. The three bears rhyme book (k-2) **811**

The **bear's** bicycle. McLeod, E. **E**

The **bears'** house. Sachs, M. **Fic**

The **bears** on Hemlock Mountain. Dalgliesh, A. **Fic**

Bears on wheels. Berenstain, S. **E**

The **bear's** toothache. McPhail, D. M. **E**

Bearskin. Pyle, H. **E**

Beast feast. Florian, D. **811**

The **beast** under the wizard's bridge. Strickland, B. *See note under* Strickland, B. John Bellair's Lewis Barnavelt in The specter from the magicians museum **Fic**

The **beasties**. Sleator, W. **Fic**

Beasts in a pit. Afanas′ev, A. N.
 In Afanas′ev, A. N. Russian fairy tales p498
            398.2

A **beasty** story. Martin, B.   **E**

Beat the turtle drum. Greene, C. C. **Fic**

Beattie, Owen
 Buried in ice (4 and up)   **998**

Beatty, Patricia, 1922-1991
 Charley Skedaddle (5 and up)   **Fic**
 Jayhawker (5 and up)   **Fic**
 Turn homeward, Hannalee (5 and up) **Fic**

Beatty, Richard
 Copper
  In The Elements [Benchmark Bks.] **546**
 Phosphorus
  In The Elements [Benchmark Bks.] **546**
 Sulfur
  In The Elements [Benchmark Bks.] **546**

The **beautiful** butterfly. Sierra, J. **398.2**

The **beautiful** Christmas tree. Zolotow, C. **E**

The **beautiful** girl of the moon tower. Hamilton, V.
 In Hamilton, V. The people could fly: American black folktales p53-59
            398.2

Beautiful warrior. McCully, E. A. **E**

Beauty. Wallace, B.   **Fic**

Beauty: a retelling of the story of Beauty & the beast. McKinley, R.   **Fic**

Beauty and the beast. Brett, J. **398.2**

Beauty and the beast. Le Prince de Beaumont, Madame
 In The Classic fairy tales p139-50 **398.2**

Beauty and the beast. Mayer, M. **398.2**

Beauty and the Beast. Steig, J.
 In Steig, J. A handful of beans p33-58
            398.2

Beauty and the beast. Villeneuve, M. de
 In The Blue fairy book p100-19 **398.2**

Beauty and the beast. Willard, N. **398.2**

The **Beauty** of the beast (4-6) **811.008**

The **Beauty** Way—the ceremony of White-Painted Woman. Bruchac, J.
 In Bruchac, J. The girl who married the Moon p84-89   **398.2**

Beaver and Muskrat change tails. Curry, J. L.
 In Curry, J. L. Turtle Island: tales of the Algonquian nations p48-49 **398.2**

Beaver at Long Pond. George, W. T. See note under George, W. T. Box Turtle at Long Pond
              E

Beaver face. Lelooska
 In Lelooska, D. Echoes of the elders p32-38
            398.2

Beavers
 Rounds, G. Beaver (k-3)   **599.3**

Because of Winn-Dixie. DiCamillo, K. **Fic**

Bechstein, Ludwig, 1801-1860
 The three dogs
  In The Green fairy book p360-66 **398.2**
 The three musicians
  In The Green fairy book p353-59 **398.2**

Becket, Thomas à *See* Thomas, à Becket, Saint, Archbishop of Canterbury, 1118?-1170

Beckett, Wendy
 A child's book of prayer in art (3-6) **242**

Become a historical detective. (6 and up) See entry in Part 2: Web Resources

Bed-knob and broomstick. Norton, M. **Fic**

Beddows, Eric, 1951-
 (il) Fleischman, P. I am phoenix: poems for two voices   **811**
 (il) Fleischman, P. Joyful noise: poems for two voices   **811**

Bedford, F. D.
 (il) Barrie, J. M. Peter Pan **Fic**

Bedore, Bernie, 1923-
 The mufferaw catfish
  In Bauer, C. F. Celebrations p85-86
            808.8

Bedtime
Fiction
Apple, M. Brave Martha   **E**
Asch, F. Barnyard lullaby   **E**
Banks, K. And if the moon could talk **E**
Brown, M. W. A child's good night book
              E
Eilenberg, M. Cowboy Kid   **E**
Emberley, E. Go away, big green monster!
              E
Fox, M. Sleepy bears   **E**
Greenstein, E. Dreaming   **E**
Hest, A. Mabel dancing   **E**
Hoban, R. Bedtime for Frances **E**
Lum, K. What! cried Granny   **E**
Murphy, J. A quiet night in   **E**
Rathmann, P. 10 minutes till bedtime **E**
Schnur, S. Night lights   **E**
Spinelli, E. Night shift daddy **E**
Thomas, S. M. Good night, Good Knight
              E
Waddell, M. Can't you sleep, Little Bear?
              E
Waddell, M. Who do you love? **E**
Wood, D. Piggies   **E**
Yolen, J. How do dinosaurs say goodnight?
              E

Bedtime for Frances. Hoban, R. **E**

Bee culture *See* Beekeeping

The **Bee-man** of Orn. Stockton, F.
 In American fairy tales p67-80 **S C**

"Bee my valentine!"**. Cohen, M. See note under Cohen, M. It's George!   **E**

The **bee** tree. Polacco, P.   **E**

Beecher family
About
Fritz, J. Harriet Beecher Stowe and the Beecher preachers (5 and up)   **92**

Beekeeping
 Gibbons, G. The honey makers (k-3) **595.7**

Beeler, Selby B.
 Throw your tooth on the roof (k-3) **398**

Been to yesterdays: poems of a life. Hopkins, L. B.   **811**

Beep beep, vroom vroom!. Murphy, S. J.
              515

Bees

See also Beekeeping

Cole, J. The magic school bus inside a beehive (2-4) **595.7**

Gibbons, G. The honey makers (k-3) **595.7**

Lavies, B. Killer bees (4 and up) **595.7**

Micucci, C. The life and times of the honeybee (2-4) **595.7**

Fiction

Polacco, P. The bee tree **E**

Beethoven, Ludwig van, 1770-1827

See/See also pages in the following book(s):

Krull, K. Lives of the musicians p24-29 (4 and up) **920**

Fiction

Nichol, B. Beethoven lives upstairs (3-5) **Fic**

Beethoven lives upstairs. Nichol, B. **Fic**

The **beetle**. Andersen, H. C.

In Andersen, H. C. The little mermaid and other fairy tales p112-20 **S C**

Beetles

See also Ladybugs

Fiction

Carle, E. The very clumsy click beetle **E**

Beezus and Ramona. Cleary, B. See note under Cleary, B. Ramona the pest **Fic**

Befana (Legendary character)

De Paola, T. The legend of Old Befana (k-3) **398.2**

Begay, Shonto

Navajo (5 and up) **811**

(il) Cohen, C. L. The mud pony **398.2**

The **Beggar** Queen. Alexander, L. **Fic**

The **beggar's** magic. Chang, M. S. **398.2**

The **beggar's** plan. Afanas'ev, A. N.

In Afanas'ev, A. N. Russian fairy tales p599 **398.2**

The **beginning** of the armadilloes. Kipling, R. **Fic**

also in Kipling, R. Just so stories **S C**

Beginning with books. DeSalvo, N. **027.62**

Beginning with the ears. Olson, A. N.

In Olson, A. N. Ask the bones: scary stories from around the world p42-45 **398.2**

Behan, Brendan, 1923-1964

The King of Ireland's son (3-5) **398.2**

Behind rebel lines: the incredible story of Emma Edmonds, Civil War spy. Reit, S. **92**

Behind the attic wall. Cassedy, S. **Fic**

Behind the mask. Heller, R. **428**

Behind the secret window. Toll, N. S. **940.53**

Behler, John L.

National Audubon Society first field guide: reptiles (4 and up) **597.9**

Behold . . . the dragons!. Gibbons, G. **398**

Beier, Ellen

(il) Bulla, C. R. The Paint Brush Kid **Fic**

(il) Walker, S. M. The 18 penny goose **E**

Beil, Karen Magnuson

Fire in their eyes (4 and up) **628.9**

Belarus

Levy, P. M. Belarus (5 and up) **947.8**

Belgium

Burgan, M. Belgium (4 and up) **949.3**

Pateman, R. Belgium (5 and up) **949.3**

Bell, Alexander Graham, 1847-1922

About

Fisher, L. E. Alexander Graham Bell (4 and up) **92**

Gearhart, S. The telephone (4 and up) **621.385**

Matthews, T. L. Always inventing: a photobiography of Alexander Graham Bell (4 and up) **92**

St. George, J. Dear Dr. Bell—your friend, Helen Keller (5 and up) **92**

Bell, Anthea

The nutcracker (2-4) **Fic**

The Snow Queen **E**

Bell, Cool Papa, 1903-1991

See/See also pages in the following book(s):

Brashler, W. The story of Negro league baseball (5 and up) **796.357**

Bell, Currer See Brontë, Charlotte, 1816-1855

Bell, David C.

(il) Pascoe, E. Scholastic kid's almanac for the 21st century **031.02**

Bell, Ellis See Brontë, Emily, 1818-1848

The **bell**. Andersen, H. C.

In Andersen, H. C. The little mermaid and other fairy tales p84-90 **S C**

The **bell**, the book and the spellbinder. Strickland, B. See note under Strickland, B. The hand of the necromancer **Fic**

Bellairs, John

The chessmen of doom. See note under Bellairs, J. The curse of the blue figurine **Fic**

The curse of the blue figurine (5 and up) **Fic**

The doom of the haunted opera. See note under Bellairs, J. The house with a clock in its walls **Fic**

The eyes of the killer robot. See note under Bellairs, J. The curse of the blue figurine **Fic**

The figure in the shadows. See note under Bellairs, J. The house with a clock in its walls **Fic**

The ghost in the mirror. See note under Bellairs, J. The house with a clock in its walls **Fic**

The house with a clock in its walls (5 and up) **Fic**

The letter, the witch, and the ring. See note under Bellairs, J. The house with a clock in its walls **Fic**

The mummy, the will and the crypt. See note under Bellairs, J. The curse of the blue figurine **Fic**

The revenge of the wizard's ghost. See note under Bellairs, J. The curse of the blue figurine **Fic**

The secret of the underground room. See note under Bellairs, J. The curse of the blue figurine **Fic**

Bellairs, John—*Continued*

The spell of the sorcerer's skull. See note under Bellairs, J. The curse of the blue figurine
Fic

The trolley to yesterday. See note under Bellairs, J. The curse of the blue figurine
Fic

The vengeance of the witch-finder. See note under Bellairs, J. The house with a clock in its walls
Fic

Bellan-Gillen, Patricia
(il) Baker, P. J. My first book of sign　419

Belle Prater's boy. White, R.　Fic

Beller, Susan Provost, 1949-
To hold this ground (5 and up)　973.7

The **Bellmaker**. Jacques, B. See note under Jacques, B. Redwall　Fic

The **bells** of Christmas. Hamilton, V.　Fic

Bellville, Cheryl Walsh, 1944-
(il) Berman, R. American bison　599.64
(il) Burns, D. L. Cranberries: fruit of the bogs
634

Belpré, Pura
Tropical memories
In You're on!: seven plays in English and Spanish p34-41　812.008

Bemelmans, Ludwig, 1898-1962
Madeline　E
Madeline and the bad hat. See note under Bemelmans, L. Madeline　E
Madeline and the gypsies. See note under Bemelmans, L. Madeline　E
Madeline in London. See note under Bemelmans, L. Madeline　E
Madeline's Christmas. See note under Bemelmans, L. Madeline　E
Madeline's rescue　E

About
Marciano, J. Bemelmans　92
See/See also pages in the following book(s):
Caldecott Medal books, 1938-1957 p255-65
028.5

Ben-Ami, Doron
(il) Byars, B. C. Tornado　Fic

Ben and me. Lawson, R.　Fic

Ben and the porcupine. Carrick, C. See note under Carrick, C. The accident　E

Ben-´Ezer, Ehud, 1936-
Hosni the dreamer (2-4)　398.2

Benchley, Nathaniel, 1915-1981
A ghost named Fred　E
Small Wolf　E

Bendall-Brunello, John
(il) Braun, T. My goose Betsy　E

Bender, Howard
(il) Pellowski, M. The art of making comic books　741.5

Bender, Lionel
Invention (4 and up)　609

Bender, Robert
(il) Greene, R. G. Barnyard song　E

Beneath a blue umbrella: rhymes. Prelutsky, J.
811

Benedict, William
(il) Hindley, J. The big red bus　E

Beneduce, Ann
Jack and the beanstalk (2-4)　398.2
The tempest　822.3

Beneficial insects
See also Insect pests

Benizara and Kakezara. MacDonald, M. R.
In MacDonald, M. R. Celebrate the world p10-19　372.6

Benjamin and the caliph. Jaffe, N.
In Jaffe, N. While standing on one foot p33-37　296.1

Benne, Mae, 1924-
Principles of children's services in public libraries　027.62

Bennett, Michelle, 1946-
Missouri
In Celebrate the states　973

Bennett, Nneka
(il) Lasky, K. Vision of beauty: the story of Sarah Breedlove Walker　92

Bennett Cerf's book of riddles. Cerf, B.
793.73

Benny bakes a cake. Rice, E.　E

Benoit, Joan *See* Samuelson, Joan

Ben's dream. Van Allsburg, C.　E

Ben's trumpet. Isadora, R.　E

Benson, Allen C.
Connecting kids and the Internet　004.6

Benson, Islay
Long live Christmas
In The Big book of Christmas plays p213-27
808.82

Benson, Kathleen, 1947-
(jt. auth) Haskins, J. African beginnings
960

(jt. auth) Haskins, J. Bound for America
326

(jt. auth) Haskins, J. Carter G. Woodson
92

(jt. auth) Haskins, J. Out of the darkness
305.8

Benson, Patrick
(il) Grahame, K. The wind in the willows
Fic

(il) Waddell, M. Owl babies　E

Bentley, Nancy
Putting on a play (4-6)　792
The young journalist's book (3-6)　070.1
The young producer's video book (4-6)
791.45

Bentley, Wilson Alwyn, 1865-1931
About
Martin, J. B. Snowflake Bentley (k-3)　92

Bently & egg. Joyce, W.　E

Benton, Thomas Hart, 1889-1975
See/See also pages in the following book(s):
Greenberg, J. The American eye p33-41 (6 and up)　920

Beowulf. Osborne, M. P.
In Osborne, M. P. Favorite medieval tales p8-16　398.2

Beowulf against Grendel. Nye, R.
 In Bauer, C. F. Celebrations p105-08
            808.8

The **berbalangs**. San Souci, R.
 In San Souci, R. Even more short & shivery
  p20-23   **398.2**

Berberick, Nancy Varian
 A song for Croaker Nordge
 In A Glory of unicorns p127-43 **S C**

Bereavement
 Brown, L. K. When dinosaurs die (k-3)
            155.9
 Fry, V. L. Part of me died, too (5 and up)
            155.9
 Krementz, J. How it feels when a parent dies (4
  and up)   **155.9**

Berends, Polly Berrien
 The case of the elevator duck (3-5) **Fic**

Berenstain, Jan, 1923-
 (jt. auth) Berenstain, S. Bears on wheels **E**

Berenstain, Stan, 1923-
 Bears on wheels   **E**

Berenzy, Alix, 1957-
 A Frog Prince   **E**
 (il) A Glory of unicorns. See A Glory of unicorns   **S C**
 (il) Guiberson, B. Z. Into the sea **597.9**

Berg, Elizabeth, 1953-
 Senegal (5 and up)   **966.3**

Berg, Leila, 1917-
 Pete and the ladybird
 In The Oxford treasury of children's stories
  p12-15   **S C**

Berger, Barbara, 1945-
 Grandfather Twilight   **E**

Berger, Gilda
 Celebrate! (4 and up)   **296.4**
 (jt. auth) Berger, M. Do stars have points?
            523
 (jt. auth) Berger, M. Do whales have belly buttons?   **599.5**
 (jt. auth) Berger, M. How do flies walk upside
  down?   **595.7**
 (jt. auth) Berger, M. Why don't haircuts hurt?
            612

Berger, Melvin, 1927-
 Chirping crickets (k-3)   **595.7**
 Do stars have points? (2-4) **523**
 Do whales have belly buttons? (2-4) **599.5**
 Germs make me sick! (k-3) **616.9**
 How do flies walk upside down? (3-5)
            595.7
 Look out for turtles! (k-3) **597.9**
 Oil spill! (k-3)   **363.7**
 Switch on, switch off (k-3) **537**
 Why don't haircuts hurt? (2-4) **612**
 Why I cough, sneeze, shiver, hiccup, and yawn.
  See Meisel, P. Why I sneeze, shiver, hiccup,
  and yawn   **612.7**
 Why I sneeze, shiver, hiccup, and yawn (k-3)
            612.7

Berger, Pam
 Internet for active learners **004.6**

Berkeley, Jon
 (il) Wallace, K. Scarlette Beane **E**

Berkowitz, Robert E.
 (jt. auth) Eisenberg, M. Teaching information &
  technology skills   **025.5**

Berlin (Germany)
 Stein, R. C. Berlin (5 and up) **943**

Berman, Ruth, 1958-
 American bison (3-6)   **599.64**
 Sharks (3-6)   **597**

The **Bermuda** Triangle. Wynne-Jones, T.
 In Wynne-Jones, T. Lord of the Fries and
  other stories p69-90   **S C**

Bernardin, James, 1966-
 (il) Walker, P. R. Big men, big country
            398.2

Bernhard, Durga
 Earth, sky, wet, dry (k-2) **578**
 (il) Bernhard, E. Eagles   **598**
 (il) Bernhard, E. Happy New Year! **394.26**
 (il) Bernhard, E. Prairie dogs **599.3**

Bernhard, Emery
 Eagles (k-3)   **598**
 Happy New Year! (3-5)   **394.26**
 Prairie dogs (2-4)   **599.3**

Bernier-Grand, Carmen T.
 Juan Bobo (k-2)   **398.2**
 Contents: The best way to carry water; A pig in Sunday
 clothes; Do not sneeze, do not scratch . . . do not eat; A dime
 a jug

Bernos de Gasztold, Carmen
 Prayers from the ark   **841**

Bernstein, Zena
 (il) O'Brien, R. C. Mrs. Frisby and the rats of
  NIMH   **Fic**

Berries
   See also Cranberries; Strawberries
        Fiction
 Degen, B. Jamberry   **E**

Berry, Holly
 (il) Bunting, E. Market Day **E**
 (il) Old MacDonald had a farm. See Old Mac-
  Donald had a farm   **782.42**
 (il) Stanley, D. Roughing it on the Oregon Trail
            Fic

Berry, James
 Bro Tiger goes dead
 In The Oxford treasury of children's stories
  p45-46   **S C**
 Celebration song (k-3)   **821**

Beshore, George W.
 Science in ancient China (4 and up) **509**
 Science in early Islamic culture (4 and up)
            509

Beskow, Elsa, 1874-1953
 Pelle's new suit   **E**

Besmehn, Bobby
 Juggling step-by-step (4 and up) **793.8**

Bess Call. San Souci, R.
 In San Souci, R. Cut from the same cloth
  p13-18   **398.2**

Besserat, Denise Schmandt- *See* Schmandt-
 Besserat, Denise

Best, Cari
 Red light, green light, mama and me **E**
 Three cheers for Catherine the Great **E**

The **best** bad thing. Uchida, Y. See note under Uchida, Y. A jar of dreams   **Fic**

The **best** birthday parties ever!. Ross, K.   **793.2**

Best books
  Adventuring with books   **011.6**
  Barstow, B. Beyond picture books   **011.6**
  Best books for children   **011.6**
  The Best in children's books   **028.1**
  Book Links   **028.505**
  Bookbird   **028.505**
  Booklist   **028.1**
  Colborn, C. What do children read next?   **016.8**
  Freeman, J. More books kids will sit still for   **011.6**
  The Horn Book Magazine   **028.505**
  Kaleidoscope   **011.6**
  Notable children's trade books in the field of social studies   **016.3**
  Outstanding science trade books for children   **016.5**

Best books for children   **011.6**

The **best** boy in the world. Schwartz, A.
  In Schwartz, A. All of our noses are here, and other noodle tales p38-57   **398.2**

The **best** Christmas pageant ever. Robinson, B.   **Fic**

Best friends. Cohen, M. See note under Cohen, M. It's George!   **E**

Best friends. Kellogg, S.   **E**

Best friends for Frances. Hoban, R. See note under Hoban, R. Bedtime for Frances   **E**

Best friends together again. Aliki   **E**

The **Best** in children's books   **028.1**

The **best** of Shakespeare. Nesbit, E.   **822.3**

The **best** of the Latino heritage. Schon, I.   **011.6**

The **best** place. Meddaugh, S.   **E**

The **best** school year ever. Robinson, B. See note under Robinson, B. The best Christmas pageant ever   **Fic**

The **best** that life has to give. Pyle, H.
  In Christmas fairy tales p112-22   **398.2**

The **best** way to carry water. Bernier-Grand, C. T.
  In Bernier-Grand, C. T. Juan Bobo p6-12   **398.2**

Best wishes. Rylant, C.   **92**

Bestiary. Hunt, J.   **398**

Bet you can! science possibilities to fool you. Cobb, V.   **793.8**

Bet you can't! science impossibilities to fool you. Cobb, V.   **793.8**

Betancourt, Jeanne, 1941-
  My name is brain Brian (4-6)   **Fic**

Betcha!. Murphy, S. J.   **519.5**

Betsy and Joe. Lovelace, M. H. See note under Lovelace, M. H. Betsy-Tacy   **Fic**

Betsy and Tacy go downtown. Lovelace, M. H. See note under Lovelace, M. H. Betsy-Tacy   **Fic**

Betsy and Tacy go over the big hill. Lovelace, M. H. See note under Lovelace, M. H. Betsy-Tacy   **Fic**

Betsy and the great world. Lovelace, M. H. See note under Lovelace, M. H. Betsy-Tacy   **Fic**

Betsy in spite of herself. Lovelace, M. H. See note under Lovelace, M. H. Betsy-Tacy   **Fic**

Betsy-Tacy. Lovelace, M. H.   **Fic**

Betsy-Tacy and Tib. Lovelace, M. H. See note under Lovelace, M. H. Betsy-Tacy   **Fic**

Betsy was a junior. Lovelace, M. H. See note under Lovelace, M. H. Betsy-Tacy   **Fic**

Betsy's wedding. Lovelace, M. H. See note under Lovelace, M. H. Betsy-Tacy   **Fic**

Better not get wet, Jesse Bear. Carlstrom, N. W. See note under Carlstrom, N. W. Jesse Bear, what will you wear?   **E**

Better wait till Martin comes. Hamilton, V.
  In Hamilton, V. The people could fly: American black folktales p133-37   **398.2**

Between earth & sky. Bruchac, J.   **398.2**

Betz, Adrienne
  (comp) Scholastic treasury of quotations for children. See Scholastic treasury of quotations for children   **808.88**

Beverages
  See also Carbonated beverages

Beware and Stogie. Haas, J. See note under Haas, J. Beware the mare   **Fic**

Beware of kissing Lizard Lips. Shalant, P.   **Fic**

Beware the mare. Haas, J.   **Fic**

The **bewitching** of Sea Pink. Climo, S.
  In Climo, S. Magic & mischief p75-84   **398.2**

Beyond picture books. Barstow, B.   **011.6**

Beyond the fringe. Maguire, G.
  In A Glory of unicorns p45-57   **S C**

Beyond the mango tree. Zemser, A. B.   **Fic**

Beyond the ridge. Goble, P.   **Fic**

The **BFG**. Dahl, R.   **Fic**

Bial, Raymond
  Amish home (3-5)   **289.7**
  A handful of dirt (3-6)   **577.5**
  Mist over the mountains (4 and up)   **974**
  One-room school (3-5)   **370.9**
  Portrait of a farm family (4 and up)   **630.1**
  Shaker home (3-5)   **289**
  The strength of these arms (4 and up)   **326**
  The Underground Railroad (4 and up)   **326**
  With needle and thread (4 and up)   **746.46**

Bianco, Margery Williams, 1880-1944
  The velveteen rabbit (2-4)   **Fic**

Bible
  The Holy Bible [King James Bible. Oxford Univ. Press]   **220.5**
  The Holy Bible: new revised standard version   **220.5**

Natural history
  Bible. Selections. Animals of the Bible (1-4)   **220.8**

Big Anthony: his story. De Paola, T. See note under De Paola, T. Strega Nona: an old tale **E**

Big bad Bruce. Peet, B. **E**

The **big** balloon race. Coerr, E. **E**

The **big** black umbrella. Leach, M.
In The Oxford book of scary tales p86-87 **808.8**

Big blue whale. Davies, N. **599.5**

The **big** book of bones. Llewellyn, C. **573.7**

The **Big** book of Christmas plays **808.82**

Big book of trains (4-6) **625.1**

The **big** brown box. Russo, M. **E**

The **big** bug book. Facklam, M. **595.7**

The **Big** cabbage
In Stockings of buttermilk: American folktales p87 **398.2**

Big cats. Simon, S. **599.75**

A **big** cheese for the White House. Fleming, C. **E**

The **big** dinin'. Van Laan, N.
In Van Laan, N. With a whoop and a holler p27-31 **398.2**

Big Dipper *See* Ursa Major

The **Big** Dipper. Branley, F. M. **523.8**

Big fat hen. Baker, K. **398.8**

Big feet of the Empress Tu Chin. Carpenter, F.
In Carpenter, F. Tales of a Chinese grandmother p81-88 **398.2**

Big game hunting *See* Hunting

Big green drawing book, Ed Emberley's. Emberley, E. **741.2**

Big head!. Rowan, P. **612.8**

Big Jabe. Nolen, J. **E**

Big Jack and Little Jack
In The Jack tales p67-75 **398.2**

Big men, big country. Walker, P. R. **398.2**

Big Mose and the Lady Washington. Walker, P. R.
In Walker, P. R. Big men, big country p29-35 **398.2**

Big numbers. Packard, E. **513**

Big old bones. Carrick, C. **E**

Big red barn. Brown, M. W. **E**

The **big** red bus. Hindley, J. **E**

Big red drawing book, Ed Emberley's. Emberley, E. **741.2**

The **big** rivers. Hiscock, B. **551.48**

Big Sixteen
In Raw Head, bloody bones p65-67 **398.2**

The **big** snow. Hader, B. **E**

Big talk. Fleischman, P. **811**

Big tracks, little tracks. Selsam, M. E. **591.5**

Big Tree People. Bruchac, J.
In Bruchac, J. When the Chenoo howls **398.2**

The **Big** worm
In Raw Head, bloody bones p51-53 **398.2**

Bigger and smaller. Cole, J.
In Ready, set, read—and laugh! p30-43 **810.8**

Bigger than T. rex. Lessem, D. **567.9**

Biggest. McCaughrean, G.
In McCaughrean, G. The bronze cauldron: myths and legends of the world p97-101 **398.2**

The **biggest** bear. Ward, L. K. **E**

The **biggest** frog in Australia. Roth, S. L. **398.2**

The **biggest** house in the world. Lionni, L. **E**

The **biggest** pumpkin ever. Kroll, S. **E**

Biggest, strongest, fastest. Jenkins, S. **590**

Bigmama's. Crews, D. **92**

The **bijli**. San Souci, R.
In San Souci, R. A terrifying taste of short & shivery p35-38 **398.2**

Bileck, Marvin, 1920-
(jt. auth) Scheer, J. Rain makes applesauce **E**

Bilingual books
English-Chinese
Lee, J. M. The song of Mu Lan **398.2**
English-Japanese
Mado, M. The magic pocket (k-3) **895.6**
Wells, R. A to Zen (3-5) **495.6**
English-Korean
Han, S. C. The rabbit's escape (k-3) **398.2**
English-Spanish
Ada, A. F. Gathering the sun (2-4) **811**
Alarcón, F. X. From the bellybutton of the moon and other summer poems (2-4) **811**
Alarcón, F. X. Laughing tomatoes and other spring poems (2-4) **811**
Ancona, G. The piñata maker: El piñatero (k-3) **745.594**
Arroz con leche (k-3) **782.42**
Brusca, M. C. Three friends. Tres amigos **E**
Cool salsa (5 and up) **811.008**
Cruz, A. The woman who outshone the sun (k-3) **398.2**
De colores and other Latin-American folk songs for children (k-3) **782.42**
Diez deditos. Ten little fingers & other play rhymes and action songs from Latin America (k-3) **782.42**
Dorros, A. Radio Man. Don Radio **E**
Eastman, P. D. Are you my mother? **E**
Ehlert, L. Cuckoo. Cucú (k-3) **398.2**
Ehlert, L. Moon rope. Un lazo a la luna (k-3) **398.2**
Garza, C. L. Family pictures **E**
Garza, C. L. In my family (k-3) **305.8**
Garza, C. L. Magic windows **305.8**
Guy, G. F. Fiesta! **E**
Hayes, J. Little Gold Star (k-3) **398.2**
Herrera, J. F. Laughing out loud, I fly **811**
Herrera, J. F. The upside down boy (k-3) **92**
Mora, P. Uno, dos, tres: one, two, three **E**
Pérez, A. I. My very own room **E**

Bird song *See* Birdsongs

The **bird** who spoke three times. Sawyer, R.
In Sawyer, R. The way of the storyteller
p297-304 **372.6**

Bird Woman *See* Sacagawea, b. 1786

Birdie's lighthouse. Hopkinson, D. **Fic**

Birds

See also classes of birds, e.g. Birds of prey;
Cage birds; Game and game birds; State
birds; Water birds; etc.; and names of specific
birds, e.g. Cranes (Birds); Penguins

Arnosky, J. Crinkleroot's guide to knowing the
birds (k-3) **598**

Bishop, N. Digging for bird-dinosaurs (4 and
up) **567.9**

Burnie, D. Bird (4 and up) **598**

George, J. C. One day in the woods (4-6)
577.3

Hickman, P. M. Starting with nature bird book
(4 and up) **598**

Latimer, J. P. Backyard birds (4 and up)
598

Latimer, J. P. Bizarre birds (4 and up) **598**

Latimer, J. P. Shorebirds (4 and up) **598**

Latimer, J. P. Songbirds (4 and up) **598**

Lerner, C. Backyard birds of summer (3-6)
598

Markle, S. Outside and inside birds (2-4)
598

National Audubon Society first field guide: birds
(4 and up) **598**

Wildsmith, B. Brian Wildsmith's birds **E**

Eggs and nests

See Birds—Nests

Fiction

Asch, F. Baby Bird's first nest **E**
Asch, F. Moonbear's dream **E**
Burgess, M. Kite (5 and up) **Fic**
Cannon, J. Stellaluna **E**
De Paola, T. Bill and Pete **E**
Eastman, P. D. Are you my mother? **E**
Ehlert, L. Feathers for lunch **E**
Fleming, C. When Agnes caws **E**
Hamilton, V. When birds could talk & bats
could sing (3-5) **398.2**
Hill, E. S. Bird Boy (2-4) **Fic**
Lewin, B. Booby hatch **E**
Lionni, L. Inch by inch **E**
Rohmann, E. Time flies **E**
Schaefer, L. M. This is the sunflower **E**
Torres, L. Subway sparrow **E**
Ward, H. The king of the birds (k-3)
398.2

Flight

See/See also pages in the following book(s):
Bishop, N. The secrets of animal flight p8-17
(3-6) **591.47**

Migration

Arnold, C. Hawk highway in the sky (4-6)
598

Gans, R. How do birds find their way? (k-3)
598

See/See also pages in the following book(s):
Simon, S. Ride the wind (4-6) **591.56**

Nests

Bash, B. Urban roosts: where birds nest in the
city (1-4) **598**

Jenkins, P. B. A nest full of eggs (k-1)
598

Poetry

Fleischman, P. I am phoenix: poems for two
voices (4 and up) **811**

Florian, D. On the wing **811**

North America

Peterson, R. T. A field guide to the birds
598

West (U.S.)

Peterson, R. T. A field guide to western birds
598

Birds, Brian Wildsmith's. Wildsmith, B. **E**

The **Bird's** Christmas Carol. Wiggin, K. D. S.
Fic

The **birds'** gift. Kimmel, E. A. **398.2**

Birds' nests *See* Birds—Nests

Birds of prey

See also names of birds of prey
Latimer, J. P. Birds of prey (4 and up)
598

Parry-Jones, J. Amazing birds of prey (2-4)
598

Birdseye, Debbie Holsclaw
Under our skin (4 and up) **305.8**
What I believe (4 and up) **200**

Birdseye, Tom
(jt. auth) Birdseye, D. H. Under our skin
305.8

(jt. auth) Birdseye, D. H. What I believe
200

Birdsongs
Latimer, J. P. Songbirds (4 and up) **598**

Birmingham, Christian
(il) Morpurgo, M. Wombat goes walkabout
E

Birth *See* Childbirth

Birth of a foal. Isenbart, H.-H. **636.1**

The **birth** of Maui. Te Kanawa, K.
In Te Kanawa, K. Land of the long white
cloud p11-16 **398.2**

A **birthday** for Frances. Hoban, R. See note under
Hoban, R. Bedtime for Frances **E**

The **birthday** of the Infanta. Wilde, O.
In Wilde, O. The fairy tales of Oscar Wilde
p76-93 **S C**

Birthday pinata. Delacre, L.
In Delacre, L. Salsa stories p44-54 **S C**

Birthday rhymes, special times (k-3) **811.008**

The **birthday** room. Henkes, K. **Fic**

Birthdays
Gibbons, G. Happy birthday! (k-3) **394.2**
Ross, K. The best birthday parties ever! (2-4)
793.2

Trawicky, B. Anniversaries and holidays
394.26

Fiction

Best, C. Three cheers for Catherine the Great
E

Bunting, E. Flower garden **E**

Black Elk, 1863-1950
See/See also pages in the following book(s):
    Krull, K. They saw the future p67-73 (4 and up)
          133.3

The **Black** experience in children's books
          016.3058

Black-eyed Susan. Armstrong, J.   **Fic**
The **black** fox. San Souci, R.
    In San Souci, R. A terrifying taste of short &
        shivery p137-40   **398.2**
The **black** geese. Lurie, A.   **398.2**
Black hair. Martin, R.
    In Martin, R. Mysterious tales of Japan
          398.2

Black hands, white sails. McKissack, P. C.
          639.2

Black hearts in Battersea. Aiken, J. See note under
    Aiken, J. The wolves of Willoughby Chase
          Fic

Black holes (Astronomy)
    Couper, H. Black holes (5 and up)   **523.8**
Black hoops. McKissack, F.   **796.323**
Black is brown is tan. Adoff, A.   **E**
Black Jack. Garfield, L.   **Fic**
Black literature (American) *See* American litera-
    ture—African American authors
Black magic (Witchcraft) *See* Magic
Black music
    See also African American music
Black musicians
    See also African American musicians
Black on white. Hoban, T.   **E**
The **black** pearl. O'Dell, S.   **Fic**
Black poetry (American) *See* American poetry—
    African American authors
Black ships before Troy. Sutcliff, R.   **883**
The **black** snake. Olson, A. N.
    In Olson, A. N. Ask the bones: scary stories
        from around world p99-104   **398.2**
The **Black** Stallion. Farley, W.   **Fic**
The **Black** Stallion and Flame. Farley, W. See
    note under Farley, W. The Black Stallion
          Fic
The **Black** Stallion returns. Farley, W. See note
    under Farley, W. The Black Stallion   **Fic**
The **Black** Stallion's ghost. Farley, W. See note
    under Farley, W. The Black Stallion   **Fic**
Black stars [series]
    Sullivan, O. R. African American inventors
          920
    Wilkinson, B. S. African American women writ-
    ers   **810.9**
Black stars in orbit. Burns, K.   **920**
Black whiteness. Burleigh, R.   **998**
Black women of the Old West. Katz, W. L.
          978

Blackberries in the dark. Jukes, M.   **Fic**
Blackboard Bear. Alexander, M. G.   **E**
Blackburn, G. Meredith
    (comp) Index to poetry for children and young
    people. See Index to poetry for children and
    young people   **808.81**

Blackburn, Lorraine A.
    (comp) Index to poetry for children and young
    people. See Index to poetry for children and
    young people   **808.81**
Blackfoot Indians *See* Siksika Indians
Blacklock, Craig
    (il) Nicholson, D. Wild boars   **599.63**
Blacks

          Bibliography
    The Black experience in children's books
          016.3058

          Biography
    See also African Americans—Biography
    Cameron, A. The kidnapped prince: the life of
    Olaudah Equiano (4 and up)   **92**
          Fiction
    Daly, N. Jamela's dress   **E**
    Daly, N. Not so fast, Songololo   **E**
    Sisulu, E. B. The day Gogo went to vote
          E

          United States
    See African Americans
Blacks in art
    See also African Americans in art
Blacks in literature
    See also African Americans in literature
The **blacksmith** and the Devil. Lester, J.
    In Lester, J. The last tales of Uncle Remus
    p141-47   **398.2**
Blacksmithing
    Fisher, L. E. The blacksmiths (4 and up)
          682

See/See also pages in the following book(s):
    Lyons, M. E. Catching the fire: Philip Simmons,
    blacksmith (4 and up)   **92**
Blackstone, Margaret
    This is soccer (k-2)   **796.334**
Blackwater. Bunting, E.   **Fic**
Blackwood, Gary L.
    The Shakespeare stealer (5 and up)   **Fic**
The **bladder,** the straw, and the shoe. Afanas´ev,
    A. N.
    In Afanas´ev, A. N. Russian fairy tales p590
          398.2

Blake, Quentin, 1932-
    Mrs. Armitage and the big wave   **E**
    (il) Dahl, R. The BFG   **Fic**
    (il) Dahl, R. The enormous crocodile   **Fic**
    (il) Dahl, R. The magic finger   **Fic**
    (il) Dahl, R. Matilda   **Fic**
    (il) Dickens, C. A Christmas carol   **Fic**
    (il) Fleischman, S. Here comes McBroom!
          Fic
    (il) Yeoman, J. The Seven voyages of Sinbad
    the Sailor   **398.2**
Blake, Robert J.
    Akiak   **E**
    (il) Turner, A. W. Mississippi mud   **811**
Blakey, Michael L.
    See/See also pages in the following book(s):
    Talking with adventurers p24-29 (4-6)   **920**
Blankets
          Fiction
    Henkes, K. Owen   **E**

Bloomers!. Blumberg, R.   305.4
Blos, Joan W., 1928-
   A gathering of days: a New England girl's jour-
      nal, 1830-32 (6 and up)   Fic
   The heroine of the Titanic: a tale both true and
      otherwise of the life of Molly Brown (k-3)
                                                92
   Old Henry   E
   See/See also pages in the following book(s):
   Newbery and Caldecott Medal books, 1976-1985
      p65-73   028.5
A **Blossom** promise. Byars, B. C. See note under
   Byars, B. C. The not-just-anybody family
                                               Fic
The **Blossoms** and the Green Phantom. Byars, B.
   C. See note under Byars, B. C. The not-just-
   anybody family   Fic
The **Blossoms** meet the Vulture Lady. Byars, B.
   C. See note under Byars, B. C. The not-just-
   anybody family   Fic
BLS Career Information. (5 and up) See entry in
   Part 2: Web Resources
Blue Beard. Perrault, C.
   In The Blue fairy book p290-95   398.2
   In The Classic fairy tales p106-09   398.2
   In Perrault, C. Cinderella, Puss in Boots, and
      other favorite tales p40-55   398.2
The **Blue** Bird. Aulnoy, Madame d'
   In The Green fairy book p1-26   398.2
A **blue-eyed** daisy. Rylant, C.   Fic
The **Blue** fairy book (4-6)   398.2
A **blue** for Beware. Haas, J. See note under Haas,
   J. Beware the mare   Fic
Blue heron. Avi   Fic
Blue Jay and Swallow take the heat. Hamilton, V.
   In Hamilton, V. When birds could talk & bats
      could sing p19-25   398.2
The **Blue** Mountains
   In The Yellow fairy book p256-64   398.2
Blue potatoes, orange tomatoes. Creasy, R.
                                                635
Blue-ribbon Henry. Calhoun, M. See note under
   Calhoun, M. Cross-country cat   E
The **blue** rose. Baring, M.
   In Shedlock, M. L. The art of the story-teller
      p204-12   372.6
Blue sea. Kalan, R.   E
Blue silver. Sandburg, C.
   In Sandburg, C. Rootabaga stories pt 2 p175-
      79   S C
   In Sandburg, C. The Sandburg treasury p159-
      60   818
Blue willow. Gates, D.   Fic
Bluebeard. Perrault, C.
   In Perrault, C. The complete fairy tales of
      Charles Perrault p35-44   398.2
Blueberries for Sal. McCloskey, R.   E
Blues music
                  Fiction
   Grifalconi, A. Tiny's hat   E
   Myers, W. D. The blues of Flats Brown   E
The **blues** of Flats Brown. Myers, W. D.   E

Bluestem. Arrington, F.   Fic
Bluford, Guion S., 1942-
   See/See also pages in the following book(s):
   Haskins, J. Black eagles p146-63 (5 and up)
                                             629.13
Blumberg, Rhoda, 1917-
   Bloomers! (k-3)   305.4
   Commodore Perry in the land of the Shogun (5
      and up)   952
   Full steam ahead (5 and up)   385.09
   The incredible journey of Lewis and Clark (5
      and up)   978
Blume, Judy
   Are you there God? it's me, Margaret (5 and
      up)   Fic
   Freckle juice (2-4)   Fic
   Fudge-a-mania. See note under Blume, J. Tales
      of a fourth grade nothing   Fic
   It's not the end of the world (4-6)   Fic
   The one in the middle is the green kangaroo
                                                E
   Otherwise known as Sheila the Great (4-6)
                                               Fic
   The Pain and the Great One   E
   Superfudge. See note under Blume, J. Tales of
      a fourth grade nothing   Fic
   Tales of a fourth grade nothing (3-6)   Fic
   See/See also pages in the following book(s):
   Author talk (4 and up)   028.5
Boadicea, Queen, d. 62
   See/See also pages in the following book(s):
   Meltzer, M. Ten queens p25-31 (5 and up)
                                                920
Boadicea. Mayer, M.
   In Mayer, M. Women warriors p51-53
                                                398
Boar out there. Rylant, C.
   In Rylant, C. Every living thing p15-18
                                               S C
Boars
   Nicholson, D. Wild boars (3-6)   599.63
Boat. Kentley, E.   387.2
Boat book. Gibbons, G.   387.2
Boatbuilding
      See also Shipbuilding
Boating. Babbitt, N.
   In Babbitt, N. The Devil's other storybook
      p25-32   S C
Boats, Submarine *See* Submarines; Submersibles
Boats. Barton, B.   387.2
Boats and boating
      See also Rafting (Sports); Sailing; Ships
   Barton, B. Boats (k-1)   387.2
   Gibbons, G. Boat book (k-3)   387.2
   Kentley, E. Boat (4 and up)   387.2
   The Visual dictionary of ships and sailing (4
      and up)   387.2
                  Fiction
   Maestro, B. Ferryboat   E
Boatwright, Phil
   (il) Van Leeuwen, J. Nothing here but trees
                                                E

Bobak, Cathy
(il) Poetry from A to Z. See Poetry from A to Z **808.1**

Bobbi Bobbi!. McCaughrean, G.
In McCaughrean, G. The bronze cauldron: myths and legends of the world p37-40 **398.2**

The **bobbin** girl. McCully, E. A. **Fic**

Bobby Baseball. Smith, R. K. **Fic**

Bock, Judy
Scholastic encyclopedia of the United States (4 and up) **973.03**

Bock, William Sauts, 1939-
(il) Bruchac, J. When the Chenoo howls **398.2**

Bodart, Joni Richards
Booktalk! 2-5. See Booktalk! 2-5 **028.5**

Bodart-Talbot, Joni
See Bodart, Joni Richards

Bode, Janet
Food fight (5 and up) **616.85**

Bodecker, N. M., 1922-1988
(il) Eager, E. Half magic **Fic**
(il) Eager, E. Magic or not? **Fic**
(il) Eager, E. Seven-day magic **Fic**

Bodeen, Stephanie Stuve- *See* Stuve-Bodeen, Stephanie, 1965-

Bodies from the bog. Deem, J. M. **930.1**

Bodkin, Odds
The crane wife (3-5) **398.2**

Bodmer, Karl, 1809-1893
(il) Freedman, R. An Indian winter **978**

Bodnar, Judit Z.
Tale of a tail **E**

The **body** atlas. Parker, S. **611**

The **body** book. Rotner, S. **E**

Bodybuilding (Weight lifting) *See* Weight lifting

Bogacki, Tomasz *See* Bogacki, Tomek

Bogacki, Tomek
My first garden **E**

The **Boggart**. Cooper, S. **Fic**

The **Boggart** and the monster. Cooper, S. See note under Cooper, S. The Boggart **Fic**

Bogs *See* Marshes; Wetlands

Boiko, Claire
We interrupt this program—
In The Big book of Christmas plays p200-12 **808.82**

Bolam, Emily
(il) Ziefert, H. Little Red Riding Hood **398.2**

The **bold** knight, the apples of youth, and the water of life. Afanas'ev, A. N.
In Afanas'ev, A. N. Russian fairy tales p314-20 **398.2**

Bolivia
Pateman, R. Bolivia (5 and up) **984**
Social life and customs
Hermes, J. The children of Bolivia (3-5) **984**

Bollard, John K.
Scholastic children's thesaurus (4 and up) **423**

Bolognese, Don
(il) Avi. Abigail takes the wheel **Fic**
(il) Brenner, B. Wagon wheels **E**

Bolton, A. C.
The friendly ghost
In The Oxford book of scary tales p137-43 **808.8**

Bomans, Godfried, 1913-1971
The thrush girl
In The Oxford treasury of children's stories p23-27 **S C**

The **bomb** in the Bessledorf bus depot. Naylor, P. R. See note under Naylor, P. R. Peril in the Bessledorf Parachute Factory **Fic**

Bonaparte, Napoleon *See* Napoleon I, Emperor of the French, 1769-1821

Bonar, Samantha
Comets (4 and up) **523.6**

Bond, Felicia, 1954-
(il) Brown, M. W. Big red barn **E**
(il) Kramer, S. How to think like a scientist **507**
(il) Numeroff, L. J. If you give a mouse a cookie **E**

Bond, Higgins, 1951-
(il) Berger, M. Do whales have belly buttons? **599.5**

Bond, Michael, 1926-
A bear called Paddington (2-5) **Fic**
More about Paddington. See note under Bond, M. A bear called Paddington **Fic**
Paddington abroad. See note under Bond, M. A bear called Paddington **Fic**
Paddington at large. See note under Bond, M. A bear called Paddington **Fic**
Paddington at work. See note under Bond, M. A bear called Paddington **Fic**
Paddington goes to town. See note under Bond, M. A bear called Paddington **Fic**
Paddington helps out. See note under Bond, M. A bear called Paddington **Fic**
Paddington marches on. See note under Bond, M. A bear called Paddington **Fic**
Paddington on screen. See note under Bond, M. A bear called Paddington **Fic**
Paddington on stage. See note under Bond, M. A bear called Paddington **Fic**
Paddington on top. See note under Bond, M. A bear called Paddington **Fic**
Paddington takes the air. See note under Bond, M. A bear called Paddington **Fic**
Paddington takes the test. See note under Bond, M. A bear called Paddington **Fic**
Paddington takes to TV. See note under Bond, M. A bear called Paddington **Fic**
Paddington's storybook (2-5) **S C**
Contents: A spot of decorating; Paddington cleans up; Paddington dines out; A visit to the bank; A day by the sea; Something nasty in the kitchen; Paddington and the "finishing touch"; Paddington steps out; Paddington and the "cold snap"; Paddington and the Christmas pantomime

Bond, Nancy, 1945-
A string in the harp (6 and up) **Fic**

Bond, Peter, 1948-
DK guide to space (4 and up)   520
Bond, Ruskin
Eyes of the cat
In The Oxford book of scary tales p76-78
    808.8

The **bone** detectives. Jackson, D.   614
The **Bone** Man. Simms, L.   398.2
Boneless. San Souci, R.
In San Souci, R. Short & shivery p127-32
    398.2

Bones
Balestrino, P. The skeleton inside you (k-3)
    611
Barner, B. Dem bones (k-3)   611
Llewellyn, C. The big book of bones (4-6)
    573.7
Simon, S. Bones (3-6)   612.7
The Visual dictionary of the skeleton (4 and up)
    591.4

Fiction
Johnston, T. The ghost of Nicholas Greebe
    E
Steig, W. The amazing bone   E
Bones, bones, dinosaur bones. Barton, B.   E
Bonetta, Sarah Forbes, b. 1843?
About
Myers, W. D. At her majesty's request (5 and up)   92
Bong Way Wong *See* El Chino
Bongo Larry. Pinkwater, D. M. See note under Pinkwater, D. M. Young Larry   E
Bonjour, Babar!. Brunhoff, J. de See note under Brunhoff, J. de. The story of Babar, the little elephant   E
Bonners, Susan, 1947-
The wooden doll   E
Bonny, Anne, b. 1700
Poetry
Yolen, J. The ballad of the pirate queens (3-5)
    811
Bonsall, Crosby Newell, 1921-1995
The case of the cat's meow. See note under Bonsall, C. N. The case of the hungry stranger   E
The case of the double cross. See note under Bonsall, C. N. The case of the hungry stranger   E
The case of the dumb bells. See note under Bonsall, C. N. The case of the hungry stranger   E
The case of the hungry stranger   E
The case of the scaredy cats. See note under Bonsall, C. N. The case of the hungry stranger   E
The day I had to play with my sister   E
Mine's the best   E
Piggle. See note under Bonsall, C. N. Who's a pest?   E
Who's a pest?   E
Who's afraid of the dark?   E
Bonson, Richard
(il) Van Rose, S. The earth atlas   550

Bonvillain, Nancy
The Navajos (4-6)   970.004
Bony-Legs. Cole, J.   398.2
Boo, Michael
The story of figure skating (5 and up)
    796.91
Boo!. Hubbell, P.   811
Boo Mama. McKissack, P. C.
In McKissack, P. C. The dark-thirty p78-94
    S C
Booby hatch. Lewin, B.   E
The **Boogey** Man's wife. Aardema, V.
In Aardema, V. Misoso p15-23   398.2
A **book** about God. Fitch, F. M.   231
Book awards *See* Literary prizes
Book illustration *See* Illustration of books
Book industry
See also Publishers and publishing
Book Links   028.505
The **book** of Adam to Moses. Segal, L. G.
    222
Book of Bible stories, Tomie dePaola's. Bible. Selections   220.9
The **book** of changes. Wynne-Jones, T.   S C
also in Wynne-Jones, T. The book of changes p47-66   S C
Book of children's verse in America, The Oxford
    811.008
Book of children's verse, The Oxford
    821.008
Book of enchantments. Wrede, P. C.   S C
The **book** of fairy tales. Andersen, H. C.
In Christmas fairy tales p17-27   398.2
Book of Greek gods and heroes, The Macmillan. Low, A.   292
The **Book** of knowledge. See The New book of knowledge   031
The **book** of North American owls. Sattler, H. R.
    598
Book of poetry for children, The Random House
    821.008
Book of popular science, The New   503
Book of riddles. Cerf, B.
In Cerf, B. Riddles and more riddles!
    793.73
Book of scary stories and songs, Diane Goode's
    398.2
The **book** of think. Burns, M.   153.4
The **book** of three. Alexander, L.   Fic
A **book** of your own. Stevens, C.   808
Book poems   811.008
Book talks
Bauer, C. F. Leading kids to books through crafts   027.62
Buzzeo, T. Terrific connections with authors, illustrators, and storytellers   372.6
The **book** that Jack wrote. Scieszka, J.   811
Bookbird   028.505
Booklist   028.1
Bookplay. MacDonald, M. R.   027.62

Born worker. Soto, G.
   In Soto, G. Petty crimes   **S C**
The **borning** room. Fleischman, P.   **Fic**
Bornstein, Ruth Lercher, 1927-
   (il) MacLachlan, P. Mama One, Mama Two
        E

Borreguita and the coyote. Aardema, V.
      398.2
The **Borrowers.** Norton, M.   **Fic**
The **Borrowers** afield. Norton, M. See note under
   Norton, M. The Borrowers   **Fic**
The **Borrowers** afloat. Norton, M. See note under
   Norton, M. The Borrowers   **Fic**
The **Borrowers** aloft. Norton, M. See note under
   Norton, M. The Borrowers   **Fic**
The **Borrowers** avenged. Norton, M. See note un-
   der Norton, M. The Borrowers   **Fic**
Borton, Elizabeth *See* Treviño, Elizabeth Borton
   de, 1904-
Bosch, Hieronymus, d. 1516
          Poetry
   Willard, N. Pish, posh, said Hieronymus Bosch
   (2-5)   **811**
Boss of the plains [biography of John Batterson
   Stetson] Carlson, L. M.   **92**
Bostock, Mike
   (il) Lasky, K. Pond year   **E**
   (il) Wallace, K. Gentle giant octopus   **594**
Boston, L. M. (Lucy Maria), 1892-1990
   The children of Green Knowe (4-6)   **Fic**
   The river at Green Knowe. See note under Bos-
   ton, L. M. The children of Green Knowe
        Fic
   A stranger at Green Knowe. See note under
   Boston, L. M. The children of Green Knowe
        Fic
Boston, Lucy Maria *See* Boston, L. M. (Lucy
   Maria), 1892-1990
Boston, Peter, 1918-
   (il) Boston, L. M. The children of Green Knowe
        Fic

Boston (Mass.)
          Fiction
   Fleischman, P. Saturnalia (6 and up)   **Fic**
   Forbes, E. Johnny Tremain (5 and up)   **Fic**
   McCloskey, R. Make way for ducklings   **E**
Boston Children's Museum activity book [series]
   Zubrowski, B. Shadow play   **778.7**
   Zubrowski, B. Soda science   **641.8**
Boston Tea Party, 1773
   Kroll, S. The Boston Tea Party (3-5)   **973.3**
Botany
   See also Plants
   VanCleave, J. P. Janice VanCleave's plants (4
   and up)   **581**
Bottner, Barbara, 1943-
   Bootsie Barker bites   **E**
Boucher, Jerry, 1941-
   (il) Powell, E. S. Rats   **599.3**
Boudicca *See* Boadicea, Queen, d. 62
Bouki dances the kokioko
   In The Magic orange tree, and other Haitian
   folktales p79-86   **398.2**

Boulanger, Nadia, 1887-1979
   See/See also pages in the following book(s):
   Krull, K. Lives of the musicians p78-81 (4 and
   up)   **920**
Boulton, Jane
   Only Opal   **E**
Bound for America. Haskins, J.   **326**
Bound for Oregon. Van Leeuwen, J.   **Fic**
Boundless Grace. Hoffman, M. See note under
   Hoffman, M. Amazing Grace   **E**
A **bouquest** of flowers. McCaughrean, G.
   In McCaughrean, G. The crystal pool: myths
   and legends of the world p24-26
        398.2
Bowden, Bob, 1954-
   (jt. auth) Levine, S. Awesome yo-yo tricks
        796.2
Bowden, Joan Chase, 1925-
   Why the tides ebb and flow (k-2)   **398.2**
Bowdish, Lynea
   Brooklyn, Bugsy, and me (3-5)   **Fic**
Bowen, Betsy
   Antler, bear, canoe   **E**
   (il) Lunge-Larsen, L. The troll with no heart in
   his body and other tales of trolls from Nor-
   way   **398.2**
   (il) Van Laan, N. Shingebiss   **398.2**
Bowen, Gary
   Stranded at Plimoth Plantation, 1626 (3-5)
        974.4
Bowermaster, Jon, 1954-
   (jt. auth) Steger, W. Over the top of the world
        998
Bowers, Tim
   (il) Numeroff, L. J. Sometimes I wonder if poo-
   dles like noodles   **811**
Bowie, James, 1799?-1836
          About
   Gaines, A. Jim Bowie (5 and up)   **92**
   See/See also pages in the following book(s):
   Calvert, P. Great lives: the American frontier
   p15-28 (5 and up)   **920**
Bowles, Ann
   See/See also pages in the following book(s):
   Talking with adventurers p30-36 (4-6)   **920**
Bowman, Leslie W.
   (il) King-Smith, D. The cuckoo child   **Fic**
   (il) Kinsey-Warnock, N. The Canada geese quilt
        Fic
The **box.** Coville, B.
   In Coville, B. Oddly enough p1-9   **S C**
Box Turtle at Long Pond. George, W. T.   **E**
Boxes
          Fiction
   Russo, M. The big brown box   **E**
The **boxes.** Sleator, W.   **Fic**
Boxing
          Fiction
   Kroeger, M. K. Paperboy   **E**
The **boxing** lesson. Soto, G.
   In Soto, G. Petty crimes   **S C**
A **boy,** a dog, and a friend. Mayer, M. See note
   under Mayer, M. A boy, a dog, and a frog
        E

A **boy**, a dog, and a frog. Mayer, M.   **E**

The **boy** and the loon. Lelooska
  In Lelooska, D. Echoes of the elders p14-21
                398.2

The **boy** and the North Wind. Lunge-Larsen, L.
  In Lunge-Larsen, L. The troll with no heart in
    his body and other tales of trolls from
    Norway p49-55   **398.2**

The **Boy** and the wolves
  In The Yellow fairy book p138-40   **398.2**

A **boy** called Slow: the true story of Sitting Bull.
  Bruchac, J.   **92**

Boy fossil. Conrad, P.
  In Conrad, P. Our house p5-11   **S C**

The **boy** of the three-year nap. Snyder, D.
                398.2

The **boy** who ate too much. Keithahn, E. L.
  In From sea to shining sea p234-35
                810.8

The **boy** who became a lion, a falcon, and an ant.
  Lunge-Larsen, L.
  In Lunge-Larsen, L. The troll with no heart in
    his body and other tales of trolls from
    Norway p23-31   **398.2**

The **boy** who drew cats. Levine, A. A.   **398.2**

The **boy** who drew cats. Martin, R.
  In Martin, R. Mysterious tales of Japan
                398.2

The **boy** who lived for a million years.
  McCaughrean, G.
  In McCaughrean, G. The bronze cauldron:
    myths and legends of the world p121-25
                398.2

The **boy** who lived with the seals. Martin, R.
                398.2

The **boy** who loved to draw: Benjamin West.
  Brenner, B.   **92**

The **boy** who took care of the pigs. Brenner, A.
  In Bauer, C. F. Celebrations p152-54
                808.8

The **boy** who tried to fool his father. Sierra, J.
  In Sierra, J. Nursery tales around the world
    p29-31   **398.2**

The **boy** who was followed home. Mahy, M.
                E

The **boy** who wouldn't obey: a Mayan legend.
  Rockwell, A. F.   **398.2**

Boyd, Candy Dawson, 1946-
  Charlie Pippin (4-6)   **Fic**

Boys
  Rand, D. Black Books Galore!—guide to great
  African American children's books about
  boys   **016.3058**
          Books and reading
  Odean, K. Great books for boys   **028.1**
              Employment
    See Child labor

Boys, Teenage *See* Teenagers

A **boy's** Thanksgiving Day. See Child, L. M. F.
  Over the river and through the wood
                811

The **boys'** war. Murphy, J.   **973.7**

Brace, Eric
  (il) Solheim, J. It's disgusting—and we ate it!
                641.3

The **bracelet**. Uchida, Y.   **E**

Bradamante. Yolen, J.
  In Yolen, J. Not one damsel in distress p84-
    94   **398.2**

Bradburn, Frances Bryant
  Output measures for school library media programs   **027.8**

Bradby, Marie
  Momma, where are you from?   **E**
  More than anything else   **E**

Bradley, Kimberly Brubaker
  Ruthie's gift (3-5)   **Fic**

Bradley, Will H., 1868-1962
  The lad and Luck's House
  In American fairy tales p129-42   **S C**

Bradshaw, Terry
  See/See also pages in the following book(s):
  Sullivan, G. Quarterbacks! p27-29 (5 and up)
                920

Brady, April A.
  Kwanzaa karamu (4-6)   **641.5**

Bragg, Linda Wallenberg
  Fundamental gymnastics (5 and up)   **796.44**

Brahms, Johannes, 1833-1897
  See/See also pages in the following book(s):
  Krull, K. Lives of the musicians p48-53 (4 and
  up)   **920**

Braille, Louis, 1809-1852
                About
  Adler, D. A. A picture book of Louis Braille
  (1-3)   **92**
  Freedman, R. Out of darkness: the story of Louis Braille (4 and up)   **92**

Brain
  Parker, S. The brain and the nervous system (4
  and up)   **612.8**
  Rowan, P. Big head! (4 and up)   **612.8**
  Simon, S. The brain (3-6)   **612.8**

The **brain** and the nervous system. Parker, S.
                612.8

The **Brain** explorer (5 and up)   **793.73**

Braine, Susan
  Drumbeat—heartbeat (3-6)   **970.004**

Brainstorm!. Tucker, T.   **609**

Braman, Arlette N., 1952-
  Kids around the world cook! (4-6)   **641.5**

Branch, Muriel Miller
  Juneteenth (5 and up)   **394.26**

Branch, Willis
  (il) Branch, M. M. Juneteenth   **394.26**

Brandenberg, Aliki *See* Aliki

Brandenburg, Jim
  An American safari (4 and up)   **577.4**
  Sand and fog (4 and up)   **968.8**
  Scruffy (2-4)   **599.77**
  To the top of the world (4 and up)   **599.77**
  (il) Swinburne, S. R. Once a wolf   **333.95**

Brandon *See* Brendan, Saint, the Voyager, ca.
  483-577

Brandt, Sue R., 1916-
State flags (5 and up)   929.9
Branford, Henrietta, 1946-
Fire, bed, & bone (5 and up)   Fic
Branley, Franklyn Mansfield, 1915-
Air is all around you (k-1)   551.5
The Big Dipper (k-1)   523.8
Day light, night light (k-3)   535
Down comes the rain (k-3)   551.57
Flash, crash, rumble, and roll (k-3)   551.55
Floating in space (k-3)   629.47
Is there life in outer space? (k-3)   576.8
Keeping time (4-6)   529
The moon seems to change (k-3)   523.3
The planets in our solar system (k-3)   523.4
Snow is falling (k-1)   551.57
The sun and the solar system (4-6)   523.2
What makes a magnet? (k-3)   538
What the moon is like (k-3)   523.3
Branton, Ann
(comp) The Children's song index, 1978-1993.
See The Children's song index, 1978-1993   782.42

Braren, Loretta Trezzo
(il) Hauser, J. F. Kids' crazy concoctions   745.5

Brashler, William
The story of Negro league baseball (5 and up)   796.357

Braun, Trudi
My goose Betsy   E
Brave as a mountain lion. Scott, A. H.   E
Brave Horace. Keller, H. See note under Keller, H. Horace   E
Brave Irene. Steig, W.   E
The **brave** laborer. Afanas'ev, A. N.
In Afanas'ev, A. N. Russian fairy tales p276-77   398.2
Brave little tailor. Grimm, J.
In The Blue fairy book p304-12   398.2
Brave Margaret. San Souci, R.   398.2
Brave Martha. Apple, M.   E
Brave potatoes. Speed, T.   E
Brave quest. McCaughrean, G.
In McCaughrean, G. The golden hoard: myths and legends of the world p29-38   398.2
Brave woman counts coup. Yolen, J.
In Yolen, J. Not one damsel in distress p38-43   398.2
Bravest ever bear. Ahlberg, A.   E
Bravo, Amelia Bedelia. Parish, H. See note under Prish, P. Amelia Bedelia   E
Bravo Tanya. Gauch, P. L. See note under Gauch, P. L. Dance, Tanya   E
Bray, Rosemary L.
Martin Luther King (2-4)   92
Brazelton, T. Berry, 1918-
Going to the doctor (k-3)   610.69
Brazil
Galvin, I. F. Brazil (4 and up)   981
Heinrichs, A. Brazil (4 and up)   981

Social life and customs
Ancona, G. Carnaval (3-6)   394.25
Bread
Jones, J. Knead it, punch it, bake it! (3-6)   641.8
Morris, A. Bread, bread, bread (k-3)   641.8
Fiction
Gershator, D. Bread is for eating   E
Bread and jam for Frances. Hoban, R. See note under Hoban, R. Bedtime for Frances   E
Bread, bread, bread. Morris, A.   641.8
Bread is for eating. Gershator, D.   E
Break-of-day book [series]
Sharmat, M. W. Nate the Great   E
Yolen, J. Sleeping ugly   E
Breckinridge, Mary, 1881-1965
About
Wells, R. Mary on horseback (4 and up)   92

Bredeson, Carmen
John Glenn returns to orbit (4 and up)   629.4
The moon (4 and up)   523.3
Texas
In Celebrate the states   973
Bredeson, Lynn Gates
(il) Bauer, C. F. Caroline Feller Bauer's new handbook for storytellers   372.6
(il) Bauer, C. F. Celebrations   808.8
Breedlove, Sarah *See* Walker, C. J., Madame, 1867-1919
The **Bremen** Town Band. Wildsmith, B.   398.2
The **Bremen** town musicians. Grimm, J.   398.2
Brenda. Spinelli, J.
In Spinelli, J. The library card   S C
Brendan, Saint, the Voyager, ca. 483-577
About
Fritz, J. Brendan the Navigator (3-5)   398.2
Brendan the Navigator. Fritz, J.   398.2
Brenner, Anita, 1905-1974
The boy who took care of the pigs
In Bauer, C. F. Celebrations p152-54   808.8

Brenner, Barbara
The boy who loved to draw: Benjamin West (k-3)   92
Chibi (k-3)   598
If you were there in 1492 (4-6)   970.01
If you were there in 1776 (4-6)   973.3
Wagon wheels   E
(ed) The Earth is painted green. See The Earth is painted green   808.81
Brenner, Fred, 1920-
(il) Monjo, F. N. The drinking gourd   E
Brent, Isabelle
(il) Andersen, H. C. The little mermaid and other fairy tales   S C
(il) Christmas fairy tales. See Christmas fairy tales   398.2
(il) Philip, N. Celtic fairy tales   398.2
(il) Wilde, O. The fairy tales of Oscar Wilde   S C

The **brown** bear of the Green Glen. Philip, N.
In Philip, N. Celtic fairy tales p36-43
398.2

Brown honey in broomwheat tea. Thomas, J. C.
811

Brown paper school book [series]
Burns, M. The book of think **153.4**
Burns, M. The I hate mathematics! book
513

Browne, Anthony
Piggybook **E**
Voices in the park **E**
Willy the champ. See note under Browne, A.
Willy the dreamer **E**
Willy the dreamer **E**
Willy the wizard. See note under Browne, A.
Willy the dreamer **E**
Willy's pictures. See note under Browne, A.
Willy the dreamer **E**

Browne, Frances, 1816-1879
The Christmas cuckoo
In Christmas fairy tales p28-46 **398.2**

Browne, George
The wonderful tar baby
In The Oxford treasury of children's stories
p47-49 **S C**

Brownell, Shawn
(il) Peacock, C. A. Mommy far, Mommy near
E

The **browney** at the grocer's. Andersen, H. C.
In Andersen, H. C. The swan's stories p99-
107 **S C**

Browning, Robert, 1812-1889
The Pied Piper of Hamelin **821**

The **Browns** take the day off. Schwartz, A.
In Schwartz, A. There is a carrot in my ear,
and other noodle tales p9-14 **398.2**

Bruchac, Joseph, 1942-
The arrow over the door (4-6) **Fic**
Between earth & sky (3-5) **398.2**
A boy called Slow: the true story of Sitting Bull
(1-3) **92**
Children of the longhouse (4 and up) **Fic**
Crazy Horse's vision **E**
The first strawberries (k-3) **398.2**
Flying with the eagle, racing the great bear (5
and up) **398.2**
Contents: The dream fast; White Weasel; Racing the great
bear; Granny Squannit and the Bad Young Man; How the game
animals were set free; The wild boy; The underwater lodge; The
wisdom of the willow tree; The Owl-Man Giant and the Monster
Elk; How the hero twins found their father; The bear boy; The
ghost society; The light-haired boy; Star Boy; Salmon Boy; Tommy's whale
The girl who married the Moon (5 and up)
398.2
Contents: Arrowhead Finger; The abandoned girl; The girl and
the Chenoo; The girl who escaped; Stonecoat; The girl who
helped Thunder; The girl who married an Osage; The girls who
almost married an owl; The poor Turkey Girl; The girl who gave
birth to Water-Jar Boy; The Bear Woman; The Beauty Way—the
ceremony of White-Painted Woman; How Pelican Girl was
saved; Where the girl rescued her brother; Chipmunk Girl and
Owl Woman; The girl who married the Moon
Gluskabe and the four wishes (k-3) **398.2**
The great ball game (k-3) **398.2**
Pushing up the sky: seven native American
plays for children (3-5) **812**

Contents: Gluskabe and Old Man Winter; Star sisters; Possum's tail; Wihio's duck dance; Pushing up the sky; The cannibal
monster; The strongest one
Sacajawea (6 and up) **Fic**
The story of the Milky Way (k-3) **398.2**
Tell me a tale (5 and up) **372.6**
Includes the following stories: Coyote's name; Bill Greenfield
and the cold day; How the Adirondacks got their name; Can you
pluck my rooster?; The wisdom of Princess Maya; Bring in the
chickens; Yiyi the Spider and the stick sap man; Straightening
the mind of Tadadaho; The seventh boy; The creation of
Gluskabe; The other half of the blanket; The three young crows
Thirteen moons on a turtle's back **811**
The Trail of Tears (2-4) **970.004**
Turtle makes war on Man
In From sea to shining sea p252-55
810.8
When the Chenoo howls (4-6) **398.2**
Contents: The Stone Giant; The Flying Head; Ugly-face;
Chenoo; Amankamek; Keewahkwee; Yakwawiak; Man Bear; The
Spreaders; Aglebemu; Big Tree People; Toad Woman
(jt. auth) Caduto, M. J. Keepers of the night
398.2

Bruh Alligator and Bruh Deer. Hamilton, V.
In Hamilton, V. The people could fly:
American black folktales p26-30
398.2

Bruh Alligator meets Trouble. Hamilton, V.
In Hamilton, V. The people could fly:
American black folktales p35-42
398.2

Bruh Buzzard and Fair Maid. Hamilton, V.
In Hamilton, V. When birds could talk & bats
could sing p27-31 **398.2**

Bruh Lizard and Bruh Rabbit. Hamilton, V.
In Hamilton, V. The people could fly:
American black folktales p31-34
398.2

Bruh Wolf and Bruh Rabbit join together. Hamilton, V.
In Hamilton, V. A ring of tricksters p39-43
398.2

Brunello, John Bendall- *See* Bendall-Brunello,
John

Brunhoff, Jean de, 1899-1937
Babar and Father Christmas. See note under
Brunhoff, J. de. The story of Babar, the little
elephant **E**
Babar and his children. See note under
Brunhoff, J. de. The story of Babar, the little
elephant **E**
Babar the king. See note under Brunhoff, J. de.
The story of Babar, the little elephant **E**
Bonjour, Babar! See note under Brunhoff, J. de.
The story of Babar, the little elephant **E**
The story of Babar, the little elephant **E**
Travels of Babar. See note under Brunhoff, J.
de. The story of Babar, the little elephant
E

Brunhoff, Laurent de, 1925-
Babar and the ghost. See note under Brunhoff,
J. de. The story of Babar, the little elephant
E
Babar and the succotash bird. See note
Brunhoff, J. de. The story of Babar, the little
elephant **E**

Brunhoff, Laurent de, 1925——*Continued*
Babar learns to cook. See note under Brunhoff, J. de. The story of Babar, the little elephant **E**
Babar saves the day. See note under Brunhoff, J. de. The story of Babar, the little elephant **E**
Babar's ABC. See note under Brunhoff, J. de. The story of Babar, the little elephant **E**
Babar's book of color. See note under Brunhoff, J. de. The story of Babar, the little elephant **E**
Babar's little girl. See note under Brunhoff, J. de. The story of Babar, the little elephant **E**
Meet Babar and his family. See note under Brunhoff, J. de. The story of Babar, the little elephant **E**

Brunkus, Denise
(il) Park, B. Junie B. Jones and her big fat mouth **Fic**

Brusca, María Cristina
Three friends. Tres amigos **E**
When jaguars ate the moon and other stories about animals and plants of the Americas (2-4) **398.2**
(il) Medearis, A. S. The zebra-riding cowboy **782.42**

Bryan, Ashley, 1923-
Ashley Bryan's African tales, uh-huh (4-6) **398.2**
Contents: The ox of the wonderful horns: Ananse the Spider in search of a fool; Frog and his two wives; Elephant and Frog go courting; Tortoise, Hare, and the sweet potatoes; The ox of the wonderful horns [story]
Beat the story-drum, pum-pum: Hen and Frog; Why Bush Cow and Elephant are bad friends; The husband who counted the spoonfuls; Why Frog and Snake never play together; How animals got their tails
Lion and the ostrich chicks: Lion and the ostrich chicks [story]; The son of the wind; Jackal's favorite game; The foolish boy
The cat's purr
In From sea to shining sea p260-63 **810.8**
Sing to the sun **811**
The story of Lightning & Thunder (3-5) **398.2**
Tortoise, Hare, and the sweet potatoes
In Bauer, C. F. Celebrations p231-34 **808.8**
(comp) All night, all day. See All night, all day **782.25**
(il) Ashley Bryan's ABC of African-American poetry. See Ashley Bryan's ABC of African-American poetry **811.008**
(il) Christmas gif'. See Christmas gif' **394.26**
(il) Giovanni, N. The sun is so quiet **811**
(il) Hughes, L. Carol of the brown king **811**
(comp) The Night has ears. See The Night has ears **398.9**
(il) Salting the ocean. See Salting the ocean **811.008**
(il) What a morning! See What a morning! **782.25**

Bryan, Mike
(jt. auth) Herman, G. Cal Ripken, Jr. **92**

Bryant, Michael
(il) Grimes, N. Come Sunday **811**
(il) McKissack, P. C. Booker T. Washington **92**
(il) McKissack, P. C. Madam C.J. Walker **92**
(il) McKissack, P. C. Sojourner Truth **92**

Bstan-'dzin-rgya-mtsho *See* Dalai Lama XIV, 1935-

Bucher, Katherine Toth, 1947-
Information technology for schools **027.8**

Buchholz, Quint, 1957-
The collector of moments (3-6) **Fic**

Buck, Pearl S. (Pearl Sydenstricker), 1892-1973
See/See also pages in the following book(s):
Faber, D. Great lives: American literature p173-82 (5 and up) **920**

Buckley, Helen E. (Helen Elizabeth), 1918-
Grandfather and I **E**
Grandmother and I **E**

Buckley, James, Jr.
America's greatest game (4 and up) **796.332**
Football (4 and up) **796.332**

Bud, not Buddy. Curtis, C. P. **Fic**

Buddha, Gautama *See* Gautama Buddha

Buddha. Demi **294.3**

The **Buddha** and the five hundred queens. Krishnaswami, U.
In Krishnaswami, U. Shower of gold: girls and women in the stories of India p24-30 **398.2**

Buddha stories. Demi **294.3**

Buddhism
Chödzin, S. The wisdom of the crows and other Buddhist tales (4 and up) **294.3**
Demi. The Dalai Lama (3-6) **92**
See/See also pages in the following book(s):
Osborne, M. P. One world, many religions p49-60 (4 and up) **291**

Budgets, Personal *See* Personal finance

Budiansky, Stephen
The world according to horses (4 and up) **636.1**

Buehner, Caralyn
Fanny's dream **E**
I did it, I'm sorry **E**

Buehner, Mark
(il) Barracca, D. The adventures of Taxi Dog **E**
(il) Buehner, C. Fanny's dream **E**
(il) Buehner, C. I did it, I'm sorry **E**
(il) Nolen, J. Harvey Potter's balloon farm **E**
(il) Schertle, A. I am the cat **811**

Buffalo, Amos Bad Heart *See* Bad Heart Buffalo, Amos, ca. 1869-1913

Buffalo, American *See* Bison

Buffalo Bill, 1846-1917
See/See also pages in the following book(s):
Calvert, P. Great lives: the American frontier p111-24 (5 and up) **920**

Buffalo days. Hoyt-Goldsmith, D. **970.004**

Buffalo gals. Miller, B. M. **978**

Buffalo hunt. Freedman, R. **970.004**

Buffalo woman. Goble, P. **398.2**

Bug in a rug. Gilson, J. **Fic**

Bugs!. Greenberg, D. **E**

Bugs! Bugs! Bugs!. Barner, B. **595.7**

Bugs! bugs! bugs!. Dussling, J. **595.7**

Buh Rabby and Bruh Gator. Hamilton, V.
In Hamilton, V. A ring of tricksters p15-23
398.2

Build a prairie. (3-6) See entry in Part 2: Web Resources

Build your own Web site. Kalbag, A. **004.6**

Building

See also Carpentry; House construction

Barton, B. Building a house (k-1) **690**

Barton, B. Machines at work (k-1) **690**

Gibbons, G. How a house is built (k-3)
690

Macaulay, D. Unbuilding (4 and up) **690**

Macaulay, D. Underground (4 and up)
624.1

Fiction

Banks, K. The night worker **E**

Building. Wilkinson, P. **690**

Building a house. Barton, B. **690**

Building a special collection of children's literature in your library **025.2**

Building an igloo. Steltzer, U. **728**

Building materials

Wilkinson, P. Building (4 and up) **690**

Building the book Cathedral. Macaulay, D.
726

Buildings

See also Apartment houses; Houses; Skyscrapers

Built for speed. Thompson, S. E. **599.75**

Bukhtan Bukhtanovich. Afanas'ev, A. N.
In Afanas'ev, A. N. Russian fairy tales p168-70 **398.2**

Bulfinch, Thomas, 1796-1867

Bulfinch's mythology (6 and up) **291.1**

Bulfinch's mythology. Bulfinch, T. **291.1**

Bull, Amos Bad Heart *See* Bad Heart Buffalo, Amos, ca. 1869-1913

Bull, Jacqueline Left Hand *See* Left Hand Bull, Jacqueline

Bull Run, 1st Battle of, 1861

Fiction

Fleischman, P. Bull Run (6 and up) **Fic**

Bulla, Clyde Robert, 1914-

The chalk box kid **E**

Daniel's duck **E**

The Paint Brush Kid (2-4) **Fic**

The story of Valentine's Day (k-3) **394.26**

The sword in the tree (3-5) **Fic**

What makes a shadow? (k-1) **535**

Bulletin of the Center for Children's Books
028.1

Bullfights

Biography

Say, A. El Chino (2-5) **92**

Fiction

Leaf, M. The story of Ferdinand **E**

Wojciechowska, M. Shadow of a bull (6 and up) **Fic**

Bulls

Fiction

Leaf, M. The story of Ferdinand **E**

Bully for you, Teddy Roosevelt!. Fritz, J. **92**

The bully of Barkham Street. Stolz, M. See note under Stolz, M. A dog on Barkham Street
Fic

Bumps in the night. Allard, H. **E**

The bun. Afanas'ev, A. N.
In Afanas'ev, A. N. Russian fairy tales p447-49 **398.2**

The bun. Sierra, J.
In Sierra, J. Nursery tales around the world p17-21 **398.2**

Bunche, Ralph J. (Ralph Johnson), 1904-1971
See/See also pages in the following book(s):
Haskins, J. One more river to cross (4 and up)
920

Bunnicula. Howe, D. **Fic**

Bunnicula strikes again!. Howe, J. See note under Howe, J. The celery stalks at midnight
Fic

Bunny cakes. Wells, R. See note under Wells, R. Max's first word **E**

The bunny who found Easter. Zolotow, C. **E**

Bunny's noisy book. Brown, M. W. **E**

Bunting, Anne Eve *See* Bunting, Eve, 1928-

Bunting, Edward

(ed) The Visual dictionary of prehistoric life. See The Visual dictionary of prehistoric life
560

Bunting, Eve, 1928-

Blackwater (5 and up) **Fic**

Butterfly house **E**

Can you do this, Old Badger? **E**

Cheyenne again **E**

Dandelions **E**

December **E**

Dreaming of America **E**

Flower garden **E**

Fly away home **E**

Ghost's hour, spook's hour **E**

How many days to America? **E**

Little Badger, terror of the seven seas. See note under Bunting, E. Can you do this, Old Badger? **E**

Market Day **E**

The Mother's Day mice **E**

Nasty, stinky sneakers (4-6) **Fic**

Night tree **E**

Once upon a time (1-3) **92**

A perfect Father's Day **E**

A picnic in October **E**

Scary, scary Halloween **E**

Secret place **E**

Smoky night **E**

So far from the sea **E**

Some frog! (2-4) **Fic**

Someday a tree **E**

Spying on Miss Müller (5 and up) **Fic**

Caldecott Medal—*Continued*

The Newbery and Caldecott awards **028.5**

Newbery and Caldecott Medal books, 1966-1975 **028.5**

Newbery and Caldecott Medal books, 1976-1985 **028.5**

Caldecott Medal books, 1938-1957 **028.5**

Caldecott Medal titles

Azarian, M. See Martin, J. B. Snowflake Bentley (1999) **92**

Bemelmans, L. See Bemelmans, L. Madeline's rescue (1954) **E**

Brown, M. See Brown, M. Once a mouse (1962) **398.2**

Brown, M. See Cendrars, B. Shadow (1983) **841**

Brown, M. See Perrault, C. Cinderella (1955) **398.2**

Burton, V. L. See Burton, V. L. The little house (1943) **E**

Cooney, B. See Cooney, B. Chanticleer and the fox (1959) **E**

Cooney, B. See Hall, D. Ox-cart man (1980) **E**

Diaz, D. See Bunting, E. Smoky night (1995) **E**

Dillon, L. and Dillon, D. See Aardema, V. Why mosquitoes buzz in people's ears (1976) **398.2**

Dillon, L. and Dillon, D. See Musgrove, M. Ashanti to Zulu: African traditions (1977) **960**

Duvoisin, R. See Tresselt, A. R. White snow, bright snow (1948) **E**

Egielski, R. See Yorinks, A. Hey, Al (1987) **E**

Emberley, E. See Emberley, B. Drummer Hoff (1968) **398.8**

Gammell, S. See Ackerman, K. Song and dance man (1989) **E**

Goble, P. See Goble, P. The girl who loved wild horses (1979) **398.2**

Hader, B. and Hader, E. See Hader, B. The big snow (1949) **E**

Haley, G. E. See Haley, G. E. A story, a story (1971) **398.2**

Hogrogian, N. See Hogrogian, N. One fine day (1972) **398.2**

Hogrogian, N. See Leodhas, S. N. Always room for one more (1966) **782.42**

Hyman, T. S. See Hodges, M. Saint George and the dragon (1985) **398.2**

Jones, E. O. See Field, R. Prayer for a child (1945) **242**

Keats, E. J. See Keats, E. J. The snowy day (1963) **E**

Lathrop, D. P. See Bible. Selections. Animals of the Bible (1938) **220.8**

Lent, B. See Mosel, A. The funny little woman (1973) **398.2**

Lobel, A. See Lobel, A. Fables (1981) **Fic**

Macauley, D. See Macaulay, D. Black and white (1990) **E**

McCloskey, R. See McCloskey, R. Make way for ducklings (1942) **E**

McCloskey, R. See McCloskey, R. Time of wonder (1958) **E**

McCully, E. See McCully, E. A. Mirette on the high wire (1993) **E**

McDermott, G. See McDermott, G. Arrow to the sun (1975) **398.2**

Montresor, B. See De Regniers, B. S. May I bring a friend? (1965) **E**

Ness, E. See Ness, E. Sam, Bangs & Moonshine (1967) **E**

Politi, L. See Politi, L. Song of the swallows (1950) **E**

Provensen, A. and Provensen, M. See Provensen, A. The glorious flight: across the Channel with Louis Blériot, July 25, 1909 (1984) **92**

Rathmann, P. See Rathmann, P. Officer Buckle and Gloria (1996) **E**

Rojankovsky, F. See Langstaff, J. M. Frog went a-courtin' (1956) **782.42**

Say, A. See Say, A. Grandfather's journey (1994) **E**

Schoenherr, J. See Yolen, J. Owl moon (1988) **E**

Sendak, M. See Sendak, M. Where the wild things are (1964) **E**

Shulevitz, U. See Ransome, A. The Fool of the World and the flying ship (1969) **398.2**

Sidjakov, N. See Robbins, R. Baboushka and the three kings (1961) **398.2**

Simont, M. See Udry, J. M. A tree is nice (1957) **E**

Slobodkin, L. See Thurber, J. Many moons (1944) **Fic**

Small, D. See St. George, J. So you want to be president (2001) **973**

Spier, P. See Spier, P. Noah's ark (1978) **222**

Steig, W. See Steig, W. Sylvester and the magic pebble (1970) **E**

Taback, S. See Taback, S. Joseph had a little overcoat (2000) **E**

Van Allsburg, C. See Van Allsburg, C. Jumanji (1982) **E**

Van Allsburg, C. See Van Allsburg, C. The Polar Express (1986) **E**

Ward, L. K. See Ward, L. K. The biggest bear (1953) **E**

Wiesner, D See Wiesner, D. Tuesday (1992) **E**

Wisniewski, D. See Wisniewski, D. Golem (1997) **398.2**

Young, E. See Young, E. Lon Po Po (1990) **398.2**

Zelinsky, P. O. See Zelinsky, P. O. Rapunzel (1998) **398.2**

Calder, Nancy Edwards

(il) Brown, M. W. On Christmas Eve **E**

Caleb & Kate. Steig, W. **E**

Calendar of events, Chase's **394.26**

Calendars

See also Days

Branley, F. M. Keeping time (4-6) **529**

Chase's calendar of events **394.26**

Maestro, B. The story of clocks and calendars (3-6) **529**

Calendars—*Continued*

Murphy, S. J. Pepper's journal   **E**

Trawicky, B. Anniversaries and holidays

394.26

See/See also pages in the following book(s):

Bauer, C. F. Celebrations p43-62   **808.8**

Calhoun, Mary, 1926-

Blue-ribbon Henry. See note under Calhoun, M.
Cross-country cat   **E**

Cross-country cat   **E**

Flood   **E**

Henry the sailor cat. See note under Calhoun, M. Cross-country cat   **E**

High-wire Henry. See note under Calhoun, M. Cross-country cat   **E**

Hot-air Henry. See note under Calhoun, M. Cross-country cat   **E**

Calico's cousins. Tildes, P. L.   **636.8**

California

Altman, L. J. California
In Celebrate the states   **973**

Heinrichs, A. California
In America the beautiful, second series

973

Antiquities

Thompson, S. E. Death trap (4 and up)

560

Fiction

Gates, D. Blue willow (4 and up)   **Fic**

Koertge, R. Tiger, tiger, burning bright (6 and up)   **Fic**

Koss, A. G. The Ashwater experiment (4 and up)   **Fic**

Politi, L. Song of the swallows   **E**

Soto, G. Baseball in April, and other stories (5 and up)   **S C**

Soto, G. Petty crimes (5 and up)   **S C**

Uchida, Y. A jar of dreams (5 and up)   **Fic**

Gold discoveries

Krensky, S. Striking it rich (2-4)   **979.4**

Murrow, L. K. The gold rush (5 and up)

979.4

Stanley, J. Hurry freedom (5 and up)

979.4

Gold discoveries—Fiction

Cushman, K. The ballad of Lucy Whipple (5 and up)   **Fic**

Fleischman, S. Bandit's moon (4-6)   **Fic**

Fleischman, S. By the Great Horn Spoon! (4-6)

Fic

Kay, V. Gold fever   **E**

Yep, L. The journal of Wong Ming-Chung (4 and up)   **Fic**

The **California** condor. Silverstein, A.   **598**

California condors *See* Condors

The **caliph** and the cobbler. Kimmel, E. A.
In Kimmel, E. A. The spotted pony: a collection of Hanukkah stories p50-55

398.2

Calisthenics *See* Gymnastics

Call down the moon (6 and up)   **821.008**

Call it courage. Sperry, A.   **Fic**

Call me Francis Tucket. Paulsen, G. See note under Paulsen, G. Mr. Tucket   **Fic**

The **call** of the sea. McCaughrean, G.
In McCaughrean, G. The crystal pool: myths and legends of the world p57-60

398.2

The **call** of the wild. London, J.   **Fic**

Callan, Lyndall
(jt. auth) Rappaport, D. Dirt on their skirts

E

Calling on dragons. Wrede, P. C. See note under Wrede, P. C. Dealing with dragons   **Fic**

Calliope [periodical]   **905**

Calmenson, Stephanie

Dinner guests
In The Read-aloud treasury p100-11

808.8

The Gator Girls. See note under Calmenson, S. Get well, Gators!   **Fic**

Gator Halloween. See note under Calmenson, S. Get well, Gators!   **Fic**

Get well, Gators! (1-3)   **Fic**

The lion and the mouse
In The Read-aloud treasury p188-89

808.8

Rockin' reptiles. See note under Calmenson, S. Get well, Gators!   **Fic**

Rosie (k-3)   **636.7**

(jt. auth) Cole, J. Crazy eights and other card games   **795.4**

(jt. auth) Cole, J. Fun on the run   **793.7**

(jt. auth) Cole, J. Marbles   **796.2**

(jt. auth) Cole, J. Pin the tail on the donkey and other party games   **793**

(jt. auth) Cole, J. The rain or shine activity book

793

(jt. auth) Cole, J. Six sick sheep   **808.88**

(jt. auth) Cole, J. Why did the chicken cross the road? and other riddles, old and new

793.73

(comp) The Eentsy, weentsy spider: fingerplays and action rhymes. See The Eentsy, weentsy spider: fingerplays and action rhymes

796.1

(comp) Miss Mary Mack and other children's street rhymes. See Miss Mary Mack and other children's street rhymes   **796.1**

(comp) Pat-a-cake and other play rhymes. See Pat-a-cake and other play rhymes   **398.8**

(comp) The Read-aloud treasury. See The Read-aloud treasury   **808.8**

(comp) Ready, set, read—and laugh! See Ready, set, read—and laugh!   **810.8**

Calvert, Patricia, 1931-

Great lives: the American frontier (5 and up)

920

Cam Jansen and the barking treasure mystery. Adler, D. A. See note under Adler, D. A. Cam Jansen and the mystery of the stolen diamonds   **Fic**

Cam Jansen and the birthday mystery. Adler, D. A. See note under Adler, D. A. Cam Jansen and the mystery of the stolen diamonds

Fic

Cam Jansen and the catnapping mystery. Adler, D. A. See note under Adler, D. A. Cam Jansen and the mystery of the stolen diamonds
Fic

Cam Jansen and the chocolate fudge mystery. Adler, D. A. See note under Adler, D. A. Cam Jansen and the mystery of the stolen diamonds
Fic

Cam Jansen and the ghostly mystery. Adler, D. A. See note under Adler, D. A. Cam Jansen and the mystery of the stolen diamonds **Fic**

Cam Jansen and the mystery at the haunted house. Adler, D. A. See note under Adler, D. A. Cam Jansen and the mystery of the stolen diamonds
Fic

Cam Jansen and the mystery at the monkey house. Adler, D. A. See note under Adler, D. A. Cam Jansen and the mystery of the stolen diamonds
Fic

Cam Jansen and the mystery of Flight 54. Adler, D. A. See note under Adler, D. A. Cam Jansen and the mystery of the stolen diamonds
Fic

Cam Jansen and the mystery of the Babe Ruth baseball. Adler, D. A. See note under Adler, D. A. Cam Jansen and the mystery of the stolen diamonds
Fic

Cam Jansen and the mystery of the carnival prize. Adler, D. A. See note under Adler, D. A. Cam Jansen and the mystery of the stolen diamonds
Fic

Cam Jansen and the mystery of the circus clown. Adler, D. A. See note under Adler, D. A. Cam Jansen and the mystery of the stolen diamonds
Fic

Cam Jansen and the mystery of the dinosaur bones. Adler, D. A. See note under Adler, D. A. Cam Jansen and the mystery of the stolen diamonds
Fic

Cam Jansen and the mystery of the gold coins. Adler, D. A. See note under Adler, D. A. Cam Jansen and the mystery of the stolen diamonds
Fic

Cam Jansen and the mystery of the monster movie. Adler, D. A. See note under Adler, D. A. Cam Jansen and the mystery of the stolen diamonds
Fic

Cam Jansen and the mystery of the stolen corn popper. Adler, D. A. See note under Adler, D. A. Cam Jansen and the mystery of the stolen diamonds
Fic

Cam Jansen and the mystery of the stolen diamonds. Adler, D. A. **Fic**

Cam Jansen and the mystery of the television dog. Adler, D. A. See note under Adler, D. A. Cam Jansen and the mystery of the stolen diamonds
Fic

Cam Jansen and the mystery of the UFO. Adler, D. A. See note under Adler, D. A. Cam Jansen and the mystery of the stolen diamonds
Fic

Cam Jansen and the scary snake mystery. Adler, D. A. See note under Adler, D. A. Cam Jansen and the mystery of the stolen diamonds
Fic

Cam Jansen and the Triceratops Pops mystery. Adler, D. A. See note under Adler, D. A. Cam Jansen and the mystery of the stolen diamonds
Fic

Cambodia
Fiction
Lee, J. M. Silent Lotus **E**

Cameras
Gibbons, G. Click! (k-3) **771**
Price, S. Click! fun with photography (4 and up) **771**

Cameron, Ann, 1943-
Gloria's way (2-4) **Fic**
Julian, dream doctor. See note under Cameron, A. The stories Julian tells **Fic**
Julian, secret agent. See note under Cameron, A. The stories Julian tells **Fic**
Julian's glorious summer. See note under Cameron, A. The stories Julian tells **Fic**
The kidnapped prince: the life of Olaudah Equiano (4 and up) **92**
More stories Huey tells. See note under Cameron, A. The stories Julian tells **Fic**
More stories Julian tells. See note under Cameron, A. The stories Julian tells **Fic**
The stories Huey tells. See note under Cameron, A. The stories Julian tells **Fic**
The stories Julian tells (2-4) **Fic**

Cameron, Eleanor, 1912-1996
The court of the stone children (5 and up) **Fic**
The seed and the vision **028.5**
The wonderful flight to the Mushroom Planet (4-6) **Fic**

Cameron, Marie
(il) Chödzin, S. The wisdom of the crows and other Buddhist tales **294.3**

Cameron, Scott
(il) De Regniers, B. S. David and Goliath **222**
(il) Nichol, B. Beethoven lives upstairs **Fic**

Cameroon
Fiction
Alexander, L. The fortune-tellers **E**

Camouflage (Biology)
Fiction
Aruego, J. We hide, you seek **E**

Camp Fat. Konigsburg, E. L.
In Konigsburg, E. L. Altogether, one at a time p29-59 **S C**

Campbell, Ann
The New York Public Library amazing space (5 and up) **520**

Campbell, Mary, fl. 1764
Fiction
Durrant, L. The beaded moccasins (5 and up) **Fic**

Campbell, Peter A.
Alien encounters (4 and up) **001.9**

Camping
Fiction
Gilson, J. 4B goes wild (4-6)   **Fic**
Locker, T. Where the river begins   **E**
McCully, E. A. Monk camps out   **E**
Naylor, P. R. The fear place (5 and up)   **Fic**
Say, A. The lost lake   **E**
Williams, V. B. Three days on a river in a red canoe   **E**

Camps
Fiction
Honey, E. Don't pat the wombat! (4-6)   **Fic**
Vail, R. Daring to be Abigail (4-6)   **Fic**

Can do, Jenny Archer. Conford, E. *See note under* Conford, E. A case for Jenny Archer   **Fic**

Can Krishna die? McCaughrean, G.
In McCaughrean, G. The silver treasure: myths and legends of the world p86-90   **398.2**

Can you do this, Old Badger? Bunting, E.   **E**

Can you pluck my rooster? Bruchac, J.
In Bruchac, J. Tell me a tale p38-42   **372.6**

Canada
Sateren, S. S. Canada (4 and up)   **971**
Children
See Children—Canada
Fiction
Burnford, S. The incredible journey (4 and up)   **Fic**
Cooper, S. The Boggart (4-6)   **Fic**
Ellis, S. Next-door neighbors (4 and up)   **Fic**
Temple, F. Grab hands and run (6 and up)   **Fic**
Wynne-Jones, T. Lord of the Fries and other stories (5 and up)   **S C**
History—0-1763 (New France)
Maestro, B. The new Americans (2-4)   **973.2**

The **Canada** geese quilt. Kinsey-Warnock, N.   **Fic**

Canada goose *See* Geese

Canady, Alexa, 1950-
See/See also pages in the following book(s):
Hansen, J. Women of hope p26-27 (4 and up)   **920**

Canals
Fiction
Howard, E. The gate in the wall (5 and up)   **Fic**

Cancer
See also Leukemia
Fiction
Borden, L. Good luck, Mrs. K!   **E**
Brisson, P. Sky memories (3-5)   **Fic**
Winthrop, E. Promises   **E**

The **candlesticks**. Kimmel, E. A.
In Kimmel, E. A. The adventures of Hershel of Ostropol p52-60   **398.2**

Candy corn. Stevenson, J.   **811**

The **cannibal** monster. Bruchac, J.
In Bruchac, J. Pushing up the sky: seven native American plays for children p67-77   **812**

Cannon, Annie
(il) Carson, J. You hold me and I'll hold you   **E**
(il) Porte, B. A. Tale of a tadpole   **E**

Cannon, Janell, 1957-
Crickwing   **E**
Stellaluna   **E**
Verdi   **E**

Canoes and canoeing
Fiction
Williams, V. B. Three days on a river in a red canoe   **E**

Can't you make them behave, King George? [biography of George III, King of Great Britain] Fritz, J.   **92**

Can't you sleep, Little Bear? Waddell, M.   **E**

Canterbury tales. Cohen, B.   **821**

The **Canterbury** tales. McCaughrean, G.   **821**

Canto familiar. Soto, G.   **811**

Cap o' Rushes. Jacobs, J.
In Jacobs, J. English fairy tales p57-62   **398.2**
In Womenfolk and fairy tales p77-82   **398.2**

Caple, Kathy
The friendship tree   **E**

Caponigro, John Paul, 1962-
(il) Cohen, D. Ghost in the house   **133.1**

Cappelloni, Nancy
Ethnic cooking the microwave way
In Easy menu ethnic cookbooks   **641.5**

Caps for sale. Slobodkina, E.   **E**

Caps, hats, socks, and mittens. Borden, L.   **E**

Captain Snap and the children of Vinegar Lane. Schotter, R.   **E**

The **captive**. Hansen, J.   **Fic**

The **captive**. O'Dell, S.   **Fic**

Capucilli, Alyssa, 1957-
Bathtime for Biscuit. *See note under* Capucilli, A. Biscuit's new trick   **E**
Biscuit. *See note under* Capucilli, A. Biscuit's new trick   **E**
Biscuit finds a friend. *See note under* Capucilli, A. Biscuit's new trick   **E**
Biscuit wants to play. *See note under* Capucilli, A. Biscuit's new trick   **E**
Biscuit's new trick   **E**
Biscuit's picnic. *See note under* Capucilli, A. Biscuit's new trick   **E**
Happy birthday, Biscuit! *See note under* Capucilli, A. Biscuit's new trick   **E**
Hello, Biscuit! *See note under* Capucilli, A. Biscuit's new trick   **E**

Carbon
Sparrow, G. Carbon
In The Elements [Benchmark Bks.]   **546**

Carbonated beverages
Zubrowski, B. Soda science (4 and up)   **641.8**

Card games
  Cole, J. Crazy eights and other card games (3-5) **795.4**

  See/See also pages in the following book(s):
  Cole, J. The rain or shine activity book p36-51 (3-5) **793**

Cardinal and Bruh Deer. Hamilton, V.
  In Hamilton, V. When birds could talk & bats could sing p47-53 **398.2**

Cardiovascular system
  See also Blood—Circulation; Heart
  Ballard, C. The heart and circulatory system (5 and up) **612.1**
  Simon, S. The heart (3-6) **612.1**

Care, Medical *See* Medical care

Career day. Rockwell, A. F. **E**

Careers *See* Occupations

Caribbean canvas. Lessac, F. **811**

Caribbean region
  Antiquities
  Macaulay, D. Ship (4 and up) **387.2**
  Fiction
  Godard, A. Mama, across the sea **E**
  Mitchell, R. P. Hue Boy **E**
  Taylor, T. The cay (5 and up) **Fic**
  Taylor, T. Timothy of the cay (5 and up) **Fic**

  Folklore
  See Folklore—Caribbean region
  Poetry
  Berry, J. Celebration song (k-3) **821**

Caribbean region in art
  Lessac, F. Caribbean canvas **811**

Caribou
  Miller, D. S. A caribou journey (2-4) **599.65**

A **caribou** journey. Miller, D. S. **599.65**

Caricatures *See* Cartoons and caricatures

Carle, Eric
  The art of Eric Carle **741.6**
  Do you want to be my friend? **E**
  Does a kangaroo have a mother, too? **E**
  Eric Carle's animals, animals **808.81**
  Eric Carle's dragons dragons and other creatures that never were **808.81**
  From head to toe **E**
  The grouchy ladybug **E**
  A house for Hermit Crab **E**
  The mixed-up chameleon **E**
  Today is Monday (k-3) **782.42**
  The very busy spider **E**
  The very clumsy click beetle **E**
  The very hungry caterpillar **E**
  The very lonely firefly **E**
  The very quiet cricket **E**
  (il) Martin, B. Brown bear, brown bear what do you see? **E**
  (il) Martin, B. Polar bear, polar bear, what do you hear? **E**

Carlson, Ann D., 1952-
  Flannelboard stories for infants and toddlers **372.6**

Carlson, Laurie M., 1952-
  Boss of the plains [biography of John Batterson Stetson] (k-3) **92**

Carlson, Lori M.
  (ed) Cool salsa. See Cool salsa **811.008**
  (comp) You're on!: seven plays in English and Spanish. See You're on!: seven plays in English and Spanish **812.008**

Carlson, Mary, 1951-
  (il) Carlson, A. D. Flannelboard stories for infants and toddlers **372.6**

Carlson, Nancy L., 1953-
  ABC I like me! See note under Carlson, N. L. I like me! **E**
  I like me! **E**

Carlson, Natalie Savage, 1906-
  The family under the bridge (3-5) **Fic**

Carlstrom, Nancy White, 1948-
  Better not get wet, Jesse Bear. See note under Carlstrom, N. W. Jesse Bear, what will you wear? **E**
  Guess who's coming, Jesse Bear. See note under Carlstrom, N. W. Jesse Bear, what will you wear? **E**
  Happy birthday, Jesse Bear. See note under Carlstrom, N. W. Jesse Bear, what will you wear? **E**
  How do you say it today, Jesse Bear? See note under Carlstrom, N. W. Jesse Bear, what will you wear? **E**
  It's about time, Jesse Bear, and other rhymes. See note under Carlstrom, N. W. Jesse Bear, what will you wear? **E**
  Jesse Bear, what will you wear? **E**
  Let's count it out, Jesse Bear. See note under Carlstrom, N. W. Jesse Bear, what will you wear? **E**
  Thanksgiving Day at our house (k-2) **811**
  What a scare, Jesse Bear! See note under Carlstrom, N. W. Jesse Bear, what will you wear? **E**
  Where is Christmas, Jesse Bear? See note under Carlstrom, N. W. Jesse Bear, what will you wear? **E**
  Who said boo? (k-3) **811**

Carmen Teresa's gift. Delacre, L.
  In Delacre, L. Salsa stories p71-75 **S C**

Carmi, Giora
  (il) Kimmel, E. A. The Chanukkah guest **E**
  (il) Penn, M. The miracle of the potato latkes **E**
  (il) Schwartz, H. A journey to paradise and other Jewish tales **398.2**

Carnival
  Ancona, G. Carnaval (3-6) **394.25**

Carol of the brown king. Hughes, L. **811**

A **Carolina** banshee. San Souci, R.
  In San Souci, R. Even more short & shivery p120-24 **398.2**

Caroline Feller Bauer's new handbook for storytellers. Bauer, C. F. **372.6**

Carolrhoda creative minds book [series]
  Crofford, E. Healing warrior: a story about Sister Elizabeth Kenny **92**

Contents: Inside the bright red gate; How Pan Ku made the world; Sisters in the sun; Gentle Gwan Yin; God that lived in the kitchen; Guardians of the gate; Painted eyebrow; Ting Lan and the lamb; Daughter of the dragon king; Big feet of the Empress Tu Chin; Grateful fox fairy; Two dutiful sons; King of the monkeys; Lady with the horse's head; Poet and the peony princess; First emperor's magic whip; Wonderful pear tree; How the eight old ones crossed the sea; White snake; Prince Chi Ti's city; Ko-Ai's lost shoe; Spinning maid and the cowherd; Lost star princess; Mandarin and the butterflies; Heng O, the moon lady; Cheng's fighting cricket; Maid in the mirror; Miss Lin, the sea goddess; Simple Seng and the parrot; Old Old One's birthday

Cats—Fiction—*Continued*
Wormell, M. Why not?   **E**
           Poetry
Curious cats in art and poetry   **808.81**
Eliot, T. S. Growltiger's last stand   **811**
Farjeon, E. Cats sleep anywhere   **821**
Galdone, P. Three little kittens   **398.8**
Schertle, A. I am the cat (k-3)   **811**
Cats, Wild *See* Wild cats
Cat's baptism
     In The Magic orange tree, and other Haitian
         folktales p123-26   **398.2**
Cat's cradle *See* String figures
Cat's cradle, owl's eyes. Gryski, C.   **793.9**
Cats in art
Curious cats in art and poetry   **808.81**
Cats: plans for perfection. (3-6) See entry in Part
     2: Web Resources
The **cat's purr.** Bryan, A.
     In From sea to shining sea p260-63
                 810.8
Cats sleep anywhere. Farjeon, E.   **821**
Catskill Mountains (N.Y.)
           Fiction
George, J. C. My side of the mountain (5 and
     up)   **Fic**
George, J. C. On the far side of the mountain
     (5 and up)   **Fic**
Catskin. Jacobs, J.
     In Jacobs, J. English fairy tales p403-08
                 398.2
Catskinella. Hamilton, V.
     In Hamilton, V. Her stories p23-27
                 398.2
Catskins
     In Grandfather tales p106-14   **398.2**
Cattle
     See also Bulls
Aliki. Milk from cow to carton (k-3)   **637**
Gibbons, G. The milk makers (k-3)   **637**
           Fiction
Cooper, S. The silver cow: a Welsh tale (1-4)
                 398.2
Cronin, D. Click, clack, moo   **E**
Egan, T. Metropolitan cow   **E**
Ernst, L. C. When Bluebell sang   **E**
Johnson, P. B. The cow who wouldn't come
     down   **E**
Lewis, K. Little calf   **E**
Milgrim, D. Cows can't fly   **E**
Seymour, T. Hunting the white cow   **E**
Van Laan, N. The tiny, tiny boy and the big,
     big cow (k-3)   **398.2**
           Poetry
Schertle, A. How now, brown cow?   **811**
Catwings. Le Guin, U. K.   **Fic**
Catwings return. Le Guin, U. K. See note under
     Le Guin, U. K. Catwings   **Fic**
Caudill, Rebecca, 1899-1985
A certain small shepherd (4 and up)   **Fic**
Did you carry the flag today, Charley? (2-4)
                 Fic
Caught in the act. Nixon, J. L. See note under
     Nixon, J. L. A family apart   **Fic**

The **Cauld** Lad of Hilton. Jacobs, J.
     In Jacobs, J. English fairy tales p200-02
                 398.2
Cauley, Lorinda Bryan, 1951-
Clap your hands   **E**
(il) Kipling, R. The beginning of the armadilloes
                 Fic
(il) Kipling, R. The elephant's child   **Fic**
Cavanaugh, Matthew
(il) Anderson, J. Batboy   **796.357**
Cave drawings and paintings
     See also Rock drawings, paintings, and en-
     gravings
Caves
Kramer, S. Caves (4-6)   **551.4**
Silver, D. M. Cave (3-5)   **577.5**
The **cay.** Taylor, T.   **Fic**
Cayce, Edgar, 1877-1945
See/See also pages in the following book(s):
Krull, K. They saw the future p83-89 (4 and up)
                 133.3
Caylus, Anne Claude Philippe de Tubières,
     comte de, 1692-1765
Fairy gifts
     In The Green fairy book p64-67   **398.2**
Heart of ice
     In The Green fairy book p106-36   **398.2**
Rosanella
     In The Green fairy book p48-55   **398.2**
Sylvain and Jocosa
     In The Green fairy book p56-63   **398.2**
Cayuga Nature Center (Ithaca, N.Y.)
Lang, S. S. Nature in your backyard   **508**
CBC *See* Children's Book Council (New York,
     N.Y.)
CD-ROMs
List of titles with CD-ROM versions:
The American Heritage children's dictionary
                 423
Children's books in print   **015.73**
Cole, J. The magic school bus at the waterworks
                 551.48
Cole, J. The magic school bus: in the time of
     the dinosaurs   **567.9**
Cole, J. The magic school bus inside a hurricane
                 551.55
Cole, J. The magic school bus inside the Earth
                 551.1
Cole, J. The magic school bus, lost in the solar
     system   **523**
Cole, J. The magic school bus on the ocean
     floor   **591.7**
Compton's encyclopedia & fact-index   **031**
The Elementary school library collection
                 011.6
Kane, J. N. Famous first facts   **031.02**
Macaulay, D. The new way things work
                 600
Macmillan dictionary for children   **423**
Subject guide to Children's books in print
                 015.73
The World Book encyclopedia   **031**

CD-ROMs—*Continued*
Catalogs
Culturally diverse videos, audios, and CD-ROMS for children and young adults **011.6**

Reviews
Adamson, L. G. Literature connections to American history, K-6 **016.973**

Adamson, L. G. Literature connections to world history, K-6 **016.9**

CD's, superglue, and salsa [series 2] **670**

Cecil, Randy
(il) Stenmark, V. The singing chick **E**

Cecil's story. Lyon, G. E. **E**

The **Cegua.** San Souci, R.
In San Souci, R. Short & shivery p41-47 **398.2**

Celebrate!. Berger, G. **296.4**

Celebrate the 50 states. Leedy, L. **973**

Celebrate the states (4 and up) **973**

Celebrate the world. MacDonald, M. R. **372.6**

Celebrating Chinese New Year. Hoyt-Goldsmith, D. **394.26**

Celebrating Hanukkah. Hoyt-Goldsmith, D. **296.4**

Celebrating Passover. Hoyt-Goldsmith, D. **296.4**

Celebration song. Berry, J. **821**

Celebrations. Bauer, C. F. **808.8**

Celebrations. Kindersley, A. **394.26**

Celebrations. Livingston, M. C. **811**

The **celery** stalks at midnight. Howe, J. **Fic**

Cello *See* Violoncellos

The **cello** of Mr. O. Cutler, J. **E**

Celtic civilization
Martell, H. M. The Celts (4 and up) **936**

Celtic fairy tales. Philip, N. **398.2**

Celts
Martell, H. M. The Celts (4 and up) **936**
Folklore
Philip, N. Celtic fairy tales (4 and up) **398.2**

Cendrars, Blaise, 1887-1961
Shadow (1-3) **841**

Cendrillon. San Souci, R. **398.2**

Censorship
Hit list: frequently challenged books for children **016.8**

Centerburg tales. McCloskey, R. See note under McCloskey, R. Homer Price **Fic**

Central High School (Little Rock, Ark.)
O'Neill, L. Little Rock (5 and up) **370**

Central Pacific Railroad
Blumberg, R. Full steam ahead (5 and up) **385.09**

Central Utah Relocation Center
Tunnell, M. O. The children of Topaz (5 and up) **940.53**

The **century.** See Jennings, P. The century for young people **909.82**

Century farm. Peterson, C. **630.1**

The **century** for young people. Jennings, P. **909.82**

Cepeda, Joe
(il) Aardema, V. Koi and the kola nuts **398.2**

(il) Cowley, J. Gracias, the Thanksgiving turkey **E**

(il) Lester, J. What a truly cool world! **E**

(il) Skorpen, L. M. We were tired of living in a house **E**

(il) Yacowitz, C. Pumpkin fiesta **E**

Cerebral palsy
Carter, A. R. Stretching ourselves (1-3) **362.4**

Pimm, P. Living with cerebral palsy (3-5) **362.4**
Fiction
Mikaelsen, B. Petey (5 and up) **Fic**

Cerf, Bennett, 1898-1971
Bennett Cerf's book of riddles (k-3) **793.73**
Book of riddles
In Cerf, B. Riddles and more riddles! **793.73**

More riddles
In Cerf, B. Riddles and more riddles! **793.73**

Riddles and more riddles! **793.73**

A **certain** small shepherd. Caudill, R. **Fic**

Cerullo, Mary M.
Coral reef (4 and up) **577.7**
Sharks (4 and up) **597**
The truth about great white sharks (4 and up) **597**

Cervantes Saavedra, Miguel de, 1547-1616
See/See also pages in the following book(s):
Krull, K. Lives of the writers p14-17 (4 and up) **920**

Cha, Chue
(il) Cha, D. Dia's story cloth **305.8**

Cha, Dia, 1962-
Dia's story cloth (3-5) **305.8**

Cha, Nhia Thao
(il) Cha, D. Dia's story cloth **305.8**

Chagoya, Enrique
See/See also pages in the following book(s):
Just like me p4-5 **920**

Chaiet, Donna
The safe zone (4 and up) **613.6**

Chaikin, Miriam, 1928-
Clouds of glory (4 and up) **296.1**
Exodus (2-4) **222**
Menorahs, mezuzas, and other Jewish symbols (5 and up) **296.4**

Chaikovsky, P. I. *See* Tchaikovsky, Peter Ilich, 1840-1893

Chain of fire. Naidoo, B. **Fic**

A **chair** for my mother. Williams, V. B. **E**

Chairs
Fiction
Williams, V. B. A chair for my mother **E**

Check. Ellis, S.
  In Ellis, S. Back of beyond   **S C**
Cheerleading
          Fiction
  Lester, H. Three cheers for Tacky   **E**
Cheese
  Peterson, C. Extra cheese, please! (k-3)
                        637
          Fiction
  Fleming, C. A big cheese for the White House
                        E
Cheetahs
  Esbensen, B. J. Swift as the wind (2-4)
                 599.75
  MacMillan, D. M. Cheetahs (3-6)   **599.75**
  Morrison, T. Cheetah! (k-3)   **599.75**
  Thompson, S. E. Built for speed (5 and up)
                 599.75
Chelm and their history, The fools of. Singer, I.
  B.   **Fic**
Chemical elements
  The Elements [Benchmark Bks.] (5 and up)
                      546
  Elements [Grolier] (5 and up)   **546**
Chemical pollution *See* Pollution
Chemistry
  Challoner, J. The visual dictionary of chemistry
    (4 and up)   **540**
  Gardner, R. Science projects about kitchen
    chemistry (5 and up)   **540.7**
  Newmark, A. Chemistry (4 and up)   **540**
          Experiments
  Kramer, A. How to make a chemical volcano
    and other mysterious experiments (4-6)
                 540.7
Chemists
  Parker, S. Marie Curie and radium (4 and up)
                      92
  Poynter, M. Marie Curie: discoverer of radium
    (4 and up)   **92**
Cheng, Pang Guek, 1950-
  Mongolia (5 and up)   **951.7**
Cheng's fighting cricket. Carpenter, F.
  In Carpenter, F. Tales of a Chinese grand-
    mother p217-25   **398.2**
Chenoo. Bruchac, J.
  In Bruchac, J. When the Chenoo howls
                 398.2
Chernoff, Goldie Taub
  Easy costumes you don't have to sew (3-5)
                   391
Cherokee Indians
  Bealer, A. W. Only the names remain (4-6)
                970.004
  Brill, M. T. The Trail of Tears (5 and up)
                970.004
  Bruchac, J. The Trail of Tears (2-4)
                970.004
  Klausner, J. Sequoyah's gift (4 and up)   **92**
  Sneve, V. D. H. The Cherokees (3-5)
                970.004
          Folklore
  Bruchac, J. The first strawberries (k-3)
                398.2

  Bruchac, J. The story of the Milky Way (k-3)
                398.2
  Ross, G. How Turtle's back was cracked (k-3)
                398.2
Cherr, Pat
  (jt. auth) Keats, E. J. My dog is lost!   **E**
Cherries and cherry pits. Williams, V. B.   **E**
Cherry, Lynne, 1952-
  Flute's journey (2-4)   **598**
  The great kapok tree   **E**
  (il) Viorst, J. If I were in charge of the world
    and other worries   **811**
Cherry pies and lullabies. Reiser, L.   **E**
Chess, Victoria, 1939-
  (il) Aardema, V. This for that   **398.2**
  (il) Lewis, J. P. A hippopotamusn't and other
    animal verses   **811**
  (il) Prelutsky, J. Rolling Harvey down the hill
                811
  (il) Prelutsky, J. The sheriff of Rottenshot: po-
    ems   **811**
  (il) Schwartz, A. Ghosts!   **398.2**
  (il) Sierra, J. The beautiful butterfly   **398.2**
  (il) Wise, W. Ten sly piranhas   **E**
  (il) Yolen, J. King Long Shanks   **E**
The **chessmen** of doom. Bellairs, J. See note under
  Bellairs, J. The curse of the blue figurine
                 Fic
Chester. Heide, F. P.
  In Thanksgiving: stories and poems p49-50
                810.8
Chester Cricket's new home. Selden, G. See note
  under Selden, G. The cricket in Times Square
                 Fic
Chester Cricket's pigeon ride. Selden, G. See note
  under Selden, G. The cricket in Times Square
                 Fic
Chester's way. Henkes, K.   **E**
Chesworth, Michael
  (il) Lewis, M. Morgy makes his move   **Fic**
Chewning, Randy
  (il) Showers, P. Where does the garbage go?
                363.7
Cheyenne again. Bunting, E.   **E**
Cheyenne Indians
  Sneve, V. D. H. The Cheyennes (3-5)
                970.004
  Viola, H. J. It is a good day to die (5 and up)
                973.8
  See/See also pages in the following book(s):
  Ehrlich, A. Wounded Knee: an Indian history of
    the American West (6 and up)   **970.004**
          Fiction
  Bunting, E. Cheyenne again   **E**
  Goble, P. Death of the iron horse   **E**
          Folklore
  Goble, P. Her seven brothers (2-4)   **398.2**
The **Ch'i-lin** purse. Fang, L.   **398.2**
  In Fang, L. The Ch'i-lin purse p3-15
                398.2
Chiappe, Luis M.
  (jt. auth) Dingus, L. The tiniest giants
                567.9
Chibi. Brenner, B.   **598**

Chicago (Ill.)
Fiction
McKissack, P. C. Color me dark (4 and up)
            Fic
Chicanos *See* Mexican Americans
Chichester-Clark, Emma, 1955-
 (il) McCaughrean, G. Greek gods and goddesses
            292
 (il) McCaughrean, G. Greek myths **292**
The **chick** and the duckling. Ginsburg, M. **E**
Chicka chicka boom boom. Martin, B. **E**
Chickadee   **505**
Chickasaw Indians
Folklore
Moroney, L. Baby rattlesnake (k-2) **398.2**
The **chicken-coop** monster. McKissack, P. C.
 In McKissack, P. C. The dark-thirty p111-122
            S C
Chicken Licken. Asbjornsen, P. C.
 In Tomie dePaola's favorite nursery tales
  p105-11   **398.2**
Chicken Little. Kellogg, S. **398.2**
The **Chicken** sisters. Numeroff, L. J. **E**
Chicken soup with rice. Sendak, M. **E**
Chicken Sunday. Polacco, P. **E**
Chickenpox
Fiction
Kelley, T. I've got chicken pox **E**
Chickens
 See also Roosters
Johnson, S. A. Inside an egg (4 and up)
            598
Fiction
Auch, M. J. Peeping Beauty   **E**
Baker, K. Big fat hen   **398.8**
Barton, B. The little red hen (k-2) **398.2**
Ernst, L. C. Zinnia and Dot   **E**
Fox, M. Hattie and the fox   **E**
Galdone, P. The little red hen (k-2) **398.2**
Ginsburg, M. The chick and the duckling
            E
Ginsburg, M. Good morning, chick **E**
Heine, H. The most wonderful egg in the world
            E
Hutchins, P. Rosie's walk   **E**
Kasza, K. The wolf's chicken stew **E**
Mathers, P. Lottie's new beach towel **E**
Numeroff, L. J. The Chicken sisters **E**
O'Connor, J. Super Cluck   **E**
Pinkwater, D. M. The Hoboken chicken emer-
 gency (3-6)   **Fic**
Reiser, L. The surprise family **E**
Stoeke, J. M. A hat for Minerva Louise **E**
Sturges, P. The Little Red Hen (makes a pizza)
 (k-3)   **398.2**
Zemach, M. The little red hen (k-2) **398.2**
Chickens aren't the only ones. Heller, R.
            591.4
Chicoine, Stephen
Spain (4 and up)   **946**
Chidi only likes blue. Onyefulu, I. **E**
Chief Joseph *See* Joseph, Nez Percé Chief, 1840-
1904

Chilcoat, George W.
 (jt. auth) Tunnell, M. O. The children of Topaz
           940.53
Child, Lydia Maria Francis, 1802-1880
Over the river and through the wood (k-2)
           811
Child abuse
 See also Child sexual abuse
Fiction
Byars, B. C. Cracker Jackson (5 and up)
           Fic
Coman, C. What Jamie saw (5 and up) **Fic**
Magorian, M. Good night, Mr. Tom (6 and up)
           Fic
Neufeld, J. Almost a hero (5 and up) **Fic**
Child and mother *See* Mother-child relationship
Child and parent *See* Parent-child relationship
Child artists
Hughes, L. The sweet and sour animal book
           811
—I never saw another butterfly— **741.9**
Periodicals
Stone Soup   **810.8**
Child care
 See also Babysitting
Child labor
Bartoletti, S. C. Growing up in coal country (5
 and up)   **331.3**
Bartoletti, S. C. Kids on strike! (5 and up)
           331.8
Freedman, R. Kids at work (5 and up)
           331.3
Fiction
Beatty, P. Turn homeward, Hannalee (5 and up)
           Fic
Howard, E. The gate in the wall (5 and up)
           Fic
Child molesting *See* Child sexual abuse
Child of Faerie. Kimberly, G.
 In A Glory of unicorns p165-82 **S C**
Child of the owl. Yep, L. **Fic**
Child of the Warsaw ghetto. Adler, D. A.
          940.53
Child sexual abuse
See/See also pages in the following book(s):
Jukes, M. It's a girl thing p104-15 (5 and up)
          305.23
Fiction
Woodson, J. I hadn't meant to tell you this (6
 and up)   **Fic**
Childbirth
Bauer, M. D. If you were born a kitten (k-1)
          591.3
Cole, J. How you were born (k-2) **612.6**
Frasier, D. On the day you were born **E**
Harris, R. H. It's so amazing! (2-4) **612.6**
Pringle, L. P. Everybody has a bellybutton (k-3)
          612.6
Rosenberg, M. B. Mommy's in the hospital hav-
 ing a baby (k-1)   **362.1**
Fiction
Harris, R. H. Happy birth day! **E**

Chinese

United States—Fiction

Namioka, L. Yang the youngest and his terrible ear (4-6) **Fic**

Yep, L. Dragon's gate (6 and up) **Fic**

Yep, L. The journal of Wong Ming-Chung (4 and up) **Fic**

The **Chinese** American family album. Hoobler, D. **305.8**

Chinese Americans

See also Chinese—United States

Hoobler, D. The Chinese American family album (5 and up) **305.8**

Kuklin, S. How my family lives in America (k-3) **305.8**

Yep, L. The lost garden (5 and up) **92**

Fiction

Chinn, K. Sam and the lucky money **E**

Coerr, E. Chang's paper pony **E**

Lee, M. Nim and the war effort **E**

Look, L. Love as strong as ginger **E**

Lord, B. B. In the Year of the Boar and Jackie Robinson (4-6) **Fic**

Peacock, C. A. Mommy far, Mommy near **E**

Yep, L. The amah (5 and up) **Fic**

Yep, L. Child of the owl (5 and up) **Fic**

Yep, L. The cook's family (5 and up) **Fic**

Yep, L. Dragonwings (5 and up) **Fic**

Yep, L. Later, gator (4-6) **Fic**

Yep, L. The magic paintbrush (3-5) **Fic**

Yep, L. The star fisher (6 and up) **Fic**

Yep, L. Thief of hearts (5 and up) **Fic**

Social life and customs

Hoyt-Goldsmith, D. Celebrating Chinese New Year (3-5) **394.26**

Waters, K. Lion dancer: Ernie Wan's Chinese New Year (k-3) **394.26**

Chinese artists *See* Artists, Chinese

The **Chinese** babies. Wynne-Jones, T.

In Wynne-Jones, T. Lord of the Fries and other stories p173-214 **S C**

Chinese civilization *See* China—Civilization

A **Chinese** fairy tale. Housman, L.

In Bauer, C. F. Celebrations p4-11 **808.8**

Chinese language

Lee, H. V. At the beach (k-3) **495.1**

Young, E. Voices of the heart **179**

The **Chinese** mirror. Ginsburg, M. **398.2**

Chinese New Year

Demi. Happy New Year! (k-3) **394.26**

Hoyt-Goldsmith, D. Celebrating Chinese New Year (3-5) **394.26**

Waters, K. Lion dancer: Ernie Wan's Chinese New Year (k-3) **394.26**

Fiction

Chinn, K. Sam and the lucky money **E**

Wong, J. S. This next New Year **E**

Chinese poetry

Lee, J. M. The song of Mu Lan **398.2**

Maples in the mist **895.1**

The **Chinese** Red Riding Hood. Chang, I. C.

In Womenfolk and fairy tales p14-19 **398.2**

Chinese science *See* Science—China

Chinn, Karen, 1959-

Sam and the lucky money **E**

Chinook Indians

Folklore

Martin, R. The boy who lived with the seals (1-4) **398.2**

Taylor, H. P. Coyote places the stars (k-3) **398.2**

Chipmunk and the Owl Sisters. Caduto, M. J.

In Caduto, M. J. Keepers of the night p93-96 **398.2**

Chipmunk Girl and Owl Woman. Bruchac, J.

In Bruchac, J. The girl who married the Moon p108-15 **398.2**

Chippewa Indians *See* Ojibwa Indians

Chips. San Souci, R.

In San Souci, R. Even more short & shivery p94-99 **398.2**

Chirping crickets. Berger, M. **595.7**

Chisholm, Shirley, 1924-

See/See also pages in the following book(s):

Haskins, J. One more river to cross (4 and up) **920**

Chita's Christmas tree. Howard, E. F. **E**

Chitty-Chitty-Bang-Bang. Fleming, I. **Fic**

Chivalry

See also Medieval civilization

Bulfinch, T. Bulfinch's mythology (6 and up) **291.1**

Chocolate, Debbi, 1954-

Kwanzaa (3-5) **394.26**

My first Kwanzaa book (k-2) **394.26**

The piano man **E**

Chocolate

See/See also pages in the following book(s):

Johnson, S. A. Tomatoes, potatoes, corn, and beans p95-109 (6 and up) **641.3**

Chocolate fever. Smith, R. K. **Fic**

Chodos-Irvine, Margaret

(il) Wong, J. S. Buzz **E**

Chödzin, Sherab

The wisdom of the crows and other Buddhist tales (4 and up) **294.3**

Choi, Sook Nyul

Echoes of the white giraffe. See note under Choi, S. N. Year of impossible goodbyes **Fic**

Gathering of pearls. See note under Choi, S. N. Year of impossible goodbyes **Fic**

Halmoni and the picnic **E**

Year of impossible goodbyes (5 and up) **Fic**

Yunmi and Halmoni's trip. See note under Choi, S. N. Halmoni and the picnic **E**

Choi, Yangsook

(il) Lee, M. Nim and the war effort **E**

(il) Wong, J. S. This next New Year **E**

Choosing books for children. Hearne, B. G. **028.5**

Chopin, Frédéric, 1810-1849

See/See also pages in the following book(s):

Krull, K. Lives of the musicians p30-35 (4 and up) **920**

Chorao, Kay, 1936-
Knock at the door and other baby action rhymes
398.8
Pig and Crow **E**
(comp) The Baby's bedtime book. See The Baby's bedtime book **808.81**
(comp) The Baby's lap book. See The Baby's lap book **398.8**
(il) Crowe, R. L. Clyde monster **E**
(comp) Jumpety-bumpety hop. See Jumpety-bumpety hop **811.008**
(il) Monster poems. See Monster poems **821.008**
(il) Viorst, J. My mama says there aren't any zombies, ghosts, vampires, creatures, demons, monsters, fiends, goblins, or things **E**

Choreographers
Glover, S. Savion!: my life in tap (5 and up) **92**

Chow, Octavio
(jt. auth) Rohmer, H. The invisible hunters **398.2**

Chrisman, Arthur Bowie, 1889-1953
See/See also pages in the following book(s):
Newbery Medal books, 1922-1955 p40-43 **028.5**

Christ *See* Jesus Christ

Christelow, Eileen, 1943-
Don't wake up Mama! See note under Christelow, E. Five little monkeys jumping on the bed **E**
Five little monkeys jumping on the bed **E**
Five little monkeys sitting in a tree. See note under Christelow, E. Five little monkeys jumping on the bed **E**
Five little monkeys wash the car. See note under Christelow, E. Five little monkeys jumping on the bed **E**
Five little monkeys with nothing to do. See note under Christelow, E. Five little monkeys jumping on the bed **E**
What do authors do? (1-3) **808**
What do illustrators do? (1-3) **741.6**
(il) Aylesworth, J. The completed hickory dickory dock **398.8**

Christian, Peggy
If you find a rock (k-3) **552**

Christian, Rebecca
Cooking the Spanish way
In Easy menu ethnic cookbooks **641.5**

Christian life
Fiction
Paterson, K. Preacher's boy (5 and up) **Fic**
Tolan, S. S. Save Halloween! (5 and up) **Fic**

Christian missions
Fiction
O'Dell, S. Zia (5 and up) **Fic**

Christian saints
Armstrong, C. Lives and legends of the saints (4 and up) **920**
De Paola, T. Patrick: patron saint of Ireland (k-3) **92**
Hodges, M. Joan of Arc (2-4) **92**

Mayo, M. Brother sun, sister moon: the life and stories of St. Francis (3-6) **92**
Mulvihill, M. The treasury of saints and martyrs (5 and up) **920**
Poole, J. Joan of Arc (2-4) **92**
Sabuda, R. Saint Valentine (1-3) **92**
Stanley, D. Joan of Arc (4 and up) **92**
Tompert, A. Saint Patrick (k-3) **92**

Christianity
See/See also pages in the following book(s):
Osborne, M. P. One world, many religions p13-22 (4 and up) **291**
Fiction
Speare, E. G. The bronze bow (6 and up) **Fic**

Christianson, Stephen G.
(ed) The American book of days. See The American book of days **394.26**

Christie, Gregory, 1971-
(il) Miller, W. Richard Wright and the library card **E**
(il) The Palm of my heart. See The Palm of my heart **811.008**

Christina, Queen of Sweden, 1626-1689
See/See also pages in the following book(s):
Meltzer, M. Ten queens p85-95 (5 and up) **920**

Christina Katerina & the box. Gauch, P. L. See note under Gauch, P. L. Christina Katerina and the time she quit the family **E**
Christina Katerina and Fats and the Great Neighborhood War. Gauch, P. L. See note under Gauch, P. L. Christina Katerina and the time she quit the family **E**
Christina Katerina and the time she quit the family. Gauch, P. L. **E**

Christmas
See also Jesus Christ—Nativity
Barth, E. Holly, reindeer, and colored lights (3-6) **394.26**
Christmas gif' (3-6) **394.26**
Cooney, B. The story of Christmas (2-4) **394.26**
Encyclopedia of Christmas **394.26**
Hoyt-Goldsmith, D. Las Posadas (3-5) **394.26**
Lankford, M. D. Christmas around the world (3-5) **394.26**
McKissack, P. C. Christmas in the big house, Christmas in the quarters (4-6) **394.26**
See/See also pages in the following book(s):
Bauer, C. F. Celebrations p257-78 **808.8**
Drama
The Big book of Christmas plays **808.82**
Fiction
Anaya, R. A. Farolitos for Abuelo **E**
Anaya, R. A. The farolitos of Christmas **E**
Bell, A. The nutcracker (2-4) **Fic**
Brett, J. The wild Christmas reindeer **E**
Briggs, R. Father Christmas **E**
Brown, M. W. On Christmas Eve **E**
Bunting, E. December **E**
Bunting, E. Night tree **E**
Carlson, N. S. The family under the bridge (3-5) **Fic**

A **Christmas** story. Wildsmith, B.   **E**

The **Christmas** tree man. Rylant, C.
  In Rylant, C. Children of Christmas p1-5
        S C

The **Christmas** turkey. Sanfield, S.
  In Sanfield, S. The adventures of High John
    the Conqueror   **398.2**

Christmas with Ida Early. Burch, R. See note under Burch, R. Ida Early comes over the
  mountain   **Fic**

Christopher, Saint, 3rd cent.?
        About
  De Paola, T. Christopher, the holy giant (k-3)
        398.2

See/See also pages in the following book(s):
  Shedlock, M. L. The art of the story-teller p168-
  72   **372.6**

Christopher, John, 1922-
  The city of gold and lead. See note under Chris-
    topher, J. The White Mountains   **Fic**
  The pool of fire. See note under Christopher, J.
    The White Mountains   **Fic**
  When the Tripods came. See note under Chris-
    topher, J. The White Mountains   **Fic**
  The White Mountains (5 and up)   **Fic**

Christopher, Matt, 1917-1997
  The dog that called the pitch (2-4)   **Fic**
  The hit-away kid (2-4)   **Fic**
  Tackle without a team (4-6)   **Fic**
  Tennis ace (3-6)   **Fic**

Christopher, the holy giant. De Paola, T.
        398.2

Chronicles of Prydain [series]
  Alexander, L. The book of three   **Fic**
  Alexander, L. The high king   **Fic**

Chrysanthemum. Henkes, K.   **E**

Chuck Close, up close. Greenberg, J.   **92**

Chukovskiĭ, Korneĭ, 1882-1969
  Ginsburg, M. Good morning, chick   **E**

Chung, Okwha
  Cooking the Korean way
  In Easy menu ethnic cookbooks   **641.5**

Chunk o' meat
  In Grandfather tales p222-25   **398.2**

Church
  See also Christianity

Church music
  See also Gospel music

Churchill, Sir Winston, 1874-1965
        About
  Severance, J. B. Winston Churchill (5 and up)
        92

Chusham and the wind. Schwartz, H.
  In Schwartz, H. The diamond tree p29-33
        398.2

Chwast, Eve
  (il) Drucker, M. Grandma's latkes   **E**

Cianciolo, Patricia J., 1929-
  Informational picture books for children
        028.1

Ciardi, John, 1916-1986
  You read to me, I'll read to you   **811**

Cigliano, Bill
  (il) Byars, B. C. Me Tarzan   **Fic**

Ciment, James
  Scholastic encyclopedia of the American Indian
  (4 and up)   **970.004**

Cincinnati (Ohio)
        Fiction
  Kroeger, M. K. Paperboy   **E**

Cinder Edna. Jackson, E. B.   **E**

Cinderella (Ballet)
See/See also pages in the following book(s):
  McCaughrean, G. The Random House book of
  stories from the ballet p36-47 (4 and up)
        792.8

Cinderella. Perrault, C.   **398.2**
  also in The Blue fairy book p64-71
        398.2
  also in The Classic fairy tales p123-27
        398.2
  also in Perrault, C. Cinderella, Puss in Boots,
    and other favorite tales p56-77
        398.2
  also in Perrault, C. The complete fairy tales
    of Charles Perrault p60-69   **398.2**

Cinderella, Puss in Boots, and other favorite tales.
  Perrault, C.   **398.2**

Cinderella, The Egyptian. Climo, S.   **398.2**

Cinderella, The Korean. Climo, S.   **398.2**

Cinderella's rat. Meddaugh, S.   **E**

Cinderellis and the glass hill. Levine, G. C. See
  note under Levine, G. C. The princess test
        Fic

Cinematography
  Hamilton, J. Special effects in film and television (4 and up)   **791.43**

Cinnamon's day out. Roth, S. L.   **E**

Cinque, 1811?-1879
        Fiction
  Chambers, V. Amistad rising   **E**

Cipher and telegraph codes
        Fiction
  Barasch, L. Radio rescue   **E**

Circle dogs. Henkes, K.   **E**

The **circle** of days. Lindbergh, R.   **242**

Circle of love. Nixon, J. L. See note under Nixon,
  J. L. A family apart   **Fic**

A **circle** of seasons. Livingston, M. C.   **811**

Circle opens quartet
  Pierce, T. Magic steps   **Fic**

The **circlemaker.** Schur, M.   **Fic**

The **circuit.** Jiménez, F.
  In Jiménez, F. The circuit: stories from the
    life of a migrant child p73-83   **S C**

The **circuit:** stories from the life of a migrant
  child. Jiménez, F.   **S C**

Circulatory system *See* Cardiovascular system

The **circulatory** system. Silverstein, A.   **612.1**

Circus
  Granfield, L. Circus (4 and up)   **791.3**
        Fiction
  Clements, A. Circus family dog   **E**
  Ehlert, L. Circus   **E**

Cleary, Brian P., 1959-
Hairy, scary, ordinary (k-3) **428**
Cleaver, Bill
(jt. auth) Cleaver, V. Where the lillies bloom
Fic
Cleaver, Vera
Where the lillies bloom (5 and up) **Fic**
Clemens, Samuel Langhorne *See* Twain, Mark, 1835-1910
Clément, Frédéric
(il) Levine, A. A. The boy who drew cats
398.2
Clemente, Roberto, 1934-1972
See/See also pages in the following book(s):
Krull, K. Lives of the athletes p67-69 (4 and up) **920**
Littlefield, B. Champions p117-29 (5 and up)
920
Clementina's cactus. Keats, E. J. **E**
Clements, Andrew, 1949-
Circus family dog **E**
Frindle (4-6) **Fic**
The janitor's boy (4-6) **Fic**
The Landry News (4-6) **Fic**
Temple cat **E**
Workshop (k-2) **621.9**
Clemesha, David
(jt. auth) Zimmerman, A. G. My dog Toby
E
(jt. auth) Zimmerman, A. G. Trashy town
E
Cleopatra, Queen of Egypt, d. 30 B.C.
About
Stanley, D. Cleopatra (4 and up) **92**
See/See also pages in the following book(s):
Meltzer, M. Ten queens p11-23 (5 and up)
920
Clever answers. Afanas'ev, A. N.
In Afanas'ev, A. N. Russian fairy tales p578-79 **398.2**
Clever cat. Collington, P. **E**
The **clever** coachman. Jaffe, N.
In Jaffe, N. While standing on one foot p66-69 **296.1**
Clever crow. DeFelice, C. C. **E**
The **clever** daughter-in-law. MacDonald, M. R.
In MacDonald, M. R. Celebrate the world p137-45 **372.6**
Clever Frog. Curry, J. L.
In Curry, J. L. Back in the beforetime p57-59
398.2
Clever Grethel. De la Mare, W.
In Womenfolk and fairy tales p71-76
398.2
The **clever** magistrate. Fang, L.
In Fang, L. The Ch'i-lin purse p63-70
398.2
Clever Manka. Fillmore, P.
In Womenfolk and fairy tales p146-55
398.2
Clever Mistress Murray. Jagendorf, M. A.
In From sea to shining sea p68-73 **810.8**
Click!. Gibbons, G. **771**

CLICK!: a story about George Eastman. Mitchell B. **92**
Click, clack, moo. Cronin, D. **E**
Click! fun with photography. Price, S. **771**
Clifford, Eth, 1915-
Help! I'm a prisoner in the library (3-5)
Fic
The remembering box (3-5) **Fic**
Clifton, Lucille, 1936-
Everett Anderson's 1-2-3 **E**
Everett Anderson's Christmas coming. See note under Clifton, L. Everett Anderson's 1-2-3
E
Everett Anderson's friend. See note under Clifton, L. Everett Anderson's 1-2-3 **E**
Everett Anderson's goodbye. See note under Clifton, L. Everett Anderson's 1-2-3 **E**
Everett Anderson's nine month long. See note under Clifton, L. Everett Anderson's 1-2-3
E
Everett Anderson's year. See note under Clifton, L. Everett Anderson's 1-2-3 **E**
The lucky stone (3-5) **Fic**
Some of the days of Everett Anderson. See note under Clifton, L. Everett Anderson's 1-2-3
E
Climate
See also Meteorology; Weather
Arnold, C. El Niño (4 and up) **551.6**
Seibert, P. Discoverning El Niño (k-3)
551.6
Climb into my lap (k-3) **808.81**
Climo, Shirley, 1928-
The cobweb Christmas **E**
The Egyptian Cinderella (k-3) **398.2**
The Korean Cinderella (k-3) **398.2**
Magic & mischief (4 and up) **398.2**
Includes the following stories: The giant of Castle Treen; The very old woman and the Piskey; The widow and the Spriggans of Trencrom Hill; Tom Treverrow and the Knackers; Pleasing Betty Stoggs; The changeling of Brea Vean; The bewitching of Sea Pink; The mermaid of Zennor; The cornish teeny-tiny; Duffy and the Bucca
Stolen thunder (3-5) **293**
Cline-Ransome, Lesa
Satchel Paige (2-4) **92**
Clinton, Catherine, 1952-
Scholastic encyclopedia of the Civil War (4 and up) **973.7**
(comp) I, too, sing America. See I, too, sing America **811.008**
The **cloak**. Jaffe, N.
In Jaffe, N. The cow of no color: riddle stories and justice tales from around the world p23-26 **398.2**
Clocks and more clocks. Hutchins, P. **E**
Clocks and watches
Branley, F. M. Keeping time (4-6) **529**
Duffy, T. The clock (4 and up) **681.1**
Maestro, B. The story of clocks and calendars (3-6) **529**
Older, J. Telling time (k-3) **529**
Fiction
Harper, D. Telling time with Big Mama Cat
E
Hutchins, P. Clocks and more clocks **E**

Clockwork. Pullman, P.   Fic

Close, Chuck, 1940-
About
Greenberg, J. Chuck Close, up close (4 and up)   92

Cloth *See* Fabrics

Clothing and dress
> *See also* Coats; Costume

Corey, S. You forgot your skirt, Amelia Bloomer (k-2)   92

Kuskin, K. The Philharmonic gets dressed   E

Rowland-Warne, L. Costume (4 and up)   391
Fiction
Brett, J. The hat   E
Daly, N. Jamela's dress   E
Gilson, J. Bug in a rug (2-4)   Fic
Neitzel, S. The dress I'll wear to the party   E

Neitzel, S. The jacket I wear in the snow   E

Taback, S. Joseph had a little overcoat   E

The cloud book. De Paola, T.   551.57

Clouds
Branley, F. M. Down comes the rain (k-3)   551.57
De Paola, T. The cloud book (k-3)   551.57
McMillan, B. The weather sky (4 and up)   551.57
Fiction
Wiesner, D. Sector 7   E

Clouds of glory. Chaikin, M.   296.1

The clown of God. De Paola, T.   398.2

Clowns
Perkins, C. The most excellent book of how to be a clown (4-6)   791.3

Club de Madres Virgen del Carmen of Lima, Peru
Dorros, A. Tonight is Carnaval   E

Clutton-Brock, Juliet
Cat (4 and up)   599.75
Horse (4 and up)   636.1

Clyde monster. Crowe, R. L.   E

Coady, Christopher
(il) Hooper, M. The drop in my drink   553.7

A coal miner's bride. Bartoletti, S. C.   Fic

Coal mines and mining
Bartoletti, S. C. Growing up in coal country (5 and up)   331.3
Fiction
Almond, D. Kit's wilderness (5 and up)   Fic
Bartoletti, S. C. A coal miner's bride (4 and up)   Fic

Coalson, Glo
(il) Scott, A. H. Brave as a mountain lion   E
(il) Scott, A. H. Hi   E
(il) Scott, A. H. On Mother's lap   E
(il) Willner-Pardo, G. Daphne Eloise Slater, who's tall for her age   Fic

A coat for the moon. Schwartz, H.
> *In* Schwartz, H. A coat for the moon and other Jewish tales p74-76   398.2

A coat for the moon and other Jewish tales. Schwartz, H.   398.2

Coat o' clay. Jacobs, J.
> *In* Jacobs, J. English fairy tales p294-99   398.2

Coats
Fiction
Hest, A. The purple coat   E
Oram, H. The wrong overcoat   E
Ziefert, H. A new coat for Anna   E

Coatsworth, Elizabeth Jane, 1893-1986
The cat who went to heaven (4 and up)   Fic

See/See also pages in the following book(s):
Newbery Medal books, 1922-1955 p94-98   028.5

Cobb, Josh
(jt. auth) Cobb, V. Light action!   535

Cobb, Mary, 1931-
The quilt-block history of pioneer days (2-5)   746.46
A sampler view of colonial life (2-5)   746.44

Cobb, Theo
(il) Cobb, V. Light action!   535

Cobb, Ty, 1886-1961
About
Jacobs, W. J. They shaped the game (4 and up)   920

Cobb, Vicki, 1938-
Bet you can! science possibilities to fool you (4 and up)   793.8
Bet you can't! science impossibilities to fool you (4 and up)   793.8
Dirt & grime, like you've never seen (4-6)   502.8
Don't try this at home! (4-6)   507.8
Follow your nose (3-6)   612.8
How to really fool yourself (5 and up)   152.1
Light action! (5 and up)   535
Magic—naturally! (4 and up)   793.8
Science experiments you can eat (5 and up)   507.8
Wanna bet! (4 and up)   793.8
Why doesn't the earth fall up? (3-5)   531
You gotta try this! (4 and up)   507.8
Your tongue can tell (3-6)   612.8

Cobblestone   973.05

Cobras
Fiction
Pinkney, J. Rikki-tikki-tavi   E

Coburn, Jewell Reinhart
Domitila (2-4)   398.2

The cobweb Christmas. Climo, S.   E

Cocca-Leffler, Maryann, 1958-
(il) Spinelli, E. Thanksgiving at the Tappletons'   E

Cochise, Apache Chief, d. 1874
See/See also pages in the following book(s):
Ehrlich, A. Wounded Knee: an Indian history of the American West (6 and up)   970.004

The **cock** and the hand mill. Afanas´ev, A. N.
In Afanas´ev, A. N. Russian fairy tales p387-89   **398.2**

The **cock** and the hen. Afanas´ev, A. N.
In Afanas´ev, A. N. Russian fairy tales p309   **398.2**

The **cock** and the jackal. Aardema, V.
In Aardema, V. Misoso p47-49   **398.2**

Cockfight. Yolen, J.
In Yolen, J. Here there be dragons p26-50   **810.8**

Cockroach cooties. Yep, L. See note under Yep, L. Later, gator   **Fic**

Cockroaches
Fiction
Cannon, J. Crickwing   **E**
James, M. Shoebag (5 and up)   **Fic**

Cocoa ice. Appelbaum, D. K.   **E**

CoConis, Constantinos *See* CoConis, Ted

CoConis, Ted
(il) Byars, B. C. The summer of the swans   **Fic**

Coconut kind of day. Joseph, L.   **811**

Cody, William Frederick *See* Buffalo Bill, 1846-1917

Cody unplugged. Duffey, B. See note under Duffey, B. Spotlight on Cody   **Fic**

Cody's secret admirer. Duffey, B. See note under Duffey, B. Spotlight on Cody   **Fic**

Coerr, Eleanor, 1922-
The big balloon race   **E**
Chang's paper pony   **E**
The Josefina story quilt   **E**
Mieko and the fifth treasure (3-5)   **Fic**
Sadako [biography of Sadako Sasaki] (1-4)   **92**
Sadako and the thousand paper cranes [biography of Sadako Sasaki] (3-6)   **92**

Cogancherry, Helen
(il) Sanders, S. R. Warm as wool   **E**

Cohen, Barbara, 1932-1992
Canterbury tales (4 and up)   **821**
Contents: The nun's priest's tale; The pardoner's tale; The wife of Bath's tale; The franklin's tale
The carp in the bathtub (2-4)   **Fic**
Molly's pilgrim   **E**
Thank you, Jackie Robinson (4-6)   **Fic**

Cohen, Caron Lee
The mud pony (k-3)   **398.2**
Sally Ann Thunder Ann Whirlwind Crockett meets Mike Fink, Snappin' Turkle
In From sea to shining sea p118-20   **810.8**

Cohen, Daniel, 1936-
Ghost in the house (4 and up)   **133.1**
Great ghosts (4 and up)   **133.1**

Cohen, Miriam, 1926-
"Bee my valentine!". See note under Cohen, M. It's George!   **E**
Best friends. See note under Cohen, M. It's George!   **E**
Don't eat too much turkey! See note under Cohen, M. It's George!   **E**
It's George!   **E**

Jim meets the thing. See note under Cohen, M. It's George!   **E**
No good in art. See note under Cohen, M. It's George!   **E**
See you tomorrow, Charles. See note under Cohen, M. It's George!   **E**
So what? See note under Cohen, M. It's George!   **E**
Starring first grade. See note under Cohen, M. It's George!   **E**
When will I read? See note under Cohen, M. It's George!   **E**
Will I have a friend? See note under Cohen, M. It's George!   **E**

Cohn, Amy
Casey Jones, railroad man
In From sea to shining sea p170-71   **810.8**
Jack and the two-bullet hunt
In From sea to shining sea p90-91   **810.8**
Strong as Annie Christmas
In From sea to shining sea p277-79   **810.8**
With a way, hey, Mister Stormalong
In From sea to shining sea p104-06   **810.8**
(comp) From sea to shining sea. See From sea to shining sea   **810.8**

Cohn, Ronald H.
(il) Patterson, F. Koko-love!   **599.8**

Coiley, John
Train (4 and up)   **625.1**

Coins
Hoban, T. 26 letters and 99 cents   **E**

Colborn, Candy, 1942-
What do children read next?   **016.8**

Cold (Disease)
Silverstein, A. Common colds (3-5)   **616.2**

The **cold** & hot winter. Hurwitz, J. See note under Hurwitz, J. The hot & cold summer   **Fic**

Cold Feet and the Lonesome Queen
In Stockings of buttermilk: American folktales p51-55   **398.2**

Cold little duck, duck, duck. Peters, L. W.   **E**

Cold Shoulder Road. Aiken, J. See note under Aiken, J. The wolves of Willoughby Chase   **Fic**

Cole, Ann
I saw a purple cow, and 100 other recipes for learning   **372**

Cole, Brock, 1938-
Buttons   **E**
(il) Banks, L. R. The Indian in the cupboard   **Fic**

Cole, Henry
I took a walk   **E**
(il) Earle, A. Zipping, zapping, zooming bats   **599.4**
(il) Edwards, P. D. Honk!   **E**
(il) Edwards, P. D. Some smug slug   **E**

Cole, Joanna
Bigger and smaller
In Ready, set, read—and laugh! p30-43   **810.8**

Collins, Joseph T.
(jt. auth) Conant, R. Peterson first guide to reptiles and amphibians   **597.9**

Collins, Mary, 1961-
The Industrial Revolution (4 and up)
    330.973

Collins, Pat Lowery, 1932-
(il) Dreams of glory. See Dreams of glory
    811.008

Collodi, Carlo, 1826-1890
The adventures of Pinocchio (3-6)   **Fic**
The adventures of Pinocchio; adaptation. See Young, E. Pinocchio   **Fic**

Colman, Penny
Girls! (5 and up)   **305.23**
Rosie the riveter (5 and up)   **331.4**

Colombia
Markham, L. Colombia (4 and up)   **986.1**
Morrison, M. Colombia (4 and up)   **986.1**

Colombo, Cristoforo See Columbus, Christopher

Colón, Raúl
(il) Burleigh, R. Hercules   **292**
(il) Gray, L. M. My mama had a dancing heart   **E**
(il) Hopkinson, D. A band of angels   **E**
(il) Mora, P. Tomás and the library lady   **E**
(il) San Souci, R. A weave of words   **398.2**

Colonial craftsmen [series]
Fisher, L. E. The architects   **720**
Fisher, L. E. The blacksmiths   **682**
Fisher, L. E. The cabinetmakers   **684.1**
Fisher, L. E. The doctors   **610.9**
Fisher, L. E. The glassmakers   **666**
Fisher, L. E. The homemakers   **640**
Fisher, L. E. The limners   **759.13**
Fisher, L. E. The peddlers   **381**
Fisher, L. E. The potters   **666**
Fisher, L. E. The printers   **686.2**
Fisher, L. E. The shipbuilders   **623.8**
Fisher, L. E. The shoemakers   **685**
Fisher, L. E. The silversmiths   **739.2**
Fisher, L. E. The tanners   **675**
Fisher, L. E. The weavers   **677**
Fisher, L. E. The wigmakers   **391**

Colonial craftsmen and the beginnings of American industry. Tunis, E.   **680**

Colonial days. King, D. C.   **973.2**

Colonial leaders [series]
Hinman, B. Benjamin Banneker   **92**

Colonial living. Tunis, E.   **973.2**

Color
Crews, D. Freight train   **E**
Ehlert, L. Color farm   **E**
Ehlert, L. Color zoo   **E**
Fleming, D. Lunch   **E**
Hoban, T. Colors everywhere   **E**
Hoban, T. Is it red? Is it yellow? Is it blue?   **E**
Hoban, T. Of colors and things   **E**
Levine, S. The optics book (4 and up)   **535**
McMillan, B. Growing colors   **E**
Onyefulu, I. Chidi only likes blue   **E**
Serfozo, M. Who said red?   **E**
Testa, F. If you take a paintbrush   **E**

Fiction
Godwin, L. Little white dog   **E**
Lionni, L. A color of his own   **E**
Lionni, L. Little blue and little yellow   **E**
Martin, B. A beasty story   **E**
Martin, B. Brown bear, brown bear what do you see?   **E**
Zolotow, C. Mr. Rabbit and the lovely present   **E**

Poetry
O'Neill, M. L. D. Hailstones and halibut bones (k-3)   **811**

Color farm. Ehlert, L.   **E**

Color me dark. McKissack, P. C.   **Fic**

A **color** of his own. Lionni, L.   **E**

Color zoo. Ehlert, L.   **E**

Colorado
Ayer, E. H. Colorado
In Celebrate the states   **973**
Blashfield, J. F. Colorado
In America the beautiful, second series   **973**

Colors everywhere. Hoban, T.   **E**

Colum, Padraic, 1881-1972
The Golden Fleece and the heroes who lived before Achilles (5 and up)   **292**
The Trojan War and the adventures of Odysseus (4 and up)   **883**

Columbus, Christopher
About
Brenner, B. If you were there in 1492 (4-6)   **970.01**
Fritz, J. Where do you think you're going, Christopher Columbus? (2-4)   **92**
Marzollo, J. In 1492 (k-2)   **970.01**
Sis, P. Follow the dream (k-3)   **92**
See/See also pages in the following book(s):
Fritz, J. Around the world in a hundred years p39-49 (4-6)   **910.4**

Coman, Carolyn
What Jamie saw (5 and up)   **Fic**

Comanche Indians
See/See also pages in the following book(s):
Freedman, R. Indian chiefs p53-71 (6 and up)   **920**

Come a stranger. Voigt, C.   **Fic**

Come a tide. Lyon, G. E.   **E**

Come all you brave soldiers. Cox, C.   **973.3**

Come along, Daisy!. Simmons, J.   **E**

Come back, Amelia Bedelia. Parish, P. See note under Parish, P. Amelia Bedelia   **E**
also in Ready, set, read—and laugh! p75-96   **810.8**

Come back, salmon. Cone, M.   **639.3**

Come on, rain!. Hesse, K.   **E**

Come out and play, little mouse. Kraus, R. See note under Kraus, R. Whose mouse are you?   **E**

Come sing, Jimmy Jo. Paterson, K.   **Fic**

Come Sunday. Grimes, N.   **811**

The **comeback** dog. Thomas, J. R.   **Fic**

Comet in Moominland. Jansson, T. See note under Jansson, T. Moominsummer madness   **Fic**

Comets

Bonar, S. Comets (4 and up)   **523.6**

Marsh, C. S. Asteroids, comets, and meteors (4-6)   **523.6**

Simon, S. Comets, meteors, and asteroids (3-6)   **523.6**

Vogt, G. Asteroids, comets, and meteors (2-4)   **523.6**

Fiction

Hopkinson, D. Maria's comet   **E**

Comets, meteors, and asteroids. Simon, S.   **523.6**

The **Comic** adventures of Old Mother Hubbard and her dog   **398.8**

Comic books, strips, etc.

See also Cartoons and caricatures

Pellowski, M. The art of making comic books (5 and up)   **741.5**

Fiction

Pinkney, B. The adventures of Sparrowboy   **E**

Coming home: from the life of Langston Hughes. Cooper, F.   **92**

The **coming** of Manabush. Curry, J. L.

In Curry, J. L. Turtle Island: tales of the Algonquian nations p23-26   **398.2**

Coming to America: the story of immigration. Maestro, B.   **325.73**

Commander Toad and the big black hole. Yolen, J. See note under Yolen, J. Commander Toad and the voyage home   **Fic**

Commander Toad and the dis-asteroid. Yolen, J. See note under Yolen, J. Commander Toad and the voyage home   **Fic**

Commander Toad and the intergalactic spy. Yolen, J. See note under Yolen, J. Commander Toad and the voyage home   **Fic**

Commander Toad and the Planet of the Grapes. Yolen, J. See note under Yolen, J. Commander Toad and the voyage home   **Fic**

Commander Toad and the space pirates. Yolen, J. See note under Yolen, J. Commander Toad and the voyage home   **Fic**

Commander Toad and the voyage home. Yolen, J.   **Fic**

Commander Toad in space. Yolen, J. See note under Yolen, J. Commander Toad and the voyage home   **Fic**

Commodore Perry in the land of the Shogun. Blumberg, R.   **952**

Common colds. Silverstein, A.   **616.2**

Commonwealth of Independent States

See also Former Soviet republics; Soviet Union

Communicable diseases

See also Sexually transmitted diseases

Communication

Aliki. Communication (k-3)   **302.2**

Aliki. Hello! good-bye! (k-3)   **395**

Communication among animals *See* Animal communication

Community development

See also City planning

Hoose, P. M. It's our world, too! (5 and up)   **302**

Company's coming. Yorinks, A.   **E**

Comparative religion *See* Religions

Competitions *See* Contests

The **complete** adventures of Tom Kitten and his friends. Potter, B. See note under Potter, B. The story of Miss Moppet   **E**

The **Complete** dog book for kids (4 and up)   **636.7**

The **complete** fairy tales of Charles Perrault. Perrault, C.   **398.2**

The **complete** nonsense of Edward Lear. Lear, E.   **821**

The **complete** poems to solve. Swenson, M.   **811**

The **complete** story of the three blind mice. Ivimey, J. W.   **E**

The **complete** tales of Winnie-the-Pooh. Milne, A. A.   **Fic**

Complete version of ye three blind mice. See Ivimey, J. W. The complete story of the three blind mice   **E**

The **complete** works of Lewis Carroll. Carroll, L.   **828**

The **completed** hickory dickory dock. Aylesworth, J.   **398.8**

Comport, Sally Wern

(il) San Souci, R. Brave Margaret   **398.2**

Composers

See also Women composers

Isadora, R. Young Mozart (2-4)   **92**

Krull, K. Lives of the musicians (4 and up)   **920**

Venezia, M. George Handel (k-3)   **92**

Winter, J. Sebastian: a book about Bach (k-3)   **92**

Compost

Glaser, L. Compost! (k-2)   **363.7**

Lavies, B. Compost critters (4 and up)   **591.7**

Compost critters. Lavies, B.   **591.7**

Compton's encyclopedia & fact-index   **031**

Compton's yearbook. See Compton's encyclopedia & fact-index   **031**

Compulsory labor *See* Slavery

Computation, Approximate *See* Approximate computation

Computer-assisted instruction

Benson, A. C. Connecting kids and the Internet   **004.6**

Berger, P. Internet for active learners   **004.6**

Eisenberg, M. Teaching information & technology skills   **025.5**

Computer-based information systems *See* Information systems

Computer modeling *See* Computer simulation

Computer models *See* Computer simulation

Computer networks

See also Internet

Computer programming
See also Computer software

Computer science
See also Data processing

Computer simulation
Baker, C. W. Scientific visualization (5 and up)
006

Jefferis, D. Cyberspace (4 and up)   **004.6**

Computer software
Catalogs
Ross, C. The frugal youth cybrarian   **025.2**

Computers
See also Data processing
Jefferis, D. Cyberspace (4 and up)   **004.6**
Dictionaries
Spencer, D. D. Illustrated computer dictionary for young people   **004**
Webster's New World dictionary of computer terms   **004**
Computers & technology in school library media centers. See Bucher, K. T. Information technology for schools   **027.8**

Conant, Roger, 1909-
Peterson first guide to reptiles and amphibians (6 and up)   **597.9**

Concentration camps
See also Holocaust, 1933-1945; Japanese Americans—Evacuation and relocation, 1942-1945

Concepts
See also Shape
The **concise** AACR2, 1998 revision. Gorman, M.
025.3

Condors
Silverstein, A. The California condor (4 and up)
598

Cone, Molly, 1918-
Come back, salmon (3-6)   **639.3**
Cone, Patricia Clapp *See* Clapp, Patricia, 1912-
Cone, Patrick
Wildfire (3-6)   **577.2**
Conestoga wagons. Ammon, R.   **388.3**

Conflict, Ethnic *See* Ethnic relations

Conford, Ellen
Annabel the actress starring in "Gorilla my dreams" (2-4)   **Fic**
Annabel the actress starring in "Just a little extra". See note under Conford, E. Annabel the actress starring in "Gorilla my dreams"   **Fic**

Can do, Jenny Archer. See note under Conford, E. A case for Jenny Archer   **Fic**
A case for Jenny Archer (2-4)   **Fic**
Get the picture, Jenny Archer. See note under Conford, E. A case for Jenny Archer   **Fic**
Jenny Archer, author. See note under Conford, E. A case for Jenny Archer   **Fic**
Jenny Archer to the rescue. See note under Conford, E. A case for Jenny Archer   **Fic**
A job for Jenny Archer. See note under Conford, E. A case for Jenny Archer   **Fic**
Nibble, nibble, Jenny Archer. See note under Conford, E. A case for Jenny Archer   **Fic**

What's cooking, Jenny Archer? See note under Conford, E. A case for Jenny Archer   **Fic**

Confucianism
See/See also pages in the following book(s):
Osborne, M. P. One world, many religions p63-69 (4 and up)   **291**

Congo (Brazzaville) *See* Congo (Republic)

Congo (Republic)
Heale, J. Democratic Republic of the Congo (5 and up)   **967.51**

Congress (U.S.) *See* United States. Congress

The **conjure** brother. McKissack, P. C.
In McKissack, P. C. The dark-thirty p66-77
S C

The **Conjure** wives
In Diane Goode's book of scary stories & songs p42-47   **398.2**
The **conjure** wives. MacDonald, M. R.
In MacDonald, M. R. When the lights go out p79-85   **372.6**

Conjuring *See* Magic tricks

Conly, Jane Leslie
Crazy lady! (5 and up)   **Fic**
Racso and the rats of NIMH (4 and up)
Fic

RT, Margaret, and the rats of NIMH. See note under Conly, J. L. Rasco and the rats of NIMH   **Fic**
While no one was watching (5 and up)   **Fic**

Conly, Robert L. *See* O'Brien, Robert C., 1918-1973

Connected university. See entry in Part 2: Web Resources

Connecticut
McNair, S. Connecticut
In America the beautiful, second series
973

Sherrow, V. Connecticut
In Celebrate the states   **973**
Fiction
Dalgliesh, A. The courage of Sarah Noble (2-4)
Fic

History—1600-1775, Colonial period—Fiction
Speare, E. G. The witch of Blackbird Pond (6 and up)   **Fic**

The **Connecticut** peddler. Leach, M.
In From sea to shining sea p218   **810.8**
Connecting kids and the Internet. Benson, A. C.
004.6

Connolly, Maureen *See* Brinker, Maureen Connolly, 1934-1969

Conrad, Pam, 1947-1996
My Daniel (5 and up)   **Fic**
Our house (4-6)   **S C**
Contents: Boy fossil; Night photograph; Dead flies; The longest summer on record; Writer's notebook; The second bad thing
Prairie songs (5 and up)   **Fic**
Stonewords (5 and up)   **Fic**
Zoe rising (5 and up)   **Fic**

Conservation of forests *See* Forest conservation
Conservation of natural resources
See also Forest conservation; Nature conservation; Wildlife conservation

Conservation of natural resources—*Continued*
Fiction
Cherry, L. The great kapok tree   E
Conservation of plants *See* Plant conservation
Consider the lilies. Paterson, J. B.   **220.8**
Constance: a story of early Plymouth. Clapp, P.   **Fic**
Constellations
VanCleave, J. P. Janice VanCleave's constellations for every kid (4 and up)   **523.8**
Constitutional history
United States
Fritz, J. Shhh! we're writing the Constitution (2-4)   **342**
Maestro, B. A more perfect union (2-4)   **342**
Constitutional rights *See* Civil rights
Construction *See* Building
Construction, House *See* House construction
Construction zone. Hoban, T.   **621.8**
Consumer credit
See/See also pages in the following book(s):
Otfinoski, S. The kid's guide to money p89-98 (4 and up)   **332.024**
Consumer education
See/See also pages in the following book(s):
Otfinoski, S. The kid's guide to money p35-58 (4 and up)   **332.024**
Contact Kids   **505**
Containers, Box *See* Boxes
The **contest.** Hogrogian, N.   **398.2**
Contests
Fiction
Lester, H. Three cheers for Tacky   E
Silverman, E. Don't fidget a feather   E
Contract labor
Fiction
Avi. Encounter at Easton (5 and up)   Fic
Avi. Night journeys (5 and up)   Fic
Contributions to the study of science fiction and fantasy [series]
Sands, K. Back in the spaceship again   **016.8**
Conundrums *See* Riddles
Cook, Deanna F., 1965-
Kids' pumpkin projects (2-4)   **745.5**
Cook, Scott
(il) Van Laan, N. With a whoop and a holler   **398**
Cook-a-doodle-doo!. Stevens, J.   E
The **cookcamp.** Paulsen, G.   Fic
Cooking
See also Baking
Brady, A. A. Kwanzaa karamu (4-6)   **641.5**
Braman, A. N. Kids around the world cook! (4-6)   **641.5**
Cobb, V. Science experiments you can eat (5 and up)   **507.8**
D'Amico, J. The healthy body cookbook (4-6)   **641.5**
D'Amico, J. The math chef (4-6)   **641.5**
D'Amico, J. The science chef (5 and up)   **641.3**

Easy menu ethnic cookbooks (5 and up)   **641.5**
Gillies, J. The Kids Can Press jumbo cookbook (4 and up)   **641.5**
The Good Housekeeping illustrated children's cookbook (4-6)   **641.5**
Kids' first cookbook (k-3)   **641.5**
McMillan, B. Eating fractions (k-2)   **513**
Perl, L. Slumps, grunts, and snickerdoodles: what Colonial America ate and why (4 and up)   **641.5**
Vezza, D. S. Passport on a plate (5 and up)   **641.5**
Walker, B. M. The Little House cookbook (5 and up)   **641.5**
Warshaw, H. The sleepover cookbook (4 and up)   **641.5**
Webb, L. S. Holidays of the world cookbook for students (5 and up)   **641.5**
Zalben, J. B. To every season (4 and up)   **641.5**
See/See also pages in the following book(s):
Cook, D. F. Kids' pumpkin projects (2-4)   **745.5**
King, D. C. Colonial days (3-6)   **973.2**
King, D. C. Pioneer days (3-6)   **978**
King, D. C. Wild West days (3-6)   **978**
Fiction
Stevens, J. Cook-a-doodle-doo!   E
The **cook's** family. Yep, L.   Fic
Cool melons—turn to frogs!: the life and poems of Issa [Kobayashi] Gollub, M.   **92**
Cool salsa (5 and up)   **811.008**
Cool sites series
Trumbauer, L. Homework help for kids on the Net   **004.6**
The **Coomacka-Tree.** Sherlock, Sir P. M.
In Sherlock, Sir P. M. West Indian folk-tales p7-12   **398.2**
Cooney, Barbara, 1917-2000
Chanticleer and the fox   E
Eleanor [biography of Eleanor Roosevelt] (k-3)   **92**
Island boy   E
Miss Rumphius   E
The story of Christmas (2-4)   **394.26**
(il) Boulton, J. Only Opal   E
(il) Hall, D. Ox-cart man   E
(il) Houston, G. The year of the perfect Christmas tree   E
(il) Kesselman, W. A. Emma   E
(il) McLerran, A. Roxaboxen   E
(il) Ray, M. L. Basket moon   E
(il) Seeger, R. C. Animal folk songs for children   **782.42**
(il) Tortillitas para mamá and other nursery rhymes. See Tortillitas para mamá and other nursery rhymes   **398.8**
(il) Yolen, J. Letting Swift River go   E
See/See also pages in the following book(s):
Newbery and Caldecott Medal books, 1976-1985 p211-19   **028.5**
Coons, Jason
(il) Levine, S. Fun with your microscope   **502.8**
(il) Levine, S. The optics book   **535**

Cooper, Elisha
Ballpark   **E**

Cooper, Floyd
Coming home: from the life of Langston
Hughes (2-4)   **92**
Mandela (2-4)   **92**
(il) Greenfield, E. Grandpa's face   **E**
(il) Grimes, N. Meet Danitra Brown   **811**
(il) Haskins, J. African beginnings   **960**
(il) Haskins, J. Bound for America   **326**
(il) How sweet the sound: African-American
songs for children. See How sweet the sound:
African-American songs for children
     782.42
(il) Howard, E. F. Chita's Christmas tree   **E**
(il) Kroll, V. L. Faraway drums   **E**
(il) McKissack, P. C. Ma Dear's aprons   **E**
(il) Merrill, J. The Girl Who Loved Caterpillars
     E
(il) Pass it on. See Pass it on   **811.008**
(il) Schroeder, A. Satchmo's blues   **E**
(il) Thomas, J. C. Brown honey in broomwheat
tea   **811**
(il) Thomas, J. C. Gingerbread days   **811**
(il) Thomas, J. C. I have heard of a land
     E
(il) Williams, K. L. When Africa was home
     E

Cooper, Helen, 1963-
Pumpkin soup   **E**

Cooper, Ilene
The Dead Sea scrolls (5 and up)   **296.1**

Cooper, James Fenimore, 1789-1851
See/See also pages in the following book(s):
Faber, D. Great lives: American literature p3-10
(5 and up)   **920**

Cooper, Martha
(il) Waters, K. Lion dancer: Ernie Wan's Chinese New Year   **394.26**

Cooper, Susan, 1935-
The Boggart (4-6)   **Fic**
The Boggart and the monster. See note under
Cooper, S. The Boggart   **Fic**
The dark is rising. See note under Cooper, S.
Over sea, under stone   **Fic**
Dawn of fear (5 and up)   **Fic**
Ghost story
In Don't read this! and other tales of the un-
natural p33-50   **S C**
Greenwitch. See note under Cooper, S. Over
sea, under stone   **Fic**
The grey king (5 and up)   **Fic**
King of shadows (5 and up)   **Fic**
Over sea, under stone (5 and up)   **Fic**
Seaward (6 and up)   **Fic**
The silver cow: a Welsh tale (1-4)   **398.2**
Silver on the tree. See note under Cooper, S.
Over sea, under stone   **Fic**
Tam Lin (1-4)   **398.2**
See/See also pages in the following book(s):
Newbery and Caldecott Medal books, 1976-1985
p6-17   **028.5**
Origins of story p60-79   **808.06**

Coppélia (Ballet)
Fonteyn, Dame M. Coppélia (3-5)   **792.8**

See/See also pages in the following book(s):
McCaughrean, G. The Random House book of
stories from the ballet p18-28 (4 and up)
     792.8
Newman, B. The illustrated book of ballet stories p32-41 (4-6)   **792.8**

Copper
Beatty, R. Copper
In The Elements [Benchmark Bks.]   **546**
Coral reef. Cerullo, M. M.   **577.7**

Coral reefs and islands
Arnold, C. A walk on the Great Barrier Reef
(3-5)   **578.7**
Cerullo, M. M. Coral reef (4 and up)
     577.7

Fiction
Barner, B. Fish wish   **E**

Corazones Valientes (Organization)
Reiser, L. Tortillas and lullabies. Tortillas y
cancioncitas   **E**

Corbella, Luciano
(il) Couper, H. Black holes   **523.8**
(il) Couper, H. Is anybody out there?
     576.8

Corbett, Scott, 1913-
The lemonade trick (3-5)   **Fic**

Corbishley, Mike
Ancient Rome (5 and up)   **937**
The Middle Ages (5 and up)   **940.1**

Corduroy. Freeman, D.   **E**
also in The Read-aloud treasury p190-206
     808.8

Coretta Scott King Award
The Coretta Scott King Awards book, 1970-
1999   **028.5**
Stephens, C. G. Coretta Scott King Award
books   **028.5**
Coretta Scott King Award books. Stephens, C. G.
     028.5
The **Coretta** Scott King Awards book, 1970-1999
     028.5

Corey, Shana
You forgot your skirt, Amelia Bloomer (k-2)
     92

Corfield, Robin Bell
(il) Levy, C. A crack in the clouds and other
poems   **811**

Corn
Aliki. Corn is maize (k-3)   **633.1**
Landau, E. Corn (2-4)   **633.1**
See/See also pages in the following book(s):
Johnson, S. A. Tomatoes, potatoes, corn, and
beans p7-25 (6 and up)   **641.3**
Corn is maize. Aliki   **633.1**

Cornell, Laura
(il) Curtis, J. L. Tell me again about the night
I was born   **E**
(il) Fleischman, S. The ghost on Saturday night
     Fic

Cornerstones of freedom [series]
Collins, M. The Industrial Revolution
     330.973
Harvey, M. The fall of the Soviet Union
     947

Counting—*Continued*

Murphy, S. J. Just enough carrots (k-1)
    513

Onyefulu, I. Emeka's gift   **E**

Pomeroy, D. One potato   **E**

Rankin, L. The handmade counting book
    419

Saul, C. P. Barn cat   **E**

Schmandt-Besserat, D. The history of counting (4 and up)   **513**

Schnur, S. Night lights   **E**

Schumaker, W. In my garden   **E**

Schwartz, D. M. On beyond a million (2-4)
    513

Sendak, M. One was Johnny   **E**

Tafuri, N. Counting to Christmas   **E**

Tudor, T. 1 is one   **E**

Van Laan, N. A tree for me   **E**

Walsh, E. S. Mouse count   **E**

Walton, R. One more bunny   **E**

Wells, R. Emily's first 100 days of school
    E

Williams, S. Let's go visiting   **E**

Winter, J. Josefina   **E**

Wise, W. Ten sly piranhas   **E**

Counting books *See* Counting

Counting kids. Golding, K.   **E**

Counting to Christmas. Tafuri, N.   **E**

Counting wildflowers. McMillan, B.   **E**

Countries of the world [series]
NgCheong-Lum, R. France   **944**

Country and western music *See* Country music

The **country** bunny and the little gold shoes. Heyward, D.   **E**

Country crossing. Aylesworth, J.   **E**

Country life

    See also Mountain life

Crews, D. Bigmama's (k-3)   **92**

Fiction

Burch, R. Ida Early comes over the mountain (4 and up)   **Fic**

Johnson, A. Down the winding road   **E**

Lyon, G. E. Come a tide   **E**

Martin, B. Barn dance!   **E**

Rylant, C. Night in the country   **E**

Schertle, A. Down the road   **E**

Winch, J. The old woman who loved to read
    E

Yolen, J. Letting Swift River go   **E**

Country music

    See also Cowhands—Songs

Fiction

Paterson, K. Come sing, Jimmy Jo (5 and up)
    Fic

Couper, Heather

Black holes (5 and up)   **523.8**

Is anybody out there? (4 and up)   **576.8**

Courage

Fiction

Hearne, B. G. Seven brave women   **E**

Peet, B. Cowardly Clyde   **E**

Spinelli, J. Wringer (4 and up)   **Fic**

The **courage** of Kazan. Walker, B. K.
  In Walker, B. K. A treasury of Turkish folktales for children p67-74   **398.2**

The **courage** of Sarah Noble. Dalgliesh, A.
    Fic

The **courier**. Delacre, L.
  In Delacre, L. Golden tales p65-68   **398.2**

Courlander, Harold, 1908-1996

Cow-tail switch, and other West African stories (4-6)   **398.2**

Coyote helps decorate the night
  In From sea to shining sea p16-17   **810.8**

Sharing the crops
  In From sea to shining sea p219-21
    810.8

The **court** jester's last wish. Jaffe, N.
  In Jaffe, N. While standing on one foot p23-25   **296.1**

The **court** of the stone children. Cameron, E.
    Fic

Courts and courtiers

    See also Princesses; Queens

Aliki. A medieval feast (2-5)   **394.1**

Courtship (Animal behavior) *See* Animal courtship

Cousins

Fiction

Greenfield, E. Easter parade (2-4)   **Fic**

Hamilton, V. Cousins (5 and up)   **Fic**

Hamilton, V. Second cousins (5 and up)
    Fic

Hest, A. Nana's birthday party   **E**

Root, P. Aunt Nancy and Cousin Lazybones
    E

White, R. Belle Prater's boy (5 and up)
    Fic

Cousins in the castle. Wallace, B. B.   **Fic**

Coverlets *See* Quilts

Coville, Bruce

The guardian of memory
  In A Glory of unicorns p1-28   **S C**

Jennifer Murdley's toad (4-6)   **Fic**

Jeremy Thatcher, dragon hatcher (4-6)   **Fic**

Oddly enough (6 and up)   **S C**
Contents: The box; Duffy's jacket; Homeward bound; With his head tucked underneath his arm; Clean as a whistle; The language of blood; Old glory; The passing of the pack; A blaze of glory

The skull of truth (4-6)   **Fic**

William Shakespeare's A midsummer night's dream   **822.3**

William Shakespeare's Macbeth   **822.3**

William Shakespeare's Romeo and Juliet
    822.3

(comp) A Glory of unicorns. See A Glory of unicorns   **S C**

Coville, Katherine

Story hour
  In A Glory of unicorns p97-112   **S C**

(il) San Souci, R. More short & shivery
    398.2

(il) San Souci, R. Short & shivery   **398.2**

The **cow**. Kimmel, E. A.
  In Kimmel, E. A. The adventures of Hershel of Ostropol p44-51   **398.2**

The **cow** of no color. Jaffe, N.
  In Jaffe, N. The cow of no color: riddle stories and justice tales from around the world p10-13   **398.2**

The **cow** of no color: riddle stories and justice tales from around the world. Jaffe, N.
    398.2

The **cow-tail** switch. Courlander, H.
  In Courlander, H. Cow-tail switch, and other West African stories p5-12   **398.2**

Cow-tail switch, and other West African stories. Courlander, H.   **398.2**

The **cow** who wouldn't come down. Johnson, P. B.   **E**

The **coward**. Kimmel, E. A.
  In Kimmel, E. A. Sword of the samurai p23-30   **Fic**

Cowardly Clyde. Peet, B.   **E**

Cowboy: an album. Granfield, L.   **978**

The **cowboy** and the black-eyed pea. Johnston, T.   **E**

Cowboy bunnies. Loomis, C.   **E**

Cowboy Charlie: the story of Charles M. Russell. Winter, J.   **92**

Cowboy country. Scott, A. H.   **978**

Cowboy dreams. Appelt, K.   **E**

Cowboy dreams. Khalsa, D. K.   **E**

Cowboy Kid. Eilenberg, M.   **E**

Cowboys. Rounds, G.   **978**

Cowboys of the wild West. Freedman, R.   **978**

Cowcher, Helen
  Jaguar   **E**
  Tigress   **E**

Cowhands
  Ancona, G. Charro (3-6)   **972**
  Freedman, R. Cowboys of the wild West (4 and up)   **978**
  Granfield, L. Cowboy: an album (5 and up)   **978**
  Kimmel, E. A. Grizz!   **E**
  Pinkney, A. D. Bill Pickett, rodeo ridin' cowboy (k-3)   **92**
  Rounds, G. Cowboys (k-2)   **978**
  Scott, A. H. Cowboy country (k-3)   **978**

            Fiction
  Appelt, K. Cowboy dreams   **E**
  Johnston, T. The cowboy and the black-eyed pea   **E**
  Khalsa, D. K. Cowboy dreams   **E**
  Kimmel, E. A. Four dollars and fifty cents   **E**
  Lester, J. Black cowboy, wild horses   **E**
  Loomis, C. Cowboy bunnies   **E**
  Myers, W. D. The journal of Joshua Loper (5 and up)   **Fic**
  Teague, M. How I spent my summer vacation   **E**

            Songs
  Medearis, A. S. The zebra-riding cowboy (k-3)   **782.42**
  Songs of the Wild West   **782.42**

Cowles, Kathleen *See* Krull, Kathleen, 1952-

Cowley, Joy
  Gracias, the Thanksgiving turkey   **E**
  Red-eyed tree frog   **E**

Cows *See* Cattle

Cows can't fly. Milgrim, D.   **E**

Cox, Clinton
  Come all you brave soldiers (6 and up)   **973.3**
  Undying glory (6 and up)   **973.7**

Cox, Judy, 1954-
  Weird stories from the Lonesome Café (2-4)   **Fic**

Coxe, Molly, 1959-
  (il) Branley, F. M. The Big Dipper   **523.8**

Coy, John
  Strong to the hoop   **E**

Coyote (Legendary character)
  Aardema, V. Borreguita and the coyote (k-3)   **398.2**
  Bierhorst, J. Doctor Coyote (1-4)   **398.2**
  Curry, J. L. Back in the beforetime (4-6)   **398.2**
  Goldin, B. D. Coyote and the firestick (3-5)   **398.2**
  Johnston, T. The tale of Rabbit and Coyote (k-3)   **398.2**
  McDermott, G. Coyote: a trickster tale from the American Southwest (k-3)   **398.2**
  Stevens, J. Coyote steals the blanket (k-3)   **398.2**
  Stevens, J. Old bag of bones (k-3)   **398.2**
  Taylor, H. P. Coyote places the stars (k-3)   **398.2**

Coyote and Badger. Curry, J. L.
  In Curry, J. L. Back in the beforetime p78-88   **398.2**

Coyote and the firestick. Goldin, B. D.   **398.2**

The **coyote** and the rabbit. Sierra, J.
  In Sierra, J. Nursery tales around the world p77-79   **398.2**

Coyote and the salmon. Curry, J. L.
  In Curry, J. L. Back in the beforetime p42-47   **398.2**

Coyote helps decorate the night. Courlander, H.
  In From sea to shining sea p16-17   **810.8**

Coyote places the stars. Taylor, H. P.   **398.2**

Coyote rides a star. Curry, J. L.
  In Curry, J. L. Back in the beforetime p48-51   **398.2**

Coyote rides the Sun. Curry, J. L.
  In Curry, J. L. Back in the beforetime p100-106   **398.2**

Coyote steals the blanket. Stevens, J.   **398.2**

Coyotes
  Swinburne, S. R. Coyote (4-6)   **599.77**

Coyote's crying song. MacDonald, M. R.
  In MacDonald, M. R. Twenty tellable tales p10-19   **372.6**

Coyote's name. Bruchac, J.
  In Bruchac, J. Tell me a tale p13-16   **372.6**

Coyote's rain song. MacDonald, M. R.
  In MacDonald, M. R. Twenty tellable tales p20-23   **372.6**

Coyote's squirrel hunt. Curry, J. L.
  In Curry, J. L. Back in the beforetime p74-77
          398.2

The **crab** that played with the sea. Kipling, R.
  In Kipling, R. Just so stories   **S C**

Crabs
  McDonald, M. Is this a house for Hermit Crab?
  (k-2)   **595.3**
        Fiction
  Carle, E. A house for Hermit Crab   **E**

A **crack** in the clouds and other poems. Levy, C.
        811

Cracker Jackson. Byars, B. C.   **Fic**

Craft, Charlotte
  King Midas and the golden touch   **398.2**

Craft, Kinuko, 1940-
  (il) Craft, C. King Midas and the golden touch
        398.2
  (il) Craft, M. Cupid and Psyche   **292**
  (il) Mayer, M. Baba Yaga and Vasilisa the
  brave   **398.2**
  (il) Mayer, M. Pegasus   **292**

Craft, Marie
  Cupid and Psyche (4 and up)   **292**

Crafts (Arts) *See* Handicraft

Crafts for Kwanzaa. Ross, K.   **745.5**

Craig, Helen
  (il) Holabird, K. Angelina ballerina   **E**
  (il) Zolotow, C. The bunny who found Easter
        E

Craine, Michael
  (il) Howe, J. Playing with words   **92**

Crampton, W. G. (William G.)
  Flag (4 and up)   **929.9**

Crampton, William G. *See* Crampton, W. G.
  (William G.)

Cranberries
  Burns, D. L. Cranberries: fruit of the bogs (3-5)
        634

The **crane** and the heron. Afanas'ev, A. N.
  In Afanas'ev, A. N. Russian fairy tales p66
        398.2

The **crane** maiden. Martin, R.
  In Martin, R. Mysterious tales of Japan
        398.2

The **crane** wife. Bodkin, O.   **398.2**

Cranes (Birds)
  DuTemple, L. A. North American cranes (3-6)
        598
        Fiction
  Byars, B. C. The house of wings (4-6)   **Fic**
  Keller, H. Grandfather's dream   **E**

Crash. Spinelli, J.   **Fic**

Cravath, Lynne Woodcock, 1951-
  (il) Giff, P. R. Kidnap at the Catfish Cafe
        Fic
  (il) Petersen, P. J. I hate weddings   **Fic**

Crawford, Andy
  (il) Hornby, H. Soccer   **796.334**
  (il) Lane, B. Crime & detection   **364**

Crawford, Ruth *See* Seeger, Ruth Crawford,
  1901-1953

Crazy eights and other card games. Cole, J.
        795.4

Crazy Horse, Sioux Chief, ca. 1842-1877
        About
  Freedman, R. The life and death of Crazy Horse
  (5 and up)   **92**
  See/See also pages in the following book(s):
  Calvert, P. Great lives: the American frontier
  p125-36 (5 and up)   **920**
        Fiction
  Bruchac, J. Crazy Horse's vision   **E**

Crazy Horse's vision. Bruchac, J.   **E**

Crazy lady!. Conly, J. L.   **Fic**

Creasy, Rosalind
  Blue potatoes, orange tomatoes (3-5)   **635**

Creation
  Bible. O.T. Genesis. Genesis   **222**
  Bible. O.T. Genesis. The story of the creation
  (k-3)   **222**
  Goble, P. I sing for the animals   **242**
  Hamilton, V. In the beginning; creation stories
  from around the world (5 and up)   **291.1**
  Lester, J. When the beginning began (4 and up)
        296.1
  Ziefert, H. First He made the sun   **E**
        Fiction
  Goble, P. Remaking the earth (2-4)   **398.2**
  Lester, J. What a truly cool world!   **E**

The **creation** of Gluskabe. Bruchac, J.
  In Bruchac, J. Tell me a tale p102-03
        372.6

Creationism
  See also Evolution

Creative sparks [series]
  Cole, J. On the bus with Joanna Cole   **92**
  McPhail, D. M. In flight with David McPhail
        92

Creative writing
  Bauer, M. D. What's your story? (5 and up)
        808.3
  Livingston, M. C. Poem-making (4 and up)
        372.6
  Young, S. Writing with style (5 and up)
        808

The **creator** makes the world. Curry, J. L.
  In Curry, J. L. Turtle Island: tales of the Algonquian nations p1-4   **398.2**

Creatures all around us [series]
  Souza, D. M. Shy salamanders   **597.8**

Credit
  See also Consumer credit

Creech, Sharon
  Absolutely normal chaos (5 and up)   **Fic**
  Bloomability (5 and up)   **Fic**
  Chasing Redbird (5 and up)   **Fic**
  Walk two moons (6 and up)   **Fic**
  The Wanderer (5 and up)   **Fic**
  See/See also pages in the following book(s):
  The Newbery & Caldecott medal books, 1986-
  2000 p227-38   **028.5**
  Origins of story p20-35   **808.06**

Creek Indians
        Fiction
  Smith, C. L. Jingle dancer   **E**

Creek Indians—*Continued*
Folklore
Bruchac, J. The great ball game (k-3)

398.2

Creepy castle. Goodall, J. S.   **E**

A **creepy** countdown. Huck, C. S.   **E**

Creepy-crawly birthday. Howe, J. See note under Howe, J. Scared silly: a Halloween treat

     E

Creepy, crawly caterpillars. Facklam, M.

595.7

Creepy riddles. Hall, K.   **793.73**

The **cremation** of Sam McGee. Service, R. W.

811

Cresswell, Helen
Ordinary Jack (5 and up)   **Fic**
Zero and the commercial
   In Bauer, C. F. Celebrations p213-18

808.8

The **crested** curassow. Sherlock, Sir P. M.
   In Sherlock, Sir P. M. West Indian folk-tales p13-20   **398.2**

Creswick, Paul, 1866-1947
Robin Hood (5 and up)   **398.2**

Crews, Donald
Bigmama's (k-3)   **92**
Carousel   **E**
Freight train   **E**
Harbor   **E**
Night at the fair   **E**
Parade   **E**
Sail away   **E**
School bus   **E**
Shortcut   **E**
Truck   **E**
(il) Giganti, P., Jr. Each orange had 8 slices

     E
(il) Giganti, P., Jr. How many snails?   **E**
(il) Kalan, R. Blue sea   **E**
(il) Kalan, R. Rain   **E**
(il) Schaefer, L. M. This is the sunflower

     E
(il) Shannon, G. Tomorrow's alphabet   **E**

Crews, Jeanne Lee
See/See also pages in the following book(s):
Thimmesh, C. Girls think of everything (5 and up)   **920**

Crews, Nina
A high, low, near, far, loud, quiet story   **E**
You are here   **E**
(il) Adler, D. A. My writing day   **92**
(il) Howard, E. F. When will Sarah come?

     E
(il) Simon, S. From paper airplanes to outer space   **92**

Cribb, Joe
Money (4 and up)   **332.4**

Cricket   **051**

Cricket and Mountain Lion. Curry, J. L.
   In Curry, J. L. Back in the beforetime p70-73

398.2

The **cricket** in Times Square. Selden, G.   **Fic**

Cricket never does. Livingston, M. C.   **811**

Crickets
Berger, M. Chirping crickets (k-3)   **595.7**
Fiction
Carle, E. The very quiet cricket   **E**
Selden, G. The cricket in Times Square (3-6)

     Fic

Crickwing. Cannon, J.   **E**

Crictor. Ungerer, T.   **E**

Crime
   See also Homicide
Lane, B. Crime & detection (4 and up)

     364

Crime & detection. Lane, B.   **364**

Criminal investigation
   See also Forensic anthropology; Forensic sciences
Jackson, D. The bone detectives (5 and up)

     614
Lane, B. Crime & detection (4 and up)

     364

Criminalistics *See* Forensic sciences

Criminals
   See also Thieves
Fiction
Kehret, P. Don't tell anyone (4 and up)

     Fic

Crinkleroot's guide to knowing animal habitats. Arnosky, J.   **591.7**

Crinkleroot's guide to knowing butterflies & moths. Arnosky, J.   **595.7**

Crinkleroot's guide to knowing the birds. Arnosky, J.   **598**

Crinkleroot's nature almanac. Arnosky, J.

     508

Crockett, Davy, 1786-1836
See/See also pages in the following book(s):
Calvert, P. Great lives: the American frontier p137-48 (5 and up)   **920**

Crockett, Sally Ann Thunder Ann Whirlwind
Fiction
Kellogg, S. Sally Ann Thunder Ann Whirlwind Crockett (k-3)   **398.2**

Crocodiles
   See also Alligators
Simon, S. Crocodiles & alligators (3-6)

     597.9
Fiction
Dahl, R. The enormous crocodile (2-4)   **Fic**
De Paola, T. Bill and Pete   **E**
Marcellino, F. I, crocodile   **E**
Waber, B. Lyle, Lyle, crocodile   **E**

Crocodiles & alligators. Simon, S.   **597.9**

Crofford, Emily
Healing warrior: a story about Sister Elizabeth Kenny (3-5)   **92**

The **Croglin** Grange vampire. San Souci, R.
   In San Souci, R. More short & shivery p51-56   **398.2**

Croll, Carolyn, 1945-
(il) Berger, M. Switch on, switch off   **537**
(il) Coerr, E. The big balloon race   **E**

Cronin, Doreen
Click, clack, moo   **E**

Crook, George, 1829-1890
See/See also pages in the following book(s):
Ehrlich, A. Wounded Knee: an Indian history of the American West (6 and up)   **970.004**

Crooker waits. San Souci, R.
In San Souci, R. A terrifying taste of short & shivery p1-5   **398.2**

Cross, Gillian, 1945-
See/See also pages in the following book(s):
Origins of story p1-19   **808.06**

Cross-country cat. Calhoun, M.   **E**

The **cross** is pledged as security. Afanas´ev, A. N.
In Afanas´ev, A. N. Russian fairy tales p159-60   **398.2**

Crossing over. Storr, C.
In The Oxford book of scary tales p16-21   **808.8**

Crossing the Starlight Bridge. Mead, A.   **Fic**

Crossley-Holland, Kevin
The dauntless girl
In The Oxford treasury of children's stories p64-71   **S C**
Slam and the ghosts
In The Oxford book of scary tales p14-15   **808.8**
The world of King Arthur and his court (5 and up)   **942.01**

The **Crow**
In The Yellow fairy book p92-94   **398.2**

The **crow** and the snake. Walker, B. K.
In Walker, B. K. A treasury of Turkish folktales for children p17-19   **398.2**

Crow Boy. Iwamatsu, A. J.   **E**

Crow chief. Goble, P.   **398.2**

Crow Fair (Crow Agency, Mont.)
Ancona, G. Powwow (3-6)   **970.004**

Crow Indians
Hoyt-Goldsmith, D. Buffalo days (3-5)   **970.004**

Crow learns a lesson. Lester, J.
In Lester, J. When the beginning began p39-42   **296.1**

Crowe, Robert L.
Clyde monster   **E**

Crows
Fiction
Chorao, K. Pig and Crow   **E**
DeFelice, C. C. Clever crow   **E**

Cruel sisters. Wrede, P. C.
In Wrede, P. C. Book of enchantments p184-203   **S C**

Cruise, Robin, 1951-
Fiona's private pages (5 and up)   **Fic**
The top-secret journal of Fiona Clare Jardin. See note under Cruise, R. Fiona's private pages   **Fic**

Crum, Robert
(il) Birdseye, D. H. Under our skin   **305.8**
(il) Birdseye, D. H. What I believe   **200**

Crummel, Susan Stevens
(jt. auth) Stevens, J. Cook-a-doodle-doo!   **E**

Crusades
See/See also pages in the following book(s):
Brooks, P. S. Queen Eleanor: independent spirit of the medieval world p31-50 (6 and up)   **92**

Crutches. Härtling, P.   **Fic**

Crutchfield, Jimmie, 1910-1993   •
See/See also pages in the following book(s):
Brashler, W. The story of Negro league baseball (5 and up)   **796.357**

Cruz, Alejandro
The woman who outshone the sun (k-3)   **398.2**

Cruz, Ray
(il) Hurwitz, J. Baseball fever   **Fic**
(il) Viorst, J. Alexander and the terrible, horrible, no good, very bad day   **E**

Crystal & gem. Symes, R. F.   **548**

The **crystal** coffin. Grimm, J.
In The Green fairy book p290-95   **398.2**

The **crystal** heart. Shepard, A.   **398.2**

The **crystal** mountain. Afanas´ev, A. N.
In Afanas´ev, A. N. Russian fairy tales p482-84   **398.2**

The **crystal** mountain. Sanderson, R.   **398.2**

The **crystal** pool. McCaughrean, G.
In McCaughrean, G. The crystal pool: myths and legends of the world p79-81   **398.2**

The **crystal** pool: myths and legends of the world. McCaughrean, G.   **398.2**

Crystallography *See* Crystals

Crystals
Stangl, J. Crystals and crystal gardens you can grow (4 and up)   **548**
Symes, R. F. Crystal & gem (4 and up)   **548**

Crystals and crystal gardens you can grow. Stangl, J.   **548**

Cuba
Sheehan, S. Cuba (5 and up)   **972.91**
Social life and customs
Ada, A. F. Under the royal palms (4 and up)   **92**
Wolf, B. Cuba: after the revolution (4 and up)   **972.91**

The **Cuban** American family album. Hoobler, D.   **305.8**

Cuban Americans
Hoobler, D. The Cuban American family album (5 and up)   **305.8**

The **cuckoo** child. King-Smith, D.   **Fic**

Cuckoo. Cucú. Ehlert, L.   **398.2**

The **cuckoo** sister. Alcock, V.   **Fic**

The **cuckoo** tree. Aiken, J. See note under Aiken, J. The wolves of Willoughby Chase   **Fic**

The **cuckoo's** child. Freeman, S. T.   **Fic**

Cuffari, Richard, 1925-1978
(il) Cohen, B. Thank you, Jackie Robinson   **Fic**
(il) Perl, L. Slumps, grunts, and snickerdoodles: what Colonial America ate and why   **641.5**

Cuffari, Richard, 1925-1978—*Continued*
(il) Pope, E. M. The Perilous Gard   **Fic**
Culloch and the big pig. McCaughrean, G.
In McCaughrean, G. The crystal pool: myths and legends of the world p107-12
    398.2

Cullum, Carolyn N.
The storytime sourcebook   **027.62**
Cultural anthropology *See* Ethnology
Cultural atlas for young people [series]
Corbishley, M. Ancient Rome   **937**
Corbishley, M. The Middle Ages   **940.1**
Cultural pluralism *See* Multiculturalism
Culturally diverse videos, audios, and CD-ROMS for children and young adults   **011.6**
Culture crafts [series]
Temko, F. Traditional crafts from Africa
    745.5
Temko, F. Traditional crafts from Mexico and Central America   **745.5**
Temko, F. Traditional crafts from native North America   **745.5**
Cultures of the past [series]
Stein, R. C. The Aztec empire   **972**
Cultures of the world [series]
Barlas, R. Bahamas   **972.96**
Barlas, R. Latvia   **947.9**
Barlas, R. Uganda   **967.6**
Bassis, V. Ukraine   **947.7**
Berg, E. Senegal   **966.3**
Brown, R. V. Tunisia   **961.1**
Cheng, P. G. Mongolia   **951.7**
Dhilawala, S. Armenia   **947.5**
Elias, M. L. Barbados   **972.98**
Falconer, K. Peru   **985**
Foley, E. Costa Rica   **972.86**
Foley, E. Ecuador   **986.6**
Foley, E. El Salvador   **972.84**
Gascoigne, I. Papua New Guinea   **995.3**
Hassig, S. M. Panama   **972.87**
Hassig, S. M. Somalia   **967.73**
Heale, J. Democratic Republic of the Congo
    967.51
Heale, J. Madagascar   **969.1**
Heale, J. Tanzania   **967.8**
Hestler, A. Yemen   **953.3**
Holmes, T. Zambia   **968.94**
Jermyn, L. Guyana   **988.1**
Jermyn, L. Paraguay   **989.2**
Jermyn, L. Uruguay   **989.5**
Kagda, F. Algeria   **965**
Kagda, F. Hong Kong   **951.25**
Kagda, S. Lithuania   **947.9**
Kott, J. Nicaragua   **972.85**
Lee, T. C. Finland   **948.97**
Levy, P. M. Belarus   **947.8**
Levy, P. M. Ghana   **966.7**
Levy, P. M. Liberia   **966.62**
Levy, P. M. Sudan   **962.4**
Mansfield, S. Laos   **959.4**
McGaffey, L. Honduras   **972.83**
NgCheong-Lum, R. Fiji   **996**
NgCheong-Lum, R. Tahiti   **996**
O'Shea, M. Kuwait   **953.67**
Pateman, R. Belgium   **949.3**

Pateman, R. Bolivia   **984**
Seffal, R. Niger   **966.26**
Sheehan, P. Côte d'Ivoire   **966.68**
Sheehan, P. Luxembourg   **949.35**
Sheehan, P. Moldova   **947.6**
Sheehan, S. Cuba   **972.91**
Sheehan, S. Guatemala   **972.81**
Sheehan, S. Lebanon   **956.92**
Sheehan, S. Malta   **945**
Sioras, E. Czech Republic   **943.7**
Smelt, R. New Zealand   **993**
South, C. Jordan   **956.95**
Spilling, M. Cyprus   **956.93**
Spilling, M. Estonia   **947.9**
Spilling, M. Georgia   **947.5**
Wilcox, J. Iceland   **949.12**
Cummings, Linda, 1948-
(comp) Talking with adventurers. See Talking with adventurers   **920**
Cummings, Pat, 1950-
Angel baby   **E**
Clean your room, Harvey Moon!   **E**
(il) Caines, J. F. Just us women   **E**
(il) MacDonald, M. R. Pickin' peas   **398.2**
(il) Stolz, M. Go fish   **Fic**
(il) Stolz, M. Storm in the night   **E**
(comp) Talking with adventurers. See Talking with adventurers   **920**
(ed) Talking with artists [I-III] See Talking with artists [I-III]   **741.6**
Cummins, Julie
(jt. auth) Munro, R. The inside-outside book of libraries   **027**
Cunnie Anansi does some good. Hamilton, V.
In Hamilton, V. A ring of tricksters p59-71
    398.2
Cunnie Rabbit and Spider make a match. Hamilton, V.
In Hamilton, V. A ring of tricksters p75-83
    398.2
Cupid (Roman deity) *See* Eros (Greek deity)
Cupid and Psyche. Craft, M.   **292**
Cupid and Psyche. McCaughrean, G.
In McCaughrean, G. The bronze cauldron: myths and legends of the world p20-25
    398.2
Curie, Marie, 1867-1934
About
Parker, S. Marie Curie and radium (4 and up)
    92
Poynter, M. Marie Curie: discoverer of radium (4 and up)   **92**
Curiosities and wonders
See also Monsters
Guiberson, B. Z. Tales of the haunted deep (4 and up)   **001.9**
Guinness book of records   **032.02**
Simon, S. Strange mysteries from around the world (4-6)   **001.9**
Wilson, C. Mysteries of the universe (4 and up)   **001.9**
Curious cats in art and poetry   **808.81**
Curious George. Rey, H. A.   **E**
Curious George flies a kite. Rey, M. See note under Rey, H. A. Curious George   **E**

Curious George gets a medal. Rey, H. A. See note under Rey, H. A. Curious George E

Curious George goes to the hospital. Rey, H. A. See note under Rey, H. A. Curious George E

Curious George goes to the hospital. Rey, M. See note under Rey, H. A. Curious George E

Curious George learns the alphabet. Rey, H. A. See note under Rey, H. A. Curious George E

Curious George rides a bike. Rey, H. A. See note under Rey, H. A. Curious George E

Curious George takes a job. Rey, H. A. See note under Rey, H. A. Curious George E

The **curious** honeybird. McCaughrean, G.
In McCaughrean, G. The crystal pool: myths and legends of the world p76-78 398.2

Curlee, Lynn, 1947-
Liberty (3-5) 974.7
Rushmore (4 and up) 730.9

Curriculum materials centers *See* Instructional materials centers

Curriculum resource center. (4 and up) See entry in Part 2: Web Resources

Curry, Jane Louise, 1932-
Back in the beforetime (4-6) 398.2
Contents: How Old Man Above created the World; Roadrunner's pack; How Coyote stole the Sun; Mountain-making; Measuring Worm's great climb; The theft of fire; Coyote and the salmon; Coyote rides a star; Gopher's revenge; Clever Frog; The lost brother; The war between beasts and birds; Cricket and Mountain Lion; Coyote's squirrel hunt; Coyote and Badger; Mole and the Sun; The making of First Man; The waking of Men; The last council; Dog's choice

A stolen life (5 and up) Fic
Turtle Island: tales of the Algonquian nations (4-6) 398.2
Contents: The Creator makes the world; Rainbow Crow; The race between Buffalo and Man; Why deer have short tails; The three cranberries; The coming of Manabush; Manabush and the monsters; The Great Flood; Turtle Island; Maushop the Giant; Wesakaychak snares the sun; Beaver and Muskrat change tails; Wesakaychak rides on the moon; Woodpecker and Sugar Maple; Why Blackfeet never kill mice; Ground Squirrel and Turtle; How summer came to the north; The White Fawn; The great bear hunt; How Glooskap defeated the Great Bullfrog; The Land of the Northern Lights; The seven wise men; The burnt-faced girl; The bear maiden; Kupahweese's luck; The mighty wasis; Glooskap's farewell gifts

Curry, Tom
(il) Lowell, S. The bootmaker and the elves 398.2

The **curse** of the blue figurine. Bellairs, J. Fic

Curtis, Christopher Paul
Bud, not Buddy (4 and up) Fic
The Watsons go to Birmingham—1963 (4 and up) Fic
See/See also pages in the following book(s):
The Newbery & Caldecott medal books, 1986-2000 p343-58 028.5

Curtis, Gavin, 1965-
The bat boy & his violin E

Curtis, Jamie Lee
Tell me again about the night I was born E

Cushman, Doug
Inspector Hopper E
(il) Wood, D. What dads can't do E

Cushman, Karen
The ballad of Lucy Whipple (5 and up) Fic
Catherine, called Birdy (6 and up) Fic
The midwife's apprentice (6 and up) Fic
See/See also pages in the following book(s):
Author talk (4 and up) 028.5
The Newbery & Caldecott medal books, 1986-2000 p245-55 028.5

Custard the dragon and the wicked knight. Nash, O. 811

Custer, George Armstrong, 1839-1876
About
Viola, H. J. It is a good day to die (5 and up) 973.8

See/See also pages in the following book(s):
Calvert, P. Great lives: the American frontier p149-60 (5 and up) 920
Fiction
Irwin, H. Jim-Dandy (5 and up) Fic

Cut from the same cloth. San Souci, R. 398.2

Cut-paper play!. Henry, S. 745.54

The **cut-ups**. Marshall, J. E

The **cut-ups** at Camp Custer. Marshall, J. See note under Marshall, J. The cut-ups E

The **cut-ups** carry on. Marshall, J. See note under Marshall, J. The cut-ups E

The **cut-ups** crack up. Marshall, J. See note under Marshall, J. The cut-ups E

Cutler, Jane
The cello of Mr. O E
'Gator aid. See note under Cutler, J. Rats! Fic
No dogs allowed. See note under Cutler, J. Rats! Fic
Rats! (3-5) Fic

Cuts, scrapes, scabs, and scars. Silverstein, A. 617.1

"Cutta cord-la". Lester, J.
In Lester, J. The last tales of Uncle Remus p115-19 398.2

Cuyler, Margery
100th day worries E

Cyberspace. Jefferis, D. 004.6

The **Cybil** war. Byars, B. C. Fic

Cycling
See also Bicycles; Motorcycles
Gibbons, G. Bicycle book (k-3) 629.227
Fiction
Burleigh, R. Messenger, messenger E
McLeod, E. The bear's bicycle E
Mills, C. Gus and Grandpa and the two-wheeled bike E
Say, A. The bicycle man E
Wolff, A. Stella & Roy E

Cyclones
See also Hurricanes

Cyclopes (Greek mythology)
Fisher, L. E. Cyclops (3-5) 292

Cyclopes (Greek mythology)—*Continued*
Hutton, W. Odysseus and the Cyclops (3-5)
292

Cyprus
Spilling, M. Cyprus (5 and up) **956.93**

Czech, Kenneth P.
Snapshot (5 and up) **770.9**

Czech Republic
Sioras, E. Czech Republic (5 and up)
943.7

Czechoslovakia
See also Czech Republic

D

D.W. all wet. Brown, M. T. **E**
D.W. flips. Brown, M. T. See note under Brown, M. T. D.W. all wet **E**
D.W. go to your room!. Brown, M. T. See note under Brown, M. T. D.W. all wet **E**
D.W. rides again. Brown, M. T. See note under Brown, M. T. D.W. all wet **E**
D.W.'s library card. Brown, M. T. See note under Brown, M. T. D.W. all wet **E**
D.W.'s lost blankie. Brown, M. T. See note under Brown, M. T. D.W. all wet **E**
D.W. the picky eater. Brown, M. T. See note under Brown, M. T. D.W. all wet **E**
D.W. thinks big. Brown, M. T. See note under Brown, M. T. D.W. all wet **E**
Da Gama, Vasco *See* Gama, Vasco da, 1469-1524
The **Da** Trang crab. Terada, A. M.
In Terada, A. M. Under the starfruit tree p37-41 **398.2**
Da Vinci, Leonardo *See* Leonardo, da Vinci, 1452-1519
Da Wei's treasure. Chang, M. S. **398.2**
Dabcovich, Lydia, 1935-
The polar bear son (k-3) **398.2**
Dacey, Bob
(il) Manushkin, F. Miriam's cup **222**
Daddy makes the best spaghetti. Hines, A. G.
E
Daggie Dogfoot. See King-Smith, D. Pigs might fly **Fic**
Dahl, Roald
The BFG (4-6) **Fic**
The enormous crocodile (2-4) **Fic**
James and the giant peach (4-6) **Fic**
The magic finger (2-4) **Fic**
Matilda (4-6) **Fic**
Daily life in a Plains Indian village, 1868. Terry, M. B. H. **970.004**
Daily life in ancient and modern Timbuktu. Brook, L. **966.23**
Daily life on a Southern plantation, 1853. Erickson, P. **975**
Dairying
Aliki. Milk from cow to carton (k-3) **637**
Gibbons, G. The milk makers (k-3) **637**
Peterson, C. Extra cheese, please! (k-3)
637

Daisy and the Beastie. Simmons, J. See note under Simmons, J. Come along, Daisy! **E**
Daisy and the egg. Simmons, J. See note under Simmons, J. Come along, Daisy! **E**
Daisy is a mommy. Kopper, L. See note under Kopper, L. Daisy knows best **E**
Daisy knows best. Kopper, L. **E**
Daisy's babies. Kopper, L. See note under Kopper, L. Daisy knows best **E**
Dakota dugout. Turner, A. W.
In From sea to shining sea p194-95
810.8

Dakota Indians
See also Oglala Indians
Bruchac, J. A boy called Slow: the true story of Sitting Bull (1-3) **92**
Sneve, V. D. H. The Sioux (3-5) **970.004**
See/See also pages in the following book(s):
Ehrlich, A. Wounded Knee: an Indian history of the American West (6 and up) **970.004**
Freedman, R. Indian chiefs p115-39 (6 and up)
920
Fiction
Sneve, V. D. H. High Elk's treasure **Fic**
Folklore
Goble, P. Adopted by the eagles (2-4)
398.2
Goble, P. Iktomi and the boulder (k-3)
398.2
Wars
Viola, H. J. It is a good day to die (5 and up)
973.8

Dalai Lama XIV, 1935-
About
Demi. The Dalai Lama (3-6) **92**
Dale, Penny
(il) Stevenson, R. L. My shadow **821**
(il) Waddell, M. Rosie's babies **E**
Dalfunka, where the rich live forever. Singer, I. B.
In Singer, I. B. Stories for children p254-59
S C

Dalgliesh, Alice, 1893-1979
The bears on Hemlock Mountain (1-4) **Fic**
The courage of Sarah Noble (2-4) **Fic**
Daly, Jude
Fair, Brown & Trembling (k-3) **398.2**
Daly, Kathleen N.
Greek and Roman mythology A to Z (5 and up)
292
Daly, Niki, 1946-
Jamela's dress **E**
My dad **E**
Not so fast, Songololo **E**
Why the Sun & Moon live in the sky (k-3)
398.2
(il) Best, C. Red light, green light, mama and me **E**
(il) Gregorowski, C. Fly, eagle, fly! **398.2**
D'Amico, Joan, 1957-
The healthy body cookbook (4-6) **641.5**
The math chef (4-6) **641.5**
The science chef (5 and up) **641.3**

Dance

See also Ballet; Tap dancing
Ancona, G. Let's dance! (k-3) **793.3**
Grau, A. Dance (4 and up) **792.8**
Jones, B. T. Dance (k-3) **792.8**
Lowery, L. Twist with a burger, jitter with a bug **E**
Fiction
Gray, L. M. My mama had a dancing heart **E**
Hest, A. Mabel dancing **E**
Lee, J. M. Silent Lotus **E**
Martin, B. Barn dance! **E**
McKissack, P. C. Mirandy and Brother Wind **E**
Schroeder, A. Ragtime Tumpie **E**
Shannon, G. Dance away! **E**
Poetry
Song and dance (k-3) **811.008**

Dance away!. Shannon, G. **E**
Dance, dance, dolly mine!. Andersen, H. C.
In Andersen, H. C. The little mermaid and other fairy tales p129-30 **S C**
The **dance** of Elegba. Jaffe, N.
In Jaffe, N. The cow of no color: riddle stories and justice tales from around the world p76-83 **398.2**
Dance of the continents. Gallant, R. A. **551.1**
Dance, Tanya. Gauch, P. L. **E**

Dancers

See also African American dancers
Tallchief, M. Tallchief (3-5) **92**
Fiction
Levy, E. Seventh grade tango (5 and up) **Fic**

Dancing *See* Dance
The **dancing** dead of Shark Island. San Souci, R.
In San Souci, R. Even more short & shivery p24-28 **398.2**
The **dancing** pig. Sierra, J. **398.2**
The **dancing** skeleton. DeFelice, C. C.
In From sea to shining sea p322-25 **810.8**
Dancing teepees: poems of American Indian youth (3-5) **897**
Dandelion. Freeman, D. **E**
Dandelions. Bunting, E. **E**
D'Andrea, Domenick
(il) Farley, W. The Black Stallion **Fic**
Dangerous games. Aiken, J. See note under Aiken, J. The wolves of Willoughby Chase **Fic**
Dangerous hill. San Souci, R.
In San Souci, R. A terrifying taste of short & shivery p73-76 **398.2**
A **dangerous** promise. Nixon, J. L. See note under Nixon, J. L. A family apart **Fic**
Daniel, Alan, 1939-
(il) Howe, D. Bunnicula **Fic**
(il) Naylor, P. R. The grand escape **Fic**
Daniel's duck. Bulla, C. R. **E**

Danilo the Luckless. Afanas´ev, A. N.
In Afanas´ev, A. N. Russian fairy tales p255-61 **398.2**
Danish authors *See* Authors, Danish
Dann, Geoff
(il) Gravett, C. Castle **728.8**
(il) Gravett, C. Knight **940.1**
(il) Greenaway, T. Jungle **577.3**
(il) Wilkinson, P. Building **690**
Danny and the dinosaur. Hoff, S. **E**
Danny and the dinosaur go to camp. Hoff, S. See note under Hoff, S. Danny and the dinosaur **E**
Danziger, Paula, 1944-
Amber Brown goes fourth. See note under Danziger, P. Amber Brown is not a crayon **Fic**
Amber Brown is feeling blue. See note under Danziger, P. Amber Brown is not a crayon **Fic**
Amber Brown is not a crayon (2-4) **Fic**
Amber Brown sees red. See note under Danziger, P. Amber Brown is not a crayon **Fic**
Amber Brown wants extra credit. See note under Danziger, P. Amber Brown is not a crayon **Fic**
Forever Amber Brown. See note under Danziger, P. Amber Brown is not a crayon **Fic**
I, Amber Brown. See note under Danziger, P. Amber Brown is not a crayon **Fic**
P.S. Longer letter later (5 and up) **Fic**
Snail mail no more (5 and up) **Fic**
You can't eat your chicken pox, Amber Brown. See note under Danziger, P. Amber Brown is not a crayon **Fic**
Daphne Eloise Slater, who's tall for her age. Willner-Pardo, G. **Fic**
Daphne's book. Hahn, M. D. **Fic**
Dare to dream: Coretta Scott King and the civil rights movement . Medearis, A. S. **92**
Dare you. Scott, R.
In The Oxford book of scary tales p88-93 **808.8**
Daring to be Abigail. Vail, R. **Fic**
Dark Ages *See* Middle Ages
A **dark,** dark tale. Brown, R. **E**
The **dark** is rising. Cooper, S. See note under Cooper, S. Over sea, under stone **Fic**
The **dark** portal. Jarvis, R. **Fic**
The **dark-thirty.** McKissack, P. C. **S C**
Darling, Kathy
Arctic babies (k-3) **591.9**
Desert babies (k-3) **591.7**
Komodo dragon on location (3-5) **597.9**
Lemurs on location (3-5) **599.8**
Lions (3-6) **599.75**
Rain forest babies (k-3) **591.9**
Seashore babies (k-3) **591.7**
(jt. auth) Cobb, V. Bet you can! science possibilities to fool you **793.8**
(jt. auth) Cobb, V. Bet you can't! science impossibilities to fool you **793.8**

Darling, Kathy—*Continued*
(jt. auth) Cobb, V. Don't try this at home!
507.8
(jt. auth) Cobb, V. Wanna bet! **793.8**
(jt. auth) Cobb, V. You gotta try this!
507.8

Darling, Louis, 1916-1970
(il) Butterworth, O. The enormous egg **Fic**
(il) Cleary, B. Ellen Tebbits **Fic**
(il) Cleary, B. Henry Huggins **Fic**
(il) Cleary, B. The mouse and the motorcycle
Fic
(il) Cleary, B. Otis Spofford **Fic**
(il) Cleary, B. Ramona the pest **Fic**

Darling, Tara
(il) Darling, K. Arctic babies **591.9**
(il) Darling, K. Desert babies **591.7**
(il) Darling, K. Komodo dragon on location
597.9
(il) Darling, K. Lemurs on location **599.8**
(il) Darling, K. Lions **599.75**
(il) Darling, K. Rain forest babies **591.9**
(il) Darling, K. Seashore babies **591.7**

The **darning** needle. Andersen, H. C.
In Andersen, H. C. The swan's stories p69-77
S C

The **darning** needle. Kimmel, E. A.
In From sea to shining sea p189-91
810.8

Darwin, Beatrice
(il) Cleary, B. Socks **Fic**

Darwin, Charles, 1809-1882
About
Parker, S. Charles Darwin and evolution (4 and up) **92**

Darwinism *See* Evolution

Darzee's chant. Kipling, R.
In Kipling, R. The jungle book: the Mowgli stories **S C**

Dasch, E. Julius (Ernest Julius), 1932-
(ed) Explorers. See Explorers **920.003**

Dasch, Ernest Julius *See* Dasch, E. Julius (Ernest Julius), 1932-

Data processing
Dictionaries
Spencer, D. D. Illustrated computer dictionary for young people **004**
Webster's New World dictionary of computer terms **004**

Data storage and retrieval systems *See* Information systems

Data transmission systems
See also Electronic mail systems

Daugherty, James Henry, 1889-1974
Andy and the lion **E**
See/See also pages in the following book(s):
Newbery Medal books, 1922-1955 p178-91
028.5

Daughter and stepdaughter. Afanas'ev, A. N.
In Afanas'ev, A. N. Russian fairy tales p278-79 **398.2**

The **daughter-in-law** who got her way. Krishnaswami, U.
In Krishnaswami, U. Shower of gold: girls and women in the stories of India p31-35
398.2

Daughter of the dragon king. Carpenter, F.
In Carpenter, F. Tales of a Chinese grandmother p72-80 **398.2**

Daughters and fathers *See* Father-daughter relationship

Daughters and mothers *See* Mother-daughter relationship

D'Aulaire, Edgar Parin, 1898-1986
(il) Key, F. S. The Star-Spangled Banner
782.42
See/See also pages in the following book(s):
Caldecott Medal books, 1938-1957 p49-62
028.5

D'Aulaire, Ingri, 1904-1980
Persephone
In Bauer, C. F. Celebrations p199-202
808.8
(il) Key, F. S. The Star-Spangled Banner
782.42
See/See also pages in the following book(s):
Caldecott Medal books, 1938-1957 p45-49, 55-62 **028.5**

D'Aulnoy, Madame *See* Aulnoy, Madame d', 1650 or 51-1705

The **dauntless** girl. Crossley-Holland, K.
In The Oxford treasury of children's stories p64-71 **S C**

Dauntless Little John
In Diane Goode's book of scary stories & songs p38-41 **398.2**

Dávalos, Felipe
(il) Markle, S. Gone forever! **591.68**
(il) Wardlaw, L. Punia and the King of Sharks
398.2

Dave at night. Levine, G. C. **Fic**

Davenier, Christine
(il) Hest, A. Mabel dancing **E**
(il) In every tiny grain of sand. See In every tiny grain of sand **291.4**

Dave's down-to-earth rock shop. Murphy, S. J.
511.3

David, King of Israel
About
De Regniers, B. S. David and Goliath **222**
Fisher, L. E. David and Goliath (k-3) **222**

David, Thomas
(il) Isenbart, H.-H. Birth of a foal **636.1**

David and Dog. See Hughes, S. Dogger **E**

David and Goliath. De Regniers, B. S. **222**

David and Goliath. Fisher, L. E. **222**

David goes to school. Shannon, D. See note under Shannon, D. No, David! **E**

David's search. Nixon, J. L. See note under Nixon, J. L. Aggie's home **Fic**

Davidson, Andrew
(il) Hughes, T. The iron giant **Fic**

Davie, Helen
(il) Bancroft, H. Animals in winter **591.56**

Davie, Helen—*Continued*
    (il) Esbensen, B. J. The star maiden: an Ojibway tale   **398.2**
    (il) Goldin, A. R. Ducks don't get wet **598**
    (il) Zoehfeld, K. W. What lives in a shell?
        591.4

Davies, Nicola, 1958-
    Big blue whale (k-3)   **599.5**

Davis, Benjamin O., Jr.
See/See also pages in the following book(s):
    Haskins, J. Black eagles p75-108 (5 and up)
        629.13

Davis, Lambert
    (il) Esbensen, B. J. Baby whales drink milk
        599.5
    (il) Hamilton, V. The bells of Christmas
        Fic

Davis, Lucile
    Alabama
    In America the beautiful, second series
        973
    Puerto Rico
    In America the beautiful, second series
        973

Davis, Nancy, 1949-
    (il) Graham, J. B. Flicker flash   **811**

Davis, Rich, 1958-
    (il) Meister, C. Tiny's bath   **E**

Davis, Stuart, 1892-1964
See/See also pages in the following book(s):
    Greenberg, J. The American eye p42-50 (6 and up)   **920**

Davis, Yvonne, 1927-
    (il) MacDonald, M. R. The girl who wore too much   **398.2**
    (il) MacDonald, M. R. The round book
        782.42

Davy Crockett. Osborne, M. P.
    In Osborne, M. P. American tall tales p3-13
        398.2

Davy Crockett teaches the steamboat a leetle patriotism. Walker, P. R.
    In Walker, P. R. Big men, big country p15-21
        398.2

Dawn. Shulevitz, U.   **E**

Dawn. Wynne-Jones, T.
    In Wynne-Jones, T. The book of changes p109-33   **S C**

Dawn, Evening, and Midnight. Afanas'ev, A. N.
    In Afanas'ev, A. N. Russian fairy tales p457-63   **398.2**

Dawn of fear. Cooper, S.   **Fic**

Dawson, Len, 1935-
See/See also pages in the following book(s):
    Sullivan, G. Quarterbacks! p39-41 (5 and up)
        920

Day, Kenrick L.
    (il) Kramer, S. Caves   **551.4**

Day
    See also Night
        Fiction
    George, J. C. Morning, noon, and night **E**
    Tafuri, N. What the sun sees   **E**

    Williams, V. B. Lucky song   **E**

A **day** by the sea. Bond, M.
    In Bond, M. Paddington's storybook p66-82
        S C

The **day** Gogo went to vote. Sisulu, E. B.   **E**

The **day** I got lost. Singer, I. B.
    In Singer, I. B. Stories for children p115-21
        S C

The **day** I had to play with my sister. Bonsall, C. N.   **E**

The **day** Jimmy's boa ate the wash. Noble, T. H.   **E**

Day light, night light. Branley, F. M. **535**

A **day** no pigs would die. Peck, R. N. **Fic**

The **day** of Ahmed's secret. Heide, F. P. **E**

Day of Atonement *See* Yom Kippur

Day of the Dead *See* All Souls' Day

Day of the Dead. Hoyt-Goldsmith, D. **394.26**

Day of the Dead. Johnston, T.   **E**

The **day** puffins netted Hid-Well. Norman, H.
    In Norman, H. The girl who dreamed only geese, and other tales of the Far North
        398.2

A **day** with Wilbur Robinson. Joyce, W. **E**

The **daydreamer.** Afanas'ev, A. N.
    In Afanas'ev, A. N. Russian fairy tales p161
        398.2

Dayrell, Elphinstone, 1869-1917
    Why the Sun and the Moon live in the sky (k-3)
        398.2

Days
        Fiction
    Lobel, A. One lighthouse, one moon   **E**

Days like this   **811.008**

Days of Awe. Kimmel, E. A.   **296.4**

Days of the Dead. Lasky, K.   **394.26**

Days with Frog and Toad. Lobel, A. See note under Lobel, A. Frog and Toad are friends
        E

De Angeli, Marguerite Lofft, 1889-1987
    The door in the wall (4-6)   **Fic**
    Thee, Hannah! (3-5)   **Fic**
See/See also pages in the following book(s):
    Newbery Medal books, 1922-1955 p337-52
        028.5

De Balboa, Vasco Núñez *See* Balboa, Vasco Núñez de, 1475-1519

De Brunhoff, Jean *See* Brunhoff, Jean de, 1899-1937

De Brunhoff, Laurent *See* Brunhoff, Laurent de, 1925-

De colores and other Latin-American folk songs for children (k-3)   **782.42**

De Coubertin, Pierre *See* Coubertin, Pierre de, baron, 1863-1937

De Groat, Diane
    Happy birthday to you, you belong in the zoo. See note under De Groat, D. Trick or treat, smell my feet   **E**
    Jingle bells, homework smells. See note under De Groat, D. Trick or treat, smell my feet
        E

De Groat, Diane—*Continued*

Roses are pink, your feet really stink. See note under De Groat, D. Trick or treat, smell my feet   **E**

Trick or treat, smell my feet   **E**

(jt. auth) Hahn, M. D. Anna all year round   **Fic**

(il) Shreve, S. R. The flunking of Joshua T. Bates   **Fic**

De Kiefte, Kees *See* Kiefte, Kees de

De La Fontaine, Jean *See* La Fontaine, Jean de, 1621-1695

De la Mare, Walter, 1873-1956

Clever Grethel

In Womenfolk and fairy tales p71-76   **398.2**

Molly Whuppie

In Womenfolk and fairy tales p20-29   **398.2**

De Larrea, Victoria

(il) Perl, L. Piñatas and paper flowers   **394.26**

De Morgan, Mary

The story of a cat

In Christmas fairy tales p123-34   **398.2**

De Paola, Thomas Anthony *See* De Paola, Tomie, 1934-

De Paola, Tomie, 1934-

26 Fairmount Avenue (2-4)   **92**

The baby sister   **E**

Big Anthony and the magic ring. See note under De Paola, T. Strega Nona: an old tale   **E**

Big Anthony: his story. See note under De Paola, T. Strega Nona: an old tale   **E**

Bill and Pete   **E**

Bill and Pete go down the Nile. See note under De Paola, T. Bill and Pete   **E**

Bill and Pete to the rescue. See note under De Paola, T. Bill and Pete   **E**

Christopher, the holy giant (k-3)   **398.2**

The cloud book (k-3)   **551.57**

The clown of God (k-3)   **398.2**

An early American Christmas   **E**

Here we all are (2-4)   **92**

Jamie O'Rourke and the big potato (k-3)   **398.2**

Jamie O'Rourke and the pooka   **E**

The kids' cat book (2-4)   **636.8**

The knight and the dragon   **E**

The legend of Old Befana (k-3)   **398.2**

The legend of the Indian paintbrush (k-3)   **398.2**

The legend of the poinsettia (k-3)   **398.2**

Mary, the mother of Jesus (3-5)   **232.91**

Merry Christmas, Strega Nona. See note under De Paola, T. Strega Nona: an old tale   **E**

The miracles of Jesus (k-3)   **232.9**

Nana Upstairs & Nana Downstairs   **E**

The night of Las Posadas   **E**

Now one foot, now the other   **E**

Patrick: patron saint of Ireland (k-3)   **92**

The popcorn book (k-3)   **641.3**

The quicksand book (k-3)   **552**

Strega Nona: an old tale   **E**

Strega Nona: her story. See note under De Paola, T. Strega Nona: an old tale   **E**

Strega Nona meets her match. See note under De Paola, T. Strega Nona: an old tale   **E**

Strega Nona takes a vacation. See note under De Paola, T. Strega Nona: an old tale   **E**

Strega Nona's magic lessons. See note under De Paola, T. Strega Nona: an old tale   **E**

Tom   **E**

Tomie dePaola's Favorite nursery tales. See Tomie dePaola's Favorite nursery tales   **398.2**

Tony's bread: an Italian folktale (k-3)   **398.2**

(il) Adler, D. A. The carsick zebra and other animal riddles   **793.73**

(il) The Comic adventures of Old Mother Hubbard and her dog. See The Comic adventures of Old Mother Hubbard and her dog   **398.8**

(il) Fritz, J. Can't you make them behave, King George? [biography of George III, King of Great Britain]   **92**

(il) Fritz, J. Shhh! we're writing the Constitution   **342**

(il) Ghost poems. See Ghost poems   **821.008**

(il) Johnston, T. Alice Nizzy Nazzy, the Witch of Santa Fe   **E**

(il) Johnston, T. The quilt story   **E**

(il) Johnston, T. The tale of Rabbit and Coyote   **398.2**

(il) Madrigal, A. H. Erandi's braids   **E**

(il) Tomie dePaola's Mother Goose. See Tomie dePaola's Mother Goose   **398.8**

About

De Paola, T. Here we all are (2-4)   **92**

Elleman, B. Tomie de Paola   **92**

De Regniers, Beatrice Schenk

David and Goliath   **222**

May I bring a friend?   **E**

What can you do with a shoe?   **E**

(comp) Sing a song of popcorn. See Sing a song of popcorn   **808.81**

De Saint-Exupéry, Antoine *See* Saint-Exupéry, Antoine de, 1900-1944

De Treviño, Elizabeth Borton *See* Treviño, Elizabeth Borton de, 1904-

De Villeneuve, Madame *See* Villeneuve, Madame de

The **deacon's** ghost. San Souci, R.

In San Souci, R. Short & shivery p88-91   **398.2**

Dead Aaron

In Raw Head, bloody bones p23-27   **398.2**

The **dead** body. Afanas´ev, A. N.

In Afanas´ev, A. N. Russian fairy tales p118-19   **398.2**

Dead flies. Conrad, P.

In Conrad, P. Our house p22-28   **S C**

The **dead** man in Indian Creek. Hahn, M. D.   **Fic**

The **dead** mother. San Souci, R.

In San Souci, R. More short & shivery p143-47   **398.2**

Dead Sea scrolls
  Cooper, I. The Dead Sea scrolls (5 and up)
    296.1

The **Dead** wife
  In The Yellow fairy book p149-51   **398.2**
The **deadly** violin. San Souci, R.
  In San Souci, R. Even more short & shivery
    p125-27   **398.2**
Deaf
  Adler, D. A. A picture book of Helen Keller
    (1-3)   **92**
  Haughton, E. Living with deafness (3-5)
    362.4
  St. George, J. Dear Dr. Bell—your friend, Helen
    Keller (5 and up)   **92**
      Fiction
  Lee, J. M. Silent Lotus   **E**
  Millman, I. Moses goes to school   **E**
  Riskind, M. Apple is my sign (5 and up)
    Fic

    Means of communication
    See also Sign language
Deafness
  Haughton, E. Living with deafness (3-5)
    362.4

Dealing with dragons. Wrede, P. C.   **Fic**
Dean, Julia
  A year on Monhegan Island (4-6)   **974.1**
Dear America [series]
  Bartoletti, S. C. A coal miner's bride   **Fic**
  Hesse, K. A light in the storm   **Fic**
  Lasky, K. Dreams in the golden country
    Fic
  McKissack, P. C. Color me dark   **Fic**
  McKissack, P. C. A picture of Freedom
    Fic

Dear Annie. Caseley, J.   **E**
Dear Benjamin Banneker. Pinkney, A. D.   **92**
Dear dog. McCaughrean, G.
  In McCaughrean, G. The crystal pool: myths
    and legends of the world p61-66
    398.2
Dear Dr. Bell—your friend, Helen Keller. St.
  George, J.   **92**
Dear Jane. Lavelle, S.
  In The Oxford book of scary tales p8-13
    808.8
Dear Juno. Pak, S.   **E**
Dear Levi. Woodruff, E.   **Fic**
Dear Mr. Henshaw. Cleary, B.   **Fic**
Death
  Brown, L. K. When dinosaurs die (k-3)
    155.9
  Fry, V. L. Part of me died, too (5 and up)
    155.9
  Krementz, J. How it feels when a parent dies (4
    and up)   **155.9**
  See/See also pages in the following book(s):
  Gellman, M. Lost & found p95-161 (4-6)
    155.9

    Fiction
  Aliki. The two of them   **E**
  Anaya, R. A. Farolitos for Abuelo   **E**

Barron, T. A. Where is Grandpa?   **E**
Brisson, P. Sky memories (3-5)   **Fic**
Brooks, B. Everywhere (4 and up)   **Fic**
Bunting, E. Blackwater (5 and up)   **Fic**
Carrick, C. The accident   **E**
Carson, J. You hold me and I'll hold you
    E
Clifford, E. The remembering box (3-5)
    Fic
Conly, J. L. Crazy lady! (5 and up)   **Fic**
Couloumbis, A. Getting near to baby (5 and up)
    Fic
Creech, S. Walk two moons (6 and up)
    Fic
De Paola, T. Nana Upstairs & Nana Downstairs
    E
DiSalvo-Ryan, D. A dog like Jack   **E**
Fletcher, R. Fig pudding (4 and up)   **Fic**
Fletcher, R. Flying solo (5 and up)   **Fic**
Fox, P. The eagle kite (6 and up)   **Fic**
Greene, C. C. Beat the turtle drum (5 and up)
    Fic
Haas, J. Unbroken (5 and up)   **Fic**
Hamilton, V. Cousins (5 and up)   **Fic**
Henkes, K. Sun & Spoon (4 and up)   **Fic**
Hughes, S. Alfie and the birthday surprise
    E
Jukes, M. Blackberries in the dark (2-4)
    Fic
Kaplan, H. Waiting to sing   **E**
Lowry, L. A summer to die (5 and up)
    Fic
MacLachlan, P. Baby (5 and up)   **Fic**
Miles, M. Annie and the Old One (1-4)
    Fic
Neufeld, J. Almost a hero (5 and up)   **Fic**
Park, B. Mick Harte was here (4-6)   **Fic**
Paterson, K. Bridge to Terabithia (4 and up)
    Fic
Polikoff, B. G. Life's a funny proposition, Hora-
  tio (5 and up)   **Fic**
Recorvits, H. Goodbye, Walter Malinski (3-6)
    Fic
Rodowsky, C. F. The Turnabout Shop (4-6)
    Fic
Ross, A. In the quiet (5 and up)   **Fic**
Rylant, C. Missing May (5 and up)   **Fic**
Schick, E. Mama   **E**
Sleator, W. Rewind (4 and up)   **Fic**
Slepian, J. The Broccoli tapes (5 and up)
    Fic
Smith, D. B. A taste of blackberries (4-6)
    Fic
Thomas, J. R. Saying good-bye to Grandma
    E
Viorst, J. The tenth good thing about Barney
    E
Yumoto, K. The friends (5 and up)   **Fic**
Zolotow, C. The old dog   **E**
Death and the two friends. San Souci, R.
  In San Souci, R. Even more short & shivery
    p110-12   **398.2**
Death forgiven. Jiménez, F.
  In Jiménez, F. The circuit: stories from the
    life of a migrant child p57-60   **S C**

Death of a miser. Afanas´ev, A. N.
In Afanas´ev, A. N. Russian fairy tales p268
398.2

The **death** of El Cid. McCaughrean, G.
In McCaughrean, G. The golden hoard: myths and legends of the world p94-99
398.2

The **death** of the cock. Afanas´ev, A. N.
In Afanas´ev, A. N. Russian fairy tales p17-19
398.2

Death of the iron horse. Goble, P.
E
also in From sea to shining sea p160-63
810.8

The **Death** of the Sun-Hero
In The Yellow fairy book p213-15
398.2

Death trap. Thompson, S. E.
560

The **death** waltz. San Souci, R.
In San Souci, R. Short & shivery p133-38
398.2

The **debate** in sign language. Lieberman, S.
In From sea to shining sea p34-35
810.8

DeBruyne-Ammon, Bette *See* Ammon, Bette D.

The **deceitful** heron. Lee, J. M.
In Lee, J. M. I once was a monkey
294.3

December. Bunting, E.
E

Decision making
See also Problem solving

Declaration of Independence *See* United States. Declaration of Independence

Decorative arts
Tunis, E. Colonial craftsmen and the beginnings of American industry (4 and up)
680

Dee, Ruby
See/See also pages in the following book(s):
Hansen, J. Women of hope p16-17 (4 and up)
920

Deem, James M.
Bodies from the bog (4 and up)
930.1

Deep diving vehicles *See* Submersibles

Deep in the jungle. Yaccarino, D.
E

Deep sea diving *See* Submarine diving

Deep-sea explorer: the story of Robert Ballard, discoverer of the Titanic. Archbold, R.
92

Deer
See also Elk; Reindeer
Patent, D. H. Deer and elk (4 and up)
599.65

Fiction
Rawlings, M. K. The yearling (6 and up)
Fic
Salten, F. Bambi (4-6)
Fic

Deer and elk. Patent, D. H.
599.65

Deer hunting. Sanfield, S.
In Sanfield, S. The adventures of High John the Conqueror
398.2

Deer woman. San Souci, R.
In San Souci, R. Even more short & shivery p5-8
398.2

Deere, John, 1804-1886
See/See also pages in the following book(s):
Calvert, P. Great lives: the American frontier p161-76 (5 and up)
920

Deere, Kathleen
(jt. auth) Feinberg, S. Running a parent/child workshop
027.62

DeFelice, Cynthia C.
The apprenticeship of Lucas Whitaker (4 and up)
Fic
Clever crow
E
The dancing skeleton
In From sea to shining sea p322-25
810.8
The ghost of Fossil Glen (4-6)
Fic
Weasel (4 and up)
Fic

Defense mechanisms (Zoology) *See* Animal defenses

Degen, Bruce, 1945-
Jamberry
E
(il) Carlstrom, N. W. Jesse Bear, what will you wear?
E
(il) Coerr, E. The Josefina story quilt
E
(il) Cole, J. The magic school bus and the electric field trip
621.3
(il) Cole, J. The magic school bus at the waterworks
551.48
(il) Cole, J. The magic school bus explores the senses
612.8
(il) Cole, J. The magic school bus: in the time of the dinosaurs
567.9
(il) Cole, J. The magic school bus inside a beehive
595.7
(il) Cole, J. The magic school bus inside a hurricane
551.55
(il) Cole, J. The magic school bus inside the Earth
551.1
(il) Cole, J. The magic school bus inside the human body
612
(il) Cole, J. The magic school bus, lost in the solar system
523
(il) Cole, J. The magic school bus on the ocean floor
591.7
(il) Yolen, J. Commander Toad and the voyage home
Fic

DeGroat, Diane, 1947-
(il) Gilson, J. Bug in a rug
Fic
(il) Koss, A. G. How I saved Hanukkah
Fic

Deities *See* Gods and goddesses

DeJong, Meindert, 1906-1991
The house of sixty fathers (4-6)
Fic
The wheel on the school (4-6)
Fic
See/See also pages in the following book(s):
Newbery Medal books, 1922-1955 p427-39
028.5

Del Negro, Janice
Lucy Dove
E

Delacre, Lulu, 1957-
Golden tales (4 and up)
398.2
Contents: How the sea was born; Guanina; The eleven thousand Virgins; The laughing skull; Sención, the Indian girl; When the sun and the moon were children; How the rainbow was born; The miracle of Our Lady of Guadalupe; El Dorado; Manco Capac and the rod of gold; Kákuy; The courier
Salsa stories (4-6)
S C

Delacre, Lulu, 1957——*Continued*
Contents: New Years Day; A carpet for Holy Week; At the beach; The night of San Juan; Teatime; Birthday piñata; The Lord of Miracles; Aguinaldo; Carmen Teresa's gift
    Arroz con leche. See Arroz con leche
                             782.42
    (il) González, L. M. Señor Cat's romance and other favorite stories from Latin America
                             398.2

Delany, Annie Elizabeth *See* Delany, Bessie
Delany, Bessie
See/See also pages in the following book(s):
    Hansen, J. Women of hope p8-9 (4 and up)
                             920

Delany, Sadie
See/See also pages in the following book(s):
    Hansen, J. Women of hope p8-9 (4 and up)
                             920

Delany, Sarah Louise *See* Delany, Sadie
Delaware
    Blashfield, J. F. Delaware
    In America the beautiful, second series
                             973

    Schuman, M. Delaware
    In Celebrate the states   **973**
               Fiction
    Hesse, K. A light in the storm (4 and up)
                             Fic

Delaware Indians
               Fiction
    Durrant, L. The beaded moccasins (5 and up)
                             Fic

Delinquency, Juvenile *See* Juvenile delinquency
Delivering Web reference services to young people. Minkel, W.   **025.04**
Delivery. Suen, A.   **E**
Delton, Judy
    Angel bites the bullet. See note under Delton, J. Angel's mother's wedding   **Fic**
    Angel in charge. See note under Delton, J. Angel's mother's wedding   **Fic**
    Angel spreads her wings. See note under Delton, J. Angel's mother's baby. See note under Delton, J. Angel's mother's wedding   **Fic**
    Angel's mother's baby. See note under Delton, J. Angel's mother's wedding   **Fic**
    Angel's mother's boyfriend. See note under Delton, J. Angel's mother's wedding   **Fic**
    Angel's mother's wedding (3-5)   **Fic**
    Back yard Angel. See note under Delton, J. Angel's mother's wedding   **Fic**
Dem bones. Barner, B.   **611**
Demarest, Chris L., 1951-
    Firefighters A to Z (k-1)   **628.9**
    (il) Murphy, S. J. Beep beep, vroom vroom!
                           515
    (il) Ziefert, H. April Fool!   **E**
Demas, Corinne, 1947-
    If ever I return again (5 and up)   **Fic**
Demi, 1942-
    Buddha (4-6)   **294.3**
    Buddha stories (3-6)   **294.3**
    The Dalai Lama (3-6)   **92**
    The donkey and the rock (k-3)   **398.2**
    The emperor's new clothes   **E**
    The empty pot (k-3)   **398.2**

    The greatest treasure (k-3)   **398.2**
    Happy New Year! (k-3)   **394.26**
    In the eyes of the cat   **895.6**
    Kites   **E**
    One grain of rice (2-4)   **398.2**
Democratic Republic of the Congo. Heale, J.
                          967.51

The **demon** in the wine cellar. Schwartz, H.
    In Schwartz, H. A coat for the moon and other Jewish tales p22-25   **398.2**
Demonstrations
    See also Riots
Demuth, Patricia, 1948-
    Those amazing ants (k-2)   **595.7**
Denman-West, Margaret W., 1926-
    Children's literature: a guide to information sources   **011.6**
Denmark
              Fiction
    Lowry, L. Number the stars (4 and up)   **Fic**
Dennis, Wesley, 1903-1966
    (il) Henry, M. Brighty of the Grand Canyon
                             Fic
    (il) Henry, M. Justin Morgan had a horse
                             Fic
Denslow, William Wallace, 1856-1915
    (il) Baum, L. F. The Wizard of Oz   **Fic**
Dentistry
    Keller, L. Open wide (k-3)   **617.6**
Dentists
             Fiction
    Steig, W. Doctor De Soto   **E**
Denton, Terry
    (il) Fox, M. Night noises   **E**
DePaola, Tomie *See* De Paola, Tomie, 1934-
Depressions
             1929
    See Great Depression, 1929-1939
Deptford mice trilogy
    Jarvis, R. The dark portal   **Fic**
DeSalvo, Nancy
    Beginning with books   **027.62**
Desegregation in education *See* School integration
Desert animals
    Arnosky, J. Watching desert wildlife (3-6)
                             591.7
    Darling, K. Desert babies (k-3)   **591.7**
Desert babies. Darling, K.   **591.7**
Desert ecology
    Bash, B. Desert giant (3-5)   **583**
    Baylor, B. The desert is theirs (1-4)   **577.5**
    Brandenburg, J. Sand and fog (4 and up)
                             968.8
    Gibbons, G. Deserts (k-3)   **577.5**
    Guiberson, B. Z. Cactus hotel (k-3)   **583**
    Lesser, C. Storm on the desert (2-4)   **577.5**
    Silver, D. M. Cactus desert (3-5)   **577.5**
    Simon, S. Deserts (3-6)   **577.5**
    Stille, D. R. Deserts (2-4)   **577.5**
    Wright-Frierson, V. A desert scrapbook (3-5)
                             577.5

Desert giant. Bash, B.   **583**

The **desert** is theirs. Baylor, B.   **577.5**

Desert plants
   See also Cactus

A **desert** scrapbook. Wright-Frierson, V.
   577.5

The **deserted** mine. Sawyer, R.
   In Sawyer, R. The way of the storyteller
   p285-94   **372.6**

Deserts
   Gibbons, G. Deserts (k-3)   **577.5**
      Fiction
   Ben-´Ezer, E. Hosni the dreamer (2-4)
      398.2
   Johnson, P. B. Lost   **E**
   Keats, E. J. Clementina's cactus   **E**
      Poetry
   Siebert, D. Mojave (1-3)   **811**

Deserts. Simon, S.   **577.5**

Deserts. Stille, D. R.   **577.5**

Design, Industrial *See* Industrial design

Desimini, Lisa, 1965-
   (il) Aardema, V. Anansi does the impossible!
      398.2
   (il) Adoff, A. Love letters   **811**
   (il) Adoff, A. Touch the poem   **811**
   (il) Lewis, J. P. Doodle dandies   **811**

Desserts
   See also Cake

Desserts around the world
   In Easy menu ethnic cookbooks   **641.5**

Destination: Jupiter. Simon, S.   **523.4**

Destination: Mars. Simon, S.   **523.4**

Destination: rain forest. Grupper, J.   **577.3**

Destiny. Grove, V.   **Fic**

Detectives
   Wormser, R. Pinkerton: America's first private
   eye (5 and up)   **92**

Deulin, Charles
   The enchanted watch
   In The Green fairy book p43-47   **398.2**
   The little soldier
   In The Green fairy book p157-74   **398.2**

Devi. Mayer, M.
   In Mayer, M. Women warriors p13-15
      398

Devil
      Fiction
   Babbitt, N. The Devil's other storybook (4-6)
      S C
   Babbitt, N. The Devil's storybook (4-6)
      S C
   Kimmel, E. A. Grizz!   **E**
   The **Devil** and his boy. Horowitz, A.   **Fic**
   The **devil** and his grandmother. Grimm, J.
   In The Yellow fairy book p38-41   **398.2**
   The **devil** and Tom Walker. San Souci, R.
   In San Souci, R. More short & shivery p88-
   92   **398.2**
   Devil boy. Kimmel, E. A.
   In Kimmel, E. A. Sword of the samurai p85-
   94   **Fic**
   The **devil** in Vienna. Orgel, D.   **Fic**

The **devil** who was a potter. Afanas´ev, A. N.
   In Afanas´ev, A. N. Russian fairy tales p576-
   77   **398.2**

The **devil's** arithmetic. Yolen, J.   **Fic**

The **Devil's** other storybook. Babbitt, N.   **S C**

The **Devil's** storybook. Babbitt, N.   **S C**

The **Devil's** trick. Singer, I. B.
   In Singer, I. B. Zlateh the goat, and other stories p71-73   **398.2**

The **devoted** friend. Wilde, O.
   In Wilde, O. The fairy tales of Oscar Wilde
   p38-49   **S C**

Dew drop dead. Howe, J.   **Fic**

Dewey, Ariane
   (jt. auth) Aruego, J. We hide, you seek   **E**
   (il) Birthday rhymes, special times. See Birthday
   rhymes, special times   **811.008**
   (il) Ginsburg, M. The chick and the duckling
      E
   (il) Kraus, R. Little Louie the baby bloomer
      E
   (il) Raffi. Five little ducks   **782.42**
   (il) Shannon, G. Dance away!   **E**
   (il) Shannon, G. Lizard's home   **E**
   (il) Sharmat, M. W. Mitchell is moving   **E**
   (il) Sharmat, M. Gregory, the terrible eater
      E
   (il) Sierra, J. Antarctic antics   **811**
   (il) Swinburne, S. R. Safe, warm, and snug
      591.56

Dewey, Jennifer
   Mud matters (4-6)   **553.6**
   Poison dart frogs (3-5)   **597.8**

Dewey, Melvil, 1851-1931
   Abridged Dewey decimal classification and relative index   **025.4**

Dewey Decimal Classification
   Dewey, M. Abridged Dewey decimal classifica-
   tion and relative index   **025.4**
   Subject headings for children   **025.4**

Dhilawala, Sakina, 1964-
   Armenia (5 and up)   **947.5**

Di Fate, Vincent, 1945-
   (il) Berger, M. Do stars have points?   **523**

Diabetes
   Peacock, C. A. Sugar was my best food (3-6)
      362.1
   Pirner, C. W. Even little kids get diabetes (k-1)
      616.4
      Fiction
   Zemser, A. B. Beyond the mango tree (5 and
   up)   **Fic**

La **Diablesse.** Joseph, L.
   In Joseph, L. The mermaid's twin sister: more
   stories from Trinidad p18-28   **398.2**

Diakité, Baba Wagué *See* Wagué Diakité, Baba

Dial easy-to-read [series]
   Ehrlich, A. Leo, Zack, and Emmie together
   again   **E**
   Hall, K. Creepy riddles   **793.73**
   Hall, K. Mummy riddles   **793.73**
   Hall, K. Snakey riddles   **793.73**
   Herman, G. Cal Ripken, Jr.   **92**
   Krensky, S. Lionel at large   **E**

Dial easy-to-read—*Continued*

Marshall, E. Fox and his friends   **E**

Marshall, E. Three by the sea   **E**

Parks, R. I am Rosa Parks   **92**

Van Leeuwen, J. Tales of Oliver Pig   **E**

Diamond, Donna, 1950-

(il) Clifford, E. The remembering box   **Fic**

(il) Greene, C. C. Beat the turtle drum   **Fic**

(il) Hautzig, E. R. A gift for Mama   **Fic**

(il) Paterson, K. Bridge to Terabithia   **Fic**

The **diamond** tree. Schwartz, H.   **398.2**

The **diamond** tree [story] Schwartz, H.

In Schwartz, H. The diamond tree p77-84   **398.2**

Diane Goode's book of scary stories & songs (2-5)   **398.2**

Dianov, Alisher

(il) Shepard, A. Forty fortunes   **398.2**

Diaries

Stevens, C. A book of your own (5 and up)   **808**

Fiction

Cruise, R. Fiona's private pages (5 and up)   **Fic**

Gantos, J. Heads or tails (5 and up)   **Fic**

The **diary** of a young girl. Frank, A.   **92**

The **diary** of a young girl: the definitive edition. Frank, A.   **92**

The **diary** of Melanie Martin; or, How I survived Matt the Brat, Michelangelo, and the Leaning Tower of Pizza. Weston, C.   **Fic**

Dias, Bartholomeu, 1450?-1500

See/See also pages in the following book(s):

Fritz, J. Around the world in a hundred years p31-37 (4-6)   **910.4**

Dias, Earl Joseph, 1916-

Video Christmas

In The Big book of Christmas plays p26-40   **808.82**

Dia's story cloth. Cha, D.   **305.8**

Diaz, Bartholomeu *See* Dias, Bartholomeu, 1450?-1500

Diaz, David

(il) Brown, M. W. The little scarecrow boy   **E**

(il) Bunting, E. December   **E**

(il) Bunting, E. Smoky night   **E**

(il) Creech, S. The Wanderer   **Fic**

(il) Kimmel, E. A. Be not far from me   **221.9**

(il) Krull, K. Wilma unlimited: how Wilma Rudolph became the world's fastest woman   **92**

(il) Soto, G. Neighborhood odes   **811**

(il) Wilbur, R. The disappearing alphabet   **811**

See/See also pages in the following book(s):

The Newbery & Caldecott medal books, 1986-2000 p220-26   **028.5**

DiCamillo, Kate

Because of Winn-Dixie (4-6)   **Fic**

Dicey and Orpus. San Souci, R.

In San Souci, R. Even more short & shivery p89-93   **398.2**

Dicey's song. Voigt, C.   **Fic**

Dickens, Charles, 1812-1870

A Christmas carol (4 and up)   **Fic**

A Christmas carol; dramatization. See Thane, A. A Christmas carol

About

Stanley, D. Charles Dickens (4 and up)   **92**

See/See also pages in the following book(s):

Krull, K. Lives of the writers p38-41 (4 and up)   **920**

Dickinson, Emily, 1830-1886

I'm nobody! who are you? (3-6)   **811**

See/See also pages in the following book(s):

Faber, D. Great lives: American literature p100-10 (5 and up)   **920**

Krull, K. Lives of the writers p48-51 (4 and up)   **920**

Dictionaries *See* Encyclopedias and dictionaries

Dictionaries, Biographical *See* Biography—Dictionaries

Dictionaries, Picture *See* Picture dictionaries

Dictionary of phrase and fable, Brewer's   **803**

Did the rabbi have a head? Kimmel, E. A.

In Kimmel, E. A. The spotted pony: a collection of Hanukkah stories p43-46   **398.2**

Did you carry the flag today, Charley? Caudill, R.   **Fic**

Didrikson, Babe *See* Zaharias, Babe Didrikson, 1911-1956

Diehn, Gwen, 1943-

Making books that fly, fold, wrap, hide, pop up, twist, and turn (4 and up)   **736**

Science crafts for kids (5 and up)   **507.8**

Diet

See also Eating customs

Fiction

Sharmat, M. Gregory, the terrible eater   **E**

Diets, Reducing *See* Weight loss

Diez deditos. Ten little fingers & other play rhymes and action songs from Latin America (k-3)   **782.42**

DiFate, Vincent *See* Di Fate, Vincent, 1945-

Dig, drill, dump, fill. Hoban, T.   **E**

Dig hole, soft mole. Lesser, C.   **E**

Digby. Hazen, B. S.   **E**

Digby and Kate. Baker, B. See note under Baker, B. Digby and Kate and the beautiful day   **E**

Digby and Kate again. Baker, B. See note under Baker, B. Digby and Kate and the beautiful day   **E**

Digby and Kate and the beautiful day. Baker, B.   **E**

Digestion

Silverstein, A. The digestive system (5 and up)   **612.3**

The **digestive** system. Silverstein, A.   **612.3**

Digging for bird-dinosaurs. Bishop, N.   **567.9**

Digital learning center for microbial ecology: the microbe zoo. (3-6) See entry in Part 2: Web Resources

Dillon, Diane
(il) Aardema, V. Who's in Rabbit's house?
398.2
(il) Aardema, V. Why mosquitoes buzz in people's ears
398.2
(il) Bible. O.T. Ecclesiastes. To every thing
there is a season
223
(il) Greenfield, E. Honey, I love, and other love
poems
811
(il) Hamilton, V. The girl who spun gold
398.2
(il) Hamilton, V. Her stories
398.2
(il) Hamilton, V. Many thousand gone
326
(il) Hamilton, V. The people could fly:
American black folktales
398.2
(il) Musgrove, M. Ashanti to Zulu: African traditions
960
(il) Norman, H. The girl who dreamed only
geese, and other tales of the Far North
398.2
(il) Paterson, K. The tale of the mandarin ducks
398.2
(il) Price, L. Aïda
792.5
(il) Verne, J. 20,000 leagues under the sea
Fic
(il) Walter, M. P. Brother to the wind
E
(il) Willard, N. Pish, posh, said Hieronymus
Bosch
811
(il) Willard, N. The sorcerer's apprentice
811
See/See also pages in the following book(s):
Newbery and Caldecott Medal books, 1976-1985
p170-92
028.5

Dillon, Eilís, 1920-1994
Saint Patrick and the snakes
In Bauer, C. F. Celebrations p170-71
808.8

Dillon, Lee, 1966-
(il) Willard, N. Pish, posh, said Hieronymus
Bosch
811

Dillon, Leo, 1933-
(il) Aardema, V. Who's in Rabbit's house?
398.2
(il) Aardema, V. Why mosquitoes buzz in people's ears
398.2
(il) Bible. O.T. Ecclesiastes. To every thing
there is a season
223
(il) Greenfield, E. Honey, I love, and other love
poems
811
(il) Hamilton, V. The girl who spun gold
398.2
(il) Hamilton, V. Her stories
398.2
(il) Hamilton, V. Many thousand gone
326
(il) Hamilton, V. The people could fly:
American black folktales
398.2
(il) Musgrove, M. Ashanti to Zulu: African traditions
960
(il) Norman, H. The girl who dreamed only
geese, and other tales of the Far North
398.2
(il) Paterson, K. The tale of the mandarin ducks
398.2
(il) Price, L. Aïda
792.5
(il) Verne, J. 20,000 leagues under the sea
Fic
(il) Walter, M. P. Brother to the wind
E

(il) Willard, N. Pish, posh, said Hieronymus
Bosch
811
(il) Willard, N. The sorcerer's apprentice
811
See/See also pages in the following book(s):
Newbery and Caldecott Medal books, 1976-1985
p170-92
028.5

A **dime** a dozen. Grimes, N.
811
A **dime** a jug. Bernier-Grand, C. T.
In Bernier-Grand, C. T. Juan Bobo p42-58
398.2

Dingle, Derek T.
First in the field: baseball hero Jackie Robinson
(3-6)
92

Dingus, Lowell
The tiniest giants (4 and up)
567.9
(jt. auth) Norell, M. A nest of dinosaurs
567.9

Dining
Fiction
Friedman, I. R. How my parents learned to eat
E
History
Aliki. A medieval feast (2-5)
394.1
Poetry
Poem stew (3-6)
811.008

Dinkins is dead. San Souci, R.
In San Souci, R. A terrifying taste of short &
shivery p82-85
398.2

Dinner guests. Calmenson, S.
In The Read-aloud treasury p100-11
808.8

Dino easy reader [series]
Brown, L. K. Rex and Lilly family time
E

Dinosaur!. Sis, P.
E

Dinosaur babies. Zoehfeld, K. W.
567.9

Dinosaur Bob and his adventures with the family
Lazardo. Joyce, W.
E

Dinosaur mountain. Arnold, C.
567.9

Dinosaur National Monument (Colo. and Utah)
Arnold, C. Dinosaur mountain (4 and up)
567.9

Dinosaur tree. Henderson, D.
560

Dinosaurs
Arnold, C. Dinosaur mountain (4 and up)
567.9
Arnold, C. Dinosaurs all around (4 and up)
567.9
Barton, B. Bones, bones, dinosaur bones
E
Barton, B. Dinosaurs, dinosaurs
E
Bausum, A. Dragon bones and dinosaur eggs: a
photobiography of Roy Chapman Andrews (5
and up)
92
Bishop, N. Digging for bird-dinosaurs (4 and
up)
567.9
Cole, J. The magic school bus: in the time of
the dinosaurs (2-4)
567.9
Dingus, L. The tiniest giants (4 and up)
567.9
Dixon, D. Dougal Dixon's amazing dinosaurs
(3-6)
567.9
Dixon, D. Dougal Dixon's dinosaurs (4 and up)
567.9

Divorce
See also Remarriage
Brown, L. K. Dinosaurs divorce (k-3)
    306.89
Krementz, J. How it feels when parents divorce
(4 and up) **306.89**
Rogers, F. Divorce (k-2) **306.89**
    Fiction
Blume, J. It's not the end of the world (4-6)
    Fic
Bunting, E. Some frog! (2-4) **Fic**
Cleary, B. Dear Mr. Henshaw (4-6) **Fic**
Cleary, B. Strider (4 and up) **Fic**
Fine, A. Step by wicked step (4-6) **Fic**
Johnson, A. Songs of faith (5 and up) **Fic**
Rodowsky, C. F. Spindrift (5 and up) **Fic**
Williams, V. B. Scooter (3-5) **Fic**
Dixon, Dougal, 1947-
Dougal Dixon's amazing dinosaurs (3-6)
    567.9
Dougal Dixon's dinosaurs (4 and up) **567.9**
Dixon, Jeane, 1918-1997
See/See also pages in the following book(s):
Krull, K. They saw the future p91-97 (4 and up)
    133.3
Dixon, Tennessee
(il) Blos, J. W. The heroine of the Titanic: a
tale both true and otherwise of the life of
Molly Brown **92**
DK eyewitness books
Barber, J. Presidents **920**
DK guide to space. Bond, P. **520**
DK illustrated Oxford dictionary **423**
DK Merriam Webster children's dictionary
    423
DK Millennium world atlas. See Millennium
world atlas **912**
DK nature encyclopedia **508**
DK riding club [series]
Henderson, C. Horse & pony care **636.1**
The **DK** science encyclopedia (5 and up) **503**
DK student atlas **912**
DK superguides [series]
Bailey, J. Fishing **799.1**
Bussell, D. Ballet **792.8**
Irwin, D. Inline skating **796.21**
Jackman, J. Gymnastics **796.44**
Mitchell, D. Martial arts **796.8**
Morrissey, P. Ice skating **796.91**
Simmons, R. Golf **796.352**
Do bananas chew gum? Gilson, J. **Fic**
Do like Kyla. Johnson, A. **E**
Do not open. Turkle, B. C. **E**
Do not sneeze, do not scratch . . . do not eat!.
Bernier-Grand, C. T.
In Bernier-Grand, C. T. Juan Bobo p26-41
    398.2
Do stars have points? Berger, M. **523**
Do whales have belly buttons? Berger, M.
    599.5
Do you remember the color blue? Alexander, S. H.
    362.4
Do you want to be my friend? Carle, E. **E**

Dobie, J. Frank (James Frank), 1888-1964
The mezcla man
In From sea to shining sea p30-32 **810.8**
Dobie, James Frank *See* Dobie, J. Frank (James
Frank), 1888-1964
Doc Rabbit, Bruh Fox, and Tar Baby. Hamilton,
V.
In Hamilton, V. The people could fly:
American Black folktales p13-19
    398.2
Dockray, Tracy
(il) Tomb, H. Microaliens **502.8**
Doctor Coyote. Bierhorst, J. **398.2**
Doctor De Soto. Steig, W. **E**
Doctor De Soto goes to Africa. Steig, W. See note
under Steig, W. Doctor De Soto **E**
Doctor Faust. McCaughrean, G.
In McCaughrean, G. The bronze cauldron:
myths and legends of the world p31-34
    398.2
Doctors *See* Physicians
The **doctors**. Fisher, L. E. **610.9**
Dodge, Mary Mapes, 1830-1905
Hans Brinker; or, The silver skates (4 and up)
    Fic
Dodgers (Baseball team) *See* Brooklyn Dodgers
(Baseball team)
Dodgson, Charles Lutwidge *See* Carroll, Lewis,
1832-1898
Dodson, Peter
An alphabet of dinosaurs (k-3) **567.9**
Does a kangaroo have a mother, too? Carle, E.
    E
The **dog** and the woodpecker. Afanas´ev, A. N.
In Afanas´ev, A. N. Russian fairy tales p499-
500 **398.2**
A **dog** called Kitty. Wallace, B. **Fic**
Dog days. Prelutsky, J. **811**
Dog Friday. McKay, H. **Fic**
A **dog** like Jack. DiSalvo-Ryan, D. **E**
A **dog** named Boye. Hausman, G.
In Hausman, G. Dogs of myth p59-62
    398.2
A **dog** on Barkham Street. Stolz, M. **Fic**
Dog racing
See also Iditarod Trail Sled Dog Race,
Alaska; Sled dog racing
Dog steals and Rooster crows. Fang, L.
In Fang, L. The Ch'i-lin purse p16-26
    398.2
The **dog** that called the pitch. Christopher, M.
    Fic
The **dog**, the cat, the snake, and the ring.
Hausman, G.
In Hausman, G. Dogs of myth p69-74
    398.2
The **dog** who married a princess. Hausman, G.
In Hausman, G. Dogs of myth p63-66
    398.2
The **dog** with the diamond foot. Hausman, G.
In Hausman, G. Dogs of myth p75-81
    398.2

Dogger. Hughes, S. **E**

Dogs

Calmenson, S. Rosie (k-3) **636.7**

Cole, J. My puppy is born (k-3) **636.7**

The Complete dog book for kids (4 and up) **636.7**

George, J. C. How to talk to your dog (2-4) **636.7**

Gibbons, G. Dogs (k-3) **636.7**

Kehret, P. Shelter dogs (3-5) **636.7**.

King-Smith, D. Puppy love (k-3) **636.7**

Paulsen, G. My life in dog years (4 and up) **92**

Paulsen, G. Puppies, dogs, and blue northers (5 and up) **798.8**

Fiction

Armstrong, W. H. Sounder (5 and up) **Fic**

Baker, B. Digby and Kate and the beautiful day **E**

Barracca, D. The adventures of Taxi Dog **E**

Bemelmans, L. Madeline's rescue **E**

Blake, Q. Mrs. Armitage and the big wave **E**

Blake, R. J. Akiak **E**

Branford, H. Fire, bed, & bone (5 and up) **Fic**

Burnford, S. The incredible journey (4 and up) **Fic**

Byars, B. C. Tornado (2-4) **Fic**

Cabrera, J. Dog's day **E**

Capucilli, A. Biscuit's new trick **E**

Carrick, C. The accident **E**

Christopher, M. The dog that called the pitch (2-4) **Fic**

Cleary, B. Strider (4 and up) **Fic**

Clements, A. Circus family dog **E**

DiCamillo, K. Because of Winn-Dixie (4-6) **Fic**

DiSalvo-Ryan, D. A dog like Jack **E**

Estes, E. Ginger Pye (4-6) **Fic**

Feiffer, J. Bark, George **E**

Fleischman, S. Jim Ugly (4 and up) **Fic**

Gackenbach, D. What's Claude doing? **E**

Gardiner, J. R. Stone Fox (2-5) **Fic**

Gipson, F. B. Old Yeller (6 and up) **Fic**

Goode, D. Mama's perfect present **E**

Gregory, N. How Smudge came **E**

Griffith, H. V. Alex and the cat (1-3) **Fic**

Harlow, J. H. Star in the storm **Fic**

Harper, I. Our new puppy **E**

Hazen, B. S. Digby **E**

Henkes, K. Circle dogs **E**

Henkes, K. Protecting Marie (5 and up) **Fic**

Hesse, K. Lester's dog **E**

Hesse, K. Sable (2-4) **Fic**

Hoberman, M. A. One of each **E**

Huneck, S. Sally goes to the beach **E**

Hurd, T. Art dog **E**

Johnson, P. B. Lost **E**

Johnston, T. The ghost of Nicholas Greebe **E**

Jonas, A. Watch William walk **E**

Keats, E. J. My dog is lost! **E**

Kellogg, S. Pinkerton, behave! **E**

Kopper, L. Daisy knows best **E**

Kuskin, K. City dog **E**

Lewis, K. Just like Floss **E**

Lexau, J. M. Go away, dog **E**

London, J. The call of the wild (5 and up) **Fic**

London, J. White Fang (5 and up) **Fic**

London, J. Shawn and Keeper: show-and-tell **E**

Lowry, L. Stay! (5 and up) **Fic**

MacLachlan, P. Three Names **E**

McKay, H. Dog Friday (4-6) **Fic**

Meddaugh, S. Martha speaks **E**

Meister, C. Tiny's bath **E**

Miller, S. S. Three more stories you can read to your dog **E**

Myers, W. D. The blues of Flats Brown **E**

Naylor, P. R. Shiloh (4-6) **Fic**

Peet, B. The whingdingdilly **E**

Pilkey, D. The Hallo-wiener **E**

Pomerantz, C. The outside dog **E**

Rathmann, P. Officer Buckle and Gloria **E**

Rawls, W. Where the red fern grows **Fic**

Reaver, C. Bill (5 and up) **Fic**

Rodowsky, C. F. Not my dog (2-4) **Fic**

Rylant, C. Henry and Mudge **E**

Rylant, C. The old woman who named things **E**

Schwartz, A. Oma and Bobo **E**

Sebestyen, O. Out of nowhere (5 and up) **Fic**

Seibold, J. O. Olive the other reindeer **E**

Sendak, M. Higglety pigglety pop! (2-4) **Fic**

Steig, W. Caleb & Kate **E**

Steig, W. Dominic (3-5) **Fic**

Stolz, M. A dog on Barkham Street (4-6) **Fic**

Taylor, T. The trouble with Tuck (5 and up) **Fic**

Thayer, J. The puppy who wanted a boy **E**

Thomas, J. R. The comeback dog (3-5) **Fic**

Van Allsburg, C. The garden of Abdul Gasazi **E**

Van Allsburg, C. The sweetest fig **E**

Vande Velde, V. Smart dog (4-6) **Fic**

Wallace, B. A dog called Kitty (4-6) **Fic**

Wells, R. McDuff moves in **E**

Wright, B. R. Nothing but trouble (4 and up) **Fic**

Yorinks, A. Harry and Lulu **E**

Ziefert, H. Pushkin meets the bundle **E**

Zimmerman, A. G. My dog Toby **E**

Zion, G. Harry the dirty dog **E**

Zolotow, C. The old dog **E**

Folklore

Hausman, G. Dogs of myth (3-6) **398.2**

Poetry

George, K. O. Little dog poems (k-2) **811**

Johnston, T. It's about dogs (2-4) **811**

Prelutsky, J. Dog days (k-1) **811**

Training

Jones, R. F. Jake (3-5) **636.7**

Dog's choice. Curry, J. L.

In Curry, J. L. Back in the beforetime p128-31 **398.2**

Dog's day. Cabrera, J.   **E**

The **dog's** nose is cold. Sherlock, Sir P. M.
    In Sherlock, Sir P. M. West Indian folk-tales p34-38   **398.2**

Dogs of myth. Hausman, G.   **398.2**

Dogsong. Paulsen, G.   **Fic**

Dōhaku's head. Kimmel, E. A.
    In Kimmel, E. A. Sword of the samurai p5-10   **Fic**

Dolan, Edward F., 1924-
    America in World War I (5 and up)   **940.3**

Dole, Patricia Pearl, 1927-
    Children's books about religion   **016.2**

The **doll** in the garden. Hahn, M. D.   **Fic**

The **doll** people. Martin, A. M.   **Fic**

The **dollar** watch and the five jack rabbits. Sandburg, C.
    In Sandburg, C. Rootabaga stories pt 1 p117-24   **S C**
    In Sandburg, C. The Sandburg treasury p57-61   **818**

The **dollhouse** murders. Wright, B. R.   **Fic**

Dollhouses
    Fiction
    Godden, R. The doll's house (2-4)   **Fic**
    Sachs, M. The bears' house (4-6)   **Fic**

Dolls
    Fiction
    Bonners, S. The wooden doll   **E**
    Cassedy, S. Behind the attic wall (5 and up)   **Fic**
    Field, R. Hitty: her first hundred years (4 and up)   **Fic**
    Fonteyn, Dame M. Coppélia (3-5)   **792.8**
    Godden, R. The doll's house (2-4)   **Fic**
    Hutchins, P. Changes, changes   **E**
    Martin, A. M. The doll people (3-5)   **Fic**
    Polacco, P. Babushka's doll   **E**
    Pomerantz, C. The chalk doll   **E**
    Waugh, S. The Mennyms (5 and up)   **Fic**
    Zolotow, C. William's doll   **E**

The **doll's** house. Godden, R.   **Fic**

Dolphin luck. McKay, H. See note under McKay, H. Dog Friday   **Fic**

Dolphins
    Berger, M. Do whales have belly buttons? (2-4)   **599.5**
    Dudzinski, K. Meeting dolphins (4 and up)   **599.5**
    Fiction
    Hesse, K. The music of dolphins (6 and up)   **Fic**

Domestic animals
    See also Pets
    Tafuri, N. Spots, feathers, and curly tails   **E**
    Fiction
    Asch, F. Barnyard lullaby   **E**
    Cronin, D. Click, clack, moo   **E**
    Greene, R. G. Barnyard song   **E**
    Hutchins, P. Ten red apples   **E**
    Plourde, L. Pigs in the mud in the middle of the rud   **E**
    Sloat, T. Farmer Brown goes round and round   **E**

Williams, S. Let's go visiting   **E**
Wormell, M. Why not?   **E**
    Poetry
Godwin, L. Barnyard prayers (k-2)   **811**

Domestic architecture
    See also House construction

Domestic economic assistance
    See also Community development

Domestic finance *See* Personal finance

Domestic relations
    See also Family

Domestic violence
    See also Child abuse; Wife abuse
    Fiction
    Hahn, M. D. Following my own footsteps (5 and up)   **Fic**

Domingo siete. MacDonald, M. R.
    In MacDonald, M. R. Look back and see p37-44   **372.6**

Dominic. Steig, W.   **Fic**

Dominican Republic
    Fiction
    Appelbaum, D. K. Cocoa ice   **E**

Dominoes around the world. Lankford, M. D.   **795.3**

Domitila. Coburn, J. R.   **398.2**

Donahue, Dorothy
    (il) Patron, S. Maybe yes, maybe no, maybe maybe   **Fic**

Doney, Todd L. W.
    (il) Otten, C. F. January rides the wind   **811**

The **donkey** and the rock. Demi   **398.2**

Donkey trouble. Young, E.   **398.2**

Donkeys
    Fiction
    Henry, M. Brighty of the Grand Canyon (4 and up)   **Fic**
    Steig, W. Sylvester and the magic pebble   **E**
    Wildsmith, B. A Christmas story   **E**

Donkeyskin. Perrault, C.
    In Perrault, C. The complete fairy tales of Charles Perrault p108-17   **398.2**

Donnelly, Marlene Hill
    (il) Selsam, M. E. Big tracks, little tracks   **591.5**

Donner party
    Calabro, M. The perilous journey of the Donner Party (5 and up)   **978**
    Lavender, D. S. Snowbound (4 and up)   **978**

Donoughue, Carol
    The mystery of the hieroglyphs (3-6)   **493**

Don't be my valentine. Lexau, J. M.   **E**

Don't eat too much turkey!. Cohen, M. See note under Cohen, M. It's George!   **E**

Don't ever look at a mermaid. Mayo, M.
    In Mayo, M. Mythical birds & beasts from many lands p22-31   **398.2**

Don't fidget a feather. Silverman, E.   **E**

Don't forget the bacon!. Hutchins, P.   **E**

Don't make me laugh. Stevenson, J.   **E**

Don't pat the wombat!. Honey, E.   **Fic**

Don't read this!. Piumini, R.
   In Don't read this! and other tales of the un-natural p51-70   **S C**

Don't read this! and other tales of the unnatural (6 and up)   **S C**

Don't shake hands with everybody. Courlander, H.
   In Courlander, H. Cow-tail switch, and other West African stories p129-32   **398.2**

Don't tell anyone. Kehret, P.   **Fic**

Don't try this at home!. Cobb, V.   **507.8**

Don't wake up Mama!. Christelow, E. See note under Christelow, E. Five little monkeys jumping on the bed   **E**

Don't you know there's a war on? Stevenson, J.   **E**

Doodle dandies. Lewis, J. P.   **811**

Dooling, Michael
   (il) Atkins, J. Mary Anning and the sea dragon   **92**
   (il) Giblin, J. The amazing life of Benjamin Franklin   **92**
   (il) Giblin, J. Thomas Jefferson   **92**
   (il) Woodruff, E. The memory coat   **E**

Doolittle, Michael J.
   (il) Goodman, S. Stones, bones, and petroglyphs   **930.1**
   (il) Goodman, S. Ultimate field trip 4: a week in the 1800s   **973.5**

The **doom** of the haunted opera. Bellairs, J. See note under Bellairs, J. The house with a clock in its walls   **Fic**

The **door** in the wall. De Angeli, M. L.   **Fic**

The **doorbell** rang. Hutchins, P.   **E**

Dork in disguise. Gorman, C.   **Fic**

The **Dorling** Kindersley science encyclopedia. See The DK science encyclopedia   **503**

Dornfeld, Margaret
   Maine
   In Celebrate the states   **973**

Dorothy & Mikey. Kasza, K.   **E**

Dorothy and the Wizard in Oz. Baum, L. F. See note under Baum, L. F. The Wizard of Oz   **Fic**

Dorris, Michael
   Morning Girl (4-6)   **Fic**
   Sees Behind Trees (4 and up)   **Fic**
   The window (4 and up)   **Fic**

Dorros, Arthur
   Abuela   **E**
   Ant cities (k-3)   **595.7**
   Feel the wind (k-3)   **551.51**
   Follow the water from brook to ocean (k-3)   **551.48**
   Isla. See note under Dorros, A. Abuela   **E**
   Radio Man. Don Radio   **E**
   Tonight is Carnaval   **E**
   A tree is growing (2-4)   **582.16**
   (il) Wyler, R. Magic secrets   **793.8**

Dots, spots, speckles, and stripes. Hoban, T.   **E**

Doty, Eldon
   (il) Muller, E. P. While you're waiting for the food to come   **507.8**

Doty, Roy, 1922-
   (il) Blume, J. Tales of a fourth grade nothing   **Fic**
   (il) Zubrowski, B. Soda science   **641.8**

Doubilet, David
   See/See also pages in the following book(s):
   Talking with adventurers p36-43 (4-6)   **920**

Double dog dare. Gilson, J. See note under Gilson, J. 4B goes wild   **Fic**

The **double** life of Pocahontas. Fritz, J.   **92**

Dougal Dixon's amazing dinosaurs. Dixon, D.   **567.9**

Dougal Dixon's dinosaurs. Dixon, D.   **567.9**

Douglas fir
   Bash, B. Ancient ones (3-5)   **585**

Douglas-Hamilton, Oria
   (il) Patent, D. H. African elephants   **599.67**

Douglass, Frederick, 1817?-1895
About
   Miller, W. Frederick Douglass (1-3)   **92**

Dove, Arthur Garfield, 1880-1946
   See/See also pages in the following book(s):
   Greenberg, J. The American eye p6-14 (6 and up)   **920**

The **dove** dove. Terban, M.   **793.73**

Doves See Pigeons

Dovey Coe. Dowell, F. O.   **Fic**

Dowden, Anne Ophelia Todd, 1907-
   (il) Paterson, J. B. Consider the lilies   **220.8**

Dowell, Frances O'Roark
   Dovey Coe (4 and up)   **Fic**

The **down** & up fall. Hurwitz, J. See note under Hurwitz, J. The hot & cold summer   **Fic**

Down by the bay. Raffi   **782.42**

Down by the station. Hillenbrand, W.   **782.42**

Down comes the rain. Branley, F. M.   **551.57**

Down the road. Schertle, A.   **E**

Down the winding road. Johnson, A.   **E**

Downen, Thomas W.
   (comp) School Library Journal's best. See School Library Journal's best   **027.8**

Downing, Julie
   (il) Rylant, C. Mr. Griggs' work   **E**

Doyle, Sir Arthur Conan, 1859-1930
   Sherlock Holmes' Christmas Goose; dramatization. See Nolan, P. T. Sherlock Holmes' Christmas goose

Doyle, Conan See Doyle, Sir Arthur Conan, 1859-1930

Dr. Seuss See Seuss, Dr.

Draanen, Wendelin van
   Sammy Keyes and the curse of Moustache Mary. See note under Draanen, W. V. Sammy Keyes and the hotel thief   **Fic**
   Sammy Keyes and the Hollywood mummy. See note under Draanen, W. V. Sammy Keyes and the hotel thief   **Fic**
   Sammy Keyes and the hotel thief (4-6)   **Fic**

Draanen, Wendelin van—*Continued*

Sammy Keyes and the runaway elf. See note under Draanen, W. V. Sammy Keyes and the hotel thief **Fic**

Sammy Keyes and the Sisters of Mercy. See note under Draanen, W. V. Sammy Keyes and the hotel thief **Fic**

Sammy Keyes and the skeleton man. See note under Draanen, W. V. Sammy Keyes and the hotel thief **Fic**

The **Drackenberg** adventure. Alexander, L. See note under Alexander, L. The Illyrian adventure **Fic**

Dragon bones and dinosaur eggs: a photobiography of Roy Chapman Andrews. Bausum, A. **92**

The **Dragon** of the north
In The Yellow fairy book p9-20 **398.2**

The **dragon** woke and stretched. Yolen, J.
In Yolen, J. Here there be dragons p23 **810.8**

Dragondrums. McCaffrey, A. See note under McCaffrey, A. Dragonsong **Fic**

Dragonfield. Yolen, J.
In Yolen, J. Here there be dragons p52-83 **810.8**

Dragonfly. (3-5) See entry in Part 2: Web Resources

Dragons
Gibbons, G. Behold . . . the dragons! (k-3) **398**

Fiction
Coville, B. Jeremy Thatcher, dragon hatcher (4-6) **Fic**
De Paola, T. The knight and the dragon **E**
Gannett, R. S. My father's dragon (1-4) **Fic**
Grahame, K. The reluctant dragon (3-5) **Fic**
Gray, L. Falcon's egg (3-5) **Fic**
Hodges, M. Saint George and the dragon (2-5) **398.2**
Nolen, J. Raising dragons **E**
Thayer, J. The popcorn dragon **E**
Thomas, S. M. Good night, Good Knight **E**
Wrede, P. C. Dealing with dragons (6 and up) **Fic**
Yolen, J. Here there be dragons (5 and up) **810.8**

Poetry
Nash, O. Custard the dragon and the wicked knight (k-3) **811**
Nash, O. The tale of Custard the Dragon (k-3) **811**
Prelutsky, J. The dragons are singing tonight (2-5) **811**

The **dragons** are singing tonight. Prelutsky, J. **811**

The **dragon's** boy. Yolen, J. **Fic**
also in Yolen, J. Here there be dragons p90-113 **810.8**

Dragons dragons and other creatures that never were, Eric Carle's. Carle, E. **808.81**

Dragon's gate. Yep, L. **Fic**

The **dragons** of Blueland. Gannett, R. S. See note under Gannett, R. S. My father's dragon **Fic**

Dragons to dine. McCaughrean, G.
In McCaughrean, G. The bronze cauldron: myths and legends of the world p1-4 **398.2**

Dragonsinger. McCaffrey, A. See note under McCaffrey, A. Dragonsong **Fic**

Dragonsong. McCaffrey, A. **Fic**

Dragonwagon, Crescent
Half a moon and one whole star **E**

Dragonwings. Yep, L. **Fic**

Drake, Sir Francis, 1540?-1596
About
Marrin, A. The sea king: Sir Francis Drake and his times (6 and up) **92**

Drake, Jane
The kids campfire book (4-6) **796.5**
The kids' summer handbook (4 and up) **790.1**
(jt. auth) Love, A. Kids and grandparents: an activity book **790.1**

Drama
See also American drama; Children's plays; One act plays
Indexes
Play index **808.82**
Periodicals
Plays: the drama magazine for young people **808.82**

Dramatists
Stanley, D. Bard of Avon: the story of William Shakespeare (4 and up) **92**

Dramatists, American
McKissack, P. C. Young, black, and determined: a biography of Lorraine Hansberry (6 and up) **92**

Dramer, Kim
People's Republic of China (4 and up) **951**

The **draug**. San Souci, R.
In San Souci, R. More short & shivery p22-26 **398.2**

[**Draw** 50 series]. Ames, L. J. **743**

Drawing
Ames, L. J. [Draw 50 series] (4 and up) **743**
Emberley, E. Ed Emberley's big green drawing book (2-5) **741.2**
Emberley, E. Ed Emberley's big red drawing book (2-5) **741.2**
Emberley, E. Ed Emberley's drawing book: make a world (2-5) **741.2**
Emberley, E. Ed Emberley's drawing book of faces (2-5) **743**
Emberley, E. Ed Emberley's great thumbprint drawing book (2-5) **743**
Fiction
Drescher, H. Simon's book **E**
Kleven, E. The paper princess **E**
Williams, V. B. Cherries and cherry pits **E**

Drawing book: make a world, Ed Emberley's. Emberley, E. **741.2**

Drawing book of faces, Ed Emberley's. Emberley, E. **743**

Drawing lessons from a bear. McPhail, D. M. **E**

The **dreadful** future of Blossom Culp. Peck, R. See note under Peck, R. The ghost belonged to me **Fic**

The **dream**. Jaffe, N.
In Jaffe, N. The mysterious visitor p13-18 **398.2**

The **dream** fast. Bruchac, J.
In Bruchac, J. Flying with the eagle, racing with the great bear p3-5 **398.2**

A **dream** in the road. Storni, A.
In You're on!: seven plays in English and Spanish p100-07 **812.008**

Dream journey. McCaughrean, G.
In McCaughrean, G. The silver treasure: myths and legends of the world p14-19 **398.2**

The **dream** keeper and other poems. Hughes, L. **811**

Dream wolf. Goble, P. **E**

Dreamcatcher. Osofsky, A. **E**

Dreaming. Greenstein, E. **E**

Dreaming of America. Bunting, E. **E**

Dreamplace. Lyon, G. E. **E**

Dreams

See also Sleep

Fiction

Appelt, K. Cowboy dreams **E**
Asch, F. Moonbear's dream **E**
Briggs, R. The snowman **E**
Browne, A. Willy the dreamer **E**
Ringgold, F. Tar Beach **E**
Stevenson, J. "Could be worse!" **E**
Van Allsburg, C. Ben's dream **E**
Van Allsburg, C. Just a dream **E**
Van Allsburg, C. The sweetest fig **E**
Wiesner, D. Free fall **E**
Wood, A. Sweet dream pie **E**

Poetry

Wong, J. S. Night garden (3-6) **811**

Dreams in the golden country. Lasky, K. **Fic**

Dreams of glory (3-5) **811.008**

Dreiser, Theodore, 1871-1945
See/See also pages in the following book(s):
Faber, D. Great lives: American literature p111-20 (5 and up) **920**

Dresang, Eliza T.
Radical change **028.5**

Drescher, Henrik, 1955-
Simon's book **E**

Dress *See* Clothing and dress

The **dress** I'll wear to the party. Neitzel, S. **E**

Dressman, Mark
(ed) Kaleidoscope. See Kaleidoscope **011.6**

Drew, Charles Richard, 1904-1950
See/See also pages in the following book(s):
Haskins, J. One more river to cross (4 and up) **920**

Drinking. Pringle, L. P. **362.292**

The **drinking** gourd. Monjo, F. N. **E**

Drinking problem *See* Alcoholism

The **dripping** cutlass. Olson, A. N.
In Olson, A. N. Ask the bones: scary stories from around the world p92-98 **398.2**

Driven from the land. Meltzer, M. **978**

Dronzek, Laura
(il) Henkes, K. Oh! **E**

The **drop** in my drink. Hooper, M. **553.7**

A **drop** of water. Wick, W. **553.7**

Drop Star. San Souci, R.
In San Souci, R. Cut from the same cloth p21-26 **398.2**

Droughts

Fiction

Aardema, V. Bringing the rain to Kapiti Plain (k-3) **398.2**
Hamilton, V. Drylongso (3-5) **Fic**
MacLachlan, P. Skylark (3-5) **Fic**

Drucker, Malka, 1945-
Grandma's latkes **E**

Drug abuse
See/See also pages in the following book(s):
Jukes, M. It's a girl thing p43-51 (5 and up) **305.23**

Drugs

Fiction

Christopher, M. Tackle without a team (4-6) **Fic**

Druids and Druidism

Fiction

Pope, E. M. The Perilous Gard (6 and up) **Fic**

Drumbeat—heartbeat. Braine, S. **970.004**

Drummer Hoff. Emberley, B. **398.8**

Drummond, Karen Eich
(jt. auth) D'Amico, J. The healthy body cookbook **641.5**
(jt. auth) D'Amico, J. The math chef **641.5**
(jt. auth) D'Amico, J. The science chef **641.3**

Drums

Fiction

James, J. A. The drums of Noto Hanto **E**
Mahy, M. Boom, baby, boom, boom! **E**

The **drums** of Noto Hanto. James, J. A. **E**

Dry-Bone and Anansi. Sherlock, Sir P. M.
In Sherlock, Sir P. M. West Indian folk-tales p77-85 **398.2**

Dry goods *See* Fabrics

Drying out. Rylant, C.
In Rylant, C. Every living thing p34-41 **S C**

Drylongso. Hamilton, V. **Fic**

Du Bois, William Pène, 1916-1993
The twenty-one balloons (5 and up) **Fic**
(il) Caudill, R. A certain small shepherd **Fic**
(il) Zolotow, C. William's doll **E**
See/See also pages in the following book(s):
Newbery Medal books, 1922-1955 p302-17 **028.5**

Duntze, Dorothée
  (il) Andersen, H. C. The princess and the pea
                            Fic

The **duppy.** San Souci, R.
  In San Souci, R. More short & shivery p11-
  15   **398.2**

Duppy ghost
  In Raw Head, bloody bones p37-40
                     398.2

Durán, Cheli
  Hildilid's night   **E**

Durbin, William, 1951-
  The journal of Sean Sullivan (5 and up)
                     Fic

Durrant, Lynda, 1956-
  The beaded moccasins (5 and up)   **Fic**

Dussling, Jennifer, 1970-
  Bugs! bugs! bugs! (1-3)   **595.7**

Dust for dinner. Turner, A. W.   **E**

Dust storms
  Meltzer, M. Driven from the land (4 and up)
                    978

             Fiction
  Hesse, K. Out of the dust (5 and up) **Fic**

Dutch sneakers and flea keepers. Brown, C.
                    811

DuTemple, Lesley A., 1952-
  North American cranes (3-6)   **598**
  North American moose (3-6) **599.65**

Dutton easy reader [series]
  Baker, B. One Saturday afternoon   **E**
  London, J. Shawn and Keeper: show-and-tell
                     E

  Thomas, S. M. Good night, Good Knight
                     E

Duvoisin, Roger, 1904-1980
  (il) Tresselt, A. R. Hide and seek fog **E**
  (il) Tresselt, A. R. White snow, bright snow
                     E

  See/See also pages in the following book(s):
  Caldecott Medal books, 1938-1957 p166-83
                 028.5

The **dwarf,** the giant, and the unicorn. Giblin, J.
                  398.2

Dyer, Jane
  (il) Appelt, K. Oh my baby, little one **E**
  (il) Here is my heart. See Here is my heart
                821.008
  (il) Talking like the rain. See Talking like the
  rain   **821.008**
  (il) Yolen, J. Piggins and the royal wedding
                     E
  (il) Yolen, J. The three bears holiday rhyme
  book   **811**
  (il) Yolen, J. The three bears rhyme book
                    811

Dypold, Pat
  (il) Lowery, L. Twist with a burger, jitter with
  a bug   **E**

Dyslexia
             Fiction
  Betancourt, J. My name is brain Brian (4-6)
                   Fic

Dyson, Marianne J.
  Space station science (4 and up)   **629.45**

E

E is for Elisa. Hurwitz, J. See note under Hurwitz,
  J. Rip-roaring Russell   **Fic**
E-mail. Brimner, L. D.   **004.6**
E-mail systems *See* Electronic mail systems
E.S.P. *See* Extrasensory perception
Each living thing. Ryder, J.   **E**
Each orange had 8 slices. Giganti, P., Jr. **E**
Each peach pear plum. Ahlberg, J.   **E**
Eagan, Eddie, 1898-1967
  See/See also pages in the following book(s):
  Knapp, R. Top 10 American men's Olympic
  gold medalists (4 and up)   **920**
Eager, Edward, 1911-1964
  Half magic (4-6)   **Fic**
  Knight's castle. See note under Cleary, B. Hen-
  ry Higgins   **Fic**
  Magic by the lake. See note under Eager, E.
  Half magic   **Fic**
  Magic or not? (4-6)   **Fic**
  Seven-day magic (4-6)   **Fic**
  The time garden. See note under Eager, E. Half
  magic   **Fic**
  The well-wishers. See note under Eager, E.
  Magic or not?   **Fic**
The **eagle** kite. Fox, P.   **Fic**
Eagles
  See also Bald eagle
  Arnold, C. Hawk highway in the sky (4-6)
                   598
  Bernhard, E. Eagles (k-3)   **598**
  Patent, D. H. Eagles of America (4 and up)
                   598

             Fiction
  Paraskevas, B. On the day the tall ships sailed
                   E

Eagles of America. Patent, D. H.   **598**
The **ear.** Babbitt, N.
  In Babbitt, N. The Devil's other storybook
  p73-81   **S C**
The **Ear,** the Eye, and the Arm. Farmer, N.
                   Fic

Earhart, Amelia, 1898-1937
             About
  Adler, D. A. A picture book of Amelia Earhart
  (1-3)   **92**
  Lauber, P. Lost star: the story of Amelia Earhart
  (5 and up)   **92**
  Szabo, C. Sky pioneer: a photobiography of
  Amelia Earhart (4 and up)   **92**
             Fiction
  Ryan, P. M. Amelia and Eleanor go for a ride
                   E

Earl Mar's daughter. Jacobs, J.
  In Jacobs, J. English fairy tales p159-63
                 398.2

Earle, Ann
  Zipping, zapping, zooming bats (k-3) **599.4**

Education

See also Elementary education; Schools; Teaching

Social aspects

Stanley, J. Children of the Dust Bowl (5 and up) **371.9**

United States—History

Bial, R. One-room school (3-5) **370.9**

Fisher, L. E. The schoolmasters (4 and up) **371.1**

Loeper, J. J. Going to school in 1776 (4 and up) **370.9**

See/See also pages in the following book(s):
Freedman, R. Children of the wild West p59-69 (4 and up) **978**

Education, Elementary *See* Elementary education

Education, Preschool *See* Preschool education

Education, Segregation in *See* Segregation in education

Educational media *See* Teaching—Aids and devices

Educational media centers *See* Instructional materials centers

Educators

See also African American educators

Edward and the pirates. McPhail, D. M. **E**

Edward in deep water. Wells, R. See note under Wells, R. Edward unready for school **E**

Edward unready for school. Wells, R. **E**

Edwards, Dorothy, 1914-1982

My naughty little sister makes a bottle-tree
In The Oxford treasury of children's stories p35-38 **S C**

Edwards, Linda

(il) Gilson, J. 4B goes wild **Fic**

Edwards, Pamela Duncan

Honk! **E**
Some smug slug **E**

Edward's overwhelming overnight. Wells, R. See note under Wells, R. Edward unready for school **E**

Eels

Landau, E. Electric fish (2-4) **597**

The **eensy-weensy** spider. Hoberman, M. A. **782.42**

The **Eentsy,** weentsy spider: fingerplays and action rhymes **796.1**

Effler, James M., 1956-

(il) Berger, M. How do flies walk upside down? **595.7**

Egan, Tim

Metropolitan cow **E**

Egg. Burton, R. **591.4**

Egg decoration

Fiction

Adams, A. The Easter egg artists **E**

Eggs

See also Eggs
Burton, R. Egg (3-5) **591.4**
Johnson, S. A. Inside an egg (4 and up) **598**

Fiction

Joyce, W. Bently & egg **E**

Polacco, P. Rechenka's eggs **E**
Schertle, A. Down the road **E**

Egielski, Richard

The gingerbread boy (k-3) **398.2**
Jazper **E**
(il) Yorinks, A. Hey, Al **E**
See/See also pages in the following book(s):
The Newbery & Caldecott medal books, 1986-2000 p47-52 **028.5**

Ego-tripping and other poems for young people. Giovanni, N. **811**

Egoff, Sheila A.

(ed) Only connect: readings on children's literature. See Only connect: readings on children's literature **028.5**

Egypt

Heinrichs, A. Egypt (4 and up) **962**
King, D. C. Egypt (4 and up) **962**

Antiquities

Perl, L. Mummies, tombs, and treasure (4 and up) **393**
Sabuda, R. Tutankhamen's gift (k-3) **92**

Civilization

Macaulay, D. Pyramid (4 and up) **726**
Tanaka, S. Secrets of the mummies (4 and up) **393**

Fiction

Clements, A. Temple cat **E**

Folklore

See Folklore—Egypt

History

Stanley, D. Cleopatra (4 and up) **92**

Science

See Science—Egypt

The **Egypt** game. Snyder, Z. K. **Fic**

The **Egyptian** Cinderella. Climo, S. **398.2**

Egyptian language

Donoughue, C. The mystery of the hieroglyphs (3-6) **493**
Giblin, J. The riddle of the Rosetta Stone (5 and up) **493**

Egyptian mythology

Fisher, L. E. The gods and goddesses of ancient Egypt (3-6) **299**
Morley, J. Egyptian myths (4 and up) **299**

Egyptian myths. Morley, J. **299**

Egyptian science *See* Science—Egypt

Ehlert, Lois, 1934-

Circus **E**
Color farm **E**
Color zoo **E**
Cuckoo. Cucú (k-3) **398.2**
Eating the alphabet **E**
Feathers for lunch **E**
Growing vegetable soup **E**
Hands **E**
Market day **E**
Mole's hill **E**
Moon rope. Un lazo a la luna (k-3) **398.2**
Nuts to you! **E**
Planting a rainbow **E**
Red leaf, yellow leaf (k-3) **582.16**
Snowballs **E**
Top cat **E**

Ehlert, Lois, 1934-—_Continued_
(il) Martin, B. Chicka chicka boom boom
E

Ehrlich, Amy, 1942-
Leo, Zack, and Emmie. See note under Ehrlich,
A. Leo, Zack, and Emmie together again
E
Leo, Zack, and Emmie together again **E**
Parents in the pigpen, pigs in the tub **E**
Wounded Knee: an Indian history of the
American West (6 and up) **970.004**

Eichenberg, Fritz, 1901-1990
Ape in a cape **E**
(il) Sandburg, C. Rainbows are made: poems
811
(il) Sewell, A. Black Beauty **Fic**

Eight cousins. Alcott, L. M. See note under Alcott, L. M. Little women **Fic**
Eight hands round. Paul, A. W. **E**
The **eight** sons of Ganga. Krishnaswami, U.
_In_ Krishnaswami, U. Shower of gold: girls
and women in the stories of India p86-89
398.2
The **eighteen** penny goose. See Walker, S. M. The
18 penny goose **E**
Eighth book of junior authors and illustrators
920.003

Eilenberg, Max
Cowboy Kid **E**

Einstein, Albert, 1879-1955
About
Parker, S. Albert Einstein and relativity (4 and
up) **92**
Severance, J. B. Einstein (5 and up) **92**

Einzig, Susan, 1922-
(il) Pearce, P. Tom's midnight garden **Fic**

Eisenberg, Lisa, 1949-
(jt. auth) Hall, K. Creepy riddles **793.73**
(jt. auth) Hall, K. Mummy riddles **793.73**
(jt. auth) Hall, K. Snakey riddles **793.73**

Eisenberg, Michael
Teaching information & technology skills
025.5

Eitan, Ora, 1940-
(il) Loomis, C. Cowboy bunnies **E**
(il) Mallett, D. Inch by inch **782.42**

El Chino
About
Say, A. El Chino (2-5) **92**
El Dorado. Delacre, L.
_In_ Delacre, L. Golden tales p47-51 **398.2**
The **El Dorado** adventure. Alexander, L. See note
under Alexander, L. The Illyrian adventure
Fic

El Niño (Ocean current)
Arnold, C. El Niño (4 and up) **551.6**
Seibert, P. Discoverning El Niño (k-3)
551.6

El Salvador
Foley, E. El Salvador (5 and up) **972.84**
Fiction
Temple, F. Grab hands and run (6 and up)
Fic

Elbert's bad word. Wood, A. **E**
Elderly
See also Old age
The **elders** of Chelm & Genendel's key. Singer, I.
B.
_In_ Singer, I. B. Stories for children p3-7
S C
_In_ Singer, I. B. When Shlemiel went to War-
saw & other stories p45-51 **398.2**
**Eleanor, of Aquitaine, Queen, consort of Henry
II, King of England, 1122?-1204**
About
Brooks, P. S. Queen Eleanor: independent spirit
of the medieval world (6 and up) **92**
See/See also pages in the following book(s):
Meltzer, M. Ten queens p43-57 (5 and up)
920

Fiction
Konigsburg, E. L. A proud taste for scarlet and
miniver (5 and up) **Fic**
Eleanor [biography of Eleanor Roosevelt] Cooney,
B. **92**
Elections
Maestro, B. The voice of the people (3-5)
324
Fiction
Sisulu, E. B. The day Gogo went to vote
E
Electric fish. Landau, E. **597**
Electric lighting
Wallace, J. The lightbulb (4 and up)
621.32

Electric lines
See/See also pages in the following book(s):
Macaulay, D. Underground p67-77 (4 and up)
624.1

Electric power
Cole, J. The magic school bus and the electric
field trip (2-4) **621.3**
Electricity
Berger, M. Switch on, switch off (k-3) **537**
Cole, J. The magic school bus and the electric
field trip (2-4) **621.3**
Dispezio, M. A. Awesome experiments in elec-
tricity & magnetism (5 and up) **537**
Levine, S. Shocking science (5 and up)
537
Parker, S. Electricity (4 and up) **537**
Experiments
VanCleave, J. P. Janice VanCleave's electricity
(4 and up) **537**
Electromagnetic waves
Skurzynski, G. Waves (3-6) **539.2**
Electron microscopes
Tomb, H. Microaliens (5 and up) **502.8**
Electronic data processing See Data processing
Electronic mail systems
Brimner, L. D. E-mail (2-4) **004.6**
Elementary education
Periodicals
Childhood Education **372.05**
Instructor **372.05**
Teaching K-8 **372.05**

E (top right corner)

Elementary English Review. *See* Language Arts
372.605

Elementary school libraries
See also Children's libraries
Exploring science in the library **027.8**
The **Elementary** school library collection
011.6
The **Elements** [Benchmark Bks.] (5 and up)
546
Elements [Grolier] (5 and up) **546**
Elena the Wise. Afanas'ev, A. N.
In Afanas'ev, A. N. Russian fairy tales p545-49 **398.2**
Elephant and Frog go courting. Bryan, A.
In Bryan, A. Ashley Bryan's African tales, uh-huh p13-19 **398.2**
Elephant woman. Pringle, L. P. **599.67**
Elephants
Patent, D. H. African elephants (3-5)
599.67
Pringle, L. P. Elephant woman (4 and up)
599.67

Fiction
Brunhoff, J. de. The story of Babar, the little elephant **E**
Hoff, S. Oliver **E**
Kipling, R. The elephant's child **Fic**
Lobel, A. Uncle Elephant **E**
Murphy, J. A quiet night in **E**
Pullman, P. The firework-maker's daughter (4 and up) **Fic**
Seuss, Dr. Horton hatches the egg **E**
Seuss, Dr. Horton hears a Who! **E**
Young, E. Seven blind mice (k-3) **398.2**
Ziefert, H. April Fool! **E**
The **elephant's** child. Kipling, R. **Fic**
also in Kipling, R. Just so stories **S C**
The **elevator** family. Evans, D. **Fic**
Elevator magic. Murphy, S. J. **513**
The **eleven** thousand Virgins. Delacre, L.
In Delacre, L. Golden tales p15-18 **398.2**
Elffers, Joost
(jt. auth) Freymann, S. How are you peeling?
E
(jt. auth) Freymann, S. One lonely sea horse
E
Eli. Peet, B. **E**
Elias (Biblical figure) *See* Elijah (Biblical figure)
Elias, Marie Louise
Barbados (5 and up) **972.98**
eLibrary elementary. (K-6) See entry in Part 2: Web Resources
Elijah (Biblical figure)
About
Goldin, B. D. Journeys with Elijah (4 and up)
222
Jaffe, N. The mysterious visitor (4-6) **398.2**
Elijah and the fisher boy. Jaffe, N.
In Jaffe, N. The mysterious visitor p43-48
398.2
Elijah and the three brothers. Goldin, B. D.
In Goldin, B. D. Journeys with Elijah p39-47
222

Elijah in the marketplace. Jaffe, N.
In Jaffe, N. The mysterious visitor p20-29
398.2
Elijah the slave. Singer, I. B.
In Singer, I. B. Stories for children p206-09
S C
Elijah's angel. Rosen, M. J. **Fic**
Elimination (Physiology) *See* Excretion
Eliot, T. S. (Thomas Stearns), 1888-1965
Growltiger's last stand **811**
Eliot, Thomas Stearns *See* Eliot, T. S. (Thomas Stearns), 1888-1965
Elisa in the middle. Hurwitz, J. *See* note under Hurwitz, J. Rip-roaring Russell **Fic**
Elish, Dan, 1960-
Vermont
In Celebrate the states **973**
Washington, D.C.
In Celebrate the states **973**
Elizabeth I, Queen of England, 1533-1603
See/See also pages in the following book(s):
Meltzer, M. Ten queens p73-83 (5 and up)
920
Fiction
Lasky, K. Elizabeth I (4 and up) **Fic**
Elizabeti's doll. Stuve-Bodeen, S. **E**
Elk
Patent, D. H. Deer and elk (4 and up)
599.65
The **elk** and the wren. MacDonald, M. R.
In MacDonald, M. R. Look back and see p103-06 **372.6**
Ella enchanted. Levine, G. C. **Fic**
Ella of all of a kind family. Taylor, S. *See* note under Taylor, S. All-of-a-kind family **Fic**
Elleman, Barbara
Tomie de Paola **92**
Ellen Tebbits. Cleary, B. **Fic**
Ellington, Duke, 1899-1974
About
Pinkney, A. D. Duke Ellington (2-4) **92**
Elliott, Mark
(il) Levine, G. C. The princess test **Fic**
Ellis, George, 1753-1815
The twelve months; adaptation. *See* Tafuri, N. Snowy flowy blowy **E**
Ellis, Gerry
(il) MacMillan, D. M. Cheetahs **599.75**
(il) Walker, S. M. Hippos **599.63**
(il) Walker, S. M. Rhinos **599.66**
Ellis, Jan Davey
(il) Cobb, M. The quilt-block history of pioneer days **746.46**
(il) Cobb, M. A sampler view of colonial life
746.44
(il) Seibert, P. Discovering El Niño **551.6**
Ellis, Sarah, 1952-
Back of beyond (6 and up) **S C**
Contents: Tunnel; Potato; Pinch; Knife; Happen; Check; Gore; Catch; Net; Sisters; Fix; Visitors
Next-door neighbors (4 and up) **Fic**
See/See also pages in the following book(s):
Origins of story p49-59 **808.06**

Ellis Island. Kroll, S.   **325.73**

An **Ellis** Island Christmas. Leighton, M. R.   **E**

Ellis Island Immigration Station

Bierman, C. Journey to Ellis Island (3-5)
    325.73

I was dreaming to come to America (4 and up)
    325.73

Kroll, S. Ellis Island (3-5)   **325.73**

Levine, E. . . . if your name was changed at
Ellis Island (3-5)   **325.73**

See/See also pages in the following book(s):

Maestro, B. Coming to America: the story of
immigration (k-3)   **325.73**

             Fiction

Woodruff, E. The memory coat   **E**

Elmer and the dragon. Gannett, R. S. See note under Gannett, R. S. My father's dragon
    Fic

Elocution *See* Public speaking

Eloise at Christmastime. Thompson, K. See note
under Thompson, K. Kay Thompson's Eloise
    Fic

Eloise in Moscow. Thompson, K. See note under
Thompson, K. Kay Thompson's Eloise
    Fic

Eloise in Paris. Thompson, K. See note under
Thompson, K. Kay Thompson's Eloise
    Fic

Eloise, Kay Thompson's. Thompson, K.   **E**

Eloise's guide to life. Thompson, K. See note under Thompson, K. Kay Thompson's Eloise
    Fic

The **elves** and the shoemaker. Galdone, P.
    398.2

The **elves** and the shoemaker. Grimm, J.

In Tomie dePaola's favorite nursery tales
p100-04   **398.2**

Elvis lives! and other anagrams. Agee, J.
    793.73

Elway, John

See/See also pages in the following book(s):

Sullivan, G. Quarterbacks! p15-17 (5 and up)
    920

Elya, Susan Middleton, 1955-

Say hola to Spanish, otra vez (1-4)   **463**

Emberley, Barbara

Drummer Hoff   **398.8**

(il) Branley, F. M. The moon seems to change
    523.3

Emberley, Ed

Ed Emberley's big green drawing book (2-5)
    741.2

Ed Emberley's big red drawing book (2-5)
    741.2

Ed Emberley's drawing book: make a world
(2-5)   **741.2**

Ed Emberley's drawing book of faces (2-5)
    743

Ed Emberley's great thumbprint drawing book
(2-5)   **743**

Go away, big green monster!   **E**

(il) Branley, F. M. The moon seems to change
    523.3

(il) Emberley, B. Drummer Hoff   **398.8**

See/See also pages in the following book(s):

Newbery and Caldecott Medal books, 1966-1975
p199-207   **028.5**

Emberley, Michael, 1960-

(il) Harris, R. H. Happy birth day!   **E**

(il) Harris, R. H. It's perfectly normal
    613.9

(il) Harris, R. H. It's so amazing!   **612.6**

Emberley, Rebecca

Three cool kids (k-3)   **398.2**

Emblems *See* Signs and symbols

Embracing *See* Hugging

Embroidery

Cobb, M. A sampler view of colonial life (2-5)
    746.44

Embryology

See also Fetus; Reproduction

Burton, R. Egg (3-5)   **591.4**

Emeka's gift. Onyefulu, I.   **E**

Emeline at the circus. Priceman, M.   **E**

Emelya the simpleton. Afanas'ev, A. N.

In Afanas'ev, A. N. Russian fairy tales p46-
48   **398.2**

Emergency!. Gibbons, G.   **363.34**

Emergency!. Masoff, J.   **616.02**

Emergency medicine

Masoff, J. Emergency! (3-6)   **616.02**

Emerson, Ralph Waldo, 1803-1882

See/See also pages in the following book(s):

Faber, D. Great lives: American literature p11-
20 (5 and up)   **920**

Emigrants *See* Immigrants

Emigration *See* Immigration and emigration

Emily's first 100 days of school. Wells, R.
    E

Emma. Kesselman, W. A.   **E**

Emma's rug. Say, A.   **E**

Emotions

Aliki. Feelings (k-3)   **152.4**

Freymann, S. How are you peeling?   **E**

Young, E. Voices of the heart   **179**

The **emperor's** egg. Jenkins, M.   **598**

The **emperor's** new clothes. Andersen, H. C.
    E

also in Andersen, H. C. The little mermaid
and other fairy tales p61-66   **S C**

also in Tomie dePaola's favorite nursery tales
p87-95   **398.2**

also in The Yellow fairy book p21-25
    398.2

The **emperor's** new clothes. Demi   **E**

The **emperor's** new clothes. See Yolen, J. King
Long Shanks   **E**

Empire State Building (New York, N.Y.)

Macaulay, D. Unbuilding (4 and up)   **690**

             Fiction

Wiesner, D. Sector 7   **E**

Employees

             Training

See also Apprentices

Employment of children *See* Child labor

Employment of women See Women—Employment

Empresses

See also Queens

The **empty** pot. Demi   **398.2**

Emrich, Marion Vallet
Johnny Appleseed! Johnny Appleseed!
In From sea to shining sea p274-76
    810.8

eNature.com. (4 and up) See entry in Part 2: Web Resources

Encarta world English dictionary   **423**

The **enchanted** cap. Osborne, M. P.
In Osborne, M. P. Mermaid tales from around the world p19-23   **398.2**

The **enchanted** castle. Nesbit, E.   **Fic**

The **Enchanted** horse
In The Arabian nights entertainments p358-89
    398.2

The **Enchanted** prince
In Stockings of buttermilk: American folktales p95-103   **398.2**

The **enchanted** princess. Afanas´ev, A. N.
In Afanas´ev, A. N. Russian fairy tales p600-11   **398.2**

The **enchanted** ring. Afanas´ev, A. N.
In Afanas´ev, A. N. Russian fairy tales p31-37   **398.2**

The **enchanted** ring. Fénelon, F. de S. de L. M.
In The Green fairy book p137-44   **398.2**

The **Enchanted** snake
In The Green fairy book p186-93   **398.2**

The **enchanted** spring. Schwartz, H.
In Schwartz, H. A coat for the moon and other Jewish tales p8-11   **398.2**

The **enchanted** watch. Deulin, C.
In The Green fairy book p43-47   **398.2**

Enchantment of the world, second series

Blashfield, J. F. England	**942**
Blauer, E. South Africa	**968**
Burgan, M. Belgium	**949.3**
Dramer, K. People's Republic of China	**951**
Foster, L. M. Iraq	**956.7**
Foster, L. M. Kuwait	**953.67**
Foster, L. M. Oman	**953**
Heinrichs, A. Australia	**994**
Heinrichs, A. Brazil	**981**
Heinrichs, A. Egypt	**962**
Heinrichs, A. Japan	**952**
Hintz, M. Argentina	**982**
Hintz, M. The Bahamas	**972.96**
Hintz, M. Haiti	**972.94**
Hintz, M. Israel	**956.94**
Hintz, M. Poland	**943.8**
McNair, S. Finland	**948.97**
McNair, S. Thailand	**959.3**
Milivojevic, J. Serbia	**949.7**
Morrison, M. Colombia	**986.1**
Morrison, M. Costa Rica	**972.86**
Nardo, D. France	**944**
Stein, R. C. Mexico	**972**
Willis, T. Libya	**961.2**
Wright, D. K. Albania	**949.65**

Encounter at Easton. Avi   **Fic**

Encyclopedia Brown and the case of Pablo's nose. Sobol, D. J. See note under Sobol, D. J. Encyclopedia Brown, boy detective   **Fic**

Encyclopedia Brown and the case of the dead eagles. Sobol, D. J. See note under Sobol, D. J. Encyclopedia Brown, boy detective   **Fic**

Encyclopedia Brown and the case of the disgusting sneakers. Sobol, D. J. See note under Sobol, D. J. Encyclopedia Brown, boy detective   **Fic**

Encyclopedia Brown and the case of the midnight visitor. Sobol, D. J. See note under Sobol, D. J. Encyclopedia Brown, boy detective   **Fic**

Encyclopedia Brown and the case of the mysterious handprints. Sobol, D. J. See note under Sobol, D. J. Encyclopedia Brown, boy detective   **Fic**

Encyclopedia Brown and the case of the secret pitch. Sobol, D. J. See note under Sobol, D. J. Encyclopedia Brown, boy detective   **Fic**

Encyclopedia Brown and the case of the sleeping dog. Sobol, D. J. See note under Sobol, D. J. Encyclopedia Brown, boy detective   **Fic**

Encyclopedia Brown and the case of the slippery salamander. Sobol, D. J. See note under Sobol, D. J. Encyclopedia Brown, boy detective   **Fic**

Encyclopedia Brown and the case of the treasure hunt. Sobol, D. J. See note under Sobol, D. J. Encyclopedia Brown, boy detective   **Fic**

Encyclopedia Brown and the case of the two spies. Sobol, D. J. See note under Sobol, D. J. Encyclopedia Brown, boy detective   **Fic**

Encyclopedia Brown, boy detective. Sobol, D. J.   **Fic**

Encyclopedia Brown finds the clues. Sobol, D. J. See note under Sobol, D. J. Encyclopedia Brown, boy detective   **Fic**

Encyclopedia Brown gets his man. Sobol, D. J. See note under Sobol, D. J. Encyclopedia Brown, boy detective   **Fic**

Encyclopedia Brown keeps the peace. Sobol, D. J. See note under Sobol, D. J. Encyclopedia Brown, boy detective   **Fic**

Encyclopedia Brown lends a hand. Sobol, D. J. See note under Sobol, D. J. Encyclopedia Brown, boy detective   **Fic**

Encyclopedia Brown saves the day. Sobol, D. J. See note under Sobol, D. J. Encyclopedia Brown, boy detective   **Fic**

Encyclopedia Brown sets the pace. Sobol, D. J. See note under Sobol, D. J. Encyclopedia Brown, boy detective   **Fic**

Encyclopedia Brown shows the way. Sobol, D. J. See note under Sobol, D. J. Encyclopedia Brown, boy detective   **Fic**

Encyclopedia Brown solves them all. Sobol, D. J. See note under Sobol, D. J. Encyclopedia Brown, boy detective   **Fic**

Encyclopedia Brown takes the cake!. Sobol, D. J. See note under Sobol, D. J. Encyclopedia Brown, boy detective   **Fic**

Encyclopedia Brown takes the case. Sobol, D. J. See note under Sobol, D. J. Encyclopedia Brown, boy detective   **Fic**

Encyclopedia Brown tracks them down. Sobol, D. J. See note under Sobol, D. J. Encyclopedia Brown, boy detective   **Fic**

Encyclopedia of Christmas   **394.26**

Encyclopedia of first ladies [series]
Santow, D. Mary Todd Lincoln, 1818-1882
92

The **encyclopedia** of Native America. Griffin-Pierce, T.   **970.004**

Encyclopedia of people and places. See The World Book encyclopedia of people and places   **910.3**

Encyclopedia of presidents [series]
Kent, Z. John Quincy Adams, sixth president of the United States   **92**
Simon, C. Chester A. Arthur: twenty-first president of the United States   **92**
Wade, L. R. James Carter: thirty-ninth president of the United States   **92**

Encyclopedia of the nations, Worldmark
910.3

Encyclopedia Smithsonian. See entry in Part 2: Web Resources

Encyclopedias and dictionaries
See also Picture dictionaries; names of languages with the subdivision *Dictionaries* and subjects with the subdivision *Dictionaries* or *Encyclopedias*
Compton's encyclopedia & fact-index   **031**
Kane, J. N. Famous first facts   **031.02**
The New book of knowledge   **031**
Pascoe, E. Scholastic kid's almanac for the 21st century (4 and up)   **031.02**
The World Book encyclopedia   **031**

Endangered in America [series]
Silverstein, A. The California condor   **598**
Silverstein, A. The Florida panther   **599.75**
Silverstein, A. The red wolf   **599.77**
Silverstein, A. The sea otter   **599.7**

Endangered species
See also Rare animals; Wildlife conservation
Galan, M. A. There's still time (3-6)
333.95
Mullins, P. V for vanishing   **E**
Patent, D. H. Back to the wild (4-6)   **639.9**
Silverstein, A. The red wolf (4 and up)
599.77
Silverstein, A. The sea otter (4 and up)
599.7
Thapar, V. Tiger (3-5)   **599.75**
Fiction
Burgess, M. Kite (5 and up)   **Fic**
George, J. C. There's an owl in the shower (3-5)   **Fic**

Endurance (Ship)
Kimmel, E. C. Ice story (4 and up)   **998**

Energy forever? [series]
Graham, I. Geothermal and bio-energy
333.8
Graham, I. Nuclear power   **333.7**

Energy resources
Parker, S. Fuels for the future (4-6)   **333.79**

Engel, Dean, 1943-
Ezra Jack Keats (3-5)   **92**

Engineering, Structural *See* Structural engineering

England
Blashfield, J. F. England (4 and up)   **942**
History
See Great Britain—History
Social life and customs
Nikola-Lisa, W. Till year's good end (2-4)
942.02

English, Karen
Francie (5 and up)   **Fic**

English fairy tales. Jacobs, J.   **398.2**

English folk songs
On Christmas Day in the morning (k-3)
782.28

English language
Dictionaries
The American Heritage children's dictionary
423
The American Heritage picture dictionary (k-1)
423
The Cat in the Hat beginner book dictionary (k-3)   **423**
DK illustrated Oxford dictionary   **423**
DK Merriam Webster children's dictionary
423
Encarta world English dictionary   **423**
Macmillan dictionary for children (3-6)   **423**
Macmillan first dictionary (1-3)   **423**
Merriam-Webster's elementary dictionary (4-6)
423
Merriam-Webster's intermediate dictionary (6 and up)   **423**
Scholastic children's dictionary (3-5)   **423**
Scholastic first dictionary (1-3)   **423**
Webster's New World children's dictionary (3-5)   **423**
Grammar
Cleary, B. P. Hairy, scary, ordinary (k-3)
428
Heller, R. Fantastic! wow! and unreal! (k-2)
428
Heller, R. Kites sail high: a book about verbs (k-2)   **428**
Heller, R. Many luscious lollipops: a book about adjectives (k-2)   **428**
Heller, R. Mine, all mine (k-2)   **428**
Heller, R. Up, up and away (k-2)   **428**
Homonyms
Terban, M. Funny you should ask (3-5)
793.73
Idioms
Terban, M. Mad as a wet hen! and other funny idioms (3-5)   **427**
Terban, M. Scholastic dictionary of idioms (4 and up)   **423**

English language—*Continued*
Spelling
See also Spellers
Study and teaching—Periodicals
Language Arts 372.605
Synonyms and antonyms
Bollard, J. K. Scholastic children's thesaurus (4 and up) 423
Crews, N. A high, low, near, far, loud, quiet story E
The Facts on File student's thesaurus 423
The Harcourt Brace student thesaurus (4 and up) 423
Hoban, T. Exactly the opposite E
Roget's children's thesaurus (3-5) 423
Roget's student thesaurus (5 and up) 423
Serfozo, M. What's what? a guessing game E
Terms and phrases
Heller, R. Behind the mask (k-2) 428
Heller, R. A cache of jewels and other collective nouns (k-2) 428
Heller, R. Merry-go-round (k-2) 428
Terban, M. Mad as a wet hen! and other funny idioms (3-5) 427
Vocabulary
See Vocabulary
English poetry
Collections
Ghost poems (1-4) 821.008
Here is my heart 821.008
I saw Esau 398.8
Knock at a star 811.008
Monster poems (1-4) 821.008
The Oxford book of children's verse 821.008
The Random House book of poetry for children 821.008
Read-aloud rhymes for the very young (k-2) 821.008
Talking like the rain (k-3) 821.008
Witch poems 821.008
Enigmas *See* Curiosities and wonders
Enik, Ted
(il) Cobb, V. Why doesn't the earth fall up? 531
The **enormous** carrot. Vagin, V. V. 398.2
The **enormous** crocodile. Dahl, R. Fic
The **enormous** egg. Butterworth, O. Fic
The **enormous** frog. Schwartz, H.
In Schwartz, H. The diamond tree p61-62 398.2
Enright, Elizabeth, 1909-1968
Gone-Away Lake (4-6) Fic
Return to Gone-Away Lake. See note under Enright, E. Gone-Away Lake Fic
See/See also pages in the following book(s):
Newbery Medal books, 1922-1955 p168-75 028.5
Entertainers
Fiction
Ackerman, K. Song and dance man E
Byars, B. C. The Golly sisters go West E
The **environmental** movement. Pringle, L. P. 363.7

Environmental pollution *See* Pollution
Environmental protection
See also Conservation of natural resources
Brown, L. K. Dinosaurs to the rescue! (k-3) 363.7
Pringle, L. P. The environmental movement (5 and up) 363.7
Fiction
Van Allsburg, C. Just a dream E
An **epidemic** of ducks. Sanfield, S.
In Sanfield, S. The adventures of High John the Conqueror 398.2
Epigrams
See also Proverbs; Quotations
Eppridge, Bill
(il) Jones, R. F. Jake 636.7
Equestrianism *See* Horsemanship
Equiano, Olaudah, b. 1745
About
Cameron, A. The kidnapped prince: the life of Olaudah Equiano (4 and up) 92
Erandi's braids. Madrigal, A. H. E
Eratosthenes, 3rd cent. B.C.
About
Lasky, K. The librarian who measured the earth (2-5) 92
Erdrich, Louise
The birchbark house (4 and up) Fic
Ereth's birthday. Avi See note under Avi. Poppy Fic
Eric Carle's animals, animals. Carle, E. 808.81
Eric Carle's dragons dragons and other creatures that never were. Carle, E. 808.81
Erickson, Darren
(il) Kelly, E. J. Paper airplanes 745.592
(il) Ross, M. E. Millipedeology 595.6
(il) Ross, M. E. Spiderology 595.4
Erickson, Paul, 1976-
Daily life on a Southern plantation, 1853 (4-6) 975
Erie Canal (N.Y.)
Harness, C. The amazing impossible Erie Canal (3-5) 386
Eriksson, Inga-Karin
(il) Björk, C. Vendela in Venice Fic
Erlbach, Arlene
The kids' invention book (4-6) 608
The kids' volunteering book (4-6) 302
Sidewalk games around the world (3-5) 796.1
Ernst, Lisa Campbell, 1957-
Goldilocks returns E
Little Red Riding Hood: a newfangled prairie tale (k-3) 398.2
Sam Johnson and the blue ribbon quilt E
When Bluebell sang E
Zinnia and Dot E
(il) Lied, K. Potato E
(il) Young, R. Who says moo? E
Eros (Greek deity)
Craft, M. Cupid and Psyche (4 and up) 292

Explorers—*Continued*

Marrin, A. The sea king: Sir Francis Drake and his times (6 and up) **92**

Marzollo, J. In 1492 (k-2) **970.01**

Sis, P. Follow the dream [biography of Christopher Columbus] (k-3) **92**

Dictionaries

Explorers (5 and up) **920.003**

Explorers & discoverers **920.003**

Explorers (5 and up) **920.003**

Explorers & discoverers **920.003**

Exploring cultures of the world [series]

Ayer, E. H. Germany **943**

Chicoine, S. Spain **946**

Galvin, I. F. Brazil **981**

Kent, D. Mexico **972**

King, D. C. Egypt **962**

King, D. C. Italy **945**

King, D. C. Kenya **967.62**

King, D. C. Peru **985**

Markham, L. Colombia **986.1**

Meisel, J. D. Australia **994**

Pickering, M. Chile **983**

Sateren, S. S. Canada **971**

Skelton, O. Vietnam **959.7**

Steins, R. Hungary **943.9**

Exploring Leonardo. (5 and up) See entry in Part 2: Web Resources

Exploring life science (4-6) **570**

Exploring science in the library **027.8**

Exploring the deep, dark sea. Gibbons, G. **551.46**

Exploring the planets. (4 and up) See entry in Part 2: Web Resources

Exploring the Titanic. Ballard, R. D. **910.4**

Extinct animals

See also Prehistoric animals; Rare animals

Lessem, D. Dinosaurs to dodos (4 and up) **560**

Markle, S. Gone forever! (k-3) **591.68**

Mullins, P. V for vanishing **E**

Extinct plants *See* Fossil plants

The **extinguished** lights. Singer, I. B.

In Singer, I. B. The power of light p13-20 **S C**

In Singer, I. B. Stories for children p15-21 **S C**

Extra cheese, please!. Peterson, C. **637**

Extra! Extra!. Granfield, L. **071**

Extra innings (4 and up) **811.008**

Extraordinary black Americans. Altman, S. **920**

An **extraordinary** egg. Lionni, L. **E**

Extraordinary friends. Rogers, F. **362.4**

An **extraordinary** life. Pringle, L. P. **595.7**

Extrasensory perception

Fiction

Christopher, M. The dog that called the pitch (2-4) **Fic**

Sleator, W. Into the dream (5 and up) **Fic**

Extraterrestrial beings

Wilson, C. UFOs and aliens (4 and up) **001.9**

Fiction

Brittain, B. Shape-changer (4 and up) **Fic**

Spinner, S. Be first in the universe (4-6) **Fic**

Weston, M. Space guys! **E**

Willis, J. Earthlets, as explained by Professor Xargle **E**

Yorinks, A. Company's coming **E**

Extravehicular activity (Space flight)

Vogt, G. Spacewalks (4 and up) **629.45**

Exupéry, Antoine de Saint- *See* Saint-Exupéry, Antoine de, 1900-1944

Exxon Valdez (Ship)

Markle, S. After the spill (4 and up) **363.7**

Eye

Showers, P. Look at your eyes (k-1) **612.8**

Eye of the storm. Kramer, S. **778.9**

Eyeglasses

Fiction

Giff, P. R. Watch out, Ronald Morgan! **E**

Smith, L. Glasses: who needs 'em? **E**

The **eyes**. Pearson, K.

In Don't read this! and other tales of the unnatural p132-48 **S C**

Eyes, nose, fingers and toes. Hindley, J. **E**

Eyes of marriage. Terada, A. M.

In Terada, A. M. Under the starfruit tree p64-68 **398.2**

The **eyes** of the Amaryllis. Babbitt, N. **Fic**

Eyes of the cat. Bond, R.

In The Oxford book of scary tales p76-78 **808.8**

The **eyes** of the killer robot. Bellairs, J. See note under Bellairs, J. The curse of the blue figurine **Fic**

Eyewitness books [series]

Ardley, N. Music **784.19**

Bender, L. Invention **609**

Brookfield, K. Book **070.5**

Buckley, J., Jr. Football **796.332**

Burnie, D. Bird **598**

Burnie, D. Tree **582.16**

Byam, M. Arms & armor **355.8**

Challoner, J. Hurricane & tornado **551.55**

Clarke, B. Amphibian **597.8**

Clutton-Brock, J. Cat **599.75**

Clutton-Brock, J. Horse **636.1**

Coiley, J. Train **625.1**

Cotterell, A. Ancient China **931**

Crampton, W. G. Flag **929.9**

Cribb, J. Money **332.4**

Early humans **930.1**

Grau, A. Dance **792.8**

Gravett, C. Castle **728.8**

Gravett, C. Knight **940.1**

Greenaway, T. Jungle **577.3**

Hill, D. Witches & magic-makers **133.4**

Hornby, H. Soccer **796.334**

Kentley, E. Boat **387.2**

Lane, B. Crime & detection **364**

Langley, A. Renaissance **940.2**

Lindsay, W. Prehistoric life **560**

Macquitty, M. Shark **597**

Margeson, S. M. Viking **948**

Eyewitness books—*Continued*

McCarthy, C. Reptile	**597.9**
McIntosh, J. Archeology	**930.1**
Mound, L. A. Insect	**595.7**
Nahum, A. Flying machine	**629.133**
Parker, S. Fish	**597**
Parker, S. Mammal	**599**
Pearson, A. Ancient Greece	**938**
Putnam, J. Mummy	**393**
Putnam, J. Pyramid	**909**
Redmond, I. Gorilla	**599.8**
Rowland-Warne, L. Costume	**391**
Symes, R. F. Crystal & gem	**548**
Symes, R. F. Rocks & minerals	**549**
Taylor, B. Arctic & Antarctic	**998**
Taylor, P. D. Fossil	**560**
Van Rose, S. Volcano & earthquake	**551.2**
Whalley, P. E. S. Butterfly & moth	**595.7**
Wilkinson, P. Building	**690**

Eyewitness explorers [series]

Feltwell, J. Butterflies and moths	**595.7**
Stott, C. Night sky	**520**

Eyewitness juniors [series]

Clarke, B. Amazing frogs & toads	**597.8**
Ling, M. Amazing fish	**597**
Parry-Jones, J. Amazing birds of prey	**598**
Parsons, A. Amazing cats	**599.75**
Parsons, A. Amazing spiders	**595.4**
Smith, T. Amazing lizards	**597.9**
Still, J. Amazing butterflies & moths	**595.7**

Eyewitness readers [series]

Dubowski, C. E. Shark attack!	**597**
Dussling, J. Bugs! bugs! bugs!	**595.7**
Maynard, C. Micromonsters	**579**
Wallace, K. Tale of a tadpole	**597.8**

Eyewitness science [series]

Burnie, D. Light	**535**
Gamblin, L. Evolution	**576.8**
Newmark, A. Chemistry	**540**
Parker, S. Electricity	**537**
Pollock, S. Ecology	**577**
Van Rose, S. Earth	**550**

Eyewitness visual dictionaries [series]

Challoner, J. The visual dictionary of chemistry	**540**
Challoner, J. The visual dictionary of physics	**530**
The Visual dictionary of ancient civilizations	**930**
The Visual dictionary of buildings	**720**
The Visual dictionary of human anatomy	**611**
The Visual dictionary of military uniforms	**355.1**
The Visual dictionary of plants	**580**
The Visual dictionary of prehistoric life	**560**
The Visual dictionary of ships and sailing	**387.2**
The Visual dictionary of the earth	**550**
The Visual dictionary of the horse	**636.1**
The Visual dictionary of the human body	**611**
The Visual dictionary of the skeleton	**591.4**
The Visual dictionary of the universe	**520**

'Ezer, Ehud Ben- *See* Ben-'Ezer, Ehud, 1936-

F

Fa Mulan. San Souci, R.	**398.2**

Faber, Doris, 1924-
Great lives: American literature (5 and up)   **920**

Faber, Harold
(jt. auth) Faber, D. Great lives: American literature   **920**

Fables

Bierhorst, J. Doctor Coyote (1-4)	**398.2**
Brett, J. Town mouse, country mouse (k-3)	**398.2**
Brown, M. Once a mouse (k-3)	**398.2**
Cooney, B. Chanticleer and the fox	**E**
Galdone, P. The monkey and the crocodile (k-2)	**398.2**
Heins, E. L. The cat and the cook and other fables of Krylov (1-4)	**398.2**
McClintock, B. Animal fables from Aesop (1-4)	**398.2**
Nolan, D. Androcles and the lion (1-3)	**398.2**
Pinkney, J. Aesop's fables	**398.2**
Poole, A. L. The ant and the grasshopper (k-3)	**398.2**
Scieszka, J. Squids will be squids	**E**
Tomie dePaola's Favorite nursery tales (k-3)	**398.2**
Ward, H. The hare and the tortoise (k-3)	**398.2**
Wildsmith, B. The hare and the tortoise (k-2)	**398.2**
Wildsmith, B. The miller, the boy and the donkey (k-2)	**398.2**
Young, E. Donkey trouble (k-3)	**398.2**
Young, E. Seven blind mice (k-3)	**398.2**

Fables. Lobel, A.   **Fic**

Fabra, Jordi Sierra i *See* Sierra i Fabra, Jordi, 1947-

Fabrics
Keeler, P. A. Unraveling fibers (3-5)   **677**

Face in art
Emberley, E. Ed Emberley's drawing book of faces (2-5)   **743**

The **face** in the Bessledorf funeral parlor. Naylor, P. R. See note under Naylor, P. R. Peril in the Bessledorf Parachute Factory   **Fic**

Faces   **306.05**

Facklam, Margery, 1927-

The big bug book (3-6)	**595.7**
Creepy, crawly caterpillars (3-6)	**595.7**

Facklam, Paul

(il) Facklam, M. The big bug book	**595.7**
(il) Facklam, M. Creepy, crawly caterpillars	**595.7**

Factorials
Anno, M. Anno's mysterious multiplying jar (2-5)   **512**

Factories

Fiction

Ackerman, K. By the dawn's early light	**E**
McCully, E. A. The bobbin girl (3-5)	**Fic**
Paterson, K. Lyddie (5 and up)	**Fic**

Fairy tales—*Continued*

Hautzig, D. The nutcracker ballet **E**

Hayes, J. Little Gold Star (k-3) **398.2**

Helldorfer, M. C. Phoebe and the River Flute **E**

Hickox, R. The golden sandal (k-3) **398.2**

Hoffmann, E. T. A. Nutcracker (4 and up) **Fic**

Hooks, W. H. Moss gown (k-3) **398.2**

Huck, C. S. Princess Furball (1-3) **398.2**

Isadora, R. Swan Lake **E**

Jackson, E. B. Cinder Edna **E**

Jacobs, J. English fairy tales (4-6) **398.2**

Johnston, T. The cowboy and the black-eyed pea **E**

Kellogg, S. Jack and the beanstalk (k-3) **398.2**

Kimmel, E. A. Bearhead (k-3) **398.2**

Kimmel, E. A. Iron John (2-5) **398.2**

Kimmel, E. A. The magic dreidels **E**

Kimmel, E. A. Seven at one blow (k-3) **398.2**

Kimmel, E. A. Three sacks of truth (2-4) **398.2**

Kingsley, C. The water babies (4-6) **Fic**

Krudop, W. The man who caught fish **E**

Lesser, R. Hansel and Gretel (k-3) **398.2**

Levine, G. C. The princess test (4 and up) **Fic**

Lewis, J. P. At the wish of the fish (k-3) **398.2**

Lindgren, A. The Tomten **E**

Louie, A.-L. Yeh-Shen (2-4) **398.2**

Lowell, S. The bootmaker and the elves (k-3) **398.2**

Lurie, A. The black geese (k-3) **398.2**

MacDonald, G. At the back of the North Wind (4-6) **Fic**

MacDonald, G. The light princess (3-6) **Fic**

MacDonald, G. The princess and the goblin (3-6) **Fic**

MacDonald, M. R. Twenty tellable tales **372.6**

Mahy, M. The seven Chinese brothers (1-3) **398.2**

Marshall, J. Hansel and Gretel (k-2) **398.2**

Martin, R. The language of birds (2-4) **398.2**

Mayer, M. Baba Yaga and Vasilisa the brave (3-5) **398.2**

Mayer, M. Beauty and the beast (1-4) **398.2**

Mayer, M. Iron John (3-6) **398.2**

McDermott, G. Tim O'Toole and the wee folk **E**

McKinley, R. Beauty: a retelling of the story of Beauty & the beast (6 and up) **Fic**

Meddaugh, S. Cinderella's rat **E**

Merrill, J. The Girl Who Loved Caterpillars **E**

Norton, M. The Borrowers (3-6) **Fic**

Osborne, M. P. Kate and the beanstalk (k-3) **398.2**

Perrault, C. Cinderella (k-3) **398.2**

Perrault, C. Cinderella, Puss in Boots, and other favorite tales (k-4) **398.2**

Perrault, C. The complete fairy tales of Charles Perrault (4-6) **398.2**

Perrault, C. Puss in boots (k-3) **398.2**

Philip, N. The Arabian nights (4 and up) **398.2**

Philip, N. Celtic fairy tales (4 and up) **398.2**

Polacco, P. Luba and the wren (k-3) **398.2**

Poole, J. Snow White (3-5) **398.2**

Prokofiev, S. Peter and the wolf **E**

Pyle, H. Bearskin **E**

Pyle, H. King Stork (2-4) **398.2**

Rogasky, B. Rapunzel (1-3) **398.2**

Rogasky, B. The water of life (1-3) **398.2**

Ruskin, J. The king of the Golden River **Fic**

San Souci, R. Brave Margaret (k-3) **398.2**

San Souci, R. Cendrillon (k-3) **398.2**

San Souci, R. The Hobyahs (k-3) **398.2**

San Souci, R. A weave of words (3-5) **398.2**

San Souci, R. The white cat (2-4) **398.2**

Sandburg, C. Rootabaga stories **S C**

Sandburg, C. Rootabaga stories **S C**

Sanderson, R. The crystal mountain (3-5) **398.2**

Sanderson, R. Papa Gatto (3-5) **398.2**

Schroeder, A. Smoky Mountain Rose **E**

Schulman, J. The nutcracker (4 and up) **Fic**

Scieszka, J. The Frog Prince continued **E**

Seidler, T. The steadfast tin soldier (1-4) **Fic**

Sendak, M. Outside over there **E**

Shepard, A. Forty fortunes (2-4) **398.2**

Shulevitz, U. The golden goose (k-3) **398.2**

Silverman, E. Raisel's riddle (k-3) **398.2**

Stanley, D. Rumpelstiltskin's daughter **E**

Steig, J. A handful of beans (k-3) **398.2**

Talbott, H. O'Sullivan stew **E**

Thurber, J. The great Quillow **E**

Thurber, J. Many moons (1-4) **Fic**

Tseng, G. White tiger, blue serpent (2-4) **398.2**

Vuong, L. D. The brocaded slipper and other Vietnamese tales (4-6) **398.2**

Waters, F. Oscar Wilde's The selfish giant (2-5) **Fic**

Watson, R. J. Tom Thumb (k-3) **398.2**

Watts, B. The ugly duckling **E**

Wilde, O. The fairy tales of Oscar Wilde (3-6) **S C**

Wilde, O. The selfish giant (2-5) **Fic**

Wildsmith, B. The Bremen Town Band (k-2) **398.2**

Willard, N. Beauty and the beast (5 and up) **398.2**

Winthrop, E. The little humpbacked horse (4-6) **398.2**

Wisniewski, D. The warrior and the wise man **E**

Wolff, P. R. The toll-bridge troll **E**

Womenfolk and fairy tales (3-6) **398.2**

Wood, A. Heckedy Peg **E**

Wrede, P. C. Dealing with dragons (6 and up) **Fic**

The Yellow fairy book (4-6) **398.2**

Fairy tales—*Continued*

Yeoman, J. The Seven voyages of Sinbad the Sailor (5 and up) **398.2**

Yolen, J. King Long Shanks **E**

Yolen, J. Not one damsel in distress (4 and up) **398.2**

Yolen, J. Sleeping ugly **E**

Yolen, J. Tam Lin (3-6) **398.2**

Young, E. Pinocchio (3-6) **Fic**

Zelinsky, P. O. Rapunzel (3-5) **398.2**

Zelinsky, P. O. Rumpelstiltskin (k-4) **398.2**

Ziefert, H. Little Red Riding Hood (k-2) **398.2**

Bibliography

Lynn, R. N. Fantasy literature for children and young adults **016.8**

History and criticism

The Oxford companion to fairy tales **398.2**

See/See also pages in the following book(s):

Only connect: readings on children's literature p122-29, 278-87 **028.5**

Indexes

Index to fairy tales **398.2**

The **fairy** tales of Oscar Wilde. Wilde, O. **S C**

The **fairy's** mistake. Levine, G. C. See note under Levine, G. C. The princess test **Fic**

The **faithful** friend. San Souci, R. **398.2**

Fake out. (3-6) See entry in Part 2: Web Resources

Falconer, Ian

Olivia **E**

Falconer, Kieran, 1970-

Peru (5 and up) **985**

Falcons

Arnold, C. Hawk highway in the sky (4-6) **598**

Fiction

George, J. C. Frightful's mountain (5 and up) **Fic**

Falcon's egg. Gray, L. **Fic**

Fall *See* Autumn

Fall. Hirschi, R. **508.2**

The **fall** and rise of Bathbone. Babbitt, N.

In Babbitt, N. The Devil's other storybook p53-61 **S C**

The **fall** of the Soviet Union. Harvey, M. **947**

The **fallen** angel. Wynne-Jones, T.

In Wynne-Jones, T. Lord of the Fries and other stories p116-49 **S C**

Falling stars *See* Meteors

Falling up. Silverstein, S. **811**

Falls, C. B. (Charles Buckles), 1874-1960

ABC book **E**

Falls, Charles Buckles *See* Falls, C. B. (Charles Buckles), 1874-1960

Falsehood *See* Truthfulness and falsehood

Familiar quotations. Bartlett, J. **808.88**

Family

See also types of family members

Morris, A. Families (k-1) **306.8**

A **family** apart. Nixon, J. L. **Fic**

Family finance *See* Personal finance

The **family** Haggadah. Schecter, E. **296.4**

Family histories *See* Genealogy

Family life

Fiction

Adoff, A. Black is brown is tan **E**

Ahlberg, J. Peek-a-boo! **E**

Alcott, L. M. Little women (5 and up) **Fic**

Alcott, L. M. An old-fashioned Thanksgiving (3-5) **Fic**

Armstrong, W. H. Sounder (5 and up) **Fic**

Avi. Blue heron (5 and up) **Fic**

Baker, B. One Saturday afternoon **E**

Blume, J. The one in the middle is the green kangaroo **E**

Blume, J. Tales of a fourth grade nothing (3-6) **Fic**

Bradley, K. B. Ruthie's gift (3-5) **Fic**

Browne, A. Piggybook **E**

Bunting, E. Dandelions **E**

Byars, B. C. The not-just-anybody family (5 and up) **Fic**

Cameron, A. Gloria's way (2-4) **Fic**

Cameron, A. The stories Julian tells (2-4) **Fic**

Cooney, B. Island boy **E**

Creech, S. Absolutely normal chaos (5 and up) **Fic**

Creech, S. Chasing Redbird (5 and up) **Fic**

Creech, S. Walk two moons (6 and up) **Fic**

Creech, S. The Wanderer (5 and up) **Fic**

Cresswell, H. Ordinary Jack (5 and up) **Fic**

Curtis, C. P. The Watsons go to Birmingham—1963 (4 and up) **Fic**

Cushman, K. The ballad of Lucy Whipple (5 and up) **Fic**

Cutler, J. Rats! (3-5) **Fic**

Delacre, L. Salsa stories (4-6) **S C**

Delton, J. Angel's mother's wedding (3-5) **Fic**

Dorris, M. The window (4 and up) **Fic**

Ellis, S. Next-door neighbors (4 and up) **Fic**

Estes, E. The Moffats (4-6) **Fic**

Fletcher, R. Fig pudding (4 and up) **Fic**

Flournoy, V. The patchwork quilt **E**

Fox, P. The stone-faced boy (4-6) **Fic**

Franklin, K. L. Lone wolf (4 and up) **Fic**

Gantos, J. Heads or tails (5 and up) **Fic**

Gauch, P. L. Christina Katerina and the time she quit the family **E**

Gibbons, F. Mama and me and the Model-T **E**

Gibbons, F. Mountain wedding **E**

Grove, V. Destiny (5 and up) **Fic**

Hahn, M. D. Anna all year round (3-5) **Fic**

Hahn, M. D. Daphne's book (5 and up) **Fic**

Hamilton, V. The bells of Christmas (4-6) **Fic**

Hamilton, V. M. C. Higgins the great (6 and up) **Fic**

Heide, F. P. Sami and the time of the troubles **E**

Family life—Fiction—*Continued*

Henkes, K. The birthday room (5 and up)　　**Fic**

Herman, C. How Yussel caught the gefilte fish　　**E**

Hesse, K. Just Juice (3-5)　　**Fic**

Hickman, J. Jericho (5 and up)　　**Fic**

Hill, E. S. Evan's corner　　**E**

Holm, J. L. Our only May Amelia (5 and up)　　**Fic**

Horvath, P. The trolls (3-6)　　**Fic**

Horvath, P. When the circus came to town (4-6)　　**Fic**

Howard, E. F. Chita's Christmas tree　　**E**

Hurwitz, J. Rip-roaring Russell (2-4)　　**Fic**

Johnson, A. Down the winding road　　**E**

Karim, R. Kindle me a riddle　　**E**

Karr, K. Man of the family (4 and up)　　**Fic**

Keller, H. Jacob's tree　　**E**

Kinsey-Warnock, N. The Canada geese quilt (3-5)　　**Fic**

Krensky, S. Lionel at large　　**E**

Kuskin, K. I am me　　**E**

L'Engle, M. Meet the Austins (5 and up)　　**Fic**

Levitin, S. Journey to America (4 and up)　　**Fic**

Little, J. From Anna (4-6)　　**Fic**

Love, D. A. A year without rain (4 and up)　　**Fic**

Lowry, L. Anastasia Krupnik (4-6)　　**Fic**

Lowry, L. Switcharound (5 and up)　　**Fic**

Lyon, G. E. One lucky girl　　**E**

MacLachlan, P. All the places to love　　**E**

MacLachlan, P. Journey (4 and up)　　**Fic**

MacLachlan, P. Seven kisses in a row (2-4)　　**Fic**

Mahy, M. The other side of silence (6 and up)　　**Fic**

Mahy, M. The rattlebang picnic　　**E**

Namioka, L. Yang the youngest and his terrible ear (4-6)　　**Fic**

Nesbit, E. The railway children (4-6)　　**Fic**

Osofsky, A. Dreamcatcher　　**E**

Paterson, K. Come sing, Jimmy Jo (5 and up)　　**Fic**

Paterson, K. Marvin's best Christmas present ever　　**E**

Paterson, K. Preacher's boy (5 and up)　　**Fic**

Pérez, A. I. My very own room　　**E**

Rattigan, J. K. Dumpling soup　　**E**

Recorvits, H. Goodbye, Walter Malinski (3-6)　　**Fic**

Rocklin, J. Strudel stories (4 and up)　　**Fic**

Rylant, C. A blue-eyed daisy (5 and up)　　**Fic**

Rylant, C. A fine white dust (5 and up)　　**Fic**

Rylant, C. The relatives came　　**E**

Sachs, M. The bears' house (4-6)　　**Fic**

Sebestyen, O. Words by heart (5 and up)　　**Fic**

Segal, L. G. Tell me a Mitzi　　**E**

Shelby, A. Homeplace　　**E**

Shreve, S. R. The flunking of Joshua T. Bates (3-5)　　**Fic**

Smith, R. K. The war with Grandpa (4-6)　　**Fic**

Turner, A. W. Dust for dinner　　**E**

Uchida, Y. A jar of dreams (5 and up)　　**Fic**

Uchida, Y. Journey home (5 and up)　　**Fic**

Van Leeuwen, J. Going West　　**E**

Van Leeuwen, J. Tales of Oliver Pig　　**E**

Voake, C. Here comes the train　　**E**

Walter, M. P. Justin and the best biscuits in the world (3-6)　　**Fic**

Warner, S. Totally confidential (4 and up)　　**Fic**

Watson, W. Thanksgiving at our house　　**E**

Waugh, S. The Mennyms (5 and up)　　**Fic**

Weston, C. The diary of Melanie Martin; or, How I survived Matt the Brat, Michelangelo, and the Leaning Tower of Pizza (3-6)　　**Fic**

Williams, V. B. A chair for my mother　　**E**

Williams, V. B. "More more more" said the baby　　**E**

Willis, P. The barn burner (5 and up)　　**Fic**

Woodson, J. We had a picnic this Sunday past　　**E**

Yep, L. The amah (5 and up)　　**Fic**

Zamorano, A. Let's eat!　　**E**

Poetry

Adoff, A. In for winter, out for spring (k-3)　　**811**

Fletcher, R. Relatively speaking (4 and up)　　**811**

Singer, M. Family reunion (k-3)　　**811**

Thomas, J. C. Gingerbread days (k-3)　　**811**

A **family** of demons. Schwartz, H.

　　In Schwartz, H. A coat for the moon and other Jewish tales p66-67　　**398.2**

Family pictures. Garza, C. L.　　**E**

Family reunion. Singer, M.　　**811**

The **family** under the bridge. Carlson, N. S.　　**Fic**

Family violence *See* Domestic violence

Famous first facts. Kane, J. N.　　**031.02**

Fancher, Lou

　　(il) Duncan, L. I walk at night　　**E**

　　(il) Fonteyn, Dame M. Coppélia　　**792.8**

Fancy dress *See* Costume

Fang, Linda

　　The Ch'i-lin purse (5 and up)　　**398.2**

　　Contents: The Ch'i-lin purse; Dog steals and Rooster crows; Two Miss Peonys; The Ho Shi jade; The prime minister and the General; The clever magistrate; Mr. Yeh's New Year; The miracle doctor; The royal bridegroom

Fanny's dream. Buehner, C.　　**E**

Fantastic fiction *See* Fantasy fiction

Fantastic! wow! and unreal!. Heller, R.　　**428**

Fantasy fiction

　　See also Fairy tales; Science fiction

Alexander, L. The Arkadians (5 and up)　　**Fic**

Alexander, L. The book of three (5 and up)　　**Fic**

Alexander, L. The foundling and other tales of Prydain (5 and up)　　**S C**

Alexander, L. Gypsy Rizka (5 and up)　　**Fic**

Fantasy fiction—_Continued_

Alexander, L. The high king (5 and up)
Fic

Almond, D. Skellig (5 and up) Fic

Avi. Perloo the bold (5 and up) Fic

Babbitt, N. Tuck everlasting (5 and up)
Fic

Banks, L. R. The Indian in the cupboard (5 and up)
Fic

Barron, T. A. The lost years of Merlin (6 and up)
Fic

Baum, L. F. The Wizard of Oz (3-6) Fic

Billingsley, F. The Folk Keeper (5 and up)
Fic

Billingsley, F. Well wished (4-6) Fic

Bond, N. A string in the harp (6 and up)
Fic

Boston, L. M. The children of Green Knowe (4-6)
Fic

Carroll, L. Alice's adventures in Wonderland (4 and up)
Fic

Carroll, L. Alice's adventures in Wonderland, and Through the looking glass (4 and up)
Fic

Cooper, S. The grey king (5 and up) Fic

Cooper, S. Over sea, under stone (5 and up)
Fic

Cooper, S. Seaward (6 and up) Fic

Corbett, S. The lemonade trick (3-5) Fic

Coville, B. Jennifer Murdley's toad (4-6)
Fic

Coville, B. Jeremy Thatcher, dragon hatcher (4-6)
Fic

Coville, B. The skull of truth (4-6) Fic

Dahl, R. James and the giant peach (4-6)
Fic

Eager, E. Half magic (4-6) Fic

Eager, E. Magic or not? (4-6) Fic

Eager, E. Seven-day magic (4-6) Fic

Etchemendy, N. The power of Un (4 and up)
Fic

Fleischman, P. Time train E

Fleischman, S. The 13th floor (4-6) Fic

Gannett, R. S. My father's dragon (1-4)
Fic

Hodges, M. Gulliver in Lilliput (3-6) Fic

Ibbotson, E. The secret of platform 13 (5 and up)
Fic

Ibbotson, E. Which witch? (4 and up) Fic

Jacques, B. Redwall (6 and up) Fic

James, M. Shoebag (5 and up) Fic

Jansson, T. Moominsummer madness (4-6)
Fic

Jarrell, R. The animal family (4 and up)
Fic

Jarvis, R. The dark portal (5 and up) Fic

Jones, D. W. Castle in the air (6 and up)
Fic

Jones, D. W. Howl's moving castle (6 and up)
Fic

Joyce, W. George shrinks E

Juster, N. The phantom tollbooth (5 and up)
Fic

Kendall, C. The Gammage Cup Fic

Langton, J. The fledgling (5 and up) Fic

Le Guin, U. K. Catwings (2-4) Fic

Le Guin, U. K. A wizard of Earthsea (6 and up)
Fic

L'Engle, M. A wrinkle in time (5 and up)
Fic

Levine, G. C. Ella enchanted (5 and up)
Fic

Lewis, C. S. The lion, the witch, and the wardrobe (4 and up) Fic

Lisle, J. T. Forest (5 and up) Fic

Mayne, W. Hob and the goblins (4 and up)
Fic

McCaffrey, A. Dragonsong (6 and up) Fic

McCaughrean, G. The stones are hatching (5 and up)
Fic

McGraw, E. J. The moorchild (4 and up)
Fic

McKinley, R. The hero and the crown (6 and up)
Fic

Nesbit, E. The enchanted castle (4-6) Fic

Nesbit, E. Five children and it (4-6) Fic

Norton, M. Bed-knob and broomstick (3-6)
Fic

Pearce, P. Tom's midnight garden (4 and up)
Fic

Philbrick, W. R. REM world (4 and up)
Fic

Pierce, T. Magic steps (5 and up) Fic

Pope, E. M. The Perilous Gard (6 and up)
Fic

Pullman, P. I was a rat! (4 and up) Fic

Rowling, J. K. Harry Potter and the sorcerer's stone (4 and up)
Fic

Scieszka, J. Knights of the kitchen table (3-5)
Fic

Sendak, M. In the night kitchen E

Sendak, M. Where the wild things are E

Tolkien, J. R. R. The hobbit (4 and up)
Fic

Travers, P. L. Mary Poppins (4-6) Fic

Winthrop, E. The castle in the attic (4-6)
Fic

Yorinks, A. Hey, Al E

Bibliography

Lynn, R. N. Fantasy literature for children and young adults 016.8

History and criticism

See/See also pages in the following book(s):

Only connect: readings on children's literature p164-91, 288-300 028.5

Fantasy for children. See Lynn, R. N. Fantasy literature for children and young adults
016.8

Fantasy literature for children and young adults. Lynn, R. N. 016.8

Faraway drums. Kroll, V. L. E

Faraway home. Kurtz, J. E

Faraway summer. Hurwitz, J. Fic

Farb, Nathan
(il) Myers, L. B. Galápagos: islands of change
508

Farjeon, Eleanor, 1881-1965
Cats sleep anywhere 821

Farley, Walter, 1915-1989
The Black Stallion (4 and up) Fic
The Black Stallion and Flame. See note under Farley, W. The Black Stallion Fic

Farrell, Kate
(comp) Talking to the sun: an illustrated anthology of poems for young people. See Talking to the sun: an illustrated anthology of poems for young people **808.81**

The **farthest** shore. Le Guin, U. K. See note under Le Guin, U. K. A wizard of Earthsea **Fic**

Fashion
See also Clothing and dress; Costume

Fasick, Adele M., 1930-
Managing children's services in the public library **027.62**

Fast Sam, Cool Clyde, and Stuff. Myers, W. D. **Fic**

Fasts and feasts
Judaism
See Jewish holidays

Fat men from space. Pinkwater, D. M. **Fic**

The **fata**. San Souci, R.
In San Souci, R. A terrifying taste of short & shivery p12-14 **398.2**

Father Bear comes home. Minarik, E. H. See note under Minarik, E. H. Little Bear **E**

Father Christmas. Briggs, R. **E**

Father Christmas and the carpenter. Prøysen, A.
In Christmas fairy tales p58-64 **398.2**

Father-daughter relationship
Fiction
Alcock, V. The monster garden (4 and up) **Fic**
Boyd, C. D. Charlie Pippin (4-6) **Fic**
Bunting, E. A perfect Father's Day **E**
Catalanotto, P. The painter **E**
Grifalconi, A. Tiny's hat **E**
Henkes, K. Protecting Marie (5 and up) **Fic**
Kurtz, J. Faraway home **E**
Nelson, T. Earthshine (5 and up) **Fic**
Reaver, C. Bill (5 and up) **Fic**
Ryder, J. My father's hands **E**
Showers, P. The listening walk **E**
Spinelli, E. Night shift daddy **E**
Yolen, J. Owl moon **E**

Father Nicholas and the thief. Afanas'ev, A. N.
In Afanas'ev, A. N. Russian fairy tales p145-46 **398.2**

Father-son relationship
Fiction
Bunting, E. Some frog! (2-4) **Fic**
Clements, A. The janitor's boy (4-6) **Fic**
Curtis, G. The bat boy & his violin **E**
Fox, P. The eagle kite (6 and up) **Fic**
Garland, S. My father's boat **E**
Hines, A. G. Daddy makes the best spaghetti **E**
Hort, L. How many stars in the sky? **E**
Hurwitz, J. Baseball fever (3-5) **Fic**
Jonell, L. Let's play rough **E**
McBratney, S. Guess how much I love you **E**
Say, A. The lost lake **E**
Smith, R. K. Bobby Baseball (4-6) **Fic**
Steig, W. Pete's a pizza **E**

Fathers
Fiction
Daly, N. My dad **E**
Isadora, R. At the crossroads **E**
Numeroff, L. J. What mommies do best **E**
Schwartz, A. Bea and Mr. Jones **E**
Wood, D. What dads can't do **E**
Poetry
In daddy's arms I am tall **811.008**

Fathers, Single parent *See* Single parent family

Fathers and sons *See* Father-son relationship

Father's Day
Fiction
Bunting, E. A perfect Father's Day **E**

Faulkner, Matt
Black belt **E**

Faulkner, William, 1897-1962
See/See also pages in the following book(s):
Faber, D. Great lives: American literature p193-202 (5 and up) **920**

Faulkner, William J.
How the slaves helped each other
In From sea to shining sea p130-31 **810.8**

Favorite Greek myths. Osborne, M. P. **292**

Favorite medieval tales. Osborne, M. P. **398.2**

Favorite Norse myths. Osborne, M. P. **293**

Favorite nursery tales, Tomie dePaola's **398.2**

Favre, Brett
See/See also pages in the following book(s):
Sullivan, G. Quarterbacks! p5-8 (5 and up) **920**

Fazio, Wende
Saudi Arabia (2-4) **953.8**
West Virginia
In America the beautiful, second series **973**

Fear
Fiction
Blegvad, L. Anna Banana and me **E**
Blume, J. Otherwise known as Sheila the Great (4-6) **Fic**
Bonsall, C. N. Who's afraid of the dark? **E**
Bunting, E. Ghost's hour, spook's hour **E**
Crowe, R. L. Clyde monster **E**
Emberley, E. Go away, big green monster! **E**
Martin, B. The ghost-eye tree **E**
Martin, J. B. Grandmother Bryant's pocket **E**
Mayer, M. There's a nightmare in my closet **E**
Polacco, P. Thunder cake **E**
Stolz, M. Storm in the night **E**

The **fear** place. Naylor, P. R. **Fic**

Fearnley, Jan
Mr. Wolf's pancakes **E**

The **fearsome** inn. Singer, I. B.
In Singer, I. B. Stories for children p290-307 **S C**

Feast of Lights *See* Hanukkah

Feast of Tabernacles *See* Sukkoth

The **feather** of Finist, the Bright Falcon. Afanas'ev, A. N.
  In Afanas'ev, A. N. Russian fairy tales p580-88   **398.2**

Feather Woman and the morning star. Mayo, M.
  In Mayo, M. Magical tales from many lands p18-24   **398.2**

Feathers for lunch. Ehlert, L.   **E**

Feathertop. Hawthorne, N.
  In American fairy tales p29-54   **S C**

Febold Feboldson. Osborne, M. P.
  In Osborne, M. P. American tall tales p63-71   **398.2**

Febold Feboldson, first citizen of Nebraska. Schmidt, S.
  In From sea to shining sea p178-79   **810.8**

Feder, Jane
  Table, chair, bear (k-2)   **413**

Federal resources for educational excellence. See entry in Part 2: Web Resources

Feel the wind. Dorros, A.   **551.51**

Feelings, Muriel, 1938-
  Jambo means hello   **E**
  Moja means one   **E**

Feelings, Tom, 1933-
  (il) Feelings, M. Jambo means hello   **E**
  (il) Feelings, M. Moja means one   **E**
  (il) Soul looks back in wonder. See Soul looks back in wonder   **811.008**
  See/See also pages in the following book(s):
  Origins of story p93-97   **808.06**

Feelings. Aliki   **152.4**

Feet *See* Foot

Feiffer, Jules
  Bark, George   **E**
  I lost my bear   **E**
  The man in the ceiling (4-6)   **Fic**
  (il) Juster, N. The phantom tollbooth   **Fic**

Feinberg, Sandra, 1946-
  Running a parent/child workshop   **027.62**

Feldman, Jane
  I am a gymnast (3-5)   **796.44**
  I am a rider (3-5)   **798.2**

Feldman, Roxanne Hsu
  (jt. auth) Minkel, W. Delivering Web reference services to young people   **025.04**

Felicia and the pot of pinks. Aulnoy, Madame d'
  In The Blue fairy book p148-56   **398.2**

Feliciana Feydra LeRoux. Thomassie, T.   **E**

Feliciana meets d'Loup Garou. Thomassie, T. See note under Thomassie, T. Feliciana Feydral LeRoux   **E**

Felita. Mohr, N. See note under Mohr, N. Going home   **Fic**

Fellenbaum, Charlie
  (il) Jackson, D. The bone detectives   **614**

Felstead, Cathie
  (il) Lindbergh, R. The circle of days   **242**

Feltwell, John
  Butterflies and moths (3-5)   **595.7**

Female role *See* Sex role

Feminism
  Adler, D. A. A picture book of Sojourner Truth (1-3)   **92**
  Corey, S. You forgot your skirt, Amelia Bloomer (k-2)   **92**
  Ferris, J. Walking the road to freedom: a story about Sojourner Truth (3-5)   **92**
  Fritz, J. You want women to vote, Lizzie Stanton? (2-4)   **92**
  McKissack, P. C. Sojourner Truth (1-3)   **92**
  Fiction
  McCully, E. A. The ballot box battle   **E**

Fénelon, François de Salignac de La Mothe-, 1651-1715
  The enchanted ring
  In The Green fairy book p137-44   **398.2**

Fenner, Carol
  The king of dragons (5 and up)   **Fic**
  Yolonda's genius (4-6)   **Fic**

Feral children *See* Wild children

Ferguson, Amos, 1920-
  (il) Greenfield, E. Under the Sunday tree   **811**

Fernandes, Eugenie *See* Eugenie

Ferrets
  Johnson, S. A. Ferrets (3-6)   **636.97**
  See/See also pages in the following book(s):
  Patent, D. H. Back to the wild p28-39 (4-6)   **639.9**

Ferrie, Richard
  The world turned upside down (5 and up)   **973.3**

Ferris, Jeri
  Arctic explorer: the story of Matthew Henson (3-6)   **92**
  Go free or die: a story about Harriet Tubman (3-5)   **92**
  Walking the road to freedom: a story about Sojourner Truth (3-5)   **92**
  What are you figuring now? a story about Benjamin Banneker (3-5)   **92**
  What I had was singing: the story of Marian Anderson (4 and up)   **92**

Ferryboat. Maestro, B.   **E**

Festivals
  Ancona, G. Fiesta fireworks (k-3)   **394.26**
  The Folklore of world holidays   **394.26**
  Jones, L. Kids around the world celebrate! (4-6)   **394.26**
  Kindersley, A. Celebrations (3-5)   **394.26**
  MacDonald, M. R. Celebrate the world   **372.6**
  Moehn, H. World holidays (3-6)   **394.26**
  Fiction
  Dorros, A. Tonight is Carnaval   **E**
  History
  Aliki. A medieval feast (2-5)   **394.1**
  Poetry
  Livingston, M. C. Festivals   **811**
  United States
  The American book of days   **394.26**
  Ancona, G. Fiesta U.S.A. (k-3)   **394.26**

Festivals [series]
  Marchant, K. Id-ul-Fitr   **297.3**

Fetus
Pringle, L. P. Everybody has a bellybutton (k-3)
612.6

Fiammenghi, Gioia
(il) Smith, R. K. Chocolate fever **Fic**

Fibers
Keeler, P. A. Unraveling fibers (3-5) **677**

Fiction
See also Adventure fiction; Fairy tales; Fantasy fiction; Historical fiction; Horror fiction; Mystery fiction; School stories; Science fiction; Sea stories; Short stories

Fiction, folklore, fantasy & poetry for children, 1876-1985 **011.6**

The **fiddler**. San Souci, R.
In San Souci, R. A terrifying taste of short & shivery p15-19 **398.2**

The **fiddler** in hell. Afanas'ev, A. N.
In Afanas'ev, A. N. Russian fairy tales p180-82 **398.2**

The **fiddler** in the cave. Philip, N.
In Philip, N. Celtic fairy tales p119-20
398.2

The **Fiddler** Man. Medearis, A. S.
In Medearis, A. S. Haunts p1-8 **S C**

Fiddling with fire. Olson, A. N.
In Olson, A. N. Ask the bones: scary stories from around the world p46-52 **398.2**

Fiedler, Joseph Daniel
(il) Shepard, A. The crystal heart **398.2**

Field, Elinor Whitney, 1889-1980
(ed) Caldecott Medal books, 1938-1957. See Caldecott Medal books, 1938-1957 **028.5**
(ed) Newbery Medal books, 1922-1955. See Newbery Medal books, 1922-1955 **028.5**

Field, Rachel, 1894-1942
Hitty: her first hundred years (4 and up)
Fic
Prayer for a child (k-3) **242**
See/See also pages in the following book(s):
Newbery Medal books, 1922-1955 p76-88
028.5

Field athletics *See* Track athletics

A **field** guide to the birds. Peterson, R. T.
598

A **field** guide to western birds. Peterson, R. T.
598

Fiesta!. Guy, G. F. **E**

Fiesta fireworks. Ancona, G. **394.26**

Fiesta U.S.A. Ancona, G. **394.26**

Fifteenth century *See* World history—15th century

Fig pudding. Fletcher, R. **Fic**

Fighting fires. Kuklin, S. **628.9**

The **fighting** ground. Avi **Fic**

The **figure** in the shadows. Bellairs, J. See note under Bellairs, J. The house with a clock in its walls **Fic**

The **figure** skating book. Wilkes, D. **796.91**

Figuring out Frances. Willner-Pardo, G. **Fic**

Fiji
NgCheong-Lum, R. Fiji (5 and up) **996**

Files and filing
ALA filing rules **025.3**

Filial piety. Shedlock, M. L.
In Shedlock, M. L. The art of the story-teller p229-32 **372.6**

Fill, bowl! Fill!
In The Jack tales p89-95 **398.2**

Fillmore, Parker
Clever Manka
In Womenfolk and fairy tales p146-55
398.2

Films *See* Motion pictures

Financial planning, Personal *See* Personal finance

Find the constellations. Rey, H. A. **523.8**

Finding Buck McHenry. Slote, A. **Fic**

Finding Providence: the story of Roger Williams. Avi **92**

Finding things *See* Lost and found possessions

Fine, Anne
Bad dreams (4-6) **Fic**
Flour babies (6 and up) **Fic**
Step by wicked step (4-6) **Fic**
The Tulip touch (6 and up) **Fic**

Fine, Howard
(il) Palatini, M. Piggie pie! **E**

A **fine** white dust. Rylant, C. **Fic**

Finger, Charles Joseph, 1869-1941
See/See also pages in the following book(s):
Newbery Medal books, 1922-1955 p37-38
028.5

The **finger**. Schwartz, H.
In Schwartz, H. A journey to paradise and other Jewish tales p32-35 **398.2**

The **finger** Lock. MacDonald, M. R.
In MacDonald, M. R. Celebrate the world p128-34 **372.6**

Finger play
Briggs, D. 101 fingerplays, stories, and songs to use with finger puppets **791.5**
Brown, M. T. Finger rhymes **796.1**
Brown, M. T. Hand rhymes **796.1**
Brown, M. T. Play rhymes **796.1**
Chorao, K. Knock at the door and other baby action rhymes **398.8**
Diez deditos. Ten little fingers & other play rhymes and action songs from Latin America (k-3) **782.42**
The Eentsy, weentsy spider: fingerplays and action rhymes **796.1**
Hoberman, M. A. The eensy-weensy spider (k-3) **782.42**
Pat-a-cake and other play rhymes **398.8**
Wilner, I. The baby's game book **398.8**

Fingers on the back of the neck. Mahy, M.
In Don't read this! and other tales of the unnatural p7-22 **S C**

Fingers on the back of the neck and other ghost stories. See Don't read this! and other tales of the unnatural **S C**

Fink, Mike, 1770-1823?
Fiction
Kellogg, S. Mike Fink (k-3) **398.2**

Finland
  Lee, T. C. Finland (5 and up)   948.97
  McNair, S. Finland (4 and up)   948.97
Finley, Carol
  The art of African masks (5 and up)   391
Finn Family Moomintroll. Jansson, T. See note
  under Jansson, T. Moominsummer madness
                                                            Fic
Finn MacCool See Finn MacCumhaill, 3rd cent.
Finn MacCool and the Scottish giant. Philip, N.
  In Philip, N. Celtic fairy tales p73-77
                                                            398.2
Finn Maccoul. Osborne, M. P.
  In Osborne, M. P. Favorite medieval tales
  p1-7   398.2
Finn MacCoul and his fearless wife. Byrd, R.
                                                            398.2
Finn MacCumhaill, 3rd cent.
                    Fiction
  Byrd, R. Finn MacCoul and his fearless wife
  (k-3)   398.2
Finnish Americans
                    Fiction
  Holm, J. L. Our only May Amelia (5 and up)
                                                            Fic
Fiona's private pages. Cruise, R.   Fic
Fiore, Carole D.
  Running summer library reading programs
                                                            027.62
Fiore, Peter M.
  (il) Hand in hand. See Hand in hand
                                                            811.008
  (il) Kroll, S. The Boston Tea Party   973.3
Fir, Douglas See Douglas fir
The **fir** tree. Andersen, H. C.
  In Andersen, H. C. The swan's stories p123-
  41   S C
  In Christmas fairy tales p92-102   398.2
Fire!. Masoff, J.   628.9
Fire, bed, & bone. Branford, H.   Fic
Fire engines
  Marston, H. I. Fire trucks (k-3)   628.9
                    Fiction
  Sis, P. Fire truck   E
Fire fighters
  Beil, K. M. Fire in their eyes (4 and up)
                                                            628.9
  Demarest, C. L. Firefighters A to Z (k-1)
                                                            628.9
  Kuklin, S. Fighting fires (k-3)   628.9
  Marston, H. I. Fire trucks (k-3)   628.9
  Masoff, J. Fire! (3-6)   628.9
Fire fighting
  Gibbons, G. Fire! Fire! (k-3)   628.9
Fire! Fire!. Gibbons, G.   628.9
Fire: friend or foe. Patent, D. H.   577.2
Fire in their eyes. Beil, K. M.   628.9
Fire on the mountain. Kurtz, J.   398.2
Fire truck. Sis, P.   E
Fire trucks. Marston, H. I.   628.9
Firearms
                    Fiction
  Fox, P. One-eyed cat (5 and up)   Fic

Firebird (Ballet)
  See/See also pages in the following book(s):
  McCaughrean, G. The Random House book of
  stories from the ballet p85-94 (4 and up)
                                                            792.8
The **Firebird** and Princess Vasilisa. Afanas'ev, A.
  N.
  In Afanas'ev, A. N. Russian fairy tales p494-
  97   398.2
Firefighters A to Z. Demarest, C. L.   628.9
Fireflies
  Hawes, J. Fireflies in the night (k-1)   595.7
  Waber, B. A firefly named Torchy   E
                    Fiction
  Carle, E. The very lonely firefly   E
Fireflies in the night. Hawes, J.   595.7
A **firefly** named Torchy. Waber, B.   E
Fires
                    Fiction
  Polacco, P. Tikvah means hope   E
                    Chicago (Ill.)
  Murphy, J. The great fire (5 and up)   977.3
The **fires** of Merlin. Barron, T. A. See note under
  Barron, T. A. The lost years of Merlin
                                                            Fic
Firetalking. Polacco, P.   92
Fireweed. Paton Walsh, J.   Fic
The **firework-maker's** daughter. Pullman, P.
                                                            Fic
Fireworks
  Ancona, G. Fiesta fireworks (k-3)   394.26
                    Fiction
  Pullman, P. The firework-maker's daughter (4
  and up)   Fic
Fireworks, picnics, and flags. Giblin, J.
                                                            394.26
First aid
  Silverstein, A. Cuts, scrapes, scabs, and scars
  (3-5)   617.1
First Americans book [series]
  Sneve, V. D. H. The Apaches   970.004
  Sneve, V. D. H. The Cherokees   970.004
  Sneve, V. D. H. The Cheyennes   970.004
  Sneve, V. D. H. The Hopis   970.004
  Sneve, V. D. H. The Iroquois   970.004
  Sneve, V. D. H. The Navajos   970.004
  Sneve, V. D. H. The Nez Percé   970.004
  Sneve, V. D. H. The Seminoles   970.004
  Sneve, V. D. H. The Sioux   970.004
First book [series]
  Aronson, B. Meteors   523.5
  Bonar, S. Comets   523.6
  Bredeson, C. The moon   523.3
  Fitzgerald, K. The story of oxygen   546
  Powell, S. I. The Pueblos   970.004
  Stangl, J. Crystals and crystal gardens you can
  grow   548
  Walsh Shepherd, D. The Klondike gold rush
                                                            971.9
The **first** Christmas. Bible. N.T. Selections
                                                            232.9
First emperor's magic whip. Carpenter, F.
  In Carpenter, F. Tales of a Chinese grand-
  mother p134-41   398.2

The **first** four years. Wilder, L. I. See note under Wilder, L. I. Little house in the big woods **Fic**

First friends. Blegvad, L. **E**

First generation children *See* Children of immigrants

First He made the sun. Ziefert, H. **E**

First human body encyclopedia, The Kingfisher. Walker, R. **612**

First in the field: baseball hero Jackie Robinson. Dingle, D. T. **92**

First man and first woman's dog. Hausman, G. *In* Hausman, G. Dogs of myth p19-24 **398.2**

First on the moon. Hehner, B. **629.45**

The **first** shlemiel. Singer, I. B. *In* Singer, I. B. Zlateh the goat, and other stories p55-65 **398.2**

First snow. McCaughrean, G. *In* McCaughrean, G. The golden hoard: myths and legends of the world p120-25 **398.2**

The **first** snowfall. Rockwell, A. F. **E**

First stepping stone book [series] Park, B. Junie B. Jones and her big fat mouth **Fic** Sachar, L. Marvin Redpost, kidnapped at birth? **Fic**

The **first** strawberries. Bruchac, J. **398.2**

First tomato. See Wells, R. Moss pillows **E**

The **first** woman to vote in the state of California. Polese, C. *In* From sea to shining sea p182-85 **810.8**

Firth, Barbara (il) Waddell, M. Can't you sleep, Little Bear? **E**

Fischer, Hans, 1909-1958 Puss in boots (k-3) **398.2** (il) Grimm, J. The Bremen town musicians **398.2**

Fish, Helen Dean (ed) Bible. Selections. Animals of the Bible **220.8**

The **fish** and the ring. Jacobs, J. *In* Jacobs, J. English fairy tales p189-92 **398.2**

Fish and Wildlife Service (U.S.) *See* U.S. Fish and Wildlife Service

The **fish** at dragon's gate. Mayo, M. *In* Mayo, M. Mythical birds & beasts from many lands p46-54 **398.2**

The **fish** cart. Manning-Sanders, R. *In* The Oxford treasury of children's stories p19-22 **S C**

Fish culture *See also* Aquariums

The **fish** husband. Osborne, M. P. *In* Osborne, M. P. Mermaid tales from around the world p33-36 **398.2**

Fish is fish. Lionni, L. **E**

A **fish** story. San Souci, R. *In* San Souci, R. A terrifying taste of short & shivery p25-29 **398.2**

Fish watching with Eugenie Clark. Ross, M. E. **92**

Fish wish. Barner, B. **E**

Fisher, Aileen Lucia, 1906- The story of Easter (3-5) **394.26** A tree to trim *In* The Big book of Christmas plays p59-79 **808.82**

Fisher, Cynthia (il) Adler, D. A. Easy math puzzles **793.73** (il) King-Smith, D. The school mouse **Fic**

Fisher, Dorothy Canfield, 1879-1958 Thanksgiving Day *In* Bauer, C. F. Celebrations p243-48 **808.8** *In* Thanksgiving: stories and poems p11-22 **810.8** Understood Betsy (4-6) **Fic**

Fisher, Jeff, 1952- (il) Adler, D. A. A picture book of Amelia Earhart **92**

Fisher, Leonard Everett, 1924- The ABC exhibit **E** Alexander Graham Bell (4 and up) **92** Anasazi (4 and up) **970.004** The architects (4 and up) **720** The blacksmiths (4 and up) **682** The cabinetmakers (4 and up) **684.1** Cyclops (3-5) **292** David and Goliath (k-3) **222** The doctors (4 and up) **610.9** Galileo (4 and up) **92** Gandhi (4 and up) **92** The glassmakers (4 and up) **666** The gods and goddesses of ancient Egypt (3-6) **299** Gods and goddesses of the ancient Maya (3-6) **299** Gutenberg (4 and up) **92** The homemakers (4 and up) **640** The limners (4 and up) **759.13** Monticello (4 and up) **975.5** Moses (k-3) **222** Niagara Falls (4 and up) **971.3** The Oregon Trail (4 and up) **979.5** The peddlers (4 and up) **381** The potters (4 and up) **666** The printers (4 and up) **686.2** The schoolmasters (4 and up) **371.1** The shipbuilders (4 and up) **623.8** The shoemakers (4 and up) **685** The silversmiths (4 and up) **739.2** The tanners (4 and up) **675** Theseus and the Minotaur (3-5) **292** To bigotry, no sanction (4 and up) **296** The weavers (4 and up) **677** The White House (4 and up) **975.3** The wigmakers (4 and up) **391** William Tell (k-3) **398.2** (il) If you ever meet a whale. See If you ever meet a whale **811.008** (il) Kimmel, E. A. The three princes **398.2**

Fisher, Leonard Everett, 1924-—*Continued*
(il) Kimmel, E. A. The two mountains
      398.2
(il) Livingston, M. C. Celebrations   **811**
(il) Livingston, M. C. A circle of seasons
      811
(il) Livingston, M. C. Festivals   **811**
(il) Livingston, M. C. Sky songs   **811**
The **Fisherman** and his soul. Wilde, O.
   In Wilde, O. The fairy tales of Oscar Wilde
   p94-123   **S C**
The **fisherman** and the bottle. McCaughrean, G.
   In The Oxford treasury of children's stories
   p114-20   **S C**
The **fisherman** and the jinni. Philip, N.
   In Philip, N. The Arabian nights p13-21
      398.2
The **fisherman** and the silver fish. Schwartz, H.
   In Schwartz, H. A coat for the moon and oth-
   er Jewish tales p54-59   **398.2**
Fishes
   See also Aquariums; Eels; Goldfish; Salm-
   on
Butts, E. Eugenie Clark (5 and up)   **92**
Evans, M. Fish (2-5)   **639.34**
Landau, E. Electric fish (2-4)   **597**
Ling, M. Amazing fish (2-4)   **597**
Parker, S. Fish (4 and up)   **597**
Pfeffer, W. What's it like to be a fish? (k-1)
      597
Ross, M. E. Fish watching with Eugenie Clark
   (4 and up)   **92**
Smith, C. L. National Audubon Society first
   field guide: fishes (4 and up)   **597**
Wildsmith, B. Brian Wildsmith's fishes   **E**
      Fiction
Cohen, B. The carp in the bathtub (2-4)
      Fic
Kalan, R. Blue sea   **E**
Lionni, L. Fish is fish   **E**
Lionni, L. Swimmy   **E**
Wise, W. Ten sly piranhas   **E**
Fishing
   See also Fly casting
Bailey, J. Fishing (4 and up)   **799.1**
McMillan, B. Salmon summer (2-4)   **639.2**
See/See also pages in the following book(s):
Bauer, C. F. Celebrations p81-102   **808.8**
      Fiction
Bodnar, J. Z. Tale of a tail   **E**
Garland, S. My father's boat   **E**
Hill, E. S. Bird Boy (2-4)   **Fic**
McKissack, P. C. A million fish—more or less
      E
Seuss, Dr. McElligot's pool   **E**
Stolz, M. Go fish (2-4)   **Fic**
Fishing for a dream   **782.42**
Fishman, Cathy, 1951-
On Hanukkah (k-3)   **296.4**
On Passover (k-3)   **296.4**
On Purim (k-3)   **296.4**
On Rosh Hashanah and Yom Kippur (k-3)
      296.4
Fisk Jubilee Singers (Musical group) *See* Jubilee
   Singers (Musical group)

Fitch, Florence Mary, 1875-1959
A book about God (k-3)   **231**
Fitcher's bird. Yolen, J.
   In Yolen, J. Not one damsel in distress p17-
   26   **398.2**
Fitzgerald, F. Scott (Francis Scott), 1896-1940
See/See also pages in the following book(s):
Faber, D. Great lives: American literature p203-
   11 (5 and up)   **920**
Fitzgerald, Francis Scott *See* Fitzgerald, F. Scott
   (Francis Scott), 1896-1940
Fitzgerald, Gerald
(il) Thayer, E. L. Casey at the bat   **811**
Fitzgerald, John D., 1907-1988
The Great Brain (4 and up)   **Fic**
The Great Brain at the academy. See note under
   Fitzgerald, J. D. The Great Brain   **Fic**
The Great Brain does it again. See note under
   Fitzgerald, J. D. The Great Brain   **Fic**
The Great Brain is back. See note under Fitzger-
   ald, J. D. The Great Brain   **Fic**
The Great Brain reforms. See note under Fitz-
   gerald, J. D. The Great Brain   **Fic**
Me and my little brain. See note under Fitzger-
   ald, J. D. The Great Brain   **Fic**
More adventures of the Great Brain. See note
   under Fitzgerald, J. D. The Great Brain
      Fic
The return of the Great Brain. See note under
   Fitzgerald, J. D. The Great Brain   **Fic**
Fitzgerald, Karen
The story of oxygen (4 and up)   **546**
Fitzhugh, Louise, 1928-1974
Harriet the spy (4 and up)   **Fic**
The long secret. See note under Fitzhugh, L.
   Harriet the spy   **Fic**
Five alien elves. Maguire, G. See note under
   Maguire, G. Seven spiders spinning   **Fic**
Five children and it. Nesbit, E.   **Fic**
The **five** hundred hats of Batholomew Cubbins.
   See Seuss, Dr. The 500 hats of Bartholomew
   Cubbins   **E**
Five little ducks. Raffi   **782.42**
Five little monkeys jumping on the bed.
   Christelow, E.   **E**
Five little monkeys sitting in a tree. Christelow, E.
   See note under Christelow, E. Five little mon-
   keys jumping on the bed   **E**
Five little monkeys wash the car. Christelow, E.
   See note under Christelow, E. Five little mon-
   keys jumping on the bed   **E**
Five little monkeys with nothing to do.
   Christelow, E. See note under Christelow, E.
   Five little monkeys jumping on the bed
      E
Five little piggies. Martin, D.   **E**
Five Owls   **028.505**
Five peas from the same pod. Andersen, H. C.
   In Andersen, H. C. The little mermaid and
   other fairy tales p107-11   **S C**
Five threads. MacDonald, M. R.
   In MacDonald, M. R. Celebrate the world
   p43-48   **372.6**

Five trucks. Floca, B.   **E**

Fix. Ellis, S.
  In Ellis, S. Back of beyond   **S C**

Flack, Marjorie, 1897-1958
  Angus and the cat
  In The Read-aloud treasury p156-78
      808.8
  Ask Mr. Bear   **E**
  (il) Heyward, D. The country bunny and the little gold shoes   **E**

Flag. Crampton, W. G.   **929.9**

Flags
  Crampton, W. G. Flag (4 and up)   **929.9**
  United States
  Brandt, S. R. State flags (5 and up)   **929.9**
  Haban, R. D. How proudly they wave (4 and up)   **929.9**
  Wallner, A. Betsy Ross (k-2)   **92**

Flamingos
  McMillan, B. Wild flamingos (3-6)   **598**
  Fiction
  Walsh, E. S. For Pete's sake   **E**

Flanagan, Alice K.
  The Pueblos (2-4)   **970.004**
  The Zunis (4 and up)   **978**

Flanagan, Kate
  (il) Cook, D. F. Kids' pumpkin projects
      745.5

Flanders, Lillian Hsu- *See* Hsu-Flanders, Lillian

The **flannel** board storytelling book. Sierra, J.
      027.62

Flannelboard stories for infants and toddlers. Carlson, A. D.   **372.6**

Flash, crash, rumble, and roll. Branley, F. M.
      551.55

Flashy fantastic rain forest frogs. Patent, D. H.
      597.8

The **flask.** Jaffe, N.
  In Jaffe, N. The cow of no color: riddle stories and justice tales from around the world p88-91   **398.2**

Flat Stanley. Brown, J.   **E**

Flavin, Teresa
  (il) Bruchac, J. Pushing up the sky: seven native American plays for children   **812**
  (il) Walter, M. P. Suitcase   **Fic**

The **fledgling.** Langton, J.   **Fic**

Fleischman, Albert Sidney *See* Fleischman, Sid, 1920-

Fleischman, Paul
  Big talk (4 and up)   **811**
  The borning room (6 and up)   **Fic**
  Bull Run (6 and up)   **Fic**
  Graven images (6 and up)   **S C**
  Contents: The binnacle boy; Saint Crispin's follower; The man of influence
  The Half-a-Moon Inn (4-6)   **Fic**
  I am phoenix: poems for two voices (4 and up)
      811
  Joyful noise: poems for two voices (4 and up)
      811
  Lost!   **Fic**
  Saturnalia (6 and up)   **Fic**
  Seedfolks (4 and up)   **Fic**

Time train   **E**
Weslandia   **E**
See/See also pages in the following book(s):
The Newbery & Caldecott medal books, 1986-2000 p90-103   **028.5**

Fleischman, Sid, 1920-
  The 13th floor (4-6)   **Fic**
  The abracadabra kid (5 and up)   **92**
  Bandit's moon (4-6)   **Fic**
  By the Great Horn Spoon! (4-6)   **Fic**
  Chancy and the grand rascal (4-6)   **Fic**
  The ghost on Saturday night (3-5)   **Fic**
  Here comes McBroom! (3-5)   **Fic**
  Jim Ugly (4 and up)   **Fic**
  McBroom and the big wind
  In The Oxford treasury of children's stories p105-13   **S C**
  McBroom tells a lie. See note under Fleischman, S. Here comes McBroom!   **Fic**
  McBroom tells the truth. See note under Fleischman, S. Here comes McBroom!
      Fic
  McBroom's wonderful one-acre farm: three tall tales. See note under Fleischman, S. Here comes McBroom!   **Fic**
  The midnight horse (3-6)   **Fic**
  Mr. Mysterious & Company (5 and up)
      Fic
  The scarebird   **E**
  The whipping boy (5 and up)   **Fic**
  See/See also pages in the following book(s):
  The Newbery & Caldecott medal books, 1986-2000 p53-62   **028.5**

Fleischner, Jennifer
  I was born a slave: the story of Harriet Jacobs (5 and up)   **92**

Fleming, Candace
  A big cheese for the White House   **E**
  Gabriella's song   **E**
  The hatmaker's sign   **E**
  When Agnes caws   **E**

Fleming, Denise, 1950-
  Barnyard banter   **E**
  Count!   **E**
  The everything book   **E**
  In the small, small pond   **E**
  In the tall, tall grass   **E**
  Lunch   **E**
  Mama cat has three kittens   **E**
  Time to sleep   **E**
  Where once there was a wood (k-2)   **639.9**

Fleming, Ian, 1908-1964
  Chitty-Chitty-Bang-Bang (4-6)   **Fic**

Fletcher, Ralph, 1953-
  Fig pudding (4 and up)   **Fic**
  Flying solo (5 and up)   **Fic**
  Ordinary things (5 and up)   **811**
  Relatively speaking (4 and up)   **811**

Fletcher, Susan, 1951-
  Shadow spinner (6 and up)   **Fic**

Flicker flash. Graham, J. B.   **811**

Flies
  Fiction
  Aylesworth, J. Old black fly   **E**

Flies in the water, fish in the air. Arnosky, J.
799.1

Flight
Bishop, N. The secrets of animal flight (3-6)
591.47
Simon, S. Ride the wind (4-6) **591.56**
Experiments
Ardley, N. The science book of air (3-5)
507.8
Fiction
Pinkney, B. The adventures of Sparrowboy
E
Walter, M. P. Brother to the wind **E**
The **flight** of the beasts. Lee, J. M.
In Lee, J. M. I once was a monkey
294.3
The **flight** of the midwife. Schwartz, H.
In Schwartz, H. A journey to paradise and
other Jewish tales p18-23 **398.2**
Flight: the journey of Charles Lindbergh. Burleigh, R.
92
Flights of fancy and other poems. Livingston, M. C.
811
Flipper, Henry O., 1856-1940
About
Pfeifer, K. Henry O. Flipper (5 and up) **92**
Floating in space. Branley, F. M. **629.47**
Floca, Brian
Dinosaurs at the ends of the earth (3-5)
567.9
Five trucks **E**
(il) Avi. Poppy **Fic**
(il) King-Smith, D. Jenius: the amazing guinea pig **Fic**
(il) Sports! sports! sports! See Sports! sports! sports! **811.008**
Flood. Calhoun, M. **E**
Floods
Hiscock, B. The big rivers (2-4) **551.48**
Lauber, P. Flood (4 and up) **551.48**
Fiction
Calhoun, M. Flood **E**
Lyon, G. E. Come a tide **E**
Florian, Douglas, 1950-
Beast feast **811**
Bing bang boing **811**
In the swim **811**
Insectlopedia **811**
Laugh-eteria **811**
Mammalabilia **811**
On the wing **811**
Turtle day **E**
Winter eyes **811**
Florida
Chang, P. Florida
In Celebrate the states **973**
Heinrichs, A. Florida
In America the beautiful, second series
973
Fiction
DiCamillo, K. Because of Winn-Dixie (4-6)
Fic
Rawlings, M. K. The yearling (6 and up)
Fic
The **Florida** panther. Silverstein, A. **599.75**

Floss. Lewis, K. See note under Lewis, K. Just like Floss **E**
Flossie & the fox. McKissack, P. C. **E**
Flour babies. Fine, A. **Fic**
Flournoy, Valerie, 1952-
The patchwork quilt **E**
Flower, Renée
(il) Yummy! See Yummy! **811.008**
Flower garden. Bunting, E. **E**
The **Flower** queen's daughter
In The Yellow fairy book p192-97 **398.2**
Flowers, Helen F., 1931-
Public relations for school library media programs **021.7**
Flowers
See also Sunflowers; Wild flowers
Fiction
Bunting, E. Flower garden **E**
De Paola, T. The legend of the poinsettia (k-3)
398.2
Ehlert, L. Planting a rainbow **E**
Lobel, A. Alison's zinnia **E**
Lobel, A. The rose in my garden **E**
The **flunking** of Joshua T. Bates. Shreve, S. R.
Fic
Flutes
Fiction
Hobbs, W. Kokopelli's flute (5 and up)
Fic
Flute's journey. Cherry, L. **598**
Fly away home. Bunting, E. **E**
Fly casting
Arnosky, J. Flies in the water, fish in the air (5 and up)
799.1
Fly, eagle, fly!. Gregorowski, C. **398.2**
Flying *See* Flight
The **Flying** Dutchman. McCaughrean, G.
In McCaughrean, G. The crystal pool: myths and legends of the world p123-27
398.2
The **Flying** Head. Bruchac, J.
In Bruchac, J. When the Chenoo howls
398.2
Flying machine. Nahum, A. **629.133**
Flying saucers *See* Unidentified flying objects
The **Flying** ship
In The Yellow fairy book p198-205
398.2
Flying solo. Fletcher, R. **Fic**
The **flying** trunk. Andersen, H. C.
In Andersen, H. C. The little mermaid and other fairy tales p74-80 **S C**
In Andersen, H. C. The swan's stories p13-25
S C
Flying with the eagle, racing the great bear. Bruchac, J.
398.2
Foa, Maryclare
(il) Philip, N. Odin's family **293**
(il) Songs are thoughts. See Songs are thoughts
897
Fodemski, Linda M.
(jt. auth) Benson, A. C. Connecting kids and the Internet **004.6**

Fog
Tresselt, A. R. Hide and seek fog   **E**

Folcarelli, Ralph J.
(jt. auth) Gillespie, J. T. Guides to collection development for children and young adults   **011.6**

Foley, Erin, 1967-
Costa Rica (5 and up)   **972.86**
Ecuador (5 and up)   **986.6**
El Salvador (5 and up)   **972.84**

Foley, Mike
Fundamental hockey (5 and up)   **796.962**

Foliage See Leaves

Folk art
See also Decorative arts

Folk dancing
See also Native American dance

The **Folk** Keeper. Billingsley, F.   **Fic**

Folk lore See Folklore

Folk music

United States

See also Country music

Folk songs
Arroz con leche (k-3)   **782.42**
De colores and other Latin-American folk songs for children (k-3)   **782.42**
Diane Goode's book of scary stories & songs (2-5)   **398.2**
Langstaff, J. M. Frog went a-courtin' (k-3)   **782.42**
Langstaff, J. M. Oh, a-hunting we will go (k-2)   **782.42**
Langstaff, J. M. Over in the meadow (k-2)   **782.42**
Leodhas, S. N. Always room for one more (k-3)   **782.42**
Priceman, M. Froggie went a-courting (k-3)   **782.42**
Taback, S. There was an old lady who swallowed a fly   **782.42**

United States

See also Spirituals (Songs)
The Farmer in the dell (k-1)   **782.42**
The Fox went out on a chilly night   **782.42**
From sea to shining sea   **810.8**
Gonna sing my head off!   **782.42**
Hush, little baby (k-2)   **782.42**
Old MacDonald had a farm   **782.42**
Seeger, R. C. Animal folk songs for children   **782.42**
Songs of the Wild West   **782.42**
Zemach, H. Mommy, buy me a china doll   **E**
Ziefert, H. When I first came to this land (k-2)   **782.42**

Folk songs, English See English folk songs

Folklore

See also Dragons; Legends; Tongue twisters; topics as themes in folklore and names of ethnic or national groups with the subdivision *Folklore*
Aylesworth, J. Aunt Pitty Patty's piggy (k-3)   **398.2**

Aylesworth, J. The Gingerbread man (k-3)   **398.2**
Barton, B. The little red hen (k-2)   **398.2**
Barton, B. The three bears (k-1)   **398.2**
The Blue fairy book (4-6)   **398.2**
Bowden, J. C. Why the tides ebb and flow (k-2)   **398.2**
Brett, J. Gingerbread baby (k-3)   **398.2**
Bruchac, J. Tell me a tale (5 and up)   **372.6**
Diane Goode's book of scary stories & songs (2-5)   **398.2**
Egielski, R. The gingerbread boy (k-3)   **398.2**
Emberley, R. Three cool kids (k-3)   **398.2**
Ernst, L. C. Little Red Riding Hood: a newfangled prairie tale (k-3)   **398.2**
The Folklore of world holidays   **394.26**
Galdone, P. The gingerbread boy (k-2)   **398.2**
Galdone, P. Henny Penny (k-2)   **398.2**
Galdone, P. The little red hen (k-2)   **398.2**
Galdone, P. The three bears (k-2)   **398.2**
Gibbons, G. Behold . . . the dragons! (k-3)   **398**
The Green fairy book (4-6)   **398.2**
Greene, E. The little golden lamb (k-3)   **398.2**
Hamilton, V. A ring of tricksters   **398.2**
Jaffe, N. The cow of no color: riddle stories and justice tales from around the world (4 and up)   **398.2**
Kellogg, S. Chicken Little (k-3)   **398.2**
Kellogg, S. The three little pigs (k-3)   **398.2**
Kimmel, E. A. The gingerbread man (k-2)   **398.2**
Lowell, S. The bootmaker and the elves (k-3)   **398.2**
MacDonald, M. R. Celebrate the world   **372.6**
MacDonald, M. R. Look back and see   **372.6**
MacDonald, M. R. The storyteller's start-up book   **372.6**
MacDonald, M. R. Twenty tellable tales   **372.6**
MacDonald, M. R. When the lights go out   **372.6**
Marshall, J. Goldilocks and the three bears (k-2)   **398.2**
Mayo, M. Magical tales from many lands (3-6)   **398.2**
Mayo, M. Mythical birds & beasts from many lands (3-6)   **398.2**
McCaughrean, G. The bronze cauldron: myths and legends of the world (4-6)   **398.2**
McCaughrean, G. The crystal pool: myths and legends of the world (4-6)   **398.2**
McCaughrean, G. The golden hoard: myths and legends of the world (4-6)   **398.2**
McCaughrean, G. The silver treasure: myths and legends of the world (4-6)   **398.2**
McGovern, A. Too much noise (k-3)   **398.2**
Olson, A. N. Ask the bones: scary stories from around the world (4 and up)   **398.2**

Folklore—*Continued*

East Africa
Aardema, V. Who's in Rabbit's house? (k-3)
398.2

Egypt
Climo, S. The Egyptian Cinderella (k-3)
398.2

England
See Folklore—Great Britain

Ethiopia
Kurtz, J. Fire on the mountain (1-4) **398.2**

Europe
Bulfinch, T. Bulfinch's mythology (6 and up)
291.1
Osborne, M. P. Favorite medieval tales (4 and up) **398.2**

France
Brett, J. Beauty and the beast (1-3) **398.2**
Brown, M. Stone soup (k-3) **398.2**
Fischer, H. Puss in boots (k-3) **398.2**
Galdone, P. Puss in boots (k-2) **398.2**
Kimmel, E. A. Three sacks of truth (2-4)
398.2
Mayer, M. Beauty and the beast (1-4)
398.2
Perrault, C. Cinderella (k-3) **398.2**
Perrault, C. Cinderella, Puss in Boots, and other favorite tales (k-4) **398.2**
Perrault, C. The complete fairy tales of Charles Perrault (4-6) **398.2**
Perrault, C. Puss in boots (k-3) **398.2**
San Souci, R. The white cat (2-4) **398.2**
Willard, N. Beauty and the beast (5 and up)
398.2

Germany
Andreasen, D. Rose Red and the bear prince (k-3) **398.2**
Babbitt, N. Ouch! (k-3) **398.2**
Galdone, P. The elves and the shoemaker (k-2)
398.2
Grimm, J. The Bremen town musicians (k-3)
398.2
Grimm, J. Hansel and Gretel [Dial Press] (k-3)
398.2
Grimm, J. Hansel and Gretel [Picture Book Studio] (k-3) **398.2**
Grimm, J. Little Red Cap (k-3) **398.2**
Grimm, J. Snow White & Rose Red (1-4)
398.2
Hodges, M. The hero of Bremen (3-5)
398.2
Hyman, T. S. Little Red Riding Hood (k-2)
398.2
Kimmel, E. A. Iron John (2-5) **398.2**
Kimmel, E. A. Seven at one blow (k-3)
398.2
Lesser, R. Hansel and Gretel (k-3) **398.2**
Marshall, J. Hansel and Gretel (k-2) **398.2**
Marshall, J. Red Riding Hood (k-2) **398.2**
Mayer, M. Iron John (3-6) **398.2**
Poole, J. Snow White (3-5) **398.2**
Rogasky, B. Rapunzel (1-3) **398.2**
Rogasky, B. The water of life (1-3) **398.2**
Shulevitz, U. The golden goose (k-3) **398.2**
Wildsmith, B. The Bremen Town Band (k-2)
398.2

Zelinsky, P. O. Rumpelstiltskin (k-4) **398.2**
Ziefert, H. Little Red Riding Hood (k-2)
398.2

Ghana
McDermott, G. Anansi the spider (k-3)
398.2
Mollel, T. M. Ananse's feast (k-3) **398.2**

Great Britain
Alderson, B. The tale of the turnip (k-3)
398.2
Beneduce, A. Jack and the beanstalk (2-4)
398.2
Climo, S. Magic & mischief (4 and up)
398.2
Galdone, P. The teeny-tiny woman (k-2)
398.2
I saw Esau **398.8**
Jacobs, J. English fairy tales (4-6) **398.2**
Kellogg, S. Jack and the beanstalk (k-3)
398.2
Kellogg, S. The three sillies (k-3) **398.2**
Marshall, J. The three little pigs (k-2)
398.2
Opie, I. A. The lore and language of schoolchildren **398**
Osborne, M. P. Kate and the beanstalk (k-3)
398.2
Philip, N. Celtic fairy tales (4 and up)
398.2
San Souci, R. The Hobyahs (k-3) **398.2**
Sewall, M. The Green Mist (k-3) **398.2**
Zemach, M. The three little pigs (k-2)
398.2

Greece
Manna, A. L. Mr. Semolina-Semolinus (1-3)
398.2

Haiti
The Magic orange tree, and other Haitian folktales (5 and up) **398.2**
Wolkstein, D. The banza (k-3) **398.2**

Hawaii
Wardlaw, L. Punia and the King of Sharks (k-3)
398.2

India
Brown, M. Once a mouse (k-3) **398.2**
Demi. One grain of rice (2-4) **398.2**
Galdone, P. The monkey and the crocodile (k-2)
398.2
Krishnaswami, U. Shower of gold: girls and women in the stories of India (5 and up)
398.2
Young, E. Seven blind mice (k-3) **398.2**

Indonesia
Sierra, J. The dancing pig (k-3) **398.2**

Iran
Shepard, A. Forty fortunes (2-4) **398.2**

Iraq
Hickox, R. The golden sandal (k-3) **398.2**

Ireland
Behan, B. The King of Ireland's son (3-5)
398.2
Byrd, R. Finn MacCoul and his fearless wife (k-3) **398.2**
Daly, J. Fair, Brown & Trembling (k-3)
398.2
De Paola, T. Jamie O'Rourke and the big potato (k-3) **398.2**

Fonteyn, Dame Margot, 1919-1991
Coppélia (3-5)   **792.8**
Food
D'Amico, J. The science chef (5 and up)
     641.3
Johnson, S. A. Tomatoes, potatoes, corn, and
beans (6 and up)   **641.3**
Rockwell, L. Good enough to eat (k-3)
     613.2
VanCleave, J. P. Janice VanCleave's food and
nutrition for every kid (4 and up)   **613.2**
Fiction
Pinkwater, D. M. Fat men from space (3-6)
     Fic
Riley, L. A. Mouse mess   **E**
Seuss, Dr. Green eggs and ham   **E**
Wells, R. Yoko   **E**
History
Solheim, J. It's disgusting—and we ate it! (4-6)
     641.3
Poetry
Never take a pig to lunch and other poems
about the fun of eating (k-3)   **811.008**
Poem stew (3-6)   **811.008**
Yummy! (k-3)   **811.008**
Food chains (Ecology)
Lauber, P. Who eats what? (k-3)   **577**
Food fight. Bode, J.   **616.85**
Food habits *See* Eating customs
Food preparation *See* Cooking
The **food** pyramid. Kalbacken, J.   **613.2**
Food service
See also Restaurants
Food supply
See also Agriculture
The **fool**. Lester, J.
In Lester, J. The last tales of Uncle Remus
p128-31   **398.2**
Fool John. Van Laan, N.
In Van Laan, N. With a whoop and a holler
p14-17   **398.2**
The **Fool** of the World and the flying ship.
Ransome, A.   **398.2**
The **foolish** boy. Bryan, A.
In Bryan, A. Ashley Bryan's African tales,
uh-huh p172-98   **398.2**
The **foolish** forest sprite. Lee, J. M.
In Lee, J. M. I once was a monkey
     294.3
The **foolish** German. Afanas'ev, A. N.
In Afanas'ev, A. N. Russian fairy tales p600
     398.2
The **foolish** wishes. Perrault, C.
In Perrault, C. The complete fairy tales of
Charles Perrault p118-22   **398.2**
The **foolish** wolf. Afanas'ev, A. N.
In Afanas'ev, A. N. Russian fairy tales p450-
52   **398.2**
The **fools** of Chelm and the stupid carp. Singer, I.
B.
In Singer, I. B. Stories for children p71-76
     S C
The **fools** of Chelm and their history. Singer, I. B.
     Fic

Fool's paradise. Singer, I. B.
In Singer, I. B. Zlateh the goat, and other sto-
ries p5-16   **398.2**
Foot
Aliki. My feet (k-1)   **612**
Fiction
Paul, A. W. Hello toes! Hello feet!   **E**
Football
See also Soccer
Buckley, J., Jr. America's greatest game (4 and
up)   **796.332**
Buckley, J., Jr. Football (4 and up)
     796.332
Gibbons, G. My football book (k-2)
     796.332
Biography
Sullivan, G. Quarterbacks! (5 and up)   **920**
Fiction
Christopher, M. Tackle without a team (4-6)
     Fic
Kessler, L. P. Kick, pass, and run   **E**
Spinelli, J. Crash (5 and up)   **Fic**
The **footless** champion and the handless champion.
Afanas'ev, A. N.
In Afanas'ev, A. N. Russian fairy tales p269-
73   **398.2**
Footsteps in time [series]
Hewitt, S. The Aztecs   **972**
Footwear *See* Shoes
For being good. Rylant, C.
In Rylant, C. Children of Christmas p13-19
     S C
For laughing out loud   **811.008**
For Pete's sake. Walsh, E. S.   **E**
Forbes, Esther, 1891-1967
Johnny Tremain (5 and up)   **Fic**
See/See also pages in the following book(s):
Newbery Medal books, 1922-1955 p245-54
     028.5
The **Forbidden** apple
In The Magic orange tree, and other Haitian
folktales p171-75   **398.2**
Forced labor *See* Slavery
Ford, George
(il) Coles, R. The story of Ruby Bridges
     370
Ford, H. J. (Henry Justice), 1860-1941
(il) The Arabian nights entertainments. See The
Arabian nights entertainments   **398.2**
(il) The Blue fairy book. See The Blue fairy
book   **398.2**
(il) The Green fairy book. See The Green fairy
book   **398.2**
(il) The Yellow fairy book. See The Yellow
fairy book   **398.2**
Ford, Harry
The young astronomer (4 and up)   **520**
Ford, Henry, 1863-1947
About
Mitchell, B. We'll race you, Henry: a story
about Henry Ford (3-5)   **92**
Ford, Henry Justice *See* Ford, H. J. (Henry Justice), 1860-1941

The **Forty** thieves
In The Blue fairy book p242-50   **398.2**
The **forty** thieves. Lang, A.
In Womenfolk and fairy tales p51-64
                                          398.2

Fossey, Dian
About
Matthews, T. L. Light shining through the mist: a photobiography of Dian Fossey (4 and up)
                                          92
Fossil hominids
Gallant, R. A. Early humans (5 and up)
                                          599.93
Fossil mammals
    See also Mastodon
Giblin, J. The mystery of the mammoth bones (4 and up)   **569**
Fossil plants
Henderson, D. Dinosaur tree (2-4)   **560**
Fossil reptiles
    See also Dinosaurs
Fossils
    See also Fossil mammals; Prehistoric animals
Aliki. Fossils tell of long ago (k-3)   **560**
Anholt, L. Stone girl, bone girl: the story of Mary Anning (k-3)   **92**
Atkins, J. Mary Anning and the sea dragon (k-3)   **92**
Bausum, A. Dragon bones and dinosaur eggs: a photobiography of Roy Chapman Andrews (5 and up)   **92**
Bishop, N. Digging for bird-dinosaurs (4 and up)   **567.9**
Brown, D. Rare treasure: Mary Anning and her remarkable discoveries (k-3)   **92**
Dingus, L. The tiniest giants (4 and up)
                                          567.9
Floca, B. Dinosaurs at the ends of the earth (3-5)   **567.9**
Lessem, D. Bigger than T. rex (4 and up)
                                          567.9
Lessem, D. Dinosaurs to dodos (4 and up)
                                          560
Lindsay, W. Prehistoric life (4 and up)   **560**
Norell, M. A nest of dinosaurs (5 and up)
                                          567.9
Tanaka, S. Graveyards of the dinosaurs (4-6)
                                          567.9
Taylor, P. D. Fossil (4 and up)   **560**
Thompson, S. E. Death trap (4 and up)
                                          560
The Visual dictionary of prehistoric life (4 and up)   **560**
Fiction
Carrick, C. Big old bones   **E**
Fossils tell of long ago. Aliki   **560**
Foster, Leila Merrell
Iraq (4 and up)   **956.7**
Kuwait (4 and up)   **953.67**
Oman (4 and up)   **953**
Foster, Stephen Collins, 1826-1864
See/See also pages in the following book(s):
Krull, K. Lives of the musicians p44-47 (4 and up)   **920**

Foster home care
Fiction
Byars, B. C. The pinballs (5 and up)   **Fic**
MacLachlan, P. Mama One, Mama Two   **E**
Nixon, J. L. A family apart (5 and up)   **Fic**
Paterson, K. The great Gilly Hopkins (5 and up)   **Fic**
Polacco, P. Welcome Comfort   **E**
Sebestyen, O. Out of nowhere (5 and up)
                                          Fic
The **founding** of London. McCaughrean, G.
    In McCaughrean, G. The bronze cauldron: myths and legends of the world p87-91
                                          398.2
The **foundling**. Alexander, L.
    In Alexander, L. The foundling and other tales of Prydain p5-14   **S C**
The **foundling** and other tales of Prydain. Alexander, L.   **S C**
Four dollars and fifty cents. Kimmel, E. A.
                                          E
The **four-footed** horror. Olson, A. N.
    In Olson, A. N. Ask the bones: scary stories from around the world p37-41   **398.2**
Four fur feet. Brown, M. W.   **E**
Four hairs from the beard of the Devil
    In The Magic orange tree, and other Haitian folktales p43-48   **398.2**
Four on the shore. Marshall, E. See note under Marshall, E. Three by the sea   **E**
Four perfect pebbles. Perl, L.   **940.53**
The **four** questions. Schwartz, L. S.   **296.4**
Four stupid cupids. Maguire, G. See note under Maguire, G. Seven spiders spinning   **Fic**
Four worlds and a broken stone. McCaughrean, G.
    In McCaughrean, G. The crystal pool: myths and legends of the world p1-7
                                          398.2
Fourth of July
Giblin, J. Fireworks, picnics, and flags (3-6)
                                          394.26
Ziefert, H. Hats off for the Fourth of July!
                                          E
Fiction
Paraskevas, B. On the day the tall ships sailed
                                          E
Fowler, Allan
A snail's pace (k-3)   **594**
Stars of the sea (k-3)   **593.9**
Fox, Dan
Go in and out the window. See Go in and out the window   **782.42**
Songs of the Wild West. See Songs of the Wild West   **782.42**
Fox, Mem, 1946-
Hattie and the fox   **E**
Koala Lou   **E**
Night noises   **E**
Sleepy bears   **E**
Sophie   **E**
Tough Boris   **E**
Wombat divine   **E**

Fox, Paula
    Amzat and his brothers: three Italian tales (3-5) **398.2**

Contents: Amzat and his brothers; Mezgalten; Olimpia, Cucol, and the door

    The eagle kite (6 and up) **Fic**
    A likely place (3-5) **Fic**
    One-eyed cat (5 and up) **Fic**
    The slave dancer (5 and up) **Fic**
    The stone-faced boy (4-6) **Fic**
    The village by the sea (5 and up) **Fic**
    See/See also pages in the following book(s):
    Newbery and Caldecott Medal books, 1966-1975 p116-25 **028.5**

Fox all week. Marshall, E. See note under Marshall, E. Fox and his friends **E**

Fox and his friends. Marshall, E. **E**

The **fox** and the crab. Sierra, J.
    In Sierra, J. Nursery tales around the world p81-83 **398.2**

The **fox** and the crane. Afanas'ev, A. N.
    In Afanas'ev, A. N. Russian fairy tales p171-72 **398.2**

The **fox** and the lobster. Afanas'ev, A. N.
    In Afanas'ev, A. N. Russian fairy tales p310 **398.2**

The **fox** and the woodcock. Afanas'ev, A. N.
    In Afanas'ev, A. N. Russian fairy tales p171 **398.2**

The **fox** and the woodpecker. Afanas'ev, A. N.
    In Afanas'ev, A. N. Russian fairy tales p199 **398.2**

The **fox** as midwife. Afanas'ev, A. N.
    In Afanas'ev, A. N. Russian fairy tales p191-92 **398.2**

The **fox** as mourner. Afanas'ev, A. N.
    In Afanas'ev, A. N. Russian fairy tales p437-38 **398.2**

Fox at school. Marshall, E. See note under Marshall, E. Fox and his friends **E**

Fox be nimble. Marshall, J. See note under Marshall, E. Fox and his friends **E**

The **fox** confessor. Afanas'ev, A. N.
    In Afanas'ev, A. N. Russian fairy tales p72-74 **398.2**

Fox in love. Marshall, E. See note under Marshall, E. Fox and his friends **E**

Fox on stage. Marshall, J. See note under Marshall, E. Fox and his friends **E**

Fox on the job. Marshall, J. See note under Marshall, E. Fox and his friends **E**

Fox on wheels. Marshall, E. See note under Marshall, E. Fox and his friends **E**

Fox outfoxed. Marshall, J. See note under Marshall, E. Fox and his friends **E**

The **fox** physician. Afanas'ev, A. N.
    In Afanas'ev, A. N. Russian fairy tales p15-17 **398.2**

The **Fox**, the goose, and the corn
    In From sea to shining sea p259-63 **810.8**

The **fox**, the hare, and the cock. Afanas'ev, A. N.
    In Afanas'ev, A. N. Russian fairy tales p192-94 **398.2**

The **Fox** went out on a chilly night **782.42**

Foxes
Fiction
Auch, M. J. Peeping Beauty **E**
Bodnar, J. Z. Tale of a tail **E**
Byars, B. C. The midnight fox (4-6) **Fic**
Cooney, B. Chanticleer and the fox **E**
Fox, M. Hattie and the fox **E**
Gliori, D. No matter what **E**
Hogrogian, N. One fine day (k-3) **398.2**
Hutchins, P. Rosie's walk **E**
Kvasnosky, L. M. Zelda and Ivy **E**
Marshall, E. Fox and his friends **E**
McKissack, P. C. Flossie & the fox **E**
Shannon, G. Dance away! **E**
Tompert, A. Grandfather Tang's story **E**

Fraction action. Leedy, L. **513**

Fraction fun. Adler, D. A. **513**

Fractions
Adler, D. A. Fraction fun (2-4) **513**
Leedy, L. Fraction action (k-3) **513**
McMillan, B. Eating fractions (k-2) **513**
Murphy, S. J. Jump, kangaroo, jump! (1-3) **513**

Fradin, Dennis B.
The Georgia colony (4 and up) **975.8**
Hiawatha: messenger of peace (3-5) **92**
Ida B. Wells (5 and up) **92**
Is there life on Mars? (4 and up) **576.8**
The New York Colony (4 and up) **974.7**
The Pennsylvania colony (4 and up) **974.8**
The planet hunters (5 and up) **523.4**
Samuel Adams (6 and up) **92**
The South Carolina Colony (4 and up) **975.7**
Washington, D.C (3-5) **975.3**

Fradin, Judith Bloom
(jt. auth) Fradin, D. B. Ida B. Wells **92**

The **fragrance** of paradise. Goldin, B. D.
    In Goldin, B. D. Journeys with Elijah p49-56 **222**

Frampton, David
(il) Aylesworth, J. My son John **E**
(il) Carrick, C. Whaling days **639.2**
(il) Chaikin, M. Clouds of glory **296.1**
(il) Fleischman, P. Bull Run **Fic**

France
Landau, E. France (2-4) **944**
Nardo, D. France (4 and up) **944**
NgCheong-Lum, R. France (4 and up) **944**
Fiction
Knight, J. Charlotte in Giverny (3-6) **Fic**
Maguire, G. The good liar (4 and up) **Fic**
Polacco, P. The butterfly (2-4) **Fic**
Schnur, S. The shadow children (5 and up) **Fic**
Yorinks, A. Harry and Lulu **E**
Folklore
See Folklore—France
History—1328-1589, House of Valois
Hodges, M. Joan of Arc (2-4) **92**
Poole, J. Joan of Arc (2-4) **92**
Stanley, D. Joan of Arc (4 and up) **92**

Friendship—Fiction—*Continued*

Hamilton, V. The planet of Junior Brown (6 and up) **Fic**

Härtling, P. Crutches (5 and up) **Fic**

Heine, H. Friends **E**

Henkes, K. Words of stone (5 and up) **Fic**

Hesse, K. Lester's dog **E**

Hoberman, M. A. And to think that we thought that we'd never be friends **E**

Hoberman, M. A. One of each **E**

Holt, K. W. When Zachary Beaver came to town (5 and up) **Fic**

Horvath, P. When the circus came to town (4-6) **Fic**

Howe, J. Horace and Morris but mostly Dolores **E**

Howe, J. Pinky and Rex **E**

Hurwitz, J. The hot & cold summer (3-5) **Fic**

James, B. Mary Ann **E**

Kasza, K. Dorothy & Mikey **E**

Kellogg, S. Best friends **E**

Kimmel, E. C. Visiting Miss Caples (6 and up) **Fic**

Konigsburg, E. L. Jennifer, Hecate, Macbeth, William McKinley, and me, Elizabeth (4-6) **Fic**

Konigsburg, E. L. The view from Saturday (4-6) **Fic**

Koss, A. G. The Ashwater experiment (4 and up) **Fic**

Koss, A. G. The girls (5 and up) **Fic**

Krumgold, J. Onion John (5 and up) **Fic**

Kurtz, J. The storyteller's beads (5 and up) **Fic**

Lasky, K. Pond year **E**

Levoy, M. Alan and Naomi (6 and up) **Fic**

Levy, E. Seventh grade tango (5 and up) **Fic**

Lionni, L. An extraordinary egg **E**

Lisle, J. T. Afternoon of the elves (4-6) **Fic**

Lovelace, M. H. Betsy-Tacy (2-4) **Fic**

Lowry, L. Autumn Street (4 and up) **Fic**

Lowry, L. Number the stars (4 and up) **Fic**

Lowry, L. Rabble Starkey (5 and up) **Fic**

Marshall, J. George and Martha **E**

Martin, A. M. Rachel Parker, kindergarten show-off **E**

Mathis, S. B. Sidewalk story (3-5) **Fic**

Myers, W. D. Fast Sam, Cool Clyde, and Stuff (6 and up) **Fic**

Myers, W. D. Me, Mop, and the Moondance Kid (4-6) **Fic**

Narahashi, K. Two girls can! **E**

Novak, M. Little Wolf, Big Wolf **E**

Orgel, D. The devil in Vienna (6 and up) **Fic**

Paterson, K. Bridge to Terabithia (4 and up) **Fic**

Peck, R. N. Soup (5 and up) **Fic**

Peet, B. Eli **E**

Perkins, L. R. All alone in the universe (5 and up) **Fic**

Polacco, P. Chicken Sunday **E**

Polacco, P. Mrs. Katz and Tush **E**

Polacco, P. Pink and Say **E**

Pomerantz, C. You're not my best friend anymore **E**

Raschka, C. Yo! Yes? **E**

Robins, J. Addie meets Max **E**

Ross, P. Meet M and M **E**

Rylant, C. A fine white dust (5 and up) **Fic**

Rylant, C. Poppleton **E**

Sachar, L. Holes (5 and up) **Fic**

Schotter, R. Captain Snap and the children of Vinegar Lane **E**

Sharmat, M. W. Mitchell is moving **E**

Silverman, E. Don't fidget a feather **E**

Smith, D. B. A taste of blackberries (4-6) **Fic**

Smith, J. L. The kid next door and other headaches (2-4) **Fic**

Snyder, Z. K. Libby on Wednesdays (5 and up) **Fic**

Speare, E. G. The sign of the beaver (5 and up) **Fic**

Spinelli, J. Crash (5 and up) **Fic**

Uchida, Y. The bracelet **E**

Warner, S. Totally confidential (4 and up) **Fic**

Williams, V. B. Scooter (3-5) **Fic**

Willner-Pardo, G. Figuring out Frances (4-6) **Fic**

Wojciechowski, S. The Christmas miracle of Jonathan Toomey **E**

Woodson, J. I hadn't meant to tell you this (6 and up) **Fic**

Yep, L. Thief of hearts (5 and up) **Fic**

Yumoto, K. The friends (5 and up) **Fic**

Zolotow, C. The hating book **E**

Zolotow, C. My friend John **E**

Poetry

Grimes, N. Meet Danitra Brown (2-4) **811**

Prelutsky, J. Rolling Harvey down the hill (1-3) **811**

The **friendship**. Taylor, M. D. **Fic**

The **friendship** tree. Caple, K. **E**

Frierson, Virginia Wright- *See* Wright-Frierson, Virginia, 1949-

The **fright** before Christmas. Howe, J. See note under Howe, J. Scared silly: a Halloween treat **E**

Frightful's mountain. George, J. C. **Fic**

Frindle. Clements, A. **Fic**

Fritz, Jean

And then what happened, Paul Revere? (2-4) **92**

Around the world in a hundred years (4-6) **910.4**

Brendan the Navigator (3-5) **398.2**

Bully for you, Teddy Roosevelt! (5 and up) **92**

The cabin faced west (3-6) **Fic**

Can't you make them behave, King George? [biography of George III, King of Great Britain] (2-4) **92**

China homecoming (6 and up) **951.05**

China's Long March (6 and up) **951.04**

The double life of Pocahontas (4 and up) **92**

Early thunder (6 and up) **Fic**

Frozen in time—*Continued*
Patent, D. H. Secrets of the ice man   **930.1**
Frozen man. Getz, D.   **930.1**
Frozen stars *See* Black holes (Astronomy)
Frozen summer. Auch, M. J.   **Fic**
The **frugal** youth cybrarian. Ross, C.   **025.2**
Fruit
  See also Apples; Berries
  Ehlert, L. Eating the alphabet   **E**
  Hughes, M. S. Yes, we have bananas (4 and up)
    634
  McMillan, B. Growing colors   **E**
Fruit culture
  Hughes, M. S. Yes, we have bananas (4 and up)
    634
Fry, Virginia Lynn, 1952-
  Part of me died, too (5 and up)   **155.9**
Ftera, Constance
  (il) Simon, S. Now you see it, now you don't
    152.14
Fuchs, Bernie
  (il) Littlefield, B. Champions   **920**
  (il) Schroeder, A. Ragtime Tumpie   **E**
  (il) Yolen, J. Raising Yoder's barn   **E**
Fudge-a-mania. Blume, J. See note under Blume,
  J. Tales of a fourth grade nothing   **Fic**
Fuel
  Parker, S. Fuels for the future (4-6)   **333.79**
Fuels for the future. Parker, S.   **333.79**
Fujiwara, Murasaki *See* Murasaki Shikibu, b.
  978?
The **full** belly bowl. Aylesworth, J.   **E**
Full steam ahead. Blumberg, R.   **385.09**
Fuller, Elizabeth
  (il) Butler, D. My brown bear Barney   **E**
Fun on the run. Cole, J.   **793.7**
Fun with your microscope. Levine, S.   **502.8**
Fund raising
  Grantsmanship for small libraries and school li-
  brary media centers   **025.1**
Fundamental baseball. Geng, D.   **796.357**
Fundamental golf. Krause, P.   **796.352**
Fundamental gymnastics. Bragg, L. W.
    796.44
Fundamental hockey. Foley, M.   **796.962**
Fundamental soccer. Coleman, L.   **796.334**
Fundamental sports [series]
  Bragg, L. W. Fundamental gymnastics
    796.44
  Coleman, L. Fundamental soccer   **796.334**
  Foley, M. Fundamental hockey   **796.962**
  Geng, D. Fundamental baseball   **796.357**
  Jensen, J. Fundamental volleyball   **796.325**
  Krause, P. Fundamental golf   **796.352**
  Miller, M. Fundamental tennis   **796.342**
Fundamental tennis. Miller, M.   **796.342**
Fundamental volleyball. Jensen, J.   **796.325**
Funeral rites and ceremonies
  Perl, L. Mummies, tombs, and treasure (4 and
  up)   **393**
  Putnam, J. Mummy (4 and up)   **393**

The **funeral** suits. Soto, G.
  In Soto, G. Petty crimes   **S C**
Fungi
  See also Mushrooms
  Pascoe, E. Slime, molds, and fungi (4 and up)
    579.5
Funicular railroads *See* Cable railroads
Funnies *See* Comic books, strips, etc.
Funny, funny Lyle. Waber, B. See note under
  Waber, B. Lyle, Lyle, crocodile   **E**
The **funny** little woman. Mosel, A.   **398.2**
Funny you should ask. Terban, M.   **793.73**
Furaha means happy. Wilson-Max, K.   **496**
Further tales of Uncle Remus. Lester, J. See note
  under Lester, J. The last tales of Uncle Re-
  mus   **398.2**

G

G.I.'s *See* Soldiers—United States
G is for googol. Schwartz, D. M.   **510**
Gabby growing up. Hest, A.   **E**
Gaber, Susan
  (il) Forest, H. The baker's dozen   **398.2**
  (il) Forest, H. The woman who flummoxed the
  fairies   **398.2**
  (il) Martin, R. The language of birds   **398.2**
  (il) Sanfield, S. Bit by bit   **398.2**
  (il) Silverman, E. Raisel's riddle   **398.2**
  (il) Small talk. See Small talk   **811.008**
Gabriella's song. Fleming, C.   **E**
Gackenbach, Dick, 1927-
  Claude the dog. See note under Gackenbach, D.
  What's Claude doing?   **E**
  What's Claude doing?   **E**
  (il) Smith, J. L. The kid next door and other
  headaches   **Fic**
Gág, Wanda, 1893-1946
  Millions of cats   **E**
Gaines, Ann
  Jim Bowie (5 and up)   **92**
Galan, Mark A.
  There's still time (3-6)   **333.95**
Galapagos Islands
  Myers, L. B. Galápagos: islands of change (4
  and up)   **508**
    Fiction
  Lewin, B. Booby hatch   **E**
    Natural history
    See Natural history—Galapagos Islands
Galaxies
  Simon, S. Galaxies (3-6)   **523.1**
Galaxy (Milky Way) *See* Milky Way
Galdone, Joanna
  The tailypo (k-3)   **398.2**
Galdone, Paul, 1914-1986
  The cat goes fiddle-i-fee (k-1)   **398.8**
  The elves and the shoemaker (k-2)   **398.2**
  The gingerbread boy (k-2)   **398.2**
  Henny Penny (k-2)   **398.2**
  The little red hen (k-2)   **398.2**

Garfield, Leon, 1921-1996—*Continued*
Smith (6 and up)   **Fic**
The **gargoyle** on the roof. Prelutsky, J.   **811**
Garland, Michael, 1952-
(il) Friedrich, E. Leah's pony   **E**
(il) Tompert, A. Saint Patrick   **92**
Garland, Sherry, 1948-
My father's boat   **E**
Voices of the Alamo (3-6)   **976.4**
Garments *See* Clothing and dress
Garner, Alan, 1934-
Glosskap and Wasis
In From sea to shining sea p210-11
    810.8
Garns, Allen
(il) Gonna sing my head off! See Gonna sing my head off!   **782.42**
Garza, Carmen Lomas
Family pictures   **E**
In my family (k-3)   **305.8**
Magic windows   **305.8**
Making magic windows (3-6)   **736**
See/See also pages in the following book(s):
Just like me p6-7   **920**
Gascoigne, Ingrid
Papua New Guinea (5 and up)   **995.3**
Gasztold, Carmen Bernos de *See* Bernos de Gasztold, Carmen
The **gate** in the wall. Howard, E.   **Fic**
Gates, Doris, 1901-1987
Blue willow (4 and up)   **Fic**
Gateway solar system [series]
Vogt, G. Asteroids, comets, and meteors
    523.6
Gath, Tracy
(ed) Exploring science in the library. See Exploring science in the library   **027.8**
Gathering blue. Lowry, L.   **Fic**
A **gathering** of days: a New England girl's journal, 1830-32. Blos, J. W.   **Fic**
Gathering of pearls. Choi, S. N. See note under Choi, S. N. Year of impossible goodbyes
    Fic
Gathering the sun. Ada, A. F.   **811**
'**Gator** aid. Cutler, J. See note under Cutler, J. Rats!   **Fic**
The **Gator** Girls. Calmenson, S. See note under Calmenson, S. Get well, Gators!   **Fic**
Gator Halloween. Calmenson, S. See note under Calmenson, S. Get well, Gators!   **Fic**
Gauch, Patricia Lee
Bravo Tanya. See note under Gauch, P. L. Dance, Tanya   **E**
Christina Katerina & the box. See note under Gauch, P. L. Christina Katerina and the time she quit the family   **E**
Christina Katerina and Fats and the Great Neighborhood War. See note under Gauch, P. L. Christina Katerina and the time she quit the family   **E**
Christina Katerina and the time she quit the family   **E**
Dance, Tanya   **E**

Presenting Tanya the Ugly Duckling. See note under Gauch, P. L. Dance, Tanya   **E**
Tanya and Emily in a dance for two. See note under Gauch, P. L. Dance, Tanya   **E**
Tanya and the magic wardrobe. See note under Gauch, P. L. Dance, Tanya   **E**
This time, Tempe Wick? (3-5)   **Fic**
Thunder at Gettysburg (3-5)   **Fic**
Gautama Buddha
About
Demi. Buddha (4-6)   **294.3**
Gauthier, Gail, 1953-
A year with Butch and Spike (4-6)   **Fic**
Gawain (Legendary character)
Hastings, S. Sir Gawain and the loathly lady (3 and up)   **398.2**
Gay, Kathlyn
Science in ancient Greece (4 and up)   **509**
World War I (5 and up)   **940.3**
Gay, Martin
(jt. auth) Gay, K. World War I   **940.3**
Gay lifestyle *See* Homosexuality
Gearhart, Sarah
The telephone (4 and up)   **621.385**
Gecko. MacDonald, M. R.
In MacDonald, M. R. The storyteller's startup book p139-44   **372.6**
Gee, Lillian
(il) Chaiet, D. The safe zone   **613.6**
Geese
Fiction
Bang, M. Goose   **E**
Braun, T. My goose Betsy   **E**
King-Smith, D. The cuckoo child (3-5)   **Fic**
Langton, J. The fledgling (5 and up)   **Fic**
McBratney, S. Just you and me   **E**
Polacco, P. Rechenka's eggs   **E**
Schoenherr, J. Rebel   **E**
Silverman, E. Don't fidget a feather   **E**
Walker, S. M. The 18 penny goose   **E**
Geese find the missing piece. Maestro, M.
    793.73
Gehm, Charles
(il) Peck, R. N. Soup   **Fic**
Gehrig, Henry Louis *See* Gehrig, Lou, 1903-1941
Gehrig, Lou, 1903-1941
About
Adler, D. A. Lou Gehrig (2-4)   **92**
Geiger, John, 1960-
(jt. auth) Beattie, O. Buried in ice   **998**
Geisel, Theodor Seuss *See* Seuss, Dr.
Geisert, Arthur
After the flood   **E**
The ark (k-3)   **222**
Oink   **E**
Oink, oink. See note under Geisert, A. Oink
    E
Pigs from 1 to 10   **E**
Pigs from A to Z   **E**
Roman numerals I to MM (k-3)   **513**
(jt. auth) Geisert, B. Mountain town   **E**
(jt. auth) Geisert, B. Prairie town   **E**
(jt. auth) Geisert, B. River town   **E**

Geisert, Bonnie, 1943-
Mountain town   E
Prairie town   E
River town   E
Gellman, Marc
How do you spell God? (5 and up)   **200**
Lost & found (4-6)   **155.9**
Gelman, Rita Golden, 1937-
Queen Esther saves her people (k-3)   **222**
Gems
    See also Precious stones
Gender identity *See* Sex role
Genealogy
Taylor, M. Through the eyes of your ancestors (4 and up)   **929**
                 Fiction
Hearne, B. G. Seven brave women   E
The **general**. Terada, A. M.
In Terada, A. M. Under the starfruit tree p78-82   **398.2**
Generals
Archer, J. A house divided: the lives of Ulysses S. Grant and Robert E. Lee (5 and up)   **92**
Fritz, J. Stonewall [biography of Stonewall Jackson] (4 and up)   **92**
Genesis, Book of *See* Bible. O.T. Genesis
Genesis. Bible. O.T. Genesis   **222**
Geng, Don
Fundamental baseball (5 and up)   **796.357**
The **genie** of Sutton Place. Selden, G.   **Fic**
Genreflecting advisory series
Volz, B. D. Junior genreflecting   **016.8**
Gentle Ben. Morey, W.   **Fic**
Gentle giant octopus. Wallace, K.   **594**
Gentle Gwan Yin. Carpenter, F.
In Carpenter, F. Tales of a Chinese grandmother p29-38   **398.2**
The **Gentleman** Outlaw and me—Eli. Hahn, M. D.   **Fic**
Geo mysteries. (3-6) See entry in Part 2: Web Resources
Geographical distribution of people *See* Human geography
Geographical myths
    See also Atlantis
Geography
    See also Maps; Voyages and travels
Jenkins, S. Hottest, coldest, highest, deepest (k-2)   **910**
Rockwell, A. F. Our earth (k-2)   **910**
                 Dictionaries
The World Book encyclopedia of people and places   **910.3**
Worldmark encyclopedia of the nations   **910.3**
                 Periodicals
National Geographic World (3-6)   **910.5**
Geography, Historical *See* Historical geography
Geology
Blobaum, C. Geology rocks! (4-6)   **551**
Cole, J. The magic school bus inside the Earth (2-4)   **551.1**

Gallant, R. A. Dance of the continents (5 and up)   **551.1**
Gibbons, G. Planet earth/inside out (k-3)   **550**
Patent, D. H. Shaping the earth (4 and up)   **550**
Van Rose, S. The earth atlas (5 and up)   **550**
Zoehfeld, K. W. How mountains are made (k-3)   **551.4**
Geology rocks!. Blobaum, C.   **551**
Geometric patterns *See* Patterns (Mathematics)
Geometry
    See also Shape
Adler, D. A. Shape up! (2-4)   **516**
VanCleave, J. P. Janice VanCleave's geometry for every kid (4 and up)   **516**
Geometry for every kid, Janice VanCleave's. VanCleave, J. P.   **516**
George III, King of Great Britain, 1738-1820
                 About
Fritz, J. Can't you make them behave, King George? (2-4)   **92**
George, Charles, 1949-
Idaho
    In America the beautiful, second series   **973**
Mississippi
    In America the beautiful, second series   **973**
Montana
    In America the beautiful, second series   **973**
George, Jean Craighead, 1919-
Everglades (2-4)   **975.9**
Frightful's mountain (5 and up)   **Fic**
How to talk to your cat (2-4)   **636.8**
How to talk to your dog (2-4)   **636.7**
Julie (6 and up)   **Fic**
Julie of the wolves (6 and up)   **Fic**
Julie's wolf pack (6 and up)   **Fic**
Look to the North   E
Morning, noon, and night   E
My side of the mountain (5 and up)   **Fic**
On the far side of the mountain (5 and up)   **Fic**
One day in the prairie (4-6)   **577.4**
One day in the tropical rain forest (4-6)   **577.3**
One day in the woods (4-6)   **577.3**
Snow Bear   E
A tarantula in my purse (4-6)   **92**
There's an owl in the shower (3-5)   **Fic**
See/See also pages in the following book(s):
Newbery and Caldecott Medal books, 1966-1975 p96-106, 109-12   **028.5**
George, Kristine O'Connell
The great frog race and other poems (3-5)   **811**
Little dog poems (k-2)   **811**
Old Elm speaks (2-4)   **811**
George, Lindsay Barrett
Around the pond: who's been here? See note under George, L. B. In the woods: who's been here?   E

George, Lindsay Barrett—*Continued*
Around the world: who's been here? See note under George, L. B. In the woods: who's been here?　**E**
In the snow: who's been here? See note under George, L. B. In the woods: who's been here?　**E**
In the woods: who's been here?　**E**
(il) George, W. T. Box Turtle at Long Pond　**E**

George, Michael, 1964-
Wolves (1-3)　**599.77**

George, Twig C., 1950-
Jellies (2-4)　**593.5**

George, William T.
Beaver at Long Pond. See note under George, W. T. Box Turtle at Long Pond　**E**
Box Turtle at Long Pond　**E**
Christmas at Long Pond. See note under George, W. T. Box Turtle at Long Pond　**E**

George and Martha. Marshall, J.　**E**
George and Martha back in town. Marshall, J. See note under Marshall, J. George and Martha　**E**
George and Martha encore. Marshall, J. See note under Marshall, J. George and Martha　**E**
George and Martha, one fine day. Marshall, J. See note under Marshall, J. George and Martha　**E**
George and Martha rise and shine. Marshall, J. See note under Marshall, J. George and Martha　**E**
George and Martha, round and round. Marshall, J. See note under Marshall, J. George and Martha　**E**
George and Martha, tons of fun. Marshall, J. See note under Marshall, J. George and Martha　**E**
George and the dragon. McCaughrean, G.
In McCaughrean, G. The golden hoard: myths and legends of the world p12-16　**398.2**

George, Saint, d. 303
About
Hodges, M. Saint George and the dragon (2-5)　**398.2**
George shrinks. Joyce, W.　**E**

George Washington Bridge (N.Y. and N.J.)
Fiction
Swift, H. H. The little red lighthouse and the great gray bridge　**E**
George Washington's breakfast. Fritz, J.　**Fic**
George Washington's cows. Small, D.　**E**
George Washington's mother. Fritz, J.　**92**
George's dream. Sanfield, S.
In Sanfield, S. The adventures of High John the Conqueror　**398.2**

Georgia
Fradin, D. B. The Georgia colony (4 and up)　**975.8**
Otfinoski, S. Georgia
In Celebrate the states　**973**

Robinson Masters, N. Georgia
In America the beautiful, second series　**973**

Fiction
Beatty, P. Turn homeward, Hannalee (5 and up)　**Fic**
Burch, R. Ida Early comes over the mountain (4 and up)　**Fic**
Burch, R. Queenie Peavy (5 and up)　**Fic**

Georgia (Republic)
Spilling, M. Georgia (5 and up)　**947.5**
Georgia (Soviet Union) *See* Georgia (Republic)
The **Georgia** colony. Fradin, D. B.　**975.8**
Georgia music. Griffith, H. V. See note under Griffith, H. V. Grandaddy's place　**E**
Geothermal and bio-energy. Graham, I.　**333.8**

Geothermal resources
Graham, I. Geothermal and bio-energy (4 and up)　**333.8**
Geraldine and Mrs. Duffy. Keller, H. See note under Keller, H. Geraldine's blanket　**E**
Geraldine first. Keller, H. See note under Keller, H. Geraldine's blanket　**E**
Geraldine's baby brother. Keller, H. See note under Keller, H. Geraldine's blanket　**E**
Geraldine's big snow. Keller, H. See note under Keller, H. Geraldine's blanket　**E**
Geraldine's blanket. Keller, H.　**E**

Gerbils
Fiction
Roth, S. L. Cinnamon's day out　**E**

Gerhardt, Lillian Noreen
(ed) School Library Journal's best. See School Library Journal's best　**027.8**

Geringer, Laura
The pomegranate seeds (3-5)　**292**
A three hat day　**E**

Germaine, Elizabeth
Cooking the Australian way
In Easy menu ethnic cookbooks　**641.5**
The **German** American family album. Hoobler, D.　**305.8**

German Americans
De Paola, T. An early American Christmas　**E**
Hoobler, D. The German American family album (5 and up)　**305.8**

German prisoners of war
Fiction
Greene, B. Summer of my German soldier (6 and up)　**Fic**

German West Africa *See* Cameroon
Germans
Canada—Fiction
Little, J. From Anna (4-6)　**Fic**

Germany
Ayer, E. H. Germany (4 and up)　**943**
Fiction
Holub, J. The robber and me (5 and up)　**Fic**

Folklore
See Folklore—Germany

Germany's lightning war. McGowen, T.   **940.54**

Germs See Bacteria

Germs make me sick!. Berger, M.   **616.9**

Geronimo, Apache Chief, 1829-1909
See/See also pages in the following book(s):
Ehrlich, A. Wounded Knee: an Indian history of the American West (6 and up)   **970.004**

Gerontology
> *See also* Old age

Gershator, David
Bread is for eating   **E**

Gershator, Phillis, 1942-
Zzzng! Zzzng! Zzzng! (k-3)   **398.2**
(jt. auth) Gershator, D. Bread is for eating   **E**

Gershon's monster. Kimmel, E. A.   **398.2**

Gershwin, George, 1898-1937
See/See also pages in the following book(s):
Krull, K. Lives of the musicians p86-89 (4 and up)   **920**

Gerson, Mary-Joan
Why the sky is far away (k-3)   **398.2**

Gerstein, Mordicai, 1935-
The mountains of Tibet   **E**
Queen Esther the morning star (1-3)   **222**
The wild boy (k-3)   **92**
(il) Kimmel, E. A. The jar of fools: eight Hanukkah stories from Chelm   **S C**

Get on board: the story of the Underground Railroad. Haskins, J.   **326**

Get the picture, Jenny Archer. Conford, E. See note under Conford, E. A case for Jenny Archer   **Fic**

Get well, Gators!. Calmenson, S.   **Fic**

Getting near to baby. Couloumbis, A.   **Fic**

Getting ready for bed See Bedtime

Getting to know the world's greatest artists [series]
Venezia, M. Georgia O'Keeffe   **92**

Getting to know the world's greatest composers [series]
Venezia, M. George Handel   **92**

Gettysburg (Pa.), Battle of, 1863
Beller, S. P. To hold this ground (5 and up)   **973.7**
Murphy, J. The long road to Gettysburg (5 and up)   **973.7**
> **Fiction**
Gauch, P. L. Thunder at Gettysburg (3-5)   **Fic**
Osborne, M. P. My brother's keeper (3-5)   **Fic**

Getz, David, 1957-
Frozen girl (5 and up)   **930.1**
Frozen man (5 and up)   **930.1**

Ghana
Levy, P. M. Ghana (5 and up)   **966.7**
> **Folklore**
See Folklore—Ghana

Ghana Empire
> **History**
McKissack, P. C. The royal kingdoms of Ghana, Mali, and Songhay (5 and up)   **966.2**

Ghazi, Suhaib Hamid
Ramadan (k-3)   **297.3**

Gherman, Beverly
The mysterious rays of Dr. Röntgen (2-4)   **92**
Norman Rockwell (4 and up)   **92**
Robert Louis Stevenson, teller of tales (5 and up)   **92**

The **Ghost** and the watermelon
In Raw Head, bloody bones p34-36   **398.2**

The **ghost** belonged to me. Peck, R.   **Fic**

Ghost dance
See/See also pages in the following book(s):
Ehrlich, A. Wounded Knee: an Indian history of the American West (6 and up)   **970.004**

The **ghost-eye** tree. Martin, B.   **E**

The **ghost** in Room 11. Wright, B. R.   **Fic**

Ghost in the house. Cohen, D.   **133.1**

The **ghost** in the mirror. Bellairs, J. See note under Bellairs, J. The house with a clock in its walls   **Fic**

Ghost liners. Ballard, R. D.   **910.4**

A **ghost** named Fred. Benchley, N.   **E**

The **ghost** of Eddy Longo. Wynne-Jones, T.
In Wynne-Jones, T. The book of changes p83-108   **S C**

The **ghost** of Fossil Glen. DeFelice, C. C.   **Fic**

The **ghost** of Jean Lafitte. Schmidt, S.
In From sea to shining sea p320-21   **810.8**

The **ghost** of Misery Hill. San Souci, R.
In San Souci, R. Short & shivery p139-43   **398.2**

The **ghost** of Nicholas Greebe. Johnston, T.   **E**

The **ghost** on Saturday night. Fleischman, S.   **Fic**

Ghost poems (1-4)   **821.008**

The **ghost** society. Bruchac, J.
In Bruchac, J. Flying with the eagle, racing with the great bear p83-90   **398.2**

Ghost stories
Allard, H. Bumps in the night   **E**
Almond, D. Kit's wilderness (5 and up)   **Fic**
Avi. Something upstairs (5 and up)   **Fic**
Benchley, N. A ghost named Fred   **E**
Cassedy, S. Behind the attic wall (5 and up)   **Fic**
Conrad, P. Stonewords (5 and up)   **Fic**
DeFelice, C. C. The ghost of Fossil Glen (4-6)   **Fic**
Diane Goode's book of scary stories & songs (2-5)   **398.2**
Dickens, C. A Christmas carol (4 and up)   **Fic**
Don't read this! and other tales of the unnatural (6 and up)   **S C**

Ghost stories—*Continued*

Fleischman, S. The ghost on Saturday night (3-5)   **Fic**

Fleischman, S. The midnight horse (3-6)   **Fic**

Galdone, P. The teeny-tiny woman (k-2)   **398.2**

Guiberson, B. Z. Tales of the haunted deep (4 and up)   **001.9**

Hahn, M. D. The doll in the garden (4-6)   **Fic**

Hahn, M. D. Time for Andrew (5 and up)   **Fic**

Hahn, M. D. Wait till Helen comes (4-6)   **Fic**

Johnston, T. The ghost of Nicholas Greebe   **E**

Kimmel, E. C. In the stone circle (5 and up)   **Fic**

Martin, B. The ghost-eye tree   **E**

McKissack, P. C. The dark-thirty (4 and up)   **S C**

Medearis, A. S. Haunts (4 and up)   **S C**

Peck, R. The ghost belonged to me (5 and up)   **Fic**

San Souci, R. Even more short & shivery (4 and up)   **398.2**

San Souci, R. More short & shivery (4 and up)   **398.2**

San Souci, R. Short & shivery (4 and up)   **398.2**

San Souci, R. A terrifying taste of short & shivery (4 and up)   **398.2**

Schnur, S. The shadow children (5 and up)   **Fic**

Schwartz, A. Ghosts! (k-2)   **398.2**

Schwartz, A. In a dark, dark room, and other scary stories (k-2)   **398.2**

Schwartz, A. More scary stories to tell in the dark (4 and up)   **398.2**

Schwartz, A. Scary stories 3 (4 and up)   **398.2**

Schwartz, A. Scary stories to tell in the dark (4 and up)   **398.2**

Vande Velde, V. There's a dead person following my sister around (4 and up)   **Fic**

Wright, B. R. The ghost in Room 11 (3-5)   **Fic**

Wright, B. R. The ghosts of Mercy Manor (4 and up)   **Fic**

Wright, B. R. The moonlight man (5 and up)   **Fic**

Ghost story. Cooper, S.

In Don't read this! and other tales of the unnatural p33-50   **S C**

A **ghost** story. Lester, J.

In Lester, J. The last tales of Uncle Remus p33-36   **398.2**

The **ghostly** little girl. San Souci, R.

In San Souci, R. Short & shivery p48-52   **398.2**

The **ghostly** weaver. Hausman, G.

In Hausman, G. Dogs of myth p33-38   **398.2**

Ghosts

Cohen, D. Ghost in the house (4 and up)   **133.1**

Cohen, D. Great ghosts (4 and up)   **133.1**

Poetry

Ghost poems (1-4)   **821.008**

Ghosts!. Schwartz, A.   **398.2**

The **ghost's** cap. San Souci, R.

In San Souci, R. Short & shivery p22-27   **398.2**

Ghost's hour, spook's hour. Bunting, E.   **E**

Ghosts I have been. Peck, R. See note under Peck, R. The ghost belonged to me   **Fic**

Ghosts in the castle. (3-6) See entry in Part 2: Web Resources

Ghosts in the gallery. Wallace, B. B.   **Fic**

The **ghosts** of Mercy Manor. Wright, B. R.   **Fic**

Giacobbe, Beppe

(il) Fleischman, P. Big talk   **811**

The **giant** jam sandwich. Lord, J. V.   **E**

The **giant** of Castle Treen. Climo, S.

In Climo, S. Magic & mischief p3-10   **398.2**

The **giant** Og and the ark. Schwartz, H.

In Schwartz, H. The diamond tree p13-20   **398.2**

Giant panda

Fiction

Wild, M. Tom goes to kindergarten   **E**

The **giant** who threw tantrums. Harrison, D. L.

In The Oxford treasury of children's stories p28-32   **S C**

Giants

See also Cyclopes (Greek mythology)

Fiction

Byrd, R. Finn MacCoul and his fearless wife (k-3)   **398.2**

Dahl, R. The BFG (4-6)   **Fic**

Kellogg, S. Jack and the beanstalk (k-3)   **398.2**

Osborne, M. P. Kate and the beanstalk (k-3)   **398.2**

Waters, F. Oscar Wilde's The selfish giant (2-5)   **Fic**

Wilde, O. The selfish giant (2-5)   **Fic**

The **Giants** and the herd-boy

In The Yellow fairy book p75-77   **398.2**

Giants in the land. Appelbaum, D. K.   **634.9**

Gib Morgan brings in the well. Walker, P. R.

In Walker, P. R. Big men, big country p62-68   **398.2**

Gibbons, Faye, 1938-

Mama and me and the Model-T   **E**

Mountain wedding   **E**

Gibbons, Gail

Apples (k-3)   **634**

The art box (k-1)   **702.8**

Bats (k-3)   **599.4**

Beacons of light: lighthouses (k-3)   **387.1**

Behold . . . the dragons! (k-3)   **398**

Bicycle book (k-3)   **629.227**

Boat book (k-3)   **387.2**

Gibbons, Gail—*Continued*

Cats (k-3)	636.8
Click! (k-3)	771
Deserts (k-3)	577.5
Dogs (k-3)	636.7
Easter (k-3)	394.26
Emergency! (k-3)	363.34
Exploring the deep, dark sea (k-3)	551.46
Fire! Fire! (k-3)	628.9
Frogs (k-3)	597.8
From seed to plant (k-3)	580
The great St. Lawrence Seaway (k-3)	386
Gulls—gulls—gulls (k-3)	598
Halloween (k-3)	394.26
Happy birthday! (k-3)	394.2
The honey makers (k-3)	595.7
How a house is built (k-3)	690
Knights in shining armor (k-3)	394
Marshes & swamps (k-3)	577.6
The milk makers (k-3)	637
Monarch butterfly (k-3)	595.7
The moon book (k-3)	523.3
My baseball book (k-2)	796.357
My basketball book (k-2)	796.323
My football book (k-2)	796.332
My soccer book (k-2)	796.334
Nature's green umbrella (k-3)	577.3
Penguins! (k-3)	598
Pigs (k-3)	636.4
Planet earth/inside out (k-3)	550
The planets (k-3)	523.4
Playgrounds (k-3)	796
The puffins are back! (k-3)	598
The pumpkin book (k-3)	635
Rabbits, rabbits, & more rabbits! (k-3)	599.3
The reasons for seasons (k-3)	525
Recycle! (k-3)	363.7
Sea turtles (k-3)	597.9
The seasons of Arnold's apple tree	E
Sharks (k-3)	597
Soaring with the wind (k-3)	598
St. Patrick's Day (k-3)	394.26
Sun up, sun down (k-3)	523.7
Sunken treasure (k-3)	910.4
Thanksgiving Day (k-3)	394.26
Valentine's Day (k-3)	394.26
Weather forecasting (k-3)	551.63
Weather words and what they mean (k-3)	551.6
Wolves (k-3)	599.77

Gibbs, Mifflin Wistar, 1823-1915
About

Stanley, J. Hurry freedom (5 and up)   979.4

Giblin, James, 1933-

The amazing life of Benjamin Franklin (4-6)   92

The dwarf, the giant, and the unicorn (3-5)   398.2

Fireworks, picnics, and flags (3-6)   394.26

The mystery of the mammoth bones (4 and up)   569

The riddle of the Rosetta Stone (5 and up)   493

Thomas Jefferson (2-4)   92

Gibson, Josh, 1911-1947
See/See also pages in the following book(s):

Brashler, W. The story of Negro league baseball p95-109 (5 and up)   796.357

Giff, Patricia Reilly

Good luck, Ronald Morgan. See note under Giff, P. R. Watch out, Ronald Morgan!   E

Happy birthday, Ronald Morgan! See note under Giff, P. R. Watch out, Ronald Morgan!   E

Kidnap at the Catfish Cafe (3-5)   Fic

Lily's crossing (4 and up)   Fic

Mary Moon is missing. See note under Giff, P. R. Kidnap at the Catfish Cafe   Fic

Ronald Morgan goes to bat. See note under Giff, P. R. Watch out, Ronald Morgan!   E

Ronald Morgan goes to camp. See note under Giff, P. R. Watchout, Ronald Morgan!   E

Today was a terrible day. See note under Giff, P. R. Watchout, Ronald Morgan!   E

Watch out, Ronald Morgan!   E

A **gift** for Mama. Hautzig, E. R.   Fic

The **gift** of fire. Hausman, G.
In Hausman, G. Dogs of myth p3-8   398.2

The **gift** of the Magi. Henry, O.   Fic

The **gift** of the sacred dog. Goble, P.   398.2
also in Goble, P. Paul Goble gallery   398.2

Gifts
Fiction

Best, C. Three cheers for Catherine the Great   E

Bunting, E. The Mother's Day mice   E

Goode, D. Mama's perfect present   E

Hall, D. Lucy's Christmas   E

Hautzig, E. R. A gift for Mama (3-6)   Fic

Helldorfer, M. C. Hog music   E

Paterson, K. Marvin's best Christmas present ever   E

Skolsky, M. W. Hannah and the whistling tea kettle   E

Giganti, Paul, Jr.

Each orange had 8 slices   E

How many snails?   E

Gila monsters meet you at the airport. Sharmat, M. W.   E

Gilbert, W. S. (William Schwenck), 1836-1911
See/See also pages in the following book(s):

Krull, K. Lives of the musicians p58-61 (4 and up)   920

Gilbert, William Schwenck *See* Gilbert, W. S. (William Schwenck), 1836-1911

Gilberto and the Wind. Ets, M. H.   E

Gilchrist, Jan Spivey
(il) Greenfield, E. Angels   811
(il) Greenfield, E. Easter parade   Fic

Gill, Margery, 1925-
(il) Cooper, S. Dawn of fear   Fic
(il) Cooper, S. Over sea, under stone   Fic

Gillen, Patricia Bellan- *See* Bellan-Gillen, Patricia

Gillespie, Jessie
  (il) Wiggin, K. D. S. The Bird's Christmas Carol   **Fic**

Gillespie, John Thomas, 1928-
  Guides to collection development for children and young adults   **011.6**
  Juniorplots 4   **028.5**
  Middleplots 4   **028.5**
  The Newbery companion   **028.5**
  (ed) Best books for children. See Best books for children   **011.6**

Gillies, Judi
  The Kids Can Press jumbo cookbook (4 and up)   **641.5**

Gilliland, Judith Heide
  Steamboat!: the story of Captain Blanche Leathers (2-4)   **92**
  (jt. auth) Heide, F. P. The day of Ahmed's secret   **E**
  (jt. auth) Heide, F. P. Sami and the time of the troubles   **E**

Gilson, Jamie, 1933-
  4B goes wild (4-6)   **Fic**
  Bug in a rug (2-4)   **Fic**
  Do bananas chew gum? (4-6)   **Fic**
  Double dog dare. See note under Gilson, J. 4B goes wild   **Fic**
  Hello, my name is Scrambled Eggs (4 and up)   **Fic**
  Hobie Hanson, you're weird. See note under Gilson, J. 4B goes wild   **Fic**
  Thirteen ways to sink a sub. See note under Gilson, J. 4B goes wild   **Fic**

Ginger. Voake, C.   **E**

Ginger Pye. Estes, E.   **Fic**

Gingerbread baby. Brett, J.   **398.2**

The **gingerbread** baby. McCaughrean, G.
  In McCaughrean, G. The bronze cauldron: myths and legends of the world p41-44   **398.2**

The **gingerbread** boy. Egielski, R.   **398.2**

The **gingerbread** boy. Galdone, P.   **398.2**

Gingerbread days. Thomas, J. C.   **811**

The **Gingerbread** man
  In The Read-aloud treasury p135-43   **808.8**

The **Gingerbread** man. Aylesworth, J.   **398.2**

The **gingerbread** man. Kimmel, E. A.   **398.2**

The **gingerbread** man. Sierra, J.
  In Sierra, J. Nursery tales around the world p3-9   **398.2**

The **gingi**. McKissack, P. C.
  In McKissack, P. C. The dark-thirty p95-110   **S C**

Ginsburg, Max
  (il) Taylor, M. D. The friendship   **Fic**
  (il) Taylor, M. D. Mississippi bridge   **Fic**

Ginsburg, Mirra
  The chick and the duckling   **E**
  The Chinese mirror (k-3)   **398.2**
  Clay boy (k-3)   **398.2**
  Good morning, chick   **E**

Ginzberg, Louis, 1873-1953
  Legends of the Bible. See Chaikin, M. Clouds of glory   **296.1**

Giovanni, Nikki
  Ego-tripping and other poems for young people (5 and up)   **811**
  Spin a soft black song: poems for children (3-6)   **811**
  The sun is so quiet (k-3)   **811**
  See/See also pages in the following book(s):
  Wilkinson, B. S. African American women writers (4 and up)   **810.9**

Gipsies *See* Gypsies

Gipson, Frederick Benjamin, 1903-1973
  Old Yeller (6 and up)   **Fic**

The **girl** and the Chenoo. Bruchac, J.
  In Bruchac, J. The girl who married the Moon p29-36   **398.2**

The **girl** and the puma. Yolen, J.
  In Yolen, J. Not one damsel in distress p27-32   **398.2**

A **girl** called Al. Greene, C. C.   **Fic**

A **girl** named Disaster. Farmer, N.   **Fic**

The **girl** who dreamed only geese. Norman, H.
  In Norman, H. The girl who dreamed only geese, and other tales of the Far North   **398.2**

The **girl** who dreamed only geese, and other tales of the Far North. Norman, H.   **398.2**

The **girl** who escaped. Bruchac, J.
  In Bruchac, J. The girl who married the Moon p37-43   **398.2**

The **girl** who gave birth to Water-Jar Boy. Bruchac, J.
  In Bruchac, J. The girl who married the Moon p69-74   **398.2**

The **girl** who helped Thunder. Bruchac, J.
  In Bruchac, J. The girl who married the Moon p51-54   **398.2**

The **Girl** Who Loved Caterpillars. Merrill, J.   **E**

The **girl** who loved wild horses. Goble, P.   **398.2**
  also in Goble, P. Paul Goble gallery   **398.2**

The **girl** who married an Osage. Bruchac, J.
  In Bruchac, J. The girl who married the Moon p55-57   **398.2**

The **girl** who married the Moon. Bruchac, J.   **398.2**

The **girl** who married the Moon [story] Bruchac, J.
  In Bruchac, J. The girl who married the Moon p116-22   **398.2**

The **girl** who spun gold. Hamilton, V.   **398.2**

The **girl** who watched in the nighttime. Norman, H.
  In Norman, H. The girl who dreamed only geese, and other tales of the Far North   **398.2**

The **girl** who waters basil and the very inquisitive prince. García Lorca, F.
  In You're on!: seven plays in English and Spanish p62-83   **812.008**

The **girl** who wore too much. MacDonald, M. R.
398.2

The **girl** with the silver eyes. Roberts, W. D.
Fic

Girls
Colman, P. Girls! (5 and up) **305.23**
Jukes, M. Growing up: it's a girl thing (4 and up) **612.6**
Jukes, M. It's a girl thing (5 and up)
305.23
Rand, D. Black Books Galore!—guide to great African American children's books about girls
016.3058

Books and reading
Bauermeister, E. Let's hear it for the girls
028.1
Odean, K. Great books for girls **028.1**

Employment
See Child labor

Poetry
Dreams of glory (3-5) **811.008**
Nash, O. The adventures of Isabel (k-3)
811

Girls, Teenage *See* Teenagers

Girls!. Colman, P. **305.23**

The **girls**. Koss, A. G. **Fic**

Girls think of everything. Thimmesh, C. **920**

The **girls** who almost married an owl. Bruchac, J.
In Bruchac, J. The girl who married the Moon p58-61 **398.2**

Girouard, Patrick
(il) Caffey, D. Yikes-lice! **616.5**

GIs *See* Soldiers—United States

Giselle (Ballet)
See/See also pages in the following book(s):
McCaughrean, G. The Random House book of stories from the ballet p29-35 (4 and up)
792.8
Newman, B. The illustrated book of ballet stories p22-31 (4-6) **792.8**

Give me a crab, John. Philip, N.
In Philip, N. Celtic fairy tales p66 **398.2**

Give me a sign!. Samoyault, T. **302.2**

The **giver**. Lowry, L. **Fic**

Giving thanks. Swamp, J. **299**

The **Gizzard**
In The Magic orange tree, and other Haitian folktales p99-112 **398.2**

Glaciers
Simon, S. Icebergs and glaciers (3-5) **551.3**

Gladiators
Watkins, R. R. Gladiator (4 and up) **937**

Glanzman, Louis S., 1922-
(il) Lindgren, A. Pippi Longstocking **Fic**

Glaser, Isabel Joshlin, 1929-
(comp) Dreams of glory. See Dreams of glory
811.008

Glaser, Linda
Compost! (k-2) **363.7**

Glass, Andrew
Folks call me Appleseed John **E**
(il) Fleischman, P. Graven images **S C**

(il) Kimmel, E. A. Grizz! **E**
(il) Mollel, T. M. Ananse's feast **398.2**

The **glass** dog. Baum, L. F.
In American fairy tales p105-15 **S C**

Glass manufacture
Fisher, L. E. The glassmakers (4 and up)
666

The **Glass** mountain
In The Yellow fairy book p114-18 **398.2**

Glasser, Robin Preiss
(il) Weitzman, J. P. You can't take a balloon into the Metropolitan Museum **E**
(il) Weitzman, J. P. You can't take a balloon into the National Gallery **E**

Glasses: who needs 'em? Smith, L. **E**

The **glassmakers**. Fisher, L. E. **666**

Gleeson, Brian
Ride 'em, round 'em, rope 'em: the story of Pecos Bill
In From sea to shining sea p286-88
810.8

Glenn, John, 1921-
About
Bredeson, C. John Glenn returns to orbit (4 and up) **629.4**

Gliori, Debi
Mr. Bear says "Are you there, Baby Bear?". See note under Gliori, D. Mr. Bear's new baby
E
Mr. Bear to the rescue. See note under Gliori, D. Mr. Bear's new baby **E**
Mr. Bear's new baby **E**
Mr. Bear's vacation. See note under Gliori, D. Mr. Bear's new baby **E**
No matter what **E**

Globe Theatre (London, England)
See also Shakespeare's Globe (London, England);
Aliki. William Shakespeare & the Globe (3-6)
792.09

Glooskap's farewell gifts. Curry, J. L.
In Curry, J. L. Turtle Island: tales of the Algonquian nations p120-26 **398.2**

Gloria. Wynne-Jones, T.
In Wynne-Jones, T. The book of changes p134-43 **S C**

Gloria's way. Cameron, A. **Fic**

The **glorious** flight: across the Channel with Louis Blériot, July 25, 1909. Provensen, A. **92**

The **Glorious** Mother Goose **398.8**

A **Glory** of unicorns (5 and up) **S C**

Glossaries *See* Encyclopedias and dictionaries

Glosskap and Wasis. Garner, A.
In From sea to shining sea p210-11
810.8

Glossop, Jennifer
(jt. auth) Gillies, J. The Kids Can Press jumbo cookbook **641.5**

Glover, Savion
Savion!: my life in tap (5 and up) **92**

Gluskabe and Old Man Winter. Bruchac, J.
In Bruchac, J. Pushing up the sky: seven native American plays for children p11-23
812

Gluskabe and the four wishes. Bruchac, J.
398.2

Go away, big green monster!. Emberley, E.
E

Go away, dog. Lexau, J. M. **E**

Go fish. Stolz, M. **Fic**

Go free or die: a story about Harriet Tubman. Ferris, J. **92**

Go hang a salami! I'm a lasagna hog! and other palindromes. Agee, J. **793.73**

Go home!. Meggs, L. P. **E**

Go I know not whither, bring back I know not what. Afanas'ev, A. N.
In Afanas'ev, A. N. Russian fairy tales p504-20 **398.2**

Go in and out the window **782.42**

The goat in the rug. Blood, C. L. **E**

The goat shedding on one side. Afanas'ev, A. N.
In Afanas'ev, A. N. Russian fairy tales p312-13 **398.2**

Goats

Fiction
Blood, C. L. The goat in the rug **E**
Emberley, R. Three cool kids (k-3) **398.2**
Galdone, P. The three Billy Goats Gruff (k-2) **398.2**
Rounds, G. Three billy goats Gruff (k-3) **398.2**
Sharmat, M. Gregory, the terrible eater **E**
Gobborn Seer. Jacobs, J.
In Jacobs, J. English fairy tales p275-78 **398.2**

Goble, Paul
Adopted by the eagles (2-4) **398.2**
Beyond the ridge (2-4) **Fic**
Buffalo woman (2-4) **398.2**
Crow chief (2-4) **398.2**
Death of the iron horse **E**
also in From sea to shining sea p160-63 **810.8**
Dream wolf **E**
The gift of the sacred dog (2-4) **398.2**
also in Goble, P. Paul Goble gallery **398.2**
The girl who loved wild horses (k-3) **398.2**
also in Goble, P. Paul Goble gallery **398.2**
The great race of the birds and animals (2-4) **398.2**
Hau kola: hello friend (1-3) **92**
Her seven brothers (2-4) **398.2**
also in Goble, P. Paul Goble gallery **398.2**
I sing for the animals **242**
Iktomi and the berries. See note under Goble, P. Iktomi and the boulder **398.2**
Iktomi and the boulder (k-3) **398.2**
Iktomi and the buffalo skull. See note under Goble, P. Iktomi and the boulder **398.2**

Iktomi and the buzzard. See note under Goble, P. Iktomi and the boulder **398.2**
Iktomi and the coyote. See note under Goble, P. Iktomi and the boulder **398.2**
Iktomi loses his eyes. See note under Goble, P. Iktomi and the boulder **398.2**
The legend of the White Buffalo Woman (3-5) **398.2**
Love flute (2-4) **398.2**
Paul Goble gallery (2-4) **398.2**
Remaking the earth (2-4) **398.2**
Star Boy (2-4) **398.2**
See/See also pages in the following book(s):
Newbery and Caldecott Medal books, 1976-1985 p205-09 **028.5**

The goblin. Schwartz, H.
In Schwartz, H. The diamond tree p97-99 **398.2**

The goblin at the grocer's. Andersen, H. C.
In Andersen, H. C. The little mermaid and other fairy tales p99-103 **S C**

The goblin spider. San Souci, R.
In San Souci, R. Short & shivery p160-65 **398.2**

The Goblins at the bathhouse
In Diane Goode's book of scary stories & songs p54-61 **398.2**

God
Fitch, F. M. A book about God (k-3) **231**
Paterson, J. B. Images of God (5 and up) **231**

Fiction
Lester, J. What a truly cool world! **E**
God battles the Queen of the Waters. Lester, J.
In Lester, J. When the beginning began p7-10 **296.1**
God confronts Adam, the Woman, and the Snake. Lester, J.
In Lester, J. When the beginning began p87-92 **296.1**
God creates Adam. Lester, J.
In Lester, J. When the beginning began p59-63 **296.1**
God creates Woman. Lester, J.
In Lester, J. When the beginning began p64-68 **296.1**
God learns how to create. Lester, J.
In Lester, J. When the beginning began p1-5 **296.1**
God makes people. Lester, J.
In Lester, J. When the beginning began p49-57 **296.1**
God moves away. McCaughrean, G.
In McCaughrean, G. The silver treasure: myths and legends of the world p57-59 **398.2**
God returns to Heaven. Lester, J.
In Lester, J. When the beginning began p93-95 **296.1**
God that lived in the kitchen. Carpenter, F.
In Carpenter, F. Tales of a Chinese grandmother p39-46 **398.2**

Godard, Alex
Mama, across the sea **E**

Goddard, Robert Hutchings, 1882-1945
About
Streissguth, T. Rocket man: the story of Robert Goddard (4 and up)   **92**
Godden, Rumer, 1907-1998
The doll's house (2-4)   **Fic**
The **goddess** and the buffalo demon. Krishnaswami, U.
  In Krishnaswami, U. Shower of gold: girls and women in the stories of India p41-46
    398.2

The **goddess** and the girl. Krishnaswami, U.
  In Krishnaswami, U. Shower of gold: girls and women in the stories of India p11-15
    398.2

Goddesses *See* Gods and goddesses
Godfrey, Neale S.
Neale S. Godfrey's ultimate kids' money book (5 and up)   **332.024**
Godkin, Celia, 1948-
What about ladybugs? (k-3)   **595.7**
Gods and goddesses
  See also Religions; names of individual gods and goddesses
See/See also pages in the following book(s):
Hamilton, E. Mythology [21-76] (6 and up)
    292

The **gods** and goddesses of ancient Egypt. Fisher, L. E.   **299**
The **gods** and goddesses of Olympus. Aliki
    292

Gods and goddesses of the ancient Maya. Fisher, L. E.   **299**
The **gods** down tools. McCaughrean, G.
  In McCaughrean, G. The crystal pool: myths and legends of the world p18-23
    398.2

God's kingdom. McCaughrean, G.   **225.9**
God's people. McCaughrean, G.   **221.9**
Godwin, Laura
Barnyard prayers (k-2)   **811**
Little white dog   **E**
(jt. auth) Martin, A. M. The doll people
    Fic

Goembel, Ponder
(il) Walter, V. A. "Hi, pizza man!"   **E**
Goggles. Keats, E. J. See note under Keats, E. J. The snowy day   **E**
Going home. Mohr, N.   **Fic**
Going to Cervières. MacDonald, M. R.
  In MacDonald, M. R. Celebrate the world p202-09   **372.6**
Going to school in 1776. Loeper, J. J.   **370.9**
Going to the doctor. Brazelton, T. B.   **610.69**
Going to the hospital. Rogers, F.   **362.1**
Going West. Van Leeuwen, J.   **E**
Gol' in the chimley
  In From sea to shining sea p95-97   **810.8**
Gold, Alison Leslie
Memories of Anne Frank (5 and up)   **92**
A special fate (5 and up)   **940.53**
Gold, Susan Dudley
Alzheimer's disease (4 and up)   **616.8**

Gold
Angliss, S. Gold
  In The Elements [Benchmark Bks.]   **546**
The **gold** Cadillac. Taylor, M. D.   **Fic**
Gold fever. Kay, V.   **E**
The **Gold** in the chimney
  In Stockings of buttermilk: American folktales p73-77   **398.2**
Gold mines and mining
  See also Klondike River valley (Yukon)—Gold discoveries
Fiction
Coerr, E. Chang's paper pony   **E**
Gold rush *See* California—Gold discoveries
The **gold** rush. Murrow, L. K.   **979.4**
Goldberg, Jake
Hawaii
  In Celebrate the states   **973**
Golden, Diana
See/See also pages in the following book(s):
Littlefield, B. Champions p105-16 (5 and up)
    920

The **golden** arm. Jacobs, J.
  In Jacobs, J. English fairy tales p138-39
    398.2

The **golden** arm. San Souci, R.
  In San Souci, R. More short & shivery p103-08   **398.2**
The **golden** ball. Jacobs, J.
  In Jacobs, J. English fairy tales p234-37
    398.2

Golden Bear. Young, R.   **E**
The **Golden** Blackbird. Sébillot, P.
  In The Green fairy book p151-56   **398.2**
The **golden** bracelet. Kherdian, D.   **398.2**
The **golden-bristled** pig, the golden-feathered duck, and the golden-maned mare. Afanas'ev, A. N.
  In Afanas'ev, A. N. Russian fairy tales p533-41   **398.2**
The **Golden** crab
  In The Yellow fairy book p26-31   **398.2**
Golden Fleece (Greek mythology) *See* Argonauts (Greek mythology)
The **Golden** Fleece and the heroes who lived before Achilles. Colum, P.   **292**
The **golden** goose. Shulevitz, U.   **398.2**
The **golden** hoard: myths and legends of the world. McCaughrean, G.   **398.2**
The **golden** lads. Grimm, J.
  In The Green fairy book p311-18   **398.2**
The **golden** mermaid. Grimm, J.
  In The Green fairy book p328-38   **398.2**
The **golden** sandal. Hickox, R.   **398.2**
The **golden** slipper. Afanas'ev, A. N.
  In Afanas'ev, A. N. Russian fairy tales p44-46   **398.2**
Golden tales. Delacre, L.   **398.2**
The **Golden** Vanity. McCaughrean, G.
  In McCaughrean, G. The bronze cauldron: myths and legends of the world p68-70
    398.2

The **golden** windows. Richards, L. E. H.
  In American fairy tales p116-19   **S C**

The **golden** wish. McCaughrean, G.
  In McCaughrean, G. The golden hoard: myths
  and legends of the world p1-6
                  398.2

Goldfish
  See/See also pages in the following book(s):
  Pfeffer, W. What's it like to be a fish? (k-1)
                  597

The **goldfish**. Afanas'ev, A. N.
  In Afanas'ev, A. N. Russian fairy tales p528-
  32   **398.2**

Goldilocks and the three bears
  In The Read-aloud treasury p214-24
                808.8

Goldilocks and the three bears. Marshall, J.
                398.2

Goldilocks returns. Ernst, L. C.   **E**

Goldin, Augusta R.
  Ducks don't get wet (k-3)   **598**

Goldin, Barbara Diamond
  Coyote and the firestick (3-5)   **398.2**
  Journeys with Elijah (4 and up)   **222**
  Contents: A journey with Elijah; Seven good years; A disor-
derly table; The weaver of Yzad; Elijah and the three brothers;
The fragrance of paradise; The blessing; Meeting Elijah
  The Passover journey (4 and up)   **296.4**
  While the candles burn (4 and up)   **296.4**
  The world's birthday   **E**

Golding, Kim
  Counting kids   **E**

Goldsmith, Diane Hoyt- *See* Hoyt-Goldsmith,
  Diane

Goldstein, Bobbye S.
  (il) Birthday rhymes, special times. See Birthday
  rhymes, special times   **811.008**

The **golem**. McCaughrean, G.
  In McCaughrean, G. The bronze cauldron:
  myths and legends of the world p109-12
                398.2

The **golem**. Rogasky, B.   **398.2**

The **golem**. San Souci, R.
  In San Souci, R. Short & shivery p149-54
                398.2

Golem. Wisniewski, D.   **398.2**

Golembe, Carla
  (il) Gerson, M.-J. Why the sky is far away
                398.2

Golenbock, Peter, 1946-
  Teammates [biography of Jackie Robinson]
  (1-4)   **92**

Golf
  Krause, P. Fundamental golf (5 and up)
                796.352
  Simmons, R. Golf (4 and up)   **796.352**
        Fiction
  Miller, W. Night golf   **E**

Goliath (Biblical figure)
        About
  De Regniers, B. S. David and Goliath   **222**
  Fisher, L. E. David and Goliath (k-3)   **222**

Gollub, Matthew, 1960-
  Cool melons—turn to frogs!: the life and poems
  of Issa [Kobayashi] (3-6)   **92**

The **Golly** sisters go West. Byars, B. C.   **E**

The **Golly** sisters ride again. Byars, B. C. See note
  under Byars, B. C. The Golly sisters go West
                E

Gómez, Elizabeth
  (il) Herrera, J. F. The upside down boy   **92**

Gone-Away Lake. Enright, E.   **Fic**

Gone forever!. Markle, S.   **591.68**

Gonna sing my head off!   **782.42**

Gonzales, Edward, 1947-
  (il) Anaya, R. A. Farolitos for Abuelo   **E**
  (il) Anaya, R. A. The farolitos of Christmas
                E

Gonzalez, Christina
  (il) Alarcón, F. X. Laughing tomatoes and other
  spring poems   **811**

González, Lucía M., 1957-
  El gallo de bodas: the rooster on the way to the
  wedding
  In From sea to shining sea p364-65
                810.8
  Juan Bobo and the buñuelos
  In From sea to shining sea p240-41
                810.8
  Señor Cat's romance and other favorite stories
  from Latin America (2-4)   **398.2**
  Contents: The little half-chick; Juan Bobo and the three-legged
pot; Martina, the little cockroach; The billy goat and the vegeta-
ble garden; How Uncle Rabbit tricked Uncle Tiger; Señor Cat's
romance

Gonzalez, Maya Christina, 1964-
  (il) Alarcón, F. X. From the bellybutton of the
  moon and other summer poems   **811**
  (il) Pérez, A. I. My very own room   **E**
  See/See also pages in the following book(s):
  Just like me p8-9   **920**

Gooch, Randall
  (il) Temko, F. Traditional crafts from Africa
                745.5
  (il) Temko, F. Traditional crafts from Mexico
  and Central America   **745.5**
  (il) Temko, F. Traditional crafts from native
  North America   **745.5**

Good advice. Afanas'ev, A. N.
  In Afanas'ev, A. N. Russian fairy tales p289-
  91   **398.2**

Good and evil
        Fiction
  Cooper, S. The grey king (5 and up)   **Fic**
  Cooper, S. Over sea, under stone (5 and up)
                Fic

Good Blanche, bad Rose, and the talking eggs.
  Hamilton, V.
  In Hamilton, V. Her stories p28-32
                398.2

Good books, good times! (1-3)   **811.008**

Good driving, Amelia Bedelia. Parish, H. See note
  under Parish, P. Amelia Bedelia   **E**

Good enough to eat. Rockwell, L.   **613.2**

The **Good** Housekeeping illustrated children's
  cookbook (4-6)   **641.5**

Good job, Little Bear. Waddell, M. See note under Waddell, M. Can't you sleep, Little Bear? **E**

The **good** liar. Maguire, G. **Fic**

Good luck, Mrs. K!. Borden, L. **E**

Good luck, Ronald Morgan. Giff, P. R. See note under Giff, P. R. Watch out, Ronald Morgan! **E**

The **Good** Master. Seredy, K. **Fic**

Good morning, chick. Ginsburg, M. **E**

Good night Baby Bear. Asch, F. See note under Asch, F. Moonbear's dream **E**

Good night, Good Knight. Thomas, S. M. **E**

Good night, Gorilla. Rathmann, P. **E**

Good night, Maman. Mazer, N. F. **Fic**

Good night, Mr. Tom. Magorian, M. **Fic**

Good-night, Owl!. Hutchins, P. **E**

Good rhymes, good times. Hopkins, L. B. **811**

The **good,** the bad, and the goofy. Scieszka, J. See note under Scieszka, J. Knights of the kitchen table **Fic**

Good work, Amelia Bedelia. Parish, P. See note under Parish, P. Amelia Bedelia **E**

Goodall, Jane, 1934-
My life with the chimpanzees (3-6) **92**
With love (4 and up) **599.8**
About
Goodall, J. My life with the chimpanzees (3-6) **92**

See/See also pages in the following book(s):
Talking with adventurers p44-51 (4-6) **920**

Goodall, John S., 1908-1996
Creepy castle **E**
Shrewbettina's birthday **E**
The surprise picnic **E**

Goodbye house. Asch, F. See note under Asch, F. Moonbear's dream **E**

Goodbye, Vietnam. Whelan, G. **Fic**

Goodbye, Walter Malinski. Recorvits, H. **Fic**

Goode, Diane
Mama's perfect present **E**
(il) Alexander, L. The House Gobbaleen **E**
(il) Diane Goode's book of scary stories & songs. See Diane Goode's book of scary stories & songs **398.2**
(il) Levinson, R. Watch the stars come out **E**
(il) Rylant, C. When I was young in the mountains **E**

Goode, J. Paul, 1862-1932
Goode's world atlas. See Goode's world atlas **912**

Goodell, Jon
(il) King-Smith, D. A mouse called Wolf **Fic**

Goode's school atlas. See Goode's world atlas **912**

Goode's world atlas **912**

Goodman, Joan E., 1950-
Hope's crossing (5 and up) **Fic**

Goodman, Susan, 1952-
Animal rescue (2-4) **639.9**

Stones, bones, and petroglyphs (4 and up) **930.1**

Ultimate field trip 4: a week in the 1800s (5 and up) **973.5**

The **goodness** of Matt Kaizer. Avi
In Avi. What do fish have to do with anything? and other stories p35-59 **S C**

Goodnight Max. Wells, R. See note under Wells, R. Max's first word **E**

Goodnight moon. Brown, M. W. **E**

Goose. Bang, M. **E**

The **goose** girl. Grimm, J.
In The Blue fairy book p266-73 **398.2**

The **goose's** foot. Kimmel, E. A.
In Kimmel, E. A. The adventures of Hershel of Ostropol p13-15 **398.2**

Gopher's revenge. Curry, J. L.
In Curry, J. L. Back in the beforetime p52-56 **398.2**

Gordon, John, 1925-
The hawk
In The Oxford book of scary tales p114-22 **808.8**

Gore, Leonid
(il) Del Negro, J. Lucy Dove **E**
(il) Geringer, L. The pomegranate seeds **292**
(il) Pullman, P. Clockwork **Fic**
(il) Simon, N. The story of Hanukkah **296.4**

Gore. Ellis, S.
In Ellis, S. Back of beyond **S C**

Gorey, Edward, 1925-2000
(il) Bellairs, J. The house with a clock in its walls **Fic**
(il) Ciardi, J. You read to me, I'll read to you **811**
(il) Heide, F. P. The shrinking of Treehorn **Fic**

Gorilla. Redmond, I. **599.8**

Gorilla walk. Lewin, T. **599.8**

Gorillas
Lewin, T. Gorilla walk (4 and up) **599.8**
Matthews, T. L. Light shining through the mist: a photobiography of Dian Fossey (4 and up) **92**
Patterson, F. Koko-love! (1-4) **599.8**
Fiction
Browne, A. Voices in the park **E**
Morozumi, A. One gorilla **E**

Gorman, Carol
Dork in disguise (4 and up) **Fic**

Gorman, Michael, 1941-
The concise AACR2, 1998 revision **025.3**

Gorski, Jason
(il) The Brain explorer. See The Brain explorer **793.73**

Goslar, Hannah Pick- *See* Pick-Goslar, Hannah

Goso the teacher. Aardema, V.
In Aardema, V. Misoso p63-69 **398.2**

Gospel music

See also Spirituals (Songs)

Fiction

Hopkinson, D. A band of angels   **E**

Gotami and the mustard seed. Krishnaswami, U.

In Krishnaswami, U. Shower of gold: girls and women in the stories of India p41-51   **398.2**

Gotcha!. Baxter, K. A.   **028.1**

Gothic architecture

Macaulay, D. Building the book Cathedral (4 and up)   **726**

Macaulay, D. Cathedral: the story of its construction (4 and up)   **726**

Gotta go! Gotta go!. Swope, S.   **E**

Gottesman, Jane

(ed) Play like a girl. See Play like a girl   **796**

Gough, Barry M.

(ed) Explorers. See Explorers   **920.003**

Gould, Philip, 1951-

(il) Joyce, W. The world of William Joyce scrapbook   **92**

Gouveia, Pedro Alvares de *See* Cabral, Pedro Alvares, 1460?-1526?

Gove, Doris

A water snake's year (3-5)   **597.9**

Govenar, Alan B., 1952-

Mays, O. Osceola [biography of Osceola Mays]   **92**

Grab hands and run. Temple, F.   **Fic**

Gracias, the Thanksgiving turkey. Cowley, J.   **E**

Graef, Renée

(il) Schulman, J. The nutcracker   **Fic**

Graham, Bette Nesmith, 1924-1980

See/See also pages in the following book(s):

Thimmesh, C. Girls think of everything (5 and up)   **920**

Vare, E. A. Women inventors & their discoveries p97-109 (5 and up)   **920**

Graham, Bob, 1942-

(il) Poems for the very young. See Poems for the very young   **821.008**

Graham, Ian, 1953-

Geothermal and bio-energy (4 and up)   **333.8**

Nuclear power (4-6)   **333.7**

Graham, Joan Bransfield

Flicker flash   **811**

Splish splash   **811**

Graham, Kennon *See* Harrison, David Lee, 1937-

Graham, Margaret Bloy, 1920-

(il) Zion, G. Harry the dirty dog   **E**

Graham, Mark, 1952-

(il) Ryder, J. My father's hands   **E**

Graham, Otto, 1921-

See/See also pages in the following book(s):

Sullivan, G. Quarterbacks! p51-53 (5 and up)   **920**

Grahame, Kenneth, 1859-1932

The reluctant dragon (3-5)   **Fic**

The wind in the willows (4-6)   **Fic**

Grail

Fiction

Sutcliff, R. The light beyond the forest (4 and up)   **398.2**

Gramatky, Hardie, 1907-1979

Little Toot   **E**

Grammar

See also English language—Grammar

Grammar gorillas. (3-6) See entry in Part 2: Web Resources

Grand, Carmen T. Bernier- *See* Bernier-Grand, Carmen T.

Grand Canyon (Ariz.)

Minor, W. Grand Canyon (4 and up)   **758**

Fiction

Henry, M. Brighty of the Grand Canyon (4 and up)   **Fic**

Grand Central Terminal (New York, N.Y.)

Kalman, M. Next stop, Grand Central   **E**

The **grand** escape. Naylor, P. R.   **Fic**

The **Grand** Inquisitor. Jaffe, N.

In Jaffe, N. While standing on one foot p7-10   **296.1**

The **grand** parade. Lester, J.

In Lester, J. When the beginning began p43-48   **296.1**

Grandaddy and Janetta. Griffith, H. V. See note under Griffith, H. V. Grandaddy's place   **E**

Grandaddy's place. Griffith, H. V.   **E**

Grandaddy's stars. Griffith, H. V. See note under Griffith, H. V. Grandaddy's place   **E**

Grandfather and I. Buckley, H. E.   **E**

Grandfather Bear is hungry. MacDonald, M. R.

In MacDonald, M. R. Look back and see p126-29   **372.6**

Grandfather tales (4 and up)   **398.2**

Grandfather Tang's story. Tompert, A.   **E**

Grandfather Twilight. Berger, B.   **E**

Grandfathers

Fiction

Ackerman, K. Song and dance man   **E**

Aliki. The two of them   **E**

Anaya, R. A. Farolitos for Abuelo   **E**

Anholt, C. Harry's home   **E**

Barron, T. A. Where is Grandpa?   **E**

Bowdish, L. Brooklyn, Bugsy, and me (3-5)   **Fic**

Brooks, B. Everywhere (4 and up)   **Fic**

Buckley, H. E. Grandfather and I   **E**

Bunting, E. Butterfly house   **E**

Byars, B. C. The house of wings (4-6)   **Fic**

Caseley, J. Dear Annie   **E**

Chocolate, D. The piano man   **E**

De Paola, T. Now one foot, now the other   **E**

De Paola, T. Tom   **E**

DiSalvo-Ryan, D. Grandpa's corner store   **E**

Fox, M. Sophie   **E**

Greenfield, E. Grandpa's face   **E**

Griffith, H. V. Grandaddy's place   **E**

Haas, J. Beware the mare (3-5)   **Fic**

Haas, J. Sugaring   **E**

Grandfathers—Fiction—*Continued*

Hest, A. Gabby growing up   E

Hest, A. The purple coat   E

Hunter, M. The mermaid summer (4 and up)   **Fic**

Johnson, A. When I am old with you   E

Keller, H. Grandfather's dream   E

Koertge, R. Tiger, tiger, burning bright (6 and up)   **Fic**

Levin, B. Shadow-catcher (4 and up)   **Fic**

Lewin, T. The storytellers   E

Locker, T. Where the river begins   E

MacLachlan, P. Three Names   E

Martin, B. Knots on a counting rope   E

Mills, C. Gus and Grandpa and the two-wheeled bike

Polikoff, B. G. Life's a funny proposition, Horatio (5 and up)   **Fic**

Pomerantz, C. The outside dog   E

Say, A. Grandfather's journey   E

Shetterly, S. H. Shelterwood   E

Slote, A. The trading game (4-6)   **Fic**

Smith, R. K. The war with Grandpa (4-6)   **Fic**

Spinelli, J. Crash (5 and up)   **Fic**

Stevenson, J. "Could be worse!"   E

Stolz, M. Go fish (2-4)   **Fic**

Stolz, M. Storm in the night   E

Tsubakiyama, M. Mei-Mei loves the morning   E

Wallace, B. B. Ghosts in the gallery (5 and up)   **Fic**

Walter, M. P. Justin and the best biscuits in the world (3-6)   **Fic**

Grandfather's clock. Reuter, B.

In Don't read this! and other tales of the unnatural p149-73   **S C**

Grandfather's dream. Keller, H.   E

Grandfather's journey. Say, A.   E

Grandma Chickenlegs. McCaughrean, G.   **398.2**

The **grandma** mix-up. McCully, E. A.   E

Grandma Moses *See* Moses, Grandma, 1860-1961

Grandmama's joy. Greenfield, E.   E

Grandmas at bat. McCully, E. A. See note under McCully, E. A. The grandma mix-up   E

Grandmas at the lake. McCully, E. A. See note under McCully, E. A. The grandma mix-up   E

Grandma's latkes. Drucker, M.   E

Grandmother and I. Buckley, H. E.   E

Grandmother Bryant's pocket. Martin, J. B.   E

Grandmother Spider. Mooney, J.

In From sea to shining sea p12-13   **810.8**

Grandmother Winter. Root, P.   E

Grandmothers

Fiction

Ackerman, K. By the dawn's early light   E

Babbitt, N. The eyes of the Amaryllis (5 and up)   **Fic**

Bawden, N. Granny the Pag (4 and up)   **Fic**

Best, C. Three cheers for Catherine the Great   E

Buckley, H. E. Grandmother and I   E

Bunting, E. The Wednesday surprise   E

Castañeda, O. S. Abuela's weave   E

Choi, S. N. Halmoni and the picnic   E

Clifford, E. The remembering box (3-5)   **Fic**

Daly, N. Not so fast, Songololo   E

De Paola, T. The baby sister   E

De Paola, T. Nana Upstairs & Nana Downstairs   E

Dorros, A. Abuela   E

Fleischman, P. Lost!   **Fic**

Greenfield, E. Grandmama's joy   E

Guback, G. Luka's quilt   E

Hahn, M. D. Following my own footsteps (5 and up)   **Fic**

Hamilton, V. Cousins (5 and up)   **Fic**

Henkes, K. Sun & Spoon (4 and up)   **Fic**

Hest, A. Nana's birthday party   E

Hest, A. When Jessie came across the sea   E

Hickman, J. Jericho (5 and up)   **Fic**

Johnson, D. Quinnie Blue   E

Jukes, M. Blackberries in the dark (2-4)   **Fic**

Kinsey-Warnock, N. The Canada geese quilt (3-5)   **Fic**

LaMarche, J. The raft   E

Look, L. Love as strong as ginger   E

Luenn, N. Nessa's fish   E

Lum, K. What! cried Granny   E

Mahy, M. Tingleberries, tuckertubs and telephones (3-5)   **Fic**

Martin, J. B. Grandmother Bryant's pocket   E

McCully, E. A. The grandma mix-up   E

McKay, H. The exiles (5 and up)   **Fic**

Pak, S. Dear Juno   E

Paulsen, G. Alida's song (5 and up)   **Fic**

Paulsen, G. The cookcamp (5 and up)   **Fic**

Peck, R. A long way from Chicago (5 and up)   **Fic**

Peck, R. A year down yonder (5 and up)   **Fic**

Plourde, L. Pigs in the mud in the middle of the rud   E

Polacco, P. Thunder cake   E

Reiser, L. Cherry pies and lullabies   E

Reiser, L. Tortillas and lullabies. Tortillas y cancioncitas   E

Schwartz, A. Oma and Bobo   E

Siegelson, K. L. In the time of the drums   E

Thomas, J. R. Saying good-bye to Grandma   E

Tunnell, M. O. Mailing May   E

Voigt, C. Dicey's song (6 and up)   **Fic**

Wild, M. Our granny   E

Willner-Pardo, G. Figuring out Frances (4-6)   **Fic**

Yep, L. Child of the owl (5 and up)   **Fic**

Yep, L. The cook's family (5 and up)   **Fic**

Yolen, J. Off we go!   E

Grandmother's tale. Singer, I. B.
  In Singer, I. B. Zlateh the goat, and other sto-
    ries p21-23 **398.2**
Grandpa buys a pumpkin egg. Schwartz, A.
  In Schwartz, A. There is a carrot in my ear,
    and other noodle tales p44-57 **398.2**
Grandpa misses the boat. Schwartz, A.
  In Schwartz, A. All of our noses are here,
    and other noodle tales p18-21 **398.2**
Grandparents
  See/See also pages in the following book(s):
    Bauer, C. F. Celebrations p63-80 **808.8**
              Fiction
    Bonners, S. The wooden doll **E**
    Creech, S. Walk two moons (6 and up)
              Fic
    Haas, J. Hurry! **E**
    Skolsky, M. W. Hannah and the whistling tea
      kettle **E**
Grandpa's corner store. DiSalvo-Ryan, D. **E**
Grandpa's face. Greenfield, E. **E**
Grandpré, Mary
  (il) Armstrong, J. Chin Yu Min and the ginger
    cat **E**
  (il) Rowling, J. K. Harry Potter and the sorcer-
    er's stone **Fic**
Granfield, Linda
  Circus (4 and up) **791.3**
  Cowboy: an album (5 and up) **978**
  Extra! Extra! (4-6) **071**
Grange, Red, 1903-1991
  See/See also pages in the following book(s):
    Krull, K. Lives of the athletes p25-27 (4 and
      up) **920**
Granny Squannit and the Bad Young Man.
    Bruchac, J.
  In Bruchac, J. Flying with the eagle, racing
    with the great bear p24-27 **398.2**
Granny the Pag. Bawden, N. **Fic**
The **Grannyman.** Schachner, J. B. **E**
Granström, Brita, 1969-
  (il) Hindley, J. Eyes, nose, fingers and toes
              E
Grant, Ulysses S. (Ulysses Simpson), 1822-1885
              About
  Archer, J. A house divided: the lives of Ulysses
    S. Grant and Robert E. Lee (5 and up)
              92
Grants *See* Subsidies
Grantsmanship for small libraries and school li-
    brary media centers **025.1**
The **graphic** alphabet. Pelletier, D. **E**
Graphic methods
  Markle, S. Discovering graph secrets (3-6)
              001.4
Grasshopper on the road. Lobel, A. **E**
Grasshopper summer. Turner, A. W. **Fic**
Grassland ecology
  Dunphy, M. Here is the African savanna (k-3)
              577.4
  Silver, D. M. African savanna (3-5) **577.4**
  Stille, D. R. Grasslands (2-4) **577.4**
Grasslands. Stille, D. R. **577.4**

Grassroots. Sandburg, C. **811**
Grassy, John
  National Audubon Society first field guide:
    mammals (4 and up) **599**
Graston, Arlene
  (il) Andersen, H. C. Thumbelina **Fic**
The **Grateful** beasts
  In The Yellow fairy book p64-74 **398.2**
Grateful fox fairy. Carpenter, F.
  In Carpenter, F. Tales of a Chinese grand-
    mother p89-97 **398.2**
The **grateful** tombstone. Terada, A. M.
  In Terada, A. M. Under the starfruit tree
    p130-31 **398.2**
Grau, Andrée
  Dance (4 and up) **792.8**
Gravelle, Jennifer
  (jt. auth) Gravelle, K. The period book
              612.6
Gravelle, Karen
  The period book (4 and up) **612.6**
Graven images. Fleischman, P. **S C**
Gravett, Christopher
  Castle (4 and up) **728.8**
  Knight (4 and up) **940.1**
The **graveyard** jumbies. Joseph, L.
  In Joseph, L. A wave in her pocket p13-19
              398.2
Graveyards of the dinosaurs. Tanaka, S.
              567.9
Gray, Elizabeth Janet *See* Vining, Elizabeth
    Gray, 1902-1999
Gray, Libba Moore
  My mama had a dancing heart **E**
  Small Green Snake **E**
Gray, Luli, 1945-
  Falcon's egg (3-5) **Fic**
Great African Americans [series]
  McKissack, P. C. Booker T. Washington
              92
  McKissack, P. C. Madam C.J. Walker **92**
  McKissack, P. C. Sojourner Truth **92**
Great athletes of the twentieth century. (5 and up)
    See entry in Part 2: Web Resources
Great-aunts *See* Aunts
The **great** ball game. Bruchac, J. **398.2**
Great Barrier Reef (Australia)
  Arnold, C. A walk on the Great Barrier Reef
    (3-5) **578.7**
The **great** bear hunt. Curry, J. L.
  In Curry, J. L. Turtle Island: tales of the Al-
    gonquian nations p77-80 **398.2**
Great books for boys. Odean, K. **028.1**
Great books for girls. Odean, K. **028.1**
The **Great** Brain. Fitzgerald, J. D. **Fic**
The **Great** Brain at the academy. Fitzgerald, J. D.
    See note under Fitzgerald, J. D. The Great
    Brain **Fic**
The **Great** Brain does it again. Fitzgerald, J. D.
    See note under Fitzgerald, J. D. The Great
    Brain **Fic**

The **Great** Brain is back. Fitzgerald, J. D. See note under Fitzgerald, J. D. The Great Brain **Fic**

The **Great** Brain reforms. Fitzgerald, J. D. See note under Fitzgerald, J. D. The Great Brain **Fic**

Great Britain

See also England

Fiction

Aiken, J. The wolves of Willoughby Chase (5 and up) **Fic**

Almond, D. Kit's wilderness (5 and up) **Fic**

Bagnold, E. National Velvet (5 and up) **Fic**

Bond, M. A bear called Paddington (2-5) **Fic**

Bond, M. Paddington's storybook (2-5) **S C**

Boston, L. M. The children of Green Knowe (4-6) **Fic**

Burgess, M. Kite (5 and up) **Fic**

Burnett, F. H. A little princess (4-6) **Fic**

Cooper, S. Dawn of fear (5 and up) **Fic**

Cooper, S. Over sea, under stone (5 and up) **Fic**

Cushman, K. Catherine, called Birdy (6 and up) **Fic**

Cushman, K. The midwife's apprentice (6 and up) **Fic**

De Angeli, M. L. The door in the wall (4-6) **Fic**

Dickens, C. A Christmas carol (4 and up) **Fic**

Howard, E. The gate in the wall (5 and up) **Fic**

King-Smith, D. Pigs might fly (3-5) **Fic**
King-Smith, D. Sophie's Tom (3-5) **Fic**
King-Smith, D. Spider Sparrow (4-6) **Fic**
Magorian, M. Good night, Mr. Tom (6 and up) **Fic**

McKay, H. Dog Friday (4-6) **Fic**
Nesbit, E. The enchanted castle (4-6) **Fic**
Nesbit, E. Five children and it (4-6) **Fic**
Nesbit, E. The railway children (4-6) **Fic**
Pope, E. M. The Perilous Gard (6 and up) **Fic**

Sewell, A. Black Beauty (4-6) **Fic**
Tomlinson, T. The Forestwife (6 and up) **Fic**

Vining, E. G. Adam of the road (5 and up) **Fic**

Waugh, S. The Mennyms (5 and up) **Fic**
Westall, R. The machine gunners (6 and up) **Fic**

Wiseman, D. Jeremy Visick (5 and up) **Fic**

Folklore

See Folklore—Great Britain

History—0-1066

Crossley-Holland, K. The world of King Arthur and his court (5 and up) **942.01**

History—1154-1399, Plantagenets—Fiction
Branford, H. Fire, bed, & bone (5 and up) **Fic**

History—1485-1603, Tudors—Fiction
Blackwood, G. L. The Shakespeare stealer (5 and up) **Fic**
Lasky, K. Elizabeth I (4 and up) **Fic**

History—1714-1837—Fiction
Lawrence, I. The smugglers (5 and up) **Fic**
Lawrence, I. The wreckers (5 and up) **Fic**

History—19th century

See also Industrial revolution; Industrial revolution

Kings and rulers

Brooks, P. S. Queen Eleanor: independent spirit of the medieval world (6 and up) **92**

Fritz, J. Can't you make them behave, King George? [biography of George III, King of Great Britain] (2-4) **92**

Politics and government—20th century
Severance, J. B. Winston Churchill (5 and up) **92**

Great Britain. Navy *See* Great Britain. Royal Navy

Great Britain. Royal Navy

Biesty, S. Stephen Biesty's cross-sections: Man-of-war (4 and up) **359.1**

Great Depression *See* Great Depression, 1929-1939

Great Depression, 1929-1939

Meltzer, M. Driven from the land (4 and up) **978**

Stanley, J. Children of the Dust Bowl (5 and up) **371.9**

Fiction

Adler, D. A. The Babe & I **E**
Burch, R. Ida Early comes over the mountain (4 and up) **Fic**
Curtis, C. P. Bud, not Buddy (4 and up) **Fic**
Friedrich, E. Leah's pony **E**
Hesse, K. Out of the dust (5 and up) **Fic**
Lied, K. Potato **E**
Peck, R. A long way from Chicago (5 and up) **Fic**
Peck, R. A year down yonder (5 and up) **Fic**
Recorvits, H. Goodbye, Walter Malinski (3-6) **Fic**
Snyder, Z. K. Cat running (4 and up) **Fic**
Stewart, S. The gardener **E**
Taylor, M. D. Let the circle be unbroken (4 and up) **Fic**
Taylor, M. D. Roll of thunder, hear my cry (4 and up) **Fic**
Taylor, M. D. Song of the trees (4 and up) **Fic**
Turner, A. W. Dust for dinner **E**
Willis, P. The barn burner (5 and up) **Fic**

The **great** dinosaur atlas. Lindsay, W. **567.9**

Great events of the twentieth century. (6 and up) See entry in Part 2: Web Resources

The **great** fire. Murphy, J. **977.3**

The **Great** Flood. Curry, J. L.
In Curry, J. L. Turtle Island: tales of the Algonquian nations p33-35 **398.2**

The **great** frog race and other poems. George, K. O. **811**

Great ghosts. Cohen, D.   **133.1**

The **great** Gilly Hopkins. Paterson, K.   **Fic**

Great-Grandfather Dragon's tale. Yolen, J.
   In Yolen, J. Here there be dragons p3-22
          810.8

Great horned owl *See* Owls

Great ice bear. Patent, D. H.   **599.78**

Great journeys [series]
   Haskins, J. Out of the darkness   **305.8**
   Meltzer, M. Driven from the land   **978**

The **great** kapok tree. Cherry, L.   **E**

The **great** Lacrosse game. Caduto, M. J.
   In Caduto, M. J. Keepers of the night p97-99
          398.2

Great Lakes region
Fiction
   Holling, H. C. Paddle-to-the-sea (4-6)   **Fic**

The **great** little Madison. Fritz, J.   **92**

Great lives: American literature. Faber, D.
          920

Great lives: the American frontier. Calvert, P.
          920

The **great** migration. Lawrence, J.   **759.13**

Great minds of science [series]
   Poynter, M. Marie Curie: discoverer of radium
          92

Great Plains
History
   Meltzer, M. Driven from the land (4 and up)
          978

The **great** pumpkin switch. McDonald, M.   **E**

The **great** Quillow. Thurber, J.   **E**

The **great** race of the birds and animals. Goble, P.
          398.2

The **Great** Red Cat. MacDonald, M. R.
   In MacDonald, M. R. When the lights go out
   p47-60   **372.6**

Great scientific achievements of the twentieth
century. (6 and up) See entry in Part 2: Web
Resources

The **great** St. Lawrence Seaway. Gibbons, G.
          386

The **Great** Swallowing Monster. McCaughrean, G.
   In The Oxford book of scary tales p64-69
          808.8

Great thumbprint drawing book, Ed Emberley's.
Emberley, E.   **743**

The **great** turkey walk. Karr, K.   **Fic**

The **great** white man-eating shark. Mahy, M.
          E

The **greatest** treasure. Demi   **398.2**

Greece
Civilization
   Hart, A. Ancient Greece! (4 and up)   **938**
   Pearson, A. Ancient Greece (4 and up)
          938
Fiction
   Harrison, B. Theo (5 and up)   **Fic**
Folklore
   See Folklore—Greece
Science
   See Science—Greece

The **greedy** daughter. San Souci, R.
   In San Souci, R. More short & shivery p93-
   96   **398.2**

The **greedy** man and the goat. Olson, A. N.
   In Olson, A. N. Ask the bones: scary stories
   from around the world p129-33
          398.2

Greek and Roman mythology A to Z. Daly, K. N.
          292

Greek gods and goddesses. McCaughrean, G.
          292

The **Greek** king and the physician Douban
   In The Arabian nights entertainments p29-31
          398.2

Greek mythology *See* Classical mythology

Greek myths. McCaughrean, G.   **292**

Greek science *See* Science—Greece

Green, Roger Lancelyn, 1918-1987
   King Arthur and his Knights of the Round Table (5 and up)   **398.2**

The **green-clawed** thunderbird. Mayo, M.
   In Mayo, M. Mythical birds & beasts from
   many lands p37-45   **398.2**

Green eggs and ham. Seuss, Dr.   **E**

The **Green** fairy book (4-6)   **398.2**

The **green** frogs. Heo, Y.   **398.2**

Green gourd
   In Grandfather tales p213-21   **398.2**

Green grass and white milk. See Aliki. Milk from
cow to carton   **637**

The **green** mist. San Souci, R.
   In San Souci, R. Short & shivery p35-40
          398.2

The **Green** Mist. Sewall, M.   **398.2**

The **Green** ribbon
   In Diane Goode's book of scary stories &
   songs p62-63   **398.2**

The **green** ribbon. Schwartz, A.
   In Schwartz, A. In a dark, dark room, and
   other scary stories p24-33   **398.2**

Green willow. Martin, R.
   In Martin, R. Mysterious tales of Japan
          398.2

Greenaway, Frank
   (il) Clarke, B. Amphibian   **597.8**
   (il) The Snake book. See The Snake book
          597.9

Greenaway, Kate, 1846-1901
   (il) Browning, R. The Pied Piper of Hamelin
          821

Greenaway, Theresa, 1947-
   Jungle (4 and up)   **577.3**

Greenberg, David
   Bugs!   **E**

Greenberg, Jan, 1942-
   The American eye (6 and up)   **920**
   Chuck Close, up close (4 and up)   **92**

Greene, Bette, 1934-
   Philip Hall likes me, I reckon maybe (4-6)
          Fic
   Summer of my German soldier (6 and up)
          Fic

Greene, Constance C.
Beat the turtle drum (5 and up) Fic
A girl called Al (5 and up) Fic

Greene, Ellin, 1927-
The little golden lamb (k-3) 398.2
Storytelling 372.6

Greene, Rhonda Gowler, 1955-
Barnyard song E

Greene, Stephanie
Owen Foote, frontiersman (2-4) Fic
Owen Foote, money man. See note under
Greene, S. Owen Foote, frontiersman Fic
Owen Foote, second grade strongman. See note
under Greene, S. Owen Foote, frontiersman
 Fic
Owen Foote, soccer star. See note under Greene,
S. Owen Foote, frontiersman Fic

Greenfeld, Howard
The hidden children (4 and up) 940.53

Greenfield, Eloise, 1929-
Africa dream E
Angels 811
Childtimes: a three-generation memoir (4 and
up) 920
Easter parade (2-4) Fic
Grandmama's joy E
Grandpa's face E
Honey, I love, and other love poems (2-4)
 811
Rosa Parks (2-4) 92
She come bringing me that little baby girl
 E
Sister (4 and up) Fic
Under the Sunday tree (2-4) 811

Greenseid, Diane
(il) Woodson, J. We had a picnic this Sunday
past E

Greenstein, Elaine, 1959-
Dreaming E
(il) Goldin, B. D. While the candles burn
 296.4

Greenstein, Susan
(il) Vezza, D. S. Passport on a plate 641.5

Greenwald, Sheila
Rosy Cole: she grows and graduates (3-5)
 Fic

Greenwillow read-alone books [series]
Jaspersohn, W. How the forest grew 577.3
Prelutsky, J. It's Christmas 811
Prelutsky, J. It's Thanksgiving 811
Prelutsky, J. It's Valentine's Day 811
Shub, E. The white stallion E

Greenwitch. Cooper, S. See note under Cooper, S.
Over sea, under stone Fic

Greenwood, Barbara
A pioneer sampler (4 and up) 971.3

Greetings from Antarctica. Wheeler, S. 998

Gregorowski, Christopher, 1940-
Fly, eagle, fly! (k-3) 398.2

Gregory, Adair
(jt. auth) Peacock, C. A. Sugar was my best
food 362.1

Gregory, Kyle Carney
(jt. auth) Peacock, C. A. Sugar was my best
food 362.1

Gregory, Nan
How Smudge came E

Gregory, the terrible eater. Sharmat, M. E

The **grey** king. Cooper, S. Fic

The **Grey** Lady and the Strawberry Snatcher.
Bang, M. E

Grief. Andersen, H. C.
In Andersen, H. C. The swan's stories p79-83
 S C

Griego, Margot C.
(comp) Tortillitas para mamá and other nursery
rhymes. See Tortillitas para mamá and other
nursery rhymes 398.8

Grifalconi, Ann
Tiny's hat E
The village of round and square houses (k-3)
 398.2
(il) Byars, B. C. The midnight fox Fic
(il) Clifton, L. Everett Anderson's 1-2-3 E
(il) McGovern, A. The secret soldier: the story
of Deborah Sampson [Gannett] 92
(il) Olaleye, I. In the Rainfield 398.2

Griffin, Adele
The other Shepards (6 and up) Fic

Griffin, Peni R.
Switching well (5 and up) Fic

Griffin, Robert, 1951-
(ed) The Folklore of world holidays. See The
Folklore of world holidays 394.26

Griffin-Pierce, Trudy
The encyclopedia of Native America
 970.004

Griffith, Gershom, 1960-
(il) Adler, D. A. A picture book of Sojourner
Truth 92

Griffith, Helen V.
Alex and the cat (1-3) Fic
Alex remembers
In Griffith, H. V. Alex and the cat Fic
Georgia music. See note under Griffith, H. V.
Grandaddy's place E
Grandaddy and Janetta. See note under Griffith,
H. V. Grandaddy's place E
Grandaddy's place E
Grandaddy's stars. See note under Griffith, H.
V. Grandaddy's place E
More Alex and the cat
In Griffith, H. V. Alex and the cat Fic

Grimes, Nikki
Come Sunday (k-3) 811
A dime a dozen (5 and up) 811
Hopscotch love (4 and up) 811
Is it far to Zanzibar? (2-4) 811
Meet Danitra Brown (2-4) 811
My man Blue (2-5) 811

Grimm, Jacob, 1785-1863
Allerleirauh
In The Green fairy book p276-81 398.2
Brave little tailor
In The Blue fairy book p304-12 398.2
The Bremen town musicians (k-3) 398.2

Grimm, Jacob, 1785-1863—*Continued*

Bremen town musicians; adaptation. See Wildsmith, B. The Bremen Town Band   **398.2**

The cabbage donkey
   In The Yellow fairy book p42-49   **398.2**

Cat and mouse in partnership
   In The Yellow fairy book p1-3   **398.2**

The crystal coffin
   In The Green fairy book p290-95   **398.2**

The devil and his grandmother
   In The Yellow fairy book p38-41   **398.2**

The devil with the three golden hairs; adaptation. See Babbitt, N. Ouch!   **398.2**

The elves and the shoemaker
   In Tomie dePaola's favorite nursery tales p100-04   **398.2**

The elves and the shoemaker; adaptation. See Galdone, P. The elves and the shoemaker   **398.2**

The frog-prince
   In The Classic fairy tales p185-87   **398.2**
   In Tomie dePaola's favorite nursery tales p21-30   **398.2**

The golden goose; adaptation. See Shulevitz, U. The golden goose   **398.2**

The golden lads
   In The Green fairy book p311-18   **398.2**

The golden mermaid
   In The Green fairy book p328-38   **398.2**

The goose girl
   In The Blue fairy book p266-73   **398.2**

Hansel and Gretel [Dial Press] (k-3)   **398.2**

Hansel and Gretel [Picture Book Studio] (k-3)   **398.2**
   also in The Classic fairy tales p238-44   **398.2**

Hansel and Grettel
   In The Blue fairy book p251-58   **398.2**

How six men travelled through the wide world
   In The Yellow fairy book p95-99   **398.2**

Iron Hans; adaptation. See Kimmel, E. A. Iron John   **398.2**

Iron Hans; adaptation. See Mayer, M. Iron John   **398.2**

The iron stove
   In The Yellow fairy book p32-37   **398.2**

Jack my Hedgehog
   In The Green fairy book p304-10   **398.2**

Jorinde and Joringel
   In The Green fairy book p271-75   **398.2**

Lazy Heinz
   In Bauer, C. F. Celebrations p140-43   **808.8**

Little One-eye, Little Two-eyes, and Little Three-eyes
   In The Green fairy book p262-70   **398.2**

Little Red Cap (k-3)   **398.2**

Little Red Riding Hood; adaptation. See Hyman, T. S. Little Red Riding Hood   **398.2**

Little Red Riding Hood; adaptation. See Marshall, J. Red Riding Hood   **398.2**

Little Red Riding Hood; adaptation. See Ziefert, H. Little Red Riding Hood   **398.2**

Rapunzel; adaptation. See Rogasky, B. Rapunzel   **398.2**

The riddle
   In The Green fairy book p300-03   **398.2**

Rumpelstiltskin
   In The Classic fairy tales p197-98   **398.2**
   In Tomie dePaola's favorite nursery tales p46-52   **398.2**

Rumpelstiltskin; adaptation. See Zelinsky, P. O. Rumpelstiltskin   **398.2**

Rumpelstiltzkin
   In The Blue fairy book p96-99   **398.2**

Seven at one blow; adaptation. See Kimmel, E. A. Seven at one blow   **398.2**

The six swans
   In The Yellow fairy book p4-8   **398.2**

Snow White & Rose Red (1-4)   **398.2**

Snow-White and Rose-Red
   In The Blue fairy book p259-65   **398.2**

Snow White and Rose Red; adaptation. See Andreasen, D. Rose Red and the bear prince   **398.2**

Snowdrop
   In The Classic Fairy tales p177-82   **398.2**

Spindle, shuttle, and needle
   In The Green fairy book p286-89   **398.2**

The story of a clever tailor
   In The Green fairy book p324-27   **398.2**

The story of the fisherman and his wife
   In The Green fairy book p343-52   **398.2**

The tale of a youth who set out to learn what fear was
   In The Blue fairy book p86-95   **398.2**

The three snake-leaves
   In The Green fairy book p296-99   **398.2**

Trusty John
   In The Blue fairy book p296-303   **398.2**

The twelve brothers
   In Womenfolk and fairy tales p36-43   **398.2**

The twelve dancing princesses
   In The Classic fairy tales p191-94   **398.2**

The twelve huntsmen
   In The Green fairy book p282-85   **398.2**

The war of the wolf and the fox
   In The Green fairy book p339-42   **398.2**

The water of life; adaptation. See Rogasky, B. The water of life   **398.2**

The white snake
   In The Green fairy book p319-23   **398.2**

Grimm, Wilhelm, 1786-1859
Fairy tales by the Brothers Grimm are listed under Jacob Grimm

Grinnell, George Bird, 1849-1938
See/See also pages in the following book(s):
Calvert, P. Great lives: the American frontier p177-92 (5 and up)   **920**

Griswold, Wendy Smith- *See* Smith-Griswold, Wendy, 1955-

Grizz!. Kimmel, E. A.   **E**

Grocery trade
                Fiction
DiSalvo-Ryan, D. Grandpa's corner store   **E**

Grogan, Brian, 1951-
(il) Ross, M. E. Millipedeology   **595.6**
(il) Ross, M. E. Spiderology   **595.4**

Grolier multimedia encyclopedia online. (5 and up) See entry in Part 2: Web Resources

The **grooming** of Alice. Naylor, P. R. See note under Naylor, P. R. The agony of Alice
    Fic

Grose, Helen Mason
  (il) Wiggin, K. D. S. Rebecca of Sunnybrook Farm   **Fic**

Grossman, Bill
  My little sister ate one hare   **E**

Grossman, Nancy, 1940-
  (il) Caudill, R. Did you carry the flag today, Charley?   **Fic**

Groth-Fleming, Candace
  See also Fleming, Candace

The **grouchy** ladybug. Carle, E.   **E**

Ground-hogs *See* Marmots

The **ground** parrot and the albatross. Te Kanawa, K.
  In Te Kanawa, K. Land of the long white cloud p113-14   **398.2**

Ground Squirrel and Turtle. Curry, J. L.
  In Curry, J. L. Turtle Island: tales of the Algonquian nations p64-65   **398.2**

Groundhog dance. MacDonald, M. R.
  In MacDonald, M. R. Twenty tellable tales p35-42   **372.6**

Groundhog's dance. Sierra, J.
  In Sierra, J. Nursery tales around the world p93-95   **398.2**

Grove, Vicki
  Destiny (5 and up)   **Fic**
  Reaching Dustin (5 and up)   **Fic**

Growing colors. McMillan, B.   **E**

Growing frogs. French, V.   **597.8**

Growing seasons. Splear, E. L.   **630**

Growing up. Singer, I. B.
  In Singer, I. B. Stories for children p217-30   **S C**

Growing up. Soto, G.
  In Soto, G. Baseball in April, and other stories p97-107   **S C**

Growing up in coal country. Bartoletti, S. C.   **331.3**

Growing up: it's a girl thing. Jukes, M.   **612.6**

Growing up wild: bears. Markle, S.   **599.78**

Growing vegetable soup. Ehlert, L.   **E**

Growltiger's last stand. Eliot, T. S.   **811**

Growth
  Martin, L. Watch them grow (k-2)   **571.8**
  Parker, S. The reproductive system (5 and up)   **612.6**

Fiction
Brown, M. W. Another important book   **E**
Cooney, B. Island boy   **E**
Henderson, K. The baby dances   **E**
James, B. Tadpoles   **E**
Keller, H. Jacob's tree   **E**
McMillan, B. Step by step   **E**
Mitchell, R. P. Hue Boy   **E**

The **grumbling** old woman. Afanas'ev, A. N.
  In Afanas'ev, A. N. Russian fairy tales p340-41   **398.2**

Grupper, Jonathan
  Destination: rain forest (1-3)   **577.3**

Gryski, Camilla, 1948-
  Cat's cradle, owl's eyes (4-6)   **793.9**

Guanina. Delacre, L.
  In Delacre, L. Golden tales p7-12   **398.2**

The **guardian** of memory. Coville, B.
  In A Glory of unicorns p1-28   **S C**

Guardians of the gate. Carpenter, F.
  In Carpenter, F. Tales of a Chinese grandmother p47-55   **398.2**

Guarino, Deborah, 1954-
  Is your mama a llama?   **E**

Guatemala
  Sheehan, S. Guatemala (5 and up)   **972.81**
       Children
    See Children—Guatemala
       Fiction
  Castañeda, O. S. Abuela's weave   **E**

Guback, Georgia
  Luka's quilt   **E**

La **güera.** Soto, G.
  In Soto, G. Petty crimes   **S C**

Guess, George *See* Sequoyah, 1770?-1843

Guess how much I love you. McBratney, S.
  E

Guess who? Miller, M.   **E**

Guess who's coming, Jesse Bear. Carlstrom, N. W. See note under Carlstrom, N. W. Jesse Bear, what will you wear?   **E**

Guests. Paterson, K.
  In Paterson, K. Angels & other strangers: family Christmas stories p17-25
    S C

Guests from Gibbet Island. San Souci, R.
  In San Souci, R. Even more short & shivery p44-48   **398.2**

Guevara, Susan
  (il) Soto, G. Chato's kitchen   **E**
  (il) Yolen, J. Not one damsel in distress   **398.2**

La **Guiablesse.** San Souci, R.
  In San Souci, R. Even more short & shivery p33-37   **398.2**

Guiberson, Brenda Z.
  Cactus hotel (k-3)   **583**
  Into the sea (k-3)   **597.9**
  Lighthouses (3-5)   **387.1**
  Tales of the haunted deep (4 and up)   **001.9**

Guide to reference books for school media centers. See Safford, B. R. Guide to reference materials for school media centers   **011.6**

Guide to reference materials for school media centers. Safford, B. R.   **011.6**

A **guided** tour of the visible human. (5 and up)
  See entry in Part 2: Web Resources

Guides to collection development for children and young adults. Gillespie, J. T.   **011.6**

Guilt
       Fiction
  Bunting, E. Blackwater (5 and up)   **Fic**

Guinea fowl

Fiction

Knutson, B. How the guinea fowl got her spots (k-3) **398.2**

Guinea Fowl and Rabbit get justice. Courlander, H.

In Courlander, H. Cow-tail switch, and other West African stories p87-94 **398.2**

Guinea pigs

Duke, K. One guinea pig is not enough **E**

Hansen, E. Guinea pigs (3-6) **636.9**

King-Smith, D. I love guinea pigs (k-3) **636.9**

Fiction

King-Smith, D. Jenius: the amazing guinea pig (2-4) **Fic**

Meade, H. John Willy and Freddy McGee **E**

Guinness book of records **032.02**

Guinness book of world records. See Guinness book of records **032.02**

Guitar solo. McCaughrean, G.

In McCaughrean, G. The bronze cauldron: myths and legends of the world p11-13 **398.2**

Gulevich, Tanya

(ed) Encyclopedia of Christmas. See Encyclopedia of Christmas **394.26**

Gull-girl. McCaughrean, G.

In McCaughrean, G. The crystal pool: myths and legends of the world p71-75 **398.2**

Gullahs

Fiction

Siegelson, K. L. In the time of the drums **E**

Gulliver in Lilliput. Hodges, M. **Fic**

Gulls

Gibbons, G. Gulls—gulls—gulls (k-3) **598**

Gulls—gulls—gulls. Gibbons, G. **598**

The **gunny** wolf. MacDonald, M. R.

In MacDonald, M. R. Twenty tellable tales p68-74 **372.6**

The **gunny** wolf. Sierra, J.

In Sierra, J. Nursery tales around the world p87-91 **398.2**

Gus and Grandpa. Mills, C. See note under Mills, C. Gus and Grandpa and the two-wheeled bike **E**

Gus and Grandpa and show-and-tell. Mills, C. See note under Mills, C. Gus and Grandpa and the two-wheeled bike **E**

Gus and Grandpa and the Christmas cookies. Mills, C. See note under Mills, C. Gus and Grandpa and the two-wheeled bike **E**

Gus and Grandpa and the two-wheeled bike. Mills, C. **E**

Gus and Grandpa at the hospital. Mills, C. See note under Mills, C. Gus and Grandpa and the two-wheeled bike **E**

Gus and Grandpa ride the train. Mills, C. See note under Mills, C. Gus and Grandpa and the two-wheeled bike **E**

Gustafson, Dana

(il) Haskins, J. Count your way through the Arab world **909**

Gustafson, Scott, 1956-

(il) Barrie, J. M. Peter Pan **Fic**

Gustavson, Adam

(il) Borden, L. Good luck, Mrs. K! **E**

Gutenberg, Johann, 1397?-1468

About

Fisher, L. E. Gutenberg (4 and up) **92**

Guthrie, Donna, 1946-

(jt. auth) Bentley, N. Putting on a play **792**

(jt. auth) Bentley, N. The young producer's video book **791.45**

Guthrie, Woody, 1912-1967

Howdi do (k-2) **782.42**

This land is your land (k-3) **782.42**

See/See also pages in the following book(s):

Krull, K. Lives of the musicians p90-93 (4 and up) **920**

Gutman, Dan

Babe and me (4 and up) **Fic**

Honus and me. See note under Gutman, D. Babe and me **Fic**

Ice skating **796.91**

Jackie and me. See note under Gutman, D. Babe and me **Fic**

Guy, Ginger Foglesong

Fiesta! **E**

Guy time. Weeks, S. See note under Weeks, S. Regular Guy **Fic**

Guyana

Jermyn, L. Guyana (5 and up) **988.1**

Gwendolen. Mayer, M.

In Mayer, M. Women warriors p43-49 **398**

Gymnastics

Bragg, L. W. Fundamental gymnastics (5 and up) **796.44**

Feldman, J. I am a gymnast (3-5) **796.44**

Jackman, J. Gymnastics (4 and up) **796.44**

Gynecology *See* Women—Health and hygiene

Gypsies

Fiction

Alexander, L. Gypsy Rizka (5 and up) **Fic**

Gypsy Rizka. Alexander, L. **Fic**

H

Haas, Jessie

Be well, Beware. See note under Haas, J. Beware the mare **Fic**

Beware and Stogie. See note under Haas, J. Beware the mare **Fic**

Beware the mare (3-5) **Fic**

A blue for Beware. See note under Haas, J. Beware the mare **Fic**

Hurry! **E**

Sugaring **E**

Unbroken (5 and up) **Fic**

Haas, Martha

(il) Haas, J. Beware the mare **Fic**

Haas, Shelly O.
(il) Ransom, C. F. Listening to crickets: a story about Rachel Carson **92**

Haban, Rita D.
How proudly they wave (4 and up) **929.9**

Habetrot and Scantlie Mab. Jacobs, J.
In Jacobs, J. English fairy tales p396-400 **398.2**

Habitat (Ecology)
Arnosky, J. Crinkleroot's guide to knowing animal habitats (k-3) **591.7**
Fleming, D. Where once there was a wood (k-2) **639.9**
Orr, R. Nature cross-sections (4 and up) **577**
VanCleave, J. P. Janice Vancleave's ecology for every kid (4 and up) **577**

Hackett, Walter, 1909-
A merry Christmas
In The Big book of Christmas plays p332-48 **808.82**

Hader, Berta, 1891-1976
The big snow **E**
See/See also pages in the following book(s):
Caldecott Medal books, 1938-1957 p185-99 **028.5**

Hader, Elmer Stanley, 1889-1973
(jt. auth) Hader, B. The big snow **E**
See/See also pages in the following book(s):
Caldecott Medal books, 1938-1957 p185-99 **028.5**

Hafiz, the stone-cutter. Shedlock, M. L.
In Shedlock, M. L. The art of the story-teller p179-82 **372.6**

Hafner, Marylin, 1925-
(il) Berger, M. Germs make me sick! **616.9**
(il) Lasky, K. Show and Tell bunnies **E**
(il) Prelutsky, J. It's Christmas **811**
(il) Prelutsky, J. It's Thanksgiving **811**
(il) Ross, P. Meet M and M **E**

The Hag
In Raw Head, bloody bones p9-12 **398.2**

Hague, Michael, 1948-
(il) Baum, L. F. The Wizard of Oz **Fic**
(il) Bianco, M. W. The velveteen rabbit **Fic**
(il) Grahame, K. The reluctant dragon **Fic**
(il) Grahame, K. The wind in the willows **Fic**
(il) Norton, M. The Borrowers **Fic**
(il) Sandburg, C. Rootabaga stories **S C**
(il) Sandburg, C. Rootabaga stories **S C**

Hahn, Mary Downing, 1937-
Anna all year round (3-5) **Fic**
Anna on the farm. See note under Hahn, M. D. Anna all year round **Fic**
As ever, Gordy (5 and up) **Fic**
Daphne's book (5 and up) **Fic**
The dead man in Indian Creek (5 and up) **Fic**
The doll in the garden (4-6) **Fic**
Following my own footsteps (5 and up) **Fic**

The Gentleman Outlaw and me—Eli (5 and up) **Fic**
Promises to the dead (5 and up) **Fic**
Stepping on the cracks (5 and up) **Fic**
Time for Andrew (5 and up) **Fic**
Wait till Helen comes (4-6) **Fic**

Haiku
Livingston, M. C. Cricket never does (4 and up) **811**
Stone bench in an empty park (4 and up) **811.008**
See/See also pages in the following book(s):
Gollub, M. Cool melons—turn to frogs!: the life and poems of Issa [Kobayashi] (3-6) **92**

Hailstones and halibut bones. O'Neill, M. L. D. **811**

Hair
Fiction
Madrigal, A. H. Erandi's braids **E**
Yarbrough, C. Cornrows **E**

Hairston, Martha
(il) Burns, M. The I hate mathematics! book **513**

The **hairy** hands. San Souci, R.
In San Souci, R. A terrifying taste of short & shivery p52-57 **398.2**

Hairy, scary, ordinary. Cleary, B. P. **428**

Haiti
Hintz, M. Haiti (4 and up) **972.94**
Fiction
Lotu, D. Running the road to ABC **E**
Temple, F. Tonight, by sea (6 and up) **Fic**
Williams, K. L. Painted dreams **E**
Folklore
See Folklore—Haiti

Hakim, Joy
A history of US (5 and up) **973**

Halala means welcome!. Wilson-Max, K. **496**

Haldane, Suzanne
(jt. auth) Left Hand Bull, J. Lakota hoop dancer **970.004**

Hale, Christy
(il) Stuve-Bodeen, S. Elizabeti's doll **E**
(il) Swenson, M. The complete poems to solve **811**

Hale, James Graham
(il) Branley, F. M. Down comes the rain **551.57**
(il) Turner, A. W. Through moon and stars and night skies **E**
(il) Zoehfeld, K. W. How mountains are made **551.4**

Hale, Sarah Josepha
Mary had a little lamb (k-2) **811**

Haley, Gail E.
A story, a story (k-3) **398.2**
(il) Konigsburg, E. L. Altogether, one at a time **S C**
See/See also pages in the following book(s):
Newbery and Caldecott Medal books, 1966-1975 p223-29, 232-35 **028.5**

Half-a-Ball-of-Kenki. Aardema, V.
In Aardema, V. Misoso p25-31 **398.2**

Half a moon and one whole star. Dragonwagon, C.   E

The **Half-a-Moon** Inn. Fleischman, P.   Fic

The **Half-chick**
  In The Green fairy book p27-31   **398.2**
Half-chick. See Barnes, H. The proud cock

Half magic. Eager, E.   Fic

Halfway home. Rylant, C.
  In Rylant, C. Children of Christmas p6-12
           S C

Hall, Donald, 1928-
  Lucy's Christmas   E
  Ox-cart man   E
  (ed) The Oxford book of children's verse in America. See The Oxford book of children's verse in America   **811.008**
  (ed) The Oxford illustrated book of American children's poems. See The Oxford illustrated book of American children's poems   **811.008**

Hall, Jacque
  What does the rabbit say?   E

Hall, Katy, 1947-
  See also McMullan, Kate, 1947-
  Creepy riddles (k-2)   **793.73**
  Mummy riddles (k-2)   **793.73**
  Snakey riddles (k-2)   **793.73**

Hall, Melanie W.
  (il) Fishman, C. On Hanukkah   **296.4**
  (il) Fishman, C. On Passover   **296.4**
  (il) Fishman, C. On Purim   **296.4**
  (il) Fishman, C. On Rosh Hashanah and Yom Kippur   **296.4**
  (il) Weather. See Weather   **811.008**

Hall, Minna

        Fiction
  Lasky, K. She's wearing a dead bird on her head!   E

Hall, Nelson
  (il) Reynolds, D. W. Star wars: the visual dictionary   **791.43**

Hall, Ruby Bridges *See* Bridges, Ruby

Hall, Susan, 1940-
  Using picture storybooks to teach literary devices   **016.8**

Hall, Zoe, 1957-
  The apple pie tree (k-1)   **634**
  It's pumpkin time!   E
  The surprise garden   E

Hallensleben, Georg
  (il) Banks, K. And if the moon could talk   E
  (il) Banks, K. Baboon   E
  (il) Banks, K. The night worker   E

The **Hallo-wiener**. Pilkey, D.   E

Halloween
  Barth, E. Witches, pumpkins, and grinning ghosts (3-6)   **394.26**
  Gibbons, G. Halloween (k-3)   **394.26**
  See/See also pages in the following book(s):
  Bauer, C. F. Celebrations p103-18   **808.8**
        Fiction
  Bunting, E. Scary, scary Halloween   E

  De Groat, D. Trick or treat, smell my feet   E
  Hall, Z. It's pumpkin time!   E
  Howe, J. Scared silly: a Halloween treat   E
  Huck, C. S. A creepy countdown   E
  Johnston, T. The soup bone   E
  Kline, S. Mary Marony, mummy girl (2-4)   Fic
  Kroll, S. The biggest pumpkin ever   E
  Marshall, E. Space case   E
  Pilkey, D. The Hallo-wiener   E
  Teague, M. One Halloween night   E
  Tolan, S. S. Save Halloween! (5 and up)   Fic

        Poetry
  Carlstrom, N. W. Who said boo? (k-3)   **811**
  Hubbell, P. Boo! (k-3)   **811**
  Merriam, E. Halloween A B C (k-2)   **811**

Halloween A B C. Merriam, E.   **811**

The **Halloween** pony. San Souci, R.
  In San Souci, R. Short & shivery p166-70   **398.2**

The **Halloween** witches. Mayo, M.
  In Mayo, M. Magical tales from many lands p95-99   **398.2**

Hallworth, Grace
  The shiner
  In The Oxford book of scary tales p52-53   **808.8**

Halmoni and the picnic. Choi, S. N.   E

Halperin, Wendy Anderson, 1952-
  (il) Aylesworth, J. The full belly bowl   E
  (il) Seymour, T. Hunting the white cow   E
  (il) Shelby, A. Homeplace   E

Halpern, Joan
  (il) Cohen, B. The carp in the bathtub   Fic

Halpern, Shari
  (il) Hall, Z. The apple pie tree   **634**
  (il) Hall, Z. It's pumpkin time!   E
  (il) Hall, Z. The surprise garden   E

Halsey, Megan
  (il) Older, J. Telling time   **529**
  (il) Rockwell, A. F. One bean   **635**

Halstead, Virginia
  (il) Spectacular science. See Spectacular science   **811.008**

Ham radio stations *See* Amateur radio stations

Hamal Hasan and the baby day. Walker, B. K.
  In Walker, B. K. A treasury of Turkish folktales for children p123-26   **398.2**

Hamanaka, Sheila
  All the colors of the earth   E
  I look like a girl   E
  The journey (5 and up)   **305.8**
  Screen of frogs (k-3)   **398.2**
  (il) Hurwitz, J. Class clown   Fic

Hamer, Fannie Lou Townsend, 1917-1977
  See/See also pages in the following book(s):
  Hansen, J. Women of hope p14-15 (4 and up)   **920**
  Haskins, J. One more river to cross (4 and up)   **920**

Hamilton, Alice
About
McPherson, S. S. The workers' detective: a story about Dr. Alice Hamilton (3-5)   **92**

Hamilton, Edith, 1867-1963
Mythology (6 and up)   **292**

Hamilton, Jake
Special effects in film and television (4 and up)   **791.43**

Hamilton, Oria Douglas- *See* Douglas-Hamilton, Oria

Hamilton, Virginia, 1936-
Anthony Burns: the defeat and triumph of a fugitive slave (5 and up)   **92**
The bells of Christmas (4-6)   **Fic**
Cousins (5 and up)   **Fic**
Drylongso (3-5)   **Fic**
The girl who spun gold (k-3)   **398.2**
Her stories (4 and up)   **398.2**
Includes the following stories: Little Girl and Buh Rabby; Lena and Big One Tiger; Marie and Redfish; Miz Hattie gets some company; Catskinella; Good Blanche, bad Rose, and the talking eggs; Mary Belle and the mermaid; Mom Bett and the little ones a-glowing; Who you!; Macie and boo hag; Lonna and Cat Woman; Malindy and little devil; Woman and Man started even; Luella and the tame parrot; The mer-woman out of the sea; Annie Christmas
The house of Dies Drear (5 and up)   **Fic**
In the beginning; creation stories from around the world (5 and up)   **291.1**
M. C. Higgins the great (6 and up)   **Fic**
Many thousand gone (5 and up)   **326**
The mystery of Drear House (5 and up)   **Fic**

The peculiar such thing
In From sea to shining sea p338-39   **810.8**

The people could fly [story]
In From sea to shining sea p144-47   **810.8**

The people could fly: American black folktales (4 and up)   **398.2**
Contents: He Lion, Bruh Bear and Bruh Rabbit; Doc Rabbit, Bruh Fox, and Tar Baby; Tappin, the land turtle; Bruh Alligator and Bruh Deer; Bruh Lizard and Bruh Rabbit; Bruh Alligator meets Trouble; Wolf and birds and the Fish-Horse; The beautiful girl of the moon tower; A wolf and Little Daughter; Manuel had a riddle; Papa John's tall tale; The two Johns; Wiley, his mama, and the Hairy Man; John and the Devil's daughter; The peculiar such thing; Little Eight John; Jack and the Devil; Better wait till Martin comes; Carrying the running-aways; How Nehemiah got free; The talking cooter; The riddle tale of freedom; The most useful slave; The people could fly
Plain City (5 and up)   **Fic**
The planet of Junior Brown (6 and up)   **Fic**
A ring of tricksters   **398.2**
Contents:Buh Rabby and Bruh Gator; Buzzard and Wren have a race; The Cat and the Rat; Bruh Wolf and Bruh Rabbit join together;That one, Anansi; Magic Anansi; Cunnie Anansi does some good; Cunnie Rabbit and Spider make a match; How Chameleon became a ride; Old Mister Turtle gets a whipping; The animals share
Second cousins (5 and up)   **Fic**
When birds could talk & bats could sing (3-5)   **398.2**
Contents: How Bruh Sparrow and Sis Wren lost out; Still and ugly Bat; Blue Jay and Swallow take the heat; Bruh Buzzard and Fair Maid; Hummingbird and Little Breeze; When Miss Bat could sing; Cardinal and Bruh Deer; Little Brown Wren
Zeely (4 and up)   **Fic**

See/See also pages in the following book(s):
Newbery and Caldecott Medal books, 1966-1975 p129-40   **028.5**
Origins of story p113-19   **808.06**

Hamley, Dennis, 1935-
Supermarket
In The Oxford book of scary tales p106-11   **808.8**

Hamlin, Janet
(il) Radin, R. Y. Escape to the forest   **Fic**

Hampton, Wilborn
Kennedy assassinated! (5 and up)   **973.922**

Hamsters
Fiction
Rathmann, P. 10 minutes till bedtime   **E**

Han, Suzanne Crowder, 1953-
The rabbit's escape (k-3)   **398.2**
The rabbit's tail (k-3)   **398.2**

Hancock, John, 1737-1793
About
Fritz, J. Will you sign here, John Hancock? (2-4)   **92**

Hand
Aliki. My hands (k-1)   **612**
Hand in hand (4 and up)   **811.008**

The **hand** of death. Olson, A. N.
In Olson, A. N. Ask the bones: scary stories from around the world p105-09   **398.2**

The **hand** of fate. San Souci, R.
In San Souci, R. Even more short & shivery p140-43   **398.2**
The **hand** of the necromancer. Strickland, B.   **Fic**

Hand rhymes. Brown, M. T.   **796.1**
Handbook for storytellers. See Bauer, C. F. Caroline Feller Bauer's new handbook for storytellers   **372.6**

Handel, George Frideric, 1685-1759
About
Venezia, M. George Handel (k-3)   **92**

Handelsman, J. B.
(il) Fritz, J. Who's that stepping on Plymouth Rock?   **974.4**

Handforth, Thomas, 1897-1948
See/See also pages in the following book(s):
Caldecott Medal books, 1938-1957 p23-43   **028.5**

A **handful** of beans. Steig, J.   **398.2**
A **handful** of dirt. Bial, R.   **577.5**

Handicapped
See also Mentally handicapped; Physically handicapped

Handicapped children
See also Mentally handicapped children; Physically handicapped children
Rogers, F. Extraordinary friends (k-2)   **362.4**

Handicraft
See also Egg decoration; Leather work; Nature craft
Bauer, C. F. Leading kids to books through crafts   **027.62**

Hanson, Peter E.—*Continued*
(il) Mitchell, B. A pocketful of goobers: a story about George Washington Carver **92**

Hanson, Rick
(il) Haskins, J. Count your way through Israel **956.94**

Hanukkah
Fishman, C. On Hanukkah (k-3) **296.4**
Goldin, B. D. While the candles burn (4 and up) **296.4**
A Hanukkah treasury **296.4**
Hoyt-Goldsmith, D. Celebrating Hanukkah (3-5) **296.4**
Podwal, M. H. The menorah story (k-3) **296.4**
Rosen, M. J. Our eight nights of Hanukkah (k-3) **296.4**
Simon, N. The story of Hanukkah (2-4) **296.4**

Fiction
Adler, D. A. Chanukah in Chelm (k-3) **398.2**
Drucker, M. Grandma's latkes **E**
Howland, N. Latkes, latkes, good to eat **E**
Jaffe, N. In the month of Kislev **E**
Kimmel, E. A. The Chanukkah guest **E**
Kimmel, E. A. Hershel and the Hanukkah goblins **E**
Kimmel, E. A. The jar of fools: eight Hanukkah stories from Chelm (3-5) **S C**
Kimmel, E. A. The magic dreidels **E**
Kimmel, E. A. The spotted pony: a collection of Hanukkah stories (3-6) **398.2**
Koss, A. G. How I saved Hanukkah (3-5) **Fic**
Manushkin, F. Latkes and applesauce **E**
Penn, M. The miracle of the potato latkes **E**
Polacco, P. The trees of the dancing goats **E**
Rosen, M. J. Elijah's angel **Fic**
Schnur, S. The tie man's miracle **E**
Singer, I. B. The power of light (4 and up) **S C**
A Hanukkah Eve in Warsaw. Singer, I. B.
In Singer, I. B. Stories for children p53-70 **S C**
A Hanukkah evening in my parents' house. Singer, I. B.
In Singer, I. B. The power of light p3-9 **S C**
In Singer, I. B. Stories for children p155-59 **S C**
Hanukkah in the poorhouse. Singer, I. B.
In Singer, I. B. The power of light p75-87 **S C**
In Singer, I. B. Stories for children p271-82 **S C**
A Hanukkah treasury **296.4**
Hapendeki and Binti the Bibi. Aardema, V.
In Aardema, V. Misoso p71-77 **398.2**
Happen. Ellis, S.
In Ellis, S. Back of beyond **S C**
Happy birth day!. Harris, R. H. **E**
Happy birthday (k-3) **811.008**

Happy birthday!. Gibbons, G. **394.2**
Happy birthday, Biscuit!. Capucilli, A. See note under Capucilli, A. Biscuit's new trick **E**
Happy birthday, Danny and the dinosaur. Hoff, S. See note under Hoff, S. Danny and the dinosaur **E**
Happy birthday, Jesse Bear. Carlstrom, N. W. See note under Carlstrom, N. W. Jesse Bear, what will you wear? **E**
Happy birthday, Lulu!. Uff, C. See note under Uff, C. Lulu's busy day **E**
Happy birthday, Martin Luther King. Marzollo, J. **92**
Happy birthday, Moon. Asch, F. See note under Asch, F. Moonbear's dream **E**
Happy birthday, Ronald Morgan!. Giff, P. R. See note under Giff, P. R. Watch out, Ronald Morgan! **E**
Happy birthday Rotten Ralph. Gantos, J. See note under Gantos, J. Rotten Ralph **E**
Happy birthday, Sam. Hutchins, P. **E**
Happy birthday to you, you belong in the zoo. De Groat, D. See note under De Groat, D. Trick or treat, smell my feet **E**
Happy Christmas to all. Nolan, J. C.
In The Big book of Christmas plays p137-50 **808.82**
Happy New Year!. Bernhard, E. **394.26**
Happy New Year!. Demi **394.26**
The **happy** prince [story] Wilde, O.
In Wilde, O. The fairy tales of Oscar Wilde p13-23 **S C**

Harbors
Crews, D. Harbor **E**
The **Harcourt** Brace student thesaurus (4 and up) **423**

Hard sell. Wynne-Jones, T.
In Wynne-Jones, T. The book of changes p67-82 **S C**

Harding, R. R., 1938-
(jt. auth) Symes, R. F. Crystal & gem **548**

Hardy Hardhead
In The Jack tales p96-105 **398.2**
The **hare** and the lion. See Aardema, V. Rabbit makes a monkey of lion **398.2**
The **hare** and the tortoise. Sierra, J.
In Sierra, J. Nursery tales around the world p75 **398.2**
The **hare** and the tortoise. Ward, H. **398.2**
The **hare** and the tortoise. Wildsmith, B. **398.2**

Hariton, Anca, 1955-
(il) Glaser, L. Compost! **363.7**
Hark, Mildred
Christmas Eve letter
In The Big book of Christmas plays p41-58 **808.82**
A star in the window
In The Big book of Christmas plays p118-33 **808.82**

Harlem (New York, N.Y.)
Fiction
Collier, B. Uptown **E**

Harlem (New York, N.Y.)—Fiction—*Continued*
Myers, W. D. Fast Sam, Cool Clyde, and Stuff
(6 and up)   Fic
Ringgold, F. Tar Beach   E
           Poetry
Myers, W. D. Harlem   811
Harlow, Joan Hiatt
Star in the storm   Fic
Harmful insects *See* Insect pests
Harmon, Charles T., 1960-
(jt. auth) Symons, A. K. Protecting the right to
read   323.44
Harmonicas
           Fiction
McCloskey, R. Lentil   E
Harms, Jeanne McLain
Picture books to enhance the curriculum
    011.6
Harness, Cheryl
Abe Lincoln goes to Washington, 1837-1865
(2-4)   92
The amazing impossible Erie Canal (3-5)
    386
George Washington (3-5)   92
Mark Twain and the queens of the Mississippi
(3-5)   92
They're off! (3-5)   383
Harold, Jerdine Nolen *See* Nolen, Jerdine
Harold & Chester in Scared silly. See Howe, J.
Scared silly: a Halloween treat   E
Harold and the purple crayon. Johnson, C.   E
Harold's ABC. Johnson, C. See note under John-
son, C. Harold and the purple crayon   E
Harold's circus. Johnson, C. See note under John-
son, C. Harold and the purple crayon   E
Harold's fairy tale. Johnson, C. See note under
Johnson, C. Harold and the purple crayon
    E
Harold's trip to the sky. Johnson, C. See note un-
der Johnson, C. Harold and the purple crayon
    E
The **harp** of Dagda. McCaughrean, G.
In McCaughrean, G. The silver treasure:
myths and legends of the world p31-37
    398.2
Harp seals. Cossi, O.   599.79
Harper, Dan, 1963-
Telling time with Big Mama Cat   E
Harper, Isabelle
Our new puppy   E
Harper, Peter
(il) Mitchelson, M. The most excellent book of
how to be a juggler   793.8
Harper growing tree [series]
Blegvad, L. First friends   E
Zolotow, C. Some things go together   E
Harpers Ferry (W. Va.)
      History—John Brown's Raid, 1859
January, B. John Brown's raid on Harpers Ferry
(4-6)   973.7
The **harps** of Heaven. Babbitt, N.
In Babbitt, N. The Devil's storybook p21-35
    S C

Harriet and the Promised Land. Lawrence, J.
    811
Harriet Beecher Stowe and the Beecher preachers.
Fritz, J.   92
Harriet the spy. Fitzhugh, L.   Fic
Harris, Jacqueline L., 1929-
Science in ancient Rome (4 and up)   509
Harris, Mary *See* Jones, Mother, 1830-1930
Harris, Robie H.
Happy birth day!   E
It's perfectly normal (4 and up)   613.9
It's so amazing! (2-4)   612.6
Harrison, Barbara
A ripple of hope: the life of Robert F. Kennedy
(6 and up)   92
Theo (5 and up)   Fic
(ed) Origins of story. See Origins of story
    808.06
Harrison, David Lee, 1937-
The giant who threw tantrums
In The Oxford treasury of children's stories
p28-32   S C
Harrison, John, 1693-1776
See/See also pages in the following book(s):
Duffy, T. The clock p34-45 (4 and up)
    681.1
Harrison, Michael, 1939-
(ed) The New Oxford treasury of children's po-
ems. See The New Oxford treasury of chil-
dren's poems   808.81
(ed) The Oxford book of animal poems. See
The Oxford book of animal poems
    808.81
(ed) The Oxford book of Christmas poems. See
The Oxford book of Christmas poems
    808.81
(comp) The Oxford treasury of children's sto-
ries. See The Oxford treasury of children's
stories   S C
Harrison, Supenn
Cooking the Thai way
In Easy menu ethnic cookbooks   641.5
Harrison, Ted, 1926-
(il) Service, R. W. The cremation of Sam
McGee   811
(il) Service, R. W. The shooting of Dan
McGrew   811
Harry and Lulu. Yorinks, A.   E
Harry and the lady next door. Zion, G. See note
under Zion, G. Harry the dirty dog   E
Harry by the sea. Zion, G. See note under Zion,
G. Harry the dirty dog   E
Harry Cat's pet puppy. Selden, G. See note under
Selden, G. The cricket in Times Square
    Fic
Harry in trouble. Porte, B. A.   E
Harry Kitten and Tucker Mouse. Selden, G. See
note under Selden, G. The cricket in Times
Square   Fic
Harry Potter and the Chamber of Secrets.
Rowling, J. K. See note under Rowling, J. K.
Harry Potter and the sorcerer's stone   Fic

The **haunted** inn. San Souci, R.
In San Souci, R. More short & shivery p40-44 **398.2**

Haunts. Medearis, A. S. **S C**

Hauser, Jill Frankel
Kids' crazy concoctions (3-6) **745.5**
Super science concoctions (3-5) **507.8**

Hausman, Gerald
Dogs of myth (3-6) **398.2**
Contents: The gift of fire; Why dogs cannot talk like people; How dog brought death into the world; First man and first woman's dog; King Herla's hound; The ghostly weaver; Prince Llewelyn's Gelert; The seven sleepers; The thunder mouth dog; A dog named Boye; The dog who married a princess; The dog, the cat, the snake, and the ring; The dog with the diamond foot

Hausman, Loretta
(jt. auth) Hausman, G. Dogs of myth **398.2**

Hautzig, Deborah, 1956-
The nutcracker ballet **E**

Hautzig, Esther Rudomin, 1930-
A gift for Mama (3-6) **Fic**

Have you seen bugs? Oppenheim, J. **595.7**

Have you seen my duckling? Tafuri, N. **E**

Haviland, Virginia, 1911-1988
Wiley and The Hairy Man
In The Oxford book of scary tales p55-61 **808.8**

Havill, Juanita
Jamaica and Brianna. See note under Havill, J. Jamaica's find **E**
Jamaica and the substitute teacher. See note under Havill, J. Jamaica's find **E**
Jamaica tag-along. See note under Havill, J. Jamaica's find **E**
Jamaica's blue marker. See note under Havill, J. Jamaica's find **E**
Jamaica's find **E**

Hawaii
Goldberg, J. Hawaii
In Celebrate the states **973**
Hintz, M. Hawaii
In America the beautiful, second series **973**

Fiction
Guback, G. Luka's quilt **E**
Rattigan, J. K. Dumpling soup **E**
Slepian, J. The Broccoli tapes (5 and up) **Fic**

Folklore
See Folklore—Hawaii
History
Stanley, F. The last princess: the story of Princess Ka'iulani of Hawai'i (4 and up) **92**

Hawes, Charles Boardman, 1889-1923
See/See also pages in the following book(s):
Newbery Medal books, 1922-1955 p30-32 **028.5**

Hawes, Judy
Fireflies in the night (k-1) **595.7**

The **hawk**. Gordon, J.
In The Oxford book of scary tales p114-22 **808.8**

Hawk highway in the sky. Arnold, C. **598**

Hawk, I'm your brother. Baylor, B. **E**

Hawkes, Kevin
(il) Bauer, M. D. Jason's bears **E**
(il) Fleischman, P. Weslandia **E**
(il) Grossman, B. My little sister ate one hare **E**
(il) Hoberman, M. A. And to think that we thought that we'd never be friends **E**
(il) Imagine that! See Imagine that! **811.008**
(il) Lasky, K. The librarian who measured the earth [biography of Eratosthenes] **92**
(il) Lasky, K. Marven of the Great North Woods **E**
(il) Pullman, P. I was a rat! **Fic**

Hawks
Arnold, C. Hawk highway in the sky (4-6) **598**

Fiction
Baylor, B. Hawk, I'm your brother **E**

Hawthorne, Nathaniel, 1804-1864
Feathertop
In American fairy tales p29-54 **S C**
Lady Eleanore's mantle; adaptation. See San Souci, R. Lady Eleanore's mantle
See/See also pages in the following book(s):
Faber, D. Great lives: American literature p21-30 (5 and up) **920**

Hayes, Ann
Meet the orchestra (k-3) **784.2**

Hayes, Joe, 1945-
Little Gold Star (k-3) **398.2**
La Llorona, the weeping woman
In From sea to shining sea p331-35 **810.8**
A spoon for every bite **E**

Hayes, Sarah
Eat up, Gemma **E**

Hayman, Peter
(il) Putnam, J. Mummy **393**
(il) Putnam, J. Pyramid **909**

The **haymeadow**. Paulsen, G. **Fic**

Hays, Michael, 1956-
(il) Schmandt-Besserat, D. The history of counting **513**
(il) Taylor, M. D. The gold Cadillac **Fic**

The **haystack** cricket and how things are different up in the moon towns. Sandburg, C.
In Sandburg, C. Rootabaga stories pt 2 p123-29 **S C**
In Sandburg, C. The Sandburg treasury p139-42 **818**

Haywood, John, 1956-
World atlas of the past **911**

The **Hazel-nut** child
In The Yellow fairy book p222-24 **398.2**

Hazel's amazing mother. Wells, R. **E**

Hazen, Barbara Shook, 1930-
Digby **E**

The **HBJ** student thesaurus. See The Harcourt Brace student thesaurus **423**

He came down. Paterson, K.
In Paterson, K. Angels & other strangers: family Christmas stories p81-89 **S C**

He is risen: the Easter story. Winthrop, E.
232.9

He Lion, Bruh Bear and Bruh Rabbit. Hamilton, V.
In Hamilton, V. The people could fly: American black folktales p5-12
398.2

Head
Rowan, P. Big head! (4 and up) **612.8**
The **headless** cupid. Snyder, Z. K. **Fic**
The **Headless** Horseman rides tonight. Prelutsky, J. **811**
The **headrest**. San Souci, R.
In San Souci, R. More short & shivery p130-33 **398.2**

Heads of state
See also Kings and rulers; Presidents
Heads or tails. Gantos, J. **Fic**
Heale, Jay
Democratic Republic of the Congo (5 and up)
967.51
Madagascar (5 and up) **969.1**
Tanzania (5 and up) **967.8**
The **healing** truth. Lay, K.
In A Glory of unicorns p145-62 **S C**
Healing warrior: a story about Sister Elizabeth Kenny. Crofford, E. **92**

Health
Kalbacken, J. The food pyramid (2-4)
613.2

Health care *See* Medical care
Health watch [series]
Gold, S. D. Alzheimer's disease **616.8**
The **healthy** body cookbook. D'Amico, J.
641.5

Heap, Sue
(il) Eilenberg, M. Cowboy Kid **E**
Hearing. Pringle, L. P.
In Pringle, L. P. Explore your senses
612.8

Hearing impaired
See also Deaf
Hearn, Lafcadio, 1850-1904
The old woman and her dumpling
In Womenfolk and fairy tales p44-50
398.2
The old woman and her dumpling; adaptation. See Mosel, A. The funny little woman
398.2

Hearne, Betsy Gould
Choosing books for children **028.5**
Seven brave women **E**
Hearne, Elizabeth G. *See* Hearne, Betsy Gould
Heart
See also Blood—Circulation
Ballard, C. The heart and circulatory system (5 and up) **612.1**
Silverstein, A. The circulatory system (5 and up) **612.1**
Simon, S. The heart (3-6) **612.1**
The **heart** and circulatory system. Ballard, C.
612.1

Heart of a tiger. Arnold, M. D. **E**
Heart of ice. Caylus, A. C. P. de T., comte de
In The Green fairy book p106-36 **398.2**
A **heart** of stone. McCaughrean, G.
In McCaughrean, G. The silver treasure: myths and legends of the world p70-74
398.2
Hearts, cupids, and red roses. Barth, E.
394.26
Heat wave at Mud Flat. Stevenson, J. See note under Stevenson, J. The Mud Flat Olympics
E
Heaven. Johnson, A. **Fic**
Heaven to Betsy. Lovelace, M. H. See note under Lovelace, M. H. Betsy-Tacy **Fic**
The **heavenly** court. Schwartz, H.
In Schwartz, H. A journey to paradise and other Jewish tales p24-25 **398.2**
Heckedy Peg. Wood, A. **E**
Hedgehogs

Fiction
Brett, J. The hat **E**
Potter, B. The tale of Mrs. Tiggy-Winkle
E

The **Hedley** Kow. Jacobs, J.
In Jacobs, J. English fairy tales p271-74
398.2

Hehner, Barbara, 1947-
First on the moon (4 and up) **629.45**
(jt. auth) Bierman, C. Journey to Ellis Island
325.73

Heide, Florence Parry, 1919-
Chester
In Thanksgiving: stories and poems p49-50
810.8
The day of Ahmed's secret **E**
Oh, grow up! (k-3) **811**
Sami and the time of the troubles **E**
The shrinking of Treehorn (2-5) **Fic**
also in The Oxford treasury of children's stories p135-43 **S C**

Heiden, Eric, 1958-
See/See also pages in the following book(s):
Knapp, R. Top 10 American men's Olympic gold medalists (4 and up) **920**
Heidi. Spyri, J. **Fic**
The **Heifer** hide
In The Jack tales p161-71 **398.2**
Heiligman, Deborah
From caterpillar to butterfly (k-1) **595.7**
The New York Public Library kid's guide to research (5 and up) **025.5**
Heine, Helme
Friends **E**
Friends go adventuring. See note under Heine, H. Friends **E**
The most wonderful egg in the world **E**
Heinemann, Sue, 1948-
The New York Public Library amazing women in American history (5 and up) **305.4**
Heinrichs, Ann
Australia (4 and up) **994**
Brazil (4 and up) **981**

Heinrichs, Ann—*Continued*
California
In America the beautiful, second series
973
Egypt (4 and up) 962
Florida
In America the beautiful, second series
973
Indiana
In America the beautiful, second series
973
Japan (4 and up) 952
New York
In America the beautiful, second series
973
Ohio
In America the beautiful, second series
973
Pennsylvania
In America the beautiful, second series
973
Texas
In America the beautiful, second series
973

Heins, Ethel L., 1918-1997
The cat and the cook and other fables of Krylov
(1-4) **398.2**

Hekeke. San Souci, R.
In San Souci, R. Cut from the same cloth
p103-09 **398.2**

Helldorfer, Mary Claire, 1954-
Hog music **E**
Phoebe and the River Flute **E**

Heller, Julek
(il) Mayer, M. Women warriors **398**

Heller, Ruth
Behind the mask (k-2) **428**
A cache of jewels and other collective nouns
(k-2) **428**
Chickens aren't the only ones (k-1) **591.4**
Fantastic! wow! and unreal! (k-2) **428**
Kites sail high: a book about verbs (k-2)
428
Many luscious lollipops: a book about adjectives
(k-2) **428**
Merry-go-round (k-2) **428**
Mine, all mine (k-2) **428**
Up, up and away (k-2) **428**
(il) Climo, S. The Egyptian Cinderella
398.2
(il) Climo, S. The Korean Cinderella **398.2**
(il) Creasy, R. Blue potatoes, orange tomatoes
635

Hello, Biscuit!. Capucilli, A. See note under
Capucilli, A. Biscuit's new trick **E**
Hello friend. Goble, P. **92**
Hello! good-bye!. Aliki **395**
Hello, Lulu. Uff, C. See note under Uff, C. Lulu's
busy day **E**
Hello, Mrs. Piggle-Wiggle. MacDonald, B. See
note under MacDonald, B. Mrs. Piggle-
Wiggle **Fic**
Hello, my name is Scrambled Eggs. Gilson, J.
Fic
Hello toes! Hello feet!. Paul, A. W. **E**

Help! I'm a prisoner in the library. Clifford, E.
Fic

Helquist, Brett
(il) Snicket, L. The bad beginning **Fic**

Hemenway, Harriet, d. 1960
Fiction
Lasky, K. She's wearing a dead bird on her
head! **E**

Hemingway, Ernest, 1899-1961
See/See also pages in the following book(s):
Faber, D. Great lives: American literature p221-
30 (5 and up) **920**

Hemmant, Lynette, 1938-
(il) King-Smith, D. Ace, the very important pig
Fic

Hen and Frog. Bryan, A.
In Bryan, A. Ashley Bryan's African tales,
uh-huh p43-53 **398.2**
The **hen** and the dove. Aardema, V.
In Aardema, V. Misoso p33-35 **398.2**
Hen Lake. Auch, M. J. See note under Auch, M.
J. Peeping Beauty **E**

Henbest, Nigel
(jt. auth) Couper, H. Black holes **523.8**
(jt. auth) Couper, H. Is anybody out there?
576.8

Henderson, Carolyn
Horse & pony care **636.1**

Henderson, Douglas
Asteroid impact (3-5) **567.9**
Dinosaur tree (2-4) **560**
(il) Lauber, P. Living with dinosaurs **567.9**

Henderson, Kathy
The baby dances **E**

Henderson, Meryl
(il) Pringle, L. P. Bats! **599.4**

Hendry, Linda
(il) Irvine, J. How to make holiday pop-ups
736
(il) Irvine, J. How to make super pop-ups
736

Heng O, the moon lady. Carpenter, F.
In Carpenter, F. Tales of a Chinese grandmother p206-16 **398.2**

Henie, Sonja, 1912-1969
See/See also pages in the following book(s):
Krull, K. Lives of the athletes p43-45 (4 and
up) **920**

Henkes, Kevin, 1960-
The birthday room (5 and up) **Fic**
Chester's way **E**
Chrysanthemum **E**
Circle dogs **E**
Jessica **E**
Julius, the baby of the world **E**
Lilly's purple plastic purse **E**
Oh! **E**
Owen **E**
Protecting Marie (5 and up) **Fic**
Sheila Rae, the brave **E**
Sun & Spoon (4 and up) **Fic**
Wemberly worried **E**
Words of stone (5 and up) **Fic**

Henneberger, Robert, 1921-
   (il) Cameron, E. The wonderful flight to the Mushroom Planet   **Fic**

Hennessy, B. G. (Barbara G.)
   Road builders (k-2)   **625.7**

Hennessy, Barbara G. *See* Hennessy, B. G. (Barbara G.)

Henny Penny. Galdone, P.   **398.2**

Henny-penny. Jacobs, J.
   In Jacobs, J. English fairy tales p116-19
      398.2

Henny-Penny. Wattenberg, J.   **398.2**

Henriquez, Elsa
   (il) The Magic orange tree, and other Haitian folktales. See The Magic orange tree, and other Haitian folktales   **398.2**

Henry, Infante of Portugal, 1394-1460
   See/See also pages in the following book(s):
   Fritz, J. Around the world in a hundred years p19-29 (4-6)   **910.4**

Henry, the Navigator *See* Henry, Infante of Portugal, 1394-1460

Henry, Marguerite, 1902-1997
   Brighty of the Grand Canyon (4 and up)   **Fic**
   Justin Morgan had a horse (4 and up)   **Fic**
   King of the wind (4 and up)   **Fic**
   Misty of Chincoteague (4 and up)   **Fic**
   Sea Star, orphan of Chincoteague. See note under Henry, M. Misty of Chincoteague   **Fic**
   Stormy, Misty's foal. See note under Henry, M. Misty of Chincoteague   **Fic**
   See/See also pages in the following book(s):
   Newbery Medal books, 1922-1955 p320-24, 327-34   **028.5**

Henry, O., 1862-1910
   The gift of the Magi (5 and up)   **Fic**
   See/See also pages in the following book(s):
   Faber, D. Great lives: American literature p121-29 (5 and up)   **920**

Henry, Patrick, 1736-1799
        About
   Fritz, J. Where was Patrick Henry on the 29th of May? (2-4)   **92**

Henry, Sandi, 1951-
   Cut-paper play!   **745.54**

Henry and Beezus. Cleary, B. See note under Bond, M. A bear called Paddington   **Fic**

Henry and Mudge. Rylant, C.   **E**

Henry and Mudge and Annie's good move. Rylant, C. See note under Rylant, C. Henry and Mudge   **E**

Henry and Mudge and Annie's perfect pet. Rylant, C. See note under Rylant, C. Henry and Mudge   **E**

Henry and Mudge and the bedtime thumps. Rylant, C. See note under Rylant, C. Henry and Mudge   **E**

Henry and Mudge and the best day of all. Rylant, C. See note under Rylant, C. Henry and Mudge   **E**

Henry and Mudge and the careful cousin. Rylant, C. See note under Rylant, C. Henry and Mudge   **E**

Henry and Mudge and the forever sea. Rylant, C. See note under Rylant, C. Henry and Mudge   **E**

Henry and Mudge and the happy cat. Rylant, C. See note under Rylant, C. Henry and Mudge   **E**

Henry and Mudge and the long weekend. Rylant, C. See note under Rylant, C. Henry and Mudge   **E**

Henry and Mudge and the sneaky crackers. Rylant, C. See note under Rylant, C. Henry and Mudge   **E**

Henry and Mudge and the Snowman plan. Rylant, C. See note under Rylant, C. Henry and Mudge   **E**

Henry and Mudge and the starry night. Rylant, C. See note under Rylant, C. Henry and Mudge   **E**

Henry and Mudge and the wild wind. Rylant, C. See note under Rylant, C. Henry and Mudge   **E**

Henry and Mudge get the cold shivers. Rylant, C. See note under Rylant, C. Henry and Mudge   **E**

Henry and Mudge in puddle trouble. Rylant, C. See note under Rylant, C. Henry and Mudge   **E**

Henry and Mudge in the family trees. Rylant, C. See note under Rylant, C. Henry and Mudge   **E**

Henry and Mudge in the green time. Rylant, C. See note under Rylant, C. Henry and Mudge   **E**

Henry and Mudge in the sparkle days. Rylant, C. See note under Rylant, C. Henry and Mudge   **E**

Henry and Mudge take the big test. Rylant, C. See note under Rylant, C. Henry and Mudge   **E**

Henry and Mudge under the yellow moon. Rylant, C. See note under Rylant, C. Henry and Mudge   **E**

Henry and Ribsy. Cleary, B. See note under Cleary, B. Henry Higgins   **Fic**

Henry and the clubhouse. Cleary, B. See note under Cleary, B. Henry Higgins   **Fic**

Henry and the paper route. Cleary, B. See note under Cleary, B. Henry Higgins   **Fic**

Henry hikes to Fitchburg. Johnson, D. B.   **E**

Henry Huggins. Cleary, B.   **Fic**

Henry Reed, Inc. Robertson, K.   **Fic**

Henry Reed's babysitting service. Robertson, K. See note under Robertson, K. Henry Reed, Inc.   **Fic**

Henry Street Settlement (New York, N.Y.)
   Wolf, B. Homeless (2-4)   **362.5**

Henry the fourth. Murphy, S. J.   **513**

Henry the sailor cat. Calhoun, M. See note under Calhoun, M. Cross-country cat   **E**

Hensel, Fanny Cécile Mendelssohn, 1805-1847
About
Kamen, G. Hidden music (4 and up)   **92**
Henson, Matthew Alexander, 1866-1955
About
Ferris, J. Arctic explorer: the story of Matthew Henson (3-6)   **92**
See/See also pages in the following book(s):
Haskins, J. One more river to cross (4 and up)   **920**

Henterly, Jamichael
(il) Arnold, M. D. Heart of a tiger   **E**
Heo, Yumi
The green frogs (k-3)   **398.2**
(il) Aardema, V. The lonely lioness and the ostrich chicks   **398.2**
(il) Han, S. C. The rabbit's escape   **398.2**
(il) Kajikawa, K. Yoshi's feast   **398.2**
Hepler, Susan Ingrid
(jt. auth) Huck, C. S. Children's literature in the elementary school   **028.5**
Her seven brothers. Goble, P.   **398.2**
also in Goble, P. Paul Goble gallery   **398.2**
Her stories. Hamilton, V.   **398.2**
Heracles (Legendary character) *See* Hercules (Legendary character)
Herb, Sara Willoughby- *See* Willoughby-Herb, Sara
Herb, Steven
Using children's books in preschool settings   **372.4**
Herbie Jones. Kline, S.   **Fic**
Herbie Jones and Hamburger Head. Kline, S. See note under Kline, S. Herbie Jones   **Fic**
Herbie Jones and the birthday showdown. Kline, S. See note under Kline, S. Herbie Jones   **Fic**
Herbie Jones and the class gift. Kline, S. See note under Kline, S. Herbie Jones   **Fic**
Herbie Jones and the dark attic. Kline, S. See note under Kline, S. Herbie Jones   **Fic**
Herbie Jones and the monster ball. Kline, S. See note under Kline, S. Herbie Jones   **Fic**
Herbst, Judith
The mystery of UFOs (2-4)   **001.9**
Hercules (Legendary character)
Burleigh, R. Hercules (3-6)   **292**
See/See also pages in the following book(s):
Colum, P. The Golden Fleece and the heroes who lived before Achilles p244-94 (5 and up)   **292**
Hamilton, E. Mythology p224-43 (6 and up)   **292**
Here comes McBroom!. Fleischman, S.   **Fic**
Here comes Mother Goose   **398.8**
Here comes Pontus!. Jeppson, A.-S.   **Fic**
Here comes the strikeout. Kessler, L. P.   **E**
Here comes the train. Voake, C.   **E**
Here is my heart   **821.008**
Here is the African savanna. Dunphy, M.   **577.4**

Here there be dragons. Yolen, J.   **810.8**
Here we all are. De Paola, T.   **92**
Hereafterthis. Jacobs, J.
In Jacobs, J. English fairy tales p230-33   **398.2**
Herman, Charlotte
How Yussel caught the gefilte fish   **E**
Herman, Gail
Cal Ripken, Jr. (1-3)   **92**
Hermes, Jules, 1962-
The children of Bolivia (3-5)   **984**
Hermes, Patricia, 1936-
Our strange new land (3-5)   **Fic**
Hermit crabs *See* Crabs
Hermod and Hadvor
In The Yellow fairy book p301-07   **398.2**
The **hero** and the crown. McKinley, R.   **Fic**
The **hero** of Bremen. Hodges, M.   **398.2**
Heroes. Mochizuki, K.   **E**
Heroes and heroines
Mayer, M. Women warriors (4 and up)   **398**
The **heroine** of the Titanic: a tale both true and otherwise of the life of Molly Brown. Blos, J. W.   **92**
Heroines *See* Heroes and heroines
Heroism *See* Courage
Herold, Maggie Rugg
A very important day   **E**
Herons
Fiction
Avi. Blue heron (5 and up)   **Fic**
The **hero's** adventure. (5 and up) See entry in Part 2: Web Resources
Herrera, Juan Felipe, 1948-
Laughing out loud, I fly   **811**
The upside down boy (k-3)   **92**
About
Herrera, J. F. The upside down boy (k-3)   **92**
Herriot, James
Moses the kitten   **E**
Hershel and the Hanukkah goblins. Kimmel, E. A.   **E**
Hershel and the nobleman. Jaffe, N.
In Jaffe, N. While standing on one foot p56-61   **296.1**
Hershel goes to heaven. Kimmel, E. A.
In Kimmel, E. A. The adventures of Hershel of Ostropol p61-62   **398.2**
Hershele and Hanukkah. Singer, I. B.
In Singer, I. B. The power of light p63-72   **S C**
In Singer, I. B. Stories for children p184-93   **S C**
Herzog, George, 1901-1984
(jt. auth) Courlander, H. Cow-tail switch, and other West African stories   **398.2**
Heslop, Michael
(il) Cooper, S. The grey king   **Fic**
Hess, Paul
(il) Helldorfer, M. C. Phoebe and the River Flute   **E**

Hesse, Eva, 1936-1970
See/See also pages in the following book(s):
Greenberg, J. The American eye p98-105 (6 and up) **920**

Hesse, Karen
Come on, rain! **E**
Just Juice (3-5) **Fic**
Lester's dog **E**
Letters from Rifka (5 and up) **Fic**
A light in the storm (4 and up) **Fic**
The music of dolphins (6 and up) **Fic**
Out of the dust (5 and up) **Fic**
Sable (2-4) **Fic**
See/See also pages in the following book(s):
The Newbery & Caldecott medal books, 1986-2000 p295-305 **028.5**

Hest, Amy
Baby Duck and the bad eyeglasses. See note under Hest, A. In the rain with Baby Duck **E**
Gabby growing up **E**
In the rain with Baby Duck **E**
Mabel dancing **E**
Nana's birthday party **E**
Off to school, Baby Duck. See note under Hest, A. In the rain with Baby Duck **E**
The purple coat **E**
When Jessie came across the sea **E**
You're the boss, Baby Duck. See note under Hest, A. In the rain with Baby Duck **E**

Hestler, Anna
Yemen (5 and up) **953.3**

Hewett, Richard
(il) Arnold, C. The ancient cliff dwellers of Mesa Verde **970.004**
(il) Arnold, C. Cats: in from the wild **599.75**
(il) Arnold, C. Dinosaur mountain **567.9**
(il) Arnold, C. Dinosaurs all around **567.9**
(il) Arnold, C. Rhino **599.66**
(il) Arnold, C. Stories in stone **709.01**

Hewitson, Jennifer
(il) Wong, J. S. The rainbow hand **811**

Hewitt, Kathryn
(il) Bunting, E. Flower garden **E**
(il) Krull, K. Lives of the athletes **920**
(il) Krull, K. Lives of the musicians **920**
(il) Krull, K. Lives of the presidents **920**
(il) Krull, K. Lives of the writers **920**

Hewitt, Richard
(il) Arnold, C. City of the Gods **972**

Hewitt, Sally
The Aztecs (1-3) **972**
Solid, liquid, or gas? (k-3) **530.4**
Time (k-3) **529**

Hey, Al. Yorinks, A. **E**
Hey! listen to this **028.5**
Hey, new kid. Duffey, B. See note under Duffey, B. Spotlight on Cody **Fic**
Hey world, here I am!. Little, J. **811**

Heyer, Carol, 1950-
(il) Pringle, L. P. Dinosaurs! **567.9**

Heyman, Ken, 1930-
(il) Morris, A. Bread, bread, bread **641.8**

(il) Morris, A. Hats, hats, hats **391**
(il) Morris, A. Houses and homes **728**

Heyward, DuBose, 1885-1940
The country bunny and the little gold shoes **E**

Hi. Scott, A. H. **E**
Hi, cat!. Keats, E. J. **E**
"Hi, pizza man!". Walter, V. A. **E**

Hiawatha, 15th cent.
About
Fradin, D. B. Hiawatha: messenger of peace (3-5) **92**

Hiawatha. Longfellow, H. W. **811**

Hibernation
Fiction
Fleming, D. Time to sleep **E**

Hic! Hic! Hic!. MacDonald, M. R.
In MacDonald, M. R. Twenty tellable tales p142-53 **372.6**

Hickman, Janet
Jericho (5 and up) **Fic**
(jt. auth) Huck, C. S. Children's literature in the elementary school **028.5**

Hickman, Pamela M.
Animals in motion (3-5) **591.47**
Starting with nature bird book (4 and up) **598**

Hickock, Martha Jane Canary *See* Calamity Jane, 1852-1903

Hickox, Rebecca
The golden sandal (k-3) **398.2**

The **hidden** children. Greenfeld, H. **940.53**
The **hidden** forest. Baker, J. **E**
Hidden music [biography of Fanny Cecile Mendelssohn Hensel] Kamen, G. **92**
Hide and seek. Vos, I. **Fic**
Hide and seek fog. Tresselt, A. R. **E**
Hiding from the Nazis. Adler, D. A. **940.53**
Hiding to survive. Rosenberg, M. B. **940.53**

Hiera. Mayer, M.
In Mayer, M. Women warriors p27-29 **398**

Hieroglyphics
See also Picture writing; Rosetta stone inscription
Donoughue, C. The mystery of the hieroglyphs (3-6) **493**
Giblin, J. The riddle of the Rosetta Stone (5 and up) **493**
Rumford, J. Seeker of knowledge (3-5) **92**

Higglety pigglety pop!. Sendak, M. **Fic**

High, Linda Oatman
Barn savers **E**

High Elk's treasure. Sneve, V. D. H. **Fic**
High John the Conquerer. Sanfield, S.
In From sea to shining sea p134-35 **810.8**
High John the Conqueror, The adventures of. Sanfield, S. **398.2**
The **high** king. Alexander, L. **Fic**
A **high,** low, near, far, loud, quiet story. Crews, N. **E**

High school libraries
See also Young adults' libraries
High tech *See* Technology
High-wire Henry. Calhoun, M. See note under Calhoun, M. Cross-country cat   **E**
A **higher** truth. Jaffe, N.
    In Jaffe, N. The cow of no color: riddle stories and justice tales from around the world p110-13   **398.2**
Highlights for Children   **051**
Highways *See* Roads
Hiiaka. San Souci, R.
    In San Souci, R. Cut from the same cloth p121-28   **398.2**
Hijuelos, Oscar
Christmas fantasy
    In You're on!: seven plays in English and Spanish p108-31   **812.008**
Hiking
    See also Walking
Hilde and Eli, children of the Holocaust. Adler, D. A.   **940.53**
Hildebrandt, Ziporah, 1956-
This is our Seder (k-3)   **296.4**
Hildegard, von Bingen, Saint, 1098-1179
See/See also pages in the following book(s):
Krull, K. They saw the future p35-41 (4 and up)   **133.3**
Hildilid's night. Durán, C.   **E**
Hill, Barbara W., 1941-
Cooking the English way
    In Easy menu ethnic cookbooks   **641.5**
Hill, Christine M.
Robert Ballard (5 and up)   **92**
Hill, Douglas, 1935-
Witches & magic-makers (4 and up)   **133.4**
Hill, Elizabeth Starr
Bird Boy (2-4)   **Fic**
Evan's corner   **E**
Hill, James Jerome, 1838-1916
See/See also pages in the following book(s):
Calvert, P. Great lives: the American frontier p193-208 (5 and up)   **920**
Hillary, Sir Edmund
See/See also pages in the following book(s):
Krull, K. Lives of the athletes p55-57 (4 and up)   **920**
Hillel the Wise. Jaffe, N.
    In Jaffe, N. While standing on one foot p91-95   **296.1**
Hillenbrand, Will
Down by the station (k-2)   **782.42**
(il) Aardema, V. Traveling to Tondo   **398.2**
(il) Goldin, B. D. Coyote and the firestick   **398.2**
(il) Hickox, R. The golden sandal   **398.2**
(il) Wooldridge, C. N. Wicked Jack   **398.2**
Hills, Alan
(il) Cotterell, A. Ancient China   **931**
Himler, Ronald
(il) Bunting, E. Fly away home   **E**
(il) Bunting, E. Someday a tree   **E**

(il) Bunting, E. Train to Somewhere   **E**
(il) Bunting, E. The Wall   **E**
(il) Coerr, E. Sadako and the thousand paper cranes [biography of Sadako Sasaki]   **92**
(il) Fritz, J. Why not, Lafayette?   **92**
(il) Garland, S. Voices of the Alamo   **976.4**
(il) Kroll, S. William Penn   **92**
(il) Oppenheim, S. L. The lily cupboard   **E**
(ed) Sneve, V. D. H. The Apaches   **970.004**
(il) Sneve, V. D. H. The Cherokees   **970.004**
(il) Sneve, V. D. H. The Cheyennes   **970.004**
(il) Sneve, V. D. H. The Hopis   **970.004**
(il) Sneve, V. D. H. The Iroquois   **970.004**
(il) Sneve, V. D. H. The Navajos   **970.004**
(il) Sneve, V. D. H. The Nez Percé   **970.004**
(il) Sneve, V. D. H. The Seminoles   **970.004**
(il) Sneve, V. D. H. The Sioux   **970.004**
(il) Turner, A. W. Katie's trunk   **E**
(il) Turner, A. W. Nettie's trip South   **Fic**
Himmelman, John, 1959-
A pill bug's life (k-2)   **595.3**
(il) Kraus, R. Mort the sport   **E**
Hindley, Judy
The big red bus   **E**
Eyes, nose, fingers and toes   **E**
Hinduism
See/See also pages in the following book(s):
Osborne, M. P. One world, many religions p37-46 (4 and up)   **291**
Hine, Lewis Wickes, 1874-1940
About
Freedman, R. Kids at work (5 and up)   **331.3**
Hinemoa and Tutanekai. Te Kanawa, K.
    In Te Kanawa, K. Land of the long white cloud p35-44   **398.2**
Hines, Anna Grossnickle, 1946-
Daddy makes the best spaghetti   **E**
What can you do in the rain?   **E**
What can you do in the snow? See note under Hines, A. G. What can you do in the rain?   **E**
What can you do in the sun? See note under Hines, A. G. What can you do in the rain?   **E**
What can you do in the wind? See note under Hines, A. G. What can you do in th rain?   **E**
Hinman, Bonnie
Benjamin Banneker (4 and up)   **92**
Hintz, Martin, 1945-
Argentina (4 and up)   **982**
The Bahamas (4 and up)   **972.96**
Haiti (4 and up)   **972.94**
Hawaii
    In America the beautiful, second series   **973**
Iowa
    In America the beautiful, second series   **973**

Hintz, Martin, 1945-—*Continued*
Israel (4 and up)   **956.94**
Louisiana
In America the beautiful, second series
                                     973
Michigan
In America the beautiful, second series
                                     973
Minnesota
In America the beautiful, second series
                                     973
Missouri
In America the beautiful, second series
                                     973
North Carolina
In America the beautiful, second series
                                     973
North Dakota
In America the beautiful, second series
                                     973
Poland (4 and up)   **943.8**
Hintz, Stephen V.
(jt. auth) Hintz, M. The Bahamas   **972.96**
(jt. auth) Hintz, M. Israel   **956.94**
Hippety-hop, hippety-hay. Dunn, O.   **398.8**
Hippopotamus
Walker, S. M. Hippos (3-6)   **599.63**
Fiction
Kasza, K. Dorothy & Mikey   **E**
Mahy, M. The boy who was followed home
                                     E
Marshall, J. George and Martha   **E**
A **hippopotamusn't** and other animal verses.
Lewis, J. P.   **811**
Hippos. Walker, S. M.   **599.63**
The **hired** hand. San Souci, R.   **398.2**
Hiroshima (Japan)
Bombardment, 1945
Coerr, E. Sadako [biography of Sadako Sasaki]
(1-4)   **92**
Coerr, E. Sadako and the thousand paper cranes
[biography of Sadako Sasaki] (3-6)   **92**
Maruki, T. Hiroshima no pika   **940.54**
Bombardment, 1945—Fiction
Yep, L. Hiroshima (4 and up)   **Fic**
Hiroshima no pika. Maruki, T.   **940.54**
Hirschfelder, Arlene B.
American Indian stereotypes in the world of
children   **970.004**
Native Americans today   **970.004**
(comp) Rising voices. See Rising voices
                                     810.8
Hirschi, Ron
Fall (k-2)   **508.2**
Spring (k-2)   **508.2**
Summer (k-2)   **508.2**
Winter (k-2)   **508.2**
Hirst, Robin
My place in space (2-4)   **520**
Hirst, Sally
(jt. auth) Hirst, R. My place in space   **520**
Hiscock, Bruce, 1940-
The big rivers (2-4)   **551.48**

Hispanic American poetry *See* American poetry—Hispanic American authors
Hispanic Americans
Wadham, T. Programming with Latino children's materials   **027.62**
Drama
You're on!: seven plays in English and Spanish
(4 and up)   **812.008**
Fiction
Dorros, A. Abuela   **E**
Garza, C. L. Family pictures   **E**
Gershator, D. Bread is for eating   **E**
Hayes, J. A spoon for every bite   **E**
Soto, G. Taking sides (5 and up)   **Fic**
Folklore
Hayes, J. Little Gold Star (k-3)   **398.2**
Poetry
Soto, G. Neighborhood odes (4-6)   **811**
Social life and customs
Ancona, G. Fiesta U.S.A. (k-3)   **394.26**
Hoyt-Goldsmith, D. Las Posadas (3-5)
                                     394.26
Hispanics of achievement [series]
O'Brien, S. Pancho Villa   **92**
Historical American biographies [series]
Gaines, A. Jim Bowie   **92**
Historical fiction
History and criticism
See/See also pages in the following book(s):
Only connect: readings on children's literature
p62-73   **028.5**
Historical geography
Haywood, J. World atlas of the past **911**
History
See also World history
Bibliography
Adamson, L. G. Literature connections to world
history, K-6   **016.9**
From biography to history   **016.8**
Periodicals
Calliope   **905**
The **history** of counting. Schmandt-Besserat, D.
                                     513
The **History** of Jack and the bean-stalk
In The Classic Fairy tales p164-74   **398.2**
The **History** of Jack and the giants
In The Classic fairy tales p51-65   **398.2**
The **History** of Jack the giant killer
In The Blue fairy book p374-79   **398.2**
The **History** of Tom Thumb
In The Classic fairy tales p33-46   **398.2**
The **history** of Tom Thumb. Jacobs, J.
In Jacobs, J. English fairy tales p140-46
                                     398.2
A **history** of US. Hakim, J.   **973**
The **History** of Whittington
In The Blue fairy book p206-13   **398.2**
The **hit-away** kid. Christopher, M.   **Fic**
Hit list: frequently challenged books for children
                                     016.8
Hitty: her first hundred years. Field, R.   **Fic**
Hitz, Demi *See* Demi, 1942-
HIV disease *See* AIDS (Disease)

Hodges, Margaret—*Continued*
The hero of Bremen (3-5)   **398.2**
Joan of Arc (2-4)   **92**
The kitchen knight (3 and up)   **398.2**
Saint George and the dragon (2-5)   **398.2**
Saint Patrick and the peddler (k-3)   **398.2**
The true tale of Johnny Appleseed (k-3)   **92**

Hodges, Sarah Margaret *See* Hodges, Margaret

Hoestlandt, Jo, 1948-
Star of fear, star of hope   **E**

Hoff, Syd, 1912-
Danny and the dinosaur   **E**
Danny and the dinosaur go to camp. See note under Hoff, S. Danny and the dinosaur   **E**
Happy birthday, Danny and the dinosaur. See note under Hoff, S. Danny and the dinosaur   **E**
Oliver   **E**
Sammy the seal   **E**
(il) Lexau, J. M. Don't be my valentine   **E**
(il) Schwartz, A. I saw you in the bathtub, and other folk rhymes   **398.2**

Hoffman, Frank W. *See* Hoffmann, Frank W. (Frank William), 1949-

Hoffman, Mary, 1945-
Amazing Grace   **E**
Boundless Grace. See note under Hoffman, M. Amazing Grace   **E**
Starring Grace. See note under Hoffman, M. Amazing Grace   **E**
Sun, moon, and stars (3-6)   **398.2**

Hoffman, Nancy, 1955-
South Carolina
In Celebrate the states   **973**
West Virginia
In Celebrate the states   **973**

Hoffmann, E. T. A. (Ernst Theodor Amadeus), 1776-1822
Nutcracker (4 and up)   **Fic**
In Christmas fairy tales p47-57   **398.2**
The nutcracker; adaptation. See Bell, A. The nutcracker   **Fic**
The nutcracker and the King of Mice; adaptation. See Schulman, J. The nutcracker   **Fic**

Hoffmann, Ernst Theodor Amadeus *See* Hoffmann, E. T. A. (Ernst Theodor Amadeus), 1776-1822

Hoffmann, Frank W. (Frank William), 1949-
(ed) Grantsmanship for small libraries and school library media centers. See Grantsmanship for small libraries and school library media centers   **025.1**

Hog-eye. Meddaugh, S.   **E**

Hog music. Helldorfer, M. C.   **E**

Hogrogian, Nonny
The contest (k-3)   **398.2**
One fine day (k-3)   **398.2**
(il) Kherdian, D. The golden bracelet   **398.2**
(il) Leodhas, S. N. Always room for one more   **782.42**

See/See also pages in the following book(s):
Newbery and Caldecott Medal books, 1966-1975 p179-85, 237-42   **028.5**

Hoichi the earless. San Souci, R.
In San Souci, R. A terrifying taste of short & shivery p118-22   **398.2**

Holabird, Katharine
Angelina and Alice. See note under Holabird, K. Angelina ballerina   **E**
Angelina and the princess. See note under Holabird, K. Angelina ballerina   **E**
Angelina at the fair. See note under Holabird, K. Angelina ballerina   **E**
Angelina ballerina   **E**
Angelina on stage. See note under Holabird, K. Angelina ballerina   **E**
Angelina's baby sister. See note under Holabird, K. Angelina ballerina   **E**
Angelina's Christmas. See note under Holabird, K. Angelina ballerina   **E**
Angelina's Halloween. See note under Holabird, K. Angelina ballerina   **E**

"Hold him, Tabb!". San Souci, R.
In San Souci, R. More short & shivery p1-4   **398.2**

Hold your horses. Meltzer, M.   **636.1**

Holes. Sachar, L.   **Fic**

Holiday cooking around the world
In Easy menu ethnic cookbooks   **641.5**

Holiday crafts for kids [series]
Ross, K. Crafts for Kwanzaa   **745.5**

Holiday House reader [series]
Caple, K. The friendship tree   **E**
Ruelle, K. G. The Thanksgiving beast feast   **E**
Weston, M. Space guys!   **E**

Holidays
See also Christmas; Father's Day; Fourth of July; Kwanzaa; New Year; Saint Patrick's Day; Thanksgiving Day; Valentine's Day
The American book of days   **394.26**
Bauer, C. F. Celebrations   **808.8**
Chase's calendar of events   **394.26**
The Folklore of world holidays   **394.26**
Irvine, J. How to make holiday pop-ups (3-6)   **736**
Jones, L. Kids around the world celebrate! (4-6)   **394.26**
Kindersley, A. Celebrations (3-5)   **394.26**
McElmeel, S. L. WWW almanac   **025.04**
Moehn, H. World holidays (3-6)   **394.26**
Perl, L. Piñatas and paper flowers (4 and up)   **394.26**
Trawicky, B. Anniversaries and holidays   **394.26**
Webb, L. S. Holidays of the world cookbook for students (5 and up)   **641.5**
Zalben, J. B. To every season (4 and up)   **641.5**

Poetry
Livingston, M. C. Celebrations   **811**
Yolen, J. The three bears holiday rhyme book (k-2)   **811**

Holidays, Jewish *See* Jewish holidays

Holidays of the world cookbook for students. Webb, L. S. **641.5**

Holland, Kevin Crossley- *See* Crossley-Holland, Kevin

Holland *See* Netherlands

Holling, Holling C., 1900-1973
Paddle-to-the-sea (4-6) **Fic**

Holly, reindeer, and colored lights. Barth, E. **394.26**

Holm, Anne, 1922-
North to freedom (6 and up) **Fic**

Holm, Jennifer L.
Our only May Amelia (5 and up) **Fic**

Holm, Sharon Lane, 1955-
(il) Erlbach, A. Sidewalk games around the world **796.1**
(il) Lang, S. S. Nature in your backyard **508**
(il) Ross, K. The best birthday parties ever! **793.2**
(il) Ross, K. Crafts for Kwanzaa **745.5**

Holman, Felice
Slake's limbo (6 and up) **Fic**

Holmes, Sally
(il) Perrault, C. The complete fairy tales of Charles Perrault **398.2**

Holmes, Timothy
Zambia (5 and up) **968.94**

Holocaust, 1933-1945
See also World War, 1939-1945—Jews
Abells, C. B. The children we remember (3-6) **940.53**
Adler, D. A. Child of the Warsaw ghetto (3-5) **940.53**
Adler, D. A. Hiding from the Nazis (2-4) **940.53**
Adler, D. A. Hilde and Eli, children of the Holocaust (3-5) **940.53**
Adler, D. A. A picture book of Anne Frank (1-3) **92**
Bachrach, S. D. Tell them we remember (5 and up) **940.53**
Gold, A. L. Memories of Anne Frank (5 and up) **92**
Gold, A. L. A special fate (5 and up) **940.53**
Hurwitz, J. Anne Frank: life in hiding (3-5) **92**
Leapman, M. Witnesses to war (5 and up) **940.53**
Meltzer, M. Never to forget: the Jews of the Holocaust (6 and up) **940.53**
Meltzer, M. Rescue: the story of how Gentiles saved Jews in the Holocaust (6 and up) **940.53**
Mochizuki, K. Passage to freedom (3-6) **940.53**
Rol, R. van der. Anne Frank, beyond the diary (5 and up) **92**
Bibliography
Sullivan, E. T. The Holocaust in literature for youth **016.94053**
Fiction
Ackerman, K. The night crossing (3-5) **Fic**
Hoestlandt, J. Star of fear, star of hope **E**

Mazer, N. F. Good night, Maman (5 and up) **Fic**
Orgel, D. The devil in Vienna (6 and up) **Fic**
Orlev, U. The island on Bird Street (5 and up) **Fic**
Orlev, U. The man from the other side (6 and up) **Fic**
Radin, R. Y. Escape to the forest (3-6) **Fic**
Schnur, S. The shadow children (5 and up) **Fic**
Vos, I. Anna is still here (4 and up) **Fic**
Vos, I. Hide and seek (4 and up) **Fic**
Vos, I. The key is lost (4 and up) **Fic**
Yolen, J. The devil's arithmetic (4 and up) **Fic**

Personal narratives
Frank, A. The diary of a young girl (6 and up) **92**
Frank, A. The diary of a young girl: the definitive edition (6 and up) **92**
Greenfeld, H. The hidden children (4 and up) **940.53**
Perl, L. Four perfect pebbles (6 and up) **940.53**
Reiss, J. The upstairs room (4 and up) **92**
Rosenberg, M. B. Hiding to survive (5 and up) **940.53**
Toll, N. S. Behind the secret window (6 and up) **940.53**

The **Holocaust** in literature for youth. Sullivan, E. T. **016.94053**

Holocaust Museum (U.S.) *See* United States Holocaust Memorial Museum

Holt, Kimberly Willis
Mister and me (3-5) **Fic**
My Louisiana sky (6 and up) **Fic**
When Zachary Beaver came to town (5 and up) **Fic**

Holub, Josef, 1926-
The robber and me (5 and up) **Fic**

The **Holy** Bible [King James Bible. Oxford Univ. Press] Bible **220.5**

The **Holy** Bible: new revised standard version. Bible **220.5**

Holy Grail *See* Grail

Hom, Nancy
(il) Blia Xiong. Nine-in-one, Grr! Grr! **398.2**
See/See also pages in the following book(s):
Just like me p10-11 **920**

Home
Fiction
Anholt, C. Harry's home **E**
Home among the giants. Norman, H.
In Norman, H. The girl who dreamed only geese, and other tales of the Far North **398.2**

Home instruction *See* Home schooling

Home life *See* Family life

Home lovely. Perkins, L. R. **E**

Home run. Burleigh, R. **E**

Home schooling
Scheps, S. G. The librarian's guide to homeschooling resources **021.2**

Home sweet home. Marzollo, J. **E**

Home video systems
See also Video recording

Homecoming. Voigt, C. **Fic**

Homeless. Wolf, B. **362.5**

Homeless bird. Whelan, G. **Fic**

Homeless persons
See also Refugees; Runaway children; Runaway teenagers; Tramps
Wolf, B. Homeless (2-4) **362.5**
Fiction
Bunting, E. December **E**
Bunting, E. Fly away home **E**
Fenner, C. The king of dragons (5 and up) **Fic**
Howe, J. Dew drop dead (4-6) **Fic**
Neufeld, J. Almost a hero (5 and up) **Fic**
Spinelli, J. Maniac Magee (5 and up) **Fic**

The **homemakers.** Fisher, L. E. **640**

Homeplace. Shelby, A. **E**

Homer
Adaptations
Colum, P. The Trojan War and the adventures of Odysseus (4 and up) **883**
Philip, N. The adventures of Odysseus (4-6) **883**
Sutcliff, R. Black ships before Troy (5 and up) **883**
Sutcliff, R. The wanderings of Odysseus (5 and up) **883**

Homer Price. McCloskey, R. **Fic**

Homeschoolers and the public library. See Scheps, S. G. The librarian's guide to homeschooling resources **021.2**

Homesick: my own story. Fritz, J. **92**

Homesteading. Patent, D. H. **978**

Homeward bound. Coville, B.
In Coville, B. Oddly enough p19-31
S C

Homework help for kids on the Net. Trumbauer, L. **004.6**

Homicide
See/See also pages in the following book(s):
Fry, V. L. Part of me died, too p185-206 (5 and up) **155.9**

Homosexuality
Fiction
Fox, P. The eagle kite (6 and up) **Fic**
Nelson, T. Earthshine (5 and up) **Fic**

Honduras
McGaffey, L. Honduras (5 and up) **972.83**

Honest pretzels. Katzen, M. **641.5**

The **honest-to-goodness** truth. McKissack, P. C. **E**

Honesty
See also Truthfulness and falsehood
Fiction
McKissack, P. C. The honest-to-goodness truth **E**

Honey, Elizabeth, 1947-
Don't pat the wombat! (4-6) **Fic**

Honey
Gibbons, G. The honey makers (k-3) **595.7**
Micucci, C. The life and times of the honeybee (2-4) **595.7**

Honey, I love, and other love poems. Greenfield, E. **811**

The **honey** makers. Gibbons, G. **595.7**

A **honey** of a day. Marshall, J. P. **E**

Honeybee culture See Beekeeping

Hong, Lily Toy, 1958-
How the ox star fell from heaven (k-3) **398.2**
Two of everything (k-3) **398.2**

Hong Kong (China)
Kagda, F. Hong Kong (5 and up) **951.25**

Honk!. Edwards, P. D. **E**

Honoring our ancestors **759.13**

Honus and me. Gutman, D. See note under Gutman, D. Babe and me **Fic**

Hoobler, Dorothy
The African American family album (5 and up) **305.8**
The Chinese American family album (5 and up) **305.8**
The Cuban American family album (5 and up) **305.8**
The German American family album (5 and up) **305.8**
The Irish American family album (5 and up) **305.8**
The Italian American family album (5 and up) **305.8**
The Japanese American family album (5 and up) **305.8**
The Jewish American family album (5 and up) **305.8**
The Mexican American family album (5 and up) **305.8**
The Scandinavian American family album (5 and up) **305.8**

Hoobler, Thomas
(jt. auth) Hoobler, D. The African American family album **305.8**
(jt. auth) Hoobler, D. The Chinese American family album **305.8**
(jt. auth) Hoobler, D. The Cuban American family album **305.8**
(jt. auth) Hoobler, D. The German American family album **305.8**
(jt. auth) Hoobler, D. The Irish American family album **305.8**
(jt. auth) Hoobler, D. The Italian American family album **305.8**
(jt. auth) Hoobler, D. The Japanese American family album **305.8**
(jt. auth) Hoobler, D. The Jewish American family album **305.8**
(jt. auth) Hoobler, D. The Mexican American family album **305.8**
(jt. auth) Hoobler, D. The Scandinavian American family album **305.8**

Hood, George Percy Jacomb- See Jacomb-Hood, George Percy, 1857-1929

Hood, Susan
National Audubon Society first field guide: wildflowers (4 and up)   **582.13**
Hood, Robin (Legendary character) *See* Robin Hood (Legendary character)
Hooks, William H.
Freedom's fruit (3-5)   **Fic**
Moss gown (k-3)   **398.2**
The three little pigs and the fox (k-3)
          398.2

Hooper, Meredith
The drop in my drink (3-5)   **553.7**
River story   **E**
Hoops. Burleigh, R.   **811**
Hooray, a piñata!. Kleven, E.   **E**
Hooray for Diffendoofer Day!. Seuss, Dr.   **E**
Hooray for me!. Charlip, R.   **E**
Hooray for the Golly sisters!. Byars, B. C. See note under Byars, B. C. The Golly sisters go West   **E**
Hoose, Phillip M., 1947-
It's our world, too! (5 and up)   **302**
Hooway for Wodney Wat. Lester, H.   **E**
Hop o' my thumb. Perrault, C.
In Perrault, C. The complete fairy tales of Charles Perrault p82-95   **398.2**
The **Hope** Bakery. Wynne-Jones, T.
In Wynne-Jones, T. Some of the kinder planets: stories p25-35   **S C**
Hope's crossing. Goodman, J. E.   **Fic**
Hopi Indians
Sneve, V. D. H. The Hopis (3-5)   **970.004**
Hopkins, Dianne McAfee
(jt. auth) Zweizig, D. Lessons from Library Power   **027.8**
Hopkins, Lee Bennett, 1938-
Been to yesterdays: poems of a life (4 and up)
          811
Good rhymes, good times (k-2)   **811**
Pass the poetry, please!   **372.6**
The writing bug (1-3)   **92**
(comp) All God's children. See All God's children   **242**
(comp) Blast off! See Blast off!   **811.008**
(comp) Climb into my lap. See Climb into my lap   **808.81**
(comp) Dinosaurs: poems. See Dinosaurs: poems   **811.008**
(comp) Extra innings. See Extra innings
          811.008
(comp) Good books, good times! See Good books, good times!   **811.008**
(comp) Hand in hand. See Hand in hand
          811.008
(comp) Happy birthday. See Happy birthday
          811.008
(comp) Lives: poems about famous Americans. See Lives: poems about famous Americans
          811.008
(comp) Marvelous math. See Marvelous math
          811.008
(comp) Opening days. See Opening days
          811.008

(comp) Side by side. See Side by side
          808.81
(comp) Small talk. See Small talk   **811.008**
(comp) Song and dance. See Song and dance
          811.008
(comp) Spectacular science. See Spectacular science   **811.008**
(comp) Sports! sports! sports! See Sports! sports! sports!   **811.008**
(comp) Surprises. See Surprises   **811.008**
(comp) Weather. See Weather   **811.008**
(ed) Yummy! See Yummy!   **811.008**
See/See also pages in the following book(s):
Author talk (4 and up)   **028.5**
Hopkinson, Deborah
A band of angels   **E**
Birdie's lighthouse (1-3)   **Fic**
Maria's comet   **E**
Sweet Clara and the freedom quilt   **E**
Hopper, Edward, 1882-1967
See/See also pages in the following book(s):
Greenberg, J. The American eye p25-32 (6 and up)   **920**
Hopper, Grace
See/See also pages in the following book(s):
Thimmesh, C. Girls think of everything (5 and up)   **920**
Vare, E. A. Women inventors & their discoveries p111-23 (5 and up)   **920**
Hopscotch
Lankford, M. D. Hopscotch around the world (3-5)   **796.2**
Hopscotch around the world. Lankford, M. D.
          796.2
Hopscotch love. Grimes, N.   **811**
Horace. Keller, H.   **E**
Horace and Morris but mostly Dolores. Howe, J.
          E
Horenstein, Henry
A is for—?   **E**
Horlbeck, Barbara
(jt. auth) Steger, W. Over the top of the world
          998
The **Horn** Book Guide to Children's and Young Adult Books   **028.505**
The **Horn** Book Magazine   **028.505**
Hornby, Hugh
Soccer (4 and up)   **796.334**
Horning, Kathleen T.
From cover to cover   **028.1**
Horns. Afanas´ev, A. N.
In Afanas´ev, A. N. Russian fairy tales p292-94   **398.2**
Horowitz, Anthony, 1955-
The Devil and his boy (5 and up)   **Fic**
Horrible Harry and the ant invasion. Kline, S. See note under Kline, S. Horrible Harry in room 2B   **Fic**
Horrible Harry and the Christmas surprise. Kline, S. See note under Kline, S. Horrible Harry in room 2B   **Fic**
Horrible Harry and the Drop of Doom. Kline, S. See note under Kline, S. Horrible Harry in room 2B   **Fic**

Horrible Harry and the dungeon. Kline, S. See note under Kline, S. Horrible Harry in room 2B **Fic**

Horrible Harry and the green slime. Kline, S. See note under Kline, S. Horrible Harry in room 2B **Fic**

Horrible Harry and the kickball wedding. Kline, S. See note under Kline, S. Horrible Harry in room 2B **Fic**

Horrible Harry and the purple people. Kline, S. See note under Kline, S. Horrible Harry in room 2B **Fic**

Horrible Harry at Halloween. Kline, S. See note under Kline, S. Horrible Harry in room 2B **Fic**

Horrible Harry goes to the moon. Kline, S. See note under Kline, S. Horrible Harry in room 2B **Fic**

Horrible Harry in room 2B. Kline, S. **Fic**

Horrible Harry moves up to third grade. Kline, S. See note under Kline, S. Horrible Harry in room 2B **Fic**

Horrible Harry's secret. Kline, S. See note under Kline, S. Horrible Harry in room 2B **Fic**

Horror fiction
  Coville, B. Oddly enough (6 and up) **S C**
  MacDonald, M. R. When the lights go out **372.6**

  Schwartz, A. In a dark, dark room, and other scary stories (k-2) **398.2**
  Schwartz, A. More scary stories to tell in the dark (4 and up) **398.2**
  Schwartz, A. Scary stories 3 (4 and up) **398.2**

  Schwartz, A. Scary stories to tell in the dark (4 and up) **398.2**
  Sleator, W. The beasties (6 and up) **Fic**

Horse & pony care. Henderson, C. **636.1**

The **horse** and his boy. Lewis, C. S. See note under Lewis, C. S. The lion, the witch, and the wardrobe **Fic**

Horse and toad
  In The Magic orange tree, and other Haitian folktales p143-50 **398.2**

The **horse** that could fly. Mayo, M.
  In Mayo, M. Mythical birds & beasts from many lands p11-21 **398.2**

Horseback riding *See* Horsemanship

Horsemanship
  See also Rodeos
  Feldman, J. I am a rider (3-5) **798.2**

Horsepower. Peterson, C. **636.1**

Horses
  See also Ponies
  Budiansky, S. The world according to horses (4 and up) **636.1**
  Clutton-Brock, J. Horse (4 and up) **636.1**
  Henderson, C. Horse & pony care **636.1**
  Isenbart, H.-H. Birth of a foal (3-6) **636.1**
  Lauber, P. The true-or-false book of horses (2-4) **636.1**

  Meltzer, M. Hold your horses (4 and up) **636.1**

Patent, D. H. Horses (3-6) **636.1**
Peterson, C. Horsepower (k-3) **636.1**
Ryden, H. Wild horses I have known (4 and up) **599.66**

The Visual dictionary of the horse (4 and up) **636.1**

Fiction
Wilson, D. L. I rode a horse of milk white jade **Fic**

Bagnold, E. National Velvet (5 and up) **Fic**

Coerr, E. Chang's paper pony **E**
Cohen, C. L. The mud pony (k-3) **398.2**
Farley, W. The Black Stallion (4 and up) **Fic**

Goble, P. The gift of the sacred dog (2-4) **398.2**

Goble, P. The girl who loved wild horses (k-3) **398.2**

Haas, J. Beware the mare (3-5) **Fic**
Haas, J. Sugaring **E**
Haas, J. Unbroken (5 and up) **Fic**
Henry, M. Justin Morgan had a horse (4 and up) **Fic**

Henry, M. King of the wind (4 and up) **Fic**

Henry, M. Misty of Chincoteague (4 and up) **Fic**

Irwin, H. Jim-Dandy (5 and up) **Fic**
Jeppson, A.-S. Here comes Pontus! (2-4) **Fic**

Lawson, R. Mr. Revere and I (5 and up) **Fic**

Lester, J. Black cowboy, wild horses **E**
Locker, T. The mare on the hill **E**
Peet, B. Cowardly Clyde **E**
Polacco, P. Mrs. Mack **E**
Rounds, G. Once we had a horse **E**
Sewell, A. Black Beauty (4-6) **Fic**
Shub, E. The white stallion **E**
Wallace, B. Beauty (4-6) **Fic**
Ward, L. K. The silver pony (2-4) **Fic**
Winthrop, E. The little humpbacked horse (4-6) **398.2**

Hort, Lenny
  How many stars in the sky? **E**
  The seals on the bus (k-2) **782.42**

Horton hatches the egg. Seuss, Dr. **E**

Horton hears a Who!. Seuss, Dr. **E**

Horvath, Polly
  The trolls (3-6) **Fic**
  When the circus came to town (4-6) **Fic**

Hosking, Joe
  (il) Friedhoffer, R. Physics lab in a hardware store **530**
  (il) Friedhoffer, R. Science lab in a supermarket **507.8**

Hosking Smith, Jan
  (il) Mitchell, B. CLICK!: a story about George Eastman **92**

Hosni the dreamer. Ben-'Ezer, E. **398.2**

Hospitals
  Rogers, F. Going to the hospital (k-2) **362.1**

How Brer Lion lost his hair. Lester, J.
In Lester, J. The last tales of Uncle Remus p131-33 **398.2**

How Bruh Sparrow and Sis Wren lost out. Hamilton, V.
In Hamilton, V. When birds could talk & bats could sing p3-9 **398.2**

How Chameleon became a ride. Hamilton, V.
In Hamilton, V. A ring of tricksters p85-89 **398.2**

How come Ol' Buzzard boards. Van Laan, N.
In Van Laan, N. With a whoop and a holler p49-52 **398.2**

How Coyote stole the sun. Curry, J. L.
In Curry, J. L. Back in the beforetime p10-21 **398.2**

How crab got a hard back. Sherlock, Sir P. M.
In Sherlock, Sir P. M. West Indian folk-tales p86-92 **398.2**

How Deep Red Roses goes back and forth between the clock and the looking glass. Sandburg, C.
In Sandburg, C. Rootabaga stories pt 2 p79-85 **S C**
In Sandburg, C. The Sandburg treasury p121-23 **818**

How Deli kept his part of the bargain. Walker, B. K.
In Walker, B. K. A treasury of Turkish folktales for children p80-84 **398.2**

How Dippy the Wisp and Slip Me Liz came in the moonshine where the Potato Face Blind Man sat with his accordion. Sandburg, C.
In Sandburg, C. Rootabaga stories pt 2 p95-102 **S C**
In Sandburg, C. The Sandburg treasury p127-31 **818**

How do apples grow? Maestro, B. **634**

How do birds find their way? Gans, R. **598**

How do dinosaurs say goodnight? Yolen, J. **E**

How do flies walk upside down? Berger, M. **595.7**

How do you say it today, Jesse Bear? Carlstrom, N. W. See note under Carlstrom, N. W. Jesse Bear, what will you wear? **E**

How do you spell God? Gellman, M. **200**

How dog brought death into the world. Hausman, G.
In Hausman, G. Dogs of myth p15-18 **398.2**

How fear came. Kipling, R.
In Kipling, R. The jungle book: the Mowgli stories **S C**

How Gimme the Ax found out about the zigzag railroad and who made it zigzag. Sandburg, C.
In Sandburg, C. Rootabaga stories pt 1 p51-56 **S C**
In Sandburg, C. The Sandburg treasury p31-32 **818**

How Glooskap defeated the Great Bullfrog. Curry, J. L.
In Curry, J. L. Turtle Island: tales of the Algonquian nations p81-88 **398.2**

How Googler and Gaggler, the two Christmas babies, came home with monkey wrenches. Sandburg, C.
In Sandburg, C. Rootabaga stories pt 2 p63-69 **S C**
In Sandburg, C. The Sandburg treasury p113-17 **818**

How Grizzly Bear climbed the mountain. Caduto, M. J.
In Caduto, M. J. Keepers of the night p121-22 **398.2**

How Henry Hagglyhoagly played the guitar with his mittens on. Sandburg, C.
In Sandburg, C. Rootabaga stories pt 1 p145-50 **S C**
In Sandburg, C. The Sandburg treasury p69-71 **818**

How Hot Balloons and his pigeon daughters crossed over into the Rootabaga Country. Sandburg, C.
In Sandburg, C. Rootabaga stories pt 2 p103-10 **S C**
In Sandburg, C. The Sandburg treasury p131-34 **818**

How I captured a dinosaur. Schwartz, H. See note under Schwartz, H. Albert goes Hollywood **E**

How I saved Hanukkah. Koss, A. G. **Fic**

How I spent my summer vacation. Teague, M. **E**

How it feels to be adopted. Krementz, J. **362.7**

How it feels when a parent dies. Krementz, J. **155.9**

How it feels when parents divorce. Krementz, J. **306.89**

How Jack went to seek his fortune. Jacobs, J.
In Jacobs, J. English fairy tales p34-36 **398.2**
In Tomie dePaola's favorite nursery tales p118-21 **398.2**

How Johnny the Wham sleeps in money all the time and Joe the Wimp shines and sees things. Sandburg, C.
In Sandburg, C. Rootabaga stories pt 2 p70-75 **S C**
In Sandburg, C. The Sandburg treasury p117-20 **818**

How many days to America? Bunting, E. **E**

How many fools? Philip, N.
In Philip, N. The Arabian nights p143-44 **398.2**

How many snails? Giganti, P., Jr. **E**

How many stars in the sky? Hort, L. **E**

How many teeth? Showers, P. **612.3**

How men and women finally agreed. McCaughrean, G.
In McCaughrean, G. The golden hoard: myths and legends of the world p114-19 **398.2**

How the guinea fowl got her spots. Knutson, B.
398.2

How the hat ashes shovel helped Snoo Foo. Sandburg, C.
In Sandburg, C. Rootabaga stories pt 1 p87-91 **S C**

How the hero twins found their father. Bruchac, J.
In Bruchac, J. Flying with the eagle, racing with the great bear p67-77 **398.2**

How the hot ashes shovel helped Snoo Foo. Sandburg, C.
In Sandburg, C. The Sandburg treasury p45-46 **818**

How the leopard got his spots. Kipling, R.
In Kipling, R. Just so stories **S C**

How the narwhal got its tusk. Norman, H.
In Norman, H. The girl who dreamed only geese, and other tales of the Far North **398.2**

How the ox star fell from heaven. Hong, L. T.
398.2

How the polar bear became. Hughes, T.
In The Oxford treasury of children's stories p130-34 **S C**

How the Potato Face Blind Man enjoyed himself on a fine spring morning. Sandburg, C.
In Sandburg, C. Rootabaga stories pt 1 p34-39 **S C**
In Sandburg, C. The Sandburg treasury p25-26 **818**

How the rainbow was born. Delacre, L.
In Delacre, L. Golden tales p37-39 **398.2**

How the rhinoceros got his skin. Kipling, R.
In Kipling, R. Just so stories **S C**
In The Oxford treasury of children's stories p127-29 **S C**

How the rooster got his crown. Poole, A. L.
398.2

How the sea was born. Delacre, L.
In Delacre, L. Golden tales p3-5 **398.2**

How the slaves helped each other. Faulkner, W. J.
In From sea to shining sea p130-31
810.8

How the three wild Babylonian Baboons went away in the rain eating bread and butter. Sandburg, C.
In Sandburg, C. Rootabaga stories pt 2 p43-47 **S C**
In Sandburg, C. The Sandburg treasury p106-07 **818**

How the tiger got its stripes. Terada, A. M.
In Terada, A. M. Under the starfruit tree p7-9
398.2

How the walls of the temple were built. Schwartz, H.
In Schwartz, H. Next year in Jerusalem p19-21 **296.1**

How the whale got his throat. Kipling, R.
In Kipling, R. Just so stories **S C**

How the witch was caught. Lester, J.
In Lester, J. The last tales of Uncle Remus p66-70 **398.2**

How they bring back the Village of Cream Puffs when the wind blows it away. Sandburg, C.
In Sandburg, C. Rootabaga stories pt 1 p13-19 **S C**
In Sandburg, C. The Sandburg treasury p17-19 **818**

How they broke away to go to the Rootabaga Country. Sandburg, C.
In American fairy tales p143-50 **S C**
In Sandburg, C. Rootabaga stories pt 1 p3-12
S C
In Sandburg, C. The Sandburg treasury p10-16 **818**

How they play driedel in Chelm. Kimmel, E. A.
In Kimmel, E. A. The jar of fools: eight Hanukkah stories from Chelm p5-8
S C

How things work. (6 and up) See entry in Part 2: Web Resources

How Tinktum Tidy recruited an army for the king. Lester, J.
In Lester, J. The last tales of Uncle Remus p82-88 **398.2**

How to be a friend. Brown, L. K. **158**

How to be a nature detective. See Selsam, M. E. Big tracks, little tracks **591.5**

How to break a bad habit. MacDonald, M. R.
In MacDonald, M. R. Twenty tellable tales p75-78 **372.6**

How to cook a gooseberry fool. Vaughan, M.
In Easy menu ethnic cookbooks **641.5**

How-to-do-it manuals for librarians [series]
Duncan, D. I-Search, you search, we all learn to research **001.4**
Feinberg, S. Running a parent/child workshop
027.62
Fiore, C. D. Running summer library reading programs **027.62**
Nespeca, S. M. Library programming for families with young children **027.62**
Symons, A. K. Protecting the right to read
323.44
Wadham, T. Programming with Latino children's materials **027.62**

How-to-do-it manuals for school and public librarians [series]
Herb, S. Using children's books in preschool settings **372.4**

How to do "The three bears" with two hands. Minkel, W. **791.5**

How to eat fried worms. Rockwell, T. **Fic**

How to make a chemical volcano and other mysterious experiments. Kramer, A. **540.7**

How to make an apple pie and see the world. Priceman, M. **E**

How to make holiday pop-ups. Irvine, J. **736**

How to make super pop-ups. Irvine, J. **736**

How to really fool yourself. Cobb, V. **152.1**

How to talk to your cat. George, J. C. **636.8**

How to talk to your dog. George, J. C.
636.7

How to tell a true princess. Andersen, H. C.
In The Yellow fairy book p254-55 **398.2**

Howliday Inn. Howe, J. *See note under* Howe, J.
  The celery stalks at midnight   **Fic**
Howl's moving castle. Jones, D. W.   **Fic**
How's the weather? [series]
  Kahl, J. D. Weather watch   **551.63**
Hoyt-Goldsmith, Diane
  Apache rodeo (3-5)   **970.004**
  Arctic hunter (3-5)   **970.004**
  Buffalo days (3-5)   **970.004**
  Celebrating Chinese New Year (3-5)
       394.26
  Celebrating Hanukkah (3-5)   **296.4**
  Celebrating Passover (3-5)   **296.4**
  Day of the Dead (3-5)   **394.26**
  Hoang Anh (3-5)   **305.8**
  Lacrosse (3-5)   **796.34**
  Mardi Gras: a Cajun country celebration (3-5)
       394.25
  Migrant worker (3-5)   **331.5**
  Las Posadas (3-5)   **394.26**
  Pueblo storyteller (3-5)   **970.004**
  Totem pole (3-5)   **970.004**
Hsu-Flanders, Lillian
  (il) Rattigan, J. K. Dumpling soup   **E**
Hu, Ying-hwa
  (il) Chinn, K. Sam and the lucky money   **E**
  (il) Make a joyful sound. *See* Make a joyful
  sound   **811.008**
  (il) Miller, W. Zora Hurston and the chinaberry
  tree   **92**
  (il) Smith, C. L. Jingle dancer   **E**
  (il) Tsubakiyama, M. Mei-Mei loves the morn-
  ing   **E**
Hubbard, Woodleigh
  (il) Brown, M. W. Four fur feet   **E**
Hubbell, Patricia
  Boo! (k-3)   **811**
Hubble Space Telescope
  Cole, M. D. Hubble Space Telescope (4 and up)
       522
  Scott, E. Adventure in space (4 and up)
       522
Huck, Charlotte S.
  Children's literature in the elementary school
       028.5
  A creepy countdown   **E**
  Princess Furball (1-3)   **398.2**
The Huckabuck family and how they raised pop-
  corn in Nebraska and quit and came back.
  Sandburg, C.   **E**
  also in Sandburg, C. Rootabaga stories pt 2
  p137-44   **S C**
  also in Sandburg, C. The Sandburg treasury
  p145-49   **818**
Hudson, Cheryl Willis
  (comp) How sweet the sound: African-American
  songs for children. *See* How sweet the sound:
  African-American songs for children
       782.42
Hudson, Wade
  (comp) How sweet the sound: African-American
  songs for children. *See* How sweet the sound:
  African-American songs for children
       782.42
Hue Boy. Mitchell, R. P.   **E**

Huffman, Tom
  (il) Terban, M. The dove dove   **793.73**
Huge Harold. Peet, B.   **E**
Hugging
       Fiction
  London, J. Snuggle wuggle   **E**
Hughes, Arizona Houston, 1876-1969
       About
  Houston, G. My great-aunt Arizona   **E**
Hughes, Arthur, 1832-1915
  (il) MacDonald, G. The princess and the goblin
       Fic
Hughes, Edward James *See* Hughes, Ted, 1930-
  1998
Hughes, George
  (il) Clifford, E. Help! I'm a prisoner in the li-
  brary   **Fic**
Hughes, Helga
  Cooking the Irish way
    In Easy menu ethnic cookbooks   **641.5**
  Cooking the Swiss way
    In Easy menu ethnic cookbooks   **641.5**
Hughes, Langston, 1902-1967
  Carol of the brown king   **811**
  The dream keeper and other poems (5 and up)
       811
  The sweet and sour animal book   **811**
       About
  Cooper, F. Coming home: from the life of
  Langston Hughes (2-4)   **92**
  Meltzer, M. Langston Hughes (6 and up)
       92
  See/See also pages in the following book(s):
  Faber, D. Great lives: American literature p231-
  39 (5 and up)   **920**
  Krull, K. Lives of the writers p86-89 (4 and up)
       920
Hughes, Meredith Sayles
  Spill the beans and pass the peanuts: legumes (4
  and up)   **583**
  Yes, we have bananas (4 and up)   **634**
Hughes, Neal
  (il) Sachar, L. Marvin Redpost, kidnapped at
  birth?   **Fic**
Hughes, Richard, 1941-
  Nothing
    In Bauer, C. F. Celebrations p144-45
       808.8
Hughes, Shirley
  Alfie and the birthday surprise   **E**
  Alfie's 1 2 3. *See note under* Hughes, S. Alfie
  and the birthday surprise   **E**
  Dogger   **E**
  Out and about   **E**
  Rhymes for Annie Rose (k-2)   **821**
  Stories by firelight   **E**
Hughes, Ted, 1930-1998
  How the polar bear became
    In The Oxford treasury of children's stories
    p130-34   **S C**
  The iron giant (4-6)   **Fic**
Hugo, Victor, 1802-1885
  Les Misérables; dramatization. *See* Thane, A.
  Little Cosette and Father Christmas

Hull, Richard, 1945-
(il) Viorst, J. Sad underwear and other complications **811**

The **hullabaloo** ABC. Cleary, B. **E**

Human anatomy
Berger, M. Why don't haircuts hurt? (2-4) **612**
Biesty, S. Stephen Biesty's incredible body (4 and up) **611**
Cole, J. The magic school bus inside the human body (2-4) **612**
Parker, S. The body atlas (5 and up) **611**
Sweeney, J. Me and my amazing body (k-2) **611**
VanCleave, J. P. Janice VanCleave's the human body for every kid (4 and up) **612**
The Visual dictionary of human anatomy (4 and up) **611**
The Visual dictionary of the human body (4 and up) **611**
Walker, R. The Kingfisher first human body encyclopedia (3-5) **612**

Human body [series]
Ballard, C. The heart and circulatory system **612.1**
Ballard, C. The skeleton and muscular system **612.7**
Parker, S. The brain and the nervous system **612.8**
Parker, S. The lungs and respiratory system **612.2**
Parker, S. The reproductive system **612.6**

Human body for every kid, Janice VanCleave's. VanCleave, J. P. **612**

Human body systems [series]
Silverstein, A. The circulatory system **612.1**
Silverstein, A. The digestive system **612.3**
Silverstein, A. The excretory system **612.4**
Silverstein, A. The reproductive system **612.6**

Human ecology
See/See also pages in the following book(s):
Swamp, J. Giving thanks (k-3) **299**
Fiction
Baker, J. Window **E**

Human geography
Encyclopedias
Junior Worldmark encyclopedia of world cultures (5 and up) **306**

Human influence on nature
See/See also pages in the following book(s):
Patent, D. H. Biodiversity p65-75 (5 and up) **333.95**

Human origins
See also Evolution; Fossil hominids; Prehistoric peoples
Gallant, R. A. Early humans (5 and up) **599.93**

Humbug. Bawden, N. **Fic**

Humbug witch. Balian, L. **E**

Hummingbird and Little Breeze. Hamilton, V.
In Hamilton, V. When birds could talk & bats could sing p33-39 **398.2**

Humor *See* Wit and humor

Humorous poetry
Brown, C. Dutch sneakers and flea keepers (2-4) **811**
Ciardi, J. You read to me, I'll read to you **811**
Florian, D. In the swim **811**
Florian, D. Laugh-eteria **811**
For laughing out loud **811.008**
Heide, F. P. Oh, grow up! (k-3) **811**
Lewis, J. P. A hippopotamusn't and other animal verses **811**
Numeroff, L. J. Sometimes I wonder if poodles like noodles (k-3) **811**
Prelutsky, J. The new kid on the block: poems (3-6) **811**
Prelutsky, J. A pizza the size of the sun (3-6) **811**
Prelutsky, J. Rolling Harvey down the hill (1-3) **811**
Prelutsky, J. Something big has been here (3-5) **811**
Shields, C. D. Lunch money and other poems about school (2-4) **811**
Silverstein, S. Falling up **811**
Silverstein, S. A light in the attic **811**
Silverstein, S. Where the sidewalk ends **811**
Viorst, J. Sad underwear and other complications (3-6) **811**

The **hundred** dresses. Estes, E. **Fic**

The **hundredth** skull. San Souci, R.
In San Souci, R. A terrifying taste of short & shivery p43-45 **398.2**

Hundreth day worries. See Cuyler, M. 100th day worries **E**

Huneck, Stephen
Sally goes to the beach **E**

Hungarian Americans
Fiction
Karr, K. Man of the family (4 and up) **Fic**

Hungary
Steins, R. Hungary (4 and up) **943.9**
Fiction
Seredy, K. The Good Master (4-6) **Fic**
Seredy, K. The white stag (4-6) **Fic**

Hungry Spider and the Turtle. Courlander, H.
In Courlander, H. Cow-tail switch, and other West African stories p107-12 **398.2**

Hunkin's experiments. (4 and up) See entry in Part 2: Web Resources

Hunt, Irene, 1907-
Across five Aprils (5 and up) **Fic**
See/See also pages in the following book(s):
Newbery and Caldecott Medal books, 1966-1975 p22-33 **028.5**

Hunt, Jonathan
Bestiary (4 and up) **398**

Hunter, Mollie, 1922-
The mermaid summer (4 and up) **Fic**
A stranger came ashore (6 and up) **Fic**

Hunter, Norman, 1899-1995
The unexpected banquet
In Bauer, C. F. Celebrations p45-51 **808.8**

Hunter, Ryan Ann, 1951-
 Take off! (k-3)   **629.13**
The **hunter**. Casanova, M.   **398.2**
The **hunter** in the haunted forest. San Souci, R.
 In San Souci, R. Short & shivery p112-16
     398.2

The **hunterman** and the crocodile. Wagué Diakité,
 B.   **398.2**
Hunting
 See also Tracking and trailing
 Fiction
 Dahl, R. The magic finger (2-4)   **Fic**
 Rosen, M. We're going on a bear hunt   **E**
The **hunting** of Death. McCaughrean, G.
 In McCaughrean, G. The bronze cauldron:
 myths and legends of the world p113-15
     398.2

The **hunting** of the snark. Carroll, L.
 In Carroll, L. The complete works of Lewis
 Carroll p677-99   **828**
Hunting song of the Seeonee pack. Kipling, R.
 In Kipling, R. The jungle book: the Mowgli
 stories   **S C**
Hunting the white cow. Seymour, T.   **E**
Hurd, Clement, 1908-1988
 (il) Brown, M. W. Goodnight moon   **E**
 (il) Brown, M. W. The runaway bunny   **E**
 (il) Hurd, E. T. Johnny Lion's book   **E**
Hurd, Edith Thacher, 1910-1997
 Johnny Lion's bad day. See note under Hurd,
 E.T. Johnny Lion's book   **E**
 Johnny Lion's book   **E**
 Johnny Lion's rubber boots. See note under
 Hurd, E.T. Johnny Lion's book   **E**
 Starfish (k-3)   **593.9**
Hurd, Thacher
 Art dog   **E**
 Little Mouse's big valentine   **E**
 Mama don't allow   **E**
 Mystery on the docks   **E**
 Zoom City   **E**
Hurray for Ali Baba Bernstein. Hurwitz, J. See
 note under Hurwitz, J. The adventures of Ali
 Baba Bernstein   **Fic**
Hurricane. Wiesner, D.   **E**
Hurricane & tornado. Challoner, J.   **551.55**
Hurricanes
 Cole, J. The magic school bus inside a hurricane
 (2-4)   **551.55**
 Lauber, P. Hurricanes (4 and up)   **551.55**
 Fiction
 Wiesner, D. Hurricane   **E**
Hurry!. Haas, J.   **E**
Hurry!. McCully, E. A.   **Fic**
Hurry freedom. Stanley, J.   **979.4**
Hurston, Zora Neale, 1891-1960
 The talking mule
 In From sea to shining sea p224-25
     810.8

About
 Miller, W. Zora Hurston and the chinaberry tree
 (k-3)   **92**
 Porter, A. P. Jump at de sun: the story of Zora
 Neale Hurston (4 and up)   **92**

See/See also pages in the following book(s):
 Krull, K. Lives of the writers p82-85 (4 and up)
     920

 Wilkinson, B. S. African American women writ-
 ers (4 and up)   **810.9**
Hurwitz, Johanna
 The adventures of Ali Baba Bernstein (2-4)
     Fic
 Aldo Applesauce. See note under Hurwitz, J.
 Much ado about Aldo   **Fic**
 Aldo Ice Cream. See note under Hurwitz, J.
 Much ado about Aldo   **Fic**
 Aldo Peanut Butter. See note under Hurwitz, J.
 Much ado about Aldo   **Fic**
 Anne Frank: life in hiding (3-5)   **92**
 Baseball fever (3-5)   **Fic**
 Busybody Nora. See note under Hurwitz, J.
 New neighbors for Nora   **Fic**
 Class clown (2-4)   **Fic**
 Class president. See note under Hurwitz, J.
 Class clown   **Fic**
 The cold & hot winter. See note under Hurwitz,
 J. The hot & cold summer   **Fic**
 The down & up fall. See note under Hurwitz, J.
 The hot & cold summer   **Fic**
 E is for Elisa. See note under Hurwitz, J. Rip-
 roaring Russell   **Fic**
 Elisa in the middle. See note under Hurwitz, J.
 Rip-roaring Russell   **Fic**
 Ever clever Elisa. See note under Hurwitz, J.
 Rip-roaring Russell   **Fic**
 Faraway summer (4-6)   **Fic**
 The hot & cold summer (3-5)   **Fic**
 Hurray for Ali Baba Bernstein. See note under
 Hurwitz, J. The adventures of Ali Baba Bern-
 stein   **Fic**
 Make room for Elisa. See note under Hurwitz,
 J. Rip-roaring Russell   **Fic**
 Much ado about Aldo (3-5)   **Fic**
 New neighbors for Nora (2-4)   **Fic**
 New shoes for Silvia   **E**
 Rip-roaring Russell (2-4)   **Fic**
 Russell and Elisa. See note under Hurwitz, J.
 Rip-roaring Russell   **Fic**
 Russell rides again. See note under Hurwitz, J.
 Rip-roaring Russell   **Fic**
 Russell sprouts. See note under Hurwitz, J. Rip-
 roaring Russell   **Fic**
 School spirit. See note under Hurwitz, J. Class
 clown   **Fic**
 School's out. See note under Hurwitz, J. Class
 clown   **Fic**
 Spring break. See note under Hurwitz, J. Class
 clown   **Fic**
 Starting school (2-4)   **Fic**
 String beans
 In Bauer, C. F. Celebrations p65-67
     808.8

 Summer with Elisa. See note under Hurwitz, J.
 Rip-roaring Russell   **Fic**
 Teacher's pet. See note under Hurwitz, J Class
 clown   **Fic**
 Thanksgiving
 In Thanksgiving: stories and poems p29-40
     810.8

 The up & down spring. See note under Hurwitz,
 J. The hot & cold summer   **Fic**

Hurwitz, Johanna—*Continued*
See/See also pages in the following book(s):
  Author talk (4 and up)   **028.5**
Husband and wife. Afanas'ev, A. N.
  In Afanas'ev, A. N. Russian fairy tales p369-
  70   **398.2**
The **husband** who counted the spoonfuls. Bryan,
A.
  In Bryan, A. Ashley Bryan's African tales,
  uh-huh p70-80   **398.2**
The **husband** who was to mind the house.
Asbjornsen, P. C.
  In Womenfolk and fairy tales p106-110
     398.2
Hush!. Ho, M.   **E**
Hush, little baby (k-2)   **782.42**
Hussar, Michael
  (il) Coville, B. Oddly enough   **S C**
Hutchins, Pat, 1942-
  1 hunter   **E**
  Changes, changes   **E**
  Clocks and more clocks   **E**
  Don't forget the bacon!   **E**
  The doorbell rang   **E**
  Good-night, Owl!   **E**
  Happy birthday, Sam   **E**
  It's my birthday! See note under Hutchins, P.
  Where's the baby?   **E**
  Rosie's walk   **E**
  Silly Billy. See note under Hutchins, P. Where's
  the baby?   **E**
  Ten red apples   **E**
  Tidy Titch. See note under Hutchins, P. Titch
     E
  Titch   **E**
  The very worst monster. See note under Hutch-
  ins, P. Where's the baby?   **E**
  Where's the baby?   **E**
  The wind blew   **E**
  You'll soon grow into them, Titch. See note un-
  der Hutchins, P. Titch   **E**
Hutchinson, Sascha
  (il) Vaughan, M. Snap!   **E**
Hutton, Warwick
  Odysseus and the Cyclops (3-5)   **292**
  Perseus (3-5)   **292**
  Theseus and the Minotaur (3-5)   **292**
  (il) Cooper, S. The silver cow: a Welsh tale
     398.2
  (il) Cooper, S. Tam Lin   **398.2**
Hutu and Pare. Te Kanawa, K.
  In Te Kanawa, K. Land of the long white
  cloud p105-10   **398.2**
Huynh, Quang Nhuong
  The land I lost: adventures of a boy in Vietnam
  (4 and up)   **92**
  Water buffalo days (3-5)   **92**
Hydrogen
  Farndon, J. Hydrogen
  In The Elements [Benchmark Bks.]   **546**
Hydrothermal vents *See* Ocean bottom
Hygiene
  See also Health

Hyman, Flo
See/See also pages in the following book(s):
  Krull, K. Lives of the athletes p91-93 (4 and
  up)   **920**
Hyman, Trina Schart, 1939-
  Little Red Riding Hood (k-2)   **398.2**
  (il) Alexander, L. The fortune-tellers   **E**
  (il) Brink, C. R. Caddie Woodlawn   **Fic**
  (il) Christmas poems. See Christmas poems
     808.81
  (il) Cohen, B. Canterbury tales   **821**
  (il) Dickens, C. A Christmas carol   **Fic**
  (il) Fritz, J. Why don't you get a horse, Sam
  Adams?   **92**
  (il) Fritz, J. Will you sign here, John Hancock?
     92
  (il) Hodges, M. The kitchen knight   **398.2**
  (il) Hodges, M. Saint George and the dragon
     398.2
  (il) Kimmel, E. A. The adventures of Hershel of
  Ostropol   **398.2**
  (il) Kimmel, E. A. Hershel and the Hanukkah
  goblins   **E**
  (il) Kimmel, E. A. Iron John   **398.2**
  (il) Lasky, K. The night journey   **Fic**
  (il) Medearis, A. S. Haunts   **S C**
  (il) Pyle, H. Bearskin   **E**
  (il) Pyle, H. King Stork   **398.2**
  (il) Rogasky, B. The golem   **398.2**
  (il) Rogasky, B. Rapunzel   **398.2**
  (il) Rogasky, B. The water of life   **398.2**
  (il) Updike, J. A child's calendar   **811**
  (il) Winter poems. See Winter poems
     808.81
  (il) Winthrop, E. The castle in the attic   **Fic**
  (il) Witch poems. See Witch poems
     821.008
See/See also pages in the following book(s):
  Newbery and Caldecott Medal books, 1976-1985
  p264-78   **028.5**
Hymns
  See also Spirituals (Songs)
Hyperactive children
  See also Attention deficit disorder
Hypnotism
Fiction
  Auch, M. J. I was a third grade science project
  (2-4)   **Fic**

I

I am a gymnast. Feldman, J.   **796.44**
I am a rider. Feldman, J.   **798.2**
I am an American. Stanley, J.   **305.8**
I am me. Kuskin, K.   **E**
I am phoenix: poems for two voices. Fleischman,
P.   **811**
I am Rosa Parks. Parks, R.   **92**
I am the cat. Schertle, A.   **811**
I am the darker brother   **811.008**
I, Amber Brown. Danziger, P. See note under
  Danziger, P. Amber Brown is not a crayon
     Fic

I can read book [series]

Benchley, N. Small Wolf   E
Bernier-Grand, C. T. Juan Bobo   **398.2**
Blast off!   **811.008**
Bonsall, C. N. The case of the hungry stranger   E
Bonsall, C. N. Who's a pest?   E
Brenner, B. Wagon wheels   E
Bulla, C. R. Daniel's duck   E
Byars, B. C. The Golly sisters go West   E
Coerr, E. The big balloon race   E
Coerr, E. Chang's paper pony   E
Coerr, E. The Josefina story quilt   E
Cushman, D. Inspector Hopper   E
Hazen, B. S. Digby   E
Hoban, L. Arthur's Christmas cookies   E
Hoban, L. Silly Tilly's Thanksgiving dinner   E
Hoff, S. Oliver   E
Hoff, S. Sammy the seal   E
Hurd, E. T. Johnny Lion's book   E
Kessler, L. P. Here comes the strikeout   E
Kessler, L. P. Kick, pass, and run   E
Kessler, L. P. Last one in is a rotten egg   E
Kuskin, K. Soap soup and other verses   **811**
Levinson, N. S. Snowshoe Thompson   E
Lexau, J. M. Don't be my valentine   E
Lobel, A. Frog and Toad are friends   E
Lobel, A. Grasshopper on the road   E
Lobel, A. Mouse soup   E
Lobel, A. Mouse tales   E
Lobel, A. Owl at home   E
Lobel, A. Small pig   E
Lobel, A. Uncle Elephant   E
Maestro, M. Geese find the missing piece   **793.73**
Maestro, M. What do you hear when cows sing?   **793.73**
McCully, E. A. The grandma mix-up   E
Minarik, E. H. Little Bear   E
Minarik, E. H. No fighting, no biting!   E
Monjo, F. N. The drinking gourd   E
Novak, M. Little Wolf, Big Wolf   E
O'Connor, J. Super Cluck   E
Paterson, K. Marvin's best Christmas present ever   E
Pomerantz, C. The outside dog   E
Sandin, J. The long way westward   E
Schwartz, A. All of our noses are here, and other noodle tales   **398.2**
Schwartz, A. Busy buzzing bumblebees and other tongue twisters   **808.88**
Schwartz, A. Ghosts!   **398.2**
Schwartz, A. I saw you in the bathtub, and other folk rhymes   **398.2**
Schwartz, A. In a dark, dark room, and other scary stories   **398.2**
Schwartz, A. There is a carrot in my ear, and other noodle tales   **398.2**
Sports! sports! sports!   **811.008**
Surprises   **811.008**
Turner, A. W. Dust for dinner   E
Walker, S. M. The 18 penny goose   E
Weather   **811.008**

Wiseman, B. Morris and Boris at the circus   E
Wyler, R. Magic secrets   **793.8**
Wyler, R. Spooky tricks   **793.8**

I can read chapter book [series]

Avi. Abigail takes the wheel   **Fic**
Avi. Finding Providence: the story of Roger Williams   **92**

I can read mystery book [series]

Benchley, N. A ghost named Fred   E

I can read picture book [series]

Hoff, S. Danny and the dinosaur   E
Parish, P. Amelia Bedelia   E

I, crocodile. Marcellino, F.   E
I did it, I'm sorry. Buehner, C.   E
I hadn't meant to tell you this. Woodson, J.   **Fic**
I hate camping. Petersen, P. J. See note under Peterson, P. J. I hate weddings   **Fic**
I hate company. Petersen, P. J. See note under Peterson, P. J. I hate weddings   **Fic**
The I hate mathematics! book. Burns, M.   **513**
I hate weddings. Petersen, P. J.   **Fic**
I have a dream. King, M. L.   **323.1**
I have a dream: the life and words of Martin Luther King, Jr. Haskins, J.   **92**
I have heard of a land. Thomas, J. C.   E
I, Juan de Pareja. Treviño, E. B. de   **Fic**
I know an old lady who swallowed a fly. Sierra, J.
  In Sierra, J. Nursery tales around the world p25-27   **398.2**
I know an old lady who swallowed a fly. See Taback, S. There was an old lady who swallowed a fly   **782.42**
I know what I'll do. Walker, B. K.
  In Walker, B. K. A treasury of Turkish folktales for children p36   **398.2**
I like me!. Carlson, N. L.   E
I look like a girl. Hamanaka, S.   E
I lost my bear. Feiffer, J.   E
I love guinea pigs. King-Smith, D.   **636.9**
"I love you, Prime Minister!". McCaughrean, G.
  In McCaughrean, G. The bronze cauldron: myths and legends of the world p102-06   **398.2**
—I never saw another butterfly—   **741.9**
I never told and other poems. Livingston, M. C.   **811**
I once was a monkey. Lee, J. M.   **294.3**
I read signs. Hoban, T.   **659.1**
I rode a horse of milk white jade. Wilson, D. L.   **Fic**
I saw a purple cow, and 100 other recipes for learning. Cole, A.   **372**
I saw Esau   **398.8**
I saw you in the bathtub, and other folk rhymes. Schwartz, A.   **398.2**
I-Search, you search, we all learn to research. Duncan, D.   **001.4**

I see the rhythm. Igus, T. **780.89**

I sing for the animals. Goble, P. **242**

I speak English for my mom. Stanek, M. **Fic**

I spy. Wick, W. **793.73**

I spy a freight train: transportation in art. Micklethwait, L. See note under Micklethwait, L. I spy: an alphabet in art **E**

I spy a lion: animals in art. Micklethwait, L. See note under Micklethwait, L. I spy: an alphabet in art **E**

I spy: an alphabet in art. Micklethwait, L. **E**

I spy Christmas. Wick, W. **793.73**

I spy extreme challenger!. Wick, W. **793.73**

I spy fantasy. Wick, W. **793.73**

I spy fun house. Wick, W. **793.73**

I spy gold challenger!. Wick, W. **793.73**

I spy mystery. Wick, W. **793.73**

I spy school days. Wick, W. **793.73**

I spy spooky night. Wick, W. **793.73**

I spy super challenger!. Wick, W. **793.73**

I spy treasure hunt. Wick, W. **793.73**

I spy two eyes: numbers in art. Micklethwait, L. See note under Micklethwait, L. I spy: an alphabet in art **E**

I sure am glad to see you, Blackboard Bear. Alexander, M. G. See note under Alexander, M. G. Blackboard Bear **E**

I, too, sing America (6 and up) **811.008**

I took a walk. Cole, H. **E**

I took my frog to the library. Kimmel, E. A. **E**

I walk at night. Duncan, L. **E**

I want to be an astronaut. Barton, B. **E**

I was a rat!. Pullman, P. **Fic**

I was a third grade science project. Auch, M. J. **Fic**

I was born a slave: the story of Harriet Jacobs. Fleischner, J. **92**

I was born about 10,000 years ago. Kellogg, S. **E**

I was dreaming to come to America (4 and up) **325.73**

I was there books [series]
Hehner, B. First on the moon **629.45**
Tanaka, S. Lost temple of the Aztecs **972**
Tanaka, S. Secrets of the mummies **393**

I went to the library
In Juba this and Juba that **372.6**

Ibbotson, Eva
The secret of platform 13 (5 and up) **Fic**
Which witch? (4 and up) **Fic**

IBBY *See* International Board on Books for Young People

Iblis. Oppenheim, S. L. **297.1**

Ibn Ezra and the archbishop. Kimmel, E. A.
In Kimmel, E. A. The spotted pony: a collection of Hanukkah stories p12-17 **398.2**

Ibo (African people) *See* Igbo (African people)

Ice
Fiction
Appelbaum, D. K. Cocoa ice **E**

Ice cream, ices, etc.
Fiction
Mahy, M. Simply delicious! **E**

Ice cream Larry. Pinkwater, D. M. See note under Pinkwater, D. M. Young Larry **E**

Ice hockey *See* Hockey

Ice skating
Boo, M. The story of figure skating (5 and up) **796.91**
Gutman, D. Ice skating **796.91**
Isadora, R. Sophie skates (k-3) **796.91**
Morrissey, P. Ice skating (4 and up) **796.91**
Wilkes, D. The figure skating book (4 and up) **796.91**
Fiction
Dodge, M. M. Hans Brinker; or, The silver skates (4 and up) **Fic**

Ice story. Kimmel, E. C. **998**

Icebergs
Simon, S. Icebergs and glaciers (3-5) **551.3**

Icebergs and glaciers. Simon, S. **551.3**

Iceland
Wilcox, J. Iceland (5 and up) **949.12**

Ichikawa, Satomi, 1949-
(il) Gauch, P. L. Dance, Tanya **E**
(il) Lisle, J. T. The lost flower children **Fic**

Ick. Wynne-Jones, T.
In Wynne-Jones, T. Lord of the Fries and other stories p45-68 **S C**

Icky, squishy science. Markle, S. **507.8**

Iconography *See* Religious art

Id-ul-Fitr. Marchant, K. **297.3**

Ida Early comes over the mountain. Burch, R. **Fic**

Idaho
George, C. Idaho
In America the beautiful, second series **973**
Stefoff, R. Idaho
In Celebrate the states **973**

Identification
See also Forensic anthropology

Idioms *See* English language—Idioms

Iditarod dream. Wood, T. **798.8**

Iditarod Trail Sled Dog Race, Alaska
Fiction
Blake, R. J. Akiak **E**

If ever I return again. Demas, C. **Fic**

If I had a paka. Pomerantz, C. **811**

If I ran the circus. Seuss, Dr. **E**

If I ran the zoo. Seuss, Dr. **E**

If I were in charge of the world and other worries. Viorst, J. **811**

If the shoe fits. Soto, G.
In Soto, G. Petty crimes **S C**

Illustrators—*Continued*
Weidt, M. N. Oh, the places he went (3-5)
92
Wings of an artist **741.6**
Dictionaries
Eighth book of junior authors and illustrators
920.003
Something about the author **920.003**
Something about the author: autobiography series **920.003**
Dictionaries—Indexes
Children's authors and illustrators: an index to biographical dictionaries **920.003**
The **Illyrian** adventure. Alexander, L. **Fic**
Ilya Muromets and the dragon. Afanas'ev, A. N.
In Afanas'ev, A. N. Russian fairy tales p569-75 **398.2**
I'm nobody! who are you? Dickinson, E. **811**
I'm not Oscar's friend anymore. Sharmat, M. W.
In Bauer, C. F. Celebrations p282-85 **808.8**
"I'm Tipingee, she's Tipingee, we're Tipingee, too"
In The Magic orange tree, and other Haitian folktales p129-34 **398.2**
Images of God. Paterson, J. B. **231**
Imaginary playmates
Fiction
Henkes, K. Jessica **E**
Howe, J. There's a dragon in my sleeping bag **E**
Imagine that! **811.008**
Imershein, Betsy, 1953-
(il) Howe, J. When you go to kindergarten **372.2**
Immigrant kids. Freedman, R. **325.73**
Immigrants
Fiction
Bartoletti, S. C. A coal miner's bride (4 and up) **Fic**
Immigration and emigration
See also Children of immigrants; Immigrants; Refugees; names of countries with the subdivision *Immigration and emigration*; and names of nationality groups
See/See also pages in the following book(s):
Bauer, C. F. Celebrations p241-56 **808.8**
Fiction
Aliki. Painted words: Marianthe's story one **E**
Bunting, E. Dreaming of America **E**
Bunting, E. A picnic in October **E**
Cohen, B. Molly's pilgrim **E**
Herold, M. R. A very important day **E**
Hesse, K. Letters from Rifka (5 and up) **Fic**
Hest, A. When Jessie came across the sea **E**
Lasky, K. Dreams in the golden country (4 and up) **Fic**
Leighton, M. R. An Ellis Island Christmas **E**
Levinson, R. Watch the stars come out **E**

Oberman, S. The always prayer shawl **E**
Rael, E. O. What Zeesie saw on Delancey Street **E**
Sandin, J. The long way westward **E**
Woodruff, E. The memory coat **E**
Imogene's antlers. Small, D. **E**
The **imp** in the basket. Babbitt, N.
In Babbitt, N. The Devil's storybook p37-46 **S C**
Imperial Trans-Antarctic Expedition (1914-1917)
Kimmel, E. C. Ice story (4 and up) **998**
Impty-Umpty and the blacksmith. Lester, J.
In Lester, J. The last tales of Uncle Remus p49-56 **398.2**
In 1492. Marzollo, J. **970.01**
In a box. Sanfield, S.
In Sanfield, S. The adventures of High John the Conqueror **398.2**
In a dark, dark room. Schwartz, A.
In Schwartz, A. In a dark, dark room, and other scary stories p34-41 **398.2**
In a dark, dark room, and other scary stories. Schwartz, A. **398.2**
In a different light. Meyer, C. **979.8**
In a thousand years' time. Andersen, H. C.
In Andersen, H. C. The little mermaid and other fairy tales p104-06 **S C**
In daddy's arms I am tall **811.008**
In every tiny grain of sand (2-5) **291.4**
In flight with David McPhail. McPhail, D. M. **92**
In for winter, out for spring. Adoff, A. **811**
In-line skating
Irwin, D. Inline skating (4 and up) **796.21**
In my family. Garza, C. L. **305.8**
In my garden. Schumaker, W. **E**
In my own words [series]
Uchida, Y. The invisible thread **92**
Yep, L. The lost garden **92**
In other words, a beginning thesaurus. See Roget's children's thesaurus **423**
In other words, a junior thesaurus. See Roget's student thesaurus **423**
In search of [series]
Caselli, G. In search of Pompeii **937**
In search of Pompeii. Caselli, G. **937**
In the beginning; creation stories from around the world. Hamilton, V. **291.1**
In the days of the Salem witchcraft trials. Roach, M. K. **133.4**
In the eyes of the cat. Demi **895.6**
In the face of danger. Nixon, J. L. See note under Nixon, J. L. A family apart **Fic**
In the graveyard. Schwartz, A.
In Schwartz, A. In a dark, dark room, and other scary stories p18-23 **398.2**
In the heart of the village. Bash, B. **583**
In the Land of Souls
In The Yellow fairy book p152-54 **398.2**
In the line of fire. St. George, J. **364.1**

Inventions—*Continued*

Vare, E. A. Women inventors & their discoveries (5 and up)   **920**

Wulffson, D. L. The kid who invented the popsicle and other surprising stories about inventions (4 and up)   **609**

Wulffson, D. L. Toys! (4 and up)   **688.7**

Inventions & inventors   **609**

Inventors

Fisher, L. E. Alexander Graham Bell (4 and up)   **92**

Inventions & inventors   **609**

Matthews, T. L. Always inventing: a photobiography of Alexander Graham Bell (4 and up)   **92**

Mitchell, B. CLICK!: a story about George Eastman (3-5)   **92**

Mitchell, B. We'll race you, Henry: a story about Henry Ford (3-5)   **92**

Nirgiotis, N. Thomas Edison (4-6)   **92**

Parker, S. Thomas Edison and electricity (4 and up)   **92**

Tucker, T. Brainstorm! (5 and up)   **609**

Inventors, African American *See* African American inventors

Investments

See/See also pages in the following book(s):

Otfinoski, S. The kid's guide to money p99-110 (4 and up)   **332.024**

The **invisible** guest. Olson, A. N.

In Olson, A. N. Ask the bones: scary stories from around the world p110-17   **398.2**

The **invisible** hunters. Rohmer, H.   **398.2**

The **invisible** thread. Uchida, Y.   **92**

Inviting Jason. Konigsburg, E. L.

In Konigsburg, E. L. Altogether, one at a time p1-12   **S C**

Iofin, Michael

(il) Schwartz, H. A coat for the moon and other Jewish tales   **398.2**

Iona and Peter Opie library of children's literature [series]

Nesbit, E. The best of Shakespeare   **822.3**

Iowa

Hintz, M. Iowa

In America the beautiful, second series   **973**

Morrice, P. A. Iowa

In Celebrate the states   **973**

Ira says goodbye. Waber, B. See note under Waber, B. Ira sleeps over   **E**

Ira sleeps over. Waber, B.   **E**

Iran

Fiction

Fletcher, S. Shadow spinner (6 and up)   **Fic**

Folklore

See Folklore—Iran

Iraq

Foster, L. M. Iraq (4 and up)   **956.7**

Folklore

See Folklore—Iraq

Science

See Science—Iraq

Ireland, Norma Olin, 1907-

(comp) Index to fairy tales. See Index to fairy tales   **398.2**

Ireland

January, B. Ireland (2-4)   **941.5**

Fiction

Bunting, E. Market Day   **E**

Bunting, E. Spying on Miss Müller (5 and up)   **Fic**

De Paola, T. Jamie O'Rourke and the pooka   **E**

McDermott, G. Tim O'Toole and the wee folk   **E**

Schmidt, G. D. Anson's way (5 and up)   **Fic**

Talbott, H. O'Sullivan stew   **E**

Folklore

See Folklore—Ireland

History

McCully, E. A. The pirate queen (k-3)   **92**

The **Irish** American family album. Hoobler, D.   **305.8**

Irish Americans

Hoobler, D. The Irish American family album (5 and up)   **305.8**

Fiction

Bunting, E. Dreaming of America   **E**

Iron

Sparrow, G. Iron

In The Elements [Benchmark Bks.]   **546**

The **iron** giant. Hughes, T.   **Fic**

Iron John. Kimmel, E. A.   **398.2**

Iron John. Mayer, M.   **398.2**

The **iron** man. See Hughes, T. The iron giant   **Fic**

The **Iron** Moonhunter. Chang, K.

In From sea to shining sea p164-66   **810.8**

The **iron** ring. Alexander, L.   **Fic**

The **iron** stove. Grimm, J.

In The Yellow fairy book p32-37   **398.2**

Iroquois Indians

Fradin, D. B. Hiawatha: messenger of peace (3-5)   **92**

Hoyt-Goldsmith, D. Lacrosse (3-5)   **796.34**

Sneve, V. D. H. The Iroquois (3-5)   **970.004**

Irraweka, mischief-maker. Sherlock, Sir P. M.

In Sherlock, Sir P. M. West Indian folk-tales p21-26   **398.2**

Irvine, Joan, 1951-

How to make holiday pop-ups (3-6)   **736**

How to make super pop-ups (3-6)   **736**

Irvine, Margaret Chodos- *See* Chodos-Irvine, Margaret

Irving, Washington, 1783-1859

The adventure of the German student; adaptation. See San Souci, R. The adventure of the German student

Irving, Washington, 1783-1859—_Continued_
Rip Van Winkle (5 and up)   **Fic**
   _In_ American fairy tales p9-28   **S C**
See/See also pages in the following book(s):
Faber, D. Great lives: American literature p31-
   39 (5 and up)   **920**

Irwin, Dawn
Inline skating (4 and up)   **796.21**

Irwin, Hadley
Jim-Dandy (5 and up)   **Fic**
The original Freddie Ackerman (5 and up)
    Fic

Is anybody out there? Couper, H.   **576.8**

Is it far to Zanzibar? Grimes, N.   **811**

Is it larger? Is it smaller? Hoban, T.   **E**

Is it red? Is it yellow? Is it blue? Hoban, T.
    E

Is it rough? Is it smooth? Is it shiny? Hoban, T.
    E

Is that a rash? Silverstein, A.   **616.5**

Is that you, winter? Gammell, S.   **E**

Is there life in outer space? Branley, F. M.
    576.8

Is there life on Mars? Fradin, D. B.   **576.8**

Is this a house for Hermit Crab? McDonald, M.
    595.3

Is underground. Aiken, J. See note under Aiken, J.
   The wolves of Willoughby Chase   **Fic**

Is your mama a llama? Guarino, D.   **E**

Isaacs, Anne, 1949-
Swamp Angel   **E**
Treehouse tales (3-5)   **Fic**

Isabel. Meyer, C.   **Fic**

Isabella I, Queen of Spain, 1451-1504
See/See also pages in the following book(s):
Meltzer, M. Ten queens p56-71 (5 and up)
    920

Meyer, C. Isabel (4 and up)   **Fic**

Isadora, Rachel
123 pop!   **E**
ABC pop!   **E**
At the crossroads   **E**
Ben's trumpet   **E**
City seen from A to Z   **E**
Lili at ballet   **E**
Lili backstage. See note under Isadora, R. Lili
   at ballet   **E**
Lili on stage. See note under Isadora, R. Lili at
   ballet   **E**
Listen to the city   **E**
Max   **E**
Sophie skates (k-3)   **796.91**
Swan Lake   **E**
Young Mozart (2-4)   **92**
(il) Andersen, H. C. The little match girl
    Fic
(il) McKissack, P. C. Flossie & the fox   **E**
(il) Shub, E. The white stallion   **E**
(il) Young, R. Golden Bear   **E**

Isenbart, Hans-Heinrich, 1923-
Birth of a foal (3-6)   **636.1**

Ishi
   About
Kroeber, T. Ishi, last of his tribe (5 and up)
    92

Isis and Osiris. McCaughrean, G.
   _In_ McCaughrean, G. The crystal pool: myths
   and legends of the world p50-56
    398.2

Isla. Dorros, A. See note under Dorros, A. Abuela
    E

Islam
Ghazi, S. H. Ramadan (k-3)   **297.3**
Marchant, K. Id-ul-Fitr (3-5)   **297.3**
See/See also pages in the following book(s):
Osborne, M. P. One world, many religions p25-
   34 (4 and up)   **291**

Islamic countries
   See also Arab countries
   Civilization
Beshore, G. W. Science in early Islamic culture
   (4 and up)   **509**
Island boy. Cooney, B.   **E**
The **island** light. See Wells, R. Moss pillows
    E

Island of fear. San Souci, R.
   _In_ San Souci, R. More short & shivery p68-
   74   **398.2**

Island of the Blue Dolphins. O'Dell, S.   **Fic**

Island of the lost children. Osborne, M. P.
   _In_ Osborne, M. P. Favorite medieval tales
   p25-33   **398.2**

The **island** on Bird Street. Orlev, U.   **Fic**

An **island** scrapbook. Wright-Frierson, V.   **508**

Islands
   Fiction
Cooney, B. Island boy   **E**
Irwin, H. The original Freddie Ackerman (5 and
   up)   **Fic**
MacLachlan, P. Baby (5 and up)   **Fic**

Isles, Joanna
(il) Stevenson, R. L. A child's garden of verses
    821

Israel
   See also Jerusalem
Haskins, J. Count your way through Israel (2-4)
    956.94
Hintz, M. Israel (4 and up)   **956.94**
Israel and the werewolf. San Souci, R.
   _In_ San Souci, R. A terrifying taste of short &
   shivery p114-17   **398.2**

It is a good day to die. Viola, H. J.   **973.8**

It is time to go to sleep. Schwartz, A.
   _In_ Schwartz, A. There is a carrot in my ear,
   and other noodle tales p58-63   **398.2**

It looked like spilt milk. Shaw, C.   **E**

The **Italian** American family album. Hoobler, D.
    305.8

Italian Americans
Hoobler, D. The Italian American family album
   (5 and up)   **305.8**
   Fiction
Bartone, E. American too   **E**
Bartone, E. Peppe the lamplighter   **E**

Italian Americans—Fiction—*Continued*
Bunting, E. A picnic in October   E
Italian artists *See* Artists, Italian
Italiano, Bob
(il) Pascoe, E. Scholastic kid's almanac for the 21st century   **031.02**
Italy
King, D. C. Italy (4 and up)   **945**
Fiction
Avi. Midnight magic (5 and up)   Fic
De Paola, T. Strega Nona: an old tale   E
Weston, C. The diary of Melanie Martin; or, How I survived Matt the Brat, Michelangelo, and the Leaning Tower of Pizza (3-6)   Fic
Folklore
See Folklore—Italy
It's a girl thing. Jukes, M.   **305.23**
It's about dogs. Johnston, T.   **811**
It's about time, Jesse Bear, and other rhymes. Carlstrom, N. W. See note under Carlstrom, N. W. Jesse Bear, what will you wear?   E
It's all Greek to me. Scieszka, J. See note under Scieszka, J. Knights of the kitchen table   Fic
It's Christmas. Prelutsky, J.   **811**
It's disgusting—and we ate it!. Solheim, J.   **641.3**
It's George!. Cohen, M.   E
It's like this, Cat. Neville, E. C.   Fic
It's mine!. Lionni, L.   E
It's my birthday!. Hutchins, P. See note under Hutchins, P. Where's the baby?   E
It's my birthday. Oxenbury, H.   E
It's my birthday, too!. Jonell, L.   E
It's not the end of the world. Blume, J.   Fic
It's our world, too!. Hoose, P. M.   **302**
It's perfectly normal. Harris, R. H.   **613.9**
It's pumpkin time!. Hall, Z.   E
It's science! [series]
Hewitt, S. Solid, liquid, or gas?   **530.4**
Hewitt, S. Time   **529**
It's snowing! It's snowing!. Prelutsky, J.   **811**
It's so amazing!. Harris, R. H.   **612.6**
It's Thanksgiving. Prelutsky, J.   **811**
It's the bear!. Alborough, J. See note under Alborough, J. My friend Bear   E
It's Valentine's Day. Prelutsky, J.   **811**
Ivan the Cow's Son. Afanas′ev, A. N.
In Afanas′ev, A. N. Russian fairy tales p234-49   **398.2**
Ivan the peasant's son and the thumb-sized man. Afanas′ev, A. N.
In Afanas′ev, A. N. Russian fairy tales p262-68   **398.2**
Ivan the Simpleton. Afanas′ev, A. N.
In Afanas′ev, A. N. Russian fairy tales p142-45   **398.2**
Ivanko the bear's son. Afanas′ev, A. N.
In Afanas′ev, A. N. Russian fairy tales p221-23   **398.2**

Ivanushka the Little Fool. Afanas′ev, A. N.
In Afanas′ev, A. N. Russian fairy tales p62-65   **398.2**
I've got chicken pox. Kelley, T.   E
Ives, Charles Edward, 1874-1954
See/See also pages in the following book(s):
Krull, K. Lives of the musicians p70-73 (4 and up)   **920**
Ivimey, John W. (John William), 1868-1961
The complete story of the three blind mice   E
Ivory Coast
Sheehan, P. Côte d'Ivoire (5 and up)   **966.68**
The **ivory** door. Biegel, P.
In Don't read this! and other tales of the unnatural p110-31   S C
Iwai, Melissa
(il) Spinelli, E. Night shift daddy   E
Iwamatsu, Atushi Jun, 1908-1994
Crow Boy   E
Umbrella   E

J

Jabar, Cynthia
(il) Evans, L. Rain song   **811**
Jack and his golden snuff-box. Jacobs, J.
In Jacobs, J. English fairy tales p85-96   **398.2**
Jack and King Marock
In The Jack tales p135-50   **398.2**
Jack and the bean tree
In The Jack tales p31-39   **398.2**
Jack and the beanstalk
In Stockings of buttermilk: American folktales p81-86   **398.2**
Jack and the beanstalk. Beneduce, A.   **398.2**
Jack and the beanstalk. Jacobs, J.
In Jacobs, J. English fairy tales p65-72   **398.2**
Jack and the beanstalk. Kellogg, S.   **398.2**
Jack and the beanstalk. Steig, J.
In Steig, J. A handful of beans p119-42   **398.2**
Jack and the bull
In The Jack tales p21-30   **398.2**
Jack and the Devil. Hamilton, V.
In Hamilton, V. The people could fly: American black folktales p126-32   **398.2**
Jack and the doctor's girl
In The Jack tales p114-26   **398.2**
Jack and the king's girl
In The Jack tales p83-88   **398.2**
Jack and the North West Wind
In The Jack tales p47-57   **398.2**
Jack and the robbers
In The Jack tales p40-46   **398.2**
Jack and the robbers. MacDonald, M. R.
In MacDonald, M. R. Twenty tellable tales p95-103   **372.6**

Jacobs, William Jay
They shaped the game (4 and up)   **920**

Jacob's sukkah. Jaffe, N.
In Jaffe, N. While standing on one foot p81-86   **296.1**

Jacob's tree. Keller, H.   **E**

Jacomb-Hood, George Percy, 1857-1929
(il) The Blue fairy book. See The Blue fairy book   **398.2**

Jacques, Brian
The Bellmaker. See note under Jacques, B. Redwall   **Fic**
The legend of Luke. See note under Jacques, B. Redwall   **Fic**
The long patrol. See note under Jacques, B. Redwall   **Fic**
Lord Brocktree. See note under Jacques, B. Redwall   **Fic**
Mariel of Redwall. See note under Jacques, B. Redwall   **Fic**
Marlfox. See note under Jacques, B. Redwall   **Fic**
Martin the Warrior. See note under Jacques, B. Redwall   **Fic**
Mattimeo. See note under Jacques, B. Redwall   **Fic**
Mossflower. See note under Jacques, B. Redwall   **Fic**
The outcast of Redwall. See note under Jacques, B. Redwall   **Fic**
Pearls of Lutra. See note under Jacques, B. Redwall   **Fic**
Redwall (6 and up)   **Fic**
Salamandastron. See note under Jacques, B. Redwall   **Fic**

Jaeger, Winifred
(jt. auth) MacDonald, M. R. The round book   **782.42**

Jaffe, Nina
The cow of no color: riddle stories and justice tales from around the world (4 and up)   **398.2**
Contents: The cow of no color; The sound of work; Ximen Bao and the river spirit; The cloak; The thief and the pig; The testimony of the fly; Susannah and the elders; The jury; The magic seed; The bird lovers; An ounce of mud; The dance of Elegba; The three wives of Nenpetro; The flask; Kim Son Dal and the water-carriers; The land; Sharing the soup; A higher truth; The walnut and the pumpkin; The wise king; Josephus in the cave; The water pot and the necklace; The test
In the month of Kislev   **E**
The mysterious visitor (4-6)   **398.2**
Contents: The dream; Elijah in the marketplace; The three brothers; Elijah and the fisher boy; The woman with the face of a donkey; The bear in the forest; The strange journey of Rabbi Joshua ben Levi; Where is Elijah
The uninvited guest and other Jewish holiday tales (4-6)   **296.4**
Includes the following stories: The never-ending song; Miracles on the sea; The magician's spell; Hannah the Joyful; The Purim trunk; The two brothers; The uninvited guest
The way meat loves salt (k-3)   **398.2**
While standing on one foot (4 and up)   **296.1**

Contents: The Grand Inquisitor; Leviathan and the fox; The case of the boiled egg; The court jester's last wish; The most precious thing; Benjamin and the caliph; The princess in the mirror; What is Talmud?; The shepherd's disguise; Hershel and the nobleman; The wise fools of Chelm; The clever coachman; Prince Rooster; On the streets of the Lower East Side; Jacob's sukkah; A bird in the hand; Hillel the Wise

Jafta. Lewin, H.   **E**

Jafta and the wedding. Lewin, H. See note under Lewin, H. Jafta   **E**

Jafta—the journey. Lewin, H. See note under Lewin, H. Jafta   **E**

Jafta—the town. Lewin, H. See note under Lewin, H. Jafta   **E**

Jafta's father. Lewin, H. See note under Lewin, H. Jafta   **E**

Jafta's mother. Lewin, H. See note under Lewin, H. Jafta   **E**

Jagendorf, M. A. (Moritz Adolph), b. 1888
Clever Mistress Murray
In From sea to shining sea p68-73   **810.8**
The sad tale of three slavers
In From sea to shining sea p138-39   **810.8**
The sad tale of Tom the catfish
In From sea to shining sea p232-33   **810.8**

Jagendorf, Moritz Adolph *See* Jagendorf, M. A. (Moritz Adolph), b. 1888

The **jaguar** and the crested curassow. Sherlock, Sir P. M.
In Sherlock, Sir P. M. West Indian folk-tales p27-33   **398.2**

Jaguars
Fiction
Cowcher, H. Jaguar   **E**

Jake. Jones, R. F.   **636.7**

Jakobsen, Kathy, 1952-
(il) Guthrie, W. This land is your land   **782.42**
(il) Lindbergh, R. Johnny Appleseed   **811**

Jamaica
Fiction
Pomerantz, C. The chalk doll   **E**
Folklore
See Folklore—Jamaica

Jamaica and Brianna. Havill, J. See note under Havill, J. Jamaica's find   **E**

Jamaica and the substitute teacher. Havill, J. See note under Havill, J. Jamaica's find   **E**

Jamaica tag-along. Havill, J. See note under Havill, J. Jamaica's find   **E**

Jamaica's blue marker. Havill, J. See note under Havill, J. Jamaica's find   **E**

Jamaica's find. Havill, J.   **E**

Jamberry. Degen, B.   **E**

Jambo means hello. Feelings, M.   **E**

Jamela's dress. Daly, N.   **E**

James, Betsy
Mary Ann   **E**
Tadpoles   **E**

James, Elizabeth
How to write super school reports (4 and up)   **808**

James, Elizabeth—*Continued*
How to write terrific book reports (4 and up) **808**

James, Henry, 1843-1916
See/See also pages in the following book(s):
Faber, D. Great lives: American literature p130-40 (5 and up) **920**

James, J. Alison
The drums of Noto Hanto **E**

James, Mary, 1927-
Shoebag (5 and up) **Fic**
Shoebag returns. See note under James, M. Shoebag **Fic**

James, Simon
(comp) Days like this. See Days like this **811.008**

James, Simon, 1957-
Ancient Rome (4 and up) **937**

James, Will, 1892-1942
See/See also pages in the following book(s):
Newbery Medal books, 1922-1955 p47-48 **028.5**

James and the giant peach. Dahl, R. **Fic**

James Marshall's Mother Goose **398.8**

Jamestown (Va.)
Fiction
Hermes, P. Our strange new land (3-5) **Fic**
History
Fritz, J. The double life of Pocahontas (4 and up) **92**

Jamie and the biggest, first, and father of all sea serpents. Mayo, M.
In Mayo, M. Mythical birds & beasts from many lands p55-66 **398.2**

Jamie O'Rourke and the big potato. De Paola, T. **398.2**

Jamie O'Rourke and the pooka. De Paola, T. **E**

Jane, Calamity *See* Calamity Jane, 1852-1903

Jane gets a donkey. Schwartz, A.
In Schwartz, A. All of our noses are here, and other noodle tales p8-17 **398.2**

Jane grows a carrot. Schwartz, A.
In Schwartz, A. There is a carrot in my ear, and other noodle tales p40-43 **398.2**

Jane on her own. Le Guin, U. K. See note under Le Guin, U. K. Catwings **Fic**

Janeczko, Paul B., 1945-
How to write poetry (5 and up) **808.1**
That sweet diamond (4-6) **811**
(comp) The Place my words are looking for. See The Place my words are looking for **811.008**
(comp) Poetry from A to Z. See Poetry from A to Z **808.1**
(ed) Stone bench in an empty park. See Stone bench in an empty park **811.008**

Janice VanCleave's 201 awesome, magical, bizarre & incredible experiments. VanCleave, J. P. **507.8**

Janice VanCleave's 202 oozing, bubbling, dripping & bouncing experiments. VanCleave, J. P. **507.8**

Janice VanCleave's 203 icy, freezing, frosty, cool & wild experiments. VanCleave, J. P. **507.8**

Janice VanCleave's constellations for every kid. VanCleave, J. P. **523.8**

Janice VanCleave's earth science for every kid. VanCleave, J. P. **550**

Janice Vancleave's ecology for every kid. VanCleave, J. P. **577**

Janice VanCleave's electricity. VanCleave, J. P. **537**

Janice VanCleave's food and nutrition for every kid. VanCleave, J. P. **613.2**

Janice VanCleave's geometry for every kid. VanCleave, J. P. **516**

Janice VanCleave's guide to more of the best science fair projects. VanCleave, J. P. **507.8**

Janice VanCleave's guide to the best science fair projects. VanCleave, J. P. **507.8**

Janice VanCleave's insects and spiders. VanCleave, J. P. **595.7**

Janice VanCleave's oceans for every kid. VanCleave, J. P. **551.46**

Janice VanCleave's plants. VanCleave, J. P. **581**

Janice VanCleave's play and find out about bugs. VanCleave, J. P. **595.7**

Janice VanCleave's play and find out about math. VanCleave, J. P. **513**

Janice VanCleave's play and find out about nature. VanCleave, J. P. **570**

Janice VanCleave's rocks and minerals. VanCleave, J. P. **552**

Janice VanCleave's the human body for every kid. VanCleave, J. P. **612**

Janice VanCleave's weather. VanCleave, J. P. **551.5**

The **janitor's** boy. Clements, A. **Fic**

Jansson, Tove, 1914-2001
Comet in Moominland. See note under Jansson, T. Moominsummer madness **Fic**
Finn Family Moomintroll. See note under Jansson, T. Moominsummer madness **Fic**
Moominland midwinter. See note under Jansson, T. Moominsummer madness **Fic**
Moominpapa at sea. See note under Jansson, T. Moominsummer madness **Fic**
Moominpapa's memoirs. See note under Jansson, T. Moominsummer madness **Fic**
Moominsummer madness (4-6) **Fic**
Tales from Moominvalley. See note under Jansson, T. Moominsummer madness **Fic**

January, Brendan, 1972-
Ireland (2-4) **941.5**
John Brown's raid on Harpers Ferry (4-6) **973.7**
Science in colonial America (4 and up) **509**
Science in the Renaissance (4 and up) **509**

January rides the wind. Otten, C. F. **811**

Japan

Haskins, J. Count your way through Japan (2-4)
952
Heinrichs, A. Japan (4 and up) **952**
See/See also pages in the following book(s):
Blumberg, R. Commodore Perry in the land of the Shogun p44-53 (5 and up) **952**

Fiction

Baker, K. The magic fan **E**
Coatsworth, E. J. The cat who went to heaven (4 and up) **Fic**
Coerr, E. Mieko and the fifth treasure (3-5) **Fic**
Faulkner, M. Black belt **E**
Friedman, I. R. How my parents learned to eat **E**
Iwamatsu, A. J. Crow Boy **E**
James, J. A. The drums of Noto Hanto **E**
Kimmel, E. A. Sword of the samurai (4 and up) **S C**
Little, M. O. Yoshiko and the foreigner **E**
Melmed, L. K. Little Oh **E**
Merrill, J. The Girl Who Loved Caterpillars **E**
Morimoto, J. The two bullies **E**
Paterson, K. The master puppeteer (6 and up) **Fic**
Paterson, K. Of nightingales that weep (6 and up) **Fic**
Say, A. The bicycle man **E**
Say, A. Grandfather's journey **E**
Say, A. Tea with milk **E**
Say, A. Tree of cranes **E**
Watkins, Y. K. My brother, my sister, and I (6 and up) **Fic**
Watkins, Y. K. So far from the bamboo grove (6 and up) **Fic**
Wisniewski, D. The warrior and the wise man **E**
Yumoto, K. The friends (5 and up) **Fic**

Folklore

See Folklore—Japan
Foreign relations—United States
Blumberg, R. Commodore Perry in the land of the Shogun (5 and up) **952**
Social life and customs
Brenner, B. Chibi (k-3) **598**
Wells, R. A to Zen (3-5) **495.6**
The **Japanese** American family album. Hoobler, D. **305.8**

Japanese Americans

Brown, T. Konnichiwa! (1-4) **305.8**
Hoobler, D. The Japanese American family album (5 and up) **305.8**
Ross, M. E. Nature art with Chiura Obata (4 and up) **92**
Uchida, Y. The invisible thread (5 and up) **92**
Evacuation and relocation, 1942-1945
Hamanaka, S. The journey (5 and up) **305.8**
Stanley, J. I am an American (5 and up) **305.8**
Tunnell, M. O. The children of Topaz (5 and up) **940.53**

Evacuation and relocation, 1942-1945—Fiction
Bunting, E. So far from the sea **E**
Mochizuki, K. Baseball saved us **E**
Uchida, Y. The bracelet **E**
Uchida, Y. Journey to Topaz (5 and up) **Fic**

Fiction
Mochizuki, K. Heroes **E**
Say, A. Allison **E**
Say, A. Grandfather's journey **E**
Say, A. Tea with milk **E**
Uchida, Y. A jar of dreams (5 and up) **Fic**
Uchida, Y. Journey home (5 and up) **Fic**
Wolff, V. E. Bat 6 (5 and up) **Fic**

Japanese-English bilingual books *See* Bilingual books—English-Japanese

Japanese language

Wells, R. A to Zen (3-5) **495.6**

Japanese paper folding *See* Origami

Japanese poetry

See/See also pages in the following book(s):
Gollub, M. Cool melons—turn to frogs!: the life and poems of Issa [Kobayashi] (3-6) **92**
Collections
Demi. In the eyes of the cat **895.6**
Mado, M. The magic pocket (k-3) **895.6**

Jaques, Faith, 1923-1997

(il) The Orchard book of nursery rhymes. See The Orchard book of nursery rhymes **398.8**

A **jar** of dreams. Uchida, Y. **Fic**
The **jar** of fools. Kimmel, E. A.
In Kimmel, E. A. The jar of fools: eight Hanukkah stories from Chelm p1-4 **S C**
The **jar** of fools: eight Hanukkah stories from Chelm. Kimmel, E. A. **S C**

Jaramillo, Raquel

(il) Barrie, J. M. Peter Pan **Fic**

Jarecka, Danuta

(il) Kassirer, S. Joseph and his coat of many colors **222**

Jarrell, Randall, 1914-1965

The animal family (4 and up) **Fic**
The bat-poet (2-4) **Fic**

Jarvis, Robin

The dark portal (5 and up) **Fic**

Jaskol, Julie

City of angels (2-4) **979.4**

Jason's bears. Bauer, M. D. **E**
Jason's gold. Hobbs, W. **Fic**

Jaspersohn, William

How the forest grew (1-3) **577.3**

Jataka stories

Demi. Buddha stories (3-6) **294.3**
Galdone, P. The monkey and the crocodile (k-2) **398.2**
Lee, J. M. I once was a monkey (2-5) **294.3**

Jay, Alison

Picture this . . . **E**

Jayhawker. Beatty, P. **Fic**
Jazper. Egielski, R. **E**

Jazz music
See also Blues music
Jazz musicians
  Pinkney, A. D. Duke Ellington (2-4)   **92**
  Raschka, C. Mysterious Thelonious   **E**
The **jealous** husband. Terada, A. M.
  In Terada, A. M. Under the starfruit tree p10-
  13   **398.2**
Jean-Bart, Leslie
  (il) Coy, J. Strong to the hoop   **E**
Jeanne d'Arc, Saint *See* Joan, of Arc, Saint,
  1412-1431
The **Jedera** adventure. Alexander, L. See note un-
  der Alexander, L. The Illyrian adventure
    Fic
Jefferis, David
  Cyberspace (4 and up)   **004.6**
Jeffers, Susan
  (il) Grimm, J. Hansel and Gretel [Dial Press]
    398.2
  (il) Longfellow, H. W. Hiawatha   **811**
  (il) Wells, R. McDuff moves in   **E**
Jefferson, Thomas, 1743-1826
About
  Adler, D. A. A picture book of Thomas Jeffer-
  son (1-3)   **92**
  Giblin, J. Thomas Jefferson (2-4)   **92**
Fiction
  Fleming, C. A big cheese for the White House
    E
  Fleming, C. The hatmaker's sign   **E**
Homes and haunts
  Fisher, L. E. Monticello (4 and up)   **975.5**
  Richards, N. Monticello (4-6)   **975.5**
Jeffery, Debby Ann
  Literate beginnings   **027.62**
Jellies. George, T. C.   **593.5**
Jelly beans for sale. McMillan, B.   **332.4**
Jellyfishes
  George, T. C. Jellies (2-4)   **593.5**
  Landau, E. Jellyfish (2-4)   **593.5**
Jemison, Mae C.
  See/See also pages in the following book(s):
  Hansen, J. Women of hope p28-29 (4 and up)
    920
Jenius: the amazing guinea pig. King-Smith, D.
    Fic
Jenkins, Leonard
  (il) Holt, K. W. Mister and me   **Fic**
  (il) Myers, W. D. Malcolm X   **92**
Jenkins, Martin
  The emperor's egg (k-3)   **598**
Jenkins, Priscilla Belz
  A nest full of eggs (k-1)   **598**
  A safe home for manatees (k-2)   **599.5**
Jenkins, Steve
  Big & little (k-2)   **591.4**
  Biggest, strongest, fastest (k-2)   **590**
  Hottest, coldest, highest, deepest (k-2)   **910**
  The top of the world (2-4)   **796.52**
  What do you do when something wants to eat
  you? (k-3)   **591.47**
  (il) Collard, S. B., III. Animal dads   **591.56**

  (il) Collard, S. B., III. Making animal babies
    571.8
  (il) Mora, P. This big sky   **811**
Jennifer, Hecate, Macbeth, William McKinley,
  and me, Elizabeth. Konigsburg, E. L.
    Fic
Jennifer Murdley's toad. Coville, B.   **Fic**
Jennings, Peter, 1938-
  The century for young people   **909.82**
Jennings, Richard W.
  Orwell's luck (5 and up)   **Fic**
Jenny Archer, author. Conford, E. See note under
  Conford, E. A case for Jenny Archer   **Fic**
Jenny Archer to the rescue. Conford, E. See note
  under Conford, E. A case for Jenny Archer
    Fic
Jensen, Julie, 1957-
  Fundamental volleyball (5 and up)   **796.325**
Jenssen, Hans, 1963-
  (il) Reynolds, D. W. Star wars: incredible cross
  sections   **791.43**
Jeppson, Ann-Sofie
  Here comes Pontus! (2-4)   **Fic**
Jeram, Anita
  (il) King-Smith, D. All pigs are beautiful
    636.4
  (il) King-Smith, D. I love guinea pigs
    636.9
  (il) King-Smith, D. Puppy love   **636.7**
  (il) McBratney, S. Guess how much I love you
    E
Jeremy Thatcher, dragon hatcher. Coville, B.
    Fic
Jeremy Visick. Wiseman, D.   **Fic**
Jericho. Hickman, J.   **Fic**
Jermyn, Leslie
  Guyana (5 and up)   **988.1**
  Paraguay (5 and up)   **989.2**
  Uruguay (5 and up)   **989.5**
Jerusalem
  Schwartz, H. Next year in Jerusalem (4 and up)
    296.1
Poetry
  Yolen, J. O Jerusalem (4 and up)   **811**
Jesse Bear, what will you wear? Carlstrom, N. W.
    E
Jessica. Henkes, K.   **E**
The **jester**. Afanas'ev, A. N.
  In Afanas'ev, A. N. Russian fairy tales p151-
  55   **398.2**
Jesus Christ
About
  Bible. N.T. Selections. The Easter story
    232.9
  De Paola, T. The miracles of Jesus (k-3)
    232.9
  Mayer, M. Young Jesus of Nazareth (4 and up)
    232.9
  McCaughrean, G. God's kingdom (4-6)
    225.9
  Osborne, M. P. The life of Jesus in masterpieces
  of art   **232.9**
  Thompson, L. Love one another (1-3)
    232.9

Jesus Christ—About—_Continued_
Winthrop, E. He is risen: the Easter story (k-3)
232.9

Birth
See Jesus Christ—Nativity
Fiction
Speare, E. G. The bronze bow (6 and up)
Fic
Nativity
Bible. N.T. Selections. The Christmas story
232.9
Bible. N.T. Selections. The first Christmas (4
and up) 232.9
Nativity—Fiction
Menotti, G. C. Amahl and the night visitors
(2-4) Fic
Wildsmith, B. A Christmas story E
Nativity—Poetry
Berry, J. Celebration song (k-3) 821
Christmas in the stable (2-4) 811.008
Hughes, L. Carol of the brown king 811
Wilner, I. B is for Bethlehem E
Resurrection
Fisher, A. L. The story of Easter (3-5)
394.26

Jewels _See_ Precious stones
The **Jewish** American family album. Hoobler, D.
305.8
The **Jewish** Americans: a history in their own
words, 1650-1950 (6 and up) 305.8
Jewish art and symbolism
Chaikin, M. Menorahs, mezuzas, and other Jew-
ish symbols (5 and up) 296.4
Jewish holidays
See also Hanukkah; Passover; Purim; Rosh
ha-Shanah; Sukkoth; Yom Kippur
Berger, G. Celebrate! (4 and up) 296.4
Jaffe, N. The uninvited guest and other Jewish
holiday tales (4-6) 296.4
Poetry
Poems for Jewish holidays (k-3) 811.008
Jewish holocaust (1933-1945) _See_ Holocaust,
1933-1945
Jewish legends
Chaikin, M. Clouds of glory (4 and up)
296.1
Goldin, B. D. Journeys with Elijah (4 and up)
222
Jaffe, N. The uninvited guest and other Jewish
holiday tales (4-6) 296.4
Jaffe, N. While standing on one foot (4 and up)
296.1
Kimmel, E. A. The adventures of Hershel of
Ostropol (3-5) 398.2
Lester, J. When the beginning began (4 and up)
296.1
Rogasky, B. The golem (4 and up) 398.2
Schwartz, H. Next year in Jerusalem (4 and up)
296.1
Wisniewski, D. Golem (3-5) 398.2
Jewish New Year _See_ Rosh ha-Shanah
Jewish refugees
Fiction
Kerr, J. When Hitler stole Pink Rabbit (4 and
up) Fic

Levitin, S. Journey to America (4 and up)
Fic
Mazer, N. F. Good night, Maman (5 and up)
Fic
Jewish wit and humor
See/See also pages in the following book(s):
Bauer, C. F. Celebrations p119-34 808.8
Jews
Biography
Stanley, J. Frontier merchants (4-6) 92
Wells, R. Streets of gold [biography of Mary
Antin] (3-6) 92
Festivals
See Jewish holidays
Fiction
Clifford, E. The remembering box (3-5)
Fic
Cohen, B. The carp in the bathtub (2-4)
Fic
Cohen, B. Molly's pilgrim E
Drucker, M. Grandma's latkes E
Goldin, B. D. The world's birthday E
Herman, C. How Yussel caught the gefilte fish
E
Hesse, K. Letters from Rifka (5 and up)
Fic
Hest, A. When Jessie came across the sea
E
Hoestlandt, J. Star of fear, star of hope E
Hurwitz, J. Faraway summer (4-6) Fic
Jaffe, N. In the month of Kislev E
Kimmel, E. A. Hershel and the Hanukkah gob-
lins E
Kimmel, E. A. The jar of fools: eight Hanukkah
stories from Chelm (3-5) S C
Kimmel, E. A. The magic dreidels E
Konigsburg, E. L. About the B'nai Bagels (4-6)
Fic
Koss, A. G. How I saved Hanukkah (3-5)
Fic
Lasky, K. Dreams in the golden country (4 and
up) Fic
Lasky, K. Marven of the Great North Woods
E
Lasky, K. The night journey (4 and up)
Fic
Levine, G. C. Dave at night (5 and up)
Fic
Levoy, M. Alan and Naomi (6 and up) Fic
Lowry, L. Number the stars (4 and up) Fic
Manushkin, F. Latkes and applesauce E
Manushkin, F. The matzah that Papa brought
home E
Oberman, S. The always prayer shawl E
Polacco, P. The keeping quilt E
Polacco, P. Mrs. Katz and Tush E
Polacco, P. Tikvah means hope E
Polacco, P. The trees of the dancing goats
E
Rael, E. O. What Zeesie saw on Delancey Street
E
Rocklin, J. Strudel stories (4 and up) Fic
Rosen, M. J. Elijah's angel Fic
Schnur, S. The tie man's miracle E
Silverman, E. Raisel's riddle (k-3) 398.2

Jews—Fiction—*Continued*

Singer, I. B. The fools of Chelm and their history (4 and up)   **Fic**

Singer, I. B. The power of light (4 and up)   **S C**

Singer, I. B. Stories for children (4 and up)   **S C**

Taback, S. Joseph had a little overcoat   **E**

Taylor, S. All-of-a-kind family (4-6)   **Fic**

Woodruff, E. The memory coat   **E**

Yolen, J. The devil's arithmetic (4 and up)   **Fic**

Zalben, J. B. Unfinished dreams (5 and up)   **Fic**

Folklore

Adler, D. A. Chanukah in Chelm (k-3)   **398.2**

Jaffe, N. The mysterious visitor (4-6)   **398.2**

Jaffe, N. The way meat loves salt (k-3)   **398.2**

Kimmel, E. A. Gershon's monster (k-3)   **398.2**

Kimmel, E. A. The spotted pony: a collection of Hanukkah stories (3-6)   **398.2**

Prose, F. The angel's mistake (k-3)   **398.2**

Prose, F. You never know (k-3)   **398.2**

Sanfield, S. Bit by bit (k-3)   **398.2**

Schwartz, H. A coat for the moon and other Jewish tales (4 and up)   **398.2**

Schwartz, H. The diamond tree (3-5)   **398.2**

Schwartz, H. A journey to paradise and other Jewish tales (3-5)   **398.2**

Singer, I. B. Mazel and Shlimazel (2-5)   **398.2**

Singer, I. B. When Shlemiel went to Warsaw & other stories (4 and up)   **398.2**

Singer, I. B. Zlateh the goat, and other stories (4 and up)   **398.2**

History

Waldman, N. Masada (4 and up)   **933**

Legends

See Jewish legends

Persecutions

See also Holocaust, 1933-1945; World War, 1939-1945—Jews—Rescue

Rites and ceremonies

See Judaism—Customs and practices

Austria—Fiction

Ackerman, K. The night crossing (3-5)   **Fic**

Orgel, D. The devil in Vienna (6 and up)   **Fic**

Ethiopia—Fiction

Levitin, S. The return (6 and up)   **Fic**

Europe

Greenfeld, H. The hidden children (4 and up)   **940.53**

Rosenberg, M. B. Hiding to survive (5 and up)   **940.53**

France—Fiction

Morpurgo, M. Waiting for Anya (5 and up)   **Fic**

Polacco, P. The butterfly (2-4)   **Fic**

Germany

Perl, L. Four perfect pebbles (6 and up)   **940.53**

Netherlands

Adler, D. A. Hiding from the Nazis (2-4)   **940.53**

Adler, D. A. A picture book of Anne Frank (1-3)   **92**

Frank, A. The diary of a young girl (6 and up)   **92**

Frank, A. The diary of a young girl: the definitive edition (6 and up)   **92**

Gold, A. L. Memories of Anne Frank (5 and up)   **92**

Hurwitz, J. Anne Frank: life in hiding (3-5)   **92**

Reiss, J. The upstairs room (4 and up)   **92**

Rol, R. van der. Anne Frank, beyond the diary (5 and up)   **92**

Netherlands—Fiction

Oppenheim, S. L. The lily cupboard   **E**

Propp, V. W. When the soldiers were gone (3-5)   **Fic**

Vos, I. Anna is still here (4 and up)   **Fic**

Vos, I. Hide and seek (4 and up)   **Fic**

Vos, I. The key is lost (4 and up)   **Fic**

Poland

Adler, D. A. Child of the Warsaw ghetto (3-5)   **940.53**

Toll, N. S. Behind the secret window (6 and up)   **940.53**

Poland—Fiction

Hautzig, E. R. A gift for Mama (3-6)   **Fic**

Orlev, U. The island on Bird Street (5 and up)   **Fic**

Radin, R. Y. Escape to the forest (3-6)   **Fic**

Russia—Fiction

Howland, N. Latkes, latkes, good to eat   **E**

Penn, M. The miracle of the potato latkes   **E**

Schur, M. The circlemaker (5 and up)   **Fic**

Schur, M. The peddler's gift   **E**

United States

Bierman, C. Journey to Ellis Island (3-5)   **325.73**

Fisher, L. E. To bigotry, no sanction (4 and up)   **296**

Hoobler, D. The Jewish American family album (5 and up)   **305.8**

United States—History—Sources

The Jewish Americans: a history in their own words, 1650-1950 (6 and up)   **305.8**

Jiang, Ji-li

Red scarf girl (6 and up)   **951.05**

Jim-Dandy. Irwin, H.   **Fic**

Jim meets the thing. Cohen, M. See note under Cohen, M. It's George!   **E**

Jim Ugly. Fleischman, S.   **Fic**

Jiménez, Francisco, 1943-

The circuit: stories from the life of a migrant child (5 and up)   **S C**

Contents: Under the wire; Soledad; Inside out; Miracle in Tent City; El angel de Oro; Christmas gift; Death forgiven; Cotton sack; The circuit; Learning the game; To have and to hold; Moving still

Jimmy's boa and the big splash birthday bash. Noble, T. H. See note under Noble, T. H. The day Jimmy's boa ate the wash   **E**

Johnson, Crockett, 1906-1975—*Continued*
Harold's trip to the sky. See note under Johnson, C. Harold and the purple crayon **E**
A picture for Harold's room. See note under Johnson, C. Harold and the purple crayon **E**
(il) Krauss, R. The carrot seed **E**

Johnson, Dinah
Quinnie Blue **E**

Johnson, Donald B. (Donald Barton), 1933-
Henry hikes to Fitchburg **E**

Johnson, James Weldon, 1871-1938
Lift every voice and sing **782.42**

Johnson, Jane, 1951-
My dear Noel: the story of a letter from Beatrix Potter (k-3) **92**

Johnson, Jinny
Simon & Schuster children's guide to insects and spiders (4-6) **595.7**
Simon & Schuster children's guide to sea creatures (4 and up) **591.7**

Johnson, Meredith
(il) Cobb, V. Wanna bet! **793.8**

Johnson, Milton, 1932-
(il) O'Dell, S. The black pearl **Fic**

Johnson, Paul Brett
The cow who wouldn't come down **E**
Lost **E**
(il) Hodges, M. Saint Patrick and the peddler **398.2**
(il) McDonald, M. Insects are my life **E**

Johnson, Stephen, 1964-
Alphabet city **E**
City by numbers **E**
(il) Burleigh, R. Hoops **811**
(il) Look, L. Love as strong as ginger **E**
(il) San Souci, R. The samurai's daughter **398.2**
(il) Schnur, S. The tie man's miracle **E**

Johnson, Steve, 1960-
(il) Duncan, L. I walk at night **E**
(il) Fonteyn, Dame M. Coppélia **792.8**
(il) Scieszka, J. The Frog Prince continued **E**

Johnson, Sylvia A.
Ferrets (3-6) **636.97**
Inside an egg (4 and up) **598**
Mapping the world (4 and up) **912**
Tomatoes, potatoes, corn, and beans (6 and up) **641.3**

Johnston, Tony
Alice Nizzy Nazzy, the Witch of Santa Fe **E**
The barn owls **E**
The cowboy and the black-eyed pea **E**
Day of the Dead **E**
The ghost of Nicholas Greebe **E**
It's about dogs (2-4) **811**
The quilt story **E**
The soup bone **E**
The tale of Rabbit and Coyote (k-3) **398.2**

Johnston, William J., b. 1850
Fiction
Wisler, G. C. Mr. Lincoln's drummer (4 and up) **Fic**

Johnstone, Leslie
(jt. auth) Levine, S. Fun with your microscope **502.8**
(jt. auth) Levine, S. The optics book **535**
(jt. auth) Levine, S. Shocking science **537**

Jokes
Cerf, B. Riddles and more riddles! **793.73**
Kessler, L. P. Old Turtle's 90 knock-knocks, jokes, and riddles (1-3) **793.73**

Jonas, Ann
The 13th clue **E**
Aardvarks, disembark! **E**
The quilt **E**
Reflections **E**
Round trip **E**
Splash! **E**
The trek **E**
Two bear cubs **E**
Watch William walk **E**

Jonell, Lynne, 1956-
It's my birthday, too! **E**
Let's play rough **E**

Jones, Mother, 1830-1930
About
Kraft, B. H. Mother Jones (4 and up) **92**
See/See also pages in the following book(s):
Bartoletti, S. C. Kids on strike! (5 and up) **331.8**

Jones, Bill T.
Dance (k-3) **792.8**

Jones, Carol, 1942-
(il) Old MacDonald had a farm. See Old MacDonald had a farm **782.42**

Jones, Charlotte Foltz, 1945-
Mistakes that worked (4-6) **609**
Yukon gold (4 and up) **971.9**

Jones, Dee *See* Jones, Dolores Blythe

Jones, Diana Wynne
Castle in the air (6 and up) **Fic**
Howl's moving castle (6 and up) **Fic**

Jones, Dolores Blythe
(ed) Building a special collection of children's literature in your library. See Building a special collection of children's literature in your library **025.2**

Jones, Elizabeth Orton, 1910-
(il) Field, R. Prayer for a child **242**
See/See also pages in the following book(s):
Caldecott Medal books, 1938-1957 p118-30 **028.5**

Jones, Evan, 1915-1996
(jt. auth) Jones, J. Knead it, punch it, bake it! **641.8**

Jones, Jemima Parry- *See* Parry-Jones, Jemima

Jones, Joe, 1896-1987
See/See also pages in the following book(s):
Haskins, J. Out of the darkness (5 and up) **305.8**

Jones, Judith
Knead it, punch it, bake it! (3-6) **641.8**

Jones, Lynda
Kids around the world celebrate! (4-6) **394.26**

Jones, Mary
(il) Peacock, C. A. Sugar was my best food
362.1

Jones, Mary Harris *See* Jones, Mother, 1830-1930

Jones, Pattie Ridley
(jt. auth) Greenfield, E. Childtimes: a three-generation memoir **920**

Jones, Raymond E.
Characters in children's literature **028.5**

Jones, Robert F., 1934-
Jake (3-5) **636.7**

Jones, Terry, 1942-
Simple Peter's mirror
In The Oxford treasury of children's stories p50-54 **S C**

Jones, Tim Wynne- *See* Wynne-Jones, Tim

Joosse, Barbara M., 1949-
Mama, do you love me? **E**

Joplin, Scott, 1868-1917
See/See also pages in the following book(s):
Krull, K. Lives of the musicians p66-69 (4 and up) **920**

Jordan, Sandra
(jt. auth) Greenberg, J. The American eye
920
(jt. auth) Greenberg, J. Chuck Close, up close
92

Jordan
South, C. Jordan (5 and up) **956.95**

Jorinde and Joringel. Grimm, J.
In The Green fairy book p271-75 **398.2**

Jo's boys. Alcott, L. M. See note under Alcott, L. M. Little women **Fic**

Josefina. Winter, J. **E**

The **Josefina** story quilt. Coerr, E. **E**

Joseph (Biblical figure)
About
Kassirer, S. Joseph and his coat of many colors (k-2) **222**

Joseph, Nez Percé Chief, 1840-1904
See/See also pages in the following book(s):
Freedman, R. Indian chiefs p90-113 (6 and up) **920**

Joseph, Saint
Fiction
De Paola, T. The night of Las Posadas **E**

Joseph, Lynn
Coconut kind of day **811**
The mermaid's twin sister: more stories from Trinidad (4 and up) **398.2**
Contents: Keeping the duennes away; The mermaid's twin sister; La Diablesse; Colin's island; Tantie's callaloo fete; The obeah woman's birthday present
A wave in her pocket (4 and up) **398.2**
Contents: A soucouyant dies; Ligahoo; The graveyard jumbies; Simon and the big joke; A wave in her pocket; The bamboo beads

Joseph & Koza. Singer, I. B.
In Singer, I. B. Stories for children p139-54 **S C**

Joseph and his coat of many colors. Kassirer, S.
222

Joseph had a little overcoat. Taback, S. **E**

Josephus in the cave. Jaffe, N.
In Jaffe, N. The cow of no color: riddle stories and justice tales from around the world p122-27 **398.2**

Joshua T. Bates in trouble again. Shreve, S. R. See note under Shreve, S. R. The flunking of Joshua T. Bates **Fic**

Joshua T. Bates takes charge. Shreve, S. R. See note under Shreve, S. R. The flunking of Joshua T. Bates **Fic**

Joslin, Sesyle
What do you do, dear? (k-2) **395**
What do you say, dear? (k-2) **395**

Joubert, Beverly
See/See also pages in the following book(s):
Talking with adventurers p52-59 (4-6) **920**

Joubert, Dereck
See/See also pages in the following book(s):
Talking with adventurers p52-59 (4-6) **920**

Jourdenais, Norma Jean
(il) Henry, S. Cut-paper play! **745.54**

The **journal** of Jasper Jonathan Pierce, a pilgrim boy. Rinaldi, A. **Fic**

The **journal** of Joshua Loper. Myers, W. D. **Fic**

The **journal** of Scott Pendleton Collins. Myers, W. D. **Fic**

The **journal** of Sean Sullivan. Durbin, W. **Fic**

The **journal** of Wong Ming-Chung. Yep, L. **Fic**

Journal of Youth Services in Libraries **027.6205**

Journalism
Bentley, N. The young journalist's book (3-6) **070.1**
Hampton, W. Kennedy assassinated! (5 and up) **973.922**

Journals *See* Periodicals

Journals (Diaries) *See* Diaries

The **journey.** Hamanaka, S. **305.8**

Journey. MacLachlan, P. **Fic**

Journey home. Uchida, Y. **Fic**

Journey of the red wolf. Smith, R. **599.77**

Journey through the northern rainforest. Pandell, K. **578.7**

Journey to America. Levitin, S. **Fic**

Journey to Ellis Island. Bierman, C. **325.73**

Journey to Jo'burg. Naidoo, B. **Fic**

Journey to nowhere. Auch, M. J. **Fic**

A **journey** to paradise. Schwartz, H.
In Schwartz, H. A journey to paradise and other Jewish tales p40-45 **398.2**

A **journey** to paradise and other Jewish tales. Schwartz, H. **398.2**

Journey to Topaz. Uchida, Y. **Fic**

A **journey** with Elijah. Goldin, B. D.
In Goldin, B. D. Journeys with Elijah p1-10 **222**

Journeys *See* Voyages and travels

Journeys with Elijah. Goldin, B. D. **222**

Joyce, William
Bently & egg   **E**
A day with Wilbur Robinson   **E**
Dinosaur Bob and his adventures with the family Lazardo   **E**
George shrinks   **E**
The world of William Joyce scrapbook (2-5)   **92**
(il) Winthrop, E. Shoes   **E**

Joyful noise: poems for two voices. Fleischman, P.   **811**

Juan, de Pareja
Fiction
Treviño, E. B. de. I, Juan de Pareja (6 and up)   **Fic**

Juan Bobo. Bernier-Grand, C. T.   **398.2**
Juan Bobo and the buñuelos. González, L. M.
In From sea to shining sea p240-41   **810.8**

Juan Bobo and the three-legged pot. González, L. M.
In González, L. M. Señor Cat's romance and other favorite stories from Latin America p15-19   **398.2**

Juba this and Juba that   **372.6**

Jubb, Kendahl Jan, 1956-
(il) Patent, D. H. Flashy fantastic rain forest frogs   **597.8**

Jubilee Singers (Musical group)
Fiction
Hopkinson, D. A band of angels   **E**

Judaism
See/See also pages in the following book(s):
Osborne, M. P. One world, many religions p1-11 (4 and up)   **291**

Customs and practices
See also Bar mitzvah
Chaikin, M. Menorahs, mezuzas, and other Jewish symbols (5 and up)   **296.4**

Judar and his brothers. Philip, N.
In Philip, N. The Arabian nights p42-64   **398.2**

The **judge**. Zemach, H.   **E**

Judges
Adler, D. A. A picture book of Thurgood Marshall (1-3)   **92**
Fiction
Zemach, H. The judge   **E**

Judkis, Jim
(il) Rogers, F. Divorce   **306.89**
(il) Rogers, F. Extraordinary friends   **362.4**
(il) Rogers, F. Going to the hospital   **362.1**
(il) Rogers, F. Making friends   **158**
(il) Rogers, F. Stepfamilies   **306.8**

Judy Moody. McDonald, M.   **Fic**

The **juggler** of Notre Dame. Sawyer, R.
In Sawyer, R. The way of the storyteller p273-81   **372.6**

Juggling
Besmehn, B. Juggling step-by-step (4 and up)   **793.8**
Mitchelson, M. The most excellent book of how to be a juggler   **793.8**

Juggling step-by-step. Besmehn, B.   **793.8**
Jukes, Mavis
Blackberries in the dark (2-4)   **Fic**
Growing up: it's a girl thing (4 and up)   **612.6**
It's a girl thing (5 and up)   **305.23**
Like Jake and me (2-4)   **Fic**

Julian, dream doctor. Cameron, A. See note under Cameron, A. The stories Julian tells   **Fic**

Julian, secret agent. Cameron, A. See note under Cameron, A. The stories Julian tells   **Fic**

Julian's glorious summer. Cameron, A. See note under Cameron, A. The stories Julian tells   **Fic**

Julie. George, J. C.   **Fic**
Julie of the wolves. George, J. C.   **Fic**
Julie's wolf pack. George, J. C.   **Fic**
Julius. Johnson, A.   **E**
Julius, the baby of the world. Henkes, K.   **E**
Jumanji. Van Allsburg, C.   **E**
Jump at de sun: the story of Zora Neale Hurston. Porter, A. P.   **92**
Jump back, Honey. Dunbar, P. L.   **811**
Jump, frog, jump!. Kalan, R.   **E**

Jump in. Ruiz, D.
In You're on!: seven plays in English and Spanish p42-61   **812.008**

Jump, kangaroo, jump!. Murphy, S. J.   **513**

Jump rope rhymes
Anna Banana: 101 jump-rope rhymes   **398.8**
See/See also pages in the following book(s):
Cole, J. The rain or shine activity book p66-81 (3-5)   **793**

Jump ship to freedom. Collier, J. L.   **Fic**

Jumpers. Andersen, H. C.
In Andersen, H. C. The swan's stories p47-51   **S C**

Jumpety-bumpety hop   **811.008**
June 29, 1999. Wiesner, D.   **E**
Junebug. Mead, A.   **Fic**
Junebug and the Reverend. Mead, A. See note under Mead, A. Junebug   **Fic**
Juneteenth. Branch, M. M.   **394.26**
Jungle. Greenaway, T.   **577.3**
The **jungle** book: the Mowgli stories. Kipling, R.   **S C**

Junie B. Jones and a little monkey business. Park, B. See note under Park, B. Junie B. Jones and her big fat mouth   **Fic**

Junie B. Jones and her big fat mouth. Park, B.   **Fic**

Junie B. Jones and some sneaky peeky spying. Park, B. See note under Park, B. Junie B. Jones and her big fat mouth   **Fic**

Junie B. Jones and that meanie Jim's birthday. Park, B. See note under Park, B. Junie B. Jones and her big fat mouth   **Fic**

Junie B. Jones and the mushy gushy valentine. Park, B. See note under Park, B. Junie B. Jones and her big fat mouth   **Fic**

Junie B. Jones and the stupid smelly bus. Park, B. See note under Park, B. Junie B. Jones and her big fat mouth **Fic**

Junie B. Jones and the yucky blucky fruitcake. Park, B. See note under Park, B. Junie B. Jones and her big fat mouth **Fic**

Junie B. Jones Captain Field Day. Park, B. See note under Park, B. Junie B. Jones and her big fat mouth **Fic**

Junie B. Jones has a monster under her bed. Park, B. See note under Park, B. Junie B. Jones and her big fat mouth **Fic**

Junie B. Jones has a peep in her pocket. Park, B. See note under Park, B. Junie B. Jones and her big fat mouth **Fic**

Junie B. Jones is a beauty shop guy. Park, B. See note under Park, B. Junie B. Jones and her big fat mouth **Fic**

Junie B. Jones is a graduation girl. Park, B. See note under Park, B. Junie B. Jones and her big fat mouth **Fic**

Junie B. Jones is a party animal. Park, B. See note under Park, B. Junie B. Jones and her big fat mouth **Fic**

Junie B. Jones is (almost) a flower girl. Park, B. See note under Park, B. Junie B. Jones and her big fat mouth **Fic**

Junie B. Jones is not a crook. Park, B. See note under Park, B. Junie B. Jones and her big fat mouth **Fic**

Junie B. Jones loves handsome Warren. Park, B. See note under Park, B. Junie B. Jones and her big fat mouth **Fic**

Junie B. Jones smells something fishy. Park, B. See note under Park, B. Junie B. Jones and her big fat mouth **Fic**

Junion-Metz, Gail, 1947-
Coaching kids for the Internet **004.6**

Junion reference collection. (4-8) See entry in Part 2: Web Resources

Junior authors & illustrators series
Eighth book of junior authors and illustrators **920.003**

Junior genreflecting. Volz, B. D. **016.8**
Junior high school library catalog. See Middle and junior high school library catalog **011.6**

Junior Worldmark encyclopedia of the states (4 and up) **973.03**

Junior Worldmark encyclopedia of world cultures (5 and up) **306**
Juniorplots 4. Gillespie, J. T. **028.5**
Juno's Roman geese. McCaughrean, G.
In McCaughrean, G. The golden hoard: myths and legends of the world p66-73
398.2

Jupiter (Planet)
Brimner, L. D. Jupiter (2-4) **523.4**
Simon, S. Destination: Jupiter (3-6) **523.4**
Jurmain, Suzanne
Freedom's sons (4 and up) **326**

The **jury.** Jaffe, N.
In Jaffe, N. The cow of no color: riddle stories and justice tales from around the world p47-51 **398.2**
Just a dream. Van Allsburg, C. **E**
Just enough carrots. Murphy, S. J. **513**
Just Juice. Hesse, K. **Fic**
Just like Daddy. Asch, F. See note under Asch, F. Moonbear's dream **E**
Just like Floss. Lewis, K. **E**
Just like me **920**
Just me. Ets, M. H. **E**
Just one ghost. Terada, A. M.
In Terada, A. M. Under the starfruit tree p128-29 **398.2**
Just plain Fancy. Polacco, P. **E**
The **just** reward. Afanas'ev, A. N.
In Afanas'ev, A. N. Russian fairy tales p39-40 **398.2**
Just say hiç!. Walker, B. K.
In Walker, B. K. A treasury of Turkish folktales for children p76-79 **398.2**
Just so stories. Kipling, R. **S C**
Just us women. Caines, J. F. **E**
Just you and me. McBratney, S. **E**
Juster, Norton, 1929-
The phantom tollbooth (5 and up) **Fic**
Justice. Babbitt, N.
In Babbitt, N. The Devil's other storybook p11-17 **S C**
Justice. McKissack, P. C.
In McKissack, P. C. The dark-thirty p22-34 **S C**
Justin and the best biscuits in the world. Walter, M. P. **Fic**
Justin Morgan had a horse. Henry, M. **Fic**
Juvenile delinquency
Fiction
Sachar, L. Holes (5 and up) **Fic**

K

Kaa's hunting. Kipling, R.
In Kipling, R. The jungle book: the Mowgli stories **S C**
The **kabil's** donkey. Kimmel, E. A.
In Kimmel, E. A. The spotted pony: a collection of Hanukkah stories p19-23 **398.2**
Kaddo's wall. Courlander, H.
In Courlander, H. Cow-tail switch, and other West African stories p13-24 **398.2**
Kadono, Eiko, 1935-
The mirror
In Don't read this! and other tales of the unnatural p85-109 **S C**
Kafirs (African people) *See* Zulu (African people)
Kagda, Falaq
Algeria (5 and up) **965**
Hong Kong (5 and up) **951.25**
Kagda, Sakina, 1939-
Lithuania (5 and up) **947.9**

Keller, Holly—*Continued*
(il) Branley, F. M. Air is all around you
551.5
(il) Branley, F. M. Snow is falling   **551.57**
(il) Esbensen, B. J. Sponges are skeletons
593.4
(il) Gans, R. Let's go rock collecting   **552**
(il) Lauber, P. Be a friend to trees   **582.16**
(il) Lauber, P. Snakes are hunters   **597.9**
(il) Lauber, P. Who eats what?   **577**
(il) Lauber, P. You're aboard Spaceship Earth
550
(il) Pfeffer, W. From tadpole to frog   **597.8**
(il) Pfeffer, W. Sounds all around   **534**
(il) Pfeffer, W. What's it like to be a fish?
597

Keller, Laurie
Open wide (k-3)   **617.6**
(il) Wulffson, D. L. Toys!   **688.7**

Kelley, Gary
(il) Coville, B. William Shakespeare's Macbeth
822.3
(il) Tallchief, M. Tallchief   **92**

Kelley, True, 1946-
I've got chicken pox   **E**
(il) Balestrino, P. The skeleton inside you
611
(il) Branley, F. M. Flash, crash, rumble, and roll
551.55
(il) Branley, F. M. Floating in space
629.47
(il) Branley, F. M. What makes a magnet?
538
(il) Branley, F. M. What the moon is like
523.3
(il) Cobb, V. Don't try this at home!
507.8
(il) Cobb, V. You gotta try this!   **507.8**
(il) Cole, A. I saw a purple cow, and 100 other recipes for learning   **372**
(il) Miller, S. S. Three more stories you can read to your dog   **E**
(il) Showers, P. How many teeth?   **612.3**
(il) Showers, P. Look at your eyes   **612.8**
(il) Zimmerman, A. G. My dog Toby   **E**

Kellogg, Steven, 1941-
A-hunting we will go! (k-2)   **782.42**
Aster Aardvark's alphabet adventures   **E**
Best friends   **E**
Chicken Little (k-3)   **398.2**
I was born about 10,000 years ago   **E**
Jack and the beanstalk (k-3)   **398.2**
Johnny Appleseed (k-3)   **92**
Mike Fink (k-3)   **398.2**
The missing mitten mystery   **E**
Much bigger than Martin   **E**
The mysterious tadpole   **E**
Paul Bunyan (k-3)   **398.2**
Pecos Bill (k-3)   **398.2**
Pinkerton, behave!   **E**
Prehistoric Pinkerton. See note under Kellogg, S. Pinkerton, behave!   **E**
A Rose for Pinkerton. See note under Kellogg, S. Pinkerton, behave!   **E**
Sally Ann Thunder Ann Whirlwind Crockett (k-3)   **398.2**

Tallyho, Pinkerton! See note under Kellogg, S. Pinkerton, behave!   **E**
The three little pigs (k-3)   **398.2**
The three sillies (k-3)   **398.2**
(il) Bayer, J. A my name is Alice   **E**
(il) Caines, J. F. Abby   **E**
(il) Ehrlich, A. Leo, Zack, and Emmie together again   **E**
(il) Ehrlich, A. Parents in the pigpen, pigs in the tub   **E**
(il) Guarino, D. Is your mama a llama?   **E**
(il) Mahy, M. The boy who was followed home
E
(il) Mahy, M. The rattlebang picnic   **E**
(jt. auth) Martin, B. A beasty story   **E**
(il) Massie, D. R. The baby beebee bird   **E**
(il) Noble, T. H. The day Jimmy's boa ate the wash   **E**
(il) Schwartz, D. M. How much is a million?
E
(il) Schwartz, D. M. If you made a million
E
(il) Thurber, J. The great Quillow   **E**
(il) Twain, M. The adventures of Huckleberry Finn   **Fic**
(il) Williams, S. Library Lil   **E**

Kelly, Emery J.
Paper airplanes (4 and up)   **745.592**

Kelly, Eric Philbrook, 1884-1960
See/See also pages in the following book(s):
Newbery Medal books, 1922-1955 p67-73
028.5

Kelly, Jim
See/See also pages in the following book(s):
Sullivan, G. Quarterbacks! p21-23 (5 and up)
920

Kelly, Sheila M.
(jt. auth) Rotner, S. About twins   **306.8**

Keloğlan and the twelve dancing princesses. Walker, B. K.
In Walker, B. K. A treasury of Turkish folktales for children p29-34   **398.2**

Kelps
Fiction
Baker, J. The hidden forest   **E**

Kemp, Moira
(il) McCaughrean, G. Grandma Chickenlegs
398.2

Kemp-Welch, Lucy Elizabeth, 1869-1958
(il) Sewell, A. Black Beauty   **Fic**

Kendall, Carol
The Gammage Cup   **Fic**
The whisper of Glocken. See note under Kendall, C. The Gammage Cup   **Fic**

Kendall, Russ
(il) Waters, K. On the Mayflower   **974.4**
(il) Waters, K. Samuel Eaton's day   **974.4**
(il) Waters, K. Sarah Morton's day   **974.4**

Kenna, Kathleen
A people apart (4 and up)   **289.7**

Kennebec Indians *See* Abnaki Indians

Kennedy, Dorothy M. (Dorothy Mintzlaff), 1931-
(comp) Knock at a star. See Knock at a star
811.008

The **kidnappers**. Roberts, W. D.   **Fic**

Kidnapping

Fiction

Fleischman, P. The Half-a-Moon Inn (4-6)
    Fic

Roberts, W. D. The kidnappers (4 and up)
    Fic

Kids and grandparents: an activity book. Love, A.
    790.1

Kids around the world celebrate!. Jones, L.
    394.26

Kids around the world cook!. Braman, A. N.
    641.5

Kids at work. Freedman, R.   **331.3**

The **kids** campfire book. Drake, J.   **796.5**

The **Kids** Can Press jumbo book of gardening.
Morris, K.   **635.9**

The **Kids** Can Press jumbo cookbook. Gillies, J.
    641.5

The **kids'** cat book. De Paola, T.   **636.8**

The **kids** cottage book. See Drake, J. The kids'
summer handbook   **790.1**

Kids' crazy concoctions. Hauser, J. F.   **745.5**

Kids dance. Varriale, J.   **792.8**

Kids' first cookbook (k-3)   **641.5**

A **kid's** guide to America's Bill of Rights. Krull,
K.   **342**

The **kid's** guide to money. Otfinoski, S.
    332.024

The **kid's** guide to social action. Lewis, B. A.
    361.2

The **kids'** invention book. Erlbach, A.   **608**

Kids on strike!. Bartoletti, S. C.   **331.8**

Kids' pumpkin projects. Cook, D. F.   **745.5**

Kids space connection. (3-6) See entry in Part 2:
Web Resources

The **kids'** summer handbook. Drake, J.   **790.1**

The **kids'** volunteering book. Erlbach, A.   **302**

KidsClick!. See entry in Part 2: Web Resources

Kiefte, Kees de
(il) Livingston, M. C. Cricket never does
    811
(il) Namioka, L. Yang the youngest and his terrible ear   **Fic**

Kiesler, Kate, 1971-
(il) Clements, A. Temple cat   **E**
(comp) Fishing for a dream. See Fishing for a
dream   **782.42**
(il) Freedman, R. Out of darkness: the story of
Louis Braille   **92**
(il) George, K. O. The great frog race and other
poems   **811**
(il) George, K. O. Old Elm speaks   **811**

Kiitos! Kiitos!. Hands, R.
In The Oxford book of scary tales p144-49
    808.8

Kilborne, Sarah S.
Leaving Vietnam (1-4)   **959.704**

Kilcup, Rick
Randy the red-horned rainmoose
In The Big book of Christmas plays p228-39
    808.82

Killer bees. Lavies, B.   **595.7**

Kim Son Dal and the water-carriers. Jaffe, N.
In Jaffe, N. The cow of no color: riddle stories and justice tales from around the
world p94-98   **398.2**

Kimberly, Gail
Child of Faerie
In A Glory of unicorns p165-82   **S C**

Kimmel, Elizabeth Cody
Balto and the great race (3-5)   **636.7**
Ice story (4 and up)   **998**
In the stone circle (5 and up)   **Fic**
Visiting Miss Caples (6 and up)   **Fic**

Kimmel, Eric A.
The adventures of Hershel of Ostropol (3-5)
    398.2
Contents: What Hershel's father did; The goose's foot; The
bandit; Money from a table; Potatoes!; The miracle; An incredi-
ble story; The cow; The candlesticks; Hershel goes to heaven
Anansi and the talking melon (k-3)   **398.2**
Anansi goes fishing (k-3)   **398.2**
Bar mitzvah (5 and up)   **296.4**
Be not far from me (5 and up)   **221.9**
Bearhead (k-3)   **398.2**
The birds' gift (k-3)   **398.2**
The Chanukkah guest   **E**
The darning needle
In From sea to shining sea p189-91
    810.8
Days of Awe (3-6)   **296.4**
Four dollars and fifty cents   **E**
Gershon's monster (k-3)   **398.2**
The gingerbread man (k-2)   **398.2**
Grizz!   **E**
Hershel and the Hanukkah goblins   **E**
I took my frog to the library   **E**
Iron John (2-5)   **398.2**
The jar of fools: eight Hanukkah stories from
Chelm (3-5)   **S C**
Contents: The jar of fools; How they play dreidel in Chelm;
Sweeter than honey, purer than oil; The Knight of the Golden
Slippers; Silent Samson, the Maccabee; The magic spoon; The
soul of a Menorah; Wisdom for sale
The magic dreidels   **E**
Montezuma and the fall of the Aztecs (3-5)
    972
The rooster's antlers (k-3)   **398.2**
Seven at one blow (k-3)   **398.2**
The spotted pony: a collection of Hanukkah sto-
ries (3-6)   **398.2**
Includes the following stories: Ibn Ezra and the archbishop;
The kabil's donkey; Leviathan and the fox; The wonderful
shamir; Did the rabbi have a head?; The caliph and the cobbler;
When Hershel eats; The spotted pony
Sword of the samurai (4 and up)   **S C**
Includes the following stories: Dōhaku's head; The samurai
and the dragon; The coward; Matajuro's training; The oxcart;
The battle of Chihaya Castle; Tomoe Gozen; The burglar; Devil
boy; The Rōnin and the tea master; No sword
Ten suns (2-4)   **398.2**
The three princes (k-3)   **398.2**
Three sacks of truth (2-4)   **398.2**
The two mountains (3-5)   **398.2**
(ed) A Hanukkah treasury. See A Hanukkah
treasury   **296.4**

Kinaaldá: a Navajo girl grows up. Roessel, M.
    970.004

Kindai and the ape. Aardema, V.
In Aardema, V. Misoso p79-87   **398.2**

King of the monkeys. Carpenter, F.
   In Carpenter, F. Tales of a Chinese grand-
     mother p107-16   **398.2**
King of the wind. Henry, M.   **Fic**
King Peacock
   In Stockings of buttermilk: American folktales
     p47-50   **398.2**
King-Smith, Dick, 1922-
   Ace, the very important pig (3-5)   **Fic**
   All pigs are beautiful (k-3)   **636.4**
   Babe: the gallant pig (3-5)   **Fic**
   The cuckoo child (3-5)   **Fic**
   I love guinea pigs (k-3)   **636.9**
   Jenius: the amazing guinea pig (2-4)   **Fic**
   A mouse called Wolf (2-4)   **Fic**
   Pigs might fly (3-5)   **Fic**
   Puppy love (k-3)   **636.7**
   The school mouse (3-5)   **Fic**
   Sophie hits six. See note under King-Smith, D.
     Sophie's Tom   **Fic**
   Sophie in the saddle. See note under King-
     Smith, D. Sophie's Tom   **Fic**
   Sophie is seven. See note under King-Smith, D.
     Sophie's Tom   **Fic**
   Sophie's Lucky. See note under King-Smith, D.
     Sophie's Tom   **Fic**
   Sophie's snail. See note under King-Smith, D.
     Sophie's Tom   **Fic**
   Sophie's Tom (3-5)   **Fic**
   Spider Sparrow (4-6)   **Fic**
   Three terrible trins (3-5)   **Fic**
   The water horse (3-5)   **Fic**
King Solomon and his magic ring. Wiesel, E.
     222
King Solomon tests fate. Schwartz, H.
   In Schwartz, H. A journey to paradise and
     other Jewish tales p14-15   **398.2**
King Stork. Pyle, H.   **398.2**
The king who wanted to touch the moon. Mayo,
M.
   In Mayo, M. Magical tales from many lands
     p54-58   **398.2**
The **Kingdom** Under the Sea. Mayo, M.
   In Mayo, M. Magical tales from many lands
     p25-34   **398.2**
The **Kingfisher** first human body encyclopedia.
   Walker, R.   **612**
Kingman, Lee, 1919-
   (ed) Newbery and Caldecott Medal books, 1966-
   1975. See Newbery and Caldecott Medal
   books, 1966-1975   **028.5**
   (ed) Newbery and Caldecott Medal books, 1976-
   1985. See Newbery and Caldecott Medal
   books, 1976-1985   **028.5**
Kings and rulers
   See also Queens
         Fiction
   Wood, A. King Bidgood's in the bathtub   **E**
The **king's** ankus. Kipling, R.
   In Kipling, R. The jungle book: the Mowgli
     stories   **S C**
The **king's** dragon. Yolen, J.
   In Yolen, J. Here there be dragons p84-86
     810.8

The **King's** fifth. O'Dell, S.   **Fic**
Kings Landing Historical Settlement (N.B.)
   Goodman, S. Ultimate field trip 4: a week in the
     1800s (5 and up)   **973.5**
The **King's** secret. Schwartz, H.
   In Schwartz, H. A coat for the moon and oth-
     er Jewish tales p48-51   **398.2**
Kingsley, Charles, 1819-1875
   The water babies (4-6)   **Fic**
Kinsey-Warnock, Natalie
   The Canada geese quilt (3-5)   **Fic**
Kiowa Indians
   See/See also pages in the following book(s):
   Freedman, R. Indian chiefs p29-51 (6 and up)
     920
Kipling, Rudyard, 1865-1936
   The beginning of the armadilloes   **Fic**
   The elephant's child   **Fic**
   How the rhinoceros got his skin
   In The Oxford treasury of children's stories
     p127-29   **S C**
   The jungle book: the Mowgli stories (4 and up)
     S C
   Contents: Mowgli's brothers; Hunting song of the Seeonee
   Pack; Kaa's hunting; Road song of the bandard-log; How fear
   came; The law of the jungle; "Tiger-Tiger!"; Mowglie's song;
   Letting in the jungle; Mowglie's song gainst people; The king's
   ankus; The song of the little hunter; Red dog; Chil's song; The
   spring running; The outsong; "Rikki-tikki-tavi"; Darzee's chant
   Just so stories (3-6)   **S C**
   Contents: How the whale got his throat; How the camel got
   his hump; How the rhinoceros got his skin; How the leopard got
   his spots; The elephant's child; The sing-song of old man kangaroo; The beginning of the armadilloes; How the first letter was
   written; How the alphabet was made; The crab that played with
   the sea; The cat that walked by himself; The butterfly that
   stamped
   Rikki-tikki-tavi
   In Kipling, R. The jungle book: the Mowgli
     stories   **S C**
   Rikki-tikki-tavi; adaptation. See Pinkney, J.
     Rikki-tikki-tavi   **E**
A **kiss** for Little Bear. Minarik, E. H. See note un-
   der Minarik, E. H. Little Bear   **E**
Kiss Me. Sandburg, C.
   In Sandburg, C. Rootabaga stories pt 2 p170-
     73   **S C**
   In Sandburg, C. The Sandburg treasury p158-
     59   **818**
Kitamura, Satoshi
   Me and my cat?   **E**
   Sheep in wolves' clothing   **E**
Kitchen, Bert
   Animal alphabet   **E**
   (il) Tagholm, S. The rabbit   **599.3**
The **kitchen** knight. Hodges, M.   **398.2**
Kite. Burgess, M.   **Fic**
The **kite** fighters. Park, L. S.   **Fic**
Kites
         Fiction
   Demi. Kites   **E**
   Park, L. S. The kite fighters (4-6)   **Fic**
   Williams, V. B. Lucky song   **E**
Kites sail high: a book about verbs. Heller, R.
     428
Kit's wilderness. Almond, D.   **Fic**

Kiuchi, Tatsuro
(il) Martin, R. Mysterious tales of Japan
398.2

Klages, Ellen, 1954-
(jt. auth) Murphy, P. The science explorer
507.8

Klause, Annette Curtis
Alien secrets (5 and up)   Fic

Klausner, Janet
Sequoyah's gift (4 and up)   92

Klein, Suzanna
(il) Womenfolk and fairy tales. See Womenfolk
and fairy tales   398.2

Klein, T. E. D., 1947-
Rhode Island
In Celebrate the states   973

Klein, Ted *See* Klein, T. E. D., 1947-

Kleven, Elisa
Hooray, a piñata!   E
The paper princess   E
(il) De colores and other Latin-American folk
songs for children. See De colores and other
Latin-American folk songs for children
782.42
(il) Diez deditos. Ten little fingers & other play
rhymes and action songs from Latin America.
See Diez deditos. Ten little fingers & other
play rhymes and action songs from Latin
America   782.42
(il) Dorros, A. Abuela   E
(il) Jaskol, J. City of angels   979.4
(il) Wilner, I. B is for Bethlehem   E

Kline, Michael P.
(il) Blobaum, C. Geology rocks!   551
(il) Hart, A. Ancient Greece!   938
(il) Hauser, J. F. Super science concoctions
507.8
(il) Johmann, C. Bridges!   624
(il) Milord, S. Mexico!   972
(il) Williamson, S. Summer fun!   790.1

Kline, Suzy, 1943-
Herbie Jones (3-5)   Fic
Herbie Jones and Hamburger Head. See note
under Kline, S. Herbie Jones   Fic
Herbie Jones and the birthday showdown. See
note under Kline, S. Herbie Jones   Fic
Herbie Jones and the class gift. See note under
Kline, S. Herbie Jones   Fic
Herbie Jones and the dark attic. See note under
Kline, S. Herbie Jones   Fic
Herbie Jones and the monster ball. See note un-
der Kline, S. Herbie Jones   Fic
Horrible Harry and the ant invasion. See note
under Kline, S. Horrible Harry in room 2B
Fic
Horrible Harry and the Christmas surprise. See
note under Kline, S. Horrible Harry in room
2B   Fic
Horrible Harry and the Drop of Doom. See note
under Kline, S. Horrible Harry in room 2B
Fic
Horrible Harry and the dungeon. See note under
Kline, S. Horrible Harry in room 2B   Fic

Horrible Harry and the green slime. See note
under Kline, S. Horrible Harry in room 2B
Fic
Horrible Harry and the kickball wedding. See
note under Kline, S. Horrible Harry in room
2B   Fic
Horrible Harry and the purple people. See note
under Kline, S. Horrible Harry in room 2B
Fic
Horrible Harry at Halloween. See note under
Kline, S. Horrible Harry in room 2B   Fic
Horrible Harry goes to the moon. See note un-
der Kline, S. Horrible Harry in room 2B
Fic
Horrible Harry in room 2B (2-4)   Fic
Horrible Harry moves up to third grade. See
note under Kline, S. Horrible Harry in room
2B   Fic
Horrible Harry's secret. See note under Kline, S.
Horrible Harry in room 2B   Fic
Marvin and the mean words. See note under
Kline, S. Mary Marony, mummy girl   Fic
Marvin and the meanest girl. See note under
Kline, S. Mary Marony, mummy girl   Fic
Mary Marony and the chocolate surprise. See
note under Kline, S. Mary Marony, mummy
girl   Fic
Mary Marony and the snake. See note under
Kline, S. Mary Marony, mummy girl   Fic
Mary Marony hides out. See note under Kline,
S. Mary Marony, mummy girl   Fic
Mary Marony, mummy girl (2-4)   Fic
Orp. See note under Kline, S. Orp and the FBI
Fic
Orp and the chop suey burgers. See note under
Kline, S. Orp and the FBI   Fic
Orp and the FBI (4-6)   Fic
Orp goes to the hoop. See note under Kline, S.
Orp and the FBI   Fic
Song Lee and Leech Man. See note under
Kline, S. Horrible Harry in room 2B   Fic
Song Lee and the hamster hunt. See note under
Kline, S. Horrible Harry in room 2B   Fic
Song Lee and the "I hate you" notes. See note
under Kline, S. Horrible Harry in room 2B
Fic
Song Lee in room 2B. See note under Kline, S.
Horrible Harry in room 2B   Fic
What's the matter with Herbie Jones? See note
under Kline, S. Herbie Jones   Fic

Kliros, Thea
(il) Hines, A. G. What can you do in the rain?
E

The **Klondike** gold rush. Walsh Shepherd, D.
971.9

Klondike River valley (Yukon)
Gold discoveries
Jones, C. F. Yukon gold (4 and up)   971.9
Walsh Shepherd, D. The Klondike gold rush (4
and up)   971.9
Gold discoveries—Fiction
Hobbs, W. Jason's gold (5 and up)   Fic

Knapp, Ron, 1952-
Top 10 American men's Olympic gold medalists
(4 and up)   920

Knead it, punch it, bake it!. Jones, J.   641.8

The **knee-high** man. Lester, J.
  In Lester, J. The knee-high man, and other tales p27-29   **398.2**
  In The Oxford treasury of children's stories p33-34   **S C**

The **knee-high** man, and other tales. Lester, J.
   398.2

Kneeknock Rise. Babbitt, N.   **Fic**

Knife. Ellis, S.
  In Ellis, S. Back of beyond   **S C**

Knight, Christopher G.
  (il) Lasky, K. Days of the Dead   **394.26**
  (il) Lasky, K. Monarchs   **595.7**
  (il) Lasky, K. The most beautiful roof in the world   **577.3**

Knight, Hilary
  (il) Happy birthday. See Happy birthday   **811.008**
  (il) MacDonald, B. Mrs. Piggle-Wiggle   **Fic**
  (il) Side by side. See Side by side   **808.81**
  (il) Thompson, K. Kay Thompson's Eloise   **E**

Knight, Joan
  Charlotte in Giverny (3-6)   **Fic**

Knight, Margaret, 1838-1914
  See/See also pages in the following book(s):
  Thimmesh, C. Girls think of everything (5 and up)   **920**

Knight, Margy Burns
  Talking walls (3-5)   **909**
  Talking walls: the stories continue (3-5)   **909**

The **knight** and the dragon. De Paola, T.   **E**

The **Knight** of the Golden Slippers. Kimmel, E. A.
  In Kimmel, E. A. The jar of fools: eight Hanukkah stories from Chelm p13-18   **S C**

Knights & castles. Hart, A.   **940.1**

Knights and knighthood
  Gibbons, G. Knights in shining armor (k-3)   **394**
  Gravett, C. Knight (4 and up)   **940.1**
  Hart, A. Knights & castles (4 and up)   **940.1**
  Yue, C. Armor (4 and up)   **355.8**
    Fiction
  Bulla, C. R. The sword in the tree (3-5)   **Fic**
  De Paola, T. The knight and the dragon   **E**
  Hodges, M. Saint George and the dragon (2-5)   **398.2**
  Thomas, S. M. Good night, Good Knight   **E**

Knight's castle. Eager, E. See note under Cleary, B. Henry Higgins   **Fic**

Knights in shining armor. Gibbons, G.   **394**

Knights of the kitchen table. Scieszka, J.   **Fic**

Knights of the Round Table *See* Arthurian romances

Knock at a star   **811.008**

Knock at the door and other baby action rhymes. Chorao, K.   **398.8**

Knock . . . knock . . . knock. San Souci, R.
  In San Souci, R. More short & shivery p148-52   **398.2**

Knots in my yo-yo string. Spinelli, J.   **92**

Knots on a counting rope. Martin, B.   **E**

Knotts, Bob
  Martial arts (2-4)   **796.8**
  The Summer Olympics (2-4)   **796.48**
  Track and field (2-4)   **796.42**
  Weightlifting (2-4)   **796.41**

Know Not. Afanas´ev, A. N.
  In Afanas´ev, A. N. Russian fairy tales p97-109   **398.2**

Knowles, Elizabeth, 1946-
  More reading connections   **028.5**

Knutson, Barbara
  How the guinea fowl got her spots (k-3)   **398.2**
  (il) Brady, A. A. Kwanzaa karamu   **641.5**

Ko-Ai's lost shoe. Carpenter, F.
  In Carpenter, F. Tales of a Chinese grandmother p175-81   **398.2**

Ko Kóngole. MacDonald, M. R.
  In MacDonald, M. R. The storyteller's start-up book p179-81   **372.6**

Koala. Mayo, M.
  In Mayo, M. Magical tales from many lands p100-04   **398.2**

Koala Lou. Fox, M.   **E**

Koalas
    Fiction
  Fox, M. Koala Lou   **E**

Kobayashi, Issa, 1763-1827
    About
  Gollub, M. Cool melons—turn to frogs!: the life and poems of Issa (3-6)   **92**

Koch, Kenneth, 1925-
  (comp) Talking to the sun: an illustrated anthology of poems for young people. See Talking to the sun: an illustrated anthology of poems for young people   **808.81**

Kochel, Marcia Agness
  (jt. auth) Baxter, K. A. Gotcha!   **028.1**

Koerber, Nora
  (il) Kimmel, E. C. Balto and the great race   **636.7**

Koertge, Ronald
  Tiger, tiger, burning bright (6 and up)   **Fic**

Kogan, Deborah *See* Ray, Deborah Kogan, 1940-

Kogi. Martin, R.
  In Martin, R. Mysterious tales of Japan   **398.2**

Koheleth *See* Bible. O.T. Ecclesiastes

Kohn, Alexandra
  (jt. auth) Chödzin, S. The wisdom of the crows and other Buddhist tales   **294.3**

Kohn, Michael H. *See* Chödzin, Sherab

Kohn, Sherab Chödzin *See* Chödzin, Sherab

Koi and the kola nuts. Aardema, V.   **398.2**

Koide, Tan, 1938-1986
  May we sleep here tonight?   **E**

Koide, Yasuko
(il) Koide, T. Mày we sleep here tonight?
    E

Koizumi, Yakumo *See* Hearn, Lafcadio, 1850-1904

Koko-love!. Patterson, F.   **599.8**

Kokopelli's flute. Hobbs, W.   **Fic**

Koller, Jackie French
One monkey too many   E

Komodo!. Sis, P.   E

Komodo dragon
Darling, K. Komodo dragon on location (3-5)
    597.9

Fiction
Sis, P. Komodo!   E

Komodo dragon on location. Darling, K.
    597.9

Konigsburg, E. L.
About the B'nai Bagels (4-6)   **Fic**
Altogether, one at a time (4-6)   **S C**
Contents: Inviting Jason; The Night of the Leonids; Camp Fat; Momma at the Pearly Gates
From the mixed-up files of Mrs. Basil E. Frankweiler (4-6)   **Fic**
Jennifer, Hecate, Macbeth, William McKinley, and me, Elizabeth (4-6)   **Fic**
A proud taste for scarlet and miniver (5 and up)   **Fic**
TalkTalk   **028.5**
Up from Jericho Tel (5 and up)   **Fic**
The view from Saturday (4-6)   **Fic**
See/See also pages in the following book(s):
Author talk (4 and up)   **028.5**
The Newbery & Caldecott medal books, 1986-2000 p266-78   **028.5**
Newbery and Caldecott Medal books, 1966-1975 p36-44   **028.5**

Konnichiwa!. Brown, T.   **305.8**

Kopper, Lisa, 1950-
Daisy is a mommy. See note under Kopper, L. Daisy knows best   E
Daisy knows best   E
Daisy's babies. See note under Kopper, L. Daisy knows best   E
(il) Lewin, H. Jafta   E

Kops, Deborah
(jt. auth) Pascoe, E. Scholastic kid's almanac for the 21st century   **031.02**

Kordon, Klaus, 1943-
The ravens
In Don't read this! and other tales of the unnatural p71-84   **S C**

Korea
Fiction
Choi, S. N. Year of impossible goodbyes (5 and up)   **Fic**
Park, F. The royal bee   E
Park, L. S. The kite fighters (4-6)   **Fic**
Watkins, Y. K. So far from the bamboo grove (6 and up)   **Fic**
Folklore
See Folklore—Korea
Korean Americans
Fiction
Bunting, E. Smoky night   E

Choi, S. N. Halmoni and the picnic   E
Pak, S. Dear Juno   E
Shalant, P. Beware of kissing Lizard Lips (4-6)
    Fic

The Korean Cinderella. Climo, S.   **398.2**

Korean-English bilingual books *See* Bilingual books—English-Korean

Korman, Gordon, 1963-
The sixth grade nickname game (4-6)   **Fic**

Koscielniak, Bruce
The story of the incredible orchestra (2-4)
    784.2

Koshchey the Deathless. Afanas'ev, A. N.
In Afanas'ev, A. N. Russian fairy tales p485-94   **398.2**

Koshkin, Alexander
(il) Climo, S. Stolen thunder   **293**
(il) Paterson, J. B. Images of God   **231**
(il) Paterson, K. The angel and the donkey
    222
(il) Winthrop, E. The little humpbacked horse
    398.2

Koslow, Philip
(jt. auth) Kranz, R. The biographical dictionary of African Americans   **920.003**

Kosovo (Serbia)
Marx, T. One boy from Kosovo (3-6)
    949.7

Koss, Amy Goldman, 1954-
The Ashwater experiment (4 and up)   **Fic**
The girls (5 and up)   **Fic**
How I saved Hanukkah (3-5)   **Fic**

Kostyal, K. M., 1951-
Trial by ice: a photobiography of Sir Ernest Shackleton (4 and up)   **92**

Kott, Jennifer, 1971-
Nicaragua (5 and up)   **972.85**

Kovacs, Deborah
Dive to the deep ocean (4 and up)   **623.8**

Kovalski, Maryann, 1951-
The wheels on the bus (k-2)   **782.42**

Kraft, Betsy Harvey
Mother Jones (4 and up)   **92**

Kramer, Alan
How to make a chemical volcano and other mysterious experiments (4-6)   **540.7**

Kramer, Dave
(il) Bradley, K. B. Ruthie's gift   **Fic**

Kramer, David Joseph *See* Kramer, Dave

Kramer, Stephen
Caves (4-6)   **551.4**
Eye of the storm (4 and up)   **778.9**
How to think like a scientist (3-5)   **507**
Lightning (4-6)   **551.56**

Kranz, Rachel
The biographical dictionary of African Americans   **920.003**
(jt. auth) Bock, J. Scholastic encyclopedia of the United States   **973.03**

Krasilovsky, Phyllis, 1926-
The man who didn't wash his dishes
In The Read-aloud treasury p179-87
    808.8

Kraske, Robert
Asteroids (5 and up)   **523.4**

Kraus, Robert, 1925-
Come out and play, little mouse. See note under Kraus, R. Whose mouse are you?   E
Little Louie the baby bloomer   E
Mort the sport   E
Mouse in love. See note under Kraus, R. Whose mouse are you?   E
Where are you going, little mouse? See note under Kraus, R. Whose mouse are you?   E
Whose mouse are you?   E

Krause, Peter, 1954-
Fundamental golf (5 and up)   **796.352**

Krauss, Ruth, 1911-1993
The carrot seed   E
A very special house   E

Krautwurst, Terry, 1946-
(jt. auth) Diehn, G. Science crafts for kids   **507.8**

Krementz, Jill
How it feels to be adopted (4 and up)   **362.7**
How it feels when a parent dies (4 and up)   **155.9**
How it feels when parents divorce (4 and up)   **306.89**

Krenina, Katya, 1968-
(il) Herman, C. How Yussel caught the gefilte fish   E
(il) Kimmel, E. A. The birds' gift   **398.2**
(il) Kimmel, E. A. The magic dreidels   E
(il) Lewis, J. P. At the wish of the fish   **398.2**

Krensky, Stephen, 1953-
How Santa got his job   E
Lionel and his friends. See note under Krensky, S. Lionel at large   E
Lionel and Louise. See note under Krensky, S. Lionel at large   E
Lionel at large   E
Lionel at school. See note under Krensky, S. Lionel at large   E
Lionel in the fall. See note under Krensky, S. Lionel at large   E
Lionel in the spring. See note under Krensky, S. Lionel at large   E
Lionel in the summer. See note under Krensky, S. Lionel at large   E
Lionel in the winter. See note under Krensky, S. Lionel at large   E
Striking it rich (2-4)   **979.4**

Kreutzer, Peter
Little League's official how-to-play baseball book (4 and up)   **796.357**

Krishnaswami, Uma, 1956-
Shower of gold: girls and women in the stories of India (5 and up)   **398.2**
Contents: The goddess and the girl; Savitri and the God of Death; The Buddha and the five hundred queens; The daughter-in-law who got her way; The mother of Karaikkal; The goddess and the buffalo demon; Gotami and the mustard seed; Sita's story; The princess who wished to be beautiful; The warrior queen of Jhansi; Vishnu's bride; The love story of Roopmati and Baz Bahadur; The eight sons of Ganga; She who showers gold; The magic tree; My name is Illusion; Kali's curse; Supriya's bowl

Kristina, Queen of Sweden, 1626-1689 *See* Christina, Queen of Sweden, 1626-1689

Kristy, Davida
Coubertin's Olympics (5 and up)   **92**

Kroeber, Theodora, 1897-1979
Ishi, last of his tribe (5 and up)   **92**

Kroeger, Mary Kay, 1950-
Paperboy   E

Kroll, Steven
The biggest pumpkin ever   E
The Boston Tea Party (3-5)   **973.3**
By the dawn's early light (3-5)   **782.42**
Ellis Island (3-5)   **325.73**
Pony Express! (3-5)   **383**
William Penn (3-5)   **92**

Kroll, Virginia L.
Faraway drums   E
Masai and I   E

Krommes, Beth
(il) Root, P. Grandmother Winter   E

Krone, Julie
See/See also pages in the following book(s):
Littlefield, B. Champions p11-24 (5 and up)   **920**

Kronquist, Burleigh *See* Burleigh, Robert, 1936-

Krudop, Walter, 1966-
The man who caught fish   E
(il) Burleigh, R. Black whiteness   **998**
(il) Fletcher, R. Ordinary things   **811**
(il) Fletcher, R. Relatively speaking   **811**

Kruidenier, Robert, 1946-
(il) Arnold, C. Hawk highway in the sky   **598**

Krull, Kathleen, 1952-
A kid's guide to America's Bill of Rights (4 and up)   **342**
Lives of the artists (4 and up)   **920**
Lives of the athletes (4 and up)   **920**
Lives of the musicians (4 and up)   **920**
Lives of the presidents (4 and up)   **920**
Lives of the writers (4 and up)   **920**
They saw the future (4 and up)   **133.3**
Wilma unlimited: how Wilma Rudolph became the world's fastest woman (2-4)   **92**
(comp) Gonna sing my head off! See Gonna sing my head off!   **782.42**

Krumgold, Joseph, 1908-1980
Onion John (5 and up)   Fic
See/See also pages in the following book(s):
Newbery Medal books, 1922-1955 p407-23   **028.5**

Krupinski, Loretta, 1940-
(il) Bianco, M. W. The velveteen rabbit   Fic
(il) Cooney, B. The story of Christmas   **394.26**
(il) Maestro, B. Why do leaves change color?   **582.16**

Krush, Beth, 1918-
(il) Enright, E. Gone-Away Lake   Fic
(il) Norton, M. The Borrowers   Fic

Krush, Joe, 1918-
(il) Enright, E. Gone-Away Lake   Fic
(il) Norton, M. The Borrowers   Fic

Lange, Dorothea, 1895-1965
About
Partridge, E. Restless spirit: the life and work of
Dorothea Lange (6 and up)   92
Langley, Andrew
Hans Christian Andersen (2-4)   92
Renaissance (4 and up)   940.2
Langstaff, John M., 1920-
Frog went a-courtin' (k-3)   782.42
Oh, a-hunting we will go (k-2)   782.42
Over in the meadow (k-2)   782.42
(ed) What a morning! See What a morning!
   782.25
Langton, Jane
The fledgling (5 and up)   Fic
Language and languages
See also Sign language
Language arts
See also Creative writing
Language Arts   372.605
The **language** of birds. Martin, R.   398.2
The **language** of blood. Coville, B.
In Coville, B. Oddly enough p61-78
   S C
The **language** of the birds. Schwartz, H.
In Schwartz, H. Next year in Jerusalem p14-
18   296.1
Languages
Vocabulary
See Vocabulary
Lanino, Deborah
(il) Hopkinson, D. Maria's comet   E
Lankford, Mary D., 1932-
Christmas around the world (3-5)   394.26
Dominoes around the world (3-5)   795.3
Hopscotch around the world (3-5)   796.2
The **lantuch**. Singer, I. B.
In Singer, I. B. Stories for children p231-36
   S C
Lantz, Paul, 1908-
(il) Gates, D. Blue willow   Fic
Laos
Mansfield, S. Laos (5 and up)   959.4
Folklore
See Folklore—Laos
Lapland
Lewin, T. The reindeer people (3-5)   948.97
Laplanders *See* Sami (European people)
The **Laplander's** drum. Olson, A. N.
In Olson, A. N. Ask the bones: scary stories
from around the world p53-59   398.2
Large, Annabel
(il) Ibbotson, E. Which witch?   Fic
Large print books
Almond, D. Kit's wilderness   Fic
Almond, D. Skellig   Fic
Billingsley, F. The Folk Keeper   Fic
Clements, A. The janitor's boy   Fic
Clements, A. The Landry News   Fic
Couloumbis, A. Getting near to baby   Fic
Curtis, C. P. Bud, not Buddy   Fic
DeFelice, C. C. The ghost of Fossil Glen
   Fic

Erdrich, L. The birchbark house   Fic
Giff, P. R. Lily's crossing   Fic
Haas, J. Unbroken   Fic
Holm, J. L. Our only May Amelia   Fic
Johnson, A. Heaven   Fic
Korman, G. The sixth grade nickname game
   Fic
Koss, A. G. The Ashwater experiment   Fic
Koss, A. G. The girls   Fic
Lawrence, I. The wreckers   Fic
Levine, G. C. Ella enchanted   Fic
Lewis, C. S. The lion, the witch, and the ward-
robe   Fic
McCaffrey, A. Dragonsong   Fic
O'Connor, B. Me and Rupert Goody   Fic
Paterson, K. Preacher's boy   Fic
Peterson, R. T. A field guide to the birds
   598
Robinet, H. G. Forty acres and maybe a mule
   Fic
Rocklin, J. Strudel stories   Fic
Rowling, J. K. Harry Potter and the sorcerer's
stone   Fic
Spinelli, J. Knots in my yo-yo string   92
Laroche, Giles
(il) Sturges, P. Bridges are to cross   624
Larsen, Janet
(il) Terada, A. M. Under the starfruit tree
   398.2
Larsen, Lise Lunge- *See* Lunge-Larsen, Lise
Lascom, Adrian
(il) Snedden, R. What is an amphibian?
   597.8
Lasker, Joe
(il) Climo, S. The cobweb Christmas   E
Lasky, Kathryn
A brilliant streak: the making of Mark Twain (4
and up)   92
Days of the Dead (4-6)   394.26
Dreams in the golden country (4 and up)
   Fic
Elizabeth I (4 and up)   Fic
The librarian who measured the earth [biography
of Eratosthenes] (2-5)   92
Lunch bunnies. See note under Lasky, K. Show
and tell bunnies   E
Marie Antoinette (4 and up)   Fic
Marven of the Great North Woods   E
Monarchs (4 and up)   595.7
The most beautiful roof in the world (4-6)
   577.3
The night journey (4 and up)   Fic
Pond year   E
Science fair bunnies. See note under Lasky, K.
Show and tell bunnies   E
She's wearing a dead bird on her head!   E
Show and Tell bunnies   E
True north (6 and up)   Fic
Vision of beauty: the story of Sarah Breedlove
Walker (3-5)   92
The **lass** who went out at the cry of dawn.
Leodhas, S. N.
In Womenfolk and fairy tales p83-92
   398.2

The **last** battle. Lewis, C. S. See note under Lewis, C. S. The lion, the witch, and the wardrobe **Fic**

The **last** council. Curry, J. L.
In Curry, J. L. Back in the beforetime p121-27 **398.2**

Last dance at the Dew Drop Inn. Medearis, A. S.
In Medearis, A. S. Haunts p16-21 **S C**

The **last** dream of the old oak tree. Andersen, H. C.
In Christmas fairy tales p135-40 **398.2**

Last one in is a rotten egg. Kessler, L. P. **E**

The **last** princess: the story of Princess Ka'iulani of Hawai'i. Stanley, F. **92**

The **last** tales of Uncle Remus. Lester, J. **398.2**

The **Last** tiger in Haiti
In The Magic orange tree, and other Haitian folktales p183-87 **398.2**

Later, gator. Yep, L. **Fic**

Lathrop, Dorothy P., 1891-1980
(il) Bible. Selections. Animals of the Bible **220.8**
(il) Field, R. Hitty: her first hundred years **Fic**
See/See also pages in the following book(s):
Caldecott Medal books, 1938-1957 p7-21 **028.5**

Latimer, Jonathan P.
Backyard birds (4 and up) **598**
Birds of prey (4 and up) **598**
Bizarre birds (4 and up) **598**
Butterflies (4 and up) **595.7**
Caterpillars (4 and up) **595.7**
Shorebirds (4 and up) **598**
Songbirds (4 and up) **598**

Latimer, Lewis Howard, 1848-1928
See/See also pages in the following book(s):
McKissack, P. C. African-American inventors p61-69 (5 and up) **920**

Latin America
Bibliography
Schon, I. The best of the Latino heritage **011.6**
Civilization
Wadham, T. Programming with Latino children's materials **027.62**
Fiction
Delacre, L. Salsa stories (4-6) **S C**
Hurwitz, J. New shoes for Silvia **E**
Folklore
See Folklore—Latin America

Latin-American folk songs for children, De colores and other **782.42**

Latin American literature
Bibliography
Schon, I. Recommended books in Spanish for children and young adults, 1996 through 1999 **011.6**

Latinos (U.S.) *See* Hispanic Americans

Latkes and applesauce. Manushkin, F. **E**

Latkes, latkes, good to eat. Howland, N. **E**

Lattimore, Deborah Nourse
Medusa (3-6) **398.2**

Latvia
Barlas, R. Latvia (5 and up) **947.9**

Lauber, Patricia, 1924-
Be a friend to trees (k-3) **582.16**
Earthworms: underground farmers (3-5) **592**
Flood (4 and up) **551.48**
Hurricanes (4 and up) **551.55**
Living with dinosaurs (3-6) **567.9**
Lost star: the story of Amelia Earhart (5 and up) **92**
Painters of the caves (4 and up) **759.01**
Snakes are hunters (k-3) **597.9**
Summer of fire (4 and up) **577.2**
The true-or-false book of cats (k-3) **636.8**
The true-or-false book of horses (2-4) **636.1**
Volcano: the eruption and healing of Mount St. Helens (4 and up) **551.2**
What you never knew about fingers, forks, & chopsticks (2-4) **394.1**
Who eats what? (k-3) **577**
You're aboard Spaceship Earth (k-3) **550**

Laugh-eteria. Florian, D. **811**

The **laughing** dragon. Wilson, R.
In The Oxford treasury of children's stories p39-44 **S C**

Laughing out loud, I fly. Herrera, J. F. **811**

The **laughing** skull. Delacre, L.
In Delacre, L. Golden tales p21-23 **398.2**

Laughing tomatoes and other spring poems. Alarcón, F. X. **811**

Laughlin, Kay
(comp) The Children's song index, 1978-1993. See The Children's song index, 1978-1993 **782.42**

Laurent, Richard
(il) Bauer, C. F. Leading kids to books through puppets **027.62**

Lauter, Richard
(il) Smith, R. K. The war with Grandpa **Fic**

Lauture, Denize *See* Lotu, Denize, 1946-

Lavallee, Barbara
(il) Joosse, B. M. Mama, do you love me? **E**
(il) Mora, P. Uno, dos, tres: one, two, three **E**

Lavelle, Sheila
Dear Jane
In The Oxford book of scary tales p8-13 **808.8**

Lavender, David Sievert, 1910-
The Santa Fe Trail (4 and up) **978**
Snowbound (4 and up) **978**

Lavender. San Souci, R.
In San souci, R. Short & shivery p155-59 **398.2**

Lavert, Gwendolyn Battle- *See* Battle-Lavert, Gwendolyn, 1951-

Lavies, Bianca
Backyard hunter: the praying mantis (2-4) **595.7**
Compost critters (4 and up) **591.7**

Learning and scholarship

See also Education

Learning disabilities

See also Attention deficit disorder

Fiction

Gilson, J. Do bananas chew gum? (4-6) **Fic**

Polacco, P. Thank you, Mr. Falker **E**

Learning resource centers *See* Instructional materials centers

Learning the game. Jiménez, F.

In Jiménez, F. The circuit: stories from the life of a migrant child p84-95 **S C**

Leary, Catherine

(il) Dispezio, M. A. Awesome experiments in electricity & magnetism **537**

Leather work

Fisher, L. E. The tanners (4 and up) **675**

Leathers, Blanche

About

Gilliland, J. H. Steamboat!: the story of Captain Blanche Leathers (2-4) **92**

Leaves

Maestro, B. Why do leaves change color? (k-3) **582.16**

Robbins, K. Autumn leaves (3-6) **582.16**

Leaving Vietnam. Kilborne, S. S. **959.704**

Lebanon

Sheehan, S. Lebanon (5 and up) **956.92**

Fiction

Heide, F. P. Sami and the time of the troubles **E**

Lee, Alan

(il) Sutcliff, R. Black ships before Troy **883**

(il) Sutcliff, R. The wanderings of Odysseus **883**

Lee, Bruce, 1940-1973

See/See also pages in the following book(s):

Krull, K. Lives of the athletes p83-85 (4 and up) **920**

Lee, Dom, 1959-

(il) Mochizuki, K. Baseball saved us **E**

(il) Mochizuki, K. Heroes **E**

(il) Mochizuki, K. Passage to freedom **940.53**

Lee, Huy Voun

At the beach (k-3) **495.1**

Lee, Jeanne M.

I once was a monkey (2-5) **294.3**

Includes the following stories: The foolish forest sprite; The deceitful heron; The monkey and the crocodile; The flight of the beasts; The wise dove; Three friends in a forest

Silent Lotus **E**

The song of Mu Lan **398.2**

Toad is the uncle of heaven (k-3) **398.2**

(il) Fang, L. The Ch'i-lin purse **398.2**

Lee, Jody A.

(il) Montgomery, L. M. Anne of Green Gables **Fic**

Lee, Milly

Nim and the war effort **E**

Lee, Paul

(il) Chambers, V. Amistad rising **E**

Lee, Robert E. (Robert Edward), 1807-1870

About

Archer, J. A house divided: the lives of Ulysses S. Grant and Robert E. Lee (5 and up) **92**

Lee, Tan Chung, 1949-

Finland (5 and up) **948.97**

Leedy, Loreen, 1959-

2 x 2 = boo! (k-3) **513**

Celebrate the 50 states (k-3) **973**

Fraction action (k-3) **513**

Measuring Penny (1-3) **530.8**

Messages in the mailbox (k-3) **808**

Mission: addition (k-3) **513**

Subtraction action (k-3) **513**

Leelee Goro. Aardema, V.

In Aardema, V. Misoso p1-7 **398.2**

Leer, Rebecca

(il) Hayes, J. A spoon for every bite **E**

Leffler, Maryann Cocca- *See* Cocca-Leffler, Maryann, 1958-

Left behind. Carrick, C. *See note under* Carrick, C. The accident **E**

Left Hand Bull, Jacqueline

Lakota hoop dancer (3-6) **970.004**

The **legend** of Luke. Jacques, B. *See note under* Jacques, B. Redwall **Fic**

The **legend** of Old Befana. De Paola, T. **398.2**

The **legend** of Pin Oak. McKissack, P. C.

In McKissack, P. C. The dark-thirty p3-16 **S C**

The **legend** of Saint Elizabeth. Sawyer, R.

In Sawyer, R. The way of the storyteller p307-15 **372.6**

The **legend** of Scotland. Carroll, L.

In Carroll, L. The complete works of Lewis Carroll p999-1005 **828**

The **Legend** of St. Christopher

In Shedlock, M. L. The art of the story-teller p168-72 **372.6**

The **legend** of the Indian paintbrush. De Paola, T. **398.2**

The **legend** of the poinsettia. De Paola, T. **398.2**

The **legend** of the White Buffalo Woman. Goble, P. **398.2**

Legends

See also Folklore; Mythology

De Paola, T. The clown of God (k-3) **398.2**

Legends, Jewish *See* Jewish legends

Legends of Charlemagne. Bulfinch, T.

In Bulfinch, T. Bulfinch's Mythology **29**

Legerdemain *See* Juggling

Legge, David, 1963-

(il) Wild, M. Tom goes to kindergarten

LeGuin, Ursula *See* Le Guin, Ursula K., 1929-

Legumes

Hughes, M. S. Spill the beans and pass the peanuts: legumes (4 and up) **583**

Leighton, Maxinne Rhea

An Ellis Island Christmas **E**

Lelooska, 1934-1996

Echoes of the elders (4-6) **398.2**
Contents: The old Owl Witch; The boy and the loon; Raven & Sea Gull; Poogweese; Beaver face

Spirit of the cedar people (4-6) **398.2**
Includes the following stories: The ant and the bear; Old Grandmother Loon; Raven & monster halibut; Puffin Rock; Young Raven & Old Raven

Lelooska, Don *See* Lelooska, 1934-1996

Lember, Barbara Hirsch, 1941-

(il) Christian, P. If you find a rock **552**

Lemel and Tzipa. Singer, I. B.

In Singer, I. B. Stories for children p103-14 **S C**

Lemieux, Michèle

(il) Menotti, G. C. Amahl and the night visitors **Fic**

Lemmons, Bob

Fiction

Lester, J. Black cowboy, wild horses **E**

The **Lemon** Princess. Mayo, M.

In Mayo, M. Magical tales from many lands p7-17 **398.2**

The **lemonade** trick. Corbett, S. **Fic**

Lemurs

Darling, K. Lemurs on location (3-5) **599.8**
See/See also pages in the following book(s):
Patent, D. H. Back to the wild p50-59 (4-6) **639.9**

Lemurs on location. Darling, K. **599.8**

Lena. Woodson, J. **Fic**

Lena and Big One Tiger. Hamilton, V.

In Hamilton, V. Her stories p7-10 **398.2**

Lenape Indians *See* Delaware Indians

L'Engle, Madeleine, 1918-

Many waters. See note under L'Engle, M. A wrinkle in time **Fic**

Meet the Austins (5 and up) **Fic**

The moon by night. See note under L'Engle, M. Meet the Austins **Fic**

A ring of endless night. See note under L'Engle, M. Meet the Austins **Fic**

A swiftly tilting planet. See note under L'Engle, M. A wrinkle in time **Fic**

Troubling a star. See note under L'Engle, M. Meet the Austins **Fic**

A wind in the door. See note under L'Engle, M. A wrinkle in time **Fic**

A wrinkle in time (5 and up) **Fic**
See/See also pages in the following book(s):
Origins of story p105-12 **808.06**

Lenski, Lois, 1893-1974

(il) Lovelace, M. H. Betsy-Tacy **Fic**
See/See also pages in the following book(s):
Newbery Medal books, 1922-1955 p270-87 **028.5**

Lent, Blair, 1930-

(il) Dayrell, E. Why the Sun and the Moon live in the sky **398.2**

(il) Mosel, A. The funny little woman **398.2**

(il) Mosel, A. Tikki Tikki Tembo **398.2**
See/See also pages in the following book(s):
Newbery and Caldecott Medal books, 1966-1975 p244-55 **028.5**

Lentil. McCloskey, R. **E**

Leo, Zack, and Emmie. Ehrlich, A. See note under Ehrlich, A. Leo, Zack, and Emmie together again **E**

Leo, Zack, and Emmie together again. Ehrlich, A. **E**

Leodhas, Sorche Nic, 1898-1968

Always room for one more (k-3) **782.42**

The lass who went out at the cry of dawn
In Womenfolk and fairy tales p83-92 **398.2**

The stolen bairn and the Sidh
In Womenfolk and fairy tales p1-13 **398.2**

The woman who flummoxed the fairies
In Womenfolk and fairy tales p135-45 **398.2**

Leon, Juan Ponce de *See* Ponce de Leon, Juan, 1460?-1521

Leonard, Alison

Bronwen and the crows
In The Oxford book of scary tales p98-105 **808.8**

Leonard, Thomas, 1955-

(il) Dunphy, M. Here is the African savanna **577.4**

Leonardo, da Vinci, 1452-1519

About

Stanley, D. Leonardo da Vinci (4 and up) **92**

See/See also pages in the following book(s):
Krull, K. They saw the future p43-49 (4 and up) **133.3**

Leonhardt, Mary

Keeping kids reading **028.5**

Leon's story. Tillage, L. **92**

The **leopard** in the rafters. Watts, M.
In The Oxford book of scary tales p132-36 **808.8**

Leplar, Anna

(il) McCaughrean, G. God's kingdom **225.9**

(il) McCaughrean, G. God's people **221.9**

Leprince de Beaumont, Madame *See* Le Prince de Beaumont, Madame, 1711-1780

Lerner, Carol, 1927-

Backyard birds of summer (3-6) **598**

My backyard garden (4-6) **635**

My indoor garden (4-6) **635.9**

Lerner natural science book [series]

Johnson, S. A. Inside an egg **598**

Lessac, Frané

Caribbean canvas **811**

(il) Gelman, R. G. Queen Esther saves her people **222**

(il) Pomerantz, C. The chalk doll **E**

(il) Singer, M. On the same day in March **551.6**

Lessem, Don
  Bigger than T. rex (4 and up)   **567.9**
  Dinosaurs to dodos (4 and up)   **560**

Lesser, Carolyn
  Dig hole, soft mole   **E**
  Storm on the desert (2-4)   **577.5**

Lesser, Rika
  Hansel and Gretel (k-3)   **398.2**

Lessons. Babbitt, N.
  In Babbitt, N. The Devil's other storybook
  p47-52   **S C**

Lessons from Library Power. Zweizig, D.
   027.8

Lester, Helen
  Author (k-3)   **92**
  Hooway for Wodney Wat   **E**
  Tacky and the emperor. See note under Lester,
  H. Three cheers for Tacky   **E**
  Tacky in trouble. See note under Lester, H.
  Three cheers for Tacky   **E**
  Tacky the penguin. See note under Lester, H.
  Three cheers for Tacky   **E**
  Three cheers for Tacky   **E**

Lester, Julius
  Black cowboy, wild horses   **E**
  Brer Rabbit in Mr. Man's garden
  In From sea to shining sea p212-15
   810.8
  From slave ship to freedom road (4 and up)
   326
  Further tales of Uncle Remus. See note under
  Lester, J. The last tales of Uncle Remus
   398.2
  John Henry (k-3)   **398.2**
  The Knee-High Man
  In The Oxford treasury of children's stories
  p33-34   **S C**
  The knee-high man, and other tales (k-3)
   398.2
  Contents: What is trouble?; Why dogs hate cats; Mr. Rabbit
  and Mr. Bear; Why the waves have whitecaps; The farmer and
  the snake; The knee-high man
    The last tales of Uncle Remus (4-6)   **398.2**
  Contents: Why the cricket has elbows on his legs; Why the
  earth is mostly water; The origin of the ocean; Brer Rabbit and
  Miss Nancy; The old king and the new king; Brer Bear comes
  to the community; The snake; A ghost story; Brer Bear exposes
  Brer Rabbit; Brer Rabbit teaches Brer Bear to comb his hair;
  Why Brer Possum has no hair on his tail; Why Brer Possum
  loves peace; The baby who loved pumpkins; Impty-Umpty and
  the blacksmith; The angry woman; Brer Rabbit throws a party;
  Why Brer Fox's legs are black; How the witch was caught; The
  man who almost married a witch; Why dogs are tame; How
  Tinktum Tidy recruited an army for the king; Why guinea fowls
  are speckled; Why the Guineas stay awake; Brer Fox and the
  white grapes; Why the hawk likes to eat chickens; The little boy
  and his dogs; The man and the wild cattle; "Cutta cord-la"; Why
  Brer Bull growls and grumbles; Brer Rabbit, King Polecat, and
  the gingercakes; The fool; How Brer Lion lost his hair; The man
  and the boots; Why the goat has a short tail; Brer Buzzard and
  Brer Crow; The blacksmith and the Devil; Why chickens scratch
  in the dirt; Brer Rabbit and Aunt Nancy; The adventures of Simon and Susanna
    More tales of Uncle Remus. See note under
  Lester, J. The last tales of Uncle Remus
   398.2
  Sam and the tigers   **E**
  The tales of Uncle Remus. See note under Lester, J. The last tales of Uncle Remus
   398.2
  To be a slave (6 and up)   **326**

What a truly cool world!   **E**
When the beginning began (4 and up)
   296.1
Contents: God learns how to create; God battles the Queen of
the Waters; Sun and Moon; Strange creatures; The Angel of
Death; Cat and Mouse; Leviathan and Fox; Crown learns a les-
son; The grand parade; God makes people; God creates Adam;
God creates Woman; Adam marries; The Snake; The Woman,
Adam, and the fruit; God confronts Adam, the Woman, and the
Snake; God returns to Heaven

Lester, Mike
  A is for salad   **E**

Lester's dog. Hesse, K.   **E**

Let my people go. McKissack, P. C.   **221.9**

Let the circle be unbroken. Taylor, M. D.
   Fic

Let the games begin!. Ajmera, M.   **796**

Let's count. Hoban, T.   **E**

Let's count it out, Jesse Bear. Carlstrom, N. W.
  See note under Carlstrom, N. W. Jesse Bear,
  what will you wear?   **E**

Let's dance!. Ancona, G.   **793.3**

Let's eat!. Zamorano, A.   **E**

Let's go Froggy. London, J. See note under London, J. Froggy learns to swim   **E**

Let's go home, Little Bear. Waddell, M. See note
  under Waddell, M. Can't you sleep, Little
  Bear?   **E**

Let's go rock collecting. Gans, R.   **552**

Let's go visiting. Williams, S.   **E**

Let's hear it for the girls. Bauermeister, E.
   028.1

Let's play rough. Jonell, L.   **E**

Let's-read-and-find-out science [series]
  Bancroft, H. Animals in winter   **591.56**
  Berger, M. Chirping crickets   **595.7**
  Berger, M. Germs make me sick!   **616.9**
  Berger, M. Oil spill!   **363.7**
  Berger, M. Why I sneeze, shiver, hiccup, and
  yawn   **612.7**
  Branley, F. M. Day light, night light   **535**
  Branley, F. M. Down comes the rain
   551.57
  Branley, F. M. Flash, crash, rumble, and roll
   551.55
  Branley, F. M. Floating in space   **629.47**
  Branley, F. M. Is there life in outer space?
   576.8
  Branley, F. M. The planets in our solar system
   523.4
  Branley, F. M. Snow is falling   **551.57**
  Branley, F. M. What makes a magnet?   **538**
  Branley, F. M. What the moon is like
   523.3
  Bulla, C. R. What makes a shadow?   **535**
  Earle, A. Zipping, zapping, zooming bats
   599.4
  Esbensen, B. J. Baby whales drink milk
   599.5
  Fraser, M. A. Where are the night animals?
   591.5
  Gans, R. How do birds find their way?
   598
  Gans, R. Let's go rock collecting   **552**
  Goldin, A. R. Ducks don't get wet   **598**

Levin, Betty, 1927-
Shadow-catcher (4 and up)   Fic
See/See also pages in the following book(s):
Origins of story p86-92   **808.06**

Levine, Arthur A., 1962-
The boy who drew cats (k-3)   **398.2**

Levine, Ellen
. . . if your name was changed at Ellis Island (3-5)   **325.73**

Levine, Gail Carson, 1947-
Cinderellis and the glass hill. See note under Levine, G. C. The princess test   Fic
Dave at night (5 and up)   Fic
Ella enchanted (5 and up)   Fic
The fairy's mistake. See note under Levine, G. C. The princess test   Fic
Princess Sonora and the long sleep. See note under Levine, G. C. The princess test   Fic
The princess test (4 and up)   Fic

Levine, Joe
(il) Hirst, R. My place in space   **520**

Levine, Shar
Awesome yo-yo tricks (4 and up)   **796.2**
Fun with your microscope   **502.8**
The optics book (4 and up)   **535**
Shocking science (5 and up)   **537**

Levinson, Nancy Smiler, 1938-
Snowshoe Thompson   E

Levinson, Riki
Watch the stars come out   E

Levitin, Sonia, 1934-
Boomtown. See note under Levitin, S. Nine for California   E
Journey to America (4 and up)   Fic
Nine for California   E
The return (6 and up)   Fic
Taking charge. See note under Levitin, S. Nine for California   E

Levittown (N.Y.)
Fiction
Conrad, P. Our house (4-6)   S C

Levoy, Myron
Alan and Naomi (6 and up)   Fic

Levy, Constance, 1931-
A crack in the clouds and other poems (3-5)   **811**

Levy, Elizabeth, 1942-
My life as a fifth-grade comedian (4-6)   Fic
Seventh grade tango (5 and up)   Fic

Levy, Matthys
Earthquake games (5 and up)   **551.2**

Levy, Patricia Marjorie, 1951-
Belarus (5 and up)   **947.8**
Ghana (5 and up)   **966.7**
Liberia (5 and up)   **966.62**
Sudan (5 and up)   **962.4**

Lewin, Betsy, 1937-
Booby hatch   E
(il) Cronin, D. Click, clack, moo   E
(il) Grimes, N. Is it far to Zanzibar?   **811**
(jt. auth) Lewin, T. Gorilla walk   **599.8**
(il) Prigger, M. S. Aunt Minnie McGranahan   E
(il) Winthrop, E. Promises   E

Lewin, Hugh, 1939-
Jafta   E
Jafta and the wedding. See note under Lewin, H. Jafta   E
Jafta—the journey. See note under Lewin, H. Jafta   E
Jafta—the town. See note under Lewin, H. Jafta   E
Jafta's father. See note under Lewin, H. Jafta   E
Jafta's mother. See note under Lewin, H. Jafta   E

Lewin, Ted, 1935-
Fair! (k-3)   **394**
Gorilla walk (4 and up)   **599.8**
Market! (k-3)   **381**
The reindeer people (3-5)   **948.97**
The storytellers   E
(il) Bartone, E. American too   E
(il) Bartone, E. Peppe the lamplighter   E
(il) Borden, L. A. Lincoln and me   E
(il) Heide, F. P. The day of Ahmed's secret   E
(il) Heide, F. P. Sami and the time of the troubles   E
(il) High, L. O. Barn savers   E
(il) Kroeger, M. K. Paperboy   E
(il) London, J. Ali, child of the desert   E
(il) McDonald, M. The great pumpkin switch   E
(il) McDonald, M. The potato man   E
(il) McNulty, F. How whales walked into the sea   **599.5**
(il) Oberman, S. The always prayer shawl   E
(il) O'Dell, S. Island of the Blue Dolphins   Fic
(il) Scott, A. H. Cowboy country   **978**

Lewis, Barbara A., 1943-
The kid's guide to social action (4 and up)   **361.2**

Lewis, Bobby *See* Moore, Bobbie, 1944-

Lewis, Brian, 1963-
(jt. auth) Jaskol, J. City of angels   **979.4**

Lewis, C. S. (Clive Staples), 1898-1963
The horse and his boy. See note under Lewis, C. S. The lion, the witch, and the wardrobe   Fic
The last battle. See note under Lewis, C. S. The lion, the witch, and the wardrobe   Fic
The lion, the witch, and the wardrobe (4 and up)   Fic
The magician's nephew. See note under Lewis, C. S. The lion, the witch, and the wardrobe   Fic
Prince Caspian. See note under Lewis, C. S. The lion, the witch, and the wardrobe   Fic
The silver chair. See note under Lewis, C. S. The lion, the witch, and the wardrobe   Fic
The voyage of the Dawn Treader. See note under Lewis, C. S. The lion, the witch, and the wardrobe   Fic

Lewis, Celeste
(jt. auth) Johnson, P. B. Lost   E

Lewis, Clive Staples *See* Lewis, C. S. (Clive Staples), 1898-1963

Lewis, Cynthia Copeland, 1960-
(il) Cobb, V. Follow your nose   **612.8**
(il) Cobb, V. Your tongue can tell   **612.8**

Lewis, E. B. (Earl B.)
(il) Curtis, G. The bat boy & his violin   **E**
(il) Echewa, T. O. The magic tree   **398.2**
(il) Howard, E. F. Virgie goes to school with us boys   **E**
(il) Kurtz, J. Faraway home   **E**
(il) Kurtz, J. Fire on the mountain   **398.2**
(il) Kurtz, J. Only a pigeon   **E**
(il) Matthews, M. Magid fasts for Ramadan   **Fic**
(il) Mollel, T. M. My rows and piles of coins   **E**
(il) Rappaport, D. Dirt on their skirts   **E**
(il) Schertle, A. Down the road   **E**
(il) Taulbert, C. L. Little Cliff and the porch people   **E**

Lewis, Earl B. *See* Lewis, E. B. (Earl B.)

Lewis, Elizabeth Foreman, 1892-1958
See/See also pages in the following book(s):
Newbery Medal books, 1922-1955 p109-13
    028.5

Lewis, J. Patrick
At the wish of the fish (k-3)   **398.2**
The bookworm's feast   **811**
Doodle dandies   **811**
A hippopotamusn't and other animal verses
    811

Lewis, Kim
Floss. See note under Lewis, K. Just like Floss
    E
Just like Floss   **E**
Little calf   **E**
Little lamb. See note under Lewis, K. Little calf
    E
Little puppy. See note under Lewis, K. Little calf   **E**

Lewis, Maggie
Morgy makes his move (2-4)   **Fic**

Lewis, Meriwether, 1774-1809
About
Blumberg, R. The incredible journey of Lewis and Clark (5 and up)   **978**
Schanzer, R. How we crossed the West (3-5)
    978
See/See also pages in the following book(s):
Calvert, P. Great lives: the American frontier p226-43 (5 and up)   **920**

Lewis, Sinclair, 1885-1951
See/See also pages in the following book(s):
Faber, D. Great lives: American literature p240-49 (5 and up)   **920**

Lewis, Valerie V.
Valerie & Walter's best books for children
    028.5

Lewis and Clark Expedition (1804-1806)
Blumberg, R. The incredible journey of Lewis and Clark (5 and up)   **978**
Schanzer, R. How we crossed the West (3-5)
    978
St. George, J. Sacagawea (4-6)   **92**

Fiction
O'Dell, S. Streams to the river, river to the sea (5 and up)   **Fic**

Lewis and Clark Expedition (1804-1806) (1804-1806)
Adler, D. A. A picture book of Sacagawea (1-3)
    92
Fiction
Bruchac, J. Sacajawea (6 and up)   **Fic**

Lewis Barnavelt in The specter from the magician's museum, John Bellairs's. Strickland, B.
    Fic

Lexau, Joan M.
Don't be my valentine   **E**
Go away, dog   **E**
Who took the farmer's [hat]?   **E**

Lexington (Mass.), Battle of, 1775
Poetry
Longfellow, H. W. Paul Revere's ride   **811**

Leyton, Lawrence
My first magic book (3-5)   **793.8**

Li Chi slays the serpent. Yolen, J.
In Yolen, J. Not one damsel in distress p33-37   **398.2**

Libby on Wednesdays. Snyder, Z. K.   **Fic**

Liberia
Levy, P. M. Liberia (5 and up)   **966.62**
Fiction
Zemser, A. B. Beyond the mango tree (5 and up)   **Fic**
Folklore
See Folklore—Liberia

Liberty. Curlee, L.   **974.7**

The librarian who measured the earth [biography of Eratosthenes] Lasky, K.   **92**

Librarians
Fiction
Williams, S. Library Lil   **E**

The librarian's guide to homeschooling resources. Scheps, S. G.   **021.2**

Libraries
See also Instructional materials centers; Public libraries
Duncan, D. I-Search, you search, we all learn to research   **001.4**
Heiligman, D. The New York Public Library kid's guide to research (5 and up)   **025.5**
Munro, R. The inside-outside book of libraries (2-4)   **027**
Scheps, S. G. The librarian's guide to homeschooling resources   **021.2**
Censorship
Intellectual freedom manual   **323.44**
Symons, A. K. Protecting the right to read
    323.44
Fiction
Alexander, M. G. How my library grew, by Dinah   **E**
Best, C. Red light, green light, mama and me
    E
Clifford, E. Help! I'm a prisoner in the library (3-5)   **Fic**
Kimmel, E. A. I took my frog to the library
    E

Lionni, Leo, 1910-1999
Alexander and the wind-up mouse   E
The biggest house in the world   E
A color of his own   E
An extraordinary egg   E
Fish is fish   E
Frederick   E
Inch by inch   E
It's mine!   E
Little blue and little yellow   E
Matthew's dream   E
Swimmy   E

Lions
Darling, K. Lions (3-6)   599.75
Fiction
Daugherty, J. H. Andy and the lion   E
Freeman, D. Dandelion   E
Hurd, E. T. Johnny Lion's book   E
Nolan, D. Androcles and the lion (1-3)   398.2
Peet, B. Eli   E
Waber, B. A lion named Shirley Williamson   E
We're going on a lion hunt   E
Yaccarino, D. Deep in the jungle   E

The **lion's** den. Walker, B. K.
In Walker, B. K. A treasury of Turkish folk-tales for children p16   398.2

Lippincott, Gary, 1953-
(il) Coville, B. Jennifer Murdley's toad   Fic
(il) Coville, B. Jeremy Thatcher, dragon hatcher   Fic
(il) Coville, B. The skull of truth   Fic

Lisa, W. Nikola- *See* Nikola-Lisa, W.

Lisker, Emily
(il) A Hanukkah treasury. See A Hanukkah treasury   296.4
(il) Lester, J. When the beginning began   296.1

Lisker, Sonia O., 1933-
(il) Blume, J. Freckle juice   Fic

Lisle, Janet Taylor, 1947-
Afternoon of the elves (4-6)   Fic
Forest (5 and up)   Fic
The lost flower children (4-6)   Fic

A **list.** Lobel, A.
In The Oxford treasury of children's stories p16-18   S C

Listen to the city. Isadora, R.   E

Listening to crickets: a story about Rachel Carson. Ransom, C. F.   92

The **listening** walk. Showers, P.   E

Literacy
Fiction
Hesse, K. Just Juice (3-5)   Fic

Literary prizes
See also Caldecott Medal; Coretta Scott King Award; Newbery Medal
Bibliography
Children's books: awards & prizes   028.5

Literary recreations
See also Word games

Literate beginnings. Jeffery, D. A.   027.62

Literature
See also African Americans in literature; Characters and characteristics in literature; Children's literature; Young adult literature; names of national literatures, e.g. *English literature*
Collections
Bauer, C. F. Celebrations   808.8
Hey! listen to this   028.5
Juba this and Juba that   372.6
The Oxford book of scary tales (5 and up)   808.8
The Read-aloud treasury   808.8
Sawyer, R. The way of the storyteller   372.6
Shedlock, M. L. The art of the story-teller   372.6
Snowy day: stories and poems (2-4)   808.8
Dictionaries
Brewer's dictionary of phrase and fable   803

History and criticism
See also Authors
Stories, plots, etc.
See Stories, plots, etc.—Collections
Study and teaching
Hall, S. Using picture storybooks to teach literary devices   016.8

Literature and technology
Dresang, E. T. Radical change   028.5

Literature connections to American history, K-6. Adamson, L. G.   016.973

Literature connections to world history, K-6. Adamson, L. G.   016.9

Lithuania
Kagda, S. Lithuania (5 and up)   947.9

Little, Jean, 1932-
From Anna (4-6)   Fic
Hey world, here I am! (4-6)   811

Little, Lessie Jones, 1906-1986
(jt. auth) Greenfield, E. Childtimes: a three-generation memoir   920

Little, Malcolm *See* Malcolm X, 1925-1965

Little, Mimi Otey
Yoshiko and the foreigner   E

Little Badger, terror of the seven seas. Bunting, E. See note under Bunting, E. Can you do this, Old Badger?   E

Little Bald-Headed
In Raw Head, bloody bones p73-77   398.2

Little Bear. Minarik, E. H.   E

Little Bear goes to the moon. Minarik, E. H.
In The Read-aloud treasury p70-83   808.8

Little Bear's baby book. Waddell, M. See note under Waddell, M. Can't you sleep, Little Bear?   E

Little Bear's friend. Minarik, E. H. See note under Minarik, E. H. Little Bear   E

Little Bear's visit. Minarik, E. H. See note under Minarik, E. H. Little Bear   E

Little Bighorn, Battle of the, 1876
Viola, H. J. It is a good day to die (5 and up)
973.8

The **little** bird. Philip, N.
In Philip, N. Celtic fairy tales p137-[38]
398.2

Little Black Sambo, The story of. See Bannerman, H. The story of Little Babaji **E**

Little blue and little yellow. Lionni, L. **E**

The **little** boy and his dogs. Lester, J.
In Lester, J. The last tales of Uncle Remus p102-10 **398.2**

Little Brown Wren. Hamilton, V.
In Hamilton, V. When birds could talk & bats could sing p55-61 **398.2**

The **little** bull-calf. Jacobs, J.
In Jacobs, J. English fairy tales p388-92
398.2

The **Little** bull with the golden horns
In Stockings of buttermilk: American folktales p62-72 **398.2**

Little Buttercup. MacDonald, M. R.
In MacDonald, M. R. When the lights go out p7-20 **372.6**

Little calf. Lewis, K. **E**

Little Cliff and the porch people. Taulbert, C. L.
E

Little Cosette and Father Christmas. Thane, A.
In The Big book of Christmas plays p313-31
808.82

Little crab and his magic eyes. MacDonald, M. R.
In MacDonald, M. R. Twenty tellable tales p24-34 **372.6**

Little Cricket's marriage. MacDonald, M. R.
In MacDonald, M. R. Look back and see p55-67 **372.6**

Little dog poems. George, K. O. **811**

Little Eight John. Hamilton, V.
In Hamilton, V. The people could fly: American black folktales p121-25
398.2

The **little** engine that could. Piper, W. **E**

Little Finger of the watermelon patch. Vuong, L. D.
In Vuong, L. D. The brocaded slipper, and other Vietnamese tales **398.2**

Little Fur family. Brown, M. W. **E**

Little Girl and Buh Rabby. Hamilton, V.
In Hamilton, V. Her stories p3-6 **398.2**

Little Gold Star. Hayes, J. **398.2**

The **little** golden lamb. Greene, E. **398.2**

A **little** green bottle. Schwartz, A.
In Schwartz, A. Ghosts! p20-37 **398.2**

The **Little** green frog
In The Yellow fairy book p50-59 **398.2**

The **little** half-chick. González, L. M.
In González, L. M. Señor Cat's romance and other favorite stories from Latin America p9-13 **398.2**

The **little** hands big fun craft book. Press, J.
745.5

The **little** house. Burton, V. L. **E**

The **Little** House cookbook. Walker, B. M.
641.5

Little house in the big woods. Wilder, L. I.
Fic

Little house on the prairie. Wilder, L. I. See note under Wilder, L. I. Little house in the big woods **Fic**

The **little** humpbacked horse. Winthrop, E.
398.2

The **Little** hunchback
In The Arabian nights entertainments p187-95
398.2

Little Ida's flowers. Andersen, H. C.
In Andersen, H. C. The little mermaid and other fairy tales p27-34 **S C**

Little lamb. Lewis, K. See note under Lewis, K. Little calf **E**

Little League Baseball, Inc.
Kreutzer, P. Little League's official how-to-play baseball book (4 and up) **796.357**

Little League's official how-to-play baseball book. Kreutzer, P. **796.357**

Little lions. Arnosky, J. **E**

Little Louie the baby bloomer. Kraus, R. **E**

The **little** match girl. Andersen, H. C. **Fic**
also in Andersen, H. C. The little mermaid and other fairy tales p91-94 **S C**

The **little** match girl. Pinkney, J. **E**

Little men. Alcott, L. M. See note under Alcott, L. M. Little women **Fic**

The **little** mermaid. Andersen, H. C.
In Andersen, H. C. The little mermaid and other fairy tales p35-60 **S C**

The **little** mermaid. Osborne, M. P.
In Osborne, M. P. Mermaid tales from around the world p71-77 **398.2**

The **little** mermaid and other fairy tales. Andersen, H. C. **S C**

Little Mouse's big valentine. Hurd, T. **E**

Little Oh. Melmed, L. K. **E**

The **little** old lady who was not afraid of anything. Williams, L. **E**

The **little** old woman who lived in a vinegar bottle. MacDonald, M. R.
In MacDonald, M. R. The storyteller's start-up book p117-23 **372.6**

Little One-eye, Little Two-eyes, and Little Three-eyes. Grimm, J.
In The Green fairy book p262-70 **398.2**

Little Poucet. Perrault, C.
In The Classic fairy tales p130-36 **398.2**

The **little** prince. Saint-Exupéry, A. de **Fic**

A **little** princess. Burnett, F. H. **Fic**

Little puppy. Lewis, K. See note under Lewis, K. Little calf **E**

Little Red Cap. Grimm, J. **398.2**

The **little** red hen. Barton, B. **398.2**

The **little** red hen. Galdone, P. **398.2**

The **little** red hen. Jacobs, J.
In Tomie dePaola's favorite nursery tales p16-19 **398.2**

Llewellyn, Claire—*Continued*
Oranges (k-3) — **641**
Tractor (k-3) — **629.225**
Truck (k-3) — **629.224**

La **Llorona,** the weeping woman. Hayes, J.
In From sea to shining sea p331-35 — **810.8**

Lloyd, Megan
(il) Berger, M. Look out for turtles! — **597.9**
(il) Guiberson, B. Z. Cactus hotel — **583**
(il) Kimmel, E. A. The gingerbread man — **398.2**
(il) Kimmel, E. A. Seven at one blow — **398.2**
(il) O'Connor, J. Super Cluck — **E**
(il) Surprises. See Surprises — **811.008**
(il) Williams, L. The little old lady who was not afraid of anything — **E**

Lobel, Anita, 1934-
Alison's zinnia — **E**
One lighthouse, one moon — **E**
(il) Heins, E. L. The cat and the cook and other fables of Krylov — **398.2**
(il) Huck, C. S. Princess Furball — **398.2**
(il) Lobel, A. On Market Street — **E**
(il) Lobel, A. The rose in my garden — **E**
(il) Lobel, A. A treeful of pigs — **E**
(il) Ziefert, H. A new coat for Anna — **E**

Lobel, Arnold
Days with Frog and Toad. See note under Lobel, A. Frog and Toad are friends — **E**
Fables (3-5) — **Fic**
Frog and Toad all year. See note under Lobel, A. Frog and Toad are friends — **E**
Frog and Toad are friends — **E**
Frog and Toad together. See note under Lobel, A. Frog and Toad are friends — **E**
Grasshopper on the road — **E**
A list
In The Oxford treasury of children's stories p16-18 — **S C**
Ming Lo moves the mountain — **E**
Mouse soup — **E**
Mouse tales — **E**
On Market Street — **E**
Owl at home — **E**
The rose in my garden — **E**
Small pig — **E**
A treeful of pigs — **E**
Uncle Elephant — **E**
Very Tall Mouse and Very Short Mouse
In The Read-aloud treasury p207-13 — **808.8**
(il) The Arnold Lobel book of Mother Goose. See The Arnold Lobel book of Mother Goose — **398.8**
(il) Durán, C. Hildilid's night — **E**
(il) Geringer, L. A three hat day — **E**
(il) Prelutsky, J. The Headless Horseman rides tonight — **811**
(il) Prelutsky, J. Nightmares: poems to trouble your sleep — **811**
(il) Prelutsky, J. Tyrannosaurus was a beast — **811**

(il) The Random House book of poetry for children. See The Random House book of poetry for children — **821.008**
(il) Van Leeuwen, J. Tales of Oliver Pig — **E**
(il) Zolotow, C. The quarreling book — **E**
See/See also pages in the following book(s):
Newbery and Caldecott Medal books, 1976-1985 p220-28 — **028.5**

Locker, Thomas, 1937-
The mare on the hill — **E**
Where the river begins — **E**
(il) Bruchac, J. Between earth & sky — **398.2**
(il) Bruchac, J. Thirteen moons on a turtle's back — **811**

Lockhart, Laura
(jt. auth) Duncan, D. I-Search, you search, we all learn to research — **001.4**

Lockouts *See* Strikes

Locusts
Fiction
Lobel, A. Grasshopper on the road — **E**

Loehle, Richard
(il) Tucker, T. Brainstorm! — **609**

Loeper, John J., 1929-
Going to school in 1776 (4 and up) — **370.9**

Loft the enchanter. San Souci, R.
In San Souci, R. More short & shivery p115-20 — **398.2**

Lofting, Hugh, 1886-1947
See/See also pages in the following book(s):
Newbery Medal books, 1922-1955 p21-27 — **028.5**

Lofts, Pamela
(il) Fox, M. Koala Lou — **E**

Logging *See* Lumber and lumbering

A **log's** life. Pfeffer, W. — **577.3**

Loh, Morag Jeanette, 1935-
Tucking Mommy in — **E**

Lomas Garza, Carmen *See* Garza, Carmen Lomas

Lon Po Po. Young, E. — **398.2**

London, Jack, 1876-1916
The call of the wild (5 and up) — **Fic**
White Fang (5 and up) — **Fic**
See/See also pages in the following book(s):
Faber, D. Great lives: American literature p141-50 (5 and up) — **920**
Krull, K. Lives of the writers p70-73 (4 and up) — **920**

London, Jonathan, 1947-
Ali, child of the desert — **E**
Baby whale's journey — **E**
Froggy bakes a cake. See note under London, J. Froggy learns to swim — **E**
Froggy gets dressed. See note under London, J. Froggy learns to swim — **E**
Froggy goes to bed. See note under London, J. Froggy learns to swim — **E**
Froggy goes to school. See note under London, J. Froggy learns to swim — **E**
Froggy learns to swim — **E**
Froggy plays soccer. See note under London, J. Froggy learns to swim — **E**

London, Jonathan, 1947-—*Continued*
Froggy's best Christmas. See note under London, J. Froggy learns to swim   E
Froggy's first kiss. See note under London, J. Froggy learns to swim   E
Froggy's Halloween. See note under London, J. Froggy learns to swim   E
Let's go Froggy. See note under London, J. Froggy learns to swim   E
Red wolf country   E
Shawn and Keeper and the birthday party. See note under London, J. Shawn and Keeper: show-and-tell   E
Shawn and Keeper: show-and-tell   E
Snuggle wuggle   E
(jt. auth) Bruchac, J. Thirteen moons on a turtle's back   **811**

London (England)
Fiction
Alcock, V. The cuckoo sister (6 and up)   **Fic**
Garfield, L. Black Jack (6 and up)   **Fic**
Garfield, L. Smith (6 and up)   **Fic**
Horowitz, A. The Devil and his boy (5 and up)   **Fic**
Newman, R. The case of the Baker Street Irregular (5 and up)   **Fic**
Paton Walsh, J. Fireweed (5 and up)   **Fic**
Lone wolf. Franklin, K. L.   **Fic**
The **lonely** lioness and the ostrich chicks. Aardema, V.   **398.2**

Long, Sylvia
(il) Sylvia Long's Mother Goose. See Sylvia Long's Mother Goose   **398.8**
Long live Christmas. Benson, I.
In The Big book of Christmas plays p213-27   **808.82**
The **long** patrol. Jacques, B. See note under Jacques, B. Redwall   **Fic**
The **long** road to Gettysburg. Murphy, J.   **973.7**
The **long** secret. Fitzhugh, L. See note under Fitzhugh, L. Harriet the spy   **Fic**
A **long** way from Chicago. Peck, R.   **Fic**
The **long** way westward. Sandin, J.   E
The **long** winter. Wilder, L. I. See note under Wilder, L. I. Little house in the big woods   **Fic**
The **longest** summer on record. Conrad, P.
In Conrad, P. Our house p29-39   **S C**

Longevity
    See also Old age

Longfellow, Henry Wadsworth, 1807-1882
Hiawatha   **811**
Paul Revere's ride   **811**
See/See also pages in the following book(s):
Faber, D. Great lives: American literature p40-48 (5 and up)   **920**
Lonna and Cat Woman. Hamilton, V.
In Hamilton, V. Her stories p56-60   **398.2**

Look, Lenore
Love as strong as ginger   E
Look-alikes. Steiner, J.   **793.73**

Look-alikes, jr. Steiner, J.   **793.73**
Look at your eyes. Showers, P.   **612.8**
Look back and see. MacDonald, M. R.   **372.6**
Look back and see [story] MacDonald, M. R.
In MacDonald, M. R. Look back and see p11-23   **372.6**
Look book. Hoban, T.   E
The **look-it-up** book of presidents. Blassingame, W.   **920**
Look out for turtles!. Berger, M.   **597.9**
Look to the North. George, J. C.   E
Look what I can do. Aruego, J.   E
Looking at bears. Patent, D. H.   **599.78**
Looking at penguins. Patent, D. H.   **598**
Looking at picture books. Stewig, J. W.   **741.6**
Looking back. Lowry, L.   **92**
Looking for home. MacDonald, M. R.
In MacDonald, M. R. When the lights go out p29-32   **372.6**

Loomis, Christine
Astro bunnies. See note under Loomis, C. Cowboy bunnies   E
Cowboy bunnies   E
Loop the loop. Dugan, B.   E

Lopez, Loretta, 1963-
(il) Elya, S. M. Say hola to Spanish, otra vez   **463**

Lorbiecki, Marybeth
Sister Anne's hands   E
Lorca, Federico García *See* García Lorca, Federico, 1898-1936

Lord, Bette Bao
In the Year of the Boar and Jackie Robinson (4-6)   **Fic**

Lord, John Vernon, 1939-
The giant jam sandwich   E
Lord Brocktree. Jacques, B. See note under Jacques, B. Redwall   **Fic**
The **Lord** of Miracles. Delacre, L.
In Delacre, L. Salsa stories p55-61   **S C**
Lord of the Fries. Wynne-Jones, T.
In Wynne-Jones, T. Lord of the Fries and other stories p1-44   **S C**
Lord of the Fries and other stories. Wynne-Jones, T.   **S C**
Lord's Day *See* Sabbath
The **lore** and language of schoolchildren. Opie, I. A.   **398**
The **Lorelei.** Wrede, P. C.
In Wrede, P. C. Book of enchantments p128-52   **S C**
Lorenzini, Carlo *See* Collodi, Carlo, 1826-1890

Los Angeles (Calif.)
Jaskol, J. City of angels (2-4)   **979.4**
Fiction
Bunting, E. Smoky night   E
Losing things *See* Lost and found possessions

Loss (Psychology)
Gellman, M. Lost & found (4-6)   **155.9**
Lost!. Fleischman, P.   **Fic**

Lost. Johnson, P. B.   E

Lost & found. Gellman, M.   155.9

Lost and found possessions
Fiction
Porte, B. A. Harry in trouble   E
The **lost** brother. Curry, J. L.
   In Curry, J. L. Back in the beforetime p60-67
                               398.2

Lost city of Pompeii. Patent, D. H.   937

The **lost** flower children. Lisle, J. T.   Fic

The **lost** garden. Yep, L.   92

Lost in cyberspace. Peck, R.   Fic

Lost in the storm. Carrick, C. See note under Carrick, C. The accident   E

The **lost** lake. Say, A.   E

Lost star princess. Carpenter, F.
   In Carpenter, F. Tales of a Chinese grandmother p190-97   398.2

Lost star: the story of Amelia Earhart. Lauber, P.
                                 92

Lost temple of the Aztecs. Tanaka, S.   972

Lost treasure of the Inca. Lourie, P.   986.6

The **lost** years of Merlin. Barron, T. A.   Fic

Lottie's new beach towel. Mathers, P.   E

Lottie's new friend. Mathers, P. See note under Mathers, P. Lottie's new beach towel   E

Lotu, Denize, 1946-
Running the road to ABC   E

Louganis, Greg
See/See also pages in the following book(s):
Knapp, R. Top 10 American men's Olympic gold medalists (4 and up)   920

Louie, Ai-Ling, 1949-
Yeh-Shen (2-4)   398.2

Louie. Keats, E. J.   E

Louie's search. Keats, E. J. See note under Keats, E. J. Louie   E

Louisiana
Hintz, M. Louisiana
   In America the beautiful, second series
                               973
LeVert, S. Louisiana
   In Celebrate the states   973
Fiction
Holt, K. W. Mister and me (3-5)   Fic
Holt, K. W. My Louisiana sky (6 and up)
                               Fic
McKissack, P. C. A million fish—more or less
                               E
Thomassie, T. Feliciana Feydra LeRoux   E

Louisiana Purchase
Sakurai, G. The Louisiana Purchase (4-6)
                             973.4

The **loup-garou**. San Souci, R.
   In San Souci, R. Short & shivery p144-48
                           398.2

Lourie, Peter
Lost treasure of the Inca (4 and up)   986.6
Rio Grande (4 and up)   976.4

Louse *See* Lice

Lovable Lyle. Waber, B. See note under Waber, B. Lyle, Lyle, crocodile   E

Love, Ann, 1947-
Kids and grandparents: an activity book (3-6)
                             790.1
(jt. auth) Drake, J. The kids campfire book
                             796.5
(jt. auth) Drake, J. The kids' summer handbook
                             790.1

Love, D. Anne
A year without rain (4 and up)   Fic

Love as strong as ginger. Look, L.   E

Love flute. Goble, P.   398.2

Love letters. Adoff, A.   811

Love one another. Thompson, L.   232.9

Love poetry
Adoff, A. Love letters (3-6)   811
Greenfield, E. Honey, I love, and other love poems (2-4)   811
Grimes, N. Hopscotch love (4 and up)   811
Here is my heart   821.008

The **love** story of Roopmati and Baz Bahadur.
Krishnaswami, U.
   In Krishnaswami, U. Shower of gold: girls and women in the stories of India p80-83
                           398.2

Lovelace, Maud Hart, 1892-1980
Betsy and Joe. See note under Lovelace, M. H. Betsy-Tacy   Fic
Betsy and Tacy go downtown. See note under Lovelace, M. H. Betsy-Tacy   Fic
Betsy and Tacy go over the big hill. See note under Lovelace, M. H. Betsy-Tacy   Fic
Betsy and the great world. See note under Lovelace, M. H. Betsy-Tacy   Fic
Betsy in spite of herself. See note under Lovelace, M. H. Betsy-Tacy   Fic
Betsy-Tacy (2-4)   Fic
Betsy-Tacy and Tib. See note under Lovelace, M. H. Betsy-Tacy   Fic
Betsy was a junior. See note under Lovelace, M. H. Betsy-Tacy   Fic
Betsy's wedding. See note under Lovelace, M. H. Betsy-Tacy   Fic
Heaven to Betsy. See note under Lovelace, M. H. Betsy-Tacy   Fic

Lovers. Andersen, H. C.
   In Andersen, H. C. The swan's stories p53-58
                             S C

The **lovers** of Dismal Swamp. San Souci, R.
   In San Souci, R. Short & shivery p123-26
                           398.2

Low, Alice, 1926-
The Macmillan book of Greek gods and heroes (3-6)   292

Low, Joseph, 1911-
Mice twice   E

Low, Madeline Slovenz- *See* Slovenz-Low, Madeline

Lowell, Susan, 1950-
The bootmaker and the elves (k-3)   398.2

Lowery, Linda
Aunt Clara Brown (2-4)   92
Twist with a burger, jitter with a bug   E

Lowman, Margaret
About
Lasky, K. The most beautiful roof in the world
(4-6)   **577.3**
Lowry, Lois
All about Sam. See note under Lowry, L.
Anastasia Krupnik   **Fic**
Anastasia, absolutely. See note under Lowry, L.
Anastasia Krupnik   **Fic**
Anastasia again! See note under Lowry, L.
Anastasia Krupnik   **Fic**
Anastasia, ask your analyst. See note under
Lowry, L. Anastasia Krupnik   **Fic**
Anastasia at this address. See note under Lowry,
L. Anastasia Krupnik   **Fic**
Anastasia at your service. See note under Low-
ry, L. Anastasia Krupnik   **Fic**
Anastasia has the answers. See note under Low-
ry, L. Anastasia Krupnik   **Fic**
Anastasia Krupnik (4-6)   **Fic**
Anastasia on her own. See note under Lowry, L.
Anastasia Krupnik   **Fic**
Anastasia's chosen career. See note under Low-
ry, L. Anastasia Krupnik   **Fic**
Attaboy, Sam! See note under Lowry, L.
Anastasia Krupnik   **Fic**
Autumn Street (4 and up)   **Fic**
Gathering blue (5 and up)   **Fic**
The giver (6 and up)   **Fic**
Looking back (5 and up)   **92**
Number the stars (4 and up)   **Fic**
The one hundredth thing about Caroline (5 and
up)   **Fic**
Rabble Starkey (5 and up)   **Fic**
See you around Sam! See note under Lowry, L.
Anastasia Krupnik   **Fic**
Stay! (5 and up)   **Fic**
A summer to die (5 and up)   **Fic**
Switcharound (5 and up)   **Fic**
Your move, J.P.! (5 and up)   **Fic**
Zooman Sam. See note under Lowry, L.
Anastasia Krupnik   **Fic**
See/See also pages in the following book(s):
Author talk (4 and up)   **028.5**
The Newbery & Caldecott medal books, 1986-
2000 p114-26, 207-19   **028.5**
Loya, Olga
Tía Miseria
In From sea to shining sea p202-05
     810.8

Loyalists, American *See* American Loyalists
Luba and the wren. Polacco, P.   **398.2**
Lubin, Leonard B., 1943-
(il) Conly, J. L. Racso and the rats of NIMH
     Fic
Luby, Thia, 1954-
Children's book of yoga   **613.7**
Lucas, Cedric
(il) Miller, W. Frederick Douglass   **92**
(il) Miller, W. Night golf   **E**
Luciani, Brigitte
How will we get to the beach?   **E**
Luck. Castedo, E.
In You're on!: seven plays in English and
Spanish p84-99   **812.008**

Luckman, Sid, 1916-1998
See/See also pages in the following book(s):
Sullivan, G. Quarterbacks! p57-59 (5 and up)
     920
Lucky song. Williams, V. B.   **E**
The **lucky** stone. Clifton, L.   **Fic**
A **lucky** thing. Schertle, A.   **811**
Lucy Dove. Del Negro, J.   **E**
Lucy's Christmas. Hall, D.   **E**
Lucy's wish. Nixon, J. L. See note under Nixon,
J. L. Aggie's home   **Fic**
Ludwig, Warren
(il) Johnston, T. The cowboy and the black-eyed
pea   **E**
Lueders, Edward
(comp) Reflections on a gift of watermelon
pickle . . . and other modern verse. See Re-
flections on a gift of watermelon pickle . . .
and other modern verse   **811.008**
Luella and the tame parrot. Hamilton, V.
In Hamilton, V. Her stories p75-77
     398.2
Luenn, Nancy, 1954-
Nessa's fish   **E**
Luka's quilt. Guback, G.   **E**
Lullabies
All the pretty little horses (k-2)   **782.42**
Appelt, K. Bayou lullaby   **E**
Asch, F. Barnyard lullaby   **E**
The Baby's bedtime book   **808.81**
Bang, M. Ten, nine, eight   **E**
Fishing for a dream   **782.42**
Ho, M. Hush! (k-3)   **E**
Hush, little baby (k-2)   **782.42**
Lullaby. San Souci, R.
In San Souci, R. Even more short & shivery
p105-09   **398.2**
Lulu's busy day. Uff, C.   **E**
Lum, Kate
What! cried Granny   **E**
Lum, Roseline NgCheong- *See* NgCheong-Lum,
Roseline, 1962-
Lumber and lumbering
Appelbaum, D. K. Giants in the land (2-4)
     634.9
Fiction
Lasky, K. Marven of the Great North Woods
     E
Lunar bases
Cole, M. D. Moon base (4 and up)   **629.4**
Lunar expeditions *See* Space flight to the moon
Lunch. Fleming, D.   **E**
Lunch bunnies. Lasky, K. See note under Lasky,
K. Show and tell bunnies   **E**
Lunch money and other poems about school.
Shields, C. D.   **811**
Lunge-Larsen, Lise
The troll with no heart in his body and other
tales of trolls from Norway (3-6)   **398.2**
Contents: The Three Billy Goats Gruff; The boy who became
a lion, a falcon, and an ant; Butterball; The handshake; The boys
and the North Wind; The white cat in the Dovre Mountain; The
sailors and the troll; The eating competition; The troll with no
heart in his body

MacDonald, George, 1824-1905
At the back of the North Wind (4-6) **Fic**
The light princess (3-6) **Fic**
The princess and the goblin (3-6) **Fic**

MacDonald, Margaret Read
Bookplay **027.62**
Celebrate the world **372.6**
Stories included are: Little rooster and the heavenly dragon; Benizara Kakezara; Todo o nada; Poule and Roach; Five threads; The pumpkin child; The old woman in a pumpkin shell; Escargot on his way to Dijon; Forget-me-not; The small yellow dragon; Little Snot Nose Boy; Nail Soup; The finger Lock; The clever daughter-in-law; Stinky spirits; Sparrow's luck!; Yao Jour; The silver pine cones; Papa God and the Pintards; Going to Cervières
The girl who wore too much (k-3) **398.2**
Look back and see **372.6**
Stories included are: The snow bunting's lullaby; Look back and see; Kanji-jo, the nestlings; Domingo siete; Turkey girl; Little Cricket's marriage; Please all . . . please none; Why Koala has no tale; Katchi Katchi Blue Jay; Biyera well; The strawberries of the little men; The elk and the wren; The bear-child; Two women hunt for ground squirrels; Quail song; Grandfather Bear is hungry; Tiny Mouse goes traveling; The singing turtle; The Teeny Weeny Bop; A penny and a half
Pickin' peas (k-3) **398.2**
The round book **782.42**
The storyteller's sourcebook **398**
The storyteller's start-up book **372.6**
Stories included are: Turtle of Koka; The little old woman who lived in a vinegar bottle; Puchika Churika; Marsh Hawk; Gecko; Kudu break!; What are their names!; Aayoga with many excuses; Kanu above and Kanu below; Ko Kóngole; Ningun; Yonjwa seeks a bride
Twenty tellable tales **372.6**
Stories included are: A whale of a tale; Coyote's crying song; Coyote's rain song; Little crab and his magic eyes; Groundhog dance; Old one-eye; Parley Garfield and the frogs; The little rooster and the Turkish Sultan; The gunny wolf; How to break a bad habit; Sody sallyrytus; Turkey tale; Jack and the robbers; Roly poly rice ball; Udala tree; The rabbit and the well; Hic! Hic! Hic!; Mr. Fox; Punia and the king of the sharks; The magic fox
When the lights go out **372.6**
Stories included are: Little Buttercup; The Wee Little Tyke; Looking for home; Wicked John and the Devil; The Great Red Cat; The wizard clip; The tinker and the ghost; The conjure wives; Sop doll; The Hobyahs; Old Ben; Sam'l; The cat with the beckoning paw; Totanguak; The red silk handkerchief; The strange visitor; Who lives in the skull?

Macdonald, Suse, 1940-
Alphabatics **E**
Peck, slither and slide **E**
Sea shapes **E**

The **machine** gunners. Westall, R. **Fic**

Machinery
See also Mills
Bingham, C. Monster machines **621.8**
Hoban, T. Construction zone (k-2) **621.8**
Hoban, T. Dig, drill, dump, fill **E**
Llewellyn, C. Truck (k-3) **629.224**
Macaulay, D. The new way things work (4 and up) **600**
Maynard, C. Airplane (k-3) **629.136**

Machines at work. Barton, B. **690**

Macie and boo hag. Hamilton, V.
In Hamilton, V. Her stories p51-55 **398.2**

MacKain, Bonnie
(il) Pinczes, E. J. One hundred hungry ants **E**

Mackay, Donald A., 1914-
(il) Fox, P. The stone-faced boy **Fic**

MacLachlan, Patricia
All the places to love **E**
Arthur, for the very first time (4-6) **Fic**
Baby (5 and up) **Fic**
The facts and fictions of Minna Pratt (4 and up) **Fic**
Journey (4 and up) **Fic**
Mama One, Mama Two **E**
Sarah, plain and tall (3-5) **Fic**
Seven kisses in a row (2-4) **Fic**
Skylark (3-5) **Fic**
Three Names **E**
See/See also pages in the following book(s):
The Newbery & Caldecott medal books, 1986-2000 p35-46 **028.5**

MacMillan, Dianne M., 1943-
Cheetahs (3-6) **599.75**

The **Macmillan** book of Greek gods and heroes. Low, A. **292**

Macmillan dictionary for children (3-6) **423**
Macmillan first dictionary (1-3) **423**
Macmillan very first dictionary. See Macmillan first dictionary **423**

Macquitty, Miranda
Shark (4 and up) **597**

Macy, Sue, 1954-
(ed) Play like a girl. See Play like a girl **796**

Mad as a wet hen! and other funny idioms. Terban, M. **427**

Madagascar
Heale, J. Madagascar (5 and up) **969.1**
Description
Bishop, N. Digging for bird-dinosaurs (4 and up) **567.9**

Madama, John
(il) Peters, R. M. Clambake **970.004**

Madeline. Bemelmans, L. **E**

Madeline and the bad hat. Bemelmans, L. See note under Bemelmans, L. Madeline **E**

Madeline and the gypsies. Bemelmans, L. See note under Bemelmans, L. Madeline **E**

Madeline in London. Bemelmans, L. See note under Bemelmans, L. Madeline **E**

Madeline's Christmas. Bemelmans, L. See note under Bemelmans, L. Madeline **E**

Madeline's rescue. Bemelmans, L. **E**

Madhouse. Wynne-Jones, T.
In Wynne-Jones, T. The book of changes p24-46 **S C**

Madison, James, 1751-1836
About
Fritz, J. The great little Madison (5 and up) **92**

Madlenka. Sis, P. **E**

Mado, Michio
The magic pocket (k-3) **895.6**

Madrigal, Antonio Hernandez
Erandi's braids **E**

Maestro, Betsy, 1944-
Coming to America: the story of immigration (k-3) **325.73**
The discovery of the Americas (2-4) **970.01**

Magic or not? Eager, E.   **Fic**

The **Magic** orange tree
   In The Magic orange tree, and other Haitian folktales p13-21   **398.2**

The **Magic** orange tree, and other Haitian folktales (5 and up)   **398.2**

The **magic** paintbrush. Yep, L.   **Fic**

The **magic** pencil. Hough, C. W.
   In Bauer, C. F. Celebrations p12-14   **808.8**

The **magic** pitcher. Schwartz, H.
   In Schwartz, H. The diamond tree p21-28   **398.2**

The **magic** pocket. Mado, M.   **895.6**

The **magic** purse. Uchida, Y.   **398.2**

The **Magic** ring
   In The Yellow fairy book p178-91   **398.2**

The **magic** sandals of Abu Kassim. Schwartz, H.
   In Schwartz, H. The diamond tree p45-52   **398.2**

The **magic** school bus and the electric field trip. Cole, J.   **621.3**

The **magic** school bus at the waterworks. Cole, J.   **551.48**

The **magic** school bus explores the senses. Cole, J.   **612.8**

The **magic** school bus: in the time of the dinosaurs. Cole, J.   **567.9**

The **magic** school bus inside a beehive. Cole, J.   **595.7**

The **magic** school bus inside a hurricane. Cole, J.   **551.55**

The **magic** school bus inside the Earth. Cole, J.   **551.1**

The **magic** school bus inside the human body. Cole, J.   **612**

The **magic** school bus, lost in the solar system. Cole, J.   **523**

The **magic** school bus on the ocean floor. Cole, J.   **591.7**

Magic secrets. Wyler, R.   **793.8**

The **magic** seed. Jaffe, N.
   In Jaffe, N. The cow of no color: riddle stories and justice tales from around the world p55-58   **398.2**

The **magic** shirt. Afanas'ev, A. N.
   In Afanas'ev, A. N. Russian fairy tales p110-13   **398.2**

The **magic** spoon. Kimmel, E. A.
   In Kimmel, E. A. The jar of fools: eight Hanukkah stories from Chelm p27-34   **S C**

Magic steps. Pierce, T.   **Fic**

The **Magic** swan
   In The Green fairy book p175-79   **398.2**

The **magic** swan geese. Afanas'ev, A. N.
   In Afanas'ev, A. N. Russian fairy tales p349-51   **398.2**

The **magic** tree. Echewa, T. O.   **398.2**

The **magic** tree. Krishnaswami, U.
   In Krishnaswami, U. Shower of gold: girls and women in the stories of India p94-99   **398.2**

Magic tricks
   Bauer, C. F. Leading kids to books through magic   **027.62**
   The Brain explorer (5 and up)   **793.73**
   Broekel, R. Hocus pocus: magic you can do (3-5)   **793.8**
   Cobb, V. Bet you can! science possibilities to fool you (4 and up)   **793.8**
   Cobb, V. Bet you can't! science impossibilities to fool you (4 and up)   **793.8**
   Cobb, V. Magic—naturally! (4 and up)   **793.8**
   Cobb, V. Wanna bet! (4 and up)   **793.8**
   Leyton, L. My first magic book (3-5)   **793.8**
   White, L. B. Math-a-magic: number tricks for magicians (3-6)   **793.8**
   White, L. B. Shazam! simple science magic (3-6)   **793.8**
   Wyler, R. Magic secrets (k-2)   **793.8**
   Wyler, R. Spooky tricks (k-2)   **793.8**
   See/See also pages in the following book(s):
   Cole, J. The rain or shine activity book p168-77 (3-5)   **793**

Magic windows. Garza, C. L.   **305.8**

Magical tales from many lands. Mayo, M.   **398.2**

Magicians
   Matthews, T. L. Spellbinder: the life of Harry Houdini (5 and up)   **92**
      Fiction
   Avi. Midnight magic (5 and up)   **Fic**
   Fleischman, S. The midnight horse (3-6)   **Fic**
      Poetry
   Willard, N. The sorcerer's apprentice (2-5)   **811**

The **magician's** nephew. Lewis, C. S. See note under Lewis, C. S. The lion, the witch, and the wardrobe   **Fic**

The **magician's** spell. Jaffe, N.
   In Jaffe, N. The uninvited guest and other Jewish holiday tales p25-31   **296.4**

Magid fasts for Ramadan. Matthews, M.   **Fic**

Magnesium
   Uttley, C. Magnesium
   In The Elements [Benchmark Bks.]   **546**

Magnetism
   Dispezio, M. A. Awesome experiments in electricity & magnetism (5 and up)   **537**

Magnets
   Branley, F. M. What makes a magnet? (k-3)   **538**

Magnuson, Diana
   (il) Bruchac, J. The Trail of Tears   **970.004**

Magorian, Michelle, 1947-
   Good night, Mr. Tom (6 and up)   **Fic**

The **magpie** and the milk. Walker, B. K.
   In Walker, B. K. A treasury of Turkish folktales for children p11-13   **398.2**

Malone, Nola Langner
(il) Viorst, J. Earrings! **E**

Malone, Peter, 1953-
(il) Crossley-Holland, K. The world of King Arthur and his court **942.01**
(il) Mayo, M. Brother sun, sister moon: the life and stories of St. Francis **92**
(il) Philip, N. The adventures of Odysseus **883**

Malory, Sir Thomas, 15th cent.
Morte d'Arthur. See Sabuda, R. Arthur and the sword **398.2**

Malta
Sheehan, S. Malta (5 and up) **945**

Mama. Schick, E. **E**

Mama, across the sea. Godard, A. **E**

Mama and me and the Model-T. Gibbons, F. **E**

Mama cat has three kittens. Fleming, D. **E**

Mama, coming and going. Caseley, J. **E**

Mama, do you love me? Joosse, B. M. **E**

Mama don't allow. Hurd, T. **E**

Mama Elizabeti. Stuve-Bodeen, S. See note under Stuve-Bodeen, S. Elizabeti's doll **E**

Mama is a miner. Lyon, G. E. **E**

Mama One, Mama Two. MacLachlan, P. **E**

Mama talks too much. Russo, M. **E**

Mama's perfect present. Goode, D. **E**

Mammalabilia. Florian, D. **811**

Mammals
See also Fossil mammals; groups of mammals; and names of mammals
Esbensen, B. J. Baby whales drink milk (k-1) **599.5**
Grassy, J. National Audubon Society first field guide: mammals (4 and up) **599**
Parker, S. Mammal (4 and up) **599**
Wildsmith, B. Brian Wildsmith's wild animals **E**

Poetry
Florian, D. Mammalabilia **811**

Mammoths
Aliki. Wild and woolly mammoths (k-3) **569**

Fiction
Martin, R. Will's mammoth **E**

Man
Influence on nature
See Human influence on nature
Origin
See Human origins

Man, Fossil *See* Fossil hominids

Man, Prehistoric *See* Prehistoric peoples

The **man** and the boots. Lester, J.
In Lester, J. The last tales of Uncle Remus p133-36 **398.2**

The **man** and the wild cattle. Lester, J.
In Lester, J. The last tales of Uncle Remus p110-14 **398.2**

Man Bear. Bruchac, J.
In Bruchac, J. When the Chenoo howls **398.2**

The **man** from the other side. Orlev, U. **Fic**

The **man** in the ceiling. Feiffer, J. **Fic**

The **man** of influence. Fleischman, P.
In Fleischman, P. Graven images p61-85 **S C**

Man of the family. Karr, K. **Fic**

Man-of-war, Stephen Biesty's cross-sections. Biesty, S. **359.1**

The **man** who almost lived forever. McCaughrean, G.
In McCaughrean, G. The golden hoard: myths and legends of the world p100-02 **398.2**

The **man** who almost married a witch. Lester, J.
In Lester, J. The last tales of Uncle Remus p71-76 **398.2**

The **man** who caught fish. Krudop, W. **E**

The **man** who did not know fear. Afanas'ev, A. N.
In Afanas'ev, A. N. Russian fairy tales p325-27 **398.2**

The **man** who didn't wash his dishes. Krasilovsky, P.
In The Read-aloud treasury p179-87 **808.8**

The **man** who married a seagull. Norman, H.
In Norman, H. The girl who dreamed only geese, and other tales of the Far North **398.2**

The **Man** who was afraid of nothing
In Diane Goode's book of scary stories & songs p26-31 **398.2**

Manabush and the monsters. Curry, J. L.
In Curry, J. L. Turtle Island: tales of the Algonquian nations p27-32 **398.2**

Managing children's services in the public library. Fasick, A. M. **027.62**

Manatees
Jenkins, P. B. A safe home for manatees (k-2) **599.5**

Manco Capac and the rod of gold. Delacre, L.
In Delacre, L. Golden tales p55-57 **398.2**

Mancrow, bird of darkness. Sherlock, Sir P. M.
In Sherlock, Sir P. M. West Indian folk-tales p65-70 **398.2**

Mandarin and the butterflies. Carpenter, F.
In Carpenter, F. Tales of a Chinese grandmother p198-205 **398.2**

Mandela, Nelson
About
Cooper, F. Mandela (2-4) **92**

Manders, John
(il) Lauber, P. What you never knew about fingers, forks, & chopsticks **394.1**

Mangelsen, Thomas D.
(il) Hirschi, R. Fall **508.2**
(il) Hirschi, R. Spring **508.2**
(il) Hirschi, R. Summer **508.2**
(il) Hirschi, R. Winter **508.2**

Maniac Magee. Spinelli, J. **Fic**

Manna, Anthony L.
Mr. Semolina-Semolinus (1-3) **398.2**

Manners *See* Etiquette

Manners. Aliki **395**

Manners and customs
See also Country life; Hugging

Manning-Sanders, Ruth, 1895-1988
The fish cart
In The Oxford treasury of children's stories
p19-22   **S C**

Mansfield, Stephen
Laos (5 and up)   **959.4**

Manslaughter *See* Homicide

Manson, Christopher
(il) Child, L. M. F. Over the river and through
the wood   **811**
(il) Nikola-Lisa, W. Till year's good end
     942.02

Mantell, Paul
(jt. auth) Hart, A. Ancient Greece!   **938**
(jt. auth) Hart, A. Knights & castles   **940.1**

Manuel had a riddle. Hamilton, V.
In Hamilton, V. The people could fly:
American black folktales p65-75
     398.2

Manufactures
Biesty, S. Stephen Biesty's incredible everything
(4 and up)   **670**
CD's, superglue, and salsa [series 2]   **670**

Manushkin, Fran
Latkes and applesauce   **E**
The matzah that Papa brought home   **E**
Miriam's cup (k-3)   **222**

Many happy reruns. Paterson, K.
In Paterson, K. Angels & other strangers:
family Christmas stories p26-39
     S C

Many luscious lollipops: a book about adjectives.
Heller, R.   **428**

Many, many weddings in one corner house. Sandburg, C.
In Sandburg, C. Rootabaga stories pt 2 p17-21   **S C**
In Sandburg, C. The Sandburg treasury p95-97   **818**

Many moons. Thurber, J.   **Fic**

Many thousand gone. Hamilton, V.   **326**

Many waters. L'Engle, M. *See* note under
L'Engle, M. A wrinkle in time   **Fic**

Maoris
     Folklore
Te Kanawa, K. Land of the long white cloud
(3-6)   **398.2**

Maple sugar
     Fiction
Haas, J. Sugaring   **E**

Maples in the mist   **895.1**

Mapping the world. Johnson, S. A.   **912**

Maps
See also Atlases
Johnson, S. A. Mapping the world (4 and up)
     912
     Fiction
Hartman, G. As the crow flies   **E**
Walters, V. Are we there yet, Daddy?   **E**

Maravich, Pete, 1948-1988
See/See also pages in the following book(s):
Krull, K. Lives of the athletes p79-81 (4 and
up)   **920**

The **marble** champ. Soto, G.
In Soto, G. Baseball in April, and other stories p90-96   **S C**

Marbles. Cole, J.   **796.2**

Marcellino, Fred, 1939-2001
I, crocodile   **E**
(il) Babbitt, N. Ouch!   **398.2**
(il) Bannerman, H. The story of Little Babaji
     E
(il) Lear, E. The pelican chorus and other nonsense   **821**
(il) Perrault, C. Puss in boots   **398.2**
(il) Seidler, T. The steadfast tin soldier   **Fic**
(il) Seidler, T. The Wainscott weasel   **Fic**
(il) White, E. B. The trumpet of the swan
     Fic

Marchant, Kerena
Id-ul-Fitr (3-5)   **297.3**

Marchesi, Stephen
(il) Gherman, B. The mysterious rays of Dr.
Röntgen   **92**

Marciano, John
Bemelmans   **92**

Marco the Rich and Vasily the Luckless.
Afanas'ev, A. N.
In Afanas'ev, A. N. Russian fairy tales p213-20   **398.2**

Marcus, Leonard S., 1950-
A Caldecott celebration   **741.6**
(ed) Author talk. *See* Author talk   **028.5**

Mardi Gras *See* Carnival

Mardi Gras: a Cajun country celebration. Hoyt-Goldsmith, D.   **394.25**

The **mare** on the hill. Locker, T.   **E**

Margeson, Susan M.
Viking (4 and up)   **948**

Maria Morevna. Afanas'ev, A. N.
In Afanas'ev, A. N. Russian fairy tales p553-62   **398.2**

Maria Theresa, Empress of Austria, 1717-1780
See/See also pages in the following book(s):
Meltzer, M. Ten queens p97-107 (5 and up)
     920

Marian, Maid (Legendary character) *See* Maid
Marian (Legendary character)

Marianthe's story. *See* Aliki. Painted words:
Marianthe's story one   **E**

Maria's comet. Hopkinson, D.   **E**

Marie and Redfish. Hamilton, V.
In Hamilton, V. Her stories p11-14
     398.2

**Marie Antoinette, Queen, consort of Louis XVI,
King of France, 1755-1793**
     Fiction
Lasky, K. Marie Antoinette (4 and up)   **Fic**

Marie Curie and radium. Parker, S.   **92**

Mariel of Redwall. Jacques, B. *See* note under
Jacques, B. Redwall   **Fic**

Marika the snowmaiden. Bauer, C. F.
  In Snowy day: stories and poems p45-49
                808.8

Marine animals
  See also Freshwater animals
  Aliki. My visit to the aquarium (k-3)
                639.34
  Arnold, C. A walk on the Great Barrier Reef
  (3-5)   **578.7**
  Cole, J. The magic school bus on the ocean
  floor (2-4)   **591.7**
  Johnson, J. Simon & Schuster children's guide
  to sea creatures (4 and up)   **591.7**
  Macdonald, S. Sea shapes   **E**
  Simon, S. They swim the seas (3-6) **578.7**
            Fiction
  Freymann, S. One lonely sea horse   **E**
            Poetry
  Florian, D. In the swim   **811**

Marine aquariums
  Aliki. My visit to the aquarium (k-3)
                639.34

Marine biology
  Gibbons, G. Exploring the deep, dark sea (k-3)
                551.46

Marine ecology
  Cerullo, M. M. Coral reef (4 and up)
                577.7

Marine mammals
  See also Dolphins; Seals (Animals); Whales

Marine plants
  See also Kelps
  Simon, S. They swim the seas (3-6) **578.7**

Marine pollution
  See also Oil spills

Marino, Dan
  See/See also pages in the following book(s):
  Sullivan, G. Quarterbacks! p18-20 (5 and up)
                920

Marino, Jane
  Mother Goose time   **027.62**

Mark, Jan
  The Midas touch   **398.2**
  No-good Claus
  In The Oxford book of scary tales p123-29
                808.8
  William's version
  In The Oxford treasury of children's stories
  p144-50   **S C**

Mark Twain and the queens of the Mississippi.
  Harness, C.   **92**

Market Day. Bunting, E.   **E**

Market day. Ehlert, L.   **E**

Markets
  Lewin, T. Market! (k-3)   **381**
            Fiction
  Bunting, E. Market Day   **E**
  Ehlert, L. Market day   **E**

Markham, Lois
  Colombia (4 and up)   **986.1**

Markle, Sandra, 1946-
  After the spill (4 and up)   **363.7**
  Discovering graph secrets (3-6) **001.4**

Gone forever! (k-3)   **591.68**
Growing up wild: bears (2-4) **599.78**
Icky, squishy science (3-5)   **507.8**
Measuring up! (4 and up)   **530.8**
Outside and inside alligators (2-4) **597.9**
Outside and inside bats (2-4) **599.4**
Outside and inside birds (2-4) **598**
Outside and inside kangaroos (2-4) **599.2**
Outside and inside sharks (2-4) **597**
Outside and inside snakes (2-4) **597.9**
Outside and inside spiders (2-4) **595.4**
A rainy day (k-2)   **551.57**

Markle, William
  (jt. auth) Markle, S. Gone forever! **591.68**

Marks, Alan
  (il) Goodall, J. With love   **599.8**

Marks, Claude, 1915-1991
  Go in and out the window. See Go in and out
  the window   **782.42**

Marlfox. Jacques, B. See note under Jacques, B.
  Redwall   **Fic**

Marmots
         Fiction
  Seidler, T. Mean Margaret (3-6) **Fic**

Marrella, Maria Pia
  (il) MacLachlan, P. Seven kisses in a row
                Fic

Marriage
  See also Divorce; Family; Remarriage;
  Weddings
         Fiction
  Buehner, C. Fanny's dream   **E**

Marriage, Interracial *See* Interracial marriage

Marriage customs and rites
  Morris, A. Weddings (k-1)   **392**

Marrin, Albert, 1936-
  The sea king: Sir Francis Drake and his times
  (6 and up)   **92**

Marriott, Pat, 1920-
  (il) Aiken, J. The wolves of Willoughby Chase
                Fic

Mars (Planet)
  Fradin, D. B. Is there life on Mars? (4 and up)
                576.8
  Ride, S. K. The mystery of Mars (4-6)
                523.4
  Simon, S. Destination: Mars (3-6) **523.4**
         Fiction
  Pinkney, B. Cosmo and the robot **E**

Marschall, Ken
  Inside the Titanic (4 and up) **910.4**
  (il) Ballard, R. D. Exploring the Titanic
                910.4
  (il) Ballard, R. D. Ghost liners **910.4**

Marsh, Carole S., 1946-
  Asteroids, comets, and meteors (4-6) **523.6**

Marsh Hawk. MacDonald, M. R.
  In MacDonald, M. R. The storyteller's start-
  up book p133-37   **372.6**

Marshall, Chris, 1962-
  (ed) Dinosaurs of the world. See Dinosaurs of
  the world   **567.9**

Martin, Ann M., 1955-—*Continued*
  Rachel Parker, kindergarten show-off   E
  (jt. auth) Danziger, P. P.S. Longer letter later
      Fic
  (jt. auth) Danziger, P. Snail mail no more
      Fic
  See/See also pages in the following book(s):
  Author talk (4 and up)   **028.5**
Martin, Bill, 1916-
  Barn dance!   E
  A beasty story   E
  Brown bear, brown bear what do you see?
      E
  Chicka chicka boom boom   E
  The ghost-eye tree   E
  Knots on a counting rope   E
  The maestro plays   E
  Polar bear, polar bear, what do you hear?
      E
Martin, David, 1944-
  Five little piggies   E
Martin, Fran
  Raven brings fresh water
  In From sea to shining sea p8-11   **810.8**
Martin, Jacqueline Briggs
  Grandmother Bryant's pocket   E
  Snowflake Bentley [biography of Wilson Alwyn
  Bentley] (k-3)   **92**
Martin, Joseph Plumb, 1760-1850
About
  Murphy, J. A young patriot (5 and up)
      973.3
Martin, Linda
  Watch them grow (k-2)   **571.8**
Martin, Patricia Miles *See* Miles, Miska, 1899-
  1986
Martin, Rafe, 1946-
  The boy who lived with the seals (1-4)
      398.2
  The language of birds (2-4)   **398.2**
  Mysterious tales of Japan (4 and up)   **398.2**
  Contents: Urashima Tarō; Green willow; Ho-Ichi the earless;
  The snow woman; Kogi; The crane maiden; The pine of Akoya;
  Snake husband, Frog friend; The boy who drew cats; Black hair
  Will's mammoth   E
Martin, William Ivan *See* Martin, Bill, 1916-
Martin the Warrior. Jacques, B. See note under
  Jacques, B. Redwall   Fic
Martina, the little cockroach. González, L. M.
  In González, L. M. Señor Cat's romance and
    other favorite stories from Latin America
    p21-27   **398.2**
Martindale, Emily
  (il) Armstrong, J. Black-eyed Susan   Fic
Martinez, Ed, 1954-
  (il) Soto, G. Too many tamales   E
Martinez, Sergio, 1937-
  (il) Meltzer, M. Weapons & warfare   **355**
Martinique
Folklore
  See Folklore—Martinique
Martins, George
  (il) Giovanni, N. Spin a soft black song: poems
    for children   **811**

Maruki, Toshi, 1912-
  Hiroshima no pika   **940.54**
The **marvelous** land of Oz. Baum, L. F. See note
  under Baum, L. F. The Wizard of Oz
      Fic
Marvelous math (3-5)   **811.008**
The **marvelous** misadventures of Sebastian. Alex-
  ander, L.   Fic
Marven of the Great North Woods. Lasky, K.
      E
Marvin and the mean words. Kline, S. See note
  under Kline, S. Mary Marony, mummy girl
      Fic
Marvin and the meanest girl. Kline, S. See note
  under Kline, S. Mary Marony, mummy girl
      Fic
Marvin Redpost, a flying birthday cake. Sachar,
  L. See note under Sachar, L. Marvin Redpost,
  kidnapped at birth?   Fic
Marvin Redpost, a magic crystal. Sachar, L. See
  note under Sachar, L. Marvin Redpost, kid-
  napped at birth?   Fic
Marvin Redpost, alone in his teacher's house.
  Sachar, L. See note under Sachar, L. Marvin
  Redpost, kidnapped at birth?   Fic
Marvin Redpost, class president. Sachar, L. See
  note under Sachar, L. Marvin Redpost, kid-
  napped at birth?   Fic
Marvin Redpost, is he a girl? Sachar, L. See note
  under Sachar, L. Marvin Redpost, kidnapped
  at birth?   Fic
Marvin Redpost, kidnapped at birth? Sachar, L.
      Fic
Marvin Redpost, superfast, out of control. Sachar,
  L. See note under Sachar, L. Marvin Redpost,
  kidnapped at birth?   Fic
Marvin Redpost, why pick on me? Sachar, L. See
  note under Sachar, L. Marvin Redpost, kid-
  napped at birth?   Fic
Marvin's best Christmas present ever. Paterson,
  K.   E
Marx, Trish, 1948-
  One boy from Kosovo (3-6)   **949.7**
Mary, Blessed Virgin, Saint
About
  De Paola, T. Mary, the mother of Jesus (3-5)
      232.91
  Mayer, M. Young Mary of Nazareth (4 and up)
      232.91
Fiction
  De Paola, T. The night of Las Posadas   E
Mary Ann. James, B.   E
Mary Anning and the sea dragon. Atkins, J.
      92
Mary Belle and the mermaid. Hamilton, V.
  In Hamilton, V. Her stories p33-37
      398.2
Mary had a little lamb. Hale, S. J.   **811**
Mary Marony and the chocolate surprise. Kline, S.
  See note under Kline, S. Mary Marony, mum-
  my girl   Fic

Mary Marony and the snake. Kline, S. See note under Kline, S. Mary Marony, mummy girl **Fic**

Mary Marony hides out. Kline, S. See note under Kline, S. Mary Marony, mummy girl **Fic**

Mary Marony, mummy girl. Kline, S. **Fic**

Mary Moon is missing. Giff, P. R. See note under Giff, P. R. Kidnap at the Catfish Cafe **Fic**

Mary on horseback [biography of Mary Breckinridge] Wells, R. **92**

Mary Poppins. Travers, P. L. **Fic**

Mary Poppins comes back. Travers, P. L. See note under Travers, P. L. Mary Poppins **Fic**

Mary Poppins in the park. Travers, P. L. See note under Travers, P. L. Mary Poppins **Fic**

Mary poppins opens the door. Travers, P. L. See note under Travers, P. L. Mary Poppins **Fic**

Mary, the mother of Jesus. De Paola, T. **232.91**

Maryland
Burgan, M. Maryland
In America the beautiful, second series **973**

Pietrzyk, L. Maryland
In Celebrate the states **973**
Fiction
Hahn, M. D. Promises to the dead (5 and up) **Fic**

Marzollo, Jean
Happy birthday, Martin Luther King (k-3) **92**

Home sweet home **E**
In 1492 (k-2) **970.01**
Pretend you're a cat **E**
(jt. auth) Wick, W. I spy **793.73**
(jt. auth) Wick, W. I spy Christmas **793.73**
(jt. auth) Wick, W. I spy extreme challenger! **793.73**
(jt. auth) Wick, W. I spy fantasy **793.73**
(jt. auth) Wick, W. I spy fun house **793.73**
(jt. auth) Wick, W. I spy gold challenger! **793.73**
(jt. auth) Wick, W. I spy mystery **793.73**
(jt. auth) Wick, W. I spy school days **793.73**
(jt. auth) Wick, W. I spy spooky night **793.73**
(jt. auth) Wick, W. I spy super challenger! **793.73**
(jt. auth) Wick, W. I spy treasure hunt **793.73**

Masada. Waldman, N. **933**
Masada Site (Israel)
Waldman, N. Masada (4 and up) **933**
Masai (African people)
Fiction
Kroll, V. L. Masai and I **E**
Folklore
Aardema, V. The lonely lioness and the ostrich chicks (k-3) **398.2**
Aardema, V. Who's in Rabbit's house? (k-3) **398.2**

Mollel, T. M. The orphan boy (k-3) **398.2**
Masai and I. Kroll, V. L. **E**
Masks (Facial)
Finley, C. The art of African masks (5 and up) **391**

Masoff, Joy, 1951-
Emergency! (3-6) **616.02**
Fire! (3-6) **628.9**
Mason, Bob
About
Montgomery, S. The snake scientist (4 and up) **597.9**

Mass communication *See* Communication
Massachusetts
LeVert, S. Massachusetts
In Celebrate the states **973**
McNair, S. Massachusetts
In America the beautiful, second series **973**
Fiction
Lewis, M. Morgy makes his move (2-4) **Fic**
McCully, E. A. The bobbin girl (3-5) **Fic**
Paterson, K. Lyddie (5 and up) **Fic**
Rinaldi, A. The journal of Jasper Jonathan Pierce, a pilgrim boy (4 and up) **Fic**
Yolen, J. Letting Swift River go **E**
History—1600-1775, Colonial period
See also Plymouth Rock
Bowen, G. Stranded at Plimoth Plantation, 1626 (3-5) **974.4**
Sewall, M. The pilgrims of Plimoth (3-6) **974.4**
Waters, K. On the Mayflower (2-4) **974.4**
Waters, K. Samuel Eaton's day (2-4) **974.4**
Waters, K. Sarah Morton's day (2-4) **974.4**
History—1600-1775, Colonial period—Fiction
Clapp, P. Constance: a story of early Plymouth (5 and up) **Fic**
Massey, Cal
(il) Chocolate, D. My first Kwanzaa book **394.26**

Massie, Diane Redfield
The baby beebee bird **E**
The **master** and his pupil. Jacobs, J.
In Jacobs, J. English fairy tales p77-80 **398.2**
Master Angelo *See* Angelo, Master, fl. ca. 1370-ca. 1405
The **master** cat. Perrault, C.
In The Blue fairy book p141-47 **398.2**
In The Classic fairy tales p113-16 **398.2**
Master Frog. Vuong, L. D.
In Vuong, L. D. The brocaded slipper, and other Vietnamese tales **398.2**
The **master-maid**. Asbjornsen, P. C.
In The Blue fairy book p120-35 **398.2**
Master of all masters. Jacobs, J.
In Jacobs, J. English fairy tales p216-17 **398.2**
In Tomie dePaola's favorite nursery tales p84-85 **398.2**
The **master** puppeteer. Paterson, K. **Fic**

The **Master** thief
> *In* The Magic orange tree, and other Haitian folktales p135-41 **398.2**

Masters, Nancy Robinson *See* Robinson Masters, Nancy

Master's walking stick. Sanfield, S.
> *In* Sanfield, S. The adventures of High John the Conqueror **398.2**

Mastodon
> Giblin, J. The mystery of the mammoth bones (4 and up) **569**

Matajuro's training. Kimmel, E. A.
> *In* Kimmel, E. A. Sword of the samurai p31-39 **Fic**

Mataora and Niwareka in the Underworld. Te Kanawa, K.
> *In* Te Kanawa, K. Land of the long white cloud p67-80 **398.2**

Materia medica
> *See also* Drugs

Math-a-magic: number tricks for magicians. White, L. B. **793.8**

The **math** chef. D'Amico, J. **641.5**

Math curse. Scieszka, J. **E**

Math for the very young **793.7**

Math forum problems. (4 and up) See entry in Part 2: Web Resources

Mathematical models
> *See also* Computer simulation

Mathematical recreations
> Adler, D. A. Easy math puzzles (2-4) **793.73**
> Math for the very young **793.7**
> White, L. B. Math-a-magic: number tricks for magicians (3-6) **793.8**

Mathematics
> *See also* Arithmetic; Fractions; Patterns (Mathematics)
> Anno, M. Anno's mysterious multiplying jar (2-5) **512**
> Anno, M. Anno's magic seeds (k-3) **513**
> Anno, M. Anno's math games (k-3) **513**
> Anno, M. Anno's math games II (k-3) **513**
> Anno, M. Anno's math games III (k-3) **513**
> Burns, M. The I hate mathematics! book (4 and up) **513**
> D'Amico, J. The math chef (4-6) **641.5**
> Giganti, P., Jr. Each orange had 8 slices **E**
> Merriam, E. 12 ways to get to 11 (k-3) **510**
> Schmandt-Besserat, D. The history of counting (4 and up) **513**
> Scholastic explains math homework (1-3) **513**
> Schwartz, D. M. G is for googol (4 and up) **510**
> VanCleave, J. P. Janice VanCleave's play and find out about math (k-2) **513**

Fiction
> Pinczes, E. J. One hundred hungry ants **E**
> Scieszka, J. Math curse **E**

Poetry
> Marvelous math (3-5) **811.008**

Mathers, Petra
> Lottie's new beach towel **E**
> Lottie's new friend. See note under Mathers, P. Lottie's new beach towel **E**
> (il) Aardema, V. Borreguita and the coyote **398.2**
> (il) Jonell, L. It's my birthday, too! **E**
> (il) Martin, J. B. Grandmother Bryant's pocket **E**

Mathis, Sharon Bell, 1937-
> Sidewalk story (3-5) **Fic**

MathStart [series]
> Murphy, S. J. Beep beep, vroom vroom! **515**
> Murphy, S. J. Betcha! **519.5**
> Murphy, S. J. Dave's down-to-earth rock shop **511.3**
> Murphy, S. J. Divide and ride **513**
> Murphy, S. J. Elevator magic **513**
> Murphy, S. J. Henry the fourth **513**
> Murphy, S. J. Jump, kangaroo, jump! **513**
> Murphy, S. J. Just enough carrots **513**
> Murphy, S. J. Pepper's journal **E**
> Murphy, S. J. Room for Ripley **530.8**

Matilda. Dahl, R. **Fic**

Mating behavior *See* Animal courtship

Matje, Martin
> (il) Yorinks, A. Harry and Lulu **E**

The **Matsuyama** mirror. Quayle, E.
> *In* Quayle, E. The shining princess, and other Japanese legends p90-96 **398.2**

Matter
> Hewitt, S. Solid, liquid, or gas? (k-3) **530.4**
> Zoehfeld, K. W. What is the world made of? (k-3) **530.4**

A **matter** of brogues. Sawyer, R.
> *In* Sawyer, R. The way of the storyteller p259-70 **372.6**

Matthews, Mary, 1928-
> Magid fasts for Ramadan (2-4) **Fic**

Matthews, Tom L., 1949-
> Always inventing: a photobiography of Alexander Graham Bell (4 and up) **92**
> Light shining through the mist: a photobiography of Dian Fossey (4 and up) **92**
> Spellbinder: the life of Harry Houdini (5 and up) **92**

Matthew's dream. Lionni, L. **E**

Mattimeo. Jacques, B. See note under Jacques, B. Redwall **Fic**

The **matzah** that Papa brought home. Manushkin, F. **E**

Matzeliger, Jan, 1852-1889
> **About**
> Mitchell, B. Shoes for everyone: a story about Jan Matzeliger (3-5) **92**
> *See/See also pages in the following book(s):*
> McKissack, P. C. African-American inventors p48-53 (5 and up) **920**

Maui and the birds. Te Kanawa, K.
> *In* Te Kanawa, K. Land of the long white cloud p117-18 **398.2**

Maui and the Great Fish. Te Kanawa, K.
In Te Kanawa, K. Land of the long white cloud p17-22 **398.2**

Maui tames the Sun. Te Kanawa, K.
In Te Kanawa, K. Land of the long white cloud p23-26 **398.2**

Maushop the Giant. Curry, J. L.
In Curry, J. L. Turtle Island: tales of the Algonquian nations p40-43 **398.2**

Maver, Salley
(il) Hale, S. J. Mary had a little lamb **811**

Max, Ken Wilson- *See* Wilson-Max, Ken, 1965-

Max. Isadora, R. **E**

Max and Ruby's first Greek myth: Pandora's box. Wells, R. See note under Wells, R. Max's first word **E**

Max and Ruby's Midas: another Greek myth. Wells, R. See note under Wells, R. Max's first word **E**

Max cleans up. Wells, R. See note under Wells, R. Max's first word **E**

Maxi, the hero. Barracca, D. See note under Barracca, D. The adventures of Taxi Dog **E**

Maxi, the star. Barracca, D. See note under Barracca, D. The adventures of Taxi Dog **E**

Maximilian, Prince of Wied-Neuwied *See* Wied, Maximilian, Prinz von, 1782-1867

Maxims *See* Proverbs

Max's bath. Wells, R. See note under Wells, R. Max's first word **E**

Max's bedtime. Wells, R. See note under Wells, R. Max's first word **E**

Max's birthday. Wells, R. See note under Wells, R. Max's first word **E**

Max's breakfast. Wells, R. See note under Wells, R. Max's first word **E**

Max's chocolate chicken. Wells, R. See note under Wells, R. Max's first word **E**

Max's Christmas. Wells, R. See note under Wells, R. Max's first word **E**

Max's dragon shirt. Wells, R. See note under Wells, R. Max's first word **E**

Max's first word. Wells, R. **E**

Max's new suit. Wells, R. See note under Wells, R. Max's first word **E**

Max's ride. Wells, R. See note under Wells, R. Max's first word **E**

Max's toys. Wells, R. See note under Wells, R. Max's first word **E**

May I bring a friend? De Regniers, B. S. **E**

May we sleep here tonight? Koide, T. **E**

Mayas
Ancona, G. Mayeros (3-6) **972**
Staub, F. J. Children of Yucatán (3-5) **972**
See/See also pages in the following book(s):
Krull, K. They saw the future p27-33 (4 and up) **133.3**

Fiction
O'Dell, S. The captive (6 and up) **Fic**
Wisniewski, D. Rain player **E**

Folklore
Ehlert, L. Cuckoo. Cucú (k-3) **398.2**
Rockwell, A. F. The boy who wouldn't obey: a Mayan legend (2-4) **398.2**

Religion
Fisher, L. E. Gods and goddesses of the ancient Maya (3-6) **299**

Maybe yes, maybe no, maybe maybe. Patron, S. **Fic**

Maybelle, the cable car. Burton, V. L. **E**

Mayer, Marianna, 1945-
Baba Yaga and Vasilisa the brave (3-5) **398.2**
Beauty and the beast (1-4) **398.2**
Iron John (3-6) **398.2**
Pegasus (4-6) **292**
Women warriors (4 and up) **398**
Contents: Devi; Rangada; Semiramis; Hiera; Scathach; Morrigan; Gwendolen; Boadicea; Mella; Yakami; Winyan Ohitika; Aliquipiso
Young Jesus of Nazareth (4 and up) **232.9**
Young Mary of Nazareth (4 and up) **232.91**

Mayer, Mercer, 1943-
A boy, a dog, and a friend. See note under Mayer, M. A boy, a dog, and a frog **E**
A boy, a dog, and a frog **E**
Frog goes to dinner. See note under Mayer, M. A boy, a dog, and a frog **E**
Frog on his own. See note under Mayer, M. A boy, a dog, and a frog **E**
Frog, where are you? See note under Mayer, M. A boy, a dog, and a frog **E**
One frog too many. See note under Mayer, M. A boy, a dog, and a frog **E**
There's a nightmare in my closet **E**
There's an alligator under my bed. See note under Mayer, M. There's a nightmare in my closet **E**
(il) Fitzgerald, J. D. The Great Brain **Fic**
(il) Mayer, M. Beauty and the beast **398.2**

Mayeros. Ancona, G. **972**

Mayes, Walter
(jt. auth) Lewis, V. V. Valerie & Walter's best books for children **028.5**

Mayflower (Ship)
Waters, K. On the Mayflower (2-4) **974.4**

Maynard, Christopher
Airplane (k-3) **629.136**
Micromonsters (2-4) **579**

Mayne, William, 1928-
Hob and the goblins (4 and up) **Fic**

Mayo, Margaret, 1935-
Brother sun, sister moon: the life and stories of St. Francis (3-6) **92**
Magical tales from many lands (3-6) **398.2**
Contents: The Lemon Princess; Feather Woman and the morning star; The Kingdom Under the Sea; Unanana and the enormous one-tusked elephant; Kate Crackernuts; The king who wanted to touch the moon; Three golden apples; The magic fruit; Seven clever brothers; The prince and the flying carpet; The Halloween witches; Koala; Baba Yaga Bony-Legs; The yellow thunder dragon

McClintock, Barbara, 1955—*Continued*
(il) Aylesworth, J. Aunt Pitty Patty's piggy
398.2
(il) Aylesworth, J. The Gingerbread man
398.2

McCloskey, Robert, 1914-
Blueberries for Sal **E**
Centerburg tales. See note under McCloskey, R.
Homer Price
Homer Price (4-6) **Fic**
Lentil **E**
Make way for ducklings **E**
One morning in Maine **E**
Time of wonder **E**
(il) Robertson, K. Henry Reed, Inc. **Fic**
See/See also pages in the following book(s):
Caldecott Medal books, 1938-1957 p80-86
028.5
Marcus, L. S. A Caldecott celebration p6-12
741.6

McCue, Lisa
(il) Brown, M. W. Bunny's noisy book **E**
(il) Thayer, J. The popcorn dragon **E**
(il) Thayer, J. The puppy who wanted a boy
E

McCully, Emily Arnold
The ballot box battle **E**
Beautiful warrior **E**
The bobbin girl (3-5) **Fic**
The grandma mix-up **E**
Grandmas at bat. See note under McCully, E. A.
The grandma mix-up **E**
Grandmas at the lake. See note under McCully,
E. A. The grandma mix-up **E**
Hurry! (2-4) **Fic**
Mirette & Bellini cross Niagra Falls. See note
under McCully, E. A. Mirette on the high
wire **E**
Mirette on the high wire **E**
Monk camps out **E**
Mouse practice. See note under McCully, E. A.
Monk camps out **E**
An outlaw Thanksgiving **E**
The pirate queen [biography of Grace O'Malley]
(k-3) **92**
Starring Mirette and Bellini. See note under
McCully, E. A. Mirette on the high wire
E
(il) Adoff, A. Black is brown is tan **E**
(il) Fox, P. Amzat and his brothers: three Italian
tales **398.2**
(il) Rockwell, T. How to eat fried worms
Fic
See/See also pages in the following book(s):
The Newbery & Caldecott medal books, 1986-
2000 p179-87 **028.5**

McCurdy, Michael
(il) Appelbaum, D. K. Giants in the land
634.9
(il) Forbes, E. Johnny Tremain **Fic**
(il) Hall, D. Lucy's Christmas **E**
(il) Osborne, M. P. American tall tales
398.2
(il) Simms, L. The Bone Man **398.2**
(il) War and the pity of war. See War and the
pity of war **808.81**

McCutcheon, Marc
(ed) The Facts on File student's thesaurus. See
The Facts on File student's thesaurus
423

McDaniel, Melissa
Arizona
In Celebrate the states **973**
New Mexico
In Celebrate the states **973**
South Dakota
In Celebrate the states **973**

McDermott, Gerald
Anansi the spider (k-3) **398.2**
Arrow to the sun (k-3) **398.2**
Coyote: a trickster tale from the American
Southwest (k-3) **398.2**
Musicians of the sun (k-3) **398.2**
Papagayo **E**
Raven (k-3) **398.2**
Tim O'Toole and the wee folk **E**
Zomo the Rabbit (k-3) **398.2**
See/See also pages in the following book(s):
Newbery and Caldecott Medal books, 1966-1975
p266-75 **028.5**

McDonald, Jill
Maggy Scraggle loves the beautiful ice-cream
man
In The Oxford treasury of children's stories
p7-11 **S C**

McDonald, John
(il) Meyer, C. In a different light **979.8**

McDonald, Megan, 1959-
The great pumpkin switch **E**
Insects are my life **E**
Is this a house for Hermit Crab? (k-2)
595.3
Judy Moody (2-4) **Fic**
The potato man **E**

McDuff and the baby. Wells, R. See note under
Wells, R. McDuff moves in **E**
McDuff comes home. Wells, R. See note under
Wells, R. McDuff moves in **E**
McDuff moves in. Wells, R. **E**
McDuff's new friend. Wells, R. See note under
Wells, R. McDuff moves in **E**

McElligot's pool. Seuss, Dr. **E**

McElmeel, Sharron L.
100 most popular children's authors **810.3**
100 most popular picture book authors and illustrators **810.3**
WWW almanac **025.04**

McElrath-Eslick, Lori
(il) Chang, M. S. Da Wei's treasure **398.2**

McGaffey, Leta
Honduras (5 and up) **972.83**

McGaw, Laurie
(il) Bierman, C. Journey to Ellis Island
325.73
(il) Spedden, D. C. S. Polar, the Titanic bear
910.4

McGill, Alice
Miles' song (6 and up) **Fic**
Molly Bannaky **E**

Medearis, Angela Shelf, 1956—*Continued*
Contents: The Fiddler Man; Scared silly; Last dance at the Dew Drop Inn; The rainmaker; Waiting for Mr. Chester
The zebra-riding cowboy (k-3)   **782.42**

Media workshop [series]
Pellowski, M. The art of making comic books
    741.5

Medical care
Brazelton, T. B. Going to the doctor (k-3)
    610.69
Rogers, F. Going to the hospital (k-2)
    362.1

Medicine
    See also Emergency medicine; types of medicine; and names of diseases and groups of diseases
         History
Fisher, L. E. The doctors (4 and up)   **610.9**

Medieval civilization
Aliki. A medieval feast (2-5)   **394.1**
Biesty, S. Stephen Biesty's cross-sections: Castle (4 and up)   **940.1**
Corbishley, M. The Middle Ages (5 and up)
    940.1
Gibbons, G. Knights in shining armor (k-3)
    394
Gravett, C. Knight (4 and up)   **940.1**
Hart, A. Knights & castles (4 and up)
    940.1

A medieval feast. Aliki   **394.1**

Medlock, Scott
(il) Bunting, E. Some frog!   **Fic**
(il) Extra innings. See Extra innings
    811.008
(il) Opening days. See Opening days
    811.008

Medusa (Greek mythology)
Hutton, W. Perseus (3-5)   **292**
Lattimore, D. N. Medusa (3-6)   **398.2**

Meet Babar and his family. Brunhoff, L. de See note under Brunhoff, J. de. The story of Babar, the little elephant   **E**

Meet Danitra Brown. Grimes, N.   **811**

Meet M and M. Ross, P.   **E**

Meet the Austins. L'Engle, M.   **Fic**

Meet the author [series]
Adler, D. A. My writing day   **92**
Asch, F. One man show   **92**
Bunting, E. Once upon a time   **92**
Goble, P. Hau kola: hello friend   **92**
Hopkins, L. B. The writing bug   **92**
Howe, J. Playing with words   **92**
Kuskin, K. Thoughts, pictures, and words
    92
Mahy, M. My mysterious world   **92**
Polacco, P. Firetalking   **92**
Rylant, C. Best wishes   **92**
Simon, S. From paper airplanes to outer space
    92

Meet the orchestra. Hayes, A.   **784.2**

Meeting dolphins. Dudzinski, K.   **599.5**

Meeting Elijah. Goldin, B. D.
In Goldin, B. D. Journeys with Elijah p65-74
    222

Megatech [series]
Jefferis, D. Cyberspace   **004.6**

Meggs, Libby Phillips
Go home!   **E**

Mei-Mei loves the morning. Tsubakiyama, M.
    E

Meigs, Cornelia Lynde, 1884-1972
See/See also pages in the following book(s):
Newbery Medal books, 1922-1955 p117-24
    028.5

Meisel, Jacqueline Drobis
Australia (4 and up)   **994**

Meisel, Paul
(jt. auth) Berger, M. Why I sneeze, shiver, hiccup, and yawn   **612.7**
(il) George, J. C. How to talk to your cat
    636.8
(il) Lexau, J. M. Go away, dog   **E**
(il) Schwartz, A. Busy buzzing bumblebees and other tongue twisters   **808.88**
(il) Schwartz, D. M. On beyond a million
    513
(il) Shields, C. D. Lunch money and other poems about school   **811**
(il) Zoehfeld, K. W. What is the world made of?   **530.4**

Meister, Cari
Tiny goes to the library. See note under Meister, C. Tiny's bath   **E**
Tiny's bath   **E**
When Tiny was tiny. See note under Meister, C. Tiny's bath   **E**

Melcher, Frederic Gershom, 1879-1963
See/See also pages in the following book(s):
Newbery Medal books, 1922-1955 p1-5
    028.5

Mella. Mayer, M.
In Mayer, M. Women warriors p55-59
    398

Melmed, Laura Krauss
Little Oh   **E**

Meltzer, Milton, 1915-
Carl Sandburg (5 and up)   **92**
Driven from the land (4 and up)   **978**
Hold your horses (4 and up)   **636.1**
Langston Hughes (6 and up)   **92**
Never to forget: the Jews of the Holocaust (6 and up)   **940.53**
Rescue: the story of how Gentiles saved Jews in the Holocaust (6 and up)   **940.53**
Ten queens (5 and up)   **920**
Weapons & warfare (5 and up)   **355**
Witches and witch-hunts (4 and up)   **133.4**
(ed) The American revolutionaries: a history in their own words, 1750-1800. See The American revolutionaries: a history in their own words, 1750-1800   **973.3**
(ed) The Black Americans: a history in their own words, 1619-1983. See The Black Americans: a history in their own words, 1619-1983   **305.8**
(ed) The Jewish Americans: a history in their own words, 1650-1950. See The Jewish Americans: a history in their own words, 1650-1950   **305.8**

The **mermaid's** twin sister. Joseph, L.
In Joseph, L. The mermaid's twin sister: more stories from Trinidad p10-17 **398.2**

The **mermaid's** twin sister: more stories from Trinidad. Joseph, L. **398.2**

Merriam, Eve, 1916-1992
12 ways to get to 11 (k-3) **510**
Bam, bam, bam (k-2) **811**
Halloween A B C (k-2) **811**
You be good and I'll be night: jump-on-the-bed poems (k-2) **811**

Merriam-Webster's biographical dictionary **920.003**

Merriam-Webster's elementary dictionary (4-6) **423**

Merriam-Webster's intermediate dictionary (6 and up) **423**

Merrill, Christine Herman
(il) George, J. C. There's an owl in the shower **Fic**

Merrill, Jean, 1923-
The Girl Who Loved Caterpillars **E**
The pushcart war (5 and up) **Fic**
The toothpaste millionaire (4-6) **Fic**

A **merry** Christmas. Hackett, W.
In The Big book of Christmas plays p332-48 **808.82**

Merry Christmas, Amelia Bedelia. Parish, P. See note under Parish, P. Amelia Bedelia **E**

Merry Christmas, Geraldine. Keller, H. See note under Keller, H. Geraldine's blanket **E**

Merry Christmas, Strega Nona. De Paola, T. See note under De Paola, T. Strega Nona: an old tale **E**

Merry-go-round. Heller, R. **428**

Mesmerism *See* Hypnotism

Mesopotamia *See* Iraq

Messages in the mailbox. Leedy, L. **808**

Messenger, Norman
(il) Mayne, W. Hob and the goblins **Fic**

A **messenger** from the World to Come. Schwartz, H.
In Schwartz, H. A journey to paradise and other Jewish tales p36-37 **398.2**

Messenger, messenger. Burleigh, R. **E**

The **messenger** to Maftam. Courlander, H.
In Courlander, H. Cow-tail switch, and other West African stories p79-86 **398.2**

Messiness *See* Cleanliness

Metals
See also Aluminum

Meteorology
See also Climate; Droughts; Weather; Weather forecasting
Cole, J. The magic school bus inside a hurricane (2-4) **551.55**
Kahl, J. D. National Audubon Society first field guide: weather (4 and up) **551.5**
Simon, S. Weather (3-6) **551.5**

Meteors
Aronson, B. Meteors (4 and up) **523.5**
Marsh, C. S. Asteroids, comets, and meteors (4-6) **523.6**

Simon, S. Comets, meteors, and asteroids (3-6) **523.6**
Vogt, G. Asteroids, comets, and meteors (2-4) **523.6**

Meteors. Aronson, B. **523.5**

Metropolitan cow. Egan, T. **E**

Metropolitan Museum of Art (New York, N.Y.)
Curious cats in art and poetry. See Curious cats in art and poetry **808.81**
Go in and out the window. See Go in and out the window **782.42**
Songs of the Wild West. See Songs of the Wild West **782.42**
Talking to the sun: an illustrated anthology of poems for young people. See Talking to the sun: an illustrated anthology of poems for young people **808.81**
Fiction
Konigsburg, E. L. From the mixed-up files of Mrs. Basil E. Frankweiler (4-6) **Fic**
Weitzman, J. P. You can't take a balloon into the Metropolitan Museum **E**

Mettger, Zak
Reconstruction (5 and up) **973.8**

Metz, Gail Junion- *See* Junion-Metz, Gail, 1947-

The **Mexican** American family album. Hoobler, D. **305.8**

Mexican Americans
Ancona, G. Barrio **305.8**
Atkin, S. B. Voices from the fields (5 and up) **331.5**
Garza, C. L. In my family (k-3) **305.8**
Hoobler, D. The Mexican American family album (5 and up) **305.8**
Hoyt-Goldsmith, D. Migrant worker (3-5) **331.5**
Biography
Herrera, J. F. The upside down boy (k-3) **92**
Fiction
Anaya, R. A. Farolitos for Abuelo **E**
Anaya, R. A. The farolitos of Christmas **E**
Bulla, C. R. The Paint Brush Kid (2-4) **Fic**
Dorros, A. Radio Man. Don Radio **E**
Jiménez, F. The circuit: stories from the life of a migrant child (5 and up) **S C**
Mora, P. Tomás and the library lady **E**
Pérez, A. I. My very own room **E**
Soto, G. Baseball in April, and other stories (5 and up) **S C**
Soto, G. Petty crimes (5 and up) **S C**
Soto, G. Snapshots from the wedding **E**
Soto, G. Too many tamales **E**
Stanek, M. I speak English for my mom (2-4) **Fic**
Poetry
Ada, A. F. Gathering the sun (2-4) **811**
Soto, G. Canto familiar (4-6) **811**
Social life and customs
Garza, C. L. Magic windows **305.8**
Hoyt-Goldsmith, D. Day of the Dead (3-5) **394.26**
King, E. Quinceañera (5 and up) **392**

Mexican artists *See* Artists, Mexican

Michigan—*Continued*
Hintz, M. Michigan
   In America the beautiful, second series
      973

Fiction
Polacco, P. Mrs. Mack   **E**
Mick Harte was here. Park, B.   **Fic**
Micklethwait, Lucy
   A child's book of art: discover great paintings
   (3-6)   **701**
   A child's book of art: great pictures, first words
   (k-2)   **701**
   A child's book of play in art (k-3) **701**
   I spy a freight train: transportation in art. See
   note under Micklethwait, L. I spy: an alpha-
   bet in art   **E**
   I spy a lion: animals in art. See note under
   Micklethwait, L. I spy: an alphabet in art
      E
   I spy: an alphabet in art   **E**
   I spy two eyes: numbers in art. See note under
   Micklethwait, L. I spy: an alphabet in art
      E
Microaliens. Tomb, H.   **502.8**
Microbes *See* Bacteria
Micromonsters. Maynard, C.   **579**
Microorganisms
   See also Bacteria
   Maynard, C. Micromonsters (2-4) **579**
Microscopes
   See also Electron microscopes
   Cobb, V. Dirt & grime, like you've never seen
   (4-6)   **502.8**
   Levine, S. Fun with your microscope **502.8**
Micucci, Charles
   The life and times of the apple (2-4) **634**
   The life and times of the honeybee (2-4)
      595.7
   The life and times of the peanut (2-4)
      641.3
Midas (Legendary character)
   Craft, C. King Midas and the golden touch
      398.2
   Mark, J. The Midas touch   **398.2**
   Stewig, J. W. King Midas   **398.2**
The Midas touch. Mark, J.   **398.2**
Middle Ages
   See also Medieval civilization; World his-
   tory—15th century
   Corbishley, M. The Middle Ages (5 and up)
      940.1
   Crossley-Holland, K. The world of King Arthur
   and his court (5 and up) **942.01**
   Hart, A. Knights & castles (4 and up)
      940.1
   Nikola-Lisa, W. Till year's good end (2-4)
      942.02
Fiction
   Branford, H. Fire, bed, & bone (5 and up)
      Fic
   Cushman, K. Catherine, called Birdy (6 and up)
      Fic
   Cushman, K. The midwife's apprentice (6 and
   up)   **Fic**

De Angeli, M. L. The door in the wall (4-6)
      Fic
Lindgren, A. Ronia, the robber's daughter (4-6)
      Fic
Platt, R. Castle diary (4 and up) **Fic**
Temple, F. The Ramsay scallop (6 and up)
      Fic
Vining, E. G. Adam of the road (5 and up)
      Fic
Williams, L. E. The executioner's daughter (6
   and up)   **Fic**
Middle and junior high school library catalog
      011.6
Middle East
   See also Arab countries
Folklore
   See Folklore—Middle East
The **middle** Moffat. Estes, E. See note under Es-
   tes, E. The Moffats   **Fic**
Middle West
   Geisert, B. Prairie town   **E**
Poetry
   Sandburg, C. Grassroots   **811**
Middleplots 4. Gillespie, J. T.   **028.5**
The **midnight** fox. Byars, B. C.   **Fic**
The **midnight** horse. Fleischman, S.   **Fic**
Midnight magic. Avi   **Fic**
The **midnight** mass of the Dead. San Souci, R.
   In San Souci, R. Short & shivery p53-57
      398.2
A **midsummer** night's dream, William Shake-
   speare's. Coville, B.   **822.3**
Midwest *See* Middle West
Midwifery *See* Midwives
The **midwife's** apprentice. Cushman, K. **Fic**
Midwives
Fiction
   Cushman, K. The midwife's apprentice (6 and
   up)   **Fic**
Mieko and the fifth treasure. Coerr, E. **Fic**
Migdale, Lawrence
   (il) Hoyt-Goldsmith, D. Apache rodeo
      970.004
   (il) Hoyt-Goldsmith, D. Arctic hunter
      970.004
   (il) Hoyt-Goldsmith, D. Buffalo days
      970.004
   (il) Hoyt-Goldsmith, D. Celebrating Chinese
   New Year   **394.26**
   (il) Hoyt-Goldsmith, D. Celebrating Hanukkah
      296.4
   (il) Hoyt-Goldsmith, D. Celebrating Passover
      296.4
   (il) Hoyt-Goldsmith, D. Day of the Dead
      394.26
   (il) Hoyt-Goldsmith, D. Hoang Anh **305.8**
   (il) Hoyt-Goldsmith, D. Lacrosse **796.34**
   (il) Hoyt-Goldsmith, D. Mardi Gras: a Cajun
   country celebration **394.25**
   (il) Hoyt-Goldsmith, D. Migrant worker
      331.5
   (il) Hoyt-Goldsmith, D. Las Posadas
      394.26

Miller, Elizabeth B.
The Internet resource directory for K-12 teachers and librarians **004.6**

Miller, Gustaf
(il) Ziefert, H. Hats off for the Fourth of July! **E**

Miller, Helen L.
A Christmas promise
In The Big book of Christmas plays p99-117 **808.82**

Red carpet Christmas
In The Big book of Christmas plays p3-25 **808.82**

Miller, Joseph
(ed) Sears list of subject headings. See Sears list of subject headings **025.4**

Miller, Marc, 1957-
Fundamental tennis (5 and up) **796.342**

Miller, Marcia
(il) Math for the very young. See Math for the very young **793.7**

Miller, Margaret, 1945-
Big and little **E**
Guess who? **E**
My five senses **E**
Who uses this? **E**
Whose shoe? **E**
(il) Cole, J. How you were born **612.6**
(il) Cole, J. My new kitten **636.8**
(il) Cole, J. My puppy is born **636.7**
(il) Cole, J. The new baby at your house **306.8**
(il) Scott, E. Adventure in space **522**
(il) Scott, E. Friends! **158**
(il) Scott, E. Twins! **306.8**

Miller, Marilyn Lea
(comp) School Library Journal's best. See School Library Journal's best **027.8**

Miller, Sara Swan
Three more stories you can read to your dog **E**

Three stories you can read to your cat. See note under Miller, S. S. Three more stories you can read to your dog **E**
Three stories you can read to your dog. See note under Miller, S. S. Three more stories you can read to your dog **E**

Miller, William, 1959-
Frederick Douglass (1-3) **92**
Night golf **E**
The piano **E**
Richard Wright and the library card **E**
Zora Hurston and the chinaberry tree (k-3) **92**

The **miller,** the boy and the donkey. Wildsmith, B. **398.2**

Millinery *See* Hats

Million (The number)
Schwartz, D. M. How much is a million? **E**

A **million** fish—more or less. McKissack, P. C. **E**

Millions of cats. Gág, W. **E**

Millipedeology. Ross, M. E. **595.6**

Millipedes
Ross, M. E. Millipedeology (3-6) **595.6**

Millman, Isaac
Moses goes to a concert. See note under Millman, I. Moses goes to school **E**
Moses goes to school **E**

Mills, Billy, 1938-
See/See also pages in the following book(s):
Knapp, R. Top 10 American men's Olympic gold medalists (4 and up) **920**

Mills, Claudia, 1954-
Gus and Grandpa. See note under Mills, C. Gus and Grandpa and the two-wheeled bike **E**

Gus and Grandpa and show-and-tell. See note under Mills, C. Gus and Grandpa and the two-wheeled bike **E**
Gus and Grandpa and the Christmas cookies. See note under Mills, C. Gus and Grandpa and the two-wheeled bike **E**
Gus and Grandpa and the two-wheeled bike **E**

Gus and Grandpa at the hospital. See note under Mills, C. Gus and Grandpa and the two-wheeled bike **E**
Gus and Grandpa ride the train. See note under Mills, C. Gus and Grandpa and the two-wheeled bike **E**
You're a brave man, Julius Zimmerman (5 and up) **Fic**

Mills, Yaroslava Surmach *See* Yaroslava, 1925-

Mills
Macaulay, D. Mill (4 and up) **690**

Mills and millwork *See* Mills

Milne, A. A. (Alan Alexander), 1882-1956
The complete tales of Winnie-the-Pooh (1-4) **Fic**
The house at Pooh Corner (1-4) **Fic**
also in Milne, A. A. The complete tales of Winnie-the-Pooh p163-344 **Fic**
also in Milne, A. A. The world of Pooh p153-314 **Fic**
Now we are six (k-3) **821**
also in Milne, A. A. The world of Christopher Robin p119-234 **821**
The Pooh story book (1-4) **Fic**
When we were very young (k-3) **821**
also in Milne, A. A. The world of Christopher Robin p1-118 **821**
Winnie-the-Pooh (1-4) **Fic**
also in Milne, A. A. The complete tales of Winnie-the-Pooh p1-159 **Fic**
also in Milne, A. A. The world of Pooh p7-149 **Fic**
The world of Christopher Robin (k-3) **821**
The world of Pooh (1-4) **Fic**

Milne, Alan Alexander *See* Milne, A. A. (Alan Alexander), 1882-1956

Milone, Karen *See* Dugan, Karen

Milord, Susan, 1954-
Mexico! **972**

Minard, Rosemary, 1939-
(ed) Womenfolk and fairy tales. See Womenfolk and fairy tales **398.2**

Minarik, Else Holmelund
Father Bear comes home. See note under
Minarik, E. H. Little Bear   **E**
A kiss for Little Bear. See note under Minarik,
E. H. Little Bear   **E**
Little Bear   **E**
Little Bear goes to the moon
In The Read-aloud treasury p70-83   **808.8**
Little Bear's friend. See note under Minarik, E.
H. Little Bear   **E**
Little Bear's visit. See note under Minarik, E.
H. Little Bear   **E**
No fighting, no biting!   **E**
Mind over matter. (5 and up) See entry in Part 2:
Web Resources
Mine, all mine. Heller, R.   **428**
Minerals
Ricciuti, E. R. National Audubon Society first
field guide: rocks and minerals (4 and up)
    552
Symes, R. F. Rocks & minerals (4 and up)
    549
VanCleave, J. P. Janice VanCleave's rocks and
minerals (4 and up)   **552**
Miners
    Fiction
Lyon, G. E. Mama is a miner   **E**
Wiseman, D. Jeremy Visick (5 and up)   **Fic**
Minerva Louise. Stoeke, J. M. See note under
Stoeke, J. M. A hat for Minerva Louise
    E
Minerva Louise at school. Stoeke, J. M. See note
under Stoeke, J. M. A hat for Minerva Louise
    E
Minerva Louise at the fair. Stoeke, J. M. See note
under Stoeke, J. M. A hat for Minerva Louise
    E
Mines and mineral resources
    See also Coal mines and mining
Mine's the best. Bonsall, C. N.   **E**
Ming Lo moves the mountain. Lobel, A.   **E**
Minkel, Walter
Delivering Web reference services to young
people   **025.04**
How to do "The three bears" with two hands
    791.5
Minnesota
Hintz, M. Minnesota
In America the beautiful, second series
    973
Schwabacher, M. Minnesota
In Celebrate the states   **973**
    Fiction
Lasky, K. Marven of the Great North Woods
    E
Lovelace, M. H. Betsy-Tacy (2-4)   **Fic**
Paulsen, G. The winter room (5 and up)
    Fic
Minor, Wendell
Grand Canyon (4 and up)   **758**
(il) Brisson, P. Sky memories   **Fic**
(il) George, J. C. Everglades   **975.9**
(il) George, J. C. Julie   **Fic**
(il) George, J. C. Julie's wolf pack   **Fic**

(il) George, J. C. Morning, noon, and night
    E
(il) George, J. C. Snow Bear   **E**
(il) Sandburg, C. Grassroots   **811**
(il) Schertle, A. A lucky thing   **811**
(il) Siebert, D. Mojave   **811**
(il) Siebert, D. Sierra   **811**
(il) Zolotow, C. The seashore book   **E**
Minorities
    See also Ethnic relations
    Bibliography
Kaleidoscope   **011.6**
Rochman, H. Against borders   **011.6**
Minotaur (Greek mythology)
Fisher, L. E. Theseus and the Minotaur (3-5)
    292
Hutton, W. Theseus and the Minotaur (3-5)
    292
Minstrels
    Fiction
Vining, E. G. Adam of the road (5 and up)
    Fic
Minter, Daniel
(il) Coleman, E. The riches of Oseola McCarty
    92
Minty: a story of young Harriet Tubman.
Schroeder, A.   **E**
The **miracle.** Kimmel, E. A.
In Kimmel, E. A. The adventures of Hershel
of Ostropol p32-36   **398.2**
The **miracle** at King David's tomb. Schwartz, H.
In Schwartz, H. Next year in Jerusalem p39-
43   **296.1**
The **miracle** doctor. Fang, L.
In Fang, L. The Ch'i-lin purse p85-100
    398.2
Miracle in Tent City. Jiménez, F.
In Jiménez, F. The circuit: stories from the
life of a migrant child p27-44   **S C**
The **miracle** of Our Lady of Guadalupe. Delacre,
L.
In Delacre, L. Golden tales p41-43   **398.2**
The **miracle** of the potato latkes. Penn, M.   **E**
Miracles
    Fiction
De Paola, T. The clown of God (k-3)
    398.2
The **miracles** of Jesus. De Paola, T.   **232.9**
Miracles on the sea. Jaffe, N.
In Jaffe, N. The uninvited guest and other
Jewish holiday tales p18-22   **296.4**
The **miraculous** pipe. Afanas'ev, A. N.
In Afanas'ev, A. N. Russian fairy tales p425-
27   **398.2**
Miranda, Anne, 1954-
To market, to market   **E**
Mirandy and Brother Wind. McKissack, P. C.
    E
Mirette & Bellini cross Niagra Falls. McCully, E.
A. See note under McCully, E. A. Mirette on
the high wire   **E**
Mirette on the high wire. McCully, E. A.   **E**

Miriam (Biblical figure)
About
Manushkin, F. Miriam's cup (k-3)   **222**
Miriam's cup. Manushkin, F.   **222**
Mirocha, Paul
(il) Berger, M. Oil spill!   **363.7**
(il) Gans, R. How do birds find their way?
   598
The **mirror**. Kadono, E.
In Don't read this! and other tales of the un-
natural p85-109   **S C**
A **mirror,** a carpet, and a lemon. Walker, B. K.
In Walker, B. K. A treasury of Turkish folk-
tales for children p132-34   **398.2**
The **mirror** of Merlin. Barron, T. A. See note un-
der Barron, T. A. The lost years of Merlin
   Fic
Miscegenation *See* Racially mixed people
Miscellaneous facts *See* Curiosities and wonders
The **miser**. Afanas'ev, A. N.
In Afanas'ev, A. N. Russian fairy tales p58-
59   **398.2**
The **miserable** mill. Snicket, L. See note under
Snicket, L. The bad beginning   **Fic**
Misery. Afanas'ev, A. N.
In Afanas'ev, A. N. Russian fairy tales p20-
24   **398.2**
Miskito Indians *See* Mosquito Indians
Misoso. Aardema, V.   **398.2**
Miss Bindergarten celebrates the 100th day of kin-
dergarten. Slate, J.   **E**
Miss Bindergarten gets ready for kindergarten.
Slate, J. See note under Slate, J. Miss
Bindergarten celebrates the 100th day of kin-
dergarten   **E**
Miss Bindergarten stays home from kindergarten.
Slate, J. See note under Slate, J. Miss
Bindergarten celebrates the 100th day of kin-
dergarten   **E**
Miss Bindergarten's craft center. Slate, J. See note
under Slate, J. Miss Bindergarten celebrates
the 100th day of kindergarten   **E**
Miss Jones. Marshall, J.
In Marshall, J. Rats on the roof, and other
stories p63-79   **S C**
Miss Lin, the sea goddess. Carpenter, F.
In Carpenter, F. Tales of a Chinese grand-
mother p235-41   **398.2**
Miss Liza and the king
In Stockings of buttermilk: American folktales
p104-11   **398.2**
Miss Mary Mack. Hoberman, M. A.   **398.8**
Miss Mary Mack and other children's street
rhymes   **796.1**
Miss Mouse. Marshall, J.
In Marshall, J. Rats on the range and other
stories p7-23   **S C**
Miss Nelson has a field day. Allard, H. See note
under Allard, H. Miss Nelson is missing!
   E
Miss Nelson is back. Allard, H. See note under
Allard, H. Miss Nelson is missing!   **E**

Miss Nelson is missing!. Allard, H.   **E**
Miss Rumphius. Cooney, B.   **E**
Missing children
See also Runaway children
Missing May. Rylant, C.   **Fic**
The **missing** mitten mystery. Kellogg, S.   **E**
Missing persons
See also Runaway teenagers
Mission: addition. Leedy, L.   **513**
Missions
Fiction
Politi, L. Song of the swallows   **E**
Missions, Christian *See* Christian missions
Mississippi
George, C. Mississippi
In America the beautiful, second series
   973
Shirley, D. Mississippi
In Celebrate the states   **973**
Fiction
Taulbert, C. L. Little Cliff and the porch people
   E
Taylor, M. D. The friendship (4 and up)
   Fic
Taylor, M. D. Let the circle be unbroken (4 and
up)   **Fic**
Taylor, M. D. Mississippi bridge (4 and up)
   Fic
Taylor, M. D. The road to Memphis (4 and up)
   Fic
Taylor, M. D. Roll of thunder, hear my cry (4
and up)   **Fic**
Taylor, M. D. Song of the trees (4 and up)
   Fic
Taylor, M. D. The well (4 and up)   **Fic**
Mississippi bridge. Taylor, M. D.   **Fic**
Mississippi mud. Turner, A. W.   **811**
Mississippi River
Harness, C. Mark Twain and the queens of the
Mississippi (3-5)   **92**
Lauber, P. Flood (4 and up)   **551.48**
Fiction
Twain, M. The adventures of Huckleberry Finn
(5 and up)   **Fic**
Twain, M. The adventures of Tom Sawyer (5
and up)   **Fic**
Mississippi River valley
Hiscock, B. The big rivers (2-4)   **551.48**
Mississippi valley *See* Mississippi River valley
Missouri
Bennett, M. Missouri
In Celebrate the states   **973**
Hintz, M. Missouri
In America the beautiful, second series
   973
Fiction
Twain, M. The adventures of Huckleberry Finn
(5 and up)   **Fic**
Twain, M. The adventures of Tom Sawyer (5
and up)   **Fic**
Missouri River valley
Description
Freedman, R. An Indian winter (6 and up)
   978

The **Monkey** who asked for Misery
In The Magic orange tree, and other Haitian
folktales p113-16 **398.2**

Monkeys

See also Baboons

Fiction

Christelow, E. Five little monkeys jumping on
the bed **E**
Koller, J. F. One monkey too many **E**
Rey, H. A. Curious George **E**
Slobodkina, E. Caps for sale **E**

Monroe, Joan Kiddell- *See* Kiddell-Monroe, Joan,
1908-1972

Monson, Dianne L., 1934-
(jt. auth) Sutherland, Z. Children and books
028.5

The **monster** garden. Alcock, V. **Fic**

The **monster** in Harry's backyard. Ruelle, K. G.
See note under Ruelle, K. G. The Thanksgiving beast feast **E**

The **monster** in the third dresser drawer and other
stories about Adam Joshua. Smith, J. L. See
note under Smith, J. L. The kid next door and
other headaches **Fic**

Monster machines. Bingham, C. **621.8**

Monster mama. Rosenberg, L. **E**

The **monster** of Baylock. San Souci, R.
In San Souci, R. Even more short & shivery
p70-75 **398.2**

Monster poems (1-4) **821.008**

The **monster** with emerald teeth. McCaughrean,
G.
In McCaughrean, G. The bronze cauldron:
myths and legends of the world p116-20
398.2

Monsters

Fiction

Alcock, V. The monster garden (4 and up)
Fic
Crowe, R. L. Clyde monster **E**
Del Negro, J. Lucy Dove **E**
Drescher, H. Simon's book **E**
Emberley, E. Go away, big green monster!
E
Hutchins, P. Where's the baby? **E**
Rosenberg, L. Monster mama **E**
Viorst, J. My mama says there aren't any zom-
bies, ghosts, vampires, creatures, demons,
monsters, fiends, goblins, or things **E**

Poetry

Monster poems (1-4) **821.008**
Prelutsky, J. The gargoyle on the roof (2-5)
811
Prelutsky, J. The Headless Horseman rides tonight (2-5) **811**
Prelutsky, J. Nightmares: poems to trouble your
sleep (2-5) **811**

Montana, Joe
See/See also pages in the following book(s):
Sullivan, G. Quarterbacks! p24-26 (5 and up)
920

Montana
George, C. Montana
In America the beautiful, second series
973

**Montezuma II, Emperor of Mexico, ca. 1480-
1520**

About

Kimmel, E. A. Montezuma and the fall of the
Aztecs (3-5) **972**

Montezuma and the fall of the Aztecs. Kimmel,
E. A. **972**

Montgomerie, Norah Mary, 1913-
Babushka and the three wise men
In Christmas fairy tales p89-90 **398.2**

Montgomery, L. M. (Lucy Maud), 1874-1942
Anne of Avonlea. See note under Montgomery,
L. M. Anne of Green Gables **Fic**
Anne of Green Gables (5 and up) **Fic**
Anne of Ingleside. See note under Montgomery,
L. M. Anne of Green Gables **Fic**
Anne of the island. See note under Mont-
gomery, L. M. Anne of Green Gables
Fic
Anne of Windy Poplars. See note under Mont-
gomery, L. M. Anne of Green Gables
Fic
Anne's house of dreams. See note under Mont-
gomery, L. M. Anne of Green Gables
Fic

Montgomery, Lucy Maud *See* Montgomery, L.
M. (Lucy Maud), 1874-1942

Montgomery, Sy
The snake scientist (4 and up) **597.9**

Months

Fiction

Lobel, A. One lighthouse, one moon **E**
Tafuri, N. Snowy flowy blowy **E**

Poetry

Otten, C. F. January rides the wind (k-3)
811
Prelutsky, J. Dog days (k-1) **811**
Updike, J. A child's calendar **811**

Monticello. Fisher, L. E. **975.5**

Monticello. Richards, N. **975.5**

Montresor, Beni, 1926-
(il) De Regniers, B. S. May I bring a friend?
E

Moominland midwinter. Jansson, T. See note under Jansson, T. Moominsummer madness
Fic

Moominpapa at sea. Jansson, T. See note under
Jansson, T. Moominsummer madness **Fic**

Moominpapa's memoirs. Jansson, T. See note under Jansson, T. Moominsummer madness
Fic

Moominsummer madness. Jansson, T. **Fic**

Moon
Branley, F. M. The moon seems to change (k-3)
523.3
Branley, F. M. What the moon is like (k-3)
523.3
Bredeson, C. The moon (4 and up) **523.3**
Gibbons, G. The moon book (k-3) **523.3**

Moon—*Continued*

Exploration

Cole, M. D. Moon base (4 and up)   **629.4**

Vogt, G. Apollo moonwalks (4 and up)
   629.45

Fiction

Banks, K. And if the moon could talk   **E**

Daly, N. Why the Sun & Moon live in the sky (k-3)   **398.2**

Dayrell, E. Why the Sun and the Moon live in the sky (k-3)   **398.2**

Ehlert, L. Moon rope. Un lazo a la luna (k-3)   **398.2**

Tafuri, N. What the sun sees   **E**

Moon, Voyages to *See* Space flight to the moon

The **moon**. Bredeson, C.   **523.3**

The **moon** and I. Byars, B. C.   **92**

Moon base. Cole, M. D.   **629.4**

Moon bases *See* Lunar bases

The **moon** book. Gibbons, G.   **523.3**

The **moon** by night. L'Engle, M. See note under L'Engle, M. Meet the Austins   **Fic**

Moon rope. Un lazo a la luna. Ehlert, L.
   398.2

The **moon** seems to change. Branley, F. M.
   523.3

Moonbear's dream. Asch, F.   **E**

Moonbear's pet. Asch, F. See note under Asch, F. Moonbear's dream   **E**

Mooncake. Asch, F. See note under Asch, F. Moonbear's dream   **E**

Moondance. Asch, F. See note under Asch, F. Moonbear's dream   **E**

Mooney, James, 1861-1921

Grandmother Spider

In From sea to shining sea p12-13   **810.8**

Moongame. Asch, F. See note under Asch, F. Moonbear's dream   **E**

The **moonlight** man. Wright, B. R.   **Fic**

The **moorchild**. McGraw, E. J.   **Fic**

Moore, Ann

See/See also pages in the following book(s):

Thimmesh, C. Girls think of everything (5 and up)   **920**

Moore, Barbara, 1934-

(jt. auth) Thomson, P. The nine-ton cat: behind the scenes at an art museum   **708**

Moore, Bobbie, 1944-

(il) King, D. C. Colonial days   **973.2**

Moore, Clement Clarke, 1779-1863

The night before Christmas (k-3)   **811**

Moore, Ella Sheppard, 1851-1914

Fiction

Hopkinson, D. A band of angels   **E**

Moore, Lilian, 1909-

(jt. auth) Charlip, R. Hooray for me!   **E**

Moose

DuTemple, L. A. North American moose (3-6)
   599.65

Fiction

Van Laan, N. Moose tales   **E**

Wiseman, B. Morris and Boris at the circus
   E

Moose tales. Van Laan, N.   **E**

Mora, Pat

This big sky   **811**

Tomás and the library lady   **E**

Uno, dos, tres: one, two, three   **E**

Moragne, Wendy

New Jersey

In Celebrate the states   **973**

Moral and philosophic stories *See* Fables

Moral philosophy *See* Ethics

Morales, Rodolfo, 1925-2001

See/See also pages in the following book(s):

Just like me p16-17   **920**

Mordan, C. B.

(il) Fleischman, P. Lost!   **Fic**

(il) Murrow, L. K. Orphan journey home
   Fic

Mordvinoff, Nicolas, 1911-1973

See/See also pages in the following book(s):

Caldecott Medal books, 1938-1957 p230-41
   028.5

More about Paddington. Bond, M. See note under Bond, M. A bear called Paddington   **Fic**

More adventures of the Great Brain. Fitzgerald, J. D. See note under Fitzgerald, J. D. The Great Brain   **Fic**

More Alex and the cat. Griffith, H. V.

In Griffith, H. V. Alex and the cat   **Fic**

More all-of-a-kind family. Taylor, S. See note under Taylor, S. All-of-a-kind family   **Fic**

More books kids will sit still for. Freeman, J.
   011.6

"**More** more more" said the baby. Williams, V. B.
   E

A **more** perfect union. Maestro, B.   **342**

More reading connections. Knowles, E.   **028.5**

More riddles. Cerf, B.

In Cerf, B. Riddles and more riddles!
   793.73

More scary stories to tell in the dark. Schwartz, A.   **398.2**

More short & shivery. San Souci, R.   **398.2**

More stories Huey tells. Cameron, A. See note under Cameron, A. The stories Julian tells
   Fic

More stories Julian tells. Cameron, A. See note under Cameron, A. The stories Julian tells
   Fic

More stories to solve. Shannon, G.   **398.2**

More tales of Amanda Pig. Van Leeuwen, J. See note under Van Leeuwen, J. Tales of Oliver Pig   **E**

More tales of Oliver Pig. Van Leeuwen, J. See note under Van Leeuwen, J. Tales of Oliver Pig   **E**

More tales of Uncle Remus. Lester, J. See note under Lester, J. The last tales of Uncle Remus   **398.2**

More than anything else. Bradby, M.   **E**

Morell, Abelardo

(il) Carroll, L. Alice's adventures in Wonderland
   Fic

Moses (Biblical figure)
About
Chaikin, M. Exodus (2-4)   **222**
Fisher, L. E. Moses (k-3)   **222**
Wildsmith, B. Exodus   **222**

Moses, Anna Mary Robertson *See* Moses, Grandma, 1860-1961

Moses, Edwin
See/See also pages in the following book(s):
Knapp, R. Top 10 American men's Olympic gold medalists (4 and up)   **920**

Moses, Grandma, 1860-1961
About
Oneal, Z. Grandma Moses: painter of rural America (4 and up)   **92**

Moses goes to a concert. Millman, I. See note under Millman, I. Moses goes to school   **E**

Moses goes to school. Millman, I.   **E**

Moses supposes his toeses are roses and 7 other silly old rhymes. Patz, N.   **398.8**

Moses the kitten. Herriot, J.   **E**

Moslem countries *See* Islamic countries

Moslemism *See* Islam

The **mosquito** and the water buffalo. Walker, B. K.
In Walker, B. K. A treasury of Turkish folktales for children p14   **398.2**

Mosquito Indians
Folklore
Rohmer, H. The invisible hunters (2-4)   **398.2**

Mosquitoes
Fiction
Aardema, V. Why mosquitoes buzz in people's ears (k-3)   **398.2**
Gershator, P. Zzzng! Zzzng! Zzzng! (k-3)   **398.2**

Moss, Carol (Carol Marie)
Science in ancient Mesopotamia (4 and up)   **509**

Moss, Cynthia
About
Pringle, L. P. Elephant woman (4 and up)   **599.67**

Moss, Francis
(jt. auth) Pedersen, T. Internet for kids!   **004.6**

Moss, Lloyd
Zin! zin! zin! a violin   **E**

Moss, Marissa
(il) Schwartz, D. M. G is for googol   **510**

Moss gown. Hooks, W. H.   **398.2**

Moss pillows. Wells, R.   **E**

Mossflower. Jacques, B. See note under Jacques, B. Redwall   **Fic**

Most, Bernard, 1937-
ABC T-Rex   **E**
How big were the dinosaurs   **E**
Whatever happened to the dinosaurs?   **E**

The **most** amazing dinosaur. Stevenson, J.   **E**

The **most** beautiful roof in the world. Lasky, K.   **577.3**

The **most** excellent book of how to be a clown. Perkins, C.   **791.3**

The **most** excellent book of how to be a juggler. Mitchelson, M.   **793.8**

The **most** precious thing. Jaffe, N.
In Jaffe, N. While standing on one foot p26-32   **296.1**

The **most** useful slave. Hamilton, V.
In Hamilton, V. The people could fly: American black folktales p160-65   **398.2**

The **most** wonderful egg in the world. Heine, H.   **E**

Motels *See* Hotels and motels

Moth, the fire dancer. Caduto, M. J.
In Caduto, M. J. Keepers of the night p43-45   **398.2**

Mother and child *See* Mother-child relationship

Mother and daughter. Soto, G.
In Soto, G. Baseball in April, and other stories p60-68   **S C**

The **mother** and death. San Souci, R.
In San Souci, R. A terrifying taste of short & shivery p141-45   **398.2**

Mother-child relationship
Fiction
Appelt, K. Oh my baby, little one   **E**
Peacock, C. A. Mommy far, Mommy near   **E**
Scott, A. H. On Mother's lap   **E**
Waddell, M. Rosie's babies   **E**

Mother-daughter relationship
Fiction
Best, C. Red light, green light, mama and me   **E**
Bradby, M. Momma, where are you from?   **E**
Brisson, P. Sky memories (3-5)   **Fic**
Conrad, P. Zoe rising (5 and up)   **Fic**
Gray, L. M. My mama had a dancing heart   **E**
Johnson, A. Tell me a story, Mama   **E**
Johnston, T. The quilt story   **E**
Joosse, B. M. Mama, do you love me?   **E**
Loh, M. J. Tucking Mommy in   **E**
Lyon, G. E. Mama is a miner   **E**
MacLachlan, P. Mama One, Mama Two   **E**
Madrigal, A. H. Erandi's braids   **E**
Pomerantz, C. The chalk doll   **E**
Reiser, L. Cherry pies and lullabies   **E**
Reiser, L. Tortillas and lullabies. Tortillas y cancioncitas   **E**
Rodowsky, C. F. Hannah in between (5 and up)   **Fic**
Russo, M. Mama talks too much   **E**
Stanek, M. I speak English for my mom (2-4)   **Fic**
Winthrop, E. Promises   **E**

Mother Goose
The Arnold Lobel book of Mother Goose
398.8
The Comic adventures of Old Mother Hubbard
and her dog **398.8**
The Glorious Mother Goose **398.8**
Here comes Mother Goose **398.8**
James Marshall's Mother Goose **398.8**
My very first Mother Goose **398.8**
The Real Mother Goose **398.8**
Sylvia Long's Mother Goose **398.8**
Tomie dePaola's Mother Goose **398.8**
Mother Goose [illus. by Brian Wildsmith]
398.8
Mother Goose time. Marino, J. **027.62**
Mother Jones See Jones, Mother, 1830-1930
The **mother** of Karaikkal. Krishnaswami, U.
In Krishnaswami, U. Shower of gold: girls
and women in the stories of India p36-40
398.2
Mother of the waters
In The Magic orange tree, and other Haitian
folktales p151-56 **398.2**
Mother-son relationship
Fiction
McKissack, P. C. Ma Dear's aprons **E**
Mills, C. You're a brave man, Julius
Zimmerman (5 and up) **Fic**
Rosenberg, L. Monster mama **E**
Say, A. Tree of cranes **E**
Zolotow, C. The seashore book **E**
Mothers
Carrick, C. Mothers are like that **E**
Fiction
Ackerman, K. By the dawn's early light **E**
Aliki. Welcome, little baby **E**
Browne, A. Piggybook **E**
Caseley, J. Mama, coming and going **E**
Charlip, R. Sleepytime rhyme **E**
Godard, A. Mama, across the sea **E**
Kaplan, H. Waiting to sing **E**
Numeroff, L. J. What mommies do best **E**
Schick, E. Mama **E**
Viorst, J. My mama says there aren't any zom-
bies, ghosts, vampires, creatures, demons,
monsters, fiends, goblins, or things **E**
Wells, R. Hazel's amazing mother **E**
Poetry
Wong, J. S. The rainbow hand (4-6) **811**
Mothers, Single parent See Single parent family
Mothers and daughters See Mother-daughter re-
lationship
Mothers and sons See Mother-son relationship
Mothers are like that. Carrick, C. **E**
Mother's clothes. Soto, G.
In Soto, G. Petty crimes **S C**
The **Mother's** Day mice. Bunting, E. **E**
Moths
See also Caterpillars
Arnosky, J. Crinkleroot's guide to knowing but-
terflies & moths (k-3) **595.7**
Feltwell, J. Butterflies and moths (3-5)
595.7

Still, J. Amazing butterflies & moths (2-4)
595.7
Whalley, P. E. S. Butterfly & moth (4 and up)
595.7
Motion
Cobb, V. Why doesn't the earth fall up? (3-5)
531
Motion picture actors See Actors
Motion picture photography See Cinematography
Motion pictures
Catalogs
Culturally diverse videos, audios, and CD-
ROMS for children and young adults
011.6
Fiction
Schwartz, H. Albert goes Hollywood **E**
Motivation (Psychology)
See also Wishes
Motorcycles
Bingham, C. Race car (k-3) **629.228**
Mound, L. A. (Laurence Alfred), 1934-
Insect (4 and up) **595.7**
Mound, Laurence Alfred See Mound, L. A.
(Laurence Alfred), 1934-
Mount Everest (China and Nepal)
Jenkins, S. The top of the world (2-4)
796.52
Mount Rushmore National Memorial (S.D.)
Curlee, L. Rushmore (4 and up) **730.9**
Mount Saint Helens (Wash.)
Lauber, P. Volcano: the eruption and healing of
Mount St. Helens (4 and up) **551.2**
The **mountain**. Mungoshi, C.
In Don't read this! and other tales of the un-
natural p23-32 **S C**
Mountain life
Bial, R. Mist over the mountains (4 and up)
974
Geisert, B. Mountain town **E**
Fiction
Ray, M. L. Basket moon **E**
Dowell, F. O. Dovey Coe (4 and up) **Fic**
Gibbons, F. Mama and me and the Model-T
E
Gibbons, F. Mountain wedding **E**
O'Connor, B. Me and Rupert Goody (4-6)
Fic
Mountain lions See Pumas
Mountain-making. Curry, J. L.
In Curry, J. L. Back in the beforetime p22-25
398.2
The **mountain** that moved. Schwartz, H.
In Schwartz, H. Next year in Jerusalem p10-
13 **296.1**
Mountain town. Geisert, B. **E**
Mountain wedding. Gibbons, F. **E**
Mountaineering
Jenkins, S. The top of the world (2-4)
796.52
Mountains
See also Catskill Mountains (N.Y.); Ozark
Mountains; Sierra Nevada Mountains
Simon, S. Mountains (3-6) **551.4**

Mountains—*Continued*

Zoehfeld, K. W. How mountains are made (k-3) **551.4**

Fiction

Lobel, A. Ming Lo moves the mountain **E**

The **mountains** of Tibet. Gerstein, M. **E**

Mouse *See* Mice

Mouse and mouser. Jacobs, J.
In Jacobs, J. English fairy tales p54-56 **398.2**

The **mouse** and the elephant. Walker, B. K.
In Walker, B. K. A treasury of Turkish folk-tales for children p1-3 **398.2**

The **mouse** and the motorcycle. Cleary, B. **Fic**

A **mouse** called Wolf. King-Smith, D. **Fic**

Mouse count. Walsh, E. S. **E**

Mouse in love. Kraus, R. See note under Kraus, R. Whose mouse are you? **E**

Mouse letters. Arnosky, J. **E**

Mouse mess. Riley, L. A. **E**

Mouse numbers. Arnosky, J. **E**

Mouse paint. Walsh, E. S. See note under Walsh, E. S. Mouse count **E**

Mouse party. Marshall, J.
In Marshall, J. Rats on the range and other stories p43-50 **S C**

Mouse practice. McCully, E. A. See note under McCully, E. A. Monk camps out **E**

Mouse soup. Lobel, A. **E**

Mouse tales. Lobel, A. **E**

The **mouse** tower. San Souci, R.
In San Souci, R. More short & shivery p83-87 **398.2**

Mouse views. McMillan, B. **E**

The **mouse** who got married. Marshall, J.
In Marshall, J. Rats on the roof, and other stories p29-39 **S C**

The **Mousehole** cat. Barber, A. **E**

The **mousetrap**. Olson, A. N.
In Olson, A. N. Ask the bones: scary stories from around the world p78-84 **398.2**

Mouth organs *See* Harmonicas

Moving

Fiction

Bowdish, L. Brooklyn, Bugsy, and me (3-5) **Fic**

Danziger, P. Amber Brown is not a crayon (2-4) **Fic**

Koss, A. G. The Ashwater experiment (4 and up) **Fic**

Lewis, M. Morgy makes his move (2-4) **Fic**

Patron, S. Maybe yes, maybe no, maybe maybe (3-5) **Fic**

Sharmat, M. W. Gila monsters meet you at the airport **E**

Sharmat, M. W. Mitchell is moving **E**

Williams, V. B. Scooter (3-5) **Fic**

Yep, L. The star fisher (6 and up) **Fic**

Moving a mountain. Schwartz, H.
In Schwartz, H. The diamond tree p85-92 **398.2**

Moving pictures *See* Motion pictures

Moving still. Jiménez, F.
In Jiménez, F. The circuit: stories from the life of a migrant child p113-34 **S C**

Mowat, Farley

Owls in the family (4 and up) **636.6**

Mowglie's song. Kipling, R.
In Kipling, R. The jungle book: the Mowgli stories **S C**

Mowglie's song gainst people. Kipling, R.
In Kipling, R. The jungle book: the Mowgli stories **S C**

Mowgli's brothers. Kipling, R.
In Kipling, R. The jungle book: the Mowgli stories **S C**

Moxley, Sheila

(il) Anholt, L. Stone girl, bone girl: the story of Mary Anning **92**

(il) Philip, N. The Arabian nights **398.2**

Mozambique

Fiction

Farmer, N. A girl named Disaster (6 and up) **Fic**

Mozart, Johann Chrysostom Wolfgang Amadeus *See* Mozart, Wolfgang Amadeus, 1756-1791

Mozart, Wolfgang Amadeus, 1756-1791

About

Isadora, R. Young Mozart (2-4) **92**
See/See also pages in the following book(s):
Krull, K. Lives of the musicians p18-23 (4 and up) **920**

The **Mozart** season. Wolff, V. E. **Fic**

Mr. Bear says "Are you there, Baby Bear?". Gliori, D. See note under Gliori, D. Mr. Bear's new baby **E**

Mr. Bear to the rescue. Gliori, D. See note under Gliori, D. Mr. Bear's new baby **E**

Mr. Bear's new baby. Gliori, D. **E**

Mr. Bear's vacation. Gliori, D. See note under Gliori, D. Mr. Bear's new baby **E**

Mr. Brown washes his underwear. Schwartz, A.
In Schwartz, A. There is a carrot in my ear, and other noodle tales p28-38 **398.2**

Mr. Fox. Jacobs, J.
In Jacobs, J. English fairy tales p145-51 **398.2**

In Womenfolk and fairy tales p30-35 **398.2**

Mr. Fox. MacDonald, M. R.
In MacDonald, M. R. Twenty tellable tales p154-62 **372.6**

Mr. Green Peas. Caseley, J. **E**

Mr. Griggs' work. Rylant, C. **E**

Mr. Gumpy's motor car. Burningham, J. See note under Burningham, J. Mr. Gumpy's outing **E**

Mr. Gumpy's outing. Burningham, J. **E**

Mr. Lincoln's drummer. Wisler, G. C. **Fic**

Mr. Miacca
In Diane Goode's book of scary stories & songs p48-51 **398.2**

Mr. Miacca. Jacobs, J.
In Jacobs, J. English fairy tales p164-66
                 398.2

Mr. Mysterious & Company. Fleischman, S.
                 Fic

Mr. Popper's penguins. Atwater, R. T.   **Fic**

Mr. Putter and Tabby bake the cake. Rylant, C.
See note under Rylant, C. Mr. Putter and
Tabby pour the tea   **E**

Mr. Putter and Tabby feed the fish. Rylant, C. See
note under Rylant, C. Mr. Putter and Tabby
pour the tea   **E**

Mr. Putter and Tabby fly the plane. Rylant, C. See
note under Rylant, C. Mr. Putter and Tabby
pour the tea   **E**

Mr. Putter and Tabby paint the porch. Rylant, C.
See note under Rylant, C. Mr. Putter and
Tabby pour the tea   **E**

Mr. Putter and Tabby pick the pears. Rylant, C.
See note under Rylant, C. Mr. Putter and
Tabby pour the tea   **E**

Mr. Putter and Tabby pour the tea. Rylant, C.
                 E

Mr. Putter and Tabby row the boat. Rylant, C. See
note under Rylant, C. Mr. Putter and Tabby
pour the tea   **E**

Mr. Putter and Tabby take the train. Rylant, C.
See note under Rylant, C. Mr. Putter and
Tabby pour the tea   **E**

Mr. Putter and Tabby toot the horn. Rylant, C.
See note under Rylant, C. Mr. Putter and
Tabby pour the tea   **E**

Mr. Putter and Tabby walk the dog. Rylant, C.
See note under Rylant, C. Mr. Putter and
Tabby pour the tea   **E**

Mr. Rabbit and Mr. Bear. Lester, J.
In Lester, J. The knee-high man, and other
tales p12-20   **398.2**

Mr. Rabbit and the lovely present. Zolotow, C.
                 E

Mr. Revere and I. Lawson, R.   **Fic**

Mr. Semolina-Semolinus. Manna, A. L.   **398.2**

Mr. Tucket. Paulsen, G.   **Fic**

Mr. Vinegar. Jacobs, J.
In Jacobs, J. English fairy tales p37-40
                 398.2

Mr. Wheeler. Sherlock, Sir P. M.
In Sherlock, Sir P. M. West Indian folk-tales
p144-51   **398.2**

Mr. Wolf's pancakes. Fearnley, J.   **E**

Mr. Yeh's New Year. Fang, L.
In Fang, L. The Ch'i-lin purse p71-84
                 398.2

Mrs. Armitage and the big wave. Blake, Q.
                 E

Mrs. Cockle's cat. Pearce, P.
In The Oxford treasury of children's stories
p91-104   **S C**

Mrs. Frisby and the rats of NIMH. O'Brien, R. C.
                 Fic

Mrs. Katz and Tush. Polacco, P.   **E**

Mrs. Mack. Polacco, P.   **E**

Mrs. Piggle-Wiggle. MacDonald, B.   **Fic**

Mrs. Piggle-Wiggle's farm. MacDonald, B. See
note under MacDonald, B. Mrs. Piggle-
Wiggle   **Fic**

Mrs. Piggle-Wiggle's magic. MacDonald, B. See
note under MacDonald, B. Mrs. Piggle-
Wiggle   **Fic**

Ms MacDonald has a class. Ormerod, J.   **E**

Much ado about Aldo. Hurwitz, J.   **Fic**

Much bigger than Martin. Kellogg, S.   **E**

Mud Flat April Fool. Stevenson, J. See note under
Stevenson, J. The Mud Flat Olympics   **E**

The Mud Flat mystery. Stevenson, J. See note under Stevenson, J. The Mud Flat Olympics
                 E

The Mud Flat Olympics. Stevenson, J.   **E**

Mud Flat spring. Stevenson, J. See note under Stevenson, J. The Mud Flat Olympics   **E**

Mud matters. Dewey, J.   **553.6**

The mud pony. Cohen, C. L.   **398.2**

Mufaro's beautiful daughters. Steptoe, J.
                 398.2

The mufferaw catfish. Bedore, B.
In Bauer, C. F. Celebrations p85-86
                 808.8

Muggie Maggie. Cleary, B.   **Fic**

Muhammedanism *See* Islam

Muir, J. (John), 1810-1882
See/See also pages in the following book(s):
Calvert, P. Great lives: the American frontier
p260-73 (5 and up)   **920**

Muir, John *See* Muir, J. (John), 1810-1882

Mukerji, Dhan Gopal, 1890-1936
See/See also pages in the following book(s):
Newbery Medal books, 1922-1955 p53-58
                 028.5

Muller, Eric Paul, 1961-
While you're waiting for the food to come (3-6)
                 507.8

Mullins, Patricia
V for vanishing   **E**
(il) Fox, M. Hattie and the fox   **E**

The mulombe. San Souci, R.
In San Souci, R. A terrifying taste of short &
shivery p95-100   **398.2**

Multicultural people *See* Racially mixed people

Multiculturalism
Bibliography
Kaleidoscope   **011.6**

Multimedia materials *See* Audiovisual materials

MultiMedia schools   **371.305**

Multiplication
Leedy, L. 2 x 2 = boo! (k-3)   **513**

Mulvihill, Margaret
The treasury of saints and martyrs (5 and up)
                 920

Mummies
Deem, J. M. Bodies from the bog (4 and up)
                 930.1
Getz, D. Frozen girl (5 and up)   **930.1**
Getz, D. Frozen man (5 and up)   **930.1**

Mummies—*Continued*

Patent, D. H. Secrets of the ice man (5 and up)
930.1

Perl, L. Mummies, tombs, and treasure (4 and up)
393

Putnam, J. Mummy (4 and up)
393

Reinhard, J. Discovering the Inca Ice Maiden (5 and up)
930.1

Tanaka, S. Secrets of the mummies (4 and up)
393

Wilcox, C. Mummies & their mysteries (4-6)
393

Mummies & their mysteries. Wilcox, C.   393

Mummies, tombs, and treasure. Perl, L.   393

Mummy riddles. Hall, K.   793.73

The **mummy,** the will and the crypt. Bellairs, J.
See note under Bellairs, J. The curse of the blue figurine   **Fic**

Munch, Philippe
(il) London, J. The call of the wild   **Fic**
(il) London, J. White Fang   **Fic**

Mungoshi, Charles
The mountain
In Don't read this! and other tales of the unnatural p23-32   **S C**

Municipal planning *See* City planning

Muñoz, William, 1949-
(il) Patent, D. H. The American alligator
597.9
(il) Patent, D. H. Back to the wild   639.9
(il) Patent, D. H. Biodiversity   333.95
(il) Patent, D. H. Deer and elk   599.65
(il) Patent, D. H. Eagles of America   598
(il) Patent, D. H. Fire: friend or foe   577.2
(il) Patent, D. H. Homesteading   978
(il) Patent, D. H. Horses   636.1
(il) Patent, D. H. Looking at bears   599.78
(il) Patent, D. H. Ospreys   598
(il) Patent, D. H. Pigeons   598
(il) Patent, D. H. Places of refuge   333.95
(il) Patent, D. H. Polar bears   599.78
(il) Patent, D. H. Prairie dogs   599.3
(il) Patent, D. H. Prairies   577.4
(il) Patent, D. H. Shaping the earth   550
(il) Patent, D. H. West by covered wagon
978
(il) Patent, D. H. Yellowstone fires   577.2

Munro, Roxie, 1945-
The inside-outside book of libraries (2-4)
027

Munsinger, Lynn, 1951-
(il) Calmenson, S. Get well, Gators!   **Fic**
(il) Greenberg, D. Bugs!   **E**
(il) Koller, J. F. One monkey too many   **E**
(il) Lester, H. Hooway for Wodney Wat   **E**
(il) Lester, H. Three cheers for Tacky   **E**
(il) Nash, O. Custard the dragon and the wicked knight   811
(il) Nash, O. The tale of Custard the Dragon
811
(il) Numeroff, L. J. What mommies do best
E
(il) Wise, W. Dinosaurs forever   811
(il) A Zooful of animals. See A Zooful of animals   808.81

The **Muppets'** big book of crafts. St. Pierre, S.
745.5

Murasaki Shikibu, b. 978?
See/See also pages in the following book(s):
Krull, K. Lives of the writers p10-13 (4 and up)
920

Murder *See* Homicide

Murdocca, Sal
(il) Clements, A. The Landry News   **Fic**
(il) Packard, E. Big numbers   513

Murdoch's rath. Ewing, J. H.
In Bauer, C. F. Celebrations p183-88
808.8

Murieta, Joaquín, d. 1853
Fiction
Fleischman, S. Bandit's moon (4-6)   **Fic**

The **murky** secret. Olson, A. N.
In Olson, A. N. Ask the bones: scary stories from around the world p10-16   398.2

Murphy, Barbara Thrash
Black authors and illustrators of books for children and young adults   920.003

Murphy, Jill, 1949-
Peace at last   **E**
A quiet night in   **E**

Murphy, Jim, 1947-
Across America on an emigrant train (5 and up)
92
The boys' war (5 and up)   973.7
The great fire (5 and up)   977.3
The long road to Gettysburg (5 and up)
973.7
A young patriot (5 and up)   973.3

Murphy, Pat, 1955-
The Brain explorer. See The Brain explorer
793.73
The science explorer (5 and up)   507.8

Murphy, Roxane
(il) MacDonald, M. R. Celebrate the world
372.6
(il) MacDonald, M. R. Look back and see
372.6
(il) MacDonald, M. R. Twenty tellable tales
372.6
(il) MacDonald, M. R. When the lights go out
372.6

Murphy, Stuart J., 1942-
Beep beep, vroom vroom! (k-1)   515
Betcha! (1-3)   519.5
Dave's down-to-earth rock shop (k-3)
511.3
Divide and ride (1-3)   513
Elevator magic (k-2)   513
Henry the fourth (k-1)   513
Jump, kangaroo, jump! (1-3)   513
Just enough carrots (k-1)   513
Pepper's journal   **E**
Room for Ripley (1-3)   530.8

Murray, Laura K.
Basic Internet for busy librarians   004.6

Murrow, Liza Ketchum, 1946-
The gold rush (5 and up)   979.4
Orphan journey home (4-6)   **Fic**

Muscles
Simon, S. Muscles (3-6)   **612.7**
Musculoskeletal system
See also Bones; Muscles
Ballard, C. The skeleton and muscular system (5 and up)   **612.7**
Museum of ancient inventions. (4 and up) See entry in Part 2: Web Resources
Museums
See also Art museums; appropriate subjects with the subdivision *Museums;* and names of galleries and museums
Norris, J. Children's museums   **069**
Fiction
Cameron, E. The court of the stone children (5 and up)   **Fic**
Howe, J. Pinky and Rex   **E**
Stevenson, J. The most amazing dinosaur
     E
Musgrove, Margaret, 1943-
Ashanti to Zulu: African traditions (3-6)
     960
Mushrooms
See also Fungi
Royston, A. Life cycle of a mushroom (k-3)
     579.6
Music
Ardley, N. A young person's guide to music (5 and up)   **780**
Sabbeth, A. Rubber-band banjos and a java jive bass (4 and up)   **781**
Analysis, appreciation
See Music appreciation
Fiction
Fleming, C. Gabriella's song   **E**
Kaplan, H. Waiting to sing   **E**
King-Smith, D. A mouse called Wolf (2-4)
     Fic
McPhail, D. M. Mole music   **E**
Schuch, S. A symphony of whales   **E**
Poetry
Call down the moon (6 and up)   **821.008**
Song and dance (k-3)   **811.008**
Music, African American *See* African American music
Music, Gospel *See* Gospel music
Music. Ardley, N.   **784.19**
Music appreciation
Ganeri, A. The young person's guide to the orchestra (4-6)   **784.2**
Music, music for everyone. Williams, V. B. See note under Williams, V. B. A chair for my mother   **E**
The **music** of dolphins. Hesse, K.   **Fic**
Musical instruments
Ardley, N. Music (4 and up)   **784.19**
Ganeri, A. The young person's guide to the orchestra (4-6)   **784.2**
Hayes, A. Meet the orchestra (k-3)   **784.2**
Koscielniak, B. The story of the incredible orchestra (2-4)   **784.2**
Moss, L. Zin! zin! zin! a violin   **E**
Sabbeth, A. Rubber-band banjos and a java jive bass (4 and up)   **781**

The **musician.** Terada, A. M.
In Terada, A. M. Under the starfruit tree p132-34   **398.2**
Musicians
See also Composers
Fiction
Alexander, L. The marvelous misadventures of Sebastian (4 and up)   **Fic**
Cutler, J. The cello of Mr. O   **E**
Fenner, C. Yolonda's genius (4-6)   **Fic**
Isadora, R. Ben's trumpet   **E**
MacLachlan, P. The facts and fictions of Minna Pratt (4 and up)   **Fic**
Martin, B. The maestro plays   **E**
Shepard, A. The sea king's daughter (3-6)
     398.2
Musicians, African American *See* African American musicians
Musicians of the sun. McDermott, G.   **398.2**
Musleah, Rahel
Why on this night?   **296.4**
Muslim countries *See* Islamic countries
Muslimism *See* Islam
Muth, Jon J.
(il) Hesse, K. Come on, rain!   **E**
(il) Kimmel, E. A. Gershon's monster
     398.2
Mutsmag
In Grandfather tales p40-51   **398.2**
My America [series]
Hermes, P. Our strange new land   **Fic**
Osborne, M. P. My brother's keeper   **Fic**
My backyard garden. Lerner, C.   **635**
My ballet book. Castle, K.   **792.8**
My baseball book. Gibbons, G.   **796.357**
My basketball book. Gibbons, G.   **796.323**
My big toe
In Diane Goode's book of scary stories & songs p12-13   **398.2**
My black me (5 and up)   **811.008**
My brother, Ant. Byars, B. C.   **E**
My brother, my sister, and I. Watkins, Y. K.
     Fic
My brother Sam is dead. Collier, J. L.   **Fic**
My brother's keeper. Osborne, M. P.   **Fic**
My brown bear Barney. Butler, D.   **E**
My brown bear Barney at the party. Butler, D. See note under Butler, D. My brown bear Barney
     E
My dad. Daly, N.   **E**
My Daniel. Conrad, P.   **Fic**
My dear Noel: the story of a letter from Beatrix Potter. Johnson, J.   **92**
My dog is lost!. Keats, E. J.   **E**
My dog Toby. Zimmerman, A. G.   **E**
My father's boat. Garland, S.   **E**
My father's dragon. Gannett, R. S.   **Fic**
My father's hands. Ryder, J.   **E**
My feet. Aliki   **612**
My first book of sign. Baker, P. J.   **419**
My first garden. Bogacki, T.   **E**

My first I can read book [series]
  Bonsall, C. N. The day I had to play with my
    sister   E
  Bonsall, C. N. Mine's the best   E
  Capucilli, A. Biscuit's new trick   E
  Lexau, J. M. Go away, dog   E
My first Kwanzaa book. Chocolate, D.
    394.26
My first magic book. Leyton, L.   793.8
My first word book. Wilkes, A.   E
My five senses. Aliki   612.8
My five senses. Miller, M.   E
My football book. Gibbons, G.   796.332
My friend Bear. Alborough, J.   E
My friend John. Zolotow, C.   E
My goose Betsy. Braun, T.   E
My great-aunt Arizona. Houston, G.   E
My great-grandfather's grave-digging. Price, S.
  In The Oxford book of scary tales p94-95
    808.8
My Guy. Weeks, S. See note under Weeks, S.
  Regular Guy   **Fic**
My hands. Aliki   612
My health [series]
  Silverstein, A. Allergies   616.97
  Silverstein, A. Common colds   616.2
  Silverstein, A. Cuts, scrapes, scabs, and scars
    617.1
  Silverstein, A. Is that a rash?   616.5
  Silverstein, A. Sleep   612.8
  Silverstein, A. Tooth decay and cavities
    617.6
My indoor garden. Lerner, C.   635.9
My life as a fifth-grade comedian. Levy, E.
    Fic
My life in dog years. Paulsen, G.   92
My life with the chimpanzees. Goodall, J.   92
My little sister ate one hare. Grossman, B.   E
My Lord Bag-o'-Rice. Quayle, E.
  In Quayle, E. The shining princess, and other
    Japanese legends p33-43   398.2
My Louisiana sky. Holt, K. W.   **Fic**
My mama had a dancing heart. Gray, L. M.
    E
My mama says there aren't any zombies, ghosts,
  vampires, creatures, demons, monsters, fiends,
  goblins, or things. Viorst, J.   E
My man Blue. Grimes, N.   811
My mother got married (and other disasters). Park,
  B.   **Fic**
My mysterious world. Mahy, M.   92
My name is America [series]
  Durbin, W. The journal of Sean Sullivan
    Fic
  Myers, W. D. The journal of Joshua Loper
    Fic
  Myers, W. D. The journal of Scott Pendleton
    Collins   **Fic**
  Rinaldi, A. The journal of Jasper Jonathan
    Pierce, a pilgrim boy   **Fic**
  Yep, L. The journal of Wong Ming-Chung
    Fic

My name is brain Brian. Betancourt, J.   **Fic**
My name is Georgia [biography of Georgia
  O'Keeffe] Winter, J.   92
My name is Illusion. Krishnaswami, U.
  In Krishnaswami, U. Shower of gold: girls
    and women in the stories of India p100-
    03   398.2
My naughty little sister makes a bottle-tree. Ed-
  wards, D.
  In The Oxford treasury of children's stories
    p35-38   **S C**
My new kitten. Cole, J.   636.8
My own self. Jacobs, J.
  In Jacobs, J. English fairy tales p238-41
    398.2
My parents think I'm sleeping: poems. Prelutsky,
  J.   811
My place in space. Hirst, R.   520
My prairie Christmas. Harvey, B.   **Fic**
My puppy is born. Cole, J.   636.7
My race car. Rex, M.   629.228
My rotten redheaded older brother. Polacco, P.
    E
My rows and piles of coins. Mollel, T. M.   E
My shadow. Stevenson, R. L.   821
My side of the mountain. George, J. C.   **Fic**
My soccer book. Gibbons, G.   796.334
My son John. Aylesworth, J.   E
My song is beautiful (k-3)   808.81
My very first Mother Goose   398.8
My very own room. Pérez, A. I.   E
My visit to the aquarium. Aliki   639.34
My visit to the zoo. Aliki   590.73
My writing day. Adler, D. A.   92
Mycology *See* Fungi
Myers, Christopher A.
  Black cat   E
  Wings   E
  (jt. auth) Myers, L. B. Galápagos: islands of
    change   508
  (il) Myers, W. D. Harlem   811
Myers, Lynne Born
  Galápagos: islands of change (4 and up)
    508
Myers, Walter Dean, 1937-
  Amistad: a long road to freedom (5 and up)
    326
  At her majesty's request [biography of Sarah
    Forbes Bonetta] (5 and up)   92
  The blues of Flats Brown   E
  Brown angels   811
  Fast Sam, Cool Clyde, and Stuff (6 and up)
    Fic
  Harlem   811
  The journal of Joshua Loper (5 and up)
    Fic
  The journal of Scott Pendleton Collins (5 and
    up)   **Fic**
  Malcolm X (3-6)   92
  Me, Mop, and the Moondance Kid (4-6)
    Fic
  Now is your time! (6 and up)   305.8

The **mysteries** of Harris Burdick. Van Allsburg, C.
E

Mysteries of the universe. Wilson, C. **001.9**

The **mysterious** disappearance of Leon (I mean Noel). Raskin, E. **Fic**

Mysterious multiplying jar, Anno's. Anno, M.
512

The **mysterious** rays of Dr. Röntgen. Gherman, B.
92

The **mysterious** tadpole. Kellogg, S. **E**

Mysterious tales of Japan. Martin, R. **398.2**

Mysterious Thelonious. Raschka, C. **E**

The **mysterious** visitor. Jaffe, N. **398.2**

Mystery and detective stories See Mystery fiction

Mystery fiction

Adler, D. A. Cam Jansen and the mystery of the stolen diamonds (2-4) **Fic**

Adler, D. A. Young Cam Jansen and the dinosaur game **E**

Bellairs, J. The curse of the blue figurine (5 and up) **Fic**

Berends, P. B. The case of the elevator duck (3-5) **Fic**

Bonsall, C. N. The case of the hungry stranger **E**

Brooks, W. R. Freddy the detective (3-5)
Fic

Cameron, E. The court of the stone children (5 and up) **Fic**

Christopher, M. Tackle without a team (4-6)
Fic

Cushman, D. Inspector Hopper **E**

Draanen, W. van. Sammy Keyes and the hotel thief (4-6) **Fic**

Giff, P. R. Kidnap at the Catfish Cafe (3-5)
Fic

Hahn, M. D. The dead man in Indian Creek (5 and up) **Fic**

Hamilton, V. The house of Dies Drear (5 and up) **Fic**

Hamilton, V. The mystery of Drear House (5 and up) **Fic**

Howe, D. Bunnicula (4-6) **Fic**

Howe, J. The celery stalks at midnight (4-6)
Fic

Howe, J. Dew drop dead (4-6) **Fic**

Hurd, T. Mystery on the docks **E**

Klause, A. C. Alien secrets (5 and up) **Fic**

Kline, S. Orp and the FBI (4-6) **Fic**

Konigsburg, E. L. Up from Jericho Tel (5 and up) **Fic**

Levin, B. Shadow-catcher (4 and up) **Fic**

Lexau, J. M. Don't be my valentine **E**

Newman, R. The case of the Baker Street Irregular (5 and up) **Fic**

Raskin, E. The mysterious disappearance of Leon (I mean Noel) (4 and up) **Fic**

Raskin, E. The Westing game (5 and up)
Fic

Roberts, W. D. Scared stiff (5 and up) **Fic**

Roberts, W. D. The view from the cherry tree (5 and up) **Fic**

Sharmat, M. W. Nate the Great **E**

Sobol, D. J. Encyclopedia Brown, boy detective (3-5) **Fic**

Strickland, B. The hand of the necromancer (5 and up) **Fic**

Wallace, B. B. Cousins in the castle (4-6)
Fic

Wallace, B. B. The twin in the tavern (4-6)
Fic

Wright, B. R. The dollhouse murders (4 and up)
Fic

Wright, B. R. The ghosts of Mercy Manor (4 and up) **Fic**

Wright, B. R. Nothing but trouble (4 and up)
Fic

Yolen, J. Piggins and the royal wedding **E**

The **mystery** of Drear House. Hamilton, V.
Fic

The **mystery** of Mars. Ride, S. K. **523.4**

The **mystery** of Melusine. Osborne, M. P.
In Osborne, M. P. Mermaid tales from around the world p1-5 **398.2**

The **mystery** of the cupboard. Banks, L. R. See note under Reid Banks, L. The Indian in the cupboard **Fic**

The **mystery** of the hieroglyphs. Donoughue, C.
493

Mystery of the Lascaux Cave. Patent, D. H.
759.01

The **mystery** of the mammoth bones. Giblin, J.
569

The **mystery** of the missing red mitten. See Kellogg, S. The missing mitten mystery **E**

The **mystery** of UFOs. Herbst, J. **001.9**

Mystery on the docks. Hurd, T. **E**

Mythical animals

See also Dragons; Mermaids and mermen

Hunt, J. Bestiary (4 and up) **398**

Fiction

Hunter, M. A stranger came ashore (6 and up)
Fic

Poetry

Carle, E. Eric Carle's dragons dragons and other creatures that never were **808.81**

Yolen, J. How beastly! (3-5) **811**

Mythical birds & beasts from many lands. Mayo, M. **398.2**

Mythology

See also Gods and goddesses; Mythical animals; mythology of particular national or ethnic groups or of particular geographic areas, e.g. Celtic mythology

Bulfinch, T. Bulfinch's mythology (6 and up)
291.1

Ganeri, A. Out of the ark (4 and up)
291.1

Hamilton, V. In the beginning; creation stories from around the world (5 and up) **291.1**

Hoffman, M. Sun, moon, and stars (3-6)
398.2

Mayo, M. Mythical birds & beasts from many lands (3-6) **398.2**

Philip, N. The illustrated book of myths (5 and up) **291.1**

Indexes

Index to fairy tales **398.2**

Mythology, Classical See Classical mythology

Mythology, Egyptian *See* Egyptian mythology
Mythology, Greek *See* Classical mythology
Mythology, Norse *See* Norse mythology
Mythology, Roman *See* Classical mythology
Mythology. Hamilton, E.   **292**
Myths and legends of the world [series]
  McCaughrean, G. The bronze cauldron: myths
    and legends of the world   **398.2**
  McCaughrean, G. The crystal pool: myths and
    legends of the world   **398.2**
  McCaughrean, G. The golden hoard: myths and
    legends of the world   **398.2**
  McCaughrean, G. The silver treasure: myths and
    legends of the world   **398.2**

N

Nabwire, Constance R.
  Cooking the African way
    In Easy menu ethnic cookbooks   **641.5**
Naden, Corinne J.
  (jt. auth) Gillespie, J. T. Juniorplots 4
        028.5
  (jt. auth) Gillespie, J. T. Middleplots 4
        028.5
  (jt. auth) Gillespie, J. T. The Newbery compan-
    ion   **028.5**
Naftali the storyteller and his horse, Sus. Singer,
  I. B.
    In Singer, I. B. Stories for children p167-83
        S C
Nagasaki (Japan)
  Bombardment, 1945—Fiction
  Coerr, E. Mieko and the fifth treasure (3-5)
        Fic
Nahum, Andrew
  Flying machine (4 and up)   **629.133**
Naidoo, Beverley
  Chain of fire (5 and up)   **Fic**
  Journey to Jo'burg (5 and up)   **Fic**
  No turning back (5 and up)   **Fic**
Nail Soup. MacDonald, M. R.
  In MacDonald, M. R. Celebrate the world
    p115-23   **372.6**
Nailling, Lee, 1917-
  About
  Warren, A. Orphan train rider (4 and up)
        362.7
Namath, Joe
  See/See also pages in the following book(s):
  Sullivan, G. Quarterbacks! p36-38 (5 and up)
        920
The Name
  In The Magic orange tree, and other Haitian
    folktales p117-22   **398.2**
Names, Personal *See* Personal names
Namibia
  Brandenburg, J. Sand and fog (4 and up)
        968.8
Namioka, Lensey
  Ties that bind, ties that break (5 and up)
        Fic

Yang the eldest and his odd jobs. See note under Namioka, L. Yang the youngest and his
  terrible ear   **Fic**
Yang the second and her secret admirers. See
  note under Namioka, L. Yang the youngest
  and his terrible ear   **Fic**
Yang the third and her impossible family. See
  note under Namioka, L. Yang the youngest
  and his terrible ear   **Fic**
Yang the youngest and his terrible ear (4-6)
        Fic
Nana Miriam. Yolen, J.
  In Yolen, J. Not one damsel in distress p11-
    16   **398.2**
Nana Upstairs & Nana Downstairs. De Paola, T.
        E
Nana's birthday party. Hest, A.   **E**
Nanye'hi *See* Ward, Nancy, 1738?-1822
Napoleon I, Emperor of the French, 1769-1821
  Fiction
  Marcellino, F. I, crocodile   **E**
Napoli, Donna Jo, 1948-
  The prince of the pond (4-6)   **Fic**
  Stones in water (5 and up)   **Fic**
The napping house. Wood, A.   **E**
Narahashi, Keiko
  Two girls can!   **E**
  (il) Serfozo, M. What's what? a guessing game
        E
  (il) Serfozo, M. Who said red?   **E**
  (il) Uchida, Y. The magic purse   **398.2**
Nardo, Don, 1947-
  France (4 and up)   **944**
Narraganset Indians
  Fiction
  Fleischman, P. Saturnalia (6 and up)   **Fic**
Narrow escape. San Souci, R.
  In San Souci, R. A terrifying taste of short &
    shivery p130-36   **398.2**
NASA explores. (4 and up) See entry in Part 2:
  Web Resources
The NASA Qwhiz. (2-6) See entry in Part 2: Web
  Resources
NASA space vehicles. Cole, M. D.   **629.44**
NASA's why files. (3-5) See entry in Part 2: Web
  Resources
Nascimbene, Yan
  (il) Zolotow, C. The beautiful Christmas tree
        E
Nash, Ogden, 1902-1971
  The adventures of Isabel (k-3)   **811**
  Custard the dragon and the wicked knight (k-3)
        811
  The tale of Custard the Dragon (k-3)   **811**
Nash, Scott, 1959-
  (il) Murphy, S. J. Henry the fourth   **513**
  (il) Shields, C. D. Martian rock   **E**
Nasreddin Hoca and the third shot. Walker, B. K.
  In Walker, B. K. A treasury of Turkish folk-
    tales for children p43-44   **398.2**
Nasreddin Hoca, seller of wisdom. Walker, B. K.
  In Walker, B. K. A treasury of Turkish folk-
    tales for children p37-42   **398.2**

Nasta, Vincent
(il) Siebert, D. Plane song **E**
Nastasia of the sea. Osborne, M. P.
In Osborne, M. P. Mermaid tales from around
the world p25-30 **398.2**
Nasty, stinky sneakers. Bunting, E. **Fic**
Natchev, Alexi
(il) San Souci, R. The Hobyahs **398.2**
Nate the Great. Sharmat, M. W. **E**
Nate the Great and me: the case of the fleeing
fang. Sharmat, M. W. See note under
Sharmat, M. W. Nate the Great **E**
Nate the Great and the boring beach bag. Sharmat,
M. W. See note under Sharmat, M. W. Nate
the Great **E**
Nate the Great and the crunchy Christmas.
Sharmat, M. W. See note under Sharmat, M.
W. Nate the Great **E**
Nate the Great and the fishy prize. Sharmat, M.
W. See note under Sharmat, M. W. Nate the
Great **E**
Nate the Great and the Halloween hunt. Sharmat,
M. W. See note under Sharmat, M. W. Nate
the Great **E**
Nate the Great and the lost list. Sharmat, M. W.
See note under Sharmat, M. W. Nate the
Great **E**
Nate the Great and the missing key. Sharmat, M.
W. See note under Sharmat, M. W. Nate the
Great **E**
Nate the Great and the monster mess. Sharmat, M.
W. See note under Sharmat, M. W. Nate the
Great **E**
Nate the Great and the mushy valentine. Sharmat,
M. W. See note under Sharmat, M. W. Nate
the Great **E**
Nate the Great and the musical note. Sharmat, M.
W. See note under Sharmat, M. W. Nate the
Great **E**
Nate the Great and the phony clue. Sharmat, M.
W. See note under Sharmat, M. W. Nate the
Great **E**
Nate the Great and the pillowcase. Sharmat, M.
W. See note under Sharmat, M. W. Nate the
Great **E**
Nate the Great and the snowy trail. Sharmat, M.
W. See note under Sharmat, M. W. Nate the
Great **E**
Nate the Great and the sticky case. Sharmat, M.
W. See note under Sharmat, M. W. Nate the
Great **E**
Nate the Great and the stolen base. Sharmat, M.
W. See note under Sharmat, M. W. Nate the
Great **E**
Nate the Great and the tardy tortoise. Sharmat, M.
W. See note under Sharmat, M. W. Nate the
Great **E**
Nate the Great goes down in the dumps. Sharmat,
M. W. See note under Sharmat, M. W. Nate
the Great **E**
Nate the Great goes undercover. Sharmat, M. W.
See note under Sharmat, M. W. Nate the
Great **E**

Nate the Great, San Francisco detective. Sharmat,
M. W. See note under Sharmat, M. W. Nate
the Great **E**
Nate the Great saves the King of Sweden.
Sharmat, M. W. See note under Sharmat, M.
W. Nate the Great **E**
Nate the Great stalks stupidweed. Sharmat, M. W.
See note under Sharmat, M. W. Nate the
Great **E**
National Audubon Society first field guide: am-
phibians. Cassie, B. **597.8**
National Audubon Society first field guide: birds
(4 and up) **598**
National Audubon Society first field guide: fishes.
Smith, C. L. **597**
National Audubon Society first field guide: in-
sects. Wilsdon, C. **595.7**
National Audubon Society first field guide: mam-
mals. Grassy, J. **599**
National Audubon Society first field guide: night
sky. Mechler, G. **520**
National Audubon Society first field guide: rep-
tiles. Behler, J. L. **597.9**
National Audubon Society first field guide: rocks
and minerals. Ricciuti, E. R. **552**
National Audubon Society first field guide: trees.
Cassie, B. **582.16**
National Audubon Society first field guide: weath-
er. Kahl, J. D. **551.5**
National Audubon Society first field guide:
wildflowers. Hood, S. **582.13**
**National Civil Rights Museum (Memphis,
Tenn.)**
Duncan, A. F. The National Civil Rights Muse-
um celebrates everyday people (3-6)
 323.1
National Council for the Social Studies
Notable children's trade books in the field of
social studies. See Notable children's trade
books in the field of social studies **016.3**
**National Council of Teachers of English. Com-
mittee to Revise the Elementary School
Booklist**
Adventuring with books. See Adventuring with
books **011.6**
**National Council of Teachers of English. Com-
mittee to Revise the Multicultural Booklist**
Kaleidoscope. See Kaleidoscope **011.6**
**National Fish and Wildlife Forensics Laborato-
ry**
Jackson, D. The wildlife detectives (4 and up)
 363.2
National Football League
Buckley, J., Jr. America's greatest game (4 and
up) **796.332**
National Gallery (Great Britain)
Bible. N.T. Selections. The first Christmas
 232.9
National Gallery of Art (U.S.)
Thomson, P. The nine-ton cat: behind the scenes
at an art museum (4 and up) **708**

National Gallery of Art (U.S.)—*Continued*
Fiction
Weitzman, J. P. You can't take a balloon into the National Gallery   **E**

National Geographic atlas of the world   **912**

National Geographic Society (U.S.)
Bausum, A. Dragon bones and dinosaur eggs: a photobiography of Roy Chapman Andrews   **92**
Earle, S. A. Dive!   **551.46**
Galan, M. A. There's still time   **333.95**
Harness, C. George Washington   **92**
Matthews, T. L. Always inventing: a photobiography of Alexander Graham Bell   **92**
National Geographic atlas of the world. See National Geographic atlas of the world   **912**
National Geographic World. See National Geographic World   **910.5**
National Geographic world atlas for young explorers. See National Geographic world atlas for young explorers   **912**
Prager, E. J. Sand   **553.6**
Reinhard, J. Discovering the Inca Ice Maiden   **930.1**
Skurzynski, G. On time   **529**

National Geographic World (3-6)   **910.5**

National Geographic world atlas for young explorers (3-6)   **912**

National Museum of the American Indian (U.S.)
When the rain sings. See When the rain sings   **811.008**

National parks and reserves
Patent, D. H. Places of refuge (4 and up)   **333.95**

National Railway Museum (Great Britain)
Big book of trains. See Big book of trains   **625.1**

National Science Teachers Association
Outstanding science trade books for children. See Outstanding science trade books for children   **016.5**

National songs
United States
Key, F. S. The Star-Spangled Banner   **782.42**

National songs, American *See* National songs—United States

National Velvet. Bagnold, E.   **Fic**

Native American art
Baylor, B. When clay sings (1-4)   **970.004**
Temko, F. Traditional crafts from native North America (4 and up)   **745.5**

Native American dance
Left Hand Bull, J. Lakota hoop dancer (3-6)   **970.004**
Fiction
Smith, C. L. Jingle dancer   **E**

Native American games
Hoyt-Goldsmith, D. Lacrosse (3-5)   **796.34**

Native American women
Tallchief, M. Tallchief (3-5)   **92**

Native Americans
See also Aztecs; Incas; Taino Indians; Zapotec Indians; names of Native American peoples and linguistic families
Hirschfelder, A. B. American Indian stereotypes in the world of children   **970.004**
Rising voices (5 and up)   **810.8**
Steins, R. Exploration and settlement (5 and up)   **970.01**
Swamp, J. Giving thanks (k-3)   **299**
Woods, G. Science of the early Americas (4 and up)   **509**
See/See also pages in the following book(s):
Freedman, R. Children of the wild West p38-57 (4 and up)   **978**
Peoples of the Americas   **970**
Antiquities
Arnold, C. Stories in stone (4 and up)   **709.01**
Sattler, H. R. The earliest Americans (5 and up)   **970.01**
Biography
Freedman, R. Indian chiefs (6 and up)   **920**
Dictionaries
Patterson, L. Indian terms of the Americas   **970.004**
Drama
Bruchac, J. Pushing up the sky: seven native American plays for children (3-5)   **812**
Encyclopedias
Ciment, J. Scholastic encyclopedia of the American Indian (4 and up)   **970.004**
Griffin-Pierce, T. The encyclopedia of Native America   **970.004**
Native Americans (4 and up)   **970.004**
Fiction
Baker, O. Where the buffaloes begin (2-4)   **Fic**
Banks, L. R. The Indian in the cupboard (5 and up)   **Fic**
Benchley, N. Small Wolf   **E**
Bruchac, J. The arrow over the door (4-6)   **Fic**
Bruchac, J. Sacajawea (6 and up)   **Fic**
Dalgliesh, A. The courage of Sarah Noble (2-4)   **Fic**
Dorris, M. Sees Behind Trees (4 and up)   **Fic**
Goble, P. Beyond the ridge (2-4)   **Fic**
Goble, P. Dream wolf   **E**
Hobbs, W. Kokopelli's flute (5 and up)   **Fic**
Martin, B. Knots on a counting rope   **E**
O'Dell, S. Island of the Blue Dolphins (5 and up)   **Fic**
O'Dell, S. Streams to the river, river to the sea (5 and up)   **Fic**
O'Dell, S. Zia (5 and up)   **Fic**
Speare, E. G. The sign of the beaver (5 and up)   **Fic**
Folklore
Bierhorst, J. The people with five fingers (k-3)   **398.2**
Bruchac, J. Between earth & sky (3-5)   **398.2**
Bruchac, J. Flying with the eagle, racing the great bear (5 and up)   **398.2**

Native Americans—Folklore—*Continued*

Bruchac, J. The girl who married the Moon (5 and up) **398.2**

Bruchac, J. Thirteen moons on a turtle's back **811**

Bruchac, J. When the Chenoo howls (4-6) **398.2**

Brusca, M. C. When jaguars ate the moon and other stories about animals and plants of the Americas (2-4) **398.2**

Caduto, M. J. Keepers of the night **398.2**

Curry, J. L. Back in the beforetime (4-6) **398.2**

De Paola, T. The legend of the Indian paintbrush (k-3) **398.2**

Delacre, L. Golden tales (4 and up) **398.2**

Goble, P. Buffalo woman (2-4) **398.2**

Goble, P. Crow chief (2-4) **398.2**

Goble, P. The gift of the sacred dog (2-4) **398.2**

Goble, P. The girl who loved wild horses (k-3) **398.2**

Goble, P. The great race of the birds and animals (2-4) **398.2**

Goble, P. The legend of the White Buffalo Woman (3-5) **398.2**

Goble, P. Love flute (2-4) **398.2**

Goble, P. Paul Goble gallery (2-4) **398.2**

Goble, P. Remaking the earth (2-4) **398.2**

Goldin, B. D. Coyote and the firestick (3-5) **398.2**

Lelooska. Echoes of the elders (4-6) **398.2**

Lelooska. Spirit of the cedar people (4-6) **398.2**

Longfellow, H. W. Hiawatha **811**

McDermott, G. Coyote: a trickster tale from the American Southwest (k-3) **398.2**

McDermott, G. Raven (k-3) **398.2**

Steptoe, J. The story of Jumping Mouse (1-3) **398.2**

Van Laan, N. The magic bean tree (k-3) **398.2**

Poetry

Bruchac, J. Thirteen moons on a turtle's back **811**

Dancing teepees: poems of American Indian youth (3-5) **897**

In the trail of the wind (5 and up) **897**

Longfellow, H. W. Hiawatha **811**

When the rain sings (4 and up) **811.008**

Religion

Fisher, L. E. Gods and goddesses of the ancient Maya (3-6) **299**

Rites and ceremonies

Ancona, G. Powwow (3-6) **970.004**

Braine, S. Drumbeat—heartbeat (3-6) **970.004**

Study and teaching

Hirschfelder, A. B. Native Americans today **970.004**

Wars

See also United States—History—1755-1763, French and Indian War

Ehrlich, A. Wounded Knee: an Indian history of the American West (6 and up) **970.004**

Central America

See also Mayas; Mosquito Indians

Great Plains

Freedman, R. Buffalo hunt (4 and up) **970.004**

Terry, M. B. H. Daily life in a Plains Indian village, 1868 (4 and up) **970.004**

Mexico

See also Aztecs; Mayas; Papago Indians; Zapotec Indians

Arnold, C. City of the Gods (4 and up) **972**

Missouri River valley

Freedman, R. An Indian winter (6 and up) **978**

Northwest Coast of North America

Hoyt-Goldsmith, D. Totem pole (3-5) **970.004**

South America

See also Incas

Southwestern States

Baylor, B. When clay sings (1-4) **970.004**

West (U.S.)

Ehrlich, A. Wounded Knee: an Indian history of the American West (6 and up) **970.004**

West Indies

See also Taino Indians

Native Americans [Grolier encyclopedia] (4 and up) **970.004**

Native Americans [series]

Andryszewski, T. The Seminoles **970.004**

Bonvillain, N. The Navajos **970.004**

Native Americans today. Hirschfelder, A. B. **970.004**

Natti, Susanna, 1948-

(il) Adler, D. A. Cam Jansen and the mystery of the stolen diamonds **Fic**

(il) Adler, D. A. Young Cam Jansen and the dinosaur game **E**

(il) Giff, P. R. Watch out, Ronald Morgan! **E**

(il) Krensky, S. Lionel at large **E**

Natural childbirth

See also Midwives

Natural disasters

See also Storms

Challoner, J. Hurricane & tornado (4 and up) **551.55**

Natural history

Dictionaries

The New book of popular science **503**

Encyclopedias

DK nature encyclopedia **508**

Periodicals

Chickadee **505**

Owl **505**

Ranger Rick **505**

Your Big Backyard **505**

Africa

Dunphy, M. Here is the African savanna (k-3) **577.4**

Silver, D. M. African savanna (3-5) **577.4**

Navajo Indians—*Continued*
See/See also pages in the following book(s):
Ehrlich, A. Wounded Knee: an Indian history of the American West (6 and up)   **970.004**

Fiction
Blood, C. L. The goat in the rug   **E**
Miles, M. Annie and the Old One (1-4)
   Fic
O'Dell, S. Sing down the moon (5 and up)
   Fic

Poetry
Begay, S. Navajo (5 and up)   **811**

Naval architecture
See also Shipbuilding

Naylor, Phyllis Reynolds, 1933-
Achingly Alice. See note under Naylor, P. R. The agony of Alice   **Fic**
The agony of Alice (5 and up)   **Fic**
Alice in April. See note under Naylor, P. R. The agony of Alice   **Fic**
Alice in-between. See note under Naylor. P. R. The agony of Alice   **Fic**
Alice in lace. See note under Naylor, P. R. The agony of Alice   **Fic**
Alice in rapture, sort of. See note under Naylor, P. R. The agony of Alice   **Fic**
Alice on the outside. See note under Naylor, P. R. The agony of Alice   **Fic**
Alice the brave. See note under Naylor, P. R. The agony of Alice   **Fic**
All but Alice. See note under Naylor. P. R. The agony of Alice   **Fic**
The bomb in the Bessledorf bus depot. See note under Naylor, P. R. Peril in the Bessledorf Parachute Factory   **Fic**
The face in the Bessledorf funeral parlor. See note under Naylor, P. R. Peril in the Bessledorf Parachute Factory   **Fic**
The fear place (5 and up)   **Fic**
The grand escape (4-6)   **Fic**
The grooming of Alice. See note under Naylor, P. R. The agony of Alice   **Fic**
Outrageously Alice. See note under Naylor, P. R. The agony of Alice   **Fic**
Peril in the Bessledorf Parachute Factory (4-6)
   Fic
Reluctantly Alice. See note under Naylor, P. R. The agony of Alice   **Fic**
Saving Shiloh. See note under Naylor, P. R. Shiloh   **Fic**
Shiloh (4-6)   **Fic**
Shiloh season. See note under Naylor, P. R. Shiloh   **Fic**
The treasure of Bessledorf. See note under Naylor, P. R. Peril in the Bessledorf Parachute Factory   **Fic**
See/See also pages in the following book(s):
The Newbery & Caldecott medal books, 1986-2000 p167-78   **028.5**

NCSS *See* National Council for the Social Studies

NCTE bibliography series
Adventuring with books   **011.6**

Neal-Schuman net-guide series
Benson, A. C. Connecting kids and the Internet
   004.6

Neale S. Godfrey's ultimate kids' money book. Godfrey, N. S.   **332.024**

Neatness *See* Cleanliness

Nebraska
McNair, S. Nebraska
In America the beautiful second series
   973

Fiction
Bunting, E. Dandelions   **E**
Conrad, P. My Daniel (5 and up)   **Fic**
Conrad, P. Prairie songs (5 and up)   **Fic**
Ruckman, I. Night of the twisters (3-6)   **Fic**

Nebulae, Extragalactic *See* Galaxies

The **needlework** teacher and the secret baby. McCaughrean, G.
In McCaughrean, G. The crystal pool: myths and legends of the world p82-87
   398.2

Negri, Rocco
(il) Byars, B. C. Trouble River   **Fic**

Negrin, Fabian
(il) Waters, F. Oscar Wilde's The selfish giant
   Fic

Neighborhood development *See* Community development

Neighborhood odes. Soto, G.   **811**

Neitzel, Shirley
The bag I'm taking to Grandma's   **E**
The dress I'll wear to the party   **E**
The jacket I wear in the snow   **E**

Nelson, Annika
(il) Soto, G. Canto familiar   **811**

Nelson, Kadir
(il) Nolen, J. Big Jabe   **E**

Nelson, S. D.
(il) Bruchac, J. Crazy Horse's vision   **E**

Nelson, Theresa, 1948-
And one for all (5 and up)   **Fic**
Earthshine (5 and up)   **Fic**

Neptune (Planet)
Brimner, L. D. Neptune (2-4)   **523.4**

Nervous system
Berger, M. Why I sneeze, shiver, hiccup, and yawn (k-3)   **612.7**
Parker, S. The brain and the nervous system (4 and up)   **612.8**
Simon, S. The brain (3-6)   **612.8**

Nesbit, E. (Edith), 1858-1924
The best of Shakespeare (4 and up)   **822.3**
The enchanted castle (4-6)   **Fic**
Five children and it (4-6)   **Fic**
The phoenix and the carpet. See note under Nesbit, E. Five children and it   **Fic**
The railway children (4-6)   **Fic**
The story of the amulet. See note under Nesbit, E. Five children and it   **Fic**

Nesbit, Edith *See* Nesbit, E. (Edith), 1858-1924

Nespeca, Sue McCleaf
Library programming for families with young children   **027.62**

Ness, Evaline, 1911-1986
Sam, Bangs & Moonshine   **E**

Ness, Evaline, 1911-1986—*Continued*
See/See also pages in the following book(s):
Newbery and Caldecott Medal books, 1966-1975
p186-98 **028.5**

Nessa's fish. Luenn, N. **E**

A **nest** and a web. McCaughrean, G.
In McCaughrean, G. The silver treasure:
myths and legends of the world p38-41 **398.2**

A **nest** full of eggs. Jenkins, P. B. **598**

A **nest** of dinosaurs. Norell, M. **567.9**

Net. Ellis, S.
In Ellis, S. Back of beyond **S C**

Netherlands
Fiction
DeJong, M. The wheel on the school (4-6) **Fic**

Dodge, M. M. Hans Brinker; or, The silver
skates (4 and up) **Fic**
Oppenheim, S. L. The lily cupboard **E**
Propp, V. W. When the soldiers were gone (3-5) **Fic**

Vos, I. Anna is still here (4 and up) **Fic**
Vos, I. Hide and seek (4 and up) **Fic**
Vos, I. The key is lost (4 and up) **Fic**

Nettie's trip South. Turner, A. W. **Fic**

Neufeld, John, 1938-
Almost a hero (5 and up) **Fic**

Neurology *See* Nervous system

**Neuwied, Maximilian Alexander Philipp, Prinz
von Wied-** *See* Wied, Maximilian, Prinz von,
1782-1867

Nevada
Stefoff, R. Nevada
In Celebrate the states **973**
Stein, R. C. Nevada
In America the beautiful, second series **973**

Fiction
Cox, J. Weird stories from the Lonesome Café
(2-4) **Fic**
Snyder, Z. K. The runaways (4 and up) **Fic**

The **never-ending** song. Jaffe, N.
In Jaffe, N. The uninvited guest and other
Jewish holiday tales p11-16 **296.4**
"**Never** far from you". San Souci, R.
In San Souci, R. Even more short & shivery
p52-56 **398.2**
Never kick a slipper at the moon. Sandburg, C.
In Sandburg, C. Rootabaga stories pt 1 p151-
55 **S C**
In Sandburg, C. The Sandburg treasury p71-
72 **818**
Never take a pig to lunch and other poems about
the fun of eating (k-3) **811.008**
Never to forget: the Jews of the Holocaust.
Meltzer, M. **940.53**

Neville, Emily Cheney, 1919-
It's like this, Cat (5 and up) **Fic**
The **new** African Americans. Ashabranner, B. K. **305.8**

The **new** Americans. Maestro, B. **973.2**

The **new** baby at your house. Cole, J. **306.8**
The **New** book of knowledge **031**
The **New** book of knowledge online. (3 and up)
See entry in Part 2: Web Resources
The **New** book of popular science **503**
The **New** book of popular science online. (5 and
up) See entry in Part 2: Web Resources
New century technology [series]
Baker, C. W. Virtual reality **006**
A **new** coat for Anna. Ziefert, H. **E**

New England
Fiction
Alcott, L. M. Little women (5 and up) **Fic**
Alcott, L. M. An old-fashioned Thanksgiving
(3-5) **Fic**
Hall, D. Ox-cart man **E**
Wiggin, K. D. S. Rebecca of Sunnybrook Farm
(4 and up) **Fic**

The **new** girl. Stewart, S.
In A Glory of unicorns p185-94 **S C**

New Hampshire
Otfinoski, S. New Hampshire
In Celebrate the states **973**
Stein, R. C. New Hampshire
In America the beautiful, second series **973**

Fiction
Blos, J. W. A gathering of days: a New England
girl's journal, 1830-32 (6 and up) **Fic**
New handbook for storytellers, Caroline Feller
Bauer's. Bauer, C. F. **372.6**

New Jersey
Moragne, W. New Jersey
In Celebrate the states **973**
Stein, R. C. New Jersey
In America the beautiful, second series **973**

Fiction
Karr, K. Man of the family (4 and up) **Fic**
Walker, S. M. The 18 penny goose **E**
The **new** kid on the block: poems. Prelutsky, J. **811**

New Mexico
Kent, D. New Mexico
In America the beautiful, second series **973**
McDaniel, M. New Mexico
In Celebrate the states **973**
Fiction
Hobbs, W. Kokopelli's flute (5 and up) **Fic**
Johnston, T. Alice Nizzy Nazzy, the Witch of
Santa Fe **E**
The **new** mother. San Souci, R.
In San Souci, R. Even more short & shivery
p76-82 **398.2**
New neighbors for Nora. Hurwitz, J. **Fic**

New Orleans (La.)
Fiction
Schroeder, A. Satchmo's blues **E**
Race relations
Bridges, R. Through my eyes: the autobiography
of Ruby Bridges (4 and up) **92**

New Orleans (La.)—Race relations—*Continued*
Coles, R. The story of Ruby Bridges (1-3)
  370

The **New** Oxford treasury of children's poems
(3-5)   **808.81**

New patches for old. Walker, B. K.
 In Walker, B. K. A treasury of Turkish folktales for children p135-38   **398.2**

New shoes for Silvia. Hurwitz, J.   **E**

New shoes, red shoes. Rollings, S.   **E**

New view almanac. (6 and up) See entry in Part
 2: Web Resources

The **new** way things work. Macaulay, D. **600**

New World dictionary of computer terms, Webster's   **004**

New Year
 Bernhard, E. Happy New Year! (3-5)
   394.26

    Fiction
 Rattigan, J. K. Dumpling soup   **E**

New Year, Chinese See Chinese New Year

New Year's Day. Delacre, L.
 In Delacre, L. Salsa stories p1-7 **S C**

New Year's hats for the statues. Uchida, Y.
 In Snowy day: stories and poems p3-11
   808.8

New York (N.Y.)
    Fiction
 Avi. Abigail takes the wheel (2-4) **Fic**
 Bartone, E. American too   **E**
 Bartone, E. Peppe the lamplighter **E**
 Cowley, J. Gracias, the Thanksgiving turkey
    E
 Egielski, R. The gingerbread boy (k-3)
   398.2
 Gray, L. Falcon's egg (3-5)   **Fic**
 Griffin, A. The other Shepards (6 and up)
    Fic
 Herold, M. R. A very important day **E**
 Holman, F. Slake's limbo (6 and up) **Fic**
 Keats, E. J. My dog is lost!   **E**
 Khalsa, D. K. How pizza came to Queens
    E
 Lasky, K. Dreams in the golden country (4 and
  up)   **Fic**
 Levine, G. C. Dave at night (5 and up)
    Fic
 Merrill, J. The pushcart war (5 and up)
    Fic
 Neville, E. C. It's like this, Cat (5 and up)
    Fic
 Paraskevas, B. On the day the tall ships sailed
    E
 Priceman, M. Froggie went a-courting (k-3)
   782.42
 Rael, E. O. What Zeesie saw on Delancey Street
    E
 Raskin, E. The mysterious disappearance of
  Leon (I mean Noel) (4 and up) **Fic**
 Ritter, J. H. Over the wall (6 and up) **Fic**
 Roberts, W. D. The kidnappers (4 and up)
    Fic
 Sawyer, R. Roller skates (4-6)   **Fic**
 Schotter, R. Nothing ever happens on 90th
  Street   **E**

 Selden, G. The cricket in Times Square (3-6)
    Fic
 Skolsky, M. W. Hannah and the whistling tea
  kettle   **E**
 Taylor, S. All-of-a-kind family (4-6) **Fic**
 Thompson, K. Kay Thompson's Eloise **E**
 Torres, L. Subway sparrow   **E**
 Waber, B. Lyle, Lyle, crocodile   **E**
 Weitzman, J. P. You can't take a balloon into
  the Metropolitan Museum   **E**
    Social conditions
 Wolf, B. Homeless (2-4)   **362.5**

New York (N.Y.). Grand Central Terminal *See*
 Grand Central Terminal (New York, N.Y.)

New York (N.Y.). Statue of Liberty *See* Statue
 of Liberty (New York, N.Y.)

New York (State)
 Heinrichs, A. New York
  In America the beautiful, second series
    973
 Schomp, V. New York
  In Celebrate the states   **973**
    Fiction
 Ray, M. L. Basket moon   **E**
 Auch, M. J. Frozen summer (4 and up)
    Fic
 Auch, M. J. Journey to nowhere (4 and up)
    Fic
 Auch, M. J. The road to home (4 and up)
    Fic
 George, J. C. Frightful's mountain (5 and up)
    Fic
 Irving, W. Rip Van Winkle (5 and up) **Fic**
 O'Dell, S. Sarah Bishop (6 and up) **Fic**
    History
 Fradin, D. B. The New York Colony (4 and up)
   974.7

New York City Public High School for Ballet
 See Ballet Tech School (New York, N.Y.)

The **New** York Colony. Fradin, D. B. **974.7**

New York Public Library
 The Black experience in children's books. See
  The Black experience in children's books
   016.3058

The **New** York Public Library amazing African
 American history. Patrick, D. **305.8**

The **New** York Public Library amazing space.
 Campbell, A.   **520**

The **New** York Public Library amazing women in
 American history. Heinemann, S. **305.4**

**New York Public Library answer books for
 kids series**
 Heinemann, S. The New York Public Library
  amazing women in American history
   305.4
 Patrick, D. The New York Public Library amazing African American history **305.8**

The **New** York Public Library kid's guide to research. Heiligman, D.   **025.5**

The **New** York Public Library science desk reference. Barnes-Svarney, P.   **500**

New Zealand

 See also Maoris
 Smelt, R. New Zealand (5 and up) **993**

New Zealand—*Continued*
Fiction
Mahy, M. The other side of silence (6 and up)
    Fic

Newberry, Clare Turlay, 1903-1970
  April's kittens   **E**
Newbery, John, 1713-1767
See/See also pages in the following book(s):
Newbery Medal books, 1922-1955 p6-9
    028.5
The **Newbery** & Caldecott medal books, 1986-
2000   **028.5**
The **Newbery** and Caldecott awards   **028.5**
Newbery and Caldecott Medal books, 1966-1975
    028.5
Newbery and Caldecott Medal books, 1976-1985
    028.5
The **Newbery** companion. Gillespie, J. T.
    028.5

Newbery Medal
Gillespie, J. T. The Newbery companion
    028.5
The Newbery & Caldecott medal books, 1986-
2000   **028.5**
The Newbery and Caldecott awards   **028.5**
Newbery and Caldecott Medal books, 1966-1975
    028.5
Newbery and Caldecott Medal books, 1976-1985
    028.5
Newbery Medal books, 1922-1955   **028.5**
Newbery Medal books, 1922-1955   **028.5**
Newbery Medal titles
Armstrong, W. H. Sounder (1970)   **Fic**
Blos, J. W. A gathering of days: a New England
  girl's journal, 1830-32 (1980)   **Fic**
Brink, C. R. Caddie Woodlawn (1936)   **Fic**
Byars, B. C. The summer of the swans (1971)
    Fic
Cleary, B. Dear Mr. Henshaw (1984)   **Fic**
Coatsworth, E. J. The cat who went to heaven
  (1931)   **Fic**
Cooper, S. The grey king (1976)   **Fic**
Creech, S. Walk two moons (1995)   **Fic**
Curtis, C. P. Bud, not Buddy (2000)   **Fic**
Cushman, K. The midwife's apprentice (1996)
    Fic
De Angeli, M. L. The door in the wall (1950)
    Fic
DeJong, M. The wheel on the school (1955)
    Fic
Du Bois, W. P. The twenty-one balloons (1948)
    Fic
Estes, E. Ginger Pye (1952)   **Fic**
Field, R. Hitty: her first hundred years (1930)
    Fic
Fleischman, P. Joyful noise: poems for two
  voices (1989)   **811**
Fleischman, S. The whipping boy (1987)
    Fic
Forbes, E. Johnny Tremain (1944)   **Fic**
Fox, P. The slave dancer (1974)   **Fic**
Freedman, R. Lincoln: a photobiography (1988)
    92
George, J. C. Julie of the wolves (1973)
    Fic

Hamilton, V. M. C. Higgins the great (1975)
    Fic
Henry, M. King of the wind (1949)   **Fic**
Hesse, K. Out of the dust (1998)   **Fic**
Keith, H. Rifles for Watie (1958)   **Fic**
Konigsburg, E. L. From the mixed-up files of
  Mrs. Basil E. Frankweiler (1968)   **Fic**
Konigsburg, E. L. The view from Saturday
  (1997)   **Fic**
Krumgold, J. Onion John (1960)   **Fic**
Lawson, R. Rabbit Hill (1945)   **Fic**
L'Engle, M. A wrinkle in time (1963)   **Fic**
Lowry, L. The giver (1994)   **Fic**
Lowry, L. Number the stars (1990)   **Fic**
MacLachlan, P. Sarah, plain and tall (1986)
    Fic
McKinley, R. The hero and the crown (1985)
    Fic
Naylor, P. R. Shiloh (1992)   **Fic**
Neville, E. C. It's like this, Cat (1964)   **Fic**
O'Brien, R. C. Mrs. Frisby and the rats of
  NIMH (1972)   **Fic**
O'Dell, S. Island of the Blue Dolphins (1961)
    Fic
Paterson, K. Bridge to Terabithia (1978)
    Fic
Peck, R. A year down yonder (2001)   **Fic**
Raskin, E. The Westing game (1979)   **Fic**
Rylant, C. Missing May (1993)   **Fic**
Sachar, L. Holes (1999)   **Fic**
Sawyer, R. Roller skates (1937)   **Fic**
Seredy, K. The white stag (1938)   **Fic**
Speare, E. G. The bronze bow (1962)   **Fic**
Speare, E. G. The witch of Blackbird Pond
  (1959)   **Fic**
Sperry, A. Call it courage (1941)   **Fic**
Spinelli, J. Maniac Magee (1991)   **Fic**
Taylor, M. D. Roll of thunder, hear my cry
  (1977)   **Fic**
Treviño, E. B. de. I, Juan de Pareja (1966)
    Fic
Vining, E. G. Adam of the road (1943)
    Fic
Voigt, C. Dicey's song (1983)   **Fic**
Willard, N. A visit to William Blake's inn
  (1982)   **811**
Wojciechowska, M. Shadow of a bull (1965)
    Fic
Yates, E. Amos Fortune, free man (1951)
    92

Newcome, Zita, 1959-
  Toddlerobics   **E**
  Toddlerobics animal fun. See note under
  Newcome, Z. Toddlerobics   **E**
Newfoundland
Fiction
Harlow, J. H. Star in the storm   **Fic**
Newman, Barbara
  The illustrated book of ballet stories (4-6)
    792.8
Newman, Deborah
  Christmas at the Cratchits
    In The Big book of Christmas plays p240-49
    808.82

Newman, Robert, 1909-1988
The case of the Baker Street Irregular (5 and up) **Fic**

Newmark, Ann
Chemistry (4 and up) **540**

News!. Jacobs, J.
In Jacobs, J. English fairy tales p384-85
398.2

Newsboys *See* Newspaper carriers

Newspaper carriers
Fiction
Kroeger, M. K. Paperboy **E**
Pilkey, D. The paperboy **E**

Newspapers
See also Periodicals
Bentley, N. The young journalist's book (3-6)
070.1
Granfield, L. Extra! Extra! (4-6) **071**
Fiction
Clements, A. The Landry News (4-6) **Fic**

Next-door neighbors. Ellis, S. **Fic**

Next-of-kin. Olson, A. N.
In Olson, A. N. Ask the bones: scary stories from around the world p17-23 **398.2**

Next stop, Grand Central. Kalman, M. **E**

Next year in Jerusalem. Schwartz, H. **296.1**

Nez Percé Indians
Sneve, V. D. H. The Nez Percé (3-5)
970.004
See/See also pages in the following book(s):
Freedman, R. Indian chiefs p91-113 (6 and up)
920

NFL *See* National Football League

NGAKids. (3-6) See entry in Part 2: Web Resources

NgCheong-Lum, Roseline, 1962-
Fiji (5 and up) **996**
France (4 and up) **944**
Tahiti (5 and up) **996**

Nguyen, Chi Thien, 1933-
Cooking the Vietnamese way
In Easy menu ethnic cookbooks **641.5**

Niagara Falls (N.Y. and Ont.)
Fisher, L. E. Niagara Falls (4 and up)
971.3

Nibble, nibble, Jenny Archer. Conford, E. See note under Conford, E. A case for Jenny Archer **Fic**

Nicaragua
Kott, J. Nicaragua (5 and up) **972.85**
Folklore
See Folklore—Nicaragua

Nichol, Barbara
Beethoven lives upstairs (3-5) **Fic**

Nichols, Judy
Storytimes for two-year-olds **027.62**

Nicholson, Darrel
Wild boars (3-6) **599.63**

Nicholson, Sir William, 1872-1949
(il) Bianco, M. W. The velveteen rabbit
Fic

Nicklaus, Carol
(il) Otfinoski, S. Speaking up, speaking out
808.5

Nicknames
Fiction
Korman, G. The sixth grade nickname game (4-6) **Fic**

Nieves, Ernesto Ramos *See* Ramos Nieves, Ernesto

Niger
Seffal, R. Niger (5 and up) **966.26**

Nigeria
Onyefulu, I. Emeka's gift **E**
Folklore
See Folklore—Nigeria
Social life and customs
Onyefulu, I. Chidi only likes blue **E**
Onyefulu, I. Ogbo (2-4) **966.9**

Night
See also Bedtime; Day
Fiction
Aylesworth, J. Country crossing **E**
Banks, K. And if the moon could talk **E**
Banks, K. The night worker **E**
Berger, B. Grandfather Twilight **E**
Bonsall, C. N. Who's afraid of the dark?
E
Brown, M. W. A child's good night book
E
Brown, M. W. Goodnight moon **E**
Bunting, E. Ghost's hour, spook's hour **E**
Caduto, M. J. Keepers of the night **398.2**
Crowe, R. L. Clyde monster **E**
Dragonwagon, C. Half a moon and one whole star **E**
Durán, C. Hildilid's night **E**
Fox, M. Night noises **E**
Murphy, J. Peace at last **E**
Rice, E. City night **E**
Rylant, C. Night in the country **E**
Schnur, S. Night lights **E**
Tafuri, N. What the sun sees **E**
Weiss, N. Where does the brown bear go?
E

Night at the fair. Crews, D. **E**
The **night** before Christmas. Moore, C. C.
811
The **night** crossing. Ackerman, K. **Fic**
The **Night** doctor
In Raw Head, bloody bones p47-50
398.2
Night garden. Wong, J. S. **811**
Night golf. Miller, W. **E**
The **Night** has ears (k-3) **398.9**
Night in the country. Rylant, C. **E**
The **night** it rained. Schwartz, A.
In Schwartz, A. In a dark, dark room, and other scary stories p42-49 **398.2**
The **night** journey. Lasky, K. **Fic**
Night journeys. Avi **Fic**
Night lights. Schnur, S. **E**
Night noises. Fox, M. **E**
The **night** of Las Posadas. De Paola, T. **E**

The **night** of San Juan. Delacre, L.
   In Delacre, L. Salsa stories p28-36   **S C**

A **night** of terror. Olson, A. N.
   In Olson, A. N. Ask the bones: scary stories
   from around the world p60-65   **398.2**

A **night** of terrors. San Souci, R.
   In San Souci, R. Even more short & shivery
   p128-35   **398.2**

The **Night** of the Leonids. Konigsburg, E. L.
   In Konigsburg, E. L. Altogether, one at a
   time p13-28   **S C**

The **night** of the pomegranate. Wynne-Jones, T.
   In Wynne-Jones, T. Some of the kinder planets: stories p1-7   **S C**

Night of the twisters. Ruckman, I.   **Fic**

Night photograph. Conrad, P.
   In Conrad, P. Our house p12-21   **S C**

Night shift daddy. Spinelli, E.   **E**

Night sky. Stott, C.   **520**

Night sky. See Mechler, G. National Audubon Society first field guide: night sky   **520**

The **night** swimmers. Byars, B. C.   **Fic**

Night tree. Bunting, E.   **E**

The **night** worker. Banks, K.   **E**

The **nightingale**. Andersen, H. C.   **Fic**
   also in Shedlock, M. L. The art of the storyteller p243-58   **372.6**
   also in The Yellow fairy book p291-300
      398.2

The **Nightingale** and the rose. Wilde, O.
   In Wilde, O. The fairy tales of Oscar Wilde
   p24-31   **S C**

Nightingales
          Fiction
Andersen, H. C. The nightingale (2-5)   **Fic**

Nightmares: poems to trouble your sleep.
   Prelutsky, J.   **811**

Nights of the pufflings. McMillan, B.   **598**

Nighty-nightmare. Howe, J. See note under
   Howe, J. The celery stalks at midnight
      Fic

Nikita the Tanner. Afanas'ev, A. N.
   In Afanas'ev, A. N. Russian fairy tales p310-
   11   **398.2**

Nikola-Lisa, W.
   Till year's good end (2-4)   **942.02**

Nim and the war effort. Lee, M.   **E**

Nine for California. Levitin, S.   **E**

Nine-in-one, Grr! Grr!. Blia Xiong   **398.2**

The **nine-ton** cat: behind the scenes at an art museum. Thomson, P.   **708**

Ningun. MacDonald, M. R.
   In MacDonald, M. R. The storyteller's start-
   up book p185-92   **372.6**

Nirgiotis, Nicholas
   Thomas Edison (4-6)   **92**

Nitrogen
   Farndon, J. Nitrogen
      In The Elements [Benchmark Bks.]   **546**

Nix nought nothing. Jacobs, J.
   In Jacobs, J. English fairy tales p41-46
      398.2

Nixon, Joan Lowery, 1927-
   Aggie's home (3-5)   **Fic**
   Caught in the act. See note under Nixon, J. L.
   A family apart   **Fic**
   Circle of love. See note under Nixon, J. L. A
   family apart   **Fic**
   A dangerous promise. See note under Nixon, J.
   L. A family apart   **Fic**
   David's search. See note under Nixon, J. L.
   Aggie's home   **Fic**
   A family apart (5 and up)   **Fic**
   In the face of danger. See note under Nixon, J.
   L. A family apart   **Fic**
   Keeping secrets. See note under Nixon, J. L. A
   family apart   **Fic**
   Lucy's wish. See note under Nixon, J. L.
   Aggie's home   **Fic**
   A place to belong. See note under Nixon, J. L.
   A family apart   **Fic**
   Will's choice. See note under Nixon, J. L.
   Aggie's home   **Fic**

The **Nixy**
   In The Yellow fairy book p108-13   **398.2**

NMAI conexus. (5 and up) See entry in Part 2:
   Web Resources

No, Boconono!. Aardema, V.
   In Aardema, V. Misoso p51-57   **398.2**

No, David!. Shannon, D.   **E**

No dogs allowed. Cutler, J. See note under Cutler,
   J. Rats!   **Fic**

No estiendo
   In Stockings of buttermilk: American folktales
   p45-46   **398.2**

No fighting, no biting!. Minarik, E. H.   **E**

No-good Claus. Mark, J.
   In The Oxford book of scary tales p123-29
      808.8

No good in art. Cohen, M. See note under Cohen,
   M. It's George!   **E**

The **no-guitar** blues. Soto, G.
   In Soto, G. Baseball in April, and other stories p43-51   **S C**

No matter what. Gliori, D.   **E**

No roses for Harry!. Zion, G. See note under Zion,
   G. Harry the dirty dog   **E**

No sword. Kimmel, E. A.
   In Kimmel, E. A. Sword of the samurai p105-
   09   **Fic**

No turning back. Naidoo, B.   **Fic**

Noah hunts a wooly mammoth. Norman, H.
   In Norman, H. The girl who dreamed only
   geese, and other tales of the Far North
      398.2

Noah's ark
   Geisert, A. The ark (k-3)   **222**
   Jonas, A. Aardvarks, disembark!   **E**
   Spier, P. Noah's ark (k-2)   **222**
          Fiction
   Geisert, A. After the flood   **E**
   Rounds, G. Washday on Noah's ark   **E**
          Poetry
   Bernos de Gasztold, C. Prayers from the ark
      841

North, Sterling, 1906-1974
  Rascal (5 and up)   **599.7**
North America
Natural history
  See Natural history—North America
North American cranes. DuTemple, L. A.
        598

North American Indians *See* Native Americans
North American moose. DuTemple, L. A.
        599.65

North Carolina
  Hintz, M. North Carolina
  In America the beautiful, second series
        973

  Shirley, D. North Carolina
  In Celebrate the states   **973**
Fiction
  Dowell, F. O. Dovey Coe (4 and up)   **Fic**
  Pinkney, G. J. Back home   **E**
Natural history
  See Natural history—North Carolina
Race relations
  Tillage, L. Leon's story (4 and up)   **92**
North Dakota
  Hintz, M. North Dakota
  In America the beautiful, second series
        973

North Pole
  See also Arctic regions
  Ferris, J. Arctic explorer: the story of Matthew
    Henson (3-6)   **92**
  Steger, W. Over the top of the world (4 and up)
        998
Fiction
  Van Allsburg, C. The Polar Express   **E**
The **North** Pole computer caper. Priore, F. V.
  In The Big book of Christmas plays p189-99
        808.82

North to freedom. Holm, A.   **Fic**
Northern lights *See* Auroras
Northern lights. Souza, D. M.   **538**
Northern Rhodesia *See* Zambia
Northmen *See* Vikings
Northwest, Pacific *See* Pacific Northwest
Norton, Mary, 1903-1992
  Bed-knob and broomstick (3-6)   **Fic**
  The Borrowers (3-6)   **Fic**
  The Borrowers afield. See note under Norton,
    M. The Borrowers   **Fic**
  The Borrowers afloat. See note under Norton,
    M. The Borrowers   **Fic**
  The Borrowers aloft. See note under Norton, M.
    The Borrowers   **Fic**
  The Borrowers avenged. See note under Norton,
    M. The Borrowers   **Fic**
  The magic bed-knob
  In Norton, M. Bed-knob and broomstick
        Fic
  Paul's tale
  In The Oxford treasury of children's stories
    p151-59   **S C**

Norway
Folklore
  See Folklore—Norway
Nose
Fiction
  Brown, M. T. Arthur's nose   **E**
Nostradamus, 1503-1566
See/See also pages in the following book(s):
  Krull, K. They saw the future p51-57 (4 and up)
        133.3

The **not-just-anybody** family. Byars, B. C.
        Fic
Not my dog. Rodowsky, C. F.   **Fic**
Not one damsel in distress. Yolen, J.   **398.2**
Not so fast, Songololo. Daly, N.   **E**
The **not-so-jolly** Roger. Scieszka, J. See note un-
  der Scieszka, J. Knights of the kitchen table
        Fic

Not so Rotten Ralph. Gantos, J. See note under
  Gantos, J. Rotten Ralph   **E**
Notable children's trade books in the field of so-
  cial studies   **016.3**
Nothing. Hughes, R.
  In Bauer, C. F. Celebrations p144-45
        808.8

Nothing but trouble. Wright, B. R.   **Fic**
Nothing ever happens on 90th Street. Schotter, R.
        E
Nothing here but trees. Van Leeuwen, J.   **E**
Noureddin and the fair Persian
  In The Arabian nights entertainments p267-94
        398.2

Novacek, Michael J.
See/See also pages in the following book(s):
  Talking with adventurers p60-67 (4-6)   **920**
Novak, Matt, 1962-
  Little Wolf, Big Wolf   **E**
NoveList. See entry in Part 2: Web Resources
Novelty and romancement. Carroll, L.
  In Carroll, L. The complete works of Lewis
    Carroll p970-78   **828**
Now is your time!. Myers, W. D.   **305.8**
Now one foot, now the other. De Paola, T.
        E
Now we are six. Milne, A. A.   **821**
  also in Milne, A. A. The world of Christo-
    pher Robin p119-234   **821**
Now you see it, now you don't. Simon, S.
        152.14

Nowhere to hide. Olson, A. N.
  In Olson, A. N. Ask the bones: scary stories
    from around the world p66-72   **398.2**
Nuckelavee. San Souci, R.
  In San Souci, R. Short & shivery p92-95
        398.2

Nuclear energy
  Graham, I. Nuclear power (4-6)   **333.7**
Nuclear physics
  Gallant, R. A. The ever changing atom (5 and
  up)   **539.7**
Nuclear power. Graham, I.   **333.7**

Nuclear power plants

See also Nuclear energy

Nuclear weapons

See also Atomic bomb

Nuestra Señora de Atocha (Ship)

Gibbons, G. Sunken treasure (k-3) **910.4**

Number patterns *See* Patterns (Mathematics)

Number systems *See* Numbers

Number the stars. Lowry, L. **Fic**

Number theory

See also Factorials

Numbers

See also Counting

Murphy, S. J. Henry the fourth (k-1) **513**

Packard, E. Big numbers (k-3) **513**

Numerals

See also Numbers; Roman numerals

Adler, D. A. Roman numerals (2-4) **513**

Numeration *See* Numbers

Numerical analysis

See also Approximate computation

Numeroff, Laura Joffe

The Chicken sisters **E**

If you give a moose a muffin. See note under Numeroff, L. J. If you give a mouse a cookie **E**

If you give a mouse a cookie **E**

If you give a pig a pancake. See note under Numeroff, L. J. If you give a mouse a cookie **E**

If you take a mouse to the movies. See note under Numeroff, L. J. If you give a mouse a cookie **E**

Sometimes I wonder if poodles like noodles (k-3) **811**

What mommies do best **E**

Numismatics

See also Coins

Nunn, Laura Silverstein

(jt. auth) Silverstein, A. Allergies **616.97**

(jt. auth) Silverstein, A. The California condor **598**

(jt. auth) Silverstein, A. Common colds **616.2**

(jt. auth) Silverstein, A. Cuts, scrapes, scabs, and scars **617.1**

(jt. auth) Silverstein, A. The Florida panther **599.75**

(jt. auth) Silverstein, A. Is that a rash? **616.5**

(jt. auth) Silverstein, A. Plate tectonics **551.1**

(jt. auth) Silverstein, A. Sleep **612.8**

(jt. auth) Silverstein, A. Tooth decay and cavities **617.6**

Nuns

Fiction

Lorbiecki, M. Sister Anne's hands **E**

The **nun's** priest's tale. Cohen, B.

In Cohen, B. Canterbury tales **821**

Nurse Corps (Army) *See* United States. Army Nurse Corps

Nursery rhymes

See also Jump rope rhymes

The Arnold Lobel book of Mother Goose (k-2) **398.8**

Aylesworth, J. The completed hickory dickory dock **398.8**

Aylesworth, J. My son John **E**

The Baby's bedtime book **808.81**

The Baby's lap book **398.8**

Baker, K. Big fat hen **398.8**

Brown, M. T. Finger rhymes **796.1**

Brown, M. T. Hand rhymes **796.1**

Brown, M. T. Play rhymes **796.1**

Chorao, K. Knock at the door and other baby action rhymes **398.8**

The Comic adventures of Old Mother Hubbard and her dog **398.8**

Dunn, O. Hippety-hop, hippety-hay **398.8**

Emberley, B. Drummer Hoff **398.8**

Galdone, P. The cat goes fiddle-i-fee (k-1) **398.8**

Galdone, P. Three little kittens **398.8**

The Glorious Mother Goose **398.8**

Hale, S. J. Mary had a little lamb (k-2) **811**

Here comes Mother Goose **398.8**

Hoberman, M. A. Miss Mary Mack **398.8**

James Marshall's Mother Goose **398.8**

Keats, E. J. Over in the meadow **E**

Marino, J. Mother Goose time **027.62**

Miss Mary Mack and other children's street rhymes **796.1**

Mother Goose [illus. by Brian Wildsmith] **398.8**

My very first Mother Goose **398.8**

Old Mother Hubbard and her wonderful dog **398.8**

The Orchard book of nursery rhymes **398.8**

Pat-a-cake and other play rhymes **398.8**

Patz, N. Moses supposes his toeses are roses and 7 other silly old rhymes **398.8**

Polacco, P. Babushka's Mother Goose **398.8**

Prelutsky, J. Beneath a blue umbrella: rhymes (k-3) **811**

Prelutsky, J. Ride a purple pelican (k-3) **811**

Read-aloud rhymes for the very young (k-2) **821.008**

The Real Mother Goose **398.8**

Scieszka, J. The book that Jack wrote (2-4) **811**

Sylvia Long's Mother Goose **398.8**

Tomie dePaola's Mother Goose **398.8**

Tortillitas para mamá and other nursery rhymes **398.8**

Wilner, I. The baby's game book **398.8**

Winter, J. The house that Jack built **398.8**

Dictionaries

The Oxford dictionary of nursery rhymes **398.8**

History and criticism

See/See also pages in the following book(s):

Only connect: readings on children's literature p110-21 **028.5**

Nursery schools
See also Preschool education
Nursery tales around the world. Sierra, J.
398.2

Nurses
Crofford, E. Healing warrior: a story about Sister Elizabeth Kenny (3-5) 92
Wells, R. Mary on horseback (4 and up)
92

Nutcracker (Ballet)
See/See also pages in the following book(s):
McCaughrean, G. The Random House book of stories from the ballet p57-69 (4 and up)
792.8
Newman, B. The illustrated book of ballet stories p52-61 (4-6) 792.8
The **nutcracker**. Bell, A. Fic
Nutcracker. Hoffmann, E. T. A. Fic
In Christmas fairy tales p47-57 398.2
The **nutcracker**. Schulman, J. Fic
The **nutcracker** ballet. Hautzig, D. E

Nutrition
See also Diet; Eating customs
D'Amico, J. The healthy body cookbook (4-6)
641.5
Kalbacken, J. The food pyramid (2-4)
613.2
Kalbacken, J. Vitamins and minerals (2-4)
613.2
Rockwell, L. Good enough to eat (k-3)
613.2
VanCleave, J. P. Janice VanCleave's food and nutrition for every kid (4 and up) 613.2
Nuts. Babbitt, N.
In Babbitt, N. The Devil's storybook p47-51
S C
Nuts! Nuts! Nuts!. Van Laan, N.
In Van Laan, N. With a whoop and a holler p61-64 398.2
Nuts to you!. Ehlert, L. E
Nutt, Ken *See* Beddows, Eric, 1951-
Nye, Naomi Shihab
(comp) Salting the ocean. See Salting the ocean
811.008

Nye, Robert, 1939-
Beowulf against Grendel
In Bauer, C. F. Celebrations p105-08
808.8

NYPL *See* New York Public Library

O

O Jerusalem. Yolen, J. 811
Oak
Morrison, G. Oak tree (3-6) 583
Pfeffer, W. A log's life (k-3) 577.3
Royston, A. Life cycle of an oak tree (k-3)
583
Oak tree. Morrison, G. 583
Obata, Chiura, 1888-1975
About
Ross, M. E. Nature art with Chiura Obata (4 and up) 92

The **obeah** woman's birthday present. Joseph, L.
In Joseph, L. The mermaid's twin sister: more stories from Trinidad p49-59 398.2
Oberman, Sheldon, 1949-
The always prayer shawl E
Obesity
Control
See Weight loss
Fiction
Holt, K. W. When Zachary Beaver came to town (5 and up) Fic
O'Brien, Anne Sibley, 1952-
(il) Havill, J. Jamaica's find E
(il) Knight, M. B. Talking walls 909
(il) Knight, M. B. Talking walls: the stories continue 909
O'Brien, Dan
See/See also pages in the following book(s):
Knapp, R. Top 10 American men's Olympic gold medalists (4 and up) 920
O'Brien, John, 1953-
(il) Blackstone, M. This is soccer 796.334
(il) Jones, C. F. Mistakes that worked 609
(il) Lewis, J. P. The bookworm's feast 811
(il) Terban, M. Funny you should ask
793.73
(il) The Twelve days of Christmas. See The Twelve days of Christmas 782.28
O'Brien, Robert C., 1918-1973
Mrs. Frisby and the rats of NIMH (4 and up)
Fic
See/See also pages in the following book(s):
Newbery and Caldecott Medal books, 1966-1975 p83-92 028.5
O'Brien, Steven
Pancho Villa (5 and up) 92
Occult sciences *See* Occultism
Occultism
See also Fortune telling; Prophecies
Fiction
Snyder, Z. K. The headless cupid (5 and up)
Fic
Occupations
Miller, M. Guess who? E
Miller, M. Who uses this? E
Fiction
Rockwell, A. F. Career day E
Ocean
See also Seashore
Cole, J. The magic school bus on the ocean floor (2-4) 591.7
Simon, S. Oceans (3-6) 551.46
Stille, D. R. Oceans (2-4) 551.46
Ocean bottom
Gibbons, G. Exploring the deep, dark sea (k-3)
551.46
Ocean currents
See also El Niño (Ocean current)
Oceanographic submersibles *See* Submersibles
Oceanography
VanCleave, J. P. Janice VanCleave's oceans for every kid (4 and up) 551.46

Old Stormalong finds a man-sized ship. Walker, P. R.
In Walker, P. R. Big men, big country p22-28
398.2

Old Testament *See* Bible. O.T.

Old Turtle's 90 knock-knocks, jokes, and riddles. Kessler, L. P.
793.73

The **old** witch. Jacobs, J.
In Jacobs, J. English fairy tales p312-17
398.2

The **old** woman and her dumpling. Hearn, L.
In Womenfolk and fairy tales p44-50
398.2

The **old** woman and her pig. Jacobs, J.
In Jacobs, J. English fairy tales p31-33
398.2

The **old** woman in a pumpkin shell. MacDonald, M. R.
In MacDonald, M. R. Celebrate the world p61-66
372.6

The **old** woman who loved to read. Winch, J.
E

The **old** woman who named things. Rylant, C.
E

The **old** woman who ran away. Afanas'ev, A. N.
In Afanas'ev, A. N. Russian fairy tales p182-83
398.2

Old Yeller. Gipson, F. B.
Fic

Older, Jules
Telling time (k-3)
529

Ole & Trufa. Singer, I. B.
In Singer, I. B. Stories for children p249-53
S C

Olfson, Lewy
Christmas coast to coast
In The Big book of Christmas plays p80-98
808.82

Olimpia, Cucol, and the door. Fox, P.
In Fox, P. Amzat and his brothers: three Italian tales p45-67
398.2

Olive the other reindeer. Seibold, J. O.
E

Oliver, Jenni
(il) Lowry, L. A summer to die
Fic

Oliver. Hoff, S.
E

Oliver, Amanda, and Grandmother Pig. Van Leeuwen, J. See note under Van Leeuwen, J. Tales of Oliver Pig
E

Oliver and Albert, friends forever. Van Leeuwen, J. See note under Van Leeuwen, J. Tales of Oliver Pig
E

Oliver and Amanda and the big snow. Van Leeuwen, J. See note under Van Leeuwen, J. Tales of Oliver Pig
E

Oliver and Amanda's Christmas. Van Leeuwen, J. See note under Van Leeuwen, J. Tales of Oliver Pig
E

Oliver and Amanda's Halloween. Van Leeuwen, J. See note under Van Leeuwen, J. Tales of Oliver Pig
E

Oliver Pig at school. Van Leeuwen, J. See note under Van Leeuwen, J. Tales of Oliver Pig
E

Olivera, Francisco E.
(il) Cruz, A. The woman who outshone the sun
398.2

Olivia. Falconer, I.
E

Ology. (4-6) See entry in Part 2: Web Resources

Olson, Arielle North, 1932-
Ask the bones: scary stories from around the world (4 and up)
398.2
Contents: The haunted forest; The murky secret; Next-of-kin; The bloody fangs; Ask the bones; The four-footed horror; Beginning with the ears; Fiddling with fire; The Laplander's drum; A night of terror; Nowhere to hide; The handkerchief; The mousetrap; The speaking head; The dripping cutlass; The black snake; The hand of death; The invisible guest; A trace of blood; The bridal gown; The greedy man and the goat; The evil eye

Olympic games
Anderson, D. The story of the Olympics (5 and up)
796.48
Knapp, R. Top 10 American men's Olympic gold medalists (4 and up)
920
Knotts, B. The Summer Olympics (2-4)
796.48
Kristy, D. Coubertin's Olympics (5 and up)
92
Woff, R. The ancient Greek Olympics (4 and up)
796.48

Oma and Bobo. Schwartz, A.
E

O'Malley, Grace, 1530?-1603?
About
McCully, E. A. The pirate queen (k-3)
92

O'Malley, Kevin, 1961-
(il) Adler, D. A. Chanukah in Chelm
398.2
(il) Branley, F. M. The planets in our solar system
523.4
(il) Jackson, E. B. Cinder Edna
E
(il) Murphy, S. J. Jump, kangaroo, jump!
513

Oman
Foster, L. M. Oman (4 and up)
953

On beyond a million. Schwartz, D. M.
513

On Christmas Day in the morning (k-3)
782.28

On Christmas Eve. Brown, M. W.
E

On Hanukkah. Fishman, C.
296.4

On Market Street. Lobel, A.
E

On Mother's lap. Scott, A. H.
E

On my honor. Bauer, M. D.
Fic

On my own biography [series]
Lowery, L. Aunt Clara Brown
92

On Passover. Fishman, C.
296.4

On Purim. Fishman, C.
296.4

On Rosh Hashanah and Yom Kippur. Fishman, C.
296.4

On the banks of Plum Creek. Wilder, L. I. See note under Wilder, L. I. Little house in the big woods
Fic

On the bus with Joanna Cole. Cole, J.
92

On the day the tall ships sailed. Paraskevas, B.
E

On the day you were born. Frasier, D.
E

On the far side of the mountain. George, J. C.
Fic

On the Mayflower. Waters, K.
974.4

Only a fair day's huntin'
  In Grandfather tales p180-85   **398.2**
Only a pigeon. Kurtz, J.   **E**
Only connect: readings on children's literature
   028.5
Only Opal. Boulton, J.   **E**
Only the names remain. Bealer, A. W.
   970.004

Ontal, Carlo
  (il) Rylant, C. Best wishes   **92**

Onyefulu, Ifeoma, 1959-
  Chidi only likes blue   **E**
  Emeka's gift   **E**
  Ogbo (2-4)   **966.9**

Ooh-la-la. Marshall, J.
  In Marshall, J. Rats on the roof, and other
    stories p55-61   **S C**

Oot-Kwah-Tah, the seven star dancers. Caduto,
  M. J.
  In Caduto, M. J. Keepers of the night p63-65
   398.2

Opal: the journey of an understanding heart. See
  Boulton, J. Only Opal   **E**

Open wide. Keller, L.   **617.6**

Opening days (4 and up)   **811.008**

Opera
    Fiction
  Auch, M. J. Bantam of the opera   **E**
    Stories, plots, etc.
  Price, L. Aïda (4 and up)   **792.5**
  Rosenberg, J. Sing me a story (4-6)   **792.5**

Opie, Iona Archibald
  The lore and language of schoolchildren
   398
  (ed) The Classic fairy tales. See The Classic
    fairy tales   **398.2**
  (ed) Here comes Mother Goose. See Here
    comes Mother Goose   **398.8**
  (ed) I saw Esau. See I saw Esau   **398.8**
  (ed) My very first Mother Goose. See My very
    first Mother Goose   **398.8**
  (ed) The Oxford book of children's verse. See
    The Oxford book of children's verse
   821.008
  (ed) The Oxford dictionary of nursery rhymes.
    See The Oxford dictionary of nursery rhymes
   398.8

Opie, Peter, 1918-1982
  (ed) The Classic fairy tales. See The Classic
    fairy tales   **398.2**
  (ed) I saw Esau. See I saw Esau   **398.8**
  (ed) The Oxford book of children's verse. See
    The Oxford book of children's verse
   821.008
  (ed) The Oxford dictionary of nursery rhymes.
    See The Oxford dictionary of nursery rhymes
   398.8

Opossums
    Fiction
  Van Laan, N. Possum come a-knockin'   **E**

Oppel, Kenneth
  Peg and the whale   **E**
  Silverwing (5 and up)   **Fic**
  Sunwing (5 and up)   **Fic**

Oppenheim, Joanne
  Have you seen bugs? (k-3)   **595.7**

Oppenheim, Shulamith Levey
  Iblis (2-4)   **297.1**
  The lily cupboard   **E**

Opposites
  Bernhard, D. Earth, sky, wet, dry (k-2)
   578

Optical illusion magic. Dispezio, M. A.
   152.14

Optical illusions
  Cobb, V. How to really fool yourself (5 and up)
   152.1
  Dispezio, M. A. Optical illusion magic (4 and
    up)   **152.14**
  Simon, S. Now you see it, now you don't (4
    and up)   **152.14**
  Westray, K. Picture puzzler (2-4)   **152.14**
  Wick, W. Walter Wick's Optical tricks (4 and
    up)   **152.14**

Optical storage devices
   See also CD-ROMs

Optics
  Cobb, V. Light action! (5 and up)   **535**
  Levine, S. The optics book (4 and up)   **535**
The **optics** book. Levine, S.   **535**

Oram, Hiawyn
  Baba Yaga & the wise doll (k-3)   **398.2**
  Princess Chamomile gets her way. See note un-
    der Oram, H. Princess Chamomile's garden
   E
  Princess Chamomile's garden   **E**
  The wrong overcoat   **E**

Oranges
  Llewellyn, C. Oranges (k-3)   **641**

Orchard book of mythical birds & beasts. See
  Mayo, M. Mythical birds & beasts from many
   lands   **398.2**

The **Orchard** book of nursery rhymes   **398.8**

The **Orchard** book of stories from the ballet. See
  McCaughrean, G. The Random House book
   of stories from the ballet   **792.8**

Orchestra
  Ardley, N. A young person's guide to music (5
    and up)   **780**
  Ganeri, A. The young person's guide to the or-
    chestra (4-6)   **784.2**
  Hayes, A. Meet the orchestra (k-3)   **784.2**
  Koscielniak, B. The story of the incredible or-
    chestra (2-4)   **784.2**
  Kuskin, K. The Philharmonic gets dressed
   E

Ordinary Jack. Cresswell, H.   **Fic**
Ordinary things. Fletcher, R.   **811**

Oregon
  Boulton, J. Only Opal   **E**
  Ingram, S. Oregon
   In America the beautiful, second series
   973
  Stefoff, R. Oregon
   In Celebrate the states   **973**

Oregon country *See* Pacific Northwest

Oregon Trail
Fisher, L. E. The Oregon Trail (4 and up)
979.5
Fiction
Stanley, D. Roughing it on the Oregon Trail
(2-4) **Fic**
Van Leeuwen, J. Bound for Oregon (4-6)
Fic

Organic farming
Paladino, C. One good apple (4 and up)
363.7

Orgel, Doris
The devil in Vienna (6 and up) **Fic**

Origami
Fiction
Melmed, L. K. Little Oh **E**

Origin of man See Human origins

Origin of species See Evolution

The **origin** of the ocean. Lester, J.
In Lester, J. The last tales of Uncle Remus
p13-16 **398.2**

The **original** Freddie Ackerman. Irwin, H.
Fic

Origins of story **808.06**

Orioles (Baseball team) See Baltimore Orioles
(Baseball team)

Orion, the Hunter. Apfel, N. H. **523.8**

Orlev, Uri, 1931-
The island on Bird Street (5 and up) **Fic**
The man from the other side (6 and up)
Fic
The song of the whales
In Don't read this! and other tales of the un-
natural p174-96 **S C**

Ormai, Stella
(il) Cobb, V. Bet you can! science possibilities
to fool you **793.8**

Ormerod, Jan
Ms MacDonald has a class **E**
(il) Buckley, H. E. Grandfather and I **E**
(il) Buckley, H. E. Grandmother and I **E**
(il) Hayes, S. Eat up, Gemma **E**
(il) Kingsley, C. The water babies **Fic**

Orozco, José-Luis
(comp) Diez deditos. Ten little fingers & other
play rhymes and action songs from Latin
America. See Diez deditos. Ten little fingers
& other play rhymes and action songs from
Latin America **782.42**

Orp. Kline, S. See note under Kline, S. Orp and
the FBI **Fic**

Orp and the chop suey burgers. Kline, S. See note
under Kline, S. Orp and the FBI **Fic**

Orp and the FBI. Kline, S. **Fic**

Orp goes to the hoop. Kline, S. See note under
Kline, S. Orp and the FBI **Fic**

The **orphan** boy. Mollel, T. M. **398.2**

Orphan journey home. Murrow, L. K. **Fic**

Orphan train children [series]
Nixon, J. L. Aggie's home **Fic**

Orphan train rider. Warren, A. **362.7**

Orphans
Warren, A. Orphan train rider (4 and up)
362.7
Fiction
Avi. Night journeys (5 and up) **Fic**
Blackwood, G. L. The Shakespeare stealer (5
and up) **Fic**
Bunting, E. Train to Somewhere **E**
Cassedy, S. Behind the attic wall (5 and up)
Fic
Cleaver, V. Where the lillies bloom (5 and up)
Fic
Curtis, C. P. Bud, not Buddy (4 and up)
Fic
Dahl, R. The BFG (4-6) **Fic**
DeFelice, C. C. The apprenticeship of Lucas
Whitaker (4 and up) **Fic**
Echewa, T. O. The magic tree (k-3) **398.2**
Fleischman, S. The midnight horse (3-6)
Fic
Haas, J. Unbroken (5 and up) **Fic**
Harrison, B. Theo (5 and up) **Fic**
Hobbs, W. Jason's gold (5 and up) **Fic**
Holub, J. The robber and me (5 and up)
Fic
Howard, E. The gate in the wall (5 and up)
Fic
Karr, K. Skullduggery (5 and up) **Fic**
L'Engle, M. Meet the Austins (5 and up)
Fic
Levine, G. C. Dave at night (5 and up)
Fic
Lunn, J. L. S. The root cellar (5 and up)
Fic
Mahy, M. Tingleberries, tuckertubs and tele-
phones (3-5) **Fic**
Murrow, L. K. Orphan journey home (4-6)
Fic
Nixon, J. L. Aggie's home (3-5) **Fic**
Prigger, M. S. Aunt Minnie McGranahan **E**
Reeder, C. Shades of gray (4 and up) **Fic**
Rodowsky, C. F. The Turnabout Shop (4-6)
Fic
Snicket, L. The bad beginning (4 and up)
Fic
Spinelli, J. Maniac Magee (5 and up) **Fic**
Stanley, D. Saving Sweetness **E**
Wallace, B. B. Cousins in the castle (4-6)
Fic
Wallace, B. B. Ghosts in the gallery (5 and up)
Fic
Wallace, B. B. The twin in the tavern (4-6)
Fic
Wright, B. R. The ghosts of Mercy Manor (4
and up) **Fic**

Orr, Richard
Nature cross-sections (4 and up) **577**

Orwell's luck. Jennings, R. W. **Fic**

Osborne, Linda Barrett, 1949-
(jt. auth) King, C. Oh, freedom! **323.1**

Osborne, Mary Pope, 1949-
Adaline Falling Star (4 and up) **Fic**
American tall tales (3-6) **398.2**
Contents: Davy Crockett; Sally Ann Thunder Ann Whirlwind;
Johnny Appleseed; Stormalong; Mose; Febold Feboldson; Pecos
Bill; John Henry; Paul Bunyan
Favorite Greek myths (3-6) **292**

Osborne, Mary Pope, 1949—*Continued*
Favorite medieval tales (4 and up) **398.2**
Contents: Finn Maccoul; Beowulf; The sword in the stone; Island of the lost children; The song of Roland; The werewolf; Sir Gawain and the Green Knight; Robin Hood and his merry men; Chanticleer and the fox
Favorite Norse myths (4 and up) **293**
Kate and the beanstalk (k-3) **398.2**
The life of Jesus in masterpieces of art
232.9
Mermaid tales from around the world (4-6)
398.2
Contents: The mystery of Melusine; Menana of the waterfall; The sea nymph and the Cyclops; The enchanted cap; Nastasia of the sea; The fish husband; The serpent and the Sea Queen; The mermaid's revenge; The princess of the Tung Lake; The sea princess of Persia; The mermaid in the millpond; The little mermaid
My brother's keeper (3-5) **Fic**
One world, many religions (4 and up) **291**
Paul Bunyan, the mightiest logger of them all
In From sea to shining sea p280-83
810.8

Oscar Wilde's The selfish giant. Waters, F.
Fic
Osceola [biography of Osceola Mays] Mays, O.
92
O'Shaughnessy, Tam
(jt. auth) Ride, S. K. The mystery of Mars
523.4
O'Shea, Maria
Kuwait (5 and up) **953.67**
O'Shea, Pat, 1931-
See/See also pages in the following book(s):
Origins of story p80-85 **808.06**
Osofsky, Audrey
Dreamcatcher **E**
Ospreys
Patent, D. H. Ospreys (4 and up) **598**
Osser, Stephanie
(il) St. Pierre, S. The Muppets' big book of crafts **745.5**
Ostriches
Fiction
King-Smith, D. The cuckoo child (3-5) **Fic**
Ostropoler, Hershele, 18th cent.
Legends
Kimmel, E. A. The adventures of Hershel of Ostropol (3-5) **398.2**
O'Sullivan stew. Talbott, H. **E**
Osuna Perez, Gloria
(il) Hayes, J. Little Gold Star **398.2**
Otani, June
(il) Brenner, B. Chibi **598**
(il) Bulla, C. R. What makes a shadow?
535
(il) George, K. O. Little dog poems **811**
Otfinoski, Steven, 1949-
Georgia
In Celebrate the states **973**
The kid's guide to money (4 and up)
332.024
New Hampshire
In Celebrate the states **973**
Speaking up, speaking out (5 and up)
808.5

The **other** half of the blanket. Bruchac, J.
In Bruchac, J. Tell me a tale p114-15
372.6
The **other** Shepards. Griffin, A. **Fic**
The **other** side. Johnson, A. **811**
The **other** side of silence. Mahy, M. **Fic**
Otherwise known as Sheila the Great. Blume, J.
Fic
Otis. Bynum, J. **E**
Otis Spofford. Cleary, B. **Fic**
Otoonah. San Souci, R.
In San Souci, R. Cut from the same cloth p111-18 **398.2**
Otten, Charlotte F.
January rides the wind (k-3) **811**
Otters
Arnosky, J. Otters under water (k-2) **599.7**
Silverstein, A. The sea otter (4 and up)
599.7
Otters under water. Arnosky, J. **599.7**
Ouch!. Babbitt, N. **398.2**
An **ounce** of mud. Jaffe, N.
In Jaffe, N. The cow of no color: riddle stories and justice tales from around the world p70-73 **398.2**
Our earth. Rockwell, A. F. **910**
Our eight nights of Hanukkah. Rosen, M. J.
296.4
Our granny. Wild, M. **E**
Our house. Conrad, P. **S C**
Our new puppy. Harper, I. **E**
Our only May Amelia. Holm, J. L. **Fic**
Our solar system. Simon, S. **523.2**
Our stars. Rockwell, A. F. **523.8**
Our strange new land. Hermes, P. **Fic**
Out and about. Hughes, S. **E**
Out of darkness: the story of Louis Braille. Freedman, R. **92**
Out of nowhere. Sebestyen, O. **Fic**
Out of sight. Simon, S. **502.8**
Out of the ark. Ganeri, A. **291.1**
Out of the darkness. Haskins, J. **305.8**
Out of the dump: writings and photographs by children from Guatemala **972.81**
Out of the dust. Hesse, K. **Fic**
The **outcast** of Redwall. Jacques, B. See note under Jacques, B. Redwall **Fic**
Outdoor life
See also Camping
Drake, J. The kids campfire book (4-6)
796.5
Fiction
George, J. C. My side of the mountain (5 and up) **Fic**
George, J. C. On the far side of the mountain (5 and up) **Fic**
Greene, S. Owen Foote, frontiersman (2-4)
Fic
Outdoor survival *See* Wilderness survival

Owls—*Continued*
Mowat, F. Owls in the family (4 and up)
636.6

Sattler, H. R. The book of North American owls (4 and up) **598**
Fiction
George, J. C. There's an owl in the shower (3-5) **Fic**
Hutchins, P. Good-night, Owl! **E**
Johnston, T. The barn owls **E**
Lobel, A. Owl at home **E**
Waddell, M. Owl babies **E**
Yolen, J. Owl moon **E**

Owls in the family. Mowat, F. **636.6**

Ox-cart man. Hall, D. **E**

The **ox** of the wonderful horns [story] Bryan, A.
In Bryan, A. Ashley Bryan's African tales, uh-huh p27-39 **398.2**

The **oxcart**. Kimmel, E. A.
In Kimmel, E. A. Sword of the samurai p41-51 **Fic**

Oxenbury, Helen, 1938-
It's my birthday **E**
Pippo gets lost **E**
Tom and Pippo and the bicycle. See note under Oxenbury, H. Pippo gets lost **E**
Tom and Pippo go for a walk. See note under Oxenbury, H. Pippo gets lost **E**
Tom and Pippo on the beach. See note under Oxenbury, H. Pippo gets lost **E**
Tom and Pippo read a story. See note under Oxenbury, H. Pippo gets lost **E**
Tom and Pippo's day. See note under Oxenbury, H. Pippo gets lost **E**
(il) Carroll, L. Alice's adventures in Wonderland **Fic**
(il) Rosen, M. We're going on a bear hunt **E**
(il) Trivizas, E. The three little wolves and the big bad pig **E**
(il) Waddell, M. Farmer duck **E**

The **Oxford** book of animal poems (5 and up) **808.81**

The **Oxford** book of children's verse **821.008**

The **Oxford** book of children's verse in America **811.008**

The **Oxford** book of Christmas poems (4 and up) **808.81**

The **Oxford** book of scary tales (5 and up) **808.8**

The **Oxford** companion to children's literature. Carpenter, H. **809**

The **Oxford** companion to fairy tales **398.2**

The **Oxford** dictionary of nursery rhymes **398.8**

The **Oxford** illustrated book of American children's poems **811.008**

Oxford myths and legends [series]
Sherlock, Sir P. M. West Indian folk-tales **398.2**

Oxford Scientific Films
Snedden, R. What is an amphibian? **597.8**

The **Oxford** treasury of children's stories (3-5) **S C**

Oxygen
Farndon, J. Oxygen
In The Elements [Benchmark Bks.] **546**
Fitzgerald, K. The story of oxygen (4 and up) **546**

Ozark Mountains
Fiction
Rawls, W. Where the red fern grows **Fic**

Ozma of Oz. Baum, L. F. See note under Baum, L. F. The Wizard of Oz **Fic**

Ozone layer
Pringle, L. P. Vanishing ozone (4 and up) **363.7**

P

P.S. Longer letter later. Danziger, P. **Fic**

Pablo remembers. Ancona, G. **394.26**

Pacific Northwest
Pandell, K. Journey through the northern rainforest (4 and up) **578.7**
Fiction
Sloat, T. There was an old lady who swallowed a trout **E**

Packaging
See also Boxes

Packard, Edward, 1931-
Big numbers (k-3) **513**

Paddington abroad. Bond, M. See note under Bond, M. A bear called Paddington **Fic**

Paddington and the Christmas pantomime. Bond, M.
In Bond, M. Paddington's storybook p146-[60] **S C**

Paddington and the "cold snap". Bond, M.
In Bond, M. Paddington's storybook p131-45 **S C**

Paddington and the "finishing touch". Bond, M.
In Bond, M. Paddington's storybook p97-111 **S C**

Paddington at large. Bond, M. See note under Bond, M. A bear called Paddington **Fic**

Paddington at work. Bond, M. See note under Bond, M. A bear called Paddington **Fic**

Paddington cleans up. Bond, M.
In Bond, M. Paddington's storybook p21-36 **S C**

Paddington dines out. Bond, M.
In Bond, M. Paddington's storybook p37-51 **S C**

Paddington goes to town. Bond, M. See note under Bond, M. A bear called Paddington **Fic**

Paddington helps out. Bond, M. See note under Bond, M. A bear called Paddington **Fic**

Paddington marches on. Bond, M. See note under Bond, M. A bear called Paddington **Fic**

Paddington on screen. Bond, M. See note under Bond, M. A bear called Paddington **Fic**

Paddington on stage. Bond, M. See note under Bond, M. A bear called Paddington **Fic**

Paddington on top. Bond, M. See note under Bond, M. A bear called Paddington   **Fic**

Paddington steps out. Bond, M.
In Bond, M. Paddington's storybook p112-30
  S C

Paddington takes the air. Bond, M. See note under Bond, M. A bear called Paddington
  Fic

Paddington takes the test. Bond, M. See note under Bond, M. A bear called Paddington
  Fic

Paddington takes to TV. Bond, M. See note under Bond, M. A bear called Paddington   **Fic**

Paddington's storybook. Bond, M.   **S C**

Paddle-to-the-sea. Holling, H. C.   **Fic**

Pageants
Fiction
Robinson, B. The best Christmas pageant ever (4-6)   **Fic**

Paige, Leroy *See* Paige, Satchel, 1906-1982

Paige, Satchel, 1906-1982
About
Cline-Ransome, L. Satchel Paige (2-4)   **92**
See/See also pages in the following book(s):
Brashler, W. The story of Negro league baseball p73-83 (5 and up)   **796.357**
Littlefield, B. Champions p1-10 (5 and up)
  920

The **Pain** and the Great One. Blume, J.   **E**
The **Paint** Brush Kid. Bulla, C. R.   **Fic**
Painted dreams. Williams, K. L.   **E**
Painted eyebrow. Carpenter, F.
In Carpenter, F. Tales of a Chinese grandmother p56-65   **398.2**
Painted words: Marianthe's story one. Aliki
  E
The **painter.** Catalanotto, P.   **E**
Painters
See also Artists
Painters of the caves. Lauber, P.   **759.01**
Painting
See also Landscape painting; Portrait painting
Fiction
Kesselman, W. A. Emma   **E**
Rylant, C. All I see   **E**
Pak, Soyung
Dear Juno   **E**
Paladino, Catherine
One good apple (4 and up)   **363.7**
Palatini, Margie
Piggie pie!   **E**
Pale-Faced Lightning. San Souci, R.
In San Souci, R. Cut from the same cloth p77-85   **398.2**
Palen, Debbie
(il) Cerf, B. Riddles and more riddles!
  793.73
(il) Gravelle, K. The period book   **612.6**
Paleobotany *See* Fossil plants
Paleontology *See* Fossils

Palestine
Fiction
Speare, E. G. The bronze bow (6 and up)
  Fic
Paley, Joan
(il) Whippo, W. Little white duck   **782.42**
A **palindrome.** Babbitt, N.
In Babbitt, N. The Devil's storybook p53-61
  S C
The **Palm** of my heart   **811.008**
Palmer, Jan
(il) Merrill, J. The toothpaste millionaire
  Fic
Palmisciano, Diane
(il) Conford, E. A case for Jenny Archer
  Fic
(il) Skolsky, M. W. Hannah and the whistling tea kettle   **E**
Panama
Hassig, S. M. Panama (5 and up)   **972.87**
The **pancake.** Sierra, J.
In Sierra, J. Nursery tales around the world p11-15   **398.2**
Panda *See* Giant panda
Pandell, Karen
Journey through the northern rainforest (4 and up)   **578.7**
Papa Gatto. Sanderson, R.   **398.2**
Papa God and General Death
In The Magic orange tree, and other Haitian folktales p75-78   **398.2**
Papa God and the Pintards. MacDonald, M. R.
In MacDonald, M. R. Celebrate the world p193-97   **372.6**
"**Papa** God first, Man next, Tiger last"
In The Magic orange tree, and other Haitian folktales p177-81   **398.2**
Papa God sends turtle doves
In The Magic orange tree, and other Haitian folktales p87-90   **398.2**
Papa John's tall tale. Hamilton, V.
In Hamilton, V. The people could fly: American black folktales p76-80
  398.2
Papa tells Chita a story. Howard, E. F. See note under Howard, E. F. Chita's Christmas tree
  E
Papagayo. McDermott, G.   **E**
Papago Indians
Baylor, B. The desert is theirs (1-4)   **577.5**
Paparone, Pamela
(il) Lindbergh, R. Nobody owns the sky   **E**
Papa's parrot. Rylant, C.
In Rylant, C. Every living thing p19-25
  S C
Papa's song. McMullan, K.   **E**
The **paper** airplane book. Simon, S.   **745.592**
Paper airplanes. Kelly, E. J.   **745.592**
Paper crafts
See also Origami
Ancona, G. The piñata maker: El piñatero (k-3)
  745.594

Park, Barbara, 1947-—*Continued*

Junie B. Jones and that meanie Jim's birthday. See note under Park, B. Junie B. Jones and her big fat mouth **Fic**

Junie B. Jones and the mushy gushy valentine. See note under Park, B. Junie B. Jones and her big fat mouth **Fic**

Junie B. Jones and the stupid smelly bus. See note under Park, B. Junie B. Jones and her big fat mouth **Fic**

Junie B. Jones and the yucky blucky fruitcake. See note under Park, B. Junie B. Jones and her big fat mouth **Fic**

Junie B. Jones Captain Field Day. See note under Park, B. Junie B. Jones and her big fat mouth **Fic**

Junie B. Jones has a monster under her bed. See note under Park, B. Junie B. Jones and her big fat mouth **Fic**

Junie B. Jones has a peep in her pocket. See note under Park, B. Junie B. Jones and her big fat mouth **Fic**

Junie B. Jones is a beauty shop guy. See note under Park, B. Junie B. Jones and her big fat mouth **Fic**

Junie B. Jones is a graduation girl. See note under Park, B. Junie B. Jones and her big fat mouth **Fic**

Junie B. Jones is a party animal. See note under Park, B. Junie B. Jones and her big fat mouth **Fic**

Junie B. Jones is (almost) a flower girl. See note under Park, B. Junie B. Jones and her big fat mouth **Fic**

Junie B. Jones is not a crook. See note under Park, B. Junie B. Jones and her big fat mouth **Fic**

Junie B. Jones loves handsome Warren. See note under Park, B. Junie B. Jones and her big fat mouth **Fic**

Junie B. Jones smells something fishy. See note under Park, B. Junie B. Jones and her big fat mouth **Fic**

Mick Harte was here (4-6) **Fic**

My mother got married (and other disasters) (4-6) **Fic**

Skinnybones (4-6) **Fic**

Park, Eung Won

(il) Park, L. S. The kite fighters **Fic**

Park, Frances

The royal bee **E**

Park, Ginger

(jt. auth) Park, F. The royal bee **E**

Park, Linda Sue

The kite fighters (4-6) **Fic**

Parker, Edward, 1961-

Forests for the future (4-6) **333.75**

Parker, Ely Samuel, 1828-1895

See/See also pages in the following book(s):

Ehrlich, A. Wounded Knee: an Indian history of the American West (6 and up) **970.004**

Parker, Nancy Winslow

Money, money, money (3-5) **769.5**

(il) Blood, C. L. The goat in the rug **E**

(il) Langstaff, J. M. Oh, a-hunting we will go **782.42**

(il) Longfellow, H. W. Paul Revere's ride **811**

(il) Neitzel, S. The bag I'm taking to Grandma's **E**

(il) Neitzel, S. The dress I'll wear to the party **E**

(il) Neitzel, S. The jacket I wear in the snow **E**

Parker, Quanah, Comanche Chief, 1854?-1911

See/See also pages in the following book(s):

Freedman, R. Indian chiefs p52-71 (6 and up) **920**

Parker, Robert Andrew, 1927-

(il) Bierhorst, J. The people with five fingers **398.2**

(il) Fleming, C. The hatmaker's sign **E**

(il) Hesse, K. Just Juice **Fic**

(il) Tompert, A. Grandfather Tang's story **E**

Parker, Robert LeRoy *See* Cassidy, Butch, b. 1866 or 7

Parker, Steve

The age of the dinosaurs (5 and up) **567.9**

Albert Einstein and relativity (4 and up) **92**

The body atlas (5 and up) **611**

The brain and the nervous system (4 and up) **612.8**

Charles Darwin and evolution (4 and up) **92**

Electricity (4 and up) **537**

Fish (4 and up) **597**

Fuels for the future (4-6) **333.79**

The lungs and respiratory system (4 and up) **612.2**

Mammal (4 and up) **599**

Marie Curie and radium (4 and up) **92**

The reproductive system (5 and up) **612.6**

Thomas Edison and electricity (4 and up) **92**

Parker, Toni Trent

(jt. auth) Rand, D. Black Books Galore!—guide to great African American children's books about boys **016.3058**

(jt. auth) Rand, D. Black Books Galore!—guide to great African American children's books about girls **016.3058**

Parkhurst, Charley, 1812-1879

See/See also pages in the following book(s):

Calvert, P. Great lives: the American frontier p274-79 (5 and up) **920**

Parkhurst, Charlotte *See* Parkhurst, Charley, 1812-1879

Parkins, David

(il) King-Smith, D. Sophie's Tom **Fic**

(il) King-Smith, D. The water horse **Fic**

(il) Root, P. Aunt Nancy and Cousin Lazybones **E**

Parkman, Francis, 1823-1893

See/See also pages in the following book(s):

Calvert, P. Great lives: the American frontier p280-94 (5 and up) **920**

Parks, Rosa, 1913-

I am Rosa Parks (1-3) **92**

Rosa Parks: my story (5 and up) **92**

Pawnee Indians
Folklore
Cohen, C. L. The mud pony (k-3) 398.2
Payne, Emmy, 1919-
Katy No-Pocket E
Payson, Dale
(il) Clifton, L. The lucky stone Fic
Peace at last. Murphy, J. E
Peacock, Carol Antoinette
Mommy far, Mommy near E
Sugar was my best food (3-6) 362.1
Peacocks
Fiction
Polacco, P. Just plain Fancy E
Peacock's ghost. San Souci, R.
In San Souci, R. A terrifying taste of short &
shivery p109-13 398.2
Peake, Mervyn Laurence, 1911-1968
(il) Stevenson, R. L. Treasure Island Fic
Peale, Charles Willson, 1741-1827
About
Giblin, J. The mystery of the mammoth bones
(4 and up) 569
Wilson, J. The ingenious Mr. Peale (4 and up)
92
Peanuts
Micucci, C. The life and times of the peanut
(2-4) 641.3
See/See also pages in the following book(s):
Johnson, S. A. Tomatoes, potatoes, corn, and
beans p51-63 (6 and up) 641.3
Pear, Nancy
(ed) Explorers & discoverers. See Explorers &
discoverers 920.003
Pearce, Philippa, 1920-
Mrs. Cockle's cat
In The Oxford treasury of children's stories
p91-104 S C
Tom's midnight garden (4 and up) Fic
Pearl fisheries
Fiction
O'Dell, S. The black pearl (6 and up) Fic
Pearls of Lutra. Jacques, B. See note under
Jacques, B. Redwall Fic
Pearson, Anne
Ancient Greece (4 and up) 938
Pearson, Kit
The eyes
In Don't read this! and other tales of the un-
natural p132-48 S C
Pearson, Tracey Campbell
Where does Joe go? E
(il) Cutler, J. Rats! Fic
The **peasant** and the corpse. Afanas'ev, A. N.
In Afanas'ev, A. N. Russian fairy tales p333-
34 398.2
The **peasant,** the bear, and the fox. Afanas'ev, A.
N.
In Afanas'ev, A. N. Russian fairy tales p288-
89 398.2
Peck, Beth
(il) Bunting, E. How many days to America?
E

(il) Woodruff, E. Dear Levi Fic
Peck, Richard, 1934-
The dreadful future of Blossom Culp. See note
under Peck, R. The ghost belonged to me
Fic
The ghost belonged to me (5 and up) Fic
Ghosts I have been. See note under Peck, R.
The ghost belonged to me Fic
A long way from Chicago (5 and up) Fic
Lost in cyberspace (5 and up) Fic
A year down yonder (5 and up) Fic
Peck, Robert Newton, 1928-
A day no pigs would die (6 and up) Fic
Soup (5 and up) Fic
Soup 1776. See note under Peck, R. N. Soup
Fic
Soup ahoy. See note under Peck, R. N. Soup
Fic
Soup for president. See note under Peck, R. N.
Soup Fic
Soup in love. See note under Peck, R. N. Soup
Fic
Soup on wheels. See note under Peck, R. N.
Soup Fic
Soup's hoop. See note under Peck, R. N. Soup
Fic
Peck, slither and slide. Macdonald, S. E
Pecos Bill (Legendary character)
Kellogg, S. Pecos Bill (k-3) 398.2
Pecos Bill. Osborne, M. P.
In Osborne, M. P. American tall tales p73-85
398.2
Pecos Bill finds a ranch but loses a wife. Walker,
P. R.
In Walker, P. R. Big men, big country p69-76
398.2
The **peculiar** such thing. Hamilton, V.
In From sea to shining sea p338-39
810.8
In Hamilton, V. The people could fly:
American black folktales p116-20
398.2
Pedagogy *See* Teaching
The **peddler** of Ballaghadereen. Sawyer, R.
In Sawyer, R. The way of the storyteller
p239-47 372.6
The **peddlers.** Fisher, L. E. 381
Peddlers and peddling
Fisher, L. E. The peddlers (4 and up) 381
Fiction
McDonald, M. The potato man E
Schur, M. The peddler's gift E
Slobodkina, E. Caps for sale E
The **peddler's** gift. Schur, M. E
Pedersen, Ted
Internet for kids! (5 and up) 004.6
Pederson, Judy
(il) Fleischman, P. Seedfolks Fic
The **pedlar** of Swaffham. Jacobs, J.
In Jacobs, J. English fairy tales p309-11
398.2
Peek-a-boo!. Ahlberg, J. E
Peeping Beauty. Auch, M. J. E
Peepo!. See Ahlberg, J. Peek-a-boo! E

The **period** book. Gravelle, K.   612.6
Periodicals
List of magazines entered in this catalog:

Appraisal	016.5
AudioFile	028.1
Book Links	028.505
Bookbird	028.505
Booklist	028.1
Bulletin of the Center for Children's Books	028.1
Calliope	905
Chickadee	505
Childhood Education	372.05
Children's Magazine Guide	051
Cobblestone	973.05
Contact Kids	505
Cricket	051
Faces	306.05
Five Owls	028.505
Highlights for Children	051
The Horn Book Guide to Children's and Young Adult Books	028.505
The Horn Book Magazine	028.505
Instructor	372.05
Journal of Youth Services in Libraries	027.6205
Ladybug	051
Language Arts	372.605
Library Talk	027.805
MultiMedia schools	371.305
National Geographic World (3-6)	910.5
Odyssey	520.5
Owl	505
Plays: the drama magazine for young people	808.82
Ranger Rick	505
The Reading Teacher	372.405
School Library Journal	027.805
Science and Children	507.05
Science Books & Films	016.5
Spider	051
Sports Illustrated for Kids	796
Stone Soup	810.8
Teaching Children Mathematics	510.7
Teaching K-8	372.05
Your Big Backyard	505
Zoonooz	590.5

Bibliography
Magazines for kids and teens   011.6
Indexes
Children's Magazine Guide   051
Perkins, Catherine
The most excellent book of how to be a clown (4-6)   791.3
Perkins, Lynne Rae
All alone in the universe (5 and up)   Fic
Home lovely   E
Perl, Lila
Four perfect pebbles (6 and up)   940.53
Mummies, tombs, and treasure (4 and up)   393
Piñatas and paper flowers (4 and up)   394.26
Slumps, grunts, and snickerdoodles: what Colonial America ate and why (4 and up)   641.5
Perloo the bold. Avi   Fic

Perrault, Charles, 1628-1703
Blue Beard
  In The Blue fairy book p290-95   398.2
  In The Classic fairy tales p106-09   398.2
Cinderella (k-3)   398.2
  also in The Blue fairy book p64-71   398.2
  also in The Classic fairy tales p123-27   398.2
Cinderella, Puss in Boots, and other favorite tales (k-4)   398.2
Contents: Little Red Riding Hood; The fairies; Puss in Boots; Blue Beard; Cinderella; Ricky of the Tuft; The Sleeping Beauty in the woods; Little Tom Thumb
The complete fairy tales of Charles Perrault (4-6)   398.2
Contents: The sleeping beauty; Little Red Riding Hood; Bluebeard; Puss-in-boots; The fairies; Cinderella; Tufty Ricky; Hop o' my thumb; Patient Griselda; Donkeyskin; The foolish wishes
The fairy
  In The Classic fairy tales p100-02   398.2
Little Poucet
  In The Classic fairy tales p130-36   398.2
The Little Red Riding-Hood
  In The Classic fairy tales p95-97   398.2
Little Thumb
  In The Blue fairy book p231-41   398.2
The master cat
  In The Blue fairy book p141-47   398.2
  In The Classic fairy tales p113-16   398.2
Puss in boots (k-3)   398.2
Puss in boots; adaptation. See Fischer, H. Puss in boots   398.2
Puss in boots; adaptation. See Galdone, P. Puss in boots   398.2
The sleeping beauty in the wood
  In The Blue fairy book p54-63   398.2
  In The Classic fairy tales p85-92   398.2
Toads and diamonds
  In The Blue fairy book p274-77   398.2
Perrin, Gerry
(il) Goble, P. Hau kola: hello friend   92
Perrone, Donna
(il) Joseph, L. The mermaid's twin sister: more stories from Trinidad   398.2
Perry, Matthew Calbraith, 1794-1858
About
Blumberg, R. Commodore Perry in the land of the Shogun (5 and up)   952
Persephone (Greek deity)
Geringer, L. The pomegranate seeds (3-5)   292
Persephone. D'Aulaire, I.
  In Bauer, C. F. Celebrations p199-202   808.8
Perseus (Greek mythology)
Hutton, W. Perseus (3-5)   292
See/See also pages in the following book(s):
The Blue fairy book p182-92 (4-6)   398.2
Hamilton, E. Mythology p197-208 (6 and up)   292
Persia *See* Iran
Personal finance
See also Consumer credit
Godfrey, N. S. Neale S. Godfrey's ultimate kids' money book (5 and up)   332.024

Personal finance—*Continued*

Otfinoski, S. The kid's guide to money (4 and up) **332.024**

Schwartz, D. M. If you made a million **E**

Personal names

Fiction

Henkes, K. Chrysanthemum **E**

Hurwitz, J. The adventures of Ali Baba Bernstein (2-4) **Fic**

Mosel, A. Tikki Tikki Tembo (k-2) **398.2**

Pertzoff, Alexander

(il) MacLachlan, P. Three Names **E**

Peru

Falconer, K. Peru (5 and up) **985**

King, D. C. Peru (4 and up) **985**

Antiquities

Getz, D. Frozen girl (5 and up) **930.1**

Reinhard, J. Discovering the Inca Ice Maiden (5 and up) **930.1**

Fiction

Dorros, A. Tonight is Carnaval **E**

Folklore

See Folklore—Peru

Pesach *See* Passover

Pesticides

Paladino, C. One good apple (4 and up) **363.7**

Pests

See also Insect pests

A **pet**. Rylant, C.

In Rylant, C. Every living thing p26-30 **S C**

Pet show!. Keats, E. J. See note under Keats, E. J. Hi cat! **E**

Pete and the ladybird. Berg, L.

In The Oxford treasury of children's stories p12-15 **S C**

Peter I, the Great, Emperor of Russia, 1672-1725

About

Stanley, D. Peter the Great (4 and up) **92**

Peter and the wolf. Prokofiev, S. **E**

Peter and Wendy. See Barrie, J. M. Peter Pan **Fic**

Peter Pan. Barrie, J. M. **Fic**

Peter Spier's circus!. Spier, P. **E**

Peters, Lisa Westberg

Cold little duck, duck, duck **E**

Peters, Russell M.

Clambake (3-6) **970.004**

Peter's chair. Keats, E. J. See note under Keats, E. J. The snowy day **E**

Petersen, David, 1946-

Australia (2-4) **994**

Petersen, P. J., 1941-

I hate camping. See note under Peterson, P. J. I hate weddings **Fic**

I hate company. See note under Peterson, P. J. I hate weddings **Fic**

I hate weddings (3-5) **Fic**

Petersham, Maud, 1890-1971

See/See also pages in the following book(s):

Caldecott Medal books, 1938-1957 p132-49 **028.5**

Petersham, Miska, 1888-1960

See/See also pages in the following book(s):

Caldecott Medal books, 1938-1957 p132-49 **028.5**

Peterson, Cris, 1952-

Century farm (k-3) **630.1**

Extra cheese, please! (k-3) **637**

Horsepower (k-3) **636.1**

Peterson, Roger Tory, 1908-1996

A field guide to the birds **598**

A field guide to western birds **598**

(il) Latimer, J. P. Backyard birds **598**

(il) Latimer, J. P. Birds of prey **598**

(il) Latimer, J. P. Bizarre birds **598**

(il) Latimer, J. P. Shorebirds **598**

(il) Latimer, J. P. Songbirds **598**

Peterson field guides for young naturalists [series]

Latimer, J. P. Backyard birds **598**

Latimer, J. P. Birds of prey **598**

Latimer, J. P. Bizarre birds **598**

Latimer, J. P. Butterflies **595.7**

Latimer, J. P. Caterpillars **595.7**

Latimer, J. P. Shorebirds **598**

Latimer, J. P. Songbirds **598**

Peterson first guide to birds of North America. See Peterson, R. T. A field guide to the birds **598**

Peterson first guide to reptiles and amphibians. Conant, R. **597.9**

Pete's a pizza. Steig, W. **E**

Petey. Mikaelsen, B. **Fic**

Petroglyphs *See* Rock drawings, paintings, and engravings

Petroleum

Pringle, L. P. Oil spills (4 and up) **363.7**

Petrouchka (Ballet)

See/See also pages in the following book(s):

McCaughrean, G. The Random House book of stories from the ballet p95-101 (4 and up) **792.8**

Petrushka (Ballet) *See* Petrouchka (Ballet)

Petry, Ann Lane

Tituba of Salem Village (6 and up) **Fic**

Pets

See also Domestic animals; names of animals, e.g. *Cats; Dogs;* etc.

George, J. C. A tarantula in my purse (4-6) **92**

Fiction

Caseley, J. Mr. Green Peas **E**

Kellogg, S. The mysterious tadpole **E**

Kimmel, E. A. I took my frog to the library **E**

Pets. Avi

In Avi. What do fish have to do with anything? and other stories p121-50 **S C**

Petty crimes. Soto, G. **S C**

Pinkney, Gloria Jean, 1941-
Back home   E

Pinkney, J. Brian *See* Pinkney, Brian

Pinkney, Jerry, 1939-
Aesop's fables   398.2
The little match girl   E
Rikki-tikki-tavi   E
The ugly duckling   E
(il) Aardema, V. Rabbit makes a monkey of lion   398.2
(il) Adoff, A. In for winter, out for spring   811
(il) Dragonwagon, C. Half a moon and one whole star   E
(il) Flournoy, V. The patchwork quilt   E
(il) Goldin, B. D. Journeys with Elijah   222
(il) Greenfield, E. Childtimes: a three-generation memoir   920
(il) Hamilton, V. Drylongso   Fic
(il) Hurwitz, J. New shoes for Silvia   E
(il) Kipling, R. The jungle book: the Mowgli stories   S C
(jt. auth) Lester, J. Black cowboy, wild horses   E
(il) Lester, J. John Henry   398.2
(il) Lester, J. The last tales of Uncle Remus   398.2
(il) Lester, J. Sam and the tigers   E
(il) Marzollo, J. Pretend you're a cat   E
(il) McKissack, P. C. Mirandy and Brother Wind   E
(il) Pinkney, G. J. Back home   E
(il) San Souci, R. The hired hand   398.2
(il) San Souci, R. The talking eggs   398.2
(il) Schroeder, A. Minty: a story of young Harriet Tubman   E
(il) Taylor, M. D. Song of the trees   Fic

Pinkwater, Daniel Manus, 1941-
At the Hotel Larry. See note under Pinkwater, D. M. Young Larry   E
Bongo Larry. See note under Pinkwater, D. M. Young Larry   E
Fat men from space (3-6)   Fic
The Hoboken chicken emergency (3-6)   Fic
Ice cream Larry. See note under Pinkwater, D. M. Young Larry   E
Lizard music (4 and up)   Fic
Young Larry   E

Pinkwater, Jill
(il) Pinkwater, D. M. The Hoboken chicken emergency   Fic
(il) Pinkwater, D. M. Young Larry   E

Pinkwater, Manus *See* Pinkwater, Daniel Manus, 1941-

Pinky and Rex. Howe, J.   E

Pinky and Rex and the bully. Howe, J. See note under Howe, J. Pinky and Rex   E

Pinky and Rex and the double-dad weekend. Howe, J. See note under Howe, J. Pinky and Rex   E

Pinky and Rex and the just-right pet. Howe, J. See note under Howe, J. Pinky and Rex   E

Pinky and Rex and the mean old witch. Howe, J. See note under Howe, J. Pinky and Rex   E

Pinky and Rex and the new baby. Howe, J. See note under Howe, J. Pinky and Rex   E

Pinky and Rex and the new neighbors. Howe, J. See note under Howe, J. Pinky and Rex   E

Pinky and Rex and the perfect pumpkin. Howe, J. See note under Howe, J. Pinky and Rex   E

Pinky and Rex and the school play. Howe, J. See note under Howe, J. Pinky and Rex   E

Pinky and Rex and the spelling bee. Howe, J. See note under Howe, J. Pinky and Rex   E

Pinky and Rex get married. Howe, J. See note under Howe, J. Pinky and Rex   E

Pinky and Rex go to camp. Howe, J. See note under Howe, J. Pinky and Rex   E

Pinky Pye. Estes, E. See note under Estes, E. Ginger Pye   Fic

Pinocchio. Young, E.   Fic
Pinocchio. See Collodi, C. The adventures of Pinocchio   Fic

Pinto, Ralph
(il) Lester, J. The knee-high man, and other tales   398.2

Pioneer days. King, D. C.   978

Pioneer girl: the story of Laura Ingalls Wilder. Anderson, W. T.   92

Pioneer life *See* Frontier and pioneer life

A **pioneer** sampler. Greenwood, B.   971.3
A **pioneer** story. See Greenwood, B. A pioneer sampler   971.3

Piper, Watty
The little engine that could   E

Pippi goes on board. Lindgren, A. See note under Lindgren, A. Pippi Longstocking   Fic

Pippi in the South Seas. Lindgren, A. See note under Lindgren, A. Pippi Longstocking   Fic

Pippi Longstocking. Lindgren, A.   Fic
Pippo gets lost. Oxenbury, H.   E

Piranhas
Landau, E. Piranhas (2-4)   597

The **pirate.** San Souci, R.
In San Souci, R. More short & shivery p97-102   398.2

The **pirate.** Schwartz, A.
In Schwartz, A. In a dark, dark room, and other scary stories p50-59   398.2

The **pirate** princess. Yolen, J.
In Yolen, J. Not one damsel in distress p64-77   398.2

The **pirate** queen [biography of Grace O'Malley] McCully, E. A.   92

Pirates
McCully, E. A. The pirate queen (k-3)   92
Fiction
Fleischman, S. The 13th floor (4-6)   Fic
Fox, M. Tough Boris   E
Mahy, M. Tingleberries, tuckertubs and telephones (3-5)   Fic

Pirates—Fiction—*Continued*
McPhail, D. M. Edward and the pirates   E
Stevenson, R. L. Treasure Island (6 and up)
     Fic

Poetry
Yolen, J. The ballad of the pirate queens (3-5)
     811

Pirner, Connie White
Even little kids get diabetes (k-1)   616.4

Pish, posh, said Hieronymus Bosch. Willard, N.
     811

Pistolis, Donna Reidy
(ed) Hit list: frequently challenged books for children. See Hit list: frequently challenged books for children   016.8

Piumini, Roberto
Don't read this!
   In Don't read this! and other tales of the unnatural p51-70   S C

A **pizza** the size of the sun. Prelutsky, J.
     811

Pizza time. Marshall, J.
   In Ready, set, read—and laugh! p44-55
     810.8

Place, François
(il) Stevenson, R. L. The strange case of Dr. Jekyll and Mr. Hyde   Fic

The **Place** my words are looking for (4 and up)
     811.008

A **place** of bird beaks. Schwartz, H.
   In Schwartz, H. The diamond tree p71-75
     398.2

A **place** to belong. Nixon, J. L. See note under Nixon, J. L. A family apart   Fic

Places of refuge. Patent, D. H.   333.95

Plain City. Hamilton, V.   Fic

Plane song. Siebert, D.   E

Planet earth/inside out. Gibbons, G.   550

The **planet** hunters. Fradin, D. B.   523.4

The **planet** of Junior Brown. Hamilton, V.
     Fic

Planets
   See also names of planets
Branley, F. M. The planets in our solar system (k-3)   523.4
Branley, F. M. The sun and the solar system (4-6)   523.2
Cole, J. The magic school bus, lost in the solar system (2-4)   523
Fradin, D. B. The planet hunters (5 and up)
     523.4
Gibbons, G. The planets (k-3)   523.4
Rockwell, A. F. Our stars (k-2)   523.8
Fiction
Shields, C. D. Martian rock   E

The **planets** in our solar system. Branley, F. M.
     523.4

Plant conservation
   See also Scarecrows
Galan, M. A. There's still time (3-6)
     333.95

Plantation life
Bial, R. The strength of these arms (4 and up)
     326
Erickson, P. Daily life on a Southern plantation, 1853 (4-6)   975
McKissack, P. C. Christmas in the big house, Christmas in the quarters (4-6)   394.26

Planting a rainbow. Ehlert, L.   E

Planting things. Rylant, C.
   In Rylant, C. Every living thing p48-55
     S C

Plants
   See also Flowers
Bernhard, D. Earth, sky, wet, dry (k-2)
     578
Björk, C. Linnea's windowsill garden (3-6)
     635
Gibbons, G. From seed to plant (k-3)   580
Paterson, J. B. Consider the lilies (5 and up)
     220.8
VanCleave, J. P. Janice VanCleave's plants (4 and up)   581
The Visual dictionary of plants (4 and up)
     580
Fiction
Fleischman, P. Weslandia   E

Plants, Fossil *See* Fossil plants

Plants, Industrial *See* Factories

Plat-eye
   In Raw Head, bloody bones p18-22
     398.2

Plate tectonics
Gallant, R. A. Dance of the continents (5 and up)   551.1
Silverstein, A. Plate tectonics (5 and up)
     551.1

Plato
Critias. See Balit, C. Atlantis   398.2
Timaeus. See Balit, C. Atlantis   398.2

Platt, Richard, 1953-
Castle diary (4 and up)   Fic
(jt. auth) Biesty, S. Stephen Biesty's cross-sections: Castle   940.1
(jt. auth) Biesty, S. Stephen Biesty's cross-sections: Man-of-war   359.1
(jt. auth) Biesty, S. Stephen Biesty's incredible body   611
(jt. auth) Biesty, S. Stephen Biesty's incredible cross-sections   600
(jt. auth) Biesty, S. Stephen Biesty's incredible everything   670
(jt. auth) Biesty, S. Stephen Biesty's incredible explosions   741.6

Play and find out about math, Janice VanCleave's. VanCleave, J. P.   513

Play ball, Amelia Bedelia. Parish, P. See note under Parish, P. Amelia Bedelia   E

Play direction (Theater) *See* Theater—Production and direction

Play index   808.82

Play like a girl (5 and up)   796

Play production *See* Theater—Production and direction

Play rhymes. Brown, M. T.   796.1

Play with me. Ets, M. H.   **E**

Playgrounds

    See also Parks

    Gibbons, G. Playgrounds (k-3)   **796**

Playing with words. Howe, J.   **92**

Playmates, Imaginary *See* Imaginary playmates

Plays *See* One act plays

Plays for children *See* Children's plays

Plays: the drama magazine for young people

                                  808.82

Playwrights *See* Dramatists

Please all . . . please none. MacDonald, M. R.

    In MacDonald, M. R. Look back and see p68-
73   **372.6**

Pleasing Betty Stoggs. Climo, S.

    In Climo, S. Magic & mischief p49-55
                                    398.2

Plecas, Jennifer

    (il) Pomerantz, C. The outside dog   **E**

    (il) Thomas, S. M. Good night, Good Knight
                                      E

Plotkin, Gregory

    Cooking the Russian way

    In Easy menu ethnic cookbooks   **641.5**

Plots (Drama, fiction, etc.) *See* Stories, plots, etc.

Plourde, Lynn

    Pigs in the mud in the middle of the rud

                                        E

Pluralism (Social sciences) *See* Multiculturalism

Pluto (Planet)

    Brimner, L. D. Pluto (2-4)   **523.4**

Plymouth Rock

    Fritz, J. Who's that stepping on Plymouth
Rock? (2-4)   **974.4**

Pocahontas, d. 1617

                About

    Fritz, J. The double life of Pocahontas (4 and
up)   **92**

A **pocket** for Corduroy. Freeman, D. See note under Freeman, D. Corduroy   **E**

A **pocketful** of goobers: a story about George
Washington Carver. Mitchell, B.   **92**

Podell, Janet

    (jt. auth) Kane, J. N. Famous first facts
                                      031.02

Podwal, Mark H., 1945-

    The menorah story (k-3)   **296.4**

    (il) Prose, F. The angel's mistake   **398.2**

    (il) Prose, F. You never know   **398.2**

    (il) Wiesel, E. King Solomon and his magic ring
                                      222

Poe, Edgar Allan, 1809-1849

See/See also pages in the following book(s):

    Faber, D. Great lives: American literature p59-
67 (5 and up)   **920**

    Krull, K. Lives of the writers p32-37 (4 and up)
                                      920

Poem-making. Livingston, M. C.   **372.6**

Poem stew (3-6)   **811.008**

Poems for Jewish holidays (k-3)   **811.008**

Poems for the very young (k-3)   **821.008**

Poet and the peony princess. Carpenter, F.

    In Carpenter, F. Tales of a Chinese grand-
mother p124-33   **398.2**

Poetics

    Janeczko, P. B. How to write poetry (5 and up)
                                      808.1

    The Place my words are looking for (4 and up)
                                      811.008

    Poetry from A to Z (5 and up)   **808.1**

Poetry

    See also American poetry; Animals—Poet-
ry; Chinese poetry; Christmas—Poetry; English poetry; French poetry; Japanese poetry;
Native Americans—Poetry; types of poetry;
subjects with the subdivision *Poetry*

See/See also pages in the following book(s):

    Bauer, C. F. This way to books p193-266
                                      028.5

    Only connect: readings on children's literature
p214-35   **028.5**

                Collections

    A. Nonny Mouse writes again! (1-3)
                                      808.81

    The Baby's bedtime book   **808.81**

    The Beauty of the beast (4-6)   **811.008**

    Call down the moon (6 and up)   **821.008**

    Carle, E. Eric Carle's animals, animals
                                      808.81

    Carle, E. Eric Carle's dragons dragons and other
creatures that never were   **808.81**

    Christmas in the stable (2-4)   **811.008**

    Christmas poems   **808.81**

    Climb into my lap (k-3)   **808.81**

    Curious cats in art and poetry   **808.81**

    The Earth is painted green (4-6)   **808.81**

    Fishing for a dream   **782.42**

    Jumpety-bumpety hop   **811.008**

    Lessac, F. Caribbean canvas   **811**

    My song is beautiful (k-3)   **808.81**

    The New Oxford treasury of children's poems
(3-5)   **808.81**

    The Oxford book of animal poems (5 and up)
                                      808.81

    The Oxford book of Christmas poems (4 and
up)   **808.81**

    Poems for the very young (k-3)   **821.008**

    Side by side   **808.81**

    Sing a song of popcorn   **808.81**

    Stone bench in an empty park (4 and up)
                                      811.008

    Talking to the sun: an illustrated anthology of
poems for young people   **808.81**

    Until I saw the sea and other poems (k-2)
                                      811.008

    Valentine poems   **808.81**

    War and the pity of war (5 and up)
                                      808.81

    Winter poems   **808.81**

    Yummy! (k-3)   **811.008**

    A Zooful of animals   **808.81**

                Fiction

    Jarrell, R. The bat-poet (2-4)   **Fic**

                Indexes

    Index to children's poetry   **808.81**

    Index to poetry for children and young people
                                      808.81

Poetry—*Continued*

Study and teaching

Bauer, C. F. The poetry break   **372.6**

Hopkins, L. B. Pass the poetry, please!   **372.6**

Livingston, M. C. Poem-making (4 and up)   **372.6**

The **poetry** break. Bauer, C. F.   **372.6**

Poetry for young people [series]

Frost, R. Robert Frost   **811**

Sandburg, C. Carl Sandburg   **811**

Poetry from A to Z (5 and up)   **808.1**

Poets

Gollub, M. Cool melons—turn to frogs!: the life and poems of Issa [Kobayashi] (3-6)   **92**

Herrera, J. F. The upside down boy (k-3)   **92**

Poets, American

Cooper, F. Coming home: from the life of Langston Hughes (2-4)   **92**

Meltzer, M. Carl Sandburg (5 and up)   **92**

Meltzer, M. Langston Hughes (6 and up)   **92**

Pogány, Willy, 1882-1955

(il) Colum, P. The Golden Fleece and the heroes who lived before Achilles   **292**

Pohaha. San Souci, R.

In San Souci, R. Cut from the same cloth p87-91   **398.2**

Pohrt, Tom

(il) Norman, H. Trickster and the fainting birds   **398.2**

Poison dart frogs. Dewey, J.   **597.8**

Poisonous animals

See also Rattlesnakes

Poker Face the Baboon and Hot Dog the Tiger. Sandburg, C.

In Sandburg, C. Rootabaga stories pt 1 p40-45   **S C**

In Sandburg, C. The Sandburg treasury p27-29   **818**

Polacco, Patricia

Babushka's doll   **E**

Babushka's Mother Goose   **398.8**

The bee tree   **E**

The butterfly (2-4)   **Fic**

Chicken Sunday   **E**

Firetalking (1-3)   **92**

Just plain Fancy   **E**

The keeping quilt   **E**

Luba and the wren (k-3)   **398.2**

Mrs. Katz and Tush   **E**

Mrs. Mack   **E**

My rotten redheaded older brother   **E**

Pink and Say   **E**

Rechenka's eggs   **E**

Thank you, Mr. Falker   **E**

Thunder cake   **E**

Tikvah means hope   **E**

The trees of the dancing goats   **E**

Welcome Comfort   **E**

(il) Thayer, E. L. Casey at the bat   **811**

Poland

Hintz, M. Poland (4 and up)   **943.8**

Fiction

Hautzig, E. R. A gift for Mama (3-6)   **Fic**

Orlev, U. The island on Bird Street (5 and up)   **Fic**

Polar bear

Miller, D. S. A polar bear journey (2-4)   **599.78**

Patent, D. H. Great ice bear (4 and up)   **599.78**

Patent, D. H. Polar bears (3-6)   **599.78**

Fiction

Dabcovich, L. The polar bear son (k-3)   **398.2**

George, J. C. Snow Bear   **E**

Pinkwater, D. M. Young Larry   **E**

A **polar** bear journey. Miller, D. S.   **599.78**

Polar bear, polar bear, what do you hear? Martin, B.   **E**

The **polar** bear son. Dabcovich, L.   **398.2**

Polar expeditions *See* Antarctica—Exploration

The **Polar** Express. Van Allsburg, C.   **E**

Polar regions

See also Antarctica; Arctic regions; North Pole

Taylor, B. Arctic & Antarctic (4 and up)   **998**

Polar, the Titanic bear. Spedden, D. C. S.   **910.4**

Polese, Carolyn, 1947-

The first woman to vote in the state of California

In From sea to shining sea p182-85   **810.8**

Polikoff, Barbara Garland

Life's a funny proposition, Horatio (5 and up)   **Fic**

Poliomyelitis

Kehret, P. Small steps: the year I got polio (4-6)   **92**

Polis, Gary A.

About

Pringle, L. P. Scorpion man (4 and up)   **595.4**

Polish Americans

Fiction

Bartoletti, S. C. A coal miner's bride (4 and up)   **Fic**

Leighton, M. R. An Ellis Island Christmas   **E**

Recorvits, H. Goodbye, Walter Malinski (3-6)   **Fic**

Polish refugees

Fiction

Serraillier, I. The silver sword (5 and up)   **Fic**

Politi, Leo, 1908-1996

Song of the swallows   **E**

See/See also pages in the following book(s):

Caldecott Medal books, 1938-1957 p201-11   **028.5**

Political refugees

Kilborne, S. S. Leaving Vietnam (1-4)   **959.704**

Powell, Ransom J., 1849-1899
Fiction
Wisler, G. C. Red Cap (4 and up)   **Fic**

Powell, Suzanne I.
The Pueblos (4 and up)   **970.004**

Powell, William J., 1899-1942
See/See also pages in the following book(s):
Haskins, J. Black eagles p51-58 (5 and up)
    629.13

Power (Mechanics)
See also Electric power
The **power** of light. Singer, I. B.   **S C**
The **power** of light [story] Singer, I. B.
In Singer, I. B. The power of light p53-60
    S C
In Singer, I. B. Stories for children p210-16
    S C
The **power** of speech. Babbitt, N.
In Babbitt, N. The Devil's storybook p91-101
    S C
The **power** of Un. Etchemendy, N.   **Fic**
Power resources *See* Energy resources
The **powers** of Congress. Stein, R. C.   **328.73**
The **powers** of the Supreme Court. Stein, R. C.
    347

Powhatan Indians
Fritz, J. The double life of Pocahontas (4 and up)   **92**
Powwow. Ancona, G.   **970.004**

Poydar, Nancy
(il) Martin, A. M. Rachel Parker, kindergarten show-off   **E**

Poynter, Margaret
Marie Curie: discoverer of radium (4 and up)
    92

Prager, Ellen J.
Sand (k-3)   **553.6**

Prairie animals
Brandenburg, J. An American safari (4 and up)
    577.4
A **prairie** boy's summer. Kurelek, W.   **971.27**
A **prairie** boy's winter. Kurelek, W.   **971.27**

Prairie dogs
Bernhard, E. Prairie dogs (2-4)   **599.3**
Patent, D. H. Prairie dogs (4 and up)
    599.3

Prairie ecology
Brandenburg, J. An American safari (4 and up)
    577.4
George, J. C. One day in the prairie (4-6):
    577.4
Patent, D. H. Prairie dogs (4 and up)
    599.3
Patent, D. H. Prairies (4 and up)   **577.4**
Staub, F. J. America's prairies (3-6)   **577.4**
Prairie songs. Conrad, P.   **Fic**
Prairie town. Geisert, B.   **E**
Prairie-town boy. Sandburg, C.
In Sandburg, C. The Sandburg treasury p263-382   **818**
Prairies. Patent, D. H.   **577.4**
Prayer for a child. Field, R.   **242**

Prayers
All God's children (k-3)   **242**
Beckett, W. A child's book of prayer in art (3-6)   **242**
Bernos de Gasztold, C. Prayers from the ark
    841
Field, R. Prayer for a child (k-3)   **242**
Godwin, L. Barnyard prayers (k-2)   **811**
In every tiny grain of sand (2-5)   **291.4**
Lindbergh, R. The circle of days (k-3)   **242**
Marzollo, J. Home sweet home   **E**
One earth, one spirit   **242**
Prayers from the ark. Bernos de Gasztold, C.
    841

Praying mantis
Lavies, B. Backyard hunter: the praying mantis (2-4)   **595.7**
Fiction
James, B. Mary Ann   **E**
Preacher's boy. Paterson, K.   **Fic**
The **precious** hide. Afanas'ev, A. N.
In Afanas'ev, A. N. Russian fairy tales p156-58   **398.2**

Precious stones
Symes, R. F. Crystal & gem (4 and up)
    548
Precipitation (Meteorology) *See* Rain; Snow
Pregnancy
Cole, J. How you were born (k-2)   **612.6**
Harris, R. H. It's so amazing! (2-4)   **612.6**
Pringle, L. P. Everybody has a bellybutton (k-3)
    612.6

Prehistoric animals
See also Dinosaurs; Extinct animals
Lessem, D. Dinosaurs to dodos (4 and up)
    560

Prehistoric art
See also Rock drawings, paintings, and engravings
Lauber, P. Painters of the caves (4 and up)
    759.01
Patent, D. H. Mystery of the Lascaux Cave (5 and up)   **759.01**
Prehistoric life. Lindsay, W.   **560**
Prehistoric man *See* Fossil hominids
Prehistoric peoples
Arnold, C. Stone Age farmers beside the sea (4 and up)   **936.1**
Deem, J. M. Bodies from the bog (4 and up)
    930.1
Early humans (4 and up)   **930.1**
Getz, D. Frozen man (5 and up)   **930.1**
Lauber, P. Painters of the caves (4 and up)
    759.01
Patent, D. H. Mystery of the Lascaux Cave (5 and up)   **759.01**
Patent, D. H. Secrets of the ice man (5 and up)
    930.1
Sattler, H. R. The earliest Americans (5 and up)
    970.01
The Visual dictionary of prehistoric life (4 and up)   **560**
Prehistoric Pinkerton. Kellogg, S. See note under Kellogg, S. Pinkerton, behave!   **E**

Preiss-Glasser, Robin *See* Glasser, Robin Preiss

Prejudices

See also Antisemitism

Fiction

Conly, J. L. Crazy lady! (5 and up)   **Fic**

Curtis, C. P. The Watsons go to Birmingham—1963 (4 and up)   **Fic**

Fleischman, P. Saturnalia (6 and up)   **Fic**

Horvath, P. When the circus came to town (4-6)   **Fic**

Kurtz, J. The storyteller's beads (5 and up)   **Fic**

Little, M. O. Yoshiko and the foreigner   **E**

Miller, W. Night golf   **E**

Mochizuki, K. Baseball saved us   **E**

Mochizuki, K. Heroes   **E**

Taylor, M. D. The gold Cadillac (4 and up)   **Fic**

Taylor, M. D. Mississippi bridge (4 and up)   **Fic**

Uchida, Y. A jar of dreams (5 and up)   **Fic**

Uchida, Y. Journey home (5 and up)   **Fic**

Wolff, V. E. Bat 6 (5 and up)   **Fic**

Yarbrough, C. The shimmershine queens (4-6)   **Fic**

Yep, L. The star fisher (6 and up)   **Fic**

Prelutsky, Jack

The baby Uggs are hatching (k-3)   **811**

Beneath a blue umbrella: rhymes (k-3)   **811**

Dog days (k-1)   **811**

The dragons are singing tonight (2-5)   **811**

The gargoyle on the roof (2-5)   **811**

The Headless Horseman rides tonight (2-5)   **811**

It's Christmas (1-3)   **811**

It's snowing! It's snowing! (1-3)   **811**

It's Thanksgiving (1-3)   **811**

It's Valentine's Day (1-3)   **811**

Monday's troll (2-5)   **811**

My parents think I'm sleeping: poems (2-4)   **811**

The new kid on the block: poems (3-6)   **811**

Nightmares: poems to trouble your sleep (2-5)   **811**

A pizza the size of the sun (3-6)   **811**

Ride a purple pelican (k-3)   **811**

Rolling Harvey down the hill (1-3)   **811**

The sheriff of Rottenshot: poems (2-5)   **811**

Something big has been here (3-5)   **811**

Tyrannosaurus was a beast (2-5)   **811**

(comp) The 20th century children's poetry treasury. See The 20th century children's poetry treasury   **811.008**

(comp) A. Nonny Mouse writes again! See A. Nonny Mouse writes again!   **808.81**

(comp) The Beauty of the beast. See The Beauty of the beast   **811.008**

(comp) For laughing out loud. See For laughing out loud   **811.008**

(comp) Imagine that! See Imagine that!   **811.008**

(ed) The Random House book of poetry for children. See The Random House book of poetry for children   **821.008**

(comp) Read-aloud rhymes for the very young. See Read-aloud rhymes for the very young   **821.008**

(jt. auth) Seuss, Dr. Hooray for Diffendoofer Day!   **E**

Preschool education

See also Kindergarten

Cole, A. I saw a purple cow, and 100 other recipes for learning   **372**

Presenting Tanya the Ugly Duckling. Gauch, P. L. See note under Gauch, P. L. Dance, Tanya   **E**

Presentneed, Bymeby, and Hereafter

In Grandfather tales p140-49   **398.2**

Preservation of wildlife See Wildlife conservation

Presidents

United States

Adler, D. A. A picture book of Abraham Lincoln (1-3)   **92**

Adler, D. A. A picture book of John F. Kennedy (1-3)   **92**

Adler, D. A. A picture book of Thomas Jefferson (1-3)   **92**

Barber, J. Presidents (3-5)   **920**

Blassingame, W. The look-it-up book of presidents (5 and up)   **920**

Freedman, R. Franklin Delano Roosevelt (5 and up)   **92**

Freedman, R. Lincoln: a photobiography (4 and up)   **92**

Fritz, J. Bully for you, Teddy Roosevelt! (5 and up)   **92**

Fritz, J. The great little Madison (5 and up)   **92**

Giblin, J. Thomas Jefferson (2-4)   **92**

Harness, C. Abe Lincoln goes to Washington, 1837-1865 (2-4)   **92**

Harness, C. George Washington (3-5)   **92**

Kent, Z. John Quincy Adams, sixth president of the United States (4 and up)   **92**

Krull, K. Lives of the presidents (4 and up)   **920**

Lincoln, in his own words (6 and up)   **92**

Simon, C. Chester A. Arthur: twenty-first president of the United States (4 and up)   **92**

St. George, J. So you want to be president (3-6)   **973**

Wade, L. R. James Carter: thirty-ninth president of the United States (4 and up)   **92**

United States—Assassination

St. George, J. In the line of fire (4 and up)   **364.1**

United States—Mothers

Fritz, J. George Washington's mother (1-3)   **92**

United States—Spouses

See Presidents' spouses—United States

Presidents. Barber, J.   **920**

Presidents' spouses

United States

Adler, D. A. A picture book of Eleanor Roosevelt (1-3)   **92**

Cooney, B. Eleanor [biography of Eleanor Roosevelt] (k-3)   **92**

Princes and princesses *See* Princesses

The **princess** and the goatherd. Walker, B. K.
In Walker, B. K. A treasury of Turkish folktales for children p118-22 **398.2**

The **princess** and the goblin. MacDonald, G. **Fic**

The **princess** and the pea. Andersen, H. C. **Fic**
also in Tomie dePaola's favorite nursery tales p64-67 **398.2**

The **princess** and the peas. Andersen, H. C.
In The Classic fairy tales p217 **398.2**

The **princess** and the pig. Walker, B. K.
In Walker, B. K. A treasury of Turkish folktales for children p114-17 **398.2**

The **princess** and the vagabone. Sawyer, R.
In Sawyer, R. The way of the storyteller p319-33 **372.6**

Princess Chamomile gets her way. Oram, H. See note under Oram, H. Princess Chamomile's garden **E**

Princess Chamomile's garden. Oram, H. **E**

Princess Furball. Huck, C. S. **398.2**

The **princess** in the mirror. Jaffe, N.
In Jaffe, N. While standing on one foot p38-44 **296.1**

Princess Nur al-Nihar, the three princes, and Peri-Banu. Philip, N.
In Philip, N. The Arabian nights p116-30 **398.2**

Princess of Canterbury. Jacobs, J.
In Jacobs, J. English fairy tales p425-28 **398.2**

The **princess** of light. Schwartz, H.
In Schwartz, H. Next year in Jerusalem p32-34 **296.1**

The **princess** of the Tung Lake. Osborne, M. P.
In Osborne, M. P. Mermaid tales from around the world p51-55 **398.2**

The **princess** on the glass hill. Asbjornsen, P. C.
In The Blue fairy book p332-41 **398.2**

The **princess** on the pea. Andersen, H. C.
In Shedlock, M. L. The art of the story-teller p259-60 **372.6**

Princess Sonora and the long sleep. Levine, G. C. See note under Levine, G. C. The princess test **Fic**

Princess tales [series]
Levine, G. C. The princess test **Fic**

The **princess** test. Levine, G. C. **Fic**

The **princess**, the cat, and the unicorn. Wrede, P. C.
In Wrede, P. C. Book of enchantments p9-26 **S C**

The **princess** who could not dance. Thompson, R. P.
In American fairy tales p120-128 **S C**

The **princess** who never smiled. Afanas´ev, A. N.
In Afanas´ev, A. N. Russian fairy tales p360-63 **398.2**

The **princess** who wanted to solve riddles. Afanas´ev, A. N.
In Afanas´ev, A. N. Russian fairy tales p115-17 **398.2**

The **princess** who wished to be beautiful. Krishnaswami, U.
In Krishnaswami, U. Shower of gold: girls and women in the stories of India p61-67 **398.2**

Princesses
Stanley, F. The last princess: the story of Princess Ka'iulani of Hawai'i (4 and up) **92**
Fiction
Oram, H. Princess Chamomile's garden **E**

Principles of children's services in public libraries. Benne, M. **027.62**

Pringle, Laurence P.
Bats! (3-5) **599.4**
Dinosaurs! (k-3) **567.9**
Drinking (5 and up) **362.292**
Elephant woman (4 and up) **599.67**
The environmental movement (5 and up) **363.7**
Everybody has a bellybutton (k-3) **612.6**
Explore your senses (3-6) **612.8**
Contents: Hearing; Sight; Smell; Taste; Touch
An extraordinary life (5 and up) **595.7**
Oil spills (4 and up) **363.7**
Scorpion man (4 and up) **595.4**
Smoking (5 and up) **362.29**
Vanishing ozone (4 and up) **363.7**

The **printers**. Fisher, L. E. **686.2**

Printing
History
Fisher, L. E. Gutenberg (4 and up) **92**
Fisher, L. E. The printers (4 and up) **686.2**

Prints
Pomeroy, D. One potato **E**

Printup, Erwin, 1956-
(il) Swamp, J. Giving thanks **299**

Priore, Frank V.
The North Pole computer caper
In The Big book of Christmas plays p189-99 **808.82**

Prisoners of war, German *See* German prisoners of war

Prizes, Literary *See* Literary prizes

Problem drinking *See* Alcoholism

Problem solving
Burns, M. The book of think (4 and up) **153.4**

Professional growth series
Bucher, K. T. Information technology for schools **027.8**
McElmeel, S. L. WWW almanac **025.04**

Professions
See also Occupations

Profiles [series]
Vare, E. A. Women inventors & their discoveries **920**

Programmed instruction
See also Computer-assisted instruction

Programming with Latino children's materials. Wadham, T. **027.62**

Purple mountain majesties: the story of Katharine Lee Bates and "America the beautiful". Younger, B.   **92**

The **pushcart** war. Merrill, J.   **Fic**

Pushing up the sky. Bruchac, J.
  In Bruchac, J. Pushing up the sky: seven native American plays for children p57-65   **812**

Pushing up the sky: seven native American plays for children. Bruchac, J.   **812**

Pushkin meets the bundle. Ziefert, H.   **E**

Pushkin minds the bundle. Ziefert, H. See note under Ziefert, H. Pushkin meets the bundle   **E**

Puss in boots. Fischer, H.   **398.2**

Puss in boots. Galdone, P.   **398.2**

Puss in boots. Perrault, C.   **398.2**
  also in Perrault, C. Cinderella, Puss in Boots, and other favorite tales p26-39
   398.2
  also in Perrault, C. The complete fairy tales of Charles Perrault p45-53   **398.2**

Put that man to bed
  In The Magic orange tree, and other Haitian folktales p37-42   **398.2**

Putawai. Te Kanawa, K.
  In Te Kanawa, K. Land of the long white cloud p91-100   **398.2**

Putnam, James
  Mummy (4 and up)   **393**
  Pyramid (4 and up)   **909**

Putting on a play. Bentley, N.   **792**

Puzzles
  See also Riddles
  The Brain explorer (5 and up)   **793.73**
  Jonas, A. The 13th clue   **E**
  Steiner, J. Look-alikes   **793.73**
  Steiner, J. Look-alikes, jr.   **793.73**
  Wick, W. I spy   **793.73**
  Wick, W. I spy Christmas   **793.73**
  Wick, W. I spy extreme challenger!   **793.73**
  Wick, W. I spy fantasy   **793.73**
  Wick, W. I spy fun house   **793.73**
  Wick, W. I spy gold challenger!   **793.73**
  Wick, W. I spy mystery   **793.73**
  Wick, W. I spy school days   **793.73**
  Wick, W. I spy spooky night   **793.73**
  Wick, W. I spy super challenger!   **793.73**
  Wick, W. I spy treasure hunt   **793.73**
  See/See also pages in the following book(s):
  Cole, J. The rain or shine activity book p142-53 (3-5)   **793**

Pyle, Howard, 1853-1911
  The apple of contentment
   In American fairy tales p81-91   **S C**
  Bearskin   **E**
  The best that life has to give
   In Christmas fairy tales p112-22   **398.2**
  King Stork (2-4)   **398.2**

Pyramids
  Macaulay, D. Pyramid (4 and up)   **726**
  Putnam, J. Pyramid (4 and up)   **909**

Q

Qin Shi Huang, Emperor of China *See* Ch'in Shih-huang, Emperor of China, 259-210 B.C.

Qoheleth *See* Bible. O.T. Ecclesiastes

Quack and count. Baker, K.   **E**

Quail song. MacDonald, M. R.
  In MacDonald, M. R. Look back and see p121-25   **372.6**

Quakers *See* Society of Friends

The **quarreling** book. Zolotow, C.   **E**

Quarrelsome Demyan. Afanas'ev, A. N.
  In Afanas'ev, A. N. Russian fairy tales p163-64   **398.2**

Quarterbacks!. Sullivan, G.   **920**

Quayle, Eric
  The shining princess, and other Japanese legends (5 and up)   **398.2**
  Contents: The shining princess; The white hare and the crocodiles; My Lord Bag-o-Rice; The tongue-cut sparrow; The adventures of a fisher lad; The old man who made dead trees bloom; Momotaro—The peach warrior; The Matsuyama mirror; The wooden bowl; The ogre of Rashomon

Queen Eleanor: independent spirit of the medieval world. Brooks, P. S.   **92**

Queen Esther saves her people. Gelman, R. G.   **222**

Queen Esther the morning star. Gerstein, M.   **222**

The **Queen** of Attolia. Turner, M. W.   **Fic**

The **Queen** of the Sea. Schwartz, H.
  In Schwartz, H. A coat for the moon and other Jewish tales p2-5   **398.2**

Queenie Peavy. Burch, R.   **Fic**

Queens
  See also names of queens and countries with the subdivision *Kings and rulers*
  Meltzer, M. Ten queens (5 and up)   **920**
  Stanley, D. Cleopatra (4 and up)   **92**

The **Quest** channel. (K-6) See entry in Part 2: Web Resources

A **question** of arithmagic. McCaughrean, G.
  In McCaughrean, G. The crystal pool: myths and legends of the world p14-17   **398.2**

A **question** of life and death. McCaughrean, G.
  In McCaughrean, G. The silver treasure: myths and legends of the world p27-30   **398.2**

Quicksand
  De Paola, T. The quicksand book (k-3)   **552**

The **quicksand** book. De Paola, T.   **552**

A **quiet** night in. Murphy, J.   **E**

The **quilt**. Jonas, A.   **E**

The **quilt-block** history of pioneer days. Cobb, M.   **746.46**

The **quilt** story. Johnston, T.   **E**

Quilting
  Bial, R. With needle and thread (4 and up)   **746.46**

Race relations—Fiction—*Continued*

Taylor, M. D. The friendship (4 and up)

    Fic

Taylor, M. D. The gold Cadillac (4 and up)

    Fic

Taylor, M. D. Mississippi bridge (4 and up)

    Fic

Taylor, M. D. The road to Memphis (4 and up)

    Fic

Taylor, M. D. The well (4 and up)   **Fic**

Taylor, T. The cay (5 and up)   **Fic**

Taylor, T. Timothy of the cay (5 and up)

    Fic

Voigt, C. Come a stranger (6 and up)   **Fic**

Race to the top. McCaughrean, G.

  In McCaughrean, G. The crystal pool: myths and legends of the world p36-40

    398.2

Races of people *See* Ethnology

Rachel Parker, kindergarten show-off. Martin, A. M.   **E**

Racial balance in schools *See* School integration

Racial intermarriage *See* Interracial marriage

Racially mixed people

Fiction

Dorris, M. The window (4 and up)   **Fic**

Hamilton, V. Plain City (5 and up)   **Fic**

O'Connor, B. Me and Rupert Goody (4-6)

    Fic

Osborne, M. P. Adaline Falling Star (4 and up)

    Fic

Paterson, K. Jip (5 and up)   **Fic**

Racing

  See also types of racing

Bingham, C. Race car (k-3)   **629.228**

Racing the great bear. Bruchac, J.

  In Bruchac, J. Flying with the eagle, racing with the great bear p15-23   **398.2**

Rackham, Arthur, 1867-1939

  (il) Irving, W. Rip Van Winkle   **Fic**

  (il) Moore, C. C. The night before Christmas

    811

Racso and the rats of NIMH. Conly, J. L.

    Fic

Radiation

Skurzynski, G. Waves (3-6)   **539.2**

Radical change. Dresang, E. T.   **028.5**

Radin, Ruth Yaffe, 1938-

  Escape to the forest (3-6)   **Fic**

Radio Man. Don Radio. Dorros, A.   **E**

Radio rescue. Barasch, L.   **E**

Radio stations, Amateur *See* Amateur radio stations

Radunsky, Vladimir

  (il) Guthrie, W. Howdi do   **782.42**

  (il) Martin, B. The maestro plays   **E**

Rael, Elsa Okon

  What Zeesie saw on Delancey Street   **E**

Raffi

Baby Beluga (k-2)   **782.42**

Down by the bay (k-2)   **782.42**

Five little ducks (k-2)   **782.42**

One light, one sun (k-2)   **782.42**

Raffi songs to read [series]

Raffi. Baby Beluga   **782.42**

Raffi. Down by the bay   **782.42**

Raffi. Five little ducks   **782.42**

Raffi. One light, one sun   **782.42**

The raft. LaMarche, J.   **E**

Rafting (Sports)

Fiction

LaMarche, J. The raft   **E**

Ragged emperor. McCaughrean, G.

  In McCaughrean, G. The bronze cauldron: myths and legends of the world p71-77

    398.2

Ragtime Tumpie. Schroeder, A.   **E**

Ragweed. Avi *See* note under Avi. Poppy

    Fic

Raible, Alton, 1918-

  (il) Snyder, Z. K. The Egypt game   **Fic**

  (il) Snyder, Z. K. The headless cupid   **Fic**

  (il) Snyder, Z. K. The witches of Worm

    Fic

Railroads

Barton, B. Trains (k-1)   **625.1**

Big book of trains (4-6)   **625.1**

Coiley, J. Train (4 and up)   **625.1**

Crews, D. Freight train   **E**

Ziefert, H. Train song   **E**

Fiction

Aylesworth, J. Country crossing   **E**

Crews, D. Shortcut   **E**

Durbin, W. The journal of Sean Sullivan (5 and up)   **Fic**

Goble, P. Death of the iron horse   **E**

McCully, E. A. An outlaw Thanksgiving   **E**

Nesbit, E. The railway children (4-6)   **Fic**

Piper, W. The little engine that could   **E**

Rylant, C. Silver packages   **E**

Siebert, D. Train song   **E**

Suen, A. Window music   **E**

Tunnell, M. O. Mailing May   **E**

Voake, C. Here comes the train   **E**

Yep, L. Dragon's gate (6 and up)   **Fic**

History

Blumberg, R. Full steam ahead (5 and up)

    385.09

Murphy, J. Across America on an emigrant train (5 and up)   **92**

Railroads, Cable *See* Cable railroads

The railway children. Nesbit, E.   **Fic**

Rain

  See also Droughts

Branley, F. M. Down comes the rain (k-3)

    551.57

Kalan, R. Rain   **E**

Markle, S. A rainy day (k-2)   **551.57**

Shulevitz, U. Rain, rain, rivers   **E**

Fiction

Hesse, K. Come on, rain!   **E**

Hest, A. In the rain with Baby Duck   **E**

Hines, A. G. What can you do in the rain?

    E

McPhail, D. M. The puddle   **E**

Ray, M. L. Red rubber boot day   **E**

Stojic, M. Rain   **E**

Rain—*Continued*

Poetry

Evans, L. Rain song (k-1)　　　　**811**

Rain. Stojic, M.　　　　**E**

Rain & hail. *See* Branley, F. M. Down comes the rain　　　　**551.57**

Rain forest babies. Darling, K.　　　　**591.9**

Rain forest ecology

George, J. C. One day in the tropical rain forest (4-6)　　　　**577.3**

Gibbons, G. Nature's green umbrella (k-3)　　　　**577.3**

Greenaway, T. Jungle (4 and up)　　　　**577.3**

Grupper, J. Destination: rain forest (1-3)　　　　**577.3**

Lasky, K. The most beautiful roof in the world (4-6)　　　　**577.3**

Pandell, K. Journey through the northern rainforest (4 and up)　　　　**578.7**

Stille, D. R. Tropical rain forest (2-4)　　　　**577.3**

Rain forests

Darling, K. Rain forest babies (k-3)　　　　**591.9**

Grupper, J. Destination: rain forest (1-3)　　　　**577.3**

Patent, D. H. Flashy fantastic rain forest frogs (k-3)　　　　**597.8**

Fiction

Baker, J. Where the forest meets the sea　　　　**E**

Cherry, L. The great kapok tree　　　　**E**

Olaleye, I. Bitter bananas　　　　**E**

Rain makes applesauce. Scheer, J.　　　　**E**

The **rain** or shine activity book. Cole, J.　　　　**793**

Rain player. Wisniewski, D.　　　　**E**

Rain, rain, rivers. Shulevitz, U.　　　　**E**

Rain song. Evans, L.　　　　**811**

Rainbow biography [series]

Medearis, A. S. Dare to dream: Coretta Scott King and the civil rights movement　　　　**92**

Rainbow Crow. Curry, J. L.

In Curry, J. L. Turtle Island: tales of the Algonquian nations p5-10　　　　**398.2**

The **rainbow** hand. Wong, J. S.　　　　**811**

Rainbow snake. McCaughrean, G.

In McCaughrean, G. The golden hoard: myths and legends of the world p60-65　　　　**398.2**

Rainbows are made: poems. Sandburg, C.　　　　**811**

Rainfall *See* Rain

The **rainmaker**. Medearis, A. S.

In Medearis, A. S. Haunts p22-31　　　　**S C**

A **rainy** day. Markle, S.　　　　**551.57**

Raisel's riddle. Silverman, E.　　　　**398.2**

Raising dragons. Nolen, J.　　　　**E**

Raising Sweetness. Stanley, D. *See* note under Stanley, D. Saving Sweetness　　　　**E**

Raising Yoder's barn. Yolen, J.　　　　**E**

Ralph S. Mouse. Cleary, B. *See* note under Cleary, B. The mouse and the motorcycle　　　　**Fic**

The **ram** in the chile patch. Sierra, J.

In Sierra, J. Nursery tales around the world p47-51　　　　**398.2**

The **ram,** the cat, and the twelve wolves. Afanas'ev, A. N.

In Afanas'ev, A. N. Russian fairy tales p196-98　　　　**398.2**

The **ram** who lost half his skin. Afanas'ev, A. N.

In Afanas'ev, A. N. Russian fairy tales p188-91　　　　**398.2**

Ramadan

Ghazi, S. H. Ramadan (k-3)　　　　**297.3**

Fiction

Matthews, M. Magid fasts for Ramadan (2-4)　　　　**Fic**

Ramona and her father. Cleary, B. *See* note under Cleary, B. Ramona the pest　　　　**Fic**

Ramona and her mother. Cleary, B. *See* note under Cleary, B. Ramona the pest　　　　**Fic**

Ramona, forever. Cleary, B. *See* note under Cleary, B. Ramona the pest　　　　**Fic**

Ramona Quimby, age 8. Cleary, B. *See* note under Cleary, B. Ramona the pest　　　　**Fic**

Ramona the brave. Cleary, B. *See* note under Cleary, B. Ramona the pest　　　　**Fic**

Ramona the pest. Cleary, B.　　　　**Fic**

Ramona's world. Cleary, B. *See* note under Cleary, B. Ramona the pest　　　　**Fic**

Ramos Nieves, Ernesto

(il) Bernier-Grand, C. T. Juan Bobo　　　　**398.2**

The **Ramsay** scallop. Temple, F.　　　　**Fic**

Ramsey, Alice Huyler, d. 1983

About

Brown, D. Alice Ramsey's grand adventure (k-3)　　　　**92**

Ranch life

King, D. C. Wild West days (3-6)　　　　**978**

Fiction

Noble, T. H. Meanwhile back at the ranch　　　　**E**

Paulsen, G. The haymeadow (6 and up)　　　　**Fic**

Rand, Donna

Black Books Galore!—guide to great African American children's books about boys　　　　**016.3058**

Black Books Galore!—guide to great African American children's books about girls　　　　**016.3058**

Rand, Ted

(il) Aylesworth, J. Country crossing　　　　**E**

(il) Bunting, E. Night tree　　　　**E**

(il) Bunting, E. Secret place　　　　**E**

(il) Cleary, B. The hullabaloo ABC　　　　**E**

(il) Garland, S. My father's boat　　　　**E**

(il) Gibbons, F. Mama and me and the Model-T　　　　**E**

(il) Gibbons, F. Mountain wedding　　　　**E**

(il) Johnston, T. It's about dogs　　　　**811**

(il) Jonell, L. Let's play rough　　　　**E**

(il) Lesser, C. Storm on the desert　　　　**577.5**

(il) Longfellow, H. W. Paul Revere's ride　　　　**811**

(il) Martin, B. Barn dance!　　　　**E**

The **rattlebang** picnic. Mahy, M.   E
Rattlesnake dance. Arnosky, J.   E
Rattlesnakes
Fiction
Arnosky, J. Rattlesnake dance   E
Moroney, L. Baby rattlesnake (k-2)   **398.2**
Rauzon, Mark J.
Water, water everywhere (k-3)   **551.48**
Raven. McDermott, G.   **398.2**
Raven & monster halibut. Lelooska
In Lelooska. Spirit of the cedar people p18-25   **398.2**

Raven & Sea Gull. Lelooska
In Lelooska, D. Echoes of the elders p22-27   **398.2**

The **raven** and the lobster. Afanas'ev, A. N.
In Afanas'ev, A. N. Russian fairy tales p612   **398.2**

The **Raven** and the moon. McCaughrean, G.
In McCaughrean, G. The silver treasure: myths and legends of the world p114-17   **398.2**

The **raven** and the star fruit tree. Tran, V. D.
In From sea to shining sea p368-69   **810.8**

Raven brings fresh water. Martin, F.
In From sea to shining sea p8-11   **810.8**
The **ravens.** Kordon, K.
In Don't read this! and other tales of the unnatural p71-84   **S C**
Raw Head, bloody bones (4-6)   **398.2**
Raw Head, Devil, and the barefoot woman
In Raw Head, bloody bones p59-64   **398.2**

Rawlings, Marjorie Kinnan, 1896-1953
The yearling (6 and up)   **Fic**
Rawlins, Donna
(il) Loh, M. J. Tucking Mommy in   E
Rawls, Wilson, 1913-
Where the red fern grows   **Fic**
Ray, Deborah Kogan, 1940-
(il) Coerr, E. Chang's paper pony   E
(il) Harvey, B. Cassie's journey   **Fic**
(il) Harvey, B. My prairie Christmas   **Fic**
(il) Johnston, T. The barn owls   E
(il) Singer, M. Sky words   **811**
Ray, Jane
(il) Bible. O.T. Genesis. The story of the creation   **222**
(il) Hoffman, M. Sun, moon, and stars   **398.2**
(il) Mayo, M. Magical tales from many lands   **398.2**
(il) Mayo, M. Mythical birds & beasts from many lands   **398.2**
Ray, Mary Lyn
Basket moon   E
Red rubber boot day   E
Rayevsky, Robert
(il) Hodges, M. Joan of Arc   **92**
(il) Kimmel, E. A. Three sacks of truth   **398.2**

Rayner, Mary, 1933-
(il) King-Smith, D. Babe: the gallant pig   **Fic**
(il) King-Smith, D. Pigs might fly   **Fic**
Rayyan, Omar
(il) Ghazi, S. H. Ramadan   **297.3**
(il) Stewig, J. W. King Midas   **398.2**
Re-zoom. Bányai, I.   E
Reaching Dustin. Grove, V.   **Fic**
Read, Mary, 1680-1721
Poetry
Yolen, J. The ballad of the pirate queens (3-5)   **811**
The **read-aloud** handbook. Trelease, J.   **028.5**
Read-aloud rhymes for the very young (k-2)   **821.008**
The **Read-aloud** treasury   **808.8**
Read and wonder [series]
King-Smith, D. All pigs are beautiful   **636.4**
King-Smith, D. I love guinea pigs   **636.9**
Read for the fun of it. Bauer, C. F.   **027.62**
Read to your bunny. Wells, R.   E
Readers' guide for young people. (4-8) See entry in Part 2: Web Resources
Reading
Herb, S. Using children's books in preschool settings   **372.4**
Leonhardt, M. Keeping kids reading   **028.5**
Fiction
Bunting, E. The Wednesday surprise   E
Gilson, J. Do bananas chew gum? (4-6)   **Fic**
Park, F. The royal bee   E
Polacco, P. Thank you, Mr. Falker   E
Periodicals
The Reading Teacher   **372.405**
The **Reading** Teacher   **372.405**
Ready, set, read—and laugh! (k-3)   **810.8**
Ready-to-read [series]
Bang, M. Wiley and the Hairy Man   **398.2**
Goodman, S. Animal rescue   **639.9**
Kassirer, S. Joseph and his coat of many colors   **222**
Kilborne, S. S. Leaving Vietnam   **959.704**
Krensky, S. Striking it rich   **979.4**
Sharmat, M. W. Mitchell is moving   E
The **Real** Mother Goose   **398.8**
The **real** thief. Steig, W.   **Fic**
The **reasons** for seasons. Gibbons, G.   **525**
Reaver, Chap, 1935-1993
Bill (5 and up)   **Fic**
Reaver, Herbert R. *See* Reaver, Chap, 1935-1993
Rebecca of Sunnybrook Farm. Wiggin, K. D. S.   **Fic**
Rebel. Schoenherr, J.   E
Rebels against slavery. McKissack, P. C.   **326**
Rechenka's eggs. Polacco, P.   E
Recipes *See* Cooking
Recipes for art and craft materials. Sattler, H. R.   **745.5**
Reclamation of land
See also Wetlands

Reconstruction (1865-1876)
Mettger, Z. Reconstruction (5 and up)
973.8
Fiction
Robinet, H. G. Forty acres and maybe a mule (4 and up) **Fic**
Recorded books *See* Audiobooks
Recordings, Sound *See* Sound recordings
Recorvits, Helen
Goodbye, Walter Malinski (3-6) **Fic**
Recreation
See also Amusements
Drake, J. The kids' summer handbook (4 and up) **790.1**
Recycle!. Gibbons, G. **363.7**
Recycling
Gibbons, G. Recycle! (k-3) **363.7**
Showers, P. Where does the garbage go? (k-3) **363.7**
See/See also pages in the following book(s):
Glaser, L. Compost! (k-2) **363.7**
The **red** balloon. Lamorisse, A. **E**
Red Cap. Wisler, G. C. **Fic**
Red carpet Christmas. Miller, H. L.
In The Big book of Christmas plays p3-25 **808.82**
Red Cloud, Sioux Chief, 1822-1909
See/See also pages in the following book(s):
Ehrlich, A. Wounded Knee: an Indian history of the American West (6 and up) **970.004**
Freedman, R. Indian chiefs p10-27 (6 and up) **920**
Red dog. Kipling, R.
In Kipling, R. The jungle book: the Mowgli stories **S C**
The **Red** Etin
In The Blue fairy book p385-90 **398.2**
The **Red** Ettin. Jacobs, J.
In Jacobs, J. English fairy tales p132-37 **398.2**
Red-eyed tree frog. Cowley, J. **E**
Red leaf, yellow leaf. Ehlert, L. **582.16**
Red light, green light, mama and me. Best, C. **E**
Red Riding Hood. Marshall, J. **398.2**
Red rubber boot day. Ray, M. L. **E**
The **red** silk handerchief. MacDonald, M. R.
In MacDonald, M. R. When the lights go out p129-32 **372.6**
The **red** wolf. Silverstein, A. **599.77**
Red wolf country. London, J. **E**
Redfeather book [series]
Guiberson, B. Z. Lighthouses **387.1**
Lauber, P. Earthworms: underground farmers **592**
Redmond, Ian
Gorilla (4 and up) **599.8**
Reducing *See* Weight loss
Redwall. Jacques, B. **Fic**

Reed, Mike, 1951-
(il) Bollard, J. K. Scholastic children's thesaurus **423**
Reeder, Carolyn, 1937-
Across the lines (5 and up) **Fic**
Shades of gray (4 and up) **Fic**
Reedy, Jerry
Oklahoma
In America the beautiful, second series **973**
Reese, Harold *See* Reese, Pee Wee, 1919-1999
Reese, Pee Wee, 1919-1999
About
Golenbock, P. Teammates [biography of Jackie Robinson] (1-4) **92**
Reference books
Bibliography
Safford, B. R. Guide to reference materials for school media centers **011.6**
Reference Books Bulletin. See Booklist **028.1**
Reference sources in the humanities series
Denman-West, M. W. Children's literature: a guide to information sources **011.6**
Reflections. Jonas, A. **E**
Reflections on a gift of watermelon pickle . . . and other modern verse (6 and up) **811.008**
Reflexes
Berger, M. Why I sneeze, shiver, hiccup, and yawn (k-3) **612.7**
Reformers
Kraft, B. H. Mother Jones (4 and up) **92**
Refugees
Marx, T. One boy from Kosovo (3-6) **949.7**
Fiction
Bunting, E. How many days to America? **E**
Holm, A. North to freedom (6 and up) **Fic**
Temple, F. Grab hands and run (6 and up) **Fic**
Temple, F. Tonight, by sea (6 and up) **Fic**
Whelan, G. Goodbye, Vietnam (4 and up) **Fic**
Refugees, Jewish *See* Jewish refugees
Refugees, Polish *See* Polish refugees
Refugees, Political *See* Political refugees
Refuges, Wildlife *See* Wildlife refuges
Refuse and refuse disposal
See also Recycling
Maass, R. Garbage (k-3) **363.7**
Showers, P. Where does the garbage go? (k-3) **363.7**
Fiction
Zimmerman, A. G. Trashy town **E**
Regan, Laura
(il) Lesser, C. Dig hole, soft mole **E**
Regan, Michael
(jt. auth) Ajmera, M. Let the games begin! **796**
Regards to the man in the moon. Keats, E. J. See note under Keats, E. J. Louie **E**

Regular Guy. Weeks, S.   **Fic**

Reich, Susanna, 1954-
Clara Schumann (5 and up)   **92**

Reid, Rob
Children's jukebox   **782.42**

Reid Banks, Lynne See Banks, Lynne Reid, 1929-

Reim, Melanie K., 1956-
(il) Fleischner, J. I was born a slave: the story of Harriet Jacobs   **92**
(il) Haskins, J. Carter G. Woodson   **92**

Reincarnation
Fiction
Gerstein, M. The mountains of Tibet   **E**

Reindeer
Fiction
Brett, J. The wild Christmas reindeer   **E**
Hansen, B. Caesar's antlers (5 and up)   **Fic**
Seibold, J. O. Olive the other reindeer   **E**

The **reindeer** people. Lewin, T.   **948.97**

Reinhard, Johan
Discovering the Inca Ice Maiden (5 and up)   **930.1**

See/See also pages in the following book(s):
Talking with adventurers p68-75 (4-6)   **920**

Reisberg, Mira, 1955-
See/See also pages in the following book(s):
Just like me p18-19   **920**

Reisberg, Veg
(il) Moroney, L. Baby rattlesnake   **398.2**
(il) Rohmer, H. Uncle Nacho's hat   **398.2**

Reiser, Lynn
Cherry pies and lullabies   **E**
The surprise family   **E**
Tortillas and lullabies. Tortillas y cancioncitas   **E**

Reiss, Johanna
The upstairs room (4 and up)   **92**

Reit, Seymour
Behind rebel lines: the incredible story of Emma Edmonds, Civil War spy (4 and up)   **92**

Relations among ethnic groups See Ethnic relations

Relatively speaking. Fletcher, R.   **811**

The **relatives** came. Rylant, C.   **E**

Religion
Fiction
Rylant, C. A fine white dust (5 and up)   **Fic**

Religions
See also Gods and goddesses; Occultism
Birdseye, D. H. What I believe (4 and up)   **200**
Dole, P. P. Children's books about religion   **016.2**
Ganeri, A. Out of the ark (4 and up)   **291.1**
Gellman, M. How do you spell God? (5 and up)   **200**
Maestro, B. The story of religion (3-5)   **291**
Osborne, M. P. One world, many religions (4 and up)   **291**

Fiction
Blume, J. Are you there God? it's me, Margaret (5 and up)   **Fic**

Religious art
See also Jewish art and symbolism
Bible. O.T. Stories from the Old Testament (5 and up)   **221.9**
Osborne, M. P. The life of Jesus in masterpieces of art   **232.9**
See/See also pages in the following book(s):
Armstrong, C. Women of the Bible (5 and up)   **220.9**

Religious holidays
See also Jewish holidays

Religious poetry
All God's children (k-3)   **242**

Relocation of Japanese Americans, 1942-1945
See Japanese Americans—Evacuation and relocation, 1942-1945

The **reluctant** dragon. Grahame, K.   **Fic**

Reluctantly Alice. Naylor, P. R. See note under Naylor, P. R. The agony of Alice   **Fic**

REM world. Philbrick, W. R.   **Fic**

Remaking the earth. Goble, P.   **398.2**

The **remarkable** journey of Prince Jen. Alexander, L.   **Fic**

The **remarkable** rocket. Wilde, O.
In Wilde, O. The fairy tales of Oscar Wilde p50-61   **S C**

Remarriage
Fiction
Clifton, L. Everett Anderson's 1-2-3   **E**
Holt, K. W. Mister and me (3-5)   **Fic**
Love, D. A. A year without rain (4 and up)   **Fic**
Petersen, P. J. I hate weddings (3-5)   **Fic**

The **remembering** box. Clifford, E.   **Fic**

Remington, Frederic, 1861-1909
See/See also pages in the following book(s):
Calvert, P. Great lives: the American frontier p311-27 (5 and up)   **920**

Remkiewicz, Frank
(il) Kline, S. Horrible Harry in room 2B   **Fic**
(il) London, J. Froggy learns to swim   **E**
(il) Murphy, S. J. Just enough carrots   **513**

Renaissance
See also World history—15th century
January, B. Science in the Renaissance (4 and up)   **509**
Langley, A. Renaissance (4 and up)   **940.2**
Wood, T. The Renaissance (4 and up)   **940.2**

Fiction
Avi. Midnight magic (5 and up)   **Fic**

Rendeiro, Charlene
(il) Hopkins, L. B. Been to yesterdays: poems of a life   **811**

Reneaux, J. J., 1955-
Why alligator hates dog
In From sea to shining sea p46-49   **810.8**

Rey, H. A. (Hans Augusto), 1898-1977—*Continued*

Curious George takes a job. See note under Rey, H. A. Curious George   E
Find the constellations   **523.8**
(il) Payne, E. Katy No-Pocket   E
(jt. auth) Rey, M. Whiteblack the penguin sees the world   E

Rey, Hans Augusto *See* Rey, H. A. (Hans Augusto), 1898-1977

Rey, Margret

Curious George flies a kite. See note under Rey, H. A. Curious George   E
Curious George goes to the hospital. See note under Rey, H. A. Curious George   E
Whiteblack the penguin sees the world   E

Reynolds, Adrian

(il) Whybrow, I. Sammy and the dinosaurs   E

Reynolds, David West

Star wars: incredible cross sections   **791.43**
Star wars: the visual dictionary   **791.43**

Reynolds, Peter

(il) McDonald, M. Judy Moody   **Fic**

Reznicki, Jack

(il) Masoff, J. Fire!   **628.9**

Rhead, Louis, 1857-1926

(il) Wyss, J. D. The Swiss family Robinson   **Fic**

Rhino. Arnold, C.   **599.66**

Rhinoceros

Arnold, C. Rhino (3-5)   **599.66**
Walker, S. M. Rhinos (3-6)   **599.66**

Rhinos. Walker, S. M.   **599.66**

Rhode Island

Klein, T. E. D. Rhode Island
In Celebrate the states   **973**
McNair, S. Rhode Island
In America the beautiful, second series   **973**

History
Avi. Finding Providence: the story of Roger Williams (2-4)   **92**

Rhodesia, Northern *See* Zambia

Rhodesia, Southern *See* Zimbabwe

Rhyme

See also Stories in rhyme

Rhymes for Annie Rose. Hughes, S.   **821**

Ribsy. Cleary, B. See note under Cleary, B. Henry Higgins   **Fic**

Ricciuti, Edward R.

National Audubon Society first field guide: rocks and minerals (4 and up)   **552**

Rice, Eve, 1951-

Benny bakes a cake   E
City night   E
Sam who never forgets   E

Rice cakes for the new year. Terada, A. M.
In Terada, A. M. Under the starfruit tree p105-08   **398.2**

Rich, Anna, 1956-

(il) Medearis, A. S. Dare to dream: Coretta Scott King and the civil rights movement   **92**

Rich, Mary Perrotta

(ed) Book poems. See Book poems   **811.008**

The **rich** man's place. Scudder, H. E.
In American fairy tales p55-62   **S C**

Richard, Maurice, 1921-2000

See/See also pages in the following book(s):
Krull, K. Lives of the athletes p59-61 (4 and up)   **920**

Richard Wright and the library card. Miller, W.   E

Richards, Laura Elizabeth Howe, 1850-1943

The golden windows
In American fairy tales p116-19   **S C**

Richards, Norman, 1932-

Monticello (4-6)   **975.5**

The **riches** of Oseola McCarty. Coleman, E.   **92**

Ricky of the Tuft. Perrault, C.
In Perrault, C. Cinderella, Puss in Boots, and other favorite tales p78-101   **398.2**

Riddell, Chris, 1962-

(il) Andersen, H. C. The swan's stories   **S C**
(il) Platt, R. Castle diary   **Fic**

Riddle, Sue, 1966-

(il) Swope, S. Gotta go! Gotta go!   E

The **riddle.** Grimm, J.
In The Green fairy book p300-03   **398.2**

The **riddle** of the Rosetta Stone. Giblin, J.   **493**

Riddle road. Spires, E.   **793.73**

Riddle roundup. Maestro, G.   **793.73**

The **riddle** tale of freedom. Hamilton, V.
In Hamilton, V. The people could fly: American black folktales p156-59   **398.2**

The **riddlemaster.** Storr, C.
In The Oxford treasury of children's stories p72-81   **S C**

Riddles

Adler, D. A. The carsick zebra and other animal riddles (1-3)   **793.73**
Adler, D. A. Easy math puzzles (2-4)   **793.73**
The Brain explorer (5 and up)   **793.73**
Cerf, B. Bennett Cerf's book of riddles (k-3)   **793.73**
Cerf, B. Riddles and more riddles!   **793.73**
Cole, J. Why did the chicken cross the road? and other riddles, old and new (3-5)   **793.73**
Hall, K. Creepy riddles (k-2)   **793.73**
Hall, K. Mummy riddles (k-2)   **793.73**
Hall, K. Snakey riddles (k-2)   **793.73**
Kessler, L. P. Old Turtle's 90 knock-knocks, jokes, and riddles (1-3)   **793.73**
Maestro, G. Riddle roundup (2-4)   **793.73**
Maestro, M. Geese find the missing piece (k-2)   **793.73**

Rivera, Tomás
Fiction

Mora, P. Tomás and the library lady   **E**

Riverdeep.net. (4 and up) See entry in Part 2: Web Resources

Rivers

    See also Mississippi River

Geisert, B. River town   **E**

LaMarche, J. The raft   **E**
Fiction

Byars, B. C. Trouble River (4-6)   **Fic**

Hooper, M. River story   **E**

Locker, T. Where the river begins   **E**

Roach, Marilynne K.

In the days of the Salem witchcraft trials (4 and up)   **133.4**

Roach (Insect) *See* Cockroaches

Road builders. Hennessy, B. G.   **625.7**

The **road** from home [biography of Veron Kherdian] Kherdian, D.   **92**

Road song of the bandard-log. Kipling, R.

   In Kipling, R. The jungle book: the Mowgli stories   **S C**

The **road** to Camlann. Sutcliff, R.   **398.2**

The **road** to home. Auch, M. J.   **Fic**

The **road** to Memphis. Taylor, M. D.   **Fic**

Roadrunner's pack. Curry, J. L.

   In Curry, J. L. Back in the beforetime p5-9   **398.2**

Roads

Hennessy, B. G. Road builders (k-2)   **625.7**
Fiction

Hindley, J. The big red bus   **E**

Lyon, G. E. Who came down that road?   **E**

The **robber** and me. Holub, J.   **Fic**

The **robber** bridegroom. San Souci, R.

   In San Souci R. Short & shivery p1-8   **398.2**

The **robbers**. Afanas´ev, A. N.

   In Afanas´ev, A. N. Russian fairy tales p419-23   **398.2**

Robbers and outlaws *See* Thieves

Robbins, Ken

Autumn leaves (3-6)   **582.16**

Trucks (k-2)   **629.224**

Robbins, Ruth

Baboushka and the three kings (1-4)   **398.2**

(il) Kroeber, T. Ishi, last of his tribe   **92**

Robert Frost. Frost, R.   **811**

Robert Louis Stevenson, teller of tales. Gherman, B.   **92**

Roberts, Willo Davis

The girl with the silver eyes (4-6)   **Fic**

The kidnappers (4 and up)   **Fic**

Scared stiff (5 and up)   **Fic**

The view from the cherry tree (5 and up)   **Fic**

Robertshaw, Andrew

A soldier's life (4 and up)   **355**

Robertson, Graham

(il) Patent, D. H. Looking at penguins   **598**

Robertson, Keith, 1914-1991

Henry Reed, Inc. (4-6)   **Fic**

Henry Reed's babysitting service. See note under Robertson, K. Henry Reed, Inc.   **Fic**

Robin Hood (Legendary character)

Creswick, P. Robin Hood (5 and up)   **398.2**
Fiction

Tomlinson, T. The Forestwife (6 and up)   **Fic**

Robin Hood and his merry men. Osborne, M. P.

   In Osborne, M. P. Favorite medieval tales p60-66   **398.2**

Robin Hood and the golden arrow. McCaughrean, G.

   In McCaughrean, G. The golden hoard: myths and legends of the world p20-28   **398.2**

Robinet, Harriette Gillem, 1931-

Forty acres and maybe a mule (4 and up)   **Fic**

Walking to the bus-rider blues (5 and up)   **Fic**

Robins, Joan

Addie meets Max   **E**

Addie's bad day. See note under Robins, J. Addie meets Max   **E**

Robins

Jenkins, P. B. A nest full of eggs (k-1)   **598**

Robinson, Aminah Brenda Lynn, 1940-

(il) Battle-Lavert, G. The shaking bag   **E**

(il) Fox, M. Sophie   **E**

(il) Rosen, M. J. Elijah's angel   **Fic**

(il) Rosen, M. J. A school for Pompey Walker   **Fic**

Robinson, Barbara

The best Christmas pageant ever (4-6)   **Fic**

The best school year ever. See note under Robinson, B. The best Christmas pageant ever   **Fic**

Robinson, Charles, 1870-1937

(il) Stevenson, R. L. A child's garden of verses   **821**

Robinson, Charles, 1931-

(il) Levitin, S. Journey to America   **Fic**

(il) Smith, D. B. A taste of blackberries   **Fic**

Robinson, Eddie

See/See also pages in the following book(s):

Haskins, J. One more river to cross (4 and up)   **920**

Robinson, Jackie, 1919-1972
About

Adler, D. A. A picture book of Jackie Robinson (1-3)   **92**

Dingle, D. T. First in the field: baseball hero Jackie Robinson (3-6)   **92**

Golenbock, P. Teammates (1-4)   **92**

Jacobs, W. J. They shaped the game (4 and up)   **920**

See/See also pages in the following book(s):

Brashler, W. The story of Negro league baseball p121-33 (5 and up)   **796.357**

Krull, K. Lives of the athletes p51-53 (4 and up)   **920**

Robinson Masters, Nancy
Georgia
In America the beautiful, second series
973
Kansas
In America the beautiful, second series
973
Robotics *See* Robots
Robotics: sensing, thinking, acting. (4 and up) See
entry in Part 2: Web Resources
Robots
Sonenklar, C. Robots rising (3-5)   629.8
Fiction
Pinkney, B. Cosmo and the robot   E
Robots rising. Sonenklar, C.   629.8
Rochman, Hazel
Against borders   011.6
Rock, Lois
(comp) Words of gold. See Words of gold
220.9
Rock and roll music *See* Rock music
Rock collecting. See Gans, R. Let's go rock col-
lecting   552
Rock drawings, paintings, and engravings
Arnold, C. Stories in stone (4 and up)
709.01
Rock music
Fiction
Appelt, K. Bats around the clock   E
Rock paintings *See* Rock drawings, paintings, and
engravings
Rocket man: the story of Robert Goddard.
Streissguth, T.   92
Rockin' reptiles. Calmenson, S. See note under
Calmenson, S. Get well, Gators!   Fic
Rocklin, Joanne
Strudel stories (4 and up)   Fic
Rockman, Connie C.
(ed) Eighth book of junior authors and illustra-
tors. See Eighth book of junior authors and il-
lustrators   920.003
Rocks
Christian, P. If you find a rock (k-3)   552
Ricciuti, E. R. National Audubon Society first
field guide: rocks and minerals (4 and up)
552
Symes, R. F. Rocks & minerals (4 and up)
549
VanCleave, J. P. Janice VanCleave's rocks and
minerals (4 and up)   552
Collectors and collecting
Gans, R. Let's go rock collecting (k-2)
552
Murphy, S. J. Dave's down-to-earth rock shop
(k-3)   511.3
Rocks & minerals. Symes, R. F.   549
Rockwell, Anne F., 1934-
At the beach   E
The boy who wouldn't obey: a Mayan legend
(2-4)   398.2
Career day   E
The first snowfall   E
One bean (k-2)   635
Our earth (k-2)   910

Our stars (k-2)   523.8
Thanksgiving Day   E
Rockwell, Harlow, 1910-1988
(jt. auth) Rockwell, A. F. At the beach   E
(jt. auth) Rockwell, A. F. The first snowfall
E
Rockwell, Lizzy
Good enough to eat (k-3)   613.2
(il) Jenkins, P. B. A nest full of eggs   598
(il) Rockwell, A. F. Career day   E
(il) Rockwell, A. F. Thanksgiving Day   E
Rockwell, Norman, 1894-1978
About
Gherman, B. Norman Rockwell (4 and up)
92
Rockwell, Thomas, 1933-
How to eat fried worms (3-6)   Fic
Rodanas, Kristina
(il) Bealer, A. W. Only the names remain
970.004
Rodeos
Hoyt-Goldsmith, D. Apache rodeo (3-5)
970.004
Pinkney, A. D. Bill Pickett, rodeo ridin' cowboy
(k-3)   92
Rodgers, Mary, 1931-
Freaky Friday (4 and up)   Fic
Rodman, Maia *See* Wojciechowska, Maia, 1927-
Rodowsky, Colby F., 1932-
Hannah in between (5 and up)   Fic
Not my dog (2-4)   Fic
Spindrift (5 and up)   Fic
The Turnabout Shop (4-6)   Fic
Roentgen, Wilhelm Conrad *See* Röntgen, Wil-
helm Conrad, 1845-1923
Roessel, Monty
Kinaaldá: a Navajo girl grows up (3-6)
970.004
Songs from the loom (3-6)   970.004
Rogasky, Barbara
The golem (4 and up)   398.2
Rapunzel (1-3)   398.2
The water of life (1-3)   398.2
(comp) Winter poems. See Winter poems
808.81
Rogers, Fred
Divorce (k-2)   306.89
Extraordinary friends (k-2)   362.4
Going to the hospital (k-2)   362.1
Making friends (k-1)   158
Stepfamilies (k-2)   306.8
Rogers, Jacqueline
(il) Byars, B. C. The not-just-anybody family
Fic
(il) San Souci, R. Even more short & shivery
398.2
(il) San Souci, R. More short & shivery
398.2
(il) Wright, B. R. The ghost in Room 11
Fic
(il) Wright, B. R. Nothing but trouble   Fic
Roget's children's thesaurus (3-5)   423
Roget's student thesaurus (5 and up)   423

Rushen Coatie. Jacobs, J.
In Jacobs, J. English fairy tales p367-71
398.2

Rushmore. Curlee, L. **730.9**

Ruskin, John, 1819-1900
The king of the Golden River **Fic**

Russell, Charles M. (Charles Marion), 1864-1926
About
Winter, J. Cowboy Charlie: the story of Charles M. Russell (k-3) **92**

Russell, Francine
(jt. auth) Chaiet, D. The safe zone **613.6**

Russell, John, 1885-1956
A saga
In Shedlock, M. L. The art of the story-teller p165-67 **372.6**

Russell and Elisa. Hurwitz, J. See note under Hurwitz, J. Rip-roaring Russell **Fic**

Russell rides again. Hurwitz, J. See note under Hurwitz, J. Rip-roaring Russell **Fic**

Russell sprouts. Hurwitz, J. See note under Hurwitz, J. Rip-roaring Russell **Fic**

Russia
See also Soviet Union
Fiction
Lasky, K. The night journey (4 and up) **Fic**
Polacco, P. Rechenka's eggs **E**
Schur, M. The circlemaker (5 and up) **Fic**
Folklore
See Folklore—Russia
Kings and rulers
Brewster, H. Anastasia's album (5 and up) **92**
Stanley, D. Peter the Great (4 and up) **92**

Russia (Federation)
See also Russia; Soviet Union

Russian Americans
Fiction
Best, C. Three cheers for Catherine the Great **E**

Russian Empire *See* Russia

Russian fairy tales. Afanas'ev, A. N. **398.2**

Russo, Marisabina
The big brown box **E**
Hannah's baby sister **E**
Mama talks too much **E**

Rustin, Bayard, 1910-1987
About
Haskins, J. Bayard Rustin: behind the scenes of the civil rights movement (5 and up) **92**

The **rusty** plate. Schwartz, H.
In Schwartz, H. A coat for the moon and other Jewish tales p28-30 **398.2**

Ruth, Babe, 1895-1948
About
Jacobs, W. J. They shaped the game (4 and up) **920**

See/See also pages in the following book(s):
Krull, K. Lives of the athletes p19-23 (4 and up) **920**
Fiction
Adler, D. A. The Babe & I **E**

Burleigh, R. Home run **E**
Gutman, D. Babe and me (4 and up) **Fic**

Ruth, George Herman *See* Ruth, Babe, 1895-1948

Ruth Law thrills a nation. Brown, D. **629.13**

Ruthie's gift. Bradley, K. B. **Fic**

Ryan, Cheli Durán *See* Durán, Cheli

Ryan, DyAnne DiSalvo- *See* DiSalvo-Ryan, DyAnne, 1954-

Ryan, Pam Muñoz
Amelia and Eleanor go for a ride **E**

Ryan, Susannah
(il) Maestro, B. Coming to America: the story of immigration **325.73**

Rydberg, Abraham Viktor *See* Rydberg, Viktor, 1828-1895

Rydberg, Viktor, 1828-1895
Lindgren, A. The Tomten **E**

Ryden, Hope
Wild horses I have known (4 and up) **599.66**

Ryder, Joanne
Each living thing **E**
My father's hands **E**

Rylant, Cynthia
All I see **E**
Appalachia **974**
Best wishes (1-3) **92**
A blue-eyed daisy (5 and up) **Fic**
Children of Christmas (4 and up) **S C**
Contents: The Christmas tree man; Halfway home; For being good; Ballerinas and bears; Silver packages; All the stars in the sky
Every living thing (5 and up) **S C**
Contents: Slower than the rest; Retired; Boar out there; Papa's parrot; A pet; Spaghetti; Drying out; Stray; Planting things; A bad road for cats; Safe; Shells
A fine white dust (5 and up) **Fic**
Henry and Mudge **E**
Henry and Mudge and Annie's good move. See note under Rylant, C. Henry and Mudge **E**
Henry and Mudge and Annie's perfect pet. See note under Rylant, C. Henry and Mudge **E**
Henry and Mudge and the bedtime thumps. See note under Rylant, C. Henry and Mudge **E**
Henry and Mudge and the best day of all. See note under Rylant, C. Henry and Mudge **E**
Henry and Mudge and the careful cousin. See note under Rylant, C. Henry and Mudge **E**
Henry and Mudge and the forever sea. See note under Rylant, C. Henry and Mudge **E**
Henry and Mudge and the happy cat. See note under Rylant, C. Henry and Mudge **E**
Henry and Mudge and the long weekend. See note under Rylant, C. Henry and Mudge **E**
Henry and Mudge and the sneaky crackers. See note under Rylant, C. Henry and Mudge **E**

Rylant, Cynthia—*Continued*

Henry and Mudge and the Snowman plan. See note under Rylant, C. Henry and Mudge
    E

Henry and Mudge and the starry night. See note under Rylant, C. Henry and Mudge **E**

Henry and Mudge and the wild wind. See note under Rylant, C. Henry and Mudge **E**

Henry and Mudge get the cold shivers. See note under Rylant, C. Henry and Mudge **E**

Henry and Mudge in puddle trouble. See note under Rylant, C. Henry and Mudge **E**

Henry and Mudge in the family trees. See note under Rylant, C. Henry and Mudge **E**

Henry and Mudge in the green time. See note under Rylant, C. Henry and Mudge **E**

Henry and Mudge in the sparkle days. See note under Rylant, C. Henry and Mudge **E**

Henry and Mudge take the big test. See note under Rylant, C. Henry and Mudge **E**

Henry and Mudge under the yellow moon. See note under Rylant, C. Henry and Mudge
    E

Missing May (5 and up) **Fic**

Mr. Griggs' work **E**

Mr. Putter and Tabby bake the cake. See note under Rylant, C. Mr. Putter and Tabby pour the tea **E**

Mr. Putter and Tabby feed the fish. See note under Rylant, C. Mr. Putter and Tabby pour the tea **E**

Mr. Putter and Tabby fly the plane. See note under Rylant, C. Mr. Putter and Tabby pour the tea **E**

Mr. Putter and Tabby paint the porch. See note under Rylant, C. Mr. Putter and Tabby pour the tea **E**

Mr. Putter and Tabby pick the pears. See note under Rylant, C. Mr. Putter and Tabby pour the tea **E**

Mr. Putter and Tabby pour the tea **E**

Mr. Putter and Tabby row the boat. See note under Rylant, C. Mr. Putter and Tabby pour the tea **E**

Mr. Putter and Tabby take the train. See note under Rylant, C. Mr. Putter and Tabby pour the tea **E**

Mr. Putter and Tabby toot the horn. See note under Rylant, C. Mr. Putter and Tabby pour the tea **E**

Mr. Putter and Tabby walk the dog. See note under Rylant, C. Mr. Putter and Tabby pour the tea **E**

Night in the country **E**

The old woman who named things **E**

Poppleton **E**

Poppleton and friends. See note under Rylant, C. Poppleton **E**

Poppleton everyday. See note under Rylant, C. Poppleton **E**

Poppleton forever. See note under Rylant, C. Poppleton **E**

Poppleton has fun. See note under Rylant, C. Poppleton **E**

Poppleton in Fall. See note under Rylant, C. Poppleton **E**

Poppleton in Spring. See note under Rylant, C. Poppleton **E**

Poppleton through and through. See note under Rylant, C. Poppleton **E**

The relatives came **E**

Silver packages **E**

This year's garden **E**

When I was young in the mountains **E**

See/See also pages in the following book(s):
The Newbery & Caldecott medal books, 1986-2000 p188-97 **028.5**

S

S.O.R. losers. Avi **Fic**

Saaf, Donald
(il) Ziefert, H. Pushkin meets the bundle **E**
(il) Ziefert, H. Train song **E**

Saar, Betye, 1926-
See/See also pages in the following book(s):
Sills, L. Visions p32-45 (5 and up) **920**

Saari, Peggy
(ed) Explorers & discoverers. See Explorers & discoverers **920.003**

Saavedra, Miguel de Cervantes *See* Cervantes Saavedra, Miguel de, 1547-1616

Sabbath

Fiction
Herman, C. How Yussel caught the gefilte fish **E**

The **Sabbath** walking stick. Schwartz, H.
In Schwartz, H. A coat for the moon and other Jewish tales p36-39 **398.2**

Sabbeth, Alex, 1950-
Rubber-band banjos and a java jive bass (4 and up) **781**

Sable. Hesse, K. **Fic**

Sabuda, Robert
Arthur and the sword (k-3) **398.2**
Saint Valentine (1-3) **92**
Tutankhamen's gift (k-3) **92**

Sacagawea, b. 1786
About
Adler, D. A. A picture book of Sacagawea (1-3) **92**
St. George, J. Sacagawea (4-6) **92**
See/See also pages in the following book(s):
Calvert, P. Great lives: the American frontier p328-38 (5 and up) **920**
Fiction
Bruchac, J. Sacajawea (6 and up) **Fic**
O'Dell, S. Streams to the river, river to the sea (5 and up) **Fic**

Sacajawea *See* Sacagawea, b. 1786

Sachar, Louis, 1954-
Holes (5 and up) **Fic**
Marvin Redpost, a flying birthday cake. See note under Sachar, L. Marvin Redpost, kidnapped at birth? **Fic**
Marvin Redpost, a magic crystal. See note under Sachar, L. Marvin Redpost, kidnapped at birth? **Fic**
Marvin Redpost, alone in his teacher's house. See note under Sachar, L. Marvin Redpost, kidnapped at birth? **Fic**

Sachar, Louis, 1954—_Continued_

Marvin Redpost, class president. See note under Sachar, L. Marvin Redpost, kidnapped at birth?   **Fic**

Marvin Redpost, is he a girl? See note under Sachar, L. Marvin Redpost, kidnapped at birth?   **Fic**

Marvin Redpost, kidnapped at birth? (2-4)   **Fic**

Marvin Redpost, superfast, out of control. See note under Sachar, L. Marvin Redpost, kidnapped at birth?   **Fic**

Marvin Redpost, why pick on me? See note under Sachar, L. Marvin Redpost, kidnapped at birth?   **Fic**

Sideways stories from Wayside School. See note under Sachar, L. Wayside School gets a little stranger   **Fic**

Wayside School gets a little stranger (3-6)   **Fic**

Wayside School is falling down. See note under Sachar, L. Wayside School gets a little stranger   **Fic**

See/See also pages in the following book(s):
The Newbery & Caldecott medal books, 1986-2000 p317-31   **028.5**

Sachs, Marilyn, 1927-
The bears' house (4-6)   **Fic**

The **sad** tale of three slavers. Jagendorf, M. A.
_In_ From sea to shining sea p138-39   **810.8**

The **sad** tale of Tom the catfish. Jagendorf, M. A.
_In_ From sea to shining sea p232-33   **810.8**

Sad underwear and other complications. Viorst, J.   **811**

Sadako [biography of Sadako Sasaki] Coerr, E.   **92**

Sadako and the thousand paper cranes [biography of Sadako Sasaki] Coerr, E.   **92**

Sadko and the Tsar of the Sea. McCaughrean, G.
_In_ McCaughrean, G. The bronze cauldron: myths and legends of the world p14-19   **398.2**

Safari. Bateman, R.   **599**

Safe. Rylant, C.
_In_ Rylant, C. Every living thing p66-72   **S C**

A **safe** home for manatees. Jenkins, P. B.   **599.5**

Safe, warm, and snug. Swinburne, S. R.   **591.56**

The **safe** zone. Chaiet, D.   **613.6**

Safety education
Chaiet, D. The safe zone (4 and up)   **613.6**
Fiction
Rathmann, P. Officer Buckle and Gloria   **E**

Safford, Barbara Ripp
Guide to reference materials for school media centers   **011.6**

A **saga**. Russell, J.
_In_ Shedlock, M. L. The art of the story-teller p165-67   **372.6**

Sahara Desert
Fiction
London, J. Ali, child of the desert   **E**

Sail away. Crews, D.   **E**

Sailing
Fiction
Creech, S. The Wanderer (5 and up)   **Fic**
Crews, D. Sail away   **E**
Mead, A. Junebug (3-5)   **Fic**

The **sailors** and the troll. Lunge-Larsen, L.
_In_ Lunge-larsen, L. The troll with no heart in his body and other tales of trolls from Norway p63-67   **398.2**

Sailors' life _See_ Seafaring life

Saint Christopher. McCaughrean, G.
_In_ McCaughrean, G. The silver treasure: myths and legends of the world p53-56   **398.2**

Saint Crispin's follower. Fleischman, P.
_In_ Fleischman, P. Graven images p25-59   **S C**

Saint-Exupéry, Antoine de, 1900-1944
The little prince   **Fic**

Saint George and the dragon. Hodges, M.   **398.2**

Saint Helens, Mount (Wash.) _See_ Mount Saint Helens (Wash.)

Saint Lawrence Seaway
Gibbons, G. The great St. Lawrence Seaway (k-3)   **386**

Saint Patrick and the peddler. Hodges, M.   **398.2**

Saint Patrick and the snakes. Dillon, E.
_In_ Bauer, C. F. Celebrations p170-71   **808.8**

Saint Patrick's Day
Barth, E. Shamrocks, harps, and shillelaghs (3-6)   **394.26**
Gibbons, G. St. Patrick's Day (k-3)   **394.26**
See/See also pages in the following book(s):
Bauer, C. F. Celebrations p167-94   **808.8**

Saint Valentine. Sabuda, R.   **92**

Saint Valentine's Day _See_ Valentine's Day

Saints
See also Christian saints

Sakurai, Gail, 1952-
Asian-Americans in the old West (4-6)   **978**
The Louisiana Purchase (4-6)   **973.4**

Sakyamuni _See_ Gautama Buddha

Sal Fink. San Souci, R.
_In_ San Souci, R. Cut from the same cloth p51-55   **398.2**

Salamandastron. Jacques, B. See note under Jacques, B. Redwall   **Fic**

Salamanders
Souza, D. M. Shy salamanders (4-6)   **597.8**

Salem (Mass.)
Fiction
Fritz, J. Early thunder (6 and up)   **Fic**
Petry, A. L. Tituba of Salem Village (6 and up)   **Fic**

Salem (Mass.)—*Continued*
History
Jackson, S. The witchcraft of Salem Village (4 and up) **133.4**
Roach, M. K. In the days of the Salem witchcraft trials (4 and up) **133.4**
The **Salem** ghost ship. Shay, F.
In From sea to shining sea p113-14
810.8
Sally Ann Thunder Ann Whirlwind. Osborne, M. P.
In Osborne, M. P. American tall tales p15-23
398.2
Sally Ann Thunder Ann Whirlwind Crockett meets Mike Fink, Snappin' Turkle. Cohen, C. L.
In From sea to shining sea p118-20
810.8
Sally goes to the beach. Huneck, S. **E**
Salmon
Cone, M. Come back, salmon (3-6) **639.3**
McMillan, B. Salmon summer (2-4) **639.2**
Salmon Boy. Bruchac, J.
In Bruchac, J. Flying with the eagle, racing with the great bear p113-17 **398.2**
Salmon summer. McMillan, B. **639.2**
Salmonson, Jessica Amanda
The ugly unicorn
In A Glory of unicorns p79-94 **S C**
Salsa stories. Delacre, L. **S C**
Salt. Afanas'ev, A. N.
In Afanas'ev, A. N. Russian fairy tales p40-44 **398.2**
The **saltcellar.** McCaughrean, G.
In McCaughrean, G. The silver treasure: myths and legends of the world p121-26
398.2
Salten, Felix, 1869-1945
Bambi (4-6) **Fic**
Salting the ocean (4 and up) **811.008**
Salvadori, Mario George, 1907-1997
(jt. auth) Levy, M. Earthquake games
551.2
Salzmann, Siegmund *See* Salten, Felix, 1869-1945
Sam, Joe *See* JoeSam
Sam and Jane go camping. Schwartz, A.
In Schwartz, A. There is a carrot in my ear, and other noodle tales p16-26 **398.2**
Sam and Sooky
In Grandfather tales p150-55 **398.2**
Sam and the lucky money. Chinn, K. **E**
Sam and the tigers. Lester, J. **E**
Sam, Bangs & Moonshine. Ness, E. **E**
Sam Johnson and the blue ribbon quilt. Ernst, L. C. **E**
Sam who never forgets. Rice, E. **E**
Sami (European people)
Lewin, T. The reindeer people (3-5) **948.97**
Sami and the time of the troubles. Heide, F. P.
E
Sam'l. MacDonald, M. R.
In MacDonald, M. R. When the lights go out p109-14 **372.6**

Sammy and the dinosaurs. Whybrow, I. **E**
Sammy Keyes and the curse of Moustache Mary. Draanen, W. van *See* note under Draanen, W. V. Sammy Keyes and the hotel thief **Fic**
Sammy Keyes and the Hollywood mummy. Draanen, W. van *See* note under Draanen, W. V. Sammy Keyes and the hotel thief **Fic**
Sammy Keyes and the hotel thief. Draanen, W. van **Fic**
Sammy Keyes and the runaway elf. Draanen, W. van *See* note under Draanen, W. V. Sammy Keyes and the hotel thief **Fic**
Sammy Keyes and the Sisters of Mercy. Draanen, W. van *See* note under Draanen, W. V. Sammy Keyes and the hotel thief **Fic**
Sammy Keyes and the skeleton man. Draanen, W. van *See* note under Draanen, W. V. Sammy Keyes and the hotel thief **Fic**
Sammy the seal. Hoff, S. **E**
Samoyault, Tiphaine
Give me a sign! (4 and up) **302.2**
A **sampler** view of colonial life. Cobb, M.
746.44
Sam's girl friend. Schwartz, A.
In Schwartz, A. All of our noses are here, and other noodle tales p58-63 **398.2**
Samton, Sheila White
(il) Van Laan, N. A tree for me **E**
Samuel Eaton's day. Waters, K. **974.4**
Samuels, Barbara
Aloha Dolores. See note under Samuels, B. Duncan & Delores **E**
Duncan & Dolores **E**
Samuelson, Joan
See/See also pages in the following book(s):
Littlefield, B. Champions p39-52 (5 and up)
920
The **samurai** and the dragon. Kimmel, E. A.
In Kimmel, E. A. Sword of the samurai p11-21 **Fic**
The **samurai** maiden. Yolen, J.
In Yolen, J. Not one damsel in distress p78-83 **398.2**
The **samurai's** daughter. San Souci, R. **398.2**
San Francisco (Calif.)
Ancona, G. Barrio **305.8**
Description
Wilder, L. I. West from home (6 and up)
92
Fiction
Burton, V. L. Maybelle, the cable car **E**
Evans, D. The elevator family (3-5) **Fic**
Freeman, M. The trouble with cats (2-4)
Fic
Yep, L. Child of the owl (5 and up) **Fic**
Yep, L. Dragonwings (5 and up) **Fic**
Yep, L. Thief of hearts (5 and up) **Fic**
Social life and customs
Brown, T. Konnichiwa! (1-4) **305.8**
San Nicolas Island (Calif.)
Fiction
O'Dell, S. Island of the Blue Dolphins (5 and up) **Fic**

San Souci, Daniel

(il) Kimmel, E. A. Montezuma and the fall of the Aztecs **972**
(il) London, J. Red wolf country **E**
(il) San Souci, R. Sootface **398.2**
(il) San Souci, R. Two bear cubs **398.2**

San Souci, Robert, 1946-

Brave Margaret (k-3) **398.2**
Cendrillon (k-3) **398.2**
Cut from the same cloth (4-6) **398.2**
Contents: The Star Maiden; Bess Call; Drop Star; Molly Cottontail; Annie Christmas; Susanna and Simon; Sal Fink; Sweet Betsey from Pike; Old Sally Cato; Pale-Face Lightning; Pohaha; Sister Fox and Brother Coyote; Hekeke; Otoonah; Hiiaka
Even more short & shivery (4 and up) **398.2**
Contents: Appointment in Samarra; Deer woman; The maggot; Witch woman; The berbalangs; The dancing dead of Shark Island; "That I see, but this I sew"; La Guiablesse; The blood-drawing ghost; Guests from Gibbet Island; The haunted house; "Never far from you"; The rose elf; The wind rider; The skull that spoke; The monster of Baylock; The new mother; Rokuro-Kubi; Dicey and Orpus; Chips; The skeleton's revenge; Lullaby; Death and the two friends; Forest ghosts; A Carolina banshee; The deadly violin; A night of terrors; The sending; The hand of fate; Old raw head
Fa Mulan (2-4) **398.2**
The faithful friend (2-4) **398.2**
The hired hand (2-4) **398.2**
The Hobyahs (k-3) **398.2**
More short & shivery (4 and up) **398.2**
Contents: "Hold him, Tabb!"; The witches' eyes; The duppy; Two snakes; The draug; The vampire cat; Windigo Island; The haunted inn; The rolling head; The Croglin Grange vampire; The Yara; "Me, myself"; Island of fear; Three who sought death; Sister Death and the healer; The mouse tower; The devil and Tom Walker; The greedy daughter; The pirate; The golden arm; The serpent woman; Loft the enchanter; The accursed house; Escape up the tree; The headrest; The thing in the woods; King of the Cats; The dead mother; Knock . . . knock . . . knock . . .; Twice surprised
The samurai's daughter (1-4) **398.2**
The secret of the stones (k-3) **398.2**
Short & shivery (4 and up) **398.2**
Contents: The robber bridegroom; Jack Frost; The waterfall of ghosts; The ghost's cap; The witch cat; The green mist; The Cegua; The ghostly little girl; The midnight mass of the Dead; Tailypo; Lady Eleanore's mantle; The soldier and the vampire; The skeleton's dance; Scared to death; Swallowed alive; The deacon's ghost; Nuckelavee; The adventure of the German student; Billy Mosby's night ride; The hunter in the haunted forest; Brother and sister; The lovers of Dismal Swamp; Boneless; The death waltz; The ghost of Misery Hill; The loup-garou; The golem; Lavender; The goblin spider; The Halloween pony
Six foolish fishermen (k-3) **398.2**
Sootface (1-4) **398.2**
Sukey and the mermaid (1-4) **398.2**
The talking eggs (k-3) **398.2**
A terrifying taste of short & shivery (4 and up) **398.2**
Contents: Crooker waits; Yara-ma-yha-who; The fata; The fiddler; Land-otter; A fish story; Apparitions; The bijli; The lutin; The hundredth skull; The ogre's arm; The hairy hands; The snow husband; The zimwi; Witchbirds; Dangerous hill; The witch's head; Dinkins is dead; Old Nan's ghost; The interrupted wedding; The mulombe; The haunted grove; The tiger woman; Peacock's ghost; Israel and the werewolf; Hoichi the earless; A snap of the fingers; Narrow escape; The black fox; The mother and death
Two bear cubs (k-3) **398.2**
A weave of words (3-5) **398.2**
The white cat (2-4) **398.2**

Sanchez, Enrique O., 1942-

(il) Castañeda, O. S. Abuela's weave **E**

Sanctuaries, Wildlife See Wildlife refuges

Sanctuary movement

See also Refugees

Sand

See also Quicksand
Prager, E. J. Sand (k-3) **553.6**

Sand and fog. Brandenburg, J. **968.8**

Sand Creek, Battle of, 1864

See/See also pages in the following book(s):
Ehrlich, A. Wounded Knee: an Indian history of the American West (6 and up) **970.004**

Sand flat shadows. Sandburg, C.
In Sandburg, C. Rootabaga stories pt 1 p159-66 **S C**

Sandburg, Carl, 1878-1967

Abe Lincoln grows up
In Sandburg, C. The Sandburg treasury p383-477 **818**
Carl Sandburg (4 and up) **811**
Early moon
In Sandburg, C. The Sandburg treasury p161-207 **818**
Grassroots **811**
The haystack cricket and how things are different up in the moon towns
In Sandburg, C. The Sandburg treasury p139-42 **818**
How Rag Bag Mammy kept her secret while the wind blew away the Village of Hat Pins
In Sandburg, C. The Sandburg treasury p100-02 **818**
How they broke away to go to the Rootabaga Country
In American fairy tales p143-50 **S C**
The Huckabuck family and how they raised popcorn in Nebraska and quit and came back **E**
Prairie-town boy
In Sandburg, C. The Sandburg treasury p263-382 **818**
Rainbows are made: poems (5 and up) **811**
Rootabaga stories **S C**
Contents pt 1: How they broke away to go to the Rootabaga Country; How they bring back the Village of Cream Puffs when the wind blows it away; How the five rusty rats helped find a new village; The Potato Face Blind Man who lost the diamond rabbit on his gold accordion; How the Potato Face Blind Man enjoyed himself on a fine spring morning; Poker Face the Baboon and Hot Dog the Tiger; The Toboggan-to-the-moon dream of the Potato Face Blind Man; How Gimme the Ax found out about the zigzag railroad and who made it zigzag; The story of Blixie Bimber and the power of the gold buckskin whincher; The story of Jason Squiff and why he had a popcorn hat, popcorn mittens, and popcorn shoes; The story of Rags Habakuk, the two blue rats, and the circus man who came with spot cash money; The wedding procession of the Rag Doll and the Broom Handle and who was in it; How the hat ashes shovel helped Snoo Foo; Three boys with jugs of molasses and secret ambitions; How Bimbo the Snip's thumb stuck to his nose when the wind changed; The two skyscrapers who decided to have a child; The dollar watch and the five jack-rabbits; The Wooden Indian and the Shaghorn Buffalo; The White Horse Girl and the Blue Wind Boy; What six girls with balloons told the Gray Man on Horseback; How Henry Hagglyhoagly played the guitar with his mittens on; Never kick a slipper at the moon; Sand flat shadows; How to tell corn fairies if you see 'em; How the animals lost their tails and got them back traveling from Philadelphia to Medicine Hat

Sandburg, Carl, 1878-1967—*Continued*

pt 2: The skyscraper to the moon and how the green rat with the rheumatism ran a thousand miles twice; Slipfoot and how he nearly always never gets what he goes after; Many, many weddings in one corner house; Shush, Shush, the big buff banty hen who laid an egg in the postmaster's hat; How Rag Bag Mammy kept her secret while the wind blew away the Village of Hat Pins; How six pigeons came back to Hatrack the Horse after many accidents and six telegrams; How the three wild Babylonian Baboons went away in the rain eating bread and butter; How six umbrellas took off their straw hats to show respect to the one big umbrella; How Bozo the Button Buster busted all his buttons when a mouse came; How Googler and Gaggler, the two Christmas babies, came home with monkey wrenches; How Johnny the Wham sleeps in money all the time and Joe the Wimp shines and sees things; How Deep Red Roses goes back and forth between the clock and the looking glass; How Pink Peony sent Spuds, the ballplayer up to pick four moons; How Dippy the Wisp and Slip Me Liz came in the moonshine where the Potato Face Blind Man sat with his accordion; How Hot Balloons and his pigeon daughters crossed over into the Rootabaga country; How two sweetheart dippies sat in the moonlight on a lumberyard fence and heard about the sooners and the boomers; The haystack cricket and how things are different up in the moon towns; Why the big ball game between Hot Grounders and the Grand Standers was a hot game; The Huckabuck family and how they raised popcorn in Nebraska and quit and came back; Yang Yang and Hoo Hoo, or the song of the left foot of the shadow of the goose in Oklahoma; How a skyscraper and a railroad train got picked up and carried away from Pig's Eye Valley far in the Pickax Mountains; Pig Wisps; Kiss Me; Blue silver

also in Sandburg, C. The Sandburg treasury
p9-160 **818**

The Sandburg treasury (5 and up) **818**

Wind song

In Sandburg, C. The Sandburg treasury p209-
61 **818**

About

Meltzer, M. Carl Sandburg (5 and up) **92**

See/See also pages in the following book(s):

Krull, K. Lives of the writers p74-77 (4 and up)
920

The **Sandburg** treasury. Sandburg, C. **818**

Sanders, Ruth Manning- *See* Manning-Sanders,
Ruth, 1895-1988

Sanders, Scott R. (Scott Russell), 1945-

Aurora means dawn **E**

Warm as wool **E**

Sanderson, Ruth, 1951-

The crystal mountain (3-5) **398.2**

Papa Gatto (3-5) **398.2**

(il) Sleator, W. Into the dream **Fic**

Sandflat shadows. Sandburg, C.

In Sandburg, C. The Sandburg treasury p73-
77 **818**

Sandford, John, 1953-

(il) Bodnar, J. Z. Tale of a tail **E**

Sandin, Joan, 1942-

The long way westward **E**

(il) Benchley, N. Small Wolf **E**

(il) Bulla, C. R. Daniel's duck **E**

(il) Levinson, N. S. Snowshoe Thompson
E

(il) Little, J. From Anna **Fic**

Sands, Karen

Back in the spaceship again **016.8**

Sanfield, Steve

The adventures of High John the Conqueror (4
and up) **398.2**

Contents: Master's walking stick; Just possum; "You better not do it"; In a box; Off limits; John wins a bet; This one and that one; Who's the fool now; George's dream; Deer hunting; John's memory; Freedom; An epidemic of ducks; John in court; Tops and bottoms; The Christmas turkey

Bit by bit (k-3) **398.2**

High John the Conquerer

In From sea to shining sea p134-35
810.8

Sanfilippo, Margaret

(il) Christopher, M. Tackle without a team
Fic

Sankey, Tom

(il) Gryski, C. Cat's cradle, owl's eyes
793.9

Santa Claus

Fiction

Briggs, R. Father Christmas **E**

Krensky, S. How Santa got his job **E**

Pearson, T. C. Where does Joe go? **E**

Polacco, P. Welcome Comfort **E**

Seibold, J. O. Olive the other reindeer **E**

Van Allsburg, C. The Polar Express **E**

Poetry

Moore, C. C. The night before Christmas (k-3)
811

Santa Claus is twins. Martens, A. C.

In The Big book of Christmas plays p169-85
808.82

Santa Fe (N.M.)

Fiction

De Paola, T. The night of Las Posadas **E**

Santa Fe Trail

Lavender, D. S. The Santa Fe Trail (4 and up)
978

Santa's magic hat. Thornton, J. F.

In The Big book of Christmas plays p253-62
808.82

Santella, Andrew

Illinois

In America the beautiful, second series
973

Santow, Dan

Mary Todd Lincoln, 1818-1882 (4 and up)
92

Saport, Linda

(il) All the pretty little horses. See All the pretty
little horses **782.42**

Sara Crewe. See Burnett, F. H. A little princess
Fic

Sarah Bishop. O'Dell, S. **Fic**

Sarah Morton's day. Waters, K. **974.4**

Sarah, plain and tall. MacLachlan, P. **Fic**

Sasaki, Sadako, 1943-1955

About

Coerr, E. Sadako (1-4) **92**

Coerr, E. Sadako and the thousand paper cranes
(3-6) **92**

Saskatchewan

Fiction

Eckert, A. W. Incident at Hawk's Hill (6 and
up) **Fic**

Sasso, Sandy Eisenberg, 1947-

But God remembered (3-5) **221.9**

Satan See Devil

Satanta, Kiowa Chief, 1820-1878

See/See also pages in the following book(s):

Freedman, R. Indian chiefs p28-51 (6 and up)
920

Satchmo's blues. Schroeder, A.   E

Sateren, Shelley Swanson
Canada (4 and up)   971

Satie, Erik, 1866-1925
See/See also pages in the following book(s):
Krull, K. Lives of the musicians p62-65 (4 and up)   920

Sattler, Helen Roney
The book of North American owls (4 and up)   598
The earliest Americans (5 and up)   970.01
Recipes for art and craft materials (4 and up)   745.5

Saturn (Planet)
Brimner, L. D. Saturn (2-4)   523.4

Saturnalia. Fleischman, P.   Fic

Saudi Arabia
Fazio, W. Saudi Arabia (2-4)   953.8

Saul, Carol P., 1947-
Barn cat   E

Saul, Wendy, 1946-
(jt. auth) Cole, J. On the bus with Joanna Cole   92

Savadier, Elivia
(il) Jaffe, N. The mysterious visitor   398.2
(il) Jaffe, N. The uninvited guest and other Jewish holiday tales   296.4

Savage, Steele
(il) Hamilton, E. Mythology   292

Save Halloween!. Tolan, S. S.   Fic

Save Queen of Sheba. Moeri, L.   Fic

Save-the-earth book [series]
Pringle, L. P. Oil spills   363.7
Pringle, L. P. Vanishing ozone   363.7

Save the moon for Kerdy Dickus. Wynne-Jones, T.
In Wynne-Jones, T. Some of the kinder planets: stories p8-24   S C

Saving and investment
Fiction
Williams, V. B. A chair for my mother   E

Saving Shiloh. Naylor, P. R. See note under Naylor, P. R. Shiloh   Fic

Saving Sweetness. Stanley, D.   E

Saving time. McCaughrean, G.
In McCaughrean, G. The golden hoard: myths and legends of the world p39-42   398.2

Savion!: my life in tap. Glover, S.   92

Savitri and the God of Death. Krishnaswami, U.
In Krishnaswami, U. Shower of gold: girls and women in the stories of India p16-23   398.2

Sawyer, Ruth, 1880-1970
The Christmas apple
In Bauer, C. F. Celebrations p259-64   808.8
Roller skates (4-6)   Fic
Schnitzle, Schnotzle, and Schnootzle
In Christmas fairy tales p103-11   398.2
The way of the storyteller   372.6

Stories included are: Wee Meg Barnileg and the fairies; The magic box; Señora, will you snip? Señora will you sew?; The peddler of Ballaghadereen; Where one is fed a hundred can dine; A matter of brogues; The juggler of Notre Dame; The deserted mine; The legend of Saint Elizabeth; The princess and the vagabone; The bird who spoke three times

See/See also pages in the following book(s):
Newbery Medal books, 1922-1955 p149-56   028.5

Say, Allen, 1937-
Allison   E
The bicycle man   E
El Chino (2-5)   92
Emma's rug   E
Grandfather's journey   E
The lost lake   E
Tea with milk   E
Tree of cranes   E
(il) Snyder, D. The boy of the three-year nap   398.2

See/See also pages in the following book(s):
The Newbery & Caldecott medal books, 1986-2000 p198-206   028.5

Say hola to Spanish, otra vez. Elya, S. M.   463

Saying good-bye to Grandma. Thomas, J. R.   E

Sayles, Elizabeth
(il) Ackerman, K. The night crossing   Fic

The **Scandinavian** American family album. Hoobler, D.   305.8

Scandinavian Americans
Hoobler, D. The Scandinavian American family album (5 and up)   305.8

Scandinavians
See also Vikings

The **scarebird**. Fleischman, S.   E

Scarecrows
Fiction
Brown, M. W. The little scarecrow boy   E

Scared silly! (k-3)   810.8

Scared silly. Medearis, A. S.
In Medearis, A. S. Haunts p9-15   S C

Scared silly: a Halloween treat. Howe, J.   E

Scared stiff. Roberts, W. D.   Fic

Scared to death. San Souci, R.
In San Souci, R. Short & shivery p78-83   398.2

Scarlette Beane. Wallace, K.   E

Scary, scary Halloween. Bunting, E.   E

Scary stories 3. Schwartz, A.   398.2

Scary stories to tell in the dark. Schwartz, A.   398.2

Scathach. Mayer, M.
In Mayer, M. Women warriors p31-36   398

Schachner, Judith Byron
The Grannyman
(il) Napoli, D. J. The prince of the pond   Fic

Schaefer, Carole Lexa
The squiggle   E

Schaefer, Lola M., 1950-
This is the sunflower   E

Science and civilization—*Continued*

Gay, K. Science in ancient Greece (4 and up) **509**

Harris, J. L. Science in ancient Rome (4 and up) **509**

January, B. Science in colonial America (4 and up) **509**

January, B. Science in the Renaissance (4 and up) **509**

Moss, C. Science in ancient Mesopotamia (4 and up) **509**

Stewart, M. Science in ancient India (4 and up) **509**

Woods, G. Science in ancient Egypt (4 and up) **509**

Woods, G. Science of the early Americas (4 and up) **509**

The **science** book of air. Ardley, N. **507.8**

Science Books & Films **016.5**

Science Books, a quarterly review. See Science Books & Films **016.5**

The **science** chef. D'Amico, J. **641.3**

Science concepts [series]

Silverstein, A. Plate tectonics **551.1**

Science crafts for kids. Diehn, G. **507.8**

Science discoveries [series]

Parker, S. Albert Einstein and relativity **92**

Parker, S. Charles Darwin and evolution **92**

Parker, S. Marie Curie and radium **92**

Parker, S. Thomas Edison and electricity **92**

Science experiments on file **507.8**

Science experiments on-line. (3 and up) See entry in Part 2: Web Resources

Science experiments you can eat. Cobb, V. **507.8**

The **science** explorer. Murphy, P. **507.8**

Science fair bunnies. Lasky, K. See note under Lasky, K. Show and tell bunnies **E**

Science fair project index, 1973-1980/1985-1989 **507.8**

Science fair projects See Science projects

Science fiction

See also Fantasy fiction

Alcock, V. The monster garden (4 and up) **Fic**

Brittain, B. Shape-changer (4 and up) **Fic**

Cameron, E. The wonderful flight to the Mushroom Planet (4-6) **Fic**

Christopher, J. The White Mountains (5 and up) **Fic**

Farmer, N. The Ear, the Eye, and the Arm (6 and up) **Fic**

Hughes, T. The iron giant (4-6) **Fic**

Klause, A. C. Alien secrets (5 and up) **Fic**

Lowry, L. Gathering blue (5 and up) **Fic**

Lowry, L. The giver (6 and up) **Fic**

Marshall, E. Space case **E**

Pinkney, B. Cosmo and the robot **E**

Pinkwater, D. M. Fat men from space (3-6) **Fic**

Pinkwater, D. M. Lizard music (4 and up) **Fic**

Service, P. F. Stinker from space (4-6) **Fic**

Skurzynski, G. The virtual war (6 and up) **Fic**

Sleator, W. The boxes (6 and up) **Fic**

Sleator, W. Interstellar pig (5 and up) **Fic**

Sleator, W. Rewind (4 and up) **Fic**

Spinner, S. Be first in the universe (4-6) **Fic**

Verne, J. 20,000 leagues under the sea (5 and up) **Fic**

Yolen, J. Commander Toad and the voyage home (1-3) **Fic**

Bibliography

Sands, K. Back in the spaceship again **016.8**

History and criticism

See/See also pages in the following book(s):

Only connect: readings on children's literature p194-212 **028.5**

Science for every kid series

VanCleave, J. P. Janice Vancleave's ecology for every kid **577**

VanCleave, J. P. Janice VanCleave's food and nutrition for every kid **613.2**

VanCleave, J. P. Janice VanCleave's oceans for every kid **551.46**

Science in ancient China. Beshore, G. W. **509**

Science in ancient Egypt. Woods, G. **509**

Science in ancient Greece. Gay, K. **509**

Science in ancient India. Stewart, M. **509**

Science in ancient Mesopotamia. Moss, C. **509**

Science in ancient Rome. Harris, J. L. **509**

Science in colonial America. January, B. **509**

Science in early Islamic culture. Beshore, G. W. **509**

Science in the Renaissance. January, B. **509**

Science lab in a supermarket. Friedhoffer, R. **507.8**

Science of the early Americas. Woods, G. **509**

Science of the past [series]

Beshore, G. W. Science in ancient China **509**

Beshore, G. W. Science in early Islamic culture **509**

Gay, K. Science in ancient Greece **509**

Harris, J. L. Science in ancient Rome **509**

January, B. Science in colonial America **509**

January, B. Science in the Renaissance **509**

Moss, C. Science in ancient Mesopotamia **509**

Stewart, M. Science in ancient India **509**

Woods, G. Science in ancient Egypt **509**

Woods, G. Science of the early Americas **509**

Science project ideas [series]

Gardner, R. Science project ideas about trees **582.16**

Science project ideas about trees. Gardner, R. **582.16**

Scott, Ann Herbert, 1926-
Brave as a mountain lion   **E**
Cowboy country (k-3)   **978**
Hi   **E**
On Mother's lap   **E**
Scott, Elaine, 1940-
Adventure in space (4 and up)   **522**
Friends! (k-3)   **158**
Twins! (k-2)   **306.8**
Scott, Michael M.
The young Oxford book of ecology (6 and up)   **577**
Scott, Robert
Bush lion
  In The Oxford book of scary tales p74-75   **808.8**
Dare you
  In The Oxford book of scary tales p88-93   **808.8**
Scott, Steve
(il) Graham, J. B. Splish splash   **811**
Scott Foresman beginning thesaurus. See Roget's children's thesaurus   **423**
Scott Foresman junior thesaurus. See Roget's student thesaurus   **423**
Scottish authors *See* Authors, Scottish
Scrapefoot. Jacobs, J.
  In Jacobs, J. English fairy tales p305-08   **398.2**
Screen of frogs. Hamanaka, S.   **398.2**
Scruffy. Brandenburg, J.   **599.77**
Scudder, Horace Elisha, 1838-1902
The rich man's place
  In American fairy tales p55-62   **S C**
Sea animals *See* Marine animals
Sea chase. McCaughrean, G.
  In McCaughrean, G. The bronze cauldron: myths and legends of the world p49-57   **398.2**
Sea horses
Landau, E. Sea horses (2-4)   **597**
The **Sea** King and Vasilisa the Wise. Afanas'ev, A. N.
  In Afanas'ev, A. N. Russian fairy tales p427-37   **398.2**
The **sea** king: Sir Francis Drake and his times. Marrin, A.   **92**
The **sea** king's daughter. Shepard, A.   **398.2**
Sea life *See* Seafaring life
Sea lions *See* Seals (Animals)
The **Sea-Mammy.** Sherlock, Sir P. M.
  In Sherlock, Sir P. M. West Indian folk-tales p130-34   **398.2**
Sea monsters
Fiction
King-Smith, D. The water horse (3-5)   **Fic**
The **sea** nymph and the Cyclops. Osborne, M. P.
  In Osborne, M. P. Mermaid tales from around the world p13-16   **398.2**
Sea otter *See* Otters
The **sea** otter. Silverstein, A.   **599.7**
Sea poetry
Fishing for a dream   **782.42**

Until I saw the sea and other poems (k-2)   **811.008**
The **sea** princess of Persia. Osborne, M. P.
  In Osborne, M. P. Mermaid tales from around the world p57-61   **398.2**
The **Sea** serpent
  In Raw Head, bloody bones p13-17   **398.2**
Sea shapes. Macdonald, S.   **E**
Sea shells *See* Shells
Sea Star, orphan of Chincoteague. Henry, M. See note under Henry, M. Misty of Chincoteague   **Fic**
Sea-stars *See* Starfishes
Sea stories
Avi. The true confessions of Charlotte Doyle (6 and up)   **Fic**
Babbitt, N. The eyes of the Amaryllis (5 and up)   **Fic**
Barber, A. The Mousehole cat   **E**
Creech, S. The Wanderer (5 and up)   **Fic**
Demas, C. If ever I return again (5 and up)   **Fic**
Fox, P. The slave dancer (5 and up)   **Fic**
Guiberson, B. Z. Tales of the haunted deep (4 and up)   **001.9**
Van Allsburg, C. The wretched stone   **E**
Sea turtles
Gibbons, G. Sea turtles (k-3)   **597.9**
Guiberson, B. Z. Into the sea (k-3)   **597.9**
Staub, F. J. Sea turtles (2-4)   **597.9**
The **Sea** View Hotel. Stevenson, J.   **E**
Seafaring life
Biesty, S. Stephen Biesty's cross-sections: Man-of-war (4 and up)   **359.1**
Seals (Animals)
Cossi, O. Harp seals (3-6)   **599.79**
Fiction
Hoff, S. Sammy the seal   **E**
Martin, R. The boy who lived with the seals (1-4)   **398.2**
The **seals** on the bus. Hort, L.   **782.42**
The **search** for delicious. Babbitt, N.   **Fic**
Searching for dragons. Wrede, P. C. See note under Wrede, P. C. Dealing with dragons   **Fic**
Sears, Lori D.
(il) Nichols, J. Storytimes for two-year-olds   **027.62**
Sears list of subject headings   **025.4**
Seashore
Darling, K. Seashore babies (k-3)   **591.7**
Fiction
Jonas, A. Reflections   **E**
Turkle, B. C. Do not open   **E**
Zolotow, C. The seashore book   **E**
Seashore. Silver, D. M.   **577.7**
Seashore babies. Darling, K.   **591.7**
The **seashore** book. Zolotow, C.   **E**
Seashore ecology
Silver, D. M. Seashore (3-5)   **577.7**

Seasons

See also Autumn; Spring; Summer; Winter
Arnosky, J. Crinkleroot's nature almanac (k-3)
508
Bowen, B. Antler, bear, canoe   **E**
Geisert, B. Mountain town   **E**
Geisert, B. Prairie town   **E**
Geisert, B. River town   **E**
Gibbons, G. The reasons for seasons (k-3)
525
Splear, E. L. Growing seasons (3-5)   **630**
Fiction
Anno, M. Anno's counting book   **E**
Borden, L. Caps, hats, socks, and mittens
E
Gibbons, G. The seasons of Arnold's apple tree
E
Gray, L. M. My mama had a dancing heart
E
Hughes, S. Out and about   **E**
Rylant, C. This year's garden   **E**
Sendak, M. Chicken soup with rice   **E**
Tafuri, N. Snowy flowy blowy   **E**
Poetry
Adoff, A. In for winter, out for spring (k-3)
811
Bruchac, J. Thirteen moons on a turtle's back
811
Giovanni, N. The sun is so quiet (k-3)   **811**
Livingston, M. C. A circle of seasons   **811**
Livingston, M. C. Cricket never does (4 and up)
811

The **seasons** of Arnold's apple tree. Gibbons, G.
E

Seaward. Cooper, S.   **Fic**

Sebastian: a book about Bach. Winter, J.   **92**

Sebestyen, Ouida, 1924-
Out of nowhere (5 and up)   **Fic**
Words by heart (5 and up)   **Fic**

Sébillot, Paul, 1846-1918
The dirty shepherdess
In The Green fairy book p180-85   **398.2**
The Golden Blackbird
In The Green fairy book p151-56   **398.2**
The snuff-box
In The Green fairy book p145-50   **398.2**

The **second** bad thing. Conrad, P.
In Conrad, P. Our house p49-63   **S C**

Second cousins. Hamilton, V.   **Fic**

The **secret** ball. Afanas'ev, A. N.
In Afanas'ev, A. N. Russian fairy tales p224-
26   **398.2**

The **secret** garden. Burnett, F. H.   **Fic**

The **secret** language. Nordstrom, U.   **Fic**

The **secret** of Gumbo Grove. Tate, E. E. See note
under Tate, E. E. Thank you, Dr. Martin Luther King, Jr.!   **Fic**

The **secret** of platform 13. Ibbotson, E.   **Fic**

The **secret** of the Indian. Banks, L. R. See note
under Reid Banks, L. The Indian in the cupboard   **Fic**

The **secret** of the stones. San Souci, R.
398.2

The **secret** of the underground room. Bellairs, J.
See note under Bellairs, J. The curse of the
blue figurine   **Fic**

Secret place. Bunting, E.   **E**

Secret service
See also Spies

The **secret** soldier: the story of Deborah Sampson
[Gannett] McGovern, A.   **92**

The **secrets** of animal flight. Bishop, N.
591.47

Secrets of space [series]
Branley, F. M. The sun and the solar system
523.2
Marsh, C. S. Asteroids, comets, and meteors
523.6

Secrets of the ice man. Patent, D. H.   **930.1**

Secrets of the mummies. Tanaka, S.   **393**

Sector 7. Wiesner, D.   **E**

Sedna, the sea goddess. Caswell, H. R.
In From sea to shining sea p18-22   **810.8**

See through history [series]
James, S. Ancient Rome   **937**
Martell, H. M. The Celts   **936**
Wood, T. The Aztecs   **972**
Wood, T. The Renaissance   **940.2**

See you around Sam!. Lowry, L. See note under
Lowry, L. Anastasia Krupnik   **Fic**

See you later, gladiator. Scieszka, J. See note under Scieszka, J. Knights of the kitchen table
Fic

See you tomorrow, Charles. Cohen, M. See note
under Cohen, M. It's George!   **E**

The **seed** and the vision. Cameron, E.   **028.5**

Seedfolks. Fleischman, P.   **Fic**

Seeds
Gibbons, G. From seed to plant (k-3)   **580**
See/See also pages in the following book(s):
Simon, S. Ride the wind (4-6)   **591.56**
Fiction
Hall, Z. The surprise garden   **E**

Seeger, Ruth Crawford, 1901-1953
Animal folk songs for children   **782.42**

Seeker of knowledge [biography of Jean François
Champollion] Rumford, J.   **92**

Sees Behind Trees. Dorris, M.   **Fic**

Seffal, Rabah
Niger (5 and up)   **966.26**

Segal, John
(il) Jaffe, N. While standing on one foot
296.1

Segal, Lore Groszmann
The book of Adam to Moses (4-6)   **222**
Tell me a Mitzi   **E**

Segregation in education
Haskins, J. Separate, but not equal (5 and up)
379

Seibert, Patricia
Discovering El Niño (k-3)   **551.6**

Seibold, J. Otto
Olive the other reindeer   **E**

Seidler, Tor, 1952-
Mean Margaret (3-6)   **Fic**

Seidler, Tor, 1952-—*Continued*

The steadfast tin soldier (1-4)   **Fic**

The Wainscott weasel (4-6)   **Fic**

Seismology *See* Earthquakes

Selden, George, 1929-1989

Chester Cricket's new home. See note under Selden, G. The cricket in Times Square

   Fic

Chester Cricket's pigeon ride. See note under Selden, G. The cricket in Times Square

   Fic

The cricket in Times Square (3-6)   **Fic**

The genie of Sutton Place (4 and up)   **Fic**

Harry Cat's pet puppy. See note under Selden, G. The cricket in Times Square   **Fic**

Harry Kitten and Tucker Mouse. See note under Selden, G. The cricket in Times Square

   Fic

The old meadow. See note under Selden, G. The cricket in Times Square   **Fic**

Tucker's countryside. See note under Selden, G. The cricket in Times Square   **Fic**

Selecting books for the elementary school library media center. Van Orden, P. J.   **025.2**

Self-defense

   See also Martial arts

Self-defense in animals *See* Animal defenses

The **self-playing** gusla. Afanas'ev, A. N.

   In Afanas'ev, A. N. Russian fairy tales p211-13   **398.2**

The **selfish** giant. Wilde, O.   **Fic**

   also in The Oxford treasury of children's stories p121-26   **S C**

   also in Wilde, O. The fairy tales of Oscar Wilde p32-37   **S C**

The **selfish** giant. See Waters, F. Oscar Wilde's The selfish giant   **Fic**

Selsam, Millicent Ellis, 1912-1996

Big tracks, little tracks (k-3)   **591.5**

Seltzer, Meyer

(il) White, L. B. Math-a-magic: number tricks for magicians   **793.8**

(il) White, L. B. Shazam! simple science magic   **793.8**

Selven, Maniam

(il) Krishnaswami, U. Shower of gold: girls and women in the stories of India   **398.2**

Selznick, Brian

(il) Clements, A. Frindle   **Fic**

(il) Conrad, P. Our house   **S C**

(il) Godwin, L. Barnyard prayers   **811**

(il) Martin, A. M. The doll people   **Fic**

(il) Ryan, P. M. Amelia and Eleanor go for a ride   **E**

Seminole Indians

Andryszewski, T. The Seminoles (4-6)

   970.004

Sneve, V. D. H. The Seminoles (3-5)

   970.004

Semiramis. Mayer, M.

   In Mayer, M. Women warriors p21-24

   398

Sención, the Indian girl. Delacre, L.

   In Delacre, L. Golden tales p25-27   **398.2**

Sendak, Maurice

Alligators all around   **E**

Chicken soup with rice   **E**

Higglety pigglety pop! (2-4)   **Fic**

In the night kitchen   **E**

One was Johnny   **E**

Outside over there   **E**

Pierre   **E**

The sign on Rosie's door   **E**

Where the wild things are   **E**

(il) De Regniers, B. S. What can you do with a shoe?   **E**

(il) DeJong, M. The house of sixty fathers

   Fic

(il) DeJong, M. The wheel on the school

   Fic

(il) Hoffmann, E. T. A. Nutcracker   **Fic**

(il) I saw Esau. See I saw Esau   **398.8**

(il) Jarrell, R. The animal family   **Fic**

(il) Jarrell, R. The bat-poet   **Fic**

(il) Joslin, S. What do you do, dear?   **395**

(il) Joslin, S. What do you say, dear?   **395**

(il) Krauss, R. A very special house   **E**

(il) MacDonald, G. The light princess   **Fic**

(il) Marshall, J. Swine Lake   **E**

(il) Minarik, E. H. Little Bear   **E**

(il) Minarik, E. H. No fighting, no biting!

   E

(il) Singer, I. B. Zlateh the goat, and other stories   **398.2**

(il) Zolotow, C. Mr. Rabbit and the lovely present   **E**

See/See also pages in the following book(s):

Marcus, L. S. A Caldecott celebration p19-25

   741.6

Origins of story p36-48   **808.06**

The **sending.** San Souci, R.

   In San Souci, R. Even more short & shivery p136-39   **398.2**

Seneca Indians

Folklore

Taylor, H. P. Brother Wolf (k-3)   **398.2**

Senegal

Berg, E. Senegal (5 and up)   **966.3**

Senn, J. A., 1941-

(comp) Quotations for kids. See Quotations for kids   **808.88**

Señor Cat's romance. González, L. M.

   In González, L. M. Señor Cat's romance and other favorite stories from Latin America p43-46   **398.2**

Señor Cat's romance and other favorite stories from Latin America. González, L. M.

   398.2

Señora, will you snip? Señora, will you sew? Sawyer, R.

   In Sawyer, R. The way of the storyteller p229-36   **372.6**

Senses and sensation

Aliki. My five senses (k-1)   **612.8**

Cobb, V. How to really fool yourself (5 and up)   **152.1**

Cole, J. The magic school bus explores the senses (2-4)   **612.8**

Miller, M. My five senses   **E**

Senses and sensation—*Continued*
Pringle, L. P. Explore your senses (3-6)
    612.8

Separate, but not equal. Haskins, J.   **379**
Separation of powers
    United States
Stein, R. C. The powers of Congress (4-6)
    328.73
Sequoyah, 1770?-1843
    About
Klausner, J. Sequoyah's gift (4 and up)   **92**
Sequoyah's gift. Klausner, J.   **92**
Serbia
Milivojevic, J. Serbia (4 and up)   **949.7**
Seredy, Kate, 1899-1975
The Good Master (4-6)   **Fic**
The white stag (4-6)   **Fic**
See/See also pages in the following book(s):
Newbery Medal books, 1922-1955 p161-65
    028.5
Serfozo, Mary
What's what? a guessing game   **E**
Who said red?   **E**
Serial publications
    See also Newspapers; Periodicals
Series of unfortunate events [series]
Snicket, L. The bad beginning   **Fic**
The **serpent** and the Sea Queen. Osborne, M. P.
In Osborne, M. P. Mermaid tales from around
    the world p39-42   **398.2**
The **serpent** woman. San Souci, R.
In San Souci, R. More short & shivery p109-
    14   **398.2**
Serraillier, Ian, 1912-1994
The silver sword (5 and up)   **Fic**
Service, Pamela F.
Stinker from space (4-6)   **Fic**
Service, Robert W., 1874-1958
The cremation of Sam McGee (4 and up)
    811
The shooting of Dan McGrew (4 and up)
    811
Servitude *See* Slavery
Set theory
Murphy, S. J. Dave's down-to-earth rock shop
    (k-3)   **511.3**
Settel, Joanne
Exploding ants (4 and up)   **591.5**
Seuss, Dr.
The 500 hats of Bartholomew Cubbins   **E**
And to think that I saw it on Mulberry Street
    E
Bartholomew and the oobleck   **E**
The cat in the hat   **E**
The Cat in the Hat beginner book dictionary.
    See The Cat in the Hat beginner book dictio-
    nary   **423**
The cat in the hat comes back! See note under
    Seuss, Dr. The cat in the hat   **E**
Green eggs and ham   **E**
Hooray for Diffendoofer Day!   **E**
Horton hatches the egg   **E**
Horton hears a Who!   **E**

How the Grinch stole Christmas   **E**
If I ran the circus   **E**
If I ran the zoo   **E**
McElligot's pool   **E**
Oh, the places you'll go!   **E**
    About
Weidt, M. N. Oh, the places he went (3-5)
    92
Seven at one blow. Kimmel, E. A.   **398.2**
Seven blind mice. Young, E.   **398.2**
Seven brave women. Hearne, B. G.   **E**
Seven candles for Kwanzaa. Pinkney, A. D.
    394.26
The **seven** Chinese brothers. Mahy, M.   **398.2**
Seven clever brothers. Mayo, M.
In Mayo, M. Magical tales from many lands
    p76-84   **398.2**
Seven-day magic. Eager, E.   **Fic**
Seven good years. Goldin, B. D.
In Goldin, B. D. Journeys with Elijah p11-19
    222
The **Seven-headed** serpent
In The Yellow fairy book p60-63   **398.2**
Seven kisses in a row. MacLachlan, P.   **Fic**
The **seven** Semyons. Afanas´ev, A. N.
In Afanas´ev, A. N. Russian fairy tales p410-
    14   **398.2**
The **seven** sleepers. Hausman, G.
In Hausman, G. Dogs of myth p45-48
    398.2
The **seven** songs of Merlin. Barron, T. A. See note
    under Barron, T. A. The lost years of Merlin
    Fic
Seven spiders spinning. Maguire, G.   **Fic**
The **Seven** voyages of Sinbad the Sailor. Yeoman,
    J.   **398.2**
The **Seven** voyages of Sindbad the Sailor
In The Arabian nights entertainments p122-86
    398.2
The **seven** wise men. Curry, J. L.
In Curry, J. L. Turtle Island: tales of the Al-
    gonquian nations p93-97   **398.2**
Seventeen kings and forty-two elephants. Mahy,
    M.   **E**
The **seventh** boy. Bruchac, J.
In Bruchac, J. Tell me a tale p89-91
    372.6
Seventh grade. Soto, G.
In Soto, G. Baseball in April, and other sto-
    ries p52-59   **S C**
Seventh grade tango. Levy, E.   **Fic**
Severance, John B.
Einstein (5 and up)   **92**
Gandhi, great soul (5 and up)   **92**
Winston Churchill (5 and up)   **92**
Sewall, Marcia, 1935-
The Green Mist (k-3)   **398.2**
The pilgrims of Plimoth (3-6)   **974.4**
(il) Gardiner, J. R. Stone Fox   **Fic**
(il) Hesse, K. Sable   **Fic**
(il) Schotter, R. Captain Snap and the children
    of Vinegar Lane   **E**

Sewall, Marcia, 1935—_Continued_
(il) Thomas, J. R. Saying good-bye to Grandma
  E

Sewell, Anna, 1820-1878
Black Beauty (4-6) Fic
Sewell, Helen Moore, 1896-1957
(il) Dalgliesh, A. The bears on Hemlock Mountain Fic
Sewerage
See/See also pages in the following book(s):
Macaulay, D. Underground p57-65 (4 and up)
  624.1

Sex crimes
See also Child sexual abuse
Sex education
Brown, L. K. What's the big secret? (k-3)
  613.9
Harris, R. H. It's perfectly normal (4 and up)
  613.9
Harris, R. H. It's so amazing! (2-4) **612.6**
Jukes, M. It's a girl thing (5 and up)
  305.23
Silverstein, A. The reproductive system (5 and up) **612.6**
Sex role
Fiction
Gibbons, F. Mama and me and the Model-T
  E
Howe, J. Horace and Morris but mostly Dolores
  E
Namioka, L. Ties that bind, ties that break (5 and up) Fic
Numeroff, L. J. What mommies do best E
Spinelli, J. There's a girl in my hammerlock (5 and up) Fic
Walter, M. P. Justin and the best biscuits in the world (3-6) Fic
Zolotow, C. William's doll E
Sexual behavior in animals
See also Animal courtship
Sexually transmitted diseases
See/See also pages in the following book(s):
Jukes, M. It's a girl thing p88-95 (5 and up)
  305.23

Seymour, Tres
Hunting the white cow E
Seymour Simon's book of trucks. Simon, S.
  629.224
Shackleton, Sir Ernest Henry, 1874-1922
About
Kimmel, E. C. Ice story (4 and up) **998**
Kostyal, K. M. Trial by ice: a photobiography of Sir Ernest Shackleton (4 and up) **92**
Shades and shadows
Bulla, C. R. What makes a shadow? (k-1)
  535
Hoban, T. Shadows and reflections E
Zubrowski, B. Shadow play (4 and up)
  778.7
Poetry
Stevenson, R. L. My shadow (k-3) **821**
Shades of gray. Reeder, C. Fic
Shadow. Cendrars, B. **841**
Shadow-catcher. Levin, B. Fic

The **shadow** children. Schnur, S. Fic
Shadow of a bull. Wojciechowska, M. Fic
Shadow play. Zubrowski, B. **778.7**
Shadow spinner. Fletcher, S. Fic
Shadows and reflections. Hoban, T. E
Shadows of night. Bash, B. **599.4**
Shahan, Sherry, 1949-
(il) Winner, C. The sunflower family **583**
Shaka _See_ Chaka, Zulu Chief, 1787?-1828
Shaka, king of the Zulus. Stanley, D. **92**
Shaker home. Bial, R. **289**
Shakers
Bial, R. Shaker home (3-5) **289**
Fiction
Peck, R. N. A day no pigs would die (6 and up)
  Fic

Shakespeare, William, 1564-1616
About
Aliki. William Shakespeare & the Globe (3-6)
  792.09
Stanley, D. Bard of Avon: the story of William Shakespeare (4 and up) **92**
See/See also pages in the following book(s):
Krull, K. Lives of the writers p18-23 (4 and up)
  920
Adaptations
Beneduce, A. The tempest **822.3**
Coville, B. William Shakespeare's A midsummer night's dream **822.3**
Coville, B. William Shakespeare's Macbeth
  822.3
Coville, B. William Shakespeare's Romeo and Juliet **822.3**
Lamb, C. Tales from Shakespeare **822.3**
McCaughrean, G. Stories from Shakespeare
  822.3
Nesbit, E. The best of Shakespeare (4 and up)
  822.3
Fiction
Blackwood, G. L. The Shakespeare stealer (5 and up) Fic
Cooper, S. King of shadows (5 and up)
  Fic

The **Shakespeare** stealer. Blackwood, G. L.
  Fic
Shakespeare's Globe (London, England)
Aliki. William Shakespeare & the Globe (3-6)
  792.09
The **shaking** bag. Battle-Lavert, G. E
Shalant, Phyllis
Bartleby of the mighty Mississippi (3-6)
  Fic
Beware of kissing Lizard Lips (4-6) Fic
Shamrocks, harps, and shillelaghs. Barth, E.
  394.26
Shannon, David, 1959-
A bad case of stripes E
David goes to school. See note under Shannon, D. No, David! E
No, David! E
(il) Martin, R. The boy who lived with the seals
  398.2
(il) Wood, A. The Bunyans E

Shattil, Wendy
(il) Jackson, D. The wildlife detectives
363.2

Shaw, Alison, 1953-
(comp) Until I saw the sea and other poems.
See Until I saw the sea and other poems
811.008

Shaw, Charles, 1892-1974
It looked like spilt milk   E

Shaw, Nancy
Sheep in a jeep   E
Sheep in a shop. See note under Shaw, N.
Sheep in a jeep   E
also in Ready, set, read—and laugh! p12-29
810.8
Sheep on a ship. See note under Shaw, N.
Sheep in a jeep   E
Sheep out to eat. See note under Shaw, N.
Sheep in a jeep   E
Sheep take a hike. See note under Shaw, N.
Sheep in a jeep   E
Sheep trick or treat. See note under Shaw, N.
Sheep in a jeep   E

Shaw-Smith, Emma
(il) Gershator, D. Bread is for eating   E

Shawn and Keeper and the birthday party. London, J. See note under London, J. Shawn and Keeper: show-and-tell   E

Shawn and Keeper: show-and-tell. London, J.
E

Shay, Frank
The Salem ghost ship
In From sea to shining sea p113-14
810.8

She come bringing me that little baby girl. Greenfield, E.   E

She who showers gold. Krishnaswami, U.
In Krishnaswami, U. Shower of gold: girls and women in the stories of India p90-93
398.2

Shecter, Ben
(il) Benchley, N. A ghost named Fred   E
(il) Zolotow, C. The hating book   E

Shed, Greg
(il) Bunting, E. Butterfly house   E
(il) Bunting, E. Dandelions   E

Shedlock, Marie L., 1854-1935
The art of the story-teller   372.6
Includes the following stories: Filial piety; The folly of panic; Hafiz, the stone-cutter; Snegourka; The true spirit of a festival day

Sheehan, Patricia, 1954-
Côte d'Ivoire (5 and up)   966.68
Luxembourg (5 and up)   949.35
Moldova (5 and up)   947.6

Sheehan, Sean, 1951-
Cuba (5 and up)   972.91
Guatemala (5 and up)   972.81
Lebanon (5 and up)   956.92
Malta (5 and up)   945

Sheep
Fiction
Aardema, V. Borreguita and the coyote (k-3)
398.2
Caple, K. The friendship tree   E

Kitamura, S. Sheep in wolves' clothing   E
Paulsen, G. The haymeadow (6 and up)
Fic
Shaw, N. Sheep in a jeep   E
Poetry
Hale, S. J. Mary had a little lamb (k-2)
811

Sheep herders *See* Shepherds

Sheep in a jeep. Shaw, N.   E

Sheep in a shop. Shaw, N. See note under Shaw, N. Sheep in a jeep   E
also in Ready, set, read—and laugh! p12-29
810.8

Sheep in wolves' clothing. Kitamura, S. E

Sheep on a ship. Shaw, N. See note under Shaw, N. Sheep in a jeep   E

Sheep out to eat. Shaw, N. See note under Shaw, N. Sheep in a jeep   E

Sheep take a hike. Shaw, N. See note under Shaw, N. Sheep in a jeep   E

The **sheep,** the fox, and the wolf. Afanas'ev, A. N.
In Afanas'ev, A. N. Russian fairy tales p275-76
398.2

Sheep trick or treat. Shaw, N. See note under Shaw, N. Sheep in a jeep   E

A **sheepish** tale. Marshall, J.
In Marshall, J. Rats on the roof, and other stories p19-27   S C

Sheila Rae, the brave. Henkes, K.   E

Shelby, Anne
Homeplace   E

Shellfish
See also Crabs

Shells
Zoehfeld, K. W. What lives in a shell? (k-1)
591.4

Shells. Rylant, C.
In Rylant, C. Every living thing p73-81
S C

Shelter dogs. Kehret, P.   636.7

Shelterwood. Shetterly, S. H.   E

Shemiaka the judge. Afanas'ev, A. N.
In Afanas'ev, A. N. Russian fairy tales p625-27
398.2

Shepard, Aaron
The crystal heart (2-4)   398.2
Forty fortunes (2-4)   398.2
The sea king's daughter (3-6)   398.2

Shepard, Ernest H. (Ernest Howard), 1879-1976
(il) Grahame, K. The reluctant dragon   Fic
(il) Milne, A. A. The complete tales of Winnie-the-Pooh   Fic
(il) Milne, A. A. The house at Pooh Corner
Fic
(il) Milne, A. A. Now we are six   821
(il) Milne, A. A. The Pooh story book   Fic
(il) Milne, A. A. When we were very young
821
(il) Milne, A. A. Winnie-the-Pooh   Fic
(il) Milne, A. A. The world of Christopher Robin   821
(il) Milne, A. A. The world of Pooh   Fic

Shepard, Mary Eleanor, 1909-2000
  (il) Travers, P. L. Mary Poppins   **Fic**
Shepherd, Donna Walsh *See* Walsh Shepherd, Donna, 1948-

The **shepherdess** and the chimney sweep. Andersen, H. C.
  In Andersen, H. C. The swan's stories p85-97
                                  S C

Shepherds
              Fiction
Ben-'Ezer, E. Hosni the dreamer (2-4)
                                  398.2

The **shepherd's** disguise. Jaffe, N.
  In Jaffe, N. While standing on one foot p50-55   **296.1**

The **sheriff** of Rottenshot: poems. Prelutsky, J.
                                    811

Sherlock, Sir Philip Manderson, 1902-
  West Indian folk-tales (4-6)   **398.2**
  Contents: The Coomacka-Tree; The crested curassow; Irraweka, mischief-maker; The jaguar and the crested curassow; The dog's nose is cold; The Warau people discover the earth; Tiger story, Anansi story; Tiger in the forest, Anansi in the web; Mancrow, bird of darkness; Anansi and Snake the postman; Dry-Bone and Anansi; How crab got a hard back; Cat and Dog; Anansi and Candlefly; Anansi's old riding-horse; Why women won't listen; Anansi hunts with Tiger; Work-let-me-see; The Sea-mammy; Born a monkey, live a monkey; Mr. Wheeler

Sherlock Holmes' Christmas goose. Nolan, P. T.
  In The Big book of Christmas plays p298-312
                                808.82

Sherman, Gale W.
  (jt. auth) Ammon, B. D. Worth a thousand words   **011.6**

Sherman, Oren
  (il) Vinge, J. D. The Random House book of Greek myths   **292**

Sherman, Ori
  (il) Schwartz, L. S. The four questions
                                  296.4

Sherman, Patsy O., 1930-
  See/See also pages in the following book(s):
  Thimmesh, C. Girls think of everything (5 and up)   **920**

Sherman, Whitney
  (il) Jaffe, N. The cow of no color: riddle stories and justice tales from around the world
                                398.2

Sherrow, Victoria
  Connecticut
    In Celebrate the states   **973**
  Ohio
    In Celebrate the states   **973**

She's wearing a dead bird on her head!. Lasky, K.
                                    E

Shetland (Scotland)
              Fiction
Hunter, M. A stranger came ashore (6 and up)
                                Fic

Shetland Islands *See* Shetland (Scotland)

Shetterly, Susan Hand, 1942-
  Shelterwood   **E**

Shhh! we're writing the Constitution. Fritz, J.
                                  342

Shields, Carol Diggory
  Lunch money and other poems about school (2-4)   **811**
  Martian rock   **E**

Shih Huang-ti, Emperor of China *See* Ch'in Shih-huang, Emperor of China, 259-210 B.C.
Shikibu, Murasaki *See* Murasaki Shikibu, b. 978?
Shiloh. Naylor, P. R.   **Fic**
Shiloh season. Naylor, P. R. See note under Naylor, P. R. Shiloh   **Fic**
Shimin, Symeon, 1902-
  (il) Hamilton, V. Zeely   **Fic**
  (il) Krumgold, J. Onion John   **Fic**
Shimizu, Kiyoshi, 1924-
  (il) Johnson, S. A. Inside an egg   **598**
The **shimmershine** queens. Yarbrough, C.   **Fic**
Shine, Andrea
  (il) Brisson, P. The summer my father was ten
                                    E

The **shiner.** Hallworth, G.
  In The Oxford book of scary tales p52-53
                                808.8

Shingebiss. Van Laan, N.   **398.2**
The **shining** princess. Quayle, E.
  In Quayle, E. The shining princess, and other Japanese legends p13-23   **398.2**
The **shining** princess, and other Japanese legends. Quayle, E.   **398.2**
Ship. Macaulay, D.   **387.2**
Ship ahoy!. Sis, P.   **E**
The **ship** that went to America. Philip, N.
  In Philip, N. Celtic fairy tales p125-36
                                398.2
The **shipbuilders.** Fisher, L. E.   **623.8**
Shipbuilding
              History
Appelbaum, D. K. Giants in the land (2-4)
                                634.9
Fisher, L. E. The shipbuilders (4 and up)
                                623.8

Ships
    See also Steamboats
Barton, B. Boats (k-1)   **387.2**
Biesty, S. Stephen Biesty's cross-sections: Man-of-war (4 and up)   **359.1**
Crews, D. Harbor   **E**
Gibbons, G. Boat book (k-3)   **387.2**
Kentley, E. Boat (4 and up)   **387.2**
Sis, P. Ship ahoy!   **E**
The Visual dictionary of ships and sailing (4 and up)   **387.2**
              Fiction
Avi. Abigail takes the wheel (2-4) **Fic**
Paraskevas, B. On the day the tall ships sailed
                                    E

Shipwrecks
Ballard, R. D. Exploring the Titanic (4 and up)
                                910.4
Ballard, R. D. Ghost liners (4 and up)
                                910.4
Gibbons, G. Sunken treasure (k-3) **910.4**
Macaulay, D. Ship (4 and up)   **387.2**
Marschall, K. Inside the Titanic (4 and up)
                                910.4

Short stories—*Continued*

Wrede, P. C. Book of enchantments (6 and up) **S C**

Wynne-Jones, T. The book of changes (4 and up) **S C**

Wynne-Jones, T. Lord of the Fries and other stories (5 and up) **S C**

Wynne-Jones, T. Some of the kinder planets: stories (4 and up) **S C**

Shortall, Leonard W.

(il) Sobol, D. J. Encyclopedia Brown, boy detective **Fic**

(il) Stolz, M. A dog on Barkham Street **Fic**

Shortcut. Crews, D. **E**

Shortcut. Macaulay, D. **E**

Shortwave radio

See also Amateur radio stations

Shoshoni Indians

Adler, D. A. A picture book of Sacagawea (1-3) **92**

St. George, J. Sacagawea (4-6) **92**

See/See also pages in the following book(s):

Freedman, R. Indian chiefs p73-89 (6 and up) **920**

Fiction

Scott, A. H. Brave as a mountain lion **E**

Folklore

Stevens, J. Old bag of bones (k-3) **398.2**

Show and Tell bunnies. Lasky, K. **E**

The **show-and-tell** war and other stories about Adam Joshua. Smith, J. L. See note under Smith, J. L. The kid next door and other headaches **Fic**

Shower of gold: girls and women in the stories of India. Krishnaswami, U. **398.2**

Showers, Paul, 1910-1999

How many teeth? (k-1) **612.3**

The listening walk **E**

Look at your eyes (k-1) **612.8**

Sleep is for everyone (k-2) **612.8**

What happens to a hamburger? (k-3) **612.3**

Where does the garbage go? (k-3) **363.7**

Your skin and mine (k-3) **612.7**

Shrader, Christine Nyburg

(il) Bruchac, J. Gluskabe and the four wishes **398.2**

Shreve, Susan Richards

The flunking of Joshua T. Bates (3-5) **Fic**

Joshua T. Bates in trouble again. See note under Shreve, S. R. The flunking of Joshua T. Bates **Fic**

Joshua T. Bates takes charge. See note under Shreve, S. R. The flunking of Joshua T. Bates **Fic**

Shrewbettina's birthday. Goodall, J. S. **E**

Shrewd Todie and Lyzer the miser. Singer, I. B.

In Bauer, C. F. Celebrations p121-25 **808.8**

In Singer, I. B. Stories for children p283-89 **S C**

In Singer, I. B. When Shlemiel went to Warsaw & other stories p3-13 **398.2**

Shrews

Fiction

Goodall, J. S. Shrewbettina's birthday **E**

The **shrinking** of Treehorn. Heide, F. P. **Fic**

also in The Oxford treasury of children's stories p135-43 **S C**

Shub, Elizabeth

The white stallion **E**

Shulevitz, Uri, 1935-

Dawn **E**

The golden goose (k-3) **398.2**

Rain, rain, rivers **E**

Snow **E**

The treasure (k-3) **398.2**

(il) Ben-´Ezer, E. Hosni the dreamer **398.2**

(il) Ransome, A. The Fool of the World and the flying ship **398.2**

(il) Schwartz, H. The diamond tree **398.2**

(il) Singer, I. B. The fools of Chelm and their history **Fic**

See/See also pages in the following book(s):

Newbery and Caldecott Medal books, 1966-1975 p209-16 **028.5**

Shulman, Fay Stanley *See* Stanley, Fay, 1925-1990

Shurgin, Ann H., 1952-

(ed) The Folklore of world holidays. See The Folklore of world holidays **394.26**

Shush, Shush, the big buff banty hen who laid an egg in the postmaster's hat. Sandburg, C.

In Sandburg, C. Rootabaga stories pt 2 p22-26 **S C**

In Sandburg, C. The Sandburg treasury p97-98 **818**

Shuttles, Space *See* Space shuttles

Shy Charles. Wells, R. **E**

Shy salamanders. Souza, D. M. **597.8**

Shyer, Marlene Fanta

Welcome home, Jellybean (5 and up) **Fic**

Siberia (Russia)

Fiction

Schuch, S. A symphony of whales **E**

Siblings

See also Twins

Cole, J. The new baby at your house (k-3) **306.8**

Fiction

Alexander, M. G. When the new baby comes, I'm moving out **E**

Beard, D. B. Twister **E**

Blume, J. The one in the middle is the green kangaroo **E**

Blume, J. The Pain and the Great One **E**

Bonsall, C. N. The day I had to play with my sister **E**

Bradley, K. B. Ruthie's gift (3-5) **Fic**

Brown, L. K. Rex and Lilly family time **E**

Brown, M. T. D.W. all wet **E**

Bruchac, J. Children of the longhouse (4 and up) **Fic**

Byars, B. C. The night swimmers (5 and up) **Fic**

Byars, B. C. The not-just-anybody family (5 and up) **Fic**

Siblings—Fiction—*Continued*

Byars, B. C. The summer of the swans (5 and up) **Fic**

Caines, J. F. Abby **E**

Caseley, J. Mama, coming and going **E**

Christopher, M. Tennis ace (3-6) **Fic**

Cleaver, V. Where the lillies bloom (5 and up) **Fic**

Cummings, P. Angel baby **E**

De Groat, D. Trick or treat, smell my feet **E**

De Paola, T. The baby sister **E**

Fenner, C. Yolonda's genius (4-6) **Fic**

Fox, P. The stone-faced boy (4-6) **Fic**

Greenfield, E. She come bringing me that little baby girl **E**

Hahn, M. D. As ever, Gordy (5 and up) **Fic**

Hoberman, M. A. And to think that we thought that we'd never be friends **E**

Horvath, P. The trolls (3-6) **Fic**

Howard, E. F. When will Sarah come? **E**

Hutchins, P. Titch **E**

James, B. Tadpoles **E**

Kehret, P. Earthquake terror (4-6) **Fic**

Lowry, L. Switcharound (5 and up) **Fic**

McDonald, M. The great pumpkin switch **E**

Moeri, L. Save Queen of Sheba (4 and up) **Fic**

Nelson, T. And one for all (5 and up) **Fic**

Nixon, J. L. A family apart (5 and up) **Fic**

Park, B. Mick Harte was here (4-6) **Fic**

Polacco, P. My rotten redheaded older brother **E**

Porte, B. A. If you ever get lost (2-4) **Fic**

Russo, M. Hannah's baby sister **E**

Shyer, M. F. Welcome home, Jellybean (5 and up) **Fic**

Stuve-Bodeen, S. Elizabeti's doll **E**

Voigt, C. Dicey's song (6 and up) **Fic**

Voigt, C. Homecoming (6 and up) **Fic**

Wells, R. Max's first word **E**

Sick

Fiction

Calmenson, S. Get well, Gators! (1-3) **Fic**

Greene, R. G. Barnyard song **E**

Kelley, T. I've got chicken pox **E**

Siddhārtha *See* Gautama Buddha

Side by side **808.81**

Sidewalk games around the world. Erlbach, A. **796.1**

Sidewalk story. Mathis, S. B. **Fic**

Sideways stories from Wayside School. Sachar, L. See note under Sachar, L. Wayside School gets a little stranger **Fic**

Sidjakov, Nicolas, 1924-

(il) Robbins, R. Baboushka and the three kings **398.2**

Siebel, Fritz, 1913-

(il) Lexau, J. M. Who took the farmer's [hat]? **E**

(il) Parish, P. Amelia Bedelia **E**

Siebert, Diane

Mojave (1-3) **811**

Plane song **E**

Sierra (1-3) **811**

Train song **E**

Truck song **E**

Siegel, Beatrice

Marian Wright Edelman (5 and up) **92**

Siegelson, Kim L., 1962-

In the time of the drums **E**

Sierra, Judy

Antarctic antics (k-3) **811**

The beautiful butterfly (k-3) **398.2**

Children's traditional games **796**

The dancing pig (k-3) **398.2**

The flannel board storytelling book **027.62**

Nursery tales around the world **398.2**

Contents: The gingerbread man; The pancake; The bun; I know an old lady who swallowed a fly; The boy who tried to fool his father; The cat and the parrot; Sody sallyraytus; The ram in the chile patch; Odon the giant; This is the house that Jack built; Anansi and the pig; The rooster and the mouse; The hare and the tortoise; The coyote and the rabbit; The fox and the crab; The gunny wolf; Groundhog's dance; The three pigs

Tasty baby belly buttons (k-3) **398.2**

Sierra. Siebert, D. **811**

Sierra i Fabra, Jordi, 1947-

Uninvited guests

In Don't read this! and other tales of the unnatural p197-213 **S C**

Sierra Nevada Mountains

Poetry

Siebert, D. Sierra (1-3) **811**

The **sight**. McKissack, P. C.

In McKissack, P. C. The dark-thirty p44-54 **S C**

Sight. Pringle, L. P.

In Pringle, L. P. Explore your senses **612.8**

Sign language

Baker, P. J. My first book of sign (k-3) **419**

Rankin, L. The handmade alphabet **419**

Rankin, L. The handmade counting book **419**

Fiction

Millman, I. Moses goes to school **E**

The **sign** of the beaver. Speare, E. G. **Fic**

The **sign** on Rosie's door. Sendak, M. **E**

The **signpost**. Babbitt, N.

In Babbitt, N. The Devil's other storybook p41-44 **S C**

Signs and signboards

Hoban, T. I read signs (k-2) **659.1**

Signs and symbols

See also Sign language

Barth, E. Hearts, cupids, and red roses (3-6) **394.26**

Barth, E. Holly, reindeer, and colored lights (3-6) **394.26**

Barth, E. Lilies, rabbits, and painted eggs (3-6) **394.26**

Barth, E. Shamrocks, harps, and shillelaghs (3-6) **394.26**

Barth, E. Turkeys, Pilgrims, and Indian corn (3-6) **394.26**

Barth, E. Witches, pumpkins, and grinning ghosts (3-6) **394.26**

Signs and symbols—*Continued*
Parker, N. W. Money, money, money (3-5)
769.5
Samoyault, T. Give me a sign! (4 and up)
302.2

Siksika Indians
Folklore
Goble, P. Star Boy (2-4)   **398.2**
Taylor, H. P. When Bear stole the chinook (k-3)
398.2

Silberman, Henri
(il) Stone bench in an empty park. See Stone bench in an empty park   **811.008**

Silent Lotus. Lee, J. M.   **E**

Silent Samson, the Maccabee. Kimmel, E. A.
In Kimmel, E. A. The jar of fools: eight Hanukkah stories from Chelm p19-26
S C

Sills, Leslie
Visions (5 and up)   **920**

Silly Billy. Hutchins, P. See note under Hutchins, P. Where's the baby?   **E**

Silly Tilly and the Easter Bunny. Hoban, L. See note under Hoban, L. Silly Tilly's Thanksgiving dinner   **E**

Silly Tilly's Thanksgiving dinner. Hoban, L.
E

Silly Tilly's valentine. Hoban, L. See note under Hoban, L. Silly Tilly's Thanksgiving dinner
E

Silva, Simon
(il) Ada, A. F. Gathering the sun   **811**

Silver, Donald M., 1947-
African savanna (3-5)   **577.4**
Arctic tundra (3-5)   **577.5**
Backyard (3-5)   **577**
Cactus desert (3-5)   **577.5**
Cave (3-5)   **577.5**
Pond (3-5)   **577.6**
Seashore (3-5)   **577.7**
Woods (3-5)   **577.3**

Silver, Stan
(il) Herman, G. Cal Ripken, Jr.   **92**

The **silver** chair. Lewis, C. S. See note under Lewis, C. S. The lion, the witch, and the wardrobe   **Fic**

The **silver** cow: a Welsh tale. Cooper, S.
398.2

The **silver-miners**. McCaughrean, G.
In McCaughrean, G. The silver treasure: myths and legends of the world p1-5
398.2

Silver on the tree. Cooper, S. See note under Cooper, S. Over sea, under stone   **Fic**

Silver packages. Rylant, C.   **E**
also in Rylant, C. Children of Christmas p26-31   **S C**

The **silver** pine cones. MacDonald, M. R.
In MacDonald, M. R. Celebrate the world p184-90   **372.6**

The **silver** pony. Ward, L. K.   **Fic**

The **silver** sword. Serraillier, I.   **Fic**

The **silver** treasure: myths and legends of the world. McCaughrean, G.   **398.2**

Silverman, Erica
Don't fidget a feather   **E**
Raisel's riddle (k-3)   **398.2**

The **silversmiths**. Fisher, L. E.   **739.2**

Silverstein, Alvin
Allergies (3-5)   **616.97**
The California condor (4 and up)   **598**
The circulatory system (5 and up)   **612.1**
Common colds (3-5)   **616.2**
Cuts, scrapes, scabs, and scars (3-5)   **617.1**
The digestive system (5 and up)   **612.3**
The excretory system (5 and up)   **612.4**
The Florida panther (4 and up)   **599.75**
Is that a rash? (3-5)   **616.5**
Plate tectonics (5 and up)   **551.1**
The red wolf (4 and up)   **599.77**
The reproductive system (5 and up)   **612.6**
The sea otter (4 and up)   **599.7**
Sleep (3-5)   **612.8**
Tooth decay and cavities (3-5)   **617.6**

Silverstein, Robert A.
(jt. auth) Silverstein, A. The circulatory system
612.1
(jt. auth) Silverstein, A. The digestive system
612.3
(jt. auth) Silverstein, A. The excretory system
612.4
(jt. auth) Silverstein, A. The red wolf
599.77
(jt. auth) Silverstein, A. The reproductive system
612.6
(jt. auth) Silverstein, A. The sea otter
599.7

Silverstein, Shel
Falling up   **811**
A light in the attic   **811**
Where the sidewalk ends   **811**

Silverstein, Virginia B.
(jt. auth) Silverstein, A. Allergies   **616.97**
(jt. auth) Silverstein, A. The California condor
598
(jt. auth) Silverstein, A. The circulatory system
612.1
(jt. auth) Silverstein, A. Common colds
616.2
(jt. auth) Silverstein, A. Cuts, scrapes, scabs, and scars   **617.1**
(jt. auth) Silverstein, A. The digestive system
612.3
(jt. auth) Silverstein, A. The excretory system
612.4
(jt. auth) Silverstein, A. The Florida panther
599.75
(jt. auth) Silverstein, A. Is that a rash?
616.5
(jt. auth) Silverstein, A. Plate tectonics
551.1
(jt. auth) Silverstein, A. The red wolf
599.77
(jt. auth) Silverstein, A. The reproductive system
612.6
(jt. auth) Silverstein, A. The sea otter
599.7
(jt. auth) Silverstein, A. Sleep   **612.8**

Silverstein, Virginia B.—*Continued*
(jt. auth) Silverstein, A. Tooth decay and cavities **617.6**

Silverwing. Oppel, K. **Fic**

Silverwork
Fisher, L. E. The silversmiths (4 and up) **739.2**

Silvey, Anita
(ed) Children's books and their creators. See Children's books and their creators **028.5**

Simmons, Elly
See/See also pages in the following book(s):
Just like me p22-23 **920**

Simmons, Jane
Come along, Daisy! **E**
Daisy and the Beastie. See note under Simmons, J. Come along, Daisy! **E**
Daisy and the egg. See note under Simmons, J. Come along, Daisy! **E**

Simmons, Philip
About
Lyons, M. E. Catching the fire: Philip Simmons, blacksmith (4 and up) **92**

Simmons, Richard
Golf (4 and up) **796.352**

Simms, Laura, 1947-
The Bone Man (2-4) **398.2**
Rotten teeth **E**

Simner, Janni Lee
Tearing down the unicorns
In A Glory of unicorns p31-42 **S C**

Simon, Charnan
Chester A. Arthur: twenty-first president of the United States (4 and up) **92**

Simon, Francesca
Toddler time (k-1) **821**

Simon, Norma, 1927-
The story of Hanukkah (2-4) **296.4**
The story of Passover (2-4) **296.4**

Simon, Seymour, 1931-
Autumn across America (3-5) **508.2**
Big cats (3-6) **599.75**
Bones (3-6) **612.7**
The brain (3-6) **612.8**
Comets, meteors, and asteroids (3-6) **523.6**
Crocodiles & alligators (3-6) **597.9**
Deserts (3-6) **577.5**
Destination: Jupiter (3-6) **523.4**
Destination: Mars (3-6) **523.4**
Earthquakes (3-6) **551.2**
From paper airplanes to outer space (1-3) **92**
Galaxies (3-6) **523.1**
The heart (3-6) **612.1**
Icebergs and glaciers (3-5) **551.3**
Lightning (3-6) **551.56**
Mountains (3-6) **551.4**
Muscles (3-6) **612.7**
Now you see it, now you don't (4 and up) **152.14**
Oceans (3-6) **551.46**
Our solar system (3-6) **523.2**
Out of sight (4 and up) **502.8**
The paper airplane book (3-5) **745.592**

Ride the wind (4-6) **591.56**
Seymour Simon's book of trucks (k-3) **629.224**
Sharks (2-4) **597**
Snakes (3-6) **597.9**
Storms (3-6) **551.55**
Strange mysteries from around the world (4-6) **001.9**
They swim the seas (3-6) **578.7**
They walk the earth (3-6) **591.56**
Tornadoes (3-6) **551.55**
The universe (3-6) **523**
Volcanoes (3-6) **551.2**
Weather (3-6) **551.5**
Wild babies (2-4) **591.3**
Wildfires (3-6) **577.2**
Wolves (3-6) **599.77**
See/See also pages in the following book(s):
Author talk (4 and up) **028.5**

Simon & Schuster children's guide to insects and spiders. Johnson, J. **595.7**

Simon & Schuster children's guide to sea creatures. Johnson, J. **591.7**

Simon and the big joke. Joseph, L.
In Joseph, L. A wave in her pocket p21-27 **398.2**

Simon's book. Drescher, H. **E**

Simont, Marc
(il) Byars, B. C. My brother, Ant **E**
(il) Kuskin, K. The Philharmonic gets dressed **E**
(il) Lord, B. B. In the Year of the Boar and Jackie Robinson **Fic**
(il) Sharmat, M. W. Nate the Great **E**
(il) Udry, J. M. A tree is nice **E**
See/See also pages in the following book(s):
Caldecott Medal books, 1938-1957 p297-306 **028.5**

Simple Peter's mirror. Jones, T.
In The Oxford treasury of children's stories p50-54 **S C**

Simple Seng and the parrot. Carpenter, F.
In Carpenter, F. Tales of a Chinese grandmother p242-51 **398.2**

Simple sentences. Babbitt, N.
In Babbitt, N. The Devil's other storybook p63-71 **S C**

Simply delicious!. Mahy, M. **E**

Sims, Blanche
(il) Kimmel, E. A. I took my frog to the library **E**
(il) Kline, S. Mary Marony, mummy girl **Fic**

SimScience. (5 and up) See entry in Part 2: Web Resources

Simulation, computer *See* Computer simulation

Sinbad the Sailor, The Seven voyages of. Yeoman, J. **398.2**

Sindbad the Porter and Sindbad the Sailor, The story of. Alderson, B.
In Alderson, B. The Arabian nights p79-91 **398.2**

Sing a new song (k-3) **223**
Sing a song of popcorn **808.81**

Sing down the moon. O'Dell, S.   **Fic**

Sing me a story. Rosenberg, J.   **792.5**

The **sing-song** of old man kangaroo. Kipling, R.
In Kipling, R. Just so stories   **S C**

Sing to the sun. Bryan, A.   **811**

Singer, Beverly R.
(comp) Rising voices. See Rising voices
    810.8

Singer, Isaac Bashevis, 1904-1991
The fools of Chelm and their history (4 and up)
    Fic

Mazel and Shlimazel (2-5)   **398.2**

The power of light (4 and up)   **S C**
Contents: A Hanukkah evening in my parents' house; The extinguished lights; The parakeet named Dreidel; Menashe and Rachel; The squire; The power of light; Hershele and Hanukkah; Hanukkah in the poorhouse

Shrewd Todie and Lyzer the miser
In Bauer, C. F. Celebrations p121-25
    808.8

The snow in Chelm
In Snowy day: stories and poems p25-29
    808.8

Stories for children (4 and up)   **S C**
Contents: The elders of Chelm & Genendel's key; A tale of three wishes; The extinguished lights; Mazel & Shlimazel; Why Noah chose the dove; Zlateh the goat; A Hanukkah Eve in Warsaw; The fools of Chelm & the stupid carp; The wicked city; Rabbi Leib & the witch Cunegunde; The parakeet named Dreidel; Lemel & Tzipa; The day I got lost; Menashe & Rachel; Shlemiel the businessman; Joseph & Koza; A Hanukkah evening in my parents' house; Tsirtsur & Peziza; Naftali the storyteller & his horse, Sus; Hershele & Hanukkah; When Shlemiel went to Warsaw; The power of light; Growing up; The Lantuch; Utzel & his daughter, Poverty; The squire; Ole & Trufa; Dalfunka, where the rich live forever; Topiel & Tekla; Hanukkah in the poorhouse; Shrewd Todie & Lyzer the miser; The fearsome inn; The cat who thought she was a dog & the dog who thought he was a cat; Menaseh's dream; Tashlik

When Shlemiel went to Warsaw & other stories (4 and up)   **398.2**
Contents: Shrewd Todie & Lyzer the miser; Tsirtsur & Peziza; Rabbi Leib & the witch Cunegunde; The elders of Chelm & Genendel's key; Shlemiel, the businessman; Utzel & his daughter Poverty; Menaseh's dream; When Shlemiel went to Warsaw

Zlateh the goat, and other stories (4 and up)
    398.2
Contents: Fool's paradise; Grandmother's tale; The snow in Chelm; The mixed-up feet and the silly bridegroom; The first shlemiel; The Devil's trick; Zlateh the goat
See/See also pages in the following book(s):
Krull, K. Lives of the writers p90-93 (4 and up)
    920

Singer, Marilyn, 1948-
Family reunion (k-3)   **811**
On the same day in March (k-3)   **551.6**
Sky words (k-3)   **811**

The **singer** above the river. McCaughrean, G.
In McCaughrean, G. The golden hoard: myths and legends of the world p77-83
    398.2

Singers
See also African American singers
Fiction
Auch, M. J. Bantam of the opera   **E**

Singing
Fiction
Stenmark, V. The singing chick   **E**

The **Singing** bone
In The Magic orange tree, and other Haitian folktales p91-97   **398.2**

The **singing** chick. Stenmark, V.   **E**

The **singing** tortoise. Courlander, H.
In Courlander, H. Cow-tail switch, and other West African stories p65-72   **398.2**

The **singing** tree and the talking bird. Afanas'ev, A. N.
In Afanas'ev, A. N. Russian fairy tales p184-88   **398.2**

The **singing** turtle. MacDonald, M. R.
In MacDonald, M. R. Look back and see p137-46   **372.6**

Single parent family
Fiction
Byars, B. C. The night swimmers (5 and up)
    Fic
Greenfield, E. Sister (4 and up)   **Fic**
Lowry, L. The one hundredth thing about Caroline (5 and up)   **Fic**

Sink the Bismarck. McGowen, T.   **940.54**

Sino-Japanese Conflict, 1937-1945
Fiction
DeJong, M. The house of sixty fathers (4-6)
    Fic

Sioras, Efstathia
Czech Republic (5 and up)   **943.7**

Siouan Indians
See also Dakota Indians; Oglala Indians

The **Sioux**. Sneve, V. D. H.   **970.004**

Sioux Indians *See* Dakota Indians

Sir Gammer Vans. Jacobs, J.
In Jacobs, J. English fairy tales p261-63
    398.2

Sir Gawain and the Green Knight. Osborne, M. P.
In Osborne, M. P. Favorite medieval tales p50-59   **398.2**

Sir Gawain and the loathly lady. Hastings, S.
    398.2

Sir Patrick Spens. McCaughrean, G.
In McCaughrean, G. The silver treasure: myths and legends of the world p118-20
    398.2

SIRS discoverer deluxe on the web. (3-8) See entry in Part 2: Web Resources

Sis, Peter
Dinosaur!   **E**
Fire truck   **E**
Follow the dream [biography of Christopher Columbus] (k-3)   **92**
Komodo!   **E**
Madlenka   **E**
Ship ahoy!   **E**
Starry messenger [biography of Galileo Galilei]
    92
Tibet   **951**
Trucks, trucks, trucks   **E**
(il) Fleischman, S. The midnight horse   **Fic**
(il) Fleischman, S. The scarebird   **E**
(il) Fleischman, S. The whipping boy   **Fic**
(il) Prelutsky, J. The dragons are singing tonight
    811

Sis, Peter—*Continued*

(il) Prelutsky, J. The gargoyle on the roof

811

(il) Prelutsky, J. Monday's troll   **811**

(il) Rice, E. City night   **E**

(il) Shannon, G. More stories to solve

398.2

(il) Shannon, G. Still more stories to solve

398.2

(il) Shannon, G. Stories to solve   **398.2**

Sister. Greenfield, E.   **Fic**

Sister Alionushka, brother Ivanushka. Afanas´ev, A. N.

In Afanas´ev, A. N. Russian fairy tales p406-10   **398.2**

Sister Anne's hands. Lorbiecki, M.   **E**

Sister Death and the healer. San Souci, R.

In San Souci, R. More short & shivery p78-82   **398.2**

Sister Fox and Brother Coyote. San Souci, R.

In San Souci, R. Cut from the same cloth p93-99   **398.2**

Sisters

Fiction

Alcock, V. The cuckoo sister (6 and up)

Fic

Arrington, F. Bluestem (4-6)   **Fic**

Couloumbis, A. Getting near to baby (5 and up)

Fic

Greene, C. C. Beat the turtle drum (5 and up)

Fic

Greenfield, E. Sister (4 and up)   **Fic**

Griffin, A. The other Shepards (6 and up)

Fic

Johnson, A. Do like Kyla   **E**

Kroll, V. L. Faraway drums   **E**

Kvasnosky, L. M. Zelda and Ivy   **E**

Lisle, J. T. The lost flower children (4-6)

Fic

Loh, M. J. Tucking Mommy in   **E**

Lowry, L. A summer to die (5 and up)

Fic

McKay, H. The exiles (5 and up)   **Fic**

Numeroff, L. J. The Chicken sisters   **E**

Patron, S. Maybe yes, maybe no, maybe maybe (3-5)   **Fic**

Rodowsky, C. F. Spindrift (5 and up)   **Fic**

Schwartz, A. Annabelle Swift, kindergartner

E

Sendak, M. Outside over there   **E**

Woodson, J. Lena (6 and up)   **Fic**

Sisters (in religious orders, congregations, etc.) *See* Nuns

Sisters. Ellis, S.

In Ellis, S. Back of beyond   **S C**

Sisters and brothers *See* Siblings

Sisters in the sun. Carpenter, F.

In Carpenter, F. Tales of a Chinese grandmother p22-28   **398.2**

Sisulu, Elinor Batezat

The day Gogo went to vote   **E**

Sit on a potato pan, Otis!. Agee, J.   **793.73**

Sita's story. Krishnaswami, U.

In Krishnaswami, U. Shower of gold: girls and women in the stories of India p52-60

398.2

Sitting Bull, Dakota Chief, 1831-1890

About

Bruchac, J. A boy called Slow: the true story of Sitting Bull (1-3)   **92**

See/See also pages in the following book(s):

Ehrlich, A. Wounded Knee: an Indian history of the American West (6 and up)   **970.004**

Freedman, R. Indian chiefs p114-39 (6 and up)

920

Six foolish fishermen. San Souci, R.   **398.2**

Six haunted hairdos. Maguire, G. See note under Maguire, G. Seven spiders spinning   **Fic**

Six sick sheep. Cole, J.   **808.88**

The **six** swans. Grimm, J.

In The Yellow fairy book p4-8   **398.2**

The **sixth** grade nickname game. Korman, G.

Fic

The **sixty-two** curses of Caliph Arenschadd. Wrede, P. C.

In Wrede, P. C. Book of enchantments p49-70   **S C**

Size

Ash, R. Incredible comparisons (4 and up)

031.02

Hoban, T. Is it larger? Is it smaller?   **E**

Hoban, T. Is it red? Is it yellow? Is it blue?

E

Miller, M. Big and little   **E**

Fiction

Joyce, W. George shrinks   **E**

Kalan, R. Blue sea   **E**

Keller, H. Jacob's tree   **E**

Size and shape *See* Shape

Skating *See* Ice skating

Skeleton

Balestrino, P. The skeleton inside you (k-3)

611

Ballard, C. The skeleton and muscular system (5 and up)   **612.7**

Barner, B. Dem bones (k-3)   **611**

Llewellyn, C. The big book of bones (4-6)

573.7

Simon, S. Bones (3-6)   **612.7**

The Visual dictionary of the skeleton (4 and up)

591.4

Fiction

Johnston, T. The soup bone   **E**

The **skeleton** and muscular system. Ballard, C.

612.7

The **skeleton** inside you. Balestrino, P.   **611**

The **skeleton's** dance. San Souci, R.

In San Souci, R. Short & shivery p73-77

398.2

The **skeleton's** revenge. San Souci, R.

In San Souci, R. Even more short & shivery p100-04   **398.2**

Skellig. Almond, D.   **Fic**

Skelton, Olivia

Vietnam (4 and up)   **959.7**

Slavery—*Continued*
History
Haskins, J. Bound for America (5 and up)
    326

United States
See also Abolitionists

Bial, R. The strength of these arms (4 and up)
    326

Bial, R. The Underground Railroad (4 and up)
    326

Erickson, P. Daily life on a Southern plantation, 1853 (4-6) **975**

Fleischner, J. I was born a slave: the story of Harriet Jacobs (5 and up) **92**

Hamilton, V. Anthony Burns: the defeat and triumph of a fugitive slave (5 and up) **92**

Hamilton, V. Many thousand gone (5 and up)
    326

Haskins, J. Get on board: the story of the Underground Railroad (5 and up) **326**

Jurmain, S. Freedom's sons (4 and up) **326**

Lester, J. From slave ship to freedom road (4 and up) **326**

Lester, J. To be a slave (6 and up) **326**

McKissack, P. C. Christmas in the big house, Christmas in the quarters (4-6) **394.26**

McKissack, P. C. Rebels against slavery (5 and up) **326**

Myers, W. D. Amistad: a long road to freedom (5 and up) **326**

Yates, E. Amos Fortune, free man (4 and up)
    92

Slavin, Bill
(il) Granfield, L. Extra! Extra! **071**

Sleator, William
The beasties (6 and up) **Fic**
The boxes (6 and up) **Fic**
Interstellar pig (5 and up) **Fic**
Into the dream (5 and up) **Fic**
Rewind (4 and up) **Fic**

Sled dog racing
See also Iditarod Trail Sled Dog Race, Alaska

Kimmel, E. C. Balto and the great race (3-5)
    636.7

Paulsen, G. Puppies, dogs, and blue northers (5 and up) **798.8**

Wood, T. Iditarod dream (4 and up) **798.8**
Fiction
Gardiner, J. R. Stone Fox (2-5) **Fic**

Sleep
See also Bedtime

Showers, P. Sleep is for everyone (k-2)
    612.8

Silverstein, A. Sleep (3-5) **612.8**
Fiction
Dragonwagon, C. Half a moon and one whole star **E**
Fox, M. Night noises **E**
Loh, M. J. Tucking Mommy in **E**
Massie, D. R. The baby beebee bird **E**
McMullan, K. Papa's song **E**
Wood, A. The napping house **E**

Poetry
Prelutsky, J. My parents think I'm sleeping: poems (2-4) **811**

Sleep is for everyone. Showers, P. **612.8**

Sleep out. Carrick, C. See note under Carrick, C. The accident **E**

Sleeping Beauty (Ballet)
See/See also pages in the following book(s):

McCaughrean, G. The Random House book of stories from the ballet p102-12 (4 and up)
    792.8

Newman, B. The illustrated book of ballet stories p10-21 (4-6) **792.8**

The sleeping beauty. Perrault, C.
  In Perrault, C. The complete fairy tales of Charles Perrault p15-29 **398.2**

The sleeping beauty in the wood. Perrault, C.
  In The Blue fairy book p54-63 **398.2**
  In The Classic fairy tales p85-92 **398.2**

The Sleeping Beauty in the woods. Perrault, C.
  In Perrault, C. Cinderella, Puss in Boots, and other favorite tales p102-31 **398.2**

Sleeping ugly. Yolen, J. **E**

The sleepover cookbook. Warshaw, H. **641.5**

Sleepy bears. Fox, M. **E**

Sleepytime rhyme. Charlip, R. **E**

Sleight of hand *See* Juggling; Magic tricks

Slepian, Jan, 1921-
The Broccoli tapes (5 and up) **Fic**

Slier, Debby
(ed) Make a joyful sound. See Make a joyful sound **811.008**

Slime, molds, and fungi. Pascoe, E. **579.5**

Slipfoot and how he nearly always never gets what he goes after. Sandburg, C.
  In Sandburg, C. Rootabaga stories pt 2 p9-13
    S C

  In Sandburg, C. The Sandburg treasury p93-95 **818**

SLJ/School Library Journal. See School Library Journal **027.805**

Sloat, Teri
Farmer Brown goes round and round **E**
Farmer Brown shears his sheep. See note under Slote, T. Farmer Brown goes round and round
    E

There was an old lady who swallowed a trout
    E

The thing that bothered Farmer Brown. See note under Slote, T. Farmer Brown goes round and round **E**

Slobodkin, Louis, 1903-1975
(il) Estes, E. The hundred dresses **Fic**
(il) Estes, E. The Moffats **Fic**
(il) Thurber, J. Many moons **Fic**
See/See also pages in the following book(s):
Caldecott Medal books, 1938-1957 p99-116
    028.5

Slobodkina, Esphyr, 1908-
Caps for sale **E**

The Sloogey Dog and the stolen aroma. Aardema, V.
  In Aardema, V. Misoso p37-45 **398.2**

Smith, Lane—*Continued*
  (il) Scieszka, J. Math curse   E
  (jt. auth) Scieszka, J. Squids will be squids
    E
  (jt. auth) Scieszka, J. The Stinky Cheese Man
    and other fairly stupid tales   E
  (il) Scieszka, J. The true story of the 3 little
    pigs   E
  (jt. auth) Seuss, Dr. Hooray for Diffendoofer
    Day!   E

Smith, Lotsee Patterson *See* Patterson, Lotsee

Smith, Martha, 1946-
  (jt. auth) Knowles, E. More reading connections
    028.5

Smith, Robert Kimmel, 1930-
  Bobby Baseball (4-6)   Fic
  Chocolate fever (4-6)   Fic
  The war with Grandpa (4-6)   Fic

Smith, Roland, 1951-
  Journey of the red wolf (4 and up)   599.77

Smith, Theresa
  (il) Gershator, P. Zzzng! Zzzng! Zzzng!
    398.2

Smith, Trevor
  Amazing lizards (2-4)   597.9

Smith, Wendy
  (il) Ross, M. E. Fish watching with Eugenie
    Clark   92
  (il) Ross, M. E. Pond watching with Ann Mor-
    gan   92

Smith, William Jay, 1918-
  Around my room (k-3)   811
  (comp) Here is my heart. See Here is my heart
    821.008

Smith. Garfield, L.   Fic

Smith-Griswold, Wendy, 1955-
  (il) Ross, M. E. Nature art with Chiura Obata
    92

The **smith,** the weaver, and the harper. Alexander,
L.
  In Alexander, L. The foundling and other
    tales of Prydian p65-72   S C

Smithsonian expeditions. (5 and up) See entry in
Part 2: Web Resources

**Smithsonian Institution. National Museum of
the American Indian** *See* National Museum
of the American Indian (U.S.)

Smoking
  See also Tobacco habit
  Pringle, L. P. Smoking (5 and up)   362.29

Smoky Mountain Rose. Schroeder, A.   E

Smoky night. Bunting, E.   E

The **smugglers.** Lawrence, I.   Fic

Smuggling
    Fiction
  Lawrence, I. The smugglers (5 and up)   Fic

Smyth, Ian
  The young baseball player (4 and up)
    796.357

Snail mail no more. Danziger, P.   Fic

Snails
  Fowler, A. A snail's pace (k-3)   594

    Fiction
Lionni, L. The biggest house in the world
    E

A **snail's** pace. Fowler, A.   594

The **snake.** Lester, J.
  In Lester, J. The last tales of Uncle Remus
    p28-33   398.2
  In Lester, J. When the beginning began p73-
    80   296.1

The **Snake** book (4-6)   597.9

Snake husband, Frog friend. Martin, R.
  In Martin, R. Mysterious tales of Japan
    398.2

The **snake** princess. Terada, A. M.
  In Terada, A. M. Under the starfruit tree p14-
    17   398.2

The **snake** scientist. Montgomery, S.   597.9

Snakes
  See also Rattlesnakes
  Gove, D. A water snake's year (3-5)   597.9
  Lauber, P. Snakes are hunters (k-3)   597.9
  Markle, S. Outside and inside snakes (2-4)
    597.9
  Montgomery, S. The snake scientist (4 and up)
    597.9
  Simon, S. Snakes (3-6)   597.9
  The Snake book (4-6)   597.9
  See/See also pages in the following book(s):
  Byars, B. C. The moon and I (4 and up)
    92

    Fiction
Cannon, J. Verdi   E
Gray, L. M. Small Green Snake   E
Noble, T. H. The day Jimmy's boa ate the wash
    E
Shannon, G. Lizard's home   E
Ungerer, T. Crictor   E
Walsh, E. S. Mouse count   E

Snakes are hunters. Lauber, P.   597.9

Snakey riddles. Hall, K.   793.73

Snap!. Vaughan, M.   E

A **snap** of the fingers. San Souci, R.
  In San Souci, R. A terrifying taste of short &
    shivery p123-29   398.2

Snapshot. Czech, K. P.   770.9

Snapshots from the wedding. Soto, G.   E

Snedden, Robert
  What is an amphibian? (3-6)   597.8

Sneed, Brad
  (il) Arnold, M. D. The pumpkin runner   E
  (il) Schroeder, A. Smoky Mountain Rose   E

Snegourka. Shedlock, M. L.
  In Shedlock, M. L. The art of the story-teller
    p195-97   372.6

Sneve, Virginia Driving Hawk
  The Apaches (3-5)   970.004
  The Cherokees (3-5)   970.004
  The Cheyennes (3-5)   970.004
  High Elk's treasure   Fic
  The Hopis (3-5)   970.004
  The Iroquois (3-5)   970.004
  The Navajos (3-5)   970.004
  The Nez Percé (3-5)   970.004

Sneve, Virginia Driving Hawk—*Continued*

The Seminoles (3-5)	**970.004**
The Sioux (3-5)	**970.004**

(comp) Dancing teepees: poems of American Indian youth. See Dancing teepees: poems of American Indian youth **897**

Snicket, Lemony

The austere academy. See note under Snicket, L. The bad beginning **Fic**

The bad beginning (4 and up) **Fic**

The ersatz elevator. See note under Snicket, L. The bad beginning **Fic**

The miserable mill. See note under Snicket, L. The bad beginning **Fic**

The reptile room. See note under Snicket, L. The bad beginning **Fic**

The vile village. See note under Snicket, L. The bad beginning **Fic**

The wide window. See note under Snicket, L. The bad beginning **Fic**

Snodgrass, Mary Ellen

(jt. auth) Patterson, L. Indian terms of the Americas **970.004**

The **Snooks** family

In Juba this and Juba that **372.6**

The **snotty** goat. Afanas'ev, A. N.

In Afanas'ev, A. N. Russian fairy tales p200-02 **398.2**

Snow

Branley, F. M. Snow is falling (k-1)

551.57

Martin, J. B. Snowflake Bentley [biography of Wilson Alwyn Bentley] (k-3) **92**

Fiction

Briggs, R. The snowman **E**

Burton, V. L. Katy and the big snow **E**

Ehlert, L. Snowballs **E**

Henkes, K. Oh! **E**

Keats, E. J. The snowy day **E**

Neitzel, S. The jacket I wear in the snow

E

Rockwell, A. F. The first snowfall **E**

Root, P. Grandmother Winter **E**

Shulevitz, U. Snow **E**

Tresselt, A. R. White snow, bright snow **E**

Poetry

Prelutsky, J. It's snowing! It's snowing! (1-3)

811

Snow Bear. George, J. C. **E**

The **snow** bunting's lullaby. MacDonald, M. R.

In MacDonald, M. R. Look back and see p3-10 **372.6**

The **Snow-daughter** and the Fire-son

In The Yellow fairy book p206-08 **398.2**

The **snow** husband. San Souci, R.

In San Souci, R. A terrifying taste of short & shivery p58-61 **398.2**

The **snow** in Chelm. Singer, I. B.

In Singer, I. B. Zlateh the goat, and other stories p29-34 **398.2**

In Snowy day: stories and poems p25-29

808.8

Snow is falling. Branley, F. M. **551.57**

The **Snow** Queen. Bell, A. **E**

Snow valentines. Ruelle, K. G. See note under Ruelle, K. G. The Thanksgiving beast feast

E

Snow White. Poole, J. **398.2**

Snow White & Rose Red. Grimm, J. **398.2**

Snow-White and Rose-Red. Grimm, J.

In The Blue fairy book p259-65 **398.2**

Snow White and the fox. Afanas'ev, A. N.

In Afanas'ev, A. N. Russian fairy tales p283-84 **398.2**

The **snow** woman. Martin, R.

In Martin, R. Myterious tales of Japan

398.2

Snowballs. Ehlert, L. **E**

Snowboarding

Sullivan, G. Snowboarding (4 and up)

796.9

Snowbound. Lavender, D. S. **978**

Snowdrop. Grimm, J.

In The Classic Fairy tales p177-82 **398.2**

Snowflake Bentley [biography of Wilson Alwyn Bentley] Martin, J. B. **92**

The **snowman**. Andersen, H. C.

In Andersen, H. C. The swan's stories p109-21 **S C**

The **snowman**. Briggs, R. **E**

Snowshoe Thompson. Levinson, N. S. **E**

The **snowy** day. Keats, E. J. **E**

Snowy day: stories and poems (2-4) **808.8**

Snowy flowy blowy. Tafuri, N. **E**

The **snuff-box**. Sébillot, P.

In The Green fairy book p145-50 **398.2**

Snuggle wuggle. London, J. **E**

Snyder, Dianne

The boy of the three-year nap (1-3) **398.2**

Snyder, Zilpha Keatley

Cat running (4 and up)	**Fic**
The Egypt game (5 and up)	**Fic**
The headless cupid (5 and up)	**Fic**
Libby on Wednesdays (5 and up)	**Fic**
The runaways (4 and up)	**Fic**
The witches of Worm (5 and up)	**Fic**

So, Meilo

(il) The 20th century children's poetry treasury. See The 20th century children's poetry treasury **811.008**

(il) The Beauty of the beast. See The Beauty of the beast **811.008**

(il) Sierra, J. Tasty baby belly buttons

398.2

So far from the bamboo grove. Watkins, Y. K.

Fic

So far from the sea. Bunting, E. **E**

So many circles, so many squares. Hoban, T.

E

So many dynamos! and other palindromes. Agee, J. **793.73**

So what? Cohen, M. See note under Cohen, M. It's George! **E**

So you want to be president. St. George, J.

973

Soap, soap, soap

In Grandfather tales p130-36 **398.2**

Soap soup and other verses. Kuskin, K. **811**

Soaring with the wind. Gibbons, G. **598**

Sobol, Donald J., 1924-

Encyclopedia Brown and the case of Pablo's nose. See note under Sobol, D. J. Encyclopedia Brown, boy detective **Fic**

Encyclopedia Brown and the case of the dead eagles. See note under Sobol, D. J. Encyclopedia Brown, boy detective **Fic**

Encyclopedia Brown and the case of the disgusting sneakers. See note under Sobol, D. J. Encyclopedia Brown, boy detective **Fic**

Encyclopedia Brown and the case of the midnight visitor. See note under Sobol, D. J. Encyclopedia Brown, boy detective **Fic**

Encyclopedia Brown and the case of the mysterious handprints. See note under Sobol, D. J. Encyclopedia Brown, boy detective **Fic**

Encyclopedia Brown and the case of the secret pitch. See note under Sobol, D. J. Encyclopedia Brown, boy detective **Fic**

Encyclopedia Brown and the case of the sleeping dog. See note under Sobol, D. J. Encyclopedia Brown, boy detective **Fic**

Encyclopedia Brown and the case of the slippery salamander. See note under Sobol, D. J. Encyclopedia Brown, boy detective **Fic**

Encyclopedia Brown and the case of the treasure hunt. See note under Sobol, D. J. Encyclopedia Brown, boy detective **Fic**

Encyclopedia Brown and the case of the two spies. See note under Sobol, D. J. Encyclopedia Brown, boy detective **Fic**

Encyclopedia Brown, boy detective (3-5) **Fic**

Encyclopedia Brown finds the clues. See note under Sobol, D. J. Encyclopedia Brown, boy detective **Fic**

Encyclopedia Brown gets his man. See note under Sobol, D. J. Encyclopedia Brown, boy detective **Fic**

Encyclopedia Brown keeps the peace. See note under Sobol, D. J. Encyclopedia Brown, boy detective **Fic**

Encyclopedia Brown lends a hand. See note under Sobol, D. J. Encyclopedia Brown, boy detective **Fic**

Encyclopedia Brown saves the day. See note under Sobol, D. J. Encyclopedia Brown, boy detective **Fic**

Encyclopedia Brown sets the pace. See note under Sobol, D. J. Encyclopedia Brown, boy detective **Fic**

Encyclopedia Brown shows the way. See note under Sobol, D. J. Encyclopedia Brown, boy detective **Fic**

Encyclopedia Brown solves them all. See note under Sobol, D. J. Encyclopedia Brown, boy detective **Fic**

Encyclopedia Brown takes the cake! See note under Sobol, D. J. Encyclopedia Brown, boy detective **Fic**

Encyclopedia Brown takes the case. See note under Sobol, D. J. Encyclopedia Brown, boy detective **Fic**

Encyclopedia Brown tracks them down. See note under Sobol, D. J. Encyclopedia Brown, boy detective **Fic**

Soccer

Baddiel, I. Ultimate soccer (4 and up) **796.334**

Blackstone, M. This is soccer (k-2) **796.334**

Coleman, L. Fundamental soccer (5 and up) **796.334**

Gibbons, G. My soccer book (k-2) **796.334**

Hornby, H. Soccer (4 and up) **796.334**

Fiction

Avi. S.O.R. losers (5 and up) **Fic**

Soccer: the ultimate World Cup companion. See Baddiel, I. Ultimate soccer **796.334**

Social action

Hoose, P. M. It's our world, too! (5 and up) **302**

Social anthropology *See* Ethnology

Social problems

Lewis, B. A. The kid's guide to social action (4 and up) **361.2**

Social sciences

Bibliography

Notable children's trade books in the field of social studies **016.3**

Society of Friends

Kroll, S. William Penn (3-5) **92**

Fiction

Avi. Night journeys (5 and up) **Fic**

Bruchac, J. The arrow over the door (4-6) **Fic**

De Angeli, M. L. Thee, Hannah! (3-5) **Fic**

Socks. Cleary, B. **Fic**

Sod houses on the Great Plains. Rounds, G. **693**

Soda science. Zubrowski, B. **641.8**

Sody saleratus

In Juba this and Juba that **372.6**

Sody Sallyraytus

In Grandfather tales p75-80 **398.2**

Sody sallyraytus. Sierra, J.

In Sierra, J. Nursery tales around the world p41-45 **398.2**

Sody sallyrytus. MacDonald, M. R.

In MacDonald, M. R. Twenty tellable tales p79-89 **372.6**

Soentpiet, Chris K.

(il) Barron, T. A. Where is Grandpa? **E**

(il) Bradby, M. Momma, where are you from? **E**

(il) Bradby, M. More than anything else **E**

(il) Bunting, E. So far from the sea **E**

(il) McGill, A. Molly Bannaky **E**

(il) Rylant, C. Silver packages **E**

Softball

Fiction

Wolff, V. E. Bat 6 (5 and up) **Fic**

Software, Computer *See* Computer software

Soil ecology
  Bial, R. A handful of dirt (3-6)   **577.5**
  Lavies, B. Compost critters (4 and up)
      591.7

Soils
  Bial, R. A handful of dirt (3-6)   **577.5**
Sojourner Truth *See* Truth, Sojourner, d. 1883
Solar system
  Berger, M. Do stars have points? (2-4)   **523**
  Branley, F. M. The planets in our solar system
    (k-3)   **523.4**
  Branley, F. M. The sun and the solar system
    (4-6)   **523.2**
  Simon, S. Our solar system (3-6)   **523.2**
  Vogt, G. The solar system (5 and up)
      523.2

The **solar** system: an A-Z guide. Wilsdon, C.
    520.3

Solbert, Ronni
  (il) Merrill, J. The pushcart war   **Fic**
The **soldier**. Babbitt, N.
  In Babbitt, N. The Devil's other storybook
    p19-23   **S C**
The **soldier** and the king. Afanas'ev, A. N.
  In Afanas'ev, A. N. Russian fairy tales p563-
    67   **398.2**
The **soldier** and the vampire. San Souci, R.
  In San Souci, R. Short & shivery p68-72
    398.2
Soldier Jack
  In The Jack tales p172-79   **398.2**
Soldiers
  See also Women soldiers; names of coun-
  tries with the subdivision *Army—Military life*
      History
  Robertshaw, A. A soldier's life (4 and up)
      355
      United States
  McGovern, A. The secret soldier: the story of
    Deborah Sampson [Gannett] (3-5)   **92**
A **soldier's** life. Robertshaw, A.   **355**
A **soldier's** riddle. Afanas'ev, A. N.
  In Afanas'ev, A. N. Russian fairy tales p117-
    18   **398.2**
Soledad. Jiménez, F.
  In Jiménez, F. The circuit: stories from the
    life of a migrant child p9-13   **S C**
Solheim, James
  It's disgusting—and we ate it! (4-6)   **641.3**
Solid, liquid, or gas? Hewitt, S.   **530.4**
Solomon, King of Israel
      About
  Wiesel, E. King Solomon and his magic ring
    (3-5)   **222**
Somalia
  Hassig, S. M. Somalia (5 and up)   **967.73**
Soman, David
  (il) Johnson, A. Tell me a story, Mama   **E**
  (il) Johnson, A. When I am old with you
      E
  (il) Pomerantz, C. You're not my best friend
    anymore   **E**
Some frog!. Bunting, E.   **Fic**

Some of the days of Everett Anderson. Clifton, L.
  See note under Clifton, L. Everett Anderson's
  1-2-3   **E**
Some of the kinder planets [story] Wynne-Jones,
  T.
  In Wynne-Jones, T. Some of the kinder plan-
    ets: stories p101-17   **S C**
Some of the kinder planets: stories. Wynne-Jones,
  T.   **S C**
Some smug slug. Edwards, P. D.   **E**
Some things go together. Zolotow, C.   **E**
Someday a tree. Bunting, E.   **E**
Something about the author   **920.003**
Something about the author: autobiography series
    920.003
Something big has been here. Prelutsky, J.
    811
Something nasty in the kitchen. Bond, M.
  In Bond, M. Paddington's storybook p83-96
    S C
Something special for me. Williams, V. B. See
  note under Williams, V. B. A chair for my
  mother   **E**
Something upstairs. Avi   **Fic**
Sometimes I wonder if poodles like noodles.
  Numeroff, L. J.   **811**
A **son** of Adam. Jacobs, J.
  In Jacobs, J. English fairy tales p328-29
    398.2
Son of Black Stallion. Farley, W. See note under
  Farley, W. The Black Stallion   **Fic**
The **son** of the wind. Bryan, A.
  In Bryan, A. Ashley Bryan's African tales,
    uh-huh p136-71   **398.2**
Sonenklar, Carol
  Robots rising (3-5)   **629.8**
Song and dance (k-3)   **811.008**
Song and dance man. Ackerman, K.   **E**
A **song** for Croaker Nordge. Berberick, N. V.
  In A Glory of unicorns p127-43   **S C**
Song Lee and Leech Man. Kline, S. See note un-
  der Kline, S. Horrible Harry in room 2B
    Fic
Song Lee and the hamster hunt. Kline, S. See note
  under Kline, S. Horrible Harry in room 2B
    Fic
Song Lee and the "I hate you" notes. Kline, S.
  See note under Kline, S. Horrible Harry in
  room 2B   **Fic**
Song Lee in room 2B. Kline, S. See note under
  Kline, S. Horrible Harry in room 2B   **Fic**
The **song** of Mu Lan. Lee, J. M.   **398.2**
The **song** of Roland. Osborne, M. P.
  In Osborne, M. P. Favorite medieval tales
    p34-41   **398.2**
The **song** of the little hunter. Kipling, R.
  In Kipling, R. The jungle book: the Mowgli
    stories   **S C**
Song of the swallows. Politi, L.   **E**
Song of the trees. Taylor, M. D.   **Fic**

The **song** of the whales. Orlev, U.
   In Don't read this! and other tales of the un-
     natural p174-96   **S C**

Songbirds. Latimer, J. P.   **598**

Songhai Empire
   McKissack, P. C. The royal kingdoms of Ghana,
     Mali, and Songhay (5 and up)   **966.2**

Songs
     See also Carols; National songs; Spirituals
     (Songs)
   Carle, E. Today is Monday (k-3)   **782.42**
   Child, L. M. F. Over the river and through the
     wood (k-2)   **811**
   Cole, J. Fun on the run (3-5)   **793.7**
   Diez deditos. Ten little fingers & other play
     rhymes and action songs from Latin America
     (k-3)   **782.42**
   The Eentsy, weentsy spider: fingerplays and ac-
     tion rhymes   **796.1**
   Gershator, D. Bread is for eating   **E**
   Go in and out the window   **782.42**
   Guthrie, W. Howdi do (k-2)   **782.42**
   Guthrie, W. This land is your land (k-3)
     782.42
   Hillenbrand, W. Down by the station (k-2)
     782.42
   Hoberman, M. A. The eensy-weensy spider
     (k-3)   **782.42**
   Hort, L. The seals on the bus (k-2)   **782.42**
   How sweet the sound: African-American songs
     for children (k-3)   **782.42**
   Johnson, J. W. Lift every voice and sing
     782.42
   Kellogg, S. A-hunting we will go! (k-2)
     782.42
   Kovalski, M. The wheels on the bus (k-2)
     782.42
   MacDonald, M. R. The round book   **782.42**
   Mallett, D. Inch by inch (k-2)   **782.42**
   Raffi. Baby Beluga (k-2)   **782.42**
   Raffi. Down by the bay (k-2)   **782.42**
   Raffi. Five little ducks (k-2)   **782.42**
   Raffi. One light, one sun (k-2)   **782.42**
   Staines, B. All God's critters got a place in the
     choir (k-2)   **782.42**
   Whippo, W. Little white duck (k-2) **782.42**
         Fiction
   Williams, V. B. Lucky song   **E**
         Indexes
   The Children's song index, 1978-1993
     782.42
   Reid, R. Children's jukebox   **782.42**

Songs are thoughts (1-3)   **897**

Songs from the loom. Roessel, M.   **970.004**

Songs of faith. Johnson, A.   **Fic**

Songs of the Wild West   **782.42**

Songwriters *See* Composers

Sonoran Desert
   Wright-Frierson, V. A desert scrapbook (3-5)
     577.5

Sons and fathers *See* Father-son relationship

Sons and mothers *See* Mother-son relationship

Sonseray. Spinelli, J.
   In Spinelli, J. The library card   **S C**

Sootface. San Souci, R.   **398.2**

Sop doll!
   In The Jack tales p76-82   **398.2**

Sop doll. MacDonald, M. R.
   In MacDonald, M. R. When the lights go out
     p86-95   **372.6**

Sophie. Fox, M.   **E**

Sophie hits six. King-Smith, D. See note under
   King-Smith, D. Sophie's Tom   **Fic**

Sophie in the saddle. King-Smith, D. See note under King-Smith, D. Sophie's Tom   **Fic**

Sophie is seven. King-Smith, D. See note under
   King-Smith, D. Sophie's Tom   **Fic**

Sophie skates. Isadora, R.   **796.91**

Sophie's Lucky. King-Smith, D. See note under
   King-Smith, D. Sophie's Tom   **Fic**

Sophie's snail. King-Smith, D. See note under
   King-Smith, D. Sophie's Tom   **Fic**

Sophie's Tom. King-Smith, D.   **Fic**

The **sorcerer's** apprentice. Willard, N.   **811**

The **sorceress.** Afanas'ev, A. N.
   In Afanas'ev, A. N. Russian fairy tales p567-
     68   **398.2**

Sorcery *See* Magic

Sorensen, Henri, 1950-
   (il) Fitch, F. M. A book about God   **231**
   (il) Frost, R. Robert Frost   **811**

SOS math. (4 and up) See entry in Part 2: Web
   Resources

Sosa, Maria
   (ed) Exploring science in the library. See Ex-
     ploring science in the library   **027.8**

Soto, Gary
   Baseball in April, and other stories (5 and up)
     S C
   Contents: Broken chain; Baseball in April; Two dreamers;
   Barbie; The no-guitar blues; Seventh grade; Mother and daughter;
   The Karate Kid; La Bamba; The marble champ; Growing up
   Canto familiar (4-6)   **811**
   Chato and the party animals. See note under
     Soto, G. Chato's kitchen   **E**
   Chato's kitchen   **E**
   Neighborhood odes (4-6)   **811**
   Petty crimes (5 and up)   **S C**
   Contents: La güera; Mother's clothes; Try to remember; The
   boxing lesson; Your turn, Norma; The funeral suits; Little scams;
   If the shoe fits; Frankie the rooster; Born worker
   Snapshots from the wedding   **E**
   Taking sides (5 and up)   **Fic**
   These shoes of mine
     In You're on!: seven plays in English and
       Spanish p12-32   **812.008**
   Too many tamales   **E**

Souci, Daniel San *See* San Souci, Daniel

A **soucouyant** dies. Joseph, L.
   In Joseph, L. A wave in her pocket p1-5
     398.2

Souhami, Jessica
   (il) Lurie, A. The black geese   **398.2**

The **soul** cages. Philip, N.
   In Philip, N. Celtic fairy tales p113-18
     398.2

Soul looks back in wonder (3-6)   **811.008**

The **soul** of a menorah. Kimmel, E. A.
  In Kimmel, E. A. The jar of fools: eight Hanukkah stories from Chelm p35-41
                  S C

Sound
  Isadora, R. Listen to the city   E
  Pfeffer, W. Sounds all around (k-3) **534**
  Sabbeth, A. Rubber-band banjos and a java jive bass (4 and up) **781**
             Fiction
  Brown, M. W. Bunny's noisy book   E
The **sound** of work. Jaffe, N.
  In Jaffe, N. The cow of no color: riddle stories and justice tales from around the world p14-17 **398.2**

Sound recordings
          Indexes
  Reid, R. Children's jukebox **782.42**
Sounder. Armstrong, W. H.   **Fic**
Sounds all around. Pfeffer, W. **534**
Soup. Peck, R. N.   **Fic**
Soup 1776. Peck, R. N. See note under Peck, R. N. Soup **Fic**
Soup ahoy. Peck, R. N. See note under Peck, R. N. Soup **Fic**
The **soup** bone. Johnston, T.   E
Soup for president. Peck, R. N. See note under Peck, R. N. Soup **Fic**
Soup in love. Peck, R. N. See note under Peck, R. N. Soup **Fic**
Soup on wheels. Peck, R. N. See note under Peck, R. N. Soup **Fic**
Soup's hoop. Peck, R. N. See note under Peck, R. N. Soup **Fic**
South, Coleman
  Jordan (5 and up) **956.95**
South (U.S.) *See* Southern States
South Africa
  Blauer, E. South Africa (4 and up) **968**
          Fiction
  Daly, N. Jamela's dress   E
  Daly, N. Not so fast, Songololo   E
  Isadora, R. At the crossroads   E
  Lewin, H. Jafta   E
  Naidoo, B. No turning back (5 and up) **Fic**
  Sisulu, E. B. The day Gogo went to vote
                  E
    Politics and government
  Cooper, F. Mandela (2-4) **92**
      Race relations
  Cooper, F. Mandela (2-4) **92**
    Race relations—Fiction
  Naidoo, B. Chain of fire (5 and up) **Fic**
  Naidoo, B. Journey to Jo'burg (5 and up)
                 Fic
    Social life and customs
  Wilson-Max, K. Halala means welcome! (k-2)
                496
South American animals. Arnold, C. **591.9**
South Carolina
  Fradin, D. B. The South Carolina Colony (4 and up) **975.7**
  Hoffman, N. South Carolina
    In Celebrate the states **973**

Stein, R. C. South Carolina
  In America the beautiful, second series
                973
The **South** Carolina Colony. Fradin, D. B.
             975.7
South Dakota
  McDaniel, M. South Dakota
    In Celebrate the states **973**
          Fiction
  Armstrong, J. Black-eyed Susan (3-5) **Fic**
  Love, D. A. A year without rain (4 and up)
                Fic
  Turner, A. W. Grasshopper summer (4-6)
                Fic
South Pole
  See also Antarctica
Southern Rhodesia *See* Zimbabwe
Southern States
          Folklore
  See Folklore—Southern States
      Race relations
  Haskins, J. Freedom Rides (5 and up)
                323.1
Southey, Robert, 1774-1843
  The story of the three bears
    In The Classic fairy tales p201-05 **398.2**
    In The Green fairy book p234-37 **398.2**
Southwest, New *See* Southwestern States
Southwestern States
          Poetry
  Mora, P. This big sky **811**
Souza, D. M. (Dorothy M.)
  Northern lights (4-6) **538**
  Shy salamanders (4-6) **597.8**
Souza, Dorothy M. *See* Souza, D. M. (Dorothy M.)
Sovak, Jan, 1953-
  (il) Lessem, D. Dinosaurs to dodos **560**
Sovereigns *See* Kings and rulers; Queens
Soviet Union
  See also Former Soviet republics; Russia
          History
  Harvey, M. The fall of the Soviet Union (4-6)
                947
Space, Outer *See* Outer space
Space and time
          Fiction
  Conrad, P. Stonewords (5 and up) **Fic**
  Conrad, P. Zoe rising (5 and up) **Fic**
  Griffin, P. R. Switching well (5 and up)
                Fic
  Hahn, M. D. The doll in the garden (4-6)
                Fic
  Hahn, M. D. Time for Andrew (5 and up)
                Fic
  Lunn, J. L. S. The root cellar (5 and up)
                Fic
  Pearce, P. Tom's midnight garden (4 and up)
                Fic
  Peck, R. Lost in cyberspace (5 and up) **Fic**
  Wiseman, D. Jeremy Visick (5 and up) **Fic**
Space case. Marshall, E.   E
Space emergency. Cole, M. D. **629.45**

Spanish language editions—*Continued*

Waber, B. Ira sleeps over	E
Waddell, M. Can't you sleep, Little Bear?	E
Waddell, M. Owl babies	E
Wells, R. McDuff moves in	E
Whalley, P. E. S. Butterfly & moth	595.7
White, E. B. Charlotte's web	Fic
White, E. B. Stuart Little	Fic
White, E. B. The trumpet of the swan	Fic
Wildsmith, B. ABC	E
Williams, L. The little old lady who was not afraid of anything	E
Williams, V. B. A chair for my mother	E
Wood, A. The napping house	E
Zelinsky, P. O. Rumpelstiltskin	398.2
Zion, G. Harry the dirty dog	E
Zolotow, C. Mr. Rabbit and the lovely present	E

Spanish literature

Bibliography

Schon, I. Recommended books in Spanish for children and young adults, 1996 through 1999　**011.6**

Sparrow, Giles

Carbon

In The Elements [Benchmark Bks.]　**546**

Iron

In The Elements [Benchmark Bks.]　**546**

Sparrows

Fiction

Hansen, B. Caesar's antlers (5 and up)　**Fic**

Sparrow's luck!. MacDonald, M. R.

In MacDonald, M. R. Celebrate the world p162-71　**372.6**

Spastic paralysis *See* Cerebral palsy

Speaking *See* Public speaking

The **speaking** bird, the singing tree, and the golden water. Philip, N.

In Philip, N. The Arabian nights p99-112　**398.2**

The **speaking** head. Olson, A. N.

In Olson, A. N. Ask the bones: scary stories from around the world p85-91　**398.2**

Speaking up, speaking out. Otfinoski, S.　**808.5**

Speare, Elizabeth George, 1908-1994

The bronze bow (6 and up)　**Fic**

The sign of the beaver (5 and up)　**Fic**

The witch of Blackbird Pond (6 and up)　**Fic**

Special collections in libraries *See* Libraries—Special collections

Special effects in film and television. Hamilton, J.　**791.43**

A **special** fate. Gold, A. L.　**940.53**

Spectacular science (2-4)　**811.008**

Spectacular science projects series

VanCleave, J. P. Janice VanCleave's insects and spiders　**595.7**

VanCleave, J. P. Janice VanCleave's plants　**581**

VanCleave, J. P. Janice VanCleave's rocks and minerals　**552**

VanCleave, J. P. Janice VanCleave's weather　**551.5**

The **specter** from the magician's museum. See Strickland, B. John Bellairs's Lewis Barnavelt in The specter from the magician's museum　**Fic**

Spedden, Daisy Corning Stone, 1872-1950

Polar, the Titanic bear (3-6)　**910.4**

Speech disorders

Fiction

Kline, S. Mary Marony, mummy girl (2-4)　**Fic**

Lester, H. Hooway for Wodney Wat　**E**

Speed, Toby

Brave potatoes　**E**

The **speedy** messenger. Afanas'ev, A. N.

In Afanas'ev, A. N. Russian fairy tales p124-30　**398.2**

Speidel, Sandra

(il) Hill, E. S. Evan's corner　**E**

(il) Joseph, L. Coconut kind of day　**811**

Speleology *See* Caves

The **spell** of the sorcerer's skull. Bellairs, J. See note under Bellairs, J. The curse of the blue figurine　**Fic**

Spellbinder: the life of Harry Houdini. Matthews, T. L.　**92**

Spellers

Terban, M. Scholastic dictionary of spelling (4 and up)　**428**

Spells *See* Charms; Magic

Spencer, Donald D., 1931-

Illustrated computer dictionary for young people　**004**

(comp) Webster's New World dictionary of computer terms. See Webster's New World dictionary of computer terms　**004**

Spenser, Edmund, 1552?-1599

Faerie Queene; adaptation. See Hodges, M. Saint George and the dragon　**398.2**

Sperry, Armstrong, 1897-1976

Call it courage (5 and up)　**Fic**

See/See also pages in the following book(s):

Newbery Medal books, 1922-1955 p194-207　**028.5**

The **spider.** Afanas'ev, A. N.

In Afanas'ev, A. N. Russian fairy tales p75-76　**398.2 051**

Spider Sparrow. King-Smith, D.　**Fic**

Spiderology. Ross, M. E.　**595.4**

Spiders

Johnson, J. Simon & Schuster children's guide to insects and spiders (4-6)　**595.7**

Markle, S. Outside and inside spiders (2-4)　**595.4**

Parsons, A. Amazing spiders (2-4)　**595.4**

Ross, M. E. Spiderology (3-6)　**595.4**

VanCleave, J. P. Janice VanCleave's insects and spiders (4 and up)　**595.7**

Fiction

Carle, E. The very busy spider　**E**

Climo, S. The cobweb Christmas　**E**

Jukes, M. Like Jake and me (2-4)　**Fic**

Lasky, K. Show and Tell bunnies　**E**

Spowart, Robin
(il) Manushkin, F. Latkes and applesauce **E**

The **Spreaders**. Bruchac, J.
In Bruchac, J. When the Chenoo howls
398.2

Spring
Hirschi, R. Spring (k-2) **508.2**
Maass, R. When spring comes (k-2) **508.2**
Schnur, S. Spring **E**
See/See also pages in the following book(s):
Bauer, C. F. Celebrations p195-210 **808.8**
Fiction
Peters, L. W. Cold little duck, duck, duck
E
Schnur, S. Spring thaw **E**
Poetry
Alarcón, F. X. Laughing tomatoes and other
spring poems (2-4) **811**
Fletcher, R. Ordinary things (5 and up)
811

Spring break. Hurwitz, J. See note under Hurwitz,
J. Class clown **Fic**

The **spring** running. Kipling, R.
In Kipling, R. The jungle book: the Mowgli
stories **S C**

Spring thaw. Schnur, S. **E**

Springboard books [series]
Conford, E. A case for Jenny Archer **Fic**

Sprug, Joseph W., 1922-
(comp) Index to fairy tales. See Index to fairy
tales **398.2**

Spying on Miss Müller. Bunting, E. **Fic**

Spyri, Johanna, 1827-1901
Heidi (4 and up) **Fic**

Squids will be squids. Scieszka, J. **E**

The **squiggle**. Schaefer, C. L. **E**

The **squire**. Singer, I. B.
In Singer, I. B. The power of light p43-50
S C
In Singer, I. B. Stories for children p242-48
S C

Squirrels
Fiction
Cooper, H. Pumpkin soup **E**
Ehlert, L. Nuts to you! **E**
Lisle, J. T. Forest (5 and up) **Fic**
Potter, B. The tale of Squirrel Nutkin **E**
Potter, B. The tale of Timmy Tiptoes **E**

St. George, Judith, 1931-
Dear Dr. Bell—your friend, Helen Keller (5 and
up) **92**
In the line of fire (4 and up) **364.1**
Sacagawea (4-6) **92**
So you want to be president (3-6) **973**

St. Patrick's Day *See* Saint Patrick's Day

St. Pierre, Stephanie
The Muppets' big book of crafts (2-5)
745.5

St. Valentine's Day *See* Valentine's Day

St. Valentine's Day. See Bulla, C. R. The story of
Valentine's Day **394.26**

Staermose, Robert
(il) Mahy, M. Tingleberries, tuckertubs and telephones **Fic**

Stage fright. Howe, J. See note under Howe, J.
Dew drop dead **Fic**

Stahl, Ben, 1910-1987
(il) Bunting, E. Dreaming of America **E**

Staines, Bill
All God's critters got a place in the choir (k-2)
782.42

Stamm, Claus
Three strong women
In Womenfolk and fairy tales p93-105
398.2

Stammen, Jo Ellen McAllister- *See* McAllister-
Stammen, Jo Ellen

Stanek, Muriel
I speak English for my mom (2-4) **Fic**

Stangl, Jean, 1928-
Crystals and crystal gardens you can grow (4
and up) **548**

Stanley, Diane, 1909-
Michelangelo (4 and up) **92**

Stanley, Diane, 1943-
Bard of Avon: the story of William Shakespeare
(4 and up) **92**
Charles Dickens (4 and up) **92**
Cleopatra (4 and up) **92**
Joan of Arc (4 and up) **92**
Leonardo da Vinci (4 and up) **92**
Peter the Great (4 and up) **92**
Raising Sweetness. See note under Stanley, D.
Saving Sweetness **E**
Roughing it on the Oregon Trail (2-4) **Fic**
Rumpelstiltskin's daughter **E**
Saving Sweetness **E**
Shaka, king of the Zulus (4 and up) **92**
(il) Stanley, F. The last princess: the story of
Princess Ka'iulani of Hawai'i **92**
(il) Yolen, J. Sleeping ugly **E**

Stanley, Fay, 1925-1990
The last princess: the story of Princess Ka'iulani
of Hawai'i (4 and up) **92**

Stanley, Jerry, 1941-
Children of the Dust Bowl (5 and up)
371.9
Frontier merchants (4-6) **92**
Hurry freedom (5 and up) **979.4**
I am an American (5 and up) **305.8**

Stanley, Jessica Wolk- *See* Wolk-Stanley, Jessica

Stanton, Elizabeth Cady, 1815-1902
About
Fritz, J. You want women to vote, Lizzie Stan-
ton? (2-4) **92**
Fiction
McCully, E. A. The ballot box battle **E**

Star Boy. Bruchac, J.
In Bruchac, J. Flying with the eagle, racing
with the great bear p104-12 **398.2**

Star Boy. Goble, P. **398.2**

The **Star-Child**. Wilde, O.
In Wilde, O. The fairy tales of Oscar Wilde
p126-41 **S C**

The **star** fisher. Yep, L. **Fic**

Star in the storm. Harlow, J. H. **Fic**

A **star** in the window. Hark, M.
   In The Big book of Christmas plays p118-33
                       808.82

Star journey. (4 and up) See entry in Part 2: Web
   Resources

The **Star** Maiden. San Souci, R.
   In San Souci, R. Cut from the same cloth p3-
   10   **398.2**

The **star** maiden: an Ojibway tale. Esbensen, B. J.
                              398.2

Star of fear, star of hope. Hoestlandt, J.   **E**

Star of night. Paterson, K.
   In Paterson, K. Angels & other strangers:
   family Christmas stories p64-80
                              S C

Star sisters. Bruchac, J.
   In Bruchac, J. Pushing up the sky: seven native American plays for children p25-36
                              812

Star spangled banner (Song)
   Key, F. S. The Star-Spangled Banner
                         782.42
   Kroll, S. By the dawn's early light (3-5)
                         782.42

Star-taker. Wynne-Jones, T.
   In Wynne-Jones, T. Some of the kinder planets: stories p118-30   **S C**

Star Wars films
   Reynolds, D. W. Star wars: incredible cross sec-
   tions   **791.43**
   Reynolds, D. W. Star wars: the visual dictionary
                         791.43

Star wars: incredible cross sections. Reynolds, D.
   W.   **791.43**

Star wars: the visual dictionary. Reynolds, D. W.
                         791.43

StarChild. (4 and up) See entry in Part 2: Web
   Resources

Starfishes
   Fowler, A. Stars of the sea (k-3)   **593.9**
   Hurd, E. T. Starfish (k-3)   **593.9**

Stargazer to the sultan. Walker, B. K.
   In Walker, B. K. A treasury of Turkish folktales for children p98-107   **398.2**

Stark, Ken
   (il) Splear, E. L. Growing seasons   **630**

Starr, Bart, 1934-
   See/See also pages in the following book(s):
   Sullivan, G. Quarterbacks! p46-48 (5 and up)
                             920

Starring first grade. Cohen, M. See note under
   Cohen, M. It's George!   **E**

Starring Grace. Hoffman, M. See note under
   Hoffman, M. Amazing Grace   **E**

Starring Mirette and Bellini. McCully, E. A. See
   note under McCully, E. A. Mirette on the
   high wire   **E**

Starry messenger [biography of Galileo Galilei]
   Sis, P.   **92**

Stars
     See also Black holes (Astronomy); Constel-
   lations

Apfel, N. H. Orion, the Hunter (4 and up)
                         523.8
Berger, M. Do stars have points? (2-4)   **523**
Gallant, R. A. When the sun dies (6 and up)
                         523.7
Rey, H. A. Find the constellations   **523.8**
Rockwell, A. F. Our stars (k-2)   **523.8**
                Fiction
Goble, P. Her seven brothers (2-4)   **398.2**
Hort, L. How many stars in the sky?   **E**
Taylor, H. P. Coyote places the stars (k-3)
                         398.2

The **stars** in the sky. Jacobs, J.
   In Jacobs, J. English fairy tales p380-83
                         398.2

Stars of the sea. Fowler, A.   **593.9**

Starting school. Hurwitz, J.   **Fic**

Starting with nature bird book. Hickman, P. M.
                         598

State flags. Brandt, S. R.   **929.9**

State geography. (4 and up) See entry in Part 2:
   Web Resources

Statesmen
    See also Politicians

Statistics
   Information please almanac, atlas & yearbook
                         031.02
   The World almanac and book of facts
                         031.02

Statue of Liberty (New York, N.Y.)
   Curlee, L. Liberty (3-5)   **974.7**
   Maestro, B. The story of the Statue of Liberty
   (k-3)   **974.7**
                Fiction
   Bunting, E. A picnic in October   **E**

Staub, Frank J.
   America's forests (3-6)   **577.3**
   America's prairies (3-6)   **577.4**
   Children of Yucatán (3-5)   **972**
   Sea turtles (2-4)   **597.9**

Staub, Leslie, 1957-
   (il) Lives: poems about famous Americans. See
   Lives: poems about famous Americans
                       811.008

Staubach, Roger, 1942-
   See/See also pages in the following book(s):
   Sullivan, G. Quarterbacks! p30-32 (5 and up)
                             920

Stawicki, Andrew
   (il) Kenna, K. A people apart   **289.7**

Stay!. Lowry, L.   **Fic**

The **steadfast** tin soldier. Andersen, H. C.
   In Andersen, H. C. The little mermaid and
   other fairy tales p67-73   **S C**
   In Andersen, H. C. The swan's stories p27-37
                         S C
   In The Yellow fairy book p308-12   **398.2**

The **steadfast** tin soldier. Seidler, T.   **Fic**

Steal away. Armstrong, J.   **Fic**

Stealing dreams. O'Neill, R.
   In A Glory of unicorns p59-73   **S C**

Stories from Central America [series]
Rohmer, H. The invisible hunters   **398.2**

Stories from Shakespeare. McCaughrean, G.
    822.3

Stories from the Old Testament. Bible. O.T.
    221.9

Stories from the Web. (3-5) See entry in Part 2:
Web Resources

The **stories** Huey tells. Cameron, A. See note under Cameron, A. The stories Julian tells
    Fic

Stories in rhyme
Aardema, V. Bringing the rain to Kapiti Plain
(k-3)   **398.2**
Adoff, A. Black is brown is tan   E
Ahlberg, J. Each peach pear plum   E
Ahlberg, J. Peek-a-boo!   E
Alborough, J. My friend Bear   E
Appelt, K. Bats around the clock   E
Appelt, K. Bayou lullaby   E
Appelt, K. Cowboy dreams   E
Appelt, K. Oh my baby, little one   E
Aylesworth, J. Old black fly   E
Barracca, D. The adventures of Taxi Dog
    E
Bayer, J. A my name is Alice   E
Bemelmans, L. Madeline   E
Bemelmans, L. Madeline's rescue   E
Blegvad, L. First friends   E
Blos, J. W. Old Henry   E
Brown, M. W. Another important book   E
Brown, M. W. Big red barn   E
Brown, M. W. Goodnight moon   E
Bunting, E. Butterfly house   E
Bunting, E. Flower garden   E
Bunting, E. Scary, scary Halloween   E
Burleigh, R. Messenger, messenger   E
Cabrera, J. Over in the meadow   E
Carlstrom, N. W. Jesse Bear, what will you
wear?   E
Cauley, L. B. Clap your hands   E
Charlip, R. Sleepytime rhyme   E
Cleary, B. The hullabaloo ABC   E
Clifton, L. Everett Anderson's 1-2-3   E
Cummings, P. Angel baby   E
Cummings, P. Clean your room, Harvey Moon!
    E
De Regniers, B. S. What can you do with a
shoe?   E
DeFelice, C. C. Clever crow   E
Degen, B. Jamberry   E
Dragonwagon, C. Half a moon and one whole
star   E
Ehlert, L. Feathers for lunch   E
Ehlert, L. Market day   E
Ehlert, L. Nuts to you!   E
Ehlert, L. Top cat   E
Fleming, D. Barnyard banter   E
Fleming, D. In the small, small pond   E
Fleming, D. In the tall, tall grass   E
Fox, M. Sleepy bears   E
Freymann, S. One lonely sea horse   E
Gliori, D. No matter what   E
Godwin, L. Little white dog   E
Greenberg, D. Bugs!   E
Greene, R. G. Barnyard song   E

Grossman, B. My little sister ate one hare
    E
Guarino, D. Is your mama a llama?   E
Hall, J. What does the rabbit say?   E
Hamanaka, S. I look like a girl   E
Hindley, J. Eyes, nose, fingers and toes   E
Hoberman, M. A. And to think that we thought
that we'd never be friends   E
Hoberman, M. A. One of each   E
Huck, C. S. A creepy countdown   E
Hughes, S. Out and about   E
Hutchins, P. Ten red apples   E
Hutchins, P. The wind blew   E
Ivimey, J. W. The complete story of the three
blind mice   E
Kalan, R. Jump, frog, jump!   E
Kellogg, S. I was born about 10,000 years ago
    E
Koller, J. F. One monkey too many   E
Kraus, R. Whose mouse are you?   E
Kuskin, K. City dog   E
Lesser, C. Dig hole, soft mole   E
Lindbergh, R. Nobody owns the sky   E
Lobel, A. On Market Street   E
Lobel, A. The rose in my garden   E
Loomis, C. Cowboy bunnies   E
Lord, J. V. The giant jam sandwich   E
Lowery, L. Twist with a burger, jitter with a
bug   E
Mahy, M. 17 kings and 42 elephants   E
Mahy, M. A summery Saturday morning   E
Manushkin, F. The matzah that Papa brought
home   E
Martin, B. Barn dance!   E
Martin, B. A beasty story   E
Martin, B. Brown bear, brown bear what do you
see?   E
Martin, B. Chicka chicka boom boom   E
Martin, B. Polar bear, polar bear, what do you
hear?   E
Marzollo, J. Pretend you're a cat   E
McPhail, D. M. Pigs aplenty, pigs galore!
    E
Milgrim, D. Cows can't fly   E
Miranda, A. To market, to market   E
Mora, P. Uno, dos, tres: one, two, three   E
Moss, L. Zin! zin! zin! a violin   E
Neitzel, S. The bag I'm taking to Grandma's
    E
Neitzel, S. The dress I'll wear to the party
    E
Neitzel, S. The jacket I wear in the snow
    E
Newcome, Z. Toddlerobics   E
Ormerod, J. Ms MacDonald has a class   E
Paul, A. W. Hello toes! Hello feet!   E
Peet, B. Huge Harold   E
Peters, L. W. Cold little duck, duck, duck
    E
Pinczes, E. J. One hundred hungry ants   E
Plourde, L. Pigs in the mud in the middle of the
rud   E
Pomerantz, C. The piggy in the puddle   E
Rice, E. City night   E
Riley, L. A. Mouse mess   E
Rollings, S. New shoes, red shoes   E
Ryder, J. Each living thing   E

Stories in rhyme—*Continued*

Saul, C. P. Barn cat	E
Schaefer, L. M. This is the sunflower	E
Schnur, S. Night lights	E
Sendak, M. Chicken soup with rice	E
Sendak, M. Pierre	E
Seuss, Dr. And to think that I saw it on Mulberry Street	E
Seuss, Dr. The cat in the hat	E
Seuss, Dr. Green eggs and ham	E
Seuss, Dr. Hooray for Diffendoofer Day!	E
Seuss, Dr. Horton hatches the egg	E
Seuss, Dr. Horton hears a Who!	E
Seuss, Dr. How the Grinch stole Christmas	E
Seuss, Dr. If I ran the circus	E
Seuss, Dr. If I ran the zoo	E
Seuss, Dr. McElligot's pool	E
Seuss, Dr. Oh, the places you'll go!	E
Shaw, N. Sheep in a jeep	E
Shields, C. D. Martian rock	E
Siebert, D. Plane song	E
Siebert, D. Train song	E
Siebert, D. Truck song	E
Slate, J. Miss Bindergarten celebrates the 100th day of kindergarten	E
Sloat, T. Farmer Brown goes round and round	E
Sloat, T. There was an old lady who swallowed a trout	E
Small, D. George Washington's cows	E
Spinelli, E. Night shift daddy	E
Stewart, S. The library	E
Suen, A. Delivery	E
Suen, A. Window music	E
Tafuri, N. Snowy flowy blowy	E
Van Laan, N. Possum come a-knockin'	E
Van Laan, N. A tree for me	E
Walters, V. Are we there yet, Daddy?	E
Walton, R. One more bunny	E
Wells, R. Noisy Nora	E
Wells, R. Read to your bunny	E
Wells, R. Shy Charles	E
Weston, M. Space guys!	E
Williams, S. Let's go visiting	E
Winthrop, E. Shoes	E
Wise, W. Ten sly piranhas	E
Yolen, J. How do dinosaurs say goodnight?	E
Yolen, J. Off we go!	E
Young, R. Golden Bear	E
Zemach, H. The judge	E
Ziefert, H. April Fool!	E
Ziefert, H. First He made the sun	E
Ziefert, H. Hats off for the Fourth of July!	E
Ziefert, H. Train song	E

Stories in stone. Arnold, C.	**709.01**
The **stories** Julian tells. Cameron, A.	**Fic**

Stories, plots, etc.

Collections

Gillespie, J. T. Juniorplots 4	**028.5**
Gillespie, J. T. Middleplots 4	**028.5**
Stories to solve. Shannon, G.	**398.2**

Stories without words

Anno, M. Anno's counting book	E
Arnosky, J. Mouse letters	E
Arnosky, J. Mouse numbers	E
Baker, J. Window	E
Bang, M. The Grey Lady and the Strawberry Snatcher	E
Bányai, I. Re-zoom	E
Bányai, I. Zoom	E
Briggs, R. The snowman	E
Carle, E. Do you want to be my friend?	E
Geisert, A. Oink	E
Goodall, J. S. Creepy castle	E
Goodall, J. S. Shrewbettina's birthday	E
Goodall, J. S. The surprise picnic	E
Hutchins, P. Changes, changes	E
Keats, E. J. Clementina's cactus	E
Mayer, M. A boy, a dog, and a frog	E
Rohmann, E. Time flies	E
Sis, P. Dinosaur!	E
Sis, P. Ship ahoy!	E
Ward, L. K. The silver pony (2-4)	**Fic**
Weitzman, J. P. You can't take a balloon into the Metropolitan Museum	E
Weitzman, J. P. You can't take a balloon into the National Gallery	E
Wiesner, D. Free fall	E
Wiesner, D. Sector 7	E

Storks

Fiction

DeJong, M. The wheel on the school (4-6)	**Fic**
Storm in the night. Stolz, M.	E
Storm on the desert. Lesser, C.	**577.5**

Stormalong. Osborne, M. P.

In Osborne, M. P. American tall tales p37-49 **398.2**

Storms

See also Dust storms; Hurricanes; Tornadoes

Kramer, S. Eye of the storm (4 and up)	**778.9**
Simon, S. Storms (3-6)	**551.55**

See/See also pages in the following book(s):

Challoner, J. Hurricane & tornado (4 and up) **551.55**

Fiction

McBratney, S. Just you and me   E

Stormy, Misty's foal. Henry, M. See note under Henry, M. Misty of Chincoteague **Fic**

Storni, Alfonsina, 1892-1938

A dream in the road

In You're on!: seven plays in English and Spanish p100-07 **812.008**

Storr, Catherine

Crossing over

In The Oxford book of scary tales p16-21 **808.8**

The riddlemaster

In The Oxford treasury of children's stories p72-81 **S C**

A **story,** a story. Haley, G. E. **398.2**

A **story** about a darning needle. Andersen, H. C.

In The Yellow fairy book p319-21 **398.2**

Story hour. Coville, K.

In A Glory of unicorns p97-112 **S C**

The **story** of a cat. De Morgan, M.

In Christmas fairy tales p123-34 **398.2**

The **story** of a clever tailor. Grimm, J.

In The Green fairy book p324-27 **398.2**

The **story** of the powers of Congress. See Stein, R. C. The powers of Congress **328.73**

The **story** of the powers of the Supreme Court. See Stein, R. C. The powers of the Supreme Court **347**

The **Story** of the second calender, son of a king
In The Arabian nights entertainments p75-85 **398.2**

The **Story** of the second old man and of the two black dogs
In The Arabian nights entertainments p19-22 **398.2**

The **story** of the Statue of Liberty. Maestro, B. **974.7**

The **Story** of the third calender, son of a king
In The Arabian nights entertainments p102-21 **398.2**

The **story** of the three bears. Jacobs, J.
In Jacobs, J. English fairy tales p97-101 **398.2**

The **story** of the three bears. Southey, R.
In The Classic fairy tales p201-05 **398.2**
In The Green fairy book p234-37 **398.2**

The **Story** of the three calenders, sons of kings, and of five ladies of Bagdad
In The Arabian nights entertainments p54-67 **398.2**

The **story** of the three little pigs. Jacobs, J.
In Jacobs, J. English fairy tales p73-76 **398.2**

The **Story** of the vizier who was punished
In The Arabian nights entertainments p34-47 **398.2**

The **Story** of the young king of the Black Isles
In The Arabian nights entertainments p48-53 **398.2**

The **Story** of two sisters who were jealous of their young sister
In The Arabian nights entertainments p390-424 **398.2**

The **story** of Valentine's Day. Bulla, C. R. **394.26**

The **story** of Valley Forge. See Stein, R. C. Valley Forge **973.3**

Story painter: the life of Jacob Lawrence. Duggleby, J. **92**

"**Story**," the old man said. Yolen, J.
In Yolen, J. Here there be dragons p24 **810.8**

The **storytellers**. Lewin, T. **E**

The **storyteller's** beads. Kurtz, J. **Fic**

The **storyteller's** sourcebook. MacDonald, M. R. **398**

The **storyteller's** start-up book. MacDonald, M. R. **372.6**

Storytelling
Bauer, C. F. Caroline Feller Bauer's new handbook for storytellers **372.6**
Briggs, D. 52 programs for preschoolers **027.62**
Bruchac, J. Tell me a tale (5 and up) **372.6**
Carlson, A. D. Flannelboard stories for infants and toddlers **372.6**

Champlin, C. Storytelling with puppets **372.6**
Cullum, C. N. The storytime sourcebook **027.62**
Greene, E. Storytelling **372.6**
Juba this and Juba that **372.6**
MacDonald, M. R. Celebrate the world **372.6**
MacDonald, M. R. Look back and see **372.6**
MacDonald, M. R. The storyteller's start-up book **372.6**
MacDonald, M. R. Twenty tellable tales **372.6**
MacDonald, M. R. When the lights go out **372.6**
Nichols, J. Storytimes for two-year-olds **027.62**
Pellowski, A. The storytelling handbook **372.6**
Pellowski, A. The world of storytelling **372.6**
Sawyer, R. The way of the storyteller **372.6**
Shedlock, M. L. The art of the story-teller **372.6**
Sierra, J. The flannel board storytelling book **027.62**

See/See also pages in the following book(s):
Bauer, C. F. This way to books p1-59 **028.5**

Fiction
Fletcher, S. Shadow spinner (6 and up) **Fic**
Lewin, T. The storytellers **E**
Rocklin, J. Strudel stories (4 and up) **Fic**

Storytelling. Greene, E. **372.6**

The **storytelling** handbook. Pellowski, A. **372.6**

Storytelling with puppets. Champlin, C. **372.6**

The **storytime** sourcebook. Cullum, C. N. **027.62**

Storytimes for two-year-olds. Nichols, J. **027.62**

Stott, Carole
Night sky (3-5) **520**

Stowe, Harriet Beecher, 1811-1896
About
Fritz, J. Harriet Beecher Stowe and the Beecher preachers (5 and up) **92**
See/See also pages in the following book(s):
Faber, D. Great lives: American literature p68-78 (5 and up) **920**

Straightening the mind of Tadadaho. Bruchac, J.
In Bruchac, J. Tell me a tale p71-76 **372.6**

Stranded at Plimoth Plantation, 1626. Bowen, G. **974.4**

The **strange** case of Dr. Jekyll and Mr. Hyde. Stevenson, R. L. **Fic**

Strange creatures. Lester, J.
In Lester, J. When the beginning began p18-24 **296.1**

A **strange** encounter. Terada, A. M.
    In Terada, A. M. Under the starfruit tree p95-98   **398.2**

The **strange** journey of Rabbi Joshua Ben Levi. Jaffe, N.
    In Jaffe, N. The mysterious visitor p77-84   **398.2**

Strange mysteries from around the world. Simon, S.   **001.9**

The **strange** visitor. Jacobs, J.
    In Jacobs, J. English fairy tales p177-80   **398.2**

The **strange** visitor. MacDonald, M. R.
    In MacDonald, M. R. When the lights go out p133-42   **372.6**

The **stranger**. Van Allsburg, C.   **E**

A **stranger** at Green Knowe. Boston, L. M. See note under Boston, L. M. The children of Green Knowe   **Fic**

A **stranger** came ashore. Hunter, M.   **Fic**

Strangers on the shore. Wynne-Jones, T.
    In Wynne-Jones, T. Some of the kinder planets: stories p49-65   **S C**

Stratospheric ozone *See* Ozone layer

Strauss, Lindy *See* Edwards, Linda

Stravinsky, Igor, 1882-1971
    See/See also pages in the following book(s):
    Krull, K. Lives of the musicians p74-77 (4 and up)   **920**

The **Straw** ox
    In Tomie dePaola's favorite nursery tales p75-82   **398.2**

Strawberries
Fiction
Bang, M. The Grey Lady and the Strawberry Snatcher   **E**
Bruchac, J. The first strawberries (k-3)   **398.2**

The **strawberries** of the little men. MacDonald, M. R.
    In MacDonald, M. R. Look back and see p95-102   **372.6**

Stray. Rylant, C.
    In Rylant, C. Every living thing p42-47   **S C**

Streams to the river, river to the sea. O'Dell, S.   **Fic**

Street, Emmet *See* Behan, Brendan, 1923-1964

Street, Michael
    (jt. auth) Cole, J. Fun on the run   **793.7**
    (jt. auth) Cole, J. Marbles   **796.2**

Street people *See* Homeless persons

Street railroads
    See also Cable railroads

Streets of gold [biography of Mary Antin] Wells, R.   **92**

Strega Nona: an old tale. De Paola, T.   **E**

Strega Nona: her story. De Paola, T. See note under De Paola, T. Strega Nona: an old tale   **E**

Strega Nona meets her match. De Paola, T. See note under De Paola, T. Strega Nona: an old tale   **E**

Strega Nona takes a vacation. De Paola, T. See note under De Paola, T. Strega Nona: an old tale   **E**

Strega Nona's magic lessons. De Paola, T. See note under De Paola, T. Strega Nona: an old tale   **E**

Streissguth, Thomas
    Rocket man: the story of Robert Goddard (4 and up)   **92**

The **strength** of these arms. Bial, R.   **326**

Stretching ourselves. Carter, A. R.   **362.4**

Strickland, Brad
    The beast under the wizard's bridge. See note under Strickland, B. John Bellair's Lewis Barnavelt in The specter from the magicians museum   **Fic**
    The bell, the book and the spellbinder. See note under Strickland, B. The hand of the necromancer   **Fic**
    The hand of the necromancer (5 and up)   **Fic**
    John Bellairs's Lewis Barnavelt in The specter from the magician's museum (5 and up)   **Fic**
    The tower at the end of the world. See note under Strickland, B. John Bellair's Lewis Barnavelt in The specter from the magicians museum   **Fic**
    The wrath of the grinning ghost. See note under Strickland, B. The hand of the necromancer   **Fic**

Strickland, Tessa
    (comp) One earth, one spirit. See One earth, one spirit   **242**

Strider. Cleary, B.   **Fic**

Strikes
    Bartoletti, S. C. Kids on strike! (5 and up)   **331.8**
Fiction
McCully, E. A. The bobbin girl (3-5)   **Fic**

Striking it rich. Krensky, S.   **979.4**

String beans. Hurwitz, J.
    In Bauer, C. F. Celebrations p65-67   **808.8**

String figures
    Gryski, C. Cat's cradle, owl's eyes (4-6)   **793.9**
Fiction
Fleischman, P. Lost!   **Fic**

A **string** in the harp. Bond, N.   **Fic**

Stringbean's trip to the shining sea. Williams, V. B.   **E**

Stringer, Lauren
    (il) Ray, M. L. Red rubber boot day   **E**

Strong as Annie Christmas. Cohn, A.
    In From sea to shining sea p277-79   **810.8**

Strong but quirky: the birth of Davy Crockett. Shapiro, I.
    In From sea to shining sea p85-87   **810.8**

Strong to the hoop. Coy, J.   **E**

Stronger than time. Wrede, P. C.
    In Wrede, P. C. Book of enchantments p153-83   **S C**

The **strongest** one. Bruchac, J.
  In Bruchac, J. Pushing up the sky: seven native American plays for children p79-90
      812

Stroud, Virginia A.
  (il) Bruchac, J. The story of the Milky Way
      398.2

Structural engineering
  Wilkinson, P. Building (4 and up)   **690**

Strudel stories. Rocklin, J.   **Fic**

Strugnell, Ann
  (il) Cameron, A. The stories Julian tells
      Fic

Stuart-Clark, Christopher
  (ed) The New Oxford treasury of children's poems. See The New Oxford treasury of children's poems   **808.81**
  (ed) The Oxford book of animal poems. See The Oxford book of animal poems
      808.81
  (ed) The Oxford book of Christmas poems. See The Oxford book of Christmas poems
      808.81
  (comp) The Oxford treasury of children's stories. See The Oxford treasury of children's stories   **S C**

Stuart Little. White, E. B.   **Fic**

The **stubborn** wife. Afanas´ev, A. N.
  In Afanas´ev, A. N. Russian fairy tales p280
      398.2

A **student** in magic. Schwartz, H.
  In Schwartz, H. A journey to paradise and other Jewish tales p28-31   **398.2**

Student resource center junior. (4-8) See entry in Part 2: Web Resources

Stupid's cries. Jacobs, J.
  In Jacobs, J. English fairy tales p409-12
      398.2

Sturges, Philemon
  Bridges are to cross (2-4)   **624**
  The Little Red Hen (makes a pizza) (k-3)
      398.2

Sturla, the historian
  In Shedlock, M. L. The art of the story-teller p161-64   **372.6**

Sturm, Brian W.
  (jt. auth) MacDonald, M. R. The storyteller's sourcebook   **398**

Stuve-Bodeen, Stephanie, 1965-
  Elizabeti's doll   **E**
  Mama Elizabeti. See note under Stuve-Bodeen, S. Elizabeti's doll   **E**

Subject catalogs
  Subject guide to Children's books in print
      015.73

Subject guide to Children's books in print
      015.73

Subject headings
  Sears list of subject headings   **025.4**
  Subject headings for children   **025.4**

Subject headings for children   **025.4**

Subject index to Children's Magazines. See Children's Magazine Guide   **051**

Submarine diving
  Earle, S. A. Dive! (4-6)   **551.46**

Submarine exploration *See* Underwater exploration

Submarines
      Fiction
  Verne, J. 20,000 leagues under the sea (5 and up)   **Fic**

Submersibles
  Kovacs, D. Dive to the deep ocean (4 and up)
      623.8

Subsidies
  Grantsmanship for small libraries and school library media centers   **025.1**

Substance abuse *See* Drug abuse

Subtraction
  Leedy, L. Subtraction action (k-3)   **513**
  Murphy, S. J. Elevator magic (k-2)   **513**

Subtraction action. Leedy, L.   **513**

Subway sparrow. Torres, L.   **E**

Subways
  See/See also pages in the following book(s):
  Macaulay, D. Underground p93-107 (4 and up)
      624.1
      Fiction
  Holman, F. Slake's limbo (6 and up)   **Fic**
  Torres, L. Subway sparrow   **E**

Succoth (Feast of Tabernacles) *See* Sukkoth

Sudan
  Levy, P. M. Sudan (5 and up)   **962.4**

Suen, Anastasia
  Delivery   **E**
  Window music   **E**

Suffrage
  See also Women—Suffrage

Sugar
  See also Maple sugar

Sugar was my best food. Peacock, C. A.
      362.1

Sugaring. Haas, J.   **E**

Sugihara, Chiune *See* Sugihara, Sempo, 1900-1986

Sugihara, Sempo, 1900-1986
      About
  Gold, A. L. A special fate (5 and up)
      940.53
  Mochizuki, K. Passage to freedom (3-6)
      940.53

Suicide
  See/See also pages in the following book(s):
  Fry, V. L. Part of me died, too p133-58 (5 and up)   **155.9**

Suitcase. Walter, M. P.   **Fic**

Sukey and the mermaid. San Souci, R.   **398.2**

Sukkoth
      Fiction
  Polacco, P. Tikvah means hope   **E**

Sulfur *See* Sulphur

Sullivan, Sir Arthur, 1842-1900
  See/See also pages in the following book(s):
  Krull, K. Lives of the musicians p58-61 (4 and up)   **920**

Sullivan, Edward T.
The Holocaust in literature for youth
        016.94053

Sullivan, George
All about hockey (5 and up)   **796.962**
Quarterbacks! (5 and up)   **920**
Snowboarding (4 and up)   **796.9**
To the bottom of the sea (5 and up)
        551.46

Sullivan, Otha Richard, 1941-
African American inventors (5 and up)   **920**

Sulphur
Beatty, R. Sulfur
In The Elements [Benchmark Bks.]   **546**

Sultanate of Oman *See* Oman

Sumerians
See/See also pages in the following book(s):
Moss, C. Science in ancient Mesopotamia (4 and up)   **509**

Summer
Hirschi, R. Summer (k-2)   **508.2**
Kurelek, W. A prairie boy's summer (3-5)
        971.27
Fiction
Hesse, K. Come on, rain!   **E**
Mahy, M. A summery Saturday morning   **E**
Poetry
Alarcón, F. X. From the bellybutton of the moon and other summer poems (2-4)
        811

Summer camps *See* Camps

Summer fun!. Williamson, S.   **790.1**

Summer ice. McMillan, B.   **508**

The **summer** my father was ten. Brisson, P.
        E

Summer of fire. Lauber, P.   **577.2**

Summer of my German soldier. Greene, B.
        Fic

The **summer** of the swans. Byars, B. C.   **Fic**

The **Summer** Olympics. Knotts, B.   **796.48**

Summer reading is killing me!. Scieszka, J. See note under Scieszka, J. Knights of the kitchen table   **Fic**

A **summer** to die. Lowry, L.   **Fic**

Summer with Elisa. Hurwitz, J. See note under Hurwitz, J. Rip-roaring Russell   **Fic**

A **summery** Saturday morning. Mahy, M.   **E**

Sun
Branley, F. M. The sun and the solar system (4-6)   **523.2**
Gallant, R. A. When the sun dies (6 and up)
        523.7
Gibbons, G. Sun up, sun down (k-3)   **523.7**
Fiction
Daly, N. Why the Sun & Moon live in the sky (k-3)   **398.2**
Dayrell, E. Why the Sun and the Moon live in the sky (k-3)   **398.2**
Tafuri, N. What the sun sees   **E**

Sun (in religion, folklore, etc.) *See* Sun worship

Sun & Spoon. Henkes, K.   **Fic**

Sun and Moon. Lester, J.
In Lester, J. When the beginning began p11-17   **296.1**

The **sun** and the solar system. Branley, F. M.
        523.2

The **sun** is so quiet. Giovanni, N.   **811**

Sun, moon, and stars. Hoffman, M.   **398.2**

The **Sun,** the Moon, and the Raven. Afanas'ev, A. N.
In Afanas'ev, A. N. Russian fairy tales p588-89   **398.2**

Sun up, sun down. Gibbons, G.   **523.7**

Sun worship
Baylor, B. The way to start a day (1-4)
        291.4

Sundiata *See* Keita, Soundiata, d. 1255

Sundiata. Wisniewski, D.   **92**

The **sunflower** family. Winner, C.   **583**

Sunflowers
Fiction
Schaefer, L. M. This is the sunflower   **E**

Sunken treasure. Gibbons, G.   **910.4**

Sun's son. McCaughrean, G.
In McCaughrean, G. The bronze cauldron: myths and legends of the world p82-86
        398.2

Sunwing. Oppel, K.   **Fic**

Super Cluck. O'Connor, J.   **E**

Super science concoctions. Hauser, J. F.
        507.8

Superfudge. Blume, J. See note under Blume, J. Tales of a fourth grade nothing   **Fic**

Supermarket. Hamley, D.
In The Oxford book of scary tales p106-11
        808.8

Supermarket Thanksgiving. Bauer, C. F.
In Thanksgiving: stories and poems p57-68
        810.8

Supermarkets
Friedhoffer, R. Science lab in a supermarket (5 and up)   **507.8**

Supernatural
Fiction
Cooper, S. The Boggart (4-6)   **Fic**
Ellis, S. Back of beyond (6 and up)   **S C**
Farmer, N. A girl named Disaster (6 and up)
        Fic
Fleischman, P. Graven images (6 and up)
        S C
The Oxford book of scary tales (5 and up)
        808.8
Pullman, P. Clockwork (4 and up)   **Fic**
Thompson, K. Switchers (6 and up)   **Fic**
Vaughan, M. Whistling Dixie   **E**
Wiseman, D. Jeremy Visick (5 and up)   **Fic**
Poetry
Prelutsky, J. Monday's troll (2-5)   **811**

Superstition
Fiction
Babbitt, N. Kneeknock Rise (4-6)   **Fic**

Supreme Court (U.S.) *See* United States. Supreme Court

Supriya's bowl. Krishnaswami, U.
In Krishnaswami, U. Shower of gold: girls and women in the stories of India p108-12   **398.2**

Surfing

Fiction

Blake, Q. Mrs. Armitage and the big wave   **E**

The **surprise** family. Reiser, L.   **E**

The **surprise** garden. Hall, Z.   **E**

The **surprise** picnic. Goodall, J. S.   **E**

Surprises (k-2)   **811.008**

Survival after airplane accidents, shipwrecks, etc.

Fiction

Moeri, L. Save Queen of Sheba (4 and up)   **Fic**

Steig, W. Abel's island (3-5)   **Fic**

Taylor, T. The cay (5 and up)   **Fic**

Taylor, T. Timothy of the cay (5 and up)   **Fic**

Wyss, J. D. The Swiss family Robinson (5 and up)   **Fic**

Susanna and Simon. San Souci, R.
In San Souci, R. Cut from the same cloth p43-48   **398.2**

Susannah and the elders. Jaffe, N.
In Jaffe, N. The cow of no color: riddle stories and justice tales from around the world p40-46   **398.2**

Susie. Schwartz, A.
In Schwartz, A. Ghosts! p13-19   **398.2**

Sutcliff, Rosemary, 1920-1992
Black ships before Troy (5 and up)   **883**
The light beyond the forest (4 and up)   **398.2**
The road to Camlann (4 and up)   **398.2**
The sword and the circle (4 and up)   **398.2**
The wanderings of Odysseus (5 and up)   **883**

Sutcliffe, Justin
(il) Calmenson, S. Rosie   **636.7**

Suteev, V. (Vladimir)
Arnold, K. Me too!   **E**
Ginsburg, M. The chick and the duckling   **E**

Suteev, Vladimir *See* Suteev, V. (Vladimir)

Suteyev, V. *See* Suteev, V. (Vladimir)

Sutherland, Zena, 1915-
Children and books   **028.5**
(ed) The Best in children's books. See The Best in children's books   **028.1**
(comp) The Orchard book of nursery rhymes. See The Orchard book of nursery rhymes   **398.8**

Svarney, Patricia Barnes- *See* Barnes-Svarney, Patricia

Swahili language
Feelings, M. Jambo means hello   **E**
Feelings, M. Moja means one   **E**
Wilson-Max, K. Furaha means happy (k-2)   **496**

Swallowed alive. San Souci, R.
In San Souci, R. Short & shivery p84-87   **398.2**

Swallows

Fiction

Politi, L. Song of the swallows   **E**

Swamp, Jake, 1941-
Giving thanks (k-3)   **299**

Swamp Angel. Isaacs, A.   **E**

Swamps *See* Marshes; Wetlands

Swan lake (Ballet)
See/See also pages in the following book(s):
McCaughrean, G. The Random House book of stories from the ballet p7-17 (4 and up)   **792.8**
Newman, B. The illustrated book of ballet stories p42-51 (4-6)   **792.8**

Swan Lake. Isadora, R.   **E**

Swan song. Marshall, J.
In Marshall, J. Rats on the roof, and other stories p49-53   **S C**

Swans

Fiction

Edwards, P. D. Honk!   **E**
Pinkney, J. The ugly duckling   **E**

The **swan's** stories. Andersen, H. C.   **S C**

Sweden

Fiction

Beskow, E. Pelle's new suit   **E**
Lindgren, A. Pippi Longstocking (3-6)   **Fic**

Swedish Americans

Fiction

Sandin, J. The long way westward   **E**

Sweeney, Joan, 1930-
Me and my amazing body (k-2)   **611**

Sweet, Melissa
(il) Appelt, K. Bats around the clock   **E**
(il) Blast off! See Blast off!   **811.008**
(il) Howe, J. Pinky and Rex   **E**
(il) Kilborne, S. S. Leaving Vietnam   **959.704**
(il) Knight, J. Charlotte in Giverny   **Fic**
(il) On Christmas Day in the morning. See On Christmas Day in the morning   **782.28**
(il) Thimmesh, C. Girls think of everything   **920**

The **sweet** and sour animal book. Hughes, L.   **811**

Sweet Betsey from Pike. San Souci, R.
In San Souci, R. Cut from the same cloth p57-64   **398.2**

Sweet Clara and the freedom quilt. Hopkinson, D.   **E**

Sweet corn. Stevenson, J.   **811**

Sweet dream pie. Wood, A.   **E**

Sweet victory: Lance Armstrong's incredible journey. Stewart, M.   **92**

Sweeter than honey, purer than oil. Kimmel, E. A.
In Kimmel, E. A. The jar of fools: eight Hanukkah stories from Chelm p9-12   **S C**

The **sweetest** fig. Van Allsburg, C.   **E**

The **sweethearts**. Andersen, H. C.
In Andersen, H. C. The little mermaid and other fairy tales p81-83 **S C**

Sweetwater, Jesse, 1952-
(il) Sierra, J. The dancing pig **398.2**

Swenson, May, 1919-1989
The complete poems to solve (5 and up) **811**

Swift, Hildegarde Hoyt, d. 1977
The little red lighthouse and the great gray bridge **E**

Swift, Jonathan, 1667-1745
Gulliver's travels; adaptation. See Hodges, M. Gulliver in Lilliput **Fic**

Swift as the wind. Esbensen, B. J. **599.75**

A **swiftly** tilting planet. L'Engle, M. See note under L'Engle, M. A wrinkle in time **Fic**

Swimming
Biography
Adler, D. A. America's champion swimmer: Gertrude Ederle (2-4) **92**
Fiction
Kessler, L. P. Last one in is a rotten egg **E**
London, J. Froggy learns to swim **E**

Swimmy. Lionni, L. **E**

Swinburne, Stephen R.
Coyote (4-6) **599.77**
Once a wolf (4 and up) **333.95**
Safe, warm, and snug (k-3) **591.56**

Swine Lake. Marshall, J. **E**

The **swineherd**. Andersen, H. C. **Fic**
also in The Classic fairy tales p232-35 **398.2**
also in Shedlock, M. L. The art of the story-teller p235-42 **372.6**
also in The Yellow fairy book p249-53 **398.2**

The **Swiss** family Robinson. Wyss, J. D. **Fic**

Switch on, switch off. Berger, M. **537**

Switcharound. Lowry, L. **Fic**

Switchers. Thompson, K. **Fic**

Switching well. Griffin, P. R. **Fic**

Switzerland
Fiction
Creech, S. Bloomability (5 and up) **Fic**
Spyri, J. Heidi (4 and up) **Fic**
Legends
See Legends—Switzerland

Swope, Sam
Gotta go! Gotta go! **E**

The **sword**. Alexander, L.
In Alexander, L. The foundling and other tales of Prydian p53-62 **S C**

The **sword** and the circle. Sutcliff, R. **398.2**

The **sword** in the stone. Osborne, M. P.
In Osborne, M. P. Favorite medieval tales p17-24 **398.2**

The **sword** in the stone. White, T. H. **Fic**

The **sword** in the tree. Bulla, C. R. **Fic**

Sword of the samurai. Kimmel, E. A. **S C**

The **sword-seller**. Wrede, P. C.
In Wrede, P. C. Book of enchantments p96-127 **S C**

Sylvada, Peter
(il) Schuch, S. A symphony of whales **E**

Sylvain and Jocosa. Caylus, A. C. P. de T., comte de
In The Green fairy book p56-63 **398.2**

Sylvester and the magic pebble. Steig, W. **E**
also in The Read-aloud treasury p112-34 **808.8**

Sylvia Long's Mother Goose **398.8**

Sylvie and Bruno. Carroll, L.
In Carroll, L. The complete works of Lewis Carroll p251-456 **828**

Sylvie and Bruno concluded. Carroll, L.
In Carroll, L. The complete works of Lewis Carroll p457-674 **828**

Symbolism of numbers
See also Numbers

Symbols *See* Signs and symbols

Symes, R. F.
Crystal & gem (4 and up) **548**
Rocks & minerals (4 and up) **549**

Symons, Ann K.
Protecting the right to read **323.44**

A **symphony** of whales. Schuch, S. **E**

Szabo, Corinne
Sky pioneer: a photobiography of Amelia Earhart (4 and up) **92**

Szilagyi, Mary
(il) Rylant, C. Night in the country **E**
(il) Rylant, C. This year's garden **E**

T

Taback, Simms, 1932-
Joseph had a little overcoat **E**
There was an old lady who swallowed a fly **782.42**
(il) Hall, K. Snakey riddles **793.73**
(il) Hennessy, B. G. Road builders **625.7**
(il) McGovern, A. Too much noise **398.2**
(il) Ziefert, H. When I first came to this land **782.42**
See/See also pages in the following book(s):
The Newbery & Caldecott medal books, 1986-2000 p332-42 **028.5**

Tabernacles, Feast of *See* Sukkoth

Table, chair, bear. Feder, J. **413**

Table etiquette
Lauber, P. What you never knew about fingers, forks, & chopsticks (2-4) **394.1**

Tableware
Lauber, P. What you never knew about fingers, forks, & chopsticks (2-4) **394.1**

Tackle without a team. Christopher, M. **Fic**

Tacky and the emperor. Lester, H. See note under Lester, H. Three cheers for Tacky **E**

Tacky in trouble. Lester, H. See note under Lester, H. Three cheers for Tacky **E**

Tacky the penguin. Lester, H. See note under Lester, H. Three cheers for Tacky   E

Tadpoles *See* Frogs

Tadpoles. James, B.   E

Tafuri, Nancy
 Counting to Christmas   E
 Have you seen my duckling?   E
 Snowy flowy blowy   E
 Spots, feathers, and curly tails   E
 This is the farmer   E
 What the sun sees   E
 (il) Pomerantz, C. If I had a paka   811

Tagholm, Sally
 The rabbit (2-4)   599.3

Tahiti (French Polynesia)
 NgCheong-Lum, R. Tahiti (5 and up)   996

The tail. Philip, N.
 In Philip, N. Celtic fairy tales p[140]
  398.2

The tailor of Gloucester. Potter, B.   E

Tailoring
   Fiction
 Potter, B. The tailor of Gloucester   E

The tailypo. Galdone, J.   398.2

Tailypo. San Souci, R.
 In San Souci, R. Short & shivery p58-61
  398.2

Taino Indians
   Fiction
 Dorris, M. Morning Girl (4-6)   Fic

'Tain't so
 In Diane Goode's book of scary stories & songs p22-25   398.2

Takahashi, Denise Y.
 (il) Pandell, K. Journey through the northern rainforest   578.7

Takaya, Julia
 (jt. auth) Brenner, B. Chibi   598

Take a look around. Varriale, J.   770

Take off!. Hunter, R. A.   629.13

Taking care of Carruthers. Marshall, J. See note under Marshall, J. Yummers!   E

Taking charge. Levitin, S. See note under Levitin, S. Nine for California   E

Taking sides. Soto, G.   Fic

Talbott, Hudson
 Excalibur (3-5)   398.2
 King Arthur and the Round Table (3-5)
  398.2
 O'Sullivan stew   E

Tale of a tadpole. Porte, B. A.   E

Tale of a tadpole. Wallace, K.   597.8

Tale of a tail. Bodnar, J. Z.   E

The tale of a youth who set out to learn what fear was. Grimm, J.
 In The Blue fairy book p86-95   398.2

The tale of Benjamin Bunny. Potter, B. See note under Potter, B. The tale of Peter Rabbit
  E

The tale of Custard the Dragon. Nash, O.
  811

The tale of Jemima Puddle-duck. Potter, B.
  E

The tale of Mr. Jeremy Fisher. Potter, B.   E

The tale of Mr. Tod. Potter, B. See note under Potter, B. The tale of Peter Rabbit   E

The tale of Mrs. Tiggy-Winkle. Potter, B.   E

The tale of Mrs. Tittlemouse. Potter, B.   E

The tale of Peter Rabbit. Potter, B.   E

The tale of Pigling Bland. Potter, B.   E

The tale of Rabbit and Coyote. Johnston, T.
  398.2

The tale of Squirrel Nutkin. Potter, B.   E

The tale of the flopsy bunnies. Potter, B. See note under Potter, B. The tale of Peter Rabbit
  E

The tale of the mandarin ducks. Paterson, K.
  398.2

The tale of the three wishes. Le Prince de Beaumont, Madame
 In The Classic fairy tales p153-55   398.2

The tale of the turnip. Alderson, B.   398.2

A tale of three wishes. Singer, I. B.
 In Singer, I. B. Stories for children p8-14
  S C

The tale of Timmy Tiptoes. Potter, B.   E

The tale of Tom Kitten. Potter, B. See note under Potter, B. The story of Miss Moppet   E

The tale of two bad mice. Potter, B.   E

A tale of two chickens. Schwartz, H.
 In Schwartz, H. The diamond tree p65-70
  398.2

Tales from Moominvalley. Jansson, T. See note under Jansson, T. Moominsummer madness
  Fic

Tales from Shakespeare. Lamb, C.   822.3

Tales of a Chinese grandmother. Carpenter, F.
  398.2

Tales of a fourth grade nothing. Blume, J.
  Fic

Tales of Amanda Pig. Van Leeuwen, J. See note under Van Leeuwen, J. Tales of Oliver Pig
  E

Tales of Oliver Pig. Van Leeuwen, J.   E

Tales of the haunted deep. Guiberson, B. Z.
  001.9

The tales of Uncle Remus. Lester, J. See note under Lester, J. The last tales of Uncle Remus
  398.2

Taliesin
   Fiction
 Bond, N. A string in the harp (6 and up)
  Fic

Talismans *See* Charms

Talk. Courlander, H.
 In Courlander, H. Cow-tail switch, and other West African stories p25-30   398.2

Talk to me. Avi
 In Avi. What do fish have to do with anything? and other stories p61-91   S C

Talking books *See* Audiobooks

The **talking** cooter. Hamilton, V.
In Hamilton, V. The people could fly: American black folktales p151-55
398.2

The **talking** eggs. San Souci, R.   398.2

Talking like the rain (k-3)   821.008

The **talking** mule. Hurston, Z. N.
In From sea to shining sea p224-25
810.8

The **talking** taniwha of Rotorua. Te Kanawa, K.
In Te Kanawa, K. Land of the long white cloud p51-60   398.2

Talking to dragons. Wrede, P. C. See note under Wrede, P. C. Dealing with dragons   Fic

Talking to the sun: an illustrated anthology of poems for young people   808.81

Talking walls. Knight, M. B.   909

Talking walls: the stories continue. Knight, M. B.
909

Talking with adventurers (4-6)   920

Talking with artists [I-III] (4 and up)   741.6

TalkTalk. Konigsburg, E. L.   028.5

Tall cornstalk
In Grandfather tales p186-94   398.2

Tall tales
Fleischman, S. Here comes McBroom! (3-5)
Fic
Isaacs, A. Swamp Angel   E
Kellogg, S. I was born about 10,000 years ago
E
Kellogg, S. Mike Fink (k-3)   398.2
Kellogg, S. Paul Bunyan (k-3)   398.2
Kellogg, S. Pecos Bill (k-3)   398.2
Kellogg, S. Sally Ann Thunder Ann Whirlwind Crockett (k-3)   398.2
McKissack, P. C. A million fish—more or less
E
Nolen, J. Harvey Potter's balloon farm   E
Oppel, K. Peg and the whale   E
Osborne, M. P. American tall tales (3-6)
398.2
Rounds, G. Washday on Noah's ark   E
San Souci, R. Cut from the same cloth (4-6)
398.2
Walker, P. R. Big men, big country (4-6)
398.2
Williams, S. Library Lil   E
Wood, A. The Bunyans   E
Wood, A. Sweet dream pie   E

Tallchief, Maria
Tallchief (3-5)   92

Tallyho, Pinkerton!. Kellogg, S. See note under Kellogg, S. Pinkerton, behave!   E

Tam and Cam. Terada, A. M.
In Terada, A. M. Under the starfruit tree p23-34   398.2

Tam Lin. Cooper, S.   398.2

Tam Lin. Yolen, J.   398.2

Tamarins
See/See also pages in the following book(s):
Patent, D. H. Back to the wild p40-49 (4-6)
639.9

The **taming** of the shrew. Afanas´ev, A. N.
In Afanas´ev, A. N. Russian fairy tales p161-62   398.2

Tamlane. Jacobs, J.
In Jacobs, J. English fairy tales p375-79
398.2

Tanaka, Shelley
Graveyards of the dinosaurs (4-6)   567.9
Lost temple of the Aztecs (4 and up)   972
Secrets of the mummies (4 and up)   393
(jt. auth) Beattie, O. Buried in ice   998

A **tangled** tale. Carroll, L.
In Carroll, L. The complete works of Lewis Carroll p882-969   828

Tanks (Military science) *See* Military tanks

The **tanners**. Fisher, L. E.   675

Tanning
Fisher, L. E. The tanners (4 and up)   675

Tantie's callaloo fete. Joseph, L.
In Joseph, L. The mermaid's twin sister: more stories from Trinidad p40-48   398.2

Tanya and Emily in a dance for two. Gauch, P. L. See note under Gauch, P. L. Dance, Tanya
E

Tanya and the magic wardrobe. Gauch, P. L. See note under Gauch, P. L. Dance, Tanya   E

Tanzania
Heale, J. Tanzania (5 and up)   967.8
Fiction
Mollel, T. M. My rows and piles of coins
E
Stuve-Bodeen, S. Elizabeti's doll   E
Poetry
Grimes, N. Is it far to Zanzibar? (2-4)   811

Taoism
See/See also pages in the following book(s):
Osborne, M. P. One world, many religions p63-69 (4 and up)   291

Tap dancing
Glover, S. Savion!: my life in tap (5 and up)
92

Tapahonso, Luci, 1953-
Navajo ABC   E

Tape recordings, Audio *See* Sound recordings

Tape recordings, Video *See* Videotapes

Tappin, the land turtle. Hamilton, V.
In Hamilton, V. The people could fly: American black folktales p20-25
398.2

Tar Beach. Ringgold, F.   E

Taran Wanderer. Alexander, L. See note under Alexander, L. The book of three   Fic

A **tarantula** in my purse. George, J. C.   92

Tarkenton, Fran, 1940-
See/See also pages in the following book(s):
Sullivan, G. Quarterbacks! p33-35 (5 and up)
920

Tarkenton, Francis A. *See* Tarkenton, Fran, 1940-

Tashjian, Virginia A.
(comp) Juba this and Juba that. See Juba this and Juba that   372.6

Tashkent. Wynne-Jones, T.
    In Wynne-Jones, T. Some of the kinder planets: stories p36-48   **S C**
Tashlik. Singer, I. B.
    In Singer, I. B. Stories for children p322-31   **S C**
Taste
    Cobb, V. Your tongue can tell (3-6)   **612.8**
Taste. Pringle, L. P.
    In Pringle, L. P. Explore your senses   **612.8**
A **taste** of blackberries. Smith, D. B.   **Fic**
Tasty baby belly buttons. Sierra, J.   **398.2**
Tate, Eleanora E., 1948-
    The secret of Gumbo Grove. See note under Tate, E. E. Thank you, Dr. Martin Luther King, Jr.!   **Fic**
    Thank you, Dr. Martin Luther King, Jr.! (4 and up)   **Fic**
Tattercoats. Jacobs, J.
    In Jacobs, J. English fairy tales p281-85   **398.2**
Taulbert, Clifton L.
    Little Cliff and the porch people   **E**
Tauss, Herbert
    (il) Schnur, S. The shadow children   **Fic**
Taxi. Maestro, B.   **E**
A **Taxi** Dog Christmas. Barracca, D. See note under Barracca, D. The adventures of Taxi Dog   **E**
Taylor, Barbara, 1954-
    Arctic & Antarctic (4 and up)   **998**
Taylor, Cheryl Munro
    (il) Song and dance. See Song and dance   **811.008**
Taylor, Harriet Peck
    Brother Wolf (k-3)   **398.2**
    Coyote places the stars (k-3)   **398.2**
    When Bear stole the chinook (k-3)   **398.2**
Taylor, Harry
    (il) Lindsay, W. Prehistoric life   **560**
Taylor, Kim
    (il) Burton, R. Egg   **591.4**
Taylor, Maureen, 1955-
    Through the eyes of your ancestors (4 and up)   **929**
Taylor, Mildred D.
    The friendship (4 and up)   **Fic**
    The gold Cadillac (4 and up)   **Fic**
    Let the circle be unbroken (4 and up)   **Fic**
    Mississippi bridge (4 and up)   **Fic**
    The road to Memphis (4 and up)   **Fic**
    Roll of thunder, hear my cry (4 and up)   **Fic**
    Song of the trees (4 and up)   **Fic**
    The well (4 and up)   **Fic**
    See/See also pages in the following book(s):
    Newbery and Caldecott Medal books, 1976-1985 p21-34   **028.5**
Taylor, Paul D., 1953-
    Fossil (4 and up)   **560**
Taylor, Sydney, 1904-1978
    All-of-a-kind family (4-6)   **Fic**

All-of-a-kind family downtown. See note under Taylor, S. All-of-a-kind family   **Fic**
All-of-a-kind family uptown. See note under Taylor, S. All-of-a-kind family   **Fic**
Ella of all of a kind family. See note under Taylor, S. All-of-a-kind family   **Fic**
More all-of-a-kind family. See note under Taylor, S. All-of-a-kind family   **Fic**
Taylor, Theodore, 1921-
    The cay (5 and up)   **Fic**
    Timothy of the cay (5 and up)   **Fic**
    The trouble with Tuck (5 and up)   **Fic**
    Tuck triumphant. See note under Taylor, T. The trouble with Tuck   **Fic**
Tayzanne
    In The Magic orange tree, and other Haitian folktales p57-63   **398.2**
Tchaikovsky, Peter Ilich, 1840-1893
    See/See also pages in the following book(s):
    Krull, K. Lives of the musicians p54-57 (4 and up)   **920**
Te Kanawa, Kiri
    Land of the long white cloud (3-6)   **398.2**
    Contents: The birth of Maui; Maui and the Great Fish; Maui tames the Sun; Kupe's discovery of Aotearoa; Hinemoa and Tutanekai; Kahukura and the fairies; The talking taniwha of Rotorua; Te Kanawa and the visitors by firelight; Mataora and Niwareka in the Underworld; The enchanted hunting-ground; The trees of the forest; Lake Te Anau; Hotu-puku; Putawai; Rona and the legend of the moon; Hutu and Pare; The ground parrot and the albatross; Kakariki and kaka; Maui and the birds
Tea for ten. Anderson, L.   **E**
The **tea** server from heaven. Terada, A. M.
    In Terada, A. M. Under the starfruit tree p83-87   **398.2**
Tea with milk. Say, A.   **E**
Teach us, Amelia Bedelia. Parish, P. See note under Parish, P. Amelia Bedelia   **E**
Teacher tamer. Avi
    In Avi. What do fish have to do with anything? and other stories p93-119   **S C**
Teachers
    Houston, G. My great-aunt Arizona   **E**
    Fiction
    Allard, H. Miss Nelson is missing!   **E**
    Borden, L. Good luck, Mrs. K!   **E**
    Clements, A. The Landry News (4-6)   **Fic**
    Naylor, P. R. The agony of Alice (5 and up)   **Fic**
    Polacco, P. Thank you, Mr. Falker   **E**
    Priceman, M. Emeline at the circus   **E**
    Shreve, S. R. The flunking of Joshua T. Bates (3-5)   **Fic**
Teacher's pet. Hurwitz, J. See note under Hurwitz, J Class clown   **Fic**
Teaching
    Fisher, L. E. The schoolmasters (4 and up)   **371.1**
    Aids and devices—Periodicals
    MultiMedia schools   **371.305**
Teaching at home *See* Home schooling
Teaching Children Mathematics   **510.7**
Teaching information & technology skills. Eisenberg, M.   **025.5**
Teaching K-8   **372.05**

Teaching Pre-K-8. See Teaching K-8   372.05

Teague, Mark, 1963-
How I spent my summer vacation   E
One Halloween night   E
Pigsty   E
(il) King-Smith, D. Three terrible trins   Fic
(il) Rylant, C. Poppleton   E
(il) Wood, A. Sweet dream pie   E
(il) Yolen, J. How do dinosaurs say goodnight?   E

Teammates [biography of Jackie Robinson] Golenbock, P.   92

Tearing down the unicorns. Simner, J. L.
In A Glory of unicorns p31-42   S C

Teatime. Delacre, L.
In Delacre, L. Salsa stories p37-43   S C

Technology
Barnes-Svarney, P. The New York Public Library science desk reference (5 and up)   500
Biesty, S. Stephen Biesty's incredible cross-sections (4 and up)   600
Contact Kids   505
Macaulay, D. The new way things work (4 and up)   600
Dictionaries
The New book of popular science   503

Technology and literature See Literature and technology

Teddy bears
Fiction
Alborough, J. My friend Bear   E
Butler, D. My brown bear Barney   E
Freeman, D. Corduroy   E

Teen age See Adolescence

Teenagers
See also Runaway teenagers
Books and reading—Bibliography
Denman-West, M. W. Children's literature: a guide to information sources   011.6

Teenagers' library services See Young adults' libraries

Teeny-tiny. Jacobs, J.
In Jacobs, J. English fairy tales p63-64   398.2

Teeny-Tiny and the witch-woman. Walker, B. K.
In Walker, B. K. A treasury of Turkish folktales for children p49-51   398.2

A **teeny,** tiny baby. Schwartz, A.   E

The **teeny-tiny** woman. Galdone, P.   398.2

The **teeny-tiny** woman. Schwartz, A.
In Schwartz, A. Ghosts! p46-59   398.2

The **Teeny** Weeny Bop. MacDonald, M. R.
In MacDonald, M. R. Look back and see p147-56   372.6

Teeth
Keller, L. Open wide (k-3)   617.6
Showers, P. How many teeth? (k-1)   612.3
Silverstein, A. Tooth decay and cavities (3-5)   617.6
Fiction
McPhail, D. M. The bear's toothache   E
Simms, L. Rotten teeth   E

Folklore
Beeler, S. B. Throw your tooth on the roof (k-3)   398

The **teeth.** Schwartz, A.
In Schwartz, A. In a dark, dark room, and other scary stories p10-17   398.2

Tehanu. Le Guin, U. K. See note under Le Guin, U. K. A wizard of Earthsea   Fic

Telander, Todd
(il) Lauber, P. Earthworms: underground farmers   592

Telecommunication
See also Electronic mail systems

Telegraph
See also Cipher and telegraph codes

Telekinesis See Psychokinesis

Telemarking See Skiing

Telephone
Gearhart, S. The telephone (4 and up)   621.385

Telescopes
See also Hubble Space Telescope

Television
See/See also pages in the following book(s):
Bauer, C. F. Celebrations p211-26   808.8
Equipment and supplies
See also Video recording

Television actors See Actors

Television in the snow. Rettich, M.
In Bauer, C. F. Celebrations p218-20   808.8

Tell, William
About
Early, M. William Tell   398.2
Fisher, L. E. William Tell (k-3)   398.2

Tell me a Mitzi. Segal, L. G.   E

Tell me a story, Mama. Johnson, A.   E

Tell me a tale. Bruchac, J.   372.6

Tell me again about the night I was born. Curtis, J. L.   E

Tell them we remember. Bachrach, S. D.   940.53

Telling time. Older, J.   529

Telling time with Big Mama Cat. Harper, D.   E

Temko, Florence
Traditional crafts from Africa (4 and up)   745.5
Traditional crafts from Mexico and Central America (4 and up)   745.5
Traditional crafts from native North America (4 and up)   745.5

Temperance
See also Prohibition

Temperate forest. Kaplan, E.   577.3

Temperton, John
(il) Rowan, P. Big head!   612.8

The **tempest.** Beneduce, A.   822.3

Temple, Frances, 1945-1995
Grab hands and run (6 and up)   Fic
The Ramsay scallop (6 and up)   Fic

Thane, Adele
A Christmas carol
In The Big book of Christmas plays p277-97
808.82

Little Cosette and Father Christmas
In The Big book of Christmas plays p313-31
808.82

Thank you, Amelia Bedelia. Parish, P. See note under Parish, P. Amelia Bedelia **E**

Thank you, Dr. Martin Luther King, Jr.!. Tate, E. E. **Fic**

Thank you, Jackie Robinson. Cohen, B. **Fic**

Thank you, Mr. Falker. Polacco, P. **E**

Thanksgiving. Hurwitz, J.
In Thanksgiving: stories and poems p29-40
810.8

Thanksgiving at our house. Watson, W. **E**

Thanksgiving at the Tappletons'. Spinelli, E.
E

The **Thanksgiving** beast feast. Ruelle, K. G.
E

Thanksgiving Day
Barth, E. Turkeys, Pilgrims, and Indian corn (3-6) **394.26**
Gibbons, G. Thanksgiving Day (k-3)
394.26
Thanksgiving: stories and poems **810.8**
See/See also pages in the following book(s):
Bauer, C. F. Celebrations p241-48 **808.8**
Fiction
Alcott, L. M. An old-fashioned Thanksgiving (3-5) **Fic**
Bunting, E. How many days to America?
E
Cohen, B. Molly's pilgrim **E**
Cowley, J. Gracias, the Thanksgiving turkey
E
Hoban, L. Silly Tilly's Thanksgiving dinner
E
McCully, E. A. An outlaw Thanksgiving **E**
Rockwell, A. F. Thanksgiving Day **E**
Ruelle, K. G. The Thanksgiving beast feast
E
Spinelli, E. Thanksgiving at the Tappletons'
E
Watson, W. Thanksgiving at our house **E**
Poetry
Carlstrom, N. W. Thanksgiving Day at our house (k-2) **811**
Child, L. M. F. Over the river and through the wood (k-2) **811**
Prelutsky, J. It's Thanksgiving (1-3) **811**
Thanksgiving Day. Fisher, D. C.
In Bauer, C. F. Celebrations p243-48
808.8
In Thanksgiving: stories and poems p11-22
810.8
Thanksgiving Day. Rockwell, A. F. **E**
Thanksgiving Day at our house. Carlstrom, N. W.
811
Thanksgiving: stories and poems **810.8**
Thapar, Valmik
Tiger (3-5) **599.75**

Tharlet, Eve
(il) Luciani, B. How will we get to the beach?
E

"That I see, but this I sew". San Souci, R.
In San Souci, R. Even more short & shivery p29-32 **398.2**

That one, Anansi. Hamilton, V.
In Hamilton, V. A ring of tricksters p47-51
398.2

That sweet diamond. Janeczko, P. B. **811**

That's mine, Horace. Keller, H. See note under Keller, H. Horace **E**

Thayer, Ernest Lawrence, 1863-1940
Casey at the bat **811**

Thayer, Jane, 1904-
The popcorn dragon **E**
The puppy who wanted a boy **E**

The, Tjong Khing, 1933-
(il) Don't read this! and other tales of the unnatural. See Don't read this! and other tales of the unnatural **S C**

Theater

See also Acting
Fiction
Blackwood, G. L. The Shakespeare stealer (5 and up) **Fic**
Hoffman, M. Amazing Grace **E**
Horowitz, A. The Devil and his boy (5 and up)
Fic

Production and direction
Bentley, N. Putting on a play (4-6) **792**

Theatrical costume *See* Costume

Thee, Hannah!. De Angeli, M. L. **Fic**

The **theft** of fire. Curry, J. L.
In Curry, J. L. Back in the beforetime p33-41
398.2

Their names to live. Ashabranner, B. K.
959.704

Thelen, Mary
(il) Broekel, R. Hocus pocus: magic you can do
793.8

Theo. Harrison, B. **Fic**

There is a carrot in my ear, and other noodle tales. Schwartz, A. **398.2**

There was an old lady who swallowed a fly. Taback, S. **782.42**

There was an old lady who swallowed a trout. Sloat, T. **E**

There's a dead person following my sister around. Vande Velde, V. **Fic**

There's a dragon in my sleeping bag. Howe, J.
E

There's a girl in my hammerlock. Spinelli, J.
Fic

There's a monster under my bed. Howe, J. See note under Howe, J. There's a dragon in my sleeping bag **E**

There's a nightmare in my closet. Mayer, M.
E

There's an alligator under my bed. Mayer, M. See note under Mayer, M. There's a nightmare in my closet **E**

There's an owl in the shower. George, J. C.
            Fic

There's still time. Galan, M. A.   **333.95**

Thermal waters *See* Geothermal resources

These happy golden years. Wilder, L. I. See note under Wilder, L. I. Little house in the big woods   **Fic**

These shoes of mine. Soto, G.
 In You're on!: seven plays in English and Spanish p12-32   **812.008**

Theseus (Greek mythology)
 Fisher, L. E. Theseus and the Minotaur (3-5)
             292

 Hutton, W. Theseus and the Minotaur (3-5)
             292

 See/See also pages in the following book(s):
 Colum, P. The Golden Fleece and the heroes who lived before Achilles p219-44 (5 and up)
             292

 Hamilton, E. Mythology p209-23 (6 and up)
             292

Theseus and the Minotaur. Fisher, L. E. **292**

Theseus and the Minotaur. Hutton, W. **292**

They saw the future. Krull, K.   **133.3**

They shaped the game. Jacobs, W. J. **920**

They swim the seas. Simon, S.   **578.7**

They walk the earth. Simon, S.   **591.56**

They're off!. Harness, C.   **383**

The **thief**. Afanas'ev, A. N.
 In Afanas'ev, A. N. Russian fairy tales p590-93   **398.2**

The **thief**. Turner, M. W.   **Fic**

The **thief** and the pig. Jaffe, N.
 In Jaffe, N. The cow of no color: riddle stories and justice tales from around the world p28-31   **398.2**

Thief of hearts. Yep, L.   **Fic**

Thieves
      Fiction
 Fleischman, S. Bandit's moon (4-6) **Fic**
 Fleischman, S. The ghost on Saturday night (3-5)   **Fic**
 Fleischman, S. The whipping boy (5 and up)
            Fic
 Garfield, L. Smith (6 and up)   **Fic**
 Lindgren, A. Ronia, the robber's daughter (4-6)
            Fic
 Steig, W. The real thief (3-5)   **Fic**
 Turner, M. W. The Queen of Attolia (6 and up)
            Fic
 Turner, M. W. The thief (6 and up) **Fic**
 Ungerer, T. The three robbers   **E**

Thimmesh, Catherine
 Girls think of everything (5 and up) **920**

The **thing** in the woods. San Souci, R.
 In San Souci, R. More short & shivery p134-38   **398.2**

The **thing** that bothered Farmer Brown. Sloat, T. See note under Slote, T. Farmer Brown goes round and round   **E**

Things that go bump in the night. Windham, K. T.
 In From sea to shining sea p340-41
           810.8

Think of a word. Aiken, J.
 In The Oxford treasury of children's stories p82-90   **S C**

Thinking *See* Thought and thinking

Thirteen moons on a turtle's back. Bruchac, J.
            811

Thirteen ways to sink a sub. Gilson, J. See note under Gilson, J. 4B goes wild   **Fic**

The **thirteenth** clue. See Jonas, A. The 13th clue
             E

The **thirteenth** floor. See Fleischman, S. The 13th floor   **Fic**

This big sky. Mora, P.   **811**

This for that. Aardema, V.   **398.2**

This is our Seder. Hildebrandt, Z. **296.4**

This is soccer. Blackstone, M. **796.334**

This is the farmer. Tafuri, N.   **E**

This is the house that Jack built. Sierra, J.
 In Sierra, J. Nursery tales around the world p59-63   **398.2**

This is the sunflower. Schaefer, L. M. **E**

This land is your land. Guthrie, W. **782.42**

This next New Year. Wong, J. S.   **E**

This one and that one. Sanfield, S.
 In Sanfield, S. The adventures of High John the Conqueror   **398.2**

This time, Tempe Wick? Gauch, P. L. **Fic**

This way to books. Bauer, C. F.   **028.5**

This year's garden. Rylant, C.   **E**

Thomas, à Becket, Saint, Archbishop of Canterbury, 1118?-1170
 See/See also pages in the following book(s):
 Brooks, P. S. Queen Eleanor: independent spirit of the medieval world p82-86, 90-95 (6 and up)   **92**

Thomas, Dylan, 1914-1953
 A child's Christmas in Wales   **828**

Thomas, Jane Resh, 1936-
 The comeback dog (3-5)   **Fic**
 Saying good-bye to Grandma   **E**

Thomas, Joyce Carol
 Brown honey in broomwheat tea (k-3) **811**
 Gingerbread days (k-3)   **811**
 I have heard of a land   **E**

Thomas, Shelley Moore
 Good night, Good Knight   **E**

Thomas, Valerie
 See/See also pages in the following book(s):
 Thimmesh, C. Girls think of everything (5 and up)   **920**

Thomas, W. Jenkyn (William Jenkyn)
 Arthur in the cave
 In Shedlock, M. L. The art of the story-teller p173-78   **372.6**

Thomas, William Jenkyn *See* Thomas, W. Jenkyn (William Jenkyn)

Thomas Edison and electricity. Parker, S. **92**

Thomassie, Tynia
 Feliciana Feydra LeRoux   **E**

Tim and Charlotte. Ardizzone, E. See note under Ardizzone, E. Little Tim and the brave sea captain **E**

Tim and Ginger. Ardizzone, E. See note under Ardizzone, E. Little Tim and the brave sea captain **E**

Tim in danger. Ardizzone, E. See note under Ardizzone, E. Little Tim and the brave sea captain **E**

Tim O'Toole and the wee folk. McDermott, G. **E**

Tim to the rescue. Ardizzone, E. See note under Ardizzone, E. Little Tim and the brave sea captain **E**

Timbuktu (Mali) See Tombouctou (Mali)

Time
  See also Day; Night
  Branley, F. M. Keeping time (4-6) **529**
  Duffy, T. The clock (4 and up) **681.1**
  Hewitt, S. Time (k-3) **529**
  Maestro, B. The story of clocks and calendars (3-6) **529**
  Older, J. Telling time (k-3) **529**
  Skurzynski, G. On time (4 and up) **529**
    Fiction
  Harper, D. Telling time with Big Mama Cat **E**

Time. Courlander, H.
  In Courlander, H. Cow-tail switch, and other West African stories p73-78 **398.2**

Time and space See Space and time

Time flies. Rohmann, E. **E**

Time for Andrew. Hahn, M. D. **Fic**

The **time** garden. Eager, E. See note under Eager, E. Half magic **Fic**

Time of wonder. McCloskey, R. **E**

Time quest book [series]
  Ballard, R. D. Exploring the Titanic **910.4**
  Beattie, O. Buried in ice **998**

Time to sleep. Fleming, D. **E**

Time train. Fleischman, P. **E**

Time-traveling twins [series]
  Stanley, D. Roughing it on the Oregon Trail **Fic**

Time Warp Trio [series]
  Scieszka, J. Knights of the kitchen table **Fic**

Timmons, Dan
  (il) Patterson, L. Indian terms of the Americas **970.004**

Timmy. Prince, A.
  In The Oxford book of scary tales p79-83 **808.8**

Timothy of the cay. Taylor, T. **Fic**

Tim's friend Towser. Ardizzone, E. See note under Ardizzone, E. Little Tim and the brave sea captain **E**

The **tin** woodsman of Oz. Baum, L. F. See note under Baum, L. F. The Wizard of Oz **Fic**

The **tinder** box. Andersen, H. C.
  In The Classic fairy tales p207-15 **398.2**
  In The Oxford treasury of children's stories p55-63 **S C**
  In The Yellow fairy book p265-73 **398.2**

The **tinderbox.** Andersen, H. C.
  In Andersen, H. C. The little mermaid and other fairy tales p19-26 **S C**

Ting Lan and the lamb. Carpenter, F.
  In Carpenter, F. Tales of a Chinese grandmother p66-71 **398.2**

Tingleberries, tuckertubs and telephones. Mahy, M. **Fic**

The **tiniest** giants. Dingus, L. **567.9**

Tinkelman, Murray, 1933-
  (il) Dinosaurs: poems. See Dinosaurs: poems **811.008**

The **tinker** and the ghost. MacDonald, M. R.
  In MacDonald, M. R. When the lights go out p69-78 **372.6**

Tiny goes to the library. Meister, C. See note under Meister, C. Tiny's bath **E**

Tiny Mouse goes traveling. MacDonald, M. R.
  In MacDonald, M. R. Look back and see p130-36 **372.6**

The **tiny,** tiny boy and the big, big cow. Van Laan, N. **398.2**

Tiny's bath. Meister, C. **E**

Tiny's hat. Grifalconi, A. **E**

Titanic (Steamship)
  Ballard, R. D. Exploring the Titanic (4 and up) **910.4**
  Blos, J. W. The heroine of the Titanic: a tale both true and otherwise of the life of Molly Brown (k-3) **92**
  Marschall, K. Inside the Titanic (4 and up) **910.4**
  Spedden, D. C. S. Polar, the Titanic bear (3-6) **910.4**

  See/See also pages in the following book(s):
  Archbold, R. Deep-sea explorer: the story of Robert Ballard, discoverer of the Titanic (6 and up) **92**
  Hill, C. M. Robert Ballard (5 and up) **92**

Titch. Hutchins, P. **E**

Titherington, Jeanne, 1951-
  Pumpkin, pumpkin **E**
  (il) Prelutsky, J. It's snowing! It's snowing! **811**

Titty Mouse and Tatty Mouse. Jacobs, J.
  In Jacobs, J. English fairy tales p81-84 **398.2**

Tituba
    Fiction
  Petry, A. L. Tituba of Salem Village (6 and up) **Fic**

Tituba of Salem Village. Petry, A. L. **Fic**

Tlingit Indians
    Fiction
  Wisniewski, D. The wave of the Sea-Wolf **E**

To be a slave. Lester, J. **326**

To bigotry, no sanction. Fisher, L. E. **296**

To every season. Zalben, J. B.   **641.5**

To every thing there is a season. Bible. O.T. Ecclesiastes   **223**

To have and to hold. Jiménez, F.
In Jiménez, F. The circuit: stories from the
life of a migrant child p96-112   **S C**

To hold this ground. Beller, S. P.   **973.7**

To market, to market. Miranda, A.   **E**

To the bottom of the sea. Sullivan, G.
          551.46

To the top of the world. Brandenburg, J.
          599.77

To your good health!
In Shedlock, M. L. The art of the story-teller
p183-90   **372.6**

The **toad**. Andersen, H. C.
In Andersen, H. C. The little mermaid and
other fairy tales p121-28   **S C**

Toad is the uncle of heaven. Lee, J. M.
          398.2

Toad Woman. Bruchac, J.
In Bruchac, J. When the Chenoo howls
          398.2

Toads
Clarke, B. Amazing frogs & toads (2-4)
          597.8

Fiction
Brown, R. Toad   **E**
Coville, B. Jennifer Murdley's toad (4-6)
          Fic
Lee, J. M. Toad is the uncle of heaven (k-3)
          398.2
Lobel, A. Frog and Toad are friends   **E**
Porte, B. A. Tale of a tadpole   **E**
Yolen, J. Commander Toad and the voyage
home (1-3)   **Fic**

Toads and diamonds. Perrault, C.
In The Blue fairy book p274-77   **398.2**

Toad's trick. Aardema, V.
In Aardema, V. Misoso p59-61   **398.2**

Tobacco habit
Pringle, L. P. Smoking (5 and up)   **362.29**

Tobago *See* Trinidad and Tobago

Tobe killed a bear
In Stockings of buttermilk: American folktales
p88-90   **398.2**

Tobin, Nancy
(il) Adler, D. A. Fraction fun   **513**
(il) Adler, D. A. How tall, how short, how faraway   **530.8**
(il) Adler, D. A. Shape up!   **516**

The **Toboggan-to-the-moon** dream of the Potato
Face Blind Man. Sandburg, C.
In Sandburg, C. Rootabaga stories pt 1 p46-
50   **S C**
In Sandburg, C. The Sandburg treasury p29-
30   **818**

Today is Monday. Carle, E.   **782.42**

Today was a terrible day. Giff, P. R. See note under Giff, P. R. Watchout, Ronald Morgan!
          E

Todd, Mary Ellen, 1843-1924
Fiction
Van Leeuwen, J. Bound for Oregon (4-6)
          Fic

Toddler time. Simon, F.   **821**

Toddlerobics. Newcome, Z.   **E**

Toddlerobics animal fun. Newcome, Z. See note
under Newcome, Z. Toddlerobics   **E**

Toddy, Irving
(il) Bunting, E. Cheyenne again   **E**

Todo o nada. MacDonald, M. R.
In MacDonald, M. R. Celebrate the world
p24-29   **372.6**

Toft, Lis
(il) Cameron, A. Gloria's way   **Fic**

Toilets, toasters & telephones. Rubin, S. G.
          683

Tolan, Stephanie S., 1942-
Save Halloween! (5 and up)   **Fic**

Tolkien, J. R. R. (John Ronald Reuel), 1892-
1973
The hobbit (4 and up)   **Fic**

Tolkien, John Ronald Reuel *See* Tolkien, J. R. R.
(John Ronald Reuel), 1892-1973

Toll, Nelly S., 1935-
Behind the secret window (6 and up)
          940.53

The **toll-bridge** troll. Wolff, P. R.   **E**

Toltecs
See also Aztecs

Tom. De Paola, T.   **E**

Tom and Pippo and the bicycle. Oxenbury, H. See
note under Oxenbury, H. Pippo gets lost
          E

Tom and Pippo go for a walk. Oxenbury, H. See
note under Oxenbury, H. Pippo gets lost
          E

Tom and Pippo on the beach. Oxenbury, H. See
note under Oxenbury, H. Pippo gets lost
          E

Tom and Pippo read a story. Oxenbury, H. See
note under Oxenbury, H. Pippo gets lost
          E

Tom and Pippo's day. Oxenbury, H. See note under Oxenbury, H. Pippo gets lost   **E**

Tom goes to kindergarten. Wild, M.   **E**

Tom Hickathrift. Jacobs, J.
In Jacobs, J. English fairy tales p264-70
          398.2

Tom Thumb. Watson, R. J.   **398.2**

Tom Tit Tot. Jacobs, J.
In Jacobs, J. English fairy tales p13-20
          398.2

Tom Treverrow and the Knackers. Climo, S.
In Climo, S. Magic & mischief p35-44
          398.2

Tomás and the library lady. Mora, P.   **E**

Tomatoes
See/See also pages in the following book(s):
Johnson, S. A. Tomatoes, potatoes, corn, and
beans p84-94 (6 and up)   **641.3**

Trillion (The number)
Schwartz, D. M. How much is a million?
E

Trimble, Stephen, 1950-
(il) Dewey, J. Mud matters **553.6**
Trinidad and Tobago
Folklore
See Folklore—Trinidad and Tobago
Poetry
Joseph, L. Coconut kind of day **811**
The **trip**. Keats, E. J. See note under Keats, E. J.
Louie **E**
Trivas, Irene
(il) Blume, J. The one in the middle is the green
kangaroo **E**
(il) Blume, J. The Pain and the Great One
E
(il) Lyon, G. E. One lucky girl **E**
Trivia *See* Curiosities and wonders
Trivizas, Eugene, 1946-
The three little wolves and the big bad pig
E

Trojan War
Colum, P. The Trojan War and the adventures
of Odysseus (4 and up) **883**
Sutcliff, R. Black ships before Troy (5 and up)
883
See/See also pages in the following book(s):
Hamilton, E. Mythology p197-342 (6 and up)
292

The **Trojan** War and the adventures of Odysseus.
Colum, P. **883**
The **troll** with no heart in his body. Lunge-Larsen,
L.
In Lunge-Larsen, L. The troll with no heart in
his body and others tales of trolls from
Norway p77-87 **398.2**
The **troll** with no heart in his body and other tales
of trolls from Norway. Lunge-Larsen, L.
398.2
The **trolley** to yesterday. Bellairs, J. See note un-
der Bellairs, J. The curse of the blue figurine
Fic
The **trolls**. Horvath, P. **Fic**
Trombley, Richard
(il) Kelly, E. J. Paper airplanes **745.592**
Tropical memories. Belpré, P.
In You're on!: seven plays in English and
Spanish p34-41 **812.008**
Tropical rain forest. Stille, D. R. **577.3**
Tropical rain forests *See* Rain forests
Trouble River. Byars, B. C. **Fic**
The **trouble** with cats. Freeman, M. **Fic**
Trouble with trolls. Brett, J. **E**
The **trouble** with Tuck. Taylor, T. **Fic**
Troubling a star. L'Engle, M. See note under
L'Engle, M. Meet the Austins **Fic**
Trousers Mehmet and the sultan's daughter.
Walker, B. K.
In Walker, B. K. A treasury of Turkish folk-
tales for children p91-96 **398.2**
Truck. Crews, D. **E**

Truck song. Siebert, D. **E**
Trucks
Barton, B. Trucks (k-1) **629.224**
Crews, D. Truck **E**
Hennessy, B. G. Road builders (k-2) **625.7**
Llewellyn, C. Truck (k-3) **629.224**
Robbins, K. Trucks (k-2) **629.224**
Simon, S. Seymour Simon's book of trucks
(k-3) **629.224**
Sis, P. Trucks, trucks, trucks **E**
Stille, D. R. Trucks (2-4) **629.224**
Fiction
Floca, B. Five trucks **E**
Merrill, J. The pushcart war (5 and up)
Fic
Siebert, D. Truck song **E**
Trucks. Robbins, K. **629.224**
Trucks. Stille, D. R. **629.224**
Trucks, trucks, trucks. Sis, P. **E**
True book [series]
Brimner, L. D. E-mail **004.6**
Brimner, L. D. Jupiter **523.4**
Brimner, L. D. Neptune **523.4**
Brimner, L. D. Pluto **523.4**
Brimner, L. D. Saturn **523.4**
Brimner, L. D. Uranus **523.4**
Brimner, L. D. The World Wide Web
004.6
Ditchfield, C. Wrestling **796.8**
Fazio, W. Saudi Arabia **953.8**
Flanagan, A. K. The Pueblos **970.004**
January, B. Ireland **941.5**
Kalbacken, J. The food pyramid **613.2**
Kalbacken, J. Vitamins and minerals **613.2**
Kazunas, C. The Internet for kids **004.6**
Knotts, B. Martial arts **796.8**
Knotts, B. The Summer Olympics **796.48**
Knotts, B. Track and field **796.42**
Knotts, B. Weightlifting **796.41**
Landau, E. Apples **634**
Landau, E. Corn **633.1**
Landau, E. Electric fish **597**
Landau, E. France **944**
Landau, E. Jellyfish **593.5**
Landau, E. Piranhas **597**
Landau, E. Sea horses **597**
Landau, E. Wheat **633.1**
Petersen, D. Australia **994**
Stille, D. R. Deserts **577.5**
Stille, D. R. Grasslands **577.4**
Stille, D. R. Oceans **551.46**
Stille, D. R. Tropical rain forest **577.3**
Stille, D. R. Trucks **629.224**
The **true** confessions of Charlotte Doyle. Avi
Fic
The **true** enchanter. Alexander, L.
In Alexander, L. The foundling and other
tales of Prydian p29-38 **S C**
True knowledge. Philip, N.
In Philip, N. The Arabian nights p113-15
398.2
True north. Lasky, K. **Fic**
The **true-or-false** book of cats. Lauber, P.
636.8

The **true-or-false** book of horses. Lauber, P.
636.1

The **true** spirit of a festival day. Shedlock, M. L.
In Shedlock, M. L. The art of the story-teller
p225-28 **372.6**

The **true** story of the 3 little pigs. Scieszka, J.
E

The **true** tale of Johnny Appleseed. Hodges, M.
92

Truesdell, Sue
(il) Byars, B. C. The Golly sisters go West
E
(il) Clements, A. Circus family dog **E**
(il) George, J. C. How to talk to your dog
636.7
(il) Little, J. Hey world, here I am! **811**
(il) Robins, J. Addie meets Max **E**
(il) Schwartz, A. And the green grass grew all
around **398.2**

Trumbauer, Lisa
Homework help for kids on the Net (4 and up)
004.6

The **trumpet** of the swan. White, E. B. **Fic**

Truong Ba and the butcher's skin. Terada, A. M.
In Terada, A. M. Under the starfruit tree p75-
77 **398.2**

Trust your children. West, M. I. **323.44**

Trusty John. Grimm, J.
In The Blue fairy book p296-303 **398.2**

Truth, Sojourner, d. 1883
About
Adler, D. A. A picture book of Sojourner Truth
(1-3) **92**
Ferris, J. Walking the road to freedom: a story
about Sojourner Truth (3-5) **92**
McKissack, P. C. Sojourner Truth (1-3) **92**

The **truth** about great white sharks. Cerullo, M.
M. **597**

The **truthful** harp. Alexander, L.
In Alexander, L. The foundling and other
tales of Prydian p87-94 **S C**

Truthfulness and falsehood
See also Honesty
Fiction
Bawden, N. Humbug (4 and up) **Fic**
Coville, B. The skull of truth (4-6) **Fic**

Try to remember. Soto, G.
In Soto, G. Petty crimes **S C**

Tryon, Leslie
Albert's alphabet. See note under Tryon, L. Al-
bert's birthday **E**
Albert's ballgame. See note under Tryon, L. Al-
bert's birthday **E**
Albert's birthday **E**
Albert's Christmas. See note under Tryon, L.
Albert's birthday **E**
Albert's field trip. See note under Tryon, L. Al-
bert's birthday **E**
Albert's Hallowween. See note under Tryon, L.
Albert's birthday **E**
Albert's play. See note under Tryon, L. Albert's
birthday **E**
Albert's Thanksgiving. See note under Tryon, L.
Albert's birthday **E**

TryScience. (5 and up) See entry in Part 2: Web
Resources

Tseng, Grace
White tiger, blue serpent (2-4) **398.2**

Tseng, Jean
(il) Huynh, Q. N. Water buffalo days **92**
(il) Mahy, M. The seven Chinese brothers
398.2
(il) Maples in the mist. See Maples in the mist
895.1
(il) San Souci, R. Fa Mulan **398.2**
(il) Tseng, G. White tiger, blue serpent
398.2
(il) Yep, L. The Khan's daughter **398.2**

Tseng, Mou-sien
(il) Huynh, Q. N. Water buffalo days **92**
(il) Mahy, M. The seven Chinese brothers
398.2
(il) Maples in the mist. See Maples in the mist
895.1
(il) San Souci, R. Fa Mulan **398.2**
(il) Tseng, G. White tiger, blue serpent
398.2
(il) Yep, L. The Khan's daughter **398.2**

Tsirtsur & Peziza. Singer, I. B.
In Singer, I. B. Stories for children p160-66
S C
In Singer, I. B. When Shlemiel went to War-
saw & other stories p17-26 **398.2**

Tsubakiyama, Margaret
Mei-Mei loves the morning **E**

**Tubières, Anne Claude Philippe de, comte de
Caylus** *See* Caylus, Anne Claude Philippe de
Tubières, comte de, 1692-1765

Tubman, Harriet, 1815?-1913
About
Adler, D. A. A picture book of Harriet Tubman
(1-3) **92**
Ferris, J. Go free or die: a story about Harriet
Tubman (3-5) **92**
See/See also pages in the following book(s):
Haskins, J. Get on board: the story of the Un-
derground Railroad p43-63 (5 and up)
326
Fiction
Ringgold, F. Aunt Harriet's Underground Rail-
road in the sky **E**
Schroeder, A. Minty: a story of young Harriet
Tubman **E**
Poetry
Lawrence, J. Harriet and the Promised Land
811

Tuck everlasting. Babbitt, N. **Fic**

Tuck triumphant. Taylor, T. See note under Taylor, T. The trouble with Tuck **Fic**

Tucker, Tom, 1944-
Brainstorm! (5 and up) **609**

Tucker's countryside. Selden, G. See note under
Selden, G. The cricket in Times Square
Fic

Tucket's gold. Paulsen, G. See note under
Paulsen, G. Mr. Tucket **Fic**

Tucket's home. Paulsen, G. See note under
Paulsen, G. Mr. Tucket **Fic**

The **uninvited** guest and other Jewish holiday tales. Jaffe, N. **296.4**

Uninvited guests. Sierra i Fabra, J.
In Don't read this! and other tales of the unnatural p197-213 **S C**

Union of Soviet Socialist Republics *See* Soviet Union

Union Pacific Railroad Company
Blumberg, R. Full steam ahead (5 and up) **385.09**

Unitas, Johnny, 1933-
See/See also pages in the following book(s):
Sullivan, G. Quarterbacks! p42-45 (5 and up) **920**

United Nations
See/See also pages in the following book(s):
Worldmark encyclopedia of the nations **910.3**

United Nations International Children's Fund
See UNICEF

United States
America the beautiful, second series **973**
Celebrate the states **973**
Leedy, L. Celebrate the 50 states (k-3) **973**
Biography—Poetry
Lives: poems about famous Americans (4 and up) **811.008**
Constitutional history
See Constitutional history—United States
Description
Brown, D. Alice Ramsey's grand adventure (k-3) **92**
Murphy, J. Across America on an emigrant train (5 and up) **92**
Dictionaries
Junior Worldmark encyclopedia of the states (4 and up) **973.03**
Emigration
See United States—Immigration and emigration
Encyclopedias
Bock, J. Scholastic encyclopedia of the United States (4 and up) **973.03**
Exploration
See also West (U.S.)—Exploration
Foreign relations—Japan
Blumberg, R. Commodore Perry in the land of the Shogun (5 and up) **952**
Government
See United States—Politics and government
History
See also West (U.S.)—History
Hakim, J. A history of US (5 and up) **973**
See/See also pages in the following book(s):
Parker, N. W. Money, money, money (3-5) **769.5**
History—1600-1775, Colonial period
Avi. Finding Providence: the story of Roger Williams (2-4) **92**
Fisher, L. E. The blacksmiths (4 and up) **682**
Fisher, L. E. The doctors (4 and up) **610.9**
Fisher, L. E. The printers (4 and up) **686.2**

Fritz, J. Where was Patrick Henry on the 29th of May? (2-4) **92**
Maestro, B. The new Americans (2-4) **973.2**
See/See also pages in the following book(s):
Brenner, B. The boy who loved to draw: Benjamin West (k-3) **92**
History—1600-1775, Colonial period—Fiction
Avi. Encounter at Easton (5 and up) **Fic**
Avi. Night journeys (5 and up) **Fic**
Benchley, N. Small Wolf **E**
Curry, J. L. A stolen life (5 and up) **Fic**
Fritz, J. Early thunder (6 and up) **Fic**
Hermes, P. Our strange new land (3-5) **Fic**
McGill, A. Molly Bannaky **E**
History—1755-1763, French and Indian War
The American revolutionaries: a history in their own words, 1750-1800 (6 and up) **973.3**
History—1775-1783, Revolution
The American revolutionaries: a history in their own words, 1750-1800 (6 and up) **973.3**
Cox, C. Come all you brave soldiers (6 and up) **973.3**
Fradin, D. B. Samuel Adams (6 and up) **92**
Fritz, J. And then what happened, Paul Revere? (2-4) **92**
Fritz, J. Why don't you get a horse, Sam Adams? (2-4) **92**
Fritz, J. Why not, Lafayette? (5 and up) **92**
Fritz, J. Will you sign here, John Hancock? (2-4) **92**
Kroll, S. The Boston Tea Party (3-5) **973.3**
McGovern, A. The secret soldier: the story of Deborah Sampson [Gannett] (3-5) **92**
Murphy, J. A young patriot (5 and up) **973.3**
Stein, R. C. Valley Forge (4-6) **973.3**
Wallner, A. Betsy Ross (k-2) **92**
See/See also pages in the following book(s):
Giblin, J. Fireworks, picnics, and flags p2-23 (3-6) **394.26**
History—1775-1783, Revolution—Fiction
Avi. The fighting ground (5 and up) **Fic**
Bruchac, J. The arrow over the door (4-6) **Fic**
Collier, J. L. My brother Sam is dead (6 and up) **Fic**
Collier, J. L. War comes to Willy Freeman (6 and up) **Fic**
Forbes, E. Johnny Tremain (5 and up) **Fic**
Gauch, P. L. This time, Tempe Wick? (3-5) **Fic**
Goodman, J. E. Hope's crossing (5 and up) **Fic**
Lawson, R. Mr. Revere and I (5 and up) **Fic**
O'Dell, S. Sarah Bishop (6 and up) **Fic**
Turner, A. W. Katie's trunk **E**
Walker, S. M. The 18 penny goose **E**
History—1783-1809
See also Louisiana Purchase
History—1783-1809—Fiction
Collier, J. L. Jump ship to freedom (6 and up) **Fic**

United States—History—1783-1809—Fiction—
Continued

Collier, J. L. Who is Carrie? (6 and up)
           Fic
      History—1783-1865—Fiction
Nixon, J. L. A family apart (5 and up) **Fic**
    History—1812-1815, War of 1812
See War of 1812
     History—1815-1861—Fiction
McCully, E. A. The bobbin girl (3-5) **Fic**
Paterson, K. Lyddie (5 and up)   **Fic**
   History—1861-1865, Civil War
Archer, J. A house divided: the lives of Ulysses
  S. Grant and Robert E. Lee (5 and up)
                  92
Cox, C. Undying glory (6 and up) **973.7**
Fritz, J. Stonewall [biography of Stonewall Jack-
  son] (4 and up)   **92**
Haskins, J. Black, blue, & gray (5 and up)
               973.7
Lincoln, in his own words (6 and up) **92**
Murphy, J. The boys' war (5 and up)
               973.7
Reit, S. Behind rebel lines: the incredible story
  of Emma Edmonds, Civil War spy (4 and up)
               92

See/See also pages in the following book(s):
Freedman, R. Lincoln: a photobiography p72-
  117 (4 and up)   **92**
History—1861-1865, Civil War—Encyclopedias
Clinton, C. Scholastic encyclopedia of the Civil
  War (4 and up)   **973.7**
   History—1861-1865, Civil War—Fiction
Beatty, P. Charley Skedaddle (5 and up)
               Fic
Beatty, P. Jayhawker (5 and up) **Fic**
Beatty, P. Turn homeward, Hannalee (5 and up)
               Fic
Fleischman, P. Bull Run (6 and up) **Fic**
Hahn, M. D. Promises to the dead (5 and up)
               Fic
Hansen, J. Which way freedom? (5 and up)
               Fic
Hesse, K. A light in the storm (4 and up)
               Fic
Hunt, I. Across five Aprils (5 and up) **Fic**
Keith, H. Rifles for Watie (6 and up) **Fic**
Lunn, J. L. S. The root cellar (5 and up)
               Fic
Lyon, G. E. Cecil's story   **E**
Osborne, M. P. My brother's keeper (3-5)
               Fic
Polacco, P. Pink and Say   **E**
Reeder, C. Across the lines (5 and up) **Fic**
Reeder, C. Shades of gray (4 and up) **Fic**
Wisler, G. C. Mr. Lincoln's drummer (4 and up)
               Fic
Wisler, G. C. Red Cap (4 and up) **Fic**

History—1861-1865, Civil War—Reconstruction
See Reconstruction (1865-1876)
    History—1865-1898—Fiction
Robinet, H. G. Forty acres and maybe a mule (4
  and up)   **Fic**

History—1914-1918, World War
See World War, 1914-1918—United States
  History—1939-1945, World War
See World War, 1939-1945—United States
    History—Bibliography
Adamson, L. G. Literature connections to
  American history, K-6   **016.973**
    History—Dictionaries
Kane, J. N. Famous first facts   **031.02**
    History—Periodicals
Cobblestone   **973.05**
    History—Poetry
Hand in hand (4 and up)   **811.008**
  Immigration and emigration
Ashabranner, B. K. The new African Americans
  (4 and up)   **305.8**
Bierman, C. Journey to Ellis Island (3-5)
              325.73
Freedman, R. Immigrant kids (4 and up)
              325.73
I was dreaming to come to America (4 and up)
              325.73
Kroll, S. Ellis Island (3-5)   **325.73**
Levine, E. . . . if your name was changed at
  Ellis Island (3-5)   **325.73**
Maestro, B. Coming to America: the story of
  immigration (k-3)   **325.73**
Wells, R. Streets of gold [biography of Mary
  Antin] (3-6)   **92**
      Maps
Rand McNally children's atlas of the United
  States (4-6)   **912**
    National songs
See National songs—United States
   Politics and government
Maestro, B. The voice of the people (3-5)
              324
  Politics and government—1865-1898
Mettger, Z. Reconstruction (5 and up)
              973.8
    Presidents
See Presidents—United States
    Race relations
Birdseye, D. H. Under our skin (4 and up)
              305.8
Duncan, A. F. The National Civil Rights Muse-
  um celebrates everyday people (3-6)
              323.1
Haskins, J. Out of the darkness (5 and up)
              305.8
King, C. Oh, freedom! (5 and up) **323.1**
King, M. L. I have a dream   **323.1**
   Separation of powers
See Separation of powers—United States
   Social life and customs
Brenner, B. If you were there in 1776 (4-6)
              973.3
Goodman, S. Ultimate field trip 4: a week in the
  1800s (5 and up)   **973.5**
Lewin, T. Fair! (k-3)   **394**
Social life and customs—1600-1775, Colonial
      period
Cobb, M. A sampler view of colonial life (2-5)
              746.44
Fisher, L. E. The architects (4 and up) **720**

Van Laan, Nancy—*Continued*
Includes the following stories: One cold day; Monkey stew; Fool John; Possum plays dead; The big dinin'; The watermillion patch; Ol' Mister Biggety; How come Ol' Buzzard boards; Mister Grumpy rides the clouds; Nuts! Nuts! Nuts!; We hunted and we hollered; Ol' Gally Mander; Jack runs off; Three Foots

Van Leeuwen, Jean
Amanda Pig and her best friend Lollipop. See note under Van Leeuwen, J. Tales of Oliver Pig   E
Amanda Pig and her big brother Oliver. See note under Van Leeuwen, J. Tales of Oliver Pig   E
Amanda Pig on her own. See note under Van Leeuwen, J. Tales of Oliver Pig   E
Amanda Pig, school girl. See note under Van Leeuwen, J. Tales of Oliver Pig   E
Bound for Oregon (4-6)   Fic
Going West   E
More tales of Amanda Pig. See note under Van Leeuwen, J. Tales of Oliver Pig   E
More tales of Oliver Pig. See note under Van Leeuwen, J. Tales of Oliver Pig   E
Nothing here but trees   E
Oliver, Amanda, and Grandmother Pig. See note under Van Leeuwen, J. Tales of Oliver Pig
                                                   E
Oliver and Albert, friends forever. See note under Van Leeuwen, J. Tales of Oliver Pig
                                                   E
Oliver and Amanda and the big snow. See note under Van Leeuwen, J. Tales of Oliver Pig
                                                   E
Oliver and Amanda's Christmas. See note under Van Leeuwen, J. Tales of Oliver Pig   E
Oliver and Amanda's Halloween. See note under Van Leeuwen, J. Tales of Oliver Pig
                                                   E
Oliver Pig at school. See note under Van Leeuwen, J. Tales of Oliver Pig   E
Tales of Amanda Pig. See note under Van Leeuwen, J. Tales of Oliver Pig   E
Tales of Oliver Pig   E

Van Loon, Hendrik Willem, 1882-1944
See/See also pages in the following book(s):
Newbery Medal books, 1922-1955 p13-16
                                              028.5

Van Orden, Phyllis J.
Selecting books for the elementary school library media center   025.2

Van Rose, Susanna
Earth (4 and up)   550
The earth atlas (5 and up)   550
Volcano & earthquake (4 and up)   551.2

Van Wright, Cornelius
(il) Chinn, K. Sam and the lucky money   E
(il) Make a joyful sound. See Make a joyful sound   811.008
(il) Miller, W. Zora Hurston and the chinaberry tree   92
(il) Smith, C. L. Jingle dancer   E
(il) Tsubakiyama, M. Mei-Mei loves the morning   E

Van Zyle, Jon, 1942-
(il) London, J. Baby whale's journey   E
(il) Miller, D. S. A caribou journey   599.65

(il) Miller, D. S. A polar bear journey
                                              599.78
(il) Miller, D. S. River of life   577.6

VanCleave, Janice Pratt
Janice VanCleave's 201 awesome, magical, bizarre & incredible experiments (4 and up)
                                              507.8
Janice VanCleave's 202 oozing, bubbling, dripping & bouncing experiments (4 and up)
                                              507.8
Janice VanCleave's 203 icy, freezing, frosty, cool & wild experiments (4 and up)
                                              507.8
Janice VanCleave's constellations for every kid (4 and up)   523.8
Janice VanCleave's earth science for every kid (4 and up)   550
Janice Vancleave's ecology for every kid (4 and up)   577
Janice VanCleave's electricity (4 and up)
                                              537
Janice VanCleave's food and nutrition for every kid (4 and up)   613.2
Janice VanCleave's geometry for every kid (4 and up)   516
Janice VanCleave's guide to more of the best science fair projects (4 and up)   507.8
Janice VanCleave's guide to the best science fair projects (4 and up)   507.8
Janice VanCleave's insects and spiders (4 and up)   595.7
Janice VanCleave's oceans for every kid (4 and up)   551.46
Janice VanCleave's plants (4 and up)   581
Janice VanCleave's play and find out about bugs (k-2)   595.7
Janice VanCleave's play and find out about math (k-2)   513
Janice VanCleave's play and find out about nature (k-2)   570
Janice VanCleave's rocks and minerals (4 and up)   552
Janice VanCleave's the human body for every kid (4 and up)   612
Janice VanCleave's weather (4 and up)
                                              551.5

Vande Velde, Vivian, 1951-
Smart dog (4-6)   Fic
There's a dead person following my sister around (4 and up)   Fic

Vanishing ozone. Pringle, L. P.   363.7

Vanishing species *See* Endangered species

Vare, Ethlie Ann
Women inventors & their discoveries (5 and up)
                                              920

Varley, Susan
(il) Oram, H. Princess Chamomile's garden
                                              E

Varriale, Jim
Kids dance (4 and up)   792.8
Take a look around (4 and up)   770

Vasconcellos, Daniel
(il) Christopher, M. The dog that called the pitch   Fic

Vasilisa the Beautiful. Afanas'ev, A. N.
  In Afanas'ev, A. N. Russian fairy tales p439-47 **398.2**
Vaughan, Marcia, 1951-
  How to cook a gooseberry fool
    In Easy menu ethnic cookbooks **641.5**
  Snap! **E**
  Whistling Dixie **E**
VCRs *See* Video recording
VD *See* Sexually transmitted diseases
Vecchi, Floriano
  (jt. auth) Fox, P. Amzat and his brothers: three Italian tales **398.2**
Vegetable gardening
  Creasy, R. Blue potatoes, orange tomatoes (3-5) **635**
  Lerner, C. My backyard garden (4-6) **635**
  See/See also pages in the following book(s):
  Cook, D. F. Kids' pumpkin projects (2-4) **745.5**
    Fiction
  Ehlert, L. Growing vegetable soup **E**
Vegetables
  See also names of vegetables
  Creasy, R. Blue potatoes, orange tomatoes (3-5) **635**
  Ehlert, L. Eating the alphabet **E**
  Johnson, S. A. Tomatoes, potatoes, corn, and beans (6 and up) **641.3**
  McMillan, B. Growing colors **E**
    Fiction
  Hall, Z. The surprise garden **E**
  Speed, T. Brave potatoes **E**
  Wallace, K. Scarlette Beane **E**
  Wiesner, D. June 29, 1999 **E**
Vegetarian cooking
  Katzen, M. Honest pretzels (4-6) **641.5**
Vegetarian cooking around the world
  In Easy menu ethnic cookbooks **641.5**
Vegetarianism
    Fiction
  Hurwitz, J. Much ado about Aldo (3-5) **Fic**
Vehicles
  Gibbons, G. Emergency! (k-3) **363.34**
    Fiction
  Hindley, J. The big red bus **E**
Velasquez, Eric
  (il) Chocolate, D. The piano man **E**
  (il) Naidoo, B. Chain of fire **Fic**
  (il) Naidoo, B. Journey to Jo'burg **Fic**
Velázquez, Diego, 1599-1660
    Fiction
  Treviño, E. B. de. I, Juan de Pareja (6 and up) **Fic**
The **velveteen** rabbit. Bianco, M. W. **Fic**
Vendela in Venice. Björk, C. **Fic**
Venereal diseases *See* Sexually transmitted diseases
Venezia, Mike
  George Handel (k-3) **92**
  Georgia O'Keeffe (k-3) **92**
Venezuela
    Fiction
  Cowcher, H. Jaguar **E**

Natural history
  See Natural history—Venezuela
The **vengeance** of the witch-finder. Bellairs, J. See note under Bellairs, J. The house with a clock in its walls **Fic**
Venice (Italy)
    Fiction
  Björk, C. Vendela in Venice (4 and up) **Fic**
  Fleming, C. Gabriella's song **E**
Vennema, Peter
  (jt. auth) Stanley, D. Bard of Avon: the story of William Shakespeare **92**
  (jt. auth) Stanley, D. Charles Dickens **92**
  (jt. auth) Stanley, D. Cleopatra **92**
  (jt. auth) Stanley, D. Shaka, king of the Zulus **92**
Venti, Anthony Bacon
  (il) Climo, S. Magic & mischief **398.2**
  (il) Fritz, J. Around the world in a hundred years **910.4**
Vera runs away. Rosenberry, V. See note under Rosenberry, V. Vera's first day of school **E**
Vera's first day of school. Rosenberry, V. **E**
Verbitsky, Alexander
  (il) Kreutzer, P. Little League's official how-to-play baseball book **796.357**
Verdi, Giuseppe, 1813-1901
  Price, L. Aïda **792.5**
  See/See also pages in the following book(s):
  Krull, K. Lives of the musicians p36-39 (4 and up) **920**
Verdi. Cannon, J. **E**
Verhoeven, Rian
  (jt. auth) Rol, R. van der. Anne Frank, beyond the diary **92**
Vermont
  Elish, D. Vermont
    In Celebrate the states **973**
    Fiction
  Fisher, D. C. Understood Betsy (4-6) **Fic**
  Henry, M. Justin Morgan had a horse (4 and up) **Fic**
  Hurwitz, J. Faraway summer (4-6) **Fic**
  Kinsey-Warnock, N. The Canada geese quilt (3-5) **Fic**
  Paterson, K. Jip (5 and up) **Fic**
  Paterson, K. Preacher's boy (5 and up) **Fic**
  Peck, R. N. A day no pigs would die (6 and up) **Fic**
  Peck, R. N. Soup (5 and up) **Fic**
Verne, Jules, 1828-1905
  20,000 leagues under the sea (5 and up) **Fic**
  See/See also pages in the following book(s):
  Krull, K. They saw the future p59-65 (4 and up) **133.3**
Verougstraete, Randy
  (il) Godfrey, N. S. Neale S. Godfrey's ultimate kids' money book **332.024**
The **very** busy spider. Carle, E. **E**
The **very** clumsy click beetle. Carle, E. **E**

A **Very** happy donkey
In The Magic orange tree, and other Haitian folktales p157-63   **398.2**

The **very** hungry caterpillar. Carle, E.   **E**

A **very** important day. Herold, M. R.   **E**

The **very** lonely firefly. Carle, E.   **E**

The **very** old woman and the Piskey. Climo, S.
In Climo, S. Magic & mischief p15-20   **398.2**

The **very** pretty lady. Babbitt, N.
In Babbitt, N. The Devil's storybook p13-20   **S C**

The **very** quiet cricket. Carle, E.   **E**

A **very** special house. Krauss, R.   **E**

Very Tall Mouse and Very Short Mouse. Lobel, A.
In The Read-aloud treasury p207-13   **808.8**

The **very** worst monster. Hutchins, P. See note under Hutchins, P. Where's the baby?   **E**

Vespucci, Amerigo, 1451-1512
See/See also pages in the following book(s):
Fritz, J. Around the world in a hundred years p69-75 (4-6)   **910.4**

Vezza, Diane Simone
Passport on a plate (5 and up)   **641.5**

Vicksburg (Miss.)
Siege, 1863
Fraser, M. A. Vicksburg—the battle that won the Civil War (4 and up)   **973.7**

Vicksburg—the battle that won the Civil War. Fraser, M. A.   **973.7**

Victor *See* Wild Boy of Aveyron, d. 1828

Victoria, Queen of Great Britain, 1819-1901
See/See also pages in the following book(s):
Myers, W. D. At her majesty's request (5 and up)   **92**

Vidal, Beatriz
(il) Van Laan, N. The magic bean tree   **398.2**

Vidaure, Morris
(jt. auth) Rohmer, H. The invisible hunters   **398.2**

Video cassette recorders and recording *See* Video recording

Video Christmas. Dias, E. J.
In The Big book of Christmas plays p26-40   **808.82**

Video recording
Bentley, N. The young producer's video book (4-6)   **791.45**

Videorecorders *See* Video recording

Videotape recorders and recording *See* Video recording

Videotapes
Catalogs
Culturally diverse videos, audios, and CD-ROMS for children and young adults   **011.6**

Vietnam
Kilborne, S. S. Leaving Vietnam (1-4)   **959.704**

Skelton, O. Vietnam (4 and up)   **959.7**
Description
Schmidt, J. Two lands, one heart (3-5)   **959.704**
Fiction
Keller, H. Grandfather's dream   **E**
Folklore
See Folklore—Vietnam
Social life and customs
Huynh, Q. N. The land I lost: adventures of a boy in Vietnam (4 and up)   **92**
Huynh, Q. N. Water buffalo days (3-5)   **92**

Vietnam Veterans Memorial (Washington, D.C.)
Ashabranner, B. K. Their names to live (6 and up)   **959.704**
Fiction
Bunting, E. The Wall   **E**

Vietnam War, 1961-1975
Fiction
Boyd, C. D. Charlie Pippin (4-6)   **Fic**
Nelson, T. And one for all (5 and up)   **Fic**

Vietnamese
Fiction
Whelan, G. Goodbye, Vietnam (4 and up)   **Fic**

United States—Fiction
Gilson, J. Hello, my name is Scrambled Eggs (4 and up)   **Fic**

Vietnamese Americans
Hoyt-Goldsmith, D. Hoang Anh (3-5)   **305.8**
Fiction
Garland, S. My father's boat   **E**
Paterson, K. Park's quest (5 and up)   **Fic**

The **view** from Saturday. Konigsburg, E. L.   **Fic**

The **view** from the cherry tree. Roberts, W. D.   **Fic**

Viking easy-to-read [series]
Adler, D. A. Young Cam Jansen and the dinosaur game   **E**
Byars, B. C. My brother, Ant   **E**
Meister, C. Tiny's bath   **E**
Ziefert, H. April Fool!   **E**
Ziefert, H. Little Red Riding Hood   **398.2**

Vikings
Margeson, S. M. Viking (4 and up)   **948**

The **vile** village. Snicket, L. See note under Snicket, L. The bad beginning   **Fic**

Villa, Pancho, 1878-1923
About
O'Brien, S. Pancho Villa (5 and up)   **92**

The **village** by the sea. Fox, P.   **Fic**

A **village** full of valentines. Stevenson, J.   **E**

The **village** of round and square houses. Grifalconi, A.   **398.2**

Villeneuve, Madame de
Beauty and the beast
In The Blue fairy book p100-19   **398.2**

Villios, Lynne W.
Cooking the Greek way
In Easy menu ethnic cookbooks   **641.5**

Vinci, Leonardo da *See* Leonardo, da Vinci, 1452-1519

Vinge, Joan D., 1948-
The Random House book of Greek myths (4 and up) **292**

Vining, Elizabeth Gray, 1902-1999
Adam of the road (5 and up) **Fic**
See/See also pages in the following book(s):
Newbery Medal books, 1922-1955 p227-41 **028.5**

Viola, Herman J.
It is a good day to die (5 and up) **973.8**

Violence
See also Domestic violence
Fiction
Spinelli, J. Wringer (4 and up) **Fic**

Violinists
Fiction
Curtis, G. The bat boy & his violin **E**
Kraus, R. Mort the sport **E**
Wolff, V. E. The Mozart season (6 and up) **Fic**
Zalben, J. B. Unfinished dreams (5 and up) **Fic**

Violins
Fiction
McPhail, D. M. Mole music **E**

Violoncellos
Fiction
Cutler, J. The cello of Mr. O **E**

Viorst, Judith
Alexander and the terrible, horrible, no good, very bad day **E**
Alexander, who is not (do you hear me?) going (I mean it) to move. See note under Viorst, J. Alexander and the terrible, horrible, no good, very bad day **E**
Alexander, who used to be rich last Sunday. See note under Viorst, J. Alexander and the terrible, horrible, no good, very bad day **E**
Earrings! **E**
If I were in charge of the world and other worries (3-6) **811**
My mama says there aren't any zombies, ghosts, vampires, creatures, demons, monsters, fiends, goblins, or things **E**
Sad underwear and other complications (3-6) **811**
The tenth good thing about Barney **E**

Virgie goes to school with us boys. Howard, E. F. **E**

Virgin Mary *See* Mary, Blessed Virgin, Saint

Virginia
Barrett, T. Virginia
In Celebrate the states **973**
Blashfield, J. F. Virginia
In America the beautiful, second series **973**
Fiction
Beatty, P. Charley Skedaddle (5 and up) **Fic**
Curry, J. L. A stolen life (5 and up) **Fic**
Paterson, K. Bridge to Terabithia (4 and up) **Fic**
White, R. Belle Prater's boy (5 and up) **Fic**

Virtual Cody. Duffey, B. See note under Duffey, B. Spotlight on Cody **Fic**

Virtual reality
Baker, C. W. Virtual reality (5 and up) **006**
Jefferis, D. Cyberspace (4 and up) **004.6**
Fiction
Skurzynski, G. The virtual war (6 and up) **Fic**

Virtual Renaissance. (6 and up) See entry in Part 2: Web Resources

The **virtual** war. Skurzynski, G. **Fic**

Viruses
See also Chickenpox
Berger, M. Germs make me sick! (k-3) **616.9**

Vishnu's bride. Krishnaswami, U.
In Krishnaswami, U. Shower of gold: girls and women in the stories of India p75-79 **398.2**

Vision disorders
Fiction
Dorris, M. Sees Behind Trees (4 and up) **Fic**
Little, J. From Anna (4-6) **Fic**

Vision of beauty: the story of Sarah Breedlove Walker. Lasky, K. **92**

Visions. Sills, L. **920**

A **visit** from St. Nicholas. See Moore, C. C. The night before Christmas **811**

A **visit** to the bank. Bond, M.
In Bond, M. Paddington's storybook p52-65 **S C**

A **visit** to William Blake's inn. Willard, N. **811**

Visiting Miss Caples. Kimmel, E. C. **Fic**

Visiting the art museum. Brown, L. K. **708**

Visitors. Ellis, S.
In Ellis, S. Back of beyond **S C**

The **Visual** dictionary of ancient civilizations (4 and up) **930**

The **Visual** dictionary of buildings (4 and up) **720**

The **visual** dictionary of chemistry. Challoner, J. **540**

The **Visual** dictionary of human anatomy (4 and up) **611**

The **Visual** dictionary of military uniforms (4 and up) **355.1**

The **visual** dictionary of physics. Challoner, J. **530**

The **Visual** dictionary of plants (4 and up) **580**

The **Visual** dictionary of prehistoric life (4 and up) **560**

The **Visual** dictionary of ships and sailing (4 and up) **387.2**

The **Visual** dictionary of the earth (4 and up) **550**

The **Visual** dictionary of the horse (4 and up) **636.1**

The **Visual** dictionary of the human body (4 and up) **611**

The **Visual** dictionary of the skeleton (4 and up)
591.4

The **Visual** dictionary of the universe (4 and up)
520

Vitale, Stefano
(il) Fisher, A. L. The story of Easter
394.26
(il) Sierra, J. Nursery tales around the world
398.2
(il) Zolotow, C. When the wind stops **E**

Vitamins
Kalbacken, J. Vitamins and minerals (2-4)
613.2

Vitamins and minerals. Kalbacken, J. **613.2**

Vittorini, Domenico
The wooden bowl
In Bauer, C. F. Celebrations p68-70
808.8

Vivaldi, Antonio, 1678-1741
See/See also pages in the following book(s):
Krull, K. Lives of the musicians p10-13 (4 and up)
920

Vivas, Julie, 1947-
(il) Wild, M. Our granny **E**
(il) Williams, S. Let's go visiting **E**
(il) Zamorano, A. Let's eat! **E**

Vo, Dinh Mai, 1933-
(il) Huynh, Q. N. The land I lost: adventures of a boy in Vietnam **92**
(il) Vuong, L. D. The brocaded slipper and other Vietnamese tales **398.2**

Voake, Charlotte
Ginger **E**
Here comes the train **E**

Vocabulary
Ahlberg, J. The baby's catalogue **E**
Feder, J. Table, chair, bear (k-2) **413**
Hoban, T. Over, under & through, and other spatial concepts **E**
Maestro, B. Taxi **E**
Micklethwait, L. A child's book of art: great pictures, first words (k-2) **701**
Wilkes, A. My first word book **E**
Fiction
Wells, R. Max's first word **E**

Vocations *See* Occupations

Vogt, Gregory
Apollo moonwalks (4 and up) **629.45**
Asteroids, comets, and meteors (2-4) **523.6**
The solar system (5 and up) **523.2**
Spacewalks (4 and up) **629.45**

The **voice** of the people. Maestro, B. **324**

Voices from the fields. Atkin, S. B. **331.5**

Voices from the past [series]
Gay, K. World War I **940.3**

Voices in the park. Browne, A. **E**

Voices of the Alamo. Garland, S. **976.4**

Voices of the heart. Young, E. **179**

Voigt, Cynthia
Come a stranger (6 and up) **Fic**
Dicey's song (6 and up) **Fic**
Homecoming (6 and up) **Fic**

See/See also pages in the following book(s):
Newbery and Caldecott Medal books, 1976-1985 p107-19 **028.5**

Vojtech, Anna, 1946-
(il) Bruchac, J. The first strawberries **398.2**
(il) Shalant, P. Bartleby of the mighty Mississippi **Fic**

Volavková, Hana
(ed) —I never saw another butterfly—. See —I never saw another butterfly— **741.9**

Volcano & earthquake. Van Rose, S. **551.2**

Volcanoes
Lauber, P. Volcano: the eruption and healing of Mount St. Helens (4 and up) **551.2**
Levy, M. Earthquake games (5 and up)
551.2
Silverstein, A. Plate tectonics (5 and up)
551.1
Simon, S. Volcanoes (3-6) **551.2**
Van Rose, S. Volcano & earthquake (4 and up)
551.2

Volleyball
Jensen, J. Fundamental volleyball (5 and up)
796.325

Volunteer work
Erlbach, A. The kids' volunteering book (4-6)
302
Hoose, P. M. It's our world, too! (5 and up)
302

Volz, Bridget Dealy
Junior genreflecting **016.8**

Von Mason, Stephen
See/See also pages in the following book(s):
Just like me p14-15 **920**

Von Schmidt, Eric, 1931-
(il) Fleischman, S. By the Great Horn Spoon!
Fic
(il) Fleischman, S. Chancy and the grand rascal
Fic
(il) Fleischman, S. Mr. Mysterious & Company
Fic

Vos, Ida, 1931-
Anna is still here (4 and up) **Fic**
Hide and seek (4 and up) **Fic**
The key is lost (4 and up) **Fic**

Voting *See* Elections

The **voyage** of the Dawn Treader. Lewis, C. S. See note under Lewis, C. S. The lion, the witch, and the wardrobe **Fic**

The **voyage** of the Ludgate Hill. Willard, N.
811

Voyage to the Bunny Planet. See Wells, R. Moss pillows **E**

Voyages and travels
Fiction
Demas, C. If ever I return again (5 and up)
Fic
Helldorfer, M. C. Hog music **E**
Hobbs, W. Jason's gold (5 and up) **Fic**
Murrow, L. K. Orphan journey home (4-6)
Fic
Priceman, M. How to make an apple pie and see the world **E**
Say, A. Grandfather's journey **E**

Voyages and travels—Fiction—*Continued*

Weston, C. The diary of Melanie Martin; or, How I survived Matt the Brat, Michelangelo, and the Leaning Tower of Pizza (3-6) Fic

Vultures

Stone, L. M. Vultures (3-6) 598

Fiction

Peet, B. Eli E

Vuong, Lynette Dyer, 1938-

The brocaded slipper and other Vietnamese tales (4-6) 398.2

Contents: The brocaded slipper; Little Finger of the watermelon patch; The fairy grotto; Master Frog; The lampstand princess

W

Waber, Bernard

A firefly named Torchy E

Funny, funny Lyle. See note under Waber, B. Lyle, Lyle, crocodile E

The house on East 88th Street. See note under Waber, B. Lyle, Lyle, crocodile E

Ira says goodbye. See note under Waber, B. Ira sleeps over E

Ira sleeps over E

A lion named Shirley Williamson E

Lovable Lyle. See note under Waber, B. Lyle, Lyle, crocodile E

Lyle and the birthday party. See note under Waber, B. Lyle, Lyle, crocodile E

Lyle at Christmas. See note under Waber, B. Lyle, Lyle, crocodile E

Lyle at the office. See note under Waber, B. Lyle, Lyle, crocodile E

Lyle finds his mother. See note under Waber, B. Lyle, Lyle, crocodile E

Lyle, Lyle, crocodile E

Wachter, Jerry

(il) Young, R. Game day 796.357

Waddell, Martin

Can't you sleep, Little Bear? E

Farmer duck E

Good job, Little Bear. See note under Waddell, M. Can't you sleep, Little Bear? E

Let's go home, Little Bear. See note under Waddell, M. Can't you sleep, Little Bear? E

Little Bear's baby book. See note under Waddell, M. Can't you sleep, Little Bear? E

Owl babies E

Rosie's babies E

Who do you love? E

You and me, Little Bear. See note under Waddell, M. Can't you sleep, Little Bear? E

Wade, Linda R.

James Carter: thirty-ninth president of the United States (4 and up) 92

Wadham, Tim

Programming with Latino children's materials 027.62

Wadsworth, Olive A.

Keats, E. J. Over in the meadow E

Wagon wheels. Brenner, B. E

Wagons *See* Carriages and carts

Wagué Diakité, Baba

The hatseller and the monkeys (k-3) 398.2

The hunterman and the crocodile (2-4) 398.2

The **Wainscott** weasel. Seidler, T. Fic

Wait till Helen comes. Hahn, M. D. Fic

Waiting for Anya. Morpurgo, M. Fic

Waiting for Mr. Chester. Medearis, A. S.
In Medearis, A. S. Haunts p32-37 S C

Waiting to sing. Kaplan, H. E

Wake up, city!. Tresselt, A. R. E

Wake up house!. Lillegard, D. 811

Wakefield, Ruth

See/See also pages in the following book(s):

Thimmesh, C. Girls think of everything (5 and up) 920

Wakim, Yvonne

Hirschfelder, A. B. American Indian stereotypes in the world of children 970.004

The **waking** of Men. Curry, J. L.
In Curry, J. L. Back in the beforetime p116 398.2

Waldee, Lynne Marie

Cooking the French way
In Easy menu ethnic cookbooks 641.5

Waldman, Neil, 1947-

Masada (4 and up) 933

(il) Appelt, K. Bayou lullaby E

(il) Goldin, B. D. The Passover journey 296.4

(il) Luenn, N. Nessa's fish E

(il) Schecter, E. The family Haggadah 296.4

(il) Schwartz, H. Next year in Jerusalem 296.1

Wales

Fiction

Bond, N. A string in the harp (6 and up) Fic

Cooper, S. The grey king (5 and up) Fic

Kimmel, E. C. In the stone circle (5 and up) Fic

Folklore

See Folklore—Wales

A **walk** on the Great Barrier Reef. Arnold, C. 578.7

Walk two moons. Creech, S. Fic

Walker, Alice, 1944-

See/See also pages in the following book(s):

Hansen, J. Women of hope p24-25 (4 and up) 920

Walker, Barbara K.

A treasury of Turkish folktales for children (4 and up) 398.2

Contents: The mouse and the elephant; Who's there? And what do you want?; Hasan, the heroic mouse-child; The magpie and the milk; The mosquito and the water buffalo; The rabbit and the wolf; The lion's den; The crow and the snake; Lazy Keloğlan and the sultan's daughter; The three brothers and the hand of fate; Keloğlan and the twelve dancing princesses; I know what I'll do; Nasreddin Hoca, seller of wisdom; Nasreddin Hoca and the third shot; The Hoca as Tamerlane's tax collector; The Hoca

Walker, Barbara K.—*Continued*
and the candle; Teeny-Tiny and the witch-woman; Karaçor and the giants; The wonderful pumpkin; The courage of Kazan; Just say hiç!; How Deli kept his part of the bargain; Two fools and the gifts for Mehmet; Three tricksters and the pot of butter; Trousers Mehmet and the sultan's daughter; Stargazer to the sultan; The bird of fortune; The princess and the pig; The princess and the goatherd; Hamal Hasan and the baby day; The round sultan and the straight answer; A mirror, a carpet, and a lemon; New patches for old; Hasan and Allah's greatness

Walker, Barbara Muhs, 1928-
The Little House cookbook (5 and up)
641.5

Walker, C. J., Madame, 1867-1919
About
Lasky, K. Vision of beauty: the story of Sarah Breedlove Walker (3-5)　92
McKissack, P. C. Madam C.J. Walker (1-3)
92

See/See also pages in the following book(s):
Haskins, J. One more river to cross (4 and up)
920
Vare, E. A. Women inventors & their discoveries p51-65 (5 and up)　920

Walker, Lester
Carpentry for children (4 and up)　694

Walker, Paul Robert
Big men, big country (4-6)　398.2
Contents: Davy Crockett teaches the steamboat a leetle patriotism; Old Stormalong finds a man-sized ship; Big Mose and the Lady Washington; John Darling and the skeeter chariot; Ol' Gabe in the valley of the Yellowstone; Paul Bunyan and the Winter of the Blue Snow; John Henry races the steam drill; Gib Morgan brings in the well; Pecos Bill finds a ranch but loses a wife

Walker, Richard
The Kingfisher first human body encyclopedia (3-5)　612

Walker, Sally M.
The 18 penny goose　E
Earthquakes (3-6)　551.2
Hippos (3-6)　599.63
Rhinos (3-6)　599.66

Walking
Fiction
Johnson, D. B. Henry hikes to Fitchburg　E
Jonas, A. Watch William walk　E
Walking the road to freedom: a story about Sojourner Truth. Ferris, J.　92
Walking to the bus-rider blues. Robinet, H. G.
Fic

The **Wall**. Bunting, E.　E

Wallace, Barbara Brooks, 1922-
Cousins in the castle (4-6)　Fic
Ghosts in the gallery (5 and up)　Fic
The twin in the tavern (4-6)　Fic

Wallace, Bill, 1947-
Beauty (4-6)　Fic
A dog called Kitty (4-6)　Fic

Wallace, Daisy
(ed) Ghost poems. See Ghost poems
821.008
(ed) Monster poems. See Monster poems
821.008
(ed) Witch poems. See Witch poems
821.008

Wallace, Joseph, 1957-
The lightbulb (4 and up)　621.32

Wallace, Karen
Gentle giant octopus (k-3)　594
Scarlette Beane　E
Tale of a tadpole (k-1)　597.8

Wallner, Alexandra, 1946-
Betsy Ross (k-2)　92
(il) Adler, D. A. A picture book of Abraham Lincoln　92
(il) Adler, D. A. A picture book of Benjamin Franklin　92
(il) Adler, D. A. A picture book of Helen Keller
92
(il) Adler, D. A. A picture book of Louis Braille
92
(il) Adler, D. A. A picture book of Thomas Jefferson　92
(il) The Farmer in the dell. See The Farmer in the dell　782.42

Wallner, John C.
(il) Adler, D. A. A picture book of Abraham Lincoln　92
(il) Adler, D. A. A picture book of Benjamin Franklin　92
(il) Adler, D. A. A picture book of Helen Keller
92
(il) Adler, D. A. A picture book of Louis Braille
92
(il) Adler, D. A. A picture book of Thomas Jefferson　92
(il) Gilson, J. Hello, my name is Scrambled Eggs　Fic
(il) Hurwitz, J. Much ado about Aldo　Fic
(il) O'Neill, M. L. D. Hailstones and halibut bones　811

Walls
Knight, M. B. Talking walls (3-5)　909
Knight, M. B. Talking walls: the stories continue (3-5)　909

The **walnut** and the pumpkin. Jaffe, N.
In Jaffe, N. The cow of no color: riddle stories and justice tales from around the world p114-16　398.2

Walrod, Amy
(il) Howe, J. Horace and Morris but mostly Dolores　E
(il) Sturges, P. The Little Red Hen (makes a pizza)　398.2

Walsh, Ellen Stoll, 1942-
For Pete's sake　E
Mouse count　E
Mouse paint. See note under Walsh, E. S. Mouse count　E

Walsh, Jill Paton *See* Paton Walsh, Jill, 1937-
Walsh, John
About
Goodman, S. Animal rescue (2-4)　639.9
Walsh, Tina Cash- *See* Cash-Walsh, Tina, 1960-
Walsh, Vivian
(il) Seibold, J. O. Olive the other reindeer
E

Walsh Shepherd, Donna, 1948-
Alaska
In America the beautiful, second series
973
The Klondike gold rush (4 and up)　971.9

Walt Disney Productions
Peet, B. Bill Peet: an autobiography (4 and up)
92

Walter, Mildred Pitts, 1922-
Brother to the wind **E**
Justin and the best biscuits in the world (3-6)
Fic
Kwanzaa: a family affair (4 and up)
394.26
Suitcase (3-6) **Fic**

Walter, Virginia A.
"Hi, pizza man!" **E**
Output measures for public library service to
children **027.62**

Walter Wick's Optical tricks. Wick, W.
152.14

Walters, Robert F.
(il) Lessem, D. Bigger than T. rex **567.9**

Walters, Virginia
Are we there yet, Daddy? **E**

Walton, Rick
One more bunny **E**

Wampanoag Indians
Peters, R. M. Clambake (3-6) **970.004**

The **Wanderer**. Creech, S. **Fic**

The **wanderings** of Odysseus. Sutcliff, R.
883

Wang, Su-ling *See* Wang Suling

Wang Suling
(il) Yep, L. The magic paintbrush **Fic**

Wanna bet!. Cobb, V. **793.8**

Wanted—Mud Blossom. Byars, B. C. See note
under Byars, B. C. The not-just-anybody family **Fic**

War
Fiction
Cutler, J. The cello of Mr. O **E**
Poetry
War and the pity of war (5 and up)
808.81

War and the pity of war (5 and up) **808.81**

The **war** between beasts and birds. Curry, J. L.
In Curry, J. L. Back in the beforetime p68-69
398.2

A **war** between gods. Terada, A. M.
In Terada, A. M. Under the starfruit tree p50-
53 **398.2**

War comes to Willy Freeman. Collier, J. L.
Fic

War of 1812
Kroll, S. By the dawn's early light (3-5)
782.42

The **war** of the wolf and the fox. Grimm, J.
In The Green fairy book p339-42 **398.2**

The **war** with Grandpa. Smith, R. K. **Fic**

The **Warau** people discover the earth. Sherlock,
Sir P. M.
In Sherlock, Sir P. M. West Indian folk-tales
p39-44 **398.2**

Ward, Helen, 1962-
The hare and the tortoise (k-3) **398.2**
The king of the birds (k-3) **398.2**

Ward, John
(il) Sanfield, S. The adventures of High John
the Conqueror **398.2**

Ward, Lynd Kendall, 1905-1985
The biggest bear **E**
The silver pony (2-4) **Fic**
(il) Coatsworth, E. J. The cat who went to heav-
en **Fic**
(il) Fritz, J. Early thunder **Fic**
(jt. auth) Swift, H. H. The little red lighthouse
and the great gray bridge **E**
(il) Wyss, J. D. The Swiss family Robinson
Fic
See/See also pages in the following book(s):
Caldecott Medal books, 1938-1957 p243-53
028.5

Ward, Nancy, 1738?-1822
See/See also pages in the following book(s):
Calvert, P. Great lives: the American frontier
p339-51 (5 and up) **920**

Wardlaw, Lee, 1955-
Punia and the King of Sharks (k-3) **398.2**

Warhol, Andy, 1928?-1987
See/See also pages in the following book(s):
Greenberg, J. The American eye p89-97 (6 and
up) **920**

Warm as wool. Sanders, S. R. **E**

Warne, L. Rowland- *See* Rowland-Warne, L.

Warner, Sally
Totally confidential (4 and up) **Fic**

Warnick, Elsa, 1942-
(il) Rubin, S. G. Toilets, toasters & telephones
683
(il) Simon, S. Ride the wind **591.56**
(il) Simon, S. They swim the seas **578.7**
(il) Simon, S. They walk the earth **591.56**

Warnock, Natalie Kinsey- *See* Kinsey-Warnock,
Natalie

Warren, Andrea
Orphan train rider (4 and up) **362.7**

The **warrior** and the wise man. Wisniewski, D.
E

The **warrior** queen of Jhansi. Krishnaswami, U.
In Krishnaswami, U. Shower of gold: girls
and women in the stories of India p68-74
398.2

Warshaw, Hallie
The sleepover cookbook (4 and up) **641.5**

Washakie, Shoshone Chief, 1797-1900
See/See also pages in the following book(s):
Freedman, R. Indian chiefs p72-89 (6 and up)
920

Washburn, Lucia
(il) George, J. C. Look to the North **E**
(il) Zoehfeld, K. W. Dinosaur babies **567.9**

Washday on Noah's ark. Rounds, G. **E**

Washington, Booker T., 1856-1915
About
McKissack, P. C. Booker T. Washington (1-3)
92
Fiction
Bradby, M. More than anything else **E**

Watling, James—*Continued*
(il) Van Leeuwen, J. Bound for Oregon
                Fic

Watson, Richard Jesse, 1951-
Tom Thumb (k-3)   **398.2**
Watson, Wendy
Thanksgiving at our house   **E**
(il) Bierhorst, J. Doctor Coyote   **398.2**
(il) Showers, P. Sleep is for everyone
              612.8
The **Watsons** go to Birmingham—1963. Curtis, C.
P.   **Fic**
Wattenberg, Jane
Henny-Penny (k-3)   **398.2**
Watts, Bernadette, 1942-
The ugly duckling   **E**
(il) Bell, A. The Snow Queen   **E**
Watts, James, 1955-
(il) Curry, J. L. Back in the beforetime
              398.2
(il) Curry, J. L. Turtle Island: tales of the Algonquian nations   **398.2**
Watts, Marilyn
The leopard in the rafters
In The Oxford book of scary tales p132-36
              808.8
Watts library [series]
McPhee, A. T. AIDS   **616.97**
Waugh, Sylvia
The Mennyms (5 and up)   **Fic**
Mennyms alive. See note under Waugh, S. The Mennyms   **Fic**
Mennyms alone. See note under Waugh, S. The Mennyms   **Fic**
Mennyms in the wilderness. See note under Waugh, S. The Mennyms   **Fic**
Mennyms under siege. See note under Waugh, S. The Mennyms   **Fic**
A **wave** in her pocket. Joseph, L. **398.2**
A **wave** in her pocket [story] Joseph, L.
In Joseph, L. A wave in her pocket p29-35
              398.2
The **wave** of the Sea-Wolf. Wisniewski, D. **E**
Waves. Skurzynski, G.   **539.2**
The **way** meat loves salt. Jaffe, N. **398.2**
The **way** of the storyteller. Sawyer, R. **372.6**
The **way** things work. See Macaulay, D. The new way things work   **600**
The **way** to start a day. Baylor, B. **291.4**
The **Ways** of Knowing Trail. (3-5) See entry in Part 2: Web Resources
Wayside School gets a little stranger. Sachar, L.
              Fic
Wayside School is falling down. Sachar, L. See note under Sachar, L. Wayside School gets a little stranger   **Fic**
We are best friends. Aliki   **E**
We are still here: Native Americans today [series]
Braine, S. Drumbeat—heartbeat **970.004**
King, S. Shannon: an Ojibway dancer
            970.004
Peters, R. M. Clambake   **970.004**

Roessel, M. Kinaaldá: a Navajo girl grows up
          970.004
Roessel, M. Songs from the loom **970.004**
We had a picnic this Sunday past. Woodson, J.
              E
We hide, you seek. Aruego, J.   **E**
We hunted and we hollered. Van Laan, N.
In Van Laan, N. With a whoop and a holler p65   **398.2**
We interrupt this program—. Boiko, C.
In The Big book of Christmas plays p200-12
          808.82
We organized. McKissack, P. C.
In McKissack, P. C. The dark-thirty p17-21
            S C
We were tired of living in a house. Skorpen, L. M.   **E**
Wealth
        Fiction
Hayes, J. A spoon for every bite **E**
Roberts, W. D. The kidnappers (4 and up)
              Fic
Weapons
    See also Armor
Meltzer, M. Weapons & warfare (5 and up)
             355
Weapons & warfare. Meltzer, M. **355**
Weasel. DeFelice, C. C.   **Fic**
Weasels
        Fiction
Seidler, T. The Wainscott weasel (4-6) **Fic**
Weate, Jeremy
A young person's guide to philosophy (5 and up)   **100**
Weather
    See also Meteorology
Challoner, J. Hurricane & tornado (4 and up)
          551.55
Cole, J. The magic school bus inside a hurricane (2-4)   **551.55**
Gibbons, G. Weather words and what they mean (k-3)   **551.6**
Kahl, J. D. National Audubon Society first field guide: weather (4 and up) **551.5**
McMillan, B. The weather sky (4 and up)
          551.57
Simon, S. Weather (3-6)   **551.5**
Singer, M. On the same day in March (k-3)
          551.6
VanCleave, J. P. Janice VanCleave's weather (4 and up)   **551.5**
        Fiction
Thompson, K. Switchers (6 and up) **Fic**
        Poetry
Weather (k-2)   **811.008**
Weather (k-2)   **811.008**
Weather forecasting
Gibbons, G. Weather forecasting (k-3)
          551.63
Kahl, J. D. Weather watch (4-6) **551.63**
The **weather** sky. McMillan, B. **551.57**
Weather watch. Kahl, J. D.   **551.63**
Weather words and what they mean. Gibbons, G.
          551.6

Westall, Robert, 1929-1993
The machine gunners (6 and up)   Fic
Westcott, Nadine Bernard, 1949-
The lady with the alligator purse   E
(il) Heide, F. P. Oh, grow up!   811
(il) Hoberman, M. A. The eensy-weensy spider
        782.42
(il) Hoberman, M. A. Miss Mary Mack
        398.8
(il) Juba this and Juba that. See Juba this and
Juba that   372.6
(comp) Never take a pig to lunch and other poems about the fun of eating. See Never take
a pig to lunch and other poems about the fun
of eating   811.008
(il) Paul, A. W. Hello toes! Hello feet!   E
(il) Pirner, C. W. Even little kids get diabetes
        616.4
(il) Raffi. Down by the bay   782.42
(il) Sloat, T. Farmer Brown goes round and
round   E
(il) Thanksgiving: stories and poems. See
Thanksgiving: stories and poems   810.8
Westcott, Patsy
Living with blindness (3-5)   362.4
Living with leukemia (3-5)   362.1
Western and country music See Country music
Western States See West (U.S.)
The **Westing** game. Raskin, E.   Fic
Westmark. Alexander, L.   Fic
Weston, Carol
The diary of Melanie Martin; or, How I sur-
vived Matt the Brat, Michelangelo, and the
Leaning Tower of Pizza (3-6)   Fic
Weston, Martha, 1947-
Space guys!   E
(il) Burns, M. The book of think   153.4
(il) Cobb, V. Bet you can't! science impossibili-
ties to fool you   793.8
(il) Greene, S. Owen Foote, frontiersman
        Fic
Weston, Reiko
Cooking the Japanese way
In Easy menu ethnic cookbooks   641.5
Westray, Kathleen
Picture puzzler (2-4)   152.14
Westward movement See West (U.S.)—History
Wetlands
        See also Marshes
Gibbons, G. Marshes & swamps (k-3)
        577.6
Whale of a tale. MacDonald, M. R.
In MacDonald, M. R. Twenty tellable tales
p1-9   372.6
Whales
Berger, M. Do whales have belly buttons? (2-4)
        599.5
Carrick, C. Whaling days (3-6)   639.2
Davies, N. Big blue whale (k-3)   599.5
Esbensen, B. J. Baby whales drink milk (k-1)
        599.5
McNulty, F. How whales walked into the sea
(2-4)   599.5

Fiction
London, J. Baby whale's journey   E
Schuch, S. A symphony of whales   E
        Poetry
If you ever meet a whale (3-5)   811.008
Whaling
Carrick, C. Whaling days (3-6)   639.2
McKissack, P. C. Black hands, white sails (5
and up)   639.2
        Fiction
Demas, C. If ever I return again (5 and up)
        Fic
Oppel, K. Peg and the whale   E
Whaling days. Carrick, C.   639.2
Whalley, Paul Ernest Sutton
Butterfly & moth (4 and up)   595.7
Wharton, Edith, 1862-1937
See/See also pages in the following book(s):
Faber, D. Great lives: American literature p268-
77 (5 and up)   920
What!. See Lum, K. What! cried Granny   E
What a morning!   782.25
What a scare, Jesse Bear!. Carlstrom, N. W. See
note under Carlstrom, N. W. Jesse Bear, what
will you wear?   E
What a truly cool world!. Lester, J.   E
What about ladybugs? Godkin, C.   595.7
What are their names!. MacDonald, M. R.
In MacDonald, M. R. The storyteller's start-
up book p155-58   372.6
What are you figuring now? a story about Benja-
min Banneker. Ferris, J.   92
What can you do in the rain? Hines, A. G.
        E
What can you do in the snow? Hines, A. G. See
note under Hines, A. G. What can you do in
the rain?   E
What can you do in the sun? Hines, A. G. See
note under Hines, A. G. What can you do in
the rain?   E
What can you do in the wind? Hines, A. G. See
note under Hines, A. G. What can you do in
the rain?   E
What can you do with a shoe? De Regniers, B. S.
        E
What! cried Granny. Lum, K.   E
What daddies do best. See Numeroff, L. J. What
mommies do best   E
What dads can't do. Wood, D.   E
What do authors do? Christelow, E.   808
What do children read next? Colborn, C.
        016.8
What do fish have to do with anything? Avi
In Avi. What do fish have to do with any-
thing? and other stories p9-32   S C
What do fish have to do with anything? and other
stories. Avi   S C
What do illustrators do? Christelow, E.   741.6
What do you do, dear? Joslin, S.   395
What do you do when something wants to eat
you? Jenkins, S.   591.47
What do you hear when cows sing? Maestro, M.
        793.73

What do you say, dear? Joslin, S. **395**

What does the rabbit say? Hall, J. **E**

What Eric knew. Howe, J. See note under Howe, J. Dew drop dead **Fic**

What happened to Patrick's dinosaurs? Carrick, C. See note under Carrick, C. Patrick's dinosaurs **E**

What happens to a hamburger? Showers, P. **612.3**

What Hershel's father did. Kimmel, E. A.
In Kimmel, E. A. The adventures of Hershel of Ostropol p9-12 **398.2**

What I believe. Birdseye, D. H. **200**

What I had was singing: the story of Marian Anderson. Ferris, J. **92**

What is an amphibian? Snedden, R. **597.8**

What is Talmud? Jaffe, N.
In Jaffe, N. While standing on one foot p45-49 **296.1**

What is the world made of? Zoehfeld, K. W. **530.4**

What is trouble? Lester, J.
In Lester, J. The knee-high man, and other tales p5-8 **398.2**

What Jamie saw. Coman, C. **Fic**

What lives in a shell? Zoehfeld, K. W. **591.4**

What makes a magnet? Branley, F. M. **538**

What makes a shadow? Bulla, C. R. **535**

What Mary Jo shared. Udry, J. M. **E**

What mommies do best. Numeroff, L. J. **E**

What six girls with balloons told the Gray Man on Horseback. Sandburg, C.
In Sandburg, C. Rootabaga stories pt 1 p138-44 **S C**
In Sandburg, C. The Sandburg treasury p65-68 **818**

What the moon is like. Branley, F. M. **523.3**

What the moon sees. See Tafuri, N. What the sun sees **E**

What the sun sees. Tafuri, N. **E**

What they did not do on the birthday of Jacob Abbott B., familiarly called Snibbuggledyboozledom
In American fairy tales p63-66 **S C**

What you never knew about fingers, forks, & chopsticks. Lauber, P. **394.1**

What Zeesie saw on Delancey Street. Rael, E. O. **E**

Whatever happened to good old Ebenezer Scrooge? Majeski, B.
In The Big book of Christmas plays p151-68 **808.82**

Whatever happened to the dinosaurs? Most, B. **E**

What's Claude doing? Gackenbach, D. **E**

What's cooking, Jenny Archer? Conford, E. See note under Conford, E. A case for Jenny Archer **Fic**

What's for lunch? [series]
Llewellyn, C. Oranges **641**

What's inside. Avi
In Avi. What do fish have to do with anything? and other stories p153-72 **S C**

What's it like to be a fish? Pfeffer, W. **597**

What's the big idea, Ben Franklin? Fritz, J. **92**

What's the big secret? Brown, L. K. **613.9**

What's the matter with Carruthers? Marshall, J. See note under Marshall, J. Yummers! **E**

What's the matter with Herbie Jones? Kline, S. See note under Kline, S. Herbie Jones **Fic**

What's their story? [series]
Langley, A. Hans Christian Andersen **92**

What's what? a guessing game. Serfozo, M. **E**

What's your story? Bauer, M. D. **808.3**

Wheat
Landau, E. Wheat (2-4) **633.1**

Wheatley, Phillis, 1753-1784
See/See also pages in the following book(s):
Wilkinson, B. S. African American women writers (4 and up) **810.9**

The wheel on the school. DeJong, M. **Fic**

Wheeler, Sara
Greetings from Antarctica **998**

The wheels on the bus. Kovalski, M. **782.42**

Wheelwright, Sidnee
(il) Cone, M. Come back, salmon **639.3**

Whelan, Gloria
Goodbye, Vietnam (4 and up) **Fic**
Homeless bird (6 and up) **Fic**

When Africa was home. Williams, K. L. **E**

When Agnes caws. Fleming, C. **E**

When Bear stole the chinook. Taylor, H. P. **398.2**

When birds could talk & bats could sing. Hamilton, V. **398.2**

When Bluebell sang. Ernst, L. C. **E**

When clay sings. Baylor, B. **970.004**

When dinosaurs die. Brown, L. K. **155.9**

When Hershel eats. Kimmel, E. A.
In Kimmel, E. A. The spotted pony: a collection of Hanukkah stories p57-60 **398.2**

When Hitler stole Pink Rabbit. Kerr, J. **Fic**

When I am old with you. Johnson, A. **E**

When I first came to this land. Ziefert, H. **782.42**

When I was young in the mountains. Rylant, C. **E**

When jaguars ate the moon and other stories about animals and plants of the Americas. Brusca, M. C. **398.2**

When Jessie came across the sea. Hest, A. **E**

When Miss Bat could sing. Hamilton, V.
In Hamilton, V. When birds could talk & bats could sing p41-45 **398.2**

When Pig got smart. Marshall, J.
In Marshall, J. Rats on the range and other stories p57-62 **S C**

When Pig took the wheel. Marshall, J.
In Marshall, J. Rats on the range and other stories p34-42 **S C**

When Pig went to heaven. Marshall, J.
In Marshall, J. Rats on the range and other stories p24-33 **S C**

When Shlemiel went to Warsaw. Singer, I. B.
In Singer, I. B. Stories for children p194-205 **S C**
In Singer, I. B. When Shlemiel went to Warsaw & other stories p99-115 **398.2**

When Shlemiel went to Warsaw & other stories. Singer, I. B. **398.2**

When Sophie gets angry—really, really angry. Bang, M. **E**

When spring comes. Maass, R. **508.2**

When the beginning began. Lester, J. **296.1**

When the Chenoo howls. Bruchac, J. **398.2**

When the circus came to town. Horvath, P. **Fic**

When the lights go out. MacDonald, M. R. **372.6**

When the new baby comes, I'm moving out. Alexander, M. G. **E**

When the rain sings (4 and up) **811.008**

When the soldiers were gone. Propp, V. W. **Fic**

When the sun and the moon were children. Delacre, L.
In Delacre, L. Golden tales p31-35 **398.2**

When the sun dies. Gallant, R. A. **523.7**

When the Tripods came. Christopher, J. See note under Christopher, J. The White Mountains **Fic**

When the wind stops. Zolotow, C. **E**

When Tiny was tiny. Meister, C. See note under Meister, C. Tiny's bath **E**

When Vera was sick. Rosenberry, V. See note under Rosenberry, V. Vera's first day of school **E**

When we were very young. Milne, A. A. **821**
also in Milne, A. A. The world of Christopher Robin p1-118 **821**

When will I read? Cohen, M. See note under Cohen, M. It's George! **E**

When will Sarah come? Howard, E. F. **E**

When you go to kindergarten. Howe, J. **372.2**

When Zachary Beaver came to town. Holt, K. W. **Fic**

Where are the night animals? Fraser, M. A. **591.5**

Where are you going, little mouse? Kraus, R. See note under Kraus, R. Whose mouse are you? **E**

Where do you think you're going, Christopher Columbus? Fritz, J. **92**

Where does Joe go? Pearson, T. C. **E**

Where does the brown bear go? Weiss, N. **E**

Where does the garbage go? Showers, P. **363.7**

Where is Christmas, Jesse Bear? Carlstrom, N. W. See note under Carlstrom, N. W. Jesse Bear, what will you wear? **E**

Where is Elijah? Jaffe, N.
In Jaffe, N. The mysterious visitor p87-91 **398.2**

Where is Grandpa? Barron, T. A. **E**

Where once there was a wood. Fleming, D. **639.9**

Where one is fed a hundred can dine. Sawyer, R.
In Sawyer, R. The way of the storyteller p251-55 **372.6**

Where the buffaloes begin. Baker, O. **Fic**

Where the forest meets the sea. Baker, J. **E**

Where the girl rescued her brother. Bruchac, J.
In Bruchac, J. The girl who married the Moon p101-07 **398.2**

Where the lillies bloom. Cleaver, V. **Fic**

Where the red fern grows. Rawls, W. **Fic**

Where the river begins. Locker, T. **E**

Where the sidewalk ends. Silverstein, S. **811**

Where the wild things are. Sendak, M. **E**

Where was Patrick Henry on the 29th of May? Fritz, J. **92**

Where will this shoe take you? Lawlor, L. **391**

Where's my teddy? Alborough, J. See note under Alborough, J. My friend Bear **E**

Where's the baby? Hutchins, P. **E**

Which way freedom? Hansen, J. **Fic**

Which witch? Ibbotson, E. **Fic**

While no one was watching. Conly, J. L. **Fic**

While standing on one foot. Jaffe, N. **296.1**

While the candles burn. Goldin, B. D. **296.4**

While you're waiting for the food to come. Muller, E. P. **507.8**

The **whingdingdilly**. Peet, B. **E**

The **whipping** boy. Fleischman, S. **Fic**

Whipple, Catherine
(il) King, S. Shannon: an Ojibway dancer **970.004**

Whipple, Laura
(comp) Carle, E. Eric Carle's dragons dragons and other creatures that never were **808.81**

Whippo, Walt
Little white duck (k-2) **782.42**

The **whisper** of Glocken. Kendall, C. See note under Kendall, C. The Gammage Cup **Fic**

Whistle for Willie. Keats, E. J. See note under Keats, E. J. The snowy day **E**

Whistling Dixie. Vaughan, M. **E**

White, E. B. (Elwyn Brooks), 1899-1985
Charlotte's web (3-6) **Fic**
Stuart Little (3-6) **Fic**
The trumpet of the swan (3-6) **Fic**
See/See also pages in the following book(s):
Faber, D. Great lives: American literature p278-86 (5 and up) **920**
Krull, K. Lives of the writers p78-81 (4 and up) **920**

Why Blackfeet never kill mice. Curry, J. L.
In Curry, J. L. Turtle Island: tales of the Algonquian nations p59-62   **398.2**

Why Brer Bull growls and grumbles. Lester, J.
In Lester, J. The last tales of Uncle Remus p119-23   **398.2**

Why Brer Fox's legs are black. Lester, J.
In Lester, J. The last tales of Uncle Remus p64-66   **398.2**

Why Brer Possum has no hair on his tail. Lester, J.
In Lester, J. The last tales of Uncle Remus p41-44   **398.2**

Why Brer Possum loves peace. Lester, J.
In Lester, J. The last tales of Uncle Remus p44-46   **398.2**

Why Bush Cow and Elephant are bad friends. Bryan, A.
In Bryan, A. Ashley Bryan's African tales, uh-huh p54-69   **398.2**

Why chickens scratch in the dirt. Lester, J.
In Lester, J. The last tales of Uncle Remus p147-49   **398.2**

Why deer have short tails. Curry, J. L.
In Curry, J. L. Turtle Island: tales of the Algonquian nations p18-20   **398.2**

Why did the chicken cross the road? and other riddles, old and new. Cole, J.   **793.73**

Why do leaves change color? Maestro, B.   **582.16**

Why doesn't the earth fall up? Cobb, V.   **531**

Why dogs are tame. Lester, J.
In Lester, J. The last tales of Uncle Remus p76-82   **398.2**

Why dogs cannot talk like people. Hausman, G.
In Hausman, G. Dogs of myth p11-14   **398.2**

Why dogs hate cats. Lester, J.
In Lester, J. The knee-high man, and other tales p9-11   **398.2**

Why don't haircuts hurt? Berger, M.   **612**

Why don't you get a horse, Sam Adams? Fritz, J.   **92**

The **why** files. (5 and up) See entry in Part 2: Web Resources

Why Frog and Snake never play together. Bryan, A.
In Bryan, A. Ashley Bryan's African tales, uh-huh p81-92   **398.2**

Why guinea fowls are speckled. Lester, J.
In Lester, J. The last tales of Uncle Remus p88-93   **398.2**

Why I cough, sneeze, shiver, hiccup & yawn. See Berger, M. Why I sneeze, shiver, hiccup, and yawn   **612.7**

Why I sneeze, shiver, hiccup, and yawn. Berger, M.   **612.7**

Why Koala has no tale. MacDonald, M. R.
In MacDonald, M. R. Look back and see p74-80   **372.6**

Why mosquitoes buzz in people's ears. Aardema, V.   **398.2**

Why Noah chose the dove. Singer, I. B.
In Singer, I. B. Stories for children p41-44   **S C**

Why not? Wormell, M.   **E**

Why not, Lafayette? Fritz, J.   **92**

Why on this night? Musleah, R.   **296.4**

Why the big ball game between Hot Grounders and the Grand Standers was a hot game. Sandburg, C.
In Sandburg, C. Rootabaga stories pt 2 p130-34   **S C**
In Sandburg, C. The Sandburg treasury p142-44   **818**

Why the chicken crossed the road. Macaulay, D.   **E**

Why the cricket has elbows on his legs. Lester, J.
In Lester, J. The last tales of Uncle Remus p3-8   **398.2**

Why the earth is mostly water. Lester, J.
In Lester, J. The last tales of Uncle Remus p8-12   **398.2**

Why the goat has a short tail. Lester, J.
In Lester, J. The last tales of Uncle Remus p136-38   **398.2**

Why the Guineas stay awake. Lester, J.
In Lester, J. The last tales of Uncle Remus p93-94   **398.2**

Why the hawk likes to eat chickens. Lester, J.
In Lester, J. The last tales of Uncle Remus p98-102   **398.2**

Why the rude visitor was flung by walrus. Norman, H.
In Norman, H. The girl who dreamed only geese, and other tales of the Far North   **398.2**

Why the sea is salt
In Christmas fairy tales p65-70   **398.2**

Why the sea is salt. Asbjornsen, P. C.
In The Blue fairy book p136-40   **398.2**

Why the sky is far away. Gerson, M.-J.   **398.2**

Why the Sun & Moon live in the sky. Daly, N.   **398.2**

Why the Sun and the Moon live in the sky. Dayrell, E.   **398.2**

Why the tides ebb and flow. Bowden, J. C.   **398.2**

Why the waves have whitecaps. Lester, J.
In Lester, J. The knee-high man, and other tales p21-23   **398.2**

Why women won't listen. Sherlock, Sir P. M.
In Sherlock, Sir P. M. West Indian folk-tales p112-17   **398.2**

Whybrow, Ian
Sammy and the dinosaurs   **E**

Wiberg, Harald, 1908-
(il) Lindgren, A. The Tomten   **E**

Wick, Walter
A drop of water (4-6)   **553.7**
I spy   **793.73**
I spy Christmas   **793.73**
I spy extreme challenger!   **793.73**
I spy fantasy   **793.73**

Wild flowers—*Continued*

Conservation

See Plant conservation

Fiction

Marshall, J. P. A honey of a day   **E**

Wild horses I have known. Ryden, H.   **599.66**

The **wild** kid. Mazer, H.   **Fic**

Wild West days. King, D. C.   **978**

Wilde, Oscar, 1854-1900

The fairy tales of Oscar Wilde (3-6)   **S C**
Contents: The happy prince; The Nightingale and the rose; The selfish Giant; The devoted friend; The remarkable rocket; The young king; The birthday of the Infanta; The Fisherman and his soul; The Star-Child

The selfish giant (2-5)   **Fic**

also in The Oxford treasury of children's stories p121-26   **S C**

Selfish giant; adaptation. See Waters, F. Oscar Wilde's The selfish giant   **Fic**

Wilder, Laura Ingalls, 1867-1957

By the shores of Silver Lake. See note under Wilder, L. I. Little house in the big woods   **Fic**

Farmer boy. See note under Wilder, L. I. Little house in the big woods   **Fic**

The first four years. See note under Wilder, L. I. Little house in the big woods   **Fic**

Little house in the big woods (4-6)   **Fic**

Little house on the prairie. See note under Wilder, L. I. Little house in the big woods   **Fic**

Little town on the prairie. See note under Wilder, L. I. Little house in the big woods   **Fic**

The long winter. See note under Wilder, L. I. Little house in the big woods   **Fic**

On the banks of Plum Creek. See note under Wilder, L. I. Little house in the big woods   **Fic**

These happy golden years. See note under Wilder, L. I. Little house in the big woods   **Fic**

West from home (6 and up)   **92**

About

Anderson, W. T. Pioneer girl: the story of Laura Ingalls Wilder (2-4)   **92**

Walker, B. M. The Little House cookbook (5 and up)   **641.5**

Wilderness survival

Fiction

Eckert, A. W. Incident at Hawk's Hill (6 and up)   **Fic**

Fleischman, P. Lost!   **Fic**

George, J. C. Julie of the wolves (6 and up)   **Fic**

Houston, J. A. Frozen fire (6 and up)   **Fic**

O'Dell, S. Island of the Blue Dolphins (5 and up)   **Fic**

Wildfire. Cone, P.   **577.2**

Wildfires. Simon, S.   **577.2**

Wildflower ABC. Pomeroy, D.   **E**

Wildlife conservation

See also Game protection

Cone, M. Come back, salmon (3-6)   **639.3**

Fleming, D. Where once there was a wood (k-2)   **639.9**

Galan, M. A. There's still time (3-6)   **333.95**

Goodman, S. Animal rescue (2-4)   **639.9**

Lasky, K. Monarchs (4 and up)   **595.7**

Patent, D. H. Back to the wild (4-6)   **639.9**

Patent, D. H. Ospreys (4 and up)   **598**

Silverstein, A. The California condor (4 and up)   **598**

Silverstein, A. The Florida panther (4 and up)   **599.75**

Smith, R. Journey of the red wolf (4 and up)   **599.77**

Swinburne, S. R. Once a wolf (4 and up)   **333.95**

See/See also pages in the following book(s):

Walker, S. M. Rhinos (3-6)   **599.66**

Fiction

George, J. C. Frightful's mountain (5 and up)   **Fic**

McCully, E. A. Hurry! (2-4)   **Fic**

The **wildlife** detectives. Jackson, D.   **363.2**

Wildlife refuges

Patent, D. H. Places of refuge (4 and up)   **333.95**

Fiction

Cowcher, H. Tigress   **E**

Wildsmith, Brian, 1930-

ABC   **E**

The Bremen Town Band (k-2)   **398.2**

Brian Wildsmith's birds   **E**

Brian Wildsmith's fishes   **E**

Brian Wildsmith's wild animals   **E**

A Christmas story   **E**

Exodus   **222**

The hare and the tortoise (k-2)   **398.2**

The miller, the boy and the donkey (k-2)   **398.2**

(il) Mother Goose. See Mother Goose [illus. by Brian Wildsmith]   **398.8**

(il) Stevenson, R. L. A child's garden of verses   **821**

Wiley and the Hairy Man. Bang, M.   **398.2**

Wiley and The Hairy Man. Haviland, V.

In The Oxford book of scary tales p55-61   **808.8**

Wiley, his mama, and the Hairy Man. Hamilton, V.

In Hamilton, V. The people could fly: American black folktales p90-103   **398.2**

Wilhelm Tell. McCaughrean, G.

In McCaughrean, G. The silver treasure: myths and legends of the world p60-69   **398.2**

Wilhelm von Schmitz. Carroll, L.

In Carroll, L. The complete works of Lewis Carroll p986-98   **828**

Wilkes, Angela

My first word book   **E**

Wilkes, Debbi

The figure skating book (4 and up)   **796.91**

Wilkins, Mary Huiskamp Calhoun See Calhoun, Mary, 1926-

Willis, Terri
Libya (4 and up) **961.2**

Willner-Pardo, Gina
Daphne Eloise Slater, who's tall for her age (2-4) **Fic**
Figuring out Frances (4-6) **Fic**

Willoughby-Herb, Sara
(jt. auth) Herb, S. Using children's books in preschool settings **372.4**

Will's choice. Nixon, J. L. See note under Nixon, J. L. Aggie's home **Fic**

Will's mammoth. Martin, R. **E**

Willy and Hugh. See note under Browne, A. Willy the dreamer **E**

Willy the champ. Browne, A. See note under Browne, A. Willy the dreamer **E**

Willy the dreamer. Browne, A. **E**

Willy the wizard. Browne, A. See note under Browne, A. Willy the dreamer **E**

Willy's pictures. Browne, A. See note under Browne, A. Willy the dreamer **E**

Wilma unlimited: how Wilma Rudolph became the world's fastest woman. Krull, K. **92**

Wilner, Isabel
B is for Bethlehem **E**
The baby's game book **398.8**

Wilsdon, Christina
National Audubon Society first field guide: insects (4 and up) **595.7**
The solar system: an A-Z guide **520.3**

Wilson, Alex
(il) Hill, D. Witches & magic-makers **133.4**

Wilson, Colin, 1931-
Mysteries of the universe (4 and up) **001.9**
UFOs and aliens (4 and up) **001.9**

Wilson, Diane L.
I rode a horse of milk white jade (6 and up) **Fic**

Wilson, Janet, 1962-
The ingenious Mr. Peale (4 and up) **92**

Wilson, Richard, 1920-1987
The laughing dragon
In The Oxford treasury of children's stories p39-44 **S C**

Wilson, Sharon Rose
(il) Sisulu, E. B. The day Gogo went to vote **E**

Wilson, Toña
(jt. auth) Brusca, M. C. Three friends. Tres amigos **E**
(jt. auth) Brusca, M. C. When jaguars ate the moon and other stories about animals and plants of the Americas **398.2**

Wilson-Max, Ken, 1965-
Furaha means happy (k-2) **496**
Halala means welcome! (k-2) **496**

Wimmer, Mike
(il) Burleigh, R. Flight: the journey of Charles Lindbergh **92**
(il) Burleigh, R. Home run **E**
(il) Fritz, J. Bully for you, Teddy Roosevelt! **92**

(il) MacLachlan, P. All the places to love **E**

(il) Siebert, D. Train song **E**

Winborn, Marsha
(il) Baker, B. Digby and Kate and the beautiful day **E**
(il) Murphy, S. J. Pepper's journal **E**

Winch, John, 1944-
The old woman who loved to read **E**

The **wind** blew. Hutchins, P. **E**

A **wind** in the door. L'Engle, M. See note under L'Engle, M. A wrinkle in time **Fic**

The **wind** in the willows. Grahame, K. **Fic**

The **wind** rider. San Souci, R.
In San Souci, R. Even more short & shivery p62-66 **398.2**

Wind song. Sandburg, C.
In Sandburg, C. The Sandburg treasury p209-61 **818**

Windham, Kathryn Tucker
Things that go bump in the night
In From sea to shining sea p340-41 **810.8**

Windigo Island. San Souci, R.
In San Souci, R. More short & shivery p33-39 **398.2**

Window. Baker, J. **E**

The **window.** Dorris, M. **Fic**

Window music. Suen, A. **E**

Winds
Dorros, A. Feel the wind (k-3) **551.51**

Fiction
Ets, M. H. Gilberto and the Wind **E**
Hutchins, P. The wind blew **E**
Karas, G. B. The windy day **E**
McKissack, P. C. Mirandy and Brother Wind **E**

The **windy** day. Karas, G. B. **E**

Wings. Myers, C. A. **E**

Wings of an artist **741.6**

The **wings** of Merlin. Barron, T. A. See note under Barron, T. A. The lost years of Merlin **Fic**

Winkel, Lois, 1939-
(ed) Subject headings for children. See Subject headings for children **025.4**

Winner, Cherie
The sunflower family (3-6) **583**

Winnie-the-Pooh. Milne, A. A. **Fic**
also in Milne, A. A. The complete tales of Winnie-the-Pooh p1-159 **Fic**
also in Milne, A. A. The world of Pooh p7-149 **Fic**

Winter, Jeanette
Cowboy Charlie: the story of Charles M. Russell (k-3) **92**
Follow the drinking gourd **E**
The house that Jack built **398.8**
Josefina **E**
My name is Georgia [biography of Georgia O'Keeffe] (k-3) **92**
Sebastian: a book about Bach (k-3) **92**
(il) Goldin, B. D. The world's birthday **E**

Winter, Jeanette—*Continued*
  (il) Johnston, T. Day of the Dead   E
  (il) Paul, A. W. Eight hands round   E
  (il) Winter, J. Diego   92
Winter, Jonah
  Diego (k-3)   92
Winter, Susan
  (il) Simon, F. Toddler time   821
Winter
  Bancroft, H. Animals in winter (k-1)
   591.56
  Hader, B. The big snow   E
  Hirschi, R. Winter (k-2)   508.2
  Kurelek, W. A prairie boy's winter (3-5)
   971.27
Fiction
  Fleming, D. Time to sleep   E
  Gammell, S. Is that you, winter?   E
  Hughes, S. Stories by firelight   E
  Lindgren, A. The Tomten   E
  Root, P. Grandmother Winter   E
Poetry
  Florian, D. Winter eyes   811
  Prelutsky, J. It's snowing! It's snowing! (1-3)
   811
  Winter poems   808.81
Winter eyes. Florian, D.   811
Winter poems   808.81
The **winter** room. Paulsen, G.   Fic
Winter sports
  See also Olympic games
Winthrop, Elizabeth
  The battle for the castle. See note under Winthrop, E. The castle in the attic   Fic
  The castle in the attic (4-6)   Fic
  He is risen: the Easter story (k-3)   232.9
  The little humpbacked horse (4-6)   398.2
  Promises   E
  Shoes   E
Winyan Ohitika. Mayer, M.
  In Mayer, M. Women warriors p67-69
   398
Wisconsin
  Blashfield, J. F. Wisconsin
  In America the beautiful, second series
   973
  Zeinert, K. Wisconsin
  In Celebrate the states   973
Fiction
  Brink, C. R. Caddie Woodlawn (4-6)   Fic
  Wilder, L. I. Little house in the big woods (4-6)
   Fic
Wisdom for sale. Kimmel, E. A.
  In Kimmel, E. A. The jar of fools: eight Hanukkah stories from Chelm p42-55
   S C
The **wisdom** of Princess Maya. Bruchac, J.
  In Bruchac, J. Tell me a tale p46-51
   372.6
The **wisdom** of the crows and other Buddhist tales. Chödzin, S.   294.3
The **wisdom** of the willow tree. Bruchac, J.
  In Bruchac, J. Flying with the eagle, racing with the great bear p54-56   398.2

Wise, William, 1923-
  Dinosaurs forever (k-3)   **811**
  Ten sly piranhas   E
The **wise** dove. Lee, J. M.
  In Lee, J. M. I once was a monkey
   294.3
The **wise** fools of Chelm. Jaffe, N.
  In Jaffe, N. While standing on one foot p62-65   296.1
The **wise** king. Jaffe, N.
  In Jaffe, N. The cow of no color: riddle stories and justice tales from around the world p118-21   398.2
The **wise** little girl. Afanas'ev, A. N.
  In Afanas'ev, A. N. Russian fairy tales p252-55   398.2
The **wise** maiden and the seven robbers. Afanas'ev, A. N.
  In Afanas'ev, A. N. Russian fairy tales p134-40   398.2
Wise men (Magi) *See* Magi
The **wise** men of Gotham. Jacobs, J.
  In Jacobs, J. English fairy tales p418-24
   398.2
The **wise** old shepherd. Rouse, W. H. D.
  In Shedlock, M. L. The art of the story-teller p216-21   372.6
The **wise** wife. Afanas'ev, A. N.
  In Afanas'ev, A. N. Russian fairy tales p521-28   398.2
Wiseman, Bernard
  Morris and Boris at the circus   E
  Morris has a cold. See note under Wiseman, B. Morris and Boris at the circus   E
  The riddles
  In Ready, set, read—and laugh! p56-74
   810.8
Wiseman, David, 1916-
  Jeremy Visick (5 and up)   Fic
Wishes
Fiction
  Billingsley, F. Well wished (4-6)   Fic
  Zemach, M. The three wishes (k-2)   398.2
Wishes. Babbitt, N.
  In Babbitt, N. The Devil's storybook p3-11
   S C
Wisler, G. Clifton, 1950-
  Mr. Lincoln's drummer (4 and up)   Fic
  Red Cap (4 and up)   Fic
Wisniewski, David
  Golem (3-5)   398.2
  Rain player   E
  Sundiata (1-4)   92
  The warrior and the wise man   E
  The wave of the Sea-Wolf   E
  (il) Clements, A. Workshop   621.9
  See/See also pages in the following book(s):
  The Newbery & Caldecott medal books, 1986-2000 p256-65   028.5
Wit and humor
  See also Humorous poetry; Jewish wit and humor; Jokes; Puns
  Schwartz, A. All of our noses are here, and other noodle tales (k-2)   398.2

A **wolf** and Little Daughter. Hamilton, V.
  In Hamilton, V. The people could fly:
    American black folktales p60-64
    398.2

The **wolf** and the goat. Afanas'ev, A. N.
  In Afanas'ev, A. N. Russian fairy tales p249-
    51 **398.2**

Wolf children *See* Wild children

Wolfe, Art, 1951-
  (il) Pandell, K. Journey through the northern
    rainforest **578.7**

Wolfe, Diane
  (il) Brady, A. A. Kwanzaa karamu **641.5**

Wolfe, Robert L.
  (il) Brady, A. A. Kwanzaa karamu **641.5**

Wolff, Ashley, 1956-
  Stella & Roy **E**
  Stella & Roy go camping. See note under
    Wolff, A. Stella & Roy **E**
  (il) Marzollo, J. Home sweet home **E**
  (il) Raffi. Baby Beluga **782.42**
  (il) Ryder, J. Each living thing **E**
  (il) Slate, J. Miss Bindergarten celebrates the
    100th day of kindergarten **E**
  (il) Zolotow, C. Some things go together **E**

Wolff, Patricia Rae
  The toll-bridge troll **E**

Wolff, Virginia Euwer
  Bat 6 (5 and up) **Fic**
  The Mozart season (6 and up) **Fic**

Wolfram, von Eschenbach, 12th cent.
  Parzival; adaptation. See Paterson, K. Parzival
    398.2

The **wolf's** chicken stew. Kasza, K. **E**

Wolk-Stanley, Jessica
  (il) Campbell, A. The New York Public Library
    amazing space **520**
  (il) Cobb, V. How to really fool yourself
    152.1

Wolkstein, Diane
  The banza (k-3) **398.2**
  Bye-bye
    In From sea to shining sea p367 **810.8**
  Esther's story (3-5) **222**
  Owl
    In From sea to shining sea p266-67
    810.8
  White wave (k-3) **398.2**
  (comp) The Magic orange tree, and other Hai-
    tian folktales. See The Magic orange tree, and
    other Haitian folktales **398.2**

The **wolverine's** secret. Norman, H.
  In Norman, H. The girl who dreamed only
    geese, and other tales of the Far North
    398.2

Wolves
  Brandenburg, J. Scruffy (2-4) **599.77**
  Brandenburg, J. To the top of the world (4 and
    up) **599.77**
  George, M. Wolves (1-3) **599.77**
  Gibbons, G. Wolves (k-3) **599.77**
  Silverstein, A. The red wolf (4 and up)
    599.77
  Simon, S. Wolves (3-6) **599.77**

Smith, R. Journey of the red wolf (4 and up)
    599.77
Swinburne, S. R. Once a wolf (4 and up)
    333.95
See/See also pages in the following book(s):
Patent, D. H. Back to the wild p12-27 (4-6)
    639.9
  Fiction
Ernst, L. C. Little Red Riding Hood: a newfan-
    gled prairie tale (k-3) **398.2**
George, J. C. Julie (6 and up) **Fic**
George, J. C. Julie of the wolves (6 and up)
    Fic
George, J. C. Julie's wolf pack (6 and up)
    Fic
George, J. C. Look to the North **E**
Goble, P. Dream wolf **E**
Grimm, J. Little Red Cap (k-3) **398.2**
Hyman, T. S. Little Red Riding Hood (k-2)
    398.2
Kasza, K. The wolf's chicken stew **E**
Kitamura, S. Sheep in wolves' clothing **E**
London, J. Red wolf country **E**
Marshall, J. Red Riding Hood (k-2) **398.2**
Marshall, J. Swine Lake **E**
Marshall, J. The three little pigs (k-2)
    398.2
Meddaugh, S. The best place **E**
Meddaugh, S. Hog-eye **E**
Novak, M. Little Wolf, Big Wolf **E**
Numeroff, L. J. The Chicken sisters **E**
Palatini, M. Piggie pie! **E**
Prokofiev, S. Peter and the wolf **E**
Scieszka, J. The true story of the 3 little pigs
    E
Trivizas, E. The three little wolves and the big
    bad pig **E**
Young, E. Lon Po Po (1-3) **398.2**
Zemach, M. The three little pigs (k-2)
    398.2

The **wolves** of Willoughby Chase. Aiken, J.
    Fic

Womack, Alfred
  (il) Brazelton, T. B. Going to the doctor
    610.69

The **Woman**, Adam, and the fruit. Lester, J.
  In Lester, J. When the beginning began p81-
    85 **296.1**

Woman and Man started even. Hamilton, V.
  In Hamilton, V. Her stories p69-74
    398.2

The **woman** in the snow. McKissack, P. C.
  In McKissack, P. C. The dark-thirty p55-65
    S C

The **woman** who flummoxed the fairies. Forest, H.
    398.2

The **woman** who flummoxed the fairies. Leodhas,
  S. N.
  In Womenfolk and fairy tales p135-45
    398.2

The **woman** who left no footprints. McCaughrean,
  G.
  In McCaughrean, G. The bronze cauldron:
    myths and legends of the world p92-96
    398.2

The **World** Book year book. See The World Book encyclopedia **031**

World geography. (6 and up) See entry in Part 2: Web Resources

World history
Haywood, J. World atlas of the past **911**
Knight, M. B. Talking walls (3-5) **909**
Knight, M. B. Talking walls: the stories continue (3-5) **909**

15th century
Brenner, B. If you were there in 1492 (4-6) **970.01**

20th century
Jennings, P. The century for young people **909.82**

Dictionaries
Worldmark encyclopedia of the nations **910.3**

World holidays. Moehn, H. **394.26**
The **world** of Christopher Robin. Milne, A. A. **821**
The **world** of King Arthur and his court. Crossley-Holland, K. **942.01**
The **world** of Pooh. Milne, A. A. **Fic**
The **world** of storytelling. Pellowski, A. **372.6**
The **world** of William Joyce scrapbook. Joyce, W. **92**

World politics
Dictionaries
Worldmark encyclopedia of the nations **910.3**

World Series. Tunis, J. R. See note under Tunis, J. R. The Kid from Tomkinsville **Fic**
The **world** turned upside down. Ferrie, R. **973.3**

World War, 1914-1918
Gay, K. World War I (5 and up) **940.3**
United States
Dolan, E. F. America in World War I (5 and up) **940.3**

World War, 1939-1945
Aerial operations
See/See also pages in the following book(s):
Haskins, J. Black eagles p74-121 (5 and up) **629.13**

Battles, sieges, etc.
See World War, 1939-1945—Aerial operations; World War, 1939-1945—Naval operations

Children
Leapman, M. Witnesses to war (5 and up) **940.53**
Tunnell, M. O. The children of Topaz (5 and up) **940.53**

Fiction
Borden, L. The little ships **E**
Bunting, E. Spying on Miss Müller (5 and up) **Fic**
Cooper, S. Dawn of fear (5 and up) **Fic**
Giff, P. R. Lily's crossing (4 and up) **Fic**
Greene, B. Summer of my German soldier (6 and up) **Fic**

Hahn, M. D. Following my own footsteps (5 and up) **Fic**
Hahn, M. D. Stepping on the cracks (5 and up) **Fic**
Harrison, B. Theo (5 and up) **Fic**
King-Smith, D. Spider Sparrow (4-6) **Fic**
Lee, M. Nim and the war effort **E**
Levitin, S. Journey to America (4 and up) **Fic**
Levoy, M. Alan and Naomi (6 and up) **Fic**
Lowry, L. Autumn Street (4 and up) **Fic**
Lowry, L. Number the stars (4 and up) **Fic**
Maguire, G. The good liar (4 and up) **Fic**
Mazer, N. F. Good night, Maman (5 and up) **Fic**
Mochizuki, K. Baseball saved us **E**
Morpurgo, M. Waiting for Anya (5 and up) **Fic**
Myers, W. D. The journal of Scott Pendleton Collins (5 and up) **Fic**
Napoli, D. J. Stones in water (5 and up) **Fic**
Oppenheim, S. L. The lily cupboard **E**
Orlev, U. The island on Bird Street (5 and up) **Fic**
Orlev, U. The man from the other side (6 and up) **Fic**
Paton Walsh, J. Fireweed (5 and up) **Fic**
Paulsen, G. The cookcamp (5 and up) **Fic**
Polacco, P. The butterfly (2-4) **Fic**
Serraillier, I. The silver sword (5 and up) **Fic**
Uchida, Y. The bracelet **E**
Watkins, Y. K. My brother, my sister, and I (6 and up) **Fic**
Watkins, Y. K. So far from the bamboo grove (6 and up) **Fic**
Westall, R. The machine gunners (6 and up) **Fic**

Jews
See also Holocaust, 1933-1945
Adler, D. A. Hiding from the Nazis (2-4) **940.53**

Jews—Rescue
Gold, A. L. A special fate (5 and up) **940.53**
Meltzer, M. Rescue: the story of how Gentiles saved Jews in the Holocaust (6 and up) **940.53**
Mochizuki, K. Passage to freedom (3-6) **940.53**

Naval operations
McGowen, T. Sink the Bismarck (5 and up) **940.54**

Women
Kuhn, B. Angels of mercy (5 and up) **940.54**

Germany
McGowen, T. Germany's lightning war (5 and up) **940.54**

Japan
Maruki, T. Hiroshima no pika **940.54**

United States
Colman, P. Rosie the riveter (5 and up) **331.4**

World War, 1939-1945—United States—*Continued*

Hamanaka, S. The journey (5 and up)
          305.8

Stanley, J. I am an American (5 and up)
          305.8

Stevenson, J. Don't you know there's a war on?
          E

World War I. Gay, K.   **940.3**

World Wide Web

Brimner, L. D. The World Wide Web (2-4)
          004.6

Jefferis, D. Cyberspace (4 and up) **004.6**
McElmeel, S. L. WWW almanac **025.04**
Minkel, W. Delivering Web reference services
to young people   **025.04**

World wide web sites *See* Web sites

Worldmark encyclopedia of the nations
          910.3

The **world's** birthday. Goldin, B. D. **E**

World's children [series]

Hermes, J. The children of Bolivia **984**
Staub, F. J. Children of Yucatán **972**

The **worm** and the snail. Terada, A. M.
 In Terada, A. M. Under the starfruit tree p59-
 63   **398.2**

Wormell, Mary

Why not?   **E**

Worms

Lauber, P. Earthworms: underground farmers
(3-5)   **592**

Fiction

Lionni, L. Inch by inch   **E**
Rockwell, T. How to eat fried worms (3-6)
          Fic

Wormser, Richard, 1933-

Pinkerton: America's first private eye (5 and up)
          92

Worse than rotten, Ralph. Gantos, J. See note under Gantos, J. Rotten Ralph **E**

Worship

Baylor, B. The way to start a day (1-4)
         291.4

In every tiny grain of sand (2-5) **291.4**

Worth, Valerie

All the small poems and fourteen more
         811

Worth a thousand words. Ammon, B. D.
         011.6

Wortis, Avi *See* Avi, 1937-

Wounded, First aid to *See* First aid

Wounded Knee: an Indian history of the American West. Ehrlich, A. **970.004**

Wounds and injuries

 See also Wounds and injuries

Silverstein, A. Cuts, scrapes, scabs, and scars
(3-5)   **617.1**

The **wrath** of the grinning ghost. Strickland, B. See note under Strickland, B. The hand of the necromancer   **Fic**

The **wreck** of the Zephyr. Van Allsburg, C.
         E

The **wreckers**. Lawrence, I. **Fic**

Wrede, Patricia C., 1953-

Book of enchantments (6 and up) **S C**
 Includes the following stories: Rikiki and the wizard; The princess, the cat, and the unicorn; Roses by moonlight; The sixty-two curses of Caliph Arenschadd; Earthwitch; The sword-seller; The Lorelei; Stronger than time; Cruel sisters; Utensile strength

Calling on dragons. See note under Wrede, P. C. Dealing with dragons **Fic**
Dealing with dragons (6 and up) **Fic**
Searching for dragons. See note under Wrede, P. C. Dealing with dragons **Fic**
Talking to dragons. See note under Wrede, P. C. Dealing with dragons **Fic**

Wrestling

Ditchfield, C. Wrestling (2-4) **796.8**

Fiction

Spinelli, J. There's a girl in my hammerlock (5 and up)   **Fic**

The **wretched** stone. Van Allsburg, C. **E**

Wright, Amy Bartlett

(il) Latimer, J. P. Butterflies **595.7**

Wright, Betty Ren

The dollhouse murders (4 and up) **Fic**
The ghost in Room 11 (3-5) **Fic**
The ghosts of Mercy Manor (4 and up)
         Fic
The moonlight man (5 and up) **Fic**
Nothing but trouble (4 and up) **Fic**

Wright, Blanche Fisher

(il) The Real Mother Goose. See The Real Mother Goose   **398.8**

Wright, David, 1939-

The Facts on File children's atlas **912**

Wright, David K., 1943-

Albania (4 and up)   **949.65**

Wright, Jill, 1942-

(jt. auth) Wright, D. The Facts on File children's atlas   **912**

Wright, Orville, 1871-1948

About

Freedman, R. The Wright brothers: how they invented the airplane (5 and up) **92**

Wright, Richard, 1908-1960

Fiction

Miller, W. Richard Wright and the library card
         E

Wright, Wilbur, 1867-1912

About

Freedman, R. The Wright brothers: how they invented the airplane (5 and up) **92**

The **Wright** brothers: how they invented the airplane. Freedman, R. **92**

Wright-Frierson, Virginia, 1949-

A desert scrapbook (3-5) **577.5**
An island scrapbook (3-5) **508**

Wringer. Spinelli, J.   **Fic**

A **wrinkle** in time. L'Engle, M. **Fic**

Writers *See* Authors

Writer's notebook. Conrad, P.
 In Conrad, P. Our house p40-48 **S C**

Writing

 See also Picture writing

Youth

See also Teenagers
Books and reading
Dresang, E. T. Radical change   **028.5**

Yu, Ling

Cooking the Chinese way
In Easy menu ethnic cookbooks   **641.5**

Yucatán (Mexico)
Social life and customs
Staub, F. J. Children of Yucatán (3-5)   **972**

The **yuckiest** site on the Internet. (3-5) See entry in Part 2: Web Resources

Yue, Charlotte

Armor (4 and up)   **355.8**
The igloo (3-6)   **728**
Shoes (4 and up)   **391**

Yue, David

(jt. auth) Yue, C. Armor   **355.8**
(jt. auth) Yue, C. The igloo   **728**
(jt. auth) Yue, C. Shoes   **391**

Yugoslavia

See also Serbia

Yukon gold. Jones, C. F.   **971.9**

Yukon Territory
History
See also Klondike River valley (Yukon)—Gold discoveries
Poetry
Service, R. W. The cremation of Sam McGee (4 and up)   **811**
Service, R. W. The shooting of Dan McGrew (4 and up)   **811**

Yummers!. Marshall, J.   **E**

Yummers too: the second course. Marshall, J. See note under Marshall, J. Yummers!   **E**

Yummy! (k-3)   **811.008**

Yumoto, Kazumi

The friends (5 and up)   **Fic**

Yunmi and Halmoni's trip. Choi, S. N. See note under Choi, S. N. Halmoni and the picnic   **E**

Z

The **Z** was zapped. Van Allsburg, C.   **E**

Zahares, Wade

(il) Suen, A. Delivery   **E**
(il) Suen, A. Window music   **E**

Zaharias, Babe Didrikson, 1911-1956
About
Freedman, R. Babe Didrikson Zaharias (5 and up)   **92**
See/See also pages in the following book(s):
Krull, K. Lives of the athletes p37-41 (4 and up)   **920**

Zalben, Jane Breskin

To every season (4 and up)   **641.5**
Unfinished dreams (5 and up)   **Fic**

Zallinger, Jean

(il) Sattler, H. R. The book of North American owls   **598**

(il) Sattler, H. R. The earliest Americans   **970.01**

Zambia

Holmes, T. Zambia (5 and up)   **968.94**
Folklore
See Folklore—Zambia

Zamorano, Ana

Let's eat!   **E**

Zanzarella, Marianne

(il) The Good Housekeeping illustrated children's cookbook. See The Good Housekeeping illustrated children's cookbook   **641.5**

Zanzibar
Folklore
See Folklore—Zanzibar

Zapotec Indians
Folklore
Cruz, A. The woman who outshone the sun (k-3)   **398.2**
Johnston, T. The tale of Rabbit and Coyote (k-3)   **398.2**

Zarins, Juris, 1945-

See/See also pages in the following book(s):
Talking with adventurers p82-89 (4-6)   **920**

Zaritzky, Bernard

(jt. auth) Whippo, W. Little white duck   **782.42**

The **zebra-riding** cowboy. Medearis, A. S.   **782.42**

Zeely. Hamilton, V.   **Fic**

Zeinert, Karen

Wisconsin
In Celebrate the states   **973**

Zeitlin, Steven J.

(jt. auth) Jaffe, N. The cow of no color: riddle stories and justice tales from around the world   **398.2**
(jt. auth) Jaffe, N. While standing on one foot   **296.1**

Zelda and Ivy. Kvasnosky, L. M.   **E**

Zelda and Ivy and the boy next door. Kvasnosky, L. M. See note under Kvasnosky, L. M. Zelda and Ivy   **E**

Zelda and Ivy at Christmas. Kvasnosky, L. M. See note under Kvasnosky, L. M. Zelda and Ivy   **E**

Zeldis, Malcah, 1931-

(il) Bray, R. L. Martin Luther King   **92**

Zelinsky, Paul O.

Rapunzel (3-5)   **398.2**
Rumpelstiltskin (k-4)   **398.2**
(il) Cleary, B. Dear Mr. Henshaw   **Fic**
(il) Cleary, B. Strider   **Fic**
(il) Isaacs, A. Swamp Angel   **E**
(il) Lesser, R. Hansel and Gretel   **398.2**
(il) Nesbit, E. The enchanted castle   **Fic**
(il) Nesbit, E. Five children and it   **Fic**
See/See also pages in the following book(s):
The Newbery & Caldecott medal books, 1986-2000 p279-94   **028.5**

Zemach, Harve

The judge   **E**
Mommy, buy me a china doll   **E**

Zemach, Margot
The little red hen (k-2)   **398.2**
The three little pigs (k-2)   **398.2**
The three wishes (k-2)   **398.2**
(il) Ginsburg, M. The Chinese mirror   **398.2**
(il) Singer, I. B. Mazel and Shlimazel
    398.2
(il) Singer, I. B. When Shlemiel went to Warsaw & other stories   **398.2**
(il) Staines, B. All God's critters got a place in the choir   **782.42**
(il) Zemach, H. The judge   **E**
(il) Zemach, H. Mommy, buy me a china doll
    E
See/See also pages in the following book(s):
Newbery and Caldecott Medal books, 1966-1975 p257-59, 272-75   **028.5**
Zemser, Amy Bronwen
Beyond the mango tree (5 and up)   **Fic**
Zenobia, Queen of Palmyra
See/See also pages in the following book(s):
Meltzer, M. Ten queens p33-41 (5 and up)
    920
Zero and the commercial. Cresswell, H.
In Bauer, C. F. Celebrations p213-18
    808.8
Zhang, Christopher Zhong-yuan, 1954-
(il) Park, F. The royal bee   **E**
Zhang, Song Nan
A little tiger in the Chinese night   **92**
Zia. O'Dell, S.   **Fic**
Ziefert, Harriet
April Fool!   **E**
First He made the sun   **E**
Hats off for the Fourth of July!   **E**
Little Red Riding Hood (k-2)   **398.2**
A new coat for Anna   **E**
Pushkin meets the bundle   **E**
Pushkin minds the bundle. See note under Ziefert, H. Pushkin meets the bundle   **E**
Train song   **E**
When I first came to this land (k-2)
    782.42
Zimbabwe
          Fiction
Farmer, N. The Ear, the Eye, and the Arm (6 and up)   **Fic**
Farmer, N. A girl named Disaster (6 and up)
    Fic
Zimmer, Dirk
(il) Cole, J. Bony-Legs   **398.2**
(il) Maguire, G. Seven spiders spinning   **Fic**
(il) Schwartz, A. In a dark, dark room, and other scary stories   **398.2**
Zimmerman, Andrea Griffing
My dog Toby   **E**
Trashy town   **E**
The **zimwi.** San Souci, R.
In San Souci, R. A terrifying taste of short & shivery p62-67   **398.2**
Zin! zin! zin! a violin. Moss, L.   **E**
Zinnia and Dot. Ernst, L. C.   **E**
Zion, Gene
Harry and the lady next door. See note under Zion, G. Harry the dirty dog   **E**

Harry by the sea. See note under Zion, G. Harry the dirty dog   **E**
Harry the dirty dog   **E**
No roses for Harry! See note under Zion, G. Harry the dirty dog   **E**
Zipes, Jack David
(ed) The Oxford companion to fairy tales. See The Oxford companion to fairy tales
    398.2
Zipping, zapping, zooming bats. Earle, A.
    599.4
Zlateh the goat. Singer, I. B.
In Singer, I. B. Stories for children p45-52
    S C
In Singer, I. B. Zlateh the goat, and other stories p79-90   **398.2**
Zlateh the goat, and other stories. Singer, I. B.
    398.2
Zodiac
Kimmel, E. A. The rooster's antlers (k-3)
    398.2
Young, E. Cat and Rat (k-3)   **398.2**
Zoe rising. Conrad, P.   **Fic**
Zoehfeld, Kathleen Weidner
Dinosaur babies (k-3)   **567.9**
How mountains are made (k-3)   **551.4**
What is the world made of? (k-3)   **530.4**
What lives in a shell? (k-1)   **591.4**
Zolotow, Charlotte, 1915-
The beautiful Christmas tree   **E**
The bunny who found Easter   **E**
The hating book   **E**
Mr. Rabbit and the lovely present   **E**
My friend John   **E**
The old dog   **E**
The quarreling book   **E**
The seashore book   **E**
Some things go together   **E**
When the wind stops   **E**
William's doll   **E**
Zomo the Rabbit. McDermott, G.   **398.2**
A **Zooful** of animals   **808.81**
Zoom. Bányai, I.   **E**
Zoom City. Hurd, T.   **E**
Zooman Sam. Lowry, L. See note under Lowry, L. Anastasia Krupnik   **Fic**
Zoonooz   **590.5**
Zoos
Aliki. My visit to the zoo (k-3)   **590.73**
          Fiction
Hoff, S. Sammy the seal   **E**
Rathmann, P. Good night, Gorilla   **E**
Rice, E. Sam who never forgets   **E**
Seuss, Dr. If I ran the zoo   **E**
Waber, B. A lion named Shirley Williamson
    E
          Periodicals
Zoonooz   **590.5**
Zora Hurston and the chinaberry tree. Miller, W.
    92
Zubizarreta, Rosalma
Cruz, A. The woman who outshone the sun
    398.2
Rohmer, H. The invisible hunters   **398.2**

DIRECTORY OF PUBLISHERS AND DISTRIBUTORS

21st Cent. Bks. (Brookfield) See Millbrook Press

21st Cent. Bks. (NY): 21st Cent. Bks., 115 W. 18th St., New York, N.Y. 10011-4113 Tel 212-886-9200 Fax 212-633-0748

Abingdon Press, 201 8th Ave. S., Nashville, Tenn. 37202-0801 Tel 615-749-6409; 800-251-3320 (orders) Fax 615-749-6056; refer orders to Ingram Bk. Co., 1 Ingram Blvd., La Vergne, Tenn. 37086-1986 Tel 615-793-5000; 800-937-8000 (orders only) Fax 800-876-0186

Abrams: Harry N. Abrams Inc., 100 5th Ave., New York, N.Y. 10011 Tel 212-206-7715; 800-345-1359 Fax 212-645-8437

Addison Wesley Longman Inc., 75 Arlington St., Boston, Mass. 02116 Tel 617-848-6000; 800-848-9500 Fax 617-848-6034

Aladdin Bks. (NY): Aladdin Bks., Simon & Schuster Bldg., 1230 Ave. of the Americas, New York, N.Y. 10020 Tel 212-698-7000; 800-223-2348; refer orders to Simon & Schuster Children's Ordering Dept., 200 Old Tappan Rd., Old Tappan, N.J. 07675 Tel 800-223-2336 Fax 800-445-6991

Aladdin Paperbacks, Simon & Schuster Bldg., 1230 Ave. of the Americas, New York, N.Y. 10020 Tel 212-698-7000; 800-223-2348; refer orders to Simon & Schuster Children's Ordering Dept., 200 Old Tappan Rd., Old Tappan, N.J. 07675 Tel 212-689-7000; 800-223-2336 (orders) Fax 800-445-6991

Amereon Ltd., 800 Wickham Ave., Mattituck, N.Y. 11952 Tel 631-298-5100 Fax 631-298-5631; refer orders to P.O. Box 1200, Mattituck, N.Y. 11952

American Assn. for the Advancement of Science, 1200 New York Ave. N.W., Washington, D.C. 20005 Tel 202-326-6400

American Cancer Soc. Inc., 1180 6th Ave., No. 6, New York, N.Y. 10036-8401 Tel 212-840-7760; refer orders to P.O. Box 102454, Atlanta, Ga. 30368-2454

American Lib. Assn., 50 E. Huron St., Chicago, Ill. 60611-2795 Tel 312-280-2425; 800-545-2433 (orders) Fax 312-280-3255; 312-826-9958 (orders)

Apple Soup Bks., 201 E. 50th St., New York, N.Y. 10022 Tel 212-751-2600; 800-726-0600 Fax 212-572-2593; refer orders to Random House Inc., 400 Hahn Rd., Westminster, Md. 21157 Tel 410-848-1900; 800-733-3000

Applewood Bks., 128 The Great Road, Bedford, Mass. 01730 Tel 781-271-0055 Fax 781-271-0056; refer orders to P.O. Box 365, Bedford, Mass. 01730 Tel 800-277-5312 Fax 781-271-0056

Arcade Pub., 141 5th Ave., New York, N.Y. 10010 Tel 212-475-2633 Fax 212-353-8148; refer orders to Time Warner Trade Pub., Customer Service, 3 Center Plaza, Boston, Mass. 02108-2084 Tel 800-343-9204 Fax 800-286-9471

Association for Childhood Educ. Int., 17904 Georgia Ave., Suite 215, Olney, Md. 20832-2277 Tel 301-570-2111; 800-423-3563 Fax 301-570-2212

Astor-Honor Inc. Pubs., 48 E. 43rd St., New York, N.Y. 10017

Atheneum Bks. for Young Readers, Simon & Schuster Bldg., 1230 Ave. of the Americas, New York, N.Y. 10020 Tel 212-698-7000; 800-257-5755; refer orders to Simon & Schuster Children's Ordering Dept., 100 Front St., Riverside, N.J. 08075 Tel 800-223-2336 (orders) Fax 800-445-6991

Atheneum Pubs., 1230 Ave. of the Americas, New York, N.Y. 10020 Tel 212-698-7000; 800-223-2348 Fax 800-445-6991; refer orders to Simon & Schuster, 100 Front St., Riverside, N.J. 08075 Tel 800-223-2336 (orders) Fax 800-445-6991

Atlantic Monthly Press See Grove/Atlantic

AudioFile Publs., 37 Silver St., P.O. Box 109, Portland, Me. 04112-0109

August House Inc., 201 E. Markham St., Little Rock, Ark. 72201 Tel 501-372-5450; 800-284-8784 Fax 501-372-5579; refer orders to Ingram Bk. Co., 1 Ingram Blvd., La Vergne, Tenn. 37086-1986 Tel 615-793-5000; 800-937-8000 (orders only) Fax 800-876-0186

August House LittleFolk, 201 E. Markham St., Little Rock, Ark. 72201 Tel 501-372-5450; 800-284-8784 Fax 501-372-5579; refer orders to Ingram Bk. Co., 1 Ingram Blvd., La Vergne, Tenn. 37086-1986 Tel 615-793-5000; 800-937-8000 (orders only) Fax 800-876-0186

Avon Bks. See HarperCollins Pubs.

Ballantine Bks., 1540 Broadway, New York, N.Y. 10036-4094 Tel 212-782-9000; 800-726-0600 Fax 800-632-9242; refer orders to Random House Inc., 400 Hahn Rd., Westminster, Md. 21157 Tel 410-848-1900; 800-733-3000 Fax 800-659-2436

Bantam Bks. Inc., 1540 Broadway, New York, N.Y. 10036-4094 Tel 212-782-9000; 800-726-0600 Fax 800-632-9242; refer orders to Random House Inc., 400 Hahn Rd., Westminster, Md. 21157 Tel 410-848-1900; 800-733-3000 Fax 800-659-2436

Bedrick Bks.: Peter Bedrick Bks. Inc., 156 5th Ave., New York, N.Y. 10010 Tel 212-206-3738 Fax 212-206-7065; refer orders to 4255 Touhy Ave., Lincolnwood, Ill. 60712-1975 Tel 800-323-4900; 847-679-5500 Fax 800-998-3103; 847-679-2494

Beech Tree Bks. See HarperCollins Pubs.

Beginner Bks., 201 E. 50th St., New York, N.Y. 10022 Tel 212-751-2600; 800-726-0600 Fax 212-872-8026; refer orders to Random House, 400 Hahn Rd., Westminster, Md. 21157 Tel 410-848-1900; 800-733-3000

Benchmark Bks. (Tarrytown): Benchmark Bks., 99 White Plains Rd., P.O. Box 2001, Tarrytown, N.Y. 10591-9001 Tel 914-332-8888; 800-821-9881 Fax 914-332-1082

Berkley Bks., 375 Hudson St., New York, N.Y. 10014-3657 Tel 212-366-2000; 800-526-0275 (orders) Fax 212-366-2666; refer orders to Penguin Putnam Inc., 405 Murray Hill Parkway, E. Rutherford, N.J. 07073 Tel 201-933-9292; 800-526-0275

Blackbirch Press Inc., 260 Amity Rd., Woodbridge, Conn. 06525 Tel 203-387-7525; 800-831-9183 Fax 203-389-1596

Blue Sky Press (NY): Blue Sky Press, 555 Broadway, New York, N.Y. 10012-3999 Tel 212-343-6100 Fax 212-343-4535; refer orders to HarperCollins Pubs., 1000 Keystone Ind. Park, Scranton, Pa. 18512-4621 Tel 800-242-7737 Fax 800-822-4090

Books of Wonder See HarperCollins Pubs.

Bowker: R.R. Bowker Co., 121 Chanlon Rd., New Providence, N.J. 07974 Tel 908-464-6800; 888-269-5372 (orders) Fax 908-508-7696; refer orders to P.O. Box 1001, Summit, N.J. 07902-1001

Boyds Mills Press, 815 Church St., Honesdale, Pa. 18431 Tel 570-253-1164; 877-512-8366 (orders) Fax 570-253-0179

Bradbury Press Inc., 1230 Ave. of the Americas, New York, N.Y. 10020 Tel 212-698-7200; 800-223-2348; refer orders to Simon & Schuster Children's Order Dept., 100 Front St., Riverside, N.J. 08075 Tel 800-223-2336 Fax 800-445-6991

BridgeWater Bks., 100 Corporate Dr., Mahwah, N.J. 07430 Tel 201-529-4000; 800-826-4216 Fax 201-529-5109; refer orders to Andrews McMeel Pub., 4520 Main St., Suite 700, Kansas City, Mo. 64111-7701 Tel 816-932-6700; 800-826-4216 Fax 800-437-8683

Brodart Co., 500 Arch St., Williamsport, Pa. 17705 Tel 717-326-2461; 800-233-8467 Fax 717-326-1479

Browndeer Press See Harcourt

Camelot Pub. Co., P.O. Box 1357, Ormond Beach, Fla. 32175-1357 Tel 904-672-5672

Candlewick Press, 2067 Massachusetts Ave., Cambridge, Mass. 02140 Tel 617-661-3330 Fax 617-661-0565

Carolrhoda Bks. Inc., 241 1st Ave. N., Minneapolis, Minn. 55401 Tel 612-332-3344; 800-328-4929 Fax 612-332-7615; 800-332-1132

Cartwheel Bks., 555 Broadway, New York, N.Y. 10012-3999 Tel 212-343-6100 Fax 212-343-4535; refer orders to HarperCollins Pubs., 1000 Keystone Ind. Park, Scranton, Pa. 18512 Tel 800-242-7737 Fax 800-822-4090

Carus Pub. Co., 332 S. Michigan Ave., Suite 1100, Chicago, Ill. 60604 Tel 312-939-1500 Fax 312-939-8150; refer orders to Publishers Group West, 1700 4th St., Berkeley, Calif. 94710 Tel 510-528-1444; 800-788-3123 Fax 510-528-3444

Charlesbridge Pub., 85 Main St., Watertown, Mass. 02472 Tel 617-926-0329; 800-225-3214 Fax 617-926-5720

Chelsea House Pubs., 1974 Sproul Rd., Suite 400, Broomall, Pa. 19008-0914 Tel 610-353-5166; 800-848-2665 Fax 610-359-1439

Children's Art Foundation, P.O. Box 83, Santa Cruz, Calif. 95063 Tel 408-426-5557; 800-447-4569

Children's Bk. Council Inc., 12 W. 37th St., 2nd Floor, New York, N.Y. 10018-7480 Tel 212-966-1990 Fax 212-966-2073

Children's Bk. Press, 246 1st St., Suite 101, San Francisco, Calif. 94105 Tel 415-995-2200 Fax 415-995-2222

Children's Press, 90 Sherman Turnpike, Danbury, Conn. 06816 Tel 203-797-3500; 800-621-1115 Fax 203-797-3143

Children's Science Bk. Review Com., 605 Commonwealth Ave., Boston, Mass. 02215

Child's World (The), P.O. Box 326, Chanhassen, Minn. 55317-0326 Tel 612-906-3939; 800-599-7323 Fax 612-906-3940

Chronicle Bks., 85 2nd St., 6th Floor, San Francisco, Calif. 94105 Tel 415-537-3730; 800-722-6657 (orders only) Fax 415-537-4460; 800-858-7787; refer orders to Ingram Bk. Co., 1 Ingram Blvd., La Vergne, Tenn. 37086-1986 Tel 615-793-5000; 800-937-8000 (orders only) Fax 800-876-0186

Cinco Puntos Press, 2709 Louisville, El Paso, Tex. 79930 Tel 915-566-9072; 800-566-9072; refer orders to Consortium Bk. Sales & Distr., 1045 Westgate Dr., Suite 90, St. Paul, Minn. 55114-1065 Tel 612-221-9035; 800-283-3572 (orders) Fax 612-221-0124

Clarion Bks., 215 Park Ave. S., New York, N.Y. 10003 Tel 212-420-5800 Fax 212-420-5855; refer orders to Houghton Mifflin Co., 181 Ballardville St., Wilmington, Mass. 01887 Tel 508-661-1300; 800-225-3362

Clear Light Pubs., 823 Don Diego, Santa Fe, N.M. 87501 Tel 505-989-9590; 800-253-2747 (orders only) Fax 505-989-9519 (orders only)

Cobblehill Bks., 375 Hudson St., New York, N.Y. 10014-3657 Tel 212-366-2000; 800-526-0275 (orders) Fax 212-366-2666; refer orders to Penguin Putnam Inc., 405 Murray Hill Parkway, E. Rutherford, N.J. 07073 Tel 201-933-9292; 800-526-0275

Cobblestone Pub. Inc., 30 Grove St., Suite C, Peterborough, N.H. 03458 Tel 603-924-7209; 800-821-0115 Fax 603-924-7380

Contemporary Bks. Inc., 2 Penn Plaza, New York, N.Y. 10121 Tel 212-206-3738; refer orders to McGraw-Hill Order Services, P.O. Box 545, Blacklick, Ohio 43004-0545

Copper Beech Bks., 2 Old New Milford Rd., Brookfield, Conn. 06804 Tel 203-740-2220; 800-462-4703 Fax 203-740-2223

Coward-McCann Inc., 375 Hudson St., New York, N.Y. 10014 Tel 212-366-2000; 800-526-0275 Fax 212-366-2666; refer orders to Penguin Putnam Inc., 405 Murray Hill Parkway, E. Rutherford, N.J. 07073 Tel 201-933-9292; 800-526-0275 Fax 201-933-2316

Coward, McCann & Geoghegan See Coward-McCann

Crabtree Pub. Co., PMB 16A, 350 5th Ave., Suite 3308, New York, N.Y. 10118 Tel 212-496-5040; 800-387-7650 (orders) Fax 800-355-7166 (orders)

Creative Art Publs., 301 Riverland Rd., Fort Lauderdale, Fla. 33312 Tel 305-583-9207

Crocodile Bks. USA, 46 Crosby St., North Hampton, Mass. 01060 Tel 413-582-7054; 800-238-5465 Fax 413-582-7057

Crowell See HarperCollins Pubs.

Crown Pubs. Inc., 299 Park Ave., New York, N.Y. 10171 Tel 212-751-2600; 800-726-0600 Fax 800-632-9242; refer orders to Random House Inc., 400 Hahn Rd., Westminster, Md. 21157 Tel 410-848-1900; 800-733-3000 Fax 800-659-2436

Delacorte Press, 1540 Broadway, New York, N.Y. 10036-4094 Tel 212-782-9000; 800-726-0600 Fax 800-632-9242; refer orders to Random House Inc., 400 Hahn Rd., Westminster, Md. 21157 Tel 410-848-1900; 800-733-3000 Fax 800-659-2436

Dell Pub. Co. Inc., 1540 Broadway, New York, N.Y. 10036-4094 Tel 212-354-6500; 800-223-6834 Fax 212-492-9698

Dial Bks., 375 Hudson St., New York, N.Y. 10014 Tel 212-366-2000 Fax 212-366-2666; refer orders to Penguin Putnam Inc., 405 Murray Hill Parkway, E. Rutherford, N.J. 07073 Tel 201-933-9292; 800-526-0275

Dial Bks. for Young Readers, 375 Hudson St., New York, N.Y. 10014 Tel 212-366-2000 Fax 212-366-2666; refer orders to Penguin Putnam Inc., 405 Murray Hill Parkway, E. Rutherford, N.J. 07073 Tel 201-933-9292; 800-526-0275

DK Ink, 95 Madison Ave., New York, N.Y. 10016 Tel 212-213-4800; 888-342-5357 Fax 212-213-5240; refer orders to Publishers Resources, 1224 Heil Quaker Blvd., La Vergne, Tenn. 37086-7001 Tel 615-793-5090; 800-937-5557 Fax 800-774-6733

DK Pub. Inc., 95 Madison Ave., New York, N.Y. 10016 Tel 212-213-4800; 888-342-5357 Fax 212-213-5240; refer orders to 501 Mason Rd., La Vergne, Tenn. 37086 Tel 877-342-5357

Dodd, Mead Out of business; children's list acquired by Putnam & Grosset Group

Dorling Kindersley Ltd., 9 Henrietta St., London WC2E 8PS, Eng. Tel (0171) 836 5411 Fax (0171) 836 7570; refer orders to International Bk. Distributors (Hemel Hempstead) Ltd., Campus 400, Maylands Ave., Hemel Hempstead, Hertfordshire HP2 7EZ, Eng. Tel (01442) 881 900; 882 016 (orders) Fax (01442) 882 099; 882 288 (orders)
Branch offices
U.S.: DK Pub.

Doubleday, 1540 Broadway, New York, N.Y. 10036-4094 Tel 212-782-9000; 800-726-0600 Fax 800-632-9242; refer orders to Random House Inc., 400 Hahn Rd., Westminster, Md. 21157 Tel 410-848-1900; 800-733-3000 Fax 800-659-2436

Doubleday Bks. for Young Readers, 1540 Broadway, New York, N.Y. 10036-4094 Tel 212-354-6500; 800-223-6834 Fax 212-492-8941; refer orders to 2451 S. Wolf Rd., Des Plaines, Ill. 60018 Tel 312-827-1111; 800-323-9872 (orders)

Dover Publs. Inc., 31 E. 2nd St., Mineola, N.Y. 11501-3582 Tel 516-294-7000; 800-223-3130 (orders) Fax 516-742-5049

Dutton, 375 Hudson St., New York, N.Y. 10014-3657 Tel 212-366-2000; 800-526-0275 (orders) Fax 212-366-2666; refer orders to Penguin Putnam Inc., 405 Murray Hill Parkway, E. Rutherford, N.J. 07073 Tel 201-933-9292; 800-526-0275 Fax 201-933-2316

Dutton Children's Bks., 375 Hudson St., New York, N.Y. 10014-3657 Tel 212-366-2000; 800-526-0275 (orders) Fax 212-366-2666; refer orders to Penguin Putnam Inc., 405 Murray Hill Parkway, E. Rutherford, N.J. 07073 Tel 201-933-9292; 800-526-0275

EDC Pub., 10302 E. 55th Pl., Tulsa, Okla. 74146 Tel 918-622-4522; 800-475-4522; refer orders to P.O. Box 470663, Tulsa, Okla. 74147

Educational Press Assn. of Am., Rowan College of N.J., 201 Mullica Hill Rd., Glassboro, N.J. 08028-1701 Tel 609-256-4610 Fax 609-256-4926

Eerdmans: Wm. B. Eerdmans Pub. Co., 255 Jefferson Ave. S.E., Grand Rapids, Mich. 49503-4554 Tel 616-459-4591; 800-253-7521 (U.S. & Can. orders only) Fax 616-459-6540

Eerdmans Bks. for Young Readers, 255 Jefferson Ave. S.E., Grand Rapids, Mich. 49503-4554 Tel 616-459-4591; 800-253-7521 (U.S. & Can. orders only) Fax 616-459-6540

Enslow Pubs., Box 398, 40 Industrial Rd., Berkeley Heights, N.J. 07922-0398 Tel 908-771-9400; 800-398-2504 Fax 908-771-0925

Everyman's Lib. Children's Classics, 201 E. 50th St., New York, N.Y. 10022 Tel 212-751-2600; 800-726-0600 FFax 212-572-2593; refer orders to Random House Inc., 400 Hahn Rd., Westminster, Md. 21157 Tel 410-848-1900; 800-733-3000

Facts on File Inc., 11 Penn Plaza, New York, N.Y. 10001-2006 Tel 212-967-8800; 800-322-8755 Fax 212-967-9196; 800-678-3633

Farrar, Straus & Giroux Inc., 19 Union Sq. W., New York, N.Y. 10003 Tel 212-741-6900 Fax 212-633-9385; refer orders to VHPS-Von Holtzbrinck Pub. Services, 16365 James Madison Highway (U.S. Route 15), Gordonsville, Va. 22942 Tel 540-672-7600; 888-330-8477 Fax 800-672-2054

Fawcett Bks., 201 E. 50th St., New York, N.Y. 10022 Tel 212-572-2713; 800-733-3000 (orders) Fax 212-572-6046; refer orders to Random House Inc., 400 Hahn Rd., Westminster, Md. 21157 Tel 410-848-1900; 800-733-3000

Firefly Bks. (Buffalo): Firefly Bks., P.O. Box 1338, Ellicott Station, Buffalo, N.Y. 14205 Tel 800-387-5085

Firefly Bks. (Willowdale): Firefly Bks. Ltd., 3680 Victoria Park Ave., Willowdale, Ont., Can. M2H 3K1 Tel 416-499-8412 Fax 416-499-8313
Branch offices
U.S.: Firefly Bks. (Buffalo)

Forest Press (Albany): Forest Press, 85 Watervliet Ave., Albany, N.Y. 12206-2082 Tel 518-489-8549 Fax 518-489-7804; 888-339-3921; refer orders to OCLC Forest Press, 6565 Frantz Rd., Dublin, Ohio 43017-3395

Foster Bks.: Frances Foster Bks., 19 Union Sq. W., New York, N.Y. 10003 Tel 212-741-6900; 888-330-8477 Fax 212-633-9385; refer orders to VHPS-Von Holtzbrinck Pub. Services, 16365 James Madison Highway (U.S. Route 15), Gordonsville, Va. 22942 Tel 540-672-7600; 888-330-8477 Fax 800-672-2054

Four Winds Press, 1230 Ave. of the Americas, New York, N.Y. 10020 Tel 212-698-7000; 800-257-5755; refer orders to Simon & Schuster Children's Ordering Dept., 100 Front St., Riverside, N.J. 08075 Tel 800-223-2336 Fax 800-445-6991

Free Spirit Pub. Inc., 400 1st Ave. N., Suite 616, Minneapolis, Minn. 55401-1730 Tel 612-338-2068; 800-735-7323 Fax 612-337-5050

Front St., 20 Battery Park Ave., Suite 403, Asheville, N.C. 28801 Tel 828-236-3097 Fax 828-236-3098; refer orders to Publishers Group West, 1700 4th St., Berkeley, Calif. 94710 Tel 510-528-1444; 800-788-3123 Fax 510-528-3444

Front St./Cricket Bks., 20 Battery Park Ave., Suite 403, Asheville, N.C. 28801 Tel 828-236-3097 Fax 828-236-3098; refer orders to Publishers Group West, 1700 4th St., Berkeley, CA 94710 Tel 510-528-1444; 800-788-3123 Fax 510-528-3444

Fulcrum Pub., 350 Indiana St., Suite 350, Golden, Colo. 80401 Tel 303-277-1623; 800-992-2908 Fax 303-279-7111; 800-726-7112

Gale Group, 27500 Drake Rd., Farmington Hills, Mich. 48331-3535 Tel 248-699-4253; 800-877-4253; refer orders to P.O. Box 9187, Farmington Hills, Mich. 48333-9187 Tel 800-877-4253 Fax 313-961-6083; 800-414-5043

Gale Res. See Gale Group

Gallaudet Univ. Press, 800 Florida Ave. N.E., Washington, D.C. 20002-3695 Tel 202-651-5488; 800-451-1073 Fax 202-651-5489; refer orders to Chicago Distr. Center, 11030 S. Langley Ave., Chicago, Ill. 60628 Tel 773-568-1550; 800-621-2736 (orders only) Fax 773-660-2235; 800-621-8476 (orders only)

Garland Pub. Inc., 29 W. 35th St., New York, N.Y. 10001 Tel 917-351-7000; Fax 212-584-7854; refer orders to Taylor & Francis Inc., 47 Runway Rd., Levittown, Pa. 19057-4700 Tel 215-269-0400; 800-821-8312 Fax 215-269-0363

Godine: David R. Godine Pub., 9 Hamilton Pl., Boston, Mass. 02108-4715 Tel 617-451-9600; Fax 617-350-0250; refer orders to Box 450, Jaffrey, New Hampshire 03452 Tel 603-532-4100 Fax 603-532-5940

Greenwillow Bks. See HarperCollins Pubs.

Greenwood Press, 88 Post Rd. W., P.O. Box 5007, Westport, Conn. 06881-5007 Tel 203-226-3571; 800-225-5800 (orders only) Fax 203-222-1502

Grolier Inc., 90 Sherman Turnpike, Danbury, Conn. 06816 Tel 203-797-3500; 800-243-7256 Fax 203-797-3285

Grolier Educ., 90 Sherman Turnpike, Danbury, Conn. 06816-0001 Tel 203-797-3500; 800-243-7256 Fax 203-797-3285

Grosset & Dunlap Pubs., 375 Hudson St., New York, N.Y. 10014 Tel 212-366-2000; 800-331-4624 Fax 212-213-6706; refer orders to Penguin Putnam Inc., 405 Murray Hill Parkway, E. Rutherford, N.J. 07073 Tel 800-526-0275 Fax 800-227-9604

Gryphon House, P.O. Box 207, Beltsville, Md. 20704-0207 Tel 301-595-9500; 800-638-0928 Fax 301-595-0051

Gulliver Bks., 525 B St., Suite 1900, San Diego, Calif. 92101-4495 Tel 619-699-6707; 800-831-7799 Fax 619-699-6542; refer orders to Harcourt Inc., 6277 Sea Harbor Dr., Orlando, Fla. 32887 Tel 619-699-6707; 800-543-1918 (orders)

Harcourt Inc., 525 B St., Suite 1900, San Diego, Calif. 92101-4495 Tel 619-699-6707; 800-831-7799 Fax 619-699-6542; refer orders to 6277 Sea Harbor Dr., Orlando, Fla. 32887 Tel 619-699-6707; 800-543-1918 (orders)

Harcourt Brace & Co. See Harcourt

Harcourt Brace College Pubs., 301 Commerce St., Suite 3700, Fort Worth, Tex. 76102 Tel 817-334-7500 Fax 817-334-8060 (orders); 800-874-6418; refer orders to 6277 Sea Harbor Dr., Orlando, Fla. 32887 Tel 800-782-4479 (orders)

Harcourt Brace Jovanovich See Harcourt

Harper & Row See HarperCollins Pubs.

HarperCollins Pubs., 10 E. 53rd St., New York, N.Y. 10022-5299 Tel 212-207-7000; 800-242-7737 Fax 212-207-7145; refer orders to 1000 Keystone Ind. Park, Scranton, Pa. 18512-4621 Tel 570-941-1500; 800-242-7737 Fax 800-822-4090

Branch offices
: HarperCollins Children's Bks., 1350 Avenue of the Americas, New York, N.Y. 10019 Tel 212-261-6500

HarperFestival, 1350 Avenue of the Americas, New York, N.Y. 10019-4703 Tel 212-261-6797 Fax 212-261-6925; refer orders to HarperCollins Pubs., 1000 Keystone Ind. Park, Scranton, Pa. 18512-4621 Tel 570-941-1500; 800-242-7737 Fax 800-822-4090

Heinemann Lib., Halley Ct., Jordan Hill, Oxford OX2 8EJ, Eng. Tel (01865) 311 366 Fax (01865) 314 107

Branch offices
U.S.: Heinemann Lib., 100 N. LaSalle, Suite 300, Chicago, Ill. 60602 Tel 312-827-1000; 888-475-7038 Fax 888-454-2279; refer orders to P.O. Box 1650, Crystal Lake, Ill. 60039-1650 Tel 815-477-3880; 888-454-2279 Fax 888-844-5329

Heinemann (Portsmouth): Heinemann, 361 Hanover St., Portsmouth, N.H. 03801-3912 Tel 603-431-7894; 800-793-2154 Fax 603-431-7840; 800-847-0938; refer orders to Greenwood Pub. Group Inc., 88 Post Rd. W., P.O. Box 5007, Westport, Conn. 06881 Tel 203-226-3571; 800-225-5800 (orders only) Fax 203-222-1502

Herald Press, 616 Walnut Ave., Scottdale, Pa. 15683-1999 Tel 724-887-8500; 800-245-7894 Fax 724-887-3111

Highsmith Press, W 5527 Highway 106, Fort Atkinson, Wis. 53538-0800 Tel 920-563-9571; 800-558-2110 Fax 920-563-4801; 800-835-2329; refer orders to P.O. Box 800, Fort Atkinson, Wis. 53538-0800

Hill & Wang Inc., 19 Union Sq. W., New York, N.Y. 10003 Tel 212-741-6900; 888-330-8477 Fax 212-741-6973

Hill Bks.: Lawrence Hill Bks., 814 N. Franklin St., Chicago, Ill. 60610 Tel 312-337-0747; 800-888-4741 Fax 312-337-5985; refer orders to Independent Pubs. Group, 814 N. Franklin St., Chicago, Ill. 60610 Tel 312-337-0747; 800-888-4741 Fax 800-337-5985

Holiday House Inc., 425 Madison Ave., New York, N.Y. 10017 Tel 212-688-0085 Fax 212-421-6134

Holt & Co.: Henry Holt & Co., 115 W. 18th St., New York, N.Y. 10011 Tel 212-886-9200 Fax 212-645-5832; refer orders to VHPS-Von Holtzbrinck Pub. Services, 16365 James Madison Highway (U.S. Route 15), Gordonsville, Va. 22942 Tel 540-672-7600; 888-330-8477 Fax 800-672-2054

Holt, Rinehart & Winston, 1120 S. Capital of Tex. Highway, No. II-100, Austin, Tex. 78746-6487 Tel 512-314-6500; 800-225-5425

Horn Bk. Inc., 56 Roland St., Suite 200, Boston, Mass. 02129 Tel 617-228-0225; 800-325-1170 Fax 617-628-0882

Houghton Mifflin Co., 222 Berkeley St., Boston, Mass. 02116 Tel 617-351-5000 Fax 617-227-5409; refer orders to 181 Ballardville St., Wilmington, Mass. 01887 Tel 508-661-1300; 800-225-3362

Humbug Bks., 310 College Ave., Watertown, Wis. 53094-4807 Tel 920-262-8988; 800-648-6284 Fax 920-262-2442

Hungry Minds Inc., 10475 Crosspoint Blvd., Indianapolis, Ind. 46256 Tel 800-762-2974

Hyperion, 77 W. 66th St., 11th floor, New York, N.Y. 10023 Tel 212-456-0100; refer orders to Time Warner Trade Pub., Customer Service, 3 Center Plaza, Boston, Mass. 02108-2084 Tel 800-759-0190 Fax 617-890-0875; 800-286-9471

Hyperion Bks. for Children, 114 5th Ave., New York, N.Y. 10011 Tel 212-633-4400 Fax 212-633-4833; refer orders to Time Warner Trade Pub., Customer Service, 3 Center Plaza, Boston, Mass. 02108-2084 Tel 800-759-0190 Fax 617-890-0875; 800-286-9471

Information Today Inc., 143 Old Marlton Pike, Medford, N.J. 08055-8750 Tel 609-654-6266; 800-300-9868 (orders) Fax 609-654-4309

International Reading Assn., 800 Barksdale Rd., P.O. Box 8139, Newark, Del. 19714-8139 Tel 302-731-1600; 800-336-7323 (orders) Fax 302-731-1057

Jane Yolen Bks., 525 B St., Suite 1900, San Diego, Calif. 92101-4495 Tel 619-699-6707; 800-831-7799 Fax 619-699-6542; refer orders to Harcourt Inc., 6277 Sea Harbor Dr., Orlando, Fla. 32887 Tel 619-699-6707; 800-543-1918 (orders)

Jewish Lights Pub., P.O. Box 237, Sunset Farm Offices, Route 4, Woodstock, Vt. 05091 Tel 802-457-4000; 800-962-4544 (orders) Fax 802-457-4004

Jewish Publ. Soc., 1930 Chestnut St., Philadelphia, Pa. 19103-4599 Tel 215-564-5925; 800-234-3151 (orders only) Fax 215-564-6640; refer orders to JPS Bks. Int., 22883 Quicksilver Dr., Dulles, Va. 20166 Tel 703-661-1500; 800-355-1165 Fax 703-661-1501

Johns Hopkins Univ. Press (The), 2715 N. Charles St., Baltimore, Md. 21218-4319 Tel 410-516-6900; 800-537-5487 (orders only) Fax 410-516-6968

Jump at the Sun, 114 5th Ave., New York, N.Y. 10011 Tel 212-633-4400 Fax 212-633-4833; refer orders to Time Warner Trade Pub., Customer Service, 3 Center Plaza, Boston, Mass. 02108-2084 Tel 800-343-9204 Fax 800-286-9471

Kar-Ben Copies Inc., 6800 Tildenwood Lane, Rockville, Md. 20852 Tel 301-984-8733; 800-452-7236 Fax 301-881-9195

Kids Can Press Ltd., 29 Birch Ave., Toronto, Ont., Can. M4V 1E2 Tel 416-925-5437 Fax 416-960-5437
Branch offices
U.S.: Kids Can Press Ltd., 2250 Military Rd., Tonawanda, N.Y. 14150

Kingfisher (NY): Kingfisher, 95 Madison Ave., Suite 1205, New York, N.Y. 10016 Tel 212-686-1060; 800-497-1657 Fax 212-686-1082

Knopf: Alfred A. Knopf Inc., 299 Park Ave., New York, N.Y. 10171 Tel 212-751-2600; 800-726-0600 Fax 800-632-9242; refer orders to Random House Inc., 400 Hahn Rd., Westminster, Md. 21157 Tel 410-848-1900; 800-733-3000 Fax 800-659-2436

Lark Bks., 50 College St., Asheville, N.C. 28801 Tel 704-253-0467; 800-284-3388 Fax 704-253-7952

Laurel-Leaf Bks., 1540 Broadway, New York, N.Y. 10036-4094 Tel 212-354-6500; 800-223-6834 Fax 212-492-8941; refer orders to 2451 S. Wolf Rd., Des Plaines, Ill. 60018 Tel 312-827-1111; 800-323-9872 (orders)

Lee & Low Bks. Inc., 95 Madison Ave., New York, N.Y. 10016 Tel 212-779-4400 Fax 212-683-1894; refer orders to Publishers Group West, 1700 4th St., Berkeley, Calif. 94710 Tel 510-528-1444; 800-788-3123 Fax 510-528-3444

Lerner Publs. Co., 241 1st Ave. N., Minneapolis, Minn. 55401 Tel 612-332-3344; 800-328-4929 Fax 612-332-7615; 800-332-1132

Levine Bks.: Arthur A. Levine Bks., 555 Broadway, New York, N.Y. 10012-3999 Tel 212-343-6100 Fax 212-343-4535; refer orders to Penguin Putnam Inc., 405 Murray Hill Parkway, E. Rutherford, N.J. 07073 Tel 201-933-9292; 800-526-0275

Libraries Unlimited Inc., P.O. Box 6633, Englewood, Colo. 80155-6633 Tel 303-770-1200; 800-237-6124 Fax 303-220-8843

Library Professional Publs., 2 Linsley St., North Haven, Conn. 06473-2517 Tel 203-239-2702 Fax 203-239-2568

Library Solutions Press, 2137 Oregon St., Berkeley, Calif. 94075 Tel 510-841-2636; refer orders to 5000 Windplay Drive, Suite 4, El Dorado Hills, Calif. 95762 Tel 916-939-2018 Fax 916-939-9626

Linnet Bks., 2 Linsley St., North Haven, Conn. 06473-2517 Tel 203-239-2702 Fax 203-239-2568

Linworth Pub. Inc., 480 E. Wilson Bridge Rd., Suite L, Worthington, Ohio 43085 Tel 614-436-7107; 800-786-5017 Fax 614-436-9490

Lippincott See HarperCollins Pubs.

Little, Brown & Co. Inc., Time & Life Bldg., 1271 Ave. of the Americas, New York, N.Y. 10020 Tel 212-522-8700; 800-343-9204 Fax 212-522-2067; refer orders to Time Warner Trade Pub., Customer Service, 3 Center Plaza, Boston, Mass. 02108-2084 Tel 800-759-0190 Fax 617-890-0875; 800-286-9471

Lodestar Bks., 375 Hudson St., New York, N.Y. 10014-3657 Tel 212-366-2000; 800-526-0275 (orders) Fax 212-366-2666; refer orders to Penguin Putnam Inc., 405 Murray Hill Parkway, E. Rutherford, N.J. 07073 Tel 201-933-9292; 800-526-0275

Lothrop, Lee & Shepard Bks. See HarperCollins Pubs.

Macmillan, 909 Third Ave., New York, N.Y. 10022 Tel 212-884-5000; 646-497-9800; refer orders to Hungry Minds Inc., 10475 Crosspoint Blvd., Indianapolis, Ind. 46256 Tel 800-762-2974

Macmillan Bks. for Young Readers, 1230 Ave. of the Americas, New York, N.Y. 10020 Tel 212-698-7000 Fax 212-698-4350; refer orders to Simon & Schuster Children's Ordering Dept., 100 Front St., Riverside, N.J. 08075 Tel 800-223-2336 Fax 800-445-6991

Macmillan Ref. USA, 1633 Broadway, 23rd Floor, New York, N.Y. 10019 Tel 646-756-2500; refer orders to Gale Group, P.O. Box 9187, Farmington Hills, Mich. 48333-9187 Tel 248-699-4255; 800-877-4253 (orders) Fax 313-961-6083; 800-414-5043 (orders)

Madison Press Bks., 40 Madison Ave., Toronto, Ont., Can. M5R 2S1 Tel 416-923-5027 Fax 416-923-7169

Margaret K. McElderry Bks., 1230 Ave. of the Americas, New York, N.Y. 10020 Tel 212-698-7200; 800-257-5755

Marshall Cavendish Bks. Ltd., 119 Wardour St., London W1V 3TD, Eng. Tel (0171) 734 6710 Fax (0171) 734 6221
Branch offices

U.S.: Marshall Cavendish Corp., 99 White Plains Rd., P.O. Box 2001, Tarrytown, N.Y. 10591-9001 Tel 914-332-8888; 800-821-9881 Fax 914-332-1888

McFarland & Co. Inc. Pubs., P.O. Box 611, Jefferson, N.C. 28640-0611 Tel 336-246-4460; 800-253-2187 (orders only) Fax 336-246-5018

McGraw-Hill Int. Bk. Co., 1221 Ave. of the Americas, New York, N.Y. 10020 Tel 212-512-2000; 800-722-4726; refer orders to 860 Taylor Station Rd., Blacklick, Ohio 43004-0545 Tel 800-722-4726 Fax 614-755-5645

Merriam-Webster Inc., 47 Federal St., P.O. Box 281, Springfield, Mass. 01102 Tel 413-734-3134; 800-828-1880 Fax 413-731-5979

Messner: Julian Messner, 299 Jefferson Rd., Parsippany, N.J. 07054 Tel 973-739-8000; 800-848-9500 Fax 973-739-8053; 800-393-3156; refer orders to Silver Burdett Press, P.O. Box 2649, 4350 Equity Dr., Columbus, Ohio 43216 Tel 614-771-7398 Fax 614-771-7361

Metropolitan Mus. of Art, 1000 5th Ave., New York, N.Y. 10028 Tel 212-879-5500 Fax 212-472-8725; refer orders to Harry N. Abrams Inc., 100 5th Ave., New York, N.Y. 10011 Tel 212-206-7715; 800-345-1359 Fax 212-645-8437

Michael Di Capua Bks., 10 E. 53rd St., New York, N.Y. 10022-5299 Tel 212-207-7000; 800-242-7737 Fax 212-207-7145; refer orders to HarperCollins Pubs., 1000 Keystone Ind. Park, Scranton, Pa. 18512-4621 Tel 717-941-1500; 800-242-7737 Fax 800-822-4090

Millbrook Press Inc. (The), 2 Old New Milford Rd., Brookfield, Conn. 06804 Tel 203-740-2220; 800-462-4703 Fax 203-740-2223

Mint Pubs., 241 Lexington Ave., Mt. Kisco, N.Y. 10549

Morrow See HarperCollins Pubs.

Morrow Junior Bks. See HarperCollins Pubs.

National Council of Teachers of English, 1111 W. Kenyon Rd., Urbana, Ill. 61801-1096 Tel 217-328-3870; 800-369-6283 Fax 217-328-0977

National Council of Teachers of Mathematics, 1906 Association Dr., Reston, Va. 22091-1593 Tel 703-620-9840; 800-235-7566 (orders only) Fax 703-476-2970

National Geographic Soc., 1145 17th St. N.W., Washington, D.C. 20036 Tel 202-857-7000; 800-647-5463 Fax 301-921-1575; refer orders to Simon & Schuster Ordering Dept., 200 Old Tappan Rd., Old Tappan, N.J. 07675 Tel 800-223-2336 (orders) Fax 800-445-6991

National Science Teachers Assn., 1840 Wilson Blvd., Arlington, Va. 22201-3000 Tel 703-243-7100; 800-722-6782 (orders) Fax 703-243-7177

National Wildlife Federation, 11100 Wildlife Center Drive, Reston, Va. 20190-5362 Tel 703-438-6000; 800-822-9919

Neal-Schuman Pubs. Inc., 100 Varick St., New York, N.Y. 10013 Tel 212-925-8650 Fax 212-219-8916; 800-584-2414

Nelson, T.: Thomas Nelson Pubs., P.O. Box 141000, Nelson Pl. at Elm Hill Pike, Nashville, Tenn. 37214-1000 Tel 615-889-9000; 800-251-4000 Fax 615-391-5225; 800-448-8403

New York Public Lib. Astor, Lenox & Tilden Foundations, 5th Ave. & 42nd St., New York, N.Y. 10018 Tel 212-512-0203; refer orders to Publications Office, 8 W. 40th St., 6th Floor, New York, N.Y. 10018 Tel 212-512-0202 Fax 212-704-8623

New York Review of Bks. Inc., 1775 Broadway, 5th Floor, New York, N.Y. 10019-3780 Tel 212-757-8070 Fax 212-333-5374; refer orders to Publishers Group West, 1700 4th St.,Berkeley, Calif. 94710 Tel 510-528-1444; 800-788-3123 Fax 510-528-3444

North-South Bks., Industriestr. 8, 8625 Gossau, Zurich, Switzerland Tel (01) 9366868 Fax (01) 9366800
Branch offices
U.S.: North-South Bks., 11 E. 26th Street, 17th floor, New York, N.Y. 10010 Tel 212-706-4545 Fax 212-706-4546; refer orders to Chronicle Bks., 85 2nd St., 6th Floor, San Francisco, Calif. 94105 Tel 415-537-3730; 800-722-6657 (orders only) Fax 415-537-4460; 800-858-7787

Oliver Press (Minneapolis): Oliver Press Inc., 5707 W. 36th St., Minneapolis, Minn. 55416-2510 Tel 612-926-8981 Fax 612-926-8965

Omnigraphics Inc., Penobscot Bldg., Detroit, Mich. 48226 Tel 313-961-1340; 800-234-1340 (orders) Fax 800-875-1340

Orca Bk. Pubs. Ltd., P.O. Box 5626, Station B, Victoria, B.C., Can. V8R 6S4 Tel 250-380-1229 Fax 250-380-1892

Orchard Bks., 95 Madison Ave., 7th Floor, New York, N.Y. 10016 Tel 212-951-2600; 800-621-1115 Fax 212-213-6435

Oryx Press (The), 4041 N. Central Ave., 7th Floor, Phoenix, Ariz. 85012-3397 Tel 602-265-2651; 800-279-6799 Fax 602-265-6250; 800-279-4663; refer orders to P.O. Box 5007, Westport, Conn. 06881-5007 Tel 203-226-3571; 800-225-5800 Fax 203-750-9790

Overlook Press (The), 386 W. Broadway, 4th Floor, New York, N.Y. 10012 Tel 212-965-8400 Fax 212-965-9834; refer orders to 2568 Route 212, Woodstock, N.Y. 12498 Tel 914-679-6838 Fax 914-679-8571

Owen, R.C.: Richard C. Owen Pubs. Inc., P.O. Box 585, Katonah, N.Y. 10536 Tel 914-232-3903; 800-336-5588 Fax 914-232-3977

Owl Bks. (Toronto): Owl Bks., 51 Front St., E., Suite 200, Toronto, Ont., Can. M5E 1B3 Tel 416-304-0702; 800-387-6192 Fax 416-340-9769; refer orders to Firefly Bks. Ltd., P.O. Box 1338, Buffalo, N.Y. 14205 Tel 800-387-5085

Oxford Univ. Press
Branch offices
U.S.: Oxford Univ. Press Inc., 198 Madison Ave., New York, N.Y. 10016-4314 Tel 212-726-6000; 800-334-4249 Fax 212-725-2972; refer orders to 2001 Evans Rd., Cary, N.C. 27513 Tel 919-677-1303; 800-451-7556 Fax 919-677-1303

Pantheon Bks. Inc., 299 Park Ave., New York, N.Y. 10171 Tel 212-751-2600; 800-726-0600 Fax 800-632-9242; refer orders to Random House Inc., 400 Hahn Rd., Westminster, Md. 21157 Tel 410-848-1900; 800-733-3000 Fax 800-659-2436

Parnassus Press, P.O. Box 8443, Emeryville, Calif. 94608

Pavilion Bks. Ltd., London House, Great Eastern Wharf, Parkgate Rd., London SW11 4NQ, Eng. Tel (0171) 350 1230 Fax (0171) 801 0315; refer orders to Biblios Pubs. Distr. Services Ltd., Star Rd., Partridge Green, W. Sussex RH13 8LD, Eng. Tel (01403) 710 971; 710 851 (orders) Fax (01403) 711 143
Distributors
U.S.: Trafalgar Sq.

Penguin Bks. Ltd.
Branch offices
U.S.: Penguin Bks., 375 Hudson St., New York, N.Y. 10014-3657 Tel 212-366-2000; 800-331-4624 Fax 212-366-2666; refer orders to Penguin Putnam Inc., 405 Murray Hill Parkway, E. Rutherford, N.J. 07073 Tel 201-933-9292; 800-526-0275

Phillips: S. G. Phillips Inc., P.O. Box 83, Chatham, N.Y. 12037 Tel 518-392-3068

Philomel Bks., 375 Hudson St., New York, N.Y. 10014 Tel 212-366-2000; 800-331-4624 Fax 212-213-6706; refer orders to Penguin Putnam Inc., Inside Sales Dept., 1 Grosset Dr., Kirkwood, N.Y. 13795 Tel 607-775-4829; 800-847-5515

Phyllis Fogelman Bks., 375 Hudson St., New York, N.Y. 10014 Tel 212-366-2000; refer orders to Penguin Putnam Inc., Order Processing Dept., 405 Murray Hill Pkwy, East Rutherford, N.J. 07073 Tel 800-526-0275; Fax 800-227-9604

Picture Bk. Studio, 1230 Ave. of the Americas, New York, N.Y. 10020 Tel 212-698-7000; 800-257-5755; refer orders to Simon & Schuster Children's Ordering Dept., 200 Old Tappan Rd., Old Tappan, N.J. 07675 Tel 800-223-2336 (orders) Fax 800-445-6991

Pitspopany Press, 40 E. 78th St., No. 16D, New York, N.Y. 10021-1830 Tel 800-232-2931

Platt & Munk Pubs., 375 Hudson St., New York, N.Y. 10014 Tel 212-366-2000; 800-331-4624 Fax 212-213-6706; refer orders to Penguin Putnam Inc., Inside Sales Dept., 1 Grosset Dr., Kirkwood, N.Y. 13795 Tel 607-775-4829; 800-847-5515

Plays Inc., 120 Boylston St., Boston, Mass. 02116 Tel 617-423-3157 Fax 617-423-2168

Pleasant Co. Publs., 8400 Fairway Pl., Middleton, Wis. 53562 Tel 608-836-4848 Fax 608-836-1999; refer orders to P.O. Box 620991, Middleton, Wis. 53562-0991 Tel 800-233-0264

Pocket Bks., Simon & Schuster Bldg., 1230 Ave. of the Americas, New York, N.Y. 10020 Tel 212-698-7000; 800-223-2348; refer orders to Simon & Schuster Ordering Dept., 100 Front St., Riverside, N.J. 08075 Tel 800-223-2336 (orders) Fax 800-445-6991

Potter: Clarkson N. Potter Inc. Pubs., 299 Park Ave., New York, N.Y. 10171 Tel 212-572-6178; 800-869-2976 Fax 212-572-6181

Prentice-Hall Inc., 1 Lake St., Upper Saddle River, N.J. 07458-9925 Tel 201-236-7000; refer orders to Prentice-Hall/Allyn & Bacon, 200 Old Tappan Rd., Old Tappan, N.J. 07675 Tel 800-223-1360 Fax 800-445-6991

Price/Stern/Sloan Inc., 375 Hudson St., New York, N.Y. 10014 Tel 212-366-2000; 800-331-4624 Fax 212-213-6706; refer orders to Penguin Putnam Inc., Inside Sales Dept., 1 Grosset Dr., Kirkwood, N.Y. 13795 Tel 607-775-4829; 800-847-5515

Puffin Bks., 27 Wrights Lane, London W8 5TZ, Eng. Tel (0171) 416 3000 Fax (0171) 416 3099; refer orders to Penguin Bks. Ltd., P.O. Box 11, W. Drayton, Middlesex UB7 0DA, Eng. Tel (0181) 899 4000 Fax (0181) 899 4099
Branch offices
U.S.: Puffin Bks., 375 Hudson St., New York, N.Y. 10014-3657 Tel 212-366-2000 Fax 212-366-2666; refer orders to Penguin Putnam Inc., 405 Murray Hill Parkway, E. Rutherford, N.J. 07073 Tel 800-526-0275 Fax 800-227-9604

Putnam: G.P. Putnam's Sons, 375 Hudson St., New York, N.Y. 10014 Tel 212-366-2000; 800-331-4624 Fax 212-213-6706; refer orders to Penguin Putnam Inc., 405 Murray Hill Parkway, E. Rutherford, N.J. 07073 Tel 800-526-0275 Fax 800-227-9604

Putnam & Grosset, 375 Hudson St., New York, N.Y. 10014 Tel 212-366-2000; 800-331-4624 Fax 212-213-6706; refer orders to Penguin Putnam Inc., Inside Sales Dept., 1 Grosset Dr., Kirkwood, N.Y. 13795 Tel 607-775-4829; 800-847-5515

Putnam Pub. Group (The), 375 Hudson St., New York, N.Y. 10014 Tel 212-366-2000; 800-331-4624 Fax 212-213-6706; refer orders to Penguin Putnam Inc., 405 Murray Hill Parkway, E. Rutherford, N.J. 07073 Tel 800-526-0275 Fax 800-227-9604

R & S Bks., P.O. Box 45022, S 104 30 Stockholm, Sweden Tel (08) 4570300 Fax (08) 45703301
Distributors
U.S.: Farrar, Straus & Giroux

Raintree Steck-Vaughn Pubs., 466 Southern Blvd., Chatham, N.J. 07928 Tel 973-514-1525; 888-363-4266 (orders) Fax 973-514-1612; 877-578-2638 (orders); refer orders to P.O. Box 26105, Austin, Tex. 78755 Tel 512-343-6854; 800-531-5015

Rand McNally, 8255 N. Central Park, Skokie, Ill. 60076-2970 Tel 847-329-8100 Fax 847-673-0813

Random House Inc., 299 Park Ave., New York, N.Y. 10171 Tel 212-751-2600; 800-726-0600 Fax 800-632-9242; refer orders to 400 Hahn Rd., Westminster, Md. 21157 Tel 410-848-1900; 800-733-3000 Fax 800-659-2436

Red Deer College Press, 56 Ave. & 32nd St., Red Deer, Alta., Can. T4N 5H5 Tel 403-342-3321 Fax 403-340-8940

Roberts Rinehart Pubs., 6309 Monarch Park Pl., Niwot, Colo. 80503-7167 Tel 303-652-2685; 800-352-1985 Fax 303-652-2689; 800-401-9705; refer orders to Publishers Group West, 1700 4th St., Berkeley, Calif. 94710 Tel 510-528-1444; 800-788-3123 Fax 510-528-3444

Runestone Press, 241 1st Ave. N., Minneapolis, Minn. 55401 Tel 612-332-3344; 800-328-4929 Fax 612-332-7615; 800-332-1132

Scarecrow Press Inc., 4720 Boston Way, Suite A, Lanham, Md. 20706-4310 Tel 301-459-3366; 800-462-6420 Fax 717-794-3803; 800-338-4550; refer orders to National Bk. Network, 15200 NBN Way, P.O. Box 190, Blue Ridge Summit, Pa. 17214 Tel 717-794-3800; 800-462-6420 Fax 800-338-4550

Schocken Bks. Inc., 299 Park Ave., New York, N.Y. 10171 Tel 212-751-2600; 800-726-0600 Fax 800-632-9242; refer orders to Random House Inc., 400 Hahn Rd., Westminster, Md. 21157 Tel 410-848-1900; 800-733-3000 Fax 800-659-2436

Scholastic Inc., 555 Broadway, New York, N.Y. 10012-3999 Tel 212-343-6100 Fax 212-343-4535; refer orders to HarperCollins Pubs., 1000 Keystone Ind. Park, Scranton, Pa. 18512-4621 Tel 800-242-7737 Fax 800-822-4090

Scholastic Press, 555 Broadway, New York, N.Y. 10012-3999 Tel 212-343-6100 Fax 212-343-4535; refer orders to HarperCollins Pubs., 1000 Keystone Ind. Park, Scranton, Pa. 18512-4621 Tel 800-242-7737 Fax 800-822-4090

Scholastic Ref., 555 Broadway, New York, N.Y. 10012-3999 Tel 212-343-6100 Fax 212-343-4535; refer orders to HarperCollins Pubs., 1000 Keystone Ind. Park, Scranton, Pa. 18512-4621 Tel 800-242-7737 Fax 800-822-4090

Scientific Am. Bks. for Young Readers, 41 Madison Ave., 37th Floor, New York, N.Y. 10010 Tel 212-576-9400 Fax 212-689-2383; refer orders to VHPS-Von Holtzbrinck Pub. Services, 16365 James Madison Highway (U.S. Route 15), Gordonsville, Va. 22942 Tel 540-672-7600; 888-330-8477 Fax 800-672-2054

Scribner, 1633 Broadway, New York, N.Y. 10019 Tel 646-756-2500; refer orders to Gale Group; Lisa Drew books, refer orders to Simon & Schuster

Scribner Classics, Simon & Schuster Bldg., 1230 Ave. of the Americas, New York, N.Y. 10020 Tel 212-698-7000; 800-223-2348; refer orders to Simon & Schuster Ordering Dept., 100 Front St., Riverside, N.J. 08075 Tel 800-223-2336 Fax 800-445-6991

SeaStar Bks., 11 E. 26th Street, New York, N.Y. 10010 Tel 212-706-4545 Fax 212-706-4546

Sesame Workshop, P.O. Box 7690, Red Oak, IA 51591-0690

Shen's Bks., 40951 Fremont Blvd., Fremont, Calif. 94538 Tel 510-668-1898; 800-456-6660 Fax 510-668-1057

Sierra Club Bks., 85 2nd St., 2nd Floor, San Francisco, Calif. 94105 Tel 415-291-1600 Fax 415-291-1602; refer orders to Random House Inc., 400 Hahn Rd., Westminster, Md. 21157 Tel 410-848-1900; 800-733-3000

Sierra Club Bks. for Children, 85 2nd St., San Francisco, Calif. 94105 Tel 415-977-5500 Fax 415-977-5793; refer orders to Time Warner Trade Pub., Customer Service, 3 Center Plaza, Boston, Mass. 02108-2084 Tel 800-343-9204 Fax 800-286-9471

Silver Moon Press, 160 5th Ave., New York, N.Y. 10010 Tel 212-242-6499; 800-874-3320 (orders) Fax 212-242-6799

Silver Whistle Bks., 525 B St., Suite 1900, San Diego, Calif. 92101-4495 Tel 619-699-6707; 800-831-7799 Fax 619-699-6542; refer orders to Harcourt Inc., 6277 Sea Harbor Dr., Orlando, Fla. 32887 Tel 619-699-6707; 800-543-1918 (orders)

Simon & Schuster Inc. Pubs., Simon & Schuster Bldg., 1230 Ave. of the Americas, New York, N.Y. 10020 Tel 212-698-7000; 800-223-2348; refer orders to Simon & Schuster Ordering Dept., 100 Front St., Riverside, N.J. 08075 Tel 800-223-2336 Fax 800-445-6991

Simon & Schuster Bks. for Young Readers, Simon & Schuster Bldg., 1230 Ave. of the Americas, New York, N.Y. 10020 Tel 212-698-7000; 800-257-5755; refer orders to Simon & Schuster Children's Ordering Dept., 100 Front St., Riverside, N.J. 08075 Tel 800-223-2336 (orders) Fax 800-445-6991

Somerville House Pub., 3080 Yonge St., Suite 5000, Toronto, Ont., Can. M4N 3N1 Tel 416-488-5938 Fax 416-488-5506

St. Martin's Press Inc., 175 5th Ave., New York, N.Y. 10010-7842 Tel 212-674-5151; 800-221-7945 Fax 212-420-9314; refer orders to VHPS-Von Holtzbrinck Pub. Services, 16365 James Madison Highway (U.S. Route 15), Gordonsville, Va. 22942 Tel 540-672-7600; 888-330-8477 Fax 800-672-2054

Stemmer House Pubs. Inc., 2627 Caves Rd., Owings Mills, Md. 21117 Tel 410-363-3690; 800-645-6958 (orders) Fax 410-363-8459

Sterling Pub. Co. Inc., 387 Park Ave. S., New York, N.Y. 10016-8810 Tel 212-532-7160; 800-367-9692 Fax 212-213-2495; 800-542-7567

Stevens, G.: Gareth Stevens Inc., 330 West Olive St., Suite 100, Milwaukee, Wis. 53212 Tel 414-332-3520; 800-542-2595 Fax 414-332-3567

Teacher Ideas Press, P.O. Box 6633, Englewood, Colo. 80155-6633 Tel 303-770-1200; 800-237-6124 Fax 303-220-8843

Thames & Hudson Ltd.
Branch offices
U.S.: Thames & Hudson Inc., 500 5th Ave., New York, N.Y. 10110 Tel 212-354-3763 Fax 212-398-1252; refer orders to W.W. Norton & Co. Inc., 500 5th Ave., New York, N.Y. 10110 Tel 212-354-5500; 800-233-4830 (orders) Fax 212-398-1252; 800-458-6515 (orders)

Ticknor & Fields, 215 Park Ave. S., New York, N.Y. 10003 Tel 212-420-5800; 800-225-3362 Fax 212-420-5855; refer orders to Houghton Mifflin Co., Wayside Rd., Burlington, Mass. 01803 Tel 617-272-1500; 800-225-3362

Ticknor & Fields Bks. for Young Readers, 215 Park Ave. S., New York, N.Y. 10003 Tel 212-420-5800; 800-225-3362 Fax 212-420-5850; refer orders to Wayside Rd., Burlington, Mass. 01803 Tel 617-272-1500; 800-225-3362

Tilbury House, 2 Mechanic St. #3, Gardiner, Me. 04345 Tel 207-582-1899; 800-582-1899 Fax 207-582-8227

Time Inc., 1271 Ave. of the Americas, New York, N.Y. 10020 Tel 212-522-1212

Trafalgar Sq. Inc., P.O. Box 257, N. Pomfret, Vt. 05053 Tel 802-457-1911; 800-423-4525 Fax 802-457-1913

Tricycle Press, 999 Harrison St., Berkeley, Calif. 94710 Tel 510-559-1600; 800-841-2665 Fax 510-559-1637; refer orders to Ten Speed Press, P.O. Box 7123, Berkeley, Calif. 94707 Tel 510-559-1600; 800-841-2665 Fax 510-559-1629

Troll Assocs., 100 Corporate Dr., Mahwah, N.J. 07430 Tel 201-529-4000; 800-826-4216 Fax 201-529-5109; refer orders to Andrews McMeel Pub., 4520 Main St., Suite 700, Kansas City, Mo. 64111-7701 Tel 816-932-6700; 800-826-4216 Fax 800-437-8683

Tundra Bks. Inc., 481 University Ave., Suite 900, Toronto, Ont., Can. M5G 2E9 Tel 416-598-4786 Fax 416-598-0247
Subsidiaries
U.S.: Tundra Bks. of Northern N.Y., P.O. Box 1030, Plattsburgh, N.Y. 12901 Tel 416-598-4786 Fax 416-598-0247

Tuttle: Charles E. Tuttle Co. Inc., 153 Milk St., 5th Floor, Boston, Mass. 02109 Tel 617-951-4080 Fax 617-951-4045; refer orders to Rural Route 1, Box 231-5, North Clarendon, Vt. 05759-9700 Tel 802-773-8930; 800-526-2778 Fax 802-773-6993

U.X.L, 27500 Drake Rd., Farmington Hills, Mich. 48331-3535 Tel 248-699-4255; 800-877-4253 (orders) Fax 313-961-6083; 800-414-5043 (orders)

University of Chicago Press, 1427 East 60th St., Chicago, Ill. 60637 Tel 773-702-7700 Fax 773-702-9756; refer orders to Chicago Distr. Center, 11030 S. Langley Ave., Chicago, Ill. 60628 Tel 773-568-1550; 800-621-2736 (orders only) Fax 773-660-2235; 800-621-8476 (orders only)

University of Hawaii Press, 2840 Kolowalu St., Honolulu, Hawaii 96822-1888 Tel 808-956-8255; 888-847-7377 Fax 808-988-6052

University of Ill. Press, 1325 S. Oak St., Champaign, Ill. 61820 Tel 217-333-0950 Fax 217-244-8082; refer orders to P.O. Box 4856, Baltimore, Md. 21211 Tel 800-545-4703 Fax 410-516-6969

University of N.M. Press, 1720 Lomas Blvd. N.E., Albuquerque, N.M. 87131-1591 Tel 505-277-4810; 800-249-7737 (orders) Fax 505-277-3350; 800-622-8667; refer orders to Order Dept., 3721 Spirit Dr., Albuquerque, N.M. 87106-5631

Viking, 375 Hudson St., New York, N.Y. 10014-3657 Tel 212-366-2000; 800-331-4624 Fax 212-366-2666; refer orders to Penguin Putnam Inc., 405 Murray Hill Parkway, E. Rutherford, N.J. 07073 Tel 201-933-9292; 800-526-0275

Viking Kestrel, 375 Hudson St., New York, N.Y. 10014-3657 Tel 212-366-2000; 800-331-4624 Fax 212-366-2666; refer orders to Penguin Putnam Inc., 405 Murray Hill Parkway, E. Rutherford, N.J. 07073 Tel 201-933-9292; 800-526-0275

Viking Penguin Inc., 375 Hudson St., New York, N.Y. 10014-3657 Tel 212-366-2000; 800-331-4624 Fax 212-366-2666; refer orders to Penguin Putnam Inc., 405 Murray Hill Parkway, E. Rutherford, N.J. 07073 Tel 201-933-9292; 800-526-0275

Walker & Co., 435 Hudson St., New York, N.Y. 10014 Tel 212-727-8300; 800-289-2553 Fax 212-727-0984

Warne: Frederick Warne Pubs. Ltd., 27 Wrights Lane, London W8 5TZ, Eng. Tel (0171) 416 3000 Fax (0171) 416 3199; refer orders to Penguin Bks. Ltd., P.O. Box 11, W. Drayton, Middlesex UB7 0DA, Eng. Tel (0181) 899 4000 Fax (0181) 899 4099

Branch offices

U.S.: Warne, 375 Hudson St., New York, N.Y. 10014-3657 Tel 212-366-2000; 800-526-0275 Fax 212-366-2666; refer orders to Penguin Putnam Inc., 405 Murray Hill Parkway, E. Rutherford, N.J. 07073 Tel 201-933-9292; 800-526-0275

Watts: Franklin Watts Inc., 90 Sherman Turnpike, Danbury, Conn. 06816 Tel 203-797-3500; 800-621-1115 Fax 203-797-3143

Whitman, A.: Albert Whitman & Co., 6340 Oakton St., Morton Grove, Ill. 60053 Tel 847-581-0033; 800-255-7675 Fax 847-581-0039

Wiley: John Wiley & Sons Inc., 605 3rd Ave., New York, N.Y. 10158-0012 Tel 212-850-6000; 800-225-5945 Fax 212-850-6088; refer orders to 1 Wiley Dr., Somerset, N.J. 08875-1272 Tel 908-469-4400; 800-225-5945 Fax 908-302-2300

Williamson Pub. Co., 1355 Church Hill Rd., P.O. Box 185, Charlotte, Vt. 05445 Tel 802-425-2102; 800-234-8791 (orders) Fax 802-425-2199; 800-304-7224 (orders)

Wilson, H.W.: The H.W. Wilson Co., 950 University Ave., Bronx, N.Y. 10452 Tel 718-588-8400; 800-367-6770 Fax 718-590-1617; 800-590-1617

Wordsong, 815 Church St., Honesdale, Pa. 18431 Tel 570-253-1164; 877-512-8366 (orders) Fax 570-253-0179 (orders)

Workman Pub. Co. Inc., 708 Broadway, New York, N.Y. 10003 Tel 212-254-5900; 800-722-7202 Fax 212-254-8098; 800-521-1832 (orders)

World Almanac: World Almanac Education, 15355 NEO Parkway, Cleveland, Ohio 44128 Tel 800-321-1147 Fax 800-321-1149

World Bk. Inc., 233 N. Michigan Ave., Suite 2000, Chicago, Ill. 60661 Tel 312-729-5800; 800-967-5325 Fax 312-729-5600

Yosemite Assn., P.O. Box 545, Yosemite National Park, Calif. 95389 Tel 209-379-2648 Fax 209-379-2486

Zoological Soc. of San Diego, P.O. Box 551, San Diego, Calif. 92112